2015 & 2016

Tax Summary

Preface

Each year in July, Taxpayers Australia publishes the *Tax Summary*, recognised by tax professionals, individuals and small businesses as one of the most comprehensive and easy-to-use tax guides.

This publication provides a concise and practical summary, in plain English, of tax and superannuation laws operating within Australia. Filled with tips and examples, it covers all areas of taxation. It includes all 2014-15 updates and also incorporates changes applying in the 2015-16 income year.

Members of Taxpayers Australia receive the *Tax Summary*, in both print and electronic format, as well as a monthly magazine *The Taxpayer,* as part of their membership. A perfect accompaniment to the *Tax Summary*, *The Taxpayer* provides comprehensive and in-depth articles, clear guidance on the application of tax law, and interpretation and commentary on both legislation and case law.

Taxpayers Australia Ltd

ABN: 96 075 950 284
Reg No: A0033789T

This book has been printed on paper certified by the Programme for the Endorsement of Forest Certification (PEFC). PEFC is committed to sustainable forest management through third party forest certification of responsibly managed forests. For more information: www.pefc.org

PEFC/21-31-16

EDUCATING TAXPAYERS.
EMPOWERING PROFESSIONALS.

Taxpayers Australia is a not-for-profit organisation providing tax and superannuation education. Since 1919, we have been campaigning for a simpler and fairer tax system. We inform and educate professionals, small businesses, and individuals nationally.

Today our growing reach of 13,000 tax professionals, investors, financial planners, business owners, SMSF trustees and students rely on our publications, presentations and helpline calls to cut through the complexity of tax and supererannuation laws.

We support taxpayers to understand the system and to manage their tax strategy and we represent our members' views through the media, the ATO and the government.

PROFESSIONAL MEMBERSHIPS AVAILABLE:

TAX MEMBERSHIP

The Taxpayer Journal
Tax Summary
6 helpline calls
10% discount on
products and services

SUPER MEMBERSHIP

DIY Superannuation
Manual and Updates
Superannuation
Quarterly and Strategies
3 helpline calls

TAIPAL MEMBERSHIP

Post-nominals &
certificate
TAI PAL e-news,
Monthly Tax Review
PLUS all Tax member
benefits

For more information:
• visit www.taxpayer.com.au
• call 1300 657 572
• email info@taxpayer.com.au

Taxpayers Australia Ltd
1405 Burke Road
Kew East, Vic 3102

Acknowledgements

A TAXPAYERS AUSTRALIA PUBLICATION.

WRITERS

Your trusted and experienced team at Taxpayers Australia: Reece Agland, Lisa Greig, Kevin Lim, Andy Nguyen, Michael Perry and Letty Tsoi, and our subject matter expert consultants: John Gaal, Kevin Lock, Ken Mansell and Weiran Wang.

DESIGN & PRODUCTION

Véronique Kopf, Marketing and Communications Manager

Leonnie Gleeson, Publishing and Marketing Officer

Contents

Please see the last section of the book for a detailed index.

Contents

Contents

Contents

Contents

Contents

These are abbreviations used commonly in this text. In most cases, they will be referred to in full at the start of the relevant section.

All references are to the *Income Tax Assessment Act 1997* (ITAA97) unless otherwise stated.

	Example
	Tip
	Warning
AAT	Administrative Appeals Tribunal
ABN	Australian Business Number
ABN Act	A New Tax System (Australian Business Number) Act 1999
ABP	Account Based Pension
ABR	Australian Business Register
ACA	Allocated Cost Amount
ACR	Auditor/Actuary Contravention Report
ADF	Approved Deposit Fund
ANTS	A New Tax System
APRA	Australian Prudential Regulatory Authority
ASIC	Australian Securities Investments Commission
ASX	Australian Securities Exchange
ATI	Adjusted Taxable Income
ATO	Australian Taxation Office
AWOTE	Average Weekly Ordinary Time Earnings
BAS	Business Activity Statement
C of T	Commissioner of Taxation
CC	Concessional Contribution
CCB	Child Care Benefit
CCR	Child Care Rebate
CCTR	Child Care Tax Rebate
CDEF	Community Development Employment Project
CFC	Controlled Foreign Corporation
CFI	Conduit Foreign Income
CGT	Capital Gains Tax
CM&C	Central Management and Control
CPC	Code of Professional Conduct
CPE	Continuing professional education
CPI	Consumer Price Index
COT	Continuity of Ownership Test
CRC	Cooperative Research Centre
CSF	Complying Superannuation Fund
CSHC	Commonwealth Senior Health Card
DA	Deferred Annuity
DASP	Departing Australia Superannuation Payment
DFISA	Defence Force Income Support Allowance
DGR	Deductible Gift Recipient

DIMIA	Department of Immigration and Multicultural Indigenous Affairs
DIS	Decision Impact Statement
DPE	Deferred Purchase Agreement
DRP	Dividend Reimbursement Plan
DTA	Double Tax Agreement
DTP	Directed Termination Payment
DVA	Department of Veterans Affairs
EC	Excessive Component
EGCS	Energy Grants Credit Scheme
ENCO	Effectively Non-contingent Obligation
ERF	Eligible Rollover Fund
ESAS	Employee Share Acquisition Scheme
ESS	Employee Share Scheme
ESVCLP	Early Stage Venture Capital Limited Partnership
ETP	Employment Termination Payment
ETR	Education Tax Refund
ETRV	Eligible Temporary Resident Visa
FBT	Fringe Benefits Tax
FBTAA	Fringe Benefits Tax Assessment Act 1986
FCA	Federal Court of Australia
FCT	Federal Commissioner of Taxation
FFC	Full Federal Court
FHSA	First Home Saver Account
FIF	Foreign Investment Fund
FITO	Foreign Income Tax Offset
FLP	Foreign Life Policy
FMD	Farm Management Deposit
FTB	Family Tax Benefit
FTC	Fuel Tax Credits
FTDT	Family Trust Distribution Tax
FTE	Family Trust Election
GCP	Greenhouse Challenge Plus
GCS	Government Co-contribution Scheme
GDP	Gross Domestic Product
GIC	General Interest Charge
GP	Growth Pension
GST	Goods and Services Tax
GST Act	A New Tax System (Goods and Services Tax) Act 1999
GSTB	Goods and Services Tax Bulletin
GSTD	Goods and Services Tax Determination
GSTR	Goods and Services Tax Ruling
GVM	Gross Vehicle Mass
GVS	General Value Shift
GVSR	General Value Shifting Regime
HCA	High Court of Australia

Glossary

HELP	Higher Education Loan Program
IAS	Instalment Activity Statement
IC	Post-June 1994 Invalidity Component
ID	Interpretative Decision
ITAA36	Income Tax Assessment Act 1936
ITAA97	Income Tax Assessment Act 1997
ITC	Income Tax Credit
IVS	Indirect Value Shift
LAFHA	Living Away From Home Allowance
LCT	Luxury Car Tax
LIC	Listed Investment Fund
LITO	Low Income Tax Offset
LPP	Legal Professional Privilege
MAWTO	Mature Age Worker Tax Offset
MCS	Member Contribution Statement
MEC	Multiple Entry Consolidated group
MEO	Medical Expenses Offset
MLP	Market linked Pension
MLS	Medicare Levy Surcharge
MSV	Market Selling Value
MT	Miscellaneous Tax Ruling
MTAWE	Male Total Average Weekly Earning
NSA	NewStart Allowance
PA	Partner Allowance
PBS	Pharmaceutical Benefit Scheme
PAYG	Pay As You Go
PAYGW	Pay As You Go Withholding
PDF	Pooled Development Fund
PE	Permanent Establishment
PI	Professional indemnity
PS LA	Practice Statement Law Administration
PSB	Personal Services Business
PSI	Personal Services Income
PSE	Personal Services Entity
PST	Pooled Superannuation Trust
PVF	Pension Valuation Factor
RBL	Reasonable Benefit Limit
RCV	Residual Capital Value
RESC	Reportable Employer Superannuation Benefit
RFBA	Reportable Fringe Benefit Amount
RITC	Reduced Input Tax Credit
RN	Relevant Number
RSA	Retirement Savings Account
RRA	Registered Research Agency
RV	Residual Value
s	Section or subsection
ss	Sections or subsections
SA	Sickness Allowance
SAF	Small APRA Fund
SATO	Senior Australian Tax Offset
SBE	Small Business Entity (formerly STS)
SBT	Same Business Test

SCHF	Super Clearing House Facility
SCT	Superannuation Complaints Tribunal
SDBLS	Superannuation Death Benefit Lump Sum
SDBIS	Superannuation Death Benefit income stream
SFN	Superannuation Fund Number
SFSS	Student Financial Supplement Scheme
SG	Superannuation Guarantee
SGAA92	Superannuation Guarantee (Administration) Act 1992
SGC	Superannuation Guarantee Charge
SGD	Superannuation Guarantee Determination
SGR	Superannuation Guarantee Ruling
SHASA	Superannuation Holding Accounts Special Account
SIC	Shortfall Interest Charge
SIS Act	Superannuation Industry (Supervision) Act 1993
SIS Reg	Superannuation Industry (Supervision) Regulations 1994
SME	Small and Medium Sized Enterprise
SMSF	Self Managed Superannuation Fund
SNI	Separate Net Income
STS	Simplified Tax System (now Small Business Entity)
TAA	Tax Administration Act 1953
TABs	State- and Territory-based Tax Agents' Boards
TAP	Term Allocated Pension
TASA	Tax Agent Services Act 2009
TBNT	Trustee Beneficiary Non-disclosure Tax
TBS	Trustee Beneficiary Statement
TD	Tax Determination
TFN	Tax File Number
TI	Test Individual
TOFA	Taxation of Financial Arrangements
TPI	Taxable Professional Income
TR	Tax Ruling
TTP	Transitional Termination Payment
UDC	Undeducted Contributions
UJV	Unincorporated Joint Venture
UPE	Unpaid Present Entitlement
UPP	Undeducted Purchase Price
UPI	Uncontrolled Partnership Income
UUPP	Unused Undeducted Purchase Price
VCLP	Venture Capital Limited Partnership
VCMP	Venture Capital Management Partnership
WET	Wine Equalisation Tax
WHT	Withholding Tax

2014-15 Tax highlights

2014-15 Tax highlights

This edition is current as at 22 June 2015.

The key developments for the 2014-15 income year are as follows:

CHAPTER 2 - REGISTERED TAX AGENT REGIME

- Tax (financial) adviser registration will be introduced progressively from 1 July 2014.

CHAPTER 3 - TAX RATES AND OFFSETS

- Income tax rates for individual taxpayers for 2015-16 remain unchanged from 2014-15 – including the low income tax offset.
- The dependant spouse tax offset is abolished from 1 July 2014.

CHAPTER 4 - TAX ADMINISTRATION

- The Tax Office is transitioning from the electronic lodgment system to Standard Business Reporting (SBR). Under SBR, tax practitioners will lodge Tax Office forms via their SBR-enabled accounting software: **4.000**
- The office of the Commonwealth Ombudsman transferred its tax complaint handling role to the Inspector-General of Taxation on 1 May 2015: **4.450**
- A Parliamentary report on an inquiry into tax disputes has been released: **4.300**
- PS LA 2015/1, the latest Code of Settlement, has been released: **4.380**

CHAPTER 5 - TAX COLLECTION SYSTEM

- Employers will be required to implement Single Touch Payroll, which enables real-time payroll-related reporting through the payroll software: **5.430**

CHAPTER 6 - COMPANIES

- The company tax rate for small business entities is 28.5% from 1 July 2015
- In March 2015, the government released a Proposal paper on a possible amendment to improve the integrity of the tax system by extending a modified form of the unrealised loss rules to Multiple Entry Consolidated groups: **6.560**
- In April 2015, the government released draft legislation to discuss various tax treatments when entities leave a consolidated group: **6.555**

CHAPTER 7 - TRUSTS

- TR 2015/D4 on release of a unpaid present entitlement and application of Division 7A ITAA36
- TR 2015/D5 on deductibility of UPE as a bad debt under s25-35 ITAA97: **7.700**
- New guidance from the ATO on reimbursement agreements: **7.700**

CHAPTER 10 - SMALL BUSINESS ENTITY FRAMEWORK

- A temporary accelerated deduction for depreciating assets costing less than $20,000 from 7:30pm AEST on 12 May 2015
- 1.5% tax cut for SBE companies from 1 July 2015
- 5% discount on tax payable by individuals for unincorporated SBEs from 1 July 2015
- An immediate deduction for professional expenses with starting a new business from 1 July 2015

- CGT roll-over relief for SBEs for changes in structure from 1 July 2016
- FBT exemption for SBE employers who provide more than one portable electronic device to their employees from 1 April 2016: **10.300**

CHAPTER 11 - ASSESSABLE INCOME

- There are proposed changes to the employee share scheme rules, including a new concession for start-ups. At time of writing, the legislation was before Parliament: **11.880**
- In the 2015-16 Federal Budget, the Government announced that individuals in Australia for a working holiday will be classified as non-residents, regardless of how long they are in Australia: **11.020**
- An amount is an assessable employment termination payment only if the payment is received 'in consequence of' the termination of the employment: **11.210**
- TR 2014/5 on the taxation effect of private companies paying money or transferring property in compliance with a Family Court order under the Family Law Act: **11.700**
- TR 2015/1 provides guidance on the special conditions attached to the definition of 'exempt entity' in Division 50: **11.910**

CHAPTER 12 - CAPITAL GAINS TAX

- Transfer of shares by husband to himself and wife jointly: *Murphy v FC of T* [2014] AATA 461: **12.021**
- CGT event C2 from deed of settlement: *Coshott v FC of T* [2014] AATA 622: **12.024**
- CGT event E1 and transfer of land: *Taras Nominees Pty Ltd as Trustee for the Burnley Street Trust v FC of T* [2015] FCAFC 4: **12.028**
- TD 2014/26: The Commissioner considers a bitcoin and similar crypto-currencies to be a 'CGT asset': **12.054**
- Earn-out arrangements – draft legislation released May 2015: **12.142**
- Scrip for scrip roll-over – draft legislation 2015 proposed from the May 2012 Budget announcement: **12.468**
- New Division 615 ITAA97: Roll-overs for business restructures: **12.500**
- CGT small business concessions and Part IVA: *Track and Ors v FC of T* [2015] AATA 45: **12.525**

CHAPTER 15 - DEDUCTIONS FOR CAPITAL EXPENDITURE

- TR 2015/2 Updated Commissioner's effective life for depreciating assets

CHAPTER 19 - SUPERANNUATION

- Amendments provide individuals with the option of withdrawing superannuation contributions in excess of the non-concessional contributions cap made from 1 July 2013, together with 85% of the associated earnings.
- The *Minerals Resource Rent Tax Repeal and Other Measures Bill 2014* has the effect of setting the Superannuation Guarantee rates up to the year 2025-26 and for subsequent years.

CHAPTER 20 - RETIREMENT

- The Low Income Superannuation Contribution is set to expire from 1 July 2017.
- Mature Aged Worker Tax Offset no longer applies.
- The Restart program for businesses employing older Australians: **20.315**

- In the 2015-16 Federal Budget, it is proposed that from 1 July 2017 the assets test will change. From 1 January 2015 full amount of superannuation income stream is included in the income test.

CHAPTER 21 - PRIMARY PRODUCERS

- In the 2015-16 Federal Budget, the Government announced several accelerated deductions for primary producers from 7:30pm AEST on 12 May 2015: **21.000**
- Legislation was enacted in July 2014 to repeal the conservation tillage refundable tax offset one year early: **21.510**
- From 1 July 2014, a taxpayer may consolidate two or more deposits into a single deposit without any tax consequences when certain conditions are met: **21.800**

CHAPTER 22 - INTERNATIONAL TAXATION

- The application of the s23AJ exemption (for non-portfolio foreign dividends received by resident companies) has been extended.
- The law has been amended to ensure that foreign pension funds can access the managed investment trust withholding tax regime and the associated lower rate of withholding tax on income from eligible Australian investments.
- The Government has proposed a non-final withholding tax on proceeds of certain taxable Australian property transactions by non-residents.
- The payment eligible as a FITO must be a foreign tax, social security contributions exclusive.
- In March 2015, the government released exposure draft legislation and explanatory memorandum to implement the third element of the IMR reforms.
- The thin capitalisation rules have been tightened.
- ATO has released a package of guidance dealing with transfer pricing documentation requirements under the new regime.
- In the 2015-16 Federal Budget, the Government announced several anti-avoidance measures for large multinationals.

CHAPTER 23 - GST OVERVIEW

- From July 2015, the references in the GST Act to 'Australia' are being replaced with references to the 'indirect tax zone'
- From July 2017, digital products and other off shore intangible products will be subject to GST pending legislative approval.
- *FC of T v MBI properties Pty Ltd* [2014] HCA 49 in relation to making a taxable supply: **23.110**
- *Rio Tinto Services Ltd v FC of T* [2015] FCA 94 in relation to creditable purpose (under appeal): **23.220**
- GSTD 2015/1 on brokerage services being GST-free: **23.416**

CHAPTER 24 - GST ADMINISTRATION & SPECIAL TOPICS

- Division 142 in relation to refunding of excess GST on or after 31 May 2014 and withdrawal of GSTD 2014/1.

CHAPTER 25 - FRINGE BENEFITS TAX

- Updated FBT rates for the 2015-16 FBT year

Registered Tax Agent Regime

2

2.000   REGISTERED TAX AGENT REGIME

Since 1 March 2010, Australia's tax services profession has been governed by the Tax Agent Services Regime (TASR). The rules are codified in the *Tax Agent Services Act 2009* (TASA), the *Tax Agent Services (Transitional Provisions and Consequential Amendments) Act 2009* (the Amendments Act) and supplemented by the *Tax Agent Services Regulations 2009* (the Regulations).

This national regime replaced various state rules that governed the provision of tax services prior to its introduction. The new national regime was also expanded to regulate professionals providing services in connection with the preparation and lodgement of Business Activity Statements (BAS).

On its introduction the Tax Agent Services Regime established the following:

- The Tax Practitioners Board (the Board) to regulate the profession at a national level
- Rules governing the eligibility framework for the registration of tax agents
- Rules that for the first time would require and govern the registration of providers of BAS services who previously may not have been required to be registered as tax agents under state based systems
- Non-exhaustive statutory definitions of the particular services and types of services which are subject to TASR
- A Code of Professional Conduct (Code) which is binding on all registered BAS agents, tax agents and tax (financial) advisers
- Several tiers of sanctions for breaches of the Code and of the TASA, and
- Safe harbour provisions to provide penalty relief for taxpayers who rely on agents registered under the TASA.

The Board has progressively issued materials offering interpretative and practical guidance in relation to a range of issues. This guidance can be found at www.tpb.gov.au.

2.100   THE TAX PRACTITIONERS BOARD

The national Tax Practitioners Board (the Board) established under the TASA replaces all of the former State- and Territory-based Tax Agents' Boards (TABs) which previously governed the tax agent regime in each respective state and territory.

Since 1 March 2010, the Board has taken over from the TABs all pending investigations and legal proceedings and anything done by a TAB prior to the commencement of the TASA.

The Board must comprise a Chair and at least six other Board members. Board members may be appointed on a full-time or part-time basis and are remunerated for their services.

The law sets out certain grounds and criteria which Board members must satisfy in relation to a number of issues, including pecuniary interests, outside employment, minimum attendance requirements, leaves of absence, bankruptcy, misbehaviour and physical or mental incapacity. In particular, interests which may conflict with the member's duties to the Board are subject to prohibition or mandatory disclosure.

The organisational structure of the Board is currently as follows:

Tax Practitioners Board

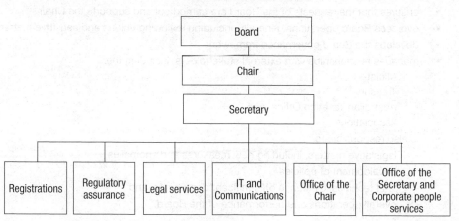

2.110 FUNCTIONAL AREAS OF THE BOARD

REGISTRATIONS

The registration area takes care of the following functions:

- processes applications for registration and supports Board committees deciding more complex registration applications
- provides information to tax practitioners on matters including registration, education and experience requirements, and
- maintains the Board register of registered and deregistered tax and BAS agents.

REGULATORY ASSURANCE

The regulatory assurance area provides for the following functions:

- provides assurance of compliance with the TASA by tax practitioners, including the Code, civil penalty provisions and fitness and propriety requirements, and
- supports the Board in conducting investigations of conduct and assuring compliance with sanctions imposed.

LEGAL SERVICES

The legal services area provides the following services:

- provides legal advice and support to the Board, including legal support for the Board and committee decisions and secretariat processes and outputs
- undertakes case management of litigation matters, and
- manages freedom of information (FOI) queries, and provides legal awareness training as required.

IT AND COMMUNICATIONS

The IT and Communications area provides the following functions:

- develops, implements and operates the systems used by the Board for registration, regulatory assurance and other support functions, including online forms and other tools for external users
- provides a broad range of communication activities (using the Board's website, advertising, community relations, the media etc) to raise community awareness of the tax agent services legislation and its objectives, and
- informs and assists tax practitioners about their obligations, and consults with relevant stakeholders.

OFFICE OF THE CHAIR

- ensures that the requests of the Board are carried out and supports the Chair
- oversees Board operations generally, including reviewing unique and sensitive matters
- develops the Board governance framework
- manages relationships with external stakeholders, including the:
  - Minister
  - Treasury
  - Australian Taxation Office, and
  - associations
- is also responsible for:
  - legislative matters, including new measures and anomalies
  - development of policies
  - final technical clearance of significant documents, and
  - overall operations and performance of the Board.

OFFICE OF THE SECRETARY AND CORPORATE PEOPLE SERVICES

- supports the Chair and the Board
- provides administrative support for the Board and Board committees, and
- provides human resources support, including workforce planning and recruitment.

The Board has a statutory right to delegate most of its powers and functions to a Board member or a committee, subject to limitations. Current and previous members of the Board or of a committee have immunity from legal action in relation to anything done, including anything omitted to be done, in good faith in the performance of the Board's functions or in the exercise of the Board's powers.

2.150   TAX AGENTS AND CONSUMER PROTECTION

The Tax Agent Services Regime was designed as a legislative regime to provide more robust consumer protections for people using a tax agent, BAS agent or tax (financial) adviser. The Tax Practitioners Board has provided details of registered practitioners to the public through their website. In accordance with previous state-based regimes, it is an offence to provide certain tax services without being registered and the Tax Practitioners Board has developed a system to facilitate the making of complaints against practitioners who breach their obligations to clients.

2.160   FINDING AND USING A REGISTERED TAX PRACTITIONER

The general public or taxpayers are able to find a tax or BAS agent, or a tax (financial) adviser using the TPB's online register at https://www.tpb.gov.au/tpb/agent_register.aspx or by contacting a professional accounting association. The register will help taxpayers filter results to find registered tax practitioner within their area.

Where a taxpayer has sourced their own tax practitioner through online or other marketing channels a degree of care and caution must be taken. A taxpayer should, when using this method, ensure a tax practitioner is appropriately registered by checking their status on the TPB's register as this provides the taxpayer with certain consumer protections. These protections include the following requirements:

- the registered practitioner has an appropriate level of professional indemnity insurance in the event the client needs to take legal action against them
- a minimum mandated level of education and experience has been obtained by the practitioner, and
- mandated professional development throughout the registration period is complied with by the practitioner.

Should a taxpayer be concerned regarding the conduct of an registered practitioner or person who purports to be a registered practitioner they should contact the TPB on 1300 362 829.

2.170 TAX AGENTS, BAS AGENTS AND TAX (FINANCIAL) ADVISERS MUST BE REGISTERED

The idea that registering a tax or BAS agent, or a tax (financial) adviser is a good protection for users of these services is not only a recommendation, it is enshrined in law. Section 50-5 *Tax Agent Services Act 2009* makes it an offence for someone to provide a tax agent service, a BAS agent service or a tax (financial) advice service when unregistered with the TPB.

This offence will lead to a civil penalty being imposed on the unregistered agent under s4AA *Crimes Act 1914* as follows:

- Individual – 250 penalty units (or $42,500)
- Body corporate – 1,250 penalty units (or $212,500)

The TPB takes its role in safeguarding consumers using these services very seriously and encourages people to contact them on 1300 362 829.

2.180 COMPLAINTS IN RELATION TO TAX AGENT, BAS AGENT AND TAX (FINANCIAL) ADVICE SERVICES

COMPLAINTS THAT CAN BE ACTED UPON

A complaint must be in relation to one of the following circumstances:

- whether or not a tax practitioner is registered
- whether or not a tax practitioner has breached the *Tax Agent Services Act 2009* including whether the practitioner:
  - is not registered and should be registered with the TPB (see 2.170)
  - has breached the professional code of conduct (see 2.410)
  - is conducting continuing professional development (see 2.420)
  - holds valid insurance cover (see 2.430)
  - is convicted of a serious taxation offence (see 2.510)
  - goes into external administration or bankruptcy (see 2.510)
  - is penalised for being the promoter of a tax exploitation scheme (see 2.510)
  - is convicted of an offence in relation to fraud or dishonesty (see 2.510)
  - is convicted of an offence in relation to misapplying a product ruling materially different from the product ruling's description (see 2.510)
  - is sentenced to a term of imprisonment (see 2.510), and
- against the TPB, including the decisions they make and their products and processes.

COMPLAINTS THAT CANNOT BE ACTED UPON

The TPB takes all complaints seriously; however not all complaints are matters that fall under their jurisdiction.

Sometimes the nature or particulars of a complaint mean it is not appropriate for the TPB to act on it. There are circumstances where a grievance would be best dealt with by another body, such as the police. The TPB will not take action on complaints that are:

- determined to be frivolous, vexatious or not made in good faith
- not relevant to their jurisdiction, including:
  - disputes over fees, where no other relevant Code of Professional Conduct (Code) issues present
  - matters encountered with an agent's provision of non-tax agent service, non-BAS services or non-tax (financial) advice services, where their fitness and propriety is not seriously called into question or there is no other relevant Code issue present, and
  - payment of taxation penalties and interest imposed by the Tax Office, however the Tax Office administers 'safe harbour' provisions set out in the *Taxation*

Administration Act 1953 (TAA), which result in taxpayers not being liable for some taxation penalties, where there would otherwise be a liability because of a registered tax agent or BAS agent's actions.

Where the TPB is unable to act in relation to a matter they encourage people making complaints to seek alternative means of resolving their disputes.

COMPLAINTS PROCESS

Complaints may be lodged using the TPB's online complaints form. This ensures they will have sufficient information to act on a taxpayer's concerns.

Once the TPB receive a complaint, they will:

- acknowledge receipt of the complaint
- make preliminary enquiries, such as contacting a taxpayer to clarify details, or to collect additional information, and
- determine whether it is a complaint they can act upon.

If they are able to act on a complaint, they will then provide details of the claims to the tax practitioner concerned. This is in line with the principles of natural justice, which means the TPB needs to give the practitioner an opportunity to respond to your claims. The TPB may also ask for further information once they receive a response from them.

They may decide to conduct a formal investigation to determine whether a breach of the TASA, including the Code, has occurred. The TPB then will provide a taxpayer with as much information about the outcome of your complaint as permitted under the law. The TPB strive to be fair in their processes by giving all parties an opportunity to provide their claims and/or an explanation. They generally request information and give a reasonable period of time to respond (usually two weeks).

Should a taxpayer not be satisfied with the TPB's handling of the complaint or the outcome of the complaint, they may then be able to either:

- notify the TPB of this matter
- discuss the matter with either the Commonwealth Ombudsman or Commonwealth Privacy Commissioner, or
- appeal a decision to the Administrative Appeals Tribunal (in terms of reviewable decisions).

2.200 SERVICES COVERED BY THE TAX AGENT SERVICES REGIME

The Tax Agent Services Regime fundamentally applies to three types of services – a 'tax agent service', a 'BAS service' and a 'tax (financial) advice service'. These services are defined in the *Tax Agent Services Act 2009* (TASA).

Practitioners providing these services where the service does not fall within the exceptions listed in the relevant regulations are required to comply with TASA. Where a practitioner provides a BAS service they are required to register as a 'BAS agent'. Also, where a practitioner provides only tax (financial) advice services they will also need to register. However, where the practitioner provides services that are wider in scope than those defined as 'BAS services' or 'tax (financial) advice services' and satisfy the definition of 'tax agent services', the practitioner is required to register under the more onerous conditions of a tax agent (where no relevant exceptions apply to their service).

Where a practitioner is not registered under TASA they are prohibited from doing the following:

- providing tax agent services, BAS agent services or tax (financial) advice services
- advertising that they provide tax agent services, BAS agent services or tax (financial) advice services, and
- making representations that they are registered under TASA when they are not.

A contravention of the above rules may be met with sanctions. These penalties are discussed on the Tax Practitioners Board website.

2.210 TAX AGENT SERVICE

A tax agent service is defined as having two main components. Both of these components must be satisfied in order for the service to be a 'tax agent service' under TASA. The definition also refers to services that are deemed not to be tax agent services. These exceptions are detailed in the *Tax Agent Services Regulations 2009* **(TASR)**.

FIRST COMPONENT – TAX AGENT SERVICE

The service should relate to at least one of the following activities:

- ascertaining liabilities, obligations or entitlements of an entity that arise, or could arise, under a taxation law
- advising an entity about liabilities, obligations or entitlements of the entity or another entity that arise, or could arise, under a taxation law, and
- representing an entity in their dealings with the Commissioner.

The term 'taxation law' is defined in s995-1 *Income Tax Assessment Act 1997* as meaning:

- an Act of which the Commissioner has the general administration (including a part of an Act to the extent to which the Commissioner has the general administration of the Act)
- legislative instruments made under such an Act (including such a part of an Act), or
- the *Tax Agent Services Act 2009* or regulations made under that Act.

This definition is therefore very wide and encompassing.

SECOND COMPONENT – TAX AGENT SERVICE

The service should be provided in circumstances where the client (or 'entity') can reasonably be expected to rely on the service for either or both of the following purposes:

- to satisfy liabilities or obligations that arise, or could arise, under a taxation law, and
- to claim entitlements that arise, or could arise, under a taxation law.

Where both of these components occur (and the exceptions below don't apply) the service will fulfil the definition and the practitioner is required to register as a tax agent.

2.220 BAS SERVICE

A BAS service (where the acronym 'BAS' stands for Business Activity Statement) is included within the definition of a tax agent service. It is also made up of two components and has a number of exceptions listed in the relevant regulations.

FIRST COMPONENT – BAS SERVICE

The service should relate to at least one of the following activities:

- ascertaining liabilities, obligations or entitlements of an entity that arise, or could arise, under a BAS provision, or
- advising an entity about liabilities, obligations or entitlements of the entity or another entity that arise, or could arise, under a BAS provision, or
- representing an entity in their dealings with the Commissioner in relation to a BAS provision.

The term 'BAS provisions' is defined in s995-1 of the *Income Tax Assessment Act 1997* as meaning:

- Part VII of the *Fringe Benefits Tax Assessment Act 1986*
- the indirect tax law (eg. GST), and
- Parts 2-5 and 2-10 in Schedule 1 to the *Taxation Administration Act 1953* (which is about the PAYG system).

SECOND COMPONENT – BAS SERVICE

The service should be provided in circumstances where the client (or 'entity') can reasonably be expected to rely on the service for either or both of the following purposes:

- to satisfy liabilities or obligations that arise, or could arise, under a BAS provision, or
- to claim entitlements that arise, or could arise, under a BAS provision.

2.225   TAX (FINANCIAL) ADVICE SERVICE

A Tax (Financial) Advice Service is a specific type of tax agent services. The service must be provided by a financial services licensee or a representative of a financial services licensee in the course of giving advice of a kind usually given by a financial services licensee or a representative of a financial services licensee. The advice should relate to:

FIRST COMPONENT – TAX (FINANCIAL) ADVICE SERVICE

The service should relate to at least one of the following activities or

- ascertaining liabilities, obligations or entitlements of an entity that arise, or could arise, under a taxation law, or
- advising an entity about liabilities, obligations or entitlements of the entity or another entity that arise, or could arise, under a taxation law.

Notice that the difference between a tax agent service and a tax (financial) advice service is that the later cannot representing an entity in their dealings with the Commissioner. This includes lodging returns for an entity.

SECOND COMPONENT – TAX (FINANCIAL) ADVICE SERVICE

The service should be provided in circumstances where the client can reasonably be expected to rely on the service to satisfy liabilities or obligations that arise, or could arise, under a taxation law.

2.230   EXCEPTIONS TO BEING CLASSIFIED A TAX SERVICE OR BAS SERVICE

The services outlined below are specifically excluded from being a 'tax agent service' (and therefore also excluded from being a 'BAS service') by the TASR. Note that financial services are only excluded up until 1 July 2014.

SERVICES EXCLUDED FROM BEING 'TAX AGENT SERVICES'

- A service provided by an auditor of a self-managed superannuation fund under the *Superannuation Industry (Supervision) Act 1993*.
- A service provided by an entity to a related entity.
- A service provided by a related entity of an entity (the *first entity*) to another related entity of the first entity.
- A service provided by a trustee of a trust (or a related entity of the trustee) to the trust in relation to the trust.
- A service provided by a trustee of a trust (or a related entity of the trustee) to a wholly owned or controlled entity of the trust in relation to the entity.
- A service provided by a responsible entity of a managed investment scheme (or a related entity of the responsible entity, the manager of the managed investment scheme or the operator of the managed investment scheme) to the scheme in relation to the scheme.
- A service provided by a partner in a partnership (or a related entity of the partner) to another partner of the partnership in relation to the partnership.
- A service provided by a member of a joint venture (or a related entity of the member) to another member of the joint venture or an entity established to pursue the joint venture:

- in accordance with a written agreement, and
- in relation to the joint venture.

- A service that is a custodial or depository service provided by a financial services licensee or an authorised representative of the licensee.

- A service provided by an entity (the *first entity*) to an entity previously owned by the first entity (the *second entity*) in relation to the second entity's obligations under a taxation law for the income year in which it was sold by the first entity.

- a service that is required, by a law of the Commonwealth or of a State or Territory, to be provided only by an actuary;

- a service provided by an actuary in relation to a defined benefit superannuation scheme or an allocation from a reserve in a superannuation scheme other than a defined benefit superannuation scheme;

- A service that is financial product advice*:

  - provided by a financial services licensee or an authorised representative of the licensee; and

  - accompanied by a statement that:

    1. the provider of the advice is not a registered tax agent under the *Tax Agent Services Act 2009*, and

    2. if the receiver of the advice intends to rely on the advice to satisfy liabilities or obligations or claim entitlements that arise, or could arise, under a taxation law, the receiver should request advice from a registered tax agent.

*This exclusion only applied up until 1 July 2014.

2.300 TAX AGENT, BAS AGENT AND TAX (FINANCIAL) ADVISER REGISTRATION

The entity providing relevant services is required to register as a tax agent, BAS agent or tax (financial) adviser. Different requirements exist depending on the type of entity and the type of registration.

2.310 TAX AGENT REGISTRATION

2.315 INDIVIDUAL (TAX AGENTS)

The individual registration is the starting point for all other registration types. It is typically a requirement that other entity types are made up of individuals registered as tax agents or BAS agents.

An individual can be registered as a tax agent if they are aged 18 or older and meet four conditions:

- they are a fit and proper person

- they meet the requirements of the regulations (such as education and experience)

- the individual maintains, or will be able to maintain, professional indemnity insurance that meets the Board's requirements, and

- in the case of a renewal of registration – the individual has completed continuing professional education that meets the Board's requirements.

Note that agents registered before the commencement of section 39 of the *Taxation Laws Amendment Act (No. 2) 1988* and registered before the commencement of the TASA regime may not need to meet the requirements under the regulations but will still be required to be a fit and proper person.

2.320 FIT AND PROPER PERSON AND REQUIREMENTS UNDER REGULATIONS FOR INDIVIDUALS

Whether a person is determined to be fit and proper by the Board depends upon whether that person is of good fame, integrity and character. Without limiting the Board's inquiry into whether someone is of good fame, integrity or character the Board must also consider, whether in the past five years:

- the individual had the status of an undischarged bankrupt at any time
- the individual served a term of imprisonment, in whole or in part, at any time
- the individual was convicted of a serious taxation offence (as described by TASA)
- the individual was convicted of an offence involving fraud or dishonesty
- the individual was penalised for being a promoter of a tax exploitation scheme
- the individual was penalised for implementing a scheme that has been promoted on the basis of conformity with a product ruling in a way that is materially different from that described in the product ruling
- the individual became an undischarged bankrupt or went into external administration, or
- the individual was sentenced to a term of imprisonment.

Further details on this condition can be found in the Board's explanatory paper TPB (EP) 02/2010.

To be eligible to register as a tax agent an applicant also needs to satisfy all the conditions contained within one of the following pathways.

2.330 PATHWAY ONE: TERTIARY QUALIFICATIONS IN ACCOUNTANCY

CONDITION 1

The individual has been awarded:

a. a degree or a post-graduate award from an Australian tertiary institution in the discipline of accountancy, or

b. a degree or award that is approved by the Board from an equivalent institution in the discipline of accountancy.

CONDITION 2

The individual has successfully completed a course in commercial law that is approved by the Board. A course in commercial law is discussed in TPB(PG) 02/2010. At a fundamental level a 'course in commercial law' is the equivalent of three tertiary level commercial law units which cover all of the following areas:

- Australian legal systems and processes
- Contracts
- The law of entities (including partnerships, corporations and trusts) and business structures, and
- Property law.

The course should also cover a number of other areas covered in TPB(PG) 02/2010.

CONDITION 3

The individual has successfully completed a course in Australian taxation law that is approved by the Board. A course in Australian taxation law is discussed in TPB(PG) 03/2010. The Board states that this course should be made up of at least two tertiary level units covering the following areas:

- the rules and principles of Australian tax law including an understanding of the legal environment in which these principles operate, including basics of the legal system, constitutional considerations, separation of powers
- the key aspects of the income tax law covering concepts of residence and source, related elements (only) of international tax, assessable income, deductions, tax rebates/offsets and tax accounting

- the key aspects of taxes that extend the ordinary income tax base including relevant principles and application of the capital gains tax and fringe benefits tax rules
- goods and services tax
- taxation of individuals and basic entities including partnerships, trusts and companies
- taxation aspects of superannuation law
- administrative aspects of the taxes identified above including returns, tax collection and withholding mechanisms, assessments, objections, rulings, penalties and audits
- rules addressing specific and general tax anti-avoidance, and
- ethical and professional responsibilities of tax agents including obligations under the TASA and TASR.

This condition is covered in greater detail in TPB (PG) 03/2010. This guidance should be reviewed before making an application under this pathway.

CONDITION 4

The individual has been engaged in the equivalent of 12 months of full-time, relevant experience in the preceding five years. Relevant experience is defined in the regulations as work performed by an individual in any of the following roles:

- as a tax agent registered under the Act
- as a tax agent registered under Part VIIA of the *Income Tax Assessment Act 1936*
- under the supervision and control of a tax agent registered under the Act
- under the supervision and control of a tax agent registered under the previous regulatory regime contained in Part VIIA of the *Income Tax Assessment Act 1936*
- as an Australian legal practitioner, or
- in another role approved by the Board.

In undertaking these roles the individual's work must include substantial involvement in one or more of the types of tax agent services described in the Act, or substantial involvement in a particular area of taxation law to which one or more of those types of tax agent services relate. See 2.210.

2.331   PATHWAY TWO: TERTIARY QUALIFICATIONS IN ANOTHER DISCIPLINE – SPECIALISTS

CONDITION 1

The individual has been awarded:

a.   a degree or a post-graduate award from an Australian tertiary institution in a discipline other than accountancy that is relevant to the tax agent services to which the application relates, or

b.   a degree or award that is approved by the Board from an equivalent institution in a discipline other than accountancy that is relevant to the tax agent services to which the application relates.

CONDITION 2

If the Board considers it relevant to the tax agent services to which the application relates, the individual has also successfully completed as many of the following courses as the Board considers necessary:

a.   a course in basic accountancy principles that is approved by the Board

b.   a course in commercial law that is approved by the Board, and

c.   a course in Australian taxation law that is approved by the Board.

Further guidance on what course of study the Board considers will be sufficient to satisfy any of the above criteria can be found in 2.330 *Pathway one: Tertiary Qualification in Accountancy* which makes reference to Board explanatory material.

CONDITION 3

The individual has been engaged in the equivalent of 12 months of full-time, relevant experience in the past five years. See 2.330 *Condition 4* of *Pathway one: Tertiary Qualification in Accountancy* for an explanation of the description of relevant experience.

NOTE: The Board may approve a degree, award or course by an approval process, an accreditation scheme, or by other means.

2.332   PATHWAY THREE: DIPLOMA OR HIGHER AWARD

CONDITION 1

The individual has been awarded a diploma or higher award from:

  a.   a registered training organisation, or

  b.   an equivalent institution in the discipline of accountancy.

CONDITION 2

The individual has successfully completed a course in Australian taxation law that is approved by the Board as discussed in 2.330 *Pathway one: Tertiary Qualification in Accountancy*.

CONDITION 3

The individual has been engaged in the equivalent of two years of full-time, relevant experience in the preceding five years. The definition of relevant experience is discussed in 2.330 *Pathway one: Tertiary Qualification in Accountancy*.

CONDITION 4

Where the application is made on or after 1 March 2013, and the individual was not previously registered under Part VIIA of the *Income Tax Assessment Act 1936*, the individual has successfully completed a course in commercial law that is approved by the Board.

2.333   PATHWAY FOUR: TERTIARY QUALIFICATIONS IN LAW

CONDITION 1

The individual has the academic qualifications required to be an Australian legal practitioner.

CONDITION 2

The individual has successfully completed a course in basic accountancy principles that is approved by the Board. Further details can be found in TPB (PG) 01/2010.

The Board is of the view that the duration of the course in basic accountancy principles should not be less than the equivalent of one quarter of a semester's full-time work load amounting to a total of 100 to 130 hours of study and tuition. This course should cover:

  • sources of regulation of accounting

  • understanding financial statements for different business structures

  • transaction analysis

  • basic understanding of double entry bookkeeping

  • cash and accrual accounting

  • key concepts and rules integral to understanding financial statements including:

    -   definition and recognition of revenues and expenses

    -   definition and recognition of assets

    -   definition and recognition of liabilities

    -   measurement of current-assets, including receivables and inventory

    -   measurement of non-current assets including depreciation and impairment

    -   measurement of liabilities, and

  • taxable income and accounting profit (loss).

CONDITION 3

The individual has successfully completed a course in Australian taxation law that is approved by the Board. For further details see 2.330 *Pathway one: Tertiary Qualification in Accountancy* and TPB(PG) 03/2010.

CONDITION 4

The individual has been engaged in the equivalent of 12 months of full-time, relevant experience in the preceding five years. The definition of relevant experience is discussed in 2.330 *Pathway one: Tertiary Qualification in Accountancy*.

NOTE: The Board may approve a course by an approval process, an accreditation scheme, or by other means.

2.334 PATHWAY FIVE: WORK EXPERIENCE

CONDITION 1

The individual has successfully completed a course in basic accountancy principles that is approved by the Board as described in TPB(PG) 01/2010 and 2.333 *Pathway four: Tertiary qualifications in law.*

CONDITION 2

The individual has successfully completed a course in Australian taxation law that is approved by the Board as described in TPB (PG) 03/2010 and 2.330 *Pathway one: Tertiary Qualification in Accountancy*.

CONDITION 3

If the application is made on or after 1 March 2013, and the individual was not previously registered under Part VIIA of the *Income Tax Assessment Act 1936*, the individual has successfully completed a course in commercial law that is approved by the Board. Further details can be found under 2.330 *Pathway one: Tertiary Qualification in Accountancy* and TPB(PG) 02/2010.

CONDITION 4

The individual has been engaged in the equivalent of eight years of full-time, relevant experience in the past 10 years. The definition of relevant experience is discussed in 2.330 *Pathway one: Tertiary qualifications in accountancy*.

NOTE: The Board may approve a course by an approval process, an accreditation scheme, or by other means.

2.335 PATHWAY SIX: MEMBERSHIP OF PROFESSIONAL ASSOCIATION

CONDITION 1

The individual is a voting member of a recognised tax agent association. A recognised tax agent association is explained in regulation 5 of the *Tax Agent Services Regulations 2009*.

Bodies that have attained this status include TAI Practitioners & Advisers Ltd (which is affiliated with Taxpayers Australia), Chartered Accountants Australia and New Zealand and CPA Australia.

CONDITION 2

The individual has been engaged in the equivalent of eight years of full-time, relevant experience in the preceding ten years. The definition of relevant experience is discussed in 2.330 *Pathway one: Tertiary qualifications in accountancy*.

2.350 BAS AGENT REGISTRATION

The main difference between the tax agent and BAS agent rules for registration apply to individuals.

For guidance on the BAS agent registration requirements for entities other than individuals, please refer to the following sections:

- Companies (2.361)
- Trustees (2.362), and
- Partnerships (2.363).

The rules for individuals are contained in Part 1 of schedule 2 of the regulations. Much like the tax agent eligibility streams, the BAS agent eligibility for individuals is broken up into a number of pathways as follows:

2.351   PATHWAY ONE: ACCOUNTING QUALIFICATION

CONDITION 1

The individual has been awarded at least a Certificate IV Financial Services (Bookkeeping), or a Certificate IV Financial Services (Accounting), from:

- a registered training organisation, or
- an equivalent institution, and

CONDITION 2

The individual has successfully completed a course in basic GST/BAS taxation principles that is approved by the Board. Further information on this course can be found in the following information sheet TPB(I) 05/2011 (which is about course assessment) and TPB(I) 04/2011 (which is about course content) on the Tax Practitioner Board's website. This course should at a minimum cover the following topics:

- collection and recovery of tax provisions in Part VII of the *Fringe Benefits Tax Assessment Act 1986*
- the indirect tax law (which means the goods and services tax (GST) law, the wine tax law, the luxury car tax law and the fuel tax law, as defined in section 995-1 of the *Income Tax Assessment Act 1997* (ITAA97))
- parts 2-5 and 2-10 of Schedule 1 to the *Taxation Administration Act 1953* (TAA) (the pay as you go system)
- relevant Australian Taxation Office (ATO) and Board requirements, including Board registration requirements, the Code of Professional Conduct (Code) and the operation of the civil penalty provisions
- relevant privacy principles as contained in the *Privacy Act 1988*
- GST terminology and appropriate application to financial transactions
- taxation requirements for business purposes and taxation parameters related to a range of business types
- relevant accounting terminology when maintaining accounting records for a variety of business types for taxation purposes
- all sections of both business activity statements and instalment activity statements for multiple entity types, including lodging statements within the allocated timeframe
- how to calculate and input data into payroll systems for the purposes of payroll is included in the definition of a BAS provision. This includes how to calculate:
  - PAYG (withholding and instalments)
  - fringe benefits tax (FBT), and
  - the collection and recovery of tax and preparation of payment summaries, and
- how to comply with organisational guidelines relating to security and confidentiality of information, (in order to be able to, or know how to, meet the Code obligations of confidentiality).

For further details about these topics, refer to the training.gov.au website.

NOTE: The Board may approve a course by an approval process, an accreditation scheme, or by other means.

CONDITION 3

The individual has undertaken at least 1,400 hours of relevant experience in the past three years. For a BAS agent 'relevant experience' means work performed by the individual in the following capacities:

- as a tax agent registered under the Act or a BAS agent registered under the Act
- as a tax agent registered under Part VIIA of the *Income Tax Assessment Act 1936*
- under the supervision and control of a tax agent registered under the Act or a BAS agent registered under the Act
- under the supervision and control of a tax agent registered under the previous regulatory regime contained in Part VIIA of the *Income Tax Assessment Act 1936*, or
- of another kind approved by the Board.

The individual's work must have included substantial involvement in one or more of the kinds of BAS services described at 2.220.

2.352 PATHWAY TWO: MEMBERSHIP OF PROFESSIONAL ASSOCIATION

CONDITION 1

The individual has been awarded at least a Certificate IV Financial Services (Bookkeeping), or a Certificate IV Financial Services (Accounting), from:

- a registered training organisation, or
- an equivalent institution.

CONDITION 2

The individual has successfully completed a course in basic GST/BAS taxation principles that is approved by the Board (see *Condition 2* of *Pathway one: Accounting Qualification* at 2.351).

CONDITION 3

The individual is a voting member of:

- a recognised BAS agent association, or
- a recognised tax agent association.

A recognised BAS agent association is explained in Regulation 4. A recognised tax agent association is explained in Regulation 5 of the *Tax Agent Services Regulations 2009*.

CONDITION 4

The individual has undertaken at least 1,000 hours of relevant experience in the past three years. See 2.351 for details of what 'relevant experience' is for a registered BAS agent.

2.353 ELIGIBILITY FOR REGISTRATION AS BAS AGENT

The following requirements apply to BAS agents in the same way as they apply to tax agents:

- maintains professional indemnity insurance (2.430), and
- performs continuing professional education (2.420).

2.354   TAX (FINANCIAL) ADVISER REGISTRATION

There are currently three options to register as a tax (financial) adviser.

The first option is the 'Notification option'. From 1 July 2014, the notification period of 18 months allows Australian financial services licensees and authorised representatives who provide tax (financial) advice services to notify the Board to become registered as a tax (financial) adviser. From 1 July 2014, AFS licensees and authorised representatives who do not notify the Board, and therefore are not registered, must provide a disclaimer when providing tax (financial) advice services for a fee or other reward. The disclaimer will only be effective until 31 December 2015.

The second option is the 'Transitional option'. From 1 January 2016, all AFS licensees and their representatives will be able to apply to register with the Board if they meet the transitional or standard eligibility requirements. This can only be used for the 2016/17 year. It is similar to the "Standard option" (discussed below). However, under the transitional option, you do not need to demonstrate that you meet the qualification requirements and companies and partnerships will not need to demonstrate that they meet the sufficient number requirement.

Under the 'Standard option', which will be the option that continues after 30 June 2017, to register you need to be (just like a tax and BAS agent) a fit and proper person, have demonstrate that you maintain, or will be able to maintain, professional indemnity insurance that meets the Board's requirements and you meet the qualifications and relevant experience requirements.

Note that under the 'Standard option' the first and main requirement is that you are, or have been, an AFS licensee or a representative of an AFS licensee within the 90 days preceding your application.

The pathways to meet the qualification and experience requirements are discussed below.

Like BAS agents, the main difference between the tax agent and tax (financial) adviser rules for registration apply to individuals. For guidance on the registration requirements for entities other than individuals as BAS agents, please refer to the following sections:

- Companies (2.361)
- Trustees (2.362), and
- Partnerships (2.363).

The rules for individuals are contained in Part 3 of Schedule 2 of the TASR. Just like the tax agent eligibility streams and the BAS agent eligibility streams for individuals, the pathways to tax (financial) adviser registration are as follows:

2.355   PATHWAY ONE: TERTIARY QUALIFICATIONS

CONDITION 1

The individual has been awarded a degree or post-graduate award from an Australian tertiary institution (or a degree or award that is approved by the Board from an equivalent institution) in a relevant discipline. 'Relevant discipline' includes finance, financial planning, commerce, economics, business, tax, accountancy or law.

CONDITION 2

The individual must has also completed a Board approved course in commercial law and have also completed a Board approved course in Australian taxation law. For further information in relation to these courses can be found on the Boards website at:

- TPB (PG) 04/2014 Course in Australian taxation law that is approved by the Board for tax (financial) advisers.
- TPB(PG) 05/2014 Course in commercial law that is approved by the Board for tax (financial) advisers.

CONDITION 3

The individual has been engaged in the equivalent of 12 months of full-time, relevant experience in the past five years.

NOTE: The Board may approve a degree, award or course by an approval process, an accreditation scheme, or by other means.

2.356 PATHWAY TWO: DIPLOMA OR HIGHER AWARD

CONDITION 1

The individual has been awarded a diploma or higher award from:

a. a registered training organisation, or
b. an equivalent institution in a relevant.

CONDITION 2

The individual must has also completed a Board approved course in commercial law and have also completed a Board approved course in Australian taxation law. For further information in relation to these courses can be found on the Boards website at:

- TPB (PG) 04/2014 Course in Australian taxation law that is approved by the Board for tax (financial) advisers.
- TPB(PG) 05/2014 Course in commercial law that is approved by the Board for tax (financial) advisers.

CONDITION 3

The individual has been engaged in the equivalent of two years of full-time, relevant experience in the preceding five years.

2.357 PATHWAY THREE: WORK EXPERIENCE

CONDITION 1

The individual must has also completed a Board approved course in commercial law and have also completed a Board approved course in Australian taxation law. For further information in relation to these courses can be found on the Boards website at:

- TPB (PG) 04/2014 Course in Australian taxation law that is approved by the Board for tax (financial) advisers
- TPB(PG) 05/2014 Course in commercial law that is approved by the Board for tax (financial) advisers.

CONDITION 2

The individual has been engaged in he equivalent of three years of full-time, relevant experience in the preceding five years.

2.358 PATHWAY FOUR: MEMBERSHIP OF PROFESSIONAL ASSOCIATION

CONDITION 1

The individual is be a voting member of a recognised tax (financial) adviser association or recognised tax agent association. A recognised association is explained in regulation 5 of the TASR.
Bodies that have attained this status include TAI Practitioners & Advisers Ltd (which is affiliated with Taxpayers Australia), Chartered Accountants Australia and New Zealand and CPA Australia.

CONDITION 2

The individual has been engaged in the equivalent of six years of full-time, relevant experience in the preceding eight years.

2.359 ELIGIBILITY FOR REGISTRATION AS A TAX (FINANCIAL) ADVISER

Note that the following requirements apply to tax (financial) advisers in the same way as they apply to tax agents:

- maintains professional indemnity insurance (2.430), and
- performs continuing professional education (2.420).

2.360   REQUIREMENTS FOR REGISTERING OTHER ENTITIES AS TAX AGENTS, BAS AGENTS OR TAX (FINANCIAL) ADVISERS

2.361   COMPANY

A company is eligible for registration as a registered tax agent, BAS agent or a tax (financial) adviser if the Board is satisfied that it meets all of the following conditions.

CONDITION 1

All of the directors of the company are fit and proper persons. The Board must consider the factors listed at 2.320 in determining whether a person meets this requirement.

CONDITION 2

The company is not under external administration.

CONDITION 3

The company has not been convicted of a serious taxation offence or an offence involving fraud or dishonesty during the previous five years.

CONDITION 4

The company has:

- in the case of registration as a registered tax agent – a sufficient number of individuals, being registered tax agents, to provide tax agent services to a competent standard and to carry out supervisory arrangements, or
- in the case of registration as a registered BAS agent – a sufficient number of individuals, being registered tax agents or BAS agents, to provide BAS services to a competent standard, and to carry out supervisory arrangements, or
- in the case of registration as a tax (financial) adviser – a sufficient number of individuals, being registered tax agents or tax (financial) advisers, to provide tax (financial) advice services to a competent standard, and to carry out supervisory arrangements.

NOTE: A company in the capacity of trustee of a trust can also be registered.

CONDITION 5

The company maintains, or will be able to maintain, professional indemnity insurance that meets the Board's requirements. For further guidance see 2.430 and the Board website.

Further guidance in relation to the registration of companies can be found on the Board website. A fact sheet titled *Registration as a company tax agent* may also assist practitioners.

2.362   TRUSTEE

The Act applies to an individual or company as the trustee of a trust in the same way as it does to the individual or company in their own capacity. This means the eligibility criteria contained at 2.310 through to 2.350 apply to a trust in the same way as they do to an individual or company. Further information can be found in TPB(I) 03/2011.

2.363   PARTNERSHIP

A partnership is eligible for registration as a registered tax agent, BAS agent or tax (financial) adviser, where it is comprised of individuals and/or companies, if the Board is satisfied that the following conditions contained in the table are met.

Conditions for registration as partnership	
Individual partner conditions	**Company partner conditions**
• Each partner who is an individual is aged 18 years or more. • Each partner who is an individual is a fit and proper person. In considering whether a person is fit and proper the Board should have regard to the factors outlined in 2.320.	• Each director of the company is a fit and proper person. • The company is not under external administration. • The company has not been convicted of a serious taxation offence or an offence involving fraud or dishonesty during the previous five years.
Conditions that apply to individuals and companies	
In the case of registration as a registered tax agent – a sufficient number of individuals, being registered tax agents, to provide tax agent services to a competent standard, and to carry out supervisory arrangements, or In the case of registration as a registered BAS agent a sufficient number of individuals, being registered tax agents or BAS agents, to provide BAS services to a competent standard, and to carry out supervisory arrangements, or In the case of registration as a registered tax (financial) adviser a sufficient number of individuals, being registered tax agents or tax (financial) advisers, to provide tax (financial) advice services to a competent standard, and to carry out supervisory arrangements. The partnership maintains, or will be able to maintain, professional indemnity insurance that meets the Board's requirements.	

NOTE: For the purposes of the TASA an individual or company trustee is treated the same as an individual or company for the purposes of registration.

2.400   REQUIREMENTS TO REMAIN REGISTERED

Once a practitioner has obtained registration as a tax agent, BAS agent or tax (financial) adviser they are required to adhere to a Code of Professional Conduct. Practitioners must also conduct professional development and ensure they are covered by a suitable amount of insurance. For companies, partnerships and trusts there is an added requirement that entities involved in providing relevant services are made up of individuals that hold a valid registration.

The following areas are explored in more detail:

- Code of Professional Conduct
- Continuing professional development, and
- Insurance requirements.

These areas are also covered in various guides released by the Board on their website http://www.tpb.gov.au.

2.410   CODE OF PROFESSIONAL CONDUCT

The Code of Professional Conduct (Code) can be found in s30-10 of the TASA. All practitioners are required to act in accordance with the Code to maintain their registration. The Code applies to registered practitioners. The requirements of the Code are broken up into specific areas of responsibility:

HONESTY AND INTEGRITY

- To act honestly and with integrity
- Comply with the taxation laws in the conduct of your personal affairs
- When you receive money or other property from or on behalf of clients and hold that money or property on trust, an agent must account to their client for the money or other property

INDEPENDENCE

- To act lawfully in the best interests of the client
- Have in place adequate arrangements for the management of conflicts of interest that may arise in relation to the activities that are undertaken in the capacity of a registered tax or BAS agent

CONFIDENTIALITY

- Unless a legal duty to do so exists, the agent must not disclose any information relating to a client's affairs to a third party without the client's permission

COMPETENCE

- Must ensure that a tax agent service provided, or provided on an agent's behalf, is provided competently
- Must maintain knowledge and skills relevant to the tax agent services provided
- Must take reasonable care in ascertaining a client's state of affairs, to the extent that ascertaining the state of those affairs is relevant to a statement made or a thing done on behalf of the client
- Must take reasonable care to ensure that taxation laws are applied correctly to the circumstances in relation to which advice to a client is being provided

OTHER

- Must not knowingly obstruct the proper administration of taxation laws
- Must advise clients of the client's rights and obligations under the taxation laws that are materially related to the tax agent services provided
- Must maintain the professional indemnity insurance that the Board requires to be maintained
- Must respond to requests and directions from the Board in a timely, responsible and reasonable manner

Sanctions and penalties for failure to comply with the Code may include termination (see 2.500).

2.420 CONTINUING PROFESSIONAL DEVELOPMENT

The requirement to be competent to perform tax agent services, BAS agent services or tax (financial) advice services is satisfied in no small part by the requirement that agents perform continuing professional development.

The number of hours of CPE required are:

- **Tax agents**
  - Complete a minimum of 90 hours of CPE within a standard three year registration period, with a minimum of 10 hours each year.
  - Tax agents with a condition of registration other than quantity surveying or fuel tax credits should complete a minimum of 45 hours of CPE within a standard three year registration period, with a minimum of five hours each year.
  - Tax agents with the condition of quantity surveying or fuel tax credits should complete a minimum of six hours of CPE within a standard three year registration period, with a minimum of two hours each year.
- **BAS agents**
  - Complete a minimum of 45 hours of CPE within a standard three year registration period, with a minimum of five hours each year.
  - BAS agents with the condition of fuel tax credits should complete a minimum of six hours of CPE within a standard three year registration period, with a minimum of two hours each year.
- **Tax financial advisers**
  - Tax (financial) advisers should complete a minimum of 60 hours of CPE within a standard three year registration period, with a minimum of seven hours each year.

- Tax (financial) advisers with a condition of registration should complete a minimum of 45 hours of CPE within a standard three year registration period, with a minimum of five hours each year.

More information on CPE requirements can be found in TPB(EP) 04/2012 titled "Continuing professional education policy requirements for tax and BAS agents" and TPB(EP) 06/2014 titled "Continuing professional education policy requirements for tax (financial) advisers" on the Boards website.

RECOGNITION OF YOUR ASSOCIATION'S CPE

If you are a member of a recognised professional association your compliance with the association's CPE requirements will be accepted as meeting the Board's CPE requirements, subject to the CPE activities:

- being relevant to the tax (financial) advice, tax agent or BAS services you provide
- being provided by persons or organisations with suitable qualifications and/or practical experience in the subject area
- meeting our minimum amount of CPE hours as mentioned above.

IMPORTANT: Registered agents should maintain a record of their CPE activities. A record keeping log is provided on the Board website.

2.430   PROFESSIONAL INDEMNITY INSURANCE

The *Tax Agent Services Act 2009* requires applicants for registration to maintain or be able to maintain professional indemnity (PI) insurance that meets our requirements. If a registered tax agent, BAS agent or tax (financial) adviser fails to maintain PI insurance that meets our requirements, they will not be meeting an ongoing registration requirement and may be in breach of the Code of Professional Conduct (Code). This can result in termination of registration.

Practitioners need to maintain a policy or have cover that meets the following requirements.

Turnover of your business (excluding GST)	Minimum amount of cover required for tax and BAS agents (incl legal and defence costs)
Up to $75,000	$250,000
$75,001 – $500,000	$500,000
Over $500,000	$1,000,000

In TPB (EP) 03/2010 *Professional indemnity insurance for tax and BAS agents* the Board summarises the minimum professional indemnity insurance requirements for tax and BAS agents.

Turnover of your business (excluding GST)	Minimum amount of cover required for tax and BAS agents (incl legal and defence costs)
Up to $2,000,000	$2,000,000
$2,000,000+	Equal to actual or expected revenue from tax (financial) advice services (up to a maximum of $20,000,000)

In TPB(EP) 05/2014 *Professional indemnity insurance requirements for tax (financial) advisers* the Board summarises the minimum professional indemnity insurance requirements for tax (financial) advisers.

The PI insurance policy or cover needs to be obtained from an insurer that meets minimum requirements. This includes insurers:

- regulated by the Australian Prudential Regulation Authority (APRA), or
- operating under an exemption within the *Insurance Act 1973* or the *Insurance Regulations 2002*.

ADVISE THE BOARD OF PROFESSIONAL INDEMNITY INSURANCE DETAILS

If an agent is newly registered, they must advise the Board of the details of how they meet the insurance requirements within 14 days of receiving notification of their registration. This would require an agent to tell the Board details of their PI insurance policy or cover, or the details of the registered agent who holds a PI insurance policy that covers them.

All registered agents must also advise the Board whenever there is a change in their policy or cover, including each and every time the policy is renewed.

The agent must also advise the Board even if they do not charge a fee or receive a reward.

2.500 TERMINATION OF REGISTRATION

The termination of a tax agent or BAS agent or tax (financial) adviser's registration can occur for all types of entities that can be registered. Termination of registration is contained in Part 4 of the TASA. Registration can generally be terminated where an event occurs that means a practitioner ceases to meet a registration requirement or breaches the Code of Professional Conduct (which they are required to abide by – see 2.410).

2.510 INDIVIDUAL PRACTITIONERS

In the case of individuals, registration can be terminated where certain events occur and the Board feels that it would be appropriate. There are also certain events that must result in termination; in other words, the Board has no choice but to terminate registration.

EVENTS THAT MAY RESULT IN TERMINATION

For an individual, the Board may terminate the registration of a tax practitioner where any of the following events occur:

- a condition imposed on a practitioner's registration is breached
- a breach of the code of conduct occurs
- an agent ceases to meet one of the tax practitioner registration requirements, or any of the following events occur:
    - an agent is convicted of a serious taxation offence
    - an agent is convicted of an offence involving fraud or dishonesty
    - an agent is penalised for being a promoter of a tax exploitation scheme an agent is penalised for implementing a scheme that has been promoted on the basis of conformity with a product ruling in a way that is materially different from that described in the product ruling
    - an agent becomes an undischarged bankrupt or goes into external administration, or
    - an agent is sentenced to a term of imprisonment.

EVENTS THAT MUST RESULT IN TERMINATION

The events that are not subject to the Board's discretion and must lead to termination are as follows:

- the registration is surrendered by notice in writing to the Board, or
- a practitioner dies.

NOTE: A registration may not be cancelled where it is surrendered in writing where the Board considers, due to a current investigation or the outcome of an investigation, it would be inappropriate to terminate the registration at that time.

2.520 PARTNERSHIPS

In the case of partnerships, registration can be terminated where certain events occur and the Board feels that it would be appropriate. There are also certain events that must result in termination, in other words the Board has no choice but to terminate registration. Additionally, the Board has the power to require the removal of a partner from the partnership.

EVENTS THAT MAY RESULT IN TERMINATION

For an partnership, the Board may terminate the registration of a tax practitioner where any of the following events occur:

- a condition imposed on a entity's registration is breached, or
- a breach of the Code of Professional Conduct occurs (by a partner).
  The Board may require the partnership to remove a partner where that partner is an agent:
  - convicted of a serious taxation offence
  - convicted of an offence involving fraud or dishonesty
  - penalised for being a promoter of a tax exploitation scheme
  - penalised for implementing a scheme that has been promoted on the basis of conformity with a product ruling in a way that is materially different from that described in the product ruling
  - that becomes an undischarged bankrupt or goes into external administration, or
  - that is sentenced to a term of imprisonment.

NOTE: Where the partner is a company, the Board may instead require the company to remove the offending director. The Board, when specifying in their notice the date by which the relevant removal must occur, must have regard to any Australian law in relation to removal of partners and the *Corporations Act 2001* when removing directors.

EVENTS THAT MUST RESULT IN TERMINATION

The event that is not subject to the Board's discretion and must lead to termination occurs where the registration of the partnership is surrendered by notice in writing to the Board.

NOTE: A registration may not be cancelled where it is surrendered in writing and the Board considers, due to a current investigation or the outcome of an investigation, it would be inappropriate to terminate the registration at that time.

2.530 COMPANIES

In the case of a company, registration can be terminated where certain events occur and the Board feels that it would be appropriate. There are also certain events that must result in termination, in other words the Board has no choice but to terminate registration. Additionally, the Board has the power to require the removal of a director from the company.

EVENTS THAT MAY RESULT IN TERMINATION

For a company, the Board may terminate the registration of a tax practitioner where any of the following events occur:

- a condition imposed on a company's registration is breached
- a breach of the Code of Professional Conduct occurs (by a director or representative of the company), or
- the Board may require the company to remove a director where that director is an agent:
  - convicted of a serious taxation offence
  - convicted of an offence involving fraud or dishonesty
  - penalised for being a promoter of a tax exploitation scheme
  - penalised for implementing a scheme that has been promoted on the basis of conformity with a product ruling in a way that is materially different from that described in the product ruling
  - that becomes an undischarged bankrupt or goes into external administration, or
  - that is sentenced to a term of imprisonment.

NOTE: Where the Board removes a director of the company and specifies in their notice the date on which the relevant removal must occur, they must have regard to the *Corporations Act 2001*.

EVENTS THAT MUST RESULT IN TERMINATION

The event that is not subject to the Board's discretion and must lead to termination occurs where the registration of the company is surrendered by notice in writing to the Board or the company ceases to exist.

NOTE: A registration may not be cancelled where it is surrendered in writing and the Board considers, due to a current investigation or the outcome of an investigation, it would be inappropriate to terminate the registration at that time.

Tax rates and offsets

3

3.000 TAX RATES AND OFFSETS

3.001 ASSESSMENT NOTICE

For individuals, a written notice of assessment must be sent to the address 'for the service of notices'. It is the taxpayer's duty to notify the Tax Office immediately of a change of address, otherwise an assessment or other notice might not be received which may have adverse consequences for the taxpayer. Companies and some other entities lodge under the full self-assessment system and therefore a notice of assessment will not ordinarily be issued (see 6.700).

All legislative references are to the *Income Tax Assessment Act 1997* (ITAA97) unless otherwise stated.

In the case of individuals or trustees, income tax is usually due for payment by the later of 21 days after the relevant due date for lodgment or 21 days after the date of issue for the notice of assessment. The Tax Office attempts to process tax returns lodged electronically within two weeks (six weeks for those lodged by post).

3.002 ELECTRONIC LODGEMENT SYSTEM (ELS)

When a tax return is lodged via ELS, it is not necessary to keep a paper signed return. The taxpayer however must provide the tax agent with a written declaration that:

- authorises the tax agent to lodge the taxpayer's return electronically, and
- records the taxpayer's agreement with the information intended for transmission to the Tax Office.

The processing of ELS returns is usually faster than paper returns. ELS services are only accessed by registered tax agents. The Tax Office also allows individual taxpayers to lodge electronic tax returns via free Etax and MyTax software (for individuals with simple tax affairs only).

3.003 TAX CHARGED AND AMOUNTS CREDITED

It is important to check assessments as sometimes a credit for instalments of tax paid is incorrectly entered into the Tax Office computer (eg. a credit of $1,213 may come out as $12.13!).
NOTE: If you are entitled to a tax refund, any outstanding taxation or child support liabilities will be deducted from the refund before it is paid to you.

3.004 EARLY AND OVERPAYMENTS OF TAX

Certain taxpayers may be entitled to receive interest from the Tax Office if they make an early payment of tax or the balance of their assessment is a credit due to overpaid tax and the Tax Office takes more than 30 days to issue a notice of assessment.

EARLY PAYMENTS

An income tax payment qualifies as an early payment if paid more than 14 days before it is due. Payments made during the year such as PAYG withholding do not attract interest. Interest is calculated and claimed by the taxpayer.

OVERPAYMENTS

An overpayment of tax will attract interest if paid by an individual or taxable trust where:

- the balance of an assessment, which is a credit, takes more than 30 days to issue after the completed return is lodged
- an amendment results in a refund, or
- a request for refund is not finalised within 30 days for:
  - variation of instalments
  - refund of advance payment of tax, and
  - remission of some penalties.

Interest is automatically calculated by the Tax Office.

Interest received on early or overpaid tax is assessable income and must be included in the taxpayer's tax return for the year in which it was received.

3.005   INTEREST RECEIVABLE

Where the taxpayer has overpaid a tax liability or paid it early, he or she may be entitled to receive interest from the Tax Office. Details of the rates that will be applicable can be obtained from www.ato.gov.au.

Interest = (Number of days payment was early or was overpaid x Amount x Interest rate)
divided by Number of days in the year

 An assessment notice for $800 is issued with a due date for payment of 1 December 2015. The taxpayer paid the amount outstanding on 1 October 2015. The taxpayer is entitled to 62 days interest, as the payment was made more than 14 days before the due date as notified.

The interest rates for early repayments and over payments of income tax are as follows:

Interest rates	2014-15	2013-14
1 July to 30 September	2.69%	2.82%
1 October to 31 December	2.63%	2.60%
1 January to 31 March	2.75%	2.59%
1 April to 30 June	2.36%	2.63%

3.010   PERSONAL INCOME TAX RATES 2014-15 & 2015-16

RESIDENT INDIVIDUALS

Resident individuals	
Up to $18,200	Nil
$18,201 to $37,000	Tax is 19% of the part over $18,200
$37,001 to $80,000	$3,572 + 32.5% of the part over $37,000
$80,001 to $180,000	$17,547 + 37% of the part over $80,000
$180,001 and over	$54,547 + 47% of the part over $180,000
Resident minors' tax rate on eligible income (Division 6AA)	
Up to $416	Nil
$417 to $1,307	66% of the part over $416
$1,308 and over	47% on the entire amount

NOTE: A Medicare levy of up to 2% may be applicable. A Low Income Tax Offset (LITO) for the full amount of $445 is available for resident taxpayers whose taxable income is below $37,000, however for minors no low income tax offset will be available on unearned income such as trust distributions, interest and dividends. The top marginal rate of 47% includes the 2% Temporary Budget Repair Levy (for three years from 1 July 2014).

NON-RESIDENT INDIVIDUALS

Non-resident individuals	
Up to $80,000	32.5%
$80,001 to $180,000	$26,000 + 37% of the part over $80,000
$180,001 and over	$63,000 + 47% of the part over $180,000

Non-resident minors' tax rate on eligible income (Division 6AA)	
Up to $416	32.5% on the entire amount
$417 to $663	$135.20 + 66% of part over $416
$663 and over	47% on the entire amount

TRUSTEE ASSESSMENT

Trustee assessed under s99*	
Up to $416	Nil
$417 to $671	50% of the part over $416
$672 and over	Ordinary rates – refer Sch 10 *Income Tax Rates Act 1986*

*For deceased estates – the person died more than three years before the end of the year of income.

TRUSTS AND TRUSTEES

The income of a trust is subject to different tax rates depending upon a number of factors. The table below gives an indication of when each rate applies:

Income rates of trust taxpayers		
Circumstances	Assessed	Rates of tax
"Trust income of minor beneficiary on unearned or 'eligible' income distributed (Resident minor)"	Trustee	Refer to rates at *Resident minors* above
"Trust income of minor beneficiary on unearned or 'eligible' income distributed (Non-resident minor)"	Trustee	Refer to rates at *Non-resident minors* above
"Trust income of minor beneficiary from deceased estate* or other 'excepted' income source (Resident minor)"	Trustee*	Refer to rates at *Resident individuals* above
"Trust income of minor beneficiary from deceased estate* or other 'excepted' income source (Non-resident minor)"	Trustee*	Refer to rates at *Non-resident individuals* above
No beneficiary is presently entitled to net income of the trust however Commissioner exercises a discretion*	Trustee	Refer to rates at *Trustee assessed under s99* above
No beneficiary is presently entitled to net income of the trust no discretion exercised by Commissioner (section 99A ITAA36)*	Trustee	47% (1 July 2014 to 30 June 2017)
Beneficiary presently entitled and not under a legal disability, including: • Individual	Beneficiary	Marginal tax rate of beneficiary
• Company	Beneficiary	30%
• Partnership	Beneficiary	To be split into the appropriate share of partnership income and taken into account when assessing partners.
• Trust	Beneficiary	Dependent upon whether the trust is ultimate beneficiary or makes another beneficiary presently entitled to the income of the trust.

* For situations in which the Commissioner may exercise his discretion see *Trusts* at 7.000.

NOTE: Add Medicare levy where applicable.

3.011   INCOME TAX READY RECKONER 2014-15 & 2015-16

This income tax ready reckoner can be used to calculate the tax liability for 2014-15 and 2015-16 for resident individuals. It does not apply for companies, or trusts assessed under ss99 or 99A, but does apply for qualifying beneficiaries assessed under s98.

Income tax payable by a taxpayer is always based on their taxable income. This reckoner shows gross tax payable before tax offsets (rebates) and other credits are allowed.

The Medicare levy has not been included as the amount payable can vary between taxpayers depending on their income, the combined income of a husband and wife and the number of dependent children (see 3.050 for Medicare levy low income thresholds). The income tax ready reckoner can be used to calculate the tax payable for resident taxpayers.

NON-RESIDENT TAXPAYERS

For the 2014-15 and 2015-16 income tax years, if the income tax ready reckoner is used by non-resident taxpayers to calculate their tax liability:

- **Taxable income from $80,000:** Add $8,453 to the amount of tax indicated as being payable by the ready reckoner.
- **Taxable income below $80,000:** Multiply taxable income by 32.5%.

LOW INCOME TAX OFFSET

For the 2014-15 and 2015-16 income tax years, a resident taxpayer whose taxable income is no more than $37,000 is entitled to the full Low Income Tax Offset (LITO) of $445. It phases out to nil at $66,667. For a reduction in PAYG see 5.650.

The effect of LITO is that a resident taxpayer's tax-free threshold is effectively increased to $20,542. This may vary if the low income taxpayer becomes or ceases to be a resident in the financial year (see reduced tax-free threshold at 3.030). The LITO is only available on assessment and is in addition to dependant and all other tax offsets allowed to a taxpayer. The LITO is only available to resident taxpayers.

TABLE 1: Income tax ready reckoner 2014-15 and 2015-16

Taxable Tax liability ($)

income($) For range of Taxable Income $18,200 – $37,000. Does not include the Medicare levy.

plus	$0	$100	$200	$300	$400	$500	$600	$700	$800	$900
$18,000		-	-	19.00	38.00	57.00	76.00	95.00	114.00	133.00
$19,000	152.00	171.00	190.00	209.00	228.00	247.00	266.00	285.00	304.00	323.00
$20,000	342.00	361.00	380.00	399.00	418.00	437.00	456.00	475.00	494.00	513.00
$21,000	532.00	551.00	570.00	589.00	608.00	627.00	646.00	665.00	684.00	703.00
$22,000	722.00	741.00	760.00	779.00	798.00	817.00	836.00	855.00	874.00	893.00
$23,000	912.00	931.00	950.00	969.00	988.00	1,007.00	1,026.00	1,045.00	1,064.00	1,083.00
$24,000	1,102.00	1,121.00	1,140.00	1,159.00	1,178.00	1,197.00	1,216.00	1,235.00	1,254.00	1,273.00
$25,000	1,292.00	1,311.00	1,330.00	1,349.00	1,368.00	1,387.00	1,406.00	1,425.00	1,444.00	1,463.00
$26,000	1,482.00	1,501.00	1,520.00	1,539.00	1,558.00	1,577.00	1,596.00	1,615.00	1,634.00	1,653.00
$27,000	1,672.00	1,691.00	1,710.00	1,729.00	1,748.00	1,767.00	1,786.00	1,805.00	1,824.00	1,843.00
$28,000	1,862.00	1,881.00	1,900.00	1,919.00	1,938.00	1,957.00	1,976.00	1,995.00	2,014.00	2,033.00
$29,000	2,052.00	2,071.00	2,090.00	2,109.00	2,128.00	2,147.00	2,166.00	2,185.00	2,204.00	2,223.00
$30,000	2,242.00	2,261.00	2,280.00	2,299.00	2,318.00	2,337.00	2,356.00	2,375.00	2,394.00	2,413.00
$31,000	2,432.00	2,451.00	2,470.00	2,489.00	2,508.00	2,527.00	2,546.00	2,565.00	2,584.00	2,603.00
$32,000	2,622.00	2,641.00	2,660.00	2,679.00	2,698.00	2,717.00	2,736.00	2,755.00	2,774.00	2,793.00
$33,000	2,812.00	2,831.00	2,850.00	2,869.00	2,888.00	2,907.00	2,926.00	2,945.00	2,964.00	2,983.00
$34,000	3,002.00	3,021.00	3,040.00	3,059.00	3,078.00	3,097.00	3,116.00	3,135.00	3,154.00	3,173.00
$35,000	3,192.00	3,211.00	3,230.00	3,249.00	3,268.00	3,287.00	3,306.00	3,325.00	3,344.00	3,363.00
$36,000	3,382.00	3,401.00	3,420.00	3,439.00	3,458.00	3,477.00	3,496.00	3,515.00	3,534.00	3,553.00
$37,000	3,572.00									

Part over $100 (When income earned is over $18,200)

plus	$0	$1	$2	$3	$4	$5	$6	$7	$8	$9
$0	0.00	0.19	0.38	0.57	0.76	0.95	1.14	1.33	1.52	1.71
$10	1.90	2.09	2.28	2.47	2.66	2.85	3.04	3.23	3.42	3.61
$20	3.80	3.99	4.18	4.37	4.56	4.75	4.94	5.13	5.32	5.51
$30	5.70	5.89	6.08	6.27	6.46	6.65	6.84	7.03	7.22	7.41
$40	7.60	7.79	7.98	8.17	8.36	8.55	8.74	8.93	9.12	9.31
$50	9.50	9.69	9.88	10.07	10.26	10.45	10.64	10.83	11.02	11.21
$60	11.40	11.59	11.78	11.97	12.16	12.35	12.54	12.73	12.92	13.11
$70	13.30	13.49	13.68	13.87	14.06	14.25	14.44	14.63	14.82	15.01
$80	15.20	15.39	15.58	15.77	15.96	16.15	16.34	16.53	16.72	16.91
$90	17.10	17.29	17.48	17.67	17.86	18.05	18.24	18.43	18.62	18.81

TABLE 2: Income tax ready reckoner 2014-15 and 2015-16

Taxable   **Tax liability($)**

For range of taxable income $37,000 – $80,000. Does not include the Medicare levy.

income($) plus	$0	$100	$200	$300	$400	$500	$600	$700	$800	$900
$37,000	3,572.00	3,604.50	3,637.00	3,669.50	3,702.00	3,734.50	3,767.00	3,799.50	3,832.00	3,864.50
$38,000	3,897.00	3,929.50	3,962.00	3,994.50	4,027.00	4,059.50	4,092.00	4,124.50	4,157.00	4,189.50
$39,000	4,222.00	4,254.50	4,287.00	4,319.50	4,352.00	4,384.50	4,417.00	4,449.50	4,482.00	4,514.50
$40,000	4,547.00	4,579.50	4,612.00	4,644.50	4,677.00	4,709.50	4,742.00	4,774.50	4,807.00	4,839.50
$41,000	4,872.00	4,904.50	4,937.00	4,969.50	5,002.00	5,034.50	5,067.00	5,099.50	5,132.00	5,164.50
$42,000	5,197.00	5,229.50	5,262.00	5,294.50	5,327.00	5,359.50	5,392.00	5,424.50	5,457.00	5,489.50
$43,000	5,522.00	5,554.50	5,587.00	5,619.50	5,652.00	5,684.50	5,717.00	5,749.50	5,782.00	5,814.50
$44,000	5,847.00	5,879.50	5,912.00	5,944.50	5,977.00	6,009.50	6,042.00	6,074.50	6,107.00	6,139.50
$45,000	6,172.00	6,204.50	6,237.00	6,269.50	6,302.00	6,334.50	6,367.00	6,399.50	6,432.00	6,464.50
$46,000	6,497.00	6,529.50	6,562.00	6,594.50	6,627.00	6,659.50	6,692.00	6,724.50	6,757.00	6,789.50
$47,000	6,822.00	6,854.50	6,887.00	6,919.50	6,952.00	6,984.50	7,017.00	7,049.50	7,082.00	7,114.50
$48,000	7,147.00	7,179.50	7,212.00	7,244.50	7,277.00	7,309.50	7,342.00	7,374.50	7,407.00	7,439.50
$49,000	7,472.00	7,504.50	7,537.00	7,569.50	7,602.00	7,634.50	7,667.00	7,699.50	7,732.00	7,764.50
$50,000	7,797.00	7,829.50	7,862.00	7,894.50	7,927.00	7,959.50	7,992.00	8,024.50	8,057.00	8,089.50
$51,000	8,122.00	8,154.50	8,187.00	8,219.50	8,252.00	8,284.50	8,317.00	8,349.50	8,382.00	8,414.50
$52,000	8,447.00	8,479.50	8,512.00	8,544.50	8,577.00	8,609.50	8,642.00	8,674.50	8,707.00	8,739.50
$53,000	8,772.00	8,804.50	8,837.00	8,869.50	8,902.00	8,934.50	8,967.00	8,999.50	9,032.00	9,064.50
$54,000	9,097.00	9,129.50	9,162.00	9,194.50	9,227.00	9,259.50	9,292.00	9,324.50	9,357.00	9,389.50
$55,000	9,422.00	9,454.50	9,487.00	9,519.50	9,552.00	9,584.50	9,617.00	9,649.50	9,682.00	9,714.50
$56,000	9,747.00	9,779.50	9,812.00	9,844.50	9,877.00	9,909.50	9,942.00	9,974.50	10,007.00	10,039.50
$57,000	10,072.00	10,104.50	10,137.00	10,169.50	10,202.00	10,234.50	10,267.00	10,299.50	10,332.00	10,364.50
$58,000	10,397.00	10,429.50	10,462.00	10,494.50	10,527.00	10,559.50	10,592.00	10,624.50	10,657.00	10,689.50
$59,000	10,722.00	10,754.50	10,787.00	10,819.50	10,852.00	10,884.50	10,917.00	10,949.50	10,982.00	11,014.50
$60,000	11,047.00	11,079.50	11,112.00	11,144.50	11,177.00	11,209.50	11,242.00	11,274.50	11,307.00	11,339.50
$61,000	11,372.00	11,404.50	11,437.00	11,469.50	11,502.00	11,534.50	11,567.00	11,599.50	11,632.00	11,664.50
$62,000	11,697.00	11,729.50	11,762.00	11,794.50	11,827.00	11,859.50	11,892.00	11,924.50	11,957.00	11,989.50
$63,000	12,022.00	12,054.50	12,087.00	12,119.50	12,152.00	12,184.50	12,217.00	12,249.50	12,282.00	12,314.50
$64,000	12,347.00	12,379.50	12,412.00	12,444.50	12,477.00	12,509.50	12,542.00	12,574.50	12,607.00	12,639.50
$65,000	12,672.00	12,704.50	12,737.00	12,769.50	12,802.00	12,834.50	12,867.00	12,899.50	12,932.00	12,964.50
$66,000	12,997.00	13,029.50	13,062.00	13,094.50	13,127.00	13,159.50	13,192.00	13,224.50	13,257.00	13,289.50
$67,000	13,322.00	13,354.50	13,387.00	13,419.50	13,452.00	13,484.50	13,517.00	13,549.50	13,582.00	13,614.50
$68,000	13,647.00	13,679.50	13,712.00	13,744.50	13,777.00	13,809.50	13,842.00	13,874.50	13,907.00	13,939.50
$69,000	13,972.00	14,004.50	14,037.00	14,069.50	14,102.00	14,134.50	14,167.00	14,199.50	14,232.00	14,264.50
$70,000	14,297.00	14,329.50	14,362.00	14,394.50	14,427.00	14,459.50	14,492.00	14,524.50	14,557.00	14,589.50
$71,000	14,622.00	14,654.50	14,687.00	14,719.50	14,752.00	14,784.50	14,817.00	14,849.50	14,882.00	14,914.50
$72,000	14,947.00	14,979.50	15,012.00	15,044.50	15,077.00	15,109.50	15,142.00	15,174.50	15,207.00	15,239.50

TABLE 2: Income tax ready reckoner 2014-15 and 2015-16 (cont)

Taxable Tax liability($)

For range of taxable income $37,000 – $80,000. Does not include the Medicare levy.

Taxable income($) plus	$0	$100	$200	$300	$400	$500	$600	$700	$800	$900
$73,000	15,272.00	15,304.50	15,337.00	15,369.50	15,402.00	15,434.50	15,467.00	15,499.50	15,532.00	15,564.50
$74,000	15,597.00	15,629.50	15,662.00	15,694.50	15,727.00	15,759.50	15,792.00	15,824.50	15,857.00	15,889.50
$75,000	15,922.00	15,954.50	15,987.00	16,019.50	16,052.00	16,084.50	16,117.00	16,149.50	16,182.00	16,214.50
$76,000	16,247.00	16,279.50	16,312.00	16,344.50	16,377.00	16,409.50	16,442.00	16,474.50	16,507.00	16,539.50
$77,000	16,572.00	16,604.50	16,637.00	16,669.50	16,702.00	16,734.50	16,767.00	16,799.50	16,832.00	16,864.50
$78,000	16,897.00	16,929.50	16,962.00	16,994.50	17,027.00	17,059.50	17,092.00	17,124.50	17,157.00	17,189.50
$79,000	17,222.00	17,254.50	17,287.00	17,319.50	17,352.00	17,384.50	17,417.00	17,449.50	17,482.00	17,514.50
$80,000	17,547.00	-	-	-	-	-	-	-	-	-

Part over $100

plus	$0	$100	$200	$300	$400	$500	$600	$700	$800	$900
$0	0.00	0.33	0.65	0.98	1.30	1.63	1.95	2.28	2.60	2.93
$10	3.25	3.58	3.90	4.23	4.55	4.88	5.20	5.53	5.85	6.18
$20	6.50	6.83	7.15	7.48	7.80	8.13	8.45	8.78	9.10	9.43
$30	9.75	10.08	10.40	10.73	11.05	11.38	11.70	12.03	12.35	12.68
$40	13.00	13.33	13.65	13.98	14.30	14.63	14.95	15.28	15.60	15.93
$50	16.25	16.58	16.90	17.23	17.55	17.88	18.20	18.53	18.85	19.18
$60	19.50	19.83	20.15	20.48	20.80	21.13	21.45	21.78	22.10	22.43
$70	22.75	23.08	23.40	23.73	24.05	24.38	24.70	25.03	25.35	25.68
$80	26.00	26.33	26.65	26.98	27.30	27.63	27.95	28.28	28.60	28.93
$90	29.25	29.58	29.90	30.23	30.55	30.88	31.20	31.53	31.85	32.18

TABLE 3: Income tax ready reckoner 2014-15 and 2015-16

Taxable Tax liability($)

For the range of Taxable Income $80,000 – $180,000. Does not include the Medicare levy

Taxable income($) plus	$0	$100	$200	$300	$400	$500	$600	$700	$800	$900
$80,000	17,547.00	17,584.00	17,621.00	17,658.00	17,695.00	17,732.00	17,769.00	17,806.00	17,843.00	17,880.00
$81,000	17,917.00	17,954.00	17,991.00	18,028.00	18,065.00	18,102.00	18,139.00	18,176.00	18,213.00	18,250.00
$82,000	18,287.00	18,324.00	18,361.00	18,398.00	18,435.00	18,472.00	18,509.00	18,546.00	18,583.00	18,620.00
$83,000	18,657.00	18,694.00	18,731.00	18,768.00	18,805.00	18,842.00	18,879.00	18,916.00	18,953.00	18,990.00
$84,000	19,027.00	19,064.00	19,101.00	19,138.00	19,175.00	19,212.00	19,249.00	19,286.00	19,323.00	19,360.00
$85,000	19,397.00	19,434.00	19,471.00	19,508.00	19,545.00	19,582.00	19,619.00	19,656.00	19,693.00	19,730.00
$86,000	19,767.00	19,804.00	19,841.00	19,878.00	19,915.00	19,952.00	19,989.00	20,026.00	20,063.00	20,100.00
$87,000	20,137.00	20,174.00	20,211.00	20,248.00	20,285.00	20,322.00	20,359.00	20,396.00	20,433.00	20,470.00
$88,000	20,507.00	20,544.00	20,581.00	20,618.00	20,655.00	20,692.00	20,729.00	20,766.00	20,803.00	20,840.00
$89,000	20,877.00	20,914.00	20,951.00	20,988.00	21,025.00	21,062.00	21,099.00	21,136.00	21,173.00	21,210.00
$90,000	21,247.00	21,284.00	21,321.00	21,358.00	21,395.00	21,432.00	21,469.00	21,506.00	21,543.00	21,580.00

TABLE 3: Income tax ready reckoner 2014-15 and 2015-16 (cont)

Taxable income($) plus   Tax liability($)
For the range of Taxable Income $80,000 – $180,000. Does not include the Medicare levy

Taxable income($) plus	$0	$100	$200	$300	$400	$500	$600	$700	$800	$900
$91,000	21,617.00	21,654.00	21,691.00	21,728.00	21,765.00	21,802.00	21,839.00	21,876.00	21,913.00	21,950.00
$92,000	21,987.00	22,024.00	22,061.00	22,098.00	22,135.00	22,172.00	22,209.00	22,246.00	22,283.00	22,320.00
$93,000	22,357.00	22,394.00	22,431.00	22,468.00	22,505.00	22,542.00	22,579.00	22,616.00	22,653.00	22,690.00
$94,000	22,727.00	22,764.00	22,801.00	22,838.00	22,875.00	22,912.00	22,949.00	22,986.00	23,023.00	23,060.00
$95,000	23,097.00	23,134.00	23,171.00	23,208.00	23,245.00	23,282.00	23,319.00	23,356.00	23,393.00	23,430.00
$96,000	23,467.00	23,504.00	23,541.00	23,578.00	23,615.00	23,652.00	23,689.00	23,726.00	23,763.00	23,800.00
$97,000	23,837.00	23,874.00	23,911.00	23,948.00	23,985.00	24,022.00	24,059.00	24,096.00	24,133.00	24,170.00
$98,000	24,207.00	24,244.00	24,281.00	24,318.00	24,355.00	24,392.00	24,429.00	24,466.00	24,503.00	24,540.00
$99,000	24,577.00	24,614.00	24,651.00	24,688.00	24,725.00	24,762.00	24,799.00	24,836.00	24,873.00	24,910.00
$100,000	24,947.00	24,984.00	25,021.00	25,058.00	25,095.00	25,132.00	25,169.00	25,206.00	25,243.00	25,280.00
$101,000	25,317.00	25,354.00	25,391.00	25,428.00	25,465.00	25,502.00	25,539.00	25,576.00	25,613.00	25,650.00
$102,000	25,687.00	25,724.00	25,761.00	25,798.00	25,835.00	25,872.00	25,909.00	25,946.00	25,983.00	26,020.00
$103,000	26,057.00	26,094.00	26,131.00	26,168.00	26,205.00	26,242.00	26,279.00	26,316.00	26,353.00	26,390.00
$104,000	26,427.00	26,464.00	26,501.00	26,538.00	26,575.00	26,612.00	26,649.00	26,686.00	26,723.00	26,760.00
$105,000	26,797.00	26,834.00	26,871.00	26,908.00	26,945.00	26,982.00	27,019.00	27,056.00	27,093.00	27,130.00
$106,000	27,167.00	27,204.00	27,241.00	27,278.00	27,315.00	27,352.00	27,389.00	27,426.00	27,463.00	27,500.00
$107,000	27,537.00	27,574.00	27,611.00	27,648.00	27,685.00	27,722.00	27,759.00	27,796.00	27,833.00	27,870.00
$108,000	27,907.00	27,944.00	27,981.00	28,018.00	28,055.00	28,092.00	28,129.00	28,166.00	28,203.00	28,240.00
$109,000	28,277.00	28,314.00	28,351.00	28,388.00	28,425.00	28,462.00	28,499.00	28,536.00	28,573.00	28,610.00
$110,000	28,647.00	28,684.00	28,721.00	28,758.00	28,795.00	28,832.00	28,869.00	28,906.00	28,943.00	28,980.00
$111,000	29,017.00	29,054.00	29,091.00	29,128.00	29,165.00	29,202.00	29,239.00	29,276.00	29,313.00	29,350.00
$112,000	29,387.00	29,424.00	29,461.00	29,498.00	29,535.00	29,572.00	29,609.00	29,646.00	29,683.00	29,720.00
$113,000	29,757.00	29,794.00	29,831.00	29,868.00	29,905.00	29,942.00	29,979.00	30,016.00	30,053.00	30,090.00
$114,000	30,127.00	30,164.00	30,201.00	30,238.00	30,275.00	30,312.00	30,349.00	30,386.00	30,423.00	30,460.00
$115,000	30,497.00	30,534.00	30,571.00	30,608.00	30,645.00	30,682.00	30,719.00	30,756.00	30,793.00	30,830.00
$116,000	30,867.00	30,904.00	30,941.00	30,978.00	31,015.00	31,052.00	31,089.00	31,126.00	31,163.00	31,200.00
$117,000	31,237.00	31,274.00	31,311.00	31,348.00	31,385.00	31,422.00	31,459.00	31,496.00	31,533.00	31,570.00
$118,000	31,607.00	31,644.00	31,681.00	31,718.00	31,755.00	31,792.00	31,829.00	31,866.00	31,903.00	31,940.00
$119,000	31,977.00	32,014.00	32,051.00	32,088.00	32,125.00	32,162.00	32,199.00	32,236.00	32,273.00	32,310.00
$120,000	32,347.00	32,384.00	32,421.00	32,458.00	32,495.00	32,532.00	32,569.00	32,606.00	32,643.00	32,680.00
$121,000	32,717.00	32,754.00	32,791.00	32,828.00	32,865.00	32,902.00	32,939.00	32,976.00	33,013.00	33,050.00
$122,000	33,087.00	33,124.00	33,161.00	33,198.00	33,235.00	33,272.00	33,309.00	33,346.00	33,383.00	33,420.00
$123,000	33,457.00	33,494.00	33,531.00	33,568.00	33,605.00	33,642.00	33,679.00	33,716.00	33,753.00	33,790.00
$124,000	33,827.00	33,864.00	33,901.00	33,938.00	33,975.00	34,012.00	34,049.00	34,086.00	34,123.00	34,160.00
$125,000	34,197.00	34,234.00	34,271.00	34,308.00	34,345.00	34,382.00	34,419.00	34,456.00	34,493.00	34,530.00
$126,000	34,567.00	34,604.00	34,641.00	34,678.00	34,715.00	34,752.00	34,789.00	34,826.00	34,863.00	34,900.00

TABLE 3: Income tax ready reckoner 2014-15 and 2015-16 (cont)

For the range of Taxable Income $80,000 – $180,000. Does not include the Medicare levy

Taxable income($) plus	Tax liability($)									
	$0	$100	$200	$300	$400	$500	$600	$700	$800	$900
$127,000	34,937.00	34,974.00	35,011.00	35,048.00	35,085.00	35,122.00	35,159.00	35,196.00	35,233.00	35,270.00
$128,000	35,307.00	35,344.00	35,381.00	35,418.00	35,455.00	35,492.00	35,529.00	35,566.00	35,603.00	35,640.00
$129,000	35,677.00	35,714.00	35,751.00	35,788.00	35,825.00	35,862.00	35,899.00	35,936.00	35,973.00	36,010.00
$130,000	36,047.00	36,084.00	36,121.00	36,158.00	36,195.00	36,232.00	36,269.00	36,306.00	36,343.00	36,380.00
$131,000	36,417.00	36,454.00	36,491.00	36,528.00	36,565.00	36,602.00	36,639.00	36,676.00	36,713.00	36,750.00
$132,000	36,787.00	36,824.00	36,861.00	36,898.00	36,935.00	36,972.00	37,009.00	37,046.00	37,083.00	37,120.00
$133,000	37,157.00	37,194.00	37,231.00	37,268.00	37,305.00	37,342.00	37,379.00	37,416.00	37,453.00	37,490.00
$134,000	37,527.00	37,564.00	37,601.00	37,638.00	37,675.00	37,712.00	37,749.00	37,786.00	37,823.00	37,860.00
$135,000	37,897.00	37,934.00	37,971.00	38,008.00	38,045.00	38,082.00	38,119.00	38,156.00	38,193.00	38,230.00
$136,000	38,267.00	38,304.00	38,341.00	38,378.00	38,415.00	38,452.00	38,489.00	38,526.00	38,563.00	38,600.00
$137,000	38,637.00	38,674.00	38,711.00	38,748.00	38,785.00	38,822.00	38,859.00	38,896.00	38,933.00	38,970.00
$138,000	39,007.00	39,044.00	39,081.00	39,118.00	39,155.00	39,192.00	39,229.00	39,266.00	39,303.00	39,340.00
$139,000	39,377.00	39,414.00	39,451.00	39,488.00	39,525.00	39,562.00	39,599.00	39,636.00	39,673.00	39,710.00
$140,000	39,747.00	39,784.00	39,821.00	39,858.00	39,895.00	39,932.00	39,969.00	40,006.00	40,043.00	40,080.00
$141,000	40,117.00	40,154.00	40,191.00	40,228.00	40,265.00	40,302.00	40,339.00	40,376.00	40,413.00	40,450.00
$142,000	40,487.00	40,524.00	40,561.00	40,598.00	40,635.00	40,672.00	40,709.00	40,746.00	40,783.00	40,820.00
$143,000	40,857.00	40,894.00	40,931.00	40,968.00	41,005.00	41,042.00	41,079.00	41,116.00	41,153.00	41,190.00
$144,000	41,227.00	41,264.00	41,301.00	41,338.00	41,375.00	41,412.00	41,449.00	41,486.00	41,523.00	41,560.00
$145,000	41,597.00	41,634.00	41,671.00	41,708.00	41,745.00	41,782.00	41,819.00	41,856.00	41,893.00	41,930.00
$146,000	41,967.00	42,004.00	42,041.00	42,078.00	42,115.00	42,152.00	42,189.00	42,226.00	42,263.00	42,300.00
$147,000	42,337.00	42,374.00	42,411.00	42,448.00	42,485.00	42,522.00	42,559.00	42,596.00	42,633.00	42,670.00
$148,000	42,707.00	42,744.00	42,781.00	42,818.00	42,855.00	42,892.00	42,929.00	42,966.00	43,003.00	43,040.00
$149,000	43,077.00	43,114.00	43,151.00	43,188.00	43,225.00	43,262.00	43,299.00	43,336.00	43,373.00	43,410.00
$150,000	43,447.00	43,484.00	43,521.00	43,558.00	43,595.00	43,632.00	43,669.00	43,706.00	43,743.00	43,780.00
$151,000	43,817.00	43,854.00	43,891.00	43,928.00	43,965.00	44,002.00	44,039.00	44,076.00	44,113.00	44,150.00
$152,000	44,187.00	44,224.00	44,261.00	44,298.00	44,335.00	44,372.00	44,409.00	44,446.00	44,483.00	44,520.00
$153,000	44,557.00	44,594.00	44,631.00	44,668.00	44,705.00	44,742.00	44,779.00	44,816.00	44,853.00	44,890.00
$154,000	44,927.00	44,964.00	45,001.00	45,038.00	45,075.00	45,112.00	45,149.00	45,186.00	45,223.00	45,260.00
$155,000	45,297.00	45,334.00	45,371.00	45,408.00	45,445.00	45,482.00	45,519.00	45,556.00	45,593.00	45,630.00
$156,000	45,667.00	45,704.00	45,741.00	45,778.00	45,815.00	45,852.00	45,889.00	45,926.00	45,963.00	46,000.00
$157,000	46,037.00	46,074.00	46,111.00	46,148.00	46,185.00	46,222.00	46,259.00	46,296.00	46,333.00	46,370.00
$158,000	46,407.00	46,444.00	46,481.00	46,518.00	46,555.00	46,592.00	46,629.00	46,666.00	46,703.00	46,740.00
$159,000	46,777.00	46,814.00	46,851.00	46,888.00	46,925.00	46,962.00	46,999.00	47,036.00	47,073.00	47,110.00
$160,000	47,147.00	47,184.00	47,221.00	47,258.00	47,295.00	47,332.00	47,369.00	47,406.00	47,443.00	47,480.00

TABLE 3: Income tax ready reckoner 2014-15 and 2015-16 (cont)

Taxable Tax liability($)
income($) For the range of Taxable Income $80,000 – $180,000. Does not include the Medicare levy

plus	$0	$100	$200	$300	$400	$500	$600	$700	$800	$900
$161,000	47,517.00	47,554.00	47,591.00	47,628.00	47,665.00	47,702.00	47,739.00	47,776.00	47,813.00	47,850.00
$162,000	47,887.00	47,924.00	47,961.00	47,998.00	48,035.00	48,072.00	48,109.00	48,146.00	48,183.00	48,220.00
$163,000	48,257.00	48,294.00	48,331.00	48,368.00	48,405.00	48,442.00	48,479.00	48,516.00	48,553.00	48,590.00
$164,000	48,627.00	48,664.00	48,701.00	48,738.00	48,775.00	48,812.00	48,849.00	48,886.00	48,923.00	48,960.00
$165,000	48,997.00	49,034.00	49,071.00	49,108.00	49,145.00	49,182.00	49,219.00	49,256.00	49,293.00	49,330.00
$166,000	49,367.00	49,404.00	49,441.00	49,478.00	49,515.00	49,552.00	49,589.00	49,626.00	49,663.00	49,700.00
$167,000	49,737.00	49,774.00	49,811.00	49,848.00	49,885.00	49,922.00	49,959.00	49,996.00	50,033.00	50,070.00
$168,000	50,107.00	50,144.00	50,181.00	50,218.00	50,255.00	50,292.00	50,329.00	50,366.00	50,403.00	50,440.00
$169,000	50,477.00	50,514.00	50,551.00	50,588.00	50,625.00	50,662.00	50,699.00	50,736.00	50,773.00	50,810.00
$170,000	50,847.00	50,884.00	50,921.00	50,958.00	50,995.00	51,032.00	51,069.00	51,106.00	51,143.00	51,180.00
$171,000	51,217.00	51,254.00	51,291.00	51,328.00	51,365.00	51,402.00	51,439.00	51,476.00	51,513.00	51,550.00
$172,000	51,587.00	51,624.00	51,661.00	51,698.00	51,735.00	51,772.00	51,809.00	51,846.00	51,883.00	51,920.00
$173,000	51,957.00	51,994.00	52,031.00	52,068.00	52,105.00	52,142.00	52,179.00	52,216.00	52,253.00	52,290.00
$174,000	52,327.00	52,364.00	52,401.00	52,438.00	52,475.00	52,512.00	52,549.00	52,586.00	52,623.00	52,660.00
$175,000	52,697.00	52,734.00	52,771.00	52,808.00	52,845.00	52,882.00	52,919.00	52,956.00	52,993.00	53,030.00
$176,000	53,067.00	53,104.00	53,141.00	53,178.00	53,215.00	53,252.00	53,289.00	53,326.00	53,363.00	53,400.00
$177,000	53,437.00	53,474.00	53,511.00	53,548.00	53,585.00	53,622.00	53,659.00	53,696.00	53,733.00	53,770.00
$178,000	53,807.00	53,844.00	53,881.00	53,918.00	53,955.00	53,992.00	54,029.00	54,066.00	54,103.00	54,140.00
$179,000	54,177.00	54,214.00	54,251.00	54,288.00	54,325.00	54,362.00	54,399.00	54,436.00	54,473.00	54,510.00
$180,000	54,547.00	54,592.00	54,637.00	54,682.00	54,727.00	54,772.00	54,817.00	54,862.00	54,907.00	54,952.00

Part over $100 The figures in this sub-table may be used for incomes from $67,000 to $180,000

plus	$0	$1	$2	$3	$4	$5	$6	$7	$8	$9
$0	$0	$0	$0	$0	$0	$0	$0	$0	$0	$0
$10	3.70	4.07	4.44	4.81	5.18	5.55	5.92	6.29	6.66	7.03
$20	7.40	7.77	8.14	8.51	8.88	9.25	9.62	9.99	10.36	10.73
$30	11.10	11.47	11.84	12.21	12.58	12.95	13.32	13.69	14.06	14.43
$40	14.80	15.17	15.54	15.91	16.28	16.65	17.02	17.39	17.76	18.13
$50	18.50	18.87	19.24	19.61	19.98	20.35	20.72	21.09	21.46	21.83
$60	22.20	22.57	22.94	23.31	23.68	24.05	24.42	24.79	25.16	25.53
$70	25.90	26.27	26.64	27.01	27.38	27.75	28.12	28.49	28.86	29.23
$80	29.60	29.97	30.34	30.71	31.08	31.45	31.82	32.19	32.56	32.93
$90	33.30	33.67	34.04	34.41	34.78	35.15	35.52	35.89	36.26	36.63

*Because the low income tax offset phases out completely at $66,667 for taxable income values above this figure use Table 3. For taxable income figures below $66,667 use Table 2.

**To calculate the tax payable on Taxable incomes above $180,000 add 45c for every dollar of taxable income over $180,000 to $54,547.

3.012   INCOME TAX READY RECKONER WITH LITO
2014-15 & 2015-16

This income tax ready reckoner can be used to calculate a resident's tax liability for 2014-15 with the Low Income Tax Offset (LITO). For a reduction in PAYG see 5.661.

A resident taxpayer whose taxable income is below a maximum of $66,667 is entitled to a LITO of up to $445 in 2014-15 and 2015-16.

Low Income Tax Offset	
Up to $37,000	flat $445
$37,000 – $66,667	$445 less 1.5% of part over $37,000
$66,667 and over	Nil

TABLE 1: Income tax ready reckoner 2014-15 and 2015-16 including Low Income Tax Offset only ($445)

For range of taxable income $15,000 – $30,000. This table does not include the Medicare levy.

Taxable income($) plus	Tax liability($) $0	$100	$200	$300	$400	$500	$600	$700	$800	$900
$17,000	(445.00)	(445.00)	(445.00)	(445.00)	(445.00)	(445.00)	(445.00)	(445.00)	(445.00)	(445.00)
$18,000	(445.00)	(445.00)	(445.00)	(426.00)	(407.00)	(388.00)	(369.00)	(350.00)	(331.00)	(312.00)
$19,000	(293.00)	(274.00)	(255.00)	(236.00)	(217.00)	(198.00)	(179.00)	(160.00)	(141.00)	(122.00)
$20,000	(103.00)	(84.00)	(65.00)	(46.00)	(27.00)	(8.00)	11.00	30.00	49.00	68.00
$21,000	87.00	106.00	125.00	144.00	163.00	182.00	201.00	220.00	239.00	258.00
$22,000	277.00	296.00	315.00	334.00	353.00	372.00	391.00	410.00	429.00	448.00
$23,000	467.00	486.00	505.00	524.00	543.00	562.00	581.00	600.00	619.00	638.00
$24,000	657.00	676.00	695.00	714.00	733.00	752.00	771.00	790.00	809.00	828.00
$25,000	847.00	866.00	885.00	904.00	923.00	942.00	961.00	980.00	999.00	1,018.00
$26,000	1,037.00	1,056.00	1,075.00	1,094.00	1,113.00	1,132.00	1,151.00	1,170.00	1,189.00	1,208.00
$27,000	1,227.00	1,246.00	1,265.00	1,284.00	1,303.00	1,322.00	1,341.00	1,360.00	1,379.00	1,398.00
$28,000	1,417.00	1,436.00	1,455.00	1,474.00	1,493.00	1,512.00	1,531.00	1,550.00	1,569.00	1,588.00
$29,000	1,607.00	1,626.00	1,645.00	1,664.00	1,683.00	1,702.00	1,721.00	1,740.00	1,759.00	1,778.00
$30,000	1,797.00	1,816.00	1,835.00	1,854.00	1,873.00	1,892.00	1,911.00	1,930.00	1,949.00	1,968.00
$31,000	1,987.00	2,006.00	2,025.00	2,044.00	2,063.00	2,082.00	2,101.00	2,120.00	2,139.00	2,158.00
$32,000	2,177.00	2,196.00	2,215.00	2,234.00	2,253.00	2,272.00	2,291.00	2,310.00	2,329.00	2,348.00
$33,000	2,367.00	2,386.00	2,405.00	2,424.00	2,443.00	2,462.00	2,481.00	2,500.00	2,519.00	2,538.00
$34,000	2,557.00	2,576.00	2,595.00	2,614.00	2,633.00	2,652.00	2,671.00	2,690.00	2,709.00	2,728.00
$35,000	2,747.00	2,766.00	2,785.00	2,804.00	2,823.00	2,842.00	2,861.00	2,880.00	2,899.00	2,918.00
$36,000	2,937.00	2,956.00	2,975.00	2,994.00	3,013.00	3,032.00	3,051.00	3,070.00	3,089.00	3,108.00
$37,000	3,127.00									

TABLE 1: Income tax ready reckoner 2014-15 and 2015-16 including Low Income Tax Offset only ($445) (cont)

Part over $100 (When income earned is over $18,200)

plus	$0	$1	$2	$3	$4	$5	$6	$7	$8	$9
$0	0.00	0.19	0.38	0.57	0.76	0.95	1.14	1.33	1.52	1.71
$10	1.90	2.09	2.28	2.47	2.66	2.85	3.04	3.23	3.42	3.61
$20	3.80	3.99	4.18	4.37	4.56	4.75	4.94	5.13	5.32	5.51
$30	5.70	5.89	6.08	6.27	6.46	6.65	6.84	7.03	7.22	7.41
$40	7.60	7.79	7.98	8.17	8.36	8.55	8.74	8.93	9.12	9.31
$50	9.50	9.69	9.88	10.07	10.26	10.45	10.64	10.83	11.02	11.21
$60	11.40	11.59	11.78	11.97	12.16	12.35	12.54	12.73	12.92	13.11
$70	13.30	13.49	13.68	13.87	14.06	14.25	14.44	14.63	14.82	15.01
$80	15.20	15.39	15.58	15.77	15.96	16.15	16.34	16.53	16.72	16.91
$90	17.10	17.29	17.48	17.67	17.86	18.05	18.24	18.43	18.62	18.81

TABLE 2: Income tax ready reckoner 2014-15 and 2015-16 including Low Income Tax Offset only (less than $445)

For range of taxable income $37,000 – $66,667, LITO phases down from $445 to nil.
This table does not include the Medicare levy.

Taxable income($)	Tax liability($)									
plus	$0	$100	$200	$300	$400	$500	$600	$700	$800	$900
$37,000	3,127.00	3,161.00	3,195.00	3,229.00	3,263.00	3,297.00	3,331.00	3,365.00	3,399.00	3,433.00
$38,000	3,467.00	3,501.00	3,535.00	3,569.00	3,603.00	3,637.00	3,671.00	3,705.00	3,739.00	3,773.00
$39,000	3,807.00	3,841.00	3,875.00	3,909.00	3,943.00	3,977.00	4,011.00	4,045.00	4,079.00	4,113.00
$40,000	4,147.00	4,181.00	4,215.00	4,249.00	4,283.00	4,317.00	4,351.00	4,385.00	4,419.00	4,453.00
$41,000	4,487.00	4,521.00	4,555.00	4,589.00	4,623.00	4,657.00	4,691.00	4,725.00	4,759.00	4,793.00
$42,000	4,827.00	4,861.00	4,895.00	4,929.00	4,963.00	4,997.00	5,031.00	5,065.00	5,099.00	5,133.00
$43,000	5,167.00	5,201.00	5,235.00	5,269.00	5,303.00	5,337.00	5,371.00	5,405.00	5,439.00	5,473.00
$44,000	5,507.00	5,541.00	5,575.00	5,609.00	5,643.00	5,677.00	5,711.00	5,745.00	5,779.00	5,813.00
$45,000	5,847.00	5,881.00	5,915.00	5,949.00	5,983.00	6,017.00	6,051.00	6,085.00	6,119.00	6,153.00
$46,000	6,187.00	6,221.00	6,255.00	6,289.00	6,323.00	6,357.00	6,391.00	6,425.00	6,459.00	6,493.00
$47,000	6,527.00	6,561.00	6,595.00	6,629.00	6,663.00	6,697.00	6,731.00	6,765.00	6,799.00	6,833.00
$48,000	6,867.00	6,901.00	6,935.00	6,969.00	7,003.00	7,037.00	7,071.00	7,105.00	7,139.00	7,173.00
$49,000	7,207.00	7,241.00	7,275.00	7,309.00	7,343.00	7,377.00	7,411.00	7,445.00	7,479.00	7,513.00
$50,000	7,547.00	7,581.00	7,615.00	7,649.00	7,683.00	7,717.00	7,751.00	7,785.00	7,819.00	7,853.00
$51,000	7,887.00	7,921.00	7,955.00	7,989.00	8,023.00	8,057.00	8,091.00	8,125.00	8,159.00	8,193.00
$52,000	8,227.00	8,261.00	8,295.00	8,329.00	8,363.00	8,397.00	8,431.00	8,465.00	8,499.00	8,533.00
$53,000	8,567.00	8,601.00	8,635.00	8,669.00	8,703.00	8,737.00	8,771.00	8,805.00	8,839.00	8,873.00
$54,000	8,907.00	8,941.00	8,975.00	9,009.00	9,043.00	9,077.00	9,111.00	9,145.00	9,179.00	9,213.00
$55,000	9,247.00	9,281.00	9,315.00	9,349.00	9,383.00	9,417.00	9,451.00	9,485.00	9,519.00	9,553.00
$56,000	9,587.00	9,621.00	9,655.00	9,689.00	9,723.00	9,757.00	9,791.00	9,825.00	9,859.00	9,893.00
$57,000	9,927.00	9,961.00	9,995.00	10,029.00	10,063.00	10,097.00	10,131.00	10,165.00	10,199.00	10,233.00

TABLE 2: Income tax ready reckoner 2014-15 and 2015-16 including Low Income Tax Offset only (less than $445) (cont)

For range of taxable income $37,000 – $66,667, LITO phases down from $445 to nil.
This table does not include the Medicare levy.

Taxable income($)	Tax liability($)									
plus	$0	$100	$200	$300	$400	$500	$600	$700	$800	$900
$58,000	10,267.00	10,301.00	10,335.00	10,369.00	10,403.00	10,437.00	10,471.00	10,505.00	10,539.00	10,573.00
$59,000	10,607.00	10,641.00	10,675.00	10,709.00	10,743.00	10,777.00	10,811.00	10,845.00	10,879.00	10,913.00
$60,000	10,947.00	10,981.00	11,015.00	11,049.00	11,083.00	11,117.00	11,151.00	11,185.00	11,219.00	11,253.00
$61,000	11,287.00	11,321.00	11,355.00	11,389.00	11,423.00	11,457.00	11,491.00	11,525.00	11,559.00	11,593.00
$62,000	11,627.00	11,661.00	11,695.00	11,729.00	11,763.00	11,797.00	11,831.00	11,865.00	11,899.00	11,933.00
$63,000	11,967.00	12,001.00	12,035.00	12,069.00	12,103.00	12,137.00	12,171.00	12,205.00	12,239.00	12,273.00
$64,000	12,307.00	12,341.00	12,375.00	12,409.00	12,443.00	12,477.00	12,511.00	12,545.00	12,579.00	12,613.00
$65,000	12,647.00	12,681.00	12,715.00	12,749.00	12,783.00	12,817.00	12,851.00	12,885.00	12,919.00	12,953.00
$66,000	12,987.00	13,021.00	13,055.00	13,089.00	13,123.00	13,157.00	13,191.00			

Part over $100

plus	$0	$1	$2	$3	$4	$5	$6	$7	$8	$9
$0	0.00	0.34	0.68	1.02	1.36	1.70	2.04	2.38	2.72	3.06
$10	3.40	3.74	4.08	4.42	4.76	5.10	5.44	5.78	6.12	6.46
$20	6.80	7.14	7.48	7.82	8.16	8.50	8.84	9.18	9.52	9.86
$30	10.20	10.54	10.88	11.22	11.56	11.90	12.24	12.58	12.92	13.26
$40	13.60	13.94	14.28	14.62	14.96	15.30	15.64	15.98	16.32	16.66
$50	17.00	17.34	17.68	18.02	18.36	18.70	19.04	19.38	19.72	20.06
$60	20.40	20.74	21.08	21.42	21.76	22.10	22.44	22.78	23.12	23.46
$70	23.80	24.14	24.48	24.82	25.16	25.50	25.84	26.18	26.52	26.86
$80	27.20	27.54	27.88	28.22	28.56	28.90	29.24	29.58	29.92	30.26
$90	30.60	30.94	31.28	31.62	31.96	32.30	32.64	32.98	33.32	33.66

TABLE 3: Income tax ready reckoner 2014-15 and 2015-16 including Low Income Tax Offset only (less than $445)

For range of taxable income $66,667 – $180,000 when LITO phases out to nil.
This table does not include the Medicare levy.

Taxable income($)	Tax liability($)									
plus	$0	$100	$200	$300	$400	$500	$600	$700	$800	$900
$66,000	-	-	-	-	-	-	13,191.00	13,224.50	13,257.00	13,289.50
$67,000	13,322.00	13,354.50	13,387.00	13,419.50	13,452.00	13,484.50	13,517.00	13,549.50	13,582.00	13,614.50
$68,000	13,647.00	13,679.50	13,712.00	13,744.50	13,777.00	13,809.50	13,842.00	13,874.50	13,907.00	13,939.50
$69,000	13,972.00	14,004.50	14,037.00	14,069.50	14,102.00	14,134.50	14,167.00	14,199.50	14,232.00	14,264.50
$70,000	14,297.00	14,329.50	14,362.00	14,394.50	14,427.00	14,459.50	14,492.00	14,524.50	14,557.00	14,589.50
$71,000	14,622.00	14,654.50	14,687.00	14,719.50	14,752.00	14,784.50	14,817.00	14,849.50	14,882.00	14,914.50
$72,000	14,947.00	14,979.50	15,012.00	15,044.50	15,077.00	15,109.50	15,142.00	15,174.50	15,207.00	15,239.50
$73,000	15,272.00	15,304.50	15,337.00	15,369.50	15,402.00	15,434.50	15,467.00	15,499.50	15,532.00	15,564.50

TABLE 3: Income tax ready reckoner 2014-15 and 2015-16 including Low Income Tax Offset only (less than $445) (cont)

For range of taxable income $66,667 – $180,000 when LITO phases out to nil.
This table does not include the Medicare levy.

Taxable income($)	Tax liability($)									
plus	$0	$100	$200	$300	$400	$500	$600	$700	$800	$900
$74,000	15,597.00	15,629.50	15,662.00	15,694.50	15,727.00	15,759.50	15,792.00	15,824.50	15,857.00	15,889.50
$75,000	15,922.00	15,954.50	15,987.00	16,019.50	16,052.00	16,084.50	16,117.00	16,149.50	16,182.00	16,214.50
$76,000	16,247.00	16,279.50	16,312.00	16,344.50	16,377.00	16,409.50	16,442.00	16,474.50	16,507.00	16,539.50
$77,000	16,572.00	16,604.50	16,637.00	16,669.50	16,702.00	16,734.50	16,767.00	16,799.50	16,832.00	16,864.50
$78,000	16,897.00	16,929.50	16,962.00	16,994.50	17,027.00	17,059.50	17,092.00	17,124.50	17,157.00	17,189.50
$79,000	17,222.00	17,254.50	17,287.00	17,319.50	17,352.00	17,384.50	17,417.00	17,449.50	17,482.00	17,514.50
$80,000	17,547.00	-	-	-	-	-	-	-	-	-

Part over $100   The figures in this sub-table may be used for incomes from $67,000 to $180,000

plus	$0	$1	$2	$3	$4	$5	$6	$7	$8	$9
$0	0.00	0.33	0.65	0.98	1.30	1.63	1.95	2.28	2.60	2.93
$10	3.40	3.58	3.90	4.23	4.55	4.88	5.20	5.53	5.85	6.18
$20	6.80	6.83	7.15	7.48	7.80	8.13	8.45	8.78	9.10	9.43
$30	10.20	10.08	10.40	10.73	11.05	11.38	11.70	12.03	12.35	12.68
$40	13.60	13.33	13.65	13.98	14.30	14.63	14.95	15.28	15.60	15.93
$50	17.00	16.58	16.90	17.23	17.55	17.88	18.20	18.53	18.85	19.18
$60	20.40	19.83	20.15	20.48	20.80	21.13	21.45	21.78	22.10	22.43
$70	23.80	23.08	23.40	23.73	24.05	24.38	24.70	25.03	25.35	25.68
$80	27.20	26.33	26.65	26.98	27.30	27.63	27.95	28.28	28.60	28.93
$90	30.60	29.58	29.90	30.23	30.55	30.88	31.20	31.53	31.85	32.18

TABLE 4: Income tax ready reckoner 2014-15 and 2015-16 including Low Income Tax Offset only (less than $445)

For range of taxable income $80,000 – $180,000 when LITO phases out to nil.
This table does not include the Medicare levy.

Taxable income($)	Tax liability($)									
plus	$0	$100	$200	$300	$400	$500	$600	$700	$800	$900
$80,000	17,547.00	17,584.00	17,621.00	17,658.00	17,695.00	17,732.00	17,769.00	17,806.00	17,843.00	17,880.00
$81,000	17,917.00	17,954.00	17,991.00	18,028.00	18,065.00	18,102.00	18,139.00	18,176.00	18,213.00	18,250.00
$82,000	18,287.00	18,324.00	18,361.00	18,398.00	18,435.00	18,472.00	18,509.00	18,546.00	18,583.00	18,620.00
$83,000	18,657.00	18,694.00	18,731.00	18,768.00	18,805.00	18,842.00	18,879.00	18,916.00	18,953.00	18,990.00
$84,000	19,027.00	19,064.00	19,101.00	19,138.00	19,175.00	19,212.00	19,249.00	19,286.00	19,323.00	19,360.00
$85,000	19,397.00	19,434.00	19,471.00	19,508.00	19,545.00	19,582.00	19,619.00	19,656.00	19,693.00	19,730.00
$86,000	19,767.00	19,804.00	19,841.00	19,878.00	19,915.00	19,952.00	19,989.00	20,026.00	20,063.00	20,100.00
$87,000	20,137.00	20,174.00	20,211.00	20,248.00	20,285.00	20,322.00	20,359.00	20,396.00	20,433.00	20,470.00
$88,000	20,507.00	20,544.00	20,581.00	20,618.00	20,655.00	20,692.00	20,729.00	20,766.00	20,803.00	20,840.00

TABLE 4: Income tax ready reckoner 2014-15 and 2015-16 including Low Income Tax Offset only (less than $445) (cont)

For range of taxable income $80,000 – $180,000 when LITO phases out to nil.
This table does not include the Medicare levy.

Taxable income($) plus	Tax liability($) $0	$100	$200	$300	$400	$500	$600	$700	$800	$900
$89,000	20,877.00	20,914.00	20,951.00	20,988.00	21,025.00	21,062.00	21,099.00	21,136.00	21,173.00	21,210.00
$90,000	21,247.00	21,284.00	21,321.00	21,358.00	21,395.00	21,432.00	21,469.00	21,506.00	21,543.00	21,580.00
$91,000	21,617.00	21,654.00	21,691.00	21,728.00	21,765.00	21,802.00	21,839.00	21,876.00	21,913.00	21,950.00
$92,000	21,987.00	22,024.00	22,061.00	22,098.00	22,135.00	22,172.00	22,209.00	22,246.00	22,283.00	22,320.00
$93,000	22,357.00	22,394.00	22,431.00	22,468.00	22,505.00	22,542.00	22,579.00	22,616.00	22,653.00	22,690.00
$94,000	22,727.00	22,764.00	22,801.00	22,838.00	22,875.00	22,912.00	22,949.00	22,986.00	23,023.00	23,060.00
$95,000	23,097.00	23,134.00	23,171.00	23,208.00	23,245.00	23,282.00	23,319.00	23,356.00	23,393.00	23,430.00
$96,000	23,467.00	23,504.00	23,541.00	23,578.00	23,615.00	23,652.00	23,689.00	23,726.00	23,763.00	23,800.00
$97,000	23,837.00	23,874.00	23,911.00	23,948.00	23,985.00	24,022.00	24,059.00	24,096.00	24,133.00	24,170.00
$98,000	24,207.00	24,244.00	24,281.00	24,318.00	24,355.00	24,392.00	24,429.00	24,466.00	24,503.00	24,540.00
$99,000	24,577.00	24,614.00	24,651.00	24,688.00	24,725.00	24,762.00	24,799.00	24,836.00	24,873.00	24,910.00
$100,000	24,947.00	24,984.00	25,021.00	25,058.00	25,095.00	25,132.00	25,169.00	25,206.00	25,243.00	25,280.00
$101,000	25,317.00	25,354.00	25,391.00	25,428.00	25,465.00	25,502.00	25,539.00	25,576.00	25,613.00	25,650.00
$102,000	25,687.00	25,724.00	25,761.00	25,798.00	25,835.00	25,872.00	25,909.00	25,946.00	25,983.00	26,020.00
$103,000	26,057.00	26,094.00	26,131.00	26,168.00	26,205.00	26,242.00	26,279.00	26,316.00	26,353.00	26,390.00
$104,000	26,427.00	26,464.00	26,501.00	26,538.00	26,575.00	26,612.00	26,649.00	26,686.00	26,723.00	26,760.00
$105,000	26,797.00	26,834.00	26,871.00	26,908.00	26,945.00	26,982.00	27,019.00	27,056.00	27,093.00	27,130.00
$106,000	27,167.00	27,204.00	27,241.00	27,278.00	27,315.00	27,352.00	27,389.00	27,426.00	27,463.00	27,500.00
$107,000	27,537.00	27,574.00	27,611.00	27,648.00	27,685.00	27,722.00	27,759.00	27,796.00	27,833.00	27,870.00
$108,000	27,907.00	27,944.00	27,981.00	28,018.00	28,055.00	28,092.00	28,129.00	28,166.00	28,203.00	28,240.00
$109,000	28,277.00	28,314.00	28,351.00	28,388.00	28,425.00	28,462.00	28,499.00	28,536.00	28,573.00	28,610.00
$110,000	28,647.00	28,684.00	28,721.00	28,758.00	28,795.00	28,832.00	28,869.00	28,906.00	28,943.00	28,980.00
$111,000	29,017.00	29,054.00	29,091.00	29,128.00	29,165.00	29,202.00	29,239.00	29,276.00	29,313.00	29,350.00
$112,000	29,387.00	29,424.00	29,461.00	29,498.00	29,535.00	29,572.00	29,609.00	29,646.00	29,683.00	29,720.00
$113,000	29,757.00	29,794.00	29,831.00	29,868.00	29,905.00	29,942.00	29,979.00	30,016.00	30,053.00	30,090.00
$114,000	30,127.00	30,164.00	30,201.00	30,238.00	30,275.00	30,312.00	30,349.00	30,386.00	30,423.00	30,460.00
$115,000	30,497.00	30,534.00	30,571.00	30,608.00	30,645.00	30,682.00	30,719.00	30,756.00	30,793.00	30,830.00
$116,000	30,867.00	30,904.00	30,941.00	30,978.00	31,015.00	31,052.00	31,089.00	31,126.00	31,163.00	31,200.00
$117,000	31,237.00	31,274.00	31,311.00	31,348.00	31,385.00	31,422.00	31,459.00	31,496.00	31,533.00	31,570.00
$118,000	31,607.00	31,644.00	31,681.00	31,718.00	31,755.00	31,792.00	31,829.00	31,866.00	31,903.00	31,940.00
$119,000	31,977.00	32,014.00	32,051.00	32,088.00	32,125.00	32,162.00	32,199.00	32,236.00	32,273.00	32,310.00
$120,000	32,347.00	32,384.00	32,421.00	32,458.00	32,495.00	32,532.00	32,569.00	32,606.00	32,643.00	32,680.00
$121,000	32,717.00	32,754.00	32,791.00	32,828.00	32,865.00	32,902.00	32,939.00	32,976.00	33,013.00	33,050.00
$122,000	33,087.00	33,124.00	33,161.00	33,198.00	33,235.00	33,272.00	33,309.00	33,346.00	33,383.00	33,420.00
$123,000	33,457.00	33,494.00	33,531.00	33,568.00	33,605.00	33,642.00	33,679.00	33,716.00	33,753.00	33,790.00
$124,000	33,827.00	33,864.00	33,901.00	33,938.00	33,975.00	34,012.00	34,049.00	34,086.00	34,123.00	34,160.00

TABLE 4: Income tax ready reckoner 2014-15 and 2015-16 including Low Income Tax Offset only (less than $445) (cont)

For range of taxable income $80,000 – $180,000 when LITO phases out to nil.
This table does not include the Medicare levy.

Taxable income($) plus	Tax liability($) $0	$100	$200	$300	$400	$500	$600	$700	$800	$900
$125,000	34,197.00	34,234.00	34,271.00	34,308.00	34,345.00	34,382.00	34,419.00	34,456.00	34,493.00	34,530.00
$126,000	34,567.00	34,604.00	34,641.00	34,678.00	34,715.00	34,752.00	34,789.00	34,826.00	34,863.00	34,900.00
$127,000	34,937.00	34,974.00	35,011.00	35,048.00	35,085.00	35,122.00	35,159.00	35,196.00	35,233.00	35,270.00
$128,000	35,307.00	35,344.00	35,381.00	35,418.00	35,455.00	35,492.00	35,529.00	35,566.00	35,603.00	35,640.00
$129,000	35,677.00	35,714.00	35,751.00	35,788.00	35,825.00	35,862.00	35,899.00	35,936.00	35,973.00	36,010.00
$130,000	36,047.00	36,084.00	36,121.00	36,158.00	36,195.00	36,232.00	36,269.00	36,306.00	36,343.00	36,380.00
$131,000	36,417.00	36,454.00	36,491.00	36,528.00	36,565.00	36,602.00	36,639.00	36,676.00	36,713.00	36,750.00
$132,000	36,787.00	36,824.00	36,861.00	36,898.00	36,935.00	36,972.00	37,009.00	37,046.00	37,083.00	37,120.00
$133,000	37,157.00	37,194.00	37,231.00	37,268.00	37,305.00	37,342.00	37,379.00	37,416.00	37,453.00	37,490.00
$134,000	37,527.00	37,564.00	37,601.00	37,638.00	37,675.00	37,712.00	37,749.00	37,786.00	37,823.00	37,860.00
$135,000	37,897.00	37,934.00	37,971.00	38,008.00	38,045.00	38,082.00	38,119.00	38,156.00	38,193.00	38,230.00
$136,000	38,267.00	38,304.00	38,341.00	38,378.00	38,415.00	38,452.00	38,489.00	38,526.00	38,563.00	38,600.00
$137,000	38,637.00	38,674.00	38,711.00	38,748.00	38,785.00	38,822.00	38,859.00	38,896.00	38,933.00	38,970.00
$138,000	39,007.00	39,044.00	39,081.00	39,118.00	39,155.00	39,192.00	39,229.00	39,266.00	39,303.00	39,340.00
$139,000	39,377.00	39,414.00	39,451.00	39,488.00	39,525.00	39,562.00	39,599.00	39,636.00	39,673.00	39,710.00
$140,000	39,747.00	39,784.00	39,821.00	39,858.00	39,895.00	39,932.00	39,969.00	40,006.00	40,043.00	40,080.00
$141,000	40,117.00	40,154.00	40,191.00	40,228.00	40,265.00	40,302.00	40,339.00	40,376.00	40,413.00	40,450.00
$142,000	40,487.00	40,524.00	40,561.00	40,598.00	40,635.00	40,672.00	40,709.00	40,746.00	40,783.00	40,820.00
$143,000	40,857.00	40,894.00	40,931.00	40,968.00	41,005.00	41,042.00	41,079.00	41,116.00	41,153.00	41,190.00
$144,000	41,227.00	41,264.00	41,301.00	41,338.00	41,375.00	41,412.00	41,449.00	41,486.00	41,523.00	41,560.00
$145,000	41,597.00	41,634.00	41,671.00	41,708.00	41,745.00	41,782.00	41,819.00	41,856.00	41,893.00	41,930.00
$146,000	41,967.00	42,004.00	42,041.00	42,078.00	42,115.00	42,152.00	42,189.00	42,226.00	42,263.00	42,300.00
$147,000	42,337.00	42,374.00	42,411.00	42,448.00	42,485.00	42,522.00	42,559.00	42,596.00	42,633.00	42,670.00
$148,000	42,707.00	42,744.00	42,781.00	42,818.00	42,855.00	42,892.00	42,929.00	42,966.00	43,003.00	43,040.00
$149,000	43,077.00	43,114.00	43,151.00	43,188.00	43,225.00	43,262.00	43,299.00	43,336.00	43,373.00	43,410.00
$150,000	43,447.00	43,484.00	43,521.00	43,558.00	43,595.00	43,632.00	43,669.00	43,706.00	43,743.00	43,780.00
$151,000	43,817.00	43,854.00	43,891.00	43,928.00	43,965.00	44,002.00	44,039.00	44,076.00	44,113.00	44,150.00
$152,000	44,187.00	44,224.00	44,261.00	44,298.00	44,335.00	44,372.00	44,409.00	44,446.00	44,483.00	44,520.00
$153,000	44,557.00	44,594.00	44,631.00	44,668.00	44,705.00	44,742.00	44,779.00	44,816.00	44,853.00	44,890.00
$154,000	44,927.00	44,964.00	45,001.00	45,038.00	45,075.00	45,112.00	45,149.00	45,186.00	45,223.00	45,260.00
$155,000	45,297.00	45,334.00	45,371.00	45,408.00	45,445.00	45,482.00	45,519.00	45,556.00	45,593.00	45,630.00
$156,000	45,667.00	45,704.00	45,741.00	45,778.00	45,815.00	45,852.00	45,889.00	45,926.00	45,963.00	46,000.00
$157,000	46,037.00	46,074.00	46,111.00	46,148.00	46,185.00	46,222.00	46,259.00	46,296.00	46,333.00	46,370.00
$158,000	46,407.00	46,444.00	46,481.00	46,518.00	46,555.00	46,592.00	46,629.00	46,666.00	46,703.00	46,740.00
$159,000	46,777.00	46,814.00	46,851.00	46,888.00	46,925.00	46,962.00	46,999.00	47,036.00	47,073.00	47,110.00
$160,000	47,147.00	47,184.00	47,221.00	47,258.00	47,295.00	47,332.00	47,369.00	47,406.00	47,443.00	47,480.00

TABLE 4: Income tax ready reckoner 2014-15 and 2015-16 including Low Income Tax Offset only (less than $445) (cont)

For range of taxable income $80,000 – $180,000 when LITO phases out to nil.
This table does not include the Medicare levy.

Taxable income($) Tax liability($) plus	$0	$100	$200	$300	$400	$500	$600	$700	$800	$900
$161,000	47,517.00	47,554.00	47,591.00	47,628.00	47,665.00	47,702.00	47,739.00	47,776.00	47,813.00	47,850.00
$162,000	47,887.00	47,924.00	47,961.00	47,998.00	48,035.00	48,072.00	48,109.00	48,146.00	48,183.00	48,220.00
$163,000	48,257.00	48,294.00	48,331.00	48,368.00	48,405.00	48,442.00	48,479.00	48,516.00	48,553.00	48,590.00
$164,000	48,627.00	48,664.00	48,701.00	48,738.00	48,775.00	48,812.00	48,849.00	48,886.00	48,923.00	48,960.00
$165,000	48,997.00	49,034.00	49,071.00	49,108.00	49,145.00	49,182.00	49,219.00	49,256.00	49,293.00	49,330.00
$166,000	49,367.00	49,404.00	49,441.00	49,478.00	49,515.00	49,552.00	49,589.00	49,626.00	49,663.00	49,700.00
$167,000	49,737.00	49,774.00	49,811.00	49,848.00	49,885.00	49,922.00	49,959.00	49,996.00	50,033.00	50,070.00
$168,000	50,107.00	50,144.00	50,181.00	50,218.00	50,255.00	50,292.00	50,329.00	50,366.00	50,403.00	50,440.00
$169,000	50,477.00	50,514.00	50,551.00	50,588.00	50,625.00	50,662.00	50,699.00	50,736.00	50,773.00	50,810.00
$170,000	50,847.00	50,884.00	50,921.00	50,958.00	50,995.00	51,032.00	51,069.00	51,106.00	51,143.00	51,180.00
$171,000	51,217.00	51,254.00	51,291.00	51,328.00	51,365.00	51,402.00	51,439.00	51,476.00	51,513.00	51,550.00
$172,000	51,587.00	51,624.00	51,661.00	51,698.00	51,735.00	51,772.00	51,809.00	51,846.00	51,883.00	51,920.00
$173,000	51,957.00	51,994.00	52,031.00	52,068.00	52,105.00	52,142.00	52,179.00	52,216.00	52,253.00	52,290.00
$174,000	52,327.00	52,364.00	52,401.00	52,438.00	52,475.00	52,512.00	52,549.00	52,586.00	52,623.00	52,660.00
$175,000	52,697.00	52,734.00	52,771.00	52,808.00	52,845.00	52,882.00	52,919.00	52,956.00	52,993.00	53,030.00
$176,000	53,067.00	53,104.00	53,141.00	53,178.00	53,215.00	53,252.00	53,289.00	53,326.00	53,363.00	53,400.00
$177,000	53,437.00	53,474.00	53,511.00	53,548.00	53,585.00	53,622.00	53,659.00	53,696.00	53,733.00	53,770.00
$178,000	53,807.00	53,844.00	53,881.00	53,918.00	53,955.00	53,992.00	54,029.00	54,066.00	54,103.00	54,140.00
$179,000	54,177.00	54,214.00	54,251.00	54,288.00	54,325.00	54,362.00	54,399.00	54,436.00	54,473.00	54,510.00
$180,000	54,547.00	54,592.00	54,637.00	54,682.00	54,727.00	54,772.00	54,817.00	54,862.00	54,907.00	54,952.00

Part over $100   The figures in this sub-table may be used for incomes from $67,000 to $180,000

plus	$0	$1	$2	$3	$4	$5	$6	$7	$8	$9
$0	0.00	0.37	0.74	1.11	1.48	1.85	2.22	2.59	2.96	3.33
$10	3.70	4.07	4.44	4.81	5.18	5.55	5.92	6.29	6.66	7.03
$20	7.40	7.77	8.14	8.51	8.88	9.25	9.62	9.99	10.36	10.73
$30	11.10	11.47	11.84	12.21	12.58	12.95	13.32	13.69	14.06	14.43
$40	14.80	15.17	15.54	15.91	16.28	16.65	17.02	17.39	17.76	18.13
$50	18.50	18.87	19.24	19.61	19.98	20.35	20.72	21.09	21.46	21.83
$60	22.20	22.57	22.94	23.31	23.68	24.05	24.42	24.79	25.16	25.53
$70	25.90	26.27	26.64	27.01	27.38	27.75	28.12	28.49	28.86	29.23
$80	29.60	29.97	30.34	30.71	31.08	31.45	31.82	32.19	32.56	32.93
$90	33.30	33.67	34.04	34.41	34.78	35.15	35.52	35.89	36.26	36.63

* Because the low income tax offset phases out completely at $66,667 for taxable income values above this figure use Table 3. For Taxable income figures below $66,667 use Table 2.
** To calculate the tax payable on Taxable incomes above $180,000 add 47c for every dollar of taxable income over $180,000 to $54,547.

3.030   REDUCED TAX-FREE THRESHOLD

The tax-free threshold of $18,200 is reduced in an income year when a taxpayer becomes or ceases to be a resident of Australia.

Reducing a taxpayer's tax-free threshold means additional tax is charged at 19c in the dollar on the difference between the reduced tax-free threshold and $18,200 (ie. the taxable income at which tax normally starts to be payable).

NOTE: The net tax payable by low income earners is reduced by the low income tax offset of $445 in 2014-15. The Medicare levy is not affected by a tax-free threshold reduction (see 3.050).

3.032   BECOMING/CEASING TO BE A RESIDENT

Non-residents are not entitled to any tax-free threshold. The amount of the tax-free threshold for a taxpayer who became, or ceased to be, a resident during the income year is calculated according to the following formula:

Tax-free threshold = $13,464 + ($4,736 x resident months / 12)

where 'resident months' is the number of part or complete months after the person arrived in Australia, up to 30 June in that year. For a taxpayer who ceased residency, it includes the month the person left Australia.

NOTE: The Tax Office administratively apportions the LITO for part year residents. The LITO only applies to individual resident taxpayers and some trusts assessed under s98 ITAA36 (see s159H and s159N ITAA36).

3.040   INCOME DERIVED BY MINORS

The 'unearned income' of minors (ie. persons under 18 years of age) is classed as 'eligible income' and taxed at punitive rates (Division 6AA ITAA36) as shown in the following tables.

Eligible income	Resident prescribed tax rate applicable (2014-15 and 2015-16)
0 – $416	Nil
$417 – $1,307	66% for amount in excess of $416
$1,308 and over	47% on the entire amount

Eligible income	Non-resident prescribed tax rate applicable (2014-15 and 2015-16)
0 – $416	32.5% on the entire amount
$417 – $663	$135.20 plus 66% for amount in excess of $416
$664 and over	47% on the entire amount

3.041   MINORS NOT AFFECTED

A minor is not liable to prescribed tax rates if any of the following apply:

- income is less than $416
- they are fully employed at the end of the year or in full time employment for at least three months during the year and later in that income year was not in full time education. In both cases, the person must intend to be in a full time occupation for most of the following financial year
- they are entitled to, or in receipt of, one of these Social Security payments:
  - carer allowance
  - disability support pension, or
  - rehabilitation allowance
- they are permanently blind
- they are not dependent on, or residing with, relatives and:

- they are a double orphan, or
- on the basis of a doctor's certificate, it is unlikely (due to permanent disability) the child will engage in a full time occupation.

NOTE: The low income tax offset is not applicable in relation to a minor's eligible income. It still applies to other 'excepted' forms of income earned by the minor (for instance an arm's length salary).

3.042   EXCEPTED INCOME* NOT AFFECTED

The following income is not liable to prescribed tax rates:

- reasonable wages or income from any services rendered, including business or partnership profits
- any pension or other income subject to the PAYG withholding provisions (eg. AUSTUDY)
- income from deceased estates
- income from will (testamentary) trusts
- income from investments made from assets transferred to a minor (or trustee, provided the minor will eventually receive the trust capital):
  - from a public fund for the relief of poverty
  - from winnings in an authorised lottery
  - received directly or indirectly through a trust from investing a court awarded (or 'out of court') settlement or compensation
  - being superannuation proceeds
  - being child support proceeds paid to a trust to facilitate support of the child following family breakdown
- from assets transferred to a minor by a person who received the assets from a deceased estate, provided the transfer to the minor is within three years of death and only if assets are no more than the minor would have received had the person died intestate (ie. if no valid will)
- from property transferred for benefit of a child as part of a legal settlement following family breakdown, and
- income from the investment and reinvestment of any of the above is excepted income

* 'Excepted income' is defined in s102 AE ITAA36.

3.043   CALCULATING TAX ON ELIGIBLE INCOME OF MINORS
FOR 2014-15 AND 2015-16

The income derived by resident minors that is subject to special rules is calculated according to the amount of 'eligible taxable income' received.

- If the eligible taxable income does not exceed the threshold of $416 it is simply subject to normal taxation together with any other taxable income.
- If the eligible taxable income exceeds $416 but does not exceed the upper threshold of $1,307 (for residents), tax on this eligible taxable income component is the greater of:
  - (i)   the tax liability calculated at a rate of 66% on the amount that exceeds $416, and
  - (ii) the difference between the tax liability calculated on the full taxable income and the liability calculated on the full taxable income less the eligible taxable income.
- If the eligible taxable income exceeds $1,307, then tax is paid at the top marginal tax rate (47% in 2014-15 and 2015-16) on the entire eligible taxable income amount over $1,307. Other taxable income is taxed separately at ordinary resident rates.

ELIGIBLE INCOME UNDER $417

(Based on normal personal tax rates – see 3.020.)

A resident minor has taxable income of $18,000 including $400 eligible income.

Since the eligible taxable income is $416 or less the entire taxable income is taxed in the normal marginal tax rates as if the special rules did not apply.

Tax at normal rates on all of the $18,000 taxable income is nil in 2014-15 and 2015-16.

ELIGIBLE INCOME BETWEEN $417 AND $1,307

Eligible taxable income is $816.

A resident minor has income that is made up entirely of eligible income of $816.

No tax is payable on the amount up to $416 but the excess is taxed at the rate of 66%.

Tax liability is ($816 – $416) x 66% = $264.

Eligible taxable income between $417 and $1,307 plus other taxable income.

A resident minor has income that is eligible taxable income of $1,216, and total taxable income of $25,000.

This involves the calculation of the tax associated with the eligible taxable income and the tax associated with the taxable income that remains.

The tax on the eligible taxable income is determined on the basis of the greater amount calculated in (i) and (ii) below.

(i)   Tax liability on the eligible taxable income ($1,216 – $416) x 66% = $528

(ii)   Normal tax on $25,000 = ($25,000 – $18,200) x 19% = $1,292

less: normal tax on ($25,000 – $1,216) = ($23,784 – $18,200) x 19% = $1,060.96

Equals: ($1,292 – $1,060.96) = $231.04

Since (i) is greater than (ii) the tax on the eligible taxable income is $528.

The tax payable on the balance of the taxable income as calculated previously is:

($25,000 – $1,216 – $18,200) x 19% = $1,060.96.

Total tax liability is made up of:

Tax payable on eligible taxable income	$528.00
Tax payable on other taxable income	$1060.96
Total tax liability	$1,588.96

ELIGIBLE INCOME EXCEEDING $1,307

Eligible taxable income exceeding $1,307.

A resident minor in the 2014-15 income year has income that is made up entirely of eligible income of $4,300. The entire amount is taxed at an effective tax rate of 47%. Tax liability is $4,300 x 47% = $2,021.

The low income tax offset is not available in respect of this type of income.

Eligible taxable income exceeding $1,307 plus other taxable income.

A resident minor in the 2014-15 income year has total taxable income of $14,000 of which $5,000 is eligible taxable income.

Since the eligible taxable income exceeds the upper threshold of $1,307 the method of tax calculation involves (as above) the use of a fixed marginal tax rate of 47% (2014-15) on the eligible taxable income and the remainder is taxed at ordinary resident tax rates that includes the lowest income tax threshold of $18,200.

This results in $9,000 being tax-free ($14,000 – $5,000).

Tax on eligible taxable income of $5,000 at 47%	$2,350
Tax on the remaining taxable income is at 0%	$0
Total tax liability = $2,350 + $0	**$2,350**

Medicare levy would not be applicable until the taxpayer exceeded the threshold. (The Medicare levy threshold in 2014-15 is $20,896). The low income tax offset is not available for this type of minors' income.

NOTE: For liability to the Medicare levy see 3.050 to 3.056.

3.044   ARM'S LENGTH RATE

The exceptions to the higher prescribed tax rates only apply if the income received (eg. wages, business income or trust distribution) is not greater than what would have been received at 'arm's length' (eg. a wage paid by someone not related to the minor).

PRESCRIBED TAX RATES COMPARED WITH 'NORMAL' TAX RATES (2014-15)

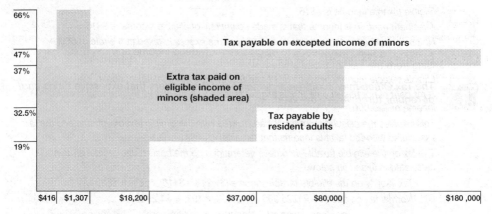

NOTE: The Temporary Budget Repair Levy of 2% for taxpayers in the top tax bracket applies for the 2014-15 to the 2016-17 income years.

3.045   CHILDRENS' BANK ACCOUNTS

Interest on childrens' bank accounts or from investments in a child's name is taxed as childrens' income where the investment or money was given (or gifted) to the child by parents, grandparents or other relatives. The income is usually subject to prescribed higher tax rates (TD 93/148). The rates of tax payable on the interest income will depend upon:

- If the money in the account, or the assets invested, came from certain special sources (ie. excepted income – see 3.042 or the child is an excepted person – see 3.041) excepted from prescribed tax rates: *Child pays the tax at resident individual rates* (see 3.010 and 3.020)

- If the money is really the child's but received in circumstances which do not satisfy the exceptions to prescribed tax rules (see 3.042): *Tax is paid at prescribed (higher) tax rates*, and

- **$1,307 and over:** *All prescribed income is taxed at top marginal tax rate of 47% (for 2014-15 and 2015-16).*

If a child is less than 16 years of age (or turns 16 in a calendar year) and their investment income is greater than $420 per year, the child must quote his or her TFN and date of birth, to prevent TFN withholding tax. If a child is aged over 16 and the investment income is greater than $120 per year, the child must quote his or her TFN to prevent TFN withholding tax.

EXTRACT FROM INCOME TAX RULING IT 2486

Children's savings accounts may be held with a bank, credit union, building society or other financial institution. They may be opened and operated by parents or grandparents and called 'trust accounts' or they may be opened or operated by the children.

Regardless of the name and the type of the account, the essential question that must be asked is: 'Whose money is it?' The answer depends on the facts of each case. If, for example, the money in the account was received by the child as pocket money, birthday or Christmas presents, etc. it should be regarded as the child's money. If the money belongs to the child, and the child's total income from all sources is under $416, no tax is payable and a tax return is not required. If the money really belongs to the parent (ie. the parent provided the money, and the parent may spend it as he or she likes, rather than as the child likes) the parent should pay tax on the interest.

3.046   CHILDREN'S SHARE INVESTMENTS

In order to decide who declares the dividends received or the net capital gain/loss from the sale of shares, you need to determine who rightfully owns and controls the shares, ie. 'whose shares are they?'

If the funds to acquire the shares were provided by a person other than a child and that person makes all decisions in relation to those shares and dividends, then that person is deemed to be the owner of the shares and that person declares any dividend income and capital gain or loss.

If the funds to acquire the shares were from money gifted to or earned by the child, and the investment decisions are made by a third party on behalf of the child, the child is considered to own the shares. The child then needs to disclose the dividend income and all capital gains and losses arising from the sale of those shares.

The Tax Office may audit the arrangement if it considers that excessive funds and/ or regular turnover are involved.

Julie purchased 1,000 shares of a publicly listed company on behalf of her son, Alexander, with money saved from his part time job and money received for his birthday.
Dividends of $200 are deposited in his bank account. The dividends are assessable to Alexander.
Capital gains and losses from the sale will also belong to him.

Rachel uses her money to purchase $5,000 worth of shares in the name of her son, John.
Dividends of $250 received are deposited into her own bank account for her personal use.
The $250 is assessable to Rachel. When the shares are sold, Rachel must declare any capital gain or loss from the sale.

The principles of trust law may apply to certain investments made on behalf of a child. If a trust is established it may be the task of the trustee to pay tax on behalf of the child and at rates which would have applied had the child directly derived the income.

3.050   MEDICARE LEVY

From 2014-15 the Medicare levy is charged at a rate of 2% of a resident taxpayer's taxable income. The levy is not payable below certain income thresholds. Non-residents are not liable to pay the levy.

Membership of a private health insurance fund, or provision of health care by an employer are irrelevant and do not result in an exemption or reduction of the Medicare levy, but can result in exemption from an additional Medicare levy surcharge (see 3.060).

3.051   WHO IS LIABLE TO PAY THE LEVY?

A Medicare levy is payable by:
- any person who is or was a 'resident' of Australia at any time during the income year based on their taxable income (which excludes the taxed element of certain superannuation lump sums received if the taxpayer is between 55 and 59 years of age)
- a trustee assessed under s98 in respect of the share of net income of the trust to which a beneficiary is presently entitled, but who is under a legal disability. The amount of the levy charged to a trustee in such circumstances is credited against any levy charged to the beneficiary on an assessment of the same income, and
- a trustee assessed under s99 or s99A on the net income of the trust estate.

When a person leaves Australia to take up permanent residence abroad or becomes a resident of Australia during the income year, the levy is charged only on income derived while an Australian resident.

NOTE: According to s251U(1A) and (1B) ITAA36, residents of Christmas or Cocos (Keeling) Islands are liable to pay the Medicare levy, however residents of Norfolk Island are exempt.

As a general rule, the Medicare levy cannot be reduced by a person's entitlement to tax offsets, even if there are unused or excess tax offsets available. The exceptions are that refundable tax offsets, such as private health insurance tax offset (see 3.220), and excess imputation credits can be used to reduce the Medicare levy.

3.052   EXEMPTIONS

Taxpayers whose income is below certain exemption thresholds (varying with the number of children and pension status) do not pay the Medicare levy (see 3.053). If a taxpayer is not eligible for exemption, the full Medicare levy is payable even though all dependants may be exempt from the Medicare levy in their own right.

Some taxpayers are exempt from the Medicare levy because of their foreign status, or the type of health care they are provided.

TAXPAYERS EXEMPT FROM LEVY

- A non-resident of Australia for the whole year, or a resident of Norfolk Island.
- War veterans entitled to full free medical treatment under repatriation legislation.
- Blind pensioners or people receiving a sickness allowance from Centrelink.
- Any foreign diplomat or staff member of a foreign government, provided that the staff member is not an Australian resident, and does not have a resident of Australia as a dependant.
- Any person not entitled to Medicare benefits for services or treatment (requires certificate from the levy exemption certification unit of the Health Insurance Commission).
- A member (or a relative of a member) of the Defence Forces who is entitled to full free medical treatment or Veterans' Affairs Repatriation Health Card (Gold Card) or repatriation arrangements.
- A trustee of a deceased estate.
- A trustee under a s98 assessment in respect of a beneficiary who is exempt from paying the Medicare levy.

PRESCRIBED PERSON

Some taxpayers pay only half the levy. This applies if the taxpayer is exempt from the levy but at least one of the taxpayer's dependants is:
- not entitled to full and free health care, and
- not liable to pay separately any Medicare levy (depends on marital status, the number of children, etc.)

If a prescribed person has a spouse who pays the levy, the spouse is treated as not being a dependant of the prescribed person and full Medicare exemption applies to the prescribed person (TD 93/103).

Further, a taxpayer in this category, with dependants, can be deemed not to have dependants and remain exempt from the levy. This applies where:
- the taxpayer has a dependant (eg. spouse) who is liable for the levy and that person is not treated as a dependant
- a child is not a dependant of the taxpayer where the taxpayer has a spouse who is liable for the levy and who contributes to the maintenance of the child, and
- a child is treated as a dependant of only one member of a married or de facto couple, where they are both prescribed persons. In that case, only one spouse is liable for half the levy on account of the child. This exemption requires the couple to enter into a 'family agreement'.

A prescribed person in this category is fully liable for the levy if they have dependants who are not prescribed persons.

 For the definition of a 'prescribed person' and further details see both s251T and s251U ITAA36.

3.053   MEDICARE LEVY RELIEF

Relief from the Medicare levy is provided for low-income earners and a full exemption applies for taxpayers whose income does not exceed the exemption threshold (see table below). Above this level of income the exemption phases out. The liability for Medicare is at a rate of 10% on the amount by which the income exceeds the full exemption threshold up to the upper threshold limit at which full Medicare becomes payable. This concessional amount approaches the normal 2% rate toward the upper threshold of the income range.

The table on the following page shows the level of taxable income before which no or a reduced amount of Medicare will be payable; below the lower limit threshold no Medicare will be payable, between the lower and upper limit the Medicare levy is calculated as the difference between the lower and upper limits multiplied by 10%.

NOTE: For non-age pensioner Medicare levy exemption thresholds see 3.055. For Medicare levy exemption threshold for pensioners eligible for the Senior Australian and Pensioner Australian Tax Offset (SAPTO) see 3.056.

 What is the Medicare levy liability in 2014-15 for an individual taxpayer with a taxable income of $21,000? Since the individual's income exceeds the low income threshold of $20,896 some Medicare levy will be payable. Because the individual's taxable income is within the phasing out range, the individual's Medicare levy is calculated as 10% of the difference between the individual's taxable income and the low income threshold. The calculation is simply 10% of ($21,000 – $20,896) = $10.40.

Medicare levy low income threshold amounts and phasing out ranges 2014-15*			
Category of taxpayer	Lower limit income threshold for Medicare levy exemption	Reduced levy in phasing out range (inclusive)	Normal 2% levy payable above upper threshold limit
Individual taxpayer	$20,896	$20,897 – $26,120	$26,121
Families[1] with the following children and/or students	Family income	Family income	Family income
0	$35,261	$35,262 – $44,076	$44,077
1	$38,499	$38,500 – $48,123	$48,124
2	$41,737	$41,738 – $52,171	$52,172
3	$44,975	$44,976 – $56,218	$56,219
4	$48,213	$48,214 – $60,266	$60,267
5	$51,451	$51,452 – $64,313	$64,314
6	$54,689[2]	$54,690[2] – $68,361[3]	$68,362[3]

*At time of writing, the 2015-16 thresholds were unavailable.

1: The figures also apply to taxpayers who are entitled to a tax offset in respect of a child-housekeeper or housekeeper, or who would have been entitled to a sole-parent rebate (had the sole parent rebate not been repealed).

2: Where there are more than six dependent children or students, add $3,238 for each extra child or student.

3: Where there are more than six dependent children or students, add $4,047 for each extra child or student.

Note that for married and sole parent taxpayers the number of children in the table is based on those who are tax dependants. In determining the income of a taxpayer for the calculation of the levy, the income of a spouse (or de facto spouse) is not combined with the taxpayer's income. This applies to each member of a couple.

Similarly the income of children is not aggregated with that of the parents, however for the child to be a dependant (for the whole year) they must:

- be a resident of Australia

- be a full time student over age 21 and less than age 25, or
- be a child under age 21, and
- the taxpayer contributes to the maintenance of the dependant, and
- satisfy the requirements of s251R(3) ITAA36.

Where a child is a dependant of parents that lived separately and the parents are eligible for FTB Part A for the period, the taxpayer must get a determination from the Families Secretary as to each parent's care percentage during a care period. The child is then taken to be a dependant for only so much of the period as corresponds with that percentage of care.

FAMILY EXEMPTION THRESHOLDS

The primary levy is based on the taxpayer's taxable income, but family income exemption thresholds apply if the taxpayer:

- on 30 June, had a spouse (or de facto spouse)
- had a spouse who died during the year and did not remarry in that income year, or
- would be entitled to a sole parent (see 3.114), child-housekeeper or housekeeper tax offset (see 3.112, 3.115 and 3.116) had they not been restricted or removed.

If there is, or was a spouse (or de facto), the test is based on the combined taxable incomes of the taxpayer and spouse. If the taxpayer had a child-housekeeper (or a 'housekeeper' caring for a child), the family income relief test is based on only the taxpayer's taxable income.

Special Medicare levy concessions apply for persons qualifying for the SAPTO (see 3.056).

NOTE: In the *Tax and Superannuation Laws Amendment (2013 Measures No.2) Bill 2013* it was announced that the dependancy spouse offsets will be consolidated into a single offset.

3.054   TRUSTEE'S LIABILITY TO MEDICARE

A resident trustee (not of a deceased estate) can be liable to the Medicare levy:

Trustee's liability to Medicare from 2014-15	
Type of trust income subject to tax	Rate of Medicare levy
Income to which a beneficiary under a legal disability is entitled. Section 98 ITAA36 (Minors)	Medicare levy (on a single-person test) is determined the same way as if the income is assessed to the beneficiary.
Income to which no beneficiary is presently entitled. Section 99A ITAA36 (Penalty rates)	2%
Income to which no beneficiary is presently entitled. Section 99 ITAA36 (Concessional rates)	<ul><li>up to $416: Nil</li><li>$417 to $520: 10% of excess over $416</li><li>$521 and above: 2% flat</li></ul>

* Deceased estates are not liable to the Medicare levy on income that is distributed to 'prescribed persons' or on income to which they are assessed under s99 or 99A. See s251U, s251S ITAA36 and 3.052.

If the beneficiary is taxed on the same income, the beneficiary will receive a credit for the amount of the Medicare levy paid by the trustee.

3.056 MEDICARE LEVY CONCESSIONS FOR SENIOR AUSTRALIANS AND PENSIONERS FROM 2014 ONWARD

In order for senior Australians and pensioners to access a Medicare exemption they need to satisfy the eligibility criteria for either the former SATO (see 3.191) or the former PTO (see 3.202). Note that these offsets were repealed and replaced with the Senior Australians and Pensioner Tax Offset (SAPTO).

Assuming the eligibility for the former SATO or PTO is met, see the table on the following page for the levels of income from which Medicare would be levied.

The lower threshold represents the level of taxable income at which no Medicare would be payable. This is aligned with the taxable income figure at which no income tax liability would arise for the taxpayer in question. This is because of the SAPTO effect on the tax payable by these taxpayers. The upper threshold represents the level of taxable income after which the full 2% Medicare levy would be payable.

The per child increase to the respective thresholds applies to couples eligible for SAPTO with dependants at the same rate as for couples without dependants.

Medicare levy concessions for those qualifying for the Senior Australians and Pensioner Tax Offset 2014-15			
Category of taxpayer claiming offset	No Medicare levy payable if taxable or family income does not exceed	Reduced Medicare levy at 10% if taxable or family income is between	2% Medicare levy payable if taxable income or family income exceeds
If are eligible for SAPTO	$ 33,044	$33,045 – $41,305	$ 41,306
Couple/sole parent with:			
Individuals with a spouse and/or dependants eligible for SAPTO	$46,000	$46,001 – $54,117	$54,118
Dependants not eligible for SAPTO	$32,743	$32,743 – $38,521	$38,521

1: Where there are dependent children or students, add $3,007 for each extra child or student.
2: Where there are dependent children or students, add $3,538 for each extra child or student.

 Single age pensioner: Ken, age 68, receives the age pension and some rental income (and is eligible for the SAPTO). In 2014-15 his taxable income is $34,000. He qualifies to receive a SAPTO. His Medicare levy liability is ($34,000 – $33,044) x 10% = $95.60.

3.060   MEDICARE LEVY SURCHARGE

Individuals with incomes in excess of a stipulated threshold who do not have private patient hospital insurance cover (including spouse and dependants) may be liable for additional tax in the form of the Medicare levy surcharge.

The measure used to determine a taxpayers liability to the surcharge is 'income for surcharge purposes'. Income for surcharge purposes is only used to determine **whether** you are liable to pay the surcharge, not **how much** surcharge you have to pay. The amount of surcharge payable by a taxpayer is calculated with reference to a taxpayer's taxable income and reportable fringe benefits see the table at 3.063. The Medicare levy surcharge is charged in addition to the 2% Medicare levy. See 3.062 and 3.063.

3.061   MEDICARE LEVY SURCHARGE RATE AND EXEMPTION

For taxpayers who are liable for the Medicare levy surcharge, the rate at which the surcharge is levied depends on which income threshold (or 'tier') the taxpayer falls into. These income tiers and the rate of surcharge are summarised in the table below.

Medicare levy surcharge threshold 2014-15*				
Income	Level of 'income for surcharge purposes'			
Tier Type	N/A	Tier 1	Tier 2	Tier 3
Single	$0 – $90,000	$90,001 – $105,000	$105,001 – $140,000	$140,001 and above
Family	$0 – 180,000	$180,001 – 210,000	$210,001 – $280,000	$280,001 and above
Surcharge rate	0%	1%	1.25%	1.5%

* The calculation of the amount of levy charged is based on the taxpayer's taxable income and reportable fringe benefits for the year.

Where the family surcharge threshold applies, the surcharge will not be imposed on an individual if their income for surcharge purposes was below $20,896 or less in the 2014-15 year.

NOTE: Private patient hospital cover is provided by an insurance policy that is issued by a registered fund and provides benefits in relation to fees and charges for hospital treatment provided in an Australian hospital or day hospital facility. However, if the policy has an annual excess of more than $500 (singles) or more than $1,000 (couples or family), then the surcharge is payable. This does not apply if the policy was purchased before 24 May 2000 and membership has been continuous since then.

INCOME FOR SURCHARGE PURPOSES

Income for surcharge purposes includes:

- taxable income for the income year (disregarding subsection 271-105(1) of Schedule 2F ITAA36)
- reportable fringe benefits total for the income year
- reportable superannuation contributions for the income year, and
- total net investment loss for the income year
- *less* any post-June 1983 elements of a cashed ETP that has a 0% tax rate after tax offset. The tax offset is the first part of a taxed element of a post-June 1983 component paid to a person of at least age 55 with a 0% tax rate.

3.062   SINGLE PERSON

A taxpayer is liable for the surcharge if their income for surcharge purposes exceeds $90,000 for the 2014-15 income year ($88,000 for 2013-14 income year). However, the surcharge itself will continue to be calculated as 1% of the total of taxable income (plus any reportable fringe benefits) up to an income of $105,000 in 2014-15. As a result, net investment losses and reportable superannuation contributions will not be subject to the surcharge; they simply will be used to determine if a taxpayer is liable for the surcharge itself.

NOTE: The *Medicare Levy Act 1986* imposes a surcharge on individuals with 'income for surcharge purposes' above a certain level. This surcharge is imposed on the taxable income of a taxpayer (even though determination of whether you are liable or not is based on 'income for surcharge purposes'. *A New Tax System (Medicare Levy Surcharge – Fringe Benefits) Act 1999* extends the imposition of the surcharge to 'reportable fringe benefits'.

Ron's taxable income is $77,000. He has a $4,000 loss from a rental property, $5,000 of reportable superannuation contributions and his reportable fringe benefits are $9,000 for the 2014-15 financial year. He is single with no dependants. He does not have private hospital cover.

Ron's 'income for surcharge purposes' is calculated as:

Taxable income	$77,000
plus	
Reportable fringe benefits	$9,000
Reportable superannuation contributions	$5,000
Net investment loss	$4,000
Income for surcharge purposes	**$95,000**

He is liable for an additional 1% Medicare levy surcharge since his 'income for surcharge purposes' of $95,000 is greater than the $90,000 threshold. His total Medicare liability will however still be based on just Ron's taxable income plus reportable fringe benefits. Thus:

Taxable income	$77,000
plus	
Reportable fringe benefits	$9,000
Total subject to surcharge	**$86,000**
Total surcharge (at 1% of $86,000)	**$860**

3.063   FAMILIES

For the 2014-15 income year the family Medicare levy surcharge threshold is increased to $180,000. The family surcharge (indexed annually) is based on the family's 'Income for surcharge purposes'.

The threshold increases by $1,500 for each additional dependent child after the first. This increase of the threshold can be calculated using the following formula:

*$1,500 * (number of dependants who are children – 1)*

 *Warren and Nancy have four dependent children, the family surcharge threshold for the 2014-15 income year will be $184,500 (ie. $1,500 * (4 – 1) + $180,000).*

The definition of 'dependant' for surcharge purposes is the same as for the Medicare levy (see 3.053) except that, for a 'dependant child' it means a child in full-time education who is 21 or more but less than 25, regardless of their separate net income.

Where parents are separated, a child can be the dependant of either parent, irrespective of whether that parent receives a family tax benefit for the child so long as they provide the child with care.

 Emily and David are separated and share custody of their son Ed. Since they share care, both Emily and David are considered to contribute to their son's maintenance. Therefore, Ed is a dependant of both Emily and David for Medicare levy surcharge purposes.

Emily has taken out private patient hospital cover for herself and Ed and she is not liable for the surcharge because all the members of her family are covered. David does not have private patient hospital cover. His 'income for surcharge purposes' of $190,000 (this income was entirely made up of his taxable income and reportable fringe benefits) in the 2014-15 financial year is greater than the $180,000 threshold and therefore he will be liable for the Medicare levy surcharge of $1,900 (ie. $190,000 x 1%).

Further, the surcharge does not apply if the person does not have any dependants and is a prescribed person under the following categories:

- war veterans entitled to full free medical treatment under repatriation legislation
- blind pensioners or people receiving a sickness allowance from Centrelink, and
- a member (or a relative of a member) of the Defence Forces who is entitled to full free medical treatment or Veteran's Affairs Repatriation Health Card (Gold Card) or repatriation arrangements.

However, if the above categories of prescribed person have dependants who are not prescribed persons, the surcharge applies. For the surcharge purposes the special rules entitling these categories of person that have dependents to half or full levy exemption do not apply (see 3.052).

 The surcharge is payable for all days in the income year that the taxpayer, a couple, or any of their dependants are not adequately covered by private hospital insurance. For those getting married, the combined surcharge rules apply from the date of marriage until the appropriate private hospital cover is obtained.

 A Medicare levy lump sum tax offset may apply to reduce the Medicare surcharge applicable to you. Certain lump sum payments in arrears applicable to previous financial years may be eligible for a lump sum in arrears tax offset (see 3.240). This offset will only apply if the lump sum constitutes 10% or more of the taxable income in the year it was paid. Broadly, the offset equals the surcharge applicable to the lump sum. The offset applies to:

- *that income eligible for the lump sum in arrears tax offset, or*
- *exempt foreign employment income which accrued for a period of more than 12 months before the date of payment to the taxpayer.*

3.070   ABOVE AVERAGE SPECIAL PROFESSIONAL INCOME

When 'above average special professional income' is derived by Australian individual residents who are special professionals such as authors of literature, drama, music or artistic works as well as inventors, performing artists, production associates and sporting persons, concessional tax rates may apply to that income.

The 'above average special professional income' rules in Division 405 ITAA97 allow taxpayers to average their income so that they are not unreasonably taxed in the years when their income is abnormally high because of the fluctuations in income of these type of taxpayers. But the opposite does not apply (ie. extra tax payable in years when their income is abnormally low).

For these rules to apply, there must be $2,500 or more of 'assessable professional income'. Once these provisions apply, they remain applicable even if the special professional income falls below $2,500.

3.071   PERSONS ELIGIBLE FOR CONCESSION – SPECIAL PROFESSIONALS

Income averaging is available to these individuals:

- **Author or artist:** the author of an artistic or literary work under the *Copyright Act 1968* (**NOTE:** Computer programmers are 'authors' – see TD 93/65).

- **Composer:** the author of a musical work under the *Copyright Act 1968*.

- **Performer:** someone who, in front of an audience (including television or radio), or on a film, tape or disc, performs music, a play, dance, entertainment, an address, display, promotional activity or exhibition.

- **Production assistant:** one with artistic input into a performer's activities:
  - art director
  - lighting designer
  - choreographer
  - musical director
  - costume designer
  - producer
  - director
  - production designer
  - film editor, and
  - set designer.

  NOTE: The occupations are not limited to the above, and may include occupations providing similar artistic services such as someone who applies elaborate make-up – but does not include a technical occupation such as a camera operator.

- **Sportsperson:** those who compete by:
  - riding animals, etc.
  - driving, piloting, or crewing motor vehicles, boats, aircraft (or other types of transport, including BMX bikes and skate boards)
  - overcoming natural obstacle (eg. mountaineering)
  - exercising physical prowess, strength or stamina (eg. playing golf, football, tennis), and
  - being a car rally navigator, coxswain in rowing or similar activities (but excludes golf caddy – ID 2004/196).

  These activities are excluded:
  - coaching or training competitors in sport
  - umpiring or refereeing sport
  - administering sport
  - being a pit crew member in motor sport being a theatrical or sports entrepreneur, and
  - owning or training animals.

EMPLOYEES USUALLY NOT ELIGIBLE

Employee sportspersons and performers are not excluded, but others who are merely employees even though their work involves the technical production of artistic, literary, dramatic or musical works or inventions, cannot average their 'special income'.

CONDITIONAL AVAILABILITY

Artists, composers, inventors or writers who enter into an arrangement to supply their service to another person cannot include as their professional income those amounts that are derived from the arrangement unless:

- the arrangement was entered into solely for the taxpayer to complete one or more specified works, and
- it is not part of a continuing or successive arrangement with the taxpayer or associate.

3.072   ASSESSABLE PROFESSIONAL INCOME

INCOME SPECIFICALLY INCLUDED

Assessable income from special professional activities relating to a taxpayer, includes:

- rewards and prizes
- income from:
  - endorsing or promoting goods or services
  - appearing/participating in an advertisement or interview, and
  - acting as a commentator
- income of composers, artists, authors, or inventors from employment or any services rendered (subject to exclusions – see *Conditional availability* above)
- income from assigning or granting patent rights
- royalties from literary, dramatic, musical or artistic work, and
- income from a patent for an invention.

The income averaging concession is available when the assessable professional income is received directly in relation to special professional activities, regardless of whether or not the person is still operating in the vocation concerned.

INCOME SPECIFICALLY EXCLUDED

Following kinds of income are specifically excluded from assessable professional income even though it may be related to the special professional activities:

- net capital gains, superannuation lump sums or Employment Termination Payments (ETPs), and
- payments for unused annual or long service leave on retirement or termination.

3.073   CALCULATING TAXABLE PROFESSIONAL INCOME

Taxable Professional Income (TPI) for an income year is the amount (if any) by which assessable professional income exceeds the following deductions for that year:

Step 1: Add up the part of the deductions that relate exclusively to assessable professional income (eg. a sportsperson's sporting equipment).

Step 2: Calculate the portion of apportionable deductions (eg. deductible donations) allocable to special professional income:

Apportionable deductions x [(assessable professional income – sum of step 1) divided by (taxable income – apportionable deductions)]

 Apportionable deductions are deductions that have no relation to the person's assessable professional income, but which are apportionable between assessable professional income and other assessable income.

Step 3: Add Step 1 to Step 2.

Step 4: TPI = Assessable professional income less Step 3 (if positive).

Evan has taxable income of $10,000 and assessable professional income of $4,000.

Step 1: Deductions relating exclusively to assessable professional income: $1,000

Step 2: Apportionable deductions: $2,000. The deduction under Step 2 is $2,000 x [($4,000 – $1,000) divided by ($10,000 + $2,000)] = $500

Step 3: $1,000 + $500 = $1,500

Step 4: Evan's TPI = $4,000 – $1,500 = $2,500

INCLUSIONS IN A TAX RETURN

Taxpayers who want their income averaged should do this in their tax return.

ASSESSABLE PROFESSIONAL INCOME LESS DEDUCTIONS THAT RELATE EXCLUSIVELY TO THAT INCOME

The amount to write at **Z** in item 24 on the tax return supplementary section is the assessable professional income less the total of deductions that reasonably relate to this income. The amount at **Z** is for disclosure purposes in order determine eligibility to averaging concession and is not added to your total taxable income. Therefore, you will not be taxed twice on this amount. Unless it has already been included as income or deductions in another item in your tax return, this amount should also be included as category 2 other income at **V** item 24 of the supplementary section of the tax return in order for it to be included as your total taxable income. Therefore, from Example 1, Evan would include $3,000 (ie. $4,000 – $1,000) in his tax returns supplementary section item 24:

- at **Z** for averaging purposes, and
- in category 2 at **V** for calculation of taxable income purposes.

NOTE: Do not include apportionable deductions in the amount included in item 24. The Tax Office will work out the part of the apportionable deductions that applies to arrive at the TPI.

3.074   CALCULATING AVERAGE TAXABLE PROFESSIONAL INCOME

Average TPI for current year = Sum of the previous 4 years TPI divided by 4.

To calculate TPI see 3.073.

NOTE: If the TPI in any income year is a negative amount, treat it as nil when calculating the person's average professional taxable income.

PHASE-IN PERIOD

If a taxpayer became entitled to the averaging provisions less than five years ago and was a resident for part of the income year immediately before professional year 1, the average TPI is calculated as follows:

Professional year	Taxable professional income (resident taxpayer)
1	Nil
2	1/3 of TPI in year 1
3	1/4 of TPI in years 1 and 2
4	1/4 of TPI in years 1, 2 and 3

A taxpayer's professional year 1 is the first income year:

- during which the taxpayer was an Australian resident (for all or part of the income year), and
- for which the taxpayer's TPI was more than $2,500.

A taxpayer can only have one professional year 1 (TD 93/33).

3.075   HOW 'SPECIAL INCOME' IS TAXED

The averaging provisions do not apply if the taxpayer's average taxable professional income exceeds their current year taxable professional income.

In 2014-15 Alice has:
- *Ordinary employment income: $10,000*
- *Taxable professional income: $30,000*
- *Average eligible income of preceding 4 years: $10,000*

  (1) Taxable income (ordinary income + taxable professional income) $40,000
  (2) Ineligible income (ordinary employment income) $10,000
  (3) Taxable professional income $30,000
  (4) Average taxable professional income of the preceding 4 years $10,000
  (5) Above average special professional income: (3) – (4) **$20,000**
  (6) Normal income: (2) + (4) $20,000
  (7) 1/5 of her special professional income (5)/5 .... $4,000
  (8) Tax on $24,000 @ 2014-15 marginal rates [(6 + 7) = $24,000] $1,102
  (9) Tax on 'normal income' $20,000 @ 2014-15 rates [(5) = $20,000] $342

Tax on special income

(10) Difference between (8) and (9)... **$760**

Tax payable

Tax on 'special income' (10), is multiplied by 5, then added to the tax on normal income [(9)].

Tax on 'special income' ie. 5 x $760... $3,800
Tax on 'normal income' (9) .... + $342
Net tax payable... **$4,142**

Tax payable on taxable income without applying the averaging provision
ie. tax on $40,000 @ 2014-15 rates.. $4,547
Therefore, applying the averaging provisions there is a tax savings
of $4,547 – $4,142... **$405**

3.100   TAX OFFSETS FOR INDIVIDUALS AND FAMILY BENEFITS

Deductions reduce taxable income, but tax offsets are subtracted from the tax payable on taxable income. Unused tax offsets (with the exception of the private health insurance tax offset and franking tax offset) are lost (ie. they are not refundable to the taxpayer).

Generally, tax offsets are only allowable to Australian residents whose dependants are also residents (see 10.020) for the definition of 'residency'). However, certain tax offsets such as dependant tax offsets and the medical expenses tax offset are available to be claimed for dependants of a migrant who lives overseas for up to five years after the migrant became an Australian resident, provided arrangements were made for the dependants to migrate to Australia as soon as possible.

Taxpayers may also be entitled to tax offsets for franking (see from 12.700), income streams (see 20.700), and superannuation contributions (see 13.400).

  The dependent spouse offset has been abolished effective 1 July 2014.

3.103   ADJUSTED TAXABLE INCOME

Claims for some dependant and concessional tax offsets are conditional upon the 'adjusted taxable income' of the taxpayer and/or dependant.

Adjusted taxable income is defined in Schedule 3 of the *A New Tax System (Family Assistance) Act 1999*. An individual's adjustable taxable income for an income year comprises the following amounts:

- taxable income
- adjusted fringe benefits total (reportable fringe benefits adjusted for FBT paid by the employer)
- target foreign income (foreign income that is not assessable and is not subject to FBT)
- total net investment loss (includes both net financial investment loss and net rental property loss)
- tax-free pensions and benefits (includes disability pensions, care payments and defence pensions), and
- reportable superannuation contributions (includes both reportable employer super contributions and deductible personal super contributions).

REPORTABLE SUPERANNUATION CONTRIBUTIONS

Reportable superannuation contributions include:

- the total of a taxpayer's deductions under Subdivision 290-C ITAA97. These deductions are likely to be the total of the taxpayer's concessional personal superannuation contributions (provided the work test is satisfied; see 19.026), and
- Reportable Employer Superannuation Contributions (RESCs).

In general, RESCs are contributions made by the employer (or an associate of the employer) to a superannuation fund or retirement savings account, on behalf of an employee during an income year (s995-1 ITAA97). The employee must also have some capacity (or reasonably be expected to have some capacity) to influence the size of the contribution or the way in which the contribution is made.

Certain salary sacrificed superannuation contributions are classified as RESCs. Under a salary sacrifice arrangement, the employee has the right to choose the amount or the percentage of their income to be contributed to their superannuation. The amount of any contribution in excess of the 9.5% required amount should be included in RESCs.

If an employer makes superannuation contributions on behalf of an employee under the terms of an industrial agreement which is higher than the 9.5% required, then the contributions can be excluded from the RESC provided the agreement has been made at arm's length with the employee and the employee has no capacity to influence the terms of the agreement.

NOTE: Employers are required to report RESCs on employees' annual or part-year payment summaries.

NET INVESTMENT LOSS

The definition of the total net investment loss includes:

- net rental property loss, and
- net losses from financial investment.

The definition of net loss from financial investment is quite broad. According to subsection 995-1(1) ITAA97, financial investments include:

- a share in a company
- an interest in a managed investment scheme (within the meaning of the *Corporations Act 2001*)
- a forestry interest in a forestry managed investment scheme
- a right or option in respect of an investment referred above, and
- an investment of a like nature of any of those referred above.

The net financial investment loss does not include capital losses (for example shares held on capital account that are subsequently sold), the losses will be the amount by which allowable deductions in respect of the particular investment exceeds gross income from those investments. For instance, if the amount of interest expense (and other allowable deductions) from a margin loan on shares exceeded the dividend income from those shares the loss would be a net financial investment loss.

SEPARATE NET INCOME

For the 2009-10 and earlier years, the income definition used for rebate purposes was 'separate net income'. The concept of separate net income (SNI) is still applicable in particular circumstances.

SNI includes income (assessable and exempt) from all sources, less all work-related allowable deductions and the costs of earning the income, even if they are not allowable tax deductions.

SNI is not reduced by donations, tax agent fees, superannuation contributions or carry forward losses.

Income included in separate net income

- All income regularly received including salary or wages, age, widows and social security pensions or allowances, including any additions made in respect of dependants (see exclusions below).
- Maintenance payments received by a spouse for his or her own support.
- Amounts to which a dependant is presently entitled from a trust, even if not received by the dependant.
- Tax-exempt amounts received (eg. tax-exempt pensions, disability support pension, war pension, defence reserve pay).
- Interest, dividends and investment income.
- Business income, and a share of profits in a partnership, or trading trust (**NOTE:** SNI is reduced by non-commercial losses).
- Rental income (after expenses and depreciation).
- Lump sums for annual leave, or long service leave.
- Lump sum severance or retirement payments of a capital nature or compensation payments for losing a job.
- Net capital gains (after claiming CGT losses).
- Payments under the Australian Government educational assistance scheme, and also the part of a scholarship or bursary to help with a dependant's living expenses after the child has reached 16 years of age.
- Pension or annuity income, reduced by any deductible amount.

Items excluded from separate net income

- Dividend imputation credits (TD 94/27).
- Amounts that are not 'income' (eg. a lump sum from any superannuation fund).
- Maintenance payments received by a spouse for his or her dependent children.
- Compensation for losing a job.
- Family tax benefit.
- Payments to educate isolated children under 16.
- Child care benefit.
- Child care rebate.
- Carer allowance and nursing care benefits.
- For a child to 16th birthday or student to 25th birthday any scholarship, bursary, exhibition or prize.
- Maternity allowance (including immunisation allowance).
- Baby Bonus.

Deductions that reduce separate net income

- Travelling expenses incurred:
  - to and from work
  - to derive or collect dividends, interest, rent or social security payments
  - to and from child care because they were working, and
  - while deriving any other income. (**NOTE:** According to TD 98/5, traveling

expenses calculation based on cents per kilometre method is acceptable and is not limited to 5000 kilometres.)

- Work-related expenses.
- Net child minding expenses (but only those incurred while working or earning income, reduced by any childcare cash tax offset received (TD 98/5)) any other expenses directly related to earning the income (whether deductible or not) eg. cost of food consumed during work hours (*Case V98* 88 ATC 642).

 A dependant's SNI cannot be reduced by amounts paid by them for gifts, donations, tax agent fees, payment of income tax (including PAYG instalments and PAYG withholding amounts), superannuation contributions, any losses brought forward from earlier income tax years, or non-deductible self-education expenses where the expenses are related only to income from Austudy, youth allowance or work that is not connected with the self-education course.

3.110   DEPENDANT (INVALID AND CARER) TAX OFFSET

The Dependant (Invalid and Carer) Tax offset applies from the 2012-13 tax year onward. This refundable tax offset is for taxpayers who contribute to the maintenance of someone who is genuinely unable to work because of invalidity or carer obligations.

IMPORTANT! The dependant spouse tax offset has been abolished effective 1 July 2014. The amending legislation also:

- expands the dependant (invalid and carer) tax offset by repealing the provision excluding spouses covered by the dependent spouse tax offset from being covered by the dependant (invalid and carer) tax offset, and
- removes the dependent spouse tax offset and instead allow the dependant (invalid and carer) tax offset to be claimed as a component of the:
  - zone tax offset (see 3.173)
  - overseas civilians tax offset (see 3.174), or
  - overseas forces tax offset (see 3.174), and

ELIGIBILITY

A taxpayer must satisfy a number of eligibility requirements before they can claim the Dependant (Invalid and Carer) Tax Offset. They are:

- maintenance of a dependant
- eligibility of the dependant (including residency requirements of both the taxpayer and the dependant)
- invalidity or carer obligations
- income requirements, and
- must not be in receipt of other entitlements (or not eligible for other entitlements in some cases).

MAINTENANCE

A taxpayer may satisfy this requirement for an income year if, during the year, they contribute to the maintenance of an eligible dependant. Determining whether a taxpayer has contributed to a dependant is open to interpretation. However it is generally accepted that if a taxpayer resides with a dependant, it will be generally accepted that they have contributed to their maintenance.

ELIGIBLE DEPENDANT

An eligible dependant of a taxpayer includes their:

- spouse
- parent

- child (aged 16 years or over)
- brother or sister (aged 16 years or over)
- spouse's parent, and
- spouse's sibling (aged 16 years or over).

The above listed dependants are only eligible if they are:

- genuinely unable to work due to invalidity or carer obligations, and
- Australian residents (see below for an exception to this general rule).

 A taxpayer can still claim a Dependant (Invalid and Carer) Tax Offset for a foreign resident spouse or child if the taxpayer is domiciled in Australia.

INVALIDITY OR CARER OBLIGATIONS

A dependant is seen to be genuinely unable to work due to invalidity where the person receives a disability support pension or a special needs disability support pension under the *Social Security Act 1991*. Alternatively this test can be passed if the dependant receives an invalidity support pension under the *Veterans' Entitlement Act 1986*.

A dependant is genuinely unable to work because of a carer obligation if they:

- receive a carer payment or carer allowance under the *Social Security Act 1991*, or
- are wholly engaged in providing care to a relative who receives one of the following entitlements:
  - a disability support pension or a special needs disability pension under the *Social Security Act 1991*, or
  - an invalidity service pension under the *Veterans' Entitlements Act 1986*.

INCOME REQUIREMENTS

The income threshold rules for the Dependant (Invalid and Carer) Tax Offset for the 2014-15 year are:

Income threshold rules for the Dependant (Invalid and Carer) Tax Offset 2014-15	
Eligibility income threshold requirement	The applicant's and his/her spouse's combined Adjusted Taxable Income (ATI) is $100,000 or less for 2014-15 (note: threshold is $150,000 for 2013-14).
Dependant's income threshold requirement	Dependant's ATI is below the cut-out point. The full rebate income is available for ATI below $10,422 for 2014-15 (below $10,166 for 2013-14) equal to $282 and below.

The definition of income used for the purposes of the income limit eligibility cap for the Dependant (Invalid and Carer) Tax Offset will be aligned with that which applies to family assistance payments for Family Tax Benefit Part B which is $100,000 for the 2014-15 income year (this is updated every year on July 1 – see 3.140.) The ATI will be used to determine whether a taxpayer passes this income test.

NOTE: Various dependant tax offsets which applied prior to 1 July 2012 have been notionally retained – refer 3.111 to 3.118.

INELIGIBILITY

A taxpayer is not entitled to a Dependant (Invalid and Carer) Tax Offset if they or their spouse received Family Tax Benefit (FTB) Part B (without shared care). The offset is reduced for the shared care percentage a taxpayer receives.

A taxpayer entitled to a zone, overseas forces or overseas civilian offset is not entitled to a Dependant (Invalid and Carer) Tax Offset.

AMOUNT OF OFFSET

The maximum offset for the 2014-15 income year is $2,535. This amount will be indexed annually in line with CPI. These indexation rules can be found in Subdivision 960-M ITAA97. The maximum offset is payable for dependants earning less than $282 in Adjusted Taxable Income (ATI). The offset reduces by $1 for every $4 of additional ATI the dependant earns.

The offset will not be available where a dependant's ATI exceeds $10,422 in 2014-15.

Josh and Tina are married. Tina cares for her invalid brother and therefore does not work for the entire income year. She has earned $5,000 in ATI. The combined ATI for both Josh and Tina is $90,000. Josh will be able to claim a Dependant (Invalid and Carer) Tax Offset of $1,355 in 2014-15. This is calculated according to the following formula:

> *Claimable Dependant (Invalid and Carer) Tax Offset =*
> *Maximum Dependant (Invalid and Carer) Tax Offset – ((ATI of Dependant – $282)/4)*
>
> *$1,355 = $2,535 – (($5,000 – $282)/4)*

REDUCTION OF OFFSET – SHARED CARE AND PART YEAR ELIGIBILITY

Reduction for shared care arrangements

A taxpayer or spouse may have shared care arrangements for a child. This occurs where two people that are not part of the same couple are eligible for FTB Part B because they care for the child between 35% and 65% of the care period. Where a taxpayer has a shared care arrangement in place and received FTB Part B then the offset is reduced by multiplying by the ratio of the shared care rate of FTB part B.

Alex and Christina are married. Christina maintains Alex as an invalid spouse who receives a part invalidity pension. Alex has a son Bill from a previous marriage. Alex is eligible for FTB Part B for his son Bill and receives it as he shares care for Bill with his previous spouse. Alex's shared care rate is determined to be 40%.

Since Alex receives a partial entitlement to FTB Part B, Christina cannot claim the full $2,535 of Dependant (Invalid and Carer) Tax Offset for Alex. The amount of the offset is reduced by Bill's shared care percentage (being 40%). The calculation of the offset would therefore be as follows:

Calculation of partial Dependant (Invalid and Carer) Tax Offset	
Shared care rate	40%
Maximum Dependant (Invalid and Carer) Tax Offset	$2,535
LESS	
Reduction due to shared care (40% x maximum Dependant (Invalid and Carer) Tax Offset	($1,014)
Pro-rata dependant (invalid and carer) tax offset claimable	$1,521

While a taxpayer who receives FTB Part B as part of shared care arrangement can claim a dependant (invalid and carer) tax offset, this offset will still be apportioned to account for the FTB Part B a taxpayer receives, a taxpayer who receives FTB Part B without it being part of a shared care arrangement will not be able to claim the offset.

REDUCTION FOR PART YEAR ELIGIBILITY

After reducing the maximum offset for shared care arrangements (where applicable) the amount of the offset otherwise available is further reduced in situations where a taxpayer may be entitled or eligible for only part of the income year. This reduction is based on the amount the Commissioner considers reasonable in the circumstances. The factors the Commissioner must have regard to when coming to this decision are as follows:

- whether the taxpayer or individuals other than the taxpayer contributed to the

maintenance of the dependant during part of the year
- the type of dependant that gave rise to the taxpayer's claim of the offset for part of the year
- whether the taxpayer is a member of a family in receipt of FTB Part B (without shared care) for part of the year, and
- whether parental leave is payable to the family under the *Paid Parental Leave Act 2010* for part of the year.

CHANGE OF SPOUSE OR DIFFERENT SPOUSES DURING AN INCOME YEAR

Where a taxpayer had a spouse for only part of an income year, the spouse's ATI is pro-rated on the proportion of the year that the spouse was a partner of the taxpayer. This rule also applies where the taxpayer has multiple spouses during an income year.

Note that it is possible to claim more than one amount of Dependant (Invalid and Carer) Tax Offset for different individuals. This can occur for example where a taxpayer maintains an invalid spouse as well as an invalid parent. However the offset cannot be claimed twice in respect of different or changing spouses.

INTERACTION WITH THE NET MEDICAL EXPENSES TAX OFFSET

In determining the amount of a net medical expenses tax offset a taxpayer is entitled to, the taxpayer is able to include net medical expenses incurred in relation to a dependant who is a relative, spouse's relative, parent or spouse's parent who is genuinely unable to work due to invalidity or care obligations. Similarly, a taxpayer may be entitled to a Medicare Levy concession by accessing the family Medicare levy low income threshold if they have a spouse or child.

Taxpayers eligible for the zone, overseas forces or overseas civilian tax offset will not experience any change to their net medical expense tax offset entitlement or Medicare levy concession.

NOTIONAL TAX OFFSETS FOR THE CALCULATION OF THE ZONE AND OVERSEAS FORCES OFFSETS

A taxpayer may be eligible to claim:
- zone tax offset if they lived or worked in a remote or isolated area of Australia (not including an offshore oil or gas rig), or
- the overseas forces offset if they served overseas as a member of the Australian Defence Force or a United Nations armed force.

Prior to 1 July 2014, a notional dependent spouse tax offset was used in the calculation of the zone and overseas forces rebates. The dependent spouse tax offset was abolished with effect from 1 July 2014. As a consequence, the dependent spouse tax offset component of each of the zone and overseas forces offsets has been replaced with a dependant (invalid and carer) tax offset component.

TWO OR MORE CAN CLAIM

If two or more people contribute to the maintenance of a dependant, they can share one tax offset between them.

PART-YEAR CLAIMS

A number of circumstances justify part-year claims, including:
- the taxpayer either became a resident, or ceased to be one (claim only for the period during which the taxpayer was a resident)
- the dependant became a resident (see 12.020 and 3.130 for some special cases), and
- the dependant satisfied the conditions of the tax offset for only part of the year.

WHO IS A DEPENDANT?

A dependant can be:
- a married or de facto spouse
- a child, including:

- an adopted child
- a step child, or
- an ex nuptial child, who is under 21 years of age and is not a student
- a student who is under age 25 and is a full-time student at school, college or university
- a child-housekeeper (ie. the taxpayer's child of any age who works full time keeping house for the taxpayer)
- an invalid relative, including:
  - a taxpayer's child, brother or sister who is 16 years of age or over and:
    * receives a disability support pension or a special needs disability support pension, or
    * receives a rehabilitation allowance and immediately before becoming eligible for this allowance was eligible to receive an invalid pension, or
    * has a certificate from a Commonwealth approved doctor certifying a continuing inability to work, and
- the taxpayer's parents or spouse's parents.

A dependant needs to be an Australian resident for tax purposes. As a general rule, the tax offset may only be claimable in respect of a dependant actually living in Australia. For a spouse, student or child only, they will be treated as a resident if the taxpayer has always lived in Australia or the taxpayer came to live in Australia permanently unless they set up a permanent home outside Australia (ATO ID 2003/405).

A taxpayer can claim a dependant rebate for spouse and dependant children who are waiting to migrate to Australia for a period of up to five years provided that arrangements have been made for the spouse and dependant children to migrate to Australia as soon as possible.

 A taxpayer can claim a dependant tax offset only if he or she is an Australian resident for tax purposes.

DEPENDANT'S INCOME IS FOR PART OF THE YEAR

Any income which a dependant derived before becoming either a resident or a dependant for tax offset purposes is ignored (IT 2453).

The tax offset is for the period in which the taxpayer contributed to the maintenance of a dependant. Regardless of the dependant's ATI, the taxpayer is presumed to have contributed to the maintenance of a dependant for the period during which the both of them reside together, unless it can be demonstrated otherwise (ie. that the dependant was self-supporting and the taxpayer contributed in no way to the maintenance of the dependant during this period).

There are no part year claims based on the dependant working for only part of the year, or the dependant deriving investment income in only part of the year.

3.111   NOTIONAL TAX OFFSETS FOR CHILDREN

A notional tax offset or rebate for children and students can be calculated for the purposes of determining entitlements to other benefits. This is important because children will not be treated as dependants for tax purposes if their ATI exceeds the ATI cut out threshold.

The tax offset is reduced by $1 for each $4 of ATI in excess of $282 during the offset period. These notional tax offsets cannot be redeemed for cash or claimed in the tax return. They only be used to increase claims for zone or overseas defence forces tax offset and child-housekeeper or housekeeper rebates. Further, the notional tax offset also helps determine whether a full-time student under the age of 25 is a dependant for medical expenses tax offset purposes (see 3.161). The notional tax offsets for children are not indexed.

The 2013-14 notional tax offset and cut out threshold is set out in the following table:

Children	Notional tax offset	Tax offset cut-out threshold above following ATI (2013-14)
Each full-time student under age 25	$376	$1,785
One non-student under age 21	$376	$1,785
Each other non-student under age 21	$282	$1,409

The 2014-15 notional tax offset and threshold have not yet been released at the time of writing.

3.112   NO NOTIONAL TAX OFFSET WITH FAMILY TAX BENEFIT PART B

A taxpayer can claim a spouse, child-housekeeper or housekeeper tax offset only for that part of the income year during which the taxpayer (or spouse where relevant) was not eligible to receive full rate FTB Part B (see 3.140).

A tax offset may be claimed:

- for the number of days of the year when the taxpayer was not entitled to FTB Part B at the full rate, or
- in the case of shared care: for the period the dependant child was not in the care of the taxpayer and this was for at least 10% of the care.

NOTE: For the purpose of calculating zone or overseas defence forces tax offsets (see 3.170) any entitlement to FTB Part B that cancels or reduces entitlement to notional spouse, housekeeper or child-housekeeper tax offset is ignored. For the purpose of determining whether a taxpayer can access the Medicare levy family income threshold in calculating their Medicare levy (see 3.053), the impact of FTB Part B in reducing or cancelling housekeeper or child-housekeeper tax offset is ignored.

James and Julie were married for the whole 2014-15 income year, so James had a spouse for 365 days. Julie had no separate net income. They agree to share the care of Julie's daughter (a full time student age 16) from 1 March (122 days) (Julie's former husband had full care before 1 March). Their shared care percentage is 40%, so they are entitled to FTB Part B at a shared care rate for 122 days.

James's dependant spouse offset is:

Number of days before the shared care started x Daily rate of spouse tax offset + (Number of days of share care x Daily rate of spouse tax offset x [100% – Shared care percentage])

= 243 days x Daily rate of spouse tax offset + (122 days x Daily rate of spouse tax offset) x (100% – 40% shared care percentage)

3.113   NOTIONAL AND PHASED-OUT DEPENDENT SPOUSE TAX OFFSET

The Dependent Spouse Tax Offset (DSTO) has been abolished from 1 July 2014. The DSTO component of each of the zone tax offset and the overseas forces tax offsets has been replaced with a dependant (invalid and carer) tax offset component.

3.114   NOTIONAL SOLE PARENT TAX OFFSET

The former sole parent tax offset is now included as part of FTB part B (see 3.140). However, this tax offset was notionally retained to calculate zone and overseas defence forces tax offsets up to 30 June 2014 (see from 3.170) and for determining the entitlement to the Medicare levy family income threshold (see 3.053).

A taxpayer is entitled to a maximum notional sole parent tax offset where during the income year the taxpayer has the sole care of a dependant and the taxpayer is entitled to a notional tax offset for a child under 21 or a full time student under 25. However, this notional tax offset is not available for the period during which the taxpayer is entitled to a spouse, child-housekeeper or housekeeper tax offset. This notional tax offset amount is indexed annually in accordance with increases in the CPI.

NOTE: This notional offset will be rewritten from the ITAA36 to the ITAA97.

3.115 NOTIONAL HOUSEKEEPER TAX OFFSET

A housekeeper tax offset is no longer available from the 2012-13 year. However it was retained as a notional offset for the calculation of the zone and overseas forces offsets up to 30 June 2014. If the housekeeper is engaged full time in keeping the taxpayer's house in Australia and in caring for:

- a child of the taxpayer who is under age 21, including an ex-nuptial child, adopted child or step-child (irrespective of the child's ATI)
- any other child under age 21 for whom the taxpayer qualifies for a notional dependant's tax offset (see 3.111)
- an invalid relative for whom the taxpayer is entitled to a dependants tax offset, or
- a spouse receiving disability support pension or rehabilitation allowance under the *Social Security Act*.

NOTE: The notional housekeeper tax offset is independent of the housekeeper's ATI including salary or wages paid by the taxpayer and any investment income.

NOTE: This notional offset will be rewritten from the ITAA36 to the ITAA97.

 A taxpayer cannot claim a notional housekeeper tax offset for any part of the financial year during which the taxpayer or spouse is eligible to receive FTB part B (see 3.140). However, a tax offset may be available for the balance of the year or for a shared care period.

PARTNERED TAXPAYERS

The notional housekeeper tax offset for married taxpayers including de facto couples can be available if there is a housekeeper who is wholly engaged in keeping house and caring for the taxpayer's invalid spouse. The notional tax offset is in addition to any notional dependants tax offset to which the taxpayer may be entitled or for any notional invalid spouse offset for a spouse or dependant receiving disability support pensions. Where a taxpayer's spouse is receiving a disability support pension, the eligibility for FTB part B does not affect the notional housekeeper tax offset. A taxpayer cannot claim both a notional spouse tax offset and a notional housekeeper tax offset for the same period. The general rule is that a housekeeper tax offset is generally not available if the taxpayer had a spouse.

A notional tax offset is available to a married taxpayer only in special circumstances such as:

- spouse deserted the taxpayer and children and the taxpayer is not living in a de facto relationship
- taxpayer's child has a severe mental disability and requires constant care, and
- taxpayer's spouse suffers from an extended mental illness and is medically certified as being unable to take part in the care of the taxpayer's children.

A person without a spouse may claim the notional housekeeper tax offset, provided the housekeeper is engaged full-time in keeping house for the taxpayer and in caring for a dependent child or invalid relative of the taxpayer.

 A housekeeper tax offset cannot be claimed if the taxpayer is entitled to a dependant tax offset for a child-housekeeper.

3.116 NOTIONAL CHILD-HOUSEKEEPER TAX OFFSET

A child-housekeeper tax offset is no longer available from the 2012-13 year. However it was retained as a notional offset for the calculation of the zone and overseas forces offsets up to 30 June 2014. Taxpayers may be able to claim a notional child-housekeeper tax offset for their child, adopted child or stepchild who kept house full-time, including responsibility for the general running of the household. This tax offset cannot be claimed if:

- the taxpayer contributes to the maintenance of a legal or de facto spouse and is entitled to a notional spouse tax offset, or would be except that the spouse's ATI exceeds the cut out point, or
- for any part of the year there is an entitlement to FTB Part B.

The notional tax offset reduces where ATI is $286 or more. Deduct $282 from ATI and divide the reduced amount by four to calculate the offset available.

There is no entitlement to any notional child-housekeeper tax offset if the ATI of the child-housekeeper exceeds the cut-off point (see table in 3.110).

 A higher notional child housekeeper offset can be claimed by a taxpayer who is eligible for a notional dependant tax offset for a child under age 21 or student under age 25 by contributing to their maintenance (see table at 3.110).

3.117 NOTIONAL INVALID RELATIVE TAX OFFSET

A notional tax offset is no longer available from the 2012-13 year. However it was retained as a notional offset for the calculation of the zone and overseas forces offsets up to 30 June 2014. A notional dependent relative tax offset can be claimed by taxpayers who maintained their child (including an adopted child, a step-child or an ex-nuptial child), brother or sister who is at least age 21 and:

- to whom a disability support pension, special needs disability support pension is paid (or would have been eligible to be paid, immediately before becoming eligible to receive a rehabilitation allowance), or
- where the taxpayer obtains a certificate by an approved medical practitioner that certifies that the relative has a continuing inability to work.

This offset will typically be replaced with the Dependant (Invalid and Carer) Tax Offset; see 3.110.

3.118 NOTIONAL PARENT OR SPOUSE'S PARENT TAX OFFSET

A notional tax offset is no longer available from the 2012-13 year. However it was retained as a notional offset for the calculation of the zone and overseas forces offsets up to 30 June 2014. A taxpayer can claim a notional dependent parent tax offset for each dependent parent or parent-in-law they maintain, including those of a de facto spouse.

3.130 CHILD CARE TAX REBATE

A tax offset for out-of-pocket child care expenses for approved care is available. This is a family assistance payment (instead of a non-refundable tax offset) administered by the Department of Human Services (DHS) and is named the Child Care Tax Rebate (CCTR).

IMPORTANT: The entitlement to this rebate is not constrained by the individual's tax liability and is made following the lodgment of the taxpayer's tax return and after the taxpayer's child care service providers have provided the DHS with the family's child care usage statement. The CCTR payment is effectively brought forward by 12 months. The maximum rebate that can be claimed for the 2014-15 income year is $7,500. The percentage of out-of-pocket expenses remains at 50%.

Out-of-pocket expenses are child care fees not already covered by the Australian Government's Child Care Benefit (CCB). Total child care fees is the amount the child care service provider charges a customer for the standard service provided for each child in care, before any adjustments for CCB. It may include non-CCB hours (hours above the CCB eligible hour limit) and other charges – meals for example – if these are part of the standard service. However, the total fee charged should not include fees charged for unapproved absence days or one-off charges such as enrolment and registration fees, and should take into account any discount provided.

 The indicative 2014-15 year rates for the Child Care Rebate can be estimated using the Centrelink's calculator, available at www.centrelink.gov.au/RateEstimatorsWeb/ publicUserCombinedStart.do

EXAMPLE: Extrapolated from Tax Office fact sheet

In the 2014-15 income year Paul and Pamela have their son Owen in approved after school child care and their daughter Grace in full-time approved child care. Paul and Pamela both work full time and Paul receives CCB which is paid direct to his child care providers.

Paul and Pamela's total fees are $36,000 (Owen $5,000 and Grace $31,000) for the year ending 30 June 2015. Their CCB entitlement for the year ending 30 June 2012 is $7,000 (Owen $1,000 and Grace $6,000).

Paul's rebate is:

	Owen	Grace
Total fees	*$5,000*	*$31,000*
less CCB	*$1,000*	*$6,000*
Out-of-pocket expense	*$4,000*	*$25,000*
50% calculation (per child)	*$4,000 x 50% = $2,000*	*$25,000 x 50% = $12,500*
50% child care rebate	*$2,000*	*$7,500*

NOTE: *Paul's rebate for Grace will be reduced to the maximum limit of $7,500. Paul's total claim in 2014-15 for the child care rebate will be $2,000 for Owen and $7,500 for Grace. This is despite 50% of out-of-pocket expenses exceeding this figure as this is the statutory cap for 2014-15.*

3.131   ELIGIBILITY

To be eligible to claim the rebate for an income year you must have:

- used approved child care during the year
- responsibility for paying the child care fees for your child
- been assessed as eligible for CCB, and
- passed the CCB work/training/study test. The CCB work/training/study test is administered by the DHS.

Approved child care is care provided by a service provider that participates satisfactorily in the Australian Government's funded quality assurance system and has been approved to receive CCB payments on behalf of eligible families. Approved care includes:

- long day care
- family day care
- in-home care
- outside school hours care
- vacation care, and
- some occasional care services.

NOTE: If you have not received CCB for approved care in an income year, you will need to lodge a CCB lump sum claim with the DHS. Lump sum claims for CCB must now be lodged within one year of the end of the financial year for which you are claiming. This means to lodge a claim for 2014-15 you have until 30 June 2016. Extensions to the one year period may be provided in special circumstances. No CCTR is available if you are not entitled to CCB.

Families with income over the following thresholds are no longer entitled to receive any CCB:

Number of children in care	Income limits 2014-15	Income limits 2015-16
1	$149,597	$152,147
2	$155,013	$157,654
3	$175,041	$178,023
Each additional child add	$33,106	$33,671

However, families that were previously receiving CCB at the minimum rate continue to be eligible for the CCTR, despite the fact that they are no longer receiving CCB for approved childcare.

3.140   FAMILY TAX BENEFIT

Family Tax Benefits (FTB) (Part A and Part B) are paid to families to help with the cost of raising dependent children. Family Tax Benefit Part A is the primary payment designed to help with the cost of raising children. It is payable to a parent/guardian or an approved care organisation for a child aged under 21 years or a dependent full-time student aged between 21 and 25 years. Family Tax Benefit Part B is designed to provide extra help to families with one main income earner, including sole parent families with a dependent full time student up to the age of 18 years. In the 2014-15 year Budget a number of reforms were proposed to this regime.

RECENT PROPOSALS

In its 2014-15 Federal Budget, the Government proposed the following measures:
- restrict FTB Part B to families with children under six years of age
- limit large family supplement to families with four or more children
- a temporary freeze on the indexation on clean energy supplements and FTB rates
- introduce new single parent benefit for eligible parents with child between 6 and 12 years old
- remove FTB Part A per child add on, and
- reducing end of year FTB supplement and freeze further indexation of payment.

From 1 July 2015, the large family supplement will only be paid to families with four or more children.

In the 2015-16 Federal Budget, the Government announced the following proposals:
- the FTB Part A large family supplement will be abolished from 1 July 2016, and
- from 1 January 2016, families will only be able to receive FTB part A for six weeks in a 12-month period while they are overseas. Currently, overseas recipients receive payments at usual rates for six weeks and at the base rate for another 50 weeks.

ELIGIBILITY

Eligibility criteria are complex. There are a number of components as follows:

NORMALLY ELIGIBLE

An individual is eligible for family tax benefit where:
- they have at least one FTB child, or
- they are not an absent overseas recipient and has at least one regular care child who is a rent assistance child.

Where this is the case the individual in question must satisfy one of the following three conditions:
- they are an Australian resident, or
- they are a special category visa holder residing in Australia, or
- where the FTB Part B for the individual is greater than nil and the individual holds a visa determined by the Minister and is in Australia or temporarily absent for no longer than 6 weeks (where that absence is deemed allowable in relation to a special benefit).

Note that a number of exceptions apply to this eligibility requirement.

FTB CHILD INCOME LIMIT

Up until 30 April 2014, a 'child income limit' applied. For the period 1 July 2013 to 30 April 2014, the taxpayer was ineligible for FTB Part A and Part B if the child earned $14,078 or more and was:
- aged 5-15 years and not studying full time, or
- aged 16-19 years and not in full time secondary study, or
- exempt from this requirement.

INCOME TEST

The payment of benefits is means tested against the family's ATI, with a progressive approach to income and level of benefit per dependent child. The definition of ATI includes an individual's total net investment loss and reportable superannuation contributions for the income year.

ASSETS TEST

No assets test is applicable to FTB Part A or B.

NOTE: Family tax benefit payments may be stopped where the family leaves Australia without notifying the Department of Human Services. Family tax benefits are not paid to a dependant who is the claimant's partner.

FTB PART A

Satisfying the 'normally eligible' requirements described above will provide access to FTB Part A. The quantum of the benefit entitlement must then be determined.

FTB Part A is paid for:

- dependent children under 16 years
- dependent children under 16-17 who have completed year 12 or an equivalent
- dependent children under 19 years of age being cared for at least 35% of the time, and
- dependent children who have resided outside Australia for not more than three years (s22, s24 *Family Assistance Act*).

MAXIMUM AND BASE RATE FTB PART A

A fixed maximum FTB Part A is paid to low income families whose income does not exceed the maximum FTB Part A threshold of $50,151 (ATI) in 2014-15 ($48,837 for the 2013-14 income year). It is paid for each dependant child whose benefit may vary with the age. (See the table below.)

Once the family income exceeds the maximum FTB part A threshold, a reduction in benefits occurs at the rate of 20 cents of benefits lost for each additional dollar of family income until a level of benefit equal to the base rate FTB Part A applies (at the threshold of $64,052.20). The base FTB Part A benefit is the family income-tested benefit paid to families on higher incomes and is also paid for each dependant child according to age. This level of benefit is maintained with increasing income until the base rate FTB Part A income threshold is reached.

NOTE: The base FTB Part A threshold increases by $3,796 for each dependent child after the first.

FAMILY INCOME LEVELS FOR FAMILY TAX BENEFIT PART A FOR ONE CHILD FAMILY

Maximum family income to get:

- Maximum FTB Part A income threshold: $50,151
- Base rate FTB Part A income threshold: $94,316

Maximum payment amounts		
For each child	**Per fortnight**	**Clean Energy Supplement**
Child, 0 – 12, each	$176.82	$3.50
Child, 13 – 19, each	$230.02	$4.48
Child up to 19 in approved care organisation	$56.70	$0.98

Base rate of Family Tax Benefit Part A		
For each child	**Per fortnight**	**Clean Energy Supplement**
Under 18 years	$56.70	$1.40
18-19 years, secondary students	$56.70	$1.40

Persons aged between 16 and 19 need to be in full time study in an approved course in order for a taxpayer to receive FTB Part A in respect of their child (unless the child is 16-17 and has completed year 12 or an equivalent).

The benefit paid for each dependent child relates to age and the primary rates applicable for the relevant year including an FTB Part A supplement of $726.35 per child for the income year. Approved care organisations are not entitled to the Family Tax Benefit Part A Supplement.

Single eligible child under 12 (2014-15)

Consider a family with a single eligible child who is under 12 years. If the family was in receipt of income below the maximum FTB Part A income threshold of $50,151 then the maximum FTB Part A of $176.82 per fortnight is paid. If the family was in receipt of income in excess of $50,151 the benefit is reduced by 20 cents for each dollar of family income above the threshold.

This reduction in benefit continues at this rate with increasing income, until the benefit is reduced from the maximum FTB Part A of $176.82 per fortnight to the base rate FTB Part A benefit of $56.70 per fortnight at an income of $94,316.

The benefit remains at this level, with increasing income until the income reaches a new threshold of $94,316, the maximum income for which the base rate FTB Part A benefit can be paid.

For this family, with further increases in income the benefit reduces at the rate of 30 cents for each additional dollar of income and ultimately cuts out at $101,787. (This example does not consider Clean Energy Supplement which is in addition to the FTB Part A paid).

The following tables are a guide and show certain threshold income limits at which FTB Part A is paid at the base level depending on the age and number of children in the family, and the income limits at which FTB Part A cuts out completely. Note that the age ranges between tables are different and incomes can be higher where rent assistance eligibility applies.

Where n/a is shown,the base rate does not usually apply for this household combination. This is because the rate calculated under the first income test for this combination is usually higher than the rate calculated under the second income test, which applies the base rate. Income limits will be higher if you are eligible for Rent Assistance.

Annual income limits for base rate FTB Part A eligibility only (DHS data) 2014-15

Number of children aged under 12	Number of children aged 13 to 15, or secondary students 16 to 19 years			
	Nil	One	Two	Three
Nil	Nil	$73,146	$96,141	N/A
One	$66,084	$89,079	N/A	N/A
Two	$82,016	N/A	N/A	N/A
Three	$97,948	N/A	N/A	N/A

Annual income level at which the FTB Part A (including supplement) ceases (DHS data) 2014-15

Number of children aged under 12	Number of children aged 13 to 15, or secondary students 16 to 19 years			
	Nil	One	Two	Three
Nil	Nil	$101,787	$118,552	$154,359
One	$101,787	$113,053	$147,296	$183,103
Two	$113,053	$140,233	$176,040	$211,846
Three	$133,171	$168,977	$204,784	$240,590

* The income limit may actually be higher than the above figures for 3 children aged 13 to 15 and for multiple birth allowances.

MAINTENANCE INCOME TEST

The following annual maintenance income thresholds apply. Above these levels FTB part A payments are reduced by 50 cents for each additional dollar of maintenance received. A reduction occurs potentially until the Base rate is received. Blind pensioners are exempt from the maintenance income test.

Maintenance income thresholds (from DHS) 2014-15	
Category	**Threshold**
One member of a couple or a single parent	$1,522.05
A couple, each receiving maintenance	$3,044.10
Each additional child	$507.35

NON-FINANCIAL ELIGIBILITY CRITERIA FOR THE FTB PART A SUPPLEMENT

To receive the FTB Part A supplement, some families may also have to meet non-financial criteria, including:

- undertaking a health check for four year old children, and
- immunising children turning 1, 2 or 5.

FTB PART B

FTB part B is paid to single income or sole parent families. It is payable until the youngest child turns 16 or until the end of the calendar year in which the youngest child turns 18 for full time students (who doesn't receive youth allowance or a similar payment). The payment is made on a per family basis unlike FTB Part A that is paid on a per dependent child basis. The rate of FTB Part B is based on an income test and is paid with reference to a family's youngest child. You also need to meet residency requirements.

BENEFIT TAPER

The ATI of the lower income earner is tested and may reach a maximum of $5,329 (2014-15 income year) to be able to obtain the full benefit of this payment. A reduction in benefit occurs at the rate of 20 cents for each dollar in excess of the threshold.

The FTB Part B will only be payable to families where the primary earner has an ATI of $150,000 or less. This income test applies to single parent families as well. Those single parent families on incomes of $150,000 or less will receive the maximum rate of payment. This income threshold will be reduced to $100,000 from 1 July 2015.

FTB Part B paid according to age of youngest child 2013-14			
Youngest child's age	Max FTB** part B payable	Income threshold for full part B payment	Income threshold* for nil part B payment
Under 5 years	$4,274.15	$5,329	$27,065
5 to 18 years	$3,091.55	$5,329	$21,043

* Lower income earner for a couple, these figures are calculated on the basis of a reduction in FTB Part B benefit of 20 cents per dollar of ATI above threshold of $5,329.

**These figures include FTB Part B supplementary benefit of $354.05 paid after the end of the income year.

 Jack and Joan (a de facto couple) have two dependent children aged 13 and 15. Joan is the main bread winner earning $80,000. Jack's income was $6,500 for the year. His income will reduce their FTB Part B by ($6,500 – $5,329) x 0.2 = $234.20 p.a. FTB Part B entitlement = $3,091.55 – $234.20 = $2,857.35.

NOTE: The definition of ATI includes an individual's total net investment loss and reportable superannuation contributions for the income year.

PAYMENT CHOICES FOR FTB

The Department of Human Services (DHS) administers the FTB Part A and Part B.

IMPORTANT: FTB claims cannot be lodged through the tax system. An eligible family can claim FTB by completing a claim form, and returning the form to the nearest Centrelink or Medicare office. The relevant forms can be obtained by:

- visiting any Centrelink or Medicare office
- downloading from the DHS website, and
- calling 13 61 50 for a postal delivery.

Alternatively, an eligible family can claim FTB online from the Centrelink website or through myGov. The claimant must register for online services with Centrelink or myGov before proceeding to the online application.

FAMILY INCOME

Most families claiming through Centrelink/DHS are required to provide an estimate of their income for the income year and the adjustments will be allowed if their circumstances change. The following are not required to provide an estimate of income:

- single people receiving an income support allowance or pension
- a family on the minimum rate of FTB Part A, if their income will not change much in the next income year
- a family receiving FTB as a lump sum from the Tax Office at the end of the income year, or
- a family receiving CCB from the DHS at the end of the income year or CCB for using registered care.

ADDITIONAL BENEFITS

Families receiving FTB may also be eligible for other payments including:

- the large family supplement of $321.20 per annum for the third (and each subsequent child) is payable in 2014-15
- multiple birth allowance of $3,854.40 for triplets and $5,131.90 for quadruplets or more children when born during the same birth
- rent assistance (if renting privately). This can only be paid by Centrelink. The amount of rent assistance is based on individual's
- newborn upfront payment and newborn supplement (to replace baby bonus) of up to $2,056.45 for the first child and $1,028.15 for each subsequent child.
- family situation which includes the number of FTB children whether the individual is single or partnered, and
- Jobs, Education and Training (JET) child care fee assistance.

3.150   SCHOOLKIDS BONUS

Important: The Schoolkids Bonus is being phased out. The last instalment will be paid in July 2016.

PAYMENT OF BONUS

You do not need to claim the Schoolkids Bonus or keep receipts for education expenses. From 1 January 2015, eligible families will receive the Schoolkids Bonus in:

- two instalments of $211 for each child in primary school – a total of $422 each year, and
- two instalments of $421 for each child in secondary school – a total of $842 each year.

If you share the care of your child with another person, you will receive a percentage of this payment, calculated based on the percentage of Family Tax Benefit you receive for the child.

The Schoolkids Bonus can be paid in different ways. If:

- you receive fortnightly payments, your Schoolkids Bonus payments will be paid in January and July
- you claim Family Tax Benefit as a lump sum, you will get your Schoolkids Bonus payment (if eligible) when your lump sum claim is assessed, and after you and your partner (if you have one) have lodged your tax returns
- you are a student and your Centrelink payment normally goes into your bank account, you will get the Schoolkids Bonus the same way
- your payments are income managed, your Schoolkids Bonus will be paid directly to your Income Management account, and
- you receive an education allowance for a child from the Department of Veterans' Affairs, they will pay your Schoolkids Bonus for that child.

If you prefer, you can change from receiving a lump sum to a fortnightly payment and receive the Schoolkids Bonus when the next payment is due (January or July). This can be done through Centrelink Online Services through myGov.

3.151 ELIGIBILITY

To be eligible for the Schoolkids Bonus, you must either be a parent or carer who gets Family Tax Benefit Part A for a dependent child attending primary or secondary education.

A child may be eligible in their own right if they are receiving a payment and undertaking primary or secondary education.

Schoolkids Bonus may also be payable where the child is undertaking an 'eligible activity' such as being home schooled, overseas study or special education.

The Schoolkids Bonus will be paid to primary and secondary students if they satisfy the income test and are:

- turning 19 years of age or younger in the calendar year, and
- receiving:
  - Youth Allowance
  - ABSTUDY (Living Allowance)
  - Disability Support Pension
  - Carer Payment
  - Parenting Payment
  - Special Benefit, or
  - an Education Allowance from the Department of Veterans' Affairs.

The Schoolkids Bonus will be paid to secondary students receiving Pensioner Education Supplement if they are:

- turning 19 years of age or younger in the calendar year, and
- receiving:
  - Disability Support Pension
  - Carer Payment
  - Parenting Payment, or
  - Special Benefit.

Children in preschool are not eligible.

3.152 DEFINITION OF PRESCHOOL, PRIMARY AND SECONDARY SCHOOL FOR SCHOOLKIDS BONUS

The names of primary and secondary school years are different depending on what state you live in. Check your child's eligibility based on your location.

State/Territory	Preschool (not eligible)	Primary school (eligible)	Secondary school (eligible)
NSW	Preschool	Kindergarten, Years 1-6	Years 7-12
VIC	Kindergarten	Preparatory, Years 1-6	Years 7-12
QLD	Kindergarten	Preparatory, Years 1-6	Years 7-12
SA	Kindergarten	Reception, Years 1-7	Years 8-12
WA	Kindergarten	Pre-primary, Years 1-6	Years 7-12
TAS	Kindergarten	Preparatory, Years 1-6	Years 7-12
NT	Preschool	Transition, Years 1-6	Years 7-12
ACT	Preschool	Kindergarten, Years 1-6	Years 7-12

3.153 INCOME TEST

From 1 January 2015, an income test will apply. Eligible families and young people with an annual adjusted taxable income of $100,000 or less will be paid the Schoolkids Bonus.

There are some exemptions to the income test. For example, people receiving Schoolkids Bonus because of their eligibility to Special Benefit, certain veterans' education allowance payments or Disability Support Pension for those who are permanently blind are exempt from the income test.

The exemption from the income test for Special Benefit and Disability Support Pension only applies where the student is receiving Schoolkids Bonus in their own right. Families receiving Schoolkids Bonus because of their eligibility to Family Tax Benefit Part A for a dependent child are not exempt from the income test.

3.160 MEDICAL EXPENSES TAX OFFSET

The net medical expense tax offset is being phased out. Taxpayers who received the offset in 2012-13 will continue to be eligible for the offset for the 2013-14 income year if they have eligible out-of-pocket medical expenses above the relevant claim threshold. Similarly, those who receive the tax offset in 2013-14 will continue to be eligible for the offset in 2014-15. The offset will continue to be available for taxpayers with out-of-pocket medical expenses relating to disability aids, attendant care or aged care expenses until 1 July 2019.

3.161 MEDICAL EXPENSE CLAIMS

ELIGIBILITY AND MEANS TESTING

Individuals with an Adjusted Taxable Income (ATI) above $90,000 for singles or $180,000 for a couple or family in 2014-15 will be means tested for this offset. The family threshold will be increased by $1,500 for each dependent child after the first. Individuals who exceed the threshold will only be able to claim a reimbursement of 10% for eligible out of pocket expenses incurred in excess of $5,233 (for 2014-15).

Taxpayers with an adjusted taxable income below these thresholds will be unaffected by the new measures. These taxpayers will continue to be able to claim a reimbursement of 20% for net medical expenses that are over $2,218 for 2014-15. Payments of medical expenses by an employer do not reduce the rebatable medical expense, but the employer may be subject to fringe benefits tax. It may also give rise to a reportable fringe benefit amount (see 25.300).

MEDICAL EXPENSE CLAIMS

A tax offset can be claimed for expenses paid by the taxpayer in the year of income in respect of:

- the taxpayer him/herself

- wife or husband (or de facto spouse). 'Spouse' does not need to be a dependant within the meaning of s159J
- any child of the taxpayer (including adopted or stepchildren) to their 21st birthday regardless of ATI, and
- any other person for whom even $1 of a notional tax offset as a dependant can be claimed, including parents, parents-in-law, child-housekeeper and invalid relatives. Note that some of these offsets have been phased out and replaced with the Dependant (Invalid and Carer) Tax Offset (see 3.110).

DEPENDANTS OVERSEAS

To qualify for the medical expenses tax offset, the medical expenses must be incurred in respect of a resident taxpayer or a resident dependant of the taxpayer.

Medical expenses can be claimed for a non-resident dependant intending to become a resident of Australia provided the person is:

- the spouse (or child up to 21 years of age) of the taxpayer, or
- a child (up to 25 years of age) receiving full time education overseas and the student has ATI below the relevant threshold per year, so some part of the 'notional tax offset' remains (see 3.111).

PAYMENTS TO A SEPARATED SPOUSE

Once divorced, a claim can no longer be made for an ex-spouse. Nor can a claim be made for a reimbursement paid to an ex-spouse if that person incurred the expenses themselves. A claim still exists for children, but maintenance payments of an undivided sum cannot be partly claimed as medical expenses. Usually the person who makes the payment is the one able to claim unless the payment is made as the agent of another.

TRUSTEE PAYING MEDICAL EXPENSES

If a trustee pays medical expenses from trust income for a resident beneficiary of a trust, the net amount after deducting reimbursements paid or payable is rebatable if:

- the trustee is assessed under s98 in that assessment, or
- the beneficiary is assessable.

If a trustee of a deceased estate pays medical expenses in respect of the liability incurred by the deceased during the deceased person's lifetime, the trustee is allowed to claim medical expenses offset in its assessment on the deceased income up to the date of death.

 To be entitled to claim a tax offset for medical expenses the person claiming must have paid for the expense.

3.162   DEFINITION OF NET MEDICAL EXPENSES

The term 'net medical expenses' is defined as the amount of payments made in respect of the following, after deducting reimbursements received or receivable from Medicare or a health fund:

- to a legally qualified medical practitioner, nurse or chemist, or a public or private hospital, in respect of an illness or operation
- to a legally qualified dentist for dental services or treatment of artificial teeth
- to a person registered under a law of a State/Territory for supply, alteration or repair of artificial teeth
- for therapeutic treatment administered by referral from a legally qualified medical practitioner (eg. physiotherapist, speech therapist)
- for the purchase or repair of an artificial limb (or part of one), an artificial eye or hearing aid
- for the purchase or repair of medical aids prescribed by legally qualified medical practitioner
- for the testing of eyes, or the prescribing of any spectacles by a person legally

qualified to perform those services, or for the supply or repair of spectacles in accordance with such a prescription

- to a person who looks after someone who is blind, or confined to bed or wheelchair
- to keep a trained guide dog for a blind person, and
- to keep a trained dog to assist or guide the hearing impaired or other disabled individuals.

 Expenses for purely cosmetic procedures are excluded from the medical expenses tax offset.

COSMETIC PROCEDURES ARE NOT MEDICAL EXPENSES

Medical and dental procedures that are cosmetic in nature do not qualify for the Medical Expenses Offset (MEO). Such expenses are called 'ineligible medical expenses'.

Payments made to a legally qualified medical practitioner, nurse or chemist for an operation that is cosmetic and for which a Medicare benefit is not available, does not qualify for the MEO. While a procedure may be cosmetic in nature, if a Medicare benefit is available, then the taxpayer can claim the MEO.

Note that if the procedure does not attract a Medicare benefit, but is not cosmetic, the taxpayer may still claim the MEO. Dental expenses have a different test because they usually do not attract a Medicare benefit. Payments to a legally qualified dentist for dental services or treatment that are solely cosmetic do not qualify for the MEO. If a procedure is not solely cosmetic, then the expense qualifies for the MEO.

 Lucy underwent reconstructive surgery for earlier surgery for breast cancer. A Medicare benefit is payable for the procedure and therefore the cost is an eligible expense for the MEO.

 Poppy has botox injections to remove wrinkles from her face. The procedure does not attract a Medicare benefit and is therefore deemed to be solely cosmetic and the MEO will not apply.

 Tony had laser surgery on both eyes. In ID 2004/51 the Tax Office took the view that the surgery changes the function but not the appearance of the eye and is therefore performed for medical reasons, not for cosmetic reasons. The expense is eligible for the MEO.

 Emily has braces fitted to her teeth. As braces are fitted for many reasons that are not solely cosmetic (eg. misaligned bite), the expense is eligible for the MEO.

 Imelda has a jewel inserted into one of her teeth by a dentist. The procedure is solely cosmetic and therefore ineligible for the MEO.

NURSING HOMES OR HOSTELS

Approved recipients of residential aged care are usually assessed as needing a particular level of personal or nursing care in a nursing home or hostel. The tax offset can be claimed for qualifying payments where care is assessed at levels 1 to 7.

Where eligible, the tax offset can be claimed for:

- basic daily fees
- income tested daily fees
- extra service fees
- accommodation charges
- amounts deducted or retained from accommodation bonds where bonds paid as a lump sum (ID 2003/360)
- interest charged on an outstanding instalment of a lump sum accommodation bond (ID 2006/251), and
- periodic payments of accommodation bonds.

The tax offset cannot be claimed for:

- lump sum payments of accommodation bonds, and
- interest derived by care providers from the investment of accommodation bonds.

Payments for respite care qualify for the tax offset on the same basis as residential care recipients where an approved provider of residential aged care provides the care.

3.163   EXPENSES THAT ARE NOT MEDICAL EXPENSES

Expenses that are not included as medical expenses for the MEO include:

- therapeutic treatment not formally referred by a doctor – a mere suggestion or recommendation by a doctor to the patient is not enough for the treatment to qualify; the patient must be referred to a particular person for specific treatment
- chemist-type items – such as tablets for pain relief – purchased in retail outlets or health food stores
- vaccinations for overseas travel
- non-prescribed vitamins or health foods
- travel or accommodation expenses associated with medical treatment
- payment for domestic services (eg. house cleaning or maintenance) rendered to a person who is blind or confined to a wheelchair or bed (ID 2007/190)
- contributions to a private health fund
- purchases from a chemist that are not related to an illness or operation
- life insurance medical examinations
- ambulance charges and subscriptions, and
- funeral expenses.

3.164   EXPENSES IN RELATION TO DISABILITY AIDS, ATTENDANT CARE AND AGED CARE

For individuals who wish to claim the net medical expense tax offset and did not claim it in 2012-13, the eligible medical expenses are limited to costs in relation to disability aids, attendant care or aged care. Note that the eligibility thresholds must still be satisfied (see 3.161).

DISABILITY AIDS

Disability aids are items of property manufactured as, or generally recognised to be, an aid to functional capacity of a person with a with a disability but, generally, will not include ordinary household or commercial appliances. Purchase of a wheelchair for a paraplegic or maintenance of a guide dog for a person who is blind are typical examples. An air conditioner to assist a bedridden person who is sensitive to temperature would typically excluded.

ATTENDANT CARE

Attendant care expenses relate to services and care provided to a person with a disability to assist with every day living, such as the provision of personal assistance, home nursing, home maintenance, and domestic services. An example is where a person with a brain injury pays for an attendant to come to their home to assist with grooming, clothing and feeding activities during the day.

AGED CARE EXPENSES

Aged care expenses relate to services and accommodation provided by an approved aged care provider to a person who is a care recipient or continuing care recipient within the meaning of the *Aged Care Act 1997*.

3.170 ZONE AND OVERSEAS DEFENCE FORCES TAX OFFSETS

A zone tax offset is available under s79A of ITAA36 for taxpayers who reside for more than half a year in prescribed areas of Australia. An overseas defence forces tax offset is available under s79B of the ITAA36 for Australian defence force members or U.N. armed forces when they serve in certain overseas localities for more than half a year. TR 94/27 explains the zone tax offset.

There is a search facility on the Tax Office's website to enable taxpayers to work out if a town is located in a prescribed area for zone tax offset purposes (it can be accessed through Practice Statement PS LA 2002/6). There is also a list of specified overseas localities for overseas defence forces tax offset purposes on the Tax Office's website. Both these offsets are in addition to the dependant tax offsets.

3.171 DESCRIPTION OF THE ZONES

DESIGNATED OR PRESCRIBED AREAS

The areas delineated are generally to the north, west, and central parts of mainland Australia and the western part of Tasmania.

- **Zone A:** Apart from areas offshore between the equator and Australian territorial limit, this also includes:
  - Macquarie Island
  - The Cocos (Keeling) Islands
  - Australian Antarctic Territory
  - Heard Island and the McDonald Islands
  - Norfolk Island and Lord Howe Island
  - Christmas Island, and
  - Islands adjacent to the Zone A coastline but excludes oil rigs located in that zone.
- **Zone B:** Islands adjacent to zone B parts of the mainland and Tasmania, with special areas including:
  - King Island, and
  - Furneaux Group of islands.
- **Special remote zone:** Some places (but not islands) are eligible for a higher basic zone tax offset if, by the shortest practical land or sea route, they are more than 250km from the centre of an urban area (whether or not that urban area is within an eligible zone) with a 1981 census population of over 2,499. The 1981 census is used only if the taxpayer is not disadvantaged by it.

3.172 RESIDENTIAL REQUIREMENTS

For zone tax offset purposes, a taxpayer is regarded as having been in a zone for the period he or she 'resided' there (ie. eats, drinks or sleeps there).

NOTE: In its 2015-16 Federal Budget, the Government proposed that from 1 July 2015 "fly-in fly-out" and "drive-in drive-out" workers will be excluded from claiming the rebate where their normal residence is not within a "zone". At the time of writing, this proposal had not been enacted.

DEATH WHILE RESIDING IN A ZONE

If a taxpayer dies in a zone while residing in it, that person will be regarded as having been in the zone and is entitled to the full tax offset in that income year.

183 TOTAL DAYS IN THE INCOME YEAR

If, in the aggregate, a taxpayer spends 183 or more days of the July to June financial year in a zone, a zone tax offset is available for that year.

183 DAYS OVER TWO ADJACENT YEARS

If the taxpayer wasn't eligible for a zone tax offset in one year, the number of days within the zone are carried forward to the next year to see if 183 days is reached. In that situation, the taxpayer becomes entitled to the zone tax offset only in the year in which the 183 days is achieved.

183 DAYS OVER FOUR YEARS

If a taxpayer resided in a zone for less than 183 days, they may still qualify if they meet each of the following criteria:

- they lived in a zone for a continuous period of less than five years after 1 July 1999
- they were unable to claim in the first year because they lived or worked there less than 183 days, and
- the total number of days they were there in the first year and in the last financial year equals 183 or more.

SUFFICIENT TIME, BUT IN MORE THAN ONE ZONE

If 183 days or more were spent in zones, but less than 183 days was spent in any one zone, a proportionate tax offset is calculated for each zone. The answers are then added together. There could be up to three components if some of the 183-plus days were spent in each of the three zone-categories discussed at 3.171.

Each component of your ultimate claim is calculated as follows:

(Eligible days in zone divided by 183) x Maximum tax offset available for zone

NOTE: If total days spent in different zones exceeds 183 days, the proportion of tax offset is calculated up to a maximum of 183 days. The zone with the least rebate is allocated the remaining days (TR 94/27).

3.173   ZONE TAX OFFSET

If more than one of the categories below are appropriate, use the one which appears first:

- **Special Zone A and Zone B areas only:** If legally a resident during the income year of either a special area of Zone A, or Zone B: *$1,173 plus 50% of the relevant tax offset amount*
- **Zone A – Ordinary area:** If a resident of zone A but did not reside in (and never was in) the special areas of zone A or Zone B during the year: *$338 plus 50% of the relevant tax offset amount*
- **Zone B – Ordinary area:** If legally a resident of zone B but didn't reside in (and never was in) Zone A or Zone B special areas during the year: *$57 plus 20% of the relevant tax offset amount*

NOTE: The relevant tax offsets amount is defined in s79A(4) to include the sum of tax offsets to which the taxpayer is entitled for the year, including tax offsets for parent, spouse's parent or invalid relative, spouse, dependent children or students, child-housekeeper and sole parent; see from 3.110. For the purpose of calculating zone tax offset (as well as overseas defence forces tax offset), any entitlement to FTB part B that would otherwise reduce or cancel entitlement to spouse, child-housekeeper or housekeeper rebate, is ignored.

3.174   OVERSEAS DEFENCE AND CIVILIAN FORCES TAX OFFSET

Service in certain localities (or with U.N. forces overseas) for more than half of the income year or where the taxpayer dies at an overseas locality during the income year, entitles Australian Defence Force (ADF) members to tax offsets like the above (but not also 'special area' tax offsets) of $338 plus 50% of the relevant tax offset amount.

A proportionate rebate is allowable if the period of service in overseas localities is not more than 182 days and is calculated as follows (TR 97/2):

(Eligible days served in overseas localities divided by 183)
x Maximum defence force tax offset available

A taxpayer that is entitled to both the zone tax offset and the defence force tax offset is only entitled to claim one of these offsets. You should claim the one with the highest tax offset.

SPECIFIED OVERSEAS LOCALITIES

Only those with service as a member of the ADF or a UN armed force in specified overseas localities are entitled to the defence force tax offset. A list of the specified overseas localities is available on the Tax Office website (search for overseas forces specified localities).

The total period of service at overseas localities excludes the period for which the ADF member is entitled to an exemption from income tax under s23AC, s23AD or s23AG.

3.190   SENIOR AUSTRALIANS AND PENSIONER TAX OFFSET

The Senior Australians and Pensioner Tax Offset (SAPTO) refers to the tax offset that is available for age and service age pensioners, and self-funded retirees of age pension age.

 The Low Income Tax Offset (LITO) of up to $445 in 2015-16 and 2014-15 may also apply (see 3.012) in conjunction with SAPTO.

The table below details the offset thresholds and maximum offset rates:

SAPTO	2014-15 Rebate income		
Eligibility condition	Threshold max. tax offset applies	Upper threshold	Max. tax offset
You did not have a spouse and your rebate income was less than	$32,279	$50,119	$2,230
You had a spouse and the combined rebate income of you and your spouse was less than	$57,948 ($28,974 each)	$83,580 ($41,790 each)	$1,602
At any time during the year you and your spouse had to live apart due to illness or because one of you was in a nursing home and the combined rebate income of you and your spouse was less than	$62,558 ($31,279 each)	$95,198 ($47,599 each)	$2,040

No change to the maximum tax offset values or the reduction rate 12.5 cents applied for every $1 over the maximum rate threshold up to the cut off threshold.

'Rebate income' is the aggregate of:
- taxable income
- adjusted fringe benefits amount
- total net investment loss (including net rental property loss), and
- reportable superannuation contributions.

3.191   ELIGIBILITY FOR THE SENIOR AUSTRALIANS & PENSIONER TAX OFFSET

TAXPAYERS ELIGIBLE

Generally, the following taxpayers are eligible for the SAPTO:
- a taxpayer who during the income year:
  - is eligible for a pension, allowance or benefit under the *Veterans' Entitlement Act 1986*
  - has reached pension age under that act, and
  - is not in gaol

- a taxpayer during the income year who:
  - is qualified for an age pension under the *Social Security Act 1991*, and
  - is not in gaol.

This definition means Veterans who were eligible for a pension but did not receive one (perhaps due to not meeting the income or asset requirements) and persons not meeting the residency requirements for an aged pension but were eligible for that pension using an alternate test could be able to access this offset.

3.192   TAX OFFSET FOR TRUSTEES OF A TRUST

Where a beneficiary of a trust would be entitled to a SAPTO but is under a legal disability, the SAPTO is available to the trustee in the trustee's assessment if the beneficiary's share of the net income of the trust is assessable under s98 (ie. bankrupts and intellectually disabled beneficiaries and the tax is paid on their behalf by the trustees. In this situation, taxable income is taken to be net income (s160AAAB)).

3.193   TRANSFER OF UNUSED SENIOR AUSTRALIAN PENSIONER TAX OFFSETS

In certain circumstances, the unused (unclaimed) portion of a taxpayer's SAPTO entitlement can be transferred to their spouse. The entitlement can be calculated according to the three-step process in the *Income Tax Assessment Regulations 1936* (ITAR36):

1. Determine a spouse's 'Maximum Rebate Amount' and then the taxpayer's 'Maximum Rebate Amount' (inclusive of any rebate transferred between spouses) (step 1)
2. Determine the 'Adjusted Rebate Threshold' for the taxpayer receiving the transferred rebate using the 'Maximum Rebate Amount' calculated in step 1 (step 2), and
3. Finally, determine the actual rebate for SAPTO including the transferred amount reduced according to the 'Adjusted Rebate Threshold' calculated in step 2 (step 3).

Refer to the ITAR36 for the necessary formulae.

Transfer of unused SAPTO

In the 2014 income year a taxpayer is able to utilise their partner's unused entitlement. The first taxpayer in the couple had a taxable income of $38,256 and their spouse had a taxable income of $16,351. Both were eligible for the SAPTO. The taxpayer and spouse had the same amount of rebate income as taxable income. The taxpayer and spouse have been together for the full income tax year.

Step 1

The spouse has a 'Maximum Rebate Amount' of $1,602 which is the 'Maximum Rebate Amount' without transferring any rebate to the spouse. The taxpayer uses the following formula to determine the maximum 'Rebate Amount' inclusive of any rebate transferred to him as follows:

> *A: Transferred 'Rebate Amount' of Spouse*
> *B: Maximum 'Rebate Amount' of Spouse*
> *S: Taxable income of spouse*
> $A = B - ((S - \$6,000) \times 0.15)$
> $A = \$1,602 - ((\$16,351 - \$6,000) \times 0.15)$
> $A = \$49.35$

The 'Maximum Rebate Amount' of the taxpayer is therefore the SAPTO transferred from their spouse plus the maximum SAPTO they could have claimed were they single as follows:

Maximum Rebate Amount of taxpayer = $1,602 + $49.35 (from above) = $1,651

Step 2

The 'Adjusted Rebate Threshold' must then be worked out for the taxpayer. This can be worked out using the following formula in this case:

A: Adjusted Rebate Threshold

D: Tax-Free Threshold in 2014-15

E: Maximum Low Income Tax Offset Available

F: Taxpayer's 'Maximum Rebate Amount' for the year (See 'Step 1')

C: Lowest marginal tax rate

$A = D + ((E+F)/C)$

$A = \$18,200 + ((\$445 + \$1,651)/19\%)$

$A = \$29,232$

This part of the formula is based on the rates and thresholds from the current income year. NOTE: The rebate amount is worked out in accordance with subregulations 150AB (2) and (2B), but may then be affected by regulations 150AE or 150AF.

Step 3

The final step in the process is then to calculate the actual SAPTO rebate taking into account both 'step 1' and 'step 2'. The formula in order to work out the actual SAPTO is as follows:

A: SAPTO Rebate

B: Taxpayer's 'Maximum Rebate Amount' (from 'Step 1')

C: Taxpayer's Rebate Income (in this case taxable income)

D: Taxpayer's 'Adjusted Rebate Threshold' (from 'Step 2')

$A = B - ((C-D) \times 12.5\%)$

$A = \$1,651 - ((\$38,256 - \$29,232) \times 12.5\%)$

$A = \$523$

 The Tax Office has a SAPTO calculator on its website.

3.210   BENEFICIARY TAX OFFSET

Taxpayers in receipt of certain Commonwealth Government payments (known as rebatable benefits) are entitled to a tax offset or rebate commonly referred to as the beneficiary tax offset (rebate) (s160 AAA(1), (3) ITAA36).

The government payments that enable taxpayers to receive this offset (ie. rebatable benefits) are:

- Newstart allowance (NSA)
- Austudy payment
- Youth allowance
- Sickness allowance (SA)
- Special benefits (SB)
- Widow allowance (WA)
- Partner allowance (PA)
- Assessable part of parenting payment (partnered), and
- Mature age allowance granted on or after 1 July 1996.

It is also available to recipients of:

- farm household support including exceptional circumstances relief or restart income support
- interim income support paid to farmers affected by drought
- Commonwealth education and training payments (except where recipient of the payment is an employee of a person who is entitled to a Commonwealth subsidy of the employment)

- payment under a Commonwealth labour market program such as enterprise incentive scheme allowance, textile, clothing and footwear special allowance, Green Corps training allowance
- ABSTUDY
- assistance for isolated children
- the veterans' children education scheme
- MRCA allowance (payment under the *Military Rehabilitation and Compensation Act 2004*), and
- Community Development Employment Projects (CDEP) scheme participant supplement.

3.212 CALCULATING THE BENEFICIARY TAX OFFSET

Beneficiary tax offsets are calculated to eliminate the tax liability on the amounts of benefit actually paid during the year over the person's tax-free threshold (or a pro-rated tax-free threshold if applicable; see 3.030). Therefore, people whose only income is from payments eligible for a beneficiary tax offset will have no tax liability.

The tax offset does not shade out when taxable income exceeds a specified threshold. However, the income level affects eligibility for Centrelink payments and benefits.

The tax offset is calculated as follows:

- If the taxpayer's rebatable benefit is $37,000 or less in 2014-15:

Tax offset = (rebatable benefit – 6,000) x 15%

- If the taxpayer's rebatable benefit is more than $37,000 in 2014-15:

Tax offset = 15% x (rebatable benefit – 6,000)
+ 15% x (rebatable benefit – $37,000)

 George receives $25,400 Newstart allowance. His beneficiary tax offset is $2,910, calculated ($25,400 – $6,000) x 15% = $2,910. His basic tax payable = $1,368 which is less than the beneficiary tax offset. The offset is not refundable.

 Christine's taxable income in 2014-15 is $44,700 of which $38,700 is rebatable benefits. Her beneficiary tax offset will be:

15% x ($38,700 – $6,000) + 15% x ($38,700 – $37,000) = $4,905 + $255 = $5,160.

Her tax liability for the 2014-15 financial year will be:

Tax payable on $44,700	$6,074.50
Less: Beneficiary tax offset	($5,160.00)
Low income tax offset: $445 – [($44,700 – $37,000) x 1.5%]	($329.50)
Net tax payable	$585.00

NOTE: If the rebate amount is calculated to be negative or zero, no rebate is available. The amount of the Beneficiary tax offset allowed is automatically calculated by the Tax Office. Recipients of social security allowances do not get any tax offset where their total rebatable benefits are $6,000 or less.

 Beneficiary tax offset entitlement is not lost because taxable income exceeds a specified threshold. Therefore, realised capital gains, termination payments, superannuation payouts and withdrawals from a rollover fund do not affect the beneficiary tax offset entitlement.

3.220   PRIVATE HEALTH INSURANCE TAX OFFSET

An incentive of between 30% and 40% of the cost of the private health insurance premiums is available to taxpayers who have taken out private health insurance. This incentive may be taken as either a fully refundable tax offset in a person's tax return, as a direct payment or as a reduced premium. The income thresholds are indexed regularly.

The taxpayer's 'income for surcharge purposes' determines the level of incentive that they are entitled to. The percentage rebate is adjusted by a rebate factor from 1 July 2014. There are three tiers of entitlement, as follows:

ENTITLEMENT BY INCOME THRESHOLD FOR 2014-15

Income thresholds*				
Singles	$90,000 or less	$90,001-105,000	$105,001-140,000	$140,001
Families	$180,000 or less	$180,001-210,000	$210,001-280,000	$280,001 or more
	Rebate entitlement : 1 July 2014 – 31 March 2015			
	Base tier (no change)	Tier 1	Tier 2	Tier 3
Under 65 years old	29.040%	19.360%	9.680%	0%
65-69 years old	33.880%	24.200%	14.520%	0%
70 years old or over	38.720%	29.040%	19.360%	0%
	Rebate entitlement : 1 April 2015 – 30 June 2015			
	Base tier (no change)	Tier 1	Tier 2	Tier 3
Under 65 years old	27.820%	18.547%	9.273%	0%
65-69 years old	32.457%	23.184%	13.910%	0%
70 years old or over	37.094%	27.820%	18.547%	0%

*Based on 'income for surcharge purposes'

The offset can only be claimed by individuals. Where an employer pays the private health insurance premiums as part of a salary sacrifice arrangement, the employee is entitled to claim the offset. To be eligible for the offset the policy must be an 'appropriate private health insurance' policy provided by a registered health fund and must provide hospital cover, ancillary cover or combined cover and each of the persons covered by the policy must be eligible to claim benefits under Medicare. The offset can only be claimed in the income year the premiums are paid.

The following persons would not be covered by a family policy:

*   students 25 years or older
*   persons 18 years or older who are not in full-time education, and
*   persons 18 years or older who are partners of other persons.

This offset is also available to a trustee who is assessed under s98 of the ITAA36 in respect of the income of a beneficiary under a legal disability who is presently entitled to trust income, and the beneficiary would have been entitled to the offset.

The percentage of tax offset entitlement is determined by the age of the oldest person covered by the policy. If the oldest person moves into the next age group during the income year, the tax offset is based on the number of days that person was in each group.

Once the policy becomes eligible for the higher tax offset, it retains this eligibility even if the person who established the eligibility comes off the policy. Additionally, this eligibility continues even if you change funds or policies after this event. However, this ongoing eligibility for higher rate is affected if a new person is added to the policy after the person who established the eligibility leaves the policy.

3.221   CLAIMING THE REBATE

The rebate can be claimed as either:

- a reduction in the private health insurance premium through the health fund; or
- a refundable tax offset at the end of the income year through the income tax return.

Taxpayers who do not receive a statement from their private health insurance fund should contact their fund to obtain the information necessary to calculate their entitlement to the tax offset.

The private health insurance tax offset is refundable, ie. any amount that remains unused in satisfying the person's tax liability is refundable.

Elise, aged 45, has a taxable income of $10,000 that is derived solely from savings.

She also contributed $1,200 in gross premiums to an approved health insurance fund in 2014-15 as follows:

- *$900 between 1 July 2014 and 31 March 2015; and*
- *$300 between 1 April 2015 and 30 June 2015.*

Her private health insurance rebate entitlement is:

Taxable income	$10,000
Tax payable on $10,000	$0
Private health insurance tax offset ($900 @ 29.04% 1 July 2014-31 March 2015)	($261)
Private health insurance tax offset ($300 @ 27.82% 1 April 2015-30 June 2015)	($83)
Low income tax offset	($445)
Total tax offset	($789)

Elise has an unused tax offset of $789 ($789 – $0). Of this amount, she is entitled to the refund of the private health insurance tax offset of $344. The excess tax offset of $445 is lost.

From a cash flow perspective, it may be better to reduce the health insurance premiums up front rather than paying a higher amount to get the refund at the end of the financial year.

3.230   DELAYED INCOME TAX OFFSET

The general rule is that employment income is assessable in the income year it is received, regardless of the period the payment covers. A tax offset is available under s159ZRA of ITAA36 to reduce the tax payable where certain types of income are received in a lump sum and the taxpayer would be disadvantaged by paying more tax than if the income had been spread over several income years.

The delayed income tax offset applies to limit the tax payable where a lump sum representing an arrears of income is paid for:

- salary or wages (only applies to the extent the salary or wages were accrued during the period earlier than 12 months before payment)
- a Commonwealth education or training payment
- salary or wages paid to a person after reinstatement to duty following a period of suspension (only to the extent the payment was for period of suspension, even if that period was within the preceding 12 months)
- deferred payment of a retiring allowance, retirement pension or annuity (or a payment which is a supplement to any of those payments)
- compensation, sickness or accident pay for incapacity to work (the concession is not available on payments made to the owner of an insurance policy under which the payment is made), and
- Social Security and repatriation pensions, benefits and allowances paid by Social Security or Veterans Affairs or similar payments made under a law of a foreign country, State or Province, but not exempt income.

The whole arrears payment is still included in the assessable income of the taxpayer in the income year it is received, but the tax offset diminishes the amount of tax payable on that component to the amount that would have been payable had the income been received in the income year it accrued.

SALARY OR WAGES

The definition of salary or wages for the purpose of the 'delayed income tax offset', include salary, wages, commissions, bonuses or allowance paid to an employee, an office-holder or a company director (excluding remuneration paid to a director who is also an associate of the company). Salary or wages does not include:

- return to work payments (paid to a taxpayer under an agreement, arrangement or understanding to resume performing work or rendering services (these payments are assessable under s26(eb))
- payments in advance for annual leave or long service leave
- lump sums paid on retiring or ceasing employment for accrued annual leave or long service leave
- eligible termination payments (ETPs)
- payments made under a contract that is wholly or principally for the labour of the recipient (and which are not otherwise subject to PAYG withholding tax purposes but for s221A(1)(a)), and
- commissions paid to an insurance or part time canvasser or collector.

3.231   ELIGIBILITY FOR TAX OFFSET

To be eligible for the tax offset, the taxpayer must satisfy the conditions set out in s159ZRA:

- a lump sum must be received from at least one of the eligible sources (see 3.230)
- the payment must have accrued in a prior income year
- the lump sum must be 10% or more of the taxpayer's taxable income in the year of receipt after deducting:
  - amounts that accrued in earlier years
  - amounts received on termination of employment in lieu of annual or long service leave and ETPs
  - net capital gains, and
  - any taxable professional income which exceeds your average taxable professional income from the preceding four years (see 3.070).

3.232   AMOUNT OF TAX OFFSET

The amount of tax offset allowed is the amount by which the tax payable on the lump sum eligible amount exceeds the tax that would have been payable if the lump sum had been included in the taxable incomes of the two most recent years of income (s159ZRB), ie:

Delayed income tax offset = tax on arrears – notional tax on arrears

where:

- **tax on arrears** is the amount of tax (excluding Medicare levy) payable in the income year of receipt. The only tax offsets taken into account when calculating the 'tax on arrears' are tax offsets for unused annual leave and long service leave (on termination of employment) and those for ETPs, and
- **notional tax on arrears** is the amount of tax that would have been payable on the eligible amount if it was taxed in the year it accrued.

The 'notional tax' has two components:

- **recent accrual years amount** (notional tax in the two most recent years before lump sum was received), and
- **distant accrual years amount** (notional tax on any accruals in the years before the two most recent years).

The notional tax for distant accrual years is calculated by multiplying the lump sum applicable for those years by the average rate of tax on the arrears for the recent accruals years.

A taxpayer receives a lump sum payment of $90,000 in November 2014 representing arrears of pay after successfully defending his suspension from service. He had been suspended from service without pay since July 2011.

The taxpayer's taxable income in the respective years (not including the lump sum) was:

> *2011-12: $7,500*
> *2012-13: $7,500*
> *2013-14: $40,000*

Of the lump sum received in the respective years, these amounts were accrued:

> *2011-12: $38,000*
> *2012-13: $32,000*
> *2013-14: $20,000*

Because the tax on arrears is the only assessable income for 2014-15 and the taxpayer had no deductions, the tax on this $90,000 would have been $21,247 in the 2014-15 year. Note that the 10% eligibility requirement is satisfied (see 3.231).

Position in 2012-13

Taxable income	*$7,500*
Plus: Accrued lump sum	*$32,000*
Adjusted taxable income	*$39,500*
Notional tax payable on $39,500	*$4,385*
Less: Tax payable on $7,500	*($0)*
EXTRA tax payable	*$4,385*
Percentage of tax payable (EXTRA tax payable/accrued lump sum)	*13.7%*

Position in 2013-14

Taxable income	*$40,000*
Plus: Accrued lump sum	*$20,000*
Adjusted taxable income	*$60,000*
Notional tax payable on $60,000	*$11,047*
Less: Tax payable on $40,000	*($4,547)*
EXTRA tax payable	*$6,500*
Percentage of tax payable (EXTRA tax payable/accrued lump sum)	*32.5%*

Position in 2011-12

This leads to an average rate to be used for 'distant accrual years' using the following formula:

> *(Year 1 % + Year 2 %)/2 = (13.7% + 32.5%)/2 = 23.1%*

Accrued lump sum	*$38,000*
Average tax rate calculated	*23.1%*
Distant accrual year amount	*$8,778*

Calculation of offset

Tax on lump sum in 2014-15	*$21,247*
Less:	
EXTRA tax payable 2012-13	*($4,385)*
EXTRA tax payable 2013-14	*($6,500)*
Distant accrual year amount	*($8,778)*
Delayed income tax offset	*$1,584*

3.240 MEDICARE LEVY SURCHARGE LUMP SUM IN ARREARS TAX OFFSET

A tax offset is available to individuals, and in some cases, their spouse, who do not have private health insurance but have a Medicare levy surcharge liability as a result of receiving lump sum payment in arrears.

The Medicare Levy Surcharge (MLS) lump sum in arrears tax offset applies to limit the MLS payable if the surcharge was as a result of a lump sum payment in arrears received in the financial year that consists of:

- eligible income for the purpose of the delayed income tax offset (see 3.220), or
- payment of 'exempt foreign employment income' (only applies to the extent this amount was accrued for a period of more than 12 months before the date on which it was paid).

3.241 ELIGIBILITY FOR TAX OFFSET

To be eligible for the tax offset, the taxpayer must be an individual and satisfy these conditions as set out in s61-580(1):

- an eligible MLS lump sum payment in arrears must be received (see above) , and
- the total MLS lump sum must be 10% or more of the taxpayer's taxable income *less:*
  - amounts that accrued in earlier years
  - amounts received on termination of employment in lieu of annual or long service leave and ETPs
  - net capital gains, and
  - any taxable professional income which exceeds your average taxable professional income from the preceding four years (see 3.070)

  plus
  - exempt foreign employment income
  - reportable fringe benefits, and
  - amount on which family trust distribution tax has been paid.

NOTE: The taxpayer's reportable superannuation contributions and total net investment loss for the current year are included in the determination of the taxpayer's eligibility for the tax offset.

3.242 SPOUSE'S ELIGIBILITY FOR TAX OFFSET

This offset is also available to a taxpayer's spouse if the taxpayer's spouse has a MLS liability as a result of the taxpayer receiving an eligible MLS lump sum payment in arrears and the taxpayer is entitled to this offset. This offset is not available to a taxpayer in the capacity of a spouse if the taxpayer is entitled to the offset in their own capacity.

In the case where the couple is already liable for MLS, even before taking into account eligible MLS lump sum in arrears received by one of the members, this offset is only available to the person in receipt of the lump sum payment (and not available to the spouse).

3.243 AMOUNT OF TAX OFFSET

The amount of tax offset allowed is equal to the amount of MLS payable attributable to the lump sum payment received (s61-585), ie:

MLS lump sum in arrears tax offset = Total MLS – total non-arrears MLS

where:

- total MLS is the amount of MLS payable for the current financial year, and
- total non-arrears MLS is the amount of MLS payable disregarding the eligible MLS lump sum payment.

Jack and Rose are a couple. They do not have private patient hospital cover. Jack receives a lump sum payment of $50,000 in November 2014 representing lump sum worker's compensation payment owed from 2012-13.

Jack's taxable income excluding the lump sum payment is $55,000 and reportable fringe benefit is $10,000 in the 2014-15 financial year. Rose's taxable income is $75,000 in the 2014-15 financial year.

Without the lump sum payment in arrears, Jack and Rose will not be liable to pay MLS in 2014-15 because their combined family income for MLS purposes is $140,000, which is less than $180,000 (for the MLS threshold for a family with two dependent children – see 3.063).

However, Jack's lump sum in arrears payment brings their total family income for MLS purposes to $190,000, which means that they have exceeded the MLS threshold. Therefore, Jack and Rose are liable for the MLS.

Jack is entitled to the MLS lump sum in arrears tax offset because he received eligible MLS lump sum payment in arrears which has resulted in a MLS liability and he meets the 10% test.

Jack's total MLS liability is $1,150 (1% of $115,000) for the 2014-15 financial year. Without the lump sum payment, Jack's MLS liability is nil. Therefore, his MLS lump sum in arrears tax offset entitlement is $1,150 – $0 = $1,150.

Rose is also entitled to the tax offset as her MLS liability arose solely due to Bruce's lump sum payment in arrears. Rose's total MLS liability for the 2014-15 financial year is $750 (1% of $75,000). Without the lump sum payment, Rose's MLS liability will be nil. Therefore, her MLS lump sum in arrears tax offset entitlement is $750 – $0 = $750.

Tax administration

4.000 TAX ADMINISTRATION

The Australian tax system is one of self-assessment. This generally means that tax returns lodged by taxpayers are accepted as being correct at the time of lodgment.

All legislative references in this chapter relate to the *Tax Administration Act 1953*, unless otherwise indicated.

4.010 INCOME TAX RETURNS

SELF-PREPARED RETURNS

Individual resident and non-resident taxpayers whose income exceeds the tax-free threshold ($18,200 in 2014-15 and 2015-16), or who is claiming a tax refund, are usually required to lodge by 31 October following the end of the income year if they are self-preparers.

Penalties are imposed for returns lodged after 31 October (see 4.650), or the next business day if 31 October falls on a weekend.

INDIVIDUALS WHO MUST LODGE A RETURN

You must lodge a return if any of the following applied to you:

- You had a reportable fringe benefits amount on your: PAYG payment summary – individual non-business, or PAYG payment summary – foreign employment.
- You had reportable employer superannuation contributions on your: PAYG payment summary – individual non-business, PAYG payment summary – foreign employment, or PAYG payment summary – business and personal services income.
- You were entitled to the private health insurance rebate.
- You carried on a business.
- You made a loss or you can claim a loss you made in a previous year.
- You were 60 years old or older and you received an Australian superannuation lump sum that included an untaxed element.
- You were under 60 years old and you received an Australian superannuation lump sum that included a taxed element or an untaxed element.
- You were entitled to a distribution from a trust or you had an interest in a partnership and the trust or partnership carried on a business of primary production.
- You were an Australian resident for tax purposes and you had exempt foreign employment income and $1 or more of other income.
- You are a special professional covered by the income averaging provisions. These provisions apply to authors of literary, dramatic, musical or artistic works, inventors, performing artists, production associates and active sportspeople.
- You received income from dividends or distributions exceeding the tax-free threshold (or $416 if you were under 18 years old on 30 June 2016) and you had: franking credits attached, or amounts withheld because you did not quote your tax file number or Australian business number to the investment body.
- You made personal contributions to a complying superannuation fund or retirement savings account and will be eligible to receive a super co-contribution for these contributions.
- You have exceeded your concessional contributions cap and may be eligible for the Refund of excess concessional contributions offer: see Super contributions (19.050).
- Concessional contributions were made to a complying superannuation fund or retirement savings account and will be eligible to receive a low income superannuation contribution, providing you have met the other eligibility criteria.
- You were a liable parent or a recipient parent under a child support assessment unless you received Australian Government allowances, pensions or payments (whether taxable or exempt), and the total of all the following payments was less than $23,523 for 2014-15:

- taxable income
- exempt Australian Government allowances, pensions and payments
- target foreign income
- reportable fringe benefits
- net financial investment loss (see IT5 Net financial investment loss)
- net rental property loss, and
- reportable superannuation contributions.

- You were either a liable parent or a recipient parent under a child support assessment. If this applies to you, you cannot use the short tax return.

- You received an Australian Government pension, allowance or payment (listed below) but were ineligible for the Senior Australian and Pensioner Tax Offset (SAPTO) and had any other non-exempt income which made his or her taxable income more than $20,542:
    - Newstart allowance
    - Youth allowance
    - Austudy payment
    - parenting payment (partnered)
    - partner allowance
    - sickness allowance
    - special benefit
    - widow allowance
    - exceptional circumstances relief payment
    - interim income support payment
    - an education payment of any of the following when a taxpayer is 16 or older: ABSTUDY living allowance, payment under the Veterans' Children Scheme, payment under the *Military Rehabilitation and Compensation Education and Training Scheme 2004* (shown as MRCA on your payment summary)
    - other taxable Commonwealth education or training payments
    - an income support component from a Community Development Employment Project (CDEP) shown as 'Community Development Employment Projects (CDEP) payments' on your PAYG payment summary – individual non-business
    - a CDEP scheme participant supplement.

- You were eligible for the senior Australians pensioner tax offset (SAPTO) and his or her taxable income (not including their spouse's) was more than the following (see table below):

Type of Senior or Pensioner	Senior Australian and Pensioner offset recipient
If you were single or widowed at any time during the year	$32,279
If you had a spouse but were separated due to illness or one of you lived in a nursing home	$31,279
If you lived with your spouse for the entire year	$28,974

- if you were ineligible for the Senior Australian and Pensioner Tax Offset (SAPTO), did not receive a payment from the table below and your taxable income was more than:
    - $18,200 for Australian residents (full year)
    - $416 under 18 at 30 June 2015 and your income was not salary and wages
    - $1 if you were a foreign resident and you had income in Australia which did not have non-resident withholding tax withheld from it, or
    - your part-year tax-free threshold amount (if you became or stopped being an Australian resident during the year).

Government allowances and payments	Australian Government pensions
Newstart allowance	Age pension
Youth allowance	Bereavement allowance
Austudy payment	Carer payment
Parenting payment (partnered)	Disability support pension, if you have reached age-pension age
Partner allowance	Education entry payment
Sickness allowance	Parenting payment (single)
Special benefit	Widow B pension
Widow allowance	Wife pension, if either you or your partner was of age-pension age
Exceptional circumstances relief payment	Age service pension
Interim income support payment	Income support supplement
An education payment of any of the following when a taxpayer is 16 or older: ABSTUDY living allowance, payment under the Veterans' Children Scheme, payment under the *Military Rehabilitation and Compensation Education and Training Scheme 2004* (shown as MRCA on your payment summary)	Defence Force income support allowance (DFISA) where the pension, payment or allowance to which it relates is taxable
Other taxable Commonwealth education or training payments	DFISA-like payment from the Department of Veterans' Affairs (DVA)
An income support component from a Community Development Employment Project (CDEP) shown as 'Community Development Employment Projects (CDEP) payments' on your PAYG payment summary – individual non-business	Invalidity service pension, if you have reached age-pension age
A CDEP scheme participant supplement.	Partner service pension.

Regardless of whether a profit or loss was made, a return (or a non-lodgment advice) must be lodged by:

- Australian tax residents
- foreign residents and temporary residents in some cases
- any person who made a loss in the previous income year
- any person in receipt of abnormal income (see 3.070)
- any person or firm either running a business or engaged in a profession
- companies
- any partnership or trust estate
- any association or club (unless exempt from tax, and written confirmation has been received from the Tax Office)
- an attorney for an absentee or non-resident
- superannuation funds, and
- Approved Deposit Funds (ADFs) and pooled superannuation trusts.

DECEASED ESTATE

If you are the executor (trustee) of the estate of someone who died during the year, consider all the above requirements on their behalf. You may need to lodge their final tax return, for the year up to the date of death. If a return is not required, complete the *Non-lodgment advice* for the relevant year.

The executor must also consider whether the deceased estate needs to submit a trust tax return for the part of the year after the date of death. For details about the tax compliance responsibilities of executors, see the Tax Office webpage *Managing the tax affairs of someone who has died*.

FRANKING CREDITS

If you don't need to lodge a tax return, but you are entitled to a refund of franking credits, you can claim the refund by using the publication *Refund of franking credit instructions and application for individuals* for the relevant year and lodging your claim by mail, or phone 13 28 65.

FIRST HOME SAVER ACCOUNT

If you had a first home saver account in 2014-15 and believe you are entitled to a first home saver account government contribution, you must lodge either:

- a tax return, or
- a notification of eligibility (if you are not required to lodge a tax return and you were an Australian resident for at least part of 2014-15) by completing the *First home saver account notification of eligibility* (NAT 72947).

NOTE: From 1 July 2015, these accounts have been repealed.

NON-LODGMENT ADVICE 2015

A *Non-lodgment advice for 2015* should be completed in the event that a taxpayer is not required to lodge an income tax return, unless one of the following applies:

- You have already lodged a non-lodgment advice or letter in a previous year telling the Tax Office that you do not need to lodge a tax return for all future years.
- You are lodging an application for a refund of franking credits for 2015.
- Your only income was from an allowance or payment listed in the relevant table above in relation to government allowances and pensions, and
  - your rebate income was less than or equal to the relevant amount in dot point 2 (if you are eligible for the Senior Australian and Pensioner Tax Offset), or
  - your 'taxable income' was less than or equal to the relevant amount in dot point 3 (the agencies that paid you have provided information for the Tax Office to determine that you do not need to lodge a tax return).

RESIDENTS INCLUDE ALL INCOME

To the extent that you were an Australian tax resident during the income year, your tax return should disclose assessable income from worldwide sources (see 11.020).

Income from overseas

Whether foreign source income is assessable is subject to the same rules in relation to the nature and timing of the income that applies to Australian sourced income. Additionally, where Australia has a tax treaty with the country concerned, the terms of the treaty should be considered (see from 22.000 and 22.220).

If you have derived income from overseas, you may be entitled to a 'foreign income tax offset' for any taxes paid overseas (see 22.400).

TAXING PROFITS ON ASSETS SOLD

A taxpayer deriving a gain from the sale of assets must ascertain whether that gain will be assessable under any provision.

Common taxing regimes are:

- trading stock (sale of assets acquired for the purposes of resale)
- capital allowances (sale of depreciating assets), and
- capital gains tax (sale of capital and investment assets).

PARTNERSHIPS AND TRUSTS (see 7.000 and 8.000)

A partner or beneficiary of a trust can be assessed on a quantum of income that is more or less than they actually receive economically and therefore care should be exercised to determine the correct amount of assessable income which must be included. If the partnership or trust return has not yet been finalised by the time the individual's tax return is due, an 'extension of time to lodge' should be obtained.

KEEP A COPY OF THE RETURN

A copy of the tax return and any accompanying schedules should be retained. That information must be available in the event of a tax audit. For record retention requirements see 4.700.

PAYMENT SUMMARY MISLAID OR NOT RECEIVED

If a Payment Summary is lost, the Tax Office accepts a signed copy from the payer (or a signed letter with full details of income and tax withheld etc). If unavailable, complete a statutory declaration for the PAYG Payment Summary and lodge it with the return.

NOTE: Payment Summaries do not need to be attached to your tax return. The only time you will need to provide a Payment Summary is if you are in receipt of an employment termination payment and the return is lodged on paper.

4.020   LODGMENT OF TAX RETURNS

The due date for the lodgement of returns for resident and foreign resident individuals, partnerships, trusts and full self-assessment taxpayers (other than those lodging through a tax agent) is 31 October. If the return is likely to be delayed, write to the Tax Office before the due date and ask for an extension, giving the reasons for the delay. The Tax Office may grant the extension depending on the reasons provided.

Individuals may self-lodge using e-tax or myTax, the Tax Office's free services for preparing and lodging a return electronically via software downloaded onto a computer.

Tax returns may still be lodged by paper. A taxpayer may prepare the return using e-tax, print it out and lodge it on paper, or they may use the paper forms and schedules provided by the Tax Office.

The timeframes for processing returns and the address for postal lodgment of returns are detailed in 4.060.

A taxpayer using e-tax to prepare their return may choose to use the pre-fill function to partially complete the return. Information is downloaded into the e-tax return, using information from certain organisations and the Tax Office's internal data.

Information that is generally available to pre-fill include the *following:*

- personal details from the previous year's tax return
- HELP/SFSS balances
- PAYG instalments
- Tax Office interest
- PAYG payment summaries
- government welfare payments
- interest income
- dividend income
- managed funds distributions
- employee share scheme statements
- share disposals
- taxable payments (building and construction industry)
- Medicare benefit tax statement, and
- Medicare levy surcharge and private health insurance policy details.

TAX AGENT LODGED RETURNS

Returns lodged by registered tax agents are due progressively according to a lodgment program. The lodgment program provides extended lodgment end dates for individuals, partnerships and trusts.

Due dates vary depending on the client type, the lodgment program of the tax agent and the tax agent's performance in respect of online and on time lodgments. Agents receive a general extension of time, and clients' returns are lodged according to the agent's lodgment program.

A comprehensive listing of due dates is available in the Tax Professionals sections of the Tax Office website.

IMPORTANT: The Tax Office is in the process of implementing Standard Business Reporting (SBR). SBR is a different way to prepare and lodge forms to the Tax Office (and other government agencies) directly from the business's accounting software. The lodger will require an AUSkey and SBR-enabled software.

Tax Office forms that can be lodged via SBR-enabled software include activity statements, some tax returns, tax file number declarations and PAYG payment summaries. More forms, including the individual tax return, will be added. SBR will not allow the user to view their tax account details, register for tax roles or make payments.

See www.sbr.gov.au to check which Tax Office forms can be lodged via SBR. The website also provides information on which software is SBR-enabled.

The Tax Office is currently transitioning from the existing electronic lodgment system (ELS) to SBR. Software developers are in the process of developing SBR-enabled software packages that will allow practitioners to upgrade to SBR. The transition from ELS to SBR is expected to be complete by July 2018.

EARLY LODGMENT FOR TARGETED TAXPAYERS

Clients who have been associated with schemes or other aggressive tax planning have been identified as specific high risk taxpayers and may be required to lodge their income tax returns by 31 October. In exceptional circumstances agents can apply for limited lodgment extensions.

Taxpayers using an agent for the first time must appoint the agent in time to be included on the agent's client list for which extensions are granted.

CLIENT TRANSFER TO ANOTHER TAX AGENT

The 'new' agent must advise the Tax Office of the transferred client by 31 December. However, if special circumstances exist (eg. the former agent becomes ill, or the taxpayer moves interstate) it may be possible to transfer a client so the return may be accepted without late lodgment penalty.

CLIENT DIDN'T USE AN AGENT IN PRIOR YEAR

If the new client did not use a tax agent for the preceding year's return, the 'new' agent must register the new client with the Tax Office by 31 October.

TAXPAYER DIES

If an individual died during the income year and a tax return is not required, complete the non-lodgment advice and send it to the Tax Office. If a tax return is required, and the deceased was normally assessed on a cash receipts basis, the deceased's first tax return up to the date of death should disclose only income actually received before the date of death. The second return for the deceased for the year of death should be lodged by the trustees in the name of the estate and will include the income which (according to the law) had been derived after the date of death and by the end of the same income year. For details of the information to be included in these returns see *Deceased estates* at 7.950.

DIRECT DEBIT AND DIRECT REFUND

Individual taxpayers can elect to use the Tax Office electronic funds transfer (EFT) to have a tax liability electronically withdrawn from a bank or building society account (but not from any credit union account). Direct debits can be arranged: information regarding this option will be shown on a notice of assessment. A direct debit request form (NAT 2284) must be completed and sent to the Tax Office.

The Tax Office does not issue tax refunds to individuals by cheque. In order to receive a refund into the taxpayer's bank (or building society or credit union) account by EFT, at the EFT election on the tax return include:

- the 6 digit BSB number (this identifies the bank, State and branch where the account is held)
- an account number of up to 9 alpha and numeric digits, and
- account name: must include taxpayer's name.

If this option was used in the prior year and there is no change to account details, then all that is needed is to place an X in the box. Otherwise complete the full details.

A direct deposit of the refund is not available on a full range of accounts. A taxpayer should confirm with their financial institution that this facility is available.

For more information, contact the EFT hot line on 1800 802 308.

NOTE: From 2014-15, individual taxpayers with a tax liability will receive a 'tax receipt' with their notice of assessment. This tax receipt shows a breakdown of how their tax money is spent.

4.030   ELECTIONS AND NOTIFICATIONS

Tax Ruling IT 2624 allows a general extension of time for companies and funds for lodging elections and notifications in all cases where the Commissioner can give an extension of time.

The Ruling extends the time for making most elections and notifications until the Commissioner specifically asks for them.

Whilst many elections and notifications are not required to be lodged with the Tax Office, they should still be made in writing, and retained with the taxpayer's records.

ELECTIONS AND NOTIFICATIONS WHICH MUST BE LODGED

UNDER ITAA36

- s73B(18) by a company to which R&D provisions do not apply (see from 15.500)
- s99A(2) request by a trustee that s99A does not apply where no beneficiary presently entitled (usually for deceased estates or bankruptcy) (see 7.700 and 7.950)
- s124ZADA(1)(3) & (5) Australian films (see 15.700)
- s297B(3) exemption from tax of income referable to current pension liabilities of a pooled superannuation trust
- former s319 and s362 elections re: controlled foreign companies (see 22.820 for CFCs)

UNDER ITAA97

- Subdiv 30-DB spread of deductions for certain cultural, environmental and heritage gifts and conservation covenants over a period of up to five income years (see from 13.800)
- s392-25 (s158A(1)) opting out of the primary production averaging system (see 21.900)

UNDER OTHER LEGISLATION

- s19 (SIS Act) election to become a regulated superannuation fund (see 19.100)
- s10(1) (FBTAA) to use cost as basis for taxable value of car fringe benefits (see from 25.350)
- s26(3) (FBTAA) re: non-remote and remote housing (see from 25.654)
- s39FA or s39GA (FBTAA) statutory formula or 12 week method for car parking fringe benefits (see 25.400).

4.040   THE ASSESSMENT

An assessment is issued on the basis of the return as lodged and the Tax Office has the right to scrutinise that assessment up to four years after it has been issued. That period is reduced to two years for certain categories of taxpayers and there is no time limit if there is fraud or evasion involved.

Companies operate under 'full' self-assessment which does not require the Tax Office to issue an assessment. A full self-assessment taxpayer also includes trustees of:

- corporate unit trusts and public trading trusts
- superannuation funds and approved deposit funds (both complying and non-complying)
- pooled superannuation trusts, and
- first home saver account trusts (from the 2009-10 income year).

For full self-assessment taxpayers, lodgment of the return is deemed to be a notice of assessment and the taxpayers must forward payment of their tax liability within the required time, which is usually upon lodgment of the return.

The tax payable by a full self-assessment taxpayer is due and payable:

- if the taxpayer's year of income ends on 30 June, on 1 December of the following income year, or
- if the taxpayer has a substituted accounting period, on the first day of the sixth month of the following income year, or
- a later date at the Commissioner's discretion.

For other taxpayers, the Tax Office must still issue a notice of assessment and the taxpayer has 21 days after the notice of assessment is given, or 21 days after the lodgment date to make payment of any tax due and payable if the return is lodged by the due date. If the return is lodged late, or not at all, the tax payable becomes due and payable 21 days after the due date for lodgement of the return.

Under self-assessment it is assumed that taxpayers have the knowledge to accurately complete their returns and that they also have the necessary knowledge and understanding to apply the law to their circumstances. However, there are 'safe harbour' provisions in Schedule 1 of the *Tax Administration Act 1953*. These provisions exempt taxpayers who utilise the services of a registered agent from liability for administrative penalties for certain mistakes and omissions where the error is solely due to the agent's mistake (see 4.600).

To facilitate the self-assessment process, the Tax Office is authorised to issue both Public and Private Rulings (see from 4.100) to provide taxpayers with certainty as to the Tax Office's application of the law on identified transactions.

Taxpayers can apply to the Tax Office for a Private Ruling where they are uncertain of the tax effect of their affairs. A Private Ruling is generally binding on the Tax Office and can be relied upon.

The Tax Office also issues Product Rulings (see 4.160) and Class Rulings (see 4.170). Product Rulings aim to provide taxpayers with certainty regarding the tax effect of publicly advertised investments only and neither sanction nor guarantee the product as an investment. Class Rulings set out how relevant tax laws apply to entities generally or to a class of entities in relation to a particular scheme or a class of schemes.

NOTE: *Under self-assessment, taxpayers can generally lodge objections against an assessment within two or four years (whichever is applicable) after the assessment notice is served on them (see 4.200 and 4.225).*

4.050   PENALTIES

Under self-assessment the onus of proof rests with the taxpayer to ensure the accuracy of the information contained in their return and to take such steps to ensure that they have considered the interpretation of the law and how it affects their personal tax affairs.

Taxpayers may face penalties and/or interest charges for various offences.

Taxpayers may face administrative penalties if:

a.   they make a false or misleading statement about a tax-related matter, or

b. they take a position that is not reasonably arguable about a tax-related matter, or

c. the Commissioner determines a tax-related liability of a taxpayer without documents they were required to provide.

Penalty amounts in respect of a. and b. (known as base penalty amounts) are calculated as a percentage of the 'shortfall amount'. The percentage applied to the shortfall amount is dependent upon the situation in which the shortfall arose. The base penalty amount may be increased or decreased.

 A tax shortfall would typically attract the General Interest Charge (GIC) or the Shortfall Interest Charge (SIC) (see 4.660).

Refer to 4.600 for commentary on the concepts of tax shortfall, reasonable care, reasonably arguable position and penalties relating to schemes.

4.060 CONTACTING THE TAX OFFICE

Below are the contact details for the Tax Office and key processing timeframes. The Tax Office web address is www.ato.gov.au. Further, various Tax Office online services are accessible to taxpayers through the myGov website, which links a range of Australian Government services.

The Tax Office can be contacted between 8am and 6pm, Monday to Friday by phoning:

Type of enquiry	Phone number
Business tax enquiries	13 28 66
Business self help (automated)	13 72 26
Complaints	1800 199 010
Fax complaints	1800 060 063
Client service feedback	1800 199 010
Superannuation	13 10 20
Electronic Funds Transfer (direct debit)	1800 802 308
Payment (BPAY and direct credit)	1800 815 886
Personal tax information	13 28 61
Personal direct (automated, including lodgement by phone)	13 28 65
Aboriginal and Islander Centre	13 10 30
Publications ordering service	1300 720 092
Speech and hearing difficulties	13 36 77
Speech to speech relay service	1300 555 727
To report tax evasion (phone freecall)	1800 060 062
To report tax evasion (fax freecall)	1800 804 544 (also online)
Tax Agent information line	13 72 86
International callers	+61 2 6216 1111
International fax	+61 2 6216 2830
Electronic products (phone)	1300 139 051
Excise	1300 657 162
Non-profit	1300 130 248
Internal administration line (switchboard for Tax Office)	13 28 69
Translating and interpreting	13 14 50
Vision Australia (tapes and disks of Tax Office material)	1800 644 885
Family Assistance Office	13 61 50
Privacy Commissioner	1300 363 992
Commonwealth Ombudsman	1300 362 072

PROCESSING RETURNS

In accordance with the Taxpayers' Charter (see 4.420), the Tax Office will generally process returns within the following time periods:

Type of lodgement	Timeframe
E-tax (on-line preparation and lodgment)	14 days
Lodgment by phone	14 days
ELS (tax agent prepared returns)	14 days
Other paper returns	6 weeks

NOTE: Only the following may be lodged by phone:
- a short tax return (available for individuals with simple tax affairs)
- an application for a refund of franking credits, or
- an on-going baby bonus claim.

Individuals may check on the progress of returns lodged with the Tax Office: phone 13 28 61.

APPOINTMENTS

The above telephone numbers can be used to access the Tax Office's information line services as well as other agencies connected with your tax affairs. For taxpayers who prefer to make their enquiries in person, the Tax Office requests that appointments are made. Appointments can be made by phoning 13 28 61 and talking to an operator from the personal tax information line.

POSTAL LODGMENT OF RETURNS

Most tax returns are lodged electronically, either through e-tax, myTax or by a tax agent via the Tax Agent Portal. However, some returns are still lodged on paper by post. Returns can be sent in a business size envelope to: Australian Taxation Office, GPO Box 9845, IN YOUR CAPITAL CITY.

NOTE: DO NOT replace the words 'IN YOUR CAPITAL CITY' with the name of your capital city and its postcode; the Tax Office has a special agreement with Australia Post.

Correspondence other than lodgment of returns can also be forwarded to GPO Box 9990, in the capital city of your state or territory.

MYGOV

Tax Office online services are accessible through the myGov website (my.gov.au). A myGov account allows the user to link a range of Australian Government services with one username and password.

Using the online services, taxpayers can:
- view and update their personal contact details
- view the progress of their original and amended income tax returns for the latest and prior financial years
- view their income tax account balance
- make or view a payment arrangement for income tax
- keep track of all their super including current, lost and ATO held accounts, and
- transfer their super into the super account they want.

4.100 RULINGS

Under self-assessment, taxpayers are responsible for ensuring the information disclosed in their returns is correct. Penalties can be imposed if a tax shortfall amount arises (see from 4.600).

To help taxpayers, the Tax Office is authorised to issue binding Rulings. Rulings are binding on the Tax Office and can be relied on by taxpayers provided their situation fully aligns with the subject matter of the Ruling. There are six types of Rulings for income tax purposes and these set out the Tax Office's interpretation of the law:

- Public Rulings (see 4.110)
- Private Rulings (see 4.120)
- Oral Rulings (see 4.150)
- Product Rulings (see 4.160)
- Class Rulings (see 4.170), and
- Tax Determinations (see 4.110).

A taxpayer can request the Tax Office to issue a Private Ruling based on specific issues and transactions which affect them. These Rulings are modified to protect the identity of the applicant.

 The Private Rulings on the Tax Office website are not binding on the Tax Office (other than in respect of the taxpayer to whom they were given). They merely represent the views of the Tax Office and there is no protection for any other taxpayer who follows them. If in doubt, request your own Private Ruling.

 Taxpayers who follow a Public Ruling are protected from having to pay any underpaid primary tax, penalties or interest charges where it is found that the Ruling does not correctly state how the relevant provision applies to them (see 4.110).

The rules concerning Rulings are found at Part 5-5 of the TAA. The object to this Part is to provide a way to find out the Commissioner's view about how certain laws administered by the Commissioner apply.

Subdivision 357-B of the TAA sets out common rules for Public, Private and Oral Rulings.

Section 357-55 provides that provisions of Acts and Regulations of which the Commissioner has the general administration are relevant for Rulings if they are about:

a.   tax (defined at s995-1 ITAA97 to mean income tax)

b.   Medicare levy

c.   fringe benefits tax

d.   franking tax

e.   withholding tax

f.   mining withholding tax

fa.   petroleum resource rent tax

g.   the administration or collection of those taxes

h.   a grant or benefit mentioned in s8 of the *Product Grants and Benefits Administration Act 2000*, or the administration or payment of such a grant or benefit

i.   a net fuel amount, or the administration, collection or payment of a net fuel amount.

NOTE: Goods and services tax is not included in this list and is discussed further below.

GST LITERATURE

The Tax Office is bound by most written advice that it has given or published in relation to GST, including formal Rulings and Determinations, fact sheets, information booklets, advice manuals, bulletins and Product Rulings *but not* GST Practice Statements or GST Case Decision Summaries or GST draft Rulings (see GSTR 1999/1 & 25.000).

The Commissioner also administers indirect taxes. The general rules relating to the administration of indirect taxes are found in Division 105 of TAA. While no specific provision exists for the Commissioner to issue GST Rulings, other than having the general administration of indirect taxes, rules are set out at s105-60 concerning a taxpayer's reliance on the Commissioner's interpretation of an indirect tax law.

Public Rulings called GST Advice deal with specific GST technical issues. The number of each advice Ruling is prefaced with 'GSTA TPP' and each states it is a Public Ruling. Other rulings on GST issues have the preface 'GSTR'.

STATUS OF RULINGS

The system of binding Rulings started on 1 July 1992 and was subjected to a major overhaul following the review of self-assessment in 2004-05. All Rulings and Determinations issued before then are treated as binding Public Rulings provided:

- there has been no legislative change
- the Administrative Appeals Tribunal (AAT), or a court has not overturned or modified an interpretation of the law on which that Ruling or Determination is predicated, and
- the Tax Office has not changed its interpretation of the law as adopted in that Ruling or Determination.

Public, Private, Oral, Product and Class Rulings are legally binding on the Tax Office if favourable to the taxpayer (ie. if the application of the Ruling would result in a lesser amount of tax payable than in accordance with the law or another Ruling). A Ruling unfavourable to the taxpayer is not binding on the taxpayer. However, the Tax Office can impose penalties if a tax shortfall results from the taxpayer's failure to abide by a Ruling (see 4.600). Product and Class Rulings are types of Public Rulings. Class Rulings relate to a specific class of taxpayer in relation to a specific scheme. Product Rulings are designed to provide certainty to investors on the tax effects of publicly available investment products but provide no opinion on viability (see 4.160). Oral Rulings are also available but there are strict conditions (see 4.150).

OBJECTION AGAINST RULINGS

Taxpayers dissatisfied with the decision in a Private Ruling can object (see *Objections* at 4.200 and *Reviews and appeals* at 4.300).

RULINGS CAN BE WITHDRAWN

Public and Private Rulings can be withdrawn, but:

- the withdrawal operates prospectively, and
- the Ruling continues to apply to any arrangements commenced before the Ruling is withdrawn.

If a Private Ruling is revised because it would put another taxpayer at a significant disadvantage (presumably commercially) the revision cannot apply to an income year which has commenced, or a scheme which has already commenced. When a Private Ruling is revised, the original Private Ruling no longer applies. The date of revision is the date the written notice, or that on which a new Public Ruling is published, or such later date as may be indicated in the Ruling.

SELF-AMEND WITHIN TWO OR FOUR YEARS

Taxpayers can self-amend (see 4.225 & 4.270) within two or four years (whichever is applicable) after the due date on the assessment to take advantage of subsequent favourable Public or Private Rulings or Court decisions (see 4.220, 4.225, 4.300 & 4.360).

INCONSISTENT RULINGS

The rules regarding the application of Rulings where inconsistent Rulings exist are as follows (s357-75):

Item	If the earlier Ruling is:	And the later inconsistent Ruling is:	The result is:
1	A Public Ruling	Any Ruling	You may rely on either Ruling.
2	A Private Ruling or an Oral Ruling	A Private Ruling or an Oral Ruling	If you informed the Commissioner about the existence of the earlier Ruling when you applied for the later Ruling, the earlier Ruling is taken not to have been made. Otherwise, the later Ruling is taken not to have been made.
3	A Private Ruling or an Oral Ruling	A Public Ruling	The earlier Ruling is taken not to have been made if, when the later Ruling is made: (a) the income year or other period to which the Rulings relate has not begun; and (b) the scheme to which the Rulings relate has not begun to be carried out. Otherwise, you may rely on either Ruling.

NOTE: The rules in this table have effect if a Ruling and a later Ruling both apply to you and the two Rulings are inconsistent. However, the rules in the table only apply to the extent of the inconsistency.

NOTE: If three or more Rulings apply to you and the Rulings are inconsistent, apply the rules in the table to each combination of two Rulings in the order in which they were made.

PRECEDENTIAL TAX OFFICE VIEW

PS LA 2003/3 provides Tax Officers with guidance regarding 'precedential ATO views'. A 'precedential ATO view' is the Tax Office's documented interpretation of any of the laws administered by the Commissioner. The Practice Statement considers when Tax Officers are required to identify and apply a precedential ATO view and various administrative issues concerning precedential ATO views.

Further, PS LA 2008/3 provides guidance to Tax Officers regarding the provision of advice and guidance by the Tax Office. The Practice Statement explains:

- the different forms of advice and guidance the Tax Office provides about the application of laws administered by the Commissioner
- the level of protection available to taxpayers who rely on each form of advice and guidance, and
- where to find further information about procedures in developing and issuing each form of advice and guidance.

4.110   PUBLIC RULINGS

Public Rulings issued by the Tax Office are binding on the Tax Office and can be relied upon by taxpayers even if it is later found that the interpretation expressed in the Ruling is not correct. Taxpayers who ignore Public Rulings face severe penalties unless they can demonstrate the inaccuracy of the Tax Office interpretation.

Taxation Ruling TR 2006/10 outlines the system of Public Rulings.

Under the law, a Ruling will only be a Public Ruling if it:

- is published, and
- states that it is a Public Ruling.

Public Rulings can, but may not necessarily, be in the form of any of the following:

- Determinations and Tax Rulings
- return form guides, including TaxPack
- information booklets
- Tax Office media releases, and
- speeches or statements by senior Officers of the Tax Office which must say that it (or selected parts of it) constitute a Public Ruling.

Public Rulings cover a number of taxes. They are most readily identified in the 'TR' series but may also be identified by another tax type – for example, a Ruling relating to fuel tax in the 'FTR' series.

Rulings are treated as binding Public Rulings when they are made available to the public (through the Tax Office website) and they contain statements that they are Public Rulings.

 Public Rulings provide taxpayers with certainty and protection if a taxpayer follows the Ruling where the Ruling applies to the taxpayer (see below). In that case there will be no increase in primary tax nor penalties nor interest.

Paragraph 30 of TR 2006/10 provides:

A public ruling binds the Commissioner if the public ruling applies to the entity and the entity relies on it.
An entity relies on a public ruling by acting (or omitting to act) in accordance with the public ruling.

Paragraph 32 continues:

A public ruling applies to an entity if the entity is a member of the class to whom the public ruling applies and the entity's circumstances come within the circumstances addressed in the public ruling.

As a general rule, only Public and Private Rulings are binding on the Tax Office, but the Tax Office will not impose penalties where incorrect information contained in other publications (eg. booklets and pamphlets, etc.) has been relied on by the taxpayer. The Commissioner has included a guarantee to that effect in TaxPack.

DATE OF EFFECT OF PUBLIC RULING

Public Rulings state the Tax Office's interpretation of the law (which is binding on the Tax Office) which is taken to have always applied unless:

- the Ruling states that it applies only after a particular date, or
- the Tax Office feels it is unfair to disturb arrangements existing before that Ruling.

DISREGARDING PUBLIC RULINGS

There is no compulsion on a taxpayer to follow a Public Ruling, however it is a relevant authority in determining whether the taxpayer has a reasonably arguable position and if reasonable care was exercised.

If there is a tax shortfall because a Ruling was not followed, penalties can be imposed unless the taxpayer can demonstrate that reasonable care was taken (and if relevant) it had a reasonably arguable position.

 If in doubt, follow the Ruling and then lodge an objection against the assessment or seek a Private Ruling. By using either of these two strategies the taxpayer protects their rights and avoids the possibility of tax shortfall penalties.

CONFLICTING RULINGS

If two Public Rulings are issued on the same topic, the earlier Ruling still applies to arrangements which started before the issue of the new Ruling.

TAXPAYER CAN CHOOSE THE MORE FAVOURABLE RULING

Rulings under each tax type (eg. income tax, FBT) are treated separately and there can be no conflict between them. If there is any conflict in interpretation of the law between two Public Rulings, the taxpayer can rely on either Ruling.

 If an arrangement had started when a Public Ruling was issued, the taxpayer can usually adopt whichever Ruling gives greatest benefit. Be careful however, as a new Public Ruling can overturn that earlier favourable interpretation.

A conflicting Public Ruling issued before the scheme to which the Rulings relate commenced and the income year or other period to which the Rulings relate has not begun will override any Private Ruling issued to the taxpayer.

WITHDRAWAL OF PART OF A PUBLIC RULING

In the case of withdrawal of part of a Public Ruling, the portion which was not withdrawn continues to have effect for both past and future arrangements. For any arrangement that started before the Public Ruling is withdrawn, the former Ruling will apply, provided it is favourable to the taxpayer.

 A Public Ruling dealing with expenditure incurred by an employer-sponsored superannuation fund says deductions are allowed if the expenses are incurred on behalf of the fund by:

- *the trustees of the superannuation fund, or*
- *the sponsoring employer.*

A further Public Ruling is issued withdrawing the previous Ruling as it affects trustees. In that case, the earlier Ruling continues to apply to expenditure incurred by sponsoring employers.

TAXATION DETERMINATIONS

A Taxation Determination (TD) is a kind of Ruling regarding a very specific point of tax law. Accordingly, TDs have exactly the same status as Public Rulings. The difference between a TD and a Public Ruling is that a TD deals with a single issue whereas a Public Ruling looks at a number of the tax implications that might be involved in an arrangement or transaction. For example, a TD might deal with the assessability of a receipt to advise whether that receipt is income under ordinary concepts. A Public Ruling on the other hand would also consider whether the receipt was a capital receipt and subject to CGT.

Tax Determinations are intended to be short and simple Rulings issued by the Tax Office and meant to only deal with specific issues. There may be other tax implications which have not been dealt with in the Tax Determination and might impact on the ultimate tax position. Those issues still apply and must be considered in working out your tax position.

A Tax Determination is not to be confused with a Legislative Determination. Legislative Determinations are issued by the Tax Office pursuant to a provision of an Act and are a form of subordinate legislation. An example is Effective Life 2006/1 - Income Tax (Effective Life of Depreciating Assets) Amendment Determination 2006 (No. 1). This Legislative Determination is made under s40-100(1) of the ITAA97 and amends the effective life of the copyright in a feature film.

4.120   PRIVATE RULINGS

Section 359-5 provides that a Private Ruling is the Commissioner's written opinion of how a relevant provision applies or would apply to you in relation to a specified scheme. 'Scheme' is defined in s995-1 of the ITAA97. Private Rulings are not limited to just a single income year.

Taxation Ruling TR 2006/11 provides guidance concerning the system of Private Rulings.

Private Rulings are strictly limited to the taxpayer(s) named in the Ruling, and will apply only to their specific dealings or arrangements. Even if some aspect of the Ruling might be applicable to the other party to a contract or arrangement, that other party cannot take advantage of any factor in the Ruling favourable to the taxpayer(s) to whom the Ruling was issued. The Commissioner is bound by a Private Ruling where a Private Ruling applies to a taxpayer and the taxpayer relies on that Private Ruling. If the scheme covered by the Ruling is not implemented as set out in the Ruling, or material facts were omitted from the Ruling or were false or misleading, the Commissioner is not bound by the Private Ruling.

The Tax Office publishes sanitised versions of Private Rulings in the Register of Private Rulings found on the Tax Office website. These are edited to remove details that may identify the persons or entities concerned and are published as part of ensuring transparency in the Private Ruling system. The Rulings published on the register are non-binding and provide no protection for taxpayers other than those to whom the Ruling was addressed. The Tax Office advises they are not an authority for the purposes of establishing a reasonably arguable position.

Private Rulings are binding on the Tax Office. Once a taxpayer receives a Private Ruling they have several choices:

- follow the Ruling if it is favourable
- object against the Ruling, or
- ignore the Ruling if it is unfavourable or if there is a more favourable position that is open under the tax law.

Unless the Tax Office agrees, a Private Ruling cannot be obtained if an audit has started (ie. when you are advised that an audit by the Tax Office will take place).

A taxpayer can object against an unfavourable Private Ruling (see from 4.200) and request that it be reviewed by the Small Taxation Claims Tribunal, the AAT or the Courts (see 4.300 and 4.360).

NOTE: A Private Ruling obtained by a trustee of a trust will also apply to the beneficiaries in respect of issues affecting the trust.

No special sanction applies merely because the taxpayer chooses not to follow the private ruling. However, penalties may apply if the taxpayer has failed to take reasonable care, does not have a reasonably arguable position or in relation to a tax avoidance scheme.

TAX OFFICE INTERPRETATIVE DECISIONS

As set out in 4.155, the Tax Office publishes Interpretative Decisions (IDs) which in some cases are sanitised Private Rulings. They are published to improve the transparency, accountability and quality of Private Rulings.

ATO IDs are not binding on the Tax Office and taxpayers should be very careful if they choose to follow these interpretations. However, IDs contain the following statement:

> *'If you reasonably apply this decision in good faith to your own circumstances (which are not materially different from those described in the decision) and the decision is later found to be incorrect you will not be liable to pay any penalty or interest'.*

Underpaid tax will require payment if time limits under the law permit.

4.125 APPLYING FOR A RULING

A taxpayer, their agent or legal personal representative may apply for a Private Ruling in respect of how a relevant provision applies to the taxpayer.

Standardised 'Private Ruling Application' forms are published by the Tax Office. The application for a Private Ruling doesn't have to be made on the standard form but must contain all the information required by the Tax Office to enable a decision to be made. If an application for a Private Ruling is to affect more than one person, each person must consent in writing.

The Private Ruling made by the Commissioner will:

- state it is a Private Ruling
- identify the taxpayer(s) to whom it applies
- give details of the arrangement to which it applies, and
- state the relevant provision to which the Ruling relates.

To avoid lengthy descriptions, the Ruling can refer to another document containing the arrangement details but only if the applicants also have access to that document. If the Ruling request is very specific, the Commissioner can confine his decision to that specific issue or broaden the Ruling to cover other applications.

A Ruling request is received regarding the assessability of a transaction under s6-5 ITAA97 only. The Tax Office may also give an opinion on the CGT effect of the transaction.

IF FACTS IN A RULING APPLICATION VARY

A Private Ruling continues to apply even if there are minor differences (but not of a material type) between an arrangement described in the application for a Ruling and the one carried out. The Private Ruling is made by the Tax Office on the particular facts of the arrangement. If the facts are materially different from those covered by the Ruling, it has no effect.

A Private Ruling was obtained about the deductibility of interest payments under a proposed loan agreement with a financial institution. The Ruling remains valid if the taxpayer obtains a substantially similar loan from another financial institution. The rate of interest is immaterial, but significant differences in the character of the loan agreement could jeopardise the validity of the Ruling.

If a Ruling relies on assumptions, the Tax Office can decline to make the Ruling and request further information from the applicant(s), or accept the appropriate assumptions. For example, a request for a Private Ruling concerning a venture involving a trust where it is not stated if the beneficiaries are residents. The Tax Office can assume they will be Australian residents. If the assumptions are subsequently proved to be incorrect, and this materially alters the facts, the Ruling will have no effect.

MATTERS/ENTITIES INVOLVED IN RULING APPLICATION

A Private Ruling may cover any matter involved in the application of the provision. This includes liability, administrative, procedural and collection matters and ultimate conclusions of fact.

Individuals, companies, partnerships, trusts, superannuation funds and unincorporated bodies may all apply for a Private Ruling. Unless a Ruling is sought on the application of Part IVA – the general anti-avoidance provisions – the Tax Office will not refer the application to the General Anti-Avoidance Rules panel for consideration (see PS LA 2005/24 in respect of Private Ruling applications and Part IVA).

IF PRIVATE AND PUBLIC RULINGS CONFLICT

Where a Private Ruling is issued subsequent to a Public Ruling and the two Rulings conflict, a taxpayer to whom both Rulings apply may apply either Ruling.

Where a Public Ruling is issued subsequent to a Private Ruling and the two Rulings conflict, a taxpayer to whom both Rulings apply may apply the earlier Private Ruling provided the income year and the scheme to which the Rulings relate have begun. If the income year and the scheme to which the Rulings relate have not begun, the earlier Private Ruling is taken not to have been made.

If you already have a Private Ruling which conflicts with a Private Ruling you are seeking you must inform the Commissioner of this. If the Commissioner issues the second Private Ruling without being so informed, the later Ruling is taken not to have been made.

SOME PRIVATE RULINGS HAVE NO EFFECT

Private Rulings will have no effect if they were issued in these situations:

- the Ruling was given about someone else's tax position without their consent (or consent was withdrawn before the request was lodged)
- the Tax Office had already ruled on that particular matter
- the matter had already been decided and was included in an assessment
- it related to withholding tax due and payable
- a tax audit had commenced and that matter was the subject of the audit, or
- the matter was already subject to objection against a self-assessment.

The Tax Office may allow these Private Rulings to remain in force if that is considered appropriate.

 A private ruling ceases to be binding on the Commissioner if the law is repealed or amended (unless the re-enacted provision "expresses the same ideas" as the old provision): s357-60.

DELAYS IN GIVING A PRIVATE RULING

An applicant may give the Commissioner a written notice requiring the Commissioner to make the Ruling, if at the end of 60 days from the date of the application, the Commissioner has neither given nor denied the Ruling. The 60 day period may be extended in certain circumstances, including if the Commissioner has requested further information (s359-50 TAA).

PRIORITY PRIVATE BINDING RULINGS

Some Private Ruling applications may be appropriately dealt with under the Priority Private Binding Rulings process. PS LA 2009/2 sets out how the process operates and to whom it is available. Generally, the process gives priority to determining Private Ruling applications where:

- the transaction is time sensitive
- the transaction is prospective
- the transaction is of major commercial significance and requiring consideration at corporate Board level
- the tax outcome is a critical element of the transaction, and
- complex law and facts need to be analysed.

This is a formalised and time sensitive process designed to attend to Ruling applications with considerable commercial significance.

4.135   PRIVATE RULING REQUEST DENIED

Generally the Tax Office must consider all requests for Private Rulings.

However, the request may be denied or ignored in a limited number of situations, such as:

- making the Ruling would prejudice or unduly restrict the administration of a taxation law
- the matter has already been or is being considered by the Commissioner for the taxpayer
- the matter is how the Commissioner would exercise a power and the Commissioner has decided or decides whether or not to exercise the power
- the Commissioner considers that the correctness of a Private Ruling would depend on which assumptions were made about a future event or other matter
- the request is made more than two years (or four years for some taxpayers) after the due date for lodging the return
- the application is frivolous or vexatious. Includes purely hypothetical situations, or where the request involves confirmation of assessability or deductibility of all the amounts in the return
- the arrangement is not being seriously contemplated (by the taxpayer), and
- the taxpayer failed to supply additional information requested. If the required information is provided, the Tax Office must issue a Ruling. Requests for more information may be made if the required information is not provided with the application.

The Commissioner must give the applicant, in writing, the reason(s) the application has been denied.

4.140   WITHDRAWAL OF RULING/REVISION OF RULING

A Private Ruling application may be withdrawn at any time before the Private Ruling is made. The Tax Office will confirm the withdrawal in writing.

An existing Private Ruling may be revised by the Commissioner if the scheme to which the existing Ruling relates has not begun to be carried out and the income year (or other accounting period) to which the existing Ruling relates has not yet begun. The revised Ruling must be provided to the taxpayer. The revised Ruling may be issued regardless of whether a revised Ruling was sought. When the revised Ruling is made, the prior Ruling stops.

NOTE: A Private Ruling is not withdrawn but may be revised.

The issue of a Public Ruling inconsistent with a Private Ruling also terminates a Private Ruling:

- from the date the Public Ruling was issued,
- but only to the extent to which it conflicts if the scheme and year of income involved has not started.

The rules concerning the review of Private Rulings are now found in s359-55.

The withdrawal or revision of a Private Ruling now occurs by the notification of the taxpayer through a revised Private Ruling or issuing a Public Ruling applicable to the taxpayer (see 4.100).

4.145   PRIVATE RULING APPLICATION CHECKLIST

Validity checklist		
This checklist may be used when applying for a Private Ruling. If the answer to each question is YES, it will help to avoid rejection of the application or a delay in its processing.		
Entity's Name: TFN/ABN:	Yes	No
1 Entity named in the Ruling identified?	☐	☐
2 Applicant identified, if they differ from the entity named in the Ruling?	☐	☐
3 If the applicant is a tax agent or tax professional applying on behalf of a client, are their details provided, including tax agent number (if applicable)?	☐	☐
4 Is/are the TFNs/ABNs supplied (where applicable)?	☐	☐

Validity checklist		
This checklist may be used when applying for a Private Ruling. If the answer to each question is YES, it will help to avoid rejection of the application or a delay in its processing.		
Entity's Name: TFN/ABN:	Yes	No
5 Is the application in the approved form?	☐	☐
6 Has the application been signed by the applicant (or an authorised entity)?	☐	☐
7 If the application is made by someone other than the applicant (eg. an agent), has written consent been obtained?	☐	☐
8 Is the application in respect of a law the Commissioner is authorised to administer?	☐	☐
9 Does the application identify a contact person for the application?	☐	☐
10 Does the application provide the required contact details including an address to which the Ruling can be sent?	☐	☐
11 Are the questions to be answered identified?	☐	☐
12 Are the issues to be considered identified?	☐	☐
13 Is a full description of the facts provided, are they reasonably certain?	☐	☐
14 Has the applicant provided an opinion of how the law applies to the scheme or circumstance?	☐	☐
15 Are the relevant sections of tax law identified as references commensurate with the applicant's opinion of how the law applies to the scheme or circumstance?	☐	☐
16 Are relevant Public Rulings and/or case law identified commensurate with the applicant's opinion of how the law applies to the scheme or circumstance?	☐	☐
17 Has the applicant clearly identified the year(s) for which Rulings are sought (if possible)?	☐	☐
18 If the arrangement is proposed, has the applicant provided a statement confirming that it is seriously contemplated?	☐	☐
19 Is there, or has there been a Tax Office audit or notification or a proposed audit on the issues raised in the application, if so have details of the audit/proposed audit been provided?	☐	☐
20 If the applicant sought an Oral or written Ruling for these issues before, have these details been provided?	☐	☐
21 Is the applicant registered for GST?	☐	☐

4.150   ORAL RULINGS

The system of Oral Rulings is available only for resident individual taxpayers (or their legal representative) seeking non-business non-complex advice on a matter which has not already been or is not being considered by the Commissioner for the applicant.

As with Private Rulings, an Oral Ruling is the Commissioner's (oral) opinion of how a relevant provision applies or would apply to you in relation to a specified scheme. 'Scheme' is defined in s995-1 of the ITAA97.

Once issued, an Oral Ruling is legally binding on the Tax Office in much the same way that a Private Ruling is binding if it is favourable to the taxpayer. Many of the rules concerning Private

Rulings also apply to Oral Rulings. Rules specific to Oral Rulings are set out at Division 360 of the TAA. Where a taxpayer relies on an Oral Ruling, they will be protected from additional primary tax, penalties and interest.

A Ruling is favourable to a taxpayer if the taxpayer's assessment in accordance with the Ruling provides a lesser tax liability than an assessment in accordance with another Ruling or the terms of the Act.

A Ruling or Determination which is unfavourable to the taxpayer is not binding on the taxpayer. However, if the failure to follow a Ruling results in a shortfall of tax (see 4.600), no penalty will automatically arise but a penalty may arise in respect of a shortfall resulting from failing to take reasonable care.

An application for an Oral Ruling must be made orally and the Ruling is provided orally. Applicants are not entitled to a written record of the oral communication, but the Tax Office will advise the taxpayer of a registration identifier number in respect of that Ruling.

The Commissioner may decline to make an Oral Ruling on the basis the matter sought to be ruled upon is:

- a business matter ('business' is defined in s995-1 of the ITAA97)
- a complex matter
- already being, or has been considered by the Commissioner for the applicant
- such that the Commissioner requests further information within a reasonable timeframe and the further information is not provided by the applicant, or
- such that the Commissioner considers the correctness of a Ruling would depend upon making assumptions.

The taxpayer cannot object or appeal against an Oral Ruling. Pursuant to s360-10, an applicant may withdraw an application for an Oral Ruling before the Commissioner makes the Oral Ruling.

Where an Oral Ruling has been made subsequent to a Public Ruling and the two Rulings are inconsistent, a taxpayer to whom both Rulings apply may apply either Ruling.

Where an Oral Ruling has been made subsequent to an earlier Oral Ruling or a Private Ruling and the two Rulings are inconsistent, a taxpayer to whom both Rulings apply may apply the later Ruling provided the taxpayer informed the Commissioner about the existence of the earlier Ruling when applying for the later Ruling.

An earlier Oral Ruling is taken not to have been made if when a later Public Ruling is made, the income year or other period to which the Rulings relate has not begun and the scheme to which the Rulings relate has not begun to be carried out. Otherwise, either Ruling may be relied upon.

APPLYING FOR ORAL BINDING ADVICE

The following steps will apply when seeking to obtain binding oral advice:

- upon making a request for binding oral advice the authorised Tax Officer will confirm your identity (including details of your tax file number and address etc) and assess your eligibility
- details of the question asked and answer provided will be recorded on your Tax Office tax record, and
- a unique registration identification number will be allocated to identify the advice given and to whom.

4.155   NON-RULING ADVICE

Where non-Ruling advice is obtained from the Tax Office, the Tax Office is not legally bound by the advice but may be administratively bound (s361-5). Administratively binding advice can protect the taxpayer relying on the advice from the general interest charge or shortfall interest charge, provided the advice is not marked as non-binding.

'Non-Ruling advice' refers to advice from the Tax Office other than Public, Private or Oral Rulings. Reliance on the Commissioner's general administrative practice also protects the taxpayer from these interest charges.

INTERPRETATIVE DECISIONS

The Tax Office also issues Interpretative Decisions (IDs). An ID is an edited and summarised version of the Tax Office's interpretation of a particular point. IDs have precedential value for Tax Officers. They provide a useful **(non-binding)** indication of the Tax Office's view on a particular point. They mostly arise as the result of an audit or review or a summarised version of a Private Ruling that has been issued by the Tax Office. They are not binding Public Rulings. Rather, they set out the question and answer without identifying the taxpayer. IDs provide a precedential Tax Office view for Tax Officers, whereas Private Rulings do not (see 4.120).

TAXPAYER ALERTS

The Tax Office also issues Taxpayer Alerts. These are located on the Tax Office website at www. ato.gov.au.

They are not Rulings but are intended to be early warning notices of emerging potentially aggressive tax planning issues or arrangements which the Tax Office has placed under risk assessment. Taxpayer Alerts provide information on the nature of the potentially risky issues or arrangements detailing how they purport to operate and those areas of the law where the Tax Office believes the arrangements are not effective for tax purposes. See PS LA 2008/15 for information on how and why a Taxpayer Alert is issued.

Tax Alerts are not Public Rulings (however the Tax Office's final view on the issue may be reflected in a Public Ruling). They are warnings only. In many cases the Tax Office is yet to finalise its view on the arrangement. Taxpayers contemplating entering into an arrangement that is the subject of a Tax Alert should seek their own independent advice or apply for a Private Ruling (see 4.120).

4.160 PRODUCT RULINGS

Product Rulings are a type of Public Ruling which provide certainty to investors on the tax consequences of publicly marketed investments. They can deal with the same taxes as other Public Rulings (s357-55) or the administration or collection of those taxes (see 4.110). PR 2007/71 sets out the system of Product Rulings – note addenda.

Except in limited circumstances, Product Rulings have prospective effect only and apply only to arrangements entered into after the date the Ruling is made. Any persons who invest in the product, investment or arrangement before the issue date of the Ruling cannot rely on a safe harbour provided by the Ruling.

A Product Ruling is legally binding on the Commissioner. Investors can rely on conditions it contains, provided that the arrangements are made in accordance with the Ruling.

A Product Ruling applies for a specified period not exceeding three years from the end of the income year in which it is made, unless exceptional circumstances exist. It will continue to apply to those persons, even following its withdrawal, for arrangements entered into prior to withdrawal of the Ruling. It will also specify the date on which it will be withdrawn and cease to have effect and it will apply to all persons within the specified class who enter into the specified investment. The product or investment will usually be identified by its product name, the applicant and the income year.

Product Rulings are designed to publicly confirm the tax benefits available through participation in the investment or arrangement. If the arrangement described in the Product Ruling is materially different from the arrangement that is actually carried out, investors lose the protection of the Product Ruling.

Be wary of publicly marketed investments that do not have a Product Ruling. The existence of a Product Ruling means that the promoters have received a sign off that the proposed structure and financing of the investment is acceptable for tax purposes. Investors will still need to be cautious however as the Tax Office has the right to withdraw a Product Ruling if there is any significant alteration to the structure or financing on which it has ruled.

Applying for a Product Ruling Promoters (or the principals of the project) may apply for a Product Ruling setting out the information required in PR 2007/71. The Tax Office website (www. ato.gov.au) provides detailed information regarding how to apply for a Product Ruling and locate an existing Product Ruling. Prior to formally applying for a Product Ruling, the promoter may notify the Tax Office of their intention by completing an *Notification of Intention to Submit a Product Ruling Application* form. In the application for a Product Ruling, the promoter must provide the draft Ruling. The Tax Office does not issue a draft Product Ruling.

PR 2007/71 provides that the Tax Office will issue a Product Ruling provided the applicant:

- acknowledges the following will be disclosed in the Ruling:
    - the name and address of the principals of the arrangement
    - the name and description of the product, and
    - description of the agreements, deeds and transactions to which the investors are parties
- obtains express consent to be named from all parties named in the Ruling
- verifies the accuracy of the Project described in the proposed Ruling, and
- agrees to provide each investor in the project shortly following the conclusion of each financial year with a statement of income derived by the investor in that financial year.

After the issue of the Ruling the promoter or principals must agree to provide the Tax Office with copies of any documents required under the Corporations Law.

WHEN A PRODUCT RULING WILL NOT BE ISSUED

The Tax Office can refuse to issue or withdraw a Product Ruling at its discretion and will generally withdraw them when they are no longer required or necessary.

PR 2007/71 provides that the Tax Office will specifically not issue a Product Ruling if:

- the anonymity of those participants cannot be guaranteed
- the application is frivolous or vexatious
- the persons who may purchase the product are not a homogeneous group such that the tax result is the same for all
- the Ruling could reasonably be misleading to potential investors
- the substantial majority of the activities are to be undertaken outside of Australia
- the clear purpose of the arrangement is to avoid or circumvent a policy intent of law, and
- it is unreasonable to comply with the application given the extent of resources available or other relevant matters.

 A Product Ruling is NOT an endorsement of the proposed investment. Investors must still seek out their own financial advice on the likely financial success of the project.

4.170   CLASS RULINGS

Class Rulings have the same status as Public Rulings (see from 4.110). They can be published in respect of the same taxes as other Public Rulings (s357-55) or the administration or collection of those taxes (see 4.110). The Ruling will apply to all of the persons specified in the class of taxpayers who participate in the scheme identified in the Ruling.

Class Rulings enable the Tax Office to provide legally binding advice in response to a request from an entity seeking advice about the application of a tax law to a specific class of persons in relation to a particular scheme. CR 2001/1 sets out what is a Class Ruling. Section 358-5 defines 'Public Ruling'. It includes in this definition a written Ruling on the way in which the Commissioner considers a relevant provision applies or would apply to a 'class of entities'. This term extends the definition of Public Ruling to include Class Ruling.

CERTAINTY FOR PARTICIPANTS

Class Rulings provide certainty to participants and obviate the need for individual participants to seek Private Rulings.

A Class Ruling is legally binding on the Commissioner and participants can rely on the statements contained in the Ruling. This provides certainty to the participants by confirming the tax consequences set out in the Ruling provided that the schemes are carried out as described. The 'safe harbour' the Ruling offers provides that the Tax Office must apply the law as set out in the Ruling where the Ruling applies to a taxpayer. A taxpayer who relies on the Ruling is protected from shortfall tax, penalties or interest in respect of matters covered by the Ruling if the Ruling is found to incorrectly state how the relevant provisions should apply.

Class Rulings may be withdrawn or modified if the arrangement carried out is materially different from that ruled upon.

 To ensure that the safe harbour applies, participants in a particular arrangement should seek assurances from the arranger that the arrangement described in the Class Ruling will be carried out.

Examples of situations set out in CR 2001/1 where a Class Ruling may be issued include:

- an employer seeks advice about the tax consequences of retention bonuses for a class of employees
- an employer seeks advice about the tax consequences of a bona fide redundancy plan for a class of employees
- an employer seeks advice about the tax consequences of an employee share acquisition plan for individual employees
- a company seeks advice about tax consequences for its shareholders of a restructure of the company, a split or consolidation of its shares, or any other proposed transaction of the company affecting the tax affairs of its shareholders
- a public company seeks advice about the application of the scrip for scrip rollover provisions to its shareholders, and
- a Commonwealth, State or Territory Government or one of their Government authorities seeks advice about a proposed transaction (eg. an industry restructure which has taxation consequences for participants in that industry).

REQUESTS FOR CLASS RULINGS

Class Rulings will not be issued in relation to investment schemes and similar products. Rulings dealing with these issues are published as Product Rulings. While the majority of issues to be published in Class Rulings will be identified by the Tax Office, taxpayers may specifically request a Class Ruling.

From a practical perspective, the Tax Office has indicated that it will treat Public Ruling requests for advice about the application of the tax law to a specific class of entities in relation to a particular scheme as a request for a Class Ruling.

CR 2001/1 provides that requests for a Class Ruling should be sent to the same mailing address as other correspondence (see from 4.060) and must include:

- a full and accurate description of the scheme including details of the principals carrying out the arrangement and any documents referred to in the scheme
- the title given to the scheme (if relevant)
- a clear and accurate description of the class of entities subject to the scheme
- a clearly articulated question/s in terms of the particular provisions that are to be ruled on; and
- a presentation of the issues to be considered together with the results of research undertaken.

Taxpayers requesting a Class Ruling must:

- acknowledge that the Tax Office will reveal in the Ruling:
    - the names and addresses of the entities involved as principals in carrying out the scheme
    - the name and description of the scheme, and
    - a description of the agreements, deeds and transactions to which the participants are parties

- obtain express consent to be named from all parties named in the Ruling, and
- verify that the description of the scheme contained in the proposed Ruling is accurate.

OBLIGATIONS AFTER ISSUE OF A CLASS RULING

Where the arrangement is relevant to or affects statutory or other Government requirements (eg. director's reports requirements), the taxpayer may be requested to provide that relevant information to the Tax Office.

Where the Tax Office is unable to issue a favourable Ruling, it will issue a Private Ruling instead to enable the taxpayer to test the issues through the relevant review processes (see 4.200 and 4.220).

CLASS RULINGS CAN BE WITHDRAWN

The Tax Office can issue and withdraw Class Rulings at its discretion. Class Rulings will generally be withdrawn when no longer needed. Withdrawal of a Class Ruling will be made public in the Gazette.

WHEN CLASS RULINGS WILL NOT BE ISSUED

The Tax Office has indicated that it will not issue Class Rulings if:

- the request is frivolous or vexatious (including hypothetical situations where there is no realistic chance of implementing the scheme); or there is no settled scheme on which the Tax Office may rule
- the Ruling could reasonably be misleading to participants, including where the Tax Office cannot give a positive clearance on general anti-avoidance provisions or the material provided in support of the application cannot reasonably be relied upon
- insufficient information has been provided despite a request by the Commissioner for additional information, and
- it is unreasonable to comply with the application given the extent of resources available etc.

4.180   PRACTICE STATEMENTS

Practice Statements are instructions to Tax Office staff from the Commissioner on how they are to administer the law. However, they are publicised and applied more broadly to provide guidance to taxpayers and their advisers on how the law will be administered. Practice Statements are not legally binding on the Commissioner in the way that Rulings are.

Care should be taken as the Tax Office can change its approach without warning. Generally where the Tax Office has changed its approach that change has been prospective.

The scope of Law Administration Practice Statements is set out in PS LA 1998/1 (revised on 27 August 2009).

WHAT ARE PRACTICE STATEMENTS?

Practice Statements provide direction and assistance to Tax Office technical staff on the approaches they are to take in performing their technical duties. They are lawful directions from the Commissioner to Tax Office staff. They are not meant to provide interpretative advice, but they are a supplement to Public Rulings.

Practice Statements will address such issues as:

- the steps to be taken after a Tribunal or Court decision
- processes or procedures for identifying and resolving significant issues (eg. the test litigation program)
- work practices to be adopted, and
- practices to be followed in the practical application and administration of the tax laws.

For example, PS LA 2009/9 provides Tax Office staff guidance on the processes when courts award costs to a legal proceeding where the Commissioner is a party.

Tax Office staff are mandated to follow the instructions contained in Practice Statements. For that reason they provide a degree of certainty for taxpayers who follow the guidelines contained in Practice Statements. If a taxpayer relies on a Practice Statement and the Practice Statement is incorrect, the taxpayer will remain liable for any tax shortfall that may result. Law Administration Practice Statements include a general administration series. These Practice Statements focus on the practical administration of the tax system, in particular in respect of compliance.

 Be aware that Practice Statements are not binding and if incorrect, any tax shortfall will remain payable, although the Commissioner's practice is to waive penalties.

 The Federal Court decision in Macquarie Bank Limited v Commissioner of Taxation [2013] FCA 887 provides judicial authority for the proposition that the views expressed by the Commissioner in a Practice Statement are not legally binding and ultimately does not have legal force. In this particular case, the taxpayers found that because PS LA 2011/27 did not have the force of law, the Court allowed the Commissioner to apply his view on a substantive matter retrospectively.

4.200   OBJECTIONS

If a taxpayer is dissatisfied with a Private Ruling issued by the Tax Office or with an assessment or amended assessment of income tax, FBT or other tax liability (see list below), the taxpayer can object against it. The objection must be in writing and lodged, usually within 60 days after the Ruling is made or within two years (four years for some taxpayers) of receiving the assessment or amended assessment. The Tax Office has issued a comprehensive Ruling about objections against income tax assessments (TR 2011/5).

NOTE: The Tax Office does not generally make an assessment in respect of GST, however, a taxpayer wishing to object may request an assessment which becomes a reviewable indirect tax decision which may be objected against pursuant to Part IVC of the TAA.

Part IVC of the TAA sets out the rules and processes of taxation objections, reviews and appeals. Importantly, a taxpayer may not seek redress under these provisions unless a provision in a relevant Act gives the taxpayer the ability to do so. Not all decisions made by the Commissioner are reviewable.

Objections are not confined to assessments. An objection can be lodged against Tax Office decisions (known as 'taxation decisions') which is defined at s14ZQ of TAA as meaning the assessment, determination, notice or decision against which a taxation objection may be or has been made. A taxpayer may object against such a decision where a provision specifically gives them the right to do so. The taxpayer must be dissatisfied with the decision.

 An objection can still be lodged even if the assessment is in accord with the return. This may be a useful strategy when a taxpayer is uncertain about the correct treatment of an item and does not want to risk penalties.

MAKE SURE IT IS AN OBJECTION

An objection differs from an amendment and other areas of review. An objection is appropriate where an issue is not straightforward. Where a simple error exists in an assessment, requesting an amendment should be sufficient, although taxpayers should ensure that the time available for an objection does not expire without the amendment issuing.

An objection is more commonly lodged against:

- an income tax assessment
- an amended income tax assessment
- an administrative penalty
- a Private Ruling, and
- a reviewable indirect tax decision.

An objection will not be valid unless the taxpayer:

- notifies the Tax Office in writing that he or she is 'objecting' to the assessment
- states fully and in detail the grounds of objection, and

- lodges the objection within the appropriate period after service (or deemed service) of the tax decision.

The Tax Office can grant extra time to lodge an objection (PS LA 2003/7), and the Administrative Appeals Tribunal (AAT) or courts hearing an appeal may allow the grounds of objection to be varied. However, the circumstances are limited and no risks should be taken in not complying with legislative requirements and time limits.

VALID OBJECTIONS

A taxation objection may be lodged against a taxation decision where a provision grants the taxpayer a right to object against it in accordance with Part IVC of the TAA. An objection cannot be lodged against any Public Ruling, including a Taxation Determination.

GROUNDS FOR OBJECTION

There is no strict format to be followed in drafting an objection, however the taxpayer must clearly indicate to the Tax Office that the taxpayer is objecting to a taxation decision and must state fully and in detail the grounds on which the taxpayer is relying (s14ZU TAA). Taxpayers are limited to the grounds stated in their objection unless the courts or AAT order otherwise. Where an amended assessment is issued, the taxpayer's right to object is limited to the alterations or amendments to the original assessment.

CLAIMS FOR COSTS OF OBJECTION

Taxpayers are entitled to claim the full cost for non-capital expenditure incurred in managing their tax affairs (see 12.900) including the cost of professional fees in preparing a taxation objection.

4.210   LODGING OBJECTIONS – TIME LIMITS

An objection may be lodged at any Tax Office. To be valid, it must be lodged within these timeframes:
- Individuals who meet certain criteria and small business entities (see 10.100): *two years*
- All other taxpayers: *four years*

Taxpayers will have a four year amendment period in some circumstances, including where:
- the taxpayer is a beneficiary of a trust estate at any time in that income year, unless the trust is a small business entity or the trustee of the trust is a full self assessment taxpayer (eg. corporate unit trust, public trading trust or superannuation fund)
- in that year, the taxpayer or another entity entered into or carried out a scheme for the sole or dominant purpose of the taxpayer obtaining a scheme benefit in relation to income tax from the scheme, or
- other high risk and special cases prescribed by regulation.

NOTE: Situations of fraud or evasion continue to have an unlimited amendment period.

IMPORTANT: These time limits apply to the time in which a taxpayer may object against an assessment or amended assessment **and** the time in which the Commissioner may reassess a taxpayer (s170 ITAA36).

An objection against an **amended** assessment must be lodged by the later of the period during which the original assessment may be objected against, as set out above, or 60 days after the notice of amended assessment has been served (see ss14ZW(1B) and 14ZW(1BA)). The review period commences from the issue date of the assessment. The issue date of an assessment for a fully self-assessed taxpayer (ie. a taxpayer who does not receive a notice of assessment) is the date of deemed assessment which is the day the return is lodged.

The time limits for lodging objections against income tax assessments are set out at s14ZW of the TAA. Specific objection time limits for amended assessments are provided for:
- objection against amended assessment (ss14ZW(1B) and 14ZW(1BA)
- objection against an assessment of an administrative penalty (under Division 284 TAA)
- objection against a reviewable indirect taxation decision, and
- objection against a Private Ruling.

PRIVATE RULINGS

Objections must be lodged by the later of:
- 60 days after the date the Ruling was issued, or
- at the end of four years from the due date of the relevant income tax return. However, if the taxpayer's time period in which an assessment may be amended is two years (s170(1) items 1,2,3, ITAA36) the objection must be lodged no later than two years from the due date of the relevant return (see 4.220).

Section 359-60 and Part IVC set out the circumstances in which a taxpayer may object against a Private Ruling.

INDIRECT TAX DECISIONS

Objections must be lodged by the later of:
- 60 days after service of notice of the decision, or
- four years after the end of the tax period, or after the importation of goods, to which the decision relates.

OTHER DECISIONS

For the purposes of the 60 day time limit, service of notice is deemed to be effected at the time it would reach the taxpayer in the normal course of the post.

The four year objection period relates to all taxpayers other than those provided for at items 1, 2 and 3 of the table in s170(1) ITAA36 and assessments including:
- foreign income tax offsets
- income tax assessments and amendments
- delayed administration (beneficiary or trustee) (Income tax and FBT assessments ie. probate or letters of administration have not been granted within six months of death), and
- FBT assessments.

All other objections needed to be lodged within 60 days after service of notice of the decision.

TIME LIMITS FOR THE COMMISSIONER

The Commissioner is required to make an objection decision by the later of the following:
- the end of the period (the 'original 60-day period') of 60 days after the later of the following:
  - the day on which the objection is lodged, and
  - if the Commissioner makes a decision to grant an extension of time - the day on which the decision is made, and
- if the Commissioner requests information, in writing and within the original 60-day period - 60 days after the Commissioner receives that information.

If the Commissioner does not make an objection decision within the relevant time limit, the taxpayer may give the Commissioner a written notice requiring the Commissioner to make an objection decision.

If the Commissioner does not make an objection decision within 60 days of being given the notice, the Commissioner is taken to have made a decision to disallow the objection.

The Full Federal Court has confirmed that a taxpayer who gives such a notice to the Commissioner may withdraw that notice before its deemed operation comes into effect (*Commissioner of Taxation v McGrouther* (2015) FCAFC 34).

AFTER OBJECTION IS DISALLOWED (ALL OR IN PART)

Reference to the AAT or Federal Court: 60 days

APPEAL TO THE FEDERAL COURT

From a decision of the AAT: 28 days

APPEAL TO THE FULL FEDERAL COURT

From a Federal Court decision: 21 days

SEEKING LEAVE TO APPEAL TO HIGH COURT

From a Full Federal Court decision: 21 days

4.220 OBJECTIONS AGAINST PRIVATE RULINGS

The objection needs to be in writing and state the grounds on which the taxpayer relies (see 4.240). If the taxpayer disagrees with a Private Ruling, an objection can be lodged with the Tax Office, in the same manner as an objection against a tax assessment. The objection must be in writing in the prescribed form and be lodged by the later of:

- 60 days after the Ruling is made, or
- four years after the last day allowed to lodge the relevant income tax return (or two years if that is the taxpayer's amendment period).

OBJECTION AGAINST PRIVATE RULING NOT POSSIBLE IN SOME CASES

An objection against a Private Ruling cannot be lodged if:

- the tax consequences of the arrangement have already been assessed by the Tax Office, or
- the Ruling relates to withholding tax that has become due and payable.

If an objection is lodged against a Private Ruling and an assessment is issued later, you cannot lodge a further objection against the same matter unless the facts on which the assessment is based are materially different from those on which the Ruling was based.

Taxpayers may choose whether to refer the matter to the Administrative Appeals Tribunal (AAT) or the Federal Court. The Small Taxation Claims Tribunal (part of AAT) is also an option if the amount of tax is less than $5,000 (see 4.360).

 In any appeal to the AAT or Federal Court against an unfavourable Private Ruling, a taxpayer is limited to the evidence presented to the Tax Office in the application for the Private Ruling. Additional evidence CANNOT be submitted to the AAT or Federal Court. This means that any request for a Private Ruling must be accompanied by comprehensive supporting evidence if the taxpayer wants to be able to present the strongest case on appeal. This problem does not arise in an appeal against an assessment as additional information, including oral evidence, can be provided.

4.223 REVIEW/APPEAL OF OBJECTION DECISION

The decision against which the taxpayer is objecting is referred to as the taxation decision. The Commissioner's decision on the taxpayer's objection is referred to as the objection decision.

Part IVC of the TAA defines an 'appealable objection decision' to be an objection decision other than one made on a taxable objection under s14E of the TAA. Section 14E of the TAA relates to the right to object against the Commissioner's refusal to issue a tax clearance certificate (see ss14B to 14E TAA).

A 'reviewable objection decision' is defined in Part IVC as an objection decision that is not an ineligible income tax remission decision. An 'ineligible income tax remission decision' is defined at s14ZS of the TAA.

If the objection decision is both reviewable and appealable, the taxpayer may apply to either the AAT or the Federal Court. If the objection decision is only reviewable, the taxpayer may only appeal to the AAT. Similarly, if the objection decision is only appealable, the taxpayer may only appeal to the Federal Court (see 4.300).

Part IVC, Division 4 sets out the provisions regarding seeking an AAT review of objection decisions and extension of time refusal decisions. Part IVC Division 5 sets out the provisions regarding Federal Court appeals against objection decisions.

4.225   SIMPLE TAX AFFAIRS

A two year period of review applies to certain taxpayers.

For an individual to be treated as a Shorter Period of Review (SPOR) taxpayer that is eligible for the two year period, the taxpayer must:

- derive income only from salary or wages, or interest, or dividends from an Australian listed company, and
- claim deductions limited to gifts or donations, account-keeping fees (including FID and debits tax), or expenses of managing their tax affairs (eg. tax agent fees).

This criteria must be applied each year to determine the status of the taxpayer. They will not qualify if they:

- were non-resident at any time during the income year
- were entitled to a foreign tax credit or derived exempt foreign service income (see 22.400 and 22.010)
- claimed a tax deduction incurred to an associate or derived income from an associate, or
- had a capital gain or capital loss.

A business taxpayer is also a SPOR taxpayer if the business has elected to apply the Small Business Entities tax concessions (see 10.000).

 The two year period affects the taxpayer's ability to lodge objections for credit amendments, but it also prevents the Tax Office from amending assessments to disallow deductions or include additional income (provided there has been no fraud or evasion involved). It also reduces the time available to request a Private Ruling.

4.230   WITHDRAWING AN OBJECTION

An objection can be withdrawn at any time before the issue is resolved. Once withdrawn, the taxpayer's right to escalate the issue to the AAT or Federal Court may be lost if the statutory objection period has elapsed.

 Don't withdraw an objection unless the Tax Office has given, in writing, a satisfactory settlement proposition. If withdrawn, it cannot be reinstated, but another objection might be lodged if the available time hasn't elapsed.

4.235   OBJECTIONS INVOLVING CARRY FORWARD LOSSES

Objections involving losses that are carried forward can only be made against the assessment in which those losses are eventually claimed. Therefore it may be many years (especially with capital losses which can only be offset against realised capital gains) before an objection in respect of losses may be lodged.

IMPORTANT: Assessments involving a nil assessment or carry forward losses are subject to a limited period of review of four years (and may be reduced to two years in some situations).

4.240   HOW TO WRITE AN OBJECTION

There is no specified legal form for an objection, however the document must clearly show:

- that it is an objection against a particular assessment or Private Ruling, identify the year to which it relates, date of issue, and assessment number or Private Ruling number
- the particular item(s) in dispute, and
- the taxpayer's reasons for believing that the assessment should be amended (eg. that the claim in dispute should be allowed, that an amount should not be assessed, a penalty should not have been imposed or interest is not payable). It is not enough to merely contend that an assessment is wrong: reasons must be set out. The Tax Office, the AAT or Courts are only required to consider the reasons stated when reviewing an assessment.

- The Tax Office provides several (optional) forms for lodging objections (such as NAT 13471 or for tax professionals NAT 13044). The Tax Office also sets out requirements for supporting documents. If an objection is lodged without using one of the Tax Office's objection forms, the information required by the forms and required supporting information should nevertheless be supplied.

FREEDOM OF INFORMATION

It may be necessary to utilise Freedom of Information laws in order to obtain some information held by the Tax Office. A *'Request under the Freedom of Information Act 1982'* form is available from the Tax Office.

SAMPLE OBJECTION NOTICE*

I, ... (taxpayer's name) hereby object to the assessment of income tax in respect of the year ended 30th June . . . . on Assessment No . . . . dated . . . .

I claim that it should be reduced by an amount not exceeding $ . . . . being home-office costs incurred in gaining my income.

My reasons for wanting that done are:

- the amount of $ . . . . or at least some part of that amount, in respect of the home office expenses is an allowable deduction in accordance with (insert section) or some other provision of the Income Tax Assessment Act.
- the amount of $ . . . . or at least some part of that amount, is not of a capital, private or domestic nature.
- the Medicare levy payable by me should be calculated by reference to a taxable income of $ . . . or alternatively, a taxable income less than that shown on the assessment.

Name . . . . Address. . . . .
. . . .
Signature . . . . Tax File Number. . . . .

*include reference to all provisions of the law which may be relevant and to the imposition of penalties (if applicable)

QUOTING CASES, RULINGS OR TAX LAW

If relevant, refer to Tax Determinations, cases, Rulings and sections in the relevant Act(s). However, be careful to specify all potentially relevant sections and information as to do otherwise may limit the scope of the objection. Technically, the taxpayer should sign but, as an agent may stand in the client's place, the Tax Office accepts objections signed by solicitors, registered tax agents or a person with Power of Attorney. That applies for certain administrative matters, not for the signing of the tax return itself, unless the agent has been given a Power of Attorney.

The Tax Office must consider every valid objection received (see from 4.200). The taxpayer can serve a notice in writing requiring a decision to be made by the Tax Office if a decision has not been made within 60 days:

- of lodgment of the objection (or extended time for lodging)
- of provision of additional information requested by the Tax Office.

If the taxpayer lodges such a notice, and the Tax Office does not make a decision on the issue within the next 60 days:

- the objection is deemed to be disallowed, and
- the Tax Office should notify the taxpayer in writing of the deemed disallowance.

4.250   DELAYED LODGMENT

An objection must be lodged with the Tax Office within defined time limits (see 4.210).

Unless it can be proved that it was delayed in the post, an assessment is deemed to have been delivered in the ordinary course of the post. The Tax Office usually posts slightly ahead of the date shown to allow for the normal postal delivery. If the issue date of 1 February appears on the assessment, it is taken as being posted that day, and by local post should normally be received by no later than 3 February.

APPLYING FOR AN EXTENSION

If an objection is not lodged within the required time, it may be sent to the Tax Office with an application in writing, asking that it be treated as lodged within time. The application must state fully and in detail the reasons for failing to lodge on time. Factors relevant to the Tax Office's decision to grant or not to grant the time extension include:

- whether the conduct of the Tax Office, the tax agent concerned, or of the taxpayer was a contributing factor to the delay
- any uncertainty created by any announcement of planned changes in the law, and
- whether the objection has merit.

It is not acceptable for the taxpayer to have been unaware of what the law requires.

IF APPLICATION FOR MORE TIME REFUSED

Within 60 days of receiving from the Tax Office a decision not to grant extra time, the AAT can be requested to review the decision (see 4.300).

4.260   DISPUTED TAX

The fact that an objection or review or appeal of an objection decision is pending in relation to a taxation decision does not defer the liability to pay an amount of tax outstanding. However, payment may be deferred pursuant to Subdivision 255-B of the TAA and IT 2569 where a part payment is made.

LATE PAYMENT PENALTY

If the objection is unsuccessful, a late payment penalty is calculated from the due date (or deemed date) on the unpaid part of an assessment (see 4.650).

4.265   INTEREST

If the taxpayer's request for amendment or objection is successful then the Tax Office will be obliged to pay interest on any overpayment of tax (see 4.660). The rate of interest payable is based on the 90 day Bank Accepted Bill rate for that period.

If the taxpayer's objection is unsuccessful or an amended assessment is issued increasing the amount their tax liability then an interest penalty (general interest charge) is payable based on a daily compounding basis. The rates are also based on the 90 day Bank Accepted Bill rate plus an additional premium of 7% or 3% depending on the circumstances (see from 4.660).

4.270 SELF-AMENDMENTS AND TAX OFFICE AMENDMENTS

Under self-assessment, both the Commissioner and taxpayers have the right to amend returns. The applicable rules depend on the nature of the taxpayer and whether the amendment is to increase or decrease the tax liability of the taxpayer.

In cases of tax avoidance due to fraud or evasion, there is no time limit on the Tax Office's ability to amend a taxpayer's assessment to increase their tax liability. In any other case involving an increase in taxpayer's liability, the time frame is limited to two or four years after the date of the assessment.

The Tax Office can apply to the Federal Court to extend that time if it has begun an investigation of the taxpayer's affairs and has been unable to complete that investigation.

The period of review for income tax assessments and amendments is:

- Individuals and small business entities (see 10.000): *two years*
- Business taxpayers who are not small business entities: *four years*
- Individuals who are beneficiaries of trusts and members of partnerships that are not small business entities (other than public trading trusts and corporate unit trusts): *four years*

   NOTE: In *Yazbeck v Commissioner of Taxation* (2013) FCA39, the Federal Court concluded that merely being a beneficiary of a trust was sufficient for an individual's amendment period to be extended to four years; it was not necessary that a distribution actually be received.

- Anti-avoidance cases (Part IVA: see 4.510): four years
- To give effect to a decision on a review or appeal or as a result of an objection made by the taxpayer or pending a review or appeal: unlimited
- Fraud or evasion: unlimited

NOTE: The time limits also apply to assessments where no tax is payable.

Section 170 ITAA36 also contains guidance concerning time limits for further amending amended assessments, applications for extensions of time to amend assessments including court orders and taxpayer consent and to give effect to a Private Ruling.

SELF-AMENDING

If self-amending your assessment, the Tax Office requires the following information:

- name, address, phone number and tax file number
- the income year in respect of which you wish to amend
- tax return item number and change to be made
- amount of income or deduction to be added or deducted
- amount of any rebate or tax offset to be increased or decreased
- relevant code type (if applicable – see tax return instructions on the Tax Office website)
- an explanation for the change, and
- attached documentary evidence to support the change and include a statement declaring that the information is true and correct.

AMENDING AMENDED ASSESSMENTS

Subsections 170(2), (3) and (4) of the ITAA36 limit the ability to further amend amended assessments. Where the amendment period applying to the original assessment has expired, the Commissioner can only amend an amended assessment if:

- the Commissioner amends the original assessment to reduce a taxpayer's liability and in doing so accepts a self-amendment by the taxpayer, the Commissioner may amend the later assessment to increase the taxpayer's liability, and
- the Commissioner amends the original assessment to increase a taxpayer's liability (or decreases it in a way other than above), the Commissioner may amend the later assessment to decrease the taxpayer's liability.

The ability to further amend amended assessments is also affected by time limits.

4.300   REVIEWS AND APPEALS

Taxpayers who are dissatisfied with a reviewable objection decision made by the Tax Office on their objection against an assessment, amended assessment, Private Ruling application or other taxation decision can have the decision reviewed by the Administrative Appeals Tribunal (AAT). Appeals from an appealable objection decision can also be lodged with the Federal Court. If the decision is both reviewable and appealable, the taxpayer may apply to either the AAT or the Federal Court. Where the amount in dispute is less than $5,000 and the taxpayer chooses the AAT, the matter will be referred to the Small Taxation Claims Tribunal (see 4.360).

All requests for review or appeal must be lodged by the taxpayer directly with the AAT or the Federal Court within 60 days of receipt of the Tax Office's decision on the objection. If the decision is only a reviewable decision, an application can only be made to the AAT for review. An application in relation to an appealable decision is made to the Federal Court.

IMPORTANT! If the Commissioner obtains judgment for an income tax debt and that judgment is not set aside, he will not sue again on the same notice of assessment. However, if the assessment is amended and the amendment gives rise to additional tax, the Commissioner may sue to recover the additional tax. The High Court confirmed the correctness of the Commissioner's approach by refusing to grant special leave for the taxpayer to appeal the Full Federal Court's decision in *Chemical Trustee Limited v Deputy Commissioner of Taxation* [2014] FCAFC 27.

4.305   PART IVC TAX DISPUTE PROCESS

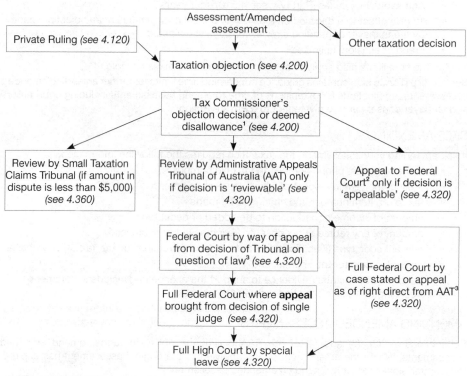

1: If an objection decision is both reviewable and appealable, the taxpayer may apply to either the AAT or Federal Court.

2: The Federal Court does not have the power to review an exercise of a discretion by the Commissioner, unless the taxpayer can show the discretion was unauthorised or the manner of exercise constituted an abuse of power.

3: Where the tribunal as constituted in a particular case includes a presidential member, any appeal from the decision by the AAT must be to the Full Federal Court. In any other case, the court on appeal may be constituted by either a single judge or by the Full Court.

Reviewable decisions are all those in which the Commissioner has exercised his discretion to impose additional tax in excess of statutory amounts. An objection decision for taxation purposes effectively means all other decisions which are not reviewable decisions.

PS LA 2009/9 provides guidance for Tax Office staff regarding disputes that are heard by a Court or Tribunal. In particular, PS LA 2009/9 sets out:

- the procedures for Tax Office staff to follow where the Commissioner has been party to legal proceedings and a Court has awarded unspecified costs. The Practice Statement addresses where the Courts have awarded costs to and against the Commissioner
- the procedures for Tax Office staff to follow in managing Court and Tribunal decisions and the risks arising form those decisions, and
- the approach for Tax Office staff to follow and the conduct of Tax Office litigation in Courts and Tribunals.

4.310   GROUNDS FOR REVIEW OR APPEAL

A taxpayer normally is limited to arguing the points raised in the original objection. Both the Federal Court and the AAT have power to approve the case being argued on points which were not in the objection, but there are no guidelines for this in the tax law. If a taxpayer has not lodged the request with the AAT or Federal Court within the 60 day limit, a request asking that it be regarded as lodged within the time can be sent directly to the appropriate body.

If the request is refused:

- the Federal Court could be asked to consider it, if the AAT made the decision, or
- seek legal advice if the Federal Court made the decision because the Federal Court does not have the power to extend the time for lodging an appeal beyond the 60 day limit.

4.320   TAXPAYER MUST PROVE CASE

Whether before the AAT or the Federal Court, the onus is on the taxpayer to prove the case, ie. if the taxpayer considers an assessment is excessive, the taxpayer must prove why the assessment is excessive and what the correct assessment should be.

FEDERAL COURT OR AAT?

If a disputed tax decision is referred to the AAT the maximum fee is $777 per reference. If more than one income tax year is involved, but the matter in dispute is the same, only one fee of $777 is required. If a taxpayer elects to have the matter dealt with in the Small Taxation Claims Tribunal, the fee is $77.

From the AAT, a direct appeal to the Full Court of the Federal Court may be possible but only on points of law, not on questions of fact. Appeals to the High Court can be made only against decisions of the Full Federal Court by 'special leave' (ie. only when the High Court agrees to hear the case).

CHOOSING THE AAT

Proceedings may be conducted in private if requested. The hearings are informal and taxpayers can represent themselves or choose to have an accountant or legal representative do so.

The AAT is able to stand in the place of the Tax Office in all matters including the exercise of discretionary powers, but some limitations exist in respect of the power to review additional tax imposed. Generally, both the taxpayer and the Tax Office bear their own costs. Costs cannot be awarded against the losing party. Unlike courts, the AAT is not bound by the rules of evidence. The AAT is bound by precedent set by Court decisions but is not bound to follow earlier AAT decisions.

If the AAT reviews an objection decision of the Commissioner, its role is only to exercise all of the powers and discretions conferred on the Commissioner. That does not involve a review of the assessment of taxable income by the Commissioner. The AAT's review does involve determining whether a taxpayer has discharged the onus of proving that the Commissioner's assessment is excessive (*Rigoli and Commissioner of Taxation* (2015) AATA 169).

The AAT's jurisdiction is confined to reviewable objection decisions - and only at the request of a person who is 'dissatisfied' in the sense intended by legislation. See: Van Gestel and Commissioner of Taxation (2014) AATA 396, in which the AAT made a distinction between the taxpayer being unhappy and the taxpayer being dissatisfied with the objection decision.

CHOOSING THE FEDERAL COURT

The Court is bound by the decisions of any higher court which can be an important factor if the case is to be a test case. Legal representation is essential, and that cost can be significant. The losing party will usually bear much of the cost of the case. Even if the case is won by the taxpayer, not all costs may be recoverable. Matters before the Court are conducted in public and published decisions will include the names of parties to the matter.

The Court is unable to review the use of a discretionary power the law gives to the Commissioner, unless the Court accepts that the decision was made contrary to law. At the discretion of the Chief Judge of the Federal Court, an appeal of an appealable objection decision including an appeal from the AAT may go to a single Judge of the Federal Court or the Full Federal Court, but normally an appeal will go to a single Judge. However, if the appeal is from an AAT decision by a Presidential Member who was a Judge, the appeal must proceed to the Full Federal Court. If a question of law is involved, a case may be referred to the Full Federal Court if, before going to the AAT, a President of the AAT consents to it.

4.325   TEST CASE LITIGATION PROGRAM

Under the Test Case Litigation program, the Tax Office provides financial assistance to taxpayers involved in litigation the Tax Office regards as important to tax administration. The program is useful for the creation of precedent in otherwise unclear areas of tax law. Taxpayers apply to the Test Case Litigation Panel to seek funding for their appeal of a decision. The Panel is comprised of members of the Tax Office and the wider taxation industry. The Panel also considers applications which seek to test an issue but where no actual case has arisen. The application in this circumstance may be made by a professional or industry group. Similarly, the Commissioner may seek to test an issue and in doing so seek agreement from a taxpayer to whom the issue relates or a professional or industry group.

Where the taxpayer wishes to appeal a tax decision, an appeal at least to the Full Federal Court will generally be funded by the Tax Office. Again, this is for the purpose of obtaining precedential guidance in unclear areas of tax law. Information on how to apply for test case funding is available from the Tax Office website: www.ato.gov.au.

4.330   COSTS OF LODGING AN APPEAL

The costs of lodging an appeal or seeking a review are as follows. Each party generally bears his or her own costs before the AAT. Before the Courts, the winning party may be awarded costs. The fees (which are GST-exempt) are:

- **Small Taxation Claims Tribunal:** $85
- **Administrative Appeals Tribunal** (AAT) – Filing the initial reference: $861
- **Federal Court**
  - To start proceedings: *Publicly listed company*: $4,980 *Corporation*: $3,320; in any other case $1,140
  - Filing notice of appeal from AAT or appeal to Full Federal Court: *Publicly listed company:* $12,405 *Corporation:* $8,270; in any other case $3,830
  - Setting down fee: *Publicly listed company:* $8,305; *Corporation:* $5,535; in any other case $2,275
  - Daily fee (including for part of a day): *Publicly listed company:* $3,310; *Corporation:* $2,205; in any other case $905
- **High Court**
  - Applications for leave to appeal, or notice to appeal to the High Court: *Individual:* $2,645; *Corporation:* $7,980; *Publicly listed company:* $11,975

- Full court first day – Hearing fee (other than special leave): *Individual:* $4,445; *Corporation:* $10,830; *Publicly listed company:* $16,250
- Full court subsequent day – Hearing fee (other than special leave): *Individual:* $1,480; *Corporation:* $3,610; *Publicly listed company:* $5,410
- Single Justice – Daily hearing fee (other than special leave): *Individual:* $495; *Corporation:* $1,205; *Publicly listed company:* $1,805

NOTE: Financial hardship provisions may apply.

4.340   LEGAL REPRESENTATION

If a case is taken to the Federal Court, the taxpayer must be represented by someone authorised to appear in that jurisdiction. At the AAT, a taxpayer can present their own case, but given the complexity of the issues involved, it may be beneficial to have competent professional representation.

 To understand what's involved in being a party to a case, seek legal advice.

4.350   REFUND OF FEES/COSTS

These are made only if:

- the taxpayer wins (in whole or in part) the case even if as part of an out-of-court settlement
- the request for reference is withdrawn before being forwarded to the AAT or the Court.

 A reduction of even $1 in the tax payable means the whole of the AAT filing fee is refundable (but not the Small Taxation Claims Tribunal fee) (see 4.360).

The Tax Office has released PS LA 2009/9 which sets out procedures for Tax Office staff to follow where the Commissioner has been party to legal proceedings and a Court has awarded unspecified costs. The Practice Statement addresses where the Courts have awarded costs to and against the Commissioner.

TAX CLAIMS FOR APPEAL COSTS

Costs for management or administration of the income tax affairs of a taxpayer are tax deductible (including any fees or any legal costs for the lodgment of an objection and for any later appeal). No deduction is allowed if the case relates to a taxation offence.

CLAIM ALLOWED, BUT SOME REFUND LATER RECEIVED

The taxpayer must show as income (in the return of the year during which the amount is received) any amount reimbursed, paid, or recouped in any way.

4.360   SMALL TAXATION CLAIMS TRIBUNAL

The Small Taxation Claims Tribunal (STCT) is set up within the taxation division of the Administrative Appeals Tribunal (AAT) and has the power to determine disputes between taxpayers and the Tax Office where the amount of tax involved is less than $5,000.

The STCT is able to review all Tax Office decisions against which an objection can be lodged including:

- assessments
- Private Rulings, and
- a decision refusing a request for an extension of time to lodge a taxation objection.

The STCT can review:

- objection decisions by the Commissioner where the amount of tax in dispute is less than $5,000
- decisions by the Tax Office refusing a request for extension of time within which to make an objection, and/or

- objection decisions by the Commissioner refusing an individual taxpayer's request to be released from paying an amount of tax (regardless of the amount involved).

 If the dispute is in respect of an issue where the amount of tax in dispute is $5,000 or more, the matter cannot be reviewed by the STCT. In that case, taxpayers must choose between a referral to the AAT or an appeal to the Federal Court (if eligible).

COST OF APPEAL

The cost of referral to the STCT is a non-refundable fee (currently $85). That amount can be waived where the taxpayer is able to demonstrate that they cannot afford the fee. The fee is payable only once by the taxpayer even if more than one application for review under the one name is lodged. If applications are lodged before both the STCT and the AAT, those issues can be dealt with together by the AAT. The cost of referral to the AAT is currently $861.

The taxpayer must state the amount of tax in dispute on the application to the AAT. Provided the amount is determined by the AAT to be below $5,000, the matter will be dealt with by the STCT. If the amount is subsequently determined to be $5,000 or more, the matter must be dealt with by the AAT and it will not proceed until the balance of the full application fee is received.

 The cost of referral to the STCT is non-refundable, but inexpensive compared to the AAT or Federal Court. The Tax Office and the taxpayer have the right to appeal a decision of the STCT to the Federal Court. Any appeal is restricted to questions of law and does not amount to a new hearing. That appeal must be made within 28 days of the initial decision.

HOW THE SMALL TAXATION CLAIMS TRIBUNAL WORKS

Taxpayers can choose not to be represented by a lawyer or tax agent at the STCT but they will be responsible for presenting their case. The STCT will assist taxpayers with all procedural matters.

 Before choosing to represent themselves, taxpayers should be very careful that they fully understand both the facts and the underlying tax laws. The Tax Office representative will be both qualified and fully conversant with the law.

On receiving the taxpayer's application for review, the matter is listed for a conference with a representative of the Tax Office. In practice, the conference should normally be held within 6-10 weeks of lodgement of the application.

The conference is designed to allow taxpayers to:

- discuss with the Tax Office why the assessment or decision is wrong
- negotiate an acceptable and agreed position on what the correct decision should be, and
- enable additional evidence to be obtained to support the case.

The conference will be conducted by a STCT Tribunal Member or Conference Registrar and each party is entitled to have support. The Tax Office will generally have two persons present. Taxpayers can choose to have a family member, a professional adviser or an interpreter present. The interpreter cannot be either a member of the taxpayer's family or a close friend. If an interpreter is needed the Tribunal should be contacted before the conference to arrange for one to be present.

The taxpayer should bring to the conference:

- all papers, letters and documents received from the Tax Office (including assessment notices and audit papers)
- any papers received from the Tribunal, and
- any other information that is important to prove the taxpayer's case (eg. account books, receipts, invoices, details of transactions, minutes and notes, and any working papers).

4.370 SETTLEMENT OF TAXATION DISPUTES

The Tax Office has developed a 'good management rule' approach to managing the tax system. Settling matters is part of this approach. Tax Office guidelines for settlements between the Tax Office and taxpayers have been developed in consultation with representatives of professional bodies, taxpayer groups and industry groups.

Disputed tax liabilities and entitlements may be resolved through a settlement process. The Tax Office will only engage in a settlement in some circumstances.

In January 2015, the Tax Office released Practice Statement PS LA 2015/1 which sets out its policy on the settlement of taxation and superannuation disputes. This is the most recent version of the Tax Office's code of settlement.

The Tax Office had also previously released PS LA 2007/5 which prescribes the mandatory use of the code of settlement by all Tax Office staff in the settlement of taxation disputes. Further, the PS LA 2007/6 sets out guidance for the settlement of widely-based tax disputes, including but not limited to, disputes involving taxpayers who have participated in tax planning arrangements.

Settlements may be made on particular issues before the audit is finalised, although a taxpayer may wish to know all of the issues before settling any of them. However, once an issue is settled it will not be re-opened during final negotiations.

The following summarises PS LA 2015/1.

WHAT ARE SETTLEMENTS?

A settlement involves an agreement between parties to resolve matters in dispute where one or more parties make concessions on what they consider is the legally correct position.

The Tax Office is legally obliged to administer the taxation system in an efficient and effective way balancing competing considerations and applying discretion and good sense.

Settlement is an important element of the administration of the tax system.

 Settlements are not a bargaining process between the parties, but the Tax Office will consider representations from the taxpayer or his or her advisors on the relevant issues. As a settlement is based on legal principles it can act as a valuable precedent for future treatment of the taxpayer by the Tax Office.

SETTLEMENT NEGOTIATIONS

Settlement negotiations or offers can be initiated by any party to the dispute. They can occur at any stage including prior to assessments being raised.

Alternative dispute resolution approaches, including mediation, may be used during settlement negotiations.

Where there are multiple taxpayers involved in the same or similar arrangement the ATO would seek to ensure consistency of treatment for taxpayers in comparable circumstances. This may include developing a widely based settlement position.

Statements made during settlement negotiations are not to be construed as an admission of liability and cannot be given in evidence. This is to ensure that, in the event that negotiations break down, parties are not prejudiced as a result of a position taken in the course of trying to resolve the matter.

SETTLEMENT CONSIDERATIONS

When deciding whether or not to settle, the Tax Office must consider **all** of the following factors:

- the relative strength of the parties' position
- the cost versus the benefits of continuing the dispute, and
- the impact on future compliance for the taxpayer and broader community.

Settlement would generally not be considered where:

- there is a contentious point of law which requires clarification
- it is in the public interest to litigate, and
- the behaviour is such that the Tax Office needs to send a strong message to the community.

SETTLEMENT DECISION

The Tax Office decision to settle or not must be a fair, effective and efficient means of resolving the matters in dispute.

A decision will be based on an informed understanding of the relevant facts and issues in dispute and any advice of a settlement advisory panel, or legal or other expert opinions relevant to the matter being considered.

A settlement can only be approved by an officer who has delegation or authorisation to do so.

RESPONSIBILITIES

During settlement negotiation parties are expected to both:

- act fairly, honestly and in good faith, and
- disclose to their best knowledge and belief, relevant and material facts which relate to the matters in dispute.

Parties must adhere to the terms of the settlement agreement unless it emerges that relevant and material facts were not disclosed.

SETTLEMENT DEED

Settlements must be finalised by the parties signing a written agreement which sets out the terms. The usual form of the agreement is a deed of settlement. A settlement agreement must reflect the final agreed position between the parties (including any payment or future obligations).

Settlement agreements are intended to resolve the matters in dispute for both parties. A settlement agreement will only be varied in exceptional circumstances if requested by the taxpayer who is party to the agreement.

The Tax Office has model deeds available to use as a basis for a deed of settlement.

FUTURE YEARS

A settlement agreement provides a reasonable basis for treating similar issues in future years unless it is specifically stated that it is not to apply to future years or transactions, or:

- the taxpayer's circumstances change materially
- the application of the law remains unclear
- there have been subsequent amendments to the law
- a taxation ruling has been subsequently released on the issue, or
- there has been a subsequent court or tribunal decision on the issue.

The Tax Office can provide greater certainty to a taxpayer for future years if required.

ALTERNATIVE DISPUTE RESOLUTION

Alternative Dispute Resolution (ADR) refers to processes, other than judicial or tribunal determination, in which an impartial person assists those in a dispute to resolve or narrow the issues between them. When disputes cannot be resolved by early engagement and direct negotiation, the Tax Office is committed to using ADR where appropriate to resolve disputes.

PS LA 2013/3 outlines the Tax Office's policies and guidelines in relation to the use of ADR in dispute resolution.

According to the PS LA, taxpayers can expect that the Tax Office will:

- identify opportunities for ADR
- consider and respond to requests for ADR
- suggest ADR where appropriate, and
- speak with and write to the taxpayer before ADR to explain the process and what they can expect from it.

Per the PS LA, the Tax Office is of the view that ADR may be appropriate when:

- there are issues that are able to be negotiated
- the Tax Office has something to give
- the taxpayer has something to give

- the dispute is capable of being settled within existing settlement policies and practices, and
- early resolution is preferable to judicial determination.

The PS LA acknowledges that there is no optimal time for ADR. It suggests that the following times may be appropriate:

- after the Tax Office issues a position paper during an audit
- during a review at the objection stage before a final decision is made, or
- during the litigation stage.

Attempting ADR too early, before key elements of the dispute have crystallised, may mean there is a lesser likelihood of success as the parties may not be in an informed position to engage in discussions to clarify, narrow or resolve the issues in dispute, increasing the overall cost to the parties and causing unnecessary delay.

The following are key categories of ADR processes:

- In a **facilitative process**, an ADR practitioner assists the parties to identify the issues in dispute, develop options, consider alternatives and endeavour to reach an agreement about part or all of the dispute. Mediation is an example of a facilitative process.
- In an **advisory process**, an ADR practitioner considers and appraises the dispute and provides advice on possible or desirable outcomes. Neutral evaluation and case appraisal are examples of advisory processes. Advisory processes, by their nature, cannot be made to be binding on any party.
- In a **determinative process**, an ADR practitioner evaluates the dispute and makes a decision. Arbitration and expert determination are examples of determinative processes.
- In a **blended process**, the ADR practitioner plays multiple roles. For example in conciliation and conferencing, the ADR practitioner may facilitate discussions as well as provide advice on the merits of the dispute.

Independent experts may be engaged to provide specialist knowledge (eg. on valuation issues).

4.380   INQUIRY INTO TAX DISPUTES

In March 2015, the House of Representatives Standing Committee on Tax and Revenue (the Committee) tabled a report on an inquiry into tax disputes. The report is available on the Australian Parliament website (www.aph.gov.au).

The general scope of the inquiry and the report is tax disputes between taxpayers and the ATO. As noted in the report, the tax laws are complex and attitudes to compliance vary. As a result, disputes are inevitable.

The Committee was tasked to inquire into and report on disputes between taxpayers and the ATO, with particular regard to:

- collecting revenues due
- fair treatment and respect of taxpayers
- efficiency, effectiveness and transparency, from the perspective of both taxpayers and the ATO, and
- how the ATO supports the outcomes of efficiency, effectiveness and transparency through the use and publication of performance information.

RECOMMENDATIONS

The Committee made 20 recommendations. These are summarised as follows:

Performance measurement and reporting	
Recommendation 1	The Committee recommends that the ATO should review its performance reporting measures and: • develop a measurable key performance indicator (KPI) of taxpayer perceptions of fairness in tax disputes • that this KPI be monitored and reviewed by the ATO executive on a regular basis, and • that the outcomes against such a KPI be reported in the ATO Annual Report.
The legal framework	
Recommendation 2	The Committee recommends that the Government amend the law and the ATO consider other administrative means by which interest charges would not act as leverage against a taxpayer during a tax dispute.
Recommendation 3	The Committee recommends that the ATO amend its internal and external guidance so that it remits interest where: • the ATO takes longer than the 60 days available to it to finalise an objection and the taxpayer has acted in good faith, and • the ATO changes arguments after assessments have been made (such as during an objection or litigation).
Recommendation 4	The Committee recommends that the ATO amend its internal guidance so that findings or allegations of fraud or evasion can only be made by an officer from the Senior Executive Service.
Recommendation 5	The Committee recommends that the ATO only make allegations of fraud against taxpayers when evidence of fraud clearly exists.
Recommendation 6	The Committee recommends the ATO should ensure that allegations of fraud or evasion are addressed as soon as practicable in an audit or review.
Recommendation 7	The Committee recommends that the Government introduce legislation to place the burden of proof on the ATO in relation to allegations of fraud and evasion after a certain period has elapsed. The change should be harmonised with the record keeping requirements. These periods could be extended, subject to concerns of regulatory costs on business and individuals.
Recommendation 8	The Committee recommends that the Government introduce legislation to require judicial approval for the Commissioner to issue a departure prohibition order.
Recommendation 9	The Committee recommends the ATO better engage with taxpayers prior to litigation so that they are aware of what the model litigant rules require, and do not require, of the ATO.
Recommendation 10	The Committee recommends the ATO approach the Australian Government Solicitor to determine if they can provide advice and assistance to the ATO in terms of best practice in complying with the model litigant rules.
Recommendation 11	The Committee recommends that the Government review the Small Taxation Claims Tribunal and determine whether it should continue. If so, there should be a one-off increase to the $5,000 limit to take account of inflation since 1997 and a system introduced so the threshold increases incrementally in future to keep pace with inflation.
Readiness to engage	
Recommendation 12	The Committee recommends that the ATO implement recommendation 3.5.2 from the Inspector-General's report on alternative dispute resolution for all taxpayers (i.e. considering whether to engage in direct conferences with taxpayers at multiple points in a dispute).
Recommendation 13	The Committee recommends that the ATO give more consideration to taxpayers when making information requests, with priority given to: • setting timeframes in practice statements, with a minimum of 28 days for all requests; • giving taxpayers the opportunity to seek an extended timeframe upon receipt of a request; and • giving reasons for an information request, typically based on a risk hypothesis.

Recommendation 14	The Committee recommends the ATO introduce a triage system for disputes so that, early in a dispute, matters can be escalated to ATO staff sufficiently senior or with the appropriate technical skills to resolve the dispute quickly and effectively. Such decisions should consider taxpayer fairness, among other criteria.
Other administrative matters	
Recommendation 15	The Committee recommends that, as much as practicable, the ATO should give taxpayers written notice of issues and topics to be raised in section 264 interviews.
Recommendation 16	The Committee recommends that the ATO invite the Commonwealth Ombudsman* to advise on improving its compensation processes, including compensation liability and amounts.
The governance framework	
Recommendation 17	The Committee recommends that the ATO ensure that the information passed between an auditor and an objection officer surrounding a dispute only consist of the factual case documents, and the audit conclusion provided to the taxpayer. Any internal auditor commentary on the dispute should remain with the audit team.
Recommendation 18	The Committee recommends that the ATO develop protocols to ensure that an individual Tax Counsel Network officer only be allowed to provide advice or contribute to the provision of advice at the audit or objection stage of a dispute.
Recommendation 19	The Committee recommends that the ATO establish a separate Appeals area: • under the leadership of a new Second Commissioner — Appeals to carry out the objection and litigation function for all cases; • establish and publicly articulate clear protocols regarding communication between Appeal officers and compliance officers, including a general prohibition against ex parte communication, save where all parties are informed of, and consent to, such communication taking place; and • empower the appeals function to independently assess and determine whether matters should be settled, litigated or otherwise resolved (for example, Alternative Dispute Resolution).
Recommendation 20	The Committee recommends that the Government establish a new position of Second Commissioner - Appeals, reporting to the Commissioner to head up the new Appeals area within the ATO.

4.400   TAX REVIEWS AND AUDITS

Tax reviews and audits are increasingly being targeted at particular industries and individuals as the Tax Office refines its data collection and data matching systems. With self-assessment, there are now techniques to check basic data and trends extracted from information shown on returns. Using industry comparisons or analysis of data on returns, computer programs indicate the likely targets.

 Taxpayers have legal as well as administrative rights. The legal rights (such as limited review periods) are set out from 4.200 and 4.300. The administrative rights are set out in the Tax Office's Taxpayers Charter (see from 4.420) and these help to safeguard against any undeserved treatment by Tax Office auditors.

AUDIT STRATEGIES

The strategies of the Tax Office are becoming ever more targeted on areas of high non-compliance and high-risk revenue areas. Penalties are imposed if taxpayers are found to have understated their assessable income or overstated their deductions.

In early 2015, the Tax Office announced that it was replacing the annual compliance program, *Compliance in focus*, with an online hub called *Building confidence*. This website contains information about the Tax Office's current compliance focus, strategies and activities.

ENHANCED THIRD PARTY REPORTING, PRE-FILLING AND DATA MATCHING

On 12 February 2014, the government released for consultation a Discussion Paper in relation to measures for enhanced third party reporting, pre-filling and data matching. This measure was announced in the 2013-14 Budget and is designed to improve taxpayer compliance by enhancing the information reported to the Tax Office by a range of third parties through the introduction of new reporting regimes.

The Discussion Paper considers the creation of new third party reporting regimes in relation to:

- sales of real property
- sales of shares and units in unit trusts
- sales through merchant debit and credit services, and
- taxable government grants and other payments.

4.410   TAX OFFICE ACCESS

The Commissioner and any of his duly authorised Officers have the right of full and free access to buildings, places, books and documents and to require a person to attend and give evidence to enable the Tax Office to carry out its statutory functions (subject to certain rules, processes and exceptions). That applies for income tax as well as FBT, GST and the other taxes administered by the Tax Office. Access extends to electronically stored records and the Tax Office expects that encryption keys, passwords, login codes, manuals for hardware and software will be made available. These rights are provided for in s263 and 264 ITAA36.

The Tax Office has issued guidelines on its access powers in its online publication *Our approach to information gathering*.

The Tax Office sets out in *Our approach to information gathering* a summary of its access and information gathering powers. This is a guideline regarding how those powers are to be exercised and taxpayers' rights and obligations are safeguarded.

Subject to a warrant allowing confiscation or the taxpayer granting permission, the Tax Office is not empowered to confiscate any original records etc but is empowered to extract details.

The Tax Office's power of access applies regardless of whether the records and documents are held personally, at the business premises or at the offices of an accountant or solicitor. In some cases 'legal professional privilege' or the 'accountants' concession' may apply to prevent access to some documents or other types of information (refer to the publication for explanation of these protection mechanisms).

An occupier of a building or any other place is specifically required to provide duly authorised Tax Office staff with all reasonable facilities and assistance to enable them to carry out their duties. A typical example of where the Tax Office would exercise its access powers is during an audit, undertaken on the taxpayer's business premises. It would be expected that the taxpayer would provide an adequate working area with access to telephones, photocopiers, computers, light and power to enable the auditor(s) to complete the examination of the business records.

Subject to the application of legal professional privilege (or the accountants' concession) to protect the requested information, it is an offence to hinder or obstruct a duly authorised Tax Officer exercising his/her right of access. In the event that there is any physical obstruction, the Tax Officers have the right to take all reasonable steps to remove that obstruction.

As a general rule, taxpayers will be advised in advance of an audit so the request for access should not come as a surprise. In exceptional circumstances Tax Officers will arrive unannounced. Where that occurs the taxpayer is entitled to temporarily delay any search of their premises while the taxpayer seeks legal advice on either the right of access itself or whether any records or documents are subject to legal professional privilege. It can be expected that where the search is temporarily delayed the Tax Office will seek to ensure that no documents or records are tampered with during the delay.

It is recommended that in the event of an unannounced audit, legal advice should be obtained.

 A Tax Officer is not entitled to remain on the premises without written authorisation signed by the Commissioner or his delegate.

4.411   LEGAL PROFESSIONAL PRIVILEGE

The Tax Office's powers of access are limited by the common law doctrine of legal professional privilege (LPP). In general, LPP applies to protect communications made between a legal advisor and his/her client for the dominant purpose of giving or receiving legal advice, or for use in existing or anticipated litigation. It generally does not apply to communications between accountants and their clients, but the Tax Office has put in place the 'accountants' concession', which is an administrative concession in respect of certain types of 'documents' that exist due to the relationship between an accountant (or other non-legal professional) and their client. As a general rule, the Tax Office abides by those administrative rules. However, the accountants' concession is not legally binding.

The privilege belongs to the client and not to the legal advisor and can only be waived by the client.

Further, it is the **communication** contained in the document that attracts the privilege, not the document itself. LPP relates to two types of privilege enabling the holder of the privilege to refuse to provide certain communications where they would otherwise be required to do so.

The two types of privilege are legal advice privilege and litigation privilege.

 For any document or record, if there is any doubt about the existence of LPP in respect of the communication contained in the document or record, the privilege should be claimed and the document withheld from the Tax Office. In this way it is up to the Tax Office to test the claim in the Courts.

It is important the claim is not arbitrarily applied and legal advice should be obtained where the taxpayer considers they may assert the privilege.

Documents that would be likely to be subject to LPP include (but are not limited to):

- solicitors' advice
- legal counsel opinion
- letters between a solicitor and client
- solicitors' notes of a conference with a client, and
- detailed bill of costs if it discloses the nature of the advice sought or given.

Legal professional privilege also extends to the Tax Office. For example, communications between the Tax Office and Australian Government Solicitor and documents held by the Australian Federal Police concerning the investigation of alleged tax offences have been held to be subject to LPP.

The Tax Office has issued the following guidelines (in agreement with the Law Council of Australia):

- as a general rule the Tax Office will give adequate notice of an intention to inspect documents
- Tax Officer(s) will not inspect documents until a legal advisor has had an opportunity to claim LPP on behalf of the client
- a list of documents on which LPP is claimed but not conceded should be prepared and endorsed by the legal advisor and the Tax Officer, and
- the disputed documents are to be placed in a sealed envelope and kept in a secure place until the claim is waived or decided by a court.

See also the Tax Office publication *Our approach to information gathering* available on the Tax Office website.

NOTE: In 2007, the Government released a discussion paper which explores the possibility of establishing a statutory tax advice privilege, based on recommendations from industry and government bodies.

4.412   THE ACCOUNTANTS' CONCESSION

Taxpayers are required by s263(3) of the ITAA36 to give all reasonable assistance and facilities to Tax Officers. The Tax Office recognises that, apart from communications with legal professionals which are eligible to be protected by legal professional privilege, taxpayers should be able to communicate confidentially with other, non-legal advisors in relation to their tax affairs.

The Tax Office's *Our approach to information gathering* sets out the Tax Office's approach regarding access to professional accounting advisors' papers. The Tax Office will follow these guidelines in respect of seeking access to specified categories of 'documents' containing communication between taxpayers and their professional accounting (or other non-legal) advisors. This is known as the accountants' concession. The following sets out excerpts of how the Tax Office will deal with different types of documents, and the extent of the concession.

The accountants' concession is purely an administrative concession offered by the Tax Office. While the courts have recognised that taxpayers generally have an entitlement to expect that the Tax Office will adhere to its own guidelines in relation to this matter, the concession certainly has no legal standing. This is a fundamental difference between the accountants' concession and legal professional privilege, which has been endorsed as a legally enforceable common law doctrine.

CATEGORIES OF DOCUMENTS

Documents will be treated differently depending on whether they are considered to be Source, Restricted source, or Non-source documents.

Source documents (record of transactions)

Tax Office auditors will seek full access to:

- papers prepared in connection with the conception, implementation and formal recording of a transaction and which explain the setting, context and purpose of transactions or arrangements
- traditional accounting records such as ledgers, journals, working papers for financial statements, profit and loss accounts and balance sheets
- permanent audit documents including those outlining the organisation's history and structure, chain of command, chart of accounts
- memorandum, articles and continuing contracts, and
- tax working papers including the tax return (eg. used to prepare trial balances and reconciliation statements).

Restricted source documents (some advice)

These documents will normally consist of tax advice prepared by an external accountant on how to structure a transaction or arrangement. They form an integral part of what has actually occurred and provide an understanding of the tax strategy or specific courses of action implemented. They are also likely to canvass issues in which frankness is an essential element. Access to restricted source documents will be sought in exceptional circumstances only.

Non-source documents (some advice)

Typically, these include advice provided after a transaction has been completed, if that advice did not affect the recording of the transaction.

Includes non-permanent papers on the current audit file obtained by an external accountant during:

- any statutory audit, or prudential audit
- due diligence report, or
- tax working papers which merely state the accountant's opinion.

Access to non-source documents will be sought in exceptional circumstances only.

Other examples of non-source documents include letters of engagement, the audit plan, letters of confirmation, test analyses, working schedules and commentaries.

Access to restricted source and non-source documents would be sought only if the:

- taxpayer or the accountant refuses to provide the source documents
- source documents are not available (for example: they are held overseas)
- source documents have been lost or destroyed

- source documents are insufficient and the opinions are considered to offer an integral understanding of the transaction involved, or
- where there are reasonable grounds to believe that fraud or evasion, or an offence under the TAA, or any other illegal activity has taken place.

OBJECTION PAPERS

Tax papers prepared by an accountant as part of an objection, appeal or review will be exempt from scrutiny by Tax Office auditors.

ACCESS TO PAPERS

Initially the Tax Office auditor as part of a tax audit may seek from the taxpayer the facts and an understanding of the consequences of a transaction. Taxpayers may be asked for that to be in writing. If the information is not given within 30 days, the Tax Office auditors may seek access to restricted source documents. If they don't reveal the required information, access can then be to non-source documents.

TIME TO SEEK ADVICE ON THE REQUEST

If access is sought, reasonable time will be allowed to enable the taxpayer to consult with advisors on the confidentiality of documents.

ACCESS TO RESTRICTED SOURCE AND NON-SOURCE DOCUMENTS

Where relevant exceptional circumstances apply and access is sought to restricted source or non-source documents, written approval of the relevant Deputy Commissioner is needed.

If the taxpayer considers that documents sought by the Tax Office attract the accountants' concession, they should complete a form 'AC1' which lists the documents the taxpayer claims attract the concession.

If the taxpayer and the Tax Office auditor disagree with a claim(s), the documents are to be placed in a sealed envelope (with contents indexed) and entrusted to the taxpayer's accountant, who is required to give an undertaking that the secured papers won't be removed for 30 days.

From this point in the process, there are inspection and independent review procedures to determine the validity of the concession claim.

4.415 KNOW YOUR RIGHTS

Under the self-assessment system you can be selected at any time for an audit by the Tax Office either before or after an assessment is issued.

YOUR RIGHTS AND ENTITLEMENTS

Your rights and entitlements in all your dealings with the Tax Office are guaranteed under the Tax Office's Taxpayers' Charter (see 4.420).

 If you are not satisfied with the service provided by the Tax Office in respect of any matter you can complain to ATO Complaints or the Taxation Ombudsman (see 4.430).

TAX OFFICE RIGHT OF ACCESS

Under s263 of the ITAA36, authorised Tax Officers must be given full and free access at all times to all buildings, places, books, documents and other papers (including computer records) provided they have evidence of delegated authority.

The taxpayer must provide Tax Officers with all reasonable facilities and assistance. That means providing reasonable office space, light and power, photocopying and telephone etc. That also means that the taxpayer might have to give details of where specific records are kept, or access computer information for the Tax Officer.

If a Tax Officer fails to produce proof of authority when asked to do so, the Officer cannot remain on the premises.

RIGHTS AND ENTITLEMENTS DURING TAX OFFICE ENQUIRIES/AUDITS

The Taxpayers' Charter (see 4.420) specifically identifies your rights and entitlements in all your dealings with the Tax Office. In respect of your rights and entitlements during a Tax Office enquiry or audit you should:

- inspect the authority of the Tax Officer or other person conducting the audit, access visit or interview. If the Tax Officer is on the taxpayer's premises and the taxpayer requests they produce a proof of authority and the Officer fails to do so, they must leave the premises
- request that your tax agent or other representative be present at the audit interview. You can discuss any point with that representative, but you are the person who must answer the questions
- expect the Tax Officer to act courteously and professionally
- ask that the audit be held at a mutually convenient time during normal business hours
- ask that reasonable time be available to enable you to collect the necessary documentary evidence before you attend the review or audit, and to answer questions posed during the review or audit
- decide whether or not you will involve your tax agent or accountant in the review or audit. As a matter of courtesy, the Tax Office should notify your tax agent or accountant that they intend to review or audit you.

 Any enquiry or audit can result in penalties. It is in your interest to have your adviser present where necessary to help answer questions accurately.

- be given the opportunity to explain any circumstances which would justify a reduction of any penalties
- take notes at the interview and also ask the Tax Officer for a copy of the record of interview
- tape record the interview. The Tax Office may also want to tape the interview. If they do, ask for a copy
- object against any assessment and penalty arising from the review or audit if you are dissatisfied with the result. The Officer should explain your rights of objection and appeal
- claim 'legal professional privilege' on any communication between you and your lawyer if you have either sought or been given advice

 Legal professional privilege does not prevent the Tax Office gaining access to the listings of clients put into particular tax arrangements (Commissioner of Taxation v Coombes [1999] FCA 842).

- ask for questions to be clear and unambiguous and for reasonable assistance or explanation if required
- receive both verbal and written notification of the Tax Office review or audit (where possible)
- be told by the Tax Officer if an error is detected which has resulted in too much tax being paid
- be given complete and honest answers and explanations to questions put to a Tax Officer (the Tax Officer may only decline to answer if giving that answer will jeopardise the conduct of the review or audit – seek the Case Manager's opinion)
- be regularly advised by the Tax Officer on the progress of the review or audit (particularly business or complex audits), and
- have reviews or audits completed in the shortest time practicable.

ANSWERING QUERIES

If a question is within the taxpayer's level of expertise, and the facts are known, give a straightforward reply. For difficult items, ask that the question be put in writing so as to allow sufficient time for an adequate answer to be given.

QUESTIONING OF STAFF MEMBERS

Problems can arise if a Tax Officer is permitted to question staff members without any restriction (eg. while inspecting premises). Designate an appropriate representative with whom the Tax Officer should deal.

Tax Officers should not discuss the review or audit with unauthorised members of the taxpayer's staff unless to clarify particular facts, and then only after notifying the taxpayer's designated representative.

CHECK AUDITOR'S IDENTITY

Be cautious. If unsure of the credentials (and bona fides) of any phone caller or visitor to your premises who purports to be from the Tax Office, phone the Tax Office to check.

Don't use any phone number provided by the suspect caller. Get a phone number from the list at 4.060 or call 13 28 69. Speak to the Tax Office case manager or to another senior officer and confirm it is safe to deal with the Tax Officer who approached you.

HANDING OVER BOOKS AND DOCUMENTS

Tax Officers have the power to inspect and copy relevant documents. You must make reasonable arrangements to enable the copying of documents to proceed. Unless a current warrant (issued by a Court, a Justice of the Peace or by some other such approved person) is produced, you need not allow books and papers to be taken from your premises.

If you accept that the documents sought by the Tax Office auditors are available for inspection and you hand over the original documents, keep a photocopy, get a receipt and agree on a date by which they must be returned.

AUDIT PLAN

During the initial interview with the Tax Officer (especially if it is a large audit) ask for a copy of the Process Plan/Audit Plan. That will identify the scope and purpose of the audit by indicating:

- the type of records to be inspected
- the expected duration of the review or audit
- any particular items relating to your industry that the Officer is interested in reviewing
- where the review or audit will be conducted, and
- which of your staff should be available to answer questions.

It may be prudent to require all Tax Office communication be made through your organisation's Public Officer or another authorised person, possibly resulting in a speedier audit.

COMMONLY SOUGHT RECORDS

With businesses, the request is most likely to be one or more of these:

- cash receipts and payments books
- general ledger and general journal
- bank statements
- pay-in books and cheque butts
- sales and purchases journals
- debtors and creditors listings
- wages and stocktake records
- other specific records (eg. repairs/maintenance)
- tax invoices (for GST purposes)
- copies of elections and other notifications (see 4.080)
- copies of trustee minutes, and
- trust deeds.

INVESTMENT AND BUSINESS PROPERTIES

The Officer may also want details of these properties. If an agent manages the property, some records may be kept by the agent.

CAPITAL GAINS, FBT AND GST RECORDS

Keep detailed records or an assets register of assets subject to CGT (purchase price, expenditure incurred, selling price and relevant dates) (see 12.200), FBT records (see 25.250) and GST records (see 4.715).

ELECTRONIC INFORMATION

The Tax Office's notice and access powers extend to information stored electronically. Documents for the purposes of these powers include anything from which sounds, images or writings can be reproduced, with or without the aid of anything else (refer s2B of the *Acts Interpretation Act 1901*).

Examples of information stored electronically that may be within the reach of the Tax Office include files stored on a computer, server, external hard drive, mobile phone or digital camera.

 For more information about the Tax Office's policies in relation to accessing electronic information, refer to the document *Our approach to information gathering* ***at www.ato.gov.au.***

The Tax Office has noted that if a taxpayer's information is to be provided electronically, the officer will usually arrange a meeting to discuss:

- the accounting systems
- the format and extent of the electronic records, and
- any documentation that may assist in the Tax Office's analysis – for example, a chart of accounts, reference tables or data dictionary.

The Tax Office encourages the attendance of the taxpayer's tax adviser and information technology specialists at this meeting.

CLOUD COMPUTING

A taxpayer's information may be stored electronically with a third party. A common example is data stored on a cloud. Cloud computing entrusts a user's data, software and computation with a remote service provider via the internet from any location. Cloud computing includes an email account or file storage arrangement.

Where the documents stored on a cloud are immediately accessible to the taxpayer, the Tax Office may obtain them by using its notice or access powers.

Further, the Tax Office may send a notice (a 's264 notice') to any other person or entity that has control of the documents, whether or not they have custody. The s264 notice can request that the person or entity is to provide the relevant documents to the taxpayer or to a third party who has custody of the documents.

Many cloud computing arrangements involve the use of parties or servers outside Australia. Where necessary, the Tax Office may invoke the information-sharing provisions of a relevant double tax agreement in order to access the information.

4.420   TAXPAYERS' CHARTER

The Charter states it is for everyone who deals with the Tax Office on tax, including superannuation, excise and the other laws the Tax Office administer. The Charter also states that 'tax' means all matters dealt with by the Tax Office.

The Charter sets out a taxpayer's rights and entitlements under the law, and the service and other standards that can be expected from the Tax Office. According to the Tax Office, it is committed to the Taxpayers' Charter and all of its staff will follow it.

If you are not satisfied with the standard or quality of service provided by the Tax Office, it is your right to lodge a complaint (see 4.430). That may involve a decision or action of the Tax Office or it may involve the actions or attitude of an individual Tax Officer.

It is in every taxpayer's interest to ensure that their rights and entitlements are protected and that the standards of service are maintained, and improved over time. If you feel that your rights or entitlements have not been satisfied, a complaint should be lodged. In some instances you may be entitled to compensation.

WHAT YOU CAN EXPECT FROM THE TAX OFFICE

As set out in the Charter, you can expect the Tax Office to:

- treat you fairly and reasonably
- treat you as being honest in your tax affairs unless you act otherwise
- offer you professional service and assistance to help you understand and meet your tax obligations
- accept that you can be represented by a person of your choice and to get advice about your tax affairs
- respect your privacy
- keep information held about you confidential, in accordance with the law
- give you access to information held about you, in accordance with the law
- give you advice and information that you can rely on
- explain to you the decisions it makes about your tax affairs
- respect your right to a review
- respect your right to make a complaint
- administer the tax system in a way that minimises your costs of compliance, and
- be accountable for what it does.

Taxpayers have the right to an independent review of a matter from outside the Tax Office and to complain to the Commonwealth Ombudsman.

The Charter also sets out the Tax Office's expectations of taxpayers. The Tax Office expects you to:

- be truthful in your dealings with the Tax Office
- keep records in accordance with the law
- take reasonable care in preparing your tax returns and other documents and in keeping records
- lodge tax returns and other required documents or information by the due date
- pay your taxes and other amounts by the due date, and
- be co-operative in your dealings with the Tax Office.

TAX OFFICE INFORMATION ON RIGHTS AND ENTITLEMENTS

A detailed explanation of your rights and entitlements are contained in the following Taxpayers' Charter explanatory booklets. They can be obtained from your nearest Tax Office, by calling freecall 1300 720 092 or on the internet at www.ato.gov.au. The Charter is available in a number of different languages.

- Taxpayers' Charter – what you need to know (abridged and expanded versions exist)
- Treating you fairly and reasonably
- Your honesty and complying with the tax laws
- Who can help you with your tax affairs
- Your privacy and the confidentiality of your tax affairs
- Accessing information under the *Freedom of Information Act*
- Getting advice from the Tax Office
- If you are not satisfied
- Fair use of our access and information gathering powers
- If you are subject to enquiry or audit

NOTE: If you are not satisfied that your rights and the standards under the Taxpayers' Charter have been met, there are various methods of seeking redress.

4.430   LODGING A COMPLAINT AGAINST THE TAX OFFICE

When you are informed of a decision, the Tax Office is required to explain that decision and to advise you of your options to have the decision reviewed by the Tax Office or another body. This applies in respect of any communication to you from the Tax Office. If you are not satisfied with the decision, or the treatment you have received from the Tax Office, or you need further help contact ATO Complaints.

 Know your rights (see also 4.410) and insist on being treated fairly and honestly. If you are not satisfied, don't be afraid to lodge a complaint either with the Tax Office or an appropriate external body.

LEGAL REVIEW

Under the law you have a right to have most decisions of the Tax Office reviewed (see 4.200 & 4.300) including:

- Private Rulings
- Assessments (including amended assessments)
- Request for issue of a tax file number
- Request for extension of time
- Penalties
- Requests for information under Freedom of Information (FOI Act)
- Conduct of audits, and
- Debt collection action.

Reviews of decisions can be conducted by the Tax Office and/or, an independent external body such as the Commonwealth Ombudsman, Privacy Commissioner, AAT, or Federal Court.

INFORMAL REVIEW BY THE TAX OFFICE

First contact should be with the person handling your case or the Tax Office where the decision was made or the action was undertaken. If you need more help, contact the ATO Complaints service on:

- Telephone: 13 28 70
- Fax: 1800 060 063
- Hearing or speech impaired: 13 36 77 (National Relay Service)

You can also make a complaint online at www.ato.gov.au or write to Locked Bag 40, Dandenong, Vic 3175.

REVIEW FROM OUTSIDE THE TAX OFFICE

There are fees and time limits for applying for a review by the AAT or Federal Court (see 4.300). For disputes involving tax in dispute of less than $5,000 there is the Small Taxation Claims Tribunal (part of AAT) (see 4.360).

Where the dispute involves administrative actions taken by the Tax Office including conduct of audits, delays in decision making, and debt collection action, contact the Inspector-General of Taxation.

Complaints about a breach of your privacy can be actioned by the Privacy Commissioner (see 4.460).

Complaints can be investigated by the Ombudsman and the Privacy Commissioner for no charge.

- Inspector-General of Taxation: 1300 44 88 29, or lodge an online form (www.igt.gov.au)
- Privacy Commissioner: 1300 363 992, or lodge an online form (www.oaic.gov.au)

TAX OFFICE SERVICE STANDARDS

The standard of service that can be expected from the Tax Office can be found in the 'Access, accountability and reporting' section of the Tax Office website. Results of their performance against those standards must be made public.

Check the 'Current year commitments to service' section for the most up-to-date commitments.

NOTE: Some timeframes are prescribed by legislation (for example, the timeframes within which the Tax Office must respond to a Private Ruling request or an objection).

4.450   INSPECTOR-GENERAL OF TAXATION

The Office of the Inspector-General of Taxation was established in 2002-03. The Inspector-General of Taxation provides a source of independent advice to Government on the effectiveness of tax administration and process. The role of the Inspector-General, current and proposed work program and published reports are available at www.igt.gov.au.

On 1 May 2015, the office of the Commonwealth Ombudsman transferred its tax complaints role to the office of the Inspector-General. Prior to that date, the Ombudsman handled specific complaints from taxpayers in relation to the conduct of the Tax Office and the Tax Practitioners Board (TPB), while the Inspector-General only focused on systemic and process issues in tax administration. In the latter capacity, the Inspector-General has a specialist review and advisory role to review tax administration systems and advise the Government on improving tax administration for the benefit of Australian taxpayers. Importantly, the Inspector-General does not impose any obligations on taxpayers.

Most tax-related complaints should now be directed to the Inspector-General. The Ombudsman will continue to receive complaints concerning Public Interest Disclosures or Freedom of Information issues about the Tax Office or the TPB.

In his systemic review role, the Inspector-General conducts reviews of tax administration and systems and invites submissions from the public and groups of taxpayers and/or tax professionals. Submissions can be received in confidence and the Inspector-General can hold meetings with taxpayers, tax professionals or their representatives. The protection of taxpayer information is designed to mirror secrecy provisions in the tax laws and to be consistent with privacy laws.

The Inspector-General has powers to compel production of documents by tax officials and to take evidence from tax officials where this proves necessary. The Inspector-General cannot direct the Tax Office, but can compel the Tax Office to disclose information for a review. Importantly, the Inspector-General can review the administration of taxation laws but cannot review the taxation policy and how that applies in the tax laws. (The Board of Taxation is responsible for advising the Government on the policy relating to taxation laws.)

The Inspector-General can conduct a review of a tax system on his or her own initiative, including where a systemic tax administration issue has been raised with the Inspector-General by taxpayers, tax professionals, the Ombudsman, or any other party. The Tax Office and/or Parliament may formally request the Inspector-General to conduct a review but may not direct the Inspector-General to conduct a review. The Minister for Revenue may direct the Inspector-General to conduct a review and the Inspector-General must comply with any such direction.

CONFIDENTIAL SUBMISSIONS

Submissions to the Inspector-General may be made in confidence and cannot be made available to the public nor can they be included in a report on a review or in the Inspector-General's annual report. The restriction on publication does not apply where the same information has been obtained by the Inspector-General or a member of the Inspector-General's staff from another source, provided the information is not itself restricted.

ANNUAL REPORT

The Inspector-General is required to prepare an annual report on the operations of the office, and the Minister is required to table the report in the Parliament within 15 sitting days of receiving the report.

4.460   PRIVACY COMMISSIONER

DISCLOSURE OF TAX FILE NUMBER

To maintain the integrity of the Tax File Number (TFN) system, the Privacy Commissioner has issued *Tax File Number Guidelines* (Guidelines). Unauthorised use or disclosure of TFNs is also an offence under the TAA as well as a breach of the Guidelines.

While the TAA protects all TFNs, not just those of natural persons, the Privacy Commissioner issues compliance notes regarding TFN compliance and also has the power to conduct audits on TFN recipients.

If a taxpayer thinks their TFN has been improperly collected, used or disclosed, they may complain to the Privacy Commissioner at www.oaic.gov.au. However, they are required to attempt to resolve the issue directly first.

DISCLOSURE OF TAXPAYER INFORMATION

The law places a general prohibition on the disclosure of taxpayer information. However, in recognition of the importance that taxpayer information can play in facilitating efficient and effective government administration and law enforcement, disclosures of taxpayer information are permitted in certain specified circumstances. As a general rule, the Act provides that the disclosure of taxpayer information should be permitted only where the public benefit associated with the disclosure clearly outweighs the need for taxpayer privacy. The Act specifically lists a range of factors which may need to be considered, which include:

- the purpose for which the information is to be used
- the potential impact on the individual from the disclosure and subsequent use of the information
- the nature and amount of information likely to be provided under any new provision
- whether the information can be obtained from other sources
- whether the new disclosure would represent a significant departure from existing disclosure provisions, and
- whether not providing the information would significantly undermine the ability of Government to effectively deliver services or enforce laws.

4.500   ANTI-AVOIDANCE RULES

The taxation laws contain anti-avoidance provisions designed to counter specifically identified arrangements or potential mischief. The Tax Office has general anti-avoidance powers to counter arrangements that have been devised for the sole or dominant purpose of obtaining a tax benefit. There are also specific anti-avoidance provisions contained in particular income tax regimes. Separate anti-avoidance rules apply for income tax, GST (see 4.520) and FBT (see 4.530).

4.510   INCOME TAX ANTI-AVOIDANCE RULES

Part IVA of ITAA36 is the 'general anti-avoidance rule' that gives the Commissioner the power to cancel any 'tax benefit' that arises from a scheme specifically designed for the dominant purpose of tax avoidance (see also 6.900).

Note: Part IVA allows the Commissioner to exercise a discretion to cancel a tax benefit. Part IVA is not a provision of automatic operation.

WILL PART IVA APPLY?

The factors to be considered in order to determine whether Part IVA will apply are:

1. Is there a scheme?

Section 177A(1) ITAA36 provides:

'Scheme' means

(a) *any agreement, arrangement, understanding, promise or undertaking, whether express or implied, and whether or not enforceable or intended to be enforceable, by legal proceedings; and*

(b) *any scheme, plan, proposal, action, course of action or course of conduct.*

Read broadly, it could cover almost anything done by the taxpayer.

2. Was the scheme entered into with the sole or dominant purpose of obtaining a tax benefit?

For Part IVA to apply, the scheme must have been entered into with the 'sole or dominant' purpose of obtaining a tax benefit (s177A(5) and s177D). 'Dominant' is not defined in the Act, however the Concise Oxford Dictionary defines 'dominant' as 'prevailing; most influential'.

3. Was a tax benefit obtained?

For Part IVA to apply, the taxpayer must, under s177C ITAA36, have obtained a tax benefit in connection with the scheme. Section 177C(1) provides that a tax benefit can arise in one of four ways. The first two are:

- an amount is not included in the taxpayer's assessable income which would have been included, or might reasonably be expected to have been included in the assessable income of the taxpayer of that year of income, if the scheme had not been entered into or carried out. (Also applies if instead, the taxpayer or another taxpayer makes a discount capital gain), or

- a deduction is allowable to the taxpayer in relation to a year of income where the whole or part of that deduction would not have been allowable, or might reasonably have been expected not to have been allowable to the taxpayer in relation to that year of income, if the scheme had not been entered into or carried out.

There is a tax benefit where the taxpayer earned less assessable income or obtained more allowable deductions than would otherwise have been the case.

The other two tax benefits in s177C(1)(ba) and (bb) are:

- a capital loss incurred by the taxpayer during a year of income where the whole or a part of that capital loss would not have been, or might reasonably be expected not to have been, incurred by the taxpayer during the income year if the scheme had not been entered into or carried out (applies to schemes entered into after 3pm on 29 April 1997), or

- a foreign tax credit being allowable to the taxpayer where the whole or a part of that foreign tax credit would not have been allowable, or might reasonably be expected not to have been allowable to the taxpayer if the scheme had not been entered into or carried out (applies to schemes entered into after 13 August 1998).

Section 177F(1) ITAA36 gives a discretionary power to the Commissioner to make certain determinations which may reduce or cancel a tax benefit. The power is conditional on these circumstances:

- a taxpayer has obtained a 'tax benefit' or would obtain such a benefit but for s177F, and

- the tax benefit has been obtained or would be obtained by the taxpayer 'in connection with a scheme' to which Part IVA applies.

The tests of whether a scheme has resulted in a tax benefit, and is therefore subject to the anti-avoidance rules contained in Part IVA set out in s177D(b) ITAA36 are:

- the manner in which the scheme was entered into or carried out
- the form and substance of the scheme
- the time at which the scheme was entered into and the length of the period of time during which the scheme was carried out

- the result in relation to the operation of the Act that, but for Part IVA, would be achieved by the scheme
- any change in the financial position of the relevant taxpayer that has resulted, or may reasonably be expected to result from the scheme
- any change in the financial position of any other person connected with the taxpayer
- any other consequences for the taxpayer or any other person connected with the taxpayer, and
- the nature and connection between the relevant taxpayer and any other person whose financial position changes as a consequence of the scheme.

Part IVA applies where a taxpayer has obtained, or would obtain if not prevented by the Commissioner's discretion to cancel or reduce a tax benefit, a tax benefit if, having regard to the above tests, it would be concluded any person(s) who entered into or carried out the scheme (or part thereof) did so for the purpose of enabling the relevant taxpayer and/or another taxpayer to obtain a tax benefit in connection with the scheme.

EXTENSION OF PART IVA TO NON-PAYMENT OF WITHHOLDING TAX

Part IVA also operates to counter schemes designed to avoid payment of withholding tax on non-resident interest, dividend and royalty payments. This includes payments to tax exempt bodies interposed between an Australian resident payer and a non-resident recipient, or dividends consisting of bonus shares issued from asset revaluation reserves. The tax benefit is the amount of unpaid withholding tax.

It does not apply to schemes where non-resident withholding tax has been paid.

APPLICATION OF PART IVA TO CERTAIN EMPLOYEE BENEFIT ARRANGEMENTS

The Tax Office has confirmed its intention to apply Part IVA to certain employee benefit trust and salary deferral arrangements and to an employee savings plan. Guidance has been issued by way of a Taxation Ruling (TR 2010/6) and draft Taxation Determinations (TD 2010/10 and TD 2010/11) clarifying the positions previously described in Taxpayer Alerts released in June 2008.

APPLICATION OF PART IVA TO DIVIDEND ACCESS SHARE ARRANGEMENTS

The Tax Office has released TD 2014/1, which considers whether a 'dividend access share' arrangement of the type described in the Determination is a scheme 'by way of or in the nature of dividend stripping' within the meaning of s177E of Part IVA.

In the opinion of the Commissioner a dividend access share arrangement of the type described in the Determination is a scheme 'by way of dividend stripping' or 'in the nature of dividend stripping' within the meaning of s177E of Part IVA. Consequently, the Commissioner's powers under s177E and s177F are enlivened. In reaching this opinion the Commissioner has assumed that other potentially relevant provisions do not apply (eg. Division 7A of the ITAA36, or Divisions 725 or 974 of the ITAA97).

TAX OFFICE GUIDANCE ON PART IVA

The Tax Office has released some broad guidance to Part IVA, including its online document *Part IVA: the general anti-avoidance rule for income tax* and practice statement PS LA 2005/24. Together, these two publications provide a useful guide regarding how the Tax Office interprets and applies Part IVA. See also the information contained on the page *Clarifying the operation of the income tax general anti-avoidance rule (Part IVA)*, which discusses Part IVA after amendments were made to the provisions in 2013.

JUDICIAL GUIDANCE ON PART IVA

THE *SPOTLESS* CASE

The High Court decision to apply Part IVA to the circumstances in *FCT v Spotless Services Ltd & Anor*, 96 ATC 5201 confirms that the anti-avoidance provisions can apply to transactions which might appear commercial in nature, but have as their dominant purpose, the obtaining of a tax benefit.

THE *GROLLO* CASE

The Full Federal Court held that Part IVA could apply to a trustee even where the trustee was not itself liable to pay tax on trust income where a consequent tax benefit to the beneficiaries and the presence of the other conditions exist (*Grollo Nominees Pty Ltd & Ors v FC of T* 97 ATC 4585).

EASTERN NITROGEN CASE

In *Eastern Nitrogen Ltd v Commissioner of Taxation* (2001) FCA 366, a case involving a sale and leaseback arrangement, the Full Federal Court concluded that, whilst a tax benefit was obtained, the dominant purpose for entering into the transaction was to generate funding on the most favourable basis available, and therefore Part IVA had no application.

HART'S CASE

In *FCT v Hart* (2004) 55 ATR 712, the High Court found the dominant purpose in a split-loan arrangement was one of obtaining a tax benefit and not a commercial benefit (as had been held by the Full Federal Court). The High Court also found a 'scheme' for the purposes of Part IVA could also be just one step in an arrangement (see 15.190 *Negative gearing*).

Legislative amendments to Part IVA were made in 2013. The amendments apply retrospectively to schemes entered into, or commenced to be carried out, on or after 16 November 2012. Most of the body of judicial authorities on Part IVA came into existence before that time. While the judicial precedents remain relevant, taxpayers and advisers need to be aware that the amendments could affect how the judicial principles now apply.

The amendments have the following effect:

- *to put it beyond doubt that the 'would have' and 'might reasonably be expected to have' limbs of each of the subs177C(1) paragraphs represent alternative bases upon which the existence of a tax benefit can be demonstrated*

- *to ensure that when obtaining a tax benefit depends on the 'would have' limb of one of the paragraphs in subs177C(1), that conclusion must be based solely on a postulate that comprises all of the events or circumstances that actually happened or existed other than those forming part of the scheme*

- *to ensure that, when obtaining a tax benefit depends on the 'might reasonably be expected to have' limb of one of the paragraphs in subs177C(1), that conclusion must be based on a postulate that is a reasonable alternative to the scheme, having particular regard to the substance of the scheme and its effect for the taxpayer, but disregarding any potential tax costs, and*

- *to require the application of Part IVA to start with a consideration of whether a person participated in the scheme for the sole or dominant purpose of securing for the taxpayer a particular tax benefit in connection with the scheme; and so emphasising the dominant purpose test in section 177D as the 'fulcrum' or 'pivot' around which Part IVA operates.*

OTHER MATTERS

In addition to consolidating its position on Part IVA in the publications of PS LA 2005/24 and the Part IVA Guide, the Tax Office has made it clear in PS LA 2005/24 that where the Tax Office has considered Part IVA as part of a Private Ruling, it will be made clear in the Ruling. Further, the Tax Office may only amend an assessment using the Part IVA provisions for a period of four years from the date of assessment.

The Tax Office maintains pages on its website dedicated to aggressive tax planning. Further, the Tax Office regularly issues Taxpayer Alerts which act as an early warning for tax professionals and investors of potential tax planning arrangements or issues the Tax Office has under risk assessment.

Further, the promoter penalties regime which has the intention of deterring the promotion of tax avoidance and tax evasion schemes (see 4.600). Part IVA is a complex area of tax law and therefore professional advice should be obtained where any doubt exists as to the possible application of the provisions.

4.520   GST ANTI-AVOIDANCE RULES

Division 165 of the GST Act (see from 23.000 and 24.000) contains anti-avoidance provisions in respect of GST, the wine tax law and the luxury car tax law that are similar to those available for income tax purposes. The rules are designed to deter schemes that would produce benefits by reducing GST, increasing refunds or altering the timing of payment of GST or refunds, and are aimed directly at artificial and contrived schemes.

Once it has established that the anti-avoidance provisions operate, the Tax Office can negate the GST benefits claimed and impose penalties. Additional penalties are also imposed for late payment of any GST obligation (see from 4.660).

For the anti-avoidance rules to apply the following conditions must be present.

- **There must be a scheme** (entered into or carried out after 2 December 1998).
  The definition of a scheme is very wide and includes arrangements, agreements, understandings, promises, and undertakings whether they are implied or expressed and they do not need to be legally enforceable. It also covers a scheme plan, proposal, action (or course of action), or course of conduct whether unilateral or otherwise.

  What is important is the timing of the scheme as it must be judged against the law in force at that time and a reconstruction of the situation that would have applied if the scheme had not been entered into.

   If an arrangement was entered into in December 2010 which will produce a GST benefit in the future and that arrangement was varied in November 2013, it is possible for that re-arrangement to be treated as a scheme for GST anti-avoidance purposes.

- **There must be a GST benefit.** This is a critical element for the GST anti-avoidance rules to apply. There must be a GST benefit that arises as a result of the scheme to the avoider from any of the following:
  - the entity does not pay GST (or pays a lower amount of GST)
  - the entity gets a GST refund (or an increased refund)
  - the entity defers their GST liability to a later time, or
  - the entity gets an earlier GST refund.

  It is not necessary for that entity to be a party to the scheme. It is sufficient that they receive a GST benefit.

- **The benefit must come from the scheme.** This requirement is very wide also as it is only necessary for the entity avoiding the GST to get the benefit as a result of the scheme. That can apply even though there was no economic alternative to the activities engaged in. This requirement will not apply however, if the entity can demonstrate that the GST benefit was attributable to a choice or election that is available under the GST rules. For example, this requirement would not be satisfied where an eligible business chooses one of the simplified accounting methods available to retail businesses (see 24.360).

- **'Reasonable' conclusion.** This is the most critical test and it involves two separate tests. If either of them is satisfied then the entity can be liable for penalties. The tests are:
  - the sole or dominant purpose test, or
  - the principal effect test.

  The **'sole or dominant purpose test'** is similar to the anti-avoidance tests set out in the income tax legislation (4.510) and seeks to determine the prevailing or most influential purpose even though it may be outweighed by all the other purposes combined. The test is satisfied if it is reasonable to conclude that an entity entered into or carried out the scheme with the sole or dominant purpose of getting a GST benefit from the scheme.

  The **'principal effect test'** is considerably wider than the dominant purpose test. The test is satisfied if it is reasonable to conclude that the principal effect of the scheme is that the avoider gets the GST benefit from the scheme. The legislation refers to '*the* principal effect' and not to '*a* principal effect'. The result is that if the GST benefit was just one of several equally important (or more important) effects then this requirement would not be satisfied.

- **Other factors.** The Tax Office will look at other factors in determining if the anti-avoidance rules apply. These include:
  - the manner in which the scheme was entered into or carried out
  - the form and substance of the scheme
  - the timing of the scheme
  - the period over which the scheme was entered into and carried out, and
  - any change in the financial position of the entities involved.

For a complete list of matters to be considered in determining purpose or effect of entering into a scheme which results in a GST benefit, see s166-15 GST Act.

THE *VCE* CASE

The first Division 165 case was heard in 2006 (*VCE v Commissioner of Taxation* [2006] AATA 821). The decision made use of existing analysis of the equivalent anti-avoidance provisions in Part IVA of the ITAA36. The case concerned an arrangement which enabled the taxpayer to claim a substantial input tax credit while deferring GST payable for 15 years in an associated party transaction. The AAT found the GST benefit was the consequence of the terms of the agreement in respect of the deferred payment.

4.530 FBT ANTI-AVOIDANCE RULES

Section 67 of the *Fringe Benefits Tax Assessment Act 1986* (FBTAA) (see from 25.000) gives the Tax Office broad anti-avoidance powers. Those powers are similar to those that operate under Part IVA of the ITAA36 for income tax purposes.

The FBT anti-avoidance rules operate where it could be concluded, on an objective view of the facts, that the arrangement was entered into by the employer for the sole or dominant purpose to avoid FBT. The anti-avoidance rule only operates where the taxable value in respect of the benefit is less than it would have been except for the arrangement. The anti-avoidance rules do not apply where additional cash wages are paid in substitution of fringe benefits, or where one benefit is substituted for another benefit (MT 2021), or the cashing out of benefits.

Government bodies are excluded from the offence provisions of the FBT legislation (FBTAA, s167).

Where the Tax Office determines that the anti-avoidance rules apply, the Commissioner is authorised to cancel the tax benefit and to increase the employer's aggregate fringe benefits amount. Similarly, corresponding adjustments may be made to the FBT returns of other employers if the benefit was declared in their return.

Where the Tax Office cancels an FBT tax benefit, it must issue an amended assessment. That amendment can be issued within 6 years from the date on which the original assessment was made. The assessment date is the date the original return was lodged (or the date of the default assessment if no return was lodged).

4.600 PENALTIES

Penalties reflect the fact that the self-assessment regime places a range of obligations on taxpayers in different situations.

In July 2014, the Inspector-General of Taxation's report *Review into the Australian Taxation Office's administration of penalties* was released.

The objective of the penalty regime is to foster voluntary compliance. The Inspector-General found that this objective may be hindered by:

- categories of taxpayer behaviours being too broad
- the inability to receive interest on unsustained penalties, and
- the broad application of false and misleading statement penalties where no tax shortfall occurs.

The Inspector-General made ten recommendations to the Tax Office. The Tax Office agreed with nine of the ten recommendations in whole, in part or in principle.

The report can be accessed on the Inspector-General's website (www.igt.gov.au).

PENALTIES ARISING FROM STATEMENTS

PS LA 2006/2 explains when a statement will give rise to an administrative penalty under s284-75(1) TAA, how the penalty is assessed and when remission under s298-20 TAA is appropriate.

Section 284-75 provides that a taxpayer is liable to an administrative penalty if the taxpayer or their agent makes a false or misleading statement resulting in a tax shortfall, the taxpayer or their agent makes a statement in relation to an income tax law which is not reasonably arguable and a tax shortfall results from that statement; or the taxpayer fails to lodge a required document with the Commissioner.

The effect of the administrative penalty regime is that a taxpayer is prima facie liable to pay an administrative penalty if the taxpayer has failed to meet their obligations under taxation laws in relation to:

- making false or misleading statements
- taking a position that is not reasonably arguable, and
- refusing to provide documents to the Commissioner and a shortfall amount has arisen.

Shortfall amounts are explained at s284-80 TAA. A shortfall amount arises where:

- a tax-related liability, worked out on the basis of the statement is less than it would be if the statement were not false or misleading
- an amount that the Commissioner must pay or credit under a taxation law, worked out on the basis of the statement is more than it would be if the statement were not false or misleading
- a tax-related liability worked out on the basis of the statement is less than it would be if the statement did not treat an income tax law as applying in a way that was not reasonably arguable, and
- an amount that the Commissioner must pay or credit under an income tax law is more than it would be if the statement did not treat an income tax law as applying in a way that was not reasonably arguable.

Taxation statements include, amongst other things, statements made in:

- a return or amendment request
- facts stated in response to a tax auditor in the course of an audit, or
- any other statement made to a Tax Officer, orally, in a document or in any other way.

They exclude statements made by the taxpayer concerning the operation of a tax law.

If assessable income is omitted from a statement it is treated as a statement that the income was not derived.

The base penalty amount is calculated as a percentage of the shortfall amount. The percentage applied depends upon the reason the shortfall resulted (see 4.660). The base penalty amount is worked out under s284-90.

Generally the base penalty amount will be calculated as follows.

1. Where the shortfall amount resulted from intentional disregard of a taxation law, the base penalty amount is 75% of the shortfall amount.
2. Where the shortfall amount resulted from recklessness as to the operation of a taxation law, the base penalty amount is 50% of the shortfall amount.
3. Where the shortfall amount resulted from a failure to take reasonable care to comply with a taxation law, the base penalty amount is 25% of the shortfall amount.
4. Where the shortfall resulted from treating an income law as applying in a particular way that was not reasonably arguable, and that amount is more than the greater of $10,000 or 1% of the income tax payable by the taxpayer for the income year, the base penalty amount is 25% of the shortfall amount.

NOTE: Where a taxpayer is liable for an administrative penalty for failing to provide required documents to the Commissioner and the Commissioner determines the tax-related liability without the documents, the base penalty is 75% of the tax-related liability concerned.

***These rules are now subject to the safe harbour provisions. See s284-75(6) of Schedule 1 to the* Tax Administration Act 1953.**

INACCURATE ADVICE GIVEN BY THE TAX OFFICE

Taxpayers will not be penalised under a scheme section (ie. tax avoidance or profit shifting) if any tax shortfall has been caused:

- by incorrect advice received from the Tax Office
- because they relied on generally accepted administrative practice of the Tax Office.

REASONABLE CARE

A taxpayer is expected to exercise the level of care a 'reasonable and ordinary' person would exercise if they were required to fulfil the taxpayer's obligations. If 'reasonable care' is not exercised by a taxpayer in preparing their tax return or in maintaining their records, a penalty of at least 25% of the tax shortfall is payable. By demonstrating reasonable care has been taken, a penalty amount of 25% may not be imposed on any or part of the tax shortfall amount.

 A taxpayer claims non-deductible interest resulting in a tax shortfall of $6,000. To avoid the penalty, the taxpayer must show that 'reasonable care' was taken.

TESTING FOR 'REASONABLE CARE'

This 'reasonable care test' requires taxpayers make a reasonable attempt to comply with their obligations and it applies to both the preparation of returns and record-keeping during the income year. The knowledge, education, experience and skill of the taxpayer is considered, but it is not a question of the taxpayer's intentions or whether they actually foresaw the problem. The test is whether an ordinary person in the same situation should have foreseen it. This means taking all reasonable steps to comply with the Tax Office's tax return instructions, and any notices issued from the Tax Office. It also involves determining whether business taxpayers can demonstrate that appropriate record keeping systems and other procedures were in place.

This test also involves deciding whether:

- the taxpayer genuinely understood the law
- the error was honestly made, isolated, an arithmetic or transposition error, or
- the taxpayer knew or could reasonably be expected to know the statement misrepresented the true position.

If there is doubt regarding the application of the law, it would be reasonable to obtain professional advice, or expert published advice including the Tax Office or other professional associations. If incorrect advice from third parties is relied on, penalties will apply only if the taxpayer was in a position to suspect that advice was wrong.

The Commissioner's view of the concept of 'reasonable care' is contained in MT 2008/1 in which the Commissioner notes that:

- 'reasonable care' does not connote the highest level of care or perfection
- using the services of a tax agent or tax adviser does not of itself mean that an entity discharges the obligation to take reasonable care
- failing to obtain a private ruling from the Tax Office on a question of interpretation does not necessarily lead to a failure to take reasonable care
- a false statement arising from an oversight or an error in adding, subtracting or transposing amounts may result from a failure to take reasonable care, but such an error is not conclusive evidence of a lack of reasonable care, and
- a failure to respond to every foreseeable risk will not necessarily mean that reasonable care is absent.

REASONABLY ARGUABLE POSITION

A minimum penalty of 25% applies if the tax shortfall exceeds the greater of $10,000 or 1% ($20,000 and 2% in case of trusts and partnerships) of the tax payable based on the taxpayer's self-assessment, unless the taxpayer's position was 'reasonably arguable'. If a tax shortfall is caused by a number of different matters, the taxpayer must satisfy only the 'reasonably arguable' test in respect of the matters causing the shortfall to exceed the $10,000 or 1% threshold.

This test allows a taxpayer to show the position taken was 'reasonably arguable' given an objective analysis of a contentious (or even a settled) area of the law. Reasonably arguable means that the position taken is more likely to be correct than incorrect or is about as likely to be correct as incorrect (as set out in s284-15). MT 2008/2 considers in depth the concept of 'reasonable arguable position'.

If a tax shortfall occurs over two or more income years because of the taxpayer's position, each shortfall is tested individually. For more information on shortfall penalties see MT 2008/2.

In 2014-15, a company taxpayer incorrectly claims a deduction which results in a carry-forward Division 36 (ITAA97) loss of $1 million. That loss is recouped over the succeeding two income years (ie. $800,000 and $200,000).

In 2015-16 there is no tax payable and $240,000 loss ($800,000 @ 30%) exceeds the tax payable on the return by $10,000. In 2016-17, the $60,000 loss ($200,000 @ 30%) exceeds the tax payable by $10,000.

To avoid penalties in either income year, the taxpayer must demonstrate a 'reasonably arguable' position to explain why the incorrectly claimed deductions were ultimately applied as losses to the 2014-15 and 2015-16 income years respectively.

PENALTIES RELATING TO SCHEMES

Legislation governing penalties relating to schemes is set out in Subdivision 284-C. A taxpayer is liable to an administrative penalty where they obtain a scheme benefit from a scheme.

A scheme is defined in s995-1 of the ITAA97 and a scheme benefit is explained in s284-150. The base penalty amount is a percentage of the scheme shortfall amount. The percentage applied depends upon the adjustment provision under which the penalty arose and whether it is reasonably arguable the adjustment provision does not apply. The base penalty amount may be increased or decreased depending upon whether the circumstances fit situations set out in ss284-220 and 284-225 respectively.

The shortfall may be reduced under s284-215 if it has been caused by incorrect advice received from the Tax Office or because of a reliance on general administrative practice by the Tax Office.

DISREGARDING A PRIVATE RULING

An automatic penalty will not be imposed where a taxpayer has failed to follow a Ruling, however penalties may still apply if by failing to follow the Ruling the taxpayer failed to take reasonable care. Further, if a position taken by taxpayer is not a reasonably arguable one, a penalty may yet be imposed.

RECKLESSNESS

Where a tax shortfall has resulted from recklessness by the taxpayer as to the operation of a taxation law, a penalty of 50% of the shortfall amount will arise (s284-90). MT 2008/1 considers the concept of 'recklessness'. This is defined as gross negligence, or disregard of, or indifference to, consequences foreseeable by a reasonable person. Even though there doesn't need to be any degree of dishonesty involved, this will result in a penalty of 50% of the tax shortfall.

It would be reckless behaviour if a taxpayer failed to declare assessable dividends after acquiring shares in a company and completely disregarding any letters from the company regarding the taxing of dividends.

INTENTIONAL DISREGARD AND DELIBERATE EVASION

If the taxpayer intentionally disregards a taxation law, a penalty of 75% of the tax shortfall applies. This includes deliberately excluding assessable income, or for claiming non-allowable deductions or rebates.

FAILURE TO PROVIDE DOCUMENTS

If the taxpayer is liable to an administrative penalty for failing to provide documents to the Commissioner pursuant to s284-75(3), a penalty of 75% of the tax-related liability concerned applies.

Section 284-75(3) provides a taxpayer is liable to a penalty if:

- they fail to give a return, notice or other document to the Commissioner by the day it is required to be given
- that document is necessary for the Commissioner to determine a tax-related liability of the taxpayer, and
- the Commissioner determines the tax-related liability without the assistance of that document.

TAX AVOIDANCE: PENALTIES ARISING FROM SCHEMES

Taxpayers are liable for a 50% penalty (of the tax shortfall) if they enter into tax schemes with the sole or dominant purpose of avoiding tax. This is a penalty relating to a scheme (Subdivision 284-C) which differs from a penalty relating to statements (Subdivision 284-B). That can be reduced to 25% if the taxpayer has a 'reasonably arguable position'.

If the scheme is found to be ineffective under ordinary provisions and anti-avoidance provisions are not invoked, the higher avoidance penalties still apply. If the tax avoidance occurs through use of a double tax agreement, or due to any non-arm's length prices in international dealings, the 25% penalty may be reduced to 10%. That reduction can apply if the taxpayer's treatment at the time of lodgment was reasonably arguable (s284-160).

PROMOTER PENALTIES

The promoter penalty provisions are set out in Division 290 of the TAA. These rules provide for the imposition of penalties for promoters of tax avoidance and tax evasion schemes (collectively referred to as tax exploitation schemes). A penalty under this provision may only be imposed by the Federal Court. The maximum penalty that may be imposed is the greater of 5,000 penalty units for an individual or 25,000 penalty units for a body corporate, and twice the consideration received or receivable directly or indirectly by the entity or its associates in respect of the scheme.

The Federal Court may also, on the application of the Commissioner, grant an injunction in relation to a tax exploitation scheme.

Two Practice Statements regarding the administration of the promoter penalty regime are:

- PS LA 2008/7: The administration of Division 290 TAA and the application of tax exploitation schemes, and
- PS LA 2008/8: The administration of Division 290 TAA and the application to schemes in relation to Product Rulings.

 The Full Federal Court decision in Commissioner of Taxation v Ludekens [2013] FCAFC 100 is a landmark decision as it was the first time that an appeal court had considered the promoter penalty provisions. The judgment is instructive as it provides the Full Federal Court's detailed commentary on a number of terms and concepts that are crucial to understanding the application of the promoter penalty provisions.

TAX AGENTS

A taxpayer who uses a registered tax agent or BAS agent may, in some circumstances, avoid administrative penalties in respect of:

- a false or misleading statement made to the Commissioner, or
- the late lodgment of a document with the Commissioner.

Administrative penalties which would otherwise arise in these circumstances will no longer be imposed if the taxpayer engages a registered tax or BAS agent, and:

- the agent is provided with all relevant information on a timely basis
- the agent makes the statement which results in a tax shortfall or is responsible for the late lodgment of the document, and
- the shortfall, or the late lodgment, does not result from an intentional disregard of the law or recklessness by the agent.

The provisions apply to:

- false or misleading statements, and
- failure to lodge.

The taxpayer is the one that must prove they provided the relevant information to the agent in order to rely on this exemption.

The activities of tax and BAS agents, including the Code of Conduct under which they must operate, are controlled by the Tax Practitioners Board. Refer: www.tpb.gov.au

PARTNERS AND TRUSTEES

A defaulting partner is liable for penalties (see table at 4.650) in respect of each partner's partnership shortfall if that tax shortfall (including any increase in tax as a result of amendment and additional tax for late payment) was caused by:

- carelessness
- recklessness
- intentional disregard of the Act or its Regulations
- incorrectly applying the law in a way that is not 'reasonably arguable' and the tax involved exceeds the greater of $20,000 (or 2% of the partnership's or trust's) net income, or
- entering into a scheme for the sole or dominant purpose of avoiding tax.

A defaulting partner (or trustee) is one who makes a statement relating to the net income (or loss) of the partnership or trust which results in an under-statement of the net income or an overstatement of any loss.

If assessable income is omitted from the return, it is taken to be a statement that the income was not derived.

A partnership (or trust) shortfall excess is the difference between:

- the tax that would have been payable by the partner (or beneficiary) based on his/her share of the net income (or loss), and
- the tax based on the defaulting partner's (or trustee's) statement (see *Voluntary disclosure* below).

TRUSTEES AND BENEFICIARIES

The whole effect shown above for the partnership and each partner's interest in it, applies in an identical way to trustees and beneficiaries.

HINDERING THE TAX OFFICE

Penalties may be increased by one-fifth (s284-220) (ie. penalty of 25% may increase to 30%) if the taxpayer acts, or omits to act in a certain manner, including:

- attempts to prevent or hinder the Tax Office from finding any tax shortfall (including any increase in tax as a result of amendment and additional tax for late payment)
- fails to inform the Tax Office within a reasonable time of finding an error (factual, or in calculating tax payable), or
- has been penalised in respect of an earlier income year for failure to take reasonable care, recklessness, intentional disregard, or for applying the law to a similar matter or in the same way.

 In 2013-14, a taxpayer claimed legal expenses incurred defending a take-over. The claim was subsequently disallowed and the taxpayer was penalised for the tax shortfall. In 2015-16, and after the earlier year's tax dispute was settled, the taxpayer claimed more legal expenses of the same type. A further penalty (uplifted by one fifth) would apply.

REMISSION OF PENALTIES

Practice Statement PS LA 2006/2 clarifies the exercise of the Commissioner's discretion to remit shortfall penalties arising from false or misleading statements.

The Commissioner's discretion to remit all or part of a penalty is set out in s298-20. PS LA 2006/2 sets out factors the Commissioner will consider when deciding whether or not to remit a penalty imposed as a result of a false or misleading statement.

Importantly, it does not apply to penalties that arise as a result of failing to have a reasonably arguable position or in situations where the person has participated in a scheme. Further, it does not deal with the general interest charge (GIC) that is imposed on any outstanding tax or penalty. The Tax Office's policy on GIC remissions in contained in the Tax Office Receivables Policy which is available on the Tax Office's website at www.ato.gov.au. Further, PS LA 2006/8 provides guidance concerning the remission of shortfall interest charge and general interest charge accrued during shortfall periods.

OBLIGATIONS UNDER NEW TAXATION LAWS

The Tax Office intends to continue with its policy of giving taxpayers the opportunity to become familiar with substantial changes to the law. Any taxpayer who genuinely attempts to comply with new statutory requirements will generally have penalties remitted:

- in the first 12 months from the commencement date of any new law, and
- during the transitional period (if applicable).

Whether a legislative measure is substantial will be based on what could reasonably be expected of the class of taxpayer under examination. There would be different expectations arising between large corporations and micro businesses. If there is evidence of a clear attempt to avoid or disregard the requirements of the law then the above remission policy will not apply.

The administrative treatment of taxpayers affected by announced but unenacted legislative measures which will apply retrospectively when enacted is guided by PS LA 2007/11.

START DATE NOT ENACTED

The Tax Office will generally remit penalties in situations where the shortfall arises as a result of the start date for a proposed law commencing prior to the date of Royal Assent.

OLD TAXATION LAWS

The principles set out in Miscellaneous Taxation Rulings MT 2008/1 and MT 2008/2 will continue to apply to the remission of penalties for failing to comply with an income tax or FBT law that existed prior to 1 July 2000. Where the taxpayer can demonstrate that efforts to comply with new rules affected their ability to comply with existing income tax and FBT rules then the new rules under PS LA 2006/2 will apply.

NOTE: While TR 94/7 has not been withdrawn, it relates to the remission of penalties payable under Part VII of the ITAA36 which is now repealed.

NEW ENTRANTS

New entrants to the tax system will generally not be penalised in their first year of operation provided there has been a genuine attempt to comply with their tax obligations.

This concession will not apply to:

- a business taxpayer whose principals have previously been involved in business operations, or
- taxpayers who use the services of a tax agent, and
  - the taxpayer has not followed the tax agent's advice, or
  - the tax agent has failed to exercise reasonable care.

4.630   REASONABLE CARE

A tax shortfall arising from the failure of a taxpayer and/or their agent to take 'reasonable care' will prima facie result in a penalty with a base penalty amount of 25% of the shortfall amount.

MT 2008/1 considers the concept of reasonable care in detail. Elements from MT 2008/1 are set out below.

The test of reasonable care is whether in making (or not making) a statement, or in acting in a particular manner (or in not acting) the taxpayer has exercised the level of care that a reasonable person in the taxpayer's circumstances would have taken to fulfil their tax obligations.

It is not a 'one size fits all' test. It is dependent on the taxpayer's background, knowledge, education, experience and skill. For a self-preparer (who lodges their own return) the test would generally be passed if a genuine attempt is made to follow the Tax Office's tax return instructions. If something in the instructions is misleading then no penalty will be payable. Similarly, if the taxpayer uses the instructions properly and makes a genuine mistake there will be no penalty payable.

Where taxpayers use the services of a tax agent, concessional treatment might only be available where both the taxpayer and the tax agent have exercised reasonable care. Additionally, the taxpayer must also have a reasonably arguable position where the tax shortfall is the greater of $10,000 or 1% of the tax payable on the taxpayer's assessment ($20,000 or 2% for trusts and partnerships).

A taxpayer who uses a tax agent will generally be entitled to remission of administrative penalties if they have:

- provided the agent with honest and complete information that is necessary for the preparation of the return, statement or document, including information that the taxpayer could reasonably be expected to have known was relevant, and
- adopted the agent's advice where it is given to the taxpayer.

If the taxpayer exercises reasonable care but the tax agent does not, the taxpayer will still be liable for administrative penalties where there is a shortfall.

Failure to take reasonable care

1. *Claiming a deduction without being able to substantiate the expense in accordance with substantiation rules.*
2. *Forgetting to include assessable income in a return.*
3. *Not making reasonable enquiries to determine the correct treatment of a tax-related matter.*
4. *Inadequate record-keeping system by a business taxpayer.*
5. *Arithmetic errors depending on the size, nature and frequency and circumstances of the person making error.*

Business taxpayers would be expected to have systems and procedures in place to prevent careless errors.

Inadvertent errors will not usually be penalised provided:

- the taxpayer's overall level of compliance is sound, and
- the taxpayer has made a genuine attempt to meet the relevant tax obligations but has made an unintentional error (eg. an isolated mistake by recording a transaction incorrectly or while having appropriate record keeping procedures, an employee makes an unintentional mistake that is not detected when the accounts are reviewed).

THE SAFE HARBOUR PROVISIONS UNDER THE TAX AGENT SERVICES REGIME

The safe harbour provisions, in certain circumstances, exempt taxpayers who engage an agent from liability for administrative penalties for certain mistakes and omissions where the error is solely due to the agent's actions or inaction.

REASONABLE CARE: TAX AGENTS

The existing standard of care expected of a tax agent is higher than that expected of a taxpayer who self prepares. The agent would be expected to:

- have the skills, knowledge and competence to prepare correct returns, statements and documents,
- be reasonably confident about a position taken on the application of a taxation law, and
- have procedures in place to ensure correct preparation.

The agent's work environment and effort to help clients comply with their tax obligations will be taken into account in determining whether the agent has exercised reasonable care.

The *Tax Agent Services Act 2009* contains a code of professional conduct by which registered tax agents and BAS agents must abide. In terms of reasonable care, the code of professional conduct requires that agents must:

- maintain knowledge and skills relevant to the tax agent services that they provide
- take reasonable care in ascertaining a client's state of affairs, and
- take reasonable care to ensure the taxation laws are applied correctly.

Refer to the TPB website (www.tpb.gov.au) for guidance on the code of professional conduct.

4.640   INCREASE/REDUCTION OF BASE PENALTY AMOUNT

The base penalty amount may be increased (s284-220) or reduced (s284-225). The base penalty amount may be increased where the taxpayer hinders the Tax Office (see 4.600). The base penalty amount may be reduced in the following circumstances:

VOLUNTARY DISCLOSURE

The voluntary disclosure to the Commissioner of a tax shortfall will result in a reduction of the base penalty amount applicable to the shortfall. Any voluntary disclosure that is made by a taxpayer before being told that an audit is to be conducted will reduce the base penalty amount by 80% if the shortfall is greater than $1,000 or is a scheme shortfall amount or to nil if the shortfall is less than $1,000. The taxpayer will generally be taken to have made an honest mistake unless there is information to indicate that the taxpayer did not make an honest mistake. The voluntary disclosure must be made in writing, be signed with the appropriate taxpayer or agent declaration and posted to the Tax Office. Any voluntary disclosure that is made after being told that an audit is to be commenced and the Commissioner has been saved significant time or resources by the disclosure, the base penalty amount is reduced by 20%. The Commissioner has the discretion to treat this disclosure as having been made prior to being told about the audit. Repeated voluntary disclosures by taxpayers or their tax agents will not be automatically entitled to the concession if there is an indication the taxpayer has not made an honest mistake or that the agent has been careless. MT 2008/3 explains this concession in greater detail.

The Tax Office undertakes many different types of reviews and audits under its compliance program. A 'tax audit' is defined in s995-1 of the ITAA97 to mean an examination by the Commissioner of an entity's financial affairs for the purposes of a taxation law.

NON-MATERIAL AMOUNTS

Penalties will not apply to non material shortfalls that result from a lack of reasonable care where it is evident that the taxpayer and agent (if any) have made a genuine attempt to comply with the taxpayer's obligations and the taxpayer's overall level of compliance is satisfactory. Consideration as to a 'material' amount will be based on the size of the shortfall relative to the taxpayer's turnover and the effect of the shortfall on the taxpayer's overall liability. The shortfall amount will continue to be payable.

CORRECTING GST MISTAKES

In certain circumstances taxpayers can correct GST mistakes on a subsequent activity statement without incurring any penalty [see correcting *GST Mistakes: Fact Sheet* (07/2004)(Nat 4700)]. In addition, where a registered tax agent prepares an income tax return and cannot reconcile the GST details in BASs prepared by the client of a bookkeeper, the GST may be corrected by including an adjustment, regardless of the amount) in the next BAS to be lodged following the lodgement of the income tax return. This concession is available only to clients with an annual turnover of under $20 million. The agent must inform the client or bookkeeper of the mistake and initiate action to prevent future occurrences.

TIMING ADJUSTMENTS

Penalties will not apply where income amounts or a supply is accidentally or unintentionally included in a period later than the period in which the amount should have been included. Penalties will apply where it is clear the taxpayer was aware of the proper treatment and sought to gain an advantage.

AMOUNTS IN ANOTHER PERSON'S RETURN

Where there has been no overall tax avoided then penalties will usually not apply if income, deductions, a credit or a supply is included in the wrong person's return. If some tax has been avoided then the penalty will be based on the net tax avoided.

4.650   CALCULATION OF PENALTIES AND INTEREST

When a taxpayer has been audited and found to have overstated their deductions or rebate (tax offset) entitlements or understated their income or income tax liability in any other manner, the income tax rules authorise the Tax Office to impose penalties based on the tax shortfall involved.

There are two components to penalties imposed:

- an administrative penalty (see from 4.600), and
- an interest component.

Each component is calculated according to different rules, but the penalty involved is based on the amount of the tax shortfall (ie. the underpayment of tax involved: see also 4.270).

ADMINISTRATIVE PENALTY

The administrative or culpability component is based on an assessment of the taxpayer's culpability. Consequently, the rate of the penalty (referred to as the base penalty rate) takes into account the co-operation of the taxpayer, their knowledge and expertise and intention or behaviour. The base penalty amount is a flat penalty (see below). Where a base penalty amount is imposed that same penalty will not also attract any interest penalty (see from 4.600).

Administrative penalties[1]			Voluntary disclosure:	
Culpable behaviour	Base penalty amount	Taxpayer hinders audit[3]	during audit[4]	before audit[5]
Intentional disregard	75%	90%	60%	15%
Recklessness	50%	60%	40%	10%
Tax avoidance/scheme benefit (s284-145(1))	$(25\%^2)$ 50%	$(30\%^2)$ 60%	$(20\%^2)$ 40%	$(5\%^2)$ 10%
Profit shifting without a predominant purpose to avoid tax (s284-145(2))	$(10\%^2)$ 25%	$(12\%^2)$ 30%	$(8\%^2)$ 20%	$(2\%^2)$ 5%
'Reasonable care' was not shown	25%	30%	20%	5%
Not having a 'reasonably arguable' case	25%	30%	20%	5%

1: If a tax shortfall can be penalised for several reasons, the highest penalty applies: eg. reckless/not having a reasonably arguable position: penalty is 50%. The minimum monetary penalty is $20.

2: In tax avoidance and profit shifting cases the lower penalties in brackets apply if $10,000 or more tax is involved and the taxpayer's position is 'reasonably arguable' – see 4.600.

3: The base penalty amount is increased by 20%.

4: The base penalty amount is decreased by 20%.

5: The base penalty amount is decreased by 80%.

NON-LODGMENT/LATE LODGMENT PENALTIES

Notwithstanding the penalty imposed pursuant to s284-75(3) where the Commissioner determines a tax-related liability without documents required from the taxpayer, failure to lodge tax returns and other documents by the due date also renders the taxpayer liable to an administrative penalty (Div. 286). The amount of penalty varies depending on classification of the taxpayer.

The base penalty is one penalty unit for each 28 days or part thereof that the return or other document remains unlodged.

In the 2015-16 Federal Budget, it was announced that the value of a penalty unit will increase from $170 to $180 from 31 July 2015.

The maximum penalty is equal to five penalty units. The effective maximum is $900 (based on a maximum of 5 penalty units x 28 days). The base penalty is applied to small entities. The penalty for medium entities is double the base penalty and large entities are penalised five times the base penalty (see table below). The amount of the penalty is determined under s286-80.

IMPORTANT: These penalty rates apply for all taxpayers and for all documents that are required to be lodged with the Tax Office. It includes returns, statements, schedules, elections, etc. It can even apply where an incomplete return or other document is returned because it did not contain all of the required information.

 The late lodgment penalty applies regardless of whether there is any primary tax liability. This is especially important for individuals as they may be penalised for late lodgment of their income tax return even if they are entitled to a refund. A penalty can also be imposed if the returns are not lodged in accordance with the Tax Office's instructions or on the approved form.

The penalty is based on the number of days the document is late beyond its due date and applies to late lodged:

* Activity Statements (see from 5.800)
* income tax returns
* FBT returns (see from 25.000)
* PAYG withholding annual reports (5.700), and
* GST annual returns and GST Information reports (see from 23.000).

Days overdue	Small entity	Medium entity	Large entity
28 or less	$180	$360	$900
29 to 56	$360	$720	$1,800
57 to 84	$540	$1,080	$2,700
85 to 112	$720	$1,440	$3,600
113 or more	$900	$1,800	$4,500

NOTE: The values in the table above are calculated based on the 2015-16 Federal Budget announcement that the value of a penalty unit will increase from $170 to $180 on 31 July 2015.

NOTE: A **small** entity is any taxpayer (including an individual) that does not qualify as a medium or large entity.

A **medium** entity is any entity that satisfies any of the following criteria:

* is treated as a medium entity for PAYG withholding purposes
* has assessable income of more than $1 million but less than $20 million for the relevant income year, or
* has a current annual turnover for GST purposes of more than $1 million but less than $20 million.

A **large** entity is any entity that satisfies any of the following criteria:

* is treated as a large entity for PAYG withholding purposes
* has assessable income in the relevant year of $20 million or more, or
* has a current annual turnover for GST purposes of $20 million or more.

Failure to lodge (FTL) penalties are generally automatically imposed, however this penalty regime is aimed at 'high risk' taxpayers. All other taxpayers can apply for the penalty to be remitted provided the taxpayer or the document required to be lodged is 'low risk'. A low risk document includes those which result in a refund or minimal debt. It also includes late lodged returns of non-taxable entities and activity statements with an overall zero liability.

A low risk taxpayer is one that:

* has no other outstanding lodgement obligations or taxation debts, and
* has a previous good compliance history, and
* is not a large taxpayer nor a member of a large taxpayer group.

The General Interest Charge (GIC) continues to be imposed on any tax liability that is outstanding after the due date (see 4.660). This penalty is tax deductible. However, any FTL penalty is not deductible.

OTHER ADMINISTRATIVE PENALTIES

These administrative penalties will also apply:

- Non-lodgment of a tax document (pursuant to s284-75(3): 75% of any tax-related liability
- Failure to keep records: 20 penalty points ($3,600)
- Failure to keep income tax or FBT declaration authorising an agent to lodge: 20 penalty points ($3,600)
- Failure to give reasonable facilities to Tax Officer carrying out their duties: 20 penalty points ($3,600)

4.660   INTEREST

Where a tax shortfall arises, the Tax Office may apply administrative penalties and/or an interest penalty. There are two types of interest penalty: the General Interest Charge and the Shortfall Interest Charge.

GENERAL INTEREST CHARGE

The GIC applies to nearly all outstanding tax debts (subject to where Shortfall Interest Charge (SIC) is imposed) including income tax and FBT. It is calculated on a daily, compounding basis and applies in addition to any culpability or other late lodgement or administrative penalty. The GIC is governed by Part IIA of the TAA.

The nominal annual interest rate is the monthly average yield of 90 day Bank Accepted Bills (the base interest rate) plus 7%. The daily effective rate is adjusted quarterly.

The GIC rate is set at a high rate (as compared with normal commercial rates) to encourage prompt payment of tax liabilities. It generally reflects the interest rate charged by financial institutions on unsecured loans.

The GIC component is a separate penalty based on the amount of tax liability, and is calculated on the unpaid daily balance from the date the tax became due and payable.

Any GIC imposed is tax deductible in the income year the notice (which includes the GIC) issues notwithstanding that the GIC was paid in a later year of income. To claim a deduction for GIC it must be more than merely impending, threatened or expected. The issue of the notice establishes that the debt has been incurred.

Daily GIC is worked out by dividing the nominal annual interest rate by the number of days in the calendar year.

Period	GIC (annual rate)	Compounding (daily rate)
July - September 2012	10.66%	0.02912568%
October - December 2012	10.62%	0.02901639%
January - March 2013	10.24%	0.02805479%
April - June 2013	9.95%	0.02726027%
July - September 2013	9.82%	0.02690411%
October - December 2013	9.60%	0.02630137%
January - March 2014	9.59%	0.02627397%
April - June 2014	9.63%	0.02638356%
July - September 2014	9.36%	0.02564383%
October - December 2014	9.75%	0.02671233%
January - March 2015	9.63%	0.02638356%
April - June 2015	9.69%	0.02654794%

If the base interest rate is 6%, the interest is: 6% + 7% = 13%. If the number of days the tax liability remains outstanding is 13, then the daily effective rate is 13/365 = 0.0356%.
(Note that in a leap year the denominator will be 366 days.)

Penalties and GIC are automatically imposed on any tax or source deduction remaining unpaid, calculated from the start of the day on which the amount is due to be paid, to the end of the day immediately before the debt (including any outstanding GIC) is totally repaid. Accordingly, the GIC compounding rate extends to most taxes, including income tax, fringe benefits tax, GST and PAYG.

NOTE: The official GIC rates for past and future periods are available on the Tax Office website www.ato.gov.au.

WHEN TAX DEBTS MUST BE PAID

Where the due date for payment of a tax debt (includes income tax, FBT, PAYG withholding, PAYG instalments, luxury car tax, wine equalisation tax etc.) falls on a weekend or public holiday the payment (and/or lodgment) may be made on the next working day.

 The Tax Office has advised that whenever there is a State based public holiday it will apply as if that holiday was nationwide. This concession will not apply to regional holidays.

 Tax debts must be paid by the due date to avoid any GIC penalties.

SHORTFALL INTEREST CHARGE

The Shortfall Interest Charge (SIC) applies where a tax shortfall is caused by an understatement of income tax liability. The SIC regime is contained in Division 280. The SIC applies only to amended assessments for 2004-05 and later years. The SIC rate is calculated on the same basis as the GIC but is four percentage points less per annum. In other words the SIC will have a three percentage point uplift over the base interest rate. The base interest rate is the monthly average yield of 90 day Bank Accepted Bills.

 If the base interest rate is 7.15% then the SIC rate is 7.15% + 3% = 10.15%. The daily effective rate is 10.15/365 = 0.0278082%.

NOTE: The official SIC rates that apply are available from the Tax Office's website at www.ato. gov.au.

The Tax Office fact sheet *ROSA in brief – shortfall interest charge* provides the following example.

 General Interest Charge and Shortfall Interest Charge
John is an office worker in the 32.5% tax bracket (plus the 2% Medicare levy).

When preparing his tax return for the 2014-15 income year, John omits to declare $800 in dividend income (unfranked). John has an income tax liability for the 2014-15 income year which is due and payable on 21 November 2015. Income matching identifies the omitted dividend income. On 2 March 2016, John is notified of an amended assessment increasing his liability by $276 (that is, 34.5% x $800) and of the SIC on that account for the 101 days from 21 November 2015 to 1 March 2016 (inclusive).

The due date for the tax liability arising from the amended assessment is 23 March 2016 (that is, 21 days after the notice is given to John). John pays the increased tax liability, SIC and the GIC in full on 30 April 2016.

John is liable for the GIC on a compounding daily basis from 23 March 2016 (the due date) to 29 April 2016 (that is, this is the last day on which at the end of the day there still remained an amount of tax, SIC or GIC that was unpaid). The day in which full payment was made (that is, 30 April 2016) is not included in the period because at the end of that day there was no tax, SIC or GIC that remained unpaid.

The SIC applies regardless of whether the taxpayer is liable for any culpability penalty. The SIC applies on a daily compounding basis from the due date for payment of the understated assessment (this will generally be the due date of the original assessment) to the day before the shortfall is corrected (ie the day before the Commissioner gives notice the assessment has been amended). In normal instances the understated assessment will be the original assessment and the SIC will apply from the date any payment is due to be made in respect of the original assessment. Where the understatement occurred as a result of an erroneous credit amendment subsequently requested by the taxpayer, the SIC commences from the date of that credit amendment. Where there are multiple amendments, the SIC applies to each amendment concurrently.

The due date for payment of the tax shortfall and the related SIC is 21 days after the date on which the Tax Office gives the notice increasing the taxpayer's liability (ie. notice of amended assessment). If payment is not made by that date then the GIC applies automatically to any unpaid tax.

The SIC is tax deductible and any recouped SIC must be included in the assessable income of the taxpayer.

The Tax Office may remit the SIC where it is fair and reasonable to do so. If the Tax Office refuses to remit the SIC it must provide written reasons for rejecting the remission request. The written reasons are intended to improve confidence in the objectivity of Tax Office remission decisions. PS LA 2006/8 sets out guidelines for Tax Office staff to follow on the remission of SIC and GIC accrued during shortfall periods. If the unremitted SIC exceeds 20% of the tax shortfall then the taxpayer has the right to lodge an objection and appeal (s280-170) (see from 4.200 and 4.300).

When considering whether to remit all or part of the SIC the Tax Office must have regard to the following:

- remission should not occur just because the benefit received from the from the temporary use of the shortfall amount is less than the SIC (eg. the taxpayer's rate of finance is lower than the SIC), and
- remission should occur where the circumstances justify the Commonwealth bearing part of the cost of delayed receipt of taxes.

PS LA 2006/8 sets out examples where remission should occur including:

- Tax Office delay (for various reasons)
- taxpayer delay (some reasons may warrant remission)
- claims for legal professional privilege or access to professional advisors' working papers
- unprompted voluntary disclosure
- advance payment of shortfall amount
- tax shortfall offset by related credit
- costs of administration (where interest charge is minimal), and
- reliance on Tax Office advice or general administrative practice.

RUNNING BALANCE ACCOUNT (RBA)

The Tax Office issues RBAs that involve the production of regular account statements showing total outstanding debts. The statements are similar to commercial credit card and cheque account statements and identify the amount of GIC (in the form of a daily interest rate) applicable to an outstanding account balance.

Part IIB of the TAA governs treatment of payments, credits and RBA surpluses and how different amounts are allocated in respect of an RBA, any outstanding debts, GIC and if an amount represents a RBA surplus.

 Taxpayers or their agents may have to deconstruct and reconstruct the individual entries in the account to find tax shortfalls and other amounts outstanding. The RBAs contain all debits and credits for all tax types and payment obligations eg. income tax, FBT, GST, PAYG withholding etc.

 When contacting the Tax Office about 'other amounts payable' shown on assessments, make sure you can identify yourself (eg. TFN, date of birth, address for service of notices shown on return) otherwise the Tax Office will refuse to talk to you.

REFUND AND INTEREST ON OVERPAID TAX

Where an amended assessment results in a tax refund and/or interest on overpaid tax, Part IIB and s172 of ITAA36 apply (see also 4.265). Overpaid tax will be applied against any RBA deficit debt, non-RBA tax debt before any remaining overpaid tax is refunded. The taxpayer is also entitled to interest on the overpaid tax pursuant to Part III of the *Taxation (Interest on Overpayments and Early Payments) Act 1983*. This interest is assessable income to the taxpayer.

PROSECUTION AND PENALTIES

The decision to prosecute rests solely with the Director of Public Prosecutions (DPP) but the Tax Office can – and does – use the threat of prosecution as a tool to enforce compliance. Tax Officers cannot give an undertaking that a prosecution will not proceed. The Tax Office may inform the taxpayer of the DPP's decision.

Further, the Tax Office warns that if a taxpayer does not lodge overdue income tax returns, a potential consequence is that the Tax Office may refer the taxpayer for prosecution without further warning.

USEFUL RULINGS AND PRACTICE STATEMENTS ON PENALTIES

- TR 94/3:Calculation of tax shortfall and allocation of additional tax
- MT 2008/1: Reasonable care, recklessness, and intentional disregard
- MT 2008/2: Reasonably arguable position
- MT 2008/3: Voluntary disclosures
- TR 94/7: Remission guidelines for tax shortfall penalties
- TR 95/4: Remission of additional tax relating to the *Fringe Benefits Tax Assessment Act*
- PS LA 2006/2: Administration of shortfall penalties for false or misleading statements
- PS LA 2006/8: Remission of SIC and GIC for shortfall periods
- PS LA 2011/12: Imposition of GIC and the circumstances in which the GIC for late payment will be remitted

NOTE: The above Rulings (except TR 95/4) relate to penalties imposed pursuant to Part VII of the ITAA36 which has now been repealed. Despite this, they have not been withdrawn and TR 94/4 (replaced by MT 2008/1) and TR 94/5 (replaced by MT 2008/2) are cited as related Rulings in PS LA 2006/2. Their application needs to be carefully considered, particularly as newer Practice Statements are released.

NOTE: A Tax Office Prosecution Policy guide is available from the Tax Office website ato.gov.au.

4.680 FINES

The Tax Office has the power to impose administrative penalties for offences committed or it can prosecute those offences in a court instead. Administrative penalties that can be automatically imposed by the Tax Office for income tax offences and other offences are set out from 4.600.

Where the option to prosecute is chosen the following fines are imposed in accordance with the TAA. In some situations the *Crimes Act (Taxation Offences) 1980* may also apply, eg. aiding, abetting in an arrangement to defraud the Commonwealth. Penalties to apply for GST are set out in Chapters 23 and 24.

Certain offences are punishable by a fine and/or imprisonment if committed by a natural person. Where committed by a company the maximum fine is five times the maximum fine that could be imposed on an individual (s8ZF TAA).

Sections 8B to 8ZN of the TAA set out penalties in monetary amounts which are converted to penalty units by dividing the monetary amount by 100 and multiplying the result with the applicable penalty unit amount (s4AB *Crimes Act 1914*). A penalty unit is currently $180 and is provided for in the *Crimes Act 1914*. The Criminal Code is applied to offences under the TAA. This is explained in greater detail in the PSCM 2007/02 Fraud Control and the Prosecution Process and the Commonwealth prosecution policy:

Offence (list not exhaustive)	No. penalty points[1]	Natural person	Corporation
Refusal/failure to comply with a requirement under a tax law to: • furnish a return or information • permit access to documents • answer questions • attend before the Tax Office • give evidence on oath or affirmation (s8C and s8D).	1st offence 2nd offence 3rd & subsequent	20 40 50^6	20 40 250
Refusal or failure to comply with a court order or to give evidence or to furnish a return or information (s8G and s8H)		50^6	250
Making a false or misleading statement or omission which makes the statement misleading[2] (s8K and s8M)	1st offence 2nd & subsequent[4]	20 40	20 40
Incorrectly keeping records (s8L and s8M)[3]	1st offence 2nd & subsequent[4]	20 40	20 40
Recklessly or knowingly making a false or misleading statement or recklessly or knowingly omitting something from a statement which makes it misleading (s8N and s8R)	1st offence 2nd & subsequent[5]	30 50^6	30 250
Recklessly or knowingly incorrectly keeping records (s8Q & s8R)	1st offence 2nd & subsequent[5]	30 50^6	30 250
Falsifying, concealing, destroying or altering records with the intent to deceive or obstruct (s8T and s8V)	1st offence 2nd & subsequent	50^6 100^7	250 500
Offences relating to Tax File Numbers	1st & subsequent	100	500
Secrecy breach (s8XB)		100^7	100

1: One penalty point is the equivalent of $180, from 31 July 2015.
2: A defence to this charge if the person can prove that on the balance of probabilities the he/she did not know and could not reasonably be expected to know that the statement was false or misleading.
3: A defence to this charge if the person can prove that on the balance of probabilities the he/she did not know and could not reasonably be expected to know that the records did not correctly record the facts.
4: The person or entity may also be ordered to pay up to 200% of the tax avoided.
5: The person or entity may also be ordered to pay up to 200% of the tax avoided for a second offence and 300% for subsequent offences.
6: And/or 12 months imprisonment.
7: And/or two years imprisonment.

Section 8W of the TAA provides that a Court may order payment of an amount in addition to a penalty imposed in relation to a statement made to a Tax Officer or in respect of relevant accounts.

OTHER FINES

Fines may be imposed in addition to any applicable GIC (see 4.660). Where an entity is found guilty of an offence, a fine will be imposed upon conviction. Should an entity be found guilty of an offence under a former collection system (PAYE, PPS, RPS or other withholding programs no longer in use) a fine may still be imposed.

Fines and penalty points measures can be found throughout the TAA, with the majority in Schedule 1.

4.700   TAX RECORDS

Records for tax purposes must be in the English language, or be capable of being readily retrieved and converted into English. The Tax Office accepts electronic records on either magnetic tape or computer disk, provided they are readily accessible and convertible.

Tax records should be kept, for tax purposes, for at least the period in which the Commissioner may amend or the taxpayer may self-amend. This is the period of review. Records may need to be kept for a period beyond the period of review for non-tax reasons (ie. Corporations law, State laws for retention of documents).

Type of taxpayer	Period of review
Individuals: SPOR (see 4.225)	**n/a**
Individuals	2 years
Small business entity taxpayers (see 10.000)	2 years
Non-small business entity taxpayers	4 years
Nil and loss taxpayers	4 years
Income from partnerships and trusts that are not small business entity taxpayers	4 years
Anti-avoidance cases (Part IVA)	4 years
Fraud and evasion	Unlimited

4.710   BUSINESS RECORDS

Every taxpayer carrying on a business must keep records explaining all business transactions and any other matter which may affect their tax liability. With self-assessment, and particularly for companies paying tax with their return, it is essential that sufficient records are available to verify the tax due.

Section 262A of the ITAA36 sets out a general requirement to keep records *'that record and explain all transactions and other acts engaged in by the person that are relevant for any purpose of the Act'*. Notably, s262A applies to a person 'carrying on a business'. In addition to s262A, there are a number of provisions within taxation law which require specific records be kept. Some of these provide for a specific length of time. Some also identify a specific penalty for not complying with the record retention provision.

Section 288-25 of the TAA imposes an administrative penalty of 20 penalty units if a taxpayer does not keep or retain a record as required by a taxation law. A penalty unit is currently $110.

The general rule is to keep records for at least five years (s262A(4) ITAA36). However, the period may be extended if:

- an amended assessment has been issued, or
- the statutory period has been amended with the taxpayer's approval, or
- the Federal Court has approved an extension on the application of the Commissioner.

Therefore in respect of most records to be kept, s262A(4) requires that those records are kept for the later of five years from when the records were prepared or obtained or when the transaction or acts to which those records relate, or, the period during which as assessment may be amended by the Commissioner, is extended.

The requirement to retain records in excess of five years is particularly relevant in respect of losses where the loss is not applied for several years. In TD 2007/2, the Tax Office advises that a taxpayer who has incurred a loss or made a capital loss for an income year should retain records until at least the later of:

- the end of the statutory record retention period, or
- the end of the statutory period of review for an assessment for the year of income when the tax loss is fully deducted or the net capital loss is fully applied.

The record retention periods have not been adjusted in line with the changes in period of review (see 4.700). Accordingly, despite having a period of review of less than four years, a taxpayer must retain tax records pursuant to s262A(4) to avoid a penalty as considered at 4.680.

WHAT RECORDS SHOULD BE KEPT?

A person must record every transaction that relates to their income and expenditure. According to the Tax Office (TR 96/7), the information needed to record a transaction depends on the circumstances of each case. TR 96/7 sets out what records are required to be kept pursuant to s262A(4). Key aspects from TR 96/7 are as follows.

The minimum information they require for each transaction is that it must be recorded in English (or be readily accessible and convertible into English, eg. magnetic tape, or disc) and must show:

- the date
- the amount, and
- its character.

In other cases, other information may be necessary to understand the relevance of the transaction to the person's business (eg. relationships between the parties to the transaction).

The Tax Office website ato.gov.au provides useful information regarding record keeping for businesses – *Record keeping essentials*. The Tax Office advises the records taxpayers are required to keep include:

- sales records
- purchase/expense records
- year-end income tax records
- records relating to payments to employees, and
- PAYG withholding records relating to business payments.

Where records are encrypted, the Tax Office considers that record keeping requirements will not be met unless:

- the encryption key and all means to decrypt the records are provided to the Tax Office, or
- the Tax Office is provided with decrypted records.

CASH REGISTERS

In the retail industry, many businesses engage in high volume/low value sales transactions and a cash register is used to record the transactions. Those cash register rolls record each individual transaction put through the register. The Tax Office accepts that as the rolls provide no additional information to the 'Z totals' produced by the register, they are unnecessary for record keeping purposes. These rolls may be discarded after one month, provided the actual sales have been reconciled with the 'Z totals' and banking for that period. The reconciliation must be retained for five years and must take into account any cash earned during the period that was used for other purposes (eg. personal drawings, minor purchases etc). If reconciliations are not done, tapes must be kept for five years.

RECEIPT BOOKS

Some businesses do not use a cash register. These businesses often record their sales as they occur in a numbered receipt book. As with cash registers, the Tax Office will accept that a person may discard their receipt book after one month provided there is a reconciliation of the summary and individual records, and the banking for that period. That reconciliation must be kept for five years.

NO SOURCE DOCUMENTS

In some situations the nature of a person's business is such that they have no records (eg. where there is high volume/low value cash sales and the person does not operate from a permanently fixed location).

The Tax Office accepts a summary record of cash takings, provided it is reconciled with the banking and takes into account any cash earned that was used for other sources. It should be done regularly and show at least:

- total cash at end of day or shift
- plus personal drawings and expenses
- less opening float.

CREDIT CARDS

Where sales are made by credit card, the bank or financial institution usually provides a summary statement of any credit transactions for the particular period. That summary records the dates when the sales transaction information was presented. The summary statement is sufficient to record the sales for the period. Once that statement has been reconciled, vouchers can be discarded provided sufficient information is disclosed on the statement. However, when a credit card sale is made in one income year and the voucher is not presented until the next income year, the voucher should be retained until the next summary so it can be annotated as a sale made in the previous income year.

COMPANIES IN LIQUIDATION

Those actually dissolved are not required to retain records except for fringe benefits which must be kept for five years.

4.715   GST RECORDS

Every entity that is registered for GST must keep the following records for five years. For commentary in relation to GST refer to 23.000 and 24.000.

The following records must be kept in English.

TAX INVOICES

It is mandatory to retain tax invoices to support claims for input tax credits for GST that have been claimed. This includes tax invoices issued by suppliers **and** those issued by the recipients of supplies (ie. recipient created tax invoices).

A tax invoice will only be required for GST exclusive acquisitions of $75 or more, to enable a GST input tax credit to be claimed.

Subdivision 382-A of the TAA concerns the retention of the records relating to indirect tax transactions. Section 382-5 sets out the records taxpayers are required to retain in respect of various indirect taxes. A penalty of 30 penalty units is imposed if an entity does not retain the required records. The provision requires an entity retain records that record and explain all transactions and other acts the entity is engaged in that are relevant to a:

> ... supply, importation, acquisition, dealing, manufacture or entitlement ...

be retained for at least five years after the completion of the transactions or acts to which they relate.

ADJUSTMENTS

GST registered entities are required to adjust their Activity Statements where events occur that affect the amount of GST payable or refundable for a tax period. Where an adjustment takes place the entity must make the necessary adjustments to their business records and report the change in the activity statement for the period when the change occurs or when the change is discovered.

4.720   SUBSTANTIATION RULES

Employees and self-employed persons (including partners) must substantiate certain claims. Refer to 13.100 for a discussion of the substantiation rules.

4.730   CAPITAL GAINS TAX RECORDS

Record-keeping requirements relating to CGT are discussed in 12.200.

4.740   FRINGE BENEFITS TAX RECORDS

Specific substantiation rules apply in relation to fringe benefits tax. For commentary on these requirements, refer to 25.250.

4.750   CONTROLLED FOREIGN COMPANIES

For a discussion of controlled foreign companies refer to 22.820.

4.760   PENALTIES IN RESPECT OF RECORDS

If adequate records are not kept, and for the required period, penalties (of $170 for each penalty point) which can be imposed are:

- Business records (including CGT and franking account first offence under the TAA): 20 points
- FBT or substantiation: 20 points
- Capital gains s121-25: 30 points
- Recklessly or knowingly keeping incorrect records: 30 points
- Intention to mislead or deceive (first offence): 50 points or 12 months jail.

Tax collection systems

5

5.000   TAX FILE NUMBER SYSTEM

A Tax File Number (TFN) is used as an unique identifier to help administer tax on income from salary or wages and income from investments of each taxpayer. Failing to notify an investment body or employer of your TFN means that for residents tax at 49% (47% plus 2% Medicare levy plus 2% budget repair levy) in 2014-15 will be deducted. The TFN system is found in Division 202 of the ITAA36.

A 'person' may apply to the Commissioner for the issue of a TFN (s202B of the ITAA36). A 'person' pursuant to s202A of the ITAA36 includes:

- a partnership
- a company, and
- a person in the capacity of trustee of a trust estate.

It is not compulsory to have a TFN or to quote a TFN to an employer and/or an investment body. However, if a person doesn't have and/or doesn't quote their TFN (or ABN, see 5.130), there are some severe consequences:

- income derived from employment and investments is taxed at up to the highest marginal tax rate (47% in 2014-15) plus Medicare levy of 2% for residents
- those entitled to Social Security payments, Military Rehabilitation and Compensation payment or Veterans' Affairs pensions are denied these entitlements, and
- a superannuation fund cannot accept a personal contribution from a member if the member has not supplied the fund with their TFN.

Any tax deducted at source because the taxpayer failed to quote their TFN can be claimed as a credit in their assessment for that income year.

5.010   TFN AND SALARY/WAGES

Employers are required to deduct PAYG withholding tax at required amounts (see 5.600) from an employee's salary or wages (see from 5.301). An employee may provide a new employer with their TFN by completing a TFN declaration form (NAT 3092).

An employer must provide a TFN declaration to be completed by an employee when they commence employment. The employer must sign and lodge this declaration with the Tax Office within 14 days after the declaration is made and retain a copy of this declaration. Failure to do so attracts a maximum of ten penalty points ($1,800). If an employee does not provide a completed TFN declaration, then the employer must withhold tax at the highest marginal rate (47% in 2014-15) from any payment made to employee, plus Medicare levy of 2% if payment were made to a resident employee, and must notify the Tax Office within 14 days of the start of the withholding obligation.

If the employee has indicated in the TFN declaration form that he/she has made a TFN application or enquiry, the employer must allow the employee 28 days to provide a TFN before deducting tax at top marginal rate.

Any TFN provided to the employer must be shown on the employee's annual payment summary (see 5.422).

TAX FILE NUMBER QUOTED

If the employee has quoted their TFN to the employer or is not required to do so, PAYG is withheld using appropriate rates (see PAYG tax tables from 5.691).

TAX FILE NUMBER NOT QUOTED

Tax at the highest marginal tax rate (47% in 2014-15 & 2015-16) plus Medicare of 2% for resident employees must be deducted, except when:

- salary or wages paid to individuals under 18 years of age of less than $112 per week ($225 fortnightly or $489 monthly) are paid to an employee who claims the tax-free threshold (no PAYG withholding is required) (TD 2000/47), or
- the employee is a resident of Norfolk Island and derives income in that Territory, or

- the taxpayer has indicated on the TFN declaration that he/she has applied for a TFN (the taxpayer must inform their employer of their TFN within 28 days of making the declaration).

NOTE: The Medicare levy is not imposed if the employee is a non-resident for tax purposes.

5.020   TFN AND INVESTMENTS

Section 12-140 of Schedule 1 to the TAA and s202D of the ITAA36 provide that if a person's TFN is not quoted for the following investments, TFN tax is withheld at a flat 47% plus 2% budget repair levy in 2014-15 from residents from:

- interest-bearing deposits and accounts
- loans to government bodies and companies (eg. bonds and debentures – but not loans made in the ordinary course of providing business or consumer finance)
- money deposited in legal practitioners' or solicitors' trust accounts for reinvestment or for on-lending
- units in unit trusts, cash and property management trusts
- farm management deposits (Division 4A, Part VA ITAA36)
- shares in public companies, and
- prizes from some investment-related lotteries.

NOTE: Closely-held trusts need to withhold amounts from trust distributions at the top marginal tax rate where taxpayers have not provided a TFN to the trustee. This will ensure that taxable distributions to a beneficiary of a closely-held trust, including a family trust, are included in the beneficiary's tax return.

5.021   INVESTORS EXEMPT FROM QUOTING TFN

Certain types of investors are exempt pursuant to Division 5, Part VA of the ITAA36 from providing a TFN to the investment body:

- investments held by non-residents if they are liable to pay withholding tax
- if the investor is a Norfolk Island resident in respect of salary or wages earned or investments in that Territory (as these types of income are tax exempt)
- companies and unincorporated associations exempted from lodging tax returns, and
- Social Security recipients. The exemption applies to recipients of these pensions: Age, Disability Support, Wife, Carer Payment, Widow B, Parenting Payment (single), a Special Benefit, Special Needs and Veterans Affairs pensions. However, application for the pension itself can be rejected if a TFN is not quoted.

NOTE: The investment body is not required to withhold amounts from investment income for the above category of taxpayers if it is unaware that the exemption from quoting the TFN no longer applies to the taxpayer (s12-160 of Schedule 1 to the TAA).

Also according to s12-170 of Schedule 1 to the TAA, withholding is not required where the TFN is not quoted if:

- the investment body is notified that the investor is under 16 years of age on 1 January before the payment date and the annual income from accounts and investments (but not shares in a public company) is less than $420 (the $420 is pro-rated if the income is for partial year), and
- for all other investors, the annual income from interest-bearing accounts or deposits is less than $120 (if income is for partial year, the $120 threshold is pro-rated).

No withholding is required where a TFN is not quoted by an investor with respect to distribution of a fully franked dividend paid by a public company (s12-165 of Schedule 1 of the TAA). Withholding at 47% (plus 2% budget repair levy) only applies to the unfranked portion of the dividend where the TFN was not quoted. Note that a shareholder is only required to quote their TFN once to a public company.

Further, persons or organisations that are in the business of lending money are exempt from quoting TFNs to borrowers (IT 2634).

5.022 QUOTING A TFN FOR INVESTMENTS

Investment bodies will accept written notification of an investor's TFN if the investor's full name, address and the details of the investment are provided. For investors exempt from quoting a TFN, they must also notify the investment body to avoid tax being withheld on income from the investment. The investor will need to give the investment body a written notification with their full name, address, nominate which investment(s) they are claiming exemption for and the reason for exemption.

NOTE: If an entity is making an investment in the course of an enterprise, it may quote its ABN instead of its TFN to avoid amounts being withheld at 47% (plus 2% budget repair levy).

JOINT INVESTMENTS

For investments held jointly by two or more persons, at least two of the investors must provide their TFNs. If not, it is treated as if a TFN had not been quoted. The partnership TFN must be quoted for any investment made by a partnership.

INVESTMENTS HELD BY TRUSTEES

If an investment is held under the name of a trustee, that person may quote the trust's or superannuation fund's TFN, or if the trust or superannuation fund does not have a TFN, the individual trustee's TFN may be quoted (TD 93/61).

INVESTMENTS HELD BY SOLICITORS OR BODY CORPORATES

When solicitors or body corporates channel funds from the primary investors to another investment body (secondary investment body), they are acting as intermediary or interposed entities. Under such circumstances, there are two options for quoting the TFN to the secondary investment body. Solicitors or body corporates may quote their TFN/ABN if they:

- are acting only in the capacity of trustee (merely a conduit or agent between their client and the investment body), and
- reinvest funds for other persons not named on the investment.

If however all the primary investors are identified in the title of the investment, the primary investors (or at least one of the primary investors if there is more than one) may quote their TFN directly, or via the solicitor or body corporate, to the investment body. In this case, the solicitor or body corporate (being the interposed entity) must not quote their TFN/ABN.

REFUND OF TAX WITHHELD

PAYG withholding tax should not be withheld from any interest, dividend or distribution income derived after a TFN is quoted.

If the bank or institution fails to record the TFN (or does so incorrectly), the Tax Office has authorised the borrower to repay the tax withheld direct to the investor. If the PAYG withholding tax withheld has been remitted to the Tax Office, the borrower's next remittance can be reduced by the amount of the repayment (s18-65 TAA).

Alternatively, under s18-70 of the TAA, the investor can apply directly to the Commissioner for a refund of the withheld amount if the borrower did not become aware of the error in withholding, or the time has lapsed for the investor to request a refund from the borrower (before 21 July in the financial year after the one in which the amount was withheld), and the payer has already paid the withheld amount to the Commissioner. This request can be made by completing an *Application by an Australian resident investor for refund of tax file number amounts deducted* form (NAT 1846).

Interest is not receivable on any PAYG withholding amount held by the Tax Office.

 There is no automatic refund of any PAYG withheld because the taxpayer did not quote their TFN. Credit for that tax must be claimed by the recipient when they lodge their tax return. Remember, it is your responsibility to claim.

REMITTING TO THE TAX OFFICE

The tax withheld must be remitted to the Tax Office (see from 5.424). Failure to comply may result in a fine or a penalty of 10 penalty units ($1,800) – see 5.426. Further, late remittance will result in general interest charged (see 5.426).

NOTIFYING INVESTORS OF TAX WITHHELD

The investor must be notified of the tax withheld:

- in an annual payment summary within 14 days after the end of a financial year, and
- within 14 days of receiving a written request (provided the request was made no later than 21 days before the end of the financial year).

The annual payment summary should be checked carefully so that all PAYG withholding tax credits are claimed in the investor's annual tax return.

5.030 TFN AND SUPERANNUATION

Significant tax consequences in relation to certain contributions may occur as a result of superannuation funds not holding their members' TFNs (see 19.060).

5.040 APPLYING FOR A TAX FILE NUMBER

Taxpayers, including individuals, companies, superannuation funds, partnerships or trusts can apply for a Tax File Number (TFN). Non-residents will not be a given a TFN for employment purposes unless they are authorised to work in Australia. If a non-resident requires a TFN for other purposes, they should use a TFN application form for individuals living outside Australia available from the Tax Office website.

Most taxpayers have a TFN and it is shown on each income tax assessment. A person's TFN, once allocated, does not change.

Those who may not have a TFN are school leavers, migrants and children getting income from estates or trusts. To apply for one online, visit the Tax Office webpage *Apply for a TFN on the web* and follow the instructions. Otherwise, applicants may ring the TFN helpline on 13 28 61 or get the application form (NAT 1432) at www.ato.gov.au.

NOTE: Secondary school students can also apply for a TFN through the secondary schools tax file number program. The program is available through most public and private secondary schools around Australia.

Superannuation entities can apply for a TFN using the *ABN Registration for superannuation entities* form (NAT 2944), which also allows the entity to register for an ABN, for GST (if required) and to elect to be a regulated fund.

There is no compulsion to have a TFN, but if you don't, tax will be deducted at source at a flat 47% plus 2% Medicare levy (see from 5.000).

5.041 PROOF OF IDENTITY

Online applicants must attend an interview at Australia Post to present their proof of identity documents within 30 days. The applicant must supply documents as follows:

- **If they are aged 16 or over:** One category A and two different category B documents.
- **If they are under 16:** One category A and one category B document.

NOTE: If the documents are in a previous name you must provide a document that shows how your name was changed (eg. marriage certificate, deed poll, change of name certificate).

CATEGORY A DOCUMENTS

- Overseas passport with evidence of immigration status
- Certificate of Australian citizenship/extract from Registrar of Citizen by Descent
- Australian full birth certificate.

CATEGORY B DOCUMENTS

- Current Australian passport
- Medicare card
- Australian firearm licence
- Current Australian driver's licence or learner's permit with photo or current international driver's permit with photo

- One of these (if less than one year old); an account statement for a bank, a building society, credit union or finance company
- tertiary student identification card with photo and signature issued from an Australian government accredited education authority
- secondary student identification card with photo and signature issued from an Australian government accredited education authority.

NOTE: For under 16-year-olds only, category B documents can include one of the following which must be less than one year old and issued by an Australian government accredited education authority:

- secondary examination certificate
- record of achievement, and
- examination report.

NOTE: If an original document is in a language other than English, you must provide a certified translation.

NOTE: Non-residents living outside Australia requiring a TFN will need to complete a different TFN application form (NAT 2628) and will need to supply different documents as proof of identity.

Companies, partnerships and trusts can obtain a TFN at the same time as an Australian Business Number (ABN). Businesses can apply for these identifiers, as well as certain others, online at the Australian Business Register (ABR) website www.abr.gov.au. Otherwise, applications can be made through a registered tax agent or using a paper application form (NAT 2939).

NOTE: TFN applications for a deceased estate use a different form: NAT 3236.

Evidence of identity is required for a non-individual applicant. The evidence required differs depending upon the entity applying. The ABR manages the application for a TFN (and other registration including ABN) for non-individual entities. The ABR provides that generally an entity's existence can be authenticated when details of the individuals or associates behind the entity seeking registration have been provided and:

- those individuals or associates can be found on the ABR database or related government systems, or
- the Registrar is satisfied, after further enquiries, that the entity is real.

See the Tax Office website www.ato.gov.au or ABR website www.abr.gov.au for more information.

5.050   TAX FILE NUMBER PRIVACY RULES

Sections 8WA to 8WC of the TAA provide rules concerning offences relating to TFNs. The following privacy guidelines have been issued by the Privacy Commissioner to protect individuals by imposing stringent requirements on those authorised to collect and use TFN information. Details of the privacy rules, the role of the Privacy Commissioner and your rights can be obtained from www.privacy.gov.au

Taxpayers affected by a breach of privacy have the right to complain to the Privacy Commissioner (see 4.460) and, if appropriate, seek compensation. The penalty for a breach of the provisions set out in ss8WA to 8WC of the TAA is a fine of up to 100 penalty points (ie. $17,000, two years imprisonment, or both).

5.051   COLLECTING TFN INFORMATION

TFN information can only be requested for an authorised purpose and all reasonable steps must be taken to ensure the individual is informed:

- of the legal basis for collection
- that not quoting their TFN is not an offence
- of the consequences of not quoting their TFN, and
- that information will only be collected if necessary and relevant for taxation or other authorised purposes.

The collection of information must not unreasonably intrude upon a person's affairs.

5.052 LIMITED USE OF TFN

Tax file number information can only be used or disclosed for an authorised purpose. These guidelines are legally binding on the recipients of TFN information.

- The TFN is not to be used as a national identification system.
- Taxpayers have the right under tax law to choose not to quote their TFN.
- The TFN is not to be used to establish or confirm the identity of an individual for any purpose, or to match personal information (either directly or indirectly) about an individual except for these purposes:
  - Income tax law including Child Support and Higher Education Funding
  - Superannuation Industry (Supervision) legislation, and
  - Data-matching under the *Child Care Act 1972, Student and Youth Assistance Act 1973, Social Security Act 1991* and *Veterans' Entitlements Act 1986.*

If a person is required, or chooses to give information containing a TFN for a purpose not connected with the authorised collection of TFN information:

- that person can have their TFN removed, and
- the recipient must not record, use or disclose the TFN if it is not removed.

5.053 OBLIGATIONS ON THE TAX OFFICE & OTHER GOVERNMENT AGENCIES

Where practicable, the following information must be published in a generally available publication (eg. major daily newspaper) before any new circumstances arise when TFN information may be requested:

- persons or bodies authorised by law to request an individual to quote their TFN
- specific purposes for making that request, and
- prohibitions on collecting, recording, use and disclosure of TFN information.

Penalties apply to unauthorised acts and practices in relation to TFN information.

5.054 STORAGE, SECURITY AND DISPOSAL

Recipients of TFN information must ensure that:

- it is protected by reasonable security safeguards to prevent loss, unauthorised access, use, modification, disclosure or misuse, and
- access to records with TFN information is restricted, where practicable, to people specifically needing to use the information.

TFN recipients may dispose of TFN information which is no longer required (eg. of past employees) but only by appropriately secure means.

5.055 STAFF MUST KNOW PRIVACY RULES

Recipients of TFN information must take all reasonable steps in the circumstances:

- to make staff aware of the need to protect the privacy of an individual's TFN, and
- to inform staff collecting or having access to TFN information of:
  - how and when information may be collected
  - prohibitions on the use and disclosure of TFN information, and
  - penalties for breaching the privacy rules.

5.100   AUSTRALIAN BUSINESS NUMBER

The Australian Business Number (ABN) is a single business identifier which is available to State, Territory and local government bodies to facilitate single entry point arrangements for all government dealings. The ABN system is governed by *A New Tax System (Australian Business Number) Act 1999* (ABN Act).

5.110   PURPOSE OF THE ABN

It is not mandatory for a business entity to have an ABN, however an entity is required to have an ABN to register for GST (see from 23.000). An enterprise that is not registered with an ABN will expose itself to a PAYG withholding deduction of 46.5% in 2013-14 (47% from 1 July 2014) from the payment for goods and services provided to another enterprise (see 5.131).

An entity that is already registered with an ABN can seek to have its registration cancelled provided the Registrar is satisfied it is appropriate to do so. A registered entity can also seek to change the details held by the Registrar.

There are severe penalties for misuse of an ABN.

5.120   AUSTRALIAN BUSINESS REGISTER (ABR)

The following persons or entities are entitled to be registered with an ABN if they are carrying on an enterprise in Australia or, in the course of furtherance of carrying on an enterprise, you make supplies that are connected with Australia:

- individuals
- body corporates
- corporations
- a body politic
- unincorporated associations
- government entity
- non-profit sub-entity
- religious practitioners and religious institutions
- partnership (include general law and tax law partnership and limited partnership)
- trustee of a trust, and
- superannuation funds.

NOTE: A non-entity joint venture is not included within the meaning of the expression 'any other unincorporated association or body of persons', and is therefore not an entity and not entitled to an ABN (s184-1(1A) of the GST Act). A 'non-entity joint venture' is defined in s995-1 of the ITAA97 to mean an arrangement that the Registrar is satisfied is a contractual arrangement:

- under which two or more parties undertake an economic activity that is subject to the joint control of the parties, and
- that is entered into to obtain individual benefits for the parties, in the form of a share of the output of the arrangement rather than joint or collective profits for all the parties.

A Corporations Act company (a body registered as a company under the *Corporations Act 2001*) is entitled to an ABN, regardless of whether it is carrying on an enterprise. Where a person or entity has a number of different legal capacities (eg. a trustee of one or more trusts) they are entitled to be registered in each of those capacities. It is the entity, not the enterprise, that is entitled to an ABN. An entity may hold an ABN but carry on multiple enterprises.

An enterprise is defined at s9-20 of the GST Act as any of the following activities that are done:

- in the form of business
- in the form of an adventure or concern in the nature of trade
- on a regular basis (eg. leasing, licencing or other granting of an interest in property)
- by the trustee of a fund or institution to which deductible gifts can be made
- by an approved charitable organisation (Subdivision 30–B), or religious institution, or

- by the Commonwealth, a State or Territory, (or one of their agencies established for a public purpose).

The meaning of enterprise does not include activities performed:

- by employees or other PAYG earners
- as a private recreational pursuit or hobby
- by an individual or a partnership of individuals without a reasonable expectation of gain or profit, or
- a member of a local governing body (other than a local body that is accepted for PAYG purposes).

Miscellaneous Taxation Ruling MT 2006/1 sets out the Tax Office's view on the meaning of an entity carrying on an enterprise for the purposes of entitlement to an ABN.

The register is publicly available and can be accessed by any person at www.abr.gov.au. The information obtained from the register can only be used for approved purposes.

For each registered entity, the register must contain:

- legal name and ABN
- registered business name, or the name it uses for business purposes
- State/Territory and postcode of the principal place of business
- date of effect of registration
- address for the service of notices and the entity's email address
- the kind of entity which is being registered
- ANZSIC (Australian New Zealand Standard Industrial Classification) code (if applicable)
- ACN or ARBN
- name of public officer or trustee (if applicable)
- date of effect of any change to the entity's ABN (if applicable)
- ABN cancellation date (if applicable)
- date and effect of any GST registration or cancellation, and
- a statement that the entity is a deductible gift recipient (if applicable).

The above information may be inspected by the public.

The registered entity must advise the registrar of any change in details within 28 days and, if requested, must provide additional information that is relevant to the entity's entitlement to registration. The Registrar may also cancel an entity's registration if it is not satisfied as to the entity's identity or entitlement to an ABN. The Registrar has the right to refuse an application for registration, but must notify the applicant in writing of the reasons for doing so. The Registrar is required to notify the applicant within 28 days. If that does not occur, the applicant can request the Registrar to treat the application as having been denied. The applicant has the right to have a decision of the Registrar regarding its ABN registration reviewed by the Administrative Appeals Tribunal.

NOTE: In January 2015, the Government released the Board of Taxation's report on taxation impediments to the success and growth of small business (*Review of Tax Impediments Facing Small Business*). The Board recommended to the ATO that it revises MT 2006/1 and other guidance material to include activities which will evidence that an applicant is intending to carry on an enterprise and is therefore eligible for an ABN. Further, the Board recommended that the ATO provides a hotline for circumstances where it is important for an ABN application to be granted or rejected urgently..

5.130   WITHHOLDING WHERE ABN IS NOT QUOTED

Not supplying an ABN in certain circumstances, such as a business not quoting an ABN/TFN when making an investment in the course of an enterprise (see 5.315), a payer not quoting an ABN in relation to a supply (see 5.131), or not quoting an ABN in relation to a voluntary agreement (see 5.305), can result in PAYG withholding from a payment made for a supply.

The PAYG withholding system is a method by which tax is collected at the source of payment and is found in the TAA Schedule 1 Part 2-5. The payments subject to this type of tax normally comprise assessable income of the recipient. In some cases, payments can be alleviated if a recipient quotes their TFN or ABN to the payer beforehand.

Under PAYG arrangements, amounts deducted from payments made to payees as required by the PAYG withholding rules are called withholding payments. As noted above, withholding payments include payment for a supply where the recipient of the payment does not quote an ABN (s12-190 TAA).

5.131   SUPPLIER FAILS TO QUOTE ABN IN RESPECT OF A SUPPLY

This concerns transactions where the supplier does not quote an ABN in respect of the supply. The ABN needs to be quoted on their invoice or other document such as a contract or lease. It may also be in an electronic format, but whichever format is used, the document must relate to a supply made. The ABN of a supplier's agent may be used instead for supplies made through an agent.

Where PAYG withholding has been deducted because the payee has not quoted their ABN and the supply was a GST taxable supply, no input tax credit may be claimed in respect of that supply. If there has been a delay in the supplier being able to obtain an ABN, the payment may be delayed until an ABN can be quoted. Regular suppliers may provide a periodic quotation of their ABN (which should be checked by the payer at least once a year for correctness). Non-resident suppliers do not need to provide an ABN unless they have a permanent establishment in Australia – this includes having an agent or branch office in Australia.

PAYMENT SUMMARIES

The payer must complete a PAYG payment summary where an ABN is not quoted and provide a copy of the payment summary to the recipient of payments subject to PAYG withholding when making the payment, or as soon as practicable afterwards (s16-167 of TAA). The payment summary covers only that particular payment. Further, an annual report must be given to the Tax Office by 31 October after the end of a financial year, for payments including where the recipient has not quoted an ABN.

5.140   ABN WITHHOLDING EXCEPTIONS

PAYG withholding is not required in certain circumstances including where:

- the supplier (or their agent) quotes the ABN
- the total payment for the goods or services is $75 or less excluding any GST (from 1 July 2007)
- the payee has quoted an ABN but it subsequently proves to be incorrect and the payer had no reasonable grounds to assume it was incorrect
- the payment is made otherwise than in the course or furtherance of an enterprise carried on in Australia by the payer (eg. payment is of a private or domestic nature or payment by an employer to an employee)
- the payee is an individual and has given the payer a written statement that states that:
- the supply is made in the course or furtherance of an activity or series of activities done as a private or recreational pursuit or hobby, or
- the supply is wholly of a private or domestic nature and the payer has no reasonable grounds to believe that the statement is false or misleading
- the payment has already been taxed under another section (eg. where an amount has been withheld for failure to quote a TFN on investment income)
- the payment would be exempt (s12-140 or s12-145) even if the entity has not quoted their TFN or ABN, and
- the supply is wholly input taxed for GST purposes (TR 2002/9).

For more information on whether to withhold amounts from payment, see TR 2002/9. Further, if a supplier is not required to quote an ABN, they should complete a statement providing reasons for not quoting their ABN so that the payer does not withhold tax at 47% (plus 2% budget repair levy) on payment made. This statement (NAT 3346) can be downloaded from www.ato.gov.au.

5.150   PAYER'S OBLIGATIONS

A payer needs to determine whether they are obliged to make a PAYG withholding.

ABN VERIFICATION

Every purchaser (who is generally the payer of the withholding payment) is required to verify:

- the supplier's ABN before making a payment, and
- that the ABN quoted by the supplier is the same as the ABN entered in the Australian Business Register for that supplier.

Verification generally only needs to be done once. However, where no further payments have been made for a period of two years or more, the supplier's ABN needs to be verified again. The penalty for failing to verify an ABN is 20 penalty points (or $3,600).

The onus is on the purchaser to prove they have verified the supplier's ABN. That may involve repeated reference to the ABN register to confirm whether an ABN has been altered, withdrawn or cancelled.

From 1 July 2012, businesses in the building and construction industry are required to report the total payments they make to each contractor for building and construction services each year (except for payments which have been the subject of tax withholding). You need to report these payments to the Australian Taxation Office on the Taxable payments annual report.

5.200   PAYG WITHHOLDING

The PAYG withholding system is a method by which tax is collected at the source of payment and is found in the *Taxation Administration Act 1953* (TAA) Schedule 1 Part 2-5 (s10-1 to s20-80). It operates by imposing upon the payers of certain amounts a requirement to withhold tax at certain published rates. The payments subject to this type of tax normally comprise assessable income of the recipient. In some cases, payments can be alleviated if a recipient quotes their Tax File Number or Australian Business Number to the payer beforehand.

5.210   WITHHOLDING PAYMENTS

Under PAYG arrangements, amounts deducted from payments made to payees as required by the PAYG withholding rules are called withholding payments. The following payments are subject to PAYG withholding:

- Payment to an employee from salary, wages, commissions, bonuses or allowance paid (excluding living-away-from-home allowance that is subject to FBT) to an individual as an employee (s12-35)
- Payment of a company director (s12-40)
- Payment of salary to an office-holder (s12-45)
- Payment to a religious practitioner (s12-47)
- Return to work payment to an individual (s12-50)
- Payments under voluntary agreement (s12-55)
- Payment under labour hire arrangements (s12-60)
- Payment of a pension or annuity (s12-80)
- Superannuation lump sums and employment termination payments (s12-85)
- Payment for unused leave on retirement or termination of employment (s12-90)
- Social security payments (s12-110)
- Commonwealth education or training payments (s12-115)
- Payment of compensation or for sickness or accident (s12-120)
- Payment from investments where a tax file number or (in certain cases) ABN not quoted (s12-140)

- Payment to an investor being presently entitled to income of a unit trust (s12-145)
- Payment for a supply where the recipient does not quote ABN (s12-190)
- Dividend payment to overseas persons (s12-210)
- Dividend payment received for a foreign resident (s12-215)
- Interest payment to an overseas person (s12-245)
- Interest payment received for a foreign resident (s12-250)
- Interest payment derived by a lender in carrying on business via an overseas permanent establishment (s12-255)
- Royalty payment to an overseas person (s12-280)
- Royalty payment received for a foreign resident (s12-285)
- A Departing Australia Superannuation Payment (DASP) (s12-305)
- An excess untaxed rollover amount (s102-312)
- Certain payments made to foreign residents (s12-315) or received for foreign residents (s12-317)
- Mining payment (s12-320)
- Natural resource payment (s12-325)
- Payment by a managed investment trust (s12-385)
- Payment by an intermediary (s12-390)
- Alienated personal services payment by personal services entity (s13-5(1))
- Non-cash benefits (s14-5(1))
- An exempt expense payment benefit (s136 and s22, FBTAA) that is the reimbursement of car expenses on basis of distance traveled (s12-1(3)).

 If more than one provision would require withholding, the provision most specific to the payment will prevail. Any payment that is not assessable or is exempt income in the hands of the recipient does not require the withholding of any PAYG withholding tax.

5.300   TYPES OF WITHHOLDING

The following types of payments are subject to the PAYG withholding rules.

5.301   PAYMENTS TO EMPLOYEES (s12-35 TAA)

An entity must withhold an amount from salary, wages, commission, bonuses or allowances it pays to an individual as an employee. This applies to common law employees only. Under the PAYG withholding system, a payer is only required to deduct amounts paid to an employee.

Payments made to contractors are only subject to PAYG withholding where they specifically fall under one of the payment types caught for PAYG withholding.

A person is an 'employee' if work is performed under the direction and control of the owner/operator or the principal contractor. This type of contractual relationship that exists is that of a 'contract **of** service'. This relationship differs from that with an independent contractor which involves a 'contract **for** services' (TR 2005/16).

In order to determine whether there is a PAYG withholding obligations for payment to employees, the payer must first consider the various indicators in order to distinguish whether the contractual relationship is a 'contract of service' (payment to employee) or a 'contract for services' (payment to independent contractor). No one indicator on its own can determine the nature of the relationship. Further, the terms of a contract cannot alter the true substance of the underlying reality.

Most allowances are within the salary or wages definition and are subject to PAYG withholding. However, an allowance that is a living away from home allowance or expense payment benefit that is subject to FBT will not be subject to PAYG withholding.

CONTROL TEST

This has traditionally been a very important factor in determining whether a person was an employee. However, while it is an important determinant of an employment relationship, it should not be a sole indicator. Other indicators should also be taken into consideration in order to determine whether the employment relationship is that of an employee or an independent contractor. Does a master-servant relationship exist? The right to control how, where, when and who is to carry out the work in question points very strongly to employee status. The greater the obligation on the person performing the work to obey the orders of the principal on how the work is to be done, the greater the implication that the person is an employee.

INTEGRATION TEST

This is used to decide if the person is performing services as an employee, or as a person in business on his or her own account. The person may not be an employee in the traditional sense but, in the way the work is performed, is effectively an employee.

A person may be caught by this test if:

- the relationship is a continuing one, or
- the individual's activities are restricted to providing service(s) to one principal, and/or
- the individual's activities are so inextricably integrated in the principal's business activities that any benefit arising from the individual's efforts would benefit the principal.

OTHER TESTS

Other factors to consider in determining whether the person is an employee or an independent contractor are:

- Results test – if the substance of the contract is to achieve a specified result, it is more likely the person is an independent contractor. In contracts to produce a result, payment is often made for a negotiated contract price (based on achieving a specified result), as opposed to an hourly rate.
- Delegation or subcontracting of work – there is a strong indication that the person is an independent contractor if the person is able to delegate/subcontract the work and is responsible in remunerating the replacement worker.
- Risk – generally independent contractors bear more risk compared to an employee.
- An individual who provides their own tools and equipment and incurs expenses is more likely to be an independent contractor.
- Right to hire or fire, rights to exclusive services of the person engaged, or the provision of benefits, eg. annual leave, sick leave or long service leave indicates that the person is more likely to be an employee.

PAYMENTS EXCLUDED

The following payments are excluded from PAYG withholding:

- a cash living away from home allowance (see 25.840) on which the employer is liable to pay FBT
- income derived by a person through a business or professional practice (not constituting salary or wages)
- payments to companies, trusts, partnerships, associations, clubs or other incorporated or unincorporated bodies
- payments made by householders for occasional services to persons not regarded as employees (eg. plumbers, electricians)
- an expense payment benefit under FBTAA (s136) that is not an exempt car expense payment benefit under s22 FBTAA
- an alienated personal services payment unless it is caught by Division 13, and
- payments of less than $210 per week for the 2011-12 financial year if made to taxpayers who quoted a TFN on their TFN declaration and have not claimed the general exemption for another job.

NOTE: Taxi operators do not have to deduct PAYG from payments made to their drivers as the relationship is one of bailment and not of employer/employee (*Deluxe Red and Yellow Cabs Co-operative (Trading) Society & Ors v FCT* 97 ATC 4770).

ANNUAL LEAVE LOADING

Some employees are entitled to annual leave loading (normally calculated at 17.5% of the person's annual leave entitlement).

From 1 July 2012, there is no longer a separate withholding scale in the tax tables for employees who are entitled to leave loading and they will no longer have higher withholding from every pay. These employees will now be taxed when the leave loading is paid.

Bob, who is paid weekly, earns $1,055 every week and is taking four weeks annual leave. He will receive a total payment of $4,220. As Bob has claimed the tax-free threshold, you refer to column 2 in the Weekly tax table for 2013 (NAT 1005).

The withholding amount for weekly earnings of $1,055 is $196.00

Multiply the withholding amount by the number of weeks leave: $196 x 4 = $784.00

The total amount to be withheld from the annual leave payment of $4,220 is $784.00

NOTE: This example is based on the figures in the Weekly tax table (NAT 1005) for payments made on or after 1 July 2012. Ensure that the applicable tax table when calculating the amount to be withheld is used.

NOTE: Lump sum payments of unused annual leave (including any annual leave loading) and long service leave are not payment of salary and wages under s12-35 Sch 1 TAA. It is instead covered under s12-90 Sch 1 TAA (see 5.312). Other payments that are employment termination payments are covered under s12-85 TAA (see 5.311).

SECOND JOB

A resident employee is entitled to claim the tax-free threshold for only one job. Second and subsequent jobs are taxed at the rate with 'no tax-free threshold' (see *No tax-free threshold* column in PAYG withholding schedules at 5.691).

It is advisable to claim the general exemption for the ongoing job with the highest remuneration.

PAYG deductions may not cover end of year tax liabilities where more than one job is involved, as the schedule rates do not account for the combined effect if a taxpayer has more than one job. If in doubt, check with your employer, or have additional PAYG deductions withheld.

BONUSES

The Tax Office has published a calculation sheet that explains how to determine the PAYG withholding attributable to bonuses. If the bonus relates to a specific period that relates to a single pay period, then it is simply added to the employee's normal gross salary for that period. If the bonus relates to more than one pay period, the amount of PAYG withholding is worked out in the following way (NAT 3348):

1. Use the withholding tax tables (see from 5.600) to work out the amount of PAYG withholding on the normal payment for the one pay period.
2. Divide the bonus by the number of pay periods it relates to, disregarding any cents. A nil answer to this step means there is no amount to withhold on the bonus.
3. Add the amount in Step 2 to the normal gross salary for a single period.
4. Use the tax tables to determine the amount to withhold on the combined payment and bonus.
5. Subtract the amount determined in Step 1 from the amount determined in Step 4.
6. Multiply the result by the number of pay periods to which the bonus relates.
7. Add result of Step 6 to Step 1.

If the bonus relates to a whole year or is a one-off payment not referrable to any pay period in a year, the period to be used is one year.

In the 2014-15 financial year, a taxpayer's normal weekly wage is $450. In that year, he receives a bonus of $800 relating to 4 weeks. Note he is not entitled to any leave loading and claimed the tax-free threshold from this payer.

1. *PAYG withholding on normal gross salary...* $24
2. *Bonus attributable to each pay period ($800/4 weeks).........................* $200
3. *Pay period's gross salary including portion of bonus ($450 + $200).......* $650
4. *PAYG withholding on combined amount..* $66
5. *PAYG attributable to bonus for a single pay period ($66 – $24)..............* $42
6. *PAYG withholding attributable to total bonus ($42 x 4 weeks)...............* $168
7. *PAYG withholding for the week when the bonus is paid ($168 + $24)..................* $192

OVERTIME

PAYG withholding is calculated on salary plus overtime as though that pay is normal income. If excessive tax is taken from overtime payments, any surplus will be refunded on the assessment. Overtime earnings increase the assumed level of continuing income, whereas an occasional higher pay period income may not lift annual income to the next tax bracket income level.

BACK PAYMENTS OF INCOME: PAYMENTS ON OR AFTER 1 JULY 2013

The amount of PAYG to be withheld from a back payment of income depends on the type of income, and the timeframe to which it relates. There are two methods of calculating PAYG withholding on back payments of income:

- **Method A** – used regardless of if the payment relates to the current or previous financial year.
- **Method B** – made up of two calculations, one for payments that relate to the current financial year, one for payments that relate to the previous financial year.

NOTE: Back payment of income may be entitled to 'Delayed income tax offset' – see 3.230.

If recipient has failed to provide the payer with their TFN, the rate of PAYG withholding is 46.5% (from 1 July 2014 this will be 47%) for a resident recipient and 45% for a non-resident.

METHOD A

1. Work out your payee's gross earnings excluding any additional payments for the current pay period. Ignore any cents.
2. Use the relevant tax table to find the amount to be withheld from your payee's gross earnings in step 1.
3. Add any additional payments to be made in the current pay period together and divide the total by the number of pay periods in the financial year (that is, 52 weekly pay periods, 26 fortnightly pay periods or 12 monthly pay periods). Ignore any cents.
4. Add the amount at step 3 to the gross earnings at step 1.
5. Use the relevant tax table to find the amount to be withheld from the amount at step 4.
6. Subtract the amount at step 2 from the amount at step 5.
7. Multiply the amount at step 6 by the number of pay periods used in step 3.
8. Multiply the additional payment being made in the current pay period by 46.5%.
9. Use the lesser amount of step 7 and step 8 for the withholding on the additional payment. Ignore any cents.
10. Work out total PAYG withholding for the current pay period by adding the withholding on the additional payment (step 9) to the withholding on the gross earnings (step 2).

METHOD B

I. CURRENT FINANCIAL YEAR

1. Work out how much of the back payment applied to each earlier pay period in the current financial year.

2. For the first affected pay period, add the back payment relevant to that period to the normal earnings previously paid to get total earnings for that period.

3. Use the relevant tax table to find the amount to be withheld from the total earnings for that period.

4. Subtract the amount previously withheld for the period from the amount at step 3.

5. repeat steps 2–4 for each pay period affected. Total the amounts calculated in step 4 for each pay period for the withholding on the back payment.

6. Use the relevant tax table to find the amount to be withheld from your payee's gross earnings (excluding additional payments) for the current pay period.

7. Work out the total PAYG withholding for the current pay period by adding the withholding on the back payment (step 5) to the withholding on the gross earnings (step 6).

II. PREVIOUS FINANCIAL YEAR

1. Calculate the 'average total earnings' paid to your payee over the current financial year to date. Ignore any cents.

2. Use the relevant tax table to find the amount to be withheld from the average total earnings in step 1.

3. Add all additional payments made in the current financial year if method B (ii) was used to calculate the withholding, to the additional payment in current pay. Then divide by the number of pay periods in the financial year (that is, 52 weekly pay periods, 26 fortnightly pay periods or 12 monthly pay periods). Ignore any cents.

4. Add the amount at step 3 to the average total earnings at step 1.

5. Use the relevant tax table to find the amount to be withheld from the amount at step 4.

6. Subtract the amount at step 2 from the amount at step 5.

7. multiply the amount in step 6 by the number of pay periods used in step 3. Subtract any amounts previously withheld from additional payments in the current financial year if method B (ii) was used, from the amount at step 7.

8. Multiply the additional payment being made in the current pay period by 46.5%.

9. Use the lesser amount of step 8 and step 9 for the withholding on the additional payment. Ignore any cents.

10. Use the relevant tax table to find the amount to be withheld from your payee's gross earnings (excluding additional payments) for the current pay period.

11. Work out the total PAYG withholding for this pay period by adding the withholding on the additional payment (step 10) to the withholding on the gross earnings (step 11).

NOTE: If you normally process payments in a pay period later than the work is performed, for example, overtime payments paid with a time lag of one pay period, they are not considered back payments. These payments are treated as part of the normal pay cycle when paid and withholding is calculated on total earnings for that period. An overtime payment is only be considered a back payment if it was meant to have been made in a prior pay period.

 The Tax Office has published NAT 3348 titled Tax table for back payments, commissions, bonuses and similar payments with more detailed information and examples of how these methods can be used.

5.302   COMPANY DIRECTORS (s12-40 TAA)

A company must withhold an amount from a payment (in the nature of remuneration: payment for services rendered) it makes to an individual:

- **if the company is incorporated:** to a director of the company, or as a person who performs the duties of a director, or

- **if the company is not incorporated:** to a member of the committee of management of the company or as a person who performs the duties of such a member.

5.303   OFFICE-HOLDERS (s12-45 TAA)

An amount is to be withheld on payments of salary, wages, commission, bonus or allowances to office-holders. This requirement applies to:

- members of Australian legislatures
- persons holding appointments under the Constitution or an Australian law
- members of the Defence Force or a Police Force
- persons who are otherwise in the service of the Commonwealth, a State or Territory, or
- members of a local governing body (where the body has resolved to be treated as an eligible local government body).

5.304   RETURN TO WORK PAYMENTS (s12-50 TAA)

A person may be provided with an inducement for the purpose of encouraging that person to resume working for an entity. The entity must withhold PAYG at 31.5% (rounded to the nearest whole dollar) from such a payment made to an individual. The payment is included in the individual's payment summary as salary/wages.

5.305   VOLUNTARY AGREEMENT TO WITHHOLD (s12-55 TAA)

This covers agreements between an entity and an individual worker which wholly or partly involve performance of work or services (whether or not performed by the individual) and not otherwise covered by the withholding system. For example, payment to an independent contractor that does not fall into any PAYG withholding categories such as non-quotation of ABN/TFN, payment that is a personal services income or payment under a labour hire arrangement, etc., can choose for tax to be withheld on that payment under a voluntary agreement to withhold.

For a voluntary agreement to exist, the worker must be an individual and:

- must have an ABN
- the agreement must be in an approved form and state that the payments made under the arrangement are subject to the voluntary agreement and must also state the worker's ABN
- each party must keep a copy of the agreement for five years after the last payment has been made to which the agreement relates, and
- either party may end the agreement by notification to the other in writing.

PAYG withholding is at a flat 20% or the amount notified by the Tax Office on the payee's instalment notice (whichever is the higher rate). If the instalment rate notified by the Tax Office is less than 20% then that Commissioner's rate can be used if both the payer and payee agree. If the payment includes GST, the withholding amount is calculated by multiplying the appropriate rate of withholding by the amount of payment excluding GST.

5.306   PAYMENT UNDER A LABOUR HIRE ARRANGEMENT (s12-60(1) TAA)

An entity conducting a business of providing staff to perform work for clients is required to withhold PAYG from the payments made to the individuals it provides to its clients.

The entity providing the staff does not agree to perform the work, as the nature of its agreement is merely to provide staff to perform duties as specified by the client of the labour hire firm. Withholding is imposed upon the labour hire firm regardless of whether the staff are employees or independent contractors to the labour hire firm.

A payment of reimbursement is when the payment compensates the recipient exactly for an actual expense already incurred. Payments of reimbursement made to workers under a labour hire arrangement may be exempt from withholding if:

- the expense incurred by the payee was related directly to the payee's work or services performed under the labour hire arrangement
- the deduction that is claimable in relation to the expense incurred must be at least equal to the amount of the reimbursement
- the payee has been advised to keep the necessary evidence to substantiate the deduction claim, and

- the amount and nature of the reimbursement is shown separately in the payer's accounting records.

Only the following allowances may be excluded from withholding under the labour hire arrangement:

- the payment of a per kilometre car allowance up to 5,000 business kilometres using the Tax Office's rates, and
- domestic and overseas travel allowances involving an overnight absence from payee's ordinary place of residence.

Note that for the above allowances to be excluded from withholding, the payee must be expected to incur deductible expenses at least equal to the amount of the allowance and have been advised to keep necessary written evidence to substantiate the claim. The payer must also show the above amount and nature of the allowance separately in its accounting records.

If the staff the labour hire firm provides are themselves working through an interposed entity (eg. a company, partnership, or trust) this would be regarded as an enterprise to enterprise supply. Under such circumstances, this type of PAYG withholding would not be applicable to the labour hire firm. However, as it is an enterprise to enterprise supply, an ABN would need to be quoted by the interposed entity to the labour hire firm, otherwise the labour hire firm will be required to withhold PAYG for failure to quote an ABN.

For GST purposes, the supply by the labour hire firm to its client is a taxable supply, as long as the criteria for a taxable supply are met. However, the supply by the individual worker to the labour hire firm and the labour hire firm's client is not a taxable supply if the worker's remuneration is subject to this PAYG withholding.

5.307   PAYMENT SPECIFIED BY REGULATIONS (s12-60(2) TAA)

There are certain payments that may come under PAYG withholding if it is specified by regulations. The purpose of this section is to provide flexibility to extend PAYG withholding to apply to types of payments for work and services that is not already considered to be under the withholding system.

The type of payments subject to PAYG withholding under the regulations (reg. 44 of the *Taxation Administration Regulations 1976*) are:

- payments for tutorial services provided for the Indigenous Tutorial Assistance Scheme (also known as ITAS) conducted by the Department of Education, Science and Training
- payments for translation and interpretation services provided for the Translating and Interpreting Service (also known as TIS) conducted by the Department of Immigration and Multicultural and Indigenous Affairs
- payments made under a contract to an individual engaged as a performing artist to perform in a promotional activity that is:
  - conducted in the presence of an audience, or
  - intended to be communicated to an audience by print or electronic media, or
  - for a film or tape, or
  - for a television or radio broadcast.

Tax is withheld at 20% on payments to resident performing artists in a promotional event in which a TFN was provided.

5.308   PERSONAL SERVICES INCOME (Division 13 TAA)

Personal services entities will have PAYG withholding obligations where they are unable to self-assess to exclude themselves from the operation of the Personal Services Income (PSI) rules, or alternatively, they have failed to obtain a Personal Services Business Determination from the Tax Office (see Chapter 16).

An entity that is caught by the personal services income rules will have additional PAYG obligations where they receive personal services income during any PAYG payment period and they have not paid the personal services income as salary or wages to the individual who performed those services.

The salary or wages must have been paid within 14 days of the end of the period. The amount in income that will be subject to PAYG withholding in the hands of the entity is called the attributed personal services income of the individual calculated using the legislative approach as follows:

The amount of personal services income for the period less any GST component less any permitted deductions less any amounts paid as salary or wages

The Commissioner has released Practice Statement PS LA 2003/6 to allow a personal services entity to use a simpler method to calculate the minimum personal services income payout that is subject to withholding, instead of using the above method. Under this alternative method, the minimum personal services payout must be equal to or greater than:

- 70%, or
- the net PSI percentage worked out based on previous income year,

applied on the gross PSI received (excluding GST) in the current PAYG payment period.

If a shortfall in withholding is as a result of applying the above method, the Commissioner will exercise discretion to remit any penalty incurred. For more information on how to use this method – see PS LA 2003/6 and NAT 3517.

NOTE: Income that is attributed to the individual is excluded from assessable income of the entity.

The personal services income paid promptly as salary/wages plus attributed personal services income (if any) should be included on Activity Statements at W1 and the withholding amount should be shown at W2.

John and Betty are directors of Spots Pty Ltd which provides John's services as a computer consultant to the Tax Office. For the quarter ended 31 October 2014, the following transactions occurred:

Consulting fees of $30,000 were received from the Tax Office for John's services.

Investment income of $5,000 was received.

Spots Pty Ltd paid John a salary of $19,000 and withheld PAYG of $108 (determined using the 2014-15 monthly PAYGW tax table – NAT 1007 (this table is also applicable to 2015-16)).

NOTE: John is not entitled to leave loading and claimed the tax-free threshold with Spots Pty Ltd.

Betty was paid a salary of $3,000 for paying the company's bills and answering phones, etc.

Spots Pty Ltd incurred other deductible expenses of $4,000 (excluding entity maintenance expenses) to generate the personal services income of John.

Entity maintenance expenses were $1,000.

Attributed personal service income:

Total personal services amount received by Spots Pty Ltd	*$30,000*
Less salary paid to John	*$19,000*
	$11,000
Less allowable deductions (excluding entity maintenance deductions)	*$4,000*
Attributed personal services income	***$7,000***
PAYG withholding on $22,000 ($19,000 + $3,000) – use monthly PAYGW table	***$828***
Less PAYG withholding already paid	*$108*
PAYG withholding on attributed personal services income	***$720***

NOTE: Salaries paid to associates, which includes spouses, will not be deductible where the associate does not perform principal work.

NOTE: Before entity maintenance deductions can contribute to the reduction, they are first exhausted against any income of the entity that is not personal services income. For the final PAYG payment period in an income year, this amount can be further reduced by the amount (if any) that entity maintenance deductions exceed other income for the year.

Entities affected by these rules are also required to:

- register for PAYG withholding
- provide the individual with an annual payment summary setting out the attributed personal services income and the amount withheld – **NOTE:** this form is different from the salary/wages payment summary, and
- complete an annual PAYG report which must be forwarded to the Tax Office by 14 August each year.

5.309 SUPERANNUATION INCOME STREAM OR ANNUITY (s12-80 TAA)

An entity may be required to withhold an amount from a payment it makes to an individual if the payment is a superannuation income stream within the meaning given by s307-70 of the ITAA97 or an annuity as defined in s995-1(1) of the ITAA97. A superannuation income stream broadly means a superannuation benefit that is paid as an income stream.

An annuity includes:

- an annuity within the meaning of the *Superannuation Industry (Supervision) Act 1993*, or
- a pension with the meaning of the *Retirement Savings Accounts Act 1997*.

The amount to withhold on payment of a superannuation income stream is dependent on the recipient's age (below age 60 or age 60 and over) and whether the payment comprises taxable or tax-free components.

The general rules of withholding for payment of a superannuation income stream are as follows:

- payments from a tax-free component regardless of the age of the recipient will not be subject to withholding
- payments made to taxpayers aged 60 and over will not be subject to withholding, except for payments from an untaxed element in which the recipient may be entitled to a 10% rebate, and
- payments from a taxable component made to taxpayers under the age of 60 will be subject to withholding and there may be an entitlement to a 15% superannuation rebate.

For more information on the calculation of PAYG withholding on payments from a superannuation income stream see NAT 70982. Also see Chapter 19 regarding the tax implications on a superannuation income stream.

5.310 SUPERANNUATION LUMP SUM PAYMENTS (s12-85(a) TAA)

The following lump sum payments from a superannuation fund, approved deposit fund, retirement savings account or any other superannuation product are subject to withholding:

- payments made to a person because they are a member of a superannuation fund, a depositer of an approved deposit fund, or a holder of a retirement savings account or any other superannuation product
- lump sum payments paid on the death of one person if paid to another person, and a payment when a superannuation pension is exchanged for a lump sum.

NOTE: Individuals who are suffering from a terminal medical condition can apply to receive their superannuation as a lump sum payment tax-free when paid from a complying superannuation plan.

In general, a superannuation lump sum payment is made up of two components – taxable and tax-free.

- the tax-free component is not subject to PAYG withholding, and
- the taxable component is subject to varying PAYG withholding rates and caps and is dependant on the type of payment and preservation age of the recipient.

For preservation age see table under *Employment termination payments* at 5.311.

No amount should be withheld where:

- taxable component of a superannuation lump sum benefit is paid to dependants (regardless of whether it is a taxed or untaxed element)
- superannuation lump sum benefit is less than $200
- superannuation lump sum benefit paid to terminally ill recipient
- the whole amount paid as a superannuation lump sum by a regulated superannuation fund, complying approved deposit fund or retirement savings account provider comprises the payee's entire benefit, and
- lump sum is paid to the trustee of a deceased estate.

NOTE: A superannuation fund must provide the payee with a PAYG payment summary within 14 days of making a superannuation lump sum payment. For more on superannuation lump sum payments see 19.600.

5.311   EMPLOYMENT TERMINATION PAYMENTS (s12-85(b) TAA)

Lump sum payments as the result of termination of employment are referred to as employment termination payments (ETPs) to a taxpayer and subject to PAYG withholding in relation to the income component table and preservation age.

Employment termination payments subject to withholding include:

- a payment in lieu of notice
- a payment for unused sick leave
- a payment for unused rostered days off
- a 'golden handshake'
- compensation for loss of employment
- compensation for wrongful dismissal (paid within 12 months)
- a redundancy payment or payment under an early retirement scheme that exceeds the tax-free limit for 2014-15 of $9,514 plus $4,758 for each year of completed service (for 2015-16 the tax-free limit is $9,780 plus $4,891 for each year of completed service)
- a payment for permanent disability (excluding compensation payment), and
- lump sum payments paid on the death of an employee.

Employment termination payments do not include:

- a payment for unused annual leave or unused long service leave (see 5.312), or
- the tax-free part of a genuine redundancy payment or an early retirement scheme payment – this payment is exempt from tax and therefore not subject to PAYG withholding.

PAYG withholding from employment termination payments is based on the type of payment, the age of the taxpayer and at varying rates of withholding (and caps) as shown in the following employment termination payment and preservation age tables.

NOTE: A payment from a superannuation fund is not an employment termination payment. Employment termination payments made after 1 July 2007 may not be contributed or rolled over into a superannuation fund.

LIFE BENEFIT EMPLOYMENT TERMINATION PAYMENTS

Any invalidity or pre-July 1983 amounts in a life benefit employment termination payment will form part of the tax-free component. The tax on any remaining, taxable component will depend on the recipient taxpayer's age, as shown in the following ETP and preservation age tables.

TRANSITIONAL TERMINATION PAYMENTS

Certain termination payments made under transitional arrangements may qualify as transitional termination payments (see 11.200).

Transitional termination payments may be rolled over into a superannuation fund if the payments are:

- contributed (in full or in part) to a super fund, or
- used (in full or in part) to buy a superannuation annuity before 1 July 2012.

If an individual taxpayer chooses to rollover a transitional termination payment into a superannuation fund it becomes a directed termination payment (see 11.200). When a directed termination payment is made on an individual taxpayer's behalf, the payment is tax-free and therefore not subject to PAYG withholding.

For transitional termination payments not rolled over into a superannuation fund, any invalidity or pre-July 1983 amounts that form part of a transitional termination payment are tax-free and not subject to PAYG withholding. The tax on any remaining, taxable component will depend on your age, as shown in the following ETP and preservation age tables and subject to withholding.

Employment termination payment table 2015-16			
Income component	Age of person at end of income year	Component subject to PAYG withholding*	Rate of withholding including Medicare levy
Life benefit ETP:	Under preservation age	Up to $195,000	32%
• taxable component	Preservation age & over	Up to $195,000	17%
	All ages	Above $195,000	49%
Death benefit ETP paid to non-dependants:	All ages	Up to $195,000	32%
• taxable component		Above $195,000	49%
Death benefit ETP paid to dependants:	All ages	Up to $195,000	Nil
• taxable component		Above $195,000	49%

* Depending on the type of ETP, the concessional tax treatment is limited to the smaller of the ETP cap and the whole of income cap. Amounts paid in excess of these caps are taxed at the top marginal rate (plus Medicare levy). The ETP cap amount for the 2015-16 income year is $195,000. This amount is indexed annually. The whole of income cap amount for the 2015-16 income year and future years is $180,000. This amount is not indexed. This cap is reduced by the other taxable payments that your employee receives in the income year; for example, salary or wages paid to the employee.

Where the ETP is paid to the trustee of a deceased estate, no amount should be withheld.

NOTE: From 1 July 2012 the whole-of-income cap of $180,000 was introduced to essentially means test the concessional taxation of ETP. Where the cap is exceeded, the ETP MYI will be taxed at marginal rates.

PRESERVATION AGE

The preservation age is determined by the date of birth of the employee to determine the rate and amount of PAYG withholding.

Date of birth	Preservation age	Date of birth	Preservation age
Before 1/7/60	55	1/7/62 – 30/6/63	58
1/7/60 – 30/6/61	56	1/7/63 – 30/6/64	59
1/7/61 – 30/6/62	57	After 30/6/64	60

EMPLOYMENT TERMINATION PAYMENT SUMMARY

Employers must provide the recipient of an ETP a *PAYG payment summary – employment termination payment* within 14 days of making the ETP.

5.312   PAYMENT FOR UNUSED ANNUAL LEAVE AND LONG SERVICE LEAVE
(s12-90 TAA)

Payments for unused annual leave and long service leave (LSL) are subject to PAYG withholding to the extent that it is included in an individual's assessable income.

ANNUAL LEAVE

Lump sum payments of annual leave and annual leave loading received on normal termination of employment, such as voluntary resignation, retirement or employment termination due to inefficiency, since 17 August 1993, are taxed this way:

- **Leave accrued before 18 August 1993:** PAYG withholding is deducted at 30% plus Medicare levy. These payments are shown at Label A on the taxpayer's payment summary (see 5.422).
- **Leave accrued after 17 August 1993:** PAYG withholding deducted at marginal tax rates (following the method statement and PAYGW tax table in 5.600) as if they were ordinary income (see following Example 1). These payments are shown as part of salary/wages on the taxpayer's payment summary.

Lump sum payments of annual leave and annual leave loading on termination of employment due to redundancy, invalidity or approved early retirement is subject to PAYG withholding at 30% plus Medicare levy. These payments are shown in Label A on the taxpayer's payment summary.

LONG SERVICE LEAVE

Lump sum payments of LSL on normal termination are split into three components and taxed as follows:

- Amount referable to service before 16 August 1978 (include amount in Label B of payment summary): *PAYG withholding on 5% of the total at marginal rate**
- Amount referable to service between 16 August 1978 and 17 August 1993 (include amount in Label A of payment summary): *PAYG withholding on the whole amount at 30% + Medicare levy*
- Amount referable to service after 17 August 1993 (include amount as salary/wages in payment summary): *PAYG withholding on the whole amount at marginal rate**

*PAYG withholding amount at marginal rate is calculated using PAYG withholding tax tables (see 5.691).

Lump sum payments of LSL on employment termination due to redundancy, invalidity or approved early retirement are split into three components and taxed in the following manner:

- Amount referable to service before 16 August 1978 (include amount in Label B of payment summary): *PAYG withholding on 5% of the total at marginal rate**
- Amount referable to service between 16 August 1978 and 17 August 1993 (include amount in Label A of payment summary): *PAYG withholding on the whole amount at 30% + Medicare levy*
- Amount referable to service after 17 August 1993 (include amount in Label A of payment summary): *PAYG withholding on the whole amount at 30% + Medicare levy*

* PAYG withholding amount at marginal rate is calculated using PAYG withholding tax tables (see 5.691).

EXAMPLE 1: Annual leave, leave loading and LSL

Barry, an employee with no dependants, resigns from his job on 1 August 2015 and receives a lump sum payout of $27,290 for accrued leave on top of his normal salary for the week of $700.

Accrued long service leave

Period referable to service:
- *before 16 August 1978 ....$12,000*
- *between 15/8/78 and 16/8/93..$13,170*
- *after 17 August 1993..$400*

Accrued annual leave: All referable to service after 17 August 1993............................$1,400

Accrued annual leave loading: All referable to service after 17 August 1993 .... $32

$27,290

Step 1. Calculate lump sum leave taxed at marginal tax rates

Annual leave referable to after 17 August 1993[1]...$1,400

Annual leave loading referable to after 17 August 1993 (over $320)[2] $0

Long service leave referable to after 17 August 1993[1]...$400

5% of long service leave referable to before 16 August 1978[3] ($12,000 x 5%).........$600

Total amount of leave taxed at marginal rates...$2,400

A. Divide total by number of pay periods in the year[5] $2,400/52.................................$46

B. Add A to normal earnings for the pay period ($700 + $46) $746

C. Calculate PAYG withholding on B (see PAYG withholding tax table in 5.691).........$94

D. PAYG withholding on normal earnings of $700
    (see PAYG withholding tax table in 5.691)..$80

E. Increase in tax for pay period (C – D)... $14

Tax on Step 1. = E x 52 (ie. the factor in A) $728

Step 2. Calculate lump sum leave taxed at 32% (max)
(if no service before 18 August 1993 go to Step 3)

Leave referable to before 18 August 1993:

Annual leave referable to before 18 August 1993[4].. $0

Annual leave loading referable to before 18 August 1993 (over $320)[2].................... $0

Long service leave referable to 16 Aug 1978-17 Aug 1993.............................. <u>$13,170</u>

Total amount of leave taxed at 32%.. $13,170

Tax on Step 2 at 32% **$4,214**

Step 3. Total PAYG withholding on lump sum leave

(Step 1 + Step 2 = $728 + $4,214).. $4,942

Add PAYG withholding on normal earnings from D... <u>$80</u>

Total PAYG withholding[6] **$5,022**

All lump sum leave paid to taxpayer due to redundancy, invalidity or early retirement accrued post-15 August 1978 is taxed at the maximum of 32% and shown at Label A of the payment summary. For LSL accrued pre-16 August 1978 PAYG is withheld at marginal rates on 5% of the payment and the whole of the pre-16 August 1978 LSL is shown at Label B on the payment summary.

EXAMPLE 2

Same facts as Example 1, except Barry is leaving due to a bona fide redundancy or approved early retirement.

Step 1. Calculate lump sum leave taxed at marginal tax rates

5% Long service leave referable to before 16 August 1978[3] ($12,000 x 5%).......... $600

A. Divide by number of pay periods in the year[5] ($600 / 52)..................... $12

B. Add A to normal earnings for the pay period ($700 + $12) $712

C. Calculate PAYG withholding on B (see PAYG withholding tax table in 5.691)...... $82

D. PAYG withholding on normal earnings of $700

    (see PAYG withholding tax table in 5.691) $80

E. Increase in tax for pay period (C – D).. <u>$2</u>

Tax on Step 1 = E x 52 (ie. the factor in A) **$104**

Step 2. Calculate lump sum leave taxed at 32%

All annual leave $1,400

All annual leave loading over $320[2] $0

Long service leave referable to after 15 Aug 1978 ($13,170 + $400)................ $13,570

Total amount of leave taxed at 32%[4]... **$14,970**

32% tax on total of Step 2. .... **$4,790**

Step 3. Total PAYG withholding on lump sum leave

(Step 1 + Step 2 = $104 + $4,790)... $4,894

Add PAYG withholding on normal earnings from D.. <u>$80</u>

Total PAYG withholding[6] **$4,974**

1: Total must be included in gross payments in the employee's payment summary.

2: Annual leave loading is included in PAYG withholding deducted from salary or wages.

3: Show the whole amount at Label B on employee's payment summary.

4: Show whole amount at Label A on the employee's payment summary.

5: 52 if paid weekly, 26 if paid fortnightly, 12 if paid monthly.

6: Round PAYG withholding up to nearest whole dollar if 50c or more if 1c to 49c round down.

5.313   SOCIAL SECURITY OR OTHER BENEFIT PAYMENTS (ss12-110 & 12-115 TAA)

This includes payments such as:

- social security payments
- veteran's affairs payments such as the age service pension and disability service payments

- occupational superannuation payments
- educational entry payments
- Commonwealth education or training payment, and
- Austudy or Abstudy.

NOTE: There is no withholding if the social security or other benefit payments are exempt from tax.

NOTE: The Tax Office has released a special PAYG tax table for aged pensioners and low income aged persons (senior Australians). This table can be downloaded from www.ato.gov.au – NAT 4466.

5.314   COMPENSATION, SICKNESS OR ACCIDENT PAYMENT (s12-120 Sch 1 TAA)

PAYG withholding applies where the payment is made to an individual because of that or another individual's incapacity for work where the payment is calculated at a periodical rate and is not made under an insurance policy to the owner of the policy.

5.315   TFN/ABN NOT QUOTED IN RESPECT OF AN INVESTMENT
(ss12-140 – 12-170 Sch 1 TAA)

The payer must withhold tax at 47% plus 2% Temporary Budget Repair Levy for a resident payee and 45% plus 2% Temporary Budget Repair Levy for a non-resident payee where some or all the payment is in respect to certain type of investment (see 5.020 and 5.130) and the payment is ordinary income or statutory income of the recipient. However there is no requirement to withhold if the following conditions apply:

- the investment is not transferable, the payee quotes its TFN in connection with the investment before the payment becomes payable
- the investment is transferable, the payee quotes its TFN in connection with the investment before it had to be registered with the investment body as the original investor is entitled to the payment
- the payee has not quoted a TFN but has quoted an ABN and the investment has been made in the course of furtherance of an enterprise
- there was an exemption from quoting the TFN by the payee and that exemption no longer applies but the payer is unaware of this
- the payment are fully franked dividends
- the payment is less than an amount set out in the regulations (*Taxation Administration Regulations 1976* Reg. 36) – that is $420 if the recipient is aged under 16 and $120 for all other recipients, and
- special rules may be used for investments which are units in a unit trust (s12-145). These rules apply where the investor becomes presently entitled to a part of the income of the trust before the investor is actually paid any of the income.

NOTE: TFN withholding also extends to arrangements to closely-held trusts, including family trusts, to ensure that assessable distributions to beneficiaries, as disclosed in the trust's income tax return, aligns with the amounts returned as assessable income by those beneficiaries. Withholding does not apply where the beneficiary has provided their TFN to the trustee or where tax is assessed to the trustee on behalf of a beneficiary (eg. minor beneficiary). Where applicable, the amount that needs to be withheld by the trustee (where a TFN has not been quoted) is 47% plus 2% Temporary Budget Repair Levy.

5.316   SUPPLIER (RECIPIENT OF THE PAYMENT) FAILS TO QUOTE ABN
IN RESPECT OF A SUPPLY (s12-190 TAA)

Generally, a supplier (recipient of the payment) needs to quote their ABN (or their agent's ABN) in respect of a supply made in the course or furtherance of the enterprise carried on in Australia by the supplier. The ABN needs to be quoted on their invoice or other document such as an order form, contract or lease, catalogue or promotional material, renewal notice or quotation, and can also be in an electronic format. Whichever format is used, the document must relate to the supply made.

Where the supplier does not quote an ABN and the total payment for the goods or services excluding GST is more than $75, the payer must deduct PAYG withholding at 47% plus 2% budget repair levy from the payment.

Where PAYG withholding has been deducted because the payee has not quoted their ABN and the supply was a GST taxable supply, no input tax credit may be claimed in respect of that supply.

For more information on withholding where a supplier fails to quote their ABN in respect of a supply and also exceptions to quoting an ABN in respect of a supply see 5.131.

 Religious practitioners will not be entitled to apply for (or quote) an ABN (or to register for GST) in respect of their religious activities. These activities performed by a religious practitioner in pursuit of his or her vocation and as a member of a religious institution, not done as an employee or agent, are taken to be the activities of the religious institution (and not activities of the religious practitioner) (MT 2006/1). The normal PAYG withholding rules that apply to employees will apply (s12-47 TAA).

5.317 DIVIDEND, INTEREST & ROYALTY PAYMENTS TO OVERSEAS PERSONS (ss12-210, 12-245 and 12-280 Sch 1 TAA)

An Australian resident company must withhold an amount from a dividend it pays if:

- the entity or any of the entities holding the shares on which the dividend is paid has an address outside Australia, or
- any of the entities holding the shares has authorised the company to pay the dividend to an entity or entities to a place outside Australia.

An Australian resident company must withhold an amount from interest or royalty it pays if:

- the recipient or any of the recipients has an address outside Australia, or
- the recipient or any of the recipients has authorised the company to pay the interest or royalty to a place outside Australia.

A payer does not have to withhold an amount from a dividend, interest or royalty if no withholding tax is payable in respect of it under s128B ITAA36 (s12-300(a) Sch 1 TAA). Further, a payer does not need to withhold more than the withholding tax payable (s12-300(b) Sch 1 TAA). See 22.140.

5.318 DIVIDEND, INTEREST OR ROYALTY PAYMENTS RECEIVED FOR FOREIGN RESIDENTS (ss12-215, 12-250 and 12-285 Sch 1 TAA)

A person in Australia or an Australian government agency must withhold from a dividend, interest or royalty received from an Australian resident company, where a foreign resident is entitled to any part of the dividend.

5.319 INTEREST PAYMENT DERIVED BY LENDER CARRYING ON BUSINESS THROUGH OVERSEAS PERMANENT ESTABLISHMENT (ss12-255 and 12-260 Sch 1 TAA)

An Australian resident (or Australian government agency) which derives interest income from carrying on a business at or through a permanent establishment in an overseas country and which the interest is payable in Australia is required to withhold an amount from that interest.

The payee (entity which derives the interest) must notify the payer in writing that withholding applies to the interest prior to entering into a transaction to derive that interest or within one month afterwards.

The Commissioner must be notified of the particulars of the transaction and the day when the notice is given to the payer immediately after the notice is given to the payer.

5.320   NON-CASH BENEFITS (Division 14 TAA)

The payer must pay the same amount of PAYG to the Tax Office before providing a non-cash benefit to the recipient if PAYG would have been required to be withheld from an amount had that payment been in the form of money. This is calculated on the market value of the non-cash benefit when it is provided. However, no PAYG is withheld if the benefit is a:

- fringe benefit or an exempt fringe benefit, or
- share or right acquired under an employee share scheme.

5.321   DEPARTING AUSTRALIA SUPERANNUATION PAYMENT
(ss12-305 & 12-310 TAA)

For full details on Departing Australia Superannuation Payments (DASPs) see 19.670.

Under Australia's Superannuation Guarantee (SG) system, Eligible Temporary Resident Visa (ETRV) holders who work in Australia will generally have superannuation contributions paid into a complying superannuation fund or Retirement Savings Account (RSA) on their behalf by their employers.

Some ETRV holders who have worked in Australia may be entitled to receive their superannuation benefits after they leave Australia in the form of a DASP.

A DASP can only be received by a person who:

- has worked in Australia while visiting on an ETRV
- has a visa that has either expired or been cancelled, and
- has permanently departed Australia.

Where a DASP is paid in accordance with the applicable regulations, it will be subject to withholding. A payer will not have to withhold an amount if no withholding tax is payable in respect of the DASP or to withhold more than the withholding tax payable in respect of the DASP.

The DASP is subject to a final PAYG withholding tax at rates in accordance with the *Superannuation (Departing Australia Superannuation Payments Tax) Act 2007*. The superannuation fund or RSA provider will determine which rate applies.

For DASP applications made prior to 1 April 2009, the rates of withholding tax are as follows:

- 0% for tax-free component
- 30% for the taxed taxable component, and
- 40% for the untaxed taxable component.

For DASP applications made on or after 1 April 2009, the various rates of withholding tax are as follows:

- 0% for tax-free component
- 35% for the taxed taxable component, and
- 45% for the untaxed taxable component.

NOTE: It is the DASP application date and not when the payment is made that determines whether to use rates prior to 1 April 2009, or rates on or after 1 April 2009.

REPORTING OBLIGATIONS

Superannuation funds and RSA providers that remit DASPs are required to report amounts withheld on an annual basis to the Tax Office. Funds must lodge their DASP reports electronically by the 31 October following the end of the financial year in which the payment was made (s16-153(1) TAA). If DASP data records are reported as part of the PAYGW payment summary annual report, funds must lodge the payment summary report by the 14 August (s16-153(2) Sch 1 TAA). In addition, a payment summary must be provided to the payee and the Tax Office within 14 days of the DASP being made (s16-166 Sch 1 TAA).

Payers who are required to pay a penalty for failing to withhold tax may recover the penalty from the individual payee concerned (s16-195(aa) Sch 1 TAA).

Crediting arrangements that normally apply in relation to PAYG withheld amounts will also apply in relation to amounts withheld from DASPs (s18-42 Sch 1 TAA).

5.400 PAYERS' OBLIGATIONS AND OTHER MATTERS

A payer making a withholding payment (see 5.210) will be required to withhold tax from the payment and remit to the Tax Office. The payer will also have other obligations in regards to PAYG withholding, such as registration and reporting obligations (see 5.420).

A payee should complete a tax or withholding declaration if receiving a withholding payment to avoid tax being withheld at the top marginal rate. The payee may vary amounts of withholding upwards or downwards depending on their circumstances (see 5.412).

5.410 DECLARATIONS AND PAYG WITHHOLDING VARIATION

5.411   TFN AND WITHHOLDING DECLARATIONS

Those who choose not to give a TFN declaration are subject to PAYG withholding on income at the top marginal rate. A TFN declaration must be forwarded to the Commissioner within 14 days after being given to the payer (see 5.000).

If a TFN declaration is not given to the payer by the recipient, the payer must notify the Tax Office of the information they hold about the recipient within 14 days of entering a relationship with that payee.

Employees are entitled to claim the tax-free threshold from only one employer at a time. If that were not done, total instalments would be insufficient to cover the year's total tax. For the same reason, tax rebates should be claimed on only one form at a time.

Taxpayers who claim the tax-free threshold, family tax benefit or tax offset (eg. dependant or zone tax offset) from more than one employer can be fined or prosecuted (see from 5.660).

A withholding declaration or a new TFN declaration should be completed when any of the following apply:

- work is started with a new employer
- entitlement to a tax offset or family tax benefit starts or finishes
- Higher Education Loan Program (HELP) debt is accumulated or repaid
- details on the completed TFN declaration are incorrect, or
- the Tax Office announces publicly that all or some declarations are no longer in force.

TFN and withholding declarations are available from any Post Office or the Tax Office or at www.ato.gov.au.

5.412   REDUCING THE PAYG WITHHOLDING AMOUNT

In special circumstances the Commissioner may vary PAYG withheld under s15-15 Sch 1 TAA. An example is where the regular withholding rate will result in a large tax credit due to large deductions.

A PAYG withholding reduction applies only for that income year.

An application for variation of amounts to be withheld under PAYG withholding must be lodged with the Tax Office.

This application requires a great deal of information and is only worth completing if there is a large tax credit involved, or you have cash flow problems.

You are required to list expected income from all sources, and estimate the various expense claims. A new application must be made each income year. You can download this form at www.ato.gov.au. For upward variation (eg. due to HECS or SFSS debt), download form NAT 5367. For downward variation (eg. due to negatively geared investments, high level of deductions, etc.), download form NAT 2036.

There are also other short application forms available on the Tax Office's website for variation in relation to entitlement to the Senior Australians and Pensioner Tax Offset, changes to HECS/SFSS debt, etc.

 An employee (or contract worker) works in one job on average eight days each month, and for another employer for three days each month. PAYG tax withheld on the income from the second job would be much higher than needed when added to the low average income from the first job. The employee can apply for a PAYG withholding reduction to have smaller amounts deducted from one (or both) of the employment sources.

PAYG WITHHOLDING VARIATION OF SUPERANNUATION INCOME STREAMS

Reduced rates of PAYG withholding can apply to payments from a taxed element of a superannuation income stream made to a taxpayer who is 59 years of age and will turn 60 in the financial year in which the payment is made.

The variation can be made due to a Legislative Instrument, *F2007L01787 Taxation Administration Act – variation to the rate of withholding for certain superannuation income stream beneficiaries who turn 60 during the financial year.* This ensures superannuation beneficiaries are not subject to excessive PAYG withholding in the year they turn 60 years of age.

5.420 PAYERS' OBLIGATIONS

Once a payment comes within the withholding rules, certain obligations apply to the payer (Div 16 Sch 1 TAA).

The payer must:
- register as a PAYG withholding payer
- withhold an amount from the payment at the required rate:
  - rounded to the nearest dollar (round 50c up) if a TFN is quoted,
  - ignoring cents when a TFN is not quoted
- give notice to the Tax Office of the amount withheld (and remit that amount to the Tax Office) by the required due date, and
- report to the Tax Office and the recipient, the amount of the payment and the amount withheld.

5.421 REGISTRATION

Entities that are required to withhold an amount are required to apply to be registered for PAYG withholding with the Commissioner in an approved form by the day on which the entity is required to withhold an amount (s16-140 Sch 1 TAA). Failure to register will incur an administrative penalty of 5 penalty units ($900).

If a taxpayer already has an ABN, the taxpayer can register for a PAYG withholding account online via the Business Portal, by phoning the Tax Office (13 28 66) or by completing a paper form NAT 2954 (order from www.ato.gov.au or by phoning 1300 720 092). You may register for PAYG withholding when you apply for an ABN. Taxpayers that are required to withhold but not required to have an ABN can register for PAYG withholding by completing the form NAT 3377.

5.422 PAYMENT SUMMARIES

The payer must provide a payment summary and a copy of the payment summary to the recipient of payments subject to PAYG withholding within 14 days of the end of the financial year (ie. normally by 14 July) if, during the income year:
- the payer made one or more withholding payments, other than:
  - superannuation lump sum or employment termination payments
  - dividend, interest or royalty payments received for a foreign resident
  - payment of a kind specified in the regulations received for a foreign resident
  - payment by a managed investment trust or an intermediary, or

- the payer received dividend, interest, royalty payment or a payment of a kind specified in the regulation received for a foreign resident, or
- payer receives personal services income that was promptly paid as salary/wages or is attributed personal services income to the person rendering the services, or
- the recipient received a reportable fringe benefits amount of more than $2,000 (ie. grossed-up amount of at least $3,740; see from 25.300).

A payment summary (and a copy) must be provided to the recipient of the following payments within 14 days of making the payments:

- superannuation lump sum payments
- employment termination payments, and
- departing Australia superannuation payment.

Further, a payment summary must be provided to recipient who does not quote their ABN at the time the payment is made or as soon as practicable afterwards. The payment summary must only cover the relevant payment.

A managed investment trust or intermediary which withholds an amount from a payment under s12-385 or s12-390 Sch 1 TAA is required to provide the payee with a payment summary not later than 14 days after the end of six months of the trust's or intermediary's income year (or a later time allowed by the Commissioner).

 Where an employee ceases employment during the year then the employer is required to provide that employee with a payment summary within 14 days of ceasing that employment if requested to do so.

Employees are required to lodge an income tax return with the Tax Office based on information contained in that payment summary and other assessable income.

5.423   ANNUAL REPORTS

An annual report must be given to the Tax Office by 31 October after the end of a financial year, for the following payments or non cash benefits:

- where the recipient has not quoted an ABN
- dividends, interest or royalties paid to or received on behalf of a non-resident
- departing Australia superannuation payments
- payments to a foreign resident, and
- mining or natural resource payment.

 Companies must lodge details of dividends and interest paid usually by 31 October each income year. Lodgment penalties will apply if statements are not lodged on time (see 4.650).

An annual report must be made to the Tax Office by 14 August after the end of the financial year, for the following payments or non cash benefits:

- payments for work and services, including salary and wages, return to work payments, voluntary agreements to withhold, payments under labour hire arrangements
- attributed personal services income
- superannuation payments and annuities
- retirement payments including accrued annual leave and long service leave
- employment termination payments
- benefits and compensation payments, and
- reportable fringe benefits in relation to employment for the income year.

5.424   REMITTING PAYGW AMOUNT TO THE TAX OFFICE

The due date for the remittance of PAYG withholding depends on the withholder's classification, and in some cases, whether it is a 'deferred BAS payer'.

DEFERRED BAS PAYER

A 'deferred BAS payer' is an entity that is **not**:
- one that has to lodge monthly GST returns, or
- one who only has to report either or both of the following amounts on their BAS:
  - an amount of PAYG withholding because they are either a medium or large withholder, or
  - an annual PAYG instalment.

An entity that meets the above criteria is called a 'non-deferred BAS payer'. This means unless an entity is GST registered with monthly tax periods, it is possible for an entity's status as a deferred or non-deferred BAS payer to change each month. This can arise if an entity has only a PAYG withholding obligation to report for a particular month (making it a non-deferred BAS payer), but in another month it has a PAYG withholding and a GST quarterly obligation to report (making it a deferred BAS payer).

A GST registered enterprise with quarterly tax periods is a medium withholder. For the month of May, it only has to report its PAYG withholding to the Tax Office. This means it is a non-deferred BAS payer, and will have to report and remit the PAYG withholding by 21 June. However, for June, it has the following to report:
- *a PAYG withholding for June, and*
- *a GST net amount in respect of its GST tax period ending on 30th June.*

As the enterprise has more than just its PAYG withholding to report to the Tax Office, it is a deferred BAS payer for June. Therefore, it needs to report and remit its total obligation to the Tax Office by 28 July.

LARGE WITHHOLDERS

An organisation is a large withholder for a particular month if:
- it withheld more than $1m PAYG withholding for the 12 months ending at least two months before the current month, or
- it was a large withholder in June 2001, or
- it was a member of a wholly-owned group and the amount withheld by the group for the 12 months ending at least two months before the current month exceeds $1m, or
- the Commissioner determines it to be a large withholder.

Large withholders must pay electronically (s16-85 TAA). Failure to do so means they will be liable to an administrative penalty of five penalty points (ie. $550) for each payment (s288-20 TAA).

A large withholder must remit their PAYG withholding as per this schedule:

Large withholders: Day of week withheld	Remit by
Saturday or Sunday	Second Monday after that day
Monday or Tuesday	The following Monday
Wednesday	Second Thursday after that day
Thursday or Friday	The following Thursday

The Tax Office will allow a large withholder to defer remitting irregular small amounts withheld until their next regular remittance day. Examples of these irregular amounts include minor ETPs, a supplier's failure to quote an ABN, or a casual's wages. The irregular amount needs to be 'small' and the Tax Office has defined this to mean an amount of PAYG withholding that does not exceed the lesser of 0.5% of the previous year's withholdings or $50,000. If the irregular amount exceeds this threshold, its remittance is not extended without a written extension from the Tax Office.

MEDIUM WITHHOLDERS

An organisation is a medium withholder for a particular month if it is not a large withholder and:
- it was a medium withholder in June 2001, or
- it withheld more than $25,000 for the 12 months ending before the current month, or
- the Commissioner determines it to be a medium withholder.

Medium withholders must remit PAYG withholding on the dates shown below.

Medium withholder	Month of withholding	Remit by
Deferred BAS payers	September, March, June	28th day of the following month
	December	Following 28 February
Non-deferred BAS payers	All months	21st day of the month after withholding month

SMALL WITHHOLDERS

All organisations that have at least withheld an amount during the month and are neither large nor medium withholders are small withholders. Small withholders must remit PAYG withholding on the dates shown below.

Small withholder	Amount withheld during quarter ending	Remit by
Deferred BAS payer	30 September	Following 28 October
	31 December	Following 28 February
	31 March	Following 28 April
	30 June	Following 28 July
Non-deferred BAS payer	All months	21st day of the month after withholding quarter

GAZETTED PUBLIC HOLIDAYS

All tax debts payable and notifications due on gazetted public holidays are extended to the next business day for all taxpayers regardless of where the taxpayer is located.

AMOUNT WITHHELD

The amounts required to be withheld from payments will vary according to the type of payment. Generally, the amounts to be withheld are set out in the PAYG withholding schedule (see 5.691). This amount may vary due to payees (recipients) circumstances such as HELP/SFSS debt, entitlement to certain tax offsets or an entitlement to a reduction in Medicare levy (see 5.600).

Special rates or special calculation methods may apply for certain payments such as return to work payments, voluntary agreement to withhold payments, superannuation lump sum, employment termination payment etc. For payments that are subject to special rates or calculation, see from 5.300. If a type of payment is subject to special rates, it will be specified under each of the type of payments.

5.425   REFUND OF AMOUNT INCORRECTLY WITHHELD

A payer may be required to refund a recipient for amounts withheld (s18-65 TAA). This may occur when amounts have been wrongly withheld. The requirement for the payer to refund the amount withheld to the recipient may not apply if:

- the payer did not become aware of the error or the recipient did not apply to the payer for the refund before the end of 21 July in the financial year after the one in which the amount was withheld incorrectly, and
- the amount withheld has already been remitted to the Commissioner.

In this case, the recipient may apply to the Commissioner for a refund (s18-70 TAA).

5.426   PENALTIES

There are penalties for not notifying the Tax Office of amounts withheld and for not remitting those amounts by the due date (see from 4.660). Other fines and penalties can also be imposed by the Court for various offences (see from 4.680). The current penalty arrangements for late payment and other obligations are based on a uniform tax-deductible general interest charge (GIC) aligned with market rates (see 4.660). The GIC is worked out daily on a compounding basis and applies from the time an unpaid amount is due to be paid.

The following are the main offences and penalties in connection with PAYG withholding obligations:

Offences	Penalty units
Failure to register	5
Failure to withhold an amount required by Div 12, 13 or 14 of Sch 1 TAA	10
Failure to provide a payment summary	20
Failure by a large withholder to remit electronically	5

Failure to lodge either an activity statement or an annual withholding summary incurs a penalty of one penalty unit for each 28 day period (or part thereof) the lodgement is outstanding to a maximum of five units.

Except for small withholders, the penalty amount also depends on the entity's PAYG classification. Large withholders will incur five times the penalty accrued. Medium withholders incur double the penalty accrued.

NOTE: Each penalty unit is equal to $180.

Failure to pay withheld amounts within the required time will result in GIC on the unpaid amount for each day starting from the day when the unpaid amount is due until the end of which any of the following amount remains unpaid:

- the unpaid amount, and
- GIC on any of the unpaid amount.

NOTE: The due date for payment will be the next business day if the due date falls on a weekend or public holiday (see 5.424).

5.430   SINGLE TOUCH PAYROLL – FROM JULY 2016

The Government originally planned to commence with Single Touch Payroll (STP) on 1 July 2016. However, feedback provided by organisations including Taxpayers Australia stated that efficiencies would not be achieved by many businesses and implementation would have cashflow implications for small business. Accordingly, the ATO has decided to consult further with industry and small business on a revised proposal.

WHAT IS SINGLE TOUCH PAYROLL?

Under STP, employers' accounting software will automatically report payroll information to the Tax Office when employees are paid. This change will remove the need for employers to report employee Pay As You Go Withholding (PAYGW) in activity statements and payment summaries. In fact, payment summaries will not be required anymore.

The government also plans to streamline Tax File Number declarations and Super Choice forms by providing digital services to simplify the process of bringing on new employees.

REPORTING CAPABILITY

Currently, employers have to undertake many steps at different points in time in order to meet payroll-related obligations.

The reporting function in STP will eliminate paper-based payroll reporting as employers will report digitally instead.

Employers would be required to report, through their payroll software, employee income, tax and SG obligations to the Tax Office via Standard Business Reporting (SBR). This would be done at the time of the payroll event. This will remove the requirement to report employees' PAYG withholding at other times through activity statements and payment summaries.

Employers would also report to the Tax Office the amount of SG contributions that they are obliged to pay to super funds. This will place the Tax Office in a better position to ensure that employers are meeting their employer super obligations.

However, the Tax Office acknowledges that the reporting functionality will not affect the payment cycle or the timing of PAYG withholding and SG obligations. Therefore, Single Touch Payroll would not address the issues associated with accruing large PAYG withholding and super obligations and some employers have difficulty meeting.

The current design of STP only includes the functionality for **reporting** payroll amounts contemporaneously with the payroll event. The consultation process will look at the potential for payments to be made in real-time as well as the reporting.

If real-time payment obligations are implemented, this will essentially bring forward the timing, and increase the frequency but reduce the amounts, of PAYGW and SG payments. Employers will typically would fall into one of the following categories in relation to the impact:

- *For businesses that already set aside their PAYG withholding and super obligations each pay cycle, the impacts should be relatively minor. However, this cash reserve will be reduced as payment will be required more frequently.*
- *For businesses that actively use the current delay between the payroll cycle and their tax or super obligation event to manage the business's cash flow, the new process may create cash flow issues.*

Further, there is a small percentage of businesses in a net GST refund position, or entitled to fuel tax credits, that are also likely to see an impact on cash flow. Currently, these GST refunds or fuel tax credits were used to offset PAYG withholding liabilities. However, under Single Touch Payroll, businesses will have to fund the PAYG withholding payment at payroll time and then receive the refund at a different point in time when they lodge their activity statement.

Also, changes to the frequency of tax and super payments may affect other business practices, such as payment of invoices.

Under STP, there will be no need to fill in PAYG withholding details in activity statements and the annual payment summary will be eliminated. However, a currently unresolved issue is how annual Reportable Fringe Benefits Amounts (RFBA) and reportable superannuation contribution amounts will now be reported. Currently these amounts appear on payment summaries which will not exist under STP. These amounts can only be calculated on an annual basis. At time of writing, the Tax Office was seeking suggestions as to an appropriate annual mechanism.

COMMENCING AND CEASING EMPLOYMENT

When a new employee commences, they are required to complete a number of forms, including a TFN Declaration and a Super Choice form. The employer then has various reporting obligations in relation to this information. Using STP, employees would have the option to supply their details electronically through an online government portal, myGov. The details are then electronically sent to the employee, their employer, the Tax Office and other relevant agencies.

STP could also allow employers to easily notify super funds, the Tax Office and other government agencies of employees that have ceased employment, through payroll software allowing for an 'employee ceased indicator to be entered'.

PENALTIES

Administrative penalties may apply for a failure to meet obligations under STP. In its discussion paper, the Tax Office committed to providing support to employers making a genuine attempt to comply with their obligations. Discretion in the administration of penalties will be necessary during the transition period and ongoing.

5.500 HELP AND SFSS

The Tax Office is responsible for collecting outstanding loan amounts for loans offered under the Higher Education Loan Program (HELP) and the Student Financial Supplement Scheme (SFSS). Taxpayers with an outstanding HELP or SFSS debt are required to make compulsory repayments once their repayment income exceeds the minimum repayment income threshold. Additional amounts are withheld through the PAYG withholding system or included in the instalment amount under the PAYG instalment system to cover for any compulsory repayments that may be calculated.

5.510   HIGHER EDUCATION LOAN PROGRAM

The Higher Education Loan Program (HELP) replaced the Higher Education Contribution Scheme (HECS) on 1 January 2005 and other student loans previously available through the Postgraduate Education Loan Scheme (PELS), Open Learning Deferred Payment Scheme (OLDPS) and Bridging for Overseas-Trained Professional Loan Scheme (BOTPLS).

WHAT IS A HELP DEBT?

When HELP was introduced, effective from 1 January 2005, any outstanding accumulated HECS debt automatically became a HELP debt from 1 June 2006 and was added together with any HELP debt incurred from 1 January 2005 to form one accumulated HELP debt.

A taxpayer is required to start repaying that HELP debt when their repayment income is above the minimum threshold for compulsory repayment.

HELP has four schemes:

- HECS-HELP: for eligible students enrolled in Commonwealth supported places. A HECS-HELP loan will cover all or part of their student contribution.
- FEE-HELP: for eligible fee-paying students enrolled at an eligible higher education provider or Open Universities Australia. FEE-HELP provides students with a loan to cover up to the full amount of their tuition fees up to a lifetime loan limit. This lifetime limit is indexed on 1 January each year and the lifetime limit for 2015 is $97,728 ($122,162 or students undertaking medicine, dentistry or veterinary science courses).
- OS-HELP: for eligible Commonwealth supported students who wish to study overseas. OS-HELP provides students with a loan to cover expenses such as accommodation and travel.
- VET FEE-HELP: for eligible full fee-paying students undertaking vocational education and training (VET) accredited diploma, advanced diploma, graduate diploma and graduate certificate courses with an approved VET provider. Similar to FEE-HELP, VET FEE-HELP provides students with a loan to cover up to the full amount of their tuition fees up to a lifetime loan limit which is indexed annually.

Repaying a HELP debt will be the same as repaying a HECS debt. There will still be:

- compulsory repayments made through income tax assessment
- additional amounts withheld through PAYG withholding or included in the calculation of PAYG instalment amounts through the PAYG instalment system to cover any compulsory repayment that may be calculated
- voluntary repayments
- a bonus on voluntary repayments, and
- indexation applied to debts on 1 June each year.

NOTE: Eligible graduates in maths and science, early childhood, education and nursing who take up employment in these professions will be eligible to apply for a HECS-HELP benefit which will reduce their HELP repayments. Refer to www.studyassist.gov.au for details.

5.511   HELP ACCOUNT

The Tax Office keeps track of any debts deferred for payment through the tax system. Debts are reported to the Tax Office twice yearly for collection through the tax system. A student incurs a debt on the census date for their unit of study. However, for administrative reasons, the Tax Office records debts for the period:

- January to June 2014 as being incurred on 31 March 2014, and
- July to December 2014 as being incurred on 31 August 2014.

Previously, in June each year the Tax Office sent an information statement to a taxpayer if there has been 'activity' on an account in the previous 15 months. This practice has now ceased.

However, a taxpayer can retrieve their HELP account balance through e-tax by using the pre-fill option, or from their tax agent. Further, at any time during the year the taxpayer can phone the Tax Office to get their balance or to order an information statement. To access this information, the taxpayer will need to provide the following identifiers to verify their identity.

If the taxpayer has ever lodged an income tax return, they must provide one of the following identifiers:

- their tax file number
- their name, or
- their ABN.

They must also provide any three of the following personal identifiers:

- their date of birth
- their business, residential, postal or email address (one only)
- their financial institution account number
- details from a Tax Office notice, or
- other identifying details – for example, correct account balance, student course code, details of a payment arrangement, or taxable income. These must be verified against their account.

NOTE: If you have never lodged an income tax return, you only need supply two personal identifiers from this list.

INDEXATION

An accumulated HELP debt is calculated on 1 June each year when indexation is applied. This is the amount on which a compulsory repayment is based. No interest is charged on an accumulated debt, but the debt is indexed each year. Indexation is applied to the part of a debt which has remained unpaid for 11 months or more. The indexation rate applied to debts on 1 June 2013 was 2.0%.

DEATH OF THE TAXPAYER

If the taxpayer dies, the trustee or executor of their estate has to lodge all outstanding income tax returns up to the date of death. Any compulsory repayment included on a notice of assessment which relates to the period before their death must be paid from their estate, but the remainder of the debt is cancelled. Neither their family nor the trustee is required to pay the rest of the accumulated debt.

BANKRUPTCY

HELP debts and a taxpayer's accumulated HELP debt are not provable under the *Bankruptcy Act 1966* and the taxpayer will have to pay them as if they had not been declared bankrupt.

5.512   COMPULSORY REPAYMENTS

The taxpayer must start repaying their debt when their repayment income is above the minimum threshold for compulsory repayment. The repayment thresholds are adjusted each year to reflect any changes in average weekly earnings. For the 2015-16 income year the minimum threshold is $54,126 ($53,345 in 2014-15).

Compulsory repayments are made through their income tax assessments. The taxpayer doesn't have to provide HECS or HELP information in their income tax return. If the taxpayer has a debt, and their repayment income is above the minimum repayment threshold, the Tax Office will automatically work out and include their compulsory repayment in their notice of assessment.

 If a taxpayer's repayment income is above the minimum threshold they must start repaying their loan, even if they are still studying.

CALCULATING REPAYMENT INCOME

A taxpayer's repayment income comprises the following:

- taxable income plus
- total net investment loss plus
- total reportable fringe benefits amounts shown on their annual PAYG payment summary plus any reportable superannuation contributions plus
- any exempt foreign employment income amounts included in their income tax return.

NOTE: Net investment losses encompass losses from rental property, financial investments in shares, managed investment schemes, forestry managed investment schemes and rights or option relating to any of the above mentioned investments. Total net investment losses exclude capital gains or losses.

NOTE: Reportable superannuation contributions are added to the calculation of repayment income and includes reportable employer superannuation contributions and personal deductible contributions. Reportable employer superannuation contributions are salary sacrificed contributions and contributions your employer made on behalf of you that are additional to the minimum contributions they must make. Therefore, superannuation guarantee contributions are not included in calculating reportable superannuation contributions.

CALCULATING COMPULSORY REPAYMENTS

The income thresholds and repayment rates for income earned during the 2014-15 and 2015-16 income years are shown below.

2014-15		2015-16	
Repayment income	**Rate**	**Repayment income**	**Rate**
Below $53,345	Nil	Below $54,126	Nil
$53,345-$59,421	4%	$54,126-$60,292	4%
$59,422-$65,497	4.5%	$60,293-$66,456	4.5%
$65,498-$68,939	5%	$66,457-$69,949	5%
$68,940-$74,105	5.5%	$69,950-$75,190	5.5%
$74,106-$80,257	6%	$75,191-$81,432	6%
$80,258-$84,481	6.5%	$81,433-$85,718	6.5%
$84,482-$92,970	7%	$85,719-$94,331	7%
$92,971-$99,069	7.5%	$94,332-$100,519	7.5%
$99,070 and above	8%	$100,520 and above	8%

When a taxpayer's repayment income is above the minimum repayment threshold for any particular year, the Tax Office will calculate their compulsory repayment for that year, applying different percentage rates for different ranges of income. Their compulsory repayment percentage increases as their repayment income increases. Their compulsory repayment is based on their income alone – not the income of their parents or spouse. Compulsory repayments continue until the taxpayer has repaid their debt.

OVERSEAS DEBTORS

It was announced in the 2015-16 Federal Budget that from 1 July 2016 the HELP repayment framework will extend to debtors residing overseas. HELP debtors residing overseas for six months or more will be required to make repayments of their HELP debt, if their worldwide income exceeds the minimum repayment threshold, at the same repayment rates as debtors in Australia. At the time of writing, these measures are yet to be introduced into Parliament.

LOW FAMILY INCOME EXEMPTION

If the taxpayer has a spouse or dependants and is entitled to a reduction of the Medicare levy or the taxpayer does not have to pay the Medicare levy due to low family income, they will be exempt from making a compulsory repayment for that year and may ask their payer not to withhold additional amounts from their pay by completing the Medicare levy variation declaration (NAT 0929).

MAKING A COMPULSORY REPAYMENT

When the taxpayer lodges their income tax return, the Tax Office will process it and send the taxpayer a notice of assessment. The amount of their compulsory repayment is calculated and included on the notice of assessment. The repayment is part of their total income tax assessment. Their notice of assessment will tell the taxpayer the amount of their:

- accumulated debt before assessment
- compulsory repayment, and
- refund or tax debt.

If the taxpayer has a tax debt, the notice of assessment will also show the date by which it must be paid.

NOTE: If the taxpayer thinks the compulsory repayment shown on their notice of assessment is wrong, they should first check the details on their notice of assessment against those in their income tax return. Then if they still think it is incorrect, the taxpayer can phone the Tax Office to request an amendment or lodge an objection with the Deputy Commissioner of Taxation. If the taxpayer is unhappy with a decision of the Deputy Commissioner of Taxation not to allow their objection, they can apply to the AAT or the Federal Court for a review of the decision.

DEFERRING A COMPULSORY REPAYMENT

If the taxpayer believes that making their compulsory repayment would cause them serious hardship or there are other special reasons why they believe that they should not make a compulsory repayment, the taxpayer can apply to defer their compulsory repayment.

The application should clearly explain the grounds and reasons for their claim and provide a detailed statement of their household income and expenditure to justify their claim.

The taxpayer who has not lodged their tax return can apply for deferment of current year, previous year or next year's compulsory repayment. Application for deferment outside these three years will not be considered by the Tax Office. If a taxpayer has already lodged their tax return and their notice of assessment includes compulsory repayment, the taxpayer can still apply to defer paying this amount. The application must be made within two years after the end of the financial year the assessment relates to.

The Deputy Commissioner of Taxation will advise the taxpayer if their application was successful or not within 28 days of the application being received. If their application is successful, the deferred amount will be added to their accumulated debt. Indexation will continue to be applied in June each year.

If the taxpayer is unhappy with a decision not to grant a deferment, they have 28 days from the time they receive the decision to apply to the Administrative Appeals Tribunal (AAT) for a review.

NOTE: If the application to defer is successful and you have additional amounts withheld from your payments, you can vary the tax withheld by completing a PAYG income tax withholding variation short application.

ADDITIONAL PAYG WITHHOLDING

Payees with accumulated HELP debt must advise their payer of that debt when completing the *Tax file number declaration* (NAT 3092) form and must have additional amounts withheld from their payment once their payments reach the minimum repayment threshold for the income year.

The payer will have an obligation to withhold additional amounts on payment to the payee for HELP debt if the payee has already notified the payer of their debt and in the 2013-14 financial year:

- if claiming tax-free threshold: the payee's income is $986 or more per week, or
- if not claiming tax-free threshold: the payee's income is $636 or more per week.

NOTE: To calculate additional withholding amount for HELP debt refer to the tax tables published by the Tax Office for weekly, fortnightly and monthly payments (NAT 2173, 2185 and 2186).

If the accumulated debt is paid off, the payee should advise their payer by completing a new Withholding declaration (NAT 3093) and answering 'NO' to the question of having any accumulated HELP debt.

If their payer does not withhold an additional amount the taxpayer may end up with a large sum to pay when their income tax return is processed and their notice of assessment is issued.

Further, you may vary upwards the additional amount of PAYG withheld if you think the amount withheld is inadequate to cover the compulsory repayment. On the contrary, you may vary the additional amount of PAYG withheld downwards if you think the amount withheld has exceeded the amount of compulsory repayment you need to make for that year. Some examples of such circumstances are:

- you have more than one job and total payments from all jobs exceed the minimum repayment threshold
- you will receive reportable fringe benefits of $2,000 or more (grossed up taxable value of $3,738 or more)
- you expect your repayment income to be much lower than your annual income as a result of deductions
- you work only part year and therefore your weekly income may exceed the threshold which requires additional withholding but your repayment income does not exceed the annual repayment threshold.

NOTE: The grossed-up taxable value of a fringe benefit is the gross salary that you would have to earn, in order to purchase the benefit from after-tax dollars. This amount is calculated by multiplying the value of the fringe benefits you received for the year ended 31 March by the Type 2 gross up rate (see 25.000).

PAYG INSTALMENTS

The PAYG instalment rate and instalment amount advised by the Commissioner (for more information on PAYG instalments see 5.700) takes into account a taxpayer accumulated HELP debt (if any). The taxpayer can vary their instalment rate or amount to take into account their personal circumstances.

If the taxpayer pays off their accumulated debt with a voluntary repayment during the year, after the taxpayer has been advised of their instalment rate or amount, they may want to vary their instalment rate or amount to take out the HECS or HELP component.

5.513   VOLUNTARY REPAYMENTS

A taxpayer receives a bonus of 10% on their HECS and 5% on their HELP debt if they:
- make voluntary repayment of $500 or more, or
- clear their debt.

 The bonus is 10% (5% for HELP debts) of the payment that the taxpayer makes, not 10% of the outstanding debt. The taxpayer will not receive a bonus on repayment amounts that are more than the balance of their account. Therefore, if you are making a voluntary payment to pay off your HELP debt, the amount of voluntary repayment you need to make is the outstanding balance divided by 1.10 rounded to the nearest dollar.

Making a voluntary repayment reduces a taxpayer's HECS-HELP debt immediately. But if, after making the voluntary repayment, the taxpayer still has an accumulated debt and their repayment income is above the minimum compulsory repayment threshold, the taxpayer may still have to make a compulsory repayment. Voluntary repayments are in addition to compulsory repayments. Voluntary repayments are not refundable.

BEST TIME TO MAKE A VOLUNTARY REPAYMENT

If the taxpayer plans to pay off their total debt with a voluntary repayment, they should make the repayment before they lodge their income tax return. If their income tax return is processed before their voluntary repayment is credited to their account, a compulsory repayment may be included in their notice of assessment and they may not receive the bonus.

The taxpayer may also benefit if they make a voluntary repayment before indexation is applied on 1 June. If the taxpayer intends to make a voluntary repayment before indexation is applied, it is important to allow enough time for the payment to be processed and credited to their account before 1 June.

The taxpayer should not make voluntary repayments to the Tax Office before they have incurred a debt. For when a debt is incurred and recorded see *HELP account* at 5.511.

SALARY PACKAGING AND VOLUNTARY REPAYMENTS

Some people make salary packaging arrangements with their payers to pay off their debts with voluntary repayments. If the taxpayer makes such an arrangement they should be aware of the following:

- the bonus on voluntary repayments only applies to individual repayments of $500 or more (after any administrative costs or fees that may be imposed by their payroll company). Two payments of $250 each will not receive a bonus, but one payment of $500 will receive a bonus
- entering into a salary sacrifice arrangement may result in their payer providing a fringe benefit to the taxpayer. The taxpayer will have a reportable fringe benefits amount stated on their annual PAYG payment summary if the total taxable value of reportable fringe benefits the taxpayer receives in a fringe benefits tax year exceeds $2,000 (grossed up value that exceeds $3,738), and
- a voluntary repayment is not refundable and therefore it is important that the payer stops making repayments as soon as the debt has been paid off.

5.514 ARE HELP DEBT REPAYMENTS TAX DEDUCTIBLE?

Any HELP debt repayment (voluntary or compulsory) made by the taxpayer or by someone other than their payer is not tax deductible. However, if a payer (the employer) chooses to reimburse the payee for their HELP repayment, the payer may be able to claim a tax deduction. But they will also be liable for fringe benefits tax on the repayment.

5.520 STUDENT FINANCIAL SUPPLEMENT SCHEME

The Student Financial Supplement Scheme (SFSS) was a voluntary loans scheme for tertiary students who were generally eligible for Youth Allowance, AUSTUDY or ABSTUDY living allowances.

The SFSS was designed to give eligible students greater choice in how they pay for living and educational expenses whilst studying. The scheme closed on 31 December 2003 and no new loans have been issued. In the fifth year of the loan being taken out the loan becomes an accumulated Financial Supplement debt and the Tax Office resumes responsibility for collecting the balance of this outstanding loan. All such remaining loans will now be in this phase.

There will be compulsory repayment if your repayment income reaches the minimum income threshold (see 5.522). You can still make voluntary repayments, but these payments will not be entitled to a discount.

5.521 VOLUNTARY REPAYMENTS

A taxpayer, or their payer, can make voluntary Financial Supplement repayments.

NOTE: You will still have to make compulsory repayments for an income year if your repayment income reaches the minimum income threshold, even though you may have already made a voluntary repayment.

5.522 COMPULSORY REPAYMENTS

A compulsory Financial Supplement repayment is calculated based on 'repayment income'. Repayment income comprises the following:

- taxable income plus
- total net investment loss plus
- total Reportable Fringe Benefits (RFB) amount shown on your annual PAYG payment summary plus
- reportable superannuation contributions plus
- any exempt foreign employment income amounts included in an income tax return.

NOTE: Net investment losses encompass losses from rental property, financial investments in shares, managed investment schemes, forestry managed investment schemes and rights or options relating to any of the above mentioned investments. Total net investment losses exclude capital gains or losses.

NOTE: Reportable superannuation contributions are added to the calculation of repayment income and includes reportable employer superannuation contributions and personal deductible contributions. Reportable employer superannuation contributions are salary sacrificed contributions and contributions your employer made on behalf of you that are additional to the minimum contributions they must make. Therefore, superannuation guarantee contributions are not included.

Annual compulsory repayments are made through the tax system once a taxpayer's repayment income reaches the minimum income type threshold for the relevant income year. The annual compulsory repayment is called the financial supplement assessment debt. The amount of the annual compulsory repayment is calculated based on the following repayment income thresholds and repayment rates.

Repayment threshold and compulsory repayment rates	
2015-16 repayment income	Rate
Below $54,126	Nil
$54,126–$66,456	2%
$66,456–$94,331	3%
$94,332 and above	4%

The Tax Office will calculate the amount of annual compulsory repayment a taxpayer needs to make which will be shown on their income tax notice of assessment. If the total outstanding loan debt is less than the compulsory repayment amount, the financial supplement assessment debt is the amount of the debt outstanding.

RELIEF FOR LOW INCOME FAMILIES

A payee will not have to make a compulsory Financial Supplement repayment if, due to low family income they:

- are entitled to a reduction of the Medicare levy, or
- do not have to pay the Medicare levy.

Payee may ask their payer not to withhold additional amount from their payments by completing the *Medicare levy variation declaration* (NAT 0929).

WHAT HAPPENS IF A PERSON DIES?

The student or taxpayer's estate will not have to repay any outstanding Financial Supplement loan debt if that person has died, unless a Financial Supplement assessment debt is included on an income tax notice of assessment issued in respect of any period prior to the date of their death. This debt must be paid from the estate.

INDEXATION

Interest is not charged on student supplement loans but the debt is indexed annually in line with the Consumer Price Index (CPI). Indexation occurs on 1 June each year, starting the year after a student took out a loan. Indexation adjustments are made automatically on any unpaid portion of the debt and are shown on the supplement statement. The indexation rate from 1 June 2013 is 2.0%.

PAYG WITHHOLDING

Payees with accumulated Financial Supplement debt must advise their payer of that debt when completing the *Tax file number declaration* (NAT 3092) form and must have an additional amount withheld from their payment once their payments reach the minimum repayment threshold for the income year.

A payer will have an obligation to withhold additional amounts on payment to their payee for SFSS if the payee has already notified the payer of their SFSS debt and in the 2015-16 financial year:

- is claiming tax-free threshold: the payee's income is $1,039 or more per week, or
- is not claiming tax-free threshold: the payee's income is $689 or more per week.

NOTE: To calculate the additional withholding amount for SFSS please refer to the tax tables published by the Tax Office for weekly, fortnightly and monthly payments (NAT 3306, NAT 3307 and NAT 3308).

If the accumulated debt is paid off, the payee should advise their payer by completing a new Withholding declaration and answering 'NO' to the question of having any accumulated SFSS debt.

If their payer does not withhold an additional amount the taxpayer may end up with a large sum to pay when their income tax return is processed and their notice of assessment is issued.

Further, you may vary upwards or downwards additional amounts of PAYG withheld in relation to your SFSS debt to best reflect your circumstances. Examples of some circumstances that may require variation of the amount withheld in relation to SFSS debt are:

- you have more than one job and total payments from all jobs exceed the minimum repayment threshold
- you will receive reportable fringe benefits of $2,000 or more (grossed up taxable value of $3,738 or more)
- you expect your repayment income to be much lower than your annual income as a result of deductions, and
- you work only part of the year and therefore your weekly income may exceed the threshold which requires additional withholding but your repayment income does not exceed the annual repayment threshold.

NOTE: The grossed-up taxable value of a fringe benefit is the gross salary which must be earned in order to purchase the benefit from after-tax dollars. This amount is calculated by multiplying the value of the fringe benefits received for the year ended 31 March by the Type 2 gross-up rate.

You may vary the additional amount of PAYG withheld. However, it is not necessary. Any excess in withholding will be refunded to you when you lodge your tax return. On the other hand, any underpayment will result in a tax debt when your tax return is lodged.

PAYG INSTALMENTS

The PAYG instalment rate and instalment amount advised by the Commissioner (for more information on PAYG instalments see 5.700) takes into account a taxpayer accumulated SFSS debt (if any). The taxpayer can vary their instalment rate or amount to take into account their personal circumstances. If the taxpayer pays off their accumulated debt with a voluntary repayment during the year, after the taxpayer has been advised of their instalment rate or amount, they may want to vary their instalment rate or amount to take out the SFSS component.

5.600 PAYG WITHHOLDING TAX TABLES

Employers are required to deduct PAYG withholding from salary and wages of their employees as well as payments for directors fees, salary and allowances to office holders, payments to labour hire workers, and compensation, sickness or accident payments calculated at a periodic rate, based on rates approved by the Tax Office. Others deemed to be employees are also subject to these rules.

The Tax Office produces tax tables based on the frequency of payment arrangements (ie. weekly, fortnightly, monthly). Those tables set out the standard amount of tax that must be deducted by the payer and remitted to the Tax Office. PAYG is rounded to the nearest dollar.

PAYG withholding tax tables have separate columns for taxpayers entitled to receive annual leave loading and for those not entitled to this loading. Special tax tables are also available to work out the PAYG withholding for certain payees. The following is a list of PAYGW tax tables that are available and corresponding publication (NAT) numbers. Copies are available from the Tax Office, or can be located using the NAT number from www.ato.gov.au.

NAT no	Title
1004	Statement of formulas for calculating amounts to be withheld
1005	Weekly tax table – incorporating Medicare levy with and without leave loading
1006	Fortnightly tax table – incorporating Medicare levy with and without leave loading
1007	Monthly tax table – incorporating Medicare levy with and without leave loading
1008	Weekly tax table with no and half Medicare levy, including weekly table for Medicare levy adjustment – half levy
1010	Medicare levy adjustment weekly tax table
1011	Medicare levy adjustment fortnightly tax table
1012	Medicare levy adjustment monthly tax table
1023	Special tax table for actors, variety artists and other entertainers
1024	Tax table for daily and casual workers – incorporating Medicare levy, including statement of formulas
2173	Higher Education Loan Program (HELP) weekly tax table, including statement of formulas
2185	Higher Education Loan Program (HELP) fortnightly tax table, including statement of formulas
2186	Higher Education Loan Program (HELP) monthly tax table, including statement of formulas
2335	Statement of formulas for calculating Higher Education Loan Program (HELP) component, including coefficients for calculating weekly withholding amounts incorporating HELP component
2446	Statement of formulas for calculating withholding amounts for members of the Defence Force
3305	Statement of formulas for calculating Student Financial Supplement Scheme (SFSS) component, including coefficients for calculating weekly withholding amounts incorporating SFSS component
3306	Student Financial Supplement Scheme (SFSS) weekly tax table, including statement of formulas
3307	Student Financial Supplement Scheme (SFSS) fortnightly tax table, including statement of formulas
3308	Student Financial Supplement Scheme (SFSS) monthly tax table, including statement of formulas
3479	Quarterly tax table – incorporating Medicare levy with and without leave loading
3539	Calculating HECS in conjunction with SFSS
4466	Special tax table for aged pensioners and low income aged persons (senior Australians)
3351	Tax table for unused leave payments on termination of employment
3348	Tax table for back payments including lump sum payments in arrears
3350	Tax table for annuities
70980	Tax table for employment termination payments
70981	Tax table for superannuation lump sums

5.610 SEASONAL WORKERS

A flat rate of withholding of 15% applies to payments made to individual employees with a Special Program (subclass 416) visa under the Seasonal Worker Program. These employees are:

- seasonal payees who are involved in the production, harvest or cultivation process in the horticultural industry on the grower's property, or
- in the shearing industry such as shearers, crutchers, wool classers, piece work cooks, shed hands, weekly wage pressers and cooks with weekly, fortnightly or monthly payments.

A seasonal worker employed under the Seasonal Worker Program is a non-resident for tax purposes. They may become a resident if they stay in Australia after they finish working on the program.

Seasonal workers are not required to lodge tax returns unless they have other Australian income outside of the Seasonal Worker Program.

5.620 HELP (PREVIOUSLY HECS) AND SFSS

Payers must calculate and withhold the HELP component where a payee has answered 'Yes' to the question 'Do you have an accumulated HECS or HELP debt?' in a TFN or withholding declaration and earns $51,308 or more a year for the 2013-14 financial year. Payers must calculate and withhold the SFSS component where a payee has said 'Yes' to the question 'Do you have an accumulated financial supplement debt?' in a TFN or withholding declaration and earns $51,308 or more a year (2013-14).

The Tax Office has produced PAYG withholding coefficients for calculating the weekly, fortnightly and monthly withholding amounts incorporating the HELP components and SFSS components (see above list for NAT number of the relevant PAYGW tax table that incorporates the HELP and SFSS components).

5.630 SENIOR AUSTRALIANS

Payers can withhold less PAYG tax from payments made to low income senior Australians and pensioners to take into account the tax offset available to people of pension age (see NAT 4466 for the relevant PAYGW tax table for senior Australians entitled to the Senior Australians and Pensioner Tax Offset (SAPTO)). To withhold tax at this lower rate, the payee must be entitled to SAPTO and have answered 'Yes' to the question 'Do you want to claim the seniors and pensioners tax offset by reducing the amount withheld from payments made to you?' in a TFN or withholding declaration. For more information on SAPTO see 3.190.

5.640 NON-RESIDENTS

Employers who employ non-residents in Australia are required to deduct PAYG withholding from their salary or wages. The rates are higher than for residents because non-residents are not entitled to the tax-free threshold (see 3.020). If the TFN is not quoted, a flat 47% (no Medicare levy) is charged. If a TFN is quoted and the 'salary and wages' (ignore cents) is:

- less than $1,538 per week: flat 32.5%
- $1,539 to $3,462 per week: $500 + 37% of the surplus over $1,538
- $3,463 or more per week: $1,212 + 45% of the surplus over $3,462

NOTE: Foreign resident payees are not entitled to claim any tax offsets. Therefore, there should not be any adjustments to the withholding amount for any tax offsets claimed.

It was announced in the 2015-16 Federal Budget that the Government intends to change the tax residency rules so that most people who are temporarily in Australia for a working holiday will be non-resident for tax purposes. At the time of writing, these measures have not been introduced into Parliament.

5.650   REDUCTION IN WITHHOLDING AMOUNT

A reduction in the tax withheld for other reasons (besides Dependant Tax Offsets, Zone Tax Offset or Medicare levy reduction) eg. because deductible expenses are high, can only occur if the Tax Office has issued an official Tax Office variation notice in respect of a payee (eg. employee) (see 5.412).

5.660   TAX OFFSETS AND FAMILY TAX BENEFITS

Concessional tax offsets (rebates) including Dependant (Invalid and Carer) Tax Offset and Zone Tax Offset can be claimed as a reduction in PAYG withholding. For entitlement and calculation of the tax offset see 3.110 and 3.170.

5.661   LOW INCOME TAX OFFSET (LITO) CLAIMED VIA PAYG WITHHOLDING

Individuals eligible for LITO can claim 70% of their LITO entitlement as a reduction in their amount of PAYG withholding and the remainder of the entitlement is then receivable upon assessment of their income tax return for the year. For the 2015-16 (and 2014-15) financial year, a full LITO entitlement of $445 is available to individuals with taxable income of less than $37,000 (see 3.010). The offset reduces at the rate of 1.5 cents for each dollar of taxable income over $37,000 and fully phases out at a taxable income of $66,667.

Sam is entitled to a full LITO of $445 in the 2014-15 financial year. Sam will be entitled to claim 70% of $445 = $311.50 as a reduction in the amount of PAYG withheld from his salary throughout the 2013-14 financial year.

As Sam is paid on a weekly basis, the reduction in the PAYG withheld from his weekly wages will be $311.50/52 weeks = $5.99 (rounded to the nearest dollar).

5.670   REPAYMENT OF OVERPAID AMOUNTS

Where an employer (or other payer) overpays an employee (or other payee), the overpaid gross amount may need to be repaid (ie. including the PAYG tax that has been withheld). Where this occurs in the same income year, the overpayment should be excluded from the payment summary. If in a later year and a payment summary has been issued, and it can be retrieved from the employee, it should be cancelled and a new one issued. If not, the employer should give the employee a letter showing the correct details and send a copy to the Tax Office.

Where the employee has already lodged a tax return they should request an amendment and attach a copy of the employer's letter with that request.

5.680   TFN NOT PROVIDED

If the taxpayer's TFN is not provided, tax is withheld at a flat 47% (plus 2% Temporary Budget Repair Levy) rate for payments made to a resident payee. For a non-resident payee, tax will be withheld at 45% (plus 2% Temporary Budget Repair Levy) (without Medicare levy component). See 5.000.

5.690   CALCULATING PAYG WITHHOLDING AMOUNTS

Using the ready reckoner in 5.691 and following the method below, you can calculate the amount to withhold on a payment taking into consideration HELP/SFSS debt, Dependent Tax Offsets, Low Income Tax Offset, Zone Tax Offset and Medicare levy reduction adjustments.

NOTE: The ready reckoner in 5.691 is for weekly payments. If you are making fortnightly payments refer to tax tables in NAT 1006 and for monthly payments use tax tables in NAT 1007.

Step 1:   Determine the payee's weekly earning including any allowances or irregular payments.

Step 2:   Match the weekly earnings to the appropriate column from the table in 5.691 to obtain the initial amount of tax to be withheld.

- Claiming the tax-free threshold and is entitled to leave loading, or

- Claiming the tax-free threshold and is not entitled to leave loading, or

- Not claiming the tax-free threshold (regardless of entitlement to leave loading).

NOTE: If TFN is not provided, tax is withheld at 49% on the payment (resident) and 47% (non-resident).

Step 3: Calculate the weekly HELP or SFSS component (if any) (using table below) using the following formula:

HELP or SFSS component rate x (weekly earning ignoring cents + 99 cents)

HELP component for weekly earnings 2015-16		
HELP component	**Weekly earnings: Tax-free threshold***	**Weekly earnings: No tax-free threshold***
0.0%	0 to $1,039	0 to $689
4.0%	$1,040 to $1,158	$690 to $808
4.5%	$1,159 to $1,277	$809 to $927
5.0%	$1,278 to $1,344	$928 to $994
5.5%	$1,345 to $1,444	$995 to $1,094
6.0%	$1,445 to $1,565	$1,095 to $1,215
6.5%	$1,566 to $1,647	$1,216 to $1,297
7.0%	$1,648 to $1,813	$1,298 to $1,463
7.5%	$1,814 to $1,932	$1,464 to $1,582
8.0%	$1,933 and over	$1,583 and over
SFSS component for weekly earnings 2015-16		
SFSS component	**Weekly earnings: Tax-free threshold***	**Weekly earnings: No tax-free threshold***
0.0%	0 to $1,039	0 to $689
2.0%	$1,040 to $1,277	$690 to $927
3.0%	$1,278 to $1,813	$928 to $1,463
4.0%	$1,814 and over	$1,464 and over

*Rounded to whole dollars.

Step 4: Calculate annual amounts of total tax offsets allowed from the prescribed rate (see 3.110 and 3.170) and use the following table to convert the annual offset amount into weekly value. The tax offsets include:

-   Dependant (Invalid and Carer) Tax Offset
-   70% of Low Income Tax Offset (see 5.661), and
-   Zone Tax Offsets.

NOTE: A payee who does not claim the tax-free threshold or does not provide a TFN to a payer is not entitled to tax offset adjustments in their amount withheld with that payer.

Ryan is entitled to a low income tax offset of $445. However, note that only 70% of the Low Income Tax Offset is entitled to be claimed as a reduction in PAYG withholding. Therefore, the adjusted annual tax offset entitlement is (70% of $445) = $311.50.

The weekly value of these offsets is worked out using the following table. If the exact amount cannot be found from the table, split the annual amount into the components that are shown on the table.

For example, for an annual tax offsets amount of $3,250 a taxpayer can split the amount into $3,000 + $200 +$50. Then find and add up the weekly value corresponding to each of these amounts.

Ready reckoner for tax offsets

Amount claimed	Weekly value	Amount claimed	Weekly value	Amount claimed	Weekly value	Amount claimed	Weekly value	Amount claimed	Weekly value
$1	0	$20	0	$200	$4	$1,000	$19	$1,500	$29
$2	0	$30	$1	$300	$6	$1,100	$21	$1,600	$30
$3	0	$40	$1	$338	$6	$1,173	$22	$1,700	$32
$4	0	$50	$1	$400	$8	$1,200	$23	$1,750	$33
$5	0	$57	$1	$500	$10	$1,300	$25	$1,800	$34
$6	0	$60	$1	$600	$11	$1,400	$27	$1,900	$36
$7	0	$70	$1	$700	$13	$1,500	$29	$2,000	$38
$8	0	$80	$2	$800	$15	$1,600	$30	$2,500	$48
$9	0	$90	$2	$850	$16	$1,700	$32	$2,535	$48
$10	0	$100	$2	$900	$17	$1,750	$33	$3,000	$57

Step 5: Work out the weekly Medicare levy reduction amount (if any). Medicare levy reduction applies only to those entitled to Medicare levy relief (see 3.050) who have provided the payer with a completed Medicare levy variation declaration (NAT 0929). The weekly Medicare levy reduction value can be worked out using the tax table in NAT 1010 available from www.ato.gov.au (NAT 1011 is Medicare levy reduction for fortnightly payments and NAT 1012 is Medicare levy reduction for monthly payments).

NOTE: If you are entitled to Medicare levy reduction or are exempt from paying Medicare levy because your income is below the Medicare levy low income threshold, you can elect for no additional withholding to apply in relation to HELP or SFSS debt by completing NAT 0929.

NOTE: A payee that does not claim the tax-free threshold or does not provide a TFN to a payer is not entitled to any Medicare levy reduction adjustment in their amount withheld with that payer.

Step 6: Work out the correct amount of tax to be withheld from the payment using the following formula:

Step 2 + Step 3 – Step 4 – Step 5

NOTE: PAYG withholding is deducted in whole dollars. Cents are rounded to the nearest whole dollar if a TFN is quoted (round 50c up), and ignored if a TFN is not quoted.

LEAVE LOADING

If an employer pays leave loading as a lump sum, they need to use the tax table for back payments, commissions, bonuses and similar payments (NAT 3348) to calculate withholding. If an employer pays leave loading on a pro-rata basis (ie. multiple payments during the year when leave is being taken), then they add the leave loading payment to earnings for the period to calculate withholding.

HOLIDAY PAY, LONG SERVICE LEAVE AND EMPLOYMENT TERMINATION PAYMENTS

The employer must include holiday pay (including any leave loading) and long service leave payments as part of normal earnings, except when they are paid on termination of employment.

TFN WITHHOLDING

The employer must withhold 49% from 1 July 2014 from any payment made to a resident payee and 47% from a foreign resident payee (ignoring any cents) if one of the following applies:

- they have not quoted their TFN, or
- they have not claimed an exemption from quoting their TFN.
- they have not advised you that they have applied for a TFN or have made an enquiry with the Tax Office.

5.691 PAYG WITHHOLDING TAX TABLE 2015-16 including Medicare levy (rounded $)

Weekly withholding amounts

Weekly earnings	With tax-free threshold	No tax-free threshold	Weekly earnings	With tax-free threshold	No tax-free threshold	Weekly earnings	With tax-free threshold	No tax-free threshold
1.00	—	—	56.00	—	11.00	111.00	—	24.00
2.00	—	—	57.00	—	12.00	112.00	—	24.00
3.00	—	1.00	58.00	—	12.00	113.00	—	25.00
4.00	—	1.00	59.00	—	12.00	114.00	—	25.00
5.00	—	1.00	60.00	—	12.00	115.00	—	25.00
6.00	—	1.00	61.00	—	12.00	116.00	—	25.00
7.00	—	1.00	62.00	—	13.00	117.00	—	25.00
8.00	—	2.00	63.00	—	13.00	118.00	—	26.00
9.00	—	2.00	64.00	—	13.00	119.00	—	26.00
10.00	—	2.00	65.00	—	13.00	120.00	—	26.00
11.00	—	2.00	66.00	—	14.00	121.00	—	26.00
12.00	—	2.00	67.00	—	14.00	122.00	—	27.00
13.00	—	2.00	68.00	—	14.00	123.00	—	27.00
14.00	—	3.00	69.00	—	14.00	124.00	—	27.00
15.00	—	3.00	70.00	—	15.00	125.00	—	27.00
16.00	—	3.00	71.00	—	15.00	126.00	—	28.00
17.00	—	3.00	72.00	—	15.00	127.00	—	28.00
18.00	—	3.00	73.00	—	15.00	128.00	—	28.00
19.00	—	4.00	74.00	—	16.00	129.00	—	28.00
20.00	—	4.00	75.00	—	16.00	130.00	—	29.00
21.00	—	4.00	76.00	—	16.00	131.00	—	29.00
22.00	—	4.00	77.00	—	16.00	132.00	—	29.00
23.00	—	4.00	78.00	—	16.00	133.00	—	29.00
24.00	—	5.00	79.00	—	17.00	134.00	—	29.00
25.00	—	5.00	80.00	—	17.00	135.00	—	30.00
26.00	—	5.00	81.00	—	17.00	136.00	—	30.00
27.00	—	5.00	82.00	—	17.00	137.00	—	30.00
28.00	—	5.00	83.00	—	18.00	138.00	—	30.00
29.00	—	6.00	84.00	—	18.00	139.00	—	31.00
30.00	—	6.00	85.00	—	18.00	140.00	—	31.00
31.00	—	6.00	86.00	—	18.00	141.00	—	31.00
32.00	—	6.00	87.00	—	19.00	142.00	—	31.00
33.00	—	6.00	88.00	—	19.00	143.00	—	32.00
34.00	—	6.00	89.00	—	19.00	144.00	—	32.00
35.00	—	7.00	90.00	—	19.00	145.00	—	32.00
36.00	—	7.00	91.00	—	19.00	146.00	—	32.00
37.00	—	7.00	92.00	—	20.00	147.00	—	32.00
38.00	—	7.00	93.00	—	20.00	148.00	—	33.00
39.00	—	7.00	94.00	—	20.00	149.00	—	33.00
40.00	—	8.00	95.00	—	20.00	150.00	—	33.00
41.00	—	8.00	96.00	—	21.00	151.00	—	33.00
42.00	—	8.00	97.00	—	21.00	152.00	—	34.00
43.00	—	8.00	98.00	—	21.00	153.00	—	34.00
44.00	—	8.00	99.00	—	21.00	154.00	—	34.00
45.00	—	9.00	100.00	—	22.00	155.00	—	34.00
46.00	—	9.00	101.00	—	22.00	156.00	—	35.00
47.00	—	9.00	102.00	—	22.00	157.00	—	35.00
48.00	—	9.00	103.00	—	22.00	158.00	—	35.00
49.00	—	10.00	104.00	—	22.00	159.00	—	35.00
50.00	—	10.00	105.00	—	23.00	160.00	—	35.00
51.00	—	10.00	106.00	—	23.00	161.00	—	36.00
52.00	—	10.00	107.00	—	23.00	162.00	—	36.00
53.00	—	11.00	108.00	—	23.00	163.00	—	36.00
54.00	—	11.00	109.00	—	24.00	164.00	—	36.00
55.00	—	11.00	110.00	—	24.00	165.00	—	37.00

Taxpayers Australia Ltd 2015 & 2016

Weekly withholding amounts

Weekly earnings	With tax-free threshold	No tax-free threshold	Weekly earnings	With tax-free threshold	No tax-free threshold	Weekly earnings	With tax-free threshold	No tax-free threshold
166.00	—	37.00	221.00	—	50.00	276.00	—	62.00
167.00	—	37.00	222.00	—	50.00	277.00	—	63.00
168.00	—	37.00	223.00	—	50.00	278.00	—	63.00
169.00	—	38.00	224.00	—	50.00	279.00	—	63.00
170.00	—	38.00	225.00	—	51.00	280.00	—	63.00
171.00	—	38.00	226.00	—	51.00	281.00	—	64.00
172.00	—	38.00	227.00	—	51.00	282.00	—	64.00
173.00	—	38.00	228.00	—	51.00	283.00	—	64.00
174.00	—	39.00	229.00	—	51.00	284.00	—	64.00
175.00	—	39.00	230.00	—	52.00	285.00	—	64.00
176.00	—	39.00	231.00	—	52.00	286.00	—	65.00
177.00	—	39.00	232.00	—	52.00	287.00	—	65.00
178.00	—	40.00	233.00	—	52.00	288.00	—	65.00
179.00	—	40.00	234.00	—	53.00	289.00	—	65.00
180.00	—	40.00	235.00	—	53.00	290.00	—	66.00
181.00	—	40.00	236.00	—	53.00	291.00	—	66.00
182.00	—	41.00	237.00	—	53.00	292.00	—	66.00
183.00	—	41.00	238.00	—	54.00	293.00	—	66.00
184.00	—	41.00	239.00	—	54.00	294.00	—	67.00
185.00	—	41.00	240.00	—	54.00	295.00	—	67.00
186.00	—	42.00	241.00	—	54.00	296.00	—	67.00
187.00	—	42.00	242.00	—	55.00	297.00	—	67.00
188.00	—	42.00	243.00	—	55.00	298.00	—	67.00
189.00	—	42.00	244.00	—	55.00	299.00	—	68.00
190.00	—	42.00	245.00	—	55.00	300.00	—	68.00
191.00	—	43.00	246.00	—	55.00	301.00	—	68.00
192.00	—	43.00	247.00	—	56.00	302.00	—	68.00
193.00	—	43.00	248.00	—	56.00	303.00	—	69.00
194.00	—	43.00	249.00	—	56.00	304.00	—	69.00
195.00	—	44.00	250.00	—	56.00	305.00	—	69.00
196.00	—	44.00	251.00	—	57.00	306.00	—	69.00
197.00	—	44.00	252.00	—	57.00	307.00	—	70.00
198.00	—	44.00	253.00	—	57.00	308.00	—	70.00
199.00	—	45.00	254.00	—	57.00	309.00	—	70.00
200.00	—	45.00	255.00	—	58.00	310.00	—	70.00
201.00	—	45.00	256.00	—	58.00	311.00	—	71.00
202.00	—	45.00	257.00	—	58.00	312.00	—	71.00
203.00	—	45.00	258.00	—	58.00	313.00	—	71.00
204.00	—	46.00	259.00	—	58.00	314.00	—	71.00
205.00	—	46.00	260.00	—	59.00	315.00	—	71.00
206.00	—	46.00	261.00	—	59.00	316.00	—	72.00
207.00	—	46.00	262.00	—	59.00	317.00	—	72.00
208.00	—	47.00	263.00	—	59.00	318.00	—	72.00
209.00	—	47.00	264.00	—	60.00	319.00	—	72.00
210.00	—	47.00	265.00	—	60.00	320.00	—	73.00
211.00	—	47.00	266.00	—	60.00	321.00	—	73.00
212.00	—	48.00	267.00	—	60.00	322.00	—	73.00
213.00	—	48.00	268.00	—	61.00	323.00	—	73.00
214.00	—	48.00	269.00	—	61.00	324.00	—	74.00
215.00	—	48.00	270.00	—	61.00	325.00	—	74.00
216.00	—	48.00	271.00	—	61.00	326.00	—	74.00
217.00	—	49.00	272.00	—	61.00	327.00	—	74.00
218.00	—	49.00	273.00	—	62.00	328.00	—	74.00
219.00	—	49.00	274.00	—	62.00	329.00	—	75.00
220.00	—	49.00	275.00	—	62.00	330.00	—	75.00

5.691 PAYG WITHHOLDING TAX TABLE 2015-16 including Medicare levy (rounded $)

Weekly withholding amounts

Weekly earnings	With tax-free threshold	No tax-free threshold	Weekly earnings	With tax-free threshold	No tax-free threshold	Weekly earnings	With tax-free threshold	No tax-free threshold
331.00	—	75.00	386.00	6.00	91.00	441.00	21.00	110.00
332.00	—	75.00	387.00	6.00	91.00	442.00	21.00	110.00
333.00	—	76.00	388.00	6.00	92.00	443.00	22.00	111.00
334.00	—	76.00	389.00	7.00	92.00	444.00	22.00	111.00
335.00	—	76.00	390.00	7.00	92.00	445.00	22.00	111.00
336.00	—	76.00	391.00	7.00	93.00	446.00	23.00	112.00
337.00	—	77.00	392.00	7.00	93.00	447.00	23.00	112.00
338.00	—	77.00	393.00	7.00	93.00	448.00	23.00	112.00
339.00	—	77.00	394.00	8.00	94.00	449.00	24.00	113.00
340.00	—	77.00	395.00	8.00	94.00	450.00	24.00	113.00
341.00	—	77.00	396.00	8.00	94.00	451.00	24.00	113.00
342.00	—	78.00	397.00	8.00	95.00	452.00	24.00	114.00
343.00	—	78.00	398.00	9.00	95.00	453.00	25.00	114.00
344.00	—	78.00	399.00	9.00	95.00	454.00	25.00	115.00
345.00	—	78.00	400.00	9.00	96.00	455.00	25.00	115.00
346.00	—	79.00	401.00	10.00	96.00	456.00	26.00	115.00
347.00	—	79.00	402.00	10.00	96.00	457.00	26.00	116.00
348.00	—	79.00	403.00	10.00	97.00	458.00	26.00	116.00
349.00	—	79.00	404.00	10.00	97.00	459.00	26.00	116.00
350.00	—	80.00	405.00	11.00	97.00	460.00	27.00	117.00
351.00	—	80.00	406.00	11.00	98.00	461.00	27.00	117.00
352.00	—	80.00	407.00	11.00	98.00	462.00	27.00	117.00
353.00	—	80.00	408.00	12.00	99.00	463.00	28.00	118.00
354.00	—	80.00	409.00	12.00	99.00	464.00	28.00	118.00
355.00	—	81.00	410.00	12.00	99.00	465.00	28.00	118.00
356.00	—	81.00	411.00	13.00	100.00	466.00	28.00	119.00
357.00	1.00	81.00	412.00	13.00	100.00	467.00	29.00	119.00
358.00	1.00	81.00	413.00	13.00	100.00	468.00	29.00	119.00
359.00	1.00	82.00	414.00	13.00	101.00	469.00	29.00	120.00
360.00	1.00	82.00	415.00	14.00	101.00	470.00	30.00	120.00
361.00	1.00	82.00	416.00	14.00	101.00	471.00	30.00	120.00
362.00	2.00	83.00	417.00	14.00	102.00	472.00	30.00	121.00
363.00	2.00	83.00	418.00	15.00	102.00	473.00	30.00	121.00
364.00	2.00	83.00	419.00	15.00	102.00	474.00	31.00	121.00
365.00	2.00	84.00	420.00	15.00	103.00	475.00	31.00	122.00
366.00	2.00	84.00	421.00	15.00	103.00	476.00	31.00	122.00
367.00	2.00	84.00	422.00	16.00	103.00	477.00	32.00	123.00
368.00	3.00	85.00	423.00	16.00	104.00	478.00	32.00	123.00
369.00	3.00	85.00	424.00	16.00	104.00	479.00	32.00	123.00
370.00	3.00	85.00	425.00	17.00	104.00	480.00	33.00	124.00
371.00	3.00	86.00	426.00	17.00	105.00	481.00	33.00	124.00
372.00	3.00	86.00	427.00	17.00	105.00	482.00	33.00	124.00
373.00	4.00	86.00	428.00	17.00	105.00	483.00	33.00	125.00
374.00	4.00	87.00	429.00	18.00	106.00	484.00	34.00	125.00
375.00	4.00	87.00	430.00	18.00	106.00	485.00	34.00	125.00
376.00	4.00	87.00	431.00	18.00	107.00	486.00	34.00	126.00
377.00	4.00	88.00	432.00	19.00	107.00	487.00	35.00	126.00
378.00	5.00	88.00	433.00	19.00	107.00	488.00	35.00	126.00
379.00	5.00	88.00	434.00	19.00	108.00	489.00	35.00	127.00
380.00	5.00	89.00	435.00	19.00	108.00	490.00	35.00	127.00
381.00	5.00	89.00	436.00	20.00	108.00	491.00	36.00	127.00
382.00	5.00	89.00	437.00	20.00	109.00	492.00	36.00	128.00
383.00	5.00	90.00	438.00	20.00	109.00	493.00	36.00	128.00
384.00	6.00	90.00	439.00	21.00	109.00	494.00	36.00	128.00
385.00	6.00	91.00	440.00	21.00	110.00	495.00	37.00	129.00

Taxpayers Australia Ltd 2015 & 2016

Weekly withholding amounts

Weekly earnings	With tax-free threshold	No tax-free threshold	Weekly earnings	With tax-free threshold	No tax-free threshold	Weekly earnings	With tax-free threshold	No tax-free threshold
496.00	37.00	129.00	551.00	48.00	148.00	606.00	60.00	167.00
497.00	37.00	129.00	552.00	49.00	149.00	607.00	60.00	168.00
498.00	37.00	130.00	553.00	49.00	149.00	608.00	60.00	168.00
499.00	38.00	130.00	554.00	49.00	149.00	609.00	61.00	168.00
500.00	38.00	131.00	555.00	49.00	150.00	610.00	61.00	169.00
501.00	38.00	131.00	556.00	50.00	150.00	611.00	61.00	169.00
502.00	38.00	131.00	557.00	50.00	150.00	612.00	61.00	169.00
503.00	38.00	132.00	558.00	50.00	151.00	613.00	61.00	170.00
504.00	39.00	132.00	559.00	50.00	151.00	614.00	62.00	170.00
505.00	39.00	132.00	560.00	50.00	151.00	615.00	62.00	170.00
506.00	39.00	133.00	561.00	51.00	152.00	616.00	62.00	171.00
507.00	39.00	133.00	562.00	51.00	152.00	617.00	62.00	171.00
508.00	39.00	133.00	563.00	51.00	152.00	618.00	63.00	172.00
509.00	40.00	134.00	564.00	51.00	153.00	619.00	63.00	172.00
510.00	40.00	134.00	565.00	51.00	153.00	620.00	63.00	172.00
511.00	40.00	134.00	566.00	52.00	153.00	621.00	63.00	173.00
512.00	40.00	135.00	567.00	52.00	154.00	622.00	63.00	173.00
513.00	40.00	135.00	568.00	52.00	154.00	623.00	64.00	173.00
514.00	41.00	135.00	569.00	52.00	154.00	624.00	64.00	174.00
515.00	41.00	136.00	570.00	52.00	155.00	625.00	64.00	174.00
516.00	41.00	136.00	571.00	53.00	155.00	626.00	64.00	174.00
517.00	41.00	136.00	572.00	53.00	156.00	627.00	64.00	175.00
518.00	42.00	137.00	573.00	53.00	156.00	628.00	65.00	175.00
519.00	42.00	137.00	574.00	53.00	156.00	629.00	65.00	175.00
520.00	42.00	137.00	575.00	53.00	157.00	630.00	65.00	176.00
521.00	42.00	138.00	576.00	54.00	157.00	631.00	65.00	176.00
522.00	42.00	138.00	577.00	54.00	157.00	632.00	65.00	176.00
523.00	43.00	139.00	578.00	54.00	158.00	633.00	66.00	177.00
524.00	43.00	139.00	579.00	54.00	158.00	634.00	66.00	177.00
525.00	43.00	139.00	580.00	55.00	158.00	635.00	66.00	177.00
526.00	43.00	140.00	581.00	55.00	159.00	636.00	66.00	178.00
527.00	43.00	140.00	582.00	55.00	159.00	637.00	67.00	178.00
528.00	44.00	140.00	583.00	55.00	159.00	638.00	67.00	178.00
529.00	44.00	141.00	584.00	55.00	160.00	639.00	67.00	179.00
530.00	44.00	141.00	585.00	56.00	160.00	640.00	67.00	179.00
531.00	44.00	141.00	586.00	56.00	160.00	641.00	67.00	180.00
532.00	44.00	142.00	587.00	56.00	161.00	642.00	68.00	180.00
533.00	45.00	142.00	588.00	56.00	161.00	643.00	68.00	180.00
534.00	45.00	142.00	589.00	56.00	161.00	644.00	68.00	181.00
535.00	45.00	143.00	590.00	57.00	162.00	645.00	68.00	181.00
536.00	45.00	143.00	591.00	57.00	162.00	646.00	68.00	181.00
537.00	46.00	143.00	592.00	57.00	162.00	647.00	69.00	182.00
538.00	46.00	144.00	593.00	57.00	163.00	648.00	69.00	182.00
539.00	46.00	144.00	594.00	57.00	163.00	649.00	69.00	182.00
540.00	46.00	144.00	595.00	58.00	164.00	650.00	69.00	183.00
541.00	46.00	145.00	596.00	58.00	164.00	651.00	69.00	183.00
542.00	47.00	145.00	597.00	58.00	164.00	652.00	70.00	183.00
543.00	47.00	145.00	598.00	58.00	165.00	653.00	70.00	184.00
544.00	47.00	146.00	599.00	59.00	165.00	654.00	70.00	184.00
545.00	47.00	146.00	600.00	59.00	165.00	655.00	70.00	184.00
546.00	47.00	146.00	601.00	59.00	166.00	656.00	71.00	185.00
547.00	48.00	147.00	602.00	59.00	166.00	657.00	71.00	185.00
548.00	48.00	147.00	603.00	59.00	166.00	658.00	71.00	185.00
549.00	48.00	148.00	604.00	60.00	167.00	659.00	71.00	186.00
550.00	48.00	148.00	605.00	60.00	167.00	660.00	71.00	186.00

5.691 PAYG WITHHOLDING TAX TABLE 2015-16 including Medicare levy (rounded $)

Weekly withholding amounts

Weekly earnings	With tax-free threshold	No tax-free threshold	Weekly earnings	With tax-free threshold	No tax-free threshold	Weekly earnings	With tax-free threshold	No tax-free threshold
661.00	72.00	186.00	716.00	84.00	206.00	771.00	103.00	225.00
662.00	72.00	187.00	717.00	84.00	206.00	772.00	103.00	225.00
663.00	72.00	187.00	718.00	85.00	206.00	773.00	104.00	225.00
664.00	72.00	188.00	719.00	85.00	207.00	774.00	104.00	226.00
665.00	72.00	188.00	720.00	85.00	207.00	775.00	104.00	226.00
666.00	73.00	188.00	721.00	86.00	207.00	776.00	105.00	226.00
667.00	73.00	189.00	722.00	86.00	208.00	777.00	105.00	227.00
668.00	73.00	189.00	723.00	86.00	208.00	778.00	105.00	227.00
669.00	73.00	189.00	724.00	87.00	208.00	779.00	106.00	228.00
670.00	73.00	190.00	725.00	87.00	209.00	780.00	106.00	228.00
671.00	74.00	190.00	726.00	87.00	209.00	781.00	106.00	228.00
672.00	74.00	190.00	727.00	88.00	209.00	782.00	107.00	229.00
673.00	74.00	191.00	728.00	88.00	210.00	783.00	107.00	229.00
674.00	74.00	191.00	729.00	88.00	210.00	784.00	107.00	229.00
675.00	74.00	191.00	730.00	89.00	210.00	785.00	108.00	230.00
676.00	75.00	192.00	731.00	89.00	211.00	786.00	108.00	230.00
677.00	75.00	192.00	732.00	89.00	211.00	787.00	109.00	230.00
678.00	75.00	192.00	733.00	90.00	212.00	788.00	109.00	231.00
679.00	75.00	193.00	734.00	90.00	212.00	789.00	109.00	231.00
680.00	76.00	193.00	735.00	90.00	212.00	790.00	110.00	231.00
681.00	76.00	193.00	736.00	91.00	213.00	791.00	110.00	232.00
682.00	76.00	194.00	737.00	91.00	213.00	792.00	110.00	232.00
683.00	76.00	194.00	738.00	92.00	213.00	793.00	111.00	232.00
684.00	76.00	194.00	739.00	92.00	214.00	794.00	111.00	233.00
685.00	77.00	195.00	740.00	92.00	214.00	795.00	111.00	233.00
686.00	77.00	195.00	741.00	93.00	214.00	796.00	112.00	233.00
687.00	77.00	196.00	742.00	93.00	215.00	797.00	112.00	234.00
688.00	77.00	196.00	743.00	93.00	215.00	798.00	112.00	234.00
689.00	77.00	196.00	744.00	94.00	215.00	799.00	113.00	234.00
690.00	78.00	197.00	745.00	94.00	216.00	800.00	113.00	235.00
691.00	78.00	197.00	746.00	94.00	216.00	801.00	113.00	235.00
692.00	78.00	197.00	747.00	95.00	216.00	802.00	114.00	236.00
693.00	78.00	198.00	748.00	95.00	217.00	803.00	114.00	236.00
694.00	78.00	198.00	749.00	95.00	217.00	804.00	114.00	236.00
695.00	79.00	198.00	750.00	96.00	217.00	805.00	115.00	237.00
696.00	79.00	199.00	751.00	96.00	218.00	806.00	115.00	237.00
697.00	79.00	199.00	752.00	96.00	218.00	807.00	115.00	237.00
698.00	79.00	199.00	753.00	97.00	218.00	808.00	116.00	238.00
699.00	80.00	200.00	754.00	97.00	219.00	809.00	116.00	238.00
700.00	80.00	200.00	755.00	97.00	219.00	810.00	117.00	238.00
701.00	80.00	200.00	756.00	98.00	220.00	811.00	117.00	239.00
702.00	80.00	201.00	757.00	98.00	220.00	812.00	117.00	239.00
703.00	80.00	201.00	758.00	98.00	220.00	813.00	118.00	239.00
704.00	81.00	201.00	759.00	99.00	221.00	814.00	118.00	240.00
705.00	81.00	202.00	760.00	99.00	221.00	815.00	118.00	240.00
706.00	81.00	202.00	761.00	100.00	221.00	816.00	119.00	240.00
707.00	81.00	202.00	762.00	100.00	222.00	817.00	119.00	241.00
708.00	81.00	203.00	763.00	100.00	222.00	818.00	119.00	241.00
709.00	82.00	203.00	764.00	101.00	222.00	819.00	120.00	241.00
710.00	82.00	204.00	765.00	101.00	223.00	820.00	120.00	242.00
711.00	82.00	204.00	766.00	101.00	223.00	821.00	120.00	242.00
712.00	82.00	204.00	767.00	102.00	223.00	822.00	121.00	242.00
713.00	83.00	205.00	768.00	102.00	224.00	823.00	121.00	243.00
714.00	83.00	205.00	769.00	102.00	224.00	824.00	121.00	243.00
715.00	84.00	205.00	770.00	103.00	224.00	825.00	122.00	244.00

PAYG WITHHOLDING TAX TABLE 2015-16 including Medicare levy (rounded $)   **5.691**

Weekly withholding amounts

Weekly earnings	With tax-free threshold	No tax-free threshold	Weekly earnings	With tax-free threshold	No tax-free threshold	Weekly earnings	With tax-free threshold	No tax-free threshold
826.00	122.00	244.00	881.00	141.00	263.00	936.00	160.00	282.00
827.00	122.00	244.00	882.00	142.00	263.00	937.00	161.00	282.00
828.00	123.00	245.00	883.00	142.00	264.00	938.00	161.00	283.00
829.00	123.00	245.00	884.00	142.00	264.00	939.00	161.00	283.00
830.00	123.00	245.00	885.00	143.00	264.00	940.00	162.00	283.00
831.00	124.00	246.00	886.00	143.00	265.00	941.00	162.00	284.00
832.00	124.00	246.00	887.00	143.00	265.00	942.00	162.00	284.00
833.00	125.00	246.00	888.00	144.00	265.00	943.00	163.00	285.00
834.00	125.00	247.00	889.00	144.00	266.00	944.00	163.00	285.00
835.00	125.00	247.00	890.00	144.00	266.00	945.00	163.00	285.00
836.00	126.00	247.00	891.00	145.00	266.00	946.00	164.00	286.00
837.00	126.00	248.00	892.00	145.00	267.00	947.00	164.00	286.00
838.00	126.00	248.00	893.00	145.00	267.00	948.00	165.00	286.00
839.00	127.00	248.00	894.00	146.00	267.00	949.00	165.00	287.00
840.00	127.00	249.00	895.00	146.00	268.00	950.00	165.00	287.00
841.00	127.00	249.00	896.00	146.00	268.00	951.00	166.00	287.00
842.00	128.00	249.00	897.00	147.00	269.00	952.00	166.00	288.00
843.00	128.00	250.00	898.00	147.00	269.00	953.00	166.00	288.00
844.00	128.00	250.00	899.00	147.00	269.00	954.00	167.00	288.00
845.00	129.00	250.00	900.00	148.00	270.00	955.00	167.00	289.00
846.00	129.00	251.00	901.00	148.00	270.00	956.00	167.00	289.00
847.00	129.00	251.00	902.00	149.00	270.00	957.00	168.00	289.00
848.00	130.00	252.00	903.00	149.00	271.00	958.00	168.00	290.00
849.00	130.00	252.00	904.00	149.00	271.00	959.00	168.00	290.00
850.00	130.00	252.00	905.00	150.00	271.00	960.00	169.00	290.00
851.00	131.00	253.00	906.00	150.00	272.00	961.00	169.00	291.00
852.00	131.00	253.00	907.00	150.00	272.00	962.00	169.00	291.00
853.00	131.00	253.00	908.00	151.00	272.00	963.00	170.00	291.00
854.00	132.00	254.00	909.00	151.00	273.00	964.00	170.00	292.00
855.00	132.00	254.00	910.00	151.00	273.00	965.00	170.00	292.00
856.00	133.00	254.00	911.00	152.00	273.00	966.00	171.00	292.00
857.00	133.00	255.00	912.00	152.00	274.00	967.00	171.00	293.00
858.00	133.00	255.00	913.00	152.00	274.00	968.00	171.00	293.00
859.00	134.00	255.00	914.00	153.00	274.00	969.00	172.00	293.00
860.00	134.00	256.00	915.00	153.00	275.00	970.00	172.00	294.00
861.00	134.00	256.00	916.00	153.00	275.00	971.00	173.00	294.00
862.00	135.00	256.00	917.00	154.00	275.00	072.00	173.00	295.00
863.00	135.00	257.00	918.00	154.00	276.00	973.00	173.00	295.00
864.00	135.00	257.00	919.00	154.00	276.00	974.00	174.00	295.00
865.00	136.00	257.00	920.00	155.00	277.00	975.00	174.00	296.00
866.00	136.00	258.00	921.00	155.00	277.00	976.00	174.00	296.00
867.00	136.00	258.00	922.00	155.00	277.00	977.00	175.00	296.00
868.00	137.00	258.00	923.00	156.00	278.00	978.00	175.00	297.00
869.00	137.00	259.00	924.00	156.00	278.00	979.00	175.00	297.00
870.00	137.00	259.00	925.00	157.00	278.00	980.00	176.00	297.00
871.00	138.00	260.00	926.00	157.00	279.00	981.00	176.00	298.00
872.00	138.00	260.00	927.00	157.00	279.00	982.00	176.00	298.00
873.00	138.00	260.00	928.00	158.00	279.00	983.00	177.00	298.00
874.00	139.00	261.00	929.00	158.00	280.00	984.00	177.00	299.00
875.00	139.00	261.00	930.00	158.00	280.00	985.00	177.00	299.00
876.00	139.00	261.00	931.00	159.00	280.00	986.00	178.00	299.00
877.00	140.00	262.00	932.00	159.00	281.00	987.00	178.00	300.00
878.00	140.00	262.00	933.00	159.00	281.00	988.00	178.00	300.00
879.00	141.00	262.00	934.00	160.00	281.00	989.00	179.00	300.00
880.00	141.00	263.00	935.00	160.00	282.00	990.00	179.00	301.00

5.691 PAYG WITHHOLDING TAX TABLE 2015-16 including Medicare levy (rounded $)

Weekly withholding amounts

Weekly earnings	With tax-free threshold	No tax-free threshold	Weekly earnings	With tax-free threshold	No tax-free threshold	Weekly earnings	With tax-free threshold	No tax-free threshold
991.00	179.00	301.00	1046.00	199.00	320.00	1101.00	218.00	339.00
992.00	180.00	301.00	1047.00	199.00	320.00	1102.00	218.00	339.00
993.00	180.00	302.00	1048.00	199.00	321.00	1103.00	218.00	340.00
994.00	181.00	302.00	1049.00	200.00	321.00	1104.00	219.00	340.00
995.00	181.00	302.00	1050.00	200.00	321.00	1105.00	219.00	340.00
996.00	181.00	303.00	1051.00	200.00	322.00	1106.00	219.00	341.00
997.00	182.00	303.00	1052.00	201.00	322.00	1107.00	220.00	341.00
998.00	182.00	303.00	1053.00	201.00	322.00	1108.00	220.00	341.00
999.00	182.00	304.00	1054.00	201.00	323.00	1109.00	221.00	342.00
1000.00	183.00	304.00	1055.00	202.00	323.00	1110.00	221.00	342.00
1001.00	183.00	305.00	1056.00	202.00	323.00	1111.00	221.00	342.00
1002.00	183.00	305.00	1057.00	202.00	324.00	1112.00	222.00	343.00
1003.00	184.00	305.00	1058.00	203.00	324.00	1113.00	222.00	343.00
1004.00	184.00	306.00	1059.00	203.00	325.00	1114.00	222.00	343.00
1005.00	184.00	306.00	1060.00	203.00	325.00	1115.00	223.00	344.00
1006.00	185.00	306.00	1061.00	204.00	325.00	1116.00	223.00	344.00
1007.00	185.00	307.00	1062.00	204.00	326.00	1117.00	223.00	345.00
1008.00	185.00	307.00	1063.00	205.00	326.00	1118.00	224.00	345.00
1009.00	186.00	307.00	1064.00	205.00	326.00	1119.00	224.00	345.00
1010.00	186.00	308.00	1065.00	205.00	327.00	1120.00	224.00	346.00
1011.00	186.00	308.00	1066.00	206.00	327.00	1121.00	225.00	346.00
1012.00	187.00	308.00	1067.00	206.00	327.00	1122.00	225.00	346.00
1013.00	187.00	309.00	1068.00	206.00	328.00	1123.00	225.00	347.00
1014.00	187.00	309.00	1069.00	207.00	328.00	1124.00	226.00	347.00
1015.00	188.00	309.00	1070.00	207.00	328.00	1125.00	226.00	347.00
1016.00	188.00	310.00	1071.00	207.00	329.00	1126.00	226.00	348.00
1017.00	189.00	310.00	1072.00	208.00	329.00	1127.00	227.00	348.00
1018.00	189.00	310.00	1073.00	208.00	329.00	1128.00	227.00	348.00
1019.00	189.00	311.00	1074.00	208.00	330.00	1129.00	227.00	349.00
1020.00	190.00	311.00	1075.00	209.00	330.00	1130.00	228.00	349.00
1021.00	190.00	311.00	1076.00	209.00	330.00	1131.00	228.00	349.00
1022.00	190.00	312.00	1077.00	209.00	331.00	1132.00	228.00	350.00
1023.00	191.00	312.00	1078.00	210.00	331.00	1133.00	229.00	350.00
1024.00	191.00	312.00	1079.00	210.00	331.00	1134.00	229.00	350.00
1025.00	191.00	313.00	1080.00	210.00	332.00	1135.00	230.00	351.00
1026.00	192.00	313.00	1081.00	211.00	332.00	1136.00	230.00	351.00
1027.00	192.00	313.00	1082.00	211.00	332.00	1137.00	230.00	351.00
1028.00	192.00	314.00	1083.00	211.00	333.00	1138.00	231.00	352.00
1029.00	193.00	314.00	1084.00	212.00	333.00	1139.00	231.00	352.00
1030.00	193.00	315.00	1085.00	212.00	333.00	1140.00	231.00	352.00
1031.00	193.00	315.00	1086.00	213.00	334.00	1141.00	232.00	353.00
1032.00	194.00	315.00	1087.00	213.00	334.00	1142.00	232.00	353.00
1033.00	194.00	316.00	1088.00	213.00	335.00	1143.00	232.00	354.00
1034.00	194.00	316.00	1089.00	214.00	335.00	1144.00	233.00	354.00
1035.00	195.00	316.00	1090.00	214.00	335.00	1145.00	233.00	354.00
1036.00	195.00	317.00	1091.00	214.00	336.00	1146.00	233.00	355.00
1037.00	195.00	317.00	1092.00	215.00	336.00	1147.00	234.00	355.00
1038.00	196.00	317.00	1093.00	215.00	336.00	1148.00	234.00	355.00
1039.00	196.00	318.00	1094.00	215.00	337.00	1149.00	234.00	356.00
1040.00	197.00	318.00	1095.00	216.00	337.00	1150.00	235.00	356.00
1041.00	197.00	318.00	1096.00	216.00	337.00	1151.00	235.00	356.00
1042.00	197.00	319.00	1097.00	216.00	338.00	1152.00	235.00	357.00
1043.00	198.00	319.00	1098.00	217.00	338.00	1153.00	236.00	357.00
1044.00	198.00	319.00	1099.00	217.00	338.00	1154.00	236.00	357.00
1045.00	198.00	320.00	1100.00	217.00	339.00	1155.00	236.00	358.00

Weekly earnings	With tax-free threshold	No tax-free threshold	Weekly earnings	With tax-free threshold	No tax-free threshold	Weekly earnings	With tax-free threshold	No tax-free threshold
1156.00	237.00	358.00	1211.00	256.00	378.00	1266.00	275.00	399.00
1157.00	237.00	358.00	1212.00	256.00	378.00	1267.00	275.00	400.00
1158.00	238.00	359.00	1213.00	257.00	379.00	1268.00	276.00	400.00
1159.00	238.00	359.00	1214.00	257.00	379.00	1269.00	276.00	401.00
1160.00	238.00	359.00	1215.00	257.00	380.00	1270.00	276.00	401.00
1161.00	239.00	360.00	1216.00	258.00	380.00	1271.00	277.00	401.00
1162.00	239.00	360.00	1217.00	258.00	380.00	1272.00	277.00	402.00
1163.00	239.00	360.00	1218.00	258.00	381.00	1273.00	278.00	402.00
1164.00	240.00	361.00	1219.00	259.00	381.00	1274.00	278.00	403.00
1165.00	240.00	361.00	1220.00	259.00	382.00	1275.00	278.00	403.00
1166.00	240.00	361.00	1221.00	259.00	382.00	1276.00	279.00	403.00
1167.00	241.00	362.00	1222.00	260.00	382.00	1277.00	279.00	404.00
1168.00	241.00	362.00	1223.00	260.00	383.00	1278.00	279.00	404.00
1169.00	241.00	362.00	1224.00	260.00	383.00	1279.00	280.00	405.00
1170.00	242.00	363.00	1225.00	261.00	383.00	1280.00	280.00	405.00
1171.00	242.00	363.00	1226.00	261.00	384.00	1281.00	280.00	405.00
1172.00	242.00	364.00	1227.00	262.00	384.00	1282.00	281.00	406.00
1173.00	243.00	364.00	1228.00	262.00	385.00	1283.00	281.00	406.00
1174.00	243.00	364.00	1229.00	262.00	385.00	1284.00	281.00	406.00
1175.00	243.00	365.00	1230.00	263.00	385.00	1285.00	282.00	407.00
1176.00	244.00	365.00	1231.00	263.00	386.00	1286.00	282.00	407.00
1177.00	244.00	365.00	1232.00	263.00	386.00	1287.00	282.00	408.00
1178.00	244.00	366.00	1233.00	264.00	387.00	1288.00	283.00	408.00
1179.00	245.00	366.00	1234.00	264.00	387.00	1289.00	283.00	408.00
1180.00	245.00	366.00	1235.00	264.00	387.00	1290.00	283.00	409.00
1181.00	246.00	367.00	1236.00	265.00	388.00	1291.00	284.00	409.00
1182.00	246.00	367.00	1237.00	265.00	388.00	1292.00	284.00	410.00
1183.00	246.00	367.00	1238.00	265.00	389.00	1293.00	284.00	410.00
1184.00	247.00	368.00	1239.00	266.00	389.00	1294.00	285.00	410.00
1185.00	247.00	368.00	1240.00	266.00	389.00	1295.00	285.00	411.00
1186.00	247.00	368.00	1241.00	266.00	390.00	1296.00	285.00	411.00
1187.00	248.00	369.00	1242.00	267.00	390.00	1297.00	286.00	412.00
1188.00	248.00	369.00	1243.00	267.00	391.00	1298.00	286.00	412.00
1189.00	248.00	369.00	1244.00	267.00	391.00	1299.00	287.00	412.00
1190.00	249.00	370.00	1245.00	268.00	391.00	1300.00	287.00	413.00
1191.00	249.00	370.00	1246.00	268.00	392.00	1301.00	287.00	413.00
1192.00	249.00	371.00	1247.00	268.00	392.00	1302.00	288.00	414.00
1193.00	250.00	371.00	1248.00	269.00	392.00	1303.00	288.00	414.00
1194.00	250.00	371.00	1249.00	269.00	393.00	1304.00	288.00	414.00
1195.00	250.00	372.00	1250.00	270.00	393.00	1305.00	289.00	415.00
1196.00	251.00	372.00	1251.00	270.00	394.00	1306.00	289.00	415.00
1197.00	251.00	373.00	1252.00	270.00	394.00	1307.00	289.00	415.00
1198.00	251.00	373.00	1253.00	271.00	394.00	1308.00	290.00	416.00
1199.00	252.00	373.00	1254.00	271.00	395.00	1309.00	290.00	416.00
1200.00	252.00	374.00	1255.00	271.00	395.00	1310.00	290.00	417.00
1201.00	252.00	374.00	1256.00	272.00	396.00	1311.00	291.00	417.00
1202.00	253.00	375.00	1257.00	272.00	396.00	1312.00	291.00	417.00
1203.00	253.00	375.00	1258.00	272.00	396.00	1313.00	291.00	418.00
1204.00	254.00	375.00	1259.00	273.00	397.00	1314.00	292.00	418.00
1205.00	254.00	376.00	1260.00	273.00	397.00	1315.00	292.00	419.00
1206.00	254.00	376.00	1261.00	273.00	398.00	1316.00	292.00	419.00
1207.00	255.00	376.00	1262.00	274.00	398.00	1317.00	293.00	419.00
1208.00	255.00	377.00	1263.00	274.00	398.00	1318.00	293.00	420.00
1209.00	255.00	377.00	1264.00	274.00	399.00	1319.00	293.00	420.00
1210.00	256.00	378.00	1265.00	275.00	399.00	1320.00	294.00	421.00

Weekly withholding amounts

Weekly earnings	With tax-free threshold	No tax-free threshold	Weekly earnings	With tax-free threshold	No tax-free threshold	Weekly earnings	With tax-free threshold	No tax-free threshold
1321.00	294.00	421.00	1376.00	313.00	442.00	1431.00	332.00	464.00
1322.00	294.00	421.00	1377.00	313.00	443.00	1432.00	332.00	464.00
1323.00	295.00	422.00	1378.00	314.00	443.00	1433.00	333.00	465.00
1324.00	295.00	422.00	1379.00	314.00	444.00	1434.00	333.00	465.00
1325.00	295.00	422.00	1380.00	314.00	444.00	1435.00	333.00	465.00
1326.00	296.00	423.00	1381.00	315.00	444.00	1436.00	334.00	466.00
1327.00	296.00	423.00	1382.00	315.00	445.00	1437.00	334.00	466.00
1328.00	297.00	424.00	1383.00	315.00	445.00	1438.00	334.00	467.00
1329.00	297.00	424.00	1384.00	316.00	445.00	1439.00	335.00	467.00
1330.00	297.00	424.00	1385.00	316.00	446.00	1440.00	335.00	467.00
1331.00	298.00	425.00	1386.00	317.00	446.00	1441.00	336.00	468.00
1332.00	298.00	425.00	1387.00	317.00	447.00	1442.00	336.00	468.00
1333.00	298.00	426.00	1388.00	317.00	447.00	1443.00	336.00	469.00
1334.00	299.00	426.00	1389.00	318.00	447.00	1444.00	337.00	469.00
1335.00	299.00	426.00	1390.00	318.00	448.00	1445.00	337.00	469.00
1336.00	299.00	427.00	1391.00	318.00	448.00	1446.00	337.00	470.00
1337.00	300.00	427.00	1392.00	319.00	449.00	1447.00	338.00	470.00
1338.00	300.00	428.00	1393.00	319.00	449.00	1448.00	338.00	470.00
1339.00	300.00	428.00	1394.00	319.00	449.00	1449.00	338.00	471.00
1340.00	301.00	428.00	1395.00	320.00	450.00	1450.00	339.00	471.00
1341.00	301.00	429.00	1396.00	320.00	450.00	1451.00	339.00	472.00
1342.00	301.00	429.00	1397.00	320.00	451.00	1452.00	339.00	472.00
1343.00	302.00	430.00	1398.00	321.00	451.00	1453.00	340.00	472.00
1344.00	302.00	430.00	1399.00	321.00	451.00	1454.00	340.00	473.00
1345.00	302.00	430.00	1400.00	321.00	452.00	1455.00	340.00	473.00
1346.00	303.00	431.00	1401.00	322.00	452.00	1456.00	341.00	474.00
1347.00	303.00	431.00	1402.00	322.00	453.00	1457.00	341.00	474.00
1348.00	303.00	431.00	1403.00	322.00	453.00	1458.00	341.00	474.00
1349.00	304.00	432.00	1404.00	323.00	453.00	1459.00	342.00	475.00
1350.00	304.00	432.00	1405.00	323.00	454.00	1460.00	342.00	475.00
1351.00	304.00	433.00	1406.00	323.00	454.00	1461.00	342.00	476.00
1352.00	305.00	433.00	1407.00	324.00	454.00	1462.00	343.00	476.00
1353.00	305.00	433.00	1408.00	324.00	455.00	1463.00	343.00	476.00
1354.00	305.00	434.00	1409.00	324.00	455.00	1464.00	343.00	477.00
1355.00	306.00	434.00	1410.00	325.00	456.00	1465.00	344.00	477.00
1356.00	306.00	435.00	1411.00	325.00	456.00	1466.00	344.00	477.00
1357.00	307.00	435.00	1412.00	326.00	456.00	1467.00	344.00	478.00
1358.00	307.00	435.00	1413.00	326.00	457.00	1468.00	345.00	478.00
1359.00	307.00	436.00	1414.00	326.00	457.00	1469.00	345.00	479.00
1360.00	308.00	436.00	1415.00	327.00	458.00	1470.00	346.00	479.00
1361.00	308.00	437.00	1416.00	327.00	458.00	1471.00	346.00	479.00
1362.00	308.00	437.00	1417.00	327.00	458.00	1472.00	346.00	480.00
1363.00	309.00	437.00	1418.00	328.00	459.00	1473.00	347.00	480.00
1364.00	309.00	438.00	1419.00	328.00	459.00	1474.00	347.00	481.00
1365.00	309.00	438.00	1420.00	328.00	460.00	1475.00	347.00	481.00
1366.00	310.00	438.00	1421.00	329.00	460.00	1476.00	348.00	481.00
1367.00	310.00	439.00	1422.00	329.00	460.00	1477.00	348.00	482.00
1368.00	310.00	439.00	1423.00	329.00	461.00	1478.00	348.00	482.00
1369.00	311.00	440.00	1424.00	330.00	461.00	1479.00	349.00	483.00
1370.00	311.00	440.00	1425.00	330.00	461.00	1480.00	349.00	483.00
1371.00	311.00	440.00	1426.00	330.00	462.00	1481.00	349.00	483.00
1372.00	312.00	441.00	1427.00	331.00	462.00	1482.00	350.00	484.00
1373.00	312.00	441.00	1428.00	331.00	463.00	1483.00	350.00	484.00
1374.00	312.00	442.00	1429.00	331.00	463.00	1484.00	350.00	484.00
1375.00	313.00	442.00	1430.00	332.00	463.00	1485.00	351.00	485.00

Weekly withholding amounts

Weekly earnings	With tax-free threshold	No tax-free threshold	Weekly earnings	With tax-free threshold	No tax-free threshold	Weekly earnings	With tax-free threshold	No tax-free threshold
1486.00	351.00	485.00	1541.00	370.00	507.00	1596.00	392.00	528.00
1487.00	351.00	486.00	1542.00	371.00	507.00	1597.00	392.00	529.00
1488.00	352.00	486.00	1543.00	371.00	508.00	1598.00	392.00	529.00
1489.00	352.00	486.00	1544.00	371.00	508.00	1599.00	393.00	529.00
1490.00	352.00	487.00	1545.00	372.00	508.00	1600.00	393.00	530.00
1491.00	353.00	487.00	1546.00	372.00	509.00	1601.00	394.00	530.00
1492.00	353.00	488.00	1547.00	373.00	509.00	1602.00	394.00	531.00
1493.00	353.00	488.00	1548.00	373.00	509.00	1603.00	394.00	531.00
1494.00	354.00	488.00	1549.00	373.00	510.00	1604.00	395.00	531.00
1495.00	354.00	489.00	1550.00	374.00	510.00	1605.00	395.00	532.00
1496.00	354.00	489.00	1551.00	374.00	511.00	1606.00	396.00	532.00
1497.00	355.00	490.00	1552.00	374.00	511.00	1607.00	396.00	532.00
1498.00	355.00	490.00	1553.00	375.00	511.00	1608.00	396.00	533.00
1499.00	356.00	490.00	1554.00	375.00	512.00	1609.00	397.00	533.00
1500.00	356.00	491.00	1555.00	376.00	512.00	1610.00	397.00	534.00
1501.00	356.00	491.00	1556.00	376.00	513.00	1611.00	397.00	534.00
1502.00	357.00	492.00	1557.00	376.00	513.00	1612.00	398.00	534.00
1503.00	357.00	492.00	1558.00	377.00	513.00	1613.00	398.00	535.00
1504.00	357.00	492.00	1559.00	377.00	514.00	1614.00	399.00	535.00
1505.00	358.00	493.00	1560.00	378.00	514.00	1615.00	399.00	536.00
1506.00	358.00	493.00	1561.00	378.00	515.00	1616.00	399.00	536.00
1507.00	358.00	493.00	1562.00	378.00	515.00	1617.00	400.00	536.00
1508.00	359.00	494.00	1563.00	379.00	515.00	1618.00	400.00	537.00
1509.00	359.00	494.00	1564.00	379.00	516.00	1619.00	401.00	537.00
1510.00	359.00	495.00	1565.00	380.00	516.00	1620.00	401.00	538.00
1511.00	360.00	495.00	1566.00	380.00	516.00	1621.00	401.00	538.00
1512.00	360.00	495.00	1567.00	380.00	517.00	1622.00	402.00	538.00
1513.00	360.00	496.00	1568.00	381.00	517.00	1623.00	402.00	539.00
1514.00	361.00	496.00	1569.00	381.00	518.00	1624.00	403.00	539.00
1515.00	361.00	497.00	1570.00	381.00	518.00	1625.00	403.00	539.00
1516.00	361.00	497.00	1571.00	382.00	518.00	1626.00	403.00	540.00
1517.00	362.00	497.00	1572.00	382.00	519.00	1627.00	404.00	540.00
1518.00	362.00	498.00	1573.00	383.00	519.00	1628.00	404.00	541.00
1519.00	362.00	498.00	1574.00	383.00	520.00	1629.00	404.00	541.00
1520.00	363.00	499.00	1575.00	383.00	520.00	1630.00	405.00	541.00
1521.00	363.00	499.00	1576.00	384.00	520.00	1631.00	405.00	542.00
1522.00	363.00	499.00	1577.00	384.00	521.00	1632.00	406.00	542.00
1523.00	364.00	500.00	1578.00	385.00	521.00	1633.00	406.00	543.00
1524.00	364.00	500.00	1579.00	385.00	522.00	1634.00	406.00	543.00
1525.00	364.00	500.00	1580.00	385.00	522.00	1635.00	407.00	543.00
1526.00	365.00	501.00	1581.00	386.00	522.00	1636.00	407.00	544.00
1527.00	365.00	501.00	1582.00	386.00	523.00	1637.00	408.00	544.00
1528.00	366.00	502.00	1583.00	387.00	523.00	1638.00	408.00	545.00
1529.00	366.00	502.00	1584.00	387.00	523.00	1639.00	408.00	545.00
1530.00	366.00	502.00	1585.00	387.00	524.00	1640.00	409.00	545.00
1531.00	367.00	503.00	1586.00	388.00	524.00	1641.00	409.00	546.00
1532.00	367.00	503.00	1587.00	388.00	525.00	1642.00	410.00	546.00
1533.00	367.00	504.00	1588.00	388.00	525.00	1643.00	410.00	547.00
1534.00	368.00	504.00	1589.00	389.00	525.00	1644.00	410.00	547.00
1535.00	368.00	504.00	1590.00	389.00	526.00	1645.00	411.00	547.00
1536.00	368.00	505.00	1591.00	390.00	526.00	1646.00	411.00	548.00
1537.00	369.00	505.00	1592.00	390.00	527.00	1647.00	412.00	548.00
1538.00	369.00	506.00	1593.00	390.00	527.00	1648.00	412.00	548.00
1539.00	369.00	506.00	1594.00	391.00	527.00	1649.00	412.00	549.00
1540.00	370.00	506.00	1595.00	391.00	528.00	1650.00	413.00	549.00

5.691 PAYG WITHHOLDING TAX TABLE 2015-16 including Medicare levy (rounded $)

Weekly withholding amounts

Weekly earnings	With tax-free threshold	No tax-free threshold	Weekly earnings	With tax-free threshold	No tax-free threshold	Weekly earnings	With tax-free threshold	No tax-free threshold
1651.00	413.00	550.00	1706.00	435.00	571.00	1761.00	456.00	593.00
1652.00	413.00	550.00	1707.00	435.00	571.00	1762.00	456.00	593.00
1653.00	414.00	550.00	1708.00	435.00	572.00	1763.00	457.00	593.00
1654.00	414.00	551.00	1709.00	436.00	572.00	1764.00	457.00	594.00
1655.00	415.00	551.00	1710.00	436.00	573.00	1765.00	458.00	594.00
1656.00	415.00	552.00	1711.00	436.00	573.00	1766.00	458.00	594.00
1657.00	415.00	552.00	1712.00	437.00	573.00	1767.00	458.00	595.00
1658.00	416.00	552.00	1713.00	437.00	574.00	1768.00	459.00	595.00
1659.00	416.00	553.00	1714.00	438.00	574.00	1769.00	459.00	596.00
1660.00	417.00	553.00	1715.00	438.00	575.00	1770.00	459.00	596.00
1661.00	417.00	554.00	1716.00	438.00	575.00	1771.00	460.00	596.00
1662.00	417.00	554.00	1717.00	439.00	575.00	1772.00	460.00	597.00
1663.00	418.00	554.00	1718.00	439.00	576.00	1773.00	461.00	597.00
1664.00	418.00	555.00	1719.00	440.00	576.00	1774.00	461.00	598.00
1665.00	419.00	555.00	1720.00	440.00	577.00	1775.00	461.00	598.00
1666.00	419.00	555.00	1721.00	440.00	577.00	1776.00	462.00	598.00
1667.00	419.00	556.00	1722.00	441.00	577.00	1777.00	462.00	599.00
1668.00	420.00	556.00	1723.00	441.00	578.00	1778.00	463.00	599.00
1669.00	420.00	557.00	1724.00	442.00	578.00	1779.00	463.00	600.00
1670.00	420.00	557.00	1725.00	442.00	578.00	1780.00	463.00	600.00
1671.00	421.00	557.00	1726.00	442.00	579.00	1781.00	464.00	600.00
1672.00	421.00	558.00	1727.00	443.00	579.00	1782.00	464.00	601.00
1673.00	422.00	558.00	1728.00	443.00	580.00	1783.00	465.00	601.00
1674.00	422.00	559.00	1729.00	443.00	580.00	1784.00	465.00	601.00
1675.00	422.00	559.00	1730.00	444.00	580.00	1785.00	465.00	602.00
1676.00	423.00	559.00	1731.00	444.00	581.00	1786.00	466.00	602.00
1677.00	423.00	560.00	1732.00	445.00	581.00	1787.00	466.00	603.00
1678.00	424.00	560.00	1733.00	445.00	582.00	1788.00	466.00	603.00
1679.00	424.00	561.00	1734.00	445.00	582.00	1789.00	467.00	603.00
1680.00	424.00	561.00	1735.00	446.00	582.00	1790.00	467.00	604.00
1681.00	425.00	561.00	1736.00	446.00	583.00	1791.00	468.00	604.00
1682.00	425.00	562.00	1737.00	447.00	583.00	1792.00	468.00	605.00
1683.00	426.00	562.00	1738.00	447.00	584.00	1793.00	468.00	605.00
1684.00	426.00	562.00	1739.00	447.00	584.00	1794.00	469.00	605.00
1685.00	426.00	563.00	1740.00	448.00	584.00	1795.00	469.00	606.00
1686.00	427.00	563.00	1741.00	448.00	585.00	1796.00	470.00	606.00
1687.00	427.00	564.00	1742.00	449.00	585.00	1797.00	470.00	607.00
1688.00	427.00	564.00	1743.00	449.00	586.00	1798.00	470.00	607.00
1689.00	428.00	564.00	1744.00	449.00	586.00	1799.00	471.00	607.00
1690.00	428.00	565.00	1745.00	450.00	586.00	1800.00	471.00	608.00
1691.00	429.00	565.00	1746.00	450.00	587.00	1801.00	472.00	608.00
1692.00	429.00	566.00	1747.00	451.00	587.00	1802.00	472.00	609.00
1693.00	429.00	566.00	1748.00	451.00	587.00	1803.00	472.00	609.00
1694.00	430.00	566.00	1749.00	451.00	588.00	1804.00	473.00	609.00
1695.00	430.00	567.00	1750.00	452.00	588.00	1805.00	473.00	610.00
1696.00	431.00	567.00	1751.00	452.00	589.00	1806.00	474.00	610.00
1697.00	431.00	568.00	1752.00	452.00	589.00	1807.00	474.00	610.00
1698.00	431.00	568.00	1753.00	453.00	589.00	1808.00	474.00	611.00
1699.00	432.00	568.00	1754.00	453.00	590.00	1809.00	475.00	611.00
1700.00	432.00	569.00	1755.00	454.00	590.00	1810.00	475.00	612.00
1701.00	433.00	569.00	1756.00	454.00	591.00	1811.00	475.00	612.00
1702.00	433.00	570.00	1757.00	454.00	591.00	1812.00	476.00	612.00
1703.00	433.00	570.00	1758.00	455.00	591.00	1813.00	476.00	613.00
1704.00	434.00	570.00	1759.00	455.00	592.00	1814.00	477.00	613.00
1705.00	434.00	571.00	1760.00	456.00	592.00	1815.00	477.00	614.00

Weekly withholding amounts

Weekly earnings	With tax-free threshold	No tax-free threshold	Weekly earnings	With tax-free threshold	No tax-free threshold	Weekly earnings	With tax-free threshold	No tax-free threshold
1816.00	477.00	614.00	1871.00	499.00	635.00	1926.00	520.00	657.00
1817.00	478.00	614.00	1872.00	499.00	636.00	1927.00	521.00	657.00
1818.00	478.00	615.00	1873.00	500.00	636.00	1928.00	521.00	658.00
1819.00	479.00	615.00	1874.00	500.00	637.00	1929.00	521.00	658.00
1820.00	479.00	616.00	1875.00	500.00	637.00	1930.00	522.00	658.00
1821.00	479.00	616.00	1876.00	501.00	637.00	1931.00	522.00	659.00
1822.00	480.00	616.00	1877.00	501.00	638.00	1932.00	523.00	659.00
1823.00	480.00	617.00	1878.00	502.00	638.00	1933.00	523.00	660.00
1824.00	481.00	617.00	1879.00	502.00	639.00	1934.00	523.00	660.00
1825.00	481.00	617.00	1880.00	502.00	639.00	1935.00	524.00	660.00
1826.00	481.00	618.00	1881.00	503.00	639.00	1936.00	524.00	661.00
1827.00	482.00	618.00	1882.00	503.00	640.00	1937.00	525.00	661.00
1828.00	482.00	619.00	1883.00	504.00	640.00	1938.00	525.00	662.00
1829.00	482.00	619.00	1884.00	504.00	640.00	1939.00	525.00	662.00
1830.00	483.00	619.00	1885.00	504.00	641.00	1940.00	526.00	662.00
1831.00	483.00	620.00	1886.00	505.00	641.00	1941.00	526.00	663.00
1832.00	484.00	620.00	1887.00	505.00	642.00	1942.00	527.00	663.00
1833.00	484.00	621.00	1888.00	505.00	642.00	1943.00	527.00	664.00
1834.00	484.00	621.00	1889.00	506.00	642.00	1944.00	527.00	664.00
1835.00	485.00	621.00	1890.00	506.00	643.00	1945.00	528.00	664.00
1836.00	485.00	622.00	1891.00	507.00	643.00	1946.00	528.00	665.00
1837.00	486.00	622.00	1892.00	507.00	644.00	1947.00	529.00	665.00
1838.00	486.00	623.00	1893.00	507.00	644.00	1948.00	529.00	665.00
1839.00	486.00	623.00	1894.00	508.00	644.00	1949.00	529.00	666.00
1840.00	487.00	623.00	1895.00	508.00	645.00	1950.00	530.00	666.00
1841.00	487.00	624.00	1896.00	509.00	645.00	1951.00	530.00	667.00
1842.00	488.00	624.00	1897.00	509.00	646.00	1952.00	530.00	667.00
1843.00	488.00	625.00	1898.00	509.00	646.00	1953.00	531.00	667.00
1844.00	488.00	625.00	1899.00	510.00	646.00	1954.00	531.00	668.00
1845.00	489.00	625.00	1900.00	510.00	647.00	1955.00	532.00	668.00
1846.00	489.00	626.00	1901.00	511.00	647.00	1956.00	532.00	669.00
1847.00	490.00	626.00	1902.00	511.00	648.00	1957.00	532.00	669.00
1848.00	490.00	626.00	1903.00	511.00	648.00	1958.00	533.00	669.00
1849.00	490.00	627.00	1904.00	512.00	648.00	1959.00	533.00	670.00
1850.00	491.00	627.00	1905.00	512.00	649.00	1960.00	534.00	670.00
1851.00	491.00	628.00	1906.00	513.00	649.00	1961.00	534.00	671.00
1852.00	491.00	628.00	1907.00	513.00	640.00	1962.00	534.00	671.00
1853.00	492.00	628.00	1908.00	513.00	650.00	1963.00	535.00	671.00
1854.00	492.00	629.00	1909.00	514.00	650.00	1964.00	535.00	672.00
1855.00	493.00	629.00	1910.00	514.00	651.00	1965.00	536.00	672.00
1856.00	493.00	630.00	1911.00	514.00	651.00	1966.00	536.00	672.00
1857.00	493.00	630.00	1912.00	515.00	651.00	1967.00	536.00	673.00
1858.00	494.00	630.00	1913.00	515.00	652.00	1968.00	537.00	673.00
1859.00	494.00	631.00	1914.00	516.00	652.00	1969.00	537.00	674.00
1860.00	495.00	631.00	1915.00	516.00	653.00	1970.00	537.00	674.00
1861.00	495.00	632.00	1916.00	516.00	653.00	1971.00	538.00	674.00
1862.00	495.00	632.00	1917.00	517.00	653.00	1972.00	538.00	675.00
1863.00	496.00	632.00	1918.00	517.00	654.00	1973.00	539.00	675.00
1864.00	496.00	633.00	1919.00	518.00	654.00	1974.00	539.00	676.00
1865.00	497.00	633.00	1920.00	518.00	655.00	1975.00	539.00	676.00
1866.00	497.00	633.00	1921.00	518.00	655.00	1976.00	540.00	676.00
1867.00	497.00	634.00	1922.00	519.00	655.00	1977.00	540.00	677.00
1868.00	498.00	634.00	1923.00	519.00	656.00	1978.00	541.00	677.00
1869.00	498.00	635.00	1924.00	520.00	656.00	1979.00	541.00	678.00
1870.00	498.00	635.00	1925.00	520.00	656.00	1980.00	541.00	678.00

Weekly withholding amounts

Weekly earnings	With tax-free threshold	No tax-free threshold	Weekly earnings	With tax-free threshold	No tax-free threshold	Weekly earnings	With tax-free threshold	No tax-free threshold
1981.00	542.00	678.00	2036.00	563.00	700.00	2091.00	585.00	721.00
1982.00	542.00	679.00	2037.00	564.00	700.00	2092.00	585.00	722.00
1983.00	543.00	679.00	2038.00	564.00	701.00	2093.00	585.00	722.00
1984.00	543.00	679.00	2039.00	564.00	701.00	2094.00	586.00	722.00
1985.00	543.00	680.00	2040.00	565.00	701.00	2095.00	586.00	723.00
1986.00	544.00	680.00	2041.00	565.00	702.00	2096.00	587.00	723.00
1987.00	544.00	681.00	2042.00	566.00	702.00	2097.00	587.00	724.00
1988.00	544.00	681.00	2043.00	566.00	703.00	2098.00	587.00	724.00
1989.00	545.00	681.00	2044.00	566.00	703.00	2099.00	588.00	724.00
1990.00	545.00	682.00	2045.00	567.00	703.00	2100.00	588.00	725.00
1991.00	546.00	682.00	2046.00	567.00	704.00	2101.00	589.00	725.00
1992.00	546.00	683.00	2047.00	568.00	704.00	2102.00	589.00	726.00
1993.00	546.00	683.00	2048.00	568.00	704.00	2103.00	589.00	726.00
1994.00	547.00	683.00	2049.00	568.00	705.00	2104.00	590.00	726.00
1995.00	547.00	684.00	2050.00	569.00	705.00	2105.00	590.00	727.00
1996.00	548.00	684.00	2051.00	569.00	706.00	2106.00	591.00	727.00
1997.00	548.00	685.00	2052.00	569.00	706.00	2107.00	591.00	727.00
1998.00	548.00	685.00	2053.00	570.00	706.00	2108.00	591.00	728.00
1999.00	549.00	685.00	2054.00	570.00	707.00	2109.00	592.00	728.00
2000.00	549.00	686.00	2055.00	571.00	707.00	2110.00	592.00	729.00
2001.00	550.00	686.00	2056.00	571.00	708.00	2111.00	592.00	729.00
2002.00	550.00	687.00	2057.00	571.00	708.00	2112.00	593.00	729.00
2003.00	550.00	687.00	2058.00	572.00	708.00	2113.00	593.00	730.00
2004.00	551.00	687.00	2059.00	572.00	709.00	2114.00	594.00	730.00
2005.00	551.00	688.00	2060.00	573.00	709.00	2115.00	594.00	731.00
2006.00	552.00	688.00	2061.00	573.00	710.00	2116.00	594.00	731.00
2007.00	552.00	688.00	2062.00	573.00	710.00	2117.00	595.00	731.00
2008.00	552.00	689.00	2063.00	574.00	710.00	2118.00	595.00	732.00
2009.00	553.00	689.00	2064.00	574.00	711.00	2119.00	596.00	732.00
2010.00	553.00	690.00	2065.00	575.00	711.00	2120.00	596.00	733.00
2011.00	553.00	690.00	2066.00	575.00	711.00	2121.00	596.00	733.00
2012.00	554.00	690.00	2067.00	575.00	712.00	2122.00	597.00	733.00
2013.00	554.00	691.00	2068.00	576.00	712.00	2123.00	597.00	734.00
2014.00	555.00	691.00	2069.00	576.00	713.00	2124.00	598.00	734.00
2015.00	555.00	692.00	2070.00	576.00	713.00	2125.00	598.00	734.00
2016.00	555.00	692.00	2071.00	577.00	713.00	2126.00	598.00	735.00
2017.00	556.00	692.00	2072.00	577.00	714.00	2127.00	599.00	735.00
2018.00	556.00	693.00	2073.00	578.00	714.00	2128.00	599.00	736.00
2019.00	557.00	693.00	2074.00	578.00	715.00	2129.00	599.00	736.00
2020.00	557.00	694.00	2075.00	578.00	715.00	2130.00	600.00	736.00
2021.00	557.00	694.00	2076.00	579.00	715.00	2131.00	600.00	737.00
2022.00	558.00	694.00	2077.00	579.00	716.00	2132.00	601.00	737.00
2023.00	558.00	695.00	2078.00	580.00	716.00	2133.00	601.00	738.00
2024.00	559.00	695.00	2079.00	580.00	717.00	2134.00	601.00	738.00
2025.00	559.00	695.00	2080.00	580.00	717.00	2135.00	602.00	738.00
2026.00	559.00	696.00	2081.00	581.00	717.00	2136.00	602.00	739.00
2027.00	560.00	696.00	2082.00	581.00	718.00	2137.00	603.00	739.00
2028.00	560.00	697.00	2083.00	582.00	718.00	2138.00	603.00	740.00
2029.00	560.00	697.00	2084.00	582.00	718.00	2139.00	603.00	740.00
2030.00	561.00	697.00	2085.00	582.00	719.00	2140.00	604.00	740.00
2031.00	561.00	698.00	2086.00	583.00	719.00	2141.00	604.00	741.00
2032.00	562.00	698.00	2087.00	583.00	720.00	2142.00	605.00	741.00
2033.00	562.00	699.00	2088.00	583.00	720.00	2143.00	605.00	742.00
2034.00	562.00	699.00	2089.00	584.00	720.00	2144.00	605.00	742.00
2035.00	563.00	699.00	2090.00	584.00	721.00	2145.00	606.00	742.00

PAYG WITHHOLDING TAX TABLE 2015-16 including Medicare levy (rounded $)   5.691

Weekly withholding amounts

Weekly earnings	With tax-free threshold	No tax-free threshold	Weekly earnings	With tax-free threshold	No tax-free threshold	Weekly earnings	With tax-free threshold	No tax-free threshold
2146.00	606.00	743.00	2201.00	628.00	764.00	2256.00	649.00	786.00
2147.00	607.00	743.00	2202.00	628.00	765.00	2257.00	649.00	786.00
2148.00	607.00	743.00	2203.00	628.00	765.00	2258.00	650.00	786.00
2149.00	607.00	744.00	2204.00	629.00	765.00	2259.00	650.00	787.00
2150.00	608.00	744.00	2205.00	629.00	766.00	2260.00	651.00	787.00
2151.00	608.00	745.00	2206.00	630.00	766.00	2261.00	651.00	788.00
2152.00	608.00	745.00	2207.00	630.00	766.00	2262.00	651.00	788.00
2153.00	609.00	745.00	2208.00	630.00	767.00	2263.00	652.00	788.00
2154.00	609.00	746.00	2209.00	631.00	767.00	2264.00	652.00	789.00
2155.00	610.00	746.00	2210.00	631.00	768.00	2265.00	653.00	789.00
2156.00	610.00	747.00	2211.00	631.00	768.00	2266.00	653.00	789.00
2157.00	610.00	747.00	2212.00	632.00	768.00	2267.00	653.00	790.00
2158.00	611.00	747.00	2213.00	632.00	769.00	2268.00	654.00	790.00
2159.00	611.00	748.00	2214.00	633.00	769.00	2269.00	654.00	791.00
2160.00	612.00	748.00	2215.00	633.00	770.00	2270.00	654.00	791.00
2161.00	612.00	749.00	2216.00	633.00	770.00	2271.00	655.00	791.00
2162.00	612.00	749.00	2217.00	634.00	770.00	2272.00	655.00	792.00
2163.00	613.00	749.00	2218.00	634.00	771.00	2273.00	656.00	792.00
2164.00	613.00	750.00	2219.00	635.00	771.00	2274.00	656.00	793.00
2165.00	614.00	750.00	2220.00	635.00	772.00	2275.00	656.00	793.00
2166.00	614.00	750.00	2221.00	635.00	772.00	2276.00	657.00	793.00
2167.00	614.00	751.00	2222.00	636.00	772.00	2277.00	657.00	794.00
2168.00	615.00	751.00	2223.00	636.00	773.00	2278.00	658.00	794.00
2169.00	615.00	752.00	2224.00	637.00	773.00	2279.00	658.00	795.00
2170.00	615.00	752.00	2225.00	637.00	773.00	2280.00	658.00	795.00
2171.00	616.00	752.00	2226.00	637.00	774.00	2281.00	659.00	795.00
2172.00	616.00	753.00	2227.00	638.00	774.00	2282.00	659.00	796.00
2173.00	617.00	753.00	2228.00	638.00	775.00	2283.00	660.00	796.00
2174.00	617.00	754.00	2229.00	638.00	775.00	2284.00	660.00	796.00
2175.00	617.00	754.00	2230.00	639.00	775.00	2285.00	660.00	797.00
2176.00	618.00	754.00	2231.00	639.00	776.00	2286.00	661.00	797.00
2177.00	618.00	755.00	2232.00	640.00	776.00	2287.00	661.00	798.00
2178.00	619.00	755.00	2233.00	640.00	777.00	2288.00	661.00	798.00
2179.00	619.00	756.00	2234.00	640.00	777.00	2289.00	662.00	798.00
2180.00	619.00	756.00	2235.00	641.00	777.00	2290.00	662.00	799.00
2181.00	620.00	756.00	2236.00	641.00	778.00	2291.00	663.00	799.00
2182.00	620.00	757.00	2237.00	642.00	778.00	2292.00	663.00	800.00
2183.00	621.00	757.00	2238.00	642.00	779.00	2293.00	663.00	800.00
2184.00	621.00	757.00	2239.00	642.00	779.00	2294.00	664.00	800.00
2185.00	621.00	758.00	2240.00	643.00	779.00	2295.00	664.00	801.00
2186.00	622.00	758.00	2241.00	643.00	780.00	2296.00	665.00	801.00
2187.00	622.00	759.00	2242.00	644.00	780.00	2297.00	665.00	802.00
2188.00	622.00	759.00	2243.00	644.00	781.00	2298.00	665.00	802.00
2189.00	623.00	759.00	2244.00	644.00	781.00	2299.00	666.00	802.00
2190.00	623.00	760.00	2245.00	645.00	781.00	2300.00	666.00	803.00
2191.00	624.00	760.00	2246.00	645.00	782.00	2301.00	667.00	803.00
2192.00	624.00	761.00	2247.00	646.00	782.00	2302.00	667.00	804.00
2193.00	624.00	761.00	2248.00	646.00	782.00	2303.00	667.00	804.00
2194.00	625.00	761.00	2249.00	646.00	783.00	2304.00	668.00	804.00
2195.00	625.00	762.00	2250.00	647.00	783.00	2305.00	668.00	805.00
2196.00	626.00	762.00	2251.00	647.00	784.00	2306.00	669.00	805.00
2197.00	626.00	763.00	2252.00	647.00	784.00	2307.00	669.00	805.00
2198.00	626.00	763.00	2253.00	648.00	784.00	2308.00	669.00	806.00
2199.00	627.00	763.00	2254.00	648.00	785.00	2309.00	670.00	806.00
2200.00	627.00	764.00	2255.00	649.00	785.00	2310.00	670.00	807.00

5.691 PAYG WITHHOLDING TAX TABLE 2015-16 including Medicare levy (rounded $)

Weekly withholding amounts

Weekly earnings	With tax-free threshold	No tax-free threshold	Weekly earnings	With tax-free threshold	No tax-free threshold	Weekly earnings	With tax-free threshold	No tax-free threshold
2311.00	670.00	807.00	2366.00	692.00	828.00	2421.00	713.00	850.00
2312.00	671.00	807.00	2367.00	692.00	829.00	2422.00	714.00	850.00
2313.00	671.00	808.00	2368.00	693.00	829.00	2423.00	714.00	851.00
2314.00	672.00	808.00	2369.00	693.00	830.00	2424.00	715.00	851.00
2315.00	672.00	809.00	2370.00	693.00	830.00	2425.00	715.00	851.00
2316.00	672.00	809.00	2371.00	694.00	830.00	2426.00	715.00	852.00
2317.00	673.00	809.00	2372.00	694.00	831.00	2427.00	716.00	852.00
2318.00	673.00	810.00	2373.00	695.00	831.00	2428.00	716.00	853.00
2319.00	674.00	810.00	2374.00	695.00	832.00	2429.00	716.00	853.00
2320.00	674.00	811.00	2375.00	695.00	832.00	2430.00	717.00	853.00
2321.00	674.00	811.00	2376.00	696.00	832.00	2431.00	717.00	854.00
2322.00	675.00	811.00	2377.00	696.00	833.00	2432.00	718.00	854.00
2323.00	675.00	812.00	2378.00	697.00	833.00	2433.00	718.00	855.00
2324.00	676.00	812.00	2379.00	697.00	834.00	2434.00	718.00	855.00
2325.00	676.00	812.00	2380.00	697.00	834.00	2435.00	719.00	855.00
2326.00	676.00	813.00	2381.00	698.00	834.00	2436.00	719.00	856.00
2327.00	677.00	813.00	2382.00	698.00	835.00	2437.00	720.00	856.00
2328.00	677.00	814.00	2383.00	699.00	835.00	2438.00	720.00	857.00
2329.00	677.00	814.00	2384.00	699.00	835.00	2439.00	720.00	857.00
2330.00	678.00	814.00	2385.00	699.00	836.00	2440.00	721.00	857.00
2331.00	678.00	815.00	2386.00	700.00	836.00	2441.00	721.00	858.00
2332.00	679.00	815.00	2387.00	700.00	837.00	2442.00	722.00	858.00
2333.00	679.00	816.00	2388.00	700.00	837.00	2443.00	722.00	859.00
2334.00	679.00	816.00	2389.00	701.00	837.00	2444.00	722.00	859.00
2335.00	680.00	816.00	2390.00	701.00	838.00	2445.00	723.00	859.00
2336.00	680.00	817.00	2391.00	702.00	838.00	2446.00	723.00	860.00
2337.00	681.00	817.00	2392.00	702.00	839.00	2447.00	724.00	860.00
2338.00	681.00	818.00	2393.00	702.00	839.00	2448.00	724.00	860.00
2339.00	681.00	818.00	2394.00	703.00	839.00	2449.00	724.00	861.00
2340.00	682.00	818.00	2395.00	703.00	840.00	2450.00	725.00	861.00
2341.00	682.00	819.00	2396.00	704.00	840.00	2451.00	725.00	862.00
2342.00	683.00	819.00	2397.00	704.00	841.00	2452.00	725.00	862.00
2343.00	683.00	820.00	2398.00	704.00	841.00	2453.00	726.00	862.00
2344.00	683.00	820.00	2399.00	705.00	841.00	2454.00	726.00	863.00
2345.00	684.00	820.00	2400.00	705.00	842.00	2455.00	727.00	863.00
2346.00	684.00	821.00	2401.00	706.00	842.00	2456.00	727.00	864.00
2347.00	685.00	821.00	2402.00	706.00	843.00	2457.00	727.00	864.00
2348.00	685.00	821.00	2403.00	706.00	843.00	2458.00	728.00	864.00
2349.00	685.00	822.00	2404.00	707.00	843.00	2459.00	728.00	865.00
2350.00	686.00	822.00	2405.00	707.00	844.00	2460.00	729.00	865.00
2351.00	686.00	823.00	2406.00	708.00	844.00	2461.00	729.00	866.00
2352.00	686.00	823.00	2407.00	708.00	844.00	2462.00	729.00	866.00
2353.00	687.00	823.00	2408.00	708.00	845.00	2463.00	730.00	866.00
2354.00	687.00	824.00	2409.00	709.00	845.00	2464.00	730.00	867.00
2355.00	688.00	824.00	2410.00	709.00	846.00	2465.00	731.00	867.00
2356.00	688.00	825.00	2411.00	709.00	846.00	2466.00	731.00	867.00
2357.00	688.00	825.00	2412.00	710.00	846.00	2467.00	731.00	868.00
2358.00	689.00	825.00	2413.00	710.00	847.00	2468.00	732.00	868.00
2359.00	689.00	826.00	2414.00	711.00	847.00	2469.00	732.00	869.00
2360.00	690.00	826.00	2415.00	711.00	848.00	2470.00	732.00	869.00
2361.00	690.00	827.00	2416.00	711.00	848.00	2471.00	733.00	869.00
2362.00	690.00	827.00	2417.00	712.00	848.00	2472.00	733.00	870.00
2363.00	691.00	827.00	2418.00	712.00	849.00	2473.00	734.00	870.00
2364.00	691.00	828.00	2419.00	713.00	849.00	2474.00	734.00	871.00
2365.00	692.00	828.00	2420.00	713.00	850.00	2475.00	734.00	871.00

Weekly withholding amounts

Weekly earnings	With tax-free threshold	No tax-free threshold	Weekly earnings	With tax-free threshold	No tax-free threshold	Weekly earnings	With tax-free threshold	No tax-free threshold
2476.00	735.00	871.00	2531.00	756.00	893.00	2586.00	778.00	914.00
2477.00	735.00	872.00	2532.00	757.00	893.00	2587.00	778.00	915.00
2478.00	736.00	872.00	2533.00	757.00	894.00	2588.00	778.00	915.00
2479.00	736.00	873.00	2534.00	757.00	894.00	2589.00	779.00	915.00
2480.00	736.00	873.00	2535.00	758.00	894.00	2590.00	779.00	916.00
2481.00	737.00	873.00	2536.00	758.00	895.00	2591.00	780.00	916.00
2482.00	737.00	874.00	2537.00	759.00	895.00	2592.00	780.00	917.00
2483.00	738.00	874.00	2538.00	759.00	896.00	2593.00	780.00	917.00
2484.00	738.00	874.00	2539.00	759.00	896.00	2594.00	781.00	917.00
2485.00	738.00	875.00	2540.00	760.00	896.00	2595.00	781.00	918.00
2486.00	739.00	875.00	2541.00	760.00	897.00	2596.00	782.00	918.00
2487.00	739.00	876.00	2542.00	761.00	897.00	2597.00	782.00	919.00
2488.00	739.00	876.00	2543.00	761.00	898.00	2598.00	782.00	919.00
2489.00	740.00	876.00	2544.00	761.00	898.00	2599.00	783.00	919.00
2490.00	740.00	877.00	2545.00	762.00	898.00	2600.00	783.00	920.00
2491.00	741.00	877.00	2546.00	762.00	899.00	2601.00	784.00	920.00
2492.00	741.00	878.00	2547.00	763.00	899.00	2602.00	784.00	921.00
2493.00	741.00	878.00	2548.00	763.00	899.00	2603.00	784.00	921.00
2494.00	742.00	878.00	2549.00	763.00	900.00	2604.00	785.00	921.00
2495.00	742.00	879.00	2550.00	764.00	900.00	2605.00	785.00	922.00
2496.00	743.00	879.00	2551.00	764.00	901.00	2606.00	786.00	922.00
2497.00	743.00	880.00	2552.00	764.00	901.00	2607.00	786.00	922.00
2498.00	743.00	880.00	2553.00	765.00	901.00	2608.00	786.00	923.00
2499.00	744.00	880.00	2554.00	765.00	902.00	2609.00	787.00	923.00
2500.00	744.00	881.00	2555.00	766.00	902.00	2610.00	787.00	924.00
2501.00	745.00	881.00	2556.00	766.00	903.00	2611.00	787.00	924.00
2502.00	745.00	882.00	2557.00	766.00	903.00	2612.00	788.00	924.00
2503.00	745.00	882.00	2558.00	767.00	903.00	2613.00	788.00	925.00
2504.00	746.00	882.00	2559.00	767.00	904.00	2614.00	789.00	925.00
2505.00	746.00	883.00	2560.00	768.00	904.00	2615.00	789.00	926.00
2506.00	747.00	883.00	2561.00	768.00	905.00	2616.00	789.00	926.00
2507.00	747.00	883.00	2562.00	768.00	905.00	2617.00	790.00	926.00
2508.00	747.00	884.00	2563.00	769.00	905.00	2618.00	790.00	927.00
2509.00	748.00	884.00	2564.00	769.00	906.00	2619.00	791.00	927.00
2510.00	748.00	885.00	2565.00	770.00	906.00	2620.00	791.00	928.00
2511.00	748.00	885.00	2566.00	770.00	906.00	2621.00	791.00	928.00
2512.00	749.00	885.00	2567.00	770.00	907.00	2622.00	792.00	928.00
2513.00	749.00	886.00	2568.00	771.00	907.00	2623.00	792.00	929.00
2514.00	750.00	886.00	2569.00	771.00	908.00	2624.00	793.00	929.00
2515.00	750.00	887.00	2570.00	771.00	908.00	2625.00	793.00	929.00
2516.00	750.00	887.00	2571.00	772.00	908.00	2626.00	793.00	930.00
2517.00	751.00	887.00	2572.00	772.00	909.00	2627.00	794.00	930.00
2518.00	751.00	888.00	2573.00	773.00	909.00	2628.00	794.00	931.00
2519.00	752.00	888.00	2574.00	773.00	910.00	2629.00	794.00	931.00
2520.00	752.00	889.00	2575.00	773.00	910.00	2630.00	795.00	931.00
2521.00	752.00	889.00	2576.00	774.00	910.00	2631.00	795.00	932.00
2522.00	753.00	889.00	2577.00	774.00	911.00	2632.00	796.00	932.00
2523.00	753.00	890.00	2578.00	775.00	911.00	2633.00	796.00	933.00
2524.00	754.00	890.00	2579.00	775.00	912.00	2634.00	796.00	933.00
2525.00	754.00	890.00	2580.00	775.00	912.00	2635.00	797.00	933.00
2526.00	754.00	891.00	2581.00	776.00	912.00	2636.00	797.00	934.00
2527.00	755.00	891.00	2582.00	776.00	913.00	2637.00	798.00	934.00
2528.00	755.00	892.00	2583.00	777.00	913.00	2638.00	798.00	935.00
2529.00	755.00	892.00	2584.00	777.00	913.00	2639.00	798.00	935.00
2530.00	756.00	892.00	2585.00	777.00	914.00	2640.00	799.00	935.00

Weekly withholding amounts

Weekly earnings	With tax-free threshold	No tax-free threshold	Weekly earnings	With tax-free threshold	No tax-free threshold	Weekly earnings	With tax-free threshold	No tax-free threshold
2641.00	799.00	936.00	2696.00	821.00	957.00	2751.00	842.00	979.00
2642.00	800.00	936.00	2697.00	821.00	958.00	2752.00	842.00	979.00
2643.00	800.00	937.00	2698.00	821.00	958.00	2753.00	843.00	979.00
2644.00	800.00	937.00	2699.00	822.00	958.00	2754.00	843.00	980.00
2645.00	801.00	937.00	2700.00	822.00	959.00	2755.00	844.00	980.00
2646.00	801.00	938.00	2701.00	823.00	959.00	2756.00	844.00	981.00
2647.00	802.00	938.00	2702.00	823.00	960.00	2757.00	844.00	981.00
2648.00	802.00	938.00	2703.00	823.00	960.00	2758.00	845.00	981.00
2649.00	802.00	939.00	2704.00	824.00	960.00	2759.00	845.00	982.00
2650.00	803.00	939.00	2705.00	824.00	961.00	2760.00	846.00	982.00
2651.00	803.00	940.00	2706.00	825.00	961.00	2761.00	846.00	983.00
2652.00	803.00	940.00	2707.00	825.00	961.00	2762.00	846.00	983.00
2653.00	804.00	940.00	2708.00	825.00	962.00	2763.00	847.00	983.00
2654.00	804.00	941.00	2709.00	826.00	962.00	2764.00	847.00	984.00
2655.00	805.00	941.00	2710.00	826.00	963.00	2765.00	848.00	984.00
2656.00	805.00	942.00	2711.00	826.00	963.00	2766.00	848.00	984.00
2657.00	805.00	942.00	2712.00	827.00	963.00	2767.00	848.00	985.00
2658.00	806.00	942.00	2713.00	827.00	964.00	2768.00	849.00	985.00
2659.00	806.00	943.00	2714.00	828.00	964.00	2769.00	849.00	986.00
2660.00	807.00	943.00	2715.00	828.00	965.00	2770.00	849.00	986.00
2661.00	807.00	944.00	2716.00	828.00	965.00	2771.00	850.00	986.00
2662.00	807.00	944.00	2717.00	829.00	965.00	2772.00	850.00	987.00
2663.00	808.00	944.00	2718.00	829.00	966.00	2773.00	851.00	987.00
2664.00	808.00	945.00	2719.00	830.00	966.00	2774.00	851.00	988.00
2665.00	809.00	945.00	2720.00	830.00	967.00	2775.00	851.00	988.00
2666.00	809.00	945.00	2721.00	830.00	967.00	2776.00	852.00	988.00
2667.00	809.00	946.00	2722.00	831.00	967.00	2777.00	852.00	989.00
2668.00	810.00	946.00	2723.00	831.00	968.00	2778.00	853.00	989.00
2669.00	810.00	947.00	2724.00	832.00	968.00	2779.00	853.00	990.00
2670.00	810.00	947.00	2725.00	832.00	968.00	2780.00	853.00	990.00
2671.00	811.00	947.00	2726.00	832.00	969.00	2781.00	854.00	990.00
2672.00	811.00	948.00	2727.00	833.00	969.00	2782.00	854.00	991.00
2673.00	812.00	948.00	2728.00	833.00	970.00	2783.00	855.00	991.00
2674.00	812.00	949.00	2729.00	833.00	970.00	2784.00	855.00	991.00
2675.00	812.00	949.00	2730.00	834.00	970.00	2785.00	855.00	992.00
2676.00	813.00	949.00	2731.00	834.00	971.00	2786.00	856.00	992.00
2677.00	813.00	950.00	2732.00	835.00	971.00	2787.00	856.00	993.00
2678.00	814.00	950.00	2733.00	835.00	972.00	2788.00	856.00	993.00
2679.00	814.00	951.00	2734.00	835.00	972.00	2789.00	857.00	993.00
2680.00	814.00	951.00	2735.00	836.00	972.00	2790.00	857.00	994.00
2681.00	815.00	951.00	2736.00	836.00	973.00	2791.00	858.00	994.00
2682.00	815.00	952.00	2737.00	837.00	973.00	2792.00	858.00	995.00
2683.00	816.00	952.00	2738.00	837.00	974.00	2793.00	858.00	995.00
2684.00	816.00	952.00	2739.00	837.00	974.00	2794.00	859.00	995.00
2685.00	816.00	953.00	2740.00	838.00	974.00	2795.00	859.00	996.00
2686.00	817.00	953.00	2741.00	838.00	975.00	2796.00	860.00	996.00
2687.00	817.00	954.00	2742.00	839.00	975.00	2797.00	860.00	997.00
2688.00	817.00	954.00	2743.00	839.00	976.00	2798.00	860.00	997.00
2689.00	818.00	954.00	2744.00	839.00	976.00	2799.00	861.00	997.00
2690.00	818.00	955.00	2745.00	840.00	976.00	2800.00	861.00	998.00
2691.00	819.00	955.00	2746.00	840.00	977.00	2801.00	862.00	998.00
2692.00	819.00	956.00	2747.00	841.00	977.00	2802.00	862.00	999.00
2693.00	819.00	956.00	2748.00	841.00	977.00	2803.00	862.00	999.00
2694.00	820.00	956.00	2749.00	841.00	978.00	2804.00	863.00	999.00
2695.00	820.00	957.00	2750.00	842.00	978.00	2805.00	863.00	1000.00

Weekly withholding amounts

Weekly earnings	With tax-free threshold	No tax-free threshold	Weekly earnings	With tax-free threshold	No tax-free threshold	Weekly earnings	With tax-free threshold	No tax-free threshold
2806.00	864.00	1000.00	2861.00	885.00	1022.00	2916.00	906.00	1043.00
2807.00	864.00	1000.00	2862.00	885.00	1022.00	2917.00	907.00	1043.00
2808.00	864.00	1001.00	2863.00	886.00	1022.00	2918.00	907.00	1044.00
2809.00	865.00	1001.00	2864.00	886.00	1023.00	2919.00	908.00	1044.00
2810.00	865.00	1002.00	2865.00	887.00	1023.00	2920.00	908.00	1045.00
2811.00	865.00	1002.00	2866.00	887.00	1023.00	2921.00	908.00	1045.00
2812.00	866.00	1002.00	2867.00	887.00	1024.00	2922.00	909.00	1045.00
2813.00	866.00	1003.00	2868.00	888.00	1024.00	2923.00	909.00	1046.00
2814.00	867.00	1003.00	2869.00	888.00	1025.00	2924.00	910.00	1046.00
2815.00	867.00	1004.00	2870.00	888.00	1025.00	2925.00	910.00	1046.00
2816.00	867.00	1004.00	2871.00	889.00	1025.00	2926.00	910.00	1047.00
2817.00	868.00	1004.00	2872.00	889.00	1026.00	2927.00	911.00	1047.00
2818.00	868.00	1005.00	2873.00	890.00	1026.00	2928.00	911.00	1048.00
2819.00	869.00	1005.00	2874.00	890.00	1027.00	2929.00	911.00	1048.00
2820.00	869.00	1006.00	2875.00	890.00	1027.00	2930.00	912.00	1048.00
2821.00	869.00	1006.00	2876.00	891.00	1027.00	2931.00	912.00	1049.00
2822.00	870.00	1006.00	2877.00	891.00	1028.00	2932.00	913.00	1049.00
2823.00	870.00	1007.00	2878.00	892.00	1028.00	2933.00	913.00	1050.00
2824.00	871.00	1007.00	2879.00	892.00	1029.00	2934.00	913.00	1050.00
2825.00	871.00	1007.00	2880.00	892.00	1029.00	2935.00	914.00	1050.00
2826.00	871.00	1008.00	2881.00	893.00	1029.00	2936.00	914.00	1051.00
2827.00	872.00	1008.00	2882.00	893.00	1030.00	2937.00	915.00	1051.00
2828.00	872.00	1009.00	2883.00	894.00	1030.00	2938.00	915.00	1052.00
2829.00	872.00	1009.00	2884.00	894.00	1030.00	2939.00	915.00	1052.00
2830.00	873.00	1009.00	2885.00	894.00	1031.00	2940.00	916.00	1052.00
2831.00	873.00	1010.00	2886.00	895.00	1031.00	2941.00	916.00	1053.00
2832.00	874.00	1010.00	2887.00	895.00	1032.00	2942.00	917.00	1053.00
2833.00	874.00	1011.00	2888.00	895.00	1032.00	2943.00	917.00	1054.00
2834.00	874.00	1011.00	2889.00	896.00	1032.00	2944.00	917.00	1054.00
2835.00	875.00	1011.00	2890.00	896.00	1033.00	2945.00	918.00	1054.00
2836.00	875.00	1012.00	2891.00	897.00	1033.00	2946.00	918.00	1055.00
2837.00	876.00	1012.00	2892.00	897.00	1034.00	2947.00	919.00	1055.00
2838.00	876.00	1013.00	2893.00	897.00	1034.00	2948.00	919.00	1055.00
2839.00	876.00	1013.00	2894.00	898.00	1034.00	2949.00	919.00	1056.00
2840.00	877.00	1013.00	2895.00	898.00	1035.00	2950.00	920.00	1056.00
2841.00	877.00	1014.00	2896.00	899.00	1035.00	2951.00	920.00	1057.00
2842.00	878.00	1014.00	2897.00	899.00	1036.00	2952.00	920.00	1057.00
2843.00	878.00	1015.00	2898.00	899.00	1036.00	2953.00	921.00	1057.00
2844.00	878.00	1015.00	2899.00	900.00	1036.00	2954.00	921.00	1058.00
2845.00	879.00	1015.00	2900.00	900.00	1037.00	2955.00	922.00	1058.00
2846.00	879.00	1016.00	2901.00	901.00	1037.00	2956.00	922.00	1059.00
2847.00	880.00	1016.00	2902.00	901.00	1038.00	2957.00	922.00	1059.00
2848.00	880.00	1016.00	2903.00	901.00	1038.00	2958.00	923.00	1059.00
2849.00	880.00	1017.00	2904.00	902.00	1038.00	2959.00	923.00	1060.00
2850.00	881.00	1017.00	2905.00	902.00	1039.00	2960.00	924.00	1060.00
2851.00	881.00	1018.00	2906.00	903.00	1039.00	2961.00	924.00	1061.00
2852.00	881.00	1018.00	2907.00	903.00	1039.00	2962.00	924.00	1061.00
2853.00	882.00	1018.00	2908.00	903.00	1040.00	2963.00	925.00	1061.00
2854.00	882.00	1019.00	2909.00	904.00	1040.00	2964.00	925.00	1062.00
2855.00	883.00	1019.00	2910.00	904.00	1041.00	2965.00	926.00	1062.00
2856.00	883.00	1020.00	2911.00	904.00	1041.00	2966.00	926.00	1062.00
2857.00	883.00	1020.00	2912.00	905.00	1041.00	2967.00	926.00	1063.00
2858.00	884.00	1020.00	2913.00	905.00	1042.00	2968.00	927.00	1063.00
2859.00	884.00	1021.00	2914.00	906.00	1042.00	2969.00	927.00	1064.00
2860.00	885.00	1021.00	2915.00	906.00	1043.00	2970.00	927.00	1064.00

5.691 PAYG WITHHOLDING TAX TABLE 2015-16 including Medicare levy (rounded $)

Weekly withholding amounts

Weekly earnings	With tax-free threshold	No tax-free threshold	Weekly earnings	With tax-free threshold	No tax-free threshold	Weekly earnings	With tax-free threshold	No tax-free threshold
2971.00	928.00	1064.00	3026.00	949.00	1086.00	3081.00	971.00	1107.00
2972.00	928.00	1065.00	3027.00	950.00	1086.00	3082.00	971.00	1108.00
2973.00	929.00	1065.00	3028.00	950.00	1087.00	3083.00	972.00	1108.00
2974.00	929.00	1066.00	3029.00	950.00	1087.00	3084.00	972.00	1108.00
2975.00	929.00	1066.00	3030.00	951.00	1087.00	3085.00	972.00	1109.00
2976.00	930.00	1066.00	3031.00	951.00	1088.00	3086.00	973.00	1109.00
2977.00	930.00	1067.00	3032.00	952.00	1088.00	3087.00	973.00	1110.00
2978.00	931.00	1067.00	3033.00	952.00	1089.00	3088.00	973.00	1110.00
2979.00	931.00	1068.00	3034.00	952.00	1089.00	3089.00	974.00	1110.00
2980.00	931.00	1068.00	3035.00	953.00	1089.00	3090.00	974.00	1111.00
2981.00	932.00	1068.00	3036.00	953.00	1090.00	3091.00	975.00	1111.00
2982.00	932.00	1069.00	3037.00	954.00	1090.00	3092.00	975.00	1112.00
2983.00	933.00	1069.00	3038.00	954.00	1091.00	3093.00	975.00	1112.00
2984.00	933.00	1069.00	3039.00	954.00	1091.00	3094.00	976.00	1112.00
2985.00	933.00	1070.00	3040.00	955.00	1091.00	3095.00	976.00	1113.00
2986.00	934.00	1070.00	3041.00	955.00	1092.00	3096.00	977.00	1113.00
2987.00	934.00	1071.00	3042.00	956.00	1092.00	3097.00	977.00	1114.00
2988.00	934.00	1071.00	3043.00	956.00	1093.00	3098.00	977.00	1114.00
2989.00	935.00	1071.00	3044.00	956.00	1093.00	3099.00	978.00	1114.00
2990.00	935.00	1072.00	3045.00	957.00	1093.00	3100.00	978.00	1115.00
2991.00	936.00	1072.00	3046.00	957.00	1094.00	3101.00	979.00	1115.00
2992.00	936.00	1073.00	3047.00	958.00	1094.00	3102.00	979.00	1116.00
2993.00	936.00	1073.00	3048.00	958.00	1094.00	3103.00	979.00	1116.00
2994.00	937.00	1073.00	3049.00	958.00	1095.00	3104.00	980.00	1116.00
2995.00	937.00	1074.00	3050.00	959.00	1095.00	3105.00	980.00	1117.00
2996.00	938.00	1074.00	3051.00	959.00	1096.00	3106.00	981.00	1117.00
2997.00	938.00	1075.00	3052.00	959.00	1096.00	3107.00	981.00	1117.00
2998.00	938.00	1075.00	3053.00	960.00	1096.00	3108.00	981.00	1118.00
2999.00	939.00	1075.00	3054.00	960.00	1097.00	3109.00	982.00	1118.00
3000.00	939.00	1076.00	3055.00	961.00	1097.00	3110.00	982.00	1119.00
3001.00	940.00	1076.00	3056.00	961.00	1098.00	3111.00	982.00	1119.00
3002.00	940.00	1077.00	3057.00	961.00	1098.00	3112.00	983.00	1120.00
3003.00	940.00	1077.00	3058.00	962.00	1098.00	3113.00	983.00	1120.00
3004.00	941.00	1077.00	3059.00	962.00	1099.00	3114.00	984.00	1121.00
3005.00	941.00	1078.00	3060.00	963.00	1099.00	3115.00	984.00	1121.00
3006.00	942.00	1078.00	3061.00	963.00	1100.00	3116.00	984.00	1122.00
3007.00	942.00	1078.00	3062.00	963.00	1100.00	3117.00	985.00	1122.00
3008.00	942.00	1079.00	3063.00	964.00	1100.00	3118.00	985.00	1122.00
3009.00	943.00	1079.00	3064.00	964.00	1101.00	3119.00	986.00	1123.00
3010.00	943.00	1080.00	3065.00	965.00	1101.00	3120.00	986.00	1123.00
3011.00	943.00	1080.00	3066.00	965.00	1101.00	3121.00	986.00	1124.00
3012.00	944.00	1080.00	3067.00	965.00	1102.00	3122.00	987.00	1124.00
3013.00	944.00	1081.00	3068.00	966.00	1102.00	3123.00	987.00	1125.00
3014.00	945.00	1081.00	3069.00	966.00	1103.00	3124.00	988.00	1125.00
3015.00	945.00	1082.00	3070.00	966.00	1103.00	3125.00	988.00	1126.00
3016.00	945.00	1082.00	3071.00	967.00	1103.00	3126.00	988.00	1126.00
3017.00	946.00	1082.00	3072.00	967.00	1104.00	3127.00	989.00	1127.00
3018.00	946.00	1083.00	3073.00	968.00	1104.00	3128.00	989.00	1127.00
3019.00	947.00	1083.00	3074.00	968.00	1105.00	3129.00	989.00	1128.00
3020.00	947.00	1084.00	3075.00	968.00	1105.00	3130.00	990.00	1128.00
3021.00	947.00	1084.00	3076.00	969.00	1105.00	3131.00	990.00	1129.00
3022.00	948.00	1084.00	3077.00	969.00	1106.00	3132.00	991.00	1129.00
3023.00	948.00	1085.00	3078.00	970.00	1106.00	3133.00	991.00	1130.00
3024.00	949.00	1085.00	3079.00	970.00	1107.00	3134.00	991.00	1130.00
3025.00	949.00	1085.00	3080.00	970.00	1107.00	3135.00	992.00	1131.00

PAYG WITHHOLDING TAX TABLE 2015-16 including Medicare levy (rounded $) 5.691

Weekly withholding amounts

Weekly earnings	With tax-free threshold	No tax-free threshold	Weekly earnings	With tax-free threshold	No tax-free threshold	Weekly earnings	With tax-free threshold	No tax-free threshold
3136.00	992.00	1131.00	3191.00	1014.00	1158.00	3246.00	1035.00	1185.00
3137.00	993.00	1132.00	3192.00	1014.00	1159.00	3247.00	1036.00	1186.00
3138.00	993.00	1132.00	3193.00	1014.00	1159.00	3248.00	1036.00	1186.00
3139.00	993.00	1133.00	3194.00	1015.00	1160.00	3249.00	1036.00	1187.00
3140.00	994.00	1133.00	3195.00	1015.00	1160.00	3250.00	1037.00	1187.00
3141.00	994.00	1134.00	3196.00	1016.00	1161.00	3251.00	1037.00	1188.00
3142.00	995.00	1134.00	3197.00	1016.00	1161.00	3252.00	1037.00	1188.00
3143.00	995.00	1135.00	3198.00	1016.00	1162.00	3253.00	1038.00	1189.00
3144.00	995.00	1135.00	3199.00	1017.00	1162.00	3254.00	1038.00	1189.00
3145.00	996.00	1136.00	3200.00	1017.00	1163.00	3255.00	1039.00	1190.00
3146.00	996.00	1136.00	3201.00	1018.00	1163.00	3256.00	1039.00	1190.00
3147.00	997.00	1137.00	3202.00	1018.00	1164.00	3257.00	1039.00	1191.00
3148.00	997.00	1137.00	3203.00	1018.00	1164.00	3258.00	1040.00	1191.00
3149.00	997.00	1138.00	3204.00	1019.00	1165.00	3259.00	1040.00	1192.00
3150.00	998.00	1138.00	3205.00	1019.00	1165.00	3260.00	1041.00	1192.00
3151.00	998.00	1139.00	3206.00	1020.00	1166.00	3261.00	1041.00	1193.00
3152.00	998.00	1139.00	3207.00	1020.00	1166.00	3262.00	1041.00	1193.00
3153.00	999.00	1140.00	3208.00	1020.00	1167.00	3263.00	1042.00	1194.00
3154.00	999.00	1140.00	3209.00	1021.00	1167.00	3264.00	1042.00	1194.00
3155.00	1000.00	1141.00	3210.00	1021.00	1168.00	3265.00	1043.00	1195.00
3156.00	1000.00	1141.00	3211.00	1021.00	1168.00	3266.00	1043.00	1195.00
3157.00	1000.00	1142.00	3212.00	1022.00	1169.00	3267.00	1043.00	1196.00
3158.00	1001.00	1142.00	3213.00	1022.00	1169.00	3268.00	1044.00	1196.00
3159.00	1001.00	1143.00	3214.00	1023.00	1170.00	3269.00	1044.00	1196.00
3160.00	1002.00	1143.00	3215.00	1023.00	1170.00	3270.00	1044.00	1197.00
3161.00	1002.00	1144.00	3216.00	1023.00	1171.00	3271.00	1045.00	1197.00
3162.00	1002.00	1144.00	3217.00	1024.00	1171.00	3272.00	1045.00	1198.00
3163.00	1003.00	1145.00	3218.00	1024.00	1171.00	3273.00	1046.00	1198.00
3164.00	1003.00	1145.00	3219.00	1025.00	1172.00	3274.00	1046.00	1199.00
3165.00	1004.00	1146.00	3220.00	1025.00	1172.00	3275.00	1046.00	1199.00
3166.00	1004.00	1146.00	3221.00	1025.00	1173.00			
3167.00	1004.00	1147.00	3222.00	1026.00	1173.00			
3168.00	1005.00	1147.00	3223.00	1026.00	1174.00			
3169.00	1005.00	1147.00	3224.00	1027.00	1174.00			
3170.00	1005.00	1148.00	3225.00	1027.00	1175.00			
3171.00	1006.00	1148.00	3226.00	1027.00	1175.00			
3172.00	1006.00	1149.00	3227.00	1028.00	1176.00			
3173.00	1007.00	1149.00	3228.00	1028.00	1176.00			
3174.00	1007.00	1150.00	3229.00	1028.00	1177.00			
3175.00	1007.00	1150.00	3230.00	1029.00	1177.00			
3176.00	1008.00	1151.00	3231.00	1029.00	1178.00			
3177.00	1008.00	1151.00	3232.00	1030.00	1178.00			
3178.00	1009.00	1152.00	3233.00	1030.00	1179.00			
3179.00	1009.00	1152.00	3234.00	1030.00	1179.00			
3180.00	1009.00	1153.00	3235.00	1031.00	1180.00			
3181.00	1010.00	1153.00	3236.00	1031.00	1180.00			
3182.00	1010.00	1154.00	3237.00	1032.00	1181.00			
3183.00	1011.00	1154.00	3238.00	1032.00	1181.00			
3184.00	1011.00	1155.00	3239.00	1032.00	1182.00			
3185.00	1011.00	1155.00	3240.00	1033.00	1182.00			
3186.00	1012.00	1156.00	3241.00	1033.00	1183.00			
3187.00	1012.00	1156.00	3242.00	1034.00	1183.00			
3188.00	1012.00	1157.00	3243.00	1034.00	1184.00			
3189.00	1013.00	1157.00	3244.00	1034.00	1184.00			
3190.00	1013.00	1158.00	3245.00	1035.00	1185.00			

NOTE: Where the tax-free threshold is claimed and the employee earns:

- more than $3,275 but less than $3,461, withhold $1,046 plus 39 cents for each $1 of earnings in excess of $3,275

- more than $3,460, withhold $1,119 plus 49 cents for each $1 of earnings in excess of $3,460.

Where the tax-free threshold is not claimed and the employee earns more than $3,275, withhold $1,199 plus 49 cents for each $1 of earnings in excess of $3,275.

For all withholding amounts calculated, round the result to the nearest dollar.

5.700 PAYG INSTALMENTS

Throughout the year, certain investors and businesses are required to pay instalments of income tax on instalment income earned. The rules governing the PAYG instalment system are in Sch 1 Division 45 of the TAA. A PAYG instalment for which an entity is liable will be credited to the entity on assessment in the same way as PAYG withholding. Unpaid instalments are subject to the General Interest Charge (GIC).

5.710   LIABILITY TO PAY PAYG INSTALMENTS

A liability to pay PAYG instalments arises if the Tax Office advises a taxpayer (in writing) of their liability. All entities are eligible to receive an instalment notification.

 Taxpayers need to be aware that the non-receipt of this notification is not an excuse, as it is open to the Commissioner to deem the notice to have been received in the ordinary course of mail. As a result, taxpayers should monitor their own liability to PAYG instalments.

Generally, individuals are liable for PAYG instalments if they have a 'base assessment instalment income' of at least $2,000 unless:

* the tax payable on their most recent notice of assessment is less than $500, or
* their notional tax is less than $250 (notional tax is the tax that would have been payable on their business and investment income (excluding capital gains) in the latest income tax assessment on current income tax rates), or
* they are entitled to the seniors and pensioners tax offset (see 3.190).

Companies and superannuation funds are liable for PAYG instalments if they have a 'base assessment instalment income' of at least $1.

However, companies and superannuation funds are not required to pay PAYG instalments if:

* their Tax Office calculated instalment rate is 0%, or their notional tax is less than $250
* gross business and investment income shown in their most recent income tax return is less than $2,000,000, and
* they are not registered for GST.

'Base assessment instalment income' is gross investment and business income (excluding any capital gains) for the base year. A 'base year' is the most recent income tax year for which a notice of assessment, or a notice of amended assessment has been made. For more information see 5.711.

5.711   KEY CONCEPTS

BASE ASSESSMENT INSTALMENT INCOME (s45-320(2) TAA)

'Base assessment instalment income' means so much of a taxpayer's assessable income, as worked out for the purposes of the base assessment, as the Commissioner determines is instalment income for the base year.

BASE ASSESSMENT (s45-320(3) TAA)

Base assessment is the latest assessment for the taxpayer's most recent income year for which an assessment has been made. However, if the Commissioner is satisfied that there is a later income year for which the taxpayer does not have taxable income, the 'base assessment' is the latest return or other information from which an assessment for that income year would have been made.

 A 'refund notice' or a 'nil tax advice' is not an assessment. Therefore, the Commissioner will go back to a year for which a notice of assessment or a notice of amended assessment exists.

BASE YEAR (S45-320(4) SCH 1 TAA)

The base year is the income year for which the taxpayer has a 'base assessment'.

INSTALMENT INCOME (s45-120 TAA)

Generally, instalment income for a period includes a taxpayer's ordinary income derived during that period but only to the extent it is assessable income of the income year that is, or includes, that period. The meaning of instalment income differs for different entities (see s45-120 TAA).

Instalment income does not include income which is subject to PAYG withholding (except for withholding due to non-quotation).

It would generally also exclude statutory income (eg. capital gains) for most entities unless taxpayer is a complying/non-complying approved deposit fund, superannuation fund, pooled superannuation trust or life insurance company.

5.720   WHEN IS A PAYG INSTALMENT DUE?

Instalment payment patterns will either be quarterly or annually. If liable to pay PAYG instalments, taxpayers will automatically become quarterly payers unless they are eligible to pay instalments on an annual basis and elect to do so.

QUARTERLY INSTALMENTS

The due dates for quarterly instalments depend on whether the entity is a GST registered enterprise with monthly tax periods.

The due dates for paying quarterly PAYG instalments are:

Instalment quarter	Instalment quarter end date	Non deferred BAS payers	Deferred BAS payers
1	30 September	21 October	28 October
2	31 December	21 January	28 February
3	31 March	21 April	28 April
4	30 June	21 July	28 July

For the definition of deferred and non-deferred BAS payers see 5.424. However, if the due dates fall on gazetted public holidays, it will be extended to the next business day.

Further, registered tax agents should check their lodgment program as the Tax Office allows them additional time to spread their workloads (see www.ato.gov.au).

DUAL INSTALMENTS

Special arrangements exist for individuals who, during the current income tax year, are either carrying on a business of primary production, or who derive 'above average special professional income' (see 3.070). To gain this concession:

- the primary producer must have carried on a primary production business during the base year, and derived a taxable income from that business for that year, and
- the person who derived 'special professional income' must have derived it during the base year, and derived a taxable income from that activity for that year.

If these tests can be satisfied, the individual is entitled to pay the third and fourth instalments only. The instalments will be amounts calculated by the Tax Office. Payment of instalment amounts calculated by the taxpayer will cause the taxpayer to become a quarterly instalment payer.

The third instalment will represent 75% of the taxpayer's annual PAYG instalment liability and the fourth payment will be the remainder. The relevant due date is determined by whether they are a 'non-deferred' or a 'deferred BAS payer' (see above table).

ANNUAL PAYERS

A taxpayer subject to PAYG instalments may choose to pay an annual PAYG instalment if, at the end of the 'instalment quarter' when they first became liable for PAYG instalments, the taxpayer:

- is neither registered nor required to be registered for GST purposes
- is not a partner of a partnership that is registered nor required to be registered for GST purposes
- has a (most recent) notional tax amount less than $8,000, and
- if a company: is not a participant in a GST joint venture or part of an 'Instalment group'.

For taxpayers already in the PAYG instalment system, the election to pay annually must be made before the date the first quarterly PAYG instalment is due for the income year. If the taxpayer becomes subject to PAYG instalments part way through the year, the election must be made before the first instalment is due, after it became liable to a PAYG instalment.

Once the election is made, it will continue through until the taxpayer's circumstances change such that they are no longer eligible to be an annual payer.

The dates for paying the annual instalment are:

Taxpayer type	Due date for payment
Taxpayers with 30 June year end	21 October after year end
Taxpayers with year end other than 30 June	21st day of 4th month following year end

Events that disqualify an entity from using the annual instalment

An entity using the annual instalment will become disqualified from using that payment method if they are notified by the Tax Office that their notional tax has reached $8,000. The entity will not be able to use the annual instalment for the current income tax year if the notification occurred between the end of the first instalment quarter of the previous year and the end of the first instalment quarter of the current year. For the previous income tax year, they will remain an annual instalment payer, but for the current income tax year quarterly instalments must be adopted.

Mr. Wilson, an annual PAYG instalment payer, lodges his 2015 income tax return on 31 October 2015. One month later he receives his notice of assessment. On the basis of this assessment, his notional tax exceeds $8,000. Mr. Wilson becomes ineligible to use the annual PAYG instalment from 1 July 2015. Therefore, he is liable to pay his first quarterly PAYG instalment in respect of the 2015-16 income year on 28 October 2015. He remains liable to pay the 2014-15 annual instalment due by 21 October 2015 as well.

An entity that chooses to adopt quarterly instalments cannot adopt the annual instalment.

5.730   AMOUNT OF PAYG INSTALMENTS

5.731   ANNUAL INSTALMENTS

Section 45-115 of Sch 1 to the TAA provides that an annual instalment may be calculated using one of these three alternatives:

- **instalment income method:** the instalment amount is worked out using the formula:
  Commissioner's instalment rate x Taxpayer's instalment income for income year
- **notional tax method:** the taxpayer's most recent notional tax notified by the Commissioner before the end of the income year, or
- **benchmark tax method:** the amount the taxpayer estimates will be its benchmark tax for that income year.

5.732   QUARTERLY INSTALMENTS

A quarterly instalment may be calculated using either:

- **instalment income method** (s45-110 Sch 1 TAA) or
- **GDP-adjusted notional tax method** (s45-112 Sch 1 TAA).

NOTE: All taxpayers are entitled to use the instalment income method. Only the following taxpayers may use the GDP-adjusted notional tax method:

- individuals
- multi-rate trustees
- companies, superannuation funds with business or investment income of $2 million or less in their most recently assessed income tax return, and
- companies and superannuation funds that have more than $2 million in instalment income for the previous income year and which are eligible to pay annual PAYG instalments but have chosen not to do so.

NOTE: Small Business Entities (SBEs) (see 10.200 and 10.300) may pay PAYG instalments based on GDP-adjusted notional tax. The concession is also available to a partner in a partnership which is a SBE and a beneficiary of a trust which is a SBE.

5.733   NOTIONAL TAX METHOD

This term relates to an entity's entitlement to adopt the 'annual PAYG instalment'.

Annual payers can pay the 'notional tax' by the due date. This amount will be notified by the Tax Office and is based on an entity's 'adjusted tax' on 'adjusted taxable income' for the 'base year', then reduced by the 'adjusted tax' on 'adjusted withholding income' for the base year (Subdivision 45-J Sch 1 TAA). Using 'notional tax' as the amount of a PAYG instalment is only available to entities entitled to adopt the 'annual PAYG instalment'.

NO WITHHOLDING INCOME IN TAXABLE INCOME FOR THE BASE YEAR

If the taxpayer's taxable income for the 'base year' contains no 'withholding income', then 'notional tax' will be the taxpayer's 'adjusted tax' on its 'adjusted taxable income' (s45-325 Sch 1 TAA).

'Adjusted tax' is the income tax payable on the taxpayer's 'adjusted taxable income' for the base year taking into account the following adjustments (s45-340 Sch 1 TAA):

- disregard the following tax offsets: private health insurance, childcare, entrepreneurs', mature age worker, Medicare levy surcharge (lump sum payment in arrears), franking deficit tax, low income rebate and superannuation contribution for spouse rebate
- include Medicare levy payable on the 'adjusted taxable income' for the 'base year', but disregard the Medicare levy surcharge applicable to individuals and trustees
- include any amount owing for the 'base year' for 'accumulated HECS/HELP debt' adjusted taxable income
- include any amount liable to be paid for the 'base year' by way of an Financial Supplement (FS) assessment debt, and
- deduct any family tax benefit worked out on the taxpayer's taxable income (rather than 'adjusted taxable income') for the 'base year'.

'Adjusted taxable income' for a 'base year' is assessable income for the base assessment less any:

- net capital gains
- allowable deductions claimed (excluding any tax losses claimed), and
- any carried forward tax losses. See s45-330 TAA.

Should the taxpayer be a complying approved deposit fund, superannuation fund, or a pooled superannuation trust, 'adjusted taxable income' for the 'base year' is calculated in the same way, except net capital gains are included in assessable income.

TAXABLE INCOME FOR THE 'BASE YEAR' CONTAINS 'WITHHOLDING INCOME'

'Notional tax' in respect of the 'base year' is worked out in the same way as it is above, but it is reduced if a taxpayer's assessable income for the 'base year' includes 'withholding income'.

The reduction is the 'adjusted tax' on the taxpayer's 'adjusted withholding income' for the 'base year', but 'notional tax' cannot be reduced to a figure that is less than zero. No reduction is available in respect of income for which PAYG withholding tax has been withheld owing to non-quotation of an ABN or a TFN.

'Adjusted withholding income' (s45-335 TAA) is the total of a taxpayer's assessable withholding payments for the base year, excluding any amounts that were subject to PAYG withholding due to non-quotation of an ABN or a TFN, for the 'base year'. It is reduced by allowable deductions claimed in the 'base year', as they reasonably relate to the earning of that income.

5.734   GDP-ADJUSTED NOTIONAL TAX METHOD

Entities liable for quarterly PAYG instalments may pay an amount that is based on a proportion of the notional tax that has been adjusted for growth in GDP.

The Tax Office will advise taxpayers of their GDP-adjusted notional tax amounts. Subdivision 45-L Sch 1 TAA sets out how the Commissioner works out an amount of quarterly instalment on the basis of GDP-adjusted notional tax. The amount payable for an instalment quarter depends whether the entity is liable for quarterly or dual instalments.

For entities liable for quarterly instalments the amount payable is worked out under s45-400 Sch 1 TAA as follows:

Instalment quarter	Amount
1	25% of GDP-adjusted notional tax
2	50% of GDP-adjusted notional tax less the amount of the instalment for the earlier instalment quarter in that income year
3	75% of GDP-adjusted notional tax less the total of the instalment for the earlier instalment quarters in that income year
4	100% of GDP-adjusted notional tax less the total of the instalments for the earlier instalment quarters in that income year

For entities liable for dual instalments the amount payable is worked out at s45-402 Sch 1 TAA as follows:

Instalment quarter	Amount
1 & 2	0% of GDP-adjusted notional tax
3	75% of GDP-adjusted notional tax
4	100% of GDP-adjusted notional tax less amount of previous instalment in that income year

If the entity is first advised of their liability to PAYG instalments during the second instalment quarter, the proportions are 50% and 75% for the third and fourth instalments.

If advised of a PAYG liability during the third instalment quarter, the proportions are 25% and 50% for the third and fourth instalments. If advised of a PAYG liability during the fourth instalment quarter, the proportion for the fourth quarter only is 25%.

The formula for calculating the 'GDP-adjusted notional tax' (set out at s45-405 Sch 1 TAA) is similar to working out notional tax. The adjusted taxable income for the base year is increased by the GDP adjustment before the adjusted tax is worked out on that increased/up-lifted taxable amount.

Any adjusted withholding income for the base year is also increased by the GDP adjustment before the adjusted tax is worked out on that increased adjusted withholding income.

GDP up-lifted adjusted taxable income = 'Adjusted taxable income'
x (1 + GDP adjustment)

GDP up-lifted adjusted withholding income = 'Adjusted withholding income'
x (1 + GDP adjustment)

The 'GDP adjustment' is a percentage figure worked out using this formula:

100 x [Sum of GDP amounts (current year) divided by sum of GDP amounts (previous year)] – 100

where the:

- 'GDP amount' for a quarter is the gross domestic product at current prices as published by the Australian Statistician (see Australian National Accounts: National Income, Expenditure and Product, ABS catalogue no. 5206)
- 'sum of GDP amounts (current year)' is the sum of 'GDP amounts' for the quarters in the last calendar year (the later calendar year) ending at least three months before the start of the current year
- 'sum of GDP amounts (previous year)' is the sum of GDP amounts for the quarters in the calendar year (the earlier calendar year) before the later year.

The 'sum of GDP amounts' are specified in the first document published by the Australian Statistician after the end of each calendar year. The GDP adjustment used to work out quarterly PAYG instalment amounts for the 2015-16 financial year is 3% (4% for 2014-15).

 Care must be taken when ascertaining which years are the 'current and the previous years'. The 'current year GDP' is the last calendar year that ends at least three months before the 'current year' of income. The 'previous year GDP' is simply the year before the 'current year GDP'.

NOTE: If the result from the calculation of the GDP adjustment is negative, it is treated as 0%.

5.735   VARIATION OF A GDP-ADJUSTED NOTIONAL TAX INSTALMENT/ ESTIMATED BENCHMARK TAX

Due to changes in an entity's circumstances during an 'instalment quarter', the 'GDP-adjusted notional tax' may become an inaccurate estimate. In view of this, an entity's PAYG quarterly instalment worked out on the basis of 'GDP-adjusted notional tax' may be varied under s45-112. Section 45-112(1)(b) Sch 1 TAA allows a taxpayer to calculate an instalment amount on the basis of their estimate of their *benchmark tax*. The amount is calculated under Subdivision 45-M.

The variation becomes effective from this time. The notification must also contain an estimate of the entity's benchmark tax. It is upon this estimated benchmark tax that the instalment should be calculated. Once notified, the Commissioner will use this estimate as the basis of determining the amount owing in respect of the following instalment quarters for the income year, unless another estimate is made for a following quarter.

The amount of each quarterly instalment is then worked out in the following way:

Instalment quarter	Amount
1	25% of estimated benchmark tax
2	50% of estimated benchmark tax less the amount of the instalment for the earlier instalment quarter in that income year
3	75% of estimated benchmark tax less the total of the instalment for the earlier instalment quarters in that income year
4	100% of the estimated benchmark tax less the total of the instalments for the earlier instalment quarters in that income year

For entities liable for dual instalments the amount payable is then worked out in the following way:

Instalment quarter	Amount
1 & 2	0% of estimate of benchmark tax
3	75% of estimate of benchmark tax
4	100% of estimate of benchmark tax less the amount of previous instalments in that income year

An annual instalment payer may also use the benchmark tax method if as a result of the changes in its circumstances during the financial year, the 'notional tax' amount (see 5.733) or the instalment rate (see 5.737) as advised by the Commissioner may become an inaccurate estimate.

5.736   BENCHMARK TAX

'Benchmark tax' is worked out at s45-365 (s45-535 for trusts) in a similar way to notional tax and depends upon whether the entity's income includes any PAYG withholding income. If none, it is the entity's 'adjusted assessed tax' on its 'adjusted assessed taxable income', otherwise this figure is reduced by the amount of PAYG withholding tax that has been withheld.

An entity's 'adjusted assessed taxable income' for a 'variation year' is its taxable income for that year less any net capital gains. It is different from 'adjusted taxable income' used to work out an entity's 'notional tax' as the 'adjusted taxable income' is worked out based on the taxpayer's 'base year'.

If the taxpayer is a complying approved deposit fund, superannuation fund, or pooled superannuation trust, adjusted assessed taxable income for the variation year includes net capital gains. Special rules exist for life insurance companies (see s45-370(3) Sch 1 TAA).

A 'variation year' is the income tax year for which its GDP-adjusted notional tax was varied.

'Adjusted assessed tax' on an entity's 'adjusted assessed taxable income' for a variation year is the income tax payable on the taxpayer's 'adjusted assessed taxable income' for the 'variation year':

- disregarding the following tax offsets:
  - child care
  - mature age worker
  - Medicare levy surcharge (lump sum payments in arrears)
  - franking deficit tax liabilities
  - private health insurance
  - low income rebate, and
  - superannuation contribution for spouse rebate
- including Medicare levy payable on the 'adjusted assessed taxable income' for the 'variation year', but disregarding the Medicare levy surcharge applicable to individuals and trustees
- including amount owing for the 'variation year' for the taxpayer's accumulated HECS or HELP debt on the basis of the taxpayer's 'adjusted assessed taxable income'
- include any amount liable to be paid for the 'base year' by way of an Financial Supplement (FS)assessment debt, and
- less any family tax benefit worked out on the taxpayer's 'adjusted assessed taxable income' for the 'variation year'.

CREDIT FOR OVERPAID INSTALMENT (S45-420 TAA)

A variation of a GDP-adjusted quarterly instalment may cause the previous payments of quarterly instalments to be overpaid (eg. if the estimate of benchmark tax is less than the GDP-adjusted notional tax as notified by the Commissioner). A credit arises if the above method of determining the amount of instalment results in a negative figure. That negative figure will be the amount of the credit.

To be entitled for this credit, a claim must be made in the approved form (activity statement) before the day on which the instalment for the current quarter is due.

UNDERESTIMATING BENCHMARK TAX

Subdivision 45-G Sch 1 TAA sets out a taxpayer's liability to pay the GIC where a shortfall has arisen in respect of a quarterly instalment worked out on the basis of a varied instalment rate (see 5.737) or estimated benchmark rate (see 5.735).

Care needs to be taken in determining 'estimated benchmark tax', as the GIC will be imposed under s45-232 if the estimate used to calculate an instalment is less than 85% of the 'benchmark tax' as determined by the Commissioner at the end of the income tax year pursuant to s45-365 Sch 1 TAA.

The amount subject to the GIC is: *Acceptable amount of instalment less actual amount*

The 'acceptable amount of instalment' depends on which instalment quarter is concerned. It is the lesser of the amount that would have been the instalment for that quarter had it not been varied or the amount worked out using the following table:

Instalment quarter	Amount
1	25% of benchmark tax
2	50% of benchmark tax less acceptable amount of prior quarter
3	75% of benchmark tax less acceptable amount of prior quarters
4	100% of benchmark tax less acceptable amount of prior quarters

The 'actual amount' is the amount of the instalment that was based on the estimate. If, as a result of the variation a credit was claimed, the figure will be negative.

The GIC is calculated from the day the PAYG instalment was due to be paid to the earlier of the date the entity's assessed tax for the year of income was due to be paid.

The Commissioner is obliged to supply a written notice of the GIC that the entity is liable to pay. It must be paid within 14 days after the notice is given. If the GIC is unpaid at the expiry of this time, the entity also becomes liable for a GIC on the GIC itself.

The period during which the GIC is levied upon the GIC starts at the end of those 14 days, and ends at the later of when the:

- original GIC is paid, or
- GIC on the GIC is paid.

In short, an unpaid GIC on an understated varied PAYG instalment begins to compound daily, if it remains unpaid after the issue of the notice. In special circumstances the Commissioner has discretion to remit the GIC if satisfied it is fair and reasonable to do so.

REDUCTION IN THE GIC (S45-233 SCH 1 TAA)

The GIC liability may be reduced if the instalment shortfall is made up in a later instalment. The shortfall on which the taxpayer is liable to pay GIC is reduced thereby reducing the GIC payable. The amount of understated quarterly instalment subject to the GIC can be reduced if the following formula produces a negative result for a later instalment quarter. That result is the amount of the reduction of the shortfall.

Acceptable amount of your instalment for the later quarter
– Actual amount of your instalment for the later quarter

If any portion of this reduction has already been applied to reduce the shortfall of an earlier instalment, the amount of the reduction itself is reduced by so much as has already been applied (s45-233(3) Sch 1 TAA).

The reduction to the shortfall amount takes effect from the payment date for the later quarterly PAYG instalment, to the earlier of:

- the date the entity's assessed tax for the year of income was due to be paid, or
- the last day when any of that tax is paid.

5.737   INSTALMENT RATE METHOD

The instalment rate method is available for both annual and quarterly instalment payers. However, the method differs slightly for the two different types of payers.

For quarterly payers, the amount of quarterly instalment worked out under the instalment rate method is as follows (s45-110 Sch 1 TAA):

The amount of the instalment = Instalment income for that quarter
x Applicable instalment rate

The applicable instalment rate for a quarterly payer will be the most recent instalment rate given by the Commissioner or a varied instalment rate under s45-205 Sch 1 TAA.

For annual payers, the amount of annual instalment worked out under the instalment rate method is as follows (s45-115 Sch 1 TAA):

The amount of the instalment = Instalment income for the income year
x Commissioner's instalment rate.

Annual PAYG instalment payers must use the most recent rate advised by the Commissioner and cannot vary the rate even though it might result in overpayment of tax. In such circumstances, an annual payer can instead work out the instalment amount using the benchmark tax method (see 5.736).

INSTALMENT INCOME

The meaning of 'instalment income' is set out at s45-120. This is the amount of ordinary income derived in the 'instalment quarter' that is assessable income. This will exclude any GST payable and income which was, or should have been, subject to PAYG withholding (other than a withholding caused by non-quotation of the TFN or ABN).

Determining when instalment income is derived is done in the same way as determining when assessable income is derived (see 11.030). 'Instalment income' for most entities is their gross ordinary income including:

- gross sales, fees for service, interest received, gross rent, dividends and royalties received
- for primary producers, deposits and withdrawals from Farm Management Deposit Funds are included in the instalment income in that quarter (s45-120(4) and (5)), and
- profit arising from a profit making scheme or undertaking.

'Instalment income' excludes statutory income, such as:

- imputation credits
- royalties
- exempt income
- deemed dividends, and
- net capital gain.

The 'instalment income' of a superannuation fund, Pooled Superannuation Trust (PST) and an Approved Deposit Fund (ADF) is comprised of ordinary and statutory income (s45-120(2)). the instalment income of a life insurance company also includes some statutory income (s45-120(2)). Special rules exist for calculating the instalment income for partnerships and trustees and beneficiaries (see 5.740, 5.750 and 5.760).

INSTALMENT RATE

The Tax Office will inform taxpayers if they have to pay PAYG instalments by providing them with a written notification of their applicable instalment rate and an activity statement. Quarterly instalment payers receiving a notification may use either the Commissioner's instalment rate or a varied rate if it is believed that the Commissioner's instalment rate incorrectly reflects current conditions. Annual payers if using the instalment rate method cannot vary the instalment rate provided by the Commissioner, but may instead choose to calculate their instalment amount using the other two methods – notional tax method or benchmark tax method.

The formula the Commissioner uses to calculate an instalment rate is set out at s45-320 as follows:

(Notional tax divided by Base assessment instalment income) x 100

The rate is a percentage worked out to two decimal places (rounded up if the third decimal place is five or more; rounding down if otherwise).

'Base assessment instalment income' is assessable income from the 'base assessment' (latest assessment) for the 'base year' (the income year the base assessment relates to) reduced by:

- income covered by PAYG withholding (other than income covered by withholding only because of failure to quote an ABN or a TFN), and
- statutory income (eg. capital gain or dividend gross-up).

The 'base assessment' is the latest assessment for an entity's most recent income tax year. If there is a later income year for which the entity does not have a taxable income (eg. it made a loss or tax losses exceeded what would otherwise have been taxable income), the base assessment is the latest return or other information from which an assessment for that income year could have been made.

For a quarterly payer, the instalment rate method may apply another instalment rate other than the Commissioner's rate if:

- the taxpayer has chosen an instalment rate under the provisions that provide for a varied instalment rate (s45-205), the taxpayer may use that rate, or
- if the taxpayer has chosen a varied instalment rate for an earlier instalment quarter in that income year and the taxpayer has not varied the rate for the current quarter pursuant to s45-205, the taxpayer may use that rate.

VARYING THE INSTALMENT RATE

The instalment rate method allows an instalment payer to vary their instalment rate should they feel it incorrectly reflects current conditions. This is provided for in Subdivision 45-F.

Once an instalment payer has chosen to use a varied instalment rate, it must be used from then on unless the instalment payer varies it again in a later instalment quarter. Notification must be given to the Tax Office of the varied instalment rate by the date the instalment is due. This is done by completing box 'T3' on an activity statement.

The varied instalment rate does not carry over into the following income tax year, as the instalment payer starts afresh at the beginning of each year.

An instalment payer needs to be careful in calculating the varied rate, as an inadequate instalment rate will cause the instalment payer to become subject to the GIC. Care is needed, as there is no prescribed method of calculating a varied rate, though the trigger for GIC effectively forces one to estimate their benchmark instalment rate (s45-230).

CREDITS FOR OVER-PAID QUARTERLY INSTALMENTS

An entity that has previously paid quarterly instalments during a particular year before adopting a varied instalment rate may claim a credit in relation to those previous instalments pursuant to s45-215 if:

- the instalment rate chosen for calculating the current quarterly instalment is less than the instalment rate used to calculate the previous instalment(s), and

- the amount that was due to be paid for prior instalments during the income tax year exceeds what they would have been had the varied instalment rate been used instead.

The claim for credit need to be made in an approved form (ie. activity statement) by the date on which the current quarter instalment is due.

 Whilst it is possible to claim a credit for unpaid instalments, the unpaid amount is subject to the GIC.

The claim for a credit is made by entering the amount of credit at box '5B' on an activity statement.

GIC ON UNDERSTATED INSTALMENT RATE

The GIC is charged under s45-230 if the varied instalment rate used for working out an instalment is less than 85% of a 'benchmark instalment rate' worked out by the Commissioner.

The GIC is calculated on the amount payable from the day the instalment was due to the earlier of:

- the day the instalment for the varied quarter was due to be paid, or

- the last day on which the assessed tax for the income year is due to be paid.

Subdivision 45-K sets out how the Commissioner works out the benchmark instalment rate and benchmark tax for a year in which the taxpayer has varied their instalment rate.

The 'benchmark instalment rate' is worked out by using the formula:

(Benchmark tax divided by Variation year instalment income) x 100
(work out to two decimal places, round up if third decimal place is five or higher)

Where:

- 'variation year instalment income' is an entity's instalment income for the year as determined by the Commissioner, for the year of income to which the instalments have been varied, and

- 'benchmark tax' means the taxpayer's adjusted assessed tax (calculated at s45-375) on their adjusted assessed taxable income (calculated under s45-370) for the year in which they have varied their instalment rate.

 If any 'varied instalment rate' used by an entity for an instalment quarter falls short of 85% of the benchmark instalment rate, it is liable for the GIC for quarters where the 'varied instalment rate' was used. The requirement to notify the Tax Office of a varied instalment rate provides the Tax Office with the means of monitoring whether the 85% threshold has been breached.

The amount subject to the GIC is calculated at s45-230(2) using this formula:

(Rate discrepancy for the quarter x Instalment income for the variation quarter) + credit adjustment

Where:

- 'rate discrepancy' is the difference between the taxpayer's chosen instalment rate and the lesser of:
  - the benchmark instalment rate for that income year, and
  - the Commissioner's most recent instalment rate given to the entity prior to the end of the variation quarter, and
- 'credit adjustment': if the taxpayer has claimed a credit because having varied an instalment rate lower than the instalment rate used to calculate previous instalments in the same income year, the credit adjustment is the lesser of:
  - the credit claimed, or
  - the amount calculated by multiplying the instalment income of the previous instalment quarters of the income year by the rate discrepancy.

If no credit is claimed, the credit adjustment is nil.

The Commissioner must supply a written notice of the GIC that the entity is liable to pay. It must be paid within 14 days after the notice is given. If the GIC is unpaid at the expiry of this time, the entity also becomes liable for a GIC on the GIC itself.

The period over which the GIC is levied upon the GIC starts from the end of those 14 days and ends at the later of when the:

- original GIC is paid, or
- the GIC on the GIC is paid.

In short, an unpaid GIC on an understated varied instalment compounds daily from 14 days after receiving notice of liability to the amount of GIC. The Commissioner has a discretion to remit the GIC if satisfied it is fair and reasonable to do so owing to special circumstances. The GIC will not apply if the instalment rate of the Commissioner is used.

5.740   IMPLICATIONS FOR PARTNERSHIPS

Subdivision 45-H sets out rules regarding instalment payments specific to partnership income. Partners using the instalment rate method are required to include their share of partnership instalment income in an activity statement each instalment quarter. A partner's share of partnership instalment income is added to any other instalment income the partner may have.

A partner who has adopted the 'instalment rate method' to determining the quarterly instalments has a prescribed method of including a share of their partnership's 'instalment income' in their own 'instalment income'. The share of instalment income that a partner needs to include in their personal instalment income is calculated by using the formula set out at s45-260:

> *(The taxpayer's assessable income from the partnership for the last income year divided by The partnership's instalment income for that income year)*
> *x Partnership's instalment income for the current period*

This formula imposes a requirement upon the partnership to notify each partner the amount of 'instalment income' the partnership derives for each instalment quarter. A partner will be given one instalment rate by the Commissioner at any one time, regardless of the number of partnerships they are in.

PRIOR YEAR LOSSES

If the partnership incurred a loss, or 'broke even' last income tax year, partners are still required to pay a 'fair and reasonable amount' of quarterly instalment amounts having regard to:

- the extent of the partner's interest in the partnership during the current period, and
- the partnership's instalment income for the current period, and
- any other relevant circumstances.

 A partner who claimed a partnership loss in their own income tax return for the previous income tax year must still include a share of their partnership's instalment income for each instalment quarter in their activity statement.

5.750   IMPLICATIONS FOR TRUST BENEFICIARIES

Beneficiaries must also include their share of trust instalment income in their personal instalment income each instalment quarter. How this is achieved depends upon the type of trust concerned. Subdivision 45-I sets out how to calculate trust income to be included in the instalment income of a beneficiary.

Bare trusts require the beneficiary to include their share of trust instalment income as it is earned by the trust.

Unit trusts require the beneficiary to adopt the 'distributions basis', meaning beneficiaries will include distributions made to them during an instalment quarter in their instalment income.

'Corporate unit trust' or 'public trading trust' beneficiaries are treated as though they are shareholders in a company.

Beneficiaries in any other type of trust must adopt a formula to work out the share of trust instalment income they are required to declare in their personal instalment income.

5.751   BARE TRUSTS (s45-280(6) Sch 1 TAA)

Beneficiaries of a bare trust (trusts whose beneficiary is absolutely entitled) are required to include an amount of trust instalment income for an instalment quarter using the following formula:

> *Beneficiary's proportion of the vested and indefeasible interest in the trust*
> *x Trust's instalment income for the current instalment quarter*

The beneficiary's proportion is the proportion of their interest in relation to the total interests in the trust property as each beneficiaries' interests in the trust property have become fixed.

5.752   RESIDENT UNIT TRUSTS – DISTRIBUTION BASIS (s45-285 TAA)

A beneficiary may adopt this basis if the trust is:

* a broadly held resident unit trust, or
* a non-broadly held resident unit trust.

 Beneficiaries of a unit trust falling outside of these two categories must use the formula applicable to other trusts. The operation of this method is explained at 'Other trusts' (see 5.753).

The instalment income for an instalment quarter of a beneficiary of either trust will include so much trust income or trust capital that the trust distributes to the beneficiary during the instalment quarter. Section 45-285(1) provides that in determining the beneficiary's instalment income, it does not matter whether the trust income or trust capital is included in the taxpayer's assessable income for the income year which is or includes that period.

 Care must be taken when determining the instalment quarter in which to declare a trust distribution. The relevant legislation is drafted in terms of when the trust distributes. This implies timing is dependent upon payment by the trust rather than receipt by the beneficiary. So, if a trustee makes a distribution on the last day of an instalment quarter, and the beneficiary receives the distribution on the day after, that beneficiary will be required to include the trust distribution in the instalment quarter that just concluded.

BROADLY HELD RESIDENT UNIT TRUSTS

A taxpayer's instalment income includes trust income or trust capital that a broadly held resident unit trust distributes/applies to them pursuant to s45-285(1).

For a trust to be a 'broadly held resident unit trust' it:

* must be a resident unit trust being:
    - either any property of the unit trust situated in Australia or the trustee carries on business in Australia, and
    - either the central management and control of the unit trust is in Australia or Australian residents hold more than 50% of the beneficial interests in the income or property of the trust

- must be 'broadly held', meaning throughout the instalment period the units in the unit trust were:
  - listed on a stock exchange in Australia or elsewhere
  - offered to the public, or
  - held by at least 50 persons
- must not have its interests concentrated, either directly or indirectly, in the hands of 20 people or less (this concept is explained at s45-287), and
- can only invest in 'eligible investment business' activities defined at s102M of the ITAA36.

Section 45-287 provides that ownership of a trust will be concentrated in the hands of up to 20 people if they hold between them (directly or indirectly, and for their own benefit) fixed entitlements to at least 75% of the trust's income, capital or voting rights. A beneficiary's associates or nominees will count as one person.

A trust's ownership will also be concentrated in the hands of up to 20 people if it reasonable to conclude so having regard to:

- any constituent document, contract, agreement or instrument that authorises the variation or abrogation of the rights attaching to any of the interests in the trust or relates to conversion, cancellation, extinguishment or redemption of those interests
- any contract, arrangement, option or instrument under which a person has power to acquire an interest in the trust, or
- any power, authority or discretion in a person in relation to the rights attaching to any of the interests in the trust.

The non-concentration of interests requirement places a compliance burden upon the trustee that is possibly more arduous than that of using the formula applicable to beneficiaries of 'other trusts'. While not the case for large managed funds that will clearly come within the requirement, it is an issue for those that are close to breaching the requirement.

A trustee is required to determine how many people ultimately hold interests in the trust's units. Unit-holders who are themselves trustees of another trust, or a company must be traced through to ascertain ultimate ownership. Unit-holders who are government bodies do not need to be traced through, as they will count as a person. The units held by a trustee of a superannuation fund that has more than 50 members will be taken to be held by more than 20 individuals rather than the trustee of the superannuation fund.

If the superannuation fund has up to 50 members, each member of the superannuation fund is taken to hold the units held by the trustee of the superannuation fund in equal proportions.

NON-BROADLY HELD RESIDENT UNIT TRUSTS

A taxpayer's instalment income also includes trust income or trust capital that a non-broadly held resident unit trust distributes/applies to them. This income or capital is not included in the taxpayer's instalment income as being distributed/applied by a broadly-held resident unit trust pursuant to s45-285(1). Subsection 445-285(2) provides for the inclusion of trust income or trust capital distributed/applied by a non-broadly held resident unit trust.

When determining whether a trust is a 'non-broadly held resident unit trust', the residency and eligible investment business requirements applicable to 'broadly held resident unit trusts' must also be satisfied in relation to 'non-broadly held resident unit trusts'. Further, the non-broadly held unit trust's activities must consist only of 'eligible business activities' as defined by s102M of the ITAA36.

Additionally, throughout an 'instalment quarter', the beneficiary must be either:

- a trustee of a trust that is a broadly held resident investment unit trust (refer to tests for 'broadly held resident unit trusts'), or
- exempt from tax, or
- a complying superannuation entity or a statutory fund of a life insurance company, or
- the trustee of a trust set out at s45-288 whose beneficiary(ies) is absolutely entitled
- that is a resident unit trust being:

- either any property of the unit trust is situated in Australia or the trustee carries on business in Australia, and
- either the central management and control of the unit trust is in Australia or Australian residents hold more than 50% of the beneficial interests in the income or property of the trust

- whose beneficiaries' directions are limited to those that are of 'eligible investment business'
- whose beneficiaries became beneficiaries as a result of a public offer, and
- has at least 50 beneficiaries. If the trustee is also the trustee of other trusts that also fit the above criteria, the beneficiaries of those other trusts will count toward the 50.

The Variety Unit Trust has over 1,000 unit-holders and invests both in shares listed on the ASX and large scale office blocks and shopping centres to derive rental income. None of the unit-holders are related to each other. Investment in the trust is open to members of the general public by completing the application form that accompanies the prospectus. Units in the trust can be redeemed for the value of the units on the day the unit-holder's redemption application is received by the unit trust.

The trust makes quarterly distributions for the 2014-15 year, the first being on 30 September 2014 and is comprised of (on a per unit basis):

Cash dividends	*$4*
Property rental	*$3*
Tax deferred amount	*$2*
Tax free amount	*$1*
Total	***$10***

For the first instalment quarter of the 2014-15 year, John holds 1,000 units. He has been notified of an instalment rate and uses the instalment rate method to work out his quarterly instalment. He must include $10,000 in his instalment income for the first instalment quarter (1,000 x $10).

5.753 OTHER TRUSTS (s45-280 TAA)

If the trust is not one that permits its beneficiaries to adopt any of the preceding methods, a beneficiary's share of their trust's instalment income is worked out at s45-280(1) as:

> **(Beneficiary's assessable income from the trust for last income year divided by trust's instalment income for last income year) x trust's instalment income for current instalment quarter**

The beneficiary's assessable income for the purposes of this calculation excludes capital gains unless the beneficiary is:

- an eligible approved deposit fund
- an eligible superannuation fund, or
- a pooled superannuation trust.

Capital gains are also included in the case of a life insurance company to the extent that the share of the trust's net income is included in the complying superannuation class of its taxable income for the income year that is or includes the current period.

TRUST INCURS OVERALL LOSS IN PRIOR YEAR

Section 45-280(3) provides that if the trust incurred a loss, or broke even last income year, beneficiaries are still required to include an amount in their 'instalment income' in respect of their interest in the trust. The amount is to be a 'fair and reasonable amount'. This 'fair and reasonable amount' has regard to:

- the extent of the beneficiary's interest in the trust, and the beneficiary's interest in the income of the trust during the current period, and
- the trust's instalment income for the current period, and
- any other relevant circumstances.

The trust must determine its instalment income for each instalment quarter, and then notify each beneficiary of the trust's instalment income for that instalment quarter. If a trust incurred a loss in prior year, beneficiaries would not be able to use the above formula, as the proportion would always work out to be zero. Therefore, to work out their share of the trust's instalment income, a beneficiary must use their share of the trust's net income as specified in the trust deed. This is an easy task if a fixed trust is involved, as the beneficiaries' interests will be stated and fixed.

However, it becomes difficult if a discretionary trust is involved. It needs to be remembered that the nature of a beneficiary's interest in a discretionary trust has been described as a 'mere expectancy'. It amounts to nothing more than a right to be considered by the trustee when exercising its discretion. A beneficiary does not gain an interest in either the trust's income or property until the trustee's discretion is exercised in the beneficiary's favour. This creates the possibility for a beneficiary of a discretionary trust to pay PAYG instalments on trust income in which they ultimately gain no interest.

TRUST DERIVES A NET INCOME IN PRIOR YEAR

The above formula poses a similar problem for discretionary trusts that derived a net income for the previous income year. Inconsistency arises where a trustee exercises its discretion in a different pattern to that of the prior year (eg. exclusion of different beneficiaries). This creates the situation where a beneficiary who held an interest in the trust's prior year net income, but none the following year, will still be required to include an amount in their quarterly PAYG instalment income. The above formula makes such a beneficiary work out their share of the trust instalment income on the basis of their previous year's entitlement. This means the beneficiary would be required to pay a PAYG instalment on income to which they gained no entitlement.

Once the subsequent income year concludes, and the beneficiary without an interest in the trust lodges their income tax return for that income year, that beneficiary would get a credit for the PAYG instalments they were liable for during the income year.

Trust derives a net income in prior year

The XYZ Discretionary Trust has three beneficiaries, and the trustee has total discretion as to the distribution of trust income and capital. The trustee makes only one declaration each year on 30 June. Each of the beneficiaries received an instalment rate notification from the Tax Office.

For the 30 June 2015 year, the trust derived a net income of $104,000 comprised as follows:

Franking credit	*$26,000*
Franked dividend	*$50,000*
Unfranked dividends	*$18,000*
Net capital gain	*$10,000*
	$104,000

The trustee distributed this in the following way:

	Franked dividend	Franking credit	Unfranked dividend	Net capital gain	Total
Kerry	$35,000	$18,200	$10,000	$8,000	$71,200
Tony	$15,000	$7,800	$8,000	$2,000	$32,800
Sam	$0	$0	$0	$0	$0
Total	$50,000	$26,000	$18,000	$10,000	$104,000

At the end of the first instalment quarter for the 2014-15 financial year, the trust derived an instalment income of $10,000. To enable each beneficiary to complete their personal Activity Statements, the trustee must notify each beneficiary of the trust's instalment income for the previous income year, and the recently concluded instalment quarter.

Each of the beneficiaries would need to declare an amount using the s45-280(1) formula:

(Beneficiary's assessable income from the trust for last income year divided by trust's instalment income for the last income year) x trust's instalment income for current instalment quarter

Kerry: $63,200/$68,000 x $10,000 .... *$9,294*
Tony: $30,800/$68,000 x $10,000 .... *$4,529*
Sam: $0/$68,000 x $10,000 .... *$0*

Sam still needs to consider declaring a 'fair and reasonable amount'.

NOTE: The calculation of the beneficiary's assessable income excludes capital gains (s45-280(2)) and the trust's instalment income for the last year of income includes ordinary income and excludes franking credits and capital gains (s45-120).

5.754   CORPORATE UNIT TRUSTS AND PUBLIC TRADING TRUSTS

The income a unit-holder (beneficiary) derives through a 'corporate unit trust', or a 'public trading trust' is excluded from the methods explained above. This arises because these trusts are taxed as though they are a company. As a result, unit-holders in these trusts are required to include only the cash distribution from the trust in their 'instalment income', in much the same way a shareholder in a company would include the cash dividend in 'instalment income'.

5.760   IMPLICATIONS FOR TRUSTEES

Subdivision 45-N sets out how trustees of a trust calculate their instalment payments. Some types of trusts will have only one instalment rate – these are called 'single-rate trustees'. Other types of trusts have more than one instalment rate – these are called 'multi-rate trustees'.

5.761   SINGLE RATE TRUSTEES (s45-450 TAA)

These rules apply to trustees of corporate unit trusts, public trading trusts, complying superannuation funds, non-complying superannuation funds, complying approved deposit funds, non-complying approved deposit funds and pooled superannuation trusts. Each of these trustees is taxed on the trust's income as if the trust is a company, so each trustee will only have one instalment rate. The trustee of a trust that is a corporate unit trust or a public trading trust is treated as if they had a taxable income for the income year, equal to the net income of the trust.

5.762   MULTI-RATE TRUSTEES (s45-455 TAA)

Certain trustees will have more than one liability to pay tax as the trustee of one particular trust, and as such there may be several liabilities to pay PAYG instalments. Section 45-455 provides that this will apply where the trustee was liable to pay tax for a previous income year in respect of a beneficiary's share of the net trust income pursuant to s98(1) or (2), s99 or s99A of the ITAA36. This applies where the trustee is assessed and liable to pay tax in respect of the share of net income of a trust estate of a beneficiary under a legal disability (s98) and where certain trust income is to be taxed as income.

 A trustee liable to pay tax under s98(1) or (2) will be exempt from PAYG instalments if the beneficiary will no longer be under a legal disability, or it is reasonable to expect that they will no longer be under a legal disability, at the end of the subsequent year.

INSTALMENT INCOME OF A TRUSTEE

A multi-rate trustee will not have to work out the share of instalment income of a particular beneficiary in regard to whom the liability to pay instalments arises. The multi-rate trustee will multiply the relevant instalment rate by the whole of the trust's instalment income for the period.

The Tax Office works out the separate instalment rates for a trustee using the trust's total base assessment instalment income. The trustee will calculate the correct instalment by matching the instalment income to the rate calculation for each of the trustee's different instalment liabilities.

GDP-ADJUSTED NOTIONAL TAX

A multi-rate trustee may choose to pay quarterly instalments on a GDP-adjusted notional tax basis if the trustee has a liability to pay instalments in respect of a beneficiary or income to which no beneficiary is entitled. This is because the beneficiaries for whom the trustee is assessed under s98 are individuals, and under s99 and s99A the trustee is taxed as an individual in respect of income to which no beneficiary is entitled.

INSTALMENT RATE AND NOTIONAL TAX

Instalment rates are calculated by the Commissioner at s45-470 as:

(Notional tax divided by base assessment instalment income) x 100

where:

- 'notional tax' is the notional tax in respect of a particular liability for a beneficiary or income to which no beneficiary is presently entitled, and
- 'base assessment instalment income' is worked out on the total base assessment instalment income of the trust – not a share of it. This enables the trustee to apply the instalment rate to the total instalment income of the trust for an instalment period. The trustee will not need to work out the beneficiary's share of the trust's instalment income. The base assessment instalment income is the assessable income of the trust worked out for the purposes of the base assessment, that the Commissioner determines is instalment income of the trust for the base year.
- 'the base assessment' is the latest assessment for the most recent income year for which an assessment has been made of the tax payable by the trustee under s98(1) or (2), s99 or s99A.

If the Tax Office deems that there is a later income year for which no tax is payable, the base assessment is the latest return from which an assessment of tax could have been made.

The notional tax for the trustee is the trustee's adjusted tax on the trustee's adjusted taxable income reduced by the adjusted tax on the trustee's adjusted withholding income (s45-475).

The adjusted taxable income for a multi-rate trustee is calculated upon a part of the adjusted net income of the trust rather than total taxable income of an entity (s45-480). The adjusted net income of the trust is the net income of the trust calculated for the base assessment:

- reduced by any net capital gain in the trust's assessable income
- increased by any deduction for tax losses made in working out the net income, and
- reduced by the amount of any tax loss, to the extent that it can be carried forward for working out the trust's net income for the next income year.

The net income which is adjusted is the net income of the trust as worked out using s95(1) of the ITAA36.

The adjusted net income of the trust is multiplied by a ratio to determine the share of the trust's adjusted net income for which the trustee is assessed:

Relevant share divided by reduced net income of the trust

where:

- 'reduced net income of the trust' is the net income of the trust, as calculated for the base assessment, reduced by any net capital gain included in the trust's assessable income.
- 'relevant share' is the 'reduced beneficiary's share', or the 'reduced no beneficiary's share', of the net income of the trust, as calculated for the purposes of the base assessment. 'Reduced beneficiary's share' is the share of net income of the trust on which the trustee is liable to pay tax under s98(1) or (2) for a particular beneficiary. It does not include a net capital gain included in the trust's assessable income. Reduced no beneficiary's share is the amount on which the trustee is liable to pay tax under s99 or 99A. It does not include a capital gain included in the trust's net income.

Where a trust has withholding income, the notional tax is reduced by the adjusted tax on the adjusted withholding income. The adjusted tax is worked out at s45-340. The adjusted withholding income for the purposes of calculating the notional tax of a multi-rate trustee is set out at s45-485 as follows:

Adjusted withholding income = net withholding income of the trust x
(relevant share divided by reduced net income of the trust)

where:

- 'net withholding income of the trust' is the sum of the amounts included in the trust's assessable income for the base assessment in respect of withholding payments (with the exception of non-quotation withholding payments) reduced by any deduction relating to those amounts.

- The Tax Office will inform the multi-rate trustee of the instalment rate and the notional tax for each of the liabilities of the trustee. The Tax Office is required to notify the notional tax so that the trustee knows how the Tax Office calculated its instalment rate and whether it may select to pay an annual instalment or pay on GDP adjusted notional tax.

5.770 PAYG INSTALMENT ADJUSTMENTS

The PAYG instalment amounts worked out by the Tax Office is adjusted for GDP so that instalments payable during the income year more accurately reflects an entity's expected income tax liability. In 2013-14 the GDP was 3%.

5.800 ACTIVITY STATEMENTS

There are two types of Activity Statement. There is the Business Activity Statement (BAS) which is required to be completed by those taxpayers registered for GST, and the Instalment Activity Statement (IAS) that applies to those not required to be registered for GST.

Within those two types there are a number of different forms tailored to different entity types and incorporating different reporting requirements. For example, a sole trader will most likely use BAS A which provides for the reporting of quarterly GST, PAYG withholding and PAYG instalments. Alternatively, an entity with no PAYG instalment requirements but with GST and PAYG withholding requirements may use BAS form F.

5.810 INSTALMENT ACTIVITY STATEMENTS

Taxpayers who are not registered for GST are required to report their tax obligations on an Instalment Activity Statement (IAS). This statement mainly applies to individuals (including trustees) with investment income (eg. rental income, dividend and interest income) or who have businesses with an annual turnover below the $75,000 GST registration threshold.

The IAS can be used for the following reporting obligations. The most common situation would be the payment of:

- PAYG instalments
- PAYG withholding, and
- FBT instalments.

Entities that are not registered (nor required to be registered) for GST but are classified as medium or large taxpayers are required to lodge monthly or quarterly statements, depending on their other reporting obligations.

Some taxpayers may be forced to complete both an IAS and a BAS. As a general rule the lodgment dates for IASs is quarterly unless an election is made to be an annual payer (see from 5.720).

The Tax Office will forward personalised statements for each tax period with some information already completed and a unique document identification number.

 The BAS/IAS you receive from the Tax Office will identify the types of tax obligations you are required to report and remit for that tax period.

5.820 BUSINESS ACTIVITY STATEMENTS

Taxpayers who are registered for GST must report their tax obligations on a Business Activity Statement (BAS). The BAS can be used for the following reporting obligations:

- Goods and services tax
- Luxury car tax and wine equalisation tax
- PAYG instalments
- PAYG withholding, and
- FBT instalments.

Taxpayers will receive only one BAS for each reporting period even if they have both monthly and quarterly reporting obligations. For example, an obligation to report GST on a monthly basis and an obligation to report PAYG instalment on a quarterly basis. A BAS can be lodged electronically or mailed to the Tax Office using the pre-paid envelope provided.

A BAS with nothing to report at any label can also be lodged by phoning 13 72 26.

Large PAYG remitters and those with a GST turnover of $20 million or more must lodge electronically (see 5.424).

The Tax Office will presume that you intend to lodge electronically if you indicated that you wanted to use the Tax Office's e-commerce system when you registered.

If you want to lodge (and pay) at Australia Post or by mail, contact the Tax Office for personalised payment advice forms.

Amounts owing to you by the Tax Office must be paid within 14 days of lodging the completed BAS. The Tax Office must pay interest on refunds not paid within 14 days. Any interest received is assessable in the year it is received. Amounts owed to the Tax Office after the due date may incur a general interest charge (GIC) (see 4.660).

The completed BAS or IAS must be signed and dated by someone with the authority to do so (s164 ITAA36). Examples of persons who may have this authority include:

- the individual in business
- a partner of a partnership
- director, or public officer of a company
- trustee of a trust, or
- office holder of an association.

Where it is prepared by a tax agent, the tax agent must also sign the required declaration.

5.830   LODGMENT DATES FOR IAS AND BAS

The lodgment date of an activity statement depends on whether the entity is a GST registered enterprise with monthly tax periods or, if not, whether the only obligation to be reported on the activity statement is PAYG withholding. In either case, the activity statement for each month must be lodged by the 21st day of the following month.

If the entity has quarterly GST tax periods and/or quarterly PAYG instalments, the activity statement must be lodged by the following dates:

Quarter	Quarter ending	Due date[1]
1	30 September 2015	28 October 2015
2	31 December 2015	28 February 2016
3	31 March 2016	28 April 2016
4	30 June 2016	28 July 2016

1: Due date can be extended if lodging through a tax agent (see 1.700). Entities entitled to adopt dual GST and PAYG instalments only need to lodge an activity statement for the third and fourth instalments, unless they are a medium or large PAYG withholder.

5.840   COMPLETING AN ACTIVITY STATEMENT

5.841   GOODS AND SERVICES TAX (GST) INFORMATION

There are two methods for completing the GST section of the BAS:

- the GST calculation sheet option, and
- the GST derived from accounts option.

For more information on the operation of the GST see from 23.000.

GST CALCULATION SHEET METHOD

Use the information from your accounts and follow the instructions to complete all of the relevant items on the calculation sheet.

- Complete items G1 to G8 to work out the GST payable at G9.
- Transfer the amount of GST payable (shown at G9) to item 1A on the front of the BAS.
- Complete G10 to G19 to work out the total input tax credits at G20.
- Transfer the amount of input tax credits (shown at G20) to item 1B on the BAS.

 This is the most complicated of the options and requires the entity to calculate for each transaction the GST effect. The simplest option is obviously to have a sophisticated accounting system as the Tax Office will accept the transposition of accounting information as representing a true reflection of the GST information. Entities with unsophisticated systems will struggle to complete the required GST information in a timely manner. The calculation sheet no longer forms part of the BAS. Instead, you will need to contact the Tax Office each tax period to obtain one if you wish to continue using this option. The calculation sheet is not to be lodged with the BAS; it is to be used in calculating items 1A and 1B of the BAS only. The GST calculation worksheet is form NAT 4203 available from the Tax Office website.

GST DERIVED FROM ACCOUNTS METHOD

This method can only be used if the entity has record keeping and accounting systems in place that have proper audit trails and can accurately provide details of the GST payable and input tax credits.

This means the system must:

- record the amount of GST payable and bring that amount to account in a GST payable control account for each transaction
- record the amount of input tax credits and bring that amount to account in an input tax credit control account for each transaction, and
- record the amount of any adjustment (amounts that both increase and decrease the net amount) and correctly record that amount in the relevant control account.

That information is then used to complete:

- Items G1, G2, G3, G10, G11 for information purposes only, and
- Report GST on sales at 1A and GST on purchases at 2B.

For more information on using this option see Tax Office's information sheet NAT 3613.

NOTE: A simplified GST accounting method may be available for certain entities – see 23.360 and NAT 3185.

REPORTING AND PAYING GST

Entities will report and pay GST in one of the following ways:

- report and pay GST monthly
- report and pay GST quarterly
- report annually and pay GST quarterly
- report annually and pay a GST instalment quarterly, or
- report and pay GST annually.

PAYING GST ANNUALLY

Annual GST periods are governed by Division 151 of the GST Act (see 24.100).

Businesses that have chosen to register for GST voluntarily but are not required to register are eligible to report GST annually if their annual turnover for GST at the time an election to report GST annually is made is less than:

- $75,000 for businesses, or
- $150,000 for non-profit bodies, and
- they have not elected to pay GST by instalments advised by the Tax Office.

The election is not available to entities who are not required to be registered because their turnover falls below the threshold because they have disregarded supplies of rights or options offshore in calculating their annual turnover pursuant to s188-15 and s188-20 of the GST Act.

To be entitled to elect to report GST annually eligible taxpayers must have no outstanding activity statements.

Eligible taxpayers wanting to make an annual tax period election must make the election in the approved form. The election must be made no later than:

- 21 August for taxpayers that were previously reporting GST on a monthly basis
- 28 October for taxpayers that were previously reporting GST on a quarterly basis, and
- six months from the date of GST registration for newly registered taxpayers.

Once a taxpayer has elected to report GST annually, there is no need to re-elect each year. However, they must determine their eligibility to report annually on 31 July each year and must notify the Tax Office if on this date:

- their projected annual turnover is greater than or equal to the registration turnover threshold
- they are required to be registered for some other reason, or
- they wish to change their reporting cycle.

The Tax Office will then change their reporting cycle to monthly or quarterly.

The projected annual turnover as at 31 July for GST purposes is the sum value (GST-exclusive price) of taxable and GST-free sales made for the month of July and those expected to be made for the next 11 months, other than sales involving the transfer of ownership of a capital asset (see 24.210).

Eligible clients that elect to report GST annually will be sent an annual GST return to complete close to the end of the financial year. The annual GST return will be for the period from the date the election takes effect to 30 June. The entity must report the GST, WET and/or LCT (if applicable) amount for this tax period on its annual GST return.

The due date for lodgment of the annual GST return and payment of any amounts due is either:

- the due date for lodgment of the client's income tax return, or
- 28 February if the client is not required to lodge an income tax return.

 If clients elect to report and pay GST annually, they are also electing to pay or claim a refund annually. This option can be detrimental if the taxpayer has a large input tax credit entitlement during the course of the year.

PAYING GST QUARTERLY

Many taxpayers will calculate, report and pay GST quarterly. This is identified as Option 1 on the BAS. This option requires calculating and reporting more information than other options on a quarterly basis and also payment on a quarterly basis. An annual reconciliation is not required.

As noted above, a taxpayer may calculate and pay GST quarterly and report annually. This is identified as option 2 on the BAS. Using this option only requires the taxpayer to report total sales, GST on those sales and GST on purchases. In an annual GST information report, export sales, other GST-free sales, capital purchases and non-capital purchases are reported.

Option 3 is to pay GST instalment quarterly and report annually. This option is only available to enterprises with an annual turnover of less than $2 million and who are required to lodge quarterly (not monthly). The quarterly payments are calculated using a GST instalment amount provided by the Tax Office. The instalment amount notified by the Commissioner is generally based on the previous year's net amount, adjusted by GDP. Where the annual GST return for the previous year has not yet been lodged, the notified instalment is the prior year's instalment amount adjusted for GDP.

NOTE: GDP adjusted GST (and PAYG) instalment amounts are explained in the Tax Office publication NAT 5094.

This GST instalment amount advised by the Commissioner can be varied, but it needs to remain within 85% of the enterprise's actual GST amount for the year, otherwise the GIC will be applied. An annual GST return must be completed when using Option 3 in order to reconcile between the quarterly GST instalment payments and the taxpayer's actual annual GST liability.

The annual GST report required to be lodged under Option 2 and the annual GST return required to be lodged under Option 3 must be lodged at the earlier of:

- when the enterprise's income tax return is lodged, or
- 28 February.

No GST refunds will be paid by the Tax Office until the annual GST report/return is lodged.

GST AND ANNUAL APPORTIONMENT

Eligible taxpayers can make an annual apportionment election. This concession is provided for at Division 131 of the GST Act. This means that instead of estimating the portion of intended non-creditable use of any purchase when claiming your GST credit the taxpayer can make a single adjustment after the end of your income year to account for the private portion of all purchases.

An annual apportionment election can be made if:

- the taxpayer's annual turnover, calculated at the time the election is made, is $2 million or less, and
- no election to pay GST by instalments or to have an annual tax period has been made.

Determination of eligibility to use annual apportionment must be made on 31 July in each year.

An annual apportionment election may be made at any time and takes effect from the beginning of the earliest tax period for which an activity statement is not yet due. The election continues to apply until you cancel your election, it is disallowed by the Tax Office, or the annual apportionment turnover threshold is exceeded on 31 July in any year. An annual apportionment election must be forwarded to the Tax Office and copy retained by the taxpayer detailing the date the election was made and the date it took effect.

For more information on annual apportionment, see 23.225.

5.842   LUXURY CAR TAX INFORMATION

For entities that are subject to Luxury Car Tax (LCT), the lodgment and remittance requirements are the same as for their GST obligations (see *Luxury car tax* from 28.200). Note that the luxury car tax threshold is different from the car limit for depreciation purposes. The GST obligation will be based on the depreciation limit of the vehicle.

When completing the BAS, the luxury car tax section must account for supplies made during the tax period. Details of luxury car tax payable should be shown at item 1E and any refundable amount should be shown at item 1F.

A refund is available when the amount of luxury car tax payable decreases due to any of the following events after the car has been supplied or imported:

- there is a decrease in the price of the car
- a bad debt has been written off which has been overdue for 12 months
- the sale is cancelled, or
- an ABN was not quoted when the car was purchased or imported and the car is now used for a quotable purpose.

See Division 15 of *A New Tax System (Luxury Car Tax) Act 1999* for adjustments that increase or decrease luxury car tax payable.

NOTE: Activity Statements will have fields for Wine Equalisation Tax (WET) and Luxury Car Tax (LCT) only if the enterprise has an obligation for those taxes.

5.843 PAY AS YOU GO WITHHOLDING INFORMATION

For Pay As You Go (PAYG) withholding obligations see 5.200 and 5.300.

The total of all salary, wages and other payments (except those specifically included in W3 and W4: see below) that are subject to withholding should be shown at item W1. This would include amounts which are subject to withholding but have a withholding amount of nil. For example, payment of salary to an employee, which after claiming the tax-free threshold, results in 'nil' amount required to be withheld. The amount withheld should be shown at item W2.

NOTE: Payment of superannuation contributions is not subject to PAYG withholding. Therefore, do not include this amount at W1.

At item W3 show the following amounts withheld from the following payment:

- payments to resident investors who have not provided their TFN in respect of investments
- interest, dividends, royalty payments or other payments as specified by the regulations made to non-residents, and
- departing Australian superannuation payments.

Suppliers who do not quote their ABN to the payer are also liable to have PAYG withholding tax deducted at a flat 46.5% including Medicare (47% from 1 July 2014). The amount withheld from such payment should be shown at item W4.

5.844 PAY AS YOU GO INSTALMENTS INFORMATION

For PAYG instalments, the taxpayer can choose one of two options. Under Option 1, the instalment amount payable is calculated by the Commissioner and is shown at T7 of your activity statement. This is also referred to as the GDP-adjusted notional tax method and is only available to some taxpayers (see 5.734). Taxpayers entitled to adopt quarterly instalments on the basis of GDP-adjusted notional tax may also be varied (see 5.735). This is done by entering an estimate of the year's benchmark tax at box T8, and the quarterly instalment worked out on this basis at boxes T9 and 5A on the front. Note that it is compulsory that if you are varying the instalment amount to also complete T4 for the reasons of varying the amount advised by the Commissioner (see 5.850 for variation code) and lodge the activity statement by the due date.

Option 2 sets out the instalment amount using the instalment income/rate method. This option is available if an instalment rate has been pre-printed at item T2. To work out the amount of your quarterly PAYG instalment under this option, it is necessary to calculate the instalment income for the quarter (see 5.737). Instalment income at T1 does not include any GST, WET or LCT charged to customers.

The instalment rate notified by the Tax Office at item T2 can be varied to take into account changes during the income year. The varied rate must be shown at item T3. You must also state the most appropriate reason for the change (select the most appropriate code – see 5.850) and lodge the activity statement by the due date. Where a varied instalment rate is used, the entity may be entitled to a refund of PAYG instalments paid in earlier tax periods. The amount of any credit can be claimed at item 5B (see 5.737).

5.845 FRINGE BENEFITS TAX INFORMATION

For entities with a Fringe Benefits Tax (FBT) liability in the previous year of $3,000 or more, the amount of FBT instalment tax to be paid in each quarterly BAS statement will be based on the instalment rate calculated and notified by the Tax Office at item F1. The due dates for payment have been aligned with the new BAS lodgement dates.

Where the amount of fringe benefits to be provided is estimated to be lower than that estimated by the Tax Office, the employer has the option of varying the instalment rate. This is done by entering an estimate of total FBT liability for the year ended 31 March at item F2, and the quarterly instalment is worked out on this basis at item F3 and 6A on the front.

A credit can also be claimed for overpaid instalments. The amount of the credit should be shown at item 6B together with the reason for the variation in F4 (choose the most appropriate code – see 5.850).

5.846   WHEN TAX OBLIGATIONS MUST BE INCLUDED IN AN ENTITY'S STATEMENT[1]

Tax obligation	Monthly	Quarterly	Annually
GST (including luxury car tax and wine equalisation tax)			
Annual turnover up to $75,000	Yes	Yes	Yes
Annual turnover more than $75,000 but less than $20m	Yes	Yes	
Annual turnover of less than $20m[2]		Yes	
Annual turnover $20m or more[3]	Yes		
PAYG withholding amounts			
Large withholders[3] (total PAYG withholdings exceed $1m)	Yes		
Medium withholders (total PAYG withholdings exceed $25,000)	Yes		
Small withholders (total PAYG withholdings do not exceed $25,000)		Yes	
PAYG instalments			
Individuals with notional tax of less than $8,000[5]		Yes	Yes[4]
Individuals deriving primary production income or 'special professional income'		Yes	Yes[4]
All other entities not using annual instalment		Yes	
FBT instalment		Yes	

1: Where two or more alternatives exist, a choice between the alternatives is available.

2: If an election to use the GST instalment option has been made.

3: Payments and statements must be lodged electronically.

4: Taxpayers who become ineligible to pay annual PAYG instalments commence paying quarterly instalments from the first quarter of the following income year.

5: Taxpayer is not registered for GST, or if partner in a partnership, the partnership is not registered for GST.

5.850   COMMON PROBLEMS WITH ACTIVITY STATEMENTS

The Tax Office has issued a number of guides to assist with completing BASs and IASs. The following is a compendium of common problems and their solutions identified in these guides. These guides are available from the Tax Office website www.ato.gov.au. Where there are problems with a completed BAS or IAS it can result in delayed refunds and or unnecessary contact from the Tax Office to correct the Statements. In the worse case scenario, the BAS or IAS may not be treated as lodged until the correct information is received.

There are also suggested solutions to prevent these problems in future Statements.

General	
Problem	**Solution**
Including wages and superannuation contributions as purchases at G11	Wages should be reported at W1. Don't report superannuation contributions.
Lodgment of blank forms	When lodging statements with nothing to report at any label (a nil statement), insert zeros where requested, otherwise leave the label blank.
Lodgment of photocopied statements	Original activity statements must be lodged with the Tax Office.
Not registering with the Tax Office for tax obligations reported in activity statement	Are you correctly registered for all your tax obligations? To register or cancel registration for PAYG withholding, goods and services tax, luxury car tax or wine equalisation tax, contact the Tax Office.

General	
Problem	**Solution**
Incorrect accounting method used	If using the cash accounting method and business turnover is expected to exceed the cash accounting threshold, change to the accrual accounting method and notify the Tax Office. Requests for continued use of the cash accounting method will be considered, however approval is dependent on circumstances.
Not including cash taken from the till to pay for purchases	Total sales (G1 on your BAS) should include all cash payments made out of the till for purchases.
Including dollars and cents	Show whole dollars only when completing activity statement. To avoid processing errors and to allow the Tax Office to issue any refund quickly, do not use cents, decimal points, commas, symbols or words such as $, nil and n/a.
Activity statement not lodged by the due date	Lodge your activity statement and pay any amounts owing by the due date. Lodgment is not required if an instalment notice has been received (they have the letter N, R, S or T in the top left-hand corner) and the pre-printed instalment amount was paid by the due date.
Not sure when to leave boxes blank and when to write a zero in a box	Generally, leave boxes blank if they do not apply to your business. For example, if you do not have exports to report, leave the box at G2 blank. However, write a zero (0) if: using GST Option 1 or Option 2, and the business hasn't traded for a tax period, and there's nothing to report, write 0 at G1 and 1A (these boxes must always be completed) using PAYG Option 2 but there isn't any instalment income, write 0 at T1 and 5A, and/or varying instalment down to 0 for either GST or PAYG, complete the appropriate variation labels and write 0 at 1A for GST and/or 5A for PAYG.
Used the wrong colour pen	Use a black pen only to complete your form(s).
Dates and details are missing	Provide a contact name and daytime phone number. Sign and date your statement before lodging it with the Tax Office by the due date.
Nothing to report	Even if there is nothing to report the Tax Office must receive the completed activity statement by the due date, unless it is an instalment notice (statements with the letter N, R, S or T in the top left hand corner), which only needs to be lodged by the advised due date if varying the instalment amounts.
Lodging activity statement late	Penalties now apply automatically for late lodged activity statements at a rate of $170 every 28 days or part thereof (to a maximum of $550). Maximum penalty for medium taxpayer is multiplied by two and for large taxpayers is multiplied by five.
Some boxes, such as 1A (GST sales or GST instalment) & 5A (PAYG income tax instalment), are frequently overlooked	Complete 1A if you're reporting a GST obligation and 5A if reporting a PAYG obligation (even when your instalment amount is zero).
Claiming input tax credits on the total price of a car that exceeds the luxury car limit including GST (ie. the luxury car limit threshold)	GST credits for cars with a GST-inclusive price that exceeds the luxury car limit is restricted to a maximum of 1/11th of that value limit.

General	
Problem	**Solution**
Not all amounts are being correctly reported at G1	Include all payments and other considerations received during the quarter for sales made in the course of business. This includes amounts shown at G2 (Export sales), G3 (GST-free) and input taxed supplies like interest on investments and rent on residential properties (shown at G4 if you are using the calculation sheet method). The following amounts should not be reported at G1: • inter-entity loans • transfers between bank accounts • private money • other entities' income (eg. rent for rental property that is in another entity's name/individual's name)
Options for GST	Complete the boxes for one option only.
G2 (Export sales) is completed incorrectly (eg. treating supplies as exports when the goods are consumed within Australia)	Report the following only at G2: • the free on board value of exported goods that meet the GST-free export rules • payments for the repairs of goods from overseas that are to be exported, and • payments for goods used in the repair of goods from overseas that are to be exported
Claiming input tax credits for bank fees and charges, third party insurance and stamp duty	Claim not allowed for bank fees and charges, third party insurance and stamp duty.
No valid tax invoice held	A claim can only be made in the period when a valid tax invoice is held (whether on a cash or accruals basis).
Not including the sale of a business	The sale price of a business, including any GST, must be reported at G1. Where the sale is a GST-free sale of a going concern, you also include this amount at G3. Where the sale is taxable, you must report the GST amount at 1A.
Not providing estimated net GST for the year when requesting a variation to your GST instalment amount	When varying GST instalments, an estimated annual net GST amount must be provided in G22.
Notifying a variation to your GST or PAYG Instalment after the due date for the instalment to be paid	Notify the Tax Office of variations by the date the instalment is due to be paid, or else variations will be denied.
Claiming input tax credits for the full amount of a purchase, even when the goods are to be used partially for private purposes	Claim input tax credits on the proportion of the expense used for business.
Not recording sale of a business asset	GST needs to be accounted for on an asset disposal that is neither input taxed or GST-free. The price of the asset sold is included at G1 and the GST payable at 1A on your activity statement. Ensure that the GST exclusive amount of the asset is included in business income in the income tax return. All income amounts included on the income tax return should be exclusive of GST.

General

Problem	Solution
GST-specific	
Claiming input tax credits where the contractor or supplier is not registered or required to be registered for GST	Input tax credits cannot be claimed where the contractor or supplier of the goods or services is not registered or required to be registered for GST as no GST is included in the price.
Changing the legal structure of your business entity and continuing to lodge activity statements under the ABN of the old entity	If the legal structure of the entity used to carry on the business has changed, apply for a new ABN and register the new entity for GST if that entity is required to be registered for GST, or chooses to register for GST. The former ABN cannot be used. Examples of changes in legal structure include changing from a sole trader to a partnership, trust or company, or vice-versa, and reconstituting a partnership.
Claiming full input tax credits on the purchase of real property (or deposit for same) at the time of entering into a standard land contract	If a tax invoice is held, claim the input tax credit for the depositor full payment of a creditable purchase of land under a completed standard land contract in the activity statement for the tax period in which settlement occurs. Applies for GST on a cash and accruals basis.
No reason code is shown if varying your instalment	If PAYG instalment amount or rate or GST amount is varied, show one of the following reason codes at label T4 (for PAYG instalments) or label G24 (for GST) on activity statement. Visit Tax Office website and obtain a copy of 'How to vary quarterly PAYG instalments' and 'Varying your GST instalments'.

Reason for varying	Reason code	Obligation
Change in investments	21	PAYG
Current business structure not continuing	22	FBT, GST and PAYG
Significant change in trading conditions	23	GST and PAYG
Internal business restructures	24	GST and PAYG
Change in legislation	25	GST and PAYG
Financial market changes	26	GST and PAYG
Use of income tax losses	27	PAYG
Entering simplified tax system	28	GST and PAYG
Leaving simplified tax system	29	GST and PAYG
Change in fringe benefits for employees	30	FBT only
Change in employees with fringe benefits	31	FBT only
Fringe benefits rebate now claimed	32	FBT only
Entering or exiting a consolidated group – only head companies should use this code	33	PAYG only

GST-specific

Problem	Solution
When accounting for GST on a cash basis, GST credits are claimed at the commencement of a hire purchase or lease contract	GST credits may only be claimed at the time a repayment is made for a hire purchase or lease contract, when accounting for GST on a cash basis and payment is made on a progressive or periodic basis.
Including private expenses when claiming GST credits and deductions on business income tax returns	Private expenses should not be included on your activity statements or income tax returns.

PAYG withholding

Problem	Solution
When reporting PAYG tax withheld the amount at W5 (total of amounts withheld) often incorrectly includes the amount at W1 (total salary, wages and other payments)	If required to report PAYG tax withheld, only add amounts at: • W2 (amount withheld from total salary, wages and other payments) • W3 (other amounts withheld), and • W4 (amount withheld where no ABN quoted) to calculate W5 (total of amounts withheld).
When offered options for your PAYG obligation don't complete boxes for more than one option.	Complete the boxes for one option only.
Not recording the amount of PAYG withholding at label 4 in the summary.	Label 4 in the summary of the activity statement should always equal the total of the amounts at labels W2, W3 and W4.
Label 4, or one of the W labels completed, even though you're not registered for PAYG withholding.	If you pay salary and wages and are not registered for PAYG withholding visit the Tax Office website and download an 'Add a New Business Account' form (NAT 2954).
Not reporting amounts withheld from payments when an ABN has not been quoted (W4).	Where an ABN has not been quoted, amounts withheld from payments must be reported at label W4.

PAYG income tax instalments

Problem	Solution
Some boxes and 5A (PAYG income tax instalment) are frequently overlooked	Complete 5A if reporting a PAYG obligation (even when your instalment amount is zero).

Problem	Solution
Incorrect recording of instalment income at T1	Include all earnings in instalment income. This includes amounts that are paid by direct credit to your bank account and all cash (even if it has not been banked or was used to pay expenses). Account for non-cash transactions (eg. those resulting from bartering) in instalment income.
Not providing estimated tax for the year when requesting a variation to the PAYG instalment amount	If using Option 1 and varying the PAYG instalment for the quarter, ensure T8 and T9 are completed. The Tax Office uses T8 to work out instalments for the remaining quarter of the income year.
PAYG instalment obligation but haven't calculated the amount at 5A correctly	PAYG instalment amount at 5A must equal: • T1 x T2 (ie. PAYG instalment income) x (PAYG instalment rate), or • T1 x T3 (ie. PAYG instalment income) x (varied PAYG instalment rate), or • T7 (ie. pre-printed instalment amount), or • T9 (ie. varied instalment amount).
Notifying a variation to your GST or PAYG Instalment after the due date for the instalment to be paid	Notification of any variations must be made by the date the instalment is due to be paid, or else variations will not be allowed.
No PAYG instalment income at label T1	If PAYG instalment amount is reported using the income x rate method (option 2) and income for the period is zero, write '0' at label T1.
Reporting net income at label T1	Total gross income must be reported at label T1.

PAYG income tax instalments

Problem	Solution
No interest and dividend income shown at T1	If calculating your own PAYG instalment on your activity statement (that is, you use option 2, instalment income x instalment rate), remember to include at label T1 any interest received or credited to your bank account, and dividends paid or re-invested on your behalf (don't include franking credits).
Variation of PAYG instalment amount requested, but relevant PAYG variation labels not completed	Complete all relevant PAYG variation labels, for example: if varying the T7 amount, complete labels T8, T9, T4 and 5A, or if varying the T2 rate, complete labels T1, T3, T11, T4 and 5A.
Not reporting instalment income at label T1 but reporting total sales at label G1	Generally, the presence of sales for GST purposes means that there must be at least that amount of instalment income reported at T1. Instalment income reported at T1 also includes other income such as dividends and interest
Not reporting instalment income at label T1 when T1 is zero	T1 must be completed if it is zero when the Commissioner rate (T2) is used for reporting instalment income.
Adjusting T1 figure to reflect a change in expected tax liability	Commissioner rate (T2) should be varied using T3 to reflect a change in expected tax liability.
Individuals lodging a quarterly PAYG instalment activity statement are not including their income from partnerships and trusts as instalment income at label T1 on a quarterly basis	Individuals who lodge a quarterly PAYG I activity statement must include their share of income from partnerships and trusts as instalment income at label T1 each quarter.
Label 5A is calculated incorrectly	Label 5A must equal: • T11 (T1 x T2), or • T11 (T1 x T3) – when varying the PAYG instalment rate, or • T7 – when using the PAYG instalment amount, or • T9 – when varying the PAYG instalment amount.

FBT

Problem	Solution
Lodging activity statements after your FBT return	If fringe benefits tax (FBT) is paid by instalments, all activity statements for the FBT year ending 31 March must be lodged before the FBT return is lodged. This includes the March quarter activity statement due on 28 April.
Claiming input tax credits on the full amount of the meal entertainment benefits	Only claim input tax credits on benefits that you pay FBT on, eg. using the 50/50 method you only claim 50% of the total input tax credits.
Not including FBT on private use of business assets (especially for cars and computers)	FBT obligations for private use of business assets must be reported in your FBT return.

Companies

6.000 COMPANIES

6.100 DEFINITION OF A COMPANY

The definition of 'company' includes all bodies or associations (whether incorporated or not), but not partnerships or joint ventures.

The definition covers not only incorporated bodies easily recognised as companies (firms with Ltd, Pty Ltd or N.L. after their names and companies with a licence to omit 'Limited' from their names) but also bodies such as unincorporated clubs, associations and similar groups that are not partnerships or joint ventures for tax purposes. A company is taxed at the corporate tax rate of 30%.

PRIVATE COMPANIES

The status of a company for tax purposes is not necessarily the same as that determined under corporate law. A company with 'Pty Ltd' after its name is not necessarily a private company for tax purposes. Similarly, the term 'Limited' does not always guarantee public company status.

For tax purposes, section 103A ITAA36 states that a company is a 'private' company if it does not satisfy the tests to be a 'public' company – see below for requirements to be a public company. Certain provisions in the tax legislation apply only to private companies, or apply to private companies more strictly than to public companies (eg. tax deductions can be denied to a private company for excessive remuneration paid to directors, shareholders and some loans, payments and debt forgivenesses to shareholders may be taxed as unfranked dividends (see 6.300). Further, the continuity of ownership test for carrying forward and deducting prior year tax losses is applied more strictly to private companies as compared to public companies (refer 6.400).

EXCESSIVE REMUNERATION

Payments (including any transfer of assets or property to the person) to any 'associated persons' (eg. directors, shareholders or their relatives – the general definition is modified in that 'spouse' and 'relative' includes a de facto spouse living in a bona fide domestic situation as husband or wife) are tax deductible to the extent that the Tax Office considers them reasonable remuneration for work and responsibility (s109 ITAA36). The company claiming the deduction must:

- evaluate their duties
- separate employment and directors' duties, and
- get information on comparable salaries.

Any part of the remuneration that is deemed to be excessive is treated as non-deductible to the company and is deemed to be the payment of an unfranked dividend to the recipient.

PAYMENTS, LOANS OR DEBT FORGIVENESS TO SHAREHOLDERS (DIVISION 7A ITAA36)

If a private company makes a loan or payment or makes some other advance (in cash or assets) on or after 4 December 1997 to a shareholder, or an 'associate' of a shareholder, it may be treated the loan as a dividend in the hands of the recipient if it is not repaid by tax return lodgment date or made subject to a written agreement complying with minimum interest rate and maximum term criteria (see from 6.300).

NOTE: Taxation Ruling TR 2010/3 and PS LA 2010/4 outlines the Commissioner's treatment of unpaid present entitlements (UPEs) from a related trust to a private company. Provided that certain conditions are satisfied, such UPEs may be deemed to 'convert' to a loan by the company to the trust for Division 7A purposes (see 6.300).

PUBLIC COMPANIES

Section 103A ITAA36 sets out the requirements companies must meet to obtain public company status.

STOCK EXCHANGE LISTING

A company whose non-preference shares are listed on any stock exchange (anywhere in the world) as at the last day of the company's income year will be treated as a public company.

This status may be lost if, at any time during the year of income, 20 or fewer persons had or could have had control over 75% or more of the company's voting, dividend-bearing or equity (rights to capital distribution) shares.

If the Commissioner is satisfied a company should have 'public company' status, he can override the 20/75% rule.

NON-PROFIT COMPANIES

If a company, including an unincorporated club or association, has never been run for the profit or gain of its individual members and (by the terms of its Rules) is prohibited from making any monetary distribution to members (or their relatives), it is a 'public company'.

CERTAIN ASSURANCE COMPANIES AND FRIENDLY SOCIETY DISPENSARIES

Mutual life assurance companies and friendly society dispensaries may be regarded as public companies if they fall within the Act's definition of such institutions.

(SEMI) GOVERNMENT BODIES

Any body established by government for public purposes, and companies controlled by governments or other public bodies, are treated as public companies.

A company in which a foreign government has a controlling interest on the last day of the income year is considered to be a public company for that income year as the term 'government' for the purposes of s103A includes a foreign government (ATO ID 2011/73).

A company in which a government has an interest via a chain of subsidiaries can amount to a 'controlling interest' for the purposes of determining whether the company is a public company. The government must have control of that company on the last day of the income year (ATO ID 2011/74).

SUBSIDIARIES OF PUBLIC COMPANIES

If, at all times during an income year, a company is wholly owned by one or more public companies, it itself is a public company.

A subsidiary that is not wholly owned by a public company may still qualify as a public company, provided it is more than 50% owned by a listed public company (or companies) and the shareholder-listed company (or companies) satisfies the 20/75% rule.

A subsidiary satisfying the strict rules for public status would usually lose that status if that subsidiary was run for the benefit of persons other than its parent company.

CO-OPERATIVE COMPANIES

Any company which meets certain criteria for a co-operative at all times during the year is a public company. To be a co-operative, a company must be set up for one or more of the following:

- the acquisition of commodities (or animals) from its shareholders/members
- the acquisition of commodities (or animals) for disposal or distribution among its shareholders/members
- the storage, marketing, packing or processing of commodities belonging to its shareholders/members
- the rendering of services to its shareholders/members, and
- the raising of funds from its shareholder/members – for the purposes of making loans to its shareholders/members – to enable them to acquire land and/or buildings to be used for the purpose of a residence, or residence and business.

If a company has a share capital and has been set up for one or more of these purposes, to be a co-operative it must ensure that its rules or articles limit the number of shares that any member may hold and prohibit the quotation of its shares for transfer at any stock exchange or any other public mode of sale or purchase.

As with listed companies, co-operatives may lose their public status if at any time during the income year they cannot satisfy the 20/75% rule.

The Commissioner has the power to ignore non-compliance with the rule and treat the co-operative as a public company.

DISCRETION OF THE COMMISSIONER TO TREAT A PRIVATE COMPANY AS A PUBLIC COMPANY

Where a company does not meet all the requirements of a public company, the Commissioner can decide that it should nevertheless be treated as a public company, if it is reasonable to do so (s103A(5) ITAA36). When determining whether this discretion should be exercised, regard is to be had to the following factors:

- the number of persons capable of controlling the company and whether any of them was a public company
- the market value of the shares listed by the company
- the number of persons who beneficially owned shares in the company at the end of the year of income, and
- any other matters the Commissioner considers relevant.

In ATO ID 2004/760, the Commissioner did not exercise the discretion to treat a private company as a public company. The Commissioner notes in the ID that whilst a company with several hundred shareholders and a paid up capital of $20 million would generally be more likely to be accepted as a public company than a company with 30 shareholders and a small amount of paid up capital, there is no specific quantum of shareholders or paid up capital that is required to have the discretion exercised.

6.150   PUBLIC UNIT TRUSTS TAXED AS COMPANIES

Certain public unit trusts called 'public trading trusts' and 'corporate unit trusts' are treated as companies for tax purposes.

PUBLIC TRADING TRUST (DIVISION 6C)

GENERAL TEST

A unit trust is a public trading trust for this purpose in an income year if at any time during that year:

- the trustee carried on a 'trading business' (see below), or
- the trustee controlled, or was able to control, either directly or indirectly, the affairs or operations of another person in respect of the carrying on by that other person of a trading business, and
- the units are:
  - listed on any stock exchange
  - available for investment by the public, or
  - held by 50 or more persons.

'Trading business' excludes 'eligible investment business' (see meaning below), so a trust with business limited to 'eligible investment business' cannot be caught by the public trading trust provisions.

A unit trust is considered to be a 'trading trust' where the trustee of the unit trust holds a veto power over matters that go to the structure, scope and management of its interest in a trading company (ATO ID 2011/11).

A trust which satisfies the above test is generally not a public unit trust if 20 or fewer persons hold a 75% or more beneficial interest in the trust unless it is reasonable for it to be treated as a public unit trust due to:

- the length of time in the income year when no more than 20 persons held or had the right to acquire units, and
- various other relevant matters (see s102P).

NOTE: The Commissioner has confirmed that the offering of units to the public in one income year does not result in the trust being a public trust in any subsequent income year.

EXEMPT ENTITIES

Alternative tests apply to unit trusts where an exempt entity (see below), including a complying superannuation fund, approved deposit fund or pooled superannuation trust, is a unit holder.

The unit trust is treated as a public unit trust if at any time during the income year one or more exempt entities:

(a) held 20% or more of the beneficial interest in the income or property of the unit trust, or

(b) received 20% or more of any money paid or credited to unit holders, or

(c) had the power to vary rights, generally via a trust instrument, a contract to acquire units, or a power, authority or discretion, etc. (or could benefit from the exercise of such a power) so that (a) applies or (b) applies, or, if no money was paid or credited, would have applied if money had been paid or credited.

An exempt entity includes a complying superannuation fund, ADF and pooled superannuation trust. It also includes:

- a Municipal corporation or other local governing body or public authority
- a religious, scientific, charitable or public educational institution
- a public hospital and non-profit hospital carried on by society or association not for the profit of the individual members
- a registered health benefits organisation
- The Thalidomide Foundation
- a trade union or employer association
- a friendly society, cultural and scientific society, sporting club, animal racing club and community service club
- an association for the development or promotion of aviation, tourism, pastoral, horticultural, viticultural, manufacturing or industrial resources of Australia
- Australian Film Finance Corporation
- an exempt life assurance fund
- an organisation exempt from tax under the *International Organisations (Privileges and Immunities) Act 1963*, and
- any other person who is not liable for income tax.

There are no discretions to the alternative tests which apply to exempt entities. Accordingly, there is a risk that unit trusts in which a trustee of a superannuation fund has acquired units, will be taxed as companies unless those unit trusts are wholly involved (ie. 100%) in eligible investment business.

Any tax paid by the public trading trust would be available to the superannuation fund unit holder as imputation credits.

TAXATION OF PUBLIC TRADING TRUSTS

Unit trusts caught by these rules are taxed as companies and the distributions will be deemed to be dividends. However, as mentioned above, if the unit trust is carrying on an 'eligible investment business', then that trust cannot be a public trading trust and will therefore not be treated as a company for tax purposes.

MEANING OF 'ELIGIBLE INVESTMENT BUSINESS'

'Eligible investment business' is either or both of the following:

(a) a business consisting of investing in land or in an interest in land for the purpose, or primarily for the purpose, of deriving rent. This includes investing in fixtures on the land and moveable property. Further, a 25% safe-harbour allowance was also introduced from the 2008-09 year for non-rental, non-trading income from investments in land, or

(b) investing or trading in secured or unsecured loans (including deposits with a bank, building society or other financial institution), bonds, debentures, stock or other securities, shares in a company, units in a unit trust or a right or option in respect of such a loan, security, share or unit or certain other financial instruments which are:

- futures contracts

- forward contracts
- currency swap contracts
- forward exchange contracts
- forward interest rate contracts
- life assurance policies
- a right or option in respect of loans, securities, shares, units covered by para (b) above, as well as a right or option in respect of the above-mentioned contracts and policies, and
- any financial instruments that arise under financial arrangements.

 Dealing in, or developing of, land for resale is not an eligible investment business.

A unit trust which is investing in land for the purpose of, or primarily for the purpose of rent will not be considered to be a 'trading business' notwithstanding realisation gains made during the term of the investment (ATO ID 2010/128).

CORPORATE UNIT TRUSTS (DIVISION 6B)

A trust is a corporate unit trust in relation to a year of income if it is both a public unit trust (see above in relation to public trading trusts) and an eligible unit trust. The latter requires, amongst other things, that the business formerly carried on by a company is transferred to a unit trust.

PUBLIC TRADING TRUSTS AND CORPORATE UNIT TRUSTS

Dividends received by such trusts and distributions made by trusts are taxed as dividends as though between companies (see *Imputation system* from 6.800).

RULES FOR TAXING

The net income of the trust is taxed as though it is a company, and the trustee pays the tax at the company tax rate of 30%.

Distributions to unitholders are treated in the same way as company dividends paid to shareholders with franking offsets for tax paid by the trust.

Primary producer averaging rules and trust income rules do not apply (see 21.800 and 21.900).

6.200   DEBT/EQUITY PROVISIONS

The debt/equity provisions in Division 974 ITAA97 are aimed at defining the border between debt and equity in taxation law. Where there is a debt interest, interest payments by the holder of that interest are generally tax deductible and the dividend imputation rules are not relevant. Where the interest is classified as an equity interest, the imputation rules will apply to distributions and amounts paid in relation to the interest will not be tax deductible to the issuer.

Classification of an arrangement as an equity interest or a debt interest under Division 974 does not mean that the arrangement has that classification for all aspects of tax law (eg. a share in a foreign company might be a debt interest but dividends on those shares may still be non-assessable/non-exempt under s23AJ ITAA36) (see Chapter 22 *International Tax*).

Division 974 ITAA97 classifies an interest in a company as equity or debt according to the economic substance of the rights and obligations of an arrangement rather than the legal form.

The debt test in essence treats an interest as debt where there is an effective obligation of an issuer to return to the investor an amount at least equal to the amount invested.

An interest will be an equity interest if it is held by an entity as a member or shareholder of the company, or is a financing arrangement that provides a return that is in substance contingent on the economic performance of the company. Further, the rules contain a table listing various schemes that as a general rule are equity interests.

The classification of hybrid interests that have the characteristics of both debt and equity is resolved through a tiebreaker test. Interests meeting both the debt and equity tests are treated as a debt interest.

DEBT INTEREST TEST

Subdivision 974-B sets out a debt test. The basic test for working out if an interest is treated as debt at the time it is issued is as follows:

Is there a scheme?
Yes ↓
Is the scheme a financing arrangement?
Yes ↓
Does the issuing entity receive, or will it receive, a financial benefit(s) under the scheme?
Yes ↓
Does the issuing entity have an effectively non-contingent obligation to provide a financial benefit(s) after receiving the first or only financial benefit under the scheme?
Yes ↓
Is it substantially more likely than not that the financial benefit(s) to be provided will be at least equal to the benefit received or to be received?
Yes ↓
Interest treated as a debt interest

NOTE: 'No' to any of these questions will mean the interest is not a debt interest. The conditions under the equity test will then need to be considered (refer below). To satisfy the debt test, the interest must have five essential elements.

1. There must be a scheme as defined in s995-1. 'Scheme' is broadly defined as any arrangement, or any scheme, plan, proposal, action, course of action or course of conduct.

2. There must be a financing arrangement (which is specifically defined as an arrangement entered into by the company to raise finance or to fund another scheme that is a financing arrangement).
    A contribution to a company of capital in some form such as a loan between an investor and a company would be an example of a financing arrangement.

3. There must be a financial benefit received by the company under the financing arrangement.
    A financial benefit is defined as being anything of economic value and includes property and services. In most cases the financial benefit received will be the issue price as specified in the terms of the financing arrangement (the amount paid to acquire the financial interest).

4. There must exist an effectively non-contingent obligation on the company to provide a future financial benefit to the investor. The terms, conditions and pricing of the financing arrangement will determine whether an effectively non-contingent obligation exists. An 'obligation' for these purposes does not have to be a legally enforceable obligation (TD 2009/1).

5. If the company has an effectively non-contingent obligation, it must be substantially more likely than not that the financial benefit to be provided to the investor will be at least equal to or exceed the financial benefit received (ie the return of the initial investment amount).

A non-contingent obligation is one that is not contingent on any event condition or situation (including the economic performance of the entity) other than the ability or willingness of the entity to meet the obligation.

CALCULATING THE VALUE OF THE FINANCIAL BENEFIT

The method of calculating the value of the financial benefit depends on the performance period of the arrangement. If the term is ten years or less, the value will be calculated in nominal terms. If the term is more than ten years, the value of the benefit will be calculated in present value terms. The performance period is the period within which, under the terms on which the interest is issued, the issuer has to meet its effectively non-contingent obligations in relation to the interest.

An obligation is treated as having to be met within ten years of the interest being issued if the terms formally exceed ten years but there is an effectively non-contingent obligation to terminate the interest within ten years. The present value of a benefit is the nominal value of the benefit, discounted using the adjusted benchmark rate of return.

The adjusted benchmark rate of return is defined as 75% of the benchmark rate of return on the test interest. The benchmark rate of return is defined as the internal rate of return on an investment if the investment were 'ordinary debt' of the issue or an equivalent entity, compounded annually and otherwise comparable with the interest under consideration (see ATO ID 2003/983 for characterisation of 15 year convertible note using the benchmark rate).

The Commissioner has a discretion under s974-65 to treat the interest as a debt interest under certain circumstances.

If an interest is a debt interest, interest payments are generally deductible under s8-1 ITAA97.

EQUITY INTEREST TEST

Subdivision 974-C sets out the equity test. It contains a table that lists schemes that are equity interests (s974-75(1)). A scheme satisfies the equity test if it gives rise to an interest listed at Items 1-4 of this table (see below).

Subject to the abovementioned tie-breaker test, a scheme gives rise to an equity interest if it is held by the entity as a member of shareholder of the company and it gives rise to an interest that:

- provides a variable or fixed return that depends on the company's economic performance
- provides a variable or fixed return at the discretion of the company, or
- may or will convert into an equity interest or share.

Item	Interest	Purpose
1	As member or shareholder of the company	Recognises the company's members or shareholders as the current class of equity interest holders in a company. Shareholders generally hold a number of rights attaching to the shares, including the right to vote, receive dividends and participate in the residual assets of the company when it is wound up.
2	That carries a right to a return effectively contingent on economic performance	Recognises an interest as equity where the holder has a right to receive a return on investment that is dependent on the company's economic performance.
3	That carries a right to a return at the discretion of the company	Recognises an interest as equity where the holder has a right to a return that is at the discretion of the company's directors.
4	That converts to, or provides a right to be issued with, an equity interest	Recognises either a convertible interest or an interest that attaches a right to an equity interest in the entity as an equity interest.

If the interest satisfies the equity test and the debt test did not apply, then the interest would be an equity interest. In such circumstances, the investor's returns will be frankable distributions under the simplified imputation system and unlike debt interests, would not be non-deductible to the company.

If both the debt test and equity test are satisfied, the tie-breaker provision results in the interest being considered to be debt.

NON-SHARE EQUITY INTEREST

Division 974 introduces the concept of a 'non-share equity interest'. A non-share equity interest in a company is an equity interest that is not solely a share (eg. an unsecured note issued by a private company to a director where the return and repayment of the investment was contingent upon the profitability of the company (ATO ID 2002/794)). The extended definition of equity is based on economic substance and will now include interest that raises finance and provides returns contingent on the economic performance of an entity, subject to the debt test. The current imputation rules apply equally to shareholders and holders of non-share equity interest as a result of the extended definition of equity. Frankable distributions may be paid to both groups in accordance with the simplified imputation provisions.

Capital raised by a company from the issue of non-share equity interest is credited to a non-share capital account (see below). A company has a non-share capital account if the company issues a non-share equity interest in the company.

NOTE: A stapled security issue, which includes a share in the company's capital account and a non-share equity interest will result in a credit to the company's share capital account and a credit to the company's non-share capital account.

NON-SHARE CAPITAL ACCOUNT

A non-share capital account contains similar information to that which is recorded in the shareholder's credit loan account, including such things as:

- the amount received as consideration for the issue of a non-share equity interest (eg. the at-call loan amount), and
- non-share distributions (eg. repayments to the shareholder).

A non-share capital account is an account maintained for tax purposes, rather than for financial accounting purposes. For example, if a company is placed in liquidation, the characterisation of the interest as an equity interest under the debt and equity rules does not change the rights attached to that interest in the liquidation process from debtor rights to shareholder rights.

RELATED PARTY 'AT-CALL' LOANS

A related party at-call loan is a loan made by a connected entity which does not have a fixed term and is repayable on demand.

All related party at-call loans are deemed to be debt interest if at the end of the income year, the borrowing company has an annual turnover of less than $20 million (a small business carve-out). Turnover is calculated as per the GST rules. This applies to loans made on or after 1 July 2005. Such at-call loans made prior to 1 July 2005 were treated as debt interests under transitional rules (irrespective of the size of the entity).

For private companies with related party at-call loans that have a turnover exceeding the $20 million limit in one year, but are below the $20 million limit the following year, deeming will apply from the start of the second year of income. However, a private company can elect in writing to treat the deeming to have occurred at the start of the first year. The election must be made before the earlier of the due date for lodgement of the income tax return for the first year or the actual date of lodgment.

Once the election is made, it can not be revoked and the interest will remain a debt interest until repaid (s974-110).

Post-1 July 2005, the debt and equity rules will determine for tax purposes whether the at-call loan is a debt or an equity interest. An at-call loan will be an equity interest if it falls within one or more items of the equity test in s974-75 and does not pass the debt test in s974-20.

Where a shareholder lends money to a company, repayable on demand, with no fixed maximum term, and the loan is either interest free or has a low interest rate, the interest will be an equity interest under the debt and equity rules. The main reason the equity test would apply is that the return of either the principal or interest is at the discretion of an associate of the company (ie. the shareholder).

The loan could also fall within the debt test, and therefore qualify as a debt interest as a result of a tie-breaker test in the debt/equity rules. However, this would be unlikely to be the case where:

- the term of the loan is greater than ten years, or the agreement is silent as to the term, and
- the interest rate is nil or very low, or is as determined by the parties from time to time (as is common in such arrangements between associated parties).

AT-CALL LOANS THAT ARE DEBT INTERESTS FOR TAX PURPOSES

At-call loans can pass the debt test in the following two scenarios:

- if the at-call loan has a maximum term of ten years or less, and there is an effectively non-contingent obligation to repay (at least) the amount that was borrowed, the at-call loan will be a debt interest. An at-call loan with a term of no more than ten years may be a debt interest even if the loan is 'interest free'. Section 974-135 defines an effectively non-contingent obligation. Briefly, an obligation is non-contingent if it is not contingent on any event, condition or situation (including the economic performance of the entity having the obligation on a connected entity of that entity), other than the ability or willingness of the entity to meet the obligation, and

- if the loan is repayable at-call and has no fixed term, then in order for it to be a debt interest, it needs to have an effectively non-contingent obligation to pay an interest rate that is high enough to pass the debt test on a present value basis (an arm's length interest rate will achieve this).

TAX CONSEQUENCES OF AN AT-CALL LOAN BEING A DEBT INTEREST

If an interest payment is made by the borrower on an at-call loan that is a debt interest, it will generally be eligible for deductibility and cannot be franked. Deductibility under the general rules will depend on the use to which the borrower puts the loan (ie. the purpose test).

TAX CONSEQUENCES OF AN AT-CALL LOAN BEING AN EQUITY INTEREST

Any payment of interest on the at-call loan treated as an equity interest will not be deductible, but may be frankable. A non-share capital account needs to be maintained (see above).

Effectively, the loan is treated no differently to a share investment. Returns in the nature of interest are frankable in much the same way as normal share dividends. Non-share dividends will be subject to simplified imputation system rules and interest will not be deductible for tax purposes. Unlike dividends paid on shares, non-share dividends can be paid even if the company has no profits. This means that a company could be paying non-share dividends when it is in a loss situation. Returns of principal, however, from a non-share equity interest (eg. a return of all or part of the principal of the at-call loan) will not be taxable as revenue in the shareholder's hands.

There are complex anti-avoidance provisions that may potentially apply if a company makes returns of non-share capital ahead of paying dividends.

DOCUMENTATION

Subsection 262A(1) ITAA36 provides that ... *a person carrying on a business must keep records that record and explain all transactions and other acts engaged in by the person that are relevant for any purpose of this Act.*

If characterisation of the at-call loan as a debt interest is desired, there should be documentation to establish that there is either an effectively non-contingent obligation to repay the arrangement within ten years from the date of issue of the loan, or that there is an effectively non-contingent obligation to pay an interest rate that is high enough to pass the debt test on a present value basis. Also, if a private company elects to treat an at-call loan as debt, the election must be in writing (s974-110(1B)).

 Taxpayers will need to have the necessary loan agreement in place from the date the interest is issued, not the relevant date from which the debt and equity rules apply.

There is no requirement under the debt and equity rules that the company pay a commercial rate of interest on at-call loans from shareholders. The debt and equity rules do however refer to a benchmark rate of return, but this is in relation to the valuation of a financial benefit for the purposes of the debt test. Effectively, only if the loan period exceeds ten years will there be a requirement to pay interest.

Generally, if the company only repays the capital originally advanced, there should not be any adverse consequences, regardless of whether the interest is classified as debt or equity for tax purposes unless the anti-avoidance provisions are triggered. If there are returns not in the nature of capital repayments (ie. interest) then there may be unintended consequences, depending on how the interest is classified.

The s45B capital streaming rules may deem a repayment of principal to be the payment of an unfranked dividend. This includes a distribution from a non-share capital account. This section therefore cannot apply to at-call loans which are treated as debt under the debt/equity rules. The Tax Office has indicated that it will not apply a profits first rule to the repayment of principal. If there is potential for the s45B rules to apply, it will be prudent to ensure that loans meet the debt tests to avoid its potential application.

To be treated as debt, at-call loans should be for a period of less than ten years from date of issue otherwise the loan will need to reflect an interest rate high enough to exceed the benchmark rate of return test (see above).

6.300 LOANS, PAYMENTS AND DEBT FORGIVENESS

Division 7A contains anti-avoidance provisions designed to prevent what are, in effect, distributions of private company profits by way of loan, a payment or the forgiveness of a debt. The provisions are broadly drafted and may potentially catch many transactions which, in substance, do not involve a distribution of profits.

Division 7A may apply to deem a private company to have paid an assessable unfranked dividend where:

- amounts are paid by the company to a shareholder or shareholder's associate (s109C), including transfers of property for less than the amount that would have been paid in an arm's length dealing
- amounts are lent by the company to a shareholder or shareholder's associate, and
- the company forgives a debt which was owed by a shareholder or shareholder's associate to the company (s109F).

There are numerous exceptions and exclusions to the above general rules, the main ones being as follows:

- payments of genuine debts
- payments or loans to other companies
- certain liquidation distributions and loans by liquidators
- payments or loans that are otherwise assessable or specifically excluded from being assessable
- loans made in the ordinary course of business on normal commercial terms, and
- loans that meet specific criteria in relation to the minimum interest rate and maximum term, where the loan agreement is put in writing before the earlier of the due date for lodgement of the company's income tax return or actual lodgement date, for the income year in which the loan was made.

Where a loan made in a particular year is repaid in full before the company's income tax return lodgment day (s109D) for that year, Division 7A will not apply to that loan.

In addition to the above, Division 7A applies to closely held corporate limited partnerships in the same way that it applies to private companies. Division 7A also applies to arrangements that involve a non-resident company making a payment, loan or debt forgiveness to a resident shareholder (or their associate). Further, the use of company assets by a shareholder can be deemed to be a Division 7A payment.

DATE OF EFFECT OF DIVISION 7A

Subject to a number of important exceptions, all loans, advances and other credits made by private companies to shareholders (or their associates) on or after 4 December 1997, and all debts owed by a shareholder or associate which are forgiven by a private company on or after 4 December 1997 are treated as dividends to the extent that the company has a 'distributable surplus' (s109Y ITAA36).

Note that where a loan is from a private company to a partnership, and there is a corporate partner, the partnership may fall within the 'inter-company' exemption.

Division 7A can also apply to pre-4 December 1997 loans because, if the terms of a pre-4 December 1997 loan are varied by either extending the term of the loan or increasing the amount, Division 7A applies to the loan as if it were made on new terms when the variation occurred (s109D(5)).

Certain loans made by trustees to shareholders or associates of private companies may also be subject to these rules as a result of the operation of Subdivision EA of Division 7A (refer 6.335).

6.310 DEEMED DIVIDENDS – OVERVIEW OF DIVISION 7A (EXCLUDING SUBDIVISIONS EA & EB)

OVERVIEW OF DIVISION 7

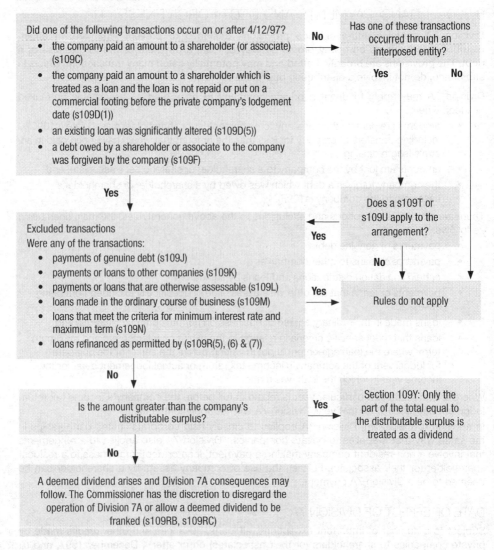

AMOUNTS PAID BY A PRIVATE COMPANY TO A SHAREHOLDER OR SHAREHOLDER ASSOCIATES (S109C)

A private company is deemed to pay a dividend to an entity at the end of the private company's year of income if the private company pays an amount to the entity during the year and either:

- the payment is made when the entity is a shareholder or an associate of such a shareholder, or

- a reasonable person would conclude (having regard to all of the circumstances) that the payment is made because the entity had been a shareholder or associate at some time.

This rule operates to deem a payment to be a dividend where an amount is paid to a current (or former) shareholder or an associate of such a person, even though the payment would not normally be treated by the company as a dividend. The amount of the payment treated as a dividend is limited to the company's distributable surplus. See below for how to calculate a company's distributable surplus.

PAYMENTS – DEFINITION

'Payment' includes payments (according to the ordinary meaning of the term) or the crediting of an amount, encompassing payments or credits to the entity, on behalf of the entity or for the benefit of the entity. The concept is also defined to include a transfer of property to the entity. Where there is a transfer of property to an entity, and therefore a 'payment', the amount of the payment is the arm's length price for the property less any consideration given by the shareholder or associate for the transfer.

The amount of the payment is deemed to be nil where the consideration given by the shareholder or associate is at least equal to the arm's length price.

TR 2014/5 sets out the Commissioner's view where an order is made under s79 of the *Family Law Act* for a private company, or a party to the matrimonial proceedings to cause the private company, to pay money or transfer property to a party to the matrimonial proceedings who is an associate of a shareholder of the private company. The Commissioner's view is that where a section 79 order requires a private company, or a party to the matrimonial proceedings to cause the private company, to pay money or transfer property to an associate of a shareholder of property in compliance with the order, the payment of money or transfer of property is a payment for the purposes of subsection 109C(3) of the ITAA 1936. Further, he states that s109J (exception for payments discharging pecuniary obligations) does not prevent the payment from being treated as a dividend.

The following example is taken from the ruling.

Section 79 orders for a private company to pay money to an associate of a shareholder
In the 2014 income year, Sam, Martha and ABC Pty Ltd are parties to matrimonial property proceedings before the Family Court. Sam is the sole shareholder of ABC Pty Ltd which is the vehicle for the family business and has retained profits of $200,000. The distributable surplus of ABC Pty Ltd as worked out under section 109Y of the ITAA 1936 is greater than $100,000.

On 29 May 2014, the Family Court makes an order pursuant to section 79 of the FLA 1975 for ABC Pty Ltd to pay Martha $100,000. On 30 June 2014, ABC Pty Ltd makes the payment of $100,000 to Martha in satisfaction of the Family Court order.

The payment to Martha is a payment as defined in paragraph 109C(3)(a) of the ITAA 1936. Section 109J of the ITAA 1936 does not prevent section 109C operating to treat the payment as a deemed dividend.

The payment is assessable to Martha as a dividend under section 44 of the ITAA 1936, by virtue of section 109C of the ITAA 1936.

USE OF COMPANY ASSETS FOR PRIVATE PURPOSES BY SHAREHOLDERS DEEMED A PAYMENT

Where an asset is available for use or lease by a shareholder (or associate) of the company, the value of a deemed payment will be determined as:

- the amount which would have been paid for the transfer, lease, licence or other right by parties dealing at arm's length: *less*

- any consideration given for the transfer, lease, licence or other right.

Therefore, unless there is any contribution towards the use of the asset, the deemed payment will be the market value of the benefit provided.

NOTE: To the extent that the use of the asset by the shareholder of the company arises in their capacity as an employee, then the Fringe Benefits Tax (FBT) provisions would apply – s109ZB(3). The FBT liability is determined having regard to the type of benefit provided (refer Chapter 25).

EXCEPTIONS

To ensure that certain taxpayers are not unduly affected, there are four exceptions available under s109CA pursuant to which a shareholder may be able to use a private company asset without the use being considered as a 'payment'.

The four exceptions are follows:

- **Exception 1: Minor benefits** Where the value of the lease, licence or right to use the asset satisfies the definition of a minor benefit as outlined under s58P of the FBTAA then use of the asset would not be deemed a payment for Division 7A purposes.

  In effect, the exception assumes that had the benefit been provided to an employee of the company (as opposed to the shareholder), it would have been exempt as a minor fringe benefit. Broadly, a 'minor benefit' arises where the benefit provided by the employer is less than $300 (GST inclusive) and, amongst other conditions, the benefit is provided on an infrequent and irregular basis.

- **Exception 2: Once-only deductible payments** The exception arises where, if the shareholder of a private company (or their associate) had paid an amount in respect of a lease, licence or other right to use an asset of the company, a once-only deduction would have been available to that shareholder (or their associate). An example of this exception is where a shareholder uses a delivery van of the private company in the conduct of their own personal business.

- **Exception 3: Dwelling owned by a private company** The third exception applies in situations where a dwelling is being used by a shareholder (or associate) of a private company and the use would not meet the once-only deductible rule under the second exception (as the use of such dwellings are normally for private purposes). A common example would be the use of a homestead on farm land.

  For this exception to apply it is necessary that:

  - the shareholder (or associate) is carrying on a business
  - the shareholder (or associate) was granted a lease, licence or other right to use the land, water or a building for the purpose of carrying on the business, and
  - the provision of the dwelling to the shareholder is connected with the use, lease, licence or other right.

Rebecca is a shareholder of a private company Health Pty Ltd. She is also a doctor who runs a surgery. Rebecca runs her surgery in a house owned by Health Pty Ltd under a licence agreement. The surgery takes up approximately 40% of the area of the house. Health Pty Ltd has also granted Rebecca a right to use the remaining 60% of the house to live in. She does not pay any rent to Health Pty Ltd under either arrangement.

Rebecca's licence to use the house to run her surgery will not be a payment because she would have been entitled to a once-only deduction if she had paid for that use.

Rebecca's use of the remainder of the house is also not a payment as she is carrying on a business, uses a building that she has been granted a licence to use and there is a connection between her carrying on the business and the use of the remainder of the house as her dwelling.

- **Exception 4: Main residence** The fourth exception applies to the provision of a dwelling if:

  - it is the main residence of a shareholder (or associate)
  - the provider of the dwelling is a private company
  - the private company acquired the dwelling before 1 July 2009, and
  - the private company satisfies the 'continuity of ownership' test in s165-12 ITAA97, commencing from the time the company acquired the dwelling.

AMOUNTS LENT BY A PRIVATE COMPANY TO A SHAREHOLDER OR SHAREHOLDER'S ASSOCIATES (S109D & S109E)

A private company is deemed to pay a dividend at the end of a year of income if the company makes a loan during that year and the loan remains outstanding by the lodgment day for the income tax return for that year – refer s109D(6).

LOANS – DEFINITION

Specifically, s109D(3) ITAA36 defines a 'loan' as:

* an advance of money
* a provision of credit or any other form of financial accommodation
* a payment of an amount for, or on account of, on behalf of or at the request of, an entity, if there is an express or implied obligation to repay the amount, and
* a transaction (whatever its terms or from) which in substance effects a loan of money.

A company's lodgment day is the earlier of the due date and the actual date of lodgment of the company's income tax return.

A loan is taken to have been made when an amount is paid by the company to an entity by way of a loan (according to the ordinary meaning of that term), or anything within the definition of 'loan' is done in relation to the entity.

Some repayments of loans made to a private company are disregarded. Specifically, s109R causes repayments to be disregarded where a reasonable person would conclude (having regard to all the circumstances) at the time of the repayment, that the borrower intended to subsequently further borrow from the private company an amount similar to, or larger than, the repayment.

The following repayments of a loan are acceptable:

* additional salary to employee shareholders being credited against the loan(s) (subject to the existing rules (ie. s109))
* the declaration of dividends (and crediting against the relevant loan(s)), or
* the transfer by shareholders (or associates) of assets to the company in satisfaction of the loan.

For the purposes of the Division 7A loan rules, a private company is taken to have made a loan to an entity, not only where such a loan is actually made by the private company, but also where an interposed entity makes the loan to the relevant entity under an arrangement with the private company (s109T).

Another category of loan which is deemed by the operation of this rule to be a dividend, is one made in the following circumstances:

* the private company made a loan to a shareholder or associate during the previous year of income
* the loan was made in the course of a winding-up of the private company by a liquidator (such loans are excluded from the operation of this rule in the year in which they are made (s109D(1A))
* the loan was not fully repaid by the end of the current year of income.

Where this rule operates to deem a private company to have paid a dividend, the amount of the dividend which the private company is taken to have paid is the amount of the loan that is treated as not having been repaid at the end of the current year, up to the amount of the company's distributable surplus.

Pre-4 December 1997 loans (see 6.350) are deemed to be loans post that date if the term is extended or the amount of the loan is increased.

Provided that certain conditions are satisfied, a loan may be excluded from the application of Division 7A if a loan agreement under s109N is in place (see *Excluded loans and repayments* below).

UNPAID PRESENT ENTITLEMENT OWED BY A TRUST TO A CORPORATE BENEFICIARY

In TR 2010/3, the Commissioner of Taxation concludes that unpaid present entitlements (UPEs) owed to corporate beneficiaries in certain circumstances may be classified as a 'loan' under the extended definition contained in s109D(3) ITAA36 (see above).

In particular, the ruling considers the application of Division 7A to certain private company loans, in circumstances where:

- the private company has a present entitlement to amounts from an associated trust that is part of the same family group of entities as the private company, and
- the funds representing the present entitlement remain intermingled with other funds of the trust estate, or are otherwise able to be used for the purposes of the trust estate.

Practice Statement PS LA 2010/4 comments on the practical application of TR 2010/3.

In summary, the Practice Statement contemplates the following types of loans:

(i) Section two loans – UPEs created prior to 16 December 2009

A Division 7A loan will arise where the UPE amount is the subject of a loan agreement between the trust and the company beneficiary (called a **section two loan**).

These loans will arise in the following circumstances:

- **Type 1 loan**
  - *There is an express loan agreement:* Arises where there is a written agreement, trust resolution or other document evidencing agreement between the trustee and the corporate beneficiary (which may be by an agreed set-off in satisfaction of the trustee's obligation to pay the entitlement to the company).
  - *There is an implied loan agreement:* Unless there is evidence to the contrary, such loans are considered to arise where the amount of the present entitlement is recorded in the financial accounts of the private company as a loan 'asset' and as a loan 'liability' in the financial accounts of the trust.
- **Type 2 loan:** Where the trustee has a power under the trust deed to pay or apply amounts on behalf of the company beneficiary and the 'financial accounts' of the trust records the UPE amount as a loan owed to the company.

Corrective action and Commissioner's discretion under s109RB for section two loans

PS LA 2010/4 states that where a company has misclassified a UPE as a loan, corrective action was available for affected taxpayers provided certain conditions were met (see para. 32 of PS LA 2010/4). This option was available until 31 December 2011.

Where a taxpayer discovers non-compliance with Division 7A in respect of section two loans, the taxpayer may request the exercise of the Commissioner's discretion under s109RB to overlook the breach under s109RB (see below).

Under normal circumstances, this would have required the taxpayer to make a written application to seek exercise of the Commissioner's discretion. However, PS LA 2010/4 permitted 'corrective action' to be taken such that a written application was not necessary provided the conditions outlined in paras 34 and 35 were satisfied by the taxpayer. Where neither of these avenues were available, it would have been necessary for taxpayers to make a formal request to the Commissioner for exercise of his discretion pursuant to s109RB.

(ii) Section three loans – UPEs created on or after 16 December 2009

A Division 7A loan will arise where a UPE owed to a private company beneficiary is not, within the required time:

- paid to the company beneficiary
- placed under a s109N complying loan agreement, or
- invested for the sole benefit of the company (ie. sub-trust arrangement (refer below)).

TIMING OF A SECTION THREE LOAN: PAYMENT OF UPE OR LOAN AGREEMENT

Case 1	
UPE created before 30 June 2010	
30 June 2010	Company becomes presently entitled to trust income
30 June 2011	If UPE unpaid and an appropriate sub-trust arrangement not established UPE becomes a Division 7A loan
15 May 2012*	UPE must become paid out or a s109N loan agreement established

Case 2	
UPE created 1 July 2010 and thereafter	
30 June 2011	Company becomes presently entitled to trust income
15 May 2012*	If UPE unpaid and no sub-trust – becomes Division 7A loan
15 May 2013*	UPE must become paid out or a s109N loan agreement established

* This date is 'lodgment day' (s109D(6) ITAA36) of the main trust (ie. the trust distributing to the company beneficiary) and therefore may differ.

NOTE: If a private company makes a loan in an income year and, in the following income year (and before the relevant lodgment day) puts in place a written loan agreement which amounts to a new loan, ATO ID 2012/60 states that s109D should apply to the original loan in the income year in which the original loan is made.

SUB-TRUST

In PSLA 2010/4 the Commissioner of Taxation states that a Division 7A loan will not arise to the extent that a sub-trust arrangement (described in the Practice Statement) is in place for the sole benefit of the company beneficiary.

The Tax Office considers that the funds are held for the sole benefit of the company beneficiary where:

- the sub-trust invests the funds representing the UPE in the main trust on commercial terms
- all the benefits from investment flow back to the company as the beneficiary of the sub-trust, and
- all the benefits from the investment are actually paid to the company beneficiary by the 'lodgment day' of the main trust for the particular income year.

Alternatively, the monies representing the sub-trust may be invested on behalf of the company in an investment which is entirely independent of the main trust.

The Tax Office will consider the sub-trust fund to be invested solely for the benefit of the company beneficiary where:

- **Option 1:** The funds representing the UPE are invested on an interest only **seven year** loan basis in the main trust (using a benchmark interest rate).
- **Option 2:** The funds are invested on an interest only **ten year** loan basis in the main trust (using a prescribed interest rate).
- **Option 3:** The funds are invested in a specific income producing asset or investment (eg. interest term deposit, investment property, etc) .

Assuming that **Option 1** (ie. seven year loan) is adopted, the timing of a sub-trust arrangement is as follows:

UPE to 30 June 2010	
30 June 2010	Company becomes presently entitled to trust income
30 June 2011[1]	Sub-trust option adopted by the trustee. Loan commences (assume 7 years).
30 June 2012	Sub-trust entitled to income which is included in company's tax return
15 May 2013[2]	Income from loan for 2012 year must be paid to the company beneficiary
30 June 2018	Final interest and loan repayment

1: One-off extension of the time available to establish the sub-trust.
2: 'Lodgment day' of the main trust and therefore the date may vary.

UPE from 1 July 2010	
30 June 2011	Company becomes presently entitled to trust income
15 May 2012*	Sub-trust option adopted by the trustee. Loan commences (assume 7 years)
30 June 2012	Sub-trust entitled to income which is included in company's tax return
15 May 2013*	Income from loan must be paid to the company beneficiary.
14 May 2019	Final interest and loan repayment

* 'Lodgment day' of the main trust and therefore the date may vary.

AMOUNTS FORGIVEN BY A PRIVATE COMPANY TO A SHAREHOLDER OR SHAREHOLDER ASSOCIATES (S109F)

Generally, if a private company forgives, wholly or partly, a debt owed to it by a shareholder or associate, the amount forgiven is treated as a dividend at the end of the private company's year of income. As with payments and loans, the amount of the dividend is the amount of the debt forgiven, to the extent of the company's distributable surplus.

A debt forgiven that was owed by a former shareholder or associate, will only be a deemed dividend to the extent it is reasonable to conclude that the amount is forgiven because of that former shareholder status.

MEANING OF DEBT FORGIVENESS

A debt is taken to be forgiven, for Division 7A purposes, in the circumstances in which a 'commercial debt' would be taken to be forgiven, assuming the amount were a debt as defined under the commercial debt provisions contained in Division 245 ITAA97. Under the commercial debt forgiveness rules, a debt is forgiven if the debtor's obligation to pay the debt is released or waived, or is otherwise extinguished. A number of other situations described in the legislation will result in the forgiveness of a debt.

FORGIVENESS BY STATUTE OF LIMITATIONS

A debt is also forgiven under s109F(3) if the period within which the creditor is entitled to sue for the recovery of the debt ends (because of the operation of a statute of limitations) without the debt having been paid.

Further, if:

- the debtor and creditor enter into an agreement or arrangement (whether or not enforceable by legal proceedings), and
- under the agreement or arrangement the debtor's obligation to pay the whole or a part of the debt is to cease at a particular future time, and
- the cessation of the obligation is to occur without the debtor incurring any financial or other obligation, or only a nominal or insignificant obligation,

then the debt, or the part of the debt, is taken to be forgiven when the agreement or arrangement is entered into.

If, after the agreement or arrangement is entered into, the debt or the part of the debt is forgiven, the last-mentioned forgiveness is disregarded for the purposes of Division 7A so that the provisions apply only to the first forgiveness (s109F(8)).

DISCHARGE OF DEBT BY TRANSFER OF PROPERTY

A forgiveness also takes place (s109F(3) and s245-35(5)) if a person subscribes for shares in a company to discharge a debt and the funds are applied as payment of the debt. The amount of debt is taken to be forgiven at the time when the money was applied against that debt. If the debt is discharged by the debtor transferring to the private company property of a value at least equal to the value of the debt, no debt forgiveness occurs for the purposes of Division 7A (s109F(4) ITAA36).

DEBT PARKING

Debt forgiveness may occur by way of 'debt parking' (s109F(5) ITAA36. The requirements are:

a. the creditor assigns the debt to a new creditor
b. the new creditor is an associate of the debtor, or the assignment occurred under an agreement or arrangement to which the new creditor and debtor were parties, and
c. a reasonable person would conclude (having regard to all the circumstances) that the new creditor will not exercise the assigned right.

In these circumstances Division 245 has effect as if the debt had been forgiven rather than assigned.

FAILURE TO RELY ON OBLIGATION TO REPAY

An amount of debt owed to a private company is also forgiven if a reasonable person would conclude that the company will not insist on the borrower repaying the amount or rely on its obligation to repay the amount (s109F(6) ITAA36).

FORGIVENESS OF AMALGAMATED DEBT

Where a private company forgives an amount of debt relating to a constituent loan forming part of an amalgamated loan, the private company is taken to forgive the same amount of debt in relation to the relevant amalgamated loan (s109F(7) ITAA36) (see 6.330 re amalgamated loans). Where the forgiven debt was a loan that was deemed to be a dividend under the Division 7A loan rules or the amalgamated loan rules, the debt forgiveness rules will not apply.

According to ATO ID 2012/77, s109F may operate to deem a private company to have paid a dividend to a deceased's legal personal representative in circumstances where a private company is taken to have made an amalgamated loan to a shareholder who dies before the amalgamated loan is repaid, and the private company forgives that loan while the shareholder's estate is in administration.

BACK-TO-BACK ARRANGEMENTS (S109T)

Subdivision E of Division 7A is an anti-avoidance provision concerned with back-to-back arrangements under which a private company pays or loans an amount to an interposed entity on the understanding that the interposed entity or another interposed entity will pay or loan an amount to the shareholder of the private company or an associate of the shareholder (the 'target entity').

In these circumstances, s109T(1) may apply to treat the private company as having made a:

* deemed payment to the target entity if the target entity is paid an amount by the interposed entity (s109V), or

* notional loan to the target entity if the target entity is loaned an amount by the interposed entity (s109W).

Specifically, s109T(1) provides that Division 7A will operate as if a private company makes a deemed payment or notional loan, as described in s109V or s109W, to the target entity if:

* the private company makes a payment or loan to another entity (the first interposed entity) that is interposed between the private company and the target entity, and

* a reasonable person would conclude (having regard to all the circumstances) that the private company made the payment or loan solely or mainly as part of an arrangement involving a payment or loan to the target entity, and either:

(i) the first interposed entity makes a payment or loan to the target entity, or

(ii) another interposed entity between the private company and the target entity makes a payment or loan to the target entity.

The amount of the deemed payment or notional loan under s109V or 109W is determined by the Commissioner. In determining the amount, the Commissioner will take into account relevant factors occurring before the earlier of the due date for lodgment and actual lodgment date of the private company's return for the relevant income year.

Section 109T can operate to treat a private company as having made a payment or loan to a shareholder or an associate of a shareholder (the target entity) in circumstances where the interposed entity is also a shareholder of the private company and the payment made to the interposed entity is the payment of an actual dividend (provided the conditions in s109T(1) (see above) are satisfied) (ATO ID 2011/104).

 EXAMPLE from ATO ID 2011/104: Application of s109T

Jack is a shareholder of Private Company A, holding 100 A class shares. He needs $100,000 to enable him to purchase a new residence. Private Company A has significant cash reserves and a distributable surplus. Private Company B is also a shareholder of Private Company A, holding 100 B class shares. Private Company A paid a fully franked dividend of $100,000 to Private Company B and on the same day Private Company B made an interest free loan of $100,000 to Jack. No repayments of the loan were made by Jack before the private company's lodgment day for the relevant year of income. Private Company B has no distributable surplus.

On the present facts, the operation of Division 7A will need to be considered in respect of:

* *the payment made by Private Company A to Private Company B*
* *the loan made by Private Company B to Jack; and*
* *any notional loan taken to be made by Private Company A to Jack.*

Loan made by private company A to private company B

Because of the operation of s109L(1) ITAA36 (which prevents a deemed dividend from being assessable), there is no prospect for the fully franked dividend paid to private company B to also be taken to be a dividend under s109C ITAA36. This is because the dividend is already included in the assessable income of Private Company B under s44 ITAA36.

Loan made by private company to Jack

Private Company B is taken to have paid a dividend to Jack under s109D ITAA36 but the amount of the dividend is capped at the company's distributable surplus. As the amount of distributable surplus is nil the amount of the dividend that Private Company B is taken to have paid to Jack is nil.

Notional loan made by Private Company A to Jack

On the present facts, the s109T(1) ITAA36 conditions are satisfied. There is a back to back arrangement in which Private Company A has made a payment to Private Company B as part of an arrangement involving a loan to Jack.

As ss109T(3) ITAA36 has no application, Division 7A can operate as if Private Company A made a loan to Jack as described in s109W ITAA36.

Under s109W ITAA36, the amount of the notional loan is the amount (if any) determined by the Commissioner. Given the facts and circumstances relating to the loan made to Jack, the Commissioner would determine that the amount of the notional loan was $100,000. There has been an informal or disguised distribution of Private Company A profits to Jack.

CONSEQUENCES OF DIVISION 7A APPLYING

If Division 7A applies, payments, loans, and forgiven amounts taken to be dividends:

- are included in the assessable income of a shareholder or an associate as an unfranked dividend (unless the Commissioner exercises his discretion to permit the dividend to be franked or the dividend arises as a result of a family law obligation)
- are taken for the purposes of ITAA36 to be paid:
  - to the entity as a shareholder in the private company, and
  - out of the private company's profits (ie. all the requirements of s44 are deemed to be satisfied, which means the transaction becomes an assessable dividend in the relevant person's hands)
- are not subject to withholding tax if deemed to be paid to a non-resident (s109ZA), and
- are not treated as a fringe benefit (s109ZB).

HOW MUCH OF THE LOAN, PAYMENT OR DEBT FORGIVENESS IS A DEEMED DIVIDEND?

DEFINITION OF 'DISTRIBUTABLE SURPLUS'

The amount taken to be a dividend cannot exceed the company's 'distributable surplus' (s109Y ITAA36) calculated at the end of the year of income. A private company's distributable surplus for a year is worked out using the following formula (s109Y(2)) and as such will not necessarily equal retained earnings:

Distributable surplus = Net assets + Division 7A amounts – Non-commercial loans – Paid up share value – Repayments of non-commercial loans

DEFINITION OF 'NET ASSETS'

'Net assets' means the amount by which the company's assets exceed 'present legal obligations' and the following provisions:

- depreciation
- annual leave and long service leave, and
- amortisation of intellectual property and trademarks.

The value of the provisions is based on the accounting records of the company however the Tax Office may apply a substituted valuation if the assets and liabilities are under or over-valued or if assets are not booked for accounting purposes such as internally generated goodwill (TD 2009/5) and that failure results in a material mis-statement of the net asset position. This may occur, for example, where financial statements record assets at historical cost but market value is significantly greater.

Net assets are determined on an accruals basis. If the company is a small business entity that prepares accounting records on a cash-basis, debtors must be included in the value of net assets (ATO ID 2003/731).

PRESENT LEGAL OBLIGATION

TD 2007/28 confirms that a 'present legal obligation' of a private company for distributable surplus purposes is an immediate obligation binding at law, whether payable and enforceable presently or at a future time. Future provisions are not included in the distributable surplus calculation unless they are one of the accounting provisions specifically set out in the definition of net assets (see above).

Z Coy Pty Ltd (Z Coy) operates a small financial services business and on 30 May 2013 receives a quarterly rates demand from the local council in respect of its business premises. The demand is due for payment by 21 June 2013 but Z Coy does not make payment for a further two weeks. The amount of the rates demand is an immediate obligation binding at law and presently enforceable. It is therefore a present legal obligation for the purposes of determining the distributable surplus at the end of the income year (30 June 2013).

M Coy Pty Ltd (M Coy) operates a small advertising agency and, in most income years, having regard to staff performance and profitability determines to pay bonuses to its employees at 30 June. The bonuses are payable during the next 6 months and are entirely at the discretion of M Coy and do not form part of the employment contract between M Coy and its employees. On 30 June 2013, M Coy determines to pay bonuses totalling $50,000 and in its financial reports for the reporting period ending 30 June 2013, takes this amount up as a 'provision for employee bonuses'. The determination to pay bonuses taken up as a provision by M Coy is not enforceable by legal action either presently or in the future. Payment of the bonuses remains at the discretion of M Coy and therefore the bonuses do not qualify as a present legal obligation for the purposes of determining the distributable surplus at the end of the income year (30 June 2013).

Note: General interest charge is a present legal obligation for each day on which tax that should have been paid remains unpaid.

OBLIGATION TO PAY INCOME TAX

In *FC of T v H* (2010) FCAFC, the Full Federal Court held that an obligation to pay income tax which is to be subsequently ascertained and assessed is a present legal obligation as at the end of the income year in respect of which the income is derived and falls within the meaning for the purposes of s109Y ITAA36. This position is confirmed in TD 2012/10.

Specifically, key comments in TD 2012/10 as to when income tax is a 'present legal obligation' are as follows:

- If a private company has a liability to pay instalments for an income year the *Taxation Administration Act 1953* (TAA), and some or all of an instalment is unpaid as at 30 June then the unpaid amount of that instalment is a 'present legal obligation' for the purposes of the distributable surplus calculation worked out at that time.

- If a private company which is a full self assessment taxpayer has an amount due and payable (after credits for instalments payable for the income year) then this amount is a present legal obligation for the purposes of the distributable surplus calculation worked out at 30 June of the income year which is subject to the deemed assessment. The fact that the tax is due on the day the return is lodged which is after the end of the year of income is not relevant for the purposes of the distributable surplus calculation.

- If the Commissioner issues a private company with an amended assessment for any income year, then amounts payable under the amended assessment will be a present legal obligation for the purposes of the distributable surplus calculation worked out at the end of the income year subject to the amended assessment.

EXAMPLE from TD 2012/10

A private company (A Pty Ltd) has correctly self assessed taxable income for the 2012-13 income year of $100,000 and the fourth quarterly PAYG instalment of $7,500 is unpaid as at the end of the income year (30 June 2013). The first three PAYG instalments totalling $22,500 have already been paid on time. The amount of the unpaid instalment at 30 June 2013 of $7,500 is a present legal obligation of A Pty Ltd for the purposes of the distributable surplus calculation at 30 June 2013.

DEFINITION OF DIVISION 7A AMOUNTS

From 2009-10, the definition of distributable surplus requires 'Division 7A amounts' to be included. Broadly, this is the total amounts of payments (s109C) or debt forgivenesses (s109F) which have occurred during the year. If these amounts are excluded (as is the case with the law which applied to 30 June 2009), the Explanatory Memorandum to the amending Bill states that it may lead to an artificial reduction in the amount of deemed dividends that a private company is considered to have paid during the year.

DEFINITION OF NON-COMMERCIAL LOANS

The distributable surplus is reduced to the extent that there have been amounts that are shown as assets in the company's accounting records at the end of the income year that have been taken under s109D, s109E and former s108 to have been paid as dividends in earlier income years (ie. as a loan or a payment). For 2009-10 income years and beyond, the definition of 'non commercial loans' is extended to include amounts that have been included in the assessable income of a shareholder (or associate), under s109XB (which relates to amounts included in assessable income where a deemed dividend arises by a trustee in favour of a shareholder of a private company with an unpaid present entitlement) (refer below).

Where an amount is included in the noncommercial loan calculation because of s109XB, it will be reduced by the total unfranked parts of any later dividends received by the shareholder (or associate) which may have been set-off under proposed s109ZCA.

Section 109ZCA prevents double taxation by ensuring that the shareholder's assessable income (or associate) does not include the amount of the later divided that is not paid to that entity (to the extent that the amount is franked).

CALCULATING THE DISTRIBUTABLE SURPLUS

Distributable surplus

Bigtop Pty Ltd, a private company, has gross assets of $250,000 and liabilities of $230,000 shown in its balance sheet at 30 June 2014. Bigtop lent $50,000 to a major shareholder on 12 December 2013. The loan was not repaid by the lodgment day and no loan agreement is entered into.

This is the first and only loan to which Division 7A has applied. Bigtop has $8,000 in its share capital account.

The gross assets of $250,000 include a block of land recorded at cost of $100,000. The market value of the property at 30 June 2014 is $150,000.

Company assets: Book value*	*$250,000*
Less company liabilities: Book value*	*($230,000)*
Net assets	*$20,000*
Add increase land to market value*	*$50,000*
Less non-commercial loans (previous Division 7A loans)	*nil*
Less paid-up share value: Paid-up capital	*$8,000*
Distributable surplus	***$62,000***

*The distributable surplus is calculated using the company's accounting records. The relevant values for assets and liabilities are the accounting or book values unless the Commissioner considers that the accounting records significantly vary from the true valuation for those assets, liabilities or provisions. Note also that the Commissioner may take into account assets not booked for accounting purposes such as internally generated goodwill.

The deemed dividend in respect of the $50,000 shareholder loan is $50,000 (being less than the distributable surplus of $62,000).

If a company does not have a distributable surplus in the year that a deemed dividend arises, but has a distributable surplus in a future year, a dividend will not arise in the future year.

A fringe benefit does not arise on a Division 7A loan where the distributable surplus is nil (ATO ID 2011/33).

DIVISION 7A AND COURT ORDERS

A private company is taken to have paid a dividend to a shareholder's spouse when there is a transfer of property made by a private company because of a court order under the Family Law Act (ID 2004/461 and ID 2004/462). A private company can frank a deemed dividend that arises due to a family law obligation. Franking can apply in the same circumstances as capital gains rollover relief applies to spouses.

TR 2014/5 sets out the Commissioner's views in relation to the tax consequences under Division 7A (and the dividend assessing provision of s44 of the ITAA36) of private companies paying money or transferring property in relation to such court orders.

EXCLUDED LOANS AND PAYMENTS

Under Division 7A a number of payments and loans will not be treated as dividends (subdivision D). These exceptions are explained below.

It is important to note that the exceptions usually have to be satisfied by reference to the entire loan, not the distributable surplus. For example, minimum repayments have to be made for the entire loan even if the distributable surplus is less than the amount advanced to a shareholder or associate of the shareholder.

PAYMENTS OR LOANS TO OTHER COMPANIES

A payment or loan by a private company to another company is not treated as a dividend under Division 7A. This exception does not extend to recipient companies acting in the capacity of trustees. However, if the recipient company pays or lends an amount to a shareholder or associate of the paying company (the company that made the original payment or loan) the amount lent back to the shareholder or associate of the paying company is likely to be treated as a dividend, pursuant to interposed entity rules.

PAYMENTS OR LOANS THAT ARE OTHERWISE ASSESSABLE

If a payment or a loan is otherwise included in assessable income by some other provision of the Act, the payment is not treated as a dividend; eg. payment of wages, directors' fees or bonuses would not be caught by Division 7A.

LOANS MADE IN THE ORDINARY COURSE OF BUSINESS ON COMMERCIAL TERMS

If a private company makes loans in the ordinary course of its business, and also makes a loan to its shareholders (or associates) on the same arm's length terms, Division 7A does not treat the loan to the shareholder as a dividend.

LOANS THAT MEET MINIMUM INTEREST RATE AND MAXIMUM TERM CRITERIA (S109N)

Division 7A does not apply to loans under a qualifying agreement that satisfies the following criteria:

- the loan is made under a written agreement. The agreement should be in place at least one day before the lodgment day of the income tax return for the year in which the loan is made. An excluded loan under s109N will be exempt from FBT.
- the rate of interest payable on the loan satisfies the benchmark interest rate requirements in s109N(1)(b).

 As the benchmark interest rate for years subsequent to that in which the loan is made will not be known until just prior to the relevant year of income, no actual figure for the interest rate should be referred to in the loan agreement. Rather, as stated in TD 98/22, the loan agreement should state that the rate of interest payable for future years must equal or exceed that required by para.109N(1)(b) ITAA36.

- the term of the loan does not exceed the maximum permitted term for a loan of that type. If 100% of the value of the loan is secured by a mortgage (over real property in Australia) that has been registered in accordance with a law of a State or Territory and if, when the loan is first made, the market value of the real property (less liabilities secured over the property in priority to the loan) is at least 110% of the amount of the loan, the maximum term is 25 years.

In any other case, the maximum term is seven years. For an unsecured loan the maximum permitted term is seven years.

INTERACTION BETWEEN EXCLUSIONS AND EXCEPTIONS AVAILABLE AND INTERPOSED ENTITY RULES

The rules that exclude certain payments and loans from being treated as a deemed dividend under Subdivision D, do not necessarily prevent Subdivision E (which relates to deeming a dividend where payments and loans are made through interposed entities from applying). This depends on the circumstances of each case (see TD 2012/12).

EXAMPLE from TD 2012/12

A private company with current year profits and a large retained profits reserve (and a large distributable surplus) lends money to a related company that has no current year earnings and several years of carried forward losses (consequently it has no distributable surplus for the purposes of s109Y). The loss company subsequently makes a loan to a shareholder of the profitable company. The shareholder does not make any repayment on the loan during the year of income. There is no commercially justifiable reason to explain why the inter-company loan was made.

It can be concluded that the profitable company made the loan to the loss company solely or mainly as part of an arrangement to make a loan to the shareholder. Accordingly under s109W, the Commissioner determines an amount of a notional loan as if the private company had made a loan to the shareholder at the time the actual loan was made to the shareholder.

Section 109K does not prevent the private company from being taken to have paid a dividend in respect of the notional loan between the private company and the shareholder under s109D because of the loan between the companies.

SECTION 109RB – THE COMMISSIONER'S DISCRETION

Section 109RB ITAA36 allows the Commissioner to either disregard a deemed dividend that arises under Division 7A or allow a private company to frank a deemed dividend.

The Commissioner can only act if the failure to satisfy the requirements of Division 7A is the result of an honest mistake or inadvertent omission by any of the following:

- the recipient (the shareholder or an associate of the shareholder)
- the private company that makes the payment or loan or is taken to pay the dividend under Division 7A, or
- any other entity whose conduct contributed to the deemed dividend arising under Division 7A (in TR 2010/8, the Commissioner indicates that this may include an interposed entity, a shareholder or associate of a shareholder who is not the recipient of what would otherwise constitute a deemed dividend, an officer or employee of the relevant entity, a tax agent).

TR 2010/8 outlines the requirements for the Commissioner's discretion to be exercised under s109RB(1) and the meaning of an honest mistake and inadvertent omission under s109RB(1)(b). PS LA 2011/29 was issued to provide practical guidance.

Whether or not there is an honest mistake or inadvertent omission is an objective question to be determined by reference to all the circumstances surrounding the failure to satisfy the requirements of Division 7A. In practice, the taxpayer will need to demonstrate to the Commissioner that the failure was the result of an honest mistake or inadvertent omission.

MEANING OF AN HONEST MISTAKE AND INADVERTENT ERROR

TR 2010/8 states that these terms take on their ordinary meaning.

The Commissioner notes that there are a wide range of possible mistakes and omissions which may occur, however merely because a mistake or omission is commonly made does not necessarily mean that there has been an honest mistake or inadvertent omission. A mistake or omission can be the result of ignorance of the law. A mistake or omission that is recurring will qualify as an honest mistake or inadvertent omission if it recurs for the same reason and the original mistake or omission qualified as an honest mistake or inadvertent omission.

Typical examples contemplated by the Commissioner include arithmetic errors in calculating minimum repayment amounts and errors arising in the course of conducting business activities.

 Mistake in carrying out activities (TR 2010/8 – paras 32-41)

Jack and Jill are the shareholders and directors of a private company. During the year the company refurbished the company premises including the office. It is Jack and Jill's practice to maintain separate business and private bank accounts and to pay business and private expenses from the appropriate account by cheque or direct debit. Jack and Jill are both signatories on each account and can sign solely. Jill does not take an active role in the company's business but is aware of the need to keep business and personal affairs separate.

One day Jill goes shopping for new household furniture at a furniture store. As she is leaving the house she unwittingly takes the business cheque book with her instead of the personal cheque book. She pays $10,000 for the private furniture using the business cheque book (again without realising her mistake) and writes 'New Furniture – Furniture Store' on the cheque butt but does not otherwise indicate whether the cheque was for business or private purposes. The amount paid for the private furniture was similar to amounts paid for office furniture. Her error goes unnoticed by Jack or by Jill.

The company's income tax return was lodged and the company was taken to have paid a dividend under s109C. During the preparation of the income tax return the company's general ledger entries were reviewed and the error was not discovered. The entry neither appeared unusual or inconsistent with other company transactions in terms of the nature of the transaction and the amount of the transaction.

Soon after the lodgment of the company's income tax return, as a result of a dispute with the supplier of the office furniture, Jack had cause to review the company's records and discovered the error. He took corrective action and repaid the money to the company from his personal bank account.

Jill's error is capable of constituting an honest mistake.

The corrective action taken by Jack is relevant for the purposes of paragraph 109RB(3) (b) when the exercise of the discretion is considered. It is irrelevant for the purposes of subsection 109RB(1).

 Arithmetic error (TR 2010/8 – paras 28-31)

A private company is taken to have paid a dividend to a shareholder because of a minimum yearly repayment shortfall. The shortfall arose because the tax agent had made an error in calculating the minimum yearly repayment for one of the amalgamated loans. No similar errors were made in respect of other amalgamated loans, either in the current year or earlier income years. The error related to the remaining term used in the minimum yearly loan repayment formula. The term used was one year longer than it should have been.

The shareholder had made repayments based on the minimum yearly loan repayment advised by the agent. Both the taxpayer and tax agent were aware of the Division 7A obligations and had attempted to comply. There is no evidence to suggest that the error was anything other than an accidental oversight.

In these circumstances, the arithmetic error is an honest mistake.

FACTORS IN MAKING DECISION

Once it is established that there is an 'honest mistake or inadvertent omission', the Commissioner is then empowered to make a decision. In considering whether to exercise his power in favour of a taxpayer, the Commissioner must have regard to the following:

- the circumstances that led to the mistake or omission which caused the deemed dividend to arise

- the extent to which the relevant taxpayer(s) had acted to try to correct the mistake or omission, and if so how quickly that action was taken after the mistake or omission was identified
- whether Division 7A had operated previously in respect of the relevant taxpayers, and if so, the circumstances in which this occurred, for example, if the Commissioner had previously exercised his power under this provision in relation to the entity that made the mistake or omission, and
- any other matters the Commissioner considers relevant, for example, the quantum of sums involved.

An examination of the circumstances that led to a mistake or omission provides an opportunity to consider both the nature and extent of the mistake or omission. There is a very wide range of possible mistakes or omissions that would result in Division 7A deeming there to be a dividend paid to a taxpayer.

If steps are taken to remedy the mistake or inadvertent omission, the Commissioner may look favourably upon this when deciding whether to exercise his discretion. For example, if the relevant mistake was a failure to enter into a written loan agreement, then the company and its shareholder could enter into a loan agreement that satisfies the requirements of s109N. Or, if the relevant mistake was a failure to pay the full amount of the minimum yearly repayment then the shareholder could repay the outstanding amount, and ensure that the correct amount is repaid in the future. According to the Commissioner *"When deciding whether or not to exercise discretion, one of the factors we consider is the extent to which corrective action has been taken and, if so, how quickly that action was taken. Alternatively, if corrective action has not been fully undertaken prior to the ATO's discretion being sought, we may exercise our discretion subject to the condition that corrective action is taken within a specified time period"*.

DECISION ISSUED

The Commissioner may make a decision subject to specified conditions. This requires that the mistake or omission that gave rise to the failure to satisfy Division 7A be corrected within a specified time period. For example, the Commissioner could require that:

- loan documentation be put in place that meets the criteria in s109N, and/or
- if the minimum yearly repayments have not been made by the due date, that the minimum amounts be paid by a later specified date.

If the conditions are not met then the deemed dividend cannot be disregarded.

The Commissioner may make a decision that the private company can choose to frank the deemed dividend. If the private company does frank the dividend, the private company's franking account will be debited as per item 1 in the table in s205-30 (see 6.800). The Commissioner's discretion to allow dividends to be franked would apply only where the dividend is made to a shareholder, not to an associate of the shareholder. The Commissioner will not be able to make a decision to permit the franking of a deemed dividend that arose before 1 July 2002, the commencement of the simplified imputation system.

6.312   BENCHMARK INTEREST RATES

The applicable benchmark interest rates are as follows.

Benchmark rates					
2003-04 year	6.55%	2007-08 year	8.05%	2012-13 year	7.05%
2004-05 year	7.05%	2008-09 year	9.45%	2013-14 year	6.20%
2005-06 year	7.30%	2009-10 year	5.75%	2014-15 year	5.95%
2005-06 year	7.30%	2010-11 year	7.40%	2015-16 year	5.45%*
2006-07 year	7.55%	2011-12 year	7.80%		

* Based on Reserve Bank of Australia: *Indicator lending rates – F5 (Housing loans; Banks; Variable; Standard)* – June 2015. At the time of writing the ATO has yet to confirm this in a Tax Determination.

6.320   EXCLUDED DEBT FORGIVENESS

Division 7A does not operate to deem a dividend to be paid by a private company in circumstances where that private company forgives a debt owed to it by another company (s109G). However, this exclusion does not apply to a debt owed by a company in the capacity of trustee. This rule now extends to subdivision EA (refer 6.335 below).

Another exclusion from Division 7A applies where a debt is forgiven because the debtor becomes a bankrupt, or because of Part X of the *Bankruptcy Act 1966* (Cth). Technically, that exclusion should really refer to the *Bankruptcy Act 1997*, as the 1966 Act has been replaced by that subsequent Act.

In addition, a private company is not taken under s109F to pay a dividend at the end of a year of income if the forgiven debt was a loan that was deemed to be a dividend under the Division 7A loans rules, under the amalgamated loan rules or under s108 ITAA36.

A further exclusion from the operation of Division 7A applies where the Commissioner is satisfied that:

- the debt was forgiven because payment of the debt would have caused the shareholder undue hardship, and
- when the shareholder incurred the debt, the shareholder had the capacity to pay the debt, and
- the shareholder lost the ability to pay the debt in the foreseeable future as a result of circumstances beyond the shareholder's control (s109Q).

The Commissioner may disregard a deemed dividend where the recipient of a private company loan (shareholder or associate) was unable to make the minimum yearly repayments because of circumstances beyond their control (s109RD). The Commissioner will specify a later time by which the minimum yearly repayments must be made if the Commissioner disregards the deemed dividend. Section 109RD does not need to consider whether the recipient will suffer undue hardship which is covered by s109Q.

6.325 LOANS THROUGH INTERPOSED ENTITIES – TRACING RULES

Tracing rules can apply where it is reasonable to conclude that there is an arrangement under which one or more entities have been interposed between the private company and the associated entity. Tracing rules can have application where for example a private company guarantees a loan made by an interposed entity to an associated entity.

6.330 AMALGAMATED LOANS

Loans are brought together to form a single 'amalgamated loan' at the end of the year if the loans:

- are not fully repaid by due date of lodgment of the income tax return
- have the same maximum term (for the purposes of s109N – see 6.310), and
- would be deemed under the normal operative rule to be dividends paid by a private company, apart from the fact that they are made under a loan agreement complying with minimum interest rate and maximum term criteria.

It should also be noted that the term of an amalgamated loan is the longest term of any loan (constituent loan) that comprises part of the amalgamated loan. A single loan may also constitute an amalgamated loan and the following applies equally if one loan only was made by the company to a shareholder (or associate) in a year of income.

Having identified loans that comprise an amalgamated loan, it is then necessary in subsequent years (not the year in which the loan was taken out) to make minimum yearly repayments in respect of the amalgamated loan to avoid the deeming of a dividend.

The formula for calculating the required minimum repayment in respect of an amalgamated loan in years subsequent to the year in which the loan was first made is as follows:

$$\frac{\text{Amount of the loan not repaid by the end of the previous year of income} \times \text{Current year's benchmark interest rate}}{1 - \frac{1}{(1 + \text{Current year's benchmark interest rate})^{\text{Remaining term}}}}$$

Where:

- **Current year's benchmark interest rate** is the benchmark interest rate for the year of income for which the minimum yearly repayment is being worked out
- **Remaining term** is the difference between:
  - the number of years in the longest term of any of the constituent loans that the amalgamated loan takes account of, and
  - the number of years between the end of the private company's year of income in which the loan was made and the end of the private company's year of income before the year of income for which the minimum yearly repayment is being worked out,

rounded up to the next higher whole number if the difference is not already a whole number.

Where the minimum annual repayment is not made and the income year is the income year in which 1 July 2006 occurred or a later year, the deemed dividend is the unpaid repayment amount for that year, subject to the company's distributable surplus.

For the purposes of Division 7A, a repayment to the private company in relation to a constituent loan in a year of income after the one in which the constituent loan was made, is taken to be a repayment in relation to the amalgamated loan that takes account of the constituent loan.

The amount of an amalgamated loan repaid by the end of a year of income is to be calculated on the basis that interest is payable on the balance of the loan from time to time in a year of income at a rate equal to the benchmark interest rate for the year of income. This determines the interest component of each instalment. The balance of all instalments constitute the total repayment for the relevant year of income.

 It should be noted that the amalgamated loan will not give rise to a dividend for that year if:

- *the minimum yearly repayment is not made, and*
- *the shareholder/associate satisfies the Commissioner that:*
  - *the amount paid was less than the requisite amount because of circumstances beyond its control, and*
  - *that treating the loan as a dividend would cause undue hardship (refer s109Q or s109RD)where the shareholder was unable to make the minimum repayment due to circumstances beyond their control.*

Where a shortfall minimum yearly repayment gives rise to a deemed dividend under s109E ITAA36, a deemed dividend does not also arise under s109D ITAA36 (see 6.310 above) in respect of the proportion of the shortfall comprising unpaid interest (ATO ID 2011/8).

6.335   LOANS, PAYMENTS AND DEBTS FORGIVEN BY A TRUST – CORPORATE BENEFICIARY – SUBDIVISION EA

Broadly, Subdivision EA applies where a trust has an unpaid present entitlement owed to a private company beneficiary, and the trust:

- makes a loan to a shareholder (or associate) of the private company on or after 12 December 2002
- pays an amount to a shareholder (or associate) of the private company on or after 12 December 2002 in reduction of a present entitlement to net income due to the shareholder (or associate) that is wholly or partly attributable to an unrealised gain, or
- forgives all or part of a debt owed by a shareholder (or associate) of the private company to the trustee, on or after 12 December 2002.

The Subdivision will apply where any of the transactions described above occur on or after 19 February 2004, if:

- a private company beneficiary becomes presently entitled to net income of a trust estate after the relevant transaction occurs
- the present entitlement arises prior to the 'lodgment day' for the trust income tax return for the particular year, and

- all of the present entitlement has not been paid to the private company by the lodgment day.

From 19 February 2004, the unpaid present entitlement may arise before or after the loan, payment or debt forgiveness occurs. For exclusions see 6.340.

IMPLICATIONS

The effect of Subdivision EA will be to treat an amount as if it were an unfranked dividend and assessable income in the hands of the shareholder or associate of the private company beneficiary unless any of the exclusions apply.

The amount to be included as a dividend will be limited to the lowest of:

- the distributable surplus of the private company beneficiary
- the actual amount of the loan, payment or debt forgiveness, and
- the unpaid present entitlement owing to the private company beneficiary.

INTERPOSED ENTITIES SUBJECT TO SUBDIVISION EA – S109XF AND S109XG

From 2009-10, where there are entities interposed between the corporate beneficiary with an unpaid present entitlement and the trust making the distribution, subdivision EA will continue to apply in those circumstances. Prior to this, the operation of Subdivision EA may be circumvented by interposing an entity (whether company or trust).

The operation of the provisions may be demonstrated diagrammatically as follows:

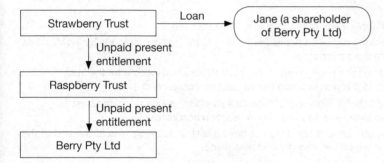

The provisions would enable the Commissioner to deem the loan to Jane as being subject to Subdivision EA.

Further, where a corporate beneficiary has a present entitlement to an amount from the net income of the trust estate and to the extent that an entity is interposed between the trust and the shareholder of a private company (or their associate), the trust will be treated as having directly paid or loaned the amount to that shareholder (or associate) for the purposes of Subdivision EA. This is achieved if:

- the trust pays (s109XF) or loans (s109XG) an amount to the interposed entity, and
- a reasonable person would conclude that the trustee made the payment or loan solely or mainly as part of an arrangement involving the target entity (ie. shareholder).

The rules state the Commissioner will be responsible for determining the amount of payment or loan from the trust to the shareholder (or associate) as the amount received may not be the same amount paid by the trustee.

The provisions will operate regardless of the number of entities interposed between the trust making the payment or loan and the shareholder (or associate) of the private company.

ENTITLEMENTS TO TRUST INCOME THROUGH INTERPOSED TRUSTS – S109XI

Subdivision EA does not apply in all circumstances where there is an unpaid present entitlement. To enable Subdivision EA to apply to a payment, loan or debt forgiveness made, s109XI of Subdivision EB, which concerns entitlements to trust income through interposed trusts, provides that the private company is taken to be or to become entitled to an amount from the net income of the 'Target Trust' provided specified conditions are satisfied.

Specifically, a private company is taken to be or to become entitled to an amount from the net income of a trust estate (the target trust) if:

- the company is or becomes presently entitled to an amount from the net income of another trust estate (the first interposed trust) that is interposed between the target trust and the company, and

- a reasonable person would conclude (having regard to all the circumstances) that the company is or becomes so entitled solely or mainly as part of an arrangement involving an entitlement to an amount from the target trust, and

- either:
  (i) the first interposed trust is or becomes presently entitled to an amount from the net income of the target trust, or
  (ii) another trust interposed between the target trust and the company is or becomes presently entitled to an amount from the net income of the target trust.

It does not matter whether the company became presently entitled to the same amount as the amount to which the interposed trust became entitled (s109XI(2)). The amount of the entitlement is determined by the Commissioner (s109XI(4)). TD 2011/15 outlines the relevant factors the Commissioner will consider in determining the amount of any deemed entitlement.

6.340   EXCLUSIONS

GENERAL EXCLUSIONS

The provisions will not apply if any of the following occurs:

a) the whole of the unpaid present entitlement owing to the private company by the trust has been paid before the earlier of:
   - the due date for the lodgment of the trustee's return of income for the trust applicable to the year in which the transaction occurs, and
   - the actual date for lodgment of the trustee's return of income for the trust applicable to the year in which the transaction occurs, or

b) the private company beneficiary does not have a distributable surplus at the end of the year of income in which the transaction takes place.

Exclusions relating to loans

Loan transactions will not be subject to the effect of the provisions if either of the following occurs:

a) the loan is repaid by the shareholder or associate before the earlier of:
   - the due date for lodgment of the trustee's return of income for the trust applicable to the year in which the loan occurs, or
   - the actual lodgment date

b) a written loan agreement is made on Division 7A terms in relation to the loan between the trust and the shareholder or associate of the private company before the earlier of the times mentioned in a) above and the minimum yearly repayments are made to the trust by the shareholder from the income year after the income year in which the loan is made.

 There does not need to be a written agreement in place at the time of the loan but it must be in place before the earlier of the due date for lodgment and the date of the lodgment of the trust's tax return for the income year in which the loan is made.

NOTE: Under changes to s109XC(8), from 2009-10, a trust withholding an amount from an employee's salary or bonus (under the PAYG withholding regime) and offsetting these amounts against the loan can be a repayment, in relation to a loan. Prior to this change, the rule applied to companies only (s109R(3)).

EXCLUSIONS RELATING TO PAYMENTS

Payment transactions caught by Division 7A will not apply if any of the following occurs:

a) the unrealised gain has been or will be included in the assessable income of the trust in:
- a year of income before the year in which the actual payment was made
- the year of income in which the actual payment was made, or
- the year of income following the year in which the payment was made. The intention is to catch any payment of an unpaid present entitlement that is attributable to long term unrealised gains

b) the payment discharges a pecuniary obligation of the trust

c) the payment of the unpaid present entitlement is attributable to a realised gain

d) the payment is a distribution of realised income or a realised gain that is sheltered from tax by tax concessions such as small business CGT concessions, or

e) the payment is of an amount that was initially gifted to a trust or previously taxed to the trust

EXCLUSIONS RELATING TO DEBT FORGIVENESS

From 2009-10, s109XD provides that where a loan from a trust has previously been included in the shareholder or associate's assessable income (under s109XB) is subsequently forgiven, then the shareholder (or their associate) would not be subject to subdivision EA in respect of the forgiveness.

6.345 ACTION LIST

1. Identify pre-4 December 1997 loans

Pre-4 December 1997 loans should be identified. This may involve ruling the books off at 3 December 1997 and running two employee loan accounts after that date.

2. Don't vary pre-4 December 1997 loans

Pre-4 December 1997 loans (old loans) should not be varied by increasing the term of the loan or the amount of the loan. If old loans are varied, they become subject to the post-3 December 1997 rules and are effectively converted into post-3 December 1997 loans (Division 7A loans).

3. Repay post-3 December 1997 loans first

Post-3 December 1997 loans should usually be repaid in preference to old loans (pre-4 December 1997 loans) as the post-3 December 1997 rules are more easily triggered than the rules in the former s108 (see 6.350).

4. Draw up loan documentation complying with the Division 7A qualifying loan rules

If loans cannot be repaid in full prior to the year end or prior to the lodgment date of the tax return, then, to the extent that there is a distributable surplus, it will usually be necessary to take the following steps to avoid the loan being treated as a deemed unfranked dividend:

- draft a written agreement at least one day before the lodgment date of the income tax return for the year in which the loan was made which specifies:
  - the maximum term (seven years (unsecured) or 25 years (secured)), and
  - the minimum benchmark interest rate to be paid on the loan, and
- make minimum repayments in years after the loan is drawn down (and repay the full amount of the loan within the maximum term of the loan).

 Company minutes setting out the term of and interest rate applying to a loan would not satisfy the requirement of a written loan agreement.

5. Identify unpaid present entitlements owed by a trust to a corporate beneficiary

Pre- and post-16 December 2009 UPEs should be identified and consideration given as to whether they constitute a 'loan' for Division 7A purposes (see 6.310).

- For pre-16 December 2009 loans (Section two loans)
  - review trust deed to ensure that there are no clauses which may themselves cause UPEs to be loans or documentation which may construe a loan

- review journal entries and financial accounts of the trust and corporate beneficiary to determine whether UPEs have been incorrectly described as loans
- For post-16 December 2009 loans (Section three loans)
  - consider implications of sub-trust arrangement for existing UPEs (using relevant options) (see 6.310)
  - consider converting a UPE to a loan which satisfies a s109N loan agreement

6.347   BOARD OF TAXATION REVIEW

In 2012, the Board of Taxation was tasked by the government to undertake a post-implementation review of Division 7A since its introduction in 1997. The Board examined whether Division 7A achieves its policy intent, examine problems associated with its current operation and to the extent that there are problems, recommend options for resolution. The Board has completed its post-implementation review of Division 7A and provided its report to the government on 12 November 2014. This report was released on 4 June 2015.

On 25 March 2014, the Board of Taxation released for consultation a discussion paper on the review. The comments below are about this discussion paper.

KEY OBSERVATIONS BY THE BOARD

In the discussion paper, the Board has made some preliminary observations about the current policy framework in which Division 7A operates, including its interactions with other areas of the tax law.

The Board's main observation is that, in its current form, Division 7A fails in achieving its policy objectives. Moreover, the Board has found that Division 7A can be a significant source of compliance costs for businesses, even for those that operate in accordance with the policy intent of the provisions.

In the discussion paper, the Board considers that protecting the progressivity of the tax system should not be at the expense of impeding the ability of businesses to reinvest their income as working capital. Facilitating this reinvestment supports improved productivity and entrepreneurial growth. By contrast, the private use of business income serves a different purpose, namely, the enjoyment and accumulation of private wealth, in which case the progressivity of the personal income tax system needs to be preserved.

POTENTIAL REFORM MODELS

The Board has developed a policy framework relevant to private business that is designed to provide an appropriate balance between these competing aims. It is designed to assist in evaluating the existing regime and in developing and evaluating possible reform models.

In doing so it has outlined four goals:

- It should ensure that the private use of company profits attracts tax at the user's progressive personal income tax rate.
- It should remove impediments to the reinvestment of business income as working capital.
- It should maximise simplicity by reducing the compliance burden on business and the administrative burden on the Commissioner and other stakeholders.
- It should not advantage the accumulation of passive investments over the reinvestment of business profits in active business activities.

The five proposed reforms from the Board are summarised in the following table:

Division 7A: Proposed reforms		
Reform	**From:**	**To:**
1. A unified set of rules based on the principle of transfers of value	A complex, unpredictable system that lacks a coherent set of guiding principles and leads to inconsistent treatment of cash based transactions (loans, payments, debt forgiveness) and transactions involving the use of company assets.	A single set of common principles for dealing with loans, payments, debt forgiveness and use of company assets.
2. A better targeted framework for calculating a company's profits	A system in which the rules for calculating company profits (or distributable surplus) are complex and costly (requiring regular revaluations of assets, formally or informally, where informal valuations may lead to disputes about the values) and can lead to either double taxation or an inappropriate failure to tax certain transactions. Under the current rules, distributable surplus is based on the values of assets. Valuing assets formally can involve significant costs to small businesses while informal valuations provide less certainty.	A simpler system in which: asset revaluations will not be required and unrealised profits will not be taken to be distributed because company assets have been used, and company profits will be tested each year to appropriately tax all transactions.
3. A simpler, more flexible and better targeted system of 'complying loans'	A system that is inflexible because it requires the principal on the loan to be repaid in equal annual instalments over the life of the loan. A system that requires loan terms that are either too restrictive (that is, 7-year terms for unsecured loans) or too generous (25 year terms for loans secured by real property).	A single 10 year loan period with more flexible requirements for the repayment of principal.
4. Greater flexibility for trusts that reinvest unpaid present entitlements (UPEs) as working capital	A system that imposes significant complexity where trusts retain funds distributed to companies as working capital (including adhering to ATO 'safe harbour' arrangements).	A 'tick the box' regime that will provide trading trusts with a simple option to retain funds that have been taxed at the corporate rate, providing important working capital. As a trade-off, trading trusts that make this election will be denied the CGT discount (like companies) except in relation to goodwill. A system that removes the uncertainty on the treatment of unpaid present entitlements (UPEs) more generally by clarifying that all UPEs are loans for Division 7A purposes.
5. A self correcting mechanism	A complex area of the tax law system that brings substantial compliance and administrative costs and where there is no ability for taxpayers to self correct mistakes and omissions and which require the exercise of the Commissioner's discretion in order to avoid a deemed dividend.	A self correction mechanism which would enable taxpayers to put in place complying loan agreements, reduce compliance and administrative costs and substantially reduce the number of cases that would require a decision by the Commissioner.

6.350   LOANS: PRE-DECEMBER 1997

Section 108 was the predecessor of Division 7A dealing with payments and loans made before 4 December 1997. If any pre-4 December 1997 loans are varied after that date, then Division 7A has application.

Section 108 has been repealed effective from 1 July 2006. However, from 4 December 1997, the provisions of Division 7A took priority over s108, leaving the section with limited application.

Section 108 dividends that have arisen in prior years are still to be taken into account in determining whether a private company has a distributable surplus under s109Y, if the actual loan that triggered the dividend is in the accounts of the company.

LOANS MADE PRE-DIVISION 7A STATUTE BARRED

Loans made to shareholders pre-Division 7A may have become unrecoverable because of the operation of State laws commonly referred to as 'the statute of limitations'.

Because of these State laws, which vary from State to State, loans may become statute barred and unrecoverable legally as the time frame within which a creditor is entitled to sue for recovery of the debt ends by the operation of a statute of limitations.

These legally unrecoverable pre-Division 7A loans could be treated as forgiven debts under Division 7A and treated as deemed dividends under such provisions.

In Practice Statement PS LA 2006/2 (GA) the Tax Office has adopted the position that statute barred private company and trustee loans made prior to the enactment of Division 7A will not be treated as giving rise to a deemed dividend under Division 7A. The Tax Office will take no active compliance action that would treat pre-4 December 1997 loans that become statute barred after this date as deemed dividends under Division 7A.

6.400   CARRY FORWARD LOSSES

A company can only deduct a tax loss from an earlier income year if it satisfies the Continuity of Ownership Test (COT), or failing that test, it satisfies the Same Business Test (SBT). Any net exempt income reduces the loss amount claimable. The rules that apply for individuals and trusts are set out at 12.950 and 7.200.

Losses incurred before 1 July 1989 could only be carried forward for seven years and are therefore now lost. Carried forward capital losses can only be offset against capital gains (see from 12.000). There is no distinction between a foreign loss and a domestic loss for the purpose of calculating taxable income. Since 2008-09, foreign losses are no longer quarantined from domestic income or from other foreign losses of a different class. A taxpayer is not required to elect to apply domestic losses against foreign income. (A transitional rule applies to foreign losses existing at 1 July 2008 up to 2012-13.)

The company tax loss rules are contained in Division 165 of the ITAA97. Less stringent modified rules apply to 'widely held companies' (see Division 166).

NOTE: In December 2013 the government committed to proceeding with changes proposed by the previous government in the 2007-08 Federal Budget. These changes are intended to improve the operation of the tax loss rules in particular circumstances (eg. where a company has non-standard classes of shares or when it joins a consolidated group).

6.405   LOSS CARRY BACK TAX OFFSET

In the 2012-13 year companies (and entities taxed like companies eg. public trading trusts and corporate limited partnerships) were able to carry back tax losses to offset profits from the 2011-12 year, so as to provide a refund of tax previously paid.

This measure has been repealed and so only applies for losses made in the 2012-13 year.

See *Tax Summary 2014 & 2015* for further information.

6.410 CONTINUITY OF OWNERSHIP TEST

To satisfy the Continuity of Ownership Test (COT), a company must be able to show that throughout the 'ownership test period' there has been a continuity of beneficial ownership of shares carrying the following rights:

- the right to exercise more than 50% of the voting power (s165-12(2))
- the right to receive more than 50% of the company's dividends (s165-12(3)), and
- the right to receive more than 50% of any capital distributions (s165-12(4)).

The COT must be satisfied in relation to each above category of ownership right but the persons who own the rights in each category may be different.

For each category of ownership right, COT must be applied under a 'primary test' or an 'alternative test'. The primary test deals with direct beneficial ownership of shares by natural persons (ie. no tracing through interposed entities is required). The alternative test applies where there is an indirect beneficial ownership of shares through interposed entities such that tracing is required. The ownership test period is the period from the start of the loss year to the end of the income year in which the loss is recouped.

Ownership rights in relation to voting power attaching to an individual's share in a company may only be taken into account if the individual owns exactly the same share throughout the relevant ownership test period (referred to as the 'same share test'). A share split or share consolidation will count as the same shares for the COT, provided that the same person remains the beneficial owner of the shares throughout the ownership period.

At the beginning of the loss year (Year 1) the shares in Company X were owned by individuals as follows: A – 12%, B – 40%, and C – 48%.

In Year 3, Company X wishes to utilise tax losses. At all times in Year 3 and during the intervening period (Year 2) the shares were beneficially owned as follows: A – 64%, B – 23%, and C – 13%.

As only the same shares held by the same person can count towards satisfying the COT, the analysis in the table below shows that the test is not satisfied, unless the saving rule applies (see below).

Shareholder	% of shares at start of test period	% of shares at end of test period	% of shares that can count
A	12	64	12
B	40	23	23
C	48	13	13
	100	100	48

Assume the same facts as in example 1, except that in Year 3 the shares in Company X are beneficially owned as follows: A – 50%, B – 25% and C – 25%.

In this case the COT is satisfied as illustrated in the table below.

Shareholder	% of shares at start of test period	% of shares at end of test period	% of shares that can count
A	12	50	12
B	40	25	25
C	48	25	25
	100	100	62

Assume the same facts as in example 1, except that in Year 3 the shares in Company X are beneficially owned by: A – 40% and BC Pty Ltd – 60%. The shareholders in BC Pty Ltd are B – 50% and C – 50%.

In this case, because there is an interposed company, the alternative test would apply. In this case the tax loss carried forward is deductible because after tracing through the shareholders of BC Pty Ltd, its individual shareholders B and C together, hold more than 50% of the same underlying rights in Company X at all times during the ownership period.

THE 'SAVINGS' RULE

The loss rules contain saving provisions that may apply where a company fails the COT but retains the same majority ownership throughout the relevant test period (ie. the same share test is not met). This situation could occur where the company issues new shares to existing shareholders or the majority shareholders no longer hold direct or indirect equity interests in the same way.

Under the saving rule, the company will be treated as having satisfied the COT if:

- the company would have satisfied the COT apart from the operation of the same share or interest rule, and

- during the test period, the company proves that less than 50% of the loss or bad debt is reflected elsewhere in deductions, capital losses or reduced assessable income arising from the disposal of direct or indirect equity interests in the company (see s165-12(7)).

Limits apply to the saving rule if 50% or more loss duplication resulting from a CGT event (such as a disposal) happens to any equity interest during the ownership test period.

At the beginning of the loss year (Year 1) A owns 70 shares (70%) and B owns 30 shares (30%) in AB Company. In Year 2 the company issues one new share for each existing share. In Year 3 the company wishes to utilise the tax loss from Year 1. Except for the saving rule, AB Company would not pass the continuity of ownership test as only 50% of the shares on issue are the same shares held by the same persons throughout the ownership period and the COT test requires more than 50%. However, in this case the saving rule will apply because A still holds a 70% interest in the company and B still holds a 30% interest, so the continuity of ownership test would have been passed except for the same share or interest rule and there has not been any loss duplication during the period as neither A nor B have sold any of their original shares.

SHARES HELD BY A DISCRETIONARY TRUST

It is not possible to trace through a discretionary trust to determine the underlying beneficial owner of the shares held by the trust as potential beneficiaries of a discretionary trust do not have any interest in the trust assets. Therefore, without any specific rules, a company cannot satisfy the COT where 50% or more of its shares are held by a discretionary trust. In these circumstances, specific rules allowing COT to be satisfied apply where:

- a trust has made a family trust election, or
- Division 165-F applies.

Where a trust has made a family trust election, the trustee of the trust is taken to be the beneficial owner of the shares for the purposes of the COT. A change in trustee does not affect this treatment.

Where a discretionary trust has not made a family trust election, Division 165-F provides an alternative tracing test for COT purposes. The alternative test broadly requires the discretionary trust to have held a fixed entitlement to 50% or more of the company's income or capital for the duration of the ownership test period and for the discretionary trust to have passed the non-fixed trust loss test rules if the loss had been incurred by the discretionary trust (see 6.900).

DEATH OF A SHAREHOLDER

Section 165-205 provides that shares a person owned beneficially at the time of their death are taken to continue to be owned by that person after they die so long as the shares are owned:

- by the trustee of the deceased person's estate, or
- beneficially by someone who received them as a beneficiary of the estate.

Until recently, this concessional treatment for deceased estates only applies in respect of ownership, not voting power and control. In 2014 this was amended so that, from the 1997-98 year, the deceased individual is considered to retain all voting power, dividend entitlements and capital distributions so long as the shares are owned by either the trustee of the deceased person's estate or by a beneficiary of the estate.

See ATO ID 2003/335 (now withdrawn as it is a straightforward application of the law) for an example of a transfer of 50% of the shares to a beneficiary of a trust estate.

An individual (A) held two of the four shares on issue in a loss company, while A's son B and another person C each held one share. A died and his 50% shareholding was subsequently transferred by the trustee of the estate to his son (B) in his capacity as a beneficiary of A's estate. B continues to hold his one share and A's two shares at all times between A's death and the company recouping its prior year losses.

In this example, s165-205(b) provides that the shares beneficially owned by A at the time of his death are taken to continue to be owned by A after his death whilst the shares continue to be owned by someone who received them as a beneficiary of A's estate.

As B continues to own A's shares as a beneficiary of A's estate, s165-205(b) provides that the deceased (A) will be taken to continue to be the beneficial owner of that 50% shareholding in the loss company which, together with the original 25% shareholding of his son (B) enables the company to satisfy the continuity of ownership test in Division 165. If B were to dispose of the shares that he received from his father's estate before the company recouped its losses then the continuity of ownership test would be failed. The continuity of ownership test would also be failed if B transferred the shares to another beneficiary of A's estate.

 Assume the same facts in the example above, except that C is also a beneficiary of A's estate. B inherits all of A's shares, but before the company recoups its losses B disposes of the shares inherited from A to C.

Upon disposal of the shares of beneficiary B to fellow beneficiary C, the necessary connection of continuing beneficial ownership of the shares in the loss company with someone who received them as a beneficiary of A's estate ceased to exist. The additional shares acquired by beneficiary C from B cannot be taken to have been received by C in their capacity as a beneficiary of A's estate, so the requirement of s165-205(b) is not met in respect of 50% of the shares in the loss company and therefore, the conditions in Division 165 are not satisfied.

FAMILY COURT ORDER

Where, during the ownership test period, shares carrying 50% of the voting, dividend, and capital rights in the company are transferred from one shareholder to another pursuant to an order of the Family Court, the company will not be able to satisfy the continuity of ownership test. There is no provision in the Act that enables this position to be considered differently to the normal disposal of shares.

6.420 'MODIFIED CONTINUITY OF OWNERSHIP TEST' FOR WIDELY HELD COMPANIES

Modified COT rules apply to 'widely held companies' and 'eligible Division 166 companies' with losses incurred on or after 1 July 2002. These modified rules are necessary because without them widely held companies would have difficulty tracing through the layers of shareholders to determine the ultimate beneficial owners of the shares that have the voting power and rights to dividend and capital distributions. The rules make it unnecessary to trace the ultimate owners of shares held by certain intermediaries and small shareholdings.

MEANING OF WIDELY HELD COMPANY

Broadly, a company is widely held if it is listed on an approved stock exchange or if it has more than 50 members, unless:

- at any time during the year, 20 or fewer people hold or have the right to acquire or become the holder of shares representing 75% or more of the value of the shares in the company, other than shares entitled to a fixed rate of dividend only
- at any time during the income year, 20 or fewer people are capable of exercising 75% or more of the voting power in the company
- in that year, 20 or fewer people receive 75% or more of any dividend paid by the company, or
- the company did not pay a dividend in that year, but the Commissioner of Taxation is of the opinion that, if a dividend had been paid by the company at any time during the income year, 20 or fewer people would have received 75% or more of that dividend.

MEANING OF ELIGIBLE DIVISION 166 COMPANY

A company is an 'eligible Division 166 company' if more than 50% of the voting power, rights to dividends or rights to capital distributions are held by one or more:

- 'widely held' companies (defined above)
- superannuation funds
- approved deposit funds
- special companies
- managed investment schemes
- entities that are prescribed under the tracing rule that deems entities to be beneficial owners
- non-profit companies, or
- charitable institutions, charitable funds or any other kind of charitable bodies.

MODIFICATIONS TO CONTINUITY OF OWNERSHIP TEST

Under the modified rules widely held companies and eligible Division 166 companies are only required to test for continuity of ownership at the start of the test period and at the end of each income year until the end of the income year in which the loss is recouped, rather than continuously as is required for other companies. There is also no requirement to test for continuity of ownership at times of abnormal trading, unless there is a 'corporate change'. If there is a known change of ownership, which may arise from take-over or a major share issue, then the COT may be failed.

Under the new modified COT tracing rules that apply to widely held companies:

- a direct stake of less than 10% is attributed to a single notional entity
- an indirect stake of less than 10% is attributed to the top interposed entity (ie. the entity in which the stakeholder with a less than 10% interest has a direct investment)
- a stake of between 10% and 50% (inclusive) held by a widely held company is attributed to the widely held company as an ultimate owner
- a stake held by an entity deemed to be a beneficial owner (a superannuation fund, approved deposit fund or managed investment scheme) is generally attributed to that entity as an ultimate owner
- an indirect stake held by way of bearer shares in a foreign listed company is attributed to a single notional entity in certain circumstances, and
- an indirect stake held by a depository entity through shares in a foreign listed company is attributed to the depository entity as an ultimate owner in certain circumstances.

The tracing rules are subject to an ordering rule, a no detriment rule and various integrity rules.

6.430   SAME BUSINESS TEST

If a company fails the COT (because of a change in ownership) it may still deduct a tax loss from an earlier income year if it satisfies the Same Business Test (SBT).

The SBT in s165-13 is satisfied where the company carries on the same business throughout the year in which the loss is deducted as it did immediately before the change in majority ownership occurred, and in all intervening years.

The SBT consists of three elements and all three must be satisfied in order to satisfy the SBT. The tests are:

1. The same business test – the company must carry on the same business that it carried on immediately before the SBT test time (ie. when COT was breached).

2. The new business test – the company must not derive assessable income from carrying on a business of a kind that it did not carry on before the SBT test time.

3. The new transaction test – the company must not derive assessable income, in the course of its business operations, from a transaction of a kind that it had not entered into before the SBT test time.

4. The Commissioner interprets the requirements of the SBT strictly. Taxation Ruling TR 1999/9 details the Commissioner's position on applying the SBT. In the case of a consolidated group, the head company must show that the one overall business carried on by the head company, was the same one overall business as carried on by the head company immediately before the test time (TR 2007/2).

The SBT can apply to a foreign resident company which carries on business both in and out of Australia (ATO ID 2006/258).

Useful same business test examples are contained in TR 1999/9 at paras 107-113.

6.440 TAX LOSSES AND FRANKING OFFSETS

Companies are not entitled to a refund of franking tax offsets (s67-25). It follows that franking tax offsets would be wasted where current year or prior year losses are offset against franked dividends if special rules relating to current year and prior year losses did not apply to companies.

Section 36-17 provides that companies are able to choose the amount of prior year losses they wish to deduct, after first having offset losses against net exempt income. There are however, the following restrictions on the amount of prior year tax losses that a company can choose to deduct:

- a company must choose not to use any of its prior year tax losses if it has excess franking tax offsets in the current year, and
- a company cannot choose to use an amount of prior year tax losses that would create excess franking tax offsets in the current year.

These are anti-avoidance rules to stop a company from utilising prior year losses and then creating current year losses by converting excess franking tax offsets into an equivalent tax loss (see below). If this were allowed, this would have the effect of 'refreshing' the losses.

CALCULATING EXCESS FRANKING OFFSETS

Step 1: Firstly, calculate the amount of franking tax offsets to which the entity is entitled (step 1).

Step 2: Secondly, calculate the amount of income tax payable. In this calculation:

- ignore the amount of franking tax offsets calculated in the step 1 as well as tax offsets subject to the refundable tax offset rules (Division 67), the carry forward tax offset rules (Division 65) and any tax offset arising from franking deficit tax liabilities (s205-70), and
- take into account all other tax offsets, if any.

If the amount from step 1 exceeds the amount from step 2, the excess is the amount of excess franking offsets.

CONVERTING THE EXCESS FRANKING OFFSET INTO A TAX LOSS

The method statement in Subdivision 36-C provides the steps to be used to convert the excess franking tax offsets into a tax loss. The amount of excess franking offset is converted into an equivalent amount of tax loss (by dividing the amount by the corporate tax rate). This tax loss needs to be added to any tax loss otherwise calculated for the income year and the aggregate amount treated as the tax loss for the income year (known as a loss year). The method statement ensures the aggregate amount of tax loss has been properly reduced by any amount of net exempt income for the income year.

XYZ Ltd has:

- *assessable income of $200 (being a fully franked dividend of $140 and the franking credit of $60)*
- *allowable deductions of $400, and*
- *net exempt income of $80.*

XYZ Ltd calculates its section 36-10 tax loss as $120 (ie. $400 – $200 – $80) and its excess franking offset amount under subsection 36-55(1) as $60.

Applying the method statement

- **Step 1:** *Work out the amount that would have been the entity's tax loss for tax year, ignoring net exempt income. Ignoring net exempt income, the tax loss of XYZ Ltd would be $200 (ie. $400 – $200).*
- **Step 2:** *Divide the amount of excess franking offsets by the corporate tax rate ie. $60 divided by 30% = $200*
- **Step 3:** *Add the result of Step 1 and 2 together ie. $200 + $200 = $400*
- **Step 4:** *Reduce the result of Step 3 by any net exempt income ie. $400 – $80 = $320. This is the amount of the company's tax loss for that year.*

6.450   UNREALISED LOSS RULES – DIVISION 165-CC

The unrealised loss rules in Division 165-CC are intended to prevent the multiplication of losses at the company and shareholder level where there has been a change in ownership of the company. The unrealised loss rules apply to disallow a deduction for a tax loss, or other deduction such as a balancing adjustment or a bad debt, or a capital loss where:

- a company has had a change in ownership (a changeover time)
- the company has an unrealised net loss at the changeover time
- the company is later entitled to a deduction, or makes a capital loss, in respect of:
  - a CGT event happening to a CGT asset held at the changeover time, or
  - trading stock, and
- the company does not satisfy the maximum net asset value test in the CGT small business concessions.

Where the rules apply, a company is required to determine the extent of its unrealised net loss at the changeover time and when it later disposes of the CGT asset or trading stock and realises the loss, the loss deduction or capital loss can only be claimed if the company satisfies the SBT. Section 165-115E sets out two method statements for calculating a company's unrealised net loss at a changeover time under:

- an asset by asset basis, or
- a global basis.

An Australian resident company undergoes a substantial ownership change as at 1 December 2013. At that time it must calculate its unrealised net loss.

Asset	Tax value	Calculation	Market value	Notional gain/loss
Business premises	$5 mil	Reduced cost base	$2 mil	($3 mil capital loss)
Shares in listed cos	$7 mil	Indexed cost base	$8 mil	$1 mil capital gain
Depreciable plant	$1 mil	Written down value	$1.6 mil	$0.6 mil revenue gain
Trading stock	$2.5 mil	Cost method	$2.9 mil	$0.4 mil revenue gain

The unrealised net loss is $1 million (ie. $3 million unrealised gross loss less $2 million unrealised gross gain).

6.460   INTER-ENTITY LOSS MULTIPLICATION RULES – DIVISION 165-CD

Subdivision 165-CD operates to prevent multiple recognition of a loss company's realised or unrealised losses, when interests that entities (other than individuals) have in the loss company are realised. When there is a change in ownership or control of a loss company, reductions may be required to:

- the reduced cost bases of direct and indirect equity or debt interests acquired by entities on or after 20 September 1985
- deductions the entity is entitled to in respect of the disposal of equity or debt which is not trading stock of the entity, and
- the cost of equity or debt that is trading stock.

An entity will be affected if:

- there is a change in the ownership or control (alteration time) of a company after 1.00 PM (ACT time) on 11 November 1999 (ie. COT is failed)
- the company has an overall loss at the alteration time (a loss company), and
- an entity has a relevant equity or debt interest in the loss company immediately before the alteration time.

The measure does not apply to an individual or a partnership of individuals, or entities in which there are no interests in respect of which a company's losses have been or can be duplicated. These entities include certain trusts and superannuation funds.

An entity has a relevant equity interest if it has:

- a direct or indirect controlling stake in the loss company, or
- direct or indirect interests that confer 10% of more of the voting power, rights to dividends or rights to capital distributions of the loss company.

An entity has a relevant debt interest where it has:

- a direct or indirect controlling stake in the loss company, and
- the loss company owes the entity at least one debt of $10,000 or more.

CALCULATING THE ADJUSTMENT AMOUNT

There are two methods available for calculating the adjustment amount. The first method, the 'formula method' should be used if:

- all shares in the loss company are of the same class and have the same market value
- the equity interest consists only of the shares in the loss company, and/or
- the debt interest consists of a single debt, or two or more debts of the same kind.

The formula to calculate the adjustment amount is set out below:

> *The number of shares in the loss company constituted by the relevant equity interest immediately before the alternation time divided by total number of shares in the loss company immediately before the alteration time*

The resulting fraction is then applied to the overall loss of the loss company (see below) and the resultant amount is then applied to the relevant equity interest to the maximum extent possible. If any amount remains, the excess overall loss is allocated to debt interests on a proportionate basis.

The overall loss of the loss company is the sum of:

- prior year tax losses or net capital losses
- current year tax losses or net capital losses, and
- adjusted unrealised losses.

Companies with aggregated net assets under $6m (as calculated under the maximum net asset value test in the CGT small business concessions) are not required to calculate unrealised losses for the purposes of calculating the adjustment amount. Below is an example of how to calculate the unrealised losses of a company.

Where the requirements for the 'formula method' are not met, an alternative method is available, the 'non-formula method' which requires the adjustment amount to be 'the amount that is appropriate' taking into account the objective of the loss duplication provisions and other factors listed in s165-115ZB(6).

6.470   PARTIAL CLAIMS

If the COT and the SBT are failed during an income year, losses incurred before the change in ownership occurred are effectively extinguished. However, the part of the tax loss that emerged after the change in ownership may be allowed as a deduction in a subsequent year, provided the COT and the SBT are satisfied for the remainder of the year and all subsequent periods within the ownership test period (see COT rules above).

 A disqualifying change of ownership and business occurred on 15 September 2013, but the continuity of ownership test was met from then on. A loss attributable to the period from 16 September 2013 to 30 June 2014 may be carried forward.

6.480 CURRENT YEAR LOSSES

If there are current year losses and a company fails both the COT and the SBT in the current year of income, special tests apply to determine taxable income for a notional period. The method used, as set out in Subdivision 165-B is:

Step 1: Divide the income year into periods for each change in ownership or control (ie. notional periods).

Step 2: Treat each period as an 'income year' to work out the notional loss or notional taxable income for that period.

Step 3: Calculate the company's taxable income for the income tax year.

Certain amounts of assessable income (s165-60(7)) and allowable deductions (s160-55(5)) are regarded as full year amounts and not included in the notional income or loss calculated under Step 2. These amounts are taken into account in Step 3.

Taxable income derived in a notional period before or after the change in ownership cannot be offset against any current year tax loss or prior year tax loss. A tax loss incurred in the notional period before the change in ownership cannot be deducted in a subsequent income tax year. However, a tax loss incurred in the notional period after the change in ownership may be carried forward for deduction in a later year of income.

6.490 ANTI-AVOIDANCE MEASURES – DIVISION 175

Anti-avoidance provisions contained in Division 175 are aimed at preventing the utilisation of a company's losses in circumstances where the company may satisfy the COT but the economic benefit of the losses is enjoyed by persons who were not shareholders in the year that the loss was incurred.

NOTE: If a company passes the SBT, these provisions do not apply.

The provisions set out case circumstances where the Commissioner may disallow the losses as follows:

- the company derived income or a capital gain which it would not have derived or sought were it not for the availability of past losses ie. income or a capital gain is injected into the loss company, or
- benefits flow to persons other than the loss company which would not have happened had the losses not been available.

TRANSFERRING LOSSES WITHIN COMPANY GROUPS

Subdivision 170A formerly allowed losses to be transferred within wholly-owned groups of companies. However, effective from 1 July 2003 the loss transfer provisions ceased to have effect for all wholly-owned groups due to the consolidation regime (see 6.535). Certain banking activities are excepted.

6.500 TAX CONSOLIDATION

Under the tax consolidation regime, wholly-owned groups can elect to consolidate for tax purposes. The effect of the election is that all of the members of the group must be included in the consolidated group. A detailed description of the consolidation rules is beyond the scope of this publication.

A group will consist of a head company, which is a resident of Australia, and all the subsidiary members of the group (see 6.520). Residency requirements also apply.

A consolidated group will be treated as a single entity for income tax purposes. The subsidiary entities are treated as elements of the head company for income tax purposes, during the time that they are members of the group. The regime mainly applies to a wholly-owned group of Australian resident entities which makes the choice to form a consolidated group. Generally, the group should be owned entirely by a company which is an Australian resident. There are exceptions to the residency rule where the conditions for a Multiple Entry Consolidated (MEC) group are met (refer below).

6.510 BASIC RULES

The head company of the consolidated group lodges a single consolidated income tax return instead of its subsidiaries lodging individual tax returns. Assets, liabilities and franking credits of each member are treated as though they belong to the head company. Transactions within the group are, to a certain extent, ignored.

An 'entry history rule' provides that in determining the head entity's tax liability or loss after a subsidiary becomes a member, everything that has happened to that subsidiary prior to joining the group is taken to have happened to the head entity. There is also a rule for exit from the group known as the 'exit history rule'. Subsidiaries which leave are given a 'fresh tax identity'.

6.515 EFFECT OF NOT CONSOLIDATING

The former grouping rules ceased to operate from 1 July 2003. This means that wholly owned groups that could and did not consolidate from that date cannot:

- transfer losses or excess foreign income tax offsets between companies that are part of the same wholly-owned group
- obtain CGT rollover relief on the transfer of assets between companies that are part of the same wholly-owned group
- receive a rebate on intercorporate dividends, or
- take advantage of the grouping provisions in the thin capitalisation regime.

6.520 MEMBERSHIP

The consolidation rules are, in general, to be restricted to groups with a resident holding company. Wholly-owned groups in Australia without a common Australian holding company between a non-resident parent and the Australian resident subsidiaries are not able to form a consolidated group under the normal rules. However, they may be able to form a Multiple Entry Consolidated (MEC) group (see 6.560) .

In general, membership is limited to an ordinary Australian resident holding company and all of its eligible resident wholly-owned companies, trusts and partnerships. Whilst consolidation itself is optional, if a group consolidates then all of the holding company's eligible resident wholly-owned companies, trusts and partnerships, including entities acquired in the future, must be included in the consolidated group, referred to as the 'one in, all in' rule. Entry into the consolidation regime is irrevocable. Once a consolidated group has formed, newly acquired or created entities may join if they satisfy the eligibility criteria. A member can also leave a consolidated group where they no longer satisfy the eligibility criteria (for example, the entity is no longer wholly-owned by the head company or its subsidiary members). Where a head company no longer holds interests in subsidiary members, a consolidated group for tax purposes may consist of only the head company.

HEAD COMPANY

In general, a head company is an entity that:

- is a company
- has an income tax rate that equals the general company tax rate applied to some or all its taxable income
- is not a type of entity that is excluded from membership of a consolidated group
- is an Australian resident but not a prescribed dual resident, and
- is not a wholly-owned subsidiary of an entity that could be a head company, or, if it is, is not a member of a consolidated or consolidatable group.

To be a head company, an entity must be a company as defined in s995-1. A corporate limited partnership will be permitted. Corporate unit trusts and public trading trusts will be allowed to head a consolidated group provided that they are taxed like companies. Also, concessionally taxed companies cannot be head companies as it is not envisaged that their tax concessions necessarily apply to the whole group. However, some companies which have a lesser tax rate applied to some of their income will still be covered by the consolidation measures where the concessional rates are only relevant to special types of income relevant to those companies (eg. life insurance companies).

Companies which cannot be members of a consolidated group include:

- an entity of any kind where the total ordinary income and statutory income of the entity is exempt from income tax under Division 50 (exempt entities)
- recognised medium credit unions (s6H of the ITAA36)
- approved credit unions not being a recognised medium credit union or a recognised large credit union
- entities that are pooled development funds (PDFs) at the end of the income year
- companies that are film licensed investment companies at the time, and
- a trust that is a complying superannuation entity or a non-complying ADF or a non-complying superannuation fund.

SUBSIDIARY MEMBER

A subsidiary member must be an Australian resident company, partnership or trust that is a wholly-owned subsidiary of the head company. It cannot be a prescribed dual resident. The following entities are specifically excluded from being subsidiary members:

- exempt entities (ie. total ordinary and statutory income is exempt)
- pooled development funds (PDFs)
- film licensed investment companies
- certain credit unions
- non-profit companies
- non-complying approved deposit funds, and
- superannuation funds.

As a general rule, an entity will be a wholly-owned subsidiary of a holding entity if all the membership interests in it are beneficially owned by either the holding entity, and/or one or more wholly-owned subsidiaries of the holding entity (this includes entities under external administration). There are some exceptions, including where there are minor holdings of shares issued under employee share schemes.

TRUSTS AS SUBSIDIARY MEMBERS

The specific Australian residence requirements for trusts depends upon the type of trust involved. Section 703-25 states that trusts must meet the following residency requirements in order to be a subsidiary member of a consolidated group:

- a trust (except a unit trust) – must be a resident trust estate for the income year for the purposes of Division 6 of Part III of the ITAA36
- a unit trust (other than a corporate unit trust or a public trading trust) – must be a resident trust estate for the income year for the purposes of Division 6 of Part III of the ITAA36 and a resident trust for CGT purposes for the income year, and
- a corporate unit trust or a public trading trust – must be a resident unit trust for the income year.

Where a trust is to be a subsidiary member of a consolidated group, all of the objects, unitholders or beneficiaries of the trust must be members of the consolidated group. A trust cannot be the head of the consolidated group.

There are also two tests for assessing whether a trust can transfer losses to the head entity. The tests apply from the beginning of the income year when the loss was incurred until just after the joining time. The tests are the 50% stake test for fixed trusts, and for trusts which are non-fixed the control test and the pattern of distribution test (with some alterations) or 50% stake test or both.

A review of trust deeds may be needed to see whether a trust can join a consolidated group.

6.525 METHOD OF CONSOLIDATION

The choice to consolidate must be in an approved form and may be made by the head company on any day in the period from the day specified in the choice to the day the group's first consolidated income tax return is lodged. The form must include:

- names, TFNs and ABNs of the head company and subsidiary members

- date the consolidation commences
- signature of the authorised person, and
- contact information of a nominated contact person.

There is a discretion in the Commissioner to deal with a notification which is incorrect as though it were correct.

The head company must also give notice to the Tax Office in an approved form within 28 days of the exit of a subsidiary from the group or within 28 days of an entity becoming a member of the group. Notice must also be given, in an approved form and by the head company, within 28 days of the group ceasing to exist.

6.530   ASSETS

When a consolidated group is formed, the head company is treated as if it purchased a subsidiary's assets for a payment that reflects the cost to the group of acquiring those assets. The tax cost setting amounts relating to assets brought to a group by subsidiary members is determined under Division 705. The object of Division 705 is to align:

- the sum of tax values of the assets of the joining entity at the time it becomes a subsidiary member of the consolidated group, and
- the sum of the cost bases of all membership interests in the joining entity held by members of the joined group, reduced by the joining entity's liabilities,

so that:

- consistent leaving values can be worked out for membership interests in a subsidiary of the joined group that are later disposed of outside the group based on the cost bases of that member's assets. The cost setting for an entity leaving the group is done under Division 711
- double taxation of gains and duplication of losses can be prevented, and
- assets can be transferred between members of the group without requiring adjustments to cost bases for membership interests to prevent value shifting.

See 6.550 and 6.555 below for details on the 'allocable cost amount' upon entry and exit of a consolidated group.

6.535   TRANSFERRING LOSSES TO A CONSOLIDATED GROUP

Losses which may be transferred to a consolidated group are tax losses (including film losses), net capital losses and foreign losses. In general, a loss can only be transferred to the head company of a consolidated group if the loss could have been used outside the group by the joining entity. The loss can be transferred if the joining entity could have deducted the loss in the period immediately before transfer, assuming it had sufficient income or gains of the relevant kind. Losses are tested at the time the joining entity becomes a member of a group (the 'joining time').

In general, the joining entity applies the general rules for deducting or applying prior year losses as though the 12 months prior to the entity joining the group were the loss claim year. For a company this will usually involve finding out whether, for the period since the loss was incurred up to the joining time, the joining entity satisfied the Continuity of Ownership Test (COT) or the Same Business Test (SBT). In applying the SBT to consolidated and MEC groups (discussed below), the Commissioner's position is outlined in TR 2007/2. The Ruling states that under the single entity rule, subsidiary members of a consolidated group are taken for the purposes of the SBT to be parts of the head company.

A transferred loss is taken to have been made by the head company to which it has been transferred. The head company may either use the loss in working out its taxable income or transfer it to another group of which it later becomes a subsidiary member. A loss transferred by a subsidiary member is no longer available for use by it, even if it later leaves the group. The transferred loss may only be used by the head company. Losses which fail the transfer test may not be used by any entity. Losses generated by the consolidated group must be used before transferred losses. The annual rate a head company can deduct or apply transferred losses is limited by their loss factor (ie. the available fraction). This is, in general, the proportion that the loss entity's market value at the joining time bears to the value of the whole group at the time.

6.540   FRANKING ACCOUNTS

There are certain imputation rules applicable to consolidated groups. During the time of consolidation, the head company will be the sole franking entity in respect of the group. It will maintain a single franking account for the consolidated group, and subsidiary members will have dormant franking accounts whilst members of the consolidated group.

When a subsidiary joins a consolidated group, any surplus in its franking account is to be transferred to the head company's franking account. If the subsidiary's franking account is in deficit at the time of joining, the subsidiary will be liable to pay franking deficit tax. Whilst the subsidiary is a member of a consolidated group, any franking credits or debits that would otherwise have arisen in its franking account are entered into the franking account of the head company. Where a subsidiary member leaves the consolidated group, the franking credits which were transferred to the head company remain with the head company.

The rules also deal with the franking of amounts distributed by a subsidiary member of a consolidated group to shareholders (and in some cases other entities) because those shareholders hold certain shares known as disregarded Employee Share Acquisition Scheme shares or hold non-share equity interests. These shares are disregarded for the purpose of eligibility for membership of a consolidated group. Distributions in relation to these interests are treated as frankable distributions made by the head company.

6.545   CONSOLIDATION AND INTERNATIONAL TAX ISSUES

FOREIGN INCOME TAX OFFSETS

Excess foreign income tax offset balances held by each member of a consolidated group are to be transferred to the head company. If an entity pays foreign tax on foreign income during the period in which it is a member of a consolidated group, the head company is assessed on the foreign income and is deemed to have paid the foreign tax.

When an entity departs from a consolidated group, any excess foreign income tax offsets will remain with the head company of the group.

TRANSFER OF ATTRIBUTION ACCOUNT AND ATTRIBUTED TAX ACCOUNT SURPLUSES

When an entity becomes a member of a consolidated group, it will transfer to the head company any attribution and attributed tax account surpluses in respect of Controlled Foreign Companies (CFCs) and Foreign Investment Fund (FIF) interests at the time of joining. These accounts record amounts that are subject to current year taxation under the CFC and FIF measures and are used to ensure the amounts are not taxed again when distributed.

The measure applies at the time a consolidated group comes into existence as well as for entities joining an existing consolidated group. The amount of the surplus to be transferred will be calculated at the formation or joining time.

Where an entity leaves a consolidated group with an interest in a FIF or CFC it can take a proportion (based on the percentage of the group's interest in the CFC or FIF held by the leaving entity) of the head company's attribution and/or attributed tax account surplus at the time it leaves the consolidated group.

NOTE: The FIF provisions have been repealed effect from 1 July 2010 with a new regime to be implemented and the CFC provisions to be re-written. At the time of writing, there is no clear indication as to when the legislation will be finalised and enacted (see 22.820).

6.550   TAX COST SETTING – ENTITIES JOINING OR BECOMING A CONSOLIDATED GROUP

When an existing consolidated group acquires an entity eligible to be a member of the consolidated group, the acquired entity becomes a subsidiary member of the consolidated group and the cost of acquiring the entity (allocable cost amount) is treated as the cost of acquiring the entity's assets (refer above).

The value of the underlying assets held by subsidiary members are reset to reflect their tax values as if the head company had purchased the assets directly as opposed to the shares in that subsidiary member (which is commonly referred to as a 'push down' of the cost). The head company itself is not required to reset the value of its assets. The tax cost setting rules for assets where entities become subsidiary members are in Division 705.

ALLOCABLE COST AMOUNT

Under the tax cost setting rules, the head company determines the underlying cost of its subsidiary members' underlying assets by calculating that entity's 'allocable cost amount' (ACA). In broad terms, the ACA is determined using the following steps as prescribed under s705-65 ITAA97:

- **Step 1:** Start with the cost of membership interest in the joining entity (ie. subsidiary member). Broadly, this is the amount paid for the interests.
- **Step 2:** Add the value of the joining entities liabilities. These values may be modified for the tax effect of any future deductions to the head company and certain adjustments for unrealised gains and losses.
- **Step 3:** Add undistributed frankable profits that accrued to the consolidated group – which generally represent profits of the subsidiary member whilst it was owned by the head company (whether directly or indirectly).
- **Step 3A:** Adjust for certain pre-joining time roll-overs from a foreign resident company to an Australian resident company.
- **Step 4:** Subtract distributions of profits that were made to the consolidated group prior to the joining time, where distributions related to pre-acquisition profits, or where the distribution recouped a loss of the consolidated group.
- **Step 5:** Subtract unutilised owned losses of any sort of the joining entity at the joining time that did not reduce owned profits taken up at Step 3 (ie. tax losses, CGT losses, etc).
- **Step 6:** Subtract 30% of the acquired losses of the joining entity that are transferred to the head company.
- **Step 7:** Subtract an amount for deductions inherited by the head company (eg. unamortised borrowing costs over five years under s25-25 of the ITAA97).
- **Step 8:** If the amount is positive after Steps 1-7, this represents the ACA. Otherwise, the ACA is nil.

The deemed payment for each of the assets held by the joining entity is calculated by allocating the ACA for the acquired entity among the entity's assets relative to those assets market values at the joining time. The deemed payment for each asset gives a basis for determining the 'cost' of the asset for trading stock, CGT and capital allowance purposes. There are specific rules in the way that the ACA is allocated depending on the types of assets held by the subsidiary member at joining time.

Acquisition by a consolidated group of another consolidated group is treated as though the acquired group were a single entity. The cost of acquiring the acquired group is treated as the cost of acquiring all its assets.

NOTE: Not all of the eight steps would typically apply when a new subsidiary joins an existing group.

RETAINED COST BASE ASSETS

Once the ACA of a joining entity has been determined using the above eight steps, it is then reduced by the sum of the tax cost setting amounts of the following retained cost base assets:

- Australian currency or a right to receive a specified amount of Australian currency
- units in cash management trust
- entitlements to pre-paid services, and
- rights to future income assets (The various rules regarding cost setting for rights to future income can be found in Taxation Determinations 2014/22 to 2014/24).

The tax cost setting amount for the above retained cost base assets is discussed under s705-25.

RESET COST BASE ASSETS

The remaining ACA, as reduced by the tax cost setting amounts of the retained cost base assets, is allocated to the reset cost base assets in proportion to their market values. A reset cost base asset is any asset of the joining entity that is not a retained cost base asset or an excluded asset (s705-35). An asset is an excluded asset if an amount has been deducted for that asset in calculating the ACA of the joining entity. No part of the ACA is allocated to excluded assets.

There are a number of special rules that apply to restrict the amount of ACA allocated to the following reset cost base assets:

- **Trading stock, depreciating assets, or other revenue assets:** The tax cost setting amount is reduced to the greater of the market value or the terminating value (s705-40).

- **Accelerated depreciation:** A head company can retain access to accelerated depreciation rates for assets of the joining entity. Where such an election is made under s701-80, the head company must reduce the reset cost of the asset to the joining entity's terminating value for that asset.

6.555   ENTITIES LEAVING A CONSOLIDATED GROUP

An entity leaves a consolidated group when it no longer satisfy the criteria as a member of the consolidated group (ie. an entity is no longer a subsidiary member). Just before an entity leaves a consolidated group, the head company is deemed to have acquired the membership interests in the leaving entity for a payment that reflects the group's cost of acquiring the net assets of the leaving entity. In other words, the cost of the shares in the subsidiary member is required to be determined. The tax cost setting rules for membership interests where entities cease to be subsidiary members are in Division 711. Under this Division, the head company is required to calculate the ACA of the leaving entity based on the following steps:

- **Step 1:** Start with the terminating value of assets (ie. cost base, tax written-down values) that the leaving entity takes with it when it ceases to be a subsidiary member.

- **Step 2:** Add the deductions inherited by the leaving entity that are not reflected in the terminating value of assets that the leaving entity takes with it (eg. unamortised borrowing cost deducted over five years under s25-25 of the ITAA97).

- **Step 3:** Add the market value of liabilities owed by members of the old group to the leaving entity at leaving time (ie. intra-group debts with other members of the group).

- **Step 4:** Subtract the accounting liabilities that the leaving entity takes with it when it ceases to be a subsidiary member (subject to certain modifications).

- **Step 5:** If the amounts are positive from Steps 1-4, then this represents the existing consolidated group's ACA in the subsidiary member, otherwise the ACA is nil (ie. cost base of membership interest is nil) and CGT event L5 is triggered. Broadly, this arises where the liabilities of the leaving entity exceed the terminating value of its assets as a result of the consolidated group no longer assuming the 'net liabilities' of the leaving entity.

Based on the deemed cost of its membership interests in the leaving entity, the head company may realise a capital gain or capital loss on disposal of those interests at or after the time of leaving (subject to any proceeds received on the entity leaving the group). The leaving entity is treated as having acquired its assets on leaving the group for a payment for each asset that, if it had been received by the group, would have resulted in a tax-neutral disposal of the asset by the group.

Where a leaving entity holds membership interests in one or more other subsidiary members of the group, those entities also will be ineligible to remain in the group. The rules for a single entity leaving are adapted to determine costs for membership interests in all such leaving entities and to provide each leaving entity with a cost for the assets it takes from the group.

Any losses and franking credits which may have been transferred to the head company upon entry into the consolidated group remain with the head company.

NOTE: In the April 2015 the government released draft legislation to:

- remove a double benefit (or double detriment) that can arise in respect of certain liabilities held by a joining entity that is acquired by a consolidated group

- remove anomalies that arise when an entity joins or leaves a consolidated group where the entity has securitised an asset

- prevent the tax costs of a joining entity's assets from being uplifted where no tax is payable by a foreign resident owner on the disposal of the joining entity in certain circumstances

- clarify the operation of the Taxation of Financial Arrangements provisions when certain intra-group assets or liabilities emerge from a consolidated group because a subsidiary member leaves the group, and

- remove anomalies that arise when an entity leaves a consolidated group holding an asset that corresponds to a liability owed to it by the old group because the value of the asset taken into account for tax cost setting purposes is not always appropriate.

6.560 MEC GROUPS: RESIDENT WHOLLY-OWNED SUBSIDIARIES OF A COMMON FOREIGN HOLDING COMPANY

Resident wholly-owned subsidiaries without a single resident holding company but with a non-resident holding company may (provided certain criteria are met) form a Multiple Entry Consolidated (MEC) group (Division 719). An MEC group is formed by two or more eligible tier-1 companies making an irrevocable choice to consolidate a potential MEC group.

In general, an eligible tier-1 company is a company that is the first level of investment in Australia by a foreign resident company. Each of the eligible tier-1 companies making the choice must be wholly-owned subsidiaries of the same non-resident holding company (the top company) on the day the choice takes effect.

The eligible tier-1 companies must identify the top company and jointly nominate one of themselves to be the provisional head company of the MEC group. An eligible tier-1 company can only be a provisional head company if all its membership interests are held by entities that are not members of the potential MEC group (ie. held by non-residents). If an MEC group is formed, eligible tier-1 companies (other than the nominated head company) do not have to join the MEC group. There are complex rules about the structure of MEC groups.

NOTE: Eligible tier-1 companies are treated similarly to the head company of a consolidated group. The cost setting rules are modified so each eligible tier-1 company is treated as though it were a part of the provisional head company and not a separate entity.

NOTE: On 16 March 2015 the government released a Proposal paper on a possible amendment to improve the integrity of the tax system by extending a modified form of the unrealised loss rules to MEC groups. This will stop MEC groups being able to retain cost bases by entering assets in entities at the tier-1 level by recovering the benefit using a modified form of the unrealised loss rules to MEC groups.

6.565 CONSOLIDATED GROUPS WITH LIFE INSURANCE COMPANIES

Subdivision 713-L provides special rules for consolidated groups containing a life insurance company as a subsidiary member.

The provisions applying to life insurance companies are designed to work so that the head company of a consolidated group that has one or more life insurance company members will be treated as a life insurance company for tax purposes. Further, certain subsidiaries of a life insurance company cannot join the consolidated group. There are also specific rules concerning losses upon joining the consolidated group, franking credits, segregated exempt assets, liabilities and tax costs setting rules upon joining or leaving the consolidated group.

The rules provide that certain assets of life insurance companies will be retained cost base assets where a joining member of the consolidated group is a life insurance company. Also, for a joining or leaving entity that is a life insurance company, the value of liabilities relating to the net risk components of life insurance policies and the net investment component of ordinary life insurance policies will be prescribed.

6.570 PAYG INSTALMENTS AND CONSOLIDATED GROUPS

In consolidated groups where the head company has not yet been assessed as head company of the group, the individual entities in the group are still liable for PAYG instalments until the head company obtains its first assessment. The head company obtains a share of credits for PAYG instalments paid by member entities from the time of consolidation.

In the period before the head company has been assessed as head company of the group, the group is said not to be a 'mature' consolidated group.

Once the head company has been assessed as a head company for the first time, the head company will pay PAYG instalments on behalf of the group.

6.575   TAX SHARING AND FUNDING AGREEMENTS

In consolidated groups, under the single entity rule, the head company is responsible for the income tax liabilities of the group. If the head company is unable to meet its income tax liabilities, the subsidiary members of the group will be jointly and severally liable for any outstanding liabilities of the group.

In order for subsidiary members to avoid such a liability, members of the group may enter into a Tax Sharing Agreement (TSA). A TSA is an agreement between the head company and its subsidiary members which, in the event of the head company defaulting on its income tax liabilities, allocates the group's tax liability to the various members based on a 'reasonable' allocation. The allocation is based on the terms of the agreement and may vary for each member (for example, an allocation may be determined on a percentage of profit of each member). In order for the TSA to be valid a number of conditions pursuant to Division 721 need to be met. The TSA is required to cover the liability of the group, be executed before the date that the tax liability is due and may need to be amended to the extent that entities either leave or exit the group.

A Tax Funding Agreement may also be required to determine how the entities within the consolidated group fund their liabilities to the head company in order to pay the consolidated group's tax. The agreement would need to adopt an acceptable allocation method.

 If purchasing a subsidiary member of a consolidated group, it is important that a TSA be sighted as part of the due diligence process to ensure that the entity would not be jointly and severally liable for any existing group liabilities after leaving the group (unless it meets the conditions for a 'clear exit').

6.600   BAD DEBTS

Deductions by companies for bad debts are subject to restrictions similar to those which restrict the deduction of prior year losses (see 6.400).

To claim a deduction for a bad debt, a company must satisfy the continuity of ownership test (COT) or same business test (SBT) requirements which override the specific deduction that may be available under s25-35 of the ITAA97 or the general deduction that may be available under s8-1 of the ITAA97 (if applicable).

6.610   CONTINUITY OF OWNERSHIP TEST

Section 165-123 requires more than 50% continuity in shareholdings measured by voting power, rights to dividends and rights to capital distribution between:

- the year in which a transaction leading to the bad debt occurred, and
- the year the bad debt was written off and claimed (s165-120).

6.620   SAME BUSINESS TEST

A bad debt is allowed in all cases if the s165-126 (see 6.400) same business test requirements are satisfied, whether or not the COT has been satisfied. Section 165-126 sets out the test periods in relation to the SBT.

6.630   DEBT FOR EQUITY SWAPS

Tax deductions are allowed as part of a debt for equity swap under s63E of the ITAA36. This section sets out various criteria to be met. If met, the deduction available is the amount by which the face value of the debt exceeds the value of the equity received. The value of the equity received is the greater of its market value and its value in the books of the creditor. Note however that the value of the equity received will be an assessable recoupment. Bad debt deductions including debt/equity swaps under s63E are considered in TR 92/18.

6.700 LODGMENTS

The tax liability of a full self-assessment taxpayer (ie. companies and superannuation funds) with a 30 June balance date is due and payable on 1 December of the following year of income (s204(1A)).

However, the date for lodgment of the associated income tax return differs as set out below:
- companies with returns two or more years outstanding: 31 October
- large/medium companies that have annual income greater than $10 million: 15 January, and
- all other companies: 28 February.

6.710 THE PAYG INSTALMENT SYSTEM

The PAYG instalment system operates to collect income tax (see 5.700 for full details of the PAYG instalments system). Under the PAYG instalment system companies pay their income tax by either annual instalment, or in quarterly instalments.

NOTE: The government announced in the May 2013 Federal Budget that it will gradually extend the requirement to make monthly PAYG income tax instalments to include all large entities in the PAYG instalment system by the end of 2016-17 income year, including trusts, superannuation funds, sole traders and large investors.

ANNUAL INSTALMENTS

The due date for paying an annual instalment is:

Tax type	Due date
Taxpayers with 30 June year end	21 October after year end
Taxpayers with year end other than 30 June	21st day of fourth month following year end

 Companies that are a member of an 'instalment group' cannot adopt the annual instalment (see 5.700).

QUARTERLY INSTALMENTS

The other method of paying PAYG instalments is either of the quarterly instalment methods, being the GDP-adjusted notional tax method or the instalment rate method. The amount of each PAYG instalment depends on the method used. Entitlement to choose the GDP-adjusted notional tax method requires meeting criteria; otherwise the instalment rate method will apply (see 5.730).

Whichever method is used, the due date for a quarterly instalment depends on whether the company or superannuation fund is GST registered with monthly tax periods.

DATES FOR PAYING PAYG INSTALMENTS

Instalment	Quarter ending	GST registered enterprise with monthly tax periods	All other entities
1	30 September	21 October	28 October
2	31 December	21 January	28 February
3	31 March	21 April	28 April
4	30 June	21 July	28 July

NOTE: These dates may vary from time to time based on lodgment programs approved by the Tax Office. They are also impacted by weekends and public holidays (see the Tax Office website at www.ato.gov.au).

 Unpaid instalments remain an outstanding debt that has to be paid which will attract late payment penalties and the GIC for the time it is outstanding.

Tax agents will be advised by the Tax Office of their lodgment program for company and superannuation fund returns.

6.720   BALANCING PAYMENT OR REFUND

On assessment, the company will either have to pay tax, or be entitled to a refund of tax, whichever the case may be. It needs to be remembered that companies are subject to the 'full self assessment system'. This means they work out their own final income tax liability without actually receiving an assessment. Instead they are deemed to have received an assessment upon lodgment of their income tax return.

Where this is the case, and a balancing payment is owing to the Tax Office, it will be due to be paid on:

- 1 December following the year end for 30 June balancers, or
- the first day of the sixth month of the year following the income tax year for entities with a balance date other than 30 June.

Due dates can be varied by the Tax Office.

6.800   DIVIDEND IMPUTATION SYSTEM

Australia operates under a full dividend imputation system. Income tax paid by a company is able to be passed on to shareholders as a franking offset. This offset is included in the shareholder's assessable income but is available to be applied against the shareholders' income tax liability. This ensures that income is not taxed twice when the company's taxed earnings are passed on to resident shareholders as dividends.

OVERVIEW

- A corporate tax entity that receives a franked dividend grosses-up that dividend to be included in its assessable income and receives an imputation credit and a tax offset similar to individuals and superannuation funds.
- All entries in the franking account are recorded on a tax paid basis rather than on an after tax distributable profits basis. Corporate tax rate changes no longer require adjustments to the franking account balance.
- The franking account is a rolling-balance account and therefore is never closed off. The balance rolls from one franking year to another.
- The franking account balance date for a private company is the same as the corporate entity's income year due to franking periods. See below for details of the franking periods for a public and private company.
- A corporate tax entity can select a preferred rate of franking for its distributions, on the proviso that the franking percentage does not exceed 100%.
- A benchmark rule replacing the required franking amount applies. The first frankable distribution in a franking period establishes benchmark franking percentage for all frankable distributions made in that period.
- Private companies can retrospectively frank distributions as they can issue distribution statements up to four months after year end. However, public companies must give a distribution statement on or before the distribution is made.
- There are various anti-streaming rules contained in Division 204 including a rule referred to as a 'disclosure rule' which applies to alert the Commissioner to potential streaming schemes where an entity's benchmark franking percentage differs significantly between franking periods.
- Rules have been introduced to ensure that franking credits attached to dividends that are paid to the trustee of a trust estate can be effectively streamed to the extent that the beneficiaries of the trust are made 'specifically entitled' to the franked distribution.

EXTENSION OF AUSTRALIAN IMPUTATION SYSTEM TO NEW ZEALAND COMPANIES

Previously, Australian shareholders investing through a New Zealand resident company, that earns income and pays taxes in Australia, were generally not able to get imputation credits arising from the payment of such Australian taxes.

Since 1 April 2003, New Zealand companies have been able to elect to maintain an Australian franking account. Australian shareholders of New Zealand companies that have elected to maintain a franking account and earn Australian income will be able to access franking benefits on a pro rata basis (in proportion to their shareholding in the New Zealand company) arising from the payment of Australian tax on that income.

Franking credits arise in New Zealand companies' franking accounts for dividend, interest and royalty withholding taxes deducted in Australia. They arise in addition to credits for Australian income tax and franking credits attached to dividends received.

The measures do not allow the recognition of New Zealand imputation credits attached to dividends received by Australian resident shareholders.

CORPORATE ENTITIES

The imputation rules apply to corporate tax entities. Corporate tax entities are:

- companies (a body corporate or any other unincorporated association or body of persons other than a partnership)
- corporate limited partnerships (Division 5A of Part III ITAA36)
- corporate unit trusts (Division 6B of Part III ITAA36), and
- public trading trusts (Division 6C of Part III ITAA36).

Corporate entities do not include mutual life insurance companies.

DIVIDEND

Broadly, s6(1) ITAA36 defines a dividend for tax purposes as including:

- any distribution made by a company to any of its shareholders, whether in money or other property, and
- any amount credited by a company to any of its shareholders as shareholders,

but does not include:

- moneys paid or credited by a company to a shareholder or any other property distributed by a company to shareholders, where the amount of the moneys paid or credited, or the amount of the value of the property, is debited against an amount standing to the credit of the share capital account of the company (subject to certain conditions)
- moneys paid or credited, or property distributed, by a company for the redemption or cancellation of a redeemable preference share (subject to certain conditions), and
- a reversionary bonus on a life assurance policy.

CHANGES TO THE DEFINITION OF DIVIDEND FOR CORPORATIONS LAW PURPOSES

The definition of dividend pursuant to s254T of the *Corporations Act* (Corps Act) was amended in June 2010. The previous definition required that dividends must be paid out of a company's profits.

Effective from 28 June 2010, the amended definition requires all of the following criteria be satisfied:

- the company's assets exceed its liabilities immediately before the dividend is declared and the excess is sufficient for the payment of the dividend
- payment of the dividend is fair and reasonable to the company's shareholders as a whole, and
- payment of the dividend does not materially prejudice the company's ability to pay its creditors.

For income tax purposes, a corporate law dividend paid in accordance with the current s254T where it is paid out of reserves or other equity accounts that do not represent 'profits' will constitute a s6(1) dividend to the extent that it is not debited against the share capital account.

All s6(1) dividends received by shareholders will be assessable under s44(1) irrespective of whether the dividend is paid out of profits (by operation of s44(1A) and s44(1B)) (see 11.700).

In Taxation Ruling TR 2012/5, the Commissioner outlines his views in relation to the franking and the assessment of dividends paid where the company has unrecovered losses:

- A company that pays a distribution to its shareholder (according to its constitution and without breaching s254T or Part 2J.1 Corps Act), out of current trading profits recognised in its accounts and available for distribution, is not prevented from franking the dividend merely because the company has unrecouped prior year accounting losses or has lost part of its share capital. That dividend will be assessable income under s44(1)(a).

  Jim Co is in an accumulated loss position as a result of prior year trading. However, in the current year, Jim Co performs more successfully, making trading profits. A meeting of the directors of the company approves financial statements in which the current year trading profits are booked.

  The current year trading profits are not offset against Jim Co's accumulated losses, and are not otherwise made unavailable for distribution. Jim Co's balance sheet is as follows:

Assets and liabilities		Equity	
Cash	$80	Share capital	$140
Property, plant and equipment	$20	Accumulated losses	($70)
		Current year profit	$30
Net assets	$100	Total equity	$100

  Jim Co determines to pay a $30 dividend to shareholders from the current year profits identified in the accounts. As the dividend is sourced from current year profits the $30 dividend will be frankable, and will be assessable income of its resident shareholders.

- A company that pays a dividend to its shareholders (according to its constitution and without breaching s254T or Part 2J.1 Corps Act), out of an unrealised capital profit of a permanent character recognised in its accounts and available for distribution, is not prevented from franking the dividend provided the company's net assets exceed its share capital by at least the amount of the dividend. That dividend will be assessable income of its resident shareholders under s44(1)(a).

- A distribution (even if it is labelled as a dividend) paid by a company to its shareholders, that does not comply with s254T or Part 2J.1 of Corps Act, is an unauthorised reduction and return of share capital that will be taxed as a CGT event under the CGT provisions, or will be taxed as an assessable unfranked dividend, depending on the particular facts and circumstances of the payment.

DISTRIBUTIONS

A distribution is defined in the context of the type of corporate entity that is making the distribution (s960-120) as follows:

- for a company – a distribution is a dividend or something taken to be so under s6(1) ITAA36
- corporate limited partnership – either a distribution made by the partnership in money or property to a partner in the partnership or something which is deemed to be a dividend by the partnership under the Act
- corporate unit trust – unit trust dividend as defined in s102D(1) ITAA36, and
- public trading trust – unit trust dividend as defined in s102M ITAA36.

A frankable distribution will include:

- general definition of dividends under s6(1) ITAA36
- bonus shares that are taken to be dividends under s6BA(5) ITAA36
- amounts taken to be dividends under the off-market share buy back provisions of s159GZZZP ITAA36
- liquidators' distributions that are deemed to be dividends under s47(1) ITAA36, and
- non-share dividends that are distributions in relation to a non-share equity interest in the company (see *Debt and equity* at 6.200).

An entity franks a distribution if it is an Australian resident franking entity at the time that it makes a frankable distribution and it allocates franking credits to that distribution. A franking entity is a corporate tax entity (see above). Franking a distribution is the means by which an entity imputes to a member tax it has paid. A member of a corporate tax entity includes:

- a member (including a shareholder) of a company
- a partner of a corporate limited partnership, or
- a unit holder in a corporate unit trust or public trading trust.

A non-resident corporate tax entity is excluded from making franked distributions. A company is a resident if either:

- it is incorporated in Australia, or
- if it is not incorporated in Australia, it carries on a business in Australia and either has its central management and control in Australia, or its voting power is controlled by shareholders who are themselves residents of Australia.

Not all distributions made by a corporate tax entity can be franked. Distributions from profits which the corporate tax entity has paid tax on are generally distributions which can be franked. A distribution is frankable (ie. those paid out of profits of the entity) unless it is specifically made unfrankable (s202-40(1) ITAA97).

The following distributions are unfrankable (s202-45 ITAA97):

- distributions made by co-operative companies where the co-operative company is able to get an income tax deduction for the distribution
- distributions from profits sourced in the Norfolk Islands from companies that are resident there
- distributions made in respect of shares that are treated as debt instruments under the debt/equity rules (see 6.200)
- distributions funded from certain capital reserves of the company
- distributions made by Approved Deposit Institutions in relation to instruments that are characterised as non-share equity under the debt/equity rules (see 6.200)
- distributions made in relation to an instrument characterised as a non-share equity interest under the debt/equity rules (see 6.200) where the distribution exceeds available frankable profits
- deemed dividends distributions under Division 7A (private company distributions)
- deemed dividends in relation to excessive payments made by a private company to its shareholders, directors and associates (s109 ITAA36)
- distributions to controlled foreign companies deemed to be dividends under s47a
- deemed dividends in relation to capital streaming and dividend substitution arrangements (s45 & 45C ITAA36)
- distributions made in relation to off-market buy backs of equity interests where the amount paid in respect of the buy-back exceeds the market value of the equity interest, and
- demerger dividends (s6(1) ITAA36).

NOTE: Amounts paid out of the company's current year profits or future retained earnings subsequent to the proposed accounting entry will not constitute an unfrankable dividend pursuant to s202-45(e) (ATO ID 2010/25).

The definition of distribution includes non-share dividends (ie. paid in relation to a non-share equity interest) which can be frankable in the same circumstances that dividends on equity interest on shares are frankable s202-40(2).

Office Pty Ltd made a loan to a Director who was also a shareholder. The loan was to be repaid over a period of seven years, with minimum yearly repayments in compliance with s109N, in order to ensure that the loan is not subject to deemed dividend provisions contained in Division 7A.

If the minimum repayments are not made prior to the end of the income year as per s109E(5), the remaining amount of the loan will be taken to be unfrankable dividend. The consequences are that the director must include the repayment shortfall as income without any imputation credit tax offset.

NOTE: A private company is not required to debit the company's franking account when a deemed dividend arises pursuant to Division 7A.

MAXIMUM FRANKING PERCENTAGE

The amount of franking credit allocated on a distribution will be the lesser of:

- the amount that is stated on the distribution statement, which must be provided to the recipient, or
- the maximum franking credit that may be allocated on the distribution (ie. 100%).

The maximum franking credit that may be allocated on a distribution is the maximum amount of income tax that the corporate tax entity could have paid on the profits it distributes. This means that, in practice, a corporate tax entity must not give its members credit for more tax than it has paid. This requirement is consistent with the former imputation system.

The maximum franking credit is calculated using the following formula:

Frankable distribution x [Corporate tax rate divided by (100% – corporate tax rate)]

where the corporate tax rate is 30%.

Frankable and unfrankable distribution

Advance Pty Ltd has $100,000 that it wants to distribute to its shareholders. Of this amount, $70,000 represents the frankable portion and $30,000 is the unfrankable component. The maximum franking credit that Advance Pty Ltd could allocate to this frankable distribution is $70,000 x [30% divided by (100% – 30%)] = $30,000.

NOTE: Where a distribution is made up of both a frankable and unfrankable portion, the maximum franking credit is calculated only in relation to the frankable portion, not on the total distribution.

Maximum franking credit

Fair Pty Ltd has after-tax profits of $70,000 available for distribution. Fair Pty Ltd decides to pay $35,000 of this after-tax profit (ie. a frankable distribution) to its shareholders. The maximum franking credit that Fair Pty Ltd can attach to this distribution is calculated as $35,000 x (30% divided by 70%) = $15,000.

The franking percentage is a measure of the extent to which a frankable distribution has been franked. It is expressed as a percentage of the frankable distribution, rather than the whole of the distribution. Thus in the circumstances where a distribution contains both a frankable and unfrankable element, the franking percentage may be 100% even where only part of the total distribution is frankable.

The franking percentage is the lesser of 100% or the amount calculated using the following formula:

*(Franking credit allocated to the frankable distribution) divided by
(Maximum franking credit for the frankable distribution) x 100*

The franking percentage in respect of the first frankable distribution made in the franking period will establish the benchmark franking percentage. Under the imputation system, all frankable distributions made within a franking period must be franked in accordance with this benchmark franking percentage (see benchmark rule below). If the entity fails to comply with the requirement that it should not frank a distribution in excess of the maximum franking credit that may be allocated:

- the entity's franking account is debited to the full extent of the franking credit allocation
- the recipient of the franked distribution will only include in assessable income the franked distribution and the amount of franking credit up to the maximum that should have been allocated on the distribution, and
- the tax offset to which the recipient is entitled to will not exceed the maximum franking credit that could be allocated on the distribution.

THE BENCHMARK RULE

A corporate tax entity has flexibility to frank (ie. allocate franking credits to) a frankable distribution to whatever extent it chooses, subject to the benchmark rule. It will be able to select the level of franking having regard to existing and expected franking account surplus and the rate at which earlier distributions were franked.

The benchmark rule provides that all frankable distributions made by a corporate tax entity during the franking period must be franked to the same extent as the benchmark franking percentage (s203-10). This differs from the previous franking rules, which required a company to frank a dividend to the maximum extent possible having regard to the surplus in its franking account at the time of its payment.

The benchmark rule applies to all corporate tax entities to ensure that the benefits of the imputation system are applied consistently to all members to ensure corporate tax entities do not direct franked and unfranked distributions to members in a way that maximises the benefits to members.

Arrangements that try to circumvent this fundamental principle constitute dividend streaming. They include situations where unfranked distributions are streamed to members who have no need for franking credits so as to preserve the credits for those who benefit most from the credits (see dividend streaming below).

Due to the limited opportunities for streaming, the benchmark rule does not apply to a company in a franking period if at all times during that period it is a listed public company or a 100% subsidiary of a public listed company, that:

- had a single class of membership interest at all times during the franking period, or
- under its constituent documents must not:
  - make a distribution on one membership interest during the franking period without making a distribution under the same resolution to all other membership interests, or
  - frank a distribution made on one membership interest during the franking period without franking distributions made on all other membership interests under the same resolution with a franking credit worked out using the same franking percentage, or
- has more than one class of membership interest but the rights in relation to distributions and the franking of distributions are the same for each class of membership interest.

The benchmark rule is intended to prevent a corporate tax entity making distributions to its members within a particular franking period that are franked to different extents. A company may apply to the Commissioner in writing for approval to depart from the benchmark franking percentage but unless the Commissioner is satisfied that there are extraordinary unforeseen circumstances, permission is unlikely to be granted (see below).

The key components of the benchmark rule are the ascertainment of the franking period and the benchmark franking percentage for that period. Once the benchmark franking percentage is established, the entity must frank all frankable distributions made within the franking period using this percentage, or face penalties (s203-50) – see below. This highlights the importance of the first frankable distribution for a period, which establishes the benchmark franking percentage for future distributions within the period.

Breaches of the benchmark rule A penalty will be imposed on the corporate tax entity for breaches of the benchmark rule. Breaches of the benchmark rule will not invalidate the allocation made to the distribution, so shareholders in receipt of dividends are generally unaffected unless the distribution has been franked in excess of 100%.

The penalty is calculated by reference to the difference between the franking credits actually allocated and the benchmark percentage. The penalty is either:

- over-franking tax: if the franking percentage for the distribution exceeds the benchmark franking percentage, or
- a franking debit (penalty debit): if the franking percentage for the distribution is less than the benchmark franking percentage (s203-50).

The penalty debit for under-franking a distribution arises on the day on which the frankable distribution is made and is in addition to the franking debit that arises from the payment of a franked distribution. It is equivalent to the extra franking credit that should have been allocated according to the benchmark rate. The additional debit effectively cancels out the unused credit. Therefore, the penalty for under-franking by the entity is that the extra franking credit that ought to have been allocated to the distribution is wasted.

The amount of over-franking tax or the penalty debit is worked out using the following formula:

Franking % differential x Amount of frankable distribution x
[Company tax rate divided by (100% – company tax rate)]

For the purposes of the formula, the franking % differential is the difference between the franking percentage for the distribution, and either:

- the entity's benchmark franking percentage for the franking period in which the distribution is made, or
- the franking percentage the Commissioner permits in a determination made under s203-55(5).

Under-franking a distribution

Butler Pty Ltd, a corporate tax entity, has a benchmark franking percentage for the current franking period of 100%. Using this benchmark means that a frankable distribution of $700 would have $300 of franking credits attached.

Butler Pty Ltd makes a franked distribution of $700 within that franking period and allocates a $240 franking credit (resulting in a franking percentage of 80%). The entity has under-franked this distribution and a penalty-franking debit will be imposed. The amount of the under-franking debit will be equivalent to the franking debit that should have been allocated to the distribution in accordance with the benchmark. It is calculated on the same basis as an over-franking tax would have been if the distribution were over-franked, that is (100% – 80%) x $700 x (30%/70%) = $60.

The franking debit that arises in the franking account results in lost imputation credits as the beneficiary of the distribution only receives an imputation credit based on the 80% franking level even though the franking account reflects the higher benchmark franking rate of 100%. This constitutes a permanent loss of franking credits to the entity. The penalty debit arises on the same day as the under-franked distribution was made.

Over-franking a distribution

Risk Ltd, a corporate tax entity, has a benchmark franking percentage for the current franking period of 80%. Using this benchmark would mean that a frankable distribution of $700 would have $240 of franking credits attached. Risk Ltd makes a fully franked distribution of $700 within that franking period. That is, it allocates a $300 franking credit (resulting in a franking percentage of 100%). The entity has over-franked this distribution and over-franking tax will be imposed.

The amount of the over-franking tax is equivalent to the franking credit allocated in excess of the benchmark, calculated on the same basis as a penalty debit would have been if the distribution were under-franked, that is (100% – 80%) x $700 x (30%/70%) = $60.

The over-franking penalty tax does not result in a franking credit to the franking account and therefore represents lost imputation credits. Over-franking results in the corporate tax entity having to lodge a franking return and pay overfranking tax.

DEPARTURE FROM BENCHMARK RULES

A corporate tax entity may apply to the Commissioner in writing, either before or after a distribution is made, for permission to depart from the benchmark rule.

The power to permit a departure from a benchmark percentage will be exercised only in extraordinary circumstances. Generally, the circumstances justifying a departure would need to be unforeseeable and beyond the control of the entity. An entity seeking permission to depart from the benchmark rule should include all relevant information in support of the application. In particular, the application should address the following factors, which must be considered by the Commissioner in making a decision (s203-55(3)):

- the entity's reasons for wanting to depart or proposing to depart from the benchmark rule
- the extent of the departure or proposed departure (the greater the departure, the greater the onus on the corporate tax entity to justify it)
- whether the entity has previously sought the exercise of the Commissioner's powers to permit the departure in the past (assuming the previous applications resulted from circumstances within the entity's control – if so, the onus on the entity to justify a departure will increase if the entity applies for a variation relatively frequently)
- whether a member of the entity will be disadvantaged by the departure or proposed departure (eg. because the member will receive a distribution with a lower franking percentage than the distribution received by another member)
- whether a member of the entity will receive franking benefits in preference to other members of the entity as a result of the departure (in such a case the departure may be motivated by a desire to stream franking credits inappropriately), and
- any other matters that the Commissioner considers relevant.

A distribution that is franked in accordance with the Commissioner's permission to depart from the relevant benchmark rules is taken to comply with the benchmark rule.

NOTE: A change in entity ownership would rarely amount to extraordinary circumstances sufficient to warrant a departure from a benchmark rule.

ASCERTAINING THE FRANKING PERIOD

The franking period rules align an entity's franking year with its income year. A corporate tax entity that is a private company for an income year will have a franking period that is the same as its income year.

Company type	Income year length	No. periods	Franking periods
Private	Irrelevant	1	Equals tax year
Not private	12 months	2	Period 1: Six months beginning at start of entities income year. Period 2: Remainder of income year.
Not private	< 6 months	1	Equals Income year
Not private	> 6 months but <12 months	2	Period 1: Six months beginning at start of entities income year. Period 2: Remainder of income year.
Not private	>12 months	3	Period 1: Six months beginning at start of entities income year. Period 2: The following six months. Period 3: Remainder of income year.

 Program Pty Ltd is a private company. Its income year is from 1 July to 30 June. Program Pty Ltd has only one franking period in its income year and it is the same as its income year.

A corporate tax entity that is not a private company for an income year will generally have two franking periods (1 July to 31 December and 1 January to 30 June) (s203-40(2)). There are special rules where the income year is more or less than a 12 month period. The benchmark franking percentage for a franking period will be the franking percentage allocated to the first frankable distribution made by the entity within that period. If no frankable distributions are made in the franking period, the entity does not have a benchmark franking percentage for the franking period (s203-30).

Franking periods

BBS Pty Ltd makes a distribution, franked to 60%, at the start of the franking period. The benchmark rule provides that BBS Pty Ltd will have to frank all its frankable distributions to 60% for that franking period.

NOTE: If all distributions made by a corporate entity are unfrankable distributions, the entity does not have a benchmark franking percentage for the franking period.

ANTI-STREAMING RULES – OVERVIEW

Streaming refers to the selective directing of the flow of franked distributions to those members who can most benefit from franking credits. The benchmark rule has been supplemented with four specific anti-streaming rules, introduced as part of the simplified imputation legislation. These rules are intended to ensure that franking credits are not streamed, or disproportionately allocated to certain members. The four rules relate to:

1. linked distributions

2. substituting tax-exempt bonus shares for franked distributions

3. an anti-streaming rule involving distributions to provide imputation benefits to members who benefit more from imputation credits than other members commonly known as dividend streaming (s204-30), and

4. a disclosure rule. This rule was brought in to help the Commissioner identify cases where the anti-streaming rules might have application. It applies where an entity's benchmark franking percentage differs significantly between franking periods.

1. STREAMING USING LINKED DISTRIBUTIONS – SUBDIVISION 204-B

This applies to streaming arrangements involving linked distributions, where a member of one entity can choose to receive a distribution from another entity that is franked to a greater or lesser extent than distributions made to other members of the first entity. To prevent this, a penalty franking debit (s204-15(1)) will arise when a member of an entity who would otherwise receive a distribution from the first entity can choose to receive a distribution with a higher or lower franking percentage from another entity. The distribution received from the other entity is called a linked distribution. The penalty debit is imposed on the entity with the higher benchmark franking percentage. The franking debit imposed is equal to the debit that would have arisen if the first entity had made the linked distribution at its benchmark franking percentage.

This rule would apply, for example, where stapled stock arrangements are used for streaming. Under these arrangements, holders of stapled stock can choose to receive either a franked or an unfranked (or a lesser franked) dividend, depending on the company paying the dividend. These arrangements might be used in an attempt to stream franked dividends to Australian resident shareholders of a company group and unfranked dividends to non-resident shareholders (who receive less benefit from imputation credits).

2. STREAMING USING TAX-EXEMPT BONUS SHARES – SUBDIVISION 204-C

The second rule applies to streaming arrangements involving tax-exempt bonus shares, where a member of an entity can choose that tax-exempt bonus shares are issued to the member, or to another member of the entity, instead of receiving a franked dividend. Tax-exempt bonus shares are shares issued by a listed public company without crediting the share capital account (s204-25(4) and (5)).

If the tax-exempt bonus shares streaming rule applies, the entity involved in the arrangement will incur a penalty franking debit. The franking debit imposed is equal to the debit that would have arisen if the entity had made the substituted distribution at its benchmark franking percentage (s204-25(2)). If the entity does not have a benchmark franking percentage for the franking period in which the shares are issued, it is taken to be 100% for that period (s204-25(6)).

3. STREAMING BENEFITS TO MEMBERS WHO BENEFIT MORE FROM IMPUTATION THAN OTHERS – SUBDIVISION 204-D

The third of the specific anti-streaming rules applies where a corporate tax entity streams distributions in such a way as to give those members who benefit most from franking credits (eg. taxable residents) a greater franking benefit than those who benefit less (eg. non-residents).

The rule applies regardless of whether the streaming occurs within a single franking period or between different franking periods (s204-30(1)).

Streaming may occur by making franked distributions to some members of the entity and unfranked (including unfrankable) distributions to others. It may also occur by making franked distributions to some members and providing non-distribution benefits (eg. superannuation contributions) to others (s204-30(2)).

If benefits are streamed the Commissioner may determine that a debit to the franking account arises and deny the franking credit to the member. However, the company may lodge an objection.

4. THE DISCLOSURE RULE – SUBDIVISION 204-E

This rule applies where an entity's benchmark franking percentage differs significantly between franking periods. Significant variations between benchmark franking rates can indicate the presence of franking credit streaming. Because of this, entities are required to disclose to the Commissioner any significant variation between successive benchmark franking rates.

The benchmark franking percentage for the current franking period varies significantly from the benchmark franking percentage for the last relevant franking period if it has increased or decreased by an amount greater than the amount worked out under the following formula:

Number of franking periods starting immediately after the last relevant franking period and ending at the end of the current franking period x 20 percentage points

The last relevant franking period is the last franking period in which a frankable distribution was made.

Disclosure rule

Grand Ltd has a benchmark percentage of 30% in the current franking period and a benchmark percentage of 0% in the immediately preceding franking period. Grand Ltd's benchmark franking percentage has increased by 30%, greater than a 20 percentage point increase (1 x 20 percentage points). As the benchmark franking percentage for the current franking period has varied significantly it has a disclosure requirement.

If a corporate tax entity's benchmark franking percentage varies significantly between franking periods, the entity must notify the Commissioner in an approved form of the following (s204-75):

- the benchmark franking percentage for the current franking period, and
- the benchmark franking percentage for the last franking period in which a frankable distribution was made

the Commissioner may request the following:

- reasons for setting the significantly varied benchmark franking percentage
- the franking percentage for all frankable distributions made in the current and last relevant franking period
- details of any other benefits given to the entity's members, either by the entity or an associate of the entity, in the period from the beginning of the last relevant franking period to the end of the current franking period
- whether any of the entity's members has derived, or will derive, a greater benefit from the imputation credits than another member of the entity as a result of the variation in the benchmark franking percentage period, and
- any other information.

Significant variation in the benchmark franking percentage does not in itself trigger penalties. It does however empower the Commissioner to seek further information to determine if the variance amounts to a breach of the anti-streaming rules.

NOTE: A corporate tax entity that triggers the disclosure rule is required to lodge a franking tax return.

DIVIDEND WASHING

In 2014, the government introduced an integrity rule to preventing 'dividend washing' arrangements, with effect from 1 July 2013. If you have distributions made before 1 July 2013, the general anti-avoidance provisions in Part IVA apply to deny franking credit benefits received through dividend washing arrangements (see Taxation Determination 2014/10).

Dividend washing is a process that allows investors to effectively trade franking credits, and can result in some shareholders receiving two sets of franking credits for the same parcel of shares. This integrity rule prevents taxpayers from obtaining two sets of franking credits, which may otherwise provide a tax benefit where the tax offset received from the additional franking credits is greater than the amount of tax payable on the additional dividend.

The integrity rule means that if you receive a dividend as a result of dividend washing, you are not entitled to a tax offset for the franking credits associated with the dividend received on the shares purchased on the special ASX trading market and not required to include the amount of the franking credits on the shares purchased on the special ASX trading market in your assessable income (however, you must still declare all assessable dividends in your assessable income).

NOTE: The integrity rule generally does not apply to individuals who receive $5,000 or less in franking credits in a year, which we call the small shareholder exemption.

FRANKING ACCOUNT

A franking account is an account that a corporate tax entity maintains to keep track of income tax credits it can pass on to members. Franking account rules apply to all corporate tax entities. The franking account is credited with franking credits and debited with franking debits. Franking credits arise upon payment of income tax and PAYG instalments, and receipt of franked distributions, directly or indirectly. Franking debits arise upon payment of franked distributions, and refunds of income tax. Franking deficit tax will be imposed if a franking account is in deficit at the end of the income year (ie. if the sum of the franking debits in the franking account exceeds the sum of the franking credits).

The significant features of the franking account include:

- entries are to be recorded on a tax paid basis, not an after-tax distributable profits basis, and
- the franking account will operate on a rolling balance account rather than a yearly account with an annual balance transfer. This removes the need for franking entries to effect the transfer of a credit balance to the following income year.

FRANKING CREDITS

Generally, a franking credit arises when a corporate tax entity:

- makes a payment of a PAYG instalment or income tax
- receives a franked distribution either directly or indirectly, or
- incurs a liability for franking deficits tax.

NOTE: Receipt of a franked distribution can also flow indirectly through a partnership or trust (s205-15, item 4 in the table below).

Detailed circumstances in which a franking credit will arise and the timing of the credit are set out in the table in s205-15. Under the simplified imputation rules, franking credits arising from income tax paid are expressed on a tax paid basis in the franking account.

FRANKING DEBITS

Generally, a franking debit arises when a corporate tax entity:

- receives a refund of income tax
- makes a franked distribution
- under-franks a distribution (that is, the corporate tax entity makes a distribution with a franking percentage that is less than the entity's benchmark franking percentage for the franking period)
- ceases to be a franking entity (to eliminate any franking surplus in the franking account)
- makes a linked distribution (s204-15)
- issues tax-exempt bonus shares (instead of making a distribution) (s204-25)
- streams imputation benefits to members most able to benefit from them (s204-30(3)(a))
- pays a distribution under the rules governing payments and loans to a shareholder (Division 7A of Part III of the ITAA36), and
- buys back a share on-market.

Circumstances in which a franking debit will arise are set out in the table that follows.

If an entity ceases to be a franking entity, a franking debit will arise to eliminate any franking surplus. The debit will ordinarily arise at the time the entity ceases to be a franking entity (s205-30). A refund of a research and development tax offset does not generate a franking debit under s205-30.

FRANKING DEFICIT TAX

It a corporate tax entity has a deficit in its franking account at the end of an income year, it has imputed to its members more tax than it has paid and it will be liable to pay franking deficit tax to account for the over-imputation of tax. An entity's franking account is in deficit at a particular time when the sum of the franking debits in the account exceeds the sum of the franking credits. The franking deficit tax payable is the amount of the entity's franking deficit at the end of the income year and is due for payment on 31 July.

Franking deficit tax can be offset against income tax, and as such,is a prepayment of income tax which is set against next year's company tax liability.

If a franking deficit would have arisen but does not because of a refund of tax that is received in the following year (within three months of the end of the previous year), the refund that arises in the following year will be treated for the purpose of franking deficit tax as though it had been refunded at the end of the preceding income year. This will result in a recalculation of franking deficit tax. The franking deficit tax, or additional amount of franking deficit tax, is payable within 14 days of the day the refund is paid or such later day as set by s205-45 ITAA97. This rule is a disincentive for an entity that might overpay tax to avoid franking deficit tax. The rule achieves the same outcome as the deficit deferral tax that is imposed under the previous law, but removes the need for a separate tax.

 If the liability for franking deficit tax that arises in the franking account for the year is greater than 10% of all franking credits in that same year, then the corporate entity's tax offset entitlement will be reduced by 30%.

RELIEF FROM EXCESSIVE OVER-FRANKING PENALTY

1. FIRST INCUR INCOME TAX LIABILITY – CONCESSION FOR PRIVATE COMPANIES

In certain situations, private companies that pay franked distributions will not have their franking deficit tax offset reduced in respect of the income year in which they first incur an income tax liability.

Generally, a company does not pay income tax until after the end of the first income year during which it derives taxable income. Consequently, the company does not generate franking credits during that income year to attach to distributions made in that year. The company will first generate franking credits after the end of the relevant income year when the company pays its income tax liability for that year. The inability of a company to generate franking credits does not restrict it from paying franked distributions during that year. However, a company that makes franked distributions in these circumstances is required to pay franking deficit tax at the end of the income year because the balance in its franking account will be in deficit at that time.

The payment of franking deficit tax allows a company to claim an offset equal to the amount of franking deficit tax paid when calculating its income tax liability for that income year. The franking deficit tax offset can also be carried forward to later income years to reduce the company's future income tax liability but will be reduced if the company's franking deficit at the end of the income year exceeds the franking credits in its franking account at that time by more than 10%.

The conditions that must be satisfied to avoid the penalty are:

- the private company must (assuming that it did not have the franking deficits tax offset) be liable to pay income tax for the income year that is sufficient to generate franking credits equal to at least 90% of the deficit in the company's franking account at the end of that income year – this 90% rule ensures that there is a close alignment between the amount of franking credits the company has paid out during the income year and the company's income tax liability for that income year, and

- the private company must not have had an income tax liability for any earlier income year – that is, it must be the private company's first income year.

Michael is the sole shareholder of Speed Pty Ltd, a private company established on 1 July 2013. The company did not generate taxable income (or become liable for income tax) for the 2013-14 income year.

Speed's franking account balance as at 1 July 2014 is zero. Speed makes a pre-tax profit of $10,000 for the 2014-15 income year and expects to pay income tax for that income year of $3,000 ($10,000 multiplied by 30%). Speed makes a franked distribution to Michael of $7,000. Speed attaches $3,000 in franking credits to the distribution. The deficit in its franking account at the end of the income year is $3,000. Speed is liable to pay $3,000 in franking deficit tax. Speed pays the franking deficit tax and therefore is entitled to a franking deficit tax offset.

As the 2014-15 income year is the first income year in which Speed derives taxable income and it satisfies the other conditions Speed's franking deficit tax offset will not be reduced by 30%. Therefore, Speed will be entitled to a franking deficit tax offset of $3,000.

2. REDUCTION IN FRANKING DEFICIT TAX OFFSET

Only franking deficit tax attributable to item 1, 3, 5 or 6 in the table in s205-30 (see *Debits in the franking account* table following) will be taken into account to determine whether the 30% franking deficit tax offset reduction applies. The intention is not to apply the reduction if the franking debit that caused the franking account to go into deficit arose because of the imposition of a penalty or because the franking deficit arose due to circumstances beyond the company's control. Franking deficit tax attributable to item 2 in the table in s205-30 will also be taken into account in some circumstances. The Commissioner has a discretion to disregard the 30% franking deficit tax offset reduction if, in the Commissioner's opinion, the deficit in the franking account of a corporate tax entity arose because of events outside of the entity's control.

The franking debits in the table in s205-30 that are taken into account to determine whether the 30% franking deficit tax offset reduction applies are:

Item 1: All franking debits that arise when an entity franks a distribution

Item 3: All franking debits that arise when an entity franks a distribution in contravention of the benchmark rule

Item 5: All franking debits that arise when a distribution by one entity is substituted for a distribution by another entity, and

Item 6: All franking debits that arise when a tax-exempt bonus share is issued in substitution for a franked distribution.

If an entity has franking debits that arise under one or more of item 1, 3, 5 or 6 in the table in s205-30, all franking debits that arise under item 2 in that table will also be taken into account to determine whether the 30% franking deficit tax offset reduction applies. Franking debits arise under item 2 in the table in s205-30 when, generally, an entity receives a refund of tax.

Franking deficit tax offset

Bigtop Pty Ltd has a franking account balance of $5,000 credit at 1 July 2013. However, by 30 June 2014 the franking account balance is $80,000 in deficit. As such Bigtop is liable to franking deficit tax.

During the year Bigtop paid pay as you go (PAYG) instalments totalling $495,000, which was recognised as a credit to the franking account. Bigtop also made the following debits to its franking account:

- *$10,000 of franking credits on distributions (item 1 franking debits)*
- *$50,000 from a refund of tax (item 2 franking debits), and*
- *$20,000 resulting from Commissioner's determination under the streaming provisions (item 7 franking debits).*

Franking deficit tax attributable only to items 1 and 2 is taken into account to determine whether the 30% franking deficit tax offset reduction applies.

The franking deficit tax is $60,000, being the total franking deficit tax ($80,000) less the franking deficit tax attributable to item 7 ($20,000). The relevant franking deficit tax amount exceeds 10% of the franking credits included in the company's franking account during the year – $49,500 (ie. $495,000 x 10%). Therefore, the 30% franking deficit tax offset reduction will apply.

Bigtop's franking deficit tax offset will be $62,000, (ie. $80,000 – ($60,000 x 30%)).

Imputation system: Maintaining the franking account on a tax-paid basis

In this example assume that Bigtop Pty Ltd has a franking account credit balance of $85,714 at 1 July 2013. During the 2013-14 year Bigtop completed the following transactions:

- *28 July 2013: Paid last PAYG instalment of $40,000 in respect of 2012-13*
- *1 August 2013: Paid a dividend of $20,000 with a franking percentage of 80%*
- *20 September 2013: Received dividend from BHP Ltd of $10,000 fully franked (imputation credit $4,286)*
- *28 October 2013: Paid first PAYG instalment for 2013-14 income year of $50,000*
- *10 December 2013: Payment of a dividend of $44,000 with a franking percentage of 100%*
- *15 December 2013: Paid final tax in respect of 2012-13 income tax year of $6,000*
- *28 February 2014: Paid second PAYG instalment of $30,000*
- *1 April 2014: Received $5,000 fully franked dividend carrying an imputation credit of $2,143*
- *28 April 2014: Paid third quarter PAYG instalment of $22,000*
- *15 June 2014: Received fully franked dividend from a trust of $1,500 carrying an imputation credit of $643*

Bigtop Pty Ltd franking account for 2013-14		Debit $	Credit $	Balance $
2013				
01 Jul				85,714cr
28 Jul	PAYG instalment $40,000		40,000	125,714cr
01 Aug	Payment for a dividend of $20,000 with a franking percentage of 80% ($20,000 x 80% x 30/70[1])	6,857		118,857cr
20 Sep	Receipt of dividend of $10,000 from BHP Ltd[2]		4,286	123,143cr
28 Oct	PAYG instalment $50,000		50,000	173,143cr
10 Dec	Payment for a fully franked dividend of $44,000 ($44,000[3] x 100% x 30/70)	18,857		154,286cr
15 Dec	Final tax liability outstanding for 2012-13 income year		6,000	160,286cr
2014				
28 Feb	PAYG instalment		30,000	190,286cr
01 Apr	Received fully franked dividend		2,143	192,429cr
28 Apr	PAYG instalment		22,000	214,429cr
15 Jun	Receipt of distribution from trust of $1,500 with share of imputation credit of $643[4]		643	215,072cr

1. This is the first frankable distribution for the franking period, as such the benchmark rate for all distributions in a franking period must be limited to 80%. Note, a private company's franking period is generally 12 months.

2. The imputation credit attached to a franked distribution received by a franking entity is generally the amount of the credit posted to the franking account. Note the Commissioner may determine otherwise.

3. The company has franked the distribution at 100% rather than the benchmark rate of 80% established by the first payment. It is now liable for overfranking tax. The overfranking penalty tax is not recognised as a credit to the franking account and as such an imputation benefit is lost. The overfranking penalty tax is calculated as: Franking % differential x Amount of frankable distribution x Company tax rate/(100% – Company tax rate). Bigtop is liable to pay overfranking tax of $3,771 (20% x $44,000 x 30/70 = $3,771).

4. A franked distribution received indirectly from a trust results in a credit in the franking account to the extent of its share of the franking credit. The date of the entry in the franking account for a distribution received from the trust.

Credits in the franking account

Item	If ...	A debit of ...	Arises ...
1	• the entity pays a PAYG instalment, and • the entity satisfies the residency requirement for the income year in relation to which the PAYG instalment is paid, and • the entity is a franking entity for the whole or part of the relevant PAYG instalment period	that part of the payment that is attributable to the period during which the entity was a franking entity	on the day on which the payment is made
2	• the entity pays income tax, and • the entity satisfies the residency requirement for the income year for which the tax is paid, and • the entity is a franking entity for the whole or part of that income year	that part of the payment that is attributable to the period during which the entity was a franking entity	on the day on which the payment is made
3	• a franked distribution is made to the entity, and • the entity satisfies the residency requirement for the income year in which the distribution is made, and • the entity is a franking entity when it receives the distribution, and • the entity is entitled to a tax offset because of the distribution under Division 207	the franking credit on the distribution	on the day on which the distribution is made
4	• a franked distribution flows indirectly to the entity through a partnership or trust, and • the entity is a franking entity when the franked distribution is made, and • the entity is entitled to a tax offset because of the distribution under Division 207	the entity's share of the franking credit on the distribution	at the end of the income year of the last partnership or trust interposed between the entity and the corporate tax entity that made the distribution
5	• the entity incurs a liability to pay franking deficit tax under s205-45 or s205-50	the amount of the liability	immediately after the liability is incurred

Debits in the franking account

Item	If ...	A debit of ...	Arises ...
1	• the entity franks a distribution	the amount of the franking credit on the distribution	on the day on which the distribution is made
2	• the entity receives a refund of income tax, and • the entity satisfies the residency requirement for the income year to which the refund relates, and • the entity was a franking entity during the whole or part of the income year to which the refund relates	that part of the refund that is attributable to the period during which the entity was a franking entity	on the day on which the refund is received
3	• a franking debit arises for the entity under paragraph 203-50(1)(b) (the entity franks a distribution in contravention of the benchmark rule)	the franking debit worked out under paragraph 203-50(2)(b)	on the day specified in subsection 203-50(4)
4	• the entity ceases to be a franking entity, and • the entity's franking account is in surplus immediately before ceasing to be a franking entity	the amount of the franking surplus	on the day on which the entity ceases to be a franking entity

Debits in the franking account			
Item	If ...	A debit of ...	Arises ...
5	• a franking debit arises for the entity under s204-15 (linked distributions)	the franking debit specified in subsection 204-15(3)	on the day specified in subsection 204-15(4)
6	• a franking debit arises under s204-25 (debit for substituting tax-exempt bonus shares for franked distributions)	the amount of the debit specified in subsection 204-25(2)	on the day specified in subsection 204-25(3)
7	• the Commissioner makes a determination under paragraph 204-30(3)(a) giving rise to a franking debit for the entity (streaming distributions)	the amount of the debit specified in the determination	on the day specified in s204-35
8	• an on-market share buy-back by a company of a membership interest in the company	an amount equal to the debit that would have arisen if: • the purchase of the interest was a frankable distribution equal to the one that would have arisen if the company had purchased the interest off-market, and • the distribution was franked at the entity's benchmark franking percentage for the franking period in which the purchase was made or, if the entity does not have a benchmark franking percentage for the period, at a franking percentage of 100%	on the day on which the interest is purchased

NOTE: From 1 July 2006, the company's franking account is no longer automatically debited when a deemed dividend arises.

EFFECT OF RECEIVING A FRANKED DISTRIBUTION

Division 207 sets out the tax effects for an entity that receives a franked distribution. The consequences vary depending on whether the distribution is received directly from a corporate tax entity or indirectly through a partnership or trust. Corporate entities in the past were not required to gross-up the distribution received and were entitled to an intercorporate dividend rebate to the extent that the distribution was franked. This ensured that the receipt of franked dividends were not taxed again. The current rules achieve the same result and bring the treatment for corporate entities into line with other taxpayer entities.

TAX OFFSET FOR DIRECT DISTRIBUTIONS FROM A COMPANY (OTHER THAN PARTNERSHIP OR TRUST)

All entities, excluding partnerships and trusts, that receive a franked distribution directly, are to include the amount of the franking credit on the distribution in the assessable income of the entity (ie. the entity's assessable income will be grossed-up) and the entity will be entitled to a tax offset equal to the amount of the franking credit (s207-20(1) and (2)). This will generally be the case where the entity is:

- an individual
- a corporate tax entity
- an eligible superannuation fund, approved deposit fund or PST, or
- an eligible income tax exempt charity or a deductible gift recipient.

NOTE: The gross-up and tax offset rules under s207-20 do not apply to a partnership or trust that receives a franked distribution directly. Nor do these rules apply to a partner or beneficiary that receives a share of a franked distribution, or to a trustee that is assessed on a share of a franked distribution, because the distribution flows indirectly to the taxpayer in these cases.

Direct distribution

Sun Pty Ltd, an Australian resident company receives a fully franked distribution of $7 million. Sun Pty Ltd also has net income from other sources of $12 million in the same income year. The consequences for Sun Pty Ltd of receiving a franked distribution directly are as follows:

Other income	*$12.0 million*
Franked distribution	*$7.0 million*
Franking credit (gross up)	*$3.0 million*
Taxable income	*$22.0 million*
Tax at company rate (30%)	*$6.6 million*
Less franking credit offset	*$3.0 million*
Tax payable by Sun Pty Ltd	*$3.6 million*

TAX OFFSET FOR INDIRECT DISTRIBUTIONS THROUGH PARTNERSHIPS AND TRUSTS

If a franked distribution is received by a partnership or a trust, the assessable income of the entity will be grossed-up by the amount of the franking credit.

A partner, beneficiary or trustee who is assessed in respect of a share of the franked distribution will be entitled to a tax offset equal to a proportionate share of the franking credit. The partner's, beneficiary's or trustee's share of franking credit on the distribution is calculated by apportioning the total franking credit according to the entity's share in the cash amount of the franked distribution (s207-55(1)).

Where a franked distribution flows through more than one partnership or trust, ultimate recipients of the distribution will be entitled to a tax offset equal to their share of the franking credit. In these circumstances the ultimate recipient's share of the franking credit is calculated by apportioning the flow through the entity's share of the franking credit. This share is apportioned according to the ultimate recipient's share of the cash amount of the distribution in relation to the flow through of the entity's share of the cash amount of the distribution (s207-55(2)).

The following entities are entitled to a tax offset for distributions that flow indirectly to them as either partners in a partnership or a beneficiary of a trust:

- an individual
- a corporate tax entity
- a trustee who is taxed on a share of net income of the trust under s98, 99 or 99A ITAA36, or
- an eligible superannuation fund, approved deposit fund or pooled superannuation trust.

GROSS-UP AND OFFSET RULES

The general gross-up and offset rules are also subject to rules relating to:

- residency requirements which must be satisfied by individuals and corporate tax entities, as set out in Subdivision 207-C
- the treatment of franked distributions which are exempt income or received by certain exempt institutions, set out in Subdivision 207-E, and
- cases where the imputation system has been manipulated, set out in Subdivision 207-F.

CONVERSION OF TAX OFFSETS INTO LOSSES FOR CORPORATE TAX ENTITIES

Corporate tax entities, other than certain income tax exempt charities and deductible gift recipients, are not entitled to refunds of excess imputation credits. Where a corporate tax entity has imputation tax offsets which exceed its income tax which results in 'excess franking offsets', there is scope for that entity to have the excess imputation credits converted into a tax loss. This is achieved by dividing the excess amount by the corporate tax rate. This converted tax loss is then aggregated with any current year tax loss and the aggregated amount becomes the tax loss for the income year (see 6.440).

REFUND OF TAX OFFSETS FOR INDIVIDUALS

Subject to certain anti-avoidance provisions not applying (the holding period rule and related payment rule – refer below), resident individual taxpayers are entitled to a refund of franking credits from the receipt of franked dividends either directly or indirectly, provided that:

- they receive those franked dividends directly or indirectly, via a partnership or trust distribution, and
- their tax liability is less than their franking credit entitlement after applying any other tax offsets to which that individual is entitled.

Michael is a student who owns shares in XYZ Ltd. During the 2013-14 income year, Michael received the following income:

- *$5,000 gross wages from his part-time job at a restaurant, and*
- *$700 dividends from XYZ Ltd which are fully franked (with a $300 franking credit attached).*

Michael had no other tax deductions and PAYG was not withheld with respect to his wage income. His taxable income for the year was $6,000 (which includes franking credit gross-up of $300).

As Michael is under the tax-free threshold, he would not be liable to an income tax liability for the year. As his basic tax liability is less than his franking credit entitlement (he is not entitled to any other offsets), he would be entitled to a refund of the franking credits amounting to $300. Michael will receive the refund following the lodgment of his 2014 income tax return.

HOLDING PERIOD RULE

In order to be entitled to a franking offset for individuals it is necessary that a shareholder has held the relevant shares substantially 'at risk' for the minimum qualification period (45 days for ordinary shares and 90 days for preference shares). This is commonly referred to as the 'holding period rule'.

Whilst the provisions applicable to the 'holding period rule' pursuant to the former Division 1A of Part IIIA ITAA36 have been repealed, these rules still have application as they are incorporated into the ITAA97.

In determining the number of days the shares have been held, the day that the shares were acquired and the day in which the shares are disposed do not count. This applies similarly for both 45 day ordinary shares and 90 days for preference shares. This rule does not apply if the $5,000 small shareholder exemption rule applies (refer below).

NOTE: The holding rule cannot be satisfied where shares are held by non-fixed trusts and franked dividends are distributed to a beneficiary. This is due to the fact that the shares are not being held 'at risk' as the beneficiary in receipt of the dividend has no interest in the trust assets and essentially does not hold the shares which give rise to the franking credits. In such instances, a family trust election may enable the holding period rule to be satisfied (refer 7.200).

RELATED PAYMENTS RULE

In addition to the holding period rule, an anti-avoidance rule applies where an individual makes, or is under an obligation to make, a 'related payment'. More specifically, a related payment is one which passes on the benefit of the franking credit to another person. This rule applies to each distribution received.

This rule applies irrespective of whether the available franking credits is less than $5,000 (refer to *Small shareholder exemption* below).

SMALL SHAREHOLDER EXEMPTION

The holding period rule does not apply where the taxpayer satisfies the small shareholder exemption. This exemption applies where the taxpayer receives **less than $5,000** in franking credits from all sources for the income year.

Where the taxpayer is not entitled to a franking credit, they will not be required to gross-up their dividend by any franking credits which may have been attached.

RESIDENCY REQUIREMENTS FOR TAX OFFSETS

The rules concerning the residency requirements for individuals and corporate tax entities to receive a tax offset for a direct distribution are set out in Subdivision 207-C. An individual or a corporate tax entity that receives a franked distribution directly must be a resident at the time the distribution is made to be eligible for a tax offset (s207-70). If the taxpayer was not a resident, the distribution would be exempt from withholding tax because it is franked and therefore exempt from income tax, removing the need for a tax offset. The taxpayer's assessable income is not grossed-up in this case because the distribution is exempt income.

NO TAX OFFSET IF DISTRIBUTION EXEMPT INCOME

An entity will generally not be entitled to a tax offset if the franked distribution or share of a franked distribution is exempt income. In this case, the entity's assessable income will not be grossed-up where the entity receives the distribution directly. If the entity has received a share of the distribution indirectly, a deduction (or reduction) will be allowed to remove the entity's share of the franking credit from the entity's assessable income (s207-110).

There are two exceptions to the rule that an offset does not arise in respect of a franked distribution that is exempt income:

- complying superannuation funds, approved deposit funds and PSTs (eligible superannuation entities) and life insurance companies are entitled to a tax offset in respect of certain exempt income, for example, income derived by a complying superannuation fund from segregated pension assets, and
- eligible income tax exempt charities and deductible gift recipients are entitled to a tax offset. Although these bodies are exempt from income tax, they are given an entitlement to an offset to make them eligible for a refund of their share of the franking credit under Division 67 (s207-110).

Eligible income tax exempt charities and deductible gift recipients entitled to a tax offset are as follows (s207-115):

- charitable institutions that are endorsed as exempt from income tax under Subdivision 50-B, that satisfy the residency requirement set out in s207-117
- deductible gift recipients that are endorsed under s30-120(a), that satisfy the residency requirement set out in s207-117
- deductible gift recipients that are specified in Subdivision 30-B and have an Australian Business Number and satisfy the residency requirement set out in s207-117
- a public fund declared by the Treasurer to be a relief fund in accordance with s30-85(2) (other than a fund prescribed in the regulations as not being eligible), and
- any income tax exempt entities prescribed in the regulations as eligible for the offset.

NO OFFSET IF THE IMPUTATION SYSTEM HAS BEEN MANIPULATED

An entity that directly or indirectly receives a franked distribution will be denied a tax offset in the following circumstances because the imputation system has been manipulated (Subdivision 207-F):

- the entity does not satisfy the holding period rule
- the Commissioner has made a determination under s204-30(3)(b) that no imputation benefit is to arise because a corporate tax entity has streamed distributions in a certain way
- the distribution is made as part of a dividend stripping operation, or
- the Commissioner has made a determination under s177EA(5)(b) that no imputation benefit is to arise because the distribution was paid as part of a scheme to obtain a franking credit benefit.

If these exceptions apply, the assessable income of an entity that receives the distribution directly will not be grossed-up. An entity that receives the distribution indirectly is allowed a deduction (or reduction) to ensure that the entity's share of the franking credit is excluded from the entity's assessable income (s207-75).

If the Commissioner has made a determination under s177EA(5)(b) that an imputation benefit is not to arise in respect of part of a franked distribution, an entity's entitlement to a tax offset is reduced proportionately (s207-145(2)).

ADJUSTMENTS FOR NON-RESIDENTS

The rules for adjustments to the assessable income of an entity receiving a distribution indirectly that is exempt from income tax because the distribution is exempt from withholding tax are set out in Subdivision 207-D.

Where an individual or a corporate tax entity receives a franked distribution indirectly, and the individual or corporate tax entity was a non-resident at the time the distribution was made (so that the distribution would be exempt from withholding tax because it is franked and therefore exempt from income tax), the assessable income of the entity will be adjusted to remove the entity's share of the franking credit from the entity's assessable income. This adjustment is necessary because, while the distribution would be exempt from income tax, the entity's share of the franking credit would otherwise be included in the entity's assessable income.

6.820   FRANKING ACCOUNT TAX RETURN

Corporate tax entities must complete a franking account tax return if certain conditions apply.

Corporate tax entities must complete a franking account tax return if any of the following circumstances apply:

- it has a liability to pay franking deficit tax, and/or
- it has a liability to pay over-franking tax, and/or
- it has triggered the disclosure obligation due to a significant variation in its benchmark franking percentages. A significant variation will occur where the benchmark franking percentage for the current franking period has increased or decreased by more than 20 percentage points from the last franking period.

If a corporate tax entity receives a refund of income tax within three months after the end of the income year and the franking account would have been in deficit or in deficit to a greater extent had the refund been received during the income year then it will be required to complete a franking account tax return.

The franking account tax return must be lodged and the franking deficit liability and/or over franking tax liability must be paid at the later of:

- the last day of the month following the end of the income year (ie. 31 July), or
- the 14th day after the refund of income tax is received.

A penalty is imposed for late returns and general interest charge is applied to the outstanding tax if not paid by the due date (see from 4.660).

NOTE: The Commissioner may amend a franking assessment within three years of the date of the first franking assessment for the entity for the income year.

6.850   DISTRIBUTION STATEMENT

 A corporate tax entity that makes a franked distribution must issue a distribution statement to the members.

DISTRIBUTION STATEMENTS

An entity that makes a frankable distribution must provide the recipient with a distribution statement that contains certain information about the entity and the distribution (s202-75).

The time at which a distribution statement must be given depends on whether, for the income year in which the distribution is made, the entity is a private company or not.

A private company is one that is not a public company, as defined in s103A ITAA36, for the income year. A company will generally be a private company if:

- it does not have its shares listed on an official stock exchange, or

- 20 or fewer persons control 75% or more of:
    - the paid up capital of the company
    - the voting rights in the company, or
    - the rights to the income of the company.

An entity that is a private company, for the income year in which the distribution was made, must give a distribution statement before the end of four months after the end of the income year in which the distribution is made, or such further time as the Commissioner allows.

As a consequence of this, private companies can, in effect, retrospectively frank a distribution. A private company has the entire income year and up to another four months (or such further time allowed by the Commissioner) after the end of its income year to make decisions on the extent to which it franks distributions made during the income year.

An entity that is not a private company (ie. a public company) for the income year in which a distribution is made is required to give a distribution statement to the recipient on or before the day on which the distribution is made (s202-75(2)(a)).

DISTRIBUTION STATEMENT: APPROVED FORM

Corporate entities must issue to shareholders distribution statements in the approved form. The distribution statement meets the requirements if it contains the following information (s202-80(2) and (3)):

- A. the name of the entity making the distribution
- B. the date on which the distribution was made
- C. the amount of the distribution
- D. the amount of franking credit allocated to the distribution
- E. the franking percentage for the distribution
- F. the amount of any withholding tax that has been deducted from the distribution, and
- G. any other information required by the approved form that is relevant to imputation generally or the distribution.

For the purpose of paragraph (g) above, the following is required on the distribution statement:

- A. the name of the shareholder
- B. where the distribution is unfranked – a statement to that effect, and
- C. where the distribution is franked – the franked amount and the unfranked amount of the distribution.

NOTE: For the purposes of recording the franking percentage on the distribution statement, the value stated should be worked out to two decimal places, rounding up if the third decimal place is five or more.

Taxpayers in Listed Investment Companies (LICs) should note the additional information on their distribution statements brought about by the Government's decision to extend the CGT discount on assets realised on or after 1 July 2001 by an LIC. They are now entitled to a deduction of 50% CGT discount on assets realised on or after 1 July 2001 when an LIC includes such gains as part of the distribution (see below).

FRANKED AMOUNT OF THE DISTRIBUTION

The franked amount, unfranked amount and franking credit recorded on the distribution statement should be rounded off to the nearest cent and are calculated as follows.

The franked amount of a distribution is the amount calculated using the following formula found in s976 ITAA97:

Franking credit on the distribution x
[(1 – Corporate tax rate) divided by Corporate tax rate]

where:

- the corporate tax rate is 30%, and

- the franking credit on the distribution is the lesser of either:
  - the amount stated on the distribution statement, or
  - the amount calculated using the following formula:

Franked amount of the distribution x company tax rate
divided by (100% – company tax rate)

UNFRANKED AMOUNT OF THE DISTRIBUTION

The unfranked amount of the distribution is the amount calculated using the following formula:

Amount of the frankable distribution – Franked amount

On 1 September 2013 Fizz International Ltd made a frankable distribution of $10,000 to its shareholders and allocated franking credits of $1,500 to the distribution. Assume all shareholders are resident for tax purposes and no shareholders have TFN withholding.

Note that for illustrative purposes the distribution statement has been completed as if the entire distribution was payable to one shareholder.

The franked amount of the distribution is calculated as follows:

Franking credit on the distribution x [(1 – Corporate tax rate) divided by Corporate tax rate]
$1,500 x (70% divided by 30%) = $3,500

The unfranked amount of the distribution is calculated as follows:

Amount of distribution – Franked amount
$10,000 – $3,500 = $6,500

Pro-forma distribution statement	
Fizz International Limited ABN/ACN XX XXXXXXXXX	
Distribution Statement	
A) Date on which the distribution was made	1 September 2013
B) Name of shareholder	Name of shareholder
C) Amount of distribution	$10,000
D) Franked amount of the distribution	$3,500
E) Unfranked amount of the distribution	$6,500
F) Amount of franking credit allocated to the distribution	$1,500
G) Franking percentage	35%
H) The amount of any withholding tax that has been deducted from the distribution (assume resident shareholder)	$Nil
I) Withholding tax withheld due to failure to quote TFN	$Nil

The franking percentage is the lesser of 100% or the amount calculated using the following formula:

(Franking credit allocated to the frankable distribution divided by Maximum franking credit for the (frankable) distribution) x 100%

LISTED INVESTMENT COMPANY (LIC): DISTRIBUTION STATEMENT

Certain shareholders of an LIC are entitled to a deduction for a LIC capital gain if all or some part of the dividend paid by the LIC is reasonably attributable to an LIC capital gain made by an LIC. To facilitate this, the LIC includes the following additional information in the distribution statements it provides to its members on payment of the final dividend:

A. the attributable part of the dividend

B. the members who are entitled to a deduction for the attributable part of the dividend, and

C. the amount of deduction that these members may claim.

From 1 July 2001, shareholders can receive a distribution which is fully franked and still receive a deduction of 50% of the attributable part disclosed on the distribution statement. This is because LICs may pass on the benefit of the 50% capital gains discount to their shareholders. Companies are not generally eligible to use the capital gains discount method when disposing of capital assets, however a exception was granted for LICs which can now pass this benefit onto shareholders.

6.900   ANTI-AVOIDANCE RULES

Section 177EA has been inserted into the Part IVA anti-avoidance provisions (see also 4.500) to deal with schemes that provide a tax advantage in relation to franking credits.

The general anti-avoidance rule applies to dividends and other distributions paid on or after 7.30pm AEST, 13 May 1997, including schemes or arrangements entered into before that time. The conditions necessary for the application of this provision are set out in s177EA(3) as follows:

1. there is a scheme for a disposition of shares or an interest in shares in a company, and
2. a frankable dividend or distribution has been paid, or is payable or expected to be payable, in respect of the shares or interest, and
3. the dividend or distribution was, or is expected to be franked, and
4. except for s177EA, a person would receive, or could reasonably expect to receive, franking credit benefits as a result of the dividend or distribution, and
5. having regard to the relevant circumstances of the scheme, it would be concluded that one of the persons who entered into or carried out the scheme did so for a purpose (whether or not the dominant purpose but not including an incidental purpose) of enabling the relevant taxpayer to obtain a franking credit benefit.

If the conditions are satisfied, the Commissioner has a choice as whether to:

- post a debit to the company's franking account if the company is a party to the scheme, or
- deny the franking credit benefit to the recipient of the dividend or distribution.

WHAT IS A 'SCHEME' FOR THE DISPOSITION OF SHARES OR AN INTEREST IN SHARES?

A 'scheme' for the disposition of shares or an interest in shares would include the issue of a dividend access share, or an arrangement whereby a person obtains an interest in a discretionary trust for the purpose of streaming franking credits to particular beneficiaries. An interest in shares includes (s177EA(13) ITAA36):

- legal or equitable interests in shares
- a partner's interest in partnership assets which includes shares, or the partnership derives dividends directly or indirectly from shares, and
- the interests of a person who is a beneficiary of a trust (including a potential beneficiary of a discretionary trust) where the shares form, or will form, part of the trust estate, or the trust directly or indirectly derives (or will derive) dividends paid on shares.

A scheme for a disposition of shares or an interest in shares includes (but is not limited to) (s177EA(14) ITAA36):

- issuing the shares or creating the interest in shares
- entering into any contract, arrangement, transaction or dealing that changes or otherwise affects the legal or equitable ownership of the shares or interest in shares
- creating, varying, or revoking a trust in relation to the shares or interest in shares
- creating, altering or extinguishing a right, power or liability attaching to or otherwise relating to the shares or interest in shares
- substantially altering any of the risks of loss or opportunities for profit or gain, involved in holding or owning the shares or having an interest in them, and

- the shares or interest beginning, or ceasing to be included in any of the insurance funds of a life assurance company.

Therefore, even the simple purchase of shares would constitute a scheme for a disposition of shares.

In ATO ID 2002/613, the Commissioner considers that the sale of shares in the taxpayer company by a director to his wife and his family trust for asset protection purposes as a result of commencing a new business venture did not constitute a franking credit scheme.

SHARES PURCHASED 'CUM-DIVIDEND'

One example of a situation where the general anti-avoidance rule may apply is where shares are purchased 'cum-dividend'. A concessionally taxed fully franked dividend is received by the purchaser and then the shares are sold ex-dividend for a deductible or capital loss (say, approximately equal to the cash dividend received). As the dividend would otherwise be concessionally taxed and the loss (if one was made due to the potential fall in share price following the dividend payment) might be fully deductible, or be able to be offset against capital gains made, these types of arrangements fall within these new rules if a 'not merely incidental' purpose of such an arrangement of acquiring the shares was to obtain a franked dividend.

SCRIP LENDING

Another example of where the general anti-avoidance provision would apply is in a scrip lending arrangement. Under these types of arrangements it is possible for a shareholder who cannot fully use franking credits to loan scrip (shares) for a fee. The borrower receives a tax deduction for the fee paid, and as a borrower of the scrip receive fully franked dividends.

DIVIDEND WASHING – PRE-1 JULY 2013

Another example of where the general anti-avoidance provision would apply is dividend washing (discussed above). In Taxation Determination TD 2014/10 the Commissioner states that section 177EA ITAA36 applies to these arrangements. However, from 1 July 2013 a specific integrity rule applies to these arrangements.

DETERMINING PURPOSE

Whether these rules apply depends on whether a purpose test is satisfied; namely whether it could be concluded that a person who entered into the contract or carried out the scheme under which the disposition of shares occurs, did so to obtain a tax advantage relating to franking credits. Unlike the test for the general application of Part IVA, the purpose does not have to be the dominant purpose but it must be more than an incidental purpose. However, a person does not enter into a scheme merely because the person acquired shares or an interest in shares in a company.

It is necessary to determine whether it was a more than an incidental purpose of a person who entered into or carried out a scheme (involving the disposition of shares or interest in shares) to obtain a tax advantage relating to franking credits. In forming that conclusion, it is necessary to consider the relevant circumstances of the scheme including (s177EA(17) ITAA36):

- the extent to which the person holding the share and the other party to the scheme is exposed to the risks and opportunities of ownership, and whether there has been any change in those risks and opportunities. The greater the exposure to such risks and opportunities, the less likely that the requisite purpose is present

- whether the relevant taxpayer would have derived in the year of income in which the dividend is paid, a greater benefit from franking credits than other persons who hold shares or interests in shares in the company. This test looks at the tax profiles of the parties to the scheme

- if the scheme involves payment of a franked dividend, whether in the absence of the scheme the company would have retained the franking credits or would have used the franking credits to pay a franked dividend to another person

- if the scheme involves making a franked distribution, whether if not for the scheme, a franked distribution would have been made to another person
- whether any consideration paid or given was calculated by reference to the franking credit benefits to be received by the relevant taxpayer
- whether a deduction is available or a capital loss incurred in connection with the paying of a dividend or the making of a distribution under a scheme
- whether the dividend paid or distribution made under the scheme is equivalent to interest or in the nature of interest
- whether the dividend paid or distribution made under the scheme is sourced from unrealised or untaxed profits
- the period for which the taxpayer held the shares or had an interest in the shares. The longer the period the shares were held the less likely that these provisions apply, and
- any of the existing factors set out in Part IVA (see s177D(b)) which are relevant in determining whether a scheme has been entered into for the sole or dominant purpose of obtaining a tax benefit.

The explanatory memorandum states that:

A purpose is an incidental purpose when it occurs fortuitously or in a subordinate conjunction with another purpose, or merely follows another purpose as its natural incident. For example, when a taxpayer holds shares in the ordinary way to obtain the benefit of any increase in their share price and the dividend income flowing from the shares, a franking credit benefit is generally no more than a natural incident of holding the shares, and generally the purpose of obtaining the benefit simply follows incidentally a purpose of obtaining the shares: it is therefore merely an incidental purpose.

The maximum debit that can be posted to the company's franking account (as a result of s177EA being involved) is determined under s160AQB as the same amount of the debit that would have arisen when the company pays the franked dividend. Alternatively, the Commissioner may deny franking credit benefits.

In *Mills v Commissioner of Taxation* (2011) FCA 205, the Federal Court, after analysing the relevant factors under s177EA(17) and s177D, held that securities issued by the financial institution under a particular scheme enabled its holders to obtain an imputation benefit that would not otherwise be available and that the Commissioner was entitled to exercise his discretion under s177EA(5)(b) to cancel the imputation credit in the hands of the relevant taxpayer.

6.950   SHARE CAPITAL TAINTING – DIVISION 197

Shareholders are taxed preferentially on distributions of share capital as opposed to distributions of profits that are generally taxed at the shareholders' marginal tax rate. The share capital tainting rules are integrity rules designed to prevent a company from disguising a distribution of profits as a tax-preferred capital distribution by transferring profits into its share capital account and subsequently making distributions from that account.

Share capital accounts will become tainted if a company transfers certain amounts to that account. The consequences of a share capital account becoming tainted will be that a franking debit arises in the company's franking account. If the company chooses to untaint its share capital account, an additional franking debit may arise and untainting tax may be payable.

An amount is transferred where that amount is moved from one account to another. This requires the balance of the first account to be reduced, while the balance of the second account is increased by the same amount.

An amount is not transferred from one account to another where the particular accounting entries result in the balances of both accounts increasing in size. Accordingly, an accounting entry that 'debits asset/expense, credits share capital account' does not represent a transfer in the relevant sense.

A company's share capital account will become tainted if it transfers an amount to its share capital account from any other account, other than:

- an amount that can be identified as share capital
- certain amounts that are transferred under debt/equity swaps (see below)

- an amount that is transferred from the share premium account by a non-Corporations Act company to remove shares with a par value
- certain amounts that are transferred from an option premium reserve (see below), and
- certain amounts that are transferred in connection with demutualisations and post-demutualisation transfers of a non-insurance company.

Under certain circumstances, the conversion of convertible debentures held by the head company of a tax consolidated group (see 6.500) in its subsidiary member into ordinary shares does not constitute a transfer to the share capital account of either subsidiary member for the purposes of the share capital tainting rules (ATO ID 2009/136).

Further, a journal entry made to a consolidated group's financial statements is not a transfer into the share capital account of the head company for the purposes of the share capital tainting rules (ATO ID 2009/94).

Certain dividend reinvestment plans provided to shareholders of a company would not ordinarily taint the issuing company's share capital account for the purposes of the share capital tainting rules (TD 2009/4).

A share capital account for the purposes of the share tainting rules is:

- any account that the company keeps of its share capital, or
- any other account (whether or not it is called a share capital account) that was created after 1 July 1998 where the first amount credited to the account was an amount of share capital.

If a company has more than one share capital account, those accounts are taken to be a single account. The concept of share capital is not defined in the ITAA97. Under its ordinary meaning, share capital includes amounts received by a company in consideration for the issue of shares.

CONSEQUENCES OF TAINTING SHARE CAPITAL ACCOUNT

If a company's share capital account becomes tainted, a franking debit arises in the company's franking account at the end of the franking period in which the transfer occurs. A tainted share capital account is treated as a profit account and any subsequent distributions from that account are unfrankable distributions (rather than returns of capital). The amount of the franking debit is calculated by applying the formula in s197-45(2):

Transferred amount x [Company tax rate divided by (100% – company tax rate)] x Franking percentage

The applicable franking percentage is the company's benchmark franking percentage (determined under s203-30 ITAA97) for the franking period in which the tainting occurs. If the company has not set a benchmark franking percentage by the end of the franking period, it is taken to be 100%.

 A company's share capital account becomes tainted when an amount of $700 is transferred to the account from another account. The company has a benchmark franking percentage for the franking period in which the tainting occurred of 80%.

Section 197-45 imposes a franking debit at the end of the franking period of $240 (ie. $700 x [(30 divided by 70 x 80%)]).

UNTAINTING A SHARE CAPITAL ACCOUNT

A company can make an irrevocable choice to untaint its share capital account. If the company chooses to untaint its share capital account, an additional franking debit may arise at the end of the franking period in which the choice to untaint is made. Untainting tax may also be payable at that time which is payable within 21 days of the end of the franking period in which the choice is made. The amount of untainting tax depends if the company is:

- a company with only lower tax members in relation to the tainting period, or
- a company with higher tax members in relation to the tainting period.

Untainting tax will only be payable by a company that only has lower tax members in the tainting period if the company's benchmark franking percentage at either the time of tainting or the time of untainting is less than 100%.

A company will only have lower tax members in the tainting period if, in that period, it only has members that are:

- other companies (including life insurance companies)
- complying superannuation entities, or
- foreign residents.

Untainting tax will always be payable by a company with higher tax members during the tainting period.

Irrespective of the kind of members a company has, the amount of untainting tax (if any) is equal to the 'applicable tax amount' less any franking debits that arose in relation to the tainting amount. The 'applicable tax amount' is the grossed up tainting amount multiplied by the 'applicable tax rate'. The 'applicable tax rate' for a higher tax member is 47.5% (ie. highest marginal tax rate + Medicare levy + Medicare levy surcharge). For a lower tax member, the rate is 30%. The formulae to calculate the untainting tax are in s197-60(3) and (4).

AMOUNTS TRANSFERRED UNDER DEBT/EQUITY SWAPS (s197-15)

A company's share capital account is not tainted if the amount is transferred under a debt for equity swap. A debt for equity swap is an arrangement under which a person discharges, releases or otherwise extinguishes the whole or part of a debt that the company owes to the person in return for shares other than redeemable preference shares.

This exclusion only applies to the transferred amount that does not exceed the lesser of:

- the market value of the shares issued, and
- the amount of the debt that is discharged, released or extinguished in return for the shares.

AMOUNTS TRANSFERRED FROM OPTION PREMIUM RESERVES (s197-25)

A company's share capital account does not become tainted if an amount is transferred from an option premium reserve to the share capital account where:

- the transfer is made because the options were exercised, and
- the amount transferred represents option premiums that were credited to the option premium reserve.

Amounts that are credited as tax assets that are greater than debited tax expenses in relation to the employee share scheme of a company employer are not considered to be option premiums under s197-25 (ATO ID 2009/87).

Trusts

7

7.000 TRUSTS

A trust is established whenever there is a separation of the legal ownership (eg. the name appearing on a land title) from the beneficial (equitable) owner of an asset (ie. the person whom the Courts would recognise as being the true owner).

A trust is established under state law and generally lasts for 80 years or the term of a life plus 21 years. There is an exception in South Australia where the law against perpetuities has been abolished.

The trustee is the legal owner of the trust property and the beneficiaries have equitable rights to the trust property. A trust establishes a relationship between trustee and beneficiaries in respect of the trust property as documented in a Trust Deed or a Will. The Tax Office is reluctant to accept the existence of any trust that has not had its terms set out in writing. The terms of trusts can, however be established by implication, conduct or a decision of the Courts.

Division 6 ITAA36 details the rules by which trust income should be calculated for tax purposes and how that income should be taxed (ie. whether in the hands of the trustee or the beneficiary) (see 7.600 and 7.700). A deceased estate (see 7.950) is a trust, as is a superannuation fund, although the latter is treated very differently for tax purposes (see from 19.000).

Where potentially appreciating assets are being acquired, discretionary trusts are usually preferable to companies and fixed trusts from a tax perspective. Pre-CGT profits of a discretionary trust can be passed to beneficiaries tax-free, in contrast to the situation where such profits are paid in the form of an unfranked dividend by a company to a shareholder which are usually assessable. In the case of a unit trust, such a distribution may have CGT event E4 implications.

ELEMENTS OF A TRUST

The essential elements required for a validly enforceable trust arrangement are:
- the trustee
- certain beneficiaries (or 'objects')
- the trust property which is clearly identifiable and capable of being held on trust, and
- the obligation in respect of the trust property referred to above.

An appointor or guardian can also be used to provided additional checks and balances. The person who initially transfers the trust property to (which could be payment of an initial sum of money to establish) the trust is known as the settlor. A settlor may also declare themselves a trustee of property which they own, as for the benefit of certain beneficiaries. It is possible that the settlor and the trustee could be one and the same person.

 An invalid settlement or nullity can occur where the trustee is the sole beneficiary or the settlor is a beneficiary. No trust relationship actually exists in such circumstances.

KEY ELEMENTS OF A TRUST DEED

The trust deed establishes the trust and sets out the rules for the governance and operation of the trust, and the powers of the trustee.

The key clauses of the trust deed are those dealing with:
- **the beneficiaries of the trust**

  Most deeds provide for primary beneficiaries (named in the trust deed), general beneficiaries (defined in terms of a class or by their relationship to the primary beneficiaries) and default beneficiaries (who are entitled to the trust's income if the trustee does not make a valid distribution to the primary or general beneficiaries).

- **the income of the trust**

  The trust deed may define the income of the trust as being equal to the trust's s95 ITAA36 income (an 'income equalisation clause') or as being determined according to trust or general concepts. In deeds where income is not defined, the income of the trust would ordinarily be according to trust or general concepts. Also, the trustee may have discretion under the trust deed to determine whether a receipt of the trust is income or capital of the trust.

- **the requirements for the trustee to make a distribution of income**

  The trust deed will usually specify that the trustee must resolve or take action to distribute the trust's income by a particular point in time (eg. 30 June).

- **the 'streaming' of income**

  If the trustee wishes to stream income in accordance with the streaming rules, the trust deed must also contain provisions that allow a beneficiary to be made specifically entitled to an amount of trust income in its character as a capital gain or a franked distribution.

- **the vesting date of the trust**

  This is the date that the trust comes to an end and the capital must be returned to the primary beneficiaries. A trust normally has a statutory life of 80 years.

TRUSTEE RESOLUTIONS

If the trustee has resolved to either pay or apply an amount of trust income to or for the benefit of a beneficiary, that beneficiary will be deemed to be presently entitled to the amount (s101 ITAA36).

See 7.170 for comment and sample trustee resolutions.

KEY CATEGORIES OF TRUSTS

- **Fixed trusts:** The beneficiaries have fixed entitlements to all the income and capital of the trust (eg. unit trusts with no trustee discretion).
- **Non-fixed trusts:** Any trust which does not meet the requirements of a fixed trust such that there is a discretionary element (eg. discretionary trusts, beneficiary testamentary trusts, unit trusts with trustee discretion, hybrid trusts, child support trusts, and superannuation proceeds trusts).
- **Deceased estates:** Including life interests and estate testamentary trusts.

CLOSELY HELD TRUSTS

If a maximum of 20 individuals beneficially hold, directly or indirectly, 75% or more of the fixed entitlements to the income or capital of the trust, the trust is closely held. Related parties are treated as a single individual. For some purposes under the tax law, a discretionary trust is also considered to be a closely held trust.

CONCESSIONALLY TAXED 'WILL' TRUSTS

Ordinarily, where a minor (ie. a beneficiary under the age of 18) is presently entitled to any trust income, that income is taxed as unearned income of minors at a higher rate (see 3.040). However, trust income resulting from a 'will' (typically referred to as a testamentary trust) will be taxed at normal rates.

CONCESSIONALLY TAXED 'DEED' TRUSTS

Certain types of 'deed' trusts also qualify for concessional tax treatment when income is distributed to minor beneficiaries (ie. those under 18 years) (see 3.040). While there is often a discretion as to who receives the income, the capital must ultimately pass to the minor beneficiary (eg. when the minor beneficiary's surviving parent has died) (s102AG(2)(c) and (2A)). Examples include:

- child support (maintenance) trusts
- compensation proceeds trusts
- estate proceeds trusts, and
- superannuation proceeds trusts.

DISCRETIONARY TRUSTS

A discretionary or non-fixed trust is the most common form of trust. It is used in tax and asset protection planning and may be set up during a person's lifetime (inter vivos), or by a person's will. A trustee of a discretionary trust may be able to elect for that trust to be a family trust.

A 'deed' discretionary trust is formally established by a settlor. Because of the operation of s102 ITAA36 (revokable trusts), the settlor is usually not a member of the family, but an unrelated person who 'settles' a small sum to create the trust. Money, assets or even whole businesses may be transferred into a trust by sale or gift. The initial trustee will normally be appointed by the deed. The class of potential beneficiaries is set out in the trust deed. Discretionary trusts can also be established by a person's will (also known as a 'testamentary trust').

A discretionary trust allows the trustee to retain control over distribution of both trust income and trust assets. The trust assets do not normally constitute personal assets for either the trustee or the beneficiaries for bankruptcy purposes.

Discretionary powers give the trustee flexibility to vary income and capital distributions each year to minimise the overall tax liability which is particularly beneficial where income of individual beneficiaries fluctuates from year to year. A decision as to which beneficiaries are to receive the income has to be made by the trustee by the end of each financial year unless the trust deed requires an earlier determination (see 7.170).

BARE TRUST

A bare trust is the most basic form of trust. The trustee only holds the property until the beneficiaries demand transfer of the property. Bare trusts are often employed where the true owner or purchaser of the property which is to become the subject of the bare trust wishes to conceal his/her identity. A bare trustee holds the legal ownership of the subject property for the express and absolute benefit of the true [beneficial] owner (ie. the beneficiary). The bare trustee has no active duties to perform and no power or discretion as to the trust property.

In property developments this use of a bare trust is common where a property developer wishes to purchase property without the vendor becoming aware that the purchaser is a person who seeks to develop their property.

FAMILY TRUSTS

For tax purposes, a trust becomes a 'family trust' if a trustee makes a Family Trust Election (FTE). Any trust may become a 'family trust' (see 7.200). If a distribution from a family trust is made outside of the family group (as defined in the deed and tax law) then the trustee is taxed at the highest marginal tax rate plus the Medicare levy (family trust distribution tax) (see 7.200).

FIXED UNIT TRUSTS

Unitholders typically have fixed entitlements to all the income and capital of the trust. The distribution of certain non-assessable amounts to unitholders (eg. a distribution of the CGT 50% active asset reduction or capital works deductions), can trigger CGT event E4 for the unitholder resulting in a reduction of the unitholders cost base in the units and potentially also a capital gain if the non-assessable amount distributed exceeds the cost base of the units. Non-assessable amounts which are not taken into account for the purposes of CGT event E4 are listed in s104-71 ITAA97.

In *Colonial First State Investments v Commissioner of Taxation* (2011) FCA16, the Court held that the investment trust under consideration was not a fixed trust because the deed contained a power which enabled amendments to be made. The court concluded that the trust will only be 'fixed' where the trustee has no power to alter the interests of the beneficiaries.

HYBRID TRUSTS

A hybrid trust is typically partly discretionary and partly fixed. This provides the trustee with considerable flexibility in respect of distributions. However, as the trust is not a fixed trust, the more rigorous non-fixed trust loss rules will apply. This can be mitigated to some extent by the hybrid trust making an FTE.

SERVICE TRUSTS

Frequently, trusts are established to provide services to operating entities such as professional practices and small businesses, enabling income-producing assets and the provision of services to be kept separate from the operating entity. If the charges for services are imposed on an arms-length basis, they should be deductible to the payer and the income generated by the service trust may be distributed to lower income beneficiaries. As service trusts generally offer limited liability protection and access to the capital gains tax concessions, these trusts may be established to hold assets with the potential to appreciate (eg. land, trademarks, copyrights, franchises).

SUB-TRUSTS

A sub-trust may be created to manage a Division 7A issue (see 6.310) where a distribution is made but not actually paid to a beneficiary. Where this occurs the distribution amount becomes the property of a sub-trust and the trustee becomes the trustee of the sub-trust. The amount must be held separately from the original trust and the funds used for trust purposes.

NOTE: In TR 2010/3, unpaid present entitlements owed by a trust to a corporate beneficiary may be treated as a sub-trust to the extent that the funds are applied solely for the benefit of that beneficiary in accordance with the requirements of PS LA 2010/4.

PUBLIC UNIT TRUSTS

Public unit trusts may be treated as public companies for tax purposes, where certain conditions are met. A unit trust is a public unit trust if at any time during the income year:

- any of the units were listed on a stock exchange
- any of the units were offered to the public
- the units were held by 50 or more persons, or
- if certain exempt or concessionally taxed entities (eg. complying super funds) held at least 20% of the units.

See 6.150 for further detailed information.

SPECIAL DISABILITY TRUSTS

Special disability trusts (SDTs) are a special form of trust given concessional treatment under the *Social Securities Act 1991* to assist families to provide for the current or future cost of care and accommodation needs of their children or close relatives with severe disabilities when the family is no longer able to care for them. Assets owned by the trust may be taken into account for the purposes of determining the beneficiary's entitlement to income support payments such as the disability support pension. Any asset balance above the exempt amount will be assessed as the beneficiary's assets. Income derived by a special disability trust and Income received by a beneficiary is exempt from the income test.

The three key benefits of establishing an SDT are:

- an SDT can spend up to $11,000 on items other than care and accommodation in the 2014-15 income year ($10,750) for 2013-14)
- immediate family members making gifts to an SDT may access a concession of up to a combined total of $500,000 from the social security or veterans' entitlements gifting rules (see below for recent amendments), and
- assets of an SDT up to $626,000 and indexed annually ($609,500 in 2013-14) plus the principal beneficiary's main residence do not impact upon the principal beneficiary's ability to access income support payments.

Sammy and Scott are an elderly couple. Their daughter Rachel is severely disabled. Sammy and Scott establish an SDT in order to provide for Rachel's care and accommodation needs.

In the 2014-15 income year, the SDT has gross income of $20,000. The SDT's net income is also $15,000. The trustee of the SDT applies $10,000 for Rachel's reasonable care and accommodation costs and retains the remaining $5,000 in the trust.

Rachel is deemed to be presently entitled to all of the $15,000 of the trust's income for the 2014-15 income year although $5,000 of the income is retained in the trust.

Unexpended income of an SDT is to be taxed at the relevant principal beneficiary's personal income tax rate.

Further, the tax law was amended to:

- provide equivalent taxation treatment amongst SDTs established under either the *Veterans' Entitlements Act 1986* and *Social Security Act 1991*
- provide a CGT exemption for assets transferred into an SDT for no consideration:
  - for inter vivos transfers, the transferor disregards any gains or losses on the asset, and
  - for testamentary transfers, the first element of the cost base and reduced cost base in the hands of the trustee is equal to the asset's market value as at date of death
- provide a CGT main residence exemption for a trustee of an SDT that holds a dwelling for use by the principal beneficiary, that would have been that beneficiary's main residence if that person had owned the interest in the dwelling directly, and
- where the principal beneficiary dies, provide a CGT main residence exemption for the intended recipient of the principal beneficiary's main residence, if the recipient disposes of the dwelling within two years of the principal beneficiary's death (or, if the dwelling was used to produce assessable income before the principal beneficiary's death, a partial exemption may apply to the trustee of the SDT).

TESTAMENTARY 'WILL' TRUSTS

Income from deceased estates and from testamentary trusts established by a will are usually taxed at normal 'adult' rates of tax, including income received by beneficiaries who are minors. Also, where a beneficiary transfers property from a deceased estate to a minor within three years of death, the income from that property is taxed at 'adult' rates of tax. This concession is limited to the amount of income that the minor beneficiary would have received directly from the deceased estate had the deceased died intestate. This limitation does not apply where the income was received by the minor directly from the deceased estate.

The trustee of a testamentary trust can distribute an asset of the deceased individual without a CGT taxing point occurring.

TRADING TRUSTS

Trusts can be a suitable structure for conducting business. A trust Tax File Number (TFN) and GST registration should be obtained and quoted, even if the trustee of the trust is a company. Stationery, invoices and contracts should show the name of the trustee. The fact that the trustee is acting on behalf of a trust normally does not have to be disclosed.

MANAGED INVESTMENT TRUSTS (MIT)

Some non-trading trusts may fall into the definition of an MIT. An MIT is a type of collective investment vehicle such as a public unit trust and include a variety of investment types including cash management and property trusts.

An MIT is a widely held trust which is centrally controlled by a resident trustee and only permitted to invest in specific assets.

The impact of being an MIT is that:

- the trustee can make a choice to treat certain passive CGT assets (primarily shares, units and real property) of the trust as being subject to the CGT provisions. If the election is not made then those assets are treated as revenue assets, and
- the trustee of an MIT may have to withhold final PAYG withholding amounts on defined fund payments to non-resident entities (similar to withholding on dividends, interest and royalties).

EMPLOYEE BENEFITS TRUSTS

Employee benefit trusts are commonly used as a tool by employers to retain and reward employees. Broadly, an employee benefit trust is a unit trust (see above) established by an employer whereby funds contributed by the employer are lent to employees to acquire ordinary units in the trust. The trust is managed by a trustee.

Bonus units can also be issued to employees which give the employee the right to redeem the units. Subject to meeting certain performance criteria and after a relevant holding period, the employee is able to redeem their units for a cash payment. The payment of cash effectively extinguishes the employee's outstanding loan to the trust.

TR 2010/6 considers the income tax, PAYG withholding, general anti-avoidance and fringe benefits tax implications of issuing, holding and redeeming bonus units under an employee benefits trust.

7.150 COMPARISON OF TRUST STRUCTURES

Comparison of trust structures			
Factor	**Discretionary trusts**	**Unit trusts**	**Hybrid trusts**
Limited liability	Yes[1]	Yes[1]	Yes[1]
Suitability for equity raising	None	Yes	Yes
Distribution flexibility	Yes	Limited to issuing different classes of units	Limited to the discretionary element and issuing different classes of units
Income splitting	Yes	Yes	Yes
'Asset protection'	Yes	Limited – assets of the trust are protected from claims by creditors of unitholders and assets of unitholders are protected from claims by creditors of the trust. But the unitholder's units are not protected from creditors of the unitholder	Limited – assets of the trust are protected from claims by creditors of unitholders and assets of unitholders are protected from claims by creditors of the trust. But the unitholder's units are not protected from creditors of the unitholder
Use of losses • generally • non-commercial loss rules • other measures	Trapped No impact Trust loss measures[2]	Trapped No impact Trust loss measures	Trapped No impact Trust loss measures[2]
Ability to stream distributions	Yes[3]	No	Limited to discretionary element[3]
Potential access to small business CGT relief on disposal of assets in form of: • 15 year exemption • 50% active asset • retirement • rollover	Yes Yes Yes Yes	Yes Yes[4] Yes Yes	Yes Yes[4] Yes Yes
Access to CGT 50% discount and/or ability to effectively pass discount on to beneficiaries	Yes	Yes	Yes

Comparison of trust structures

Factor	Discretionary trusts	Unit trusts	Hybrid trusts
Tax free threshold if trustee is assessed	No	No	No
Small business entity regime applicable	Yes	Yes	Yes
Entitled to a refund of excess imputation credits	May be available to a beneficiary depending upon the identity of the beneficiary and to a trustee taxed under s99 on a resident beneficiary's share of trust income	May be available to a unitholder depending upon the identity of the unitholder	May be available to a unitholder depending upon the identity of the unitholder and to a trustee taxed under s99 on a resident beneficiary's share of trust income
CGT relief available on transfer of assets from the trust to a company	Yes	Yes	Yes
PAYG applies to trust and/or beneficiaries	Yes	Yes	Yes
Potential loss of franking credits when dividends distributed to beneficiaries (45 day holding period rule)	Yes, unless a family trust election is made (subject to small shareholder exemption)	No, provided unitholders have a fixed interest in the corpus of the trust	Yes, unless a family trust election is made (subject to small shareholder exemption)
Income can be accumulated in entity	Yes but income taxed in hands of trustee at penalty rates	No (unless the deed provides for accumulation)	Yes but income taxed in hands of trustee at penalty rates
Trustee beneficiary statements (see 7.300)	Yes, unless a family trust election is made	Yes, unless a family trust election is made	Yes, unless a family trust election is made
TFN withholding by trust where beneficiary fails to provide TFN (see 7.350)	Yes[6]	Yes[6]	Yes[6]
Deductibility of superannuation contributions	Fully deductible[5] by the trust in relation to any employees of the trust	Fully deductible[5] by the trust in relation to any employees of the trust	Fully deductible[5] by the trust in relation to any employees of the trust

1: Subject to directors, shareholders, beneficiaries and others giving guarantees.
2: A family trust election can limit the operation of the trust loss measures to only the income injection test.
3: Care needs to be taken when streaming dividends as numerous integrity provisions can apply to cancel the tax benefit (eg. Division 204 ITAA97 and Part IVA ITAA36); limitations which may exist in the Deed should be considered. The application of subdivision 115-C and 207-B ITAA97 in relation to the streaming of capital gains and franked distributions should also be considered.
4: Distribution of the tax-free amount has implications for CGT event E4.
5: For eligible contributions. Also see 19.020 for contribution caps.
6: Provided that closely-held trust (see 7.300) and the nature of the payment made (see 7.350).

7.170   TRUSTEE DISTRIBUTION RESOLUTIONS BY 30 JUNE

TRUSTEE RESOLUTIONS MUST BE MADE BY 30 JUNE

Trustee resolutions must be to be made by 30 June each year to make a beneficiary entitled to income of the trust (or such earlier date as required by the deed). Failure to effect a resolution by 30 June may result in no beneficiary of the trust being presently entitled to income of the trust (in the absence of a default beneficiary). The trustee would then be assessed under s99A ITAA36 (see 7.700).

Tax Office guidelines for making resolutions before year end

In making a trustee resolution before year end, the Tax Office has issued the following guidance:

- **Standard format:** The Tax Office cannot provide a standard format for trustee resolutions due to the wide variety of trust deeds with different requirements for resolutions.

- **Resolution in writing:** Whether a resolution has to be in writing depends on the terms of the trust deed. If the deed does not require a resolution to be in writing, an unwritten decision made by the trustee would create a valid entitlement at that time and be effective for tax purposes. However, the Tax Office advises that a written record will provide better evidence of the resolution and help trustees to avoid a later dispute with the Tax Office or with beneficiaries as to whether any resolution was made by 30 June.

- **Streaming capital gains and franked distributions:** A written record is essential in order to effectively stream capital gains or franked distributions for tax purposes.
  The entitlement to capital gains or franked distributions must be recorded in writing in the trust records by 30 June for franked dividends and 31 August for capital gains (see 7.700).

- **Resolution formalised after 30 June:** The Tax Office advises that it will accept official minutes prepared after 30 June as evidence of actions undertaken by the trustee before 30 June to create present entitlement in the beneficiaries by that date (it would be unwise for the actions undertaken by 30 June to not be documented).

- **Effective resolutions:** The resolution does not need to specify a dollar amount unless the trust deed specifically requires it. A resolution is effective if it prescribes a clear methodology for calculating the entitlement (eg. expressed as a specified percentage of the income). Alternatively, if it is known that the income of the trust will be at least a certain amount, the trustee may choose to make one or more beneficiaries presently entitled to the certain amount, and other beneficiaries entitled to the balance that is unknown as at 30 June.

- **If no resolution made:** If no beneficiary (including a default beneficiary) was presently entitled to trust income as at 30 June, the trustee will be assessed on the trust's net (taxable) income at the highest marginal tax rate plus the Medical levy (currently a total rate of 49%).

IMPORTANT: From the 2010-11 year, in order to enable capital gains and franked distributions to be streamed, the law requires 'specific entitlement' to be recorded in the trustee's trust records (eg. resolution) by 31 August for capital gains and 30 June for franked distributions. Notwithstanding the 31 August deadline in relation to capital gains under the streaming provisions, if such a capital gain formed part of trust income, the Commissioner's approach would seem to require a resolution by 30 June.

DISTRIBUTION RESOLUTIONS

In the case of discretionary trusts there are different forms of distribution resolutions which may be effective, including those which seek to have particular beneficiaries entitled to a fixed sum. For example, a resolution may be framed in a manner which attempts to limit the entitlement of a minor beneficiary to an amount equivalent to the minor's tax-free threshold. Alternatively, an income distribution resolution may specify income entitlements as a percentage of trust income.

The decision of the High Court in the *Bamford case* provided conclusive authority for the proposition that the 'proportionate view' (see 7.600) must be adopted in determining the amount of the trust's net income that is assessable to a beneficiary. It does not matter whether the resolution confers the present entitlement to trust income in dollar terms or percentage terms, for tax purposes, the law is clear that the beneficiary's entitlement will be to a proportion (or fraction) of trust income.

If no streaming of a capital gain or franked distribution occurs, a trustee resolution on or before 30 June might be framed as follows:

1. *Resolved: Pursuant to the powers conferred on the trustee by clause .... of the trust deed, the income of the trust estate for the year ended 30 June .... is appointed as follows:*

Beneficiary A	20%
Beneficiary B	30%
Beneficiary C	50%

    Further, that the amounts so appointed be credited to or set aside for the benefit of the beneficiary, in the books and records of the trust.

Alternative styles of resolution

2. *Resolved: Pursuant to the powers conferred on the trustee by clause .... of the trust deed, the income of the trust estate for the year ended 30 June .... is appointed as follows:*

Beneficiary D	The first $10,000
Beneficiary E	The next $20,000
Beneficiary F	The balance

    Further, that the amounts so appointed be credited to or set aside for the benefit of the beneficiary, in the books and records of the trust.

3. *Pursuant to the powers conferred on the trustee by clause .... of the trust deed, the income of the trust estate for the year ended 30 June .... is appointed as follows:*

    Beneficiary G ....that proportion of the income of the trust estate which when that proportion is applied to the net income of the trust calculated in accordance with s95 ITAA36 produces an amount of $416
    Beneficiary H ....the next $10,000 of trust income
    Beneficiary I .... the balance

    Further, that the amounts so appointed be credited to or set aside for the benefit of the beneficiary, in the books and records of the trust.

SAMPLE TRUSTEE RESOLUTION (INCLUDING STREAMING)

TRUSTEE: Name

TRUSTEE OF: Name of Trust

Minutes of meeting of directors held on .... day of ....

PRESENT:

DETERMINATION OF TRUST INCOME:

Resolved that income of the trust estate for the year ended 30 June .... be determined in accordance with clause..........of the trust deed as follows:

- an amount equal to the net income of the trust estate as defined in s95(1) ITAA36, or
- an amount calculated after taking into account discretions exercised by the trustee:
    - to include all realised capital gains in the income of the trust estate,
    - to recoup capital losses of prior years against current year capital gains and include the net amount in the income of the trust of the trust estate,
    - (include other relevant terms), or
- (include other relevant terms)

APPOINTMENT OF TRUST INCOME:

Resolved that income of the trust estate for the year ended 30 June .... be appointed to the beneficiaries in the proportions and with the tax attributes as follows:

1. Specific entitlement to capital gains:

Pursuant to the powers conferred on the trustee by clause.... of the trust deed, in respect of the capital gains arising from the sale of BHP Billiton Ltd shares during the year ended 30 June ......, the following beneficiaries are in respect of the capital gain specifically entitled to the share indicated and each beneficiary has an equivalent share of the 'net financial benefit' that is referable to the capital gain:

- 50% to Beneficiary A
- 50% to Beneficiary B

Further, that the relevant amounts will be set aside in the trust records for the absolute benefit of each beneficiary.

Further, that this resolution records the character of the amount attributable to each beneficiary as being referable to the capital gain.

2. Specific entitlement to franked dividends:

Pursuant to the powers conferred on the trustee by clause ...... of the trust deed, in respect of franked dividends received during the year ended 30 June ......, the following beneficiaries are in respect of the franked dividends specifically entitled to the share indicated and each beneficiary has an equivalent share of the 'net financial benefit' that is referable to the franked dividends:

- 50% to Beneficiary C
- 50% to Beneficiary D

Further, that the relevant amounts will be set aside in the trust records for the absolute benefit of each beneficiary.

Further, that this resolution records the character of the amount attributable to each beneficiary as being referable to the franked dividends.

3. Other income of the trust:

Pursuant to the powers conferred on the trustee by clause.... of the trust deed, the income of the trust estate for the year ended 30 June ......, (other than capital gains and franked dividends previously appointed) is appointed as follows:

- 50% to Beneficiary E
- 50% to Beneficiary F

Further, that the amounts so appointed (less any amounts previously paid or applied for the benefit of a beneficiary) be credited to or set aside for the benefit of the beneficiary in the books and records of the trust.

CLOSURE: There being no further business the meeting was closed.

....
Chairman

IMPORTANT:

1. When framing a distribution resolution it is imperative that the requirements of the particular deed are followed, which may mean that the approach adopted in the sample resolution requires modification.

2. The sample resolution adopts the percentage approach. Other approaches may achieve the same objective of establishing a beneficiary's proportionate share of trust income. For example, provided that the trust deed allows, dollar amounts may be allocated with the balance distributed to a default beneficiary (see above).

SAMPLE TRUSTEE RESOLUTION (NO STREAMING)

TRUSTEE: Name

CAPACITY: The company is acting in its capacity as trustee of (name of trust)

Minutes of meeting of directors held on day of ....

PRESENT:

DETERMINATION OF TRUST INCOME:

RESOLVED that income of the trust estate for the year ended 30 June ..... be determined in accordance with clause .... of the trust deed as follows:

- an amount equal to the net income of the trust estate as defined in s95(1) ITAA 1936, or
- all amounts determined by the trustee to be income of the trust estate (including realised capital gains), or
  - (include other relevant terms), or
- (include other relevant terms)

APPOINTMENT OF TRUST INCOME:

RESOLVED that income of the trust estate for the year ended 30 June .... be appointed to the beneficiaries in the proportions and with the tax attributes as follows:

Pursuant to the powers conferred on the trustee by clause.....of the trust deed, the income of the trust estate for the year is appointed as follows:

- 50% to Beneficiary X
- 50% to Beneficiary Y

Further, that the amounts so appointed (less any amounts previously paid to or applied for the benefit of the beneficiary) be credited to or set aside for the benefit of the beneficiary in the books of account of the trust.

CLOSURE: There being no further business the meeting was closed.

....
Chairman

IMPORTANT:

1. When framing a distribution resolution it is imperative that the requirements of the particular deed are followed, which may mean that the approach adopted in the sample resolution required modification.

7.200   FAMILY TRUSTS

A Family Trust Election (FTE) is made by a fixed or non-fixed trustee to either simplify the tests for deducting prior year tax losses, to enable a trust shareholding to be taken into account when considering the continuity of ownership test for a company or to assist a beneficiary to utilise franking credits distributed by the trust. The disadvantage of making an FTE is that distributions to beneficiaries outside the family group created by the FTE will be subject to tax at maximum marginal rates.

OVERVIEW OF FAMILY TRUST ELECTIONS

The relevant legislation requires an individual to be specified in an FTE. This individual is referred to as the Primary Individual (PI) for the purposes of establishing the members of the 'family group'. The election must specify a person as the PI, which will enable the 'family group' of the person to be identified (refer below).

The FTE can only be made in a prescribed form, available from the Tax Office. An FTE should be considered in the circumstances described above.

Originally the FTE was required to be lodged with the trust income tax return in the year to which it first related, however, with effect from the 2004-05 income year, the election may be lodged in a subsequent income year provided that, for the year specified in the notice until the end of the year immediately preceding the year in which the election is actually made, the trust:

- passed the family control test, and
- only conferred present entitlement to, or made actual distributions of income or capital to the PI or members of the PI's family group. Broadly, a trust passes the family control test if the PI and/or their defined family members and/or one or more legal or financial advisers, 'control' the trust.

A group is taken to 'control' the trust if the group:

- has the power, by means of the exercise of a power of appointment or revocation or otherwise, to obtain beneficial enjoyment of the capital or income of the trust
- is able to control the application of the income or capital of the trust
- is capable, under a scheme, of gaining the beneficial enjoyment or control of the capital and income of the trust
- directs, instructs or wishes for the trustee to act in a certain manner which the trustee is generally accustomed to follow
- is able to remove or appoint the trustee
- has more than a 50% stake in the income or capital, or
- includes persons who are the only persons who can obtain beneficial enjoyment of the income and capital.

The choice to make an FTE is generally irrevocable but can be revoked under certain circumstances (refer below).

NOTE: The nominated individual is referred to as the 'primary individual' in defining the family group (s272-90 ITAA97) and the 'test individual' for the purposes of defining the family of that person (s272-95 ITAA97).

'FAMILY GROUP'

The family group of the TI is important as distributions to persons or entities outside of the family group will attract family trust distribution tax at 49% (refer below). The family group includes:

- the TI
- other defined family members (see diagram below)
- companies wholly owned by TI and/or other family group members
- fixed trusts wholly owned by the TI and/or other family group members
- family trusts with the same TI
- entities covered by interposed entity elections (refer below)
- estates of the TI or defined family members if all are deceased
- Division 30 (s78) 'deductible' entities, and
- Division 50 (s23) exempt entities.

DEFINED FAMILY MEMBERS FOR DISTRIBUTION PURPOSES*

* Including:

- all current spouses of these family members
- former spouses
- former widows/ widowers, and
- former step-children.

VARIATION OF TEST INDIVIDUAL

There is scope for the trust for vary the TI (on a once only basis) provided that certain circumstances are met. These circumstances require that:

- the new specified TI must be a member of the original TI's family at the time the election is first made, and

- there have been no conferrals of present entitlement to, and distributions of, income or capital made (by the trust or an interposed entity) outside the new TI's family group during the period in which the election has been in force.

Alternatively, a TI may be varied if, as a result of a family law order, agreement or award arising from a marriage breakdown, the 'control' of the trust passes to the new SI and/or members of their family (refer above for meaning of 'control' of the trust).

ADVANTAGES OF FAMILY TRUST ELECTIONS

If an FTE is made, the family trust will have the following advantages:

- an ability for a beneficiary to utilise franking credits in respect of shares acquired post-31 December 1997 by satisfying the 45/90 day holding period rule (see 11.745)
- easier utilisation of carry forward income losses – a non-family discretionary trust (ie. a non-fixed trust) will need to satisfy the 50% stake test (if applicable), the control test and the pattern of distribution test (see table at 7.900) as well as the income injection test before it can carry forward its losses. A family trust only needs to satisfy the income injection test, and
- assists a company or fixed trust with losses to pass the continuity of ownership test or the 50% stake test where a non-fixed trust holds at least 50% of the shares or units, by treating the family trust as a 'person' for tax purposes.

DISADVANTAGE OF FAMILY TRUST ELECTIONS

The primary disadvantage of making an FTE is the trust's restricted ability to distribute to any person or entity outside of the trust's family group (see above). Distributions outside the family group are subject to family trust distribution tax.

FAMILY TRUST DISTRIBUTION TAX

Family Trust Distributions Tax (FTDT) is levied at the top marginal rate for individuals plus Medicare levy (49% from 1 July 2014). The trustee of the family trust is normally liable to pay the tax.

The FTDT is part of the self-assessment regime and a payment advice is completed for each distribution made by the family trust or interposed entity. Payment for the this tax must be accompanied by the Family Trust Distribution Tax Payment Advice available from the Tax Office. Payment is generally required to be made within 21 days after the distribution is made. If the distribution is made before an FTE is made, the trustee is not required to pay until 21 days after the FTE is made.

REVOKING FAMILY TRUST ELECTIONS

An FTE can be revoked in certain circumstances. Essentially, an FTE can be revoked where the election was not relied upon at any time up to the year of revocation. However, if because of the FTE tax losses have been recouped, bad debts deducted or franking credits claimed the FTE cannot be revoked.

The trustee of a fixed trust may seek to revoke the election where some or all of the interests in the trust are disposed of to non-family members, or persons holding interests in the trust cease to be family members.

An FTE commencing in the 2005 income year or earlier must have been revoked in the period from 1 July 2007 to 30 June 2009. An FTE commencing in the 2006 income year onwards can be revoked no later than the income year ending four years after the FTE commencement year end. In practice, for fixed trusts, the revocation must be made in the trust's return for the income year in which the change in fixed entitlement occurs. If the trustee is not required to lodge a return for the income year the revocation must be given to the Commissioner within two months of the end of the income year in which that change occurs or such later day as the Commissioner allows.

For other trusts, the revocation must be made in the trust's return for the income year from which the revocation is to be effective. If the trustee is not required to lodge a return for the income year, the revocation must be given to the Commissioner within two months of the end of the income year from which the revocation is to be effective or such later day as the Commissioner allows.

Where an FTE has been revoked, a trustee must not make more than one election under s272-80(11) Schedule 2F ITAA36 in relation to the same trust. This may arise where an FTE is made in a prior year, it then satisfies the relevant conditions to be revoked and then an FTE is made for an income year subsequent to that (refer ATO ID 2008/73)).

INTERPOSED ENTITIES

The purposes of an interposed entity election are:

- Firstly, an election made allows an entity to be included as part of the 'family group' and therefore, any distributions made to that entity will not be subject to family trust distributions tax (refer ATO ID 2003/164).
- Secondly, the making of an election will exclude a trust from having to comply with the trustee beneficiary reporting rules (refer to 7.300).

A company, trust or partnership is required to make an interposed entity election before it can be included as part of a family group. The interposed entity election can be made in a later year than the FTE but must specify the income year that it takes effect. However, the entity must pass the family control test at the end of the income year that the election is being made.

In some instances, an interposed entity election may not be necessary for membership of a family group (eg. a fixed trust or company which is 100% owned by family group members or another family trust with the same SI).

Other matters for interposed entity elections include:

- a company, partnership or trust can make more than one interposed entity election provided each family trust with which the entity is interposed, has the same SI specified in its FTE
- an entity cannot make an interposed entity election in respect of two family trusts where the SI specified in the FTE are different, and
- a trustee of a family trust can make an interposed entity election to be included in the family group of another family trust where the SIs are not the same provided the respective family control tests are passed (eg. where the SIs are siblings).

REVOKING AN INTERPOSED ENTITY ELECTION

An interposed entity election can be revoked where:

- the election was made for an entity that was already included in the family group of the SI, or
- the election relates to an entity that became wholly-owned by members of the family group (via fixed entitlement to all the income and capital of the entity) (s272-85(5A) ITAA36).

If an FTE is revoked, the related interposed entity election is automatically revoked (s272-85(5B) ITAA36). An entity revokes the interposed entity election in the tax return for the year of the revocation. If a tax return in not required, the revocation must be sent to the Commissioner within two months of the end of the income year from which the revocation is to be effective.

An interposed entity election commencing in the 2005 income year or earlier must be revoked in the period from 1 July 2007 to 30 June 2009. An interposed entity election commencing in the 2006 income year onwards can be revoked no later than the income year ending four years after the end of the year in which the interposed entity election commenced.

7.300 TRUSTEE BENEFICIARY REPORTING

The trustee of a 'closely held trust' must use the approved form to advise the Tax Office of the details of each trustee beneficiary, including TFN, that is presently entitled to a share of the trust's net income or a tax-preferred amount. A correct Trustee Beneficiary Statement (TBS) must be lodged to avoid Trustee Beneficiary Non-disclosure Tax (TBNT) levied at 49% on the trustee beneficiary's share of net trust income. Further, in order to discourage the use of chains of trusts to make it difficult to identify the ultimate beneficiary of the net income, TBNT is also imposed on a share of net income of a 'closely held trust' included in the assessable income of the trustee beneficiary, to which the 'closely held trust' itself becomes presently entitled.

EXCLUDED TRUSTS

Certain trusts (known as 'excluded trusts') are excluded from the trustee beneficiary reporting requirements such as:

- family trusts (ie. a trust which has made an FTE (refer 7.200))
- trusts covered by an interposed entity election
- trusts wholly owned by a family trusts and/or family members
- complying super funds, approved deposit funds and pooled superannuation trusts
- deceased estates for five years after death
- fixed trusts wholly owned by tax-exempt entities, and
- listed unit trusts.

 These rules only apply to a chain of trusts where one trust is distributing to another trust (eg. unit trust distributes to a discretionary trust).

CLOSELY HELD TRUSTS

The obligation to disclose details of the identity of a trustee beneficiary arises only where a 'closely held trust' distributes to another trust.

There are two limbs to the definition of 'closely held trust' (s102UC ITAA36):

1. a trust where, at most, 20 individuals have fixed entitlements to at least 75% of the income or capital of the trust, or
2. a discretionary trust.

For the purposes of the first limb, an individual and his/her relatives and their nominees are treated as one individual. This is to avoid a situation where the threshold of 20 could be exceeded by including more than 20 relatives as beneficiaries of a trust.

Further, where a trustee of a discretionary trust holds a fixed entitlement to a share of the income or capital of a trust (directly or indirectly) and no person holds that fixed entitlement (directly or indirectly) through the discretionary trust, then that trustee is taken to hold the interest in that fixed entitlement as an individual (s102UC(2)).

TRUSTEE BENEFICIARY

A person is a trustee beneficiary of a 'closely held trust' if the person is acting in the capacity of trustee of another trust.

CORRECT TRUSTEE BENEFICIARY STATEMENT (TBS)

A correct TBS in the approved form must be provided where the trustee beneficiary's share of net income includes an untaxed or a tax-preferred amount.

If the trustee beneficiary is a resident at the end of the year of income, the TBS must contain:

- the name and TFN of the trustee beneficiary and the amount of the 'untaxed part' of their share or the amount of their share of the tax-preferred amount, or
- if the trustee beneficiary is a non-resident at the end of the year of income, the TBS must contain the name and address of the trustee beneficiary and the amount of the 'untaxed part' of their share or the amount of their share of the tax-preferred amount.

If the 'closely held trust' has multiple beneficiaries the reporting applies for each trustee beneficiary of the 'closely held trust'.

DUE DATE FOR TRUSTEE BENEFICIARY STATEMENT

Where the trustee of a closely held trust is required to complete a TBS, it must be given within the TBS period. The TBS period is the period from the end of the year of income up to the lodgement due date for the trust's return. If the information in the TBS cannot be provided on time, the Commissioner has the power to grant extensions of time in certain circumstances.

LIABILITY FOR TRUSTEE BENEFICIARY NON-DISCLOSURE TAX

Where a share of the net income of a closely held trust for a year of income is included in the assessable income of a trustee beneficiary of the trust and, during the TBS period, the trustee of the closely held trust is required but fails to provide the Commissioner with a correct TBS, TBNT at 49% is imposed on the share of the net income and must be paid within 21 days of the due date for lodgement of the trust return, or such later day as the Tax Office, in special circumstances allows (s102UO ITAA36). If the tax is outstanding 60 days after the due date, GIC will be payable.

Where the corporate trustee of a 'closely held trust' becomes liable for TBNT, the directors of that company become jointly and severally liable to pay the tax (s102UK(2) and (3) ITAA36). However, a director may be excused from such a liability where it would be unreasonable to impose such a liability. The rules (s102UL ITAA36) set out particular circumstances where a director would be relieved from such a joint and several liability for TBNT.

UNTAXED AMOUNT

An untaxed part of a share of net income is the share of the net income of a closely held trust less any part of the share of net income that has been taxed under:

- s98(4) ITAA36 (a non-resident beneficiary of a trust estate)
- subdivision 12-H in schedule 1 of the *Taxation Administration Act 1953* (TAA) (which relates to distributions of managed investment trust income), or
- division 6D (trustee beneficiary non-disclosure tax) (refer above).

TAX-PREFERRED AMOUNT

A trustee of a 'closely held trust' is also required to disclose certain details as to the identity of trustee beneficiaries who are entitled to a share of a tax-preferred amount in respect of the 'closely held trust' (s102UT ITAA36). A 'tax-preferred amount' is any income of the trust not included in the trust's assessable income (eg. an exempt capital gain due to the application of the CGT small business concessions).

Where the trustee fails to discharge that obligation, the trustee may be found guilty of an offence under s8C of the TAA. However, this will not be the case where the trustee:

- did not have all of the information required to be included in the TBS
- took reasonable steps to obtain that information, and
- included in a statement sent to the Commissioner during the TBS period, any of the required information which the trustee did have.

RELIEF FOR TRUSTEES

AMENDMENT OF STATEMENTS

Trustees can amend a TBS but only in the following circumstances:

- within four years of the time the TBNT became due and payable
- where the amendment only corrects an error in the original statement where the trustee believed on reasonable grounds that the statement was correct, and
- the reason for the change could not reasonably have been foreseen by the trustee.

POWER TO RECOVER TAX FROM BENEFICIARIES

The trustee of a closely held trust may sue to recover TBNT from a trustee beneficiary where the beneficiary has received their full distribution and:

- the trustee beneficiary refused or failed to give information to the trustee of the closely held trust, or
- the trustee beneficiary provided incorrect information and the trustee of the closely held trust honestly believed on reasonable grounds that the information was correct.

7.350   TFN TRUST WITHHOLDING RULES

Trustees of closely-held trusts must withhold tax from trust distributions at the rate of 49% where beneficiaries have not provided a tax file number (TFN) to the trustee by the time present entitlement is created. This ensures that a beneficiary of a closely-held trust (including a family trust), reports taxable distributions in their tax return.

The rules apply to 'closely held trusts' (refer 7.300 for definition) and the beneficiaries of such trusts (irrespective of whether they are an individual, company, partnership, trust or superannuation fund). The rules do not apply to 'excluded trusts' (see 7.300) and 'excluded beneficiaries'.

An **excluded beneficiary** includes beneficiaries that are non-resident for tax purposes, that are exempt entities for tax purposes (eg. tax concession charities) and those under a legal disability (such as minors).

FEATURES OF THE TFN WITHHOLDING RULES

The rules apply as follows:

- all beneficiaries may quote their TFN to the trustee
- the trustee must provide to the Commissioner a **TFN report** where a beneficiary has provided their TFN to the trustee
- the trustee must report the TFN to the Commissioner in the **TFN report** by the last day of the month following the end of the quarter. to which it relates or within such further time as the Commissioner allows. For example, for the quarter ended 30 June, the report would be due on 31 July.

  The TFN report must include the beneficiary's:
  - TFN
  - full name
  - date of birth (for individuals only)
  - postal address
  - business or residential address
  - entity type, and
  - Australian Business Number
- the trustee will need to withhold tax from distributions made to beneficiaries at 49% where the beneficiaries have not provided their TFN to the trustee when the entitlement is created
- a payment is:
  - a distribution from the ordinary or statutory income of the trust, or
  - a beneficiary's share of the net income of a trust where they are presently entitled to a share of trust income
- TFN withholding tax must be remitted to the Tax Office annually (by the 20th of the month following the month in which the **annual trustee payment report** must be lodged)
- the trustee is required to annually report all payments and amounts withheld (if any) in the **annual trustee payment report** (lodged with the trust tax return) and issue a payment summary to a beneficiary even where they have reported a TFN. The annual trustee payment report must include all the payments made to each beneficiary during the year irrespective of whether TFNs have been quoted and there are no withholding obligations, and
- beneficiaries are entitled to claim a credit for amounts withheld in their income tax return
- all trusts must comply or the trustee will be subject to significant penalties which include failure to withhold penalties amounting to 49% of the amount paid to a beneficiary, plus penalties for failing to:
  - issue an annual trustee withholding report
  - lodge a trustee payment report annually, and
  - issue payment summaries.

The ABC Trust is a closely held trust that has only one beneficiary, B Co Pty Ltd (B Co). The company provided the trustee with its TFN before any payments were made so the trustee does not have an obligation to withhold from payments it makes to B Co Pty Ltd.

As the trustee of the ABC Trust has not withheld any amounts, they do not need to lodge an Annual TFN withholding report. However, as the trustee has made payments to B Co Pty Ltd, the trustee must lodge an Annual trustee payment report which is included in the trust's income tax return (in the distribution statement in the return).

PAYMENTS NOT SUBJECT TO WITHHOLDING

There are circumstances where the TFN withholding rules do not apply to certain payments, these include:

- where a family trust makes a distribution to a beneficiary who is outside the 'family group' (see 7.200), the trustee of the trust is subject to family trust distributions tax (FTDT) at 49%. The trustee is not required to withhold payments where the FTDT is payable
- where the trustee is required to lodge a TBS (refer 7.300), the TFN withholding rules do not apply for that beneficiary. The TFN withholding rules will still apply to non-trustee beneficiaries, and
- for unit trusts, withholding only applies once when a payment is made which is subject to withholding for investments and the TFN trust withholding rules. Withholding for investments will take precedence under these circumstances.

Other payments which are excluded from TFN withholding include:

- payments which are less than thresholds set by the regulations
- payments in respect of income of the trust that were subject to the TFN withholding rules in an earlier year – that is, amounts that a beneficiary was presently entitled to but which the trustee did not distribute, and
- payments in respect of income of the trust that the beneficiary was presently entitled to and related to an income year before the TFN withholding rules applied.

7.400   SERVICE TRUSTS

A service trust is established to separate business assets and employment obligations from the operations of a professional business to minimise risk and provide asset protection. However, from a tax perspective the service arrangement must be carried out on an arm's-length basis. Service costs incurred by the business may be denied deductibility to the extent that costs incurred are not at arm's length.

The ability to claim a deduction for a service fee paid by the professional business was argued in *Phillips v FCT* (1971). However, the Tax Office do not accept *Phillips case* as authority that service fees calculated using the mark-ups stated in that case will always be deductible (see TR 2006/2).

Tax Ruling TR 2006/2 states that a service arrangement typically has some or all of the following features:

- a business taxpayer providing professional or other services to clients
- a service entity being an entity owned or controlled by the business taxpayer
- the business taxpayer agrees to pay fees to the service entity in return for the supply of services such as staff hire, recruitment, clerical and administrative services, premises, plant and equipment
- a mark-up or fixed charge is calculated on the costs of the service entity
- the business taxpayer claims a deduction for the service fees as expenditure incurred in the ordinary course of business, and
- the service entity derives profits from the arrangement, for both accounting and tax purposes which is for the immediate or future benefit of persons who are typically associated with the owners of the business.

The flowchart below indicates the steps to determine if the deduction will be allowed.

WILL SERVICE FEES BE DEDUCTIBLE?

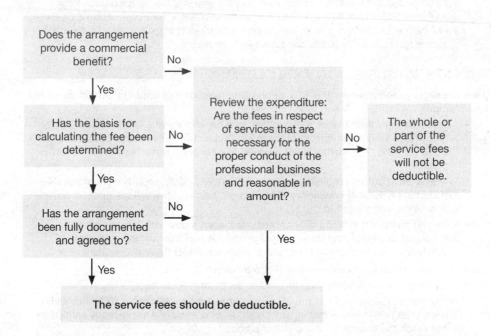

The service fees should be deductible.

For services fees to be deductible, the taxpayer should be able to demonstrate that the arrangement provides a commercial benefit to the professional business (see TR 2006/2).

The Tax Office guide *Your Service Entity Arrangements* (NAT 13086) lists the following comparable and indicative mark-up rates as being reasonable.

Service	Comparable mark-up rates	Indicative mark-up rates	
	Net	Net	Gross
Temporary staff[1]	5%	10%	30%
Permanent staff[1]	3.5%	10%	30%
Recruitment[1]	5%	10%	N/A
Expense payment[1]	5%	10%	N/A
Equipment hire	7.5%[2]	N/A	10%[3]
Rental	0%[4]	0%[4]	0%[4]

1: Net mark-up on direct and indirect operating costs
2: Return on opening written down value of assets
3: Gross mark-up on cost of equipment to service trust.
4: Charged at market rate although may add a finders fee.

 While a trust is a flexible entity to conduct a service arrangement, a company may also be used.

7.500 TRADING TRUSTS

Trusts can provide a flexible structure for trading activities, and on disposal of the units or the business assets, allow access to the small business CGT concessions. A trust also provides a certain amount of anonymity as the fact that the trustee is acting on behalf of a trust normally does not have to be disclosed, and may be useful for asset protection purposes.

PERSONAL EXERTION INCOME

Case law makes it clear that trusts, like companies, cannot be used as a means of diverting income from the person whose personal exertion generated the income (see IT 2121 and IT 2330). Income derived by an entity from the personal services of an individual may be assessed for tax purposes, to the individual performing the work, under the Personal Services Income (PSI) rules. The PSI rules will not apply if the income is derived by a Personal Services Business (PSB). Division 87 ITAA97 contains four tests, one of which must be met, for a PSB to exist (see 16.200).

UNIT TRUST V COMPANY

By retaining profits, a company limits the tax rate to the company tax rate (ie. 30%), whereas unit trust profits are typically distributed to either the individual, trustee or corporate unitholders as pre-tax income, and taxed in their 'hands'.

In a company, tax-preferred income (eg. the indexation component of a capital gain, building allowance, etc.) can only be passed to shareholders as an unfranked dividend. That is, concessions available at the entity level are lost at the shareholder level. Capital gains made by a company do not attract the CGT general discount. This contrasts with the position for unit trusts where distributions of tax-free amounts remain tax free and the beneficiary is entitled to the CGT general discount on any distribution of a capital gain where the asset has been held for 12 months or more.

However, in the case of a unit trust, CGT event E4 can apply when certain tax-free amounts are distributed to unitholders. If CGT event E4 applies, the CGT cost base of the unitholder's units is reduced and any excess tax-free distributions over the cost base of the units will cause a capital gain to be realised (see 11.028) even though no disposal of the units has occurred. Tax-free amounts which do not reduce cost base are set out in s104-71(4) ITAA97.

Both beneficiaries and shareholders can receive refunds of excess imputation credits.

7.600 CALCULATING TRUST INCOME

The income of a trust is calculated in accordance with the definition of 'income' in the trust deed which may result in discrepancies between taxable income calculated in accordance with s95 ITAA36 and trust/accounting income (distributable trust income).

A discrepancy between trust income and taxable income could arise for a number of reasons, such as:

- capital gains are assessable for tax purposes but treated as corpus in the trust deed
- discount capital gains are derived
- expenses incurred are either non-deductible or deductible to a greater or lesser extent for tax purposes, or
- a different basis is used for valuing trading stock or depreciable assets for accounting purposes than that used for taxation purposes.

The treatment of such discrepancies for tax purposes requires an understanding of the following terms:

- income of the trust estate
- share of net income, and
- net income of the trust estate.

TRUST INCOME

The provisions which deal with the taxation of trusts are primarily contained in Division 6 ITAA36. Section 95 ITAA36 defines 'net income' of the trust as assessable income less allowable deductions of the trust estate, calculated as if the trustee were a resident taxpayer. Thus, 'net income' is taxable income. The residency of the trust is the residency of the trustee of the trust.

Where beneficiaries are presently entitled to the income of a trust estate (typically referred to as 'distributable income'), those beneficiaries will most commonly become assessable pursuant to s97 however, beneficiaries may also be assessed pursuant to sub divisions 115-C (capital gains) and 207-B (franked dividends) ITAA97.

Net income of a trust estate which is not included in the assessable income of a beneficiary will be assessable to the trustee under s99A ITAA36, unless the Commissioner considers this unreasonable, in which case s99 ITAA36 will apply.

ASSESSING BENEFICIARIES: S97

The principal provision assessing trust beneficiaries is s97 ITAA36, a section which can create particular difficulties and inequitable outcomes for beneficiaries returning assessable income pursuant to that provision.

Section 97 provides that:

> ... where a beneficiary of a trust estate is presently entitled to a share of the income of the trust estate:
> (a) The assessable income of the beneficiary shall include:
>   (i) So much of that share of the net income of the trust estate ...

'SHARE OF THE INCOME OF THE TRUST ESTATE'

Considerable debate has occurred over many years as to the correct interpretation of the word 'share'. The High Court in the case of *Commissioner of Taxation v Bamford* (2010) HCA10 confirmed that 'share' means a proportion, or fraction (commonly referred to as the proportionate approach).

The term 'income of the trust estate' was considered by the High Court in *Bamford* and by the Commissioner of Taxation in draft tax ruling TR 2012/D1 (see below).

Proportionate view

Under the proportionate view, the trustee firstly determines the proportion, or fraction, of the trust income to which a beneficiary is presently entitled; that proportion or fraction ('share') is then applied to the net (taxable) income of the trust to determine the amount of assessable income to be returned by the beneficiary.

This approach was explained in *Zeta Force Pty Ltd v FCT* (1998) 98 ATC 4681 as follows:

> *Once the share of the distributable income to which the beneficiary is presently entitled is worked out, the notion of present entitlement has served its purpose, and the beneficiary is taxed on that share (or proportion) of the taxable income of the trust estate.*

The High Court in the *Bamford* case noted what it indicated was the intention of s97(1) ITAA36 by referring to the *Zeta Force* decision:

> *The contrast between the expressions 'share of the income of the trust estate' and 'that share of the net income of the trust estate' shows that the draftsman has sought to relate the concept of present entitlement to distributable income, and not to taxable income, which is, after all, an artificial tax amount. Once the share of the distributable income to which the beneficiary is presently entitled is worked out, the notion of present entitlement has served its purpose, and the beneficiary is to be taxed on that share (or proportion) of the taxable income of the trust estate.*

An illustration of the application of the proportionate view is set out below.

Illustration – Proportionate view

The Bright Discretionary Trust – Year ended 30 June 2015

Trust income.....$100,000 Net (taxable) income....$150,000

The trustee resolves to distribute in the following proportions: A: 10%; B: 10%; C: 80%

	Distribution of trust income	Taxable income: Proportionate view[1]
Beneficiary A	$10,000	$15,000[2]
Beneficiary B	$10,000	$15,000
Beneficiary C	$80,000	$120,000
TOTAL	$100,000	$150,000

1: The proportionate interest of the beneficiary in the trust income is applied to taxable income to determine the amount upon which each beneficiary is assessable (s97).

2: $\dfrac{\$10,000 \ x \ \$150,000}{100,000} = \$15,000$

INCOME OF THE TRUST ESTATE' (TRUST INCOME)

'Income of the trust estate' is not defined in the tax laws and has been developed by case law, specifically the decision of the High Court in the *Bamford case*.

The term 'income of the trust estate' is typically defined in a trust deed and might be, for example:

- income according to ordinary concepts
- income according to ordinary concepts and amounts deemed to be income for tax purposes
- all profits or gains taken into account in calculating the net income of the trust under s95 ITAA36 and any other amounts which the trustee may determine from time to time to be income
- an amount equal to the net income of the trust under s95 ITAA36, or
- an amount equal to the net income of the trust under s95 ITAA36, unless otherwise determined by the trustee.

The trust income is commonly referred to as the distributable income.

The High Court in *Bamford's case* concluded that 'income of the trust estate' is based on trust law principles, to be ascertained by the trustee applying:

- appropriate accounting principles, and
- the relevant terms of the trust deed.

If the trust deed contains no definition of 'income' and no powers are vested in the trustee in that regard, it would be reasonable to conclude that 'income according to ordinary concepts' (in a trust law context) would be the appropriate measure.

TAX RULING TR 2012/D1: MEANING OF 'INCOME OF THE TRUST ESTATE'

The Commissioner of Taxation has considered the term 'Income of the trust estate' for the purposes of Division 6 ITAA36, and expressed views which are inconsistent with those expressed by the High Court in the *Bamford case*.

A joint submission from five professional bodies representing the accounting and tax professions criticised the draft ruling in that 'it does not represent an appropriate interpretation of the High Court's comments in *Commissioner of Taxation v Bamford* (2010) HCA 10 ...'. The submission called for the draft ruling to be withdrawn, however that has not occurred.

The draft ruling concludes that the 'income of the trust estate' cannot exceed the net amount of income to which beneficiaries could be made presently entitled or the trustee could accumulate.

Importantly, whilst acknowledging that the term is based on trust law principles, the Commissioner rejects the view that 'income of the trust estate' is determined solely on the basis of the relevant definition in the trust deed.

The ruling states that notional income amounts cannot be taken into account in calculating the 'income of the trust estate' (subject to an exception)*. Notional income is defined as:

> *An amount of assessable income taken into account in calculating the net income of an income year that either does not represent any accretion (of either cash or value) to the trust estate in that year or that represents an accretion coupled with a corresponding depletion (in cash or value) of the fund.*

Examples of what the Commissioner refers to as 'notional income amounts' are set out below.

* the exception being where notional income amounts are matched by notional expense amounts (refer: paragraph 16 of the Ruling).

NOTIONAL INCOME AMOUNTS

The following examples of notional income are provided in the ruling:

- **Franking credits**: The Commissioner expresses the view that a franking credit 'does not represent an accretion to the trust estate nor an accounting asset of the trust (that is, it is not a future economic benefit of the trust) that can itself be dealt with by the trustee'. It is merely a feature of the income tax law which confers benefits at the time of assessment. The conclusion is therefore reached that a franking credit cannot form part of trust income.

- **CGT: Market value substitution rule**: In certain circumstances a capital gain will be calculated taking into account the market value of the asset rather than the actual capital proceeds (s116-30 ITAA97).
  To the extent that capital proceeds are deemed rather than actual, that amount does not represent an accretion to the trust estate and therefore cannot form part of the income of the trust estate.

- **Distributions from other trusts**: If a trust distributes income to a beneficiary trust and the net (taxable) income is greater than the income of the trust, the beneficiary trust will not be able to include the excess in its own distributable income as it does not represent an accretion to the trust estate.

EXAMPLE

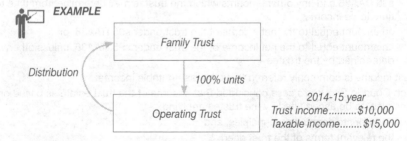

For the 2014-15 year, the 'income of the trust estate' of Family Trust would include an amount of $10,000 from Operating Trust (according to TR 2012/D1).

Division 7A dividends

A trust estate may become assessable in respect of a deemed dividend pursuant to Division 7A ITAA36. For example: a loan from a private company which contravenes s109D ITAA36. In these circumstances the deemed dividend is described as notional income and therefore not able to be included in the distributable income of the trust estate.

Attributable income

If a trustee is an attributable taxpayer pursuant to the transferor trust or controlled foreign company rules, the attributed amount will be considered to be notional income and therefore excluded from the calculation of income of the trust estate.

Ruling commentary

The ruling describes 'income of the trust estate' in these terms:

> *The income, being a product of, or a flow from, the trust estate, must represent, in total, an actual accretion to the trust estate for the relevant period. In other words, that which is 'income' cannot in total exceed (although it can be less than) the yield or accretion to the fund for the relevant period. And it must represent an accretion that, following its production, is capable of adhering to, or forming part of, the trust estate. However, in this context an accretion need not be a realised gain – it may in appropriate cases reflect an unrealised gain which represents an increase in value which has accrued to the trust.*

Income equalisation clauses

The ruling acknowledges the widespread practice of trust deeds defining 'income' as being equal to the net income of the trust for tax purposes.

Notwithstanding the adoption of this definition, the Commissioner is of the view that 'an amount which is included in the net income of the trust but which is not represented by a net accretion to the trust fund (for example, notional income amounts) cannot generally form part of the distributable income of that trust estate'.

Having reached that conclusion the Commissioner goes on to state that *"... notional income amounts ... do not represent any amount to which a beneficiary could be made presently entitled.*

Issues with income equalisation clauses

A trust which defined 'income' as being the net (taxable) income pursuant to s95 ITAA36 had the following:

Trading loss	($90)
Franked dividend	$70
Franking credits	$30
Taxable income	$10

Based on TR 2012/10, no distribution could occur as there would be no income of the trust estate (loss of $20).

Adapted from TR 2012/D1: Income equalisation clause – notional income

The Melbourne Family Trust deed defines 'income' to mean the net income of the Fund in any Financial Year determined in accordance with s95(1).

For the 2013-14 income year, the trust's net income as defined in s95 is $100,000, made up of franked dividend of $70,000 and franking credit of $30,000. The trustee has no other relevant income or expenses for that income year.

The trustee resolves to distribute the trust income to resident beneficiaries (two of whom, Beth and Jim, are under a legal disability) as follows:

Beth Melbourne	$416
Jim Melbourne	$416
Charitable Melbourne Inc	$20,000
Deal Melbourne Pty Ltd	$Balance

Despite the terms of the deed, the $30,000 franking credit does not represent an accretion of the trust fund and therefore does not form part of the distributable income of the trust. The trust's distributable income is $70,000.

Applying the proportionate approach, each beneficiary's share of the trust's distributable income and their corresponding proportionate share of the trust's net income, is as calculated in the table below:

Entity assessed	Share of distributable income	Share of net income
Beth	$416 of $70,000 (ie. 0.59%)	0.59% x $100,000 = $594
Jim	$416 of $70,000 (ie. 0.59%)	0.59% x $100,000 = $594
Charitable Melbourne	$20,000 of $70,000 (ie. 28.57%)	28.57% x $100,000 = $28,571
Deal Melbourne	$49,168 of $70,000 (ie. 70.24%)	70.24% x $100,000 = $70,240
Trustee	$0	$0

As Beth and Jim are under a legal disability, the trustee will be assessed in respect of their share of the net income of the Melbourne Family Trust (as set out in the table above) under s98.

Both Charitable Melbourne and Deal Melbourne will be assessed on their share of the net income of the Melbourne Family Trust (as set out in the table above) under s97.

ACTION POINTS TO DEAL WITH APPROACH ADOPTED IN TR 2012/D1

- Review the definition of 'income' in trust deeds.
- If the definition equates income to the net (taxable) income, consider the implications and whether an amendment to the deed is appropriate.
- If an amendment to the deed is contemplated, obtain legal advice confirming that the amendment will not constitute a resettlement (see 7.850).
- If the trust deed provides the trustee with the power to determine whether income is equated to net (taxable) income or, alternatively some other basis, identify what is required in order to evidence the trustees decision in this regard.
- Establish a procedure to ensure that notional amounts which arise in future years are identified.
- Where necessary, review prior year distributions to ascertain whether any trustee actions would contravene the approach described in TR 2012/D1.

SUBSEQUENT INCREASE IN TRUST TAXABLE INCOME

The Commissioner of Taxation has considered this situation in TD 2012/22. The determination contains numerous examples.

The outcome of a subsequent increase in the taxable income of a trust will be impacted by:
- how 'income of the trust estate' is determined
- whether the trust deed contains default beneficiaries who would become presently entitled to income in the event the trustee fails to appoint trust income for the year in accordance with the deed, and
- the style of income distribution resolution adopted by the trustee.

7.700 TAXING TRUSTS AND BENEFICIARIES

Division 6 ITAA36 provides the primary laws which tax trustees and/or beneficiaries are to be taxed. Rates of tax vary according to the circumstances of the trust and the beneficiary.

The trustee must ensure that beneficiaries become presently entitled to trust income at or before year end to avoid income being assessed to the trustee (usually under s99A ITAA36.)

PRESENT ENTITLEMENT

As noted, a beneficiary would be assessed on a distribution of income of the trust to the extent that there is a present entitlement conferred on that beneficiary. *Harmer v FCT* defined present entitlement by stating that a beneficiary would be entitled, if and only if:

(a) the beneficiary had an interest in the income which is both vested in interest and vested in possession, and

(b) the beneficiary has the present legal right to demand and receive payment of income,

whether or not the precise entitlement can be ascertained before the end of the relevant financial year of income and whether or not the trustee has the funds available for immediate payment. A beneficiary is 'presently entitled' to the income of a trust if they are in a position to call for the income (require the trustee to pay the income to them, or for their benefit), or would be in such a position if not for the fact that they are under a legal disability (see *Whiting's case* (1943) 68 CLR 199 and *Taylor's case* (1970) 199 CLR 444).

Where the beneficiary made presently entitled is a company, and the entitlement remains unpaid, TR 2010/3 may apply in order to determine that an entitlement be converted to a loan for the purposes of Division 7A ITAA36 (refer 6.310).

If a beneficiary is a non-resident, the liability to tax in respect of the trust income distributed falls to the trustee under s98(3) ITAA36 (refer below).

The decision of the High Court in the *Bamford case* and subsequent removal of TR 95/29 has impacted the ability of those carrying on a primary production business via a loss trust to access the income averaging provisions (21.900) and farm management deposits concessions (see 21.800) because in a loss year there are no beneficiaries presently entitled to primary production income. As a result, legislation has been enacted to allow such beneficiaries to access these concessions in certain circumstances (see Chapter 21).

LEGAL DISABILITY

The trustee is assessable on the beneficiary's income (s98(1) ITAA36) if the beneficiary is presently entitled to income and is under a legal disability by reason of:

* mental incapacity
* being under age 18 at end of the financial year, or
* bankruptcy.

BENEFICIARIES UNDER 18 YEARS OF AGE

The trust income to which a beneficiary under 18 years of age at the end of the financial year is presently entitled may be subject to tax at the maximum marginal rate depending on the type of income received (see 3.040). If the income is from a deceased estate, normal personal tax rates generally apply (see 7.950). Usually, a minor beneficiary does not have to lodge a separate tax return if that person is not deriving income from other sources.

A beneficiary under 18 years of age is considered to be under a legal disability and therefore the trustee would be assessable (s98 ITAA36) in respect of trust income to which the beneficiary was presently entitled.

NON-RESIDENT BENEFICIARIES

Generally, the net trust income is taxed to beneficiaries under s97 ITAA36. However, ss98 and 98A ITAA36 apply to certain distributions made to a non-resident beneficiary.

The general principles where distributions are made to non-resident beneficiaries are:

* **Trustee liable to tax:** A non-resident beneficiary, who is not under a legal disability and who is presently entitled to a share of the net income of the trust, would not be assessed on that share under s97(2)(b) ITAA36. Instead, the non-resident beneficiary's share of net income comprising Australian sourced income would be assessed in the hands of the trustee as if it were the income of the individual and were not subject to any deduction (s98(2A) and s98(3) ITAA36). The trustee is also liable to tax on foreign source income attributable to a period that the beneficiary was a resident. The amount of tax payable would be in accordance with non-resident tax rates for individuals.
* **Non-resident beneficiary also assessed:** The share of net income which is assessed to the trustee would also be assessable to the non-resident beneficiary (s98A(1) ITAA36). The tax which is assessed to the non-resident beneficiary would be reduced by the tax paid by the trustee for that beneficiary's share of net income (s98A(2)(a) ITAA36). Any excess tax paid by the trustee would be refundable to the beneficiary (s98A(2)(b) ITAA36).
* **Distribution of foreign source income is NANE:** Normally, a distribution of foreign sourced income would be non-assessable to a non-resident beneficiary. A non-resident beneficiary can apply for a refund for tax paid by the trustee on that income if it can be demonstrated that the share of income to which they are presently entitled comprises of any foreign sourced income (s99D ITAA36).
* **Trustee not liable to tax under s98 ITAA36 in certain circumstances:** As a general rule, distributions of certain income such as interest, dividends and royalties to non-resident beneficiaries will attract withholding tax to which the trustee would be required to deduct and remit the withholding tax.

Therefore, there are certain situations where income distributed would not be assessed at non-resident rates to the trustee. In IT 2680, the Commissioner accepts that where an unfranked dividend or interest is distributed to a non-resident beneficiary, the withholding tax provisions will have application and the beneficiary would be liable for withholding tax when the income is derived per s128A(3) ITAA36. The withholding still applies even if the trust has no net income or has incurred a loss for the income year (IT 2680). The obligation to deduct and remit the withholding tax is placed on the trustee.

OTHER CONSIDERATIONS

Affected taxpayers should also be aware of specific rules which:

- work out the share of franking credits for franked dividends which flow through a trust to a beneficiary (sub-division 207-B ITAA97) (see 7.600 and 6.800)
- can reduce the amount of non-resident tax payable under s98(4) ITAA36 by the trustee for distributions of discounted capital gains (s115-222 ITAA97), and
- allow a non-resident beneficiary to disregard capital gains from non-taxable Australian property distributed by a fixed trust (s855-40 ITAA97).

STREAMING TRUST INCOME

The trustee is permitted to 'stream' capital gains and/or franked distributions, provided the trustee is empowered to do so under the terms of the relevant trust deed and the legislative requirements are satisfied as follows:

- capital gains and franked distributions (including franking credits) to be 'streamed' to particular beneficiaries where:
  - the trust deed empowers the trustee to take such action
  - the particular beneficiaries are made 'specifically entitled' to the capital gain or franked distribution
  - the particular beneficiaries have, or it is reasonable to believe they will, receive the net financial benefit which is referable to the capital gain or franked distribution, and
  - the entitlement is appropriately recorded in the records of the trust (for example by trustee resolution) by
    - in the case of a capital gain – 31 August
    - in the case of a franked distribution – 30 June
- a trustee to elect to be assessed on a capital gain on behalf of beneficiaries of the trust in circumstances where:
  - an income beneficiary cannot benefit from the capital gain, or
  - a capital beneficiary is unable to immediately benefit from the capital gain.

Refer to 7.170 for comment regarding the need for resolutions to be prepared by 30 June.

NOTE: The streaming rules apply strictly to net capital gains and franked distributions only. Other income types cannot be streamed.

APPLICATION OF DIVISION 6E

Whilst trust income is generally determined solely in accordance with Division 6 ITAA36, where capital gains and/or franked distributions are included in the definition of trust income then Division 6E will also need to be considered.

Division 6E ITAA36 applies if:

a. the trust has a positive taxable income (ie. net income), and
b. capital gains (after applying capital losses, discounts if applicable and any small business CGT concessions)
c. franked distributions (after deducting directly relevant expenses), and/or
d. franking credits are taken into account in working out that taxable income.

Assessable distributions received by a beneficiary may be included in taxable income pursuant to:

- Division 6 (being the Division 6E income ie. exclusive of capital gains and franked distributions)
- Subdivision 115-C in respect of capital gains
  - s115-227 (a) where there is specific entitlement
  - s115-227 (b) for other capital gains
- Subdivision 207-B in respect of franked distributions
  - s207-55(4)(a) where there is specific entitlement
  - s207-55(4)(b) for other franked distributions

The provisions do not alter the requirement to adopt the 'proportionate approach' (see 7.600) to all trust income other than capital gains and franked distributions for which specific entitlement has been created under the streaming provisions.

KEY TERMS

The following key terms are used in establishing a beneficiary's entitlement to a capital gain or franked distribution:

- **Division 6 percentage** is the share of the income of the trust estate (distributable income) to which a beneficiary or trustee is presently entitled. The share is expressed as a percentage. If the income of a trust estate is nil, a beneficiary will have a Division 6 percentage of nil and the trustee will have a Division 6 percentage of 100%.

- **Adjusted Division 6 percentage** is the Division 6 percentage of a beneficiary or trustee calculated on the assumption that the amount of any capital gain or franked distribution to which a beneficiary or trustee is specifically entitled has been disregarded in working out the income of the trust estate. In effect, capital gains are transferred from Division 6 ITAA36 to subdivision 115-C ITAA97 whilst franked distributions are transferred to subdivision 207-B ITAA97.

REQUIREMENTS FOR STREAMING

Streaming can only be effective if the trustee makes a beneficiary specifically entitled to a share of the net financial benefit in respect of a capital gain or franked dividend, and:
- the beneficiary has received, or c**an be reasonably expected to receive**, the **financial benefit**
- the benefit is referable to the capital gain or franked distribution, and
- it is recorded in its character, as **referable to the capital gain or franked distribution** in the accounts.

The highlighted terms are discussed below at *Implementing a streamed distribution*.

The XYZ trust derived the following in the 2014-15 year:

Rental income	*$1,000*
Capital gain (discount)	*$400*
Franked dividend	*$700*
Franking credit	*$300*
Trust income 2014-15 year*	*$2,100*
Net (taxable) income 2014-15 year	*$2,200*

Division 6E application

Taxable income	*$2,200*
Less: Capital gain	*($200)*
Franked dividend	*($700)*
Franking credit	*($300)*
Division 6E net income	*$1,000*

The Division 6E net income becomes assessable pursuant to Division 6.
Beneficiaries to whom distributions are made may be assessable pursuant to:

Division 6: the Division 6E amount	*$1,000*
Subdivision 115-C: Capital gains	*$200*
Subdivision 207-B: Franked distributions	*$700 plus franking credits*

*exclusion of franking credits from trust income is the approach adopted in TR 2012/D1 (see 7.600) and is consistent with the examples contained in the EM which accompanied the amending legislation.

NO BENEFICIARY SPECIFICALLY ENTITLED

Continuing with the assumptions from the previous example, assume the XYZ trust for the 2014-15 year has:

Trust income.. $2,100

Taxable income

Business profits... $1,000
Capital gain $200
Franked dividend... $700
Franking credit $300
                                                          $2,200

The trustee resolves that the trust income will be distributed to:

- Kathy: 50%
- Kenny: 50%

(In these circumstances there would be no income to which a beneficiary was specifically entitled.)

The beneficiaries' position would be:

	Kathy	Kenny	Total
Division 6 (s97 ITAA36)	$500	$500	$1,000
Subdivision 115-C ITAA97	$100	$100	$200
Subdivision 207-B ITAA97			
Franked distribution	$350	$350	$700
Franking credit	$150	$150	$300
Assessable amount	$1,100	$1,100	$2,200
Present entitlement	$1,050	$1,050	$2,100

STREAMING A CAPITAL GAIN

Assume the following position for the Bell Family Trust for the year ended 30 June 2015:

	Trust income	Taxable income
Trading profit	$100,000	$100,000
Discount capital gain	$300,000	$150,000
	$400,000	$250,000

Trustees distribution resolution

- Specific entitlement:
  Kathy: 50% of capital gain

- Remaining income:
  Kathy: 50%
  Ben: 50%

Implementing the terms of the trustee resolution

STEP 1 – Division 6 percentages

- Trust income is $400,000
  Kathy: $150,000 + $75,000 + $50,000 = 68.75%*
  Ben: $75,000 + $50,000 = 31.25%**

STEP 2 – Adjust: Division 6E

Exclude capital gains and franked distributions for which specific entitlement has been created to the extent they are included in trust taxable income.

Kathy:

$$\frac{\$275,000 - \$150,000}{\$400,000 - \$150,000} = 50\%$$

Ben:

$$\frac{\$75,000 + \$50,000}{\$250,000} = 50\%$$

STEP 3 – Apply subdivision 115-C

a. Determine each beneficiary's share of the capital gain

	Specific entitlement	Unallocated gain	Total	%
Kathy	$150,000	$75,000*	$225,000	75%
Ben	$0	$75,000*	$75,000	25%
	$150,000	$150,000	$300,000	

*$150,000 x 50% = $75,000

b. Determine each beneficiary's attributable capital gain

	Share of capital gain	Taxable capital gain
Kathy	75%	$112,500
Ben	25%	$37,500
Total		$150,000

c. Gross up the capital gain where applicable

	Share of capital gain	Gross up	Total assessable gain
Kathy	$112,500	$112,500	$225,000
Ben	$37,500	$37,500	$75,000
	$150,000	$150,000	$300,000

STEP 4 – Assessable amounts Division 6E

The Division 6E income is $100,000 Division 6E percentages: Kathy and Ben each 50%

- Kathy: 50% x $100,000 = $50,000
- Ben: 50% x $100,000 = $50,000

STEP 5 – Overall beneficiary's assessable income

	Division 6 (s97)	Subdivision 115-C	Gross up capital gain	Total
Kathy	$50,000	$112.500	$112,500	$275,000
Ben	$50,000	$37,500	$37,500	$125,000
	$100,000	$150,000	$150,000	$400,000

Note: Beneficiaries may be eligible to apply the 50% discount to the capital gain distributed from the trust.

IMPLEMENTING A STREAMED DISTRIBUTION

1. Trust deed terms

The trust deed must empower the trustee to:

- separately account for different classes of income, specifically capital gains and franked distributions, and
- distribute the different classes of income separately to particular beneficiaries.

If consideration is given to amending the trust deed to create a streaming capability, trustees should:

- consider the definition of 'income' in the deed in light of the views expressed in tax ruling TR 2012/D1 (see 7.600 above), and
- confirm that proposed amendments would not result in a resettlement of the trust (see 7.850).

2. The trust must have net (taxable) income for the year which includes capital gains and/or franked dividends.

3. Specific entitlement

The beneficiaries must be 'specifically entitled' to the streamed capital gain and/or franked distribution. Such entitlement can be created by formula with the exact amounts being determined at a later time.

In order to be 'specifically entitled', the beneficiary:

- must receive, or can reasonably be expected to receive, an amount equal to their share of the 'net financial benefit' referable to the capital gain or franked distribution in the trust, and
- the entitlement must be recorded in its character as such in the accounts or records of the trust.

Therefore, it will not be possible to stream distributions where:

- a capital gain has arisen as a result of the application of the market value substitution rule, or
- the gross benefit has been reduced to zero by losses or directly relevant expenses (eg. interest on borrowed funds directly applicable to franked distributions received).

If a beneficiary's entitlement has not been physically paid, it should follow that the 'specifically entitled' requirements would be satisfied if:

- the relevant amount was credited to an account in the beneficiary's name, or
- the amount was credited to an unpaid present entitlement account for the beneficiary.

4. Share of net financial benefit

The 'share of the net financial benefit' to which a beneficiary is entitled is that part of the benefit that:

- the beneficiary has received or can reasonably be expected to receive,
- is referable to the capital gain or franked distribution, and
- is recorded 'in its character as referable to a capital gain or franked distribution in the accounts or records of the trust'.

NOTE: 'Accounts or records of the trust' would include resolutions and distribution statements. A record merely for tax purposes (such as a tax return schedule) would not suffice. An appropriately worded trustee distribution supported by corresponding entries in the books of account should satisfy this requirement.

- **Reasonably expected to receive:** The term 'can reasonably be expected to receive' has been considered in TD 2012/11. The TD contemplated a situation where a CGT event occurs prior to year-end (eg. May, when a contract is executed) but the existence of a capital gain is not established until after year-end (eg. December, when the contract is settled). The Commissioner concludes that it is possible (depending on the circumstances) for a beneficiary of a trust estate to be reasonably expected to receive an amount of a financial benefit referable to such a gain.
- **'Net financial benefit' of a franked distribution – directly relevant expenses:** Expenditure that is directly relevant to the derivation of franked distributions is required to be deducted from those distributions for the purposes of the streaming provisions. Franked distributions can only be taken into account for Division 6E to the extent that there is an amount of franked distribution remaining after reducing it by deductions that were directly relevant to it (s102UW). Common examples of expenses which might be 'directly relevant' would include interest and portfolio management fees. There is no requirement to apportion expenses which are not direct.

5. Character of capital gain or franked distribution

The capital gain or franked distribution must be recorded in its character as being referable to the capital gain or franked distribution in the accounts or records of the trust.

The recording must occur:

- **for a capital gain:** no later than two months after year-end (ie. 31 August), and
- **for a franked distribution:** no later than year-end (ie. 30 June).

Streaming of capital gains and franked distributions will occur on a quantum basis.

- **Rateable reduction:** The streaming of capital gains and franked distributions on a quantum basis could result in beneficiaries being taxed on amounts greater than the taxable income of the trust. In these circumstances a rateable reduction of the taxable amount occurs. The rateable reduction would have application where net capital gains and total franked distributions (net of directly relevant expenses) together exceed the taxable income of the trust (excluding franking credits). The rateable reduction formula is designed to enable beneficiaries to retain franking credits notwithstanding a reduction in the assessable franked distribution.

Assume a trust derived the following:

Royalty income	*$5,000*
Franked distribution	*$7,000*
Franking credits	*$3,000*
Trading loss	*($10,000)*
Taxable income	**$5,000**

The trustee resolves to distribute 100% of franked distributions to Kathy and 100% of remaining income to Kenny.

Beneficiaries' position

Kathy – entitlement .....$7,000 franked distribution
$3,000 franking credits

Trust taxable income **$5,000**

If Kathy was assessed on the streamed distribution of $7,000, it would exceed the taxable income of the trust.

Rateable reduction formula

Trust taxable income (excl. franking credits)
Net capital gain + net franked distribution

$$\frac{\$2,000}{0 + \$7,000} = 0.2857$$

Beneficiaries' tax outcome

Kathy

Franked distribution: $7,000 x 0.2857	*$2,000*
Franking credits	*$3,000*
Taxable income	**$5,000**

6. Franked distributions: In relation to franked distributions:

- it will not be possible to flow franking credits through a trust if there is no overall trust net income to which beneficiaries can become entitled (which continues the position under the previous law),
- provided there is overall trust net income to which beneficiaries can become entitled, it will be possible to flow franking credits through a trust, and
- it is not possible to stream franking credits separately from franked distributions.

7. Trustee may choose to become specifically entitled to a capital gain

A trustee may make a choice to be assessed on a capital gain provided:

- the capital gain was taken into account in working out the net capital gain of the trust for an income year, and
- trust property representing all or part of that capital gain has not been paid to or applied for the benefit of a beneficiary of the trust by the end of two months after the end of the income year.

In such circumstances, the trustee would be treated as being specifically entitled to the capital gain and assessed under s99A ITAA36 or alternatively, s99 ITAA36. A choice of this type was previously only available to the trustee of a testamentary trust.

8. Specific anti-avoidance – tax sheltering arrangements

Specific anti-avoidance measures have been introduced that prevent the inappropriate use of exempt beneficiaries (such as charitable organisations) to 'shelter' taxable income of a trust. Broadly, the anti-avoidance rules apply where a beneficiary that is an exempt entity is not notified or paid their present entitlement to income of the trust; or where an exempt beneficiary would otherwise be assessed on a share of a trust's taxable income that is disproportionate to their overall trust entitlement (s100AA and s100AB ITAA36). These rules do not apply to a trust that is an MIT (see 7.000).

AVOID WASTING TAX CREDITS / OFFSETS

To be of any benefit to an individual beneficiary or unitholder, foreign income tax offsets must be utilised by the beneficiary or unitholder in the tax year in which they are distributed. Franking credits on franked dividends are refundable to non-corporate beneficiaries and every effort should be made to ensure that the trust has a net income which is able to be distributed to the beneficiaries as franking credits can be lost if the trust does not or cannot make a distribution.

UTILISING TAX OFFSETS TO ADVANTAGE

A distribution of dividend income may carry with it imputation credits applicable to franked dividends paid by companies. This can create important planning opportunities.

Particular care is needed to ensure that the proposed beneficiary or unitholder can fully utilise the tax credits. Distribution of franked distributions will need to be in line with the requirements for streaming of franked distributions (see *Implementing a streamed distribution* above). Otherwise the franked distribution would be proportionally allocated amongst beneficiaries.

A trust's assessable income for this tax year comprises dividend payments totalling $15,000, including franking credits of $4,500, and rental income of $8,000. If $24,000 of deductible expenses (eg. interest on borrowings to acquire shares, and repairs to the rental property) are incurred, there would be no net income of the trust for the trustee to distribute. The $4,500 in franking credits would be forfeited.

However, if it is possible for sufficient expenses to be delayed until the next tax year, there would be net income in the trust which could be distributed along with the imputation credits. For instance, if repairs of $2,000 were delayed then there would be $1,000 net income to distribute to beneficiaries along with the imputation credits. The beneficiaries could use the imputation credits to partially or totally offset their own tax assessment, depending on their circumstances.

If the $1,000 of net trust income was distributed to beneficiary X, that beneficiary would also receive $4,500 of franking credits.

TRUST DISTRIBUTIONS TO COMPANIES

The top marginal tax rate for individuals is higher than the corporate tax rate. This natural arbitrage has encouraged the trustees of many trusts to distribute trust income to company beneficiaries. The tax effectiveness of such distributions depends on the particular facts and circumstances. Distributions to corporate beneficiaries which remain unpaid may have Division 7A implications.

UNPAID PRESENT ENTITLEMENTS AND DIVISION 7A

TR 2010/3 addresses the circumstances in which an Unpaid Present Entitlement (UPE) owed to a corporate beneficiary may constitute a loan for the purposes of Division 7A ITAA36.

TR 2010/3 contemplates two types of loans:

1. Those arising as a result of:
   - an actual or implied agreement between the trust and the corporate beneficiary, and
   - the trustee crediting the UPE amount to an account in favour of the corporate beneficiary in accordance with a power contained in the trust deed.

   For loans arising in these circumstances the ruling applies both before and after the date of issue (16 December 2009).

2. A loan arising as a result of a UPE being 'converted' into a loan.

   In this instance the ruling applies to UPEs created from 26 December 2009.

PS LA 2010/4 has also been issued which provides practical guidance on how such unpaid present entitlements should be treated for Division 7A purposes. For further information, see 6.310.

Division 7A may apply if an unpaid present entitlement is released by a private company (see TD 2015/D4). Further, a beneficiary is not entitled to a bad debt deduction for a UPE under s25-35 ITAA97 as the requirement of s25-35(1)(a) cannot be met as the amount is not included in the beneficiary's assessable income (TD 2015/D5). The amount is instead used in determining the net income of the trust.

REDUCTION OF CREDIT LOAN ACCOUNTS

Where a trust has outstanding loans from individuals or other trusts and has unpaid company entitlements, a payment to the individual or other trust to reduce the loan account balance will not trigger a deemed dividend for Division 7A purposes.

TAXATION OF CAPITAL GAINS

Trusts have access to both the general CGT discount (at 50%) and the small business CGT concessions where applicable (see 12.525).

SMALL BUSINESS CGT CONCESSIONS – UNIT TRUSTS

The CGT small business concessions may apply to reduce a capital gain realised by a trust. However, where a fixed trust distributes a tax-free amount to a beneficiary, CGT event E4 may apply to reduce the cost base of the units by the tax-free amount distributed. If the cost base is reduced to nil, any excess will be a capital gain, although an eligible beneficiary may apply the general CGT 50% discount if the units have been held for more than 12 months.

The tax-free amounts which may trigger CGT event E4 include:

- frozen indexation amount
- 50% active asset reduction
- capital works allowance (special building write-off), and
- a return of trust capital.

NOTE: The general discount amount does not impact the cost base (see 12.165).

RENOUNCING INTEREST

A beneficiary of a discretionary trust may renounce their interest in the trust. A renunciation triggers CGT event C2 for the beneficiary because it is an abandonment, surrender or forfeiture of the interest (s104-25 ITAA97). However, there will generally be no capital gain unless the market value of any capital proceeds on renunciation exceeds the cost base of the trust interest. A capital gain is more likely to arise if the trustee has allocated assets or income to the beneficiary, before the renunciation.

There are usually no CGT consequences for the trustee if a discretionary beneficiary renounces their interest in the trust. Amending clauses in a discretionary trust deed to specifically exclude a beneficiary may result in a resettlement of the trust (refer 7.850) which may have adverse CGT consequences.

SAMPLE RENUNCIATION BY BENEFICIARY

I . . . . renounce my interest in the. . . . . Trust

and my entitlement to any further benefits from the . . . . Trust, whether

those benefits be income or capital or of any other nature.   I request that the trustee of the

. . . . . Trust recognise my request that I receive no further benefits

from the . . . . Trust and furthermore recognise that this renunciation

of my beneficial interest in the. . . . . Trust is irrevocable.

NOTE: Taxpayers in receipt of a government pension will be affected by the gifting rules if they renounce their interest. An interest in a trust will count towards the income and assets tests.

DEDUCTIBILITY OF INTEREST EXPENSES ON BENEFICIARY DISTRIBUTIONS

In Tax Ruling TR 2005/12, the Commissioner states that interest incurred by a trustee on funds borrowed to pay a monetary distribution to a beneficiary is deductible if the funds are used to refinance a 'returnable amount'. This would arise where the amount:

- is employed by the trustee in gaining or producing the assessable income of the trust estate, or in carrying on business for that purpose, and
- a beneficiary of the trust estate is entitled to require the amount to be returned to that beneficiary, and that
- it is or represents money or property that was either:
  - previously transferred by the beneficiary to the trustee of the trust estate, or
  - previously retained by the trustee out of funds to which the beneficiary was presently entitled.

REIMBURSEMENT AGREEMENTS

Where a beneficiary of a trust estate is not under a legal disability and is presently entitled to a share of the trust income, but the beneficiary's present entitlement arose out of a 'reimbursement agreement', the beneficiary is deemed not to be presently entitled and taxed under the special rate determined under s99A.

A 'reimbursement agreement' is an agreement that provides for money to be paid, or property to be transferred, or services or other benefits to be provided, to or for 'a person or persons other than the beneficiary or the beneficiary and another person or other persons'.

Reimbursement agreements do not include arrangements entered into in the course of ordinary family or commercial dealings.

The ATO has identified that this concept has either not been identified or otherwise misunderstood by taxpayers. They have published practical guidance to further explain possible scenarios where this issue applies.

EXAMPLE 1: Trust Estate (from the ATO website)

Consider the following arrangement:

- *the trustee of a trust estate makes a beneficiary entitled to distributable income*
- *the presently entitled beneficiary's assessable income includes a share of the trust's taxable income*
- *instead of paying the amount of distributable income to the presently entitled beneficiary, the trustee gives, or lends on interest-free terms, the money to another person*
- *the other person benefits from the distributable income of trust, but is not assessed on any part of the trust's taxable income.*

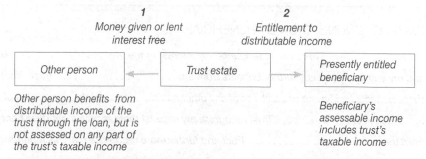

If this arrangement was entered into in the course of an ordinary family or commercial dealing (discussed below), section 100A will have no application.

If it was not entered into in the course of an ordinary family or commercial dealing, it will generally be a reimbursement agreement if it was intended that the beneficiary who was made presently entitled to the distributable income pay a lower amount of tax than would otherwise have been payable – for example, by the person who actually enjoyed the economic benefits of that income.

In Example 1, the presently entitled beneficiary may pay less (or no) tax because it:

- *is a tax-exempt entity*
- *is a foreign resident and the assessable income of the trust includes foreign source income or income subject to withholding tax in Australia*
- *has tax losses or excess deductions or capital losses or an unapplied net capital loss, or*
- *is otherwise subject to a lower rate of tax.*

Another scenario where this situation could apply is in relation to loans made through ordinary commercial and family dealings. Where a trustee lends money on terms that require repayments of principal and interest, this would go towards indicating an ordinary commercial dealing. However, loans made in the course of ordinary family dealings may not be commercial loans – for example, where money is lent by a trustee to a family member on terms that require repayments of principal only (and such repayments are intended to be made) this could still indicate an ordinary family dealing when considered together with all the other relevant facts.

EXAMPLE 5: Commissioner considers section 100A applies (from the ATO website)

The Commissioner considers that the following arrangement would constitute a reimbursement agreement:

- *the trustee of a trust owns all of the shares in a private company. The company is also a beneficiary of the trust and undertakes no activity, but derives a small amount of bank interest on its own account*
- *the directors of the trustee company and the beneficiary company are the same (or related) individuals*
- *the trustee resolves to make the company presently entitled to all, or some part of, the distributable income of the trust at the end of year 1*
- *the company includes its share of the trust taxable income in its assessable income for year 1 and pays tax at the corporate rate. The year 1 trust income is distributed to the company in year 2 prior to the lodgment of the company's year 1 income tax return. (Division 7A does not apply because the company's entitlement is paid prior to the lodgment of the company's income tax return for the year in which the entitlement arose.)*
- *the company pays a fully franked dividend to the trustee in year 2, sourced from the trust income*
- *the dividend forms part of the distributable income and taxable income of the trust in year 2*
- *the trustee makes the company presently entitled to all, or some part of, the income of the trust at the end of year 2 (possibly including the franked distribution).*
  [The arrangement is repeated.]

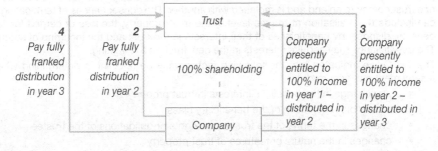

The reimbursement agreement results in relevant funds benefitting persons other than the beneficiary. In this case, money is paid to the trustee. The reimbursement agreement is the payment of income from the trustee to the company on the understanding (implied from the repetition in each income year and their common control) that the company would pay a dividend to the trustee of a corresponding amount (less the tax paid).

The agreement is designed to secure the reduction in tax that would otherwise be payable had the trustee simply accumulated the income.

This agreement is not an ordinary commercial dealing because the ownership structure and, particularly, the perpetual circulation of funds, serves no commercial purpose.

7.800   OTHER CGT CONSEQUENCES

Trustees may have the power to vary the terms of a trust deed. Certain decisions can cause a resettlement of the trust which may trigger the capital gains tax provisions, cause losses to be forfeited and have stamp duty implications.

7.820   CLONING TRUSTS

The trust cloning provisions have now been repealed. Trust cloning describes the CGT exception to CGT events E1 and E2 arising when assets are transferred between two trusts with the same beneficiaries and terms. The test of sameness has strict application and any differences between the trusts will trigger the CGT provisions. The repealed exceptions apply to CGT events happening on or after 1 November 2008. Therefore, trustees cannot rely on the sameness test in order to be exempt from CGT where CGT event E1 or E2 is triggered. Nonetheless, a capital gain in relation to CGT event E1 or E2 may be disregarded if there is a sole beneficiary of a non-unit trust who is absolutely entitled to the asset of the trust as against the trustee (disregarding any legal disability) (refer 12.028).

Generally, CGT event E1 occurs when a person declares or settles a trust over a CGT asset. However, s104-55(5) ITAA97 provides an exception where the trust is created by transferring the asset from another trust and the beneficiaries and the terms of both trusts are the same. CGT event E2 occurs when a person transfers a CGT asset into an existing trust. A similar exception applies under s104-60(5) ITAA97 if the beneficiaries and the terms of the existing trusts are the same.

The sameness test must be met at the time the asset is transferred. Where the asset is transferred to a new trust, the test time for the original trust is immediately before the asset is transferred and for the new trust immediately after the asset is transferred. Taxation ruling TR 2006/4 (withdrawn) outlined the indicators of sameness.

7.850   RESETTLEMENT (CREATION OF A NEW TRUST)

Care should be taken if making any changes to the terms of a trust arrangement. Depending on the nature and extent, the change may amount to more than a variation. If a change fundamentally alters a trust relationship or a change in the essential nature and character of the trust, then the trust may resettle and a new trust is created. In effect, this triggers CGT Event E1 (a trust is created over a CGT asset by declaration or settlement of a trust) (refer 12.028).

The Tax Office had published *Creation of a new trust – Statement of Principles August 2001* (withdrawn on 20 April 2012) which provided guidelines to clarify changes to a trust such that one trust comes to an end and is replaced with another. The consequences of terminating a trust can include the realisation at trustee level of the trust property, the loss of carried forward tax benefits, disposal by beneficiaries of their interests in the trust and the incurring of stamp duty. The beneficiaries may acquire interests in the new trust on the vesting.

The Tax Office indicated that the following factors may be relevant in determining whether a resettlement has occurred:

- any change in the beneficial interests in trust property
- a possible redefinition of the beneficiary class
- changes in the terms of the trust or the rights or obligations of the trustee
- changes in the nature or features of trust property

- additions of property which could amount to a new and separate settlement
- depletion of the trust property
- a change to the trust that is outside of the terms of the original trust
- a change in the essential nature and purpose of the trust, and/or
- a merger of two or more trusts or a splitting of a trust into two or more trusts.

The Tax Office indicated that this Statement of Principles has been withdrawn due to the decision in *Federal Commissioner of Taxation v Clark and Anor* [2011] FCAFC 5 and the High Court's refusal to grant the Commissioner leave to appeal that decision. Clark established the principle that, at least in the context of recoupment of losses, continuity of a trust estate will be maintained so long as the trust is not terminated for trust law purposes. As such, in the absence of termination, tax losses being carried forward by a trustee will as a general rule remain available to be recouped against relevant trust income derived in future years of income.

TAX DETERMINATION TD 2012/21

The statement of principles has to some degree been replaced by TD 2012/21 which considers whether CGT event E1 or E2 (see 7.820) (ie. a resettlement) happens if, pursuant to a valid exercise of a power contained within the trust's constituent document, the terms of the trust are changed.

In the TD, the Commissioner states that unless an amendment to a trust deed causes the trust to terminate for trust law purposes, or the effect of the amendment is to lead to a particular asset being subject to a separate charter of rights and obligations such as to give rise to the conclusion that the asset has been settled on terms of a different trust, neither CGT event E1 nor CGT event E2 happen (see 7.820 above).

The TD provides examples in relation to:

- addition of new entities to class of objects (see below)
- expansion of power to invest
- addition of definition of income and power to stream, and
- settling of trust asset on new trust.

FROM TD: Addition of new entities to class of objects

The Acorn Trust is a family discretionary trust that was settled to benefit the members of the Squirrel Family. Under the terms of the trust deed the trustee, a private company of which Mr and Mrs Squirrel are directors, has the power at its absolute discretion to appoint income to any one or more of the General Beneficiaries defined to include Mr Squirrel, his wife, their children, their grandchildren, and entities associated with the family. The trust deed for the Acorn Trust provides for a procedure for the trust to be amended, namely by trustee resolution recorded in writing.

Pursuant to this procedure the trustee resolves in writing to amend the deed to add to the class of General Beneficiaries the respective spouses of the children. The making of the resolution, being a valid exercise of a power of amendment contained within the deed, does not give rise to the happening of a CGT event

7.870   TRUST BECOMES A COMPANY

Trustees may resolve that a corporate structure would be a more suitable vehicle for commercial operations. Usually transferring assets including the business operations from a trust into a company would trigger capital gains tax. However, three rollover relief rules are contained in the CGT provisions to defer any capital gain to a later taxing point. Subdivision 124-H allows rollover relief on the exchange of units for shares in an interposed company. Subdivision 124-N provides rollover relief on the disposal of trust assets to a company as part of a trust restructure (refer 12.487). Subdivision 122-A provides roll-over relief where assets of a trust are disposed of to a wholly-owned company (refer 12.480).

7.900   TRUST LOSSES AND BAD DEBTS

If a trust incurs a tax loss, that loss cannot be distributed and must be carried forward. In order to deduct carried-forward and current year losses (and bad debts), there are various tests which must be satisfied.

CAPITAL LOSSES NOT AFFECTED

The trust loss rules do not apply to capital losses.

BAD DEBTS

For bad debts incurred post-20 August 1996, the trust also has to satisfy the trust loss tests described below.

TYPES OF TRUSTS

There are three main types of trusts for the purposes of the trust loss rules:

1. **Fixed trusts** – a trust in which the beneficiaries have fixed entitlements to all of the income and capital of the trust (eg. a fixed unit trust)

2. **Non-fixed trusts** – trusts which are not fixed trusts or excepted trusts eg discretionary trusts and hybrid trusts, and

3. **Excepted trusts** – family trusts, deceased estates within a five year administration period and superannuation funds.

SUMMARY OF TRUST LOSS RULES

Requirements for claiming trust losses					
Type of private trust	Income injection	50% stake	Pattern of distribution	Control	Same business
Fixed trust (not widely held)	Yes	Yes[1]	No	No	No
Non-fixed trust	Yes	Yes[2]	Yes	Yes	No
Family trust	Yes	No	No	No	No

1: Where an interest of at least 50% in a fixed trust is held by one or more trustees of discretionary trusts, it is not possible for it to satisfy the 50% stake test (see below). Accordingly, the rules provide an alternative test which requires, amongst other things, that each discretionary trust satisfies the tests that would apply if it was in a tax loss position instead of the fixed trust (refer s266-45).

2: Only applies to non-fixed trusts which confer a beneficiary with a fixed entitlement.

FIXED TRUSTS

Generally, a fixed trust must satisfy the income injection and 50% stake tests. For the purposes of the trust loss rules, a fixed trust with 50% or more of its units held by the trustees of non-fixed trusts (ie. discretionary trusts and superannuation funds) is not able to satisfy the 50% stake test, because the test requires the entitlements to be held as an individual for its own benefit.

However, if the trustee of any discretionary trust unitholder makes a family trust election (refer 7.200), the trustee of the family trust is deemed to hold any entitlements as an individual for its own benefit.

As a concession, an alternative to the 50% stake test is available which requires, among other things, that all of the non-fixed trust unitholders each satisfy the four tests which would apply if each non-fixed trust unitholder were in a tax loss position. The 50% stake test is used in determining whether there has been a change in ownership of a trust with fixed entitlements.

 The terms of the relevant trust deed generally determine the type of trust for tax purposes. What may be perceived to be a fixed trust (such as a unit trust) may be a non-fixed trust if not all the income and capital of the trust are the subject of fixed entitlements.

NON-FIXED TRUSTS

A trust with discretionary income or capital entitlements is subject to all four tests (eg. a discretionary trusts or a hybrid trust).

Unlike the corresponding tests that apply to companies, the trust loss rules permanently deny a deduction for income losses if any of the relevant tests (other than the income injection test) are not satisfied.

50% STAKE TEST

The 50% stake test assesses whether there has been a change in ownership in a trust with fixed entitlements. The test is satisfied where individuals have direct or indirect fixed entitlements to more than a 50% share of the income or capital of the trust during the test period. The test period commences from the start of the loss year to the end of the income year in which the loss is recouped.

NOTE: The individuals with fixed entitlements to income and those with fixed entitlements to capital do not have to be the same persons. The test applies independently to income and capital.

INCOME INJECTION TEST

The income injection test is an anti-avoidance provision intended to prevent schemes that seek to take advantage of tax losses or other deductions by injecting assessable income into the trust and sheltering that income from tax with the losses or deductions.

The test applies where:

- a trust derives assessable income
- any 'outsider' to the trust directly or indirectly provides a 'benefit' to the trustee, a beneficiary or any 'associate' of the trustee or beneficiary
- the trustee, beneficiary or associate directly or indirectly provides a benefit to the 'outsider' to the trust or to an 'associate' of the 'outsider', and
- it is reasonable to conclude that the derivation of the assessable income or the provision of the benefit was wholly or partly due to the availability of deductions.

An advantage of a trust making a family trust election is that the definition of 'outsider' is much narrower in the case of a family trust, than it is with any other trust.

For a **family trust,** an outsider is defined as a person other than:

- the trustee of the trust
- a person with a fixed entitlement to a share of the income or capital of the trust
- the test individual (SI) specified in the trust's family trust election (FTE)
- a member of the SI's family
- a trust with the same SI specified in its FTE
- a company, partnership or trust which has made an interposed entity election, and
- a fixed trust, partnership or company which the SI and/or members of the SI's family or trustees of the family trusts with the same SI hold fixed entitlements to all of the income and capital.

For **trusts other than a family trust**, an outsider is defined as a person other than:

- the trustee of the trust, and
- a person with a fixed entitlement to a share of the income or capital of the trust.

PATTERN OF DISTRIBUTIONS TEST

This test is applicable only if the trust has distributed income or capital in the income year and in at least one of the previous six years.

The pattern of distribution test is passed if, within two months of year end of the income year, the same individuals receive directly or indirectly, and for their own benefit (not in the capacity of trustee):

- more than 50% of every 'test year distribution' of income, or
- more than 50% of every 'test year distribution' of capital.

A 'test year distribution' of income or capital refers to years including:

1. the income year under examination and two months after that year end
2. the earliest of the following:
   - the closest income year prior to the loss year the trust distributed accounting income
   - the loss year if the trust distributed accounting income, and
   - the closest income year after the loss year, and
3. each intervening year between the above two years (see s269-65 ITAA36).

The relevant percentage to be taken into account is the percentage of total income or capital an individual is directly or indirectly entitled to as a percentage of the total distributed in a given year. Where a beneficiary has received different percentage distributions in test years, the smallest percentage is counted, making the test potentially harder to satisfy.

The same individuals are not entitled to receive more than 50% of income (or capital) under the patterns of distributions test and therefore lose their claim for income losses, unless an election is made to become a family trust.

Entitlements	Mother	Father	Child turns 18 in year 3
Year 1 (year before loss occurs)	30%	69%	1%
Year 3 (year loss is recouped)	50%	15%	35%
Lowest percentage	30%	15%	1%

The trust loss rules provide for special tracing rules for indirect entitlements and for situations where entitlements do not eventually flow through the interposed entity to the individual.

For hybrid and discretionary trusts that have income losses and choose or have to remain non-fixed trusts, the pattern of distributions test implications should be carefully considered before any distributions are made.

CONTROL TEST

The control test only applies to non-fixed trusts that have not made a family trust election. No group must begin to control the trust, directly or indirectly, during the test period. A non-fixed trust is controlled if a group has the power to direct, instruct, appoint or remove the trustee or alternatively controls the income or capital of the trust. A group also gains control of a trust if they hold over a 50% stake in the income or capital of the trust. A 'group' consists of a least one person (s269-95(5) ITAA36). Control of a trust will not be taken to have changed where a member of the controlling group has died, becomes incapacitated or suffered a marriage breakdown.

7.940   TRUSTS TREATED AS COMPANIES

Corporate unit trusts and public trading trusts are taxed as companies. These rules arose to prevent companies structuring as a unit trust to prevent being taxed at both the company level and at the shareholder level, and instead achieve taxation at only the unit holder level.

Although the simplified imputation system addresses the problem of two-tier corporate taxation to some extent, there are still situations where a company would prefer to distribute gross rather than net income. For example, the difference in the imputation system for residents and non-residents, the interaction of tax losses carried forward, the selective nature of refunding imputation credits and the availability of the CGT discount for all capital gains all compound to make taxation as a company less attractive.

7.950   DECEASED ESTATES

Deceased estates are treated as trusts for taxation purposes, and qualify for some concessional tax treatment. Payments in consequence of death might be made directly to beneficiaries or via the deceased estate.

OVERVIEW OF DECEASED ESTATES

A deceased estate is a trust comprising:

- assets of a deceased person (the trust property)
- beneficiaries (usually those named in the deceased's Will), and
- the trustee (usually the Legal Personal Representative (LPR)) appointed by the deceased's Will.

The LPR should:

- notify the Tax Office of the death
- lodge an individual tax return for the deceased from 1 July to the date of death where assessable income is received, or where a tax return has not been lodged in the previous year, such as when the deceased had been receiving the age pension, disability support pension or Department of Veteran's Affairs pension, write to the Tax Office and advise the facts, and
- apply for a trust TFN and lodge a trust tax return for assessable income received after the taxpayer's death to the end of that income year.

RETURNS TO BE LODGED

FINAL INDIVIDUAL RETURN OF DECEASED

The LPR includes in this return all assessable income derived and allowable deduction incurred by the deceased up to the date of death (eg. any salary or wages and other income actually received up to the date of death), including any business income derived by the deceased (even if not received) during his or her lifetime and any tax agent fees and deductible expenses paid by the LPR. A medical expense offset may be available for the deceased's medical expenses paid by the LPR.

If the deceased had been in business then any business income receivable up to the date of death will be included in the individual return. If the deceased had been a member of a partnership, the final return of the deceased would show a share of partnership profit or loss to that date.

FIRST TRUST RETURN

The first trust return will include the income from the date of death to the end of the income year. Include in this return income received after the taxpayer's death, such as salary and wage entitlements, interest, dividends, rent, business income and capital gains from the sale of shares, land or other assets which would have been assessed in the hands of the deceased (see 12.650).

Unused annual leave and long service leave entitlements paid to a deceased estate are exempt from income tax. The tax treatment of lump sum death benefit termination payments depends on whether the recipient of the benefits was a dependant of the deceased and the amount paid. Any death benefit termination payment to dependants which accrued before 1 July 1983 or an amount up to the employment termination payment cap of $185,000 will be tax-free. Any amount paid above the employment termination cap is taxed at 49%.

Lump sum superannuation death benefits paid to death benefit dependants will be tax-free. Note that there are different rules where a superannuation death benefit is paid as an income stream or if paid to a non-dependant. Payments from friendly society funeral policies are exempt from tax if the policy was taken out before 1 January 2003. If the policy was issued after 31 December 2002 the investment income is included as assessable income in the estate return if the estate's trustee instructs the friendly society to pay for the funeral or is reimbursed for the funeral expenses.

The trust estate return for the deceased should be lodged by the trustee in the name of the estate and a separate TFN should be obtained for the estate. The name of the trust is 'The Estate of 'name of deceased' Deceased'.

At law, the trustee cannot distribute the income or assets of a deceased estate to the beneficiaries until all debts of the deceased have been settled. This includes any outstanding tax liabilities. This requires a notice of assessment. Once the notice of assessment has been issued, and other debts provided for, the trustee can proceed to deal with the assets in accordance with the deceased's Will.

During this period of administration no beneficiary will be presently entitled to trust income and the trustee will be taxed under s99A ITAA36 at the highest marginal tax rate unless the trustee makes a written request to the Commissioner for him to exercise his discretion to tax the estate under s99 ITAA36.

It is expected that this discretion would be exercised unless the Commissioner considers that there is a tax avoidance motive.

ESTATE ASSETS

Estate assets are assets which were owned by the deceased at death and pass to the deceased estate, as well as assets received by the estate in consequence of death. Examples include:

- assets owned solely
- assets owned as tenants-in-common (see 12.350)
- loans to companies, trusts and other entities
- outstanding trust entitlements
- insurance policies owned by the deceased, and
- remainder interests (see 12.650).

NON-ESTATE ASSETS

Among the assets that will usually not form part of a deceased person's estate are:

- death benefits paid directly to dependants (eg. superannuation death benefits (see 11.210))
- insurance payments (unless owned by deceased)
- joint tenancies – ownership passes to the survivor (see 12.350)
- unallocated discretionary trust assets
- pensions, allocated pensions and annuities – which may terminate on death or continue to be paid to a dependant rather than the estate, and
- compensation payments which pass to dependants rather than the estate.

TAXING DECEASED ESTATES

There are four main ways in which the income of a deceased estate is assessed. The rate of tax depends on whether:

- the beneficiary is presently entitled to the income of the estate or the trust (s97 ITAA36)
- the beneficiary is under a legal disability (s98 and s102AG)
- some part of the net income is subject to tax in the trustee's hands, because no beneficiary is presently entitled to that portion of the income. This situation occurs where an estate is not yet fully administered (s99 or s99A) – where s99 applies, normal tax rates apply to the estate for the first three years after death, thereafter higher tax rates apply (see 3.010), and
- the trustee is assessed on the net income which is fully administered but the income is accumulating in the estate, rather than being allocated to beneficiaries (s99A); the top marginal tax rate (plus Medicare) applies.

Deceased estates sometimes need to become family trusts (see 7.200).

Provided that certain conditions are met, the executor (ie. trustee) of a deceased estate can access the small business CGT concessions in respect business assets of the deceased (see 12.525).

For example, a trustee of a deceased estate can choose to have the retirement exemption apply for the purposes of the small business CGT concessions under certain circumstances (ATO ID 2012/39).

TAX RATES APPLICABLE TO DECEASED ESTATES

- **The estate itself:** During the income years the last day of which occurs prior to the third anniversary of the date of death of the deceased, accumulated income is generally taxed under s99 at normal tax rates. For the rates applicable to subsequent income years (see 3.020). Where artificial arrangements are involved the Commissioner is unlikely to exercise his discretion to apply s99 rather than s99A.

- **Beneficiaries:** All estate beneficiaries and beneficiaries of trusts resulting from a Will, including minors under 18 years of age, are taxed at normal tax rates. Will (testamentary) trusts might therefore be a useful strategy in tax and estate planning (see also 7.000).

EXAMPLE: 2014-15 YEAR

Share of estate paid to and invested by beneficiary $180,000
Income earned each year (say at 10% pa) $18,000
Beneficiary pays tax at rates of up to 46.5%.
Tax payable on beneficiary's additional income each year...........................up to $8,370

EXAMPLE

Share of estate received and held on a discretionary Will trust $180,000
Income earned each year (say at 10% pa) $18,000
Distribution of estate income to the primary beneficiary's two children under the Will.
Income tax payable (including low income tax offsets) on $9,000 per child................ Nil
Tax saved each year .... up to $8,370

PRESENTLY ENTITLED

Technically, the beneficiary of a deceased estate cannot be presently entitled to the income of a deceased estate until the estate has been fully administered. However, the Commissioner states in IT 2622 that where the LPR actually pays some of the income to a beneficiary, the beneficiary will be presently entitled to that amount and taxed accordingly.

THE INITIAL STAGE OF TRUSTEE ADMINISTRATION

Both the capital and income are held on trust and no beneficiary is presently entitled.

INTERMEDIATE STAGE OF ADMINISTRATION

If part of the estate's net income is not needed to pay outstanding debts, the executor may decide to distribute some of this surplus. In such a case, as mentioned above, the beneficiary is presently entitled to the amount actually allocated. The balance of the income that may be needed for outstanding debts can be accumulated and taxed to the trustee under s99 or s99A.

FINAL STAGE OF TRUSTEE ADMINISTRATION

Once all estate debts are paid and distribution of specific assets has occurred (and any legacies have been provided for) the beneficiaries become presently entitled to any income derived by the estate. Some estates continue to derive income for many years after this final stage has been reached, because there are estate testamentary trusts or fixed or discretionary life interests involved, or there are minor, bankrupt,or intellectually disabled beneficiaries.

In the year in which the final stage occurs, the net income of a trust estate (and a beneficiary's present entitlement to any of that income) is usually determined on the last day of the financial year. The High Court confirmed that basis in *Union Fidelity Trustee Co v FC of T* (1969) ATC 4084.

However, where requested, the Commissioner may apply an alternative administrative practice whereby the net income of the estate will be apportioned between the LPR and beneficiaries for the income year in which the estate was fully administered. Note that this approach requires that accounts be drawn up at the conclusion of administration to support the apportionment.

STAGES OF ADMINISTRATION OF A DECEASED PERSON

- Date of death
- Period of administration
- Executor or administrator appointed by Will or by the court.
- Probate applied for and granted by the court ie. the court recognises the Will as being both valid and authentic
- Assets vest in executor or administrator who pays debts and expenses
- Initial stage: Net income applied to reduce debts
- Intermediate stage: Part of net income not required to pay debts may be paid to beneficiaries
- Final stage: Debts paid, net income is available for distribution
- Administration complete

CGT and death is discussed at 12.650.

Partnerships

8.000 PARTNERSHIPS

A partnership can be an effective structure to split income within the tax rules. This structure also offers investors freedom to pool capital, skill and expertise. However, caution is advised as the liability of a partnership is also unlimited in respect of the individual partners to the arrangement and extends to debts incurred by any partner without consent of the other partners.

Legislative references below relate to the *Income Tax Assessment Act 1997* (ITAA97) or *Income Tax Assessment Act 1936* (ITAA36) unless otherwise specified.

A partnership generally has the following characteristics:

- a partnership is not a separate legal entity and partners are assessed individually on their share of any profit
- partners are responsible for their own superannuation arrangements as they are not employees of the partnership. Partners may be able to claim a deduction for personal superannuation contributions
- unlike in companies and trusts, partnership losses are not quarantined within the partnership. Instead, the losses are distributed to the partners, and
- each partner is jointly and severally liable for the debts of the partnership. One partner may be required to pay all the partnership debts if the other partners are insolvent or cannot be traced.

8.100 DEFINITION OF PARTNERSHIP

The term 'partnership' is defined differently under general law and tax law. The tax law definition is generally broader than the term defined under various state based statutes.

GENERAL LAW PARTNERSHIP

For general law purposes, the term 'partnership' is defined under each state's respective Partnership Act. Similar provisions define a partnership as 'the relationship between people carrying on a business with a view to profit'.

TAX LAW PARTNERSHIP

The following definition of a partnership, for tax law purposes, is contained in ss995-1(1) ITAA97:

- an association of persons (other than a company or a limited partnership) carrying on business as partners
- an association of persons (other than a company or a limited partnership) in receipt of ordinary income or statutory income jointly, or
- a limited partnership.

As the definitions suggest, the tax law partnership covers not only persons carrying on business with a view to profit, but also extends the tax law meaning of the words to persons in receipt of income jointly. In other words, certain joint investments such as an investment by more than one person in a rental property may result in a tax law partnership being formed (see 8.110).

8.110 JOINTLY DERIVED INCOME

If investments are held jointly, this is generally considered a partnership for tax purposes (as the owners are in receipt of income jointly).

8.111 COMBINED OWNERSHIP OF INVESTMENTS

Combined ownership of rental properties (or other investments) is a tax law partnership because the owners receive income jointly, but it is not a general law partnership unless the ownership amounts to the carrying on of a business (*Cripps and Commissioner of Taxation* (1999) 43 ATR 1202; 99 ATC 2428). For this reason, a partnership return is generally not required where a general law partnership is not in existence. However, the income or losses must be shared appropriately between respective partners in receipt of income jointly and reported in their individual tax returns (see 18.100).

The Commissioner considers the issue of division of net income or loss between the co-owners of a rental property in TR 93/32. In the Commissioner's view, it is the legal interest which ultimately determines, among co-owners of property, the division of the net income or loss from the property.

NOTE: For ABN/GST registration purposes, joint tenants need to register as a partnership even though no general law partnership exists.

8.112   UNINCORPORATED JOINT VENTURES (UJV)

Unincorporated joint ventures are purely contractual arrangements and are generally not a partnership arrangement under either general or taxation law. Unincorporated joint ventures are intended to avoid the disadvantages of partnerships, such as joint and several liability, and to retain as much flexibility as possible for the parties involved. The joint venture parties are taxed separately.

The essential difference between a UJV and a partnership is the absence of an agreement to share profits and losses and the absence of mutual agency. However, if the UJV does stipulate receipt of income jointly, then the UJV is a tax law partnership.

In a UJV where product, rather than income, is shared, there is no tax partnership and each UJV party includes their own income and claims their own expenses in their own tax return.

Unincorporated joint ventures are common in the mining industry and other projects based businesses like property development.

8.113   UNCONTROLLED PARTNERSHIP INCOME (UPI)

Generally, partners pay tax on their individual share of the profits at their tax rate (see 3.010 and 3.020 for personal marginal tax rates).

Further tax at the top marginal rate plus Medicare levy may be imposed if income is derived by a nominal party not having real and effective control and disposal of their share of UPI where they are not:

- a company
- a person in their capacity as trustee, or
- a person who is under 18 years of age on the last day of the income year

Those partners under 18 years of age would be subject to the penalty tax rules that apply to the unearned income of minors (see from 3.040).

A non-primary producer taxpayer has taxable income of $30,000 which includes $3,000 of UPI in 2014-15. No other deductions are available.

Total tax payable is calculated:

Primary Tax payable on $30,000	*$2,242*
Plus further tax on UPI ($3,000 x 37.53%*)	*$1,126*
Plus 2% Medicare levy on $30,000	*$600*
Less Low Income Tax Offset	*($445)*
Total tax payable	***$3,523***

* Grossed up tax rate for UPI = 45% – (Gross tax on taxable income divided by total taxable income) x 100 = 45% – ($2,242 divided by $30,000) x 100 = 37.53%

In determining if a partner has real and effective control, the Tax Office will consider:

- the terms of the partnership agreement
- control of partnership having regard to its management and how the business is conducted, and
- the operations of the partnership.

These rules apply in limited circumstances because, in essence, the partner must be prevented from dealing with their share of the net income because they have been forced to deal with that share in another way. This is more likely to occur in family partnerships.

8.120   EXISTENCE OF A PARTNERSHIP

When a partnership is formed, professional advice should be obtained to ensure that the Tax Office will be satisfied that it is a bona fide arrangement. The Tax Office's view of what constitutes a partnership is set out in Taxation Ruling TR 94/8.

According to TR 94/8, the Tax Office will look at the following factors in deciding whether a business is being carried on in a partnership:

- **Intention: the essential element is the** mutual assent and intention to act as partners
- **Conduct:**
  - joint ownership of business assets
  - registration of business name
  - joint business account and power to operate it
  - extent to which parties are involved in the conduct of the business
  - extent of capital contributions
  - entitlements to a share of net profits
  - business records, and
  - trading in joint names and public recognition of the partnership.

The list is not exhaustive and no single factor is decisive. Note that the ruling does not apply to situations where persons are in receipt of income jointly (a tax law partnership) unless the income is derived from carrying on a business or to limited partnerships.

 Transfer of assets into a partnership may result in turning a pre-CGT asset into a post-CGT asset, or a disposal of an interest in a post-CGT asset may trigger a capital gain and/or stamp duty. This is the case even though a partnership cannot hold CGT assets for tax purposes, only individual partners can hold a CGT asset (see 8.300).

SPECIAL SITUATIONS

Some professions are controlled by State law, making it difficult or impossible to set up a partnership where all partners are not legally qualified to practice.

PARTNERS HAVE UNEQUAL SHARES

Some partnerships include a 'salaried' partner – ie. a partner with a predetermined share of the expected partnership profit, but with no right to share in the balance of the profits. A 'salaried' partner is not subject to PAYG withholding, as you cannot employ yourself. Being a salaried partner, however, offers no protection from creditors. Indeed, if one is held out to 'all the world' as a partner, a Court may hold that you are liable as a partner.

Note that if an arrangement is merely a tax partnership, rather than a general law partnership, a Court will not uphold an agreement between the partners to share income on an unequal basis (refer *FCT v McDonald* 87 ATC 4541 (McDonald)).

REQUIREMENTS FOR VALID PARTNERSHIP

There is no legal requirement for there to be a partnership agreement however the existence of an agreement will assist in:

- identifying the terms under which the partners agree to carry on business, and
- establishing the bona fides of the arrangement to the Tax Office.

The relationship between the partners should be documented before the partnership commences although a retrospective agreement can be written stating the commencement date.

Note, however, that a partnership can never be formed retrospectively. The partnership agreement does not need to be lodged with the Tax Office.

8.200   TAX TREATMENT OF A PARTNERSHIP

As a general rule, a partnership does not pay income tax, rather it is required to furnish a tax return which discloses the final net income derived by the partnership during the income year. Each partner is then taxed in their individual capacity on their share of the net partnership income at applicable tax rates. Alternatively, if the partnership has a tax loss, a partner's share of that loss is deductible in the partner's tax return.

8.210   SHARE OF NET INCOME

A partner's share of the net profit of the partnership is taxable even if not all of the profit is withdrawn. Technically, the partner is entitled to a share of the 'net income' of the partnership, and Court decisions have confirmed that the income isn't assessable to the partners until it is quantifiable (eg. at year-end). If a partner decides to leave some of the profit in the business, it is still 'income' and is assessed to the partner in the year the partnership did the work and derived the profit. In other words a partnership cannot assist a partner to defer the taxation of 'net income' derived.

NET INCOME OR LOSS OF PARTNERSHIP

A partnership is generally treated as if it was a taxpayer and a partnership tax return must be lodged disclosing the net income or loss derived by the partnership during the income year. The net income (or loss) is calculated by ascertaining all of the assessable income of the partnership less any allowable deductions.

In addition to the partner's share of the partnership profit or loss, the following should be included in the partner's return:

- any share of capital gain on disposal of assets (whether held jointly or solely)
- deductions allowed for investment in Australian films
- superannuation contributions, and
- insurance premiums (where the proceeds would be assessable).

Whether a partnership is required to disclose its assessable income on a cash or accruals basis is dependent on whether or not the partnership is carrying on a business (see from 11.030).

Each partner is entitled to claim a share of any tax offsets (eg. franking tax offsets or foreign income tax offsets) based on their share of the net income of the partnership.

Partnership income retains its character in the hands of the partners. The effect of this rule is that where the partner's share of the net income contains different characteristics (eg. business income, dividends etc.) then that share is apportioned to reflect those components when assessing each partner's individual return.

An individual carrying on business as a partner in a partnership will be subject to the non-commercial loss provisions in Division 35 ITAA97.

8.220   SALARIES OF PARTNERS

Ruling TR 2005/7 states in part:

A 'partnership salary' is not truly a salary, nor is it an expense of the partnership, but instead is a distribution of partnership profits to the recipient partner. It is not an allowable deduction and '... cannot result in or increase a partnership loss'.

It continues:

The recipient partner's interest in the net income will include the partnership salary to the extent that there is available net income. ... If in a particular year the 'partnership salary' drawn by a partner exceeds the recipient partner's interest in the available net income of the partnership, the excess advanced to the partner is not, at that time, assessable income of the partner ... an advance of future profits is assessable to the partner in a future income year when sufficient profits are available. An agreement by the partners ... to allow a partner to draw a 'partnership salary' is ... contractual ... For such an agreement to be effective for tax purposes in an income year the agreement must be entered into before the end of that income year.

Examples from the ruling are reproduced as follows.

Anna and Robert formed a general law partnership under which it was agreed that they share the profits and losses of the partnership equally. The partnership agreement allowed the partners to draw a salary if the partners so agreed. It was agreed at the beginning of the income year that Anna would draw a salary of $20,000 for managing the business and that the balance of profits and losses would be shared equally.
The 2014-15 year's net profit after paying Anna's salary was $35,000.
Determination of the net income, for the partnership return is as follows.

Partnership profit (after deducting salary)	$35,000
Plus Anna's salary	$20,000
Net income	**$55,000**

The net income is then distributed in accordance with the partnership agreement, being 50% as follows:

Anna

Salary	$20,000
Plus interest's balance of net income: 50% of ($55,000 – $20,000)	$17,500
Distribution (inclusive of salary)	$37,500

Robert

Interest in balance of net income: 50% of ($55,000 – $20,000)	$17,500
Total distribution	**$55,000**

Christine and Julia formed a general law partnership under which it was agreed that they share the profits and losses of the partnership equally. The partnership agreement provided that in addition to this Christine would be entitled to draw $20,000 a year for managing the business. The 2014-15 year's net (accounting) loss, after paying Christine's salary, was $10,000.

Determination of the net income, for the purpose of completing the Statement of Distribution on the partnership return, is as follows:

Partnership net loss (after deducting salaries)	($10,000)
Plus Christine's salary	$20,000
Net income	$10,000

The net income is then distributed, in accordance with the partnership agreement, being 50%, as follows:

Christine

Salary	$10,000
Interest in partnership's net income 50% of ($10,000 – $10,000)	$0
Distribution	$10,000

Julia

Interest in partnership net income 50% of ($10,000 – $10,000)	$0
Total distribution	$10,000

The $20,000 was taken by Christine as drawings in advance of profits. Christine's drawings do not affect her liability to tax, other than to determine her individual interest in the net income and loss of the partnership under ss92(I) ITAA36. The $10,000 drawn in excess of available profits will be met from profits in future years and be assessable to Christine in that future year when sufficient profits are available. If the partnership is wound up before this time, the $10,000 excess is repayable by her and thus not assessable.

8.230   PARTNERSHIP WITH NON-RESIDENT

The net income or loss of a partnership is calculated on the basis that the partnership is a separate legal entity and is a resident taxpayer. The assessable income must include income from all sources both within and outside Australia. Each partner is then assessed on their share of the net income or loss of the partnership.

In the case of non-resident partners special rules apply to ensure that the non-resident is generally not assessed on any foreign income for the period when the partner was a non-resident. In essence the non-resident partner is assessed on only their share of:

- the Australian sourced net income or loss, and
- any foreign sourced income for the period he or she was actually a resident of Australia.

8.240   MINORS AS PARTNERS

As a general rule, income derived by a minor is taxed at normal individual rates (see 3.010 and 3.020 for rates).   Where excessive partnership income is derived by a partner who is a minor or where partnership income is included in the net income of a trust estate, special children's tax rates can apply (see 3.040).

8.250   INTEREST ON MONEY LENT BY A PARTNER & REFINANCING LOANS

Interest credited by the partnership to individual partners on their capital account does not represent income of the partnership. Similarly, interest on capital accounts is not deductible to the partnership, as it merely represents the allocation of profit to the partners. This issue is similar to partner salaries in that it raises questions of dealing with or contracting with yourself.

However, in *FCT v Beville* [1953] ALR 490, the interest on the loan made to the partnership was deductible to the partnership and assessable as interest income to the partner. While there are some difficulties in reconciling this situation with the concept of not contracting with yourself, practice seems to accept that it is possible to act in more than one capacity. The partner acts as partner on one hand and acts as a third party lender on the other hand.

In the case where partnerships refinance working capital to release capital from the partnership for use by the individual partners, interest expense on the loan can be deductible to the partnership. Partnerships may borrow funds from third parties, where the loan is effectively used to replace the working capital used in the business – this is commonly referred to as the 'refinancing principle'. In *FCT v Roberts and Smith* [1992] 37 ATC 4380 the partnership was allowed deductions for interest on loans to provide capital on the admission of a new partner. Subsequently the ATO issued TR 95/25 which acknowledges that interest on loans used to replace capital contributed to the partnership will be deductible.

8.260   DRAWINGS

Drawings are not taken into account when determining a partner's share of net income (or loss) of the partnership and are merely prepayments of partnership profits. Subject to the terms of the partnership agreement, drawings can include income and/or capital of the partnership.

8.270   ELECTIONS OF PARTNERSHIPS

Any election concerning the calculation of net income or loss of a partnership must be made by the partnership and not by the partners individually. Once made, the elections apply to all of the partners.

The type of elections include:

- valuation of trading stock
- method of depreciation to be used
- spread or defer the profit on sale of forced livestock sales
- spread insurance recoveries for losses of livestock and trees, and
- defer the profit on a second wool clip for a year.

8.280   PAYG INSTALMENTS

Even though a partnership does not pay tax itself, the net income or loss of the partnership is calculated as if the partnership were a taxpayer in its own right. It is the partners themselves that are required to include in their returns their share of net income or loss of the partnership. Similarly, the partnership is not required to remit PAYG instalments in respect of the partnership.

That is the responsibility of the partners. However the partnership is required to calculate its position at the end of each reporting period so that the partners can prepare and return their Business or Investment Activity Statements including any PAYG instalments (see from 5.700).

8.290   FRINGE BENEFITS TAX

Since partners are not employees, the fringe benefit tax provisions do not apply to them (see TD 95/57).

8.300   CAPITAL GAINS TAX

A 'look-through' approach is adopted under the general capital gains tax (CGT) provisions so that the partners rather than the partnership are identified as the relevant taxpayer holding CGT assets.

Where a CGT event occurs in respect of a partnership asset, there is a CGT event in respect of each partner's proportionate interest in the asset. Each partner must keep records of their interest in partnership assets, ie. acquisition dates and cost bases such that any resultant capital gains or losses may be determined (see 12.550). Where eligible, each partner is also entitled to CGT rollover relief and any concessional treatment on disposals of their interest in an asset such as the small business CGT concessions (see 12.160 and 12.525). That also applies where a partner disposes of his/her interest in the partnership (CGT event A1), as that leads to a disposal of their interest in each of the underlying assets of the partnership. A partner's interest in an asset of the partnership is a CGT asset (s108-5(2)(c) ITAA97).

In an Everett-type assignment, a partner in a partnership assigns to their spouse or some related entity a portion of their share in the partnership. The assignment is treated by the partner as the disposal of their beneficial interest in the partnership assets. The deemed consideration for such an assignment is the market value of the interest. Based on the valuation method used in *Reynolds v Commissioner of State Taxation* (WA) (1986) 17 ATR 987 that value would be based on the value of the right to future partnership income.

The Small Business Entity (SBE) test for the purposes of the CGT small business concessions has been extended to include partners owning a CGT asset used in the partnership business. The operation of the CGT provisions in relation to dealings in partnership interests is considered in tax ruling IT 2540.

8.400   PARTNERSHIP CHANGES

Where a partner retires from a partnership and receives a payment for work in progress, that payment must be included in the assessable income of the retiring partner. The partnership is entitled to a deduction for the payment. The amounts subsequently received from clients/customers by the reconstituted partnership when the work in progress is completed and billed are fully assessable to the reconstituted partnership.

VARYING ENTITLEMENTS

Variation in the partnership allocations of ordinary profits and losses, either in respect of the current income year or future income years, has frequently been held by the Courts and AAT to be ineffective for tax purposes. Income allocations will not be accepted where it is apparent that the partnership agreement (or a variation in that partnership) is merely a device to enable distributions to be made that are out of proportion with the partners' true interests in the partnership assets or participation in the partnership. (See IT 2316 and the earlier reference to *McDonald's case* at 8.120.) The partner's interests, as specified in the partnership agreement, can be varied. This would need to be done at the beginning of the income year and would need to reflect the interests of the partners and to represent their input to the operations of the partnership.

Alternatively, where partnership interests are formally altered during an income year, it would be necessary to account for partnership profits or losses both before and after the change. Changes to a partnership agreement solely to gain a tax advantage are likely to attract the operation of the anti-avoidance rules in Part IVA (see from 4.500).

CHANGES IN PARTNERSHIP PROPERTY

Every time there is a formation, dissolution or change in the constitution of a partnership there are subsequent changes in the ownership of partnership property (including trading stock) that must be taken into account (see 12.550, 14.230 and 21.460). In relation to depreciable property, the change in ownership upon formation, dissolution or change in the constitution of a partnership is deemed to take place at market value. Balancing adjustment roll-over relief is available if all partners so choose.

Special rules also apply to disposals of trading stock outside of normal family or commercial dealings (see 14.200). Special trading stock rules also apply on the death of a partner, and changes in a partnership where the former partners retain a 25% interest in the new partnership (see 14.230).

VOLUNTARY PAYMENTS TO RETIRED PARTNERS

Payments made to former partners may still constitute ordinary income and therefore be assessable to the former partner. In the decision of *Mews v FCT* [2008] ACT 10-025, it was determined that even though the taxpayer was no longer a partner and had no enforceable right to a share of the partnership profit, the voluntary payment was ordinary income paid to the taxpayer because of the former business relationship.

8.500   CORPORATE LIMITED PARTNERSHIPS

Corporate limited partnerships (CLP) have general partners and limited partners. General partners operate in the same way and have the same responsibilities as normal partners. Limited partners are not allowed to participate in management decisions and have limited liability to the extent of their initial contribution to the partnership. If limited partners participate in the management of the partnership, their liability becomes unlimited.

Corporate limited partnerships are treated as companies for tax purposes. These entities lodge a company tax returns, and not partnership tax return. Losses are trapped in the CLP, and the CGT rules apply as to a company. Capital gains or losses are taxed in the hands of the CLP.

8.600   TAX RETURNS

A partnership is required to lodge a tax return, but the partnership itself is not required to pay tax. The net income (or loss) of the partnership is assessable in the hands of each partner based on their share of that net income or loss. For partnerships that derive income jointly (eg. joint investments, rental property) a partnership return does not need to be lodged. Each partner can disclose details of their share of any jointly derived investment or rental income in their individual tax returns. If rental income is involved, each partner should also include a schedule of the total income and any allowable deductions in their tax return.

PENALTY TAX

No assessment is raised in respect of a partnership with the net income or loss disclosed in the individual tax return of each partner. There are situations, however, where a partner's share of the net income of a partnership can be further taxed to lift the effective tax rate to the top marginal rate (eg. s94 ITAA36). That occurs where the partner does not have real and effective control of their share of the partnership income or they are unable to dispose of their interest in the partnership. This rule does not apply to a partner that is a company, but can apply to a trustee of a trust who is a partner. That effect can also flow through to any beneficiary (who is not under any legal liability) entitled to a share of the net income of the trust where the trustee does not have effective control over the partnership income.

Minors are taxed under child taxing rules (see 3.040), but the effect is the same.

NOTES

Comparison of structures

9.000 COMPARISON OF STRUCTURES

The following tables provide an overview of tax issues to consider when choosing or reviewing investment and business structures.

Issue	Sole trader	Partnership (see 8.000)
Unsecured business debts	Personally liable for all debts	Personally liable for all partnership debts
Potential for splitting income	No, except for payments to associated parties	Between partners (according to partnership agreement)
Streaming of income	N/A	No
Offset of entity's losses against personal income	N/A	Yes (subject to non-commercial loss rules)
Retention and taxing of income at company tax rate[6]	N/A	Only possible if partner is a company
Taxable capital gains	Returned by individual	Returned by partners
CGT roll-over relief to a company (see 12.450)	Yes[1]	Available to partners[1]
Distribution of capital gain	N/A	Capital gains are made by partners (see 12.550)
Distribution of pre-CGT capital profits	N/A	Pre-CGT capital gains are made by partners
Indexation of capital profits[2]	Yes, but frozen at September 1999	Yes, but frozen at September 1999
Access to CGT general discount	Yes – 50% discount[1]	Yes, if partner is an individuals or an entity that is otherwise eligible[1]
Access to CGT small business concessions (see 12.525)	Yes[1]	Available to partners[1]
Administration: specific external regulator	State authority regulating business names registration. Fair trading and trade practices legislation and general law	State authority regulating business names registration. Fair trading and trade practices legislation and general law
Franking tax offset	Refundable	Refundability of excess franking credits to each partner depends upon the partner's identity
Deductible superannuation contributions (see 13.400)	Fully deductible[5]	Fully deductible[5] in relation to employees of the partnership. Partners are responsible for their own superannuation arrangements
Loan from the entity	N/A	Yes
R&D concessions (see 15.500)	No	No
Admission of new parties	New structure required	Usually permitted[3]
Interest that can be disposed	N/A	Partnership interest
CGT on disposal of interest	N/A	Yes[4]
Transfers on death	By will	By will (for partners who are individuals)

1: Subject to certain conditions and requirements.

2: For assets acquired before 21 September 1999 the entity can still use the indexation method to index the cost base. However the indexation factor is frozen as at 30 September 1999. The CGT general discount does not apply if the indexation method is chosen.

3: CGT implications for continuing partners. They will be treated as disposing of fractional interests in underlying assets.

4: For CGT purposes, the relevant CGT assets are generally the fractional interests in the underlying assets.

5: Subject to eligibility criteria.

6: The Government announced in the Federal Budget 2015-16 that the company tax rate will be decreased to 28.5% for eligible small businesses. At time of writing, the amending legislation was before Parliament.

Issue	Private company / shareholder (see 6.000)	Fixed unit trust / unitholder (see 7.000)
Unsecured business debts	Limited liability protection[1]	Limited liability (unless trustee personally liable)
Potential for splitting income	Between shareholders[7]	Between unitholders[7]
Streaming of income	No – all distributions of profit received as dividends: Note anti-streaming rules	Yes, if trust deed permits[6]: Note general anti-streaming rules
Offset of entity's tax losses against personal income	No	No
Retention and taxing of income at company tax rate[8]	Yes	Yes, if there is a company unitholder
Taxable capital gains	Tax paid by company	Distributed to unit holders
CGT roll-over relief to a company (see 12.450)	Yes[2]	Yes[2]
Distribution of capital gain	Taxed as dividend even on winding up (see 11.720)	Taxed as capital gain
Distribution of pre-CGT capital profits	Taxed as dividend except on formal liquidation	Tax-free[3]
Indexation of capital profits[4]	Yes, but frozen at September 1999	Yes, but frozen at September 1999
Access to CGT general discount	No for the company, availability for a shareholder selling shares in a private company will depend upon the identity of the shareholder and period of ownership	Yes – 50% discount if held for greater than 12 months
Access to CGT small business concessions (see 12.525)	Yes[2]	Yes[2]
Administration: specific external regulator	ASIC, fair trading and trade practices legislation and general law	ASIC if a corporate trustee, Prudent person rules, other trust, fair trading and trade practices law
Franking tax offset	Refundability of excess franking offsets to shareholder depends on identity of shareholder Available to a private company but excess franking credits converted to tax losses	Refundability of excess franking offsets to unitholder depends on identity of unitholder
Deductible superannuation contributions (see 13.400)	Fully deductible[5] by private company in relation to employees of the company	Fully deductible[5] by unit trust in relation to employees of the trust
Loan from the entity	Subject to Division 7A (see 6.300)	Not taxed as income, may be subject to Division 7A (see 6.300)
R&D concessions (see 15.500)	Eligible	No
Admission of new parties	Usually permitted	Usually permitted
Interest that can be disposed	Shares	Units
CGT on disposal of interest	Yes	Yes
Transfers on death	By will (for individual shareholders interests)	By power of appointment

1: Unless a director who gives a personal guarantee in respect of debts of the company. Director penalty regime can apply in respect of certain tax and super liabilities.

2: Subject to certain conditions and requirements.

3: Cost base adjustments required for certain distributions (see 12.600).

4: For assets acquired before 21 September 1999 the indexation method may be used to index the cost base. However the indexation factor is frozen as at 30 September 1999. The CGT general discount does not apply if this method is chosen.

5: Subject to eligibility criteria.

6: The ability of a trust to effectively 'stream' franked distributions and capital gains to certain beneficiaries is determined under Division 6E ITAA36 and Subdivisions 115-C and 207-B ITAA97 (see 7.700).

7: Depending on the rights attached to the classes of shares/units.

8. The Government announced in the Federal Budget 2015-16 that the company tax rate will be decreased to 28.5% for eligible small businesses. At time of writing, the amending legislation was before Parliament.

Issue	Discretionary trust / beneficiary (see 7.000)	Member of unincorporated joint venture (UJV) (see 8.112)	Member of super fund (see 19.300)
Unsecured business debts	Limited liability (unless individual trustee personally liable)	Individual liability for each JV member	N/A
Potential for splitting income	Between potential beneficiaries: can be varied from year to year	N/A as JV members share the output of the JV not the JV income[2]	N/A
Streaming of income	Yes, if trust deed permits:[6] Note general anti-streaming rule	Depends upon the type of entity which is a JV member	No
Offset of entity's losses against personal income	No	Yes	No
Retention and taxing of income at company tax rate	Yes, if able to distribute to company beneficiary	Yes, if JV member is company	Qualifies for own concessional rate
Taxable capital gains	Paid by beneficiaries if capital gain distributed [6]	Paid by JV members	Paid by trustee
CGT roll-over relief to company (see 12.450)	No	Depends upon the type of entity which is a JV member	No
Distribution of capital gain	Taxed as capital gain	Taxed as capital gain	Special rules apply
Distribution of pre-CGT capital profits	Tax-free	Tax-free	Potentially taxed on distribution to member
Indexation of capital profits[3]	Yes but frozen at September 1999	Yes but frozen at September 1999	Yes but frozen at September 1999
Access to CGT general discount	Yes – 50% discount	Yes, if JV members are individuals or entities who qualify	Yes – 33 1/3% discount
Access to CGT small business concessions (see 12.525)	Yes[1]	Yes[1]	Not available
Administration: specific external regulator	ASIC if a corporate trustee. Prudent person rules. Other trust, fair trading and trade practices law	State authority regulating business name registration Fair trading and trade practices legislation and general law	Tax Office if SMSF; APRA if non-SMSF. *Superannuation Industry (Supervision) Act 1993* & related laws
Franking tax offset	Available – refundability of excess franking offsets depends upon identity of beneficiary.	N/A	Available – refundable
Deductible super contributions (see 13.400)	Fully deductible[5] by discretionary trust in relation to employees of the trust	N/A	N/A
Loan from the entity	Not taxed as income – may be subject to Division 7A - eg unpaid present entitlement to a corporate beneficiary (see 6.300)	Not taxed as income – subject to Division 7A if the JV member is a company or a trust (see 6.300)	Not permitted
R&D concessions (see 15.500)	No	No, unless the JV member is a company	No
Admission of new parties	May be difficult – subject to trust deed and consider whether a resettlement of the trust may occur	Usually permitted	Usually permitted
Interest that can be disposed	N/A	Joint venture interest	N/A
CGT on disposal of interest	N/A	Yes	Special rules apply
Transfers on death	Refer to trust deed. Typically, trust assets not an asset of individual trustee's estate. The appointer determines new trustee.	By trustee discretion	By trustee discretion[4]

NOTE: See following page for associated footnotes.

1: Subject to certain conditions and requirements.
2: If the joint venturers derive income jointly, the joint venture is a partnership for tax purposes.
3: For assets acquired before 21 September 1999 the entity can still use the indexation method to index the cost base. However the indexation factor is frozen as at 30 September 1999. The CGT general discount does not apply if the indexation method is chosen.
4: If there is no valid Binding Death Benefit Nomination (BDBN).
5: For eligible contributions.
6: The ability of a trust to effectively 'stream' franked distributions and capital gains to certain beneficiaries is determined under Division 6E ITAA36 and Subdivisions 115-C and 207-B ITAA97 (see 7.700).

9.020   OVERVIEW OF STRUCTURES

Choosing the right business structure to maximise the return and to minimise the legal and economic risk for the owner(s) is important. Choice of structure can significantly affect the tax liability arising from various transactions. The comparison tables (see 9.000) highlight the key differences between the various structures.

SOLE TRADER

A sole trader is subject to income tax on all sources of assessable income whether from business, salary and wages and/or investment. Such individuals are taxed at their relevant marginal tax rate (plus Medicare levy).

Income derived by an individual taxpayer would not be assessable to the extent they are conducting a hobby. Where the taxpayer demonstrates the characteristics of running a business such as maintenance of records, repetition of transactions, establishment of business premises, creation of a business plan, etc (refer to TR 97/11, TR 2005/1 and TR 2008/2) income from such activities will be assessable.

Consideration should also be given as to whether income derived should be assessed on a cash or an accruals basis (refer 11.035 and 11.040).

Provided that certain conditions are met, predominantly having an 'aggregated turnover' of less than $2 million (refer to 10.200), a sole trader may be classified as a 'small business entity' and entitled to a number of small business concessions (refer 10.300).

COMPANY

For tax purposes, a company includes a body or an association corporate or unincorporate, but does not include a partnership or a non-entity joint venture.

A company is treated as a resident of Australia if one of the following applies:

- it is incorporated in Australia
- it carries on business in Australia and has its central management and control in Australia, or
- it carries on business in Australia and has its voting power controlled by shareholders who are residents of Australia (see 11.020).

Subject to special rules, the taxable income of associations, clubs and body corporates are taxed as if they were companies (see 9.400 and 9.500). Shareholders are assessed on the dividends they receive from the company, including any franking tax offsets. Shareholders who are individuals are taxed on dividends at their marginal rate (including Medicare levy where applicable) and can claim any tax paid by the company on the profits underlying the dividends as a franking tax offset. Individual shareholders are also entitled to a refund of excess franking credits where their basic tax liability is less than the amount of the tax offsets available (see 11.700).

PARTNERSHIPS

For tax purposes, a partnership includes an association of persons (other than a company or a 'limited partnership') carrying on business as partners or a limited partnership. This incorporates the definition of a partnership under general law. The tax law definition also includes an association of persons who are in receipt of income jointly (see 8.110).

Under general law and state-based legislation, a partnership exists between persons carrying on a business in common, with a view to profit. Whether the relationship is a partnership depends on the mutual assent and intention of the parties, including their conduct. The existence of a partnership agreement normally provides evidence of the existence of a common law partnership. The general definition is extended for taxation purposes and the partnership rules apply where income is derived jointly. Receipt of income jointly usually applies to the joint owners of property who share the rental or investment income produced as joint tenants or tenants in common. For tax purposes, each partner is taxed at their marginal rate on their share of the net income (and losses) of the partnership, except where partners do not have control over their partnership entitlement (see 8.110).

Division 830 ITAA97 extends the definition of 'partnership' to include certain 'foreign hybrid' entities that are treated as partnerships for the purposes of foreign income tax, but as companies for Australian tax purposes. Special rules under this Division apply to these entities in addition to those that normally apply to partnerships.

TRUSTS

Trusts may include discretionary trusts, unit trusts, fixed trusts, testamentary trusts and inter vivos trusts (ie. between the living).

For a trust to exist there must be five elements:

- a settlor who provides trust property
- an appointer (who appoints a Trustee)
- a trustee
- beneficiaries, and
- obligations and rights created in respect of the trust property.

In general law, a trust is not recognised as a separate legal entity. However, trusts are recognised as such for tax purposes (see 7.000). The trust deed sets out the obligations imposed on, and the discretions allowed to, the trustee and the relationship between the trustee, the beneficiaries and the trust property. The trustee (who may also be a beneficiary, but not the sole beneficiary) has a fiduciary duty and a duty of care to the beneficiaries to exercise due care and skill in the exercise of decisions over the trust property. Each beneficiary is taxed on their present entitlement to the 'net income' of the trust (including capital gains). In other cases, the trustee may be assessed on the net income of the trust (eg. distributions to minors, those under a legal disability, non-resident taxpayers, or in respect of income to which no beneficiary is presently entitled) (see 7.600 and 7.700).

9.050 TAX RATES

The company tax rate is 30%. Complying superannuation funds and approved deposit funds pay tax at a rate of 15% on both 'income' derived and concessional contributions received (refer 19.300).

PRIVATE, PUBLIC COMPANIES AND PUBLIC TRADING TRUSTS

For private companies, public companies, including co-operatives (see 9.400), bodies corporate (see 9.500), trustees of corporate unit trusts and public trading trusts (see 6.150) and corporate limited partnerships, the tax rate is **30%**.

IMPORTANT! In the 2015-16 Federal Budget, the Government announced a 1.5% reduction to the company tax rate to **28.5%** for eligible small business entities, see Chapter 10. At the time of writing, the amending legislation was before Parliament.

COMPANY PROFITS

All company profits (including pre-CGT and post-CGT capital profits and goodwill) paid or allocated to members are generally taxed as dividends if distributed to shareholders.

For private companies, there are also rules which deem certain loans, excess remuneration, payments and debt forgiveness involving shareholders or associates of shareholders, to be assessable dividends pursuant to Division 7A ITAA36 (see 6.300).

LIFE INSURANCE COMPANIES, FRIENDLY SOCIETIES AND CREDIT UNIONS

Life insurance companies and friendly societies	
On ordinary income from life business:	
• friendly societies	30%
• other life insurance companies	30%
On income referable to policies of superannuation funds and rollover annuities:	
• complying	15%
• non-complying	45%

Credit unions	
Small credit unions (where notional taxable income is less than $50,000)	30%
Medium credit unions (where notional taxable income is from $50,000 to $149,999 on income exceeding $49,999)	45%
Large credit unions (where notional taxable income is at least $150,000 on all income)	30%

NON-PROFIT BODIES

Many, but not all, non-profit bodies are exempt from income tax under Division 50 ITAA97 (see 11.900).

All entities are exempt on their 'mutual' receipts (ie. membership subscriptions and revenue from sales to members and certain services provided to members). Specific rates apply where the non-profit body is not exempt from income tax (see below).

9.300   EARLY STAGE VENTURE CAPITAL LIMITED PARTNERSHIP

An Early Stage Venture Capital Limited Partnership (ESVCLP) is an investment vehicle providing tax concessions for both Australian resident partners and foreign resident partners. An ESVCLP must be registered with Innovation Australia.

An ESVCLP is treated as an ordinary partnership for tax purposes with the partners exempt from tax on their share of the income and gains derived from, or from disposal of, eligible ESVC investments.

TAX ON ESVCLP INCOME

Income from an ESVCLP flows through to the partners proportionately; it is not taxed as a corporate limited partnership. This means each partner is responsible for the tax on their respective share of ESVCLP income.

INCOME DERIVED FROM ELIGIBLE VENTURE CAPITAL INVESTMENTS

A partner's share of income derived from an eligible venture capital investment will be tax exempt if:

- the ESVCLP was unconditionally registered when the entity made the eligible investment

- the partner is an Australian resident or a resident of a country with a double tax agreement with Australia, and
- the ESVCLP owned the eligible investment and was unconditionally registered when the income was derived.

CAPITAL GAINS AND LOSSES

A partner's share of capital gains and losses arising from an eligible venture capital investment is exempt from income tax if the following are met:

- the ESVCLP was unconditionally registered when the entity made the eligible investment and at the time of the CGT event
- the partner is an Australian resident or a resident of a country with a double tax agreement with Australia, and
- the ESVCLP owned the eligible investment at risk for at least 12 months.

NO TAX CONSEQUENCE ON DISPOSAL

A partner's gain or profit on the disposal of an eligible venture capital investment is also exempt from income tax if the above conditions are met. A partner's loss is not deductible.

9.400   CLUBS, SOCIETIES AND ASSOCIATIONS

Some organisations are exempt from tax on all income, such as public educational institutions and those promoting Australian business (see 11.910 for exempt status). 'Not-for-profit' associations do not pay tax on member income but may pay tax on income from non-member sources such as investment income.

TAX-EXEMPT ORGANISATIONS

Division 50 ITAA97 exempts a variety of not-for-profit funds and organisations from tax. They include:

- charitable, public educational, religious, scientific, cultural and industrial institutions
- societies, associations or clubs established for community service purposes excluding political or lobbying purposes
- any employer and employee associations registered under a State, Territorial or Commonwealth Act which relates to the settling of industrial disputes
- a trade union
- municipal corporations, local government bodies and certain public authorities
- public hospitals and non-profit hospitals, medical or health benefits organisations
- organisations established to promote the development of information and communications technology
- organisations established to promote tourism, aviation, agriculture, horticulture, industry, manufacturing, and other resources in Australia
- bodies formed to promote sport, music, the arts and animal races
- bodies set up to promote Australian business (eg. the Business Council of Australia)
- organisations providing childcare to the public on a non-profit basis
- self-help bodies with open and non-discriminatory membership, and
- closed or contemplative religious orders that offer prayerful intervention to the public.

TAX-EXEMPT STATUS

In order to be granted tax-exempt status, the manager or committee of the organisation must receive endorsement from the Tax Office.

An organisation is required to have an Australian Business Number (ABN) before they seek endorsement with the Tax Office. In addition to having an ABN, charities must also be registered with the Australian Charities and Not-for-profits Commission (ACNC). If the organisation is a charity and is not registered with the ACNC, it must apply for charity registration before seeking endorsement for charity tax concessions. Registration can be made by visiting the ACNC website.

If an organisation is registered with the ACNC, it can apply to the Tax Office using the application form entitled *Application for endorsement as a tax concession charity* available on the Tax Office website.

The application requires the organisation to provide information which includes: its main purpose and areas of its main activities, governing documents such the organisation's Rules, or Memorandum and Articles of Association (if a company) and its latest financial statements including receipts and outgoings. The Tax Office will either accept or reject the application. If rejected, an objection may be lodged.

NOTE: The provision of social facilities may not necessarily disqualify a club or association from being tax exempt.

NON-PROFIT CLUBS AND COMMUNITY SERVICE GROUPS

Non-profits clubs, associations and community groups which are not tax exempt under Division 50 may still be able to exclude member income from assessable income (see *Principle of Mutuality*).

To establish the non-profit status, it is usual for the company's Articles of Association and/or Rules to say that members cannot receive distributions of profit or income, and that any distribution of assets on winding up be made to another non-profit organisation with similar interests and activities.

PRINCIPLE OF MUTUALITY

The principle of mutuality is an extension of the principle that a taxpayer's income includes moneys derived from sources outside him or herself. Specifically, the principle provides that where a number of persons contribute to a common fund created and controlled by them for a common purpose, any surplus arising from the use of that fund for the common purpose is not assessable income. This principle does not extend to include income that is derived from sources outside that group. Where the aim of a club is to provide and improve facilities to its members, the principle of mutuality will apply to all transactions between that club and its members. For example, membership subscriptions and profits on sales to club members are not assessable income. Any expenses incurred in deriving non-assessable member income would typically be non-deductible.

A club or association may be a company: it is generally accepted that being incorporated does not affect the principle of mutuality.

An unincorporated club and the club members are treated as if they were the same person. Just as a person does not make a profit from him or herself, a club does not derive 'income' from activities with its own members.

The types of income which require distinction by a mutual entity include:

MEMBER INCOME SOURCES

Membership subscriptions, payments for services rendered to members and donations are typically exempt from tax under the principal of mutuality. Mutual receipts do not form part of 'exempt income' in the context of general domestic current year losses and undeducted prior year losses (see TD 92/181).

NON-MEMBER INCOME SOURCES

Interest on bank accounts, income from investments, income from sales to a non-member, receipts from temporary or honorary members for goods and services and betting and lottery facilities are not within the principle of mutuality. They are received from outside the Club member grouping, and are typically assessable to the entity.

Commission income derived from Keno operations, the TAB (or similar bodies) and vending machines is not mutual income (see TD 1999/38).

MIXED SOURCED GROSS RECEIPTS

Individual receipts may need to be dissected where the receipt comprises of member and non-member income sources (refer below). A typical example is the use of restaurant and dining facilities by members and non-members of a licensed club.

Licensed clubs can adopt alternative measurement techniques, provided they are reasonable and reflect the club's income for that year.

ESTABLISHING TAXABLE AND NON-TAXABLE AMOUNTS

The principle of mutuality does not extend to income derived from sources outside the membership. For tax purposes, receipts derived and expenditure incurred by a club can be:

- **Wholly exempt**

  Receipts from or payments on behalf of members (eg. subscriptions, cost of membership badges) and receipts which are exempt or non-assessable, non-exempt income under tax law.

- **Wholly assessable or deductible**

  Income or expenditure from sources outside the club or its members (eg. interest on investments, an arrangement with an external party for betting facilities, catering, entertainment activities, vending and gaming machines).

- **Partly assessable or deductible (apportionable)**

  Income or expenditure resulting from general club trading activities which cannot be identified as being from members or non-members (eg. from the club's machines, bar and meals). Section 25-75 ITAA97 however allows a full tax deduction to a body to which the principle of mutuality applies, in respect of rates and land tax incurred on premises used for producing mutual receipts, or in carrying on a business for the purpose of producing mutual receipts.

To help clubs to calculate the percentage of partly assessable income and allowable deductions attributable to non-members, TD 93/194 provides this 'rule of thumb' formula:

$$[(B \times 75\%) + C] / [(R \times S \times T)] + A] \times 100$$

Where:

A = total visitors for the income year including temporary and honorary members (calculation is made from a summation of the visitors book, or, if the club does not have permanent door staff, from a survey over representative average trading periods)

B = members' guests (ie. visitors accompanied and signed into the club by a member)

C = A − B

R = average number of subscribed members in that income year

S = average daily percentage of members that attend the club

T = number of trading days for the income year

NOTE: Clubs must ensure that variables used in the formula reflect their own club circumstances. Alternative methods can be used which reasonably and accurately reflect the club's income.

Clubs which are gaming machine operators are not entitled to claim a deduction for accumulated jackpot amounts until players win the jackpots as the outgoing has not been incurred.

For the Tax Office view on apportionment of expenses by a licensed club, see TD 93/194.

A social club has 857 full members, and estimates that 60 attend the club daily (ie. 7%). The records showed that 7,000 visitors attended the club during the year, of which one third were members' guests. The club opens on 331 days of the income year.

Receipts	Total	Member: Non-assessable/ Non-deductible	Non-member: Assessable/ Deductible	Mixed: Apportionable
Subscriptions and fees	$40,000	$40,000		
Donations received	$2,500	$2,500		
Meals	$6,000			$6,000
Bar trading, etc.	$100,000			$100,000
Gross receipts	**$148,500**	**$42,500**		**$106,000**
Less expenses:				
Rent	$10,000			$10,000
Badges and trophies	$300	$300		
Postage and stationery	$1,300			$1,300
Accountancy/tax fees	$600		$300	$300
Depreciation	$2,700			$2,700
Subscription expenses	$5,000	$5,000		
Insurance and interest	$6,700			$6,700
Crockery, linen	$13,300			$13,300
Salaries and wages	$30,000			$30,000
Lighting and heating	$5,500			$5,500
Rates and taxes	$1,500		$1,500	
Superannuation	$1,800		$1,800	
Donations paid	$700		$700	
Expenses	**$79,400**	**$5,300**	**$4,300**	**$69,800**
Net receipts	**$69,100**	**$37,200**	**($4,300)**	**$36,200**

Applying the formula from TD 93/194, the percentage of non-member income and expenditure is:

$$[(B \times 75\%) + C \text{ divided by } [(R \times S) \times T] + A] \times 100$$

Non-member net income % is:

$$[(1/3 \times 7,000 \text{ members}) \times 75\% + 4,667] \text{ divided by}$$
$$[(857 \times 7\% \times 331) + 7,000 \text{ members}] \times 100 = 23.9\%$$

Taxable income is calculated:

Assessable income

23.9% of $106,000 (apportionable receipts) $25,334

Allowable deductions

23.9% of $69,800 (apportionable expenses)............................$16,682

Non-member loss...$4,300 .... $20,982

Taxable income **$4,352**

The club's activities for the year resulted in a trading income of $100,000 and investment income of $5,000. The non-member ratio was 25% and total expenses for the year was $60,000 comprising:

- *$50,000 unidentified as either member or non-member*
- *$2,000 for donations and superannuation*
- *$3,000 member only expenses*
- *$4,000 non-member only expenses, and*
- *$1,000 expenses relating to investment income.*

1. Determine apportionable income and expenses

Gross income	$105,000
Less investment income	($5,000)
Apportionable income	**$100,000**
Gross expenditure	$60,000

Less

Member only expenditure	($3,000)	
Donations and superannuation	($2,000)	
Investment expenses	($1,000)	
Non-member only expenses	($4,000)	($10,000)
Apportionable expenses		**$50,000**

2. Calculate taxable income

Apportionable income (25% of $100,000)	$25,000
Investment income	$5,000
	$30,000

Less

Apportionable expenses (25% of $50,000)	($12,500)	
Donations and superannuation	($2,000)	
Investment expenses	($1,000)	
Non-member only expenses	($4,000)	$19,500
Taxable income		**$10,500**

TAX RATES

Clubs and associations that are not exempt from income tax are treated as companies and must calculate their own tax liability under self-assessment on any taxable income (ie. their non-mutual income and expenses).

Tax returns must be lodged, and their tax liability paid, by the dates applying to companies (see 6.700).

The tax rates payable by a non-profit company are as follows:

- **Taxable income up to $416:** Nil%
- **Taxable income from $417 to $915:** 55% on the part over $416
- **Taxable income of $916 or more:** 30% on entire amount

9.500   BODIES CORPORATE

With strata titles, a company is usually the holder of the residual land and those parts of the building which are available for access and common use by owners. The ownership laws affecting this vary from state to state. Strata title schemes are governed by each state and territory.

BODY CORPORATE

A common feature under the various State and Territory schemes is the creation (on the registration of the strata scheme) of a 'body corporate'.

On registration, the schedule of lot entitlements records the number(s) on the lot plan allocated to each proprietor.

The body corporate is a separate legal entity responsible for maintaining common areas (such as land, unallocated parts of the buildings (eg. gardens and stairways) and mechanical devices providing a service to more than one area). Draft Ruling TR 2015/D1 considers the income tax matters relating to bodies constituted under strata title legislation.

TAX RETURNS AND TAX RATE

A body corporate is treated as a public company for income tax purposes and is required to lodge an income tax return for any year of income in which it has derived assessable income or when requested by the Commissioner (see TR 2015/D1). The tax rate is 30%.

TAXATION OF BODY CORPORATES

CONTRIBUTIONS FROM PROPRIETORS

Despite the body corporate being a separate legal entity from its proprietors, the levies paid by proprietors are nevertheless non-assessable income to the body corporate under the principle of mutuality. This includes interest received on late levies (see TR 2015/D1 – see example 2).

The principle of mutuality operates to treat such amounts as not being assessable income of the body corporate. Where proprietors have contributed to any administration, reserve or special purpose fund to meet common expenses, and any surplus contributions are returned to those proprietors in their capacity as contributors, such surpluses are not taken to be assessable income (see TR 2015/D1). However, any distributions to proprietors out of profits derived by the body corporate constitute dividends which are assessable income of the proprietors under s44(1) ITAA36.

Payments made by members of a body corporate in respect of their membership may be subject to PAYG withholding (eg. when the body corporate does not quote an ABN). Some exceptions apply however (see TD 2000/49). The exceptions apply where the payment does not exceed $82.50, or the payment is not in the course or furtherance of the payer carrying on an enterprise in Australia, (eg. if it is solely in respect of the payer's private residence).

INVESTMENT INCOME AND INCOME FROM NON-MEMBERS

As these are not covered by the principle of mutuality, the body corporate is assessed on investment income.

If any part of moneys borrowed is referable to investment income, a proportion of the interest is allowable as a deduction.

A body corporate is not taxed as a non-profit company just because it includes non-profit clauses in its by laws (see TR 2015/D1). The body corporate is liable for tax on any transaction with outsiders, and any lot-holders, if it is outside the scope of normal mutual activities.

The mutuality principle does not extend to non-essential transactions with members of the company – such as renting an item the company owns. If the company provides gardening equipment and other items to lot-holders, any charge made in relation to the use of the equipment would be assessable to the body corporate, but depreciation and other expenses incurred are allowable as a deduction.

BODY CORPORATE EXPENDITURE

As the contributions and levies are items of mutual receipt, most expenses the body corporate incurs are generally non-deductible.

However, where expenditure can be apportioned between mutual (non-assessable) and non-mutual (assessable) income, (eg. where management and audit fees can be attributed to investment income), the deductible portion of the expenditure is determined in accordance with the formula:

((Non-mutual income) / (Total income)) x (Apportionable expenditure)

where:

- **Total income** comprises contributors' levies plus all non-mutual Income, and
- **Apportionable expenditure** does not include insurance, rates and taxes, maintenance and upkeep of the grounds, building or their contents.

See TR 2015/D1 for further information.

Small business entity framework

10

10.000 SBE FRAMEWORK

The Small Business Entity (SBE) framework seeks to reduce the compliance burden on small business by providing tax concessions to qualifying entities. It achieves this by standardising eligibility criteria used to access a range of small business concessions including certain CGT, GST, PAYG withholding and FBT concessions.

All references are to the *Income Tax Assessment Act 1997* (ITAA97) unless stated otherwise.

10.100 OVERVIEW

An SBE is an entity that satisfies the $2 million aggregated turnover test (see 10.220). Entities that meet this criteria are entitled to access a range of small business concessions (see 10.300). For some of these concessions, additional or alternative tests may be applicable. For example, if an entity fails the $2 million aggregated turnover test, it may still apply the maximum net asset value test, which has a $6 million threshold, to access the small business CGT concessions (see 12.525).

IMPORTANT: In the 2015-16 Federal Budget, the Government announced measures to assist small businesses (see 10.300 for list of announced measures). At time of writing, the amending legislation to implement some of these measures has been passed into law and others are before Parliament.

10.200 ELIGIBILITY

Subdivision 328-C provides a single definition of an SBE for the purpose of accessing any of the small business tax concessions listed in s328-10 (see 10.300).

Under Subdivision 328-C, an entity is a **small business entity** if it:

- carries on a business, and
- satisfies the $2 million aggregated turnover test.

An entity will satisfy the $2 million aggregated turnover test if any one of the following three tests are met:

(i) its aggregated turnover for the previous income year (ie. before the current income year) was less than $2 million, or

(ii) its aggregated turnover for the current income year, based on its state of affairs as at the first day of the income year is likely to be less than $2 million and the aggregated turnover for each of the two previous income years was less than $2 million, or

(iii) its actual aggregated turnover for the current income year, worked out as at the end of the current income year, is less than $2 million.

An entity that starts carrying on a business part-way through an income year must calculate what its turnover would have been had the entity carried on the business for the entire income year (s328-120(5)).

NOTE: For the purposes of the small business CGT provisions (see 12.525), the SBE rules extend to cover business structures where:

- the CGT asset is owned by a non-business entity but is used in the business of an affiliate (see 10.231) or connected entity (see 10.232) of the taxpayer (the affiliate or connected entity must be a small business entity), and
- situations where the CGT asset is owned by a partner or partners (although not a partnership asset) but is used in the partnership business (the partnership must be a small business entity).

10.210 CARRYING ON A BUSINESS

As a general rule, an entity will be treated as carrying on a business if it satisfies the criteria set out in *TR 97/11: Am I carrying on a business of primary production?* (see also 21.100 for details).

The ruling states that the following indicators are relevant in determining whether a 'business' is being conducted by the taxpayer:

- there is significant commercial activity
- the purpose and intent of the taxpayer in engaging in the activity
- an intention to make a profit from the activity
- the activity is or will be profitable
- repetition and regularity of activity
- the activity is carried on in a similar manner to that of ordinary trade
- the activity is organised and carried on systematically in a business-like manner
- the size and scale of the activity
- the activity is not a hobby, recreation or sporting activity
- a business plan exists
- there are commercial sales of the goods or services being provided, and
- the taxpayer has the knowledge and skill to conduct a business of that type.

An entity will be deemed to be carrying on a business in an income year when the business is wound up or ceases to be carried on, provided the above criteria were satisfied for the relevant part of the income year (s328-110(5)).

10.220 AGGREGATED TURNOVER

Aggregated turnover is the 'annual turnover' of the entity plus the annual turnover of:

- affiliates (see 10.231), and/or
- connected entities (see 10.232).

IMPORTANT: The same method must be adopted (ie. one of the three tests above) in determining the aggregated turnover for all entities which are required to be included.

The annual turnovers are aggregated to prevent a business from splitting its activities in order to access the small business concessions.

An entity's **annual turnover** is the total ordinary income (exclusive of GST) that it derives in the income year in the ordinary course of carrying on a business (s328-120(1)). This means that statutory income (such as capital gains and dividend income) is excluded, as is non-business ordinary income (such as passive investment income or wages).

Where a business is not carried on for the entire income year, a reasonable estimate of annual turnover must be made based on what the entity's annual turnover would be if the business was conducted for the entire year (s328-120(5)). Where there are two businesses and one of those businesses ceases during the year, in calculating the aggregate turnover, a reasonable estimate of what would have been the full year turnover of the business which had ceased is required (ATO ID 2009/49).

TRANSACTIONS WITH CONNECTED ENTITIES AND AFFILIATES EXCLUDED

To avoid double counting, transactions between related entities are not included in aggregated turnover (s328-115(3)). Further, only income derived by an entity while it is connected to (see 10.232), or an affiliate of (see 10.231), the other entity is required to be included in the entity's aggregated turnover.

Lucy is connected with Ball Pty Ltd. Dezzie is an affiliate of Lucy. Their current annual turnovers during the 2015 year are as follows:

Lucy	*$500,000*
Ball Pty Ltd	*$1,500,000*
Dezzie	*$300,000*

These figures include sales from Ball Pty Ltd to Dezzie of $100,000.

Lucy's aggregated turnover is $2.2 million ($500,000 + $1.5 million + $300,000 – $100,000). Lucy is not an SBE based on current turnover for 2015 (although she could be an SBE if her aggregated turnover for the 2014 year was less than $2 million).

NON-ARM'S LENGTH TRANSACTIONS WITH ASSOCIATES

When an entity deals with an associate and that dealing is not at arm's length, the entity must account for the transaction on an arm's length basis (s328-120(4)). The term 'associate' is defined under s318 ITAA36 (see 16.110 for meaning). If it happens that the associate is an affiliate or a connected entity of the relevant entity, the non-arm's length transaction amount is subtracted from the calculation of the entity's aggregated turnover.

DETERMINING TURNOVER

For the purposes of these tests, the term 'annual turnover' is defined as *the total ordinary income that the entity derives in the income year in the ordinary course of carrying on a business*. See 10.210 above for meaning of carrying on a business.

Examples of what should be included and excluded from the meaning of turnover are follows:

- **Included:**
  - trading stock sales
  - fees for services
  - interest from business bank accounts, and
  - receipts to replace something that would have had the character of business income; for example, a payment for loss of earnings.
- **Excluded:**
  - GST charged on a transaction
  - amounts borrowed for the business
  - proceeds from selling business capital assets (ie. depreciating assets or CGT assets)
  - insurance proceeds for the loss or destruction of a business asset, and
  - amounts received from farm management deposit repayments.

In addition, the following rules should also be applied when calculating turnover:

- if the taxpayer operates multiple businesses, income from all those businesses activities must be included in determining aggregated turnover (eg. a sole trader who works as a retailer and part-time consultancy must include income from both activities)
- amounts derived from dealing with 'associates' (as defined under s318 ITAA36 – see 16.110) are excluded, and
- amounts derived from the sale of retail fuel are also excluded.

10.230 GROUPING PROVISIONS

The grouping provisions combine the annual turnovers of affiliates and connected entities with the relevant entity when calculating aggregated turnover. The concepts of 'affiliates' and 'connected entities' are discussed below.

10.231 AFFILIATES

An individual or company is an affiliate of an entity where that individual or company acts, or could reasonably be expected to act:

- in accordance with the entity's directions or wishes in relation to the affairs of that individual or company's business, or
- in concert with the entity in relation to the affairs of the individual or company's business (s328-130(1)).

An individual or company is not an affiliate of an entity merely because of the nature of their business relationship (s328-130(2)). A spouse or a child under the age of 18 years will therefore not automatically be an affiliate. Similarly, co-directors of a company, partners in a partnership, franchisee and franchisor etc. do not automatically become affiliates unless there are indicators that the parties are acting in concert with one another.

 Tim and Jim are in a partnership of providing business and bookkeeping services. Tim also has a business of preparing tax returns. Tim manages and runs his tax return preparation business independently from the partnership. Tim and Jim are not affiliates merely because they are

acting in concert in relation to the affairs of their bookkeeping partnership. However, Tim's tax return preparation business is said to act in concert with the partnership if, for example, clients that engage Tim's services must also employ the partnership to provide necessary bookkeeping services. In such circumstances Tim and Jim would be considered affiliates.

Only an individual or a company can be an affiliate of another entity. Other entities, such as trusts, partnerships, and superannuation funds, are not capable of being affiliates.

For the purposes of accessing the small business CGT concessions, there is a special affiliate rule which may deem a spouse or child under 18 years of age to be an affiliate in order to satisfy the 'active asset test' (see 12.525).

10.232   CONNECTED ENTITIES

An entity is connected with another entity if:

* either entity controls the other entity, or
* both entities are controlled by the same third entity (s328-125(1)).

The concept of 'control' is discussed below (see 10.233).

10.233   CONTROL TESTS

Control tests apply to measure whether two or more entities are connected with one another. The test differs according to whether or not the entity under control is a discretionary trust or another entity.

ENTITIES OTHER THAN DISCRETIONARY TRUSTS

Except where the other entity is a discretionary trust, an entity controls another entity where the first entity and/or its affiliates beneficially own, or have the right to acquire the beneficial ownership of, interests in the other entity that give the right to receive at least 40% of any distribution by the other entity of either income or capital.

There is an additional control test that applies if the other entity is a company. This test requires control of at least 40% of the voting power of the company.

DISCRETIONARY TRUSTS

An entity controls a discretionary trust for an income year if:

(1) For any of the four years prior to the year of income:

   - the trustee paid or applied any income or capital of the trust to or for the benefit of the first entity, and/or its affiliates, and
   - the amount paid or applied is at least 40% of the total amount of income or capital paid or applied by the trustee for that income year

   Amounts paid to, or applied for the benefit of, exempt entities or deductible gift recipients are not relevant in determining whether these entities control discretionary trusts (s328-125(5)).

   The Kendall Family Trust is a discretionary trust. In 2010, the trustee of the Kendall Family Trust distributed 25% of income to Carl, 25% to Liz and 50% to a church (a tax-exempt entity). In 2011, the trustee of the Kendall Family Trust distributed 50% of its income to Carl, 30% to Liz and 20% to a church. None of the entities are connected to or affiliated with one another. Carl controlled the Kendall Family Trust in 2012, 2013, 2014, and 2015, but did not control the trust in 2011. Although the church received a distribution of greater than 40% in 2010, it cannot control the trust as it is an exempt entity.

(2) An entity controls a discretionary trust if the trustee of the trust acts, or could reasonably be expected to act, in accordance with the directions or wishes of that entity and/or its affiliates (s328-125(3)).

   The Administrative Appeals Tribunal held that an individual was not 'controller' of a discretionary trust notwithstanding that she was the sole shareholder and director of the trustee company (*Gutteridge v Commissioner of Taxation* [2013] AATA 947). The Tribunal concluded that the trustee company was not accustomed to act in accordance with her wishes. Instead, the individual's father was considered to have controlled the trustee company in his capacity as a shadow or de facto director of the company. She was not considered to be a 'connected entity' and her assets were to be excluded for the purposes of the maximum net asset value test under the small business CGT concessions (see 12.525 – Division 152). See Tax Office Decision Impact Statement for further information.

(3) The trustee of a discretionary trust may nominate up to four beneficiaries to be controllers of the trust for an income year for which the trustee did not make a distribution of capital or income if the trust had a tax loss or no taxable income for that year. The nominated beneficiaries will be considered controllers for the purposes of the SBE tests and applying the CGT small business concession provisions in Division 152.

Indirect control

Generally, a 'look through' rule applies where there are interposed entities. Where one entity directly controls a second entity, and that second entity controls a third entity, the first entity is taken to control the third entity. However, this look through rule will not apply to a public company, publicly traded unit trust, mutual insurance company, mutual affiliate company or a company in which all shares are beneficially owned by one or more of the entities mentioned above.

Suzie and Fidel both own 50% each of the shares in Channel Pty Ltd, which owns 50% of the shares in Yves Pty Ltd. Both Suzie and Fidel control Channel Pty Ltd. Because Channel Pty Ltd controls Yves Pty Ltd, Suzie and Fidel will be taken to also control Yves Pty Ltd indirectly.

COMMISSIONER'S DISCRETION

Where an entity's interest in another entity is at least 40% but less than 50% the Commissioner may choose to ignore the interest of that entity in the other entity when determining its aggregated turnover if he determines that a third entity has actual control of the other entity (s328-125(6)).

Nancy owns 40% of the shares in Acme Pty Ltd. The remaining 60% of shares are held by Sidney. Nancy may apply to the Commissioner requesting that his discretion be exercised in ignoring Acme Pty Ltd when determining her aggregated turnover. This is on the basis that a third party, Sidney, has actual control of Acme Pty Ltd.

10.300 SMALL BUSINESS ENTITY CONCESSIONS

An entity that satisfies the small business entity test may be able to access the following concessions:

Income tax and capital gains tax

- Small business CGT concessions (see 12.525)
  - CGT 15-year asset exemption
  - CGT 50% active asset reduction
  - CGT retirement exemption
  - CGT roll-over
- Simplified depreciation rules (see 10.600)
- Simplified trading stock rules (see 10.500), and
- Immediate deduction for certain prepaid business expenses (see 10.700)

Fringe benefits tax

- FBT car parking exemption (see 24.403)

Tax administration

- Standard two year income tax assessment amendment period applies (s328-10(2)) (see 4.270).

Goods and services tax

- Accounting for GST on a cash basis (see 24.121)
- Annual apportionment of GST input tax credits for acquisitions and importations that are partly creditable (see 23.200)
- Paying GST by quarterly instalments (see 5.840), and
- Simplified accounting methods for SBEs that make mixed supplies or mixed purchases (see 10.400)

PAYG withholding
- PAYG instalments based on gross domestic product (GDP) adjusted notional tax (see 5.700).

The GST and PAYG withholding concessions outlined above cannot be chosen by an entity that is an SBE as a result of the third test being satisfied by that entity (ie. actual turnover at the end of the current year is less than $2 million) (see 10.200). This is due to the third test being assessed only at the end of the income year which denies the application of the concessions that are used throughout that income year.

FEDERAL BUDGET 2015-16: SMALL BUSINESS MEASURES

On 12 May 2015, the Government announced a *Growing Jobs and Small Business* package which contains a number of tax concessions for 'Small business entities' – with aggregated turnover of less than $2 million (see 10.200).

The proposed concessions include:
- Tax cuts for small business to apply from 1 July 2015.
  - For small companies: a 1.5% tax cut from 30% to 28.5%.
  - For unincorporated small business entities: a 5% discount on tax payable on income from such entities. This is capped at $1,000 per individual for each income year and delivered as a tax offset.
- Temporary accelerated depreciation for assets costing less than $20,000 (until 30 June 2017)
  - An immediate deduction for depreciating assets costing less than $20,000 that a business starts to use or install ready for use between 7:30pm (AEST) 12 May 2015 and 30 June 2017 (see 10.605).
  - The current 'lock out' laws for the simplified depreciation rules will be suspended until 30 June 2017 (see 10.660).
- Immediate deduction for professional expenses associated with starting a new business, such as professional, legal and accounting advice, from 2015-16.
- CGT roll-over relief for changes to entity structure from 2016-17.
- FBT exemption for employers who provide their employees with more than one qualifying work-related portable electronic device, even when they have substantially similar functions. This applies from 1 April 2016.

The 28.5% tax rate and $20,000 immediate write-off have been enacted. The other measures are yet to be enacted at the time of writing.

10.400 ACCOUNTING METHODS AND TRANSITIONAL MEASURES (STS TAXPAYERS)

From 1 July 2005 all SBEs must account for their business taxable income using the general income derivation rules, that is, according to an accrual basis of accounting or the traditional cash accounting method, whichever is the most appropriate method.

Transitional provisions were introduced to enable taxpayers that were in the former STS before 1 July 2005 to choose to either:
- continue to use the 'STS accounting method' while remaining eligible, or
- change either to the traditional cash method or the accrual method, whichever method is the most appropriate for the business to calculate its taxable income.

These transitional provisions have been carried into the SBE framework for entities which:
- were in the former STS in the 2006-07 income year
- were using the STS accounting method continuously since before 1 July 2005, and
- are SBEs from the 2007-08 income year.

A taxpayer using the 'STS accounting method' can continue to do so until it chooses to change its accounting method or it is no longer eligible to be an SBE.

NOTE: Where a business was in the former STS at 30 June 2005 and later changes to accrual accounting, the transitional provisions ensure that business income and expenses that have not been recognised under the 'STS accounting method' (because they had not been received or paid) are recognised in the year the business changes its accounting method.

10.500 SIMPLIFIED TRADING STOCK RULES

The general trading stock rules (see 14.200) are simplified for SBEs.

An SBE has the choice to apply the simplified trading stock rules if the difference between:

- the value of all its trading stock on hand at the start of the year, and
- the reasonable estimated value of its trading stock at the end of the year,

is not more than $5,000.

A reasonable estimate is an approximation of the value by the taxpayer that is reasonable in all circumstances. For example, some taxpayers may maintain a constant level of stock each year and will know the value of stock on hand, while others with fluctuating stock levels may keep comprehensive records from which the estimate can be derived.

If the SBE qualifies and elects to account for trading stock using the simplified trading stock rules it will not be required to undertake a stocktake at the end of the income year, or include adjustments to its income for changes in the value of trading stock. The effect of this rule is that the closing value and the opening value of trading stock in a particular financial year are deemed to be the same for tax purposes, and this value will become the trading stock opening value in the next income year.

However, if the difference between the closing and opening values of trading stock is over $5,000 it is mandatory for the SBE to do a stocktake and account for the change in accordance with the usual trading stock valuation method pursuant to s70-45 (eg. cost, market selling value, replacement or obsolescence where applicable) (also see 14.200, 21.200 and 21.400).

10.600 SIMPLIFIED DEPRECIATION RULES

An SBE can calculate its deduction for the decline in value of depreciating assets held for a taxable purpose under Subdivision 328-D rather than the general rules under the capital allowance provisions contained in Division 40 (see 15.000). For assets purchased prior to 1 July 2012, refer to the Tax Summary 2013-14.

The simplified depreciation rules are summarised as follows:

Concession	Income years from 1 July 2012	From 1 January 2014 and later income years
Immediate write-off – see 10.605	Claim an immediate deduction for most depreciating assets costing less than $6,500	Claim an immediate deduction for most depreciating assets costing less than $1,000.
Pooling – see 10.610	General business pool: Pool and deduct at a rate of 30% on a diminishing value basis in a general small business pool. A rate of 15% applies to newly acquired assets regardless of when the asset was acquired during that income year.	Unchanged since 30 June 2012: General small business pool applies.
Motor vehicle write-off – see 10.615	Special rules for the acquisition of motor vehicles where an immediate deduction is available for up to $5,000 of the vehicle's cost.	Not available
Private use of depreciating assets	Simplified arrangements for accounting for the private use of depreciating assets	Simplified arrangements for accounting for the private use of depreciating assets
Disposal of depreciating assets	Simplified arrangements for accounting for the disposal of depreciating assets	Simplified arrangements for accounting for the disposal of depreciating assets

NOTE: The simplified depreciation rules uses terminology which are the same as that contained in the Uniform Capital Allowance provisions contained in Division 40, such as 'taxable purpose', 'balancing adjustment event', 'adjustable value', 'termination value', etc. The meaning of these terms can be found in Chapter 15 (15.000-15.090).

10.605   IMMEDIATE WRITE-OFF OF DEPRECIATING ASSETS

From 1 January 2014, the amount that a small business is allowed to claim as an immediate deduction for the purchase of depreciating assets has decreased from $6,500 to $1,000. A special rule in respect of motor vehicles was also abolished from 1 January 2014 (see 10.615).

POST 1 JANUARY 2014: ASSETS COSTING LESS THAN $1,000

Where an SBE chooses to access the simplified depreciation rules, an immediate deduction can be claimed for the taxable purpose proportion of a depreciating asset with a cost of less than $1,000 in the year that it was first used or installed ready for use (s328-180(1)).

The taxable purpose proportion is the estimate (as a percentage) of how much the asset will be used for a taxable purpose.

A second element cost addition of $1,000 or less to such an asset is also deductible in the year of purchase. However, if the second element cost is $1,000 or more or there were any subsequent cost additions, the cost additions and underlying low value asset must be added to the general small business pool (s328-180(2) and (3)) (see 10.610).

 During the 2014-15 income year, an SBE taxpayer applying Subdivision 328-D purchased a fax machine for $900, estimating that 70% of its use will be for business purposes. The taxpayer can claim $630 ($900 x 70%) as an immediate deduction under the simplified depreciation regime. If the fax machine had cost $1,300, the taxpayer is unable to claim an immediate deduction because the total cost of the asset exceeded $999, even though the business use estimate would have reduced the deductible amount to below $1,000.

Low cost depreciating assets that were held, or used for a taxable purpose, prior to the taxpayer utilising the simplified depreciation regime do not qualify for the immediate deduction for low-cost assets, even if the cost of the asset was less than $1,000. This is because the immediate deduction is only available for business assets acquired by taxpayers after choosing to utilise the simplified depreciation regime. However, such assets may be pooled (see 10.610).

On disposal of a low cost asset, the taxable purpose proportion of the termination value of the asset is assessable income (s328-215(4)). The termination value is the amount received, or taken to be received, for the asset when a balancing adjustment event occurs (normally the sale proceeds, but market value may be substituted in certain circumstances).

1 JULY 2012 TO 31 DECEMBER 2013: ASSETS COSTING LESS THAN $6,500

Between 1 July 2012 and 31 December 2013, SBEs that chose to access the simplified depreciation rules could claim an immediate deduction for depreciating assets costing less than $6,500 in the income year the asset was first used or installed ready for use for a taxable purpose (ie. used by the SBE in producing assessable income).

$1,000 WRITE-OFF THRESHOLD INCREASED TO $20,000

The government announced in the Federal Budget 2015-16 that from 7:30pm (AEST) 12 May 2015 to 30 June 2017 an immediate write-off of $20,000 is available for depreciating assets which are first used or installed ready for use by the business during that period. This is increased from the current threshold of $1,000. This law was passed on 22 June 2015.

10.610   SMALL BUSINESS POOLS: GENERAL CONCEPTS

* **For income years that commenced prior to 1 July 2012:** Where an SBE chooses to access the simplified depreciation rules, it must pool and deduct at a rate of 30% (or 5% for long life assets) most depreciating assets. A rate of 15% (or 2.5% for long life assets) applies to newly acquired assets in the first year regardless of when the asset was acquired during that year. For information on the small business pool before 1 July 2012, see The Tax Summary 2013-14.

- **For income years commencing on or after 1 July 2012:** Instead of managing two pools, being the general and long-life small business pools, SBE taxpayers will be able to allocate their assets to a single general small business pool (with the exception of buildings) and claim depreciation at a rate of 30%.

See 10.630 for comments on the operation of a small business pool.

SINGLE GENERAL SMALL BUSINESS POOL

For income years commencing on or after 1 July 2012, small businesses can allocate depreciating assets costing $6,500 or more to the general small business pool to be depreciated at a rate of 15% in the year of allocation and 30% in other income years on a diminishing value basis irrespective of the effective life of the asset. From 1 January 2014, assets costing $1,000 or more must be allocated to the general small business pool.

Even if the taxable purpose use of the assets determines the amount to be depreciated to be less than $6,500, the asset must still be allocated to the single general small business pool.

Jim's Graphic Design is an SBE. During 2014-15, the entity buys a new computer for $1,200 that Jim uses 80% for business purposes and 20% for personal purposes. Although the taxable purpose proportion of the computer is $960 ($80% of $1,200), the business cannot claim an immediate deduction for the asset. To depreciate this asset, Jim allocates $960 to the general small business pool for the 2014-15 income year.

ASSETS HELD AT THE TIME OF CHOOSING THE SIMPLIFIED DEPRECIATION RULES

When an SBE chooses to access the simplified depreciation rules, it must allocate the taxable purpose proportion of the adjustable values of assets held at the start of the income year to the relevant pool at the beginning of that year. The adjustable value of an asset is generally its cost less any decline in value of the asset to date, regardless of whether the decline in value amounts were deductible for tax purposes. The taxable purpose proportion is the estimate (as a percentage) of how much a depreciating asset will be used for a taxable purpose (ie. for an income producing purpose).

Assets allocated to a software development pool (see 15.050) or to a low-value pool (see 15.040) before the taxpayer elects to apply the simplified depreciation rules are excluded from the small business pool(s).

Depreciating assets used or installed ready for use prior to choosing to use the simplified depreciation rules qualify for a deduction at the full pool rate of 30%.

Craig is an SBE who chose to apply the simplified depreciation rules from 1 July 2014. He owns a specialised mainframe computer in his app development business. The computer was purchased for $30,000 in the 2013 year, and decline in value to date amounts to $6,000. Craig estimates that the asset will be used 90% of the time for the purpose of producing assessable income. This means the taxable purpose proportion of the computer's adjustable value is $21,600 (90% of ($30,000 – $6,000)). This amount should be allocated to Craig's general small business pool at the beginning of that year and depreciated at a rate of 30% for the 2014-15 income year.

NEWLY ACQUIRED ASSETS

Depreciating assets costing $6,500 or more (between 1 July 2012 and 31 December 2013) or $1,000 or more (from 1 January 2014) that an SBE first uses or has installed ready for use during an income year in which it is an SBE and chose to use the simplified depreciation rules must be allocated to a small business pool at the end of the year. The SBE will qualify for a deduction at half the pool's normal rate in that first income year, irrespective of when during that first year the asset is first used or installed ready for use. The rate that would apply is 15% (ie. half of 30%). See 10.630 for operation of a general pool.

This reduced rate does not apply to depreciating assets used or installed ready for use prior to choosing to use the simplified depreciation rules. The full pool deduction rate would apply in these circumstances.

POOL BALANCE FALLS BELOW INSTANT ASSET WRITE-OFF THRESHOLD

If the value of a small business pool before subtracting the depreciation deduction for the year is less than $6,500 (from 1 July 2012) or $1,000 (from 1 January 2014), the SBE may claim a low pool value deduction (ie. a deduction for the entire pool balance) and the pool's closing balance for that income year then becomes zero (s328-210).

10.615 SPECIAL MOTOR VEHICLE RULES (FROM 1 JULY 2012 TO 31 DECEMBER 2014)

IMMEDIATE DEDUCTION UP TO $5,000 FOR MOTOR VEHICLES PURCHASED

From 1 July 2012: After allocating a motor vehicle to a single general small business pool, an SBE can claim up to $5,000 as an immediate deduction in the income year in which they start to use the motor vehicle or have it installed ready for use.

The remaining value is depreciated through the general small business pool at a rate of 15% in the first year and 30% in later income years. If the motor vehicle is under the instant asset write-off threshold of $6,500 (from 1 July 2012 to 31 December 2014), a small business can claim a deduction under that rule instead of the specific rule applying to motor vehicles.

Cost of vehicle immediately deductible under instant asset write-off: Bob's Landscaping is an SBE and in the 2012-13 income year, purchases a second-hand ute for $6,000 to transport tools. The vehicle is used only for business purposes. The business is able to claim a deduction for the full value of the ute ($6,000) under the instant asset write-off rules instead of the special rules for motor vehicles.

SPECIAL MOTOR VEHICLE RULE ABOLISHED (FROM 1 JANUARY 2014)

The special rule for motor vehicle has been abolished effective 1 January 2014, and an immediate deduction is not available. Motor vehicles with a cost of $1,000 or more must be allocated to the general business pool (see 10.610).

OTHER CONSIDERATIONS

Other considerations in relation to the special rules for motor vehicles include:

- **Adjustment for taxable purpose in general pool:** once a motor vehicle is allocated to the single general small business pool, the deduction available is subject to adjustments for taxable purpose proportion of the adjustable value of the vehicle
- **Deduction for start year in general pool:** where the taxable proportion of the adjustable value of the motor vehicle is more than $5,000, the deduction available in the income year that the asset is used or installed ready for use is: $5,000 + 15% x ((taxable purpose proportion x adjustable value of motor vehicle) – $5,000)

Philip's Courier Services is an SBE and in the 2012-13 income year purchases a small second-hand vehicle for $14,000 to assist with deliveries. The vehicle is only used for business purposes. The business calculates its start year deduction as follows: $5,000 + $15% x ((100% x $14,000) – $5,000) = $6,350

The total deduction for the 2012-13 income year for the motor vehicle is $6,350. The closing balance of the small business general pool for the 2012-13 income year (assuming that there are no other depreciating assets) is $7,650 (ie. 15% x $9,000).

In the 2013-14 income year, the business purchases a new vehicle for $30,000 to assist with large deliveries. Philip estimates that 20% of his use of the vehicle will be for private purposes and 80% for a taxable purpose. The business calculates its start year deductions as follows: $5,000 + $15% x ((80% x $30,000) – $5,000) = $7,850

The deduction for the 2013-14 income year in respect of new vehicle is $7,850.

The deduction for the 2013-14 income year in respect of second hand vehicle acquired in the 2012-13 income year would be: $7,650 x 30% = $2,295

The total deduction for the 2013-14 income year for both vehicles is $10,145 ($7,850 + $2,295).

- **Adjustment for taxable purpose to deduction in start year:** if an SBE purchases a motor vehicle which is allocated to a general small business pool and the taxable purpose proportion of the adjustable value of vehicle is $5,000 or less, the deduction in the start year is that amount. For example, a deduction would be available for a vehicle that costs $8,000, has a taxable use proportion of 60% and has an adjustable value of $4,800. The immediate deduction would be $4,800.

See 10.630 for method statement in relation to operating a general pool.

10.620   EXCEPTIONS TO SIMPLIFIED DEPRECIATION RULES

Exceptions to the simplified depreciation rules are as follows:

- **Primary producers:** A primary producer who is an SBE can elect to claim deductions under the simplified depreciation provisions in Subdivision 328-D or under the primary production provisions in Subdivisions 40-F or 40-G. The choice is available in respect of each depreciating asset. Once made the taxpayer cannot change that choice (s328-175(3) and (4))

- **Assets acquired before 1 July 2001:** An SBE can elect not to pool assets that were used or installed ready for use for a taxable purpose before 1 July 2001 and have an effective life of 25 years or greater (s328-185(5)). This election must be made in the first year that a taxpayer is an SBE and chooses for the simplified depreciation rules under Subdivision 328-D to apply. This election is irrevocable (s328-185(6)). Assets not allocated to a long life pool continue to be depreciated under Division 40 ITAA97 (see 15.000)

- **Buildings and structural improvements:** Buildings and structural improvements are specifically excluded from the small business pool unless the building or structural improvement would qualify for a deduction under Division 40 (see 15.000); eg. water tanks (s328-175(2))

- **Horticultural plants:** Horticultural plants (including grapevines) cannot be deducted under the simplified depreciation rules (s328-175(5))

- **Leased depreciating assets:** Leased depreciating assets are excluded from the concessional small business depreciation treatment (s328-175(6)). This exclusion would apply to depreciating assets in a rented property. This exclusion does not apply to depreciating assets leased out under a hire purchase or short term hire agreement. **Note:** The hiring out of scaffolding by a SBE taxpayer to an unrelated entity for a total period of hire of nine weeks including extensions of the initial term, is not considered to be a 'depreciating asset lease' as the hiring out is a 'short-term hire agreement' as defined in s995-1(1) ITAA97 (see ATO ID 2011/72). Under the circumstances outlined in the ID, the taxpayer and customer agreed to a weekly hire for an initial four week period followed by an additional four weeks and then one week. Having regard to these agreements, the ATO ID concluded that the hiring out of the scaffolding for a total period of nine weeks does not amount to a substantial continuity of hiring and therefore will be a short-term hire agreement

- **Low value pool:** Depreciating assets previously allocated to a low-value pool (see 15.040) are excluded from the simplified depreciation rules (s328-175(7)). The SBE must continue to use the rules in Subdivision 40-E for assets allocated to a low-value pool prior to electing the application of these rules. However, low cost assets acquired after choosing to utilise the simplified depreciation rules are subject to the low-cost asset rules in s328-180 (see 10.605), and

- **Software development pool:** Expenditure previously allocated to a software development pool (see 15.050) is also excluded from the simplified depreciation rules (s328-175(7)) and remains in that pool on entry to the simplified depreciation regime. Software development expenditure incurred thereon must continue to be allocated to the existing software development pool according to the rules in Division 40 (s328-175(8)). Where an SBE incurs software development expenditure after entry to the simplified depreciation regime and did not have a software development pool on entry, that SBE taxpayer may either:
  - create software development pools under Division 40 and allocate all future software development expenditure to such pools, or
  - choose not to create a software development pool, and allocate the software to

a small business pool in the income year it is first used, or installed ready for use, for a taxable purpose.

10.630   SMALL BUSINESS POOLS: METHOD STATEMENT

Set out below is a method statement to assist in calculating opening and closing balances of a small business general pool:

1. CALCULATE THE OPENING BALANCE OF EACH POOL

The opening balance of a pool will be:

- **For the first year that the taxpayer utilises the small business pool:** The sum of the taxable purpose proportions of the adjustable value of each depreciating asset that is allocated to that pool (s328-195(1)).

- **For a later income year:** The pool's closing pool balance from the previous year, unless an adjustment is made to reflect the change in business use of a pooled asset (s328-195(2)) (see 10.631 below).

- **On re-electing the simplified depreciation rules:** The closing pool balance for the previous year plus the taxable purpose proportion of the adjustable value of any depreciating assets not yet allocated to a pool (excluding assets to which an exception applies). This means that on re-entry, an SBE will need to allocate, to the appropriate pool, assets they have begun to use, or have installed ready for use, for a taxable purpose since choosing to no longer utilise the simplified depreciation rules (s328-195(3)).

Evan is an SBE who chose to apply the simplified depreciation rules from 1 July 2014 He owns two assets that are used in his printing business. He has a van with an effective life of five years and its adjustable value is $28,000. Evan estimates that the van will be used 90% of the time for the purpose of producing assessable income. This means the taxable purpose proportion of the van's adjustable value is $25,200 (90% of $28,000).

The other asset is a printing press, which has an effective life of four years and its adjustable value is $15,000. The press is used solely for the purpose of producing assessable income. Evan expects this rate of usage to continue. This means the taxable purpose proportion of the press's adjustable value is $15,000 (100% of $15,000).

The depreciation deduction will be $40,200 x 30% = $12,060.

If Evan chose to apply the simplified depreciation rules from 1 July 2014 the van and the printing press will both be allocated to a small business general pool and a deduction claimed based on 30% (being $12,060 as per the above example).

2. DETERMINE ADDITIONS

Add to the opening pool balance at end of year:

- the sum of the taxable purpose proportions of the adjustable values of depreciating assets used or installed for use during the year, and

- the taxable purpose proportion of any cost addition amounts.

Taxable purpose: *During the 2012-13 income year, Evan purchases a specialised computer for his printing business for $8,000. Its effective life is three years and, as it has not been used, its adjusted value (cost less amount deducted) is $8,000. Evan estimated the computer will be used 80% for producing assessable income. The taxable purpose proportion of the computer is $6,400 (80% of $8,000).*

As the depreciating asset was acquired during the year its depreciation rate in that first year is half the normal rate (15% rather than 30%). The depreciation deduction will be $960 ($6,400 x 15%). This computer is allocated to the general small business pool in the 2012-13 closing balance calculation.

NOTE: The instant asset write-off rules do not apply even if the taxable purpose proportion reduces the adjustable value below the immediate write-off threshold ie $6,500 for 1 July 2012 to 31 December 2013, and $1,000 from 1 January 2014).

3. DETERMINE DISPOSALS

When a balancing adjustment event occurs for a depreciating asset that has been or will be allocated in that income year to a pool, the taxable purpose proportion of the asset's termination value is deducted from the pool (s328-200) (see 10.640).

Based on the example above in relation to calculating the opening pool balance, if Evan sold the van used in his printing business during the 2015-16 income year for $20,000, he would reduce the general small business pool by $18,000 ($20,000 x 90% – the estimated taxable purpose of the van).

Where the business use estimate of a pooled asset has previously been adjusted because it has changed by more than 10% (see 10.631), the taxable purpose proportion of the asset's termination value must reflect the average of the business use estimates made for that asset (s328-205(4)(b)).

4. DETERMINE THE CLOSING BALANCE

The closing balance is determined by following the method statement in s328-200.

In brief, the method statement is:

Opening pool balance, plus
- *the sum of the taxable purpose proportions of the adjustable values of depreciating assets used or installed for use during the year, and*
- *the taxable purpose proportion of any cost addition amounts, less*
- *the sum of the taxable purpose proportions of termination values, and*
- *deductions for decline in value of pooled assets*

equals the closing pool balance.

In respect to Evan's printing business (see above), if he had chosen the simplified depreciation rules to apply from 1 July 2014, the closing balance of Evan's general small business pool for the 2014-15 income year would be:

Opening balance		*$40,200*
Add addition: computer		*$6,400**
		$46,600
Less disposal: van	*$18,000*	
deductions: $40,200 x 30%	*$12,060*	
$6,400 x 15%	*$960*	*$31,020*
Closing balance of general small business pool		*$15,580*

Adjusted value is $6,400.

*Total cost $8,000 (taxable use 80%)

NEGATIVE POOL BALANCE AMOUNT

If an amount is deducted from the pool due to a balancing adjustment event (such as a disposal), the closing pool balance may be a negative amount. Where this occurs, the amount below zero is included in assessable income (s328-215(2)) and the closing pool balance then becomes zero (s328-215(3)).

POOL BALANCE LESS THAN INSTANT ASSET WRITE-OFF AMOUNT

If the value of a small business pool before subtracting the depreciation deduction for the year is less than the instant asset write-off threshold (either $6,500 from 1 July 2012 or $1,000 from 1 January 2014), the SBE may claim a low pool value deduction and the pool's closing balance for that income year then becomes zero (s328-210).

10.631   CHANGE IN ASSET'S BUSINESS USE

Where a taxpayer's estimate of an asset's use for a taxable purpose increases or decreases by more than 10%, an adjustment to the opening balance of the pool must be made to reflect the changed business use of the asset allocated to it (s328-225(1A)). No adjustment is made for an asset where the business use estimate changes by 10% or less or where the change occurs three years after an asset was allocated to a general small business pool (s328-225(5)).

Where an adjustment is necessary, it must be made in the income year for which the change occurs and it must be made to the opening pool balance before calculating the deduction (s328-225(1) and (2)). The adjustment is:

Reduction factor x asset value x (present year estimate – last estimate)

The adjustment to an asset value can lead to either an increase or a decrease to the pool value. The terms in this adjustment are as follows:

(i) **Asset value** is the adjustable asset value at the start of the income year in which the asset was allocated to a pool.

(ii) **Present and last year estimates** are estimates of the taxable proportion of the assets.

(iii) The **reduction factor** assists in determining the asset's pool value for that income year. It is applied to the asset value to calculate the taxable purpose proportion of the pooled asset's adjustable value at the start of the income year. It differs depending upon:

- whether the asset was used, or installed for use, before or after the taxpayer opted to apply the simplified depreciation rules, and
- the number of years that an asset has been in the small business pool.

REDUCTION FACTORS FOR GENERAL POOL

For assets that were first used, or installed ready for use, for a taxable purpose while the taxpayer was an SBE and chose to use the simplified depreciation rules, the reduction factor for assets in the general pool is:

- **0.85** in the **second year** deductions are calculated under the simplified rules
- **0.595** in the **third year** deductions are calculated under the simplified rules, and
- **0.417** in the **fourth year** deductions are calculated under the simplified rules.

For assets that were first used, or installed ready for use, for a taxable purpose while the taxpayer was **not** an SBE or did not choose to use the simplified depreciation rules, the reduction factor for assets in the general pool is:

- **0.70** in the **second year** deductions are calculated under the simplified rules
- **0.49** in the **third year** deductions are calculated under the simplified rules, and
- **0.343** in the **fourth year** deductions are calculated under the simplified rules.

Assuming facts above: During 2014-15, Evan estimates that the taxable purpose proportion of his computer increases from 80% to 95%. Before Evan can calculate the 2014-15 deduction for the general small business pool, he must adjust the 2014-15 opening pool balance to reflect the computer's new business use estimate. The closing pool balance for 2013-14 was $15,580. This is the opening pool balance for 2014-15.

The adjustment that is required is:

Reduction factor x asset value x (present year estimate – last estimate)

As Evan was depreciating the computer after he elected to apply the simplified depreciation rules, the 'reduction factor' is 0.85.

The 'asset value' of the computer is $8,000 (its adjustable value when Evan started to use the computer). The present year estimate less the last estimate is 0.15, ie. (0.95 – 0.80). As a result, the 2014-15 opening general small business pool balance is increased by 0.85 x $8,000 x 0.15 = $1,020.

The adjusted opening general small business pool balance is $15,580 (2014-15 opening pool balance) + $1,020 (positive adjustment to the 2014-15 opening pool balance) = $16,600.

Once Evan's 2014-15 general small business opening pool balance has been adjusted, the pool deduction can be calculated. The deduction is 30% x $16,600 = $4,980.

If Evan did not acquire or dispose of any assets during 2014-15, the closing balance calculation is:

2014-15 adjusted opening pool balance $16,600
Less general small business pool deduction (30% x $16,600) .... ($4,980)
Opening pool balance of 2015-16 general small business pool $11,620

NOTE: *If Evan had depreciated the computer before he chose the simplified depreciation rules, the 'reduction factor' would have been 0.7.*

10.640 DISPOSALS OF ASSETS IN SMALL BUSINESS POOLS

When an SBE stops using a depreciating asset for any purpose or the asset has been disposed of, sold, lost, or destroyed, a balancing adjustment event has occurred (s325-215) (see 15.070). The taxable purpose proportion of the termination value must be deducted from the pool balance at the end of the income year. The termination value could be monies received from the sale of an asset or insurance monies received as the result of the loss or destruction of an asset. If the disposal is a taxable supply, the termination value must be reduced by the amount of GST payable (except where the termination value is deemed to be the market value of the asset).

If an SBE disposes of an asset and the taxable purpose proportion has been changed, then the termination value must also be adjusted. The taxable purpose proportion must be recalculated to reflect the average taxable purpose proportion applied during the income years in which the asset was in a small business pool (s328-205(4)(b)).

Where an immediate deduction has been claimed for a low-cost asset and it is later disposed of, the taxable purpose proportion of the termination value must be included in assessable income (s328-215(4)). Where an amount is deducted from the pool balance on disposal of an asset and this results in a negative pool balance, the amount of the balance is treated as assessable income (s328-215(2)). The closing pool balance then becomes zero (s328-215(3)).

Bill is an SBE. During the income year, he disposes of the following assets from the general small business pool:

- *a computer desk, used 100% in the business and sold for $200, and*
- *a station wagon, traded in for $10,000 on a new vehicle – the station wagon was used 80% for business purposes, so the taxable purpose proportion of its termination value is: $10,000 x 80% = $8,000.*

Bill must reduce the closing balance of his general small business pool by the taxable purpose proportion of the termination values of the computer desk ($200) and the station wagon ($8,000).

If the closing balance of the pool was $6,000 before deducting the taxable purpose proportion of the termination values of the computer desk and station wagon ($200 + $8,000 = $8,200), then the pool will have a negative value of $2,200 and this amount will be treated as assessable income.

Roll-over relief is available to certain balancing adjustment events such as changes in a partnership structure, marriage/relationship breakdown and disposal of assets to wholly-owned company (see 10.670). If chosen, the effect of the roll-over relief is that the balancing adjustment event is ignored for the asset until the asset is involved in another balancing adjustment event.

No capital gains tax liability arises in respect of the disposal of a depreciating asset that has been deducted under the simplified depreciation rules.

10.650 DEDUCTION PROHIBITED BY ANOTHER PROVISION

If another provision of the income tax law denies a deduction that could be claimed under Division 328, the SBE is deemed to have made a business use estimate of zero for that depreciating asset for the income year (s328-230).

10.660 CEASING TO USE THE SIMPLIFIED DEPRECIATION RULES

If a taxpayer chooses to stop using the simplified depreciation rules or is no longer an SBE, the relevant rules which may apply are as follows:

- The taxpayer continues to claim deductions under the simplified depreciation rules for the small business general pool, provided the entity continues to exist and has a positive opening pool balance (s328-220(1)). This is so regardless of whether the entity has ceased to carry on business and/or hold the depreciating assets allocated to the small business pools in a later year.

- In the later year in which the pool value falls to less than the instant asset write-off threshold (ie. $1,000 from 1 January 2014 or $6,500 from 1 July 2012 to 31 December 2013), the entity can deduct the full remaining pool balance and treat the pool as exhausted.

- For the rule in s328-220(1) to apply, the SBE taxpayer must continue to exist for tax purposes in the later year so it is able to utilise the allowable deduction. Where a partnership is dissolved and then reconstituted, the original partnership ceases to exist for tax purposes and the new partnership cannot take over the deductions for the original partnership's small business pool.

- Depreciating assets that are first used, or installed ready for use, for a taxable purpose while the taxpayer did not choose to use the simplified depreciation rules cannot be added to existing pools until the taxpayer starts to apply Subdivision 328-D again (s328-220(2)).

- An entity that claimed deductions under the simplified depreciation rules in an income year and then voluntarily opts out of the simplified depreciation rules, cannot use the simplified depreciation rules again until at least five years after the last income year in which these rules applied. The five year period does not apply to an entity that ceases using the simplified depreciation rules because it fails to qualify as an SBE. Such entities can choose to use these rules as soon as they once again qualify as an SBE (even within five years from the time the entity stopped using the simplified depreciation rules).

NOTE: Under proposed 2015-16 Budget measures, the Government has suspended the 'lock out' measure for the simplified depreciation rules until 30 June 2017. This will allow entities that are otherwise 'locked out' during that period access to the '$20,000 immediate write off'.

10.670 ROLL-OVER RELIEF

Roll-over relief is typically allowed under the simplified depreciation rules in the following situations:

- a balancing adjustment event (BAE) (eg. disposal) occurs as a result of partial ownership change involving a partnership (s328-243(1))(see example below)

- a sole trader, trustee or partnership who is an SBE disposes of all of the assets in a small business pool to a wholly-owned company (s328-243(1A), and

- a small business pool is transferred as a result of a court order or binding agreement upon a marriage/relationship breakdown (items 1, 2 or 3 of the table in s40-340(1)) (s328-243(1A)).

CONDITIONS FOR ROLL-OVER RELIEF

The roll-over relief is available where the following conditions contained is s328-243 are satisfied:

- the capital allowance deductions are worked out under the simplified depreciation rules

- both the transferor entity and the transferee entity make a joint election for roll-over relief in writing, and

- all the depreciating assets that, before the BAE occurred, were held in the transferor's general small business pool (from 1 July 2012) are held by the transferee after the BAE (s328-243).

The transferee does not have to be an SBE taxpayer that has applied Subdivision 328-D in order to elect to apply the roll-over relief. If the transferee has not elected to use the simplified depreciation rules, s328-220(3) deems that they will be treated as if they have used the simplified depreciation rules and then ceased to do so immediately after the BAE. This means that the assets eligible for roll-over relief will remain in the small business pool and continue to be depreciated under Subdivision 328-D even though the transferee has never elected to use the simplified depreciation rules.

CONSEQUENCES OF ROLL-OVER RELIEF

Where roll-over relief is chosen, it effectively defers the BAE until a later time when another BAE happens to the asset (eg. when the asset is ultimately disposed of by the transferee entity). The transferor does not need to subtract any termination values from its small business pools, nor must it include an amount in its assessable income if the pool balance would otherwise be less than zero. In addition, the transferor will not include the taxable purpose proportion of a low cost asset in its assessable income due to the BAE (s328-245).

Where roll-over is chosen, the capital allowance deductions for pooled assets are split equally amongst the entities involved in the income year in which the BAE occurred (s328-247(1)).

Further, where the closing balance of the transferor's small business general pool for the BAE year is less than zero (due to a BAE happening to a pool asset during that year) the amount included in assessable income is split equally between the transferor and transferee (s328-255).

Jan and Ted (the transferor partnership) have operated a small business as a partnership since 1 July 2010. In December 2014, their son Mark became a partner, forming a new partnership of Jan, Ted and Mark (the transferee partnership).

The new partnership elects to apply the simplified depreciation rules under the SBE framework for the 2014-15 income year. There are no further variations in the constitution of the partnership or in the interests of the partners during the balancing adjustment year. Assume the opening balance of the transferor's small business general pool is $60,000.

The transferor partnership would have been able to deduct an amount equal to $18,000 ($60,000 x 30% pool rate) from its general small business pool. However by both transferor and transferee choosing to apply the roll-over jointly, the deduction is split equally between the 'old' partnership and 'new' partnership in the year of the BAE and each receives a deduction of $9,000.

In the income year after the BAE (2015-16) the transferor entity will not be able to continue to deduct amounts from the general pool (s328-247(2)).

The transferee must continue to use the same taxable purpose proportion as the transferor (s328-257).

Roll-over relief cannot be chosen under s328-243(1) if all the assets allocated to a partnership's general small business pool are disposed of to former partners and, just after the disposal, no former partner has an interest in each of the assets that were allocated to the pool (ATO ID 2011/99). Under these circumstances, the requirements under s328-243(1)(c) are not met as the transferee was not considered to have had an interest in the assets just after the BAE occurred.

DEDUCTIONS FOR LOW COST ASSETS FIRST USED IN BAE YEAR

Where an asset acquired in the BAE year has a cost less than $1,000 (from 1 January 2014) or has a cost less than $6,500 (from 1 July 2012 to 31 December 2013), or an asset that is pooled or a motor vehicle to which the special motor vehicle rules apply (see 10.615) and roll-over is chosen:

- if the asset was first used by transferor the immediate write-off deduction is split equally among the transferor and transferee, and
- if the asset is first used by transferee, the transferor cannot deduct an amount for the asset for the BAE year and transferee is entitled to the full deduction (s328-250).

The same rules apply for deducting any cost addition amounts for the BAE year (s328-253).

The choice for roll-over relief must be made in writing, contain sufficient information about the transferor's holding of the depreciating assets for the transferee to determine the effect of the roll-over, and be made within six months after the end of the transferee's income year in which the BAE occurs. The Commissioner of Taxation may extend the period.

A copy of the written election must be retained for five years (s40-340).

10.700 PREPAYMENTS

Where a taxpayer is eligible to claim a deduction under the general deduction provision (s8-1), a deduction is usually permitted in the year the expense is incurred. However, rules are in place to alter the timing of a deduction for prepayments – where the expenditure relates to a period extending beyond the end of the relevant income year.

See 14.170 for a details of the prepayment rules and special rules applying to SBEs.

Assessable income

11

11.000 ASSESSABLE INCOME

'Income according to ordinary concepts' is not defined in the income tax legislation. The Macquarie Dictionary defines income as 'the returns that come in periodically from one's work, property or business. For instance revenue, receipts or something that comes in'.

All section and division references in this Chapter are to the *Income Tax Assessment Act 1997* (ITAA97) unless otherwise stated.

11.005 CHARACTERISTICS OF ASSESSABLE INCOME

Assessable income includes income under ordinary concepts plus statutory income (ie. amounts specifically made assessable by the provisions of the income tax legislation).

INCOME UNDER ORDINARY CONCEPTS

Section 6-5(1) provides that a taxpayer's assessable income includes income according to ordinary concepts (ie. ordinary income).

The Courts have indicated that ordinary income usually possesses the following characteristics:

- **recurrence:** periodicity, recurrence or regularity are usual, although not essential for an amount to be considered income.
- **convertibility:** it must be in money or in a form capable of conversion into money (or deemed to be convertible in the case of s21A ITAA36 which relates to non-cash business benefits derived by a taxpayer), and
- **it must be a reward for:**
  - services rendered
  - use of property, or
  - proceeds of a business.
- **isolated transactions:** profit from an isolated transaction is generally income where the transaction is entered into with a profit making purpose and is in the furtherance of a business or commercial transaction.

Income according to ordinary concepts includes:

- salary and wages
- business and professional earnings
- primary production income
- share of the net income from a partnership
- insurance receipts to replace loss of wages, profits and/or trading stock (note that assessable income from insurance receipts is not limited to the items mentioned here; the general rule is that insurance proceeds will be assessable if the item they replace would have been assessable)
- workers compensation receipts
- non-exempt social security and veteran affairs pensions, allowances and benefits
- dividends
- rents, and
- royalties.

Certain types of income may satisfy the requirements to be considered income according to ordinary concepts whilst also being statutory income eg. dividend income.

RESIDENCY

An Australian resident taxpayer includes in assessable income amounts derived from worldwide sources (ss6-5(2)). A non-resident taxpayer is, broadly, assessed on only income from Australian sources (ss6-5(3)). Refer to 11.020.

CONSTRUCTIVE RECEIPT

In working out whether a taxpayer has 'derived' an amount of ordinary income, and when it has been derived, a taxpayer is taken to have received an amount as soon as it is applied or dealt with in any way on the taxpayer's behalf (s6-5(4)) (see 11.030). In other words, the taxpayer is deemed to have received the amount even though no actual receipt has occurred.

A common example is where an employee asks that salary and wage income be directed to a family member's bank account instead. The income is still considered to be derived by the taxpayer.

In *Sent v Commissioner of Taxation* (2012) FCAFC 187, the Full Court was of the view that future and past bonuses of an executive that was replaced by an entitlement to five million ordinary shares which were placed in an executive share trust was assessable income to the taxpayer. The fact that the payment was made to a nominee of the trust and not the taxpayer would trigger s6-5(4) in that the payment was made to the trustee at the direction of, or on behalf of, the taxpayer.

In *Howard v Commissioner of Taxation* [2014] HCA 21, the High Court discusses fundamental concepts in relation to whether a constructive trust exists, and the difference between assigning a right to future income and assigning the actual future income.

GST AND ASSESSABLE INCOME

As a general principle, the assessable income of a GST registered enterprise excludes the GST payable on the taxable supplies it makes (see from 24.000).

STATUTORY INCOME

Statutory income includes amounts which do not comprise income as it is ordinarily understood, but are deemed by the tax law to be income, including:

- allowances (eg. uniform allowance, gratuities, compensations, and other benefits, in relation to employment or services rendered, other than fringe benefits which are taxable to the employer)
- employee share acquisition scheme benefits
- dividend franking credits
- lump sum retirement payments for:
  - annual leave
  - all post-15 August 1978 long service leave
  - 5% of pre-16 August 1978 long service leave
  - the taxable portion of an employment termination payment
  - the value of certain benefits to an employee, and
- net capital gains (see 12.000).

 In the view of the Commissioner, a commission paid to a taxpayer for acting as the executor of a deceased estate is assessable as statutory income under s6-10 (ATO ID 2014/44).

Where an amount is specifically deemed to be assessable by the legislation and also would constitute income according to ordinary concepts, the amount would normally be characterised as ordinary income and not as statutory income (see s6-25). The s6-10 definition of statutory income excludes amounts that are ordinary income.

REVENUE VERSUS CAPITAL

It may be necessary to determine whether a gain is assessable on revenue or capital account. The distinction may not always be clear.

Whilst one of the characteristics of income is recurrence, the 'Myer principle' may be invoked to determine that a one-off transaction resulted in a revenue gain (see 11.770 – *Profit-making undertaking*). TR 92/3 sets out the Commissioner's interpretation of the decision in *FCT v The Myer Emporium Ltd*, which may be summarised as follows:

Taxpayers carrying on a business

If a taxpayer makes a profit from a transaction or operation, that profit will be on income account if the transaction or operation:

- is in the course of the taxpayer's business, although not in the ordinary course of that business, and the taxpayer entered into the transaction or operation with the intention or purpose of making a profit (see TR 97/11 for factors in relation to conducting a business), or
- is not in the course of the taxpayer's business, but

    - the intention or purpose of the taxpayer in entering into the transaction or operation was to make a profit or gain, and

    - the transaction or operation was entered into, and the profit was made, in carrying out a business operation or commercial transaction.

Taxpayers not carrying on business

In these circumstances a profit from a transaction or operation would be on income account if:

- the intention or purpose of the taxpayer entering into the profit-making transaction or operation was to make a profit or gain, and
- the transaction was entered into, and the profit was made, in carrying out a business operation or commercial transaction.

ASSESSABLE RECOUPMENTS

Assessable recoupments include any kind of recoupment, reimbursement, refund, insurance, indemnity or recovery, or a grant in respect of a loss or outgoing. The provisions can be found in Subdivision 20A and cover situations such as where a taxpayer:

- receives an amount that recoups previously deducted expenditure, or
- makes a profit on the disposal of a previously leased car for which lease payments have been deducted.

The amount received may be:

- ordinary income
- statutory income, or
- an assessable recoupment that is treated as statutory income under Subdivision 20A.

Some of the statutory provisions which designate particular types of recouped amounts to be assessable income impose a requirement that there be a nexus between the recouped amount and an amount that has been, is or otherwise would be deductible before the amount becomes statutory income. This includes all recoupments covered by Subdivision 20A. However, be mindful that even where a recouped amount does not satisfy the assessability requirements of a statutory provision, it may still be assessable as ordinary income.

Statutorily assessable recoupments can arise from:

- a balancing charge for property (s40-285)
- an amount received from insurance or an indemnity for a loss of trading stock (s70-115)
- the termination of a limited recourse debt (s243-40) (see 15.800)
- an amount received in respect of petroleum resource rent tax paid (s40-750(3))
- an amount received from a partial realisation of intellectual property (former s373-50)
- an amount received in respect of research and development activities (s73B(27A) ITAA36)
- recouped election expenses (s25-65)
- certain returned superannuation contributions (s290-100 ITAA97), and
- recouped expenses, eg. bad debts (see 14.160), grape vine establishment expenditure, Landcare operations expenditure (see 15.090). Where the deduction was claimed:

    - in a single year: the recoupment is generally assessable income in the year of receipt, and

    - over several income years: the recoupment included in assessable income is limited to the total amount deducted to date.

NOTE: Where a deduction for legal costs is available to the recipient under the general deduction rules under s8-1 (see Chapter 14), a settlement or award in respect of legal costs will be included in the recipient's assessable income as an assessable recoupment under Subdivision 20-A (see TR 2012/8).

EXEMPT INCOME AND NON-ASSESSABLE NON-EXEMPT INCOME

There are certain items of income which are specifically exempted from being included in assessable income. The exemption may be due to the identity of the taxpayer or the nature of the income or both. Refer 11.900 and 11.950 for details.

THE PATHWAY TO ASSESSABLE INCOME

The following flowchart can be used to determine whether an amount of income is assessable income and, if so, whether an exemption applies pursuant to a statutory provision.

For example, there is no specific section to assess salary, but salary is 'income' under ordinary concepts for most people and is not removed by any of the exempting provisions, and therefore is assessable income.

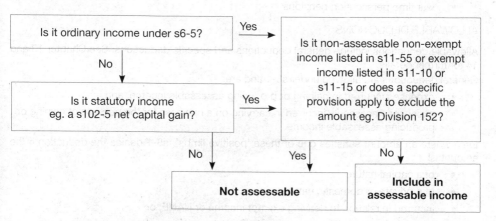

11.010 CALCULATING TAXABLE INCOME

The method for calculating taxable income of a taxpayer is contained in s4-15.

Generally, taxable income is worked out using the formula below:

Taxable income = Assessable income – Deductions

That is:

Step 1: **Add up all the assessable income for the income year.**

Step 2: **Add up the deductions for the income year.**

Step 3: Subtract the deductions from the assessable income (unless they exceed it). The result is taxable income. (If the deductions equal or exceed the assessable income, then there is no taxable income).

ASSESSABLE INCOME

Assessable income includes income from ordinary concepts (salary or wages, interest, business takings etc) as well as statutory income. Statutory income includes income that is not 'ordinary income' but is included in assessable income under a specific provision of the legislation. This may include:

- non-cash business benefits (see 11.060)
- lump sum payments (see 11.200)
- bonuses from life insurance policies (see 11.800)
- traditional securities (see 11.300)

- dividend franking credits (see 11.700)
- profit making undertakings (see 11.770)
- employee share scheme discounts (see 11.850), and
- net capital gains (see 12.000).

Exempt income and non-assessable non-exempt income (NANE) (see 11.900) should be excluded from a taxpayer's assessable income as these amounts are not subject to income tax. Examples include:

- pay and allowances for some defence force personnel on overseas activities (eg. East Timor or Afghanistan)
- Commonwealth education or training payments
- maintenance payments
- certain overseas employment income
- gifts
- structured compensation settlements, and
- war time persecution pensions.

ALLOWABLE DEDUCTIONS

Allowable deductions include general deductions and specific deductions. See Chapter 13 and 14 for further details.

General deductions are allowed under s8-1 and are:

- expenses incurred in gaining or producing assessable income, and
- expenses necessarily incurred in carrying on a business for the purpose of gaining or producing assessable income.

Even where an amount satisfies one of these 'positive limbs', s8-1 denies the deduction if the amount is:

- of a capital nature
- of a private or domestic nature
- incurred in relation to deriving exempt income or NANE, or
- non-deductible pursuant to a specific provision of the tax law.

If an amount is non-deductible under s8-1, it may still be a 'specific deduction' under a particular provision of the law. For example, amounts of a capital nature are specifically deductible under various regimes, including:

- capital allowance deductions (or claims based on the decline in value) (see from 15.000)
- capital works deductions (see 15.200)
- research and development (see 15.500)
- environmental expenditure (see 15.600)
- investments in Australian films (see 15.700)
- primary production capital costs for land care and water conservation (see 15.090), and
- farm management deposits (see 21.800).

The excess of assessable income over allowable deductions is taxable income.

The excess of allowable deductions over assessable income is a tax loss.

NOTE: Subdivision 36-A deals with deductions for tax losses of earlier income years.

CALCULATION OF TAX PAYABLE

For a taxpayer, the taxable income and tax payable is calculated by the steps set out in the following flowchart.

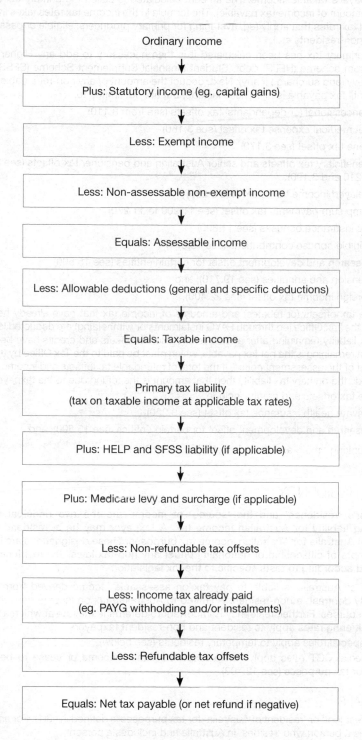

Ordinary income

↓

Plus: Statutory income (eg. capital gains)

↓

Less: Exempt income

↓

Less: Non-assessable non-exempt income

↓

Equals: Assessable income

↓

Less: Allowable deductions (general and specific deductions)

↓

Equals: Taxable income

↓

Primary tax liability
(tax on taxable income at applicable tax rates)

↓

Plus: HELP and SFSS liability (if applicable)

↓

Plus: Medicare levy and surcharge (if applicable)

↓

Less: Non-refundable tax offsets

↓

Less: Income tax already paid
(eg. PAYG withholding and/or instalments)

↓

Less: Refundable tax offsets

↓

Equals: Net tax payable (or net refund if negative)

CALCULATING TAX PAYABLE

The tax liability is calculated by applying the rates as set out in the *Income Tax Rates Act 1986* to the taxpayer's taxable income. The amount calculated is called the primary tax payable (or the gross amount of income tax payable). The formula in the income tax rates takes into account any special tax rates that apply (eg. averaging for primary producers, eligible or passive income of minors, non-residents etc).

Once the primary tax has been calculated it is then necessary to add any Higher Education Loan Program scheme (HELP) debt, Student Financial Supplement Scheme (SFSS) debt and Medicare levy (and surcharge if any). Next, deduct the amount of any non-refundable tax offsets (but only until tax payable is nil). These include, but are not limited to:

- concessional (or dependants) tax offsets (see from 3.110)
- net medical expense tax offset (see 3.160)
- zone tax offset (see 3.170)
- beneficiary tax offsets and senior Australian and pensioner tax offsets (see 3.200, 3.210 and 3.190)
- delayed income tax offset (see 3.230)
- lump sum payments tax offset (see 11.200 to 11.270)
- life insurance bonuses (see 11.800)
- eligible spouse contributions (see 19.074)
- research and development offset for certain entities (see 15.500)
- pension and annuities (see 19.710), and
- foreign income tax offset (see 22.400).

Refundable tax offsets (or rebates) and amounts of income tax that have already been paid or remitted to the Tax Office (eg through PAYG instalments or withholding) are deducted last from the primary tax liability remaining after all non-refundable tax offsets and credits have been applied. Any amount remaining is the net tax payable, which must be paid to the Tax Office by the due date for payment of the assessment notice. If the total of refundable tax offsets and income tax already paid exceeds the primary tax liability then that amount is the refund due to the taxpayer.

Refundable tax offsets and credits include:

- private health insurance tax offset (see 3.220)
- research and development offset for certain entities (see 15.500), and
- franking credit tax offsets (see 11.700 and 6.800).

11.020 RESIDENCY

A taxpayer's 'residence' and the 'source' of income are the two principal criteria for determining liability for Australian income tax. A taxpayer may be a 'resident' or a 'non-resident' of Australia for Australian income tax purposes. These designations are not aligned with concepts of citizenship or nationality under any non-tax laws. Tax residency status is determined according to tests specific to the tax legislation.

A resident of Australia is liable to pay tax on assessable income derived from worldwide sources. By contrast, a non-resident is limited to Australian tax on income derived only from Australian sources. Further, residency is important to determine the rate at which a taxpayer is taxed as differing rates apply to resident and non-resident taxpayers.

Note that special rules apply to temporary residents (see below).

NOTE: Special CGT rules apply where taxpayers either become or cease to be Australian residents for tax purposes (see 12.700).

INDIVIDUALS

The term 'resident' or 'resident of Australia' for tax purposes is defined in s6(1). For an individual, a resident is a person who 'resides' in Australia and includes a person:

- whose domicile is in Australia unless the Commissioner is satisfied their usual place of residence is outside Australia, or
- who has actually been in Australia, continuously or intermittently, during more than half the year of income unless the Commissioner is satisfied that the person's usual place of abode is outside Australia and that the taxpayer does not intend to take up residence in Australia, or
- is a member of, or is eligible to join, a Commonwealth superannuation scheme.

An individual may be a resident of Australia and another country simultaneously as Australia's residency tests are not affected by the taxpayer's residency status in any other country.

Australia's Double Tax Agreements (DTAs) with other countries (see 22.200) generally contain residency tie-breaker rules. Where a taxpayer is a dual resident, he or she is deemed to solely be a resident of only one of the countries under the tie-breaker rules in the relevant DTA. Therefore, a dual resident taxpayer who is an Australian resident under domestic laws may be treated as a non-resident because of the tie-breaker. Note that the tie-breaker rules are only contained in the DTAs.

Furthermore, a double tax agreement may preclude or limit Australia's taxing rights over certain classes of income derived by an individual even where the rights exist under domestic law (TR 98/17).

 When determining the residence of a taxpayer or the tax treatment of a transaction the specific double tax agreement in place should always be consulted.

(i) 'Resides in Australia' test

The resides under ordinary concepts test is the primary test to determine tax residency. The three statutory tests need to be examined only where this test cannot be passed.

As there is no definition of 'reside' in the Act, its ordinary meaning must be considered. The Shorter Oxford Dictionary defines reside as:

> *... to dwell permanently, or for a considerable time, to have one's settled or usual abode, to live in particular place ...*

TR 98/17 sets out the Commissioner's guidance as to whether someone entering Australia is considered a resident for tax purposes. The ruling states that while the length of time a person is present in Australia is not determinative (although it is a factor), their behaviour may indicate a continuity, routine or habit consistent with someone who is residing in Australia. The factors examined by the Tax Office are:

- intention or purpose of presence
- family and business/employment ties
- maintenance and location of assets, and
- social and living arrangements.

The ruling also indicates that, as a rule of thumb, behavioural patterns over a six month period would be sufficient to determine whether the behaviour was consistent with residing in Australia. However, it is possible to establish Australian tax residency in a period of less than six months, or non-residency where a person is present in Australia for more than six months. All relevant facts and circumstances have to be taken into consideration and no single factor is determinative.

(ii) Domicile in Australia

Under this test, a person is treated as a resident if the person lives in Australia and/or the individual's circumstances indicate that their permanent place of abode is not outside Australia.

'Permanent' does not mean 'everlasting' but is used in contrast to temporary. A person remains a resident of Australia unless that person adopts a permanent place of abode outside Australia. This test generally applies to individuals who have been residents of Australia and have departed the country.

A resident who travels abroad, even on an extended holiday, is likely to retain residency status if he or she has no permanent place of abode outside Australia.

There are various cases dealing with the issue of domicile. In a landmark case, *Commissioner of Taxation v Applegate* 79 ATC 4307, the taxpayer left Australia with his wife to set up an office in the New Hebrides (now Vanuatu). He gave up tenancy of his flat and left no other assets except for a life policy. He always intended to return after an indefinite period of time. He returned 21 months later due to his wife's ill health. He was held to be a non-resident during his period of absence as his permanent place of abode was outside Australia.

The general rule for seafarers is that residency applies to the country where the seafarer maintains a permanent home and lives whenever they return from sea duty.

(iii) The 183-day test

A person who resides in Australia for more than 50% (ie. more than 183 days) of the financial year is treated as a resident unless the Commissioner of Taxation is satisfied that:

- the person's usual place of abode is outside Australia, and
- he or she does not intend to take up residence in Australia.

The emphasis is on the person's 'usual' rather than their permanent place of abode.

This test generally applies to non-residents entering Australia. The intended outcome is to treat as residents certain persons who live here for more than six months, (eg. overseas students undertaking courses of study in Australia). The criteria in the test also removes the possibility of treating as residents those who are purely visitors (eg. tourists) and those who are here for short term vocational experience (TD 93/223).

(iv) Commonwealth superannuation scheme

A member of a public sector superannuation scheme, or an eligible employee, is treated as a resident regardless of where they reside under ordinary concepts or where their usual place of abode is located. This applies to Commonwealth employees working overseas, irrespective of where they may have been recruited.

The residency status is also conferred upon the spouse or a child under 16 years of age of the member or eligible employee.

Refer: *Baker and Commissioner of Taxation* (2012) AATA 168.

IMPORTANT! In the 2015-16 Federal Budget, the Government announced its intention to amend the law so that individuals in Australia for a working holiday will be classified as non-residents, regardless of how long they are in Australia. Under the current residency tests, many of these working holiday makers are treated as residents despite the fact that they do not intend to settle in Australia. Holders of 457 visas and other temporary visas who qualify as temporary residents will not be affected. At time of writing, no legislation has been released.

RESIDENT FOR PART OF AN INCOME YEAR

Where a taxpayer becomes a resident or ceases to be a resident for tax purposes during an income year, he or she is a part-year resident. As such, his or her assessable income for the year includes the following:

- Australian source income derived during the period of non-residency, and
- income derived from worldwide sources during the period of Australian residency.

Income tax is *not* payable in Australia on foreign source income derived before the person becomes an Australian tax resident or after the person ceases to be an Australian tax resident. This treatment is subject to the provisions of any relevant double tax agreement (see 22.200).

 It would be necessary to apportion the tax-free threshold where an individual taxpayer is an Australian tax resident for only part of the income year.

NON-RESIDENT WITHHOLDING TAX

If a non-resident derives certain types of Australian source income (most commonly interest and dividends), non-resident withholding tax is deducted from the income before it is remitted to the non-resident (see 22.140). The withholding tax is a final tax on that income in Australia in the hands of the non-resident. The non-resident does not have to include the income as assessable income for Australian tax purposes and no more Australian tax is payable on the income.

TEMPORARY RESIDENTS

The law exempts those qualifying as 'temporary residents' from Australian income tax on all ordinary and statutory income from a foreign source (Subdivision 768-R). The exemption does not apply to foreign employment remuneration earned during the period of temporary residency. Temporary residents are also treated as non-residents for CGT purposes, with some modifications (see 12.721).

A person Is a temporary resident if:

- they hold a temporary visa granted under the *Migration Act 1958* (a temporary visa is a visa to travel to and remain in Australia during a specified period, until a specified event happens or while the holder has a specified status. Such a visa does not permit a person to remain in Australia indefinitely)
- they are not an Australian resident within the meaning of the *Social Security Act 1991*, and
- their spouse (if applicable) is not an Australian resident within the meaning of the *Social Security Act 1991*.

Under the *Social Security Act 1991*, an Australian resident is generally a person who resides in Australia and is either an Australian citizen or holds a permanent resident visa. Taxpayers who hold a protected special category visa and were in Australia on or before 26 February 2001 are also included.

PARTNERSHIPS

For income tax purposes, partnerships are not taxpaying entities with an identity separate to the partners. Consequently, there are no specific rules to determine the residency of a partnership. Whether Australian taxation is imposed on the income derived through a partnership is determined solely by reference to the residency status of the partners themselves. Each partner is taxed on their respective share of the partnership's net income as though they derived it directly (see from 8.100). That is, a non-resident partner generally would not be taxed on foreign sourced partnership income.

TRUSTS

A trust estate is a resident trust estate for an income year if *at any time during the income year* a trustee of a trust estate was a resident of Australia or the central management and control of the trust estate was in Australia (see from 7.000).

Trust estates are required to calculate their net income as if they were a resident of Australia (s95(1) ITAA36). This is the case even if the trust is a non-resident trust as a trust estate is generally a flow-through entity for Australian tax purposes. Australian residents that are required to include their share of trust income in their assessable income must do so under Australian tax principles applying to them. However, some key modifications to the tax law apply including:

- where the trustee is taxed under sections 99 and 99A on income to which no beneficiary is presently entitled, the trustee of a non-resident trust estate will only be subject to tax on net income from Australian sources, and
- the transferor trust rules (Division 6AAA) which are intended to apply to residents that have transferred property or services to trusts in low-tax jurisdictions used to accumulate income free from tax in Australia (see 22.830).

 The taxing of trusts and beneficiaries have been amended in relation to the streaming of net capital gains and franked distributions. See 7.700.

COMPANIES

Under the definition of residency in s6(1) of the ITAA36, there are three tests to determine whether a company is a resident of Australia for tax purposes. The tests are:

- place of incorporation
- place of central management and control (if carrying on business in Australia), and
- residence of controlling shareholders (if carrying on business in Australia).

COMPANIES INCORPORATED IN AUSTRALIA

If a company is incorporated in Australia then it will be treated as a resident for Australian taxation purposes regardless of any other factors (see from 6.000).

COMPANIES NOT INCORPORATED IN AUSTRALIA

For a company that is not incorporated in Australia to be treated as a resident of Australia for tax purposes it must be carrying on business in Australia **and** either have its central management and control (CM&C) in Australia or have its voting power controlled by shareholders who are residents of Australia. See TR 2004/15 for the Tax Office's views on carrying on a business in Australia and CM&C.

If no business is carried on in Australia, the company cannot meet the requirements of the second statutory test and, in these circumstances, it is not a resident of Australia based on that fact alone. There is then no need to determine the location of the company's CM&C or the residency of shareholders.

The fact that a company, not incorporated in Australia, is carrying on a business in Australia does not, of itself, necessarily mean that the company has its CM&C in Australia.

CARRIES ON BUSINESS IN AUSTRALIA

The question of where business is carried on is one of fact. It requires a consideration of where the activities of the company are carried on and is dependent on the facts and circumstances of each case. However, the Tax Office's approach to this factual determination is to draw a distinction between a company with operational activities (for example trading, service provision, manufacturing or mining activities) and a company which is more passive in its dealings (for example, investment in income-producing assets such as shares in other companies or interest-bearing financial instruments).

For the purposes of the second statutory test relating to CM&C, a company that has major operational activities (relative to the whole of its business) carries on business wherever those activities take place and not necessarily where its CM&C is likely to be located. Operational activities include major trading, service provision, manufacturing or mining activities (eg. the place of business of a large industrial concern is wherever its offices, factories or mines are situated). On the other hand, a company whose income earning outcomes are largely dependent on the investment decisions made in respect of its assets, is usually deemed to be carrying on its business where these decisions are made. This is often where its CM&C is located.

According to the Tax Office, the concept of carrying on a business may be wider than its ordinary meaning and extends to undertakings of a business or a commercial character. For example, for the purposes of the second statutory test, a company may be carrying on business even if its only activity is the management of its investment assets.

CENTRAL MANAGEMENT AND CONTROL

The second statutory test focuses on management and control decisions that guide and control the company's business activities. This level of management and control involves the high level decision making processes, including activities involving high level company matters such as general policies and strategic directions, major agreements and significant financial matters. It also includes activities such as the monitoring of the company's overall corporate performance and the review of strategic recommendations made in the light of the company's performance.

Possession of the mere legal right to exercise central management and control of a company is not, of itself, sufficient to constitute CM&C of the company. Someone who has the 'mere legal right to CM&C' is a person with the legal right to make these decisions involving CM&C but who for one reason or another does not exercise this right. However, a person with the legal right to CM&C may participate in the CM&C of the company even if they delegate all or part of that power to another, provided that they at least review or consider the actions of the delegated decision maker before deciding whether any further or different action is required.

LOCATION OF CENTRAL MANAGEMENT AND CONTROL

The location of the company's CM&C is a question of fact to be determined in light of all the relevant facts and circumstances. In order to reduce uncertainty, the Tax Office, as a matter of practical compliance, accepts that for those companies whose CM&C is exercised by a board of directors at board meetings the CM&C is in Australia if the majority of the board meetings are held in Australia. The exception to this is cases where the circumstances indicate an artificial or contrived CM&C outcome (eg. where there is no business reason for the location of the meeting or where the decisions are made by someone other than the board).

A board meeting is treated as being held in Australia when the majority of directors of the company meet in Australia. If the location of the directors at board meetings is evenly split within and outside Australia, then the location of any directors with special powers may be decisive. This is also subject to the exception for cases where the circumstances indicate an artificial or contrived CM&C outcome. If a majority of board meetings are held in a particular jurisdiction outside Australia, the company's CM&C will not be located in Australia. This would apply regardless of whether the directors are Australian residents but is subject to the exception for cases where the circumstances indicate an artificial or contrived CM&C outcome. As long as the high level decisions of the company are made at specific board meetings, the fact that less pressing business of the board is often conducted by circulating resolutions will not impact on the location of CM&C.

A parent company that does not involve itself in the CM&C of a subsidiary but ultimately has the power to remove the board in a manner consistent with the constitution of the company does not, for this reason alone, exercise the CM&C of the subsidiary for the purpose of the residence test. Where a parent company in Australia exercises CM&C in relation to a subsidiary (but does not conduct the day-to-day activities of the business), the subsidiary would need to also be carrying on business in Australia for it to be a resident under the second statutory test.

LOCATION OF CENTRAL MANAGEMENT AND CONTROL IN MORE THAN ONE COUNTRY

It is possible for CM&C to exist in more than one country. Therefore the company can have CM&C in Australia notwithstanding that it also has its CM&C in another country. CM&C can be located where there is some part of the superior or directing authority by means of which the relevant affairs of the company are controlled. However, it is necessary that the exercise of that power and authority is to some substantial degree found in a place for the CM&C to be located there (and elsewhere).

11.030 DERIVING INCOME

Most individual taxpayers are assessed on a 'cash receipts basis'; that is, their income is taxed in the income year it is received, not the income year the relevant services are performed. Business taxpayers (except for some small businesses) are generally required to return their income on an 'accruals basis' (ie. when it is earned, rather than received). When income is not directly received in cash, it can be deemed to have been derived if it is reinvested, accumulated, capitalised or otherwise dealt with on behalf of the earner as they direct.

There is no definitive rule regarding whether particular taxpayers should account for income using the cash basis or the accruals basis. A taxpayer is generally required to return income on the basis that is most appropriate in their circumstances. The Commissioner's view on which method is most appropriate for business taxpayers is outlined in TR 98/1 having regard to:

- the size of the business
- the type of business
- the method of accounting
- the current practice in the industry
- overhead costs, and
- the policy for recovery of outstanding debts.

The correct method must be used and once adopted it must be maintained, unless there are substantial changes to the activity.

WHAT CONSTITUTES A BUSINESS

The question of whether a taxpayer is carrying on a business is one of fact. A number of factors have been considered by the courts to characterise an activity or group of activities as a business (also see TR 97/11 for indicia of a business). They include whether:

- the activity has a significant commercial purpose
- the taxpayer has an intention to engage in the business in question
- the prospect as well as the intention is to derive profit
- repetition and regularity of the activity (or activities) in question is evident
- the activity is one normally carried out by a similar business in that industry and is carried out in a similar way
- the degree to which the activity is planned, organised and carried on in is businesslike in manner
- the size, scale and permanency of the activity is consistent with a business, and
- the activity would not be better described as a hobby, recreational or sporting pastime.

In determining if a business activity is being undertaken the above factors should be taken into account. Both the cash and accruals methods are now discussed below.

11.035 CASH RECEIPTS BASIS

Under a cash receipts basis, income is derived (and therefore declared) in the income year in which it is received. 'Income' is constructively received and therefore derived when it is *'reinvested, accumulated, capitalised, carried to a reserve, sinking fund or insurance fund however designated or otherwise dealt with on the taxpayer's behalf or as the taxpayer directs'*. In other words, if a taxpayer exercises control over income, it is taxed in the year the taxpayer first exercised control over it.

The cash receipts basis would generally be considered more appropriate than the accruals basis for the derivation of:

- salary and wages
- income derived from a person's personal exertion, the provision of knowledge or the exercise of skill (including business income of small professional practices), and
- investment income (subject to some exceptions).

EMPLOYMENT INCOME

Employees and those who derive income through their own personal exertion should declare their income on a cash receipts basis. This would generally occur when the payment is received.

If an employee works the last week of June and wages are paid the first week of July, these wages should be included in the assessable income for the year commencing in July (ie. when the payment is made).

LONG SERVICE LEAVE

Employees taking long service leave are assessed on the income in the year the money is received.

If the period of leave straddles two income years, the payment may be split between those years to reduce the tax and exposure to superannuation and Medicare levy surcharges by ensuring that money due next year is received next year.

DIVIDENDS

Dividends are generally assessed in the year they are received (or, if not received, when they are dealt with on the taxpayer's behalf, such as the funds being applied to purchase more shares through a dividend reinvestment plan).

INTEREST

Normally, interest is taxed in the year it is received, or is credited to a bank account or similar. Special rules apply to securities where interest is not paid at least every 12 months, or where securities are acquired at a discount. In these cases, accrued interest must be declared as income. Statutory provisions apply to calculate the accrued interest and when that interest must be returned as income (Division 16E of ITAA36).

Any disposal of the security is usually dealt with under the CGT provisions.

NOTE: Division 230 of ITAA97 will provide the tax treatment for most of the gains and losses on discounted and deferred interest securities that are acquired or issued on or after 1 July 2010, or 1 July 2009 should the taxpayer so elect, that would otherwise have been taxed under Division 16E (refer TOFA 3 and 4). Refer 17.550.

CASH OR CHEQUES IN TRANSIT

If a taxpayer uses a cash receipts basis, and a cheque is posted before the end of the income year but received after the end of the income year, the income should be included in the income year it is received.

The payer is eligible to claim a deduction for the amount paid in the earlier income year.

Through electronic data matching, companies and financial institutions provide the Tax Office with details of interest and/or dividends paid to taxpayers during a financial year. This assists the Tax Office in checking if the relevant income has been disclosed.

 Taxpayers may consider retaining envelopes of cheques received early in July. The date shown on the postmark may help establish that the payment was not received in June.

Other situations where the cash receipts basis may be appropriate include:

- non-business income derived from the provision of knowledge or the exercise of skill possessed by the taxpayer (eg. a barrister), and
- interest derived by taxpayers whose other income is calculated on an accruals basis.

SMALL BUSINESS ENTITIES

Special rules apply for a taxpayer that qualifies as a Small Business Entity (SBE). A full explanation of the SBE rules can be found at 10.000.

11.040   ACCRUALS BASIS

For many businesses, the derivation of income using the cash receipts basis is not appropriate. In essence, these taxpayers are required to return their income as it is earned (on an accruals basis). Under an accruals basis of taxation, income is derived where a recoverable debt is created. This is the time when the taxpayer is legally entitled to an ascertainable amount after goods are provided or services are performed. Accordingly, amounts included in trade debtors at year end, where the entitlement to those amounts arose during the year (eg. when a sale was made) are included in assessable income for that year. Whether a debt is a recoverable debt is dependant upon the arrangement for billing. Where an amount is to be billed only on completion of the project, none is considered to be recoverable earlier.

The accruals basis would generally be considered more appropriate for the derivation of:

- trading income (where the taxpayer is in the business of selling goods)
- manufacturing income
- income from larger professional practices, and
- interest earned by financial institutions.

In TR 98/1, the Commissioner is of the view that in borderline cases, the accruals method should be selected.

 Returning income on a cash or accruals basis does not necessarily mean expenses are returned on the same basis. Expenses are subject to the definition of 'incurred' under s8-1 or the timing rules prescribed by various statutory provisions.

PROFESSIONAL PRACTICES

While sole professional practitioners and small professional firms may record income on a cash basis, the accruals basis is more appropriate for larger professional practices (such as legal or accounting practices that employ staff). Generally, the nature of the work will determine which method is to be used.

The following cases demonstrate this distinction:

- *Dunn's case* (1989) and *Firstenburg's case* (1976) involved sole practitioners deriving their income through personal exertion. Dunn was a chartered accountant; Firstenburg, a solicitor in sole practice. The cash receipts basis was held to be appropriate.

- *Henderson's case* (1970) involved a large firm with 295 employees. The accruals basis was held to be appropriate.

A medical practitioner with personal services income (see 16.000) can use the cash receipts basis, as established in *Commissioner of Taxes (SA) v Executor Trustee & Agency Coy of SA* (1938) HCA 69 – *Carden's case*. However, *Barratt's case* 92 ATC 4275 established that a pathologist (using costly equipment monitored by staff) should use the accruals basis.

WORK-IN-PROGRESS

Taxpayers using an accruals basis are not required to return income in respect of work in progress until a recoverable debt is created. If the arrangement is for an account to be sent only when the job is completed, the taxpayer is not assessed on the income until the year in which all the work is done and the bill or invoice is issued.

SHARE OF PARTNERSHIP INCOME

There is an accepted legal argument in the context of partnership law and tax law that a share of partnership profits is income of the partner only when it is calculated at the end of the income year and not at any other time during the year. Each partner is assessed in their share of the net income of the partnership as calculated as to 30 June each year (unless the partnership terminates at an earlier date). The partnership agreement determines how profits are to be split between the partners (see also 8.100).

 The salary and wages paid to partners are considered a share of profit not an expense of the partnership (see TR 2005/7).

TRUST DISTRIBUTIONS

A beneficiary 'presently entitled' to income derived by a trust in respect of an income year is usually personally liable for tax on that income in the same year, whether or not it was received by the beneficiary in the year of income. The trustee of the trust generally has no obligation to pay tax on the net income of the trust if all of the net income is distributed to beneficiaries, subject to certain exceptions such as non-resident beneficiaries and beneficiaries under a legal disability. If there is no beneficiary presently entitled to an amount of income, it is assessed to the trustee in the year it is derived (see also 7.000).

In the case of certain trusts such as public trading trusts (which are treated as companies – see 7.100), distributions are assessed in the income year they are received.

Where there is no absolute entitlement to a distribution or a contractual payment (as with an income stream payable under a will) the benefit is derived by the beneficiary either when the trustee pays the amount or credits it to an account accessible by the beneficiary.

Note that a taxable distribution can be larger than the accounting profit made for the year.

 There are specific rules in relation to the streaming of capital gains and franked distributions (see 7.000).

LONG TERM CONSTRUCTION PROJECTS

A long term construction project is one that spans more than one financial year. This generally applies to the building industry, demolition, major refurbishment, civil engineering projects and ship building. The Tax Office accepts two methods for the derivation and calculation of profits on long term construction projects (IT 2450):

- **The billings basis:** requires all progress and final payments received in a year to be returned as income as well as amounts which have been or are entitled to be billed in the year. All deductible losses and outgoings for the year are also taken into account as incurred.

- **Estimated profits basis:** the ultimate profit or loss can be spread over the years taken to complete the contract, provided the basis is reasonable and in accord with established accounting principles. This is also known as the 'percentage complete method'. 'Ultimate profit or loss' in this context refers to the overall taxable income or loss expected to arise from a particular contract.

The adopted method must be applied consistently to all years during which the particular contract runs and to all similar contracts entered into by the taxpayer.

There are many small businesses associated with the construction industry (eg. minor subcontractors and 'spec' home builders) who return income on an accruals basis: receivables, expenditure incurred, work-in progress and any trading stock on hand. Although some operations may overlap two income years, the Tax Office says there is no need to disturb that basis of returning income.

 In applying IT 2450, have regard to TD 94/39 in relation to the timing of income derived and expenses incurred.

INCOME RECEIVED IN ADVANCE

The case *Arthur Murray (NSW) Pty Ltd v FCT* (1965) 114 CLR 314 established the principle that income received in advance of services being rendered is not earned until the relevant services are performed, therefore delaying the derivation of income until that time.

The case involved a taxpayer in the business of providing dancing tuition. Payment for courses was often received in advance. Students did not have a contractual right to refunds, however refunds were occasionally made. The Court held that the amounts received in advance for dancing lessons were not derived until the lessons were actually given. This principle would apply to other services with the characteristics of payment being received in advance of the services being rendered.

11.050 EMPLOYMENT INCOME AND ALLOWANCES

Discussed below are the various forms of remuneration and allowances typically received by employees.

REWARD FOR EMPLOYMENT

Salary and wages are assessable under ordinary concepts (s6-5). Allowances, commissions, bonuses and any special or gratuitous amounts received during a period of employment are taxable (see s15-2). Lump sums received upon retirement are generally taxed concessionally (see 11.200). However, wages relating to the final working period are taxed at normal rates even if it is paid with a retirement lump sum.

HONORARIUMS

Sometimes those helping out organisations are given a small cash 'honorarium'. The fact that it is small does not mean that it is not subject to tax. However, in *Case Z16*, 92 ATC 183 it was held that a $100 honorarium was not assessable income and therefore $3,510 expenses were not deductible. The assessability of such amounts will depend upon the facts of each case.

ALLOWANCES

Assessable income includes lump sums or periodic allowances paid to an employee towards meeting the cost to the employee of any travelling, tools, uniforms etc. If the allowances are spent in the course of the job, or under the terms of a contract (whether written or verbal) of employment, the employee may be able to deduct these expenses provided the employee can substantiate them (see 13.100) and the expense is deductible under s8-1 or another statutory provision. Note that PAYG withholding is required to be made on this income by the employer.

 If the employee is able to claim a deduction in relation to the allowance and the allowance disclosed is shown separately the employer may be able to reduce the amount of PAYG withholding to be collected as long as the employee requests a variation in the approved form.

Living away from home allowances meeting certain criteria are dealt with under the fringe benefits tax (FBT) provisions (see 25.840) and should not be included in the employee's income.

MEAL ALLOWANCES

Meal allowances are taxed in full as ordinary income. If a reasonable overtime meal allowance is paid under an industrial instrument (eg. an award) of up to $28.20 in 2014-15 per overtime meal (the reasonable amount), the employee may claim a deduction for overtime meals up to the reasonable amount (see TD 2014/19). If the employee wishes to claim in excess of the reasonable amount, the full meal cost must be substantiated (see 13.140). If no award allowance is paid, no claim can be made. Also see TR 2004/6 about claiming travel allowance expenses and overtime meal allowance expenses. The 2015-16 amount had not been released at the time of writing.

TRAVEL ALLOWANCES

Where an employee travels away from home overnight and the employer pays the employee an allowance in respect of that travel, the allowance is assessable and the costs deductible (subject to the usual deductibility rules) in the hands of the employee. Written evidence of expenses is generally required. However, where the employer pays the employee a travel allowance for such travel, written evidence need not be kept provided the deduction does not exceed the 'reasonable allowance' amount (published by the Commissioner each year). The 'reasonable amount' is dependent upon the employee's salary and the place of travel. Reasonable travel expense amounts for 2015-16 had not been released at the time of writing.

BENEFITS PROVIDED TO EMPLOYEES

Benefits received by an employee or their associate in respect of the employee's employment are dealt with in the FBT provisions (see from 25.000). Note that such benefit are non-assessable, non exempt income (s23L – see 11.950).

GIFTS FROM THE EMPLOYER

In some cases, gifts to the employee from the employer are tax-free (eg. wedding present or personal gift when the employee leaves). Certain gifts may also fall within the FBT provisions (see 25.000).

Performance bonuses or a share of the business profits are fully assessable as employment income.

When leaving a job, an employer payment (eg. a 'golden handshake') is assessable as an Employment Termination Payment (ETP) (see 11.210).

GRATUITIES FROM CUSTOMERS

Gratuities and tips gained in the course of employment are assessable.

COMPENSATION

Whether an amount of compensation received is income or capital in nature may generally be determined by reference to the underlying thing for which the amount is compensating.

An amount received as compensation for the loss of a capital asset is capital in nature, whereas an amount received for the loss of revenue is income in nature. An amount received in compensation for loss of earning capacity is generally capital in nature. Further, a lump sum in full satisfaction of all entitlements or claims is generally capital in nature; that is, if an amount cannot be apportioned between income and capital components, it is deemed to be capital. Where damages are to compensate a taxpayer for the loss of business suffered as a result of its wounded reputation, the amount will be capital in nature, even where the compensation is calculated with reference to lost profits (*Commissioner of Taxation v Sydney Refractive Surgery Centre Pty Ltd* [2008] FCAFC 190). The calculation methodology was deemed to have no bearing on the underlying nature of the amount in this case.

Periodic amounts of workers' compensation (in lieu of wages) are taxed as income even where tax instalments are not deducted and they may not be shown on a PAYG payment summary.

Lump sums received as compensation for personal injury or wrong doing are considered private, capital receipts and not taxable (see 11.950).

A lump sum payment was received by a taxpayer under the *Workers Compensation Act 1987* to compensate her for giving up her employment in order to provide domestic assistance to her spouse who was seriously injured in the course of his employment. The Tribunal determined that the payment was given in respect of a loss of her income and it was therefore assessable as ordinary income (*Coshott and Commissioner of Taxation* (2014) AATA 622).

ANNUAL OR LONG SERVICE LEAVE

If an employee takes annual or long service leave, any amount received during the leave period is treated as salary or wages. However, special tax rules apply to lump sums paid in lieu of leave entitlements on termination of employment (see from 11.200).

SICK PAY

Sick pay is taxable if received by a current employee. If accrued amounts are paid to the employee upon ceasing employment permanently, such amounts are taxed as an ETP (see 11.200).

OVERTIME PAYMENTS

Overtime payments are assessable as an addition to normal earnings of an employee.

NOT INCLUDED IN ASSESSABLE INCOME

REPORTABLE FRINGE BENEFITS AMOUNT

Payment summaries issued by employers are required to include the reportable fringe benefits amount (see 25.300) applying to that employee. The amount is not included in assessable income however it is reported on an employee's payment summary. It may however affect other liabilities such as HELP repayments, and means testing for certain government benefits (eg. Family Tax Benefit amounts).

REPORTABLE EMPLOYER SUPERANNUATION CONTRIBUTIONS

Reportable Employer Superannuation Contributions (RESCs) are reportable on payment summaries. These are employer superannuation contributions, but only to the extent the employee has the capacity to influence the size of the contribution or the way the amount was contributed so as to reduce the assessable income of the employee.

11.060 NON-CASH BUSINESS BENEFITS

Non-cash benefits received in respect of a business relationship totaling no more than $300 in a year are exempt from tax. If the benefit exceeds $300, the total amount is assessable (see s21A of the ITAA36) unless the benefit is dealt with under the fringe benefits tax provisions (see 25.000).

WHAT IS A NON-CASH BUSINESS BENEFIT?

A 'non-cash business benefit' means a benefit provided as property or service that is provided wholly or partly, directly or indirectly, in respect of a business relationship. 'Services' themselves are defined very widely to include any benefit, right, privilege or facility.

WHAT IS ASSESSABLE?

Non-cash business benefits are assessable as ordinary income whether or not they are convertible to cash (see from 11.050). The amount assessable to the taxpayer is the arm's length value, which is the amount the recipient could reasonably be expected to pay to get the benefit from the provider if the parties were dealing with each other at arm's length. This amount is adjusted for the following:

- the value is reduced by any amount the recipient was required to pay to the provider in respect of the benefit, but increased by any reimbursement to the recipient

- the assessable amount is reduced or eliminated if the recipient would have been eligible for a once-only deduction if the recipient had (hypothetically) incurred the expenditure directly (eg. an interest-free business loan). Note a depreciation claim is not a once-only deduction, and

- the assessable amount is also reduced by the amount of the provider's costs which are not tax deductible to the provider (eg. entertainment) (see 13.500).

 The supplier of a computer gives a crate of wine to a good customer. The wine is a non-deductible 'entertainment expense' and the business customer is not taxed on the value.

A benefit's value is included in assessable income in the income year in which the benefit is taken.

Based on the total of all benefits in an income year, the amount assessable is:

- if under $300: treated as exempt income, and

- if $300 or more: the total is assessable.

If a value cannot be determined, the Tax Office may determine an amount.

Conditions or limitations which would prevent or restrict the conversion of the benefit to cash are disregarded in calculating the value of the benefit.

Note that while s21A ITAA36 deems non-cash business benefits to be assessable income, if the total of the non-cash business benefits earned during the year does not exceed $300 s23L(2) of the ITAA36 will exclude the benefit from assessable income.

APPORTIONING EXPENDITURE

If the taxpayer purchased an item for business, and received something else either free or at a reduced price, the cost must be apportioned realistically between the item purchased and the business benefit. If trading stock is purchased and, as part of the deal, a non-business item is acquired, no claim can be made for the non-business item (s51AK ITAA36).

 A taxpayer bought a business computer for $5,000 and was given a watch worth $500 as a bonus. The depreciation claim is based on $4,500. The watch is a non-deductible private cost.

PAY AS YOU GO (PAYG) WITHHOLDING

Under the PAYG withholding rules, the provider of a non-cash benefit must pay an amount to the Tax Office if the payment is subject to withholding before the benefit is provided to the payee. For example, where the payee has not provided their ABN, the required rate of withholding is 47% for resident taxpayers. The payer has the right to recover that remittance from the payee.

For more information on the PAYG withholding requirements see 5.200 and 5.300.

11.100 FREQUENT FLYER, REWARD PROGRAMS AND CLUB BENEFITS

Many businesses offer their customers loyalty award-based incentives programs. These programs, such as the 'Frequent Flyer' and 'Fly Buys' program are designed to reward customers for purchasing or using their goods and services (or those of their affiliates).

As a result of *Payne v FC of T* (1996) 66 FCR 299 (Payne's case), the Tax Office has accepted that flight rewards received by employees in their personal capacities in respect of expenditure paid by their employer are not assessable income (TR 1999/6). The reward is not assessable as it arises from the personal (ie. non service/non-business) contractual relationship with the program administrator. In *Payne's case,* an employee who had accumulated points as a result of travel on behalf of her employer converted those points into airline tickets for her parents. The points were not convertible to money. The Court held that the points related to her membership of the program which was privately paid for by the member and that there was no contractual relationship between the employer and the program administrator. Consequently, it was irrelevant that the employer had paid for the cost of the original travel.

One exception to this rule is when a person renders a service on the basis that there will be an entitlement to a flight reward (eg. a person enters into a service contract understanding they will receive a flight reward).

The Tax Office also accepts (TD 1999/35) that with consumer loyalty programs such as 'Fly Buys' aimed primarily at domestic purchases by an employee, no amount is assessable income. Also, no FBT liability arises.

 In Practice Statement PS LA 2004/4 (GA) the Tax Office has stated that they may take a different view of situations where the number of points accumulated in a year exceeds 250,000 from a business relationship or business expenditure and the arrangement has no commercial purpose other than to allow the recipient to receive reward points.

DEDUCTIONS FOR CLUB MEMBERSHIP

Joining or annual fees for a program membership are only deductible for employers as a cost of employing a person or for self-employed persons provided it is directly related to their business activities (TD 1999/35).

Where the cost of other loyalty programs is paid or reimbursed by the member's employer (or an associate of that employer) the FBT rules apply and the employer will generally be liable for FBT on the value of that membership fee. However, the cost may be exempt from FBT if it is a 'minor benefit' (refer 25.000).

The cost of the membership will then be deductible to the employer as a cost of employing the person.

 TD 2003/20 discusses the timing of deductions for the provision of awards points from the perspective of the reward provider.

11.200 LUMP SUM PAYMENTS ON TERMINATION OF EMPLOYMENT

Some payments which are made as a result of termination of employment fall within the definition of an Employment Termination Payment (ETP). A specific tax regime applies to ETPs. However, not all lump sums paid on termination or cessation of employment are taxed as an ETP. Lump sum payments of accrued annual leave, annual leave loading or long service leave paid on ceasing employment are taxed under different rules.

If the employee is a current employee and receives a lump sum payment for annual leave, annual leave loading or long service leave, it is included in the employee's gross earnings and tax is withheld in accordance with PAYG withholding schedules.

 The relevant PAYG withholding schedules for employment termination payments is NAT 70980. For the withholding rates associated with unused leave payments on termination have reference to NAT 3351.

11.210 EMPLOYMENT TERMINATION PAYMENTS

An ETP is defined in s82-130 as a payment received by the taxpayer in consequence of the termination of his or her employment, or after another person's death, in consequence of the termination of that other person's employment.

ETPs include:

- amounts for unused rostered days off
- amounts in lieu of notice
- a gratuity or 'golden handshake'
- an employee's invalidity payment (for permanent disability, other than compensation for personal injury), and

- certain payments after the death of an employee (ie. death benefit employment termination payments – see below).

Certain types of payments are excluded by s82-135. These include the following:

- a payment for unused annual leave or unused long service leave, or
- the tax-free part of a genuine redundancy payment or an early retirement scheme payment.

An ETP is subject to concessional tax treatment. To be eligible for the concessional treatment, the payment will generally need to be received within 12 months of the termination of employment. It cannot be rolled over into a superannuation fund. The tax treatment is dependent upon whether the ETP is a 'life benefit ETP' or a 'death benefit ETP' (refer discussion below).

 An amount is an assessable ETP only if the payment is received 'in consequence of' the termination of the employment. The Federal Court has confirmed that the words 'in consequence of' require more than a temporal connection; they require some causal relationship (see Bond v Commissioner of Taxation (2015) FCA 245).

THE '12 MONTH RULE'

The payment must be received within 12 months of employment termination to qualify as an ETP. Payments received outside of the 12 month period will usually be taxed as ordinary income at marginal tax rates.

The Tax Office however may allow a payment received after this period to be treated as an ETP for tax purposes, if any of the following apply (s82-130(4)):

- the payment is a genuine redundancy payment
- the payment is an early retirement scheme payment
- the payment is made as a result of legal action being commenced within 12 months of the termination of employment, where the legal action concerned entitlement to the payment or the amount of the payment
- the payment is made by a liquidator, receiver or trustee in bankruptcy, who was appointed, within 12 months of employment termination, to a business or organisation that is liable to make the payment, or
- the Tax Office determines, in writing, that the timeframe is reasonable having regard to all relevant circumstances.

NOTE: An amount received in relation to a dispute concerning termination of employment is not an ETP, nor forms part of an ETP, where the amount is capable of being identified as relating specifically to the reimbursement of legal costs. Further, If the amount of a settlement or court award received is a lump sum where the component of the receipt that relates to legal costs has not been and cannot be determined, then the whole amount is treated as being received in consequence of termination of employment (see TR 2012/8).

LIFE BENEFIT EMPLOYMENT TERMINATION PAYMENTS

Any invalidity segment (refer 11.250) or pre-1 July 1983 amounts in a life benefit ETP will form part of the tax-free component.

The tax on any remaining balance (ie. the taxable component) will depend on the recipient taxpayer's age, as shown in the following table.

Life benefit employment termination payments			
Age		**Tax on taxable component 2014-15**	**Tax on taxable component 2015-16**
Under preservation age* on the last day of the income year in which the payment is made	Up to ETP cap amount	*Up to $185,000:* Taxed at a max. rate of 30% plus Medicare levy#	*Up to $195,000:* Taxed at a max. rate of 30% plus Medicare levy#
	Above ETP cap amount	*Amount over $185,000:* Taxed at the top marginal rate^ plus Medicare levy#	*Amount over $195,000:* Taxed at the top marginal rate^ plus Medicare levy#
Preservation age* or over on the last day of the income year in which the payment is made	Up to ETP cap amount	*Up to $185,000:* Taxed at a max. rate of 15% plus Medicare levy#	*Up to $195,000:* Taxed at a max. rate of 15% plus Medicare levy#
	Above ETP cap amount	*Amount over $185,000:* Taxed at the top marginal rate^ plus Medicare levy#	*Amount over $195,000:* Taxed at the top marginal rate^ plus Medicare levy#

* Preservation age is the age at which retirees can generally access their super benefits on retirement (see 19.700).

The Medicare levy is 2%.

^ The top marginal rate for 2014-15 and 2015-16 is 47%, which includes the 2% Temporary Budget Repair Levy.

Two different ETP caps can apply, namely:

- the ETP cap, and
- the whole-of-income cap – this is a non-indexed cap that applies to some ETPs and is applied together with the ETP cap

CONCESSIONAL CAP ON LIFE BENEFIT EMPLOYMENT TERMINATION PAYMENTS

The ETP cap on concessionally taxed ETPs is $195,000 in 2015-16 ($185,000 in 2014-15). The concessional cap is indexed annually in line with Average Weekly Ordinary Time Earnings (AWOTE) and will increase in increments of $5,000. The taxable components of all life benefit ETPs received in an income year are counted towards this cap.

As shown in the above table, the taxable components of any payments in excess of the cap are taxed at the top marginal rate plus the Medicare levy. This rate applies regardless of the age of the taxpayer.

Life benefit ETPs include:

- a 'golden handshake' payment
- amounts paid in lieu of notice
- unused sick leave
- compensation for wrongful dismissal, and
- genuine redundancy payments which exceed the tax-free threshold.

Payments must be made 'in consequence of' the employees termination of employment.

Items which are not ETPs include:

- superannuation benefits
- unused annual leave amounts
- unused long service leave amounts, and
- the tax-free part of a genuine redundancy payment.

 Concessional rates of taxation described above are subject to a whole-of-income cap. The cap removes the tax offset for an ETP if the ETP together with a taxpayer's other taxable income exceeds $180,000 for the income year.

WHOLE-OF-INCOME CAP

The whole-of-income cap is $180,000 for 2015-16 (the same amount applied for 2014-15). This cap is not indexed.

The cap applies to the following types of ETPs (referred to as 'non excluded payments'):

- payments that do not meet the genuine redundancy rules (gratuities)
- golden handshakes
- payments for rostered days off
- payments for unused sick leave, and
- gratuities.

Note that genuine redundancy payments made to those who have exceeded preservation age (eg. a person aged 65 or older) are not included in the whole-of-income cap.

INTERACTION BETWEEN WHOLE-OF-INCOME CAP AND ETP CAP

The whole-of-income cap is $180,000 less certain amounts of other taxable income earned during the relevant year. The taxable component of the ETP is taxed at either 17% or 32% (inclusive of the Medicare levy) up to the whole-of-income cap amount. ETP amounts in excess of the cap are taxed at the top marginal rate plus Medicare levy (47% for the 2014-15, 2015-16 and 2016-17 income year, which includes the Temporary Budget Repair Levy).

MEANING OF 'OTHER TAXABLE INCOME'

'Other taxable income' commonly includes, but is not limited to, the following:

- salary and wage income
- bank interest
- bonuses
- accrued leave paid upon termination, and
- other investment income.

It does not include the following:

- reportable fringe benefits
- salary sacrifice items
- superannuation guarantee
- reportable employer superannuation contributions, or
- reimbursement of work expenses.

The examples below illustrate the application of the whole-life-cap and its interaction with the ETP cap:

EXAMPLE 1: Whole-of-income cap

Jim is a 61 year old former engineer who retired from his job in December 2015. His taxable income from his wages in 2015-16 up to that point was $100,000. His employer paid him an ETP of $50,000 in the form of a gratuity.

Jim's ETP was a non-excluded ETP so the lesser of the two caps applied. His whole-of-income cap was reduced from $180,000 to $80,000 because Jim had earned $100,000 in that income year.

As Jim's calculated whole-of-income cap of $80 000 was less than his ETP cap of $180,000 (for 2015-16), the calculated whole-of-income cap was applied to his ETP. As his ETP ($50,000) is less than his calculated whole-of-income cap ($80,000), the entire ETP will be taxed at concessional (lower) tax rates. Jim has reached his preservation age so his employer will withhold tax at a rate of 17% from his ETP.

EXAMPLE 2: ETP cap

Ray is a 61 year old computer programmer who retired from his job on 1 July 2015. As he retired at the start of an income year he had not received any salary or wage income from his employer; however, his employer paid him a termination payment (that is, an ETP) of $50,000 in the form of a gratuity. Ray's ETP was a non-excluded ETP and the lesser of the two caps was applied. His whole-of-income cap remained at $180,000 because he had no other income.

As Ray's ETP cap ($180,000 for 2015-16) was less than his calculated whole-of-income cap, the ETP cap applied to his ETP. As his ETP ($50,000) was less than the ETP cap ($180,000 for 2015-16), his entire ETP was taxed at concessional (lower) tax rates.

Ray had reached his preservation age so his employer withheld tax at a rate of 17% from his ETP.

EXAMPLE 3: Whole-of-income cap

In August 2015, Sam is terminated from his job and receives a $100,000 gratuity and $20,000 for accrued leave. His employer also paid him $5,000 in salary for the period 1 July 2015 to date of termination.

When working out the tax on Sam's ETP of $100,000, his employer calculates his whole-of-income cap as $155,000, being $180,000 less $25,000 (salary plus accrued leave payment). The calculated whole-of-income cap is less than the ETP cap ($180,000 for 2015-16) and, as he has not reached his preservation age, his employer withholds 32% in tax from the $100,000 ETP, totalling $32,000.

Sam gets a new job in September 2015 and earns a further $60,000 salary in the 2015-16 income year. When calculating the tax on his ETP at the end of the financial year, his taxable income for the purposes of the whole-of-income cap is $85,000 calculated as the sum of:

- $5,000 salary from his first job
- $20,000 accrued leave payment, and
- $60,000 salary from his second job.

Therefore, Sam's calculated whole-of-income cap is $95,000, which means $5,000 of his $100,000 ETP will be taxed at 47%. This is because the whole-of-income cap is reduced by his other taxable income (that is, $180,000 – $85,000).

Sam will need to pay an additional 15% tax on the $5,000 (that is, 47% less 32% already withheld by his employer). This means he will have a tax debt of $750.

DEATH BENEFIT EMPLOYMENT TERMINATION PAYMENTS

The tax treatment of the taxable component of a death benefit ETP is dependent upon whether the payment is made to a 'death benefits dependant' and the amount paid. See below for the definition of a 'death benefits dependant'.

PAYMENT TO A 'DEATH BENEFITS DEPENDANT'

A 'death benefits dependant' (s302-195) includes:

- the deceased person's legal spouse (which may be of either gender and also includes a de facto partner) or former spouse
- the deceased person's child aged less than 18
- any other person with whom the deceased person had an interdependency relationship (as defined in s302-200) with just before he or she died, or
- any other person who was a dependant of the deceased person just before he or she died.

The taxable component of a death benefit ETP paid to a dependant that is within the recipient's cap on concessionally taxed ETPs is tax-free. The remainder of the taxable component (if any) will be taxed at the top marginal tax rate plus the Medicare levy.

An employer has no PAYG withholding obligation in respect of the death benefit ETP if the death benefit ETP is paid to the trustee of the deceased employee's estate.

Employers are not required to withhold PAYG on taxable components paid to dependants for a death benefit up to the ETP cap amount.

PAYMENT TO A NON-DEPENDANT

The taxable component of a death benefit ETP paid to a non-dependant that is within the recipient's cap on concessionally taxed ETPs is taxed at a maximum rate of 30% plus the Medicare levy. The remainder of the taxable component (if any) is taxed at the top marginal tax rate plus Medicare levy.

The table below sets out the tax treatment for death benefit ETPs.

Death benefit employment termination payments			
Recipient		**Tax on taxable component 2014-15**	**Tax on taxable component 2015-16**
Dependant	Up to ETP cap amount	Up to $185,000: Tax-free	Up to $195,000: Tax-free
	Above ETP cap amount	Over $185,000: Taxed at the top marginal rate^ plus Medicare levy#	Over $195,000: Taxed at the top marginal rate^ plus Medicare levy#
Non-dependant	Up to ETP cap amount	Up to $185,000: Taxed at a max. rate of 30% plus Medicare levy#	Up to $195,000: Taxed at a max. rate of 30% plus Medicare levy#
	Above ETP cap amount	Over $185,000: Taxed at the top marginal rate^ plus Medicare levy#	Over $195,000: Taxed at the top marginal rate^ plus Medicare levy#

\# The Medicare levy is 2%.
^ The top marginal rate for 2014-15 and 2015-16 is 47%, which includes the 2% Temporary Budget Repair Levy.

CONCESSIONAL CAP ON DEATH BENEFIT EMPLOYMENT TERMINATION PAYMENTS

The cap on death benefit ETPs is $195,000 in 2015-16 ($185,000 in 2014-15). The cap is indexed in line with AWOTE in increments of $5,000. The cap limits the amount of death benefit ETPs payable for the same employment termination that are concessionally taxed. The death benefit ETP cap operates independently from the life benefit ETP cap. That is, any death benefit ETPs an individual taxpayer receives do not count towards their life benefit ETP cap, and vice versa.

Michael's spouse dies and he receives a death benefit ETP from his spouse's employer. Michael resigns from his job and receives a life benefit ETP. The death benefit ETP cap and the life benefit ETP cap apply separately to each respective ETP.

Tax-free amounts are not counted towards the cap.

11.240 GENUINE REDUNDANCY AND EARLY RETIREMENT SCHEME PAYMENTS

Division 83 of ITAA97 contains the provisions relating to genuine redundancy and early retirement scheme payments made as a consequence of termination of employment.

Genuine redundancy and early retirement scheme payments are received tax-free up to an indexed threshold. These amounts:

- cannot be rolled over in to superannuation
- cannot be paid in lieu of superannuation benefits, and
- are not classified as ETPs.

The thresholds for the tax-free amount of a genuine redundancy payment and an early retirement scheme payment are:

Tax-free part of genuine redundancy payments and early retirement scheme payments		
Income year	**Base limit**	**For each complete year of service**
2015-16	$9,780	$4,891
2014-15	$9,514	$4,758

These amounts are currently indexed each year to movements in Average Weekly Ordinary Time Earnings (AWOTE). Any amount paid in excess of these thresholds is an ETP and is apportioned according to the pre-1 July 1983 segment (tax-free) and *the taxable component (taxed up to the top marginal rate plus the Medicare levy)*.

For PAYG withholding obligations of the employer in respect of these payments, see 5.400.

Thelma, aged 56, receives her first genuine redundancy payment of $60,000 in January 2015 after completing ten years of service. Therefore $57,094 ($9,514 plus [10 x $4,758]) is tax-free. The remaining $2,906 all relates to post-1 July 1983 employment days and is treated as an ETP.

NOTE: The application of the ETP caps would need to be considered in working out the amount of tax liability and extent of any ETP tax offset noting that genuine redundancy payments are excluded in working out the whole-of-life cap (see 11.210 above).

GENUINE REDUNDANCY PAYMENTS

To be eligible for concessional tax treatment, special conditions must be satisfied for genuine redundancy payments (s83-175):

- the payment must be due to the termination of employment or dismissal
- the termination of employment or dismissal must be caused by a genuine redundancy of the employee's position
- the payment must be in addition to any ETP the person could reasonably have expected to receive on voluntary resignation on that day
- the time of termination must take place before the earlier of age 65 and the earliest date that the employee's employment would have terminated (ie. by reaching a particular age, or completing a specified period of service)
- if the parties are not dealing with each other at arm's length, the payment must not exceed an arm's length amount, and
- there must be no arrangement at the time of termination for the employer or another person to re-employ that person.

The Commissioner considers each of these conditions in TR 2009/2.

Payments from a superannuation fund are not genuine redundancy payments.

GENUINE REDUNDANCY

Redundancy is where an employer no longer requires employees to carry out particular work. The employer must initiate the termination, and it must be the position that becomes redundant, not the employee. This occurs when:

- the employer decides the job of an employee is no longer to be done by anyone (replacement by another employee with similar skills indicates the employee's dismissal is not a genuine redundancy)
- the employer's decision is not due to general turnover of labour
- the employer's decision results in the termination of the employee's employment, and
- the termination is not due to an issue peculiar to the employee, including personal or disciplinary reasons.

In *Weeks v Commissioner of Taxation* [2013] FCAFC 2, the Full Federal Court upheld an earlier decision of the Federal Court, concluding that an executive's payout did not amount to a genuine redundancy payment under s83-175. The executive in this case worked for the Tax Office and was terminated under s29(3)(a) of the Public Service Act because she was deemed 'excess to requirements'. The Court found that being 'excess to requirements' under the Public Service Act was not the same as being genuinely redundant.

Generally, a genuine redundancy is evidenced by the dismissal of similarly classified employees.

Both voluntary and involuntary payments made to redundant and retrenched employees usually qualify, including:

- payments in lieu of notice
- severance payments based on period of service, and
- lump sum gratuitous payments.

Mandy started work for GE Security on 10 July 1994. Her employment contract stated that if she is dismissed or resigns for any reason she will be paid one month's severance pay of $5,000.

Mandy was dismissed on 30 June 2015 due to the loss of a major contract by her employer. There was no agreement to re-hire Mandy at a later time. Mandy was aged 50 when she received a redundancy payment of $12,000 including the amount of $5,000 stated in her employment contract. The severance pay of $5,000 is not a genuine redundancy payment because GE Security had a pre-existing obligation to make this payment. However, the payment does qualify as an ETP. This leaves $7,000 ($12,000 – $5,000), which may be treated as a tax-free genuine redundancy payment provided it does not exceed the relevant threshold.

The tax-free limit available to Mandy was $9,514 + $85,644 (18 years x $4,758) = $95,158. The entire amount of $7,000 is tax-free, as it is under this limit. The tax liable in respect of the ETP would need to be considered in light of the ETP and whole of life caps. Any amounts not exceeding the caps would be taxed at a rate of 32% (including Medicare levy)

In April 2015, Mary's employment is terminated and she is paid two weeks wages in lieu of notice immediately after her employer discovered that she had been taking stock for her own use.

The termination of employment did not occur because of the position becoming redundant. Therefore the payment is not a genuine redundancy payment. However, it is still an ETP and is split into the pre-1 July 1983 tax-free component and a post-30 June 1983 taxable component as required.

CONSTRUCTIVE DISMISSAL

The concept of dismissal includes 'constructive dismissal', which is where an employee has little choice but to resign. This may occur where replacement employment is offered in a position which is inconsistent with the employee's qualifications and experience or a reduction in pay.

In *Case 12/98,* 98 ATC 183, the employer (the Tax Office) merged five managerial positions into two and the taxpayer, who was not selected for one of the new positions, was given a position beneath his level of experience. The taxpayer subsequently retired as an 'excess officer' under the Tax Office's 'Voluntary Staff Separation Scheme'.

The Tax Office determined that the payment was not a genuine redundancy payment. However, the AAT held that, as the job previously held by the taxpayer was no longer done by anyone, this led to the ultimate termination and was 'constructive dismissal'.

However the AAT decided in *Long and Commissioner of Taxation* (2007) AATA 1269 that a payment was for genuine redundancy even though the payment was made to a person who could reasonably be expected to be involved in the decision to terminate employment. This was determined on the basis that the company provided services under contract to a third party. The contract was terminated and the business ceased to exist. It was considered reasonable that the person become redundant as a result of a third party action and that the payment made was in respect of redundancy.

DISMISSAL OF DIRECTOR/EMPLOYEE INDIVIDUALS

In TR 2009/2, the Commissioner considers the dismissal of employees who are also directors. Where an employee is also a director, it may be difficult to show the dismissal was without the employee's consent and that any amount received is limited to an arm's length amount. The Commissioner lists the following factors which suggest that the genuine redundancy conditions have been met on the termination of employment of a director/employee:

- the recipient of the payment did not agree with the decision of their co-directors
- there was a legal or economic compulsion that caused the genuine redundancy (eg. insolvency of the business), and
- other employees received similar payments.

EARLY RETIREMENT SCHEME PAYMENTS

To be eligible for concessional tax treatment, an early retirement scheme must satisfy the following conditions (s83-180):

- the scheme must be offered to all employees in a class approved by the Tax Office

- the scheme must be due to rationalisation or re-organisation of the employer's operations. Acceptable objectives of a qualifying scheme include:
  - replacement of employees with particular skills with those of different skills
  - replacement of employees who have reached a particular age or particular ages (at least 55), with younger employees
  - cessation or reduction in output of whole or part of the employer's operations
  - introduction of new technology, processes or systems or productivity increases, or
  - any other change approved by the Tax Office
- the Tax Office must approve the scheme prior to its implementation, or exercise its discretion to overlook the scheme's non-compliance with any of the conditions if special circumstances exist (eg. the employer did not realise that the income tax treatment of payments made under the scheme could be affected)
- the payment must be in addition to any ETP the person could reasonably have expected to receive on voluntary resignation on that day
- the time of retirement must take place before the earlier of age 65 and the earliest date that the employee's employment would have terminated (ie. by reaching a particular age, or completing a specified period of service)
- if the parties are not dealing with each other at arm's length, the payment must not exceed an arm's length amount, and
- there must be no arrangement at the time of retirement for the employer or another party to re-employ that person.

In March 2015, an employee received an early retirement scheme payment of $80,000, but would have received $15,000 had retirement been voluntary. The employer arranged for the employee to be employed later by an unrelated firm.

The $65,000 surplus over the $15,000 will not be an early retirement scheme payment on the basis that the employer had made an arrangement for the person to be employed by another firm. It will be taxed as an ETP and apportioned according to the taxpayer's employment days. If the taxpayer's employment started after 30 June 1983, the entire amount is a taxable component.

11.250 INVALIDITY PAYMENTS

An invalidity payment is the notional future service component of an amount paid on termination of employment. It is the part of the ETP paid in respect of the period between the time of actual retirement and the time the person would normally have retired to the extent that it is paid as a consequence of permanent invalidity. That part of the ETP that forms the 'invalidity segment' is tax-free.

The payment must be made as a result of the termination of employment due to the disability of the employee.

For the future service component to be classified as an invalidity payment, the recipient's disability must be verified by two legally qualified medical practitioners as being likely to result in the taxpayer being unable to ever be employed in a capacity in keeping with their education, training or experience. Disability can be physical or mental and it is not limited to total incapacity but covers incapacity for that employment.

The termination of employment must have happened before the 'last retirement date' (ie. the date the taxpayer's employment would have normally ended). The taxpayer's 65th birthday (for both men and women) is the 'last retirement date' under the terms of employment or an award, if no other date can be determined.

The invalidity component of an ETP is tax-free, and cannot be rolled over into superannuation.

CALCULATION

To calculate the invalidity component, the following formula should be used:

$$(A \times B) \text{ divided by } C$$

where:

- A is the amount of the employment termination payment
- B is the number of whole days from the actual termination date to normal last retirement date, and
- C is the number of employment days in the employment termination payment, plus the number of days in B.

Jane started work on 1 January 1987 and has an earliest normal retirement date of 1 January 2015, but due to a disability, retires on 1 January 2014.

If the taxpayer receives an employment termination payment of $100,000, the invalidity component is:

A: Amount of employment termination payment $100,000

B: No. of days from termination to normal retirement date

(2 January 2014 to 1 January 2015) .... 365 days

C: No. of employment days + B (1 January 1987 to 1 January 2015) .... 10,227 days

Invalidity segment of the employment termination payment:

(A x B) divided by C = ($100,000 x 365) divided by 10,227 = $3,569

This $3,569 is tax-free. The remaining $96,431 of the ETP is apportioned between the pre-1 July 1983 segment (also tax-free) and the taxable component. In this case there is no pre-1 July 1983 component.

11.255 EMPLOYMENT DAYS

'Employment days' is the total number of days of employment to which the ETP relates (s82-150(2)).

For seasonal workers who receive an ETP, the 'employment days' is usually the period of that season's work. For casual or part-time workers, the 'employment days' is the number of days in the period of employment to which the payment relates, not the number of days actually worked.

A taxpayer was employed for 20 hours a week for 28 years. Her 'employment days' is 28 years, regardless of whether the 20 hours is worked over five days or a lesser number of days each week.

An employee started work with her employer on 1 July 1990 and took unpaid sick leave from 1 July 2001 to 31 December 2001. She then worked 20 hours a week until she left her employment on 30 June 2014.

Her 'employment days' for employer payment purposes is:

1 July 1990 to 30 June 2001 .... 4,017 days

1 January 2001 to 30 June 2014 .... 4,929 days

Aggregate 'employment days' .... 8,946 days

NOTE: This illustrates the exclusion of unpaid sick leave from the 'employment days' calculation.

11.260 UNUSED ANNUAL LEAVE

Division 83 of the ITAA97 contains provisions relating to the tax treatment of payments for unused annual leave on termination of employment.

Lump sum payments of annual leave (AL) and annual leave loading (ALL) received on termination of employment are assessable income (s83-10 ITAA97) and are taxed in the following way (also see 11.210 for PAYG withholding requirements):

ORDINARY TERMINATION OF EMPLOYMENT

- **Leave accrued before 18 August 1993:** The amount is assessable income but the tax payable is limited (by rebate) to a maximum of 30% plus the Medicare levy. A tax offset (rebate) reduces any additional tax payable. The amount should be shown at Label A on the former employee's PAYG payment summary.

- **Leave accrued after 17 August 1993:** The amount is taxed as ordinary income at the taxpayer's marginal rate of tax (up to the top marginal rate plus Medicare levy – 49% for the 2014-15 to 2015-17 income years).The amount should be shown in gross payments on the PAYG payment summary.

REDUNDANCY, EARLY RETIREMENT OR INVALIDITY

When employment terminates due to a genuine redundancy, invalidity or early retirement scheme, the whole amount of the relevant payment (including the amount received in respect of AL and ALL) is assessable income, but the tax (and PAYG withholding) is limited to a maximum of 30% plus the Medicare levy. It is included in lump sum payments at Label A on the former employee's PAYG payment summary.

DEATH

A lump sum received by the trustee of the estate of a deceased person for accrued annual leave and annual leave loading is exempt from tax (s101A(2) of ITAA36). Such payments are not to be shown on the PAYG payment summary of any deceased payees.

11.270 UNUSED LONG SERVICE LEAVE

Long Service Leave (LSL) is calculated as if the leave was taken on a last-in-first-out basis. The payment is assessable income (s83-80 ITAA97) and is also subject to PAYG withholding.

Long service leave taken after 15 August 1978 is first deducted from the entitlement accrued after 15 August 1978. It is only deducted from the pre-15 August 1978 entitlement once the post-15 August 1978 entitlement has been extinguished. The effect is that the unused pre-15 August 1978 entitlement is used last.

Lump sum payments of LSL received on termination of employment are assessable income and are taxed in the following way (also see 11.210 for PAYG withholding requirements):

ORDINARY TERMINATION OF EMPLOYMENT

Lump sum payments of LSL are split into three components and each is taxed differently.

- **Amount referable to service before 16 August 1978:** 5% is assessable as ordinary income (ie. PAYG withholding is deducted at marginal tax rates – up to 45% plus Medicare levy). The amount should be shown at Label B on the former employee's PAYG payment summary.
- **Amount referable to service between 16 August 1978 and 17 August 1993:** The entire amount is assessable as ordinary income, but tax (and PAYG withholding) is limited to 30% plus the Medicare levy. The amount should be shown at Label A on the former employee's PAYG payment summary.
- **Amount referable to service on or after 18 August 1993:** All of this amount is assessable as ordinary income (ie. PAYG withholding is deducted at marginal tax rates – up to the top marginal rate plus Medicare levy- 49% for the 2014-15 to 2016-17 income years). The amount should be included in the former employee's gross payments on the PAYG payment summary.

 Long service leave entitlement legislation usually does not allow any leave to be taken until a certain length of service has been reached. Voluntary payments (ie. those not paid under an industrial award or employment contract) are not LSL for the purposes of the governing law. If an employer is not required to pay LSL but does so, that payment is taxed as an ETP.

CALCULATING LSL COMPONENTS

STEP 1: POST-15 AUGUST 1978 (AND POST-17 AUGUST 1993) AMOUNT

Unused long service attributable to service from 16 August 1978 (and 17 August 1993) is calculated:
$$(A \text{ divided by } B) \times \{ \ ([C \ (B + D)] \text{ divided by } E) - F \}$$
(ignore fraction from the product of this part of formula)

Where:
- A is the lump sum of unused LSL
- B is the number of whole days relating to the lump sum
- C is the number of employment days that occurred after 15 August 1978
- D is the number of whole days of LSL used before retirement
- E is the total number of employment days
- F is the lesser of:
  - the number of days of long service leave used after 15 August 1978, and
  - the product of: [C (B + D) divided by E] and [C^1 (B + D) divided by E] where C^1 is the number of employment days that occurred after 17 August 1993.

NOTE: A nil or negative answer means the post-15 August 1978 component of the lump sum is nil, ie. all the payment is treated as a pre-16 August 1978 component.

STEP 2: PRE-16 AUGUST 1978 AMOUNT

Unused long service attributable to service before 16 August 1978 is calculated as follows:

The lump sum less the post-15 August 1978 component

STEP 3: POST-17 AUGUST 1993 AMOUNT

Unused long service attributable to service from 17 August 1993 is calculated as follows:

(A divided by B) x { ([C^1 (B + D)] divided by E) – F^1}

where:

- C^1 is the number of employment days that occurred after 17 August 1993 (**NOTE:** C = 5,481 days + C^1), and
- F^1 is the number of days of long service leave used after 17 August 1993.

STEP 4: 16 AUGUST 1978 TO 17 AUGUST 1993 AMOUNT

Unused long service attributable to service from 16 August 1978 to 17 August 1993 is calculated as follows:

Post-15 August 1978 amount less post-17 August 1993 amount

An employee started employment before 16 August 1978 and the following apply on his retirement:

A = Lump sum LSL $25,000
B = Days of unused LSL 175
C = Days from 16 August 1978 to retirement date 10,206
C^1 = Days after 17 August 1993 4,725
D = Days of leave used before retirement 8
E = Total period of service (in days) 10,732
F = Days of LSL used after 15 August 1978 (includes five days used after 17/8/93) 8
F^1 = Days of LSL used after 17 August 1993 5

Step 1: Calculate post-15 August 1978 LSL component

(A divided by B) x { ([C (B + D)] divided by E) – F}

= ($25,000 divided by 175) x { ([10,206 (175 + 8)] divided by 10,732) – 8}

= $142.86 x (174.03 – 8)

= $142.86 x 166 (rounded down to whole number)

Total post-15 August 1978 component = $23,715

Step 2: Calculate pre-16 August 1978 LSL component

$25,000 – $23,715 = $1,285

Step 3: Calculate post-17 August 1993 LSL component

(A divided by B) x { ([C^1 (B + D)] divided by E) – F^1}

= ($25,000 divided by 175) x { ([4,725 (175 + 8)] divided by 10,732) – 5}

= $142.86 x (80 – 5)

= $142.86 x 75 (rounded down to whole number)

Total post-17 August 1993 component = $10,715

Step 4: Calculate 16 August 1978 to 17 August 1993 LSL component

Post-15 August 1978 amount less post-17 August 1993 amount:
$23,715 – $10,715 = $13,000

Summary of assessable income and tax payable:

- *Pre-16 August 1978 LSL component: 5% x $1,285 x taxpayer's marginal rate (ie. up to 47% plus Medicare levy)*
- *16 August 1978 to 17 August 1993 LSL component: $13,000 x (30% plus Medicare levy) (maximum tax payable)*
- *Post-17 August 1993 LSL component: $10,715 x taxpayer's marginal rate plus Medicare levy*

Include in payment summary:
$13,000 at label A; $1,285 at Label B; $10,715 in gross payments.

For PAYG withholding consequences see from 11.200.

TERMINATION DUE TO GENUINE REDUNDANCY, EARLY RETIREMENT SCHEME OR INVALIDITY

If lump sum LSL is paid to a taxpayer in relation to a genuine redundancy, invalidity, or an early retirement scheme there is no need to calculate the post-17 August 1993 component, as tax on all the post-15 August 1978 component is limited to a maximum of 30% plus the Medicare levy.

From the previous example, the employee's payment summary must show at:
- **Label A:** *post-15 August 1978, amount of $23,715, and*
- **Label B:** *pre-16 August 1978 amount of $1,285.*

DEATH

Lump sums received by the trustee of the estate of a deceased person for long service leave (as well as annual leave and loading) are exempt from tax (s101A(2) ITAA36). Such payments are not shown on the PAYG payment summary of the deceased payee.

11.300 INVESTMENT INCOME

Investment income can be derived from a variety of sources including interest, rent, royalties, dividends, sale of leased cars, traditional securities, lease incentives, short-term life insurance policies etc. This list is not exhaustive. These types of income are generally referred to as income from property.

NOTE: Chapter 17 provides more detail with regard to investment income and outlines the tax issues relating to some specific investment activities.

As a general rule, the sale of investments including shares and other financial instruments (which are held for long-term gain in value and not for short-term profits) are transactions of a capital nature and the capital gains tax rules may apply (see from 12.000). However, the income derived from those investments during the period of ownership is usually income under ordinary concepts. If the income is not ordinary income, it may be statutory income under certain provisions (eg. certain distributions or receipts in respect of equity interests in companies are deemed to be dividend income even if the amounts are not dividends for legal or commercial purposes). In some instances, there are special rules for calculating the amount of assessable income that must be declared and the amount of any deductions that may be claimed.

For guidance on deciding if an amount received should be treated as capital or revenue in nature refer to 17.100.

RIGHTS ISSUES ON SHARES

The issue to shareholders of rights to buy or sell additional shares has been considered, in some situations, to be assessable income when not otherwise assessable as a dividend (*C of T v McNeil* [2007] HCA 5). The law was amended subsequent to this decision to ensure that call options issued by companies to investor shareholders to raise capital are instead dealt with under the CGT provisions. See 12.800, 12.820 and 12.830.

Note that special rules apply to rights or options issued under an employee option plan (see 12.816).

11.400 INTEREST

An Australian resident is taxed on interest income earned from sources both within Australia and outside of Australia. For income earned outside of Australia, a foreign income tax offset is generally allowed for any foreign tax paid (see from 22.400).

As a general rule, income from interest is treated as income from property unless the taxpayer's principal business consists of the lending of money (eg. financial institutions, banks and mortgage houses) or it is derived in respect of a business debt. In each of those cases the interest income is treated as business income.

For a discussion relating to international aspects of the taxation of interest refer to 22.110.

Interest is usually derived on a cash receipts basis (ie. when it is received). Derivation includes when *it is applied or dealt with in any way on the taxpayer's behalf* (for example, where the funds are directed to somebody else). This is known as constructive receipt.

INTEREST FROM EARLY OR OVERPAYMENT OF TAX DEBTS

The Tax Office is required to pay interest (at the applicable 13 Week Treasury Note rate) for any early payment or overpayment of tax. This is to be included as assessable income.

LOANS TO FRIENDS AND RELATED PARTIES

Interest earned on any loan is assessable, even if it is unusual for the taxpayer to lend money. A taxpayer should be careful however, if money is lent at interest rates that are not commensurate with the prevailing commercial rate of interest at that time, this may infer an income shifting motive, especially where a corresponding deduction is claimed by the related party member and a difference exists between the rates of tax the interest income and expense are subject to respectively. The use to which the funds are put will be important in determining if the deduction will be allowable.

 The loan if made by a company may be subject to the provisions of Division 7A ITAA36.

CHILDREN'S BANK ACCOUNTS

For children under the age of 18 years as at 30 June of the relevant income year, there are special taxing rules that apply to any interest they earn on investments (as well as other investment income). Essentially, the income may be subject to higher tax rates to discourage adults from streaming income that would otherwise be derived by the adult to a child who is in a lower marginal tax bracket.

Before the punitive tax regime is applied to the income, it is necessary to establish the ownership of the income in order to determine whether it will be taxed under general marginal tax rates or whether the prescribed higher tax rates will apply (see from 3.040 and 3.045). The Tax Office will look at the following criteria to determine if the interest belongs to the child or to the parent (or other adult):

- if the parent(s) provided the money and can spend it as they like, the interest income will normally be taxed to the parent(s)
- if the account contains a large sum of money, the interest income will normally be taxed to the parent(s) unless the source of the funds is an exempt source
- if the account is comprised of money from presents, pocket money or casual work performed by the child, the interest income will generally be taxed to the child, and

- if the account is comprised of income from investments made from assets that were transferred to the minor from the following sources then the interest income will be taxed to the child
  - from a public fund for the relief of poverty
  - from winnings in an authorised lottery
  - received directly or indirectly through a trust from investing a Court awarded (or 'out of court') settlement or compensation
  - superannuation proceeds, or
  - child support proceeds paid to a trust to facilitate the support of the child following a family breakdown.

Where interest income is taxed to the child, it will be taxed at the rates set out in Chapter 3 (see 3.020).

Ordinary marginal rates of tax however will apply to certain types of investment income, including income derived from:

- property from a deceased person's estate, or
- property transferred to the child as a result of the death of another person or family breakdown, or income in the form of damages for an injury they suffer.

NOTE: Net capital gains from the disposal of the above items of property or investments are also subject to ordinary marginal rates of tax.

Where income from active pursuits is earned, such as salary or wage income, income from running a business or partnership distributions where the child was an active partner, these amounts will also be subject to ordinary marginal tax rates and the low income tax offset. Such income is known as 'excepted income'. Furthermore, a child that qualifies as an 'excepted person' is taxed at ordinary marginal rates in respect of all of their income, including investment income (ie. the special provisions do not apply). There are a number of categories of excepted persons, including children who work full-time and children on particular disability pensions.

 The low income tax offset is available to reduce a minor's tax payable only on excepted income, such as salary and wage, compensation and inheritance income. It is not available to offset tax payable on other types of income derived by a minor, including interest, dividends, rent and trust distributions.

MORTGAGE OR INTEREST OFFSET ARRANGEMENTS

Interest offset accounts allow borrowers to apply savings towards an effective reduction of their home mortgage or other debts rather than derive interest income.

As a general rule, the savings and borrowing accounts are linked and deposits and withdrawals can be made in the normal manner. However, the deposit account does not earn interest. Instead, a reduction in the interest payable on the borrowed funds applies. These types of accounts are acceptable to the Tax Office (see TR 93/6) and will not be treated as structures with a tax minimisation purpose with which the Tax Office is concerned.

INTEREST ON COMPENSATION AND DAMAGES

Pre-judgment interest on damages for personal injury is not assessable. Post-judgment interest is assessable.

A judgment is finalised when the final judgment takes effect. The final judgment takes effect after any appeals (or after the appeal period expires if there are no appeals) or when any appeal is settled or discontinued.

In non-personal injury cases, interest is assessable provided there is an identifiable amount on which the interest is paid. If the amount paid is an undissected amount which comprises both capital and income components then any interest is treated as amounts of capital and not as interest of an income nature.

DISCOUNTED OR DEFERRED INTEREST SECURITIES

The yield on discounted and deferred interest securities is generally taxed on an accrual basis (Div 16E ITAA36).

NOTE: Division 230 ITAA97 will provide the tax treatment for most of the gains and losses on discounted and deferred interest securities that are acquired or issued on or after 1 July 2010, or 1 July 2009 should the taxpayer so elect, that would otherwise have been taxed under Division 16E (refer TOFA 3 and 4). Refer 17.550.

 A common security that this rule may apply to is a term deposits with a maturity in excess of 12 months, where interest accrues for a period greater than 12 months. The interest earned would be returned as income on an accrual basis over the period. The application of these rules will depend on the terms as stated in the documentation of the security in question.

11.500 RENTAL INCOME

Rental income is generally assessable as ordinary income on a receipts basis. It is normally treated as income from property unless the taxpayer is carrying on a business of renting properties (where the taxpayer had multiple properties which were managed by the taxpayer). The rules for rental properties are set out from 18.000.

The location of the property normally determines the source of rental income. It should be noted that amounts received by a landlord, or former landlord, for a tenant failing to comply with a lease obligation to repair premises are assessable income where the tenant used the premises for producing assessable income (s15-25).

Rental bond money is included as assessable income once a taxpayer is entitled to retain it (eg. a tenant defaulted on the rent).

11.600 ROYALTY INCOME

Income from royalties arises from arrangements conferring a right to use property, including fees received in relation to the licensing of copyright, patents or intellectual property. There is also an extended definition of royalties for income tax purposes in s6(1) ITAA36 that broadens the scope of assessable payments beyond that reached by the ordinary meaning of 'royalty'.

A royalty is generally assessable as either ordinary income or statutory income. A royalty is included in ordinary income and is assessable under s6-5. To the extent that a receipt is not assessable under its ordinary meaning it will be assessable under s15-20.

The ordinary meaning of royalties encompasses two categories:

- payments by licence to the owners of patents and copyrights, and
- payments to landowners for the taking of some special thing forming part of or attached to the land, such as minerals by miners or timber.

The extended definition (s6(1) ITAA36) includes any amount paid for:

- the use of, or the right to use, any copyright, patent, design or model, plan, secret formula or process, trademark, or other like property or right
- the use of, or the right to use, any industrial, commercial or other equipment
- the supply of scientific, technical, industrial, or commercial knowledge or information
- the supply of any assistance that is ancillary and subsidiary to, and is furnished as a means of enabling that application or enjoyment of, any such property or right mentioned in the previous items
- the use of, or the right to use motion picture films, television films or video tapes or tapes for use in connection with radio broadcasting, or
- the total or partial forbearance of any of the above items.

If a royalty payment is not assessable as income then it may be subject to tax under the CGT rules (see from 12.000). Royalties are generally assessable only when they are actually received (or constructively received).

In IT 2660, the Tax Office sets out its view of what types of payments fall under the definition of royalty. As a general rule, payments for services are not royalties unless those services are ancillary to, or are part of enabling relevant technology, information, know-how, copyright, machinery or equipment to be transferred or used. According to the Tax Office a contract for services is likely to involve a much greater level of expenditure. Where both elements are present under the same contract then an apportionment of both income and expenses relating to royalties and to services will be required.

Where there is an outright sale of rights (as distinct from the granting of a licence to use property) for a fixed sum then as a general rule the transaction will be treated as a capital payment rather than income.

In TR 93/12 the Tax Office considers the taxation of royalties in relation to computer software. The following payments are considered to be royalties:

- the granting of a licence to reproduce or modify a computer program in a manner that would infringe copyright if such a licence was not available (including the right to manufacture copies from a master and the right to modify or adapt a program), and
- the supply of know-how (eg. the supply of source code or algorithms).

The following payments would not be considered to be royalties for income tax purposes:

- payments for the transfer of all rights relating to copyright
- payments for the granting of a licence which allows simple use of the software
- payments for the provision of services in the modification or creation of the software, and
- the proceeds from a sale of goods (eg. the unbundled sale of hardware and software).

The payment from a taxpayer to a company for the surrender of data licensing rights is typically not a 'royalty' under ss6(1) ITAA36 (see ATO ID 2007/4).

Foreign sourced royalties derived by Australian tax residents are subject to Australian income tax. Generally, the royalty income would be subject to withholding tax in the foreign country. The taxpayer would generally be eligible for a foreign income tax offset (see 22.400) in respect of foreign taxes paid on the royalty income against the Australian tax liability that arises in respect of the same income. Australian sourced royalties derived by non-residents are subject to Australian withholding tax (refer 22.140).

 If the relevant country has a double tax treaty with Australia, check the treaty definition of the term 'royalties'. It may differ from the domestic law meaning in s6 ITAA36.

11.700 DIVIDENDS

As a general rule, an Australian resident shareholder is assessed on dividends received plus any franking credits attached to those dividends. The shareholder is assessed on the 'grossed-up' income and then allowed a 'franking tax offset' in respect of the corporate tax paid by the company on the profits from which those dividends are paid (see from 6.800). This system is referred to as the dividend imputation system.

Under the Australian dividend imputation system, shareholders who receive franked dividends (including franked distributions received indirectly through trusts or partnerships) are entitled to a franking credit based on the franked amount of the dividend they received. That credit represents the tax that has previously been paid by the company on the profits underlying the dividend.

Excess franking tax offsets are refundable to certain taxpayers (ie. individuals, superannuation funds). Taxpayers who are not required to lodge an income tax return (such as eligible endorsed income tax exempt entities) can obtain a refund of imputation credits by completing a Refund of Imputation Credits claim form from the Tax Office. For a company, excess franking credits are not refundable but may be converted into an equivalent tax loss and carried forward to use in a subsequent income year.

 For an illustration of how the franking credit will increase a taxable loss see 6.440.

NOTE: Australian sourced dividend income derived by non-residents are subject to non-resident dividend withholding tax on the unfranked portion of the dividend (refer 22.140).

NOTE: Where an Australian resident derives foreign sourced dividend income, the other country may impose withholding tax on the amount. The gross dividend (comprising the amount received net of withholding tax plus the tax withheld) is assessable income. The taxpayer may be able to claim a foreign income tax offset (see 22.400) in respect of the foreign tax paid.

IMPORTANT! In Taxation Ruling TR 2014/5, the Commissioner outlines the taxation effect of private companies paying money or transferring property in compliance with a Family Court order under the *Family Law Act*. Where the order requires a private company, or a party to the matrimonial proceedings to cause the private company, to pay money or transfer property to a shareholder of the private company, the payment or transfer is an ordinary dividend to the extent that it is paid out of the company's profits. The dividend is assessable to the shareholder. The ruling also considers the franking, Division 7A and CGT roll-over implications.

11.710   FRANKING A DIVIDEND

The imputation system is designed so that the ultimate individual shareholders of companies that receive dividends (including where dividends are passed through partnerships to partners or through trusts to beneficiaries) will receive a credit for the tax already paid by the company on the profits from which the dividend was paid. The result is that the pre-tax profits of the company is ultimately taxed at the shareholders' marginal tax rate. Franking credits (or imputation credits), representing the corporate tax paid, are of a non-cash nature and are attached to the 'franked dividends' paid to the company's shareholders. A franking tax offset is allowed to the shareholder based on the amount of franking credits included in their assessable income.

See 6.800 for an explanation of the dividend imputation system.

UNFRANKED DIVIDENDS

Unfranked dividends are dividends with no franking credits attached. Shareholders in receipt of unfranked dividends only include the actual amount of the dividend received as assessable income. As no franked credits are attached, there is no requirement to 'gross-up' the dividend.

11.720   SHAREHOLDERS RECEIVING DIVIDENDS

As a general rule, a shareholder receiving a fully franked (or partly franked) dividend can claim a franking tax offset for the tax already paid by the company on the profits attaching to the dividend.

The shareholder is entitled to a franking tax offset up to the amount of the franking credit included in their assessable income. The tax offset is equal to 30% of the total of the franked amount and the imputation credit. The tax offset reduces the shareholder's tax payable on those dividends. Where the taxpayer's marginal rate of tax is below the corporate tax rate, the excess credit can be used to reduce the tax payable on the taxable income from other sources. Any unused franking credits are refundable for individuals (and other qualifying taxpayers).

 A company earned the following amount of taxable income and after tax profit:

Taxable income	*$15,000*
Income tax paid (30% by company)	*$4,500*
After tax profit	*$10,500*

The company tax paid resulted in the following entry in the franking account:

Franking credit	*$4,500*

An individual shareholder of the company receives a fully franked dividend. The following table sets out the primary tax payable to shareholders on the dividend income at various tax rates (the example utilises the 2014-15 marginal tax rates to show the impact of the dividend at different marginal rates and ignores the Medicare levy).

Note: The top marginal tax rate is 47% due to imposition of the Temporary Budget Repair Levy.

Marginal rate	47%	37%	32.5%	19%	0%
Dividend received (cash component)	$10,500	$10,500	$10,500	$10,500	$10,500
Add: Franking credit	$4,500	$4,500	$4,500	$4,500	$4,500
Assessable income	$15,000	$15,000	$15,000	$15,000	$15,000
Personal primary tax assessed (Rate x assessable income)	$7,050	$5,550	$4,875	$2,850	0
Less: franking tax offset	($4,500)	($4,500)	($4,500)	($4,500)	($4,500)
Tax payable	$2,550	$1,050	$375	Nil	Nil
Excess credit refundable	Nil	Nil	Nil	$1,650	$4,500

If a franked dividend is paid to a trust or partnership, the franking credit is 'grossed-up' and included in the trust or partnership's income. Each beneficiary or partner is typically entitled to utilise those credits based on their share of the net income subject to satisfying the holding period rule (see 11.745 for discussion). For discretionary trusts, satisfying the holding period rule may entail the trust making a family trust election (see 7.200). Further, special rules apply in relation to ensuring the franked dividends can be streamed to beneficiaries (see 11.730 and 7.700).

Where a company is in receipt of franked dividends, the franking credit is included in the recipient company's assessable income and a franking credit tax offset is allowed (subject to the holding period rule). The franking credit is then credited to the recipient company's franking account, available to be attached to the recipient company's own frankable distributions.

Note that franking tax offsets can sometimes be denied or limited because the entitlement to franking tax offsets or a refund of franking credits is subject to:

- the 'qualified person' requirement (franking credit trading rules) (see from 11.740)
- anti -avoidance rules (see from 6.900), and
- anti-streaming rules (see from 6.800).

If shareholders do not qualify for a franking tax offset, they do not 'gross-up' (include the imputation credit in assessable income) and are not entitled to a franking tax offset. Shareholders must satisfy the 'holding period rule' to qualify for the franking tax offset. (see 11.745) An individual taxpayer is exempt from the holding period rule if they satisfy 'small shareholder exemption' (see 11.750). Superannuation funds may also be entitled to certain concessions in respect of the holding period rule.

INDIVIDUAL, PARTNERSHIP AND TRUST SHAREHOLDERS

INDIVIDUAL SHAREHOLDERS

When franked dividends are paid to an individual, a partnership or the trustee of a trust estate, the dividend is 'grossed up' by the franking credit and the total is included in assessable income.

A company paid $640 fully franked and $200 unfranked dividends to a single individual shareholder.

The shareholder's assessable dividend would be as follows:

Franked dividend	$640
Franking credit $640 x 30/70	$274
Unfranked dividend	$200
Assessable income	**$1,114**

PARTNERSHIP SHAREHOLDERS

For partnerships, proportionate imputation credits flow through to each partner in receipt of a taxable distribution from the partnership. The imputation credits flowed through to the partners are proportional to the amount of franked dividends that are included in their taxable distribution pursuant to the relevant partnership agreement.

A resident partner is then entitled to a tax offset equal to their share of the franking credit. This credit must be in exact proportion to the recipient's share of the total franked dividends included in net income.

Special rules apply to franked dividends received from pooled development funds.

 A partnership received a fully franked dividend of $2,100 with franking credit of $900.

Two partners in the partnership are entitled to receive 40% and 60% of the partnership's net profits respectively.

On distribution of partnership income, the tax implications (ignoring Medicare levy and assuming the partners are in the top marginal tax rate) of the receipt of dividend income to each partner is as follows:

	Partner 1 (60%)	Partner 2 (40%)
Dividend received	$1,260	$840
Add: Franking credit	$540	$360
Assessable income	$1,800	$1,200
Basic tax payable (47% x assessable income)	$846	$564
Less: franking tax offset	($540)	($360)
Additional tax payable by each partner on assessment	$306	$204

CORPORATE SHAREHOLDERS

When franked dividends are paid to a company, the dividend is 'grossed up' by the franking credit and the total is included in assessable income of the recipient company (see from 6.800). The company is entitled to a franking tax offset. This effectively results in no additional tax being payable on fully franked shares paid to Australian resident companies as the recipient company's tax rate of 30% is the same rate of tax that is imputed into the franked dividend. In other words, although the grossed up dividend is included in assessable income, the additional tax paid on that grossed-up amount is reduced by the company's franking credit entitlement in respect of that dividend. Therefore, no additional tax is payable. Further, the franking credits attached to dividends received are also credited to the recipient company's franking account to be attached to dividends paid to the recipient company's shareholders (see 6.800).

SUPERANNUATION FUND SHAREHOLDERS

Complying superannuation funds, Approved Deposit Funds (ADFs) and Pooled Superannuation Trusts (PSTs) are entitled to a franking tax offset in respect of franked dividends. The offset applies even where the entity is partly or fully exempt from income tax on that income (as would typically be the case after the fund had commenced to pay a pension to a member). See 19.000.

REFUNDABLE FRANKING CREDITS

Where the relevant shareholder is a resident individual and has franking credits for the income year which exceed their total tax payable, a refund may be available for the excess.

An individual would typically be entitled to a refund of excess franking credits if:

- franked dividends are received either directly or through a trust or partnership, and
- the individual's basic tax liability is less than their franking credits after taking into account any other tax offsets they are entitled to.

Individuals who are not liable to lodge an income tax return or whose tax liability is less than the amount of the tax offset available are generally entitled to a refund of those franking credits. A special form is available for taxpayers not required to complete a tax return so that they may claim a refund (see 11.700).

Other taxpayers eligible for the refund are resident:

- trustees liable to be assessed
- superannuation funds

- approved deposit funds
- life assurance companies (in respect of their superannuation business)
- registered organisations (in respect of their superannuation business)
- pooled superannuation trusts, and
- certain registered charitable and gift deductible organisations.

NON-RESIDENT SHAREHOLDERS

Non-resident shareholders who receive franked dividends cannot utilise franking credits and cannot claim any refund in relation to franking credits associated with a franked dividend. That is, franking credits are 'wasted' in the hands of the non-resident. However, a franked dividend that is paid to a non-resident shareholder is generally exempt from non-resident withholding tax (under the PAYG withholding system) and is not subject to any other Australian income tax. The unfranked part of a dividend are generally subject to non-resident withholding tax at 30%. The rate may be lower if a double tax agreement applies – see from 22.200.

11.730 FRANKED DISTRIBUTIONS FROM TRUSTS

As a general rule, the income distributed by a trustee of a trust to a beneficiary retains the character it had when it was derived by the trustee.

Where the trustee is in receipt of a franked distribution, the franking credits are included as part of the trust's net income.

Resident beneficiaries who are presently entitled to a share of a trust's net income also include in their assessable income their share of the franking credits attached to that income, to the extent that the present entitlement includes a present entitlement to franked dividends (pursuant to the trust deed and/or the relevant distribution minutes).

They are also entitled (subject to the qualification expressed below) to the corresponding franking tax offset on assessment if some or all of that net income includes franked dividends.

STREAMING OF FRANKED DISTRIBUTIONS

There are specific rules to deal with the streaming of franked distributions (dividends) by a trustee to beneficiaries. Broadly, the mechanics of streaming of franked dividends (and also net capital gains) are as follows:

- requiring the trustee to make a beneficiary 'specifically entitled' to a franked dividend derived by the trust
- removing the dividend from the operation of Division 6 ITAA36 where the requirements to create a 'specific entitlement' to the beneficiary are met
- assessing the streamed franked dividend under subdivision 207-B on a quantum basis: that is, the beneficiary is assessed on the amount streamed, net of 'directly relevant expenses'.

For more details regarding the amendments and streaming of franked dividends see from 7.700. Also see the example below.

DISTRIBUTIONS TO A RESIDENT COMPANY

When a company receives a franked distribution from a trust, the recipient company includes that distribution as part of its assessable income and is entitled to a tax offset (see from 6.800). The company recipient is required to gross up the amount of any franked distribution received and is then entitled to claim a franking tax offset. The franking credits attached to the trust distribution are credited to the franking account of the recipient company (see 6.800). This increases the franking credits in the franking account that can flow through to shareholders (see example at 11.720).

NOTE: In the hands of the company, the amount credited to the franking account may be more than the proportional amount of net income in the form of a dividend to which it is presently entitled, and in respect of which it will be taxed if trust losses or directly attributable expenses reduced the distributable amount. Note that in cases where the trust is in a 'Division 6E' loss situation, a 'rateable reduction' will apply to reduce the amount of dividend distributed to the company without a loss of franking credits.

During the year the Big Wind Trust suffered a trading loss of $2,000 and received a fully franked dividend of $6,300. The net trust income is distributed to a company beneficiary, Westerly Pty Ltd.

Net loss of the trust from trading	($2,000)
Add Net fully franked dividends	$6,300
Accounting income	**$4,300**
Add franking credits	$2,700
Net income of trust (for tax purposes)	**$7,000**

Distribution of 'Division 6E income of the Trust Estate'		Distribution of 'Division 207-B income of the Trust Estate'	
Net income of trust (for tax purposes)	$7,000	Net franked dividend	$6,300
Less		Add	
Removal of net franked dividend	($6,300)	Franking credit attached to dividend	$2,700
Removal of franking credit attached to dividends	($2,700)		
Division 6E income of the Trust Estate/(Carried forward loss)	**($2,000)**	Division 207-B income of the Trust Estate/(Carried forward loss)	**$9,000**

Distribution to beneficiary of Division 207-B income

Division 207-B income	$9,000
Less Rateable reduction	
[Div 207-B income – Net income of the Trust (tax purposes)]	($2,000)
Assessable distribution	$7,000
Less Franking credit (not reduced by rateable reduction)	($2,700)
Net franked distribution	**$4,300**

Beneficiary (Westerly Pty Ltd) receives 100% of the distributable income, ie. a cash amount of $4,300.

Present entitlement to the net income is conferred within the appropriate timeframes.

The tax implications to the beneficiary are as follows:

Westerly Pty Ltd: Calculation of taxable income and tax payable

Div 207-B income	$9,000
Less Rateable reduction	($2,000)
Grossed up distribution	$7,000
Company tax ($7,000 x 30%)	$2,100
Franking tax offset (maximum permitted)	$2,100
Tax payable	**Nil**
Excess franking credit	**$600**

Companies can only use as much of the franking tax offset which reduces their tax liability to nil. Excess franking credits are not refundable. However, excess franking credits can be converted to tax losses (see 6.800) that can be carried forward to use in future years. If the beneficiary was an individual they ordinarily would be eligible to a refund of the excess franking credit.

Further to the above example, the following shows the franking account entries required by Westerly Pty Ltd on the receipt of the franked distribution. The company is allowed to credit the total available franking credit:

Westerly Pty Ltd – franking account entry			
	Debit	Credit	Balance
Franking credit $2,700	–	$2,700	$2,700

11.740 FRANKING CREDIT TRADING RULES

The franking credit trading rules prevent taxpayers from claiming franking credit tax offsets unless they have held the relevant shares for the requisite minimum time period, excluding the purchase and sale dates.

The franking credit trading rules are an integrity measure to prevent taxpayers from buying and selling arrangements involving short periods of ownership by parties which can benefit the most from franking credits attached to dividends where those parties benefitting from the franking credits are not in substance bearing the economic risks of ownership.

To claim a franking tax offset, the relevant taxpayer must be a 'qualified person'. A 'qualified person' is defined in the former s160APHO ITAA36 (also see TD 2007/11 stating that the former law has application for this purpose). The definition has four components, the most commonly applicable being the 'holding period rule' (see 11.745) and the 'small shareholder exemption' (see 11.750).

IMPORTANT: These rules generally apply in respect of shares acquired on or after 1 July 1997. However, special rules specific to trusts only apply to shares acquired by the trustee after 3.00pm EST on 31 December 1997.

QUALIFIED PERSON

To be entitled to a franking credit or a franking tax offset in relation to a particular dividend, a taxpayer must be a 'qualified person' in relation to the dividend.

One requirement to be a 'qualified person' and obtain franking credits or access tax offsets is for taxpayers to be exposed to at least 30% of the risk of share price movements for at least 45 days for ordinary shares (90 days for preference shares) acquired after 30 June 1997.

This rule is modified for discretionary trusts (and other non-fixed trusts) that are not widely held. The operative date is 3pm on 31 December 1997.

Where the dividend is received through a trust or partnership, the taxpayer does not receive the dividend as such, but receives a trust or partnership amount that is attributable to the dividend. In these cases the beneficiary or partner must determine what component of the trust or partnership distribution is attributable to a particular dividend, and then determine whether, in relation to that dividend, the taxpayer is a 'qualified person'.

Where a taxpayer is not a qualified person, the franking tax offset on the dividend or distribution will be denied.

Dividend recipient	Consequences where taxpayer is not a 'qualified person'	
Corporate partner, company shareholder or corporate beneficiary	No credit in the relevant franking account	
	No imputation gross up	No franking tax offset
Trust, partnership or individual	No imputation gross up	No franking tax offset

Where a taxpayer is able to satisfy the 'holding period rule', the taxpayer will be a 'qualified person'.

11.745   HOLDING PERIOD RULE

A taxpayer who holds shares or an interest in shares on which a dividend or distribution has been paid is a 'qualified person' in relation to the dividend if the taxpayer has held the shares or interest in shares at risk to market forces for 45 days (or 90 days for certain preference shares). This is known as the 'qualification period'. The qualification period does not include the day of acquisition or disposal. Each dividend paid on a share must be tested.

Shares are considered to be held 'at risk' where the shareholder is exposed to at least 30% of the normal risks of share ownership. The risk factor is determined in reference to the delta (a financial planning concept) of the underlying financial instrument and associated derivative instruments. Upside and downside risks are taken into account and the threshold delta is +0.3. Days during which the shares are not held 'at risk' or at a diminished risk are not counted.

The holding period rule is tested on a last-in-first-out (LIFO) basis in respect of the purchase and sale of shares.

Specific anti-avoidance rules apply if shares which are substantially the same as the shares under consideration are disposed of by the taxpayer or an associate during the holding period.

HOLDING AN INTEREST IN SHARES

A person is taken to hold an interest in shares or other property if that person:

- has or had a legal or equitable interest in the shares or other property
- is a partner in a partnership that holds or held the shares or other property
- is a beneficiary of a trust that holds or held the shares or other property, or
- is a partner in a partnership or a beneficiary of a trust that derives or derived dividend income through interposed entities from dividends paid on the shares or distributions of the other property.

'DIVIDEND WASHING' ARRANGEMENTS

The law contains an integrity measure to prevent investors from engaging in 'dividend washing'. Dividend washing results in two sets of franking credits being claimed on what is effectively the same parcel of shares in publicly listed companies.

The arrangement being contemplated by the Government can be illustrated as follows:

- Investor X holds a parcel A of shares in a listed public company Z. It sells those shares just before they go ex-dividend (the right to the dividend and any franking credits remains with the seller).
- Investor X immediately purchases another parcel B of shares in company Z, equivalent to the shares in A, in the cum-dividend market (the right to the dividend and any franking credits remains with the buyer).

Historically, a rule of the market has allowed a two-day period for settlement of option trades which has been exploited by sophisticated investors to buy shares which carry a dividend to claim two sets of franking credits.

From 1 July 2013, the integrity rule is activated during the period between the dividend date and the record date of a membership interest, where a membership interest is disposed of on an ex dividend basis and a substantially identical membership interest is acquired cum-dividend. The rules will deny franking benefits in respect of the newly acquired shares.

This only applies to investors that have franking credit tax offset entitlements in excess of $5,000, so the typical 'mum and dad' investors are not affected.

QUALIFICATION PERIOD

The holding period requirement must be met during the qualification period which begins the day after the taxpayer acquires the shares or interest and ends on day 45 (day 90 for preference shares) after the shares or interests become 'ex-dividend'.

In practice, to satisfy the statutory 45-day test, ordinary shares must be held for 47 calendar days (ie. 45 days plus the acquisition day plus the disposal day). The holding period rule is only relevant if the shares go ex-dividend during the first 45 days after the day of acquisition.

A share or interest becomes *ex-dividend* on the day after the last day on which the shares or interest in shares can be acquired by a taxpayer so as to become entitled to a dividend or distribution on the shares or interest.

Note that a secondary qualification period must be satisfied where a related payment in respect of a dividend is or may be made. A *related payment* obligation essentially occurs where a person is under an obligation to pass the benefit of a dividend to another person. Where there is such a related payment obligation, the 45 day holding period (for ordinary shares) must occur within the period starting 45 days before, and ending 45 days after, the shares become ex-dividend.

'RISK DIMINISHED' DAYS

In calculating whether a taxpayer has satisfied the requisite holding period, any days during which there is a materially diminished risk in relation to the relevant shares or interest are not counted. For example, this would occur if the taxpayer has short sold the shares or has taken a position in derivatives which eliminates the upside and downside risk of holding the shares. A taxpayer's risk is considered materially diminished, if the net position reduces the exposure to less than 30% of the risks and gains relating to the shareholding (ie. a delta of less than +0.3).

Mary buys shares in Black Sheep Co on 1 June 2015 and a franked dividend is declared on the shares on 5 July 2015. On 6 July 2015, Mary buys a put option on the shares and exercises the option on 18 August 2015.

Mary cannot satisfy the holding period rule. While she has held the shares for a total of 77 days, the purchase of the put option has diminished her risk with respect to the shares. This means the shares are only held at risk for 34 days. This is because the put option guarantees Mary a certain sale price for her shares, and she will not be exposed to falls in the market price of the shares from the time the put option was acquired.

Mary is not a qualified person and is not entitled to utilise the franking credits unless she can satisfy the small shareholder exemption.

DEFINING 'RISK' – A 'POSITION' IN RELATION TO SHARES

A 'position' in relation to shares or an interest in shares is anything that has a 'delta' in relation to the shares or interest. *'Delta'* is the measure of correlation of a derivative to a share price movement. Shares held are allocated a delta of 1. If a derivative in relation to a share has a delta of 1, there is a 1:1 correlation between the derivative and the shares or the non-'fixed interest' in a trust. This means that if the share price increases by 15% the underlying instrument (ie. the derivative) increases by 15%.

If a taxpayer writes or buys a call option over shares in a company, that taxpayer has taken a position in relation to those shares because the obligation or right under the option provides an opportunity for profit or loss by reference to the market value of the shares.

A call option over shares gives the grantee of the option or the right (but not the obligation) to purchase shares at a predetermined price in the future. If the value of shares increases, the value of the call option will also increase. As discussed below, this position is known as a long position or a positive position.

SHORT POSITION

A 'short' position, in relation to shares, is a position which has a negative delta in relation to those shares. This includes, for example, a short sale, a futures contract to sell shares, a sold call option or a bought put option, and a futures contract to sell a particular share index.

The value of these derivatives increases if the price of the share falls or vice versa. For example, a short sale is a short position (or a position with a negative delta) that occurs when a person sells shares before they are required to purchase them. If it was expected that the share price would fall, a sale of shares at today's price followed by a purchase at tomorrow's lower price would result in a profit to the short seller. The greater the fall in the share value, the greater the value of the short position (see TD 2007/29).

LONG POSITION

A 'long' position, in relation to shares, is a position which has a positive delta in relation to those shares, eg. a share purchase, a bought future, a bought call option and a sold put option and a futures contract to buy a particular index are long positions.

It is noted that a bought future over a parcel of shares gives the purchaser of the future both the right and obligation to purchase the shares at a predetermined price over a given period of time in the future. The greater the rise in the price of the shares the greater the value of the derivative, being the bought future, as the price at which shares may be acquired in the future remains fixed.

'NET POSITION'

The 'net position' of a taxpayer in relation to shares is calculated by adding the sum of the taxpayer's long positions to the sum of the taxpayer's short positions.

If an associate of the taxpayer enters into a short position in relation to shares held by the taxpayer, the taxpayer is deemed to have taken the position entered into by the associate.

POSITION OF A TRUST BENEFICIARY

Beneficiaries of certain types of trusts (where the beneficiary has a fixed interest in the underlying shares held by the trust) are taken to have acquired or disposed of a shareholding at the time the trustee acquired or disposed of the shareholding. Therefore if the trustee satisfies the holding period rules, so will the beneficiaries.

To determine whether risk has been reduced materially (except under a family trust or deceased estate, but not a testamentary trust) in the case of shares acquired by a trustee after 31 December 1997, certain deeming rules apply:

- the beneficiary is deemed to have a long position of +1 in relation to its notional interest (see below) and to have an equal and offsetting short position (of –1) in relation to that interest, and

- the beneficiary is also deemed to have a long position or if its interest is an actual fixed interest, if any, in corpus consisting of shares.

An interest is fixed if it is vested and indefeasible.

The interest of the beneficiary in shares is deemed to be a notional interest in the holding of the trustee, worked out as the proportion of the trust's dividend income from the relevant shares to which the beneficiary is entitled.

DISCRETIONARY TRUST

A beneficiary (discretionary object) of a discretionary trust does not have a fixed interest (defined as vested and indefeasible) because the beneficiary only has a right to be considered by the trustee in exercising its discretion to distribute trust corpus or income. Similarly, a default beneficiary has a vested but defeasible interest (that is, does not have a fixed interest). This also applies to beneficiaries of hybrid trusts that do not have the requisite fixed interest.

In the case of a discretionary trust, there will always be a material diminution of risk in the absence of that trust electing to be a 'family trust' for the purposes of the trust loss provisions regardless of how long the trustee actually holds the shares (see 7.900). That is, the beneficiary will have a delta of zero (+1–1) in relation to its notional interest and has no fixed interest (see ATO ID 2002/604).

 The 45 day holding period rule can never be satisfied by a beneficiary in a discretionary trust unless the trustee elects for the trust to be a 'family trust' (see from 7.200). The small shareholder exemption is also available where the amount of franking tax offset is no more than $5,000 for a beneficiary and the rule will not be applicable where the relevant shares were acquired prior to 31 December 1997.

In the case of a family trust (see *Trust loss rules* from 7.900), the beneficiary is deemed to have a long position of +1 in relation to its notional interest, but is not deemed to have an equal and offsetting short position in respect of that notional interest.

The beneficiary will not have a materially diminished risk unless the beneficiary (or trustee) specifically enters into other risk reduction strategies (derivative transactions).

DECEASED ESTATES AND TESTAMENTARY TRUSTS

Deceased estates (deemed to be a trust for tax purposes) are also not deemed to have a material diminished risk in shares or an interest in shares. However, this exception does not extend to trusts created by a will (testamentary trusts), and only applies to estates administered by executors or administrators.

FRANKING CREDITS FOR LIFE TENANTS

A life tenant of a testamentary trust is not entitled to the benefit of franking credits which are attributable to shares acquired by the trust after 31 December 1997 and distributed from that trust unless the trust makes a family trust election. The life tenant does not have a vested and indefeasible interest in the corpus of the trust and as a result of s160APHL of ITAA36, the life tenant will have a nil net position. As this is less than 0.3, the taxpayer will not be a qualified person and will not be entitled to any franking credits where the trust has not made a family trust election (ATO ID 2002/122).

CLOSELY HELD TRUSTS

A trust is a closely held trust for tax purposes if 20 persons or less (none of whom is an associate of any of the others) have interests in the trust that together entitle them to 75% or more of the beneficial interests in the income or property of the trust.

Where a trustee of a closely held trust enters into a position with respect to shares or an interest in shares (relevant shares) which form the property of the trust, all beneficiaries of the trust are deemed to have entered into a proportionate position with respect to their interests in the relevant shares at the later of the time the trustee entered into the position, or at the time that the beneficiary acquired the interest in the trust.

A closely-held trust established in 1996 has two beneficiaries entitled to share equally in the trust income. The trust holds 1,000 shares in a company acquired at the time of the trust's establishment.

In October 2000, the trustee appoints a third beneficiary who shares in the trust income equally with the original beneficiaries. At the same time the trustee buys a put option with a delta of –0.8 as against the shares so that the risk with regards to the shares is materially diminished.

The result is that the original beneficiaries are still eligible for franking credits because they have held the shares for the required period. However, the position entered into by the trustee in respect of the shares is deemed to be the position of the beneficiaries. As a result, the new beneficiary is not entitled to franking benefits because they are unable to satisfy the holding period rule because his delta is below 0.3.

A beneficiary with a post-1 July 1997 interest cannot be a 'qualified person' unless the trustee is a qualified person.

WIDELY HELD TRUSTS

A widely held trust is a fixed trust that is not a 'closely held trust'.

A taxpayer who holds an interest in shares as a beneficiary of a widely held trust on which a distribution has been paid is a 'qualified person' in relation to any dividend paid on the shares (from which the distribution is derived) if the taxpayer has held the interest in shares during the qualification period in relation to the interest (not counting the day of acquisition or disposal) for 45 days.

Beneficiaries of widely-held trusts do not have to be concerned whether the trustee of the trust has taken a position with respect to the shares in the trust property. Provided the beneficiary personally satisfies the holding period requirements, the beneficiary will be a qualified person.

11.750   SMALL SHAREHOLDER EXEMPTION

Individuals with total franking credits of $5,000 or less from all sources (direct shareholdings and distributions from trusts and partnerships) in respect of an income year are excluded from the franking credit trading rules for the year. The Commissioner also allows beneficiaries of discretionary trusts, where the individuals do not own or hold an interest in the underlying shares of the entity, access to the small shareholder exemption as an administrative concession.

This exemption does not apply to other entities such as companies, partnerships and superannuation funds.

Where the amount of franking credits exceeds $5,000, the individual must satisfy the holding period rules (see 11.745) in respect of the entire amount (ie. not just the excess over $5,000).

On 1 August, Sally bought shares in her own name 30 days before they became ex-dividend on 30 August. The shares were sold on 5 September. The franking credit attached to the dividend was $4,500.

The small shareholder exemption automatically applies provided that Sally does not have other affected franking credits of more than $500, ie. no more than $5,000 in total.

 Continuing from the previous example, if the franking credit attached to the dividends were $5,500 then the taxpayer would be denied the entire amount of the franking tax offset as the shares were not held for the minimum holding period.

 Continuing from the previous example, Sally instead buys the shares through a discretionary trust. The franking credit attached to the dividend was $4,500. In this case the franking tax offsets would be denied because the trustee of the discretionary trust has not satisfied the holding period requirement.

Even if the shares had been held by the trustee for more than 45 days, the individual would still not be entitled to the franking credits unless the trust lodged an irrevocable election to be a family trust.

The small shareholder exemption automatically applies provided that Sally does not have other affected franking credits of more than $500, ie. no more than $5,000 in total.

 Where a taxpayer is denied a franking tax offset there is no requirement for those imputation credits to be included in the taxpayer's assessable income.

11.755 WINDING UP A COMPANY

If shares are issued and cancelled in the course of winding up a company and a dividend is paid in relation to those shares, it is necessary to test whether the taxpayer who holds the shares or an interest in the shares is a qualified person in relation to the dividend. If, for example, shares are issued in the course of winding up and then within 45 days are disposed of to a third party (as opposed to the issuing company), the taxpayer will not be a 'qualified person' in relation to any dividends paid on the shares.

11.760 OTHER ASSESSABLE INCOME

11.770 PROFIT-MAKING UNDERTAKING

A profit that arises from the carrying out of a profit-making undertaking or plan (that is, one with a profit-making intention) will be assessable as statutory income under s15-15 of the ITAA97 where the proceeds of the profit-making undertaking or plan are not otherwise assessable as ordinary income under s6-5 of the ITAA97.

Any capital profit on the disposal of assets acquired before 20 September 1985 is generally received tax-free (see from 12.020 and 12.070 for variations) unless the taxpayer acquired the asset with the intention of reselling it at a profit or using that asset as part of a profit-making venture. Section 15-15 operates to assess any profit on disposal of an asset if the asset was acquired for a profit making intention before 20 September 1985 but only if the proceeds from the venture are not otherwise assessable as ordinary income. Any profit made on the disposal is assessed on the same basis as ordinary income pursuant to s25A ITAA36 (ie. the assessable profit is calculated after deducting all expenses incurred in deriving that profit).

A change of intention may subject a profit to s15-15; for example, where the owner of a block of pre-CGT land subsequently decides to significantly improve the land, sub-divide it, build residential units on the lots with the purpose of selling the blocks for profit. However, profits arising from a 'mere realisation' of a capital asset to its best advantage are not subject to s15-15. Whether a capital asset is sold as part of a profit-making plan or as a mere realisation of the asset is a matter of fact and degree.

In the case of *Whitfords Beach Pty Ltd* (1982) 12 ATR 692, the taxpayer company owned land that had been acquired as a capital asset. When another company subsequently purchased all the shares in the company, the taxpayer developed and sold the land at the direction of the new shareholders. The Federal Court looked through the corporate veil to the intentions of the shareholders and determined that the profit-making intention of the new shareholders should be attributable to the taxpayer company, thereby signalling a change in intention.

Note that the intention of the original owner of the asset can be attributed to subsequent owners. For transfers of assets under a will or to a recipient in a non-arm's length transaction, the recipient is deemed to have acquired the asset for:

- the same purpose as the original owner (ie. profit motive), and
- the same cost at which the original owner acquired the asset.

The recipient is taxed on the profit on the disposal of the asset as if they had acquired the asset.

A parcel of land was acquired in 1983 by the taxpayer's late grandfather for $10,000. The grandfather's original intention was to subdivide the property and to dispose of each separate parcel of land at a profit.

In 1993 the land was bequeathed to the deceased's grandson. Its market value at that time was $600,000 even though there were no improvements made to the property. Over the years a total of $35,500 in rates and taxes were incurred. The grandson sold the property in 2015 for $1,000,000.

Because the property was originally acquired with a profit-making intention, the grandson is deemed to have acquired the property with the same intention. The grandson will be assessed on a profit of $954,500.

Sale price		$1,000,000
Less Cost of land	($10,000)	
Rates and taxes	($35,500)	($45,500)
Assessable profit		**$954,500**

NOTE: If the land had not been acquired by the grandfather with the intention of making a profit on disposal of the land, the grandson would have been assessed under the CGT rules (the asset is deemed to be acquired by the grandson at the date of death for its market value at that time). The cost base would have been $600,000 and the assessable profit significantly less. Further, the grandson would have been eligible for the CGT discount.

11.780   LAND SOLD UNDER CONDITIONAL OR INSTALMENT CONTRACTS

The general rule for a business taxpayer is that income (under ordinary concepts) is derived on an accruals basis. Following the decision of the Federal Court in **Gasparin v F C of T** (1994) 28 ATR 130, it is accepted that business income earned under conditional or instalment contracts for the sale of land is not derived until the date of settlement.

In that case the Court also held that the land (including each parcel of land) remained trading stock of the vendor until settlement because it was only at that time that the vendor finally lost all dispositive power over the land. This means the point in time where any contingencies that may have prevented the sale to proceed cease to exist. There may also be GST implications in relation to how and when you account for the land or property transaction (see from 23.000).

An instalment contract would generally have the following features:

- the sale price represents a profit over the taxpayer's purchase price after purchase expenses
- the payment of a deposit by a third party purchaser
- vendor finance is provided to the third party purchaser and interest charged on the sale price at a premium above the rate of interest paid by the taxpayer on their mortgage on the property
- the payment of the balance of the sale price, plus interest, is by instalments over a substantial period, such as 25 years
- the third party purchaser is licensed to occupy the property during the term of the instalment contract
- the contract states that this occupation is not by way of lease
- the third party purchaser is required to pay the rates, taxes and insurance premiums

on the property and is responsible for the repair and maintenance of the property

- the taxpayer retains title to the property until the final instalment is paid and the contract is completed, at which time the title is transferred to the third party purchaser, and

- if the third party purchaser defaults on the contract, deposit and instalments paid are forfeited to the taxpayer.

11.790 INCOME FROM LEASING ARRANGEMENTS

LUXURY CAR LEASES

Normally, the lessor of a motor vehicle is subject to tax on lease payments received. The lessee is allowed a corresponding tax deduction for lease payments where the requirements for deductibility are satisfied. However, special rules apply where the lease is a 'luxury car lease'.

A car is a luxury car where its cost exceeds the annually indexed 'car cost limit'. The limit for 2014-15 is $57,466 (unchanged since the 2010-11 year). Leases of luxury cars entered into after 20 August 1996, other than short term hire arrangements, are treated as if they are a notional sale and loan transaction (see 14.088).

SALE OF LEASED CAR

Where a car has been used wholly or partly for income-producing purposes by either the taxpayer or an associate then the taxpayer is required to declare any profit on the disposal of the leased car in their assessable income (see from 15.070, 15.085 and 11.000). The amount to be included in assessable income is the lesser of:

- the profit on the disposal

- the total of deductible lease payments for the entire lease period, and

- the notional amounts that could have been claimed for decline in value of the vehicle if it were owned (and not leased) and used wholly for income producing purposes.

A car that has been held for private purposes (ie. has not been used to produce income) and is acquired by the lessee and sold at a profit is excluded from the above rule. Any profit arising from the sale is not treated as assessable income.

NOTE: Subdivision 20-B operates to assess as income the calculated recoupment. It does not calculate or allow for a loss. See 15.070 for balancing adjustment events.

LEASE INCENTIVES

Lease incentives are inducements that are offered by lessors to potential lessees to enter into leases. The most common type of lease incentive relates to new tenancies in commercial office buildings and can include such inducements as the provision of cars or boats, free fit-out of the premises, rent free periods, up-front cash payments or combinations thereof. The assessability of lease incentives as ordinary income have been determined by case law over time. Some leading cases include the following.

Cooling's case

In *FCT v Cooling* 90 ATC 4472 a firm of solicitors were offered a lump sum cash lease incentive payment to sign guarantees and procure the taxpayer to enter into the lease of new office premises. The Full Federal Court held that the payment constituted income according to ordinary concepts assessable under former s25(1) ITAA36 (ie. the predecessor to s6-5 ITAA97). In reaching its decision, the Court was of the view that the payment was correctly characterised as an incentive to the taxpayer which caused it to move premises. Further, the Court believed that the transaction entered into by the firm was a commercial transaction that formed part of the ordinary business activities of the taxpayer.

Montgomery's case (Montgomery v FC of T 98 ATC 4120)

Montgomery's case involved a firm of solicitors who were required to move out of their leased premises due to asbestos removal works being conducted. They had the option of temporarily relocating to other floors in the building until the works were completed, but chose to move to new premises in another building. As an incentive to move to the new building a cash payments was made in three tranches by the landlord. Some of these funds were used to pay for the fit-out of the new premises.

The High Court, adopting similar principles to those of the Full Federal Court in *Cooling's case*, decided that the payments constituted income according to ordinary concepts. The argument that the receipts were on capital account was rejected on the basis that there had been no addition to the profit-yielding structure of the business.

Selleck's case (Selleck v FC of T (1997) 36 ATR 558)

In *Selleck's case*, two existing legal firms merged necessitating a move to larger premises. The landlord contributed a substantial sum towards the fit-out of the new premises. The Court accepted that the payments were not received in the ordinary course of business, as the firm was newly created, and that there was no profit-making purpose connected to the incentive. The new firm's only purpose in entering into the lease (and receiving the incentive) was to establish appropriate premises from which to conduct business.

IT 2631

In IT 2631, the Tax Office considers the tax treatment of various types of lease incentives based on such case law. The ruling provides the general rule that lease incentives in the form of cash, or non-cash incentives that are convertible into cash, would be income. Further, if a non-cash incentive is received in similar circumstances, that is, a business taxpayer receives a non-cash incentive to enter into or vary a lease of business premises, it will have an income character provided that it is convertible to cash, either as a matter of fact or through the operation of s21A (see 11.060).

There is also an otherwise deductible rule, whereby a lease incentive would have no tax consequences if the cost of the incentive would have been deductible to the lessee had the lessee incurred the expenditure themselves.

The following table sets out the tax treatment in respect of certain types of lease incentives according to the Tax Office.

Lease incentive	Tax treatment
Cash payment	Assessable
Rent free period	Not assessable
Rent discount	Not assessable
Interest-free loan	Tax-free provided it is a genuine business loan
Free fit-out: If landlord owns fit-out	Not assessable
If tenant owns fit-out	Assessable but capital allowance deductions may be permitted
Free plant	Assessable but capital allowance deductions may be permitted
Holiday packages	Tax-free to tenant (note costs non-deductible to landlord)
Removal expenses	Assessable
Surrender payments	Assessable

 There are also GST implications which may apply when providing and receiving lease incentives. These implications are considered in GSTR 2003/16.

11.800 LIFE POLICY BONUSES

When a life insurance policy has been held by the taxpayer for ten years or longer, reversionary bonuses received on that policy are tax-free. For policies held for less than ten years, stipulated amounts are included in the taxpayer's assessable income, and a tax offset is available.

A bonus is not assessable income if it is received:

- at least ten years after the policy was first acquired
- under a life assurance policy that was part of a superannuation fund or scheme when the person on whose life the policy was effected dies, has an accident, illness or other disability, or

- as a result of serious financial difficulties, provided the policy was not taken out with a plan to mature or be terminated within ten years.

ASSESSABLE AMOUNT

The assessable amount of a bonus on short-term life policy is:

- the full bonus if received during the first eight years of the policy
- 2/3 of the bonus if received in the ninth year of the policy
- 1/3 of the bonus if received in the tenth year of the policy, or
- nil if received ten or more years after the policy started.

Losses on policies cannot be claimed as a deduction.

RESETTING OF POLICY COMMENCEMENT DATE

Where a policy risk started after 27 August 1982, and premiums are increased by more than 25% of the premium payable in the preceding year, the policy is deemed to recommence on the anniversary of the date it started (in the year that increased premium was paid). This has the effect of resetting the start date of the policy and results in bonuses being fully or partially assessable within ten years from the new start date. That effect can be avoided if the excess premium (the part that exceeds a 25% increase) is paid into a new policy rather than the existing policy.

NOTE: IT 2346 states that fixed premiums are not taken to have increased just because they are paid in advance or arrears.

 If a policy started on 1 June 2010, and the policy owner paid a $500 premium in 2012, 2013 and 2014 respectively, and an $800 premium in 2015, the deemed date of commencement would become 1 June 2015.

If an income bond is converted to a life insurance policy, the income bond is terminated and the commencement date can not be carried over to the insurance policy (ATO ID 2003/767).

TAX OFFSETS

When bonuses are included in a taxpayer's assessable income, the taxpayer may be entitled to a non-refundable tax offset. These offsets are as follows:

- **Life company:** The tax offset for life assurance bonuses is 30%.
- **Friendly Society:** The tax offset for friendly society bonuses is 30%.

 If a policy with a $5,000 bonus is surrendered in Year 7, the tax payable if the person has other taxable income of $48,000 is (using 2014-15 rates):

	Without surrender	With surrender
Tax on $48,000	$7,147	$7,147
Tax on $5,000 bonuses	–	$1,625
Total income	$7,147	$8,772
less tax offset @ 30%	–	($1,500)
Tax payable	$7,147	$7,272
plus 2% Medicare (on total income)	$960	$1,060
Total tax payable	**$8,107**	**$8,332**

If the policy continued for ten years, the bonus would be tax-free.

 Taxpayers considering surrendering a policy early to use the tax offset against income tax payable should consider all other factors, for example:

- *impact on the income amount that is tested against thresholds for liability to surcharges and entitlement to benefits (including future child support liability and support from Centrelink and Department of Veterans Affairs), and*
- *whether the surrender will result in a tax offset which reduces total tax otherwise payable after other tax offsets to nil.*

11.850 EMPLOYEE SHARE SCHEMES

Division 83A of the ITAA97 governs the income tax treatment of shares or rights granted to an employee under a qualifying Employee Share Scheme (ESS). Division 83A applies to shares and other interests acquired under an ESS on or after 1 July 2009.

Division 83A replaced Division 13A of Pt II of the ITAA36. Division 83A also applies to interests acquired before 1 July 2009 where the taxing point had been deferred until at least after that date pursuant to Division 13A.

PURPOSE OF ESS RULES

The aims of the Division 83A ESS regime are to align the taxation of employment remuneration received in different forms (whether as cash salary or as a discount from the market value of a share or right).

Division 83A provides that, where a taxpayer receives a share or right under an ESS at a discount to market value, that discount is assessable income to the taxpayer upfront (as would be the case had that discount been received as cash remuneration). Generally, the discount is assessable at the time the share or right is acquired (ie. at the time of receipt). A $1,000 reduction of the assessable amount is available for taxpayers whose 'adjusted taxable incomes' are no greater than $180,000 (see below for discussion). A deferral of the taxing point is also available if certain conditions are satisfied.

DEFINITIONS OF 'ESS INTEREST' AND 'ESS'

Division 83A only applies to benefits received by the employee that are 'ESS interests'.

An ESS interest in a company is a beneficial interest in either (s83A-10(1)):

- a share in a the company, or
- a right to acquire a beneficial interest in a share in the company.

Note that an ESS interest is defined with reference to a company only and therefore does not include units in a unit trust or an opportunity to buy into a partnership (with the exception of limited liability partnerships which are treated as companies for tax purposes).

The concept of a 'right to acquire shares in a company' extends to rights, other than options, which may give rise to an acquisition of shares rather than being confined to the acquisition of shares by the exercise of options (*Commissioner of Taxation v McWilliam* (2012) FCAFC 105).

An 'employee share scheme' is defined as being a scheme under which ESS interests in a company are provided to past, present or prospective employees (or their associates). The ESS interests must be provided under the scheme in relation to the employees' employment by the company in respect which the interests are issued or the subsidiaries of the company (that is, employees may acquire interests in the employer's holding company).

INCOME TAX CONSEQUENCES FOR EMPLOYEE

Section 83A-25 includes in the taxpayer's assessable income the discount received in relation to the acquisition of the ESS interest resulting in upfront taxation (ie. assessable in the year of the acquisition) unless deferral applies.

A contractual right to acquire options may constitute a right to acquire shares for the purposes of the former ESS provision under Division 13A ITAA36 (*Commissioner of Taxation v McWilliam*). This proposition remains relevant under the current rules also.

For any purposes of the income tax law other than Division 83A, such as the application of the CGT regime to the share or right acquired under the ESS (eg. upon a subsequent disposal), the share or the right is deemed to have been acquired for market value rather than for the discounted value (s83A-30) at the time of the taxing point (be it deferred or upfront).

INTERNATIONAL CONSIDERATIONS

Pursuant to s83A-25(2), where the assessable amount arises in relation to employment outside Australia, the income is deemed to be foreign sourced income. As with other types of employment remuneration, Australian tax residents are subject to tax on foreign sourced income but non-residents are not (see 22.010).

NOTE: Temporary residents are generally taxed in the same way as non-residents but there is a specific exemption for foreign sourced employment remuneration. Where the income is otherwise ordinary or statutory income and is derived in relation to employment during the period of temporary residency, that income is included in assessable income (s768-910(3)(a) and (b) of the ITAA97). This means that a temporary resident may be subject to tax on discounts received on ESS interests under an ESS in relation to foreign employment.

The Division 83A provisions do not appear to restrict their application to interests in Australian resident companies nor do they require a nexus to an Australian resident employer. Therefore, the measures should apply even where the employer is a non-resident or the company (the employer or the employer's holding company) in which the interests are issued is a non-resident.

INCOME TAX CONSEQUENCES FOR EMPLOYER

DEDUCTION FOR EMPLOYERS

Section 83A-205 allows the employer to claim a tax deduction in limited circumstances. A deduction may be claimed by the employer providing the ESS interests where the employee taxpayer is eligible for the upfront concession. The deduction available is equal to the concession to which the employee is entitled – ie. a maximum of $1,000 in respect of that employee.

For the purposes of the deductibility test, the income threshold test (currently $180,000) imposed on the employee in the upfront concession rules is ignored. That means if the employee is ineligible for the upfront concession only because of breaching the income test, the employee is treated as being eligible for the purposes of determining the employer's eligibility for the tax deduction.

REPORTING REQUIREMENTS FOR EMPLOYERS

Under Division 83A, employers are subject to annual reporting requirements in respect of ESS interests issued. Furthermore, employers must now withhold tax where the employee has not provided a TFN or an ABN at the taxing point.

Specifically, the relevant reporting requirements include:

- **Reporting to employees:** An *ESS Statement* is required to be issued to the employee by 14 July after the end of the financial year. A statement is required where
    - (i) the employee (or their associate) have acquired ESS interests at a discount and is taxed upfront during the income year (see below for discussion) or
    - (ii) the deferred taxing point has been triggered during the income year in respect of ESS interests in which taxation has been deferred. A sample ESS Statement is available on the Tax Office website.
- **Reporting to the Tax Office:** Employers are also require to provide the Tax Office with an *ESS annual report* by 14 August after the end of the financial year. The report requires information to be disclosed such as each employee participating in an ESS, and ESS the employee is participating in. It also requires information such as ESS interest which have either been taxed upfront or deferred, the number of interests issued and the discounts and reductions available. A sample copy of the annual report is available on the Tax Office website.

UPFRONT TAXATION – $1,000 EXEMPTION

Section 83A-35 provides a exemption for up to $1,000 of an assessable discount, where the taxpayer is assessed on the discount upfront. This exemption was also available under the superseded law. However, amongst other conditions, it will only be available to employees whose Adjusted Taxable Income (ATI) for the year is no greater than $180,000.

 For further discussion and a definition of ATI refer to 3.104.

The other conditions which must be satisfied in order to access the tax exemption are:

- all the ESS interests available for acquisition under the ESS have to be ordinary shares (ie. a granted right is eligible so long as the right is in relation to an ordinary share)
- the taxpayer has to be employed by the company in which the shares are issued or a subsidiary of the company at the time of acquisition of the shares (note that the ESS

rules generally also apply to past and prospective employees and associates of past, present and prospective employees)

- the share trading and investment company integrity rule is not breached; a breach occurs where:
  - the predominant business of the company is the acquisition, sale or holding of shares or other Investments
  - the taxpayer is employed by the company, and
  - the taxpayer is also employed by a subsidiary of the company, the holding company of the company or another subsidiary of the holding company of the company
- the ESS must be non-discriminatory, which means that the scheme operates in relation to at least 75% of permanent employees who have completed at least three years of service and who are Australian residents
- there is no real risk of forfeiture:
- in the case of a share – there is no real risk of forfeiture other than by disposing of it
- in the case of a right – there is no real risk of forfeiture other than by:
  - disposing of it, exercising it or letting it lapse, or
  - under the conditions of the scheme, if the right is exercised the employee will forfeit the resulting share or lose it other than by disposal
- the 'minimum holding period' requirements are met at all times between the time of acquisition of the interest and the earlier of three years later and cessation of employment:
  - the taxpayer is not permitted to dispose of either the ESS interest or a beneficial interest in a share acquired as a result of an ESS interest, and
  - all other people who acquire ESS interests under the scheme are subject to the same restriction, and
- immediately after the interest is acquired, the taxpayer:
  - does not hold a beneficial interest in more than 5% of the shares in the company, and
  - the taxpayer does not have more than 5% of the voting rights in the company.

Amendments to these rules have been proposed. See 11.880.

DEFERRAL OF TAXING POINT

Where a discount is subject to taxation under Division 83A, the default taxing point is the year of acquisition of the ESS interest unless the taxpayer qualifies for a deferred taxing point pursuant to Subdivison 83A-C.

A deferral will be allowed only where the interests under the scheme:

- satisfies the 'real risk of forfeiture' test, or
- are acquired under a 'salary sacrificed based employee share scheme' offering interests to an employee with a market value of no more than $5,000.

Therefore, the deferral of any discount gains is dependent on the structure of the scheme, as opposed to a choice made by the employee (as was the case under the former Division 13A).

The maximum period for deferral is seven years (decreased from the ten years available under the former law). During that seven year period, the employee may be subject to tax in an earlier year if:

- the employee ceases their employment in respect of which the ESS interest was acquired, or
- there ceases to be a risk of forfeiture of the interests and any restrictions on the sale of the shares or exercise of rights are lifted.

Amendments to these rules have been proposed. See 11.880.

REAL RISK OF FORFEITURE TEST

An employee is allowed to defer a discount received on the shares or rights to the extent that there is a real risk the benefits of the shares or rights may never in fact be received by the employee.

A 'real risk of forfeiture' exists if a reasonable person would consider that there is a real risk that the employee will:

- in the case of a share – forfeit the share or lose it other than by disposing of it, and
- in the case of a right:
  - forfeit the right or lose it other than by disposing of it, exercising it or letting it lapse, or
  - under the conditions of the scheme, if the right is exercised the employee will forfeit the resulting share or lose it other than by disposal.

 Amendments to these rules have been proposed. See 11.880.

The table below summarises the potential application of the real risk of forfeiture test to particular scenarios:

No.	Scenario	Example	Real risk of forfeiture?
1	Legal compulsion to transfer the ownership of the interests back to the employer	The return of an interest to an employee share trust because the employee did not meet certain sales targets.	Yes
2	Employee share plan contrived to create nominal risk of forfeiture	Conditions in the scheme which state that the shares are forfeited if the company's value falls by 95% during the next 12 months or the shares are forfeited upon request – these are not considered 'real risks'.	No
3	A condition that restricts an employee from disposing of their interest	An employee purchases some shares in their employer. At the same time, an option was provided by the employer to the employee whereby an equivalent number of free shares will be provided in two years' time if the employee does not sell those purchased shares.	No
4	Fraud or gross misconduct	An employee receives shares but will forfeit them if dismissed for fraud or gross misconduct in the next three years.	No
5	Performance hurdles – market share	An employee under an employee share plan receives a certain amount of shares in one year, if the employer's market share has increased by 10% in 12 months time. The employer's market share was steady in the previous 12 months.	Yes
6	Performance hurdles – market price increasing	An employee under an employee share plan receives a certain amount of shares in one year, if the employer's share price has increased by 10% in 24 months time. The employer's share price has performed broadly in line with the sector index in the last five years, but has outperformed the CPI by an average of 2%.	No
7	Performance hurdles – market price maintained	An employee under an employee share plan receives a certain amount of shares in one year, if the employer's share price has maintained its value in 24 months time.	Yes
8	Employee controlled risk	An employee is granted options which require that person to regularly save a certain amount of post-tax money in an approved savings account. The options will lapse if this condition is no longer met.	No
9	Forfeiture on cessation of employment	An employee under an employee share plan will receive a certain number of shares in 12 months time if still employed by the employer at that time.	Yes
10	Forfeiture on cessation of employment – good leaver clause	An employee under an employee share plan will receive a certain number of shares in three years if still employed by the employer at that time. However, shares will be granted if the employee leaves before three years for reasons outside their control, such as sickness, invalidity, being made redundant, etc under a 'good leaver' clause.	Yes

In ATO ID 2010/61 the Commissioner considered that a condition imposing a minimum employment period of 12 months before the rights vest would give rise to more than a 'rare' possibility of forfeiture and is a genuine condition to retain employees. In other words, there is a real risk of forfeiture if the employee chooses to leave their employment. The ATO ID also discusses 'good leaver' conditions.

INTERESTS ACQUIRED UNDER SALARY SACRIFICE

A tax deferral is also available where the ESS interest is provided as part of a salary sacrifice arrangement. To be entitled to the deferral, the interest must be provided:

- because the employee agreed to acquire the interest in return for a reduction in salary or wages that would not have happened apart from the agreement, or
- as part of the remuneration package, in circumstances where it is reasonable to conclude that the employee's salary or wages would be greater if the interest was not part of that package.

In addition, the following conditions must also be satisfied:

- the interest under the salary sacrifice arrangement must be shares (not rights); however, rights and shares may be provided separately subject to a 'real risk of forfeiture' under the same scheme (eg. matching rights attached to shares salary sacrificed)
- the interest provided must be for no consideration (other than salary foregone)
- the governing rules of the scheme must state that a deferral of taxation will arise under the scheme, and
- the total market value of the shares acquired during an income year under the salary sacrifice arrangement must not exceed $5,000.

NOTE: The limit is allowed per employee per employee relationship. If an employee has an employee relationship with more than one employer which are part of the same corporate group, the employee is limited to a $5,000 cap.

INVOLUNTARY FORFEITURE OR LOSS OF ESS INTEREST

Pursuant to s83A-310, the ESS provisions do not apply in relation to an ESS interest if the taxpayer forfeits or loses the interest other than by disposal or by exercise of the right (where the interest is a beneficial interest in a right) if the forfeiture or loss did not arise from either:

- a choice made by the taxpayer, other than a choice to cease employment, or
- a condition of the ESS that protects (wholly or partly) the taxpayer against a fall in the market value of the interest.

 Amendments to these rules have been proposed. See 11.880.

OTHER CONSIDERATIONS

Division 83A also contains provisions covering the application of the main rules to the following:

- takeovers and restructures
- acquisitions of ESS interests by associates of employees
- where the taxpayer holds interests in a trust that holds shares
- relationships similar to employment
- stapled securities, and
- indeterminate rights.

11.860 PRE-1 JULY 2009 ESS INTERESTS

Division 83A may apply to interests acquired prior to 1 July 2009 where they had been subject to deferred taxation under the superseded rules.

The key transitional rules are summarised as follows:

INTERESTS WHERE TAXING POINT DEFERRED

Interests acquired before 1 July 2009 under an ESS pursuant to Division 13A with the assessable discount being deferred to a date later than 30 June 2009 will become subject to Division 83A rules (refer below for rules regarding the taxing point).

INTERESTS WHERE DISCOUNT ALREADY TAXED

ESS interests which have been assessed under Div 13A will remain subject to those rules. For example, rights in respect of which no election was made to defer the taxing point would continue to be subject to the application of Div 13A.

NOTE: Where the interests are deemed to be acquired pre-1 July 2009 under the former rules and the new rules deem the interest to be acquired post-1 July 2009, a tie-breaker rule gives priority to the Div 13A provisions.

TAXING POINT DETERMINED BY FORMER RULES

Shares or rights acquired before 1 July 2009 under either of the former measures (Division 13A or s26AAC of the ITAA36) will continue to be subject to tax at the time determined by reference to those previous rules. For example: ESS interests for which no 'cessation time' event had occurred after seven years (the maximum period available under Division 83A) would have no taxing point until such an event did occur (which may be after ten years, the maximum deferral available under the DIvision 13A rules).

REFUND OF TAX PAID UNDER OLD RULES

Taxpayers who paid tax on rights acquired under an ESS prior to 1 July 2010 will still be entitled to a refund of tax if the employee subsequently forfeits those rights and a refund would have been available under the former rules. The refund in this case would be available if the employee loses the right without having exercised it.

TFN WITHHOLDING REQUIREMENT NOT APPLICABLE

The TFN withholding requirement does not apply to shares and rights which have been transitioned to the new rules and the employee has not quoted their TFN and/or ABN to their employer. Reporting will apply to transitioned interests.

The new rules relating to, among other things, employer reporting and calculating the amount to include in assessable income will apply to those shares or rights which have been brought within the new rules. The Commissioner will formulate the manner in which this information is to be reported.

11.870   INTERACTION BETWEEN ESS RULES AND CGT

As a general rule, the ESS provision is the primary taxing provision and will apply in preference to the CGT provisions (or any other provision in tax law). Therefore, to avoid double taxation, once an ESS interest has been taxed under the ESS rules, it is subsequently taxed consistent with other capital assets, typically under the CGT regime, but possibly under regimes such as the trading stock provisions. Subdivision 130-D contained in the CGT provisions achieves this outcome by preventing any overlap (see 12.800).

As such, the CGT implications to an employee for ESS interests (ie. shares or options) acquired and disposed of under an ESS are as follows:

(I) TAXED-UPFRONT ESS

Under these circumstances, the ESS interests are taken to be acquired at their market value irrespective of whether the employee is eligible for the $1,000 reduction or consideration has been made in acquiring those interests. In other words, for CGT purposes, the interests will have a market value cost base at that time.

NOTE: The cost base also takes into account any expense such as brokerage and interest which may be paid.

As the discount is taxed upfront, the CGT rules will apply from the time the ESS interests are acquired.

For the purposes of determining entitlement to the CGT discount (see 12.165) if the ESS interests were to be disposed, the interests are deemed to have been acquired at the time of acquisition.

(II) TAX DEFERRED

Under these circumstances, the ESS interests are taken to be 're-acquired' at their market value immediately after the 'ESS deferred taxing point' (discussed above). This market value will be the cost base of the interests at that time. The CGT rules will apply from the ESS deferred taxing point.

For the purposes of determining entitlement to the CGT discount (see 12.165) if the ESS interests were to be disposed, the interests are deemed to have been acquired immediately after the ESS deferred taxing point.

WHERE ESS INTEREST ARE RIGHTS OR OPTIONS

In additlon to the above CGT implications, where rights are acquired under an ESS, the CGT implications which apply if the rights lapse or are exercised by the employee are follows:

- **If rights lapse:** A capital loss equal to the cost base of the rights would be triggered at the time pursuant to CGT event C2 (see 12.024).
- **If rights exercised:**
    - Any capital gain or loss upon exercise would typically be disregarded.
    - The cost base of the shares acquired would be the cost base of the rights acquired plus the exercise price.
    - For the purposes of determining entitlement to the CGT discount (see 12.165) if the shares were to be disposed, the acquisition date of the shares will be at the time the shares were allotted.

11.880 PROPOSED CHANGES TO ESS

On 25 March 2015, the *Tax and Superannuation laws Amendment (Employee Share Schemes) Bill 2015* was introduced into Parliament. At time of writing, the Bill has not been enacted.

The Bill contains a number of proposed amendments to the ESS rules. These amendments will apply to ESS interests acquired on or after 1 July 2015.

The proposed changes are summarised below.

CONCESSION FOR SMALL START-UP COMPANIES

There will be a tax exemption for discounts on ESS interests acquired in eligible 'small start-up companies'. **Where the interest is a share**, the discount is exempt from tax. The share is then subject to the CGT regime, with a market value cost base.

Where the interest is a **right**, the discount is no subject to upfront taxation. The right, and the resulting share once acquired, are then subject to the CGT regime, with a cost base equal to the employee's cost of acquiring the right.

The tax concession is available only if certain conditions are met.

EMPLOYER CONDITIONS

The company which the ESS interest is in – the employer (or its holding company) – must satisfy the following conditions:

- No equity interests in the employer can be listed on an approved stock or securities exchange at the end of the income year before the acquisition of the ESS interest. For integrity reasons, this rule also applies to a subsidiary of the employer company, a holding company and any other subsidiary of a holding company.
- The employer must be a company that was incorporated less than 10 years before the end of the income year prior to when the ESS interest was acquired. For integrity reasons, this rule also applies to a subsidiary of the employer company, a holding company and any other subsidiary of a holding company.
- The company's aggregated turnover (as defined in s328-115 ITAA97) for the income year prior to the income year in which the ESS interest was acquired must not exceed $50 million.
- The employing company (which may or may not be the company issuing the ESS interest) must be an Australian tax resident.

ESS INTEREST CONDITIONS

The ESS interest must meet the following conditions:

- In the case of a share – it must be acquired with a discount of less than 15% of the market value of the share when acquired.

- In the case of a right – it must have an exercise price that is greater than or equal to the market value of an ordinary share in the issuing company at the time the right is acquired.

The Explanatory Memorandum contains examples of how the start-up concession will operate.

EXAMPLE 1.1: Shares

Tracy is issued with 10,000 shares in a small Australian start-up entity under an ESS. The shares at issue have a market value of $1 per share. Tracy contributes 85¢ per share under the scheme. Tracy and the ESS meet all the rules for her 10,000 shares to be covered by the small start-up ESS tax concession.

After 5 years, the Australian start-up entity is sold under a trade sale where Tracy receives $1.50 per share for each of shares. On acquisition, Tracy receives a discount of $1,500 which is not included in her assessable income (ie., not subject to income tax). Her shares will then have a cost base for capital gains tax purposes of $10,000.

When Tracy sells her shares she has a discount capital gain of $2,500 this is included in her net capital gain or loss for the income year. If she has no other capital gains or losses for that year, and no capital losses carried forward from a previous year, the $2,500 is then included in her assessable income.

EXAMPLE 1.2: Rights

Tim is issued with 10,000 'out of the money' options under an ESS operated by his small Australian start-up employer for no consideration. The options allow Tim to acquire 10,000 ordinary shares in his employer after paying an exercise price of $1.50 per right (which is more than the current market value of each share – $1 per share).

Tim and the ESS meet all the rules for his 10,000 rights to be covered by the small start-up ESS tax concession.

After 5 years, Tim exercises each right by paying $15,000. Tim then immediately sells each share for $2.00 with his total proceeds being $20,000. On acquisition, Tim does not include any amount in his assessable income in relation to the discount received on his options. His options will have a nil cost base for capital gains tax purposes.

There will be no capital gains tax on exercise of his rights and receipt of his shares (due to the availability of a capital gains tax rollover). However, on exercise, the cost base of his shares will be $1.50 per share.

On sale of his shares Tim will have a discount capital gain of $2,500 that is included in his net capital gain or loss for the income year. If he has no other capital gains or losses for that year, and no capital losses carried forward from a previous year, the $2,500 is then included in his assessable income.

CHANGES TO SOME DEFERRED TAXING POINTS

Increase in maximum deferral period

The maximum deferral period will increase from 7 years to 15 years.

Deferral for rights

The ability to defer the taxing point for rights has been expanded. Under the proposed law, the taxing point does not occur merely once the restrictions on the exercise of the right are lifted; the taxpayer must actually have exercised the right in order to trigger the taxing point.

CHANGES TO GENERAL CONDITIONS

Ownership and voting rights

The Bill raises the ownership and voting rights limitation thresholds from 5% to 10%. This doubling of the thresholds will be accompanied by new integrity provisions:

- The ownership and voting rights tests will become associate-inclusive tests. There is an exception if the associate acquired their interests in relation to their own employment.
- The ownership and voting rights tests will include beneficial interests in shares that the taxpayer could obtain by exercising rights, whether or not those rights are ESS interests. Further, it is assumed that the taxpayer would be entitled to cast votes as a result of holding those beneficial interests in shares. This rule is also associate-inclusive.

Minimum holding period

The Commissioner will be allowed to reduce the minimum holding period (3 years) in situations in which all employees are effectively required to exercise and/or dispose of their ESS interests (eg. where there is an initial public offering of the company).

The reduction is at the discretion of the Commissioner. In applying the discretion, the Commissioner will need to have regard to whether, when employees acquired their interest, there was a genuine intention for the interests to be held for the minimum holding period.

Scheme rules in relation to rights

The Bill will insert a provision in relation to scheme rules. Under the proposal, the general conditions for deferred taxation in relation to a right include a situation where all of the following are met at the time that the taxpayer acquired the interest:

- the scheme genuinely restricted the taxpayer immediately disposing of the right, and
- the governing rules of the scheme expressly stated that Subdivision 83A-C (ie. the deferral provisions) applies to the scheme.

REFUNDS OF INCOME TAX

The current law provides for a refund of income tax paid in relation to an ESS interest in circumstances where the interest is forfeited after the taxpayer has been assessed on the discount.

The Bill proposes an amendment to ensure that the following choices in relation to a beneficial interest in a right will not prevent the application of the refund provision:

- a choice not to exercise the right before it lapsed, or
- a choice to allow the right to be cancelled.

A refund is not available where the forfeiture or loss is a result of:

- a condition of the scheme that has the effect of protecting the taxpayer against downside market risk, or
- a choice made by the taxpayer (eg. a choice not to exercise a right or to allow a right to be cancelled).

STANDARDISED DOCUMENTATION

The ATO is required to work with industry and ASIC to develop and approve and approve new standardised documentation that streamlines the establishment and administration of an ESS. The standard documentation will be issued under the Commissioner's general powers of administration. The ATO has undertaken consultation in relation to this matter.

SAFE HARBOUR VALUATION METHODS

The Bill introduces a new power for the Commissioner to approve market valuation methodologies that can be used by taxpayers to comply more easily with the law and to reduce compliance costs.

The Commissioner can, by legislative instrument, approve a method for determining the market value of an asset or non-cash benefit for income tax law purposes (proposed s960-412).

An approved methodology is binding on the Commissioner so long as the taxpayer has complied with any relevant conditions.

While the new approved safe harbour valuation methodology applies more broadly in relation to the tax law than just the ESS regime, it is anticipated that the Commissioner will initially only exercise this new power with regard to ESS arrangements for small unlisted corporate tax entities only.

The Commissioner's safe harbour market valuation methodologies will apply from the date specified by the Commissioner in a legislative instrument.

The ATO has undertaken consultation in relation to this matter.

CONSEQUENTIAL AMENDMENTS

CGT for temporary residents and foreign residents

The CGT concessions that apply to temporary residents and foreign residents will be removed in relation to ESS interests which qualify for the new start-up concession.

Fringe benefits tax

The Bill amends Division 83A to fix a technical defect and ensure that certain ESS interests that are issued at a discount remains within the scope of Division 83A and not be subject to FBT.

11.900 EXEMPT INCOME

Exempt income is not included in assessable income (s6-20 of the ITAA97), and accordingly expenses incurred in deriving exempt income are not allowable deductions (s8-1(2)(c) of the ITAA97). However, carried forward losses must be offset against net exempt income prior to being offset against assessable income. Subdivision 11-A of the ITAA97 provides a list of classes of exempt income. Many of the exempting provisions are found in Divisions 51 and 52 of the ITAA97, while Division 50 outlines entities that are exempt from income tax.

Exempt income is statutorily defined as being ordinary income or statutory income that is designated as exempt income by a provision of the Tax Acts. Therefore, amounts that are not prima facie of an 'income' nature (ie. are not ordinary or statutory income) will also not be exempt income. Examples of items that are not assessable or exempt income include lottery prizes and gifts that are not received in relation to income-earning activities.

Types of exempt income include the following (note this is not an exhaustive list):

EXEMPT AUSTRALIAN GOVERNMENT PENSIONS, ALLOWANCES AND PAYMENTS

- Carer payment where:
  - both the carer and either the care receiver or all of the care receivers are under age-pension age, or
  - the carer is under age-pension age and any of the care receivers has died
- Defence Force Income Support Allowance (DFISA) payable where the whole of another social security pension or benefit is exempt from income tax under s52-10 ITAA97
- Disability support pension paid by Centrelink to a person who is under age-pension age
- Double orphan pension
- Invalidity service pension where the veteran is under age-pension age
- Partner service pension where either:
  - the partner (excluding the non-illness separated spouse of a veteran) and the veteran are under age-pension age and the veteran receives an invalidity service pension, or
  - the partner is under age-pension age and the veteran has died and was receiving an invalidity service pension at the time of death
- Veterans' Affairs disability pension and allowances, war widows and war widowers pension
- Wife pension where both the recipient and their partner are under age-pension age or the recipient is under age-pension age and their partner has died.

EXEMPT AUSTRALIAN GOVERNMENT EDUCATION PAYMENTS

- Allowances for students under 16 years of age including those paid under ABSTUDY, austudy payment, youth allowance, Assistance for Isolated Children Scheme, Commonwealth secondary education assistance and the Veterans' Children Education Scheme
- Apprenticeship wage top-up
- Australian–American Educational Foundation grant
- Commonwealth scholarships or bursaries provided to foreign students
- Commonwealth secondary education assistance other than that already referred to
- Commonwealth Trade Learning Scholarship
- Early completion bonuses for apprentices
- Language, literacy and numeracy supplement
  - Payments under the Military Rehabilitation and Compensation Act Education and Training Scheme 2004 for eligible young persons whose eligibility was determined

under: paragraph 258 (1)(a) of the *Military Rehabilitation and Compensation Act 2004* and the eligible young person was under 16 years of age, or
- paragraph 258 (1)(b) of the *Military Rehabilitation and Compensation Act 2004*
- Pensioner education supplement and fares allowance paid by Centrelink
- Some scholarships and bursaries received by full-time students
- Supplementary allowances for students paid under the Assistance for Isolated Children Scheme.

OTHER EXEMPT AUSTRALIAN GOVERNMENT PAYMENTS

- Australian Government disaster recovery payments
- Baby bonus paid by Centrelink
- Back to school bonus or single income family bonus
- Carer allowance paid under the *Social Security Act 1991*
- Child care benefit
- Child care tax rebate
- Child disability assistance under Part 2 19AA of the *Social Security Act 1991*
- DFISA bonus and DFISA bonus bereavement payment under Part VIIAB of the *Veterans' Entitlement Act 1986*
- Disaster relief payment
- Employment entry payment
- F-111 deseal/reseal ex-gratia lump sum payments
- Family tax benefit
- Farm household support payments that have been converted to a grant
- Loss of earnings allowance paid under the *Veterans' Entitlements Act 1986*
- Lump sum pension bonus paid under the *Social Security Act 1991* or the *Veterans' Entitlements Act 1986*
- Maternity immunisation allowance
- Maternity payment
- Mobility allowance paid under the *Social Security Act 1991*
- One-off payment to families
- Open employment incentive bonus under the *Handicapped Persons Assistance Act 1974*
- Payments from the Australian Government under the incentive payments scheme relating to certain private health insurance policies
- Payments to carers under the scheme determined under Schedule 4 to the *Social Security and Veterans' Affairs Legislation Amendment (One-off Payments and Other 2007 Measures) Act 2007*
- Pension bonus and pension bonus bereavement payment under Part 2.2A of the *Social Security Act 1991* or Part IIIAB of the *Veterans' Entitlement Act 1986*
- Pharmaceutical allowances paid under the *Social Security Act 1991* or the *Veterans' Entitlements Act 1986*
- Phone allowance paid under the *Social Security Act 1991* or the *Veterans' Entitlements Act 1986*
- Remote area allowance
- Rent assistance
- Seniors concession allowance paid under the *Social Security Act 1991* or the *Veterans' Entitlements Act 1986*
- Sugar industry exit grants where conditions are met
- Super Co-contributions
- Tobacco industry exit grant where you complied with a condition of the grant not to own or operate any agricultural business within five years after receiving the grant
- Utilities allowance paid under the *Social Security Act 1991* or the *Veterans' Entitlements Act 1986*.

EXEMPT AUSTRALIAN DEFENCE FORCE AND UNITED NATIONS PAYMENTS

- Certain pay and allowances for Australian Defence Force personnel
- Compensation payments for impairment or incapacity resulting from service with a United Nations armed force
- Compensation payments made under the *Military Rehabilitation and Compensation Act 2004,* except those that are income-related payments
- Pay and allowances for part-time service in the Australian Naval, Army or Air Force Reserve
- Some allowances paid to Australian Defence Force personnel who served in prescribed overseas areas.

OTHER EXEMPT AMOUNTS

- Certain annuities and lump sums which are paid to an injured person under a structured settlement
- Mortgage and Rent Relief Scheme payments
- Certain distributions from an early stage venture capital limited partnership
- Certain distributions from a pooled development fund
- Certain payments relating to persecution during the Second World War
- Japanese internment compensation payments made under the *Compensation (Japanese Internment) Act 2001* or the *Veterans' Entitlements Act 1986.*
- A payment by company or trust arising from application of the small business retirement exemption
- Income of a superannuation fund from assets used to meet current pension liabilities or segregated current pensions assets
- Benefits from non-complying superannuation fund
- Maintenance and child support payments
- Salary and wages earned overseas by certain Australian resident aid workers and defence force personnel where the period of continuous foreign service is at least 91 days (s23AG of the ITAA36 – see from 22.010)
- Income earned in relation to approved overseas projects.

11.910 ORGANISATIONS EXEMPT FROM INCOME TAX

The income of certain categories of organisations is specifically exempted from tax. This includes deductible gift recipients (ie. those to whom a gift or donation is tax deductible to the donor) – see from 13.890.

While Division 50 of the ITAA97 governs the tax-exempt status of certain types of organisations, the provisions interact with Division 30 of the ITAA97 which sets out the categories of organisations to which gifts are tax-deductible.

ORGANISATIONS THAT ARE EXEMPT

Division 50 of the ITAA97 sets out specific categories of organisations which are tax-exempt, including:

- religious, scientific, charitable and public educational institutions
- public or not-for-profit hospitals
- not-for-profit cultural, sporting and friendly societies but not a friendly society dispensary
- public charitable and scientific research funds
- registered associations of employers
- trade unions
- certain employer or employee associations

- bodies promoting development of aviation, tourism, agricultural, pastoral, horticultural or viticultural resources
- bodies established to promote manufacturing or industrial resources etc. in Australia
- registered not-for-profit medical, health or hospital benefits organisations
- public hospitals or not-for-profit hospitals carried on by a society or association
- groups established for musical purposes, or to encourage music, art, science or literature
- not-for-profit clubs, societies and associations established to promote or encourage a sport or game – but social clubs are taxable
- bodies established for the encouragement or the promotion of animal races
- local government businesses that become companies to improve their efficiency and service delivery
- bodies established for community services purposes (eg. Apex and Rotary Clubs) (but not for political or lobbying purposes), and
- municipalities, other local governing bodies and public authorities.

Organisations in the listed categories will often also need to satisfy 'special conditions', legislated in Division 50, in order to qualify for tax-exempt status (see below).

Some, but not all, of the above will also be exempt from fringe benefits tax and GST.

The deductible gift tables can be found on the Tax Office's website at www.ato.gov.au. Details of prescribed organisation are set out in the regulations (Reg. 50-50.01, 50-55.01 and 50.70.01) and in the ITAA97.

 An exempt body receiving income from a trust is not taxed on that income. The trustee of a trust deriving investment or trading income may therefore be able to make tax-effective donations to a preferred charity or cause if the trust deed provides that ability.

SPECIAL CONDITIONS

To be entitled to exemption under Division 50, the relevant organisation would generally be required to satisfy other special conditions. Generally it is required that the organisation:

- has a physical presence in Australia, incurs its expenditure and conduct its activities in Australia
- be listed in one of the deductible gift tables in Division 30
- be a prescribed organisation located outside Australia and exempt in the country of residence, or
- be a prescribed organisation with a physical presence in Australia but incurring its expenditure and conducting its activities outside Australia.

 Taxation Ruling TR 2015/1 provides guidance on the special conditions attached to the definition of 'exempt entity' in Division 50.

OTHER NOT-FOR-PROFIT ORGANISATIONS

Note that a not-for-profit organisation that does not satisfy the criteria for obtaining tax-exempt status would only be taxed on its non-member income (eg. interest or dividend income from external investments or income from sales of goods to third parties). This outcome is due to the principle of mutuality. The principle of mutuality is based on the notion that a taxpayer cannot make profit out of themselves and therefore such an organisation should not be assessed on receipts from members (such as membership fees). As a corollary, expenditures that the organisation pays to itself (its members) are not allowed as deductions. Therefore, even if an organisation is not exempt from income tax, it will only be liable to income tax on the income it derives from sources outside of the organisation (see 9.400 and 9.500).

In the Commissioner's view, the principle of mutuality does not apply to a penalty amount received by a strata corporation. The amount is ordinary income.

11.950 NON-ASSESSABLE NON-EXEMPT INCOME

Non-assessable non-exempt (NANE) income is ordinary or statutory income that is designated as being neither assessable nor exempt income by a specific provision of the Tax Acts (s6-23 of the ITAA97). In the same way as exempt income, NANE is not subject to income tax, but unlike exempt income, it does not reduce carry forward losses nor is it taken into account for income threshold tests in respect of certain government benefits or tax surcharges. Expenses incurred in deriving NANE income are not allowed as deductions (s8-1(2)(c) of the ITAA97).

Division 11-B of the ITAA97 lists the types of NANE income contained in the Tax Acts. NANE income includes (this list is not exhaustive):

IN THE ITAA36

- Fringe benefits (s23L(1))
- Dividend, royalty or interest income subject to withholding tax (s128D)
- Demerger dividends (s44(4)) and later dividend set off against an amount taken to be dividends (s109ZC(3))
- For corporate taxpayers – non-portfolio dividends sourced from a foreign country (s23AJ)
- Attributable controlled foreign company income (s23AI)
- Attributable foreign investment fund income (s23AK)
- Foreign branch income (s23AH).

IN THE ITAA97

- GST payable on a taxable supply (s17-5)
- Bonus payments made to older Australians (s59-5)
- Tax Bonus for Working Australians (s59-45)
- Compensation under s59-10 for firearms surrender arrangements
- Payments to Aboriginals and distributing bodies subject to mining withholding tax (s59-15)
- Amounts that must be repaid (s59-30)
- Payments by personal services entity or associate of personal services income already assessable to an individual (s86-35(1))
- Income from the disposal of small business assets arising from CGT event that a company or trust owned continuously for 15 years (s152-110(2))
- Amounts subject to family trust distribution tax (s271-105(3) in Sch 2F)
- Payments by taxed superannuation funds to members 60 and over or to reversionaries 60 or over (Div 301)
- Superannuation lump sum for recipient having terminal medical condition (s303-10)
- Either of the following under a demutualisation of a private health insurer:
    - the market value of shares and rights at time of issue, or
    - payments received in exchange for cancellation or variation of interests under the demutualisation (s315-310)
- Tax-free amount of a genuine redundancy or early retirement scheme payment (s83-235, 83-240 & 83-170)
- Credits to and payments from first home saver accounts (s345-50)
- Foreign income derived by temporary resident (s768-910)
- Managed investment fund withholding tax (s840-815)
- Payments made, and non-cash benefits provided, by a State or Territory governmental body in relation to participation in the National Rental Affordability Scheme (s380-35)
- Lease payments that the lessor receives for luxury car leases (subdivision 242-B)
- Amounts received from related entities in excess of reasonable amount (s26-35(4)).

Capital gains tax

12

HOW CAPITAL GAINS TAX WORKS

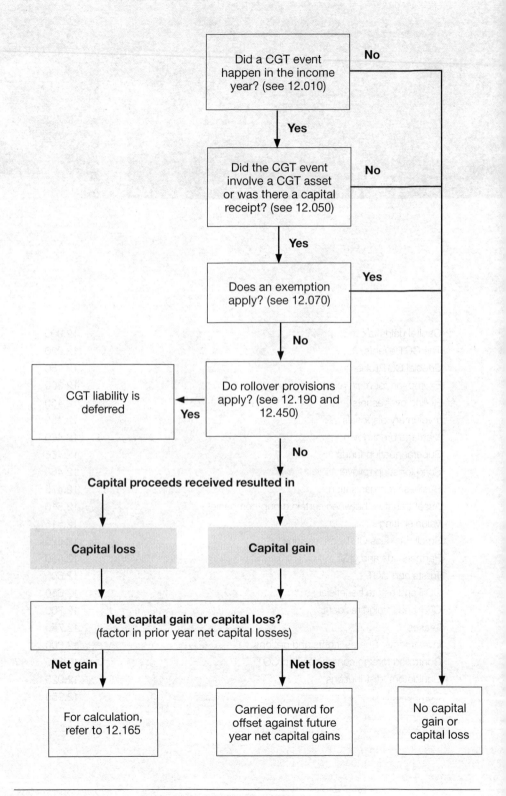

Did a CGT event happen in the income year? (see 12.010) — **No**

Yes

Did the CGT event involve a CGT asset or was there a capital receipt? (see 12.050) — **No**

Yes

Does an exemption apply? (see 12.070) — **Yes**

No

Do rollover provisions apply? (see 12.190 and 12.450) — **Yes** → CGT liability is deferred

No

Capital proceeds received resulted in

Capital loss | **Capital gain**

Net capital gain or capital loss?
(factor in prior year net capital losses)

Net gain → For calculation, refer to 12.165

Net loss → Carried forward for offset against future year net capital gains

No capital gain or capital loss

12.000 CAPITAL GAINS TAX

Capital Gains Tax (CGT) is a tax on the realisation of an asset acquired after 19 September 1985 (or deemed to be acquired after that date) where the realisation of the asset was not undertaken in a manner which would result in a gain being considered ordinary income (and assessable under s6-5). The provisions also tax certain capital amounts received by a taxpayer. Not all assets are subject to the CGT regime and provisions exist to defer the tax in some circumstances.

NOTE: All legislative references are to the *Income Tax Assessment Act 1997* (ITAA97) unless otherwise stated.

Generally, a capital gain arises where a 'CGT event' occurs after 19 September 1985 and the capital amount received (or receivable) from the CGT event, exceeds the total costs associated with that event (s100-35). Any net capital gain that results from a CGT event is included in assessable income (s102-5(1)).

Determining whether a CGT event has occurred and if so, which CGT event has occurred, is central to the CGT provisions and is the first step in the decision process. The legislation separately sets out how the net capital gain is determined and the timing of each of the CGT events.

The CGT legislation operates in accordance with the preceding diagrammatic outline.

12.010 STEP 1: DID A CGT EVENT HAPPEN?

The first step is to determine whether a CGT event has happened (s102-20).

WHAT IS A CGT EVENT?

The ITAA97 currently lists 53 CGT events. Some of these events will happen frequently whilst other events will have limited application. The CGT events are discussed later in this chapter. For each CGT event the legislation sets out:

- the cause of the event
- the timing of the event, and
- how the capital gain or capital loss resulting from the event is determined.

The CGT events summarised in s104-5 are in no particular order.

WHICH IS THE APPROPRIATE CGT EVENT?

To resolve any conflict that may arise in determining the most appropriate CGT event, s102-25 sets out the applicable rules.

The steps for selecting the applicable CGT event are:

- Select which of the CGT events apply (initially ignore D1 and H2 which are considered later).
- If more than one event applies, select the most specific to the situation.
- There are three exceptions:
  - Where the circumstances that give rise to CGT event J2 constitute another CGT event, CGT event J2 applies in addition to the other event, and
  - CGT event K5 depends on CGT events A1, C2 or E8 happening. In that case, event K5 applies in addition to the other event, and
  - CGT event K12 happens in addition to the individual CGT events that gave rise in the end to a foreign hybrid net capital loss.
- If no previously considered CGT event applies, then consider if CGT event D1 applies.
- If CGT event D1 does not apply, then consider if CGT event H2 applies.

As a general rule the most specific event is used, but there are exceptions.

As the happening of a CGT event is essential to determining whether a taxpayer is subject to tax, s102-25 requires that all CGT events be considered. CGT events D1 and H2 are considered last because they only apply if no other CGT event triggers a capital gain or loss (ie. catch-all provisions).

No guidelines exist to assist taxpayers in determining the most specific CGT event. This is consistent with the legal principle that where there is a conflict between a general provision and a specific provision, the specific provision prevails.

Importance of choosing the correct CGT event

Selection of the correct CGT event is critical because:

- each CGT event has its own timing rules
- the capital gain or capital loss calculated under different CGT events may vary, and
- concessions and exemptions apply only to some CGT events.

For example, if a factory that was insured was completely destroyed by fire, both CGT events A1 and C1 could apply. If the taxpayer incorrectly selected CGT event A1 as the most appropriate event, the taxpayer could be disadvantaged because CGT event A1 would recognise the disposal at the time of the change in ownership, while in the case of event C1 the disposal is deferred until compensation is received. Further, different timing rules may impact the amount of tax payable on the capital gain where differing tax rates over more than one financial year apply due to fluctuating taxable income levels or rate changes. Alternatively, if the fire had resulted in a capital loss, the taxpayer may be disadvantaged by CGT event C1 because the loss is not available to shelter gains in the intervening period.

As the CGT event is the first essential element in determining whether a taxpayer is liable for CGT, it is important to have knowledge of each CGT event and when it might apply.

Section 104-5 provides a description of each CGT event, its timing and how to calculate the capital gain or loss. While s104-5 provides a convenient overview, it is only a summary. It does not indicate whether there is an exemption or whether any rollover provisions apply. It is therefore important to read the operative provision of each specific event.

12.020 THE CGT EVENTS

12.021   CGT EVENT A1: DISPOSAL OF A CGT ASSET

CGT event A1 is the most common event. It covers the disposal or part disposal of a CGT asset (defined in s108-5) that was acquired (or is deemed to be acquired) after 19 September 1985 (s104-10). A disposal of a CGT asset occurs where there is a change in beneficial ownership of that asset (s104-10(2)). Consequently, CGT event A1 would not apply where:

- the asset is lost or destroyed etc: event C1 would apply
- there is a creation of rights, which on creation vest in another entity: event D1 would apply
- there is no change in beneficial ownership: event E2 may apply, or
- there is merely a change in trustee (ie. merely a change in the legal ownership of the asset).

There is also no change of ownership where land is subdivided or titles to land are amalgamated (Taxation Determination TD 7 and TD 8).

CGT event A1 generally occurs at the making of the contract (written or oral) which subsequently leads to a change of ownership. If there is no contract, the timing of the CGT event is when there is a change of ownership. Section 104-10(6) outlines some special timing rules where an asset is compulsorily acquired.

TD 94/89 deals with the scenario where an exchange of contracts occurs in one year of income, but settlement occurs in a subsequent year of income. It is the view of the Commissioner that CGT Event A1 is triggered at settlement because a change of ownership occurs at this time, however the CGT event would be recognised at the contract date. Therefore, the Commissioner accepts that a taxpayer may lodge a return for the earlier year of income (when the contract was made) without including the capital gain where settlement has not yet occurred. Once settlement occurs, the taxpayer would be required to amend that return within a reasonable period to include the capital gain. The Commissioner states that a period of one month after settlement would generally be considered reasonable. This means that the actual payment of

CGT will be deferred until settlement proceeds are received. Any late payment penalties should generally be waived, although care must be exercised to ensure that the amended return is submitted immediately after settlement occurs.

The Commissioner also suggests that as an alternative (and to ensure that no penalties or interest are incurred), a taxpayer may include the capital gain in the return for the earlier year of income notwithstanding that settlement has not yet occurred. In the event that settlement never occurs, the taxpayer would be able to amend their return to exclude the capital gain.

 Julie sells land under a contract made on 30 June 2013. The contract is settled on 31 January 2014. A capital gain of $50,000 accrues to her on the disposal. Julie is required to include the $50,000 in her tax return for the 2012-13 income year (not the 2014-15 income year).

If Julie had already lodged her 2012-13 tax return before the date of settlement without including the capital gain, she should, within a reasonable period of time after settlement, take any action necessary to have her assessment amended to include the capital gain.

With some contracts (eg. a mandatory buy/sell agreement) it is noted that many years may elapse between the date of contract and date of settlement.

A change of ownership generally occurs when the transfer of title occurs on physical delivery of the asset. If the property is intangible, such as a legal right, title will usually pass on the execution and delivery of the instrument effecting the assignment.

If there is more than one contract, it is necessary to consider which is the appropriate contract. The appropriate contract is the one which is the source of the obligations to effect the disposal (*FC of T v Sara Lee Household & Bodycare (Aust) Pty Ltd* 2000 ATC 4378, *Elmslie & Ors v FC of T* 93 ATC 4964). Further, the appropriate contract is not required to be specifically enforceable when made: it can be subject to subsequent conditions such as obtaining statutory approval (*Kiwi Brands Pty Ltd v FC of T* 99 ATC 4001).

In the case of a contract to sell land, a written contract is required by law, the signing and exchange of the written contract is the time of the CGT event (*McDonald & Anor v FC of T* 2001 ATC 4146).

Where a written contract exists, the date of the CGT event is the date that the contract is signed. However, if the contract falls through before its completion, CGT event A1 does not apply because there would not be a change of ownership (although a breach of contract may create contractual or other rights causing CGT event D1 to happen).

The disposal of rights under an assumption agreement occurs at the time the assumption payments are made and not when the assumption agreement is entered into (*FC of T v Dulux Holdings Pty Ltd & Anor* 2001 ATC 4658). In *Corin v Patton* 1990 169 CLR 540, the High Court said that for a change in ownership to have occurred, the donor is required to have done everything necessary to enable the donee to achieve legal ownership.

In the case of a gift of shares, the handing over of a signed share transfer form and the share scrip would constitute a disposal of shares by the donor, even though the transfer is not registered (*Case V156* 88 ATC 1005).

The change of ownership from a husband, to a husband and wife jointly can be a CGT event A1 (AAT Case [2014] AATA 461, Re Murphy v FC of T)

A capital gain arises under CGT event A1 if the capital proceeds from the disposal of the CGT asset are more than the asset's cost base (12.092), and a capital loss arises if those proceeds are less than the asset's reduced cost base (12.102).

A capital gain or loss is disregarded under event A1 where the asset was acquired prior to 20 September 1985.

Exclusions: Subsection 104-10(7) provides that CGT event A1 does not happen if the disposal of the asset was done:

- to provide or redeem a security
- to vest the asset in a trustee under Bankruptcy laws (or similar foreign laws), or
- to vest the asset in a liquidator of a company (or the holder of a similar office under foreign law).

If land is mortgaged and the mortgage paid out, the mortgagor neither disposes of the land nor acquires the land and the mortgagee neither acquires nor disposes of the land.

NOTE: In *Confidential and Commissioner of Taxation* (2013) AATA 76, the taxpayer disposed of business assets by way of:

- a Heads of Agreement executed on 7 August 2008, and
- a Contract of Sale executed on 17 December 2008.

The AAT concluded that CGT event A1 occurred on 7 August 2008 as the Heads of Agreement bound the parties to the transaction and therefore a 'disposal' of the assets occurred.

12.022   CGT EVENT B1: USE AND ENJOYMENT BEFORE TITLE PASSES

CGT event B1 applies if the use and enjoyment of a CGT asset passes (without title passing) and title will or may pass at or before the 'end of the agreement'. The term 'end of the agreement' presupposes that there is a period for which the agreement runs and title will or may pass either during the agreement period or at the end of the agreement period (TD 1999/78).

CGT event B1 will not happen if, under a loose family arrangement, title to an asset may pass at an unspecified time in the future.

CGT event B1 can also happen to real estate if a terms contract is entered into (being a contract where the purchaser is entitled to possession of the land before becoming entitled to a transfer of the land). CGT event B1 occurs and not CGT event A1 where a taxpayer transfers a property to their adult children where it had been agreed that the children could use and enjoy the property for a specified period after which title to the property would be transferred to them (ATO ID 2005/216).

Where CGT event B1 applies, the CGT event occurs at the time the use and enjoyment of the asset occurs, even though title may not and will not pass until the property is paid for in full.

A capital gain arises for the grantor of the right if the capital proceeds from the agreement are more than the asset's cost base, and a capital loss arises if those proceeds are less than the asset's reduced cost base (s104-15(3)).

Any capital gain or loss made when the agreement was entered into is disregarded if the title to the asset does not pass at the end of the agreement (s104-15(4)). From a practical point of view, the grantor will need to include any capital gain as assessable income in the year the asset is first used, and if title does not pass at the end of the agreement, an amended assessment will be required to exclude the capital gain previously assessed.

A capital gain or loss will also not arise where the relevant asset was acquired before 20 September 1985.

12.024   CGT EVENTS C1 TO C3: END OF A CGT ASSET

CGT EVENT C1: LOSS OR DESTRUCTION OF A CGT ASSET

CGT event C1 applies to CGT assets that have been lost or destroyed. TD 1999/79 states that CGT event C1 does not distinguish between tangible and intangible assets.

The word 'loss' suggests an involuntary rather than a voluntary act (eg. theft), while the word 'destruction' contemplates both voluntary and involuntary actions (eg. natural disasters, acts by others over which the taxpayer has no control or the voluntary destruction of the asset by the taxpayer). CGT event C1 does not cover an economic loss, nor does C1 cover damages to an asset without the asset being wholly lost or destroyed (TD 1999/79).

The sale of shares without the owner's consent, to a bona fide purchaser of the shares for value and without notice of the owner's prior interest in the shares, means that the shares are lost and CGT event C1 will happen (ATO ID 2010/116).

Any compensation received for the loss or destruction is capital proceeds (s116-20(1)). The compensation could be either money or a replacement asset.

The rollover relief provisions in Subdivision 124-B may also apply (12.190 and 12.455).

CGT event C1 occurs when the compensation is received, or if no compensation is received, the timing of the event is when the loss is discovered (s104-20(2)).

A taxpayer makes a capital gain if the capital proceeds from the loss or destruction are more than the asset's cost base, and a capital loss if those proceeds are less than the asset's reduced cost base (s104-20(3)).

Any such gain or loss is ignored if the lost or destroyed asset was acquired prior to 20 September 1985.

For CGT event C1, the modification rule under which market value is substituted for actual capital proceeds does not apply (s116-25 and s116-30).

CGT EVENT C2: CANCELLATION, SURRENDER OR SIMILAR ENDINGS

CGT event C2 relates to the extinction of a taxpayer's ownership of an intangible CGT asset.

An intangible CGT asset is one that has no physical form such as an option, lease or a share in a company. Although there is no physical property, intangible assets are property because of the rights attached to the relevant agreement. For example, the rights attached to a share in a company are not bound to the share certificate, but are related to the agreement. Therefore, if the share certificate is destroyed, the property (rights to dividends etc.) has not been affected. This is in contrast to tangible assets where, if destroyed, the asset is also lost.

Intangible assets will no longer exist when the rights are given up or lost. Therefore, CGT event C2 includes such events as:

- a share being 'redeemed or cancelled'
- a debt being 'released, discharged or satisfied'
- a contract 'expiring' (expiry does not include voluntary termination of assets, but is limited to a lapse of time - TD 1999/76)
- a lease being 'abandoned, surrendered or forfeited'
- a cancellation or satisfaction of a right to compensation
- an option being exercised, and
- a convertible interest being converted.

The close-out of an exchange traded option is considered to trigger CGT event C2 (ATO ID 2005/164).

The timing of CGT event C2 is either when the taxpayer enters into the contract that results in the asset ending or, if there is no contract, when the asset ends.

A capital gain arises if the capital proceeds on the ending of the asset are more than the asset's cost base, whereas a capital loss arises if those proceeds are less than its reduced cost base. No capital gain arises where the asset was acquired prior to 20 September 1985. Accordingly, where the asset is a lease it will not result in a capital gain or loss under CGT event C2 if it was granted before 20 September 1985 or was last renewed or extended before that date (s104-25(5)).

Further, a legislative note to s104-25(5) alerts taxpayers to the various exceptions to CGT event C2.

CGT event C2 will not occur on the maturity of an unsecured note if the company that issued the note defaults on repayment of the amount the note represents. In these circumstances the underlying debt subject to the note may continue to exist despite the maturity of the note even where the relevant company is placed in administration. Thus, CGT event C2 will only happen if the taxpayer executes a deed of release in favour of the company so that the taxpayer is legally barred from collecting the debt or where the company is deregistered (ATO ID 2008/58).

Conversely, CGT event C2 will occur in respect of an investor's rights under a Deferred Purchase Agreement (DPA) warrant on the delivery of 'delivery assets' typically being securities issued on the Australian Securities Exchange (TD 2008/22). That is, the investor's rights under the warrant will be satisfied once the issuer of the warrant transfers the relevant securities to the investor in accordance with the terms of the DPA warrant.

CGT event C2 will occur when the deed of settlement covering a legal dispute is executed because the CGT assets, being the causes of action or 'choses in action', ended by "release, discharge or satisfaction or by being surrendered" as required by CGT event C2 (AAT Case [2014] AATA 622, Re *Coshott v FCT*). Taxation Ruling TR 95/35 states that compensation will be considered to be capital proceeds for the right to sue, if it is not received in relation to an underlying asset or is received as an undissected lump sum.

CGT EVENT C3: END OF AN OPTION TO ACQUIRE SHARES ETC

CGT event C3 happens if a company or the trustee of a unit trust grants to an entity an option to acquire shares or debentures in the company, or units or debentures in the unit trust, and the option ends because it is not exercised, is cancelled, or the entity releases or abandons it (s104-30(1)).

The timing of the event is when the option ends (s104-30(2)).

The company or trustee makes a capital gain if the capital proceeds from the granting of the option are more than the costs incurred in granting it. Conversely, a capital loss arises if those proceeds are less than the expenditure incurred in granting the option.

CGT event C3 does not apply to an option granted before 20 September 1985.

12.026 CGT EVENTS D1 TO D4: BRINGING A CGT ASSET INTO EXISTENCE

EVENT D1: CREATING CONTRACTUAL OR OTHER RIGHTS

CGT events D1 and D2 are the reverse of CGT events C1 to C3, and attempt to bring into the scope of CGT the disposal of legal rights through their creation. For example, in *Hepples v Federal Commissioner of Taxation* 91 ATC 4808 no property or asset existed before the signing of a restrictive covenant not to disclose trade secrets. After signing the agreement, the taxpayer received cash and his employer had a right to sue if the agreement was breached. Property had been created and disposed of to the employer on the signing of the agreement.

CGT event D1 only applies if no other CGT event happens, other than CGT event H2 (s102-25).

CGT event D1 may have wide application because it arises if a contractual right or other legal or equitable rights are created in another entity. The event still occurs even if there is no capital gain or loss for the entity creating the right (s102-23(a) and TD 1999/82).

CGT event D1 would apply where a person enters into a contractual agreement with another entity which acquired the rights under that agreement. An example is a cricketer accepting $20,000 in return for agreeing not to play for another club. The cricketer brings into existence a CGT asset, the contractual rights under the agreement, and CGT event D1 happens. If the agreement is breached, the other party to that agreement can enforce that right.

The provision of the right to use a depreciating asset by the taxpayer to another party is considered to trigger CGT event D1 (as the asset is not considered to be used for a 'taxable purpose' in terms of Division 40 ITAA97) and therefore the taxpayer was not entitled to a depreciation deduction under Division 40 ITAA97 (ATO ID 2009/137).

CGT event D1 will bring into the CGT net any capital proceeds received when a contractual right is created, such as a restrictive covenant. The only costs that can be applied against the capital proceeds are the incidental costs incurred in relation to the event (s104-35(3)).

As CGT event D1 only applies where another CGT event (other than CGT event H2) does not happen, if a taxpayer enters into a contract to sell land, CGT event A1 takes precedence over CGT event D1. The signing of the contract of sale constitutes the time of disposal of that land. Even though the buyer has a contractual right to enforce the contract, CGT event A1 would apply to the disposal of the land and therefore CGT event D1 is disregarded (s104-35(5)).

The timing of CGT event D1 is when the contract is entered into. If there is no contract, the time of the event is when the right is created (s104-35(2)). As the right is created when the legal or equitable right is enforceable, the exact timing of the event may not be easy to establish.

CGT event D1 does not apply on the creation of a loan although the lender would have acquired a debt for CGT purposes. Without this exclusion, the creation of a loan would be subject to CGT (s104-35(5)(a)).

In addition, if the right requires the taxpayer to do something that triggers another CGT event, then CGT event D1 also does not apply.

Section 104-35(5) also excludes from the application of CGT event D1 the allotment of equity or non-equity shares by a company, the issuing by the trustee of units in a unit trust, and the granting by the entities of an option to acquire equity interests, units or debentures.

NOTE: The market value substitution rule does not apply where CGT event D1 is triggered (s112-20(1)(a)(i)).

CGT EVENT D2: GRANTING AN OPTION

CGT event D2 refers to the granting of an option and the renewal or extension of an option. An option is a right over property that requires one of the parties to transfer or acquire the property if the option is exercised. Note that CGT event D1 would also cover this transaction, although CGT event D2 takes precedence as the more specific event.

A common example of an option is an agreement between a buyer and seller that allows the buyer more time to make a decision with respect to the purchase, allowing the buyer time to make relevant investigations without fear of the property being sold in the meantime. The buyer would pay an amount of consideration to the seller in return for this privilege. This agreement is termed a 'call option' (s134-1) and binds the grantor (seller) to transfer the property to the grantee (buyer) if the purchaser so requests within the time agreed. The reverse of a call option is termed a 'put option' (s134-1) which binds the grantor to purchase the property which is the subject of the option. Where the grantee acts on the option, this process is termed 'exercising' the option. If the time allowed in the option expires without the option being exercised, the option is said to 'lapse'.

When options granted under a business succession agreement are enforceable in the event of death or disablement, CGT event D2 is considered to be triggered upon death or disablement occurring and not at the time that the agreement was entered into (ATO ID 2003/1190).

CGT event D2 would also cover situations where an option requires an asset to be created.

As an option is a CGT asset under s108-5 it can also be sold by the grantee to another person (provided the agreement does not preclude this) thereby transferring the rights to a new owner giving rise to the possible application of CGT event A1.

The timing of CGT event D2 is when the grantor grants, renews or extends the option (s104-40(2)).

A capital gain occurs if the capital proceeds from the grant of the option are more than the expenditure incurred in granting it whereas a capital loss occurs where the capital proceeds are less than the expenditure incurred (s140-40(3)).

CGT event D2 also recognises that separate rules are required where the option is exercised so that there is a sale and purchase of the asset over which the option is created (s104-40(5)). In effect, where an option is created and then exercised, any capital gain or capital loss in relation to the grant of the option is disregarded for CGT purposes. Instead, the consideration for the grant of the option forms part of the total consideration for the underlying asset to which the option relates. Where this event straddles more than one income year, any capital gain returned in the year of the option may be later withdrawn by an amended assessment if the option is exercised in a later year.

Similarly, the cost of the option becomes part of the cost base of the asset over which the option was created (s134-1 sets out the cost bases applicable on the exercise of an option).

CGT event D2 does not apply to options created by a company or trustee of a unit trust to acquire a CGT asset being shares, debentures, or units in the relevant company or unit trust (s104-40(6)). This exception allows for specific rules that simplify the CGT treatment of options over shares etc. as these options are frequently traded before the option is either exercised or lapses.

Options over shares etc. are only subject to CGT when the option ceases to exist (CGT event C3, s104-30) or when the options are sold (CGT event A1).

CGT event D2 does not apply to an option over a personal use asset or collectable (s104-35(7)).

CGT EVENT D3: GRANTING A RIGHT TO INCOME FROM MINING

CGT event D3 happens if the taxpayer owns a prospecting entitlement or mining entitlement, or an interest in one, and grants another entity the right to receive ordinary income or statutory income from the operations permitted to be carried on by the entitlement.

The time of this event is either when the contract is entered into or, if there is no contract, when the right to receive the income is granted (s104-45(2)).

A capital gain arises if the capital proceeds from granting the right are more than the expenditure incurred in granting it. Conversely, a capital loss arises where those proceeds are less than the costs incurred (s104-45(3)).

CGT EVENT D4: CONSERVATION COVENANTS

Governments, environmental and philanthropic organisations enter into covenants with landowners to conserve their property in perpetuity, in order to maintain its environmental value for all Australians. For such covenants entered into on or after 15 June 2000 and approved by the Minister for the Environment, CGT event D4 rather than CGT event D1 may apply.

Under CGT event D4, at the time of entering into the covenant the landowner is required to apportion the cost base of the property between that part subject to the covenant and the remaining property. The event has the effect of a part disposal of the land subject to the covenant. CGT is payable on the difference between the capital proceeds and the cost base of that part of the land which is subject to the covenant.

If the land-owner has not received any capital proceeds, CGT event D4 does not apply unless all of the requirements for a deduction under Division 31 are satisfied. Capital proceeds are then taken to be the amount of the deduction under Division 31 for the decline in market value of the land (note that where no capital proceeds are received, a deduction under Division 31 is only available for covenants entered into on or after 1 July 2002).

If CGT event D4 does not apply, then CGT event D1 will apply to the covenant and the land-owner will have a capital loss equivalent to the incidental costs of entering into the covenant. When the land is subsequently sold, any capital gain will be calculated on the difference between the sale price and the remaining cost base of the property.

The capital gain made from the covenant will attract a pre-CGT exemption, or a CGT discount, where applicable. In addition to these benefits, small business landowners who enter into conservation covenants may be able to access the small business CGT concessions where the land was used as an active asset. The market value substitution rule does not apply to CGT event D4.

12.028   CGT EVENTS E1 TO E9: TRUSTS

To understand CGT events E1 to E9, it is necessary to understand the legal concept of a trust.

Where a trust relationship exists, the rights of ownership of trust property are divided between:

- a legal owner – the trustee, and
- an equitable owner – the beneficiary.

The trust holds the trust property for the benefit of its beneficiary(ies).

As an equitable owner, the beneficiary may have certain rights under a deed of settlement, such as a right to use or occupy trust property or a right to a share of trust income. In the case of a discretionary trust, there is no equitable owner because the trustee has the discretionary power to allocate the income and capital among the potential beneficiaries.

If a beneficiary becomes absolutely entitled to trust property as against the trustee, s106-50 provides that any act done by the trustee in relation to an asset is taken to be an act done by the person absolutely entitled to that asset. If a CGT event occurs in relation to that asset, the person that is absolutely entitled will be subject to the CGT liability, not the trustee.

Where a trustee makes a capital gain it is included in the calculation of net trust income (s95 ITAA36). This may result in the trust net income being different from the distributed accounting trust income. The trustee may then be able to allocate the capital gain to selected beneficiaries of a discretionary trust (refer to 12.600 for a discussion of trust streaming measures).

It should be noted that capital gains arising from CGT events E1 to E8 may be potentially eligible for the CGT discount while any gain from CGT event E9 is ineligible for such relief.

CGT EVENT E1: CREATING A TRUST OVER A CGT ASSET

CGT event E1 happens where a trust is created over a CGT asset by declaration or settlement (s104-55 (1)). The time of the event is when the trust over the asset is created.

A capital gain arises if the capital proceeds from the event exceed the asset's cost base, whilst a capital loss occurs if those capital proceeds are less than the asset's reduced cost base (s104-55(3)). However, such a gain or loss will not arise where the asset subject to the trust was acquired prior to 20 September 1985 (s104-55(6)).

Where a taxpayer does not receive any capital proceeds upon the creation of a trust over the asset (or from any CGT event), the taxpayer is taken to have received the market value of the asset at the time of the event (s116-30(1)). The trustee is also taken to have paid the market value of the asset at the date the trust is created if no beneficiary is presently entitled to the asset (disregarding any legal disability) as against the trustee (s104-55(4)). This value becomes the first element of the asset's cost base or reduced cost base.

The effect of CGT event E1 is that the trustee is taken to have acquired the asset when the trust is created (s109-5(2)).

CGT event E1 does not happen where the taxpayer is the sole beneficiary of a non-unit trust and is absolutely entitled to the asset as against the trustee (disregarding any legal disability). In this case, the acts of the trustee are taken to be the acts of the taxpayer (s106-50), so the asset effectively continues to be beneficially owned by the taxpayer rather than the trustee. Accordingly, if the trustee sold the asset, CGT event A1 would apply and any resulting capital gain would be assessed to the taxpayer.

The Full Federal Court has confirmed that a transaction effecting the transfer of land from a taxpayer to a joint-venture trust that the taxpayer is a beneficiary of, for the purposes of redevelopment was a "resettlement" that triggered CGT event E1 (Taras Nominees Pty Ltd as Trustee for the *Burnley Street Trust v FCT* [2015] FCAFC 4).

Prior to 1 November 2008, CGT event E1 also did not happen where the trust is created by transferring the asset from another trust, and the beneficiaries and terms of both trusts are the same (s104-55(5)(b)) (referred to as the trust cloning exemption). From 1 November 2008, trustees cannot rely on the exception where CGT event E1 or E2 is triggered. Nonetheless, an exception has been retained for circumstances where a sole beneficiary is absolutely entitled to trust assets and an optional CGT rollover has been established for eligible fixed trusts (Division 126-G).The Commissioner has considered the application of CGT event E1 where the terms of a trust are varied pursuant to a valid exercise of a power contained in the deed (see TD 2012/21).

CGT EVENT E2: TRANSFERRING A CGT ASSET TO A TRUST

CGT event E2 happens where a CGT asset is transferred to an existing trust (ss104-60(1)). The time of the event is when the asset is transferred.

A capital gain arises for the transferor to the extent that the capital proceeds on the transfer are more than the asset's cost base. Conversely, a capital loss arises where those proceeds are less than the asset's reduced cost base (ss104-60(3). However, no such gain or loss will arise if the asset transferred was acquired by the transferor before 20 September 1985.

Where no beneficiary is absolutely entitled to the asset as against the trustee, the first element in the trustee's cost base is the market value of the asset at date of transfer (ss104-60(4)).

Like CGT event E1, CGT event E2 will not apply where the taxpayer is the sole beneficiary of the trust and is absolutely entitled to the assets as against the trustee and the trust is not a unit trust.

Prior to 1 November 2008, CGT event E2 applied where a trust is created by transferring the asset from another trust, and the beneficiary(ies) and the terms of both trusts are the same (trust closing exception) (s104-60(5)). From 1 November 2008, the trust cloning exception will no longer apply. Nonetheless, a capital gain in relation to CGT event E1 or E2 may be disregarded if there is a sole beneficiary of a non-unit trust who is absolutely entitled to the asset of the trust as against the trustee (disregarding any legal disability) or a mere change of trustee of a single trust. The Commissioner has considered the application of CGT event E2 where the terms of a trust are varied pursuant to a valid exercise of a power contained in the deed (see TD 2012/21).

CGT EVENT E3: CONVERTING A TRUST TO A UNIT TRUST

CGT event E3 happens where a trust over a CGT asset is converted to a unit trust and, immediately before the conversion, a beneficiary was absolutely entitled to the asset as against the trustee (ss104-65(1)). CGT event E3 occurs when the trust is converted.

In this case, the beneficiary makes a capital gain if the market value of the asset is more than its cost base at the time the trust is converted, and a capital loss applies if that market value is less than the asset's reduced cost base (ss104-65(3)).

Such a gain or loss is disregarded where the asset was acquired prior to 20 September 1985 (ss104-65(4)).

CGT EVENT E4: CAPITAL PAYMENT FOR TRUST INTEREST

CGT event E4 applies where a payment of non-assessable income (referred to as the 'non-assessable part') is made by the trustee to a beneficiary who has a unit or an interest in a trust (ss104-70 (1)). The event will not occur if CGT events A1, C2, E1, E2, E6 or E7 also occur in relation to a taxpayer's unit or interest in a trust.

See below for inclusions and exclusions from the 'non-assessable part'.The amount of the 'non-assessable part' then reduces the cost base of the asset. When the 'non-assessable part' eventually, or, even initially, exceeds the cost base, a capital gain will arise (ss104-70(4)). The timing of CGT event E4 is at the end of the income tax year, or when another CGT event applies to the trust interest (ss104-70(3)).

The requirement that the beneficiary have an 'interest in the trust' suggests that CGT event E4 would not apply to a discretionary trust (TD 2003/28 supports this conclusion).

From 21 March 2005, CGT event E4 does not apply to a distribution of foreign source income from the trustee of a trust to a beneficiary that is a foreign resident. This exception however does not apply if the trust is a corporate trust or a public trading trust (ss104-70(9)).

THE NON-ASSESSABLE PART

CGT event E4 would apply where a trust distribution includes such non-assessable amounts as:

- the excess of trust income for trust law purposes over net income of the trust for tax purposes (unless the excess arose as a result of an amount which was itself excluded)
- the frozen amount of CGT indexation
- the CGT small business 50% reduction
- the tax-free amount relating to capital works deductions, or
- a return of trust capital.

The Commissioner has concluded that timing differences ie, where expenses are deductible for taxation purposes in a different year than for trust law purposes, can result in the application of CGT event E4 (see ATO ID 2012/63).

NOTE: The 'non-assessable part' is reduced by the amount of the CGT discount allowed to the trustee that is paid to a beneficiary. Other adjustments are permitted (see below). This means that a beneficiary of a unit trust or a beneficiary with an interest in a trust does not have to adjust their cost base of the CGT asset for the CGT discount amount.

In March 2014, Mary received a payment of $600 from a unit trust. The trustee advised her that this amount comprised $150 that was included in the net income of the unit trust after claiming the 50% CGT discount ($300) and the small business 50% reduction ($150).

In applying CGT event E4 to the payment, Mary first reduces the $600 payment by $150, being the amount of the net income assessed to her under s97. She then reduces the remaining $450 balance by a further $300, being the amount that represents the CGT discount allowed against the capital gain made by the trust. Mary's non-assessable part is $150, which represents the amount of the small business 50% reduction.

If Mary's cost base of her units in the trust is $90, she makes a capital gain of $60 ($150 – $90) under CGT event E4. If Mary had owned her units for more than 12 months, the CGT discount will reduce her capital gain on this transaction under CGT event E4 to $30.

If Mary satisfies the conditions in Division 152, she may be able to reduce her capital gain further under the small business CGT concessions (see examples in TD 2006/71 where the beneficiary is assumed to satisfy the conditions in s152-10).

The 'non-assessable part' is also adjusted to exclude any:

- income which is exempt because it arises from shares in a Pooled Development Fund (PDF)
- income which is exempt as a payment relating to certain infrastructure borrowings
- payments for compensation or damages paid through a trust to a beneficiary to which paragraph 118-37(1)(ba) and subsection 118-300(1A) apply (paragraphs 104-71(1)(da) and (db))

- proceeds from a CGT event that happens in relation to shares in a company that was a PDF when that event happened (ss104-71(3)), or
- the discount amount arising from a discount capital gain (ss104-71(4)).

In working out the non-assessable part, the following amounts are disregarded:

- payments of non-assessable non-exempt income
- amounts paid from an amount that has been assessed to the trustee
- personal service income included in assessable income under s86-15
- a payment of a small business 15 year exemption amount, or
- a repayment (ss104-71(1)).

However, the 'non-assessable part' is not reduced by any part of the payment that is deductible (ss104-71(2)).

The 'non-assessable part' is also reduced to reflect the difference (if any) between the CGT concessions (frozen indexation amount, small business 50% reduction or both) claimed by the trustee and the CGT concessions claimed by the beneficiary, as well as for the application of capital losses by the trustee before applying the CGT concessions (refer TD 2006/71 in relation the small business 50% reduction).

Stable Unit Trust made a capital gain of $1,800 in the 2013-14 tax year. The trust also made a capital loss of $500.

After offsetting the capital loss, the trustee applied the CGT discount to the balance of the gain ($1,300) resulting in the trust having a net capital gain of $650.

Smith, a beneficiary of the trust, was presently entitled to all the trust income.

On 1 June 2015, the trustee paid Smith $1,800, and advised him that this amount comprised $650 net income, the remainder being sheltered from tax due to the CGT discount ($650) and the capital loss applied by the trustee against the capital gain ($500).

In applying CGT event E4 to the payment, Smith reduces the $1,800 payment by the following amounts:

- *$650, being the amount of the capital gain included in the net trust income assessed to him under section 97 ITAA36 (paragraph 104-70(1)(b))*
- *$650, being the amount that represents the CGT discount allowed against the capital gain made by the trust (item 1 in the table in ss104-71(4)), and*
- *$500, being the amount of the loss applied against the capital gain made by the trust and reflected in the payment to Smith (item 7 in the table in ss104-71(4)).*

Smith's adjusted non-assessable part is nil [$1,800 − ($650 + $650 + $500)].

CGT EVENT E5: BENEFICIARY BECOMES ENTITLED TO A TRUST ASSET

CGT event E5 applies where a beneficiary becomes absolutely entitled to a CGT asset of the trust (ss104-75(1)). The time of the event is when the beneficiary becomes so entitled.

Essentially, CGT event E5 can apply both to the trustee (in respect of the asset to which the beneficiary has become absolutely entitled) and to the beneficiary (in respect of the beneficiary's interest in the trust). In these circumstances both the beneficiary and the trustee of the trust may separately recognise a capital gain or a capital loss.

The beneficiary is taken to have received the market value of the asset in exchange for the interest the beneficiary has in the trust. If the market value of the CGT asset exceeds the cost base of the beneficiary's interest in the trust capital (to the extent it relates to the asset), the beneficiary makes a capital gain. Conversely, the beneficiary will incur a capital loss if the reduced cost base of the interest exceeds the market value of the asset (ss104-75(5)). Such a gain is disregarded if the beneficiary's interest in the trust was acquired prior to 20 September 1985, or was acquired for nil expenditure other than by way of assignment, such as an interest in an asset bequeathed in a will or the interest of a beneficiary in a discretionary trust (s104-75(6)).

By contrast the trustee makes a capital gain if the market value of the CGT asset (at the time of the event) is more than its cost base, and a capital loss if that market value is less than that asset's reduced cost base (ss104-75(3)). However, any such gain or loss is disregarded if the trustee acquired the asset before 20 September 1985 (ss104-75(4)).

CGT event E5 does not apply to a unit trust or a deceased estate to which Division 128 ITAA97 applies.

CGT EVENT E6: DISPOSAL TO BENEFICIARY TO END INCOME RIGHT

CGT event E6 applies to the disposal of a CGT asset by the trustee to a beneficiary in return for the beneficiary's right to receive trust income (ss104-80(1)). It applies where the beneficiary has a right to income which is either wholly or partly satisfied by the transfer of a CGT asset.

The timing of CGT event E6 is when the asset disposal occurs. CGT event E6 can affect both the trustee and the beneficiary because the trustee is disposing of an asset and the beneficiary is disposing of rights to trust income.

The trustee is taken to have disposed of the asset at its market value and a capital gain arises if the asset's market value exceeds its cost base (ss104-80(3)). A capital loss occurs if the market value is more than the asset's reduced cost base (ss104-80(3)). The gain or loss is disregarded if the trustee acquired the asset prior to 20 September 1985.

The beneficiary makes a capital gain if the market value of the asset at the time of its disposal exceeds the cost base of the beneficiary's right to trust income, and a capital loss if that market value is less than the reduced cost base of that right (ss104-80(5)). Such a gain or loss is ignored if the beneficiary acquired the right before 20 September 1985 (ss104-80(6)).

CGT event E6 does not apply to a unit trust or to a deceased estate.

NOTE: Unlike CGT events E5 and E7, the capital gain or loss is not disregarded if the beneficiary's interest was acquired for nil consideration.

CGT EVENT E7: DISPOSAL TO BENEFICIARY TO END CAPITAL INTEREST

CGT event E7 has a similar effect to CGT event E6. The difference is that CGT event E7 applies where the consideration for the trustee disposing of a CGT asset of the trust to the beneficiary is the full or partial disposal of the beneficiary's interest to trust capital to the trustee (ss104-85(1)) (as opposed to income rights). The time of the event is when the disposal of the CGT asset occurs.

As is the case with CGT event E6, both the trustee and the beneficiary may realise a capital gain or loss as a result of CGT event E7.

The trustee makes a capital gain if the asset's market value at the time of disposal exceeds its cost base, and a capital loss if that market value is less than the asset's reduced cost base (ss104-85(3)). Such gains and losses will not arise if the trustee acquired the asset before 20 September 1985 (ss104-85(4)).

The beneficiary makes a capital gain if the market value of the asset at the time of its disposal exceeds the cost base of the beneficiary's interest in trust capital, and a capital loss if that market value is less than the reduced cost base of the interest (ss104-85(5)). This gain or loss is disregarded if the beneficiary's interest in trust capital was acquired before 20 September 1985, or acquired other than by way of assignment for nil consideration (ss104-85(6)).

In addition to the beneficiary making a capital gain, is it likely that an amount will be included in the beneficiary's assessable income under s97 ITAA36 in respect of the capital gain made by the trustee because the capital gain will form part of the net income of the trust estate. Where this situation occurs, the anti-overlap rule in s118-20 will apply to reduce the beneficiary's capital gain by the amount of the trust capital gain included in the beneficiary's assessable income (see TR 2006/14).

CGT event E7 does not apply to a unit trust or a deceased estate to which Division 128 ITAA97 applies.

CGT EVENT E8: DISPOSAL BY BENEFICIARY OF CAPITAL INTEREST

While CGT event E7 applies to a disposal of a beneficiary's interest in the capital of the trust to the trustee, CGT event E8 applies where a beneficiary, who did not give any money or property to acquire their interest in the capital of the trust and who did not acquire their interest by assignment, disposes of an interest (or part interest) in the capital of the trust to a third party not being the trustee (ss104-90(1)). The time of the event is when the beneficiary enters into the contract for the disposal or, if there is no contract, when the beneficiary stops owning the interest (or part thereof).

An example of where CGT event E8 might apply would be where a beneficiary disposes of their interest in the capital of a trust that they acquired from the settlement of the original trust without making any payment.

The specific calculation of any capital gain or loss arising under CGT event E8 will depend on the number of beneficiaries holding such trust interests, and the extent to which these interests are disposed of to third parties. Essentially, a beneficiary makes a capital gain to the extent capital proceeds for their pro rata interest in trust capital exceeds their commensurate interest in the 'net asset amount'. The net asset amount is the aggregate of the cost bases of the trust's post CGT acquired assets, the market value of the trust's pre-CGT acquired assets, money held by the trust less any trust liabilities at the time of disposal (s104-95).

Broadly, a capital loss is incurred if the beneficiary's share of the 'net asset amount' is greater than their interest in trust capital (s104-100).

Any gains or losses are disregarded to the extent that the interest in trust capital was acquired before 20 September 1985.

As with CGT events E5, E6 and E7, CGT event E8 will not apply where the trust is a unit trust or a deceased estate to which Division 128 ITAA97 applies.

NOTE: A taker in default of trust capital does not have an 'interest in the trust capital' of the kind contemplated by CGT event E8 in s104-90 (refer TD 2009/19). This is because the interest which a taker in default has in the trust capital is defeasible.

CGT EVENT E9: CREATING A TRUST OVER FUTURE PROPERTY

CGT event E9 happens if the taxpayer enters into an agreement in return for consideration that when property comes into existence, it will be held on trust (ss104-105(1)). However, for CGT event E9 to apply at the time of the agreement, no potential beneficiary of the trust must have a beneficial interest in the rights created under the agreement. The timing of this event is when the agreement is made (s104-105).

An example of where CGT event E9 would apply includes an assignment by a partner of part of his or her interest in a partnership to a discretionary trust so that the right to the partnership share is not created in another person. If the assignment however was made to a particular person, so that a beneficial interest in the partner's share in a partnership is created in that person, then CGT event D1 would apply (see *FC of T v Everett* 80 ATC 4076).

The capital gain is the difference between the market value of the property if it had existed when the taxpayer made the agreement and any incidental costs incurred by the taxpayer. A capital loss arises if those incidental costs exceed that market value (ss104-105(3)).

As discussed, a capital gain arising under event E9 cannot be reduced by the CGT discount.

12.030   CGT EVENTS F1 TO F5: LEASES

One of the rights of ownership is the right of possession. This right of possession can be granted to another entity. A lease confers a right to exclusive possession (subject to native title rights).

A lease can be granted by the owner (head-lease) or by an entity that has a right to exclusive possession (sub-lease).

The lessor is the person who grants the lease, and is usually the owner of the property. The lessee is the person who takes exclusive possession of the property for the duration of the lease.

The lessee may pay a lease premium, rent or both. The premium, if paid at all, is the amount paid for obtaining the lease, rather than for the use of the property. There may be CGT implications where a lease premium exists.

A lease is a CGT asset under s108-5 and would be subject to CGT event D1 on creation. However, specific CGT events F1 to F5 clarify how leases are treated for CGT purposes. In general terms, these events deem the granting of a lease to be a CGT event for the lessor and deal with certain other transactions in respect of a lease.

CGT events F1, F2 and F5 are not eligible for the CGT discount.

CGT EVENT F1: GRANTING A LEASE

The granting, renewal or extension of a lease constitutes CGT event F1 (ss104-110(1)).

CGT event F1 occurs when the lessor grants a lease, or at the start of the renewal or extension of a lease. This means that if a pre-CGT lease is renewed or extended after 19 September 1985, the new lease may attract CGT.

The capital proceeds for CGT event F1 are defined as the premium paid (ss116-20(2)), while the cost base is restricted to the expenditure the lessor incurred on the grant, renewal or extension of the lease.

A capital gain will arise for the lessor if the capital proceeds are greater than the cost of granting, renewing or extending the lease. A capital loss arises where the capital proceeds are less than those costs (ss104-110(3)).

Lease premiums should be distinguished from payments for goodwill (*Krakos Investments Pty Ltd v FC of T* 96 ATC 4063). If the lessee received a cash incentive to enter the lease of premises, this sum is assessable income to the lessee under s6-5 (*FC of T v Montgomery* 99 ATC 4749) and would be a deduction to the lessor under s8-1 on the basis that it was an outgoing incurred in earning assessable income. These amounts would be excluded from the cost base (ss104-110(4)).

As a result of CGT event F1, the lessee will have acquired a CGT asset (the lease) for a cost base equal to the value of any premium paid. If the lease is later transferred to another entity, CGT event A1 would apply as there is a disposal of a CGT asset. On the other hand, if the lease ends, the lessee will be subject to CGT event C2 as the lease, being an intangible asset, has expired. Capital proceeds will be nil, and as the market value substitution rule does not apply to CGT event C2 (ss116-30(3)), a capital loss may result subject to s118-40.

CGT event F1 does not apply if the lessor can and does choose CGT event F2.

NOTE: CGT event F1 may qualify for small business CGT relief on the basis that the CGT event happens 'in relation to' the underlying asset (in this case, the premises over which the lease is granted) (refer ATO ID 2004/650).

CGT EVENT F2: GRANTING A LONG-TERM LEASE

Where a lease over land is a long-term lease (50 years or more), the lessor may elect for CGT event F2 to apply (s104-115) in place of CGT event F1 (s104-110). Again, CGT event F2 may apply to the grant, renewal or extension of a lease. The timing of the event is when the lease is granted, or when it is renewed or extended.

The lessor makes a capital gain if the capital proceeds from the event exceed the cost base of the interest in the land, and a capital loss if those proceeds are less than the reduced cost base of that interest (s104-115(3)).

By choosing CGT event F2, the cost base for any later CGT event on a disposal of the underlying land and buildings excludes any expenditure incurred before CGT event F2 happened. The grant of the lease itself is effectively ignored (s132-10(2)).

When determining whether a lease is for at least 50 years, the original lease term does not include the period of any renewal of the lease (ie. any renewal of the lease cannot be added to the original lease term and must be considered separately) (ATO ID 2007/175).

Where there are circumstances that a lease which has a term of 50 years or more may be terminated before that period has elapsed, the Commissioner of Taxation considers that lease would not be a long term lease (ATO ID 2003/906).

CGT EVENTS F3, F4 AND F5: PAYMENTS FOR CHANGING A LEASE

CGT events F3, F4 and F5 bring into the scope of CGT amounts paid and/or received by the lessor or lessee to alter the lease agreement (see s104-120, s104-25 and s104-130).CGT event F3 applies where a lessor pays the lessee to have the lease varied or a term waived. The amount paid by the lessor in varying the lease is a capital loss (ss104-120(1)). The time of the event is when the term is varied or waived.

The amount received by the lessee on a variation may give rise to a capital gain under CGT event F4 (ss104-125(3)). A capital gain will arise where the capital proceeds are greater than the lease's cost base at the time of the variation of the lease.

CGT event F5 applies if the lessor receives a payment from the lessee for agreeing to vary or waive the lease. The lessor makes a capital gain if the amount received is greater than the expenditure incurred by the lessor in relation to the variation or waiver of the lease. A capital loss arises if the capital proceeds are less than those costs (ss104-130(3)).

12.032 CGT EVENTS G1 TO G3: SHARES

Where there is a simple acquisition and disposal of shares, CGT event A1 happens because there is a change of beneficial ownership of the shares. If a share is redeemed or cancelled, CGT event C2 would apply. CGT events A1 and C2 therefore apply before CGT event G1 (ss104-135(1)).

By contrast CGT events G1 to G3 deal with capital returns, value shifting before 1 July 2002 and companies going into liquidation.

CGT EVENT G1: CAPITAL PAYMENT FOR SHARES

CGT event G1 happens if a company makes a non-assessable distribution to a shareholder which is not a dividend under section 6 of the ITAA36 or a deemed dividend under s47 of the ITAA36 (ss104-135(1)).

CGT event G1 applies where a liquidator's interim distribution (that is not a dividend) is made more than 18 months before the company is dissolved (TD 2001/27), or where there is a return of capital to shareholders. CGT event G1 does not apply to a payment by a liquidator if the company is dissolved within 18 months of the payment. In such a case the payment of the interim distribution forms part of the shareholders' capital proceeds for CGT event C2 which happens when the shares end (see ss104-136(6) and TD 2001/27).

It is unlikely that CGT event G1 applies to the redemption of shares and share buy-backs as CGT event C2 covers these situations and CGT event G1 does not apply if CGT event C2 happens.

Note that any assessable dividend arising from a dividend reinvestment plan would not trigger CGT event G1.

TD 2000/2 states that CGT event G1 does not apply to bonus shares issued out of a share capital account because Subdivision 130-A deals specifically with the treatment of bonus shares.

Event G1 also does not apply to a payment that is personal services income included in assessable income under s86-15 (see 16.000).

Where CGT event G1 applies, each distribution reduces the cost base of the shares (ss104-135(4)) with a capital gain arising when the 'non-assessable part' exceeds the cost base (ss104-135(3)). However, any gain is disregarded where the shares were acquired prior to 20 September 1985 (ss104-135(5)).

The timing of the event is when the company makes the payment (ss104-135(2)).

 Robins owns a share in a company. The share currently has a cost base of $20. Robins receives $200 from the company, which includes a non-assessable part of $56. As a result, CGT event G1 happens and Robins makes a capital gain of $36 (ie. $56 – $20). If Robins acquired the share at least 12 months earlier he is eligible for the 50% CGT discount so the assessable capital gain is reduced by 50% to $18.

CGT EVENT G3: LIQUIDATOR OR ADMINISTRATOR DECLARES SHARES OR FINANCIAL INSTRUMENTS WORTHLESS

CGT event G3 applies where a liquidator or administrator declares shares or financial instruments worthless. Prior to 22 March 2005, CGT event G3 only happened when the liquidator of a company declared in writing that the company's shares were worthless. Such a written declaration could not be made until the liquidator had reasonable grounds to believe that there was no likelihood that shareholders would receive any further distribution on the winding up of the company (ss104-145(1) and TD 2000/52).

From 22 March 2005, CGT event G3 was extended under ss104-145(1) to apply to a written declaration by an administrator (in addition to a liquidator). It was also extended to apply to a declaration that financial instruments (in addition to shares) issued or created by a company had nil or negligible value. Examples of financial instruments include debentures, bonds and promissory notes issued by a company, loans to a company and futures contracts, forward contracts or currency swap contracts relating to a company.

The time of the event is when the liquidator or administrator makes the declaration.

When CGT event G3 occurs, the taxpayer can choose to recognise a capital loss equal to the reduced cost base of their shares or financial instruments at the time of the declaration (ss104-145(4)). However, where such a choice is made the shares or financial instruments will thereafter have a nil cost base on any subsequent CGT event (ss104-45(5)). Broadly, the choice cannot be made in respect of shares or financial instruments that were acquired before 20 September 1985.

12.034   CGT EVENTS H1 AND H2: SPECIAL CAPITAL RECEIPTS

CGT EVENT H1: FORFEITURE OF DEPOSIT

Where a deposit on a prospective sale or other transaction is forfeited because the transaction does not proceed, CGT event H1 happens (ss104-150(1)). The time of the event is when the deposit is forfeited (ss104-150(2)).

A capital gain arises if the deposit received exceeds the costs incurred in connection with the prospective sale, whereas a capital loss arises where the amount of those costs exceeds the deposit received (ss104-150(3)). However, the amount of the deposit must be reduced by any non-deductible repayments made (ss104-150(1A)).

Prior to the rewriting of the CGT provisions, ss160ZZC(12) ITAA36 contained a similar provision but the effect of this was challenged in *Guy v FC of T* 96 ATC 4520. In this case, the deposit received was in relation to a contract of sale of a private residence. The Court held that the forfeited deposit was not subject to CGT because it was received as part of an immediately operative purchase contract. It was not in the nature of an option or holding deposit for a prospective purchase as required by the former ss160ZZC(12) and that section did not deem a contract for sale to be an option.

The Full Federal Court in *Brooks v Commissioner of Taxation* (2000) FCA 72 (Brooks) however departed from the decision in *Guy* and held that the former ss160ZZC(12) could apply to a deposit forfeited under an ordinary contract of sale, because the contract is not completed until the purchase price has been paid, and until that time, the contract is a future contract and the purchaser is a prospective purchaser.

Following the decision in *Brooks*, the Commissioner issued an addendum to TR 1999/19 which provides that where the forfeiture of a deposit under a contract for the sale of real estate does not occur within a continuum of events, the forfeited deposit will be assessable under s104-150 (CGT event H1) and CGT event C2 will not apply. This is the case whether the contract is for the sale of pre-CGT real estate, post-CGT real estate or a main residence.

If a deposit is forfeited under a contract for the sale of a main residence or pre-CGT real estate where the forfeiture occurs within a continuum of events resulting in the later disposal of the main-residence or pre-CGT real estate, the deposit will remain not assessable. However, if the deposit is forfeited under a contract for the sale of post-CGT real estate and the forfeiture occurs within a continuum of events that results in the later disposal of the post-CGT real estate, then the forfeited deposit forms part of the capital proceeds from CGT event A1 happening to the post-CGT real estate.

A taxpayer may still be able to access the small business CGT concessions from the triggering of CGT event H1 in relation to an underlying asset (eg. the forfeiture from the sale of property) (ATO ID 2003/346).

CGT EVENT H2: RECEIPT FOR AN EVENT RELATING TO A CGT ASSET

CGT event H2 happens if an act, transaction or event occurs in relation to a CGT asset, and there is no disposal of the asset or adjustment to the asset's cost base (ss104-155(1)). It aims to bring into the CGT net any proceeds received by a taxpayer in relation to a CGT asset that the taxpayer owns where there is no disposal or cost base adjustment. It is essentially, a catch all provision for capital receipts.

The time of the event is when the act, transaction or event occurs (s104-155(2)).

Where the event is triggered, the taxpayer makes a capital gain if the capital proceeds for the event exceed any incidental costs incurred which relate to that event (ss104-155(3)). The taxpayer cannot, however, make a capital loss under event H2.

As discussed, ss102-25(3) states that CGT event H2 is a provision of last resort and only applies if no other CGT event is applicable. Subsection 104-155(1) provides an example of when event H2 would apply whilst some exceptions are outlined in ss104-155(5). It should be noted that the market substitution rule does not apply to capital proceeds received from CGT event H2.

ATO ID 2006/222 examines the application of CGT event H2. This ATO ID deals with a resolution by an insurer to allow a premium rebate to a policy holder under an insurance policy. As this resolution affects the rights of the policy holder (a CGT asset), the resolution was an act or event that happened in relation to the policy holder's bundle of rights under the insurance policy. As the insurer's resolution did not result in any adjustment to the cost base of the policy holder's bundle of rights under the policies, CGT event H2 applies.

12.036   CGT EVENTS I1 AND I2: AUSTRALIAN RESIDENCY ENDS

A capital gain or capital loss may occur for each asset owned which is not 'taxable Australian property' where an individual or a company ceases to be a resident of Australia for tax purposes (CGT event I1) or a trust ceases to be a resident trust (CGT event I2) (see ss104-160(1) and ss104-170(1) and further commentary at 12.700 for the meaning of 'taxable Australian property').

The rationale for these CGT events is that foreign residents do not pay tax on assets that are not taxable Australian property (as defined in s855-15) so in the absence of these events, these assets would escape the Australian 'tax net' when they were later sold.

The time of the event is when the relevant taxpayer ceases to be an Australian resident.

Under CGT events I1 and I2, a capital gain will arise if the market value of the asset at the time the taxpayer ceases residency is more than its cost base. Conversely, a capital loss arises where the asset's reduced cost base is more than the asset's market value at that time.

A capital gain or capital loss from I1 is disregarded if the taxpayer was a 'temporary resident' (see 12.721) at the time of the CGT event and would not have made a capital gain or capital loss if he or she had been a foreign resident (s768-915). For CGT purposes, a temporary resident is therefore treated in the same way as a foreign resident.

An individual ceasing Australian residency can elect to disregard making a capital gain or capital loss under CGT event I1. If they make this choice, it must be made for all affected assets which will then be taken to be 'taxable Australian property' for CGT purposes until the earlier of:

- a CGT event happening in relation to the asset, if the CGT event involves the taxpayer ceasing to own the asset, or
- the person again becoming an Australian resident (ss104-165(2) and (3)).

A trust ceases to be a resident when it no longer satisfies the definition of a 'resident trust' under s995-1 (eg. the trustee stops being an Australian resident or the central management and control of the trust is no longer in Australia (see s104-170 and TD 1999/83).

A capital gain or capital loss arising under either of CGT events I1 or I2 is disregarded if the relevant asset was acquired before 20 September 1985 . Refer to 12.715 for an example on the application of CGT event I1.

12.038   CGT EVENTS J1 TO J6: REVERSAL OF ROLLOVERS

CGT EVENT J1: COMPANY CEASING TO BE A MEMBER OF WHOLLY-OWNED GROUP AFTER ROLLOVER

CGT event J1 applies where a company transfers a CGT asset to another company in a wholly-owned company group that has elected for rollover relief under Sub-Division 126-B in respect of the asset transfer, and the recipient company later ceases to be a member of that wholly owned group whilst continuing to own that asset (ss104-175(1)). The time of the event is the break-up time when the recipient company ceases to be a wholly owned member of the company group.

The recipient company makes a capital gain if the market value of the rolled over asset at the break-up time is more than its cost base, and a capital loss if that market value is less than the asset's reduced cost base (ss104-175(5)). As a corollary, the recipient company will acquire a cost base for the rolled over asset equal to its market value at the break-up time which will be its cost base in determining any gain or loss on any subsequent CGT event (s104-75(8)).

A capital gain or loss will be disregarded if the rolled over asset was an asset acquired by the transferor company prior to 20 September 1985.

CGT event J1 will also not apply if:

- a sub-group within the wholly-owned group leaves the group and the asset has been rolled over in the sub-group (s104-175(6) and s104-180), or

- the recipient company ceases to be subsidiary member of a consolidated group at the break up time (s104-182). In this latter case, CGT event L5 may apply.

CGT EVENT J2: CHANGE IN RELATION TO REPLACEMENT ASSET OR IMPROVED ASSET AFTER A ROLLOVER UNDER SUBDIVISION 152-E

CGT event J2 happens if there is a change in the status of a replacement asset acquired under the small business rollover concession under Subdivision 152-E after the end of the replacement period (s104-185(1)).

The time of the event is when the change in the status of the asset happens (s104-185(4)).

A replacement asset can change status by ceasing to be an active asset in the taxpayer's business or, in the case of a share in a company or a unit in a unit trust, CGT event G3 or I1 happens in relation to it or the conditions in s104-182(1)(c) stop being satisfied. CGT event J2 will also be triggered if:

- the asset becomes trading stock
- the taxpayer makes a testamentary gift of the asset under the Cultural Bequests Program, or
- the taxpayer starts to use the asset solely to produce exempt income or non-assessable non-exempt income.

It might be that an asset will cease to be an active asset either by ceasing to be used in the business (and still remaining within the ownership of the relevant taxpayer) or by being sold. However, it is not entirely clear because the general provisions state that an asset need be active only for half the period of ownership or $7^{1}/_{2}$ years, whichever is less.

If the replacement asset is sold, CGT event A1 would occur in respect of the replacement asset. In addition, the pre-rollover capital gains would be taxed under CGT event J2 as CGT event J2 applies in addition to the other event (s102-25(2A)).

Note that CGT event J2 only applies to a rollover under Subdivision 152-E. It does not apply to a capital gain rolled over under the Subdivision 124-B replacement asset rollover. Any gain arising under CGT event J2 cannot be reduced under the CGT discount.

NOTE: CGT event J3 was repealed from 1 July 2006.

CGT EVENT J4: TRUST FAILING TO CEASE TO EXIST AFTER ROLLOVER UNDER SUBDIVISION 124-N

Where a fixed trust transfers all of its assets (apart from assets retained to pay existing or expected debts) to a resident Australian company and claims CGT rollover relief under subdivision 124-N, that trust must cease to exist within six months of the time it transferred the first asset to the company.

Where this does not happen and the company owns the asset when the trust fails to cease to exist, CGT event J4 occurs (s104-195(1)). The time of the event is at the end of the six month trust restructuring period when the trust ceases to exist.

Where CGT event J4 occurs, the company (not the trust) will make a capital gain if the CGT asset's market value is more than its cost base at the time the company acquired it from the trust. The company will incur a capital loss if that market value is less than the asset's reduced cost base at that time (s104-195(4)).

Similarly, following the trust restructure, a shareholder would make a capital gain under CGT event J4 if the market value of the shares that the shareholder has acquired in exchange for their interest in the trust is more than their cost-base at that time (see s104-195(2) and s104-195(6)).

CGT EVENT J5: FAILURE TO ACQUIRE REPLACEMENT ASSET OR TO INCUR FOURTH ELEMENT EXPENDITURE AFTER A ROLLOVER UNDER SUBDIVISION 152-E

CGT event J5 will happen two years after the last CGT event in the year in which small business rollover relief is chosen under Subdivision 152-E (refer 12.525) if no replacement asset has been acquired by the end of that two year replacement period (s104-197(1)). The time of the event is at the end of the two year replacement period (which can be modified or extended in certain circumstances (s104-190)).

The replacement asset can either be a new asset or an improvement to an existing asset (the incurring of fourth element expenditure).

CGT event J5 will also happen if a replacement asset is not an active asset at the end of that period.

Further, if the replacement asset is a share in a company or an interest in a trust, the asset must be owned by either:

- a CGT concession stakeholder of the company or trust
- an entity connected with a CGT concession stakeholder, or
- a company or trust that meets the 90% small business participation test at the end of the replacement period

otherwise CGT event J5 will apply.

Where CGT event J5 applies the capital gain is equal to the amount of the previous capital gain that was rolled over under subdivision 152-E. Such a gain is not eligible for the CGT discount.

 In the 2012 income year, Sandra makes a capital gain of $30,000 on an active asset. She satisfies the conditions of Division 152. Sandra elects to use Subdivision 152-E rollover and disregards the whole capital gain. By the end of the replacement asset period Sandra does not have any replacement assets. CGT event J5 happens and Sandra makes a capital gain of $30,000 in the 2014 income year.

NOTE: Effective for CGT events from the 2006-07 income year, when a gain from CGT events J5 or J6 occur, it will not be necessary to satisfy the basic conditions for the small business retirement exemption (refer to 12.525 on commentary on small business CGT concessions).

CGT EVENT J6: COST OF ACQUISITION OF REPLACEMENT ASSET OR AMOUNT OF FOURTH ELEMENT EXPENDITURE, OR BOTH, NOT SUFFICIENT TO COVER DISREGARDED CAPITAL GAIN

CGT event J6 will happen two years after the last CGT event in the year that the small business replacement rollover is chosen if expenditure on the replacement asset, or improvements to existing assets, is insufficient to cover the capital gain rolled over. CGT event J6 will also happen if the replacement asset is not the taxpayer's active asset at the end of the two year period. The two year period can be extended.

Further, if the replacement asset is a share in a company or an interest in a trust, the asset must be owned by either:

- a CGT concession stakeholder of the company or trust
- an entity connected with a CGT concession stakeholder, or
- a company or trust that meets the 90% small business participation test at the end of the replacement period

otherwise CGT event J6 can apply.

Where CGT event J6 applies, the capital gain is the difference between the original capital gain that was rolled over and the amount of expenditure incurred on the replacement asset. This expenditure is made up of:

- the costs that would be included in the first element of cost base of a replacement asset
- the incidental costs of acquisition of a replacement asset, and
- the costs that would be included in the fourth element of cost base of a replacement asset.

 In the 2012 income year, Jack makes a capital gain of $900,000 on an active asset. As Jack satisfies the conditions of Division 152-E he chooses to disregard the whole capital gain.

In the 2013 income year, Jack purchased new business premises for $500,000 and spent $100,000 on improving some other assets. The replacement assets meet all of the relevant conditions. However, the amount of expenditure on the replacement assets is only $600,000 and the capital gain that was rolled over was $900,000.

In the 2014 income year, two years after the last CGT event in the income year of the rollover, CGT event J6 happens because there has been insufficient expenditure and Jack makes a capital gain of $300,000. The rollover of $600,000 of the original capital gain continues.

NOTE: Effective for CGT events from the 2006-07 income year, when a gain from CGT events J5 or J6 occur, it will not be necessary to satisfy the basic conditions for the small business retirement exemption (refer to 12.525 on commentary on small business CGT concessions).

12.040 EVENTS K2-K11: OTHER CGT EVENTS

This group of CGT events are miscellaneous events that may give rise to a capital gain or capital loss.

NOTE: Event K1 was repealed from 1 July 2001.

CGT EVENT K2: PAYMENT OF DEBT BY BANKRUPT

Any net capital loss of a person who is a bankrupt is disregarded (s102-5(2)).

CGT event K2 re-instates part of the capital loss previously disallowed if part of the debt is repaid (s104-210).

The time of the event is when the payment is made.

CGT EVENT K3: ASSET PASSING TO A TAX-ADVANTAGED ENTITY

CGT event K3 happens on the death of a taxpayer where a CGT asset is transferred to a tax advantaged entity (s104-215(1)). The time of the event is just before the taxpayer's death so that any resulting capital gain is included in the deceased's return to date of death.

This event prevents assets going untaxed (or being subject to a reduced rate of tax) where the assets pass after a taxpayer's death to:

- a beneficiary who is a tax exempt entity
- a trustee of a complying superannuation entity, or
- a foreign resident.

For an asset passing to a foreign resident beneficiary, CGT event K3 will only apply where the deceased was a resident of Australia and the asset (in the hands of the beneficiary) is not 'taxable Australian property' (s855-15).

Although CGT event K3 applies to a bequest of property to a gift deductible entity, by virtue of s118-60(1) a capital gain or capital loss from a testamentary gift of property under the Cultural Bequests Program or what would have been deductible under s30-15 if it had not been a testamentary gift, is disregarded.

Where CGT event K3 occurs, a capital gain arises if the market value of the asset at the date of death of the deceased is more than its cost base, and a capital loss occurs where that market value is less than the asset's reduced cost base (s104-215(4)).

CGT event K3 is disregarded if the deceased acquired the asset before 20 September 1985.

CGT EVENT K4: CGT ASSET BECOMES TRADING STOCK

As trading stock is exempt from CGT (s118-25), CGT event K4 will apply where an entity begins to hold a former CGT asset as trading stock and the entity elects under s70-30 to treat that asset as having been sold for its market value s104-220(1) (refer 14.200).

The time of the event is when the entity starts to hold the asset as trading stock.

A capital gain will arise if the asset's market value exceeds its cost base at that time, and a capital loss if that market value is less than its reduced cost base.

Any capital gain or loss is disregarded if the asset was acquired before 20 September 1985.

CGT event K4 will not apply where the entity elects to value the asset at cost.

CGT EVENT K5: SPECIAL COLLECTABLE LOSSES

The effect of CGT event K5 is to re-characterise a capital gain or capital loss arising from disposal of shares or an interest in a trust as a capital gain or capital loss from a collectable.

CGT event K5 would arise where there is a fall in the underlying value of a collectable owned by the entity that is indirectly realised by the taxpayer when either CGT events A1, C2 or E8 occur in relation to the taxpayer's shares in a company or interest in a trust (s104-225(1)). The time of CGT event K5 is when CGT event A1, C2 or E8 happens. In these circumstances, the capital loss from the collectable is the difference between the market value of the shares or interest in the trust and the actual capital proceeds from the event. A capital gain cannot arise under this event. Section 104-225 gives an example of CGT event K5.

A capital loss on a collectable can only be offset against a capital gain from a collectable (s108-10).

CGT EVEN I K6: PRE-CGT SHARES OR TRUST INTEREST

CGT event K6 prevents the control of post-CGT assets changing hands through the sale of pre-CGT shares or units, rather than the sale of the post-CGT assets owned by the entity. The time of CGT event K6 is when that sale (or certain other prescribed events) happens.

Broadly CGT event K6 occurs where an interest in an entity held by the taxpayer (such as shares in a company) is a pre-CGT asset, but more than 75% of the net market value of the underlying assets of the entity (excluding trading stock) has been acquired post-CGT (s104-230(1)).

For the purpose of the 75% test, the 'net value' of a company or trust includes the market value of trading stock (because trading stock comes within the word 'assets' in the definition of 'net value') but the market value with which it is compared is the post-CGT property that does not include trading stock (s104-230(2)(a) and (b) and TR 2004/18).

Where CGT event K6 occurs, the taxpayer may derive a capital gain on the shares or units sold even though they were acquired prior to 20 September 1985. The capital gain will be equal to the amount of capital proceeds received for the shares or units that is reasonably attributable to the difference between the market value and cost base of the underlying post CGT acquired assets owned by the company or trust as at the date of sale. The Commissioner provides a detailed explanation of the calculation of the capital gain under CGT event K6 in TR 2004/18. A capital loss cannot arise under this event.

CGT event K6 does not apply to shares in a company or to units in a public unit trust which are listed for quotation on an official stock exchange at all times for five years before the event triggering CGT event K6 (see conditions in s104-230(9)). The same applies to interests in a demerged entity when the combined period that the head entity and the demerged entity have been continuously listed on an official stock exchange is at least five years (s104-230(9A)&(9B)).

 A taxpayer owns shares in a company which has been listed on an official stock exchange for three years. The company is the head entity of a demerger group. As part of a demerger, the taxpayer receives new interests in a demerged entity. The demerged entity then lists in its own right.

Since the head entity was listed for only three years, the demerged entity must remain listed for two years before the taxpayer's new interests become eligible for the exception from CGT event K6.

NOTE: CGT event K6 does not apply where the transfer of shares in a pre-CGT company or interest in a trust are the subject of a roll-over under Division 128 (refer ATO ID 2006/139). Division 128 relates to the transfer of assets upon death and deceased estates (refer 12.650).

CGT EVENT K7: BALANCING ADJUSTMENT EVENTS FOR DEPRECIATING ASSETS

This event applies if a balancing adjustment event happens to a depreciating asset that has been used, either wholly or partly, for a non-taxable purpose (s104-235(1)).

A capital gain or capital loss under CGT event K7 is calculated by reference to the Division 40 capital allowances concepts of cost and termination value, not the CGT concepts of cost base and capital proceeds.

A capital gain will arise if the termination value of a depreciating asset used for a non-taxable purpose is greater than the cost of the depreciating asset at the asset's start time. If the asset is used partially for a taxable purpose, the taxable use fraction is excluded from the capital gain.

Conversely, a capital loss will arise if the termination value is below the cost of the depreciating asset. The taxable use fraction is excluded from any capital loss. The capital gain or capital loss will arise in the same year as any balancing adjustment calculated under Subdivision 40-D.

The calculation(s) required when a balancing adjustment happens to a depreciating asset are as follows:

Use of asset	Calculation
100% taxable use	Balancing adjustment only
Mixed use	Balancing adjustment and capital gain/loss
100% non-taxable use	Capital gain or capital loss only

If the depreciating asset was acquired before 20 September 1985, any capital gain or capital loss is disregarded. Similarly, any capital gain from a collectable costing $500 or less or personal use asset costing $10,000 or less is disregarded.

If a balancing adjustment event happens to a depreciating asset that has been used 100% for taxable purposes, the taxpayer will not make any capital gain or capital loss, and any balancing adjustment will be assessable or deductible under s40-285.

Importantly, if a balancing adjustment happens to a depreciating asset that may be caught by another CGT event (other than CGT event J2), that event is disregarded and only CGT event K7 applies (s118-24).

CGT event K7 does not apply:

- to assets covered by Subdivision 40-F (water facilities or horticultural plants) or Subdivision 40-G (Landcare operations, electricity connections or telephone lines)
- to depreciating assets used in carrying on research and development activities, or
- where there is rollover relief for the balancing adjustment event under s40-340.

As the capital gain or capital loss under CGT event K7 is determined by Division 40 capital allowance concepts, when CGT event K7 happens to a partnership asset, the capital gain or capital loss is calculated by reference to the partnership as the holder of the depreciating asset rather than by an individual partner. Consequently, under s106-5, the partners have an interest in the capital gain or capital loss as calculated by reference to the partnership as the holder of the depreciating asset, rather than by having an individual interest in the depreciating asset (ATO ID 2006/200).

A capital gain from CGT event K7 may qualify for the 50% CGT discount if the conditions in Division 115 are satisfied, but will not qualify for any of the small business CGT concessions because CGT event K7 arises only from the private use of an asset.

CGT EVENT K8: DIRECT VALUE SHIFTS

CGT event K8 happens where there is a capital gain on a 'down interest' under s725-245 from a direct value shift that materially affects a taxpayer's equity or loan interest in a company or trust. The time of the event is when the decrease in market value in the equity or loan interest happens.

CGT event K8 applies where the event happens on or after 22 August 2002 and effectively replaces the former CGT event G2

CGT event K8 is disregarded if the 'down interest' is an entity's revenue asset, trading stock or a pre-CGT asset. There are de minimis exceptions for direct value shifts that total less than $150,000 in respect of the overall scheme.

There is no taxing event allowing a capital loss on a direct value shift.

CGT EVENT K9: CARRIED INTERESTS

CGT event K9 happens where a venture capital manager is entitled to a share of the gains made by a Venture Capital Management Partnership (VCMP), a Venture Capital Limited Partnership (VCLP), an Early Stage Venture Capital Limited Partnership (ESVCLP) or an Australian Venture Capital Fund or funds on the sale of eligible venture capital investments.

The venture capital manager's share of these gains is called 'carried interest' and is taxed as a capital gain (s104-255).

CGT event K9 happens at the time the venture capital manager is entitled to receive a payment.

The capital gain is a discount capital gain if the 'carried interest' arises under a partnership agreement that was entered into at least 12 months before the CGT event happened and the other requirements for the discount are met (s115-25(2A)).

CGT EVENTS K10 AND K11: CERTAIN SHORT TERM FOREIGN EXCHANGE ('FOREX') REALISATION GAINS AND LOSSES AFTER 30 JUNE 2003

As a general rule a foreign currency gain is assessable income and a foreign currency loss is an allowable deduction. Division 775 refers to these gains and losses as 'forex realisation gains' and 'forex realisation losses'. An exception to this general rule applies to certain short term realisation gains and losses that occur where the time between the acquisition or disposal of a capital asset and the due date for payment is 12 months or less. Such short-term gains or losses are integrated into the tax treatment of capital assets as CGT events K10 (gains) and K11 (losses).The time of CGT events K10 and K11 is when the forex realisation event happens.

Where there is a gain or loss on a *right to receive* foreign currency arising from realising a non-depreciating CGT asset (forex realisation event 2):

- the gain is not assessable under s775-15, but CGT event K10 will happen and assess the forex realisation gain as a non-discountable capital gain, and
- the loss is not deductible under s775-30 but CGT event K11 will happen and the taxpayer will make a capital loss equal to the forex realisation loss.

Where the gain or loss arises from an *obligation to pay* foreign currency to acquire a CGT asset (forex realisation event 4):

- the gain is not assessable under s775-15, but the cost base and reduced cost base of the CGT asset is reduced by the forex realisation gain (item 25 s112-97), and
- the loss is not deductible under s775-30, but the cost base and reduced cost base of the CGT asset is increased by the forex realisation loss (item 26 s112-97).

An entity can choose not to apply the short-term realisation rules in which case the normal Division 775 rules apply. This choice must be made in writing and is irrevocable (s775-80). Section 775-80(3) outlines the time limits for making this choice. Alternatively, an entity may make the 'limited balance election' or the 'retranslation election'. Under the 'limited balance election', entities that maintain the balance of their qualifying forex accounts in the foreign currency range of plus or minus A$250,000 can elect, in writing, to disregard any capital gain or capital loss from forex realisation events 2 and 4 (ie. the gain or loss that would have arisen when an entity stops having a right to receive or pay foreign currency) (s775-250). There is a buffer provision which allows the balance to exceed A$250,000 for not more than two 15 day periods in any income year.

The 'retranslation' option allows an entity to bring to account the foreign currency gains and losses arising in respect of their qualifying forex accounts by annually restating the balance by reference to deposits, withdrawals and the exchange rate prevailing at the beginning and end of each year. This alternative option removes the requirement for an entity to calculate a foreign currency gain or loss on each deposit to, or withdrawal from, the account. Where the retranslation option is chosen, any forex realisation gain or loss from forex realisation events 2 or 4 is disregarded (s775-280).

CGT EVENT K12: FOREIGN HYBRIDS

From 1 July 2003, certain foreign hybrids (defined in Subdivision 830-A) are to be treated as partnerships rather than as companies. All shareholders in a foreign hybrid company will be treated as a partner and each partner will have an interest in each asset of the partnership. Consequently, the partners will make any capital gain or capital loss in respect of a CGT event happening to a foreign hybrid or one of its CGT assets. As a consequence, any outstanding foreign hybrid net capital losses may be available to the partners. In this situation, CGT event K12 will allow the limited partner to use this capital loss in calculating its net capital gain or capital loss for the income year.

The time of CGT event K12 is just before the end of the income year (s104-270).

12.042   CGT EVENTS L1 TO L8: CONSOLIDATED GROUPS AND MULTIPLE ENTRY CONSOLIDATED GROUPS

When an existing consolidated group completes the acquisition of an entity that is eligible to become a member of that consolidated group, the cost of acquiring the entity (the Allocable Cost Amount (ACA)) is treated as the cost to the group of the entity's assets. The group's cost for each asset for CGT purposes is then determined by allocating the ACA for the acquired entity to the entity's assets.

The application of the ACA calculation when an entity joins or leaves a consolidated group may result in a capital gain or capital loss for the head company of the consolidated group. The following CGT events prescribe the conditions under which a capital gain or capital loss will arise.

The CGT events that apply to consolidated groups also apply to Multiple Entry Consolidated groups (MEC groups) that would not qualify as consolidated groups under Division 701.

In each of the 'L' events the capital gain or capital loss is made by the head company of the consolidated group, or head company of the MEC group.

CGT EVENT L1: LOSS OF PRE-CGT STATUS OF MEMBERSHIP INTERESTS IN ENTITY BECOMING A SUBSIDIARY MEMBER

CGT event L1 happens if there is a reduction in the tax cost setting amount of assets of an entity that becomes a subsidiary member of a consolidated group or MEC group (s104-500(1)).

The capital loss is calculated with reference to the consolidation concepts in Part 3-90 and not the CGT concepts of capital proceeds and cost base (s104-500). The capital loss is used to calculate the head company's net capital loss for the year in which the entity becomes a group member (ss104-500(3)). However, the head company is only able to utilise up to 1/5th of the CGT loss from CGT event L1 each year, over five years.

The time of the event is just after an entity becomes a subsidiary member of the group.

CGT EVENT L2: WHERE PRE-FORMATION INTRA-GROUP ROLLOVER REDUCTION RESULTS IN NEGATIVE ALLOCABLE COST AMOUNT

CGT event L2 will happen where an entity brings into a consolidated group or a MEC group an asset that was subject to pre-formation intra-group rollover (ss104-505(1)).

As the capital gain deferred as a result of this rollover may be sheltered from tax as a result of the tax cost setting process, an adjustment is necessary to the ACA. If the reduction results in a negative ACA, the head company will make a capital gain equal to the negative amount (ss104-505(3)).

The time of the event is just after the entity becomes a subsidiary member of the group or MEC group.

CGT EVENT L3: WHERE TAX COST SETTING AMOUNTS FOR RETAINED COST BASE ASSETS EXCEED JOINING ALLOCABLE COST AMOUNT

CGT event L3 will happen if the total amount to be treated as the head company's cost for retained cost base assets of an entity joining the consolidated group or MEC group exceeds the group's ACA for the joining entity (ss104-510(1)). Where CGT event L3 happens, the head company of the consolidated group or MEC group will make a capital gain equal to the excess (ss104-510(3)).

The time of CGT event L3 is just after the joining entity joins the consolidated group or MEC group.

CGT EVENT L4: WHERE NO RESET COST BASE ASSETS AND EXCESS OF NET ALLOCABLE COST AMOUNT ON JOINING

CGT event L4 happens where the ACA exceeds the retained cost base assets of the joining entity and there are no reset cost base assets of the joining entity against which to allocate the excess (ss104-515(1)). A 'reset cost base asset' is any asset that is not a retained cost base asset (s104-515). CGT event L4 will always result in a capital loss (ss104-515(3)).

The time of CGT event L4 is just after the entity joins the consolidated group or MEC group.

CGT EVENT L5: WHERE AMOUNT REMAINING AFTER STEP 4 OF LEAVING ALLOCABLE COST AMOUNT IS NEGATIVE

CGT event L5 will happen when an entity leaves a consolidated group or MEC group and the liabilities of that entity exceed its assets. In that case, when determining the group's ACA for the entity that is leaving the group, the amount remaining after applying step 4 of the table in s711-20 will be negative and the head company will make a capital gain equal to the negative amount (ss104-520(1)). CGT event L5 will always result in a capital gain (s104-520(3)).

The time of CGT event L5 is when the entity ceases to be a subsidiary member of the consolidated group or MEC group.

CGT event L5 effectively replaces CGT event J1.

CGT EVENT L6: ERROR IN CALCULATION OF TAX COST SETTING AMOUNT FOR JOINING ENTITY'S ASSETS

CGT event L6 will happen where the Commissioner becomes aware that a head company of a consolidated group or MEC group has a net overstated amount or a net understated amount for the subsidiary member (ss104-525(1)). The net overstated amount (capital gain) or net understated amount (capital loss) is determined by using the table in ss104-525(3). The effect of CGT event L6 is that after the net error is taken into account as a capital gain or capital loss, the calculation error is preserved. Consequently, any subsequent gain or loss on disposal of the asset or depreciation of the asset will not have to be adjusted for the earlier calculation error.

The time of CGT event L6 is the start of the income year in which the Commissioner becomes aware of the error.

CGT EVENT L7: DISCHARGED AMOUNT OF LIABILITY DIFFERS FROM AMOUNT FOR ALLOCABLE COST AMOUNT PURPOSES

CGT event L7 is repealed with effect from 1 July 2002.

CGT EVENT L8: WHERE REDUCTION IN TAX COST SETTING AMOUNTS FOR RESET COST BASE ASSETS CANNOT BE ALLOCATED

Under the consolidation rules, the ACA is allocated first to retained cost base assets and then to reset cost base assets. The head company will make a capital loss if after an entity joins a consolidated group or MEC group there is an excess of ACA that cannot be allocated to reset cost base assets because of the restriction on the cost that can be allocated to reset cost base assets held on revenue account in s705-40 (see s104-535(1)). In effect, CGT event L8 will only apply where the entity does not hold any reset cost base assets on capital account because there are no restrictions on the amount of ACA which can be allocated to reset cost base assets on capital account. The capital loss is equal to the unallocated amount (s104-535).

The time of CGT event L8 is just after the entity joins the consolidated group or MEC group.

12.050 STEP 2: DID THE CGT EVENT INVOLVE A CGT ASSET?

Before there can be a capital gain or capital loss, most of the CGT events require something to happen to a 'CGT asset' that was acquired on or after 20 September 1985. Events that do not require there to be a CGT asset require there to be a receipt of capital arising from the CGT event. Understanding the meaning of a CGT asset is therefore an essential step in the CGT process.

12.052 MEANING OF CGT ASSET

Subsection 108-5(1) defines a CGT asset in general terms to mean ... *any kind of property, or a legal or equitable right that is not property.*

Subsection 108-5(2) specifically includes in the definition of a CGT asset:

- part of, or an interest in, a CGT asset covered by ss108-5(1)
- goodwill or an interest in goodwill
- an interest in an asset of a partnership, and
- an interest in a partnership not covered in (c).

A note to s108-5 provides the following examples of CGT assets:

- land and buildings

- shares in a company and units in a unit trust
- options
- debts owed to a taxpayer
- a right to enforce a contractual obligation, and
- foreign currency.

12.054   ORDINARY MEANING OF 'PROPERTY'

As the definition of CGT asset includes any kind of property, it is necessary to first consider the ordinary meaning of the term 'property'.

'Property' is a broad term and encompasses tangible items and intangible rights, in each case, capable of being transferred between two persons, and in respect of which the law recognises legally enforceable rights of ownership. For example, shares, land, rights and options, and an interest in a trust are all 'property'. Items of tangible property such as land, buildings, and chattels are clearly property. They are capable of possession, ownership, may be transferred, and the right of ownership may be defended in a court of law.

In contrast, intangible property may not be so easily identified as a CGT asset. For example, the purchase of a share in a company gives the owner a set of rights (the right to vote, right to share in profits and the right to a share of the assets on liquidation) which are not physically identifiable but are nevertheless property. The property in this case is the right to take legal action to protect rights where they are breached.

The ordinary meaning of property does not normally include rights that cannot be transferred, or rights that are not exclusively held by a person.

NOTE: A non-exclusive licence to occupy property or to use intellectual property may be an exception. For example, the right to freedom of trade cannot be transferred to another person and the right to freedom of speech is not the possession of one person to the exclusion of others.

In *Hepples* it was held that property did not include personal rights that could not be transferred (eg. the right to freedom of trade) nor civil rights (eg. the right to freedom of speech or religion) as these are not possessed by any one person, however *Hepples* was decided under the previous CGT provisions in ITAA36.

Know-how is not a CGT asset because it is not a form of property, nor a legal or equitable right. A contractual right however to require the disclosure or non-disclosure of know-how or a licence to use know-how would be a CGT asset (TD 2000/33).

NOTE: Bitcoin is a "CGT asset" as the Commissioner considers that Bitcoin holding rights amount to property. Therefore, the disposal of Bitcoin to a third party will usually give rise to CGT event A1 (TD 2014/26).

12.056   STATUTORY MEANING OF 'PROPERTY'

Paragraph 108-5(1)(b) extends the meaning of CGT asset to include legal and equitable rights that are not property.

The extension to the definition of 'CGT asset' to include certain non-proprietary rights brings into the scope of CGT any right that a court of law or a court of equity would uphold (for example, the right to compensation arising out of an injury or other event).

Where a patent or other industrial property over an idea or knowledge is created, property exists in the patent as it is transferable and may be the subject of legal action.

Where the patent is sold to another person, the right to use that idea has been given up and therefore the property has been transferred to a new owner.

12.058   CHANGE IN DEFINITION OF 'ASSET'

Following *Hepples* case, the definition of asset was amended (effective 26 June 1992) to include legal or equitable rights that are not property. Assets created prior to 26 June 1992 are still subject to the previous definition.

It was required that an asset acquired before 26 June 1992 was property according to its ordinary meaning before it could be an asset under the former s160A ITAA36. This means that an agreement that restricted personal rights entered into before 26 June 1992 is not a CGT asset for CGT purposes (see ss108-5(2) note 2).

Another item, which may be affected by the change in definition of asset, is goodwill.

Paragraph 108-5(2)(b) specifically includes goodwill as a CGT asset. Prior to the 26 June 1992 amendment, goodwill was only an asset if it was property. This limited the application of CGT to goodwill that was transferable. Personal goodwill could not be transferred and therefore was not property under the former definition (*FC of T v Krakos Investments Pty Ltd* 96 ATC 4063).

12.060   CLASSIFICATION OF ASSETS

For CGT purposes, assets are categorised as either collectables, personal-use assets or other assets.

COLLECTABLES (SUBDIVISION 108-B)

A collectable is any of the following, that is used or kept mainly for the taxpayer's (or associate's) personal use or enjoyment (ss108-10(2)):

- artwork, jewellery, an antique, or a coin or medallion
- a rare folio, manuscript or book, or
- a postage stamp or first day cover.

The Commissioner considers that an 'antique' is an object of artistic and historical significance that is over 100 years old (TD 1999/40).

Any capital gain or loss is disregarded if the first element of the collectable's cost on acquisition is $500 or less (s118-10(1)).

When applying the $500 threshold, any GST input tax credit in respect of the acquisition is excluded. When applying the $500 limit, a set of collectables is taken to be a single collectable. Accordingly, if a seller sells a set as individual separate assets for no more than $500 each, this would not stop the total acquisition being treated as a collectable acquired for more than $500 (s108-15).

Note that capital losses from collectables can only be offset against realised capital gains on other collectables in the current or future years of income (ss108-10(1) and (4)).

PERSONAL USE ASSETS (SUBDIVISION 108-C)

A personal-use asset is a non-collectable asset, other than land or buildings, used or kept for the personal use or enjoyment of the taxpayer or associate (ss108-20(2) and (3)). An asset that is not used for business or profit making purpose is, by default, used or kept mainly for personal use and enjoyment (ATO ID 2003/451).

Any capital gain is disregarded where the first element of the personal use asset's cost is $10,000 or less (s118-10(3)). The $10,000 threshold excludes any GST input tax credit in respect of the acquisition.

Note that any capital loss on a personal use asset is disregarded for CGT purposes (ss108-20(1)).

Where personal use assets would ordinarily be disposed of as a set, for the purpose of the $10,000 threshold, a set of personal use assets is taken to be a single asset and any disposal of part of the set is taken to be a disposal of part of a personal-use asset (s108-25).

ASSETS OTHER THAN COLLECTABLES OR PERSONAL USE ASSETS

The ordinary CGT rules apply to an asset that is not a collectable or a personal use asset.

12.062   SEPARATE CGT ASSETS: SUBDIVISION 108-D

Under common law, when an accessory is annexed to a principal asset (such as land) the accessory becomes part of that principal asset. Accordingly, if the principal asset had been acquired pre-CGT (before 20 September 1985), any building on that land or any addition to that land would also be regarded as a pre-CGT asset even though the building or addition to that land had been acquired post-CGT.

Subdivision 108-D modifies this rule for CGT purposes and treats an asset as being a separate CGT asset from the principal asset where the asset is:

- a building or structure on post-CGT land which would be subject to a balancing adjustment under Subdivision 40-D (depreciating assets) or s73B ITAA36 (research and development) (ss108-55(1)). A building or structure is not a separate asset merely because it is subject to a capital works deduction under Division 43
- a building or structure erected post-CGT on land acquired pre-CGT (ss108-55(2))
- a depreciating asset that is part of the building or structure (s108-60)
- post-CGT land acquired adjacent to pre-CGT land, even if the titles were subsequently amalgamated (s108-65), or
- a capital improvement that is made to a pre-CGT asset where the cost base of that improvement (assuming it were a separate CGT asset) is beyond a specified limit (s108-70 and s108-85).

Broadly, a post CGT improvement to a pre-CGT acquired asset will taken to be a separate CGT asset if its cost base when a CGT event happens in relation to the pre-CGT acquired asset is:

- more than the improvement threshold in the year the CGT event occurs (**$140,443** for the 2014-15 income year and **$136,884** for the 2013-14 income year), and
- more than 5% of the capital proceeds from the event.

For separate improvements, the threshold applies for each improvement.

Section 108-80 outlines the factors to be considered in determining whether improvements are to be aggregated or treated as separate assets. For example, improvements are likely to be aggregated where they are part of an overall project or made within a reasonable period of each other.

Where the improvements need to be aggregated, the threshold levels apply to the total of all costs.

When a CGT event happens involving a CGT asset acquired before 20 September 1985, it is critical to check whether the cost base of the asset includes any post-19 September 1985 improvements. Where a disposal of a CGT asset comprises two or more separate assets, the capital proceeds will need to be apportioned between the separate assets (s116-40).

Where a taxpayer has an interest in a CGT asset and acquired another interest in the same asset, the two interests remain separate CGT assets for CGT purposes (TD 2000/31).

IMPROVEMENTS TO PRE-CGT ASSETS

These limits are used to determine whether an improvement must be treated as a separate asset (s108-70(3)(a)).

Year	Limit for treatment as a separate asset	Year	Limit for treatment as a separate asset
1985-86	$50,000	2001-02	$97,721
1986-87	$53,950	2002-03	$101,239
1987-88	$58,859	2003-04	$104,377
1988-89	$63,450	2004-05	$106,882
1989-90	$68,018	2005-06	$109,447
1990-91	$73,459	2006-07	$112,512
1991-92	$78,160	2007-08	$116,337
1992-93	$80,036	2008-09	$119,594
1993-94	$80,756	2009-10	$124,258
1994-95	$82,290	2010-11	$126,619
1995-96	$84,347	2011-12	$130,418
1996-97	$88,227	2012-13	$134,200
1997-98	$89,992	2013-14	$136,884
1998-99	$89,992	2014-15	$140,443
1999-00	$91,072	2014-15	$140,443
2000-01	$92,802	2015-16	$143,392

Where a pre-CGT building is relocated to post-CGT land, the exceptions to the common law principle do not apply and the result is a single post-CGT asset that comprises both the land and the building (ATO ID 2003/626).

12.070 STEP 3: DOES AN EXEMPTION OR CONCESSION APPLY?

Where a CGT event has been triggered, there are often exemptions or concessions that may apply with the effect that any capital gain or loss is either disregarded or reduced.

12.072 ASSET ACQUIRED BEFORE 20 SEPTEMBER 1985

Essentially, CGT only applies where a CGT event happens in relation to a CGT asset that was acquired (or was deemed to have been acquired) after 19 September 1985. Therefore, a CGT event affecting an asset acquired before 20 September 1985 will not involve any CGT liability. However, there are integrity rules in place deeming certain pre-CGT assets to have been acquired post-CGT. Therefore, it is necessary to determine the date on which an asset was acquired.

The timing of the acquisition may vary depending upon the nature of the CGT event. However, as a general rule, a CGT asset is acquired when the taxpayer becomes the asset's owner as a result of:

- a CGT event (s109-5) (eg. the transfer of an asset or the creation of a right)
- other events (s109-10) (eg. the issue of shares by a company or creating a new CGT asset), or
- the application of special rules (s109-55) (eg. assets acquired as a beneficiary of a deceased estate).

Generally, if an asset is acquired under a contract, the date of acquisition is the date the contract is made even if the contract was unenforceable.

The date of making the contract may, in some cases, be prior to the date of exchange of contracts. This may occur where there is an oral contract provided it constitutes a contract under the common law. Further, it is the date of the contract that results in change of ownership which is the relevant contract, not the date of agreements that have imposed an obligation to enter the final contract (*Elmslie & Ors v FC of T* 93 ATC 4964).

The date of acquisition appearing on a land title (the date of settlement) is often a later date than the date of acquisition for CGT purposes. If an asset was not acquired under a contract, the date of acquisition is generally the date ownership changed.

An asset can also be acquired if it is constructed by, or created by or for a person, or if shares or units in a unit trust are allotted or issued to a person. If an asset is constructed or created by a person for their own use, the date of acquisition is the date on which the construction or creation commenced. If the construction or creation is undertaken by another person under a contract, the date of acquisition is the date on which a contract is made.

Below is a summary of the general timing rules for assets acquired as a result of the main CGT events (ss109-5(2)), although the rule for the specific CGT event may deviate from these general rules. The time of acquisition is important because:

- CGT does not generally apply to assets acquired before 20 September 1985
- where applicable, the CGT discount or indexation only applies where the asset was acquired at least 12 months before the CGT event happened, and
- the cost base is sometimes based upon market value of the asset.

General rules (main CGT events only)	Time of acquisition
If contract exists (A1)	Date of contract
If no contract (A1)	
• asset compulsorily acquired by law (A1)	Date ownership changed unless: Asset acquired at the earlier of: • payment of compensation • acquirer becoming the owner • acquirer entering on the asset • acquirer taking possession
• asset first used (B1)	When the taxpayer first obtained use and enjoyment[1] of the asset
An entity creates contractual or other rights in the taxpayer (D1)	When contract entered into, or the right created
An entity grants an option to the taxpayer (D2)	When the option is granted
A trust created over a CGT asset (E1)	When the trust is created
A CGT asset is transferred to the trust (E2)	When the asset is transferred
Beneficiary becomes absolutely entitled[2] to a CGT asset	When beneficiary becomes absolutely entitled

1: Unless title does not pass when the agreement ends.　2: Disregarding any legal disability.

IMPORTANT: A CGT asset acquired before 20 September 1985 may still may be subject to CGT (ie. treated as a post-CGT asset), in the following circumstances:
- CGT event K6 is triggered (refer 12.040) which treats a pre-CGT shares in a company or interest in a unit trust as a post CGT share or unit to the extent that at least 75% of the market value of the underlying assets in the entity are post CGT assets relative to the total assets of the entity (refer 12.250).
- Division 149 applies. Broadly, this applies where the majority underlying ownership interests in a pre-CGT asset are no longer held by owners who had majority interests in the asset immediately before 20 September 1985.

GOODWILL OF A BUSINESS

Goodwill is treated as having been acquired on the day the business was either purchased or started. Therefore, no CGT is payable on the disposal of internally generated goodwill of a business started before 20 September 1985. However, this is provided the business can truly be said to be the same business, albeit that it has evolved over time. If a business is expanded after 19 September 1985 by acquiring the goodwill of another business, the goodwill of the original pre-September 1985 business remains a pre-CGT asset.

Any capital gain on goodwill may be eligible for the small business CGT concessions (see 12.525). Note a 50% goodwill exemption applied to CGT events prior to 11.45am on 21 September 1999 (former s118-250).

The definition of goodwill of a business was considered in *FC of T v Murry* 98 ATC 4585; (1998) 39 ATR 129 (Murry). TR 1999/16 adopts the legal meaning taken in Murry as to the meaning of goodwill which is not necessarily the same as the goodwill which may be ascertained by an application of accounting principles.

The meaning of goodwill as described in Murry and TR 1999/16 is taken to mean:

> *The product of combining and using the tangible, intangible and human assets of a business for such purposes and in such ways that custom is drawn to it. The attraction of custom is central to the legal concept of goodwill. Goodwill is a quality or attribute that derives among other things from using or applying other assets of a business. It may be site, personality, service, price or habit that obtains custom. It is more accurate to refer to goodwill as having sources than it is to refer to it as being composed of elements. Goodwill is a composite thing. It is one whole. It is an indivisible item of property that is legally distinct from the sources from which it emanates. It is something*

that attaches to a business and is inseparable from the conduct of a business. It cannot be dealt with separately from the business with which it is associated.

In terms of measuring goodwill, the ruling states that the parties to a sale of a business need to determine how much of the capital proceeds is properly attributable, and able to be allocated, to:

(a) goodwill, and

(b) off balance sheet assets and identifiable assets (including work in progress, the get-up of the business and scientific, technical, industrial or commercial knowledge or information, eg., know-how and mining, or prospecting information) of the business in terms of the accounting standards.

In terms of valuing goodwill, the ruling states that the preferred approach to valuing goodwill on the sale of a profitable business or a business expected to be profitable is the difference between:

(a) the present value of the predicted earnings of the business, and

(b) the sum of the market values of off balance sheet assets and all identifiable net assets (in terms of the accounting standards) other than goodwill of the business disposed of.

PATENT OR COPYRIGHT

A patent or copyright is taken to have been created when the research and development work started on the project (IT 2484).

If the work started before 20 September 1985, any capital gain from the sale of the rights is disregarded as a pre-CGT asset. As with creating a lease, however, should a licence be granted after 19 September 1985, that licence is a separate CGT asset. The asset is created at the time it is granted and (except for associated legal and other costs) is taken to have been acquired at nil cost.

NOTE: A patent, copyright, registered design or license to use such assets are treated as depreciating assets under the Uniform Capital Allowances provisions contained under Division 40. Note that a trade mark does not satisfy the definition of a depreciating asset and is commonly treated as a CGT asset (ATO ID 2004/858).

12.074   EXEMPTIONS AND CONCESSIONS

In addition to the pre-CGT asset exemption, subdivision 118-A sets out the general exemptions from CGT for certain CGT assets acquired on or after 20 September 1985.

An exemption from CGT may arise either because the post-CGT asset is exempt, the CGT event is taxed under another provision of the Act, or the transaction is exempt. In other cases, the CGT event is disregarded. In each case the taxpayer can disregard any capital gain or loss arising from the following CGT assets or CGT events.

EXEMPT ASSETS

A capital gain or loss on the following assets is disregarded:

- a motor vehicle designed to carry less than one tonne or fewer than nine passengers, a motorcycle or a similar vehicle (paragraph 118-5(a)). As motor vehicles generally decrease in value their exclusion denies most taxpayers a capital loss. The gain on any motor vehicle that increases in value is disregarded unless its capacity exceeds the relevant threshold (TD 2000/35)
- a decoration awarded for valour or brave conduct, unless purchased by the taxpayer (paragraph 118-5(b))
- a collectable where the first element of its cost is $500 or less, excluding the net GST input tax credit (ss118-10(1)). Where a taxpayer acquired an interest in a collectable after 15 December 1995, it is the market value of the collectable itself that must be $500 or less for this exemption to apply and not the value of the taxpayer's interest. Before 16 December 1995, the exemption applied if the taxpayer's interest in the collectable had been acquired below the $500 threshold
- a personal use where the first element of its cost is $10,000 or less, excluding the net GST input tax credit (ss118-10(3)), and
- a CGT asset used solely to produce exempt income or non-assessable non-exempt income (s118-12). However, ss118-12(2) contains a list of non-assessable income

amounts to which the CGT exemption does not apply. The non-assessable non-exempt amounts in the list are there to prevent double taxation and there is no justification for disregarding capital gains or losses on assets used to produce such income.
- shares in a pooled development fund (s118-13).

ANTI-OVERLAP PROVISIONS PREVENTING DOUBLE TAXATION

Generally, a capital gain is reduced to the extent to which another provision of the tax law includes an amount in assessable or exempt income (s118-20) (note that including a balancing adjustment in assessable income is one exception to this rule). This means that CGT is generally a residual provision and all other provisions of the Act should be considered before CGT.

There are no CGT implications where as a result of a CGT event, an amount is included in assessable income under a provision relating to:
- a superannuation lump sum or Employment Termination Payment (ETP) (s118-22)
- depreciating assets except for certain primary production assets depreciated under Subdivisions 40F and 40G (however, note that CGT event K7 can apply where a depreciating asset is used wholly or partially for a non-taxable purpose) (s118-24)
- trading stock (s118-25)
- film copyright (s118-30), and
- eligible research and development tax concession projects where an amount is included in assessable income under sections 73B(27A),73BF(4) or 73BM(4) of the ITAA36 (s118-35).

In each case, the amount included in assessable income under these provisions does not have to equate to the notional capital gain for the exemption to apply. Trade debts which arise as a result of provision of services, which have been included in assessable income of the taxpayer, would be reduced under the anti-overlap rules upon the extinguishment of that debt (ATO ID 2008/110).

During the 2012-13 income year, Alistair received an ETP as a consequence of having his long standing employment terminated. A significant component of the payment relates to Alistair's pre-July 1983 service which will be regarded as a life benefit termination payment. Alistair's receipt of this portion of the ETP will be treated as non-assessable and non exempt income under ss82-10(1). Prima facie the payment would also be a capital gain. However, for CGT purposes the total amount received is excluded (s118-22).

12.090 STEP 4: IS THERE A CAPITAL GAIN OR CAPITAL LOSS?

Each CGT event contains rules governing the method of calculating any resulting capital gain or loss.

In the case of CGT event A1, a capital gain arises if the capital proceeds from disposal of the CGT asset are more than the asset's 'cost base'. A capital loss will arise if the capital proceeds are less than the asset's 'reduced cost base'.

The definition of 'capital proceeds', 'cost base' and 'reduced cost base' are therefore important in determining the capital gain or loss arising under the various CGT events. Section 110-10 contains a list of the CGT events for which it is not necessary to determine the cost base (12.150).

Divisions 110 to 114 define the elements needed to determine the cost base and reduced cost base. Division 116 defines capital proceeds. Each of these elements are considered below.

12.092   COST BASE

Division 110 defines cost base by first defining it in general terms, and then providing modifications to these rules for some situations.

Cost base is the sum of these five elements:

1. CONSIDERATION GIVEN ON ACQUISITION OF THE CGT ASSET

The consideration is either:
- the amount of money paid (or required to be paid) and the market value of any other property given to acquire the asset (ss110-25(2)), or

- modified to the market value of the asset, if:
  - no expenditure was incurred, unless CGT event D1 happened (eg. by gift) or another entity did something that did not constitute a CGT event happening
  - some or all of the expenditure cannot be valued, or
  - the transaction was not at arm's length (ss112-20)(1)). Where a taxpayer accepts an unconditional takeover offer from a 'bidder' company for their shares in the 'target' company, the first element in the cost base of the shares acquired in the 'bidder' company is the market value of the taxpayer's shares in the 'target' company at the time the taxpayer entered into the contract to acquired the bidder company's shares (see TD 2002/4).

The first element does not include formation costs incurred by prospective shareholders when establishing a company (ATO ID 2009/1).

2. INCIDENTAL COSTS INCURRED

Valuation fees, stamp duty, remuneration for professional services, transfer costs, advertising etc or costs that relate to the CGT event, where no deduction has been or will be allowed for these expenses (ss110-25(3) and s110-35). Refer to 12.094 for further commentary.

3. COSTS OF OWNING A CGT ASSET ACQUIRED AFTER 20 AUGUST 1991

Where no deduction has been (or will be) allowed for these expenses (ss110-25(4)). Costs of owning include interest on borrowings, insurance, repairs and maintenance, rates and land tax and costs of travel to the property to carry out maintenance and repairs. An example of an interest cost required to be capitalised may arise where a taxpayer acquires land for capital appreciation purposes (refer s51AAA ITAA36). This element of the cost base does not apply to assets acquired before 21 August 1991. Where the asset is a collectable or a personal use asset, the third element is not included in the cost base (s108-17 and s108-30). After 30 June 2002, debt deductions disallowed by the thin capitalisation rules cannot be included as a cost of ownership (s110-54). Where a cost of ownership arises from a tax benefit in connection with a scheme to which Part IVA applies, the deduction disallowed under Part IVA does not form part of the cost base of the asset unless the Commissioner makes a compensating adjustment to that effect. An example of a disallowed tax benefit is the additional interest obtained from entering into a split loan arrangement to provide funds for the purchase of both a rental property and a home (TD 2005/33).

4. CAPITAL EXPENDITURE INCURRED

The fourth element is capital expenditure incurred by the taxpayer:

- for the purpose or expected purpose of increasing or preserving the asset's value, or
- that relates to installing or moving the asset

Prior to 1 July 2005, it was necessary that the purpose of the expenditure was to increase the asset's value and that the expenditure be reflected in the state or nature of the asset at the time of the CGT event. The current provision extended the element to including capital expenditure incurred to preserve the asset value. This ensures that, for example, legal costs incurred to preserve the value of a property by opposing a nearby development that would adversely affect the property's value and costs incurred in unsuccessfully applying for zoning changes can form part of the fourth element of an asset's cost base.

There is no longer a requirement that the expenditure be reflected in the state or nature of the asset at the time of the CGT event.

The fourth element does not apply to capital expenditure incurred in relation to goodwill.

5. CAPITAL EXPENDITURE TO ESTABLISH, PRESERVE OR DEFEND TITLE TO THE ASSET OR A RIGHT OVER THE ASSET (SS110-25(6))

The fifth element would include a compensation payment made by the vendor of a CGT asset to a potential purchaser to terminate a contract of sale (ATO ID 2008/147). Similarly, legal costs incurred by the executor of a deceased estate to defend a claim for the control of the estate forms part of the cost base of the estate's assets as the fifth element of cost base (ATO ID 2001/730).

IMPACT OF ACQUISITION TIME ON ELEMENTS OF COST BASE

For CGT assets acquired between 7.30pm on 13 May 1997 and 19 February 2004 only the first, second and third elements of the cost base were reduced by the amount of any GST net input tax credit (ss110-45(3A)). All elements however are reduced by any GST net input tax credit from 20 February 2004 (s103-30). Note that if the asset was acquired before 7.30pm on 13 May 1997, unlike the second and third elements, the first, fourth and fifth elements are not required to be reduced if part of that cost is an allowable deduction. For example, this means the acquisition cost of an asset (the first element) is not reduced by the capital allowance for buildings under Division 43 if the building was acquired before 7.30 on 13 May 1997.

For assets acquired after 7.30pm on 13 May 1997, however, expenditure that is:

- deductible
- eligible for a heritage conservation expenditure tax offset, or
- landcare and water facility tax offset under the former s388-55

will not form part of the cost base of an asset.

The wording of the cost base provisions is important because deductible expenditure forming part of the second or third element is never included in the cost base, while deductible expenditure relating to the first, fourth or fifth element in the cost base of a CGT asset acquired after 7.30pm on 13 May 1997 is initially included in the asset's cost base and then excluded at the time of the CGT event (s110-37). This means that a taxpayer can receive the benefit of any indexation component on deductible expenditure initially included in the first, fourth or fifth element of a post-13 May 1997 CGT asset should an eligible taxpayer choose to apply CGT indexation.

These provisions do not apply to a deemed separate asset acquired after 13 May 1997 but before 1 July 1999, where the underlying asset is land or buildings acquired before 7.30pm on 13 May 1997. An exception is the deduction under Division 243 (limited recourse debt) which will be included in the cost base (ss110-40(4)).

Expenditure on illegal activities, entertainment, penalties and bribes to a foreign public official or public official are also specifically excluded from the cost base of a CGT asset (s110-38).

Where the deduction provision has rules that require the recoupment of these deductions on the sale of the asset (eg. Division 40 balancing adjustment), it is correct not to take account of the deduction for CGT because it is assessable elsewhere in the Act.

Two new buildings were constructed at a cost of $100,000 each. There are two identical investors – Investor 1 acquired one of the properties before 7.30pm on 13 May 1997 and Investor 2 acquired the other property after that date. A 2.5% capital works deduction was claimed by both taxpayers for 15 years. The buildings were then each sold for $200,000. Both taxpayers (individuals) choose to use the CGT discount method to determine the capital gain.

Investor 1. Building acquired before 7.30pm on 13 May 1997

Capital proceeds		$200,000
Cost	$100,000	
Tax claim ($37,500 over 15 years)		
Reduction in cost base	Nil	$100,000
		$100,000
less CGT discount (50%)		$50,000
Taxable capital gain		**$50,000**

Investor 2. Building acquired on or after 7.30pm on 13 May 1997

Capital proceeds		$200,000
Cost base		$100,000
Tax claim ($37,500 over 15 years)		
Reduction in cost base	$37,500	$62,500
		$137,500
less CGT discount (50%)		$68,750
Taxable capital gain		**$68,750**

Increased CGT payable by Investor 2 (assuming top marginal tax rate plus Medicare levy plus 2% budget repair) = 49% of ($68,750 – $50,000) = $9,187.50

Note that TD 2005/47 states that where a taxpayer failed to claim capital works deductions but was eligible to do so, the taxpayer is only required to reduce the cost base if the taxpayer can deduct these amounts at the time of lodging an income tax return for the relevant income year in question. This means that if the time period prescribed for amending assessments for those income years has lapsed, cost base adjustments are not necessary. In PS LA 2006/1 (GA), the Tax Office states that, as a concessional measure, where a taxpayer does not have sufficient information to determine the amount and nature of capital works expenditure and does not seek to claim a deduction for the capital works, cost base adjustments will not be necessary.

12.094   INCIDENTAL COSTS

For an incidental cost to be included in the cost base, the cost must have been incurred:

- to acquire a CGT asset, or
- relate to a CGT event.

This requirement does not however apply to the 'ninth' element.

Costs that do not meet these tests would not be included in the second element (e.g. auctioneer's costs where the property was not sold at the auction would not be eligible for inclusion in the property's cost base as no CGT event happened). 'Incidental costs' are defined as having ten elements (s110-35):

- remuneration for the services of a surveyor, valuer, auctioneer, accountant, broker, agent, consultant or legal adviser. This first element includes professional advice about the operation of the ITAA97, but only if the advice is provided by a recognised tax adviser who is defined in s995-1(1) as a registered tax agent or a legal practitioner
- costs of transfer
- stamp duty or other similar duty
- cost of advertising or marketing to find a seller (if the taxpayer is buying the asset) or buyer (if the taxpayer is selling the asset)
- costs in making any valuation or apportionment for CGT purposes
- search fees (which are essentially related to checking land titles)
- the cost of a conveyancing kit (or similar cost)
- borrowing expenses, such as loan application fees and mortgage discharge fees, and
- costs incurred by a head company of a consolidated group or MEC group relating to a CGT asset because of a transaction between members of the group. Whilst there are no tax consequences arising from this intra-group transfer any relevant incidental costs such as stamp duty should be included in the cost base of the asset (even thought there is no acquisition or disposal of a CGT asset outside the group)
- termination or other similar fees incurred as a direct result of your ownership of a CGT asset ending.

The payment of a foreign gift tax on the transfer of shares would form part of the second element of the cost base because it is an incidental cost in acquiring the shares (ATO ID 2005/39). The payment of UK inheritance tax however on the acquisition of shares is not part of the cost base because the tax is not imposed on the transfer of property but on the estate of the deceased if the deceased's total assets exceed the inheritance threshold (ATO ID 2005/40). Remuneration paid by the taxpayer, as seller, to a legal adviser as a result of an action for damages brought by the purchaser in connection with the consideration paid for the sale are incidental costs which relate to a CGT event (ATO ID 2006/179).

12.096   INDEXATION OF COST BASE

The use of an indexed cost base (frozen at 30 September 1999) in determining a capital gain is available to all taxpayers who acquired the CGT asset at or before 11.45am on 21 September 1999, and held the asset for at least 12 months before the CGT event happened (s114-10(1)).

SIX EXCEPTIONS TO THE 12 MONTH OWNERSHIP RULE

- Where CGT event E8 applies (ss114-10(3)).

- Same-asset rollovers where the transferor and transferee's ownership period are aggregated in determining whether the asset has been held for at least 12 months (ss114-10(4)).
- Replacement-asset rollovers where the combined ownership of the original asset and the replacement asset together are at least 12 months (ss114-10(5)).
- Deceased estates where the 12 months rule applies to the trustee or beneficiary as if the asset was acquired when the deceased acquired it (ss114-10(6)).
- Joint tenancy where a surviving joint tenant is taken to acquire the deceased's joint tenant's interest in an asset when the deceased acquired it (ss114-10(7)).
- Where CGT event J1 applies the company who owns the rollover asset ignores the acquisition rule in ss104-175(8) (ss114-10(8)).

Where an eligible taxpayer chooses to use the indexation method to determine the capital gain, the indexed cost base includes elements 1, 2, 4 and 5 inflated by the all groups Consumer Price Index (CPI), which is frozen at 30 September 1999, plus the unindexed third element (costs of ownership) (s110-35 and ss960-275(4)).

An example in s114-1 illustrates the application of the indexation process.

Expenditure incurred in the same quarter as the CGT event has an indexation factor of 1.

Shares acquired in the Telstra 1 float are indexed from December 1997 quarter, the quarter in which the shares were allocated to an investor; not from the final instalment for the shares (*Dolby v FC of T* (2002) FCA 1065).

12.098   CGT INDEX FACTORS

The capital gain from a CGT event happening to an asset acquired between 20 September 1985 and 11.45am on 21 September 1999 and held by the taxpayer for at least 12 months may in certain circumstances be calculated by comparing the asset's indexed cost base and the capital proceeds received (or receivable).

Indexation applies to all assets held for 12 months or more. It also applies to 'improvements' that can be treated as 'separate assets' even if the original improved asset was acquired before 20 September 1985.

Where it is appropriate for a taxpayer to elect to use the indexation method, the first, second, fourth and fifth elements in the cost base cannot be indexed beyond the September 1999 quarter, even if the CGT event occurred after that time (Division 114 and ss960-275(2)).The index factor was 123.4 when frozen at 30 September 1999.

12.102   REDUCED COST BASE

Capital gains are determined by comparing the capital proceeds and the cost base (indexed if appropriate and elected). Capital losses however are determined by comparing the capital proceeds with the asset's reduced cost base.

In essence, the definition of reduced cost base in s110-55 is similar to the definition of cost base. However, the following important differences must be noted:

- no element included in the reduced cost base is indexed (s110-55(1)), and
- any part of the cost that has been allowed as a deduction is not included in the reduced cost base (ss110-55(4)).

The reduced cost base has five elements:

- elements 1, 2, 4 and 5 are the same as for the 'cost base' (see 12.092) but are never indexed (ss110-55(2))
- the non-capital cost of ownership is not included when determining the reduced cost base. Instead, the third element is any amount that is assessable because of a balancing adjustment, or would be assessable if the taxpayer had not elected to take balancing adjustment relief (ss110-55(3)).

For CGT assets acquired before 20 February 2004, no element in the reduced cost base was reduced by any GST net input tax credit. For CGT assets acquired after 19 February 2004, however, all elements in the reduced cost base are reduced by any GST net input credit (s103-30).

These costs are not included in the reduced cost base:

- an amount to the extent that it is deductible. This includes balancing adjustments and eligible heritage conservation expenditure that would have qualified as construction expenditure but for paragraph 43-70(2)(h) (ss110-55(4))
- amounts that could have been deducted for a CGT asset had it been used wholly for producing assessable income (ss110-55(5))
- any cost that has been recouped and not included in assessable income (ss110-55(6))
- expenditure to the extent that the taxpayer chooses a landcare and water facility tax offset for it under the former s388-55 rather than deducting it (ss110-55(6A))
- if the CGT asset is a share, certain sums attributable to amounts derived by the company before the share was acquired (ss110-55(7)). This provision only applies where there is a distribution wholly or partly out of pre-acquisition profits and the company makes the distribution to a corporate shareholder entitled to a tax offset under Division 207, and the corporate shareholder is the controller (or an associate of the controller) of a company. (See ss110-55(7), ss100-55(8) and s975-155 which defines the term 'controller'), and
- an amount the taxpayer has deducted, can deduct or could have deducted except for Subdivision 170-D (transactions by a company that is a member of a linked group) as a result of a CGT event that happened in relation to a CGT asset (ss110-55(9)).

Also, expenditure on illegal activities, entertainment, bribes to a foreign public official or public official, penalties and excess boat expenditure under s26-47 are respectively excluded from the reduced cost base of a CGT asset (refer ss110-55(9A) to (9E)).

Capital works

A taxpayer acquired a hotel on 1 December 2012 for $1,500,000, and two years later sold it for $1,400,000 (selling costs: $40,000). The taxpayer was entitled to claim 2.5% capital works allowance write-off based on the construction cost of the building $1,000,000.

Cost of hotel	$1,500,000
plus Incidental disposal costs	$40,000
less 2.5% capital allowance	($50,000)
Reduced cost base	$1,490,000
less Capital proceeds: CGT event A1	$1,400,000
Capital loss	**$90,000**

NOTE: In PS LA 2006/1 (GA), for the purposes of working out the cost base and reduced cost base of a CGT asset under Division 110, the Commissioner states that he will accept that a taxpayer cannot deduct the capital works write-off under Division 43 for construction expenditure where the taxpayer does not have sufficient information to work out the deduction and has not claimed a deduction in respect of the capital works. In this case, the cost base and reduced cost base will not be adjusted for any capital works deductions.

Unclaimed holding costs

A holiday house cost $200,000 and was sold for $190,000 (CGT event A1 happens). During the period of ownership unclaimed expenses for interest and rates amounted to $16,000. The capital loss (ignoring non-deductible holding costs) is: $200,000 – $190,000 = $10,000. Unclaimed non-capital holding costs on post-20 August 1991 assets do not increase a capital loss.

12.120 SPECIAL 'REDUCED COST BASE' PROVISIONS

SHARES

A reduction in the cost base of shares can occur if a taxpayer acquired shares after 19 September 1985 and there is a payment by the company to the taxpayer that is not a dividend under s6 or s47 ITAA36 (refer CGT event G1 and ss104-135(1)). For example, a return of capital (other than on disposal of shares or a distribution of bonus shares from an untainted share capital account) constitutes a payment by a company that is not a dividend.

Such payments impact on the cost base as follows:

- if the payment does not exceed the asset's cost base, the cost base is reduced by the 'non-assessable part' of the capital distribution (ss104-135(4))
- where a 'non-assessable part' of the capital payment exceeds the cost base the excess is a capital gain at the time when the company makes the payment (ss104-135(3)), and
- when CGT event G1 happens, it cannot result in a capital loss.

A taxpayer acquired shares in a company for $15,000 on 1 May 1999. On 1 October 2014, the taxpayer receives a non-assessable cash distribution of $3,000 which was paid out of the company's untainted share capital account.

Cost base	$15,000
less Non-assessable part of distribution	($3,000)
New cost base	**$12,000**

Any payment by a liquidator if the company is dissolved within 18 months of the payment is disregarded for the purposes of CGT event G1, but would be part of the taxpayer's capital proceeds for CGT event C2 when the shares end (ss104-135(6)).

TRUSTS

A reduction in the cost base of a fixed interest in a trust (such as units) acquired after 19 September 1985 may occur where all or part of a trust distribution is non-assessable (CGT event E4 happens, see s104-70).

The timing of CGT event E4 (12.028) is generally just prior to the end of the year of income in which the non-assessable distribution occurs. This means that the adjustment of the cost base only occurs once, whereas under former s160ZM of ITAA36, numerous adjustments of the cost base of units or interests in trusts could occur because a deemed disposal and re-acquisition occurred each time a non-assessable distribution was received by a beneficiary. The one exception to this rule is if another CGT event (other than E4) occurs after the trustee makes the payment, but before 30 June. In that case, CGT event E4 occurs just before the earlier CGT event occurs (ss104-70(3)).

The Commissioner has confirmed that CGT event E4 has no application to a beneficiary of a discretionary trust because the beneficiaries have no 'interest' in the trust (TD 2003/28). The TD however does not address the potential application of s104-70 to takers in default of appointment (or default beneficiaries). Such persons have either a vested interest subject to defeasance (when the trust exercises the discretion to apply the income or capital of the trust to one or more discretionary beneficiaries) or a contingent interest. That is, it will only exist if the trustee fails to exercise his discretion in favour of one or more discretionary beneficiaries.

A taxpayer cannot make a capital loss from CGT event E4.

For further discussion of reduction in cost base due to a non assessable distribution from a unit trust see 12.605.

12.124   CGT EVENTS AFFECTING SHARES OR UNITS

If a CGT event occurs in respect of shares or units within 12 months of acquisition, the 'cost base' is not indexed and the CGT general discount is not available. When the shares or units are held for 12 months (or more) before the CGT event, and there is a return of capital, the reduction in the cost base is applied to the 'cost base' just prior to 30 June as discussed above in 12.120.

For more information on the operation and effect of these rules as they apply to property trusts under s104-70, see 12.600.

Units in a unit trust were acquired by an individual taxpayer in February 2010 at a cost of $3,500. The first and following distributions were received during the 2013-14 income year.

	Total distribution	Payment attributable to Div 43 (capital works) deductions	Tax-deferred allowance
July 2013	$400	$34	$38
October 2013	$250	$21	$24
January 2014	$300	$28	$29
March 2014	$350	$31	$33
Totals	**$1,300**	**$114**	**$124**

The amount included in assessable income of the beneficiary is $1,300 – $114 – $124 = $1,062.

If the units are disposed of in April 2014 for $4,000, CGT event A1 happens.

As this CGT event occurs after the non-assessable payment by the trustee in March 2014 but before 30 June, CGT event E4 would be taken to have occurred just prior to the occurrence of CGT event A1.

The cost base is calculated by deducting the non-assessable part, which includes the building allowance:

> *Original cost base: $3,500 – 114 – 124 = $3,262*

If the units are disposed of in April 2014 for $4,000 the capital gain using the CGT discount method is:

> *$4,000 less 3,262 = $738 less 50% CGT discount ($369) = $369*

The reduced cost base is: $3,500 – $114 – $124 = $3,262

If the units had been sold for $3,000, then the capital loss is: $3,262 – $3,000 = $262.

12.140 MODIFICATIONS TO THE COST BASE

Both the general definition of cost base and reduced cost base may be modified by the operation of Division 112.

The most important of these modifications relate to:

- the replacement of actual cost with market value: s112-20.
- split and merged assets: s112-25.
- apportionment rules: s112-30.
- assumption of liabilities: s112-35.

MARKET VALUE SUBSTITUTION RULE

This rule impacts on the first element of the cost base (the consideration on acquisition).

Where an asset is acquired from another entity and:

- there was no expenditure incurred in acquiring the asset (except where the acquisition resulted from CGT event D1 or another entity doing something that did not constitute a CGT event happening), or
- some or all of the expenditure incurred to acquire it cannot be valued, or
- the taxpayer did not deal at arm's length with the other entity in connection with the acquisition

the cost of acquisition is taken to be the market value of the CGT asset (at the time of acquisition) (ss112-20(1)).

This modification to the cost base is important when determining the cost base of an asset that has been gifted, has been transferred in a family situation, or is a transfer of property which is not at arm's length, eg. where a family business is restructured.

The term 'market value' is not defined in ITAA97 but in *Spencer v The Commonwealth of Australia* (1907) 5 CLR 418, market value was defined as the price agreed between two parties who are willing to trade, but neither of them so anxious to do so that he would overlook ordinary business considerations. That is, the price that would be agreed between a willing but not anxious buyer, and a willing but not anxious seller. However, this test may not always be appropriate. For example, when land is subdivided it is normal for the roads to be transferred to the local government authority for no consideration and it could be argued that there is no normal market value which may be applied. The test in Spencer's case requires that there is a willing buyer which may not always be the case.

An issue also arises as to what constitutes not dealing at arm's length (this same issue also arises with capital proceeds, discussed later). The relevant issue is not a test of whether the two parties are at arm's length (eg. a husband and wife), but is a test of whether the parties are *dealing* at arm's length (*Elmslie & Ors v FC of T* (1993) 93 ATC 4964). For this reason it is possible for non-arm's length taxpayers to deal at arm's length and vice versa. Broadly, the test of an arm's length transaction is whether the agreed price is similar to an open market price.

In *Granby Pty Ltd v FC of T* (1995) 95 ATC 4240 Lee J stated:

What is asked is whether the parties behaved in the manner in which parties at arm's length would be expected to behave in conducting their affairs.

Dealing at arm's length can be equated to a test of market value.

The Tax Office has also outlined its views on market valuations on its website under the heading *Market Valuation for tax purposes*.

The market value substitution rule is further modified where the acquisition of a CGT asset on or after 16 August 1989 results from:

- the issue or allotment of shares in a company, or
- the issue of units in a unit trust by the trustee.

In these two cases, market value is only substituted if what is paid to acquire the asset is more than its market value at the time of acquisition.

The market substitution rule will not apply to the situations set out in the following table (see ss112-20(3)).

MARKET SUBSTITUTION RULE WILL NOT APPLY IN THESE SITUATIONS

Item	The taxpayer acquired this CGT asset:	. . . . in this situation
1	A right to receive ordinary income or statutory income from a trust (except a unit trust or a trust that arises because of someone's death)	(a) The taxpayer did not pay or give anything for the right, and (b) The taxpayer did not acquire the right by way of an assignment from another entity
2	A decoration awarded for valour or brave conduct	The taxpayer did not pay or give anything for it
3	A contractual or other legal or equitable right resulting from CGT event D1 happening (12.026)	The taxpayer did not pay or give anything for it
4	Rights to acquire: (a) shares, or options to acquire shares in a company, or (b) units, or options to acquire units, in a unit trust: in a situation covered by Subdivision 130-B	The taxpayer did not pay or give anything for the rights
5	A share in a company or a right to acquire a share or debenture in a company	It was issued or allotted to the taxpayer by the company and the taxpayer did not pay or give anything for it
6	A unit in a unit trust or a right to acquire a unit or debenture in a unit trust	It was issued to the taxpayer by the trustee of the unit trust and the taxpayer did not pay or give anything for it
7	Shares in a 'no goodwill' incorporated professional practice (TD 2011/26)	Where the share is the subject of an arms length dealing but for which no amount is received as capital proceeds or paid as cost base is nil

SPLIT, CHANGED OR MERGED ASSETS

A modification of the cost base occurs where CGT assets are split or merged and the taxpayer remains the beneficial owner of the new asset after the change.

The splitting or merging of a CGT asset is not a CGT event. Each element in the cost base is simply added where assets are merged, and apportioned 'in a reasonable way' where an asset is split into two or more assets (s112-25).

TD 97/3 indicates that if a parcel of post-CGT land is subdivided into lots, the subdivided are treated as separate assets under s112-25 and therefore, requires a reasonable apportionment of the cost. In such circumstances, the Commissioner will accept any approach that is appropriate, such as an area basis or relative market value basis.

 In 1990, Barry purchases 10 hectares of land for $200,000. In February 2013 he subdivides the land into five two-hectare blocks. The cost base of each block is 1/5 x $200,000 = $40,000.

Any other elements in the cost base would also need to be apportioned.

If a company converts its shares into a larger or smaller number of shares, no CGT event happens in respect of those shares. To the extent that those converted shares are post CGT shares, s112-25 applies to attribute a proportionate cost base to the converted shares (refer TD 2000/10).

APPORTIONMENT RULES

The elements in the asset's cost base may need to be apportioned where an asset is acquired and only part of the asset is subject to CGT on the happening of a CGT event (s112-30). An example would be where the taxpayer disposes of 100 hectares of land which includes his main residence, or where the taxpayer disposes of standing timber on the land.

However, no apportionment is required if an amount forming part of the 'cost base' or 'reduced cost base' of the asset is wholly attributable to either the part of the asset affected if a CGT event happens or to the remaining part (ss112-30(5)).

ASSUMPTION OF LIABILITY RULE

If a CGT asset is acquired from another entity, and it is subject to a liability, the first element in the cost base or reduced cost base of the asset includes the amount of liability assumed (s112-35).

For example, if $100,000 is paid for a block of land that includes a $40,000 mortgage also assumed, the first element in the cost base is $140,000.

12.142   CAPITAL PROCEEDS

The approach to defining 'capital proceeds' is similar to 'cost base' in that Division 116 starts with a general definition (s116-20), and then gives six modifications that may need to be applied which are summarised in s116-25.

Capital proceeds from CGT events are:

- the money a taxpayer receives, or is entitled to receive, for the CGT event happening, and
- the market value of any other property a taxpayer receives, or is entitled to receive, in respect of the event happening (ss116-20(1)).

From 1 July 2000, capital proceeds do not include the net GST on any supply (ss116-20(5)). The net GST is the GST payable on the supply, net of any increasing and decreasing adjustments of GST in relation to the supply (ss995-1(1)).

Capital proceeds may be in the form of cash and/or other property and will be taken into account at the time the CGT event occurs regardless of whether they have been actually received. For example, if land is sold for $400,000 with payment to be made in four equal annual payments of $100,000 each, the total amount of any capital gain will be assessable in the year of the CGT event, notwithstanding that the taxpayer has only actually received one quarter of the total capital proceeds in that year.

Where the market value of property is relevant to the calculation of a capital gain or loss, it is the market value at the time of the CGT event that is included as capital proceeds.

 A contracts to sell land valued at $150,000 in exchange for 30,000 shares in B Ltd to be delivered in six months time. At the time of the CGT event (the sale of the land), shares in B Ltd had a market value of $5 each. By the time the shares were delivered six months later their value had declined to $1 each.

The capital proceeds from such a CGT event would be $150,000 (30,000 x $5) notwithstanding that the value of shares on delivery is only $30,000 (30,000 x $1) (ie. the value at the time of the CGT event – see s116-20(1)).

It should be noted that non-cash receipts are only included in 'capital proceeds' if they are property.

EARN-OUT ARRANGEMENTS

Problems can arise where the total amount of consideration is unascertainable or contingent on other factors. For example, the consideration for the sale of a business may be the payment of a fixed sum on the signing of the contract, plus a percentage of turnover for a period of up to five years which may be generated from the use of the business assets sold.

The actual consideration received by the seller is dependent upon the future turnover of the business. These are known as 'earnout arrangements'.

Over seven years ago the Commissioner released a draft Ruling on how CGT applied to an earnout arrangement (TR 2007/D10). This draft Ruling had a series of unwanted outcomes and so the Government indicated it would amend the CGT law so it applied appropriately to earnout arrangements. In May 2015, the Government released draft legislation.

In summary, the draft legislation will give earnout arrangements a "look-through" CGT treatment. This means that capital gains and losses arising on these earnout rights will be disregarded. Instead, taxpayers will be required to include financial benefits provided or received under or in relation to such rights in determining the capital proceeds of the disposal of the underlying asset for the seller or the cost base and reduced cost base of the underlying asset for the buyer. The amounts are effectively treated as additional consideration for the underlying asset.

For these new rules to apply, the following conditions must be met:

- the disposal must cause CGT event A1 to happen
- the asset being sold initially must be an "active asset" of the business before it is sold
- the rights must be created as part of arrangements entered into on an arm's-length basis
- for a right to be a look-through earnout right, future financial benefits provided under the right must be linked to the future economic performance of the asset or a business in which the asset is used and must provide for financial benefits the value of which reasonably relates to this performance
- the financial benefits provided must not be able to be reasonably ascertained at the time the right is created, and
- the right must not require financial benefits to be provided more than four years after CGT event A1 occurs in relation to the disposal of the relevant active asset.

It should also be noted that amendment periods are extended for taxpayers who have these arrangements so that any payment made over the four years can be taken into account when working out the capital gain on the underlying asset.

There is one interesting change where the asset being sold under an earnout arrangement is a share or a unit. There are some additional rules. These are:

- the entity holding the share or unit must either be a CGT concession stakeholder in relation to the company or trust or otherwise own a sufficient share of the business that they would be a CGT concession stakeholder were they an individual
- the trust or company must carry on a business and have carried on a business or businesses for at least one prior income year, and
- for the immediately preceding income year, at least 80% of the income of the trust or company must have come from the carrying on a business or businesses and not been derived as an annuity, interest, rent, royalties or foreign exchange gains, or derived from or in relation to financial instruments.

These proposed amendments will apply to all earnout arrangements entered into on or after 23 April 2015, however the Commissioner has effectively been accepting this treatment in lodged income tax returns as if this was law for the past five years.

Leigh proposes to sell shares in his regional wholesale petroleum distributorship company to David for $6,000,000. The company's business has significant goodwill and turns over $20,000,000 annually. However, David, only offers Leigh $5,000,000 for the shares as he is not sure the turnover is sustainable. The parties ultimately negotiate a sale price on 28 June 2015 whereby the business will be sold for a lump sum of $5,000,000 and 50% of the business turnover to the extent its turnover exceeds $18,000,000 for the 2016 financial year.

CGT event A1 happens on the sale of Leigh's shares. His capital proceeds from the event are $5,000,000.

At the end of the June 2016 year it is determined that the company's turnover for the financial year was $21,000,000.

Under the sale contract Leigh will be entitled to $1,500,000 being 50% of the excess of $3,000,000 over the $18,000,000 turnover threshold established under the earnout right. This is merely additional consideration for the initial A1 event.

12.144 MODIFICATIONS TO CAPITAL PROCEEDS

The six modifications to the general rules with respect to capital proceeds are summarised in s116-10. They are:

1. MARKET VALUE SUBSTITUTION RULE

Market value is substituted for the actual capital proceeds if:

- there are no capital proceeds from the CGT event (eg. a gift of a CGT asset)
- some or all of the capital proceeds cannot be valued (see TD 1999/84)
- the actual capital proceeds are more or less than market value, and
  - the parties to the event were not dealing at arm's length, or
  - the CGT event is C2 (about cancellation, surrender or similar ending of the asset) (s116-30).

The Tax Office has also outlined its views on market valuations on its website under the heading *Market Valuation for tax purposes*.

There are some exceptions to this rule. The market value substitution rule does not apply where the expiry of a CGT asset or the cancellation of a statutory licence happens under CGT event C2 or where CGT event D1 (the creation of contractual and other rights) happens (ss116-30(3)). The purpose of ss116-30(3) is to prevent the market value substitution rule applying when the market value of an asset has diminished through the normal course of events to zero, for example on the expiry of a lease agreement.

The market value substitution rule does not apply where shares in a widely held company or a widely held trust are cancelled under CGT event C2 (from the 2007 income year).

Broadly, a company or unit trust will be 'widely held' where the entity has at least 300 members or unitholders who do not hold any concentrated ownership in the relevant entity. Such concentrated ownership will arise where up to 20 individuals have more than 75% fixed entitlements to capital, income and voting rights in the entity (or the rights attaching to the interests in the entity can be varied or abrogated to create such a concentration of ownership). Where widely held entities exist it is assumed that any cancellation of shares or units will be on an arms length basis as the parties are at arms length in the absence of concentrated ownership and the cancellation price will often be agreed before the shares are cancelled. In these circumstances there is no need to apply the market value substitution rule.

The market value substitution rule also does not apply to CGT event D4. (see s116-105).

The Commissioner's view on the application of the market value substitution rule where a share in a 'no goodwill' incorporated professional practice is disposed of for no consideration is contained in TD 2011/26.

2. APPORTIONMENT RULE

Capital proceeds are apportioned if:

- there is more than one CGT event, or
- only part of the proceeds related to the CGT event (s116-40).

 Ewan sells a block of land and a boat (both acquired after 19 September 1985) for $100,000. There are two CGT events and accordingly, the capital proceeds of $100,000 must be divided between both assets on the basis of what is reasonably attributable to each CGT event.

The legislation does not give any guidelines on how this apportionment is to be made but the Commissioner has issued TD 9 and TD 98/24 to provide guidance. TD 9 states that each taxpayer should take whatever steps are appropriate to determine the valuation of a particular asset and be able to justify the estimate. TD 98/24 says that the apportionment should be based upon market values of the separate assets at the time of the contract.

The taxpayer should keep records of the approach used to show it was 'reasonable' in the circumstances. If the assets are sold under a contract and the parties are dealing at arm's length, the Commissioner will accept the allocation in that contract or even an allocation between the same parties in a later contract.

3. NON-RECEIPT RULE

Capital proceeds are reduced by any amount unpaid after reasonable steps have been taken to recover the unpaid amount (s116-45). The non-receipt must not be attributable to anything that the taxpayer or taxpayer's associate has done or omitted to do.

If the capital proceeds are reduced and subsequently all or part of the amount is received, the capital proceeds must be increased by that amount.

4. REPAID RULE

Capital proceeds are reduced by any non-deductible amount a taxpayer has to repay (s116-50).

5. ASSUMPTION OF LIABILITY RULE

Capital proceeds are increased by the amount of any liability by way of security over the asset that the other entity assumes in connection with the asset (s116-55). The increase is equal to the amount of the liability the other party assumes.

6. MISAPPROPRIATION RULE

The final modification relates to misappropriation by an employee or agent of the taxpayer (whether by theft, embezzlement, larceny or otherwise) of all or part of the capital proceeds. The capital proceeds are reduced by any amount misappropriated (s116-60). However, where any of the misappropriated amount is later recouped, the capital proceeds must be increased by the recouped amount.

MODIFICATIONS TO THE GENERAL RULES

The table below from s116-25 outlines to which CGT event each modification may be relevant.

Capital proceeds modifications			
Event	Description of event	Only these modifications can apply	Special rules
A1	Disposal of a CGT asset	1,2,3,4,5	If disposal is because another entity exercises an option see s116-65. If disposal is of shares or interest in a trust see s116-80. If disposal is a gift for which a s30-212 valuation is obtained, see s116-100
B1	Use and enjoyment before title passes	1,2,3,4,5,6	None
C1	Loss or destruction of a CGT asset	2,3,4,6	None
C2	Cancellation, surrender and similar endings	1,2,3,4,6	See ss116-75 and 116-80
C3	End of option to acquire shares etc.	2,3,4,6	None
D1	Creating contractual or other rights	1,2,3,4,6	None
D2	Granting an option	1,2,3,4,6	See s116-70

Capital proceeds modifications			
D3	Granting a right to income from mining	1,2,3,4,6	None
D4	Entering into a conservation covenant	2,3,4,5,6	See s116-105
E1	Creating a trust over a CGT asset	1,2,3,4,5,6	None
E2	Transferring a CGT asset to a trust	1,2,3,4,5,6	None
E8	Disposal by beneficiary of capital interest	1,2,3,4,5,6	See s116-80
F1	Granting a lease	2,3,4,6	None
F2	Granting a long-term lease	2,3,4,6	None
F4	Lessee receives payment for changing lease	2,3,4,6	None
F5	Lessor receives payment for changing lease	2,3,4,6	None
H2	Receipt for event relating to a CGT asset	2,3,4,6	None
K6	Pre-CGT shares or trust interest	1,2,3,4,5,6	None
K9	Entitlement to receive payment of a carried interest	2,3,4,6	None

12.150   OTHER CGT EVENTS

For some CGT events the capital gain or capital loss is worked out by reference to an amount other than the cost base or reduced cost base. For example:

- for CGT events C3, D2, D3, F1, F5 and H1, the capital gain or capital loss is calculated by comparing capital proceeds with relevant specific expenditure.
- for CGT events D1, E9 and H2 the capital gain or capital loss is calculated by comparing capital proceeds with incidental costs.

Any GST net input credit must be excluded from these amounts.

12.160 STEP 5: CALCULATING THE CAPITAL GAIN OR CAPITAL LOSS

A capital gain arises where the capital proceeds from a CGT event are greater than the 'cost base' of the CGT asset. A capital loss only occurs if the capital proceeds from a CGT event are less than the 'reduced cost base' of a CGT asset (see 12.102 and 12.120).

CAPITAL GAIN

A capital gain will arise where the capital proceeds from a CGT event are greater than the cost base of the CGT asset. This cost base can be indexed or discounted if the CGT event occurs at least 12 months after the date the asset was acquired and the taxpayer is permitted to, and chooses to use the indexation method or discount method to calculate the capital gain (see 12.165). The capital gain is included in the taxpayer's assessable income, unless there are offsetting capital losses.

 Tax losses on revenue account may typically be applied against assessable income which includes a capital gain.

CAPITAL LOSS

In determining a capital loss, indexation of the cost base is not permitted. Unclaimed holding costs (see 12.092 and 12.102) cannot increase a capital loss.

A capital loss cannot be claimed as a deduction against assessable income. It can only be offset against realised capital gains in the current year, or carried forward indefinitely, and offset against future realised capital gains. Capital losses carried forward are lost when a person dies.

A capital loss cannot result from a CGT event in relation to a 'personal use asset'.

Shares in ABC Ltd were acquired on 1 May 1994 for $4,000. The shares were sold on 10 June 2014 for $2,900.

Capital proceeds... $2,900
less Reduced cost base... $4,000
Capital loss.. ($1,100)

The capital loss of $1,100 can be applied against any capital gains. If there are no capital gains against which to apply the capital loss, the capital loss is carried forward and accumulated with capital losses from previous years.

There are three main exceptions to the basic rule that capital losses can be applied to reduce any capital gain:

- capital losses from a CGT event relating to a collectable may only be offset against a capital gain from a collectable (ss108-10(1))

- capital losses of a company are subject to the continuity of ownership and control test from the start of the loss year to the end of the income year or the same business test (s165-93). A company can transfer a surplus amount of its net capital losses to another wholly-owned group company so that the other company can apply the amount in working out its net capital gain for the income year in which the loss is transferred. However, one of the companies must be an Australian branch of a foreign bank and both companies must be members of the same wholly-owned group. (see s170-105)), and

- net capital losses from prior years are disregarded in determining a net capital gain in the income year or later year where a taxpayer became bankrupt or was released from debts under a law relating to bankruptcy during the income year (ss102-5(2)).

NEITHER A CAPITAL GAIN NOR A CAPITAL LOSS

Where the taxpayer uses the indexation method and the capital proceeds from a CGT event fall between the reduced cost base and the indexed cost base, there is neither a capital gain nor a capital loss.

CALCULATION OF A NET CAPITAL GAIN OR CAPITAL LOSS

Where a non-corporate taxpayer has not elected to use the indexation method (see 12.096 and 12.098) the net capital gain for the current income year is calculated using the method statement in ss102-5(1).

In brief the method statement is as follows:

Current year capital gain(s)
less .... **Current year capital loss(es)**
less .... **Unrecouped previous year capital loss(es)**
equals ...... **Notional net capital gain:**
less .... **Discount percentage (if applicable)**
equals ...... **Discount capital gain (not applicable to companies)**
less .... **Small business CGT concessions under Division 152 (if applicable)**
equals ...... **Net capital gain**

The CGT discount method does not apply to companies.

These rules are modified if the taxpayer became bankrupt or was released from bankruptcy debts during the income year (see ss102-5(2)).

The discount method only applies to a CGT event which happens after 11.45am on 21 September 1999. Before that date, where the CGT asset had been held for at least 12 months before the CGT event, the capital gain was determined with reference to the indexed cost base of the asset (see 12.096 and 12.165).

A capital loss is determined by following the method statement in s102-10. This method statement requires the taxpayer to:

- **Step 1:** Add up the capital losses made during the year, and add up the capital gains.
- **Step 2:** Subtract capital gains from capital losses.
- **Step 3:** If the step 2 amount is more than zero, the difference is the net capital loss for the income year.

The net capital loss cannot be claimed as a deduction, but can be carried forward and offset against capital gains in future years.

12.165   DETERMINING THE CAPITAL GAIN

The rules with respect to different taxpayers are as follows.

INDIVIDUALS

Where an individual acquired a CGT asset at least 12 months before the CGT event, the rules for calculating the capital gain are as follows:

ASSET ACQUIRED AT OR BEFORE AND CGT EVENT OCCURRED AFTER 11.45AM ON 21 SEPTEMBER 1999

Rules: The individual taxpayer has the choice of including in assessable income the capital gain that results from either:

- **Indexation:** the capital gain with a cost base which includes indexation frozen at 30 September 1999, or
- **CGT discount:** the capital gain without indexation and then reducing the notional capital gain by the CGT discount (50% for individuals) (sections 115-5, 115-10, 115-15, 115-20, 115-25 & 115-100).

(NOTE: CGT averaging is no longer available).

On 12 November 1995, Ralph acquired shares for $4,000. Ralph sold the shares on 20 May 2014 for $14,164. Ralph has a choice to either apply indexation or the CGT discount.

Option 1: Indexation method

Under this option, the assessable capital gain is $10,000.

Ralph's capital gain is:

Capital proceeds	$14,164
less Indexed cost base $4,000 x 1.041 (123.4/118.5)	$4,164
Capital gain	**$10,000**

Note that even though the shares were sold in May 2014, the index for the September quarter of 1999 is used as under this method the index is frozen at 30 September 1999.

Option 2: Discount method

Under option 2 Ralph's capital gain is determined using the method statement in ss102-5(1); namely:

Capital proceeds	$14,164
less Unindexed cost base	$4,000
Pre-discount capital gain	$10,164
less CGT discount (50% for an individual)	$5,082
Capital gain	**$5,082**

Ralph would choose the CGT discount option as it gives the lower capital gain.

ASSET ACQUIRED AND CGT EVENT OCCURRED AFTER 11.45AM ON 21 SEPTEMBER 1999

Rules: The non-indexed gain is reduced by the CGT discount, which is 50% for individual taxpayers.

On 28 November 1999, Ralph acquired shares for $8,000. Ralph sold these shares on 2 June 2014 for $14,164. Ralph will have made a gain of $6,164. After applying the CGT discount, half this gain ($3,082) will be included in his assessable income.

Foreign individuals no longer entitled to CGT discount (also see 22.130)

As a general rule, the CGT 50% discount no longer applies to foreign resident individuals on taxable Australian property (eg. Australian real property). These can also include an individual in partnership or as a beneficiary of a trust.

Specifically, from 8 May 2012, foreign or temporary resident individuals must meet certain eligibility conditions to apply the CGT discount.

For CGT events occurring after 8 May 2012, the application of a CGT discount percentage will depend on:
- whether the CGT asset was held before or after 8 May 2012, and
- the residency status of the individual who has the capital gain.

The rules also apply to Australian resident individuals who, after 8 May 2012, have a capital gain from a CGT event and a period of foreign or temporary residency. Special calculations apply in working out a discount capital gain where an foreign or temporary resident individual has derived a discount capital gain from a CGT event that occurred after 8 May 2012. See 22.130 for details.

ASSET WAS OWNED FOR LESS THAN 12 MONTHS

In the examples above, the individual had acquired the asset at least 12 months before the CGT event. If the asset was acquired less than 12 months before the CGT event then indexation does not apply, and for CGT events happening after 11.45am on 21 September 1999, the 50% discount option is not available (s115-25).

In May 2013, Karen acquired 1,000 ordinary shares in a listed public company for $10 per share. She sells these shares in April 2014 for $14 per share.

At the date of the contract of sale (the CGT event), Karen had acquired the shares less than 12 months earlier. Therefore she is unable to claim the CGT discount. Karen must therefore include in her assessable income a net capital gain of $4,000 ($4 per share for 1,000 shares).

COMPLYING SUPERANNUATION FUNDS

Similar rules to those outlined above for an individual apply to a complying superannuation fund, except that the CGT discount for a complying superannuation fund is 33⅓%, not 50% as for individuals (paragraph 115-100)(b)).

TRUSTS

The CGT tax treatment of most trusts (other than a complying fund) is similar to individuals. However, special rules apply where there is a concentration of ownership in the trust (s115-45 and s115-50).

Where the net income of a trust includes a discounted capital gain, that part of a beneficiary's share of the net trust income that is attributable to a discounted capital gain must be grossed up by applying a gross-up factor of 100%. This grossed-up amount is treated as the beneficiary's capital gain for the purposes of applying the beneficiary's capital losses before the CGT discount is applied, if applicable (ss115-215(3)).

No CGT discount is allowed for a trustee assessed under paragraph 98(3)(b), s98(4) or s99A of ITAA36 (s115-220, s115-222 and s115-225).

During the 2014-15 income tax year, a trust derived $40,000 net income from trading activities and in addition, as a result of a CGT event occurring on 1 December 2014, also made a capital gain of $2,000.

If the trustee elects to choose the 50% CGT discount option, the trustee will include a capital gain of $1,000 as part of net trust income. The net trust income is $41,000. If the trustee distributed this income to one beneficiary who was presently entitled to trust income, that beneficiary will gross up the discounted capital gain component of the distribution to $2,000.

If that beneficiary was a company, which is not eligible for the 50% CGT discount, the company would include in its assessable income the net trust distribution of $40,000 and the capital gain of $2,000. If the beneficiary was an individual who is eligible for the 50% CGT discount and did not have any capital losses to offset, that beneficiary would apply the 50% discount against the $2,000 capital gain and include in his or her assessable income the net trust distribution of $40,000 and the capital gain of $1,000.

The same 100% gross up is applied where the trust's capital gain is reduced by another concession, such as the small business 50% reduction concession, and not reduced by the general 50% CGT discount. If both the general 50% CGT discount and the small business 50% reduction reduce the trust's capital gain, the capital gain is multiplied by 4. The beneficiary can then apply its capital losses to the capital gain before applying the appropriate CGT discount percentage and/or the small business 50% reduction (See Subdivision 115-C and s102-5(1)).

COMPANIES

Where a company derives a capital gain:

- the CGT discount is not available
- if the asset was acquired after 11.45am on 21 September 1999, indexation of its cost base is not available, and
- if the asset was acquired at or before 11.45am on 21 September 1999, indexation of its cost base, frozen at 30 September 1999 is used to calculate the capital gain if the asset has been acquired for at least 12 months before the CGT event.

A net capital loss cannot be applied unless:

- the same people maintained majority ownership of the company during the loss year, the income year and any intervening year, and
- no person controlled the company's voting power at any time during the income year who did not also control it during the whole of the loss year and any intervening year, or
- the company has satisfied the same business test (s102-30 item 5 and s165-13).

THE 12 MONTH RULE

As noted above, to qualify for the CGT discount, a CGT asset must have been acquired by the taxpayer at least 12 months before the CGT event (ss115-25(1) and (2)). Both the day of acquisition and the day of the CGT event are excluded in determining the 12 month period.

Certain CGT events, such as those that create a new asset, cannot qualify for the CGT discount because the asset was not acquired at least 12 months before the CGT event. The CGT events for which the CGT discount cannot apply are CGT events D1, D2, D3, E9, F1, F2, F5, H2, J2, J5, J6 and K10 (ss115-25(3)).

In some cases, a taxpayer that acquires an asset within 12 months of the CGT event will be eligible for the CGT discount for any capital gain that arises. This will occur where certain assets are acquired under the same asset or replacement asset rollover provisions or under the rules applying to deceased persons. In these cases, the taxpayer will be treated for CGT purposes as having acquired the asset for at least 12 months if the collective period of ownership is at least 12 months (see s115-30). Assets owned by a taxpayer before becoming an Australian resident are treated as having been acquired at the date they become an Australian resident, so the 12-month rule will commence from the date of residency. This rule does not apply to assets that are 'taxable Australian property' before the person becomes a resident.

The 12 month rule is subject to two other provisions that can negate the CGT discount.

The CGT discount will not apply to a capital gain if the CGT event that occurred later than 12 months after acquisition was the result of an agreement entered into within that 12 month period (s115-40). This rule aims to prevent taxpayers from taking advantage of the CGT discount by seeking to artificially extend the period of acquisition of the asset that produces the capital gain. The Act does not define what constitutes an agreement, but it must be less than a binding contract otherwise a CGT event would occur at that time.

The CGT discount is not available for capital gains arising from certain CGT events happening to equity interests in a company or trust if all of the following three conditions are satisfied:

- the taxpayer and/or associates owned at least 10% of the equity in the entity before the CGT event
- more than half of the cost bases of CGT assets owned by the underlying company or trust were acquired within the 12 month period before the sale of the equity interests, and
- a notional net capital gain made on assets held by the company or trust just before the CGT event, and acquired less than 12 months before, is greater than 50% of the notional net capital gain on all assets held by the company or trust at that time (s115-45).

If any one of the above three conditions in s115-45 is not met, the capital gain is a discount capital gain.

Ed sold his 9% shareholding in a non-widely held entity making a capital gain of $10,000. Ed had owned the shares for four years. Ed has access to the CGT discount because the 10% ownership condition in s115-45 was not met.

However, the CGT discount can apply to such capital gains from CGT events happening to:

- shares in a company with at least 300 members, or
- interests in a fixed trust with at least 300 beneficiaries

unless the concentrated ownership rules apply (s115-50).

Concentrated ownership occurs if:

- one or up to 20 individuals own (directly or indirectly) shares with fixed entitlements to at least 75% of the income or capital, or at least 75% of the voting rights in the company, or
- one or up to 20 individuals own (directly or indirectly) interests in the trust with fixed entitlements to at least 75% of the income or capital, or at least 75% of the voting rights in the trust (if any) (ss115-50(3) and (4)).

For the purpose of the concentration of the ownership test, one individual together with associates, and any nominees of the individual or their associates will be counted as one individual (ss115-50(5)).

Special rules apply to capital gains made by a trust (Subdivision 115-C: see 12.600) and a listed investment company (Subdivision 115-D: see 12.675).

DISCOUNT CAPITAL GAINS MUST NOT BE INDEXED

When determining the discount capital gain, the cost base must have been calculated without reference to indexation at any time. In some circumstances however another provision of the Act will include indexation in the cost base. An example is the acquisition of an asset under a replacement asset rollover where the cost base of original asset includes indexation and becomes the cost base of the replacement asset. In such a circumstance, an entity can recalculate the cost base to exclude indexation, so that the entity can use the CGT discount in determining the capital gain if the other tests are met (s115-20).

In June 1995 Wendy acquired shares in A Ltd under the asset replacement rollover provisions in former s160ZZN ITAA36. Wendy would have been deemed to have acquired her shares for $33,000, being the indexed cost base of the assets she transferred to A Ltd. The cost base of the assets at the time was $25,000. Wendy sold her shares in May 2014 for $100,000. If Wendy elects to use the CGT discount method to determine her capital gain, her discount capital gain is $75,000 (capital proceeds of $100,000 less cost base of $25,000).

CALCULATING THE NET CAPITAL GAIN WHERE CAPITAL LOSSES ARE APPLIED

Where a capital gain is determined using the CGT discount method, any capital losses are applied against the capital gain before it is reduced by the CGT discount or other concession (ss102-5(1)).

Assume that the beneficiary of a trust received a distribution which consists of a capital gain from the trust of $1,000, after it has applied the 50% discount. The beneficiary has a current year capital loss of $600 which has arisen from shares. This loss is applied against his grossed-up trust capital gain of $2,000 to give a net capital gain of $1,400. The 50% CGT discount is then applied against the $1,400 so that the beneficiary is assessed on a net capital gain of $700.

Section 102-5(1) provides a method statement for determining the net capital gain.

If the indexation method is used, any capital losses are applied against the net capital gain as determined after deducting the indexed cost base of the asset from the capital proceeds arising from the CGT event.

If a capital gain was made during the income year, where appropriate, realise capital losses on other assets held to offset the tax liability to reduce or eliminate the impact of the Medicare levy surcharge (see 3.060).

FOREIGN CURRENCY CONVERSION

Where a CGT event involves a foreign currency, the amount or the market value of property must be translated into Australian currency at the exchange rate applicable at the time of the transaction or event (ss960-50(6)). This means that the foreign currency conversion must be made for each transaction relevant to the calculation of a capital gain or capital loss at the time of the transaction or event (for example, on the acquisition, improvement or disposal of a CGT asset).

CASE STUDIES

WHERE CGT EVENT OCCURS AT OR BEFORE 11.45AM ON 21 SEPTEMBER 1999

Capital proceeds exceed CPI increase

An asset acquired for $200,000 in March 1989, is sold on 1 September 1999 for $420,000 (CGT event A1 happened). Acquisition costs were $20,000. Improvements costing $50,000 were made to the property in September 1990. At the auction in June 1999, the property was passed in and auction costs of $3,000 were paid at the time. The property was later sold by private treaty. The contract was signed on 1 September 1999 and sale costs of $15,000 were incurred.

To determine the cost base (indexed), each cost associated with the CGT event must be multiplied by its own indexation factor. The results, added together, give the indexed cost base for the asset.

Capital proceeds		$420,000
less Cost base (indexed) (each quarter):		
Mar 1989: Purchase price (including legal costs)		
$220,000 indexed by 1.328 (123.4/92.9)		$292,160
Sep 1990: Improvements $50,000 indexed by 1.195		
(123.4/103.3)	$59,750	
June 1999: Incidental costs of disposal $15,000 x 1.000		
(123.4/123.4)	$15,000	$366,910
Capital gain		**$53,090**

NOTE: In determining the cost base, the cost of the unsuccessful auction is not included. The only incidental costs included are costs incurred to acquire the CGT asset or that relate to the CGT event (in this case the actual disposal of the property).

WHERE ASSET ACQUIRED PRE-SEPTEMBER 1999 AND THE CGT EVENT HAPPENS AFTER 11.45AM ON 21 SEPTEMBER 1999

Contract signed on 1 March 2000

Assume the same facts as example 1 except the contract for sale was signed on 1 March 2000. As the CGT event occurred after 11.45am on 21 September 1999, the taxpayer (if an individual, complying superannuation fund, or trustee) will have the choice of including in assessable income the capital gain that results from either:

- *Calculating the capital gain with a cost base which includes indexation frozen at 30 September 1999, or*
- *Calculating the capital gain without indexation and then reducing the notional capital gain by the relevant CGT discount (50% for individuals).*

Calculating for the indexation method is the same as in case study 1 and the capital gain is $53,090.

Using the CGT discount method, the capital gain is calculated as follows.

Capital proceeds	$420,000
less Unindexed cost base ($200,000 + 20,000 + 50,000 + 15,000)	$285,000
Notional capital gain	$135,000
less Relevant CGT discount (50% for individuals)	$67,500
Capital gain	**$67,500**

As the capital gain is lower using the indexation method, the taxpayer would choose that method.

Where a CGT event occurs after 11.45am on 21 September 1999, the taxpayer needs to make both the indexation and the CGT discount calculations to determine which gives the lower capital gain and select that method.

WHERE THE ASSET WAS ACQUIRED AFTER 11.45AM ON 21 SEPTEMBER 1999

Asset acquired after 11.45am on 21 September 1999

On 2 November 1999 an individual acquires shares for $60,000. The shares are sold in May 2014 for $100,000. The costs of acquisition were $100 and the cost of disposal was $80. As the asset was acquired after 11.45am on 21 September 1999 the non-indexed gain is reduced by the relevant CGT discount (note indexation and CGT averaging are not available). The assessable capital gain is:

Capital proceeds	$100,000
less Cost base ($60,000 + $100 + $80)	$60,180
Notional capital gain	$39,820
less CGT discount (50% for an individual)	$19,910
Capital gain	**$19,910**

OTHER EXAMPLES

Asset disposed of at loss

An investment property was acquired in March 2008 for $250,000 and disposed of in March 2014 for $220,000 (CGT event A1 occurs). Costs of acquisition and disposal were $30,000. Capital works deductions of 2.5% pa. on the building (which cost $150,000 to construct) were claimed in the taxpayer's income tax return.

Finding the 'reduced cost base'

Original purchase price	$250,000
plus Incidental costs of acquisition and disposal	+ $30,000
less Capital works deduction	– $15,000
Reduced cost base	$265,000
Capital proceeds	$220,000
Capital loss	**$45,000**

NOTE: *A capital loss can only be offset against a capital gain derived by the taxpayer in the same, or a later tax year. For example, if the taxpayer in example 4 also incurred an assessable gain from the CGT event in example 1, the taxpayer's net capital gain is:*

Assessable capital gain (from example 1)	$53,090
less Capital loss (from example 5)	$45,000
Net capital gain	**$8,090**

Capital gain and trading loss

A taxpayer in business made a trading loss of $20,000, but had an $80,000 assessable net capital gain on a CGT asset acquired after 19 September 1985. Although capital losses can

only be offset against capital gains, as net capital gains are included in assessable income there is no restriction on the utilisation of trading losses which may be offset to reduce the net capital gains.

Capital gains (including in assessable income)	$80,000
less Net trading loss	$20,000
Taxable income	**$60,000**

As taxable income is a positive figure, no tax loss is carried forward.

Note that the CGT discount amount is not exempt income.

Cost base (indexed) more than capital proceeds

In March 1988, the taxpayer bought a block of land for $100,000 (including incidentals) and sold it on 1 June 2014 for $137,000 (net of disposal costs). CPI index was 87.0 when acquired and 123.4 at 30 September 1999 when the index is frozen: CPI index factor of 1.418.

Net proceeds on disposal	$137,000
less Original cost CPI indexed 1.418 x $100,000 (asset cost)	$141,800
Net 'real' loss (due to inflation)	$4,800
Assessable capital gain/loss	**Nil**

As the capital proceeds ($137,000) are less than the 'indexed cost base' ($141,800) but more than the reduced cost base ($100,000), there is no assessable capital gain and no capital loss.

12.190 STEP 6: DOES A ROLLOVER PROVISION APPLY?

The Act provides for deferral of CGT in limited 'rollover' circumstances. This includes situations where there is a change in the entity owning the asset without a change in the underlying beneficial ownership of the asset. The main rollover provisions are described below.

Refer to 12.468 for amending legislation that makes it easier for takeovers and mergers regulated by the *Corporations Act 2001* to qualify for CGT scrip for scrip rollover.

ROLLOVER FOR THE DISPOSAL OF ASSETS TO, OR THE CREATION OF ASSETS IN, A WHOLLY-OWNED COMPANY

Transfer of an asset(s) to a wholly-owned company where the consideration is non-redeemable shares in the company of substantially the same market value as the net assets transferred is a rollover event (Subdivision 122A - individuals and trustee, Subdivision 122B - partners). After the event the transferor must own all the shares in the company and the company must not be exempt from tax in the year of the CGT event (s122-25).

Subsection 122-25(2) lists assets not subject to rollover, eg. depreciating assets, trading stock, collectables and personal use assets (see 12.475).

ROLLOVER EVENTS

Replacement asset rollover events and same asset rollover events are listed at 12.450.

12.200 STEP 7: MAINTAIN APPROPRIATE CGT RECORDS

As is the case with the substantiation rules, record keeping is of vital importance for CGT.

The Act requires the taxpayer to *'keep records of every act, transaction, event or circumstance that can reasonably be expected to be relevant to working out whether you have made a capital gain or capital loss from a CGT event'* (s121-20). A taxpayer does not have to keep records for an event where any capital gain or capital loss is disregarded, except because of a rollover. Examples include assets acquired before 20 September 1985, and assets exempt from CGT such as cars. The taxpayer has the option of maintaining records or an asset register.

CAPITAL GAINS TAX CHECKLIST

If you answer YES to any of the following questions you must keep records including details of acquisitions, disposals, deferred capital amounts, additions, improvements and other expenditure.

	Y/N
If main residence acquired after 19 September 1985:	
Have you used it to produce income? (eg. carried on a business from it or rented part or all of it)[1] Does its land exceed two hectares (4.94 acres)? or Have you or your spouse had another main residence for more than six months since you acquired your current main residence?	☐ ☐ ☐ ☐
Do you own any other land or property which you acquired after 19 September 1985? **(eg. rental property, holiday home, offices)**	☐
Have you made any improvements after 19 September 1985:	

• to land acquired prior to 20 September 1985, including:
   – demolishing and then erecting a new building
   – constructing a building
   – acquiring adjacent land
   – other improvements where the cost exceeded the indexed threshold
	☐

• to buildings or parts of buildings that are treated as separate assets under the Act	☐
• other post-19/9/85 improvements to property acquired prior to 20/9/85, where the cost of the improvement exceeded the indexed threshold (see 12.062)	☐
Do you own any shares in a company or units in a unit trust that you acquired after 19 September 1985?	☐
Have you acquired, or acquired an interest in, any of the following collectables **after 19 September 1985 for more than $500:**	☐
• a painting, sculpture, drawing, engraving, photograph, reproduction or similar work of art • jewellery, a coin or medallion, an antique • a rare folio, manuscript or book • a postage stamp or first day cover • an interest, debt, or right or option in respect of any of the above?	
Have you acquired any assets used primarily for personal use and enjoyment **that you acquired for more than $10,000[2]?**	☐
Since 19/9/85, have you acquired any motor vehicles designed to carry more than eight **passengers or loads exceeding one tonne?**	☐
Have you received a capital amount after 19 September 1985 including:	☐
• a payment for giving up amateur status • a forfeited deposit (other than one payable on exchange of contracts) • a restrictive covenant or compensation payment	
Have you acquired any rights, options or other assets **(but see assets specifically excluded; 12.074) since 19 September 1985?**	☐
Have you received a capital distribution or a distribution that includes a **non-assessable payment from a trust?**	☐
Have you acquired any assets as a result of a marriage breakdown?	☐
Have you acquired any business assets?	☐
Have you received an asset from a deceased estate?	☐

1: In certain circumstances, no CGT will be payable when a CGT event occurs, notwithstanding that the entire property (house) was rented out for a period, provided that the house had, at one point, been the taxpayer's main residence and the taxpayer chooses to continue to treat it as their main residence (s118-145; see 12.330).

2: For personal use assets acquired on or after 1 July 1998, no CGT will arise, provided that those assets are acquired for $10,000 or less.

RECORDS

Under this option the taxpayer must keep details of the date of:

- acquiring the asset, and its cost (including all incidental costs)
- the CGT event happening and any incidental costs involved, and
- the capital proceeds in respect of the CGT event.

Further records are required where assets are transferred between companies in the same wholly-owned group and one is a foreign resident or where the former CGT event G2 (a shift in share value) happened (ss121-20(1)).

Records must be kept in English or readily accessible and convertible to English (ss121-20(2)). For the principles associated with the retention of electronic records see TR 2005/9. Where records must be kept, they must be retained for five years after it becomes certain that no CGT event (or no further CGT event) can happen (ss121-25(2)).

Where a taxpayer has made a net capital loss, records should be retained to the end of the statutory period of review for an assessment for the income year when the net capital loss is fully applied, if that is a later date (TD 2007/2). The absence of appropriate records may mean that the quantum of a capital gain or loss cannot be adequately proven.

 Failure to keep records may incur 30 penalty points (s121-25). Each penalty point is currently $180.

ASSET REGISTER

Taxpayers can transfer all or some of the information they are required to retain for CGT purposes into an asset register that has been certified as correct by a registered tax agent or other person approved by the Commissioner (s121-35). Where the information is entered on to an asset register, the original record must be kept for at least five years from the date the entry is certified, rather than the period referred to above under 'Records'. Entries must be in English. See the sample register on the next page. Refer also to TR 2002/10.

SEPARATE ASSETS

Significant improvements to an asset may be treated as separate assets for which records must also be maintained (see 12.062). Investors should record the date and number of all acquisitions of shares, including those received by participation in dividend reinvestment plans, and by way of bonus issues, especially those acquired after 20 September 1985 (see also 12.820).

12.250 SPECIAL CGT RULES

When calculating the CGT effect on a transaction, the following special rules may apply.

ANTI-OVERLAP RULES

Section 118-20 prevents an amount being taxed as a capital gain when an amount is already required to be included in the taxpayer's assessable income under another provision of the Act in any income year. The capital gain will be reduced to nil provided that the other amount is at least equal to the capital gain. Were it not for s118-20, a profit might be taxed both as ordinary income and as a capital gain.

The section operates by reducing the amount of a capital gain by the amount included in the taxpayer's assessable income under another (non-CGT) provision. This reduction does not apply to amounts included in assessable income due to a balancing adjustment, a dividend under an off-market share buy back, the gross-up of a franked dividend or an amount included in non-assessable, non-exempt income under s23AJ ITAA36 (certain non-portfolio dividends paid by non-resident companies) (see ss118-20(1B) and ss118-20(4),(5) and (6)).

Where the method of accounting changes from cash to accruals, income earned in the previous (cash) year but received in the current (accruals) year would not be assessable under s6-5 but would be taxed under CGT event C2 (ATO ID 2014/1). The anti-overlap rule under s118-20 does not apply under this situation. The debt owed is taken to be a CGT asset.

A company acquires an asset on 1 July 1983 for $150,000 with the intention of reselling it at a profit. On 1 July 1987, ownership of the company changes hands and as a result there is a more than 50% change in the ownership of the shares and all of the company's underlying pre-CGT acquired assets are deemed to be post-CGT acquired assets from that date under Division 149. The asset is taken to be acquired at its (then) market value of $220,000. The asset is sold for $350,000 in June 2014. At the time of sale the cost base (indexed to September 1999) of the asset was $323,180.

Assuming there are no expenses, the profit on disposal under s15-15 is $200,000 (ie. $350,000 less $150,000). The notional capital gain is $26,820 (ie. $350,000 less $323,180). This is the capital gain that would have accrued to the taxpayer if it were not for the operation of s118-20 (the CGT discount method does not apply to a company).

As the capital gain does not exceed the amount that is already included in the company's assessable income under s15-15, the effect under s118-20 is that no capital gain is deemed to have accrued to the company.

PRE-CGT ASSET DEEMED TO BE POST-CGT

While it is generally accepted that an asset acquired before 20 September 1985 is exempt from CGT on the happening of a CGT event, there are exceptions where a pre-CGT asset can be deemed to be post-CGT. These situations are discussed below.

CHANGE IN OWNERSHIP OF NON-PUBLIC ENTITIES

If an asset is owned by an entity, the underlying ownership of that asset changes as equity-holders change.

Unless 'majority underlying interests' in assets held by a non-public entity (eg. a private company or trust) continue to be held post-19 September 1985 by the same persons who held them prior to 20 September 1985, all pre-CGT assets of the entity will stop being pre-CGT assets and become post-CGT assets (s149-30). 'Majority underlying interests' in a CGT asset means that the ultimate owners have more than 50% of the beneficial interests (whether directly or indirectly) in the asset, *and* in any ordinary income that may be derived from the asset (s149-15). An individual, as a member of a superannuation fund, is the 'ultimate owner' under paragraph 149-15(3)(a), not the superannuation fund (ATO ID 2006/219).

If there is a 50% change in the underlying interests in assets *or* income from the non-public entity in question, compared to the pre-CGT position, all pre-CGT assets are deemed to be acquired at their market value when the change in the majority underlying interest occurred (s149-35). Thus, s149-30 is not a taxing provision. It operates to convert pre-CGT assets of non-public entities into post-CGT assets.

Without s149-30, a new group of persons who acquired control of a non-public entity after 20 September 1985 could take advantage of the entity's separate legal existence (ie. that of a company to its shareholders, or a trustee to the beneficiaries of the trust) and dispose of pre-CGT assets free of CGT notwithstanding the change in control of the entity.

Section 149-30 does not apply to changes in interests in superannuation funds or partnerships. Nor does it apply to public entities which are subject to their own rules as set out below.

In a company where all of the shares carry a discretionary right to dividends, majority underlying interests in a pre-CGT asset of the company are held by ultimate owners who had such interests in the asset immediately before 20 September 1985 if after that date there has been no new shareholders in the company (see ATO ID 2011/101). However for the situation where a new share with discretionary rights to dividends is issued to a new shareholder after 20 September 1985 and Division 149 is considered to have application (see ATO ID 2011/107).

CHANGE OF OWNERSHIP ON DEATH

If assets of a deceased estate had been acquired by the deceased before 20 September 1985, these assets are deemed to be acquired by the legal personal representative or beneficiary at the date of the deceased's death for a consideration equal to the assets' market values at that date. The assets will then be post-CGT assets of the beneficiary. This means any capital gain that accrued prior to the deceased's death will remain exempt.

CAPITAL GAINS TAX ASSET REGISTER

Record all costs you incur in respect of each asset. Use a separate page for each asset.

Date[1]	Description of expenditure[2]	Amount $	Documents held[3]	CPI figure[4]	Indexation figure[5]	Indexed cost base	Allowed as a deduction[7]	Reduced cost base

Cost base $ _____   Indexed cost base $ _____   Reduced cost base $ _____

Asset owned for less than 12 months
Indexation method

Capital proceeds

less cost base[8]

Capital gain

Asset owned for 12 months or more
CGT discount method

Capital proceeds

less cost base (indexed)[8]

Notional gain[9]

Less CGT discount

Capital gain

Reduced cost base exceeds capital proceeds

Reduced cost base

less capital proceeds

Capital loss

Entry certified by ....
(signature of suitably qualified person)

1: Date costs incurred 2: Eg. purchase price, capital improvements 3: Eg. receipts, share certificate 4: From table at 12.098 5: Indexation factor (see 11.098)
6: Cost base multiplied by index factor 7: Amounts a) owed (or allowable) as tax deductions are reduced by any amount recouped or included as assessable income on disposal
8: Where assets are acquired post-7.30pm 13 May 1997; see 12.092 for changes to the calculation of a capital gain
9: Capital losses are applied against the notional gain before they are reduced by the CGT discount.

PUBLIC ENTITIES

If a public entity (public companies, publicly traded unit trusts and mutual insurance organisations) with pre-CGT assets wishes to retain the pre-CGT status of those assets it must, within six months after each 'test date', give the Commissioner written evidence about the majority underlying interests in the asset on the test date.

A test date is any of the following:

* 30 June 1999
* every five years from that date, and
* a day where abnormal trading of shares or units occurs (s149-55).

If a public entity fails to provide evidence to support that there has not been a change in majority underlying interest within the required period of six months, the asset will cease to be a pre-CGT asset from the test date and become a post-CGT asset, with a cost base equal to its market value at the relevant test date.

Reference should be made to Subdivision 149-C for further clarification.

CHANGE IN UNDERLYING ASSETS

When a taxpayer owns shares in a private company or units in a unit trust, it should not be assumed that when a CGT event happens in respect to shares or units acquired before 20 September 1985, that there will not be any liability for CGT.

Section 104-230 operates to 'look through' pre-CGT shareholdings or unitholdings to determine if assets (other than trading stock) acquired after 19 September 1985 equal at least 75% of the 'net value' of the private company or trust. 'Net value' is the market value of the assets less liabilities.

Where this threshold is met, s104-230 (CGT event K6) is triggered and a capital gain may arise, notwithstanding the pre-CGT status of the shares or units (see 12.040 for further commentary on CGT event K6).

Where liabilities have been discharged to increase the net value of the business to avoid s104-230, the Commissioner may disregard the discharge of the liabilities.

CGT EXEMPTION ON AN ASSET TRANSFERRED INTO A SPECIAL DISABILITY TRUST

ITAA97 has been amended to extend CGT concessions for Special Disability Trusts (SDTs). These amendments apply to income tax assessments for the 2006-07 income year and later income years.

AN ASSET TRANSFERRED DIRECTLY TO AN SPECIAL DISABILITY TRUST

Under the CGT legislation, generally when there is a change of ownership of an asset for no consideration, the market value substitution rule in s116-30 applies and the taxpayer will determine a capital gain or loss based on the difference between the cost base (or reduced cost base) of the asset and its market value at the time of the CGT event. However, under the rules which apply to a SDT any capital gain or loss that the taxpayer would have made is disregarded when the asset is transferred into the SDT for no consideration.

When determining whether a taxpayer receives consideration for transferring an asset into an SDT, any interest in the trust is disregarded. This ensures that where an asset is transferred into an SDT and the transferor is entitled to receive the asset at the ending of the trust, a CGT exemption is still available.

If an asset is transferred into a trust that is not yet an SDT, a CGT exemption will still be available provided the trust becomes an SDT as soon as practicable after the asset is transferred into it. Whether a trust satisfies this requirement will depend on the circumstances of each case. For example, a trust will satisfy this requirement if it applies to become an SDT within a reasonable time and the application is later approved.

Bright Pty Ltd (Bright) is the trustee of an SDT established for Jessica, who is the principal beneficiary. In 2007, Suban, Jessica's father, transfers ownership of a townhouse for no consideration to Bright as trustee of the SDT. Suban acquired the townhouse in 1990 and it was not his main residence during his ownership period. Suban may be entitled to receive the asset back when the SDT comes to an end. Based on the market value of the townhouse,

Suban would make a capital gain of $100,000 (apart from these amendments) at the time the townhouse is transferred to the SDT. As Suban has transferred the townhouse to an SDT, he disregards the capital gain of $100,000.

AN ASSET PASSES TO A SPECIAL DISABILITY TRUST FROM A DECEASED PERSON'S ESTATE

Typically, where an asset with an unrealised capital gain or loss passes from a deceased person's estate to a beneficiary of the estate, there is no taxing point for the deceased person or their legal personal representative. Instead, any unrealised capital gain or loss is typically deferred until a later dealing with the asset by the beneficiary or the trustee of the estate.

To ensure that a trustee of an SDT disregards any unrealised capital gain or loss when an asset passes to the trustee from a deceased person's estate, the trustee will use the market value of the asset on the day the deceased died as the first element of its cost base (and reduced cost base). This effectively exempts any unrealised capital gain or capital loss that has accrued up until the transferor's death.

If the trust is not an SDT at the time the asset passes to it from the deceased person's estate, the trust must become an SDT as soon as it is practicable after the asset passes to it. If the trust is not an SDT or does not become an SDT as soon as practicable, the normal deceased estate cost base rules will apply.

Following on from the example above, Jessica's grandfather, Ron passes away and leaves shares in his will to Bright as trustee of the SDT, who is a beneficiary of Ron's estate. The shares are worth $20,000 at the time of Ron's death. Ron and his legal personal representative disregard any capital gains or losses on the shares using the normal deceased estate provisions. These amendments ensure Bright obtains a market value cost base (and reduced cost base) of $20,000 for the shares. One year later, Bright sells the shares for $21,000. Assuming that Bright has not incurred any other costs in relation to the shares, Bright makes a capital gain of $1,000 on the shares.

12.300 EXEMPTION FOR MAIN RESIDENCE

A taxpayer's dwelling, owned by an individual and normally occupied as the taxpayer's main residence is generally exempt from CGT. If the dwelling is also used for income earning activities, it may be partially subject to CGT on disposal (see 12.320).

DWELLING OWNED BY INDIVIDUALS

A capital gain or loss made from a CGT event (typically, a disposal under CGT A1) by an individual in relation to a dwelling or an interest in the dwelling is disregarded if the

- the dwelling was that individual's 'main residence' throughout the individual's period of ownership, and
- the interest in the dwelling did not pass to the individual as a beneficiary and was not acquired by the individual as a trustee of a deceased estate (other rules may apply in these circumstances). (see s118-110). See main residence issues on death below.

The main residence exemption only applies to these CGT events: A1, B1, C1, C2, E1, E2, F2, I1, I2, K3, K4 and certain CGT events that involve forfeiting a deposit.

DWELLING OWNED BY COMPANY/TRUST

If a dwelling is owned by a trustee or company, the main residence exemption does not apply unless:

- beneficial ownership is via a home-unit company, a strata title company, or a retirement village company
- a trustee of a deceased estate holds the home for certain beneficiaries (see 12.310), and
- a beneficiary of a trust is absolutely entitled as against the trustee to the dwelling used as the main residence of the beneficiary.

CGT may apply where a dwelling is transferred from an entity to a spouse on marriage breakdown.

A company acquired a dwelling on or after 20 September 1985, and the dwelling is transferred to a person following marriage breakdown. Rollover relief is available to the company under Subdivision 126A. The dwelling cannot be treated as a main residence of the person who acquired it during the time it was owned by the company even if that person lived in the dwelling during the time it was owned by the company (s118-180(2)). This means that on subsequent disposal of the dwelling, only a partial exemption under s118-185 will apply. If the dwelling was owned by a private company, the property transfer could be taxed as a dividend under Division 7A.

This dividend would not be frankable unless the transfer took place pursuant to a court order under the Family Law Act 1975 or a corresponding foreign law, an approved maintenance agreement or a court order under state law, territory law or foreign law relating to de facto marriage breakdowns (from 1 July 2006) (see from 7.300).

DWELLING OWNED BY SPECIAL DISABILITY TRUST (SDT)

The CGT main residence exemption extends to a residence owned by an SDT.

Under these rules, if a trustee of an SDT holds a dwelling (or an ownership interest in the dwelling) for the benefit of the principal beneficiary, the trustee will be eligible for the CGT main residence exemption if the principal beneficiary used the dwelling as their main residence and the dwelling was not used to produce assessable income.

The trustee of the SDT will be eligible for the CGT main residence exemption in the same way as the principal beneficiary would have been had they owned the dwelling directly. This is achieved by treating the trustee of the SDT as holding the dwelling personally and using it in the same particular way as the principal beneficiary on each day that the trust is an SDT. Where the trustee is not an individual, they are treated as if they were an individual.

NOTE: In the ITAA97, 'special disability trust' and 'principal beneficiary' have the meanings given by ss1209L and 1209M *Social Security Act 1991* respectively. It also includes SDTs established under the *Veterans' Entitlements Act 1986*.

Debbie and Marina are the trustees of an SDT established for Jack, who is the principal beneficiary. The trustees purchase a dwelling for the benefit of Jack. Settlement occurs on 1 January 2008 and Jack moves in as soon as practicable after minor modifications are made to the dwelling to assist Jack with his independent occupation of the dwelling. The trustees later sell the dwelling, making a capital gain of $20,000 (apart from these amendments). Jack continues to live in the dwelling until settlement occurs on 31 December 2011. The dwelling was never used to produce assessable income and the trust is an SDT throughout the entire ownership period. If Jack owned the dwelling directly, he would have been able to disregard the entire capital gain. Therefore, the trustees will be able to disregard the entire capital gain.

A trustee of an SDT can also access the extensions to the main residence exemption contained in ss118-135 to 118-160, to the extent that the principal beneficiary could access them if they owned the dwelling (or interest in the dwelling directly).

Further to the above example, assume that in mid-2010, Jack moved out of the dwelling into a nursing home, with the dwelling being rented out at market value until the dwelling was sold in 2011. The trust remains an SDT for all of the ownership period. If Jack owned the dwelling directly, he could access the absence rule under section 118-145. Therefore, the trustees can decide to continue to treat the dwelling as a main residence during this period under the absence rule and disregard the $20,000 capital gain when the dwelling is sold.

For any day that a trust is not an SDT, that day will be treated as a non-main residence day for the purposes of the CGT main residence exemption. Accordingly, only a partial main residence exemption will be available on disposal of the dwelling. This treatment will not apply where the trust becomes an SDT as soon as practicable after a dwelling is transferred into it or after the trustee purchases a dwelling. Thus, where the dwelling is the principal beneficiary's main residence in the time leading up to the trust becoming an SDT, those days will be main residence days.

Respect Pty Ltd (Respect) is the trustee of an SDT established for Mark. Respect, in its capacity as trustee, purchases a dwelling for the benefit of Mark, with settlement occurring on 1 January 2007. Mark moves in on this day. Respect sells the dwelling with settlement occurring on 31 December 2010. Mark moves out on this day. Respect would make a capital gain of $15,000 (apart from these amendments). The trust is not an SDT during the calendar year of 2010 (including at the time of the CGT event) as during this period, the trustee paid a weekly allowance of $200 to Mark's mother for her personal expenditure. When Respect sells the dwelling in 2010, the trustee is required to use the partial main residence formula in ss118-185(2) or the year of 2010, the days are counted as non-main residence days.

Therefore, Respect will be taken to have made a capital gain of $3,747 calculated as follows:

$$\text{CG amount} = \frac{\text{Non-main residence days}}{\text{Days in Respect's ownership period}}$$

$$\$15,000 = \frac{365}{1,461}$$

$$= \$3,747$$

The list of CGT events that is required to happen in order for a taxpayer to access a CGT main residence exemption is expanded for SDT cases to include CGT event E5 (where a beneficiary becomes absolutely entitled to a dwelling held in an SDT) and CGT event E7 (where the trustee disposes of the dwelling in satisfaction of the beneficiary's interest in the SDT). To ensure that the main residence exemption at the trustee level is not unwound at the beneficiary level, the beneficiary will disregard any capital gain or loss on their interest in the trust ending.

NOTE: The trustee will disregard the use of their personal dwelling when determining whether they are eligible for the CGT main residence exemption in their capacity as trustee of an SDT. Under ss960-100(3), the trustee of an SDT is taken to be a different entity for tax purposes to the individual who accesses the main residence exemption in their personal capacity. For the same reason, the trustee can ignore the deemed use of the dwelling held in the SDT when the trustee accesses the CGT main residence exemption in their personal capacity.

WHAT IS A 'DWELLING'?

Generally, a 'dwelling' is a unit of residential accommodation owned by the taxpayer and includes a flat, home unit, caravan, houseboat, or other mobile home, and the land immediately under the unit of accommodation (ss118-115(1)).

Consequently, if a unit of accommodation is removed from land and the land is then sold, the land does not come within the definition of 'dwelling' in ss118-115(1) and is not exempt under the main residence provisions. The land is only exempt if it and the unit of accommodation are sold together as a dwelling (TD 1999/73).

A person is regarded as having an ownership interest in a dwelling:

- if it is not a flat or home unit, and the person has:
    - a legal or equitable interest in the land on which the dwelling is erected, or
    - a licence or right to occupy the dwelling.
- if it is a flat or home unit, the taxpayer must have:
    - a legal or equitable interest in a stratum unit in relation to the flat or unit,
    - a licence or right to occupy the flat or home unit, or
    - a share in a company that owns a legal or equitable interest in the land on which the building containing the flat or home unit is erected, being a share entitling the holder to the right of occupancy of the flat or home unit (see s118-130).

A dwelling can include more than one unit of accommodation if the units of accommodation are used together as one place of residence or abode (TD 1999/69). An example would be a house and a caravan used as family sleeping quarters where the caravan is connected to electricity from the house.

ATTACHED LAND EXEMPTION

A dwelling includes a maximum of two hectares of adjacent land when it is used primarily for private or domestic purposes (ss118-120(1)). Land does not have to be touching or in contact with land on which the dwelling is situated to be 'adjacent' for s118-120 purposes.

The main residence exemption will apply to the adjacent land as long as the 'adjacent' land is:

- close to or near the dwelling
- is used primarily for private or domestic purposes in association with the dwelling
- the total area does not exceed two hectares (including the land on which the dwelling is built), and
- the same CGT event happens in relation to both the dwelling and adjacent land (see TD 1999/68).

TD 1999/68 gives the following examples of 'adjacent' land.

Robert owns a 1.5 hectare property on which he has a house, swimming pool and tennis court. A public access laneway beside the house separates the tennis court from the rest of the property.

The land on which the tennis court is situated is considered to be adjacent land for the purposes of s118-120.

Bob and Lyn own a house in a country town. Lyn owns a horse which she rides in local horse competitions. There is no room for the horse in the backyard of the house, so Bob and Lyn bought a block of land two street blocks away on which to run the horse. The total area of the land on which the house is situated and the horse yard is less than two hectares.

The horse yard, which is used by Lyn primarily for private or domestic purposes in association with her house, is considered to be adjacent land for the purposes of s118-120.

Where the taxpayer's land exceeds two hectares, the taxpayer can select the two hectares to which the main residence exemption applies (TD 1999/67). To the extent that any land is not used for private purposes (even within the two hectare limit), any gain from a CGT event happening in respect to the property may be liable for CGT.

COMPULSORY ACQUISITION

An exemption is available where land adjacent to a main residence is compulsorily acquired, but not the main residence itself. The requirements of s118-250 must be satisfied.

WHAT IS A MAIN RESIDENCE?

Whether a dwelling is a taxpayer's main residence is a question of fact. The Tax Office publication *Guide to Capital Gains Tax* indicates that the following factors are relevant in deciding if a dwelling is the taxpayer's main residence:

- the length of time the taxpayer has lived in the dwelling
- the place of residence of the taxpayer's family
- whether the taxpayer has moved his or her personal belongings into the dwelling
- the address to which the taxpayer has his or her mail delivered
- the taxpayer's address on the Electoral Roll
- the connection of services such as telephone, gas and electricity, and
- the taxpayer's intention in occupying the dwelling.

The mere intention to construct a dwelling or to occupy a dwelling as a main residence, but without actually doing so, is insufficient to obtain the exemption (*Couch and Federal Commissioner of Taxation* [2009] AATA 41).

The Administrative Appeals Tribunal (AAT) relied on former TD 51 in the case of *Re Erdelyi v FCT* (2007) AATA 1388 as providing 'useful guidance' on whether a dwelling was used as a main residence or was constructed for some other purpose. In that case, the low use of electricity and the absence of furniture and other than bare necessities were persuasive factors in the AAT concluding that the dwelling was not used as a main residence.

In certain circumstances, a taxpayer may elect which of two or more dwellings is the main residence. On changing main residences a taxpayer can have two main residences for a maximum period of six months (s118-140). The potential maximum period of exemption available for each dwelling must be determined.

PRE-CGT RESIDENCES

CGT does not apply to land acquired before 20 September 1985. If substantial improvements are made on the pre-CGT land, the improvements may be treated as separate CGT assets (see 12.062).

PRE-OCCUPATION EXEMPTION

A dwelling may qualify for the main residence exemption before the dwelling actually becomes the taxpayer's main residence.

This can occur in the following circumstances, if the taxpayer so chooses:

- where a taxpayer acquired some vacant land after 19 September 1985 and later erects a dwelling on it
- where there was an existing dwelling on the site which was:
  - demolished, and a new dwelling erected, or
  - renovated, repaired, or finished before being occupied as the taxpayer's main residence.

In these circumstances, the taxpayer can choose to treat the original dwelling as his or her main residence for a period of up to four years before occupancy of the dwelling so that the main residence exemption will apply. In this period no other property can be treated as the taxpayer's main residence.

If the taxpayer acquired vacant land, the four year period runs from the date the taxpayer acquired his or her ownership interest in the land to the date the taxpayer started to occupy the new dwelling (ss118-150(4)).

If there was an existing dwelling on the land when the taxpayer acquired their ownership interest and either the taxpayer or another person occupied that dwelling, the pre-occupation exemption period starts from when the dwelling ceased to be occupied to build, repair, renovate or finish building the dwelling (ss118-150(5)).

To be eligible to make these choices, the dwelling must become the taxpayer's main residence as soon as practicable after completion of the work and continue as the taxpayer's main residence for at least three months (ss118-150(3)).

See TD 2000/16 for further commentary on the application of the above four year period rule.

THE 'PRE-OCCUPATION PERIOD'

During the 'pre-occupation period', no other dwelling can be treated as the taxpayer's main residence, except if the six months double exemption applies on the change of main residence under s118-150.

For the pre-occupation period to be eligible to be added to that of occupancy:

- the taxpayer must take up occupancy as soon as practicable after the work is finished, and
- the dwelling must be the taxpayer's main residence for at least three months (ss118-150(3)).

If those conditions are satisfied, any capital gain from a CGT event happening in relation to the asset (even covering the period when it was vacant land, or the dwelling was being built) is exempt from CGT. If the period of four years is exceeded, a partial exemption will apply to the taxpayer if the dwelling is subsequently disposed.

According to TD 92/147, the Commissioner states that the following factors would indicate that work to the building is considered finished:

- the date the Certificate of Occupancy (if applicable) is issued
- the date of the final building inspection approval is given
- the date of the dwelling becomes structurally complete, and

- the connection of services (eg. electricity, gas, etc).

The exemption does not apply where an individual is unable to move in because the property is rented out (refer ATO ID 2001/744).

If the new dwelling is not occupied for three months after completion, the potential full exemption is lost because the pre-occupation period cannot be added to the post-completion occupation time during which it was the taxpayer's main residence (unless the occupation was terminated by death in that three month period (see 118-155)). Whether a taxpayer has moved into a property 'as soon as practicable' once the work is finished needs to be considered on a case by case basis (refer TD 92/147 for examples).

The exemption does not apply during any period in which the taxpayer was a dependent child of another taxpayer.

MAIN RESIDENCE ACCIDENTALLY DESTROYED

If a dwelling that is a taxpayer's main residence is accidentally destroyed, and a CGT event happens in relation to the land before another dwelling is erected on the land, the taxpayer can choose to apply the main residence exemption to the land as if the dwelling had not been destroyed and continued to be the taxpayer's main residence until the taxpayer's ownership in the land ceases (see s118-160). However, the same taxpayer will be precluded from claiming the main residence exemption in respect of any other dwelling during such a period.

CHOICE OF MAIN RESIDENCE

Where two or more properties (or vacant land) acquired after 19 September 1985 could qualify as a taxpayer's main residence, the taxpayer must select which property is to be treated as his or her main residence for CGT purposes. The choice is made when the taxpayer's income tax return is prepared for the year in which the residence is sold.

 If a taxpayer owns two properties, one of which was acquired before 20 September 1985, that dwelling should not be selected as the taxpayer's main residence because it would be exempt from CGT in its own right. The property purchased post-CGT should be chosen as the taxpayer's main residence, and both properties would then be exempt from CGT.

CHANGING MAIN RESIDENCE

Where a dwelling is acquired with the intention that it become the taxpayer's main residence and the taxpayer still owns an existing main residence, both dwellings may be treated as main residence for the shorter of:

- six months ending when ownership of the existing main residence ends, or
- the time between the acquisition of the new main residence and ownership of the old main residence ending (see ss118-140(1)).

This exemption only applies where the previous main residence was the taxpayer's main residence for a continuous period of at least three months in the twelve month period ending when the taxpayer's ownership interest in that dwelling ends, and it was not used for income-producing purposes during that time (ss118-140(2)).

Section 118-140 can apply in conjunction with s118-145 (absence rule) and s118-150 (building, repairing or renovating).

The following examples are adapted from TD 1999/43 and ATO ID 2003/232.

 Anne acquired a dwelling on 1 January 1986 that was her existing main residence until she acquired a second dwelling on 1 March 2012. She moved into the second dwelling on 1 May 2012 but did not dispose of the first dwelling until 1 August 2012.

In accordance with s118-145 (absence rule), Anne chooses to treat the first dwelling as her main residence for the entire period of ownership. Any gain on disposal of the first dwelling is disregarded for CGT purposes.

In addition, s118-140 allows her second dwelling to be treated as her main residence for the five month period from 1 March 2012 to 1 August 2012, provided Anne meets the conditions of s118-140, because she is able to treat both dwellings as her main residence for up to six months, ending when she ceased to have an ownership interest in the first dwelling.

If Anne had used her first dwelling to produce income after she moved into her second dwelling, s118-140 would not allow both dwellings to be treated as her main residence for this five month period as the conditions of ss118-140(2) would not be met.

David acquired his first dwelling on 1 July 1993. Before he disposed of it on 1 December 2011, he acquired a vacant block of land on 1 March 2007 on which he erected a new dwelling. The new dwelling was completed on 31 October 2011. He moved in on 30 November 2011 (which was as soon as was practicable after construction) and continues to live there. In accordance with s118-150, David chose to treat the new dwelling as his main residence for the period 1 March 2007 to 30 November 2011.

David can also treat his first dwelling as his main residence from 1 July 1993 to 1 March 2007.

As David owned two dwellings at the same time, he can also choose to apply both s118-150 and s118-140. As a result of this choice, David can treat both dwellings as his main residence for the six month period from 1 June 2011 to 30 November 2011 inclusive. However, he cannot treat his first dwelling as his main residence for the period 1 March 2007 to 31 May 2011.

Thomas purchased a dwelling in 1998. He lived in the dwelling as his main residence until January 2002 when he rented it for two years while he travelled overseas. Thomas returned on 1 January 2004 and resided in the dwelling until December 2004 when the dwelling was demolished. Thomas built a new dwelling on the land and it became his main residence in June 2005 (as soon as practicable after the construction of the dwelling was completed) and he lived in the new dwelling until January 2011 when it was sold.

Thomas could make a main residence exemption choice under s118-145 in respect of the old dwelling and a main residence construction choice under s118-150. Because there was no more than four years between demolition and construction, and the new dwelling became his main residence as soon as practicable after the building work was finished, and it continues to be his main residence for more than the minimum period of three months, the two dwellings may be treated as one and the main residence usage of the former dwelling will count towards the main residence exemption for the new dwelling and land.

Consequently, Thomas would not incur any CGT on disposal of the new dwelling.

OWNERSHIP INTEREST

For the purposes of determining when a taxpayer's ownership interest in a dwelling begins and ends, the relevant date is generally the date legal ownership changes. Under a normal property contract, legal ownership usually transfers at settlement, not on payment of the deposit or exchange of contracts. However, the relevant date may be earlier if the taxpayer has a contractual right to occupy the dwelling before obtaining legal ownership (ss118-130(2)).

IF A FAMILY OWNS TWO HOMES

If a taxpayer buys another residence before disposing of the former one, both can be taken to be the main residence for up to six months (see above on 'changing main residence').

If a taxpayer occupies a dwelling as their main residence and a dependent child who is aged under 18 years occupies another dwelling as their main residence, the taxpayer must choose one dwelling to be the main residence for the purposes of the exemption (s118-175). A child will be a dependant when they are under 18 years of age and are dependant on the parent for economic support.

If the taxpayer and their spouse are occupying different main residences, they must choose which of those dwellings is main residence of both. Alternatively, they can nominate both as main residences. In the latter case, each property will benefit from no more than a 50% exemption.

Where the spouse has more than a 50% interest in the dwelling it is taken to be that spouse's main residence for one-half of the period (ss118-170(3) and (4)). If the spouse's interest is 50% or less then the dwelling is taken to be the spouse's main residence to that extent. These rules mean that a family cannot end up with more than one main residence, but may end up with less than a 100% exemption where different main residences are chosen and the spouse's interests in those dwellings are not equal.

NOTE: A spouse from 1 July 2009 means:

- another individual (whether of the same sex or different sex) with whom the individual is in a relationship registered under State or Territory law, and
- although not legally married, an individual who lives with another individual on a genuine domestic basis in a relationship as a couple (ie. a de facto relationship).

MAIN RESIDENCE ISSUES ON DEATH

TAXPAYER DIES BEFORE LIVING IN NEW HOME OR BEFORE SATISFYING THREE MONTH OCCUPATION REQUIREMENT

If a taxpayer dies after construction of the dwelling commenced but before the three months qualifying period of residency (the 'pre-occupation period'), the law allows that period to be added to the period of actual occupation if the trustee of the estate or the surviving joint tenant so elects (s118-155).

Relief is also available where the individual dies after the work began, or the individual entered into a contract for it to be done but dies before it was finished.

Another circumstance where relief is available is where the individual dies after the work was finished but before it was practicable for the dwelling to become the individual's main residence.

If death occurred before construction started, no exemption is available.

AFTER THE TAXPAYER'S DEATH

Where an individual acquired a dwelling that was his or her main residence just before death, any capital gain or capital loss made by an individual beneficiary or trustee of the deceased's estate is disregarded where a CGT event happens to that dwelling and the following conditions are satisfied:

A. The dwelling was acquired by the deceased before 20 September 1985 (pre-CGT) and

- the beneficiary's or trustee's ownership interest in the dwelling ends within two years of the deceased's death, or
- the deceased's spouse living with the deceased at death, an individual who has a right to occupancy under the will, or an individual to whom the ownership interest passes as a beneficiary, continues to use the dwelling as their main residence and then it is disposed of.

B. The dwelling had been acquired by the deceased on or after 20 September 1985 (post-CGT) and was their main residence and was not immediately before death being used for an income-producing purpose and the beneficiary's or trustee's ownership interest in the dwelling ends within two years of the deceased's death, or the deceased's spouse living with the deceased at death, an individual who has a right to occupancy under the will, or an individual to whom the ownership interest passes as a beneficiary, continues to use the dwelling as their main residence and then it is disposed of.

If these conditions are not met then a CGT event in respect to the dwelling may be subject to CGT (s118-195). In some cases a partial exemption applies (s118-200).

Further, these exemption conditions only apply to the following specific CGT events: A1, B1, C1, C2, E1, E2, F2, I1, I2, K3, K4, and K6. If the CGT event involves the forfeiture of a deposit, the exemption only applies if the forfeiture is part of an uninterrupted sequence of transactions ending in one of the CGT events specified above (ss118-195(2)).

Also, the Commissioner can extend the two year period at his discretion and will generally do this in situations where the beneficiary has attempted unsuccessfully to sell the residence.

The following examples will help clarify the rules.

Bob Martin died on 1 July 2010. His estate included a dwelling, which was his main residence that he acquired on 1 July 1985. Under Bob's will the dwelling passed to his son, James. James rents out the property for 18 months and then sells the property, with settlement occurring on 4 June 2012.

As the dwelling was acquired by the deceased pre-CGT, the assessable income-producing use to which the dwelling was put by the beneficiary is irrelevant if the beneficiary's ownership of the dwelling ends within two years of the deceased's death. The sale is exempt from CGT.

The requirement in s118-195 that the beneficiary's ownership interest end within two years of the deceased's death means that the sale of the dwelling must be completed within the two year period. Accordingly, it is not sufficient that the contract of sale was signed within the two year period.

Bill Morris died on 1 July 2006. His estate included a dwelling, which was his main residence. Bill acquired this dwelling on 1 July 1985. The trustee of Bill's estate rents the dwelling from 1 September 2006 to
1 July 2011 when the trustee's ownership ceases on sale of the dwelling.

In this situation the full exemption does not apply because the conditions in s118-195 are not satisfied, namely that the trustee's ownership did not cease within two years of Bill's death and the main residence was not occupied by a spouse, an individual with a right to occupancy or an individual beneficiary. If the capital gain amount is $100,000, the capital gain would also be $100,000 [$100,000 x 1,763 (days post-death when the house was not the main residence of spouse or individual beneficiary) divided by 1,763 (days from death until sale)].

Sue Harris died on 1 September 2009 and her estate included a dwelling, her main residence, which was acquired by her on 1 October 2000. The dwelling is sold by the trustee of her estate on 1 October 2011. Between 1 October 2007 and 1 October 2011, the dwelling was rented out. She did not adopt the absence rule.

As the deceased acquired the dwelling post-CGT and was using the post-CGT property for an income-producing purpose at the time of her death, the full exemption conditions of s118-195 do not apply. A partial exemption under s118-200 applies.

If the capital gain amount is $100,000, the capital gain under s118-200 is $36,370, calculated as: $100,000 x 1,461 (days when the house was not the main residence of the deceased, spouse or beneficiary) divided by 4,017 (days from acquisition by deceased until sale).

Where the requirements of s118-195 are not satisfied, a partial exemption may be available under s118-200 if the taxpayer is an individual who acquired their ownership interest in the dwelling as a beneficiary in, or trustee of, a deceased estate.

SPECIAL DISABILITY TRUSTS (SDTS) AND DEATH OF THE PRINCIPAL BENEFICIARY

The social security and veterans' entitlements rules provide that an SDT ends on the death of the principal beneficiary, with assets being disposed of by a trustee or passed to the relevant beneficiary as determined by the trust deed. An implied trust may arise over the assets of the SDT with the assets then being transferred out of the implied trust to the beneficiary.

THE DWELLING IS DISPOSED OF BY EITHER A TRUSTEE OF THE SDT OR A TRUSTEE OF THE IMPLIED TRUST WITH PROCEEDS GIVEN TO THE BENEFICIARY

After the death of the principal beneficiary, the terms of the trust deed may require the dwelling to be disposed of, with the proceeds being distributed to the beneficiary or beneficiaries. This disposal may be by a trustee of the SDT or a trustee of the implied trust. The trustee will access a complete or partial CGT main residence exemption, based on the use of the dwelling by the principal beneficiary during the ownership period.

In order for the trustee to qualify for the treatment available following a principal beneficiary's death, the following basic conditions must be satisfied:

- the CGT event must happen at or after the principal beneficiary's death
- the dwelling must have been owned by a trust that was an SDT at some point in the dwelling's ownership period (at or before the principal beneficiary's death), and
- when the CGT event happens, the dwelling must be owned by a trustee of the SDT or a trustee of an implied trust arising because of the principal beneficiary's death.

Prior to determining whether a full or partial CGT main residence exemption is available, to work out the amount of the capital gain or capital loss, the trustee will use the following as the first element of the cost base (and reduced cost base) as appropriate:

- where the trustee of the SDT disposes of the dwelling and distributes the proceeds to a beneficiary, the trustee will retain its original cost base, unless it satisfies the requirements of a market value cost base (see below)

- where the trustee of the implied trust disposes of the dwelling and distributes the proceeds to a beneficiary, the trustee will use the trustee of the SDT's cost base of the asset just before the deceased's death (unless the market value cost base rule applies).

The trustee of the SDT or the implied trust will use the market value of the asset just before the principal beneficiary's death as the first element of the asset's cost base where the following conditions are met:

- the dwelling was used by the principal beneficiary as their main residence ie. it was not used to produce assessable income, and
- the dwelling was owned by the trust that was an SDT just before the principal beneficiary's death.

Where the trustee of the implied trust acquires the dwelling from the trustee of the SDT, any capital gain or loss is disregarded by the trustee of the SDT. This ensures that any CGT liability is deferred until the trustee of the implied trust disposes of the asset.

The trustee of the SDT or implied trust that ultimately disposes of the dwelling will determine their eligibility for the CGT main residence exemption by decreasing the amount of the capital gain or loss they would have made by an amount that is reasonable. In determining what is a reasonable decrease in the capital gain or capital loss, the taxpayer should have regard to the principles applying in s118-195, assuming the dwelling passed to the trustee as a trustee in a deceased person's estate.

The 'relevant period' for the trustee is generally the period starting when the trustee of the SDT first acquired the dwelling and ending when the relevant trustee disposes of the dwelling.

Caring Pty Ltd (Caring) is the trustee of an SDT established for Peter, who is the principal beneficiary. Caring purchases a dwelling for the benefit of Peter. Settlement occurs on 1 January 2008 and Peter moves in on that day. On 31 December 2013, Peter dies. Immediately, the trustee of an implied trust acquires the dwelling from the trustee of the SDT. Six months later, the trustee of the implied trust disposes of the dwelling and gives the proceeds to John. In this situation, the trustee of the SDT disregards any capital gain or loss when the trustee of the implied trust acquires the dwelling. Using the principles of s118-195, the trustee of the implied trust determines that it is reasonable to disregard any capital gain or capital loss on the dwelling because:

- *the trustee's ownership interest ends within two years of Peter's death, and*
- *just before Peter's death:*
  - *the dwelling was Peter's main residence*
  - *it was not used to produce assessable income, and*
  - *the trust was an SDT.*

THE TRUSTEE PASSES THE DWELLING TO THE BENEFICIARY

When a beneficiary acquires the dwelling, no CGT taxing point will occur for a trustee of the SDT or a trustee of an implied trust. This ensures that where there is an unrealised CGT liability in the hands of the trustee, this is deferred until a later dealing with the asset by the beneficiary.

To ensure that any applicable CGT liability flows through to a beneficiary, the trustee of the SDT or implied trust will disregard any capital gain or loss on the dwelling. This is on the condition that the relevant trustee satisfies the basic condition above.

In order for a beneficiary to qualify for the treatment available following the principal beneficiary's death, the beneficiary must acquire the dwelling from a trustee of an SDT or implied trust. Prior to determining whether a complete or partial CGT main residence exemption is available, to work out the amount of the capital gain or capital loss, the beneficiary will use the following as first element of cost base (and reduced cost base) as appropriate:

- where the beneficiary acquires the dwelling from a trustee of an implied trust, the trustee's cost base for the asset, just before the beneficiary acquired the asset, or
- where the beneficiary acquires the asset directly from a trustee of an SDT, the trustee of the SDT's cost base for the asset just before the beneficiary acquired the asset.

The relevant trust will use the market value of the asset just before the principal beneficiary's death for the first element of the asset's cost base where the conditions stated above are met.

The beneficiary determines the extent of their main residence exemption by decreasing the amount of capital gain or capital loss they would have made without the exemption by an amount that is reasonable using the principles of s118-195.

Health Pty Ltd (Health) is the trustee of an SDT established for John, who is the principal beneficiary. Health purchases a dwelling for the benefit of John. Settlement occurs on 1 January 2008 and John moves in on that date. On 31 December 2013, John dies. Immediately, the trustee of the implied trust acquires the dwelling from the trustee of the SDT, as the SDT ends on the death of the principal beneficiary. Three months later, the beneficiary of the trust, Casey, acquires the dwelling. Casey later disposes of the dwelling, with settlement occurring on 1 July 2015. Both the trustee of the SDT and the trustee of the implied trust will disregard any capital gain or capital loss as a result of the CGT event happening to the dwelling.

In addition, using the principles of section 118-195, Casey determines that it is reasonable to disregard any capital gain or loss on the dwelling because:

- *Casey's ownership interest ends within two years of John's death, and*
- *just before John's death:*
  - *the dwelling was John's main residence*
  - *it was not used to produce assessable income, and*
  - *the trust was an SDT.*

12.310 TRUSTEE ACQUIRES DWELLING UNDER A WILL

Where under a deceased's will, the trustee of a deceased estate acquires an ownership interest in a dwelling for occupation by an individual, special rules apply.

If the trustee disposes of the dwelling to the individual and no consideration is received by the trustee:

- any capital gain to the trustee from the CGT event is disregarded, and
- the individual acquires the dwelling at the date it had been acquired by the trustee for the same cost base or reduced cost base as the trustee (ss118-210(2)).

If the trustee disposes of the dwelling to the individual for consideration, and the dwelling was the main residence of the individual from the date it was acquired by the trustee until the date of the CGT event, any capital gain or capital loss to the trustee is disregarded (ss118-210(3)).

Where the dwelling was the main residence of the individual for only part of the time, there is only a pro-rata exemption from CGT based on the percentage of the period which the property was the individual's main residence (ss118-210(4)).

12.315 RESIDENCE TRANSFER FROM COMPANY OR TRUST ON MARRIAGE BREAKDOWN

If rollover relief applies on breakdown of a marriage and a dwelling is transferred by a company or trustee after 19 September 1985 to a spouse, mandatory rollover relief applies, so that there is no CGT event for CGT purposes.

If the dwelling was a pre-CGT asset, it retains that status. If the dwelling was a post-CGT asset, the spouse inherits the company's or trustee's former cost base. If the dwelling was the main residence, the exemption applies only for the period during which the spouse owned the dwelling.

The effect of this is that the original purchase date is retained. This means that if the trust or company acquired the dwelling before 20 September 1985 the dwelling would remain exempt from CGT.

If the company or trust had acquired the dwelling after 19 September 1985, the spouse acquiring the dwelling assumes any CGT liability for the proportionate period during which the company or trust owned it. The dwelling cannot be treated as a main residence during the period of ownership by the company or trust (s118-180).

For the rules where a main residence is transferred between individuals on breakdown of a marriage (see 12.460).

12.320   PART INCOME-PRODUCING USE

Where a place of business is conducted in part of a taxpayer's home and that portion of the home would satisfy the interest deductibility test (even where no borrowing exists on the home), that proportion of the home (normally based on the floor area, but see TD 1999/66) is subject to CGT when a CGT event happens.

If the main residence was acquired after 19 September 1985 and was first used to produce income after 20 August 1996, then in calculating the capital gain, the residence is taken to have been acquired for its market value at the time it was first used to produce income (s118-192). This means that the period before the residence is used for income-producing purposes is not taken into account in determining any capital gain or capital loss and the taxpayer is not required to keep records of expenditure on a dwelling used solely as a main residence until it becomes income-producing.

If the income produced from the dwelling is rental income during a period of absence not exceeding six years, there is no CGT liability if an election is made under s118-145. Where the income-producing use exceeds six years, a partial exemption applies (see 12.330).

Sally purchased a dwelling for $200,000 under a contract that was settled on 1 June 1997. She occupied the dwelling from that date until 18 May 2004 when she left to take up a position in the London office of her employer. Sally did not have another main residence and chose to treat the property as her main residence during her period of absence. Sally rented out her main residence from 1 May 2005. At that time the market value of the property had increased to $300,000.

After seven years Sally was still working in London, so she sold her main residence on 1 May 2012 for $500,000.

Although Sally had elected to treat her dwelling as her main residence during her period of absence, the full exemption under s118-145 does not apply because Sally's seven year period of absence has exceeded the six year maximum. As the property first became income-producing after 20 August 1996, s118-192 will apply and Sally will be deemed to have acquired the dwelling for its market value of $300,000 on 1 June 2005 - the day it was first used to produce income.

Sally's total capital gain on disposal of the property is $500,000 less $300,000 = $200,000. Sally taxable capital gain is determined by the formula: [Capital gain amount ($200,000) x Non-main residence days (365)] divided by days in the ownership period (2,558 days- 1 May 2005 to 1 May 2012) = $28,538

As she has owned the property for at least 12 months she is entitled to the 50% CGT discount and her assessable capital gain is $14,269. Although Sally may be a foreign resident she is still assessed on the capital gain because the dwelling is taxable Australian property.

Note: *If the property was sold on or after 8 May 2012, the full 50% general discount may need to be reduced as the discount no longer applies to foreign residents from that date. Special calculations apply.*

Like Sally in Example 1, Jean purchased a dwelling for $200,000 under a contract that was settled on 1 May 1990. She occupied the dwelling from that date until 1 May 1995 when she left to take up a position in the New York office of her employer. Like Sally, Jean did not have another main residence and chose to treat the property as her main residence during her period of absence. Jean rented out her main residence from 1 May 1996. After 12 years Jean was still working in New York, so she sold her main residence on 1 May 2008 for $500,000.

Unlike Sally in Example 1, Jean is not subject to s118-192 because she first used her home to produce income before 7.30pm on 20 August 1996. This means that the market value of the dwelling when it is first used to produce income is ignored and the capital gain is determined on the original cost base of the dwelling.

Jean's total capital gain is $500,000 – $200,000 = $300,000. The part of the capital gain that is taxable is $100,000 ($300,000 x 2,192 - ie. 1 May 2002 to 1 May 2008 divided by 6,576 - ie. 1 May 1990 to 1 May 2008).

As the property has been owned for at least 12 months the CGT discount applies and the assessable capital gain is $50,000. As the property was acquired before 21 September 1999

Jean could have opted to use the indexation method but this would have produced a higher taxable capital gain.

Note: *If the property was sold on or after 8 May 2012, the full 50% general discount may need to be reduced as the discount no longer applies to foreign residents from that date. Special calculations apply.*

12.325   PART EXEMPTION FOR HOME

If a dwelling is used partly as a main residence, and partly as a place of business, any capital gain is determined by apportioning the whole gain between the residential use and income-producing use (usually on an area/time basis – see TD 1999/66).

Whether a place of business (as opposed to a home office) exists is a question of fact. The test is whether a particular part of a dwelling is:

- set aside for exclusive use as a place of business
- clearly identifiable and used as a place of business, or
- not readily suitable or adaptable for use for private or domestic purposes in association with the dwelling generally.

A self-employed architect buys a home on 1 January 2005 and uses 1/5th of it as an office. He ceases business on 1 January 2007 and becomes employed.

Provided the use of a home-study whilst employed was not sufficient to justify a claim for part of the home as a place of business, any incidental use as a home study is immaterial.

The house was sold on 1 January 2013. On the trigger of CGT event A1, the home is partially subject to CGT being 10% of any gain made (as one fifth of the home was used to carry on business for half of the period of ownership) (see ss118-190(3) for further elaboration on how this apportionment criteria applies).

12.330   ABSENCE FROM MAIN RESIDENCE

If a main residence is acquired after 19 September 1985, the following rules determine whether any capital gain from a CGT event is taxed or whether a capital loss can be offset against capital gains in the current or future tax years.

RULES OF ABSENCE

A taxpayer who initially occupies a dwelling as a main residence and then ceases to occupy it, can choose to continue to have the dwelling treated as the main residence (s118-145).

The main residence exemption can still apply:

- for a maximum of six years if the dwelling is used to produce assessable income while the taxpayer is absent. The taxpayer is entitled to another maximum period of six years each time the dwelling again becomes and ceases to be the taxpayer's main residence (ss118-145(2)), and
- indefinitely if the dwelling is not used to produce assessable income (ss118-145(3)).

Continuing to treat the dwelling as the taxpayer's main residence can only apply if the taxpayer does not have another main residence (unless the change of main residence rules apply (see 12.300).

An example is where the taxpayer moves overseas, is provided accommodation by their employer and rents out their main residence whilst absent. The property is no longer the taxpayer's main residence if the taxpayer purchases a property overseas and treats that overseas property as their main residence.

A taxpayer does not have to re-occupy the dwelling before a CGT event happens to retain the main residence exemption.

A house is occupied as a taxpayer's main residence for three years. The taxpayer is sent overseas for five years and rents out his house. He moves back to Australia after the five year absence and re-occupies the house for two years. He is sent overseas again and leases the house for a further four years. The taxpayer then sells the house. If the taxpayer has no other main residence while overseas, he can choose to continue to treat the house as the main residence during both absences; each absence being for less than six years.

On disposal of the house, any capital gain is exempt from CGT.

John owned a main residence for 10 years in total. He lived in it for three years and rented it out for seven consecutive years whilst absent. As John's absence was greater than six years a full exemption is not available. Further, as the dwelling first became income-producing after 20 August 1996, the special rule in s118-192 applies and John's cost base for determining the capital gain will be the market value of the dwelling on the day it was first used for income-producing purposes. If John sells the dwelling for $600,000 and its market value seven years earlier when the dwelling was first used to produce income was $300,000, then John's capital gain is:

(Capital gain amount x Non-main residence days divided by Days in ownership period (since deemed acquisition).

[$600,000 – $300,000] x 365 divided by 2,555 (ie. 365 x 7)= $42,857

As he has owned the property for at least 12 months John is entitled to the 50% CGT discount and his assessable capital gain is $21,429.

John in this case can still have another main residence and apply the absence rule under s118-145 in regards to this property.

DERIVING INCOME AFTER ABSENCE

The exemption period is also apportioned if, before the dwelling ceases to be the main residence, it is used partly to produce assessable income. Where this applies and the dwelling continues to be the main residence of the taxpayer under the absences rule, the exemption available during the absence period is no greater than the exemption that was available when the dwelling ceased to be the main residence.

A taxpayer uses 20% of his home as a place of business. He later accepts a position interstate and rents the house for five years. After five years he decides not to return and sells the house. If he chooses this dwelling as his main residence, he is entitled to an exemption for the five years the home was rented, but any capital gain is calculated on the basis that the dwelling continued to have a 20% business use.

ONE MAIN RESIDENCE ONLY

A taxpayer cannot elect to have two or more main residences during the period of exemption, except where a new dwelling is purchased, and then, only for a maximum of six months (see above on changing main residence).

If the conditions for exemption are met, the dwelling from which the taxpayer is absent may be elected as the taxpayer's main residence, even if the taxpayer occupies another dwelling.

Mary buys a second house and occupies it while absent from the first one. Mary may elect that the first house be treated as the main residence and, in this case, the second house is ineligible for exemption. Under s118-145 Mary may choose that the main residence exemption applies to the first dwelling from which she is absent. This choice must be made on or before lodgement of the income tax return for the income year in which the dwelling is sold.

NOTE: The six months overlapping on changing main residence exemption does not apply where the first residence is rented out during the whole period of absence that ended on disposal of the first residence.

If the taxpayer has died, the trustee or surviving joint tenant should make the choice by the date of lodgement of the tax return for the deceased taxpayer's estate return for the year of income in which the taxpayer died.

12.350 JOINT TENANTS AND TENANTS IN COMMON

The tax implications with respect to the ownership of property varies depending on whether individual taxpayers hold the property as joint tenants or tenants in common. In addition, the CGT implications on the death of one co-owner varies depending on the relationship between the owners.

ASSET OWNED BY JOINT TENANTS

A joint tenancy exists if the parties jointly own the property and survivors automatically assume ownership on death of one or more parties (eg. a family home, as it is normally held by husband and wife).

For each owner, five elements must exist for there to be a joint tenancy:
- they must have acquired their current share(s) in the asset at the same time
- their legal entitlement to the asset must occur at the same time (eg. a common transfer)
- the legal entitlement must be identical
- each owner must have the right to (shared) exclusive possession of each and every part of the asset, and
- there must be a right of survivorship.

For CGT purposes, individuals who own a CGT asset as joint tenants are treated as if they each own a separate CGT asset constituted by an equal interest in the asset, and as if each individual held that interest as a tenant in common (s108-7).

Provided that there is no change in ownership, a conversion from a joint tenancy in common in equal shares would not amount to a disposal for CGT purposes. No CGT event arises. The rules apply as if the joint tenants owned the property as tenants in common in equal shares.

DEATH OF A JOINT TENANT

Where a joint tenant dies, the interest of the deceased automatically devolves to the remaining joint tenant(s) (s128-50). This means that if joint tenants own a main residence and one dies, the surviving joint tenants are taken to have acquired the deceased's interest in the main residence. This means that the interest in the main residence does not devolve to the deceased's legal personal representative or pass to a beneficiary of the deceased's estate as s128-50 will apply (s118-197 and TD 1999/72).

INTEREST ACQUIRED BEFORE 20 SEPTEMBER 1985

On death, the survivor(s) is deemed to have:
- acquired the deceased's interest at date of death, and
- acquired the interest at a cost base equal to the market value of the interest at that date (consideration is calculated as if the deceased disposed of the asset just before death).

If there are two or more survivors, the deceased's (notional) separate interest is deemed to be acquired by the survivors in equal shares (ss128-50(4)).

INTEREST ACQUIRED AFTER 19 SEPTEMBER 1985

The survivor(s) are deemed to have:
- acquired the deceased's interest at date of death, and
- acquired the interest at a cost base equal to the deceased's cost base at that date.

If a capital loss results from a CGT event, the survivor's interest in the asset is taken to have been acquired at the deceased's 'reduced cost base' (ss128-50(3)).

ASSETS OWNED BY TENANTS IN COMMON

Tenants in common effectively own a separate (though undivided) interest in the asset, and may dispose of the interest without affecting other tenants in common (eg. partners can each hold separate and unequal interests in assets of the partnership). The main difference between 'joint tenants' and 'tenants in common' is the effect on survivors.

With a tenancy in common, upon death of one of the co-owners, the deceased's share of the property passes in accordance with their instructions as set out in their will. A surviving spouse would not automatically obtain the deceased's interest in the matrimonial home.

Any CGT is calculated as for other assets (other than main residence).

TD 45 provides that, where a taxpayer, being a tenant in common, acquires the interest of the other tenant in common, the co-ownership ceases. Typically the interest already held and the new interests acquired are treated separately by the continuing owner.

For the purchaser, the CGT implications depends on when the interest is acquired, as follows:

- to the extent that the original interest of the continuing owner was acquired before 20 September 1985, then such interest will retain its pre-CGT status as a separate CGT asset whilst the newly acquired interest would be a separate post-CGT asset, and
- to the extent that both interests are acquired post-CGT, then the total cost base of the property would be equal to the sum of the separate interests.

12.450 ROLLING OVER ASSETS

Rollover relief allows a taxpayer to choose to preserve 'pre-CGT status' of some CGT assets, or defer CGT in respect of post-CGT assets if certain CGT events happen.

A rollover occurs when a CGT asset is transferred from one owner to another, but the CGT status of the asset (eg. cost base and pre/post-CGT status) is usually preserved.

Generally, rollover relief applies where:

- there is a change in the CGT asset without a change in the underlying ownership of that asset, or
- there is a change in the entity owning the asset without there being a change in the underlying ownership of the asset, such a business reorganisation, or
- there are merely changes in legal formalities.

The Act classifies rollover relief in five categories. The rollover provisions in each category and their paragraph reference in this Summary are as follows:

12.455 INVOLUNTARY DISPOSALS

Pursuant to ss124-70(1) a taxpayer may choose rollover relief where compensation (either as money or a replacement asset, other than a car or motor cycle) is received and a capital gain would have resulted from the CGT event for a CGT asset that is:

- compulsorily acquired by an Australian government agency
- wholly or partly lost or destroyed (not merely damaged (see TD 2000/38)
- a lease, granted by an Australian government agency, which expires and is not renewed
- compulsorily acquired by a private acquirer under statutory power of compulsory acquisition, other than compulsory acquisition of minority interest under corporations law
- disposed of to an entity (other than a foreign government agency) after notice was served inviting negotiations and informing that if the negotiations are unsuccessful the asset would be compulsorily acquired by the entity under a statutory power
- land compulsorily subject to a mining lease and disposed of to the lessee (other than a foreign government agency), or
- land disposed of to an entity that would have been the lessee (other than a foreign government agency) in circumstances where a mining lease would have been compulsorily granted if the land had not been disposed of and the lease would have significantly affected the taxpayer's use of the land.

Rollover relief is not available where the taxpayer was required to dispose of the property due to financial difficulties (TD 93/82W). For foreign residents, the original asset must be 'taxable Australian property' for rollover relief to be available (see ss124-70(4)).

REPLACEMENT ASSET AS COMPENSATION

If the taxpayer receives a replacement asset, rather than money to purchase a replacement asset, s124-90 applies. Any capital gain on the original asset is disregarded, and the replacement asset inherits the CGT characteristics of the original asset.

If the original asset was acquired before 20 September 1985, the replacement asset is taken to be acquired before that date. Alternatively, if the original asset was acquired after 19 September 1985, the replacement asset inherits the original asset's cost base at the time of the event (s124-90).

For s124-90 to apply:

- the replacement asset cannot be trading stock
- the replacement asset cannot be a depreciating asset under Division 40 or Division 328, and
- the market value of the replacement asset must exceed the cost base of the original asset just before the CGT event (s124-80).

WHAT IS A 'REPLACEMENT ASSET'?

If all the tests are satisfied, an asset is a 'replacement asset' only if:

- immediately before the event happened, the original asset was used (or installed ready for use) in a business carried on by the taxpayer, and the replacement asset is used by the taxpayer for a reasonable time after acquisition in the same business, or
- the original asset was a non-business asset and the new asset is used by the taxpayer for a reasonable time after acquisition for the same or similar purpose as the original asset
- the new asset is not trading stock immediately after acquisition, and
- the new asset is not a depreciating asset.

There is no restriction on the number of CGT assets which may be treated as replacement assets for the original CGT asset in the replacement asset rollover, provided the relevant conditions in Subdivision 124-B are satisfied (TD 2000/41).

MONETARY COMPENSATION

If the taxpayer receives money as compensation, these conditions must be met before the rollover election is available to the taxpayer:

- the money must be spent to acquire a replacement CGT asset (except a depreciating asset) or in restoring or repairing the original asset
- some of the expenditure must be incurred between one year before and one year after the CGT event (unless the Commissioner allows an extension of time in special circumstances: TD 2000/40)
- the replacement asset must be used for the same or similar purpose to the original asset (see *What is a replacement asset?* above)
- the replacement asset cannot be trading stock, and
- where the original asset is pre-CGT, the replacement asset cannot exceed 120% of the market value of the original asset when the event happened, unless the CGT event was due to a 'natural disaster'. The '120% test' does not apply if the disposal is due to a natural disaster (bushfire, cyclone, earthquake, flood and storm) and the replacement asset is substantially the same as the original asset (TD 2000/45 gives examples of what is and is not 'substantially the same' asset when replacement is due to a natural disaster.)

WHAT IS A NATURAL DISASTER?

ITAA97 does not define a 'natural disaster', but ss160ZZK(7D) ITAA36 defined it to include bushfire, earthquake, cyclone, flood or storm. The test for determining this is to take into account all relevant circumstances, including the location, size, value, quality, composition and utility of the original asset and the replacement asset.

CONSEQUENCE OF RECEIVING MONETARY COMPENSATION

If the original asset was acquired:

- **Before 20 September 1985:** *the replacement asset or repaired asset is pre-CGT (s124-85(3) &(4)).*
- **On or after 20 September 1985 and the taxpayer makes a notional capital gain from the event:** *ss124-85(2) applies.*

Subsection 124-85(2) takes into account the fact that when cash compensation is received for the loss, the compensation may not be fully used to replace the lost asset. In this case, the rollover provisions may allow only a partial rollover or none at all. The intention of ss124-85(2) is to only allow rollover to the extent that the potential gain resulting from the loss is used to replace the asset.

The following example illustrates the possible results from the application of ss124-85(2).

A company's CGT asset with a cost base (indexed frozen at 30/9/99) of $200,000 has been destroyed and the insurance recovery (capital proceeds) is $300,000 so there is a potential or notional capital gain of $100,000.

Set out below are four alternative replacement costs which illustrate the effect of each on the amount of rollover available.

Case 1: Replacement cost $180,000

As the excess compensation ($300,000 – $180,000 = $120,000) is higher than the notional capital gain ($100,000), no rollover is permitted. The capital gain of $100,000 is assessable and the cost base of the new asset is $180,000.

Case 2: Replacement cost $220,000

As the excess compensation ($80,000) is $20,000 less than the notional capital gain ($100,000), a partial rollover is allowed. In this case, the capital gain is reduced by $20,000 to $80,000 and the cost base of the new asset is $200,000 (the $220,000 replacement reduced by the $20,000 by which the gain exceeds the excess compensation).

Case 3: Replacement cost $300,000

As the replacement cost is equal to the compensation, full rollover is permitted so that there is no capital gain at the time of the CGT event (the loss of the asset).

The cost base of the new asset is $200,000 (the cost base of the asset lost).

Case 4: Replacement cost $400,000

As the replacement cost is more than the compensation, full rollover is permitted at the time of the CGT event.

The capital gain is disregarded. The cost base of the replacement asset is $300,000 (the $400,000 replacement cost reduced by notional gain of $100,000).

Under Subdivision 124-M a taxpayer may be able to claim rollover relief if as a result of a takeover (including a scheme of arrangement) the acquiring company becomes the owner of at least 80% of voting shares in the original entity and in return, shareholders in the original entity receive shares in the acquirer company on substantially the same terms as their shares in the original entity (scrip for scrip rollover relief) (see 12.468).

BOTH ASSET AND MONEY AS COMPENSATION

If the taxpayer receives both money and another CGT asset for a CGT event and the taxpayer chooses to obtain rollover relief, the asset compensation and the money compensation are required to be treated separately (ss124-95(1)).

The replacement asset and the money must be apportioned to the cost base of the original asset by reference to the market value of the replacement asset and the amount of money received. After the apportionment, the same principles apply as if only a replacement asset alone or money alone had been received as compensation.

For the replacement asset, rollover relief is only available where its market value is greater than the part of the cost base of the original asset attributable to the replacement asset (s124-95(4)).

IF ROLLOVER RELIEF IS NOT AUTOMATIC

In some cases, rollover relief is allowed only if the taxpayer chooses (that is, it is not automatic). The election must be in writing and made no later than the day the income tax return was lodged for the year the CGT event happened, or within such further period as the Tax Office allows.

Generally, the choice is reflected in how the tax return is prepared (s103-25). For example, if a choice to access rollover relief has been made then any net capital gain arising would not be shown from that particular CGT event.

Taxpayers do not have to lodge most elections, but they should be made and retained on file (see 4.070).

12.460 MARRIAGE BREAKDOWN

Automatic rollover relief applies if assets are transferred between spouses due to a marriage breakdown under the following conditions.

NOTE: Prior to 13 December 2006 rollover only applied where the transfer was the result of a Court order or maintenance agreement under s87 *Family Law Act 1975* or a court order under a state, territory or foreign law relating to de facto marriages. However, after 12 December 2006 rollover relief will also automatically occur where assets are transferred to a spouse or former spouse because of:

- a financial agreement that is binding on the parties to the agreement under Part VIIA *Family Law Act 1975* or a corresponding written agreement that is binding because of a corresponding foreign law

- an award made in an arbitration of a property or financial dispute under section 13H *Family Law Act 1975* or a corresponding arbitral award under a corresponding state, territory or foreign law, or

- a written agreement that is binding because of a state, territory or foreign law relating to de facto marriage breakdowns and that, because of such a law, a court is prevented from making an order about matters to which the agreement applies, or which are inconsistent with the terms of that written agreement unless the agreement is varied or set aside. (An amendment has been made to ensure that the rollover applies to transfers of assets pursuant to written agreements made under Western Australian, Tasmanian, Queensland or Northern Territory laws relating to de facto marriage breakdown).

Under the income tax law, the term 'spouse' includes two persons who, although not legally married, live together on a genuine domestic basis as husband and wife.

From 1 July 2009, the meaning of spouse is defined as:

- another individual (whether of the same sex or different sex) with whom the individual is in a relationship registered under State or Territory law, and
- although not legally married, an individual who lives with another individual on a genuine domestic basis in a relationship as a couple (ie. a de facto relationship).

The CGT rollover can only apply where the definition of spouse is met.

For automatic rollover to be available, the following conditions in ss126-25(1) must be met, namely:

- at the time of the trigger event, the spouses involved are separated and there is no reasonable likelihood of cohabitation being resumed, and
- the trigger event happened because of reasons directly connected with the marriage or de facto marriage breakdown.

The question of whether spouses have separated is to be determined in the same way as it is for the purposes of s48 of the *Family Law Act 1975*, as affected by s49 and s50 of that Act (ss126-25(2)).

Where the conditions are met the rollover is automatic; it does not have to be elected. Automatic rollover ensures that a capital gain or capital loss that would otherwise be made by an individual, a company or a trustee is deferred until the transferee spouse or former spouse disposes of the CGT asset. The transferee spouse is taken to also have acquired the asset before that date so the pre-CGT status of the asset is preserved where the asset was acquired before 20 September 1985.

Kate receives $200,000 from Liam as a settlement directly related to their marriage breakdown. Without the automatic rollover CGT event C2 would have happened when Kate receives satisfaction for her legally enforceable right (her CGT event D1 asset) to receive that amount. Because of the automatic rollover any capital gain or capital loss that Kate makes from the marriage breakdown is disregarded (s118-75).

ROLLOVER EVENTS

The marriage breakdown rollover provisions only relate to certain CGT events, namely:

- Disposal cases – CGT events A1 and B1
- Creation cases – CGT events D1, D2, D3 and F1

There is no rollover where the CGT asset involved is trading stock of the transferor, or for CGT event B1, if title in the CGT asset does not pass to the transferee at or before the end of the agreement. While trading stock is within the definition of CGT asset, capital gains or capital losses arising from a CGT event in respect of trading stock are disregarded (s118-25).

Because rollover is mandatory for transfers subject to orders made under the Family Law Act 1975 or pursuant to a binding financial arrangement, it may, in some instances, be wise to avoid its operations by transferring assets outside these events – seek professional tax advice where relevant! For example, most accrued CGT liabilities are transferred to the new owner, so it may be better to sell an asset or to agree to compensation for the anticipated CGT liabilities.

It may also be possible to change the ownership of the underlying assets by transferring shares or an interest in a trust and so trigger CGT event K6 (s104-230) (see 12.040). In the case of marital breakdown, ss149-30(4) deems there to be continuity of ownership by the recipient spouse on transfer of the asset so Division 149 (when an asset stops being pre-CGT) will not be triggered on a change in majority underlying ownership interests.

Automatic CGT rollover relief also applies where assets are transferred from a company or trust to the spouse. However, while the company obtains CGT rollover relief, the transfer of assets by a private company to a spouse who is also a shareholder or an associate of a shareholder will be treated as a deemed dividend under Division 7A of the ITAA36, and the spouse will be assessed on the value of the asset. From 1 July 2006, where the transfer is made pursuant to a Subdivision 126-A rollover, any such dividend can be franked by the private company subject to the same conditions that would apply to other dividends (eg. compliance with the company's franking benchmark percentage).

The automatic rollover relief on marriage breakdown is only available where the asset is transferred to the spouse or former spouse. Rollover relief would not apply where an asset is transferred by the taxpayer and their former spouse to an unrelated third party (*Kok Yong Tey and C of T* 2004 AATA 1210).

If rollover relief does not apply the capital proceeds for the transferor and the first element of the cost base of the transferee spouse will be the market value of the asset transferred.

ASSET ACQUIRED BEFORE 20 SEPTEMBER 1985

Where the asset was acquired before 20 September 1985, the spouse receiving the asset is treated as having acquired the asset before that date. A subsequent CGT event happening in relation to that asset would not result in any CGT liability because its acquisition date is taken to be pre-20 September 1985.

ASSET ACQUIRED AFTER 19 SEPTEMBER 1985

For a transfer of an asset acquired after 19 September 1985, any capital gain or capital loss made by the transferor is disregarded. The transferee spouse inherits the transferor's cost base or reduced cost base when the transferee spouse acquires the asset (s126-5(5)).

Costs of transfer (conveyancing fees, stamp duty, etc.) of a CGT asset transferred between spouses because of a court order arising on a marriage breakdown are included in the cost base of the transferor which becomes the first element of the transferee's cost base (TD 1999/57).

However, the transferor's general legal costs of the marriage breakdown property settlement do not satisfy the cost base rules (TD 1999/57).

The transferor could be a company or trust if the asset was held in those entities.

Any CGT liability is deferred until there is a subsequent CGT event in relation to the asset. That is, the spouse receiving the CGT asset on transfer will potentially be liable for CGT on the whole of an assessable gain arising from a subsequent CGT event, calculated from the date the transferor (spouse, trust or company) originally acquired the asset.

There is no separate calculation of tax to the date the transferor transferred the asset. However, if the transferor were a company or trustee, as value in the form of the asset has been shifted out of the company or trust, adjustments are necessary to reduce the cost base of a taxpayer's share or interest in the company or trust, or loan to the company or trust, by an amount that reasonably reflects the fall in its market value due to the transfer of the asset (ss126-15(3)).

The cost base adjustments required reflect either the value or cost base of the asset transferred to the spouse or former spouse, less any amount that, as a result of the disposal by the company or trustee, is included in the second taxpayer's assessable income under the non-CGT rules (eg. the cost base of the share or interest of the transferee spouse (where that person holds a shares or interest in the company or trust) is increased for an amount assessable under Division 7A).

COLLECTABLES AND PERSONAL USE ASSETS

Where a collectable or personal use asset is transferred, it retains those characteristic in the hands of the recipient spouse. Any loss on a collectable is quarantined and any loss on a personal use asset is disregarded (ss126-5(7)).

MAIN RESIDENCE EXEMPTION

Effective from 12 December 2006, s118-178 ensures that where a main residence is transferred as a direct result of a breakdown of a marriage, the CGT main residence exemption rules take into account the way in which both the transferor and transferee spouse used the dwelling when determining the transferee spouse's eligibility for the main residence exemption on a future disposal of the property (refer 12.300).

Liam (the transferor spouse) was the sole owner of a dwelling that he used as rental property for three years then as a main residence for three years before transferring it to his former spouse Kate (the transferee spouse) because of a marriage breakdown which satisfied the conditions for automatic rollover relief. Kate uses the dwelling only as a rental property for six years before disposing of it.

Kate will be eligible for a 25% main residence exemption having regard to the collective manner in which both she and Liam used the dwelling.

Where a dwelling had been used as a main residence from its acquisition and then first used for an income-producing purpose after 20 August 1996 the special rule in s118-192 applies and the transferee spouse is taken to have acquired the ownership interest in the dwelling for its market value at the time it is first used to produce income.

Carol (the transferor spouse) was the sole owner of a dwelling that she acquired for $200,000 in 2000. Carol used the dwelling as a main residence for three years. In 2003, Carol decided to use the dwelling to produce income. At this time the market value of the dwelling was $300,000. On the breakdown of their marriage Carol transferred the dwelling to William (the transferee spouse). William is taken to have acquired the ownership interest in the dwelling in 2003 for its market value at that time ($300,000).

The marriage breakdown main residence rules do not prevent the operation of s103-25 which gives the transferor spouse a right to choose to treat a dwelling as their main residence during periods of absence (s118-145), building, repair or renovation (s118-150) and accidental destruction (s118-160).

If there was a period when the transferor and transferee spouse had different main residences before they separated, they need to make a choice under s118-170 to:

- treat one of the dwellings as the main residence of both of them for the period, or
- nominate the different dwellings as their main residences.

While there is automatic rollover relief on the breakdown of a marriage and the relevant choices generally do not need to be made until the transferor spouse lodges an income tax return for the income year in which a CGT event happens to the property, the choices that a transferor spouse may make about the transfer of an ownership interest may form part of the negotiations between the transferor spouse and transferee spouse. If so, a signed statement evidencing the choice could form part of the settlement.

If the main residence is owned and acquired by a company or trust after 19 September 1985, the main residence is not exempt from CGT for the period it was owned by a company or by a trust (s118-110(1)). The main residence exemption is only available to an individual (defined in s995-1(1) as a natural person). Subsection 960-100(4) goes on to provide that if a provision refers to an entity of a particular kind, it refers to the entity in its capacity as that kind of entity and not in any other capacity (see TD 58W). Section 118-195 indicates where the exemption would apply to deceased estates (see 12.650).

RECORD KEEPING

As the recipient spouse acquires a post-CGT asset at the cost base of the transferor (indexed if appropriate), the recipient will require this information from the former spouse.

The costs of the asset's transfer (including legal costs other than from the marriage or de facto relationship breakdown itself) must also be recorded as they form part of the cost base of the asset in the hands of the recipient spouse.

12.465 STRATA TITLE CONVERSIONS

A taxpayer may choose for rollover relief to apply if a building is subdivided into stratum units and the taxpayer surrenders their rights of occupancy in that building in exchange for a stratum unit (s124-190 and TR 97/4). A 'stratum unit' is a lot or unit and any accompanying common property.

ROLLOVER CONDITIONS

Rollover relief applies if:

- the taxpayer owns property that gives a right to occupy a unit in a building, and
- the building's owner subdivides it into 'stratum' units, and
- the owner transfers to the taxpayer the stratum unit that corresponds to the unit that person had the right to occupy just before the subdivision (s124-190(1)).

APPLY FOR ROLLOVER RELIEF

A taxpayer wishing to apply this deferral must choose for rollover relief to apply (refer s103-25 – the choice is evidenced by the manner that the income tax return is prepared).

Where rollover relief is chosen, any capital gain or capital loss on surrender of the taxpayer's right to occupy the building is disregarded (ss124-10(2)).

If the original asset (the property that gave the taxpayer the right to occupy a unit in the building) was acquired prior to 20 September 1985, the new asset (the stratum unit) will be deemed to be acquired before that date (ss124-10(4)).

If the original asset was acquired after 19 September 1985, the new asset will assume the 'cost base' or the 'reduced cost base' attributable to the taxpayer's original interest at the time of the conversion (ss124-10(3)).

12.466 SUPERANNUATION FUNDS

Trustees of complying superannuation funds are taxed on capital gains at an effective maximum rate of 10% where the asset has been held for at least 12 months excluding days of acquisition and disposal (ie. after the one-third CGT discount is applied).

Rollover relief is available under Subdivision 126-C for a complying superannuation fund or complying approved deposit fund (ADF) where CGT events E1 or E2 happen because the trust deed is amended or replaced for certain events, and there is no change in the assets or the members of the fund as a consequence of the amendment or replacement to the trust deed. One relevant event will be where the amendment or replacement was done for the purpose of complying with the *Superannuation Industry (Supervision) Act 1993* or to enable a complying approved deposit fund to become a complying superannuation fund. Further, a CGT event may apply where the amendment and replacement of a trust deed is done for the purpose of having the fund qualify as an approved worker entitlement fund under s58PH of the *Fringe Benefits Tax Assessment Act 1986*.

Apart from the above exception where one superannuation fund transfers an asset to another superannuation fund, CGT event E2 will happen unless the beneficiaries and the trust deeds of both superannuation funds are the same, so that the exception in s104-60(5)(b) applies (subject to the comments below).

Where superannuation funds merge as a consequence of complying with the new licensing requirements there will be automatic rollover relief under Subdivision 126-F. Automatic rollover relief will occur where the assets of a superannuation fund are transferred to one or more superannuation funds between 30 June 2004 and 1 July 2006 because the trustee of the first fund was not licensed by 1 July 2006 and registrable superannuation entities merge to comply with the licensing requirements under the superannuation safety reforms.

A registrable superannuation fund does not include a self managed superannuation fund. If superannuation fund assets are transferred to the trustee of a registrable superannuation entity that is not licensed by 1 July 2006, the automatic rollover is treated as is if it had never happened.

It should also be noted that the transfer of an asset from the trustee of a fund to:

- a member of the fund
- a dependant of a deceased member
- a trust for a dependant of a member, or
- a deceased member's estate

is treated as a CGT event for CGT purposes (but note the exemptions for superannuation payments to members set out in s118-305).

OPTIONAL CGT LOSS ROLL-OVER FOR COMPLYING SUPERANNUATION FUNDS AND ADFS

A company superannuation fund or complying ADF can choose to roll-over capital losses and transfer revenue losses (including losses realised under the merger and previously realised losses) when they merge with a complying superannuation fund with five or more members between 24 December 2008 and 30 September 2011.

 These provisions do not apply to Self Managed Superannuation Funds.

IMPORTANT: The enactment of the *Superannuation Laws Amendment (Capital Gains Tax Relief and Other Efficiency Measures) Act 2012* should ensure that tax considerations are not an impediment to superannuation funds seeking to merge and consolidate in response to the Stronger Super reforms. The taxation relief will also ensure that default members of superannuation funds are not adversely affected if their superannuation benefits and relevant assets are transferred under the MySuper reforms (see 19.285).

NO PRE-CGT EXEMPTION

Trustees of a complying superannuation fund, complying ADF or pooled superannuation trust are not exempt from CGT where a capital gain is made on an asset acquired prior to 20 September 1985. However, the cost base for the calculation of the capital gain or capital loss will be either the market value of the asset at 30 June 1988 or the actual cost, whichever yields the lower capital gain or capital loss from the CGT event.

12.467 SUPERANNUATION AND SEPARATION REFORMS

Generally, when rights are created or certain rights come to an end, a capital gain or capital loss may arise. However, if the actual transfer of an asset or making of a payment is under a superannuation agreement or court order, a CGT exemption and CGT rollover may apply.

EXEMPTIONS

- **CGT exemption for rights connected to superannuation payments:** Section 118-305(3) extends the exemption for payments to members of a superannuation fund to allow for a capital gain or capital loss to be disregarded where a spouse, who is not a member of the fund, receives a payment or property from the fund as a result of either a superannuation agreement or court order. This extension allows the exemption to apply if a non-member spouse acquired their right to the payment or property for consideration. The consideration is the spouse's foregoing of a right to a property settlement in respect of his or her superannuation interests through the Family Court under the *Family Law Act 1975*.
- **CGT exemption for rights of the parties:** Any capital gain or capital loss is disregarded if that gain or loss is made on either:
  - creating a contractual right or other legal or equitable right in another person (CGT event D1), or
  - having a right coming to an end (CGT event C2) as a result of a superannuation agreement (s118-313).

ROLLOVER

Subdivision 126-D provides CGT same-asset rollover relief where, as a result of a payments split under the *Family Law Act* or *Superannuation Industry (Supervision) Regulations*, the trustee of a small superannuation fund (four or less members) transfers an asset to another small superannuation fund in which the non-member spouse is a member. In these circumstances any capital gain or capital loss arising on an in-specie transfer of an asset is automatically deferred (see s126-140(1) and s126-140(2)).

Where the trustee who transferred the asset acquired the asset before 20 September 1985, the trustee who acquires the asset on transfer will also be taken to have acquired the asset before that day. Where the asset transferred was originally acquired post-CGT, the first element of the cost base or reduced cost base of the asset for the trustee who acquires the asset on transfer will be the cost base or reduced cost base of the asset to the trustee who transferred the asset (see s126-140(4) and s126-140(5)).

For CGT events that happen on or after 1 July 2007, a rollover is extended to marriage breakdown transfers of CGT assets reflecting the personal interest of either spouse (but not both) in a small superannuation fund to another complying superannuation fund if that transfer satisfies certain conditions. The transfer must be in accordance with certain arbitration awards, court orders or binding financial agreements. There must be a genuine marriage breakdown. The effect is to defer the making of a capital gain or capital loss from a relevant asset transfer, until a later CGT event happens to the relevant asset. The pre-existing marriage breakdown rollover is extended to transfers from a small superannuation fund to another complying superannuation fund.

12.468 SCRIP FOR SCRIP ROLLOVER

For interests in companies and fixed trusts, Subdivision 124-M allows a CGT rollover when post-CGT original equity interests in one entity are exchanged for replacement equity interests, typically because of a takeover or scheme of arrangement. The rollover defers recognition of any capital gain (but not a capital loss) until a CGT event happens to the replacement interests. The scrip for scrip rollover does not apply to a pre-CGT interest.

2010 AMENDMENTS

In 2010, the Act was amended to make it easier for takeovers and mergers regulated by the *Corporations Act 2001* to qualify for CGT scrip for scrip rollover relief. The amendments apply to CGT events that happen on or after 6 January 2010.

The amendments carve out arrangements from having to meet the rollover requirements, in paragraphs 124-780(2)(b) and (c), that the arrangement be one in which the target company's shareholders can participate on substantially the same terms, if the arrangement includes:

- a takeover bid that does not contravene key provisions in Chapter 6 *Corporations Act 2001*, and/or
- a compromise or arrangement approved by a court under Part 5.1 *Corporations Act 2001* (scheme of arrangement).

There are similar amendments which will be made for certain trust arrangements. However, as trusts cannot undertake schemes of arrangements, the amendment will apply in relation to complying takeover bids.

2013 AMENDMENTS

In 2013, the Act was amended to ensure that certain integrity rules in the scrip for scrip roll-over apply to life insurance companies, superannuation funds and trusts in the same way that they apply to other types of entities. Specifically, the amendments to the scrip for scrip rollover rules enable the scrip for scrip roll-over stakeholder tests to be based on who owns an interest in an entity, rather than who benefits from the interest.

The integrity rule changes that affect the CGT provisions take effect for CGT events that happen after 7:30 pm on 10 May 2011.

2015 PROPOSED AMENDMENTS

In 2015, the government released draft legislation to amend the CGT scrip for scrip roll-over rules. There have been a series of problems identified with the integrity rules that apply in relation to this rollover. Each of these changes is designed to rectify these problems.

To ensure these rules apply appropriately, the following changes are proposed:

- Expand the 'significant' and 'common stakeholder' tests to include any entitlements that interest holders have to acquire additional rights
- Provide that a capital gain arising on the settlement of a debt owed by an acquiring entity to its parent company as part of the scrip for scrip acquisition is no longer disregarded
- Extend the application of the cost base allocation rules regardless of whether the interest is issued to the group's parent company or to another member of the group
- Introduce a new condition on the availability of scrip for scrip roll-over relief in downstream acquisitions, and
- Extend the application of the restructure provisions to trusts restructures.

These changes were first announced in the May 2012 Budget and so are widely anticipated.

APPLICATION

The scrip for scrip rollover is available for CGT events happening on or after 10 December 1999 where the exchange results in an acquiring entity becoming the owner of 80% or more of the voting shares (in the case of a company), or trust voting interests (in the case of a trust), or units or other interest (where there are no trust voting interests) (ss124-780(2) and ss124-781(2)).

In the context of a wholly-owned group of companies, the arrangement must result in a company in the group (an acquiring entity) increasing the percentage of voting shares that it owns in the original entity and the members of the group becoming the owners of 80% or more of those interests (paragraphs 124-780(2)(a) and s124-781(2)(a)).

For companies, the arrangement must be one in which at least all owners of voting shares in the original entity can participate (paragraph 124-780(2)(b)).

For trusts, the arrangement must be one in which at least all owners of trust voting interests (or, where there are no voting interests, of units or other fixed interests) in the original entity can participate (paragraph 124-781(2)(b)).

Participation in the arrangement must have been on substantially the same terms for all of the owners of interests of a particular type in the original entity (paragraphs 124-780(2)(c) and s124-781(2)(c)).

A taxpayer was not entitled to partial CGT roll-over relief in *Commissioner of Taxation v Fabig* [2013] FCAFC 99 because the arrangement was not substantially on the same terms for all owners of the interests in the entity. The Shareholders' Agreement was not open to the shareholders to accept the offer on the same terms and the legal obligations of the shareholders were different.

The acquiring entity must enter into a single arrangement and must exchange replacement interests that are similar to the entity's original interest (shares for shares, options for options etc) (s124-780(1)). If the capital proceeds were to consist of a replacement interest and something else (eg. shares and cash) then the original interest holder can obtain partial rollover relief (s124-790).

80% test

B Ltd proposes a scrip for scrip takeover of A Ltd. A Ltd has two classes of voting shares and options on issue. In respect of each type of interest, B Ltd makes an identical takeover offer to each holder. B Ltd acquires 62% of the shares in A Ltd through acceptances of the offer. Rollover is not available to the shareholders in A Ltd because under this arrangement B Ltd did not acquire 80% of the shares.

Six months later B Ltd makes a second scrip for scrip offer to A Ltd shareholders (a new arrangement) and as a consequence increases its shareholding to 85%. Coincidentally the terms of the offer are substantially the same as the original arrangement.

The shareholders in A Ltd who accepted the offer under the second arrangement are eligible for scrip for scrip rollover. Rollover is still not available for the shareholders that participated in the first arrangement as the 80% threshold was not reached as a result of that arrangement even though both arrangements were on substantially the same terms.

Partial rollover

Johnson owns 1,000 shares in A Ltd each with a cost base of $9 per share. The shares were acquired on 1 October 2004. On 12 May 2009 he accepts a takeover offer from B Ltd, whereby he receives one share in B Ltd plus $10 cash for each share in A Ltd. On 1 June 2009 Johnson receives 1,000 shares in B Ltd, with a market value of $20 each, and $10,000 cash.

As Johnson has received $10 cash for each of his 1,000 shares in A Ltd he has proceeds of $10,000 that are not a replacement interest in the acquiring entity. These proceeds are ineligible for rollover.

To work out the amount of any capital gain or capital loss made on disposing of the ineligible part of Johnson's original interest in A Ltd, a proportion of the cost base of his interest in A Ltd reduces the ineligible proceeds. The apportionment is done on a reasonable basis (s124-790). In this example it is reasonable to allocate a portion of the cost base of the original shares having regard to the proportion that the ineligible proceeds bears to the total proceeds ($30,000). That is: ($10,000 x $9,000) divided by $30,000 = $3,000.

Johnson will make a capital gain of:

Ineligible proceeds	$10,000
Less cost base	($3,000)
Notional capital gain	($7,000)
Less CGT discount (50%)	($3,500)
Assessable capital gain	**$3,500**

If the interest-holder and the acquiring entity are not dealing at arm's length, and there are less than 300 members or beneficiaries in either the original entity or the acquiring entity, special rules apply. The market value of the capital proceeds for the exchange must be at least substantially the same as the market value of the original interest and the replacement interest must carry the same kind of rights and obligations as the original interest.

Rollover is extended in company cases to 'downstream acquisitions'. A downstream acquisition is where a subsidiary of a group of companies acquires its shares in the original entity with shares in its ultimate holding company being issued as consideration. Rollover will be available if an acquiring entity is a 100% subsidiary of another member of its wholly-owned company group and the replacement interest is a share or other relevant interest in the ultimate holding company (s124-780(3)(c)). This measure is at present limited to companies.

While the rollover provisions generally do not extend to a CGT event if the original interest was acquired before 20 September 1985, a CGT liability can arise if the disposal of a pre-CGT original interest results in a capital gain under CGT event K6. That event applies on the disposal of interests in certain private companies and trusts if at least 75% of the net value of the company or trust is represented by post-CGT acquired property. Where this occurs, a limited form of rollover applies. The rollover will:

- disregard a capital gain under CGT event K6 to the extent that rollover would have been available had the original interest been acquired on or after 20 September 1985 (s104-230(10)), and
- reduce the cost base of the replacement interests by the amount of the CGT event K6 gain that is disregarded (s124-800(2)).

COST BASE RULES FOR ACQUIRING ENTITY

Normally, the interests acquired by an acquiring entity have a CGT cost base equal to the market value of the interests issued by the acquiring entity in return for the original interests.

This normal cost base rule continues to apply to determine the acquisition cost of interests acquired by an acquiring entity in the original entity, except where an interest holder, together with associates, has either:

- a 30% or more stake in the original entity and in the entity in which the replacement interest is issued, or
- at least part of an 80% or more holding common to both entities (but only if both entities are not widely-held).

In these cases, as the original interest holders are likely to have some influence over the acquiring entity, where the original interest holder and the replacement entity jointly elect for the rollover, the cost base is to be transferred from the original interest holders to the acquiring entity.

The rules are modified if an acquiring entity is an original interest holder at the start of the arrangement.

For arrangements entered into after 7.30 pm (ACT time) on 13 May 2008, modifications to the CGT provisions prevent a market value cost base from arising when shares and certain other interests in a company are acquired by another company following a scrip for scrip CGT rollover under an arrangement that is taken to be a restructure. An arrangement will be taken to be a restructure if, just after the arrangement was completed, the market value of the replacement interests issued by the acquiring entity under the arrangement in exchange for qualifying interests in the original entity is more than 80% of the market value of all the shares (including options, rights and similar interests to acquire shares) issued by the replacement entity.

ROLLOVER FOR A FOREIGN RESIDENT

Rollover is not available to a foreign resident unless, just after the exchange, the replacement interest is 'taxable Australian property'.

CHOICE TO APPLY ROLLOVER

As each share or interest in a company or trust is treated as a separate asset for CGT purposes, where the scrip for scrip rollover conditions are satisfied, a taxpayer can choose to apply rollover in respect to some (not all) interests exchanged under the arrangement. There is no formal requirement for choosing scrip for scrip rollover. The way the taxpayer prepares their tax return is sufficient evidence of the making of a choice (s103-25(2)).

12.470   TAX RELIEF FOR DEMERGERS

Division 125 allows CGT rollover relief for demergers.

MEANING OF DEMERGER

A demerger involves the restructure of a company or unit or fixed trust by splitting the entity into two or more entities or groups, with the underlying owners holding one or more of those entities or groups directly.

For example, a demerger would happen if A Pty Ltd, which wholly owns B Pty Ltd, transfers its shareholding in B Pty Ltd to its shareholders. If the conditions of Division 125 are met the original shareholders in A Pty Ltd could claim demerger rollover relief as a result of the CGT event in respect of their original shareholding in A Pty Ltd (see following diagram).

Importantly in this example, after the demerger, shareholders A and B hold ownership interests in the same proportion in the demerged entity as they owned in the head entity of the demerged group.

A demerger of this type might also offer some tax benefits.

For example, assume the assets owned by A Pty Ltd comprised property and its shares in B Pty Ltd. The value of these assets is $4 million. B Pty Ltd conducts the business which is valued at $3 million. If A Pty Ltd sold its shares in B Pty Ltd it would be ineligible for the 50% CGT discount (which only applies to individuals and trusts).

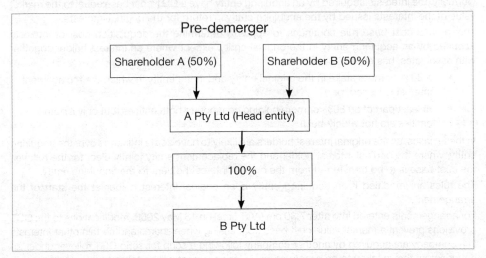

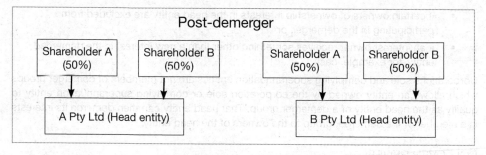

If A and B sell their shares in B Pty Ltd (after a demerger) they may be eligible for the 50% CGT discount. However, if access to the concession was the only reason for the restructure, it may not be regarded as a genuine demerger and any tax benefit obtained may be regarded as an unfranked dividend under s45B and s45C ITAA36.

Broadly, a company or trust is only the head entity of a demerger group if no other company or fixed trust member of the group holds ownership interests in the head entity (see ss125-65(3)).

 It is important that taxpayers in complex group structures correctly identify the head entity of the demerger group, otherwise no CGT rollover would be available upon restructure of the group.

ENTITIES THAT ARE ELIGIBLE FOR DEMERGER RELIEF

Demerger rollover is available to all entities, other than discretionary trusts and superannuation funds, when a demerging entity transfers or issues:

- at least 80% of the demerger group's ownership interests in a demerged entity to the interest owners of the head entity (the entity of the demerged group that no other member of the group owns any interest in), and
- the underlying ownership of the head entity is maintained as tested by examining proportional interests and market values of ownership interests.

TRIGGER FOR A DEMERGER

A demerger happens when a group of companies or trusts comprising a head entity and at least one demerger subsidiary (a demerger group) restructures and under that restructure:

- a demerger group transfers or issues at least 80% of the interests it owns in an entity (the demerged entity) to the owners of interests in the group's head entity
- a CGT event happens to the owners of original interests in the head entity or the owners simply acquire a new interest
- just after the demerger, each head entity interest owner owns the same proportion of ownership interests in the demerged entity as they owned in the head entity of the demerger group just before the demerger (proportion test)
- just after the demerger, the market value of the remaining original interests and the new interests must not be less than the market value of the original interests just before the demerger (market value test), and
- the new interests must be of a similar kind as the original interests. For example, if the original interest is a share in a company the new interest must be a share, it cannot be a unit or trust interest.

EXCEPTIONS

Rollover relief for a demerger will not apply:

- if the interest owner is a foreign resident and the new interests acquired under the demerger are not 'taxable Australian property' just after they were acquired (ss125-55(2))
- if another CGT rollover can be utilised

- if certain owners of ownership interests in the head entity are excluded from participating in the demerger, or
- if an interest owner receives something other than a new interest in the demerged entity, for example, cash.

Corporations sole and complying superannuation entities are not members of demerger groups which allows an entity owned by the corporation sole or complying superannuation entity to qualify as the head entity of a demerger group. That head entity can then demerge its interests in a member of the demerger group to the owners of the head entity.

ROLLOVER RELIEF

FOR OWNERS OF INTERESTS

Where an interest owner chooses demerger rollover relief, any capital gain or capital loss made from an original interest is disregarded (s125-80). This means:

- the pre-CGT status of ownership interests is maintained, subject to CGT event K6, and
- the original cost bases of the ownership interest are apportioned between an entity's ownership interest in the original entity and in the demerged entity, based upon their market values.

While CGT event K6 normally does not apply to shares listed on an official stock exchange, it does apply where those shares have not been listed on an official stock exchange at all times in the period of five years before disposal. Companies formed as a result of a demerger are usually not listed on a stock exchange until the demerger happens. Consequently, CGT event K6 could apply to change a pre-CGT interest to a post-CGT interest if a shareholder with pre-CGT shares disposes of the shares that they have acquired in the new post-demerger company and the combined period that the head entity and the demerged entity have been continuously listed on an official stock exchange is not at least five years. If the combined period is five years or more, then CGT event K6 does not apply to a demerger.

If an interest owner does not choose the rollover, the cost base and reduced cost base of those interests must be adjusted to reflect the change in value caused by the demerger (s125-85, 125-90 and 125-95).

However, it should be noted that where a demerger happens to a demerger group and no CGT event happens to a pre-CGT interest, there is no CGT rollover relief and the new interest acquired in the demerged entity will not be treated as a pre-CGT interest.

FOR MEMBERS OF DEMERGER GROUP

A demerging entity disregards a capital gain or capital loss made from CGT event A1, C2, C3 or K6 happening to its ownership interests in a demerged entity under a demerger (s125-155).

CGT event J1 does not happen to a demerged entity or to any other member of the demerger group when CGT event A1 or C2 happens to a demerging entity under a demerger (s125-160).

ADJUSTMENTS REQUIRED AFTER THE DEMERGER

CAPITAL LOSS ADJUSTMENTS

If a capital loss is ultimately made by a member of a demerger group because the demerger decreased the market value of an asset, the capital loss is reduced by the amount reasonably attributable to the reduction in the market value of that asset caused by the demerger (s125-165).

COST BASE REDUCTIONS

If, because of a demerger, the value of an asset is reduced and that asset is transferred after the demerger, the reduced cost base of the asset is reduced by the decrease in value caused by the demerger (s125-170).

12.472 DEMUTUALISATION

Where a member of a life or general insurance company agrees to surrender their rights in exchange for shares in the demutualised entity and the demutualisation is in accordance with one of seven specified methods in Division 9AA ITAA36:

- any capital gain or capital loss arising from this CGT event is disregarded
- no CGT liability will arise for the member until a subsequent CGT event happens to the demutualisation shares, and
- for CGT purposes, members will receive an enhanced cost base for the demutualisation shares that broadly reflects their market value (see Subdivision 126-E).

From 1 July 2007, Division 315 was introduced to the ITAA97 extending the exemption from capital gains and losses to policyholders on the demutualisation of private health insurers. Policyholders who receive shares or rights in the demutualised health insurer receive a market value cost base, and the acquisition date of the shares will be when the shares were received, not when the policy under the health insurance policy commenced.

NOTE: It has been announced that similar CGT relief will be legislated for the demutualisation of friendly societies. A discussion paper has been issued for this purpose seeking comments regarding the proposal.

12.475 BUSINESS REORGANISATION

Rollover relief may be available where a business or other entity is reorganised, thus deferring the CGT liability.

12.480   SOLE TRADER OR TRUSTEE TO COMPANY TRANSFERS

An individual or a trustee may transfer an asset to a company without incurring a CGT liability at the time of transfer where CGT events A1, D1, D2, D3 or F1 happen (Subdivision 122-A), if a choice is made for the subdivision to apply.

Rollover relief only applies to:

- a resident (including a trustee of a trust estate) transferring an asset to a resident company
- a foreign resident transferring an asset that is 'taxable Australian property' at the time of the transfer to a resident company, or
- a foreign resident transferring an asset that is 'taxable Australian property' at the time of the transfer to a foreign resident company.

Rollover relief is not available for a collectable, personal use asset or a decoration awarded for valour or brave conduct (unless the taxpayer provided consideration for it) or an asset that will become trading stock after the disposal. Certain other assets known as 'precluded assets' cannot be individually rolled over although they may be subject to a rollover where all the assets are transferred. 'Precluded assets' include depreciating assets, trading stock and an interest in a film copyright.

Other requirements which must be satisfied before an asset can be rolled over are:

- any consideration for the CGT event must consist only of non-redeemable shares in the company
- the market value of the shares must be substantially the same as that of the rollover asset, reduced by the value of liabilities assumed in respect of the asset, and
- immediately after the CGT event happening (the trigger event) the taxpayer must be the beneficial owner of all the shares in the company, or if a trustee, held upon the same trust (see ss122-20 and ss120-25(1)).

Subdivision 122-A can still apply where:

- a taxpayer disposes of an asset to a company in which they hold all the existing issued shares and do not receive any additional shares or other consideration for the disposal (ATO ID 2004/94)

- a taxpayer disposes of an asset to a company and the current shareholders transfer all their shares to the taxpayer as consideration for the disposal, without the company issuing any additional shares.

 If two or more individuals jointly own an asset there is no rollover relief available because neither will own all the shares in the company just after the disposal. Joint trustees are treated as a single entity for rollover purposes (ATO ID 2004/8). For partners, see 12.485.

If the taxpayer chooses rollover relief, any capital gain or loss made from the trigger event is disregarded.

If the asset was acquired before 20 September 1985, the taxpayer will be taken to have acquired the shares before that day assuming no precluded assets were transferred.

However, where precluded assets have been transferred such shares will not be regarded as pre-CGT acquired shares to the extent that the market value of the precluded assets comprised part of the total market value of assets transferred. In these circumstances the portion of the shares issued in respect of the precluded assets transferred will be taken to be post CGT acquired shares which will have a cost base reflecting the net market value of the precluded assets transferred.

Pre-CGT acquired assets transferred by an individual or trustee to a company retain their pre-CGT status. If a company makes a profit on disposal of a pre-CGT asset, it is still assessable to a shareholder when distributed as a pre-liquidation dividend. Any gain or loss from the disposal of a precluded asset are not subject to CGT.

Note also that when an individual or trustee chooses a roll-over under Subdivision 122-A for the disposal of pre-CGT assets to a company, the cost base of the pre-CGT assets acquired by the company is worked out based on an acquisition time of before 20 September 1985 and not the day the pre-CGT assets were transferred (see ATO ID 2014/4 for details).

For an asset acquired after 19 September 1985, the first element in each share's cost base is the asset's cost base when disposed of (less any liabilities assumed) and the market value of any precluded assets transferred divided by the number of shares.

The company acquires the asset at a cost base equal to the individual's or trustee's cost base (indexed but frozen at 30 September 1999) (or if a loss, the reduced cost base) at the date of disposal to the company. For a disposal by the company within 12 months of the date of acquisition by the individual or trustee, that individual's or trustee's unindexed cost base is used to calculate any gain. Any gain or loss from the on disposal of precluded assets will not be subject to CGT.

Where the asset transferred by an individual or trustee to a company is one that has been created, so that CGT event D1, D2, D3 or F1 is the trigger event, the first element in determining the cost base of each share is the incidental costs involved in creating the asset divided by the number of shares, plus any cost in transferring the property to the company (s122-65).

12.485 PARTNERSHIP TO COMPANY TRANSFERS

If *all* partners so choose, the partners in a partnership may transfer an asset to a company without incurring a CGT liability at the time of transfer where CGT events A1, D1, D2, D3 or F1 happen (Subdivision 122-B). See 12.550 for discussion of the CGT treatment of partnerships.

WHEN DOES ROLLOVER RELIEF APPLY?

For rollover relief to apply:

- the choice to rollover must have been made by all partners
- the consideration for the disposal of each partner's interest in a CGT asset must consist only of non-redeemable shares in the company
- the market value of the shares which each partner receives for the trigger event happening must be substantially the same as the market value of their interests in the asset or assets transferred to the company, reduced by the total amount of any liabilities which the company assumed in connection with the transfer

- immediately after the transfer of the asset all of the shares in the company are beneficially owned by the ex-partners and each ex-partner owns shares in the company in the same proportions that they held their interests in the partnership assets before the transfer. If partners are trustees, shares must be held upon the same trust

- if the ex-partner or company receiving the asset is a foreign resident, the asset must be 'taxable Australian property' at the time of transfer (ss122-135(6) and (7)).

WHEN DOES ROLLOVER RELIEF NOT APPLY?

Rollover relief is not available for a collectable, personal use asset or a decoration awarded for valour or brave conduct (unless the taxpayer provided consideration for it) or an asset that will become trading stock after the disposal. Certain other assets known as 'precluded assets' cannot be individually rolled over although they may be subject to a rollover where all the assets are transferred. 'Precluded assets' include depreciating assets, trading stock and an interest in a film copyright.

ACQUISITION DATES AND COST BASES OF TRANSFERRED ASSETS

The dates of acquisition and the cost bases of the assets which were transferred to the company are determined according to the particular dates of acquisition and cost bases to the individual ex-partners of their interest in the transferred asset.

Broadly, where the partners held pre-20 September 1985 interests in the transferred assets, that proportion will be taken to be pre-CGT acquired assets in the hands of the company. However, where the interest in the partnership asset transferred comprised an interest in a precluded asset, the shares will be deemed to have been acquired post CGT with a cost base calculated according to the proportional market value of the precluded assets vis a vis the total assets transferred.

Interests in pre-CGT acquired assets transferred by each partner are taken to be pre-CGT assets acquired by the company which will not be subject to CGT if a subsequent CGT event happens. Any gain or loss on the disposal of precluded assets will not be subject to CGT.

For an interest in a partnership asset acquired after 19 September 1985, the first element in each share's cost base is the asset's cost base when disposed of (less any liabilities assumed) and the net market value of any precluded assets transferred divided by the number of shares.

The company acquires the post CGT acquired assets at a cost base equal to the total of each individual's partner's cost base (or reduced cost base) for the post CGT acquired assets transferred.

12.487   FIXED TRUST TO COMPANY TRANSFERS

Subdivision 124-N provides for CGT rollover relief where the assets of a fixed trust are transferred to a company (from 11 November 1999).

In brief, to qualify for CGT rollover, after commencement of the trust restructuring period (see below):

- a trust (or two or more trusts) must dispose of all of its assets (apart from assets retained to pay existing or expected debts) to a single Australian resident company

- CGT event E4 must be capable of applying to all the units and interests in the trust(s)

- the beneficiaries' units and interests in the trust(s) must be exchanged for shares in the new company in the same proportion as they held units or an interest in the trust,

- the market value of beneficiaries' interests in the trust and market value of their shares in the company must be at least substantially the same, and

- the entities involved must choose the rollover.

The trust restructuring period starts just before the first asset is disposed of by the trust to the company under a trust restructure, and ends when the last CGT asset is disposed of to the company. The first disposal must be on or after 11 November 1999 to be eligible for CGT rollover relief.

The new company will generally be a shelf company because the company must:

- never have carried on any commercial activities

- have no CGT assets other than small amounts of cash or debt
- have no losses of any kind, and
- not be an entity exempt from income tax (ss124-860(4)).

However, the entity receiving the asset may hold rights under an arrangement that facilitates the transfer of assets to that entity. These rights, when treated collectively, must only be used to facilitate the transfer of assets from the transferring entity to the receiving entity. This requirement would be satisfied where the receiving entity holds any rights that only have a function of facilitating the transfer of assets to that entity, including:

- rights that stipulate that particular assets will be transferred to the receiving entity;
- rights that are required to be held by the receiving entity, to the extent they are required to facilitate the transfer of assets to that entity; and
- ancillary rights arising from other rights, whereby these other rights facilitate the transfer of assets to the receiving entity.

Green Trust (Green) plans to dispose of its assets to a newly established company, Yellow Pty Ltd (Yellow). Yellow holds a deed which stipulates that as a result of the restructure the ownership of Green's assets will be transferred to Yellow at a particular point in time.

As all of these rights under the deed facilitate the transfer of assets from Green to Yellow, they are ignored for the purposes of determining whether the roll-over conditions in Subdivision 124-N are satisfied.

Where the trustee of the trust is itself a company (a corporate trustee), rather than establish a new company for the purposes of the rollover, the trust can dispose of its assets to the corporate trustee and be eligible for the rollover without the conditions in ss124-860(4) having to apply (ss124-860(5)). However, there is a problem if the corporate trustee already owns CGT assets before the start of the trust restructuring period. If this occurs the proportionate interest test in ss124-860(6) may not be satisfied because the market value of the interests in the trust may be less than the market value of the shares in the company.

An election to rollover means that any capital gain or capital loss made in respect of

- a trust disposing of an asset to a company, and
- a beneficiary's interest in the trust being exchanged for a share in the company

is disregarded.

This will mean that the pre-CGT and post-CGT characteristics of trust interests will be transferred proportionately to the shares acquired. Shares acquired by a beneficiary are acquired on the date of the contract, or if there is no contract, on the date that the shares were allocated (s109-10). However, for the purpose of applying the CGT discount to a subsequent CGT event, ss115-30(1) Item 2 provides that the ownership period commences from the date of acquisition of the original trust interest that was replaced by shares.

Rollover is not available where an asset is trading stock of the trust or will be trading stock of the company when it acquires it from the trust (ss124-870(5)).

The trust must cease to exist within six months from the disposal of the first asset to the company, otherwise CGT event J4 will reverse the rollover if the company owns the asset when the trust fails to cease to exist (s104-195). In limited circumstances, the 6-month period can be extended. An example would be if the trustee is involved in litigation concerning the trust and cannot wind up the trust until litigation is finished.

If CGT event J4 applies, it is the company (not the trust) that will make the capital gain or capital loss under CGT event J4. The company makes a capital gain if the CGT asset's market value at the time the company acquired the asset from the trust is more than its cost base at that time. The company makes a capital loss if that market value is less than the asset's reduced cost base at the time the company acquired the asset (ss104-195(4)).

As with the company, the shareholder (former beneficiary) will make a capital gain under CGT event J4 if the market value of the shares acquired by the shareholder under the trust restructure is more than the share's cost base at the time the shares were acquired. A capital loss will arise if the market value of the shares is less than the shares' reduced cost base at the time the shareholder acquired them (ss104-195(6)).

12.489 AUSTRALIAN PROPERTY TRUSTS AND STAPLED SECURITIES

A CGT rollover applies to holders of ownership interests of stapled entities where interest-holders dispose of their interests in the stapled entities, in exchange for a proportionate number of ownership interests in a public unit trust which is placed in between the interest-holder and the stapled entity. This will allow Australian listed property trusts to re-organise their stapled structures to allow a head trust to be inserted so that they are treated as a single entity for the purposes of overseas acquisitions. The rollover applies to CGT events that happen on or after 1 July 2006 (see Subdivision 124-Q).

12.490 CONVERSION BY A BODY TO AN INCORPORATED COMPANY

The ITAA97 has been amended to expand the existing CGT roll-over for the change of a body to an incorporated company.
The amendments:

- allow Indigenous bodies to incorporate as *Corporations (Aboriginal and Torres Strait Islander) Act 2006* corporations without immediate CGT consequences for the body's members
- allow Indigenous companies incorporated under the Corporations Act to change their incorporation to the *Corporations (Aboriginal and Torres Strait Islander) Act 2006* without immediate CGT consequences
- extend the existing roll-over by allowing the value of rights associated with a body to be reflected in the shares issued by the company, when the body changes its incorporation
- allow members to access the roll-over where the body winds up and is replaced by a new company incorporated under a different law (the 'reincorporation roll-over')
- provide a tax neutral outcome for the CGT, depreciating, revenue and trading stock assets of a body that winds up and is replaced by a company incorporated under a different law.

CHANGE OF INCORPORATION WITHOUT CHANGE IN ENTITY

These amendments provide a CGT roll-over for members of bodies that change their incorporation from one law to another without forming a new legal entity where:

- a body incorporated under a law other than the Corporations Act (or a similar foreign law relating to companies) changes its incorporation to either the Corporations Act or a similar foreign law — this roll-over is a continuation of the roll-over currently available under Subdivision 124-I, or
- a body incorporated under a law other than the *Corporations (Aboriginal and Torres Strait Islander) Act 2006* changes its incorporation to that Act.

In order for the roll-over to apply, it must be reasonable to conclude that there is no significant difference between the ownership, or the mix of the ownership, of the body just before and just after the conversion. The first part of this ownership test requires that it is reasonable to conclude that there is no significant difference between the ownership of the body and rights relating to the body (held by the entities that owned the body) just before conversion occurs, and the ownership of the company just after conversion. The second part of this ownership test, which concerns the mix of ownership, requires the owners of the body to have no significant difference between their proportional ownership of the company just after the conversion and their proportional ownership of the body just before the conversion occurred.

If the conditions for the roll-over to apply are met, the taxpayer may choose the roll-over where certain other conditions are satisfied. First, the taxpayer must receive only shares in the new company. Therefore, any rights relating to the body that were held by the taxpayer prior to the conversion, must be reflected in new shares that replicate their value to the taxpayer. Second, the taxpayer must be an Australian resident at the time the body is converted to a company or, if the taxpayer is a foreign resident, the interests in the body and any rights related to the body that they held must have been taxable Australian property just before the conversion time, and the shares in the company they receive must be taxable Australian property when they are issued.

If these other conditions are met, the taxpayer may choose to obtain the roll-over, with the standard roll-over consequences set out in Subdivision 124-A applying. Generally, this means a taxpayer that satisfies the conditions for the roll-over disregards any capital gains or capital losses arising from the ending of their membership interests in the body or rights relating to the body. However, these amendments make specific modifications to the standard roll-over consequences for this roll-over where the taxpayer has a mix of pre-CGT and post-CGT interests and rights.

Corporations (Aboriginal and Torres Strait Islander) Act 2006 corporations do not issue shares to their members but issue 'rights as a member of the Corporations (Aboriginal and Torres Strait Islander) Act 2006 corporation'. Thus the taxpayer's previously held ownership interests and any rights relating to the original body should be replaced by rights as a member of the Corporations (Aboriginal and Torres Strait Islander) Act 2006 corporation.

OLD CORPORATION IS WOUND UP

This CGT roll-over requires the original body to cease to exist and the company which is replacing it to continue to exist after the time the members of the original body have received shares in the new company, or, if it is a *Corporations (Aboriginal and Torres Strait Islander) Act 2006* corporation, received rights as a member of the *Corporations (Aboriginal and Torres Strait Islander) Act 2006* corporation.

Similar to the CGT roll-over for conversions of incorporation described above, the members of the original body must receive only shares in the new converted company, or, rights as a member of the *Corporations (Aboriginal and Torres Strait Islander) Act 2006* corporation. The shares or rights as a member of the *Corporations (Aboriginal and Torres Strait Islander) Act 2006* corporation must be received in exchange for the member's interests and rights ending, and not for any other reasons.

Similar to the CGT roll-over for conversions of incorporation, there must be consistency in the ownership of the entities subject to the roll-over. Also, the provision takes both the ownership of the body, that is, membership interests in the body, and rights relating to the body that were held by owners of the body, into account when assessing the continuity of ownership.

For the roll-over to apply the original body must dispose of all of its CGT assets to the new company. This ensures that the new company is the entity that continues to carry on the business. However, there is a limited exception to this requirement which allows the original body to retain some assets in order to meet existing or expected liabilities on winding-up.

If the conditions for the roll-over to apply are met, the taxpayer may choose the roll-over for their interest in the original body and any associated rights where certain other conditions apply. The other conditions are that:

- the taxpayer must have been a member of the original body just before the 'switch time' (the 'switch time' is the time when the members receive the shares in the company or their rights in the *Corporations (Aboriginal and Torres Strait Islander) Act 2006* corporation)
- the taxpayer's ownership interest in the original body must end after the switch time (known as the 'end time')
- at the end time, the taxpayer must have the shares in the new company that they received at the switch time, and
- the taxpayer must be an Australian resident, or if they are a foreign resident, the interests (or any rights) in the original body held just before the end time must be taxable Australian property and the shares in the new company received at the switch time must be taxable Australian property at the end time.

CONSEQUENCES OF THE ROLL-OVERS

If a taxpayer is entitled to choose the conversion of incorporation or the reincorporation roll-over, the standard roll-over consequences set out in Subdivision 124-A apply (see 12.450). However, these amendments make specific modifications to the standard roll-over consequences where the taxpayer has a mix of pre-CGT and post-CGT interests and rights.

If a taxpayer has chosen the conversion of incorporation or reincorporation roll-over and their interests in the original body or rights relating to the original body - the original assets - that they held were a mix of pre-CGT and post-CGT assets, there are special consequences for the shares that replaced the original assets. If some of the original assets that were replaced by shares in the company were pre-CGT assets and some were post-CGT assets, some of the shares in the new company are taken to be pre-CGT assets as is reasonable having regard to the number and market value of the:

- original assets, and
- shares in the new company.

For the shares which are not pre-CGT assets, the taxpayer calculates the first element of the cost base of each post-CGT share as is reasonable having regard to the:

- total cost bases of the original post-CGT assets, and
- number and market value of the replacement post-CGT shares.

The reduced cost base of the post-CGT shares is worked out similarly.

If the taxpayer has chosen the conversion of incorporation or reincorporation roll-over and, under the conversion or reincorporation, they receive rights as a member of a *Corporations (Aboriginal and Torres Strait Islander) Act 2006* corporation, there is a special rule where the original assets are a mix of pre-CGT and post-CGT assets. Under the special rule, if the taxpayer has acquired any of the original assets before 20 September 1985, they are taken to have acquired all of their replacement assets before that day. This means that the rights they receive in the *Corporations (Aboriginal and Torres Strait Islander) Act 2006* corporation are pre-CGT assets.

A ROLL-OVER FOR ASSETS OF AN ENTITY WINDING UP

Where an original body disposes of a CGT asset to the company replacing it because the body ceases to exist, the capital gain or loss the body makes on the transfer of that CGT asset is disregarded.

Where an original body disposes of a CGT asset to the new company and the body ceases to exist, the first element of the CGT asset's cost base for the new company is the asset's cost base when it was disposed of by the original body. The first element of the reduced cost base for the CGT asset for the new company is worked out similarly. If the original body acquired the asset before 20 September 1985, it will retain its pre-CGT status for the new company.

The disposal of a depreciating asset to a new company will cause a 'balancing adjustment event' (as defined by s40-295) to occur. A balancing adjustment event may require the original body disposing of the depreciating asset to adjust its taxable income.

Where there is a difference between the asset's termination value (that is, the final sale price) and its adjustable value (that is, the original cost less the decline in value while it was held by the taxpayer) a balancing adjustment may be assessable or deductible under s40-285. However, s40-285 will not apply if the roll-over provided by s40-340 applies. The ITAA97 applies as if there was roll-over relief under ss40-340(1) and the original body was the transferor and the new company was the transferee mentioned in that subsection and ss328-243(1A). This formulation means there is automatic roll-over relief under ss40-340(1) for a body that is not a small business entity for any assessable balancing adjustment arising from the transfer of a depreciating asset to the new company (if the body is a SBE the roll-over relief under ss40-340(1) is contingent on the conditions in ss328-243(1A) being met apart from paragraph 328-243(1A)(c). The effects of the ITAA97 applying as if there were roll-over relief under ss40-340(1) include that:

- the balancing adjustment event does not affect the original body's assessable income or deductions (ss40-345(1))
- the new company can claim depreciation deductions for the depreciating asset's decline in value on the same basis that the original body did (ss40-345(2)), and
- the new company is treated as if it had carried out any acts that the original body had carried out in relation to the asset and the application of Division 45, which concerns the disposal of leases and leased plant (ss40-350(1)).

The company is taken to have held the item as trading stock from the date it bought the item from the original body which has the effect of giving the original body a nil profit and a nil loss for the income year it ceased to hold the item of trading stock. The company, is taken to have acquired the trading stock held by the original body for the same value that the original body was taken to have received for the trading stock.

A revenue asset is defined in s977-50 as an asset for which a profit or loss on disposal, on ceasing to own the asset, or other realisation is taken into account in calculating assessable income other than as a capital gain or loss and is neither trading stock nor a depreciating asset. The original body is taken to have disposed of revenue assets to the new company for an amount that would result in the original body not making a profit or loss because of the disposal. The new company is taken to have paid the original body the amount to acquire the asset that resulted in that body not making a profit or loss.

12.495   EXCHANGE OF SHARES, UNITS, RIGHTS OR OPTIONS

Rollover relief can apply where there is a reorganisation of share or unit capital within a company or unit trust (s124-240 and s124-245).

The reorganisation must achieve a consolidation or splitting of the share or unit holdings. The company or trustee redeems or cancels all shares or units and issues new shares or units (and nothing else) in substitution for the original shares or units.

The taxpayer may choose rollover relief where these conditions are satisfied and:

- the market value of the new shares or units after issue is at least equal to the market value of the original shares or units before they were redeemed or cancelled
- there is no change in the paid-up share capital (this rule does not apply to an exchange of units), and
- the taxpayer is a resident, or if not, the original shares or units were 'taxable Australian property' and the new shares or units are 'taxable Australian property' when issued.

Similar rules apply to exchange of rights or options for new rights or options (s124-295 and s124-300).

12.500   EXCHANGE OF SHARES BETWEEN TWO COMPANIES

Rollover relief can apply if a resident company is interposed between a shareholder and the resident company in which the shares are held (Division 615. Formerly Subdivision 124-G).

Division 615 allows taxpayers to choose for transactions under a scheme to restructure a company's or unit trust's business to be tax neutral if, under the scheme, they cease to own shares in the company or units in the trust and in exchange, they become the owner of new shares in another company. This Division deals with two cases of company reorganisations:

- the disposal of shares in one company to another company (the interposed company) in exchange for new shares in an interposed company (disposal case), and
- the redemption or cancellation of shares held in one company and the issue of new shares in the other company (redemption or cancellation case).

But unlike the previous subdivision 124-G, this Division will apply to trading stock and revenue assets as well.

You can choose to obtain Division 615 roll-over if:

- you are a member of a company or a unit trust (the original entity), and
- you and at least one other entity (the exchanging members) own all the shares or units in it, and
- under a scheme for reorganising its affairs, the exchanging members dispose of all their shares or units in it to a company (the interposed company) in exchange for shares in the interposed company (and nothing else).

The interposed company must own all the shares or units in the original entity immediately after the completion time all the exchanging members have had their shares or units in the original entity disposed of, redeemed or cancelled under the scheme.

Also, immediately after the completion time, each exchanging member must own:

- a whole number of shares in the interposed company, and
- a percentage of the shares in the interposed company that were issued to all the exchanging members that is equal to the percentage of the shares or units in the original entity that were owned by the member and disposed of, redeemed or cancelled under the scheme.

The following ratios must also be equal:

- the market value of each exchanging member's shares in the interposed company, **to**
- the market value of the shares in the interposed company issued to all the exchanging members (worked out immediately after the completion time)

and:

- the market value of that member's shares or units in the original entity that were disposed of, redeemed or cancelled under the scheme, **to**
- the market value of all the shares or units in the original entity that were disposed of, redeemed or cancelled under the scheme (worked out immediately before the first disposal, redemption or cancellation).

EXAMPLE

There are 100 shares in A Pty Ltd (the original entity), all having the same rights. B Pty Ltd (the interposed company) acquires all the shares in A by issuing each shareholder in A 10 shares in itself for each share they have in A. All shares in B have the same rights. Bill owned 15 shares in A and received 150 shares in B in exchange.

EXAMPLE

There are 1,000 units in the A unit trust (the original entity), all having the same rights. Two new units in A are issued to B Pty Ltd (the interposed company), and all other units in A are cancelled. Each unitholder in A is issued 10 shares in B for each 100 units they have in A. All shares in B have the same rights. Alison owned 200 units in A and received 20 shares in B in exchange.

Generally, a choice to apply the rollover must be made within two months of the transfer.

Division 615 applies to exchange of units in a unit trust for shares in a company (formerly subdivision 124-H).

12.510 ASSET TRANSFERS BETWEEN CERTAIN GROUP COMPANIES

Subdivision 126-B allows, in limited circumstances, a company to obtain rollover relief if it transfers a CGT asset between wholly-owned group companies as a result of CGT events A1 and B1 (disposal cases) or CGT events D1, D2, D3 and F1 (creation cases).

This rollover relief ceased to apply to asset transfers between resident companies in a wholly owned group after 30 June 2003, or before 1 July 2004 for a group of companies with a substituted accounting period, apparently due to the introduction of the tax consolidation regime.

The rollover relief still applies after these dates where the assets are transferred between:

- foreign resident companies
- a foreign resident company and the head company of a consolidated group, or
- a foreign resident company and a resident company that is not a member of a consolidated group.

Where CGT event B1 happens, title in the CGT asset must pass to the transferee at or before the end of the agreement, otherwise rollover is unavailable.

Rollover relief can apply provided:

- the transferee and the transferor companies are members of the same 'wholly-owned group' of companies at the time of the trigger event. ('Wholly-owned group' is defined in Subdivision 975-W of the ITAA, and the 'trigger event' is the transfer of the asset to, or the creation of a CGT asset in, another company that is a member of the same wholly-owned group)
- the transferred asset cannot be trading stock, or a right, option or convertible note that if exercised would result in the acquisition of trading stock in the hands of the transferee
- the recipient company must not be exempt from income tax because it is an exempt entity in the income year that the transfer occurred

- the asset must be transferred by, or to, a foreign resident company, and be 'taxable Australian property' in the hands of both the company which transfers it, and the company which receives it, and

- both the transferee and the transferor companies must choose to obtain rollover relief.

The choice is made when the income tax return is lodged in the year of the CGT event. The way entities prepare their returns is generally evidence of the choice having been made, although there are exceptions in ss103-25(3). While it will be evident by the transferor not claiming the capital gain, there will be no evidence in the return of the transferee until a subsequent CGT event happens. For this reason it is recommended that a formal written election be made.

From 21 October 1999, amendments to Subdivision 126-B ensure that rollover will not apply where the transfer would have resulted in a capital loss or deduction, unless it is a pre-CGT asset, in which case the only effect of the rollover is the preserve that pre-CGT status.

IMPORTANT: The ITAA97 has been amended to allow resident shareholders in a company which uses a share or interest sale facility in a restructure involving foreign shareholders to access a range of CGT roll-overs previously denied to them. The amendments apply to CGT events happening after 7.30 pm (AEST) on 11 May 2010. These amendments facilitate the use of share sale facilities in the CGT entity restructure roll-overs in Subdivisions 124-G, 124-H, 124-I, 124-N, 124-Q and 126-G and Division 125. These amendments do this by treating a foreign interest holder as owning an interest in a relevant entity at a time where the share sale facility owns that interest, provided the following conditions are satisfied:

- the foreign interest holder owns an interest in a relevant entity (or for Subdivision 124-I cases, owns an interest in a body, with or without rights relating to the body)

- a transaction happens to the original interest

- a foreign law impedes an entity's ability to issue or transfer an interest to the foreign interest holder, or alternatively, it would be impractical or unreasonably onerous to determine whether a foreign law impedes the entity's ability to issue or transfer the interest to the foreign interest holder

- a share sale facility will acquire the interest instead of the foreign interest holder, and

- under the share sale facility, the foreign interest holder is entitled to receive the capital proceeds (less any expenses or taxes) when the share sale facility disposes of the interest.

Under these amendments, using a share sale facility ensures that Australian residents for tax purposes (or foreign residents with taxable Australian property) can satisfy the same ownership requirements in each of the relevant roll-overs.

12.515 VALUE SHIFTING

The General Value Shifting Regime (GVSR) (contained in Division 725) applies from 1 July 2002. Generally, the GVSR will affect equity and loan interests in companies and trusts where the owners of the interests satisfy a controller/associate test and the entities are not consolidated under the consolidations regime. A value shift occurs when something is done that results in the market value of one thing increasing (or being issued at a discount to market value), and the market value of another thing decreasing. The GVSR consists of three main areas.

DIRECT VALUE SHIFTING INVOLVING EQUITY AND LOAN INTERESTS IN A SINGLE COMPANY OR TRUST (DIV 725)

Direct Value Shifting (DVS) rules apply where under a scheme value is shifted from an equity or loan interest held directly in a company or trust that is controlled. Such a value shift might arise from a scheme that involves the issue of new shares or trust units at a discount to market value, buying back shares at less than market value or varying the rights attached to an existing interest. The value shift can be to a different owner or to the same owner, such as a shift in interest from a post-CGT asset to a pre-CGT asset or from trading stock to a CGT asset that is not trading stock. To be a direct value shift:

- there must be a scheme
- there must be a control requirement affecting controllers and their associates
- under the scheme there must be a decrease in the market value of one or more equity or loan interests in the target entity (a down interest) and an increase in the market value of one or more equity or loan interests in the target entity (an up interest)
- the direct value shift will not be reversed within four years under the same scheme, and
- the total value shift must be greater than $150,000 (or otherwise a de minimis exclusion applies).

Where these conditions are satisfied and the company or trust is closely held, any active participants may be affected, not just the affected owners and associates.

If value is shifted between affected owners' interests, Division 725 will generally result in a rearrangement to the cost base and reduced cost base of those interests to prevent inappropriate losses or gains when the interests are realised.

Under Division 725, the following consequences can arise for particular types of value shift:

- for shifts between interests held by the same affected owner – the adjustable value of the down and up interests are realigned, unless value is shifted from post-CGT to pre-CGT interests or between interests of a different tax character, in which case the pre-shift gains may be taxed
- for shifts between interests held by different affected owners – the adjustable value of the interests are realigned (in some cases, pre-shift gains may be taxed), or
- for shifts involving interests held by owners that are not affected owners – there are no consequences.

*Adjustable value is the cost base or reduced cost base as appropriate.

Tom, the sole owner and controller of a resident private company (holding the company's two ordinary shares each worth $1 million but with a cost base of $1,000 each), rather than sell 50% of his shareholding (1 ordinary share) to his son for $1,000 and incur a CGT liability, has his company issue two ordinary shares to his son, Jim, for $1,000 each. Under this arrangement, Tom as the individual controller has not disposed of anything to affect capital gains tax (CGT), but would have effectively shifted $999,000 in value to his son (an associate) without any tax effect, but for the GVSR.

After the value shift Tom's shares would be worth 2 x ($2.002 million/4) = $1.001 million and Jim's shares, (for which he paid $2,000), would also be worth $1.001 million.

Under the direct value shifting rules, the amount of gain assessed to Tom is based on the value shifted from the shares less a pro-rata allocation of their adjustable values. As Tom shifted $999,000 in value to his son, which represents 49.95% of the pre-shift value of his interests ($2 million), that proportion of cost base of Tom's shares is allowed as a reduction (ie. 49.95% x $2,000 = $999). Tom's assessable gain is $998,001 ($999,000 – $999).

The cost base of Jim's shares would be $1,001,000 ($2,000 (the price paid) + $999,000 (the value shifted to him).

A similar result would have followed if Tom and his son had both owned shares in the company from its incorporation and a shift were achieved by varying the rights attaching to their shares. As the GVSR also applies to trusts, there would be a similar result if the entity were a unit trust and either units were issued at undervalue to an associate or unit rights were varied and a new trust does not result.

DIRECT VALUE SHIFTING: CREATION OF RIGHTS OUT OF, OR OVER, A NON-DEPRECIATING ASSET

A direct value shift out of a non-depreciating asset occurs where:

- rights are created over a non-depreciating asset owned by any entity
- the rights to that asset are held by an associate of the entity at the time the entity realises the underlying asset at a loss
- the rights were acquired for less than market value and the market value of the right exceeded the consideration by more than $50,000 (the de minimis threshold), and

- the entity that created the rights then realised the non-depreciating asset at a loss where the loss (or part of it) arises because of a right created over the asset in an associate, and the market value of the right was not fully brought to tax on creation. There are back-up provisions if the asset has been subject to a CGT rollover (including a replacement-asset rollover), or if those replacement assets are themselves rolled over (Division 723).

X Co owns land with a reduced cost base of $60 million and a market value of $70 million. X Co grants an associated company (Y Co) a five year lease for no premium and no rental. This transaction allows Y Co unrestricted and exclusive use of the land for five years. Existing tax laws do not impute a market value consideration to the creator of this right. As a result of the creation of this right the market value of the land decreases by $15 million to $55 million. X Co then disposes of its reversionary interest in the land to a third party in an arm's length transaction for $55 million.

This transaction ensures X Co and its associate retain rent-free use of the land for the five years, and that a capital loss of $5 million would, but for this DVS rule, be realised. However, no economic loss has been suffered, so this DVS rule denies X Co the $5 million capital loss because this loss would not have arisen on realisation of the land if the right had not existed.

Division 723 can apply whether the underlying asset is dealt with on capital account, or is an item of trading stock or a revenue asset. There are special rules to reduce or remove the impact of the Division where the right has been realised and a capital gain or assessable income accrues to an associate. There are also special rules to deal with situations where the underlying asset is rolled over.

Division 723 does not apply:

- where an associate gives consideration of at least market value
- if the right was created upon the death of the owner of the underlying property, or is a conservation covenant over the land, or
- where the creation of the right effects a part realisation or disposal in part of the underlying asset, or where a more specific provision of the tax law treats the granting of the right as a disposal of the underlying asset, such as CGT event F2.

INDIRECT VALUE SHIFTS

An Indirect Value Shift (IVS) involves a reduction in the value of equity or loan interests in a company or trust (the losing entity) and an increase in the value of equity or loan interests in a related entity (the gaining entity), that results from an unequal exchange of value between those entities. The gaining entity can be any entity, including an individual (Division 727).

For an indirect value shift to occur:

- the economic benefits provided by one entity to another (whether or not it receives anything in return) must be 'in connection with' a scheme
- the entities must not be dealing at arm's length
- the market value of the benefits received must not equal the market value of the benefits provided, so that there is a losing entity and a gaining entity
- the losing entity and the gaining entity satisfy either the control test or common ownership test that applies only to closely-held entities, and
- the indirect value shift is more than $50,000.

The IVS rules are not attracted if parties deal at arm's length, where economic benefits are exchanged for market value, or where the indirect value shift does not exceed $50,000 (the de minimis threshold).

Where the IVS rules apply, no assessable gain or loss will arise but there will be an adjustment to the adjustable values of the equity or loan interests in the entities affected by the IVS.

Helen owns all the shares in A Co and B Co. In a non-arm's length dealing, A Co transfers an asset with a market value of $500,000 to B Co for a cash payment of $100,000. As a consequence, the market value of Helen's shares in A Co has declined by $400,000 and the market value of her interests in B Co has increased by $400,000.

There has been an indirect value shift of $400,000 from Helen's shares in A Co to her interests in B Co.

CONSEQUENCES OF A VALUE SHIFT

In summary, the consequences of a value shift are as follows.

- A direct value shift can result in:
    - a deemed gain (as if the asset had been partly disposed of) but not a loss
    - adjustments to adjustable values (cost bases) to realign the relationship of that value to market value, or
    - (under the special created rights rule) a reduction in a loss on realisation of a non-depreciating asset, whose market value was affected by created rights, or an adjustment to prevent such a loss arising on replacement interests if the non-depreciating asset was rolled over.
- An indirect value shift does not cause a deemed gain or loss to arise but can result in adjustments to realised losses and gains or adjustments to adjustable values (cost bases) to realign these values in accordance with shifts in market value.

12.525 SMALL BUSINESS CGT CONCESSIONS

There are four small business CGT concessions that may apply to reduce the CGT payable on a CGT event where the conditions in Division 152 are met.

The four concessions are:

- The 15-year exemption (Subdivision 152-B)
- The 50% reduction (Subdivision 152-C)
- The retirement concession (Subdivision 152-D)
- Rollover relief (Subdivision 152-E)

 There have been significant changes in recent years to both the basic conditions as well as the requirements for individual concessions. Below is an outline of the current rules.

BASIC CONDITIONS

For a business to qualify for any of these concessions the basic conditions in Subdivision 152-A must be met.

The basic conditions are:

- a capital gain would have resulted from a CGT event happening (except CGT event K7) in relation to a post CGT acquired asset owned or created by the entity (see ss152-10(1) and (s152-12)).
- the entity
    - is a 'small business entity' for the income year in which the event occurs being an entity carrying on a business which satisfies the $2 million aggregate turnover test (see s328-110), or
    - satisfies the maximum $6 million net asset value test (see s152-15), or
    - is a partnership that is a small business entity for the income year and the CGT asset is an asset of the partnership, or
    - satisfies the asset use and ownership arrangements set out in ss152-10(1A) or ss152-10(1B)
    - the CGT asset must satisfy the active asset test (see s152-35 and s152-40), and
- where the asset is a share in a company or interest in a trust, one of following two additional conditions must be met:
    - the entity claiming the concession must be a CGT concession stakeholder in the object company or trust just before the CGT event, or

-    the CGT concession stakeholders in the object company or trust must together have a small business participation percentage of at least 90% in the entity claiming the concession just before the CGT event (ss152-10(2)).

In addition to these basic conditions each of the four concessions may have extra conditions contained in the relevant subdivision.

Subdivision 152-A examines each of the above basic conditions by defining such terms as 'net value' of the CGT asset (s152-20) and active asset (s152-35). The definitions of 'small business entity' (s328-110), 'aggregate turnover' (s328-115), 'connected entity' (s328-125) and 'affiliate' (s328-130) are set out under Division 328 dealing with the small business entity regime. Each of these concepts is discussed further below.

The small business entity rules are discussed in Chapter 10.

SMALL BUSINESS ENTITY

Under Subdivision 328-C an entity is a **small business entity** if it:

- carries on a business, and
- satisfies the $2 million aggregated turnover test.

These concepts are discussed at 10.200.

NOTE: Previously, where an active asset is held by a non-business entity (and the asset is used in the business of an affiliate or connected entity), the relevant taxpayer did not have access to the '$2 million aggregated turnover' test. This is because the taxpayer is not in business and cannot qualify as a 'small business entity'. The law has been amended such that a 'non-business owner rule' allows a non-business taxpayer access to the $2 million aggregated turnover test where the non-business owner's affiliate or connected entity is a small business entity which uses the asset in its business. Further, the rule is available to a non-business asset owner who is a partner in a partnership which is a small business entity that uses the particular asset in the conduct of its business. This rule applies for CGT events happening from the 2007-08 income year. The relevant provisions are contained in ss152-10(1A) and ss152-10(1B).

MAXIMUM NET ASSET VALUE TEST: $6 MILLION THRESHOLD

A taxpayer satisfies this test if the total net value of the CGT assets owned by:

- the taxpayer
- any 'affiliate' of the taxpayer
- any entities 'connected with' the taxpayer, and
- any entities connected with the affiliate of the taxpayer

do not exceed $6 million just before the CGT event (see s152-15).

The assets of an affiliate, or entity connected with an affiliate (see below), should only be included if they are used or held ready for use in a business carried on by the taxpayer or an entity connected with the taxpayer.

Ted operates a garage as a sole proprietor. His wife, Mary operates a gift shop that is unrelated to the garage. Mary owns the land and the building from which Ted's garage operates and she leases it to Ted. Mary is Ted's affiliate. In determining Ted's net asset value, the market value of the land and building owned by Mary are included (as it is used in Ted's business), but the assets of Mary's gift shop are not included.

When identifying the CGT assets of a business taxpayer which is not a reporting entity, taxpayers should ensure that intangible assets such as goodwill and other items of intellectual property which are not recorded in the balance sheet for accounting purposes are taken into account for the purpose of this test.

In applying the net asset value test, 'net value' means the sum of the market values of CGT assets less the sum of the liabilities 'related to the assets' and any provisions for annual leave, long service leave, unearned income and taxes (ss152-20(1)). The term market value takes on its ordinary meaning, being the price that would be negotiated in an open and unrestricted market between a knowledgeable, willing but not anxious buyer and a knowledgeable, willing but not anxious seller acting at arm's length. This calculation can result in a negative value and that negative value can be taken into account in determining if another entity satisfies the test. See *Venturi and Commissioner of Taxation* [2011] AATA 588 and *Sytadell and Holdings Pty Ltd and Commissioner of Taxation* [2011] AATA 589 for examples of where taxpayers failed to discharge the onus of establishing the correctness of market valuations used for the purposes of the Maximum Net Asset Value (MNAV) test in s152-15. See also *Commissioner of Taxation v Byrne Hotels Qld Pty Ltd* [2011] FCAFC for an example of where the costs of sale relating to the disposal of a hotel business constituted liabilities for the purposes of the maximum net asset value test.

The issue of when liabilities are 'related to the assets' was considered in *Bell v Commissioner of Taxation (2012) FCAFC32 and Scanlon v Commissioner of Taxation [2014] AATA 725.*

Joel has CGT assets with a value of $9.3 million and liabilities relating to the assets of $2.3 million. Joel has made provisions of $200,000 for employee's annual leave, $10,000 for unearned income and $60,000 for tax liabilities for the financial year. Joel has a net asset value of $6.73 million.

If X Co has CGT assets with a value of $3 million and liabilities relating to those assets of $4 million, its net asset value is negative $1 million. If Joel in the above example owns 70% of the shares in X Co it would be a connected entity and Joel's net asset value is reduced by $1 million to $5.73 million. Accordingly, Joel would pass the $6 million net asset value test.

It is also worth noting that the Commissioner has successfully applied Part IVA to schemes undertaken by taxpayers to get their maximum net assets under $6 million (Re *Track and Ors v FCT* [2015] AATA 45).

When working out the net value of the CGT assets, shares, units or other interests (except debt) in a connected entity or affiliate are disregarded (as the underlying assets are included). Where the taxpayer is an individual, the following assets are also disregarded when determining the net value of assets:

- assets used solely for the personal use and enjoyment of the individual or the individual's affiliate
- rights to amounts payable out of a superannuation fund or approved deposit fund, and
- policies of insurance on the life of the individual.

If the individual's main residence is not used solely for personal use and enjoyment and the individual would have been entitled to an interest deduction on a portion of the home (even where no borrowing exists on the home), the percentage of the income-producing use is multiplied by the current market value to work out the value of the dwelling that should be included in net value of CGT assets. This calculation will take into account the length of time and percentage of income-producing use of the dwelling (ss152-20(2A)).

Although a depreciating asset (as defined under Division 40) used wholly for a taxable purpose has been removed from the CGT regime, a depreciating asset is still a CGT asset and must be included in the maximum net asset value test. Similarly, all assets like investments generating a passive income stream should be included.

Under the previous law, liabilities relating to excluded shares units and similar interests were excluded when applying the $6 million net asset value test because the excluded interests do not form part of the 'net value of CGT assets'.
The law has now been amended to allow such borrowings to be subtracted when determining the net value of CGT assets on the basis that they indirectly relate to the net asset value of connected entities or affiliates counted under the test. This is to prevent double counting. This provision applies from 23 June 2009.

CONNECTED ENTITY

An entity is connected with another entity if:

- either entity controls the other entity, or
- both entities are controlled by the same third entity (ss328-125(1)).

These concepts are taken from the small business entity regime (Division 328) and are discussed at 10.232 and in *AAT Case* [2013] AATA 947, *Re Gutteridge v FCT.*

NOTE: The trustee of a discretionary trust may nominate up to four beneficiaries as being controllers of the trust in order to achieve 'connected entity' status for the purposes of subdivisions 152-A and 328-C ITAA97. This is only possible in an income year in which the trustee did not make a distribution due to a tax loss or no taxable income of the trust (which would prevent the trust from being controlled in that year). The nomination must be in writing and signed by the trustee and each nominated beneficiary.

This nomination will have effect for the active asset test only from the 2007-08 income year (the nomination is ignored for the purposes of the $6 million net asset value test and the $2 million aggregated turnover test).

NOTE: The Government has amended the small business tax concessions so that trusts cannot avoid being treated as connected entities for the purpose of testing eligibility for the concessions. This is because trusts do not own assets for their own benefit. These amendments have effect for capital gains tax events happening after 7.30pm (AEST) on 10 May 2011.

In particular, the amendments ensure that the provisions concerning absolutely entitled beneficiaries, bankrupt individuals, security providers and companies in liquidation interact appropriately with the capital gains tax provisions and with the connected entity test in the small business entity provisions. These changes apply at the option of taxpayers from the 2008-09 income year, and automatically from Royal Assent (in this case, being 29 June 2013).

AFFILIATE

An individual or company is an affiliate of an entity where that individual or company acts, or could reasonably be expected to act:

- in accordance with the entity's directions or wishes in relation to the affairs of that individual or company's business, or
- in concert with the entity in relation to the affairs of the individual or company's business (ss328-130(1)).

These concepts are taken from the small business entity regime (Division 328) and are discussed at 10.231.

Spouses and children under 18 years are not automatically affiliates of one another. This may cause problems, for example, in passing the active asset test where connected entity or affiliate status cannot be achieved. Amended legislation has introduced a 'New Affiliate Rule'. The rule adopts a two step process:

- **Step 1:** Consider the spouse and child under 18 years of a taxpayer to be their affiliate for the purposes of determining whether the entity using a CGT asset is an affiliate or connected entity of the taxpayer.
- **Step 2:** If step 1 results in an asset being considered an active asset, treat the spouse or child under 18 years as an affiliate of the taxpayer for the purposes of subdivision 152-A and ss325-110 to 328-125.

THE 'ACTIVE ASSET' TEST

The active asset test will be satisfied if:

- the taxpayer owned the asset for 15 years or less and the asset was an active asset of the taxpayer for a total of at least half of the relevant period (see below), or
- the taxpayer owned the asset for more than 15 years and the asset was an active asset of the taxpayer for a total of at least $7^{1}/2$ years during the relevant period (see below) (ss152-35(1)).

For these purposes, the relevant period begins when the asset was acquired and ends at the earlier of:

- the CGT event, and
- the cessation of the business where the relevant business ceased to be carried on in the 12 months before the CGT event (or any longer period that the Commissioner allows) (ss152-35(2)).

NOTE: The effect of the active asset test is that, for assets owned for more than 15 years, once the asset has been 'active' for a minimum of seven and a half years, it will not lose that status irrespective of the use to which it is put.

MEANING OF 'ACTIVE ASSET'

An 'active asset' is an asset that the taxpayer owns and uses (or holds ready for use) in carrying on a business, and includes an intangible asset, such as goodwill or the benefit from a restrictive covenant, that is inherently connected to the business. Where the asset is used for business purposes by an affiliate of the taxpayer or by an entity connected with the taxpayer, the asset will also be an active asset (ss152-40(1)).

Shares in an Australian company or an interest in an Australian resident trust are only active assets if 80% or more of the market value of all company or trust assets are active assets. In determining whether 80% of the company's or trust's assets are active assets, cash and financial instruments, although not themselves active assets, do count towards satisfaction of the 80% test where they are inherently connected with the business (such as amounts set aside for working capital purposes) (paragraph 152-40(3)(b)). Shares in a foreign company do not qualify as active assets.

Once the 80% test has been satisfied, the test does not need to be applied on a continuous basis. Retesting is only required when it is reasonable to consider that there has been a change in the active assets (ss152-40(3A) and (3B)).

Subsection 152-40(4) outlines the CGT assets that are not regarded as active assets. The list includes assets that are held to produce passive investment income.

The following cannot be active assets:

(i)   interests in an entity that is connected with the taxpayer, unless the 80% rule is met

(ii)   shares in companies, unless the 80% rule is met

(iii) interests in trusts unless the 80% rule is met

(iv) financial instruments such as loans, debentures, bonds, promissory notes, futures contracts, forward contracts, currency swap contracts and a right or option in respect of a share, security, loan or contract

(v)   an asset whose main use is to derive interest, an annuity, rent, royalties or foreign exchange gains unless the asset is an intangible asset which has been substantially developed, altered or improved by the relevant taxpayer so that its market value has been substantially enhanced, or the asset's main use for deriving rent was only temporary. For example, investment properties from which rental income is derived are not 'active assets' (also see TD 2006/78).

Commercial properties which a taxpayer had used in carrying on a business of leasing properties were held not to be 'active assets' as their main use were to derive rent (see *Jakjoy Pty Ltd v FC of T* [2013] AATA 526). Such properties are expressly excluded from being active assets under s152-40(4)(e).

Where an individual dies, their legal personal representative or beneficiary can access the small business CGT concessions – to the extent that the deceased would have been able to just before their death – if a CGT event happens to the assets in the hands of the legal personal representative or beneficiary within two years of the death of the individual (s152-80). This is also extend to surviving joint tenants and testamentary trusts, effective from the 2006-07 year.

See *Vaughan and Commissioner of Taxation* [2011] AATA 758 for an example of where the 'active asset' test was failed, the property having been used during the period of its ownership to derive rental income.

ADDITIONAL CONDITIONS FOR CGT EVENTS INVOLVING SHARE OR TRUST INTERESTS

If the CGT asset being sold is a share in a company or an interest in a trust (the object company or trust), one of these additional conditions must be satisfied (in addition to the basic conditions mentioned above) just before the CGT event:

- the taxpayer making the gain is a CGT concession stakeholder in the object company or trust, or

- CGT concession stakeholders in the object company or trust together have a small business participation percentage of at least 90% in the taxpayer entity.

Thus, irrespective of whether shares or interests are directly or indirectly held in entities, it will be paramount to consider whether there is a CGT concession stakeholder in the object company or trust.

CGT CONCESSION STAKEHOLDER

An individual is a CGT concession stakeholder of a company or trust at a time if the individual is:

- a significant individual in the company or trust, or
- a spouse of a significant individual if the spouse has a small business participation percentage in the company or trust at that time that is greater than zero.

Ted and his wife Alice carry on a small business through a company in which Ted owns 85% of the shares (and is a significant individual of the company) and Alice owns 15%. Alice disposes of her shares. On the sale of her shares, Alice is potentially entitled to claim the small business CGT concessions because Ted, her spouse, is a significant individual of the company which ensures that Alice is a CGT concession stakeholder in the company (she is the spouse of a significant individual and she has a small business participation percentage in the company of 15% which is greater than zero).

If there is no significant individual, there can be no CGT concession stakeholder. A company or a trust can have up to eight CGT concession stakeholders, comprising four significant individuals and their four spouses, each with a small business participation percentage greater than zero.

SIGNIFICANT INDIVIDUAL TEST

Given the breadth of the CGT concession stakeholder definition, it is necessary to ultimately identify the significant individuals of a company or trust. The significant individual test is also relevant because a company or a trust that makes a capital gain:

- cannot qualify for the small business 15 year exemption unless it has a significant individual for at least 15 years of its ownership of the active asset, and
- cannot qualify for the small business retirement exemption unless a payment was made in connection with a CGT concession stakeholder (a significant individual or his or her spouse with a small business participation percentage in the company or trust of greater than zero).

An entity satisfies the significant individual test if the entity has at least one significant individual just before the CGT event. An individual is a significant individual in a company or trust if the individual has a Small Business Participation Percentage (SBPP) in the company or trust of at least 20% at that time. The 20% can be made up of direct and indirect percentages so it is possible to trace interests in a company or trust through one or more interposed entities. An entity's SBPP is the sum of its direct SBPP and its indirect SBPP (s152-65).

These concepts are discussed below.

DIRECT SMALL BUSINESS PARTICIPATION PERCENTAGE

The direct small business participation percentage in a company or a trust is determined by applying the rules in s152-70, namely:

- **A company:** An entity's direct small business participation percentage in a company is the smaller or smallest percentage of:
    - the voting power that the entity is entitled to exercise
    - any dividend payment that the entity is entitled to receive, or
    - any capital distribution that the entity is entitled to receive.

    In many cases the small business participation percentage will be the same on all three accounts.

- **A trust (where entities have entitlements to all the income and capital of the trust):** An entity's direct small business participation percentage in a trust (where entities have entitlements to all the income and capital of the trust) is the smaller percentage of the income or capital of the trust that the entity is beneficially entitled to receive.

- **A trust (where entities do not have entitlements to all the income and capital of the trust):** An entity's direct small business participation percentage in a trust (where entities do not have entitlements to all the income and capital of the trust) is the smaller of the percentage of the distribution of income or capital that the entity is beneficially entitled to during the income year.

The meaning of the term 'income' in the context of an entity's direct small business participation percentage in a trust was considered in ATO ID 2012/99.

Helen holds shares in ABC Pty Ltd. Her shareholding entitles her to 15% of any dividends and capital distributions, but she has no voting rights.

Helen's direct small business participation percentage in ABC Pty Ltd is the smaller percentage (0%) being her voting rights.

Bill receives 40% of the income distribution and 20% of the capital distribution from a discretionary trust. Bill has a 20% direct small business participation percentage in the trust (the smaller of his two distributions).

INDIRECT SMALL BUSINESS PARTICIPATION PERCENTAGE

An entity's indirect small business participation percentage in a company or trust is calculated by multiplying together the entity's direct participation percentage in an interposed entity, and the interposed entity's total participation percentage (both direct and indirect) in the company or trust (s152-75).

A discretionary trust that distributes to three beneficiaries owns 80% of the shares in an Operating Company. It therefore has an 80% direct interest (and no indirect interest) in Operating Company.

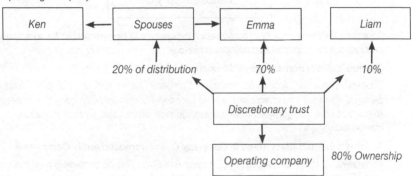

As Emma receives 70% of the distributions from the Discretionary Trust, her direct participation percentage in Discretionary Trust is 70%.

To determine Emma's participation percentage in Operating Company, it is necessary to multiply together her direct participation percentage in Discretionary Trust and Discretionary Trust's total participation percentage in Operating Company: 70% x 80% = 56%.

Emma has a 56% indirect participation percentage in Operating Company and is therefore a significant individual of Operating Company.

As Ken receives 20% of the distributions from Discretionary Trust his direct participation percentage in Discretionary Trust is 20% and his total participation percentage in Operating Company will be 20% x 80% =16%. As this percentage is less than 20%, Ken is not a significant individual of Operating Company. However, as a spouse of a significant individual with a participation percentage in Operating Company greater than zero, Ken will be a CGT concession stakeholder.

Liam receives 10% of the distributions from Discretionary Trust. Liam has a participation percentage of 10% in Discretionary Trust and his total participation percentage in Operating Company will be 10% x 80% = 8%. As this percentage is less than 20%, Liam is not a significant individual of Operating Company. As Liam is not a spouse of a significant individual, he is not a CGT concession stakeholder.

In the previous example there was only one interposed entity: a Distribution Trust interposed between the Operating Company and the beneficiaries of the trust. An indirect interest can be held through one or more interposed entities. Consider the next example.

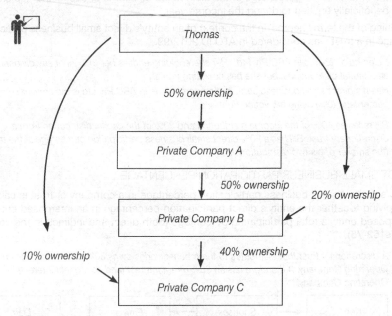

Thomas's total small business participation percentage in Company C is the sum of his direct and indirect participation percentages (s152-65).

Thomas's direct percentage in Company C

Thomas's direct participation percentage in Company C is his 10% ownership of Company C. Because there are two interposed entities between Thomas and Company C, it is necessary to calculate the indirect small business participation percentage in respect of each interposed entity.

Thomas's indirect percentage in Company C via interposed entity Company A

Thomas has a direct percentage in Company A of 50%. This percentage is multiplied by the sum of Company A's direct and indirect percentage in Company C. Company A has a direct percentage in Company C of 0% and an indirect percentage in Company C of 20% (50% of 40%).

Therefore Thomas's indirect percentage in Company C via interposed entity Company A is 50% x [0% + 20%] = 10%.

Thomas's indirect percentage in Company C via interposed entity Company B

Thomas has a direct percentage in Company B of 20%. This amount is multiplied by the sum of Company B's direct and indirect percentage in Company C. Company B has a direct percentage in Company C of 40% and no indirect percentage in Company C. Thomas's indirect interest in Company C via interposed entity Company B is 20% x [40% + 0%] = 8%.

The total of Thomas's direct and indirect percentages in Company C is 10% + 10% + 8% = 28%. As this sum is greater than 20% Thomas is a significant individual in Company C.

90% Test rule

Two individuals, Liam and Brooke both receive 50% of the income and capital distributions from a discretionary trust. In turn the discretionary trust holds 50% of the units in a unit trust.

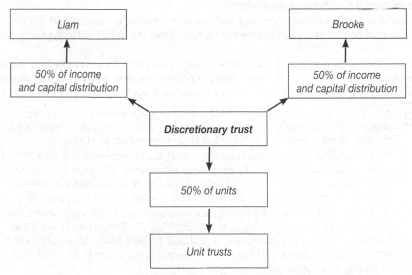

Liam's 50% direct SBPP in the discretionary trust multiplied by the discretionary trust's 50% direct SBPP in the unit trust gives Liam a 25% indirect SBPP in the unit trust. Liam is therefore a significant individual in respect of the unit trust. Similarly, Brooke will also be a significant individual in respect of the unit trust.

As both Liam and Brooke are CGT concession stakeholders in respect to the unit trust and have a combined SBPP in the discretionary trust of 100%, which is more than 90%, the 90% rule is satisfied. This means that a capital gain made by the discretionary trust in selling its units in the unit trust can (all other conditions being satisfied) qualify for the small business CGT concessions.

THE FOUR SMALL BUSINESS CGT CONCESSIONS

1. SMALL BUSINESS 15-YEAR EXEMPTION

CONDITIONS

A taxpayer can disregard a capital gain arising from a CGT event in relation to a CGT asset that it has owned for at least 15 years if:

- the basic conditions in Subdivision 152-A are met, and
- the entity continuously owned the CGT asset for 15 years before the CGT event, and
- if the entity is an individual, the individual retires or is permanently incapacitated, or
- if the entity is a company or trust, the entity had a significant individual for a total of at least 15 years throughout its period of ownership and the individual who was the significant individual just before the CGT event retires or is permanently incapacitated. The 15 year period does not have to be continuous and the significant individual does not have to be the same significant individual during that 15 year period (Subdivision 152-B).

A requirement for retirement is that the individual is aged 55 or over at the time of the CGT event (s152-105).

Note the concepts of 'retirement' and 'permanent incapacity' are addressed by the Tax Office in its publication *Advanced guide to capital gains tax concessions for small business*.

For an individual, there is an additional condition if the CGT asset is a share in a company or an interest in a trust. The company or trust must have had a significant individual for a total of at least 15 years (even if not continuous and not the same significant individual) during which the taxpayer owned the shares or trust interest.

In a year that a discretionary trust has no taxable income or a tax loss and did not make a distribution of income or capital, it is treated as having met the significant individual requirement (s152-120).

Note that it may be possible to apply the 15 year exemption to some pre-CGT assets of a company or trust (s152-125). This may assist in passing tax-free amounts out to shareholders without attracting tax on a dividend, or to unit holders without triggering CGT event E4 (12.605).

X Co acquired land and buildings in 1978 and immediately operated a business from those premises. The company had 3 equal shareholders, A, B and C. All shares issued by X Co had the same rights. Accordingly, A, B and C are significant individuals of X Co.

On 30 May 2004, A, B and C sold their shares to D, E and F who then each hold 33.3% of the shares. Consequently, D, E and F are significant individuals of X Co from that time. This event also caused a change in the majority underlying interests in the business premises with the effect that the premises stopped being a pre-CGT asset of X Co under Division 149.

On 30 May 2013, X Co sold the business premises and made a capital gain. As X Co has continuously owned the premises from 1978 to 30 May 2013 (more than 15 years) and has had a significant individual for a total of at least 15 years during the period it owned the premises, the 15-year CGT exemption will be available if the other conditions for the exemption are satisfied.

Y Co acquired land and buildings in 1980 and operated a business from those premises from that time. Y Co has two equal shareholders, A and B who have held their shares from that time. On 30 March 2013, Y Co sold the business premises and made a capital gain. Y Co has continuously owned the premises from 1980 to 30 March 2013 (more than 15 years). It has also had a significant individual during the entire period of ownership (more than 15 years). Consequently, the 15-year exemption is available.

The capital gain is exempt from tax to the company as the sale of a pre-CGT asset. However, if the company wishes to make distributions to A and B of these tax-free amounts, the distributions will be taxed in the hands of A and B as an unfranked dividend (assuming the company is not liquidated). However, if the 15-year exemption is applied, the tax-free capital gain can be passed to A and B without attracting additional tax.

IMPLICATIONS

Where the 15 year exemption concession applies, there is no need to apply the other three small business CGT concessions. The capital gain is disregarded. Thus, capital losses do not have to be applied against a capital gain arising from the 15-year exemption concession. If a capital loss were to arise, the capital loss is not disregarded and may be used to reduce other capital gains.

Where a capital gain made by a company or trust qualifies for the small business 15-year exemption and is disregarded for CGT purposes, the company or trust may distribute the gain to a CGT concession stakeholder within two years of the CGT event as an exempt amount if the conditions in s152-125 are satisfied. The Commissioner has a discretion to extend this period.

Where this amount is distributed, payments that relate to that exempt capital gain are non assessable non exempt in the hands of the CGT concession stakeholder and any interposed entity that facilitates the payment of the amount. This applies to the extent that the payments are equal to or less than the stakeholder's participation percentage.

The stakeholder's participation percentage for a company or a trust is generally the person's small business participation percentage. However, for a trust, where entities do not have entitlements to all the income and capital of the trust, it is 100% divided by the number of CGT concession stakeholders (s152-125). This payment will not constitute a dividend and will not be a frankable distribution (ss152-125(3)). Nor will the payment cause CGT event G1 to happen.

The 15-year exemption concession does not apply to CGT events J2, J5 or J6 (s152-10(4) or a balancing adjustment amount (ss152-110(3)).

IMPORTANT: SUPERANNUATION CGT CONTRIBUTION CAPS

From 1 July 2007, for those contributing a 15-year exemption amount to a superannuation fund or RSA, the amount is generally a non-concessional contribution. To exclude the amount from the non-concessional contributions cap and have it count towards the superannuation CGT cap instead the fund must be notified by way of election (see 19.079).

2. SMALL BUSINESS 50% REDUCTION

If a small business entity does not qualify for the 15-year exemption, but the basic conditions in Subdivision 152-A apply, the net capital gain after applying step 3 in the method statement in ss102-5(1) is reduced by 50% (**if the taxpayer elects to adopt this concession**). The earlier steps require the taxpayer to apply any current year capital losses (step 1), and any unapplied net capital losses (step 2) against the capital gain the taxpayer has made during the current year. Step 3 is the application of the CGT discount percentage (depends on eligibility and the type of taxpayer, eg. individual, superannuation fund, etc and is not available to company taxpayers).

Sutton operated a newsagency for 10 years as sole proprietor. On 2 April 2014 he sells the business for $700,000 and makes a capital gain of $80,000. All assets were 'active assets'. Sutton has prior year capital losses totalling $20,000.

Assuming all the conditions of Subdivision 152-A are met and Sutton chooses the CGT discount method rather than the indexation method for calculating his capital gain, Sutton's gain is calculated as follows:

Capital gain	*$80,000*
less Current year losses	*0*
	$80,000
less Prior years losses	*($20,000)*
	$60,000
less 50% CGT discount	*($30,000)*
	$30,000
less 50% small business active asset reduction	*($15,000)*
Assessable net capital gain	***$15,000***

This capital gain may be further reduced by applying the small business retirement exemption or small business rollover, or both. If the taxpayer qualifies for both concessions the taxpayer can choose the order in which those concessions are to be applied (s152-210). Further, pursuant to s152-220 a taxpayer may choose not to apply the small business 50% reduction. This may allow a company or a trust to make a larger tax-free payment under the small business retirement exemption (tax-free amounts relating to the small business 50% reduction are taxed as a dividend when paid out by a company to CGT concession stakeholders, except in certain cases involving liquidation. Further, such amounts when paid out to CGT concession stakeholders by a trust could trigger CGT event E4)

The small business 50% reduction concession does not apply to CGT events J2, J5 or J6 (ss152-10(4)).

On 30 June 2014, a beneficiary of the Ralph Unit Trust receives a distribution of $4,000, which includes net income of $500 after a capital gain of $2,000 made by the trustee of the unit trust was reduced by the 50% CGT discount and the small business 50% active asset reduction. This capital gain arose from the disposal of a CGT asset on 1 December 2009. The CGT asset was acquired in September 2001.

As the trustee has claimed both the 50% CGT discount and the small business 50% active asset reduction, the beneficiary multiplies the capital gain of $500 by 4. The resulting capital gain of $2,000 is then subject to the ss102-5(1) method statement. The beneficiary has incurred a capital loss of $200 on the disposal of another asset.

If the beneficiary was an individual who had a capital loss from another CGT event of $200, the method statement calculation is:

Step 1: $2,000 – $200 (current year capital loss) $1,800
Step 2: $1,800 – nil (no unapplied prior year capital losses) .... Nil
Step 3: $1,800 – (50% x $1800) (CGT discount) $900
Step 4: 900 – (50% x $900) (small business active asset reduction) $450

The individual beneficiary's net capital gain is $450. The beneficiary must also include in assessable income the other net trust amount of $3,500. If the beneficiary had been a company, the CGT discount does not apply so the net capital gain would be $900. If the trust had only been entitled to one 50% discount/reduction, the beneficiary would multiply the capital gain by 2 rather than 4.

3. SMALL BUSINESS RETIREMENT EXEMPTION

Under the small business retirement provisions, a taxpayer may be able to claim an exemption up to a maximum capital gain of $500,000 (lifetime limit) where the capital proceeds of sale of a small business are used for retirement (although it is not necessary to actually retire).

Assuming the basic conditions in Subdivision 152-A are met, the capital gain can be disregarded where certain other conditions are met. The conditions are dependent upon whether the capital gain is made by an individual or a company or trust.

INDIVIDUALS

An individual taxpayer can apply the retirement exemption if:

- the basic conditions of Subdivision 152-A are met
- the taxpayer makes a written election which specifies the amount the taxpayer chooses to disregard (the CGT exempt amount), and
- where the taxpayer is aged 55 or older at the time the choice is made to use the retirement exemption (generally on lodgement of the relevant income tax return), there is no requirement to pay an amount into a complying superannuation fund or RSA. However, where the individual is aged under 55 at the time the choice is made to use the retirement exemption, the CGT exempt amount must be rolled over to a complying superannuation fund or an RSA (s152-305).

An arrangement whereby the taxpayer disposes of a property to a superannuation fund and redirects the sales proceeds under the retirement exemption to the taxpayer's superannuation fund account with that fund is not considered to be a scheme under the anti-avoidance provisions of Part IVA ITAA36 (ATO ID 2003/505).

 Lawrie sells his factory on 1 November 2013, satisfies the basic conditions and makes a capital gain of $480,000. Lawrie is aged 54 when he receives capital proceeds from the sale on 1 February 2014. Lawrie turns 55 on 7 June 2014 and decides when lodging his income tax return for 2013-14 year that he wants to use the retirement exemption. Lawrie is not required to pay the money into a superannuation fund because he was aged 55 when he made the choice to apply the retirement exemption.

The CGT exempt amount cannot exceed $500,000 (the retirement exemption 'lifetime limit').

 Barbara, aged 57, sells her business for $500,000 and retires. The amount she received is solely for the goodwill of the business she established in 1990. The goodwill has a zero cost base.

Assuming that all of the criteria for the small business CGT concessions are satisfied, the following CGT implications arise:

Capital gain	$500,000
less CGT discount for an individual (50%)	$(250,000)
	$250,000
less 50% business reduction for active asset	$(125,000)
CGT exempt amount for retirement exemption	**$125,000**

Barbara can elect in writing that the amount of $125,000 be treated as her CGT exempt amount.

 Sale of a small business

Alex is aged 60. He established a small business in April 1991. Alex sold that business on 4 May 2014, making the following capital gains (see table below). If Alex had net capital losses of $10,000 carried forward from an earlier year, to calculate his net capital gain, the carried forward capital losses must be applied against his total capital gains before applying the 50% discount or the small business CGT concessions.

As Alex can reduce his capital gains by the capital losses in any order that he elects to give the best tax outcome, he elects to apply the capital losses against the restrictive covenant as it is not eligible for the CGT discount.

The notional capital gain on the restrictive covenant becomes $50,000 – $10,000 = $40,000. The 50% small business reduction is then applied to the $40 000 to give a capital gain of $20,000.

Alex's net capital gain is $37,500 + $45,000 + $20,000 = $102,500.

If Alex's exempt capital gain has not exceeded his $500,000 retirement exemption lifetime limit, he can chose to apply the small business retirement exemption to his capital gain of $102,500 and reduce the capital gain to nil.

Asset	Cost	Capital proceeds	Notional capital gain	Eligible for 50% discount [1]	Eligible for 50% active asset reduction [2]	Assessable capital gain
Land	$200,000	$350,000	$150,000	Yes	Yes	$37,500
Goodwill	0	$180,000	$180,000	Yes	Yes	$45,000
Restrictive covenant	0	$ 50,000	$ 50,000	No	Yes	$20,000 [4]
Depreciating assets	$100,000	$130,000	Nil [3]	No	No	

1: To be eligible for the 50% discount the asset must be held for at least 12 months.

2: An asset does not have to be held for at least 12 months before the small business 50% reduction can apply.

3: Depreciating assets used wholly for business are exempt from CGT (s118-24), but a balancing adjustment under s40-285 will include the difference between the adjustable value and termination value as other business income in the taxpayer's return.

4: After applying net capital losses carried forward from a prior year of $10,000.

Since 1 July 2006, it is no longer a requirement that a taxpayer must receive actual capital proceeds from a CGT event to qualify for this concession. This means the retirement exemption is available where a capital gain is made when an active asset is gifted and the market value substitution rule applies.

COMPANIES AND TRUSTS

Broadly, a company or trust can also choose to disregard an amount under the retirement exemption if:

- the basic conditions of Subdivision 152-A are met
- the company or trust satisfies the significant individual test
- the company or trust makes a written choice to apply the retirement exemption in Subdivision 152-D. The choice must specify the amount the company or trust chooses to disregard (the exempt amount) and each CGT concession stakeholder's percentage of the exempt amount (which must total 100%)
- the company or trust makes a payment of any capital gain exempted under the retirement exemption to CGT concession stakeholder(s) by the later of seven days after the choice is made by the company or trust to disregard the capital gain, or seven days after an amount of capital proceeds is received by the CGT concession stakeholder. The payment must be calculated by reference to each individual's percentage of the exempt amount, and
- if the CGT concession stakeholders is under 55 before the payment is made it must be made to a complying superannuation fund or an RSA (see s152-325).

Where there is more than one CGT concession stakeholder, the company or trust must specify in writing the percentage of each CGT asset's CGT exempt amount that is attributable to each stakeholder. One specified percentage may be nil, but they must add up to 100%.

The CGT exempt amount cannot exceed $500,000 per individual (the lifetime limit per individual (s152-320)). This means that where a company or a trust has eight CGT concession stakeholders, it is possible to apply to retirement exemption to exempt $4 million ($500,000 for each stakeholder). Any capital gain that exceeds this limit does not qualify for this exemption (ss152-310(1)).

Payment of the retirement exemption amounts to CGT concession stakeholders through interposed entity/ies will not be treated as a dividend, a frankable amount or a deemed dividend under Division 7A ITAA36.

IMPORTANT: SUPERANNUATION CGT CONTRIBUTION CAPS

From 1 July 2007, for those contributing a retirement exemption amount to a superannuation fund or RSA, the amount is generally a non-concessional contribution. To exclude the amount from the non-concessional contributions cap and have it count towards the superannuation CGT cap instead the fund must be notified by way of election (see 19.079).

4. SMALL BUSINESS ROLLOVER

To ensure that a CGT liability does not constrain development of small business by reducing the capital available to acquire a replacement asset, Subdivision 152-E gives owners of a small business the opportunity to claim rollover relief by acquiring one or more replacement assets or improvements to existing assets that the taxpayer already owns (both treated as 'replacement assets') within the 'replacement asset period'.

The 'replacement asset period' is the period starting one year before and ending two years after the last CGT event in the income year for which the taxpayer obtains the rollover. This period can be modified or extended (see s104-190).

To obtain the rollover, the basic conditions in Subdivision 152-A must be satisfied and the replacement asset must be an active asset at the end of the replacement period. Where the replacement asset is a share in a company or an interest in a trust, there is a further condition to be satisfied at the end of the replacement period. The taxpayer (or an entity connected with the taxpayer) must be a CGT concession stakeholder in the company or trust, or the CGT concession stakeholders in the company or trust must have a small business participation percentage in the small business entity of at least 90%. Where rollover is chosen, the taxpayer can choose to disregard all or part of the capital gain to which Subdivision 152-E applies.

CONDITIONS NOT SATISFIED AT THE END OF THE REPLACEMENT PERIOD

Having elected to rollover the CGT liability, if the relevant conditions are not satisfied at the end of the replacement period, CGT events J5 or J6 may apply. The time of the event is at the end of the replacement asset period (that is, two years from the CGT event).

CGT event J5 will apply if there is no replacement asset or the conditions above are not satisfied. The capital gain is the amount of the previous capital gain that was rolled over (ie. previously disregarded).

When CGT events J5 or J6 occur, it will now no longer be necessary to satisfy the basic conditions in s152-10 for CGT events happening from the 2006-07 income year.

CRYSTALLISING THE CAPITAL GAIN ROLLED OVER

Where there is a change in status of the replacement asset, the original capital gain rolled over will crystallise. For example, if the replacement asset is subsequently put to a disqualifying use, CGT event J2 will occur and the entity will make a capital gain equal to the capital gain previously deferred.

For example, CGT event J2 applies where the replacement asset:

- stops being an active asset
- becomes trading stock
- is a testamentary gift under the Cultural Bequests program, or
- is used solely to produce exempt income or non-assessable non-exempt income.

Brian sold the business premises from which he operated his small business since 1995. He made a capital gain of $100,000. Assuming Brian qualifies for all the small business CGT concessions, this capital gain is reduced by the 50% CGT discount and then reduced by the 50% small business reduction to $25,000. If Brian considers that he may acquire a replacement asset within the replacement asset period he can disregard the $25,000 capital gain. If after two years Brian has only spent $20,000 on a replacement active asset, CGT event J6 will happen and Brian will incur a capital gain of $5,000 (the difference between the original capital gain rolled over and the amount of expenditure incurred.

Where CGT event J2 occurs to crystallise a deferred capital gain, the capital gain that is crystallised may be eligible for the retirement exemption or a further small business rollover (where the conditions are satisfied), but cannot be eligible for the CGT discount or small business 50% active asset reduction as these concessions would have been applied to the capital gain prior to rollover.

Ian disposes of an active asset for $10,000, making a capital gain of $2,000. He buys two replacement assets for $5,000 each and chooses the small business rollover. $1,000 of the capital gain is disregarded for each replacement asset.

If one of the replacement assets is later sold for $7,500 (CGT event A1 occurs) and Ian makes a capital gain of $2,500.

Ian will also make a capital gain of $1,000 as the sale of the replacement asset results in that asset no longer being an active asset and CGT event J2 happens. The $1,000 capital gain represents the capital gain made on the disposal of the active asset that was rolled over in respect of this replacement asset.

Both capital gains ($2,500 made from CGT event A1 and $1,000 made from CGT event J2 crystallising the deferred capital gain) may be eligible for further rollover relief under Subdivision 152-E.

12.535 CAPITAL LOSSES TRANSFERRED WITHIN A WHOLLY-OWNED GROUP OF COMPANIES

The transfer of net capital losses within wholly-owned groups of companies will only be permitted where one of the companies is an Australian branch of a foreign bank and both companies are members of the same wholly-owned group.

Company groups that have consolidated no longer need to transfer net capital losses within the group as these losses are automatically pooled to the head company of the consolidated group.

12.550 PARTNERSHIPS AND CGT

The net income or loss of a partnership is calculated without taking into account any capital gains or losses, because a partnership is not treated as a taxpayer under the CGT regime (s106-5). CGT therefore applies at the partner level.

CGT AND PARTNERSHIP ASSETS

For CGT purposes, generally the partners themselves (not the partnership) are the relevant taxpayers. An exception to this rule is CGT event K7 because Division 40 treats the partnership as owning depreciating assets. Further, the relevant asset for CGT purposes is each partner's fractional interest in each partnership asset (paragraph 108-5(2)(c) of the definition of 'CGT asset'). This is referred to as a 'look through' approach.

The one exception to this approach is that each partner's interest in the partnership can also be an asset for CGT purposes, but only to the extent to which that interest has not already been implicitly taken into account in the 'look through' approach (paragraph 108-5(2)(d) of the definition of CGT asset).

Each partner's capital gain or loss is calculated by reference to the partnership agreement or partnership law if there is no agreement (ss106-5(1)). Each partner has a separate cost base and reduced cost base for his or her interest in each CGT asset of the partnership (ss106-5(2)).

A partnership with ten partners sells a block of land for $150,000 which was originally purchased for $90,000. Each partner is taken to have disposed of his or her interest in the land; however, individual partners may have acquired their interests at different times (some before 20 September 1985 and others on or after that date) and may have paid different amounts as consideration for the acquisition of those interests.

If the partners own equal interests in the land, each will be taken as receiving $15,000 as capital proceeds.

If the land was acquired after 19 September 1985, at a time when there were only nine partners, each member who was a partner at the time of acquisition would have a cost base of $10,000 in respect of the acquisition of his or her interest (approximately 11.11%) in the land, and the capital gain would be calculated using $10,000 as the cost base.

If the tenth partner entered the partnership after the land had been acquired and paid $12,000 for his or her interest in the land, that partner would have a cost base of $12,000 and would therefore realise a notional capital gain of $3,000. This notional capital gain might need to be adjusted for indexation or the CGT discount to determine the assessable capital gain. At the time of that partner's entry into the partnership, the original nine partners would each be treated as having disposed of a 1.11% interest for $1,333.33.

The cost base of each 1.11% interest would be 10% of $10,000 (ie. $1,000). Accordingly, each continuing partner would have a $333.33 notional capital gain at the time of entry of the new partner. This notional capital gain might need to be adjusted for indexation or CGT discount to determine the actual capital gain.

CHANGE OF INTEREST

Another possibility is that the interest of an individual partner in a partnership asset may have changed since the asset was originally acquired by the partnership, eg. by the admission or retirement of a partner.

If the asset was acquired before 20 September 1985, but admissions or retirements to the partnership have since occurred, an individual partner's interest in the asset may have changed and a proportion of that interest may have a post-19 September 1985 acquisition date.

Assume the land in the previous example was acquired by the ten partner partnership before 20 September 1985 and that there were ten partners initially. If there were no change in the composition of the partnership, when the land was subsequently sold there would be no capital gain or loss to any of the partners as each partner's interest in the partnership asset was acquired prior to 20 September 1985. However, if one of the partners retired after 19 September 1985 and the remaining 9 partners each acquired a proportion of the retiring partner's interest in the land for $1,000, the other partners have each acquired a new post-19 September 1985 interest in the asset (ie. one-ninth of the retiring partner's 10% interest in the land: 1.11% interest approximately).

On the subsequent sale of the land for $150,000, each partner would realise a capital gain in respect of that new interest. Similarly, where a new partner is admitted to a partnership, each of the old partners disposes of part of their share of each asset acquired by the new partner (see previous example).

ROLLOVER RELIEF

Rollover relief applies to a transfer of a partner's interest in a partnership asset to a company wholly-owned by the partners. The consideration for the transfer must be non-redeemable shares in the company of substantially the same market value as the net asset(s) transferred (see 12.485).

Where the partners in a partnership dispose of their interests in a CGT asset of the partnership to a company, and receive shares in the company as consideration for their disposal, the partners are entitled to roll-over relief under ss122-135(1) (ATO ID 2010/114). Even if the partners are not issued with shares in the company until completion of the disposal contract and are taken to have owned the shares in the company from the time they enter into the disposal contract rollover relief is still available.

EVERETT ASSIGNMENT

An Everett assignment (an assignment of part of a partner's interest in a partnership) creates a CGT asset being an interest in a partnership under paragraph 108-5(2)(d). The assignment is treated as a part disposal of the partner's interest in the partnership asset at market value.

According to IT 2608, where a partner assigns a share of an interest in a partnership, expenses incurred by the assignor partner in connection with the partnership may have to be apportioned in order to determine the deduction allowable to the assignor. Where the expenditure incurred relates to the partner's proportionate interest in the partnership, a deduction is only allowable to the assignor partner for the share of the partnership interest not assigned. However, where the expenditure incurred by the assignor partner is unrelated to the partner's proportionate interest in the partnership (such as professional subscriptions), a deduction is allowable in full.

FOREIGN RESIDENT PARTNERS

Foreign resident partners are liable for CGT only on disposal of a fractional interest in a partnership asset which constitutes 'taxable Australian property' (12.700 below).

CGT DISCOUNT OR INDEXATION

As the CGT liability in respect of a CGT event affecting a partnership asset falls on partners as individuals rather than the partnership itself, each non-corporate partner gets the benefit of the 50% CGT discount where the CGT event occurs after 11.45am on 21 September 1999 and the asset has been held for at least 12 months. Alternatively, where the asset was acquired at or before 11.45am on 21 September 1999 the partner could select to determine a capital gain by indexing the cost base (frozen at 30 September 1999).

In this respect, a partnership can effectively distribute the tax-free CGT discount or indexation component of a capital gain to the partners, without the distribution being subject to further tax.

This contrasts with the case in respect of a company where the benefit of such tax concessions is lost at the shareholder level.

12.600 TRUSTS AND CGT

The CGT position of trusts can be quite different to that of individuals, partnerships and companies. A trustee could stream a capital gain to a particular unitholder or beneficiary (see 7.700) provided the trust deed permits and the legislative requirements are satisfied.

CAPITAL GAINS MADE BY TRUSTS

Refer to 7.700.

UNITS IN UNIT TRUSTS

CGT applies to any units held in a unit trust acquired by the taxpayer after 19 September 1985.

12.605   REDUCTIONS OF UNIT TRUST CAPITAL

Section 104-70 provides that non-assessable capital distributions to unitholders in a unit trust (and to beneficiaries of a fixed trust or beneficiaries holding fixed entitlements within discretionary trusts) will reduce the cost base of the units of those unitholders (or beneficiaries).

The section only applies to units or beneficial interests acquired, or deemed to be acquired, after 19 September 1985.

CGT event E4 would not apply to a non-assessable payment by a trustee to a beneficiary of a discretionary trust as that beneficiary does not have an interest in the trust in terms of s104-70.

The Act refers to these non-assessable capital distributions as the 'non-assessable part'.

The 'non-assessable part' would include:

- a return of trust capital
- a distribution of accounting income which is not deemed to be net income of the trust for the purposes of ss95(1)
- a distribution of the frozen indexed amount
- a distribution of the small business 50% CGT reduction
- a distribution of a building allowance after 30 June 2001, and
- certain timing differences (refer: ATO ID 2012/63).

However the 'non-assessable part' does not include the CGT discount amount. Nor does it include:

- non-assessable non-exempt income
- payments from an amount that has been assessable to the trustee
- a payment of a small business 15 year exempt amount
- personal service income included in assessable income, or
- a repayment (s104-71).

The 'non-assessable part' of a distribution reduces the beneficiary's cost base. A capital gain will arise where the 'non-assessable part' of the distribution exceeds the cost base of the beneficiary's unit or fixed interest in the trust (s104-70(4)). See examples under CGT event E4 at 12.028.

A distribution statement issued by a managed fund will often describe non-assessable payments as:

- tax-free amounts
- tax-deferred amounts
- CGT concession amounts, and
- tax-exempted amounts.

The tax-exempted amounts and CGT concession amounts are excluded from the 'non-assessable part' so these payments do not affect the cost base or reduced cost base of a taxpayer's units. However, a taxpayer's cost base is reduced by any tax-deferred amounts and a taxpayer's reduced cost base will be reduced by both the tax-deferred amounts and tax-free amounts.

TREATMENT WHERE THE PAYMENT TO A BENEFICIARY IS A CGT CONCESSION AMOUNT

Section 104-70 may incorrectly calculate the 'non-assessable part' of a payment to a beneficiary where the trustee has claimed a CGT concession. In this case, s104-71 determines the maximum reduction necessary to reflect the difference between the CGT concessions claimed by the trustee and the CGT concessions able to be claimed by the beneficiary. The reduction also takes into account the capital losses claimed by the beneficiary.

The Martin Unit Trust made a capital gain of $18,000 in 2012-13 that was eligible for the 50% CGT discount and the small business 50% reduction. Its net capital gain is:

Trust gain	*$18,000*
less 50% CGT discount	*$9,000*
	$9,000
less Small business 50% reduction	*$4,500*
Net capital gain	**$4,500**

Peter has owned one of the three units in the trust for five years. The cost base of Peter's unit is $500. Peter is presently entitled to the income of the trust. He also has a current year capital loss of $1,000. The trustee pays Peter $6,000 and advises him that the amount comprises $3,000 CGT discount, $1500 small business reduction and $1,500 net income from the capital gain made by the trust.

Applying the rules in Subdivision 115-C ITAA97

Peter's share of the net capital gain is $1,500 (1/3 of $4,500). His notional gain is $6,000 (4 x $1,500) (paragraph 115-215(3)(c)).

Peter calculates his net capital gain in the 2012-13 year of income as:

Notional gain	*$6,000*
less Capital loss	*$1,000*
	$5,000
less 50% CGT discount	*$2,500*
	$2,500
less Small business 50% reduction	*$1,250*
Net capital gain	**$1,250**

Applying the rules of CGT event E4, the payment of $6,000 to Peter is reduced as follows:

Payment from trustee...	*$6,000*
less Net trust income assessed under s 97 ITAA36......................................	*$1,500*
	$4,500
less CGT discount to trustee (ss104-71(4) item 1).......................................	*$3,000*
	$1,500
less Proportion of Peter's capital loss reflected in the payment.....................	*$250*
Non-assessable part	*$1,250*
less Cost base...	*$500*
Notional capital gain under CGT event E4...	*$750*
less CGT discount (50%)	*$375*
Capital gain from CGT event E4...	**$375**

If payments out of a concession amount pass through a chain of fixed trusts before being paid to the beneficiary there is potential for multiple taxation from CGT event E4 applying to each trustee in the chain. This outcome is removed by reducing the non-assessable part by the CGT discount and small business reduction amounts flowing through trusts (s104-72).

Note the small business CGT concessions may be applied to a capital gain from CGT event E4 where the units in the trust qualify as an active asset and the other conditions for relief are satisfied.

DISCRETIONARY TRUSTS

CGT event E4 (s104-70) does not have any application in respect of the unallocated funds of a discretionary trust, as discretionary beneficiaries do not hold an interest in the trust fund. Assets transferred to a beneficiary of a discretionary trust give rise to CGT event E5 (s104-75). The beneficiary will be taken to have received the market value of the asset in exchange for the interest the beneficiary has in the trust.

No capital gain or loss will arise for the beneficiary, provided they:

- acquired the interest in the trust (except by way of assignment from another entity) for no expenditure, or
- acquired it before 20 September 1985 (ss104-75(6)).

CGT event E5 will give rise to a capital gain on the part of the trustee if the market value of the asset transferred exceeds its cost base.

A beneficiary can be specifically entitledentitled to a capital gain of a deceased estate where the trustee of the estate makes a capital gain by reason of CGT event E5 and a beneficiary becomes absolutely entitled to an asset of the trust (see ATO ID 2013/33).

UNIT TRUST DISTRIBUTIONS

Many unit trusts hold capital assets. During an income year, a CGT event may occur in relation to an asset held by a unit trust and a capital gain may arise. A unit holder's proportionate share of any taxable capital gain will be shown on that unit holder's trust tax statement issued by the unit trust. How this information should be treated for income tax purposes is best illustrated by the following example.

 A unit holder acquired 1,000 units in the ABC Trust for $10 per unit in 1991. Since then the receipt of tax deferred amounts has reduced the cost base of their units from $10,000 to $1,000 at 30 June 2013. On 25 August 2013, the unit holder received a tax statement from the ABC Trust which contained the following CGT information for the tax year ended 30 June 2013.

Capital gains distributed	Distribution components
Discounted gains[1]	$465 (50%)
CGT discount	$465 (50%)
Other gains[2]	$10
Indexed gains[3]	$0
Tax deferred	$1,220

1: Discounted capital gains are capital gains made on investments that have been held by the trust for more than 12 months.

2: Other capital gains are gains on assets held for 12 months or less.

3: Indexed capital gains are gains on investments acquired prior to 21 September 1999 and held for more than 12 months. The trustee would have compared these gains with the gains calculated under the discount method and used the indexation method because it gave the lower capital gain for these CGT events.

Tax treatment

Discounted capital gain: The discounted capital gain would have been calculated on the basis that the trust was entitled to a 50% CGT discount on a CGT event happening to assets that it had held for longer than 12 months. All unit holders may not be entitled to the same discount rate. Consequently, the unit holder must gross up the discounted capital gain to remove the 50% discount ($465 x 2 = $930) before offsetting any capital losses and applying the relevant discount percentage.

Individuals: If the unit holder is an individual, they would also be entitled to a 50% CGT discount on a CGT event happening to an asset held for at least 12 months. If they had any offsetting current year or prior year capital losses, these losses are first offset against the grossed up capital gain of $930 before applying the 50% CGT discount. For example, if an individual had a current year capital loss of $200 from disposal of shares this sum is first offset against the capital gain of $930 from the trust and the 50% CGT discount is then applied to the residual ($930 – $200 = $730) to give an assessable capital gain of $365.

Companies: A company is not eligible to use the CGT discount method so the grossed up capital gain of $930 is its assessable capital gain from the unit trust. Any current year or prior year capital losses carried forward will reduce this assessable gain.

Superannuation funds: A superannuation fund is eligible for a CGT discount but the discount rate is 33.33% not 50%. If the superannuation fund did not have any current and prior year capital losses to offset, then its current year assessable capital gain is $620 ($930 less its 33.33% CGT discount).

Another trust (other than a superannuation fund): Trusts (other than a superannuation fund) are eligible for a 50% CGT discount so the result would be the same as for an individual.

Other gains

Other gains refer to capital gains from assets held for less than 12 months so there is no CGT discount or indexation available. These amounts are included in full in the tax return as a capital gain regardless of the entity that is the unit holder. In our example the 'other capital gain' is $10.

CGT concession amount

The CGT concession is the 'non-assessable' component of the capital gains. This component includes the discount amount of the capital gain made by the trust. The CGT concession amount does not affect the unit holder's tax nor does it reduce the cost base of the unit holder's units in the trust.

Tax deferred amount

The tax deferred amount reduces the cost base of the unit holder's units. At 30 June 2013, the cost base of the unit holder's units was $1,000. The distribution of the tax deferred amount of $1,220 reduces the cost base of the unit holder's units to $0 and the excess distribution ($220) will give rise to a capital gain because CGT event E4 will have happened. The CGT event E4 capital gain of $220 may be reduced if the unit holder is eligible for a CGT discount. For example, if the unit holder is an individual, the CGT event E4 capital gain of $220 is reduced by 50% to $110 because the unit holder has held the units for at least 12 months.

Recording the information in the tax return

If the unit holder is an individual without any current year or prior year capital losses, they would record:

- *Yes – to the question 'Did you have a capital gains tax event for the year?'*
- *$1,160 ($930 + 10 + 220) as the 'total current year capital gain'. This amount is the sum of the discounted capital gains (x 2) plus other capital gains plus indexed capital gains plus the non-discounted capital gain from CGT event E4.*
- *$585 ($465 + 10 + 110) as the 'net capital gain'. This amount is the sum of the discounted capital gains plus other capital gains plus indexed capital gains plus the discounted capital gain from CGT event E4.*

DISCREPANCIES BETWEEN DISTRIBUTED AND TAXABLE NET INCOME OF A TRUST

The net income of a trust which the trustee is permitted to distribute to beneficiaries or unit holders is calculated in accordance with the trust deed (distributable trust income). This may differ from the net income calculated for taxation purposes in accordance with s95 ITAA36. This discrepancy could arise for a number of reasons, such as:

- capital gains are assessable for tax purposes but treated as corpus in the trust deed
- expenses in accordance with the trust deed are either non-deductible or deductible to a greater or lesser extent for tax purposes, or
- a different basis is used for valuing trading stock or depreciable assets for accounting purposes than that used for taxation purposes.

For taxation purposes, a beneficiary or unit holder will be assessed on their proportionate share of the net taxable income of the trust calculated in accordance with s95 ITAA36. This amount may be either greater or less than the distributed amount (see *Zeta Force Pty Ltd v FC of T* 98 ATC 4681).

Some trusts retain capital profits in the trust and do not distribute capital gains to beneficiaries. This may be because the definition of distributable income per the deed does not include capital gains (that may form part of corpus). However for tax purposes each unit holder will be assessed on their proportionate share of the capital gains even though they are not actually received from the trust. See 12.630 where there are different income and capital beneficiaries.

Where distributable income exceeds s95 net income (for tax purposes), CGT event E4 should be considered (see 12.605). Note that this will not be an issue where the definition of distributable 'income' per the deed is aligned with s95 income for tax purposes. It is possible for a trust deed to define income available for distribution, and this may override concepts of income determined in accordance with ordinary accounting principles (*Bamford v Commissioner of Taxation* [2010] HCA 10 (Bamford)). In aligning trust income with taxable income there may be other adjusting items where the position is less clear. For example, the application of the market value substitution rule in calculating a capital gain arising from a CGT event would impact the calculation of trust income. It is unclear whether the Commissioner of Taxation would accept that a beneficiary can be presently entitled to such an amount.

RENOUNCEMENT OF A TRUST INTEREST

The income and assets of private trusts are attributed to controlling individuals for the purposes of the means testing provisions. Accordingly, an affected beneficiary of a discretionary trust may wish to renounce their interest in the trust. The renouncement of such an interest would give rise to CGT event C2, as the beneficiary has surrendered or forfeited their interest in the trust.

Whether there is a capital gain would depend upon whether the beneficiary received any capital proceeds for renouncing their interest in the discretionary trust and the market value of the interest at the time it is renounced. A capital gain will only arise if the market value exceeds the cost base of their trust interest. Generally, as a beneficiary of a discretionary trust has no interest in the assets or income of the trust, the market value of their interest will be nil.

Specifically, TD 2001/26 states that the renunciation by a discretionary beneficiary would not normally have any CGT consequences for the trustee or for the trust. An amendment to the trust deed to exclude a beneficiary from the discretionary trust may result in the creation of a new trust with CGT event E1 happening.

12.615 TRUST DECLARATIONS/SETTLEMENTS

CGT event E1 is taken to have occurred where a trust is created over a CGT asset by declaration or settlement of a discretionary trust (s104-55). The effect of the CGT event is that the trustee is taken to have acquired the asset at the time of the trust's creation.

The trust cloning exception under CGT event E1 and E2 ceased to apply from 1 November 2008. Trustees cannot rely on the exception to be exempt from CGT where either of these events is triggered. Nonetheless, a capital gain in relation to CGT event E1 or E2 may be disregarded if there is a sole beneficiary of a non-unit trust who is absolutely entitled to the asset of the trust as against the trustee (disregarding any legal disability) or a mere change of trustee of a single trust (ie. a share split).

12.620 OTHER CAPITAL GAINS ISSUES

There are also pitfalls where the trust deed has been drafted without consideration of the capital gains provisions. Note that it is possible for a trust deed to define income available for distribution, and this may override concepts of income determined in accordance with ordinary accounting principles (*Bamford*). This means that the definition of distributable income per the deed may include capital gains, even though such gains are not considered ordinary income in accordance with generally accepted accounting principles.

Where the definition of 'income' in the trust deed does include income by way of capital gains the capital gain may be able to be 'streamed' to particular beneficiaries in accordance with the amending legislation which applies from the 2010-11 year (see 7.700). Otherwise, where capital gains form part of trust income and are distributed to beneficiaries, the 'proportionate approach' must be applied by the trustee (see 7.600).

12.640 CORPORATE UNIT TRUSTS AND PUBLIC TRADING TRUSTS

Where a corporate unit trust or a public trading trust distributes a capital gain to its unit holders, that capital gain is not adjusted in terms of s115-215 for the CGT discount or small business CGT concessions. Section 115-215 only applies where the beneficiary's assessable income includes an amount in calculating s95 net trust income. A distribution to a unit holder from a corporate unit trust or public trading trust is not s95 net trust income, but a 'unit trust dividend' which is included in a beneficiary's income in terms of s44(1) (ATO ID 2003/798).

12.650 CGT AND ESTATE BENEFICIARIES

Assets can be transferred under a will or by virtue of the laws of intestacy if no valid will was made.

Any capital gain or loss from a CGT event in relation to a CGT asset owned by the deceased at the time of death is disregarded by the trustee of the deceased's estate, unless CGT event K3 happens.

The beneficiary (or estate trustee) who actually owns the property when there is a subsequent CGT event in relation to the asset will bear the CGT liability, if any (see below).

EXCEPTIONS

CGT event K3 will occur if a CGT asset owned by the deceased passes to a tax advantaged entity, such as:

- a tax exempt entity (other than certain gifts of property (see s118-60)
- a foreign resident beneficiary (if a foreign resident beneficiary acquires any CGT asset that is not 'taxable Australian property' from a deceased estate, CGT arises only on a subsequent CGT event happening in respect to the CGT asset)
- the trustee of a complying superannuation entity (s104-215).

The practical implication of this exception is that it will often be preferable to make cash rather than asset bequests to tax-exempt entities and foreign residents. Asset bequests that attract CGT leave less to be distributed to other beneficiaries.

PASSING OF ASSET TO BENEFICIARY

While s128-20 makes it clear that a CGT asset passes to a beneficiary of a deceased estate once the beneficiary becomes the owner of the asset, the Commissioner considers that an asset can pass to a beneficiary prior to its transfer if the beneficiary becomes absolutely entitled to the asset as against the trustee (TD 2004/3). This means that if the trustee of a deceased estate, at a beneficiary's suggestion, sold an asset to which that beneficiary had a vested, indefeasible and absolute interest, then any capital gain would be made by that beneficiary because at the time the asset was sold it had passed to that beneficiary.

ASSETS BOUGHT FROM THE ESTATE

If a beneficiary buys (rather than receives) an asset from a deceased estate, CGT event A1 would happen. There is a disposal, for CGT purposes, by the trustee of the estate and an acquisition by the beneficiary.

DEATH BEFORE 20 SEPTEMBER 1985

The deceased's asset is taken to have been acquired at their date of death by the beneficiary or estate trustee. As this date is before the start of the CGT law, a subsequent CGT event in relation to the asset will not result in any CGT for the new owner. This is the case even if someone else had a life interest in the asset, such as a right to occupy the family home, and the new owner did not receive the remainder interest until after 19 September 1985.

DEATH AFTER 19 SEPTEMBER 1985

The tax consequences are dependent upon when the relevant asset was acquired. Where the:

- asset was acquired by the deceased before 20 September 1985: the asset is deemed to be acquired by the trustee (or beneficiary) on the date of death at its market value, or
- asset was acquired by the deceased after 19 September 1985: the beneficiary is deemed to have acquired the asset at the deceased's 'cost base' (indexed if appropriate) or 'reduced cost base' on the date of death.

NOTE: The beneficiary of such a post-CGT estate asset may be liable not only for CGT on an increment in value since taking over the asset, but on any gain which occurred during the former ownership.

CGT EVENT OCCURS WITHIN 12 MONTHS OF DEATH

If a trustee of a deceased person's estate or a beneficiary acquires an asset from a deceased estate, and then a CGT event happens to that asset within 12 months of the person's death, special rules apply.

For post-CGT assets, provided any one or more of the deceased, the trustee, and the beneficiary, held the asset for a total of at least 12 months before the CGT event, the 12 months holding period is satisfied for the purpose of calculating the capital gain.

Pre-CGT assets are deemed to be acquired by the beneficiary at the date of the deceased's death.

Where a trustee of the estate of a deceased person transmits a CGT asset of the deceased person's estate to a beneficiary under that will, this transaction does not constitute a CGT event. The beneficiary stands in the trustee's 'shoes' in the sense that the entire cost base of the trustee is included in the beneficiary's cost base for the asset.

DISPOSAL AT A LOSS

If the asset is subsequently sold at a loss, it is taken to have been acquired by the beneficiary at the deceased's 'reduced cost base' at the date of death (however, see 12.102 and 12.120).

MAIN RESIDENCE

Special rules apply to a property that was the main residence of the deceased (see from 12.300). If a deceased's main residence was:

- not being used for income-producing purposes at the time of death and was acquired by a beneficiary or trustee of a deceased estate after 20 August 1996, or
- acquired by the deceased before 20 September 1985

The first element in the cost base to calculate any future capital gain or loss is the market value of the home at the deceased's date of death.

The main residence exemption (or partial exemption where the residence was used as the deceased's main residence for only part of the period of ownership) applies where a deceased's main residence is disposed of, and settlement occurs within two years of the deceased's death. This exemption is also available notwithstanding that there is a disposal of this asset more than two years after the date of the death of the deceased, provided that the widow/widower, or a person who had been granted a right of occupancy of the property under the will, or a beneficiary occupied the property as his or her main residence at all times after the date of death of the deceased up to the date the ownership interest ends.

A partial exemption applies where the deceased did not use a dwelling as a main residence, but his or her spouse, or a beneficiary, or a person entitled to live in a home under the deceased's will uses that home as their main residence after the deceased's death (s118-200).

The capital gain or capital loss is calculated using the formula:

(CG or CL amount x Non-main residence days) divided by Total days

COLLECTABLE AND PERSONAL USE ASSETS

Collectables and personal use assets of the deceased retain that characteristic in the hands of the legal representative or beneficiary (s128-15(6)). See 12.060 for a discussion of the characteristics of these CGT assets.

TRANSFER OF CAPITAL LOSSES

There is no provision in the Act that would enable the deceased to transfer any unrecouped capital losses to the trustee or beneficiaries. Any unrecouped capital losses lapse on death (TD 95/47).

For a taxpayer with unrecouped capital losses, it may be advantageous to realise some capital gains before death rather than to retain the asset as part of their estate. Alternatively, an asset with a potential capital gain could be bequeathed to a tax exempt charity so the capital gain is taxed to the deceased.

REMAINDER AND LIFE INTERESTS

The date of acquisition for a remainder person inheriting assets is the deceased's date of death. Note that the trustee of a resident testamentary trust can choose to be assessed on capital gains of the trust where the capital gains would otherwise be assessed to an income beneficiary (or to the trustee on behalf of such a beneficiary) (s115-230). Otherwise, a beneficiary who was presently entitled to a share of the income of the trust estate may be assessed on a share of capital gains for which the beneficiary would not benefit.

The trustee may choose to be assessed on those gains if:

- the beneficiary that would otherwise be assessed, or on whose behalf the trustee is assessed, does not have a vested and indefeasible interest in trust property representing the capital gain, and
- the gains have not been paid or applied for the benefit of the beneficiary.

Generally the trustee must make the choice within two months after the end of an income year.

Refer TR 2006/14 for the consequences of creating life and remainder interests in property and of later events affecting those interests.

TESTAMENTARY TRUST DISTRIBUTING CGT ASSETS

Law Administration Practice Statement PS LA 2003/12 states the Commissioner's long-standing practice of treating the trustee of a testamentary trust in the same way that a legal personal representative is treated for the purposes of Division 128. That is, a testamentary trust can distribute an asset of a deceased person without a CGT taxing point occurring.

12.675 LISTED INVESTMENT COMPANIES AND CGT

Generally, a capital gain made by a company is not reduced by the CGT discount, and its shareholders receiving a distribution of a capital gain as a dividend do not benefit from the CGT discount that may have been available if the shareholder had made the capital gain directly.

Subdivision 115-D enables certain shareholders in Listed Investment Companies (LICs) to effectively reduce the eligible capital gain component of a dividend by the CGT discount. Subdivision 115-D achieves this end by:

- treating certain capital gains made by a LIC as a notional discount capital gain (LIC capital gain is defined in s115-285), and
- allowing certain shareholders in a LIC, on receiving a dividend that includes a LIC capital gain amount, a deduction that reflects the CGT discount the shareholder could have claimed if they had made the LIC capital gain directly.

The amount of the deduction allowed to the shareholder in the income year in which the dividend is paid is:

- 50% of the attributable part if the shareholder is an individual, a trust or a partnership, or
- $33^{1}/3\%$ of the attributable part if the shareholder is a complying superannuation entity or a life insurance company (s115-280(2)).

The attributable part is determined by the LIC using the formula in s115-280(3). The LIC is required to advise its shareholders of their share of the attributable part included in the dividend at the time the dividend is paid.

Georgina received a fully franked dividend of $420 from a LIC on 23 June 2013. The dividend statement stated that her share of the attributable part paid to shareholders was $140.

In completing her income tax return for the 2012-13 income year, Georgina would include in assessable income a franked dividend of $420 and imputation credit of $180. Georgina would claim a deduction of $70, being 50% of the $140 attributable part included in the dividend.

Where the shareholder in a LIC is a trust or a partnership, and the beneficiary or partner ultimately receiving the LIC dividend is not an individual, the beneficiary or partner may have to include an amount in assessable income (as they are entitled to a lesser benefit than the 50% discount claimed by the trust or partnership). This will occur where a beneficiary or partner is a complying superannuation entity or a life assurance company entitled to a $33^{1}/3\%$ discount or a company that is not entitled to any discount.

The mechanism to reduce or to deny the benefit of the deduction included in the net income of the trust or partnership, is to include in assessable income:

- that part of the deduction allowed to the trust or partnership that is reflected in the share of the net income of a beneficiary or partner that is a company, trust (except a complying superannuation entity) or partnership, or
- one-third of that part of the deduction allowed to the trust or partnership that is reflected in the share of the net income of a beneficiary or partner that is a complying superannuation entity or life insurance company (s115-280(5)).

The following example is taken from the Explanatory Memorandum.

The Robbie Partnership received a $210 fully franked dividend from a LIC that also contained an attributable part of $180. The partnership has three equal partners, Joe Robbie, Robbie Limited and the Robbie Superannuation Fund, a complying superannuation entity. The partnership claimed a deduction of $90 in respect of the attributable part in working out its net income of $12,000, including the dividend. Each partner's share of the net income is $4,000 and their reduction amount is $30 (one-third of $90). Each partner includes $4,000 in their assessable income.

The partners must also include the following additional amounts in their assessable income:

- *Joe Robbie: nil. Joe is an individual partner in the partnership*
- *Robbie Limited: $30 (the reduction amount), and*
- *Robbie Superannuation Fund: $10 (one-third of the reduction amount).*

The end result will mean that a shareholder in a LIC will receives a similar tax outcome to a payment of a similar amount to a member of a managed fund, without disturbing the operations of the company tax or imputation systems.

CGT event E4 does not happen to a payment attributable to a LIC capital gain (s104-70(8)).

LIC CAPITAL GAIN

To be a LIC capital gain:

- the CGT event must happen on or after 1 Juiy 2001 to a permitted asset
- the gain must satisfy the discount capital gain eligibility tests, and
- the LIC capital gain must be included in both the company's net capital gain and taxable income for the income year in which the capital gain is made (s115-285).

BENEFITING SHAREHOLDERS

The shareholders that can benefit from Subdivision 115-D are:

- an individual, a complying superannuation entity, a trust, a partnership, or
- a life insurance company where the dividend is in respect of shares that are virtual PST assets.

These shareholders must be Australian residents.

MEANING OF 'LISTED INVESTMENT COMPANY'

A company is an LIC if:

- it is an Australian resident
- it is listed on the Australian Securities Exchange or any other approved Australian stock exchange, and
- at least 90% of the market value of its CGT assets consist of permitted investments (as listed in s115-290(4)).

A wholly-owned subsidiary of a LIC can itself be treated as a LIC if it satisfies the requirements in s115-290(2).

12.700 CGT AND FOREIGN RESIDENTS

Under Division 855 a foreign resident can disregard for Australian tax purposes any capital gain or loss made from a CGT event unless the event relates to an asset that is 'taxable Australian property'.

Section 855-10 of that Division provides that a foreign resident, or trustee of a foreign trust, can disregard for Australian income tax purposes any capital gain or capital loss made from a CGT event unless the event relates to an asset that is 'taxable Australian property'.

Section 855-15 lists five categories of CGT assets that are 'taxable Australian property':

- taxable Australian real property
- an indirect Australian real property interest
- a business asset of an Australian permanent establishment
- an option or a right over the above items, or
- assets on which a taxpayer has made an election under s104-165(2) to disregard a capital gain or capital loss on ceasing to be a resident of Australia.

AUSTRALIAN REAL PROPERTY

The term 'taxable Australian real property' is defined in s855-20. It covers real property situated in Australia or a mining, quarrying or prospecting right (to the extent that the right is not real property) where the minerals, petroleum or quarry materials are situated in Australia.

The term 'real property' is not defined in the Act. The Explanatory Memorandum states that 'taxable Australian real property generally refers to real property, within the ordinary meaning of the term, that is situated in Australia' (paragraph 5.28). The term real property is defined in Osborn's Concise Law Dictionary as 'Lands, tenements and hereditaments. Immovable property which could be recovered by a real action'.

If the taxable Australian real property was a depreciating asset, s118-24 may apply and the capital gain or capital loss would be disregarded.

A leasehold interest in real property is 'real property' and therefore taxable Australian real property for the purposes of ss855-20(1) (TD 2009/18).

INDIRECT REAL PROPERTY INTEREST

Capital gains tax will also apply where a foreign resident disposes of a membership interest (held directly or indirectly through a chain of interposed entities) in an entity whose assets consist principally of Australian real property and that interest passes the non-portfolio test and the principal asset test (s855-25).

A membership interest passes the non-portfolio test if the sum of the direct participating interests held by a holding entity and its associates in the test entity is 10% or more. This non-portfolio test excludes from CGT the disposal of a membership interest of less than 10%.

A membership interest held by a foreign resident (holding entity) in another entity (test entity) passes the principal asset test if more than 50% of the market value of the test entity's assets is attributable to taxable Australian real property (s855-30).

As many indirect real property interests of foreign residents were not subject to CGT prior to 12 December 2006, the cost base of such interests is reset to the market value on 10 May 2005, the date the Treasurer announced the measure (ss855-25(3)). This ensures that unrealised accumulated capital gains or losses from interests in land-rich foreign interposed entities that were not previously within Australia's tax regime are not subject to CGT.

PERMANENT ESTABLISHMENT IN AUSTRALIA

A CGT event that occurs in relation to an asset used by a foreign resident in carrying on a business through an Australian permanent establishment will be subject to Australian CGT. A proportionate reduction is made to the capital gain or capital loss if the foreign resident used the asset in carrying on a trade or business through a permanent establishment in Australia for only part of the relevant period (s855-35).

If the business assets of an Australian permanent establishment include either taxable Australian real property, indirect Australian real property interests or relate to assets that are covered by a choice made by a person ceasing to be a resident of Australia (ss104-165(3)), then those assets are treated as 'taxable Australian property' under those categories, rather than as business assets of the Australian permanent establishment (s855-15 Item 3).

12.710   DOUBLE TAX TREATIES APPLY

Usually the foreign resident's tax will increase only to the extent the Australian tax rate exceeds that charged in their country of residence. See 12.840 for the CGT effect on controlled foreign corporations. For example, under Article 13(6) of the USA treaty with Australia, where a taxpayer leaves Australia with CGT assets which are not taxable Australian property (eg. Australian shares) and a deferral under CGT event I1 has been chosen, any gain on disposal would be subject to tax only in the United States. Consequently, any Australian capital gains (as a result of the asset being deemed taxable Australian property) would be disregarded as the terms of the treaty provide the taxing rights to the United States, and the treaty overrides the domestic provisions which govern the operation of CGT event I1.

In other jurisdictions, there may not be a similar clause in the relevant treaty or there may not be a treaty at all. In such circumstances, any subsequent disposal by the non-resident taxpayer may be subject to tax in Australia and the other jurisdiction.

12.715   CEASING TO BE AN AUSTRALIAN RESIDENT

Assets acquired after 19 September 1985 that are not 'taxable Australian property' are taken to have been disposed of at market value when a person ceases to be an Australian resident (CGT event I1 occurs) unless an election is made pursuant to ss104-65(2). As CGT assets that are 'taxable Australian property' remain subject to CGT regardless of a taxpayer's residency status, there are no CGT implications with respect to these assets when a taxpayer ceases to be an Australian resident. CGT event I1 will only affect post-CGT assets that are not 'taxable Australian property'.

An individual taxpayer ceasing to be a resident may choose that CGT event I1 does not apply. By making this choice, all assets owned by the taxpayer are taken to be 'taxable Australian property'. The assets will continue to be 'taxable Australian property' until the earlier of:

(a)   a CGT event happening in relation to the asset, or

(b)   the taxpayer again becoming an Australian resident.

If this choice is made (at the time of lodgement of the income tax return for the year residency changed), no CGT event will occur by virtue of the change of residency. However, a CGT liability may arise when a subsequent CGT event happens.

Note that prior to 12 December 2006, similar rules applied to a non-resident's assets that did not have the 'necessary connection with Australia'. Where a taxpayer, prior to 12 December 2006, made a s104-165 election to disregard the capital gain or capital loss on assets covered by CGT event I1 upon ceasing to be an Australian resident, the effect of that election remains. This means assets that were taken to have the 'necessary connection with Australia' became 'taxable Australian property' until either a CGT happens in relation to the assets or the taxpayer again becomes an Australian resident (s104-165 of the *Income Tax (Transitional Provisions) Act 1999*).

Tom Collins decides to permanently leave Australia to work with his brother in New York on 1 August 2011. At that time, Tom has no intention to return to Australia and prima facie, will not satisfy the definition of a 'resident' for income tax purposes. In addition, Tom does not have any carry forward tax losses from prior years and has not derived any capital gains for the 2011-12 income year.

At the time that Tom leaves Australia, he owned the following assets:

- *A townhouse in Melbourne, which he purchased for $500,000 in March 2003. The townhouse is now worth $900,000. Tom was living in the property as his home before he left and was able to find a tenant to live in the property soon after arriving in New York. Whilst in New York, Tom intends to live with his brother.*

- *An apartment in London, which he purchased in July 2007 for A$300,000. He is currently renting this property to a tenant and is deriving rental income. Surprisingly, the property now has a market value of A$280,000*

- *Shares in XYZ Ltd which he acquired in May 2010 for $100,000. The market value at 1 August 2011 is $150,000.*

- *A speedboat which he has left in storage in Australia as he was unable to find a buyer prior to leaving. The boat was purchased in March 2006 for $11,000. It was subsequently sold on eBay for $4,000 in September 2011.*

What are the tax implications for Tom Collins with respect to his Australian and foreign based assets?

CGT event I1 is triggered with respect of the CGT assets owned by Tom, but for his townhouse in Melbourne (which is taxable Australian property (see 12.700)). On that basis, there would a capital gain on the XYZ Ltd shares of $50,000. A capital loss would arise with respect to the London apartment of $20,000 and a capital loss on the speedboat of $7,000 (in any case, the loss on the boat would be disregarded as it is a 'personal use asset').

On 1 August 2011, Tom may choose to defer the capital gains or losses for all the eligible CGT assets as a result of him becoming a non-resident.

If he chooses to defer the capital gain, the choice will apply to all the CGT assets which he owns at that time. Therefore, no capital gains will immediately arise in respect of Tom's shares in XYZ Ltd as a result of making that choice. On this basis, the capital loss from the London apartment is also disregarded. As noted, the deferral does not apply to Tom's Melbourne townhouse as this is 'taxable Australian property'.

To the extent that the choice is made, all CGT assets are deemed to be taxable Australian property. This means that any subsequent disposal of, say the London apartment or shares in XYZ Ltd would be subject to the Australian CGT provisions notwithstanding that Tom is a non-resident.

To the extent that the Melbourne townhouse was Tom's main residence prior to him leaving, he can apply the six year absence rule from the date of him leaving to live with his brother (ie. he has no other main residence). If the property is subsequently sold, a partial exemption may be available if the absence period exceeds six years or if he has another main residence (eg. he acquires a property in New York).

If a choice to defer is not made, exemptions aside, Tom would be assessed on a capital gain of $30,000 (ie. $50,000 gain from the XYZ Ltd shares less $20,000 loss from the London apartment), upon becoming a non-resident.

12.721   TEMPORARY RESIDENTS

Individuals who are considered to be temporary residents of Australia are exempt from Australian tax on non-Australian sourced income.

A person is a temporary resident if that person:

* holds a temporary visa granted under the *Migration Act 1958* (a temporary visa is a visa to travel to and remain in Australia during a specified period, until a specified event happens or while the holder has a specified status. Such a visa does not permit a person to remain in Australia indefinitely), or

* or their spouse (if applicable) is not an Australian resident within the meaning of the Social Security Act 1991 (This includes a person who resides in Australia and is either an Australian citizen or holds a permanent resident visa. Note that taxpayers that hold a protected special category visa and who were in Australia on or before 26 February 2001 are also included).

An individual Australian resident who later holds a temporary visa is not eligible for the temporary residents exemption.

Apart from the income sources noted below, a temporary resident is not subject to tax on:

* ordinary income (other than employment income) and statutory income (other than a net capital gain) from a foreign source

* net capital gains from assets that are not 'taxable Australian property', and

* interest withholding tax obligations associated with amounts owing to foreign lenders.

Expenses or losses incurred in earning this exempt income are not deductible and will not reduce tax losses.

* The tax exemption for a temporary resident noted above does not apply to: any non-Australian source remuneration received for or associated with employment or for services performed while a temporary resident

* assessable income under Division 86 (alienated personal services income), or

* any discount on employee shares or rights.

A temporary resident is subject to tax on Australian sourced income.

For CGT purposes, a temporary resident is subject to the same treatment as a foreign resident. The temporary resident is exempt from Australian tax on the same capital gains as a foreign resident (s768-915) and is liable for Australian tax on the net capital gains on which a foreign resident would be taxable. A temporary resident is still liable for net capital gains arising from some employee shares or rights to the same extent that the discount is taxed under Division 13A of Part III ITAA36.

When a foreign resident becomes an Australian resident, s855-45 would normally apply to fix a cost base for the person's assets that are not 'taxable Australian property'. This rule will not apply when a foreign resident person becomes a temporary resident immediately after becoming an Australian resident (the rule will only apply when that person becomes a permanent resident (s768-950)). Similarly, CGT event I1 will only apply when a permanent Australian resident becomes a foreign resident. It will not apply when a temporary resident becomes a foreign resident.

12.725   BECOMING AN AUSTRALIAN RESIDENT

Certain assets owned at the date of becoming an Australian resident are taken to have been acquired for their market value on that date. Accordingly, increases in value before that date are disregarded.

However, this rule does not apply to any asset:

- acquired before 20 September 1985 (which remains free of CGT), or
- that is 'taxable Australian property'.

Therefore, if a choice had previously been made under CGT event I1 to defer the capital gain or loss for assets owned by a taxpayer who was previously a resident, there is no deemed asset acquisition upon the taxpayer becoming a resident. The asset merely retains its original cost base (as opposed to a market value cost base).

Where the CGT asset is foreign real property which is the taxpayer's main residence, the main residence exemption may apply from the time the asset was purchased until the time the taxpayer becomes an Australian resident and begins to reside in another property which they treat as their main residence.

Although s855-45 deems assets that are not 'taxable Australian property' to have been acquired for their market value at the date a foreign resident becomes an Australian resident taxpayer, this does not mean that the assets were not owned by the taxpayer before the taxpayer became a resident. Therefore, if the taxpayer owned a dwelling overseas and it ceased to be the taxpayer's main residence, the taxpayer can be exempt from any capital gain if the conditions of s118-145 apply (TD 95/7).

In March 2004, Susan, a UK resident, moved permanently to Australia. She was unable to sell her UK main residence (which she acquired in 1995) before her departure. As a result, Susan decided to rent the UK property. She did not acquire a main residence in Australia.

In April 2014, Susan sold the UK property to her tenant. Susan can make an election to exempt from tax the capital gain that accrued in relation to the UK property from March 2004.

Returning to Australia

After spending five years in New York, John Collins decides to return to Australia to settle down with his fiancé in December 2011. At the time that he left for New York, John had no intention of returning to Australia and was considered to be a non-resident for Australian tax purposes at that time. He had made a choice to defer his capital gains which would have arisen as a result of CGT event I1.

At the time that John leaves the United States, he owned the following assets:

- *A house in Sydney which he had purchased prior to departing. Similar to his brother, he had lived in the property as his main residence and rented out the property just prior to leaving for New York. The property was purchased in February 2001 for $400,000. The current market value of the property is $800,000. The tenant has left the property and John intends to live in the property with his fiancé upon his return.*

- *An apartment in New York which he purchased and lived in upon arriving in New York. He purchased the apartment for US$750,000 in January 2006. The apartment is worth A$1,000,000 in December 2011. His brother, Tom, who is living in New York has made an offer for the property, however, John has mixed feelings about selling this.*

- *Shares in Pear Inc which he bought for US$10,000 in February 2008. The market value of those shares in December 2010 is A$8,000.*

- *Shares in BHP Billiton which were purchased for A$10,000 in May 2011. The market value of those shares in December 2011 is A$20,000. The shares were then subsequently sold in March 2012.*

- *A rare antique cocktail shaker which was purchased in Australia in May 2002 and which John had taken with him when he left Australia. The cocktail shaker was acquired for $1,000 and has a market value of $1,500 in December 2011.*

Australian tax implications for John Collins with respect to his Australian and foreign based assets

John's property in Sydney would retain its original cost base of $400,000 as the asset was taxable Australian property and therefore CGT event I1 had no application. As this property was previously John's main residence prior to him leaving for New York, he may be entitled to a partial main residence exemption.

Given that John's New York apartment was his main residence at the time of acquisition, upon his return to Australia, he would be entitled to the main residence exemption from the date of acquisition time until he moves into his Melbourne property. If he chooses to sell the property the asset would have a deemed market value cost base of $1,000,000 (being the market value at the time residency commenced).

The shares in Pear Inc are deemed to have a market value cost base of $8,000 as at December 2011 (ie. the date residency commences.

The shares in BHP Billiton are deemed to have a market value cost base of $20,000 as at December 2011. The cost base would be used in determining the extent of any capital gain or loss when the shares are disposed in January 2011. He would be able to benefit from any franking credits attached to any dividends paid prior to disposal (subject to the 45 day holding rule). No CGT discount would be available as the shares have not been held for at least 12 months from the date of deemed acquisition.

The antique cocktail shaker is a CGT asset. It would have a cost base of $1,000 as a choice under CGT event I1 had been made. This cost base would be used to calculate any future capital gains or losses upon disposal.

Note: If taxable Australian property was sold on or after 8 May 2012, the full 50% general discount in respect of certain assets may need to be reduced as the discount no longer applies during the period that the taxpayer was a non-resident. Special calculations apply (see 22.130 for details).

12.730 ASSETS USED BY FOREIGN RESIDENTS

Under s855-15, a CGT asset is taken to be 'taxable Australian property' if the asset has been used at any time by the taxpayer in carrying on a business through a permanent establishment in Australia.

A capital gain or capital loss on an asset used in carrying on a business through a permanent establishment is calculated by reference only to the period it was used in the permanent establishment.

A foreign resident taxpayer acquires an asset on 2 February 2011 for $21,000. It is first used in carrying on business at or through the foreign resident's permanent establishment in Australia on 1 June 2011. The asset is sold on 10 November 2011 for $30,000 and was owned for 284 days but used in the permanent establishment for 163 days. The capital gain is ($9,000 x 163) divided by 284 = $5,165

Under s855-35 the capital gain is actually calculated and then reduced by the period in which the foreign resident taxpayer did not use the asset in the permanent establishment.

The capital gain of $9,000 is reduced by ($9,000 x 121) divided by 284 = $3,835 so the actual capital gain is $9,000 – $3,835 = $5,165. The CGT discount not is applicable because the CGT event has occurred within 12 months of acquiring the asset.

12.732 CGT DISCOUNT AND SMALL BUSINESS CGT CONCESSIONS

Provided that all the requirements for the CGT discount and small business CGT concessions are met, a foreign resident is entitled to both the CGT discount (up to 8 May 2012) and the small business CGT concessions to a capital gain made on an asset that is 'taxable Australian property' (see 22.130).

Where CGT assets are deemed to be acquired from the date on which the taxpayer becomes an Australian tax resident, the CGT discount would be available to individual taxpayers from the date of becoming a resident and not when the asset was actually acquired.

Note that from 8 May 2012, foreign or temporary resident individuals must meet certain eligibility conditions to apply the CGT discount.

For CGT events occurring after 8 May 2012, the application of a CGT discount percentage will depend on:

- whether the CGT asset was held before or after 8 May 2012, and
- the residency status of the individual who has the capital gain.

The rules also apply to Australian resident individuals who, after 8 May 2012, have a capital gain from a CGT event and a period of foreign or temporary residency. Special calculations apply in working out a discount capital gain where an foreign or temporary resident individual has derived a discount capital gain from a CGT event that occurred after 8 May 2012. See 22.130 for details.

12.733 CAPITAL GAINS AND LOSSES FOR FOREIGN RESIDENTS THROUGH FIXED TRUSTS

To provide comparable taxation treatment between direct and indirect ownership by foreign residents through a fixed trust of assets that are not taxable Australian property, a capital gain in respect of an interest in a fixed trust is disregarded if:

- the taxpayer is a foreign resident when the gain is made
- the gain is attributable to a CGT event happening to a CGT asset of a trust that is the fixed trust or another fixed trust in which that trust has an interest, and
- either:
  - the asset is not taxable Australian property for the trust, or
  - at least 90% (by market value) of the trust's assets underlying the interest in the trust are not 'taxable Australian property' or 90% of the trust's assets held by other fixed trusts in which the first trust has an interest (directly, or indirectly through a chain of fixed trusts) are not 'taxable Australian property'.

Further, the trustee of a fixed trust is also not liable to pay tax on an amount that is disregarded for a beneficiary in the situations above (s855-40).

12.750 LEASES

Leases and any leasehold improvements are treated as CGT assets. Special conditions apply to Crown leases.

GRANT OF LEASE IS TREATED AS A DISPOSAL OF AN ASSET

In brief, the granting, renewal or extension of a lease constitutes a CGT event under event F1 (see 12.030).

A capital gain will arise if the capital proceeds are greater than the cost of granting, renewing or extending the lease (ss104-110(3)).

The capital proceeds are the premium paid, while the cost base is restricted to the expenditure the lessor incurred on the grant, renewal or extension of the lease.

As a result of CGT event F1, the lessee will have acquired a CGT asset (the lease) for a cost base equal to the value of any premium paid. If the lease is later transferred to another person, CGT event A1 would apply as there is a disposal of a CGT asset. On the other hand, if the lease ends, the lessee will be subject to CGT event C2 as the lease has expired. The capital proceeds will be nil, as the market value modification does not apply to event C2 (ss116-30(3)) and a capital loss may result subject to s118-40.

LEASE CONVERTED TO FREEHOLD

Special provisions apply if a leasehold interest in land is converted to a freehold interest after 19 September 1985. If a lease is converted after that date, CGT applies only when the freehold is sold.

LEASE OF AT LEAST 99 YEARS

For a lease with a term of at least 99 years, the lessee is taken to acquire the land at the time the lease was granted. This means that if the lease was acquired before 20 September 1985, CGT will not apply to the disposal of leasehold or freehold interest. Where the lease is acquired post-CGT, the cost base will be any premium paid for the grant of the lease plus the amount the lessee paid to acquire the revisionary interest (s132-15).

LEASE OF LESS THAN 99 YEARS

If the lease term is less than 99 years, the lessee acquires the land at the time the lessee acquired the reversionary interest. This means that if the lease is pre-CGT but the reversionary interest was acquired post-CGT, CGT may apply to a dealing with the asset.

In the case of a pre-CGT lease but post-CGT acquisition of the reversionary interest, the cost base of the land will be its market value at the time the lessee acquired it. Where the lease is post-CGT, the cost base is any premium paid for the grant of the lease, plus the amount paid to acquire the reversionary interest (s132-15).

A payment to surrender a lease is a CGT event, and CGT will not apply if the lease was granted before 20 September 1985. However, if an amount is received by a lessee for a surrender of a lease granted after 19 September 1985, CGT event C2 happens and a capital gain may arise.

GRANT OF A LONG-TERM LEASE

A taxpayer that grants a long-term lease or sublease over any land (50 years or more) may choose to have CGT event F2 apply, rather than CGT event F1. Where CGT event F2 is chosen, the CGT provisions apply on the basis that there is a disposal of the underlying asset (ie. the freehold, or leasehold interest in the land covered by the lease) (ss104-115(1)).

The choice is available only if the lease/sub-lease is granted for at least 50 years on terms substantially the same as those under which the lessor owned the land or held the head lease.

- **If the freehold or leasehold interest was acquired before 20 September 1985:** CGT will not apply unless a major capital improvement made after 19 September 1985 was treated as a separate asset (see 12.062)
- **If the freehold or leasehold interest was acquired after 19 September 1985:** a capital gain subject to CGT may arise if the capital proceeds from the event (as defined in ss116-20(2)) are more than the cost base (capital expenditure in obtaining the leasehold interest forms part of the cost base)

PAYMENTS TO VARY OR WAIVE THE TERMS OF A LEASE

CGT event F3 happens where a lessor incurs expenditure in obtaining the consent of the lessee to the variation or waiver of any of the terms of a lease. The lessor makes a capital loss equal to the payment. The time of the event is when the term of the lease is varied or waived.

For the lessee, CGT event F4 happens:

- **If the amount received by the lessee exceeds the cost base of the lease:** the surplus will be assessable as a capital gain and the cost base reduced to nil.
- **If the amount received is less than the 'cost base' of the lease:** the lessee's 'cost base' and reduced cost base' are reduced by amount received.

Where the lessor receives money or property from the lessee for agreeing to vary or waive a term of the lease CGT event F5 happens. The lessor makes a capital gain if the capital proceeds are greater than the expenditure incurred by the lessor in varying or waiving the lease.

12.755   CROWN LEASES

Automatic rollover relief applies on the expiry or surrender of one (or more) Crown leases of land when they are replaced with new Crown leases or freehold interests. A Crown lease means a lease of land granted by the Crown under a statutory law of the Commonwealth, or of a State or Territory, or of a similar law of a foreign country (including a republic) (s124-580).

CONDITIONS FOR ROLLOVER RELIEF

Rollover relief applies only if the original rights expire and the lessee is granted one or more new Crown leases with rights relating to the same land. The new rights must be granted in one of these ways:

- the original Crown lease is renewed or extended, and the renewal is mainly due to the taxpayer's prior ownership of the original Crown lease, or
- the purpose for which the land covered by the original lease may be used, is changed, or

- the original Crown lease is converted to a Crown lease in perpetuity, or converted to freehold, or
- the original Crown leases are either consolidated (or consolidated and divided) or simply divided, or
- part of the area of land of the original lease is excised or relinquished, or
- the area of land (of the original lease) is expanded (s124-575).

IF A TRUSTEE HOLDS THE CROWN LEASE

Where the original Crown lease is held by a trustee, rollover relief applies only if (immediately after the grant of new lease or freehold interest) the trustee holds the new interest on the same trust as for the original Crown lease.

CAPITAL PROCEEDS

Any payment received for land not covered by the new leasehold or freehold interest is subject to CGT.

IF NEW LEASE IS OF DIFFERENT LAND

If the new Crown lease relates to an area of land different from the preceding lease and one of the conditions of s124-585 applies (such as there is no significant difference in the area or its market value) rollover relief can still be available.

GOVERNMENT-ACQUIRED LEASE

A new lease is treated as a renewal of the original lease if land held under a Crown lease becomes vested in, or is held by a government authority (other than the one that granted the original right), and that new authority grants a new lease over:

- the original land, or
- the original land less an excised area, or
- the original land and other land.

If, pending the grant of a fresh lease, the taxpayer continues to occupy the original land under a permission, licence or authority, any lapse of time between the original and new lease is disregarded and the new lease is accepted as a renewal of the old one (s124-605).

ROLLOVER OF REPLACEMENT CROWN LEASE

If the original lease been acquired before 20 September 1985, the CGT exemption is preserved for the new lease or freehold. If the original Crown lease was acquired after 19 September 1985, the CGT event is disregarded until the lease is either disposed of to a third party, or otherwise terminated. The cost base of the new lease is that of the old one.

ROLLOVER RELIEF FOR DEPRECIABLE PROPERTY ON CROWN LEASES

Automatic rollover relief applies to disposals of a lessee's interest (or partner's interest if a partnership) in a depreciating asset affixed to a Crown lease (Subdivision 124-K).

The rollover relief applies only to the depreciating asset (not to a disposal of the leasehold interest in the land itself) if the provisions of s40-40 treat the lessee as the holder of the depreciating asset even though the lessee has received a fresh interest as either quasi-owner or lessee of the land.

Rollover will not apply if either Subdivision 124-J (rollover or conversion of Crown lease) or Subdivision 124-L (rollover of prospecting or mining rights) apply to the expiry, surrender or termination of a Crown lease. The effect of the rollover is to prevent a capital loss or capital gain arising in respect of a depreciating asset installed on a Crown lease where the lease is terminated but the lessee is granted a new quasi-ownership right over the land.

NOTE: A CGT event affecting a depreciating asset used wholly for a taxable purpose does not fall within the CGT regime (s118-24).

12.757   PROSPECTING AND MINING ENTITLEMENTS

Subdivision 124-L provides for a rollover if a prospecting or mining entitlement expires or is surrendered and it is replaced by a new entitlement that relates to the same land as the original entitlement.

For rollover relief the new entitlement must be granted in one of these ways:

- by renewing or extending the term of the original entitlement where the renewal or extension is mainly due to the taxpayer having held the original entitlement, or
- by consolidating, or consolidating and dividing, the original entitlement, or
- by subdividing the original entitlement, or
- by converting a prospecting entitlement to a mining entitlement, or a mining entitlement to a prospecting entitlement, or
- by excising or relinquishing a part of the land to which the original entitlement related, or
- by expanding the area of that land.

A partial rollover can apply where the land to which the new entitlement relates is different in area to the original land entitlement because a part of the land to which the original entitlement related was excised or the taxpayer relinquished it, and received a payment for the expiry or surrender of the original entitlement.

12.758   DEPRECIATING ASSETS

Section 124-655 provides rollover for depreciating assets in the limited circumstances where a Crown lease rollover under Subdivision 124-J cannot apply because a quasi-ownership right over land covers more than a Crown lease, such as an easement over the land. For example, a s124-655 rollover may be available where an easement over land expires and a new easement is granted.

For s124-655 to apply all of the following conditions must be satisfied:

- the asset is attached to land that the taxpayer holds under a quasi-ownership right granted by an exempt Australian or foreign government agency
- the taxpayer holds the asset under s40-40
- the quasi-ownership right expires, is terminated or is surrendered by the taxpayer
- the taxpayer is granted a new quasi-ownership right over the land or an estate in fee simple in the land, and
- rollover is not available under Subdivision 124-J (Crown leases) or Subdivision 124-L (prospecting and mining entitlements).

Where s124-655 applies the replacement asset rollover rules in Subdivision 124-A apply.

12.800 INVESTMENTS: SHARES, RIGHTS AND OPTIONS

OPTIONS

In general terms, an option is a right granted or acquired under an agreement in return for valuable consideration. An option is a CGT asset.

'Option' is not defined in the legislation. Case law provides two views on its meaning:

- **Traditional:** There are two contracts: one complete, one incomplete.
- **Alternative:** There is one conditional contract.

The grantor of the option gives a right to another person to enter into a particular transaction for a limited time period that is specified in the agreement. If the option is not exercised within that time period, it lapses.

$80,000 is paid to the owner of a property (the grantor) for an option (call option) to purchase that property at a particular price within two years. If the person who paid for the option (the grantee) does not exercise the option (by purchasing the property) within the specified time, the grantor keeps the $80,000, and can sell the property to another buyer.

The grant of an option relating to an existing asset triggers CGT event D2. A capital gain arises to the grantor if the capital proceeds from the granting of the option are more than the expenditure incurred (s104-40). If the option is later exercised, CGT rules in effect negate the original capital gain on the grant of the option (CGT event D2 is disregarded) and substitute a single transaction treatment for the CGT events (ss104-40(5)). That is, the only asset disposed of for CGT purposes is the underlying asset which was the subject of the option (CGT event A1 happens).

After the death of her mother in December 1998, Anna inherited her mother's home. At the time of her mother's death the market value of the home was $165,000. Her mother had purchased the home in 1980. On 30 June 2013, Anna granted an option to Max to purchase the house for $300,000 before 1 January 2014.

Max paid Anna $5,000 for the option, which he exercised on 7 December 2013.

Tax position for the grantor

- *When the option is granted: Assuming the amount Anna received for the option is net of legal fees, Anna includes the $5,000 as a capital gain in her tax return in the year she granted the option, ie. the year ended 30 June 2013.*

- *When the option is exercised: As Anna's mother had initially acquired the property before 20 September 1985 (ie. it was a pre-CGT asset) Anna is taken to have acquired the house at its market value of $165,000 at the date of her mother's death in December 1998.*

The tax implications under ss104-40(5) for the grantor, Anna, are:

Year ended 30 June 2013

Anna's income tax assessment for the year ended 30 June 2013 needs to be amended to remove the capital gain of $5,000 from assessable income.

Year ended 30 June 2014

Anna's capital gain on disposal of the property is:

Capital proceeds on disposal of the asset

Exercise price s116-20	*$300,000*
plus Option fee ss104-40(5)	*$5,000*
Capital proceeds	*$305,000*
less Cost base	*($165,000)*
Notional capital gain	*$140,000*
less CGT discount (50%)	*($70,000)*
Capital gain	**$70,000**

If an option is exercised, the date of acquisition of the asset that is the subject of the option is the date of the transaction that arises from the exercise of the option (TD 16). For example, if shares are acquired upon the exercise of an option, the shares are acquired when the contract resulting from the exercise of the option is entered into and not when the contract for the acquisition of the option was entered into (also see ATO ID 2003/128).

NOTE: The tax treatment of share rights and options, including:

- rights to acquire units in a unit trust
- options to unitholders to acquire unissued units, and
- options issued by companies to their shareholders to acquire unissued shares

are subject to their own rules. See 12.815.

The grant (or renewal or extension) of an option is treated the same as a disposal of the option from the grantor to the grantee. On that basis, the rules in Division 134 for modifying the cost base and reduced cost base of the asset when the option is exercised by the grantee apply.

The capital proceeds from the creation (including grant or issue) or disposal of an option will include any payment received for granting, renewing or extending the option. For example, where a grantee exercises an option that binds the grantor to grant it a lease, the amendments will allow for the inclusion in the CGT cost base of the lease the amount paid for the option plus any amount paid to exercise it.

LOSSES ON UNEXERCISED OPTIONS CAN BE CLAIMED AGAINST OTHER CAPITAL PROFITS

If an option issued after 19 September 1985 expires unexercised, CGT event C2 happens. The cost of the option can be claimed against any assessable current or future capital gain as a capital loss – it cannot be claimed against income from other sources.

 Assume Max (from example above) did not exercise his option and it lapsed on 1 January 2014. At that date Max would have incurred a capital loss of $5,000.

12.805   SALE OF SHARES, RIGHTS AND OPTIONS

The sale of shares, rights and options may be taxed as assessable income, or dealt with under the CGT provisions.

PROFITS

- **CGT:** CGT applies when a CGT event happens to a CGT asset acquired after 19 September 1985, but only if the vendor is not in the business of trading in the items.
- **Section 15-15:** If shares or rights were acquired before 20 September 1985 with an intention of profit-making by sale, s15-15 can tax the profit.
  Section 15-15 does not apply to the sale of assets acquired after 19 September 1985, but s6-5 may apply to tax the profit as ordinary income.
- **Cost base:** For CGT purposes, where a CGT event happens within less than 12 months of acquiring an asset, the acquisition costs are not indexed (s114-10) and the CGT discount does not apply (s115-25). If the CGT happens at least 12 months from acquisition, the capital gain is calculated in accordance with step 5 (see 12.160).
- **Losses:** A loss on an isolated transaction involving an asset acquired with the intention of profit making on resale may be deductible under s8-1 or s 25-40. If CGT applies, any capital loss (calculated without indexing acquisition and other costs) can be offset only against capital gains in the same or in a later year; there is no time limit on carrying-forward capital losses.

12.810   SHARES ACQUIRED AND SOLD (OTHER THAN BONUS SHARES OR EMPLOYEE SHARES)

- **Acquired before 20 September 1985:** Where the sale of shares occurs in the ordinary course of conducting a business, any profit is assessable under s6-5. If the sale is not in the ordinary course of business, the profit is only assessable if the taxpayer's conduct involved a profit-making undertaking or plan (s15-15).
- **Acquired after 19 September 1985:** If the sale of shares is in the ordinary course of carrying on a business or part of a profit-making undertaking or plan, any profit is assessable under s6-5. If the sale is not in the ordinary course of business the CGT regime (Part 3-1) will assess the capital gain on disposal of the shares.

Where there is a partial disposal of a taxpayer's shareholding, for tax purposes the taxpayer must generally either identify the lot sold or use the 'first-in first-out' method (TD 33). The Tax Office will also accept the use of average cost to work out the acquisition cost of shares provided that the shares are in the same company, were acquired on the same day, and the shares confer identical rights and impose identical obligations (TD 33A - Addendum).

12.815   ISSUE OF RIGHTS AND OPTIONS

Rights are issued to existing shareholders or unit holders, usually at no cost to them, and are normally exercisable within a short time. It should be noted that some rights may be assessable as income rather than being covered by CGT (eg. sell-back rights (see *FC of T v McNeil* (2007) ATC 4223). The law has however been amended to ensure that call options issued by companies to shareholders to raise capital are dealt with under the CGT provisions from the 2001-02 income year. Specifically, s59-40 ensures that the market value of the rights, as at the time of issue, will be non-assessable non-exempt income provided:

- at the time of issue, the taxpayer must already own an interest in the issuing entity (known as original interests)
- the rights must be issued to the taxpayer because of their ownership of the original interests
- the original interests and the rights must not be revenue assets or trading stock at the time the rights are issued
- the rights must not have been acquired under an employee share scheme
- the original interests and rights must not be traditional securities, and

the original interests must not be convertible interests.

By contrast, options can be offered to any person or company and need not be linked to shareholdings.

SHAREHOLDERS: RIGHTS OR OPTIONS IF COVERED BY CGT

- **Issued by a company**: Where the rights or options to acquire shares have been issued by a company to its shareholders for no consideration and:

    - Rights or options are sold by the original shareholder. The rights or options are taken for CGT purposes to have been acquired at the time the original shares were acquired (ss130-45(1)). Capital gains may apply if the original shares were acquired after 19 September 1985. As there is no consideration paid for the issue of the rights or options, the cost base is zero (note: this is one of the listed exceptions to the market value substitution rule) (ss112-20(3)).

    - Rights or options exercised by the original shareholder. Again, the rights or options are taken to have been acquired at the time the original shares were acquired (ss130-45(1)). The exercising of the rights or options is deemed not to be a CGT event and any capital gain or capital loss from the exercise of the rights is disregarded (s130-40(7)). The new shares are acquired when the rights or options are exercised (s130-45(2)), not when the options are granted (*Van v FC of T* [2002] AATA 1313). The cost base of the new shares (s130-40) will be:
        * where the original shares were acquired after 19 September 1985: *the amount paid on exercise of the option (ie. the exercise price).*
        * where the original shares were acquired before 20 September 1985: *the amount paid on exercise of the option (ie. the exercise price) plus the market value of the right or option at the date when exercised.*

- **Purchased**: Where a shareholder purchases an option or a right to acquire shares, and:

    - Options or rights purchased are resold. The options and rights are themselves CGT assets. The purchase and sale of options or rights is subject to the general CGT provisions.

    - Options or rights purchased and then exercised. The exercise of the right or option is taken not to be a disposal of the right or option and any capital gain or capital loss is disregarded. The new shares are taken to be acquired on the day the option or right is exercised. Generally, the cost base of the shares is the cost base of the options plus the amount paid to exercise the option (ie. the exercise price of the shares) (s130-40).

    An exception to this rule is where the option or right is acquired pre-CGT, in which case the cost base will be the market value of the option or right on the day it is exercised plus the amount paid on exercising the option.

- **Rights or options issued to shareholders of a company within the same group:** If a company issues rights or options to shareholders of a related company, they are treated in the same way as if a company issued them to one of its own shareholders. To determine whether the other company is related (ie. a wholly-owned group company), the issue of the rights or options is not taken into account.

OPTIONS GENERALLY

For the CGT treatment of options generally, or options not issued by a company (or related company) to its shareholders, see 12.800.

12.816   EMPLOYEE SHARE SCHEMES

The Employee Share Scheme (ESS) provisions are contained within Division 83A ITAA97. These measures include the following key features:

- the eligibility to defer taxation is removed except in limited circumstances ie. in most cases discount will be taxed upfront as the default position
- deferral is only available where there is a 'real risk of forfeiture' or acquired under a salary sacrifice based employment share scheme
- the maximum time for deferral of tax (where applicable) is reduced from ten years to seven years, and
- the $1,000 tax exemption is only available to taxpayers with an adjusted taxable income of less than $180,000.

DEFERRAL OF DISCOUNT

A deferral of the taxing point for a discount on receipt of interests under an ESS is only available where:

- there is a 'real risk of forfeiture' of the interests acquired, or
- interests with a market value of up to $5,000 are acquired under a salary sacrifice arrangement.

ELIGIBILITY TO BE AN ESS

In order to take advantage of both the upfront and deferred tax concessions, the ESS must satisfy the following requirements:

- the employee must be employed by the company offering the scheme, or a subsidiary
- the scheme must relate to ordinary shares
- the scheme must be offered to at least 75 per cent of resident permanent employees with at least three years service
- the ESS interest provided cannot be disposed of within three years unless the employee ceases to be employed at an earlier time, and
- no more than five per cent ownership or control of the company can be obtained by an employee from participation in an ESS.

WHERE SHARES OR RIGHTS ACQUIRED AT A DISCOUNT

The first element in the cost base or reduced cost base is the market value of the share or right at the time it was acquired (s130-80).

QUALIFYING SHARES AND RIGHTS

For qualifying shares and rights, where the taxpayer does not elect for an amount to be included in assessable income when the share or right is acquired, an amount is included in assessable income at the deferred taxing point. In these situations, where CGT event A1, E1, E2, E5 or I1 applies on disposal of the shares or rights in an arm's length transaction at cessation time or within 30 days after the cessation time, any capital gain or capital loss the taxpayer makes from the event is ignored (ss130-83(2)). If these conditions are not satisfied, then the taxpayer is taken to have acquired the shares or rights at the cessation time for their market value (ss130-83(3)).

REAL RISK OF FORFEITURE

Examples of circumstances which would satisfy the 'real risk of forfeiture' requirement are contained in the Tax Office publication *ESS – guide for employers*.

DEFERRED TAXING POINT

The deferred discount on acquisition of an ESS interest would become assessable at the earliest of:

- Shares
  - when there is no real risk of forfeiture
  - cessation of employment, and
  - seven years from the date of acquisition.
- Rights
  - when there is no real risk that the right will be forfeited
  - cessation of employment
  - seven years from the date of acquisition
  - the earliest time when:
    * there is no real risk of forfeiture, and
    * restrictions on exercising the right no longer exist, and
    * if you exercise the right there is no real risk that you will forfeit the share, and
    * restrictions on disposing of the share acquired as a result of exercising the right no longer exist.

PROPOSED CHANGES FROM 1 JULY 2015

In April 2015, the government introduced the *Tax and Superannuation Laws Amendment (Employee Share Schemes) Bill 2015* into Parliament. In summary, this Bill makes three changes to the taxation of employee share schemes. First it reverses some of the changes made in 2009 to the rules on employee share schemes. Second, it creates a new taxation concession for employees of certain small start-up companies. And third, it allows the Commissioner to develop and approve safe harbour valuation methods and standardised documentation.

In relation to reversing some changes from the 2009, where an employee share scheme right is subject to deferred taxation, currently the taxing point is at the earliest of one of the following times:

- when the employee ceases their employment
- seven years after the employee acquired the right
- when there are no longer any genuine restrictions on the disposal of the right, and there is no real risk of the employee forfeiting the right, or
- when there are no longer any genuine restrictions on the exercise of the right, or resulting share being disposed of, and there is no real risk of the employee forfeiting the right or underlying share.

This Bill amends two of these conditions so that, from 1 July 2015, taxation of any discount will be deferred until the earliest of:

- when the employee ceases their employment
- 15 years after the employee acquired the right
- when there are no longer any genuine restrictions on the disposal of the right, and there is no real risk of the employee forfeiting the right, or
- when the right is exercised and there is no real risk of the employee forfeiting the resulting share and there is no genuine restriction on the disposal of the resulting share.

The Bill will also change the maximum ownership and voting rights limitations to 10%, rather than the current 5%.

In relation to the new employee share scheme concession for 'start-up' companies, where the employer meets the conditions of being a 'start-up' company, it can provide discounted employee share scheme interests to employees and the employees will not be subject to tax on the discount.

In relation to providing shares to an employee, if the discount is not more than 15% of the market value of the shares when acquired, nothing is included in the employee's tax return. Further the employee is given a market value cost base – even though they did not pay market value for the shares.

In relation to providing rights to acquire shares to an employee, if the exercise price is greater than or equal to the market value of an ordinary share at the time the right is acquired, nothing is included in the employee's tax return until a future CGT event.

The conditions to be a start-up company are:

- The scheme must be operated so that all the employees must hold the shares or rights for three years, or until the employee ceases employment.

  - The scheme must be offered on a non-discriminatory basis to at least 75% of the company's Australian-resident permanent employees with at least three years of service.
  - The company, and all companies in the group, must have been incorporated less than 10 years ago.
  - The company, and all companies in the group, must not be listed.
  - No employee owns more than 10% of the company who took part in the scheme.
  - The company is not a share trading company.
  - And, the aggregated turnover of the group does not exceed $50 million in the prior income year prior to the income year.

EMPLOYEE SHARE TRUSTS

If qualifying shares or rights are acquired though an employee share trust and the taxpayer has made an election to be assessed on the discount at the time the shares or rights are acquired, the taxpayer acquires the shares or rights at their market value at the time the taxpayer acquired a beneficial interest in the shares or rights. The time the taxpayer acquires a beneficial interest is the time that the trustee first holds the shares or rights for the taxpayer. This will mean that the taxpayer and not the trustee will incur any capital gain or capital loss on the disposal of the shares or rights and the 12 month rule for determining the 50% CGT discount will start from the time the taxpayer acquired the beneficial interest.

Similar rules apply where an associate of an employee acquires the shares or rights.

12.820   ISSUE OF BONUS SHARES

The source of the bonus issue will generally determine whether it is taxed as a dividend. In turn, the date of the bonus issue and whether the bonus issue is a dividend will affect the CGT treatment (see s130-15).

BONUS SHARES ISSUED BEFORE JULY 1987

Provided the original shares were acquired before 20 September 1985, bonus shares are exempt from CGT on acquisition if sourced wholly from one or more of:

- a share premium account, or from the issue at a premium of certain convertible notes, or
- profits from the sale (or revaluation) of assets not acquired for resale at a profit.

For CGT purposes, bonus shares issued before 1 July 1987 are taken to have been acquired on the same date as the original shares from which they arose. Where the original shares were acquired after 19 September 1985, the cost is averaged over all the shares then held.

	Number	Cost
Original shares	1,000	$6,000
Bonus shares	200	nil
	1,200	($5 per share) $6,000

BONUS SHARES ISSUED AFTER JUNE 1987

- **As a dividend:** The paid-up value of bonus shares issued after 30 June 1987 from a source other than an untainted share capital account will generally be taxed as a dividend. The bonus shares are acquired at date of issue. The cost base of the bonus shares is any part that is treated as a dividend (ss130-20(2)).

- **From an untainted share capital account:** Bonus shares financed wholly out of an untainted share capital account are deemed to have been acquired when the original shares giving rise to the bonus shares were acquired. On that basis, if the original shares were acquired before 20 September 1985, the bonus shares will be exempt from CGT on disposal or other CGT event. If the original shares were acquired after 19 September 1985, the cost base of the original and bonus shares is determined by pro-rating the cost of the original shares over the total holding (see example above) (ss130-20(3)).

PARTLY PAID BONUS ISSUES MADE AFTER 10 DECEMBER 1986

For any bonus shares issued after 1pm on 10 December 1986 (provided they arise from shares acquired before 19 September 1985), if the shareholder is liable to pay a call upon the shares, the acquisition date is when the liability arose to pay the money required.

The cost base is the market value of the share when the first call liability for the share arises plus the cost of the call (ss130-20(3)). Section 130-15 provides a flow chart of the possible events in relation to bonus shares.

12.826   CONVERSION OF SHARES

No CGT event happens to the shareholder's original shares where a company converts its shares into a larger or smaller number of shares in accordance with s254H of the *Corporations Act 2001* provided:

- (a) the original shares are not cancelled or redeemed in terms of the *Corporations Act*
- (b) there is no change in the total amount allocated to the share capital account of the company, and
- (c) the proportion of equity owned by each shareholder in the share capital account is maintained.

While there is a change in the form of the original shares, there is no change in their beneficial ownership. The issue of rollover relief under s124-240 does not arise because no CGT event happens in respect of the shares.

The converted shares have the same date of acquisition as the original shares to which they relate.

Cancelling original share certificates and replacing them with new certificates as part of any conversion process does not change the result above, unless there is also a cancellation or redemption of the original shares in which case CGT event C2 (s104-25) happens. In this case, rollover relief is available under s124-240 if the other requirements of s124-240 are satisfied.

12.830   ISSUE OF BONUS UNITS

The taxation treatment of bonus units issued by a unit trust essentially mirrors the rules in respect of bonus shares issued before July 1987.

Broadly, bonus units are taken to be acquired at the same date as the underlying (original) units out of which they are issued, and their cost base is spread over the original and bonus units.

Identical rules also apply for partly paid bonus unit issues made after 10 December 1986 as those that apply for partly paid bonus share issues made after 10 December 1986 (see 12.820).

12.835   RIGHTS IN A UNIT TRUST

It should also be noted that some rights may be assessable as income rather than being covered by CGT (e.g. sell-back rights and possibly others) (see *FC of T v McNeil* (2007) ATC 4223). However, the law has been amended to ensure that call options issued by companies to shareholders to raise capital will typically be dealt with under the CGT provisions.

If the trustee of a unit trust (for no consideration, and after 28 January 1988) issues either rights to acquire units, or rights to acquire an option, in a unit trust:

- **If sold as rights:** They are deemed to have been acquired when the original units were acquired (there will only be a CGT liability if the original units had been acquired after 19 September 1985).

- **If the right is exercised:** the date of acquisition is the date on which the right was exercised, with the cost base equal to the consideration, if any.
- **If a person purchases rights and exercises them:** The new units are acquired on the date the right is exercised, and the cost base is the amount paid for the right plus the amount paid to exercise it.
- **If the original units were acquired before 20 September 1985, and exercised after 28 January 1988:** The unit holder is deemed to have acquired the rights before 20 September 1985.
- **For units not deemed to be acquired before 20 September 1985:** The cost base is the cost base of the right, plus the exercise price (purchase price of the units).

RIGHTS ISSUED TO HOLDERS OF CONVERTIBLE INTEREST IN A UNIT TRUST

The same rules apply as for rights to acquire units in a unit trust.

OPTIONS TO ACQUIRE UNISSUED UNITS IN A UNIT TRUST

The rules are the same as those applicable to rights to acquire units in a unit trust. They relate to transactions after 28 January 1988, and apply also to convertible interests.

12.836   CONVERTIBLE INTEREST IN A UNIT TRUST

The rollover relief available on rights or options to acquire units in a unit trust extends to convertible interests issued after 28 January 1988 on the same basis as for comparable transactions by companies. The conversion into units is not a disposal at that time. CGT arises on disposal of the units obtained on conversion. A taxpayer acquires the units when the conversion happens. The 'cost base' is:

- any amount the taxpayer paid for the convertible interest, plus
- any amount paid for conversion.

12.837   EXCHANGEABLE INTERESTS

An exchangeable interest is a traditional security or qualifying security that was issued on the basis that it will be disposed of or redeemed in exchange for shares in a company (not the issuing company nor a related entity of the issuing company). Any taxing point is deferred until the ultimate disposal of the ordinary shares (ss130-105(4)).

For purposes of the CGT discount, a taxpayer acquires the shares on disposal or redemption of the exchangeable interest, not when the exchangeable interest was purchased.

Under Subdivision 130-E the cost base of the shares acquired on disposal or redemption of an exchangeable interest is modified so that it is the total of:

- the cost base of the exchangeable interest at the time of disposal or redemption
- an amount (if any) paid for the exchange, and
- an amount (if any) by which a capital gain from the exchangeable interest has been reduced under s118-20 by inclusion of an amount in assessable income, even though the capital gain from this event is disregarded.

12.840 CONTROLLED FOREIGN COMPANIES AND CGT

For the rules for taxing these companies, see 22.820.

To calculate the 'attributable income' of a Controlled Foreign Company (CFC), the capital gains tax provisions do not apply to the disposal of an asset that is 'taxable Australian property' from 12 December 2006 (or an asset with the 'necessary connection with Australia' before 12 December 2006), nor to capital losses made on disposal of assets before 1 July 1990. There is no blanket pre-19 September 1985 exemption. Assets acquired earlier are caught if owned at 30 June 1990.

CFC BECOMES A RESIDENT AFTER 30 JUNE 1990

Where a CFC becomes a resident of Australia, the company is deemed to have acquired any relevant asset on 30 June 1990. This means that there is no tax on any gain accruing before that date if after June 1990, a CFC becomes a resident of Australia:

- after ceasing to be resident of a 'listed country' or an 'unlisted country', and
- it disposes of an asset which at 30 June 1990 is not 'taxable Australian property'.

CGT applies to gains accruing:

- between 30 June 1990 and when the company became a resident of Australia, but only if the gain over that period would not have been subject to tax in a tax comparable country before the residence change time, and
- between the time of becoming a resident and the later disposal date.

If the asset was acquired before 30 June 1990, the cost base is determined by actual cost, or the market value of the asset as at 30 June 1990 – whichever results in the lower capital gain or capital loss on actual disposal. If the asset was acquired on 30 June 1990 or later, the normal cost base rules apply.

CHANGE OF RESIDENCE

FROM AUSTRALIA TO A LISTED COUNTRY OR UNLISTED COUNTRY

On change of residence, all assets which are not 'taxable Australian property' are taken to have been acquired on the date of change of residence.

In certain situations, s418A ITAA36 applies to fix a 'cost base' (for 'attributable income' purposes) that excludes any notional gain or loss referable to the period the company was an Australian resident for tax purposes.

FROM A BROAD-EXEMPTION LISTED COUNTRY TO ANOTHER BROAD-EXEMPTION LISTED COUNTRY

If a CFC changes residence from a broad exemption listed country (which does not levy capital gains tax) to another broad exemption listed country (which taxes capital gains made while a resident of that country) the difference between the cost base to the CFC of the asset and its market value at time of change of residence is taken as not having been subject to tax in any listed country. Australian tax will then be payable on the untaxed part. Similar treatment also applies to a trust.

'COST BASE' ADJUSTED ON RETURN OF CAPITAL

Special rules reduce the 'cost base' of shares, or an interest or unit in a trust (s413).

ROLLOVER RELIEF AND CFCS

In calculating the 'attributable income' of a CFC, an asset may be rolled over in accordance with s126-60.

12.845   CAPITAL GAINS TAX CONCESSION FOR ACTIVE FOREIGN COMPANIES

Under the former legislation, Australian companies were subject to tax on capital gains arising from the disposal of shares in foreign companies, including disposals of shares in foreign companies with underlying active businesses. However, where the underlying active business assets of the foreign company were sold, any gain arising on that sale escaped attribution under the accruals regime and could have been repatriated to Australia free from Australian tax if distributed through a non-portfolio dividend.

To enable Australian multinational companies and their controlled foreign companies to compete more effectively, Subdivision 768-G was inserted into the ITAA97. This Subdivision amended the income tax law with effect from 1 April 2004 to reduce any capital gain or capital loss arising from CGT events A1, B1, C2, E1, E2, G3, J1, K4, K6, K10 or K11 happening to shares in a foreign company that has an underlying active business, where the shares are held either by an Australian company or by a controlled foreign company (item 12 in s102-30).

To be eligible for the CGT concession:

- the company must hold a direct voting percentage in the foreign company of at least 10%. The company must directly hold the voting interest. If a trust or partnership is interposed between the shareholder entity and the foreign company, the direct voting percentage is zero
- the requisite interest must have been held by the company for a continuous period of at least 12 months in the two years before the CGT event, and
- the shares in the foreign resident company must not be an eligible finance share or a widely distributed finance share. (These shares are more equivalent to a debt rather than an equity investment.)

Note that a company is taken to have a voting interest in another company if share are beneficially owned in the non-resident company that carry the right to exercise voting power and there is no arrangement in force putting a person in a position to affect that right. Note that a contract for the sale of shares (which has not yet settled) is an 'arrangement' which affects voting rights and may prevent those shares from constituting voting interests (ATO ID 2009/22).

The active assets of a partnership, in which a foreign company is a partner, are not active foreign business assets of the foreign company for the purposes of Subdivision 768-G (TD 2008/23).

Where the conditions are satisfied the capital gains and capital losses will be reduced to the extent of the foreign company's 'active foreign business asset percentage' at the time of the CGT event. Broadly, the 'active foreign business asset percentage' is the value of active business assets owned by the foreign company as a percentage of its total assets. Either market value or book value may be chosen to value these assets in determining the active foreign asset percentage, otherwise the default foreign business asset percentage applies (s768-510).

Where the active foreign asset percentage is 90% or more, the percentage is taken to be 100% and any capital gain is reduced to zero and any capital loss is disregarded. If the percentage is less than 10%, the percentage reduction is taken to be zero and the capital gain is fully taxable and any capital loss is available to offset against any capital gain. Where the percentage is between 10% and 89% the capital gain or capital loss is reduced by the actual percentage.

12.900 RENEWAL OR DISPOSAL OF STATUTORY LICENCES

A statutory licence is defined as an authority, licence, permit or quota granted by a government or government authority. The licence can be granted under a Commonwealth, State or Territorial law, or law of a foreign country.

Statutory rights can seldom be transferred: the authority generally rescinds the existing authority and issues a new one if it approves of the proposed licencee. Examples include radio and television broadcasting licences, taxi licences, import and export quotas, but not a mining lease, or a prospecting or mining right. Such licences are created by the application of statutory powers, and the rights attaching to the grant are subject to renewal or extension.

If the holder of the asset has complied with the terms and conditions of the grant, there is normally an expectation of (but not a legal right to) renewal or extension.

ROLLOVER RELIEF

Following the expiry or surrender of an original licence or authority and the issue of a new statutory licence, rollover relief will apply automatically (s124-140). The new licence must be granted by way of a renewal or extension of the term of the original licence and must be due mainly to the ownership of the original licence.

If the owner is a trustee, immediately after the new licence is granted, it must be held upon the same trust as was the original licence.

EFFECT OF THE ROLLOVER

- **If the original statutory licence was acquired before 20 September 1985:** There is no CGT liability and the new licence is treated as having been acquired before 20 September 1985. Consequently there will be no CGT liability on any subsequent CGT event in relation to any and all subsequent renewals of the statutory licence.

- **If the original licence was acquired after 19 September 1985:** Any capital gain or capital loss on expiry or surrender of the old licence is disregarded. The date of acquisition of the new licence for CGT purposes is its date of issue.

COST BASE OF NEW STATUTORY LICENCE

Where the old licence was acquired after 19 September 1985:

- **If a capital gain is made:** The 'cost base' is the 'cost base' of the old licence plus any amount paid for the new licence. The 'cost base' is indexed if appropriate.
- **If a capital loss is made:** The 'cost base' is the 'reduced cost base' of the old licence at the time it expired (or was surrendered) plus anything paid to acquire the new licence.
- **If a disposal of a new licence occurs within 12 months of renewal:** The 'cost base' is that of the old licence plus anything paid for the new licence.

The renewal or extension of a statutory licence is a 'replacement-asset rollover' (s112-115). Accordingly, where appropriate, indexation or the CGT discount will be available where a CGT event occurs in respect of the new licence provided the combined period of the entity's ownership of the original licence and of the new licence is at least 12 months (refer ss114-10(5)). For CGT events which happen in the 2006-07 income year or later, rollover relief is extended to situations where one or more similar new licences are issued in consequence of the ending of one or more licences. Rollover is also extended to partial relief where the replacement licence or licences are granted in addition to other proceeds such as money (Subdivision 124-C).

12.925 LIQUIDATORS' DISTRIBUTIONS

FINAL DISTRIBUTION

The full amount of a liquidator's final distribution on the winding-up of a company constitutes capital proceeds from the cancellation or ending of the shareholders' shares (CGT event C2).

Any part of a final distribution that is deemed a dividend under ss47(1) ITAA36 and assessable does not reduce the capital proceeds. However, the rule in ss118-20(1) ITAA97 (which reduces capital gains if an amount is otherwise assessable) will reduce the capital gain by the amount taxed as a dividend.

Ben acquired 100 shares in A Ltd in 1990. The shares have a cost base of $10,000 at the time they are cancelled following the winding-up of the company in March 2012. Ben receives a final distribution on 1 July 2012 of $18,000 of which $7,000 is deemed to be a dividend by ss47(1) ITAA36.

Ben makes a capital gain in the year ended 30 June 2013 of $1,000 (that is, $8,000 [distribution – cost base] less the amount of $7,000 assessed as a dividend under ss44(1) ITAA36). As Ben held the shares for at least 12 months, he will be entitled to the 50% CGT discount, and the assessable capital gain will be $500.

If the ss47(1) deemed dividend had been $8,000 or more, Ben would have made no capital gain or loss on the cancellation of his shares.

INTERIM LIQUIDATION DISTRIBUTION

If the company does not cease to exist within 18 months of an interim distribution, CGT event G1 happens (to the extent the distribution is not a dividend) in respect of post-CGT shares. Under CGT event G1, the interim payment that is not a dividend reduces the cost base and reduced cost base of the shareholder's shares as at the time of the payment. If the non-dividend payment exceeds the shareholder's cost base, the excess is a capital gain.

If the company ceases to exist within 18 months, the interim distribution treated as a dividend will form part of the shareholder's capital proceeds for CGT event C2 happening when the shares end.

Where at the time of the interim distribution the shareholder does not know when the company is to cease to exist, TD 2001/27 gives the shareholder the choice to either:

- assume that the company will cease within 18 months, or

- apply CGT event G1 to the interim distribution on the assumption that the company will not cease within the 18 month period.

If the shareholder is advised in writing by the liquidator that the company will not cease to exist within 18 months of the distribution, the shareholder must initially apply CGT event G1 to the interim distribution.

In the absence of any such written advice from the liquidator, the shareholder may assume that the company will cease to exist within 18 months and disregard CGT event G1. In such a case, the payment will be part of the capital proceeds for CGT event C2 happening when the shares end.

If having assumed that the company will cease within 18 months, the company does not cease within 18 months of the interim liquidation payment, the shareholder will need to amend their return for the year in which the payment is made if a capital gain would have resulted from CGT event G1 occurring.

If having been told, or chosen to assume, that the company will not cease within 18 months, and the company does cease within 18 months, the shareholder will need to request an amended assessment to remove any CGT event G1 capital gain from their assessable income in the income year of the payment (the shareholder will be entitled to receive interest for the overpayment). The interim liquidation distribution would form part of the capital proceeds for CGT event C2 happening when the shares end. No cost base or reduced cost base reductions are required by CGT event G1 in respect of the interim distribution.

On 12 March 2014, Brett, who has no capital losses or tax losses, is paid an interim liquidation distribution of $50,000 in respect of his shares in Desert Co, which are held on capital account. An amount of $8,000 of the interim distribution is deemed to be a dividend under ss47(1) ITAA36 for the purposes of s44 ITAA36. The shares were acquired by Brett in October 2005 for $25,000.

Assuming that the liquidator of Desert Co does not advise Brett in writing that Desert Co will not cease to exist within 18 months of the 12 March 2013 distribution, Brett may assume that Desert Co will cease to exist and not initially apply CGT event G1 in relation to the distribution (on the facts given, there would be a capital gain of $17,000 under event G1 were it to apply).

If Desert Co is not dissolved within the 18 month period, Brett should request an amendment to include the capital gain of $17,000 in his assessable income for the year of income in which the distribution was made. If the company does cease within that period, Brett should include the full $50,000 distributed as capital proceeds for cancellation of the shares under CGT event C2 (other amounts distributed, including a final distribution, may also form part of the capital proceeds.) Subsection 118-20(1), when read with ss118-20(1A), will ensure that no part of the $8,000 dividend component of the $50,000 is taxed both as a dividend and as a capital gain.

If Brett acquired his shares at least 12 months before CGT event C2, he may be entitled to the 50% CGT discount.

'EXEMPT' COMPONENTS OF A CAPITAL GAIN

A distribution by a liquidator of an 'exempt' component of a capital gain (attributable to the small business 50% reduction under s152-205, or pre-CGT gains) is not deemed to be a dividend under s47(1). The 'exempt' component is not 'income derived by the company' according to ordinary concepts for the purposes of ss47(1) ITAA36, nor is it 'income derived by the company' under the extended definition of that expression in ss47(1A) ITAA36. The 'exempt' component is a 'capital gain that is disregarded' from the expression 'income derived by a company' in ss47(1A) ITAA36. The distribution by the liquidator of the 'exempt' component will represent:

- the capital proceeds for the cancellation of the shares (CGT event C2) in the case of a final distribution or an interim distribution which is followed within 18 months by the dissolution of the company, or
- the capital proceeds under CGT event G1 in the case of other interim liquidation distributions in respect of post-CGT shares if the company is dissolved more than 18 months after payment of the distribution (see TD 2001/14).

The following example is adapted from the TD:

Company's position

X Pty Ltd, a resident company, was incorporated and acquired a business after 19 September 1985. The business was acquired for $1,100,000 and of that amount its goodwill was acquired for $100,000. The business was sold and the goodwill disposed of for $200,000 in the company's 2013-14 income year.

Assuming the cost base of the goodwill after indexation was $110,000, the company made a capital gain of $90,000 of which $45,000 is exempt under s152-205 (the 50% active asset reduction). The company paid tax of $13,500 on the gain (that is 30% x $45,000).

The company transferred the after-tax amount of $86,500 to its capital profits reserve. The company was placed into liquidation. The liquidator distributed $86,500 appropriated from the capital profits reserve.

Shareholder's position

Subsection 47(1) ITAA36, read with ss47(1A), deems a shareholder to have received a dividend to the extent that an amount would have been a capital gain to the company disregarding indexation.

In this particular case, the capital gain to the company (disregarding indexation, as ss47(1A) requires) would have been $100,000. Fifty percent ($50,000) would have qualified for exemption under s152-205. The balance of the distribution ($36,500 – that is, $50,000 less $13,500 tax paid) is deemed by ss47(1) to be a dividend.

If the distribution is a final distribution or an interim distribution followed within 18 months by the dissolution of the company, the full amount of $86,500 would represent capital proceeds for the cancellation of the shares and would need to be taken into account in calculating the extent of any capital gain or capital loss in respect of the cancellation. Subsection 152-205 would operate to ensure an appropriate reduction is made to any capital gain that would otherwise arise to the extent of the $36,500 deemed dividend.

If the distribution is an interim distribution not followed within 18 months by the dissolution of the company, the application of s104-135 would need to be considered in relation to the amount of the distribution that is not deemed to be a dividend [that is, $50,000 ($86,500 – $36,500)].

12.950   COMPENSATION

Compensation or damages for personal injury or wrongdoing (such as defamation of an individual's good name) are exempt from CGT (s118-37).

There has always been confusion over other forms of compensation, such as the receipt of a payment on agreeing not to exercise the taxpayer's right to sue. Taxation Ruling TR 95/35 deals with the CGT consequences where compensation payments are received. The following is a summary of that ruling, and examples below are based on those in TR 95/35.

Care should be taken with compensation payments because they may be subject to tax under s6-5 where they represent compensation for lost income. However, where damages are to compensate a taxpayer for the loss of business suffered as a result of its wounded reputation, the amount will be capital in nature, even where the compensation is calculated with reference to lost income or profits (*Commissioner v Sydney Refractive Surgery Centre Pty Ltd* [2008] FCAFC 190).

12.955   DISPOSAL OF UNDERLYING ASSET

Where compensation represents a disposal of an underlying asset of the taxpayer, the Tax Office will not treat the consideration as being received for the disposal of any other asset, such as the right to receive compensation.

The Tax Office adopts a 'look through' approach, which means that the taxpayer must be able to show that the compensation receipt has a direct and substantial link with the underlying asset.

Joan purchased a two hectare property in January 1987 for $300,000. Since that date, the house situated on that property has been used as Joan's main residence and has not been used for income-producing purposes. One hectare was compulsorily acquired by the State Government on 1 September 2011 to complete improvements to the highway that runs beside the property. Following negotiations, the State Authority paid $195,000 in compensation for the land. Joan engaged the services of a qualified and independent valuer who estimated the value of the one hectare strip in January 1987 at $120,000.

Result: The compensation was received for a part disposal of the land. The one hectare if sold with the taxpayer's main residence would normally be exempt from CGT. However as it was sold separately from the main residence, s118-165 operates to impose CGT on the disposal of the land.

Indexation of the part of the land disposed of applies from January 1987.

Capital proceeds	$195,000
less Indexed cost base ($120,000 x 1.516)	$181,920
Capital gain	**$13,080**

(The taxpayer could have elected to use the CGT discount method instead of the indexation method but the capital gain would have been $37,500 rather than $13,080.)

NOTE: If a replacement block of land was acquired, s124-70 rollover relief may be available (see 12.455).

- Where there is an actual disposal of the whole or a part of the underlying asset, if the original asset: was acquired before 20 September 1985, there are no CGT consequences.

- Was acquired after 19 September 1985, the general CGT provisions will apply including rollover relief and exemptions.

Compensation received from the sale of shares without the owner's consent by a mortgagor was considered to be a capital gain under CGT event C1 (ATO ID 2010/116).

NOTE: The CGT main residence exemption also applies to the compulsory acquisition of part of an individual's main residence, without the actual dwelling being acquired. This became law on 29 June 2011 and apply to CGT events that happen from this date. Individuals can also choose to apply these rules to CGT events that happened at any time from the start of the 2004–05 income year up until 28 June 2011.

12.960   PERMANENT DAMAGE

Where there has been no disposal of an underlying asset (either in whole or in part) but compensation is received for permanent damage to, or a permanent reduction in the value of a post-CGT underlying asset, the compensation received will be treated as a recoupment of all or part of the total acquisition costs of the asset (ss110-45(3)).

Accordingly, the total acquisition costs of the post-CGT underlying asset should be reduced by the amount of the compensation. The effect is to treat those costs as if they had not been incurred. If the compensation amount exceeds the total acquisition costs of the underlying asset, there are no CGT consequences in respect of the excess compensation amount. It is tax-free.

No capital gain or capital loss arises in respect of the underlying asset until the taxpayer actually disposes of it, and that capital gain or capital loss will be calculated by taking into account the cost base (indexed if appropriate) of the adjusted value of the asset. If the underlying asset was acquired before 20 September 1985, or is an exempt CGT asset, the compensation received for the permanent damage to the asset will have no CGT consequences. The amount received is tax-free.

A landlord and tenant negotiate the renewal of a commercial lease on cessation of the current lease. The tenant believes, after numerous conversations, that an agreement exists for the lease to be extended. However, the landlord believes there is no such agreement. The tenant incurs $50,000 legal expenses in successfully fighting for the continuation of the lease. The settlement documents provide that the new lease will commence from cessation of the current lease and the landlord agrees to pay the tenant $40,000 in respect of his legal expenses.

Result: On the surrender of the old lease, CGT event C2 happens. On the grant of the new lease, CGT event F1 will happen and the cost base of the new lease is $10,000 (ie. $50,000 less the compensation of $40,000) (ss104-110(4)). The recoupment results in the reduction of the cost base of the new asset.

NOTE: On expiry of the new lease (if there is no consideration received), the tenant will incur a capital loss of $10,000.

12.965 EXCESSIVE CONSIDERATION

If a taxpayer is compensated for having paid excessive consideration to acquire an asset, any compensation received will represent a recoupment of all or part of the total acquisition costs of the asset.

In May 1996, Bill purchased land for $150,000 on the basis that the local council had approved the land for subdivision. In October 2009, Bill lodged a development application and was advised that the original approval for subdivision was refused due to inaccurate information submitted on the application. The taxpayer sued the seller for damages and in February 2012 received $15,000 compensation.

Result: The cost base of the underlying asset is reduced to $135,000 (ie. $150,000 less the compensation received of $15,000). The $15,000 relates to the permanent reduction in the land value. The cost base adjustment is made to the unindexed total acquisition cost of the asset.

12.970 RIGHT TO SEEK COMPENSATION

In many cases there is no underlying asset involved when compensation is sought. The asset in respect of which the compensation is paid is the right to sue (or seek compensation) and it is acquired at the time the damage or injury occurs. Accordingly, any capital gain arising from a CGT event in respect of that right is calculated using the cost base of that right. The cost base of the right to seek compensation includes legal fees and charges incurred during the course of the proceedings (s110-25). It also includes the sum of money and the market value of property given as consideration for the creation of the asset. Where the costs relate to several assets equally, the costs should be apportioned between those assets. The legal costs connected with pursuing the right to seek compensation are most directly attributable to that right and should be included in the cost base of that right. This may mean that the taxpayer incurs a capital loss from a CGT event in respect of their right to seek compensation if the damages paid are less than the total cost base of that right.

On 4 July 2007, Mary acquired a rental property. In October 2013, she decided to sell the property. A buyer indicated on 15 November 2013 his willingness to acquire the property for $400,000. The contracts were exchanged on 10 December 2013, with a requirement that the sale be settled five months later on 10 May 2014, but the sale was not finalised because of a delay in receiving a clearance from one of the local authorities.

The buyer later exercised his right under the contract to repudiate it and claim a refund of his deposit.

Mary started legal action against her legal advisers seeking damages for negligence. On 27 June 2014, she received compensation of $95,000 by way of settlement of the claim.

Result: There is no CGT event in respect of, nor permanent damage to the underlying asset (the property), but there is the creation and disposal of the right to seek compensation (CGT event D1). The relevant asset is the taxpayer's right to seek compensation which was acquired in May 2014 when the action arose. The cost base of the right to sue was nil plus legal costs.

The balance ($95,000 less the cost base) will be a capital gain to Mary in the 2013-14 income year.

Taxpayers should be wary about accepting a lump sum settlement in cases involving an action where there is no underlying asset and they are seeking compensation. Where the lump sum settlement is not dissected, there is a risk the entire amount could be subject to tax, particularly where there is no directly relevant underlying asset involved. Where the compensation received relates to

several factors, the amount of compensation and the nature of its source should be identified, especially where there are any existing assets involved which may permit a cost base adjustment.

12.975   DISPOSAL OF NOTIONAL ASSET

Generally, the amount of compensation is received by a taxpayer in respect of either:

*   an underlying asset, or
*   the surrender of the right to seek compensation (CGT event C2: surrender of the right acquired when CGT event D1 happened) (s104-25).

Where CGT event C2 applies, CGT event H2 will not apply. If the amount does not relate to either an underlying asset or a right to seek compensation (eg. unsolicited compensation) CGT event H2 may apply to the payment received (s104-155).

Barbara is an interior designer who works from spacious offices, showrooms and workshops attached to her home. The business started in 1990 and has a substantial client base. The property also had ample customer parking. Substantial roadworks were started by the council in May 2014 and lasted for 14 weeks. During this time, vehicular access to Barbara's premises was denied. The council offered the taxpayer $12,000 compensation for the inconvenience. While Barbara did not seek the compensation, payment was accepted in May 2014.

Result: A notional asset with no cost base was created in May 2013 (s104-155). The gain would not be assessable under s104-35 as there was no underlying asset and Barbara did not seek the right to compensation (creation of a contractual right – CGT event D1). However, the gain would be assessable under s104-155 (CGT event H2) as:

*   *a CGT asset (the goodwill of the business) has been affected by an act or event occurring (ie. the local council blocking access to the taxpayer's premises)*
*   *there is no adjustment to the cost base of the underlying asset (goodwill), and*
*   *the taxpayer received $12,000 as a result of that act or event.*

12.980   COMPENSATION RECEIVED UNDER INSURANCE POLICY

Compensation received under a policy of insurance also relates to a right to seek compensation (see 12.970 'Right to seek compensation'). The insured's right of indemnification by the insurer is an asset and falls within the meaning of a right to seek compensation. The payment of the claim by the insurer results in CGT event C2 happening (the surrender of the right) under s104-25. The Tax Office accepts that the cost base of this right is the amount the insured is required to pay to the claimant. The capital proceeds in respect of the surrender of this right is the amount paid out by the insurer, adjusted by any additional amounts received by the insured.

Jane was a pedestrian who was badly injured when hit by a motor vehicle. A dancer with a promising career, Jane was unable to continue dancing as a result of her injuries. The driver of the car was insured by Emu Insurance who made a $1m payment to cover all her claims for loss of earning capacity, physiotherapy, hospital and other care costs and non-pecuniary loss. The lump sum was not dissected.

Result: The right to seek compensation for the losses arose when the injury was suffered (CGT event D1). Jane's cost base was legal and medical costs incurred and the right was disposed of when the claim was settled (CGT event C2). However in this case, the net capital gain is wholly exempt under paragraph 118-37(1)(b) as Jane can prove that the whole amount of the compensation relates only to the right to seek compensation for personal injury.

EXTENDING THE CGT EXEMPTION FOR CERTAIN COMPENSATION PAYMENTS AND INSURANCE POLICIES

The CGT exemption under paragraph 118-37(1)(b) is available in respect of compensation or damages received by:

*   A trustee (other than a trustee of a complying superannuation entity) for a wrong or injury a beneficiary suffers in their occupation, or a wrong, injury or illness

a beneficiary or their relative suffers personally – and that a beneficiary that subsequently receives a distribution that is attributable to such compensation or damages from the trustee

- A taxpayer (other than a trustee of a complying superannuation entity) for a policy of insurance on the life of an individual or an annuity instrument if the taxpayer is the original owner of the policy or instrument, and
- A trustee of a complying superannuation entity for a policy of insurance for an individual's illness or injury.

Also, capital gains and capital losses are disregarded by complying superannuation entities arising from injury and illness insurance policies, life insurance policies and annuity instruments.

Robert is the beneficiary of ABC trust, which was established after Robert fell off a roof whilst working for Roofing Inc and suffered serious injuries. Patrick, as trustee of ABC trust, seeks compensation on behalf of Robert from Roofing Inc's insurance company, and receives compensation for the accident. The capital gain made by Patrick in relation to the compensation received is disregarded. Assume Robert recovers from his injuries, but requires substantial further medical and other support. Patrick, as trustee of ABC trust, distributes the compensation to Robert to assist in paying his hospital bills. Any capital gain made by Robert in relation to the compensation received is disregarded.

Lake Super Fund holds total and permanent disability insurance for its members, through Insurance Co. Tony, a member of Lake Super Fund, is injured at work and applies to be paid a total and permanent incapacity benefit from Lake Super Fund. Insurance Co is satisfied it must pay the insured amount to Lake Super Fund in respect of Tony's injury. Any capital gain made by Lake Super Fund on the payment from Insurance Co is disregarded.

12.985   EXEMPT ASSETS

As a general rule, there are no CGT consequences if compensation is received in respect of an underlying asset which is exempt from CGT (ie. a person's main residence, a motor car or an asset acquired before 20 September 1985). Compensation received by a company or trustee for any wrong or injury suffered by the company or trust is not exempt.

Robert, a doctor has a small practice which was acquired in 1982. One of his patients suffered due to his professional negligence and successfully sued Robert for malpractice in March 2014. Robert paid the agreed settlement sum to the former patient in December 2010, then sought recovery from his insurance company of the equivalent amount ($100,000) of the settlement under the terms of his professional indemnity insurance policy.
Result: The patient has a CGT event in respect of a CGT asset, being the patient's right to receive compensation for Robert's negligence. However, Robert also has a CGT asset being his right to seek indemnity under the professional indemnity insurance policy which was acquired in March 2014. Robert's cost base includes the legal costs connected with the claim. It also includes the payment to his former patient. No capital gain or capital loss arises.

While compensation in respect of an underlying exempt asset remains exempt from CGT, compensation could nonetheless be subject to CGT if it is paid in respect of:

- **some other underlying asset**
- **a right to seek compensation, or**
- **a notional asset.**

The CGT effect on those types of assets is explained earlier.

12.987   COMPENSATION FOR COMPULSORY ACQUISITION OF PART OF A CGT ASSET

Where part of a CGT asset is compulsorily acquired, the compensation received may consist of:

- an amount for the value of the asset acquired, and
- an additional amount for the decline in the value of the remaining asset.

Both these amounts form part of the capital proceeds from the CGT event that happens to that part of the asset that is compulsorily acquired (CGT event A1 happens because there is a disposal of an asset). The cost base of the asset owned before compulsory acquisition is apportioned in accordance with s112-30(3), having regard to the compensation received and market value of the remaining part of the asset.

If the market value of the remaining part of the CGT asset has been reduced by the compulsory acquisition, it is necessary to calculate the cost base of the part of the asset that is compulsorily acquired, taking into account the total compensation received (s112-30(3)). Once the cost base of the compulsorily acquired part of the CGT asset is determined, the balance of the cost base is attributed to the remaining part of the asset (s112-30(4)). The following example is extracted from TD 2001/9.

Lila has part of her wildlife park compulsorily acquired, seriously affecting the value of the remaining land. The cost base of the entire land is $600,000. The market value of the land remaining after the compulsory acquisition is $1 million. Compensation paid for the compulsorily acquired land is $1.1 million of which $100,000 reflects the reduction in value of the remaining land caused by the compulsory acquisition.

Applying the apportionment formula in s112-30(3), the cost base of the part to which the CGT event happened (the compulsorily acquired part) is:

> *Cost base x [Capital proceeds for the compulsory acquisition of the acquired part divided by (Proceeds + market value of the remaining part)]*

$600,000 x [$1,100,000 divided by ($1,100,000 + $1,000,000)] = $314 286 where:

- *Proceeds = Capital proceeds (compensation) for the compulsory acquisition*
- *Market value = Market value of remaining land (after taking into account the effect of compulsory acquisition)*

The cost base of the compulsorily acquired part is $314,286. The cost base of the part which remains is $285,714 (being $600,000 – $314,286).

APPORTIONING RECEIPT

If the compensation relates directly to more than one asset, the compensation must be apportioned between the most relevant assets.

UNDISSECTED LUMP SUM COMPENSATION

Where a lump sum is received in satisfaction of multiple claims but no specific allocation occurs, the full amount will be capital in nature; *McLaurin v FCT* (1961) 104 CLR 381.

Compensation received by an individual for a wrong or injury suffered to his or her person, or profession or vocation, is exempt from CGT (ss118-37(1)). However if the lump sum payment is made in settlement of a number of claims including a personal injury claim, the Tax Office's approach is to treat no part of the payment as exempt from CGT unless the individual components can be reasonably determined.

Advisers and taxpayers should consider carefully itemising the respective components of a settlement arrangement. Failure to do so may result in a higher amount being caught for CGT purposes.

ROLLOVER RELIEF

Where certain conditions are satisfied, rollover relief may be available under Subdivision 124-B. The compensation may be in the form of a replacement asset, money, or a combination of both. Rollover relief was discussed at 12.450.

GOODWILL

Goodwill of a business continually fluctuates in value and a taxpayer is not entitled to reduce the cost of that goodwill for those temporary fluctuations (TR 1999/16). In certain limited circumstances, a taxpayer may be able to demonstrate that he or she has suffered some permanent damage to his or her goodwill or that it has been permanently reduced in value.

In those cases, the total acquisition cost of the goodwill can be reduced by so much of the compensation that relates to the permanent damage or permanent reduction in value.

INTEREST

It is not uncommon for interest to be awarded as part of the settlement of an action. In *Whitaker v FC of T* 98 ATC 4285, the Full Federal Court held that post-judgement interest (interest that accrues from the date of judgement until the date of payment) is assessable income, but pre-judgement interest (interest that accrues from the date a cause of action arises until judgment) simply forms part of the global amount for which judgement is entered. Post-judgment interest in personal injury cases is exempt from tax (s51-57). If the interest is received as part of undissected lump sum compensation and it cannot be separately identified, no part of the payment will be treated as interest. The entire amount will be in respect of the compensation.

General deductions

13

13.000 CHECKLIST OF EMPLOYMENT-RELATED CLAIMS

This checklist is a guide only. The results may vary depending on individual circumstances.

The *Income Tax Assessment Act 1997* (ITAA97) categorises deductions into general deductions and specific deductions.

Broadly, in accordance with s8-1 of the ITAA97, a deduction may only be claimed if:

- the expense has been incurred in earning the person's assessable income, or incurred in carrying on a business for the purpose of earning assessable income (see Chapter 14 *Business deductions*), and
- it is not private (domestic) or capital expenditure, and
- it is not capital in nature, and
- a specific provision of the ITAA97 or *Income Tax Assessment Act 1936* (ITAA36) does not preclude the expense from deduction, and
- the person holds the relevant written evidence where required (see *Written evidence* at 13.120).

NOTE: How much of the expense is allowed as a tax deduction will depend on the extent the expenses are incurred in earning the person's assessable income.

NOTE: All section and division references are to the ITAA97 unless otherwise stated.

Tax deductible?	
Admission fees: For lawyers and other professionals. Disallowed as capital cost.	No
Airport lounge membership: Deductions to the extent used for work-related purposes.	Yes
Annual practising certificate: Applies to professional persons and other contractors who must pay an annual fee to practice in their chosen field.	Yes
Bank charges: Deductions are allowed if account earns interest. Not private transaction fees.	Yes
Bribes to government officials and foreign government officials: Also exclude from the cost base and reduced cost base of CGT assets and cost of depreciating assets.	No
Briefcase: If used for work and/or business purposes the cost is fully deductible if $300 or less. If more than $300, it must be depreciated.	Yes
Calculators and electronic organisers: If used for work and/or business purposes the cost is fully deductible if $300 or less. If more than $300, it must be depreciated.	Yes
Car: See 'Travel' and 13.220.	
Child care fees	No
Cleaning: Of protective clothing and uniforms – see *Laundry* at 13.150.	Yes

Clothing, uniforms and footwear
     • **Compulsory uniform:** Uniform must be unique and particular to an organisation (eg. corporate uniform).
     • **Non-compulsory uniform:** If on a register kept by the Department of Industry, Science and Tourism.
     • **Occupational specific:** The clothing identifies a particular trade, vocation or profession (eg. chefs and nurses).
     • **Protective:** Must be used to protect the person or their conventional clothing. May include sunscreen.
	Yes

Club membership fees	No
Coaching classes: Allowed to performing artists to maintain existing skills or obtain related skills.	Yes

Tax deductible?

Computers and software (see 13.155): Software is deductible if it costs less than $300, otherwise deductible over 2.5 years. Except in-house developed software which is over four years.	Yes
Conferences, seminars and training courses: Allowed if designed to maintain or increase employee's knowledge, skills or ability.	Yes
Conventional clothing	No
Depreciation: Tools, equipment, and plant used for work purposes for each item costing more than $300. Items costing $300 or less are deductible outright in the year of acquisition.	Yes
Donations: See *Gifts* at 13.800.	
Driver's licence: Cost of acquiring and renewing.	No
Dry cleaning: Allowed if the cost of the clothing is also deductible. See also *Laundry* at 13.150.	Yes
Election expenses of candidates: No limit for Federal, State and Territory. Limit of $1,000 for local government.	Yes
Employment agreements: Existing employer (see TR 2000/5). Not available for new business/employer.	Yes
Entertainment expenses	No
Fines: Imposed by court, or under law of Commonwealth, State, Territory or foreign country (s26-5).	No
First Aid course: Provided it is directly related to employment or business activities.	Yes
Gaming licence: Hospitality and gaming industry.	Yes
Gifts of $2 or more (see from 13.800): If made to approved 'deductible gift recipient' body or fund. See ato.gov.au for a full list. Gifts to clients are deductible if employees can demonstrate a direct connection with earning assessable income.	Yes
Glasses and contact lenses (prescribed): These would qualify as medical expenses (see from 3.160). Deductible if 'protective clothing'.	No
Glasses and goggles: Protective only.	Yes
Grooming	No
HELP/HECS repayments	No
Home office expenses (see from 13.600): Utility expenses (for example, heat, light, power and depreciation on depreciating assets). **Occupancy expenses:** For example, rent, insurance, rates and land tax. Deductible only to the extent that home or study is used for income-producing purposes.	Yes
Income continuance insurance: Allowed only if the proceeds are assessable.	Yes
Insurance – sickness or accident: When benefits would be assessable income.	Yes
Interest: Allowed if money borrowed for work-related purposes or to finance income earning assets. Interest paid on underpayment of tax (eg. general interest charge) is deductible (see 4.660). Fines and administrative penalties are not deductible. Interest on capital protected loans deductible except for non-deductible capital protection component (see 14.600).	Yes
Internet and computer equipment (see 13.155): Expenses allowed to the extent incurred in deriving individual's work-related income, carrying on a business or earning investment income (eg. share investing).	Yes
Laundry and maintenance: Allowed if the cost of clothing is allowable (see *Work related clothing*). Reasonable claims of laundry expenses up to $150 do not need to be substantiated (see *Laundry* at 13.150).	Yes
Legal expenses: Renewal of existing employment contract.	Yes

Tax deductible?	
Meals	
• Eaten during normal working day.	No
• Meals acquired when travelling overnight for work-related purpose.	Yes
• Meals when travelling (not overnight).	No
• Overtime meals: If allowance received under award.	Yes
Medical examination: Only if from the referral of a work-related business licence.	Yes
Motor vehicle expenses: See 'Travel expenses'.	
Newspapers: Claims may be allowed in limited cases if the publication is directly related to income-producing activities.	No
Overtime meal expenses: Only if award overtime meal allowance received (see 13.140).	Yes
Parking fees and tolls: Includes bridge and road tolls (but not fines) paid while travelling for work-related purposes.	Yes
Photographs (performing arts – with income producing purpose)	
• Cost of maintaining portfolio.	Yes
• Cost of preparing portfolio.	No
Practising certificate: Applies to professional employees.	Yes
Prepaid expenditure for tax shelter arrangements: They must be spread over the period in which the services are provided (see 14.170).	Yes
Prepaid expenses: Non-business individuals and SBE taxpayers claim is fully deductible if services are to be performed in period not exceeding 12 months. All other taxpayers must apportion claim over the period of service (see 14.170).	Yes
Professional association fees: Maximum of $42 if no longer gaining assessable income from that profession.	Yes
Professional library (books, CDs, videos etc) Established library (depreciation allowed)	Yes
• New books: Full claim if cost $300 or less (includes a set if total cost is $300 or less).	Yes
• New books: Depreciation if cost over $300 (includes a set if total cost is more than $300).	Yes
Protective equipment Includes harnesses, goggles, safety glasses, breathing masks, helmets, boots. Claims for sunscreens, sunglasses and wet weather gear allowed if used to provide protection from natural environment (see 13.147).	Yes
Removal and relocation costs If paid by the employer, may be exempt from FBT, but deductible.	No
Repairs (income producing property/or work-related equipment).	Yes
Self-education costs: Claims for fees, books, travel (see below) and equipment etc. only allowed if there is a direct connection between the course and the person's income earning activities. No claim for the first $250 if course is undertaken at school or other educational institution and the course confers a qualification. However, that first $250 can be offset against private expenses, eg. travel, child minding fees, etc. (see 13.700).	Yes
Seminars Including conference and training courses if sufficiently connected to work activities.	Yes
Social functions	No
Stationery (diaries, log books etc.)	Yes
Subscriptions	
• Publications If a direct connection between publication and income earned by taxpayer.	Yes
• Sports clubs.	No

Tax deductible?

Sun protection Claims for sunglasses, hats and sunscreen allowed for taxpayers who work outside.	**Yes**
Superannuation contributions Claims allowed in respect of employees. Substantially self-employed persons if their assessable income, reportable fringe benefits plus reportable employer superannuation contributions is less than 10% of their total assessable income from all sources, reportable fringe benefits plus reportable employer superannuation contributions total (see 19.026). No deduction is available for interest on borrowed monies used to finance deductible personal superannuation contributions.	**Yes**
Supreme Court library fees Applies to barristers and solicitors if paid on annual basis.	**Yes**
Tax agent fees (deduction can be claimed in the income year the expense is incurred). • Travel and accommodation expenses if for travel to a tax agent or other recognised tax adviser to obtain tax advice, have returns prepared, be present at audit or object against an assessment. • Cost of other incidentals if incurred in having tax return prepared, lodging an objection or appeal or defending an audit.	**Yes**
Technical and professional publications	**Yes**
Telephones and other telecommunications equipment (see 13.155) (including mobiles, pagers and beepers.) Cost of telephone calls (related to work purposes). • Installation or connection. • Rental charges (if 'on call' or required to use on regular basis). • Silent telephone number.	**Yes** **No** **Yes** **No**
Tools (work related only) If cost is $300 or less. • If cost more than $300, the amount would be depreciable, and the amount deductible equals to the decline in value).	**Yes** **Yes**
Trauma insurance If benefits capital in nature.	**No**
Travel expenses Including public transport, motor vehicles and motor cycles, fares, accommodation, meals and incidentals (see also 13.160). • Travel between home and work. • Where employee has no usual place of employment (eg. travelling salesperson). • If 'on call'. • If actually working before leaving home (eg. doctor giving instructions over phone from home. Note that this applies in limited circumstances only). • Must transport bulky equipment (eg. builder with bulky tools). • Travel from home (which is a place of business) to usual place of employment. • Travel from home to alternate work place (for work-related purposes) and return to normal work place (or directly home). • Travel between normal work place and alternate place of employment (or place of business) and return (or directly home). • Travel between two work places. • Travel in course of employment: See Substantiation rules at 13.210. • Travel accompanied by relative (may be allowed if relative is also performing work-related duties).	**No** **Yes** **No** **Yes** **Yes** **No** **Yes** **Yes** **Yes** **Yes** **No**
Union and professional association fees	**Yes**
Vaccinations	**No**
Union levees	**No**
Watch: Unless job specific such as a nurse's job watch.	**No**

13.100 SUBSTANTIATION

Claims for work-related expenses, car expenses, and travelling expenses incurred by an individual must be substantiated if the claims are to be allowed (Division 900 of ITAA97). As well as the requirement to incur deductible expenditure, the 'Substantiation' rules impose a strict evidentiary requirement that must be satisfied if claims are to be allowed.

Under the primary test in s8-1, the taxpayer must be able to show that they incurred the relevant expenses and that those expenses were incurred in earning their assessable income, or were incurred in carrying on a business.

Once the primary test has been satisfied (ie. the expense has been incurred and is allowable) the 'substantiation rules' impose a mandatory level of record keeping. If those records are not kept, the claim may be disallowed unless the relief rules apply (see below).

13.105 RECORDS

Substantiation records must be retained for five years from the later of the due date for lodging the relevant return or when it is lodged. As a general rule, employees are not required to substantiate:

- employment related expenses where the total claim is less than $300 (see 13.145)
- laundry expenses, up to a maximum of $150 (see 13.150). **NOTE:** This amount forms part of the $300 limit
- sunscreen, sunglasses and hats if their job requires them to work in the sun (see 13.147)
- reasonable travel claims where a travel allowance has been received (see from 13.160)
- overtime meal claims up to $28.80 in 2015-16 (TD 2015/14) and $28.20 in 2014-15 (TD 2014/19) for allowances paid under an Industrial Award (see 13.140)
- some car expenses (see from 13.225).

Even though the strict substantiation rules do not need to be satisfied for the above expenses (see 13.120), employees must be able to show that those expenses were incurred and how they calculated their claims.

 Self-employed persons, partners and individual trustees must have written evidence to prove all of their claims.

The five year period can be further extended automatically if any of the following are unresolved when the five years ends:

- an objection
- a review or appeal arising from an objection, or
- a request for amendment.

The extended period lasts until the dispute is resolved. The Tax Office can require you to produce your records. The Commissioner must give you 28 days notice to comply, but you may be allowed additional time.

If you receive such a notice you must produce in English:

- the required written records (or documents), and
- a summary containing this information:
    - a cross-reference to the written evidence
    - a summary of the particulars of the written evidence, and
    - the amount of the expense in Australian currency (if the expense is in a foreign currency).

The claims will be disallowed if you fail to produce these records.

13.110 RELIEF FROM SUBSTANTIATION

The Tax Office has a discretion to allow a deduction for expenditure even if there is no written evidence to substantiate the expense if the Tax Office is satisfied you incurred the expense and that you are entitled to a deduction for that amount.

In respect of work related expenses, business travel expenses and car expenses calculated under the '1/3rd of actual cost' or 'log book' methods, Subdivision 900-H says relief will be granted where expenses have not been substantiated if:

- there is sufficient evidence to satisfy the Tax Office that a deductible expense was incurred
- there was a reasonable expectation substantiation was not needed, or
- documents were lost or destroyed after reasonable precautions had been taken and reasonable efforts are made to get a substitute document (unless not reasonably possible).

This only applies to individuals and partnerships where at least one partner is an individual.

IMPORTANT: The Tax Office has further modified the strict substantiation rules to account for technology changes and the way taxpayers pay for and record financial information (see 13.120).

13.115 SUBSTANTIATION FLOWCHART

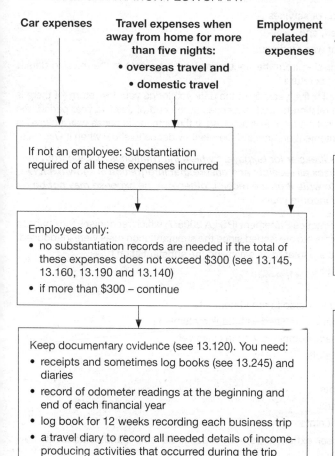

Car expenses

Travel expenses when away from home for more than five nights:
- **overseas travel and**
- **domestic travel**

Employment related expenses

Employment expenses
- **overtime meal allowance (see 13.140)**
- **domestic travel allowance (see 13.160 and 13.180)**

If not an employee: Substantiation required of all these expenses incurred

Employees only:
- no substantiation records are needed if the total of these expenses does not exceed $300 (see 13.145, 13.160, 13.190 and 13.140)
- if more than $300 – continue

No substantiation required if:
- an allowance is paid to an employee
- the expenses claimed are limited to reasonable amount

Keep documentary evidence (see 13.120). You need:
- receipts and sometimes log books (see 13.245) and diaries
- record of odometer readings at the beginning and end of each financial year
- log book for 12 weeks recording each business trip
- a travel diary to record all needed details of income-producing activities that occurred during the trip

If those conditions on the allowances are not met:
- the expenses relating to the travel allowance must be substantiated by receipts and documentary evidence and a travel diary
- the expenses relating to the meal allowance must be substantiated by receipts and documentary evidence

OR Select from three other methods of calculating car expenses (see from 13.225)

Depending on method chosen, substantiation requirements are substantially reduced

13.120   WRITTEN EVIDENCE

Deductions must be claimed in the income year the expense is incurred, and generally you must have the written evidence when you lodge your tax return. There are some situations where the evidence can be obtained in a later year – see below. In other cases, you are denied a deduction in the year the expense was incurred until you have obtained the necessary written evidence. In that case you must self-amend your original assessment.

The exception to this rule is where you have good reasons to expect to get written evidence within a reasonable time of lodging your income tax return.

Written evidence must be obtained from the supplier of the goods or services and it must be in English. However, if the expense was incurred in a country other than Australia, it can be in that country's language. The document must contain:

- the name (or business name) of the supplier
- the amount of the expense (expressed in the currency in which it was incurred)
- the nature of the goods or services
- the date it was incurred, and
- the date the document was made out.

If the nature of the goods is missing from the document, you may write in the missing details yourself before you lodge your tax return.

You must keep written evidence for five years from the date you lodge your tax return. If there is a dispute with the Tax Office in relation to work expenses at the end of this five year period, the relevant records must be kept until the dispute is resolved. If the date the expense was incurred is missing, you can use a bank statement or other independent evidence to show when it was paid.

 This exception makes it easier for taxpayers where information is missing from the written document. Check all receipts and ensure that information is shown. If it is not, get the supplier to write it on the receipt, otherwise the expense may not be claimable until a later income year.

The Tax Office has published a Practice Statement (PS LA 2005/7) which recognises the changes in technology and the way receipts etc are issued since the substantiation rules were introduced. The following types of evidence are treated as satisfying the substantiation rules:

- bank statements
- credit card statements
- internet-generated bank or credit card statements
- BPAY reference numbers, combined with bank statements
- BPAY reference numbers, combined with tax invoices
- internet generated receipts
- email receipts
- paper copies of receipts
- electronic receipts, and
- electronic copies of receipts.

The following examples have been extracted from the Practice Statement and demonstrate how the new rules will work in practice.

 Use of a bank or credit card statement only

Daniel, who is employed by a large firm of solicitors, receives a bill for his annual professional subscription fees, which he pays using his credit card. His credit card statement bears the date of the transaction, the name of the professional association and the amount paid. Before he lodges his income tax return, Daniel makes a note on his credit card statement to the effect that the transaction related to his professional subscription fees.

The Tax Office will accept the credit card statement as sufficient evidence to substantiate Daniel's claim for a deduction for the fees.

Use of electronic verification of purchase

Minh, a computer programmer, purchased some USB flash drives for work over the internet. When he ordered the USB flash drives, he received an automatic response via email that quoted an order reference number, the nature of the goods, and the amount due to be paid. He paid by sending a money order to the supplier and kept the stub of the money order, which included the supplier name and the amount paid.

Minh stored the email in an electronic folder labelled 'Tax', which he also backed up on disc. The Tax Office will accept the combination of the automatic email response and money order stub as sufficient evidence to substantiate Minh's expense.

Evidence under various methods of payment

Louise is an apprentice plumber employed by a small plumbing business. As part of her employment she needs to provide her own tools. She purchased $250 worth of tools from her local hardware store. As she is a regular customer, the hardware store issues her with a tax invoice requesting payment within 30 days, which she pays at the end of the month by way of an electronic transfer from her bank account. The Tax Office will accept the combination of the tax invoice and bank statement showing the electronic transfer as sufficient evidence to substantiate the claim for the purchases from the local hardware store.

Receipts received in electronic format

Amanda, a computer programmer, retains her internet-generated receipt for work expenses, including supplier details and purchase amount, on her computer. If necessary, the receipt could be printed and may be able to be verified as being a genuine receipt by the Tax Office through communications with the issuer of the receipt. The Tax Office will accept the electronic receipt as sufficient evidence to substantiate Amanda's expense as it meets the requirements of the substantiation legislation.

SMALL EXPENSES

If there are small expenses involved you have a choice to obtain the required written evidence or record the same information in a document (eg. diary). This option is only available for:

- separate expenses of $10 or less and if the total of all those expenses in the income year is $200 or less. The information must be in English and must be recorded as soon as possible after incurring the expense.

- if taxpayers have been unable to obtain written evidence (ie. for example, for toll or parking fees where a receipt cannot be obtained).

If the expense is a capital allowance (see Chapter 15), this information should be available as soon as possible after the last day of the income year.

The way s900-125 reads, taxpayers must have receipts for all their small expenses if the total of ALL expenses that are minor (ie. $10 or less) is $200 or more. If the total of all small expenses exceeds $200, no deduction is allowed for expenses that had been recorded by the taxpayer unless they also have a 'receipt'.

If the small expense is for a capital allowance claim, the record must show:

- the nature of the property
- the amount of the capital allowance
- who made the record, and
- the day the record was made.

DECLINE IN VALUE (DEPRECIATION OR CAPITAL ALLOWANCE)

Special rules apply when claiming a capital allowance for an asset based on its decline in value. You must obtain a document from the supplier showing:

- the name (or business name) of the supplier
- the cost of the property
- the nature of the property
- the day you acquired it, and
- the day the document was made out.

If the nature of the property is missing you can write in those details before you lodge your return when you first claim a deduction for capital allowances on that property.

EXCEPTIONS

If amounts are shown on a payment summary, you can use that as written evidence of the expense. There is no need for expenses of the same nature to be separately itemised (s900-135). The Tax Office will also accept as evidence a self-prepared record of an expense if it is unreasonable to expect you to have obtained written evidence (where for example it is not customary for the vendor to issue receipts eg. car parking).

You must record in a diary the same details as required for small expenses. Those expenses can be higher than $10 per expense and they do not count towards the $10 and $200 limits (see *Small expenses* above). For details as to when the Tax Office is able to give relief from substantiation, see TR 97/24.

13.140 OVERTIME MEAL ALLOWANCES

The Tax Office accepts an overtime meal expense claim of up to $28.80 for 2015-16 to be reasonable (TD 2015/14). The reasonable amount is $28.20 for 2014-15 (TD 2014/19).

Expenses incurred for food or drink can be claimed without written evidence if:

- an overtime meal allowance has been paid
- the allowance is to enable the employee to buy food or drink in connection with overtime
- it is paid or payable under a Commonwealth, State or Territory law, or under an Award, order, Determination or industrial agreement in force under such a law, and
- the total of the claim is considered reasonable by the Tax Office.

IMPORTANT: A claim can only be made if the allowance is included in assessable income.

Allowances must be included in assessable income unless:

- a genuine overtime meal allowance or genuine travel allowance
- the allowance is no more than the 'reasonable amount', and
- the allowance has been fully expended on deductible expenses.

If an 'overtime meal allowance' is incorporated into salary under a workplace agreement, the 'allowance' forms part of salary whether or not overtime is worked. No allowance is paid in this circumstance and no deduction is allowable.

NOTE: According to the *Tax Office PAYG Bulletin No.1*, valid from 1 July 2000, if an overtime meal allowance paid to an employee is no higher than the reasonable amount the employer is not required to show the allowance on the employee's payment summary.

 To be eligible for a claim, overtime meal allowances must be paid under a law, an award or agreement. A deduction is allowable provided the expense claimed was actually incurred to buy food or drink in connection with overtime worked. It does not include allowances negotiated privately between an employer and employee or amounts forming part of an employee's normal salary and wages.

13.145 MINOR WORK EXPENSES ($300 THRESHOLD)

A work expense is any expense incurred by an employee in earning or producing their assessable income from employment related activities. No written evidence is required if the total of all work expenses is $300 or less.

 Taxpayers must have written evidence to prove their claims if the total claims exceed $300. The records must prove the total amount, not just the amount over $300.

This includes claims for:
- laundry expenses
- depreciation of property owned and used (or installed ready for use)
- election expenses for candidates for Federal, State or Territory Parliaments, or local government
- taxi fares or similar expenses, and
- car expenses in respect of overseas travel.

For claims to be allowed, the employee must obtain written evidence (see 13.120).

The $300 threshold does not include:
- car expenses in Australia
- award transport expenses
- travel allowance expenses, and
- reasonable overtime meal allowance expenses.

 An employee incurred $285 for work expenses and also travelled 4,000kms for employment purposes. The employee elected to claim using the cents per km basis (see 13.230). In this case, the employee can claim those work related expenses without requiring written evidence because the amount is under $300 however if the claim for the motor vehicle means that the total of deductible expenses for the employee is over $300 the $285 would then need to be substantiated with written evidence.

13.147   OUTDOOR WORKERS

Expenses for sunscreen, sunglasses and hats etc. are deductible for outdoor workers.

The Tax Office accepts, following the decision of the Federal Court in *Morris Ors v FC of T* (2002) ATC 4404, that deductions may be allowable for the cost of sunscreens, sunglasses and sunhats. A deduction is allowable when these items are used because the worker is obliged to work in an environment where they are exposed to the harmful effects of the sun. This would generally require that exposure would be for sustained periods, not for example for a short walk between different employers' premises (see TR 2003/16).

Examples of occupations where people work in the sun for sustained periods (for either part or all of the day) include:
- building and construction
- delivery and courier services
- farming, agriculture and horticulture
- fishing
- forestry and logging
- landscaping and gardening services
- open air mineral, oil and gas extraction and exploration
- outdoor sports, and
- other outdoor services.

13.150   LAUNDRY EXPENSES

Employees can claim up to $150 for laundry expenses (ie. washing, drying and ironing work-related uniforms and protective clothing) without written evidence (TR 98/5). Where the total amount of work expenses incurred in the income year is $300 or less, there is no need for written evidence to be kept for laundry or other work-related expenses even if the laundry expenses are more than $150. However, where the total amount of work-related expenses is more than $300, then to claim laundry expenses that total more than $150, a taxpayer must keep written evidence of all their laundry expenses (not just the amount above $150)

The Tax Office will accept as reasonable expenses for washing, ironing and drying work-related clothing etc:
- $1 per wash (if washed separately), and
- 50c per wash (if washed with other clothes).

13.155   PHONE, COMPUTER AND INTERNET EXPENSES

Employees may be able to claim some of their home telephone, mobile phone, computer and internet expenses. As a general rule the claim is limited to the amount that relates directly to their employment.

The cost of installing a home phone or maintaining a silent number is not deductible. The cost of telephone rental may be partly deductible for employees who can demonstrate they are either 'on call' or are required to contact their employer on a regular basis whilst they are away from the workplace. The cost of work-related calls made is deductible and can be identified from the itemised account, or can be estimated by maintaining diary entries made over a four week period and claiming the relevant percentage of costs. Receipts or other documentary evidence of the total cost of calls must be maintained.

Claims for depreciation of computer and other computer equipment (eg. printers, modems, scanners) should be based on a reasonable estimate of their business or work-related usage. The Tax Office will accept an estimate based on a diary record of both private usage and work-related usage that is maintained. Internet expenses can be similarly based. Receipts or other documentary expenses must be maintained to support claims.

13.160 TRAVEL EXPENSES

As a general rule, travel expenses incidental and relevant to gaining or producing assessable income are deductible under the ordinary provisions of s8-1 ITAA97 to the extent that the expenses are not of a private, domestic or capital nature. The following rules apply when claims for business travel expenses incurred (inside or outside Australia) are made by self-employed persons, partners and employees.

13.165   BUSINESS TRAVEL: DOMESTIC AND OVERSEAS

All taxpayers must obtain documentary evidence of their business travel expenses if they are away from their ordinary residence for one night or greater (see *Written evidence* at 13.120).

There are exceptions for employees who receive an allowance from their employer and who claim no more than the amount set out at 13.180, 13.185, 13.190, 13.200 and 13.205.

Whether for overseas or domestic travel, if the travel is for six nights or more, additional records must be kept. You must record in a diary (or similar document):

- the nature of the activity
- the day and approximate time it began
- how long it lasted, and
- where you engaged in it.

 Diary entries must be made before the activity ends or as soon as possible afterwards.

Receipts are also required for accommodation expenses. You do not need to record non-business activities.

Travel expenses do not include motor vehicle expenses, which must be claimed separately (see *Car expenses* from 13.220), but taxi fares (or similar expenses) and motor vehicle expenses are treated as travel expenses if they relate to overseas travel. If your travel expenses include claims for fuel and oil, you have a choice of either getting written evidence or keeping odometer records for the period you owned or leased the car (see 13.242).

13.168   EMPLOYEE DOMESTIC TRAVEL

A travel diary or similar document must be maintained for travel within Australia or overseas if the employee is travelling away from their 'ordinary residence' for six nights or more. No written evidence and no travel records are required for travel within Australia if the employee receives a travel allowance and claims no more than the amount considered reasonable by the Tax Office.

If no travel allowance is received by an employee from their employer, or the employee claims more than the amount considered reasonable by the Tax Office (see 13.180), all travel expenses must be substantiated.

Written records (see 13.120) must be obtained for all expenses for accommodation, food and drink and incidental expenses incurred for travel away from an employee's ordinary residence, in the course of their duties.

TD 2014/19 provides the full list of reasonable allowances for meals and incidental expenses for travel within Australia during the 2014-15 year (see 13.185) and overseas (see 13.190 and 13.200).

 It is the expenditure which must not exceed what the Tax Office considers reasonable (see 13.190). This means that employers can pay higher allowances to their employees and the substantiation exemption will still apply, provided the employee's claim is limited to the 'reasonable amount' and the amount paid as an allowance is bona fide and paid to cover specific travel in performing duties as an employee.

The mere receipt of a travel allowance does not mean a deduction will be automatically allowed. If using the 'reasonable allowance' basis of claiming, a taxpayer may still be required to show the basis for the claim and that the expense was actually incurred for work-related purposes.

13.170   TRAVEL BETWEEN HOME AND WORK

The cost of travel between home and work may only be deductible where:

- home is the 'place of employment' and travel is between two places of employment
- the taxpayer's employment effectively starts before leaving home (eg. consultant who services clients from home by telephone; a surgeon at a hospital giving treatment advice to staff before leaving home for the hospital)
- bulky employment-related equipment must be transported between home and work
- taxpayer's employment is of an itinerant nature (eg. different location each day), or
- a break in the journey is needed for employment duties (other than insignificant tasks such as mail collection).

In *John Holland Group Pty Ltd v Commissioner of Taxation* [2015] FCAFC 82 the Full Federal Court held that flights paid by an employer from Perth to Geraldton (WA) for a rail upgrade project would have been deductible under s8-1 ITAA97 had the cost been incurred by the employees directly. The travel was not considered to be home to work travel based on the principles in *Lunney v FCT* [1958] HCA5 as the travel was required as part of each employee's employment to a remote location.

13.172   EMPLOYEE OVERSEAS TRAVEL

Employees travelling overseas who receive a travel allowance must still obtain written evidence of their accommodation expenses. They must also keep a travel record (or similar document) if they are away from their ordinary residence for six nights or more.

NOTE: This 'travel record' records activities undertaken while travelling, not expenses incurred while travelling. This is to prove activities were in relation to producing assessable income.

Crew members on international flights who receive travel allowances are excepted from this rule if:

- they travel principally outside Australia, and
- the total expenses claimed do not exceed the Tax Office reasonable limits (see 13.190).

13.175   ALLOWANCES NOT DECLARED

If an allowance is not required to be returned as assessable income in accordance with the exceptions set out in TR 2004/6, and is not returned, a deduction for the expense cannot be claimed in the tax return.

13.180 TRAVEL CLAIMS WITHIN AUSTRALIA 2015-16

The substantiation requirements do not apply to 'travel expenses' incurred by an employee who receives an allowance for travel costs within Australia and the costs incurred for accommodation, food, drink and incidental expenses do not exceed the following reasonable amounts as determined by the Tax Office. If the cost incurred is less than the reasonable amount, then the employee can only claim the amount incurred. This can apply to company directors and office holders (TD 2004/19).

These amounts, set out in TD 2015/14, are only applicable for employees who comply with the rules from 13.160 to 13.175 and 13.185. Claims in excess of the limit must be substantiated (see TR 2004/6 for details).

NOTE: Details of amounts applicable to the 2014-15 year can be found at 13.185.

NOTE: Please read ALL of 13.185 and TR 2004/6 to ensure you understand the requirements.

2015-16 Salary levels $115,450 or below

Location	Accomm ($)	B'fast ($)	Lunch ($)	Dinner ($)	Incidentals ($)	TOTAL ($)
Adelaide	157	25.90	29.15	49.65	18.75	280.45
Brisbane	205	25.90	29.15	49.65	18.75	328.45
Canberra	168	25.90	29.15	49.65	18.75	291.45
Darwin	216	25.90	29.15	49.65	18.75	339.45
Hobart	132	25.90	29.15	49.65	18.75	255.45
Melbourne	173	25.90	29.15	49.65	18.75	196.45
Perth	233	25.90	29.15	49.65	18.75	356.45
Sydney	185	25.90	29.15	49.65	18.75	308.45
High cost country	Variable[1]	25.90	29.15	49.65	18.75	Variable[1]
TIER 2 country centres	132	23.20	26.50	45.70	18.75	246.15
Other country centres	110	23.20	26.50	45.70	18.75	224.15

2015-16 Salary range $115.451 to $205,300

Location	Accomm ($)	B'fast ($)	Lunch ($)	Dinner ($)	Incidentals ($)	TOTAL ($)
Adelaide	208	28.20	39.90	55.90	26.80	358.80
Brisbane	257	28.20	39.90	55.90	26.80	407.80
Canberra	223	28.20	39.90	55.90	26.80	373.80
Darwin	287	28.20	39.90	55.90	26.80	437.80
Hobart	176	28.20	39.90	55.90	26.80	326.80
Melbourne	228	28.20	39.90	55.90	26.80	378.80
Perth	260	28.20	39.90	55.90	26.80	410.80
Sydney	246	28.20	39.90	55.90	26.80	396.80
High cost country	Variable[1]	28.20	39.90	55.90	26.80	Variable[1]
TIER 2 country centres	152	25.90	26.50	51.60	26.80	282.80
Other country centres	127	25.90	26.50	51.60	26.80	257.80

2015-16 Salary $205,301 and above

Location	Accomm ($)	B'fast ($)	Lunch ($)	Dinner ($)	Incidentals ($)	TOTAL ($)
Adelaide	209	33.25	47.00	65.95	26.80	382
Brisbane	257	33.25	47.00	65.95	26.80	430
Canberra	246	33.25	47.00	65.95	26.80	419
Darwin	287	33.25	47.00	65.95	26.80	460
Hobart	195	33.25	47.00	65.95	26.80	368
Melbourne	265	33.25	47.00	65.95	26.80	438
Perth	299	33.25	47.00	65.95	26.80	472
Sydney	265	33.25	47.00	65.95	26.80	438
Country centres	$195[2]	33.25	47.00	65.95	26.80	Variable[3]

1: See *High cost country centres* table (over the page).

2: Or the relevant amount in *High cost country centres* table over the page if higher.

3: See *High cost country centres* table (over the page) if applicable.

High cost country centres – accommodation expenses

Albany (WA) $179	Esperance (WA) $135	Newman (WA) $195
Alice Springs (NT) $150	Exmouth (WA) $255	Norfolk Island $329
Bordertown (SA) $135	Geraldton (WA) $175	Northam (WA) $163
Bourke (NSW) $165	Gladstone (QLD) $187	Orange (NSW) $155
Bright (VIC) $152	Gold Coast (QLD) $149	Port Hedland (WA) $295
Broome (WA) $260	Gosford (NSW) $140	Port Lincoln (WA) $170
Bunbury (WA) $155	Halls Creek (WA) $199	Port Macquarie (NSW) $140
Burnie (TAS) $160	Hervey Bay (QLD) $157	Port Pirie (SA) $140
Cairns (QLD) $140	Horn Island (QLD) $200	Queanbeyan (NSW) $133
Carnarvon (WA) $151	Jabiru (NT) $192	Roma (QLD) $139
Castlemaine (VIC) $140	Kalgoorlie (WA) $159	Thursday Is (QLD) $200
Chinchilla (QLD) $143	Karratha (WA) $347	Wagga Wagga (NSW) $141
Christmas Island (WA) $180	Katherine (NT) $134	Weipa (QLD) $138
Cocos (Keeling) Islands (WA) $285	Kingaroy (QLD) $134	Whyalla (SA) $156
Colac (VIC) $138	Kununurra (WA) $202	Wilpena Pound (SA) $167
Dalby (QLD) $144	Mackay (QLD) $161	Wollongong (NSW) $136
Dampier (WA) $175	Maitland (NSW) $152	Wonthaggi (VIC) $138
Derby (WA) $190	Mount Isa (QLD) $160	Yulara (NT) $280
Devonport (TAS) $140	Mudgee (NSW) $135	
Emerald (QLD) $156	Newcastle (NSW) $155	

Tier 2 country centres

Albury (NSW)	Esperance (WA)	Port Pirie (SA)
Ararat (VIC)	Geelong (VIC)	Portland (VIC)
Armidale (NSW)	Goulburn (NSW)	Queanbeyan (NSW)
Ayr (QLD)	Griffith (NSW)	Queenstown (TAS)
Bairnsdale (VIC)	Gunnedah (NSW)	Renmark (SA)
Ballarat (VIC)	Hamilton (VIC)	Rockhampton (QLD)
Bathurst (NSW)	Horsham (VIC)	Sale (VIC)
Bega (NSW)	Innisfail (QLD)	Seymour (VIC)
Benalla (VIC)	Kadina (SA)	Shepparton (VIC)
Bendigo (VIC)	Launceston (TAS)	Swan Hill (VIC)
Broken Hill (NSW)	Mildura (VIC)	Tamworth (NSW)
Bundaberg (QLD)	Mount Gambier (SA)	Tennant Creek (NT)
Ceduna (SA)	Muswellbrook (NSW)	Toowoomba (QLD)
Charters Towers (QLD)	Naracoorte (SA)	Townsville (QLD)
Coffs Harbour (NSW)	Nowra (NSW)	Tumut (NSW)
Cooma (NSW)	Port Augusta (SA)	Wangaratta (VIC)
Dubbo (NSW)	Port Lincoln (SA)	Warrnambool (VIC)
Echuca (VIC)	Port Macquarie (NSW)	

13.185 TRAVEL CLAIMS WITHIN AUSTRALIA 2014-15

The substantiation requirements do not apply to 'travel expenses' incurred by an employee who receives an allowance for travel costs within Australia and the costs incurred for accommodation, food, drink and incidental expenses do not exceed the following reasonable amounts as determined by the Tax Office. If the cost incurred is less than the reasonable amount, then the employee can only claim the amount incurred. This can apply to company directors and office holders (TD 2004/19).

These amounts, set out in TD 2014/19, are only applicable for employees who comply with the rules from 13.160 to 13.175. Claims in excess of the limit must be substantiated (see TR 2004/6).

NOTE: Please read ALL of 13.185 and TR 2004/6 to ensure you understand the requirements.

2014-15 Salary levels $112,610 or below

Location	Accomm ($)	B'fast ($)	Lunch ($)	Dinner ($)	Incidentals ($)	TOTAL ($)
Adelaide	157	25.35	28.55	48.65	18.70	278.25
Brisbane	201	25.35	28.55	48.65	18.70	322.25
Canberra	168	25.35	28.55	48.65	18.70	289.25
Darwin	216	25.35	28.55	48.65	18.70	337.25
Hobart	132	25.35	28.55	48.65	18.70	253.25
Melbourne	173	25.35	28.55	48.65	18.70	294.25
Perth	233	25.35	28.55	48.65	18.70	354.25
Sydney	185	25.35	28.55	48.65	18.70	306.25
High cost country	Variable[1]	25.35	28.55	48.65	18.70	Variable[1]
TIER 2 country centres	132	22.70	25.95	44.75	18.70	244.10
Other country centres	110	22.70	25.95	44.75	18.70	222.10

2014-15 Salary range $112,611 to $200,290

Location	Accomm ($)	B'fast ($)	Lunch ($)	Dinner ($)	Incidentals ($)	TOTAL ($)
Adelaide	208	27.60	39.10	54.75	26.75	356.20
Brisbane	257	27.60	39.10	54.75	26.75	405.20
Canberra	223	27.60	39.10	54.75	26.75	371.20
Darwin	287	27.60	39.10	54.75	26.75	435.20
Hobart	176	27.60	39.10	54.75	26.75	324.20
Melbourne	228	27.60	39.10	54.75	26.75	376.20
Perth	260	27.60	39.10	54.75	26.75	408.20
Sydney	246	27.60	39.10	54.75	26.75	379.20
High cost country	Variable[1]	27.60	39.10	54.75	26.75	Variable[1]
TIER 2 country centres	152	25.35	25.95	50.55	26.75	280.60
Other country centres	127	25.35	25.95	50.55	26.75	255.60

2014-15 Salary $200,291 and above

Location	Accomm ($)	B'fast ($)	Lunch ($)	Dinner ($)	Incidentals ($)	TOTAL ($)
Adelaide	209	32.55	46.10	64.60	26.75	379
Brisbane	257	32.55	46.10	64.60	26.75	427
Canberra	246	32.55	46.10	64.60	26.75	416
Darwin	287	32.55	46.10	64.60	26.75	457
Hobart	195	32.55	46.10	64.60	26.75	365
Melbourne	265	32.55	46.10	64.60	26.75	435
Perth	299	32.55	46.10	64.60	26.75	469
Sydney	265	32.55	46.10	64.60	26.75	435
Country centres	$190[2]	32.55	46.10	64.60	26.75	Variable[3]

1: See *High cost country centres* table (over the page).

2: Or the relevant amount in *High cost country centres* table over the page if higher.

3: See *High cost country centres* table (over the page) if applicable.

High cost country centres – accommodation expenses

Albany (WA) $179	Emerald (QLD) $156	Newcastle (NSW) $152
Alice Springs (NT) $150	Exmouth (WA) $255	Newman (WA) $195
Bordertown (SA) $135	Geraldton (WA) $175	Norfolk Island $329
Bourke (NSW) $165	Gladstone (QLD) $187	Northam (WA) $163
Bright (VIC) $152	Gold Coast (QLD) $149	Orange (NSW) $149
Broome (WA) $233	Gosford (NSW) $140	Port Hedland (WA) $295
Bunbury (WA) $155	Halls Creek (WA) $199	Port Pirie (SA) $140
Burnie (TAS) $149	Hervey Bay (QLD) $157	Queanbeyan (NSW) $133
Cairns (QLD) $140	Horn Island (QLD) $180	Roma (QLD) $139
Carnarvon (WA) $151	Jabiru (NT) $192	Thursday Is (QLD) $200
Castlemaine (VIC) $133	Kalgoorlie (WA) $159	Wagga Wagga (NSW) $141
Chinchilla (QLD) $143	Karratha (WA) $347	Weipa (QLD) $138
Christmas Island (WA) $150	Katherine (NT) $134	Whyalla (SA) $145
Cocos (Keeling) Islands (WA) $285	Kingaroy (QLD) $134	Wilpena Pound (SA) $167
Colac (VIC) $138	Kununurra (WA) $202	Wollongong (NSW) $136
Dalby (QLD) $144	Mackay (QLD) $161	Wonthaggi (VIC) $138
Dampier (WA) $175	Maitland (NSW) $152	Yulara (NT) $244
Derby (WA) $190	Mount Isa (QLD) $160	
Devonport (TAS) $135	Mudgee (NSW) $135	

Tier 2 country centres

Albury (NSW)	Echuca (VIC)	Portland (VIC)
Ararat (VIC)	Esperance (WA)	Port Lincoln (SA)
Armidale (NSW)	Geelong (VIC)	Port Macquarie (NSW)
Ayr (QLD)	Goulburn (NSW)	Queenstown (TAS)
Bairnsdale (VIC)	Gunnedah (NSW)	Renmark (SA)
Ballarat (VIC)	Hamilton (VIC)	Rockhampton (QLD)
Bathurst (NSW)	Horsham (VIC)	Sale (VIC)
Benalla (VIC)	Innisfail (QLD)	Seymour (VIC)
Bendigo (VIC)	Kadina (SA)	Shepparton (VIC)
Broken Hill (NSW)	Launceston (TAS)	Swan Hill (VIC)
Bundaberg (QLD)	Mildura (VIC)	Tamworth (NSW)
Ceduna (SA)	Mount Gambier (SA)	Tennant Creek (NT)
Charters Towers (QLD)	Muswellbrook (NSW)	Toowoomba (QLD)
Coffs Harbour (NSW)	Naracoorte (SA)	Townsville (QLD)
Cooma (NSW)	Nowra (NSW)	Tumut (NSW)
Dubbo (NSW)	Port Augusta (SA)	Warrnambool (VIC)

TRAVEL ALLOWANCE

As a general rule, an allowance is treated as being in respect of travel if the period away does not exceed 21 days. For longer periods, the payment may be a living away from home allowance (see 25.840).

SUBSTANTIATION

Claims up to these limits are allowed without receipts or other written documentary evidence, but only if an allowance was received from the employer. All expenses must be actually incurred by the employees before a claim can be made and apportioned between business and private expenses where appropriate (TR 2004/6 and TR 2004/6A).

If no allowance was received, or a claim more than the reasonable amount is made, all expenses must be substantiated (see 13.120).

Part day travel allowances not involving sleeping away from home are included in assessable income. Any work related claim is subject to substantiation (TR 2004/6 and TR 2004/6A).

VERIFICATION OF REASONABLE CLAIMS

In appropriate cases where the substantiation exception is relied on, the Tax Office may still require an employee to show that they are entitled to the substantiation exception, the reasonable rate used, and entitlement to a deduction. That could mean showing that work-related travel was undertaken, a bona fide travel allowance was paid, the claim is below the reasonable amount for the destination, and that commercial accommodation was used.

The nature and degree of evidence required will depend on the circumstances, eg. the circumstances under which the employer pays allowances, the occupation of the employee and the total amount of allowances received and claimed during the year by the employee.

TAX RETURN TREATMENT

Neither the allowance nor the expenses have to be included in the employee's tax return if the allowance does not exceed the reasonable amounts and has been fully expended on deductible expenses. If an amount less than the allowance has been expended, then the employee's income tax return must include the allowance and the expenses claimed. If a deduction is claimed, then the allowance must be included in the tax return.

13.187 CLAIMS BY LONG DISTANCE TRUCK DRIVERS

Employee long distance truck drivers who receive travel allowances and are required to sleep away from home can claim food and drink expenses to set amounts without substantiating those claims. Where no travel allowance is paid, all expenses must be substantiated.

EMPLOYEE DRIVERS

Long distance truck drivers who are required to sleep away from home for a minimum of one night or more can claim the cost of accommodation, food and drink, and other incidental expenses while they are travelling as part of their duties.

The employee driver can only claim the actual amount incurred. However the driver would need to obtain and retain receipts or other documentary evidence, or maintain a diary if:

- they receive no allowance from their employer, or
- the claim exceeds the amount considered reasonable by the Tax Office (below).

All employees are required to keep a diary (see 13.160) if they are away from their usual place of residence for six nights or more.

Employees who receive a daily travel allowance can claim up to the food and drink component only of the reasonable daily travel amounts listed below, without substantiating them. This does not include incidental expenses.

Note that if a higher claim is made, the total claim must be substantiated, not just the excess.

Employee truck drivers: acceptable daily rates					
Year	Salary range	Breakfast	Lunch	Dinner	Total
2015-2016:	Not applicable	$23.20	$26.50	$45.70	$95.40 per day
2014-2015:	$112,610 and below	$22.70	$25.95	$44.75	$93.40 per day
	$112,611 and above	$25.35	$25.95	$50.55	$101.85 per day

The treatment of employee truck drivers' allowances, reimbursements and work related deductions are discussed in full in taxation ruling TR 95/18. See also TR 2004/6 and TR 2004/6A.

IF NO DAILY TRAVEL ALLOWANCE

All of the expenses must be substantiated by the appropriate written evidence for accommodation, meals and other work-related travel expenses. Travel records must be kept for work-related travel of six or more consecutive nights. If it is not possible to obtain receipts, expenses must be recorded in a diary.

OWNER-DRIVERS

Owner-drivers are treated the same as employee truck drivers who do not receive an allowance.

The Tax Office takes the view that in most cases a receipt can be obtained for the cost of a meal (eg. at a roadhouse). It is considered that it is reasonable for a truck driver to get receipts for meals from roadhouses, diners or fast food chains.

For food and drink purchases from vending machines or roadside caravans, the expenses are considered 'otherwise too hard to substantiate' and expenditure must be supported by a diary or similar record containing details.

All owner drivers are required to keep a diary (see 13.160) if they are away from their usual place of residence for six or more nights in a row.

13.190   OVERSEAS TRAVEL ALLOWANCES

Claims for travel expenses by non-employees on business trips overseas must be fully substantiated for claims to be deductible. You must keep receipts or other documentary evidence as well as a diary. Special rules apply to employees only, provided a reasonable travel allowance was paid.

For those employees who receive a reasonable travel allowance, there is no need to substantiate costs for food, drink and incidental expenses. If a deduction is claimed for more than the reasonable amount, the whole claim must be substantiated. For Tax Office substantiation and tax return treatment see 13.180. Written evidence is required for all accommodation expenses and a diary must still be maintained if away for six nights or more.

 Reasonable claims for meals and incidentals when travelling overseas (see 13.200) are available only for employees who receive an allowance (see also 13.160).

SPECIAL LOCATIONS

If an employee travels to a location for which the reasonable overseas travel allowance does not include a meals component, a reasonable amount is added to the incidental component.

Special rules apply to places not covered in TD 2015/14 for employees receiving travel allowances.

For 2015-16 if an employee travels to a country that is not shown in Table 1 at 13.200 the Tax Office will accept the reasonable allowance amounts in Cost Group 1 (see Table 2 at 13.200 for entire listing).

The relevant amounts per day are as follows.

Overseas Travel: acceptable daily rates $				
Year	Salary range	Meals	Incidentals	Total
2015-2016	$115,450 and below	$60	$25	$85
	$115,450 to $205,300	$75	$25	$100
	$205,301 and above	$95	$30	$125
2014-2015	$112,610 and above	$60	$25	$85
	$112,611 to $200,290	$75	$25	$100
	$200,291 and above	$95	$30	$125

CONVERTING ALLOWANCE TO AUSTRALIA DOLLARS ($AUD)

The reasonable allowance amounts must be converted into $AUD. To find whether the allowance would be considered reasonable, convert into $AUD using the foreign exchange rate at the time of travel:

Value of allowance in $AUD = Overseas allowance divided by prevailing exchange rate

NOTE: Claims for meals will not need to be substantiated (see 13.120) provided the reasonable allowance amounts are not exceeded, and provided a diary and receipts for accommodation expenses have been maintained. An allowance must be received by the employee.

NO TRAVEL ALLOWANCE PAID

If there was no allowance (or it was not bona fide) and the employee was away for more than five nights, both written evidence and a travel diary is required. In similar circumstances, if the employee is away for five or less nights, a travel diary is not required but written evidence of spending must be obtained (see 13.120).

TRAVEL BY SPOUSE OR RELATIVE

While a taxpayer may seek to make a claim based on the reasonable allowance rules, s26-30 (ITAA97) operates to deny a claim for travel expenses attributable to a relative accompanying an employee who is travelling in the course of performing their duties as an employee, or a person who is travelling in the course of carrying on a business for the purpose of producing assessable income.

However, this rule under s26-30 will not apply if:

- the relative accompanying the taxpayer making the claim performed substantial employment duties for that employer or taxpayer as an employee of that employer or taxpayer, and
- it is reasonable to conclude that the relative would still have accompanied the taxpayer even if a personal relationship did not exist.

In addition, a deduction is still allowed if the expenditure was in respect of providing a fringe benefit.

 Employers can claim deductions for the cost of a spouse or relative if they accompany the taxpayer, but that cost is then taxed as a fringe benefit (see 25.002).

13.200 TRAVEL CLAIMS: OVERSEAS 2015-16

These 'reasonable amounts' are available for employees only. Non-employees must substantiate all claims. The countries named in Table 1 represent the most frequented locations. The list is contained in TD 2015/14.

 These limits are available only to employees who comply with the rules at 13.190. Table 1 sets out the cost group for each destination and Table 2 sets out the reasonable allowance in Australian dollars. If a country is not listed in Table 1, use the amount for cost group 1 in Table 2. The amounts are determined solely for the purpose of the exception of obtaining written evidence (see TR 2004/6 para 33).

NOTE: Details of cost groups and reasonable allowance amounts for the 2015-16 year can be found at 13.205.

Table 1: Cost groups 2015-16

Country		Country		Country		Country	
Albania	2	Ecuador	3	Lebanon	4	Saint Vincent	3
Algeria	4	Egypt	3	Lithuania	3	Samoa	4
Angola	6	El Salvador	2	Luxembourg	5	Saudi Arabia	4
Antigua and Barbuda	4	Eritrea	2	Macedonia	2	Senegal	4
Argentina	2	Estonia	3	Malawi	2	Serbia	2
Austria	5	Ethiopia	2	Malaysia	3	Sierra Leone	3
Azerbaijan	4	Fiji	2	Mali	4	Singapore	5
Bahamas	6	Finland	5	Malta	3	Slovakia	3
Bahrain	4	France	5	Mauritius	3	Slovenia	3
Bangladesh	3	Gabon	5	Mexico	3	Solomon Islands	3
Barbados	5	Gambia	2	Monaco	6	South Africa	2
Belarus	3	Georgia	3	Morocco	3	Spain	4
Belgium	5	Germany	5	Mozambique	3	Sri Lanka	2
Bermuda	5	Ghana	3	Myanmar	3	Sudan	2
Bolivia	1	Gibraltar	4	Namibia	2	Surinam	3
Bosnia	2	Greece	4	Nepal	2	Sweden	5
Brazil	3	Guatemala	3	Netherlands	5	Switzerland	6
Brunei	2	Guyana	3	New Caledonia	5	Taiwan	4
Bulgaria	3	Hungary	3	New Zealand	4	Tanzania	3
Burkina Faso	3	Iceland	5	Nicaragua	2	Thailand	3
Cambodia	2	India	3	Nigeria	5	Tonga	3
Cameroon	4	Indonesia	3	Norway	6	Trinidad and Tobago	5
Canada	5	Iran	2	Oman	5	Tunisia	2
Chile	2	Ireland	5	Pakistan	1	Turkey	4
China*	5	Israel	5	Panama	3	Uganda	2
Colombia	4	Italy	5	Papua New Guinea	5	Ukraine	2
Congo Dem Rep	4	Jamaica	3	Paraguay	1	United Arab Emirates	5
Cook Islands	4	Japan	5	Peru	3	United Kingdom	5
Costa Rica	3	Jordan	5	Philippines	3	USA	4
Cote D'Ivoire	4	Kazakhstan	3	Poland	3	Uruguay	3
Croatia	3	Kenya	4	Portugal	3	Vanuatu	4
Cuba	3	Korea Republic	5	Puerto Rico	5	Venezuela	5
Cyprus	4	Kosovo	2	Qatar	5	Vietnam	2
Czech Republic	3	Kuwait	4	Romania	2	Zambia	3
Denmark	6	Kyrgyzstan	3	Russia	5		
Dominican Republic	4	Laos	2	Rwanda	3		
East Timor	2	Latvia	3	Saint Lucia	3		

*Includes Macau and Hong Kong

Table 2: Reasonable allowances by cost groups 2015-16 ($AUD)

Cost group	Salary $115,450 and below			Salary $115,451 to $205,300			Salary $205,301 and above		
	Meals	Incidentals	Total	Meals	Incidentals	Total	Meals	Incidentals	Total
1	$60	$25	$85	$75	$25	$100	$95	$30	$125
2	$95	$30	$125	$110	$35	$145	$140	$40	$180
3	$120	$35	$155	$150	$40	$190	$185	$45	$230
4	$140	$35	$175	$170	$45	$215	$215	$50	$265
5	$190	$40	$230	$240	$50	$290	$295	$60	$355
6	$240	$45	$285	$295	$50	$345	$340	$60	$400

13.205 TRAVEL CLAIMS: OVERSEAS 2014-15

These 'reasonable amounts' are available for employees only. Non-employees must substantiate all claims. The countries named in Table 1 represent the most frequented locations. The list is contained in TD 2014/19.

These limits are available only to employees who comply with the rules at 13.190. Table 1 sets out the cost group for each destination and Table 2 sets out the reasonable allowance in Australian dollars. If a country is not listed in Table 1, use the amount for cost group 1 in Table 2. The amounts are determined solely for the purpose of the exception of obtaining written evidence (see TR 2004/6 para 33).

Table 1: Cost groups 2014-15

Albania	2	Ecuador	3	Lebanon	4	Saint Lucia	3
Algeria	4	Egypt	3	Libya	3	Saint Vincent	3
Angola	6	El Salvador	2	Lithuania	3	Samoa	4
Antigua and Barbuda	4	Eritrea	2	Luxembourg	5	Saudi Arabia	3
Argentina	2	Estonia	3	Macedonia	2	Senegal	4
Austria	5	Ethiopia	2	Malawi	1	Serbia	2
Azerbaijan	4	Fiji	2	Malaysia	3	Sierra Leone	3
Bahamas	5	Finland	5	Mali	4	Singapore	5
Bahrain	4	France	5	Malta	3	Slovakia	4
Bangladesh	3	Gabon	5	Mauritius	3	Slovenia	4
Barbados	5	Gambia	2	Mexico	3	Solomon Islands	3
Belarus	3	Georgia	3	Monaco	6	South Africa	2
Belgium	5	Germany	5	Morocco	3	Spain	4
Bermuda	5	Ghana	3	Mozambique	3	Sri Lanka	2
Bolivia	1	Gibraltar	3	Myanmar	3	Sudan	2
Bosnia	2	Greece	4	Namibia	2	Surinam	3
Brazil	4	Guatemala	3	Nepal	2	Sweden	5
Brunei	2	Guyana	3	Netherlands	5	Switzerland	6
Bulgaria	3	Hungary	3	New Caledonia	5	Taiwan	3
Burkina Faso	3	Iceland	5	New Zealand	4	Tanzania	3
Cambodia	2	India	3	Nicaragua	2	Thailand	3
Cameroon	4	Indonesia	3	Nigeria	5	Tonga	3
Canada	5	Iran	2	Norway	6	Trinidad and Tobago	5
Chile	2	Ireland	5	Oman	5	Tunisia	2
China*	5	Israel	5	Pakistan	1	Turkey	4
Colombia	4	Italy	5	Panama	2	Uganda	2
Congo Dem Rep	4	Jamaica	3	Papua New Guinea	4	Ukraine	3
Cook Islands	4	Japan	5	Paraguay	1	United Arab Emirates	5
Costa Rica	2	Jordan	5	Peru	3	United Kingdom	5
Cote D'Ivoire	4	Kazakhstan	3	Philippines	3	United States of America	4
Croatia	3	Kenya	4	Poland	3	Uruguay	3
Cuba	3	Korea Republic	5	Portugal	3	Vanuatu	4
Cyprus	4	Kosovo	2	Puerto Rico	4	Venezuela	5
Czech Republic	3	Kuwait	4	Qatar	5	Vietnam	2
Denmark	6	Kyrgyzstan	2	Romania	3	Zambia	3
Dominican Republic	3	Laos	2	Russia	5		
East Timor	2	Latvia	4	Rwanda	3		

*Includes Macau and Hong Kong

Table 2: Reasonable allowances by cost groups 2014-15 ($AUD)								
Cost group	Salary $112,610 and below			Salary $112,611 to $200,290			Salary $200,291 and above		
	Meals	Incidentals	Total	Meals	Incidentals	Total	Meals	Incidentals	Total
1	$60	$25	$85	$75	$25	$100	$95	$30	$125
2	$90	$30	$120	$110	$35	$145	$140	$40	$180
3	$115	$35	$150	$150	$40	$190	$185	$45	$230
4	$135	$35	$170	$170	$45	$215	$215	$50	$265
5	$175	$40	$215	$240	$50	$290	$295	$60	$355
6	$240	$45	$285	$295	$50	$345	$340	$60	$400

13.210 SUMMARY OF SUBSTANTIATION REQUIREMENTS

The following table contained in TR 2004/6 provides a summary of the substantiation requirement for claims for those work-related travel allowance expenses covered by the allowance where the taxpayer is required to sleep away from home when travelling for work purposes:

Travel allowance received and:	Domestic travel		Overseas travel	
	Written evidence	Travel diary	Written evidence	Travel diary
The amount claimed does not exceed the reasonable allowance amount:				
• travel less than six nights in a row	No	No	No*	No
• travel six or more nights in a row	No	No	No*	Yes**
The amount claimed exceeds the reasonable allowance amount:				
• travel less than six nights in a row	Yes – for the whole claim	No	Yes	No
• travel six or more nights in a row	Yes – for the whole claim	Yes	Yes	Yes**

* Regardless of the length of the trip, written evidence is required for overseas accommodation expenses – but not for food, drink and incidentals.

** Members of international air crews do not need to keep a travel diary (travel record) if they limit their claim to the amount of the allowance received.

13.220 CAR EXPENSES

According to s28-13 ITAA97, a car expense is a loss or outgoing to do with a car, including costs to operate a car (such as fuel, repair, registration and insurance)and depreciation of a car. However, expenses made in respect of travel outside Australia and taxi fare or similar expenses are not car expenses.

NOTE: Car parking expenses and certain road toll or e-tag expenses are not classified as car expenses under s28-13. However, these expenses can still be deductible as general deductions under general work-related expenses substantiation rules (see. 13.290 and 13.295).

NOTE: In the Federal Budget 2015-16 the Government announced its intention to change the method of calculating work-related car expenses for the 2015-16 income year. The 12% of original value and the one third of actual expenses method will be removed. At the time of writing, these measures have not yet been enacted into law.

13.225 CAR EXPENSE SUBSTANTIATION

The rules for substantiating car claims apply to all individuals (ie. employees and non-employees) and partnerships where there is at least one partner who is a natural person. These taxpayers have to substantiate their car claims if they own, lease, or hire under hire purchase, a car that is used for business or income producing purposes. The rules do not apply to claims made by companies or a trustee of a trust. Note that there are proposed changes to working out work-related car expenses (see below).

 Asset acquisition financed by hire purchase transactions and limited recourse debt may result in the clawback of capital allowances where the claim is excessive (see 15.800).

The general rule is that taxpayers must choose one of the following four methods unless an exception applies:
- cents per kilometre method
- 12% of original value method
- 1/3rd of actual expenses method, or
- log book method.

NOTE: Unlike work-related expenses, the $300 substantiation threshold does not apply to car expenses.

The rules apply to the following vehicles (including four-wheel drive vehicles):
- motor cars, station wagons, panel vans, utility trucks or similar vehicles, and
- any other road vehicle designed to carry a load of less than one tonne or fewer than nine passengers.

For each car, taxpayers can choose, in each income year, only one of the four methods to claim their car expenses. Each method has different record keeping requirements and can result in higher or lower claims. The method chosen in an income year can be changed, provided the taxpayer would have been entitled to claim deductions using an alternative method.

 Choose the method that gives the highest claim provided you are able to discharge any record keeping requirements attached to that method. If you're registered for GST see 23.200 for calculation of GST credits for each method.

 A taxpayer used the log book method and claimed car expenses of $1,000. Following an audit, the Tax Office reduced the claim to $500. Under the cents per kilometre method the taxpayer would have been entitled to claim $700. In that case the taxpayer can change the method chosen and would be allowed to claim $700.

These four methods cannot be used for:
- a motor cycle or similar vehicle
- a taxi (on hire)
- a motor vehicle hired on an intermittent basis (eg. hourly, daily, weekly or short-term) (note that a motor vehicle on hire will be subject to these substantiation rules if it is

hired under successive agreements that results (or is likely to result) in substantial continuity of that hiring arrangement), or

- panel vans and utility trucks designed to carry a load of one tonne or more.

See *Exemptions from substantiation* at 13.265.

 When using the 'one third of actual expenses' method or the 'log book' method you must keep odometer readings for the start and end of the period you leased or owned the car in the income year.

WHAT ARE 'BUSINESS KILOMETRES'?

Business kilometres are those kilometres travelled by the car in the course of producing your assessable income or travelling between workplaces. The number of business kilometres is calculated by making a reasonable estimate. However, when using the 'log book method' (see 13.245) the estimate must take into account:

- log books, odometer or other records
- variations in pattern of the use of the car, and
- any changes in the number of cars used to produce your assessable income.

Summary of the four methods

	Cents per km	12% of original cost	1/3rd of actual expenses	Log book
Eligibility rules	None but limited to a claim of 5,000kms	Business and employment use must exceed 5,000kms	Business and employment use must exceed 5,000kms	Car must have been owned or leased
Expense base	Business kms	Original value	Cost of car expenses, eg. fuel, tyres, maintenance	
Calculate deduction	Multiply by cents per km	Multiply by 12%	Multiply by 1/3rd	Multiply by % business use
Have to substantiate expenses?	NO	NO	YES	YES

 Changes to methods of calculating work-related car expense deductions
In the 2015-16 Federal Budget, the Government announced its intention to change the methods of calculating work-related car expense deductions from the 2015-16 income year.
The '12% of original value method' and the 'one-third of actual expenses method', which are used by less than 2% of those who claim work-related car expenses, will be removed. The 'cents per kilometre method' will be modernised by replacing the three current rates based on engine size with one rate set at 66c per kilometre to apply for all motor vehicles, with the Commissioner responsible for updating the rate in following years.
The 'logbook method' of calculating expenses will be retained. These changes will not affect leasing and salary sacrifice arrangements. At the time of writing, these changes have not been legislated.

13.230   CENTS PER KM METHOD

Under this method, there is no need to substantiate any of the car expenses. A taxpayer can claim car expenses based on the number of business kms the car travelled during the income year. The claim is limited to a maximum of 5,000 business kms per car, regardless of the number of cars involved. The business travel should be based on a reasonable estimate. No documentation is required to be maintained if this method is used. However the person must still satisfy the Tax Office that the travel was undertaken for income producing purposes and that the expense was calculated on a reasonable basis.

The claim is calculated by multiplying:

Business kms travelled in the income year (limited to 5,000 kms)
x rate based on car's engine capacity

This method is available even if the car has travelled more than 5,000 business kms – however the business kms in excess of 5,000 are ignored and the claim is limited to 5,000 kilometres.

Rates for 2014-15

Engine capacity		Rate per km
Non-rotary	Rotary	
Up to 1,600cc	Up to 800cc	65c
1,601 to 2,600cc	801 to 1,300cc	76c
Over 2,600cc	Over 1,300cc	77c

 A taxpayer estimates travel of 8,000 kms during the 2014-15 income year in the course of earning assessable income. The car's engine capacity was 2500cc and the number of business kms was a reasonable estimate. The claim (using the 2014-15 rates) is 5,000 kms x 76 cents = $3,800.

 A taxpayer uses two cars for business purposes. Both are over 2,600cc. The first travelled 8,000 business kms and the second travelled 3,500 kms. Using the cents per km method the claim is $6,545 (ie. 5,000 kms at 77 cents + 3,500 kms at 77 cents).

If claims have been made using the cents per km method, special rules apply to calculate the profit or loss on disposal when the car is subsequently disposed of, lost or destroyed (see 13.280).

In the 2015-16 Federal Budget, the Government has proposed replacing the three current rates based on engine size with one rate set at 66c per kilometre to apply for all motor vehicles. This will apply from the 2015-16 income year if legislated.

CAR USED BY MORE THAN ONE PERSON

Where two or more taxpayers own or lease a car and each uses that car separately for income producing purposes, each person is entitled to claim a deduction using the cents per kilometre method (see PS LA 1999/2).

 Evan uses the car during the day for business purposes. His partner uses the same car at night, also for producing assessable income. Both can claim a deduction using the cents per km method, up to 5,000 kms each.

If two or more persons own or lease a car and the car is used jointly, (one drives and the other is a passenger) for income producing purposes, each can claim a deduction based on the cents per kilometre method, but the total deduction cannot exceed the set rate multiplied by 5,000.

13.235   12% OF ORIGINAL VALUE METHOD

Under this method, there is no need to substantiate any of the car expenses (including operating expenses and depreciation). This method is available only if the car has travelled more than 5,000 kilometres in the course of producing the taxpayer's assessable income. The taxpayer must have a reasonable basis upon which to conclude that the 'business' kilometres exceed 5,000.

The taxpayer claims 12% of the cost of the car when it was originally acquired (or of its market value when first leased – see 15.060).

The cost of the car (or market value if leased) is limited to the motor vehicle depreciation cost limit of the car when it was first used for any purpose (or when it was first leased). The 'cost' of a car is generally the purchase price (see 15.060), plus dealer charges and stamp duty (inclusive of GST if not registered; if registered see 23.200).

For a car obtained by inheritance, gift or prize, the cost of the car under this method is based on its notional depreciated value immediately before it was acquired.

The maximum deduction a taxpayer can claim is 12% of the depreciation car limit in the year in which they first used or leased the car. The depreciation car limit for the 2014-15 and 2015-16 income years is $57,466.

WHERE THE OWNER IS REGISTERED FOR GST

A GST input tax credit may apply if the car is used for a creditable purpose (see 23.200).

The Tax Office's view on how to claim input tax credits for car expenses is set out in GST Bulletin GSTB 2006/1. According to the Bulletin, the 12% method assumes a 1/3rd business use (ie. a 1/3rd creditable purpose). Where an input tax credit is claimed in respect of the purchase of a car, its original purchase price should be reduced by this amount when calculating the deduction.

Jeff, a sole trader who is registered for GST, purchased a new car on 1 August 2014 for $33,000 (including $3,000 GST). He used the car for more than 5,000 kms in his business. He decides to use the 12% of original cost method to calculate his deduction for the car and claims a GST input tax credit of $1,000 (1/3rd of $3,000) because the vehicle was used for a creditable purpose.

The 'purchase price' used to calculate the deduction for the car is $32,000.(ie. $33,000 – $1,000 input tax credit) plus stamp duty on the GST inclusive price of $33,000. The deduction must be apportioned in 2014-15 income year to reflect the part year period of ownership.

PART-YEAR CLAIM

The deduction under this method is apportioned if the car was not owned or leased for the full year. In that case the reduced claim is calculated:

Deduction for full year x no. days car was owned during income year (ignoring leap years)

A new car was purchased by a GST registered business on 1 December 2014 for $57,000 (net of GST input credit) and travelled more than 5,000 kms during the balance of the income year. Deduction allowed for the full year: $6,840 (12% of $57,000).

Claim for 2014-15 is $6,840 x 212 divided by 365 (ownership days) = $3,972.

13.240   ONE-THIRD OF ACTUAL EXPENSES METHOD

Where the number of business kilometres travelled by the car in the income year exceeds 5,000 (or would have exceeded that amount if the car had been used for the whole year), the taxpayer can use as an alternative the 'one third car expenses method'. This method cannot be used unless the actual (or annualised) business travel for the car exceeds 5,000kms. The number of business kms can be based on a reasonable estimate, but odometer readings must be kept for the car for the start and end of the period owned or leased for the income year.

Under this method the taxpayer can claim one third of the car expenses for that car, including operating expenses and depreciation, provided the expenses can be substantiated (see *Written evidence*, 13.120). Where only part of an expense would normally be allowed as a deduction, under this method only one third of that part may be claimed.

Claims for car parking (see 13.290) or toll fees are **not** car expenses and should be claimed separately.

The taxpayer leases a car with a market value of $50,000. The taxpayer estimates travel of 15,000 kilometres in earning assessable income during the income year. Car expenses of $12,300 (including lease charges) were incurred during the income year and the taxpayer has retained the required receipts and other documentary evidence necessary to substantiate the claim. The deduction allowed under this method is:

$12,300 x 1/3 = $4,100

NOTE: The Government has proposed removal of this method in the Federal Budget from the 2015-16 income year.

LUXURY LEASED VEHICLES

Claims for lease charges for luxury cars (ie. cars valued above the depreciation cost limit in their first year of use, see 15.060 and 15.088) are not allowed under this method. Instead the expenses to be included are:

- depreciation of the leased car (limited to the depreciation cost limit which is $57,466 for 2014-15 and 2015-16 income years (see 15.085), and
- financing charges (eg. interest).

13.242   CLAIMS FOR FUEL AND OIL

Documentary evidence is not required to claim fuel and oil expenses, but the claim must be based on a reasonable estimate of those expenses and the business kilometres travelled.

The Tax Office stated in TD 97/19 that claims will be accepted if based on:

- the business kilometres travelled
- the average fuel cost, and
- the average fuel consumption.

Under that Determination, odometer readings must be maintained if no other records are available.

The monthly average cost of fuel within the capital cities can be obtained from the Australian Automotive Association website. Those travelling in the country must obtain another form of independent verification (eg. average price from area distributor). The average fuel consumption can be based on the figures contained in the Green Vehicle Guide- see http://www.greenvehicleguide.gov.au.

 The average fuel consumption figures in the guide are generally lower than under real conditions, leading taxpayers to inadvertently under-claim for the cost of fuel.

The figures below have been compiled from monthly data published by the Australian Automotive Association for metropolitan capital cities. Users of premium petrol or diesel may need to determine the price differential from retailers in their area. Similarly, a different average rate may apply to taxpayers living in remote or rural areas.

Average retail price of unleaded petrol (cents per litre) 2014-15 - Metro capital cities					
Location	Quarter				
	Sep 2014	Dec 2014	Mar 2015	Jun 2015*	Average 2015**
Sydney	146.0	138.2	120.1	N/A	134.8
Melbourne	145.8	132.4	117.3	N/A	131.8
Brisbane	149.3	140.5	121.9	N/A	137.2
Adelaide	143.5	133.4	116.9	N/A	131.3
Perth	148.3	136.9	121.3	N/A	135.5
Hobart	160.2	150.2	129.6	N/A	146.7
Darwin	173.5	157.7	132.4	N/A	154.5
Canberra	153.7	147.6	124.2	N/A	141.8

*Not available at time of writing. See www.aaa.asn.au/issues/petrol.htm.

**Average for the three quarters published to date (excludes June 2015 quarter).

13.245   LOG BOOK METHOD

If the number of business kilometres travelled by a vehicle in the year exceeds 5,000 the taxpayer may choose to use either the '12% of cost' (see 13.235), the 'one third of car expenses' method (see 13.240) or the log book method. The log book method can be used whether or not the vehicle travels 5,000 business kilometres, but the car must be either owned or leased by the taxpayer.

Taxpayers must substantiate all of their car expenses under this method including:

- registration and insurance
- repairs and maintenance
- fuel and oil (see 13.242)
- depreciation (if owned or on hire purchase) (see from 15.010 for details of the depreciation rules), and
- lease charges – luxury car rules may apply (see 15.085).

A deduction is allowed based on the business percentage of the total kms travelled by the car during the income year:

Business kms divided by total kms x Total car expenses

An employee purchased a car on 1 December 2014 for $40,000 (GST inclusive) and travelled 15,000 kms (of which 12,000 kms were for business travel) for the balance of the income year. Total car expenses (including depreciation) for the income year were $9,800.

Assuming the taxpayer has maintained all of the necessary substantiation records, a claim could be made in 2014-15 for 80% of $9,800 = $7,840.

NOTE: The Government has proposed this method in the Federal Budget from the 2015-16 income year.

KEEPING A LOG BOOK

A log book must be kept for the first income year when a claim is made and it must be maintained for a continuous 12 week period. The taxpayer can choose which 12 consecutive weeks to maintain the log book, but for a claim to be made under this method, the log book period must be commenced in the income year (or an earlier year: see below).

If the car is held by the taxpayer for less than 12 weeks during the income year, the log book period must cover that entire period. If claims are to be made using the log book method for two or more cars in the same income year, the log books for those cars must cover the same 12 week period.

Once a log book has been maintained for the required 12 week period, the next log book is only required to be completed in five years time unless:

- a notification is sent before the income year from the Tax Office
- a second car is acquired during an income year and you plan to claim using the log book method, or
- you vary the business percentage of your claim.

Even though a log book has been kept for 12 weeks, in a non log book year, a reasonable estimate must still be made of the business kms travelled by the car, taking into account any variation in use of the car and changes in the number of cars used to earn income. Car expense claims in that non log book year must be based on that estimate.

The log book should be in English and it must be retained for five years after the last income year that the log book is used to claim car expenses for the car. The five years start on the later of the due date for lodging the return and the lodgement date. The retention period can be extended by a further five years if there is a dispute with the Tax Office involving the business percentage claimed.

A log book was completed in 2008-2009 and the taxpayer last claimed car expenses using that log book in 2013-14. The 2013-14 income tax return was lodged on 1 October 2013. The log book must be retained until 30 September 2019.

The log book must record all business journeys made in the car during the selected 12 week period and record:

- when the log book period starts and ends
- the car's odometer readings at the start and end of the period
- the total kilometres travelled
- the total business kilometres travelled, and
- the business percentage.

For each journey the following must be recorded:

- the day the journey began and ended
- the car's odometer reading at the start and end of the journey
- the total kilometres travelled on the journey
- why the journey was made, and
- the total number of business kilometres travelled.

NOTE: If a taxpayer made two or more journeys in a row on the same day, the taxpayer can record them as a single journey.

Entries in the log book do not need to be signed.

There is no need to keep a log book for a replacement car if it is nominated as a replacement car, but the existing car (if retained) will be treated as a new car. This means the replacement car can continue to be claimed for using the old log book (provided the log book method is not also used for the old car). A new log book must be kept for both cars for a new concurrent 12 weeks if claims for both the old car and the replacement car are to be made using the log book method. The replacement nomination must be made before lodging your income tax return (or such later time allowed by the Tax Office) and must be retained until the end of the log book period.

The nomination must record for both cars:

- odometer readings at the start and end of the period
- make, model and registration, and
- engine capacity.

Log book pro forma					
Vehicle registration no					
Period covered by log book: From			to		
Odometer readings for period: Start			end		
Odometer readings per journey		Date of travel		Kilometres travelled	Reason for journey
Start	End	Start	End		
Total kilometres for period					
Total business kilometres			%		

13.250   SWITCHING METHODS

The same method of claiming motor vehicle expenses does not have to be used every year. Even though the log book method has been used in one year, the taxpayer has the right to choose a different method in each subsequent year and for each motor vehicle. That means the taxpayer can switch between the log book method, the 12% method or one third of expenses method in following years (provided more than 5,000 business kilometres have been travelled in that year by the car) or the cents per kilometre method.

If switching back to the log book method, a new log book does not have to be used until the 5th year of the original log has expired.

13.260   LOG BOOK METHOD: WORKED EXAMPLE

The log book method can be used whether business kilometres exceed 5,000 or not, but only if the car is either leased or owned by the taxpayer and is used to produce assessable income. See example on the following page.

A commercial traveller traded-in his car for $14,500 on 31 October 2014, buying another the same day on hire-purchase (the old contract was then paid out). A car allowance of $16,170 was received (ie. based on 48 weeks at $55 per week plus 76c per km including home to-work non-tax deductible travel).

The car allowance received must be included as assessable income. The profit on trade-in of the vehicle of $1,118 must also be included as an assessable balancing adjustment (assessable income).

For the year, the total travel was 19,610 kms but the business kms were only 10,800: continuing the earlier years' claims on an income-producing ratio of 55%, as established from a log book. The taxpayer's estimate of actual usage during the year confirmed the business percentage of 55%.

NOTE: A 25% diminishing value rate applies if a car is purchased under a contract entered into after 10 May 2006.

Depreciation on the traded-in car to the date of sale

Written down value at the beginning of the year $13,600
25% (diminishing-balance) depreciation (4 months out of 12 months) .... 1,133 ....**$1,133**
Written-down value on disposal (adjusted below) $12,467

Depreciation on replacement vehicle

GST exclusive cash price (Note: depreciation cost limit can apply) $35,400
25% (diminishing-balance) depreciation (8 months out of 12 months) .... 5,900 .... **$5,900**
Written-down value $29,500

Carry-forward claims and running expenses for both cars

Registration and third party insurance (old car) $320
Comprehensive insurance after refund (old car) 630
Registration and third party insurance (new car) 370
Comprehensive insurance (new car) 810

Interest and finance contract charges (new car)

Interest and finance charges for 8 months 2,800
Interest and charges on H.P. contract (old car) $1,730
less credit allowed when paid out .... (460) 1,270
Petrol and oil (both cars) 2,910
Service, repairs and oil changes 600
Motoring organisation service subscription 120
Interest on private loan towards car deposit
(ie. $3,000 @ 15% for 8 months) 300 300
Deductible costs .... $10,130 ..... **$10,130**
Total of depreciation and apportionable expenses **$17,163**

DEPRECIATION ADJUSTMENT ON TRADED-IN CAR   *W/D VALUE*
Original cost was $26,000
Calculated depreciation over the years ....(13,533)
Written down value $12,467
Sale price **$14,500**
Profit on sale **$2,033**
Amount to be added back as assessable income (ie. 55% of $2,033) **$1,118**

Business claim

Income-producing use is: 10,800kms divided by 19,610kms = 55%
The claim is: 55% of $17,163 .... $ 9,440
plus parking fees and tolls (clearly attributable to business use of car) 2,225
CLAIM IN 2014-15 TAX RETURN .... **$ 11,665**

13.265 EXEMPTIONS FROM SUBSTANTIATION

There are circumstances where certain cars are exempt from the need to substantiate car expense claims. In these situations, the taxpayer can choose to use one of the four methods or calculate the deduction under the normal rules applicable under s8-1.

If the latter is chosen, the claim will be allowed based on the extent that expenses were incurred in carrying on a business or necessarily incurred in earning the person's assessable income.

If you are covered by one of the following exceptions to the car expenses rules you can calculate your deductions under normal principles, for example s8-1 (General deductions) or Division 40 (Depreciation) or use one of the four methods (if no other method is available).

Type of car	Details of exempt circumstances	When circumstances must be satisfied
Any type	You provide the car for the exclusive use of your employees (except partners in a partnership) or their relatives and any of them were entitled to use it for private purposes.	Whenever the car is used in the income year.
Any type	You let the car on hire or lease in the course of carrying on a business of hiring or leasing cars.	Whenever the car is used in the income year.
Any type	During the period you owned or leased a car for use in producing your income: you used it principally for that purpose and it was unregistered.	Whenever the car is used in the income year.
Any type	The car was part of the trading stock of a business you carried on, and you used it in the course of that business.	Whenever the car is used in the income year.
Panel van and utility truck*, taxi, any road vehicle designed to carry less than one tonne but not a vehicle designed principally to carry passengers	You use the car only: a. for travel in the course of producing your assessable income, and/or b. for travel that is incidental to a), and/or c. for travel between your residence and where you use the car for the purpose in a), and/or d. by giving it to someone else for travel by them between their residence and where the car is used for the purpose in a), and/or e. for private travel by you or someone else that was minor, infrequent and irregular.	Whenever the car is used in the income year.
Any type	The car is unregistered and you use it principally in producing your assessable income.	Whenever the car is used in the income year.
Any type	a. The car is trading stock of your business of selling cars, and b. you didn't use the car.	a. At some time in the income year b. at any time in the year
Any type	The expense is to do with repairs or other work on the car and you incurred it in your business of doing repairs or other work on cars	Any time

*Applies only to vehicles not usually subject to the substantiation rules (see from 13.225).

13.280 DISPOSAL OF CAR

When a car is disposed of, lost or destroyed, the taxpayer may need to calculate the balancing charge (ie. profit or loss on disposal) for the car under Subdivision 40 of ITAA97. To calculate the balance adjustment charge, the four methods of substantiation generally fall into one of the following two categories.

NOTE: In the Federal Budget 2015-16 the Government announced its intention to change the method of calculating work-related car expenses for the 2015-16 income year. The 12% of original value and the one third of actual expenses method will be removed. At the time of writing, these measures have not yet been enacted into law.

ONE THIRD OF ACTUAL EXPENSES METHOD OR LOG BOOK ONLY

If deductions have been claimed using only the one third of actual expenses method and/or the log book method, depreciation allowed as a deduction is known and a balancing charge is calculated (see 15.070).

CENTS PER KM OR 12% OF COST ONLY

If expenses for a car have only ever been claimed under the cents per km and/or 12% of cost methods, there is no balancing charge because no deduction has been claimed for depreciation.

COMBINATION OF METHODS

If expenses have been claimed using a mix between the cent per km/12% method and the log book/one third of actual expenses method, s40-370 applies and depreciation claimed under cent per km and/or 12% is deemed to be:

Method used	Deemed depreciation
Cents per kilometre	20%
12% of car cost	33.3%

NOTE: The deemed business percentages are used because the deduction calculated using these two methods is only an arbitrary basis of deduction.

A taxpayer purchased a car on 1 August 2011 for $30,000 and sells it on 30 April 2015. Depreciation rates for cars acquired from 10 May 2006 is 25% for the diminishing value method.

In this case, using diminishing value method, depreciation at 25% is:

2011-2012 (11 months)	*$6,875*
2012-2013 (full year)	*$5,781*
2013-2014 (full year)	*$4,336*
2014-2015 (10 months)	*$2,710*

Deemed business use

Car claims were based on 12% of car cost method and the cents per km method.

Cost of car		*$30,000*
2011-2012 (33.3% of $6,875)	*$2,289*	
2012-2013 (33.3% of $5,781)	*$1,925*	
2013-2014 (20% of $4,336)	*$867*	
2014-2015 (20% of $2,710)	*$542*	*$5,623*
Actual depreciated value		***$19,702***

See *Balancing adjustment events* from 15.070 for a complete example.

13.290   CAR PARKING EXPENSES

Car parking fees incurred in the course of producing assessable income are generally deductible but special rules apply if the car is used by an employee to commute between home and work or the car is provided to the employee by the employer.

NON-EMPLOYEES

Self-employed persons, partnerships or trusts are entitled to claim deductions for expenses incurred for car parking fees, provided those fees are incurred in the course of producing their assessable income or as part of the ongoing operations of their business.

EMPLOYEES

Employees who use their own cars for work-related purposes are generally entitled to claim deductions for the cost of travel and car parking, provided those costs are incurred as part of employment related activities.

A deduction for car parking is denied, however, for the cost of car parking if the car:

- is parked at or near the employee's principal place of employment for more than four hours between 7am and 7pm, and
- was used to travel between either home and work, or work and home.

Other car parking expenses incurred during the day are allowed if the car is being used for work related purposes.

A deduction is not denied, however, if the employee is the driver of, or a passenger of the car and:

- they are entitled (under State or Territory law) to use a disabled person's car parking space, and
- a valid disabled person's car parking permit is displayed on the car.

NOTE: These rules do not apply if the vehicle is not a 'car' as defined in s176 (FBTAA86). See 25.350 and 25.354.

EMPLOYER-PROVIDED CAR

If the employer provides the employee with a car, any expenses incurred by the employee in maintaining the car (eg. fuel, oil) cannot be claimed as deductions. Those expenses can be used to reduce the amount of any Fringe Benefits Tax (FBT) payable on the car (see 25.350 and 25.401). Where the employee incurs car parking expenses that are not paid or reimbursed by the employer, a claim is allowed provided he/she satisfies the rules above.

If an employer provides an employee with a car park, FBT may be payable by the employer – see 25.400.

13.295   ROAD TOLL AND E-TAG EXPENSES

If an employee incurs a road toll expense when using either their own car or their employer's car while travelling when deriving assessable income, a deduction is allowable. However, if the purpose of the travel is private (eg. home to work), or the employer either pays the expense or reimburses the employee, the employee is not entitled to a deduction. (FBT may apply: see 25.600.)

13.300 WORK-RELATED CLOTHING

Expenditure on work-related clothing (and the cleaning and maintenance thereof) is tax deductible provided the clothing is used specifically in connection with the earning of the person's assessable income. There are five categories which may apply, but certain conditions must be satisfied.

A claim is allowable for the cost of buying, renting or replacing clothing, uniforms and footwear if the clothing is:

*   protective in nature
*   occupation specific (and is not conventional clothing)
*   conventional but there are special circumstances and the taxpayer can show there is a direct connection with their employment activity
*   a compulsory uniform, or
*   a non-compulsory uniform or wardrobe that has been entered on the Textile, Clothing and Footwear (TCF) Corporatewear register of AusIndustry.

The cost of maintaining and cleaning clothing can also be claimed, but only if the cost of the clothing is allowed as a tax deduction.

Any expenditure incurred forms part of the employee's work expenses and claims are allowed only if the taxpayer satisfies the substantiation rules (see from 13.100).

TAXATION RULING

The circumstances in which work related clothing, uniform, footwear and associated maintenance costs are deductible are set out in TR 97/12 and TR 2003/16.

FBT CONSEQUENCES

If clothing is provided by an employer to an employee, or the employee is reimbursed for expenses he/she incurs, the employer is not subject to FBT if:

*   the clothes are approved and listed on the register kept by AusIndustry (see 13.350)
*   the employee would have been entitled to claim a deduction had he/she incurred the expenses (the 'otherwise deductible rule' reduces the FBT liability to nil. FBT will apply, however, if the employee would not have been entitled to a deduction), or
*   the clothing is an item of protective clothing required for the employment of the employee.

Taxation ruling TR 97/12 details the consequences for employers providing clothing to employees. See also 13.360.

Moreover, subsidies paid to employees towards the cost of the uniform are exempt income in the employee's hands but are expense payment fringe benefits to the employer (see 25.550). FBT may be reduced by the 'otherwise deductible' rule if the employee would have been entitled to a tax deduction had they incurred the expense (see 25.455).

13.310   PROTECTIVE CLOTHING

Claims for expenditure on protective clothing are allowed where the item satisfies these criteria (TR 2003/16):

*   the taxpayer is exposed to the risk of illness or injury as part of their income earning activities
*   the risk is a real risk to anyone working where the taxpayer is required to work (ie. the risk is not remote or negligible)
*   the protective item provides protection from that risk and would normally be expected to be used in the given circumstances, and
*   the item is used by the taxpayer in the course of undertaking his/her income earning activities.

However, claims would be allowed for protective clothing that reduces the risk of:

- death, injury or disease (including aggravation, acceleration or recurrence of any injury or disease whether or not work-related) to the wearer or other person (eg. clothing for food preparers to prevent food contamination), or

- loss, damage or destruction of other clothing, artificial limbs, surgical or similar aids worn by the wearer.

Claims for protective footwear (eg. steel-capped boots, rubber boots and special non-slip shoes) are allowed, but not for conventional footwear (eg. running, sport or casual shoes and jeans etc that lack protective qualities). Claims are generally not allowed for the cost of items to protect from the natural environment, eg. wet weather gear or umbrellas for an office worker and thermal underwear or heavy weight suit. However, see 13.147 and 13.330 regarding sunscreen, sunhats and sunglasses. However, protective items which are clearly identifiable as principally protective items, such as heavy duty occupational wet weather gear, are deductible (TR 2003/16). For example the Tax Office considers that an umbrella and raincoat used by a parking inspector in a wet and cold climate would be considered deductible protective clothing (TR 2003/16). This ruling also sets out criteria for deductibility of clothing normally associated with private or domestic use.

Other examples of deductible clothing include:

- fire-resistant and sun-protection clothing

- safety-coloured vests

- non-slip nurse's shoes

- rubber boots for concreters

- steel-capped boots, hard hats, gloves, overalls, and heavy-duty shirts and trousers, and

- overalls, smocks and aprons you wear to avoid damage or soiling to your ordinary clothes during your income-earning activities.

Claims are allowed if the nature of the work rather than the environment creates the necessary conditions (eg. using chemicals).

13.320   OCCUPATION-SPECIFIC

Claims are allowed if the clothing distinctly identifies that the employee belongs to a particular trade, profession, calling or occupation. This would include a female nurse's traditional uniform, religious cleric's ceremonial robes and chef's checked pants. It does not include conventional clothing even if commonly worn by employees in that industry (eg. white shirt and black trousers worn by waiters).

13.330   CONVENTIONAL CLOTHING

Generally claims are not allowed for conventional clothing as they are not considered to relate specifically to a person's income earning activities, but rather complying with social customs or fashion.

Expenditure on such items as business suits and any other conventional clothing (eg. non-specific uniforms worn by employees in restaurants) is not deductible as they are not 'peculiar' to the person's particular employer or occupation, and are freely available for use by the general public.

Non-deductible items include casual footwear, sports shoes and heavy duty clothing eg. drill trousers and shorts (*Case T103*, 86 ATC 1182) even if worn to prevent injury at work. That rule applies even if they are not worn outside work.

Claims for conventional clothing may be made, but only in exceptional cases (eg. if the taxpayer's occupation requires exceptional expense in relation to clothing or there is excessive wear and tear). The onus rests on the taxpayer to demonstrate that expenses are exceptional (ie. above and beyond the norm for that occupation or circumstance). It is rarely decided in the taxpayer's favour.

Outdoor workers may claim for a sun hat (see 13.147) and possibly protective clothing required in a harsh climate (see 13.310).

For the Tax Office view on conventional clothing see taxation ruling TR 94/22. For further information about the deductibility of expenditure on clothing, uniforms and footwear see taxation ruling TR 97/12.

13.340 COMPULSORY UNIFORMS

Claims for uniforms and corporate wardrobes are deductible if certain conditions are satisfied. These rules affect claims made by both employers (and their associates, see 25.002) and employees who purchase and maintain uniforms and corporate wardrobes (see TR 97/12).

The requirement or compulsion to wear the uniform or wardrobe must be a strictly enforced policy of the employer (also see TD 1999/62). It need not be in writing, but it must be consistently enforced and all employees of the same class must be compelled to wear the uniform in its entirety.

An 'employee' is defined as an employee for PAYG withholding purposes (see 5.301). Class of employee relates to the level or category of work carried out by such a discrete body of employees. There may be different corporate collections based on various employee categories within a firm and each may have a different collection (eg. service staff may have a compulsory uniform, but executives may not).

The uniform must distinctively identify the employer organisation (or a group consisting of the employer and any of the employer's associates). It must be a collection of inter-related items of clothing and accessories positively identifying that employer (or group). It must be unique, distinctive and peculiar to the organisation and must identify the wearer as being directly or indirectly associated with that employer. The uniform must be worn in its entirety and cannot be mixed with private clothing. If only part of the clothing worn by an employee qualifies as a compulsory uniform, only the cost of that part and its cleaning is deductible.

Deductions for corporate uniform costs would only be allowed for bank managers if all the bank's managers were required to wear that uniform. Deductions would be denied if some managers chose not to wear the uniform. This indicates the bank doesn't have an express policy, or that it isn't being enforced.

A bus driver is required to wear a brown shirt with the company logo at all times when at work. There is no other requirement for clothing or footwear. In this case, claims for acquiring and cleaning the shirt only would be deductible.

The cost of acquiring and maintaining a compulsory uniform is deductible if the clothing is:

- not conventional clothing, and clearly adapted to, or directly related to, the occupational character of the employee
- unique, distinctive and peculiar to the organisation with a timeless quality unaffected by short-term changes in fashion, and:
  - it identifies and enhances the firm's public image and allows easy identification of employees
  - the whole garment (not just individual pieces) would be worn only while on official duty
  - the range of styles, fabrics and colours used is limited (they should identify and be unique but can be adaptable to account for variances in climate and geographical region)
  - corporate identifiers are not compulsory, but if used they should be in a distinctive and contrasting colour to distinguish and contrast the uniforms from conventional clothing, and
  - accessories (eg. shoes, handbags, trenchcoats) are allowed only if they bear distinguishable features such as a corporate identifier or logo.

Further information on compulsory uniforms is in TR 97/12 and TR 2003/16.

SPECIAL CIRCUMSTANCES

The rules recognise there are cases when even a compulsory uniform cannot be worn. Specifically, deductions are not denied when:

- temporary or relief staff (not required to have a uniform) are engaged for a short time, or
- special circumstances exist (such as when a bank teller as a witness in a court case wears a suit instead of the corporate uniform).

13.350   NON-COMPULSORY UNIFORMS

Claims can still be allowed if the employer has registered the design of the uniform in the register of Approved Occupational Clothing (kept by AusIndustry) before the employee purchases the uniform. Applications for registration must be made on the approved form available from AusIndustry at www.ausindustry.gov.au 'AusIndustry Products'. The application form is in Textile, Clothing and Footwear Corporate Wear Register. Alternatively, phone 13 28 46 for an application form. Incomplete forms will be returned, delaying registration until all information is provided. Applications must be approved or rejected within 90 days of receipt and applicants informed in writing. These decisions are reviewable by the AAT.

SINGLE ITEMS

The *Approved Occupational Clothing Guidelines* (November 2006) preclude the registration of single items of clothing, unless these are full body garments, eg. a dress. A single item such as a shirt would not be eligible. Expenditure on such single items of clothing is not tax deductible.

NATURE OF EMPLOYER'S BUSINESS

The nature of the employer's business or activities will be considered when determining the suitability of the designs that make up the approved occupational clothing. For example, items of clothing that may be suitable for a business operating in an office environment may not be suitable for activities carried on at a plant nursery or a boat building factory. 'Design' of a uniform includes features such as colouring, construction, durability, ornamentation, pattern and shape.

If an organisation operates over a wide climatic area it may be necessary for the design of the occupational clothing to take into account the climate for which it is intended. An employer who has operations in both southern Tasmania and far north Queensland may wish to submit four designs (one summer and one winter design for each region). A design may be used to distinguish between various staffing groups within an organisation (eg. office staff could be different from field staff). In that case the factors making up the Guidelines should be considered in the context of the collection which applies to each staffing group and be separately registered.

CORPORATE, PRODUCT OR SERVICE IDENTIFIERS

Corporate product or service identifiers are features which readily identify a particular organisation, product or service and includes well known, specific or registered trade marks logos, initials, insignia, emblems, arms and patterns. These features can be 'stand alone' (eg. insignia on a blazer) or a common feature such as a pattern in fabric which incorporates the employer's logo). An identifier does not include outlines or boxes which are not part of the logo.

Corporate, product, or service identifiers are a compulsory requirement for any design which is to be registered. There are two types of identifiers:

- stand alone – a corporate, product or service identifier which is a discreet symbol, logo, initial, form of words etc. and which is distinct from the item of clothing to which it is affixed, and
- pattern – a corporate, product or service identifier which is used in the form of a distinctive pattern over the entire item of clothing and which forms an integral part of that clothing.

An identifier must appear at least once on the external surface of each item of occupational clothing, including accessories. The clothing must be designed to ensure that when two or more items are worn together at least one 'stand alone' identifier or an approved identifier pattern are plainly visible to the casual observer. After addition of the identifiers the clothing must not be available for rental or purchase by the general public.

STAND ALONE IDENTIFIERS

The identifier must be in a contrasting colour or shade to that used for the item to which it is attached. The identifier, employer, product or service depicted must be big enough to be plainly visible to a casual observer from two metres. The minimum size for stand alone identifiers are:

- for clothing items the stand alone identifier should cover 80% of a four square centimetre area (eg. 2 cm x 2 cm, or 1 cm x 4 cm), and
- for accessories, the stand alone identifier should cover a one square centimetre area.

A stand alone identifier must be permanently affixed. This could be sewn down on all sides, ironed on, embroidered into, or printed on to an item of clothing. Detachable badges, pins, buttons and flag tags sewn into seams are not acceptable and will bar clothing from being registered.

PATTERN IDENTIFIERS

Pattern identifiers can be used as an alternative to a stand alone identifier provided that:

- identifiers used in the pattern are of a contrasting colour to the main background colour, and are of a minimum size of 1 cm x 1 cm and there are a minimum of three such identifiers in an area of material measuring 15 cm x 15 cm, and
- the employer, product or service depicted is easily identifiable from a distance of two metres.

It is not sufficient that a pattern is used exclusively by an employer if the employer, product or service cannot be distinguished by that pattern. The pattern must be used by the employer in a manner similar to advertising so that the public readily recognises it (eg. the red bullseye used by a retailer).

COLOUR USED IN UNIFORM DESIGN

The total number of colours or shades used in the design (including highlight colours but not colours used in identifiers) is limited to eight, including black and white. There must be a common theme of colours, patterns and prints applying between male and female designs and the designs for each class of employee. In general that criterion applies in respect of an employer, with the only exceptions being if it is a requirement for safety reasons for employees in different classes to be easily identifiable, or the employer maintains separate public identities for parts of the organisation. The employer may elect for this criterion to apply separately to each part of the organisation. The number of colour/pattern/print combinations available for use is limited by the number of employees in the class that the clothing has been designed for.

The following sets out how many combinations are allowed for an employer with a particular number of employees in the class that the clothing has been designed for.

Non-compulsory uniforms: Allowable number of colour, pattern and print combinations				
Total number of male and female employees in the class:	1 to 100	101 to 3000	3001 to 10,000	Over 10,000
MALES				
Full body garments: Overalls	2	3	4	6
Outer, upper body garments: Jackets, knitwear, etc.	2	3	4	5
Inner, upper body garments: Shirts, T-shirts, etc.	3	5	7	8
Lower body garments: Pants, trousers, shorts, etc.	2	3	4	5
FEMALES				
Full body garments: Dresses, overall etc.	2	3	4	6
Outer, upper body garments: Jackets, knitwear, etc.	2	3	4	5
Inner, upper body garments: Shirts, T-shirts, blouses etc.	3	5	6	8
Lower body garments: Pants, skirts, shorts etc.	2	4	6	7

RANGE OF STYLES ALLOWED

There is no limit to the range of styles that can be used for any item of clothing, provided each item has an approved identifier, but there is a limit on the number of colour, pattern and print combinations allowed for each class of employee (see table above).

DURABILITY OF STYLE

The overall look or concept of a design must be able to last between three to five years and cannot be changed merely to follow the latest fashion. This requirement will not prevent gradual changes to any design that does not disturb the overall look of the design, or prevent totally changing the design(s) if it wishes to change its 'corporate' identity or consumer/public perceptions about the employing organisation or its employees.

CHANGES TO THE DESIGN

Each change or variation of a design must be approved by AusIndustry. Once a design is changed, the employer is expected to request removal of the old design within 12 months. Tax claims for expenses incurred by employees in acquiring, replacing or maintaining superseded designs are denied from the date the registration is removed from the register.

ACCESSORIES

Accessories may be approved as part of the design if they:

- are made of the same distinctively patterned fabrics as other items in the design, or
- have a stand-alone identifier.

Permissible accessories include belts, ties, handkerchiefs, long walk socks, handbags, trench coats, scarves and hats but never shoes, short socks, stockings or underwear.

13.360   FBT LIABILITY

Some employers provide work-related uniforms to employees even though it is not compulsory to wear them. If the designs have not been registered with the AusIndustry, the initial cost, maintenance and cost of replacements is claimable by those employers and subject to FBT on the value of benefits provided (see from 25.000).

13.400 SUPERANNUATION DEDUCTIONS

The key characteristics of the superannuation laws as they relate to contributions are:

- all employers are able to claim a full deduction for all contributions made on behalf of eligible employees ('concessional contributions'), although contributions in excess of the designated annual cap will result in additional tax being incurred by way of excess contributions tax
- the substantially self-employed will be able to claim a full deduction for their eligible contributions (subject to compliance with the '10% rule' and providing the necessary notification to the trustee), and
- the ability to make deductible contributions has been extended in that no age limit applies in respect of superannuation guarantee contributions whilst for mandated contributions the age limit is now 75.

The taxation rules relating to the deductibility of employer and personal superannuation contributions are summarised in Chapter 19. Also covered in that chapter are eligible spouse contributions and the government co-contribution.

For further details on concessional contributions see 19.020.

For further details on spouse contributions see 19.074, and for government co-contributions see 19.076.

NOTE: Contributions in excess of the relevant cap will be subject to excess contributions tax (see 19.050).

13.500 ENTERTAINMENT EXPENSES

Except in limited circumstances, deductions are not allowable for entertainment expenses (Division 32).

'Entertainment' is defined in s32-10 as:
- (a) entertainment by way of food, drink or recreation, or
- (b) accommodation or travel to do with providing entertainment by way of food, drink or recreation.

'Recreation' includes amusement, sport or similar leisure time pursuits (eg. box at the tennis or races).

Entertainment may be deemed to have been provided even if business discussions or transactions occur. Further, promotional or advertising activities may constitute entertainment depending on the nature of the activity.

Expenses incurred to either obtain or maintain membership of a recreational club (ie. a company which mainly provides facilities for members for drinking, dining, recreation or entertainment) for the use or benefit of its members is not deductible (s26-45). Examples include league clubs, tennis clubs, etc. A deduction is allowed if providing a fringe benefit.

Membership of an airport lounge is considered by the Tax Office not to be an entertainment expense and is deductible if the expense is incurred on work-related activities (TR 1999/10). Payment by an employer is deductible and is an exempt benefit for FBT purposes.

Depreciation, maintenance or repair of equipment or plant which is used to provide non-deductible entertainment is not deductible.

The cost of providing a complete holiday package as part of a base incentive payment is also considered to be non-deductible (the taxable value of the base incentive would be reduced by a corresponding amount) (see IT 2631).

Entertainment expenses are deductible if provided to employees (or their associates) and those expenses are taxed as fringe benefits (see 25.900).

 For these rules to apply the food and drink must be provided as part of entertainment. Normal sustenance is not entertainment (see 25.940 for a list of entertainment and non-entertainment).

Food and drink provided as part of a seminar of at least four hours, excluding meal breaks, or at some staff training sessions, are claimable.

ENTERTAINMENT EXPENSE AS DEDUCTIONS

Claims for expenses which would fall within the definition of entertainment are allowed in the following limited categories. Each of these is discussed more fully under their respective topic headings:

- taxpayers in the business of providing entertainment, (eg. hotels, resorts, motels)
- overtime meals paid under an Industrial Award
- meals while travelling on business (applies for both employees and persons in business, but a deduction does not apply for other persons they entertain while travelling)
- meals provided in an in-house dining facility on a 'working day' (for employees and non-employees)
- conferences, meetings, seminars where the entertainment component is merely ancillary
- training sessions (if they aren't conducted on the employer's premises)
- advertising and product launches (but only if open to the public or under a contract)
- entertainment allowances an employer pays (they are assessable to the employee)
- entertainment provided for the sick, disabled, poor or otherwise disadvantaged
- recreational facilities within employer's premises
- giving a firm's own products to the public

and these, provided FBT applies to the benefits:

- meal entertainment fringe benefits (see full list at 25.940), and
- external entertainment provided for employees, or their associates (eg. club and association fees, payment or reimbursement of leisure facility subscription).

13.510   'BUSINESS OF ENTERTAINMENT'

Tax deductions are allowed for entertainment expenses if the expenses are incurred in the ordinary course of carrying on that business and:

- the business is directly involved in the entertainment industry (eg. restaurants, amusement parks and theatres), or
- the business is indirectly involved because their operations include the provision of entertainment for an inclusive charge (eg. motels providing in-house videos; airlines providing in-flight meals).

13.515   OVERTIME MEALS

Claims are allowed for the costs of providing an employee with an overtime meal allowance. Food and drink provided to employees:

- while working overtime, and
- provided and consumed on the employer's business premises

is both deductible to the employer and FBT exempt.

The Tax Office does not consider a meal to be entertainment merely because alcohol is served (TR 97/17).

 If you can show that the provision of alcohol formed only an incidental part of a meal and was not part of a social occasion or an entertainment event, it is probable that the claim would not be denied. For example, if a glass of wine was provided with a light meal (finger food) during a training session, the cost should still be deductible.

Overtime meal allowances not paid by an employer under an Industrial Instrument must be included in the employee's assessable income.

If the allowance is not paid under an Industrial Award, the employee must substantiate all claims, and the employer must deduct PAYG withholding. When an allowance exceeds the limit set by the Tax Office (see 13.140). PAYG must be deducted from the amount exceeding the limit.

If the allowance is paid under an Industrial Instrument, the employee does not need to substantiate the claim, provided the deduction for the meal is below the overtime meal allowance limit approved by the Tax Office (see 13.140). If the claim is a higher amount than the allowance it must be included in the employee's assessable income and the full claim must be substantiated.

An Industrial Instrument is a law of the Commonwealth or an award, order, determination or industrial agreement made under Australian law.

13.520   TRAVELLING ON BUSINESS

Claims for sustenance (ie. food and drink) are allowed for employees, self-employed persons and partners in a partnership for meals and accommodation expenses, provided they are incurred while travelling in the course of business (eg. a salesperson's meals taken in a restaurant while travelling overnight on business).

If an employee dines with a client, the employee's cost is deductible to the employer but may be liable for FBT (see full list at 25.940). The cost of the client's meal is not deductible.

Expenses incurred by employees receiving travelling allowances do not need to be substantiated if the employee is claiming no more than the amount considered by the Tax Office to be reasonable (see details from 13.180 and 13.200). Claims made by those not receiving an allowance must be fully substantiated (see 13.160 and 13.190).

Meal expenses are not deductible unless the taxpayer sleeps away from home (TR 95/18).

Entertainment costs incurred by a self-employed person, director or trustee are not deductible if incurred while entertaining another person; eg, dining with prospective clients, or taking them to an event such as a show or the football. Travelling expenses for the purpose of providing the entertainment are also not deductible. However, one exception is when the expense is incurred while travelling away overnight from home (not for the purpose of entertaining) and a meal is supplied to a client. While the meal for the client is not deductible, the meal for the self-employed person (etc) is deductible as a travelling expense.

 A owns an accounting practice and travels interstate (overnight) to consult with clients planning a major restructure of their business. A invites the principals of that business to a restaurant for an evening meal and afterwards he takes them to the ballet. A pays all costs of the entertainment. While A could claim a deduction for the cost of his own meal, all other expenses would not be deductible.

13.525   MEALS PROVIDED BY EMPLOYER

The rules differ depending on whether or not the person consuming the meal is an employee.

EMPLOYEES

Food and drink provided to employees (and company directors) of an employer or related company are tax-deductible (and are exempt from FBT) if provided in an in-house dining and recreational facility on working days on the employer's (or on a related company's) business premises as long as the premises are:

- not open to the public at any time, and
- operate wholly and principally to give food and drink to employees on working days.

Tax deductions apply to meals provided in that situation to all employees (or company directors) of that taxpayer (or of a related company).

For a full list of expenses classed as meal entertainment, see 25.940.

NON-EMPLOYEES

Section 32-70 ITAA97 provides that meals provided in an in-house dining facility to clients, contractors and suppliers of the firm are deductible, but if the firm claims a deduction, it must add $30 to its assessable income for each meal provided to a non-employee. Alternatively, the taxpayer can choose to treat those expenses as non-tax deductible. That choice can be separately made for each dining facility and for each income year.

13.530   CONFERENCES AND SEMINARS

The cost of food and drink provided as part of an eligible seminar is tax-deductible (TD 93/195) if that seminar runs for a minimum continuous period of four hours (excluding meal breaks). The total cost for employees attending conferences and seminars is tax-deductible, but the non-training component (eg. golf day or other entertainment) may be subject to FBT. That applies to conferences and meetings (including those involving the presentation of awards), speeches, question and answer sessions and training and education courses, but not those whose sole or dominant purpose is to:

- give or receive information about the business
- discuss matters relating to the business
- promote or advertise the business or its goods, or
- provide entertainment.

TRAINING SEMINARS NOT CONDUCTED ON EMPLOYER'S PREMISES

The cost of food and drink provided as part of a seminar organised by (or on behalf of) the employer is also deductible if it is to:

- provide training relevant to the employer's business, and/or
- discuss policy issues relevant to the internal management of the employer's business, and
- runs for at least four hours (excluding meal breaks).

Costs incurred for entertainment at business discussions (includes meetings involving agents, employees, partners, shareholders, financiers and advisers) undertaken in the normal course of business to discuss or exchange information (eg. AGM, sales strategy meeting or briefing of managers) must be apportioned between the employee (or their associates) and the client costs. The employee's (and associate's) costs are an allowable deduction, but are liable for FBT, unless a minor benefit (see 25.200). The cost of the client's meal remains non-deductible (see from 25.900).

13.540   ADVERTISING AND PRODUCT LAUNCHES

Entertainment costs are tax-deductible if provided in the following circumstances.

PROMOTIONAL GIVE-AWAYS

The expenditure must be incurred as part of a public promotion of the taxpayer's business or the goods or services provided by them. The entertainment must be provided under the terms and conditions of a contract for the supply of goods or services with that firm. For example, a holiday given to the purchaser of a new car would be deductible. See 'Public access makes claims allowable' below.

PUBLIC EXHIBITION OF GOODS/SERVICES

Costs incurred by a firm to promote or exhibit to the public its own goods or services is tax-deductible (eg. free drinks provided at a winery for wine tasting, or a cinema giving free passes). However in other cases, unless made freely available to the public, there is no deduction allowed for drinks, food and other entertainment provided as part of a firm's promotion (eg. meals provided to guests at a film premier or drinks provided by a design house at the opening of its new season's fashions).

Public access makes claims allowable. Claims can be made for entertainment to promote the goods and services (whether of the taxpayer or of others) provided the level of entertainment for the public is the same as that provided to customers, suppliers, clients, employees (or associates, journalists, or any other class of 'special' person). That is, a deduction will not apply if persons have a greater opportunity to get the benefits of the entertainment than ordinary members of the public.

13.550   IN-HOUSE RECREATION FACILITIES

The cost of providing recreational facilities (ie. for amusement, sport or similar leisure time activities) on the employer's premises for use by employees may be tax deductible. That includes tennis courts, swimming pools, gymnasium, and games rooms. Facilities must be wholly and principally for use by the employees on working days and be located on the employer's premises.

13.560   ENTERTAINMENT ALLOWANCES

The payment of entertainment allowances to employees is deductible to the employer, but is assessable income of the employee. The expenditure of the allowance for the purpose of entertainment would not give rise to a tax deduction for the employee.

Employees are assessed on allowances received but the availability of a deduction against the allowance will depend upon individual circumstances; examples of deductible expenditure include:

- meals while working overtime when in receipt of an overtime meal allowance (see 13.515)
- certain meals while travelling on business provided they are away from home overnight. Special rules apply if in receipt of a travelling allowance (see 13.520), or
- when attending eligible seminars (see 13.530).

Any entertainment expenses paid directly (or reimbursed) by the employer are tax-deductible to the employer unless the employer is a tax-exempt body (see 25.005 and 25.200). FBT is payable on those expenses.

HOSTESS ALLOWANCES

No deduction is allowed to the employer for entertainment allowances paid to an eligible relative of the employee. This includes the employee's spouse (or de facto) as well as any other relative of the taxpayer. However, such allowances would typically be assessable in the hands of the recipient.

13.570 MORNING AND AFTERNOON TEA

Providing morning and afternoon teas and light lunches to employees (or their 'associates') and visitors on the taxpayer's premises or worksite is tax-deductible to the employer. In TR 97/17 (see also TR 97/17A) the Tax Office ruled that this is not 'entertainment'. If the firm has no employees (eg. a partnership) claims for light refreshments are not allowed unless also provided to visitors to that firm.

13.580 ENTERTAINMENT FOR THE DISADVANTAGED

A tax deduction is allowed for entertainment provided gratuitously to members of the public who are sick, poor, disabled or otherwise disadvantaged.

13.600 HOME OFFICE EXPENSES

Claims for expenditure relating to a home office can be made if a taxpayer is able to demonstrate that part of the home is used for income producing purposes and has the character of a place of business, or alternatively is used in connection with income earning activities, but is not a place of business (TR 93/30).

The general rule is that expenses associated with a person's home are of a private nature, and therefore no tax deduction is allowed.

An individual taxpayer may claim a deduction for home office expenses where additional running costs are incurred because of income producing activities, based on:

- actual expenses, or
- diary records for a representative four week period that establish a pattern of use for the entire year. A new diary must be kept for each financial year and each of these diaries must be kept for five years after lodgement of the return for that year or the due date for lodgement, whichever is later. Where there is no regular pattern of use to establish a representative pattern, records must be kept of the duration and purpose of each use of a home office during the year (PS LA 2001/6).

13.610 WHAT CLAIMS ARE ALLOWED?

Broadly, the expenses fall into the following categories:

- 'running expenses' (eg. heating, lighting) relating to income earning activities (typically used by employees)
- telephone expenses
- depreciation on equipment (see 15.030 and 15.035), and
- occupancy expenses (eg. rent, interest, house insurance and rates) where the home is a place of business.

RUNNING EXPENSES – NOT IN BUSINESS

A deduction may be claimed for office running expenses comprising electricity, gas and depreciation on office furniture (eg. desks, tables, chairs, cabinets and shelves and professional library (see TR 93/30)) in the amount of:

- the actual expenses incurred, or
- 34 cents per hour.

No deduction is available where:

- no additional cost is incurred (eg. if the taxpayer works in a room where others are watching television), or
- the income producing use of the home office is incidental, rather than substantial (eg. a deduction would not be allowed for a fax machine permanently left on to receive business documents).

Claiming 'running expenses' does not affect the 'main residence exemption' (see from 12.300). Professional libraries may be depreciated.

TELEPHONE AND INTERNET EXPENSES

If the work or business telephone calls can be identified from an itemised telephone account (see also 13.155), then the deductions can be claimed for the work or business related portion of the telephone account. If an itemised telephone account is not available, a representative four week period will be accepted as establishing a pattern of use for the entire year to make a reasonable estimate of the portion of call expenses for work or business. Telephone rental expenses may be partly deductible for taxpayers who are either 'on call' or required to contact their employer or clients on a regular basis. The deductible portion can be calculated (TR 98/14):

Business calls (incoming and outgoing) divided by total calls (incoming and outgoing)

OCCUPANCY AND RUNNING EXPENSES – PLACE OF BUSINESS

Claims for both running and occupancy expenses are allowed only if an area of the home is set aside exclusively for business activities. The actual deduction is dependent on the taxpayer's circumstances. In most cases, the claim can be made as an apportionment of total expenses incurred on a floor area basis, and time basis (if the area was used as a place of business for only part of the income year). Taxpayers may use any other method to calculate occupancy expense claims provided that method can be justified.

 Being able to claim these occupancy expenses may affect a person's 'main residence exemption' for capital gains tax purposes (see from 12.300).

DEPRECIATION OF EQUIPMENT

Depreciation of home office equipment (including office furniture, carpets, computer, printer, photocopier, scanners, modem etc.) used only partly for work or business purposes, is apportioned. The claim can be based on a diary record of the income-related and non-income related use covering a representative four week period (see 13.155).

The diary needs to show:

* the nature of each use of the equipment
* whether that use was for an income-producing or non-income-producing purpose, and
* the period of time for which it was used.

 Kate is an employee accountant working for a city-based firm. She has arranged to do some of her work at night so she can spend more time with her family. Kate spends an average of ten hours a week working in her home office.

Option 1: Actual expenses

Kate has the following home office running expenses (including energy expenses which have been calculated using electricity authority hourly costs per appliance). The apportionment has been based on four weeks' diary entries as follows:

Item	Calculation	Deduction
Depreciation (desk)	Value $450 over 10 years	$45.00
Electricity for: • light • computer • heating/cooling	0.7c per hour x 10 hours per week x 48 weeks 1c per hour x 10 hours per week x 48 weeks 9c per hour x 10 hours per week x 48 weeks	$3.36 $4.80 $43.20
Total deduction		$96.36

Option 2: Estimated running expenses

Item	Calculation	Deduction
Running expenses	34c per hour 10 hours per week x 48 weeks	$163.20

Option 2 provides a simpler calculation with a similar deductible amount if future use and electricity costs remain the same.

ALIENATION RULES

The alienation of personal services income rules (see 16.000) deny a deduction for rent, mortgage interest, rates and land tax for the taxpayer's (or his or her associate's) residence that relate to gaining or producing the taxpayer's personal services income (s85-15).

A deduction can be claimed to the extent that the expense relates to income from the taxpayer conducting a personal services business (s85-30).

13.615 WHEN IS HOME A 'PLACE OF BUSINESS'?

Whether the home is a place of business, is a question of fact (TR 93/30). The broad test to be applied is whether a particular part of the dwelling:

- is clearly identifiable as a place of business
- is not readily suitable or convertible for private use as part of the home
- is used exclusively for carrying on a business, or
- is used regularly for client or customer visits.

The Courts and Tribunals have accepted part of a person's residence as being a place of business if there is no alternative place for carrying out that person's income-producing activities, but only if:

- the taxpayer needs a place of business from which to carry out their income producing activities
- there is no alternative to the taxpayer working from home, and
- that area of the home is used exclusively for business purposes.

13.700 SELF-EDUCATION EXPENSES

Self-education includes courses undertaken at an educational institution (whether leading to a formal qualification or not), attendance at work-related seminars or conferences, self-paced learning and study tours (overseas or within Australia). However certain self-education expenses under s8-1 may be subject to the limitation rule under s82A. TR 98/9 details the Tax Office's views on the deductibility of the self-education expenses.

Self-education expenses are tax deductible provided that a direct nexus can be demonstrated between the education being undertaken and how that person derives their assessable income. In general terms, it is necessary to satisfy any of the following tests to be entitled to a tax deduction:

- the expense has a relevant connection to the taxpayer's current income earning activities (ie. the course must be relevant or incidental to how the taxpayer derives his/her assessable income)
- the self-education program being undertaken enables the taxpayer to maintain or improve the skills or knowledge necessary to carry out his/her income earning activities
- the self-education leads to, or is likely to lead to, an increase in the taxpayer's income from his/her current income earning activities in the future.

Deductions for self-education expenses are not allowed if the course of study is designed to:

- get employment in a new field of endeavour (eg. a teacher studying law to become a lawyer)
- get employment or obtain a qualification to enable the taxpayer to enter a restricted field of endeavour (eg. obtaining a degree to be able to practice as a surveyor), or
- open up new income earning opportunities in the future (whether in business or in the taxpayer's current employment) because they are incurred at a point too soon to be regarded as being incurred in gaining or producing the assessable income of the individual.

It is possible for courses undertaken to have both deductible and non-deductible elements (eg. a plumber who runs his own business who undertakes a business management course where completion of the course will enable the plumber to also practice as a qualified business administrator). In that situation, the deductibility of the expenses will be determined by the intention of the taxpayer when the course was undertaken.

If the taxpayer can show that the course is incidental and relevant to his existing income earning activities, the cost is deductible. Creation of other opportunities is irrelevant. Alternatively, if the course was undertaken with the specific intention of changing the taxpayer's income earning activity, expenses would not be allowed.

13.705   EXPENSES WHICH ARE TAX-DEDUCTIBLE

Subject to the general tests of s8-1 ITAA97, these expenses are allowable:

- course or tuition fees (including student union fees)
- textbooks, professional or trade journals, technical instruments and clerical expenses such as word-processing or photocopying
- depreciation on professional libraries, desks, computers and filing cabinets, etc.
- fares, accommodation and meals (if away from home overnight) incurred on study tours, work-related seminars or conferences away from the taxpayer's home
- stationery or postage
- home office running costs
- internet usage (excluding connection fees)
- interest on money borrowed to pay the above expenses or purchase plant or equipment on which depreciation is allowable, and
- travel costs (including motor vehicle and fares etc. – see below).

13.710   EXPENSES WHICH ARE NOT TAX-DEDUCTIBLE

- Contributions made under the *Higher Education Support Act 2003* and *Student Assistance Act 1973*, such as HELP (previously HECS) payment (unless paid or reimbursed by the employer: HELP payments are generally not tax deductible, however if they are paid or reimbursed by an employer they are tax deductible to the employer but FBT is payable – see from 25.000)
- Education expenses against income received under various Commonwealth educational assistance schemes, such as the Youth Allowance (see below)
- Home office occupancy expenses
- Meals purchased while on normal travel between home and an educational institution
- Travel expenses between home and an educational institution at which the taxpayer works

13.715   EDUCATION EXPENSES AGAINST YOUTH ALLOWANCE PAYMENTS

In *FC of T v Anstis* [2010] HCA 40, the High Court considered the deductibility of costs incurred by a student in connection with university study to achieve a teaching degree. The deductions were allowed against income received by the student as a recipient of the Federal Government's Youth Allowance payments. The High Court was of the view that Youth Allowance payments were ordinary income in the hands of recipients.

In response to the decision, the law was amended to prevent self-education deductions from being claimed against all government assistance payments from 1 July 2011 by inserting s26-19 ITAA97. This section disallows a deduction for education expenses where the relevant assessable income derived includes Youth Allowance, Austudy and ANSTUDY payments from the 2011-12 income year onward.

13.715   TRAVEL EXPENSES

The cost of travel between the taxpayer's home and place of work is not allowable.

Claims are generally allowed for travel between:

- the taxpayer's home and an educational institution (including a library for research), and
- the taxpayer's place of employment and an educational institution (ie. school).

Note that travel expenses (and/or fares) between the taxpayer's home and an educational institution are not allowable if the taxpayer carries out income-earning activities at the institution; that becomes travel between work and home.

Travel expenses: Deductible as self-education expense?

Home	Yes →	Place of education	Yes →	Home
Home	Yes →	Place of education	No →	Work
Work	Yes →	Place of education	No →	Home
Work	Yes →	Place of education	Yes →	Work
Home	← No →	Work	← Yes →	Place of education

13.720 WORK-RELATED EDUCATION PROGRAMS

As a general rule, costs of certain education programs (such as seminars, professional development courses, and tertiary studies while in employment) are deductible provided the requisite nexus to the earning of assessable income can be established. However, the costs of certain tertiary studies undertaken before the commencement of any employment are generally not deductible.

$250 LIMITATION UNDER S82A ITAA36

According to s82A ITAA36, only the excess over the limit of $250 can be deductible if the amount of self-education expenses allowable under s8-1 is necessarily incurred by the taxpayer for or in connection with a course of education provided by a school, college, university or other place of education. Consequently, it is necessary to classify whether claims are deductible and if they are also self-education expenses (as defined in s82A ITAA36). Note that there is no requirement to substantiate that $250 (see TD 93/97). The table below illustrates the Tax Office views on a number of different expenses.

There is no requirement to apply the first $250 rule for any courses such as work-related seminars, conferences, in-house training programs, continuing professional education programs or any other course that is not undertaken at a place of education.

This rule also does not apply to professional programs undertaken by professional organisations.

 Where a course of education assists with your current employment but also provides an entry point into another profession or income earning activity, always record your intention. That will minimise any future dispute with the Tax Office.

Summary of education expenses

Type of expenditure	Included for s82A?	Allowed under s8-1 ?
Course or tuition fees (including union fees, but excluding HELP fees)	YES	YES
Books, journals and other stationery	YES	YES if applicable to course of study in year of purchase
Meals (to and from school or at school)	NO	NO
Accommodation and meals (if taxpayer required to live away from home overnight)	YES	YES
Depreciation of equipment	NO	NO. Allowed under Division 40 ITAA97
Transport expenses (includes car expenses and public transport)	YES	YES/NO see above
Interest on borrowed funds (ie. for self-education expenses)	YES	YES
Childcare costs	YES	NO
Repairs of equipment	NO	NO. Allowed under s25-10 ITAA97
Motor vehicle expenses (using cents per km method)	YES	NO. Allowed under substantiation rules

 Warren studied part-time at a university and the course was directly related to his current income earning activity. The relevant self-education expenses are summarised in the table below:

Self-education costs	Amount	Included for s82A ITAA36?	Allowed under s8-1?
Stationery	$100	YES	YES
Textbooks	$420	YES	YES
Course fees	$2,000	YES	YES
Bus fares	$150	YES	YES
Repair to home printer	$70	NO	NO (allowed under s25-10)
Childcare costs	$1,520	YES	NO

As a result, the total allowable deduction is $2,740 (ie. $100+$420+$2,000+$150 +$70).

Warren does not have to reduce his allowable deduction by $250 as the total of his repair costs ($70) and child care costs ($1,520) is more than $250. Angus can claim $2,740 – his Category A and C amounts.

However, if Warren had no child care costs then his claim would be worked out as follows:

Step 1: *$250 less repair cost ($70) = $180*

Step 2: *$2,670 (total allowable deduction less repair cost) less $180 (step 1 amount) = $2,490*

Step 3: *$2,490 (step 2 amount) plus $70 (repair costs) = $2,560*

Warren could claim $2,560 as his self-eduction expenses deduction.

13.800 DONATIONS AND GIFTS

Taxpayers are entitled to claim deductions for gifts and donations made during the income year to Deductible Gift Recipients (DGRs), but there are special rules that apply. Donations of property can also be made for philanthropic purposes.

Deductions for gifts or donations are not allowed unless the recipient:

- is endorsed by the Tax Office as a DGR (see 13.890), or
- is specifically named in ITAA97 or the regulations as an eligible recipient.

Approved recipients must have an ABN (see 5.100) and maintain a gift fund.

Receipts issued for donations made to the DGR (see 13.890) must state:

- the name of the fund, authority or institution receiving the gift
- the ABN of the DGR, and
- that the receipt is for a gift.

For the Tax Office view on what constitutes a gift see TR 2005/13.

13.810   BUSINESS

As a general rule, businesses are entitled to claim for gifts or donations made during the course of carrying on business. For a claim to be allowed however, the gift must be directly related to the activities of the business and be undertaken with the intention of promoting their business activities. That would include gifts and donations of cash, property and even of trading stock. Those deductions are allowed under s8-1. As an alternative, the claim can be spread over five years (see 13.888 for general rules, and 13.880 for property donations over $5,000). This would include expenses incurred in advertising, image promotion etc. Donees of these types of gifts and donations do not need to be approved donees under Division 30.

Similarly, tax-free distributions of income can be made to tax-exempt beneficiaries by trustees of discretionary and certain other trusts. Trust loss rules may have an impact; see 13.950 for further information.

Other deductions are allowed under Division 30, provided special rules are followed (see 13.830).

CLAIMS UNDER DIVISION 30

For claims made to approved donees under Division 30, losses resulting from those donations cannot be carried forward or claimed in later income years. The excess of those losses are effectively lost.

Where a donation of property is made, the business can only claim a deduction if the property was purchased within the preceding 12 months. This restriction does not apply for gifts made under the Cultural Bequests Program (see 13.870). The deduction allowed is limited to the lesser of the market value of the gift (on the day the gift is made), and its cost.

Where the gift is made from the trading stock of the business, the deduction is limited to the market value of the item on the day the gift was made (unless an election is made as a primary producer relating to forced disposal of livestock).

Joint owners of donated property can claim a tax deduction based on their share of the value of the property.

Special rules apply for donations of works of art, cultural bequests and assets that were originally acquired with the intention of reselling them to make a profit. These rules will be dealt with later.

13.820   INDIVIDUALS

Unless a gift is made in the course of carrying on a business (see 13.810), claims for gifts and donations of $2 or more are only deductible if they are made to approved donees under Division 30.

A comprehensive list of approved donees is published by the Tax Office and can be accessed:

- at www.business.gov.au; or for the Register of Cultural Organisations: www.arts.gov. au, or
- by phoning the Tax Office on 13 24 78.

Deductions are only allowed where the gift is made voluntarily. They are not allowed where there is a contractual obligation or the person receives some material reward for making the donation. For example, no deduction would be allowed if a donation is made to a charity and the donor receives a free ticket as a result of the donation, to attend a gala function being held for that charity.

There is no limit on the amount for claims made to approved donees under Division 30, however losses resulting from those donations cannot be carried forward or claimed in later income years. The excess of those losses are effectively lost.

Since 1 July 2003 taxpayers have been able to spread their claim over five years (see 13.880 for property donations over $5,000, and 13.888 for general rules).

Testamentary gifts (ie. made through a deceased estate) are deductible provided they are made under the Cultural Bequest Program. There may be CGT implications for any other gifts of property that do not qualify as donations of works of art or under this program (see 13.870). Unless made under this program, testamentary gifts are not tax deductible. Donations of property to approved donees for philanthropic purposes are also deductible (see 13.830).

The Tax Office has also approved administrative arrangements by which employees donate to DGRs via payroll deductions. For details of these requirements, see Tax Office Practice Statement PS LA 2002/15.

13.822   FUNDRAISING EVENTS

From 1 January 2007 a deduction for a donation of cash or property is allowable if:

- the value of the contribution is more than $150, and
- the minor benefit received by the contributor in return does not exceed the lesser of 20% of the value of the contribution and $150.

 Annabelle pays $500 for a ticket, which has a market value of $75, to attend a ballet hosted by a DGR. As the market value of the ticket is less than $150 and less than 20% of her contribution, Annabelle can deduct $425 (ie. $500 less $75).

Victor successfully bids $2,000 for a bottle of wine at a fund raising auction conducted by a DGR. The wine has a market value of no more than $125. Because the market value of the wine is under $150 and is less than 20% of the 'contribution', Victor can deduct $1,875 (ie. $2,000 less $125).

SHARES DONATED FOR FUNDRAISING EVENTS

A deduction is allowable for the contribution of shares by an individual in return for a right which permits the donor or some other individual to attend or participate in a particular fundraising event. The event must be in Australia.

The shares must have been acquired at least 12 months before the donation is made, be in a listed public company and have a market value on the day of donation of more than $150 but no more than $5,000.

The GST-inclusive market value of the particular fundraising event cannot exceed 20% of the value of the shares and $150, whichever is the less. The market value of the donation is reduced by the GST inclusive market value of the right to attend the event.

See also 13.830 for donation of listed shares.

13.828   LOSS CARRIED FORWARD

Claims for gifts and donations are deductible in the income year they are made, and any losses resulting from those claims allowed under Division 30 cannot be carried forward or claimed in later income years. (See the tip at 13.820.) However, deductions may be spread over five years (see 13.888).

13.830   DONATION OF PROPERTY

Deductions are allowed only for assets purchased in the 12 months before making the gift, unless made under the Cultural Bequests Program (see 13.870).

'Purchase' does not cover acquisition by gift, bequest or other non-purchase method.

The tax deduction, determined at the time the gift is made is limited to the lesser of:

- the value (ie. market value) of the gift, and
- its cost.

If the gift is the taxpayer's trading stock, its value is the amount (based on cost, market or replacement value) included in the taxpayer's assessable income. See 13.845.

DEDUCTIONS FOR JOINT OWNERS

Joint owners of donated property can claim a tax deduction based on their share of the value of the property (ie. the interest they own).

DONATION OF LISTED SHARES

A deduction is allowable where a taxpayer gifts shares to a DGR. The donor can claim a deduction for the market value of the shares on the day that the shares were gifted, provided that:

- the shares were acquired at least 12 months before the gift was made
- the shares have a market value of $2 or more but $5,000 or less
- the shares are listed public company shares, and
- are listed for quotation on the official list of an Australian stock exchange.

The shares may have been purchased by the taxpayer, or inherited, won as a prize, or received as a gift or bonus. The deduction applies only to shares and does not include derivatives or securities that are not shares, or shares that have been suspended from trading (other than a mere trading halt). If the donation of shares is in different companies and gifted at the same time, then they are treated as separate donations.

A taxpayer donates publicly listed shares, which he had held for 18 months, worth $4,000 in ZA Ltd and $4,500 in XB Ltd on the same day to a DGR. Although the total value exceeds $5,000, each is deductible as they are treated as separate gifts.

The donor is still subject to any capital gain that may be made on the disposal of the shares and is entitled to a capital loss if applicable.

Kitty purchased $3,000 of shares in Shiny Gold Ltd, a public company listed on the Melbourne Stock Exchange. After 18 months they have a market value of $2,000 and she donates them to a DGR. While Kitty will be entitled to claim a deduction for the gift of $2,000, she will be have a capital loss of $1,000 because the reduced cost base is $2,000.

See also 13.822 for shares donated for fund raising events.

13.835   CULTURAL GIFTS PROGRAM

Gifts of money or property over $2 are deductible when made to:

- Australiana fund
- Artbank
- National Trust, and
- Public libraries, museums and art galleries.

However, this excludes testamentary gifts, land or buildings. The property must be accepted by the DGR (or the Commonwealth, if Artbank) for inclusion in the collection. Gifts made under this program would usually be works of art, manuscripts, books, furniture, historical items etc. The donor can make a written election to spread the deduction over the current year and up to four following years (see 13.888).

Mr Brown donates a unique historical painting to the National Gallery. He elects to deduct over four years with 40% in the year of donation and 20% in each of the following three years.

Three valuation methods apply, depending on how the asset was acquired and whether any restrictions or conditions are imposed by the donor. When claiming for any of these donations, consideration has to be given as to the appropriate method of valuation. Particular valuation methods apply to particular circumstances and there may be GST consequences (see 13.885).

Method 1 applies if the taxpayer would have been required to return the proceeds (or profit) as assessable income if the property had been sold. Unlike Method 2, there are no restrictions on when or how the property was acquired. The value of the property is the market value of the property at the time the gift is made, but the taxpayer must get two written valuations (from approved valuers) stating the value of the property at the time of gifting or the day the valuation was made. The Tax Office can reduce the 'value' of the gift to an amount considered reasonable at the time the gift was made, particularly if the gift is conditional (see Method 3).

If the market value applies to the day of valuation, the valuation must have been made at a date within 90 days before or after the gifting of the property. The Tax Office can extend this period in appropriate cases.

Method 2 applies if the taxpayer would have been required to return the proceeds (or profit) as assessable income if the property had been sold, and it had been acquired by the taxpayer:

- within 12 months of the gifting under the terms of a Will, intestacy or varied Court Order, and
- with the purpose of making such donation.

The value of the property is the lesser of:

- the cost of the property, and
- its value (ie. market value).

Method 3 applies if the gift contains conditions that the recipient does not:

- receive immediate custody or control of the property
- have the uncontrolled right to retain custody or control of the property in perpetuity, or
- get an immediate, indefeasible and unencumbered legal and equitable title to the property.

The value of the property is the same as Method 1. See 13.885 for the GST effect.

HERITAGE CONSERVATION

A tax offset of 20% is available for expenditure of $5,000 or more on buildings or structures listed on a Commonwealth, State or Territory heritage register provided a final certificate has been issued by the Department of Environment and Heritage.

13.840 PROFIT MAKING PURCHASES

Special rules apply where the asset that has been donated was originally acquired by the taxpayer for resale to make a profit. If an asset was acquired before 20 September 1985 with the intention of resale to make a profit, the profit is taxed regardless of when the disposal occurs. This applies when assets are gifted or transferred in a non-arm's length transaction (eg. to a relative or other related person).

The recipient is treated as having acquired the asset for the same:

- purpose (profit-motive) as the donor, and
- cost at which the donor acquired it

and is assessed on any profit on disposal of the asset.

13.845 GIFTS OF TRADING STOCK

Gifts of trading stock valued at $2 or more to a DGR are deductible to the donor. The gift is treated as being a disposal outside of the normal course of business with the value being the market value of the trading stock at the time of the donation. The donor is also required to bring into account as assessable income that same value. If the Tax Office has given a valuation for the gift under s30-212, that valuation may be substituted for the market value provided that the valuation was made no more than ninety days before or after the date of the disposal.

13.850 CGT IMPLICATIONS

For assets that were not originally acquired with a profit making motive, under the current rules, donations of such property have CGT implications unless the asset qualifies under the Cultural Bequests program or would have been deductible under s30-15 if it had not been a testamentary gift. The implications vary depending on the date of acquisition of the asset and they also affect testamentary gifts. See also 13.830, 13.880 and 13.885.

ASSETS ACQUIRED BEFORE 20 SEPTEMBER 1985

Assets acquired before 20 September 1985 and transferred or gifted to a non-arm's length party are deemed to be disposed of at market value. The new owner acquires the asset at its market value at the transfer date, and the original owner is free of any CGT. Any capital gain or loss on disposal is assessed to the new owner.

ASSETS ACQUIRED AFTER 19 SEPTEMBER 1985

CGT can be payable by both the original owner and recipient if the asset was acquired after 19 September 1985.

For each transfer or gift (for no or inadequate consideration), the original owner is deemed to have disposed of the asset for consideration equal to its market value. For the recipient, the asset's cost base is deemed to be its market value. The person making the gift has a capital gain if consideration (market value) exceeds the cost base of the asset gifted.

13.860 SCHOOL AND COLLEGE BUILDING FUNDS

Gifts to school or college building funds can be tax deductible if the proposed buildings are for a purpose connected with the curriculum.

The fund must be dispersed exclusively for:

- acquisition, construction, maintenance and capital improvements, or
- installation and maintenance of fixtures of a building used or to be used as a school or college (see TR 96/8 for details of eligibility).

13.870   CULTURAL BEQUESTS PROGRAM

The cultural bequests program under sub-division 30-D was repealed in March 2012. Testamentary gifts are no longer deductible under s30-15(2). See 13.870 in the *Tax Summary 2014 & 2015.*

13.875   PRESCRIBED PRIVATE FUNDS

Certain private funds may be prescribed in the Regulations. Unlike most other categories of funds referred to in Division 30, they do not have to seek donations or receive donations from the public or be controlled by persons considered to have a responsibility to the public. These funds are intended to receive donations and then to disburse the capital and /or income of the fund to other deductible gift recipients.

The Tax Office guidelines for prescribed private funds can be found at www.ato.gov.au.

13.880   PROPERTY OVER $5,000

Deductions are allowable for donations of property regardless of when the property was acquired, provided the market value of the property is more than $5,000.

The valuation is made by the Tax Office (a fee may be charged). Market value is reduced by 1/11th if the donor is entitled to a GST input tax credit (see 13.885).

For donations of property costing less than $5,000, property would have to be donated within 12 months of purchase to be deductible. If property is valued at over $5,000, but is gifted within 12 months of purchase, the amount deductible is the lesser of the amount paid or its market value.

Where the Tax Office values a gift of property made to any DGR to be more than $5000, the donor can spread the deduction over five years (see also 13.888).

Deductions are allowed when the gift is made to public funds, etc. included in Subdivision 30-B. Also, deductibility is extended to 'prescribed private funds' (ie. prescribed by Regulation).

13.883   CONSERVATION COVENANTS

A deduction is available for taxpayers who enter into a conservation covenant with government agencies (eg. State departments of parks and wildlife). A conservation covenant over land is one that restricts or prohibits certain activities on land that could degrade the environmental value of the land. It must be permanent and registered (if registration is possible) on the title to the land, and is approved in writing by the Minister for Environment and Heritage. The covenant must be over land owned by the taxpayer.

The following conditions must be met:

- the covenant is perpetual
- the taxpayer must not receive any money, property or other material benefit for entering into the covenant
- the covenant is entered into with a fund, authority or institution that meets the requirements of Division 31 (broadly those that have deductibility under Division 30 and are in Australia)
- the market value of the land must decrease as a result of the covenant, and
- one or both of these conditions must apply:
  - the change in the market value of the land as a result of entering into the covenant is more than $5,000
  - the taxpayer must have entered into a contract to acquire the land not more than twelve months before the covenant was entered into, and
  - the amount that can be deducted is the difference between the market value of the land just before the covenant was entered into and its decreased market value just after entering into the covenant (to the extent attributable to entering into the covenant). See also 12.026 and 13.888.

13.885 GST AND CGT IMPLICATIONS

If a donor of a property gift is neither registered nor required to be registered for GST purposes, no adjustment to the value is required. As a general rule, if the donor is either registered or required to be registered for GST purposes, and the gift is either one of property less than 12 months old or was trading stock of the donor, the market value is reduced by the GST input credits. The same applies if the value related to property less than 12 months old purchased by the donor, or is a donation of shares made for a fundraising event (see 13.822).

A large accounting firm buys some computers for $22,000 but finding them unsuitable, gifts them shortly afterwards to a public university (a DGR). Because the firm would have been entitled to an input tax credit of $2,000, the value of the gift is $20,000.

A CGT exemption applies to disregard a capital gain or loss for gifts of property made under the Cultural Bequest Program (such as the Australiana Fund, public libraries, museums and art galleries, and Artbank), or for testamentary gifts. The exemption will not apply if the donor re-acquires the property for less than its market value. From 1 July 2005 testamentary gifts of property do not have to be valued at more than $5,000 to qualify for the CGT exemption (s118-60(1A)). See 13.870.

To be eligible for approval, private charitable funds must meet all of the criteria required to qualify as a public fund, as well as the new approved recipient criteria (see 13.800) but without the need to seek contributions from the public. These rules allow businesses, families and individuals greater freedom to set up their own trusts for philanthropic purposes.

For donations made under the Cultural Gifts Program, taxpayers will be able to elect to apportion their entitlement to a deduction up to a period of five years (see also 13.888).

Although these funds need not seek and receive donations from the public and do not need public control, they have to comply with all other requirements of a public fund. The guidelines for prescribed private funds and the approved trust deed are available on the website www.ato. gov.au under 'Non-profit organisations'.

13.888 SPREADING DEDUCTION OVER FIVE YEARS

Taxpayers who make a cash gift to a fund have been able to make a written election to spread the deduction over the current income year and up to four of the following income years. The conditions applying and the effect of the election are the same as for gifts of property (see 13.880) valued at over $5,000 (but not environmental, heritage and certain cultural property gifts), and conservation covenants. The amendment effectively amalgamates provisions in Division 30 relating to spreading of deductions.

The election must be made before the lodgement of the donor's income tax return for the income year in which the gift was made. In the election the donor will have to specify the percentage (if any) that is to be deducted in each income year. The election may be varied at any time, but only as to the percentage that will be deducted in income years for which returns have not been lodged.

In December 2010 Susie gives the National Gallery a painting valued at $150,000. She elects to spread the deduction over 5 years as follows: 30% in 2011-12, 35% in 2012-13, 0% in 2013-14, 25% in 2014-15 and 10% in 2015-16. Susie must make the election, and send a copy to the Arts Secretary, before lodging her return for 2011-12. The amounts deductible should be: $45,000 in 2011-12, $52,500 in 2012-13, nothing in 2013-14, $37,500 in 2014-15 and $15,000 in 2015-16.

13.890 DEDUCTIBLE GIFT RECIPIENTS

Division 30 sets out which entities are Deductible Gift Recipients (DGRs): that is, entities authorised to receive gifts which are income tax deductible. Some DGRs are specifically named in the Act (eg. Australian Conservation Foundation). Others fall into a specific category (eg. public library). This also incudes deductible donations to all entities providing volunteer based emergency services, including Volunteer Fire Brigades (VFBs). The measure also extends deductible gift recipient (DGR) status to all state and territory (state) government bodies that coordinate VFBs and State Emergency Service units.

SOME ENDORSEMENT REQUIREMENTS

There are two types of endorsement as a DGR. There are those which fall within a DGR category (eg. a public benevolent institution) and those where a fund, authority or institution that is operated by an organisation falls within a DGR category (eg. a fund for the relief of persons in necessitous circumstances operated by a church).

To be endorsed as a DGR an entity must apply to the Tax Office for endorsement and:

- have an Australian Business Number (ABN)
- be a fund, authority or institution of a type which falls within a general DGR category specified in
  Division 30 (that is, it is not specified by name in the legislation)
- maintain records relevant to their status as a DGR
- be situated in Australia unless it is an ancillary fund, and
- maintain a gift fund. Until 12 April 2007 all DGRs had to maintain a gift fund to hold deductible gifts or contributions. From that date an entity that is itself endorsed as a DGR will not have to maintain a gift fund (although it may choose to do so). However, an entity that is not eligible for endorsement but is endorsed to operate a deductible fund, authority or institution, will still be required to maintain a gift fund. These entities are able to consolidate multiple gift funds. A gift fund can only be used for the principal purposes of the entity and cannot receive any other gifts.

Application forms for endorsement can be obtained by telephoning the Tax Office on 13 24 78.

13.900 TAX-RELATED DEDUCTIONS

A deduction for expenditure incurred (whether or not the taxpayer is carrying on a business) for the management or administration of income tax affairs is a specific deduction allowed under s25-5 ITAA97.

The claim is allowable for expenses related to:

- Income tax
- PAYG instalments (or company tax)
- Goods and services tax
- Capital gains tax
- Fringe benefits tax
- Medicare levy
- a GIC charge imposed under s170AA (ITAA36)
- Franking deficit tax, and
- PAYG withholding tax.

OTHER LEVIES

The Superannuation Guarantee Charge (SGC) is not 'income tax'; and therefore costs concerning disputes as to liability, etc. might only be deductible under s8-1.

13.905   ALLOWABLE EXPENSES

Expenditure is tax-deductible under s25-5 if incurred by the taxpayer in:

- finding the extent of the taxpayer's income tax liability
- managing or administering the income tax affairs of the taxpayer
- complying with the legal obligations imposed on a taxpayer in respect of his/her income tax affairs
- disputing an assessment, determination or ruling issued by the Tax Commissioner, or
- attending to matters during, and arising from, an audit of the taxpayer's tax affairs.

Section 25-5 allows specific deduction for:

- fees paid by a taxpayer to a recognised tax adviser for professional advice in relation to the income tax affairs of the taxpayer

- costs associated with disputing assessments or any decision made by the Tax Commissioner

- lodgement fees paid to the Administrative Appeals Tribunal (AAT), or the Courts (any refunds will be assessable in the financial year during which they are received)

- costs incurred in attending to a Tax Office audit

- costs associated with tax planning

- costs of attempting to get an extension of time to pay an outstanding tax debt, including the cost of having a financial statement prepared to demonstrate the taxpayer's inability to pay the full tax liability by the due date

- costs of giving information about some other taxpayer where that is demanded by the Tax Office, or

- the cost (for example) of deducting and remitting PAYG withholding tax on contract work or even for work done privately for the taxpayer.

 This includes the cost of travel, and where appropriate, also accommodation. Any claim under s25-5 can include expenses which, in any other situation, might be private expenses.

 Membership fees and cost of the Tax Summary books paid to Taxpayers Australia Ltd and similar organisations should be deductible under s25-5.

 Contributions to a fighting fund are tax deductible as tax related expenditure if the fund has been set up to fund litigation, negotiate a settlement, or otherwise manage tax disputes arising from investments or schemes (TD 2002/1). The contributor must be a participant in the scheme, and has claimed, or will claim, a deduction which has or will be allowed.

13.910　CLAIMS NOT ALLOWABLE

Claims are not allowable for:

- capital expenditure (may form part of an asset's 'cost base', see 13.930), and

- expenditure which would be precluded as an 'entertainment expense' (such as payment for a meal with a professional tax adviser) whatever the reason for a meal and discussion.

'RECOGNISED TAX ADVISER'

The definition is:

- a registered tax agent, BAS agent or tax (financial adviser) – as defined under the _Tax Agents Services Act 2009_, or

- legal practitioner – being a person who is enrolled as a barrister, a solicitor or a barrister and solicitor of a federal court, or a court of a State or Territory.

OTHER ALLOWABLE AMOUNTS

Even capital expenditure can qualify for a deduction as tax-related provided the item is used for approved purposes. The claim allowed is limited to the applicable amount of depreciation for the income year, eg. a computer used to meet a taxpayer's tax obligations. However, when the item is used by a private person partly to assist in the administration of the taxpayer's tax affairs, depreciation would be allowed only to the extent to which the property is used by a taxpayer in ascertaining or meeting the taxpayer's 'income tax' (as it is defined) obligations. Double deductions are not allowed if the equipment is already being used and claimed for business or income earning purposes. The actual tax claim is the non-private part of overall depreciation and other costs.

OFFENCES AGAINST LAW

Deductions will not be allowed for costs associated with an offence against any law of the Commonwealth, State, Territory or foreign country.

13.915   REFUNDS OF TAX-RELATED EXPENSES

Claims for tax-related expenditure will not be an allowable deduction to the extent it is ultimately not borne by the taxpayer. This applies to any amount that was (or is) tax-deductible, but is:

- reimbursed to the taxpayer
- paid by another taxpayer after the taxpayer has technically incurred the expenditure, or
- recouped (even indirectly) by the taxpayer.

If expenditure is incurred by a taxpayer who is in business, it may be claimed in that year even though paid later (whether or not it is reimbursed later). If an amount of 'tax-related' expenditure is reimbursed or recouped, the amount is assessable income of the year in which recompense occurs.

Filing fees paid to the AAT on the lodgement of a reference. See 'Objections and Appeals' at 4.200 and 4.300. If there is any reduction in the tax liability arising from the objection, the AAT filing fees are refunded in full and are assessable in the year refunds are received.

13.920   TAXPAYER DIES DURING YEAR

Expenditure on any 'tax-related matters' is treated as incurred during the taxpayer's lifetime. A deduction is allowed in the final return to the date of death for expenditure incurred by a trustee which would have been allowable to the taxpayer had it been incurred and paid by the deceased.

13.925   PARTNERSHIPS AND TRUSTS

Section 25-5 expenditure incurred by a partnership or by a trust is an allowable deduction in calculating net income. TD 94/91 says only the trustee can claim a s25-5 ITAA97 deduction for expenses for management or administration of the income tax affairs of the trust, and a deduction is allowed for this expenditure in the tax return of the trust.

13.930   CGT COST BASE

The following expenses can generally be included in the 'cost base' of an asset (but see 12.092 and 12.120), also forming part of the 'reduced cost base':

- fees paid to a 'recognised professional tax adviser' for professional advice concerning the impact of the income tax law on the acquisition or disposal of an asset
- fees paid for professional advice on the impact of taxes other than income tax (eg. stamp duty, etc.) on the acquisition or disposal of an asset.

Expenses incurred on tax-related matters are not treated as capital merely because the income tax affairs to which the expenditure relates are of a capital nature.

To calculate a gain or loss, costs incidental to the acquisition or disposal of an asset may be eligible to be included in:

- the asset's 'cost base'
- the 'reduced cost base', or
- the 'indexed cost base'.

Incidental acquisition and disposal costs for the relevant cost base of the asset are:

- fees, commission or remuneration for the professional services of a surveyor, valuer, auctioneer, accountant, broker, agent, consultant or legal adviser: but not any paid to a 'recognised professional tax adviser' for a wider range of services allowable under s25-5
- costs of transfer (including stamp duty or similar duty)
- purchase: advertising or marketing costs to find a seller

- sale: advertising or marketing costs to find a buyer
- costs of making any valuation or apportionment of acquisition costs
- search fees
- cost of a conveyancing kit, or
- borrowing expenses (such as loan application fees and mortgage discharge fees).

Some costs are deductible under s25-5 ITAA97, while others are to be included in the 'cost base' of the asset (and indexed, if applicable) when calculating any capital gain.

NOTE: Any expenditure incurred before 1 July 1989 for tax advice does not form part of the cost base.

13.950 CARRY FORWARD TAX LOSSES

A tax loss occurs when a taxpayer's deductions for an income year exceed their income (called a 'loss year'). A tax loss may be able to be carried forward and deducted in subsequent income years, but some restrictions apply (see Division 36 and 14.450).

A loss is incurred if allowable deductions (but not unused losses from earlier years) exceed the taxpayer's assessable income and net exempt income for that income year.

'Net exempt income' is the amount by which total exempt income from all sources exceeds the total of:

- revenue (ie. not capital) expenses incurred in deriving that income, and
- any (foreign) taxes payable on that exempt income.

TAX OFFSETS IN YEAR LOSS INCURRED

Tax offsets claimed on a tax return normally will reduce the tax payable. Unused tax offsets are lost and also some of the past losses will have been used up. Unused tax offsets for franking credits are refundable to individuals.

13.955 DEDUCTING TAX LOSSES

As a general rule, loss year tax losses are deducted in the order they were incurred from:

- firstly, net exempt income (if any), and
- secondly, the part of total assessable income that exceeds total deductions for the current year other than tax losses.

From the 1989-90 year, both primary production and non-primary production tax losses can be carried forward indefinitely.

Special rules apply to:

- companies wishing to claim for past year losses (see 6.400)
- trusts wishing to claim for past year losses (see 7.900)
- capital losses (see 12.160 and 12.535)
- forgiveness of debts (see 14.400)
- non-commercial business activities (see 14.450)
- foreign losses (see 22.420)
- transfer of losses within wholly owned company groups (see 6.400), and
- claims for bad debts (see 14.160).

However, a taxpayer cannot elect the year in which to apply a prior year tax loss and they are carried forward until fully absorbed. The losses are able to be claimed by the taxpayer who incurred the losses, even though they may no longer be in business. Unrecouped losses cannot be transferred to another taxpayer; for example the vendor when selling their business cannot transfer unrecouped losses to the purchaser. The accumulated tax losses to the date of death of a deceased taxpayer cannot be carried forward and deducted by the trustee of a deceased estate (ID 2003/557).

A taxpayer who becomes a bankrupt cannot deduct a tax loss incurred before becoming bankrupt or being released.

NOTE: The carry forward loss regime is different for companies (see 'no wasting rule' below).

There are general loss limitation rules where a 'foreign hybrid' is treated as a partnership (Division 830 ITAA97). There is a limitation on the use of some losses by limited partners against income other than income from the foreign hybrid. The rules are different to those dealing with ordinary partnerships. The rules apply to partnership losses and any net capital loss attributable to the foreign hybrid. Professional advice should be sought if these rules may apply.

NOTE: From 1 July 2008 foreign losses can be claimed against any domestic income and is no longer subjected to 'specific categories' on quarantining (see 22.420).

13.960 CLAIM ONLY IF NO LOSS GENERATED

Section 26-55 ITAA97 prevents the following deductions from generating a tax loss that can be deducted in a later year:

- **Division 30 ITAA97:** gifts or contributions made to approved or listed DGRs
- **s25-50 ITAA97:** payment of pensions, gratuities or retiring allowances
- **Division 31 ITAA97:** deductions for conservation covenants
- **s78B ITAA36:** promoters recoupment tax
- **Division 3 of Pt III ITAA36:** development allowance so far as it applies to a leasing company
- **Subdivision 290-C:** deductions for personal superannuation contributions, and
- **Division 3 of Part XII ITAA36:** development and drought investment allowances of a leasing company.

If a deduction can be claimed under a more general provision such as s8-1, then it can add to a carry-forward loss (provided that s8-10 does not apply to prevent a double deduction). It would also seem that if carry forward losses already exist, then any specified deductions (eg. s290-150 ITAA97) have to be taken into account first. An example given is as follows.

A taxpayer has an assessable income of $10,000 with s290-150 ITAA97 deductions of $1,500 and carry forward losses of $20,000. The s290-150 deduction is taken into account as follows:

Assessable income		$10,000
less s290-150 deduction	$1,500	
Prior year losses	$8,500	$10,000
Taxable income		**Nil**

If the taxpayer had other expenditure deductible under s8-1 ITAA97, the effect would be as follows:

Assessable income		$10,000
less other allowable deductions	$9,500	
s290-150 claim limited to	$500	$10,000
Taxable income		**Nil**

The carry forward loss would remain at $20,000.

Expenses incurred on gifts and donations, and deductible personal superannuation contributions cannot be used to increase or create a tax loss. Hence, in this example the claim for those expenses has been limited to the amount that does not create a tax loss.

13.970 BANKRUPTCY

A deduction is allowed for what is spent or owing, but not for any debt which does not have to be paid (eg. forgiveness of debt).

A tax loss incurred before becoming bankrupt cannot be deducted if the bankruptcy is annulled later and:

- the taxpayer comes to an 'arrangement' with creditors, and
- the taxpayer may be released from some or all of the debts.

A taxpayer may be able to claim a deduction in the year of income from voluntary payments that they make towards debts from which they have been released (see TD 93/10).

Business deductions

14

14.000 CHECKLIST OF BUSINESS DEDUCTIONS

This non-exhaustive checklist is designed to provide an easy reference guide to the types of deductions that might be claimed by businesses. It should be read in conjunction with a similar checklist for employees (see from 13.000). Before deciding on the deductibility of an outgoing the taxpayer's particular circumstances should be taken into account.

All businesses are required to maintain records of every transaction that relate to their income and expenditure as well as CGT transactions, GST, FBT and other requirements. The rules for recording those transactions are summarised from 4.700. If there is any private use element, that should also be noted in the records.

Car and travel expenses must be substantiated (see 13.160, 13.190 & 13.225).

NOTE: All section and division references are to the *Income Tax Assessment Act 1997* (ITAA97) unless otherwise stated.

- **Accident insurance premiums**
- **Accounting fees** Preparation of income tax and FBT returns etc. (s25-5) including costs relating to investigations, objections and appeals (see from 13.900)
- **Advertising expenses**
- **Agent's commission** Collection of rent
- **Annual leave** If actually paid by the employer (but not on accruing liabilities)
- **Audit fees**
- **Bad debts** See from 14.160 and 6.600
- **Bank charges** Including Debits tax
- **Borrowing expenses** Claim in full if $100 or less, otherwise over the period of the loan or one fifth each year if five years is shorter commencing from the date finance is acquired (see 14.135)
- **Bribes** (public officials) No deduction is allowed, nor can the amount form part of CGT cost base
- **Business trips** See 13.160
- **Business-related cost** See 15.110 for business related costs of a capital nature that can be written-off in equal amounts over five years commencing from the first day in the income year that the expense was incurred
- **Capital works** On buildings and structural improvements (see 15.200)
- **Car expenses** Applies to employees, partners and self employed persons (see 13.220)
- **Car parking** 13.290 but see 25.300
- **Cleaning expenses**
- **Clothing** See 13.300
- **Conference expenses** see 13.700
- **Copyrights, patents and designs** See Capital allowance provisions (Division 40) (see 15.060) also consider the R&D concessions for companies
- **Cultural bequests** If made to Australian fund, public art gallery museum or library (see 13.835 & 13.870)
- **Decline in value** (depreciation) Of plant or articles used in business (see from 15.000 and 10.600)
- **Directors' fees**
- **Discharge of mortgage expenses** Where loan money used to derive assessable income (s25-30) (see 14.140)
- **Distributions by co-operatives** To members
- **Donations of property to deductible gift recipient** If market value is greater than $5,000 (see 13.880)
- **Education expenses** If paid for employees (see 13.700) but FBT may apply (see 25.000)

- **Electricity connection costs** To business premises (see 14.185). Capital allowance provisions (Division 40)
- **Entertainment of employees** But FBT payable (see 25.900)
- **Environmental impact studies** Pooled and treated under the Uniform Capital Allowance system (decline in value) (see from 15.000 and 15.600)
- **Environment protection expenditure** See 15.600
- **Equipment service fees**
- **Exploration or prospecting** For minerals (including petroleum) and quarry materials (see 15.100)
- **Film investment** 100% deduction for investment in certain Australian made films (see 14.700)
- **Freight costs**
- **Fringe benefits tax** See from 25.000
- **Fuel and oil**
- **Gifts of $2 or more** To certain prescribed or approved organisations (see 13.800)
- **Gifts to clients, etc** But not if entertainment (see 25.900)
- **Gratuities to employees** Recognition of past services (s25-30)
- **GST** Claims should be GST exclusive for those businesses that are registered for GST. The GST-inclusive price is deductible for those taxpayers not registered or required to be registered for GST
- **Home office expenses** Apportionment of interest, rates, etc. only if a business is carried out on the premises and where an area is set aside exclusively for that purpose (see 13.600)
- **Illegal activities** Where taxpayer convicted of indictable offences (no deduction allowed nor can the amount form part of CGT cost base – see 14.166).
- **Insurance premiums** Accident insurance paid by employees, and other insurance paid in relation to a business or some income-producing property. This is subject to the prepayment rules (see 14.170)
- **Interest paid** See 14.130
- **Internet and data access costs** Share investing and business websites – see also 14.000 for capital expenditure
- **Land tax** Business or rental premises. Deductible when incurred. The Tax Office has released guidance specifying that land tax is incurred in the year to which it refers, not when it is paid (see ATO ID 2010/192)
- **Lease payments** See 14.155 and 14.178
- **Lease preparation, registration or stamping expenses** Paid by either the landlord or (a business) tenant (s25-20) (see 14.115)
- **Leave payments** Paid by employer (but not on accruing liabilities)
- **Legal expenses** Unless capital expenditure, including discharge of a mortgage (s25-30) or relating to borrowing expenses (s26-40) (see 14.115 and 14.135) the nexus with ordinary activities of the business in producing assessable income will determine deductibility
- **Licenses to operate business** Prepayment rules may apply (see 14.170)
- **Losses, current year** Loss claims by companies may be limited in certain situations (Division 165), (s170-10) (see 13.950 and 7.400) Losses by trusts are subject to Trust Loss Provisions (see 7.900)
- **Losses, previous years** Company losses brought forward may be limited unless the company can pass the continuity of ownership test (s165-12) or the 'same business' test (s160-10); no time limit for losses incurred after 30 June 1989 (s36-10) (see 13.950 and 7.400) Losses by trusts are subject to Trust Loss Provisions (see 7.900)
- **Loss (book loss) on disposal of depreciable assets** (s40-285(2))

- **Loss on sale of property** If acquired before 20/09/85 for resale at a profit (s25-40); if property is sold in the ordinary course of business the loss will be on revenue account (see TR 92/3), otherwise a capital loss arises pursuant to Part 3 of ITAA97
- **Loss through misappropriation by employees, or by theft** (s25-45) See 14.165
- **Maintenance expenses** (s8-1)
- **Management expenses** Annual fees but not the capital cost of subscribing to some income-earning investments
- **Managing tax affairs** Costs of travel, accommodation, advice, booklets, seminars etc, depreciation on computers, software and other capital expenditure is deductible if incurred in managing tax affairs (see 13.900)
- **Mortgage protection insurance** (s8-1)
- **Moving trading stock**
- **Newspapers for employees** Depends on occupation. Share traders (and maybe investors) can claim
- **Overseas travel expenses** Substantiation rules apply (see 13.160 and 13.205)
- **Payroll tax** See from 26.000
- **Petrol and oil** Not subject to substantiation rules (see 13.242)
- **Petroleum resource rent tax**
- **Postage** For investors or businesses
- **Power, lighting and heating**
- **Primary producers** See from 21.000
- **Printing and stationery**
- **Professional or business association subscriptions and fees** (see 13.000) Prepayment rules may apply (see 14.170)
- **Project expenditure** To be written-off over life of project (see 15.100)
- **Protective clothing** See 13.310
- **Rates and taxes** On income-producing or business properties (see 14.125)
- **Rebates and discounts** Given to customers
- **Rent of business premises** Including part of the costs for a home used for a business (say, trading stock is stored in an area set aside exclusively for that purpose); but with a home office (or a study) rent cannot be apportioned, but some associated costs are claimable (see 13.600)
- **Repairs to cars, equipment, or to an income-producing property** (s25-10) See 14.150
- **Research & Development costs** See 15.500
- **Retiring allowance**s Paid to ex-employee (or their dependent) for past services (s25-50) (see 14.120)
- **Royalties** Paid for use of equipment etc. – withholding tax may apply
- **Salaries and wages paid to employees**
- **Scientific research related to business** If incurred before July 1995 and R&D claim is not available: accelerated write-offs for capital expenditure into scientific research (s73A ITAA36)
- **Self-education expenses** Only if related to employment/business (see 13.700)
- **Seminars** see 13.700
- **Sickness/accident premiums In some cases**
- **Solicitor's fees** (see 14.115)
- **Storage expenses**
- **Structural improvements** (see 15.200)
- **Subcontractors** May be considered employees and subject to the 9.5% superannuation guarantee provisions in certain circumstances (see 19.516)

- **Superannuation contributions**
- **Support payments to a subsidiary** (see 14.169)
- **Tax agents fees** Preparation of income tax, fringe benefits tax returns, GST etc. (s25-5) including costs relating to investigations, objections and appeals (see from 13.900)
- **Telephone expenses**
- **Telephone line installation** See 21.650
- **Tool replacement** Depreciation (see 15.030)
- **Trade journals**
- **Trading stock purchases** See 14.200 and 21.400
- **Travelling expenses** Domestic and overseas, but note the substantiation provisions (see 13.160)
- **Traveller accommodation buildings** See 15.200
- **Uniforms** See 13.340 and from 25.000 (FBT)
- **Workcover/Workers compensation premium**
- **Worker entitlement funds** Only if fund approved under regulations

14.050 BUSINESS DEDUCTIONS

This chapter deals with specific deductions that may be allowed to those carrying on business. They are in addition to the general deductions outlined in Chapter 13. For those taxpayers who have elected to take advantage of the small business entity tax concessions (formerly the simplified tax system) see Chapter 10 for additional provisions which may be relevant.

TR 97/11 outlines factors which have been established by the courts as indicators of whether the business of primary production is being carried on. However, these factors also apply to the general question of whether a business is being carried on. The factors are:

- whether the activity has a significant commercial purpose or character
- whether the taxpayer has more than just an intention to engage in business
- whether the taxpayer has a purpose of profit and prospect of profit from the activity
- whether there is repetition and regularity of the activity
- whether the activity is of the same kind and carried on in a similar manner to that of ordinary trade in that line of business
- whether the activity is planned, organised and carried on in a businesslike manner such that it is directed at making a profit
- the size, scale and permanency of the activity, and
- whether the activity is better described as a hobby, a form of recreation or a sporting activity.

No one indicator is decisive and therefore analysis of all the factors is necessary to determine if a taxpayer's activities constitute a business. These factors are more fully explained in *Primary Producers* from 21.000.

14.055 COSTS OF A NEW BUSINESS

Acquiring or commencing a business is a capital transaction. Costs incurred may form part of the 'cost base' of particular assets for capital gains tax purposes. Alternatively, a deduction equivalent to 20% per annum may be available under s40-880 as a cost in establishing a business (see 15.110). Note proposed 2015 & 2016 Federal Budget measures to allow an immediate deduction for professional fees in relation to starting up a business (see 15.110).

Examples of new business related costs included in capital expenditure include:

- the cost of feasibility studies and setting up the business entity
- business restructuring costs, and
- legal expenses incurred to acquire the business.

Once the business is established and operating, expenses of a revenue nature incurred are allowable (eg. rent, light, power) unless denied by the application of a particular provision of the tax law.

Capital expenditure incurred to prepare the new premises for occupation is not deductible under the standard provisions. Such capital costs include:

- initial repairs required when an asset is acquired
- alterations to a building (see 15.200)
- removal costs (but see 15.060 'second element of cost'), and
- any money paid to a former tenant so the taxpayer can gain possession of premises from which the business Is to be operated.

NOTE: With new and second-hand equipment (whether or not as part of the overall business), removal and installation costs are additions to capital costs. Depreciation can be claimed on the higher total.

14.105   GENERAL RUNNING EXPENSES

A checklist of deductible expenses available to taxpayers in various businesses is available at 14.000. Also see *Checklist for employees* from 13.000.

PRESENTLY EXISTING OBLIGATION

INSURANCE INDUSTRY TAXPAYERS

Once an event has occurred which gives rise to a legal liability to pay, a deduction may be claimed for the present value of the obligation to pay in the future *(FCT v MMI (Workers Compensation) Ltd* 99 ATC 4404 involving the liability of an insurance company for outstanding insurance claims reported but not settled and incurred but not reported).

OTHER TAXPAYERS

Once a legal liability to pay exists, a deduction will be available in respect of the amount payable even though the amount cannot be precisely ascertained and the debt may be defeasible in certain circumstances. No deduction is available in respect of provisions for such things as employee leave entitlements on the basis that no amount has been 'incurred' at that time *(FCT v James Flood Pty Ltd* 88 CLR 492).

Specific provisions impacting deductibility, such as the prepayment rules, may require consideration.

14.110   DECLINE IN VALUE (DEPRECIATION)

Taxpayers claiming deductions for the decline in value of assets may adopt the safe harbour of the Commissioner's rates of effective life (see TR 2015/2 from 1 July 2015) or alternatively, self-assess the life of the asset. Evidence as to the appropriateness of a self-assessed effective life may be requested by the Tax Office. Depreciation claims are covered from 15.000. Some special rules are set out at 15.060 and 15.800. The rules for the simplified tax system are detailed from 10.000. A listing of the depreciation rates that apply to depreciable assets in rental properties is contained at 18.360.

 An immediate write off of assets under $100 (GST Inclusive value) is allowed for business taxpayers in accordance with PS LA 2003/8. This threshold for immediate write-off is different for small business (see 10.600).

14.115   LEGAL EXPENSES

The deductibility of legal expenses incurred by businesses is generally determined under s8-1. When a legal expense is incurred in the operation of a business to produce assessable income (ie. when the expense satisfies the second positive limb of this section) it is generally allowable as a deduction. Exceptions are when the legal fee is capital, domestic or private in nature (negative limbs of this section), specifically excluded by another section of the income tax legislation or incurred in earning exempt and non-assessable non-exempt income.

In addition, the following types of legal expenses are not deductible under s8-1 because of their capital and private nature, instead they are made deductible under a specific provision of the ITAA97:

- the preparation of an income tax return, the disputing of a tax assessment and the obtaining of professional tax advice (s25-5)
- the preparation of leases (s25-20) (see below)
- certain borrowing expenses (s25-25)(see 14.135), and
- certain mortgage discharge expenses (s25-30) (see 14.140).

BUSINESS LEASE EXPENSE

The cost of preparing, registering and stamping a lease is deductible under s25-20 if the taxpayer is using or will use the property for earning assessable income. The lease payments themselves will be deductible under s8-1 and are therefore subject to the prepayment rules (see 14.170).

EVICTING A TENANT

A taxpayer may acquire premises (all or a portion of) which were leased to a tenant of the former owner. Any expenses incurred trying to evict the tenant will not be deductible. This expense becomes part of the cost of acquiring the property and a capital expense for income tax purposes. Arguably, it would form part of the 'cost base' of the property, being expenditure of a capital nature incurred in establishing the taxpayer's title to, or a right over, the asset (ss110-30(6)).

VALUATION EXPENSES

If valuation fees are paid to help decide whether to buy a business, these are generally capital costs and not an allowable deduction under s8-1. However, if the valuation is used to support an application to borrow money for use in the business, those expenses can be claimed as borrowing costs immediately if under $100 or over the life of the loan or 5 years from the date of the loan whichever is shorter (s25-25) (see 14.135).

FINES AND BREACHES OF LAW

Deductions are specifically denied for fines or penalties (however described) that are imposed as a consequence of a breach of any Australian or foreign law (s26-5). This rule does not apply to administratively imposed penalties such as General Interest Charge (GIC) and penalties for under estimating GST instalments. While the fines and penalties may be specifically disallowed, the costs incurred in defending the action may be deductible.

LEGAL EXPENSES THAT CAN BE CLAIMED

Circumstances where legal fees are usually deductible include:

- negotiating current employment contracts (including disputes) in respect of existing employment arrangements (see TR 2000/5)
- defending a wrongful dismissal action bought by former employees or directors
- defending a defamation action bought against a company board
- arbitration in settling disputes (depending on the facts)
- recovering misappropriated funds of the business
- opposing neighborhood developments that are likely to adversely affect the taxpayer's business (depending on the facts of the case)
- evicting a rent-defaulting tenant
- recovering wages of an employee as a result of a dishonored cheque
- defending a libel action provided the case was directly related to comments in pursuit of the company's business
- pursuing claims for workers compensation, and
- defending the unauthorised use of trademarks (depending on the facts of the case).

LEGAL EXPENSES THAT CANNOT BE CLAIMED

Circumstances where legal fees are generally not deductible include:

- the cost of negotiating employment contracts with a new employer
- defending driving charges (regardless of whether the transgression occurred while driving on company business)
- defending charges of sexual harassment or racial vilification which occurred in the workplace
- eviction of a tenant whose term had expired
- resisting land resumption, rezoning or disputing the amount of compensation, and
- disputing redundancy payout or seeking to increase the amount of any redundancy payout (TD 93/29).

Common examples of legal fees that may be deductible under other provisions of the Act (and therefore not deductible under s8-1) include s40-880 'Business related' expenditure (see 15.110).

14.120   PAYMENTS MUST BE REASONABLE

Payments for any services rendered, the purchase of goods or any other outgoings, made to a relative or partnership in which a relative is a partner ('related entity' s26-35), are deductible only to the extent they would be considered reasonable. (See also *Personal services income* from 16.000.) Any amount disallowed as a deduction is deemed not to be assessable or exempt income of the related party (s26-35).

 A property owned by a taxpayer's spouse is rented to a business operated by the taxpayer: the amount of rent claimed must be reasonable. The interest paid on money borrowed from a relative must also be reasonable (ie. no greater than a fair commercial rate) s26-35.

LUMP SUMS ON CEASING EMPLOYMENT

As a general rule an employer is entitled to claim a deduction for lump sum payments to employees when they retire or cease employment. However, that deduction may be limited if the amount is excessive. Irrespective of whether the amount is paid as a pension, gratuity or retiring allowance to an employee (or a dependant of an employee), the payment must be reasonable and made in good faith for the past services of the employee to the business. If the amount is excessive, under s25-50, the Tax Office can deny a deduction for that excessive amount. The amount allowed is limited to what is reasonable based on the employee's service.

These arrangements would not typically affect the concessional taxing of that payment in the hands of the employee (see ETPs etc. from 11.210).

 Employers should be mindful when paying gratuities to retiring employees that this type of expense cannot create or increase a tax loss.

Any part allowable only under s25-50 (eg. where there is a loss) not claimed in the year it is incurred cannot be carried forward to the next year (see 13.950 and 6.400).

14.125   RATES AND LAND TAXES

Claims for rates and land taxes incurred in respect of properties which are used to produce assessable income are allowable under s8-1.

RATES AND LAND TAXES PAID ON PURCHASE

The purchase price is adjusted by certain rates and taxes:

- some already paid by the vendor, to which the purchaser contributes. That part can be claimed, and
- others left for the purchaser to pay, and for which the vendor 'allows' a reduction to cover part of what you will pay. The tax claim is the full expense less the amount reimbursed by the vendor.

The 'rate adjustment' notice shows the expenses for which a taxpayer is liable.

Whether or not paid at settlement, or adjusted some other way, rates and land tax costs can be claimed as a deduction if the property is used for income-producing activities.

14.130 INTEREST

Interest incurred as an expense of running a business or to acquire other income-producing assets or investments is allowed as a tax deduction at the time the liability is 'incurred' (see also *Negative gearing* from 14.190). For business taxpayers under the accruals accounting method, a claim can be made for the calculated interest liability to the end of the income year (usually 30 June), provided the interest on the debt accrues on a daily basis (which would usually be the case).

NOTE: The prepayment rules may impact the time at which a deduction is available (see 14.170).

DEDUCTIONS FOR INTEREST INCURRED

The availability of deductions for interest are typically impacted by the following factors:

- interest must have a sufficient connection with the income earning operations or activities of the taxpayer
- the character of the interest will generally be determined by the use to which the borrowed funds are put
- interest on borrowings will not continue to be deductible if the borrowings cease to be employed in the borrower's business or for some income producing activity, or which are used to earn exempt income
- interest on a new loan is deductible if the new loan is used to repay an existing loan, which, at the time of the second loan, was used to produce assessable income or as part of a business to produce assessable income
- interest may still be deductible even if the borrower's business has ceased (refer to: *Brown* 99 ATC 4600 and *Jones* 2000 ATC 2103). This rule can apply to other assessable income-producing activities but would not apply to the derivation of exempt income
- interest may be deductible if incurred prior to business commencing or assessable income being derived (see TR 2004/4 and *Steele v FC of T* 99 ATC 4242 (Steele))
- the 'rule of 78' may be used in limited circumstances to calculate the interest component of instalments paid under a fixed term loan or extended credit transaction. For details of when the Tax Office accepts use of the rule see TR 93/16 and TR 93/16A, and
- penalty interest for early repayment of a loan may be deductible; see TR 93/7.

 The High Court has ruled that the additional interest incurred under split or linked loans (see below) arising in the circumstances evident in Hart's case is not deductible because of the anti-avoidance rules of Part IVA (see 4.510).

NOTE: In *Hart's case* the split or linked loan was both a private loan (to finance a home) and a business loan (to finance an investment or business). All of the interest payments are applied against the private loan leaving the taxpayer to claim compounding interest deductions on the business loan.

GENERAL LAW PARTNERSHIPS

Interest on borrowings by a common law partnership is deductible if it is to fund repayment of moneys originally advanced by a partner, used as partnership capital and was used to earn assessable income. This is seen as effectively refinancing the working capital of the partnership business. No claim is allowed for interest on borrowings used to replace capital which is represented by internally generated goodwill or an unrealised asset revaluation.

 The taxpayer borrows $25,000 which is used as capital invested in a business with several other partners (ie. general law partnership). The partnership later borrows $25,000 to return the taxpayer's initial capital contribution. At the time of borrowing, the initial capital was being used to derive assessable income in the partnership, so the interest on those borrowed funds is deductible.

Claims for interest on borrowings used to replace capital used in a business which is a tax partnership but not a common law partnership may not be deductible. See from 8.000, TR 95/25, TR 95/25A and TR 95/25A2.

COMPANIES

Interest incurred by companies may be deductible if the funds are used to:

- repay share capital to the shareholders if that capital was employed as working capital in the company business and is used to derive assessable income, or
- fund the payment of a declared dividend to the shareholders where the funds representing that dividend are employed as working capital in the company business and it is used to derive assessable income.

A deduction is not allowed if the borrowed funds are used to:

- repay share capital to shareholders to the extent it represents bonus shares paid out of an unrealised asset revaluation reserve or other equity account (eg. internally generated goodwill), or
- pay dividends out of unrealised profit reserves.

Also, interest incurred by a foreign bank on borrowings that fund the bank's general reserve liquid assets, managed and controlled for use outside Australia, is not deductible (ATO ID 2012/92).

The High Court has confirmed that interest is usually on revenue rather than capital account. The decision in Steele's case *concluded that interest incurred before a business starts operations (eg. during the construction or establishment phase) can be deductible provided that at all times the taxpayer's intention was to use the borrowed funds for the purposes of generating assessable income. See also TR 2004/4. Interest on borrowed funds must be apportioned between income-producing and non-income-producing purposes. An example of where interest was held to be on capital account arose in* Macquarie Finance Ltd v FCT *(2005) FCAFC 205.*

14.135   BORROWING EXPENSES

If costs are incurred to obtain a loan, the costs of arranging it are allowable as a deduction to the extent the loan is used to produce assessable income (s25-25). Expenses claimable under this heading include:

- legal expenses associated with the mortgage documents (see 14.115)
- valuation fees incurred (see 14.115)
- procuration fees and mortgage insurance (*Case R116* 84 ATC 761) (if any)
- stamp duty payable on mortgage documents, and
- any other cost items for taking the loan.

If the total cost is less than $100, it can be claimed in the income year the expense is incurred.

Costs over $100 – claim is spread

The deduction of borrowing expenses is spread equally over the lesser of the loan term, and five years commencing from the date the facility or loan was entered into.

If you incur borrowing costs on a number of dates for different facilities you cannot simply add them to the opening balance of your undeducted borrowing costs for that year. It is necessary to do a separate calculation for these new borrowing costs.

EARLY REPAYMENT

When this occurs, and some of the 'costs of borrowing' have not been claimed, these may be deducted in the year in which the borrowings are paid out. Generally any so-called 'rebate' given when a loan is paid out is merely a figure to adjust the interest. Any refund would diminish the final claim for the 'costs of borrowing'.

Mortgage protection insurance for a bank loan used to purchase an income-producing asset is deductible under s25-25. Penalty interest on early repayment of the loan may also be deductible.

14.140   DISCHARGING A MORTGAGE

As noted at 14.135, a claim may be made for the costs of arranging to borrow money to be used in a business or to produce assessable income. Section 25-30 allows a taxpayer to claim in full the cost of discharging a mortgage where the money was used (whether or not in a business) for producing assessable income.

If only part of the borrowings were used for that purpose, apportion the discharge expenses.

14.145   BILLS OF EXCHANGE DISCOUNT

When the proceeds of a bill of exchange are used in the conduct of a business for the purposes of deriving assessable income, a deduction will typically be available in respect of the discount, which represents a liability at the time the bill is negotiated. The Tax Office position is that, whilst the deduction is 'incurred' when the bill is negotiated, it must be taken over the life of the instrument, calculated on a straight line basis. Where the bill is issued on, say, 1 June for a period of 90 days, a deduction equal to one-third of the discount would be available in year one with the balance in the subsequent year, as the taxpayer has applied the funds to their business operations in both years. This approach reflects the views expressed by the High Court in *Coles Myer Finance Ltd v FCT* (1993) HCA 29. Further information outlining the Tax Office arguments is available in TR 93/21. An exception to this approach arises when bill proceeds are applied directly to the extinguishment of an existing or future liability of the taxpayer. In these circumstances the full deduction should be available at the time of payment (see TR 94/25). This approach is consistent with the reasoning of the *High Court in FCT v Energy Resources of Australia Ltd* (1996) HCA 10.

14.150   REPAIRS

A deduction is allowed for the cost of a repair to premises, part of premises or a depreciating asset (as defined in s40-30) held for the purpose of producing assessable income. If the property is held or used only partly for that purpose, a deduction is allowable for so much as is reasonable in the circumstances (s25-10). The tax law does not require that the property or depreciating asset be owned by the taxpayer. It may be owned by another entity, such as a landlord. However, where the expenditure is on a repair and the taxpayer holds or uses the property or depreciating asset in the income year for the purpose of producing assessable income, then a deduction is allowable provided that the expenditure is:

- incurred by the taxpayer claiming the deduction
- incurred in the year of income that the deduction is claimed, and
- incurred in respect of premises or a depreciating asset.

A 'depreciating asset' is defined in s40-30 to be an asset that has a limited effective life and can reasonably be expected to decline in value over the time it is used. For a detailed definition and exclusions as to what constitutes a depreciating asset refer to 15.010. Capital expenditure cannot be deducted under s25-10. This would include improvements, initial repairs, additions and alterations. However, such expenditure may be deductible by way of decline in value (depreciation) under Division 40 (see 15.000) capital works (15.200), or the small business tax system (10.000).

WHAT IS A 'REPAIR'?

On the face of it, deciding whether a claim can be made under s25-10 should be relatively simple, but in reality there are significant difficulties present when deciding whether or not the 'repair' is of a capital nature. ITAA97 does not define the term 'repair' and therefore it takes on its ordinary meaning. The Shorter Oxford Dictionary states that it is the *... restoration of some material thing, by the removal of some decayed or worn out parts*. In practice, it is often difficult to assess whether expenditure is really for repairs and it is therefore necessary to determine if the expense is:

- an improvement
- the replacement of a subsidiary part or of an entirety, or
- a capital expense in respect of recently acquired property.

Renewal, replacement or reconstruction of the entirety of premises or plant etc. would not be a repair. The same may apply where there is a renewal, replacement or reconstruction of a substantial portion of an asset.

While a repair obviously improves the condition of an item which existed before the repair took place, a repair essentially involves the restoration of a thing to the condition it formerly had without changing its character.

In deciding whether the work carried out is a repair or not, it is more important to decide whether there has been a restoration of efficiency or function rather than an exact repetition of form or material.

For example, if a rental property is repainted because the paint has flaked off, it would not matter that the paint is of a different colour and better quality than the original. Similarly, if a car (used to produce assessable income) has a broken windscreen replaced and the replacement windscreen is only available with a band tint and is laminated (neither feature available with the original windscreen), that is a repair because there has been a restoration of efficiency of function, although not exactly of the same material as the original.

A repair will always be the renewal of a part of capital equipment or a structure, with the portion being replaced being no more than a subordinate part of the whole. For example, a building is considered to be an entirety, rather than a subordinate part, but the components that make up that building are subordinate parts.

The following are listed in TR 97/23, as tests (each applying separately) to identify an entirety:

- *is the property (eg. a chimney) physically, commercially and functionally an inseparable part of an entirety (eg. a factory)?*
- *is the property separately identifiable as a principal item of capital equipment?*
- *is the thing or structure (eg. a timber staircase) an integral part of the entire premises, and is it capable of providing a useful function without regard to any other part of the premises?*
- *is the thing or structure (eg. meters and pumping plant) a separate and distinct item of plant in itself from the thing or structure (eg. a light and power station) to which it supplied something (eg. electric light and power) or an integral part of some larger item of plant?*
- *is the property a unit of 'property' (for depreciation purposes) bearing in mind that, to be such a 'unit', the thing or structure must be 'functionally' separate and independent?*

For example, if a window (consisting of frame and glass) in a block of flats was blown out as a result of a gas explosion and had to be rebuilt, even though the window is restored in its entirety, the restoration would be a repair to the premises. The same principle applies to an item of machinery. In TR 97/23 the Tax Office accepts that if a taxpayer uses a truck for the purposes of producing assessable income or carrying on a business for that purpose, then a deduction is allowed for the cost of replacing the vehicle's engine as it is a functional part of a motor vehicle and the cost of replacing a worn out engine with one of the same description or its modern equivalent returns the vehicle to its former condition without changing its character. This concept is confirmed in ss40-30(4) example 1 which states: A *car is made up of many separate components, but usually a car is a depreciating asset rather than each component.*

However, if for example a petrol engine is replaced with a diesel engine, this would be an improvement because of increased efficiency and likely longevity (see *Case C73* (1953) 3 TBRD). Similarly, if the engine was unserviceable when the truck was purchased and a new engine had to be installed, the cost would be capital.

MAINTENANCE

Maintenance is usually accepted as being for the conservation, preservation, protection or upkeep of an object. Maintenance is about keeping something in a state of good repair rather than actually carrying out repair work.

Expenditure incurred on maintenance of machinery such as greasing and cleaning would not be a repair because the plant is in good working condition and it is done to prevent a future problem and to allow the machine to operate. Such expenditure would usually be deductible under s8-1.

INITIAL REPAIRS

No deduction is allowed to remedy any defects, damage or deterioration existing at the date of acquisition of the asset.

Initial repairs of an asset after its acquisition must be included in the asset's cost base (see 12.094) if:

- the repair is capital in nature, or
- it enhances or improves the value of the asset either immediately or at the time of its disposal.

The basic principle is that the need for repairs existed when the asset was acquired and did not arise from the taxpayer's use, so a deduction is denied. In substance the expenses are part of the cost of acquisition. The denial of the deduction occurs even if the taxpayer was not aware of the need for repairs when the asset was acquired.

CONTROL OF HEALTH RISKS

The Tax Office takes the view in TR 97/23 that *... work done to property in controlling health risks associated with the use of dangerous substances ...* such as asbestos, pesticides, arsenic etc. are not repairs unless the work remedies or makes good defects in or damage or deterioration 'in a mechanical or physical sense of the property'.

Note, however, that a deduction may be allowable under either subdivisions 40C, 40H or 40I as environment protection expenditure.

IMPROVEMENTS

The Tax Office often targets for audit, claims for repairs to rental properties because commonly the 'repairs' being claimed as a deduction are in fact 'improvements'. It is therefore essential to determine if expenditure is a deductible repair, a non-deductible improvement or is subject to a capital works claim under Division 43. Refer to TR 97/23 and *Structural improvements* at 14.250.

In TR 97/23 the Tax Office sets out relevant considerations in deciding whether or not an expense is an improvement:

- whether or not the thing replaced or renewed was a major and important part of the structure of the property
- whether the work performed did more than meet the need for restoration of efficiency of function, bearing in mind that 'repair' involves a restoration of a thing to a condition it formerly had without changing its character
- whether the thing was replaced with a new and better one, and
- whether the new thing has considerable advantages over the old one, including the advantage that it reduces the likelihood of repair bills in the future.

For example, a shop has a wood framed single glass sheet front display window. The glass is broken by a vandal and in the course of replacing it, it is discovered that the frame has rotted and new glass cannot be successfully fitted. If the frame is replaced with the same material and new glass fitted, a deduction would be allowable as a repair. That would also probably apply if the frame is aluminium (as a modern equivalent of wood serving the same function) provided that it does no more than the old frame. However, let us assume that the owner took the opportunity to install a bay window in a 'colonial' style, which she believed would assist in window presentation.

In such a case the work exceeds the need for efficiency and function because it is better than the old window and substantially changes the appearance of the facade. The expense is non-deductible capital expenditure but a deduction may exist for capital works under Division 43 ITAA97 (see 15.200).

The Tax Office also states that landscaping and/or insulating a house are considered improvements rather than repair.

 A fence is repaired by adding new palings, or even replacing all of them. But if posts and rails are also replaced, it is a 'different' fence and the cost is not allowable as a repair (but a replacement of the entirety). Taking out an old shop front, and putting in a newer one, is not a repair.

USE OF DIFFERENT MATERIALS

There is a common belief that a deduction for repairs cannot be allowed if the material used to carry out the 'repair' is not the same as the original. However, this is not always the case. There have been numerous cases where the Board of Review, AAT or the Courts have allowed claims even though the material used in carrying out the repair was entirely different. The test to determine deductibility is whether there has been a ... *restoration of a thing's efficiency of function (without changing its character) rather than exact repetition of form or material.*

A non-deductible repair

In AAT case J24 (77 ATC 222) a wooden fence at the rear of a shop had fallen into a bad state of disrepair and was replaced with a fence made of cement blocks. The new fence constituted a substantial improvement in that it became a retaining wall and required no maintenance. In addition, the AAT considered that because the whole fence was replaced, the work done did not meet the description of a repair to a subsidiary part of a whole, and therefore was not a repair.

REPAIRS TO PROPERTY PREVIOUSLY USED FOR NON-INCOME-PRODUCING PURPOSES

A deduction may also be allowed for repairs if plant has been previously used by the taxpayer for non-income-producing purposes provided the expenditure is incurred on repairs to plant while the property is being used to produce assessable income.

In TR 97/23, the Tax Office accepts that a deduction is allowable (provided the expenditure is not of a capital nature), even though some or all of the deterioration or damage giving rise to the repairs may be attributable to use of the asset by the taxpayer prior to its use for the purpose of producing assessable income.

An employee purchased a second hand van in January 2010 and used it only for private purposes until January 2013 when he became self-employed as a carrier. The van was used only in his business.

In June 2014, the motor of the van became unserviceable and repairs had to be carried out. The account was paid before 30 June 2014. The repairs are deductible under s25-10 as they were incurred when the van was being used only for the purposes of producing assessable income. It does not matter that a portion of the repairs by way of deterioration may relate to when the van was used only for private purposes.

Note that a deduction would not be allowed if it was an initial repair or capital in nature.

REPAIRS TO PROPERTY NOT OWNED BY THE TAXPAYER

Section 25-10 does not require that property be owned by the taxpayer for a claim for repairs to be made. However, the property must be held or used for the purposes of producing assessable income. That means that a lessee of premises or plant can claim a deduction provided that the expenditure is not capital in nature and the property was being held for the purpose of producing assessable income at the time the expenditure was incurred.

Apportionment is required when property is used only partially to produce income.

Also, a taxpayer may deduct an amount paid for failing to comply with a lease obligation to repair premises if the premises were used to produce assessable income (s25-15).

ASSETS USED PARTLY TO PRODUCE INCOME

If an asset is used wholly for income-producing purposes in the income year when the claim is made, the cost of any repair is fully deductible in that year even if the asset was not wholly used to produce assessable income in the earlier years. Alternatively, if the asset is used only partly to produce assessable income in the year of the repair, the claim will be limited to the income-producing use of the asset in that income year.

14.155   LEASING AND HIRE PURCHASE

LEASING

A deduction is typically allowed in the year the expense is incurred for all the costs of obtaining a lease of premises or properties to be used for income-producing purposes. Section 25-20 allows a claim for expenditure incurred by the taxpayer for the preparation, registration and stamping of a lease, or an assignment or surrender of a lease, of property (that is to be, or has been) held, to the extent it is for the purpose of producing assessable income. Generally this is regarded as applying to leases of premises, but 'property' could apply to plant and equipment also. Balloon payments (or up-front deposits) may be deductible (see TR 98/15) but the claim will be subject to the Prepayment rules (see 14.170).

In addition, s25-20(2) provides that if the property has been, or will be, used only partly for the purpose of producing assessable income, an apportionment is required so that the expenditure is deductible only to the extent that it has been or will be so used. ATO ID 2012/36 clarifies that the phrase 'will use' is a reference to actual use rather than the intended use of the property.

HIRE PURCHASE

Before making a claim for lease expenses, it is important to determine whether those payments are deductible rental expenses or an arrangement to buy or retain the particular asset after the lease is terminated.

Income Tax ruling IT 28 sets out the Tax Office's view and guidelines for determining whether payments are deductible as lease payments, or are in substance consideration for the sale of the goods purported to be leased. In the latter case the payments would largely be capital in nature and non-deductible for income tax purposes (note that a finance or interest charge may still be deductible with payments of these types). The capital cost of the particular item may then be considered for depreciation.

The Tax Office considers that if the arrangement confers on the lessee a right which, if the lessee chose to exercise the option, would have the property in the goods pass to the lessee from the lessor at any point of time, this would for all practical purposes constitute a contract for sale.

Similarly, the Tax Office would not regard as a normal commercial lease an arrangement whereby at the termination of the lease the lessee is permitted or enabled to retain the use of the goods. If the agreement contains provisions that would enable disposal of the goods at termination of the lease other than at a public auction, this would raise the presumption that the lessee has rights of purchase.

A residual value which does not reasonably reflect market value in leases of relatively short term (eg. up to five years) would raise a strong presumption that the transaction was not an ordinary commercial lease.

The following table from TD 93/142 (as modified by ATO ID 2002/1004), illustrates the acceptable minimum residual values for various categories of plant and machinery (classified according to effective life in years) at the end of leases ranging from one to five years. Different residual values may be acceptable based on particular circumstances.

Minimum residual values – percentage of cost: Plant and machinery classified according to effective lives in years						
Term of lease	5	6.66	8	10	13.3	20
1st year	60.00	63.75	65.63	67.50	68.50	70.00
2nd year	45.00	52.50	56.25	60.00	62.50	65.00
3rd year	30.00	41.25	46.88	52.50	55.00	60.00
4th year	15.00	30.00	37.50	45.00	50.00	55.00
5th year	nil	18.75	28.13	37.50	45.00	50.00

Expenditure incurred on items of property (including plant or equipment) under hire purchase agreements is deductible, however special rules apply.

While the hirer does not become the legal owner of the property until such time as the final payment is made, for tax purposes the transaction is treated as a sale of property by the financier to the buyer financed by a loan from the financier to the buyer. The buyer would be considered the 'holder' of the asset for the purposes of s40-40 and therefore entitled to deductions for the decline in value of the asset. The rules covering hire purchase and similar transactions are set out in Division 240.

Based on the business use of the asset, the buyer is entitled to deduct the interest component of the hire purchase payment. The holder of the asset is similarly entitled to claim depreciation for the decline in value of the asset (see from 15.000 and special rules from 15.800). There are also GST implications (see from 23.110, 23.230 and 23.300).

14.160 BAD DEBTS

The debt has to be more than doubtful and certain conditions must be satisfied (see TR 92/18). There is no claim for mere provision of doubtful debts and a debt is not necessarily bad merely because time has passed without payment being made.

The deduction is available under s25-35 for a debt that is written-off as a bad debt in the income year, if:

- it was included in the taxpayer's assessable income in the current or former income years, or
- it is in respect of money lent in the ordinary course of a business of lending money by a taxpayer who carries on that business.

To claim a tax deduction, the debt must:

- be in existence (eg. no deed of release has been executed)
- be bad, and
- be written-off as a bad debt in the year of income the deduction is claimed.

If a debt is 'bad' based on a commercial judgment, it is also bad for s25-35 purposes. It is not essential that a creditor take all legally available steps to recover the debt.

A debt is considered to be 'bad' if:

- the debtor has died leaving no, or insufficient, assets to meet the debt
- the debtor cannot be traced and the creditor cannot find the existence of (or location of) assets against which action could be taken
- the debt has become statute barred and the debtor is relying on this defence (or it is reasonable to assume so) for non payment
- the debtor is a company in liquidation or receivership and there are insufficient funds to pay the whole debt, or the part claimed as a bad debt, or
- if, on an objective view of the facts or probabilities existing at the time, there is little or no chance of the debt (or part of it) being recovered.

A debt will generally be accepted as 'bad' (depending on the particular facts of the case) if the taxpayer has taken all reasonable steps to try to recover the debt and not simply written it off as bad.

 If all or part of a debt earlier written-off is recovered, the amount recovered must be shown as income in the year it is received.

PARTIAL DEBT 'WRITE-OFFS'

The entire debt does not have to be written-off to get a deduction under s25-35. A deduction may be obtained for the part which is bad and written-off. A partial debt would be deductible only if and when it is found that the remaining debt could not be recovered from the debtor. The same tests for deductibility apply as for the whole of the debt.

DEDUCTION ALLOWED

A deduction for a bad debt is allowable in the year in which the debt is written-off. The debt must actually be written-off before the income year ends, subject to the arrangements outlined in tax ruling TR 92/18. Making a general provision is not appropriate. It is not sufficient to decide to write off the debt after the income year ends, such as when the annual accounts are prepared.

A deduction is allowed if (TR 92/18):

- a board meeting authorises the writing-off of the debt and there is a physical recording of the debt and of the board's decision before the end of the income year, but the writing off in the books of account occurs after year's end, and
- a written recommendation by the financial controller to write off a debt is agreed to by the managing director in writing before year end, followed by a physical writing off after year end.

CLAIMS UNDER S8-1

If a deduction for a bad debt is not allowable under s25-35, a deduction may, in limited circumstances, be available under s8-1. To obtain a s8-1 deduction it would be necessary to demonstrate that the loss was incurred in the course of carrying on business for the purposes of deriving assessable income. Refer: (1968) 14 CTBR (NS) Case 80. Note that the debt would be subject to the negative limbs of s8-1 in this case.

COMPANIES

Companies wishing to claim bad debts must meet stringent tests laid down to avoid 'trafficking' in bad debts (ss25-35(5) and Subdivision 165). These tests require that a company satisfy either a more than 50% continuity of ownership test or a same business test, comparing the year in which the deduction is claimed with the one in which the debt was incurred (see also 6.400). In addition, a deduction is reduced if a debt is forgiven and the debtor and creditor are companies under common ownership and have agreed that the creditor forgo the deduction to a specified amount (s245-90 Schedule 2C ITAA36) (See 6.600).

NOTE: A company cannot deduct a debt that it writes off as bad on the last day of the year if the debt was incurred on that day (ss165-120(3)).

TRUSTS

Certain trusts cannot deduct a bad debt under s25 if there has been either a change of ownership or control or an abnormal trading in the units of the trust (Divisions 266 and 267 ITAA36; s25-35) (see 7.900).

Any bad debt for which an amount is recouped may be included in assessable income.

14.165 LOSS BY THEFT

Losses incurred by theft or stealing by an employee or agent are allowable unless committed by a person who is only employed for private or domestic purposes (s25-45). The operation of s25-45 was considered in detail by the Federal Court in *FCT v Lean* (2009) FCA 490.

14.166 ILLEGAL ACTIVITIES

Effective for expenditure incurred from 30 April 2005, deductions are denied for losses and outgoings to the extent that they were incurred in the furtherance of, or directly in relation to, activities where the taxpayer is convicted of an indictable offence. Similar expenditure will also be excluded from the taxpayer's cost base or reduced cost base for CGT purposes.

NOTE: In a situation where the taxpayer is undertaking a lawful business but is convicted of an illegal activity while carrying out that business, deductions will only be denied for expenditure which directly relates to entering into and carrying out the actual illegal activity. If the expenditure would have been incurred in any case, regardless of the illegal activity, then deductions will still be allowed.

14.167 BOATS

Deductions for ownership and operation of boats were generally not available unless the boat was held as trading stock or otherwise used for business purposes (s26-50). Merely providing the boat to an operator for a fee is not necessarily the carrying on of a business, see TR 2003/4 for details. Deductions are not prevented where a fringe benefit is provided. For related capital allowance claims, see 15.010.

RULES FROM 1 JULY 2007

From 1 July 2007 a deduction is allowed in respect of boats if the taxpayer holds a boat as trading stock, or uses a boat (or holds it) mainly for letting it out on hire in the ordinary course of a business. A deduction is also allowed if a taxpayer uses the boat (or holds it) mainly for transporting the public or goods for payment in the ordinary course of business, or otherwise using the boat for a purpose that is essential to the efficient conduct of a business being carried on. There are also deductions allowed for provision of fringe benefits in relation to boats.

Where none of the above exclusions apply, the changes operate to 'quarantine' each year's losses from using or holding boats so that they apply to the following income years where there is a profit from the activity in those following years. That is, the quarantined amount/s can be set off against future otherwise taxable income from the boat. The quarantined losses can also be used to reduce a capital gain from a CGT event happening in relation to a boat. Should a capital loss be made on a boat, the reduced cost base will not include amounts which s26-47 quarantines.

Sue is the owner of a boat and leases it to a charter operator. In the first year of operation she has $80,000 in deductions relating to income-earning use of the boat (though not qualifying as business use) in regard to interest, depreciation, running costs and management fees. Income of $50,000 is obtained in that year from leasing the boat. The result is that a loss of $30,000 is quarantined and carried forward.

In the second year, Sue has $100,000 of boat deductions and no income from the boat. The amount quarantined will now be $130,000 and can be carried forward.

In the third year, Sue has $50,000 of boat deductions and $140,000 income from the boat. Therefore, Sue can claim $140,000 in deductions (ie. matching the income earned in the third year), and the amount of $40,000 will be quarantined and carried forward for future use against assessable income from the boat and/or reducing any capital gain from sale of the boat.

Fred operates a boat chartering business and has $100,000 in boat deductions for the year. The income from the boat for that year is $50,000. As Fred is actually conducting a business, the $50,000 loss is not quarantined and may be offset against other assessable income for the year.

14.168   LEISURE FACILITIES

A leisure facility is land, a building, or part of a building or other structure, that is used (or held for use) for holidays or recreation (eg. tennis courts, golf courses, holiday cottages, swimming pools, and related buildings). Deductions are restricted by s26-50 unless certain conditions are met: ss26-50(3) and (4). Deductions are not prevented where a fringe benefit is provided. For depreciation see ss40-25(3) and (4). There may also be Division 7A ITAA36 implications if these types of assets are held in a company and no payment is made for use of the assets by shareholders (or associates) of the company (see 6.300).

14.169   SUPPORT PAYMENTS TO SUBSIDIARY ENTITIES

A support payment is a payment made by a parent entity to a subsidiary in circumstances where the payment is objectively made because the subsidiary has made a loss or losses or have not been sufficiently profitable.

NOTE: A support payment does not include a payment by the parent entity by way of a genuine loan to the subsidiary.

According to TD 2014/14, support payments are not deductible for the partner entity under s8-1 as they are capital in nature. Instead, they are included in the cost base and reduced cost base of the parent's investment in the subsidiary and are therefore not deductible under s40-880.

14.170 PREPAYMENT OF EXPENSES

The treatment of prepaid deductible expenditure varies depending upon the status of the taxpayer, the nature of the expense, and if the taxpayer is a Small Business Entity (SBE) (see Chapter 10).

As a general rule, prepaid expenditure must be apportioned over the period in which the relevant service is provided. Special rules apply to tax avoidance arrangements, non-business taxpayers, small business entity taxpayers and forestry plantations. The prepayment rules do not apply to excluded expenditure.

EXCLUSIONS

The following expenses are excluded from the prepaid expenditure rules and are deductible in the year that they are incurred:

- amounts less than $1,000 (GST exclusive amount – see ATO ID 2004/398)
- amounts required to be paid by Court order or Government legislation, and
- payments under a contract for service (payments of salary or wages).

Expenditure is also excluded from the prepayment rules if it is of a capital, private or domestic nature, or is incurred in meeting an obligation incurred on or before 11.45am on 21 September 1999.

SBE TAXPAYERS AND INDIVIDUALS INCURRING NON-BUSINESS EXPENDITURE

For SBE taxpayers (see Chapter 10) and individual taxpayers incurring non-business expenditure (eg. employees, investment and property owners) a 12-month rule allows an immediate deduction for prepayments where:

- the payment is incurred for a period of service, referred to as the Eligible Service Period (ESP) not exceeding 12-months, and
- the period of service ends in the next income year.

Where the ESP does not meet these requirements, the deduction for the prepaid expenditure is claimed proportionately over each income year during which the services are to be provided, to a maximum period of ten years.

Brownlow owns a rental property that is negatively geared. He is not carrying on a business activity and his income tax year ends on 30 June. On 30 November 2013 he made an interest only payment of $7,000 in relation to a loan used to finance the acquisition of the rental property.

If the prepayment was for the period 1 December 2013 to 1 November 2014, Brownlow is entitled to an immediate deduction of the $7,000, because the ESP was not longer than 12 months (it was for 11 months) and the ESP ends before 30 June 2015 (end of the income year). If the prepayment was for the period 1 December 2014 to 31 March 2015, the ESP is longer than 12 months and the prepaid expenditure needs to be apportioned over the ESP. In this case the deductions would be:

- *year ended 30 June 2014: $7,000 x 211 days divided by 484 days (1 Dec 13 to 30 June 14) = $3,052, and*
- *year ended 30 June 2015: $7,000 x 273 days divided by 484 days (1 July 14 to 31 Mar 15) = $3,948.*

OTHER TAXPAYERS

For all other taxpayers who are not small business entity taxpayers or individuals incurring non-business expenditure, there is no immediate deduction for prepaid expenditure and the expenditure must be apportioned over the eligible service period. The deduction is claimed proportionately over each income year to a maximum of ten years.

PREPAID PLANTATION FORESTRY EXPENDITURE

From 1 July 2007, Division 394 allows initial participants in a forestry managed investment scheme an immediate deduction for contributions provided certain conditions are satisfied. They may be summarised as:

- the existence of a reasonable expectation that at least 70% of contributions will be spent on direct forestry expenditure over the life of the project
- the trees must be established within 18 months of the end of the year in which the contribution is made
- the initial participants holding their investments for a minimum of four years.

Tax Laws Amendment (2010 Measures No. 1) Act 2010 introduced amendments to ensure that failing the four year rule does not lead to the denial of a previously allowed deduction, where:

- a capital gains tax (CGT) event happens because of circumstances genuinely outside the initial investor's control, and
- the initial investor could not have reasonably anticipated this CGT event happening, at the time they acquired the forestry interest.

FLOWCHART OF PREPAID EXPENSES

The following flowchart sets out the rules for prepaid expenditure.

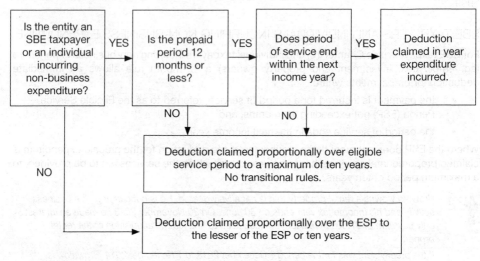

SOME EXPENSES ARE NOT ALLOWABLE

Section 82KJ ITAA36 denies a deduction where expenditure has the following attributes:

- it was incurred under (or in connection with) a tax avoidance arrangement, and
- it exceeds (at the time it was incurred) what was reasonable having regard to the benefits hoped to be obtained, and
- the taxpayer (or 'associate', see 25.002) has acquired an asset, or might reasonably be expected to acquire an asset, at a cost which is less than that which would have been incurred had the advance payment not been made.

SOME DEDUCTIONS ARE DEFERRED

Where expenditure incurred by a taxpayer is to an 'associate', s82KK ITAA36 provides that:

- if a deduction will be allowable to the taxpayer in respect of the expenditure, but
- the amount will not be included in the assessable income of the associate until a subsequent year,

the deduction will be deemed to have been incurred by the taxpayer in the year the relevant amount is included in the assessable income of the associate.

INTEREST

Interest payments (or those of a nature similar to interest) made in return for making available loan funds, will be for the period of time over which the interest is payable, not for the period of the loan.

A loan agreement is for ten years with monthly repayments of principal and interest. However, the borrower chooses to make 36 payments at the start of the loan. The deduction allowable for the interest component of the advance payment is spread over 36 months, not the full ten year period.

RENT OR LEASE PAYMENTS

Similar to payments of interest, payments of rent, leasing or similar payments are taken to relate to the period over which the payments are to be made, and not over the period of the lease.

IF INITIAL LEASE PAYMENTS ARE HIGH

If the initial lease payments are high compared with later payments required under the lease, this may indicate that the payments are capital and not deductible, unless it merely reflects the decrease in value of the item over the specific period covered by the payment, which should not exceed 13 months. Also, if plant is leased for a short initial period at a high rate of rental, with a provision for renewal at a nominal rental for a further period that corresponds with the remaining useful life of the asset, this would indicate that the lease payments are capital in nature.

 If the lessee has equity in an asset by way of an initial deposit or down payment, the Tax Office will generally not consider that the arrangement constitutes a lease (see TR 98/15).

LEASING BALLOON PAYMENT

A balloon payment on revenue account covering a period not exceeding 13 months which reflects a decrease in the market value of the asset over the period covered by the payment will be deductible when incurred. Detailed commentary from the Tax Office regarding the tax treatment of lease payments is contained in TR 98/15.

INSURANCE PREMIUMS

Claims for insurance premiums are deductible when incurred, however the prepayment rules may apply to apportion this expense based on the period over which the insurance cover is provided, even though the insurer's obligations on claims may be met after the end of the insurance period.

DISCHARGE/TRANSFER OF RIGHTS

If expenditure which has not been claimed as a deduction is brought forward, it will be deductible in the year the taxpayer discharges the prepaid agreement or transfers the rights to a third party. However, the prepaid expense provisions apply independently to expenditure incurred by the person acquiring the remaining rights.

Provided the expense is allowable under s8-1, prorating will apply where the necessary conditions are fulfilled.

TRANSFER OF PARTNERSHIP RIGHTS

If rights under a prepaid agreement are transferred on the formation, reconstitution or dissolution of a partnership, the person or partnership holding the rights after the change will be entitled to the deductions that would have been available to the person or partnership that incurred the expenditure. However, at least one of the original partners must have an interest in the rights after the partnership change. A proportionate deduction will be allowed in the year of change. Note that the negative limb of s8-1 may apply to limit a deduction in this case.

PREPAYMENT OF TRADING STOCK

Deductions for prepayment of trading stock can be denied in some circumstances.

Deductions will not be available unless the goods purchased are reflected in either:

* trading stock sold or destroyed during the financial year, or
* trading stock on hand at the end of that financial year (see from 14.230).

TAX SHELTERS

The tax shelter provisions deny an immediate deduction for certain prepaid expenditure incurred in respect of a tax shelter arrangement. Broadly, the deduction is spread over the period to which the service relates.

Tax shelter arrangements are those where all significant aspects of the management of the arrangement during that income year are conducted by people (the manager) other than the taxpayer and either more than one taxpayer participates in the arrangement or the manager, (or associate) manages similar arrangements on behalf of others.

Refer: s82KZME ITAA36 for the definition of 'tax shelter' arrangements and details of the five exceptions to the general rule.

14.178 LEASE PREMIUMS AND IMPROVEMENTS BY LESSEES

An outgoing paid as a lease premium is usually a non-deductible capital outgoing. Depreciation deductions may be available in respect of plant owned by a lessee and installed and used by the lessee for income-producing purposes (see 15.010). A deduction can be claimed for construction expenditure for capital works incurred by a lessee or holder of quasi-ownership rights (see 15.200).

14.180 INTEREST ON MONEY BORROWED TO PAY TAX

If the taxpayer carries on a business, a deduction can be claimed for interest on money borrowed for the business, even if borrowings are used to pay tax (see IT 2582). Contrast this with the situation for partners below.

PARTNERS OR INDIVIDUALS NOT IN BUSINESS

Section 8-1 denies a deduction for borrowings of a partner to fund their individual income tax liability even if the assessable income earned by the partnership was derived from a business, if in the view of the Tax Office the tax liability is a personal expense, regardless of the source of the taxpayer's income. The Tax Office view is that the interest expense incurred to fund the individual partner's income tax liability lacks a sufficient nexus with the earning of assessable income of the partnership business (see TD 2000/24). The same situation arises for individual taxpayers who do not run a business.

14.185 CONNECTING ELECTRICITY

Taxpayers who are carrying on business or other income producing activities can claim deductions pursuant to the uniform capital allowance provisions for the costs incurred in connecting electricity to premises that are used (in whole or in part) for income-producing purposes, or to carry on a business, provided the requirements of Division 40 are satisfied.

14.190 NEGATIVE GEARING

Negative gearing is the term given when interest paid on funds borrowed to finance acquisition of an income-generating investment (eg. a rental property, shares which generate dividends, or any other investment that generates assessable income) exceeds income received in the short-term, ie. produces a tax loss.

There is no limit on interest deductions allowed if the investment is a passive investment (eg. property, financial instruments, shares etc.) provided the borrowed funds were applied to the acquisition of the income-producing asset. Losses incurred on rental properties or other income-producing investments can be offset against other assessable income, thereby reducing the amount of tax payable.

In 2014-15 income year, a taxpayer has a net salary (after tax deductions) of $50,000 and borrowed $102,000 at 10% interest pa to buy a rental property. Rental received for the current year is $6,240 (ie. after deductible expenses other than interest).

Taxable salary	*$50,000.00*
plus net rental receipts	*$6,240.00*
Total assessable income	*$56,240.00*
less interest deduction	*($10,200.00)*
Taxable income	*$46,040.00*
Tax payable (excluding Medicare)	*$6,510*

The tax payable (excluding Medicare) on the $50,000 net salary without the negatively geared rental property would otherwise be $7,797

DEDUCTIBILITY OF INTEREST

For interest to be fully deductible the property or other investment to which the borrowed funds relate, must be used for an income-producing purpose.

Some of the principles relevant in determining the deductibility of interest are contained in TR 95/25:

* the interest must have a sufficient connection with the income earning operations or activities if the expenses are to be deductible under s8-1
* the character of the interest will generally be determined by the use of the borrowed funds
* interest on borrowings will not continue to be deductible if the borrowings cease to be employed for some assessable income earning activity (but see 14.130), and
* interest on a new loan will be deductible if the new loan is used to repay an existing loan, which at the time of the second loan, was used to derive assessable income.

The loss from a rental property must be shared according to the legal interest of the owners (except in situations where there is sufficient evidence to establish that the equitable interest is different to the legal interest). The legal owner of the property is recorded on the deed of title.

 Taxation Ruling TR 98/22 (see also TR 98/22A) which deals with certain fully drawn loan products deliberately structured to increase the level of interest deductions, and TR 2000/2 which deals with line of credit and redraw facilities, should be considered when arranging finance for the acquisition of income producing property.

DIFFERENT LOAN FACILITIES

LINE OF CREDIT FACILITIES

There are a number of different facilities available. The facility may operate with one account that is used for all draw downs or alternatively, it may be divided into a number of sub-accounts by agreement between the lender and the borrower. Funds may be drawn down from each sub-account up to an allocated portion of the overall credit limit.

Interest is fully deductible where funds drawn down on an investment sub-account continue to be used exclusively for an income-producing purpose. Interest is not deductible where funds drawn down on a private sub-account are used for a non-income-producing purpose.

The original application of the borrowed funds will not determine deductibility where funds borrowed under a line of credit facility have been repaid and subsequently reapplied to a different use, eg. upon sale of an asset purchased with borrowed funds. In that case the new application of the borrowed funds will determine the deductibility of interest. Interest will be deductible under s8-1 to the extent that it is incurred on that part of the outstanding borrowed money used at that time for an income-producing purpose.

Where a taxpayer has a mixed purpose sub-account, interest must be apportioned between the income-producing and non-income-producing purposes. Apportionment must be made on a fair and reasonable basis.

Any repayment of principal is applied proportionally against the outstanding balance of amounts applied to income-producing and non-income-producing purposes respectively, at the time the repayment is made except **refinancing mixed purpose debt.** A taxpayer may choose to refinance a debt outstanding on a mixed purpose sub-account by borrowing an equivalent amount under two separate accounts or sub-accounts. If the sums borrowed under those two separate accounts are equivalent to the respective income-producing and non-income-producing parts of the existing outstanding debt, the Tax Office will accept that interest accrued on the debt incurred in refinancing the income-producing portion of the mixed purpose debt will be deductible.

The Tax Office allows interest to be apportioned, where it would normally accrue on the loan on a daily basis, on the following monthly basis:

$$[(A + B) \text{ divided by } (C + D)] \times 100$$

where:

* A = opening balance (beginning of month) of outstanding principal used for income-producing purposes

- B = closing balance (end of month) of outstanding principal used for income-producing purposes
- C = opening balance of total outstanding principal, and
- D = closing balance of total outstanding principal.

NOTE: The closing balance for one month is the opening balance for the next month.

Where a taxpayer makes repayments over and above the required minimum payment and the line of credit facility comprises one mixed purpose sub-account only, the taxpayer cannot choose to notionally allocate the repayments to a particular portion of the total debt, eg. the non-income-producing portion.

SPLIT LOANS AND LINKED LOANS

Split loans and linked loans generally involve financing arrangements that allow a taxpayer to combine the repayments associated with separate loans. The loans would typically be used for financing the simultaneous acquisition of private and income-producing assets. Taxpayers utilising this type of facility should ensure that the arrangements are not structured in the same manner as occurred in *Hart's case.*

In that case the Court held that the compounding interest on a split loan that was used to finance the taxpayer's home as well as an income-producing property was not deductible due to the operation of Part IVA (the anti-avoidance rules) as the dominant purpose in setting up the structure was the obtaining of a tax benefit by way of increased interest deductions.

LOAN ACCOUNT OFFSET FACILITY

Where the facility constitutes an acceptable 'loan account offset arrangement' (as prescribed in TR 93/6), the availability of an interest deduction where funds are withdrawn for a private purpose differs to that of a line of credit facility.

According to TR 93/6, under a loan account offset facility arrangement, the borrower typically operates two accounts:

- a loan account, and
- a deposit account.

There is no entitlement to receive interest payments or payments in the nature of interest on the amounts credited to the deposit account. The reduction in the loan account interest is achieved by offsetting the balances of the two accounts.

As a general rule, the Commissioner considers that a taxpayer with an acceptable loan account offset arrangement with dual accounts is entitled to claim a deduction for the full amount of interest whilst the loan is used wholly for income producing purposes.

Any reduction to the interest payable would typically not be assessable as no amount of interest has been received or credited to the borrower (see PBR 50720).

Significantly, in a number of private rulings (see PBR 80150, 19859), the Commissioner accepts that interest of the loan account will continue to remain fully deductible if funds are withdrawn from the 'deposit account' and used for non-income producing purposes.

The Commissioner's rationale for this position is that:

- depositing funds into the deposit account will decrease the interest payable on the loan account but will not decrease of the balance of the loan account, and
- withdrawing funds from the deposit account will increase the interest payable on the loan account but again, will not impact the loan account balance.

 From a tax perspective, the offset account arrangement provides a more flexible and favourable tax outcome where funds are accessed for private use. Essentially, taxpayers will need to evaluate these facilities in line with their commercial objectives.

TRUSTS AND COMPANIES

Negative gearing is usually only an attractive proposition if the company or trust has sufficient other income to enable the losses to be applied to that other income. Losses in a trust or company must be carried forward; unit holders, discretionary beneficiaries and shareholders cannot benefit from those losses (see 7.900).

Where a taxpayer has a discretionary trust and would like to negatively gear an asset (ie. an investment property), make sure the trust receives sufficient other income to ensure the losses are utilised, as a family trust cannot distribute losses on an annual basis.

The deductibility of the losses in future years will be dependent on the company or trust satisfying the requirements of Division 165 or 166 in the case of companies and Schedule 2F ITAA36 in the case of trusts. If a trust has franking credits which it is unable to distribute to beneficiaries, those credits will be lost.

14.200 TRADING STOCK

Costs of acquiring trading stock are usually deductible, including the cost of the stock itself, transport, storage, insurance, packaging, taxes and government charges (eg. inspection fees). Expenses incurred or deemed to have been incurred to purchase trading stock are not considered to be capital (s70-25). See rules for primary producers from 21.260 and 21.400. There are separate rules for those who have elected to adopt the 'small business entity' regime in Division 328 (see from 10.000).

WHAT IS TRADING STOCK?

The definition in s70-10 is:

... trading stock includes anything produced, manufactured or acquired that is held for purposes of manufacture, sale or exchange in the ordinary course of the business and live stock.

For livestock see 21.400.

Items which become part of articles produced for sale or further manufacture (raw materials, containers, labels, etc.) are trading stock; see TR 98/7.

It also includes anything that is held for the purpose of manufacture, sale or exchange and includes containers, labels, packing or binding materials (paper, string, glue, etc.) and accessories held by the business are trading stock if:

- the materials form part of the product manufactured, sold or exchanged, or
- the materials are held for the purposes of sale, or to be provided to the customer as part of the core goods sold in the course of business (TR 98/7).

In either of the cases above, ownership of the materials transfers to the purchaser.

Materials and spare parts held by persons carrying on a business providing service for reward (eg. a builder, tradesperson or repairer) may be trading stock. For details of the circumstances see TR 98/7.

The definition of trading stock also encompasses items which were originally acquired for non-trading purposes but became trading stock (eg. a farm which is entered into a land development project. In this case the stock is valued under s70-30).

Special rules apply where the taxpayer dies (see 14.230).

Racehorses kept solely or mainly for resale or to sell their offspring are trading stock; see from 21.490.

Taxpayers may choose between four methods to value their trading stock at the end of the year of income (see below).

Matters relating to trading stock are specifically covered by Division 70.

Section 70-35 states that where a taxpayer carries on any business, the value of all trading stock on hand at the beginning and the end of the income year, must be taken into account to determine taxable income.

If the value of all trading stock on hand at the end of the income year exceeds the value at the beginning of that year, the excess is assessable income (see s70-35(2)).

When the opening value of all trading stock on hand at the beginning of the income year exceeds the closing value, the excess is an allowable deduction (see s70-35(3)). The value of trading stock on hand must include any which is in transit but owned by the taxpayer.

NOT INCLUDED IN TRADING STOCK

The following are not trading stock (s70-10):

- financial arrangements under the TOFA rules (referred to as 'Division 230 financial arrangements'), and
- CGT assets owned by a complying superannuation fund, complying ADF or a PST, or which are complying superannuation/FHSA assets of a life insurance company, which are subject to capital treatment under Subdiv 275-B (managed investment trusts) (applicable in relation to CGT assets owned after 7.30 pm, by legal time in the ACT, on 10 May 2011, unless owned and held as trading stock before that time).

In addition, trading stock does not include:

- standing or growing crops or trees
- fruit still attached to the tree (included as trading stock only when actually harvested or picked)
- fodder purchased or harvested for 'own use' by the farmer
- any animals used as beasts of burden or which do not work in a primary production business
- tobacco leaf on hand but not ready for sale (it is not a commodity and therefore not trading stock (TR 94/9)): tobacco leaf ready for sale is divested in a statutory tobacco marketing board and therefore not trading stock of the grower
- land (eg. a farm) not originally acquired for resale where the land is not returned into a business or profit-making undertaking but is subdivided for later sale (see s70-30)
- stocks of spare parts held for the repair or maintenance of your own plant. This does not apply if the taxpayer is in the business of selling the particular spare parts: deductibility will usually be in the year used
- building materials purchased by a building contractor for the purpose of fulfilling a building contract on another person's land
- new plant or equipment held on standby to replace existing plant
- goods used to earn income by hire or rental not for manufacture, sale or exchange (eg. rental videos of a video lending library). (Under the ITAA97 when items which move between trading stock and stock used for other purposes, the items are deemed to be acquired if disposed of at cost. When these items become trading stock, the effect is the amount is added to assessable income. When the item is used for other purposes, it is deemed to have been bought back for the same amount. That amount will be the cost for depreciation purposes)
- consumable aids to manufacture (eg. cleaning or bleaching agents, sandpaper)
- goods in transit where a bill of lading has not been made out so the goods are not yet legally owned by the taxpayer (see below), and
- materials or spare parts supplied to customers, but only as a minor and incidental aspect of providing services for the customer (TR 98/8).

TRADING STOCK IN TRANSIT

Whether a deduction is available to a business for trading stock acquired for an income year depends on whether the trading stock is 'on-hand'. The interpretation of the term 'trading stock on-hand' was established by the Courts and has been considered by the Commissioner of Taxation (the Commissioner) in tax ruling IT 2670.

The generally accepted proposition is that goods are trading stock 'on hand' where the taxpayer is in a position to dispose of the goods. This is the case notwithstanding that they have not been physically delivered to the taxpayer's business premises or outlet (IT 2670). This is referred to as having 'dispositive power'.

This proposition is supported by the Full Federal Court decision in *All States Frozen Foods Pty Ltd v. FC of T (1990) 21 FCR 457*. In that decision, the taxpayer was found to be the owner of goods en-route even though it did not have physical possession because they were on board vessels at sea at the time.

The Court reasoned that because the taxpayer had accepted the bills of lading (see below for discussion), they were considered to be its owners as:

- the goods were held 'at risk'
- they were entitled to possession of them, and
- they had control over them.

Where goods are in transit, the passing of the goods to the purchaser is determined by the intention of the parties to the transaction (see IT 2670). Those intentions, according to the Commissioner, are reflected by:

- the contract terms (including implied terms)
- the conduct of the parties (including their practice over a course of dealing), and
- the circumstances of the case (including commercial practice in that industry and assumption of risk).

Moreover, in TD 93/138, the Tax Office states that there is no hard and fast rule for when there is a presently existing liability in respect of the purchase of trading stock in transit. There is often no presently existing liability until the purchaser either:

- accepts the shipping documents (bill of lading), or
- accepts or endorses the financial documents relating to the liability for payment of the goods (unless conditional upon further actions by the supplier).

STOCKTAKING

A physical count is generally accepted as the most accurate method of determining the value of stock on hand. It also gives an estimate of the spoilage or theft of stock.

In TD 93/125, the Tax Office states that while the Act does not stipulate it is necessary to do a physical stocktake, in the majority of cases, it is the only way to arrive at an accurate value. It is not acceptable to guess the value of trading stock or estimate the value based on a stocktake of an earlier year.

In some businesses, purchases and sales of trading stock are recorded in a perpetual system ie. a continuous record of stock on hand is kept. This is adjusted if physical stocktakes during the year show discrepancies caused by losses or errors in the system. If such a record is properly maintained, and:

- stocktakes are done regularly during the year, and
- all items of stock are counted at least once during the year

the value of stock on hand can be determined without the need to complete a year end stocktake. It is important that stocktakes are carried out appropriately. The accuracy of stocktakes and the methods of valuing stock for tax purposes will typically form part of a tax audit.

SBEs can choose not to conduct a stocktake (and account for changes in the value of your trading stock) if there is a difference of $5,000 or less between:

- the value of your stock on hand at the start of the income year, and
- a reasonable estimate of the value of your stock on hand at the end of the income year.

CHOOSING HOW TO VALUE TRADING STOCK

You must show on the 'income side' of your return, the value of trading stock at the end of the income year. That closing stock value is in effect added to the sales figure for the year, and then a deduction is allowed for the cost of trading stock on purchases: the result is the gross profit on sale of goods.

 Choose the method of valuation carefully because the gross profit can be altered depending on the method used. The valuation method adopted can be a useful tool to bring forward or delay the taxing of income and/or claiming surplus deductions and carry forward losses. If cost price is adopted, the taxable gross profit includes the difference between sales and the cost of the stock sold. Whereas if market value is adopted, the effect is to tax a profit which is computed as if all of the stock on hand was sold.

There are three primary methods given in s70-45. Any method may be chosen for each item of stock. A fourth method may be used if an election is made and the value is reasonable. If adopting a mixture of valuing methods, be sure to prove the closing stock value shown was properly based. The available methods are:

1. cost price to the taxpayer
2. replacement value at the end of the year
3. market selling value, and
4. a lower value where that is reasonable due to obsolescence or other special circumstances (s70-50).

Adopting 'cost price' is the usual way of valuing stock, because it reflects what was the profit on the business done during the year; but here are some comments on the various methods. Also, see below for entities of $10 million turnover.

1. COST PRICE

Sometimes it is not possible to identify the actual cost of the item left on the shelf, unless the owner of the store includes the cost price in a code attached to the article.

Any increase in the stock value above the actual historical cost has the effect of increasing your taxable income in the current income year and correspondingly reduces the profit to be taxed when the item is eventually sold. With quick moving items, this may not matter, but being legally able to defer any book profit until a slow moving item is sold would be a distinct advantage.

All overheads should be included in the cost of production. For work-in-progress and manufactured goods, full absorption costing must be used when 'cost price' is adopted (see IT 2350). Retailers and wholesalers are both to use absorption costing when valuing stock at cost. The specific requirements and costing is found in TR 2006/8. For taxpayers with an annual turnover of less than $10 million, a reasonable estimate of overheads to be absorbed is acceptable.

The Tax Office will not accept the direct cost method (after the decision in the *Philip Morris case*). Absorption costing includes the cost of labour and materials, plus an appropriate proportion of variable and fixed overheads, (eg. power, rates, rent and factory administration costs); see IT 2350 and TR 2006/8.

Set out in IT 2350 is the Tax Office approach to determining the cost price of trading stock on hand at the end of a year of income where the taxpayer is a manufacturer.

The Tax Office view is that the absorption cost method is the correct one for determining the cost of trading stock on hand at the end of a year in a manufacturing business. Absorption costing deals with costs of materials and direct labour and also indirect costs such as factory overheads. Relevant will be material costs, direct labour and production overhead costs (variable such as light and power, and fixed such as factory rent). Only the part of total production overheads costs relating to manufacturing operations should be absorbed into product cost.

IT 2350 deals in detail with what items are included in production overheads costs. For the Tax Office view on use of the cost basis for taxpayers including consolidated groups with gross turnover of $10 million or more see PS LA 2003/13. Taxpayers not covered by the statement are still expected to use a reasonable and practical basis to correctly bring into account their trading stock.

As a general rule, the Commissioner accepts the following valuation methods:

- **FIFO:** the first items purchased are assumed to be disposed of first and the cost of trading stock on hand at the end of the year is the cost of the items most recently acquired
- **Average cost** (if the actual cost of stock cannot be ascertained): the cost of each item of a particular type on hand at the end of the year is the weighted average of the cost of all such items that were on hand at the beginning of the year and all those acquired during the year.
- **Standard cost** (if standards are reviewed regularly to equate with current prices): a predetermined standard cost per unit is used.
- **Retail inventory** (if old stock is not marked down as it falls in value): goods in stock are marked at their retail selling prices, the marked prices are added together in the course of stocktaking and this figure is then reduced by the amount of the mark-up to arrive at the cost of the goods on hand.

2. REPLACEMENT VALUE

This is a simple method in many cases. Rather than keep records of what items cost, simply check the replacement cost as at the end of the income year.

NOTE: TD 92/198 states that to be able to use replacement value, the relevant items must be available in the market and be substantially identical to the replaced items.

3. MARKET SELLING VALUE

Value the closing stock at the market selling value (ie. the market value in the person's selling market) applicable at year-end. This method would most commonly be used when an item of stock has fallen in value to a level below cost.

4. THE SPECIAL VALUATION METHOD

In some instances (eg. where stock is obsolete), none of the three methods contemplated by s70-45 may be appropriate (eg. fashion clothing). When trading stock becomes obsolete (eg. spare parts held for a sporadic market or the line is discontinued etc.) a taxpayer may elect to use a reasonable value which is lower than the lowest value which could be determined using any of the three methods. The Tax Office view is set out in TR 93/23.

Section 70-50 allows the taxpayer to elect to value an item of trading stock at a lower value if ... *warranted because of obsolescence ... or other special circumstances.* Previously, the value was to be determined by the Commissioner.

The value given to closing stock must be reasonable. To determine a 'reasonable' value, take into account:

- the quantity of trading stock on hand at the end of the income year
- the quantity of trading stock sold, exchanged or used in manufacture after the end of the income year and the future prospects for the disposal of further quantities
- the quantity of the same kind of trading stock sold, exchanged or used in manufacture during the year of income and the preceding years of income, and
- any other matters considered relevant.

TRADING STOCK PURCHASED WITH FOREIGN CURRENCY

The rate of exchange used to translate trading stock on hand at the end of a year of income to Australian dollar terms for Australian income tax purposes depends on the basis of trading stock valuation elected by the taxpayer.

Where the taxpayer chooses to value closing stock on an actual cost basis, the relevant rate of exchange will be the rate applying at the date of acquisition of the stock.

Use of market selling value or replacement cost would require translation at the rate of exchange on the last day of the accounting period (IT 2498 and IT 2498A).

14.230   VALUING STOCK UNDER SPECIAL CONDITIONS

Taxpayers have a choice of four methods to value trading stock (see from 14.200). However, in certain situations contemplated by the tax laws, other requirements may arise.

DISPOSAL NOT MADE IN THE ORDINARY COURSE OF BUSINESS

Sometimes stock is disposed of other than by sale in the ordinary course of business (eg. a sale of business which includes trading stock). Section 70-90 provides that the market value of the stock is included in the assessable income of the taxpayer.

Section 70-85 provides that certain property will be deemed to be trading stock and the market value brought to account as assessable income under s70-90 where:

- a taxpayer disposes by sale, gift, or other means, property which is trading stock, standing or growing crops, crop stools, or trees which were planted and tended for sale
- that property constitutes or constituted the whole or part of the assets of a business which is or was carried on by the taxpayer, and
- the disposal was not in the ordinary course of carrying on that business.

A person who acquires that trading stock is deemed to have acquired it at the same value. If there is insufficient evidence of market value, the Tax Office may include a value which it considers 'fair and reasonable'.

NOTE: Market value is the price at which goods can be purchased in this particular market and does not include any input tax credit to which the taxpayer might be entitled.

ITEMS BECOMING TRADING STOCK

If an asset held for another purpose subsequently becomes trading stock, the taxpayer is treated as having sold the item in an arm's length transaction just before it became trading stock and immediately bought it back.

The taxpayer may elect the deemed sale to be at either:

- its cost (worked out under ss70-30(3) or (4), or
- its market value.

IF A BUSINESS IS 'WOUND UP'

Trading stock is considered to have been disposed of 'other than in the normal course of business' where a business is wound up and there is an in specie distribution of the stock at market value by the liquidator (see *FC of T v St Huberts Island* 78 ATC 4104).

PURCHASES AT NON-ARM'S LENGTH

If the vendor and purchaser were not dealing with each other at arm's length in respect of the sale of trading stock (see s70-20) and the transaction price is greater than its market value, the transaction price is deemed to be the market value of the trading stock (ie. its arm's length price). The effect on the purchaser is that the value of the deduction for trading stock is reduced whilst the vendor's assessable income is decreased by the difference between the actual price and the market value of the stock.

DONATIONS TO TAX DEDUCTIBLE BODY

If a gift of trading stock of $2 or more is made to a body which is tax deductible under Division 30, s30-15 allows a deduction of the market value included in assessable income under s70-90.

TRADING STOCK LOST OR DESTROYED

Trading stock lost through fire, flooding, theft, spoilage etc. is not specifically covered. However, because the losses will be reflected in the value of trading stock on hand at the end of the year, a deduction is effectively allowed. Any insurance compensation received for loss of stock is returned as ordinary income under s6-5. If not, it is assessable under s70-115.

DEATH OF TAXPAYER

Section 70-105 provides that, upon the death of a taxpayer carrying on business, assessable income to the date of death will include the market value of trading stock on hand at that date, however in certain circumstances the Legal Personal Representative (LPR) of the taxpayer may elect to value trading stock on hand at the date of death in accordance with s70-45.

Where an asset of the business of the deceased taxpayer was standing or growing crops, crop stools or trees planted and tended for sale, the LPR of the taxpayer may elect to include no amount in assessable income.

Elections can only be made by the LPR of the taxpayer where:

- the business continues after the date of death, and
- the trading stock or other asset continues to be held as part of that business.

CHANGES IN PARTNERSHIPS

Where the composition of a partnership changes, there Is a deemed disposal and reacquisition of trading stock at market value. However, provided the members of the former partnership retain a 25% interest in the new partnership, an election can be made to account for the deemed transaction on the basis of the valuation methods contained in s70-45. The stock must remain an asset of the business and the market price must be greater than the ordinary value to be used

PREPAYMENTS OF TRADING STOCK

Section 70-15 denies a deduction for the prepayment of trading stock which is not on hand at the end of the year of income in which the payment is made. A deduction only applies to the portion of a prepayment relating to stock actually on hand. The Tax Office considers this does not apply to expenditure incurred in bringing trading stock into existence through manufacturing or production processes of the taxpayer (except as it relates to the acquisition of inputs to the manufacturing or production process which are themselves trading stock) (see TR 93/9). Section 70-15 would therefore not apply to:

* expenditure of a primary producer on seed for planting or the purchase price of an orchard which has a growing crop, or

* livestock breeding arrangements where it is part of a livestock breeding business of the taxpayer.

Section 70-15 provides that if an item becomes part of trading stock on hand either before or during the income year in which the outgoing is incurred, it is deductible in that year. Otherwise, the deduction is made in the year:

* when the item becomes part of trading stock on hand, or

* an amount is included in assessable income in connection with the disposal of that item.

COST OF ACQUIRING TREES

Special rules apply (s70-120) which allow a deduction for the capital cost of acquiring land carrying trees or acquiring a right to fell trees, to the extent that the felled trees are for sale or use in manufacture by the owner. This occurs because the trees are trading stock.

VALUING TRADING STOCK AT COST FOR ENTITIES WITH $10 MILLION OR MORE TURNOVER

The Tax Office has released Practice Statement PS LA 2003/13 relating to taxpayers (including consolidated groups) in the retail and wholesale industries where the consolidated gross operating turnover for the financial year is $10 million or more. Taxpayers not covered by the Practice Statement will be expected to use a reasonable and practical basis to correctly bring to account their trading stock. (Note that valuing stock at cost is a choice rather than compulsory).

The Practice Statement provides guidance in determining what costs to include in valuing trading stock on hand at cost applying full absorption costing. Costs to which the absorption rules must be applied include purchase, distribution centre costs, warehousing costs and freight (from supplier's premises to retail premises and from retail warehouse to retail outlet).

14.280   STOCK TAKEN FOR PRIVATE USE

The value of trading stock taken for private use is accounted for by including the market value in sales. It is necessary to be able to demonstrate that the value attributed to goods taken from stock for private use was fair and reasonable. Under self-assessment (see from 4.000) the value of stock taken for private use must be added back as income and declared in the business tax return. Taxpayers must keep accurate records to calculate the value of goods taken from stock that they have applied for their own (or dependant's) use.

The Tax Office released a guide for the value of goods taken from trading stock for private use in the 2014-15 income year (TD 2015/9). See TD 2014/2 for amounts for the 2013-14 income year. Note also that if a partner in a partnership takes trading stock for private use, Division 130 GST Act provides for an increasing adjustment (see from 24.260).

Business	Adult/Child over 16[1]	Child 4-16[1]
Bakery	$1,330	$655
Butcher	$790	$395
Restaurant/Cafe (licensed)	$4,490	$1,730
Restaurant/Cafe (unlicensed)	$3,460	$1,730
Caterer	$3,740	$1,870
Delicatessen	$3,460	$1,730
Fruiterer/greengrocer	$760	$390
Takeaway food shop	$3,350	$1,675
Mixed business[2]	$4,170	$2,085

1: GST exclusive   2: Includes milk bar, general store and convenience store

If a taxpayer considers the values in the table above do not reflect their particular circumstances, then they may elect to maintain their own records of items taken from trading stock for personal use. Practice Statement PS LA 2004/3(GA) sets out the records the Tax Office will accept. These include:

- the date the item was taken from stock
- the reason the item was taken from stock
- a description of the item, and
- the cost or market value of the item (as required).

14.400 DEBT FORGIVENESS

The Commercial Debt Forgiveness (CDF) provisions apply where certain debt is forgiven. The effect of these rules is not to assess the economic benefit of the debt forgiven to the debtor but to deny future income tax benefits.

COMMERCIAL DEBT

A commercial debt is defined in s245-10 as a debt in respect of which interest, (or amounts akin to interest) if it was paid or payable in respect of the debt, would be deductible under s8-1 even if disallowed under another section.

 Ensure that what is forgiven is actually a debt and not, say, a disputed claim that may not be a legally enforceable debt.

WHAT IS 'FORGIVENESS'?

A debt is considered to be forgiven if:

- the obligation to pay is released, waived or otherwise extinguished
- the right to sue for recovery ceases due to the statute of limitations
- 'debt parking' occurs, or
- a subscription for shares occurs to enable the company to discharge some or all of the debt.

The debt forgiveness rules do not apply to debts forgiven:

- if the debt waiver constitutes a fringe benefit
- the amount of the debt has been, or will be, included in the assessable income of the debtor
- under an Act relating to bankruptcy
- where forgiveness is effected by will, or
- for reasons of natural love and affection.

CALCULATING NET AMOUNT FORGIVEN

The legislation requires calculation of the 'net forgiven amount' of the debt. This amount is calculated as:

> *Gross forgiven amount of the debt:*
> - *less amounts included in assessable income*
> - *less reductions in allowable deductions*
> - *less reductions in cost bases of assets*
> - *less certain group company adjustments*
> = *Net forgiven amount of the debt*

The total net forgiven amount is applied successively to reduce the debtor's:

- deductible prior year revenue losses
- carry forward capital losses from income years prior to the forgiveness year
- undeducted balances of deductible expenditure for the forgiveness year or any later year (eg. opening tax depreciation written down values, capital allowance amounts, pooled software expenditure, certain borrowing expenses (s25-25), telephone line expenditure for primary producers, electricity connection expenditure, scientific research expenditure, R&D expenditure, clearing expenditure for primary producers, grape vine establishment expenditure, water plant/structure expenditure, certain plant or equipment in large development projects, environmental impact assessment expenditure, certain advance revenue expenditure, mining and quarrying expenditure, mineral exploration expenditure, mineral transportation expenditure, forestry road expenditure, certain timber milling buildings, certain industrial property expenditure, intellectual property expenditure, Australian film expenditure, building allowance, horticultural plant expenditure and spectrum licence expenditure)
- cost bases of certain assets for CGT purposes with some exclusions like certain private dwellings, goodwill, trading stock, personal use assets and with some restrictions as to investment assets in associated entities like certain shares in companies or units in trusts.

Once amounts are exhausted any excess is disregarded.

GROSS FORGIVEN AMOUNT

The gross forgiven amount of the debt is calculated by working out the notional value of the debt less consideration in respect of the forgiveness. The notional value is the lesser of:

- the value of the debt if the debtor's ability to repay at the time of forgiveness was the same as at the time the debt was incurred, where either the debt was a money lending debt or the debtor and creditor were dealing with each other at arm's length, and
- the market adjusted value of the debt.

 If the exchange rate was $US1:$A1.30 when a $100 debt was incurred, and $US1:$A1.40 when the debt was forgiven, the first amount would be $140 and the second $130. The notional value of the debt is the lesser of the two applicable amounts, ie. $130.

For non-recourse debts (see below) the notional value is the lesser of:

- the amount of the debt when it is forgiven, and
- market value of the rights to which the creditor has recourse at the same time.

A non-recourse debt is a debt incurred directly in respect of financing the cost of the debtor's acquisition, construction or development of property and the rights of the creditor against the debtor are limited to the property itself or rights in relation to the property, or goods or services provided by the property.

For debts previously parked, the notional value will usually be any consideration paid by the debtor for the assignment of the debt, plus any consideration paid by the new creditor for the debt.

Otherwise, where the assigned debt was not a money lending debt and the original and new creditors were not dealing with each other at arm's length, the notional value is the market value of the debt at the time of assignment.

CONSIDERATION

Consideration is the amount of money and/or property the debtor is required to give in respect of the forgiveness. If the debt is for 'money' (from a loan made in the ordinary course of a money lending business) the consideration also includes the market value of any obligation of the debtor to pay amounts in the future.

As with CGT, market value rules may apply to determine consideration in respect of the forgiveness of a 'non-money' debt. Specific rules also apply to determine consideration for the purposes of the debt forgiveness provisions where debt parking applies or where there is a debt for equity swap.

AMOUNTS INCLUDED IN ASSESSABLE INCOME

An amount may have been included in the debtor's assessable income under Division 7A (see 6.300) for example, upon forgiveness of a loan from a private company. In such a case, the net forgiven amount of the debt does not include any such amount.

According to ATO ID 2014/33, where a creditor forgives a commercial debt as part of a settlement agreement and also pays the debtor an additional amount under the agreement that is assessable income of the debtor, the additional amount will not reduce the gross forgiven amount of the debt.

APPLICATION OF THE NET FORGIVEN AMOUNT

PRIOR YEAR REVENUE LOSSES

Reduce prior year revenue losses available under s36-15 or s36-17 ITAA97.

If the net forgiven amount is less than the amount of prior year revenue losses, the debtor may choose the order and the amount of losses to be reduced up to the total net forgiven amount. If the net forgiven amount exceeds prior year revenue losses, the excess is applied next against deductible carry forward capital losses.

CARRY FORWARD CAPITAL LOSSES

A deductible net capital loss means a net capital loss that:

- the debtor had for an income year earlier than the forgiveness year of income, and
- apart from the subdivision, could be applied in working out the debtor's net capital gain for the forgiveness year of income (assuming the debtor had enough capital gains).

The taxpayer may elect the order in which the net forgiven amount is deducted against capital losses.

UNDEDUCTED BALANCES OF DEDUCTIBLE EXPENDITURE

The net forgiven amount is next applied, to the maximum extent possible, in reducing deductible expenditure, as identified in s245-145 ITAA97.

 See from 11.005 if previously claimed expenditure has been recouped as that recoupment is assessable.

These expenses are excluded from deductible expenditure:

- expenditure incurred in respect of assets:
    - disposed of by the debtor in an arm's length dealing
    - disposed of before the forgiveness of a debt
    - no amount is included in assessable income or is allowed as a deduction to the debtor as a result of the disposal
- expenditure incurred in respect of an asset disposed of, lost or destroyed on or before start day of the debt forgiveness provisions, and
- expenditure recouped on or before the start of the debt forgiveness provisions.

The debtor may choose the order to which and the amount to which the residual forgiven amount is to apply to deductible expenditure. If the residual forgiven amount exceeds all deductible expenditure the excess is applied to reduce the cost base of assets.

 As a tax planning measure a debtor would usually choose to reduce the opening tax written down value of, say, a work of art (prime cost depreciation rate of 1%) in preference to the opening written down value of an asset that depreciates, say, at a rate of 20% per annum prime cost over five years. It is generally preferable to defer the deduction denied to the maximum extent possible.

COST BASE OF CGT ASSET

To the extent to which the total net forgiven amount cannot be applied as above, it is to be used according to sections 245-165 to 245-190 (in reduction of the relevant cost bases of certain assets of the debtor at the beginning of the forgiveness year of income). The taxpayer can choose the assets in respect of which the cost base is reduced and the extent of the reduction.

 When purchasing a company or other legal entity, check to ensure that the debt forgiveness provisions have not previously applied or will not apply on purchase. The entity purchased may have less revenue or capital losses, less future tax benefits in the form of future deductions or hidden CGT exposures on the subsequent disposal of reducible assets for CGT purposes.

REMAINDER

Any remaining unapplied net forgiven amount is disregarded (after applying to the various tax benefits) (s245-195).

NOTE: Companies under common ownership may choose for the creditor company to forgo a capital loss or deduction if both parties enter into an agreement provided certain conditions are met (s245-90).

PARTNERSHIPS

Partnerships are treated in the same manner as other taxpayers. However, a partnership would not have carried forward revenue and/or capital losses as they are distributed to partners on an annual basis. If the total net forgiven amount is unable to be applied fully against the partnership's reducible amounts, the excess is allocated to the respective partners to the extent that the partner shares in the net partnership income or loss (Sub-division 245-F).

TRUSTS

The former s245-26 Schedule 2C ITAA36 specifically provided that the CDF rules apply to a trustee of a trust estate (in their capacity as trustee and not in their personal capacity) in respect of the trust estate's debts.

This provision has not been imported into the ITAA97 rewrite and the current CDF provisions are silent as to the treatment of trusts. However, paragraph 960-100(1)(f) specifies that a trust is an entity for the general purposes of the ITAA97. By extension, the CDF regime applies to a trust as to any other 'entity'. There has been no practical change in the treatment of forgiven debts of trusts.

RELATED COMPANIES UNDER COMMON OWNERSHIP

A creditor and a debtor may choose to enter into an agreement under s245-90 ITAA97, whereby the debtor's net forgiven amount is reduced by a particular amount in return for the creditor forgoing its entitlement to claim that same amount as either:

- a capital loss arising from the forgiveness
- a general deduction under s8 1 arising from the forgiveness, or
- a specific deduction (for a bad debt) under s25-35 arising from the forgiveness.

This choice is available if the following conditions are met:

- the debtor and the creditor are both companies
- from the time when the debt was incurred until the time when the debt is forgiven, the debtor and the creditor are 'under common ownership', defined in s995-1 as either:
  - members of the same wholly-owned group, or
  - ultimately owned (directly or indirectly) by the same individuals in the same proportions, and
- the debtor and creditor enter into a written agreement

  The written agreement must be signed by the public officer of each company, and is made before the earlier of:
  - the date of lodgment of the income tax return of the creditor for the year in which the forgiveness occurred
  - the date of lodgment of the income tax return of the debtor for the year in which the forgiveness occurred, and
  - any later date as determined by the Commissioner.

14.450 LOSSES FROM NON-COMMERCIAL BUSINESS ACTIVITIES

Losses from non-commercial activities carried on by individuals are only deductible against other income in that income year if the taxpayer satisfies at least one of four tests and they have an adjusted taxable income (ATI) as defined in ss35-10(2E) of less than $250,000. Alternatively, the Tax Office may exercise a discretion to allow the deduction. This can be done where the activity is affected by a situation outside the taxpayer's control or where an activity has been started and it is to be expected that it will meet one of the tests or generate taxable income within a period that is commercially viable; see TR 2001/14 and TR 2001/14A.

14.460   COMMERCIALITY TESTS

Before the 2009-10 income year, under the non-commercial losses rules contained in Division 35, an individual taxpayer carrying on a business activity either alone or in partnership could only claim a loss from that activity against their other income in an income year if they satisfy at least one of the four objective tests in that year. The four tests are:

- **Test 1: Assessable income test** – assessable income from a business activity is $20,000 or more.

- **Test 2: Profits test** – the business activity has produced a tax profit in at least three out of the last five income years, including the current year.

- **Test 3: Real property test** – the value of real property assets (excluding any private dwelling) used in carrying on a business is $500,000 or more.

- **Test 4: Other assets test** – the value of other assets (excluding cars, motorcycles and similar vehicles) used in carrying on a business is $100,000 or more.

Losses that are quarantined are not lost, they are merely deferred until the next income year. If a similar business makes a profit in a subsequent year, the deferred losses can be applied against the current year profit (up to the amount of the profit). Otherwise the individual must satisfy at least one of the four tests or the Tax Office has favourably exercised its discretion to allow the deferred losses to be recouped against any income.

Future claims for non-commercial losses carried forward will need to be offset first against any exempt income before they can be claimed. Similarly, losses are forfeited where the individual is declared bankrupt and the losses are not retrieved until such time as all tax debts have been paid.

EXCEPTIONS

If the activity is a primary production or professional arts business, the taxpayer will be able to claim the losses from that business provided the taxpayer's assessable income (excluding any net capital gains) from other sources is under $40,000. For primary production partnerships, this rule applies separately for each individual partner.

THE ASSESSABLE INCOME TEST

Under this test, the taxpayer must be able to demonstrate that the assessable income derived from the business activity is $20,000 or more for the year.

For those carrying on business activities in partnership, there is a requirement to determine the proportion of assessable income that is attributable to each partner for the purpose of this test. A taxpayer may include that part of the partnership's assessable income attributable to other individual partners. That is, if a taxpayer is a partner in a partnership and all other partners are individuals, the assessable income of the whole partnership must be $20,000 or more. This test is based on assessable income for the entire year. Where a business activity commences or ceases during an income year, the taxpayer is entitled to make a reasonable estimate of what the assessable income would have been for the full year. Where there are seasonal variations, the taxpayer may use an estimate rather than pro-rating.

In year 1 the taxpayer incurs a loss of $10,000. The income derived from the business activity was $15,000. In year 2, the taxpayer derives assessable income of $40,000 from the same business activity resulting in a net profit of $5,500. The taxpayer derived other taxable income of $15,000.

Applying the assessable income test, the taxpayer is not entitled to claim any deduction for the loss incurred in year 1. The loss of $10,000 is deferred.

In year 2 test 1 is satisfied as the assessable income is above $20,000 and therefore $5,500 of the carry forward loss is deductible against the business activity income and the balance (ie. $4,500) is allowed as a deduction against the taxpayer's other taxable income.

THE PROFITS TEST

Under this test a taxpayer must have earned a profit in any three of the past five income years (including the current income year in which the loss occurs). There is no minimum taxable income threshold.

Taxable income applicable from the business activity is simply the difference between the assessable income derived from the activity and the sum of deductions allowed in that income year.

Special rules apply for partners. They must aggregate their share of income and any deductions from the business activities conducted in the partnership with any income and deductions applicable in their own hands.

Income year	1	2	3	4
Business activity	$5,000	$5,000	($6,000)	$4,000
Loss deferred	Nil	Nil	Nil	($6,000)
Current year result	$5,000	$5,000	($6,000)	($2,000)
Other taxable income	$40,000	$30,000	$20,000	$35,000
Loss for current year (quarantined)	Nil	Nil	($6,000)	Nil
Taxable income	$45,000	$35,000	$20,000	$33,000

Using only test 2 the taxpayer would not qualify for deduction in year 3 as the taxpayer does not have three profitable years during the past five years. The non-commercial loss is deferred. In year 4, however, that test is now satisfied as the taxpayer can demonstrate a profit in three of the past four years (refer: TR 2001/14).

THE REAL PROPERTY TEST

The taxpayer will satisfy this test if the value of real property, which is used on a continuing basis in carrying on the business activity, is $500,000 or more at the end of the income year. When valuing the property the value to be used is the greater of:

- market value, and
- CGT reduced cost base.

Only the real property (including any fixtures whether they are depreciable or not) used mainly in the business activity is counted. Private dwellings and adjacent land used in conjunction with a private dwelling are specifically excluded.

If a business ceases during an income year, the value of the real property is to be calculated at the time when the business ceased.

Fixtures are included under the other assets test.

A taxpayer has a five hectare property that is used partly for private purposes and partly for storing car bodies that are used for spare parts for his newly established business. The total market vale of the property is $800,000 of which $450,000 relates to the private dwelling and adjacent land used in association with the private dwelling. No other real property is owned or used by the taxpayer in his business.

The taxpayer would not satisfy Test 3.

THE OTHER ASSETS TEST

This test deals with assets used on a continuing basis in carrying on the business activity, excluding real property (which is dealt with under Test 3). This test is satisfied when the value of those assets is $100,000 or more. Assets included under the real property test cannot be used when evaluating compliance with this test.

Assets included under this test are:

- an asset for which a capital allowance deduction is available
- an item of trading stock
- an asset leased from another entity, and
- trademarks, patents, copyright etc.

 Assets allocated to an SBE/STS pool cannot be included under the 'Other assets test' because they are not deductible under Division 40 (see s35-45).

COMMISSIONER'S DISCRETION

If a taxpayer fails to satisfy any of the tests and would therefore be denied a deduction, the Tax Office has a discretion to overlook the non-compliance if it would be unreasonable to do so. For that discretion to be exercised, either of the following conditions must be satisfied:

- there were special circumstances outside the taxpayer's control (eg. natural disaster such as drought, bushfire, floods, power plant shutdowns, oil spills, government restriction on land use or illness of key personnel), or
- the nature of the business activity is such that there is a lead time between the activity commencing and the production of assessable income (eg. grape growing, plantations etc) and there is an expectation that within a period of time reasonable for the particular industry, the taxpayer will satisfy one of the four tests or be profitable.

Normal economic or market fluctuations do not constitute special circumstances.

14.470   ADDITIONAL RULES FROM 1 JULY 2009

New rules were introduced from 1 July 2009 in order to deny certain high income earners the ability to offset their business losses against other income, notwithstanding that one or more of the four objective tests described above may have been satisfied. As a result, for 2009-10 and later income years, taxpayers with an ATI of at least $250,000 will not be able to offset losses from their business activities against income from other sources such as salary and investment income. The business losses will be quarantined and carried forward for deduction against future income from the same source.

Therefore, for the 2009-10 and later income years, a taxpayer can only offset business losses against assessable income from other sources if:

- the taxpayer's ATI is less than $250,000
- one of the four tests is satisfied (profits test, assessable income test, real property asset test, other assets test) (see above)
- one of the exceptions for primary production or professional arts businesses apply (see above), or
- the Commissioner has exercised his discretion to allow the loss to be deducted.

 Any excess deductions from the non-commercial business activity must be excluded when calculating the taxpayer's ATI.

 The non-commercial loss rules only apply to individuals and individuals in partnership.

COMMISSIONER'S FURTHER DISCRETION

In addition to the existing Commissioner's discretion, from the 2010 year, the Commissioner may exercise his discretion in:

- cases where the individual's ATI exceeds $250,000 but can independently demonstrate that the business is genuinely commercial and will, within a period that is commercially viable, produce profits, and
- cases where the business losses were caused solely by deductions claimed for the small business and general business tax break (Division 41).

14.600 CAPITAL PROTECTED BORROWINGS

Capital Protected Borrowings (CPB) are financing arrangements which are used to mitigate some of the investment risk of holding securities such as listed shares. CPBs are dealt with by Division 247.

A CPB involves an investor borrowing funds to enable the purchase of investment assets such as tradeable securities. A distinguishing feature of a CPB is the ability of the borrower to repay the loan by simply transferring the securities purchased back to the lender if the market value of the shares falls below the borrowing. The borrower is not required to make any further repayments under the facility and by transferring the securities back to the lender may fully satisfy the debt outstanding. A CPB borrowing will typically attract a higher interest rate than borrowings without the capital protection element.

Investors may claim a deduction for the interest paid on a CPB where the borrowing is used to acquire income producing assets. However, following the decision of the Full Federal Court in *Federal Commissioner of Taxation v Firth* (2002) 120 FCR 450, there have been limitations on the extent to which interest on a CPB will be deductible.

NOTE: TD 2013/1 states that the CPB rules do not apply to a full recourse loan (interest loan) to fund the prepayment of interest on a capital protected borrowing to which Div 247 applies.

TRANSITIONAL RULES COVERING 16 APRIL 2003 TO 13 MAY 2008

There are two methods for calculating the non-deductible interest component for a CPB under the transitional rules. These methods are the indicator method and the percentage method. The borrower must use the method that results in the greater non-deductible amount.

The details of the transitional rules are contained at 13.600 of the 2013-14 *Tax Summary.*

CAPITAL PROTECTED BORROWINGS ENTERED INTO FROM 13 MAY 2008

The appropriate benchmark interest rates for an original CPB entered into or an amendment extension made after 31 May 2008 is the Reserve Bank indicator variable rate for standard housing loans plus 100 basis points. An interest component exceeding this rate is not deductible.

TAX TREATMENT OF THE NON-DEDUCTIBLE INTEREST COMPONENT OF A CAPITAL PROTECTED BORROWING

The non-deductible interest component under a CPB is treated as an amount paid by the borrower to acquire a put option from the lender. The put option gives the borrower the ability to transfer the shares back to the lender in full satisfaction of the debt. The put option is as issued to the borrower at the commencement of the CPB and will normally cease at the conclusion or expiry of the CPB.

PUT OPTION NOT EXERCISED (MARKET VALUE EQUALS OR EXCEEDS OUTSTANDING LOAN BALANCE)

If the put option expires without being exercised, CGT event C2 will mostly likely apply. A capital loss arises where the capital proceeds received for the put option are less than assets reduced cost base.

The borrower will not normally receive any capital proceeds on the expiry of the put option and therefore realises a capital loss equal to the capital protection amount (ie. non-deductible interest component). The investor can offset the capital loss against capital gains.

PUT OPTION EXERCISED (MARKET VALUE LESS THAN OUTSTANDING LOAN BALANCE)

The borrower is taken to have disposed of the put option at the time it is exercised triggering CGT event C2 which is normally at the end of the agreement. However a special CGT rule requires the capital loss to be disregarded where a taxpayer exercises an option over an asset that is subsequently sold.

The CGT consequences are that when the taxpayer exercises the put option for the lender to acquire the shares, there is no separate CGT event for the put option. Instead, the whole series of events is treated as one sale transaction, with the cost base of the (borrower) taxpayer's interest in the shares comprising:

- the original purchase cost of the shares, and
- the non-deductible capital-protection component of the 'interest' on the loan.

In the case of CPBs, the shares are effectively sold back to the lender at the market price at the time of the transfer. The non-deductible component of the interest which is deemed the consideration for the put option is added to the second element of the borrowers cost base of the shares. The capital cost of the put option is effectively rolled into the cost base of the shares. The shares are in turn sold for their market value when handed back (deemed consideration) triggering CGT event A1.

NOTE: The cost base of the original shares also needs to be adjusted for the recoupment of the loan balance shortfall which does not need to be paid back to the lender (CGT recoupment rule) (ss110-45(3)).

14.700 FORESTRY MANAGED INVESTMENT SCHEMES

Special rules contained in Division 394 provide for deductibility of investments in forestry Managed Investment Schemes (MIS) whose purpose is for establishing and tending trees for felling only in Australia.

Initial investors in forestry schemes receive a 100% tax deduction for their contributions (both initial and ongoing) under s394-10. Initial investors are those who first contribute to a forestry scheme that is set up for the first tree planting and initial forestry operations. Secondary investors (those purchasing an investment from an initial investor) in forestry schemes receive a 100% tax deduction for their ongoing contributions in the year they pay amounts under the scheme (on the basis that the amounts would be deductible if paid by initial investors) but cannot obtain a deduction for their acquisition costs.

See 17.460 for a detailed summary of relevant rules in relation to the deductibility of MIS contributions.

Deductions for capital expenditure

15

15.000 CAPITAL ALLOWANCE WRITE-OFFS
FOR NON-SBE REGIME TAXPAYERS

Where a taxpayer uses a capital asset for a taxable purpose, the taxpayer may be able to claim a deduction for the decline in value of that asset. This chapter does not cover taxpayers that adopt the small business entity (SBE) regime which has its own simplified and concessional capital allowances rules (see 10.600).

NOTE: All references in this chapter are to the ITAA97 unless stated otherwise.

NOTE: The Government announced in the 2015 Budget that it will significantly expand accelerated depreciation for small businesses by allowing small business entities with aggregated annual turnover of less than $2 million to immediately deduct assets they start to use or install ready for use, provided the asset costs less than $20,000 (see Chapter 10 for details).

15.010 DEPRECIATION (DECLINE IN VALUE)

A taxpayer can deduct an amount equal to the decline in value of a depreciating asset that the taxpayer holds and uses, or has installed ready for use, for a taxable purpose during a year (s40-25). The deduction is worked out using the provisions in Division 40.

Division 40 implements the Uniform Capital Allowance system (UCA). It contains the capital expenditure deduction rules for:

- plant
- software
- intellectual property (patents, design and copyright)
- mining and exploration
- primary production, and
- business related capital costs (blackhole expenditure).

These rules are discussed in this chapter.

 There are very different rules that apply to those taxpayers that have elected to use the SBE regime. All of the relevant rules, including how to claim deductions for decline in value (commonly called depreciation) are discussed in Chapter 10.

Deductions for construction expenditure on building and structural improvements (capital works) under Division 43 are discussed in 15.200.

WHAT IS A DEPRECIATING ASSET?

A depreciating asset is defined in s40-30(1) as *an asset that has a limited effective life and can reasonably be expected to decline in value over the time it is used.*

Land, trading stock and any intangible assets not mentioned in s40-30(2) are not depreciating assets.

Intangible assets are not depreciating assets unless they are specifically listed. Section 40-30(2) states that the following intangible assets are depreciating assets if they are not trading stock:

- mining, quarrying or prospecting rights
- mining, quarrying or prospecting information
- items of intellectual property. Intellectual property includes a patent, registered design or copyright. It does not include a trade mark. A trade mark is outside Division 40
- in-house software
- IRUs
- spectrum licences
- datacasting transmitter licences
- telecommunications site access rights, and
- Geothermal exploration rights and geothermal exploration information (where the start time is on or after 1 July 2012).

The Minerals Resource Rent Tax and other related measures was repealed by the Government on 5 September 2014. As such, geothermal energy exploration and prospecting expenditure will no longer be immediately deductible.

While land is excluded as a depreciating asset because it does not have a limited effective life, improvements to land or fixtures on land are treated as separate from the land and thus depreciating assets, regardless of whether the improvement or fixture is removable from the land or permanently attached (s40-30(3)). In the Commissioner's view, an improvement to land generally constitutes any alteration to land that is considered an enhancement to the user (TR 2012/7).

The test of whether an asset is 'plant' is one of functionality. If the function of the asset is to provide a setting or environment within which income-producing activities are conducted such as a building, the asset will not be 'plant'. However, if the function of the asset is to provide the means or apparatus whereby income is produced, such as a machine or equipment, the asset is plant and a depreciating asset.

For part of a building to qualify as plant its structure must play a part in the manufacturing process rather than provide the settling for business operations (*Wangaratta Woollen Mills v FC of T* 69 ATC 4095).

The 'functionality test' is also used when determining whether composite items are a single depreciating asset or the components are separate depreciating assets (s40-30(4)). Generally where an item is separately identifiable and capable of performing its own intended discrete function it is a separate depreciating asset (see TR 94/11). The fact that an item has no commercial utility unless linked to other items does not preclude it from being a separate depreciating asset. For example, for a photographer, a flash generator, flash head, light shaping tool and modelling glass protector are separate depreciating assets (ATO ID 2002/930).

The Tax Office considers that rights to use software are not items of 'in-house software' and therefore are not 'depreciating assets' where the annual licence fees are deductible under s8-1 ITAA97 (ATO ID 2010/14).

DEPRECIATING ASSETS EXCLUDED FROM DIVISION 40

The following depreciating assets are specifically excluded from the UCA regime:

- depreciating assets that are capital works deductible under Division 43, or would have been deductible had the expenditure not been incurred before the operative dates or the capital works not been used for a non-relevant purpose (s40-45(2))
- depreciating assets associated with investments in Australian films (s40-45(5))
- depreciating assets that are cars where the deductions on those cars have been substantiated using the 'cents per kilometre' method or the '12% of original value method' (these methods already take into account the decline in value of the car) (s40-55), and
- certain work related assets (such as portable computer devices, mobile phones and personal protective equipment etc) provided to employees that are exempt from FBT under s58X of the FBT Act, if the item is provided as an expense payment benefit or a property benefit (s40-45(1)).

WHO HOLDS A DEPRECIATING ASSET?

Only an entity that held the depreciating asset at any time during the year can claim a deduction for its decline in value (s40-25(1)). The entity that holds the depreciating asset will be its economic owner(s). The economic owner(s) is the entity that is able to access the asset's economic benefits while stopping other entities from doing the same (see table in s40-40). There may be several economic owners, each with its own cost of the asset, so the legislation recognises joint holding of depreciating assets.

In most cases, the legal owner of a depreciating asset will also be its economic owner and the entity entitled to the deduction for the decline in value of the depreciating asset. However, this is not always the case and therefore reference should be made to the table in s40-40 which identifies the holder of an asset. In ATO ID 2011/71, the Commissioner concludes that the sole beneficiary of a trust estate is not the holder of an asset legally owned by the trustee, pursuant to Item 6 of the table, until the beneficiary demands ownership of the asset be transferred to them.

NOTE: ATO ID 2012/9 clarifies that the 'right to remove' in Item 2 is not limited to the right to remove assets at the end of the term of a quasi-ownership right and Item 2 may cover a right to remove the assets during the term of the quasi-ownership right where the right ceases at the end of the term. In addition, ATO ID 2012/80 clarifies that, under a hire purchase arrangement where the purchaser has a right to sell the asset to the owner at a predetermined price at the end of the term of the arrangement, the purchaser starts to hold the asset under Item 6 of the table.

SECTION 40-40

Identifying the holder of a depreciating asset		
Item	This kind of depreciating asset:	Is held by this entity:
1	A luxury car in respect of which a lease has been granted	The lessee (while the lessee has the right to use the car) and not the lessor
2	A depreciating asset that is fixed to land subject to a quasi-ownership right (including any extension or renewal of such a right) where the owner of the right has a right to remove the asset	The owner of the quasi-ownership right (while the right to remove exists)
3	An improvement to land (whether a fixture or not) subject to a quasi-ownership right (including any extension or renewal of such a right) made, or itself improved, by any owner of the right for the owner's own use where the owner of the right has no right to remove the asset	The owner of the quasi-ownership right (while it exists)
4	A depreciating asset that is subject to a lease where the asset is fixed to land and the lessor has the right to recover the asset	The lessor (while the right to recover exists)
5	A right that an entity legally owns but which another entity (the **economic owner**) exercises or has a right to exercise immediately, where the economic owner has a right to become its legal owner and it is reasonable to expect that: (a) the economic owner will become its legal owner, or (b) it will be disposed of at the direction and for the benefit of the economic owner	The economic owner and not the legal owner
6	A depreciating asset that an entity (the **former holder**) would, apart from this item, hold under this table (including by another application of this item) where a second entity (also the **economic owner**): (a) possesses the asset, or has a right as against the former holder to possess the asset immediately, and (b) has a right as against the former holder the exercise of which would make the economic owner the holder under any item of this table, and it is reasonable to expect that the economic owner will become its holder by exercising the right, or that the asset will be disposed of at the direction and for the benefit of the economic owner	The economic owner and not the former holder
7	A depreciating asset that is a partnership asset	The partnership and not any particular partner
8	Mining, quarrying or prospecting information that an entity has and that is relevant to: (a) mining operations carried on, or proposed to be carried on by the entity, or (b) a business carried on by the entity that includes exploration or prospecting for minerals or quarry materials obtainable by such operations, whether or not it is generally available	The entity
9	Other mining quarrying or prospecting information that an entity has and that is not generally available	The entity

Identifying the holder of a depreciating asset		
Item	This kind of depreciating asset:	Is held by this entity:
9A	Geothermal exploration information that an entity has and is relevant to: (a) geothermal energy extraction carried on, or proposed to be carried on, by the entity, or (b) a business carried on by the entity that includes exploration or prospecting for geothermal energy resources from which energy can be extracted by geothermal energy extraction. whether or not it is generally available. **NOTE:** This item is repealed by the *Minerals Resource Rent Tax Repeal and Other Measures Act 2013*.	The entity
10	Any depreciating asset	The owner, or the legal owner if there is both a legal and equitable owner

JOINTLY HELD DEPRECIATING ASSETS

When applying the table in s40-40, there may be more than one holder of a depreciating asset. This may occur in cases of:

- **Joint ownership:** Depreciate according to the use made of the asset by each owner.
- **Multiple interest holders** who have contributed to the cost of a depreciating asset: Depreciate on the basis of that portion of the cost of the underlying asset contributed by each interest holder.
- **Both lessee and lessor contributing to the cost of a depreciating asset:** Depreciate by reference to their contributions to the asset's cost.

A depreciating asset is 'jointly held' by the taxpayer and other entities where the taxpayer owns some of the parts of the depreciating asset and the remaining parts are owned by the other entities (ATO ID 2011/1).

When the jointly held depreciating asset provisions in s40-35(1) apply, the decline in value of the actual underlying asset is otherwise disregarded by the entity holding the interest (s40-35(2)). Rather the decline in value of each asset is determined by reference to an entity's interest in the underlying asset. This means that the effective life of the interest is that of the underlying asset.

However, because each holder's interest is dealt with as if it were the asset, changes to one holder's interest do not have to affect another holder. For example, if there are three joint owners of an asset and one sells all or part of an interest in the underlying asset to a new co-owner, the other original owners have no change to their asset and no balancing adjustment event occurs for them.

The recognition of joint holding of a depreciating asset means that a taxpayer can depreciate the cost of their interest in a depreciating asset. This in turn means that if the taxpayer's interest in the asset cost $300 or less or cost less than $1,000, then if the other conditions are satisfied the asset will be eligible for an immediate write off (see 15.030) or allocation to a low-value pool (see 15.040), even if the total cost of the asset exceeds those thresholds (see ATO ID 2003/439).

 A taxpayer jointly owns a rental property to the extent of 50%. The joint owners purchase a new washing machine for $490. As each taxpayer's interest in the asset cost $300 or less each taxpayer will be entitled to an immediate write off, if the other conditions in 15.030 are satisfied.

WHEN DOES A DEPRECIATING ASSET START TO DECLINE IN VALUE?

The decline in value of a depreciating asset held by a taxpayer commences at the 'start time'. The 'start time' is the earlier date of the following events:

- when the taxpayer first uses the asset, or
- when the taxpayer has the asset installed ready for use for any purpose (s40-60(2)).

Note that under UCA the decline in value commences when you use or hold the asset in reserve regardless of the purpose for which the asset is to be used. It is irrelevant that the depreciating asset may first be used for a non-taxable purpose.

Merely holding an asset in anticipation of using that asset in a business that has not yet commenced does not constitute a use, or being held ready for use, that would cause the asset to decline in value under s40-60. Under s40-60 the asset must be used or held ready for use in an existing income-producing operation (TD 2007/5).

Ralph acquires a car on 28 January 2015 and commences to use the vehicle for private purposes. On 15 July 2015 he starts to use the car jointly for business and private purposes. The 'start time' for the car is 28 January 2015.

Further, where an asset (eg. a trailer) is required to be registered under relevant legislation, the asset is not considered to be in the state required for it to be ready to perform its function and would not be installed ready for use in the absence of the registration (ATO ID 2010/171).

If a depreciating asset is not used for a taxable purpose from its 'start time' then there is no deduction for its decline in value. If at a later time the asset is used for a taxable purpose, the decline in value from 'start time' to taxable use time must be determined to calculate the deduction for the decline in value of the asset once it has commenced being used for a taxable purpose.

When a depreciating asset is used for both a taxable purpose and another purpose, apportionment applies to allow a deduction for the decline in value attributable to a taxable purpose.

Section 40-60(3) provides for a further 'start time' in situations when a taxpayer commences using an asset again after a balancing adjustment event has occurred for that asset. In this situation, 'start time' is when the taxpayer begins using that asset again.

15.020   DEPRECIATION FLOW CHART

The depreciation flow chart (and footnotes) summarises the decision process and applicable depreciation rates for a depreciating asset under UCA. The text that follows the flow chart provides a more detailed outline of the legislation supporting each decision. The specialist areas of primary production and mining and quarrying are discussed separately later in this chapter.

NOTE: The rules for taxpayers utilising the small business entity regime are detailed in Chapter 10.

15.030   DEPRECIATING ASSETS COSTING $300 OR LESS

The immediate deduction for depreciating assets costing $300 or less is restricted to assets predominantly used for the purpose of producing assessable income from activities that do not amount to carrying on a business (for example, work related expenditure by an employee on a depreciating asset, such as a briefcase, and depreciating assets acquired for a rental property).

In addition, to qualify for the immediate deduction:

- the asset cannot be acquired as part of a set of assets costing more than $300 in an income year, and
- the taxpayer cannot acquire one or more assets that are either identical or substantially identical in an income year where the total cost of these acquisitions is more than $300 (eg. the owner of a furnished rental property cannot buy two identical lamps which individually cost $290 and claim the immediate deduction (s40-80(2)).

An employee purchases a calculator for $120. The asset is used 70% for work-related purposes and 30% for private purposes. As the calculator is used predominately (more than 50%) for a taxable purpose the employee can claim an immediate deduction of 70% of $120 = $84.

Outright claims for depreciating assets costing $300 or less can only be made by non-business taxpayers. This includes employees, investors and landlords (who are not in a business of renting properties). 'Small business entity' taxpayers can write off the cost of a depreciating asset that is less than $20,000 from 7.30pm AEST 12 May 2015 until 30 June 2017 (see Chapter 10).

DEPRECIATION UNDER THE UNIFORM CAPITAL ALLOWANCE SYSTEM

For entities other than small business entities (see Chapter 10) adopting the simplified capital allowance rules and those engaged in primary production, exploration or prospecting.

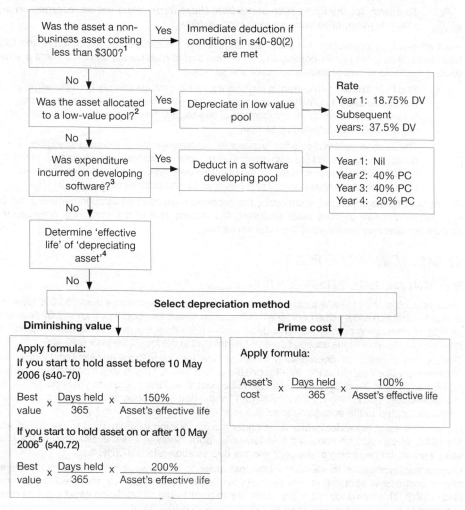

1: The immediate deduction for a depreciating asset costing $300 or less is restricted to a non-business asset. If the asset is part of a set of assets, the total cost of the set must not exceed $300. Further, if an identical or substantially identical asset is acquired in the same year the immediate deduction only applies if the sum of the cost of these assets does not exceed $300 (s40-80(2)). Assets acquired by the owner of a rental property would be an example of a non-business asset.

2: A low-value pool can be created for assets that cost less than $1,000 or have declined in value under the diminishing value method to below $1,000.

3: A taxpayer can elect to create a software development pool for expenditure incurred on developing computer software. Once the choice is made it is irrevocable. Only software to be used solely for a taxable purpose can be pooled (s40-450).

4: A taxpayer can either self-assess an asset's effective life or use the Commissioner's determination, unless an exception applies (see s40-95).

5: To start to hold the asset on or after 10 May 2006 the taxpayer must have:
- entered into the contract on or after 10 May 2006, or
- started construction of the asset on or after 10 May 2006, or
- started to hold the asset in some other way on or after 10 May 2006.

15.035   ASSETS COSTING $100 OR LESS

In PS LA 2003/8, the Tax Office announced that it will allow (subject to qualifications) expenditure of $100 or less (inclusive of GST) on tangible assets to be treated by all taxpayers as expenditure of a revenue nature and deductible outright in the year incurred.

 To qualify for the immediate deduction, these items must not be recorded on an asset register, otherwise an exclusion applies.

Alternatively, a taxpayer can use statistical sampling to determine the proportion of the total purchases of tangible assets costing $1,000 or less that is revenue expenditure. There are two options available to businesses to calculate the sample.

- **The first option** is to extract a representative percentage sample from the eligible purchases of an income year, and from this sample determine the percentage that is deemed to be revenue. Ten percent of eligible purchases is considered by the Tax Office to be a representative sample.

- **The second option** allows the taxpayer to choose a sample comprising all eligible purchases for a period (eg. two months) in an income year that is representative of the capital and revenue purchases for the business over the course of the year. From this sample the percentage deemed to be revenue can be determined.

Where statistical sampling is acceptable, the proportion established through sampling will be valid for a maximum of three years (including the income year of the sampling), provided the sample remains representative of the total population.

15.040 LOW-VALUE POOL

ELECTION AND RATE OF DEPRECIATION

Taxpayers, other than those adopting the small business entity regime (see from 10.200), have the choice to establish a low-value pool for all depreciating assets that cost less than $1,000 (low-cost assets). Depreciating assets that have declined in value under the diminishing value method to less than $1,000 (low-value assets) can also be included in the low-value pool (s40-425).

The decline in value of depreciating assets in the low-value pool is calculated under the diminishing value method using an effective life of four years. This means that the depreciation rate for a low cost asset allocated to a low-value pool is 18.75% in the first year and 37.5% for the subsequent years. Halving the 37.5% rate for the first year recognises that low cost assets may be allocated to the pool throughout the year.

A low-value asset (an asset depreciated under the diminishing value method to a value of less than $1,000) can also be allocated to a low-value pool. Such an asset is allocated to the low-value pool at the beginning of the year and the depreciation rate is 37.5%.

Once a taxpayer elects to allocate a low-cost asset to a low-value pool for an income year, all low-cost assets acquired in that year and subsequent years must be allocated to that pool (s40-430(1)). This rule does not apply to low-value assets. Any depreciating asset that has been allocated to the low-value pool must remain in the pool (s40-430(2)).

Any taxpayer that elects not to use a low-value pool must work out the decline in value of each low-cost asset according to its effective life.

ASSETS THAT CANNOT BE ALLOCATED TO LOW-VALUE POOLS

- horticultural plant, as these assets are excluded by the definitions of 'low-cost asset' and 'low-value asset'
- assets depreciated by a small business taxpayer under the capital allowances rules in Division 328D
- non-business related depreciating assets costing less than $300 that are immediately deductible
- assets where decline in value is determined using the prime cost method, and
- certain depreciating assets used in carrying out research and development activities which are entitled to a R&D tax offset under Division 355 (or a R&D deduction under the pre-2011-12 R&D provisions (s73BA ITAA36)).

It is imperative to note that a low cost asset can only be allocated to the low-value pool in the year it was first used or installed for a taxable purpose. It cannot be allocated to the low-value pool in a subsequent year (s40-425(5)(c)). Consequently, where an asset has declined in value using the diminishing value method to below $1,000 you need to check that its original cost was $1,000 or more before allocating it to the low-value pool.

DETERMINING THE DECLINE IN VALUE OF THE LOW-VALUE POOL

Taxpayers who allocate a depreciating asset to a low-value pool must make a reasonable estimate of the percentage of its use that will be for a taxable purpose over either its effective life (for a low-cost asset) or its remaining effective life (for a low-value asset). This percentage is called the 'taxable use percentage' (s40-435).

Zena Ltd buys a printer for $780. It allocates the printer to a low-value pool and estimates that it will be used for taxable purposes 80% in the first year, 80% in the second year and 40% in the third and fourth year of its four years of effective life. The 'taxable use percentage' for the printer is 60% (ie. 240%/4).

Once an asset is allocated to a low-value pool its estimated taxable use percentage cannot be varied.

CALCULATION OF DECLINE IN VALUE OF ASSETS IN A LOW-VALUE POOL

The decline in value of assets in a low-value pool is calculated by following the method statement in s40-440(1). This method statement requires the taxpayer to:

Step 1: Take 18.75% of the taxable use percentage of the cost of each low-cost asset allocated to the pool for that year. Add those amounts. The 18.75% rate represents half of the 37.5% which is the diminishing value rate on an effective life of four years. Halving this rate is in recognition that assets may be allocated to the pool throughout the income year.

Step 2: Add to the step 1 amount, 18.75% of the taxable use percentage of any amounts:
- included in the second element of the cost (see 15.060) for that year of assets allocated to the pool for an earlier income year, and
- low-value assets allocated to the pool for the current year.

Again, the halved rate of 18.75% is in recognition that these costs may be incurred at any time throughout the income year.

Step 3: Add to the step 2 amount, 37.5% of the sum of:
- the pool closing balance for the previous income year, and
- the taxable use percentage of the opening adjustable values of low-value assets, at the start of the income year that were allocated to the pool for that year.

Step 4: The result of adding step 3 and step 2 is the decline in value of the depreciating assets in the low-value pool.

The closing balance of the low-value pool of Zed Ltd for the year ended 30 June 2014 was $2,700. During the 2014-15 income year Zed Ltd acquired a depreciating asset for $800. Its taxable use percentage is 80% and Zed Ltd also chose to allocate to its low-value pool a low-value asset with an opening adjustable value of $920 as at 1 July 2014. Its taxable use percentage is 100%.
The decline in value of the depreciating assets in the low-value pool for the 2014-15 income year is determined as follows:

Asset	Calculation	Amount
Low-cost asset allocated to the pool for the 2014-15 income year	18.75% x ($800 x 80%)	$120.00
Pool closing balance from previous year ($2,700) plus low-value assets allocated to the pool for that year ($920)	37.5% x ($2,700 + $920)	$1,357.50
Total decline in value		$1,477.50

CALCULATION OF THE CLOSING BALANCE OF A LOW-VALUE POOL

The closing balance of the low-value pool for an income year is the sum of:

- the closing balance of the pool for the previous income year, plus
- the taxable use percentage of the costs of low-cost assets allocated to the pool for that year, plus
- the taxable use percentage of the opening adjustable values of any low-value assets allocated to the pool for that year as at the start of that year, plus
- the taxable use percentage of any amounts included in the second element of the cost for the income year of assets allocated to the pool for an earlier income year and low-value assets allocated to the pool for the current year, less
- the decline in value of the depreciating assets in the pool worked out under s40-440(1) (see above).

Continuing the example above, the closing balance of Zed Ltd's low-value pool at 30 June 2015 would be:

Closing balance at 30 June 2014	*$2,700*
Taxable use percentage of low-cost asset ($800 x 80%)	*$640*
Taxable use percentage of low-value asset ($920 x 100%)	*$920*
	$4,260
Less decline in value of assets for the year	*$1,478*
Closing balance of low-value pool at 30 June 2015	***$2,782***

BALANCING ADJUSTMENT EVENTS IN A LOW-VALUE POOL

If a balancing adjustment event happens to a depreciating asset in a low-value pool, the pool closing balance for that year is reduced (but not below zero) by the taxable use percentage of the asset's termination value (s40-445(1)).

The consequences of this approach (instead of the usual balancing adjustment rules and the apportionment rule applying) are that the depreciating asset that is disposed of effectively attracts a full year's depreciation in the pool and a lesser amount is available for the depreciation of the assets allocated to the pool in the following income years. This is the equivalent of including an amount in assessable income.

If Zena Ltd sold the printer it had acquired for $780 for $400, the closing balance of its low-value pool will be reduced by $240 (ie. $400 x 60% the taxable use percentage of the printer).

If the termination value of a pooled asset exceeded the pool closing balance the excess is included in the taxpayer's assessable income (s40-445(2)).

Where a taxpayer sells a business and there is balance remaining in the taxpayer's low-value pool, that balance can continue to be written-off notwithstanding the taxpayer is no longer in business.

NOTE: *The proportion of non-taxable use is only taken into account in calculating the cost of the asset to be entered into the low value pool but not in calculating the annual depreciation charge. Balancing adjustments take it into account and a pro-rated value is removed from the pool.*

15.050   SOFTWARE DEVELOPMENT POOL

A taxpayer who has incurred expenditure on in-house software that is intended to be used solely for a taxable purpose may choose to allocate such expenditure to a software development pool rather than capitalise the expenditure until the asset is created and then depreciate the software once it is used or held ready for use (s40-450(1)).

IN-HOUSE SOFTWARE

The term 'in-house' software is defined as computer software, or a right to use, computer software that is acquired, developed or another entity develops, mainly for use by the taxpayer in performing the functions for which the software was developed.

NOTE: Software is not 'in-house software' if expenditure on the software is deductible under any provision of the income tax legislation outside Div 40 (the UCA system) or Div 328 (small business entity concessions).

If software is not in-house software, it will be depreciable under the general rules in Div 40 as it is an item of intellectual property (which is a depreciating asset), and the decline in value would be calculated using an effective life of 25 years and the prime cost method.

In ATO ID 2010/14, annual software licence fees were considered to be expenditure of a revenue nature and thus deductible under s8-1.

NOTE: Expenditure in developing software for exploitation of copyright is not in-house software.

RATE OF DEDUCTION FOR SOFTWARE DEVELOPMENT POOL

A taxpayer can choose to allocate expenditure incurred on developing, or having another entity develop, in-house software in an income year to a software development pool provided that the in-house software is to be used solely for a taxable purpose. Once a taxpayer elects to create a software development pool the choice is irrevocable and any expenditure incurred on developing in-house software must be allocated to the software development pool (s40-450(2)). Once allocated to a pool, if the project is abandoned the expenditure cannot be written off at that time, it must continue to be written off in the pool.

Any consideration for disposal of pooled software is included in assessable income unless roll-over relief applies (s40-460).

The rate of deduction for assets in a software development pool is:

- First year: *Nil*
- Second year: *40%*
- Third year: *40%*
- Fourth year: *20%*

The prime cost method is used (s40-455).

Due to the rate of deduction there will be a separate pool for each year, with a maximum of four pools at any one time (s40-450(4)).

Expenditure incurred on software development projects that commenced before the income year in which the choice to pool is made must continue to be capitalised until the particular item of software is used or installed for use. So must expenditure incurred on software development projects that are not intended solely for a taxable purpose.

NOTE: Legislation is currently before Parliament which will amend the law such that expenditure allocated to software development pools is to be claimed over five years at the following rates:

- First year: *Nil*
- Second year: *30%*
- Third year: *30%*
- Fourth year: *30%*
- Fourth year: *10%*

This is to apply from 1 July 2015. At the time of writing, this amendment is not yet enacted.

NON-POOL IN-HOUSE SOFTWARE

Computer software that is acquired (off the shelf) or a right to use computer software although both covered by the definition of 'in-house software' cannot be allocated to a software development pool, but can be treated as a depreciating asset. Under the UCA rules acquired computer software is depreciated over **four years** using the prime cost method (see s40-95(7), s40-70(2) and s40-72(2)).

Upgrades to software held as at 7.30pm on 13 May 2008 remain subject to the former effective life of 2.5 years provided no new asset is created.

NOTE: Legislation is currently before Parliament that will increase the statutory effective life of in-house software from four to five years for assets acquired from 1 July 2015. At the time of writing this is yet to be enacted.

15.060 SELECTION OF DEPRECIATION METHOD

For all depreciating assets that are either not deductible immediately or allocated to a low-value pool or software development pool, the taxpayer must determine the decline in value by using the appropriate formula, which in turn depends upon the depreciation method selected.

DETERMINING DECLINE IN VALUE

For most depreciating assets the taxpayer must select to use either the diminishing value method or prime cost method (s40-65(1)). However, there are some exceptions:

- you can only use the prime cost method to work out the decline in value of in-house software expenditure, intellectual property (except copyright in a film), a spectrum licence, a datacasting transmitter licence and a telecommunications site access right (s40-70(2) and s40-72(2)).
- special rules apply:
  - where the asset is acquired from an associate, or
  - where the end-user does not change (eg. a sale and lease back arrangement or lessee purchasing the asset from the lessor), or
  - where the effective life of the former holder cannot be ascertained (s40-95).

  In these special cases, when calculating depreciation a taxpayer must:
  - use the same method that their associate was using when they acquire a depreciating asset from that associate (s40-65(2) and s40-95(4))
  - use the same method that the previous holder was using where the end-user of the depreciating asset does not change (s40-65(3) and s40-95(5))
  - use the diminishing value method where the method used by the former holder cannot be ascertained (s40-65(4))
  - where the depreciating asset forms part of a low-value pool or a software development pool, the taxpayer must calculate the decline in value using the rules provided under Subdivision 40-E (low-value and software development pools) rather than Subdivision 40-B (core provisions), and
  - where a company could deduct an amount for assets used for research and development purposes under s355-305 (or former s73BA ITAA36), the same depreciation method must be used for the notional Division 40 deduction (s40-65(6)).

Once a taxpayer makes a choice of a method for a depreciating asset it cannot be changed (s40-130(2)).

DECLINE IN VALUE FORMULA

The choice of method determines the formula to be used. There are three common elements in each formula:

- cost or base value
- days held, and
- effective life or remaining effective life.

DIMINISHING VALUE METHOD

If the diminishing value method is selected the formula is:

- If you start to hold the depreciable asset before 10 May 2006

  Base value x (days held divided by 365) x (150% divided by asset's effective life) (s40-70)

- If you start to hold the depreciable asset on or after 10 May 2006

  Base value x (days held divided by 365) x (200% divided by asset's effective life) (s40-72)

To start to hold the asset on or after 10 May 2006 the taxpayer must have:

- entered into the contract on or after 10 May 2006, or
- started construction of the asset on or after 10 May 2006, or

- started to hold the asset in some other way on or after 10 May 2006.

The Act contains integrity measures to ensure that taxpayers who dispose of and reacquire their assets held before 10 May 2006 for the main purpose of qualifying for the new 200% diminishing value rate, or acquire substitute assets for that purpose, must continue to use the 150% rate. The 200% rate will also not apply if the effective life of an asset held before 10 May 2006 is recalculated after that date.

PRIME COST METHOD

The general formula for the prime cost method is:

> *Asset's cost x (days held divided by 365) x (100% divided by asset's effective life)*
> *(s40-75)*

However, the prime cost method formula must be adjusted in a later income year if any of the following circumstances occur:

- the asset's effective life must be recalculated
- a second element cost is incurred after start time
- there is an application of the commercial debt forgiveness provisions that reduces the asset's opening adjustable value
- the taxpayer obtains rollover relief for an involuntary disposal
- GST adjustments are made under Subdivision 27-B, and
- foreign currency gains or losses arising under s770-70 or 770-75 which cause the opening adjustable value to increase or decrease. In these circumstances, the prime cost formula is changed.

Instead of 'cost' use the asset's 'opening adjustable value' for the change year plus any amount included in the second element of cost for the year; and instead of the asset's 'effective life', use the asset's 'remaining effective life', where:

> *Remaining effective life = Original calculation of effective life – Period of time*
> *that has elapsed from the asset's start time, up until the beginning*
> *of the income year for which the decline in value is being calculated*

However, where effective life has been recalculated, the 'remaining effective life' formula is:

> *Remaining effective life = Most recent calculation – Period of time*
> *that has elapsed from the asset's start time, up until the beginning*
> *of the income year for which the decline in value is being calculated.*

MEANING OF TERMS IN THE FORMULA

Base value

The term 'base value' is only relevant where the diminishing value formula is selected. For the year in which start time occurs, 'base value' is the cost of the asset. For a later year, 'base value' is the asset's adjusted value at that time, plus any improvements to the asset during the year, less the amount of any commercial debt forgiven that has been applied in reduction of the value of the depreciating asset.

Because any improvements are simply added to base value, the improvements are (in effect) given the benefit of a whole year's decline rather than being apportioned in some way.

Matt buys a business asset on 1 July 2014 for $20,000 financed through instalment payments. If the depreciation rate is 25%, the decline in value in the first year is $20,000 x 25% = $5,000.

The opening adjustable value at 1 July 2015 will be $15,000 ($20,000 – $5,000).

If on 1 July 2015 Matt has $1,000 of the debt forgiven in relation to this asset, the opening adjustable value for the 2015-16 income year is $14,000 (ie. $15,000 – $1,000). The decline in value for the 2015-16 year would be 25% of $14,000 = $3,500 and the closing adjustable value is $10,500.

If Matt improved the asset on 2 March 2016 at the cost of $700, the base value for the 2016-17 year is the opening adjustable value plus the improvement ($10,500 + $700 = $11,200) and the decline in value for the 2016-17 year is 25% x $11,200 = $2,800.

Cost

Unless an amount is specified in the table in s40-180(2), the cost of a depreciating asset is the sum of two elements, called the first element and the second element.

First element of 'cost'

The first element is what it cost the taxpayer to start holding the depreciable asset. This is always worked out at the time the taxpayer began holding the asset (s40-180). The first element includes the acquisition price of the asset and any incidental expenses incurred to acquire the asset or create a new asset. Generally this is the amount the taxpayer has paid or is taken to have paid for the asset, and would include payments incidental to start holding the asset, eg. stamp duty and any costs to transport and install it in position to be ready for use (s40-180(1)).

'Cost' also includes an amount that a taxpayer has paid or is taken to have paid in relation to starting to hold a depreciating asset if that amount is directly connected with holding the asset (s40-180(3)). For example, if a taxpayer travels overseas to purchase a specialised depreciating asset for their business or trade and the sole purpose of the trip was the acquisition of that asset, then the cost of the airfare and accommodation are included in the cost of the depreciating asset because the costs are in relation to starting to hold the depreciating asset.

The Tax Office has released a suite of ATO IDs in relation to certain expenses incurred in respect of employees that are engaged on the self-construction of depreciating assets. The ATO IDs discuss whether those expenses are deductible under s8-1 ITAA97 or whether they form part of the 'cost' of the asset for Division 40 purposes:

- ATO ID 2011/42 – in relation to salary or wages
- ATO ID 2011/43 – in relation to labour on-costs, and
- ATO ID 2011/44 – in relation to vehicle running costs.

The first element of cost of a depreciating asset does not include any amount that forms part of the second element of cost of any other depreciating asset (s40-180(4)).

Cost excludes any input tax credit and any increasing or decreasing GST adjustment in relation to the asset.

'Cost' may include any of the following:

- the amount paid
- the market value of any non-cash benefits provided by the taxpayer
- the amount of any liabilities assumed, and
- any amount included in assessable income as a result of starting to hold the asset.

Bill, a gardener, buys a panel van (a depreciating asset) from James. The agreement provides that in exchange for ownership of the panel van Bill will:

- *pay James $2,000 in cash*
- *landcare James's garden – market value of this service is $3,000, and*
- *undertake maintenance work in James's garden for the next three years – market value $1,500 per year.*

The cost of the panel van is $2,000 + $3,000 + $1,500 + $1,500 + $1,500 = $9,500.

A Ltd manufactures some furniture for B in return for a fabric-cutting machine. The furniture has a market value of $20,000, but as the fabric-cutting machine has an arm's length value of $60,000, A contributes $35,000 towards the cost of acquiring the machine.

Pursuant to s21A ITAA36, A Ltd would have included the non-cash benefit ($60,000 – $35,000 = $25,000) in its assessable income.

The first element in A Ltd's cost base is the greater of:

- *the amount it paid ($35,000) plus market value of the non-cash benefit it provided ($20,000), which is $55,000, and*
- *the amount that is assessable income from receiving the machine ($25,000) plus the amount by which the assessable income was reduced by the payment A made to B ($35,000), which is $60,000.*

In this case the first element of the fabric-cutting machine is $60,000.

In certain circumstances 'cost' will be a particular amount attributed under the cost rules rather than the amount actually paid. For example, where the asset is a luxury car, the first element is increased by part of any discount that relates to the disposal of another depreciating asset at less than its market value, and/or reduced to the car limit ($57,466 for 2014-15, 2013-14, 2012-13, 2011-12 and 2010-11).

Cars that are specially fitted for disabled persons are not subject to the car limit (s40-230(2)).

In May 2015, Fred acquires a new car from a car dealer that would have normally cost $60,000. However, the car dealer is prepared to reduce the cost to $50,000 if Fred accepts $15,000 as trade-in for his old car that had a market value of $25,000, so that the changeover price remains at $35,000.

For depreciation purposes, the new car is taken have cost $70,000 and then reduced to the 2014-15 car limit of $57,466. The termination value of the car traded-in will be $25,000.

If the acquirer of the car had been an entity entitled to an input tax credit, the cost of the car is reduced by the input tax credit before it is reduced by the car limit.

Second element of 'cost'

The second element of 'cost' is the additional cost to bring the asset to its current condition and location after the taxpayer starts to hold the asset (eg. transportation and installation costs to relocate the asset and the cost of any improvements made to the asset) and expenditure reasonably attributable to a balancing adjustment event occurring for the asset, such as the cost of its demolition (s40-190(2)). There are some exceptions to this rule (see s40-190(2A)).

The second element of the depreciating asset's cost is either:

- the amount a taxpayer has paid or is taken to have paid under s40-185 (s40-190(2)), or
- the market value of any benefits received in cases where the parties are not dealing at arm's length or receive benefits under a private or domestic arrangement (s40-190(3)).

AMOUNTS NOT INCLUDED IN 'COST'?

The cost of a depreciating asset will not include the following:

- GST input credits and decreasing adjustments (Subdivision 27-B)
- amounts incurred before 1 July 2001 (or under a contract entered into before that date) on a depreciating asset that is not plant (s40-200)
- amounts deductible for expenditure on mining, quarrying or prospecting information
- amounts deductible outside Division 40 (s40-215(1))
- expenditure allowable under the R&D provisions (s40-215(2)), and
- expenses not of a capital nature such as repairs (s40-220).

A company purchases a car. The contract of sale provides the following details:

Purchase price	*$36,669*
Leather trim	*$1,639*
Carpet mats	*$115*
Headlight covers	*$65*
Delivery fee	*$1,095*
Sub total (includes GST)	*$39,583*
Stamp duty	*$1,584*
Registration	*$500*
Total purchase price	*$41,667*

If the company is entitled to a full input tax credit for the GST, the cost of the car for depreciation purposes is:

Sub total $39,583 – GST $3,598 = $35,985 + stamp duty $1,584 = $37,569 (cost).

The GST and the registration, a revenue item, are excluded from the cost of the depreciating asset.

SPECIFIED 'COST' IN PARTICULAR CASES

For a number of special cases, such as where an asset is split or merged, or a balancing adjustment event occurs, the table in s40-180(2) specifies the 'cost' of a depreciating asset, regardless of the amount actually paid or benefit provided. In special cases the table in s40-180(2) should always be consulted when determining 'cost'. Some of these cases are discussed below.

Split assets

When a depreciating asset that a taxpayer holds is split, the taxpayer is taken to have stopped holding that original asset and to have begun to hold the new assets into which it is split (s40-115(1)).

As the split assets are essentially created out of the original asset, the first element of cost for each of these newly split assets is a reasonable proportion of the sum of:

- the adjustable value of the original asset just before it was split, and
- any expenses that the taxpayer incurred to split the original asset (s40-180(2) item 1 and s40-205).

Bill owns a cement truck with an adjustable value of $80,000. He removes the cement mixer from the truck, costing him $8,000. Bill has split the original asset into two new depreciating assets, the truck and the mixer.

The first element of cost for each of the two new assets is determined by apportioning the total of the adjustable value of the original asset and the cost of splitting it between the two assets, that is, $88,000. On the basis of the relative market values of these two new assets Bill determines that the cost of the truck is $40,000 and the cost of the cement mixer is $48,000.

Merged assets

When depreciating assets are merged into another depreciating asset, the taxpayer is taken to have stopped holding the original assets and to have begun to hold the new asset into which they are merged (s40-125).

The first element of cost for that single merged asset is the sum of:

- the adjustable value of the original assets just before they were merged, and
- any expenses that the taxpayer incurs to merge the original assets (s40-180(2) item 2 and s40-210).

If Bill, in the example above, purchased a new truck for $100,000 and spent $10,000 to have the cement mixer attached to it, he has merged two depreciating assets into a single depreciating asset, a new cement truck. The first element in the cost is $158,000 being the sum of:

- *the adjustable value of the cement mixer ($48,000)*
- *the adjustable value of the new truck before both assets were merged ($100,000), and*
- *the expense of attaching the cement mixed to the new truck ($10,000).*

Asset used again after ceasing use

Where a taxpayer expects not to use a depreciating asset ever again, there is a balancing adjustment event even though they continue to hold the asset. If that asset is used again, the first element of its cost is its termination value at the time it ceased to be used (s40-180(2), items 3 and 4).

Rollover relief

Where rollover relief is available on transfer of an asset, the first element of its cost for the transferee is the adjusted value of the asset for the transferor at the time of the transfer. This effectively means that the transferee continues to deduct the decline in value of the depreciating asset using the same method and effective life as the transferor (s40-180(2), item 6).

Partnership assets

A partnership, rather than an individual partner, is the holder of a depreciating asset that is a partnership asset. Where a partnership buys a partnership asset from an entity other than a partner, the first element of its cost to the partnership is the amount the partnership paid. However, where a depreciating asset was previously held by a partner or a differently constituted partnership, the first element of cost for the partnership is the market value of the asset when the partnership became the holder (s40-180(2), item 5).

Hire purchase agreements

While the hirer of a depreciating asset uses that asset and has a right under the agreement to become the legal owner, the hirer can depreciate the asset as the 'holder' under s40-40.

This right will end if the hirer does not become the legal owner by exercising that right under the agreement. If this happens the legal owner of the asset will become the holder and the first element of cost for the legal owner will be the market value of the asset when they become the holder (s40-180(2) item 7).

NOTE: ATO ID 2012/40 provides that the 'cost of the acquisition of the property' for the purposes of hire purchase agreements is limited to amounts which the taxpayer has a presently existing legal liability to pay in order to acquire the property. It does not include a contingent amount which is merely impending, threatened or expected.

Non-arm's length arrangements

Where a taxpayer becomes the holder of a depreciating asset under an arrangement in which they:

- did not deal at arm's length with one or more of the other parties to that arrangement, and
- paid (or are taken to have paid) more than the market value of the asset,

the first element of cost is the market value of the asset when they started to hold it (s40-180(2) item 8).

 A son buys a car from his father. The son pays $12,000 for a car that has a market value of $8,000. The first element in the son's cost of the car will be its market value of $8,000.

Private or domestic arrangements

Where a taxpayer begins to hold a depreciating asset under a private or domestic arrangement, such as where the taxpayer receives the asset as a gift, the first element of cost will be the market value of the asset, rather than any amount that the taxpayer has paid, which might be nil in the case of a gift (s40-180(2) item 9).

Death

When a person holding a depreciating asset dies and the deceased's legal personal representative becomes the holder, the first element of cost to the legal personal representative is the asset's adjustable value to the deceased on the day of death or if the asset is allocated to a low value pool, the amount of the closing pool balance reasonably attributable to the asset (s40-180(2) item 12).

If the depreciating asset of the deceased passes to a joint tenant or beneficiary, the first element of cost to the joint tenant or beneficiary is equal to the market value of the asset at the time of the deceased's death. This amount is reduced by any capital gain that was disregarded as a result of the CGT rules dealing with death (s40-180(2) item 13)).

COST OF DEPRECIATING ASSET ACQUIRED THROUGH SALARY SACRIFICE

Where an employee receives a depreciating asset, such as a desktop computer, as a property fringe benefit through an effective salary sacrifice arrangement, that employee becomes the legal owner and holder of that depreciating asset (s40-40 item 10).

As the holder of the depreciating asset, the employee can claim a deduction for the decline in value of the 'cost' of that asset under s40-25, to the extent that the asset is used for a taxable purpose.

As no item in the table in s40-180(2) applies, 'cost' is determined under s40-185.

As the employee is providing services to the employer, which constitute a non-cash benefit, in exchange for the depreciating asset, the 'cost' of the depreciating asset will be the market value of the non-cash benefit when it is provided.

No deduction will be available for the decline in value of an eligible work-related item (such as a laptop or portable computer) where the item is provided as an expense payment or property fringe benefit and is exempt from FBT pursuant to s58X of the FBT Act. This applies to items acquired after 7.30pm on 13 May 2008.

Where an item was acquired prior to that date, a deduction for decline in value was available for the 2007-08 year, but not later years.

DAYS HELD

The number of days that a taxpayer held a depreciating asset in an income year is worked out from the start of the income year, and then reduced by the number of days that the taxpayer did not use the asset, or have it installed ready for use, for any purpose (s40-70(1)).

Ed acquired a depreciating asset on 3 August 2014 and immediately used it for a taxable purpose. The days held in the 2014-15 income year are 365 – 33 = 332.

EFFECTIVE LIFE

'Effective life' is the estimated period a depreciating asset can be used by any entity for a taxable purpose or for the purpose of producing exempt income, or non-assessable non-exempt income. In making the estimate, assume that the asset will be subject to wear and tear at a rate that is reasonable for the taxpayer's expected usage and will be maintained in reasonably good order and condition (s40-105).

'Effective life' is expressed in years and can include a fraction of a year, such as 41/3 years.

The 'reasonable test' means an asset's 'effective life' will end if it is scrapped, abandoned, or it is no longer economical to maintain the asset, even though embarking on repairs might extend the effective life.

There are two methods to determine effective life. A taxpayer can either:

- make their own estimate of effective life, based on relevant factors affecting the asset and its usage, or
- adopt the Commissioner's determination of effective life of an asset (s40-95(1)) (see 15.160).

Where a taxpayer elects to adopt the Commissioner's determination, the appropriate determination to be applied is that which is in force at the earlier of the following times:

- the time the taxpayer enters into a contract to acquire the asset
- the time the taxpayer otherwise acquires the asset, and
- the time the taxpayer begins construction of the asset,

provided that the asset is first used or installed ready for use within five years of the relevant time. In other situations, the appropriate determination is the one in force at the asset's start time (s40-95(2)(a)). However, where the depreciating asset is plant that was acquired or its construction commenced before 11.45 am on 21 September 1999 the appropriate determination is that which was in force at that time. There is no restriction on the period within which this plant must be first used or held ready for use (s40-95(2)(b)).

 Care is needed when a taxpayer makes their own estimate of an asset's effective life, as the taxpayer must be able to show they took all relevant information into account and that the effective life chosen was reasonable.

The Commissioner only determines the effective life of new assets. A taxpayer who acquires a secondhand depreciating asset and decides that its condition justifies a shorter life should self-assess. The choice to either self-assess the effective life of a depreciating asset or to adopt the effective life determined by the Commissioner must be made in the year the asset's start time occurs (s40-95(3)).

There are statutory caps on the Commissioner's determination of effective life of certain assets (gas supply, oil and gas extraction and aircraft) with a 1 July 2002 'start time'; transport assets, such as buses, light commercial vehicles, trucks and truck trailers with a 1 January 2005 'start time' and harvesters and tractors with a 1 July 2007 'start time'. For example, from 1 July 2007 tractors and harvesters will be capped at 61/3 years even though the Tax Office has increased the effective life to 12 years for new tractors and 10 to 12 years for larger, new tractors. Depreciating assets with a capped effective life are listed in s40-102. Where there is a statutory cap and a taxpayer elects to use the Commissioner's determination of effective life, that taxpayer can use the statutory cap if the capped life is shorter than that determined by the Commissioner.

EXCEPTIONS

While a taxpayer generally has the choice of self-assessing or adopting the Commissioner's determination of a depreciating asset's effective life, special rules apply:

- where the taxpayer acquired the asset from an associate, or
- where the end-user does not change, or
- where the effective life of the former holder cannot be ascertained (s40-95).

In these special cases, when calculating depreciation a taxpayer must:

- use the same effective life for the diminishing value method that their associate was using or use the remaining effective life for the prime cost method (s40-95(4))
- use the same effective life for the diminishing value method that the previous holder was using where the end-user of the depreciating asset does not change, or use the remaining effective life if the prime cost method was used (s40-95(5)). Examples of this situation are a sale and lease back arrangement or lessee purchasing the asset from the lessor, and
- use the Commissioner's determination of effective life where the effective life that the former holder was using cannot be ascertained (s40-95(6)).

In addition, a taxpayer cannot elect to self-assess for the intangible assets in the table below that have a statutory effective life (s40-95(7)).

The effective life of an intangible asset not covered by the table below and not an IRU (indefeasible right to use a telecommunications cable system) cannot be shortened by a term that excludes any renewal or extension of those rights or longer than any reasonably assured extension or renewal (s40-95(8)).

INTANGIBLE ASSETS THAT HAVE A STATUTORY EFFECTIVE LIFE[1]

Item	Asset	Effective Life
1	Standard patent	20 years
2	Innovation patent	8 years
3	Petty patent	6 years
4	Registered design	15 years
5	Copyright	The shorter of: (a) 25 years, or (b) the period until the copyright ends
6	A licence (except one relating to a copyright or in-house software[2])	The term of the licence
7	A licence relating to a copyright	The shorter of: (a) 25 years, or (b) the period until the licence ends
8	In-house software[2]	2.5 years prior to 13 May 2008 and 4 years thereafter
9	Spectrum licence	The term of the licence
10	Datacasting transmitter licence	15 years

1: These assets are depreciated under the prime cost method (see s40-70(2)).

2: In-house software is computer software, or a right to use computer software, that you acquire, develop or have another entity develop. Proposed increase to 5 years from 1 July 2015.

In *Primary Health Care Limited v FCT* (2010) FCA 419, the Federal Court considered the issue of whether the taxpayer was entitled to claim deductions in respect of the decline in value of copyright in patient records. This copyright was said to be acquired from the purchase of medical and dental practices as part of goodwill. The taxpayer was a listed company and operated various medical centres through a unit trust.

The Court was of the view that:

- with limited exceptions, there was no copyright existing in the majority of the patient records in evidence. However this does not imply that copyright can never subsist in medical or similar records
- only one of a number of contracts of sale expressly provided for the transfer of copyright, and in the case of that contract only, the taxpayer acquired copyright in some referral letters. The Court found that the transfer of the patient records to certain practices did not require the implied creation of a license to use the copyright in those patient records

- on the facts of this case, there was no consideration provided for the transfer of copyright. The Court considered that where the parties had agreed to allocate the sale proceeds between goodwill and certain listed assets, there was no reason why the Court should interfere to allocate any portion of the sale proceeds to the copyright transferred (when the agreements had not done so), and

- for the purposes of determining whether the copyright was being used by the taxpayer in its business, the requirement that the copyright be available for use is satisfied by the availability of the physical records.

On the facts, the Court found that some of the medical practices would have 'used' the copyright in the material by copying the patient records to a new record or new patient database and that others would have 'used' the patient records by having physically delivered the patient records to the taxpayer thus making the records available for copying. The Court held that the taxpayer was not entitled to deductions in respect of decline in value of copyright in patient records, either because the copyright had not been acquired, or no consideration had been provided for it.

In the Decision Impact Statement issued in relation to the case, the Commissioner considers that the decision of the Court supports his view on the meaning of goodwill as set out in TR 1999/16 and the application of the capital allowance provisions to the sale of a medical practice as relevantly set out in TD 2005/1.

NOTE: TD 2005/1 has been reviewed and subsequently updated to ensure that it is consistent with the Court's reasoning in *Primary Health Care Limited v FCT* [2010] FCA 419.

RECALCULATING EFFECTIVE LIFE

The effective life of a depreciating asset may be recalculated in a later year at the election of the holder where a change in circumstance means that the original estimate is no longer accurate (s40-110(1)). However, the holder must recalculate the effective life of a depreciating asset in a later year where the cost of that depreciating asset has increased by at least 10% in that year and:

- the taxpayer has self-assessed its effective life, or

- the taxpayer has used the Commissioner's determination of effective life or capped life and uses the prime cost method to calculate the asset's decline in value, or

- the taxpayer acquired the asset from an associate or the holder changed but the user is the same or an associate (eg. a sale and leaseback arrangement) (s40-110(2)).

These situations are likely to occur where a taxpayer improves a depreciating asset. Repairs to an asset (as distinct from an improvement) will not result in a recalculation of effective life, even if the repair exceeds the cost by over 10%, because repairs of a non-capital nature do not increase the cost of a depreciating asset (s40-220).

An improvement to a depreciating asset is part of its second element of cost (s40-190).

A taxpayer cannot re-assess the effective life of an intangible depreciating asset listed in s40-95(7) (see table above) (s40-110(5)).

REMAINING EFFECTIVE LIFE

The remaining effective life of a depreciating asset is any period of its effective life that is yet to elapse as:

- at the start of the change year, or

- in the case of a rollover, the time when the balancing adjustment event occurs for the transferor (s40-75(4)).

ADJUSTABLE VALUE

The term 'adjustable value' is used to signify the cost of the asset that has yet to decline at a particular time (s40-85). 'Adjustable value' replaces the concept of 'undeducted cost', which replaced the term 'written down value'.

Where an asset has yet to be used or installed ready for use for any purpose, the 'adjustable value' is the asset's cost (s40-85(1)(a)). This rule enables a balancing adjustment to be determined when an asset is destroyed before use or is never used.

For a time in the income year in which you first use the asset or have it installed ready for use, the 'adjustable value' is the asset's cost less its decline in value up to that time (s40-85(1)(b)). For a time in a later income year, the 'adjustable value' is the asset's opening adjusted value for that year, plus any amount included in the second element of its cost for that year, less the asset's decline in value for that year up to that time (s40-85(1)(c)). The 'adjustable value' as determined above is reduced if there is any debt forgiveness amount (s40-90).

Data Pty Ltd purchases a machine for $60,000 on 22 October 2014 and first used it on the same day to produce assessable income. The estimated effective life of the machine is 8 years and the company elects to use the prime cost method.

The decline in value for the 2014-15 income year is:

$60,000 x [(365 – 113 days) divided by 365 days] x (100% divided by 8) = $5,178

The amount of $54,816 ($60,000 – $5,184) will be carried forward as the 'opening adjustable value' for the 2015-16 income year.

A taxpayer will need to know the 'adjustable value' of an asset:

- when there is a balancing adjustment event
- when there is a splitting or merging of a depreciating asset, or
- at the end of the income year.

Adjustable value may be modified by:

- certain GST adjustments
- certain balancing adjustments (see s40-285(4))
- a debt forgiveness amount
- an involuntary disposal rollover, and
- a short-term foreign exchange realisation gain or loss.

CALCULATION OF DECLINE IN VALUE

EXAMPLE 1: 100% taxable purpose

A taxpayer purchases a machine for $10,000 on 1 September 2014 and commences to use the asset on that day. The machine is used 100% for a taxable purpose.

Its effective life is ten years and the taxpayer elects to use the diminishing balance method. The decline in value for the 2014-15 tax year is:

$10,000 x [(365– 62 days) divided by 365] x (200% divided by 10) = $1,660

The adjustable value of the asset at 30 June 2015 would be $10,000 – $1,660 = $8,340.

EXAMPLE 2: Partly non-taxable purpose

A taxpayer purchases a laptop computer on 1 March 2015 for $3000 and commences to use the asset on the day of purchase. It is used 60% for a taxable purpose. The effective life of the laptop is three years and the taxpayer elects to use the prime cost method. The decline in value for the 2014-15 tax year is:

$3,000 x [(365 – 244) divided by 365] x (100% divided by 3) = $331

As the laptop had a 40% non-taxable use the taxpayer's deduction is reduced by 40% of $334 to $199.

The adjusted value at the end of the year is $2,669, irrespective of the extent of the taxpayer's non-taxable use of the computer.

15.065   FOREIGN EXCHANGE (FOREX) GAINS AND LOSSES

As a general principle foreign currency gains and losses are treated as on revenue account so foreign currency gains are assessable income and foreign currency losses are deductible when realised. One exception to this rule applies to short-term realisation gains and losses (also see 22.320).

GAINS

A short-term forex realisation gain may arise under forex realisation event 4 as a result of the cessation of an obligation to pay foreign currency for a depreciating asset that you have started to hold or a project amount that you have incurred. Where that occurs:

- the forex realisation gain is not assessable under s775-15, and
- the asset's cost, adjustable value, or the opening value of the pool in which the asset resides (as appropriate) is reduced by the gain (s775-70 item 3).

The downward adjustment to the cost, adjustable value or pool value of a depreciating asset as a result of a short-term forex gain cannot go below zero. Where the adjustment would result in a cost less than zero, the cost is taken to be reduced to zero and any excess in the forex realisation gain is included in the entity's assessable income (s775-70(2)).

On 7 April 2014, Mainline Pty Ltd contracts to purchase a depreciating asset from Foreign Country for USD $100,000. At that time, A$1 was equivalent to USD $0.92. Mainline immediately begins to 'hold' the depreciating asset and starts to use it. The cost of the depreciating asset at that time translates to A$108,696. Mainline does not pay for the depreciating asset until 8 December 2014, by which time A$1 has risen to USD $0.98. Mainline pays A$102,041, and has a forex realisation gain of A$6,655 (ie. $98,696 – $6,655).

Assuming the depreciating asset declined in value by A$10,000 during the 2013-14 tax year, its opening adjustable value at 1 July 2014 is A$98,696. However, because of the forex realisation gain Mainline must reduce this opening value to A$92,041 for the purposes of calculating its decline in value for 2014-15 and later years.

To be a short-term forex transaction involving a depreciating asset the time of payment must be a 24 month period beginning 12 months before the taxpayer begins holding the asset.

LOSSES

Similarly, a short-term forex realisation loss may arise under forex realisation event 4 as a result of starting to hold a depreciating asset. Where that occurs:

- the forex realisation loss is not deductible under s775-30, and
- the asset's cost, adjustable value, or the opening value of the pool in which the asset resides (as appropriate) is increased by the loss (s775-75 item 3).

An entity can choose not to apply the short-term realisation rules, in which case the normal Division 775 rules apply. This choice must be made in writing and is irrevocable (s775-80). Section 775-80(3) outlines the time limits for making this choice.

Alternatively, forex realisation events 2 and 4 are disregarded where the entity elects that the limited balance exemption or retranslation option applies.

15.070 BALANCING ADJUSTMENT EVENTS

ASSESSABLE INCOME OR DEDUCTION

An adjustment to a taxpayer's assessable income or deductions, may be necessary where a taxpayer:

- stops holding a depreciating asset (eg. disposal, loss or theft, depreciating asset converted to trading stock, death of taxpayer)
- stops using a depreciating asset for any purpose and expects never to use it again (eg. cessation of business activity)
- has not used a depreciating asset and expects never to use it, or
- where there is a change in the holding of an asset, or in the interest of entities in the asset, and one of the entities that has an interest after the change, held the depreciating partnership asset before the change.

A balancing adjustment event only applies to depreciable assets whose decline in value is worked out under Subdivision 40-B. This means that the balancing adjustment provisions do not apply to some primary production assets such as water facilities and horticultural plants (see 15.090).

Splitting an asset into two or more depreciating assets or the merger of depreciating assets is not a balancing adjustment event (s40-295(3)). Where a balancing adjustment event occurs, the asset's adjustable value (original cost less past decline) is compared with its termination value.

In brief, when the termination value of a depreciating asset is greater than its adjustable value the excess is included in assessable income in the year that the balancing adjustment event occurred. If the termination value of a depreciating asset is less than its adjustable value, the excess is deductible.

A Ltd acquired a machine for $40,000. The company disposed of the machine for $15,000. If the adjusted value of the machine at the time of its disposal was $13,000, then the $2,000 difference is assessable income in the year of disposal.

However, if the adjusted value at the time of disposal had been $20,000, then the company would be entitled to a deduction of $5,000 from the balancing adjustment event.

If a depreciating asset is not wholly used for a taxable purpose, the amount included in assessable income, or the amount deducted, is reduced in proportion to the extent that the depreciating asset was used for purposes other than a taxable purpose. There is a further reduction for leisure facilities and boats.

DETERMINING TERMINATION VALUE

The termination value of a depreciating asset is calculated using the table in s40-300 and this table should be referred to in all circumstances. While termination is generally the amount the taxpayer received or is taken to have received (including the market value of non-cash benefits), in other special circumstances termination value can be:

- the market value of the asset where a taxpayer stops using non-in house software and expects to never use it again
- the deceased's adjustable value where the asset passes to a legal personal representative on death
- the market value of the asset at the time of death where the asset passes to a joint tenant or beneficiary on a taxpayer's death
- the Government's determined value in the case of airport leasing
- zero in the case of in-house software not used or never to be used again, and
- the market value of the asset when the transfer is not at arms length. The Tax Office considers that when an asset passes from a legal personal representative to a beneficiary of a deceased estate it is not an arms length transaction and the transfer is at market value (ATO ID 2002/618).

A sole trader purchased a depreciating asset for $30,000. It was used solely for a taxable purpose.

The sole trader died and the asset passed to the Legal Personal Representative (LPR). At the date of death the asset's adjusted value was $16,000.

When the LPR passed the asset to a beneficiary of the sole trader its market value was $18,000.

There will not be any balancing adjustment under s40-285 when the asset passes from the deceased to the LPR because the termination value at s40-300(2) item 9 is the asset's adjusted value at the time. However, there will be a balancing adjustment of $2,000 (ie. $18,000 – $16,000) when the asset passes from the LPR to the beneficiary because under s40-300(2) item 6 the termination value is the asset's market value.

As termination value exceeds adjusted value by $2,000 the difference is included in assessable income under s40-285(1).

See s40-300 and 40-305 for the full list of special circumstances and the termination value of the asset in these circumstances.

The adjustment to termination value does not apply to taxpayers that:

- cease to be the holder under a non-arm's length arrangement, or
- transfer assets as part of a privatisation scheme to lease an airport.

Termination value is reduced if the balancing adjustment event is a taxable supply. The amount of the reduction is the GST payable on the supply. However, there is no GST reduction if the termination value is modified by Division 40 to market value. Termination value is also adjusted for any increasing or decreasing adjustments under GST law (s27-95).

Andrew sells a panel van to Barbara, a painter, in exchange for Barbara painting Andrew's home:

- *market value of this service is $4,000*
- *terminating a $1,000 debt owed to her by Andrew*

- *undertaking to re-paint Andrew's home again in 7 years: a non-cash benefit with a market value of $3,500, and*
- *incurring a liability to pay Andrew $2,000.*

It cost Andrew $50 to advertise his panel van for sale and this amount is not deductible to Andrew.
Andrew's termination value on disposal of his van is $4,000 + $1,000 + $3,500 + $2,000 – $50 = $10,450.

Where the depreciating asset is a car, its termination value may need to be adjusted where the car was acquired at a discount or its cost is affected by the car limit (s40-320 and s40-325).

Tom acquires a car in 2014-15 for $110,000, when the cost limit is $57,466. He incurs $10,000 of second element costs while he holds the car. He sells the car for $70,000.
The termination value is $70,000 x [($57,466 + $10,000) divided by $120,000] = $39,355.
This adjustment recognises that the car limit has restricted the proportion of the car's cost that has been available to be depreciated, and recognises only that same proportion of the asset's termination value for the purposes of a balancing adjustment. If there was any input tax credit, the cost of the car is reduced by the credit.

X Ltd is registered for GST. It acquired a car for $100,000 GST-inclusive on 1 July 2014. The car is used solely for a taxable purpose.
The first element of cost is reduced by the maximum input tax credit ($5,224) to $94,776. The first element of cost is then further reduced to the 2014-15 car limit of $57,466. The car is sold on 30 June 2015 for $56,000 including GST. There were no second elements of the car's cost. The car's termination value is determined as follows:

Termination value $56,000
Less GST.. $5,091
                                                            $50,909

Reduction under s40-325: ($50,909 x $57,466) divided by $94,776 = $30,868
The termination value of the car is $30,868.

To avoid double taxation, s40-300(3) provides that termination value of a depreciating asset does not include an amount that is included as ordinary income under s6-5 or as statutory income under s6-10 (except an amount that is statutory income under Division 40).

REDUCTION FOR NON-TAXABLE USE

The balancing adjustment is reduced by the amount that is attributable to the use of the asset other than for a taxable purpose – eg. using the depreciating asset for private purposes or for gaining exempt income. Further, there are other reductions for leisure facilities and boats (s40-25 and s40-290).

The reduction formula is:

[Sum of reductions for an asset under s40-25 (ie. reduction for non-taxable use) divided by Total decline in the value of the depreciating asset since it was held by the taxpayer] x Balancing adjustment amount

Ed disposes of a car that he had used 70% for business and 30% for private purposes. The car cost $40,000 and declined in value to $10,000 (its adjustable value). Its termination value was $5,000.
The balancing adjustment is $5,000 but this amount is reduced by the private usage $1,500 (30% of $5,000) so the deductible amount is $3,500.
If the termination value had been $50,000 rather than $5,000, then the amount assessable as a balancing adjustment is $50,000 – $10,000 = $40,000 reduced by 30% private usage = $28,000.

Although no balancing adjustment event occurs when a depreciating asset is split or merged, where a balancing adjustment event occurs to a depreciating asset (or assets) that has been merged or split, the amount of the balancing adjustment to be included in the taxpayer's assessable income or the amount that can be deducted is reduced by:

- the amount that is attributable to the use of the asset for non-taxable purposes, and

- the amount that can reasonably be attributable to the use of the original depreciating asset (before its split or merger) for non-taxable purposes (s40-290(3)).

However, there is no reduction required where the depreciating asset is mining, quarrying or prospecting information (s40-290(5)).

While a disposal of a depreciating asset that is used wholly for a taxable purpose is excluded from the capital gains regime, the disposal of a depreciating asset that is used partly or wholly for a non-taxable use is subject to CGT event K7 (see 12.040).

BALANCING ADJUSTMENTS WHERE DIFFERENT CAR EXPENSE METHODS USED

There is no balancing adjustment where a taxpayer has used only the 'cents per kilometre' method or the '12% of original value' method for deducting car expenses, or a mix of these two methods, because under these methods there has been no deduction for decline in value of the car (s40-55 and s40-370(1) note 2).

There is a balancing adjustment if the 'log book' method or 'one-third of actual expenses' method has been used. Under the 'one-third of actual expenses' method, two-thirds of the balancing adjustment is excluded because of the apportionment rule in s40-290.

 Meg uses a log book to establish that the business usage of a car is 80%. The adjustable value of the car is $20,000 and it is sold for $26,000. The assessable balancing adjustment is $4,800 (80% of the difference between the termination value ($26,000) and the adjustable value of the car ($20,000)).

If Meg had used the 'one-third of actual expenses' method then her assessable balancing adjustment would be reduced by two-thirds to reflect the amount attributable to her use of the car for a non-taxable purpose. Meg's assessable balancing adjustment would be one third of $6,000 = $2,000.

However, where there has been a mix of methods between the 'cents per kilometre' method or the '12% of original value' method on the one hand with the 'one-third of actual expenses' method or the 'log book' method on the other hand, the balancing adjustment is calculated using the method statement in s40-370(2) and not the formula in s40-285.

Steps in the s40-370(2) method statement are:

Step 1: Subtract the car's adjustable value just before the balancing adjustment event from its termination value.

Step 2: Reduce the amount from step 1, by the amount attributable to the use of the asset for non-taxable purposes. Use the formula:

[Sum of reductions for an asset under s40-25 (reduction for non-taxable use) divided by Total decline in the value of the depreciating asset since it was held by the taxpayer] x Balancing adjustment amount

In determining the amount that is attributable for non-taxable purposes, for the years for which the 'cents per kilometre' or the '12% of original value' methods were used to calculate car expenses, you use as the non-taxable purpose:

- 80% where the 'cents per kilometre' method has been used, and
- two-thirds, if the '12% of original value' method has been used (s40-370(4)).

Step 3: Multiply the step 2 amount by the total number of days for which the taxpayer deducted the decline in value of the car using the 'log book' or 'one-third of actual expenses' methods.

Step 4: Divide the step 3 amount by the total number of days the car was held by the taxpayer.

Step 5: If the step 4 amount is a negative number it is a deduction, and if positive, assessable income. (See TD 2006/49 for a worked example.)

When determining 'adjustable value' you assume that the decline in value for the years in which the 'cents per kilometre' and the '12% of original value' methods applied was calculated on the same basis as when the 'one-third of actual expenses' and/or the 'log book' methods were used (s40-370(3)).

IN-HOUSE SOFTWARE

A taxpayer can claim a balancing adjustment for the cost of in-house software where the expenditure was incurred with the intention of using the software for a taxable purpose, but before being able to use the software, or before installing it ready for use, the taxpayer decides the software will never be used or will never be installed ready for use (s40-335). To obtain this deduction, the expenditure must not be allocated to a software development pool.

The balancing adjustment deduction is the taxpayer's expenditure on in-house software less any consideration, reduced to the taxable purpose proportion of intended usage of the software (s40-335(2)).

RELIEF FOR INVOLUNTARY DISPOSALS

Where a depreciating asset ceases to be held by a taxpayer because it is:

- lost or destroyed
- compulsorily acquired by an Australian government agency
- disposed of to an Australian government agency after compulsory negotiations
- disposed of to a private acquirer under a statutory power other than a compulsory acquisition of minority interests under company law, or
- land (and any depreciating asset fixed to land) which is compulsorily subject to a mining lease and is disposed of to the lessee,

the taxpayer can choose whether to include a balancing adjustment in assessable income or apply some or all of the balancing adjustment amount as a reduction in the cost, or in the base value, of one or more replacement assets (s40-365(1) and (2)).

If making the latter choice, the taxpayer must incur the cost of the replacement asset, or must start to hold it:

- no earlier than one year (or any further period the Commissioner allows) before the involuntary disposal occurred, and
- no later than one year (or any further period the Commissioner allows) after the end of the income year in which the involuntary disposal occurred (s40-365(3)), and

the taxpayer must:

- have used the replacement asset, or have it installed ready for use, wholly for a taxable purpose by the end of the income year in which the taxpayer incurred expenditure on the asset, or started to hold it, and
- be able to deduct an amount for it (s40-365(4)).

The amount covered by the choice is applied in reduction of:

- the cost of the replacement asset, if the replacement asset's start time occurs in the current year, or
- the sum of the replacement asset's opening adjustable value for that year and any amount included in the second element of its cost for that year, for a later year replacement asset (s40-365(5)).

If a taxpayer is making the choice for two or more replacement assets, the amount must be apportioned between those assets in proportion to their cost (s40-365(4)). There is no other balancing adjustment relief.

PARTNERSHIPS

A depreciating asset that is a partnership asset is held by the partnership and not by any particular partner (item 7 of the table in s40-40). Where there is a change in the holding of, or interest in, an asset of a partnership a balancing adjustment event will occur under s40-295(2) unless the transferor entity and the transferee entity jointly elect that rollover relief apply (s40-340).

The transferor entity and transferee entity do not both have to be a partnership. Only one of the entities has to be a partnership meaning rollover relief is available where a sole trader takes on a partner or a partner retires from a partnership and the remaining partner continues operating the business as a sole trader. For example, where there is a variation in a partnership (eg. a partner retiring or a new partner being admitted), unless the transferor (the partners in the old partnership) and transferee (the partners in the new partnership) jointly elect that rollover relief under s40-340 applies, a balancing adjustment event will occur for the old partnership (s40-295(2)). The old partnership will be taken to have disposed of the asset to the new partnership and the termination value will be the market value of the asset when the balancing adjustment event occurred (item 5 of the table in ss40-300(2)). The old partnership will work out the balancing adjustment amount by comparing the adjustable value to the termination value of the depreciating asset. The balancing adjustment amount is then taken into account when calculating net income or loss of the old partnership. The first element in the cost base of the depreciating asset for the new partnership is its market value (item 5 of the table in ss40-180(2)).

15.080 ROLLOVER RELIEF FOR CERTAIN CGT EVENTS

Where a depreciable asset is transferred between related entities and CGT rollover relief is available, the balancing adjustment can be deferred until the next balancing adjustment event occurs.

The conditions for automatic rollover relief are:

- there is a balancing adjustment event because an entity disposes of a depreciating asset in an income year to another entity
- the disposal involves a CGT event, and
- the conditions relating to the item in the following table are satisfied:

Type of CGT rollover	Legislation
Disposal of asset by an individual or trustee to a wholly-owned company	The transferor is able to choose rollover under Subdivision 122-A
Disposal of asset by partners to a wholly-owned company	The transferors (the partners) are able to choose rollover relief under Subdivision 122-B.
Transfer of CGT asset of a trust to a company under a trust restructure	The transferor and transferee are able to choose a roll-over under Subdivision 124-N for the CGT event (applies to balancing adjustment events happening in 2008-09 or a later income year).
Marriage breakdown	Rollover relief is provided under Subdivision 126-A.
Disposal of asset to another member of the same wholly owned group	The transferor is able to choose a roll-over under Subdivision 126-B for the CGT event
Disposal of asset from one fixed trust to another fixed trust	The trustees of the trusts are able to choose to obtain a roll-over under Subdivision 126-G in relation to the disposal
Disposal of asset as part of merger of superannuation funds	The transferor is able to choose a roll-over under Subdivision 310-D in relation to the disposal
Disposal of asset as part of transfer to a MySuper product	The transferor is able to choose a roll-over under Subdivision 310-D in relation to the disposal

The capital allowance rollover provisions do not apply if Subdivision 170-D (transactions by companies within linked groups) applies to the disposal of the depreciating asset or the change in interests in it (s40-340(8)).

In determining whether the CGT rollover provisions apply, you ignore the fact that Division 118 and s122-25(3) exclude certain depreciating assets from the CGT regime (s40-340(2)). Rollover relief is also available where there is a change in a business structure involving a partnership, the transferor retains an interest in the depreciating asset after the change in holding, and both the transferor and transferee agree in writing to rollover relief (s40-340(3)).

Where the rollover relief provisions apply, the transferor is not required to include any balancing adjustment in assessable income and the transferee will use the same method of calculating the decline in value and effective life that the transferor used. Where the transferee had used the prime cost method, the transferee must use the remaining effective life of the asset when calculating its deduction. Further, the 'cost' to the transferee will be the adjustable value of the depreciating asset when it was in the hands of the transferor just before the balancing adjustment event occurred (s40-345). To enable the transferee to continue the depreciation method of the transferor, the transferor must provide the transferee with the necessary information in writing within six months after the end of the transferee's income year within which the balancing adjustment event occurred, or within a longer period allowed by the Commissioner (s40-340(4)). The transferor must keep this record for five years after the balancing adjustment event, while the transferee must keep the record until five years after the next balancing adjustment event for the depreciating asset.

If either the transferor or transferee dies before the end of the six months period the trustee of the deceased's estate may be a party to the choice (s40-340(5)).

In some cases, there are additional rollover consequences if the asset is leased (see s40-350).

15.085 LUXURY VEHICLES

Depreciation claims for luxury cars are based on a depreciation limit (s40-230). The limit that applies to each car is based on the limit in the year that the owner of the car first uses the car. Special rules may apply to hire purchase or limited recourse debt arrangements (see 15.800).

IMPORTANT: The luxury car cost limit does not apply to:
- cars that are fitted for transporting disabled persons in wheelchairs for profit
- cars whose first element of cost exceeds the car limit only because of modifications to enable persons with a disability to use the car for a taxable purpose, and
- a hearse (TD 2006/39).

DEPRECIATION COST LIMIT

Depreciation on luxury cars can only be claimed up to the limits below. When a luxury car is sold, only a recoupment of depreciation up to the cost limit needs to be accounted for in the year of disposal. These rules apply to cars, station wagons, including four wheel drives, but exclude vehicles specially fitted out for transporting disabled persons in wheel chairs and a hearse. The depreciation limit is based on the cost of the car, stamp duty, delivery charges but not registration and third party insurance.

Where a luxury car is held by one or more entities, the car limit is applied to the cost of the car and not to the cost of each entity's interest in the car (s40-230). Section 40-35 then applies to apportion the cost of the car, as reduced to the car limit, between the holders.

The following car limits apply based on the income year the car is first used by the taxpayer.

Depreciation limit for income year car first used by taxpayer									
1985-86	$26,660	1992-93	$47,280	1999-00	$55,134	2006-07	$57,009	2013-14	$57,466
1986-87	$29,646	1993-94	$48,415	2000-01	$55,134	2007-08	$57,123	2014-15	$57,466
1987-88	$34,775	1994-95	$51,271	2001-02	$55,134	2008-09	$57,180	2015-16	$57,466*
1988-89	$39,331	1995-96	$52,912	2002-03	$57,009	2009-10	$57,180		
1989-90	$42,910	1996-97	$55,134	2003-04	$57,009	2010-11	$57,466		
1990-91	$45,056	1997-98	$55,134	2004-05	$57,009	2011-12	$57,466		
1991-92	$45,462	1998-99	$55,134	2005-06	$57,009	2012-13	$57,466		

*Preliminary calculations using Australian Bureau of Statistics – *Motor vehicle sub-group of the Consumer Price Index – weighted average of the eight capital cities* – indicate that there is no indexing of the car limit for 2015-16. The ATO has yet to confirm the car limit in a Tax Determination at the time of writing.

 Luxury car limit for depreciation purposes is different from the luxury car tax threshold which is used to calculate the 33% luxury car tax liability.

DISPOSAL ABOVE DEPRECIATION COST LIMIT

Car or station wagon purchased

Where the cost of a car is above the depreciation car limit (for the income year it was first used) the balancing adjustment is determined by the formula:

Termination value x [(Car limit in year of first use + amounts included in the second element of the car's cost) divided by Total cost of the car (ignoring car limit)]

On 1 July 2011 a car cost $60,000 after excluding the GST input credit. Depreciation limit in year of first use was $57,466. Termination value was $36,000 (on 30 June 2015). The car was used 100% for business purposes. There were no second element costs. The effective life is 8 years and the prime cost depreciation method is used.

Decline in value under the prime cost method

The termination value is reduced to:

$36,000 x ($57,466 divided by $60,000) = adjusted sale price	$34,480
Adjusted value on car limit	$57,466
less decline in value for four years	$28,733
Adjusted value	$28,733
Adjusted depreciation deemed recouped	**$5,747**

$5,718 is the amount included in the taxpayer's assessable income as a balancing adjustment.

CAR OR STATION WAGON WAS FORMERLY LEASED

Details as above, and at the end of the four year lease, the residual amount paid (by the lessee to buy the car from the lessor) was $36,000. Lease charges are $1,000 per month. The amount assessable is nil: ie. the smallest of:

Actual profit on sale	nil
Deductible lease charges 36 x $ 1,000 per month	$36,000
Adjusted deemed depreciation (from previous example)	**$5,747**

Using the same facts, except the purchaser incurred expenditure on improving or enhancing the vehicle.

Second element cost – immediate capital improvements on acquisition	$2,000
Disposal price 17 weeks after acquisition	$46,000
Depreciation for 17 weeks:	
$38,000 x [(365 – 246) divided by 365] x (100 divided by 8)	**$1,549**

The assessable amount on the subsequent disposal is calculated as above, but the actual profit on sale is $46,000 – ($2,000 + $36,000) = $8,000.

The adjusted deemed depreciation of $5,747 is the lowest of the three outcomes. Therefore, the amount to be included as assessable income is $5,747 plus depreciation recouped of $1,549.

The whole of the recouped depreciation is included because the car was used wholly to produce income and was sold for more than acquisition price. Thus all depreciation claimed is recouped and assessable.

Had the car only been used partly to produce assessable income, see 15.070.

15.088 LEASES OF LUXURY CARS

The rules in Division 42A of Schedule 2E ITAA36 for claiming deductions for luxury cars affect the amount of leasing charges (and depreciation) that can be claimed on vehicles that exceed the depreciation cost limit in the year they are first used by the lessee ($57,466 for 2014-15, 2013-14 and 2012-13).

LESSOR'S TAX TREATMENT

The lessor is treated as having disposed of the luxury car at the start of the lease for consideration generally equal to the cost of the vehicle. The lessor is then denied deductions for depreciation.

The lessor is taken to have made a loan to the lessee equal to the cost of the luxury car for the term of the lease. The lessor returns income based on the finance charge which is based on the notional loan. That is, each lease payment is broken up between an interest and principal component.

The interest or finance component (which must be calculated on an accruals basis) is treated as assessable to the lessor and as deductible to the lessee. The principal or capital component is treated as a capital reduction to the notional loan. The interest payment or accrual amount is worked out by multiplying the 'outstanding notional loan principal' by the 'implicit interest rate'. If leases are being paid monthly, it is necessary to determine the monthly implicit interest rate.

EXAMPLE 1: *If the annual implicit interest rate per annum is 9.1%, the monthly implicit interest rate is 0.7583%. Using the car in example 2 on the next page, for July to August 2014, the interest payment accrual amount is calculated as: $76,290.18 x (9.1%pa divided by 12 months) = $578.53.*

The lessor would return assessable income of $3,367.07 in respect of the year ended 30 June 2014 which represents the finance or interest component of each 6 lease payment (from July to December 2014).

LESSEE'S TAX TREATMENT

The lessee is treated as the notional owner of the car who has taken out a notional loan from the lessor. The lessee is entitled to depreciation (subject to the depreciation cost limit) and notional finance charges (calculated on an accruals basis) but does not obtain a tax deduction for lease payments.

The cost of a previously owned car is worked out using the rules in Subdivision 40-C and is generally the amount paid for the car subject to the car limit.

TERMINATION OF THE LEASE

The following rules apply when a lease is terminated.

- Upon termination of the lease, if by the lessee paying out the lease, the transfer of the luxury motor vehicle from the lessor to the lessee is not treated as a disposal for the purposes of the Act, including the depreciation provisions. Further, there is no balancing adjustment event because the lessee does not stop being the holder of the car (ID 2003/756). On becoming the actual owner of the car, the former lessee would continue to depreciate the motor vehicle.

- When the motor vehicle is sold by the former lessee, the depreciation balancing adjustment provisions apply as if the vehicle was owned for the entire period of the lease and any period from the termination of the lease until the date of sale.

- If the lease is assigned by the lessee to a new lessee (eg. where the new lessee simply takes over the obligations of the former lessee), then there has been a termination of the lease (other than by the old lessee paying out the lease) for the purposes of these rules.

  The former lessee is deemed to have disposed of the car for consideration equal to:

  - the balance of notional loan less payable amount plus refundable amount, or
  - if it is impractical to work out the above, for the market value of the car at that time.

The following example looks at where a lease is paid out and the vehicle is sold by the vendor to an arm's length purchaser.

ITAA97 has been amended to ensure Division 42A of Schedule 2E ITAA36 continues to apply after 30 June 1997.

EXAMPLE 2: *A car worth $120,000 is leased for a four year period from 15 December 2012 to 15 December 2016. Lease payments are $2,090.15 per month and the residual value is $51,063.18. The motor vehicle depreciation cost limit is $57,466 for the 2012-13 income year. The taxpayer estimates the effective life of the car at seven years, using the diminishing value method (the rate being 28.57% pa).*

On 15 December 2015 the leased motor vehicle is sold. To effect the sale, the vendor/lessee purchases the vehicle for $70,174 (the payout or adjusted residual value after three years) from the lessor and sells the car for $75,000 to an arms length purchaser.

As the leased car was a luxury vehicle and treated as owned by the lessee, depreciation and finance charges available as a deduction to the lessee to date of actual sale would be:

Depreciation

Year ended	Original cost	Depreciation cost limit	Opening WDV	Depreciation[1] 28.57% pa	Adjusted value
30/6/2013	$120,000	$57,466	$57,466	$8,791	$48,675
30/6/2014			$48,675	$13,777	$34,898
30/6/2015			$34,898	$9,840	$25,058
15/12/2016			$25,058	$3,235	$21,823
Total				$35,643	

Finance charges – Accruals basis: Nominal interest rate – 9.1% pa

Date	Payments	Finance component	Capital reduction	Notional principal outstanding (start of period)
15/12/2012	0.00	0.00	0.00	$120,000.00
15/12/2012	$2,090.15	0.00	$2,090.15	$117,909.85
15/01/2013	$2,090.15	$894.15	$1,196.00	$116,713.85
15/02/2013	$2,090.15	$885.08	$1,205.07	$115,508.78
15/03/2013	$2,090.15	$875.94	$1,214.21	$114,294.57
15/04/2013	$2,090.15	$866.73	$1,223.42	$113,071.15
15/05/2013	$2,090.15	$857.46	$1,232.69	$111,838.46
15/06/2013	$2,090.15	$848.11	$1,242.04	$110,596.42
	$14,631.05	$5,227.47	$9,403.58	
15/7/13 to 15/6/14	$25,081.80	$9,421.81	$15,659.99	$109,344.96
15/7/14 to 15/6/15	$25,081.80	$7,935.79	$17,146.01	$93,566.21
15/07/2015	$2,090.15	$589.91	$1,500.24	$76,290.18
15/08/2015	$2,090.15	$578.53	$1,511.62	$74,778.56
15/09/2015	$2,090.15	$567.07	$1,523.08	$73,255.48
15/10/2015	$2,090.15	$555.52	$1,534.63	$71,720.85
15/11/2015	$2,090.15	$543.88	$1,546.27	$70,174.58
15/12/2015	$70,706.74	$532.16	$70,174.58	0.00
Total	$145,952.14	$25,952.14	$120,000.00	

1: In this example, the taxpayer has self-assessed the effective life of the car at seven years. The Commissioner's effective life is eight years. As the car was acquired after 9 May 2006, the diminishing value rate is 200 per cent.

As the lessee is able to sell the car for $75,000 a balancing adjustment would be calculated:

Adjusted sale price = $75,000 x $57,466 divided by $120,000 = $35,916

less adjusted value at date of sale ($57,466 – $35,643) = $21,823

Balancing adjustment to be included in assessable income: **$14,093**

TAX PREFERRED USE – ANTI-AVOIDANCE PROVISIONS

Division 250 ITAA97 applies to leasing and similar arrangements entered into between a taxpayer and a 'tax preferred end-user' for the financing of infrastructure and other assets.

Broadly, Division 250 applies where the particular asset is used by or for the benefit of a tax-exempt entity or a non-resident:

- the financing arrangement in relation to the asset is for a period greater than 12 months
- financial benefits are provided in relation to the tax-preferred use of the asset – eg. an agreement for the payment of a guaranteed residual value by the tax preferred entity
- apart from Division 250, the taxpayer would be entitled to capital allowance deductions for the decline in value of the asset, and
- the taxpayer lacks a predominant economic interest in the asset – eg. more than 80% of the cost of acquiring the asset was financed by limited recourse debt.

Where Division 250 has application, the Commissioner may:

- deny or reduce capital allowance deductions in respect of the particular asset, and
- treat the arrangement as a loan that is taxed as a financing arrangement.

EXCLUSIONS

Certain arrangements are excluded from the operation of Division 250, including:

- those which do not exceed 12 months in duration
- arrangements entered into by small business entities, and
- where the financial benefits arising from the arrangement do not exceed $5 million.

15.090 PRIMARY PRODUCTION

DECLINE IN VALUE OF DEPRECIATING ASSETS

For certain depreciating assets used in primary production, Subdivision 40-F provides special rules. SBE taxpayers have a choice of using Subdivision 40-F or Division 328.

For a partnership, deductions under Subdivision 40-F are available to the partners and not the partnership. A partnership must disregard any Subdivision 40-F deductions when determining its net partnership income or partnership loss.

SUMMARY OF DEDUCTIONS UNDER SUBDIVISION 40-F

Primary production event	Depreciating asset	Start time	Rate
Capital expenditure on a water facility	Water facility	When capital expenditure incurred	$33^1/3$% each year for 3 years
Capital expenditure on the cultivation and propagation of plants, fungi, seeds, bulbs, spores and similar things	Horticultural plant	If first owner when first commercial season starts. If not: when conditions in 40-525(2) are satisfied and first commercial season starts	If effective life less than three years: immediate write off. If effective life three years or more: see formula and table of rates in s40-545
Capital expenditure on the establishment of a grapevine before 1 October 2004	Grapevine	When first used	25% pa commencing from date asset first used
Established thereafter	Grapevine	When first used	Effective life (Subdivision 40-F)

WATER FACILITIES

The term 'water facility' is defined in s40-520 as:

(a) *... plant or a structural improvement or a repair of a capital nature, or an alteration, addition or extension to a plant or a structural improvement that is primarily and principally for the purpose of conserving or conveying water ...*

or

(b) *a structural improvement, or a repair of a capital nature, or an alteration, addition or extension to a structural improvement, that is reasonably incidental to conserving or conveying water.*

Part (a) of this definition would mean that capital expenditure on the construction, manufacture, installation, acquisition or initial repair (see below) of:

- dams and irrigation channels
- a tank and tank stand
- bores and wells, and
- pipes, pumps, water towers and windmills

is depreciated in equal instalments over three years where the expenditure was incurred in a primary production business on land in Australia.

(Note that while non-capital repairs to a water facility are deductible under s25-10, initial repairs are treated as part of the cost of a depreciable asset.)

In ATO ID 2011/3, the Commissioner determined that an overhead sprinkler system used by the taxpayer solely for frost protection is a water facility as defined in s40-520(1)(a) because the system is plant that is primarily and principally for the purpose of conveying water.

Part (b) of the definition of 'water facility' means that a bridge over an irrigation channel, a culvert, or a fence preventing livestock entering an Irrigation channel can also be depreciated in equal instalments over three years.

For primary producers the deduction is reduced by the extent that the water facility was:

- not wholly used in carrying on a primary production business on land in Australia, or
- not wholly used for a taxable purpose; for example partly used for domestic purposes.

For water irrigation providers the deduction is only reduced where the water facility is not used wholly for a taxable purpose. The deduction cannot exceed the amount of capital expenditure incurred on the water facility (s40-515(3)) and if the expenditure was not an arm's length dealing the deduction is based on the asset's market value (s40-560). The deduction accrues to the partners, not the partnership (s40-570).

HORTICULTURAL PLANTS

A 'horticultural plant' is defined in s40-520(2) as *'a live plant or fungus that is cultivated or propagated for any of its products or parts'.*

The deduction can be claimed by the owner of the land or by the lessee or licensees. At any one time only one taxpayer can claim the deduction for horticultural plants. The claim for depreciation is based on the capital expenditure for horticultural plants and would include the capital costs of:

- acquiring the plants or seeds
- planting the plants or seeds
- preparing to plant, such as ploughing, contouring, top dressing, fertilising, stone removal, top soil enhancement, but not including the initial clearing of land
- grafting trees
- maintaining plants until they are ready to be planted, and
- pots and potting mixture (see TD 2006/46).

Expenditure on draining swamp or low-lying land and clearing land does not qualify for the s40-545 write-off (s40-555(3)). Further, the deduction cannot exceed the amount of capital expenditure incurred on the depreciating asset (s40-515(3)) and if the expenditure was not an arm's length dealing the deduction is based on the asset's market value (s40-560). An additional deduction applies for a horticultural plant destroyed before it is written off (s40-565). Expenditure on revenue account, eg. some costs of replacing plants in an existing plantation or nursery, planting seeds in punnets to produce stock for sale, would be an immediate deduction.

The Tax Commissioner has issued TR 2013/4 which gives the effective life of horticultural plants (see 15.160). A taxpayer can self-assess the effective life but all relevant circumstances must be considered when determining effective life.

The taxpayer receives an immediate deduction where the effective life of a horticultural plant is less than three years. Where effective life is three years or more the deduction is worked out using the formula:

Establishment expenditure x write-off days in income year divided by 365 x write-off rate

The 'write-off days' is the number of days in the income year that the plant is owned and used for commercial horticultural purposes or held ready for that use.

The 'write-off rate' is the appropriate statutory rate in the table below and the taxpayer can claim a deduction during the horticultural plant's 'maximum write-off' ie. the period beginning when the plant can first be used for commercial horticulture.

Years in effective life of plant	Annual write-off rate	Maximum write-off period
3 to fewer than 5	40%	2 years and 183 days
5 to fewer than $6^{1}/3$	27%	3 years and 257 days
$6^{2}/3$ to fewer than 10	20%	5 years
10 to fewer than 13	17%	5 years and 323 days
13 to fewer than 30	13%	7 years and 253 days
30 or more	7%	14 years and 105 days

A subsequent owner can claim a deduction based on the original taxpayer's expenditure on establishing the plant, within the maximum period specified and must be provided with the necessary information (s40-575).

GRAPEVINES

Grapevines are subject to the Subdivision 40-F treatment of horticultural plants (see table above).

Taxpayers may either estimate the effective life of their grapevines or use the Commissioner's effective life:

- Grapevines: dried: 15 years
- Grapevines: table: 15 years
- Grapevines: wine: 20 years

The tax write-off of grapevines can only be claimed from when the plant is first used in a primary production business to produce assessable income, and not from the date of planting.

SPECIAL DEDUCTIONS FOR PRIMARY PRODUCERS AND RURAL BUSINESSES

A primary producer and rural business may qualify for a special deduction for landcare, electricity and telephone lines. These concessions are contained in Subdivision 40-G. An SBE taxpayer can use either Subdivision 40-G or the SBE depreciation provisions in Division 328.

In brief, Subdivision 40-G will generally allow an eligible taxpayer to claim:

- an immediate deduction for capital expenditure incurred on landcare operations (fencing, dams, levies, drainage works and operations to prevent land degradation – s40-630 – see comments below in relation to fencing)
- a deduction of 10% for the income year and next nine years of capital expenditure incurred in the connection of a mains electricity cable to a metering point or the upgrading of a connection, provided the electricity is used for a taxable purpose (s40-645(1)), and
- a deduction of 10% for the income year and next 9 years of capital expenditure incurred on a telephone line brought onto land the taxpayer uses in a primary production business (s40-645(3)).

If the capital expenditure qualifies for a deduction under Division 40G:

- another deduction cannot be claimed under another income tax law
- the deduction is limited to the market value of the expenditure if the dealings are non-arm's length (s40-660)
- any expenditure recouped is included in the assessable income under s20-30, and
- any expenditure incurred by a partnership is allocated to each partner and not included in determining net partnership income or net partnership loss under s90 ITAA36 (see rules in s40-665).

FODDER STORAGE ASSETS

Primary producers are able to deduct expenditure on fodder storage assets over three income years incurred, at or after 7:30pm AEST, 12 May 2015 (s40-548). Previously, this was 10-50 years using the Commissioner's effective life rates, depending on the asset.

A fodder storage asset is an asset that is primarily and principally for the purpose of storing fodder. This is also a structural improvement, a repair of a capital nature, or an alteration, addition or extension, to an asset or structural improvement used for that purpose.

WATER FACILITIES

Primary producers are able to deduct expenditure or water facilities immediately in the year in which the expenditure is incurred at or after 7:30pm AEST, 12 May 2015. This was previously three years. A water facility is a plant or structural improvement that is primarily or principally for the purpose of conserving or conveying water. It can also include a capital repair, alteration, addition or extension to such an asset.

LANDCARE

A primary producer, a business using rural land or a rural land irrigation water provider can claim an immediate deduction for capital expenditure incurred on a landcare operation on land in Australia.

A landcare operation is one of the following operations:

- eradicating or exterminating animal pests from the land
- eradicating, exterminating or destroying plant growth detrimental to the land
- preventing or combating land degradation other than by the use of fences
- erecting fences to keep out animals from areas affected by land degradation to prevent or limit further damage and assist in reclaiming the areas (see *Fencing* below)
- erecting fences to separate different land classes according to an approved land management plan
- constructing a levee or similar improvement
- constructing drainage works – other than the draining of swamps or low-lying areas – to control salinity or assist in drainage control, or
- expenditure incurred on a structural improvement or an alteration, addition, extension or repair of a capital nature to a structural improvement that is reasonably incidental to the last two operations (ie. the construction of a levee or drainage works).

ELECTRICITY AND TELEPHONE LINES

Capital expenditure incurred on the following is deductible in equal instalments over ten years:

- connecting power to land
- upgrading a connection of power to land, and
- a telephone line.

Refer 21.650 for detailed discussion.

FENCING ASSETS

Primary producers are able to immediately deduct capital expenditure on fences immediately in the year in which the expenditure is incurred from 7:30pm AEST, 12 May 2015. It is no longer necessary for the expenditure to be in relation to landcare (see above) or as part of a water facility (over three years). A fencing asset takes on its ordinary meaning (ie. an enclosure or barrier, usually metal or wood, as around or along a field, or paddock). It can also include a capital repair, alteration, addition or extension to such assets.

NO BALANCING ADJUSTMENTS

Where a deduction is claimed for water facilities, grapevines or horticultural plants under Subdivision 40-F, or for landcare operations, electricity connections or telephone lines under Subdivisions 40-G there is no deduction under Subdivision 40-B. This will mean that the balancing adjustment and rollover provisions will not apply to water facilities, horticultural plant, landcare operations, electricity connections or telephone lines, and these depreciable assets are not excluded from the capital gains tax provisions (see s118-24(2)).

If a horticultural plant is destroyed, s40-565 provided for an additional deduction.

If a taxpayer were to stop owning horticultural plant or leasing the land, then the next taxpayer to use the plant for commercial horticulture continues to be entitled to the deduction (s40-525 and s40-575). There are no special provisions relating to a water facility but the deduction over three years continues to be available to the taxpayer who incurred the expenditure on the water facility even if the facility has been destroyed or disposed of. Similarly, there are no special provisions relating to expenditure on electricity and telephone lines. The deduction over ten years would appear to continue to be available to the taxpayer who incurred the expenditure even if the taxpayer was no longer carrying on a business of primary production.

However, a recoupment of expenditure may need to be included in assessable income (see Subdivision 20-A).

15.100 MINING, INFRASTRUCTURE AND ENVIRONMENTAL PROTECTION

CAPITAL EXPENDITURE DEDUCTIBLE OVER TIME

PROJECT EXPENDITURE

Subdivision 40-I permits expenditure that does not form part of the cost of a depreciating asset, but does relate to a project to be written off over the life of the project where the project is for a taxable purpose. This is achieved by allocating 'project amounts' to a project pool.

A 'project amount' may consist of two types of expenditure each being expenditure:

- that does not form part of the cost of a depreciating asset
- is not deductible under another provision of the income tax law
- is not denied a deduction by a provision of the tax law, and
- is directly connected with the business or project.

The two types of expenditure are:

- mining capital expenditure (defined in s40-860) and transport capital expenditure (defined in s40-865), and
- project expenditure, specifically capital expenditure incurred:
  - to create or upgrade community infrastructure
  - for site preparation costs for a depreciating asset (except for horticultural plants and grapevines, expenditure in draining swamp or low-lying land, or expenditure in clearing land)
  - for feasibility studies for the project
  - for environmental assessments for the project (noise, ecological and traffic assessments, soil testing, stormwater management)
  - for obtaining information associated with the project
  - in seeking to obtain a right to intellectual property, and
  - for ornamental trees or shrubs (s40-840(2)) (see ATO ID 2009/35).

To claim the deduction under Subdivision 40-I, the project expenditure must not form part of the cost of a depreciating asset and must not be deductible or denied as a deduction to the taxpayer outside of Subdivision 40-I. In addition, the project expenditure must be directly connected with a project that the taxpayer carries on or proposes to carry on for a taxable purpose (s40-840(2)(c)). Expenditure in looking for a business to acquire is not, of itself, project expenditure (ATO ID 2003/206). To satisfy the 'direct connection' requirement, it is important to identify the particular undertaking to which the relevant expenditure belongs (ATO ID 2012/17).

In ATO ID 2015/12, the Commissioner held that capital expenditure on relocating utilities, such as electricity lines and water pipelines is an amount incurred for site preparation costs for a depreciating asset for the purpose of subparagraph 40-840(2), because this expenditure was necessary in making the site ready for the construction of the depreciating asset.

The deduction for a project pool commences in the year that the project starts to operate (s40-855).

Calculate your deduction for an income year by using the diminishing value method and the following formula:

- Where the project amount is incurred before 10 May 2006 the formula is:
  (Pool value x 150%) divided by DV project pool life (s40-830)
- Where the project amount is incurred on or after 10 May 2006 the formula is:
  (Pool value x 200%) divided by DV project pool life (s40-832)

Where:

- 'DV project pool life' is the effective life of the project or its most recently recalculated effective life, and
- 'pool value' is:
  - for the first year in which an amount is allocated to the pool: the total of those amounts so allocated

- for any subsequent year: the closing pool value plus any further amounts allocated in that year (s40-830).

The Act has an integrity measure to ensure any taxpayer who abandons, sells or otherwise disposes of a pre-10 May 2006 project for the purpose of reviving that project to obtain the higher 200% rate can only use the 150% rate.

XYZ Ltd conducts a feasibility study prior to commencing construction of an item of plant to be used in the company's income-producing business activities. Following construction, a government licence, required in order to use the item of plant, is issued for a twenty year period. Feasibility costs of $50,000 were incurred in the 2014-15 year.

Deductions available to the company are:

- *2014-15:* $\dfrac{\$50,000 \times 200\%}{20} = \$5,000$

- *2015-16:* $\dfrac{\$45,000 \times 200\%}{20} = \$4,500$

with deductions being claimed in this basis over the remaining 18 years.

The deduction must be reduced by a reasonable amount for the extent to which the project does not operate for a taxable purpose (s40-835).

If a project that has a project pool is abandoned, sold or otherwise disposed of, the project pool value at that time is deductible (s40-830(4)). Any proceeds received for the abandonment, sale or otherwise disposal of a pooled project are assessable income (s40-830(5) and (6)).

Although there is no explicit statement in the legislation, the Tax Office maintains that a project must have a finite project life. Therefore, for capital expenditure to be a project amount, a project with a finite project life must exist at or before the time at which the expenditure is incurred. Without a finite life that can be estimated there is no figure to insert in the equation (TR 2005/4). Where a project does not have a 'finite life' the project expenditure may be deductible under s40-880 (see *Business-related capital expenditure* below).

MINING, QUARRYING OR PROSPECTING RIGHTS

Mining, quarrying or prospecting rights are classified as depreciating assets (s40-30(2)) that can be depreciated over their effective life. The term is defined under s995-1(1) as an authority, licence, permit, lease of land or right under an Australian law to mine, quarry or prospect for minerals, petroleum or quarry materials. An interest in such rights is also included in the definition.

The effective life of a mining, quarrying or prospecting right is the estimated period until the end of the life of the relevant mine, petroleum field or quarry (or proposed mine, petroleum field or quarry) (s40-95(10)). The estimated period is worked out as the period over which the reserves are expected to be extracted from the mine in accordance with an appropriately accepted industry practice (s40-95(11)).

NOTE: If there is more than one mine or quarry, the effective life is worked out by reference to the mine or quarry that has the longest estimated life.

NOTE: Before 15 May 2013, an immediate deduction may be available under s40-80 for mining, quarrying or prospecting rights and information first used for exploration or prospecting (see below).

MINE DEVELOPMENT EXPENDITURE

Certain capital mine development expenditure (eg. cost to construct an open pit mine or an underground decline) forms part of the cost of a depreciating asset and cannot be allocated to a project pool.

In the Commissioner's view, an open mine pit is an improvement to land for the purposes of s40-30(3) that meets the conditions to be a depreciating asset, as it enhances the usefulness of the land to the user of the pit (TR 2012/7). The term 'open pit mine' generally refers to the changed configuration of land from its natural state, as it exists from time-to-time, that comes into being through the conduct of an open pit mining operation. It encompasses all of the variously described structural elements of a typical pit, such as batters, berms, and haulage roads.

NOTE: Where a mining operation has within its boundaries two or more separate and distinct pits, each pit would constitute a separate depreciating asset. Each pit in this scenario will have its own effective life which will typically equate to the planned and therefore predictable useful life of that individual pit (TR 2012/7).

IMMEDIATELY DEDUCTIBLE CAPITAL EXPENDITURE

Subdivision 40-H allows an immediate deduction for expenditure (whether capital or not) on:

- exploration or prospecting for minerals (including petroleum) and quarry materials (does not include expenditure on developing or operating a mining or quarrying site)
- rehabilitation of mining or quarrying sites
- petroleum rent resource tax, and
- environmental protection.

EXPLORATION OR PROSPECTING

The term 'exploration or prospecting' is defined in s40-730(4). Qualifying taxpayers can obtain an immediate deduction for expenditure on exploration or prospecting for minerals (including petroleum) and quarry materials as well as for expenditure on acquiring mining, quarrying or prospecting rights and/or information for use in exploration or prospecting activities.

Exploration or prospecting expenditure (both capital and revenue expenditure) is deductible provided that at least one of the following 'activity tests' is satisfied during the income year:

- the taxpayer carries on mining operations
- it would be reasonable to conclude that the taxpayer proposed to carry on mining operations, or
- the taxpayer carries on a business of exploration or prospecting for minerals or quarry materials obtainable by mining operations, and the expenditure on the asset was necessarily incurred in carrying on that business (s40-80(1)(c)). (Note that a taxpayer contracted to provide geophysical surveying services is not considered to be carrying on such a business: ID 2011/25.)

In addition, the cost of a depreciating asset first used in exploration or prospecting is fully deductible, subject to the following conditions:

- the asset when first used is not used for development drilling for petroleum, or operations in the course of working a mining property, petroleum field or quarrying property. These assets are subject to the general depreciation provisions in Subdivision 40-B (s40-80(1)(b)), and
- the taxpayer satisfies at least one of the activity tests above at the asset's 'start time'.

The immediate deduction is only available during the exploration stage of a mining or quarrying project. The exploration stage continues until a decision to undertake the development stage is made. Whether a taxpayer is in the exploration or development stage is a question of fact, having regard to the nature and purpose of the expenditure being incurred (TR 98/23).

NOTE: An immediate deduction was available for expenditure on geothermal energy exploration incurred on or after 1 July 2012 and before 1 July 2014.

The Government announced measures to limit the immediate deduction for this kind of expenditure for acquisitions of mining rights and information incurred after 7.30 pm AEST, 14 May 2013. Before the changes to the rules from 15 May 2013, an immediate deduction was available under s40-80 for mining, quarrying or prospecting rights and information first used for exploration or prospecting.

For acquisitions of mining rights and mining information after 14 May 2013, an immediate deduction is limited under s 40-80 to the following expenditure:

- expenditure incurred in acquiring a mining right from an Australian Government agency or entity
- expenditure on acquisition of mining information in an geological or geophysical data package, from an entity whose main business is providing that information, or
- expenditure to create new mining information or to enhance mining information.

MINING SITE REHABILITATION

An eligible taxpayer is entitled to an immediate deduction for expenditure, whether capital or not, on rehabilitating mining or quarrying sites, sites of exploration or prospecting activities, sites of ancillary activities (defined in s40-740), or a mining building site (s40-735(1)). The immediate deduction is not available under s40-735 for:

- depreciating assets used in rehabilitation (s40-735(3)). The cost of such assets may be deductible over their effective life under Subdivision 40-B or deductlble under Division 43 (capital works), or
- expenditure on:
  - acquiring land, an interest in the land, or any right, power or privilege to do with the land
  - a bond or security, or
  - housing and welfare (s40-745).

PETROLEUM RESOURCE RENT TAX

A taxpayer can claim an immediate deduction for the payment of petroleum resource rent tax, imposed by the *Petroleum Resource Rent Tax Assessment Act 1987*, other than payment of certain penalties under paragraph 99(c) of that Act. Any refunds, credits, or amounts paid or applied of the tax are included in assessable income (s40-750(3)).

ENVIRONMENTAL PROTECTION ACTIVITIES

A taxpayer is entitled to an immediate deduction for expenditure incurred for the sole or dominant purpose of carrying out environmental protection activities (see 15.600).

15.110 BLACKHOLE EXPENDITURE

A deduction is available under s40-880 for certain business-related costs which are not otherwise eligible for tax relief under any other provision of the Tax Acts.

NOTE: The Government announced in the 2015-16 Federal Budget that small businesses and individuals can immediately deduct certain costs incurred in starting up a business which includes the cost of advice or services relating to the structure or operation of the proposed business. This measure, if enacted, is effective from 1 July 2015. See Chapter 10.

BUSINESS-RELATED CAPITAL EXPENDITURE

Section 40-880 allows you to deduct, in equal proportions over five years, capital expenditure that you incur:

a. in relation to your business, or
b. in relation to a business that used to be carried on, or
c. in relation to a business proposed to be carried on, or
d. to liquidate or deregister a company of which you are a member, to wind up a partnership of which you are a partner or to wind up a trust of which you were a beneficiary, that carried on a business.

Note that in relation to (a) the business to which the expenditure relates must be your business, whereas under (b) or (c) the business can be any business provided that the taxpayer incurs the expenditure in connection with deriving assessable income from that business. This means that the deduction for 'blackhole expenditure' may be available to a former business, a prospective business, or a business that is currently operating provided that the business is, was or is proposed to be carried on for a taxable purpose.

The deduction is over five years at the rate of 20% in the year that the business capital expenditure is incurred and 20% of the expenditure in each of the following four income years. There is no balancing adjustment. If the business were to cease after two years then the deduction continues in the remaining three tax years.

For capital expenditure to be deductible over five years under s40-880:

- the expenditure must not otherwise be taken into account in some way elsewhere in the income tax law (ie. the expenditure is not already deductible, capitalised, amortised or capped in some way under another provision)

- a deduction must not be denied by some other provision, and
- the business must either be, was, or is proposed to be carried on for a taxable purpose.

In addition, shareholders, beneficiaries of trusts and partners are able to deduct liquidation and deregistration costs where the company, trust or partnership carried on a business. Shareholders can only deduct their own expenses, and are not entitled to a share in those that the company has incurred (s40-880(2)(d)).

The recognition of pre-business expenditure in s40-880 means that:

- expenditures to investigate the viability of the business, such as feasibility studies and market research
- establishment costs, such as the costs of establishing the business structure, and
- expenses that are a necessary precedent to the business being carried on, such as costs of market testing or putting in a tender

may be deductible.

For pre-business capital expenditure to be deductible it must be *reasonable to conclude that the business is proposed to be carried on within a reasonable time* (s40-880(7)). This is a test of the taxpayer's commitment to commencing a business and could be shown by such activities as a business plan, market research, and capital expenditure on business assets. While the deduction for pre-business expenditure will be available before the business is carried on s40-880(7) requires some evidence of a commitment to carrying on the business at the time the expenditure was incurred. Similarly, the recognition of post-business expenditure incurred in relation to a past income-producing business activity means that capital expenses incurred for the purpose of ceasing to carry on the business or capital expenses incurred as a consequence of the business ceasing will be deductible under s40-880.

 Section 40-880 explicitly states that it is only the party that incurred the expenditure that can claim the deduction. While s40-880(4) recognises that an individual may incur expenditure to establish or wind up a business operated as a company and be able to claim the deduction against their own income it does not apply to an existing business. In relation to capital expenditure incurred by an individual, s40-880 only applies to pre-commencement and post-cessation expenditure. If an individual were to incur expenditure on their own account in relation to an existing business operated through a company, the individual would not qualify for the deduction and neither would the company because it did not incur the expenditure on its own account.

LIMITATIONS AND EXCEPTIONS

Section 40-880 contains the following limitations and exceptions:

- the expenditure must be business capital expenditure and the business is, was or is proposed to be carried on for a taxable purpose (s40-880(3)(4)). This means that the deduction must be reduced to the extent that the business is not carried on for a taxable purpose. Further, only the entity that incurred the expenditure is entitled to the deduction. This means that if an individual who is carrying on a business as a sole proprietor decides to incorporate and become the sole shareholder, then s40-880(4) enables the individual to claim the deduction for incorporation expenses that would be denied by s40-880(3) because the individual has the requisite connection to the company to be entitled to the deduction, and
- section 40-880 operates as a provision of last resort. Consequently, there is no deduction under s40-880 to the extent that the expenditure falls within the scope of any of the paragraphs in subs40-880(5):
  - (a) forms part of the cost of a depreciating asset that you hold, used to hold or will hold
  - (b) is deductible under another provision of the income tax law
  - (c) forms part of the cost of land
  - (d) is in relation to a lease or other legal or equitable right
  - (e) would be taken into account in working out an assessable profit or deductible loss
  - (f) could be taken into account in working out a capital gain or capital loss
  - (g) is expressly made non-deductible under another provision of income tax lax

(h)   is expressly prevented from a deduction for a reason other than the expenditure is of a capital nature (for example, entertainment expenses)

(i)   is of a private or domestic nature, or

(j)   is incurred in gaining or producing exempt income or non-assessable non-exempt income.

Where a lease is not obtained, capital expenditure incurred in trying to obtain the lease is not expenditure incurred in relation to a lease for the purposes of para (d) (ATO ID 2010/157).

Note that in relation to para (f), the Tax Office is of the view that the exclusion applies where the capital gain or capital loss is calculated under the now repealed ITAA36 CGT provisions (ATO ID 2010/91).

In addition, you cannot deduct under s40-880 an amount of expenditure excluded from the cost of a depreciating asset or the cost base or reduced cost base of a CGT asset because of the market value substitution rule (s40-880(8)) nor can you deduct a return of capital (s40-880(9)). Further, the non-commercial loss provisions in Division 35 may prevent individuals, either alone or in partnership from deducting pre- and post-business expenditures from other assessable income in the year that the expenditure was incurred (s35-5(1) and s35-10)).

A salary earner incurs $2,500 of pre-business capital expenditure during the 2014 income year (otherwise deductible under s40-880 in equal proportions for the 2014 to 2018 income years apart from Division 35 ITAA36) for the purpose of establishing a business in the 2014 income year. Section 35-10(2B) will prevent the taxpayer from deducting the amounts arising from the pre-business expenditure in the 2013 and 2014 income years. These deductions under s40-880 ($500 + $500) are quarantined until the business commences in 2015.

If the business passes the assessable income test in Division 35 for the 2016 income year, the taxpayer can offset the two amounts ($500 + $500) quarantined from the 2014 and 2015 income years against the income from their business and against their salary income in the 2015 income year.

 Section 40-880 does not cover non-business blackhole expenditure.

In May 2011, the Tax Office released a suite of Taxation Determinations which convey the Commissioner's views in relation to whether the s40-880(5)(f) exclusion for expenditure that could be taken into account in working out a capital gain or capital loss applies to prevent the deduction of particular types of expenditure that the head company of a consolidated group or MEC group incurs. The following table summarises the Commissioner's views:

TD	Type of expenditure	Deductible under s40-880 (Commissioner's view)
2011/08	Incidental costs described in subs110-35(2) (ie. professional fees) that the head company of a consolidated group or MEC group incurs, in acquiring shares in an entity, before that entity joins the group	No as these costs are included in the second element of the cost bases (or reduced cost bases) of the shares
2011/09	Incidental costs described in subs110-35(2) (ie. professional fees) that the head company of a consolidated group or MEC group incurs, in acquiring shares in an entity, after that entity joins the group	Yes – as these costs are not included in the cost bases (or reduced cost bases) of the shares
2011/10	Incidental costs described in subs110-35(2) (ie. professional fees) that the head company of a consolidated group or MEC group incurs, in disposing of shares in a subsidiary member to an entity outside the group, after the member leaves the group	No – as these costs are included in the second element of the cost bases (or reduced cost bases) of the shares

The Rulings apply both retrospectively and prospectively.

The Tax Office has also released Taxation Ruling TR 2011/6 which sets out the Commissioner's views on the interpretation and scope of elements of s40-880 and considers the following issues:

- the type of expenditure to which the provisions apply
- the nexus required for capital expenditure to be 'in relation to' a current, former or proposed business
- the 'taxable purpose' requirement, and

- limitations and exceptions.

The key views expressed in the Ruling are summarised as follows:

- the meaning of 'incurred' for the purposes of s40-880 is governed by established case law principles: a taxpayer incurs expenditure at the time they owe a present money debt that they cannot avoid paying
- the meaning of 'capital expenditure' for s40-880 purposes is also governed by case law
- the expression 'in relation to' denotes the proximity required between the expenditure and the business; there must be a sufficient and relevant connection
- business related capital expenditure does not include expenditure relating to non-business activities (eg. passive investment or occupation as an employee)
- the reference in paragraph 40-880(2)(a) to 'your business' is a reference to the taxpayer's overall business rather than a particular undertaking or enterprise within the overall business. Where the taxpayer is the head company of a consolidated group, 'your business' refers to the overall business of the head company
- the expression 'to the extent that' in subs40-880(3), (4) and (5) indicates that apportionment may be required where the expenditure serves more than one purpose. In the Commissioner's view, the absence of the expression in subs40-880(2) does not prevent an apportionment
- the 'taxable purpose' test which limits deductibility is applied to the business rather than the expenditure – ie. expenditure is apportioned on the basis of the income earning activities of the business rather than on the basis of what the expenditure is for
- in relation to the taxable purpose test for a former business, the Commissioner will generally accept a test period of the five years before the taxpayer permanently ceased operating the business or ended their association with the business
- the legislation and extrinsic material do not prescribe a particular methodology to determine the extent of the taxable purpose. In the absence of such, the Commissioner will accept an apportionment made on a fair and reasonable basis
- as a general rule, the extent of the taxable purpose may be determined by a comparison of the amount of exempt income and non-assessable non-exempt income with total income derived, although the Commissioner acknowledges that this may not always be the most appropriate method
- in relation to the s40-880(5)(c) exclusion for expenditure that forms part of the cost of land, the Commissioner is of the opinion that this paragraph excludes from deductibility expenditure incurred to acquire land where the cost of acquiring land does not form part of the cost base or reduced cost base of the land (which is covered by the exclusion in paragraph (f)), which may occur if the land was acquired for someone other than the taxpayer
- the Commissioner is of the opinion that the s40-880(5)(c) exclusion for expenditure relating to a lease or other legal or equitable right has limited practical application, given the existence of s40-880(5)(a) (depreciating asset), s40-880(5)(f) (CGT) and s25-110 ITAA97 (deductibility of lease termination capital expenditure)
- the Commissioner is of the view that since capital proceeds and cost base (or reduced cost base) are generally taken into account in working out the amount of a capital gain or capital loss, capital expenditure which reduces capital proceeds or forms part of cost base (or reduced cost base) could be taken into account in working out the amount of a capital gain or capital loss for the purposes of the exemption in s40-880(5)(f)
- non-commercial losses – where an individual taxpayer has incurred business capital expenditure in relation to a former business and the activity does not satisfy the commerciality tests or the Commissioner does not exercise his discretion, the s40-880 deduction will be denied rather than deferred, and
- personal services income – a taxpayer that is a 'personal services entity' which carries on business and is in receipt of personal services income may be entitled to a deduction under s40-880, even though it does not meet any of the personal services business tests and has not reserved a personal services business determination.

The Ruling applies to arrangements begun to be carried out from 1 July 2005 except insofar as a view in the Ruling differs from an Interpretative Decision (ATO ID). Where a view in the Ruling differs from that in the ATO ID, the Ruling applies from 8 December 2010.

In ATO ID 2010/132, the Commissioner expresses his view that the expenditure to compensate for the early termination of an employment contract was not incurred 'in relation to' the business because it does not have the character of an expense that satisfies an objective or requirement of the business. Rather, the payment was made to satisfy the taxpayer's personal obligations under his employment contract.

15.160 EFFECTIVE LIFE TABLES FOR DEPRECIATING ASSETS

Taxpayers utilising depreciating assets in the course of earning assessable income are entitled to a deduction under Division 40 for the diminution in value of those assets over their effective life.

Taxpayers may either self-assess the effective life of an asset or adopt the determination by the Commissioner of Taxation which is issued in an annual Ruling.

The effective life tables contained in the annual Rulings apply only where a taxpayer chooses to use the Commissioner's determination rather than self-assess the effective life. Further, the tables are only relevant for calculating Division 40 amounts and not for calculating capital works deductions for assets that qualify for Division 43 treatment.

Tax Ruling TR 2015/2 applies to assets acquired from 1 July 2015, and replaces TR 2014/4 which applied to assets acquired between 1 July 2014 and 30 June 2015. The effective life determination in force at the time a particular asset is acquired continues to apply for the life of that asset.

The Commissioner only makes determinations of the effective life of new assets and only takes account of the normal industry practice when estimating effective life. The purchaser of a second hand asset or an asset with a usage pattern outside of normal industry practice may wish to self-assess the asset's effective life.

THE TABLES

The tables contain only effective lives. Rates have not been included. To work out the appropriate depreciation rate, refer 15.060.

Table A is an *industry* table which lists, under industry headings, assets that are peculiar to that industry or for which a special effective life is justified because of the use to which those assets are put by the industry. Some industry headings also contain a general grouping or class of assets that is identified by reference to the specific industry function or process for which the assets are used. The industry headings have, where possible, been drawn from the Australian New Zealand Standard Industry Classification subject categories. **Table B** is an *asset* table which contains generic assets which may be used by more than one industry.

HOW TO USE THIS SCHEDULE

The entries for the effective life of assets listed under a particular industry in Table A must only be used by members of that industry.

If an asset is listed in Table A under a particular industry heading and also in Table B, you must use the industry table if you are a member of that industry. Taxpayers not in the industry must use Table B.

If an asset used by an industry member is not listed under its industry heading, either specifically or under the general functional group/class, the member should use the effective life of the asset listed in Table B.

If an asset is not listed in either Table A or B, the Commissioner has not determined its effective life and the taxpayer will have to self-assess its effective life.

STATUTORY CAPS

Certain assets have a statutorily capped life. Where the Commissioner has determined an effective life in excess of the statutory life, # is shown beside the asset in Tables A and B.

Asset	Life (yrs)	Date of application

AGRICULTURE, FORESTRY & FISHING

Asset	Life (yrs)	Date of application
All terrain vehicles (ATVs) used in primary production activities	5	1/7/07
Environmental control structures (including glasshouses, hothouses, germination rooms, plastic clad tunnels & igloos)	20	1/7/06
Fences (excluding stockyard, pen & portable fences): Being fencing constructed at a time for a particular function (eg a line of fencing forming a side of a boundary or paddock) not being in the nature of a repair:		
General (incorporating anchor assemblies, intermediate posts, rails, wires, wire mesh & droppers)	30	1/7/08
Electric	20	1/7/08
Fence energisers for electric fences:		
Mains power	10	1/7/08
Portable	5	1/7/08
Fertigation systems:		
Pumps	3	1/7/08
Tanks	10	1/7/08
Grading & packing line assets used on farm:		
Banana assets:		
Air rams	3	1/7/08
Bunch lines	10	1/7/08
Choppers/mulchers	8	1/7/08
Rails (including points)	15	1/7/08
Scrap conveyors	5	1/7/08
Tops	8	1/7/08
Water troughs	10	1/7/08
Coffee assets:		
Dryers	15	1/7/08
Processors (including pulpers)	10	1/7/08
Fermentation tanks	10	1/7/08
Hullers	12	1/7/08
Washers/separators	10	1/7/08
General assets:		
Bin tippers	15	1/7/08
Conveyors (including elevators)	10	1/7/08
Drying tunnels	15	1/7/08
Fungicide units	12	1/7/08
Receival hoppers (including water dumps)	15	1/7/08
Tables (including packing & sorting tables)	15	1/7/08
Washing assets (including brush & barrel washers)	10	1/7/08
Waxing assets	12	1/7/08
Graders:		
Electronic	10	1/7/08
Mechanical	15	1/7/08
Optical	8	1/7/08
Labelling assets:		
Labelling applicators (including in line labellers)	8	1/7/08
Labelling guns	3	1/7/08
Olive oil processing assets – see Table A Oil & fat manufacturing)		
Packing assets (including bagging & wrapping machines)	10	1/7/08
Scales (excluding platform scales)	5	1/7/08
Tree nut assets:		
De husking units	8	1/7/08
Drying silos	20	1/7/08
Trommels	15	1/7/08
Livestock grids	40	1/7/08
Motorcycles used in primary production activities	5	1/7/07
Post drivers/hole diggers	10	1/7/08
Protective structures (including shade houses & netting constructions)	20	1/7/06
Sheds on land that is used for agricultural or pastoral operations (including machinery sheds, workshop sheds & farm production sheds)	40	1/1/07
Tractors	12#	1/7/07
Water assets:		
Bores	30	1/7/08
Dams (including earth or rock fill & turkey nests)	40	1/7/08
Dam liners & covers	20	1/7/08
Effluent channels	40	1/7/08
Effluent recycle tanks	12	1/7/08
Effluent sedimentation ponds	40	1/7/08

Asset	Life (yrs)	Date of application
Irrigation assets:		
Drip, micro spray or mini sprinkler systems:		
Above ground polyethylene pipes	10	1/7/08
Drippers, micro sprays & mini sprinklers	5	1/7/08
Control systems	10	1/7/08
Filtration systems	15	1/7/08
Pumps	12	1/7/08
Variable speed drives	15	1/7/08
Irrigation earth channels	40	1/7/08
Irrigators (including centre pivot, lateral & travelling guns):		
Fresh water	20	1/7/08
Effluent	10	1/7/08
Pumps:		
Bore pumps, effluent & manure pumps	7	1/7/08
Other	12	1/7/08
Water mains:		
Aluminium	20	1/7/08
Galvanised steel	25	1/7/08
Polyethylene	20	1/7/08
PVC	30	1/7/08
Water tanks:		
Concrete	30	1/7/08
Galvanised steel	25	1/7/08
Polyethylene	15	1/7/08
Water troughs:		
Concrete	25	1/7/08
Galvanised steel	15	1/7/08
Polyethylene	10	1/7/08
Windmills	30	1/7/08
Water pressure cleaners	5	1/7/08

AGRICULTURE

Asset	Life (yrs)	Date of application
Bee farming plant:		
Beehives	$13^{1}/_{3}$	1/1/01
Processing plant	20	1/1/01
Bridges (wooden)	20	1/1/01
Grain, cotton, peanut & rice assets:		
Chemical spraying assets:		
Generally (including broad acre trailed or linkage boom & utility)	10	1/1/07
Self-propelled	8	1/1/07
General assets:		
Aeration assets:		
Controllers	10	1/1/07
Kits	15	1/1/07
Augers (including conveyors)	15	1/1/07
Dryers	20	1/1/07
Moisture meters	5	1/1/07
Mulchers	10	1/1/07
Peanut pre-cleaners	10	1/1/07
Slashers	7	1/1/07
Harvesting assets:		
Boll buggies	15	1/1/07
Chaser bins	15	1/1/07
Combine harvesters	12#	1/7/07
Cotton picker/strippers	10#	1/7/07
Field bins	20	1/1/07
Fuel trailers	15	1/1/07
Module builders	15	1/1/07
Module tarpaulins	5	1/1/07
Peanut diggers (including peanut pullers)	10#	1/7/07
Peanut threshers	12#	1/7/07
Precision farming assets (including GPS, controllers, lightbars, variable rate technology assets, but excl hydraulic automated steering)	5	1/1/07
Seeding & fertilizing assets:		
Fertilizer spreaders (including linkage & trailed)	10	1/1/07
Planters (incl bar, box, combined seeders, precision planters & row crop planters)	15	1/1/07
Seed & fertilizer bins	15	1/1/07
Tillage assets:		
Generally	15	1/1/07
Harrows	5	1/1/07
Laser controlled scraping assets:		
Buckets	10	1/1/07
Transmitters	7	1/1/07
Rippers	10	1/1/07
Harvesters/sweepers	$6^{2}/_{3}$#	1/1/01

Asset	Life (yrs)	Date of application
Hay & foraging assets:		
Bale handling attachments (including accumulator grabs, bale stackers, hay forks/spikes/spears (incorporating metal frame), round bale grabs)	12	1/1/07
Balers	10	1/1/07
Bale wrappers	10	1/1/07
Baler & wrappers	10	1/1/07
Forage harvesters	10#	1/7/07
Hay rakes (including finger wheel, rotary & parallel)	10	1/1/07
Moisture probes	5	1/1/07
Mower conditioners:		
Self-propelled:		
Attachments	8	1/1/07
Prime movers	12	1/1/07
Trailed	8	1/1/07
Super conditioners (hay re-conditioners)	8	1/1/07
Tedders	10	1/1/07
Trailed bale handling assets:		
Big square bale stackers	10	1/1/07
Generally (including accumulators & bale carriers)	15	1/1/07
Windrowers:		
Self-propelled:		
Attachments	8	1/1/07
Prime movers	12	1/1/07
Trailed	8	1/1/07
Hop growers' plant:		
Hop picking machines	$13\frac{1}{3}$	1/1/01
Kilns	20	1/1/01
Horse stalls (Breeze way, Shed row)	$33\frac{1}{3}$	1/1/01
Horticultural plants:		
Citrus:		
Grapefruits	30	1/1/01
Lemons	20	1/1/01
Limes	20	1/1/01
Mandarins	25	1/1/01
Oranges	30	1/1/01
Grapevines, dried	15	1/10/04
Grapevines, table	15	1/10/04
Grapevines, wine	20	1/10/04
Nuts:		
Almonds	25	1/7/01
Cashews	25	1/7/01
Chestnuts	25	1/7/01
Hazelnuts	25	1/7/01
Jojoba	30	1/7/01
Macadamia	25	1/7/01
Pecans	25	1/7/01
Pistachios	25	1/7/01
Walnuts	25	1/7/01
Pome:		
Apples	20	1/1/01
Pears	25	1/1/01
Stone Fruit:		
Apricots	10	1/1/01
Cherries	18	1/1/01
Nectarines	10	1/1/01
Olives	30	1/1/01
Peaches	10	1/1/01
Plums	15	1/1/01
Prunes	20	1/1/01
Tropical:		
Avocados	20	1/1/01
Mangoes	30	1/1/01
Levee banks & revetments	40	1/1/01
Pea-viners, pea cleaners, vine & straw conveyors	10	1/1/01
Silos:		
Ancillary equipment	20	1/1/01
Grain (metal)	30	1/7/01
Stud stock & thoroughbred horses	10	1/1/01
Trellis	20	1/1/01

NURSERY & FLORICULTURE PRODUCTION

Asset	Life (yrs)	Date of application
Chemical spraying assets:		
Generally (including broad acre trailed or linkage boom & utility)	10	1/7/06
Environmental control assets:		
Boilers (including piping)	20	1/7/06
Control systems	10	1/7/06
Evaporative coolers	10	1/7/06
Heating assets	10	1/7/06
Instruments (including sensors)	10	1/7/06
Retractable screens	8	1/7/06
Ventilation fans	5	1/7/06
Fertigation system assets (incorporating control systems, pumps & tanks)	10	1/7/06
General assets:		
Bins & pallets	5	1/7/06
Fertiliser spreaders	10	1/7/06
Fumigation assets	5	1/7/06
Pasteurisation assets:		
Pasteurisation rooms	20	1/7/06
Steam boilers	15	1/7/06
Racks	15	1/7/06
Ride on mowers	5	1/7/06
Refrigeration assets:		
Insulation panels used in cool rooms	40	1/7/06
Refrigeration generally	10	1/7/06
Trailers	15	1/7/06
Trolleys	15	1/7/06
Weed mats	5	1/7/06
Harvesting assets:		
Bed lifters & diggers	10	1/7/06
Tree spades	15#	1/7/06
Packaging assets:		
Bunching & bundling machines	15	1/7/06
Deleafers	15	1/7/06
Grading machines	15	1/7/06
Planting assets:		
Benches & tables	10	1/7/06
Conveyors	15	1/7/06
Dibblers & seeders	15	1/7/06
Hoppers	15	1/7/06
Pot, punnet & tray dispensers	12	1/7/06
Potting machines (including pot & bag fillers)	10	1/7/06
Soil elevators	10	1/7/06
Soil mixers	10	1/7/06
Transplanters (plugs & seedlings)	8	1/7/06
Tray & punnet fillers	10	1/7/06
Tray washers	15	1/7/06
Vermiculite dispensers & coverers	15	1/7/06
Propagation assets:		
Heated propagators	10	1/7/06
Seedling & punnet trays, reusable	3	1/7/06
Turf growing assets:		
Chemical spraying assets:		
Generally (including broad acre trailed or linkage boom & utility)	10	1/7/06
Fertiliser spreaders	10	1/7/06
Field top makers	10	1/7/06
Land planes	25	1/7/06
Line planters	10	1/7/06
Mowers (including reel & rotary mowers)	10	1/7/06
Net layers	10	1/7/06
Power harrows	10	1/7/06
Roll layers	10	1/7/06
Soil aerators	10	1/7/06
Trailers	15	1/7/06
Turf harvesters (including pedestrian & tractor mounted harvesters)	10#	1/7/06
Turf rollers	15	1/7/06
Turf seeders	15	1/7/06
Turf vacuums	10	1/7/06

MUSHROOM GROWING

Asset	Life (yrs)	Date of application
Air handling systems (incorporating cooling coils, filter blowers, mixing boxes, environment sensors & air ducting)	10	1/7/08
Boilers (used for humidification & pasteurisation)	10	1/7/08
Casing machines (includes casing mixers)	10	1/7/08
Compost phase 1 assets:		
Bunkers	10	1/7/08
Machinery (including forklifts, front end loaders, bunker fillers & pre wet turners)	4	1/7/08
Protective structures	10	1/7/08
Pumps	3	1/7/08
Control systems (excluding personal computers)	10	1/7/08
Filling & emptying machines (including bag fillers, bed winches, cassette fillers & tunnel fillers)	10	1/7/08

Asset	Life (yrs)	Date of application
Growing systems:		
Shelves:		
Aluminium	15	1/7/08
Other materials	10	1/7/08
Trays:		
Wood	5	1/7/08
Mushroom graders	5	1/7/08
Sheds	40	1/7/08
Slicing machines	5	1/7/08
Spawning machines (including supplement machines)	12	1/7/08
Trolleys	10	1/7/08
Tunnels/rooms (incorporating doors, floors, drains, frames, insulation, lighting, roofs & walls):		
Growing	15	1/7/08
Peak heat & spawn running	10	1/7/08
Vacuum coolers	10	1/7/08
Weighing machines	10	1/7/08

VEGETABLE GROWING (UNDER COVER)

(Hydroponic growing assets (including cut flower growing):

Asset	Life (yrs)	Date of application
Hanging gutters	10	1/7/07
Troughs	10	1/7/07

Hydroponics growers may also use the effective life for relevant assets shown in Nursery & floriculture production

VEGETABLE GROWING (OUTDOORS) & SUGAR CANE GROWING

Asset	Life (yrs)	Date of application
Chemical spraying assets:		
Generally	10	1/7/07
Self propelled	8	1/7/07
Fertilizer spreaders:		
Generally	10	1/7/07
Spinner	5	1/7/07
General assets:		
Bins:		
Plastic	10	1/7/07
Timber	5	1/7/07
Mulch layers	12	1/7/07
Mulch lifters	12	1/7/07
Mulchers	8	1/7/07
Rakes (eg cane trash rakes)	10	1/7/07
Slashers	8	1/7/07
Harvesting assets:		
Cane haul out bins	12	1/7/07
Harvesters (including cane, carrot, onion, potato & tomato)	10#	1/7/07
Harvesting aids (incorporating trailers & conveyor belts)	15	1/7/07
Onion lifters	10#	1/7/07
Trailers	15	1/7/07
Windrowers (including potato diggers, onion & potato windrowers)	10#	1/7/07
Planting assets:		
Billet planters	12	1/7/07
Potato cutters	15	1/7/07
Potato planters	10	1/7/07
Precision seeders	10	1/7/07
Transplanters:		
Automated	7	1/7/07
Manual	10	1/7/07
Tillage assets:		
Generally	15	1/7/07
PTO operated (including rotary hoes & power harrows)	8	1/7/07
Trellising assets:		
Stake drivers	12	1/7/07
Stake pullers	12	1/7/07
Trellising (incorporating stakes & wire)	5	1/7/07
Wire winders	15	1/7/07

FRUIT GROWING

Asset	Life (yrs)	Date of application
Cleaning & mulching assets:		
Mowers (including zero turn & ride on)	8	1/7/08
Mulchers	6	1/7/08
Slashers	8	1/7/08
Sweeper attachments	10	1/7/08
Crop protection assets:		
Applicators (including temporary bird netting applicators & vine cover rollers)	15	1/7/08
Banana bagging machines	10	1/7/08
Banana ripening bags	3	1/7/08

Asset	Life (yrs)	Date of application
Sprayers	10	1/7/08
Temporary bird netting	5	1/7/08
Under vine weeder	10	1/7/08
Vine covers	3	1/7/08
Dried fruit assets:		
Generally (including bin dryers, boxing machines, dehydration tunnels, dippers, rack dehydrators, scrapers, trolleys & wetting machines)	15	1/7/08
Drying sheets (including ground sheets)	10	1/7/08
Trays	10	1/7/08
Fertilising assets:		
Fertigation systems:		
Pumps	3	1/7/08
Tanks	10	1/7/08
Spreaders:		
Generally	10	1/7/08
Spinners	5	1/7/08
General assets:		
Bins:		
Plastic	10	1/7/08
Timber	5	1/7/08
Crates (including picking lugs)	5	1/7/08
Elevating work platforms	10	1/7/08
Frost fans	15	1/7/08
Mulch layers	12	1/7/08
Mulch lifters	12	1/7/08
Orchard ladders	10	1/7/08
Post driver/hole diggers	10	1/7/08
Refractometers	10	1/7/08
Water pressure cleaners	5	1/7/08
Harvesting assets:		
Grape harvesters	10#	1/7/08
Harvest aids	15	1/7/08
Picking bags	3	1/7/08
Picking platforms	10	1/7/08
Picking trolleys	5	1/7/08
Trailers (including grape chaser bins)	15	1/7/08
Tree shakers	10#	1/7/08
Planting assets:		
Hole burners	10	1/7/08
Planters	12	1/7/08
Tree guards	2	1/7/08
Trellising	20	1/7/08
Weed matting	5	1/7/08
Pruning assets:		
Chain saws	3	1/7/08
Electric Hand pruners	3	1/7/08
Manual Hand pruners	2	1/7/08
Mechanical pruning assets (incl cutter bars & cane strippers, but excluding vine leaf removers)	10	1/7/08
Pneumatic pruners:		
Compressors	10	1/7/08
Hand tools	5	1/7/08
Vine leaf removers	15	1/7/08
Tillage assets:		
Generally	15	1/7/08
PTO operated (including rotary hoes & power harrows)	8	1/7/08

COFFEE, OLIVE & TREE NUT GROWING

Asset	Life (yrs)	Date of application
Chemical spraying assets (including air blast sprayers & linkage sprayers)	10	1/7/07
Cleaning & mulching assets:		
Blowers	10	1/7/07
Mowers (including zero turn & ride on)	8	1/7/07
Mulchers	8	1/7/07
Slashers	10	1/7/07
Sweeper attachments	10	1/7/07
Fertilizer spreaders	10	1/7/07
General assets:		
Bins:		
Plastic	10	1/7/07
Timber	5	1/7/07
Stakes (including trellising)	3	1/7/07
Harvesting assets:		
Bankouts (almonds)	15	1/7/07
Catcher nets	10	1/7/07
Elevators (almonds)	12	1/7/07
Harvesters:		
Coffee	10#	1/7/07
Olive	10#	1/7/07

Asset	Life (yrs)	Date of application
Nuts:		
Generally	10#	1/7/07
Macadamia mower mounted	8	1/7/07
Pick ups (eg almonds)	12#	1/7/07
Sweepers	12#	1/7/07
Tree shakers	10#	1/7/07
Reservoir carts (almonds)	15	1/7/07
Harvesting pole rakes	5	1/7/07
Trailers	15	1/7/07
Pruning assets:		
Chain saws	5	1/7/07
Electric Hand pruners	3	1/7/07
Manual Hand pruners	2	1/7/07
Pneumatic pruners:		
Compressor	10	1/7/07
Hand tools	5	1/7/07

SHEEP FARMING

Asset	Life (yrs)	Date of application
Crutching machines, portable type	10	1/1/07
Dipping & spraying assets for parasite control:		
Jet spray system assets (including the race or handler dedicated to the jet spray system)	10	1/1/07
Mobile plunge dips	5	1/1/07
Feeders (including grain feeders, oat feeders, hay feeders)	15	1/1/07
Footbaths	10	1/1/07
Instruments for measuring wool fibre fineness, laser type	10	1/1/07
Instruments for measuring backfat or eye muscle or detecting pregnancy, ultrasound type (incorporating probe & monitor)	5	1/1/07
Sheep handling assets (including autodrafter, conveyor, cradle, crate, crutching trailer, elevator, ewe lifter, handler, hydraulic lift, rollover unit, shearing table, weigh crate, winch used to lift sheep)	15	1/1/07
Weigh bars, weigh indicators & weigh platforms	10	1/1/07
Yards, races, leadup systems & loading ramps:		
Permanent types	40	1/1/07
Portable types	25	1/1/07
Woolshed assets:		
Grinding machines for sharpening cutters	30	1/1/07
Shearing machines	30	1/1/07
Shearing or crutching Handpieces	10	1/1/07
Wool bale movers	10	1/1/07
Wool presses	20	1/1/07
Woolsheds & shearing sheds	50	1/1/07
Wool tables, steel types	20	1/1/07

BEEF CATTLE FARMING

Asset	Life (yrs)	Date of application
Cattle handling assets:		
Calf cradles	10	1/1/07
Cattle crushes (hydraulic & manual)	10	1/1/07
NLIS & other readers	5	1/1/07
Scales, weigh indicators & loading bars	5	1/1/07
Cattle yards including races & coolers (steel & timber):		
Permanent types	30	1/1/07
Portable types	20	1/1/07
Feed bins including hay racks	15	1/1/07
Feed handling assets:		
Bale feeders	10	1/1/07
Feed mixers	10	1/1/07
Silage & feedout wagons	10	1/1/07
Loading ramps	20	1/1/07
Manure & fertilizer spreaders	10	1/1/07
Saddlery & harness	10	1/1/07

BEEF CATTLE FEEDLOTS

Asset	Life (yrs)	Date of application
Cattle handling assets:		
Cattle crushes (hydraulic & manual)	6	1/1/07
Cattle induction & transfer yards (steel & timber)	20	1/1/07
Cattle treatment yards (steel & timber)	20	1/1/07
Cattle wash yards (steel & timber)	20	1/1/07
NLIS & other readers	5	1/1/07
Scales, weigh indicators & loading bars	5	1/1/07
Cattle pen assets:		
Bunk sweepers	8	1/1/07
Cattle pen infrastructure assets:		
Feed bunks or troughs & aprons	20	1/1/07
Feed roads	20	1/1/07
Pen earthworks	20	1/1/07

Asset	Life (yrs)	Date of application
Pen fences & gates (steel & timber)	20	1/1/07
Shade structures	20	1/1/07
Pen scrapers	10	1/1/07
Feed milling & handling assets:		
Ancillary grain handling equipment:		
Augers	10	1/1/07
Conveyors & elevators	15	1/1/07
Bulk & segregated commodity storage facilities (incorporating bunkers)	30	1/1/07
Feed mixers	7	1/1/07
Feed mixer trucks	7	1/1/07
Grain cleaners	10	1/1/07
Grain processing assets:		
Roller mills	15	1/1/07
Steam flaking chests	15	1/1/07
Steam flaking surge bins	15	1/1/07
Tempering silos:		
Glass fused to steel	50	1/1/07
Stainless steel	15	1/1/07
Galvanised steel	12	1/1/07
Receival pits & hoppers	25	1/1/07
Roughage processing assets (incl tub rinders)	7	1/1/07
Sampling & testing assets	5	1/1/07
Silos & bins used for storing dry grain:		
Concrete	50	1/1/07
Steel	20	1/1/07
Tank storages for liquid feed supplements	15	1/1/07
Loading ramps	20	1/1/07
Manure composting & screening machines	15	1/1/07

DAIRY CATTLE FARMING

Asset	Life (yrs)	Date of application
Automatic calf feeders	10	1/7/07
Barn fed dairy farms:		
Bulk & segregated commodity storage facilities (incorporating bunkers)	30	1/7/07
Exercise yards	20	1/7/07
Feeding barns & maternity barns (incorporating cow beds, fans, & feed alleys)	20	1/7/07
Cattle handling assets:		
Air operated gates	10	1/7/07
All terrain vehicles (ATVs)	3	1/7/07
Automatic drafting systems	7	1/7/07
Automatic ID systems	7	1/7/07
Automatic weighing systems & cattle scales	5	1/7/07
Backing gates	15	1/7/07
Calf cradles	10	1/7/07
Cattle crushes	10	1/7/07
Cattle laneways	30	1/7/07
Cattle yards (including loading ramps)	30	1/7/07
Dairy milking sheds	30	1/7/07
Dairy yards & races	20	1/7/07
Teat spraying systems:		
Automatic	7	1/7/07
Manual	10	1/7/07
Clean up assets:		
High pressure pumps & hoses	10	1/7/07
Hot water services	10	1/7/07
Milk line washing systems:		
Automatic	10	1/7/07
Manual	10	1/7/07
Feed milling & handling assets:		
Augers	10	1/7/07
Conveyors & elevators	15	1/7/07
Feed pads & bunkers	30	1/7/07
Feeding systems:		
Automatic	12	1/7/07
Manual	15	1/7/07
Feed mixers	7	1/7/07
Grain mills (including roller mills, disc mills & hammer mills)	15	1/7/07
Manure spreaders	10	1/7/07
Silage pits	40	1/7/07
Silage wagons	10	1/7/07
Silos (steel)	20	1/7/07
Telescopic handlers	10	1/7/07
Tub grinders	7	1/7/07
Milking & milk handling assets:		
Automatic cluster removers	10	1/7/07
Bailing systems:		
Herringbone (including swing over, double up & rapid exit)	15	1/7/07

Asset	Life (yrs)	Date of application
Rotary	15	1/7/07
Walk through	15	1/7/07
Filters	15	1/7/07
Milking systems (incorporating clusters, swing over arms, hoses, pipes, pulsators, vacuum pumps, variable speed control)	15	1/7/07
Milk meters & recording jars (including conductivity sensors)	10	1/7/07
Milk vats	25	1/7/07
Plate coolers	15	1/7/07
Receivers	15	1/7/07
Refrigeration compressors	10	1/7/07

POULTRY FARMING FOR BREEDING, EGGS & MEAT

Asset	Life (yrs)	Date of application
Animal housing environmental control assets:		
Control systems (excluding personal computers)	10	1/1/07
Curtains:		
Baffles, brooders	10	1/1/07
Sidewalls	5	1/1/07
Tunnel inlets	10	1/1/07
Evaporative cooling systems (including frames, pipes, pumps, tanks & coolpads)	10	1/1/07
Foggers	10	1/1/07
Heaters	15	1/1/07
Minimum vents (including cabling)	12	1/1/07
Sensors	4	1/1/07
Tunnel inlet panels	15	1/1/07
Ventilation fans:		
Exhaust fans (tunnel, minivent)	12	1/1/07
Stirrer fans	15	1/1/07
Animal housing structures (incorporating frames, walls, rooves, insulation, doors, floors & lighting)	20	1/1/07
Cages (for egg layers)	20	1/1/07
Egg belt systems (under cage/nest housing) (including belts, rollers, tensioners & drive units)	15	1/1/07
Egg conveyors (including drive units)	15	1/1/07
Egg counters	15	1/1/07
Egg elevators (including drive units)	15	1/1/07
Egg grading & packing assets:		
Egg grader & packing systems (including box erectors, box sealers, candling machines, conveyors, crack, dirt, leak & blood detectors, denesters (egg inners & trays), egg loaders, egg oilers, egg tray stackers, egg washers, egg weigher & transfer systems, imprinters (egg & box), packers (inners, trays & boxes) & wrappers)	10	1/1/07
Pallet levellers (coil spring)	25	1/1/07
Palletisers	10	1/1/07
Trolley lifters	15	1/1/07
Farm trolleys:		
Chicken transport	10	1/1/07
Egg transport	10	1/1/07
Feeding systems (including troughs, trolleys, chains, hoppers, pans, tubes with auger & drive units)	10	1/1/07
Generators (emergency)	20	1/1/07
Hanging cable systems (for feeders, drinkers & nest housing)	15	1/1/07
Manure belt systems (under cage/nest housing) (including polypropylene belts, scrapers, rollers, tensioners & drive units)	15	1/1/07
Manure conveyors (including drive units)	10	1/1/07
Nest housing (including slatted walkways)	15	1/1/07
Silos for feed:		
Metal	20	1/1/07
Ancillary equipment:		
Augers	10	1/1/07
Conveyors & elevators	15	1/1/07
Water assets:		
Drinking systems (incl tubing, nipple drinkers, drinking cups, pressure regulators & filter units)	10	1/1/07
Winches	10	1/1/07

POULTRY HATCHERIES

Asset	Life (yrs)	Date of application
Air handlers	20	1/1/07
Boilers	20	1/1/07
Candling equipment	20	1/1/07
Chick counters	20	1/1/07
Chilled water plants	20	1/1/07
Control systems (excluding personal computers)	10	1/1/07
Condensers/heat exchangers	10	1/1/07
Conveyors	20	1/1/07

Asset	Life (yrs)	Date of application
Generators (emergency)	20	1/1/07
Hatcher trolleys/dollies	10	1/1/07
Hatcher baskets	10	1/1/07
Hatchers (including integrated controller units)	20	1/1/07
Hatchery buildings (incorporating frames, walls, rooves, insulation, doors, floors & lighting)	40	1/1/07
Macerators	20	1/1/07
Separators – chick & egg	20	1/1/07
Setter trays	10	1/1/07
Setter trolley unloaders	20	1/1/07
Setter trolleys	10	1/1/07
Setters/incubators (incl integrated controller unit)	20	1/1/07
Stacker/destacker systems	20	1/1/07
Transfer machines – farm trolley to setter trolley	20	1/1/07
Transfer machines – setter tray to hatcher basket	20	1/1/07
Vaccinators	15	1/1/07
Vacuum/auger systems (waste)	20	1/1/07
Washing assets	20	1/1/07

PIG FARMING

Asset	Life (yrs)	Date of application
Animal housing assets:		
Animal housing structures (incorporating frames, covers, walls, roof, insulation, shutters & doors)	20	1/7/08
Curtains - sidewalls	10	1/7/08
Floors (suspended types):		
Concrete	10	1/7/08
Plastic	10	1/7/08
Steel	5	1/7/08
Control systems (excluding personal computers)	10	1/7/08
Dry feed systems (incorporating troughs, trolleys, chains, hoppers, pans, tubers with auger & drive units)	10	1/7/08
Effluent separators/effluent fan extractors	10	1/7/08
Evaporative cooling systems (incorporating frames, pipes, pumps, tanks & coolpads)	10	1/7/08
Fans:		
Exhaust (tunnel, minivent)	10	1/7/08
Stirrer	10	1/7/08
Farrowing crates	10	1/7/08
Generators (emergency)	20	1/7/08
Heaters & heat lamps	5	1/7/08
High pressure cleaners	3	1/7/08
Instruments for measuring backfat or detecting pregnancy, ultrasound types (incorporating probes & monitors)	5	1/7/08
Liquid feed systems (incorporating feed valves, tanks, pumps, pipelines, mixers & troughs)	10	1/7/08
Milling assets	10	1/7/08
Mixing assets	10	1/7/08
Pens (including fences, gates, stalls, farrowing crates, ramps)	10	1/7/08
Silos:		
Grain storage	20	1/7/08
Readyfeed	10	1/7/08
Tank storage for liquid feed supplements	20	1/7/08
Water assets:		
Drinking systems (incorporating tubing, nipple drinkers, drinking cups, pressure regulators & filter units)	10	1/7/08
Effluent tanks (concrete)	20	1/7/08
Weigh bars, weigh indicators & weigh platforms	5	1/7/08

AQUACULTURE

Asset	Life (yrs)	Date of application
Aeration assets:		
Direct supply systems (including paddlewheels & aspirators):		
Fresh water	6	1/7/07
Salt water	3	1/7/07
Remote or indirect supply systems (incorporating blowers, diaphragm pumps, diffusers, upwellers & pipelines)	10	1/7/07
Aquaculture tanks:		
Concrete	20	1/7/07
Fibreglass	15	1/7/07
Polyethylene	20	1/7/07
Raceways	20	1/7/07
Transport of live products	10	1/7/07
Bins & crates	5	1/7/07
Commercial vessels & support assets – see Table A		
Water transport & support services		
Cooling assets (including water chillers)	10	1/7/07
Control systems	10	1/7/07

Asset	Life (yrs)	Date of application
Environmental control structures & protective structures used in salt water environment	15	1/7/07
Feeders (including belt, pendulum, scatter & blower)	5	1/7/07
Graders	10	1/7/07
Harvesting nets	4	1/7/07
Hatching assets (including hatching containers)	10	1/7/07
Heating assets:		
Direct heating system (including immersion heaters):		
Fresh water	10	1/7/07
Salt water	5	1/7/07
Indirect heating system (incl heat exchangers & passive heating)	10	1/7/07
Instruments (incl sensors & water quality meters)	5	1/7/07
Oyster farming assets:		
Baskets	8	1/7/07
Oyster growing structures (incorporating posts & racks or lines)	10	1/7/07
Rumblers	10	1/7/07
Sticks	5	1/7/07
Trays:		
Plastic	8	1/7/07
Timber	5	1/7/07
Vats, treatment	15	1/7/07
Power supply assets, emergency or standby:		
Generators (incorporating attached engine management & generator monitoring instruments)	15	1/7/07
Processing assets:		
Conveyors, elevators & hoppers	10	1/7/07
Cookers	10	1/7/07
Packaging assets (including vacuum & modified atmospheric packing)	10	1/7/07
Refrigeration assets:		
Insulation panels in cool or freezer rooms used in salt water environment	20	1/7/07
Sea cages (incorporating rings, nets, ropes, anchors, weights & stanchions)	10	1/7/07
Water assets:		
Aquaculture channels & ponds	20	1/7/07
Liners & erosion matting for ponds & channels	15	1/7/07
Pipes & pipelines:		
Above ground (polyethylene & polyvinylchloride including lay flat hoses)	10	1/7/07
In ground (polyethylene & polyvinylchloride)	30	1/7/07
Pumps:		
Generally:		
Fresh water	10	1/7/07
Salt water	5	1/7/07
Single phase transfer pumps:		
Fresh water	5	1/7/07
Salt water	3	1/7/07
Water treatment assets (including filtration assets, foam fractionators, oxygen & ozone generators & UV sterilizers)	10	1/7/07
Weighing machines	5	1/7/07

FORESTRY & LOGGING

Asset	Life (yrs)	Date of application
Logging plant:		
Cable systems (including winches & high leads)	8	1/1/01
Forwarders	8	1/1/01
Harvesters & feller bunchers (includes heads)	7	1/1/01
Log trailers	10	1/1/01
Saws:		
Mobile	8	1/1/01
Portable chain	2	1/1/01
Snigging plant (including cable & grapple skidders, wheel loaders with log grabs, bulldozers, excavators, arches & winches)	7	1/1/01

FISHING

Asset	Life (yrs)	Date of application
Fishing plant:		
Commercial vessels & support assets – see Table A Water transport & support services		
Fish holding baskets	10	1/1/01
Purse seine fishing net	5	1/1/01

MINING

Asset	Life (yrs)	Date of application
Crushing & milling assets:		
Crushers:		
Cone & gyratory	25	1/7/03

Asset	Life (yrs)	Date of application
Feeder breaker	20	1/7/03
Generally	25	1/7/03
Impact & rotary	20	1/7/03
Jaw	25	1/7/03
Roller (including roll sizers)	20	1/7/03
Grinding mills:		
Ball & rod	25	1/7/03
Generally	25	1/7/03
Hammer	15	1/7/03
SAG (autogenous)	25	1/7/03
Hydrometallurgy & Pyrometallurgy assets:		
Adsorption process assets	20	1/7/03
Agglomeration (pelletizing) assets	25	1/7/03
Calcination process assets (including kilns)	25	1/7/03
Casting process assets for casting billets or ingots	30	1/7/03
Converting process assets (including rotatable cylindrical furnaces)	30	1/7/03
Cooling process assets (including cooling towers)	25	1/7/03
Counter current decantation (CCD) process assets	20	1/7/03
Drying process assets (including rotary dryers, spray dryers & indirect heat exchanger dryers)	25	1/7/03
Electrolysis process assets (including electrowinning process & electro refining process assets including tanks)	20	1/7/03
Filtration process assets	15	1/7/03
Gas cleaning process assets (incl electrostatic precipitators & baghouses)	20	1/7/03
Gas recovery process assets (including stripping & absorption assets)	25	1/7/03
Ion exchange process assets	15	1/7/03
Leaching process assets:		
Atmospheric	15	1/7/03
Generally	25	1/7/03
Pressure	25	1/7/03
Neutralisation process assets	20	1/7/03
Pots & ladles used for molten materials	30	1/7/03
Precipitation process assets (including tanks & agitators)	20	1/7/03
Pressure vessels	30	1/7/03
Roasting process assets (including kilns & furnaces)	30	1/7/03
Sintering process assets (including continuous sintering machines)	30	1/7/03
Smelting process assets (including furnaces)	25	1/7/03
Solution treatment & metal recovery assets	20	1/7/03
Solvent extraction process assets (including mixer settler units)	20	1/7/03
Tailings stills	20	1/7/03
Infrastructure support assets:		
Compressors	15	1/7/03
Control systems & communication systems assets:		
Generally	10	1/7/03
Instruments	10	1/7/03
Towers or other supporting structures	30	1/7/03
Electrical infrastructure assets (including power reticulation, substations, switchgear & transformers)	25	1/7/03
Mineral treatment structure	40	1/7/03
Pipes & pipelines (including valves & fittings):		
Generally	25	1/7/03
Slurry pipework within processing facility (including slurry pipe to thickener)	10	1/1/06
Pumps:		
Generally	20	1/7/03
Positive displacement pumps	15	1/7/03
Materials handling assets:		
Belt magnets, samplers, metal detectors & analysers	15	1/7/03
Bins, chutes, hoppers, bunkers & silos	30	1/7/03
Bucket elevators	25	1/7/03
Conveyors	25	1/7/03
Feeders:		
Generally (including apron & belt)	20	1/7/03
Vibrating	15	1/7/03
Fuel storage tanks	30	1/7/03
Gas storage tanks & spheres	25	1/7/03
Grizzly bars & scalpers	25	1/7/03
Overhead cranes/gantries	30	1/7/03
Stacks (chimney)	30	1/7/03
Stockpile assets:		
Reclaim tunnel flow valves & activators	25	1/7/03

Asset	Life (yrs)	Date of application
Stackers, reclaimers & stacker/reclaimers	25	1/7/03
Train loaders	30	1/7/03
Trippers/stackers & stacking conveyor systems	25	1/7/03
Tunnel vent & exhaust fans	15	1/7/03
Water recycling facilities	20	1/7/03
Water storage tanks	30	1/7/03
Weighing machines (including weighers for feeders & conveyors)	20	1/7/04
Mineral dressing assets:		
Classification, gravity separation & dewatering assets:		
Centrifuges	15	1/7/03
Cyclones:		
Dense medium & heavy medium	8	1/7/03
Generally (including classifying, desliming, & hydrocyclones)	15	1/7/03
Generally	18	1/7/03
Hydraulic classifiers & teetered bed separators	20	1/7/03
Jigs	25	1/7/03
Pneumatic tables & air separators	25	1/7/03
Settling cones	25	1/7/03
Shaking tables	25	1/7/03
Sluices & cone concentrators	25	1/7/03
Spirals	12	1/7/03
Electrostatic separation assets	20	1/7/03
Filtration assets (including pressure filtration & vacuum filtration equipment)	15	1/7/03
Flotation assets (including tanks, launders, agitators, air supply & reagent dosing equipment)	20	1/7/03
Magnetic separation assets (including cross belt, drum & disc types)	20	1/7/03
Screening assets	15	1/7/03
Thickening assets	25	1/7/03
Port assets – see Table A		
Water transport & support services		
Railway infrastructure assets & rolling stock – see Table A		
Rail freight & passenger transport services		
Surface mobile mining machines:		
Bucket wheel excavators	30	1/7/02
Compressors	20	1/7/02
Cranes	20	1/7/02
Dozers	9	1/7/02
Draglines	30	1/7/02
Drill rigs (Production)	10	1/7/02
Electric rope shovels	25	1/7/02
Generators	10	1/7/02
Graders	10	1/7/02
Hydraulic excavators (incl hydraulic front shovels)	10	1/7/02
Lighting systems	10	1/7/02
Off highway trucks (incl articulated, rigid dump, service, fuel & water trucks)	10	1/7/02
Rollers	15	1/7/02
Scrapers	7	1/7/02
Skid steer loader	7	1/7/02
Tool carriers	10	1/7/02
Wheel loaders	8	1/7/02
Tailings dams	20	1/1/01
Underground mobile mining machines:		
Compressors	10	1/7/02
Continuous haulage systems	10	1/7/02
Continuous miners	10	1/7/02
Drill rigs:		
Diamond	20	1/7/02
Production	7	1/7/02
Feeder breakers	15	1/7/02
Graders	10	1/7/02
Jumbos	10	1/7/02
Load haul dump machines	6	1/7/02
Long wall equipment:		
Armoured face conveyors	6	1/7/02
Beam stage loaders	7	1/7/02
Hydraulic pump modules	15	1/7/02
Hydraulic roof supports	10	1/7/02
Impact crushers	10	1/7/02
Mobile conveyors tail end	5	1/7/02
Roof support relocation vehicles	10	1/7/02
Shearers	7	1/7/02
Shearer carriers	10	1/7/02
Maintenance vehicles	8	1/7/02

Asset	Life (yrs)	Date of application
Personnel transporters	8	1/7/02
Raise borers & down reamers	20	1/7/02
Roof bolters	8	1/7/02
Scissor lifts	6	1/7/02
Shuttle cars	12	1/7/02
Skid steer loaders	12	1/7/02
Underground haulage trucks	6	1/7/02
Wheel loaders	6	1/7/02
Workshop plant	20	1/1/01
COAL MINING		
Coal preparation assets:		
Centrifuges	15	1/7/03
Crushing assets (including feeder breakers, impact, roller & rotary crushers)	20	1/7/03
Cyclones:		
Dense medium, heavy medium	6	1/7/03
Generally (including classifying, desliming & hydrocyclones)	10	1/7/03
Filtration assets (incl belt, drum & vacuum filters)	15	1/7/03
Flotation assets (incl agitation air supply systems, launders, reagent dosing systems & tanks)	20	1/7/03
Grizzly bars & scalpers	25	1/7/03
Jigs & heavy medium baths	25	1/7/03
Magnetic separators	20	1/7/03
Spirals	12	1/7/03
Thickening assets	25	1/7/03
Infrastructure support assets:		
Analysers, belt magnets, grinding mills, metal detectors & samplers	15	1/7/03
Coal preparation facility framework/structure	40	1/7/03
Compressors	15	1/7/03
Control systems & communication systems assets:		
Generally	10	1/7/03
Instruments	10	1/7/03
Towers or other supporting structures	30	1/7/03
Electrical infrastructure assets (incl reticulation assets, substations, switch gear & transformers)	25	1/7/03
Fuel storage tanks	30	1/7/03
Gas storage tanks	25	1/7/03
Overhead cranes/gantries	30	1/7/03
Pipes & pipelines (including valves & fittings):		
Generally	25	1/7/03
Slurry pipework within processing facility (including slurry pipe to thickener)	10	1/1/06
Pumps:		
Generally (including centrifugal pumps)	20	1/7/03
Positive displacement pumps	15	1/7/03
Train loaders	30	1/7/03
Tunnel vent or exhaust fans	15	1/7/03
Valves & other non pipe fittings	10	1/7/03
Water recycling facility	20	1/7/03
Water storage dams (including fire services dams & water storage dams generally)	30	1/7/03
Water storage tanks	30	1/7/03
Materials handling assets:		
Bins, chutes, hoppers, silos & storage bunkers	30	1/7/03
Bucket elevators	25	1/7/03
Conveyors	25	1/7/03
Feeders:		
Generally (including apron & belt feeders)	20	1/7/03
Vibrating feeders	15	1/7/03
Stockpile spraying system	20	1/7/03
Stockpile stackers, reclaimers & stacker reclaimers:		
Generally (including all machinery)	25	1/7/03
Reclaim tunnels	25	1/7/03
Trippers/stackers	25	1/7/03
OIL & GAS EXTRACTION		
Assets used to manufacture condensate, crude oil, domestic gas, liquid natural gas (LNG) or liquid petroleum gas (LPG) but not if the manufacture occurs in an oil refinery:		
Control systems	10	1/7/02
Domestic gas processing assets (including centrifugal compressor, column, gas turbine, heat exchanger, piping & turbo expander)	30#	1/7/02
Electricity generation assets – see Table A Electricity supply		
Flare towers for gas flares	25#	1/7/02

Asset	Life (yrs)	Date of application
Fractionation train assets (including air coolers, columns, compressors, heat exchangers, piping & pumps)	30#	1/7/02
Hot water system assets	17¹/₂#	1/7/02
Instruments	12¹/₂	1/7/02
LNG holding facility assets (incl boil off gas compressors, cryogenic storage tanks, loading arms, pumps & tanks)	30#	1/7/02
LNG train assets (incl centrifugal compressors, columns, cryogenic heat exchangers, gas turbine drivers & other heat exchangers)	30#	1/7/02
Stabiliser process assets (incl columns, heat exchangers, pumps & reciprocating compressors)	30#	1/7/02
Storage & loading assets (incl cryogenic storage tanks, jetties, loading arms, LPG chillers & pumps)	30#	1/7/02
Trunkline onshore terminal (TOT) assets:		
Flash tanks	20#	1/7/02
Slugcatcher & associated piping	30#	1/7/02
Valves including control valves	12¹/₂	1/7/02
Gas production assets:		
Central production facility assets:		
Boilers	10	1/7/02
Cabling for power & control systems	30#	1/7/02
Diesel systems	15	1/7/02
Drains systems	20#	1/7/02
Drill rigs	10	1/7/02
Flare system assets:		
Carbon steel piping	15	1/7/02
Flare tips	5	1/7/02
Stainless steel piping	30#	1/7/02
Fuel gas systems	30#	1/7/02
Gas compression & reinjection assets:		
Gas compressors used offshore	10	1/7/02
Gas turbine drivers used offshore	12¹/₂	1/7/02
Generally (including piping, skid, vessels & assets used onshore)	30#	1/7/02
Power turbines used offshore	12¹/₂	1/7/02
Heat exchangers	30#	1/7/02
Major carbon steel vessels	12¹/₂	1/7/02
Major stainless steel (or lined) vessels	30#	1/7/02
Offshore platforms:		
Generally (including accommodation modules, flare structures, helidecks, jackets, primary steel work & topsides secondary steel work)	30#	1/7/02
Topsides tertiary steelwork (including handrails, ladders & stairs)	15	1/7/02
Piping	30#	1/7/02
Pumps:		
Circulation pump	12¹/₂	1/7/02
Generally	20#	1/7/02
Seawater lift pumps	15	1/7/02
Shutdown & fire/gas systems	15	1/7/02
Tempered water system assets:		
Chemical treatment assets	12¹/₂	1/7/02
Piping & vessels	30#	1/7/02
Utility air compressors	15	1/7/02
Control systems	10	1/7/02
Electricity generation assets – see Table A Electricity supply		
Floating production storage & offloading (FPSO) vessels (incorporating mooring systems)	20#	1/7/02
Floating storage & offloading (FSO) vessels (incorporating mooring systems)	20#	1/7/02
Infield pipeline	30#	1/7/02
Instruments (including level, pressure & temperature indicators)	12¹/₂	1/7/02
Offshore bulk loading transfer systems	10	1/7/02
Subsea production assets (including control umbilical, flowline & manifold)	20#	1/7/02
Trunklines	30#	1/7/02
Valves	12¹/₂	1/7/02
Wells & downhole equipment	15	1/7/02
Wellheads & christmas trees	30#	1/7/02
Oil production assets:		
Central production facility assets (excl FPSOs):		
Boilers	10	1/7/02
Circulation pumps	12¹/₂	1/7/02
Drill rigs	10	1/7/02
Flare tips	5	1/7/02

Asset	Life (yrs)	Date of application
Gas compression & reinjection assets:		
Gas compressors used offshore	10	1/7/02
Gas turbine drivers used offshore	12¹/₂	1/7/02
Generally (including piping, skids, vessels & assets used onshore)	15	1/7/02
Power turbines used offshore	12¹/₂	1/7/02
Generally (including offshore platforms)	15	1/7/02
Major carbon steel vessels	12¹/₂	1/7/02
Pumps:		
Circulation pumps	12¹/₂	1/7/02
Other	15	1/7/02
Tempered water system assets:		
Chemical treatment assets	12¹/₂	1/7/02
Piping & vessels	15	1/7/02
Control systems	10	1/7/02
Electricity generation assets – see Table A Electricity supply		
Floating production storage & offloading (FPSO) vessels (incorporating mooring system)	20#	1/7/02
Floating storage & offloading (FSO) vessels (incorporating mooring system)	20#	1/7/02
Infield pipelines	15	1/7/02
Instruments (including level, pressure & temperature indicators)	12¹/₂	1/7/02
Offshore bulk loading transfer systems	10	1/7/02
Subsea production assets (including control umbilical, flowline & manifold)	15	1/7/02
Trunklines	30#	1/7/02
Valves	12¹/₂	1/7/02
Wells & downhole equipment	10	1/7/02
Wellheads & christmas trees	15	1/7/02
Port assets – see Table A Water transport & support services		

IRON ORE MINING

Asset	Life (yrs)	Date of application
Infrastructure support assets:		
Blowers, high pressure	15	1/1/06
Dust suppression/control equipment	15	1/1/06
Materials handling assets:		
Feeders:		
Vibrating	10	1/1/06
Mineral dressing assets:		
Cyclones, dense/heavy medium (unlined nihard)	1	1/1/06
Dense medium separation assets (including baths & drums)	20	1/1/06
Magnetic separation assets:		
LIMS (low intensity magnetic separators)	20	1/1/06
WHIMS (wet high intensity magnetic separators)	15	1/1/06
Screening assets	10	1/1/06

GOLD ORE MINING

Asset	Life (yrs)	Date of application
Gold ore processing assets:		
Adsorption process assets	15	1/7/04
Carbon regeneration kilns	12	1/7/04
Concentrators (including inline pressure jigs & mechanical concentrators)	10	1/7/04
Crushing assets:		
Cone/gyratory crushers	20	1/7/04
Hydraulic rock breakers	12	1/7/04
Jaw crushers	20	1/7/04
Electrowinning/electrorefining assets	17	1/7/04
Elution columns	12	1/7/04
Elution storage tanks	17	1/7/04
Laboratory assets:		
Atmospheric adsorption spectrometers	10	1/7/04
Generally (including drying ovens, pulverisers, crushers, gas fired ovens, fume cupboards)	15	1/7/04
Leaching process assets (incl carbon in pulp & carbon in leach processes)	15	1/7/04
Shaking tables	12	1/7/04
Smelting furnaces	15	1/7/04
Thickening assets	20	1/7/04

MINERAL SAND MINING

Asset	Life (yrs)	Date of application
Aeration assets (including aerators, attritioners, blowers & turbine impeller agitated vessels)	20	1/1/03
Classification & gravity separation assets (including centrifuges, cones, cyclones, screw classifiers, spirals & tables)	15	1/1/03
Crushing assets (including drum scrubbers)	30	1/1/03

Asset	Life (yrs)	Date of application
Dredges	20	1/7/09
Drying assets:		
Generally (including flash & fluid bed dryers & fluid bed heaters)	20	1/1/03
Rotary dryer kilns	30	1/1/03
Dust management assets:		
Baghouse filters & extractors	30	1/1/03
Cyclones	15	1/1/03
Multiclones	20	1/1/03
Electrostatic separation assets (incl curve plates, electrostatic roll separators, high tension roll separators & screen plates)	20	1/1/03
Filtration/dewatering assets (including candle filter presses, dewatering towers, horizontal belt filters & hydrocyclones)	15	1/1/03
Magnetic separation assets (including belt & drum separators, electromagnetic separators, induced roll & rare earth magnetic separators & wet high intensity magnets)	20	1/1/03
Materials handling assets (including bins, bucket & conveying elevators, conveyors, feeders, hoppers, loading systems, paddle mixers & tailings stackers)	30	1/1/03
Screening assets (including screens & trommels)	15	1/1/03
Support assets:		
Control systems	10	1/1/03
Pipes & pipelines (including valves & fittings):		
Generally	20	1/1/03
Slurry pipework within processing facility (including slurry pipe to thickener)	10	1/1/06
Pumps	20	1/1/03
Tanks:		
Constant density & thickening	20	1/1/03
Generally (including acid leaching & water)	15	1/1/03
Thermal reduction assets (including cooler kilns, cooling towers, heat exchangers & reduction kilns)	30	1/1/03
Waste gas handling assets:		
Afterburners	20	1/1/03
Cyclones	15	1/1/03
Electrostatic precipitators	30	1/1/03
Scrubbers & stacks	20	1/1/03

NICKEL ORE MINING

Asset	Life (yrs)	Date of application
Nickel ore processing assets:		
Mineral treatment structures (including structure holding walkways, supporting assets & thoroughfares)	20	1/7/04
Reagent pumps (including high pressure acid leach pumps)	5	1/7/04

CONSTRUCTION MATERIAL MINING

Asset	Life (yrs)	Date of application
Control systems (for conveying, crushing & screening assets)	10	1/7/03
Conveyors:		
Gravity take up	25	1/7/03
Screw take up	15	1/7/03
Crushers:		
Generally	20	1/7/03
Mobile (track or wheel mounted machinery incl screening & conveying components)	15	1/7/03
Cyclones	15	1/7/03
Dredges	20	1/7/09
Drill rigs	8	1/7/03
Electrical switching assets	20	1/7/03
Graders	15	1/7/03
Heavy mobile quarry assets not specifically listed – see Table A Mining		
Hydraulic oversize rock breakers (mounted above primary crusher)	8	1/7/03
Material handling assets (including chutes, feeders, hoppers, product bins & surge bins)	20	1/7/03
Pug mills	15	1/7/03
Screening assets	12	1/7/03
Wheel loaders	10	1/7/03
Wire saws	10	1/7/03

PETROLEUM EXPLORATION SERVICES

Asset	Life (yrs)	Date of application
Exploration assets used offshore:		
Down hole geophysics units – skid mounted	10	1/1/07
Drill strings	3	1/1/07

Asset	Life (yrs)	Date of application
Offshore drilling rigs (incl blow out preventers, drilling fluid circulation systems, hoisting & rotary systems, platforms, rig powering & transmissions)	20	1/1/07
Exploration assets used onshore:		
Down hole geophysics units – truck mounted	12	1/1/07
Drill strings	4	1/1/07
Onshore surface drilling rigs (including blow out preventers, derricks, drilling fluid circulation systems, hoisting & rotary systems, rig powering & transmissions)	15	1/1/07
Portable messing & sleeping huts	7	1/1/07
Seismic survey assets:		
Airguns	5	1/1/07
Hydrophones	5	1/1/07

MINERAL EXPLORATION SERVICES

Asset	Life (yrs)	Date of application
Exploration assets:		
Drill rigs:		
Surface (including blow out preventers, drilling fluid circulation systems, hoisting & rotary systems, rig powering & transmission & trucks)	10	1/1/07
Underground	5	1/1/07
Geophysical survey assets:		
Airborne geophysical assets (incl magnetometers, receivers & transmitters):		
Aircraft integrated	10	1/1/07
Aircraft demountable	8	1/1/07
Down hole geophysical assets (including acoustic televiewers, callipers, density tools, dipmeters, draw works, neutron probes, sonic probes, receiver/transmitter modules & sondes):		
Portable assets	5	1/1/07
Vehicle integrated assets	8	1/1/07
Ground geophysical assets (incl gravity instruments, resistivity receivers & transmitters, scintillometers & spectrometers)	5	1/1/07
Portable ground geophysical assets (incl electromagnetics, ground magnetics, ground penetrating radars & radiometrics)	5	1/1/07
Seismic survey assets:		
Cabling	3	1/1/07
Geophones	5	1/1/07
Global positioning systems	5	1/1/07
Processing systems	3	1/1/07
Recording systems	10	1/1/07
Total stations (including mechanical, manual, motorised, auto lock, robotic, universal & multi-stations)	5	1/7/15
Vibration source assets:		
Buggy mounted shear wave vibrators	10	1/1/07
Drilling rigs – shot hole	10	1/1/07
Ground impactors	4	1/1/07
Portable messing & sleeping huts	7	1/1/07

MANUFACTURING

MEAT PROCESSING

Asset	Life (yrs)	Date of application
Boning room assets:		
Boneless meat packing stations	20	1/7/13
Boning & slicing stations	20	1/7/13
Boning hoists	5	1/7/13
Chine bone removal machines	10	1/7/13
De-sinewed mince meat machines	10	1/7/13
Dicing & mincing machines	10	1/7/13
Dump & product bins	15	1/7/13
Frenching machines	8	1/7/13
Knuckle & aitch bone pullers	5	1/7/13
Loin/saddle deboning machines	10	1/7/13
Overhead in-feed carcass conveyors (incorporating housings, handles, chains & motors)	20	1/7/13
Pneumatic knives (including meat trimmers/round knives & de-fatting knives)	2	1/7/13
Pork brine & marinade mixers	10	1/7/13
Pork de-rinders	10	1/7/13
Pork marinade injectors	10	1/7/13
Rise & fall platforms	15	1/7/13
Sausage filling machines	10	1/7/13

Asset	Life (yrs)	Date of application	Asset	Life (yrs)	Date of application
Saws:			Bins (includes raw material bins, charging		
Band saws	10	1/7/13	hopper/feedbins, cake bins & holding bins)	15	1/1/01
Bone saws	5	1/7/13	Blood drying equipment (includes blood holding		
Breaking saws:			tanks, agitated holding tanks, coagulators, driers,		
Circular electric	3	1/7/13	decanters & dried blood hoppers)	10	1/1/01
Circular hydraulic	2	1/7/13	Cookers & driers (includes batch cookers,		
Reciprocating electric	5	1/7/13	continuous cookers, continuous driers		
Reciprocating pneumatic	3	1/7/13	& pre heater)	15	1/1/01
Skinning or denuding machines	10	1/7/13	Decanters/centrifuges	12	1/1/01
Transfer belt & screw conveyors (incorporating			Environmental control equipment (including		
belt, drive motors & supporting structure)	10	1/7/13	condensers & associated equipment, bio filters,		
Weight graders	5	1/7/13	air scrubbers, after burners & dissolved air		
X-ray & chemical lean analysis machines	10	1/7/13	flotation systems)	10	1/1/01
Cold storage assets:			Feathrolysers/feather hydrolysers	10	1/1/01
Air curtains	5	1/7/13	Magnets	15	1/1/01
Ammonia condensers	10	1/7/13	Mills	10	1/1/01
Blast freezer tunnels	20	1/7/13	Mincers/grinders	5	1/1/01
Blast freezers	20	1/7/13	Pans & screens (includes percolator pans/screen		
Carbon dioxide snow making machines	10	1/7/13	& shaker screens)	15	1/1/01
Carton conveyors (incorporating belt, drive motors			Pre breakers/pre hoggers	10	1/1/01
& supporting structure)	10	1/7/13	Screw & bucket elevators	10	1/1/01
Chiller tunnels	20	1/7/13	Screw presses/expeller presses	13	1/1/01
Chillers (incorporating pneumatic gates)	15	1/7/13	Separators/polishers	15	1/1/01
De-humidifiers:			Tallow storage tanks	15	1/1/01
Desiccant	10	1/7/13	Waste heat evaporators	15	1/1/01
Refrigerant	15	1/7/13	**Slaughter floor assets:**		
Door controls & motor drive systems for automatic			Beef hide pullers (fixed & traversing)	15	1/7/13
opening doors (incorporating controls, motors &			Bung ring expanders:		
sensors, but excluding doors)	5	1/7/13	Pneumatic	3	1/7/13
Evaporators	15	1/7/13	Manual Hand held	5	1/7/13
Freezers	20	1/7/13	Cattle restrainers incorporating centre track belly		
Load out bays (incorporating air tight truck pads			conveyors	12	1/7/13
& hydraulic platforms)	15	1/7/13	Carcass cleaning systems:		
Overhead carcass conveyors (incorporating			Cutting line sanitising systems (incorporating		
housings, handles, chains & motors)	20	1/7/13	vacuum pumps & collection tanks)	8	1/7/13
Plate freezers	20	1/7/13	Decontamination chambers	20	1/7/13
Pressure vessels	20	1/7/13	Dehorners	5	1/7/13
Refrigeration compressors	15	1/7/13	Electrical immobilisers	12	1/7/13
Storage racking & stillages	10	1/7/13	Electrical stimulators	12	1/7/13
Transfer roller conveyors	10	1/7/13	Evisceration tables incorporating organ pans	15	1/7/13
Livestock handling assets:			Head cutters & droppers:		
Cattle soaker pens	15	1/7/13	Automatic	10	1/7/13
Cattle wash/soaker control systems	10	1/7/13	Hand held hydraulic	5	1/7/13
Cattle washes	15	1/7/13	Hock cutters	5	1/7/13
Cattle yards (incorporating concrete base			Knife blade sharpening machines	5	1/7/13
& galvanised steel posts & rails)	20	1/7/13	Knocking boxes incorporating head restrainers	12	1/7/13
Feed auger systems	10	1/7/13	Landing tables & bleed slat conveyors	15	1/7/13
Hydraulic forcing pen gates	10	1/7/13	NLIS readers:		
Lead-up races	20	1/7/13	Hand held wands	2	1/7/13
Loading ramps stationary & height adjustable			Fixed gate readers	10	1/7/13
(hydraulic, pneumatic & electronic)	15	1/7/13	Swinging gate readers	5	1/7/13
Pig lairages (incorporating concrete slat floor			Offal processing assets:		
& concrete panel walls or concrete floor			Chilled water systems	10	1/7/13
& galvanised steel posts & rails)	20	1/7/13	Fat vacuum transfer systems	10	1/7/13
Sheep lairages (incorporating galvanised web			Head splitters	7	1/7/13
mesh base & galvanised steel posts & rails)	10	1/7/13	Intestine processing machines	10	1/7/13
Water troughs	12	1/7/13	Jaw breakers	5	1/7/13
Packaging assets:			Offal bins	15	1/7/13
Automatic carton erecting & lidding machines	10	1/7/13	Offal chutes	15	1/7/13
Bagging machines	5	1/7/13	Offal cutting tables	15	1/7/13
Bar code label printers	3	1/7/13	Offal packing stations	15	1/7/13
Bar code readers	4	1/7/13	Offal transfer conveyors (incorporating belts,		
Carton weigh label stations	7	1/7/13	drives, motors & supporting structure)	10	1/7/13
Flow wrappers	10	1/7/13	Offal tumblers	10	1/7/13
Labelling machines	5	1/7/13	Offal washers	10	1/7/13
Meat compactors	10	1/7/13	Tongue cleaners	10	1/7/13
Metal detectors	10	1/7/13	Tripe cookers/centrifuges	10	1/7/13
Netting machines	5	1/7/13	Overhead bleed, dressing & trim conveyors		
Palletisers & de-palletisers	10	1/7/13	(incorporating housings, handles, chains &		
Shrink wrappers	10	1/7/13	motors) including elevators & lowerators	20	1/7/13
Strapping machines	5	1/7/13	Pneumatic knives:		
Transfer belt conveyors (incorporating belts,			De-hiding knives	2	1/7/13
drive motors & supporting structures)	10	1/7/13	Meat trimmers/round knives & de-fatting		
Vacuum packaging systems (incorporating			knives	2	1/7/13
vacuum pumps & booster pumps):			Preparation & trimming stations	15	1/7/13
Rotary systems	12	1/7/13	Rise & fall platforms	15	1/7/13
Tunnel systems	12	1/7/13	Saws:		
Weighing scales	4	1/7/13	Brisket saws	5	1/7/13
Rendering plant:			Splitting saws	5	1/7/13
Bagging/weigh batching machines	10	1/1/01	Scribing saws	3	1/7/13
			Sheep brisket scissors	5	1/7/13

Asset	Life (yrs)	Date of application
Sheep restrainers incorporating belts, pulleys, drives & motors	10	1/7/13
Sheep skin pullers	10	1/7/13
Specialised pork slaughter floor assets:		
Carbon dioxide stunning chambers incorporating carousels	10	1/7/13
Carcass grading probes	4	1/7/13
De-hairing machines	10	1/7/13
Gambrel tables	15	1/7/13
Polishers	10	1/7/13
Scalding tanks	15	1/7/13
Singers	10	1/7/13
Spinal cord removal systems (incorporating hand pieces, vacuum pumps & tanks)	8	1/7/13
Stunners:		
Electric stunners	5	1/7/13
Manual bolt stunners with cartridges	5	1/7/13
Pneumatic bolt stunners	7	1/7/13
Waste belt conveyors (incorporating drives, motors & supporting structure)	10	1/7/13
Waste screw conveyors (incorporating drives, motors & supporting structure)	10	1/7/13
Support assets:		
Air & spring balancers & counter weights	5	1/7/13
Compressed air assets:		
Air compressors	10	1/7/13
Air dryers	10	1/7/13
Air receivers	20	1/7/13
Control systems	10	1/7/13
Control systems assets:		
Flow meters	10	1/7/13
Instruments & sensors	10	1/7/13
Turbidity meters	7	1/7/13
Variable speed drives	10	1/7/13
Fire protection systems	15	1/7/13
Hand air driers	3	1/7/13
Hand wash basins	15	1/7/13
Hide preparation assets:		
Bale presses	10	1/7/13
Sheep skin & hide mixers, salt tumblers & agitators	6	1/7/13
Hydraulic power packs	10	1/7/13
Laboratory assets	10	1/7/13
Sterilisers	15	1/7/13
Truck & livestock crate washes	20	1/7/13
Waste water assets:		
Aerators & agitators	10	1/7/13
Aerobic ponds	30	1/7/13
Anaerobic ponds	30	1/7/13
Belt filter presses	15	1/7/13
Chlorine dosing systems	10	1/7/13
Dissolved air flotation systems	15	1/7/13
Effluent distribution pipes	15	1/7/13
Effluent drum filters	10	1/7/13
Effluent irrigators (including centre pivot, lateral & travelling gun)	10	1/7/13
Effluent pumps	7	1/7/13
Effluent screens	10	1/7/13
Effluent storage tanks	15	1/7/13
Methane gas cogeneration assets - see Table A Electricity supply & Gas supply		
Pond covers	10	1/7/13
Pond liners	10	1/7/13
Sequential batch reactors	10	1/7/13
Settling ponds	30	1/7/13
Solids dewatering presses	10	1/7/13
Water assets:		
Boilers	20	1/7/13
Bore pumps	7	1/7/13
Bores	30	1/7/13
Chlorine dosing systems	10	1/7/13
Clarifiers	20	1/7/13
High stage pump sets	7	1/7/13
Hot water systems	10	1/7/13
Heat exchangers	10	1/7/13
Raw water filters	15	1/7/13
Raw water in-feed pump sets	10	1/7/13
Reverse osmosis systems incorporating pumps, pipe work, membranes & controls	10	1/7/13
Water distribution pipes	20	1/7/13
Water softeners	10	1/7/13

Asset	Life (yrs)	Date of application
Water storage tanks	20	1/7/13
Water tank liners	15	1/7/13
POULTRY PROCESSING		
Conveyor systems & troughing	20	1/1/01
General plant	13 1/3	1/1/01
Refrigeration plant & boiler	10	1/1/01
CURED MEAT & SMALLGOODS MANUFACTURING		
Bacon manufacture:		
Bacon bins (demountable pig confinement units):		
Galvanised iron components of structure	33 1/3	1/1/01
Plant installed in structure	20	1/1/01
Curing plant:		
Fixtures (including overhead tracking)	20	1/1/01
Other	13 1/3	1/1/01
DAIRY PRODUCT MANUFACTURING		
Dairy product manufacturing:		
Centrifuges (includes separators, decanters, clarifiers & bactofuges)	15	1/1/01
Cheese blockformers	15	1/1/01
Churns (includes continuous buttermakers, butter reworkers & ice cream freezers)	15	1/1/01
Continuous cheddaring machines	15	1/1/01
Conveyors	10	1/1/01
Driers (includes drum, fluidised bed & spray)	20	1/1/01
Evaporators (includes circulation/vacuum chamber & falling film)	20	1/1/01
Heat exchangers	15	1/1/01
Homogenisers	15	1/1/01
Membrane filtration plant:		
Filter membranes	1 1/2	1/1/01
Membrane holding tanks	15	1/1/01
Pumps (brine & cream)	10	1/1/01
Tanks (includes storage, mixing, process & balance tanks)	20	1/1/01
Water cooling & aerating plant	8	1/1/01
FRUIT & VEGETABLE PROCESSING		
Fruit & vegetable canning plant	20	1/1/01
Fruit juice & fruit juice drink manufacturing assets:		
Evaporators (used in concentrate manufacture)	20	1/7/10
Extraction assets:		
Break tanks	20	1/7/10
Centrifugal decanters	15	1/7/10
Crushing & milling assets (incl hammer mills)	15	1/7/10
Extractors (including presses & reamers)	20	1/7/10
Filters (including membrane, pressure & vacuum filters)	20	1/7/10
Finishers	20	1/7/10
Fruit sizing assets (incl sizing belts/heads & sorting tables)	10	1/7/10
Pulp & rind mincers	20	1/7/10
Pulper finishers	15	1/7/10
Roller/spreaders	20	1/7/10
Tomato choppers	15	1/7/10
Washers (including brush washers, flume tanks & pre clean water hoppers)	15	1/7/10
Filling & sealing assets:		
Bottle inverters	20	1/7/10
Capping machines	15	1/7/10
Cap sorters	10	1/7/10
Container dryers (incorporating air knives & blowers)	10	1/7/10
Cooling & warming tunnels (including bottle warmers & water spray cooling tunnels)	15	1/7/10
Filling machines (including aseptic fillers, bag in box fillers, cup fillers, gable top carton fillers & plastic bottle fillers)	20	1/7/10
Handling assets:		
Bottle rinsing machines	20	1/7/10
Bottle unscramblers	15	1/7/10
Depalletisers	20	1/7/10
Palletisers	20	1/7/10
Stretch wrappers (pallet wrappers)	15	1/7/10
Inspection assets:		
Checkweighers	10	1/7/10
Vacuum seal testers	10	1/7/10

Asset	Life (yrs)	Date of application
Vision inspection assets (including cap inspection/rejection systems & label inspection machines)	6	1/7/10
Packing assets:		
Cartoning assets (including carton & case erectors, carton sealers, case packers & overpackers)	15	1/7/10
Coding machines (including container coders & outer date coders)	7	1/7/10
Hot melt adhesive (spot glue) applicators	10	1/7/10
Label applicators	7	1/7/10
Labellers	10	1/7/10
Multipack machines	10	1/7/10
Shrink sleeve applicators	15	1/7/10
Shrinkwrappers	15	1/7/10
Straw applicators	20	1/7/10
Support assets:		
Air compressors & receivers	20	1/7/10
Bins, cages & hoppers	20	1/7/10
Boilers	20	1/7/10
Clean in place (CIP) system assets (including pipes, pumps & tanks)	15	1/7/10
Control system assets (excluding personal computers but including program logic controllers & switchgear)	10	1/7/10
Conveyors (including augers, belt conveyors & bucket elevators)	15	1/7/10
Fruit concentrate drum tippers	15	1/7/10
Laboratory equipment:		
Electronic (including high performance liquid chromatography or HPLC machines, refractometers, spectrometry machines & titrimetric analysers)	7	1/7/10
Non electronic	10	1/7/10
Pasteurisation assets:		
Pasteurisers (including heat exchangers)	15	1/7/10
Tunnel pasteurisers	10	1/7/10
Pipes	25	1/7/10
Pumps:		
Cavity pumps	10	1/7/10
Others (including centrifugal pumps)	15	1/7/10
Refrigeration assets (including compressors, cooling towers, condensers & pumps)	15	1/7/10
Valves	10	1/7/10
Water treatment filters:		
Carbon filters	15	1/7/10
Membrane filters generally including microfiltration (MF), nanofiltration (NF) & reverse osmosis (RO) membrane filters	7	1/7/10
UF membrane filters	5	1/7/10
Weighbridges	20	1/7/10
Tanks:		
Blending & mixing tanks	25	1/7/10
Debittering tanks	30	1/7/10
Storage tanks:		
Generally	30	1/7/10
Jacketed	20	1/7/10
Refrigerated	20	1/7/10
Waste water storage/treatment tanks	20	1/7/10
Jam making plant	20	1/1/01

OIL & FAT MANUFACTURING

Asset	Life (yrs)	Date of application
Edible oil or fat, blended, manufacturing assets:		
Preparatory & extraction assets:		
Preparatory & mechanical extraction assets:		
Breaking assets (including dehullers & crackers)	20	1/7/12
Cookers (including conditioners & preheaters)	25	1/7/12
Extruders (including screw presses)	20	1/7/12
Milling & grinding assets (incl flakers, hammer mills & roller mills)	20	1/7/12
Pumps	8	1/7/12
Vibratory screens	15	1/7/12
Solvent extraction system assets:		
Distillation system assets (incorporating distillation columns, steam economisers, condensers, evaporators & oil strippers)	30	1/7/12
Meal & cake processing assets (incorporating desolventisers, toasters, drying & cooling assets)	30	1/7/12

Asset	Life (yrs)	Date of application
Mineral oil recovery system assets (incorporating heat exchangers, mineral oil scrubbers & oil strippers)	30	1/7/12
Solvent extractors (including hoppers &conveyors)	30	1/7/12
Solvent water separation system assets (incorporating condensers, solvent water separators, steam ejectors & solvent receivers)	30	1/7/12
Margarine & shortening processing assets:		
Pasteurisers	15	1/7/12
Pin rotor machines (including plasticators & complectors)	25	1/7/12
Refrigeration assets (including compressors, condensers, evaporators & pumps)	15	1/7/12
Scraped surface heat exchangers (including perfectors & crystallisers)	25	1/7/12
Measuring, monitoring & quality control assets:		
Belt weighers	15	1/7/12
Control systems	10	1/7/12
Flow meters	10	1/7/12
Laboratory assets:		
Colorimeters	10	1/7/12
Furnace ovens	15	1/7/12
Gas chromatograph analysers	10	1/7/12
Moisture & protein analysers, electronic (including near infra red analysers)	10	1/7/12
Spectrophotometers	15	1/7/12
Vacuum separators	10	1/7/12
Quality control assets (including metal detectors & magnets)	10	1/7/12
Seed samplers, hydraulic driven	10	1/7/12
Weighbridges	20	1/7/12
Packaging assets:		
Capping machines	15	1/7/12
Cartoning assets (including carton & case erecting, packing & closing machines)	15	1/7/12
Coding machines	10	1/7/12
Filling machines	20	1/7/12
Labellers	10	1/7/12
Palletisers & depalletisers	20	1/7/12
Robots (pick & place packaging machines)	10	1/7/12
Wrapping machines (incl shrink & stretch wrappers)	15	1/7/12
Receiving & storage assets:		
Bins & containers	20	1/7/12
Silos:		
Meal	20	1/7/12
Seed	30	1/7/12
Underground seed storage assets (including concrete dump pits)	40	1/7/12
Seed & product handling assets:		
Augers, conveyors, elevators & hoppers	15	1/7/12
Support assets:		
Centrifuges, decanters & separators	20	1/7/12
Cooling towers (including packaged type)	20	1/7/12
Deodorisers	30	1/7/12
Drying assets (including vacuum dryers)	20	1/7/12
Emission control assets:		
Dust collection assets (incl ductwork, dust collectors, scrubbers & fans)	20	1/7/12
Environmental control assets (including scrubbers, ductwork, fans, biofilters & concrete containers)	20	1/7/12
Filtration assets:		
Plate & frame presses & polished filters	30	1/7/12
Pressure leaf filters	20	1/7/12
Heat exchangers	15	1/7/12
Pipes & pipelines	25	1/7/12
Pumps	15	1/7/12
Stacks (steel flues)	20	1/7/12
Tanks & vessels:		
Bulk oil storage tanks	30	1/7/12
Other:		
Steel	20	1/7/12
Stainless steel	30	1/7/12
Olive oil processing assets	15	1/7/08

Asset	Life (yrs)	Date of application
GRAIN MILL PRODUCT MANUFACTURING		
Flour milling plant:		
Bins (wooden)	$33^{1}/_{3}$	1/1/01
General plant	$13^{1}/_{3}$	1/1/01
Silos, concrete	50	1/1/04
Silos, galvanised	30	1/1/04
Silos, steel	40	1/1/04
Linseed oil manufacturing plant	$13^{1}/_{3}$	1/1/01
Malt manufacturing assets:		
Barley & malt cleaning assets (including declumers, dust extractors, indented cylinders, magnetic cleaners, malt shakers, screeners)	15	1/7/08
Barley & malt handling assets:		
Augers, conveyors & elevators	15	1/7/08
Silos:		
Galvanised construction	30	1/7/08
Steel construction	40	1/7/08
Weighbridges/weighers	20	1/7/08
Clean in place (CIP) system assets (incl pipes, pumps & tanks)	15	1/7/08
Control systems (excluding personal computers)	10	1/7/08
Germination assets:		
Above/below floor cleaning systems	15	1/7/08
Aeration blowers	15	1/7/08
CO2 extraction units	15	1/7/08
Loaders/unloaders/turners	15	1/7/08
Vessels:		
Concrete	40	1/7/08
Rotating drums	20	1/7/08
Stainless steel	25	1/7/08
Kiln assets:		
Fans	15	1/7/08
Gas burners	15	1/7/08
Heat exchanger systems	20	1/7/08
Heat recovery systems	20	1/7/08
Kilns:		
Concrete	40	1/7/08
Stainless steel	25	1/7/08
Loaders/unloaders/turners	15	1/7/08
Refrigeration assets (including chillers, compressors, condensers, evaporative coolers & pumps)	15	1/7/08
Steeping assets:		
Above floor/below floor cleaning systems	15	1/7/08
Slurry tanks	25	1/7/08
Steeping vessels:		
Concrete	40	1/7/08
Rotating drums	20	1/7/08
Stainless steel	25	1/7/08
Waste water treatment assets:		
Aerators	20	1/7/08
Blowers	20	1/7/08
Clarifiers	20	1/7/08
Digester/aeration tanks	25	1/7/08
Reverse osmosis system assets	20	1/7/08
Rice milling plant	$13^{1}/_{3}$	1/1/01
CEREAL & PASTA PRODUCT MANUFACTURING		
Ancillary assets:		
Bin washers	15	1/7/08
Blowers & fans:		
Generally	25	1/7/08
Used in materials handling	15	1/7/08
Clean in place (CIP) systems	15	1/7/08
Control systems (excluding personal computers)	10	1/7/08
Dust collection assets (including cyclones)	20	1/7/08
Extrusion die washers	5	1/7/08
Racks & shelving	20	1/7/08
Scales (electronic scales & load cells)	10	1/7/08
Water chillers	20	1/7/08
Water filtration & softening assets (including reverse osmosis assets)	15	1/7/08
Cereal food manufacturing assets:		
Baked cereal bar product manufacturing assets – see Table A Bakery product manufacturing		
Cold formed & nut based cereal bar manufacturing assets:		
Cooling tunnels	20	1/7/08
Enrobers	$12^{1}/_{2}$	1/7/08
Guillotines	15	1/7/08
Slab formers (sheeters)	15	1/7/08

Asset	Life (yrs)	Date of application
Slitters	15	1/7/08
Spreaders	15	1/7/08
Syrup cookers & kettles (incl fire cookers)	15	1/7/08
Tempering machines	15	1/7/08
General cereal food processing assets:		
Blenders & mixers (including drum mixers, paddle blenders/mixers & ribbon blenders/mixers)	15	1/7/08
Ovens (electric & gas fired)	20	1/7/08
Ready to eat cereal manufacturing assets (incl extruded, co extruded, flaked & puffed cereal manufacturing assets):		
Coating assets (incl coating applicators & drum coaters)	15	1/7/08
Cookers	15	1/7/08
Delumpers (lump breakers)	10	1/7/08
Dryers:		
Flite dryers	30	1/7/08
Fluid bed dryers	20	1/7/08
Others (including belt & coating dryers)	15	1/7/08
Extruders	20	1/7/08
Feeders (incl loss in weight & screwtype feeders)	10	1/7/08
Milling machines (incl flaking mills, pellet mills & shredding mills)	20	1/7/08
Steam preconditioners	10	1/7/08
Packaging assets (including cartoners, casepackers, case palletisers, checkweighers, fillers, label applicators, robotic pick & place packaging machines, shrink wrappers & stretch wrappers etc)	12	1/7/08
Pasta manufacturing assets:		
Blenders & mixers	15	1/7/08
Cooling assets (including chillers & coolers)	10	1/7/08
Dryers	15	1/7/08
Extrusion dies	2	1/7/08
Fill preparation assets:		
Cookers/kettles	15	1/7/08
Mincers	15	1/7/08
Long goods/short goods pasta making assets (including blanchers/cookers, formers, gnocchi making machines, laminators, presses, ravioli making machines, sheeters etc)	$12^{1}/_{2}$	1/7/08
Pasteurisers	15	1/7/08
Product & raw material receiving & handling assets:		
Aspirators	20	1/7/08
Bins & hoppers (including tote bins, intermediate bulk containers, scaling bins etc):		
Mild & stainless steel	15	1/7/08
Others (including plastic & fibreglass)	10	1/7/08
Bulker bag unloaders (incl electric hoist, forklift & trolley based unloaders)	15	1/7/08
Conveyors (including belt, bucket, roller & screw conveyors)	15	1/7/08
Silos:		
Steel	30	1/7/08
Used for flour (semolina)	25	1/7/08
Storage tanks (including jacketed tanks)	20	1/7/08
Tipping stations (tote bin dumpers)	15	1/7/08
Quality control assets:		
Metal detectors	10	1/7/08
X ray detectors	5	1/7/08
BAKERY PRODUCT MANUFACTURING		
Baking assets used by large scale manufacturers of biscuits, bread, cakes, pastries & pies:		
Ancillary assets (including basket/crate washers, basket stack movers, crate/pan stackers & unstackers, depanners/detinners, foil handling denesters, oil spray units, pan cleaners, & topping applicators)	15	1/1/02
Automatic pan storage units	20	1/1/02
Automatic product handling assets (incl basket loaders & basket stackers)	15	1/1/02
Bread crumb assets (incl baggers, debaggers, hammer mills, ovens, screw conveyors & sifters)	20	1/1/02
Conveyors:		
Generally	15	1/1/02
Infloor	12	1/1/02
Cooling & refrigeration assets:		
Cooling tunnels, tray & vacuum coolers	20	1/1/02
Freezers (incl blast freezer, plate freezer)	15	1/1/02

Asset	Life (yrs)	Date of application
Spiral coolers, spiral freezers	10	1/1/02
Final provers (mechanical type)	15	1/1/02
Final provers (rack type)	8	1/1/02
Make up assets (including croissant making machines, crumpet making machines, crumbers, cutters, depositors, dividers, dough pumps, dough piece check weighers, extruders, final moulder/panners, first/intermediate provers, gauge rolls, laminators, meat cookers, meat extruders, moulders, muffin making machines, pie making machines, roll making machines, rounder/airflow handers, sheeters & stampers)	12½	1/1/02
Mixing assets (incl bowl/dough hoists/tippers, meat mincers, meat mincer/blenders, mixers generally & mixer water assets)	15	1/1/02
Ovens:		
Rack ovens	8	1/1/02
Tray type ovens (including swing tray)	20	1/1/02
Tunnel ovens:		
Generally	20	1/1/02
Lidding systems	10	1/1/02
Packaging assets (including accumulators, bag closers, bread baggers, box & carton making machines, finished product check weighers, flow wrappers, metal detectors, robotic pick & place assets & shrink wrappers)	10	1/1/02
Proof & bake systems:		
Spiral oven	15	1/1/02
Spiral prover	10	1/1/02
Secondary process assets (including cake folders, creamers, depositors, enrobers, icing machines, sandwiching machines & sprinklers)	12½	1/1/02
Slicers (including bread band slicers, cake slicers & reciprocating blade slicers)	10	1/1/02
Storage, feeding & ingredient handling assets:		
Flour silos	25	1/1/02
Blowers, flour sifters & grain soak systems	15	1/1/02
Weighers	10	1/1/02

BAKERY PRODUCT MANUFACTURING (NON FACTORY BASED)

Asset	Life (yrs)	Date of application
Retail bread, biscuit, cake & pastry baking assets:		
Bread slicers	7	1/1/02
Bun dividers/rounders	8	1/1/02
Fixed bowl spiral mixers	7	1/1/02
Hydraulic dough dividers	7	1/1/02
Moulders	8	1/1/02
Ovens (convection)	8	1/1/02
Ovens (multi decked, rotating rack or static rack, rotating deck)	10	1/1/02
Planetary mixers	7	1/1/02
Provers/prover retarders	6	1/1/02
Semi automated baguette, bread & bread roll making assets	12	1/1/02
Semi automated doughnut making assets	8	1/1/02

SUGAR MANUFACTURING

Asset	Life (yrs)	Date of application
Sugar milling assets:		
Cane delivery assets:		
Cane bin assets:		
Rail bins	20	1/7/11
Rail bin automatic coupling/de coupling devices	12	1/7/11
Road bins	12	1/7/11
Rail assets (excluding cane bin assets) – see Table A Rail freight & passenger transport services		
Receival station assets:		
Cane levellers	20	1/7/11
Cane receival hoppers	25	1/7/11
Tipplers	25	1/7/11
Weighbridges	20	1/7/11
Cane juice extraction assets:		
Cane shredding machines (incorporating drives)	30	1/7/11
Crushing mills (incorporating drives)	30	1/7/11
Rotary juice screens	15	1/7/11
Cane juice filtration & clarification assets:		
Clarifiers	25	1/7/11
Flash tanks	20	1/7/11
Juice heaters	20	1/7/11
Lime & mud storage bins	25	1/7/11

Asset	Life (yrs)	Date of application
Lime slakers	20	1/7/11
Mud mixers/minglers	20	1/7/11
Rotary vacuum mud filters	20	1/7/11
Evaporation & crystallisation assets:		
Centrifugals	25	1/7/11
Crystallisers	20	1/7/11
Evaporators	30	1/7/11
Magma mixers	20	1/7/11
Magma/massecuite distributors & receivers	20	1/7/11
Massecuite re heaters	20	1/7/11
Seed vessels	20	1/7/11
Sugar melters	20	1/7/11
Vacuum pans	30	1/7/11
Vapour condensers:		
Mild steel	20	1/7/11
Stainless steel	30	1/7/11
Molasses storage assets:		
Coolers	15	1/7/11
Dams (earthworks only)	40	1/7/11
Dam bladders & covers	12	1/7/11
Tanks	30	1/7/11
Power generation assets:		
Ash filters (including rotary & horizontal belt vacuum filters)	15	1/7/11
Bagasse handling assets:		
Bagacillo collection systems	15	1/7/11
Bagasse bins (incorporating stacking & reclaim systems)	30	1/7/11
Other power generation assets – see Table A Electricity supply		
Sugar drying & storage assets:		
Hoppers (weigh & feed)	25	1/7/11
Lump breakers	15	1/7/11
Rotary sugar dryers	25	1/7/11
Sugar storage bins & silos	30	1/7/11
Vibratory screens	15	1/7/11
Support assets:		
Air compression assets:		
Air dryers	12	1/7/11
Air receivers	20	1/7/11
Compressors	12	1/7/11
Packaged air compression systems	12	1/7/11
Blowers & fans	15	1/7/11
Control system assets:		
Control cabinets & switchgear	10	1/7/11
Instrumentation	10	1/7/11
Programmable logic controllers	10	1/7/11
Switchboards	20	1/7/11
Variable speed drives	10	1/7/11
Conveyors (incl framework & enclosures)	20	1/7/11
Conveyor belt weighers	15	1/7/11
Dust collectors (including ducting, but excluding bagacillo collection systems)	20	1/7/11
Heat exchangers	15	1/7/11
Laboratory assets:		
Cutter grinders	15	1/7/11
Moisture determination ovens	10	1/7/11
Polarimeters	10	1/7/11
Rotary juice samplers	15	1/7/11
Spectrometers	10	1/7/11
Wet disintegrators	15	1/7/11
Overhead cranes - see Table B Cranes		
Piping & valves:		
Piping:		
Mild steel	15	1/7/11
Non ferrous	20	1/7/11
Stainless steel	25	1/7/11
Valves	10	1/7/11
Pumps	15	1/7/11
Tanks (excluding molasses storage tanks):		
Water storage tanks	25	1/7/11
Other tanks:		
Mild steel	20	1/7/11
Plastic	15	1/7/11
Stainless steel	30	1/7/11
Water treatment & cooling assets:		
Clarifiers	25	1/7/11
Cooling & effluent ponds	40	1/7/11
Cooling towers:		
Field erected	25	1/7/11
Packaged	15	1/7/11

Asset	Life (yrs)	Date of application
Ion exchange systems	15	1/7/11
Sugar refining assets:		
Affination assets:		
Centrifugals	25	1/7/11
Magma mixers	20	1/7/11
Melter liquor screens	15	1/7/11
Sugar melters	20	1/7/11
Clarification & de colourising assets:		
Carbon regeneration kilns	15	1/7/11
Clarifiers	25	1/7/11
Deep bed filters	30	1/7/11
De colourising columns:		
Carbon based	30	1/7/11
Resin based	20	1/7/11
Evaporation & crystallisation assets:		
Centrifugals	25	1/7/11
Evaporators	30	1/7/11
Magma/massecuite distributors & receivers	20	1/7/11
Vacuum pans	30	1/7/11
Vapour condensers:		
Mild steel	20	1/7/11
Stainless steel	30	1/7/11
Packaging assets:		
Bagging machines (incl flow wrappers, form fill & seal machines, & roll wrapping machines)	15	1/7/11
Bottling assets:		
Bottle capping, filling & unscrambling machines	15	1/7/11
Syrup & treacle filter presses	15	1/7/11
UV disinfectors	15	1/7/11
Carton erecting, packing & closing machines (including cartoners)	15	1/7/11
Case erecting, packing & closing machines (including casepackers)	15	1/7/11
Inspection equipment (incl check weighers, metal detectors, counting machines)	10	1/7/11
Multihead & singlehead weighers	15	1/7/11
Palletisers & de palletisers	15	1/7/11
Product identification labellers including decorating, applicator & coding machines	10	1/7/11
Wrapping machines including shrink wrappers, stretch wrappers & strapping machines	15	1/7/11
Sugar receival, drying, screening, & storage assets:		
Bins, hoppers & silos	30	1/7/11
Lump breakers	15	1/7/11
Rotary sugar dryers	25	1/7/11
Sugar throwers	15	1/7/11
Vibratory screens (incl graders & scalpers)	15	1/7/11
Support assets:		
Air compression assets:		
Air dryers	12	1/7/11
Air receivers	20	1/7/11
Compressors	12	1/7/11
Packaged air compression systems	12	1/7/11
Blowers & fans	15	1/7/11
Boilers (packaged type only)	20	1/7/11
Control system assets:		
Control cabinets & switchgear	10	1/7/11
Instrumentation	10	1/7/11
Program logic controllers (PLCs)	10	1/7/11
Switchboards	20	1/7/11
Variable speed drives (VSDs)	10	1/7/11
Conveyors (incl framework & enclosures):		
Packaging conveyors	15	1/7/11
Other conveyors	20	1/7/11
Cooling towers:		
Field erected	25	1/7/11
Packaged	15	1/7/11
Dust collectors (including ducting)	20	1/7/11
Heat exchangers	15	1/7/11
Pipes & valves:		
Pipes:		
Mild steel	15	1/7/11
Non ferrous	20	1/7/11
Stainless steel	25	1/7/11
Valves	10	1/7/11
Pumps	15	1/7/11
Refractometers	10	1/7/11
Spectrometers	10	1/7/11

Asset	Life (yrs)	Date of application
Tanks:		
Water storage tanks	25	1/7/11
Other tanks:		
Mild steel	20	1/7/11
Plastic	15	1/7/11
Stainless steel	30	1/7/11
Weighbridges	20	1/7/11
CONFECTIONERY MANUFACTURING		
Confectioners' machinery	20	1/1/01
PREPARED ANIMAL & BIRD FEED MANUFACTURING		
Pet food manufacturing assets:		
Dry process assets:		
Batching systems	15	1/7/13
Blowing systems	15	1/7/13
Coating assets (including oil, tumble & vacuum coaters)	10	1/7/13
Coolers (incl counterflow, horizontal & vertical)	15	1/7/13
Cooling systems (including fans & cyclones)	10	1/7/13
Dehumidifying systems (incl silo munters)	10	1/7/13
Dosing systems (including liquid)	10	1/7/13
Dryers	15	1/7/13
Extruders	15	1/7/13
Hammer mills	15	1/7/13
Hoppers (including batch & surge)	15	1/7/13
Mixers (including batch & paddle)	15	1/7/13
Ovens (including horizontal, tunnel & vertical)	15	1/7/13
Pre-conditioners	10	1/7/13
Packaging assets:		
Bagging machines (incl flow wrappers, form fill & seal machines & roll wrapping machines)	10	1/7/13
Can & tray labelling assets	10	1/7/13
Case erecting, packing & closing machines (including cartoners)	10	1/7/13
Inspection equipment (incl checkweighers, metal detectors, counting machines etc)	10	1/7/13
Multihead & singlehead weighers	10	1/7/13
Palletisers & depalletisers	15	1/7/13
Robotic lid, tray & sealing assets	10	1/7/13
Robotic pick & place assets	10	1/7/13
Wrapping machines (incl shrink wrappers, stretch wrappers & strapping machines)	10	1/7/13
Raw material receiving, storage & handling assets:		
Chutes	15	1/7/13
Conveyors (including belt, chain, drag, screw & walking beam conveyors)	15	1/7/13
Elevators & distributors (including bucket & transfer elevators)	15	1/7/13
Hoppers (including batch & weigh hoppers)	15	1/7/13
Receival assets	15	1/7/13
Screw & weigh belt feeders	10	1/7/13
Silos	20	1/7/13
Storage bins	20	1/7/13
Tanks (incl holding, liquid storage & water)	20	1/7/13
Support assets:		
Access platforms	20	1/7/13
Air compressors & receivers	10	1/7/13
Bins (including tippers & raw material bins)	15	1/7/13
Boilers	20	1/7/13
Cleaning systems (including vacuum)	15	1/7/13
Contra shears & drum filters	10	1/7/13
Control systems	10	1/7/13
Dust management assets (including bag & dust filters, dust collectors, dust extraction hood & ducting & exhaust fans & socks)	15	1/7/13
Effluent pumps	10	1/7/13
Effluent screens & filters	10	1/7/13
Emissions & odour control systems (incorporating exhaust fans, ducting & biofilters)	15	1/7/13
Fire prevention systems (incorporating fire protection system & water tanks)	20	1/7/13
Laboratory & analysing assets (including probes & samplers)	10	1/7/13
Pumps (including liquid feed)	10	1/7/13
Racking	20	1/7/13
Safety systems	20	1/7/13
Waste water ponds	25	1/7/13
Waste water treatment assets	20	1/7/13

Asset	Life (yrs)	Date of application
Weighing assets (including weigh cells, heads & hoppers)	10	1/7/13
Wet process assets:		
Air purification & recycling systems	10	1/7/13
Basket tippers	10	1/7/13
Blending, dicing & mincing assets	10	1/7/13
Blowers	15	1/7/13
Canning & tray assets including closers & fillers	10	1/7/13
Chillers	15	1/7/13
Cooling towers	15	1/7/13
Cool rooms	15	1/7/13
Cutting assets (including knife & blade assemblies)	10	1/7/13
Dewatering assets	10	1/7/13
Drying assets	15	1/7/13
Extruders	15	1/7/13
Freezers	15	1/7/13
Frozen block warmers	10	1/7/13
Gravy make-up stations	15	1/7/13
Grinders	10	1/7/13
Hoppers (including batch & surge)	15	1/7/13
Mix slides & chutes	15	1/7/13
Mixers (including batch & paddle)	15	1/7/13
Pallet lifters & hoists	10	1/7/13
Refrigeration compressors	15	1/7/13
Retort cooking vessels	15	1/7/13
Retort trays	15	1/7/13
Seal thickness testing assets	10	1/7/13
Slicing & shredding assets	10	1/7/13
Stacking assets	15	1/7/13
Prepared animal & bird feed manufacturing assets generally:		
Batching, grinding & mixing assets:		
Bins (including mash, outloading, surge, supply & raw material bins)	30	1/7/12
Control systems (including batching systems)	10	1/7/12
Dressers	10	1/7/12
Drum magnets	10	1/7/12
Evaporative coolers	10	1/7/12
Grinders	10	1/7/12
Hammer & roller mills	15	1/7/12
Heating chambers (including coils & heat exchangers)	12	1/7/12
Hoppers (including expansion, grinder, weigh & surge hoppers)	25	1/7/12
Liquid tanks (including molasses & tallow)	20	1/7/12
Load cells	10	1/7/12
Mixers (including paddle, premix & ribbon screw)	20	1/7/12
Pumps (including heat, molasses & water pumps)	7	1/7/12
Rotary valves	15	1/7/12
Shears	15	1/7/12
Turn heads	20	1/7/12
Drying, coating, cooling & addition assets:		
Coating assets (including oil, tumble & vacuum coaters)	12	1/7/12
Coolers (including counterflow, horizontal & vertical)	15	1/7/12
Cooling fans & cyclones	10	1/7/12
Dryers	15	1/7/12
Injection systems (including tallow)	15	1/7/12
Meters (including counterflow meters)	10	1/7/12
Post pellet addition systems (incorporating mixers)	10	1/7/12
Screening & sieving assets	10	1/7/12
Vacuum pump & piping	15	1/7/12
Liquid feed assets:		
Augers, conveyors & elevators	7	1/7/12
Bladders for molasses ponds	10	1/7/12
Bulk bag hangers	10	1/7/12
Covers for molasses ponds	10	1/7/12
Hoppers	10	1/7/12
Liners for tanks	5	1/7/12
Micro scales	7	1/7/12
Mixers	10	1/7/12
Mixing tanks for clay & other products	15	1/7/12
Pumps:		
Acid & urea pumps	3	1/7/12
Heat, molasses & water pumps	10	1/7/12

Asset	Life (yrs)	Date of application
Silos (including PVC & steel construction)	15	1/7/12
Storage tanks (including PVC & steel construction)	15	1/7/12
Packaging assets:		
Bagging machines (including flow wrappers, form fill & seal machines & roll wrapping machines)	10	1/7/12
Case erecting, packing & closing machines (including cartoners)	10	1/7/12
Inspection equipment (including checkweighers, metal detectors, counting machines)	10	1/7/12
Multihead & singlehead weighers	10	1/7/12
Palletisers & depalletisers	15	1/7/12
Robotic pick & place, lid, tray & sealing assets	10	1/7/12
Wrapping machines (incl shrink wrappers, stretch wrappers & strapping machines)	10	1/7/12
Pre-conditioning & extrusion assets:		
Boilers	20	1/7/12
Conditioners	10	1/7/12
Crumble rollers	20	1/7/12
Extruders	15	1/7/12
Pellet presses (including air flow & die feeder presses)	15	1/7/12
Pellet testers	10	1/7/12
Raw material receiving, storage & handling assets:		
Augers	10	1/7/12
Bulkheads	20	1/7/12
Chutes, deadboxes & diverters	10	1/7/12
Conveyors (incl belt, drag, grain & screw conveyors)	15	1/7/12
Elevators & distributors (including bucket transfer elevators)	15	1/7/12
Grain cleaning & shifting assets (including grain blowers & grain shifters)	15	1/7/12
Grain transfer drag chains	15	1/7/12
Portable conveying assets (including augers & belt conveyors)	5	1/7/12
Receival pits	30	1/7/12
Rotary & slide gates	10	1/7/12
Silos	30	1/7/12
Storage bins	20	1/7/12
Support assets:		
Air compressors	10	1/7/12
Dust management assets (incl bag & dust filters, dust collectors, dust extraction hood & ducting & exhaust fans & socks)	15	1/7/12
Emissions & odour control systems (incorporating exhaust fans, ducting & biofilters)	15	1/7/12
Feed delivery bins	15	1/7/12
Fire prevention systems (incorporating fire protection system & water tanks)	20	1/7/12
Grain vacuum & silo sampling probes	5	1/7/12
Laboratory assets (incl grain testing assets)	10	1/7/12
Near infrared transmission systems & analysers	7	1/7/12
Racking	20	1/7/12
Waste water treatment assets	20	1/7/12
Weighbridges	25	1/7/12

OTHER FOOD PRODUCT MANUFACTURING N.E.C.

Asset	Life (yrs)	Date of application
(Coffee processing assets:		
Bins & hoppers (including gravity bins holding bins)	20	1/7/12
De-stoners, gravity separators & magnetic separators	20	1/7/12
Extraction & evaporation assets (including decanters, evaporators/finishers, flash vessels/stripping columns, pressure vessels/cells, separators/clarifiers, spray driers, strainers & wet scrubbers)	20	1/7/12
Grinders	20	1/7/12
Material handling assets (including augers, belt conveyors, bucket elevators, elevators & vibratory conveyors)	15	1/7/12
Packaging assets:		
Form fill & seal packaging machines (including flat bottom, flat top & bottom, pillow shape, stand up & vacuum brick pack packaging machines)	12	1/7/12

Asset	Life (yrs)	Date of application
Inspection equipment incl checkweighers, metal detectors, counting machines etc	12	1/7/12
Multihead weighers	12	1/7/12
Process control valves	10	1/7/12
Roasters (including cooling trays)	20	1/7/12
Sample roasters	15	1/7/12
Silos	25	1/7/12
Smoke/odour elimination systems (incorporating afterburners, housing & piping)	15	1/7/12
Support assets:		
Air compressors	12	1/7/12
Boiler house assets	20	1/7/12
Clean-in-place (CIP) systems	15	1/7/12
Control system assets (including & programmable logic controllers variable speed drives)	10	1/7/12
Laboratory assets:		
Electronic (including analysers & spectrometers)	7	1/7/12
Generally	10	1/7/12
Pipes	20	1/7/12
Pumps	20	1/7/12
Racks	20	1/7/12
Scales	10	1/7/12
Tanks	30	1/7/12
Waste water treatment assets	20	1/7/12
Weighbridges	25	1/7/12
Frozen pre-prepared food manufacturing assets (including frozen appetisers & finger foods such as dim sims & spring rolls, frozen french fries/potato chips, frozen pizzas & frozen pre-prepared meals):		
Ancillary & support assets:		
Air compression assets:		
Air dryers	10	1/7/12
Air receivers	20	1/7/12
Compressors & packaged air compression systems	15	1/7/12
Blowers & fans	15	1/7/12
Boilers	20	1/7/12
Clean in place (CIP) assets	10	1/7/12
Control systems generally	10	1/7/12
Conveyors (including auger conveyors, belt conveyors, bucket elevators, flume conveyors roller conveyors, web conveyors etc)	15	1/7/12
Dust collection systems	20	1/7/12
Fire control assets - use any relevant determination in Table B		
Frying oil reclaiming & cleansing systems incorporating filtration equipment, storage tanks & ventilation hoods	20	1/7/12
Heat exchangers	15	1/7/12
Holding & storage tanks generally (including water storage tanks)	20	1/7/12
Piping & reticulation lines (excl fire water pipes)	25	1/7/12
Pumps (including cavity pumps, centrifugal pumps, lobe pumps etc)	10	1/7/12
Refrigeration & freezing assets:		
Chilled water systems generally (incl chillers, condensers & cooling towers)	15	1/7/12
Cooling tunnels	20	1/7/12
Freezers:		
Generally (including blast freezers & plate freezers)	15	1/7/12
Spiral freezers	10	1/7/12
Insulation panels used in cold stores, cool rooms, freezer rooms etc - see Table B		
Refrigeration assets		
Uninterruptible power supply (UPS) assets - see Table B Power supply assets		
Valves	10	1/7/12
Waste water treatment assets:		
Aerators	20	1/7/12
Biogas system assets (excl lagoon & pond covers)	25	1/7/12
Blowers	20	1/7/12
Clarifiers (incl dissolved air floatation equipment & screens)	20	1/7/12
Digester/aeration tanks	25	1/7/12
Lagoons & ponds	40	1/7/12
Lagoon & pond covers	12	1/7/12
Lagoon & pond liners	20	1/7/12
Reverse osmosis system assets	20	1/7/12
Sludge dewatering assets (incl filters, separators etc)	15	1/7/12
Water treatment filters (incl carbon filters & membrane filters)	10	1/7/12
Frozen appetiser & finger food manufacturing assets:		
Appetiser forming machines	15	1/7/12
Cookers	12	1/7/12
Fryers	12	1/7/12
Mixing assets (including meat mincers, meat mincer/blenders, mixer/grinding machines & mixers generally)	15	1/7/12
Frozen lasagne manufacturing assets generally (including cookers, cutters, depositors, extruders, lasagne making machines, mixers & sheeters)	15	1/7/12
Frozen pasta product manufacturing assets generally - use any relevant determination made for pasta manufacturing assets in Table A Cereal & pasta product manufacturing		
Frozen pizza manufacturing assets:		
Pizza base making assets:		
Dough mixers	15	1/7/12
Ovens	20	1/7/12
Pizza base forming & sheeting assets (incl chunking units, cutters, extruders, laminators, spiker rollers etc)	15	1/7/12
Proofers	15	1/7/12
Pizza sauce & topping application assets (including can opening machines, cheese shredding assets, depositors, enrobers, topping applicators & water coating sprayers)	15	1/7/12
Pocket pizza making machines	15	1/7/12
Frozen potato product manufacturing assets (including french fries/potato chips, potato flake, potato shred & shred product manufacturing assets):		
Pre-processing assets:		
Deskinners & peelers:		
Abrasive/brush peelers	12	1/7/12
Steam peelers	10	1/7/12
Destoners	20	1/7/12
Sizing & sorting assets:		
Electronic sorters	10	1/7/12
Mechanical sizers (incl roller sizers & screen shaker sizers)	15	1/7/12
Trim tables (roller inspection tables)	20	1/7/12
Washers & brushers (including barrel washers, flat bed brushers, polishers & pre-cleaner wet hopper washers)	12	1/7/12
Processing assets generally:		
Batter enrobers	10	1/7/12
Blanchers	15	1/7/12
Cookers	12	1/7/12
Cutters:		
Mechanical cutters	10	1/7/12
Water based (hydro) cutters	15	1/7/12
Dicers	10	1/7/12
Dosing systems for dextrose & SAPP application etc	15	1/7/12
Dryers:		
Flake drum dryers	20	1/7/12
Generally (incl dewatering dryers)	15	1/7/12
Flake breakers	10	1/7/12
Forming drums/machines	10	1/7/12
Fryers	12	1/7/12
Mixers	15	1/7/12
Pre-heaters	15	1/7/12
Shredders	10	1/7/12
Trimming & grading assets (including shaker screen tables used in grading finished products & nubbin removal, sliver removers etc)	10	1/7/12
Frozen pre-prepared meal manufacturing assets (including cookers & kettles, depositors, fillers, meat injectors & tenderisers, mixers, multihead weighers, ovens, particle & sauce applicators & rice/pasta cookers)	15	1/7/12
Ingredient receiving & handling assets:		
Bins & hoppers (including holding bins, intermediate bulk containers, tote bins etc):		

Asset	Life (yrs)	Date of application
Mild & stainless steel.	15	1/7/12
Others (including plastic & fibreglass) . . .	8	1/7/12
Potato storage assets:		
Air handling system assets used in potato storage structures:		
Aeration pipes	25	1/7/12
Control systems	15	1/7/12
Fans	15	1/7/12
Humidification assets (humidifiers etc)	10	1/7/12
Refrigeration assets (refrigeration units etc).	12	1/7/12
Potato pilers (bin pilers)	20	1/7/12
Silos (flour).	25	1/7/12
Tippers & unloaders (including bin tippers & unloaders, bulker bag unloaders & tote tippers & unloaders)	12	1/7/12
Trolleys (for cooked rice etc)	5	1/7/12
Packaging & quality control assets:		
Accumulators	12	1/7/12
Adhesive applicators.	7	1/7/12
Cartoners (including inner & outer cartoning machines).	15	1/7/12
Case erecting, packing & closing machines (including casepackers)	15	1/7/12
Case sealing machines	10	1/7/12
Checkweighers	10	1/7/12
Coding machines (incl laser coding machines)	8	1/7/12
Flow wrappers	10	1/7/12
Form fill & seal assets (incl bagging units & multihead weighers)	15	1/7/12
Heat shrink tunnels.	10	1/7/12
Metal detectors.	10	1/7/12
Palletisers.	12	1/7/12
Palletising robots	10	1/7/12
Pallet wrappers.	12	1/7/12
Product loaders & stackers	15	1/7/12
Tray denesters	15	1/7/12
Tray sealers	15	1/7/12
Weighbridges	20	1/7/12
X-ray detectors.	10	1/7/12
Peanut processing assets:		
Aeration units	15	1/7/09
Aspirators	10	1/7/09
Bins & hoppers (including gravity bins, holding bins, shell bins, surge bins etc)	15	1/7/09
Blanchers	10	1/7/09
Cleaning assets:		
De stoners & gravity separators	20	1/7/09
Pre cleaners (intake cleaners)	15	1/7/09
Control systems.	10	1/7/09
Door controls & motor drive systems for rapid roller doors (incorporating chains, controls, motors & sensors, but excluding doors)	10	1/7/09
Dust collection assets (including ductwork, dust collectors, extraction fans etc)	20	1/7/09
Fryers	10	1/7/09
Granulators	12	1/7/09
Laboratory assets:		
Generally	10	1/7/09
Laboratory analysers	5	1/7/09
Materials handling assets (including augers, belt conveyors, bucket elevators, elevators & vibratory conveyors)	15	1/7/09
Ovens (including roasters & dryers)	10	1/7/09
Packaging assets (including packers, palletisers, shrink wrappers & strapping machines).	10	1/7/09
Peanut oil crushing assets:		
Cookers	15	1/7/09
Screw presses/expeller presses	13	1/7/09
Quality control assets:		
Magnets & magnetic separators	7	1/7/09
Metal detectors.	10	1/7/09
X ray units	5	1/7/09
Refrigeration units	20	1/7/09
Sampling assets:		
Sample grinders & shellers	10	1/7/09
Sieve tables & picking belt decks	20	1/7/09
Moisture meters	5	1/7/09
Scales	5	1/7/09
Shellers	20	1/7/09

Asset	Life (yrs)	Date of application
Silos (metal)	30	1/7/09
Sorting & sizing assets:		
Electronic/laser sorters (incl colour sorters). . .	10	1/7/09
Generally (incl vibrating sieves, shaker decks & sizing shakers)	20	1/7/09
Tipping units	20	1/7/09
Transformers	40	1/7/09
Tea processing assets:		
Bins (including receiving & refrigerated).	15	1/7/12
Bin tippers	20	1/7/12
Classifiers & shredders	20	1/7/12
Dryers (including primary, secondary & final)	20	1/7/12
Fermenters (oxidizers)	20	1/7/12
Fibre extractors	20	1/7/12
Laboratory assets:		
Generally	15	1/7/12
Laboratory analysers	10	1/7/12
Materials handling assets (including augers, belt conveyors, bucket elevators, vibratory conveyors, structures, gearboxes & motors)	15	1/7/12
Packaging assets:		
Bagging machines (incl flow wrappers & roll wrapping machines)	15	1/7/12
Packaging machines:		
Form fill & seal packaging machines	15	1/7/12
Generally (incl flat bottom, flat top & bottom, pillow shape & stand up packaging machines).	15	1/7/12
Vacuum brick pack packaging machines .	15	1/7/12
Tea packaging assets generally (including cartoners, casepackers, case palletisers, checkweighers, fillers, label applicators, shrink wrappers & stretch wrappers etc).	15	1/7/12
Pre dryers	20	1/7/12
Rollers (including crush tear & curl (CTC), electrostatic, secondary & final).	20	1/7/12
Rotovanes	20	1/7/12
Support assets:		
Air compression assets (incl air dryers, air receivers & compressors)	12	1/7/12
Blowers & fans	15	1/7/12
Boilers	20	1/7/12
Bulka bags	5	1/7/12
Control system assets (including control cabinets & switchgear, instrumentation, programmable logic controllers (PLCs) & variable speed drives (VSDs)).	10	1/7/12
Switchboards	20	1/7/12
Vibratory screens.	20	1/7/12
Withering troughs (incorporating controls & sensors)	25	1/7/12
SOFT DRINK, CORDIAL & SYRUP MANUFACTURING		
De aerated water system assets (including pipes, pumps & tanks)	20	1/7/09
Filter assets (including bag filters, carbon filters, cartridge filters, ozone filters & ultra violet filters)	15	1/7/09
Fruit juice drink manufacturing assets – see Table A Fruit & vegetable processing		
Ice making machinery:		
Condensers	13 1/3	1/1/01
Expansion pipes.	40	1/1/01
General machinery.	13 1/3	1/1/01
Ice moulds	5	1/1/01
Packaging assets:		
Filling & sealing assets:		
Capping machines	15	1/7/09
Container dryers (incorporating air knives & blowers)	10	1/7/09
Cooling & warming tunnels	10	1/7/09
Filling machines (incl bag in box fillers, cup fillers & aseptic fillers)	20	1/7/09
Induction sealers.	10	1/7/09
Inspection machines.	10	1/7/09
Handling assets:		
Bottle & can rinsing machines.	20	1/7/09
Depalletisers.	20	1/7/09
Pallet binders	10	1/7/09
Palletisers.	20	1/7/09
Strap cutting machines.	10	1/7/09
Stretch wrappers	15	1/7/09

Asset	Life (yrs)	Date of application
Packing assets:		
Carton packers	15	1/7/09
Coding machines (including container coders		
& outer date coders)	7	1/7/09
Label applicators	7	1/7/09
Labellers	15	1/7/09
Multipack machines	10	1/7/09
Shrink wrappers	15	1/7/09
Tunnel pasteurisers	10	1/7/09
Support assets:		
Additive dosing systems assets (including pipes,		
pumps & tanks)	20	1/7/09
Air compressors & receivers	20	1/7/09
Boilers	20	1/7/09
Carbonators (including controls, pumps & valves)	20	1/7/09
Centrifuges	15	1/7/09
Clean in place system (CIP) assets (including pipes,		
pumps & tanks)	15	1/7/09
Control system assets (excluding personal		
computers, but incl program logic controllers		
& switchgear)	10	1/7/09
Conveyers	15	1/7/09
Heat exchangers	15	1/7/09
Laboratory equipment	10	1/7/09
Refrigeration assets (incl compressors, cooling		
towers, condensers, evaporators & pumps)	15	1/7/09
Pipes	25	1/7/09
Pumps	15	1/7/09
Syrup preparation assets (including tanks)	15	1/7/09
Valves	10	1/7/09
Waste water treatment assets:		
Aerators	20	1/7/09
Anaerobic bio gas system assets	25	1/7/09
Blowers	20	1/7/09
Clarifiers	20	1/7/09
Digester/aeration tanks	25	1/7/09
Reverse osmosis system assets	20	1/7/09
Weighers	20	1/7/09
Tanks:		
Hot water	25	1/7/09
Liquid CO2 storage	20	1/7/09
Storage:		
Chemical storage	20	1/7/09
Generally	30	1/7/09

BEER MANUFACTURING (EXCEPT NON ALCOHOLIC BEER)

Asset	Life (yrs)	Date of application
Beer filtration assets:		
Beer filters	20	1/7/08
Filter media make up assets	20	1/7/08
Mash filters	20	1/7/08
Brewing assets:		
Grist hoppers	25	1/7/08
Mash tuns	25	1/7/08
Lauter tuns	25	1/7/08
Spent grains transfer system assets	20	1/7/08
Wort kettles	25	1/7/08
Whirlpool vessels	25	1/7/08
Cellaring assets:		
Carbonators (including controls, pumps & valves)	20	1/7/08
Centrifuges	15	1/7/08
De aerated water system assets (including pipes,		
pumps & tanks)	20	1/7/08
Yeast filters/dryers	15	1/7/08
Yeast propagators	20	1/7/08
Malt handling & cleaning assets:		
Augers/conveyers & elevators	15	1/7/08
Dust extractors	20	1/7/08
Grain cleaning assets (including screeners,		
destoners & magnetic separators)	20	1/7/08
Malt milling machines (incl hammer & roller mills)	20	1/7/08
Silos:		
Galvanised construction	30	1/7/08
Steel construction	40	1/7/08
Weighers	20	1/7/08
Packaging assets:		
Bottle & can filling & sealing assets:		
Filling machines	20	1/7/08
Inspection machines	10	1/7/08
Bottle & can handling assets:		
Bottle & can rinsing machines	20	1/7/08
Depalletisers	20	1/7/08

Asset	Life (yrs)	Date of application
Palletisers	20	1/7/08
Bottle & can packing assets:		
Carton packers	15	1/7/08
Date coders	7	1/7/08
Labellers	15	1/7/08
Multipack machines	10	1/7/08
Outer date coders	7	1/7/08
Shrink wrappers	15	1/7/08
Tunnel pasteurisers	10	1/7/08
Conveyers	15	1/7/08
Keg line assets:		
Capping machines	15	1/7/08
Coding machines	7	1/7/08
External washing machines	20	1/7/08
Internal washer & filler machines	20	1/7/08
Kegs (stainless steel)	15	1/7/13
Pasteurisers	20	1/7/08
Support assets:		
Additive & hops dosing systems assets (incl		
pipes, pumps & tanks)	20	1/7/08
Air compressors & receivers	20	1/7/08
Boilers	20	1/7/08
Carbon dioxide recovery system assets:		
Gas collection & storage assets (including		
pipes bladders & tanks)	25	1/7/08
Gas processing assets	20	1/7/08
Vaporisation system assets	20	1/7/08
Clean in place system (CIP) assets (incl pipes,		
pumps & tanks)	15	1/7/08
Control system assets (excluding personal		
computers)	10	1/7/08
Heat exchangers	15	1/7/08
Refrigeration assets (including compressors,		
condensers, evaporators & pumps)	15	1/7/08
Pipes	25	1/7/08
Pumps	15	1/7/08
Valves	10	1/7/08
Vapour condensers	15	1/7/08
Waste water treatment assets:		
Aerators	20	1/7/08
Anaerobic bio gas system assets	25	1/7/08
Blowers	20	1/7/08
Clarifiers	20	1/7/08
Digester/aeration tanks	25	1/7/08
Reverse osmosis system assets	20	1/7/08
Tanks:		
Beer fermentation & storage	30	1/7/08
Chemical storage	20	1/7/08
Cold service storage	25	1/7/08
Condensate collection	25	1/7/08
Hot service storage	25	1/7/08
Liquid CO2 storage	20	1/7/08
Trub	25	1/7/08
Yeast storage	25	1/7/08

SPIRIT MANUFACTURING

Asset	Life (yrs)	Date of application
Distillery plant (brandy etc)	13$\frac{1}{3}$	1/1/01

WINE & OTHER ALCOHOLIC BEVERAGE MANUFACTURING

Asset	Life (yrs)	Date of application
Barrel assets:		
Barrel racks	20	1/7/08
Barrel washers	7	1/7/08
Oak barrels	4	1/7/08
Grape handling assets:		
Conveyors & elevators	15	1/7/08
Crushers/destemmers	15	1/7/08
Electronic scales (mobile)	10	1/7/08
Grape bins (plastic)	5	1/7/08
Grape receival hoppers	20	1/7/08
Grape waste pits (concrete)	20	1/7/08
Presses:		
Basket	20	1/7/08
Continuous (screw)	15	1/7/08
Pneumatic (airbag)	15	1/7/08
Weighbridges/weighers	20	1/7/08
Packaging assets:		
Bottle & cask filling, sealing & coding assets:		
Cap feed systems	15	1/7/08
Cappers	15	1/7/08
Carton packing machines	15	1/7/08
Corkers	15	1/7/08

Asset	Life (yrs)	Date of application
Crown sealers (sparkling wine)	15	1/7/08
Date coders	7	1/7/08
Fillers	15	1/7/08
Foilers	15	1/7/08
Inspection machines	10	1/7/08
Labellers	10	1/7/08
Rinsers	15	1/7/08
Handling & packing assets:		
Carton erectors/sealers/tapers	15	1/7/08
Conveyors (loose bottle, carton & pallet)	15	1/7/08
Depalletisers	15	1/7/08
Outer date coders	5	1/7/08
Palletisers	15	1/7/08
Shrink wrappers	15	1/7/08
Separation/filtration assets:		
Centrifuges	10	1/7/08
Filtration units (incorporating housing & filters):		
Cross flow filter units	10	1/7/08
Diatomaceous earth filter units (including earth make up system)	10	1/7/08
Lees filter units	10	1/7/08
Membrane cartridge filter units (including lenticular)	10	1/7/08
Plate & frame filter units	15	1/7/08
Rotary drum vacuum filter units	15	1/7/08
Sparkling wine equipment:		
Carbonation equipment	10	1/7/08
Corking/wiring equipment	15	1/7/08
Disgorging & dosing equipment	10	1/7/08
Riddling equipment	15	1/7/08
Support assets:		
Additive liquid dosing systems	10	1/7/08
Air compressors	15	1/7/08
Air receivers	20	1/7/08
Boilers	15	1/7/08
Cooling towers	15	1/7/08
Electrical & Process control systems:		
Control cabinets, switchgear	10	1/7/08
Programmed logic controllers (PLCs)	10	1/7/08
Transformers	40	1/7/08
Flow meters	10	1/7/08
Grape/wine testing equipment:		
Grape must analyzers	10	1/7/08
Laboratory – glassware	2	1/7/08
Laboratory – other equipment	10	1/7/08
Heat exchangers	15	1/7/08
Hoses	5	1/7/08
Hot water systems	10	1/7/08
Inert gas systems:		
Dry ice machines	10	1/7/08
Gas storage pressure tanks	20	1/7/08
Nitrogen generators	10	1/7/08
Pipes & fittings:		
Mild steel	10	1/7/08
Non ferrous	20	1/7/08
Stainless steel	25	1/7/08
Valves	10	1/7/08
Pumps	15	1/7/08
Refrigeration assets (including compressors, condensors, evaporators & storage tanks)	15	1/7/08
Reverse osmosis plant	10	1/7/08
Waste water treatment assets:		
Aerators	10	1/7/08
Blowers	10	1/7/08
Clarifiers	10	1/7/08
Digesters	10	1/7/08
Tanks (including insulation, agitators, pump over systems & monitoring instrumentation):		
Pressure tanks (for sparkling wine)	20	1/7/08
Waste water storage/treatment tanks	15	1/7/08
Water storage tanks	30	1/7/08
Wine fermenters:		
Open	30	1/7/08
Rotary	30	1/7/08
Static	30	1/7/08
Sweeping arm	30	1/7/08
Wine storage tanks	30	1/7/08
Tank accessories:		
Micro oxygenation systems	5	1/7/08
Tank plungers	10	1/7/08

Asset	Life (yrs)	Date of application
CIGARETTE & TOBACCO PRODUCT MANUFACTURING		
Tobacco kilns	20	1/1/01
TEXTILE, LEATHER, CLOTHING & FOOTWEAR MANUFACTURING		
Boot & shoe making machinery:		
Machinery & general plant	13$^1/_3$	1/1/01
Moulds for plastic heels	3	1/1/01
Vulcanising moulds	5	1/1/01
Clothing & millinery manufacturing plant:		
General plant	20	1/1/01
Hat manufacturing plant & machinery	13$^1/_3$	1/1/01
Sewing machines	10	1/1/01
Cotton manufacturers' machinery:		
Conveyors	10	1/1/01
Engines, gas	20	1/1/01
Gas producer plant	13$^1/_3$	1/1/01
Gins	10	1/1/01
Flock manufacturing plant:		
Carding machines	13$^1/_3$	1/1/01
General plant	20	1/1/01
Knitting machines	13$^1/_3$	1/1/01
Rope & twine manufacturers' plant	20	1/1/01
Tanners' plant:		
General plant	20	1/1/01
Modern plant used in 'wet' process	13$^1/_3$	1/1/01
Weaving machinery (silk & cotton)	13$^1/_3$	1/1/01
Wool dumping machinery	13$^1/_3$	1/1/01
Wool scouring machinery	16$^2/_3$	1/1/01
Woollen manufacturers' machinery	16$^2/_3$	1/1/01
LOG SAWMILLING & TIMBER DRESSING		
Saw milling equipment:		
Dry or planner mill plant:		
Generally (includes multi saw/trimmer, pack docker, planner/molder, resaw or optimiser docker, stress grader & tilt hoist)	10	1/1/01
Stackers	15	1/1/01
Tray sorters	15	1/1/01
Green mill plant:		
Edger line plant (includes board edger & resaw)	10	1/1/01
Heating plant (includes storage bins/silos)	15	1/1/01
Kiln drying plant:		
Generally (incl kiln trolleys/carriages, traverser & weights)	10	1/1/01
Timber drying kilns & reconditioners	15	1/1/01
Main saw line plant (includes saws, chipper canter, board separator & cant turner)	10	1/1/01
Sorter & trimming line plant:		
Generally (includes grade mark reader & multi trimmer)	10	1/1/01
Stackers	15	1/1/01
Vertical bin sorters	15	1/1/01
Log debarking plant (incl decks, carriages, hydraulic grabs & fixed cranes, butt reducer, debarker, kicker sorter & bins/pockets)	10	1/1/01
Log, lumber & waste transfer equipment	15	1/1/01
Log yard equipment:		
Fixed & mobile cranes	12	1/1/01
Mobile equipment (including log loaders with log grabs)	7	1/1/01
Watering systems	15	1/1/01
Miscellaneous plant:		
Generally (includes air compressors, extraction systems & pollution & air monitoring equipment)	10	1/1/01
Moisture meters	3	1/1/01
Saw & knife sharpening equipment	10	1/1/01
Walkways	15	1/1/01
Waste processing equipment:		
Bins – waste, chip & fuel	15	1/1/01
Chippers, shakers/screens & hoggers	10	1/1/01
PLYWOOD & VENEER MANUFACTURING		
Debarking assets	15	1/1/05
Dry clipping assets	25	1/1/05
Heating unit assets	20	1/1/05
Glue mixing assets	25	1/1/05
Lay up & glue spreading assets (including roller, curtains, & spray coaters, liquid & foam extruders)	25	1/1/05

Asset	Life (yrs)	Date of application
Log conditioning, heating & steaming assets.	25	1/1/05
Log sizing assets	20	1/1/05
Log yard assets (see Table A Log sawmilling & timber dressing, saw milling equipment)		
Materials handling assets (including belt, chain & screw conveyors)	20	1/1/05
Packaging assets	20	1/1/05
Presses	25	1/1/05
Sanding & finishing assets	25	1/1/05
Sharpening assets	30	1/1/05
Trimming & sawing assets	25	1/1/05
Veneer composing, jointing & splicing assets	20	1/1/05
Veneer dryers	25	1/1/05
Veneer patching & grading assets	20	1/1/05
Veneer peeling & slicing assets (including rotary peelers, longitudinal, crosscut, & staylog lathe slicers, log chargers & reelers)	20	1/1/05
Veneer reconditioning assets	25	1/1/05
Veneer sorting assets	20	1/1/05
Wet clipping assets	25	1/1/05

RECONSTITUTED WOOD PRODUCT MANUFACTURING

Asset	Life (yrs)	Date of application
Board coolers	25	1/1/05
Board curing assets	20	1/1/05
Board storage assets	25	1/1/05
Chipping, milling & flaking assets	15	1/1/05
Debarking assets	15	1/1/05
Driers	15	1/1/05
Fibre sifters	15	1/1/05
Flake & fibre storage assets	25	1/1/05
Glue, resin & wax mixing & blending assets	15	1/1/05
Heat plant & boiler assets	25	1/1/05
Lamination assets.	15	1/1/05
Log conditioning, heating & steaming assets.	25	1/1/05
Log sizing assets	20	1/1/05
Log yard assets (see Table A Log sawmilling & timber dressing, saw milling equipment)		
Magnetic separators	25	1/1/05
Mat forming & weighing assets (including pendistor)	20	1/1/05
Materials handling assets (including belt, chain & screw conveyors)	20	1/1/05
Packaging assets	20	1/1/05
Presses (including pre press, hot & cold presses)	25	1/1/05
Quality measuring assets (including blow detectors, thickness detectors & weighing bridges)	15	1/1/05
Refiner assets	20	1/1/05
Sanding & finishing assets	25	1/1/05
Trimming & sawing assets	25	1/1/05
Ventilation & dust extraction assets.	15	1/1/05
Woodchip screening & washing assets	15	1/1/05

OTHER WOOD PRODUCT MANUFACTURING

Asset	Life (yrs)	Date of application
Clothes peg manufacturing plant (wood)	13$^{1}/_{3}$	1/1/01
Case making plant	13$^{1}/_{3}$	1/1/01
Cork manufacturers' plant	10	1/1/01
Frame (picture) manufacturing plant	13$^{1}/_{3}$	1/1/01
Joinery plant	13$^{1}/_{3}$	1/1/01
Moulding machinery (wood)	13$^{1}/_{3}$	1/1/01
Wood working plant	13$^{1}/_{3}$	1/1/01

PULP, PAPER & CONVERTED PAPER PRODUCT MANUFACTURING

Asset	Life (yrs)	Date of application
Cigarette paper cutting & folding plant	10	1/1/01
Pulp & paper mill assets:		
Auxiliary assets (including agitators, blowers/fans conveyors, heat exchangers & condensers, pipes & pumps)	15	1/1/02
Box & carton making assets (including box converting assets & corrugators)	10	1/1/02
Chemical preparation assets (including tanks & pipes used for chemical preparation)	10	1/1/02
Electrical & instrumentation assets:		
Control systems	10	1/1/02
Control valves	15	1/1/02
Local indicators (pressure, level & temperature).	15	1/1/02
Power plant assets (including switchgear, transformers & turbo generators) – see Table A Electricity supply		
Sensors:		
Specialised	8	1/1/02
Standard	15	1/1/02

Asset	Life (yrs)	Date of application
Paper machine assets:		
Dry end assets (including calenders, coaters & reelers)	15	1/1/02
Dryers (including MG cylinder & yankee cylinder)	25	1/1/02
Size press.	15	1/1/02
Wet end assets (including forming section, head box & press section)	10	1/1/02
Pulp process assets:		
Major assets (including bleaching towers, digesters, electrostatic precipitators, evaporators, lime kilns, pulp baling lines, recovery boilers, & strippers)	20	1/1/02
Other assets (including cleaners, flotation cells, pulpers & repulpers, refiners, screens & washers/thickeners)	15	1/1/02
Stock preparation assets (including cleaners, flotation cells, pulpers & repulpers, refiners, screens & washers/thickeners)	15	1/1/02
Tanks	20	1/1/02
Wood yard assets (including chip screens, chippers, reclaimers/live bottom scrappers & rotating drum debarkers)	10	1/1/02

PAPER STATIONERY MANUFACTURING

Asset	Life (yrs)	Date of application
Stationers' manufacturing plant	13$^{1}/_{3}$	1/1/01

SANITARY PAPER PRODUCT MANUFACTURING

Asset	Life (yrs)	Date of application
Finishing & converted paper product manufacturing assets:		
Generally (including machines for manufacturing disposable facial & toilet tissues, paper tablecloths, paper table napkins, interleaved & rolled paper towels)	15	1/7/13
Rolled paper core manufacturing assets (including feeder racks, glue applicators & cutting carriages).	10	1/7/13
Hygienic paper product manufacturing assets:		
Fluff preparation assets (including hammer mills, cutting machines, fluff forming drums, compacting rollers & carding machines)	13	1/7/13
Generally (including machines for manufacturing disposable nappies, sanitary napkins, sanitary liners & tampons)	13	1/7/13
Packaging assets:		
Cartoning assets (including bundlers, carton & case erectors, packing & closing machines)	10	1/7/13
Coding & labelling machines	10	1/7/13
Robots (including automatic guided vehicles (AGVs) & pick & place packaging machines)	10	1/7/13
Stackers & baggers	10	1/7/13
Wrapping machines (including shrink & stretch wrappers)	10	1/7/13
Support assets:		
Air compressors & air dryers	15	1/7/13
Control system & monitoring assets (including programmable logic controllers, variable speed drives, instruments & sensors)	10	1/7/13
Dust control assets (including ductwork, dust collectors, scrubbers & fans)	15	1/7/13
Laboratory assets (including quality control & material testing assets)	10	1/7/13
Material handling assets (including conveyors, elevators, hoists, feeders & hoppers)	15	1/7/13
Metal detectors	10	1/7/13
Storage assets (including bins & trolleys)	10	1/7/13

PRINTING

Asset	Life (yrs)	Date of application
Digital printing assets (including flatbed digital printers, ink based thermal imaging printers, ink jet printers, spray jet digital printers & toner based printers).	5	1/1/06
Flexographic printing assets:		
Ancillary assets:		
Anilox roll cleaning machines	15	1/7/06
Anilox trolley tugs	10	1/7/06
Ink dispensing systems	10	1/7/06
Sleeve mounting machines	10	1/7/06
Sleeves	2	1/7/06
Printing assets:		
Die cutters, flexo/folder/gluers (see Table A Pulp, paper & converted paper product manufacturing, box & carton making assets)		

Asset	Life (yrs)	Date of application
Presses (including mid web, narrow web, very wide web & wide web flexographic presses)	12½	1/7/06
Newspaper printing assets:		
Ancillary assets:		
Automated guided vehicles (including laser guided vehicles & track mounted automated vehicles)	10	1/1/07
Gripper conveyor systems (incorporating drive chains, grippers & tracks)	15	1/1/07
Ink pumps (mechanical)	6	1/1/07
Buffering/print line storage assets:		
Storage devices (including discs, rolls, spools & associated mountings)	15	1/1/07
Unwinders & winders (including single, double & triple stations & buffer docking stations)	15	1/1/07
Newspaper wrapping machines – see Table A Other store-based retailing		
Offset lithography printing presses:		
Hybrid heatset & non heatset webfed offset presses (incorporating integrated control systems, dryers & other peripheral equipment)	15	1/1/07
Non heatset (coldset) webfed offset presses (incorporating integrated control systems, folders, pasters, reelstands & other peripheral equipment)	15	1/1/07
Reel processing, storage & transport assets:		
Conveyors	12½	1/1/07
Racks	20	1/1/07
Reel trolleys (incorporating controls & drive chains)	15	1/1/07
Shredders	15	1/1/07
Stripping machines	15	1/1/07
Offset lithography printing presses used in commercial printing generally:		
Heatset webfed offset presses (incorporating integrated control systems, coaters & other peripheral equipment)	15	1/1/06
Sheetfed presses (incorporating integrated control systems, coaters & other peripheral equipment)	12½	1/1/06
Post press (finishing) trade services assets – see Table A Printing support services		
Pre press trade services assets – see Table A Printing support services		
Quality control assets:		
Automatic web inspection systems	6	1/7/06
Gas Chromatograph (GC) testers	8	1/7/06
Others (including densitometers, plate readers & spectrophotometers)	5	1/7/06
Screen printing assets:		
Ancillary assets:		
Dryers (including conventional air dryers, flash curers & UV dryers)	12½	1/1/06
Drying racks	20	1/1/06
Emulsion coaters	10	1/1/06
Exposure lights	5	1/7/06
Screen frames	10	1/1/06
Sign cutting machines	5	1/1/06
Squeegee cutters	10	1/1/06
Vacuum frames	20	1/1/06
Press assets:		
Heat presses used in sublimation finishing	25	1/1/06
Pen & pad print machines	20	1/1/06
Screen printing presses:		
Automatic presses (including in line multicolour presses)	15	1/1/06
Cylinder presses	15	1/1/06
Others (including manual, semi automatic & three quarter automatic carousel, flatbed & rotary screen printing presses)	20	1/1/06
Screen reclamation assets:		
Screen cleaning bays	10	1/1/06
Screen washers (automatic)	6	1/1/06
Water blasters	4	1/1/06
Support assets:		
Afterburners	10	1/1/06
Dust/waste extraction systems:		
Compactors	12½	1/1/07
Ducting	15	1/1/07
Vacuum pumps	6	1/1/07
PRINTING SUPPORT SERVICES		
Post press (finishing) trade services assets:		
Addressing & mailing assets:		
Combination addressing, folding & gluing mailing units	10	1/1/06
Inkjet addressing printers	5	1/1/06
Bagging & wrapping machines (incl palletisers)	10	1/1/06
Banding & tying machines	12½	1/1/06
Benchtop finishing assets used in small printing establishments (including benchtop guillotines, coil, plastic comb & spiral binders, portable banding & tying machines, small roll laminators & tabletop folders)	5	1/1/06
Binding assets:		
Binding lines (including case binding lines & perfect binding lines)	15	1/1/06
Perfect binders – standalone	10	1/1/06
Stitchers:		
Generally (including drum stitchers, saddle stitching lines & side stitchers)	12½	1/1/06
Saddle stitchers – standalone (bookletmakers)	7½	1/1/06
Casemakers	10	1/1/06
Collators	15	1/1/06
Die cutters	15	1/1/06
Drilling units	10	1/1/06
Foil stamping machines	10	1/1/06
Folders	12½	1/1/06
Guillotines & ancillary assets (including joggers, stackers & transomats)	15	1/1/06
Laminators	10	1/1/06
Mail inserters	5	1/1/06
Newspaper mailroom assets:		
Bundle conveying & sorting systems (including bundle sorting & barcode reading stations & bundle conveyors)	12½	1/1/07
Inserters & inserting systems (incorporating feeders & feeder chains)	10	1/1/07
Stackers	15	1/1/07
Trimmers (including rotary & scissor action trimmers)	15	1/1/07
Perforators	10	1/1/06
Sewing machines	15	1/1/06
Three knife trimmers	15	1/1/06
Pre press trade services assets:		
Conventional flexographic plate making assets (including combination units, dryers, post exposure units, ultra violet (UV) light exposure units & washout units)	7	1/1/06
Film & plate processors	6	1/1/06
Film projection camera systems (including backing board & processing assets)	10	1/1/06
Platesetters:		
Computer to plate (CtP) platesetters (including thermal & visible light platesetters) & Direct to plate flexographic platesetters (Computer digital imagers)	5	1/1/06
Film image platesetters (imagesetters)	7	1/1/06
Plate punch benders:		
Automatic (optical)	5	1/1/07
Manual	10	1/1/07
Plotters	5	1/1/06
Proofers:		
Analogue film or photographic proofers	7	1/1/06
Digital & ink jet proofers	5	1/1/06
Scanners:		
Drum	10	1/1/06
Flatbed	5	1/1/06
PETROLEUM REFINING		
Oil refinery assets:		
Assets used in acid, caustic or clay treating, alkylation, polymerisation or sour water stripping	15	1/7/02
Assets used in sulphur recovery:		
Generally	15	1/7/02
Sulphur pits	10	1/7/02
Assets used in other processes:		
Air compressors	30	1/7/02
Catalyst regenerators	20	1/7/02
Chemical injection systems	5	1/7/02
Coke drums	20	1/7/02

Asset	Life (yrs)	Date of application
Distillation columns	30	1/7/02
Drums:		
Generally	20	1/7/02
Used in amine treating, bitumen blowing, potassium carbonate treating or vacuum distillation	15	1/7/02
Electric desalters	25	1/7/02
Expansion turbines	25	1/7/02
Fans/blowers	30	1/7/02
Filters/coalescers:		
Generally	25	1/7/02
Used in amine treating, continuous coking, delayed coking, potassium carbonate treating, visbreaking or vacuum distillation	20	1/7/02
Flare stacks	25	1/7/02
Flare tips	5	1/7/02
Fractionating columns	30	1/7/02
Furnaces:		
Generally	25	1/7/02
Used in continuous coking, delayed coking or visbreaking	20	1/7/02
Gas absorbers:		
Generally	25	1/7/02
Used in amine treating or potassium carbonate treating	20	1/7/02
Gas adsorbers	25	1/7/02
Heat exchangers:		
Generally	25	1/7/02
Used in amine treating, bitumen blowing, catalytic de waxing, continuous coking, delayed coking, hydrodesulphurisation, hydrotreating, potassium carbonate treating, vacuum distillation or visbreaking	20	1/7/02
Jet ejectors	20	1/7/02
Liquid extraction columns:		
Generally	25	1/7/02
Used in amine treating	20	1/7/02
Piping	30	1/7/02
Process gas compressors	30	1/7/02
Pumps:		
Generally	25	1/7/02
Used in amine treating, bitumen blowing, catalytic de waxing, continuous coking, delayed coking, potassium carbonate treating, vacuum distillation or visbreaking	20	1/7/02
Reactors	25	1/7/02
Rotary filters	20	1/7/02
Scrubbers	25	1/7/02
Side stream strippers	25	1/7/02
Storage tanks:		
Generally	25	1/7/02
Used in amine treating, merox extraction, merox sweetening or potassium carbonate treating	20	1/7/02
Strippers:		
Generally	25	1/7/02
Used in amine treating or potassium carbonate treating	20	1/7/02
Bunds (other than formed with earth)	100	1/1/01
Control systems assets (excluding computers)	10	1/7/02
Effluent separators (concrete)	40	1/1/01
Laboratory equipment	20	1/1/01

INDUSTRIAL GAS MANUFACTURING

Asset	Life (yrs)	Date of application
Industrial gas – general manufacturing assets:		
Air & gas cooling & heating assets:		
Heat exchangers	15	1/7/11
Moisture condensers	20	1/7/11
Quench drums	20	1/7/11
Refrigeration units	20	1/7/11
Air & gas purification assets:		
Adsorption systems	25	1/7/11
Gas scrubbers	20	1/7/11
Reactors	25	1/7/11
Compressors	25	1/7/11
Gas buffer & surge tanks	25	1/7/11
Silencers/mufflers	20	1/7/11
Industrial gas – manufacturing assets for specific gases:		
Acetylene manufacturing assets (carbide process):		

Asset	Life (yrs)	Date of application
Acetylene compressors	25	1/7/11
Acetylene generators (incorporating hoppers)	30	1/7/11
Acetylene purification assets (including cooling condensers, driers, purifier vessels & scrubbers)	20	1/7/11
Calcium hydroxide settling ponds & tanks	20	1/7/11
Carbide handling assets (including carry skips, drum conveyor system & drum opening, lifting & tipping apparatus)	12	1/7/11
Dust collection systems	20	1/7/11
Flashback arrestors	10	1/7/11
Ammonia manufacturing assets - see Table A		
Basic chemical & chemical product manufacturing		
Argon, nitrogen & oxygen manufacturing assets (cryogenic process):		
Air filtering units for process air (incorporating housing & filters)	20	1/7/11
Cold boxes (incorporating distillation columns, expansion valves, heat exchangers, piping, separators & vacuum insulated enclosures)	30	1/7/11
Evaporative coolers (nitrogen cooled) & spray coolers	20	1/7/11
Nitrogen liquefiers (incorporating expansion valves, heat exchangers, piping, separators & vacuum insulated enclosures)	30	1/7/11
Turbine expansion engines	25	1/7/11
Carbon dioxide (CO2) manufacturing assets:		
Amine based absorption/desorption systems	20	1/7/11
Liquefaction assets (including condensers, condensate receivers & separators)	25	1/7/11
Dry ice manufacturing assets:		
Dry ice cutting machines	10	1/7/11
Dry ice packaging systems (incorporating conveyors, shrink tunnels & wrapping & sealing machines)	10	1/7/11
Dry ice presses	20	1/7/11
Dry ice shipping boxes	10	1/7/11
Extraction fans for waste CO2	10	1/7/11
Pelletisers	15	1/7/11
Helium manufacturing assets:		
Helium liquefiers (incorporating cryogenic adsorbers, expansion valves, heat exchangers, piping, separators & vacuum insulated enclosures)	30	1/7/11
Turbine expansion engines	25	1/7/11
Hydrogen manufacturing assets:		
Gasifiers & steam reformer furnaces	25	1/7/11
Industrial gas distribution assets:		
Compressor assets:		
Air receivers	20	1/7/11
Compressors (including those for helium gas, industrial air & medical air)	15	1/7/11
Cylinder filling assets:		
Cylinder filling station assets:		
High pressure hoses	10	1/7/11
Manifolds & piping (incorporating flashback arrestors):		
Acetylene gas	10	1/7/11
Other gases	20	1/7/11
Water cooling system for acetylene cylinders (incorporating piping & spray nozzles)	20	1/7/11
Cylinder frames (incorporating manifolds & piping)	15	1/7/11
Cylinders:		
Gas cylinders	30	1/7/11
Liquid gas cylinders:		
Flasks	7	1/7/11
Other liquid gas cylinders	15	1/7/11
Cylinder valves	10	1/7/11
Cylinder handling assets:		
Baskets, crates, & pallets	12	1/7/11
Tippers & trolleys	10	1/7/11
Cylinder preparation assets:		
Boilers	10	1/7/11
Cylinder brushing machines	10	1/7/11
Cylinder drying cabinets (incorporating heaters & fans)	15	1/7/11
Cylinder inspection lights	10	1/7/11
Cylinder spray booths	15	1/7/11
Cylinder stamping machines	10	1/7/11

Asset	Life (yrs)	Date of application
Cylinder testing machines	10	1/7/11
Cylinder valving machines (incorporating safety enclosures)	15	1/7/11
Tank truck assets:		
Gas storage tanks	20	1/7/11
Hoses	5	1/7/11
Metering systems	7	1/7/11
Pipes & valves	10	1/7/11
Pumps	10	1/7/11
Tanker filling station assets:		
Breakaway couplings	12	1/7/11
Framework, manifolds & piping	20	1/7/11
Tanker filling hoses	10	1/7/11
Weighbridges	20	1/7/11
Vapourisers	20	1/7/11
Support & other assets:		
Air drying systems for industrial & instrument air	15	1/7/11
Control system assets:		
Control cabinets & panels, programmable logic controllers (PLCs) & variable speed drives (VSDs)	10	1/7/11
System monitoring assets (including instrumentation & sensors & transmitters for level, pressure, speed & temperature measurement)	10	1/7/11
Cooling towers:		
Field erected	20	1/7/11
Packaged	15	1/7/11
Customer installations assets:		
Adsorption based nitrogen & oxygen generation systems (skid type) assets:		
Membrane systems	10	1/7/11
Pressure swing adsorption (PSA) systems	12	1/7/11
Vacuum swing adsorption (VSA) systems	15	1/7/11
Blowers & compressors	15	1/7/11
Freezers (including batch freezers, freeze tunnels, & tumble freezers)	15	1/7/11
Gas supply metering, monitoring & control systems (incorporating meters, telemetry assets, sensors, transmitters & supply switching devices)	4	1/7/11
Gas analysis assets:		
Chromatographs	15	1/7/11
Other analysers	10	1/7/11
Gas storage assets:		
Liquid CO2 storage assets:		
Tanks	30	1/7/11
Tank refrigeration units	10	1/7/11
Vacuum insulated tanks	30	1/7/11
Piping assets:		
Flow meters	10	1/7/11
Pipes:		
Carbon steel	20	1/7/11
Stainless steel	30	1/7/11
Pipelines	30	1/7/11
Valves	10	1/7/11
Platform scales	20	1/7/11
Pumps:		
Cryogenic pumps	15	1/7/11
Liquid CO2 pumps	15	1/7/11
Other pumps	15	1/7/11
Safety assets:		
Fire control & alarm assets (see Table B)		
Gas leakage monitors:		
Fixed	10	1/7/11
Portable	4	1/7/11

BASIC CHEMICAL & CHEMICAL PRODUCT MANUFACTURING

Ammonia manufacturing assets:

Asset	Life (yrs)	Date of application
Air & gas reforming & separation assets:		
Adsorption systems (including pressure & thermal swing)	25	1/7/13
Carbon dioxide absorption systems (incorporating absorber & stripping columns, flash drums, heat exchangers, piping, pumps & tanks)	20	1/7/13
Cryogenic separation process assets:		
Air cooling & drying assets (excluding adsorption systems shown above)	20	1/7/13
Cold boxes (incorporating cryogenic distillation columns, expansion valves, heat exchangers, piping, separators & vacuuminsulated enclosures)	30	1/7/13
Desulphurisers	25	1/7/13
Methanators	25	1/7/13
Pre-heaters (for air & gas feedstock)	25	1/7/13
Pre-reformers	25	1/7/13
Primary reformers	20	1/7/13
Secondary reformers	25	1/7/13
Shift converters (high & low temperature)	25	1/7/13
Compressor assets:		
Air filtering units (incorporating filters & housing filters)	25	1/7/13
Blowers & compressors (incorporating drives)	25	1/7/13
Conversion & liquefaction assets:		
Ammonia converters	25	1/7/13
Chillers, condensers, flash drums, receivers & separators	25	1/7/13
Purge gas recovery systems (incorporating heat exchangers, membranes, packing, piping pumps & vessels)	25	1/7/13
Distribution, handling & storage assets:		
Ammonia bullet tanks (including storage & surge tanks)	30	1/7/13
Ammonia deluge & vapour suppression systems	30	1/7/13
Ammonia pipelines (incorporating fittings & valves)	30	1/7/13
Ammonia pumps	15	1/7/13
Ammonia storage tank refrigeration systems (incorporating compressors, condensers, flash drums & receivers)	20	1/7/13
Ammonia storage tanks	30	1/7/13
Ammonia vapour scrubber systems	25	1/7/13
ISOtainers & portable tanks	15	1/7/13
Loading arm systems - marine	25	1/7/13
Rail & road tank filling assets:		
Breakaway couplings	10	1/7/13
Filling hoses	10	1/7/13
Loading arm systems	10	1/7/13
Gas pipelines (incorporating fittings & valves)	30	1/7/13
Heat exchangers:		
Process gas	20	1/7/13
Waste heat boilers	20	1/7/13
Support assets:		
Air compression assets (for industrial air & instrument air):		
Air compressors (incorporating air drying & filtering assets)	15	1/7/13
Air receivers	20	1/7/13
Blowers & fans (generally)	20	1/7/13
Boiler assets:		
Boilers	25	1/7/13
De-aerators	25	1/7/13
Economisers	25	1/7/13
Steam drums	25	1/7/13
Chemical storage tanks:		
Polyethylene	12	1/7/13
Other	20	1/7/13
Control system assets:		
Control cabinets & panels, program logic controllers (PLCs), switchgear & variable speed drives (VSDs)	10	1/7/13
System monitoring assets (including instrumentation & sensors & transmitters for level, pressure, speed & temperature measurement)	10	1/7/13
Cooling towers	20	1/7/13
Electricity supply assets:		
Emergency supply assets - see Table B		
Power supply assets, emergency or standby		
Steam turbine generators	25	1/7/13
Other electricity supply assets - see Table A Electricity supply		
Emission control assets:		
Flare tips	10	1/7/13
Silencers	20	1/7/13
Stacks (exhaust, vent & flare)	20	1/7/13
Fire control & alarm systems:		
Fire fighting systems (incorporating hose boxes, hydrants & ring mains)	30	1/7/13

Asset	Life (yrs)	Date of application
Other fire control & alarm assets		
- see Table B Fire control & alarm assets		
Gas detectors:		
Fixed	10	1/7/13
Portable	4	1/7/13
Heat exchangers (not specified elsewhere)	20	1/7/13
Laboratory assets:		
Analysers	10	1/7/13
Other laboratory equipment (including centrifuges, drying ovens, fume cupboards etc)	10	1/7/13
Overhead cranes	25	1/7/13
Piping assets:		
Flow meters	10	1/7/13
Pipes & fittings	25	1/7/13
Valves	10	1/7/13
Pumps:		
Boiler feedwater & cooling water pumps	20	1/7/13
Dosing pumps	5	1/7/13
Other pumps (not specified elsewhere)	15	1/7/13
Safety showers & eye wash stations	20	1/7/13
Water storage & treatment assets:		
Clarifiers & settling tanks	20	1/7/13
Dam & pond liners	20	1/7/13
Dams & effluent ponds	40	1/7/13
Ion exchange systems	20	1/7/13
Reverse osmosis systems	15	1/7/13
Water storage tanks:		
Polyethylene	15	1/7/13
Other	25	1/7/13
Weighbridges	20	1/7/13
Ammonium nitrate manufacturing assets:		
Ammonia handling & storage assets - see above in Ammonia manufacturing assets, distribution, handling & storage assets		
Ammonium nitrate prill manufacturing assets:		
Coating, cooling, drying & screening assets:		
Bulk flow coolers	20	1/7/13
Chilling systems (incorporating chillers, ducting & piping)	20	1/7/13
Coating product tanks	25	1/7/13
Fluid bed coolers	20	1/7/13
Rotary drum machines (incl coaters, coolers, driers & granulators)	20	1/7/13
Screeners	20	1/7/13
Distribution, handling & storage assets:		
Bagging machines	15	1/7/13
Conveyor belt weighers	15	1/7/13
Conveyors & elevators	15	1/7/13
Load out bins/silos	25	1/7/13
Reclaim hoppers	20	1/7/13
Scales	15	1/7/13
Prill tower blowers & fans	20	1/7/13
Prill towers (incorporating head tanks & lifts)	25	1/7/13
Scrubber systems (incorporating ducting, fans, scrubbers & tanks)	20	1/7/13
Ammonia nitrate solution manufacturing assets:		
Evaporation assets:		
Condensate tanks, flash drums & separators	20	1/7/13
Evaporators	20	1/7/13
Neutralisers	25	1/7/13
Pipe reactors (titanium)	3	1/7/13
Remelt & solution storage tanks (incorporating heating coils & stirrers)	25	1/7/13
Solution filters	20	1/7/13
Solution pumps	15	1/7/13
Nitric acid manufacturing assets:		
Ammonia liquid filtering vessels (incorporating filters)	25	1/7/13
Ammonia vapour filtering vessels (incorporating filters)	20	1/7/13
Ammonia/air mixers	20	1/7/13
Compressor assets:		
Air filtering units (incorporating housing & filters)	25	1/7/13
Compressors (incorporating drives)	25	1/7/13
Tail gas expanders	25	1/7/13
Conversion & absorption assets:		
Absorber columns (including bleachers)	25	1/7/13
Catalyst filters	25	1/7/13

Asset	Life (yrs)	Date of application
Converters	25	1/7/13
Cooler condensers:		
Zirconium	25	1/7/13
Other	10	1/7/13
Nitric acid heaters:		
Zirconium	20	1/7/13
Other	10	1/7/13
Nitric acid pumps	15	1/7/13
Nitrous oxide (NOx) abaters	25	1/7/13
Weak acid tanks	30	1/7/13
Heat exchangers:		
Air coolers & heaters	25	1/7/13
Ammonia vapourisers	20	1/7/13
Gas coolers & heaters	20	1/7/13
Superheaters	15	1/7/13
Waste heat boilers	20	1/7/13
Nitric acid storage assets:		
Scrubbers	20	1/7/13
Tanks	25	1/7/13
Support assets - see above in Ammonia manufacturing assets, support assets		
Chemical manufacturing plant (not listed elsewhere):		
General plant	$13\frac{1}{3}$	1/1/01
Organic peroxides explosion (cell block)	20	1/1/01
Ethanol manufacturing assets:		
Cooking assets:		
Filters & strainers	15	1/7/12
Flash tanks	20	1/7/12
Jet cookers	10	1/7/12
Liquefaction tanks (including cook tubes & slurry tanks)	20	1/7/12
Meal mixers	15	1/7/12
Distillation & purification assets:		
Distillation columns	25	1/7/12
Molecular sieve adsorption systems (incorporating condensers, control systems, coolers, heaters, molecular sieves, pumps, tanks & vacuum equipment)	25	1/7/12
Reboilers	20	1/7/12
Side stream strippers	20	1/7/12
Feedstock handling & storage assets:		
Grain assets:		
Cleaning assets (including magnetic separators, screeners & sieves)	20	1/7/12
Conveyor belt weighers	15	1/7/12
Conveyors (including belt, drag & screw conveyors, bucket & rake elevators & chutes)	15	1/7/12
Hoppers (including weigh hoppers)	25	1/7/12
Milling machines (including hammer & roller mills)	20	1/7/12
Silo aerators	15	1/7/12
Silos	30	1/7/12
Starch tanks	25	1/7/12
Molasses assets:		
Dam covers	12	1/7/12
Dam liners	20	1/7/12
Dams	40	1/7/12
Pipelines (incorporating fittings & valves)	25	1/7/12
Receival station control systems	10	1/7/12
Receival troughs (incorporating protective cladding, rails & roofing)	40	1/7/12
Tanks	30	1/7/12
Fermentation assets:		
Chillers	20	1/7/12
Fermentation tanks	30	1/7/12
Scrubbers	20	1/7/12
Yeast propagation vessels	20	1/7/12
Yeast recovery assets (molasses feedstock):		
Centrifugal separators	20	1/7/12
Filtering assets (incl feed tanks, filtering vessels & hydrocyclone systems)	20	1/7/12
Hoppers, mixing tanks & storage tanks	25	1/7/12
Stillage assets:		
Distillers grain assets:		
Centrifugal decanters	15	1/7/12
Conveyors	15	1/7/12
Cooling assets for dried distillers grain (including blowers & fans, chillers, ducting & other cooling assets)	20	1/7/12
Evaporators	25	1/7/12

Asset	Life (yrs)	Date of application
Mixers	15	1/7/12
Rotary drum dryers	20	1/7/12
Stillage & syrup tanks	25	1/7/12
Dunder & stillage assets (molasses feedstock):		
Conveyors & hoppers for fertiliser additives	15	1/7/12
Dam covers	12	1/7/12
Dams	40	1/7/12
Pipelines (incorporating fittings & valves)	25	1/7/12
Tanks (including fertiliser additive mixing & buffer tanks)	20	1/7/12
Support & other assets:		
Additive dosing systems (including pipes, pumps & tanks):		
Plastic	5	1/7/12
Other	20	1/7/12
Air compression assets:		
Air compressors	15	1/7/12
Air drying & filtering systems	12	1/7/12
Air receivers	20	1/7/12
Blowers & fans	20	1/7/12
Boilers	20	1/7/12
Control system assets:		
Control cabinets & panels, programmable logic controllers (PLCs), switchgear & variable speed drives (VSDs)	10	1/7/12
System monitoring assets (including instrumentation & sensors & transmitters for level, pressure, speed & temperature measurement)	10	1/7/12
Cooling towers	20	1/7/12
Dust collection systems (including baghouses, cyclones & other dust collection assets)	20	1/7/12
Heat exchangers (excluding column reboilers)	15	1/7/12
Laboratory assets:		
Analysers	10	1/7/12
Other laboratory equipment (including autoclaves, centrifuges, drying ovens, fume cupboards & UV sterilisers)	10	1/7/12
Piping assets:		
Flow meters	10	1/7/12
Pipes	25	1/7/12
Valves	10	1/7/12
Pumps	15	1/7/12
Safety assets:		
Fire control & alarm assets - see Table B		
Gas detectors:		
Fixed	10	1/7/12
Portable	4	1/7/12
Tanker filling assets:		
Automated dispensing systems	10	1/7/12
Automatic tank gauges	10	1/7/12
Fire protection systems (incorporating auxiliary monitors, fire & ultraviolet detectors, fire indicator panels, fire retardant lines & foam storage tanks)	15	1/7/12
Hoses	2	1/7/12
Loading & unloading arms (incorporating balance mechanisms, couplers, drop hoses & swivels)	10	1/7/12
Meters & metering systems	7	1/7/12
Overfill protection systems	10	1/7/12
Tanks:		
Chemical tanks (incl clean in place tanks):		
Plastic	15	1/7/12
Other	20	1/7/12
Ethanol & petroleum tanks:		
Stainless steel	30	1/7/12
Other	25	1/7/12
Water tanks (including condensate collection tanks)	25	1/7/12
Vapour condensers	20	1/7/12
Waste water treatment assets:		
Aerators	20	1/7/12
Biogas system assets (excl effluent pond covers)	25	1/7/12
Digester/aeration tanks	25	1/7/12
Effluent channels & ponds	40	1/7/12
Pond covers	12	1/7/12
Pond liners	20	1/7/12
Water filtration assets (incl ion exchange		

Asset	Life (yrs)	Date of application
assets & reverse osmosis assets)	15	1/7/12
Weighbridges	20	1/7/12
Fertiliser manufacturing plant (excluding ammonia manufacturing assets & ammonium nitrate manufacturing assets listed in Table A Basic chemical & chemical product manufacturing	20	1/1/01
Salt manufacturing & refining plant	10	1/1/01
Sulphuric acid plant:		
Acid chambers (irrespective of raw material used)	20	1/1/01
Plant:		
Where pyrites used in manufacture of the acid	10	1/1/01
Where natural sulphur (brimstone) so used	$13\frac{1}{3}$	1/1/01

HUMAN PHARMACEUTICAL & MEDICINAL PRODUCT MANUFACTURING

Asset	Life (yrs)	Date of application
Laboratory assets:		
Bench top autoclaves	5	1/1/04
Incubators	6	1/1/04
Laboratory analysers (including coagulators, carbon analysers, colour readers, gas chromatographs, high performance liquid chromatographs (HPLCs), & spectrophotometers)	5	1/1/04
Particle sizers	5	1/1/04
Packaging assets:		
Accumulators	10	1/1/04
Batch, barcode, label, & volume readers	10	1/1/04
Blister pack packaging machines	10	1/1/04
Blow fill seal (BFS) machines	12	1/1/04
Bottle & vial inverters & blowers	10	1/1/04
Bottle & vial unscramblers	10	1/1/04
Bundlers & bundle packing machines	10	1/1/04
Cappers & sealers (including tamper proof sealers)	10	1/1/04
Cartoners	10	1/1/04
Check weighers	10	1/1/04
Cream, liquid & powder filling & sealing machines (including bag, bottle, syringe & tube fillers & sealers)	12	1/1/04
Desiccant & cotton wool depositors/inserters	10	1/1/04
Dropper & leaflet inserters	10	1/1/04
Flaming stations	10	1/1/04
Flow wrappers & shrink wrappers	10	1/1/04
Ink jet batch label printers	7	1/1/04
Labelling machines	10	1/1/04
Palletisers	10	1/1/04
Pinhole inspectors	10	1/1/04
Robotic pick & place packaging machines	10	1/1/04
Sleevers	10	1/1/04
Tablet/capsule fillers, feeders & counters	10	1/1/04
Production assets:		
Autoclaves (for terminal sterilisation)	10	1/1/04
Drying ovens	10	1/1/04
Encapsulators	10	1/1/04
Fluid bed dryers	12	1/1/04
Granulators & mixer/granulators	12	1/1/04
Homogenisers	7	1/1/04
Intermediate bulk containers, bins & vessels (including instruments, pipes, pumps & valves) used to hold & transfer formulations during various stages of production	10	1/1/04
Metal detectors	10	1/1/04
Mixers & blenders (including cream, liquid, powder, & syrup mixers & blenders)	10	1/1/04
Sizing mills	10	1/1/04
Tablet & capsule coating machines, coating drums & coating pans	12	1/1/04
Tablet dedusters	10	1/1/04
Tablet presses	10	1/1/04
Vibrating sieves	10	1/1/04
Raw material storage & dispensing assets:		
Demountable strong rooms	20	1/1/04
Dispensing booths & associated air filtration systems	10	1/1/04
Laminar flow benches & biohazard cabinets	8	1/1/04
Safes	20	1/1/04
Weighing scales	10	1/1/04
Scientific medical & pharmaceutical research assets – see Table A Scientific research services		
Services:		
Air filtration systems	10	1/1/04
Water purification plant	10	1/1/04

Asset	Life (yrs)	Date of application
CLEANING COMPOUND & TOILETRY PREPARATION MANUFACTURING		
Boot & shoe polish manufacturing plant	13¹/₃	1/1/01
OTHER BASIC CHEMICAL PRODUCT MANUFACTURING		
Eucalyptus oil plant:		
Stills (coolers)	40	1/1/01
Tanks	40	1/1/01
Explosives manufacturing & chemical plant (excl ammonia manufacturing assets & ammonium nitrate manufacturing assets listed in Table A		
Basic chemical & chemical product manufacturing	13¹/₃	1/1/01
POLYMER FILM & SHEET PACKAGING MATERIAL MANUFACTURING		
Extrusion assets:		
Extruder dies	15	1/7/14
Extruders & co-extruders (incorporating barrels, screws, towers & treatment units, but excluding dies)	20	1/7/14
Heat exchangers	15	1/7/14
Laminating machines	20	1/7/14
Packaging assets:		
Labelling machines	7	1/7/14
Palletisers	12	1/7/14
Wrapping machines (including shrink & stretch wrappers)	10	1/7/14
Pouch & bag making machines	10	1/7/14
Printing assets – see Table A Printing		
Racking machines	25	1/7/14
Recycling machines	10	1/7/14
Resin preparation assets (including hoppers mixers/blenders & weigh batchers)	15	1/7/14
Slitting machines & perforation units	15	1/7/14
Support assets:		
Air compressors & receivers	15	1/7/14
Boilers	20	1/7/14
Control system assets (including control cabinets & panels, programmable logic controllers (PLCs), switchgear & variable speed drives (VSDs))	10	1/7/14
Jib cranes	15	1/7/14
Laboratory assets:		
Generally	15	1/7/14
Laboratory analysers	10	1/7/14
Silos	25	1/7/14
Vacuum transfer system assets (incorporating blowers, ductwork, fans & pumps)	10	1/7/14
POLYMER PRODUCT & RUBBER PRODUCT MANUFACTURING		
Clothes peg manufacturing plant (plastic)	13¹/₃	1/1/01
Gelatine & glue manufacturing plant	13¹/₃	1/1/01
Polymer (plastic) product manufacturing assets (not elsewhere listed):		
Blow moulders	13¹/₃	1/1/01
Dies	4	1/1/01
General plant	20	1/1/01
Hydraulic presses, injection moulding machines, extrusion machines & bottle blowing machines	13¹/₃	1/1/01
Moulds:		
Glass blowing	2	1/1/01
High usage	5	1/1/01
Low usage	10	1/1/01
Once only	1	1/1/01
Rubber manufacturers' plant:		
Moulds	5	1/1/01
Process plant	13¹/₃	1/1/01
PAINT & COATINGS MANUFACTURING		
Ink factory plant	20	1/1/01
Paint & coatings manufacturing assets:		
Air compressors	10	1/7/13
Bead mills	20	1/7/13
Bulk storage tanks	25	1/7/13
Control system assets	10	1/7/13
Disperser & mixer motors	15	1/7/13
Dispersers	20	1/7/13
Dust collectors & fume extracting assets (including bag dust collectors, blowers, cyclones & fans)	20	1/7/13
Filling & packing assets:		
Conveyors	15	1/7/13

Asset	Life (yrs)	Date of application
Denesters	10	1/7/13
Filling machines	15	1/7/13
Filtration assets	15	1/7/13
Labellers (including laser coders & label applicators)	7	1/7/13
Printers	7	1/7/13
Robotic palletisers	10	1/7/13
Wrappers	10	1/7/13
Gantry cranes	25	1/7/13
Hoists	10	1/7/13
Mixers	20	1/7/13
Paint tinting & colour blending machines (manual & automatic)	7	1/7/14
Piping assets:		
Manifolds	20	1/7/13
Meters	10	1/7/13
Piping	25	1/7/13
Pumps	10	1/7/13
Racking:		
External	15	1/7/13
Internal	20	1/7/13
Scales	10	1/7/13
Spray booths	15	1/7/13
Testing assets:		
Air conditioning assets (incl room units & split systems)	8	1/7/13
Gloss meters	10	1/7/13
Ovens	15	1/7/13
Spectrometers	10	1/7/13
Viscometers	10	1/7/13
Vacuum lifters	10	1/7/13
GLASS & GLASS PRODUCT MANUFACTURING		
Container glass & flat (float) glass manufacturing assets:		
Ancillary assets:		
Blowers & fans	25	1/7/08
Conveyors generally (incl bottle conveyors, bucket elevators, pallet transport conveyors & pneumatic conveyors)	25	1/7/08
Ducting, pipes & piping	40	1/7/08
Steelwork structures (including gantries, platforms & walkways)	40	1/7/08
Vacuum pumps:		
Liquid ring pumps	10	1/7/08
Oil sealed pumps	20	1/7/08
Annealing lehrs	25	1/7/08
Batch house assets:		
Cullet handling & return assets:		
Cullet crushers	25	1/7/08
Scraping conveyor systems:		
Container glass	12	1/7/08
Flat glass	25	1/7/08
Other assets (incl batch conveyors, batch mixers, bins, hoppers & weigh hoppers)	25	1/7/08
Silos	40	1/7/08
Coating assets (cold & hot end)	12	1/7/08
Control systems (excluding personal computers)	10	1/7/08
Flat glass ribbon cutting assets (including cross cutters, longitudinal cutters & snap rolls)	25	1/7/08
Float baths	25	1/7/08
Forehearths	12	1/7/08
Forming machines (incorporating shearing & distribution systems)	12	1/7/08
Glass furnace assets:		
Batch chargers	12	1/7/08
Exhaust stacks:		
Brick lined	40	1/7/08
Steel	12	1/7/08
Furnace support assets (including bubbler systems & electro boost systems)	12	1/7/08
Furnace tanks	12	1/7/08
Regenerators & recuperators	12	1/7/08
Glass product handling & packaging assets (including case packers, flat glass lifters & stackers, palletisers, strapping machines, shrink wrappers, stretch wrappers & trolley shuttle cars)	12	1/7/08
Inspection assets	10	1/7/08
Lehr stackers	12	1/7/08
Moulds	2	1/7/08
Glass product manufacturing assets:		
Automotive glass product manufacturing assets:		

Asset	Life (yrs)	Date of application
CNC controlled edgers & grinders	15	1/7/09
CNC controlled scorers & cutters	15	1/7/09
Inspection assets:		
Automotive laminated glass product inspection assets (including automated distortion checking assets & conveyors)..	15	1/7/09
Automotive toughened glass product inspection assets (including thermal imaging testing assets)	10	1/7/09
Post processing assets used in automotive laminated glass production & toughened glass production processes:		
Automated back window soldering units .	10	1/7/09
Others including conveyor handling assets, encapsulation presses, hot melt adhesive applicators, robots & tooling	15	1/7/09
CNC machines	7	1/7/09
Control systems (excluding personal computers) ..	10	1/7/09
Cutting tables:		
Automated cutting & break out tables.......	10	1/7/09
Laminated glass cutting tables	10	1/7/09
Manual cutting tables (incl air float tables) ...	15	1/7/09
Digital printing assets:		
Digital printers	5	1/7/09
Dryers	12½	1/7/09
Double glazing assets (including butyl coating machines, conveyors, presses, sealing machines & spacer robots)	15	1/7/09
Drilling &/or milling machines (incl horizontal & vertical drilling machines)...............	10	1/7/09
Edgers:		
Arrissing machines....................	8	1/7/09
Horizontal double edgers	10	1/7/09
Straight line edgers & bevellers.	7	1/7/09
Glass handling & storage assets:		
Automated loaders & unloaders (used with automated cutting tables, laminating lines, toughening lines etc)....................	10	1/7/09
Bulk glass handling assets:		
Straddle carriers	10	1/7/09
Vertical glass handlers (sideloaders, tuning forks)	17	1/7/09
Cranes (gantry & overhead)...............	25	1/7/14
Racks (including A frame racks, hydraulic concertina racks & freefall racks)	20	1/7/09
Steel grabs.........................	12	1/7/09
Trolleys	7	1/7/09
Vacuum lifters & scissor grabs	8	1/7/09
Vertical masts & other elevating work platforms - see Table A Rental & hiring services (except real estate), elevating work platforms (EWPs)		
Glass laminating assets (including assembly clean room assets, autoclaves, heaters, laminating lehr furnaces, ovens, pre presses, presses & vacuum bag furnacoo)	15	1/7/09
Glass toughening (tempering) assets:		
Furnaces & quenches used in toughening, bending/toughening & bending/slumping	20	1/7/09
Heat soaking ovens....................	20	1/7/09
Glass washing machines	10	1/7/09
Plastic film applicators (spotstick machines)	8	1/7/09
Screen printing assets – see Table A Printing		
Support assets:		
Air compressors	20	1/7/14
Boilers	20	1/7/14
Waterjet cutting machines	10	1/7/09

NON METALLIC MINERAL PRODUCT MANUFACTURING

Asset	Life (yrs)	Date of application
Monumental masons' plant....................	13⅓	1/1/01
Slate works plant	20	1/1/01

CERAMIC PRODUCT MANUFACTURING

Note: Determinations for assets used in mining clay are shown under the Construction material mining sub-category

Asset	Life (yrs)	Date of application
Clay brick & paver manufacturing assets:		
Box feeders	20	1/7/11
Control systems	10	1/7/11
Conveyors	20	1/7/11
Cutters	15	1/7/11
De hackers (excluding robots)	20	1/7/11

Asset	Life (yrs)	Date of application
Dryers	25	1/7/11
Extruders	15	1/7/11
Kiln/dryer car cable hauler system assets (incorporating cable, gearbox, pulling wheels & motors)	10	1/7/11
Kiln/dryer/transfer car track work	12	1/7/11
Kiln/dryer cars	10	1/7/11
Kilns	20	1/7/11
Robots	10	1/7/11
Setting assets (excluding robots)	20	1/7/11
Transfer cars	15	1/7/11
Wrapping & strapping machines	10	1/7/11
Pottery plant	20	1/1/01
Rapid fire shuttle kilns (used in the manufacture of ceramic tiles)	13⅓	1/1/01

CEMENT MANUFACTURING

Asset	Life (yrs)	Date of application
Cooling assets:		
Air to air coolers	20	1/7/11
Evaporation coolers:		
Cement coolers..................	20	1/7/11
Conditioning towers (incorporating spray systems).....................	20	1/7/11
Grate coolers (incorporating grate conveyor & quenching fans)	25	1/7/11
Drying assets:		
Fluid bed dryers.....................	20	1/7/11
Hot gas generators	15	1/7/11
Rotary dryers.......................	20	1/7/11
Electrical installation assets (including cabling):		
Power generators	15	1/7/11
Switchboards.......................	20	1/7/11
Transformers.......................	20	1/7/11
Emissions control assets:		
Dedusting fans	20	1/7/11
Particulate filtering assets (excluding filter units incorporated in kiln bypass systems):		
Bagfilter systems (incorporating housing & filters)	20	1/7/11
Electrostatic precipitators	20	1/7/11
Stacks (excluding stacks incorporated in kiln bypass systems)......................	25	1/7/11
Milling assets (used for raw material & cement milling including gearbox & drives):		
Ball mills (including dryer systems & separators/classifiers where incorporated in the mill)	25	1/7/11
Hammer mills (including dryer systems & separators/classifiers where incorporated in the mill)	20	1/7/11
Roller mills (vertical) (including dryer systems & separators/classifiers where incorporated in the mill)	25	1/7/11
Roller presses	20	1/7/11
Separators/classifiers (including single & multi cyclones).........................	15	1/7/11
Preheat & clinker production assets:		
Cyclone preheaters (incorporating tower structure, lifts, cyclones, precalciners, ducts, inlet chambers & meal pipes)	20	1/7/11
Kilns (incorporating kiln shell, inlet chamber, roller stations, thrust unit, kiln hood, burner & drive)....	25	1/7/11
Kiln bypass systems (incorporating bypass ducts, heat exchangers, spray towers, filter units, ID fans & stacks)......................	10	1/7/11
Kiln guns	5	1/7/11
Kiln shell scanners....................	10	1/7/11
Quarrying assets:		
Construction material mining assets – see Table A Construction material mining		
Scrapers	7	1/7/11
Storage, handling & packing assets:		
Conveyor systems (mechanical & pneumatic types incorporating structures, moving media, gearboxes, motors, fans, feeders, flowgates, feed valves & weighers):		
Mechanical:		
Belt, screw, drag chain, apron/pan conveyors	15	1/7/11
Bucket elevators	20	1/7/11
Pneumatic:		

Asset	Life (yrs)	Date of application
Air lift elevators	15	1/7/11
Air slides	15	1/7/11
Hoppers, bins & tanks	20	1/7/11
Packaging assets:		
Packing/bagging machines	15	1/7/11
Palletisers	15	1/7/11
Wrappers	10	1/7/11
Pressure vessels (other than air/shock blast units)	25	1/7/11
Silos:		
Concrete, generally	50	1/1/04
Concrete (used for gypsum or wetslag, or at port facilities)	40	1/1/04
Steel, generally	30	1/1/04
Steel (used for gypsum or wet slag, or at port facilities)	20	1/1/04
Stockpile assets:		
Reclaim tunnels	25	1/7/11
Reclaimers	25	1/7/11
Stackers	25	1/7/11
Unloading/loading assets:		
Bulk loading devices (including loading spouts & telescopic chutes)	10	1/7/11
Railcar & truck unloaders (including pump unloading & vacuum pressure unloading systems)	20	1/7/11
Ship unloading/loading assets – see Table A Water transport & support services		
Weighbridges	20	1/7/11
Support assets:		
Air compression assets:		
Packaged air compressors (compressor, drier & receiver in one integrated unit)	10	1/7/11
Other air compressor systems	15	1/7/11
Air/shock blast units	8	1/7/11
Control systems (process & safety control systems incorporating PLCs, cabling, monitors, sensors & switchgear, but excluding software)	10	1/7/11
Cranes	20	1/7/11
Hoists	20	1/7/11
ID (induced draught) fans	15	1/7/11
Pumps	15	1/7/11
Testing equipment:		
Generally (including spectrometers, gas chromatographs, titrators, calorimeters, laser granulometers, photometers, moisture analysers, drying ovens)	8	1/7/11
Raw material analysers	5	1/7/11
XRF/XRD analysers	5	1/7/11

PLASTER PRODUCT MANUFACTURING

Asset	Life (yrs)	Date of application
Plasterboard & cornice manufacturing assets:		
General:		
Bins	20	1/7/11
Control systems	10	1/7/11
Conveyors (including belt conveyors, belt stacker conveyors, bucket elevators & screw conveyors)	20	1/7/11
Dust collection assets (including bag dust collectors, blowers, cyclones & fans)	20	1/7/11
Dust detectors	5	1/7/11
Fans/blowers (excluding blowers used with hot pits)	20	1/7/11
Feeders	15	1/7/11
Flow meters	10	1/7/11
Hoppers	20	1/7/11
Lump breakers	20	1/7/11
Pumps	10	1/7/11
Rotary valves	15	1/7/11
Silos (steel)	20	1/7/11
Tanks	20	1/7/11
Plaster milling assets:		
Bulk bag handling assets	20	1/7/11
Calciners	20	1/7/11
Grinding/hammer mills	20	1/7/11
Heat generators	15	1/7/11
Hot pits:		
Blowers	12	1/7/11
Vessels	20	1/7/11
Stucco coolers	20	1/7/11
Plasterboard/cornice plant assets:		
Chillers (volumetric air cooled)	15	1/7/11

Asset	Life (yrs)	Date of application
Dry end handling assets (including bookers, cascades, conveyors & stackers)	20	1/7/11
Dryers	25	1/7/11
Dunnage assets used to make dunnage	25	1/7/11
Forming line assets (including belt conveyors & roller conveyors)	20	1/7/11
Forming plates	10	1/7/11
Forming station assets (excluding forming plates & pin mixers)	20	1/7/11
Hydropulpers	25	1/7/11
Knives (used for plasterboard or cornice)	25	1/7/11
Paper & tape assets (including creasers, magazines, splicing assets, tape rollers, tension stations & unwinders)	20	1/7/11
Pin mixers	13	1/7/11
Printers	5	1/7/11
Start up pullers (used for cornice)	20	1/7/11
Wet end transfer assets (including conveyors, dryer in feeds, turners)	20	1/7/11

READY-MIXED CONCRETE MANUFACTURING

Asset	Life (yrs)	Date of application
Air compressors	10	1/7/14
Air dryers	10	1/7/14
Bins (including weigh bins, but excl concrete bins)	15	1/7/14
CCTV systems	5	1/7/14
Cement tankers (incorporating tank & trailer) - see Table B Motor vehicles & trailers, trailers having a gross vehicle mass greater than 4.5 tonnes		
Chillers	15	1/7/14
Control systems	10	1/7/14
Conveyors	20	1/7/14
Dust extraction systems	15	1/7/14
Fuel storage assets:		
Card reading systems	6	1/7/14
Dispensers (incorporating electronic circuitry, hoses, LCD displays, meters & nozzles)	10	1/7/14
Pumps	10	1/7/14
Tanks	25	1/7/14
Hoppers (including weigh hoppers)	15	1/7/14
Mixers used in wet ready-mixed plants	15	1/7/14
Mobile concrete batching plants (incorporating bins, conveyors, tanks, hoppers & trailers, but excluding demountable plant)	10	1/7/14
Silos	30	1/7/14
Slump stands	10	1/7/14
Testing assets:		
Concrete testers	10	1/7/14
Ovens	8	1/7/14
Truck transit mixers:		
Mixers (incorporating barrel, chutes, frame & hydraulic pumps)	5	1/7/14
Trucks - see Table B Motor vehicles & trailers		
Volumetric concrete batching trucks:		
Trucks - see Table B Motor vehicles & trailers		
Volumetric concrete batching units (incorporating bins, hoppers, mixing augurs & water tanks)	10	1/7/14
Waste water treatment assets:		
Catchment & settlement ponds	20	1/7/14
Concrete slurry pumps	3	1/7/14
Polyethylene water tanks	8	1/7/14
Water pumps	5	1/7/14

CONCRETE PRODUCT MANUFACTURING

Asset	Life (yrs)	Date of application
Concrete block, brick & paver manufacturing assets:		
Batching & mixing assets:		
Bins (excluding concrete bins)	15	1/7/11
Colour dosing assets	12	1/7/11
Colour tanks (incorporating stirrers)	15	1/7/11
Hoppers	15	1/7/11
Mixers	15	1/7/11
Block/brick/paver making assets:		
Block/brick/paver making machines	15	1/7/11
Moulds	5	1/7/11
Splitters	10	1/7/11
Curing assets:		
Boilers (including steam generators)	20	1/7/11
Drying chambers	25	1/7/11
Elevators/lowerators (including loaders/unloaders)	15	1/7/11
Racks (excluding racks fixed to drying chambers)	5	1/7/11

Asset	Life (yrs)	Date of application
Transfer car (incorporating finger cars) track works	15	1/7/11
Transfer cars (incorporating finger cars)	15	1/7/11
General assets:		
Control systems	10	1/7/11
Conveyors	15	1/7/11
Plates	10	1/7/11
Palletising & packaging assets:		
Cubing assets (including cubers, doublers & squeezers)	15	1/7/11
Robots	10	1/7/11
Wrapping & strapping machines	10	1/7/11
Concrete roof tile manufacturing assets:		
Air compressors (rotary screw)	10	1/7/12
Applicator batching assets (including hoppers, mixers & tanks, but excluding batching assets for anti-scuff hot glue/max applicators & oil applicators)	15	1/7/12
Applicators:		
Anti-scuff hot glue/wax	10	1/7/12
General (including colour, sealer & sheen)	20	1/7/12
Oil (excluding oil tanks)	10	1/7/12
Bins	15	1/7/12
Control systems	10	1/7/12
Conveyors	20	1/7/12
Curing assets:		
Boilers	20	1/7/12
Curing bays:		
Concrete	25	1/7/12
Foam sandwich (incorporating insulated panel walls, roof & doors)	10	1/7/12
Rackers/derackers (incl loaders/unloaders)	20	1/7/12
Racks (used in curing bays)	10	1/7/12
Depalleters	20	1/7/12
Extruders	15	1/7/12
Hoppers	15	1/7/12
Mixers	15	1/7/12
Oil tanks	30	1/7/12
Packaging assets:		
General (including collectors, compilers & cranes)	20	1/7/12
Robots	10	1/7/12
Shrink wrappers	10	1/7/12
Strapping assets	10	1/7/12
Wrapping assets	10	1/7/12
Plates:		
General	7	1/7/12
Trim (including plates used for barge & ridge tiles)	5	1/7/12
Fibre cement building boards manufacturing assets:		
Curing assets:		
Autoclaves (incorporating rails)	30	1/7/12
Boilers	20	1/7/12
Chargers (including traversers)	15	1/7/12
Trackwork	20	1/7/12
Trolley chain hauling systems (incorporating chains, gearboxes, motors & tappets)	15	1/7/12
Trolley transfer platforms (including transversals)	20	1/7/12
Trolleys (including trucks) used inside & outside autoclaves	10	1/7/12
Trolleys (including trucks) used only outside autoclaves	20	1/7/12
Tunnels (including steamers)	25	1/7/12
Finishing line & packaging assets:		
Applicators (including coating & sealing applicators)	7	1/7/12
Drying tunnels (including heating ovens)	10	1/7/12
Machining assets (including sanding & trimming assets)	15	1/7/12
Printers	5	1/7/12
Robots	10	1/7/12
General assets:		
Air compressors (rotary screw)	10	1/7/12
Control systems	10	1/7/12
Conveyors	20	1/7/12
Dust collection assets	20	1/7/12
Oil tanks	30	1/7/12
Stackers/unstackers (incl pilers/unpilers)	15	1/7/12
Steel templates	7	1/7/12
Manufacturing, trimming & pressing assets:		

Asset	Life (yrs)	Date of application
Cranes (used to load boards into presses & unload boards from presses)	15	1/7/12
Guillotines	20	1/7/12
Hatschek machines (including tub machines)	25	1/7/12
Presses	20	1/7/12
Scrap return assets (including pulpers & shredders)	15	1/7/12
Trimmers	20	1/7/12
Storage, preparation & mixing assets:		
Ball mills	25	1/7/12
Batching vessels (including feeding vessels) (excluding silica thickener vessels)	20	1/7/12
Classifiers (including cyclones)	15	1/7/12
Hoppers	20	1/7/12
Hydropulpers	20	1/7/12
Mixers	15	1/7/12
Refiners	20	1/7/12
Storage tanks (including silica thickener vessels)	25	1/7/12
Prefabricated concrete product manufacturing assets:		
Air compressors	10	1/7/13
Automated panel manufacturing assets:		
Automated trowel machines (incorporating crane & trowel)	15	1/7/13
Concrete distribution stations:		
Distributors	10	1/7/13
Flying buckets	10	1/7/13
Hoppers	15	1/7/13
Curing chambers	25	1/7/13
Laser beam alignment systems	10	1/7/13
Pallet cleaning machines	15	1/7/13
Pallet receivable stands (excluding pallet vibrating stands)	20	1/7/13
Pallet transport systems:		
Pallet drive mechanisms (incorporating drive units, motors, sensors & wheels)	10	1/7/13
Track work	20	1/7/13
Transversals (including continuous transfer wagons)	10	1/7/13
Pallet vibrating stands	10	1/7/13
Pallets	15	1/7/13
Rack feeders	15	1/7/13
Shutter cleaning machines	15	1/7/13
Shutter transporting assets (incl automated roller conveyors)	15	1/7/13
Shutters	8	1/7/13
Turning machines (incl flippers & tilting assets)	20	1/7/13
Buckets (including kibbles, skips & tippers)	6	1/7/13
Casting tables	10	1/7/13
Concrete manufacturing assets:		
Bins (excluding concrete bins)	15	1/7/13
Conveyors	20	1/7/13
Hoppers	15	1/7/13
Mixers	15	1/7/13
Concrete testers	10	1/7/13
Control system assets	10	1/7/13
Gantry cranes	25	1/7/13
Lifting gear (including chains, lugs & swivels)	7	1/7/13
Moulds	10	1/7/13
Pipe manufacturing assets:		
Cage machines	20	1/7/13
Load testers	25	1/7/13
Moulds	7	1/7/13
Pallets	15	1/7/13
Pipe making machines	20	1/7/13
Prestressing assets	10˙	1/7/13
Shutter saws	7	1/7/13
Steel cutters & benders	7	1/7/13
Trowel machines	4	1/7/13
Work tables	10	1/7/13
Silos	30	1/7/12
Tile manufacturing plant (cement & concrete, but excluding concrete roof tiles):		
General plant	10	1/1/01
Pallets (aluminium used in extrusion process)	5	1/1/01

IRON SMELTING & STEEL MANUFACTURING

Asset	Life (yrs)	Date of application
Assets used in common in iron smelting & steel manufacturing processes:		
Automated guided vehicles	20	1/7/10

Asset	Life (yrs)	Date of application
Closed circuit television (CCTV) systems	3	1/7/10
Coil cars including hydraulic sliding floor plates	13	1/7/10
Coil car tracks & rails	7	1/7/10
Control systems assets:		
Instruments (including temperature probes, control panels, gas analysers, location sensors, carbon monoxide monitors, pressure controls, temperature controls, pyrometers, strip position sensors, gamma ray detectors, hot metal detectors, x ray gauges, width gauges, thickness gauges)	7	1/7/10
Programmable logic controllers (PLCs) & distributed control systems (DCS)	10	1/7/10
Uninterruptible power supplies	5	1/7/10
Cranes & gantries	20	1/7/10
Electricity distribution, generation or transmission assets:		
Aerials or underground cables	30	1/7/10
Electronic protection relays	10	1/7/10
High voltage switchgear	25	1/7/10
Transformers	20	1/7/10
Use any relevant determinations made in Electricity supply for any other electricity distribution, generation or transmission assets		
Gasometers	30	1/7/10
Rail infrastructure & rolling stock except torpedo cars – use any relevant determinations made for Rail freight & passenger transport services		
Rolls for mill roll stands (including roughing mill rolls, finishing mill rolls & skin conditioning mill rolls)	2	1/7/10
Roller tables (incorporating gearboxes, motors, drives, rolls, table frames, aprons, side guards & foundations)	15	1/7/10
Scale or transfer car rail tracks & turntables	20	1/7/10
Scale or transfer cars (incorporating cable reel & drive units)	20	1/7/10
Ship ore unloaders	20	1/7/10
Slag processing assets:		
Crushers	20	1/7/10
Granulators	15	1/7/10
Slag pots	20	1/7/10
Slag pot carriers	10	1/7/10
Stacks including flare off stacks (incorporating burners & derricks)	20	1/7/10
Stackers, reclaimers, stacker/reclaimers & sequencers	25	1/7/10
Basic oxygen steelmaking (BOS) & electric arc furnace (EAF) steel making assets:		
BOS vessels (incorporating motors, gearboxes, bull gear, vessel, torsion bar, lube pumps, pulse generators, tacho generators, brakes, limit switches, pressure switches & support structures)	10	1/7/10
Desulphurising lances (incorporating masts, winch control boxes, hydraulic cylinders carriage system, motors, gearboxes, brake lance carriages, lance guides, lances & switches)	10	1/7/10
Electric arc furnaces (EAFs)	10	1/7/10
Electrode control arms	10	1/7/10
Emissions control assets:		
Baghouses	20	1/7/10
De-dusting ducts & mains	15	1/7/10
Electrostatic precipitators	15	1/7/10
Primary & secondary scrubbers (incorporating support structure & spray systems)	20	1/7/10
Waste gas radiation cooling systems (incorporating water sprays & ducts)	20	1/7/10
Waste gas extractor fans & silencers	20	1/7/10
Flux making assets:		
Kiln contact coolers (including agitator, agitator hydraulic system & rotary valves)	15	1/7/10
Kiln burner units (incorporating gas & firing systems)	15	1/7/10
Lime kiln discharge conveyors (incorporating structures, belts, pulleys, motors & gearboxes)	15	1/7/10
Lime kilns (incorporating rollers, tyres, support structures, drives, motors & gearboxes)	25	1/7/10
Raw material crushers & ball mills	15	1/7/10
Grinders (incorporating motors, drive pullies & belts, drive shafts, roller crusher units & whizzer separators)	15	1/7/10
Heat shielding for vessels incorporating supports	30	1/7/10
Hot metal pots	20	1/7/10
Lance pumps & motor assemblies	15	1/7/10
Liquid oxygen lances (incorporating carriage system, motors, gearboxes, brake lance carriages, lance guides, lances & switches)	10	1/7/10
Liquid oxygen supply pipes	10	1/7/10
Materials handling assets:		
Air blowers	15	1/7/10
Bins	20	1/7/10
Bucket elevators	20	1/7/10
Conveyor systems (incorporating structures, belts, gearboxes & motors)	20	1/7/10
Cyclones	10	1/7/10
Hoppers, weigh hoppers, chutes, silos	20	1/7/10
Scrap metal buckets, skips & stands	20	1/7/10
Screens & weighing systems	15	1/7/10
Vibro feeders	15	1/7/10
Vibrators	15	1/7/10
Weighbridges incorporating load cells	20	1/7/10
Pneumatic air tube systems (incorporating blower units)	20	1/7/10
Scull breakers	10	1/7/10
Secondary treatment assets:		
Composition adjustment stations (including Injection Reheating Up Temperature (IRUT) stations incorporating snorkels, support structures & motors)	20	1/7/10
Ladle metallurgical furnaces (LMFs)	20	1/7/10
Vacuum degassers (incorporating steam pumps & vacuum pumps)	10	1/7/10
Slag rakes	10	1/7/10
Steel ladles (incorporating tilting bales, thrusters, cassettes, shells, lids & linings)	20	1/7/10
Sub or sampling lances (incorporating motors, drives, gearboxes, limit switches, over speed switches, drums, cables & slow motors)	10	1/7/10
Water treatment assets:		
Cooling towers (incorporating fans, motors, access platforms & stairs)	20	1/7/10
Heat exchangers	10	1/7/10
Launder distribution & collection systems	15	1/7/10
Pipes & pipelines:		
Slurry disposal pipelines	15	1/7/10
Water pipes	20	1/7/10
Valves & other non pipe fittings	10	1/7/10
Pumps including slurry disposal pumps	15	1/7/10
Settling ponds	30	1/7/10
Tanks:		
Conditioner, slurry, polymer, liquid flocculants & mixer tanks	20	1/7/10
Water tanks	25	1/7/10
Thickeners & clarifiers (incorporating tanks, rakes & access platforms)	30	1/7/10
Blast furnace assets:		
Cast house assets:		
Cast house floor iron & slag runner systems, covers, & tilting spouts	5	1/7/10
Cast house structure	40	1/7/10
Common hydraulic systems	15	1/7/10
Manipulators	15	1/7/10
Mud guns	15	1/7/10
Taphole drills	15	1/7/10
Emissions control assets:		
Baghouses	20	1/7/10
Chimney mains	30	1/7/10
De-dusting ducts & mains	15	1/7/10
Dust catchers (incorporating supporting structures)	15	1/7/10
Excess gas bleeder systems	20	1/7/10
Furnace top recovery turbine systems (incorporating hydraulic system, inlet & outlet mains & valves)	20	1/7/10
Scrubbers (incorporating support structure & spray systems)	15	1/7/10
Uptakes, bleeders & platforms, downcomers, dust dumping, valves & hydraulics	15	1/7/10
Waste gas collector mains & ducts	15	1/7/10
Furnace proper assets:		

Asset	Life (yrs)	Date of application
Furnace charging tops (incorporating charging valves & hydraulics)	15	1/7/10
Furnace elevators	15	1/7/10
Furnace shells (incorporating hearths, refractory linings, staves, probes, profile meters & sondes)	15	1/7/10
Furnace support assets (incl maintenance platforms & control & switch rooms)	15	1/7/10
Furnace support structure (incorporating foundations)	40	1/7/10
Hot blast system assets:		
Cold blast mains (incorporating snorts & mixer valves)	15	1/7/10
Hot blast mains (incorporating bustle mains, back draught mains & tuyere stock)	15	1/7/10
Stoves (incorporating refractory, shell, foundations, fan & valves)	30	1/7/10
Stoves mixed gas main systems	15	1/7/10
Materials handling assets:		
Furnace charging bins	15	1/7/10
Furnace charging conveyor systems (incorporating structures, belts, gearboxes & motors)	20	1/7/10
Furnace charging skip hoist	20	1/7/10
Furnace charging skip tracks	30	1/7/10
Furnace charging skips	15	1/7/10
Screens & weighing systems	15	1/7/10
Torpedo cars	17	1/7/10
Water treatment assets:		
Basins	30	1/7/10
Cooling towers (incorporating fans, motors, access platforms & stairs)	20	1/7/10
Heat exchangers	10	1/7/10
Thickeners & clarifiers (incorporating tanks, rakes & access platforms)	30	1/7/10
Valves & other non pipe fittings	8	1/7/10
Water distribution systems	10	1/7/10
Water pumps	10	1/7/10
Coke making assets:		
Coal screening assets:		
Crushers	20	1/7/09
Hammer mills	15	1/7/09
Hydrowashers	20	1/7/09
Primary, secondary & tertiary screens & chutes	10	1/7/09
Coke ovens batteries assets:		
Breeze basins	30	1/7/09
Charging car rails	20	1/7/09
Charging cars	20	1/7/09
Coke ovens batteries (including ovens, doors, individual oven gas off takes from supply & extraction mains)	30	1/7/09
Coke ploughs	15	1/7/09
Coke transfer cars	25	1/7/09
Coke wharves (including concrete end barriers & skids)	30	1/7/09
Hot car spur lines	30	1/7/09
Hot cars incorporating locomotive, wagon, tray & bogies	15	1/7/09
Quenchers (incorporating stack structures, water tanks, pipes, pumps, sprays, pneumatic systems & water pump pits)	15	1/7/09
Ram tracks & live rails	30	1/7/09
Rams	30	1/7/09
Coke ovens gas by products assets:		
Acid compound assets:		
Acid compound structures, pumps, overflow & storage tanks	15	1/7/09
Ammonia absorbers (including pumps, ammonia storage tanks, & distribution pipes including valves)	15	1/7/09
Ammonia plant assets:		
Ammonia incinerators, ammonia stills, tanks, decanters, pumps, condensers (including support structures, stacks)	15	1/7/09
Benzine, toluene & xylene plant assets:		
Distillation columns, dephlegorators, pumps, tanks, coolers, condensers & pre heaters	30	1/7/09
Benzol scrubbers (including pumps & distribution pipe work including valves)	35	1/7/09
Exhausters (including support structures & hydraulic systems)	5	1/7/09
Final coolers	35	1/7/09
Napthalene plant assets:		
Sludge tanks, pre heaters, distillation columns, tanks, decanters, condensers, & pumps	35	1/7/09
Primary cooler assets:		
Electric & steam pumps, tar tanks, strainers, salt water coolers (including supporting structures & distribution pipes to cooler off takes including valves)	40	1/7/09
Sulphate plant assets:		
Feed tanks, evaporators, centrifuge units, conveyors (including belts, structures, drives & chutes, jet condensers, hot water tanks, driers including chutes, drives, & support structures, pumps, vibrating screens, cyclones, & scraper conveyors)	10	1/7/09
Tar plant assets:		
Decanters, make tanks (incorporating scrapers & drives, storage tanks, steam & electric pumps, liquor tank & strainers)	15	1/7/09
Tar precipitators	20	1/7/09
Emissions control assets:		
Waste gas cleaning & dedusting assets:		
Baghouses	20	1/7/09
Dedusting fans (including extraction dusting incorporating gearboxes & drives)	20	1/7/09
Dust collection systems, dust drop out boxes & dust disposal rotary valves (incorporating motors & gearboxes)	20	1/7/09
Fume extraction hoods	20	1/7/09
Waste gas collector mains & ducts	25	1/7/09
Materials handling assets:		
Bins (including furnace coke, dust disposal bins)	20	1/7/09
Conveyor systems (incorporating structures, belts, gearboxes & motors)	15	1/7/09
Conveyor systems transfer houses	15	1/7/09
Feed bunkers	15	1/7/09
Motorised feeders	15	1/7/09
Water treatment assets:		
Cooling towers incorporating fans, motors, access platforms & stairs	25	1/7/09
Hot strip mill assets:		
Coil & slab weighers	15	1/7/10
Coil box & crop shear assets:		
Coil boxes (incorporating side guard drives & transfer mechanism assemblies)	8	1/7/10
Coil box shear & scale breakers	17	1/7/10
Crop shears (incorporating assemblies & main drive motors)	17	1/7/10
Crop shear maintenance jigs & pinch rolls	15	1/7/10
Transfer bed oxy cutting stations	15	1/7/10
Coil handling assets:		
Cooling tunnel ventilation fans	10	1/7/10
Cooling tunnel conveyors	13	1/7/10
Marking machines	15	1/7/10
De scaling systems (incorporating scale breakers, nozzles, pipe works, valves & high pressure pumps)	10	1/7/10
Down coiler assets including coilers (incorporating side guards, mandrel, mandrel drives, wrappers & unit roll drives)	15	1/7/10
Finishing mill assets:		
Finishing mill flumes	20	1/7/10
Finishing mills (incorporating mill stands, side guides, strippers, screw downs, drive shafts, pinion boxes, main drive motors, transformers, loopers, grease systems, oil circulation systems, & hydraulic systems)	20	1/7/10
Laminar flow cooling systems	15	1/7/10
Mill roll shop assets:		
Bearing washing machines	10	1/7/10
Chuck changers	15	1/7/10
Floor plate or checker plate machines	15	1/7/10
Roll grinders	15	1/7/10
Roll lathes	20	1/7/10
Roll racks & sleds	20	1/7/10
Reversing roughing mill assets:		

Asset	Life (yrs)	Date of application
Reversing roughing mills (incorporating mill stands, entry side guards, delivery side guards, main drive motors & hydraulic systems)	20	1/7/10
Vertical edgers (incorporating drive motors, gearboxes & edger adjustments)	20	1/7/10
Roll changing assets	20	1/7/10
Scale scrapers	15	1/7/10
Skin pass mill assets:		
Skin pass mills (incorporating mill entry assets,gap control & auxiliary hydraulics, main drive motors, payoff reel, un coiler mandrels & re coiler mandrels)	20	1/7/10
Tension reels & belt wrappers	15	1/7/10
Laser systems mill entry	5	1/7/10
Slab tracking systems	5	1/7/10
Strapping machines (including radial & circumferential)	13	1/7/10
Walking beam furnace assets:		
Air dilution manifolds	20	1/7/10
Air ducts	10	1/7/10
Coke ovens gas systems	15	1/7/10
Cold combustion air systems	20	1/7/10
Dilution blowers	10	1/7/10
Extractors	10	1/7/10
Furnaces (incorporating structure, charging machines with synchronising drive trains, refractories, walking beam floors, furnace hydraulic systems, & charge & discharge doors)	20	1/7/10
Nitrogen purge systems	15	1/7/10
Tracking lasers (incorporating cables & adapters)	5	1/7/10
Pellet making assets:		
Balling assets:		
Balling drums	20	1/7/10
Bentonite tanks	20	1/7/10
Mixers	20	1/7/10
Seed screens	10	1/7/10
Cooler assets:		
Cooler fans	10	1/7/10
Annular coolers (incorporating pans, pan conveyors & drives)	25	1/7/10
Roller screens	10	1/7/10
Dewatering assets:		
Launders	20	1/7/10
Pressure filter pumps	5	1/7/10
Process water tanks	20	1/7/10
Return water pipes	20	1/7/10
Slurry feed pipes	10	1/7/10
Slurry pumps	10	1/7/10
Slurry tanks incorporating agitators	15	1/7/10
Sumps	20	1/7/10
Thickeners (incorporating tanks, rakes & access platforms)	20	1/7/10
Vertical plate pressure filters (incorporating filters, plates, membranes, water sprays, ladders, bomb bay doors)	20	1/7/10
Emissions control assets:		
Compressors	20	1/7/10
Dust collection system	20	1/7/10
Multi cone	20	1/7/10
Scrubbers	20	1/7/10
Waste gas collector mains & ducts	20	1/7/10
Waste gas extractor fans	20	1/7/10
Fluxing tanks	20	1/7/10
Grinding mills	15	1/7/10
Induration assets:		
Kiln burner units (incorporating gas & firing systems)	15	1/7/10
Rotary kilns (incorporating bearings, drive gear & drive system)	30	1/7/10
Travelling grates (incorporating motors, gearboxes or drives & rollers)	30	1/7/10
Waste heat recovery ducts	15	1/7/10
Waste heat recovery fans	10	1/7/10
Materials handling assets:		
Conveyor systems (incorporating structures, belts, gearboxes & motors):		
Conveyors to & from balling drums	20	1/7/10
Filter cake conveyors	20	1/7/10
Finished pellet conveyor	20	1/7/10

Asset	Life (yrs)	Date of application
Flux bins	20	1/7/10
Roller feeders	10	1/7/10
Table feeders	10	1/7/10
Vibrating feeders	10	1/7/10
Weigh feeders	10	1/7/10
Plate mill assets:		
Cold levellers (incorporating motor, gearbox spindles, hydraulic traverse cylinders, fill in table rolls, motor, gearbox, rolls & catenaries)	30	1/7/10
De scaling boxes (incorporating sprays, mechanicals, control valves pipe work after isolation valves, de scaling box table rolls, tables, chains, covers, side guides & covers)	10	1/7/10
Edgers (incorporating motors, hydraulic controls, mechanical controls, anvil (carryover table), hand rails & walkways)	20	1/7/10
Furnace entry skids	20	1/7/10
Furnaces (incorporating slab pushers, bumpers, pyrometers, off takes from king valve to outlets & all structures & equipment from after entry skids up to & including circular apron skids)	20	1/7/10
Hot levellers (incorporating motors, gearboxes, spindles, rolls, leveller AGC capsules, screws, crowning device, de scaling header & valves)	20	1/7/10
Inter roll stand cooling sprays	15	1/7/10
Reversing finishing mill (incorporating housing, side guides & covers, guards, motors, drives, spindles, water sprays, gearboxes, screw down, spindles, AGC capsules, hydraulics, mill de scaling, filler plates, & oil systems within the mill)	20	1/7/10
Reversing roughing mill (incorporating housing, side guides & covers, guards, motors, drives, spindles, water sprays, gearboxes, screw down, spindles, AGC capsules, hydraulics, mill de scaling, filler plates, & oil systems within the mill)	20	1/7/10
Rope driven cooling transfer bed	20	1/7/10
Shears (including crop, divide, scrap, rotary trim, guillotine & end shears)	20	1/7/10
Slab sizing systems (incorporating side guard measuring devices & stands, slab sizing unit supports, cameras & light banks)	5	1/7/10
Turnover inspection table (incorporating barriers & hydraulics)	20	1/7/10
Walking beam cooling beds incorporating carry on section, carry off section, moving (walking) section, chain drives & hydraulics	20	1/7/10
Primary metal product casting assets:		
Continuous casting machines (incorporating turrets, tundishes (incorporating lids & cassettes), tundish cars, moulds, dummy bars, segments, oscillators, rolls, water sprays, hydraulics, motors & gearboxes):		
Billet casters	17	1/7/10
Combination casters	17	1/7/10
Slab casters	17	1/7/10
Cooler transfer arms (incorporating motors, gearboxes & drive shafts)	17	1/7/10
Crop removal machines	20	1/7/10
Cut to length machines & torch cutters	15	1/7/10
De burring machines incorporating fixed drives	15	1/7/10
Emissions control assets:		
Baghouses	20	1/7/10
Dedusting fans (including extraction dusting incorporating gearboxes & drives)	15	1/7/10
Dedusting ducts & mains	15	1/7/10
Steam exhaust fans	10	1/7/10
Hydraulic shears	17	1/7/10
Materials handling assets:		
Conveyor systems (including structures, belts, gearboxes & motors)	20	1/7/10
Mould powder bins	23	1/7/10
Screw feeders	15	1/7/10
Scarfing machines (incorporating catenary system of hoses, power supply cables & support structures)	20	1/7/10
Slab or billet cooler tanks (incorporating grid stands)	30	1/7/10
Slab or billet marking machines	17	1/7/10
Transfer beds	17	1/7/10
Up enders including hydraulics	17	1/7/10
Walking beam cooling beds & run out tables	17	1/7/10

Asset	Life (yrs)	Date of application
Water treatment assets:		
Basins & ponds	30	1/7/10
Cooling towers (incorporating fans, motors, access platforms & stairs)	20	1/7/10
Gravel & sand filters	25	1/7/10
Heat exchangers	10	1/7/10
Pipelines:		
Water pipelines	20	1/7/10
Valves & other non pipe fittings	10	1/7/10
Pumps:		
Water pumps	10	1/7/10
Chemical dosing pumps	5	1/7/10
Skimmers & scrapers	15	1/7/10
Tanks:		
Sludge, chemical storage & dosing tanks	20	1/7/10
Water tanks	25	1/7/10
Thickeners & clarifiers (incorporating tanks, rakes & access platforms)	30	1/7/10
Rod, bar, structural & rail mill assets:		
Controlled tempering quenching cars	10	1/7/10
Cut to length machines	17	1/7/10
De scaling systems (incorporating scale breaker, nozzles, pipe work, valves & high pressure pump)	10	1/7/10
Finishing mills (incorporating motors, gearboxes, drives, guides & cassettes)	20	1/7/10
Furnace charging skids	20	1/7/10
Intermediate mills (incorporating motors, gearboxes, drives, guides & cassettes)	20	1/7/10
Reversing roughing mills (incorporating motors, gearboxes, drives, guides & cassettes)	20	1/7/10
Roughing mills (incorporating motors, gearboxes, drives, guides & cassettes)	20	1/7/10
Shears incorporating motors & drives	17	1/7/10
Stacker/bundlers	12	1/7/10
Straighteners	20	1/7/10
Walking beam cooling beds	20	1/7/10
Walking beam, natural gas furnaces (incorporating structure, refractories, walking beam floors, furnace hydraulic systems, & charge & discharge doors)	20	1/7/10
Sinter making assets:		
Cooler assets:		
Cooler fans	10	1/7/09
Coolers (incorporating pan conveyors & drives)	25	1/7/09
Emissions control assets:		
Waste gas cleaning & dedusting assets:		
Activated carbon packed bed filters	15	1/7/09
Dedusting fans	10	1/7/09
Electrostatic precipitators & scraper chains	20	1/7/09
Waste gas collector mains & ducts	20	1/7/09
Feed sequence assets:		
Feed rolls	7	1/7/09
Mixing & rolling drums	30	1/7/09
Materials handling assets:		
Belt weighers	5	1/7/09
Bins:		
Coke bins	15	1/7/09
Ore bins	23	1/7/09
Sinter bins	17	1/7/09
Chutes	15	1/7/09
Conveyor systems (incorporating structures, belts, gearboxes & motors)	17	1/7/09
Feeders:		
Coke	15	1/7/09
Ore	23	1/7/09
Sinter	17	1/7/09
Weigh feeders:		
Coke	15	1/7/09
Ore	23	1/7/09
Strand assets:		
Ignition furnaces (incorporating associated air & gas mains)	15	1/7/09
Preheat hoods (incorporating waste heat recovery fans & mains)	7	1/7/09
Spike roll crushers (incorporating bogey flex, electric motors, primary gearboxes, fluid couplings, grillage bars & crash decks)	10	1/7/09
Strand structures & drives (including conveyors, wind legs & dust troughs)	20	1/7/09
Water treatment assets:		

Asset	Life (yrs)	Date of application
Thickeners & clarifiers (incorporating tanks, rakes & access platforms)	30	1/7/09
Steel railway track product manufacturing assets:		
Steel railway clip manufacturing assets:		
Anti corrosion dip tanks	20	1/7/11
Coil transfer arms incorporating motors, gearboxes & drive shafts	15	1/7/11
End spades	20	1/7/11
Gas temper furnaces	20	1/7/11
Induction heaters	20	1/7/11
Noise reduction enclosures	30	1/7/11
Presses	20	1/7/11
Quench systems incorporating heat exchangers, transfer arms, tanks, pipes & pumps	20	1/7/11
Shears	20	1/7/11
Tooling	15	1/7/11
Transfer systems incorporating flat bed transfer table	30	1/7/11
Quality control test rigs	30	1/7/11
Materials handling assets:		
Conveyor systems	20	1/7/11
Hoppers	20	1/7/11
Racks for storage	20	1/7/11
Weigh scales	15	1/7/11
Water treatment assets:		
Cooling towers	20	1/7/11
Pumps	10	1/7/11
Tanks	20	1/7/11
Steel railway sleeper manufacturing assets:		
Crop shear & presses	20	1/7/11
Form presses	20	1/7/11
Punch presses	20	1/7/11
Steel strip metallic coating assets:		
Accumulators (incorporating rolls, drive gear, winches & rope)	17	1/7/10
Air knife assemblies	13	1/7/10
Crop shears	17	1/7/10
Curing ovens	15	1/7/10
Horizontal air coolers (incorporating ducting fans & nozzles)	15	1/7/10
Horizontal furnaces	20	1/7/10
Levellers (incorporating gearboxes & drives)	15	1/7/10
Metal coating pots	15	1/7/10
Passivators (incorporating tanks & pumps)	17	1/7/10
Payoff reels	15	1/7/10
Pot hardware (incorporating zinc roll frames & roll assemblies)	13	1/7/10
Pre melt pots	5	1/7/10
Quench systems (incorporating rolls, spray bars & tanks)	10	1/7/10
Re coilers	15	1/7/10
Resin coaters	15	1/7/10
Scrapers	13	1/7/10
Skin conditioning mills (incorporating entry & exit tension rolls)	20	1/7/10
Steering rolls & bridles (incorporating motors, gearboxes & rolls)	15	1/7/10
Vertical air coolers (incorporating ducting, fans & motors)	15	1/7/10
Vertical preheat furnaces	15	1/7/10
Welders	17	1/7/10
Steel strip organic coating assets:		
Accumulators (incorporating rolls, drive gear, winches & rope)	17	1/7/10
Banders	15	1/7/10
Branders	10	1/7/10
Chemical rinsing, cleaning & pre treatment assets	15	1/7/10
Cooler & cooling assets	15	1/7/10
Curing ovens	15	1/7/10
Finishing assets	15	1/7/10
Inspection assets	17	1/7/10
Payoff reels	15	1/7/10
Primer & main coaters	13	1/7/10
Quench systems	10	1/7/10
Re coilers	15	1/7/10
Shears	15	1/7/10
Stitchers	17	1/7/10
Tin plating mill assets:		
Accumulators & loopers	17	1/7/11

Asset	Life (yrs)	Date of application
Acid & alkaline cleaning baths including scrubbing units, rolls & electrical grids	13	1/7/11
Batch annealing assets:		
Annealing furnaces	6	1/7/11
Bases	4	1/7/11
Convector plates	4	1/7/11
Inner covers	4	1/7/11
Cold reduction mills	20	1/7/11
Continuous annealing furnaces	15	1/7/11
Crop shears	15	1/7/11
Dryers	15	1/7/11
Electro plating baths including scrubbing units, rolls & electrical grids	13	1/7/11
Pickling tanks including scrubbing units & rolls & electrical grids	13	1/7/11
Preheat furnaces	20	1/7/11
Recoilers, bridles & uncoilers	15	1/7/11
Rinse tanks	15	1/7/11
Side trimmers	15	1/7/11
Temper mills	20	1/7/11
Tension control system including steering	10	1/7/11
Welders	17	1/7/11

ALUMINA PRODUCTION

Asset	Life (yrs)	Date of application
Alumina manufacturing (including bauxite refining & calcined alumina manufacturing):		
Bauxite crushing & handling assets:		
Conveyors	30	1/1/03
Crushing assets	30	1/1/03
Screening assets	15	1/1/03
Stockpile reclaimers, stackers & stacker/reclaimers	30	1/1/03
Train loading assets (including conveyors, product bins & towers)	30	1/1/03
Bauxite residue disposal assets:		
Initial containment areas	20	1/1/01
Mudlakes	10	1/1/01
Calcination assets:		
Calciners & kilns	25	1/1/03
Generally (including alumina cooling assets, hydrate storage tanks & hydrate washing assets)	30	1/1/03
Clarification of liquor stream assets (including counter current washing tanks, flash tanks, lime burning assets, lime handling assets, lime slaking assets, settling tanks & other tanks & vessels)	30	1/1/03
Control systems assets	10	1/1/03
Digestion assets (including desilication tanks, digester vessels, flash tanks, heat exchangers, heaters, mills & trihydrate bauxite treatment assets)	30	1/1/03
Emissions control assets (including baghouse filters & electrostatic precipitators)	20	1/1/03
Filtration assets for hydrate & slurry (including filters used for clarification of liquor & filters used for coarse hydrate)	15	1/1/03
Pipework (including slurry pipes)	30	1/1/03
Precipitation assets (incl classification assets, cooling towers, crystallisation assets, heat exchangers, tanks & vessels)	30	1/1/03
Pumps	20	1/1/03
Steam raising & electrical infrastructure assets (including switchgear & transformers)	30	1/1/03

ALUMINIUM SMELTING

Asset	Life (yrs)	Date of application
Anode baking assets (including crucibles & furnaces)	20	1/1/03
Anode (green) pasting assets:		
Crushing assets	30	1/1/03
Mixing & forming assets	15	1/1/03
Screening assets	15	1/1/03
Anode rodding assets (including aluminium spray station assets, furnaces & metal casting assets)	20	1/1/03
Compressors	20	1/1/03
Control systems assets	10	1/1/03
Cranes & gantries (including cell tending machines)	20	1/1/03
Emissions control assets (including baghouse filters & electrostatic precipitators)	20	1/1/03
Materials handling assets:		
Anode transport vehicles & hot metal carriers	10	1/1/03
Generally (including conveyors, silos & stockpile reclaiming assets)	30	1/1/03

Asset	Life (yrs)	Date of application
Metal casting assets (including casting machines, casting wheels, crucibles, foam filters, furnaces, in line metal treatment assets, stacking machines & weighing machines)	20	1/1/03
Pot line/reduction line assets (excluding cell tending machines, cranes & gantries)	25	1/1/03
Pumps	20	1/1/03
Steam raising & electrical infrastructure assets:		
Generally (including switchgear & transformers)	30	1/1/03
Rectiformers	20	1/1/03

NON FERROUS METAL CASTING

Asset	Life (yrs)	Date of application
Metal casting assets (non ferrous eg aluminium, brass & magnesium):		
Cooling assets (incl tables, conveyors, towers)	15	1/1/04
Deodorising machines/fume extraction systems	15	1/7/13
Die casting machines (including high pressure, low pressure & gravity type machines)	15	1/1/04
Die tools (moulds used for casting)	4	1/1/04
Heating assets:		
Degassing assets	5	1/1/04
Furnaces (incl dosing, holding & melting)	15	1/1/04
Heat treatment baskets	5	1/1/04
Heat treatment ovens	20	1/1/04
Ingot pre heaters	20	1/1/04
Quenching tanks	20	1/1/04
Impregnation machines	10	1/7/13
Machining/finishing assets:		
Blast machines (including shot, sand, bead)	20	1/1/04
CNC lathes	10	1/1/04
CNC machining centres	10	1/1/04
CNC milling machines	10	1/1/04
Drilling machines	15	1/1/04
Linishing belt machines	10	1/1/04
Trim presses (hydraulic type & crank type)	15	1/1/04
Trim tools used in trim press machines	4	1/1/04
Vibrating machines (including rumbling & knock out machines)	10	1/1/04
Materials handling conveyors	10	1/1/04
Molten metal transfer ladles	3	1/1/04
Paint line conveyors	15	1/1/04
Robots	10	1/1/04
Sand casting assets:		
Core boxes	4	1/1/04
Core making machines (core blowers)	15	1/1/04
Gas generators for sand curing	15	1/1/04
Sand core dies	7	1/7/13
Sand core making machines	15	1/7/13
Testing assets:		
Co ordinate measurement machines	10	1/1/04
Leak & pressure testing machines	4	1/1/04
Spectrometers	10	1/1/04
X ray machines	15	1/1/04
Tinsmiths' plant	20	1/1/01

FABRICATED METAL PRODUCT MANUFACTURING

Asset	Life (yrs)	Date of application
Galvanising plant	10	1/1/01
Metal crushing plant (core fragmentised)	13$^{1}/_3$	1/1/01
Nail manufacturing plant	20	1/1/01
Saw making plant	20	1/1/01
Spring manufacturers' plant:		
Cooling furnaces	10	1/1/01
Power presses, rotary cambering, scale testing & scragging machines	20	1/1/01
Tank manufacturing plant	20	1/1/01

STEEL COIL ROLL FORMING, SLITTING & BLANKING & SHEET METAL FORMING

Asset	Life (yrs)	Date of application
Steel coil blanking or shear line assets:		
Coil cars (including stationary coil cars)	15	1/7/12
Cut to length shears & guillotines	15	1/7/12
De-coilers/un-coilers (incorporating drives, motors, mandrels, gearboxes, snubbers & brakes)	15	1/7/12
Flying shears	10	1/7/12
Grip feeders	10	1/7/12
Levellers	15	1/7/12
Meter wheels	7	1/7/12
Peeler tables	15	1/7/12
Run out tables	15	1/7/12
Scissor lifts	15	1/7/12
Stackers	15	1/7/12

Asset	Life (yrs)	Date of application
Steel coil roll forming assets:		
Auto banders	10	1/7/12
Closed section induction welders	15	1/7/12
Closed section laser welders	10	1/7/12
CNC laser cutting units	10	1/7/12
Coil cars	15	1/7/12
Coil joining welding units	15	1/7/12
Coil levellers & straighteners	15	1/7/12
Coil magazines	15	1/7/12
Coil tilters	15	1/7/12
Coil tilting coil cars	15	1/7/12
Control systems assets:		
Motion controllers	10	1/7/12
PLCs	10	1/7/12
Potentiometers	5	1/7/12
Variable speed drives	10	1/7/12
Control systems including roll former control systems (incorporating end coders), de-coiler/un-coiler control systems & snubber control systems	10	1/7/12
De-coilers/un-coilers (incorporating drives, motors, mandrels, gearboxes, snubbers & brakes)	15	1/7/12
Embossing units	5	1/7/12
Flying shears	10	1/7/12
In-line presses & punches	15	1/7/12
In-line printers & labellers	7	1/7/12
Metal saws:		
Band saws	10	1/7/12
Rotary cut off saws	10	1/7/12
Roll former tooling	8	1/7/12
Roll formers (incorporating entry guides, fixed & height adjustable pinch rollers, drive motor & gearboxes, base & power supply unit):		
Fixed	15	1/7/12
Mobile	10	1/7/12
Run out tables	15	1/7/12
Shears & guillotines	15	1/7/12
Snubbers (incorporating drives, motors & gearboxes)	15	1/7/12
Strip lubricators	10	1/7/12
Support assets:		
Controlled access gates	10	1/7/12
Conveyors:		
Gravity feed conveyors (incorporating belts, rollers & shafts)	15	1/7/12
Motorised conveyors (incorporating gearboxes, belts, rollers, bearings, motors, frames & controls)	15	1/7/12
Engineering workshop assets:		
CNC & NC lathes	10	1/7/12
Drilling machines	10	1/7/12
Keyway broaching presses	15	1/7/12
Guard lights (incorporating red eye guard lights & stands)	7	1/7/12
Lifting assets:		
C-hooks	15	1/7/12
Overhead cranes & gantries	25	1/7/12
Spreader bars	10	1/7/12
Manual strapping machines	7	1/7/12
Measuring assets (including micrometers, protractors, tapes, & vernier callipers)	7	1/7/12
Perimeter fencing	15	1/7/12
Pneumatic systems assets:		
Air compressors	7	1/7/12
Air driers	7	1/7/12
Air receivers	15	1/7/12
Racking	20	1/7/12
Stackers (drop & suction)	15	1/7/12
Stretch wrappers	10	1/7/12
Tunnel guarding (including safety cages)	15	1/7/12
Steel coil slitting assets:		
Anti-flutter rolls	10	1/7/12
Auto banders (incorporating conveyors, strapping heads, coil lift systems, strapping dispensers, accumulators & controls)	10	1/7/12
Carryover tables	15	1/7/12
Coil cars	15	1/7/12
Coil stacking systems	20	1/7/12
Control systems	10	1/7/12
Controlled access gates	10	1/7/12
Conveyors:		

Asset	Life (yrs)	Date of application
Gravity feed conveyors (incorporating belts, rollers & frames)	15	1/7/12
Motorised conveyors (incorporating gearboxes, belts, rollers, bearings, motors, frames & controls)	15	1/7/12
De-coiler/un-coiler edge guides	10	1/7/12
De-coilers/un-coilers (incorporating drives, motors, mandrels, gearboxes, snubbers & brakes)	15	1/7/12
Downenders (incorporating conveyors, hydraulics & controls)	20	1/7/12
Entry & exit coil carousels/capstans	20	1/7/12
Entry shears	15	1/7/12
Exit edge guides	10	1/7/12
Exit feed up units (incorporating deflector & lift rolls, shears, separators, tables & traverse drives)	20	1/7/12
Exit turnstile/coil stackers	20	1/7/12
Lifting assets:		
C-hooks	15	1/7/12
Magnet cranes	20	1/7/12
Overhead cranes & gantries	25	1/7/12
Main hydraulic power pack (incorporating interconnecting pipe work to valve stands)	15	1/7/12
Pallet conveyor monorails	10	1/7/12
Peeler tables	15	1/7/12
Perimeter guarding	15	1/7/12
Pinch rollers/breakers	20	1/7/12
Pneumatic systems assets:		
Air compressors	7	1/7/12
Air driers	7	1/7/12
Air receivers	15	1/7/12
Re-coilers (incorporating drives, motors, mandrels, gearboxes, snubbers, & brakes)	15	1/7/12
Scrap baller	15	1/7/12
Scrap chopper bins & carriages	20	1/7/12
Scrap chopper conveyors (incorporating gearboxes, belts, rollers, bearings, motors, frames & controls)	15	1/7/12
Scrap choppers	20	1/7/12
Separator blades	10	1/7/12
Slitter tooling (incorporating blades, rubbers & spacers)	5	1/7/12
Slitting head building stations (incorporating rotating rigs)	20	1/7/12
Slitting head entry side guides	10	1/7/12
Slitting heads (incorporating electric motors, gearboxes & drive shafts)	15	1/7/12
Tension units (incorporating entry & exit quadrants, rolls, separators, drag pads, motors, gearboxes & drives)	15	1/7/12
Weighing scales (incorporating load cells & controls)	20	1/7/12
Steel sheet metal forming assets:		
Blankers	15	1/7/12
Brake presses	20	1/7/12
CNC multi head combined slitter/blankers	15	1/7/12
Control systems	10	1/7/12
Folders	10	1/7/12
Guillotines	10	1/7/12
Mini slitters	15	1/7/12

BOILER, TANK & OTHER HEAVY GAUGE METAL CONTAINER MANUFACTURING

Asset	Life (yrs)	Date of application
Sheet metal tanks manufacturing assets:		
Band saws	5	1/7/12
Coil holders	10	1/7/12
Curving rollers	10	1/7/12
Drilling machines (including bench & radial drills)	5	1/7/12
Gang & turret punching machines	15	1/7/12
Hand tools	5	1/7/12
Hoists:		
Electric	5	1/7/12
Hydraulic	15	1/7/12
Hooks (including c-hooks & slinger hooks)	5	1/7/12
Jib cranes	15	1/7/12
Laser cutters	7	1/7/12
Overhead cranes & gantries	25	1/7/12
Pallet jacks	10	1/7/12
Plate grabs	5	1/7/12
Racking	20	1/7/12
Riveting machines	15	1/7/12
Shears:		
Hand-held type	3	1/7/12

Asset	Life (yrs)	Date of application	Asset	Life (yrs)	Date of application
Guillotine type	15	1/7/12	Stud welding machines	15	1/7/11
Spreader bars	15	1/7/12	TIG welders	15	1/7/11
Trolleys	5	1/7/12	Vertical electric welders		
Welders	5	1/7/12	(pedestal welders)	15	1/7/11
			Welding reels	7	1/7/11

MOTOR VEHICLE MANUFACTURING

Bus & truck manufacturing assets (including bus vehicle body assembling assets & truck body manufacturing assets):

Asset	Life (yrs)	Date of application	Asset	Life (yrs)	Date of application
Ancillary & support assets:			Handling assets:		
Air compressors	15	1/7/11	Conveyors:		
Battery assets for warehouse vehicles (including pallet trucks & forklifts) – see Table B			Floor & in floor conveyors (including belt conveyors, skid conveyors, skillet conveyors, slat conveyors, turntables etc)	15	1/7/11
Warehouse & distribution centre equipment & machines			Monorails & overhead conveyors	20	1/7/11
Brake hose cleaning machines	10	1/7/11	Cranes (including gantry cranes, overhead cranes & turnover cranes)	25	1/7/11
Calibration assets	10	1/7/11	Elevating work platforms – see Table A Rental & hiring services (except real estate), Elevating work platforms (EWPs)		
Control systems	10	1/7/11	Forklift trucks (including pallet jacks, pallet stackers & reach trucks) – see Table B Forklifts		
Door controls & motor drive systems for rapid roller doors (incorporating chains, controls, motors & sensors, but excluding doors)	10	1/7/11	Mobile hoists/floor cranes (including engine & radiator hoists)	15	1/7/11
Dust & fume extraction assets:			Pushers, rollers & tug units	10	1/7/11
Fixed extraction systems (incorporating ducting, extraction arms etc)	15	1/7/11	Vehicle hoists/lifters (including column lifters & post hoists)	25	1/7/11
Mobile	7	1/7/11	Paint shop assets:		
Floor sweepers/scrubbers	10	1/7/11	Booths & ovens:		
Glycol & water mixing plant assets	15	1/7/11	Generally (including baking/curing ovens, paint mixing booths/rooms, pre treatment/sanding booths & wash down booths including cab degreasers)	20	1/7/11
Hose reels	7	1/7/11	Spray booths & combination spray booth baking ovens	15	1/7/11
Power supply assets including generators – use any relevant determinations made for Power supply assets in Table B			Dip tank electro coating assets (including alkaline cleaner tanks, electro application tanks, surface conditioner tanks & water rinse tanks)	15	1/7/11
Racks & shelving	20	1/7/11	Infrared paint dryers	7	1/7/11
Stillages, storage bins tote boxes & trolleys	15	1/7/11	Paint proportioning assets:		
Storage tanks:			Electronic component proportioning systems	10	1/7/11
Fuel storage tanks	20	1/7/11	Paint tinting & colour blending machines	5	1/7/11
Gas storage tanks (including argon, CNG & nitrogen gas storage tanks)	30	1/7/11	Press shop assets:		
Lubricant storage tanks	20	1/7/11	Bending machines:		
Tooling:			Chassis rail/frame bending machines	20	1/7/11
Dies (for press brakes)	12	1/7/11	Folders (including pan brakes)	20	1/7/11
Jigs & fixtures	7	1/7/11	Press brakes (brake presses)	25	1/7/11
Moulds (including fibreglass moulds)	7	1/7/11	Tube benders	12	1/7/11
Vehicle platforms & runways (used in wheel alignment etc)	20	1/7/11	Chassis rail drilling/punching machines:		
Ventilation fans	20	1/7/11	Chassis rail processing machines incorporating drilling & profiling	20	1/7/11
Waste oil collection & storage assets	10	1/7/11	Punching machines	20	1/7/11
Waste water treatment assets:			CNC milling machines	10	1/7/11
Meters	5	1/7/11	CNC routing machines	10	1/7/11
Pipework	15	1/7/11	Drilling machines (bench drills, pedestal drills & pillar drills)	12	1/7/11
Pumps	12	1/7/11	Guillotine shears	20	1/7/11
Separators	15	1/7/11	Lathes:		
Tanks	30	1/7/11	CNC lathes	10	1/7/11
Water demineralising plant assets including containers, pipework, pumps & reverse osmosis assets	15	1/7/11	Conventional or non CNC lathes	15	1/7/11
Weighers:			Plasma cutters	15	1/7/11
Fixed (weighbridges)	20	1/7/11	Scribing & number stamping machines (including chassis number scribing/stamping machines & vehicle identification number stamping machines)	10	1/7/11
Mobile	10	1/7/11	Trim & final shop assets:		
Assembly & body shop assets:			Air conditioning charging units	10	1/7/11
Adhesive mixing & dispensing assets	15	1/7/11	Brake testing units	20	1/7/11
Alignment, positioning & verification assets:			Bus & truck wash assets - see Table A Automotive body, paint & interior repair n.e.c. large vehicle wash assets		
Axle & frame alignment assets (including frame presses)	15	1/7/11	Electrical systems testing assets	15	1/7/11
Computer & laser based contact & non contact devices (including 'Faro arms')	10	1/7/11	Fluid filling assets:		
Dumpy levels	7	1/7/11	Fluid filling machines (including coolant, fuel, lubrication & power steering fluid filling machines)	10	1/7/11
Coupling assets	15	1/7/11	Urea dispensing systems incorporating intermediate bulk containers, hose reels, meters & pumps	10	1/7/11
Power tool & rivet gun power packs & rigs	15	1/7/11	Headlight aiming equipment	10	1/7/11
Power tools:			Torque testing machines (including chassis dynamometers & engine dynamometers)	12	1/7/11
Nut runners (including cables & controllers)	7	1/7/11	Wheel alignment assets:		
Others (including angle grinders, fastening tools, Hand operated saws, rivet guns etc) – see Table B Power tools, Hand tools					
Sawing machines (including aluminium cutting saws, bandsaws & cold saws)	12	1/7/11			
Welding assets:					
Automatic stud well bowl feeder units	10	1/7/11			
Hand held & portable spot welders (including transformers)	10	1/7/11			
MIG welders	15	1/7/11			

Asset	Life (yrs)	Date of application
Wheel alignment lasers	4	1/7/11
Wheel alignment systems incorporating alignment machines housing computer hardware & software, probes & sensors	15	1/7/11
Metal stamping & blanking assets:		
Ancillary assets (incl building & services assets):		
Air compressors	15	1/7/12
Air dryers	10	1/7/12
Generally (including air conditioning assets, air cooling assets, fencing (removable), fire control & alarm assets, power supply assets) - use any applicable determination in Table B		
Steelwork structures (including access & storage platforms, bollards, ladders etc)	15	1/7/12
Blanking & stamping press assets:		
Presses (including production presses & production supporting presses such as die spotting presses, tryout presses etc)	15	1/7/12
Support assets (including decoilers, loaders, unloaders, pallet transfer, sheet feeders, crane savers etc)	15	1/7/12
Die change over assets (die trailers, die trucks, die trolleys etc)	15	1/7/12
Die racks	15	1/7/12
Dies (stamping dies)	7	1/7/12
Inspection & measuring assets (including accelerometers, accuracy measurement tools, desktop friction & wear testers, dualscopes & measuring & evaluation machines generally)	10	1/7/12
Maintenance workshop & tool room assets:		
Benches & cutting tables (including magnetic field benches, marking out tables, welding benches etc)	15	1/7/12
Cutting machines (including gas cutters & plasma cutting machines)	10	1/7/12
Exhaust fans	10	1/7/12
Fixtures (including rotary work fixtures & set up fixtures)	10	1/7/12
Hand tools (including portable power tools, sealer guns & spray guns)	3	1/7/12
Heat treatment assets (including furnaces & quench tanks etc)	15	1/7/12
Lifting equipment (including vertical elevators & hoists)	15	1/7/12
Maintenance machines & tool room assets generally (including boring machines, folding machines, grinding machines, guillotines, hydraulic benders & presses, lapping machines, lathes, milling machines, NC machines & pipe threaders)	15	1/7/12
Measuring assets (including height gauges, micrometers, surface measuring machines & vernier calipers)	10	1/7/12
Washing machines & tanks (including ultrasonic cleaners/washers & other hot solvent small parts washing assets)	15	1/7/12
Welders (including ARC welders, MIG welders & TIG welders)	10	1/7/12
Pallets	10	1/7/12
Production control systems	10	1/7/12
Robots (including press tending robots, press transfer robots & pressed parts rack loading robots)	10	1/7/12
Scrap metal baling assets (including balers & conveying systems)	15	1/7/12
Steel coil & steel sheet handling assets:		
Automated guided vehicles (AGVs used in blank/stamped parts handling)	10	1/7/12
Coil loaders including hydraulic carts, lift tables & platforms	15	1/7/12
Conveyors	15	1/7/12
Forklifts - see Table B		
Overhead cranes & hoists	20	1/7/12
Steel coil & steel sheet processing assets:		
Blank/sheet turnover machines	15	1/7/12
Destacking/stacking machines	10	1/7/12
Washing machines	10	1/7/12
Motor car engine assembly & manufacturing assets:		
Ancillary & support assets:		
Air compressors	15	1/7/12
Air curtains	10	1/7/12
Control systems (including mimic panels)	10	1/7/12
Cooling water supply assets (including cooling towers, storage tanks & water conditioning/dosing assets)	15	1/7/12
Dust & fume extraction assets (including ducting, extraction fans, hoppers etc)	15	1/7/12
Engine lubrication storage, filtration & feed plant assets	15	1/7/12
Engine pallets	10	1/7/12
Lighting (production)	15	1/7/12
Racks, shelving, stands & tables generally	15	1/7/12
Robots generally (including assembly robots, gantry robots & pick & place robots etc)	10	1/7/12
Safety assets generally (including guarding, matting, railing etc, where separately identifiable & not incorporated into an existing asset)	10	1/7/12
Stillages, storage bins, tote boxes & trolleys	10	1/7/12
Swarf & machining line coolant separation & refrigeration systems (incorporating coolant circulation pumps & tanks, outfeed extractors, refrigeration chiller packs, separators & swarf tote excavators)	15	1/7/12
Tooling assets:		
Electronic & laser tool pre-setting & setting machines (including coordinate measurement machines)	10	1/7/12
Tooling (for drills, lathes, mills etc)	3	1/7/12
Engine assembly & engine component sub-assembly assets:		
Adhesive application assets used in form-in-place gasket systems etc (including adhesive unloading equipment & robots)	10	1/7/12
Assembly & sub-assembly assets generally (including assembly machines, balancing machines, bearing shell detection assets, crank & piston spin test machines, oil filling machines etc)	10	1/7/12
Coding assets (including automated ink or spray jet coders & automated pin coding stamping machines)	10	1/7/12
Nut runner assets:		
Automated nut runner & fastening systems incorporating cables & controllers, & including bolt torquing robots	10	1/7/12
Manually operated nut runners (pre-torque applications etc)	5	1/7/12
Power tools generally	3	1/7/12
Engine component machining line assets (including broaching machines, deburring machines, gauging machines, honing machines, leak testing machines, machining centres, pallet loading systems, surface grinding machines, transfer machines, washing machines etc)	15	1/7/12
Engine function testing assets (including cold test machines, engine dynamometers, engine ignition testing machines & hot test machines)	10	1/7/12
Handling assets:		
Conveyors:		
Elevating conveyors (including engine block elevating conveying assets etc)	15	1/7/12
Floor & in-floor standalone conveyors (including belt conveyors, infeed & outfeed conveyors)	15	1/7/12
Monorails & overhead conveyors	15	1/7/12
Cranes & hoists (including bridge cranes, gantry cranes, overhead cranes & turnover cranes)	20	1/7/12
Lifting fixtures, magnets, slings etc	10	1/7/12
Quality control assets generally (including cylinder head thickness testers, digital torque wrenches, gauges, inspection equipment generally, measuring equipment generally, microscopes, scales, scanners, testing equipment generally, thermometers, vibration meters etc)	10	1/7/12
Toolroom assets:		
Benches & cutting tables (including magnetic field benches, marking out tables, welding benches etc)	15	1/7/12
Degreasing plant systems (incorporating float valves, hoists, monorails, pumps etc)	15	1/7/12

Asset	Life (yrs)	Date of application
Fixtures (including rotary work fixtures & set up fixtures)	10	1/7/12
Heat treatment assets (including furnaces & quench tanks)	15	1/7/12
Tool grinding & maintenance machines (including boring machines, broach sharpening machines, grinding machines, guillotines, lapping machines, milling machines, toolroom lathes etc)	15	1/7/12
Washing machines & tanks (including ultrasonic cleaners/washers & other hot solvent small parts washing assets)	15	1/7/12
Welders (ARC welders, MIG welders etc)	10	1/7/12
Waste treatment assets:		
Laboratory equipment (including balancers, chart recorders, dryers, pH sampling devices, rotameters & simulators etc)	10	1/7/12
Meters & sensors (including chart recorders, dosing meters, level meters, level sensors & pH method meters & sensors etc)	10	1/7/12
Pumps (including dosing pumps, recirculation pumps etc)	10	1/7/12
Tanks & pools (including recycling tanks, sludge tanks & pools, storage tanks etc)	20	1/7/12
Waste treatment assets generally (including dosing systems, flotation waste treatment systems, heaters, oil removing systems, skimmers & sludge presses etc)	15	1/7/12
Motor vehicle manufacturing plant (not listed elsewhere):		
Basic machinery	10	1/1/01
Tooling (ie jigs, dies, press tools & specialty attachments such as working heads & work holding tools)	3	1/1/01
Non ferrous metal casting assets – see Table A Non ferrous metal casting		

MOTOR VEHICLE BODY & TRAILER MANUFACTURING

Bus vehicle body assembly assets (on supplied motor & chassis) – see Table A Motor vehicle manufacturing, bus & truck manufacturing assets (including bus vehicle body assembling assets & truck body manufacturing assets)

Truck body manufacturing assets – see Table A Motor vehicle manufacturing, bus & truck manufacturing assets (including bus vehicle body assembling assets & truck body manufacturing assets)

OTHER MOTOR VEHICLE PARTS MANUFACTURING

Metal stamping & blanking assets - see Table A Motor vehicle manufacturing, metal stamping & blanking assets

Asset	Life (yrs)	Date of application
Piston ring manufacturing plant:		
Engineering works plant	20	1/1/01
Motors	20	1/1/01
Overhead gear, equipment, belting etc	20	1/1/01
Precision machines	13⅓	1/1/01

RAILWAY ROLLING STOCK MANUFACTURING & REPAIR SERVICES

Asset	Life (yrs)	Date of application
Assembly assets:		
Access & assembly platforms	15	1/7/14
Alignment assets (including gearbox alignment assets)	10	1/7/14
Bearing puller assets	10	1/7/14
Blast chamber assets (incorporating shot recovery systems)	10	1/7/14
Cutting assets (including plate profilers, profile cutters & saws)	10	1/7/14
De-coiling assets	15	1/7/14
Drilling assets (including radial drills)	10	1/7/14
Foam filling station assets	10	1/7/14
Furnaces & ovens (including ladles & stress relief ovens)	20	1/7/14
Jigs (including rollover jigs & lifting jigs)	15	1/7/14
Lathes (including above floor & under floor wheel lathes)	20	1/7/14
Milling machines (including gantry)	20	1/7/14
Pipe & tube bending assets	10	1/7/14
Presses (incl bearing mounting, bench, brake, hydraulic power & wheel presses)	20	1/7/14
Riveting assets	5	1/7/14
Specialised hydraulic tool assets	10	1/7/14
Stretch formers	10	1/7/14

Asset	Life (yrs)	Date of application
Sweeping assets	10	1/7/14
Turning assets	10	1/7/14
Wash bay assets	10	1/7/14
Welding assets (including robot welders & spot welding towers)	10	1/7/14
Wire cutting & stripping assets	10	1/7/14
Handling assets:		
Cranes (including overhead gantry cranes)	25	1/7/14
Lifting assets generally (incl hydraulic double lift jacks, locomotive jacks & stands)	20	1/7/14
Pallet lifters	10	1/7/14
Scissor lifts	10	1/7/14
Maintenance & refurbishment assets:		
Boring assets	10	1/7/14
Cutting assets (incl guillotines, plasma cutters & profilers)	15	1/7/14
Detecting assets (including flaw detectors)	10	1/7/14
Drilling assets (including radial drills)	10	1/7/14
Grinding & milling assets	20	1/7/14
Hydraulic drop & work tables	10	1/7/14
Lathes (including above floor & under floor wheel lathes)	20	1/7/14
Paint spraying booths (incorporating baking ovens, extractor fans & gas heaters)	15	1/7/14
Portable presses (including hydraulic power presses)	10	1/7/14
Presses (including bearing mounting, bench, brake, hydraulic power & wheel presses)	20	1/7/14
Tanks (including washing & water tanks)	20	1/7/14
Vacuum assets	10	1/7/14
Washing assets (including bearing & bogie washers)	10	1/7/14
Welding assets (including robot welders & spot welding towers)	10	1/7/14
Wheel condition monitoring systems	7	1/7/14
Support assets:		
Cleaning assets (including high pressure cleaners)	5	1/7/14
Compressed air system assets (including compressors, dryers & filters & receivers)	10	1/7/14
Computer measuring & monitoring assets (including load & pressure indicators)	7	1/7/14
Control system assets (including supervisory control & data acquisition (SCADA) systems & vehicle preparation systems)	10	1/7/14
Cooling towers	15	1/7/14
Dust & fume extraction system assets	15	1/7/14
Electricity supply assets – see Table A Electricity supply		
Fastening & riveting assets	5	1/7/14
Fire prevention systems (incorporating fire protection systems & water tanks)	15	1/7/14
Induction heaters	10	1/7/14
Portable train weighing assets	10	1/7/14
Pumps (including hydraulic pumps)	10	1/7/14
Racking & storage assets	20	1/7/14
Rail vehicle moving & placing assets (including crabs, shunting locomotives & trackmobiles)	10	1/7/14
Railway tracks – see Table A Rail freight & passenger transport services		
Refrigerant recovery assets	10	1/7/14
Traversers & turntables	20	1/7/14
Vehicle progression systems assets (incl rabbits)	10	1/7/14
Waste water & effluent treatment assets	10	1/7/14
Weighing assets for carriages & locomotives	20	1/7/14
Testing assets:		
Bogie, brake & spring testing assets	10	1/7/14
Cab test benches & CRC cable testing assets	5	1/7/14
Earth testing assets	10	1/7/14
Electrical testing assets (including multimeters)	10	1/7/14
Post production testing assets (excluding weighing assets – see above in support assets):		
Water test facility assets (incorporating control systems, gantries, pipes, pumps etc)	10	1/7/14
Other post production testing assets	5	1/7/14
Test sheds for testing locomotives & other rolling stock	30	1/7/14

OTHER TRANSPORT EQUIPMENT MANUFACTURING N.E.C.

Asset	Life (yrs)	Date of application
Motor cycle building plant	10	1/1/01

Asset	Life (yrs)	Date of application
PHOTOGRAPHIC, OPTICAL & OPHTHALMIC EQUIPMENT MANUFACTURING		
Optical lens grinding & contact lens manufacturing:		
CNC milling machines	7	1/7/04
Combined surface generators & grinders & finers	10	1/7/04
Deblocking & lens cleaning machines (including ultrasonic washers)	9	1/7/04
Finers	10	1/7/04
Finishing blockers	8	1/7/04
Frame tracers	5	1/7/04
Lap tools	10	1/7/04
Layout blockers	8	1/7/04
Lens coating machines	10	1/7/04
Lens curing & drying ovens	10	1/7/04
Lens edgers	7	1/7/04
Lens tinting machines	8	1/7/04
Lensmeters:		
Automated	5	1/7/04
Manual	10	1/7/04
Polishers	10	1/7/04
Protective lacquering or surface saver taping machines	9	1/7/04
Surface generators & grinders	10	1/7/04
Surface lathes	8	1/7/04
OTHER PROFESSIONAL & SCIENTIFIC EQUIPMENT MANUFACTURING N.E.C.		
Watchmakers' plant	10	1/1/01
FURNITURE & OTHER MANUFACTURING		
Broom & brush manufacturing plant	13⅓	1/1/01
Furniture making plant	13⅓	1/1/01
Jewellers' plant	10	1/1/01
Umbrella manufacturers' plant:		
Cutting boards	10	1/1/01
Lathes	13⅓	1/1/01
Motors	20	1/1/01

ELECTRICITY, GAS, WATER & WASTE SERVICES

Asset	Life (yrs)	Date of application
ELECTRICITY SUPPLY		
Electricity distribution:		
Control, monitoring, communications & protection systems	10	1/1/02
Customer meters (incorporating load & time switches if fitted)	25	1/1/02
Customer service mains or cable, above ground	40	1/1/02
Customer service mains or cable, underground	50	1/1/02
Distribution lines:		
Above ground (incorporating conductors; cross arms, insulators & fittings; poles – concrete, wood, steel or stobie; & transformers – pole or ground pad mounted)	45	1/1/02
Combination of above ground & underground	47½	1/1/02
Underground (incorporating cables, fittings & ground pad mounted transformers)	50	1/1/02
Distribution substations/transformers, pole or ground pad mounted	40	1/1/02
Distribution zone substations (excluding control, monitoring, communications & protection systems)	40	1/1/02
Nightwatchman's lights	15	1/1/02
Street lights	15	1/1/02
Electricity generation:		
Ash & dust handling & disposal:		
Ash dams	20	1/1/02
Ash slurry systems	15	1/1/02
Conveyors	30	1/1/02
Crushers	15	1/1/02
On site storage silos, concrete or steel	30	1/1/02
Fuel supply & handling:		
On site gaseous fuel supply systems (incorporating downstream delivery pipelines)	30	1/1/02
On site liquid fuel supply systems (incorporating downstream delivery pipelines)	30	1/1/02
Solid fuels:		
Coal handling assets (including conveyors, slot bunker, transfer towers, & weighers)	30	1/1/02
Day bunkers & silos, concrete or steel (incorporating top side conveyor system)	30	1/1/02

Asset	Life (yrs)	Date of application
On site coal storage assets (including stacking & reclaiming assets)	30	1/1/02
On site storage silos, concrete or steel	30	1/1/02
Quality control assets (including coal sampling assets & secondary crushers)	30	1/1/02
Power generators:		
Co generation:		
Condensing & feed heating assets	30	1/1/02
Control & monitoring system	15	1/1/02
Emergency power supply assets (incl batteries & uninterruptible power supply assets)	15	1/1/02
Gas turbine generators	30	1/1/02
Generator transformers & unit transformers in sub tropical areas	30	1/1/02
Generator transformers & unit transformers in tropical areas	25	1/1/02
Heat recovery steam generators	30	1/1/02
Miscellaneous assets	30	1/1/02
On site switchyards with conventional outdoor switchgear	30	1/1/02
On site switchyards with gas insulated switchgear	30	1/1/02
Reciprocating engines, diesel fired	20	1/1/02
Reciprocating engines, gas spark ignition	20	1/1/02
Station & auxiliary electrical systems within the power station	30	1/1/02
Steam turbine generators	30	1/1/02
Combined cycle:		
Condensing & feed heating assets	30	1/1/02
Control & monitoring systems	15	1/1/02
Emergency power supply assets (including batteries & uninterruptible power supply assets)	15	1/1/02
Gas turbine generators	30	1/1/02
Generator transformers & unit transformers in sub tropical areas	30	1/1/02
Generator transformers & unit transformers in tropical areas	25	1/1/02
Heat recovery steam generators	30	1/1/02
Miscellaneous assets	30	1/1/02
On site switchyards with conventional outdoor switchgear	30	1/1/02
On site switchyards with gas insulated switchgear	30	1/1/02
Station & auxiliary electrical systems within the power station	30	1/1/02
Steam turbine generators	30	1/1/02
Diesel or gas engine:		
Control & monitoring systems	15	1/1/02
Diesel reciprocating engines	20	1/1/02
Emergency power supply assets (including batteries & uninterruptible power supply assets)	15	1/1/02
Gas spark ignition reciprocating engines	20	1/1/02
Generator transformers & unit transformers in sub tropical areas	30	1/1/02
Generator transformers & unit transformers in tropical areas	25	1/1/02
Miscellaneous assets	30	1/1/02
On site switchyards with conventional outdoor switchgear	30	1/1/02
On site switchyards with gas insulated switchgear	30	1/1/02
Station & auxiliary electrical systems within the power station	30	1/1/02
Gas turbine:		
Control & monitoring systems	15	1/1/02
Emergency power supply assets (including batteries & uninterruptible power supply assets)	15	1/1/02
Gas turbine generators	30	1/1/02
Generator transformers & unit transformers in sub tropical areas	30	1/1/02
Generator transformers & unit transformers in tropical areas	25	1/1/02
Miscellaneous assets	30	1/1/02
On site switchyards with conventional outdoor switchgear	30	1/1/02
On site switchyards with gas insulated switchgear	30	1/1/02

Asset	Life (yrs)	Date of application
Station & auxiliary electrical systems within the power station	30	1/1/02
Hydro electric:		
Control & monitoring system	15	1/1/02
Emergency power supply assets (including batteries & uninterruptible power supply assets)	15	1/1/02
Generator transformers & unit transformers in sub tropical area	30	1/1/02
Generator transformers & unit transformers in tropical areas	25	1/1/02
Hydro turbines & generators	40	1/1/02
Miscellaneous assets	40	1/1/02
On site switchyards with conventional outdoor switchgear	40	1/1/02
On site switchyards with gas insulated switchgear	35	1/1/02
Station & auxiliary electrical systems within the power station	40	1/1/02
Solar:		
Photovoltaic electricity generating system assets (incorporating photovoltaic panels, mounting frames & inverters)	20	1/7/11
Thermal:		
Condensing & feed heating assets	30	1/1/02
Control & monitoring systems	15	1/1/02
Emergency power supply assets (including batteries & uninterruptible power supply assets)	15	1/1/02
Generator transformers & unit transformers in sub tropical areas	30	1/1/02
Generator transformers & unit transformers in tropical areas	25	1/1/02
Miscellaneous assets	30	1/1/02
On site switchyards with conventional outdoor switchgear	30	1/1/02
On site switchyards with gas insulated switchgear	30	1/1/02
Primary dust collection systems (incorporating electrostatic precipitators or baghouse filters)	30	1/1/02
Solid fuel preparation assets (including fuel feeders & milling assets)	30	1/1/02
Station & auxiliary electrical systems within the power station	30	1/1/02
Steam generators	30	1/1/02
Steam turbine generators	30	1/1/02
Wind:		
Generator transformers & unit transformers in sub tropical areas	30	1/1/02
Generator transformers & unit transformers in tropical areas	25	1/1/02
Wind turbines	20	1/1/02
Power station civil & structural works:		
Chimney stacks:		
Concrete surrounds	30	1/1/02
Steel flues	20	1/1/02
Cooling towers (concrete or timber)	30	1/1/02
Cooling water systems (excluding cooling towers & condensing assets)	30	1/1/02
Power station buildings, to the extent that they form an integral part of plant	30	1/1/02
Workshop machinery & tools	20	1/1/02
Electricity transmission:		
Control, monitoring, communications & protection systems	12½	1/1/02
Power transformers	40	1/1/02
Transmission lines (incorporating conductors, insulators & towers)	47½	1/1/02
Transmission substations (excluding power transformers & control, monitoring, communications & protection systems)	40	1/1/02

GAS SUPPLY

Asset	Life (yrs)	Date of application
Gas distribution:		
Control systems (excluding computers)	10	1/7/02
Gas meters	15	1/7/02
Low pressure (LP) gas storage holders	40#	1/7/02
Pigging devices	5	1/7/02
Pipelines (including high, medium or low pressure trunk, primary or secondary mains or services):		
Generally	50#	1/7/02
PVC pipelines	30#	1/7/02
Regulators (including gate stations, subgate stations, block valve stations, pressure regulating stations & district regulating stations)	40#	1/7/02
Gas transmission:		
Compressor gas turbine (GT) drivers	20	1/7/02
Compressor station assets	30#	1/7/02
Control systems (excluding computers)	10	1/7/02
Gas meters	15	1/7/02
Gas pipeline LNG station assets	30#	1/7/02
Pigging devices	5	1/7/02
Pipelines – transmission, spur or lateral	50#	1/7/02
Regulators (including gate stations, subgate stations, block valve stations, pressure regulating stations & district regulating stations)	40#	1/7/02
Underground gas storage asset	40#	1/7/02

IRRIGATION WATER PROVIDERS

Asset	Life (yrs)	Date of application
Channel regulators	80	1/1/05
Cranes (including gantries)	40	1/1/05
Dams & weirs ((incorporating gates & actuators) consisting of a barrier to obstruct the flow of water constructed from any or all of the following: concrete, earth & rockfill)	100	1/1/05
Drain inlet	50	1/1/05
Drainage channels (measured from the point of intersection with another drainage channel to the following intersection)	100	1/1/05
Escapes	50	1/1/05
Flow meters	20	1/1/05
Irrigation channels (incorporating siphons & subways) measured from offtake or regulator to regulator:		
Concrete	50	1/1/05
Earth	80	1/1/05
Measurement flumes	50	1/1/05
Metered outlets:		
Electronic	40	1/1/05
Mechanical	50	1/1/05
Piped	40	1/1/05
Offtakes	80	1/1/05
Pipes: measured from valve to valve, that are of the same age & same material (not being in the nature of a repair)	80	1/1/05
Pump inlets	50	1/1/05
Pump sets (incorporating switchboards, starters, motors & pumps)	40	1/1/05
Reservoirs & tanks	80	1/1/05
Valves	40	1/1/05

WATER SUPPLY

Asset	Life (yrs)	Date of application
Aerators & blowers	20	1/1/05
Cathodic protection systems	20	1/1/05
Chemical dosing pumps	25	1/1/05
Pump sets (incorporating switch boards, starters, motors & pumps)	25	1/1/05
Raw water storage & supply assets:		
Bores	30	1/1/05
Dam or weir intake structures	100	1/1/05
Dams & weirs	100	1/1/05
Reservoirs, elevated tanks & standpipes: whether made from steel or concrete	80	1/1/05
Service connections:		
Water meters	20	1/1/05
Valves:		
Generally	30	1/1/05
Pressure reducing valves	25	1/1/05
Water mains: Being lengths of trunk, distribution & reticulation mains within a section, measured from valve to valve that are of the same age & same material (not being in the nature of a repair)	80	1/1/05
Water supply control systems assets:		
Air scour flow meters, level sensors, transmitters & meters	10	1/1/05
Chlorine analysers, mini labs, PH meters, turbidity analysers & meters	7	1/1/05
Flow meters	20	1/1/05
Pressure sensors, transmitters & meters	10	1/1/05
Telemetry (including modems & remote transfer units)	10	1/1/05
Variable speed drives	15	1/1/05

Asset	Life (yrs)	Date of application
Water supply pumping station detention tanks	80	1/1/05
Water treatment assets:		
Balance tanks	80	1/1/05
Bore water treatment assets:		
Aerators & blowers	20	1/1/05
Lime silos	50	1/1/05
Batching tanks	80	1/1/05
Lime pump sets (incorporating switch boards, starters, motors & pumps)	25	1/1/05
Reactors	25	1/1/05
Filtration tanks	80	1/1/05
Backwash pumps	25	1/1/05
Clear water tanks	80	1/1/05
Sludge thickeners	50	1/1/05
Drying beds	50	1/1/05
Chemical blowers	15	1/1/05
Chemical dosing systems	15	1/1/05
Chemical feeders & hoppers	25	1/1/05
Chemical mixers & blenders	25	1/1/05
Chemical storage tanks	30	1/1/05
Clarifiers (incorporating scrapers)	80	1/1/05
Clear water tanks	80	1/1/05
Dissolved air flotation systems	25	1/1/05
Filtration tanks (incorporating scrapers)	80	1/1/05
Flocculation tanks (incorporating scrapers)	80	1/1/05
Inline mixers	15	1/1/05
Penstocks	25	1/1/05
Raw water inlet screening systems	25	1/1/05
Sludge treatment lagoons	50	1/1/05
Wash water holding tanks	80	1/1/05

SEWERAGE & DRAINAGE SERVICES

Asset	Life (yrs)	Date of application
Chemical dosing pumps	25	1/1/05
Dams:		
Lined earth dams	100	1/1/05
Dam covers	20	1/1/05
Effluent outfalls:		
Shoreline ocean	100	1/1/05
Extended ocean	100	1/1/05
River or estuary	100	1/1/05
Methane gas & cogeneration assets - see Table A Electricity supply & Gas supply		
Pump sets (incorporating switch boards, starters, motors & pumps)	25	1/1/05
Sewage pump station assets:		
Detention tanks	80	1/1/05
Overflow screens	25	1/1/05
Sewage service connection assets:		
Low pressure pumps	25	1/1/05
Vacuum pumps	25	1/1/05
Sewage treatment assets:		
Air filtration systems	20	1/1/05
Air scrubbers	10	1/1/05
Chemical blowers	15	1/1/05
Chemical feeders & hoppers	25	1/1/06
Chemical mixers & blenders	25	1/1/05
Chemical storage tanks	30	1/1/05
Grit removal assets	25	1/1/05
Penstocks	25	1/1/05
Screenings removal assets	25	1/1/05
Sludge processing assets:		
Anaerobic digesters	80	1/1/05
Anaerobic digester gas handling & blowing systems	25	1/1/05
Anaerobic digester heating systems	25	1/1/05
Bio filters	80	1/1/05
Dissolved air flotation systems	25	1/1/05
Lime disinfection dosing units	25	1/1/05
Sludge dewatering assets:		
Belt presses	15	1/1/05
Centrifuges	20	1/1/05
Screw conveyors	25	1/1/05
Screw presses	20	1/1/05
Sludge driers	20	1/1/05
Sludge heating units	20	1/1/05
Sludge thickening tanks (incorporating scrapers)	80	1/1/05
Treatment assets:		
Primary treatment assets:		
Primary clarifiers (incorporating scrapers)	80	1/1/05
Primary sedimentation lagoons	50	1/1/05

Asset	Life (yrs)	Date of application
Primary sedimentation tanks (incorporating scrapers & weirs)	80	1/1/05
Scum collection & transfer systems	25	1/1/05
Secondary treatment assets:		
Biological nutrient removal (BNR) assets:		
Aerators & blowers	20	1/1/05
BNR tanks (incorporating mixed liquor stream, anoxic, anaerobic & swing zones & diffusers)	80	1/1/05
Mixers	25	1/1/05
Secondary clarifiers (incorporating scrapers)	80	1/1/05
Secondary treatment lagoons	50	1/1/05
Secondary treatment tanks (incorporating scrapers & weirs)	80	1/1/05
Sequenced batch reactors	80	1/1/05
Sludge aerators & blowers	80	1/1/05
Tertiary treatment assets:		
Backwash air blowers	20	1/1/05
Chlorine contact tanks	80	1/1/05
Filtration tanks	80	1/1/05
Reverse osmosis assets:		
Fine screening systems	15	1/1/05
Micro filtration units	15	1/1/05
Reverse osmosis membrane filtration units	10	1/1/05
UV disinfectors	25	1/1/05
Water storage tanks	80	1/1/05
Sewerage control systems assets:		
Chlorine residual analysers & PH meters	7	1/1/05
Dissolved oxygen probes, level sensors, transmitters & meters	10	1/1/05
Flow meters	20	1/1/05
Telemetry (including modems & remote transfer units)	10	1/1/05
Variable speed drives	15	1/1/05
Sewer mains: Being lengths of collection sewers measured from manhole to manhole (including branch, main, pressure, reticulation, sub main & trunk sewers) (not being in the nature of a repair)	80	1/1/05
Valves:		
Generally	25	1/1/05
Pressure reducing valves	30	1/1/05

SOLID WASTE COLLECTION SERVICES

Asset	Life (yrs)	Date of application
Air compressors & receivers	7	1/7/15
Balers	7	1/7/15
Bins:		
Domestic mobile bins (plastic)	10	1/7/15
Industrial mobile rubbish bins (metal)	8	1/7/15
Industrial mobile rubbish bins (plastic)	5	1/7/15
Metal skips for hire	8	1/7/15
Roll-on roll-off containers	10	1/7/15
Stationary & portable compactor bins	8	1/7/15
Bin delivery vehicle cranes/bin & skip lifters	10	1/7/15
Compactors & collection bodies on trucks (including lifting arms)	8	1/7/15
Fans	10	1/7/15
Forklifts	11	1/7/15
Garbage compactor trucks (excl the compactor)	10#	1/7/15
Hook lifts on truck body	10	1/7/15
Truck hoists	20	1/7/15
Washing assets including pressure washers	4	1/7/15
Waste water treatment systems	10	1/7/15

WASTE TREATMENT & DISPOSAL SERVICES

Asset	Life (yrs)	Date of application
Transfer stations & landfill operation assets:		
Air compressors & receivers	7	1/7/15
Balers	7	1/7/15
Bins:		
Bins generally (including metal bins)	7	1/7/15
Compactor bins	6	1/7/15
Mobile bins (including rubbish bins)	5	1/7/15
Bulk fuel above ground tanks	20	1/7/15
Bulldozers & drotts (including landfill compaction assets)	5	1/7/15
CCTV & security systems	4	1/7/15
Concrete crushing assets	15	1/7/15
Dust & odour control assets	12	1/7/15
Excavators & front end loaders	5	1/7/15
Fans	10	1/7/15

Asset	Life (yrs)	Date of application
Forklifts used in waste handling	5	1/7/15
Forklifts not used in waste handling	11	1/7/15
Gas capture assets:		
Extraction assets including wells, laterals & headers, & condensate systems	8	1/7/15
Flare skid assets generally including blowers, monitoring systems & flame arresters, but excluding flare stacks	7½	1/7/15
Flare stacks - continuous use	15	1/7/15
Flare stacks - standby stacks	7½	1/7/15
Monitoring systems (excluding wells)	5	1/7/15
Off-site monitoring wells	15	1/7/15
Green waste mulchers & shredders	7	1/7/15
Hoppers	7	1/7/15
Push pits	15	1/7/15
Sweepers – road sweepers	10	1/7/15
Transfer trailers	10	1/7/15
Water treatment systems	10	1/7/15
Weighbridges	15	1/7/15

WASTE REMEDIATION & MATERIALS RECOVERY SERVICES

Asset	Life (yrs)	Date of application
Materials recovery facility (MRF) assets:		
Air compressors & receivers	7	1/7/14
Balers	7	1/7/14
Ballistic separators	10	1/7/14
Bins:		
Bins generally (including metal bins)	7	1/7/14
Compactor bins	6	1/7/14
Mobile bins (including rubbish bins)	5	1/7/14
Bunkers	10	1/7/14
CCTV & security systems	4	1/7/14
Chippers & shredders	7	1/7/14
Control systems	10	1/7/14
Conveyors & conveyor systems:		
Bounce conveyors & feeders	10	1/7/14
Conveyors generally (incorporating belt, drive, motors & supporting structure) including walking floor conveyors	9	1/7/14
Hand sort conveyors	10	1/7/14
Door controls & motor drive systems for automatic opening doors (incorporating controls, motors & sensors, but excluding doors)	10	1/7/14
Ducted air transfer system assets	10	1/7/14
Dust collectors	12	1/7/14
Eddy current separators	7	1/7/14
Excavators & front end loaders	5	1/7/14
Fans	10	1/7/14
Feed hoppers (incorporating steel drag chain, conveyor belt, metering feed roller, motor & gearbox)	5	1/7/14
Ferrous & magnetic separators	10	1/7/14
Food separation & screening assets	10	1/7/14
Forklifts	5	1/7/14
Glass breakers & crushers	6	1/7/14
Hoppers	7	1/7/14
Leachate pumps & filters	10	1/7/14
Lifting assets (including pallet jacks)	10	1/7/14
Optical sorters	5	1/7/14
Screen separators	10	1/7/14
Sweepers & scrubbers	10	1/7/14
Trommels (incorporating wheels, motors & gearboxes):		
Fixed	7	1/7/14
Portable	7	1/7/14
Vacuum extraction & cleaning assets	10	1/7/14
Vibrating screen separators	10	1/7/14
Waste compactors	9	1/7/14
Weighbridges	15	1/7/14

CONSTRUCTION

Asset	Life (yrs)	Date of application
Air compressors:		
Compressors – reciprocating	7	1/7/08
Compressors – rotary screw	10	1/7/08
Backhoe loaders	9	1/7/02
Bending machines (bar, angle or rod)	10	1/7/08
Block & brick elevators (portable)	10	1/7/08
Chain blocks, rod shears, jacks etc	13⅓	1/1/01
Compaction:		
Compactors – flat plate	8	1/7/08
Compactors – vertical rammer	6	1/7/08

Asset	Life (yrs)	Date of application
Concreting assets:		
Brick & paving saws	5	1/7/08
Concrete demolition saws	3	1/7/08
Concrete kibble buckets	15	1/7/08
Concrete mixers	4	1/7/08
Concrete surface preparation assets (incl floor grinders, planers & scarifiers)	5	1/7/08
Concrete trowels:		
Ride on	7	1/7/08
Walk behind	5	1/7/08
Concrete vibrating screeders	5	1/7/08
Concrete vibrators:		
Brushcutter style	5	1/7/08
Drive units	6	1/7/08
Flexible shaft pumps	6	1/7/08
Vibrating shaft	3	1/7/08
Concrete wheeled saws	6	1/7/08
Concreting plant:		
Buggies or dumpers (motorised)	5	1/1/01
Hoppers, skips & hoist buckets	10	1/1/01
Mobile concrete pumping units	6⅔	1/1/01
Cranes (mobile):		
Light & medium	15	1/7/02
Heavy (over 15.24 tonnes lift)	20	1/7/02
Tower & hoists	10	1/1/01
Dozers/front end loaders	9	1/7/02
Forklifts	11	1/7/02
Formwork, beams & props, steel	10	1/7/08
Hydraulic excavators	10	1/7/02
Lift slab assets (incorporating spreader bars, clutches, pulleys & cables)	5	1/7/08
Mini excavators	8	1/7/02
Motor graders	10	1/7/02
Pavers	12	1/7/02
Power supply assets:		
Generators, portable (incorporating attached engine management & generator monitoring instruments):		
Diesel	10	1/7/08
Petrol	5	1/7/08
Power tools:		
Chain saws	3	1/7/08
Hand tools:		
Air	5	1/7/08
Battery	3	1/7/08
Electric	5	1/7/08
Jack hammers:		
Air	7	1/7/08
Electric	3	1/7/08
Nail guns – air	3	1/7/08
Profilers	10	1/7/02
Pumps	10	1/1/01
Road rollers	15	1/7/02
Saws, bench & mitre, portable	7	1/7/08
Scrapers	8	1/7/02
Skid steer loaders	7	1/7/02
Stabiliser recyclers	12	1/7/02
Surveying assets including levels - see Table A Surveying & mapping services		
Telescopic handlers	10	1/7/02
Tool carriers	10	1/7/02
Track loaders	9	1/7/02
Traffic management assets (use the relevant lives given under Table A Rental & hiring services, whether or not the assets are in fact hired or leased)		
Welders:		
Diesel	10	1/7/08
Electric	5	1/7/08
Wheel loaders	8	1/7/02
Winches	13⅓	1/1/01

OTHER HEAVY & CIVIL ENGINEERING CONSTRUCTION N.E.C.

Asset	Life (yrs)	Date of application
Automatic welding machines (used at sea in construction of submarine pipelines)	10	1/1/01

WHOLESALE TRADE

WOOL WHOLESALING

Asset	Life (yrs)	Date of application
Wool presses	20	1/7/06

Asset	Life (yrs)	Date of application
PETROLEUM PRODUCT WHOLESALING		
Bulk fuel regional depot assets (excluding LPG assets):		
Cathodic protection systems:		
Sacrificial anode	10	1/7/10
Impressed current	20	1/7/10
Effluent treatment system (incorporating pumps, motors & electronic circuitry)	15	1/7/10
Electric pumps	10	1/7/10
Hoses	2	1/7/10
Loading gantries & racks (incorporating meters & metering systems)	15	1/7/10
Petroleum product storage tanks – fibreglass & steel	20	1/7/10
Rigid fuel tank truck assets:		
Aluminium tanks or barrels	10	1/7/10
Filters	5	1/7/10
Metering systems	5	1/7/10
Overfill protection systems	10	1/7/10
Pumping systems:		
Guns & nozzles	3	1/7/10
Hose reels	7	1/7/10
Hoses	2	1/7/10
Hydraulically driven pumps	8	1/7/10
Pipes & fittings	10	1/7/10
Tailgate loaders	15	1/7/10
Single or multi product gasoline & diesoline dispensers (incorporating meters, electronic circuitry, LCD displays, cash presets, hoses, automatic nozzles & steel cabinets &, where applicable, vapour recovery monitoring & collection systems)	10	1/7/10
Single or multi product gasoline & diesoline pumps (incorporating pump units, meter, electronic circuitry, LCD displays, cash presets, hoses, automatic nozzles, steel cabinets &, where applicable, vapour recovery monitoring & collection systems)	10	1/7/10
Submersible turbine pumps	8	1/7/10
Underground distribution piping systems (incorporating pipes, fittings & manholes) fibreglass & steel	20	1/7/10
Bulk fuel terminal assets (excluding LPG assets):		
Automatic tank gauges	10	1/7/10
Effluent treatment systems (incorporating air pump, pipes, separator & tank)	10	1/7/10
Fire protection systems (incorporating auxiliary monitors, fire & ultraviolet detectors, fire indicator anels, fire retardant lines & foam storage tank)	15	1/7/10
Hoses	2	1/7/10
Loading & unloading arms (incorporating balance mechanisms, couplers, drop hoses & swivels)	10	1/7/10
Marketing pumps	7	1/7/10
Meters & metering systems	7	1/7/10
Overfill protection systems	10	1/7/10
Product piping (steel)	20	1/7/10
Terminal automation equipment	10	1/7/10
Vapour recovery units	15	1/7/10
LPG depot & terminal assets:		
Automatic tank gauges	10	1/7/10
Cathodic protection systems:		
Sacrificial anode	10	1/7/10
Impressed current	20	1/7/10
Depot & terminal storage vessels – aboveground & underground	30	1/7/10
Electronic scales	10	1/7/10
Forklift fuel tanks:		
Galvanised steel or steel tanks coated with zinc rich enamel	15	1/7/10
Aluminium tanks	12	1/7/10
Hoses	5	1/7/10
In situ permanently installed cylinders	30	1/7/10
Leak detection systems	8	1/7/10
Leisure market cylinders (4.5 & 9 kgs capacity)	15	1/7/10
Loading arms:		
Terminal	10	1/7/10
Marine	25	1/7/10
LPG fleet refuelling facility:		
Dispenser	10	1/7/10
Guns & nozzles	3	1/7/10
Hoses	5	1/7/10
Meters	7	1/7/10

Asset	Life (yrs)	Date of application
Piping	20	1/7/10
Pump sets	10	1/7/10
Storage tanks	30	1/7/10
Valves	10	1/7/10
LPG tank truck assets:		
LPG storage tanks	20	1/7/10
Metering systems	7	1/7/10
Pumping systems:		
Guns & nozzles	3	1/7/10
Hoses	5	1/7/10
Hose reels	7	1/7/10
Pipes & fittings	7	1/7/10
Pumps	7	1/7/10
Valves	7	1/7/10
Product piping systems:		
Pipes	20	1/7/10
Valves	10	1/7/10
Pumps	7	1/7/10
Stillages	5	1/7/10
Vapour recovery units & vapour compressors	7	1/7/10
Weighbridges	25	1/7/10
COMMISSION-BASED WHOLESALING		
Sale yards (used by stock & station agents)	30	1/7/14
RETAIL TRADE		
Counters, freestanding (including check out & service counters)	10	1/7/05
Electronic article surveillance (EAS) system assets (including barcodes or tag deactivators & detachers, door pedestals, electronic tag release assets, receivers & transmitters)	5	1/7/05
Floor coverings (removable without damage):		
Carpet	8	1/7/05
Floating timber	10	1/7/05
Linoleum	10	1/7/05
Vinyl	10	1/7/05
Furniture, freestanding (including chairs, cupboards, racks, showcases & tables)	10	1/7/05
Hot food display assets (including bain marie)	10	1/7/05
Overhead track scales (including meat rail scales)	10	1/7/05
Refrigeration assets:		
Generally (including blast chillers, condensers, evaporators, refrigeration cabinets, standalone freezers & standalone refrigerators)	10	1/7/14
Ice making machines	8	1/7/14
Insulation panels used in cool or freezer rooms	40	1/7/14
Roller shutter electric motors	20	1/7/05
Shelving	10	1/7/05
Trolleys, customer shopping type	7	1/7/05
Trolleys, stock type	10	1/7/05
Visual display assets (including body forms, head displayers, mannequins & seasonal decorations)	7	1/7/05
MOTOR VEHICLE TYRE OR TUBE RETAILING		
Air tools including ratchet guns	2	1/7/11
Compressed air assets:		
Air compressors:		
Reciprocating	10	1/7/11
Rotary screw	10	1/7/11
Rotary vane	10	1/7/11
Air receivers	10	1/7/11
Air driers & dehumidifiers	10	1/7/11
Hose reels	3	1/7/11
Reticulation lines:		
Aluminium	15	1/7/11
Copper	20	1/7/11
Polyethylene	15	1/7/11
Steel	10	1/7/11
Floor jacks:		
Used for car & light truck repairs	3	1/7/11
Used for heavy vehicle repairs	5	1/7/11
Hand tools	10	1/7/11
Stillages	15	1/7/11
Storage shelving	10	1/7/11
Tyre conveyors:		
Horizontal	10	1/7/11
Vertical	8	1/7/11
Tyre fitting machines	5	1/7/11
Tyre inflation cages	10	1/7/11
Tyre inflators (automatic & manual)	3	1/7/11

Asset	Life (yrs)	Date of application
Tyre spreaders	8	1/7/11
Vehicle hoists:		
Used for car & light truck repairs	10	1/7/11
Used for heavy vehicle repairs	20	1/7/11
Wheel alignment machines	7	1/7/11
Wheel balancing machines	5	1/7/11
Wheel balancing plates, flanges & finger adaptors	5	1/7/11
Wheel lifters	5	1/7/11
Wheel lifters incorporating tyre spreaders	8	1/7/11

FUEL RETAILING

Asset	Life (yrs)	Date of application
Air compressors & air lines	7	1/7/10
Automatic tank gauges	10	1/7/10
Canopy lighting:		
Liquid emitting diode	10	1/7/10
Radiant gas positive	5	1/7/10
Convenience store assets:		
Air conditioning systems	7	1/7/10
Back loading refrigerated cabinets (incorporating fans, boosters & compressors)	10	1/7/10
CCTV video surveillance systems	4	1/7/10
Coffee making machines including espresso & drip filter type machines	5	1/7/10
Counters – freestanding	10	1/7/10
Display shelving & racking	10	1/7/10
Door controls & motor drive systems for automatic opening doors (incorporating controls, motors & sensors, but excluding doors)	7	1/7/10
Hot food display assets including bain maries	10	1/7/10
Microwave ovens	5	1/7/10
Pie warmers & heating units	10	1/7/10
Refrigerated cabinets & freezers	10	1/7/10
PA systems	12	1/7/10
Point of sale assets:		
Barcode scanners	6	1/7/10
Electronic funds transfer point of sale machines (EFTPOS)	6	1/7/10
Forecourt controllers	6	1/7/10
Safes:		
Cash storage	10	1/7/10
Cash vending	7	1/7/10
Cigarette safes	7	1/7/10
Emergency shut off systems	10	1/7/10
Facility signs	7	1/7/10
Gasoline & diesoline assets:		
Effluent treatment systems (incorporating motors, electronic circuitry, pumps, & separators)	8	1/7/10
Leak protection pressure systems	8	1/7/10
Single or multi product gasoline & diesoline dispensers (incorporating meters, electronic circuitry, LCD displays, cash presets, hoses, automatic nozzles, steel cabinets &, where applicable, vapour recovery monitoring & collection systems)	10	1/7/10
Single or multi product gasoline & diesoline pumps (incorporating pump units, meters, electronic circuitry, LCD displays, cash presets, hoses, automatic nozzles, steel cabinets &, where applicable, vapour recovery monitoring & collection systems	7	1/7/10
Pay at pump card reading systems	6	1/7/10
Submersible turbine pumps	8	1/7/10
Underground fuel distribution & containment piping systems (incorporating pipes, fittings & manholes)	20	1/7/10
Underground fuel storage tanks – steel & fibreglass	20	1/7/10
Hot water systems	10	1/7/10
LPG assets:		
LPG pumps	7	1/7/10
LPG dispensers (incorporating meters, electronic circuitry, LCD displays, cash presets, hoses, automatic nozzles & steel cabinets)	10	1/7/10
LPG storage tanks – aboveground & underground	30	1/7/10
Underground steel piping systems (incorporating pipes, fittings & manholes)	20	1/7/10

FOOD RETAILING

Asset	Life (yrs)	Date of application
Butchers' plant	20	1/1/01

Asset	Life (yrs)	Date of application
OTHER STORE BASED RETAILING		
Newspaper wrapping machines	10	1/1/01
Paint tinting & colour blending machines (manual & automatic)	7	1/7/14

ACCOMMODATION & FOOD SERVICES

ACCOMMODATION

Accommodation providers using assets not listed here may rely on determinations shown for Residential property operators.
Accommodation providers who operate a pub, tavern, bar, cafe, restaurant or club within their premises should use the effective life determinations shown for cafes, restaurants, takeaway food services, pubs, taverns, bars & clubs (hospitality) for assets used in that business

Asset	Life (yrs)	Date of application
Audio visual entertainment assets including those used in conference & function rooms (including amplifier, audio speaker, digital disc player, microphone, television, turntable, video projection equipment)	5	1/7/05
Carpets	7	1/7/05
Door control & motor drive system for automatic sliding doors & revolving doors (incorporating chains, controls, motors & sensors, but excluding doors)	10	1/7/05
Furniture, freestanding:		
Generally (including guestrooms)	7	1/7/05
Outdoor	5	1/7/05
Garage doors, electric (excluding doors):		
Controls & motors	5	1/7/05
Gates, electric (excluding gates):		
Controls & motors	5	1/7/05
Guestroom assets:		
Bathroom assets:		
Accessories, freestanding (incl sanitary assets, shower caddies, soap holders & toilet brushes)	1	1/7/05
Hair dryers	3	1/7/05
Heated towel rails, electric	5	1/7/05
Scales	5	1/7/05
Spa bath pumps	7	1/7/05
Towels	1	1/7/05
Bedding (including mattress protectors, pillows & sheets)	2	1/7/05
Bed mattresses	7	1/7/05
Beds:		
Generally (including ensembles)	7	1/7/05
Foldout & rollaway beds (excluding sofas)	3	1/7/05
Bed spreads, blankets & quilts	5	1/7/05
Clocks & clock radios	5	1/7/05
Kitchen assets:		
Bar refrigerators	10	1/7/05
Cooking utensils (incl electric jugs, kettles, pans, pots & toasters, but excluding portable cook tops & ovens)	2	1/7/05
Crockery & cutlery	4	1/7/05
Glassware	2	1/7/05
Microwave ovens	5	1/7/05
Laundry assets in guestrooms:		
Clothes dryers	7	1/7/05
Irons & ironing boards	3	1/7/05
Washing machines	7	1/7/05
Window blinds & curtains	6	1/7/05
Hot water systems (excl commercial boilers & piping)	10	1/7/05
Housekeeping assets (including bins, buckets, floor signs & toilet brushes)	1	1/7/05
Laundry assets used by hotel/motel operators:		
Dryers	10	1/7/05
Linen bins	15	1/7/05
Pressers	15	1/7/05
Roller irons	20	1/7/05
Washing machines	10	1/7/05
Public address & paging system assets (including amplifiers, audio speakers & microphones)	10	1/7/05
Sauna heating assets	10	1/7/05
Swimming pools & spas:		
Chlorinators	8	1/7/05
Filtration assets (including pumps)	8	1/7/05
Heaters	10	1/7/05
Trolleys	10	1/7/05
Vacuum cleaners	3	1/7/05
Water pumps used to deliver water to residences above ground level	10	1/7/05

Asset	Life (yrs)	Date of application

CAFES, RESTAURANTS, TAKEAWAY FOOD SERVICES, PUBS, TAVERNS, BARS & CLUBS (HOSPITALITY)

Asset	Life (yrs)	Date of application
Audio visual entertainment assets (incl amplifiers, audio speakers, digital disc players, microphones, televisions, turntables & video projection equipment)	5	1/7/05
Bars, freestanding (incl drink service counters & wet bars)	15	1/7/05
Beer dispensing system assets (including, tanks, taps tubes & valves)	15	1/7/05
Coffee making machines (including espresso & drip filter type machines)	5	1/7/05
Counters for customer service, freestanding	15	1/7/05
Dance floor assets, freestanding (incl wooden surface, fog & smoke machines, strobe lights & disco balls)	5	1/7/05
Dishwasher machines	8	1/7/05
Drink blenders	3	1/7/05
Drink dispensing machines (incl hot water urns, post mix dispensers, refrigerated & frozen drink dispensers & dairy dispensers, but excl beer dispensing systems)	10	1/7/05
Electronic spirits dispensers	5	1/7/05
Floor coverings, removable without damage:		
Carpet	5	1/7/05
Rubber safety mats	5	1/7/05
Food preparation & service assets:		
Bench top appliances – small portable type (including blenders, food processors, grills, rice cookers & toasters)	3	1/7/05
Cooking appliances, large commercial type (including cook tops, deep fryers, grills, kebab machines, ovens & salamanders)	10	1/7/05
Cookware, Handheld (including frypans, pans, pots, trays & woks)	2	1/7/05
Crockery, cutlery & glassware	1	1/7/05
Hot food display assets (including bain marie)	10	1/7/05
Microwave ovens	5	1/7/05
Preparation benches, freestanding	20	1/7/05
Wok burners, large commercial type	8	1/7/05
Furniture, freestanding, for customer use:		
In drinking areas of pubs, bars, clubs	5	1/7/05
In dining areas	8	1/7/05
Furniture, not freestanding:		
Chairs & tables fixed to ground or building	20	1/7/05
Glassware	1	1/7/05
Glass washer machines	5	1/7/05
Kitchen exhaust fans	5	1/7/05
Menu boards	5	1/7/05
Poker/gaming machines	7	1/7/09
Refrigeration assets:		
Generally (including blast chillers, condensers, evaporators, refrigeration cabinets, standalone freezers & standalone refrigerators)	10	1/7/14
Ice making machines	8	1/7/14
Insulation panels used in cool or freezer rooms	40	1/7/14

TRANSPORT, POSTAL & WAREHOUSING

ROAD TRANSPORT

Asset	Life (yrs)	Date of application
Containers, transportable (used to transport goods by road, rail & sea)	10	1/1/01
Taxis	4	1/7/15

TRAMWAY & LIGHT RAIL PASSENGER TRANSPORT SERVICES

Asset	Life (yrs)	Date of application
Infrastructure assets:		
Communication, computer & passenger support assets:		
Automatic vehicle monitoring computer systems	10	1/7/10
Automatic vehicle monitoring tram borne equipment including transponders	10	1/7/10
CCTV systems	4	1/7/10
Control systems	10	1/7/10
Hand held passenger ticketing machines	5	1/7/10
Passenger information displays	10	1/7/10
Passenger ticketing machines	15	1/7/10
Radio base stations, intercoms	7	1/7/10
Electrification assets:		
Lighting	15	1/7/10

Asset	Life (yrs)	Date of application
Overhead distribution lines (incorporating conductors, cross arms, feeders, insulators, inverters, fittings & poles)	30	1/7/10
Power transformers	40	1/7/10
Substations (incorporating switchgear & circuit breakers)	40	1/7/10
Signalling assets (including automatic points)	15	1/7/10
Track maintenance assets:		
Truck mounted maintenance assets (including points cleaning, sweeping & welding machines)	15	1/7/10
Trackwork (incorporating track drainage):		
Ballasted track	25	1/7/10
Curved track	20	1/7/10
Embedded track	30	1/7/10
Points (excl automatic points) & crossings	20	1/7/10
Track within depots	40	1/7/10
Tramway & light rail rolling stock:		
Bogies	30	1/7/10
Carriages, modules, saloons	30	1/7/10
Pantographs	15	1/7/10

RAIL FREIGHT & PASSENGER TRANSPORT SERVICES

Asset	Life (yrs)	Date of application
Containers, transportable (used to transport goods by road, rail & sea)	10	1/1/01
Infrastructure assets:		
Electrification assets:		
Overhead distribution lines (incorporating conductors, contact catenary, cross arms, insulators & fittings, & poles)	33$\frac{1}{3}$	1/1/02
Power transformers	30	1/1/02
Substations (incorporating switchgear & circuit breakers)	40	1/1/02
Passenger information & ticketing system	15	1/1/02
Signalling assets (including axle detectors, block signals, dragging equipment detector, hot boxes, interlockings, level crossings, & train control & train describer)	15	1/1/02
Trackwork (incorporating rails, sleepers, ballast, permanent way/top 600, & integral bridges, culverts & tunnels):		
Freight (trackwork used by vehicles with gross axle loads of 30 tonnes & below per vehicle):		
Heavy haul (trackwork carrying >20 GMT per annum)	30	1/1/02
Light haul (trackwork carrying <1 GMT per annum)	50	1/1/02
Medium haul (trackwork carrying between 1GMT & 20 GMT per annum)	40	1/1/02
Freight (trackwork used by vehicles with gross axle loads above 30 tonnes per vehicle)	20	1/1/02
Passenger	40	1/1/02
Turnouts & crossings	20	1/1/02
Monorail operation assets:		
Infrastructure assets:		
Communication, computer & passenger assets:		
CCTV systems	4	1/7/10
Control systems including commutators	10	1/7/10
Hand held passenger ticketing machines	5	1/7/10
Passenger information displays	10	1/7/10
Passenger ticketing machines	15	1/7/10
Phones, radio base stations, intercoms	7	1/7/10
Rescue & recovery vehicles	30	1/7/10
Electrification assets:		
Collector rails	30	1/7/10
Lighting	15	1/7/10
Power transformers	40	1/7/10
Standby generators	25	1/7/10
Substations (incorporating switchgear & circuit breakers)	40	1/7/10
Uninterruptible power supply systems	5	1/7/10
Track & maintenance assets:		
Beams & columns	30	1/7/10
Maintenance vehicles	15	1/7/10
Track	30	1/7/10
Track switches	30	1/7/10
Traversers	30	1/7/10
Monorail rolling stock:		
Bogies	30	1/7/10
Carriages, modules, saloons	30	1/7/10

Asset	Life (yrs)	Date of application
Railway rolling stock:		
Locomotives:		
Generally (including diesel electric & electric)	25	1/1/02
Heavy haul (bulk minerals/coal)	20	1/1/02
Underground (diesel battery)	15	1/1/02
Passenger:		
Electric/diesel power cars & trailers	30	1/1/02
Locomotive hauled carriages (incl baggage vans, diners, mail vans, sit up cars, & sleepers)	30	1/1/02
Power vans	15	1/1/02
Rail mounted track infrastructure assets:		
Generally (including ballast wagons/cleaners/ regulators, rail grinders, sleeper laying machines & track recorders)	20	1/1/02
Mainline & switch tampers	15	1/1/02
Wagons – bulk freight:		
Mineral ores & coal:		
Carbon steel	20	1/1/02
Ferritic steel	30	1/1/02
Other:		
Coke quenchers	15	1/1/02
Grain hoppers	20	1/1/02
Limestone	20	1/1/02
Pneumatic discharge – cement	20	1/1/02
Used on tram lines	40	1/1/01
Tank cars	20	1/1/02
Wagons – non bulk freight (including all wagons used for general & inter modal freight)	30	1/1/02

Note: From the 2012-13 income year, a capped life of 10 years is available for the decline in value of eligible shipping vessels but only if certain conditions are met (see subsection 40-102(4) item 10 & subsection 40-102(4A))

WATER TRANSPORT & SUPPORT SERVICES

Asset	Life (yrs)	Date of application
Commercial vessels:		
Canoes	10	1/7/09
Dinghies & punts (not longer than 6 metres)	12	1/7/09
Fishing vessels (including trawlers, long liners, seiners, fin fish boats, pearling boats, lobster boats, aquaculture & other fishing boats):		
Longer than 10 metres	20	1/7/09
Not longer than 10 metres	15	1/7/09
Houseboats	20	1/7/09
Inflatable boats (excl rigid hull inflatable boats)	7	1/7/09
Jet skis	4	1/7/09
Kayaks	5	1/7/09
Offshore supply & support vessels	20	1/7/09
Passenger vessels (including cruise vessels, skippered charter vessels, vehicle & passenger ferries, semi submersible vessels & water taxis):		
Longer than 10 metres	20	1/7/09
Not longer than 10 metres	15	1/7/09
Pedal boats	10	1/7/09
Pontoon boats (excluding pontoons or floating jetties used for storage or walkway only)	15	1/7/09
Sail boats (not longer than 6 metres & including 'off the beach' boats)	10	1/7/09
Ski boats	10	1/7/09
Thrill boats (including jet boats)	10	1/7/09
Trading ships:		
Bulk carriers	20	1/7/09
Cargo ships	20	1/7/09
Container ships	20	1/7/09
Roll on/roll off ships	20	1/7/09
Tankers:		
Oil & chemical	20	1/7/09
LNG & LPG	30	1/7/09
Work vessels (including barges, coastal supply boats, dredges, general work boats, landing craft, launches, lighters, line boats, pilot boats, runabouts & tug boats):		
Longer than 10 metres	20	1/7/09
Not longer than 10 metres	15	1/7/09
Yachts & motor cruisers – bare boat charter (including monohulls, catamarans & trimarans)	15	1/7/09
Support assets (acquired separately from the vessel):		
Desalinators	10	1/7/09
Hot water units:		
Domestic	5	1/7/09
Marine	10	1/7/09

Asset	Life (yrs)	Date of application
Lifting assets:		
Hoists & winches:		
Electric	5	1/7/09
Hydraulic & mechanical	10	1/7/09
Navigational & communication assets acquired separately from the vessel (including autopilots, chart plotters, depth sounders, global positioning systems [GPS], radar systems & marine radios)	5	1/7/09
Outboard motors	5	1/7/09
Power supply assets:		
Batteries (deep cycle)	3	1/7/09
Generators (stand alone)	10	1/7/09
Inverters	6	1/7/09
Safety assets:		
Emergency signalling assets (incl EPIRBS)	5	1/7/09
Life rafts	10	1/7/09
Trailers	8	1/7/09
Port assets:		
Cargo handling equipment:		
Containers, transportable (used to transport goods by road, rail & sea)	10	1/1/01
Cranes:		
Container/portainer	20	1/7/02
Fixed	25	1/7/02
Mobile (over 15.24 tonnes lift)	20	1/7/02
Dozers	9	1/7/02
Forklifts:		
Container handling	7½	1/7/02
General handling	11	1/7/02
Rail mounted gantries	15	1/7/02
Reach stackers	10	1/7/02
Ship loaders	30	1/7/02
Ship unloaders	20	1/7/02
Spreaders	5	1/7/02
Stackers, reclaimers & stackers/reclaimers	25	1/7/02
Straddle carriers	12½	1/7/02
Wheel loaders	8	1/7/02
Control systems:		
Control system assets – PLCs & hardware	10	1/7/02
Motor control centre & motor control field devices	20	1/7/02
Environmental equipment:		
Current, tidal, wave & wind monitoring systems	5	1/7/02
Oil spill containment boom	10	1/7/02
Intermodal facilities:		
Receival station assets (incl belt feeder, hopper & tippler)	30	1/7/02
Truck & rail receival dump pit	50	1/7/02
Land based facilities:		
Concrete rail beams & rails	30	1/7/02
Conveyor systems (incorporating chutes, gravity take up assemblies, headframes, structures, surge bins, transfer towers & weigh towers)	30	1/7/02
Dust suppression systems	30	1/7/02
Electricity supply assets – see Table A Electricity supply		
Storage sheds, to the extent they form an integral part of bulk handling equipment	40	1/7/02
Navigational aids:		
Land based navigational aids	20	1/7/02
Offshore beacons, channel markers & lead lights:		
Floating buoys	10	1/7/02
Piled structures	20	1/7/02
Other facilities:		
Cathodic protection:		
Impressed current system	30	1/7/02
Sacrificial system	15	1/7/02
Dry docks (including floating dry docks)	40	1/7/13
Fender systems:		
Elastomeric	20	1/7/02
Timber	10	1/7/02
Gangways – removable	10	1/7/02
Mooring facilities (including bollards)	40	1/7/02
Mooring quick release hooks	20	1/7/02
Pontoons – floating	20	1/7/02
Slipways (incorporating rails, ramps, runners & winching systems)	30	1/7/02
Wharves, dolphins & jetties	40	1/7/02

Asset	Life (yrs)	Date of application
Salvage machinery:		
Boilers, vertical	40	1/1/01
Engine hoisting	40	1/1/01
Pumps:		
Centrifugal, direct acting, & connections	40	1/1/01
Duplex boiler feed	40	1/1/01
SCENIC & SIGHTSEEING TRANSPORT		
Gliders (including motor gliders)	20	1/7/13
Hot air balloon ride operation assets:		
Flight instruments	10	1/7/13
Hot air balloon assets:		
Baskets	6	1/7/13
Burners	10	1/7/13
Envelopes	5	1/7/13
Fuel cylinders & tanks (incorporating shut off valves)	20	1/7/13
Inflator fans	15	1/7/13
Monocable circulating detachable, reversible & fixed ropeway assets operated in non snowfield areas:		
Cabins including carriers	25	1/7/09
Communications assets:		
Communications cables	10	1/7/09
Radios	5	1/7/09
Drive & return station assets (including braking systems, drive systems, gear boxes, motors, variable speed drives & tensioning systems)	15	1/7/09
Rescue vehicles	30	1/7/09
Ropes:		
Haul ropes	10	1/7/09
Track ropes	20	1/7/09
Standby power drives	25	1/7/09
Towers:		
Tower heads	15	1/7/09
Tower structures	30	1/7/09
Transportation systems incorporating drives & belts	3	1/7/09
Monocable circulating fixed grip & detachable ropeway assets operated in snowfield areas including double, triple & quad chair lifts, T bar, poma & surface lifts:		
Chair head grips	15	1/7/09
Chairs, T bars & pomas	25	1/7/09
Communication assets:		
Communications cables – above ground	10	1/7/09
Communications cables – under ground	25	1/7/09
Radios & telephone systems	5	1/7/09
Covered moving walkways including covered walkways & carpets	10	1/7/09
Drive & return station assets (including braking system, drive system, gear boxes, motors, variable speed drives & tensioning systems)	20	1/7/09
Oversnow transport assets:		
Oversnow transporters	8	1/7/09
Skidoos	5	1/7/09
Ropes:		
Main hauling rope for detachable lifts etc	15	1/7/09
Main hauling rope for fixed grip, t bars lifts etc	20	1/7/09
Snow grooming assets (including free groomers, snow blowers & winches)	8	1/7/09
Snowmaking assets including:		
Air water guns & fan guns	10	1/7/09
Compressors, pumps, water mains & pipes	20	1/7/09
Cooling towers	15	1/7/09
Electrical cables – above ground	10	1/7/09
Electrical cables – under ground	25	1/7/09
Weather stations	5	1/7/09
Standby power drives	25	1/7/09
Tower heads & structures	30	1/7/09
POSTAL SERVICES		
Mail house assets:		
Envelope inserters	7	1/7/15
Folders	12½	1/7/15
Guillotines	15	1/7/15
Heat sealers	10	1/7/15
Printers	5	1/7/15
Racks	20	1/7/15
Scales	5	1/7/15
Scanners	5	1/7/15
Trolleys	8	1/7/15

Asset	Life (yrs)	Date of application
COURIER PICK UP & DELIVERY SERVICES		
Inspection assets:		
Scales:		
Bench	10	1/7/11
Floor (platform)	20	1/7/11
Weight dimension capture system assets (incl checkweighers, in motion scales & readers)	10	1/7/11
Materials handling equipment:		
Ball transfer mats & castor decks	20	1/7/11
Conveyors (including shoe sorters)	15	1/7/11
Forklifts – see Table B		
Scissor lifts	10	1/7/15
Storage racks	20	1/7/11
Trolleys, freight barrows, cages & bins	10	1/7/11
Pick up & delivery equipment:		
Barcode label printers	5	1/7/11
Portable Hand held barcode readers (including point of delivery capture devices & delivery information acquisition devices)	4	1/7/11
AIRPORT OPERATIONS & OTHER AIR TRANSPORT SUPPORT SERVICES		
Aircraft maintenance assets:		
Aircraft testing equipment	13⅓	1/1/01
General plant & machinery	20	1/1/01
Hangar fixtures & fittings	20	1/1/01
Plant subject to excessive corrosion	10	1/1/01
Precision machines & plant	10	1/1/01
Aircraft training assets:		
Flight simulators	8	1/1/01
Link trainers	8	1/1/01
Airport assets:		
Aerobridges	20	1/1/03
Baggage handling assets:		
Baggage check in stations (incorporating scales & check in conveyors)	10	1/1/03
Baggage outbound conveyor systems (incorporating belts, diverters, gearboxes, motors, ploughs, rollers, structures & tag readers)	15	1/1/03
Baggage reclaim conveyor systems (incorporating belts, gearboxes, motors, rollers & structures)	15	1/1/03
Control systems (excluding computers)	10	1/1/03
Fire safety & rescue assets:		
Breathing units	10	1/1/03
Drills, air powered	10	1/1/03
Fire fighting vehicles	20	1/1/03
Rescue boats:		
Aluminium	20	1/1/03
Inflatable	8	1/1/03
Rescue units (jaws of life)	15	1/1/03
Fuel supply assets:		
Aircraft fueller vehicles	15	1/1/03
Aircraft hydrant dispenser vehicles	15	1/1/03
Filters, fuel	25	1/1/03
Fire fighting systems	25	1/1/03
Piping	25	1/1/03
Pumps, fuel	25	1/1/03
Tanks	25	1/1/03
Ground support assets:		
Aircraft loader/unloader vehicles	15	1/1/03
Aircraft stairs:		
Manual	20	1/1/03
Vehicle mounted	15	1/1/03
Airstart units	15	1/1/03
Containers, air cargo (used to transport goods by air)	5	1/1/01
Ground power units	15	1/1/03
High lift service vehicles (including catering, lavatory, maintenance & water vehicles)	15	1/1/03
Tow tractors	20	1/1/03
Tractors, baggage	15	1/1/03
Tractor trolleys (including baggage & container trolleys, & dollies)	10	1/1/03
Navigation aids:		
Distance measuring assets	15	1/1/03
Instrument landing systems	10	1/1/03
Non directional beacons (excluding towers)	15	1/1/03
Radar sensors	15	1/1/03
Towers	30	1/1/03

Asset	Life (yrs)	Date of application
VHF omni range assets (excluding towers)	15	1/1/03
Runway sweepers	15	1/1/03
Terminal building assets:		
Flight information display signs (including monitors & LED screens)	7	1/1/03
Security scanning assets (including explosive detection systems, Hand held & walk through detectors, & x ray screening systems)	5	1/1/03
Visual aids assets:		
Docking guidance systems	10	1/1/03
Lighting systems (incl apron floodlighting, runway lighting & taxiway lighting)	15	1/1/03
Movement area guidance signs	10	1/1/03
Visual approach slope indicator systems (PAPI)	15	1/1/03
Wind direction indicators, illuminated	10	1/1/03

OTHER TRANSPORT SUPPORT SERVICES N.E.C.

Asset	Life (yrs)	Date of application
Electronic toll collection assets:		
Digital measuring instruments (including vehicle classifiers (laser or infra red) & electronic toll collection readers (radio frequency))	4	1/7/05
Electronic toll collection transponders	4	1/7/05
Optical character recognition cameras	4	1/7/05

OTHER WAREHOUSING & STORAGE SERVICES

Asset	Life (yrs)	Date of application
Warehouse & distribution centre equipment & machines:		
Automated storage & retrieval machines	20	1/7/11
Balers	15	1/7/11
Battery assets for warehouse vehicles (including pallet trucks & forklifts):		
Batteries (detachable for recharging)	5	1/7/11
Battery chargers:		
Forklifts	11	1/7/11
Other	10	1/7/11
Handling assets:		
Battery tuggers	10	1/7/11
Racking roller beds	15	1/7/11
Transfer carts	10	1/7/11
Washers	10	1/7/11
Carts/buggies	15	1/7/11
Conveyors	15	1/7/11
Dock levellers, pallet jacks, pallet trucks & scissor lifts – see Table B Loading bay assets		
Door control & motor drive systems (incorporating chains, controls, motor & sensors, but excl doors):		
External	20	1/7/11
Internal	10	1/7/11
Floor sweepers/scrubbers	10	1/7/11
Forklift attachments:		
Cages	10	1/7/11
Push pull units	11	1/7/11
Inflatable dock bags/seals/shelters	10	1/7/11
Packaging machines & wrapping machines – see Table B Packaging machines		
Pallet assets:		
Dispensers	15	1/7/11
Lift tables	10	1/7/11
Racks	20	1/7/11
Radio frequency terminal assets:		
Barcode readers/scanners	5	1/7/11
Portable/Handheld & vehicle mounted terminal devices	4	1/7/11
Refrigeration assets – see Table B		
Roll cages	10	1/7/11
Trolleys	10	1/7/11
Voice picking assets:		
Battery chargers	4	1/7/11
Headsets	4	1/7/11
Terminals (on person)	4	1/7/11
Waste compactors (used for cardboard & plastic):		
Electric	15	1/7/11
Hydraulic	20	1/7/11

INFORMATION MEDIA & TELECOMMUNICATIONS

MOTION PICTURE & VIDEO ACTIVITIES

Asset	Life (yrs)	Date of application
Camera accessories:		
Aspect ratio converters	12	1/1/06
Digital or electronic time code slates	5	1/1/06
Speed control, time lapse & phase adjustment controls	10	1/1/06
Time code generators & master clocks	10	1/1/06
Underwater & marine housings & rain deflectors	12	1/1/06
Video assist systems (incorporating monitors, video recorder with playback, transmitters & receivers)	3	1/1/06
Cameras:		
16mm & 35mm film cameras	10	1/1/06
Digital cameras	5	1/1/06
Camera lens accessories:		
Coloured & graduated filters & filter stages	3	1/1/06
Fish eye & wide angle lens adapters	10	1/1/06
Follow focus, remote focus, shutter & zoom controls	10	1/1/06
Image stabilisers, matte boxes, & teleprompters	10	1/1/06
Camera lenses	10	1/1/06
Camera supports (inclheads, legs mounts & tripods)	10	1/1/06
Copyright in a feature film (not including a licence relating to a copyright in a feature film)	5	1/7/04
Grips' assets:		
Camera cranes	10	1/1/06
Camera heads	10	1/1/06
Car rigs, sea rigs & other specialised rigs	2	1/1/06
Communications systems	5	1/1/06
Dollies	12	1/1/06
Dolly & camera attachments	10	1/1/06
Dolly track	5	1/1/06
Remote camera control systems	10	1/1/06
Towers, rigging, & dance floors	10	1/1/06
Tracking vehicles & insert trailers – see Table B Motor vehicles & trailers		
Lighting assets:		
Accessories (including gaffer grips, clamps, mounts, & stands)	10	1/1/06
Portable lights	10	1/1/06
Studio lights – fixed	15	1/1/06
Lighting control systems	10	1/1/06
Lighting grids – fixed	20	1/1/06
Lighting hoists	15	1/1/06
Motion picture film processing assets:		
Chemical agitators & mixers	10	1/1/06
Chemical storage tanks	15	1/1/06
Film cleaning machines	10	1/1/06
Film colour analysers & colour grading machines	8	1/1/06
Film densitometers	10	1/1/06
Film printing machines	10	1/1/06
Film processing machines	10	1/1/06
Film re winders	15	1/1/06
Flat bed & rear projection film viewers	15	1/1/06
Mixed chemical pumps	10	1/1/06
Optical sound camera systems (incorporating soundtrack & time code generators)	10	1/1/06
Silver recovery units	8	1/1/06
Sound quality control processors	5	1/1/06
Waste water treatment assets	10	1/1/06
Post production sound assets:		
Amplifiers & pre amplifiers	5	1/1/06
Audio effects units (incorporating aural exciters, compressors, delay & effects control processors graphic equalisers, harmonisers, limiters, noise reduction processors, reverberation processors, telephone simulators & time controllers)	5	1/1/06
Digital audio players & recorders (including CD, DVD, DAT (digital audio tape), mini disc & hard disc players & recorders)	3	1/1/06
Digital film projectors	5	1/1/06
Digital sound conversion processors (including encoders & decoders)	5	1/1/06
Hard disc video players & recorders	3	1/1/06
Microphones & microphone accessories	10	1/1/06
Motion picture film projectors	10	1/1/06
Screens	5	1/1/06
Sound mixing desks & consoles	5	1/1/06
Speakers	7	1/1/06
Time code synchronisation units	5	1/1/06
Video routers & servers	5	1/1/06
Post production video assets:		
DVD players	3	1/1/06
Edit controllers (used in linear editing)	4	1/1/06
High definition digital film scanners	4	1/1/06

Asset	Life (yrs)	Date of application
High definition laser film recorders	5	1/1/06
Monitors	5	1/1/06
Motion capture & analysis systems	5	1/1/06
Non linear editing systems (incorporating computer control, interface & hard disc system)	5	1/1/06
Telecine chains (incorporating colour correctors, film time code readers, grain & noise reduction systems & telecine machines)	7	1/1/06
VHS video cassette players & recorders	2	1/1/06
Video routers & servers	5	1/1/06
Videotape players & recorders	5	1/1/06
Screening theatre assets:		
Audio amplification & processing equipment (includes component racks systems)	5	1/1/06
Digital audio players, digital film projectors & digital sound conversion processors	5	1/1/06
Motion picture film projectors	10	1/1/06
Screens	8	1/1/06
Speakers	10	1/1/06
Sound recording assets:		
Amplifiers & pre amplifiers	5	1/1/06
Sound mixing consoles	5	1/1/06
Boom poles	2	1/1/06
Compressors, expanders & limiters	5	1/1/06
Digital audio players & recorders (including CD, DVD, DAT (digital audio tape), mini disc & hard disc players & recorders)	2	1/1/06
Digital or electronic time code slates	5	1/1/06
Headphones:		
Generally	2	1/1/06
Miniature in ear headphones	1	1/1/06
Microphones:		
Field or boom microphones	7	1/1/06
Lapel microphones	1	1/1/06
Microphone accessories (including adapters, connectors, stands, suspension mounts, pistol grips, windscreens & windjammers)	5	1/1/06
Microphone cables	2	1/1/06
Radio microphone systems (incorporating & antennas, miniature microphones, receivers transmitters)	5	1/1/06
Studio microphones	10	1/1/06
Monitors	2	1/1/06
Speakers	5	1/1/06
Vision switchers	5	1/1/06
Video monitors	5	1/1/06

MOTION PICTURE EXHIBITION

Asset	Life (yrs)	Date of application
Audio amplification & processing equipment (including component rack systems)	10	1/1/01
Carpets	5	1/1/01
Cinema automation systems	10	1/1/01
Cinema & sound processors	8	1/1/01
Cinema seating (incl frames, seat bodies & covers)	7	1/1/01
Curtains, wall & acoustic treatments	7	1/1/01
Drive in plant:		
Sound transmission equipment	10	1/1/01
Listening units (including posts, wiring & speaker equipment)	10	1/1/01
Screens & screen framing	15	1/1/01
Film handling & maintenance equipment (including splicers, footage counters, spools & reels, stripper plates, rewinders, spinners, trolleys & cleaners)	10	1/1/01
Film transport systems (including platter systems, tower, make up tables & interlock systems)	15	1/1/01
Lighting (including dimmers, aisle & seat)	10	1/1/01
Loud speakers & sound reproduction equipment	10	1/1/01
Motion picture & slide projection equipment:		
Motion picture projectors	10	1/1/01
Projector heat extraction systems	10	1/1/01
Projection ports	20	1/1/01
Slide projectors	10	1/1/01
Screen installations (including screens, framing & masking equipment)	8	1/1/01

RADIO BROADCASTING

Asset	Life (yrs)	Date of application
Amplifiers & pre-amplifiers	10	1/7/12
Audio monitors	10	1/7/12
Audio processing assets (including rack mounted effects units etc)	10	1/7/12
Audio routers	10	1/7/12

Asset	Life (yrs)	Date of application
Automation systems (including broadcast playout automation systems, content creation systems, music scheduling systems & traffic & billing automation systems)	6	1/7/12
Consoles:		
Broadcast consoles (incorporating audio logging & routing, intercommunication etc)	7	1/7/12
Production consoles	10	1/7/12
Control room assets generally:		
Electronically based assets (including audio processors, audio switchers, aural studio to transmitter linkage assets, distribution amplifiers, monitor receivers etc)	10	1/7/12
PC based assets (including, delay units, logging units, program fail detectors, RDS generators etc)	6	1/7/12
Digital audio players & recorders (including CD, DVD, mini disc, hard disc & solid state players & recorders)	5	1/7/12
Headphones & headsets	2	1/7/12
Intercommunication systems (standalone)	10	1/7/12
Microphones:		
Field & portable microphones	5	1/7/12
Studio based microphones (including recording microphones)	10	1/7/12
Microwave & satellite telecommunications assets - see Table A Telecommunications services		
Mobile production vehicles (excluding the assets contained within) - see Table B		
Motor vehicles & trailers		
On air lights	15	1/7/12
Racks	20	1/7/12
Servers, domain controllers, switches, transcoders etc	6	1/7/12
Studio based digital audio broadcasting infrastructure (encoding assets etc)	10	1/7/12
Telephone systems:		
Telephone interface assets generally (used for sending & receiving audio to & from connected telephone lines)	10	1/7/12
Telephone screening systems & other PC based telephone systems (excluding software)	6	1/7/12
Voice over internet protocol (VoIP) based systems	7	1/7/12
Time code generators	10	1/7/12
Transmission assets:		
Antennas	20	1/7/12
Codecs	10	1/7/12
Fibre optic terminal equipment generally	10	1/7/12
Generators (backup)	15	1/7/12
Obstruction lighting	15	1/7/12
Power conditioners	15	1/7/12
RF switching units	15	1/7/12
Signal receiving & monitoring assets (including audio processors, decoders, modulation monitors, spectrum analysers etc)	10	1/7/12
Silence detection & switching units	10	1/7/12
Surge arresters	10	1/7/12
Translators	15	1/7/12
Transmission towers	40	1/7/12
Transmitters	15	1/7/12
Uninterruptible power supply (UPS) assets - see Table B Power supply assets		

TELEVISION BROADCASTING

Asset	Life (yrs)	Date of application
Audio boards, consoles & mixers	12	1/7/05
Audio delay units	10	1/7/05
Audio effects units (including compression units, delay units, graphic equalisers & reverberation units)	12	1/7/05
Automated tape library systems (incorporating robotic controls & tape drives)	10	1/7/05
Broadcast antennas	20	1/7/05
Broadcast interfacing assets (including aspect ratio converters, distribution amplifiers, sync pulse generators, timecode generators & readers & other 'glue' assets)	12	1/7/05
Cameras:		
Portable cameras (including camcorders, electronic field production (EFP) & electronic news gathering (ENG) cameras)	8	1/7/05
Studio cameras	10	1/7/05
Camera control units	10	1/7/05

Asset	Life (yrs)	Date of application
Camera lens accessories (including adapters, filters, matte boxes & stabilisers)	12	1/7/05
Camera lenses	12	1/7/05
Camera mounting heads	15	1/7/05
Camera mounts (including cranes, jibs, pedestals & tripods)	25	1/7/05
Camera pan tilt & pedestal robotic systems (incorporating integrated hardware & control unit)	12	1/7/05
Character & graphics generating assets – standalone (including character generators, paintboxes & stillstores)	10	1/7/05
Digital audio players & recorders (including CD players & recorders, DAT players, DVD players & recorders, & Mini disc players & recorders)	5	1/7/05
Digital video effects (DVE) units – standalone	10	1/7/05
Edit controllers (used in linear editing & audio post production)	8	1/7/05
Hard disk recorders	5	1/7/05
Intercommunication systems	15	1/7/05
Lighting:		
Portable lighting	12	1/7/05
Studio lighting	15	1/7/05
Lighting control systems	10	1/7/05
Lighting grids – fixed	40	1/7/05
Lighting hoists	15	1/7/05
Microphones:		
Field or boom microphones	5	1/7/05
Miniature or 'lapel' microphones	5	1/7/05
Radio microphone systems (incorporating antennas, miniature microphones, receivers & transmitters)	5	1/7/05
Studio or fixed microphones	10	1/7/05
Microphone booms	10	1/7/05
Microwave telecommunications assets – see Table A Telecommunications services		
Mobile production vehicles (excluding the assets contained within) – see Table B Motor vehicles & trailers		
Monitors:		
Audio monitors	10	1/7/05
Video monitors:		
Cathode ray tube (CRT) monitors	8	1/7/05
LCD & Plasma monitors	5	1/7/05
Virtual monitor wall systems (including rear projection monitor walls)	5	1/7/05
Non linear editing systems (incorporating computer control, interface & hard disk system)	4	1/7/05
Presentation automation systems	10	1/7/05
Racks	20	1/7/05
RF Modulation units	12	1/7/05
Routing systems (incorporating control panels, hardware & switchers)	11	1/7/05
Satellite telecommunications assets – see Table A Telecommunications services		
Servers (excluding data servers)	8	1/7/05
Signal measurement, monitoring & testing assets (including modulation monitors, RF analysers, test signal generators, vectorscopes & waveform monitors)	12	1/7/05
Slow motion controllers	10	1/7/05
Switchers (including master control, presentation & production switchers)	10	1/7/05
Teleprompters	10	1/7/05
Translators	15	1/7/05
Transmission towers	40	1/7/05
Transmitters	15	1/7/05
Transmitting masts (for mobile production vehicles)	10	1/7/05
Under monitor & tally display systems	10	1/7/05
Videocassette recorders	5	1/7/05
Videotape players & recorders	8	1/7/05

INTERNET PUBLISHING & BROADCASTING

Internet only audio broadcasting assets - use any relevant determination in Table A Radio broadcasting

TELECOMMUNICATIONS SERVICES

Asset	Life (yrs)	Date of application
Backbone network assets:		
Conduits	40	1/7/03
Cross connects (including digital & optical)	15	1/7/03
Multiplexers (including wave division, terminal, & add drop)	15	1/7/03
Optical amplifiers	15	1/7/03
Optical fibre cables	25	1/7/03

Asset	Life (yrs)	Date of application
Optical patch panels	25	1/7/03
Regenerators	15	1/7/03
International telecommunications submarine cables	15	1/7/02
Microwave radio telecommunications assets:		
Antennas (incorporating wave guide, pressurisation unit, dehydrator & data cable):		
High capacity licensed microwave radio	10	1/7/04
Medium capacity licensed microwave radio	8	1/7/04
Low capacity licensed microwave radio	5	1/7/04
Microwave radio system including modulator, demodulator, receiver, transmitter, monitoring/supervisory system, RF filter:		
High capacity licensed microwave radio system ≥ 68Mb	10	1/7/04
Medium capacity licensed microwave radio system ≥ 16Mb to <68Mb	8	1/7/04
Low capacity licensed microwave radio system < 16Mb	5	1/7/04
Class licence microwave radio system (including antenna)	3	1/7/04
Multiplexers	10	1/7/04
Towers (including guyed, lattice & steel or concrete poles)	25	1/7/04
Mobile telecommunications assets:		
Base station assets:		
Antennas, battery backup, radio transmitters/receivers & rectifiers	6	1/7/02
Towers	25	1/7/02
Base station controller hardware	10	1/7/02
Microwave assets (including antennas, electronic multiplexers & transmitters/receivers)	10	1/7/02
Mobile switching centre hardware	10	1/7/02
Payphones (public telephones)	10	1/1/01
Satellite communication assets:		
Communications satellites (geosynchronous orbit)	15	1/1/05
High power amplifiers	12	1/1/05
Multiplexers	10	1/1/05
Satellite antennas:		
Electronic components, external (incl low noise amplifiers)	8	1/1/05
Non tracking antenna systems (incorporating data cables, dehydrators, pressurisation units, & wave guides)	8	1/1/05
Tracking antenna systems (incorporating antenna tracking motors, controllers, data cables, dehydrators, gearboxes, pressurisation units & wave guides)	20	1/1/05
Satellite earth station electronic assets (incl bandwidth managers, decoders, demodulators downconverters, encoders, filters, modulators, receivers, transmitters & upconverters)	10	1/1/05
Satellite telemetry & control systems	15	1/1/05
Telecommunications assets:		
Air conditioning units	5	1/7/02
Batteries, rectifiers	6	1/7/02
Racks	20	1/7/03
Equipment shelters (transportable)	25	1/7/03

LIBRARY & OTHER INFORMATION SERVICES

Asset	Life (yrs)	Date of application
Libraries:		
Circulating (all classes of books)	10	1/1/01
Music lending	$6^{2}/_{3}$	1/1/01

FINANCIAL & INSURANCE SERVICES

Asset	Life (yrs)	Date of application
Banks:		
Demountable strongrooms	100	1/1/01
Portable safes	40	1/1/01
Strongroom doors	100	1/1/01

RENTAL, HIRING & REAL ESTATE SERVICES

Note: If the asset is hired or leased to & used predominantly by a particular industry & not listed below, see the entry under Table A for that industry

RENTAL & HIRING SERVICES (EXCEPT REAL ESTATE)

Asset	Life (yrs)	Date of application
Air Compressors:		
Compressors – reciprocating	7	1/7/05
Compressors – rotary screw	10	1/7/05
Compaction:		
Compactors – flat plate	8	1/7/05

Asset	Life (yrs)	Date of application
Compactors – vertical rammer	6	1/7/05
Concreting assets:		
Brick/paving saws	5	1/7/05
Concrete demolition saws	3	1/7/05
Concrete kibble buckets	15	1/7/05
Concrete mixers	4	1/7/08
Concrete trowels:		
Ride on	7	1/7/08
Walk behind	5	1/7/08
Concrete surface preparation assets (incl floor grinders, planers & scarifers)	5	1/7/08
Concrete vibrators:		
Brushcutter style	5	1/7/08
Drive units	6	1/7/08
Flexible shaft pumps	6	1/7/08
Vibrating shafts	3	1/7/08
Concrete wheeled saws	6	1/7/05
Elevating work platforms (EWPs):		
Boom lifts (including knuckle & telescopic boom lifts)	15	1/7/15
Personnel lifts	10	1/7/15
Scissor lifts	10	1/7/15
Generators:		
Cables	5	1/7/05
Distribution boards	10	1/7/05
Diesel	10	1/7/05
Petrol	5	1/7/05
Generator with attached lighting plant	10	1/7/05
Household assets:		
Clothes dryers	5	1/1/06
Digital video display (DVD) players	5	1/1/06
Dishwashers	8	1/1/06
Evaporative coolers, portable	5	1/1/06
Freezers	6	1/1/06
Microwave ovens	6	1/1/06
Refrigerators	6	1/1/06
Stereo systems (incorporating amplifiers, cassette players, compact disc players, radios & speakers)	5	1/1/06
Surround sound systems (incorporating audio video receivers & speakers)	5	1/1/06
Television sets	8	1/1/06
Vacuum cleaners, portable	5	1/1/06
Video cassette recorder systems (VCR)	5	1/1/06
Washing machines	6	1/1/06
Ladders (including stepladders, work platforms extension ladders, trestles & planks):		
Aluminium	4	1/7/15
Fibreglass	4	1/7/15
Portable structures (sheds, site office trailers, portable toilets & washrooms etc) used for a temporary period in offsite locations (eg construction sites)	10	1/7/14
Power tools:		
Chainsaws	3	1/7/05
Hand tools – air	5	1/7/05
Hand tools – battery	3	1/7/08
Hand tools – electric	5	1/7/05
Jackhammers – air	7	1/7/05
Jackhammers – electric	3	1/7/05
Nail guns – air	3	1/7/05
Recreational vehicles:		
Campervans & motorhomes:		
Vehicles having a gross vehicle mass greater than 3 tonnes & 4WD vehicles	5	1/7/15
Vehicles having a gross vehicle mass of 3 tonnes or less	8	1/7/15
Caravans & camper trailers	12	1/7/15
Scaffolding:		
Aluminium	5	1/7/15
Fibreglass	5	1/7/15
Steel	15	1/7/15
Traffic management assets:		
Crash prevention assets:		
Barriers:		
Concrete	30	1/1/06
Plastic	5	1/1/06
Crash attenuators (truck mounted)	10	1/1/06
Road marking assets:		
< 100 litre capacity	5	1/1/06
100 to 500 litre capacity	9	1/1/06
> 500 litre capacity	11	1/1/06

Asset	Life (yrs)	Date of application
Line grinders (walk behind)	5	1/1/06
Traffic management signs:		
Arrow boards	10	1/1/06
Speed observation signs	10	1/1/06
Traffic lights – mobile	10	1/1/06
Variable message signs	10	1/1/06
Static signage (incl safety cones, barricades, warning signs & bollards)	3	1/1/06
Video recorder or equipment hiring	$6^2/_3$	1/1/01
Video tapes & games hiring	$^1/_2$	1/1/01
Welders:		
Diesel	10	1/7/05
Electric	5	1/7/05

Note where the terms 'freestanding' & 'fixed' are used in entries for residential property operators, they have the following meaning. Freestanding – items designed to be portable or movable. Any attachment to the premises is only for the item's temporary stability. Fixed – annexed or attached by any means, for example screws, nails, bolts, glue, adhesive, grout or cement, but not merely for temporary stability.

RESIDENTIAL PROPERTY OPERATORS

Asset	Life (yrs)	Date of application
Assets generally:		
Air conditioning assets (excluding ducting, pipes & vents):		
Air handling units	20	1/7/03
Chillers:		
Absorption	25	1/7/03
Centrifugal	20	1/7/03
Volumetrics (incl reciprocating, rotary, screw, scroll):		
Air cooled	15	1/7/03
Water cooled	20	1/7/03
Condensing sets	15	1/7/03
Cooling towers	15	1/7/03
Damper motors (including variable air volume box controller)	10	1/7/03
Fan coil units (connected to condensing set)	15	1/7/03
Mini split systems up to 20KW (incl ceiling, floor & high wall split system)	10	1/7/03
Packaged air conditioning units	15	1/7/03
Pumps	20	1/7/03
Room units	10	1/7/03
Ceiling fans	5	1/7/04
Clocks, electric	10	1/7/04
Digital video display (DVD) players	5	1/7/04
Door closers	10	1/7/04
Door stops, freestanding	10	1/7/04
Escalators (machinery & moving parts)	20	1/1/03
Evaporative coolers:		
Fixed (excluding ducting & vents)	20	1/7/05
Portable	10	1/7/05
Floor coverings (removable without damage):		
Carpet	10	1/1/01
Floating timber	15	1/7/04
Linoleum	10	1/1/01
Vinyl	10	1/1/01
Furniture, freestanding	$13^1/_3$	1/1/01
Garbage bins	10	1/7/04
Garbage compacting systems (excluding chutes)	$6^2/_3$	1/1/01
Generators	20	1/1/01
Gym assets:		
Cardiovascular	5	1/7/04
Resistance	10	1/7/04
Hand dryers, electrical	10	1/1/01
Heaters:		
Fixed:		
Electric	15	1/7/04
Gas:		
Ducted central heating unit	20	1/7/04
Other	15	1/7/04
Freestanding	15	1/7/04
Hot water systems (excluding piping):		
Electric	12	1/7/04
Gas	12	1/7/04
Solar	15	1/7/04
Intercom system assets	10	1/7/04
Lifts (including hydraulic & traction lifts)	30	1/1/03
Lights:		
Fittings (excluding hardwired)	5	1/7/04
Freestanding	5	1/7/04

Asset	Life (yrs)	Date of application
Shades, removable	5	1/7/04
Linen	5	1/7/04
Master antenna television (MATV) assets:		
Amplifiers	10	1/7/04
Modulators	10	1/7/04
Power sources	10	1/7/04
Mirrors, freestanding	15	1/7/04
Radios	10	1/1/01
Rugs	7	1/7/04
Solar power generating system assets	20	1/7/04
Stereo systems (incorporating amplifiers, cassette players, compact disc players, radios & speakers)	7	1/7/04
Surround sound systems (incorporating audio video receivers & speakers)	10	1/7/04
Telecommunications assets:		
Cordless phones	4	1/7/04
Telephone Hand sets	10	1/7/04
Telephone systems – see Table B Telephony		
Television antennas, freestanding	5	1/7/04
Television sets	10	1/7/04
Vacuum cleaners:		
Ducted:		
Hoses	10	1/7/04
Motors	10	1/7/04
Wands	10	1/7/04
Portable	10	1/1/01
Ventilation fans	20	1/7/04
Video cassette recorder systems (VCRs)	5	1/7/04
Water pumps	20	1/1/01
Window blinds, internal	10	1/7/04
Window curtains	6	1/7/04
Window shutters, automatic:		
Controls	10	1/7/04
Motors	10	1/7/04
Bathroom assets:		
Accessories, freestanding (including shower caddies, soap holders, toilet brushes)	5	1/7/04
Exhaust fans (including light/heating)	10	1/7/04
Heated towel rails, electric	10	1/7/04
Shower curtains (excl curtain rods & screens)	2	1/7/04
Spa bath pumps	20	1/7/04
Fire control assets:		
Alarms:		
Heat	6	1/7/04
Smoke	6	1/7/04
Detection & alarm systems:		
Alarm bells	12	1/7/04
Detectors (including addressable manual call points, heat, multi type & smoke)	20	1/7/04
Fire indicator panels	12	1/7/04
Emergency warning & intercommunication systems (EWIS):		
Master emergency control panels	12	1/7/04
Speakers	12	1/7/04
Strobe lights	12	1/7/04
Warden intercom phones (WIPs)	12	1/7/04
Extinguishers	15	1/7/04
Hoses & nozzles	10	1/7/04
Pumps (including diesel & electric)	25	1/7/04
Stair pressurisation assets:		
AC variable speed drives	10	1/7/04
Pressurisation & extraction fans	25	1/7/04
Sensors	10	1/7/04
Kitchen assets:		
Cook tops	12	1/7/04
Crockery	5	1/7/04
Cutlery	5	1/7/04
Dishwashers	10	1/7/04
Freezers	12	1/7/04
Garbage disposal units	10	1/7/04
Microwave ovens	10	1/7/04
Ovens	12	1/7/04
Range hoods	12	1/7/04
Refrigerators	12	1/7/04
Stoves	12	1/7/04
Water filters, electrical	15	1/7/04
Laundry assets:		
Clothes dryers	10	1/7/04
Ironing boards, freestanding	7	1/7/04
Irons	5	1/7/04
Washing machines	10	1/7/04

Asset	Life (yrs)	Date of application
Outdoor assets:		
Automatic garage doors:		
Controls	5	1/7/04
Motors	10	1/7/04
Barbecue assets:		
Fixed barbecue assets:		
Sliding trays & cookers	10	1/7/04
Freestanding barbecues	5	1/7/04
Floor carpet (including artificial grass & matting)	5	1/7/04
Furniture, freestanding	5	1/7/04
Gardening watering installations:		
Control panels	5	1/7/04
Pumps	5	1/7/04
Timing devices	5	1/7/04
Garden lights, solar	8	1/7/04
Garden sheds, freestanding	15	1/7/04
Gates, electrical:		
Controls	5	1/7/04
Motors	10	1/7/04
Operable pergola louvres:		
Controls	15	1/7/04
Motors	15	1/7/04
Sauna heating assets	15	1/7/04
Sewage treatment assets:		
Controls	8	1/7/04
Motors	8	1/7/04
Spas:		
Fixed spa assets:		
Chlorinators	12	1/7/04
Filtration assets (including pumps)	12	1/7/04
Heaters (electric or gas)	15	1/7/04
Freestanding spas (incorporating blowers, controls, filters, heaters & pumps)	17	1/7/04
Swimming pool assets:		
Chlorinators	12	1/7/04
Cleaning assets	7	1/7/04
Filtration assets (including pumps)	12	1/7/04
Heaters:		
Electric	15	1/7/04
Gas	15	1/7/04
Solar	20	1/7/04
Tennis court assets:		
Cleaners	3	1/7/04
Drag brooms	3	1/7/04
Nets	5	1/7/04
Rollers	3	1/7/04
Umpire chairs	15	1/7/04
Security & monitoring assets:		
Access control systems:		
Code pads	5	1/7/04
Door controllers	5	1/7/04
Readers:		
Proximity	7	1/7/04
Swipe card	3	1/7/04
Closed circuit television systems:		
Cameras	4	1/7/04
Monitors	4	1/7/04
Recorders:		
Digital	4	1/7/04
Time lapse	2	1/7/04
Switching units (including multiplexes)	5	1/7/04
Security systems:		
Code pads	5	1/7/04
Control panels	5	1/7/04
Detectors (including passive infra red, photo sensors & vibration)	5	1/7/04
Global System for Mobiles (GSM) Units	5	1/7/04
Noise makers (including bells & sirens)	5	1/7/04
NON-RESIDENTIAL PROPERTY OPERATORS		
Commercial office building assets:		
Boilers	20	1/7/05
Boiler pumps	5	1/7/05
Building maintenance units	35	1/7/05
Carpets	8	1/7/05
Door control & motor drive system for automatic sliding doors (incorporating chains, controls, motors & sensors, but excluding doors)	15	1/7/05
Hot water installations (excluding commercial boilers & piping)	15	1/7/05
Power supply assets:		

Asset	Life (yrs)	Date of application
Emergency or standby:		
Generator assets:		
Acoustic hoods & canopies	20	1/7/05
Generators (incorporating attached engine management & generator monitoring instruments)	25	1/7/05
Power management units	15	1/7/05
Lighting control systems (microprocessor based)	5	1/7/14
Uninterruptible power supply (UPS) systems:		
Line interactive types	5	1/7/13
On line double conversion types	10	1/7/13
Window blinds	20	1/7/05

PROFESSIONAL, SCIENTIFIC & TECHNICAL SERVICES

SCIENTIFIC RESEARCH SERVICES

Asset	Life (yrs)	Date of application
Scientific, medical & pharmaceutical research assets:		
Autoclaves:		
Bench top autoclaves	5	1/7/14
Others	10	1/7/14
Automated cell counters	5	1/7/14
Automated colony pickers	5	1/7/14
Balances	10	1/7/14
Biological safety cabinets	10	1/7/14
Cell harvesters	10	1/7/14
Centrifuges:		
Bench top centrifuges	5	1/7/14
Others	10	1/7/14
Computed tomography (CT) scanners	10	1/7/14
Digital cameras	3	1/7/14
DNA sequencers	5	1/7/14
Electrophoresis systems (incorporating power supplies & tanks)	7	1/7/14
Electroporators	8	1/7/14
Fermenters	10	1/7/14
Flow cytometers	8	1/7/14
Freeze dryers	10	1/7/14
Freezers	10	1/7/14
Gel documentation systems	5	1/7/14
Glassware washers	8	1/7/14
Heating blocks	10	1/7/14
Homogenisers	7	1/7/14
Incubators	6	1/7/14
Liquid chromatography systems	5	1/7/14
Liquid nitrogen assets (including dewars & tanks)	10	1/7/14
Microscopes	10	1/7/14
Microtomes	10	1/7/14
Mixers	7	1/7/14
Nano spectrophotometers	8	1/7/14
Ovens	6	1/7/14
Peristaltic pumps	7	1/7/14
PH meters	7	1/7/14
Plate readers	5	1/7/14
Polymerase chain reaction (PCR) thermal cyclers	8	1/7/14
Real-time PCR detection machines	5	1/7/14
Refrigerators	8	1/7/14
Robotic systems (including robotic liquid handling systems & robotic sampler systems)	5	1/7/14
Shakers	7	1/7/14
Sonicators (including water bath sonicators & sonicators with probes)	7	1/7/14
Spectrophotometers (excluding nano spectrophotometers)	10	1/7/14
Surface plasmon resonance (SPR) machines	5	1/7/14
Vacuum concentrators	7	1/7/14
Water baths (including refrigerated & shaking water baths)	7	1/7/14
Water purification systems	8	1/7/14

SURVEYING & MAPPING SERVICES

Asset	Life (yrs)	Date of application
Airborne imaging (cameras)	7	1/7/15
Automatic optical levels (dumpy levels)	7	1/7/15
Controllers	4	1/7/15
Digital (electronic) levels	5	1/7/15
Echo sounders	5	1/7/15
GNSS/GIS Handhelds (asset receivers)	3	1/7/15
GNSS/GPS survey equipment (including reference/base stations, rover receivers, data radios, antennas & integrated GNSS)	5	1/7/15

Asset	Life (yrs)	Date of application
Ground imaging (pole cameras)	5	1/7/15
Laser detectors/receivers (rod-eye receivers)	4	1/7/15
Laser distance measurers/meters (DISTOs)	4	1/7/15
Laser levels:		
Grade laying (dial-in grade)	6	1/7/15
Laser plummets	5	1/7/15
Line & plumb/point & cross line	4	1/7/15
Pipe laying	6	1/7/15
Rotating	6	1/7/15
Tunnelling & plumbing	6	1/7/15
Laser scanners – 3D (high definition surveying) - ground LIDAR	5	1/7/15
Laser scanners - vehicle mounted - ground LIDAR	5	1/7/15
LIDAR (airborne)	7	1/7/15
Rail surveying assets:		
Mobile rail surveying equipment	5	1/7/15
Platform clearance gauges	6	1/7/15
Rail profile gauges	6	1/7/15
Stereoplotters – digital/softcopy (hardware only)	10	1/7/15
Tablets	4	1/7/15
Theodolites (digital)	7	1/7/15
Total stations (including mechanical, manual, motorised, auto lock, robotic, universal & multi-stations)	5	1/7/15
Traverse kits (incorporating tripods, tribrachs, prisms, poles & optical plummets)	5	1/7/15
Unmanned aerial vehicles (drones):		
Fixed wing	3	1/7/15
Rotary wing	2	1/7/15
Unmanned surface vehicles	4	1/7/15
Utility locator (underground service locator) assets:		
Ground penetrating radars (GPRs)	5	1/7/15
Magnetic locators	5	1/7/15
Service locators	5	1/7/15
Signal generators	5	1/7/15
Signal tracer for locators	4	1/7/15

ADVERTISING SERVICES

Advertising signs - see Table B Advertising signs

VETERINARY SERVICES

Asset	Life (yrs)	Date of application
Veterinarians' assets:		
Anaesthesia machines	10	1/1/04
Animal blow dryers	5	1/1/04
Animal cages:		
Fibreglass, plastic & polyethylene cages	10	1/1/04
Stainless steel cages	20	1/1/04
Animal patient monitoring assets (including blood pressure monitors, CO2 end tidal monitors, ECGs & pulse oximeters)	7	1/1/04
Animal scales	7	1/1/04
Dental assets:		
Dental units	10	1/1/04
Ultrasonic scalers (standalone)	10	1/1/04
Diagnostic assets (including ophthalmoscope, otoscope, handles & power supply)	10	1/1/04
Electrocautery units	10	1/1/04
Electroejaculators	6	1/1/04
Hydrobaths	8	1/1/04
Pathology assets:		
Centrifuges	5	1/1/04
Laboratory analysers:		
Electrolyte analysers	4	1/1/04
Generally	5	1/1/04
Microscopes	10	1/1/04
Surgery lights	10	1/1/04
Tables & tubs	20	1/1/04
Ultrasound systems (incorporating scanner, transducers, integrated computer & integrated software)	5	1/1/04
X ray assets (excluding direct radiography assets):		
Mobile or portable x ray units	10	1/1/04
X ray processors – automatic	10	1/1/04

PROFESSIONAL PHOTOGRAPHIC SERVICES

Asset	Life (yrs)	Date of application
Audio assets (including microphones, preamplifiers, sound recording devices, transmitters & receivers)	3	1/7/15
Camera lenses	5	1/7/15
Digital cameras:		
Compact cameras (including point & shoot cameras)	3	1/7/15

Asset	Life (yrs)	Date of application
Compact system cameras (including bridge cameras, micro four-thirds cameras, mirrorless cameras)	3	1/7/15
Medium format single lens reflex (SLR) camera systems (including camera bodies & digital backs)	4	1/7/15
SLR cameras (including full-frame SLR cameras)	3	1/7/15
Lighting assets:		
Electronic flash units (including compact flash heads, monolights):		
Portable	3	1/7/15
Studio lightings	5	1/7/15
Light meters	5	1/7/15
Light shaping tools (including modelling glass protectors, reflectors & scrims, softboxes & umbrellas)	3	1/7/15
Portable flash units (including flashguns)	2	1/7/15
Power packs (including battery packs & compact flash generators)	4	1/7/15
Support assets:		
Backdrop support systems (including background elevation systems)	10	1/7/15
Bags & cases	5	1/7/15
Camera track sliders	2	1/7/15
Light stands (including boom arms)	5	1/7/15
Photographic printers/plotters	4	1/7/15
Tent & shooting tables	2	1/7/15
Tripods	5	1/7/15
Unmanned aerial vehicles (UAVs) - rotary	2	1/7/15
Wind machines	5	1/7/15

ADMINISTRATIVE & SUPPORT SERVICES

BUILDING & OTHER INDUSTRIAL CLEANING SERVICES

Asset	Life (yrs)	Date of application
Air purifiers, deodorising & mould remediation assets (including air filtering machines, air scrubbers & ozone generators)	5	1/7/10
Batteries, deep cycle (including those used in ride on polishers, scrubbers, sweepers & vacuum cleaners)	2	1/7/10
Drying & restoration assets (including air movers & dehumidifiers)	5	1/7/10
Extractors for carpet & upholstery cleaning:		
Spot extractors (including portable handheld & brief case size extractors for stain removal)	3	1/7/10
Other (including walk behind & self contained carpet extractors)	5	1/7/10
Truck or van mounted	10	1/7/10
Polishing, carpet cleaning & floor stripping assets (including floor polishers, burnishers, rotary scrubbers, encapsulation machines & floor strippers):		
Portable	5	1/7/10
Ride on	5	1/7/10
Pressure washers:		
Portable	4	1/7/10
Trailer or truck mounted	7	1/7/10
Scrubbers, hard floor:		
Portable	5	1/7/10
Ride on	7	1/7/10
Steam cleaners for sanitising floor & surfaces	5	1/7/10
Sweepers, hard floor:		
Portable	5	1/7/10
Ride on	7	1/7/10
Road sweeper trucks (including sweepers)	10#	1/7/10
Vacuum cleaners:		
Backpack & pull along machines	3	1/7/10
Other portable (including upright machines)	5	1/7/10
Ride on or stand on	7	1/7/10

GARDENING SERVICES

Asset	Life (yrs)	Date of application
Arboriculture & gardening services:		
Blowers	3	1/1/04
Brushcutters (including whipper snippers)	2	1/1/04
Chainsaws (including pole pruners)	2	1/1/04
Elevating work platforms	15	1/1/04
Hand tools (including pruner, rake, hedge shears, loppers & tree saws)	3	1/1/04
Hedge trimmers	4	1/1/04
Lawn edgers (excluding brushcutters)	4	1/1/04
Lawn mowers:		
Cylinder	7	1/1/04
Push (rotary)	2	1/1/04

Asset	Life (yrs)	Date of application
Ride ons	5	1/1/04
Self propelled (rotary)	2	1/1/04
Stump grinders	5	1/1/04
Tractors	8	1/1/04
Tractor attachments:		
Roller mowers	4	1/1/04
Slashers	4	1/1/04
Trailers used to carry tree & grass clippings	5	1/1/04
Tree climbing assets:		
Climbing hardware (including carabineers, figure of 8 & lowering pullies)	1	1/1/04
Climbing spurs	10	1/1/04
Friction lowering devices	10	1/1/04
Harness	3	1/1/04
Ropes	1	1/1/04
Wood chippers	8	1/1/04

PACKAGING SERVICES

Asset	Life (yrs)	Date of application
Fruit & vegetables pack houses assets used off farm:		
Banana assets:		
Air rams	3	1/7/08
Bunch lines	10	1/7/08
Choppers/mulchers	4	1/7/08
Rails (including points)	15	1/7/08
Scrap conveyors	5	1/7/08
Tops	8	1/7/08
Water troughs	10	1/7/08
General assets:		
Bins	5	1/7/08
Bin tippers	15	1/7/08
Conveyors (including elevators)	10	1/7/08
Drying tunnels	15	1/7/08
Fungicide units	10	1/7/08
Receival hoppers (including water dumps)	10	1/7/08
Tables (including packing & sorting tables)	15	1/7/08
Washing assets (including brush & barrel washers)	10	1/7/08
Waxing assets	10	1/7/08
Graders:		
Electronic	10	1/7/08
Mechanical	15	1/7/08
Optical	8	1/7/08
Labelling assets:		
Labelling applicators (incl in line labellers)	8	1/7/08
Labelling guns	3	1/7/08
Packing assets (incl bagging & wrapping machines)	10	1/7/08
Scales (excluding platform scales)	5	1/7/08
Tree nuts assets:		
Crackers	7	1/7/08
Drying silos	15	1/7/08
Separating assets (including air separators, trommels & vibrating screens)	10	1/7/08

EDUCATION & TRAINING

Asset	Life (yrs)	Date of application
Kindergarten furniture & play equipment	5	1/1/01

HEALTH CARE & SOCIAL ASSISTANCE

Asset	Life (yrs)	Date of application
Medical assets (used in common across all health care industry segments):		
Benchtop sterilisers	5	1/7/03
Benchtop ultrasonic cleaners	7	1/7/03
Clinical furniture	10	1/7/03
X ray viewers	10	1/7/03

HOSPITALS

Asset	Life (yrs)	Date of application
Hospital assets:		
Anaesthesia machines	10	1/1/03
Angiography assets:		
Image acquisition systems (incorporating computers with digital subtraction capability, digital cameras, monitors & integrated software)	4	1/7/02
Image intensifiers	7	1/7/02
Patient gantries or tables, patient monitoring assets, positioning assets & pressure injectors	10	1/7/02
Cell savers & cell separators	7	1/1/03
Colposcopes	10	1/1/03
Defibrillators	10	1/1/03
Diathermy & cautery machines/electrosurgical generators	10	1/1/03

Asset	Life (yrs)	Date of application
Endoscopic surgery assets (excluding disposable accessories):		
Arthroscopic fluid management systems	7	1/1/03
Endoscopes (flexible & rigid) & endoscopic surgical instruments	4	1/1/03
Endoscopic camera systems:		
Beam splitters & light sources	10	1/1/03
Printers, video cameras, video camera adaptors, couplers & heads, video image capture systems & video processors	5	1/1/03
Still cameras	7	1/1/03
Video monitors & video recorders	7	1/1/03
Endoscopic electrosurgical generators	10	1/1/03
Endoscopic lasers	10	1/1/03
Endoscopic ultrasound systems (incorporating scanner, transducers/probes, integrated computer & integrated software)	5	1/1/03
Haemodialysis machines	7	1/1/03
Head lights	7	1/1/03
Hospital furniture:		
Beds:		
Electronic	7	1/1/03
Mechanical	10	1/1/03
Bedside cabinets/lockers, carts & poles, blanket warming cabinets, blood warming cabinets, medical refrigerators & overbed tables	10	1/1/03
Infusion pumps:		
General, pain management & rapid	8	1/1/03
Syringe driven	6	1/1/03
Insufflators	10	1/1/03
Lithotriptors used for extra corporeal shock wave lithotripsy	7	1/1/03
Mechanical assist assets:		
Calf & cuff compression devices	8	1/1/03
Cardiac bypass & heart lung machines	8	1/1/03
Intra aortic balloon pumps	8	1/1/03
Ventricular assist heart pumps	8	1/1/03
Natal care assets (including incubators, infant warmers & mobile infant warmers)	7	1/1/03
Operating tables & attachments:		
Electronic	10	1/1/03
Mechanical	13	1/1/03
Operating theatre lights	8	1/1/03
Pan flushers	10	1/1/03
Patient hoists & lifters	10	1/1/03
Patient monitoring assets:		
Bedside monitoring systems	7	1/1/03
Cardiac monitors	7	1/1/03
ECGs (electrocardiographs)	7	1/1/03
Foetal monitors	7	1/1/03
Pulse oximeters	7	1/1/03
Vital signs monitors	7	1/1/03
Patient warming assets (excluding disposable accessories):		
Fluid warmers	10	1/1/03
Forced air patient warmers	10	1/1/03
Smoke evacuators	8	1/1/03
Sterilisation & autoclave processing assets:		
Drying cabinets	10	1/1/03
Endoscope sterilisers & disinfectors	5	1/1/03
Flash sterilisers	10	1/1/03
Instrument washers	10	1/1/03
Pre vacuum sterilisers	10	1/1/03
Ultrasonic cleaners & baths	7	1/1/03
Surgical instruments:		
Hand held manually operated instruments	8	1/1/03
Powered instruments (including drills, saws, shavers, non disposable instrument accessories & power sources)	7	1/1/03
Ultrasonic aspirators	10	1/1/03
Ultrasonic scalpels	10	1/1/03
Surgical lasers (excluding ophthalmic surgical lasers)	10	1/1/03
Surgical microscopes	10	1/1/03
Ultrasonic bladder scanners	10	1/1/03
Ultrasonic needle guides	10	1/1/03
Ultrasound systems (incorporating scanner, transducers, integrated computer & integrated software) used by cardiologists, obstetricians & vascular surgeons	5	1/7/02

Asset	Life (yrs)	Date of application
Ventilators:		
Fixed	7	1/1/03
Portable	5	1/1/03
Wheelchairs	10	1/1/03
DENTAL SERVICES		
Dentists' assets:		
Air abrasion units	10	1/7/03
Air compressors	10	1/7/03
Amalgamators	7	1/7/03
Amalgam separators	7	1/7/03
Computerised (CAD/CAM) ceramic restoration systems:		
Imaging units	7	1/7/03
Milling units	5	1/7/03
Curing lights (halogen)	5	1/7/03
Dental chairs	10	1/7/03
Dental instruments:		
Hand held manually operated instruments	3	1/7/03
Handpieces (driven by compressed air, compressed gas or electricity)	3	1/7/03
Dental lasers:		
Hard tissue & soft tissue lasers	7	1/7/03
Soft tissue & whitening lasers	7	1/7/03
Soft tissue lasers	10	1/7/03
Dental loupes	10	1/7/03
Dental operating lights	10	1/7/03
Dental units	10	1/7/03
Dental x ray assets:		
Conventional x ray film systems (incorporating control boxes, swing arms & x ray heads, but excluding OPG systems)	15	1/7/03
Digital x ray systems (including intra oral storage phosphor plate systems & intra oral digital sensor systems)	7	1/7/03
Intra oral x ray film processors	10	1/7/03
Handpiece cleaners	5	1/7/03
Intra oral camera systems (incorporating camera & integrated processor/docking station)	7	1/7/03
Nitrous oxide sedation units	20	1/7/03
Oral surgical motors	5	1/7/03
Suction units	10	1/7/03
Ultrasonic scalers (standalone)	10	1/7/03
OPTOMETRY & OPTICAL DISPENSING		
Optical assets:		
Automatic refractometers/keratometers	5	1/1/04
Cameras (including anterior segment cameras, retinal cameras, fundus cameras):		
Analogue	8	1/1/04
Digital	4	1/1/04
Colour vision testers (automated)	8	1/1/04
Corneal topography systems	5	1/1/04
Examination chairs	10	1/1/04
Glaucoma diagnostic assets (including ocular coherence tomographs (OCTs), scanning laser ophthalmoscopes & scanning laser polarimeters)	5	1/1/04
Keratometers (Ophthalmometers):		
Automated	5	1/1/04
Manual	12	1/1/04
Ophthalmic surgery assets:		
Microkeratome	3	1/1/04
Ophthalmic cryo surgery systems	5	1/1/04
Ophthalmic diathermy surgery systems	5	1/1/04
Ophthalmic lasers:		
Non refractive	10	1/1/04
Refractive (including eye tracking systems)	4	1/1/04
Phacoemulsification systems	4	1/1/04
Pupillometers (used for refractive surgery)	5	1/1/04
Vitrectomy systems	4	1/1/04
Wave front analysers	4	1/1/04
Ophthalmic viewers	5	1/1/04
Ophthalmoscopes:		
Direct (including power supply)	8	1/1/04
Indirect	9	1/1/04
Optical dispensing assets – see Table A Photographic, optical & ophthalmic equipment manufacturing		
Refraction units (including examination chair, instrument arms, table & light source)	10	1/1/04

Asset	Life (yrs)	Date of application
Refractometers (automated)	5	1/1/04
Slit lamp biomicroscopes:		
Hand held	9	1/1/04
Mounted	12	1/1/04
Telemedicine digital imaging systems (excluding imaging devices)	4	1/1/04
Tonometers:		
Contact tonometers:		
Applanation:		
Hand held	6	1/1/04
Mounted	8	1/1/04
Electronic	6	1/1/04
Non contact tonometers:		
Hand held	5	1/1/04
Table mounted	8	1/1/04
Trial lens sets	20	1/1/04
Ultrasound diagnostic assets (including A scan biometers, A/B scan biometers, B scan biometers, laser interference biometers, pachymeters & ultrasound biomicroscopes (UBMs))	5	1/1/04
Visual acuity testing assets:		
Automated vision testers	6	1/1/04
Manual vision testers (phoropters)	12	1/1/04
Visual acuity charts (illuminated)	10	1/1/04
Visual acuity chart projectors (automated)	8	1/1/04
Visual field testing assets (perimeters) – automated	5	1/1/04

PATHOLOGIST & OTHER PATHOLOGY SERVICES

Asset	Life (yrs)	Date of application
Pathologists' assets:		
Batch slide stainer	6	1/1/02
Bio hazard chambers	10	1/1/02
Centrifuges	5	1/1/02
Incubators	6	1/1/02
Laboratory analysers	5	1/1/02
Microscopes	10	1/1/02
Rotary microtomes	6	1/1/02
Tissue embedding systems	6	1/1/02
Tissue processors	6	1/1/02

PODIATRY SERVICES

Asset	Life (yrs)	Date of application
Podiatrists' assets:		
Computerised orthoses manufacturing assets:		
Carving mills	7	1/7/03
Contact pin digitisers	7	1/7/03
Doppler vascularscopes	5	1/7/03
Electric nail drills:		
Dust extraction drills	7	1/7/03
Portable dust extraction drills	5	1/7/03
Water & alcohol based spray drills	4	1/7/03
Examination/magnifying lamps	10	1/7/03
Footrests	10	1/7/03
Gait analysis assets:		
Computerised systems (incorporating in shoe pressure analysis or platform based pressure mats, integrated hardware & integrated software)	4	1/7/03
Non computerised:		
Treadmills	10	1/7/03
Video cameras	5	1/7/03
Video monitors & video recorders	7	1/7/03
Orthotic benchtop grinders	6	1/7/03
Patient chairs	12	1/7/03
Podiatric instruments	3	1/7/03
Vacuum presses	3	1/7/03
Vascular neurological assessment assets:		
Monofilaments	2	1/7/03
Tuning forks	10	1/7/03

RADIOLOGY & DIAGNOSTIC IMAGING SERVICES

Asset	Life (yrs)	Date of application
Radiologists' diagnostic imaging assets:		
Bone densitometry (BMD) systems (incorporating either whole body scanners, integrated computer & integrated software, or spine & hip scanners, holding devices, integrated computers & integrated software)	10	1/7/02
Computed radiography (CR) digitisers	4	1/7/02
Computed tomography (CT) systems (incorporating scanners, integrated computers & integrated software)	10	1/7/02
Film digitisers	4	1/7/02

Asset	Life (yrs)	Date of application
Fluoroscopy assets (excluding direct radiography assets):		
Fixed systems (incorporating buckies, generators, screening tables & suspensions)	15	1/7/02
Image acquisition systems (incorporating computers, digital cameras, integrated software & monitors)	4	1/7/02
Image intensifiers	7	1/7/02
Mobile systems (incorporating buckies, generators, screening tables & suspensions)	10	1/7/02
Magnetic resonance imaging (MRI) systems (incorporating scanners, cooling systems, radio frequency coil accessories, integrated computer & integrated software)	7	1/7/02
Mammography systems (incorporating either prone core biopsy scanners, quality assurance equipment, stereotaxis, integrated computers & integrated software, or conventional upright scanners, quality assurance equipment, stereotaxis, integrated computer & integrated software)	7	1/7/02
Nuclear medicine systems (incorporating cameras, gantries, collimators, integrated computers, integrated software & hot lab equipment, but excluding Positron Emission Tomography (PET) systems)	10	1/7/02
Orthopantomography (OPG) systems (incorporating scanners, integrated computers & integrated software)	15	1/7/02
Patient archival & communication systems (PACS)	4	1/7/02
Processing assets:		
Daylight imaging processors	9	1/7/02
Dry laser imaging processors	8	1/7/02
Wet laser imaging processors	10	1/7/02
Teleradiology assets (excl the imaging device)	4	1/7/02
Ultrasound systems (incorporating scanner, transducers, integrated computer & integrated software)	5	1/7/02
X ray assets (excluding direct radiography assets):		
Fixed systems (incorporating buckies, control panels, generators, screening table, suspensions, tube column & x ray tube)	15	1/7/02
Image intensifier	7	1/7/02
Mobile systems (incorporating buckies, control panels, generators, screening table, suspensions, tube column & x ray tube)	10	1/7/02

SPECIALIST MEDICAL SERVICES N.E.C

Asset	Life (yrs)	Date of application
Neurologists' assets:		
Electroencephalography (EEG) systems (incorporating electrodes, amplifiers, integrated software & integrated computers)	5	1/7/03
Electromyography (EMG) systems (incorporating electrodes, amplifiers, integrated software & integrated computers)	5	1/7/03
Thoracic physicians' assets:		
Body plethysmographs (incorporating flow sensors, gas analysers, integrated software & integrated computers)	7	1/7/03
Continuous positive airway pressure (CPAP) & variable positive airway pressure (VPAP) systems	7	1/7/03
Lung function analysis exercise systems (incorporating flow sensors, treadmills or ergometers, ECGs, pulse oximeters, integrated software & integrated computers)	7	1/7/03
Lung function analysis systems (incorporating flow sensors, gas analysers, integrated software & integrated computers)	7	1/7/03
Spirometers	7	1/7/03
Sleep laboratory systems (incorporating amplifiers, sensors, integrated CPAP monitors, integrated carbon dioxide monitors, integrated pulse oximeters, integrated computers & integrated software)	7	1/7/03

Asset	Life (yrs)	Date of application
NURSING HOME OPERATION		
Beds:		
Electronic	7	1/7/04
Mechanical	10	1/7/04
Bedside cabinets/lockers, carts & poles & overbed tables	10	1/7/04
Commodes	10	1/7/04
Nurse call systems	7	1/7/04
Pan flushers	10	1/7/04
Patient hoists & lifters	10	1/7/04
Patient monitoring assets	7	1/7/04
Patient scales	10	1/7/04
Shower chairs	7	1/7/04
Trolleys	10	1/7/04
Wheelchairs	10	1/7/04

ARTS & RECREATION SERVICES

Asset	Life (yrs)	Date of application
HERITAGE ACTIVITIES		
Museum displays in aircraft/war museums	100	1/1/01
Parks & gardens:		
Lion parks:		
Animal cages & sheds	20	1/1/01
Animal huts	10	1/1/01
Planetarium domes	33$^1/_3$	1/1/01
Sea life centres:		
Fibreglass aquarium tanks	20	1/1/01
Ketches	13$^1/_3$	1/1/01
TV audio systems	10	1/1/01
CREATIVE & PERFORMING ARTS ACTIVITIES		
Theatre equipment:		
Accessories (theatrical – wigs, costumes etc)	5	1/1/01
HEALTH & FITNESS CENTRES & GYMNASIA OPERATION		
Health & fitness centre operation assets:		
Cardiovascular training machines:		
Cross trainers, steppers & treadmills	4	1/7/12
Exercise bicycles (including spin bicycles, upright & recumbent bicycles)	4	1/7/12
Rowing machines	5	1/7/12
Free weight training assets:		
Barbells, dumbbells, kettle bells, weight plates & storage racks	6	1/7/12
Benches (including abdominal crunch, adjustable, declined, inclined & flat benches)	8	1/7/12
Resistance training machines (including abdomen, arm, back, chest, hip, leg, shoulder & multiple training machines)	8	1/7/12
Support assets:		
Audio visual entertainment assets (including amplifiers, audio speakers, digital disc players & televisions)	4	1/7/12
Fans (including wall mounted)	5	1/7/12
Lockers	8	1/7/12
Platform scales	5	1/7/12
SPORT & RECREATION SERVICES		
Amusement machines & equipment:		
Coin-operated amusement machines:		
Children's rides	5	1/7/01
Convertible video games/simulators (cabinet)	5$^1/_2$	1/7/01
Dedicated video games/simulators	3$^1/_2$	1/7/01
Interchangeable video game kits	1	1/7/01
Juke boxes (compact disc)	10	1/7/01
Photo-image machines	3$^1/_2$	1/7/01
Pinball machines	3$^1/_2$	1/7/01
Pool/billiard tables	10	1/7/01
Redemption games (prizes/tickets)	5$^1/_2$	1/7/01
Table games (incl air hockey, soccer etc)	5$^1/_2$	1/7/01
Billiard tables	40	1/1/01
Rides & devices (fixed or mobile):		
Chair-o-planes	15	1/1/02
Children's indoor soft playgrounds	5	1/1/02
Children's rides (designed for the carriage of children less than 8 years old)	15	1/1/02

Asset	Life (yrs)	Date of application
Ferris wheels	25	1/1/02
Free falls (including giant drop & tower of terror)	25	1/1/02
Inflatables (including jumping castles)	5	1/1/02
Overhead transit devices (including chair lifts & cabin lifts)	25	1/1/02
Roller coasters:		
Non-powered (including corkscrew loop, looping coasters & mini roller coasters – wild cat, madmouse)	25	1/1/02
Powered (including tornado)	15	1/1/02
Round rides with or without additional motions (including merry-go-rounds)	15	1/1/02
Self-drive non-powered gravity rides (including toboggans & bob-sleds):		
Track	20	1/1/02
Vehicle	5	1/1/02
Self-drive powered rides (including dodgems & go-karts):		
Track	15	1/1/02
Vehicle	5	1/1/02
Simulators	10	1/1/02
Swinging rides (including pirate ship, spaceloop, & rainbow)	15	1/1/02
Trains, tracked or trackless (including tractor trains & miniature railways)	10	1/1/02
Water rides	20	1/1/02
Water slides (gravity powered)	20	1/1/02
Bowling centres (plant & equipment):		
Bowling alleys (timber – including ball return tracks, gutters, pit signals & terminals)	13$^1/_3$	1/1/01
Bowling balls	5	1/1/01
Carpets	4	1/1/01
Masking units	10	1/1/01
Pin setters & pin spotters	10	1/1/01
Other equipment	13$^1/_3$	1/1/01
Golf courses (miniature):		
Carpets on stairways	3	1/1/01
Lighting plant, electric motors, moving parts	20	1/1/01
Lighting standards	40	1/1/01
Marina operation:		
Boat cradles	10	1/7/02
Boat storage racks	10	1/7/02
Forklifts	11	1/7/02
Marina – wet berths (incorporating piling, decking & floating pontoons)	20	1/7/02
Mooring buoys	10	1/7/02
Travel lifts	15	1/7/02
Racehorses	10	1/1/01
Racing cars	2	1/1/01
Shuffle boards	10	1/1/01
Skating rink plant:		
Fittings (open air)	20	1/1/01
General freezing plant & equipment	13$^1/_3$	1/1/01
Hired ice skating boots	5	1/1/01
Roller skates	5	1/1/01
Surface (synthetic panels)	10	1/1/01
Ski equipment (skis, boots & stocks for hiring to public)	3	1/1/01
Ski maintenance machines	13$^1/_3$	1/1/01
Space theatre domes	33$^1/_3$	1/1/01
Tennis court surfaces:		
Bitumen	20	1/1/01
Plexipave	20	1/1/01
Synthetic lawn	10	1/1/01
Trampolines	10	1/1/01
GAMBLING ACTIVITIES		
Poker/gaming machines	7	1/7/09
Totalisators:		
Computer equipment	10	1/1/01
Ancillary equipment (eg ticket issuing machines)	13$^1/_3$	1/1/01

Asset	Life (yrs)	Date of application	Asset	Life (yrs)	Date of application

OTHER SERVICES

AUTOMOTIVE REPAIR & MAINTENANCE

Automotive & heavy vehicle repair & maintenance assets:

Asset	Life (yrs)	Date of application
Air conditioning assets:		
Refrigerant leak detectors	3	1/7/11
Refrigerant management systems	5	1/7/11
Refrigerant recovery machine	5	1/7/11
Refrigerant recovery & recycling machines	5	1/7/11
Vacuum pumps	5	1/7/11
Air tools including ratchet guns	2	1/7/11
Automatic transmission flush & fill machines	5	1/7/11
Axle & ball joint play testers or shakers	10	1/7/11
Battery chargers	5	1/7/11
Battery testers	5	1/7/11
Brake disc & drum grinding lathes:		
Fixed	10	1/7/11
Portable on car	5	1/7/11
Brake fluid testers	5	1/7/11
Brake shoe riveters	5	1/7/11
Brake system flushers	5	1/7/11
Compressed air assets:		
Air compressors:		
Reciprocating	10	1/7/11
Rotary screw	10	1/7/11
Rotary vane	10	1/7/11
Air driers & dehumidifiers	10	1/7/11
Air receivers	10	1/7/11
Hose reels	3	1/7/11
Reticulation lines:		
Aluminium	15	1/7/11
Copper	20	1/7/11
Polyethylene	15	1/7/11
Steel	10	1/7/11
Continuous diesel engine particulate testers	5	1/7/11
Cooling system flushers	5	1/7/11
Decelerometer brake testers	7	1/7/11
Diagnostic assets:		
Diagnostic & roller dynamometers, performance & emissions testers	10	1/7/11
Engine analysers	5	1/7/11
Electrical test benches	10	1/7/11
Fuel injection pump test benches	5	1/7/11
Oscilloscopes	10	1/7/11
Scan tools	5	1/7/11
Diesel engine emission testers	5	1/7/11
Drill presses	15	1/7/11
Drive-on plate brake, steering & suspension testing machines	10	1/7/11
Drive-on shock absorber testers	10	1/7/11
Dual wheel removers	8	1/7/11
Effluent treatment systems incorporating motors, electronic circuitry, pumps, & separators	8	1/7/11
Engine cranes	10	1/7/11
Exhaust gas analysers for petrol engines:		
Computer operated	5	1/7/11
Standalone	10	1/7/11
Exhaust stands	11	1/7/11
Flywheel grinders	13	1/7/11
Hand tools	10	1/7/11
Headlight testers	7	1/7/11
Hydraulic brake hose machines	5	1/7/11
Hydraulic presses	10	1/7/11
Jacks:		
Floor jacks:		
Used for car & light truck repairs	3	1/7/11
Used for heavy vehicle repairs	5	1/7/11
Transmission jacks:		
Used for car & light truck repairs	8	1/7/11
Used for heavy vehicle repairs	5	1/7/11
Vehicle positioning jacks	3	1/7/11
Lathes	20	1/7/11
Measuring assets:		
Micrometers	10	1/7/11
Tension wrenches	5	1/7/11
Tyre pressure gauges	5	1/7/11
Noise level meters	5	1/7/11

Asset	Life (yrs)	Date of application
Oil & grease delivery systems:		
Bunding:		
Polyethylene pallets	5	1/7/11
Rubber	3	1/7/11
Distribution lines:		
Polyethylene	5	1/7/11
Rubber	3	1/7/11
Steel	10	1/7/11
Guns & pumps	3	1/7/11
Reels:		
Plastic	3	1/7/11
Steel	7	1/7/11
Tanks (including waste oil tanks)	20	1/7/11
Oil filter crushers	10	1/7/11
Parts cleaners & washers	7	1/7/11
Pipe & tube benders	10	1/7/11
Pipe & tube saws & cutters	10	1/7/11
Power steering flushing systems	5	1/7/11
Pressure washers	4	1/7/11
Sand blasters	7	1/7/11
Spring compressors	5	1/7/11
Stillages	15	1/7/11
Storage shelving	10	1/7/11
Toolbox roller cabinets	7	1/7/11
Trolleys	10	1/7/11
Truck brake imbalance testers	5	1/7/11
Tyre conveyors:		
Horizontal	10	1/7/11
Vertical	8	1/7/11
Tyre fitting machines	5	1/7/11
Tyre inflation cages	10	1/7/11
Tyre inflators (automatic & manual)	3	1/7/11
Tyre spreaders	8	1/7/11
Vehicle hoists:		
Used for car & light truck repairs	10	1/7/11
Used for heavy vehicle repairs	20	1/7/11
Vehicle service & inspection lane assets:		
Control consoles	10	1/7/11
Data collection devices (including bar code readers, mobile recorders & transponders)	5	1/7/11
Floor unit assets:		
Axle & ball joint play testers or shakers	10	1/7/11
Roller brake testers	10	1/7/11
Shock absorber testers	10	1/7/11
Side slip testers	10	1/7/11
Speedometer tester	10	1/7/11
Suspension play detectors	10	1/7/11
Vehicle special tools	5	1/7/11
Waste oil evacuators	5	1/7/11
Welders:		
Electric	10	1/7/11
Oxy acetylene	10	1/7/11
Wheel alignment machines	7	1/7/11
Wheel balancing machines	5	1/7/11
Wheel balancing plates, flanges & finger adaptors	5	1/7/11
Wheel lifters	5	1/7/11
Wheel lifter incorporating tyre spreaders	8	1/7/11
Work platform ladders	10	1/7/11

AUTOMOTIVE BODY, PAINT & INTERIOR REPAIR N.E.C.

Asset	Life (yrs)	Date of application
Car wash & detailing assets:		
Activation & entry station assets including bay controllers, pay station assets & bank note change machines	10	1/7/09
Automatic car wash assets including rollover & tunnel washes:		
Friction washer system assets including gantry, rails & arches & driers	10	1/7/09
Touch free pressure washer system assets including gantry, rails & arches & driers	10	1/7/09
Car conveyor system assets (incorporating correlators, sensors, tracks & rails)	15	1/7/09
Detailing assets:		
Steam cleaners	10	1/7/09
Vacuum cleaners	10	1/7/09
Hand & self serve car wash assets:		
Ceiling & wall booms	10	1/7/09
Large vehicle wash assets:		
Hoists	20	1/7/09
Side brush cleaning system assets	10	1/7/09

Asset	Life (yrs)	Date of application
Support assets:		
Door controls & motor drive systems for rapid roller doors (incorporating chains, controls, motors & sensors, but excluding doors)	10	1/7/09
Plant room assets:		
Air compressors		
Compressors – reciprocating	7	1/7/09
Compressors – screw	10	1/7/09
Boilers	20	1/7/09
Control systems	10	1/7/09
Pumps	12	1/7/09
Water treatment assets:		
Filter system assets including reverse osmosis	10	1/7/09
Tanks	20	1/7/09
Vending machines	5	1/7/09
Smash repair assets:		
Air compressors	10	1/7/09
Dust extraction systems:		
Metal arms	15	1/7/09
Stationary vacuum dust collection units	5	1/7/09
Frame straightening assets:		
Aligning benches	15	1/7/09
Chassis measuring assets:		
Computerised	10	1/7/09
Manual	10	1/7/09
Hoists	20	1/7/09
Painting assets:		
Buffing machines	3	1/7/09
Infrared paint dryers:		
Heating arches	20	1/7/09
Mobile	7	1/7/09
Sanders	3	1/7/09
Spectrophotometers	4	1/7/09
Spray bake ovens	12	1/7/09
Spray guns	3	1/7/09
Spray gun washing machines	5	1/7/09
Vacuum dust collection mobile units	3	1/7/09
Waste water filtering system assets:		
Oil & water separators	15	1/7/09
Pumps	5	1/7/09
Tanks	15	1/7/09
Water pressure cleaners	3	1/7/09
Welders	5	1/7/09

OTHER MACHINERY & EQUIPMENT REPAIR & MAINTENANCE

Asset	Life (yrs)	Date of application
Agriculture, construction & mining heavy machinery & equipment repair & maintenance assets:		
Field service assets:		
Assets used in field service that are not listed under this sub-heading - use any relevant determination listed under Workshop assets below		
Air compressors	8	1/7/15
Cranes	10	1/7/15
Cutting machines	8	1/7/15
Diagnostic assets	5	1/7/15
Lathes	5	1/7/15
Line boring machines	10	1/7/15
Milling machines	8	1/7/15
Turning machines	8	1/7/15
Trailers:		
Generally (including comb trailers & tilt trailers) – see Table B Motor vehicles & trailers		
Service trailers (incorporating built-in hoses, built-in pumps, built-in tanks etc)	10	1/7/15
Workshop assets:		
Air conditioning service assets (including refrigerant management/charging stations, refrigerant recovery machines, refrigerant recovery & recycling machines & vacuum pumps)	5	1/7/15
Air compression assets (including air dryers, air receivers, compressors & packaged air compression systems)	10	1/7/15

Asset	Life (yrs)	Date of application
Battery chargers	5	1/7/15
Battery load testers	5	1/7/15
Bending machines:		
Folders	15	1/7/15
Pipe & tube benders	10	1/7/15
Press brakes	20	1/7/15
Brake shoe riveting machines	5	1/7/15
Brake testers (including in-ground & mobile roller brake testers)	10	1/7/15
Boring machines (including floor borers, jib borers, horizontal & vertical boring machines)	15	1/7/15
Diagnostic, measuring & testing assets:		
Generally (including co-ordinate measuring machines, dynamometers, electrical testers, flow meters, hardness testers, hydraulic testers & multimeters)	10	1/7/15
Laptop diagnostic systems:		
Laptops - see Table B Computers, Laptops		
Machine interface units	3	1/7/15
Tyre pressure gauges	5	1/7/15
Vehicle specific diagnostic assets	5	1/7/15
Drilling machines (including drill presses, magnetic drills, pedestal drills & radial arm drills)	10	1/7/15
Flange facers	5	1/7/15
Forklift attachments	10	1/7/15
Forklifts	11	1/7/15
Grinding machines (including gear grinding machines)	10	1/7/15
Guillotine shears	15	1/7/15
Heat treatment assets (including furnaces & quenches)	15	1/7/15
Hydraulic hose crimpers	10	1/7/15
Lathes:		
CNC lathes	10	1/7/15
Manual lathes	20	1/7/15
Lifting assets:		
Cranes:		
Jib cranes (incl column/wall mounted, floor mounted/freestanding & portable jib cranes)	15	1/7/15
Overhead cranes	25	1/7/15
Pick & carry cranes/yard cranes	10	1/7/15
Portable cranes generally (including engine cranes, engine hoists, floor cranes, mobile gantries, shop cranes etc)	15	1/7/15
Hoists	10	1/7/15
Jacks (incl air hydraulic jacks, hydro pneumatic jacks, floor jacks, transmission jacks, trolley jacks & truck jacks)	5	1/7/15
Scissor lifts	15	1/7/15
Vehicle lifters (including mobile column lifts & post hoists)	20	1/7/15
Machining centres	10	1/7/15
Milling machines (including bed mills & universal mills)	10	1/7/15
Oil recovery, service & treatment assets:		
Collection vessels/tanks	20	1/7/15
Dangerous goods containers	15	1/7/15
Pumps	5	1/7/15
Painting assets:		
Buffing machines	3	1/7/15
Paint agitators	3	1/7/15
Space heaters	10	1/7/15
Spray booths	15	1/7/15
Spray gun washing machines	5	1/7/15
Parts washing machines	7	1/7/15
Pipe cutting machines	10	1/7/15
Plasma cutters	10	1/7/15
Presses:		
Hydraulic presses	10	1/7/15
Punch & shear machines	15	1/7/15
Saws (including band saws & cold cut saws)	10	1/7/15
Stands (including axle stands, engine stands & transmission stands)	10	1/7/15
Storage assets (including racking, shelving, safety cabinets & storage cabinets)	10	1/7/15

Asset	Life (yrs)	Date of application
Surface preparation assets:		
Abrasive blasting assets:		
Abrasive blasting machines (incorporating blasting pots, hoses, nozzles, valves etc)	10	1/7/15
Abrasive recovery/recycling machines & associated equipment (including storage hoppers)	12	1/7/15
Blast booths/chambers	12	1/7/15
Dust collection & ventilation systems	12	1/7/15
Pressure cleaners/washers	4	1/7/15
Toolboxes & toolbox roller cabinets	7	1/7/15
Tooling:		
Moulds	7	1/7/15
Press brake dies	10	1/7/15
Tooling for lathes, machining centres, milling machines & other machine tools	7	1/7/15
Vehicle specific specialised tooling	5	1/7/15
Workholding devices (including jigs & fixtures)	7	1/7/15
Tools:		
Hand tools (manually operated)	10	1/7/15
Hand held power tools (air, battery & electric)	3	1/7/15
Power packs	5	1/7/15
Torque/tension wrenches	5	1/7/15
Torque wrench pumps (pneumatic & electric driven)	5	1/7/15
Trolleys (incl powered & electrodrive trolleys)	10	1/7/15
Turning machines	10	1/7/15
Waste water recovery & treatment assets:		
Grease traps	10	1/7/15
Pumps	5	1/7/15
Tanks & separators	15	1/7/15
Waterjet cutting machines	10	1/7/15
Weight scales(corner weight)	10	1/7/15
Welding assets:		
Welders (including arc, MIG, TIG, multi process & oxy-acetylene welders/cutters)	10	1/7/15
Weld tables & positioners (including rotary tables)	10	1/7/15
Welding helmets incorporating respirators	3	1/7/15
Wire feeders	5	1/7/15
Wheel service assets:		
Bead breaker kits	5	1/7/15
Tyre changers	5	1/7/15
Wheel aligners	7	1/7/15
Wheel balancers	5	1/7/15
Wheel handlers & lifters	5	1/7/15
Wheel play detectors	10	1/7/15
Work benches & tables	15	1/7/15
HAIRDRESSING & BEAUTY SERVICES		
Beauty industry assets:		
Electrical treatment assets:		
Faradic, galvanic, high frequency & multi function units	10	1/7/10
Light therapy units (including intense pulse light systems)	10	1/7/10
Micro dermabrasion units	5	1/7/10
Hydrotherapy assets:		
Spa capsules	10	1/7/10
Vichy shower units	10	1/7/10
Wet tables	10	1/7/10
Massage & treatments beds:		
Dry hydrotherapy (including flotation)	7	1/7/10
Electronic	7	1/7/10
Non electronic (including folding)	10	1/7/10
Reception furniture, freestanding (including lobby chairs, desks, lounges, sofas & tables)	10	1/7/10
Sterilisation processing assets (incl autoclaves & hot towel cabinets)	5	1/7/10
Hairdressing industry assets:		
Barber chairs	15	1/7/10
Coffee making machines (including espresso & drip filter type)	5	1/7/10
Cutting chairs (including styling chairs & cutting stools)	10	1/7/10
Cutting & styling workstations, freestanding	10	1/7/10
Display shelving, freestanding	10	1/7/10
Hairdryers & heat accelerator machines		

Asset	Life (yrs)	Date of application
(excluding Hand held)	15	1/7/10
Reception furniture (including lobby chairs, desks, lounges, sofas & tables)	10	1/7/10
Shampoo units & wash lounges, freestanding	10	1/7/10
FUNERAL, CREMATORIUM & CEMETERY SERVICES		
Funeral directors' plant	20	1/1/01
LAUNDRY & DRY CLEANING SERVICES		
Carpet, upholstery & rug cleaning services assets:		
Air purifiers, deodorising & mould remediation assets (including air filtering machines, air scrubbers & ozone generators)	5	1/7/10
Carpet cleaning assets, portable (including rotary scrubbers & encapsulation machines)	5	1/7/10
Drying & restoration assets (including air movers & dehumidifiers)	5	1/7/10
Extractors for carpet & upholstery cleaning:		
Spot extractors (incl portable handheld & brief case size extractors for stain removal)	3	1/7/10
Others (including walk behind & self contained carpet extractors)	5	1/7/10
Truck or van mounted	10	1/7/10
Vacuum cleaners:		
Backpack & pull along machines	3	1/7/10
Other portable cleaners (incl upright machines)	5	1/7/10
Dry cleaning & laundry assets:		
Dry cleaning machines	12	1/7/11
Washers:		
Continuous batch washer systems (including washers, moisture extraction units & dryers)	17	1/7/11
Extractors, standalone	12	1/7/11
Drying assets:		
Tumble dryers, standalone	12	1/7/11
Tunnel dryers & garment finishers (including steam cabinets)	15	1/7/11
Finishing assets:		
Flatwork processing assets (including automatic pickers, feeders, folders & stackers)	13	1/7/11
Garment finishers (incl collar & cuff presses, form finishers, pant toppers & puff irons)	10	1/7/11
Presses (including flat, utility & scissor legger presses):		
Air operated, semi automatic	15	1/7/11
Manual	20	1/7/11
Roller ironers	17	1/7/11
Support assets:		
Air vacuum units, standalone	10	1/7/11
Control systems	10	1/7/11
Heat seal machines for labelling laundry items	10	1/7/11
Hot water systems	12	1/7/11
Ironing & spotting boards & tables:		
Vacuum operated	10	1/7/11
Non vacuum operated	15	1/7/11
Laundry handling assets:		
Conveyors & garment sorting & storage systems	15	1/7/11
Hoppers	20	1/7/11
Monorail & bag loading systems	20	1/7/11
Tipplers	10	1/7/11
Pipes	20	1/7/11
Soap dispenser machines	20	1/7/11
Trolleys & bins:		
Generally	10	1/7/11
Stainless steel	15	1/7/11
Waste water treatment & recycling system assets:		
Filters (including carbon & sand)	10	1/7/11
Lint shakers (including circular vibratory screens)	20	1/7/11
Ozone generators & ultra violet sterilisers	7	1/7/11
Pumps	5	1/7/11
Tanks	20	1/7/11
PHOTOGRAPHIC FILM PROCESSING		
Mini lab	10	1/1/01
Photo engraving plant:		
Automatic (dark room) cameras	10	1/1/01
General plant	20	1/1/01
Powderless etching machines	10	1/1/01
Power operated proofing presses	$13\frac{1}{3}$	1/1/01
Photo lab (one-hour service)	10	1/1/01

Asset	Life (yrs)	Date of application

A

Accommodation units in caravan/tourist parks being articles, not fixtures, & used for a specified purpose:

Asset	Life (yrs)	Date of application
Relocatable homes & tourist park cabins constructed with chassis	20	1/7/15
Other accommodation units (eg manufactured homes)	30	1/7/15

Advertising signs:
Billboard assets:
Billboard lighting:

Asset	Life (yrs)	Date of application
HID/Metal halide lighting systems	5	1/7/15
LED lighting systems (including solar powered LED lighting systems)	10	1/7/15
Solar power generating assets – see Table B Solar photovoltaic electricity generation system assets		
Billboard steel structures (incorporating electrical systems, footings, scaffolding & walking platforms & steel frame sign panels)	20	1/7/15
Computer hardware – see Table B Computers		
Digital LED screens	6	1/7/15
Electronic message centre (EMC) units	3	1/7/15
Mobile billboard assets:		
Digital LED screens	4	1/7/15
Mobile billboard trucks & trailers - see Table B Motor vehicles & trailers		
Floor mounted internal advertising panels (used in airports & shopping centres etc)	7	1/7/15
Kiosks & other external standalone advertising panel structures	15	1/7/15
LED advertising screens (used in office tower foyers etc)	5	1/7/15
Wall mounted advertising panels (used in airports, rail concourses & platforms, shopping centres etc):		
Digital LED advertising panels	5	1/7/15
Static advertising panels	10	1/7/15

Air compression assets:

Asset	Life (yrs)	Date of application
Air compression assets generally (including air compressors, air dryers & air receivers)	15	1/7/14
Air compressors (portable):		
Compressors – reciprocating	7	1/7/14
Compressors – rotary screw	10	1/7/14

Air conditioning assets (excluding pipes, duct work & vents):

Asset	Life (yrs)	Date of application
Air handling units	20	1/7/03
Cooling towers	15	1/7/03
Condensing sets	15	1/7/03
Chillers:		
Absorption	25	1/7/03
Centrifugal	20	1/7/03
Volumetrics (including reciprocating, rotary, screw, scroll):		
Air cooled	15	1/7/03
Water cooled	20	1/7/03
Damper motors (including variable air volume box controllers)	10	1/7/03
Fan coil units (connected to a condensing set)	15	1/7/03
Humidifiers (steam generator)	10	1/7/03
Mini split systems up to 20KW (including ceiling, floor & high wall split systems)	10	1/7/03
Packaged air conditioning units	15	1/7/03
Pumps	20	1/7/03
Room units	10	1/7/03

Aircraft:
Aeroplanes:

Asset	Life (yrs)	Date of application
General use	20#	1/7/02
Used predominantly for agricultural spraying or agricultural dusting	10#	1/7/02
Helicopters:		
General use	20#	1/7/02
Used predominantly for mustering, agricultural spraying or agricultural dusting	10#	1/7/02

Airless sprayers (used in painting, epoxy &

polyurethane coating, priming etc):

Asset	Life (yrs)	Date of application
Electrically & petrol-driven units	7	1/7/13
Pneumatically-driven units	15	1/7/13
Artworks qualifying as depreciating assets (restricted to works of art & reproductions of artwork that are tangible in nature, such as paintings, sculptures, drawings, engravings & photographs, that are displayed in open viewing areas in premises used for taxable purposes including reception areas, waiting rooms & foyers)	100	1/7/13
Automatic teller machines	8	1/7/01

B

Asset	Life (yrs)	Date of application
Bending machines (bar, angle & rod)	10	1/7/08
Block & brick elevators, portable	10	1/7/08
Boilers	20	1/7/05
Boom gates:		
Electromechanically operated boom gates	7	1/7/13
Hydraulically operated boom gates	10	1/7/13

C

Asset	Life (yrs)	Date of application
Car parking (hydraulic elevated platforms & hoists including control equipment)	10	1/1/01
Compaction:		
Compactors – flat plate	8	1/7/08
Compactors – vertical rammer	6	1/7/08
Computers:		
Generally	4	1/1/01
Laptops	3	1/1/01
Raised access floors in computer data rooms & server rooms	40	1/7/14
Concrete truck mixers (incorporating barrel, chutes, frame & hydraulic pumps)	5	1/7/14
Concreting assets:		
Brick & paving saws	5	1/7/08
Concrete demolition saws	3	1/7/08
Concrete kibble buckets	15	1/7/08
Concrete mixers	4	1/7/08
Concrete surface preparation assets (including floor grinders, planers & scarifers)	5	1/7/08
Concrete trowels:		
Walk behind	5	1/7/08
Ride on	7	1/7/08
Concrete vibrating screeders	5	1/7/08
Concrete vibrators:		
Brushcutter style	5	1/7/08
Drive units	6	1/7/08
Flexible shaft pumps	6	1/7/08
Vibrating shafts	3	1/7/08
Concrete wheeled saws	6	1/7/08
Control systems & control system assets (including control cabinets & panels, instruments, programmable logic controllers (PLCs), sensors, switchgear telemetry & variable speed drives)	10	1/7/15
Cranes (gantry & overhead)	25	1/7/14
Curtains & drapes	6	1/7/04

D

Asset	Life (yrs)	Date of application
Digital cameras:		
Camera lenses	5	1/7/15
Medium format single lens reflex (SLR) system (including camera bodies & digital backs)	4	1/7/15
Others	3	1/7/15
Door control & motor drive system for automatic sliding doors (incorporating chains, controls, motors & sensors, but excluding doors)	15	1/7/05
Dozers/front end loaders	9	1/7/02
Drink dispensing machines	10	1/7/05
Drones – see Table B Unmanned aerial vehicles		

Asset	Life (yrs)	Date of application
E		
Employee time & attendance recorders (including bundy clocks, time clocks etc):		
Computerised time & attendance recorders (including fingerprint & face recognition systems & swipe card digital time clock systems)	10	1/7/13
Standalone electronic time & attendance recorders (card based etc)	10	1/7/13
Escalators (machinery & their moving parts)	20	1/1/03
F		
Fences:		
Portable electric fences	20	1/7/14
Wire mesh (demountable used for partitioning purposes, including portable electric fences)	20	1/7/14
Fire control & alarm assets:		
Alarms:		
Heat	6	1/7/04
Smoke	6	1/7/04
Detection & alarm systems:		
Alarm bells	12	1/7/04
Detectors:		
Aspirated smoke	12	1/7/04
Heat	20	1/7/04
Manual call point (addressable type only)	20	1/7/04
Multi type	20	1/7/04
Smoke	20	1/7/04
Fire indicator panels	12	1/7/04
Gas suppression cylinders	25	1/7/04
Emergency warning & intercommunication systems:		
Master emergency control panels	12	1/7/04
Speakers	12	1/7/04
Strobe lights	12	1/7/04
Warden intercom phones	12	1/7/04
Extinguishers	15	1/7/04
Hoses & nozzles	10	1/7/04
Pumps (including diesel & electric)	25	1/7/04
Stair pressurisation assets:		
AC variable speed drives	10	1/7/04
Pressurisation & extraction fans	25	1/7/04
Sensors	10	1/7/04
Floor coverings - linoleum & vinyl (removable without damage)	10	1/7/13
Fogging machines (insecticide), including cold foggers & thermal foggers:		
Portable	6	1/7/13
Vehicle mounted	10	1/7/13
Forklifts	11	1/7/02
Forklift battery chargers	11	1/7/13
Formwork, beams & props, steel	10	1/7/08
Foundations for plant & machinery (integral to the operation of such plant & machinery, but not incorporated into the plant & machinery itself)	40	1/7/14
G		
Generators (see Table B Power supply assets)		
H		
Hand dryers (electrical)	10	1/7/13
Hand tools (manually operated)	10	1/7/14
J		
Judges' robes:		
Ceremonial robes	15	1/7/13
Working robes	10	1/7/13

Asset	Life (yrs)	Date of application
L		
Laboratory assets used in quality control, sample checking etc:		
Automated & electronically based laboratory assets (including analysers, refractometers, spectrometry machines etc)	7	1/7/14
Other laboratory assets (including autoclaves, centrifuges, microscopes, ovens etc)	10	1/7/14
Laser cutting machines	10	1/7/14
Levels:		
Automatic optical levels (dumpy levels)	7	1/7/15
Laser levels:		
Grade laying (dial-in grade)	6	1/7/15
Laser plummets	5	1/7/15
Line & plumb/point & cross line	4	1/7/15
Pipe laying	6	1/7/15
Rotating	6	1/7/15
Tunnelling & plumbing	6	1/7/15
Lift slab assets (incorporating spreader bars, clutches, pulleys & cables)	5	1/7/08
Libraries (professional)	10	1/7/14
Lifts (including dumbwaiters, hydraulic lifts & traction lifts)	30	1/1/03
Lighting control systems (microprocessor based)	5	1/7/14
Livestock, being working beasts & beasts of burden (including camels & horses) used in a business other than primary production	15	1/7/14
Loading bay assets:		
Dock levellers	20	1/7/05
Pallet jacks & pallet trucks	10	1/7/05
Scissor lifts	15	1/7/05
M		
Machine tools (grinding machines, lathes, milling machines etc):		
CNC & NC based machines	10	1/7/14
Conventional or manual machines	20	1/7/14
Mini skid steer loaders (with a carrying capacity less than or equal to 1100 kg)	5	1/7/05
Mini skid steer loader attachments:		
Others (including auger & bucket)	5	1/1/04
Stump grinders	2	1/1/04
Motor graders	10	1/7/02
Motor vehicles & trailers:		
Buses having a gross vehicle mass of more than 3.5 tonnes	15#	1/1/05
Cars (motor vehicles designed to carry a load of less than one tonne & fewer than 9 passengers):		
Generally	8	1/1/06
Hire & travellers' cars	5	1/1/01
Taxis	4	1/7/15
Garbage compactor trucks - see Table A Solid waste collection services (29110)		
Light commercial vehicles designed to carry a load of one tonne or greater & having a gross vehicle mass of 3.5 tonnes or less	12#	1/1/05
Minibuses having a gross vehicle mass of 3.5 tonnes or less & designed to carry 9 or more passengers	12#	1/1/05
Motorcycles (including courier motorcycles & mailbox delivery motorcycles)	7	1/7/15
Scooters	3	1/7/15
Trailers having a gross vehicle mass greater than 4.5 tonnes	15#	1/1/05
Trailers having a gross vehicle mass of 4.5 tonnes or less:		
Aluminium, galvanised steel, galvanised hot dipped steel & powder coated trailers	10	1/7/15
Mild steel trailers (painted & unpainted)	5	1/7/15
Trucks having a gross vehicle mass greater than 3.5 tonnes (excluding off highway trucks used in mining operations)	15#	1/1/05
Moving walks	20	1/1/03

Asset	Life (yrs)	Date of application	Asset	Life (yrs)	Date of application
Musical instruments & associated equipment:			Tapware (including taps, mixers & shower heads & assemblies)	15	1/7/15
Associated portable equipment (including amplifiers, microphones, speakers, mixers & music stands)	6²/₃	1/1/01	Pneumatic air tube systems	10	1/7/13
Brass instruments	10	1/1/01	**Point of sale assets:**		
Keyboard instruments (acoustic)	10	1/1/01	Cash registers, standalone type	10	1/7/05
Keyboard instruments (electric)	5	1/1/01	Cash transfer system assets, pneumatic type (including printer circuit board, transfer pipes & turbines)	10	1/7/05
Percussion instruments	5	1/1/01			
Stringed instruments	10	1/1/01	Generally (including barcode scanners, cash drawers, dedicated computers, electronic funds transfer point of sale (EFTPOS) machines, keyboards, monitors, printers & terminals)	6	1/7/05
Woodwind instruments	10	1/1/01			

O

Asset	Life (yrs)	Date of application	Asset	Life (yrs)	Date of application
Office furniture, freestanding:			Weighing machines & scales (including weigh labelling machines)	10	1/7/05
Bookcases:			Portable structures (sheds, site office trailers, portable toilets & washrooms etc) used for a temporary period in offsite locations (eg construction sites)	15	1/7/14
Metal	20	1/7/05			
Timber	15	1/7/05			
Cabinets (including credenzas, cupboards, filing, mapping, mobile, stationery & storage type):			Powder coating machines & systems (automatic & manual)	10	1/7/14
Metal	20	1/7/05	**Power supply assets:**		
Timber/laminated	15	1/7/05	Emergency or standby:		
Chairs	10	1/7/05	Generator assets:		
Desks	20	1/7/05	Acoustic hoods & canopies	20	1/7/05
Mobile storage units (compactus type)	25	1/7/05	Generators (incorporating attached engine management & generator monitoring instruments)	25	1/7/05
Reception assets (including lobby chairs, desks, lounges, sofas & tables)	10	1/7/05			
Screens	20	1/7/05	Power management units	15	1/7/05
Tables:			Uninterruptible power supply (UPS) systems	15	1/7/13
Boardroom	20	1/7/05	Generators, portable (incorporating attached engine management & generator monitoring instruments):		
General	10	1/7/05			
Workstations (including desks & partitions)	20	1/7/05	Diesel	10	1/7/08
Office machines & equipment:			Petrol	5	1/7/08
Electronic whiteboards	6	1/1/01	Private electricity line assets (where used for a specified purpose):		
Enveloping machines	6	1/1/01	Distribution lines:		
Facsimile machines	5	1/1/01	Combination of overhead & underground	47½	1/7/14
Letter folding & inserting machines (including envelope inserters & letter inserters - desktop/low volume units)	5	1/7/13	Overhead (incorporating poles - concrete, wood, steel or stobie - & electrical equipment the responsibility of the private landholder such as conductors; cross arms etc)	45	1/7/14
Mailing machines	5	1/1/01			
Multi function machines (includes fax, copy, print & scan functions)	5	1/1/01	Underground (incorporating cables, & ground pad mounted transformers)	50	1/7/14
Photo copying machines	5	1/1/01	Service cables, overhead	40	1/7/14
Projectors (including lenses)	5	1/7/14	Service cables, underground	50	1/7/14
Shredders	15	1/7/05	Storage batteries	15	1/7/13
Trolleys	15	1/7/05	**Power tools:**		
Whiteboards	10	1/7/05	Chain saws	3	1/7/08
			Hand tools:		

P

Asset	Life (yrs)	Date of application	Asset	Life (yrs)	Date of application
Packaging machines:			Air	5	1/7/08
Bagging machines (including flow wrappers, form fill & seal machines, & roll wrapping machines)	10	1/7/09	Battery	3	1/7/08
			Electric	5	1/7/08
Carton erecting, packing & closing machines (including cartoners)	10	1/7/09	Jack hammers:		
			Air	7	1/7/08
Case erecting, packing & closing machines (including casepackers)	10	1/7/09	Electric	3	1/7/08
			Nail guns - air	3	1/7/08
Inspection equipment including checkweighers, metal detectors, counting machines etc	10	1/7/09	Power transformers	45	1/1/02
Multihead & singlehead weighers	10	1/7/09	Public address & paging system assets (including amplifiers, audio speakers & microphones)	12	1/7/05
Palletisers & depalletisers	12	1/7/09			
Product identification labellers including decorating, applicators & coding machines	8	1/7/09	**R**		
Robotic pick & place packaging machines	10	1/7/09	**Refrigeration assets:**		
Wrapping machines including shrink wrappers, stretch wrappers & strapping machines	10	1/7/09	Compressors, condensers, evaporators etc	15	1/7/14
Partitions (demountable)	20	1/7/05	Insulation panels used in cool or freezer rooms	40	1/7/14
Platform scales	15	1/7/14	Robots (industrial)	10	1/7/14
Plumbing fixtures & fittings (including wall & floor tiles) provided mainly for employees &/or children of employees of an entity carrying on a business for the purpose of producing assessable income:			**S**		
			Saws, bench & mitre, portable	7	1/7/08
Floor & wall tiles	20	1/7/15	**Security & monitoring assets:**		
Generally (including basins, bidets, sinks, toilets, urinals etc)	20	1/7/15	Access control systems:		
			Code pads	5	1/7/04

Asset	Life (yrs)	Date of application
Door controllers	5	1/7/04
Readers:		
Proximity	7	1/7/04
Swipe card	3	1/7/04
Ballistic & blast resistant screens & barriers (including fixed & rising types) not forming part of the building	20	1/7/14
Closed circuit television systems:		
Cameras	4	1/7/04
Monitors	4	1/7/04
Recorders:		
Digital	4	1/7/04
Time lapse	2	1/7/04
Switching units (including multiplexers)	5	1/7/04
Security systems:		
Code pads	5	1/7/04
Control panels	5	1/7/04
Detectors (including glass, passive infra-red & vibration)	5	1/7/04
Global system for mobiles (GSM) units	5	1/7/04
Noise maker (including alarms & bells)	5	1/7/04
Sewing machines	10	1/1/14
Signage for business identification (including lighting for signs)	10	1/7/05
Silos:		
Bulk handling:		
Ancillary mechanical assets (incl augers, bucket elevators, conveyors etc)	15	1/7/14
Concrete construction	50	1/1/04
Galvanised construction	30	1/1/04
Steel construction	40	1/1/04
Solar photovoltaic electricity generation system assets	20	1/7/11
Spas used as plant in a business (incorporating blowers, controls, filters, heaters & pumps)	17	1/7/14
Spray booths	15	1/7/14
Stacks (chimney stacks, exhaust stacks, flues etc):		
Concrete stacks (including concrete reinforced stacks)	30	1/7/14
Flare stacks	25	1/7/14
Reinforced plastic stacks	25	1/7/14
Steel stacks (steel flues)	20	1/7/14
Suitcases	10	1/7/13
Swimming pool assets:		
Chlorinators	12	1/7/04
Cleaning assets	7	1/7/04
Filtration assets (including pumps)	12	1/7/04
Heaters:		
Electric	15	1/7/04
Gas	15	1/7/04
Solar	20	1/7/04
Swimming pools (used as plant in a business):		
Above-ground	10	1/7/05
Concrete	50	1/7/05
Fibreglass	20	1/7/05
Switchboards	20	1/7/14
Synthetic lawn surfaces	5	1/7/14

T

Asset	Life (yrs)	Date of application
Tarpaulins	5	1/7/14
Telephony:		
Mobile phones	3	1/7/14
Telephone systems (including analogue & digital telephone systems, PABX/PBX systems, key/commander systems, VoIP systems & hybrid telephone systems such as IP-PBX systems etc)	7	1/7/15
Television sets	10	1/7/14
Tractors	12	1/7/07
Trailers – see Table B Motor vehicles & trailers		
Two-way radios:		
Base stations	6	1/7/14
Mobile units	6	1/7/14
Portable units	3	1/7/14
Repeaters	7	1/7/14

U

Asset	Life (yrs)	Date of application
Unmanned aerial vehicles (drones):		
Fixed wing	3	1/7/15
Rotary wing	2	1/7/15

V

Asset	Life (yrs)	Date of application
Vending machines	5	1/7/01
Ventilation fans (excluding ducting, piping & vents)	20	1/1/05

W

Asset	Life (yrs)	Date of application
Warehouse & distribution centre equipment & machines:		
Automated storage & retrieval machines	20	1/7/11
Balers	15	1/7/11
Battery assets for warehouse vehicles (including pallet trucks & forklifts):		
Batteries (detachable for recharging)	5	1/7/11
Battery chargers:		
Forklifts	11	1/7/11
Other	10	1/7/11
Handling assets:		
Battery tuggers	10	1/7/11
Racking roller beds	15	1/7/11
Transfer carts	10	1/7/11
Washers	10	1/7/11
Carts/buggies	15	1/7/11
Conveyors	15	1/7/11
Dock levellers, pallet jacks, pallet trucks & scissor lifts – see Table B Loading bay assets		
Door control & motor drive systems (incorporating chains, controls, motor & sensors, but excluding doors):		
External	20	1/7/11
Internal	10	1/7/11
Floor sweepers/scrubbers	10	1/7/11
Forklift attachments:		
Cages	10	1/7/11
Push pull units	11	1/7/11
Inflatable dock bags/seals/shelters	10	1/7/11
Packaging machines & wrapping machines – see Table B Packaging machines		
Pallet assets:		
Dispensers	15	1/7/11
Lift tables	10	1/7/11
Racks	20	1/7/11
Radio frequency terminal assets:		
Barcode readers/scanners	5	1/7/11
Portable/Handheld & vehicle mounted terminal devices	4	1/7/11
Refrigeration assets – see Table B Refrigeration assets		
Roll cages	10	1/7/11
Trolleys	10	1/7/11
Voice picking assets:		
Battery chargers	4	1/7/11
Headsets	4	1/7/11
Terminals (on person)	4	1/7/11
Waste compactors (used for cardboard & plastic):		
Electric	15	1/7/11
Hydraulic	20	1/7/11
Waste storage & disposal bins (industrial)	10	1/1/01
Weighbridges	20	1/7/14
Welders:		
Diesel	10	1/7/08
Electric	5	1/7/08
Oxygen welders & cutters	10	1/7/14

15.200 CAPITAL WORKS

Division 43 ITAA97 allows a deduction for construction expenditure on capital works. The term 'capital works' includes buildings, structural improvements and environmental protection earthworks that are used for an income-producing purpose. The rate of the annual deduction depends upon the type of capital works and the date its construction commenced (see 15.205).

The deduction for capital works commenced after 21 August 1979 and is a special tax concession. It is not a claim for depreciation of the capital works as the deduction is not based on effective life. The capital works need not be constructed in Australia to qualify for the deduction if started after 21 August 1990.

For capital works started before 1 July 1997, there is a requirement that the intended use of the structure qualified for the deduction at the time of its completion.

A table in s43-90 outlines the meaning of 'intended use at time of completion of construction' for capital works started before 1 July 1997. In that table, the intended use requirement for residential accommodation is satisfied even if the accommodation was first used for private purposes after its completion.

For capital works started after 30 June 1997, a deduction can be claimed during the time the capital works are used in a deductible way (either for producing assessable income or research and development).

The building write-off concession can be applied to display homes used for income-producing purposes after 30 June 1997. The deduction is not based on the cost to the taxpayer, but on the original construction cost.

For the Division 43 deduction, the cost of construction expenditure is reduced by the amount of any input tax credit entitlement related to that expenditure (ATO ID 2003/553).

While the rate for the deduction is determined at the date the construction commenced (pouring of the foundations or the sinking of pilings), the actual capital works deduction period cannot commence before the construction of the capital works is completed, even if the taxpayer has used the capital works, or part thereof, for an income-producing purpose before the construction was completed (s43-30). When the capital works are completed the deduction period commences (ie. 25 years or 40 years). Within this period the deduction is only allowed when the building is being used for an income-producing or research and development purpose.

On change of ownership, the new owner is entitled to claim deductions based on the original construction cost.

Unlike depreciation, there is no balancing adjustment on disposal of buildings unless the building is destroyed. The residue of any deduction passes to the new owners, provided that the building continues to be used for the purpose of producing assessable income.

If the capital works had been destroyed, then the balancing deduction is equal to the undeducted construction expenditure at the date of destruction less the amount the taxpayer has received, or has a right to receive, for the destruction of the capital works.

Where a building is held on revenue account and disposed of at a profit, capital works deductions claimed are not added back in determining the profit (*MLC Limited and Anors v DFC of T* 2002 ATC 5105). However, if the building is held on capital account and the building was acquired after 7.30pm on 13 May 1997 any capital works deduction may reduce the cost base of the building for the purpose of calculating any capital gain (see below).

15.205   CAPITAL ALLOWANCES: DEDUCTIONS FOR CAPITAL WORKS

The table below summarises relevant dates of construction and annual prime cost percentage rates of deduction for the various types of construction costs. If construction started after 26 February 1992, the number of years may alter if the deduction rate varies, because the building use has changed. The total deductions are calculated at 4% or 2.5% until used up (ie. deductions cannot exceed the cost of construction).

 A 'clawback' may occur for hire purchase arrangements or limited recourse debt. Hirers under a hire purchase agreement may be treated as notional owners (see 15.800).

For expenditure incurred after 7.30pm ACT legal time on 13 May 1997, deductions for capital works allowed under these rules will generally reduce the cost base when calculating any capital gain or capital loss on disposal (s110-45). No reduction was required in respect of such expenditure incurred prior to that date.

Deductible expenditure incurred after 30 June 1999 on land or a building which was acquired at or before 7.30pm on 13 May 1997 does not form part of the fourth element (enhancement costs) of the cost base of the property. Where a capital loss is made on the property, the reduced cost base does not include amounts for which a deduction can be claimed (without reference to the date of acquisition of the property).

It should be noted that there is no fixed time for determining when amounts can be 'deducted' for the purposes of adjusting the CGT cost base: for example, the amendment period for claiming the deduction may have expired, so preventing the deduction being claimed (see TD 2005/47 in general). The cost base will then not have to be adjusted. It should also be noted, in regard to construction expenditure that where in relation to Division 43 (capital works) the taxpayer does not have sufficient information to determine the amount and nature of the expenditure and in addition does not seek to deduct the amount, the CGT cost base or reduced cost base does not have to be adjusted (Practice Statement PS LA 2006/1 (GA)).

Expenditure on any extensions, alterations or improvements is regarded as a 'separate building' and the applicable (2.5% or 4%) rate applies.

Type of construction	Start date	Rate (%)	Years
Short-term traveller accommodation[1]	22/8/79 – 21/8/84	2.5	40
	22/8/84 – 17/7/85[1]	4	25
	18/7/85 – 15/9/87[2]	4	25
	16/9/87 – 26/2/92	2.5	40
	27/2/92[1]	4	25
Non-residential income-producing buildings[3]	20/7/82 – 21/8/84	2.5	40
	22/8/84 – 15/9/87[2]	4	25
	16/9/87 –	2.5	40
Buildings used for eligible industrial activities	27/2/92 –	4	25
Residential income-producing building	18/7/85 – 15/9/87[2]	4	25
	16/9/87 –	2.5	40
Income-producing structural improvements	27/2/92 –	2.5	40
R&D buildings	21/11/87[2] –	2.5	40
Environment protection earthworks	19/8/92 –	2.5	40

1: If the building is being used for another purpose, or had less than 10 accommodation units, there is:
- no deduction for pre-18 July 1985 constructions, and
- 2.5% deduction for post-26 February 1992 constructions.

2: Or a contract was entered into before this date.

3: The 4% rate may apply if construction commenced after 26 February 1992 and the income-producing building was used mainly for industrial activities.

Deductions are available in respect of buildings used to produce assessable income, or available to do so, but not on those held as trading stock. The deduction rate is fixed according to contract or construction dates. However, a claim can be made only from the time when the construction is complete. Construction of a new building, or the alteration or extension to a building is considered to have started when construction begins (ie. pouring of foundations or the sinking of pilings).

LESSEES CAN CLAIM EXPENDITURE

Lessees can claim a deduction for improvements they made during the term of the lease (or extension) or during any continuous replacement lease, subject to satisfying the requirements of Division 43 as they relate to lessees.

EARTHWORKS

The cost of the building includes the cost of any earthworks which are an integral part of the construction of the building (such as earthworks for foundations). These costs are eligible for the higher 4% rate if for short-term traveller accommodation or as a building used wholly or mainly for industrial activities (defined in s43-150): see *Core industrial activities* at 15.230 and *Ancillary industrial activities* at 15.235.

CERTAIN IMPROVEMENTS NOT ELIGIBLE

Some improvements, which are mere changes to the landscape, typically do not lose value (eg. golf courses, landscaping and grass sports fields) and are not eligible for the capital works write-off.

DEPRECIABLE ITEMS ARE NOT ELIGIBLE

It is an overriding rule that any asset on which depreciation is allowed (including certain structural improvements such as parts of a building which are integral to a manufacturing process) are not eligible for a capital works deduction.

TENANT IMPROVEMENTS

Where a lessee improves a building that is being used by the lessee for producing assessable income, that lessee is entitled to a capital works deduction for the improvements. If these improvements are scrapped during the term of the lease, the lessee would be entitled to a deduction under s43-40 for destruction of capital works. Where a lessee gives up the lease or the lease ends, the owner/lessor of the premises gets the right to the unrecouped capital works deductions and any later re-letting of the premises does not vest this right in the new tenant. However, a tenant who obtains an assignment of a continuing lease where an earlier tenant constructed capital works may obtain the balance of the deductions.

If a lessee who owned improvements walked away at the termination of the lease, there is a disposal of the improvements by the lessee to the lessor (CGT event A1). If the parties are not dealing at arm's length or no consideration is received, the lessor is deemed to have paid the market value for the improvements and a capital gain or loss may arise to the lessee (with the cost of the improvements being the cost base) (see TD 98/23). If the lessee did not own the improvements but did pay for them, the amount may be included in the cost base of the lease itself and CGT event C2 happens when the lease expires or is terminated. A capital gain or loss may then be made by the lessee on the lease itself, with the cost base being adjusted for any non-assessable amount the lessee recovers.

15.210 SHORT-TERM TRAVELLER ACCOMMODATION

The write-off rate for buildings providing short-term traveller accommodation is 4% pa where construction of the building, extensions or improvements started after 26 February 1992.

The 4% (of construction cost) tax deduction is allowed only if the building (or part of it) and associated facilities are used wholly or principally for short-term traveller accommodation and:

- if a hotel, motel or guest house, it must have at least 10 bedrooms, or
- contain at least 10 apartments, flats or units that are owned by the one entity (s43-145).

A deduction of 2.5% of the construction costs is allowed if significant income from any other source is derived from the complex (ie. the facilities are not used wholly or principally in operating short-term traveller accommodation).

A cinema or amusement park are not commonly provided in hotels, motels or guest houses in Australia. However, if there were such a complex, the 4% may well be denied for this part of the complex because these buildings are not primarily used for short-term traveller accommodation. The rate for these buildings would drop from 4% to 2.5% as they are still used for income-producing purposes.

If a building is converted to provide both traveller accommodation and offices or shops, a 4% deduction is allowed for the part used wholly or principally for the short-term traveller, but only 2.5% is allowed for the rest.

For pre-18 July 1985 constructions, the deduction ceases once the short-term accommodation requirement ceased to be met.

Costs incurred by owners, shareholders, partners or beneficiaries for their own private accommodation in a complex providing short-term traveller accommodation (or depreciating assets on which depreciation can be claimed) are excluded from the building's construction costs and no claim for capital works is allowed. A 4% building allowance claim is allowed on the cost of the rest of that facility if used for short-term traveller accommodation.

Buildings used for producing assessable income that are also used as part of an individual's home will not qualify (eg. a doctor's surgery that is part of the doctor's residential house).

15.225   CAPITAL EXPENDITURE ON INDUSTRIAL BUILDINGS

The capital cost of buildings, or extensions, alterations or improvements to buildings used in industrial activities is deductible at 4% pa if the construction commenced after 26 February 1992.

The 4% rate applies to the extent to which a building (or part of it) is used wholly or principally:

- to produce assessable income
- whether by the owner or another person for eligible industrial activities (see *Core industrial activities* and *Ancillary industrial activities* below), and
- for meal rooms, rest rooms, first-aid rooms, change rooms or similar facilities for use by:
  - workers engaged wholly or principally to undertake the work directly involved in carrying out eligible industrial activities, or
  - the immediate supervisors of those workers, or
  - as office accommodation for immediate supervisors.

15.230   CORE INDUSTRIAL ACTIVITIES

Eligible industrial activities are extensively defined in s43-150 and include these core activities:

- manufacturing operations carried out by a person or others performing services on that person's behalf
- other manufacturing processes in which the goods are brought into the form or condition in which they are sold or used by that person or other persons, (but not mere packing, placing in containers or labelling of goods)
- concentration of a metal
- treatment/processing of a metal after concentration
- if the metal does not require concentration, the process which would normally have been applied after concentration
- refining of petroleum
- scouring or carbonising of wool
- milling of timber
- freezing of primary products
- printing, lithographing, engraving or any similar process in the course of carrying on those types of businesses
- curing of meat or fish
- production of chilled or frozen meat
- pasteurising of milk
- canning or bottling of foodstuffs, or
- production of electric current, hydraulic power, steam, compressed air or gases (not natural gas), for sale or use wholly or principally in carrying on any of the activities above.

15.235   ANCILLARY INDUSTRIAL ACTIVITIES

In addition, these activities also qualify as eligible industrial activities when carried out as part of their core activities:

- packing, placing in containers or labelling of goods
- disposal of waste substances
- assembly, maintenance, cleansing, sterilising or repair of property
- cleansing or sterilising of bottles, vats or other containers used by the person to store goods:
  - to be used by the person in carrying on core activities, or
  - resulting from the carrying on by the person of core activities, and
- storage (on premises where the taxpayer carries on core activities, or premises contiguous to those premises) of goods:
  - to be used by the person or goods on which the taxpayer has started but not completed, carrying on of core activities, or
  - resulting from core activities carried on by the person.

15.240   INELIGIBLE ACTIVITIES

Preparation of food and drink in hotels, motels, restaurants and similar retail outlets is ineligible to be an industrial activity. However, the preparation of food or drink in factories and breweries qualifies.

15.245   APPORTIONMENT

The 4% rate applies only to the proportion of the overall construction cost in respect of which a building is used in an 'eligible industrial manner'. An apportionment is made where there is multiple use, or if some part isn't used. If a taxpayer conducts retailing and manufacturing activities in the one building, the 4% rate applies to the part used for manufacturing, while the 2.5% rate applies to other income-producing areas. No deduction is allowed for any part not used to gain assessable income. If eligible industrial activities and other activities are conducted in the same area, the dominant activity determines whether the 4% or 2.5% rate applies.

An engineering firm manufactures high performance car parts (an eligible industrial activity) and also performs ineligible repair work. Unless the two activities are performed in separate areas of the workshop, the use of the facility as a whole is determined by the dominant activity.

TWO OR MORE OWNERS

If there are two or more owners of separate parts of a building, qualifying expenditure is apportioned to the various parts. Deductions for each share are separately calculated according to the use of the building.

SPREAD OF DEDUCTIONS

As in the case of buildings used for short-term traveller accommodation, the deduction is not spread over a fixed term, but is calculated according to the use of the building. The calculation (either 4% pa, or 2.5% pa if not used for an industrial activity) starts from when the capital works are completed (see s43-30) and the deduction is only allowed where the building is being used for an income-producing or a research development purpose (see 15.200 and 15.205).

15.250   ASSOCIATED STRUCTURAL IMPROVEMENTS

A structural improvement started after 26 February 1992 is treated as though it were a building and the capital cost, not claimable under another section, is deductible at 2.5% pa over 40 years when used to produce assessable income.

A factory boundary fence (usually for security) or car park is not eligible for depreciation because it is not a depreciating asset, but qualifies as an associated structural improvement and is eligible for the capital works deduction of 2.5% pa.

'STRUCTURAL IMPROVEMENTS'

There is no definition of a 'structural improvement' but broadly it means property on land, constructed from material or related parts to improve the land. Examples of structural improvements eligible for the 2.5% pa deduction include any earthworks integral to the installation of a building or structure:

- roads, driveways, carparks or airport runways (if these are sealed)
- bridges
- pipelines
- lined road tunnels
- retaining walls
- fences
- concrete or rock dams, and
- artificial sports fields.

Cuttings, culverts and embankments for a road and foundation excavations for a tunnel or bridge, qualify. In constructing a carpark, the cost of stone, gravel, underlay and concrete or bitumen surfacing is allowable, but the cost of site clearing (removal of trees or existing structures) and levelling are not. The cost of excavating foundations for a seawall or similar structure as part of a marina would qualify, as would an ornamental lake, as these excavations are integral to the installation of a structure.

INELIGIBLE STRUCTURAL IMPROVEMENTS

Earthworks that are:

- not integral to the installation or construction of a structure, non-wasting if appropriately maintained, and which can be maintained economically for an indefinite period, eg. unlined channels, unlined basins, earth tanks and dirt tracks, and
- artificial landscapes such as grass golf fairways and greens, grass sports fields such as bowling greens, ovals, etc. and gardens

do not qualify as capital works.

15.260   COST OF CONSTRUCTION

There are three categories of capital works and a deduction is calculated for each of the categories. They include:

- buildings, or extensions, alterations or improvements to buildings
- structural improvements or extensions or improvements to them, and
- environmental protection works.

Construction expenditure that is eligible for a deduction as capital works includes:

- preliminary expenses such as architect fees, engineering fees, foundation excavation expenses and costs of building permits
- cost of structural features that are an integral part of the income-producing buildings (or income-producing structural improvements eg. atriums and lift wells), and
- some proportion of indirect costs. This includes costs that (based on accounting records or other documentation) cannot be allocated wholly to an individual element of a construction project (eg. the cost of site accommodation erected for the use of all construction workers working on the project).

Construction expenditure excludes the cost of:

- acquiring land
- demolishing existing structures
- preparing a construction site (eg. clearing, levelling, filling or draining) before carrying out excavation works
- landscaping, and
- depreciable assets or property for which a deduction is (or could have been) allowable under another part of the law.

The Tax Office also considers that the value of an owner/builder's contribution to the works (such as labour and expertise and any notional profit) are excluded from the cost of construction.

A speculative builder constructing a building for sale is considered by the Tax Office to incur expenditure on revenue rather than capital account. Without any capital expenditure on the building, the builder should not be entitled to a deduction under Division 43. However, under the ITAA97, s43-75(3) and s43-85, purchase from a speculative builder is dealt with, allowing a deduction to a taxpayer purchasing capital works from an entity that:

- is not an associate of the taxpayer, and
- incurred expenditure in constructing the capital works on land it owned or leased in the course of a business that included the construction and sale of such capital works (see TR 97/25).

Excluded from construction expenditure are the value of the builder's own contributions to the construction process and any profit element on the sale transaction. If the purchase price of the capital works exceeds the actual construction cost, the purchaser is only entitled to claim deductions based on the actual cost of construction. If the construction cost exceeds the purchase price, the deduction is based on the actual construction cost and not the purchase price.

A property developer constructs a condominium of 45 units in a popular holiday resort. All of the units are intended for sale. During the construction phase 30 units are sold off the plan. After completion of the project, real estate prices decrease significantly and the developer sells the remaining units below cost. A taxpayer buys one of those units for $106,000 when the actual construction cost was $115,000. If the building is used for producing assessable income the taxpayer will be entitled to claim a deduction for capital works based on $115,000.

Where an entity purchases capital works from an associate the capital works are not taken to have a construction expenditure area (see s43-75(3)).

CONSTRUCTION ESTIMATES

TR 97/25 states that where the taxpayer is genuinely unable to precisely determine the actual cost of construction, the Tax Office will accept estimates from:

- a clerk of works (ie. a project manager for major building projects)
- a supervising architect who approves payments at each stage in major projects and who may approve individual payments to subcontractors in smaller contracts
- a builder who is experienced in estimating costs of similar building projects, and
- quantity surveyors.

Real estate valuers, estate agents, accountants and solicitors will not be accepted unless they have other relevant qualifications. The Tax Office will also not accept the use of published building cost guides unless used merely as a guide by a suitable qualified person.

A purchaser should include a requirement in the terms of the contract of purchase to gain the relevant information for buildings eligible to claim under these rules. See *Record keeping* at 15.280.

15.265   ENVIRONMENT PROTECTION EARTHWORKS

Capital works which are earthworks as a result of carrying out an eligible environment protection activity which commenced after 18 August 1992 are deductible over 40 years at 2.5% (also see 15.600).

15.270   CALCULATING THE DEDUCTION

The cost of a building or structural improvement includes expenses such as architects' and engineers' fees, building permit fees, etc. but not the cost of land, or the cost of site cleaning, levelling and landscaping. The claim may be made by the owner, lessor or lessee. The deduction period can only begin once the capital works are completed (s43-30). No deduction can be claimed before construction is completed, even though the taxpayer may have used the capital works, or part thereof, for an income-producing purpose before construction was completed. Within the deduction period (usually 25 or 40 years) the deduction can be claimed when the capital works are being used for an income-producing or research and development purpose.

The claim is based on the number of days the building is used for income-producing purposes using the following formulae.

- If two or more persons own separate parts of the same building, the 'qualifying' cost of the building is apportioned between two parts.
  - *(Portion of short-term traveller cost x Days used x 0.04) divided by 365,* and/or
  - *(Portion of other building costs x Days used x 0.025) divided by 365*

NOTE: The 4% building allowance is allowed for that portion (on a daily basis) of the building or facility used for short-term accommodation or an eligible industrial activity where construction commenced after 26 February 1992. If the building or facility produces assessable income (other than these uses) a 2.5% claim is allowed on that part.

A country motel has 20 units and associated facilities. Usually all units are available to travellers. Qualifying expenditure is $500,000. To accommodate its employees, a mining company takes a 12 month lease (from 1 January) on 15 of the 20 units.

Calculation of motel owner's claim: *From 1 July to 31 December (184 days) the whole of the motel was used for traveller accommodation. The deduction allowed is ($500,000 x 0.04 x 184 days) divided by 365 = $10,082*

From 1 January to 30 June (181 days) only five units were used as traveller accommodation. As this is less than the 10 minimum required, the claim-rate is 2.5%.

Deduction is ($500,000 x 0.025 x 181 days) divided by 365 = $6,199.

Total deduction = $16,281

CLAIM YEARS NOT FIXED

Because the rate of deduction can vary according to the use to which the facility is put, a deduction is not spread over a fixed term. The deduction is calculated at the appropriate rate for the current use of either 4% or 2.5% pa until used up, but the maximum time limit for the deduction will be 25 years if the rate is 4% pa and 40 years if the rate is 2.5% pa (s43-15). The total amount of deductions cannot exceed the allowed cost of the building or facility.

If, during that period, the building is not used to earn income, the total cost is reduced by the amount that would otherwise have been allowed as a deduction during that time.

CLAIM IF BUILDING IS DESTROYED

The general rule is, if a building or structural improvement is fully or partly demolished or destroyed, a balancing deduction is allowed for any capital cost remaining on the destroyed part, minus any compensation received (eg. from insurance or salvaging). If the building was only partially eligible for the capital works deduction, the amount is reduced to what is reasonable.

For short-term traveller accommodation built after 26 February 1992, the deduction is available only if the last use before destruction was to produce assessable income. If building started before 18 July 1985, its last use prior to destruction must have been for short-term traveller accommodation.

15.280   RECORD KEEPING

For traveller accommodation and other qualifying buildings or structures (if construction started after 26 February 1992) a person selling a building or the lease of such a building, must inform the purchaser of the amount of qualifying expenditure and the remaining tax deductible balance to enable that person to ascertain the deduction that will apply.

The information (including the cost of construction of the original building and any capital expenses such as extensions, additions, alterations, and the amount of the capital allowance still to be claimed) must be passed on within six months of the end of the income year in which the disposal occurs, or within such further period as the Commissioner allows (s262A(4AF), (4AG) (4AH) and (4AJ) of ITAA36).

The purchaser will have to keep that information for five years after the earlier of:

- ceasing to be the owner of the building, or
- the destruction of the building.

15.500 RESEARCH AND DEVELOPMENT

The Research and Development (R&D) tax incentive regime became effective from 1 July 2011. The tax incentive replaces the former R&D tax concession. The provisions are contained in Division 355 ITAA97.

The R&D tax incentive provides a tax offset to eligible companies that engage in R&D activities. The scheme is administered jointly by AusIndustry (on behalf of Innovation Australia) and the Tax Office. Applications can be made at www.business.gov.au.

15.510   R&D TAX INCENTIVE – OVERVIEW

Entities engaged in R&D may be eligible for either:

- a 45% **refundable** tax offset – for eligible entities with an aggregated annual turnover of less than $20 million which are not controlled by income tax exempt entities (eligible entities in a tax loss position will receive an upfront cash refund), or
- a 40% **non-refundable** tax offset – for all other eligible entities (any unused credits can also be carried forward for use in future years).

AusIndustry manages the registration of R&D activities and checks that they comply with the law. The Tax Office determines the eligibility of the expenditure claimed in the tax return.

RECENT R&D LEGISLATION UPDATE

The *Tax Laws Amendment (Research and Development) Bill 2013* (the Bill) was passed by the House of Representatives on 17 June 2015. The Bill was before the Senate at the time of writing.

The Bill proposes that the rate of the R&D tax offset is reduced to the company tax rate (currently 30%) for that portion of an entity's notional R&D deductions that exceeds $100 million for an income year. This change applies in relation to assessments for income years commencing on or after 1 July 2014 and before 1 July 2024.

15.520   ELIGIBILITY

Entities self-assess their eligibility for the tax offset.

ELIGIBLE ENTITIES

An eligible entity is:

- a company incorporated under Australian law
- a company incorporated under foreign law, but which is an Australian resident for tax purposes
- a foreign company that:
  - is a resident of a country with which Australia has a double tax agreement, and
  - carries on R&D activities through a permanent establishment in Australia, and
- a public trading trust with a corporate trustee.

The following are not eligible entities:

- a corporate limited partnership
- a tax-exempt entity, and
- trusts other than a public trading trust with a corporate trustee.

The offset will also be made directly available to partners in a R&D partnership but it will not be taken into account in calculating the partnership net income or loss.

NOTE: The R&D tax incentive applies to a consolidated group as if it is a single entity conducting all R&D activities within the group. As such, only the head company of the group should register for, and claim, the tax incentive for these R&D activities.

FOR WHOM THE ACTIVITIES ARE BEING CONDUCTED

The tax offset is available to an Australian resident R&D entity if the R&D activities were conducted for one of the following:

- the R&D entity itself, or
- a foreign company:
    - that is a tax resident of a country with which Australia has a double tax agreement, and
    - the activities are conducted under a written agreement between the entities.

The tax offset is available to a foreign company carrying on business through a permanent establishment in Australia if:

- the R&D activities are conducted for itself (the foreign company), and
- the R&D activities are not also conducted for the Australian permanent establishment.

REGISTRATION

To claim an R&D tax offset, an eligible entity must register its R&D activities with AusIndustry. Registration takes place in the income year after the R&D activities are undertaken. An R&D entity must register its R&D activities:

- in respect of every income year that it wants to claim the tax offset
- within ten months after the end of the income year (registering for the income year in which the offset is to be claimed), and
- prior to claiming the R&D tax offset in the tax return.

The R&D tax incentive applies to activities and expenditure in income years beginning on or after 1 July 2011. For activities and expenditure in years commencing before that date, the former R&D tax concession applies.

For the 2014-15 income year, 30 June balancers may submit their application between 1 July 2015 and 30 April 2016 using the approved forms which are available from the AusIndustry website.

15.530   ELIGIBLE ACTIVITIES

Eligible R&D activities must be either:

- 'core R&D activities', or
- 'supporting R&D activities'.

The following definitions of core R&D activities and supporting R&D activities have been taken from the Tax Office's *Guide to the Research and development tax incentive*.

The AusIndustry website (http://www.ausindustry.gov.au) contains further information about core R&D activities and supporting R&D activities.

CORE R&D ACTIVITIES

Subsection 355-25(1) ITAA97 defines core R&D activities as being experimental activities:

- whose outcome cannot be known or determined in advance on the basis of current knowledge, information or experience, but can only be determined by applying a systematic progression of work that:
    - is based on principles of established science
    - proceeds from hypothesis to experiment, observation and evaluation, and leads to logical conclusions, and
- conducted for the purpose of generating new knowledge (including about creating new knowledge or improved materials, products, devices, processes or services).

EXCLUSIONS

The following activities are specifically excluded from the definition of core R&D activities by the operation of s355-25(2) ITAA97:

- market research, market testing or market development, or sales promotion (including consumer surveys)
- prospecting, exploring or drilling activities for the purposes of discovering and/or quantifying minerals or petroleum deposits

- management studies or efficiency surveys
- research in social sciences, arts or humanities
- commercial, legal and administrative aspects of patenting, licensing or other activities
- activities associated with complying with statutory requirements or standards
- certain activities related to the reproduction of a commercial product or process, and
- developing, modifying or customising computer software for the dominant purpose of use by the entity (the developer) and/or their affiliate for their internal administration (including the internal administration of their business functions).

NOTE: This definition ensures that software developed as an integral part of an electrical or mechanical device is capable of meeting the core R&D activity definition.

Supporting R&D activities

A supporting activity is one that is directly related to core R&D activities or, for certain activities, has been undertaken for the dominant purpose of supporting core R&D activities. Activities that must satisfy the dominant purpose requirement are those that produce – or are directly related to producing – goods or services; or are specifically excluded from being core R&D activities.

15.540   ELIGIBLE NOTIONAL DEDUCTIONS

An R&D entity will be entitled to an offset if its total notional deductions are at least $20,000 for the relevant year.

ELIGIBLE EXPENDITURE

Notional deductions may include:

- expenditure incurred on R&D activities, including expenditure on overseas activities covered by an advance finding from Innovation Australia, amounts paid to associates and expenditure to a Research Service Provider (RSP)
- the decline in value of assets used for conducting R&D activities (including R&D partnership assets)
- balancing adjustments for assets used only for conducting R&D activities (including R&D partnership assets)
- expenditure in relation to goods and materials transformed or processed during R&D activities to produce marketable products (feedstock expenditure), and
- monetary contributions under the Co-operative Research Centre (CRC) program.

An R&D entity is entitled to a R&D notional deduction in relation to eligible expenditure to the extent that:

- the expenditure is eligible for the R&D tax incentive, and
- the R&D entity incurs the expenditure during the income year on one or more registered R&D activities, except when:
  - an amount of expenditure is incurred but not paid to an associate, and
  - the prepayment rules apply in relation to expenditure for services to be provided over a period.

INELIGIBLE EXPENDITURE

Notional deductions cannot include the following:

- interest expenditure (within the meaning of interest in the withholding tax rules)
- expenditure that is not at risk
- core technology expenditure
- expenditure included in the cost of a depreciating asset (decline in value notional deductions may apply however), and
- expenditure incurred to acquire or construct a building (or part of a building or an extension, alteration or improvement to a building).

 If an amount of expenditure is eligible for the R&D tax incentive under Division 355, it cannot be claimed as a deduction under any other provision of the tax law even if the entity does not choose to claim the tax incentive.

TOTAL NOTIONAL DEDUCTIONS LESS THAN $20,000

Where total notional deductions are less than $20,000, the R&D entity will only be able to claim the R&D tax offset for the following:

- expenditure incurred to a RSP for services within a research field for which the RSP is registered under the *Industry Research and Development Act 1986* (IR&D Act), where that RSP is not an associate of the R&D entity, and
- expenditure incurred as a monetary contribution under the CRC program.

15.550 ADJUSTMENTS

CLAWBACK ADJUSTMENTS

Clawback applies where the R&D entity receives a government (Commonwealth or State/Territory) recoupment (such as a grant or reimbursement) that relates to expenditure that is eligible for the R&D tax incentive. The clawback adjustment increases the income tax liability on the recoupment. The clawback does not decrease the amount of the grant or offset.

This extra income tax liability equals 10% of the recoupment. Where the recoupment covers a project that is broader than the R&D expenditure, the additional income tax payable is capped by the proportion of the R&D expenditure to total project expenditure and reduced by any repayments of the recoupment. (s355-450(3)). This cap is reduced to the extent that any part of the recoupment is repaid.

FEEDSTOCK ADJUSTMENTS

A feedstock adjustment is included in assessable income. It applies when an R&D tax offset is received for feedstock expenditure incurred on R&D activities which produce either:

- marketable products, or
- products the R&D entity applies to its own use.

The feedstock adjustment applies to expenditure on the following:

- goods or materials (feedstock inputs) that are transformed or processed during R&D activities in producing one or more tangible products (feedstock outputs), and
- energy that is input directly into that transformation or processing.

A feedstock adjustment may arise in the current or a future income year, depending on when the output is sold or applied.

NOTE: Feedstock adjustment provisions are considered by the Commissioner in TR 2013/3.

15.560 RECORD KEEPING

Eligible R&D entities must keep records that sufficiently demonstrate to the Tax Office and Innovation Australia that it has conducted eligible R&D activities and incurred eligible expenditure that meet all legislative requirements.

BUSINESS RECORDS

Business records must show:

- the amount of the expenditure incurred on R&D activities
- the nature of the R&D activities
- the relationship of the expenditure to the activities, and
- the method of apportionment of the expenditure between core R&D activities and supporting R&D activities as opposed to non-R&D activities.

The taxpayer must use accurate methods to differentiate between expenditure on R&D activities and expenditure on non-R&D activities.

SPECIFIC R&D RECORDS

Specific R&D records must be kept for a minimum of five years. Records must detail:

- the R&D activities carried out
- who conducted the R&D activities, and
- the time that the R&D entity's staff spent on the R&D activities.

15.600 ENVIRONMENTAL EXPENDITURE

Claims cannot be made for expenditure to beautify or otherwise improve the appearance of a disused industrial site. However, deductions are allowed under s40-755 for capital expenditure incurred in preventing and cleaning up pollution of the environment resulting from the taxpayer's business activities.

IMMEDIATE DEDUCTION ALLOWED

According to s40-755(2), the expenditure must be incurred for the sole or dominant purposes of:
- preventing, combating or rectifying pollution of the environment by the taxpayer's business (or on the site of the business), or
- treating, cleaning up, removing or storing waste produced by the taxpayer's business (or on the site of the business).

The following expenditure cannot be deducted as environment protection activities (s40-760(1)):
- expenditure on acquiring land
- capital expenditure on buildings, structures or structural improvements (or extensions, alterations or improvement thereto)
- a bond or security for performing environmental protection activities
- expenditure in carrying out an environmental impact assessment of your project activity, and
- expenditure deductible under another provision of the Act outside Subdivision 40-H.

Expenditure incurred by the taxpayer for the removal of a redundant structure will be eligible only if the sole or dominant purpose is to control pollution or manage waste. Examples of environmental protection activities are the demolishing and removal of a shed constructed of asbestos (ATO ID 2004/720) and the cleaning up and removal of waste material (ATO ID 2006/276).

ELIGIBLE EXPENDITURE DEDUCTIBLE OVER 40 YEARS

Building, structural improvements (including earthworks) for environment protection purposes can be written off as per normal rules for structural improvements (ie. 40 years). See 15.200.

A taxpayer buys a swamp on which to build a steelworks. Before constructing the steelworks, the taxpayer spends money to reclaim the swamp and clean up the site. Costs include:
- *special equipment and any reclamation plant: Depreciable*
- *chemicals to neutralise the waste and remove heavy metals, power and other infrastructure costs, wages and consultancy fees: Allowable in full*
- *cost of actually reclaiming the swamp: Not allowed (capital costs on the site) and not predominantly to control pollution*

CLAWBACK OF CLAIMS

A clawback may occur for hire purchase arrangements or limited recourse debt where hire purchasers are treated as notional owners (see 15.800).

15.700 AUSTRALIAN FILM INVESTMENTS

Division 376 of ITAA97 contains the tax incentives available in relation to the Australian film industry. The incentives are only available to corporate entities.

TAX INCENTIVES IN RESPECT OF AUSTRALIAN FILMS AND TELEMOVIES

The main tax incentives comprise the following three tax offsets:
- **Producer Offset:** 40% of the company's **Qualifying Australian Production Expenditure** (QAPE) if the film is a feature film and 20% of such expenditure if the film is not a feature film – ie TV series, mini-series, telemovie, short-form animation, non-

feature documentary or direct-to-DVD or web-distributed programming (s376-55 to s376-75). Depending on the project, there are minimum expenditure thresholds required to access the Producer Offset. There is no entitlement to the producer offset where the film has been granted a final certificate for either the location offset or the PDV offset.

- **Location Offset:** 16.5% of the company's QAPE (s376-10 to s376-30). The Location offset is available to a production company that commenced principal photography on or after 10 May 2011. A minimum $15 million of QAPE on a film is required to access the Location Offset.

- **Post, Digital and Visual effects production (PDV) Offset:** From 1 July 2011, 30% of the company's QAPE on the film that relates to post, digital and visual effects production for the film (s376-35 to 376-50). A minimum threshold of $500,000 qualifying PDV expenditure applies.

NOTE: The Australian Government also introduced the Location Incentive for International Film and Television Productions (the Location Incentive) to attract large-budget international productions to Australia. To be eligible for the Location Incentive applicants will be required to have a minimum level of qualifying Australian production expenditure of AUD$30 million, rather than the AUD$15 million minimum for the Location Offset. Applicants may apply for funding under the Location Incentive up to a maximum of 13.5 per cent of the production's qualifying Australian production expenditure for productions commenced principal photography on or after 1 July 2013.

Section 376-145 ITAA97 defines 'qualifying Australian production expenditure' as:

... production expenditure on the film to the extent to which it is incurred for, or is reasonably attributable to:

(a) goods and services provided in Australia; or

(b) the use of land located in Australia; or

(c) the use of goods that are located in Australia at the time they are used in the making of the film.

Tax deductions for Australian films previously available under Division 10BA ITAA36 have been phased out, effective 30 June 2009. Deductions previously available under Division 10B ITAA36 were phased out as at 30 June 2010.

15.800 CAPITAL ALLOWANCE CLAWBACK

Taxpayers who acquire an asset that has been financed by a hire purchase arrangement or limited recourse debt that results in excessive capital allowance deductions because the full amount is not paid, have to make adjustments to reflect the actual cost of the depreciating asset. This process claws back the excess of capital allowance deductions claimed.

HIRE PURCHASE ARRANGEMENTS AND LIMITED RECOURSE DEBT ADJUSTMENTS

These rules affect expenditure that has been financed by hire purchase or limited recourse finance and the debtor does not fully pay out the capital amounts owing. The rules:

- include an amount in the assessable income of a taxpayer where amounts are unpaid on the termination of a hire purchase or limited recourse debt arrangement. The adjustment will apply where hire purchase or limited recourse debt has financed capital expenditure but, because amounts remain unpaid, deductions have been allowed that exceed the deductions that would be allowable if based on actual outlays

- treat taxpayers who acquire capital assets by hire purchase as the owners of those assets in determining eligibility for capital allowance deductions, and

- treat a hire purchase agreement as a loan transaction. If the asset is used for income-producing purposes, the hire purchaser can deduct the finance charge component of hire purchase payments, and the financier is taxed on that component of the payments, but not the payments themselves.

HIRE PURCHASE ARRANGEMENTS TREATED AS A SALE AND LOAN

All hire purchase arrangements for goods are treated as limited recourse debt arrangements and a taxpayer cannot claim capital allowances in excess of the cost of an asset. Additionally, hire purchase arrangements are deemed to be a sale of property and concurrent loan agreement (Division 240). The notional seller (the financier) is treated as having sold the property to the notional buyer (the person receiving the finance) to pay for the goods. A notional loan (the consideration for the sale of the property) is treated as having been made by the notional seller to the notional buyer.

The notional seller's income includes the notional interest on the notional loan and the notional buyer is generally entitled to a deduction for notional interest. If the property is not the notional seller's trading stock, the seller's profit on the transaction is included.

INCOME RECONCILIATION RULES FOR A NOTIONAL SELLER

If the sum of the amounts included in the notional seller's assessable income differs from the finance charge determined at the end of the arrangement for the notional loan, an adjustment to the seller's assessable income will be made. This adjustment takes into account all the finance charges over the life of the loan.

If the sum of the amount paid to the notional seller and any amounts payable because an arrangement ends is:

- **More than notional loan principal** (the consideration for the sale of the property) plus assessed notional interest (the notional income that has been included in the notional seller's assessable income): *The difference will be included in the notional seller's assessable income.*
- **Less than notional loan principal** plus assessed notional interest: *The notional seller can claim a deduction for the difference.*

LIMITED RECOURSE DEBT

Division 243 applies if the net capital allowances have been excessive, having regard to the amount of unpaid debt. Investment allowances and drought investment allowances are not included in the operation of Division 243.

Where deductions for capital allowances exceed the actual cost of the asset to the taxpayer, the taxpayer is required to treat the difference between the deductions and the debt repaid as assessable income in the year the loan is terminated. The criteria for this to apply are:

- a limited recourse debt has been used to finance expenditure
- the debt has not been fully discharged by the debtor at the termination of the debt arrangement, and
- the debtor has claimed deductions for capital allowances.

A taxpayer must:

- determine the sum of net capital allowances obtained, and
- compare the sum to the entitlement of capital deductions if the amount of unpaid debt had been taken into account.

The capital allowances received by a taxpayer will be treated as having been excessive if the amount calculated would have resulted in additional tax benefits because the loan had not been fully discharged.

FOUR TYPES OF LIMITED RECOURSE DEBT

- Limitations imposed on a creditor in the case of default (eg. where the lender's rights are limited to the property acquired with the debt, even though the value of the property may be significantly less than the outstanding principal and interest that result in the lender not having the right to seek recovery of any outstanding amounts).
- A loan is treated as a limited recourse loan even if there is no express limitation in the loan but it would be expected that the creditor's rights would be limited to the property rights (eg. because debtor does not have sufficient other assets).
- A loan has no security provided for the debt & it is reasonable to conclude that the rights of the creditor are limited.

- A notional loan under a hire purchase agreement.

In *Commissioner of Taxation v BHP Billiton Limited & Ors* [2011] HCA 17, the High Court considered the issue of what is encompassed by the statement in s243-20(2) that the rights of a creditor as against a debtor, in the event of default, 'are capable of being limited in the way mentioned in subsection (1)' having regard to certain specified matters. The Court concluded that the correct interpretation of the subsection is that it 'is not directed to possibilities for a limitation of a creditor's rights of recourse which may arise in the future'.

TERMINATION OF A DEBT ARRANGEMENT

A debt is treated as being terminated if:

- it is actually terminated
- it is waived
- an agreement is made to waive or change it
- the creditor ceases to have an entitlement to recover it
- the property acquired with it is given to the creditor and part of the loan remains outstanding, or
- it becomes a bad debt.

Capital allowances in the form of depreciation can be claimed on a machine costing $10,000, whether or not it was acquired under a finance agreement, the purchaser bases the claim on a starting value of $10,000. If the machine is repossessed for non-payment when it has been depreciated for tax purposes by $6,000, but the taxpayer has paid only $3,500 of the hire purchase cost, the taxpayer would have obtained a tax benefit of $2,500 more than the cost incurred. The $6,500 unpaid cost under the hire purchase arrangement would be treated as consideration on disposal, leaving a balancing adjustment of $2,500 ($6,500 less $4,000 adjusted value). The taxpayer's net tax deductions then would be $3,500 (ie. equal to net outlays).

LUXURY CARS

Clawback of capital allowances arise where an asset is held under a hire purchase arrangement (see below). In this arrangement the owner of the goods will be treated as a 'notional seller' and the user of the goods as a 'notional buyer'.

NOTE: A hire purchase agreement includes instalment sales. It includes a contract for the hire of goods where the hirer has an obligation to buy the goods and the charge for the hire plus any other amounts payable under the contract exceeds the price of the goods. For the purposes of the division, a 'hire purchase' contract will only exist if the notional buyer is likely to buy the property. The effect of this Division is to claw back depreciation which has been allowed as a deduction where the 'notional buyer' has disposed of the property and a deduction greater than the actual expenditure in acquiring the property has been obtained.

Where the car is subject to the luxury car limit (see 15.085) at the start of the 'hire purchase' arrangement, and it is later acquired by an associate of the notional buyer, either as a notional buyer or by actual ownership, the associate calculates depreciation on the lesser of:

- the adjusted value applicable to the associate notional buyer as if they were the notional buyer of the car, adjusted for any balancing charge applicable because the car is deemed to have been disposed of by the associate notional buyer, and
- the acquisition cost of the car to the associate.

The personal services income rules

16

16.000 THE PERSONAL SERVICES INCOME RULES

The personal services income regime taxes individual contractors on a similar basis as employees where income is derived mainly from the individual's own skills, expertise or the provision of personal services. The measures also apply to companies, trusts and partnerships where income is derived by the entity primarily as a result of an individual's personal efforts or skills. These provisions are contained in Divisions 84 to 87 ITAA97.

The Personal Services Income (PSI) rules restrict:

- the availability of tax deductions to affected individuals over and above deductions ordinarily available to employees providing the same or similar services, and
- the alienation of PSI through an interposed entity to utilise lower tax rates through entities or related parties, by treating the relevant income as income earned by the individual from the provision of their personal services. The individual is taxed on the attributed income at his or her marginal rates.

The provisions apply where the individual or interposed entity is deemed to be earning PSI. However, where the relevant individual or entity can meet one of a number of carve-out tests, the rules have no application.

Those caught by the PSI rules are specifically excluded from being treated as employees for any other purposes under Australian law (s84-10). However, PAYG withholding obligations are imposed on any interposed entity which is subject to the rules (see 16.500).

The flowchart following sets out in simple terms how the PSI rules operate.

Generally, the PSI rules will not affect those individuals or interposed entities that qualify as a personal services business (PSB) – see 16.200. PSBs comprise the following:

- individuals (or interposed entities) that contract on a results basis (see 16.205)
- individuals (or interposed entities) that derive less than 80% of their PSI from a single source and satisfies one of the following tests:
    - the unrelated clients test (see 16.215)
    - the employment test (see 16.225), or
    - the business premises test (see 16.230), or
- individuals or interposed entities that obtain a personal services business determination (PSB determination) from the Tax Office (see 16.240).

NOTE: Where income is earned by an entity and one or more of the personal service business tests is passed, Part IVA ITAA36 may still be applied to the use of the entity to derive the income.

16.100 PERSONAL SERVICES INCOME

Ordinary or statutory income will be treated as PSI if it is mainly a reward for a person's personal efforts or skills. Where the income is derived by an entity other than a person, the test requires an examination of whether the income would mainly be a reward for that person's personal efforts or skills had it been derived directly by the individual.

Subsection 84-5(1) states:

Your ordinary income or statutory income, or the ordinary income or statutory income of any other entity, is your personal services income if the income is mainly a reward for your personal efforts or skills (or would mainly be such a reward if it was your income).

In TR 2001/7 the Tax Office provides its interpretation of 'mainly':

Implicit in the use of the word 'mainly' is that more than half of the relevant amount of the ordinary or statutory income is a reward for the personal efforts or skills of an individual.

Whether an amount of income is mainly a reward for an individual's personal efforts or skills is a question of fact.

Income derived from the use of an asset cannot be PSI. However, according to TR 2001/7, income derived from the provision of personal services involving the use of some equipment may nevertheless be PSI. Where the substance of an agreement is the provision by an individual of his or her personal efforts or the exercise of his or her skills, or the production of a result from those efforts or skills, income would be regarded as PSI.

Income that is derived mainly for the sale and supply of goods or for granting a right to use property is not PSI.

Income derived as a result of a business structure is also not PSI. TR 2001/7 states that when determining whether income is mainly a reward for the personal efforts or skills of an individual or from a business structure, consideration should be given to the relative values of the efforts or skills of the individual and other inputs, such as the efforts of other workers, and the use of plant and equipment, intellectual or other property and goodwill. Factors relevant to making this determination include:

- the nature of the activities being conducted that generate the income
- the extent to which the amounts paid under an agreement (whether directly to an individual or to an interposed entity) is primarily for the personal efforts or skills of a particular individual
- the extent to which the contract price has been calculated having regard to the costs to be borne by an individual or entity in providing assets to use in the performance of contractual obligations
- the market price of using any equipment, plant or tools as compared with the market price of hiring the relevant labour or skills for the same period
- the nature, size and significance of the assets used by the individual or entity in relation to the activity
- the value of the asset in relation to the total income generated under the agreement
- the uniqueness and degree to which an asset is specialised in the performance of a particular function
- the uniqueness, level of skill or degree of specialisation of an individual to provide the particular services contracted
- whether the payments made to an individual or a entity is for the transfer of the ownership or a right in respect of items produced by the individual or entity
- the existence of goodwill
- the existence of substantial income-producing assets
- the size of the business operation, and
- the contribution of other workers to the income-earning activities.

NOTE: The Full Federal Court held in *Russell v FCT* (2011) 79 ATR 315 that the PSI rules applied to the personal services income of an Australian resident derived from a New Zealand company (a non-resident). The Court also held that no double taxation arose under the Australia-NZ double tax agreement as the PSI was effectively excluded from the New Zealand company's taxable income because it was a deduction from assessable income.

 A taxpayer owns one semi trailer and he is the only person who drives it. The income derived from driving the truck is not PSI because it is mainly produced by the use of the truck and not mainly as a reward for the personal services of the taxpayer.

 A taxpayer provides a computer programming service but she does all of the work involved in providing those services and uses the client's equipment and software to do the work. The income derived would be treated as PSI as it is a reward for her personal efforts or skills.

 A taxpayer works as an accountant with a large accounting firm. None of the firm's ordinary or statutory income is PSI because it is produced mainly by the firm's structure and not mainly for his personal efforts or skills.

ALIENATION OF PERSONAL SERVICES INCOME

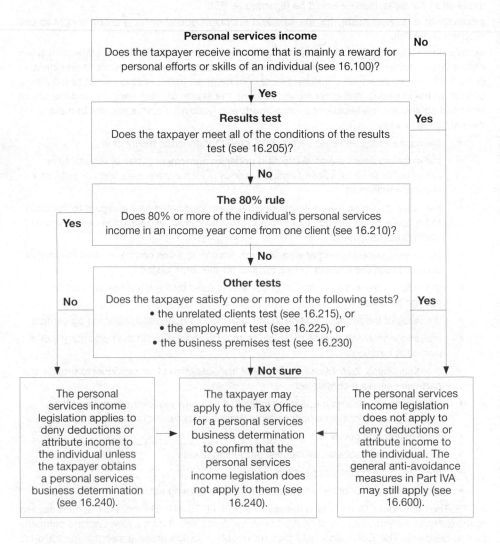

16.105   PERSONAL SERVICES ENTITY

A company, partnership or trust that derives PSI is a Personal Services Entity (PSE). Generally, a PSE would exist where the entity derives income from the end client or customer and the work is performed by an individual who, in turn, has a contract with the entity in relation to the performance of that work.

16.110   DEFINITION OF ASSOCIATES

The various tests contained in the PSI rules often include the 'associates' of the test's object. Associates are defined in s318 ITAA36 and comprise the following:

- associates of an individual:
  - a relative
  - a spouse
  - a partner of the individual in a partnership
  - a partnership of which the individual is a partner

- the spouse or child of a partner that is an individual other than in the capacity of a trustee
- a trustee of a trust under which the individual or another associate of the individual benefits
- a company which is sufficiently influenced by one or more of:
- the individual, another associate of the individual or another company that is an associate of the individual, and
- a company in which a majority voting interest is held by one or more of:
  - ○ the individual, and
  - ○ other associates of the individual
- associates of a company:
  - a partner of the company in a partnership
  - a partnership of which the company is a partner
  - the spouse or child of a partner that is an individual other than in the capacity of a trustee
  - a trustee of a trust under which the company or another associate of the company benefits
  - an entity which controls the company, either alone or jointly with another entity or other entities (the other entities would also be associates)
  - an entity which holds a majority voting interest in the company and associates of that entity
  - a company that is sufficiently influenced by one or more of:
    - ○ the company, or
    - ○ another associate of the company, and
  - a company in which the majority voting interest is held by one or more of:
    - ○ the company, or
    - ○ another associate of the company
- associates of a trustee of a trust:
  - a beneficiary of the trust
  - any associate of a beneficiary that is an individual, and
  - any associate of a beneficiary that is a company, and
- associates of a partnership:
  - a partner in the partnership
  - any associate of a partner that is an individual, and
  - any associate of a partner that is a company

AUSTRALIAN GOVERNMENT AGENCIES

The PSI legislation specifically provides that an Australian government agency is treated as a separate entity from any other government agency. Government agencies generally have no legal identity separate from the government. Furthermore, each agency is not treated as an associate of any other agency.

These provisions apply to Commonwealth, State and Territorial government agencies and only apply in relation to the 80% test (see 16.210) and the unrelated clients test (see 16.215).

16.200 PERSONAL SERVICES BUSINESS

Once it has been determined that an individual or a PSE has derived PSI, Divisions 85 and 86 may apply to deny deductions and/or attribute assessable income to the individual to be taxed at marginal rates unless the individual or the PSE is deemed to be carrying on a personal services business (PSB).

A taxpayer (whether an individual or a PSE) will be a PSB if one of four alternative tests is satisfied or if there is a PSB determination in place. The alternative tests are subject to self-assessment but a PSB determination may only be made by the Commissioner.

The four tests are:
- the results test
- the unrelated clients test
- the employment test, or
- the business premises test.

NOTE: While the four tests are alternative tests in that only one has to be satisfied for the taxpayer to qualify as a PSB, they are to be applied sequentially in the order in which they are listed. Furthermore, where the results test is failed, the subsequent three tests are available only if the taxpayer passes the 80% test (see 16.210).

 Where the results test and the 80% test are failed, the individual or PSE will not be treated as a PSB unless a PSB determination is obtained.

16.205 RESULTS TEST

The results test is satisfied if at least 75% of the PSI derived for the year meets the following criteria.

1. THE CONTRACTOR IS PAID FOR PRODUCING A RESULT.

In TR 2001/8, the Commissioner states that the phrase 'producing a result' means the performance of a service by one party for another where the first-mentioned party is free to employ his/her own means to achieve the contractually specified outcome. Payment is often made for a negotiated contract price as opposed to a fee for time (such as an hourly rate). Where payment is only made when contractual conditions have been fulfilled, generally that payment is considered to be for producing a given result. For example, a contract to build an earth dam for a set price would be a contract for a result. In contrast, the payment on an hourly basis to dig the hole is probably a contract for personal services and would not satisfy this criterion.

Satisfying the common law criteria for determining whether a person is an independent contractor does not by default mean that the statutory test has been met (*Confidential and Commissioner of Taxation* (2011) AATA 682).

NOTE: *Re Taneja and Commissioner of Taxation* [2009] AATA 87 and *Park and Commissioner of Taxation* [2011] AATA 567 espoused the principle that in determining whether the contractor is paid for producing a result, the relevant factor is not how the fee is calculated, but rather, what the contractor is paid for (ie. his responsibilities to the clients and what he has to do to satisfy the obligations he has under the agreement and to justify payment). These decisions confirmed that industry custom and practice where it is common for income to be for producing a result may be used to support an argument that a taxpayer was paid for producing a result; but conversely, industry custom and practice where it is uncommon to be paid for producing a result cannot come to a person's aid where there is a written agreement specifying that the person is entitled to payment for doing something that does not amount to producing a result.

2. THE CONTRACTOR IS REQUIRED TO PROVIDE THE TOOLS, PLANT AND EQUIPMENT NECESSARY (IF ANY) TO PRODUCE THE RESULT.

Where plant and equipment not needed by the individual or PSE to perform the agreed upon work is provided (eg. where scaffolding is provided at a building site for a carpenter to access the particular work area), this will not cause the contractor to fail this condition. Further, the condition will be met where no tools or equipment is supplied by the contractor simply because none are required to do the work. In TR 2001/8, the Tax Office also provides that a substantive approach should be taken in assessing whether this requirement is satisfied. A 'de minimis' usage of others' equipment (eg. borrowing a phone or stationery) or a temporary use of tools of trade (eg. where the contractor's own tools are not accessible at that time) would not, on their own, cause the test to be failed.

3. THE CONTRACTOR IS (OR WOULD BE) LIABLE FOR THE COST OF RECTIFYING ANY DEFECTIVE WORK.

This looks at whether the individual or entity is exposed to commercial risk for the cost of rectifying defective work. There is no requirement that the individual or entity actually performs the work to rectify defects provided they are exposed to the costs of doing so. This could include a rectification achieved by the acquirer of the services pursuing a legal remedy for damages where the defect is incapable of repair.

While a contractual clause to the effect that the contractor is liable for the cost of rectifying defective work would prima facie support a conclusion that the requisite commercial risk is borne by the contractor, the Tax Office in TR 2001/8 warns against including such a clause where it is merely 'window dressing' and that all relevant circumstances should be taken into account in forming a conclusion in relation to whether the commercial risk and potential liability does exist.

NOTE: In determining whether the contractor satisfies the results test, the custom and practice in the particular industry will be taken into account. For example, if the custom is for the contractor to rectify their work, that will be sufficient for the contract to be treated as a contract for a result. If there is any doubt, it would be wise to set out in writing the terms and conditions.

It is not essential that the terms and conditions of the 'work' to be performed are specifically included in a written contract. The Tax Office and the legislation requires an examination of all relevant facts and circumstances. This also means that 'legal form' compliance with the requirements by inserting relevant contractual clauses is insufficient.

The Federal Court decided in the case of **IRG Technical Services Pty Ltd v Deputy Commissioner of Taxation** *[2007] FCA 1867 that activities carried out by a taxpayer as part of a team did not satisfy the requirement that the taxpayer must be engaged to produce a result. If there was an engagement to produce a result, that result would be achieved by the team rather than the taxpayer. See also* **Confidential and Commissioner of Taxation** *(2011) AATA 682 in which the Tribunal arrived at a similar conclusion.*

An individual and a PSE are subject to different results tests. The three elements relating to results, tools and commercial risk are the same for both. Where the taxpayer being tested is a PSE which has derived PSI in relation to one or more individuals, the 75% threshold test appears to be applied on an aggregate basis (where there is more than one individual) and not on an individual-by-individual basis (subs87-18(3)). Where the taxpayer being tested is an individual, the 75% requirement does not apply to any income received by the individual in their capacity as an employee or an office holder (eg. a director of a company) nor income derived by religious practitioners in relation to religious activities (subs87-18(2)).

In TR 2008/1, the Commissioner considers when a taxpayer is, or would be, liable for the cost of rectifying any defect in the work performed:

An independent contractor in a genuine business undertaking assumes the entrepreneurial risks associated with the relevant activities. This will include liability for the cost of rectifying defective work, where rectification in the narrow sense is possible, and/or would be liable to an action for damages for negligent performance of the contact.

Where physical rectification is not possible, the purpose of the provision would be satisfied where a right to claim for damages exists in respect of faulty or negligent performance of contractual obligations and the individual or PSE is or would be liable for the relevant component of damages awarded for the faulty or defective work.

The results test was failed in *Re Scimitar Systems Pty Ltd v DCT* (2004) 56 ATR 1162, where a company controlled by an IT consultant hired out the consultant's services to essentially only one client. The AAT held that the relevant contract was for the efforts and skill of the particular consultant and not for producing a result. The other legislative requirements (supplying equipment and being liable for the cost of rectifying defects) were also absent.

Similarly, in *Nguyen v FCT* (2005) 60 ATR 1178 where the services of an IT consultant were hired out by his family company. the AAT held that the contracts were for work and not for producing a result as the fees were payable at a specified hourly rate, the work performed was at the direction of the client, there was little discretion in the way the work was carried out and there was no scope for substitution or delegation.

NOTE: The Tax Office will generally consider an industry's customs and practices when applying the above criteria.

16.210   THE 80% TEST

If the individual or PSE cannot satisfy the results test, they may be able to rely on one of the three other tests (the unrelated clients test, the business premises test or the employment test) if the 80% test (s87-15(3)) is satisfied.

The 80% test is passed if 80% or more of the PSI does not come from one source, including that source's associates.

Where the 80% threshold is breached, the individual or entity cannot employ any of the other self-assessed tests and would have to apply to the Tax Office for a PSB determination in order to achieve PSB status (see 16.240).

Note that the following categories of income under s87-15(4) are not taken into account in determining whether the 80% threshold is exceeded (nor for the purposes of the results test):

- income the individual receives as an employee (ie salary and wages);
- income the individual receives as an office holder (ie payments to an office holder that are subject to the PAYG withholding arrangements), and
- income received by a religious practitioner that is subject to the PAYG withholding arrangements.

NOTE: Special rules apply to agents (see 16.220).

According to TR 2001/8, the source of the PSI is determined by reference to the contract under which the services are rendered. The source is not necessarily the entity that physically pays the income. For example, a doctor has contractual relations with each of his patients, even though he/she may actually be paid by a single medical fund.

16.215   THE UNRELATED CLIENTS TEST

To satisfy the unrelated clients test (s87-20), the individual or PSE must derive income from providing services to two or more entities that are not associates of each other and are also not associates of the individual or the PSE (as appropriate). The test also requires that the services are provided as a direct result of the individual or PSE making offers or invitations (eg. advertising) to the public at large or to a section of the public. The Commissioner's view is that making an offer to the public would include advertising, tendering for work, maintaining a web site or word of mouth referrals. Services offered through labour hire companies and other such businesses that arrange to provide services directly for clients do not qualify as services which would satisfy this test.

In *Yalos Engineering Pty Ltd v FC of T* (2010) ATC 10-139, the Tribunal found that where the particular expertise is relevant only to a very small number of businesses, advertising in a general sense in newspapers, brochures or other such medium would be inappropriate and the small number of businesses would constitute the requisite *section of the public*. Further, regular personal contact with those companies to assess their needs and the opportunity to provide specialised services via word of mouth and personal recommendations constitute *making offers or invitations to provide services*. The Commissioner has issued a Decision Impact Statement in relation to the *Yalos Engineering* case.

The Federal Court in *Cameron v Commissioner of Taxation* (2012) FCA 1378 noted that an invitation or offer to a section of the public may or may not constitute an invitation or offer to the public at large. In this case, the Court observed that the manner of the communication cannot be the sole focus and regard must be had to the nature or character of the taxpayer's invitations or offers in determining whether the services were provided as a direct result of offers or invitations to a section of the public.

16.220   SPECIAL RULES FOR AGENTS

Special rules apply in relation to agents who bear entrepreneurial risk in the provision of the particular services. The rules, contained in s87-40, operate on a 'look through' basis to treat income that the agent receives from the principal in respect of services that the agent provided to the principal's clients as though the income is earned directly from the clients. The rules do not apply to employees of the principal. The principal beneficiaries of this special rule include financial planners and insurance agents who derive their income from fees and commissions.

The special rules assist agents in passing the unrelated clients test (see 16.215) and the 80% test (see 16.210).

To be subject to the special rules the agent must satisfy the following criteria:

- the agent receives income (eg. fees for service or commissions) from the principal for services the agent has provided to the principal's clients on the principal's behalf

- at least 75% of that income is commissions or fees based on the agent's performance in providing those services, and

- the agent actively seeks new clients to whom the agent can provide services on behalf of the principal, and

- the agent does not provide the services to clients from premises that are either:
  - owned by the principal or an associate of the principal, or
  - in which the principal or an associate has a leasehold interest

unless the premises are used under an arrangement made at arm's length on commercial terms.

An agent is permitted to have a fixed remuneration (such as a retainer or salary-like payment) of up to 25%. Any fixed remuneration in excess of this figure would cause the agent to breach the requirement that at least 75% of the agent's income from the principal must be based on the agent's performance in providing services to clients on the principal's behalf. In other words, the agent's income must be at risk. The agent must also actively seek new clients to whom they can provide services on behalf of the principal. It will be incumbent on the agent to demonstrate that they are making an active effort (eg. by advertising) to obtain clients. The active test is not satisfied by receiving referrals from the principal or allowing the principal to take the responsibility for obtaining clients. In determining whether an agent satisfies the 80% test (see 16.210), the income received from the principal for providing services to the client will be treated as income derived from the client if the above conditions are satisfied. The clients are in effect treated as clients of the agent. As a consequence, each client is treated as a separate 'source' of PSI for the agent instead of the principal being treated as one single source in relation to the same income. So long as there is more than one end client and none of the clients are associates of each other or of any of the agent's other PSI sources, these provisions may assist the agent in satisfying the 80% test.

In determining whether an agent satisfies the unrelated clients test (see 16.215), the legislation provides that any PSI-producing services that the agent provided to clients on the principal's behalf is deemed to have been provided directly by the agent to the clients and not by the principal to the clients. As a consequence, where the agent has at least two unrelated clients (which may all be clients of the principal which are deemed to be clients of the agent under these rules) and can demonstrate that the services provided to their clients directly resulted from making offers or invitations to the public at large or to a section of the public, the conditions of the test will be satisfied and the agent will be treated as a PSB.

The following example is modified from the Explanatory Memorandum.

Gordon is a financial planner who holds a proper authority under the Corporations Law to act as agent for Champagne Financial Services (Champagne), a licensed securities dealer. Gordon receives 85% of his income from Champagne as commissions, dependent on the level of services Gordon provides to clients of Champagne. Gordon advertises his services once a month in financial papers and in professional associations. Champagne operates from five floors of an office block which they lease, and one of those floors is dedicated for Champagne proper authority holders. Gordon uses an office and has access to other facilities under an arm's length commercial agreement.

Gordon satisfies the requirements in s87-40(1) and is consequently entitled to use the special test for agents. He would also be treated as having derived less than 80% of his PSI from one source. Gordon satisfies the unrelated clients test as he advertises to the public and does not receive referrals from Champagne. Gordon would be entitled to self-assess as a PSB.

16.225   THE EMPLOYMENT TEST

The employment test (s87-25) will be satisfied if the individual or the PSE engages one or more entities during the income year, and that entity performs or those entities together perform at least 20% of the market value of the principal work for the year.

Some entities which are engaged by the individual or the PSE are not included in this test. These entities are:

- if the taxpayer being tested is an individual - associates of the individual that are themselves not individuals, and
- if the taxpayer being tested is a PSE - associates of the individual that are themselves not individuals and any individuals whose PSI is included in the PSE's assessable income (disregarding any application of the PSI rules).

Where the PSE is a partnership, work performed by a partner is deemed to be work which the PSE has engaged another entity to perform.

The employment test does not require the hiring of labour on an employee basis. Hiring staff on a contractor basis to perform the work will suffice.

The employment test can be passed where relatives are engaged to perform principal work. However, where an associated entity (for example, the spouse's company) is engaged to perform principal work, that work is not counted toward the 20% threshold test.

 There are deduction restrictions that apply to payments to associates (see 16.305). Only amounts that specifically relate to principal work that associates have undertaken are deductible to an entity that is not a PSB. Principal work is the work essential to generating PSI (eg. a bricklayer's principal work would be bricklaying services). Principal work does not include the individual or PSE's own administrative work.

As an alternative to the 20% market value of principal work test, the employment test may also be satisfied if the individual or the PSE has one or more apprentices for at least 50% of the income year.

16.230   THE BUSINESS PREMISES TEST

The business premises test (s87-30) will be satisfied by either an individual or a PSE if at all times during the income year they maintain and use business premises:

- at which the individual or the PSE mainly conducts activities from which PSI is gained or produced
- which are used exclusively by the individual or PSE
- which are physically separate from any other premises that is used for private purposes by the individual or PSE or any of their associates, and
- which are physically separate from the premises of any of their clients (or associates of those clients) to which they provide services.

IMPORTANT: The test must be satisfied over the entire income year. The test is failed if any of the criteria is not satisfied during any part of the year. However, the test does not require the same business premises to be maintained and used throughout the year – the individual or PSE may change premises during the year.

In *C of T v Dixon Consulting Pty Ltd* [2006] FCA 1748, the Federal Court emphasised that it is important to consider whether the premises are subject to private use, unless the private use is 'minimal'. For example, private parking on the premises may indicate private use. Use for family purposes, such as private storage, may also be relevant. Physical separation from private premises is also necessary (eg. street address, a shared entrance etc. although these factors may not always be decisive).

In *Cameron and Commissioner of Taxation* [2012] FCA 1378, the Federal Court held that the business premises test requires consideration and comparison of both of the following aspects:

- the physical aspect – the area of the premises used for providing each type of service, and
- the temporal aspect – the time that the taxpayer had used the premises for providing each type of service.

The Commissioner provides further guidelines in TR 2001/8 in relation to the business premises test, which includes:

- the individual or personal services entity is required to have business premises on each day during the income year in which activities producing the individual's PSI are conducted

- the exclusive use requirement does not disqualify the shared use of common areas if they are the subject of separate arrangements;

- an individual or entity does not have exclusive use of premises if they are occupied under licence or mere possession, and

- if the business premises are within a larger building, in certain circumstances they may be regarded as physically separate from the rest of the building (the ruling lists various factors to be taken into account).

The Commissioner states in TR 2001/8 that a car of a travelling salesperson does not qualify as business premises.

16.240   PERSONAL SERVICES BUSINESS DETERMINATIONS

The Commissioner is empowered to issue a written personal services business determination (PSB determination) in certain circumstances. The Commissioner also has the power to vary a PSB determination that has already been made.

The effect of a PSB determination is that the relevant individual or PSE will be regarded as conducting a PSB during the period the determination is in force. Where an individual or an entity seeks to avoid application of the PSI rules by achieving PSB status, a PSB determination will be required in the following circumstances:

- where the results test and the 80% test have both been failed

- the results test, employment test or business premises test was failed for the year due to unusual circumstances in that year

- the unrelated clients test was met but the 80% test was failed due to unusual circumstances in that year

- the unrelated clients test was failed for the year due to unusual circumstances in that year; if the 80% test was also failed, it was also due to unusual circumstances in that year, or

- the individual or PSE is uncertain whether any of the relevant tests can be passed or is seeking confirmation that one of the PSB tests is passed if the results test, employment test or business premises test can reasonably be expected to be met.

An application for a PSB determination must be made on the approved form (NAT 72465) and the Tax Office has 60 days to respond to the application. If a decision is not made within that time, the applicant can request the Tax Office to treat the application as having been refused. Any application for a PSB determination that is refused by the Tax Office is a reviewable decision and the applicant has the right to object against that decision.

This process also applies in relation to a request for a variation of a PSB determination.

The Tax Office has the right to request further specified information to decide the application.

An application for a PSB determination can be made prior to, during or after the relevant income year. The PSB determination (or variation of it) has effect from the day specified in the notice (or if no date is specified, the date of the notice). It ceases to have effect at the earliest of when:

- any condition of the notice is not met

- the Tax Office revokes the PSB determination, or

- the period for which the PSB determination has effect has come to an end.

The Tax Office must revoke the determination by written notice if the Commissioner is no longer satisfied that there are grounds on which the determination could be made.

WHEN CAN THE COMMISSIONER ISSUE A PSB DETERMINATION?

Before issuing a PSB determination, the Commissioner must be satisfied that:

- the individual or entity does meet, or could reasonably be expected to meet, the results test, the employment test, or the business premises test

- the individual or entity could reasonably have been expected to meet or would have met the results test, the employment test or the business premises test but for unusual circumstances applying in that year

- the individual or entity does meet the unrelated clients test but unusual circumstances prevent the 80% rule from being met, or
- the individual or entity could reasonably have been expected to meet or would have met the unrelated clients test but for unusual circumstances applying in that year; and if the 80% test is also failed, that is also due to unusual circumstances applying in that year.

Note that where both the results test and the 80% test are failed, and the 80% test is failed due to unusual circumstances, the Commissioner may make a PSB determination only in relation to the unrelated clients test. If the unrelated client test is not deemed to have been failed due to the requisite unusual circumstances, there is no recourse to rely upon a PSB determination in respect of the employment test or the business premises test where the 80% test has not been met.

UNUSUAL CIRCUMSTANCES

The Commissioner states in TR 2001/8 that the term 'unusual circumstances' refers to circumstances that are exceptional and temporary, with the likelihood that usual circumstances will resume in the short term. Unusual circumstances may include:

- securing a one-off large contract for a temporary period only, and
- loss of business premises part way through a year due to circumstances outside of the taxpayer's control, or loss of an employee and inability to find a replacement despite best efforts.

In *Creaton Pty Ltd v FCT* (2002) 51 ATR 1047, the AAT specifically rejected the Commissioner's contention that unusual circumstances cannot last for more than one income year.

Moreover, the prevailing economic conditions, either in the industry in question or the place where the taxpayer is located, were held not to amount to unusual circumstances in *Scimitar Systems Pty Ltd v DCT* (2004) 56 ATR 1162. Whereas, in *The Engineering Company v FCT* (2008) 74 ATR 272, a long-term client indicating that it had no plans to engage the taxpayer's services for the foreseeable future and the resignation of a key employee who took another client with him were considered to be unusual circumstances.

16.300 EFFECT OF THE PSI RULES

Where an individual or PSE which has derived PSI cannot meet any of the self-assessment PSB tests and does not have a PSB determination in force, the PSI rules affect the income tax treatment of the PSI.

If the PSI is derived by a company, trust or partnership, that PSI is treated as having been derived by the individual whose personal efforts gave rise to the PSI (s86-15). The income is then taxed in the hands of the relevant individual at marginal rates (see 16.400). This attribution of the entity's income to the individual only applies to amounts which would be assessable to the PSE but for the PSI rules. Amounts which have been paid by the PSE to the individual as salary or wages within statutory timeframes are not attributed (see 16.400) as such amounts are already treated as employment income derived by the individual.

NOTE: In ATO ID 2010/214, the Commissioner concludes that where an Australian resident PSE derives foreign sourced income that is the PSI of a non-resident individual, the income is NOT included in the individual's assessable included under subs6-10(5) ITAA97 on the basis that:

(a) the PSI is not Australian sourced, and

(b) the Commissioner does not consider subs86-15(1) to be a provision that includes amounts in assessable income on a basis other than having an Australian source. The ID concludes that if the contrary view was accepted, foreign sourced income of a foreign resident would be assessable income in Australia and this would not be an appropriate alternative to the ordinary source rule.

The foreign employment income exemption in s23AG ITAA36 (refer 22.010) cannot apply to income attributed to a person under the PSI rules (*Clark v FC of T* (2010) AATA 392 and *Lopez v Deputy Commissioner of Taxation* (2004) FCA 756).

The individual will not be treated as an employee for any purpose outside the PSI rules. Further, the PSI rules do not have any GST effect, and do not affect any legal, contractual or workplace arrangements.

16.305   THE DEDUCTION RULES

Where an individual earns the PSI directly, or is treated as having earned PSI, Division 85 limits the type and amount of income tax deductions to which they will be entitled. Broadly, the deductions available to persons earning PSI will be limited to those that would have been allowable if that person was an employee.

A person who works as an independent architect for one firm and who fails the PSB tests would not be conducting a PSB and as such would not be entitled to claim a deduction for the cost of travelling from home to the client's business premises. The cost of a home office would be allowed, but the claim would be limited to running costs such as heat, light and power plus consumables and depreciation on plant and equipment.

No claim would be allowed for interest or any other occupancy expenses. The extent of the claims for expenses incurred in gaining the PSI would be limited to those claims allowed to an employee undertaking similar work.

The deduction rules contained in Division 85 affects individuals deriving PSI directly and individuals who have been attributed PSI amounts from a PSE.

SUMMARY OF PSI DEDUCTION RULES

The table following is reproduced from the Tax Office fact sheet *Alienation of personal services income – deductions*. It provides a summary of the deductibility or non-deductibility of particular items of expenditure in relation to those whose tax outcomes are affected by the PSI rules (PSI rules apply) and to those whose tax outcomes are not affected by the PSI rules, such as PSBs and those outside the PSI regime (PSI rules do not apply).

Deduction	PSI rules apply	PSI rules do not apply
Premiums for workers compensation, public liability and professional indemnity insurance	Yes	Yes
Bank and other account-keeping fees and charges	Yes	Yes
Tax-related expenses, eg. the cost of preparing and lodging tax returns or activity statements	Yes	Yes
Registration or licensing fees	Yes	Yes
Expenses for advertising, tendering and quoting for work	Yes	Yes
Depreciation	Yes	Yes
Running expenses for your home office (not including rent, mortgage interest, rates or land taxes, see next page)	Yes	Yes
Rent, mortgage interest, rates or land tax for your home that is a place of business	No	Yes
If you are a personal services entity, expenses or fringe benefits tax for more than one car that is used partly or solely for private purposes	No	Yes
Salary and wages for an arm's length employee (not an associate)	Yes	Yes
Salary and wages paid to the principal worker within 14 days of the end of each PAYG withholding payment period	Yes	Yes
Contributions to a super fund on behalf of the principal worker or an arm's length employee (not an associate)	Yes	Yes
Reasonable amounts paid to an associate for principal work	Yes	Yes
Contributions up to the super guarantee amount for an associate doing up to, but less than, 20% of the principal work	Yes	Yes
Reasonable amounts paid to an associate for non-principal work	No	Yes
Reasonable contributions to a super fund for an associate doing solely non-principal work	No	Yes

GENERAL RULES – INDIVIDUALS

The general rule under Division 85 is that an individual taxpayer who must include an amount of PSI in their assessable income cannot deduct expenditure relating to earning that PSI if he or she would not have been able to deduct the amount had he or she derived the same income as an employee. There are some exceptions to this general rule. Claims continue to be deductible for the cost of (s85-10):

- gaining work (eg. advertising, tendering, and quoting for work)
- insuring against loss of income or earning capacity (eg. sickness, accident and disability insurance)
- liability insurance (eg. public liability and professional indemnity insurance)
- engaging an entity that is not an associate to perform work
- engaging an associate to perform work that forms part of the principal work in relation to which the PSI is derived (warning: there are limitations on the amount that can be claimed)
- superannuation contributions for the individual (or their dependants in the event of death)
- workers compensation premiums and similar payments required under the law or payments made to an employee in respect of compensable work-related trauma, and
- meeting obligations, or exercising rights, under GST law.

PAYMENTS TO ASSOCIATES

Allowable deductions for payments made to associates are limited under s85-20. As a general rule, payments to an associate are only deductible to the extent that they relate to engaging an associate to perform work that forms part of the principal work for which the PSI is gained.

Non-principal work is incidental or subsidiary work that is not central to meeting the obligations under the contract (that is, not the main work for which the business gets paid). Examples of non-principal work include bookkeeping for the business, issuing invoices, secretarial duties and running a home office.

Deductions are also allowed in relation to superannuation contributions made in respect of an associate to the extent that the associate's work forms part of the principal work which gives rise to the PSI (s85-25(2)). The deduction available is limited to the amount necessary to avoid paying the superannuation guarantee charge (ie. 9.50% in 2014-15 and 2015-16 – see 19.500 and 19.530), calculated as though Division 85 did not operate to deny deductions for any of the salary or wages paid to the associate.

Deductions are specifically denied for all other payments to associates and for any amount incurred arising from an obligation to associates.

Any payment to an associate which is non-deductible under Division 85 is non-assessable non-exempt income in the hands of the associate.

RESIDENTIAL EXPENSES

Deductions are disallowed in relation to rent, mortgage interest, rates and land tax in respect of the individual's residence or the residence of an associate to the extent that the expenditure relates to gaining or producing the individual's PSI.

GENERAL RULE – PSEs

Section 86-60 provides that a PSE cannot deduct an amount relating to the derivation of an individual's PSI unless:

- the amount would have been deductible to the individual had the circumstances giving rise to the deduction applied to the individual instead of the PSE, and
- the PSE receives the individual's PSI in the course of conducting a PSB. In *Russell v FC of T* (2009) ATC 20-143, the PSE made payments to a partnership that was an associate of the individual who derived the PSI. The primary judge held that the PSE could not deduct the amount as neither limb of s86-20 was satisfied.

CAR EXPENSES

Division 86 does not limit the deduction which would be allowable under the tax law for car expenses in relation to a car for which there is no private use.

Where the car is not used solely for business purposes, car expenses and fringe benefits tax payable for a car fringe benefit are deductible to the extent allowable under the tax law but the deductions are restricted to one car for each individual whose work gives rise to PSI. Where there is more than one car in relation to an individual, the car in respect of which the deductions are taken is the taxpayer's choice.

Note that the car expense deduction rules only apply in relation to PSEs (and not to individuals directly deriving PSI).

16.400 PSI EARNED THROUGH PSEs: THE ATTRIBUTION RULES

Unless the PSE is carrying on a PSB, the income of the entity derived as a result of an individual providing personal services (excluding any GST component) will be treated as the relevant individual's PSI unless it is promptly paid as salary and wages to that individual.

The PSE has until the 14th day after the end of the PAYG payment period in which to pay the income (excluding any GST component) as salary to the individual, otherwise it is treated as the PSI of the individual.

Where an entity makes a payment of salary or wages to an individual by 14 July following the year of income and that amount would otherwise have been treated as PSI, then that payment is treated as having been received by the individual in the previous income year. The individual must include that amount in their assessable income for that preceding income year. However, the PSE's PAYG withholding tax obligations in relation to this amount (see 16.500) is still determined on the basis of the actual payment date; the deemed payment date is only applicable for the purposes of the PSI rules.

 It is possible for an entity to derive both PSI and non-PSI (eg. interest, rent, dividends). The PSI rules do not affect any non-PSI. Also, any GST that has been collected by the entity is excluded from the calculation of a person's PSI. GST is neither assessable income nor exempt income.

In calculating the amount of income derived by a PSE that must be treated as the PSI of an individual, the gross PSI is reduced by the amount of certain deductions which are deductible in the hands of PSE. The method statement contained in s86-20 ensures that the extent of those deductions can never be greater than the amount of the income. However, where the personal services deduction amount exceed the gross PSI, the provisions allow for a deduction of the excess in the hands of the individual (s86-27).

Listed below are the steps to work out the deductions that can be claimed to reduce the amount of PSI to be attributed to the relevant individual:

Step 1: Work out the amount of deductions allowed (other than entity maintenance deductions and salary or wages paid to the individual) against the PSI. As a general rule a PSE can only claim deductions for expenses that relate to the earning of the individual's PSI. In broad terms this means that only those expenses that would be deductible to an individual are also deductible to the entity. For a summary of the deduction rules, see 16.305.

Step 2: Work out the total entity maintenance deductions to which the PSE is entitled. These are (s86-65):
- any fee or charge payable for opening, operating or closing an account with a financial institution
- any tax-related expenses (allowed under s25-5)
- losses or outgoings incurred in preparing or lodging any document as required under the *Corporations Act 2001*, and
- any fee payable to an Australian government agency for any licence, permission, approval, certification etc granted or given under an Australian law.

Step 3: Work out the PSE's assessable income for the income year that does not constitute PSI.

Step 4: Subtract Step 3 from Step 2. (**NOTE:** This step is designed to ensure that entity maintenance deductions are first deducted from non-PSI income.)

Step 5: If the amount in Step 4 is greater than nil, the amount of the reduction is the aggregate of Steps 1 & 4.

Step 6: If the amount in Step 4 is nil or less, the amount of the reduction is limited to the amount in Step 1.

Where multiple individuals derive PSI through an entity, the reduction allowed under Step 4 must be apportioned in accordance with the amount of PSI income earned in relation to each person relative to the PSE's total PSI.

If the above calculation results in a loss (ie. the individual's PSI is less than the deductions allowed) then that loss is an allowable deduction to the relevant individual in that income year. Any unused loss is able to be carried forward (s86-27).

An individual is able to deduct a net PSI loss from other income (the loss is calculated according to s86-27 and s86-87).

The taxpayer's company has derived $120,000 of income that has been directly derived through the personal services of the taxpayer.
The company is entitled to claim $50,000 of deductions (ie. superannuation contributions paid to a complying superannuation fund) (Step 1). The company is entitled to entity maintenance deductions (ie. lodgement fees and tax agent fees) of $3,000 (Step 2). The company has also separately derived investment income of $20,000 (Step 3). As Step 4 (ie. Step 2 less Step 3) is less than nil, Step 5 is not applicable.
The company is entitled to a reduction of only $50,000 (ie. the Step 1 amount). Consequently, the taxpayer's PSI is $70,000 (ie. $120,000 less $50,000).

In the above example, if the amount of other income (ie. Step 3) was $2,000, the company would have been entitled to a reduction of $51,000 (being the amount in Step 1 (ie. $50,000) plus the difference between Step 3 and Step 2 (ie. $3,000 less $2,000). In that case, the taxpayer's PSI would have been $69,000 (ie. $120,000 less $51,000).

In the above example, if another person also derived $180,000 PSI in the company, the entitlement to a reduction for each person would need to be calculated in accordance with each person's PSI.
In the case of the taxpayer in the first example, the reduction would be 40% (ie. $120,000/$300,000) of the Step 4 amount of $1,000 (being that taxpayer's share of total PSI).
The balance would be allowed as a reduction for the second individual.

Once an entity has calculated the amount of income to be included as PSI of an individual, that amount is non-assessable non-exempt income of the PSE. In that way the entity is neither taxed on that income (which is taxed in the individual's hands) nor is it required to take it into account when claiming losses. Furthermore, the income is not a capital gain (s118-20(4)).

Under s86-35, a payment by the PSE or (an associate of the taxpayer) to the taxpayer (or an associate of the taxpayer) of PSI that is assessable income or any other amount attributable to that PSI is non-assessable non-exempt income to the recipient and is not deductible to the payer. In *Russell v FC of T* [2009] ATC 20-143, it was held that since a partnership was an associate of the taxpayer who derived PSI, the PSE could not deduct amounts paid to that partnership where the payments were attributable to the PSI.

16.500 PAYG WITHHOLDING OBLIGATIONS

Where a PSE is caught by the PSI provisions, the entity will have additional PAYG withholding obligations in relation to any PSI amounts attributable to individuals. However, where the PSE is promptly paying PSI amounts to the relevant individual as salary or wages, these additional PAYG withholding obligations will not apply. Instead, the entity will have the usual PAYG withholding obligations that apply to salary or wages.

The PSE must calculate the amount of PSI on which the PAYG withholding liability applies using one of three methods:

- calculating the attributable amount of PSI each reporting period (the legislative approach)

- using a PSI amount of 70% of the gross PSI of the period, or
- applying a percentage based on the entity's net PSI for the prior year to the gross PSI for the period.

The PAYG withholding amount in respect of attributed PSI should be reported on the PSE's BAS or IAS for the relevant period. The entity should issue the relevant individual with a *PAYG payment summary – business and personal services income* (NAT 72545).

NOTE: If the PSE has already lodged some of its activity statements and has not been withholding as required, this must be corrected by lodging a revised activity statement. It cannot simply correct the withholding understatement on a future activity statement.

16.600 APPLICATION OF THE GENERAL ANTI-AVOIDANCE PROVISIONS TO PSBs

Where a taxpayer is treated as conducting a PSB and is therefore excluded from the PSI rules, the Tax Office has indicated that it may apply its anti-avoidance powers (under Part IVA ITAA36) to prevent the splitting of income through the use of the taxpayer's entity (including the retention of personal services income in a company beyond the end of the income year) or with other members of the family, especially through trusts and companies.

Entities with minimal business infrastructure or plant and equipment used to derive the income of the entity will be at risk as will entities which focus on diverting income away from the primary individual (income splitting using a trust) or retaining profits in a company to attract the lower corporate rate of tax.

Tax Office publications which provide insight into the Commissioners approach to the use of Part IVA in these circumstances include:

- Part IVA: the general anti-avoidance rule for income tax, and
- General anti-avoidance rules and how they apply to a personal services business.

Taxation Rulings that were issued prior to the enactment of the PSI regime dealing with the alienation of income and the application of anti-avoidance rules under Part IVA (eg. IT 2639, IT 2503, IT 2503A, IT 2639, IT 2121, IT 2330 and IT 2501) remain in force. The Tax Office has established a test case program that is aimed at income splitting arrangements. It has also released a fact sheet (*General anti-avoidance rules and how they may apply to a personal services business*) drawing together all of the information from previous Rulings.

PSI ARRANGEMENTS TARGETED

The Tax Office focus is primarily on arrangements where an interposed entity, such as a company or trust, does not satisfy the PSI rules, but the taxpayer is able to obtain a tax benefit because the income in that entity is able to be streamed to others (eg. to family members or a 'dump' company).

The 'plain vanilla' scenario where the Commissioner would apply Part IVA is as follows:

- a discretionary trust derives PSI
- the principal of the business is not remunerated with a salary which is commensurate with the value of services provided, and
- the retained profits are distributed by the trust to associates of the principal who are on lower tax rates or entities with carry forward tax losses.

Other scenarios to which the Tax Office considers Part IVA may apply include:

- where there is a variation of distributions paid to the principal and/or their associates from year to year by the interposed company or trust
- profits are purportedly retained in the entity on commercial grounds but in fact are available for the private use of the principal and their associates in a company
- profits are purportedly to be retained in an entity on commercial grounds but the principal has little opportunity to benefit from the business in the future – for example, the principal either holds a minority interest in the company or is a potential beneficiary of a discretionary trust, and

- excessive amounts are distributed by the company or trust to associates of the principal (such as spouse or children) where those amounts bear little relationship to the value of the services which they may provide.

The Commissioner listed the relevant factors in determining whether Part IVA applies to the above arrangements in TR 2001/8 which include the following:

- the interposed entity derives income from sources other than from the services provided by an individual who controls, or is associated with that entity, that is, the service provider

- the expenses claimed by the interposed entity may demonstrate the existence of a business operation or structure (eg rented premises, employs others to provide services)

- the services provided may be unique to the taxpayer in that the services are of a type which cannot be provided by any other person

- whether the interposed entity is, at law, unable to provide the services to the service requirer (where, for example, the law prevents incorporation of particular types of practices)

- whether the salary or wages paid to the service provider is commensurate with the skills exercised or services provided and with the income received by the interposed entity for those services, and

- whether there has been a substantial change in the activities which the individual performed prior to incorporation or any other significant external indicators that the arrangements have changed.

LABOUR HIRE ARRANGEMENTS

The Tax Office has released Taxpayer Alert TA 2011/2 regarding its focus on certain labour hire arrangements which involve the use of a discretionary trust to split income.

The TA covers arrangements with broadly the following features:

- a labour hire firm offers remuneration structures for an individual (the service provider) who provides services or performs work

- the service provider becomes a beneficiary of a discretionary trust which is associated with the labour hire firm

- the discretionary trust agreement identifies additional beneficiaries, such as the service provider's spouse, and the basis on which the trustee will allocate distributions

- the service provider or the labour hire firm contracts for services with a client (the end user) or a recruitment agency used by the end user

- the labour hire firm may enter into such contracts either in its own capacity or in its capacity as trustee of the discretionary trust

- the labour hire firm invoices either the end user or the recruitment agency

- payment for work performed or services provided are paid by the labour hire firm via the discretionary trust

- the discretionary trust makes payments to the service provider and/or an associate of the service provider, typically the spouse

- trust distributions are purportedly discretionary; however, in reality, the total amount of distributions are consistent with the service provider's set rate of remuneration less management fees of the labour hire firm, and

- there is limited economic rationale for the arrangement other than the avoidance of taxation or superannuation guarantee obligations.

The Tax Office considers that such arrangements may give rise to PSI and Part IVA issues. In addition, the TA identifies other areas of potential concern, including the following:

- issues relating to the correct identification of the relationship as an employee/employer relationship or a contractor/principal relationship

- the PAYG withholding provisions

- the superannuation guarantee charge regime, and

- the promoter of tax exploitation scheme provisions.

Investments

17

17.000 INVESTMENTS

Investors must consider a range of tax laws dealing with income, assets and deductions. This chapter is designed to provide a general summary of the relevant tax issues that should be considered when investing in various asset categories.

17.100 REVENUE OR CAPITAL

Investment returns are assessable either on revenue or capital account. The distinction between revenue and capital is not always clear and characterisation of a receipt will ultimately depend on the circumstances which apply to the taxpayer.

The distinction between an income and capital receipt has been likened to the fruit and the tree, where the capital amount is the tree and the fruit being the return of income from the capital. Generally an income receipt is regarded as an amount that is regular, recurrent or periodic and income tax applies to a net amount of income. A good example is dividend returns from a shareholding.

However, it is not always clear whether an amount should be treated as income or capital. What may appear to be a capital gain for example may in fact be classified more correctly as income where the taxpayer had entered into a profit-making venture. The intention of the taxpayer when the asset is acquired (or any subsequent change of intention) and the length of the ownership period may be relevant in determining whether a gain is on revenue or capital account. Note also where the amount is a capital return, the investor may have access to the CGT discount provisions which provides a better tax result than would be the case where it is fully taxed as assessable income.

Similarly the treatment of an outgoing is important to determine whether an immediate deduction is allowable or whether the outgoing forms part of the cost base of a CGT asset.

Matters to be considered when deciding whether an outgoing is revenue or capital in nature include:

- the character of the advantage sought by the outgoing
- the advantage sought by the taxpayer, and
- how the advantage comes about, eg. recurrent payments (refer *Sun Newspapers Case*).

Generally, those holding investment products fall into two categories – traders and longer term investors.

TRADERS ON REVENUE ACCOUNT

Generally, where the holder of an investment product carries on activities for the purpose of earning income from buying and selling investments, that holder will be in the business of trading. Generally, a trader:

- holds investment products as trading stock
- includes gross receipts from the sale of investment products as income
- recognises expenses incurred in relation to trading activities as allowable deductions, and
- includes in assessable income investment returns such as interest, dividends and distributions.

NOTE: Where the holder of an investment product enters into an isolated transaction with a profit making intention, they will not be in the business of trading. However, any net profit from the transaction will be assessable on revenue account. See TR 92/3 for further guidance on whether profits from isolated transactions are on revenue account.

INVESTORS ON CAPITAL ACCOUNT

Where investments are held with the intention of earning regular income from those investments, the investor may be seen as generally not carrying on a business. This type of investor generally:

- does not include gross receipts from the sale of investments as income. Any net gain is assessable under the capital gains tax provisions

- cannot include capital losses from the sale of investments against income from any other sources except current or future capital gains (in other words, quarantining these losses)
- cannot include expenses incurred in relation to buying and selling investments as a deduction when incurred. These are taken into account in determining the amount of any capital gain or loss instead, and
- includes investment returns such as interest, dividends and distributions in assessable income.

NOTE: In determining whether the holder of an investment product is a trader or a longer term investor, the intention, frequency and volume of the taxpayer's investing activities must be considered. Additional guidance on this issue is contained in the Decision Impact Statement of *The Taxpayer and Commissioner of Taxation* 2011 ATC 1-037.

NOTE: Tax Determination TD 2011/21 considers the factors which may be relevant in deciding whether gains and losses from the disposal of securities would be on capital or revenue account for the trustee of a trust.

17.200 INVESTMENT EARNINGS

Assessable investment income includes both ordinary and statutory income. Investment income earnings such as dividends and interest are typically considered ordinary income. Franking credits, net capital gains and net trust distributions are statutory income.

Australian resident taxpayers include investment earnings from both Australian and foreign sources in their assessable income under s6-5(2). However, Australian resident taxpayers who are temporary residents do not include in their assessable income investment income from foreign sources (see 11.020). Non-resident taxpayers generally only include Australian sourced investment income in their assessable income.

17.210   ORDINARY OR STATUTORY INCOME

Ordinary income is typically income that is regular, periodic or recurrent (*FTC v Dixon* (1952) 86 CLR 540). Returns on property such as interest, rent or dividends are considered ordinary income. Statutory income is income that is not ordinary income but is recognised because of a provision of the tax law (Refer 6-10(2) ITAA97).

While not an exhaustive list, the following table shows some of the taxing provisions for ordinary and statutory income from investments:

Income item	Provision
Interest	s6-1 ITAA97
Rent	s6-1 ITAA97
Dividend	s44 ITAA97
Imputation credit	s207-20 ITAA97
Listed investment company dividend	s115-280 ITAA97
Forestry managed investment schemes returns	Division 394 ITAA97
Yields – traditional securities	s26BB ITAA36
Distributions – trusts	s97 ITAA36

17.300 CAPITAL GAINS

Capital gains as a result of a CGT event are included in the assessable income of the taxpayer. CGT events most commonly occur as a result of the realisation of assets acquired (or deemed to be acquired) after 19 September 1985, where the realisation is not in the course of carrying on a business or a profit making venture. The assets to which CGT applies are indicated at 12.050 – 12.062 and would include shares, units in a unit trust, rights, options, investment properties, and business goodwill.

A capital gain is generally the sale proceeds (or market value of certain transactions) less their 'cost base' (see 12.092). There are certain concessions which may reduce the taxable amount of a capital gain such as a 50% discount for individuals and trusts (12.165) and concessions for certain active business assets of eligible taxpayers (12.525). There are specific exemptions such as a taxpayer's main residence, most motor vehicles, some types of collectable, personal use assets, and compensation payments for certain forms of personal injury. It should be noted that some types of transaction involving assets which might otherwise be subject to the CGT provisions may be instead taxed as income (eg. property bought and sold in a development business or profit-making arrangement) (see from 12.000).

Generally, investors are subject to the CGT provisions on the disposal of investment assets, unless carrying on a business or where the investment is sold as a profit making undertaking. Expenses incurred in relation to buying and selling investments are included in the asset's cost base.

17.400 TYPICAL INVESTMENT PRODUCTS

In examining the tax treatment of returns on or dealings in investments, it is first necessary to examine different types of investment products. The basic investment products include cash, shares and managed investments and property. Listed below is a description of the more common investment products and tax issues faced by investors in those products. For the purposes of this analysis, it will be assumed that the relevant investors are not in the business of trading in investment products.

17.410   CASH AND FIXED INTEREST INVESTMENTS

Interest bearing accounts are the most basic of the investment products and represent a form of lending by the investor in return for an interest payment. The deposit may take the form of either direct or indirect lending. Direct lending generally includes interest bearing deposits with a financial institution, debentures, unsecured notes, bank bills or government and corporate bonds. Indirect lending generally occurs through managed funds such as cash management trusts, bond trusts and mortgage trusts.

NOTE: Division 974 of ITAA97 provides guidelines as to whether a particular investment is classed as debt or equity. This may impact whether a return paid on the investment may be frankable and non-deductible to the payer (like a dividend) or may be deductible to the payer and not frankable (like interest). (See 6.200).

17.415   TAX ISSUES FACING INVESTORS IN CASH AND FIXED INTEREST
INVESTMENTS

INTEREST INCOME

Interest income is typically recognised on a receipts basis and is assessable to the taxpayer in the year the interest is received. Typically, interest is received on bank deposits and from savings accounts as well as on term deposits.

For the tax treatment of interest from a cash managed trust, see *trust distributions* at 7.000.

DISCOUNTED OR DEFERRED INTEREST SECURITIES

Not all investment returns are based solely on the regular payment of interest. Some debt securities instead defer income to a future period. The yield on such discounted or deferred interest securities may be taxed on an accrual basis under Division 230 Part 3-10 of the ITAA97. Effectively, Division 230 taxes the return on discount and deferred interest securities issued after 16 December 1984 on an accruals basis where tax would otherwise be deferred to a future period. The division alters the timing of income and deductions.

Note that Division 230 does not apply to a qualifying security held as trading stock.

To be subject to these rules, 'qualifying securities' must have ALL of the following attributes:

- the security has a term of greater than one year (or a term beyond one year is anticipated)
- there is either no interest payable, or if there is, it is at intervals of greater than one year, and
- apart from periodic interest paid, the investor receives (including the maturity payout) more than the initial investment and that extra amount is more than 1.5% pa of the initial investment.

Division 230 only applies if the 'eligible return' of all amounts from the borrower (excluding any periodical interest) exceeds (or is likely to exceed) the amount determined by the following formula:

> *Total payments over term (other than interest) including return of capital x term of deposit x 1.5%*

A security is purchased for $1,000 with an indexed value at maturity of $1,500 in six years and interest at 3% pa.

Eligible return ($1,500 less $1,000) $500
Formula amount ($1,500 x 6 years x 1.5%) $135

The security is a 'qualifying security' because the 'eligible return' of $500 exceeds the yardstick amount determined by the formula ($135).

TAXING OF YIELD INTEREST

Regardless of when interest is received by the investor, tax is payable each income year on an accrual basis. The amount taxed is each year's increase in value. In simple terms, the increase in value is measured at six monthly intervals counted back from the maturity date.

GAINS AND LOSSES ON DISCOUNTED OR DEFERRED INTEREST SECURITIES

Gains (or losses) on these securities (if acquired after 19 September 1985) are assessed under CGT rules (see from 12.000). This assumes that the taxpayer is a non-business investor.

NOTE: The tax implications of a security that meets the definition of a 'traditional security' are discussed at 17.530.

DISCOUNTED OR DEFERRED INTEREST SECURITIES FROM 1 JULY 2010 (OR 1 JULY 2009 BY ELECTION)

Note that Division 230 of ITAA97 will provide the tax treatment for most of the gains and losses on discounted and deferred interest securities that are acquired or issued on or after 1 July 2010, or 1 July 2009 should the taxpayer so elect.

FIRST HOME SAVER ACCOUNTS

An individual can invest through a 'first home saver account' to save for the purchase of their first home through a combination of government contributions and concessional tax rates. Certain financial institutions, including banks and credit unions offer these products. Generally, the funds can only be used to buy or build the person's first home.

Holders of such accounts receive a government contribution based on that person's personal contributions to the account during an income year. The government contribution is 17% of personal contributions up to a maximum amount of $1,020 (2013-14 income year). To receive the contribution, the holder must lodge an income tax return and the account provider must report personal contributions to the Tax Office.

Earnings on the accounts are taxed at 15% and the tax is paid by the account provider.

To be eligible to open a first home saver account, an individual person must:

- be aged over 18 and under 65 years
- have a tax file number
- not have previously owned a home in Australia that has been their main residence, and
- not have previously had a first home saver account.

The account cannot be held as a joint account.

The holder of the account:

- must make personal contributions of at least $1,000 for each of four financial years before being able to withdraw the savings (not necessarily consecutive years), and
- can make contributions to the account up to a maximum cap of $90,000 (2013-14 income year) over the life of the account.

Other persons can make contributions on the holder's behalf. However, contributions cannot be made from pre-taxed salary.

A first home saver account holder may transfer funds from their account into an approved mortgage where the holder acquires a home before the end of the four year period.

IMPORTANT! *Abolition of First Home Saver Account Scheme.* In the 2014-15 Budget, the government announced the following changes to abolish the first home saver accounts scheme.

- New accounts from 7.30pm, Tuesday 13 May 2014 will not be able to access any concessions or the government contribution.
- Eligibility for a government contribution will cease from 1 July 2014. Existing account holders will continue to receive the government contribution for personal contributions made during the 2013-14 income year.
- Tax and social security concessions will cease from 1 July 2015. Existing account holders will continue to receive all tax and social security concessions associated with these accounts for the 2013-14 and 2014-15 income years.
- Restrictions on withdrawals will be removed from 1 July 2015.

Once the first home saver account scheme is abolished from 1 July 2015, these accounts will be treated like any other account held with a provider. The existing rules will continue to apply until the law is changed.

At the time of writing, the legislation for the abolition of this scheme was before Parliament and was not yet enacted.

17.420   AUSTRALIAN SHARES

Many investors hold shares in Australian companies. The return on shares is in the form of a dividend, although some investors trade in shares or buy and sell share parcels with a profit making intention.

As mentioned above, Division 974 of ITAA97 provides guidelines as to whether a particular investment in a company is classed as debt or equity. This may impact whether a return paid on the investment may be frankable and non-deductible to the payer (like a dividend) or may be deductible to the payer and not frankable (like interest). (See 6.200).

17.425   TAX ISSUES FACING SHAREHOLDERS

DIVIDENDS

These are taxable distributions by companies to shareholders, whether in money or shares or other property. Generally, dividends are sourced from retained profits (including some profits on sale of capital assets). Some distributions are excluded, for example where another provision of the tax law expressly deals with the distribution, such as s23AJ, s23AI, s23AK and s128D of the ITAA36.

FRANKED DIVIDENDS AND FRANKING OFFSETS

Dividends may be franked by a company. This means the dividend can carry a tax credit (known as the franking offset) which may be utilised by certain taxpayers to offset tax on the dividend (and/or other income). An investor in a company who is a 'qualified person' who receives a franked dividend will add the franking credit to the amount of the dividend, include the total as assessable income and then claim a tax offset for the franking credit (this method is known as 'gross-up and offset'). This means that the franking credit is included as assessable income.

If the investor is a resident individual and has franking credits for the income year which exceed their total tax payable, a refund may be available for the excess (note that in limited circumstances, certain entities also qualify for the refund).

While Australian taxpayers are generally entitled to the franking credit offset, there are anti-avoidance rules which may prevent the taxpayer from using the franking credit as a tax offset. One such measure is the 'holding period rule' which applies to each shareholding (or unitholding when franking credits are received indirectly through a trust). The holding period rule varies depending on whether the relevant shares are ordinary shares or preference shares.

The rule requires that ordinary shares must be held at risk to market forces (increasing or decreasing the share value) for at least 45 days (plus days of acquisition and disposal). The rule requires that preference shares must be held at risk for at least 90 days (plus days of acquisition and disposal). The holding period rule operates on a last-in-first-out basis so that a shareholder will be deemed for the purpose of applying the holding period rule to have disposed of their most recently acquired shares first.

An exception to the holding period applies to individual taxpayers where the total franking credits received from all sources during the year are $5,000 or less (the 'small shareholder exemption'). See 11.750 and 6.800. Such individuals include the franking credit in assessable income and are eligible to claim the franking credit tax offset.

Where a taxpayer is ineligible to claim a franking credit offset as a result of the holding period rule, there is no need to 'gross up' the dividend. This means that the franking credit disallowed is not included in the taxpayers assessable income.

Note that while franking credits are typically attached to franked dividends, trust distributions can also carry franking credits (see 11.730).

For the tax treatment of foreign income from an investment in a foreign company, see Chapter 22.

NOTE: Non-resident shareholders will be subject to the withholding tax provisions on any unfranked portion of the dividend (see 11.710 and 22.100).

DIVIDEND REINVESTMENT PLANS

Shareholders often have the option of reinvesting their dividends in the acquisition of more shares. For tax purposes, the dividend must still be included in assessable income as if the shareholder had received dividends in cash, and used the cash to acquire additional shares. For CGT purposes, the amount of the dividend applied to acquire the shares forms part of the cost base (excluding the imputation credit).

SALES AND PURCHASES OF SHARES

Where the shares are not trading stock or part of a profit-making undertaking, gains on the disposal of shares may be subject to CGT (see Chapter 12) and in this instance their cost is not deductible but forms part of the cost base of the shares.

Division 315 disregards a capital gain or loss incurred by a private health policy holder where shares or rights to acquire shares (generally in the demutualised private health insurer) are received by policy holders on demutualisation. The investor will receive a market value cost base for those shares or rights. Any subsequent disposal of those shares may then be subject to CGT.

Where the shares are trading stock or part of a profit-making undertaking, proceeds on the disposal of shares are included in assessable income. Taxpayers who are share traders may claim a deduction for shares disposed of each year in the course of trading. Those engaged in a profit making undertaking are taxed on the net gain.

Note that special rules apply to shares issued under an employee share scheme (see 11.850).

IS THE TAXPAYER CARRYING ON A BUSINESS OF SHARE-TRADING?

A taxpayer may successfully argue that a business exists and recognise profits and losses on share trading on a revenue basis. Rather than acquiring shares to obtain an income stream in the form of dividends, a share-trader seeks to obtain a profit through the purchase and sale of shares. Whether a person is a share trader has been considered in a number of cases (*Shields v DFCT* 99 ATC 2037, Case X86, Case W8, Case X31).

Income derived from share-trading activities is revenue in nature and assessed to taxation as ordinary income under s6-5 of the ITAA97, while losses are deductible under s8-1 of the ITAA97. Share traders apply the trading stock rules in Division 70 of the ITAA97 to shares purchased and sold (see 14.200).

NOTE: For those investment products (shares) held by traders as trading stock or revenue assets on hand at end of the year, the relevant price method is contained in TR 96/4.

Profits derived by non-resident share-traders whose trading involves Australian entities may be assessable under subsection 6-5(3). Regardless of whether a non-resident investor maintains an Australian office or staff, if the contracts for the purchase or sale of shares are concluded in Australia, the income will be considered Australian source income (ID 2004/904). However, the profits derived by a non-resident investor on capital account can be disregarded for Australian tax purposes, unless the CGT even relates to an asset that is 'taxable Australian property' (see 12.700).

The following factors are considered relevant in determining whether a share-trading business exists (refer ID 2001/745 and ID 2001/746):

Share trader	Investor
• The nature of the activities and whether they have the purpose of profit-making • The complexity and magnitude of the undertaking and intention to engage in trade regularly, routinely or systematically • Operating in a business-like manner and the degree of sophistication involved • Whether any profit/loss is regarded as arising from a discernible pattern of trading • The volume of the taxpayer's operations and the amount of capital employed • Repetition and regularity in the buying and selling of shares • Turnover • Whether the taxpayer is operating to a plan, setting budgets and targets, keeping records • Maintenance of an office • Accounting for the share transactions on a gross receipts basis • Whether the taxpayer is engaged in another full-time profession	• Shares typically held for longer terms • The taxpayer predominantly relies on professional advice to make investment decisions • Limited time spent on the activity • The method of operation is simple • No trading plan developed • No contingency plan in place to absorb market downturns • Inability to source funding required for continuing the activity for an indefinite period • Limited record-keeping • No home office maintained

TRADING STOCK VERSUS CAPITAL ASSET

Investment products may be held as trading stock by a taxpayer carrying on a business of share trading or options trading. However, whether a particular parcel should be treated as trading stock must be determined on a case by case basis. Generally, the tax issues facing share traders versus passive investors are summarised below.

How share transactions are taxed

Transaction	Share trader	Shareholder (passive investor)
Gain on disposal	Sale on trading account	Capital gain
Loss on disposal	Sale on trading account	Capital loss
Share buy-backs	Sale on trading account	Capital gain or loss/usually a dividend component
Dividends received	Assessable income When received but may be accounted for when derived (ie. when dividend is declared)	Assessable income When received
Share acquisition	Purchases on trading account Allowable deduction	Capital cost No immediate deduction allowed
Broker fees	Purchases Allowable deduction	Capital cost No immediate deduction
GST on broker fees	Financial supply Reduced input tax credits	Capital cost No immediate deduction No reduced input tax credits as no enterprise
Share investment course pre-ownership	If business commenced then allowable deduction, however nexus must be established	Capital cost No immediate deduction
Share investment course post-ownership	Professional development Allowable deduction	Investment expenses Allowable deduction
Technical books	Professional development Allowable deduction	Investment expenses Allowable deduction
Share trading software	Business expense Allowable deduction (if not an establishment cost)	Investment expenses Allowable deduction
Interest on margin loan	Interest expense Allowable deduction incurred to obtain assessable income	Investment expenses Allowable deduction
Prepaid interest	Deduction up to 12 months if s82KZM satisfied	Deduction up to 12 months if s82KZM satisfied
Bank charges on margin loan	Bank fees Allowable deduction	Investment expenses Allowable deduction
Costs to establish loan	Borrowing costs Allowable deduction available over five years	Investment expenses Allowable deduction available over five years

ISSUE OF RIGHTS OR OPTIONS

An investor who holds shares may be issued with rights or options to acquire additional shares at a specified price (call options) or rights or options to sell their existing shares back to the company involved (put options).

In the High Court decision in *FCT v McNeil* (2007) 64 ATR 431, the market value of rights to sell shares back to the company issued to the taxpayer were held to be assessable income. This put into doubt the treatment of call options often issued by companies seeking to raise capital. The law was subsequently to ensure that such call options issued by companies to investor shareholders to raise capital are dealt with under the CGT provisions. See 12.800, 12.820 and 12.830.

NOTE: Special rules apply to rights or options issued under an employee option plan (see 12.816).

EXERCISE OF RIGHTS OR OPTIONS

The tax implications of exercising rights or options to buy or sell investments are dealt with at 12.815.

EXPIRY OF RIGHTS OR OPTIONS

Generally, as there are no capital proceeds received on the expiry of shares or rights, a capital loss will be triggered (CGT event C2). See 12.024.

BONUS SHARES

Bonus shares are additional shares received by a shareholder for an existing holding of shares in a company. Generally, from 1 July 1998, the paid-up value of bonus shares issued is not assessable as a dividend unless part of the dividend was paid in cash as part of a dividend reinvestment plan or otherwise represented a capitalisation of profits.

For CGT purposes, the bonus shares are taken to have been acquired at the time that the original shares were acquired. The cost base and the reduced cost base of the original shares are apportioned over both the original parcel of shares and the bonus shares to provide the cost base of the bonus shares. This means that the cost base and reduced cost base of the original shares is reduced accordingly. Where the original shares are pre-CGT assets, any capital gain or loss on a subsequent sale of the bonus shares is disregarded.

Generally, where the bonus shares are assessable as a dividend, the shares are taken to have been acquired for CGT purposes at the time that the shares were issued. The amount of the dividend forms part of the cost base. This is regardless of whether the original shares were pre or post-CGT shares. Note that bonus shares may be franked when assessable as a dividend.

SHARE BUY-BACKS

A share buy-back is an arrangement where a company makes an offer to shareholders to buy back some or all of their shares in the company.

An 'off-market' buy-back is where the company buys back shares directly from the shareholder rather than buying them through the Australian Securities Exchange. Most share buy-back arrangements will constitute an 'off-market' buy-back for tax purposes. A shareholder participating in the buy-back arrangement will be taken, for CGT purposes, to have disposed of their shares when the company accepts their application.

Where the share purchase price under the buy-back arrangement exceeds the amount debited to the share capital account, the excess is taken to be a dividend. The balance is the capital component. The deemed dividend can be franked except to the extent that the purchase price exceeds the market value of the share.

For tax purposes, shareholders will be treated as disposing of their shares for the capital component plus the amount (if any) by which the tax value (see below) exceeds the buy-back price. This effectively means that a market value substitution rule applies.

The ordinary CGT rules apply to an 'on-market buy-back' of shares. The consideration received is the purchase price of the shares. No amount of the purchase price is a deemed dividend.

TAX IMPLICATIONS OF AN OFF-MARKET SHARE BUY BACK – DIVIDEND COMPONENT OF THE BUY BACK PRICE

The buy-back price in an 'off-market share buy-back' usually consists of a capital component and a fully franked dividend (an unfranked dividend will only arise where the buy-back price exceeds the market value of the share). The deemed dividend is included in the individual's assessable income in the same way as an ordinary dividend. If a shareholder, whose shares are bought back, is entitled to the benefit of franking credits on the deemed dividend the shareholder will also:

- include the franking credit on the deemed dividend in their assessable income, and
- be entitled to a franking credit offset equal to the franking credit.

The franking credit offset may reduce the total tax payable by the shareholder on their taxable income. If the shareholder's total tax offset exceeds the total tax payable on his or her taxable income, the shareholder, if eligible, may be entitled to a cash refund of that excess (see 11.720).

NOTE: Non-resident shareholders will be subject to the withholding tax provisions on any unfranked portion of the dividend.

TAX IMPLICATIONS OF AN OFF-MARKET SHARE BUY BACK – CAPITAL COMPONENT OF THE BUY BACK PRICE

This summary of the income tax implications of participating in a buy-back is limited to shareholders who hold their shares on capital account and therefore will be assessed for tax under the CGT provisions. Shareholders, who carry on a business in dealing with shares, may be assessed on their dealings on revenue account rather than under the CGT provisions.

An investor participating in the buy-back will be deemed for CGT purposes to have disposed of each share for the capital proceeds component of the buyback price plus the amount (if any) by which the tax value exceeds the buy-back price. The calculation of any capital gain in respect of shares bought back will depend on when the shares were acquired. If a shareholder has held their shares for less than 12 months, any capital gain will be calculated as the excess of the deemed capital proceeds over the CGT cost base of the shares.

However, where the shareholder is an individual or trust that has held their shares for at least 12 months, then:

- if the share was acquired at or before 11.45am (ACT time) on 21 September 1999, the shareholder may choose whether to index the cost base to 30 September 1999 or to apply the CGT discount (which reduces the gain, net of any capital losses, by 50%), and

- if the shares were acquired after 11.45am (ACT time) on 21 September 1999 the shareholder may apply the CGT discount in calculating any capital gain on disposal.

Where the shareholder is a superannuation fund that has held their shares for at least 12 months, then:

- if the share was acquired at or before 11.45am (ACT time) on 21 September 1999, the fund may choose whether to index the cost base to 30 September 1999 or apply a one-third CGT discount (which reduces the gain, net of any capital losses, by one-third), and

- if the shares were acquired after 11.45am (ACT time) on 21 September 1999, the fund may apply the one-third CGT discount.

The CGT discount is not available to companies.

Generally, the CGT cost base for the shares will be the amount the shareholder paid to acquire the shares together with certain incidental costs of acquisition, for example stamp duty and brokerage, and certain incidental costs of disposal.

A capital loss for a share disposed of under the buy-back will be the excess of the reduced cost base of the share over the deemed capital proceeds. No allowance for indexation or non-capital costs is made in determining the reduced cost base of the shares for this purpose.

The capital gain which arises under the buy-back may be lower than the capital gain which may have arisen under an equivalent sale of the shares on-market. This is because the capital proceeds under the buy-back are limited to the capital component of the buy back price plus the amount (if any) by which the tax value exceeds the buy-back price, rather than the price at which the shareholder would have sold their shares on-market. The lower deemed capital proceeds also means that any capital loss on disposal of the shares may be higher than might otherwise have arisen.

A capital loss that arises from the buy-back can only be used to offset capital gains made by the shareholder.

Any capital loss arising from the buy-back cannot be offset against the deemed dividend or any franking credit included in the shareholder's assessable income.

For superannuation fund investors that acquired their shares before 1 July 1988, the CGT cost base may be adjusted to the market value of the shares on 30 June 1988.

NOTE: As these components will vary for each shareholder, the tax implications will be unique to each participant in the buy back.

CALCULATION OF THE TAX VALUE

TD 2004/22 sets out the Tax Office's methodology in determining the tax value of shares bought back off-market. The determination provides that the tax value should be determined as the volume weighted average price of the shares over the last five trading days before the first announcement of the buy-back, adjusted for the movement in the S&P/ASX 200 Index. Irrespective of the actual buy-back price received by shareholders, for CGT purposes shareholders are deemed to have received an extra capital amount if the tax value exceeds the buy back price. This amount if any is added to the capital component of the buy back price for CGT purposes.

LIMIT ON AVAILABILITY OF FRANKING CREDITS

There are a number of anti-avoidance rules which may prevent shareholders participating in a buy-back from claiming franking credits on the deemed dividend component of the buy-back price. These rules are designed to discourage franking credit streaming and trading in franking credits. These rules may deny the benefit of franking credits to shareholders generally, or because of their particular circumstances.

The 'holding period rule' and the 'small shareholders exemption' (see 11.750) apply to dividends from share buy-backs in the same way as they apply to franking credits on ordinary dividends.

17.430   LISTED INVESTMENT COMPANY INVESTMENTS

A Listed Investment Company (LIC) is a company (or wholly owned subsidiary) that:

- is an Australian resident for tax purposes
- is listed on the Australian Securities Exchange, and
- has 90% of the market value of its CGT assets as 'permitted investments' (including shares, units, options, financial instruments, passive investment assets, goodwill, etc).

TAX ISSUES FACING INVESTORS IN A LIC

Investors in a LIC must declare dividends earned in the usual way (see 12.675). However, a concession may apply where the dividends paid by a LIC include a capital gain component.

The portion of the LIC dividend attributable to the capital gain component may be recognised as an income tax deduction. This allows shareholders of LICs to obtain a benefit similar to the discount on capital gains giving the investor access to the benefit that would have been available had the investor made the capital gain directly. The deduction is only available if:

- the dividend is paid to an individual, trust, partnership, or complying superannuation fund, and
- the shareholder is an Australian resident when the dividend was paid or a non-resident with permanent establishment in Australia.

The deduction amount is equal to the general capital gains discount, being 50% of the LIC capital gain amount for individuals and $33^{1}/3\%$ for complying superannuation funds. The deduction is generally recorded as an interest and dividend deduction. The LIC must notify the shareholders of the capital gain component of a LIC dividend by recording the amount on the distribution statement.

Tom, an Australian resident, received a distribution from LIC Ltd. During the income year, Tom received a fully franked dividend from LIC Ltd of $70,000, with an eligible capital gain amount (attributable part) of $50,000. The following amounts should be included in Tom's tax return:

Franked dividend... $70,000
Plus franking credit $30,000
Assessable income $100,000
Less 50% deduction for LIC gain amount ....($25,000)
Taxable income for Tom $75,000

Tom may be entitled to a franking tax offset equal to his franking credit.

17.435   FIXED TRUSTS

Fixed trusts provide investors with a fixed entitlement to both the income and capital of the trust. A unit trust is a type of fixed trust where the investor is the owner of a specific number of units in the trust in accordance with their investment. While investment may occur through a private fixed trust, investors are likely to be more familiar with public trusts.

A public unit trust is a listed trust or has units offered to the public or has at least 50 unit-holders. A public trust may be unlisted or listed. Listed trusts will have a readily available market valuation for the units available for sale. Valuation of units in unlisted trusts will be dependent on an appraised valuation of the underlying assets.

Public unit trusts that conduct a trading business are taxed at the corporate tax rate of 30%. Public trusts that conduct an investment business are generally not taxed unless the trust retains undistributed taxable income.

Generally, investors receive trust distributions in proportion to the number of units held over the total issued units of the trust. Whether the distribution is assessable to a beneficiary is wholly dependent on the nature of the trust's income and the tax status of the beneficiary.

17.440   MANAGED INVESTMENTS

A managed investment is the pooling together of monies from many investors to purchase investment assets. The investor receives an interest in the scheme, normally units in a unit trust. The number of units an investor receives is dependent on the amount invested in the scheme. Generally, a professional investment manager operates the scheme (the fund manager or 'responsible entity'). Many investors are attracted to managed investments for professional management and diversification of investments.

Managed investments cover a wide variety of different investment products. Some of the more popular managed investments include:

- cash management trusts
- property trusts
- Australian equity trusts, and
- international equity trusts.

17.445   TAX ISSUES FACING INVESTORS IN TRUSTS

TAX TREATMENT OF TRUST DISTRIBUTIONS

Distributions from a trust are taxed on an accruals basis. This means that a beneficiary presently entitled to trust income in respect of a particular year will be assessable in respect of that income even though it is not received until after the end of that year. The cash received by the investor (beneficiary or unit holder) from a trust distribution often differs from the amount to be included in taxable income. An annual taxation summary sent to beneficiaries or investors advises of the taxable component.

A trust distribution is generally made up of various types of income (for example, interest, dividends, capital gains or foreign income) and these income amounts retain their character as they flow from the trust through to the investor. This means the investor may record a portion of the distribution as a capital gain or foreign income in their income tax return and the balance as income from a trust. A trust distribution may comprise various components including:

- primary production income
- non-primary production income (includes Australian interest income, franked and unfranked dividends)
- capital gains
- foreign source income, and
- tax-deferred distributions.

Where a trust distribution includes a tax-deferred component, this amount is not included in the assessable income of the investor. The annual tax statement will state the tax-deferred component included in the trust distribution. While the amount is not taxable, the cost base of any units held in the trust must be reduced by the tax-deferred amount received. Receipt of the tax-deferred component therefore impacts the calculation of the capital gain or loss on units when they are eventually disposed of (see 12.120 and 12.605).

Where a trust distribution includes a tax-free amount, the investor will be required to apply that amount against their cost base in the units unless the amount is to be excluded pursuant to s104-71 of ITAA97. If the non-assessable amounts exceed the investor's cost base in the units, CGT event E4 will occur.

Where a trust has earned franked income, it may pay a franked distribution to its investors. Where the investor receives a franked distribution which flows to it indirectly, the investor, if eligible, is entitled to a tax offset equal to its share of the franking credits attached to the distribution (s207-45 ITAA97). Generally, an investor will only be eligible to utilise the franking credits attached to the franked distribution if both the trustee and the investor are 'qualified persons' (see 11.740). As the investor in this case does not directly hold shares, special 'holding period rules' are applicable. The investor must have a minimum 30% fixed interest in the trust and have held that interest for the requisite 45 days to be eligible to claim the franking credit tax offset.

NOTE: Where the investor is merely a discretionary beneficiary, they will not have a fixed interest in the trust and therefore will be unable to satisfy the 'holding period rule'. In this case, a franking credit tax offset will only be available if:

- the beneficiary is an individual that satisfies the 'small shareholder exemption' (see 12.750)
- the relevant trust has made a family trust election (see 7.200), or
- the relevant shares were acquired by the trust before 31 December 1997.

For the tax treatment of foreign income from a trust, (see 22.500).

CAPITAL GAINS COMPONENT OF DISTRIBUTION FROM MANAGED FUNDS AND TRUST INVESTMENTS

Many managed funds and trusts hold CGT assets. During a tax year a CGT event may happen in relation to those assets resulting in a capital gain to the trust. Where this event occurs, an investor (unit holder or beneficiary) is likely to receive a trust distribution comprising the investor's share of that capital gain and this will be shown on the investor's tax statement issued by the trust.

The capital gains component of the trust distribution retains its character as it flows from the trust through to the beneficiary. The tax treatment on such items as discounted gains, other gains, indexed gains, the CGT concession amount, and tax deferred amounts is outlined at 12.605 along with the cost base reduction rules for the distribution of a non-assessable amount.

SALE OF UNITS

Where the units are not trading stock or sold as part of a profit-making undertaking, gains on the disposal of trust units may be subject to CGT (see Chapter 12) and in this instance their cost is not deductible but forms part of the cost base of the units. It may be necessary to reduce the cost base of the units for any tax-deferred amounts received (see 12.605). Where the units are trading stock or part of a profit-making undertaking, then the proceeds will be on revenue account.

17.450   FOREIGN INVESTMENT INCOME

Where foreign investment income (such as foreign dividends or the foreign income component of a trust distribution) is received, these amounts must be included in the assessable income of an Australian resident taxpayer. A non-resident taxpayer is not subject to tax on income from foreign sources, even if that foreign income has been received indirectly through an Australian trust.

NOTE: Special rules may apply where an Australian resident has a substantial interest in a foreign entity by way of an accruals regime. The rules may attribute to the taxpayer a share of specified income and gains to be included in the taxpayer's assessable income. Similar rules apply where an Australian resident taxpayer has transferred property or services to a non-resident trust estate (see 22.500).

FOREIGN INCOME TAX OFFSET

Where foreign tax has been paid on the foreign income, the investor will generally receive a credit for the foreign tax paid known as a Foreign Income Tax Offset (FITO). In some circumstances, there is a cap imposed on the amount of FITO available to taxpayers (see 22.400).

FOREIGN LOSSES

A foreign loss may be offset against Australian income (see 22.420).

17.455   MANAGED INVESTMENT SCHEMES

Managed Investment Schemes (MISs) have been a popular structure for investments in agricultural projects. Historically, taxpayers have enjoyed beneficial tax treatment with respect to contributions to MISs, even though a return on the investment was often delayed for many years. Generally, such a scheme must be registered if it has more than 20 members or it is promoted by someone in the business of promoting investment schemes. Generally, members do not have control of the day-to-day operations of the scheme.

TAX ISSUES FACING INVESTORS IN NON-FORESTRY MANAGED INVESTMENT SCHEMES

Prior to 1 July 2008, investors in MISs were generally permitted to claim upfront general deductions for lease and management fees and debt deductions to the scheme manager on the basis that the investor was conducting a business regarding the scheme. This was regardless of the fact that the investor generally had little involvement with the activities of the scheme. The Commissioner's view prior to this time was expressed in TR 2000/8 (which dealt with afforestation schemes) and applied where:

- the investor had an interest in the relevant product, and
- the manager was conducting activities in a business-like manner on the investor's behalf.

From 1 July 2008, the Tax Office reconsidered its view. As a result, it withdrew TR 2000/8 and issued its revised opinion in TR 2007/8. In this ruling, the Commissioner's revised view was that the investor's contribution to a non-forestry MIS was as a passive investor rather than the carrying on of a business. As such, the investor's contribution to non-forestry MISs would, in his opinion, generally form the first element of the cost base of a CGT asset and would not be an allowable deduction. However at this time, the Tax Office gave an undertaking to test the issue through the Courts. Note this reconsidered view did not impact forestry MISs. Special statutory provisions relating to forestry MISs were introduced with effect from 1 July 2007.

The relevant test case decision, *Hance v Commissioner of Taxation* (2008) FCAFC 196, was handed down by the Full Federal Court on 19 December 2008. The Court held that deductions were permitted for investment in an almond growing MIS on the basis that each taxpayer participant was carrying on a business. Following this decision, TR 2007/8 was withdrawn. The Commissioner decided not to seek special leave to appeal to the High Court.

 See 17.470 for the Commissioner's recent guidance regarding collapsed non-forestry MISs.

To provide protection to investors, many scheme managers will apply to the Tax Office for a 'product ruling' in relation to their particular MIS. Generally, a product ruling outlines the Commissioner's opinion as to the amount allowable as a deduction under a particular scheme, as well as other tax issues pertaining to the scheme. A product ruling is a binding public ruling that investors may rely upon. However, if the scheme actually carried out is materially different from the scheme that is described in the product ruling, it is not binding on the Commissioner and may be withdrawn. Furthermore, changes to the law will impact on the ruling.

An investor who is contemplating investing in a MIS should consult any relevant product ruling where the tax implications may affect the investor's decision.

NOTE: The Commissioner makes no comment in a product ruling as to the commercial viability of the relevant MIS. Investors should seek their own financial advice with respect to this issue.

17.460   FORESTRY MANAGED INVESTMENT SCHEMES

One type of managed investment is the forestry Managed Investment Scheme (forestry MIS). A forestry MIS is established for the purpose of establishing a plantation for the future felling and harvesting of trees. Special tax rules apply to such schemes to encourage the expansion of commercial plantation forestry in Australia through the establishment and tending of new plantations for felling.

Investors participating in a forestry MIS receive an interest in the scheme either as an initial participant (those who acquired their investment from the forestry manager of the scheme) or a secondary investor (those who acquired their investment through secondary market trading by purchasing that interest from an initial participant).

TAX ISSUES FACING INVESTORS IN FORESTRY MANAGED INVESTMENT SCHEMES

Contributions to forestry managed investment schemes

Division 394 sets out the tax treatment of contributions to forestry MISs, proceeds from harvesting trees under forestry MISs and proceeds from the sale of interests in such schemes. Investors do not need to prove that they are carrying on a business in order to claim a tax deduction for contributions to a forestry MIS. Different tax outcomes arise depending on whether the participant is an initial investor (having acquired their investment from the manager of the scheme) or a secondary investor (having purchased their investment through secondary market trading by purchasing that interest from an initial participant).

Division 394 enables initial participants to claim an immediate deduction for the contribution into the scheme, provided the scheme meets the following conditions:

- there is a reasonable expectation that at least 70% of participant contributions will be spent on 'direct forestry expenditure' on 30 June in an income year (the 70% DFE rule). Direct Forestry Expenditure (DFE) includes the costs of establishing, tending and felling trees for harvest. Specifically excluded from DFE are marketing costs, insurance, contingency funds or provisions (other than for employee entitlements), financing, lobbying, general business overheads (but not overheads directly attributable to forestry), subscriptions to industry bodies, financial planning or advisory costs including commissions, compliance fees, legal fees and auditing. The 70% DFE rule is calculated using the net present value of cash flows and market values apply

- the trees must be established within 18 months after the year the contributions were received (an extension applies to the 18 month rule for the replanting of unsuccessful seedlings), and

- initial participants retain ownership of the interest for at least **four** years.

In addition, it is necessary that the plantation under the forestry MIS is established in Australia and that the scheme manager maintains the day-to-day control over the operations.

NOTE: Even if the contribution is a prepaid amount the deduction is available in the year paid.

 If an initial investor sells their interest in a forestry MIS within four years, the deductions claimed will be denied and any relevant tax returns will require amendment. The amendment may take place up to two years after the disposal effectively extending the amendment period. The four year holding period rule under Division 394 has been amended as part of the **Tax Laws Amendment (2010 Measures No.1) Act 2010** *(see 17.470). The amendment ensures that no loss of deduction occurs where the investor ceases to hold the interest for reasons outside the control of the investor and where the investor could not have foreseen the circumstances.*

The upfront deduction will not apply to secondary investors who generally hold their interests as a capital asset with the purchase price forming part of the cost base of their investment. Any costs incurred by the secondary investor such as lease fees, annual management fees or costs of felling are deductible expenses. However, these deductions affect the CGT calculation in relation to that interest.

Even though forestry MISs are covered by specific legislation, the manager or promoter will typically apply for a product ruling in respect of the scheme. The Commissioner will make a public ruling which applies until the completion of the first clear-fell harvest of the trees. PS

LA 2008/2 outlines guidelines followed by the Tax Office before issuing a forestry MIS product ruling.

Shareholdings in forestry companies or unitholdings in a forestry unit trust are not investments in forestry MISs. Investments of these types are capital acquisitions that fall outside the scope of Division 394.

Proceeds from forestry managed investment schemes

The tax treatment under Division 394 for income relating to forestry MISs will differ for initial investors and secondary investors. The income received by an initial investor is on revenue account, typically including sale or harvest proceeds and the disposal of their interest in the scheme to a secondary investor.

Income received by the secondary investor will generally be treated as a capital receipt. However, an exception is income received from the harvest of immature trees (thinning) which will be a revenue receipt for both the initial and secondary investor.

Disposal of a forestry scheme interest by a secondary investor will be treated as assessable income, but only to the extent that the proceeds represent the value of (or 'match') deductions obtained for ongoing contributions (in relation to lease fees, annual management fees or costs of felling for example). As the initial purchase of a secondary interest is on capital account for most investors (assuming the interest is held as a capital asset), the proceeds would also be capital account, only modified to the extent that some deductions have been claimed on revenue account. This means that harvest proceeds received by a secondary investor may have a revenue and a capital component. Where the sale proceeds are less than the deductions claimed, the proceeds are fully assessable.

Further, the CGT rules are modified to ensure the rules apply appropriately when secondary investors return some of the proceeds received as assessable income.

17.470   CHANGES FOR FORESTRY MANAGED INVESTMENT SCHEMES

Changes were made to key tax rules for MISs in order to protect investors in the collapsed schemes from unintended adverse tax outcomes. These changes have retrospective application from 1 July 2007.

Before the changes, for an initial investor in a forestry MIS to claim a deduction under Division 394, the four year holding period rule requires that a CGT event does not happen in relation to the investor's forestry interest within four years after the end of the income year in which an amount is first incurred by the investor.

The amendments ensure that failing the four year rule does not lead to the denial of a previously allowed deduction, where:

* a CGT event happens because of circumstances genuinely outside the initial investor's control, and
* the initial investor could not have reasonably anticipated this CGT event happening, at the time they acquired the forestry interest.

Situations that could be genuinely outside the initial investor's control include:

* the accidental death of the initial investor
* the interest in the scheme being compulsorily transferred, because of marriage breakdown or compulsory acquisition by a government
* the initial investor becoming insolvent
* the interest in the scheme being cancelled, because of trees being destroyed by fire, flood or drought, and
* the insolvency of the manager of the scheme, leading to the winding up of the scheme.

NOTE: Events that could not have been anticipated are defined by the legislation as events that could not have been anticipated by a reasonable person with knowledge of the relevant circumstances.

CHANGES FOR NON-FORESTRY MISs

The Commissioner provided guidance to affected MIS participants with the issue of three Taxation Determinations (TDs) in relation to non-forestry MISs which deal with:

- TD 2010/7: when a change of 'responsible entity' for the MIS activities occurs
- TD 2010/8: the impact of a termination of an MIS on deductions which have previously been allowed, and
- TD 2010/9: the treatment of monies received by a participant on winding up an MIS.

17.500 SPECIALISED INVESTMENT PRODUCTS

Investment products have become increasingly complex and specialised over recent decades. The following paragraphs outline a range of specialised products available in the market, including contracts for difference, stapled securities, traditional securities and warrants. Taxpayers investing in these products may require specialist investment and taxation advice.

17.510   CONTRACTS FOR DIFFERENCE

A Contract For Difference (CFD) is a high-risk speculative investment from which investors make a profit or loss on the price movement of underlying financial assets without owning those assets. CFDs typically relate to shares, but are also used for share price indices, commodity prices, interest rates, currencies and futures contracts. Under such a contract, the investor takes a position that the underlying share price, for example, will or will not exceed a given price at some time in the future.

The CFD holder may take a short position, a long position or both. A short position is taken where the CFD holder believes the value of the underlying assets will fall. A long position is taken where the CFD holder believes the value will increase. The investor receives or pays the difference in price of the underlying security multiplied by the number of units between the time the CFD contract opens and closes.

If the investor makes a gain, the provider pays the investor an amount equal to the gain. Conversely, if the investor makes a loss, the investor pays the amount of the loss to the provider.

 CFDs are leveraged instruments. This means that a CFD holder is fully exposed to price movements of the underlying instrument without having to pay the full price of that instrument. CFDs therefore have the potential to incur a larger loss than the holder's initial outlay.

17.520   TAX ISSUES FOR HOLDERS OF CONTRACTS FOR DIFFERENCES

In TR 2005/15, the Commissioner states that income received from CFDs will be classified in accordance with the activity that produced the receipt. TR 2005/15 makes it clear that the Commissioner will treat the following types of income from a CFD as follows:

- where a transaction is entered into as an ordinary incident of carrying on a business, or in a business operation or commercial transaction for the purpose of profit making: a gain from a CFD is assessable as ordinary income under s6-5 ITAA97, and a loss is allowable as a deduction under s8-1 ITAA97
- where a CFD is entered into in carrying out a profit-making scheme or plan: a gain from a CFD is assessable on the capital account as statutory income under s15-15 ITAA97 and the loss is an allowable deduction under s25-40 ITAA97, and
- from a gambling or recreational pursuit: not assessable if the gain or loss arose.

Generally, a CFD would be entered into as a business transaction or profit making scheme. However, the Commissioner states in TR 2005/15 that where the CFD is not entered into with a purpose of business or profit-making, it is likely that the purpose with which it is entered into will be as an unusual form of recreational gambling. On that basis, no capital gain or loss would arise due to the gambling exemption in s118-37(1)(c) ITAA97. However, the Commissioner has given an undertaking to test this issue (termed 'spread betting') through a suitable test case being placed before the Administrative Appeals Tribunal or a Court.

CONTRACTS FOR DIFFERENCE-RELATED INTERESTS AND DIVIDENDS

Interest is calculated on contracts that remain open at the end of each day. Holders of CFDs pay interest on open buy contracts and receive interest on open sell contracts. Typically these amounts will be taxable as ordinary assessable income and an allowable deduction available for any interest paid.

Other revenue amounts may arise by certain events occurring in respect of the underlying shares, such as the share going ex-dividend, bonus shares issue and rights issues. CFD holders pay an amount equivalent to the cash dividend declared on sell contracts that were open prior to the day the underlying shares go ex-dividend. Conversely, investors receive an amount equivalent to the cash dividend declared on buy contracts that were open prior to the day the underlying shares go ex-dividend.

17.520   STAPLED SECURITIES

A stapled security combines at least two securities, typically a company share and a trust unit, which are contractually bound together as a single entity and cannot be sold separately. While the stapled security can only be bought or sold as a single unit, the investor maintains the rights and obligations attached to each individual security. Income received may include both a dividend and a trust distribution. If the dividend is paid by an Australian company, the dividend is frankable and a franking credit offset may be available to Australian resident taxpayers. Where the dividend or distribution is paid from a non-Australian company or trust, the amount will be treated as foreign income.

Stapling of securities is not limited to companies and trusts interests. Other securities such as convertible notes and preference shares have also been traded as a stapled security.

17.525   TAX ISSUES FACING INVESTORS IN STAPLED SECURITIES

DISTRIBUTIONS ON STAPLED SECURITIES

Investors can receive at the one time separate payments for dividends and trust distributions paid on the interests in the companies and unit trusts underlying the stapled securities. These components retain their separate legal character for tax purposes and must be recorded and reported separately. The company dividend component is assessed in the tax year received whereas the trust distribution is assessed on an accruals basis in the income year it relates to. It can be quite common for a stapled security to have an underlying company dividend and trust distribution taxed in separate income years.

Trust distributions may include a tax deferred component which is not subject to tax. The annual tax statement will state the tax deferred amount included in the trust distribution. This amount must be used to reduce the cost base of any units held in the trust, therefore impacting the calculation of any capital gain or loss on units on a subsequent disposal.

DISPOSAL OF STAPLED SECURITIES

Capital gains or losses on the disposal of stapled securities are treated separately for each of the underlying securities. The CGT consequences are calculated by apportioning the purchase costs and sale proceeds to each underlying company and/or trust holding. This allocation should be made on a reasonable basis. Calculating the cost base of each underlying security will include:

- the value of the original securities
- the value of any securities received via the reinvestment of income, and
- where applicable, a reduction of the cost base for the tax-deferred component of any trust distribution received.

Once this allocation has been made, the usual CGT rules will apply to the disposal of the components of a stapled security.

Scrip for scrip roll-over relief may be available to allow a shareholder to disregard a capital gain where a share is disposed of as part of a corporate takeover or merger and the shareholder receives a replacement share in exchange. Where shares are exchanged for stapled securities comprising shares and units, scrip for scrip rollover is only available to the extent that the shareholder receives replacement shares.

Refer TA 2008/1 warning taxpayers with respect to certain stapled securities involving notes and preference shares.

17.530   TRADITIONAL SECURITIES

For tax purposes, a traditional security includes certain securities acquired by the taxpayer after 10 May 1989. 'Securities' for these purposes include stocks, bonds, debentures, certificates of entitlement, bills of exchange, promissory notes, bank or financial institution deposits and secured or unsecured loans. Generally, it is required that a traditional security must not have an eligible return unless two further conditions are satisfied:

- the precise amount of the eligible return must be ascertainable at the time of issue, and

- the security must not be issued at a discount of greater than 1.5% multiplied by the number of years, including fractions of a year, of the term of the security.

Further, a traditional security must not bear deferred interest and must not be capital indexed.

NOTE: A unit in a property or cash management public trust is not a security. Intercompany loans where there are deposits and withdrawals fall within the definition of a security.

17.535   TAX ISSUES OF HOLDERS OF TRADITIONAL SECURITIES

GAINS OR LOSSES ON THE DISPOSAL OF TRADITIONAL SECURITIES

Gains and losses on the disposal of 'traditional securities' acquired after 10 May 1989 are taxed under special rules (s26BB, s70B ITAA36).

A gain made on the disposal or redemption of a traditional security is included in assessable income under s26BB in the income year in which the disposal or redemption takes place. Section 70B provides that a loss on disposal or redemption of a traditional security may be an allowable deduction in the income year in which the disposal or redemption takes place. Note that the issuer's gain or loss on redemption is not assessable under s26BB or deductible under s70B as these provisions only affect holders of traditional securities.

When the disposal of traditional securities is for non-cash consideration (such as shares), the consideration is deemed to be the market value of the property given (s21 ITAA36).

NOTE: Death of a traditional security holder is not a disposal of that security. A disposal occurs when the executor or beneficiary disposes of the security.

CALCULATION OF THE GAIN OR LOSS ON TRADITIONAL SECURITIES

The gain or loss on disposal or redemption is calculated as the difference between any consideration received on disposal or redemption and the acquisition cost plus relevant costs of acquisition or disposal. Unlike the CGT rules, there is no indexation of the cost of the security or discount of the gain. The gain on partial disposal or redemption of the traditional security would be calculated on a proportional basis.

 A traditional security was acquired on 15 August 2015 for $10,000. A 50% interest was sold for $6,000 in the current year of income. $1,000 is assessable in the current year calculated as $6,000 less 50% of $10,000.

Refer TA 2008/1 warning taxpayers with respect to certain stapled securities involving notes and preference shares.

REMOVAL OF THE TAXING POINT ON CONVERSION OR EXCHANGE OF CERTAIN TRADITIONAL SECURITIES

Section 26BB and s70B ITAA36 will not apply when a traditional security converts or exchanges into ordinary shares where the traditional securities were issued after 7.30 pm, legal time in the Australian Capital Territory, on 14 May 2002. This means there will be no taxing point or no deduction allowable for a gain or loss when a traditional security converts or exchanges into ordinary shares.

The holder of the interest that is exchanged into shares of a company acquires the shares when the exchange of the interest happens. For the purpose of the CGT discount in Subdivision 115-A

ITAA97, the period of ownership of a share acquired on exchange commences when the share is acquired on exchange, not when the original security is purchased.

NOTE: This does not apply where traditional securities convert or exchange into interests other than ordinary shares.

A taxpayer in year 1 acquires on issue an exchangeable note for $100 which has a face value of $100. The interest is acquired on 1 July 2013. The exchangeable interest has a term of five years, subject to the holder's annual option to exchange it into one ordinary share. In each of the years the exchangeable interest is not exchanged the taxpayer will receive $5 interest income. The exchangeable note is a traditional security and is an exchangeable interest under s130-100 of the ITAA97.

At the beginning of year 3, the taxpayer exchanges the interest for a share with a market value of $110.

Due to the application of s26BB(5) of ITAA36, the gain of $10 is not included in the taxpayer's assessable income at the time of exchange. There will be no need to avoid double taxation occurring on the eventual sale of the share because there is no taxing point in relation to disposal of the share prior to that time. Accordingly, when working out the first element of the cost base of the share there is no need to increase the cost base by an amount that has reduced a capital gain made on the exchangeable interest. The exchange of the interest leads to the taxpayer making a capital gain (even though the capital gain is disregarded).

Subsection 118-20(1) of ITAA97 does not reduce that capital gain because there is no s26BB ITAA36 amount.

As a result, the first element of the cost base of the share would be $100. This is the $100 purchase price of the exchangeable interest (assuming this is the cost base of the interest at the time of conversion).

The $5 interest the taxpayer receives annually on the exchangeable interest does not form part of the cost base of the share. This is because s118-20 does not reduce the capital gain by those amounts.

If the taxpayer then sells the share for $120, the taxpayer will have a capital gain of $20.

NOTE: Forgiveness or waiver of a debt is not a disposal of a traditional security for traditional security purposes (s70B(5)) (see 14.400).

A loss is not deductible when disposals or redemptions occur because of the issuer's financial difficulties. When a security was previously issued by an insolvent company, a disposal does not occur under s70(B) when a traditional security matures. A disposal only occurs when the issuer redeems the securities (via a Court-approved scheme or otherwise) at a loss. A traditional security issued by a company that has gone into liquidation is not disposed of when the liquidator has made a final payment to the holder of the security or where no payments are to be made by the liquidator.

Section 110-55 ITAA97 operates to modify the reduced cost base of a security by any capital loss deductible under s70B. Note that a loss incurred on the waiver or release of a debt classified as a traditional security does not give rise to a deduction.

INTEREST DERIVED ON A TRADITIONAL SECURITY

Interest derived on a traditional security is assessable to the holder as ordinary income under s6-5. It is not affected by the operation of s26BB.

17.540   WARRANTS

Instalment warrants are a geared lending product offered by certain institutions which allow an investor to take an interest in underlying assets, such as listed shares. Investors pay some of the cost upfront, and take the balance of the asset price as a loan which is limited recourse (for example, if the share value falls the investor does not suffer the loss). The underlying assets are held in trust until the investor pays out the warrant or exercises an option to buy the asset at the higher of the loan balance or the current market price of the asset. The investor is entitled to receive the income from the underlying asset (eg. dividends on the shares).

Alternatively, the investor may roll-over the warrant and not change the underlying asset, or do nothing in which case the asset is sold without recourse to the investor if the sale proceeds do not meet the outstanding debt. The warrant may be accessed by cash application to the issuing institution (eg. about 50% of the share price up-front), by application by certain holders of existing shares or by investors rolling over earlier instalment warrants.

17.545   TAX ISSUES FACED BY INVESTORS IN WARRANTS

DEDUCTIBILITY OF INTEREST

Interest under the loan component of a warrant is generally tax-deductible for amounts pre-paid for up to 12 months (non-business individual investors), provided the interest period ends by the last day of the income year following the expenditure year and the dominant purpose of the investor in entering the arrangement is to derive assessable income from the investment (eg. dividends on shares).

CGT ISSUES

CGT is also relevant. The part of the purchase price which relates to purchasing the right to sell the asset back to the issuer (the 'put option') can form part of the cost base of the relevant underlying asset (eg. the shares) if the option is exercised and the asset is sold back (see Chapter 12). The cost base of the underlying asset is adjusted to remove the amount of any shortfall on the loan amount which the investor does not have to repay. If the put option expires without being exercised, a capital loss is made equivalent to the option fee.

The tax implications may also be different if the investor is a trader or not an Australian resident. Dealings between the investor and the institution must also be at arm's length.

17.550   FINANCIAL ARRANGEMENTS FROM 1 JULY 2010 (OR 1 JULY 2009 BY ELECTION)

Division 230 of the ITAA97 contains stages 3 and 4 of the Taxation of Financial Arrangements (TOFA 3 and 4) measures.

The purpose of this Division is to provide consistent taxation treatment of financial arrangements. The law defines a 'financial arrangement' and sets out different methods for bringing gains and losses on financial arrangements to account for tax purposes. Under the Division 230 rules, the gains from financial arrangements are generally assessable and losses are generally deductible on **revenue account on an accrual basis**.

Division 230 applies to financial arrangements entered into on or after 1 July 2010 (or 1 July 2009 by election).

A financial arrangement for these purposes is defined as a cash settleable right to receive, or an obligation to provide, a financial benefit which exists under an arrangement. The right or obligation will be cash settleable where the financial benefit is money or a money equivalent. Arrangements commonly coming within the definition of 'financial arrangement' include bank deposits, bonds, convertible notes and loans.

Generally, individuals are excluded from the rules, as are other entities that meet certain thresholds (that is superannuation entities or MISs with less than $100 million in assets, financial sector entities with less than $20 million aggregated turnover or other entities with:

- aggregated turnover of less than $100 million
- financial assets less than $100 million, and
- total assets of less than $300 million.

Individuals and SMEs can elect to have the TOFA rules apply. Once this election is made, it is irrevocable. As such, the benefits and disadvantages should be weighed by individuals and SMEs before committing to the TOFA regime.

However, where a financial arrangement is a qualifying security (as defined in Division 16E) of more than 12 months duration, the above taxpayers will not be excluded. The types of securities which may be a qualifying security include:

- a stock, a bond, debenture, certificate of entitlement, bill of exchange, promissory note or other security

- a deposit with a bank or other financial institution
- a secured or unsecured loan, or
- any other contract, whether or not in writing, under which a person is liable to pay an amount or amounts, whether or not the liability is secured.

17.600 COMMON DEDUCTIONS ALLOWABLE TO INVESTORS

To be deductible, a loss or outgoing must be incurred in gaining or producing assessable income or in carrying on a business for the purpose of gaining or producing assessable income. Further, the expenditure cannot be private expenditure or capital in nature. A general checklist is set out at 13.000. See also 18.000 (rental properties).

Discussed below are some of the typical deductions issues on losses or outgoings incurred by investors.

17.610   BORROWING COSTS

Borrowing costs may be claimed on certain loans for an income-producing purpose. Typically, borrowing costs include legal expenses on preparing and filing mortgage documents, loan establishment fees, mortgage insurance, stamp duty on mortgage documents, title search and valuation fees charged by the lender, mortgage broker fees and other costs on the taking out of the loan. If the costs are greater than $100, the deduction is spread over the lesser of the term of the loan or five years. See 14.135.

17.615   CAPITAL PROTECTED LOANS – INTEREST AND FEES

A capital protected borrowing is usually a limited recourse loan facility to fund the purchase of listed shares, units in a unit trust or managed fund or stapled securities. Typically, investors are protected from a fall in the price of the shares as the investor has the right to transfer the shares back to the lender for the outstanding balance on the loan. This means that should the asset value fall below the principal, a portion of the principal does not have to be repaid. Instalment warrants are a form of capital protected borrowing. Capital protected loans generally attract a fee for capital protection or a higher rate of interest.

Generally, the treatment of capital protected products or borrowings is dependent upon whether the investor entered into or extended the arrangement before 9.30am on 16 April 2003, between 9.30am on 16 April 2003 and 30 June 2007, between 1 July 2007 and 7.30pm 13 May 2008 and arrangements entered into after 7:30pm 13 May 2008. Note that Division 247 ITAA97 was amended to establish a benchmark interest rate based on Reserve Bank of Australia indicator lending rates.

See 13.600 for a detailed summary of tax treatment of capital protected loans, their entering time and adjusted appropriate benchmark interest rates.

17.620   DEPRECIATION

Certain items of equipment or other assets used to produce assessable income may be depreciated, such as the computer and software used to manage an investment portfolio. This means a gradual claim is made for these items over their effective lives or low-value pooling may be available (see 15.040). See 15.160 for listed items.

17.625   DISCHARGE OF MORTGAGE EXPENSES

The costs involved in discharging a mortgage are deductible where the mortgage was security for the repayment of money borrowed to produce assessable income. Amounts may include penalty interest for early repayment of a loan (see 14.140).

17.630 HOME OFFICE EXPENSES

A portion of home office running costs can be claimed where a distinct part of a home is used for income-production. The Commissioner will accept diary records covering a representative four week period as establishing a pattern of use for the entire year. As an alternative to claiming the actual costs incurred, the Commissioner also accepts a claim of 34 cents per hour for heating, cooling, lighting and decline in value of furniture (see PS LA 2001/6). The decline in value of office equipment such as computers is calculated separately.

Occupancy expenses (such as rent, mortgage interest, rates and insurance) cannot be claimed unless a portion of the home is set aside as a place of business. Generally, mere investors will be unable to satisfy this requirement.

NOTE: Where a property or a portion of the property is occupied as a main residence but also used for income producing purposes, the full main residence exemption may not be available.

17.635 INTEREST DEDUCTIONS

Interest may be claimed as a deduction in certain cases when the loan funds were applied to income-producing purposes. This means the loan must have been used in a genuine attempt to produce assessable income (eg. purchase of a rental property, purchase of income-producing shares or purchase of a business). Interest cannot be claimed if the relevant property was owned prior to the loan, unless other circumstances exist allowing deductibility (such as a company borrower using the borrowed funds to maintain business working capital). It should be reasonable to expect at the time the borrowed funds are first used, that the use will generate assessable income. If borrowed funds are merely used to generate the same or a lower rate of interest as is being paid to the lender (eg. on-lending to a friend or relative at a discounted rate), then deductions are limited to the amount of income actually produced. See generally 14.130 and 14.190.

Note that the deductibility of compound interest is determined according to the same principles as the deductibility of other interest (TD 2008/27).

17.640 INTEREST ON A LINE OF CREDIT

A line of credit is a borrowing facility which allows the borrower to draw on funds up to an agreed limit. If interest is paid on a mixed purpose line of credit (that is for both income producing and non-income producing purposes), the deductibility of interest is determined by considering the purpose of each drawdown. Where funds are repaid and then redrawn, the new application of that drawdown must be considered to determine the deductibility of interest. This requires taxpayers with many mixed purpose drawdowns to keep accurate records of the use of the funds to determine interest deductibility. Any principal repayments are applied proportionately to outstanding balances at that time of amounts applied to both deductible and non-deductible purposes.

17.645 INTEREST ON LINKED SPLIT LOANS AND OFFSET ACCOUNT FACILITY

LINKED LOAN

A linked loan is a credit facility taken out with a financial institution under which there are two or more loans with an account being maintained in respect of each loan. A split loan is a credit facility taken out with a financial institution under which there is one loan with sub-accounts being maintained in respect of that loan. A linked or split loan facility allows investors to combine a home loan and an investment loan, for example, under one umbrella facility with two or more loans or sub-accounts. Under such a facility, payments may be made to different loan or sub-accounts on a combined basis. Often, one loan account relates to private uses (eg. a private residence) and the other to income-producing use.

Where the arrangement is structured in a manner similar to that in *FC of T v Hart* (2004) HCA 26, where interest on a debt used for income producing purposes was capitalised whilst available cash was applied to reduce the amount of a loan used for private purposes, Part IVA may be applied to deny interest deductions.

LOAN ACCOUNT OFFSET FACILITY

Commonly referred to as a 'dual account facility', the borrower typically operates two accounts:

- a loan account, and
- a deposit account.

There is no entitlement, either in law or in equity, to receive interest payments or payments in the nature of interest on the amounts credited to the deposit account. The reduction in the loan account interest should be achieved by offsetting the balances of the two accounts.

As a general rule, the Commissioner considers that a taxpayer with an acceptable loan account offset arrangement with dual accounts is entitled to claim a deduction for the full amount of interest whilst the loan is used wholly for income producing purposes.

Any reduction to the interest payable would typically not be assessable as no amount of interest has been received or credited to the borrower. In a number of private rulings (see PBR 80150, 19859), the Commissioner accepts that interest deductions will continue to remain fully deductible if funds are withdrawn from the 'deposit account' and used for income producing purposes.

The Commissioner's rationale for this position is that:

- depositing funds into the deposit account will decrease the interest payable on the loan account but will not decrease of the balance of the loan account, and
- withdrawing funds from the deposit account will increase the interest payable on the loan account but again, will not impact the loan account balance.

17.650 NEGATIVE GEARING/MARGIN LENDING

A negatively geared investment is one purchased with the assistance of borrowed funds where the net investment income is less than the interest on the borrowings such that a net investment loss arises. Current year income losses arising from the negative gearing of investment income can be offset against other current year income. Where current year income is insufficient to fully use the investment losses, income losses may be carried forward to be offset against future income. See 14.190.

17.655 PREPAID EXPENSES

A prepaid expense is expenditure incurred in respect of a later income year. Small business entity taxpayers (see 10.700) or individuals incurring deductible non-business expenditure can claim an immediate deduction for prepaid expenses such as interest where the payment is incurred for an eligible service period not exceeding 12 months and the eligible service period ends in the following income year. Certain types of expenditure are excluded from the prepayment rules and will be deductible when incurred. These include amounts of less than $1,000, amounts required to be incurred by a law or by an order of a Court and payments of salary or wages (under a contract of service).

17.670 STAMP DUTY

Stamp duty is a State tax on certain transactions such as real estate and motor vehicle transfers (see Chapters 27 and 28.). Stamp duty is deductible in certain instances (eg. stamping leases on income-producing property). Where not deductible it may in some cases be added to the cost base of CGT assets (see 12.094).

17.675 TAX ADVICE

A deduction may be claimed for items such as the fees of recognised tax advisers including the costs of travel, meals and accommodation to obtain such tax services.

17.680 TELEPHONE, COMPUTER, INTERNET EXPENSES

A portion of these costs may be claimed as a deduction to the extent that they are associated with producing assessable income. The Commissioner will accept diary records covering a representative four week period as establishing a pattern of use for the entire year.

However, costs of installing telephone or broadband connections are capital in nature and not deductible (see 13.155).

17.700 COMMON MISTAKES

Taxpayers should take care when completing tax returns to ensure that the income and deductions are recorded correctly. Errors in the return may lead to an underpayment of tax and trigger a general interest charge.

Listed below are some common mistakes made by investors when preparing their income tax returns:

- Cash management trust income is often declared in the income tax return as interest rather than a trust distribution. Cash management trusts distribute net income in the same manner as other trusts. A statement should be obtained at year end from the financial service provider indicating the gross distribution and any management fees deducted attributable to the tax year (see 11.730).

- Listed investment trust dividends often include a LIC capital gain. A deduction is available to investors that have access to the CGT discount rate. The deduction is equal to 50% of the capital gain for individuals and trusts and 33 1/3% for superannuation funds (see 12.165).

- Trust distributions often record the taxable distribution on the annual tax statement using the 50% CGT discount. However the statement may not accurately reflect the taxpayer's investment structure and period of ownership. Make sure that:
  - the taxpayer has held the asset for at least 12 months
  - the taxpayer is eligible to use the 50% CGT discount rate, and
  - the capital gain is grossed up in the tax return before the discount is applied.

Those who receive franked distributions often fail to consider the 'holding period rule' when determining their entitlement to franking credits.

Taxpayers often incorrectly apply the 'small shareholder exemption' to entities other than individuals when determining eligibility to franking credits, and investors often fail to adjust the cost base of their units in a unit trust or managed fund for tax deferred distributions received.

17.800 INVESTMENT STRUCTURES

Investors are usually able to choose an investment structure that is appropriate to their circumstances. This may be through investment as an individual, partnership, company, trust or complying superannuation fund. Each of these structures has advantages and disadvantages from both a tax and commercial perspective.

The tax characteristics of investment entities such as companies, trusts and partnerships are contained in Chapter 9 - *Comparison of structures*.

17.900 OTHER TAXATION ISSUES

Other tax issues facing those in receipt of investment income are listed below.

AGGRESSIVE TAX PLANNING

While certain strategies are effective in minimising a tax liability, the Tax Office may deny a deduction for aggressive tax planning arrangements designed specifically to obtain a tax deduction.

PS LA 2008/15 indicates that existence of the following features in a tax planning scheme are of concern:

- improper creation of deductions, increasing credits or offsets, reduction or deferral of income or capital gains and circumventing withholding tax
- suppression or deliberate understatement of income
- contrivance and artificiality in the method of execution

- little or no real underlying business activity or purpose
- the claimed tax benefit may be significant in realising an economic return
- complete or substantial removal of any risk to a taxpayer
- limited or non-recourse financing associated with a round-robin flow of funds
- little cash outlay associated with borrowing of funds under a capitalising debt facility
- a mechanism for winding up or exiting an arrangement before net income is generated for an investor
- assumptions, including 'blue sky' projections, that can lead to seemingly excessive valuations of assets for example, resulting in inflated deduction claims
- use of tax-exempt entities, especially charities, to wash income
- transactions involving tax havens
- use of superannuation funds for purposes other than superannuation benefits
- interposed entities which have no substantial commercial rationale except to create a tax benefit, and
- transactions which do not appear to be legitimate business dealings.

FOREIGN TAX ISSUES

In some instances, investments by residents in one country made in another country may be taxed in both countries (subject to any Double Tax Agreement between the relevant countries). To prevent double taxation, Australian taxpayers are entitled to claim a non-refundable foreign income tax offset for foreign tax paid on an amount included in their assessable income. From 1 July 2008, the tax offset is limited to the lesser of foreign income tax paid and the 'foreign tax offset cap'. The cap is calculated by determining the Australian tax payable on the taxpayer's double-taxed amounts and other foreign income. As an alternative to calculating the cap, the taxpayer can choose to use a $1,000 minimum cap (see 22.400).

GOODS AND SERVICES TAX

Share traders are generally not required to register for GST. Although share traders are carrying on an enterprise because GST turnover is defined to exclude input taxed supplies (generally share sales are input taxed), the requirement to register will only exist if taxable supplies from other sources exceed the $75,000 threshold. Where an enterprise is being carried on, an investor can register for GST voluntarily where the registration threshold is not met. However, there may be limits on the refund of input tax credits for financial supplies (see 23.310).

LOSSES

Current year income losses arising from the negative gearing of investment income can generally be offset against other current year income. If current year income is insufficient to fully use the investment losses, income losses may be carried forward to be offset against future income subject to loss rules (ie. trust, company). Capital losses may only be offset against capital gains. If there is insufficient capital gain in a year to absorb a capital loss, the excess capital loss may also be carried forward and used by the taxpayer in later years. See 13.950 and 6.400-6.500.

These will not be quarantined into separate classes nor will they be quarantined from domestic assessable income (see 22.420).

NON-RESIDENT WITHHOLDING

Non-residents are not required to provide a TFN to investment bodies as TFN withholding rules do not apply. However, they will need to advise the investment body that they are a non-resident.

Non-residents are subject to non-resident withholding tax on specified types of income. Withholding tax is payable on interest, unfranked dividends, royalties or fund payments to non-resident unitholders of managed funds. Generally the payer is responsible for withholding, reporting and remitting the amounts to the Tax Office (see 22.140).

PARTIES NOT DEALING AT ARM'S LENGTH

If not dealing with each other on an arm's length basis, the Tax Office can substitute an arm's length price (eg. market value). If there is no available market value, a discounted cash flow analysis is used to determine losses.

PAYG INSTALMENTS

Investors and traders are subject to the PAYG instalment system.

RECORDS AND SUBSTANTIATION OF EXPENSES

Taxpayers are required to keep records for taxation purposes for five years. Typically the records to be retained include receipts, accounts, property records and other documents which relate to assessable income (eg. PAYG payment summaries, interest and dividend statements). Failure to keep records may attract a penalty from the Tax Office (refer PS LA 2005/2).

TAX FILE NUMBER

Australian taxpayers in receipt of investment income who lodge returns with the Tax Office are allocated a TFN. See 5.000.

Non-resident investors from a country that has a double tax agreement with Australia will have withholding tax deducted at the applicable tax rate which is typically lower than for residents of a country with which Australia has no double tax agreement. An Australian TFN is not required if the investment income relates to interest, dividends or royalties or certain managed fund distributions. Non-residents in receipt of this type of income do not usually prepare an Australian tax return. This differs from investments in other types of income, such as income from real property where a TFN and tax return are required.

TAX FILE NUMBER WITHHOLDING

Investment bodies such as banks are required to withhold tax from investment earnings where the taxpayer does not quote a TFN or Australian Business Number. See 5.315.

TFN withholding tax is refundable on provision of a valid TFN or on lodgement of the income tax return.

NOTE: Closely-held trusts (including a family trust) need to withhold amounts from trust distributions at the top marginal tax rate where beneficiaries have not provided a TFN to the trustee by the time of the entitlement. The trustee is required to report to the Tax Office the TFN details of beneficiaries who become presently entitled to trust income.

TAX RULINGS

Class and product rulings are issued in respect of certain schemes. Generally, a product ruling describes a managed investment scheme and indicates the tax implications including the amount allowable as a deduction. A class ruling provides information about the tax consequences for corporate events such as employee share schemes, corporate restructures or scrip for scrip rollovers and events concerning government authorities.

Typically, a class or product ruling is a public ruling that investors may rely upon. However, if the scheme actually carried out is materially different from the scheme that is described in the ruling it is not binding on the Commissioner and may be withdrawn. Furthermore, changes to the law will impact on the ruling and take precedence over the ruling.

 Investors should seek advice to ensure that a particular arrangement is covered by a class or product ruling before investing in a scheme.

WASH SALES

A wash sale is an arrangement in which essentially the same asset is sold and immediately repurchased or where an asset is sold to an associated taxpayer such as a spouse or family trust so that, broadly, the investor's economic position is unchanged. Where the dominant purpose of a 'wash sale' is to crystallise a capital loss, the Tax Office indicates in Taxation Ruling TR 2008/1 that Part IVA may be applied to deny a deduction for the loss.

Rental property

18

18.000 RENTAL PROPERTY

Investing in a rental property has taxation implications. The rental income and any capital gain on disposal are assessable income. Financing and ongoing maintenance costs are generally deductible. Residential rent is input taxed for GST purposes whilst commercial rental income is subject to GST where the owner is required to be registered for GST. For the impact of GST on rent see 18.600 and 23.330.

All legislative references are to the *Income Tax Assessment Act 1997* (ITAA97) unless otherwise stated.

18.100 ASSESSABLE INCOME

GROSS RENT

Rental income is usually assessable under s6-5 as ordinary income. Where a taxpayer (a person, company or trust) owns one or more rental properties, whether by themselves or with others, they are usually regarded as investors. However, if substantial rental property interests are owned by the taxpayer, it is possible that the Tax Office will accept that there is a rental business being carried on. It would be unwise for a taxpayer to treat their rental activity as being a business without receiving suitable professional advice or a private binding ruling from the Tax Office.

If the taxpayer is not considered to be carrying on a rental business, rental income is generally assessed on a cash basis, ie. in the year of receipt. Where an estate agent manages the property, the rental income received by the agent during the year is assessable to the landlord in that year, not when the rent statement is received.

If the property is owned by more than one person, rental income and expenses must be proportionally attributed to each co-owner according to their legal ownership interest in the property, despite any agreement between co-owners, either orally or in writing (TR 93/32).

For example, taxpayers generally own properties as either (see *Joint Ownership*):

- **joint tenants** (ie. there is a right of survivorship), they each hold an equal interest in the property, or
- **tenants-in-common** where they may hold unequal interests in the property – for example, one may hold a 20% interest and the other an 80% interest.

If the property is held as joint tenants, then the net income, or loss, will be split equally according to the number of owners. Such an arrangement is typically referred to as a tax law partnership, and in these circumstances the owners cannot agree to an apportionment of income on a basis different to that of the ownership interests.

 Ned and Narelle own a rental property as joint tenants. Each will be entitled to and must declare as assessable income 50% of the gross income and will claim 50% of the deductions relating to the property. If Ned and Narelle sold an interest to their daughter Nell, the percentage would become 33.33% each.

 Mary and her partner John and Carol and her partner Dave, decide to invest in a rental property and buy a $1 million house which they believe will be easily rented to foreign companies. Mary and Carol are able to invest $400,000 each, and John and Dave each invest $100,000. The investment is to be held as tenants in common. On the certificate of title, Mary and Carol are each registered as having a 40% interest and John and Dave 10% each. Income and expenses will be attributable to each party on the basis of their percentage of ownership interest.

Other rental-related income includes:

- compensation for lost rent (eg. an insurance payment)
- reimbursements or recoupments, for example:
    - a reimbursement by a tenant for the cost of repairs to a property or s15-25 amounts received from a tenant for failure to comply with a lease obligation to repair (provided the property was used by the tenant to produce assessable income)

- a government rebate for the purchase of a depreciating asset, such as a solar hot-water system
- lease surrender receipt
- lease premium receipt, and
- rental bond amounts returned to compensate for damages or lost rent.

Depending on whether or not the taxpayer is considered to be conducting a business, receipts such as those for a lease surrender may be ordinary income or a capital gain. For more information see TR 2005/6.

BOND MONEY LODGED BY TENANT

A residential tenancy bond is not 'income' and refunds cannot therefore be claimed as a deduction. If part of the bond is retained for, say, repairs or cleaning, the amount kept must be returned as income in the year retained and a deduction claimed for relevant expenditure when incurred.

CAPITAL GAIN FROM A CGT EVENT IN RESPECT OF THE PROPERTY

If a CGT event occurs in respect of rental property acquired after 19 September 1985 and the capital proceeds exceed its cost base, a capital gain will arise. Capital losses may be offset against the gain, and where the property has been owned by a person for at least 12 months, a CGT discount may be available (see 12.165). The net amount of capital gain (calculated in accordance with each co-owners interest in the property) is then included in the taxpayer's assessable income (see 12.000).

NOTE: A foreign resident cannot access the CGT discount accrued after 8 May 2012.

For details of the elements that make up the cost base see 12.092 and 12.094.

CAPITAL GAINS TAX TIPS

- Keep records of every circumstance or event that may be relevant to working out capital gains or losses. Records must be kept for at least five years. If the CGT event relates to a disposal of property, then the records must be kept from the date of acquisition up to the date of sale and then for five years after the relevant time (eg. after the last CGT event in respect of the asset).
- If appropriate, consider delaying CGT events until the next income year in order to delay the derivation of assessable income.
- Keep records of other matters which may be relevant to calculating capital gains and losses, such as capital allowance deductions.
- If a capital gain has been crystallised, consider realising capital losses in the same year to offset the capital gain(s).
- Where CGT assets are owned by an individual, partners in a partnership, trust or complying superannuation fund, be conscious of the need to hold them for at least 12 clear months in order to qualify for the CGT discount.
- When disposing of a rental property, it is necessary to account separately for depreciating assets sold with the property, as they are subject to separate balancing adjustment calculations which are on revenue account.

RENTAL INCOME FROM OVERSEAS

Income from an overseas rental property owned by an Australian resident is assessable in Australia, unless a Double Tax Agreement determines otherwise.

The deductions used to calculate the net income (or loss) are calculated according to Australian tax law, not according to the rules of the other country. Any taxes levied against that income (eg. a non-resident withholding tax) should be added back to give gross rental income. Foreign losses may be deducted against domestic income as they are no longer quarantined.

Taxpayers subject to Australian tax on foreign rental profits will usually be able to claim a Foreign Income Tax Offset (FITO) in respect of any foreign income tax paid on the rental income.

CAPITAL GAINS TAX ON OVERSEAS PROPERTY

Australian resident taxpayers owning real property in a foreign country should ascertain whether that country imposes CGT (eg. New Zealand does not have a capital gains tax) as the property will still be subject to the Australian CGT regime on disposal. For more details see 12.700.

FOREIGN RESIDENTS TAXED ON AUSTRALIAN PROPERTY

Foreign residents will be subject to tax on their taxable Australian source income. This includes rental income and CGT on the disposal of 'taxable Australian property' (which includes real property). For more details see Chapter 12.

18.150 RENTAL BUSINESS

Taxpayers who own rental properties, whether in partnership or on their own account, are typically not considered to be carrying on a business.

Whilst there is no legislation which deals with the question of whether a business is being carried on, there are a number of indicators developed from relevant case law which are set out in taxation ruling TR 97/11. They include:

- the purpose and intention of the taxpayer in engaging in the activity
- whether there is an intention to make a profit from the activity
- whether the activity is or will be profitable
- the repetition and regularity of the activity
- whether the activity is carried on in a businesslike and systematic manner
- the size and scale of the activity
- the activity does not display the characteristics of a hobby, and
- whether a business plan has been prepared.

For taxpayers owning rental properties to be considered to be carrying on business, it would be necessary to own multiple properties and have an active involvement in the income earning activities.

Andy and Lily own a number of rental properties, either as joint tenants or tenants in common. They own eight houses and three apartment blocks (each apartment block comprising six residential units) making a total of 26 properties. They actively manage all of the properties and devote a significant amount of time, an average of 25 hours per week each, to these activities. They undertake all financial planning and decision making in relation to the properties. They interview all prospective tenants and conduct all of the rent collections. They carry out regular property inspections and attend to all of the everyday maintenance and repairs themselves or organise for them to be done on their behalf. Apart from income Andy's earns from shares, they have no other sources of income.

They are carrying on a rental property business. This is demonstrated by:
- *the significant size and scale of the rental property activities*
- *the number of hours the they spend on the activities*
- *their extensive personal involvement in the activities, and*
- *the business-like manner in which the activities are planned, organised and carried on.*

18.200 DEDUCTIONS

INTEREST

Interest can be claimed for the cost of funds borrowed to purchase a rental property and to meet maintenance costs or running expenses while the rental property is being let (or is available to be let) under a commercial arrangement to generate assessable income. In these circumstances the interest paid is deductible even if it exceeds the income generated. The deductibility of interest is to be determined from the purpose for the borrowing and the use to which the borrowed funds are put.

Philip borrows $300,000 with the intention that it be used to acquire a unit in a new apartment building. He intends to lease the unit out to derive rental income. The builder has financial difficulties and Philip is able to acquire the unit for $275,000 which he then makes available for rental. Philip uses the balance of $25,000 to have an extended overseas holiday.

Philip would be entitled to deduct interest applicable to the $275,000 because it will be incurred in gaining assessable income. The interest applicable to the $25,000 will not be deductible because it is used for private purposes. That is so even though it was originally borrowed to acquire the unit.

A deduction for interest is also available on a loan taken out to:
- carry out renovations
- purchase depreciating assets (eg. furniture)
- make repairs or carry out maintenance, and
- purchase land on which to build a rental property.

REDRAW ON AN EXISTING LOAN

It is common practice for financial institutions to offer redraw facilities against existing loans. Under this loan facility, a borrower may redraw previous repayments of a loan principal. The loan may be for income producing purposes, non-income producing purposes or mixed purposes. In this case, the interest on the loan must be apportioned into deductible and non-deductible components in accordance with the amounts borrowed for the rental property and for private purposes. This is best illustrated by example.

George borrows $250,000 from a bank to buy a house which is rented out. After five years of renting out the house, the balance owing on the loan is $120,000. The bank notes George's excellent repayment record and asks whether he might like to re-borrow against the house for other purposes. George does so, drawing down $50,000 to buy a car (private use only) returning the account balance to $170,000.

George wants to claim a tax deduction for all of the interest on the loan on the basis that the loan was originally taken out to acquire the rental property. However, George can only claim interest on the loan of $120,000 because the $50,000 loan was for private purposes. Any interest paid in the future will be apportioned between the percentage applicable to the rental property (deductible) and that applicable to the car (non-deductible). The original application of the borrowed funds will not determine deductibility where funds borrowed under a line of credit have been recouped or withdrawn from the original use and are reapplied for a new use. This might also occur upon sale of an asset purchased with borrowed funds. In this example, George can claim a deduction for 70.59% of the interest paid.

For more details about the deductibility of interest on moneys drawn down under a line of credit or redraw facilities and the apportionment of interest where sub accounts are used for mixed purpose loans, see TR 2000/2.

NOTE: If a partnership borrowed to purchase a rental property, the interest incurred on the redraw of previous repayments of the loan principal may still be deductible, provided that the redraw amount is used to repay capital initially contributed by the partners (*FCT v Roberts; FCT v Smith* 92 ATC 4380).

Given the difficulties in apportioning interest that accrued on a daily basis, the Commissioner accepts a monthly calculation using an apportionment approach based on the average outstanding principal used that month for income producing purposes. This is calculated as follows:

Total interest accrued for the month x Deductible interest %

The deductible interest % is calculated as follows:

$$((A + B) / (C + D)) \times 100$$

Where:
- A = opening balance (beginning of month) of outstanding principal used for income producing purposes
- B = closing balance (end of month) of outstanding principal used for income producing purposes

- C = opening balance of total outstanding principal
- D = closing balance of total outstanding principal

SPLIT OR LINKED LOANS

According to TR 98/22, a linked loan is *... a credit facility taken out with a financial institution under which there are two or more loans with an account being maintained in respect of each loan. A split loan ... is a credit facility taken out with a financial institution under which there is one loan with sub-accounts being maintained in respect of that loan.*

In *FCT v Hart* (2004) ATC 4599, Part IVA was applied by the Commissioner to strike down the use of such a facility in the manner adopted by the taxpayer. The taxpayer capitalised interest accruing on the investment component of the loan and applied all cash to the repayment of the private component (the interest in respect of which was non-deductible). Thus, the effect of the arrangement was to re-characterise interest (on the home loan) that would have been otherwise non deductible, as deductible. See also TD 2012/1 for the Commissioner's view on the application of Part IVA to 'investment loan repayment arrangements'.

Any person taking out a loan to purchase a rental property should carefully consider their financing arrangements. In particular avoid the mixing of accounts which have both deductible and non-deductible components. Professional advice should be sought before signing up to the loan as it is difficult to unwind arrangements which may turn out to be non effective for tax purposes.

LOAN ACCOUNT OFFSET FACILITY

Where the facility constitutes an acceptable 'loan account offset arrangement' (as prescribed in TR 93/6), the availability of an interest deduction where funds are withdrawn for a private purpose differs to that of a redraw facility.

According to TR 93/6, under a loan account offset facility arrangement, the borrower typically operates two accounts:

- a loan account, and
- a deposit account.

There is no entitlement to receive interest payments or payments in the nature of interest on the amounts credited to the deposit account. The reduction in the loan account interest is achieved by offsetting the balances of the two accounts.

As a general rule, the Commissioner considers that a taxpayer with an acceptable loan account offset arrangement with dual accounts is entitled to claim a deduction for the full amount of interest whilst the loan is used wholly for income producing purposes. Any reduction to the interest payable would typically not be assessable as no amount of interest has been received or credited to the borrower (see PBR 50720). Significantly, in a number of private rulings (see PBR 80150, 19859), the Commissioner accepts that interest on the loan account will remain fully deductible if funds are withdrawn from the 'deposit account' and used for non-income producing purposes. The Commissioner's rationale for this position is that:

- depositing funds into the deposit account will decrease the interest payable on the loan account but will not decrease of the balance of the loan account, and
- withdrawing funds from the deposit account will increase the interest payable on the loan account but again, will not impact the loan account balance.

From a tax perspective, the offset account arrangement provides a more flexible and favourable tax outcome where funds are accessed for private use. Essentially, taxpayers will need to evaluate these facilities in line with their commercial objectives.

On 1 July 2015, Jimmy acquired a rental property which was funded by way of a 25 year loan. The initial loan amount was $300,000 and provides a loan offset facility such that any repayments can be made to deposit account. Interest is charged at the end of the month on the net balance between the loan account and the deposit account. During the 2015-16 income year, Jimmy made total repayment of $100,000 into the deposit account. Interest will be charged on the net amount of $200,000 (net balance between the loan account and the

offset account), and Jimmy can deduct interest incurred on the net balance.

Subsequently, on 1 July 2016, Jimmy redrew an amount of $100,000 from the deposit account to fund the purchase of a private motor vehicle. Provided that no repayments were made to the deposit account during the 2015-16 income year, Jimmy is entitled to a deduction for the interest incurred on the entire loan balance of $300,000.

PENALTY INTEREST PAYMENTS

Penalty interest payments are typically considered to be a mortgage discharge expense. The Tax Office accepts that penalty interest payments on a loan relating to a rental property are deductible when:

- the loan is secured by a mortgage over the rental property and the payment effects the discharge of the mortgage, or
- the payment is made so as to remove a recurring obligation of the taxpayer to pay interest on the loan.

INTEREST PRIOR TO RENT BEING RECEIVED

Interest may also be claimed for a period prior to rent being received. In TR 2004/4, the Tax Office accepts that:

... interest incurred in a period prior to the derivation of relevant assessable income will be 'incurred in gaining or producing the assessable income' in the following circumstances:

- *the interest is not preliminary to the income earning activities*
- *the interest is not private or domestic*
- *the period of interest outgoings before the derivation of assessable income is not so long that the necessary connection between the outgoings and assessable income is lost*
- *the interest is incurred with one end in view, the gaining or producing of assessable income, and*
- *continuing efforts are undertaken in pursuit of that end.*

This means that a deduction for interest can be claimed before income is derived, such as in the construction phase of a building where it is being constructed for income-producing purposes (see *Steele v FCT* 99 ATC 4242).

Marge borrows $150,000 from a bank with the vague idea that she will use the funds to buy a rental property. Having looked at a couple of places she loses interest and does not look further. She then has an idea that she could perhaps acquire a small business at a popular beach resort. She approaches business brokers in the area but finds nothing of interest. Marge is then made redundant from her employment and, having received a substantial payout, she repays the loan to the bank.

A deduction is not allowable for the interest because there was no continuing effort to acquire an income-producing asset, the borrowing was made too soon in the process and no asset was ever ultimately acquired.

It is possible that a deduction may be allowable even though no income is ever received from an acquired rental property provided that the intention of generating assessable income existed at all times; see *Ormiston and Commissioner of Taxation* (2005) AATA 978 where a taxpayer was allowed a deduction for interest paid on a loan taken out to acquire a 'rental' property, even though no income was received between the date of acquisition and the eventual sale of the property.

Generally, interest cannot be claimed as a deduction once the property has ceased to produce assessable income. However, the Tax Office has accepted that interest may be deductible even though assessable income is no longer being received in certain circumstances; see the Federal Court decisions in *FCT v Brown* 1999 FCA 721 and *FCT v Jones* 2002 FCA 204. In TR 2004/4, the Tax Office accepts that even though the assets representing the borrowings are no longer held by the taxpayer and therefore that the income earning activities have ceased (whether business or non-business):

... the outgoing will still have been incurred in gaining or producing 'the assessable income' if the occasion for the outgoing is to be found in whatever was productive of assessable income of an earlier period.

Judgement is required in determining whether a nexus still exists between the interest outgoing and the former income earning activity. Interest will not fail to be deductible however merely because:

- the loan is not for a fixed term
- the taxpayer has a legal entitlement to repay the principal before maturity (whether a penalty is payable or not), or
- the original loan is refinanced.

However, the Commissioner asserts that the nexus between the interest outgoing and the income earning activity is broken if the taxpayer:

- retains the loan for reasons unassociated with the receipt of the rental income, or
- extends the loan in such as way that there is an ongoing advantage to be gained from the extension which is unrelated to the gaining of assessable income for which the debt was originally incurred.

Taxation Ruling 2004/4 goes on to state that a legal or economic inability to repay the loan would suggest that it has been retained because of the former income earning activities.

PART YEAR DEDUCTIONS

Where a property is used for both private and rental purposes during an income year, expenses are generally apportioned based on the time that the property is available for the production of assessable income. Usually this is the number of days that the property is available for rental or where a taxpayer is actively marketing for a new tenancy. No deduction is available for expenses incurred in respect of a period during which the property is applied to private use. See also *Holiday homes let for part of the year* at 18.400.

David and Michelle own a unit in a high rise building in a holiday resort. They occupy it for 90 days during winter but the unit is genuinely available at all other times for rent through the building manager. It is usually fully let for most of the other 275 days of the year. They incur interest, rates and taxes, insurance and management fees, and telephone rental (which is blocked to calls other than when they are in residence). While occupied by tenants, weekly cleaning of the unit takes place.

David and Michelle can claim deductions for all expenses except for the telephone expenditure apportioned 275/365 days. A 100% deduction can be claimed for the cleaning as it relates only to the period when the property was occupied by tenants whilst no deduction can be claimed for the telephone expenditure.

PARTIAL CLAIMS

A partial interest deduction may be available if part of a property is used solely and exclusively to produce assessable income. Generally, apportionment should be made on a floor-area basis.

Maria wants to open a restaurant in a vacant two storey building that has been used as a storage facility by a local trader. She has the building renovated and fitted out as a restaurant on the ground floor whilst the first floor is converted into a residence for herself. Interest has to be apportioned on a reasonable basis between the private area and the restaurant.

You can claim a tax deduction for the interest expense of borrowing to finance rental property expenses.

If a property, or part of a property is let at less than normal commercial rates, this may limit the amount of deductions can be claimed (IT 2167).

JOINT OWNERSHIP

If the property is owned by more than one person, rental income and expenses must be attributed to each co-owner according to their legal ownership interest in the property, despite any agreement between co-owners, either orally or in writing.

As a general rule, a property would be owned by taxpayers as joint tenants or as tenants-in-common.

JOINT TENANCY

Under a joint tenancy, each owner effectively owns the whole asset. In other words, each owner shares ownership equally. On the death of one joint tenant, the asset automatically passes to the other or others, regardless of the terms of the will of the joint tenant who died.

If two people hold equal shares in an investment property as joint tenants, any separate agreement that the interest deduction should be claimed on the basis of a different ratio would be ineffective for taxation purposes.

This is consistent with the Tax Office's view that income and expenses should be returned in the same proportion as the legal interests of the owners in the property. In other words, each party is entitled to an equal share of the rent and profits and accordingly the entitlement to interest deductions should also be equal. The fact that one partner might assume greater financial liability is a private arrangement and therefore the portion of interest that exceeds the 50% partnership share should not be deductible.

TENANTS IN COMMON

Under this ownership structure, each owner may hold an unequal interest in the property, for example, one owner might own 60% and the other would then own 40%. Where two or more people own an asset as tenants in common each owner holds their share of the asset outright. On the death of one of two tenants in common the survivor retains their interest and the deceased's interest passes with his Will. There is no automatic transfer to the other.

NOTE: Each tenant in common is free to sell or otherwise deal with their interest in a property at anytime (unless there is in place a co-ownership agreement which contains terms restricting this).

Co-ownership and receipt of income jointly from property constitutes a tax law partnership. The deduction allowable to each partner for a net rental loss is limited to 'so much of the individual interest of the partner' (s92 ITAA36).

Where the parties are carrying on business in partnership (ie. a general law partnership), the terms of the partnership agreement determines the distribution of profits and losses.

TRAVELLING EXPENSES

You cannot claim the cost of travelling expenses whilst in search of a rental property to purchase. However, once the property has been purchased and is income-producing, travel expenses are deductible if incurred in:

*   inspecting the property
*   collecting rents
*   showing prospective tenants through the property
*   carrying out repairs, including travel to acquire materials for those repairs, or
*   visiting the estate agents for purposes such as leaving keys, signing lease agreements or discussing matters relevant to the letting.

A full deduction is allowable when the sole purpose of the trip relates to the rental property. However, if the trip also includes a private purpose, only a partial deduction would be allowed. If a property has already been acquired and is not used for income production but is subject to CGT (eg. a holiday home), travel costs for matters such as maintenance may form part of the cost base (third element costs) (see ATO ID 2003/772).

NOTE: Where travel related to a rental property is combined with a holiday or other private activities, taxpayers may need to apportion the expenses.

LEGAL COSTS

Stamp duty and legal costs incurred in buying and/or selling a rental property are capital expenses and not deductible. However there is an exception for rental properties purchased in the Australian Capital Territory (ACT). Freehold title cannot be obtained for properties in the ACT

– they are commonly acquired under a 99 year crown lease. Therefore stamp duty, preparation and registration costs incurred on the purchase of an ACT property are deductible to the extent that property is used as a rental property. In other cases,where the property was acquired after 19 September 1985, non-deductible legal costs will form part of the asset's cost base (second element costs) for CGT purposes (see 12.092).

DRAWING UP LEASES

The costs of drawing up a lease are typically deductible. Section 25-20 ITAA97 allows a deduction for the cost of preparing, registering or stamping a lease of a property (including costs associated with an assignment or surrender of a lease) where the property is used solely for the purpose of producing assessable income. This means that the cost of arranging for the stamp duty and registration on transfer of a crown lease of 99 years (eg. in the ACT) are deductible to the extent that the property is income-producing.

REPAIRS AND MAINTENANCE

The commentary below is only of a general nature. For a more detailed commentary about 'repairs' see 14.150.

Section 25-10 ITAA97 allows a deduction for expenditure which is incurred for repairs to premises or a depreciating asset held for the purposes of producing assessable income.

A non-capital repair to correct a defective or worn-out part, or to return a deteriorated part to its condition when first acquired, is deductible. However, the renewal or replacement of the whole of an item is usually considered to be a capital expense and not deductible (the cost might qualify to be added to the asset's cost base for CGT purposes – see 12.092). Care should be exercised when the materials used in conducting a repair are superior to the original product as the expenditure may be considered capital in nature on the basis that the asset has been 'improved' (see TR 97/23). However, it is acknowledged in TR 97/23 that to repair property improves to some extent the condition it was in immediately before repair. A minor and incidental degree of improvement, addition or alteration may be done to property and still be a repair. If the work done to a property involves an enhancement arising from the use of more modern materials and it does not change the property's character, the expenditure can still be characterised as a repair (e.g. replacement of timber stumps with concrete stumps).

Apportionment is needed if the premises, or depreciable plant, were not solely used to produce income in the year the repairs occur.

REPAIRS AFTER CEASING TO PRODUCE INCOME

Repairs may still be allowable as a deduction even though the property is no longer available for rent. A deduction may be allowable provided it can be demonstrated that the repairs are related to the period when the property was used to produce assessable income (see IT 180). The Tax Office also takes the view that the premises must have produced assessable income in the year that the expenditure was incurred.

Graeme owned and rented out a unit for some 15 years and decided to sell it. After the tenants vacated the unit in October 2014, it was found that a leaking water pipe had damaged flooring, and the tenants had smashed the ceramic stove-top and broken plaster on internal walls. In November 2014 Graeme had these faults repaired and then put the unit up for sale.

Although the unit will no longer be used to produce assessable income, the approach adopted in IT 180 would allow a deduction because the repairs relate to events which occurred while the property was used to derive assessable income and the relevant expenditure was incurred during the income year in which the property ceased to be income-producing.

INITIAL REPAIRS

Repairs to a property shortly after acquisition will be treated as a capital expense if the repair is to rectify a defect which existed at the time of purchase. This applies whether or not the purchase price would have been higher had the property been in better condition at the time of purchase. If it can be shown that repairs were necessary to fix damage caused by tenants after acquisition of the property, the expenses will be deductible.

NON-DEDUCTIBLE REPAIRS

Even though a repair may be regarded as capital expenditure because it was, for example, an initial repair, or was the replacement of a whole structure, consideration should be given to other provisions of the ITAA97.

If the work constitutes an initial repair, consider whether it may be added to the cost base of the asset for CGT purposes (see 12.092). If the work constitutes a structural improvement, eg. reconstruction of a garage destroyed by a fire, a deduction may be allowable for capital works under Division 43 (see 15.200).

Carpets are usually replaced when worn, but the replacement is not regarded as a repair; the replacement carpet is depreciated. However, the Tax Office have taken the view that a deduction is allowable as a repair when worn carpets are removed and the existing floorboards are polished on the basis that they perform substantially the same function as the carpet (see ATO ID 2002/330).

Generally, the replacement of a complete structure would not be deductible as a repair. For example, a fence is completely replaced or a stove is scrapped and replaced with a new one.

For more information about repairs see from 14.150.

EXAMPLES

Examples of deductible repairs	Examples of non-deductible improvements
• Replacing broken windows • Maintaining plumbing • Repairing electrical appliances	• Landscaping • Insulating a house/unit • Replacing an entire roof

SUNDRY COSTS

While none of the following costs (except motor vehicle expenses – see 13.225) are subject to the substantiation rules, expenses still need to be proved in the event of a request from the Tax Office.

RATES AND LAND TAX

If the property is fully let (or available to let), the cost is deductible. On purchase, solicitors prepare rate adjustments to apportion the rates and taxes for the year between the different ownership periods. Any net amount payable by a purchaser as a rate adjustment can be claimed as a deduction. Alternatively, if a vendor receives a credit adjustment, it is to be treated as assessable income.

COSTS OF OBTAINING FINANCE

The costs of obtaining finance (ie. borrowing costs) are capital expenses, however a deduction may be available under s25-25 ITAA97. Examples are:

- legal expenses associated with the mortgage documents and stamp duty payable
- valuation, survey, overdraft guarantee fees, and
- procuration, search fees, etc.

Claims are made on the following basis:

- If under $100: *Claim in full when spent*
- If $100 or more: *Spread the claim over the shorter of the period of the loan or five years. (The method statement in s25-25 requires the loan period to be calculated in days)*
- If the loan is repaid early: *Claim any remaining borrowing expenses in that year*
- If the loan is obtained part way through the year: *Apportion the deduction according to the number of days in the year you had the loan.*

The cost of discharging a mortgage on a property used as security for an income-producing loan is also deductible.

PROPERTY INSPECTION AND RENT COLLECTION

Costs of travelling to inspect an income producing property is usually deductible. Car expenses may be claimed as a deduction but are subject to the substantiation rules. Claims may be made using one of four methods: the one third actual costs method (see 13.240), the 12% of original value method (see 13.235), the cents-per-kilometre method (see 12.230) and the log book method (see 13.245).

IMPORTANT: In the 2015-16 Federal Budget, the Government announced its intention to remove the 12% of original value method and the one-third of actual costs method. Further, the Government intends to change the cents-per-kilometre method. These amendments, once legislated, are to commence 1 July 2015.

INSURANCE

Premiums paid for building, contents or public liability insurance are deductible when incurred subject to the prepayment provisions.

TELEPHONE, STATIONERY AND POSTAL EXPENSES

Calls or letters to tenants, estate agents or tradesmen are deductible.

MANAGEMENT FEES

Claims are allowed for fees and commissions paid to real estate agents to let properties and collect rent.

OWNERS CORPORATION FEES

Owners corporation fees, such as the cost of administration, maintenance of the gardens and insurance on the building are deductible, however payments to a special-purpose sinking fund to cover the cost of capital improvements or capital repairs are not immediately deductible but constitute capital works for the purposes of Division 43 (see TR 97/23).

FURTHER SUNDRY COSTS

The following sundry costs are deductible:

- advertising for tenants
- cleaning expenses including rubbish removal
- gardening and mowing expenses including tree trimming or felling
- secretary and bookkeeping fees where associated with the collection of rent and payment of expenses
- bank charges on the account used to receive rental income and pay rental expenses
- pest control
- fees charged by a solicitor or bank for safekeeping of title documents of the property
- rent paid if subletting
- advice about taxation matters relevant to the property
- legal expenses to eject a tenant for non payment of rent
- cost of services of a debt collector to collect arrears of rent
- cutting new keys
- services of trades persons where the expenditure is not capital in nature
- servicing costs (eg. heating systems)
- water supply charges (if not paid by tenant)
- quantity surveyor fees
- security patrols, and
- security system monitoring and maintenance.

LETTING RESIDENCE WHILE ON TRANSFER OF EMPLOYMENT

If the property is let on an arm's length commercial basis during the transfer of employment, losses and outgoings in relation to the letting of the residence during that time are deductible. This includes deductions for interest incurred during that time. The repair of faults which existed at the time of first being let are not deductible. For the CGT consequences of such letting, see 12.330.

Depreciation is also deductible on furniture and fittings for the period that the house is let (see Chapter 15 and 19.350 for more details). In addition, a capital works deduction may be available in respect of the house (see 15.200 and 19.300 for details).

WHEN TO CLAIM A DEDUCTION

For some deductions a claim is made when the expense is incurred. In most cases this would mean that an amount will be payable because there is a legal obligation to do so (rates), a contract requires payment (security) or the work or service has been performed and you have been billed for that service (eg. fire equipment maintenance).

Other expenses would only be deductible when paid because there is no legal obligation or commitment to pay. For example, an insurance renewal may be received on 25 June, however, a taxpayer may decide not to renew an insurance cover or may elect to reinsure with a different insurance company. In contrast, the receipt of an electricity account or council rates notice would result in a deduction because of the obligation created to pay these liabilities.

PREPAYMENT OF EXPENSES

It is not unusual for owners of rental properties to seek to maximise tax deductions in a particular year by prepaying expenses at the end of an income year. Care needs to be taken if this is contemplated because special deductibility rules apply for prepayments.

Generally, if rental property expenses are prepaid (such as insurance or interest) they will be immediately deductible provided the service period is no longer than 12 months and ends before the end of the income year following the expenditure year. A prepayment that does not meet these criteria and is $1,000 or more may have to be spread over two or more years. For more information see 14.170.

NON-DEDUCTIBLE EXPENSES

Expenses which are not able to be claimed as deductions include:
- acquisition and disposal costs of the property
- expenses not actually incurred by the landlord, such as water or electricity charges borne by tenants, and
- expenses not related to the rental of a property, such as expenses connected with the personal use of a holiday home that is rented out for part of the year.

18.300 CAPITAL WORKS

Where construction of a rental property was commenced after 21 August 1984, a capital works deduction may be available. Deductions are based on the original cost of the construction. Where the construction commenced between 22 August 1984 and 15 September 1987 the deduction is 4% per annum. Where construction commenced after 15 September 1987 the deduction is 2.5% per annum.

The manner in which the cost of capital works is ascertained is as follows. A taxpayer contracts a builder to construct what will be a rental property; the builder's costs total $450,000 and the contract price paid by the purchaser is $500,000. The construction cost for capital works purposes is $500,000. However, if the builder had constructed that property for sale, and it was subsequently purchased for $500,000 by the taxpayers, the construction cost for capital works purposes would be $450,000.

Where the property was constructed during a period when a claim for capital works is allowed, subsequent purchasers can claim for the balance of the period, because unlike a depreciating asset there is no balancing adjustment on disposal of the property, unless the building is destroyed. The balance of any claim is passed on, on the same basis, to any later owners (see *Capital works* at 15.200). For adjustments to the CGT cost base see 15.205.

Any structural improvements to your rental property that were commenced after 26 February 1992 are also deductible at 2.5% per annum as capital works. The items in the *Residential rental property assets* list at 18.360 that are designated 'Div. 43' are items treated by the Tax Office as structural improvements. The capital works deduction must be apportioned between the income-producing and non-income-producing uses of the property.

The commencement of construction is the date that the capital works starts (pouring of the foundations or the sinking of pilings). The actual capital works deduction period cannot commence before the construction of the capital works is completed, even if the taxpayer has used the capital works, or part thereof, for an income-producing purpose before the construction was completed (s43-30 ITAA97). When the capital works are completed the deduction period commences (ie. 25 years in the case of a 4% deduction or 40 years in the case of a 2.5% deduction). During this period the deduction is only allowed when the building is being used for an income-producing purpose and may be pro-rated if construction was completed part way through the year.

The seller of a property is required by s262A(4AJA) ITAA36 to provide the buyer with the cost of construction of the original building and any structural improvements, however this does not always occur and there is no enforcement mechanism in the legislation. Where necessary the Tax Office will accept valuation estimates from appropriately qualified persons (TR 97/25).

On 1 August 2015 Bill acquires a rental property for $400,000. The property is rented for the entire year. The contract of sale states that the $400,000 comprises land ($280,000), construction cost of building ($100,000) and depreciating assets as per schedule ($20,000). Records provided by the seller show that he had acquired the land in 1988 and constructed the building in 1989 at a cost of $60,000. The construction was completed on 1 December 1989 and the building was first used for an income-producing purpose from that date.

As the building was constructed in 1989 the capital works deduction is at the rate of 2.5% per annum based on the original cost ($60,000). Bill's capital works deduction for 2015-16 is $60,000 x 2.5% x 334/365 = $1,373. Bill's deduction for 2015-16 will be $1,500. Eligibility for the deduction will cease on 1 December 2029 (40 years after construction was completed).

CONSTRUCTION EXPENDITURE THAT CAN BE CLAIMED

Some costs that may be included in construction expenditure are:

- preliminary expenses such as architects' fees, engineering fees and the cost of foundation excavations
- payments to carpenters, bricklayers and other tradespeople for construction of the building, and
- payments for the construction of retaining walls, fences and in-ground swimming pools.

CONSTRUCTION EXPENDITURE THAT CANNOT BE CLAIMED

Some costs that are not included in construction expenditure are:

- the cost of the land on which the rental property is built
- expenditure on clearing the land prior to construction
- earthworks that are permanent, can be economically maintained and are not integral to the installation or construction of a structure, and
- expenditure on landscaping.

ADJUSTMENTS TO THE CGT COST BASE

In calculating a capital gain or capital loss from a rental property, the cost base and reduced cost base of the property may need to be reduced to the extent that it includes construction expenditure which has been claimed or can be claimed as a capital works deduction. For adjustments to the cost base see 15.205.

However, the Commissioner states in PS LA 2006/1 that it will accept that a taxpayer cannot deduct an amount under Division 43 for construction expenditure in respect of a rental property if the taxpayer:

- does not (as a question of fact) have sufficient information to determine the amount and nature of the expenditure, and
- does not seek to deduct an amount in relation to the expenditure under Division 43 (or any other provision).

This means that in working out a capital gain or capital loss arising from a CGT event happening in relation to the rental property, the taxpayer is not required to reduce the asset's cost base and reduced cost base by the amount not deducted under Division 43 in relation to the asset.

18.350 DECLINE IN VALUE OF A DEPRECIATING ASSET

Where a depreciating asset is used to produce rental income, a deduction is available for its decline in value. If the depreciating asset cost $300 or less and was not part of a set, an immediate deduction may be available (see 15.030).

If a depreciating asset costs less than $1,000 it can be allocated to a low value pool and be depreciated under the diminishing value method over four years with a depreciation rate of 18.75% in the year of acquisition and 37.5% in subsequent years (see 15.040). For depreciating assets that cost $1,000 or more the deduction is based upon the cost of the asset and its effective life. Taxpayers may self-assess an asset's effective life or use the Tax Office effective life tables for rental property assets (refer TR 2010/2 and 15.160).

 The decline in value of an asset held jointly with others is calculated based on the cost of each owners interest in the asset.

The following formulae (discussed at 15.060) applies to calculate the deduction for depreciation:

- **For the diminishing value method:**

  If you start to hold the asset before 10 May 2006:

  Base value x (days held divided by 365)
  x (150% divided by asset's effective life)

  If you start to hold the asset on or after 10 May 2006:

  Base value x (days held divided by 365)
  x (200% divided by asset's effective life)

- **For prime cost method:**

  Asset's cost x (days held divided by 365)
  x (100% divided by asset's effective life)

 On 13 May 2015, Bill paid $1,000 for a new gas hot water system for his rental property. Its effective life is 12 years. Bill elects to use the prime cost method.
Bill's deduction for the decline in value of this asset in 2015-16 is $1,000 x (49 divided by 365) x (100% divided by 12) = $11.

It is important when buying a rental property for a 'walk-in-walk-out figure' to agree with the vendor on an allocation of consideration between the building structure and the depreciating assets contained within. The amount paid for depreciating assets must be used to ascertain the ongoing depreciation deduction available.

Depreciation is allowed on fixtures and fittings although items such as tiles or parquetry may not be depreciable and therefore require consideration under the capital works provisions (see 15.200). Coverings which can be removed without damage to the building, such as carpet, floating timber or vinyl are depreciable (see 18.360).

18.360 RESIDENTIAL RENTAL PROPERTY ASSETS

This list, extracted from TR 2015/2 *Income tax: effective life of depreciating assets (applicable from 1 July 2015)*, identifies the most common items in a residential rental property for which deductions can be claimed for decline in value or depreciation. See 15.160 for a complete list of all depreciable assets.

Items with an effective life are depreciable under Division 40: see from 15.000. Items shown without an effective life may be eligible for a capital works deduction under Division 43: see from 15.200.

Freestanding means items designed to be portable or movable. Any attachment to the premises is only for the item's temporary stability. Fixed means items annexed or attached by any means, for example screws, nails, bolts, glue, adhesive, grout, or cement, but not merely for temporary stability.

Asset	Life (yrs)	Date of application

RESIDENTIAL PROPERTY OPERATORS

Assets generally:

Asset	Life (yrs)	Date of application
Air conditioning assets (excluding ducting, pipes and vents):		
Air handling units	20	1/7/03
Chillers:		
Absorption	25	1/7/03
Centrifugal	20	1/7/03
Volumetrics (including reciprocating, rotary, screw, scroll):		
Air cooled	15	1/7/03
Water cooled	20	1/7/03
Condensing sets	15	1/7/03
Cooling towers	15	1/7/03
Damper motors (including variable air volume box controller)	10	1/7/03
Fan coil units (connected to condensing set)	15	1/7/03
Mini split systems up to 20KW (including ceiling, floor and high wall split system)	10	1/7/03
Packaged air conditioning units	15	1/7/03
Pumps	20	1/7/03
Room units	10	1/7/03
Ceiling fans	5	1/7/04
Clocks, electric	10	1/7/04
Digital video display (DVD) players	5	1/7/04
Door closers	10	1/7/04
Door stops, freestanding	10	1/7/04
Escalators (machinery and moving parts)	20	1/1/03
Evaporative coolers:		
Fixed (excluding ducting and vents)	20	1/7/05
Portable	10	1/7/05
Floor coverings (removable without damage):		
Carpet	10	1/1/01
Floating timber	15	1/7/04
Linoleum	10	1/1/01
Vinyl	10	1/1/01
Furniture, freestanding	13 1/3	1/1/01
Garbage bins	10	1/7/04
Garbage compacting systems (excluding chutes)	6 2/3	1/1/01
Generators	20	1/1/01
Gym assets:		
Cardiovascular	5	1/7/04
Resistance	10	1/7/04
Hand dryers, electrical	10	1/1/01
Heaters:		
Fixed:		
Electric	15	1/7/04
Gas:		
Ducted central heating unit	20	1/7/04
Other	15	1/7/04
Freestanding	15	1/7/04

Asset	Life (yrs)	Date of application
Hot water systems (excluding piping):		
Electric	12	1/7/04
Gas	12	1/7/04
Solar	15	1/7/04
Intercom system assets	10	1/7/04
Lifts (including hydraulic and traction lifts)	30	1/1/03
Lights:		
Fittings (excluding hardwired)	5	1/7/04
Freestanding	5	1/7/04
Shades, removable	5	1/7/04
Linen	5	1/7/04
Master antenna television (MATV) assets:		
Amplifiers	10	1/7/04
Modulators	10	1/7/04
Power sources	10	1/7/04
Mirrors, freestanding	15	1/7/04
Radios	10	1/1/01
Rugs	7	1/7/04
Solar power generating system assets	20	1/7/04
Stereo systems (incorporating amplifiers, cassette players, compact disc players, radios and speakers)	7	1/7/04
Surround sound systems (incorporating audio video receivers and speakers)	10	1/7/04
Telecommunications assets:		
Cordless phones	4	1/7/04
Telephone Hand sets	10	1/7/04
Telephone systems – see Table B Telephony		
Television antennas, freestanding	5	1/7/04
Television sets	10	1/7/04
Vacuum cleaners:		
Ducted:		
Hoses	10	1/7/04
Motors	10	1/7/04
Wands	10	1/7/04
Portable	10	1/1/01
Ventilation fans	20	1/7/04
Video cassette recorder systems (VCRs)	5	1/7/04
Water pumps	20	1/1/01
Window blinds, internal	10	1/7/04
Window curtains	6	1/7/04
Window shutters, automatic:		
Controls	10	1/7/04
Motors	10	1/7/04
Bathroom assets:		
Accessories, freestanding (including shower caddies, soap holders, toilet brushes)	5	1/7/04
Exhaust fans (including light/heating)	10	1/7/04
Heated towel rails, electric	10	1/7/04
Shower curtains (excluding curtain rods and screens)	2	1/7/04

Asset	Life (yrs)	Date of application	Asset	Life (yrs)	Date of application
Spa bath pumps	20	1/7/04	Garden sheds, freestanding	15	1/7/04
Fire control assets:			Gates, electrical:		
Alarms:			Controls	5	1/7/04
Heat	6	1/7/04	Motors	10	1/7/04
Smoke	6	1/7/04	Operable pergola louvres:		
Detection and alarm systems:			Controls	15	1/7/04
Alarm bells	12	1/7/04	Motors	15	1/7/04
Detectors (including addressable manual call points, heat, multi type and smoke)	20	1/7/04	Sauna heating assets	15	1/7/04
			Sewage treatment assets:		
Fire indicator panels	12	1/7/04	Controls	8	1/7/04
Emergency warning and intercommunication systems (EWIS):			Motors	8	1/7/04
			Spas:		
Master emergency control panels	12	1/7/04	Fixed spa assets:		
			Chlorinators	12	1/7/04
Speakers	12	1/7/04	Filtration assets (including pumps)	12	1/7/04
Strobe lights	12	1/7/04			
Warden intercom phones (WIPs)	12	1/7/04	Heaters (electric or gas)	15	1/7/04
Extinguishers	15	1/7/04	Freestanding spas (incorporating blowers, controls, filters, heaters and pumps)	17	1/7/04
Hoses and nozzles	10	1/7/04			
Pumps (including diesel and electric)	25	1/7/04			
			Swimming pool assets:		
Stair pressurisation assets:			Chlorinators	12	1/7/04
AC variable speed drives	10	1/7/04	Cleaning assets	7	1/7/04
Pressurisation and extraction fans	25	1/7/04	Filtration assets (including pumps)	12	1/7/04
Sensors	10	1/7/04	Heaters:		
Kitchen assets:			Electric	15	1/7/04
Cook tops	12	1/7/04	Gas	15	1/7/04
Crockery	5	1/7/04	Solar	20	1/7/04
Cutlery	5	1/7/04	Tennis court assets:		
Dishwashers	10	1/7/04	Cleaners	3	1/7/04
Freezers	12	1/7/04	Drag brooms	3	1/7/04
Garbage disposal units	10	1/7/04	Nets	5	1/7/04
Microwave ovens	10	1/7/04	Rollers	3	1/7/04
Ovens	12	1/7/04	Umpire chairs	15	1/7/04
Range hoods	12	1/7/04	Security and monitoring assets:		
Refrigerators	12	1/7/04	Access control systems:		
Stoves	12	1/7/04	Code pads	5	1/7/04
Water filters, electrical	15	1/7/04	Door controllers	5	1/7/04
Laundry assets:			Readers:		
Clothes dryers	10	1/7/04	Proximity	7	1/7/04
Ironing boards, freestanding	7	1/7/04	Swipe card	3	1/7/04
Irons	5	1/7/04	Closed circuit television systems:		
Washing machines	10	1/7/04	Cameras	4	1/7/04
Outdoor assets:			Monitors	4	1/7/04
Automatic garage doors:			Recorders:		
Controls	5	1/7/04	Digital	4	1/7/04
Motors	10	1/7/04	Time lapse	2	1/7/04
Barbecue assets:			Switching units (including multiplexes)	5	1/7/04
Fixed barbecue assets:					
Sliding trays and cookers	10	1/7/04	Security systems:		
Freestanding barbecues	5	1/7/04	Code pads	5	1/7/04
Floor carpet (including artificial grass and matting)	5	1/7/04	Control panels	5	1/7/04
			Detectors (including passive infra red, photo sensors and vibration)	5	1/7/04
Furniture, freestanding	5	1/7/04			
Gardening watering installations:					
Control panels	5	1/7/04	Global System for Mobiles (GSM) Units	5	1/7/04
Pumps	5	1/7/04			
Timing devices	5	1/7/04	Noise makers (including bells and sirens)	5	1/7/04
Garden lights, solar	8	1/7/04			

18.400 HOLIDAY HOUSES AND FAMILY ARRANGEMENTS

Following is a summary of the Tax Office's views as set out in Income Tax Ruling IT 2167. It explains the rules for disclosing income and claiming deductions where non-economic rental arrangements occur involving the use of holiday homes and arrangements with family members.

LETTING OF PROPERTY TO RELATIVES

Where the property is let to relatives on a commercial basis (ie. consistent with normal commercial practice) the owner of the property would return assessable income and be entitled to normal deductions as would be available in an arms length situation. If the property is let at less than commercial rent then as a general rule income tax deductions for losses and outgoings incurred in connection with the rented property may be allowed up to the amount of rent received. Claims beyond that limit would depend upon individual circumstances.

BOARD AND LODGING

Arrangements of this nature are considered to be of a domestic nature and there should be no income tax consequences. The income received is not assessable and the owner is not entitled to claim any deductions.

OCCUPANCY ON BASIS OF SHARING HOUSEHOLD COSTS

As a general rule such arrangements are considered to be of a domestic nature and there should be no income tax consequences. The income received is not assessable and the owner is not entitled to claim any deductions.

HOLIDAY HOME LET FOR PART YEAR

The rent received from letting the property, at a commercial rental, is assessable income. Where friends or relatives of an owner occupy a property for holidays at no or minimal cost or the property is either occupied by the owner for short periods or remains unoccupied then if minimal amounts are received from friends or relatives in these cases the income would not be considered assessable.

Deductions in respect of the property are only available for those periods where the property is available for letting (ie. where active and bona fide efforts to let the property at a commercial rental have been made). In Case No. 49, 26 CTBR (NS) 372, a property was let for 16 days during the year of income and occupied by the owners for 107 days and vacant for the balance of the year. The Taxation Board of Review apportioned the losses and outgoings attributable to the property on a time basis and allowed a deduction for the proportion of the year that the property was let (ie. 4.4%).

Travelling expenses incurred by the owner of a property in inspecting and maintaining the property are typically allowable deductions. The cost of travel undertaken to prepare the property for incoming tenants or to inspect the property at the conclusion of the tenancy, should be deductible.

PURCHASE OF A RESIDENCE BY A FAMILY TRUST

Where a family's residence is owned by their family trust, and rent is paid for the right to occupy the property, it often follows that the trust will occur a net loss from the arrangement. In these circumstances it would be necessary to identify a dominant purpose of the arrangement other than the tax benefit which accrues to the trust as a result of the rental losses. An example of an alternative purpose might be asset protection in the event of litigation and to protect assets in the event of the taxpayer being made bankrupt.

In the case of *FCT v Janmor Nominees Pty Ltd* 87 ATC 4813, the Federal Court allowed deductions for rental losses incurred by a family trust in these circumstances, however it should be noted that the case was decided under the previous general anti-avoidance provision (s260 ITAA36) rather than Part IVA ITAA97.

SHORT-TERM ACCOMMODATION AND THE ACTIVE ASSET RULES

In certain circumstances holiday apartments may satisfy the active asset test for CGT purposes (see TD 2006/78).

A CGT asset is an active asset if the owner uses the asset in the course of carrying on a business. The CGT rules specifically exclude rental property unless the main use for deriving rent was only temporary (s152-40 ITAA97). Whether a rental arrangement exists or alternatively the activities give rise to business income will depend on the particular circumstances. The issues that indicate whether a rental arrangement exists include:

- the tenant's right to exclusive possession
- the degree of control retained by the owner, and
- the extent of the services provided by the owner.

Exclusive possession is a contractual arrangement whereby the premises are leased to a tenant and the landlord must obtain permission to enter the property. Short-term accommodation generally provides the guest with a temporary licence to occupy the premises.

The following example has been adapted from TD 2006/78.

Jenny owns a holiday apartment complex with ten suites. The apartments are advertised collectively as a motel and are booked for periods ranging from one to two weeks. The majority of bookings are from one to seven nights. Jenny, as the owner-manager, is responsible for bookings, checking guests in and out and cleaning the apartments. She also provides clean linen and meal facilities to guests.

The arrangements indicate that the guests do not have exclusive possession but rather only the right to occupy the apartment. The guests stay for a relatively short-term and the services and facilities provided by Jenny are significant. These facts indicate that the income derived is not rent, but rather business income and therefore the property will be considered an active asset.

Whether a property owner is carrying on a business will depend on the particular activities involved. Factors such as size and scale provide a good indication (see 10.010 and 18.150). Activities such as financing the property, appointing a property agent, attending to body corporate matters, undertaking periodic repairs and maintenance, maintenance of accounting and tax records have not been considered commercial activities but rather no more than any real property investor would carry out in monitoring and maintaining an income producing investment (*AAT Case 5857* [1990] 21 ATR 3389; *Carson and Anor v FCT* [2008]).

18.500 FBT AND RENTAL PROPERTIES

For the purposes of the 'otherwise deductible rule', a fringe benefit provided jointly to an employee and any associates of the employee, are deemed provided solely to the employee. See also from 25.000.

The otherwise deductible rule applies where, had the employee incurred the outgoing a once-only deduction would have been available. For example, an employer can reduce the taxable value of the low interest loan fringe benefit provided to an employee to the extent the interest would have been 'otherwise deductible' to the employee.

However, for new loans entered into from 7.30pm on 13 May 2008, or from 1 April 2009 for existing loans at that date, the 'otherwise deductible rule' will only apply to benefits provided to employees (not associates). Employers must adjust the taxable value of a fringe benefit provided jointly in relation to a jointly owned property, so that the taxable value of the fringe benefit is only reduced by the employee's percentage of interest in the asset.

Katie's employer provided a $700,000 low interest loan to both herself and her spouse Paul. The loan fringe benefit has a taxable value of $70,000. Katie and Paul use the loan to purchase a $700,000 investment property which they will own equally. The notional deduction of $70,000 is reduced by Katie's proportionate interest in the property, (ie. the taxable value of the loan fringe benefit is reduced by $35,000).

Katie's employer will have an FBT liability on $35,000 to reflect the share of the loan fringe benefit provided to Paul (as an associate).

18.600 GST AND RENTAL PROPERTIES

SUMMARY OF GST TREATMENT

Transaction	GST treatment
Sale of residential premises: • Newly built • Substantially renovated/built to replace • Not new	• Taxable if sold by entity required to be registered • Taxable if sold by entity required to be registered • Input taxed regardless of whether or not entity registered
Sale of residential land	Taxable if sold by an entity required to be registered
Rental of residential premises	Input taxed regardless of GST registration status
Rental of display home	Input taxed regardless of GST registration status
Rental of commercial residential premises	Taxable if leased by an entity required to be registered
Expenses connected with rental of residential property (insurance, repairs, agency, commission)	No input tax entitlement regardless of GST registration status

For full details of how GST affects property transactions see 24.340 to 24.344.

Superannuation

19

19.000 SUPERANNUATION: AN OVERVIEW

The *Superannuation Industry (Supervision) Act 1993* (SISA93) and the *Superannuation Industry (Supervision) Regulations 1994* (SISR94) provide the key prudential framework within which Australia's superannuation industry operates. Unless otherwise stated, all section and division references are to the *Income Tax Assessment Act 1997* (ITAA97).

The powers conferred on the trustee of a superannuation fund are governed by the fund trust deed. These powers are however constrained in that they may not override the framework of the legal provisions. It is important for trustees to review their deeds and where appropriate consider updating them to incorporate the full extent of the powers available under existing provisions. This has particular significance for trustees of SMSFs. When complying with the relevant provisions, fund trustees must act lawfully at all times. They should follow accepted principles under trust law and adhere to the administrative procedures as set out by the Australian Tax Office.

19.001 MEASURES ANNOUNCED IN 2015-16 BUDGET

The 2015-16 Budget proposed the following new superannuation measures.

- Early super access for terminal illness: from 1 July 2015, the life expectancy period for full access to superannuation benefits for those with a terminal medical condition to be extended from 12 to 24 months.

- Defined benefit super schemes: from 1 January 2016 a 10% cap to be applied to the deductible amount of defined benefit income streams for the social security income test.

- Supervisory levies: for the 2015-16 year and beyond, use of a full cost model to apply for supervisory levies, with the amount increasing accordingly.

- Lost and unclaimed superannuation: from 1 January 2016 the reporting obligations are to be streamlined.

The two key superannuation changes proposed in the 2014-15 Budget were passed into law.

- Provision of an option to withdraw excess non-concessional contributions from superannuation to apply from 1 July 2013, and

- Confirmation of the Superannuation Guarantee rate for current and future years.

NOTE: The government's stated position to rescind the Low Income Superannuation Contribution (LISC) was modified under a deal to secure parliamentary passage of the repeal of the Mineral Resource Rent Tax. Under this deal the LISC will continue to be payable for the years 2012-13 to 2016-17 inclusive. It will cease for the 2017-18 and subsequent years.

Footnotes for Thresholds table (19.002)

1: Indexed to AWOTE.

2: Rounded down to the nearest multiple of $5,000.

3: Available to eligible individuals over the age of 50 up to 30 June 2012. See previous editions for relevant cap.

4: Equal to six times the concessional cap.

5: Available to eligible persons to bring forward two years' worth of future non-concessional contributions (note: once triggered, the bring forward amount is fixed and does not benefit from indexation).

6: *The Minerals Resource Rent Tax Repeal and Other Measures Bill 2014* received Royal Assent on 5 September 2014. It replaces the *Minerals Resource Rent Tax Repeal and Other Measures Bill 2013 [No. 2]* which will not proceed. The measure has the effect of fixing the SG rate at 9.5% p.a. for the years 2014-15 to 2020-21 and 10% p.a. for the year 2021-22. Thereafter increments of 0.5% per year raise the rate to 12% p.a. for the year 2025-26 and for subsequent years.

7: The higher income threshold is set at $15,000 above the lower income threshold.

8: The indexation of the lower income threshold Is frozen from 1 July 2009 until 30 June 2013 (see 19.077).

9: The SG employee upper age limit is removed from 1 July 2013.

10: Indexation of the concessional cap is paused. for 2012-13 and 2013-14.

11: A higher non-indexed concessional cap of $35,000 in 2013-14 for eligible members 60 and over extends from 2014-15 to those 50 and over.   *CONT →*

19.002 THRESHOLDS

The tax provisions apply concessional treatment for superannuation savings to encourage taxpayers to save for retirement. Government policy is also aimed at preventing excessive superannuation concessions for individual taxpayers through the application of limits to a number of superannuation parameters. The thresholds for these parameters are shown below.

	2014-15	2015-16
Low rate cap amount (indexed) [1, 2]	$185,000	$195,000
Untaxed plan cap amount (indexed) [1, 2]	$1,355,000	$1,395,000
Life benefit employment termination payment cap (indexed) [1, 2]	$185,000	$195,000
Death benefit employment termination payment cap (indexed) [1, 2]	$185,000	$195,000
Tax-free part of a genuine redundancy payment or early retirement scheme payment (indexed) [1] Base amount [14]	$9,514	$9,780
For each completed year of service add [14]	$4,758	$4,891
Government co-contribution scheme [8] (see 19.076)		
Lower income threshold	$34,488	$35,454
Higher income threshold [7]	$49,488	$50,454
Matching rate	50%	50%
Maximum payable	$500	$500
Low income superannuation contribution [12] (see 19.077)		
Maximum adjusted taxable income	$37,000	$37,000
Maximum payable	$500	$500
Contribution caps		
Concessional (indexed) [1, 2, 10]	$30,000	$30,000
Fixed higher cap (from 1 July 2013 for age 60 and over, and from 1 July 2014 for age 50 and over) [11] or Transitional concessional to 30 June 2012 (non-indexed) [3]	$35,000	$35,000
Non-concessional (non-indexed) [4]	$180,000	$180,000
Non-concessional with bring forward option (non-indexed) [5]	$540,000	$540,000
CGT cap (indexed) [1, 2]	$1,355,000	$1,395,000
Superannuation Guarantee (SG)		
Prescribed minimum employer contribution rate [6]	9.5%	9.5%
Employee upper age limit obligation [9]	NA	NA
Maximum contribution base on which contributions have to be made (per quarter) [1]	$49,430	$50,810
Departing Australia Superannuation Payment (DASP) rate of tax		
Tax-free component	nil	nil
Taxed element of the taxable component [13]	38%	38%
Untaxed element of the taxable component [13]	47%	47%

Continued from previous page ...

12: In November 2013 the government confirmed its intention to rescind this measure. But following negotiations in the Senate in support of the passage of various Bills, the payment of LISC will be maintained in respect of concessional contributions that are made up-to and including 30 June 2017. Payment of LISC will cease in respect of concessional contributions made on or after 1 July 2017. While LISC will continue to be payable in respect of concessional contributions made up-to and including the 2016-17 income year, determinations of LISC will cease at 30 June 2019.

13: Maximum rate of tax for years prior to 2014-15 is 35% (taxable component) and 45% (untaxed element of taxable component).

14: The calculation of the tax-free amount of a genuine redundancy payment or early retirement scheme is made up of a base amount plus an amount for each completed year of service.

19.008   CONTRIBUTION [1] ACCEPTANCE AND DEDUCTIBILITY TABLE 2015-16

Contr. type	Criteria
Age	**Up to 65 years**
Employer (Concessional) (see 19.015, 19.022)	• Mandated and non-mandated: No 'gainful employment test'. • Employer: Full deduction for all eligible contributions. • Employee: Capped at $30,000 (indexed). A higher non-indexed cap of $35,000 from 1 July 2013 for those aged 60 and over. From 1 July 2014 this higher cap extended to those aged 50 and over. It will be phased out when it aligns with the lower, indexed cap, following any future indexation increment.
Personal (Concessional) (see 19.015, 19.026)	• Eligible persons (see 10% rule: 19.026) can claim full deduction for all eligible concessional contributions. • Capped at $30,000 or $35,000 for older Australians as for Employer (Concessional) above. • A person under 18 at the end of the income year must have derived 'employment' or 'business income' during the year. • Fund must be notified in writing of intention to claim a deduction. • No 'gainful employment test'
Personal (Non-concess.) (see 19.015, 19.030)	• Capped at $180,000, however a 'bring forward' option can be triggered to allow up to two years of future contributions to be brought forward, giving a cap of $540,000 attributable to three years [2]. • No 'gainful employment test'.
Spouse contribution (Non-concess.) (see 19.015, 19.074)	• Capped at $180,000, however a 'bring forward' option can be triggered to allow up to two years of future contributions to be brought forward, giving a cap of $540,000 attributable to three years [2]. • No 'gainful employment test'.
Government co-contribution (see 19.076)	• Co-contribution applies only to eligible non-concessional contributions of up to $1,000. • Maximum co-contribution is $500 for 2015-16 and 2014-15. • The co-contribution matching rate is 50% for 2015-16 and 2014-15. • The co-contribution benefit paid is reduced by 3.333 cents for every dollar above the lower income threshold. It is reduced to nil for incomes at or above the higher income threshold of $50,454 for 2015-16 or $49,488 in 2014-15. • 10% or more of 'total income' attributable to either or both of 'eligible employment' and 'carrying on a business'. • Income tax return for the income year must be lodged • Must be less than 71 years of age at end of the income year • Must not have held a prescribed visa at any time during income year • No 'gainful employment test'
Government low income superannuation contribution (see 19.077)	• Based on 15% of concessional contributions.(See Note 12 of Table 19.002) • Capped at $500. • 'Adjusted taxable income' must be less than $37,000. • 10% or more of 'total income' attributable to either or both of 'eligible employment' and 'carrying on a business'. • Must not have held a prescribed visa at any time during income year. • No 'gainful employment test'.
Personal injury contributions (no cap applies) (see 19.079)	Contributions arising from: • personal injury settlement relating to workers compensation, personal injury compensation, damages claim or right under statute in writing (court order or otherwise), and • where the contribution is made within 90 days of the later of receipt of payment or date of effect of settlement or order, and • two medical practitioners certify unlikely to ever be gainfully employed in a capacity where reasonably qualified by education, experience or training.
CGT cap (Small business concessions) (see 19.079)	Contributions up to a indexed lifetime limit of $1.395million for 2015-16 ($1.355million 2014-15) made from: • capital proceeds of asset sales that satisfy the requirements for the CGT small business 15 year exemption (or would have if a capital gain had arisen), or • capital gain that satisfies requirements for CGT small business retirement exemption, and • must be made by later of date of lodgement of tax return or 30 days from receipt of capital proceeds. Note: Different timing requirements are contained in the retirement exemption provisions (s152-305(1) and s152-325(4)).

Age-based tests

65 to 69	70 to 71	71 to 75	75 and over
• Mandated: No 'gainful employment test'. • Non-mandated: 'Gainful employment test'. • Employer: Full deduction for all eligible contributions. • From 1 July 2013 upper age limit of 70 no longer to apply for SG cover with contributions fully deductible to employer			Mandated: Only if required under an Industrial Award or Determination. From 1 July 2013, the upper age restriction of 70 for SG cover is overturned & employer cover is compulsory with contributions for those over 70 deductible.
• Eligible persons (see 10% rule at 19.026) can claim a full deduction for all eligible concessional contributions. • Fund must be notified in writing of intention to claim a deduction. • 'Gainful employment test'.			Not eligible to contribute.
• Capped at $180,000. [2] Bring forward not available. • 'Gainful employment test'			Not eligible to contribute
• Capped at $180,000[2] • 'Gainful employment test' for member spouse	Not eligible to contribute to superannuation on member spouse's behalf.		
• Co-contribution only applies to eligible contributions of up to $1,000. • Co-contribution matching rate is 50%. • 'Total income' must be less than the higher income threshold when co-contribution phases out to nil. • Co-contribution reduced by 3.333 cents for every dollar over lower income threshold of $35,454 in 2015-16. • 10% or more of 'total income' attributable to either or both of 'eligible employment' and 'carrying on a business'. • Income tax return for the income year must be lodged. • Must be less than 71 years of age at end of the income year. • Must not have held a prescribed visa at any time during income year. • 'Gainful employment test' applies.	No entitlement if age 71 or more in relevant income year.		
'Gainful employment test' applies.			
'Gainful employment test' applies.			

1. Non-concessional contributions cannot be accepted where the member's TFN has not been quoted. If a single non-concessional contribution, on its own, exceeds the relevant cap, the amount in excess of the cap must not be accepted by the fund, but returned within 30 days of the trustee becoming aware of the contribution.
2. The bring forward arrangement is available to individuals under 65 during the relevant financial year. However on the day that a contribution is made and the individual is 65 years or older, eligibility for making the contribution is subject to meeting the work test in the year of contribution (see 19.015).

19.010 CONTRIBUTIONS

Superannuation contributions include contributions made by employers on behalf of their employees, personal post-tax or pre-tax contributions, spouse contributions, other third party contributions and payments of the SG shortfall component. They do not include benefits 'rolled over' or 'transferred' to a superannuation fund. A superannuation fund may only accept contributions made in accordance with the *Superannuation Industry (Supervision) Regulations 1994* (SISR94). The *Income Tax Assessment Act 1997* (ITAA97) deals with the taxation treatment of contributions.

19.015 ACCEPTANCE OF CONTRIBUTIONS

The contribution acceptance rules are contained in SISR94. These rules take into account the type of contribution, the age of the contributor for whom the contributions are made, satisfying a *gainful employment test*, quotation of TFNs and contributions caps. (Also see table at 19.002.)

 Contributions do not include benefits 'rolled over' or 'transferred' to a superannuation fund.

Regulation r7.04(1) of the SISR94 specifies that a superannuation fund can only accept contributions for members. (Please note that additional rules in r7.04A apply if the fund is a public offer superannuation fund.)

Taxation Ruling TR 2010/1, explains the Commissioner's view on the ordinary meaning of 'contribution', how a contribution can be made, and when a contribution is made for the purposes of the *Superannuation Industry (Supervision) Act 1993* (SISA93) and the SISR94. However, it should be noted that the SISR94 contains a definition of 'contribution' that modifies its ordinary meaning.

MANDATED CONTRIBUTIONS r7.04(1) SISR94

All mandated employer contributions for a member of any age (ie. a contribution to satisfy an employer Superannuation Guarantee (SG), or an award based superannuation obligation, (including shortfall components)), are not subject to restrictions.

Under the provisions that apply to the end of June 2013, SG obligations cease when a member reaches age 70 unless:

- made within 28 days after the end of the month in which the member turned age 70, or
- they relate to a period before the member turned age 70.

From 1 July 2013, amendments to the SG provisions have removed the upper age limit of 70, for entitlement to SG payments.

NOTE: This mandated contribution must be paid to eligible employees including those age 70 or over, from this date.

NON-MANDATED CONTRIBUTIONS r7.04(1) SISR94

A contribution that is not a mandated employer contribution is subject to age based and related rules as follows.

- **Under age 65:** All contributions may be accepted without restriction. However refer r7.04(2) and r7.04(3) of the SISR94 (see below).
- **Age 65 to under age 75:** Non-mandated contributions can be accepted subject to the member meeting a gainful employment test (see below). Also refer r7.04(2) and r7.04(3) of SISR94 (see below).
- **Age 75 and over:** Non-mandated contributions cannot be accepted.

GAINFUL EMPLOYMENT TEST

The *gainful employment test* requires the member to have been gainfully employed. This may be on a part time basis for at least 40 hours over a continuous 30 day period during the relevant financial year in which the contribution is to be made and accepted by the fund (r7.01(3)).

QUOTATION OF TAX FILE NUMBER

Under r7.04(2) of the SISR94 a superannuation fund is required to return member non-concessional contributions where the member's Tax File Number (TFN) has not been quoted to the trustee of the superannuation fund. This prevents a person from avoiding the non-concessional contributions cap and any tax liability that may arise thereof. The Tax Office is otherwise unable to match a person to their contributions for purposes of excess contributions without a taxpayers TFN being quoted.

FUND-CAPPED CONTRIBUTION LIMITS

Under r7.04(3) of the SISR94 a superannuation fund may only accept a member contribution that is less than, or equal to, the member's fund-capped contribution limit. This applies to non-concessional contributions. The fund-capped amount does not include any amount that the member notifies their fund that they intend to claim as a personal superannuation deduction.

The fund-capped contribution limits are:

- $180,000 (for 2015-16 & 2014-15) if the member is 65 years of age or older on 1 July of the relevant financial year, and
- $540,000 (for 2015-16 & 2014-15) if the member is not yet 65 years of age on 1 July of the relevant financial year (ie. 'bring forward' option).

NOTE: If a fund receives a member contribution that exceeds their fund-capped contribution limit, the fund must return the excess to the contributor within 30 days of becoming aware of it. These rules are covered in r7.04(3) and r7.04(4) of the SISR94. Funds do not have to report any excess part of a contribution they have returned under these rules.

 The fund-capped regulation applies per contribution, not to total member contributions made to the fund.

A fund is considered to be aware that a contribution is in breach of the fund-capped contribution limit when the fund becomes aware of the contribution itself. When a fund becomes aware of a contribution is a matter of fact but will generally be on the day the contribution is received.

The Tax Office expects that trustees will act with care, skill and diligence and within 30 days of becoming aware of the contribution will:

- know that a contribution breaches the fund-capped contributions limit, or
- have a process to work out if the contribution breaches the fund-capped contributions limit.

A superannuation fund cannot use ignorance of the law as an excuse. It must have procedures in place to ensure that it knows about information relevant to its operations within a reasonable time of the information being available.

The Commissioner still requires an SMSF to return a contribution or part of a contribution if more than 30 days has expired since the trustee became aware that the contribution standards in r7.04(1), r7.04(2) or r7.04(3) were not met (see ATO ID 2009/29).

 For more information about fund-capped contribution limits, please also refer to ATO IDs 2007/225, 2008/90 and 2009/29.

CONTRIBUTIONS MADE AFTER THE RELEVANT PERIOD

An administrative provision allows late acceptance of contributions providing the fund trustee is reasonably satisfied that they relate to a period when the fund was able to accept them on behalf of the member.

CO-CONTRIBUTIONS

Please see 19.076 if the contribution is made under the government co-contribution scheme.

LOW INCOME SUPERANNUATION CONTRIBUTION

Please see 19.077 if the contribution is made under the Low Income Superannuation Contribution (LISC) scheme.

CONTRIBUTING TO MORE THAN ONE ENTITY

There is no restriction on the number of superannuation funds or Retirement Savings Accounts (RSAs) into which contributions can be made. However, this may result in greater complexity and higher administrative charges, reducing overall benefits.

19.020 CONCESSIONAL (BEFORE-TAX) CONTRIBUTIONS

Contributions for which a tax deduction is claimed are called Concessional Contributions (CCs). An individual's concessional contributions in a financial year are generally contributions made by or for that individual in that year that are included in the assessable income of a superannuation provider.

An individual's concessional contributions do not include:

- rollover superannuation benefits
- the amount of a superannuation benefit transferred from a foreign superannuation fund, and
- any contributions made to constitutionally protected superannuation funds.

Types of contributions that count towards the concessional contribution cap are:

- employer contributions (see 19.022)
- personal deductible contributions (see 19.026)
- SG shortfall payments (see 19.530), and
- small account payments.

Also see Taxation Ruling TR 2010/1, which explains the Commissioner's view of the ordinary meaning of the word 'contribution' when used in relation to a superannuation fund, ADF or RSA in the *Income Tax Assessment Act 1997* (ITAA97). In particular the Ruling explains aspects of the rules in Division 290 of ITAA97 that apply when a superannuation contribution is deductible.

19.022   EMPLOYER CONTRIBUTIONS (CONCESSIONAL)

Division 290 ITAA97 sets out the specific deduction rules that apply when an employer makes superannuation contributions. Providing certain conditions are met (see below), an employer is entitled to a full deduction for all contributions to a complying superannuation fund on behalf of an employee, regardless of whether the benefits are payable to a 'SIS dependant' (s995-1 ITAA97) of the employee or their Legal Personal Representative (LPR), even if the employee has died before or after becoming entitled to receive their superannuation benefits (ss290-60 to 290-100).

Although the amount of the employer's deduction is not limited, the employee may be liable to excess contributions tax if contributions by the employer on behalf of the employee exceed the relevant contributions cap (see 19.040 and 19.050).

From 1 July 2009 certain employer contributions may fall within the definition of Reportable Employer Superannuation Contributions (see 19.026 & 19.065).

EMPLOYEE

The meaning of 'employee' (s290-65 ITAA97) refers to the expanded definition found in s12 of the *Superannuation Guarantee (Administration) Act 1992* (SGAA92). For example, the expanded definition ensures a person who works under a contract that is wholly or principally for their labour is an employee. Directors are also statutory employees (s12(2) SGAA92) under the expanded definition.

UPPER AGE 75 RESTRICTION

Deductions for contributions are generally limited to those made in respect of employees who are less than 75 years old (s290-80).

An employer can claim a deduction for contributions made on behalf of an employee over age 75 where:

- made for the eligible employee within 28 days after the end of the month in which the employee turned age 75 (s290-80(1)(a)), or

- made to meet the actual amount of contribution required by law under an industrial award or determination (s290-80(1)(b) & (2)).

NOTE: The upper age restriction limiting SG contributions to those not yet 70 was removed from 1 July 2013.

OTHER CONDITIONS

The following conditions must also be satisfied:
- the contribution is made to a complying superannuation fund (s290-75), and
- the employee must be engaged in producing the employer's assessable income or be an Australian resident who is engaged in the employer's business (s290-70).

A contribution for a former employee may also be deductible, if it reduces the employer's SGC liability in respect of the employee (s290-85).

Jim's employer pays 12% superannuation in accordance with an industrial award. He turns 76 on 9 September 2015. His employer can claim a full tax deduction for all superannuation contributions made for him. These concessional contributions are assessable income of the fund.

19.026   PERSONAL CONCESSIONAL CONTRIBUTIONS

A person may deduct a contribution made to a superannuation fund if certain conditions are satisfied (s290-150). There is no limit on the amount of the contribution or on the deduction, but excess contributions tax may be payable if the contribution exceeds the relevant cap amount (see 19.050).

Personal contributions are only deductible if the following conditions are satisfied:
- the contribution is made to a complying superannuation fund (s290-155)
- if the contributor engages in work and this results in the contributor being treated as an employee for superannuation guarantee (SG) purposes (see below), less than 10% of the total sum of their assessable income plus reportable fringe benefits plus Reportable Employer Superannuation Contributions (RESCs) for the income year is attributable to those employment activities (s290-160) (If there is no SG related employment income then the need to meet the 10% test on income does not arise)
- a contributor aged under 18 at end of the income year must have derived income during the year from carrying on a business or from employment-related activities (s290-165(1))
- the contribution must be made by the 28th day after the month in which the contributor turns 75 (s290-165(2)), and
- the contributor must notify the fund trustee in writing of their intention to claim the deduction. The notice must be given by the earlier of when the contributor lodges their income tax return for the year or the end of the financial year following the year the contribution is made. The fund trustee must acknowledge receipt of the notice, and the contributor cannot deduct more than the amount stated in the notice (s290-170).

MADE TO A COMPLYING SUPERANNUATION FUND (s290-155)

The contribution must be made to a Complying Superannuation Fund (CSF). This definition of a CSF is for tax purposes only, and is in accordance with s45 of the SISA93.

THE '10% RULE' (S290-160)

A person who is engaged in work that results in them being treated as an employee for superannuation guarantee (SG) purposes may still be able to claim a tax deduction for personal superannuation contributions, providing less than 10% of their total assessable income, reportable fringe benefits and reportable employer superannuation contributions (RESCs) (see below) for the income year in which the contributions are made comes from 'employee activities' (s290-160(2)). The person must also satisfy a requirement that allows a superannuation fund to accept such contributions (see 19.015).

If you are aged between 18 and 65 and are solely in receipt of passive income, you may be eligible to a deduction for personal superannuation contributions.

'Employee activities' of a person means (s290-160(1)):

- holding an office or appointment
- performing functions or duties
- engaging in work, or
- doing acts or things,

that results in the person being treated as an employee under the SGAA92 (see 19.500), or being paid to do work of a private or domestic nature (ie. s12(11) SGAA92 is ignored).

In *Van Prooyen and Commissioner of Taxation* (2010) AATA 281, the AAT held that a person in receipt of workers compensation payments from 1 July 2007 to 12 July 2007, when he retired from the Australian Electoral Commission on grounds of invalidity, was engaged in the activity of holding an office or appointment for the purposes of s290-160 of ITAA97. Section 290-160 contains the 10% rule which restricts the eligibility for deductions for personal contributions.

REPORTABLE EMPLOYER SUPERANNUATION CONTRIBUTIONS

From 1 July 2009, certain employer contributions may fall within the definition of a RESC. For more information on RESCs, see 19.065.

This RESC change affects those employees who previously used superannuation based Salary Sacrifice Arrangements (SSSAs) to qualify for deductible personal superannuation contributions under the '10% rule'.

Jane, age 34, derived the following amounts for the 2015-16 income year:

Income attributable to employment activities

- *Salary and wages – assessable income* *$17,000*
- *Reportable fringe benefits total* *$2,140*
- *Reportable employer superannuation contributions* *$5,000*

          $24,140

From other sources

- *Gross rent (before deductions)* *$80,000*
- *Interest income* *$10,000*
- *Assessable capital gain* *$91,200*

          $181,200

The sum of assessable income, total reportable fringe benefits and reportable employer superannuation contributions from employee activities is $24,140.

For eligibility to make concessional contributions this income of $24,140 from employee activities may not be greater than 10% of the sum of the following three components; total assessable income (salary and wages plus income from other sources =$198,200), total reportable fringe benefits of $2,140 and reportable employer superannuation contributions of $5,000. This gives $205,340 and 10% of this amount is $20,534.

Since the total from employee activity of $24,140 is greater than 10% of all her income namely $20,534, she is therefore ineligible to claim a deduction for superannuation contributions.

INTENTION TO CLAIM A DEDUCTION FOR PERSONAL CONTRIBUTIONS (s290-170)

If a person who is making, or has made a personal contribution to a superannuation fund wishes to claim a tax deduction, a written notice must be given to the trustee of the fund stating that the person intends to claim a deduction under this section for all, or a specified part, of the contribution. The notice must be given before the earlier of the lodgment of the person's income tax return for the income year in which the contribution was made and the end of the following income year. The trustee must, without delay, acknowledge receipt of the notice.

Under s290-170(2), a person cannot:

- give a notice that is not in respect of the contribution
- covers the whole or any part of an amount covered by a previous notice

- give a notice to the trustee of a fund when not a member of the fund, or the fund no longer holds the contribution, or the trustee has begun paying an income stream based on whole or part of the contribution.

Under s290-180, a person cannot revoke or withdraw a notice, but they can vary it (see below).

SUPERANNUATION CONTRIBUTIONS SPLITTING

Persons intending to claim a tax deduction for personal contributions made to their fund during the financial year, will need to lodge a notice before lodging a contributions splitting application. This notice is in accordance with s290-170 (see 19.075).

DEDUCTION LIMITS

The maximum deduction for personal superannuation contributions cannot exceed the taxpayer's taxable income as calculated ignoring the personal contribution (ie. a loss cannot arise from a personal superannuation deduction claim) (s26-55).

In addition, a person cannot deduct more for their personal contribution or part thereof, than the amount stated in their written notice (s290-175).

VARIATION OF THE AMOUNT COVERED BY A PREVIOUS NOTICE

A notice can only be varied and cannot be revoked or withdrawn. The variation can only be to reduce (including to nil) the amount stated in relation to the contribution (s290-180(1) and (2)). The variation is not effective if the individual is not at that time a member of the fund, or the trustee no longer holds the contribution or has commenced to pay a superannuation income stream based on the contribution (s290-180(3A)).

NOTICE RECEIVED AFTER LODGEMENT OF THE MEMBER'S TAX RETURN

A valid notice cannot be varied after the earlier of the time a person lodges their income tax return and the end of the financial year following the year the contribution was made (s290-180(3)). These time limits do not apply to a variation where a deduction was disallowed for all or part of the contribution and the variation reduces the amount stated in relation to the contribution by the amount disallowed (s290-180(4)).

 Trustees should treat any personal contributions not claimed as tax deductions as non-concessional (after-tax) contributions.

19.030 NON-CONCESSIONAL (AFTER-TAX) CONTRIBUTIONS

Contributions for which a tax deduction is not available are called Non-Concessional Contributions (NCCs).

An individual's non-concessional contributions in a financial year are generally contributions made by or for that individual in that year that are not included in the assessable income of the superannuation fund.

The following types of contributions are included:

- excess concessional contributions, ie. amounts above the applicable cap
- contributions made for the benefit of a person under 18 years of age that are not employer contributions
- personal contributions for which an income tax deduction is not claimed
- contributions made to a constitutionally protected fund
- contributions which are included in the assessable income of the fund but are not allowed as a deduction (eg. where the '10% rule' is not satisfied)

 Rodney gives a notice to his fund indicating that he intends to claim his personal contribution of $10,000 as a tax deduction. This claim is later denied by the Tax Office as Rodney did not satisfy the '10% rule'. Rodney has not lodged a notice of variation, so his fund will treat his personal contributions as assessable income which will be taxed at 15%. However, these contributions will only be counted towards Rodney's non-concessional contributions cap.

- amounts transferred from foreign superannuation funds (excluding amounts included in the fund's assessable income)
- contributions a person's spouse makes to their superannuation fund account, and
- contributions in excess of an individual's Capital Gains Tax Cap (CGTC) amount.

However, an individual's non-concessional contributions do not include:

- the government superannuation co-contribution
- certain contributions relating to personal injury payments (see 19.079)
- amounts from the disposal of certain small business assets that are within the CGTC
- contributions that are made to a constitutionally protected fund that are not included in the contributions segment of your superannuation interest in the fund
- contributions that are paid out as a superannuation benefit in the same year that they are contributed as an element untaxed in the fund
- rollover superannuation benefits
- amounts not included in a provider's assessable income because of Division 295-D. These amounts are included in a person's concessional contributions cap, and
- contributions made before 10 May 2006.

19.040 CONTRIBUTION CAPS

19.041 CONCESSIONAL CAPS

The (indexed) Concessional Contributions Cap (CCC) is $30,000 in both 2015-16 and 2014-15. The Transitional Concessional Contributions Cap (TCCC) for those aged at least 50 was phased out after 30 June 2012 with a higher fixed cap being introduced subsequently for older Australians from 1 July 2013 (see below). For excess concessional contributions see 19.055.

INDEXATION

Concessional contribution caps, except those related to the transitional arrangements (and the higher fixed cap for older Australians) are indexed to Average Weekly Ordinary Time Earnings (AWOTE). Increases to the cap may only occur in increments of $5,000. Indexation amounts must therefore total at least $5,000 before they are reflected in a higher contribution cap. Any indexation amount that exceeds the increment applied to the cap is not lost but is available for future years.

TRANSITIONAL PROVISIONS

 The TCCC ended on 30 June 2012.

The five year TCCC applied from 1 July 2007 until 30 June 2012 for those aged 50 to 74 years. It was set at $100,000 for the years ended 30 June 2008 and 30 June 2009, and $50,000 for each of the years ended 30 June 2010, 30 June 2011 and 30 June 2012. The TCCC is not indexed.

HIGHER FIXED CAP FOR OLDER AUSTRALIANS

A higher annual cap of $35,000 applies in the year 2013-14.

From 1 July 2013 this higher, fixed cap of $35,000 applies for those 60* and over.

From 1 July 2014 this higher cap applies to those aged 50** and over.

At a future date this higher cap is to be phased out when the lower indexed cap has increased to $35,000 through indexation.

* The eligibility test is based on the member having reached 59 years on 30 June 2013, that is at least age 60 in the year of contribution.

** Similarly at least age 49 on 30 June of the year when the higher contribution is to be made, on or after 1 July 2014.

Graeme turns 50 on 9 September 2011 with the following concessional caps for the years ending 30 June 2012 to 30 June 2016 (assume the higher annual cap follows the projections above and that the CCC does not exceed $35,000).
- *30 June 2012: $50,000*
- *30 June 2013: $25,000*
- *30 June 2014: $25,000 (he is not yet 60, so the higher cap does not apply)*
- *30 June 2015: $35,000 (he is over 50 so the higher cap applies).*
- *30 June 2016: $35,000 (he is over 50 so the higher cap applies).*

TIPS TO HELP KEEP SUPER CONTRIBUTIONS UNDER THE CONCESSIONAL CONTRIBUTIONS CAP

- A taxpayer expecting to exceed the concessional contributions cap in the current financial year, may:
  - stop or reduce any voluntary contributions, such as salary sacrifice; but may not request a change to compulsory SG amounts or amounts paid under a contract or industrial agreement.
  - delay personal superannuation contributions they intend to claim as a deduction to a future year.
- Check details of when contributions are received by the super fund. Generally, the contribution counts towards a cap in the year in which the fund actually receives the money (but see ATO ID 2012/16 below).
- Ensure that costs such as administration fees and insurance premiums paid by employers are included in the concessional contributions cap calculation.
- If a taxpayer has more than one job or pays money into more than one super fund, they should include all of these amounts when calculating annual contributions. Remember that compulsory SG amounts are concessional contributions.
- If a taxpayer is eligible to claim an income tax deduction for their personal super contributions, only the amount the Tax Office allows as a deduction will count towards the taxpayer's concessional contributions cap.
- Consider the use of a reserve account.

19.042   NON-CONCESSIONAL CAPS

Ignoring transitional arrangements, the non-concessional contributions cap of $150,000 applied until the year ending 2013-14. For 2014-15 and 2015-16 this cap is $180,000. Non-concessional contributions in excess of the relevant cap are taxed at top marginal tax rates plus Medicare levy under the excess contributions provisions.

NOTE: An option currently exists and applies from 1 July 2013, to withdraw the excess non-concessional contributions from superannuation to avoid the impost of top marginal rates.

Contributions made directly by an individual into their spouse's account are counted against the receiving spouse's non-concessional contributions cap.

INDEXATION

The cap on non-concessional contributions is indexed indirectly, and is currently set at six times the indexed cap on concessional contributions.

BRING-FORWARD

As a concession to accommodate larger contributions, people under age 65 during a financial year are able to 'bring-forward' two years' contribution entitlements, giving them an aggregate cap over three years of three times the current non-concessional cap. In 2015-16 and 2014-15 this is $540,000.

The 'bring-forward' provisions are triggered automatically when contributions in excess of the annual cap are made in a financial year by a person who, at any time in the financial year, is under 65 and where the 'bring-forward' provisions are not already in play.

The 'bring-forward' provisions only apply to a member under age 65 on 1 July of the relevant financial year.

Mario, who turned 64 on 2 June 2015, makes the following non-concessional contributions:
- *1 June 2015: $540,000*
- *1 June 2016: $0*
- *1 June 2017: $0*

No excess contribution occurs due to the operation of the bring-forward rule, and the need to meet the work test does not arise.

Alternatively, if the following contributions were made on 1 June of each of the following years:
- *1 June 2014: $250,000*
- *1 June 2015: $100,000*
- *1 June 2016: $100,000*

No excess contribution occurs due to the bring-forward provisions.

Since Mario commenced the bring-forward arrangements in 2013-14 an amount equal to three times the commencing NCC of $150,000 (or $450,000) is available for the duration when the bring-forward applies. The increased non-concessional cap of $180,000 in 2014-15 and 2015-16 is unavailable to Mario.

EXEMPTIONS

Certain contributions arising from payments for personal injuries that result in permanent incapacity and amounts of up to a lifetime indexed limit of $1.395 million in 2015-16 ($1.355 million for 2014-15) from the disposal of qualifying small business assets are not counted towards the non-concessional contributions cap (see 19.079).

TIPS FOR THE NON-CONCESSIONAL CONTRIBUTIONS CAP

The six reminders below may assist taxpayers to keep within the non-concessional contributions cap, and avoid paying extra tax. Excess concessional contributions also count against the non-concessional contributions cap.

- Amounts that a taxpayer cashes out and re-contributes into a super fund is a personal contribution.
- Contributions are counted against the caps in the year they are allocated by the fund trustee under the provisions and the terms of the trust deed.
- Taxpayers may bring forward two succeeding years' contributions if they are 64 years old or younger on 1 July of the financial year when the annual cap is exceeded.
- If a taxpayer is at least age 65 years and is less than 75, to be eligible to contribute they must pass the work test of at least 40 hours over a consecutive, 30 day period in the year in which the contribution is made.
- A taxpayer must provide an election form to their fund before or when they make the contribution if it is to be excluded from the non-concessional cap when made in connection with:
  - contributions arising from personal injury payments (see 19.079)
  - contributions derived from the proceeds of the disposal of certain small business assets, up to their lifetime CGT cap amount (see 19.079).

NOTE: An option to withdraw excess non-concessional contributions from superannuation to avoid paying top marginal tax rates on the excess is available under legislation that applies from 1 July 2013.

19.050 EXCESS CONTRIBUTIONS AND EXCESS CONTRIBUTIONS TAX

The Excess Contributions Tax (ECT) measure was introduced from 1 July 2007 as part of the overhaul of superannuation to dissuade taxpayers from gaining disproportionate concessions from excessive superannuation contributions made into a concessionally taxed structure. Contributions in excess of the relevant cap became subject to ECT being imposed on the person for whom the contributions are made. The person may, and in some cases, must withdraw an amount equal to their tax liability from their superannuation fund.

EXCESS CONCESSIONAL CONTRIBUTIONS

When the regime was introduced, concessional contributions in excess of the cap became liable for ECT. A tax rate of 30% plus Medicare levy applied leading to the top marginal tax rate when the contributions tax rate (15%) was included. Various changes have been made to the provisions since 2007.

Major amendments were introduced covering the 2011-12 and 2012-13 years where a refund of excess concessional contributions was permitted to the taxpayer, with the income assessed at the taxpayer's marginal tax rate. These provisions were in response to the draconian impact the ECT regime was having on members who exceeded their concessional cap. It included a number of conditions that had to be met. (See *Refund of excess concessional contributions* below).

Extensive further amendments were made to the excess concessional contributions provisions. These amendments were also in response to the unfair and often unsatisfactory nature of the existing ECT regime These provisions apply for the 2013-14 and subsequent years. Under the changes excess concessional contributions are deemed to be assessable income of the taxpayer and taxed accordingly. (See *Excess concessional contributions from 2013-14.*)

 An outline of the provisions that relate to excess concessional contributions in the 2013-14 and subsequent years is provided under Excess concessional contributions from 2013-14. The remainder of the discussion under 19.050 to 19.060 covers the Excess concessional contributions tax provisions applying prior to 2013-14. It should be noted that the provisions applying from 2013-14 no longer refer to excess concessional contributions tax.

EXCESS NON-CONCESSIONAL CONTRIBUTIONS TAX

Similarly excess non-concessional contributions are liable for tax at a rate equal to the top marginal tax rate plus Medicare levy. The ECT provisions for non-concessional contributions have remained largely unchanged except for the recent change allowing taxpayers the option to withdraw the excess and avoid paying top marginal tax plus Medicare on the excess. This applies to excess non-contributions for the 2013-14 and subsequent years. See 19.053.

REFUND OF EXCESS CONCESSIONAL CONTRIBUTIONS (2011-12 AND 2012-13)

The refund provisions apply for contributions made from 1 July 2011 and allow in certain limited circumstances for eligible individuals with excess concessional contributions to withdraw the excess amount from their superannuation fund and have this amount assessed as income at their marginal rate of tax. This avoids a need for the excess to be assessed under the ECT regime. The measure only applies where an individual has made excess concessional contributions of up to $10,000 (not indexed) in a particular year. It is only available for breaches in respect of 2011-12 or later years, and only for the first year in which a breach occurs. However following subsequent amendments to the provisions as outlined below, the existing provisions have been superseded for the 2013-14 and subsequent years as outlined below.

EXCESS CONCESSIONAL CONTRIBUTIONS TAX FOR 2013-14 AND BEYOND

The *Tax Laws Amendment (Fairer Taxation of Excess Concessional Contributions) Bill 2013* and *Superannuation (Excess Concessional Contributions Charge) Bill 2013* amended the *Income Tax Assessment Act 1997* (ITAA97) and *Taxation Administration Act 1953* to establish a system for the taxation of individuals with concessional contributions in excess of their annual cap. These changes enable:

- excess concessional contributions to be included in the individual's assessable income and taxed at the taxpayer's marginal tax rate, rather than necessarily at the top marginal tax rate as applied previously.
- individuals to pay the ECT personally or elect to have released an amount up to 85% of the excess concessional contributions (made from 1 July 2013) from their superannuation account.
- the released amounts proportionately reduce the individual's NCCs.
- the imposition of an excess concessional contributions charge (ECCC) to account for a delayed payment of tax, being dependent on a determination following receipt of the taxpayer's tax return and Member Contribution Statement (MCS) from the fund.

Income tax and excess concessional contributions

Jerry has a concessional contributions cap of $30,000 for the 2014-15 financial year. His concessional contributions for the financial year total $55,000. He therefore has excess concessional contributions of $25,000.

The entire $25,000 of the excess concessional contributions are included in Jerry's assessable income for 2014-15. Jerry is also entitled to a tax offset equal to 15% of his excess concessional contributions of (15% of $25,000) = $3,750.

Calculating the increase in tax liability

In 2013-14, Mary's taxable income is $80,000, which includes excess concessional contributions of $10,000.

Mary's marginal tax rate is 32.5% and she must also pay the Medicare levy of 1.5%.

As a result of her excess concessional contributions, Mary's taxable income has increased by $10,000, on which she pays income tax (including Medicare levy) at her effective marginal rate (34%), resulting in additional tax of $3,400. However, she is also entitled to a tax offset equal to 15% of her excess concessional contributions, decreasing her tax liability by $1,500. The amount of Mary's tax liability that is attributable to her excess concessional contributions is $3,400 − $1,500 = $1,900. (An excess concessional contribution charge applies as well.)

EXCESS CONCESSIONAL CONTRIBUTION CHARGE

An Excess Concessional Contributions Charge (ECCC) is applied to concessional contributions in excess of the cap since the tax is collected later than normal income tax. The charge is payable on the increase in tax liability in the year a person makes excess concessional contributions. This applies for the 2013-14 and later income years.

The relevant period is calculated from the start of the income year in which the excess concessional contributions were made. It ends just before the tax is due to be paid under the first income tax assessment for the year that includes the excess concessional contributions.

The formula for calculating the ECCC is provided for under section 4 of the *Superannuation (Excess Concessional Contributions Charge) Act 2013*. It uses a base interest rate for the day plus an uplift factor of 3%. The base interest rate is defined under section 5 of the same Act and is the monthly average yield of 90-day Bank Accepted Bills published by the Reserve Bank of Australia.

The ECC charge rates are updated quarterly and listed in the table below.

Excess concessional contributions charge rates		
Quarter	Annual rate	Daily rate
April – June 2015	5.36%	0.014684931506849%
January – March 2015	5.75%	0.015753424657534%
October – December 2014	5.63%	0.015424657534247%
July – September 2014	5.69%	0.015589041095890%
April – June 2014	5.63%	0.015424657534247%
January – March 2014	5.59%	0.015315068493151%
October – December 2013	5.6%	0.015342465753425%
July – September 2013	5.82%	0.015945205479452%

Period of application of excess concessional contributions charge, SIC (shortfall interest charge) and GIC (general interest charge).

Matthew lodges his income tax return for the 2014-15 income year on 31 August 2015 and pays his outstanding tax liability in respect of this return on 21 September 2015. Later, on 30 November 2015, the Commissioner determines Matthew has excess concessional contributions for the 2014-15 financial year. The Commissioner amends Matthew's income tax assessment and provides him with notice of his determination that he has excess concessional contributions and the amended assessment. Matthew receives this notice on 30 November 2015.

As Matthew has excess concessional contributions in the 2014-15 financial year, he is also liable for excess concessional contributions charge. This charge applies for the period beginning on the first day of the 2014-15 financial year until the date when he was first due to pay his income tax liability for 2014-15 – 21 September 2015.

Matthew is also liable for the SIC on the shortfall between the amount he originally paid and the amount of tax identified in his amended assessment. He must pay SIC on the value of the shortfall for the period beginning from the day his liability under his original tax assessment was payable, 21 September 2015, and ending on the day when he pays his liability under the amended assessment or no later than 21 December 2015 (the date this payment is due).

All of this shortfall is due to the same amount of excess concessional contributions that resulted in Matthew being liable for excess concessional contributions charge. As a result, when determining the amount of SIC he must pay, the amount of the shortfall is increased by the amount of his excess concessional contributions charge liability.

Matthew must pay the additional amounts of income tax and excess concessional contributions charge, as well as the amount of SIC within 21 days of receiving notice of liability. If he does not pay on time he must pay GIC on any unpaid amount of income tax, excess concessional contributions charge or SIC.

ELECTING TO RELEASE EXCESS CONCESSIONAL CONTRIBUTIONS FOR 2013-14 AND LATER YEARS

Following receipt of a notice of excess concessional contributions determination, an individual may elect to release up to 85% of the amount of their excess concessional contributions for that financial year from their superannuation.

The choice of how much to release is the individual's (up to the 85% limit, the remaining 15% represents the concessional contributions tax liability incurred by the fund). The amount released as a result of this election is not assessable income or exempt income.

The election to release must be made by the individual within 21 days of receiving the excess concessional contributions notice, or such further time as the Commissioner may allow. If the Commissioner issues an amended excess concessional contributions notice, this extends the period in which the election can be made until 21 days after the issue of the amended notice.

The election must be made in the approved form, and specify the amount to be released and the superannuation interest or interests from which the amount is to be released.

Once made, the election cannot be revoked and any amounts released may only be returned to superannuation by making further concessional or non-concessional contributions.

It is also not possible to seek to vary the amount or the superannuation interests nominated in the election. However, if the Commissioner is not able to obtain the requested amount from the nominated superannuation interest, the individual has the option to nominate another superannuation interest or interests.

Upon receipt of a valid election to release, the Commissioner must provide a release authority (or release authorities) in respect of the specified amount (or amounts) to the relevant superannuation provider (or providers).

Generally, a superannuation provider must pay to the Commissioner within seven days of receiving the release authority an amount equal to the lesser of:

- that specified in the release authority, and
- the total that can be released from the specified superannuation interests (the maximum available release amount).

Superannuation providers who do not comply with a release authority are subject to an administrative penalty of 20 penalty units.

However, for certain interests, termed voluntary release interests, the superannuation provider is not obliged to comply with the release authority, but instead may choose whether or not to release the specified amount. An interest is a voluntary release interest if it is a:

- defined benefit interest
- superannuation interest in a non-complying superannuation fund, or
- superannuation interest that supports a superannuation income stream.

A superannuation provider that receives a release authority must notify the Commissioner within seven days of:

- any amounts they have paid, and
- if they are not required to make a payment or may make a lower payment, that they are not required to comply in full with the release authority.

The notice must be provided in the approved form. The Commissioner must notify the individual if a superannuation provider notifies the Commissioner that they have not released the full amount specified. However the Commissioner must credit any amounts paid by superannuation providers to the individual. If the amount released exceeds the individual's outstanding tax liabilities, the Commissioner must refund the excess to the individual. Any unreasonable delay in the excess being refunded to the individual will result in the Commissioner paying interest.

Electing to release amounts

The Commissioner makes a determination that Luke has excess concessional contributions of $1,500 in the 2014-15 financial year. He amends Luke's income tax assessment accordingly, resulting in an increase in Luke's tax liability of $225 plus an additional $20 of SIC.

Luke receives notice of this determination and his amended assessment on 18 November 2015. Luke is entitled to elect to release up to a maximum of $1,275 or 85 per cent of his excess concessional contributions by notifying the Commissioner within 21 days (or such further time as the Commissioner may allow).

On 20 November 2015, he elects to release $750 from his superannuation interest held by ABC Superannuation. The Commissioner issues a release authority to ABC Superannuation on 21 November 2015, identifying the relevant interest and the requested amount. On 25 November 2015, ABC Superannuation pays $500 to the Commissioner. ABC Superannuation notifies the Commissioner of the payment and that the payment was $250 less than the $750 identified in the release authority as this $500 was the maximum available release amount.

The Commissioner credits the $500 to Luke. After accounting for his outstanding liabilities of $245, Luke is entitled to a refund of $255. The Commissioner also notifies Luke that ABC Superannuation has not released the full amount he identified in his election. Luke is entitled to nominate a further superannuation interest from which to release the remaining $250. He provides a further election identifying his interest in XYZ Superannuation on 13 December 2015.

The Commissioner issues a release authority to XYZ Superannuation and XYZ Superannuation pays $250 to the Commissioner on 19 December 2015.

The Commissioner credits the $250 to Luke. As Luke has no further outstanding tax debts, he is entitled to a refund of the full $250.

In total, Luke has released $750 from his superannuation interests, receiving $505 after meeting his tax liabilities of $245.

NON-CONCESSIONAL CONTRIBUTIONS AND EXCESS CONCESSIONAL CONTRIBUTIONS

An individual's excess concessional contributions count towards the individual's non-concessional cap. Where the individual elects to release an amount of their excess concessional contributions, the amount of their excess concessional contributions is reduced for the purpose of determining their non-concessional contributions. The amount of the reduction is equal to 100/85 of the amount released (or the amount released divided by 85%).

Release of the maximum 85% of excess concessional contributions permitted, means that there are no excess concessional contributions to be counted for purposes of excess non-concessional contributions.

This ensures that an individual always has the option to avoid being in a position where their excess concessional contributions result in them having excess non-concessional contributions. In addition, the release may prevent the automatic bring forward provisions for those aged under 65 years in certain circumstances.

Non-concessional contributions and releasing superannuation

In 2014-15, Lucy has excess concessional contributions of $10,000. With the inclusion of these excess concessional contributions, she has non-concessional contributions for the financial year of $185,000. Lucy's non-concessional contributions cap for the 2014-15 financial year is $180,000, so she has excess non-concessional contributions of $5,000.

Lucy elects to release $4,500 of her excess concessional contributions from superannuation. This reduces her non-concessional contributions by ($4500) / (85%) = $5,294.12 (to the nearest cent) or just under $5295.

Lucy's non-concessional contributions are therefore reduced as a result of her election to release $4,500 of her excess concessional contributions from superannuation. When translated to the impact on the amount of her non-concessional contributions, they are reduced by $5,294.12 to ($185,000 – $5,294.12) = $179,705.88. She no longer exceeds the $180,000 cap and therefore does not have to pay excess non-concessional contributions tax.

19.052 EXCESS CONCESSIONAL CONTRIBUTIONS TAX

The ECT regime for excess concessional contributions applied up to and including the 2012-13 year, and the individual is liable to excess concessional contributions tax (ECCCT) of 31.5% if their concessional contributions for the year exceeds the concessional contributions cap. A cap of $25,000 applies for the 2012-13 year. For the treatment of excess concessional contributions in subsequent years see 19.050.

The rules on the excess concessional contributions tax are in Subdivision 292-B (ss292-10 to 292-25).

Concessional contributions are generally contributions that are deductible to the contributor (eg. SG contributions, employer contributions made under a salary sacrifice arrangement and deductible contributions made by a self-employed person).

In Interpretative Decision ATO ID 2010/104: Excess contributions tax: restitution of a mistaken contribution, the Tax Office decided that a personal contribution may still be included in an individual's non-concessional contributions for the financial year even if a trustee has repaid it to the member in restitution of a purported mistaken payment.

An individual is liable to excess concessional contributions tax of 31.5% if their concessional contributions for the year exceed the concessional contributions cap for that year. The cap is $25,000 for the 2012-13 year.

An employer contributes $45,000 to a complying superannuation fund on behalf of an employee aged 45. The contribution is made up of $8,000 SG contributions, $17,000 additional employer contributions and $20,000 salary sacrificed by the employee. Assuming all relevant conditions are met, the $45,000 would be deductible to the employer. The concessional contributions cap of $25,000, is exceeded by $20,000 and in 2012-13 is taxed at 31.5% in addition to the 15% contributions tax. (Note that in 2013-14 and in subsequent years the excess amount is taxed as assessable income of the employee, plus ECCC. See 19.050)

ALLOCATION OF CONCESSIONAL CONTRIBUTIONS

In ATO ID 2012/16, the Tax Office concluded that when calculating a person's concessional contributions under s292-25 of the ITAA97 for ECT purposes, a concessional contribution made to a superannuation fund in one financial year, but allocated to the member in accordance with the *Superannuation Industry (Supervision) Regulations 1994* (SISR94) in the subsequent financial year, is counted as a concessional contribution in the year it is allocated.

19.055   EXCESS CONCESSIONAL CONTRIBUTIONS TAX ASSESSMENT (UP TO AND INCLUDING 2012-13)

The following applies to the period prior to 1 July 2013. (For the post 30 June 2013 provisions refer to 19.050.)

HOW IS EXCESS CONCESSIONAL CONTRIBUTIONS TAX ASSESSED?

Superannuation funds are required to report contributions to the Tax Office each financial year who then determine whether the concessional contributions cap has been exceeded.

If a fund member has exceeded their concessional contributions cap, the Tax Office will send them a notice of assessment for the relevant year which will include the amount that they have to pay. At the same time, the Tax Office will send a Voluntary Release Authority (VRA) for the amount of the excess concessional contributions tax liability, which the fund member can use to authorise the release of up to the tax amount from their superannuation fund.

TAX PAYABLE

Excess concessional contributions tax is payable on excess concessional contributions at a rate of 31.5%. This is on top of the 15% paid by the fund on its taxable income.

The fund member is liable to pay the excess contributions tax, not their superannuation fund.

A fund member's excess concessional contributions will also count towards their non-concessional contributions cap. If their contributions exceed both the concessional and non-concessional contributions caps in a financial year, they could pay 93% tax on the excess amount.

WHAT IS A VOLUNTARY RELEASE AUTHORITY?

If the Tax Office assess that a fund member has to pay excess concessional contributions tax, the fund member may withdraw an amount up to the amount of this tax from their superannuation fund to help them meet their obligation to pay the tax. To withdraw the amount, a fund member can use the VRA that the Tax Office will send them with their notice of assessment. This allows the member's superannuation fund to pay the money out of the member's super, even if the member wouldn't otherwise be eligible to take the money out. If a fund member intends to use a VRA, they must give it to their fund or funds within 90 days after the date on the release authority.

WHAT DOES A SUPERANNUATION FUND DO WITH A VOLUNTARY RELEASE AUTHORITY?

When a superannuation fund receives a VRA from their member within 90 days after the issue date, they must release (or pay) to the member or to the Tax Office the lesser of the following:

- the amount of excess concessional contributions tax stated in the release authority
- the amount the member nominates, and
- the total value of the member's balance in the fund (excluding any defined benefit interest).

A fund cannot pay money to a member unless a condition of release is satisfied. A release authority satisfies a condition of release. If the member's fund does not receive the release authority within 90 days after the date of the release authority, it cannot release the money.

A fund must release the amount within 30 days after receiving the release authority and send the member and the Tax Office a release authority statement within 30 days after paying the money out of the member's super.

A fund is liable for penalties if they:

- release the wrong amount
- do not release an amount within 30 days after receiving a valid release authority, or
- do not provide their member and the Tax Office with a statement within 30 days after paying the money.

The Tax Office has issued Practice Statement PS LA 2011/24, which provides guidelines for remitting administrative penalties where an individual or superannuation provider does not comply with their ECT release authority obligations. The practice statement provides examples that show what the Tax Office will consider when working out whether to impose or remit these penalties.

HOW TO PAY EXCESS CONCESSIONAL CONTRIBUTIONS TAX

Excess concessional contributions tax can be paid in a number of ways. A member can:

- pay the tax personally without drawing on their superannuation
- pay the tax personally and use the VRA to direct their superannuation fund to release the money to them
- use the VRA to instruct their fund to pay the money to the Tax Office on their behalf, or
- pay using a combination of these options.

IF EXCESS CONCESSIONAL CONTRIBUTIONS TAX IS NOT PAID ON TIME

The excess concessional contributions tax is due and payable 21 days after the Tax Office gives a notice of the assessment. If the member does not pay the amount of the excess concessional contributions tax by the due date, General Interest Charge (GIC) will apply. However, a member can request the Tax Office to remit any GIC they incur if they do not pay by the due date. Generally, if a member gives a release authority to their fund within the time allowed for payment, and their fund makes the payment within 30 days (or any delay in payment was not within the member's control), the Tax Office will remit any GIC.

Any money paid to a member under a VRA is tax-free unless it is greater than their excess concessional contributions tax liability. If they withdraw more money from their superannuation than the amount of the excess concessional contributions tax stated in the release authority, they may have to pay tax on the extra amount at their marginal rate. They may also be liable for an administrative penalty.

IF THERE IS NOT ENOUGH SUPERANNUATION IN ONE FUND

If a fund member doesn't have enough money in one superannuation fund to pay their excess concessional contributions tax liability, the member can photocopy the release authority and give it to more than one of their superannuation funds. If they do this, they must sign each copy with an original signature.

The member must ensure that the total amount released is not greater than their excess concessional contributions tax liability, otherwise they may be penalised. Any additional amount released will also be counted towards the member's assessable income for the year in which they received it.

DEFINED BENEFIT INTERESTS

A release authority cannot be used to release an amount from a defined benefit interest. However, a fund member can use a release authority to obtain money from another superannuation fund even if they didn't make contributions to that superannuation fund in the year.

If all of a member's superannuation is in a defined benefit interest, they won't be able to use the release authority. Instead, they will need to pay the excess concessional contributions tax from their own money.

19.056   EXCESS NON-CONCESSIONAL CONTRIBUTIONS TAX

The rules that apply to excess non-concessional contributions tax apply from 1 July 2007. The tax itself is imposed by the *Superannuation (Excess Non-concessional Contributions Tax) Act 2007*. The rate is set at the top marginal rate plus Medicare.

The tax rate of 45% is increased by 2% to include the Temporary Budget Repair Levy for a 3 year period commencing 1 July 2014. The Medicare levy of 1.5% applies for the period ending 30 June 2014, after which it increases to 2%, to fund Disability Care Australia.

Legislation was enacted to amend the law relating to excess non-concessional contributions tax under *Tax and Superannuation Laws Amendment (2014 Measures No 7) Act 2015*. It allows individuals the option of withdrawing super contributions in excess of the non-concessional contributions cap, together with 85% of the associated earnings of the excess. The change applies from 1 July 2013.

The full notional earnings are included in the individual's assessable income and taxed at marginal tax rates. It is subject to a 15% non-refundable tax offset.

 If the excess non-concessional contributions are not withdrawn from the fund, then the 'full' ECT provisions apply to the excess and taxed at top marginal tax rates plus Medicare levy. This liability must be withdrawn from the fund.

 The associated earnings from excess non-concessional contributions are only included as part of an individual's assessable income when the individual elects to withdraw the excess.

 Individuals are not permitted to make 'voluntary' releases from their superannuation in relation to excess non-concessional contributions. They must follow the withdrawal approach outlined below, using an election and release authority to release the funds. Otherwise the Tax Office is likely to view the withdrawal as an illegal early access benefit payment.

ASSOCIATED EARNINGS

While the excess contributions are invested in the fund, the income earned is dependent on the rate of fund earnings. Funds experience different rates of return, including negative returns.

The provisions allow for the calculation of notional fund earnings using a rate corresponding to an average of the general interest charge (GIC) rate for each of the quarters of the financial year in which the excess contributions were made. This is to standardise and simplify calculations of the earnings received on the excess amounts in a fund. The rate is converted to an equivalent daily rate and applied from 1 July of the financial year in which the excess contributions were made to the day the Australian Taxation Office makes its first determination of excess non-concessional contributions for the relevant year.

The notional rate applicable to the 2013-14 year is 9.66%. This translates to a daily rate 0.02646575% for calculation of the associated earnings amount.

NOTE: Regardless of whether the refund option is selected, the superannuation interests will be subject to tax on actual earnings as per current practice.

Minimise associated earnings

Individuals may be able to minimise their 'associated earnings amount' when withdrawing the excess contributions by:

- lodging their personal income tax return (for year of excess contributions) as soon as possible after the end of the financial year, and
- as trustees of their SMSF, also lodging the Annual Return (which includes the member contribution statement) as soon as possible after the end of the financial year.

WITHDRAWAL

The withdrawal procedure depends upon lodgment by the individual of their income tax return and the member contribution/s statements by the fund/s receiving the member contributions.

Where excess non-concessional contributions apply, the ATO issues the individual with an excess non-concessional contributions determination, specifying:

- the amount of the excess
- the associated earnings figure, and
- the amount to be released (the excess amount plus 85% of the associated earnings amount).

The individual receiving an excess non-concessional contributions determination must adopt one of the following courses of action.
Either:

- ignore the release option and incur additional tax at the top marginal tax rate plus Medicare levy under the ECT provisions, or
- adopt the release option for the total amount of the determination and avoid application of the ECT provisions, with tax applied at marginal tax rate plus Medicare levy on the associated earnings.

Where an individual chooses the release option:

- this must be made to the Tax Office within 60 days of the date of issue of the determination
- once made, this selection becomes irrevocable
- the member's election must specify one or more super interests from which the amount/s are to be released, and
- the specified interests need not be the same one/s that received the excess contributions.

Following receipt of an election from the member, the ATO issues the fund/s with a release authority. Following receipt of a release authority a superannuation fund must pay the amount stated in the release authority to the individual within 21 days of the date of issue of the release authority.

PAYMENT COMPONENTS

The payment made to the individual by the superannuation fund comprises the excess non-concessional contributions, plus 85% of the associated earnings amount. The amount of excess non-concessional contributions will not incur an income tax liability for the individual. It is non-assessable non-exempt income.

One hundred per cent of the 'associated earnings amount' is included in the individual's assessable income for the year in which the excess contributions were made. A non-refundable tax-offset equal to 15% of the associated earnings amount applies.

When making a release from the fund the trustee will not apply the proportioning rule to the withdrawal.

If the release option is ignored the following applies.

TAX PAYABLE

Excess non-concessional contributions tax is imposed at the top marginal tax rate plus Medicare on non-concessional contributions in excess of the relevant cap for the individual. The tax liability arising must be released from the member's superannuation interest.

NOTE: From 1 July 2013 a taxpayer has the option of withdrawing the excess plus 85% of any notional earnings of the fund. If the taxpayer does not avail of this, the excess contributions tax provisions apply at top the marginal tax rate plus Medicare.

PAYING 93% OR 95% TAX

A member's excess concessional contributions also count towards their non-concessional contributions cap. Prior to 1 July 2013, if contributions exceed both concessional and non-concessional contributions caps in a financial year, the excess amount may be taxed at 93% overall. This potential scenario is shown in the following example. Under the provisions that apply from 1 July 2013, a cap of 95% is placed on the maximum rate of tax that may be applied.

Sally is an employee aged 68 years. Her concessional contributions cap is $25,000 and her non-concessional contributions cap is $150,000 for the 2012-13 financial year. Her salary sacrifice of $29,000 to super remained unchanged and her employer contributes $9,000 including SG. Total employer (concessional) contributions are $38,000.

The fund must pay 15% tax on all employer contributions it receives. Sally must pay excess concessional contributions tax on her excess concessional contributions of $13,000 at a tax rate of 31.5%.

The tax on her concessional contributions is calculated as follows:
- *$25,000 is taxed at 15% in the fund*
- *$13,000 is taxed at 15% in the fund + 31.5%.*

The $13,000 will also be counted towards Sally's non-concessional contributions cap.

Sally also contributes $140,000 in non-concessional contributions after downsizing her house. Her non-concessional contributions for the year are assessed at $153,000. The excess amount is $3,000. Being over 65, she may not use the bring-forward provisions. She must pay excess non-concessional contributions tax at 46.5%.

As a result, $3,000 of Sally's contributions is subject to tax at an overall rate of 93% (ie. 15% + 31.5% + 46.5%).

Given the same scenario, but in a later year. Sally's concessional contributions cap is $35,000 and her non-concessional contributions cap is $180,000. Total employer (concessional) contributions are $48,000.

The fund must pay 15% tax on all employer contributions it receives. Sally must pay excess concessional contributions tax on her excess concessional contributions of $13,000 at her marginal tax rate of 47% plus Medicare.

The tax on her concessional contributions is calculated as follows:

- *$35,000 is taxed at 15% in the fund*
- *$13,000 is taxed at 15% in the fund + 30%+2%.*

The $13,000 will also be counted towards Sally's non-concessional contributions cap.

Sally also contributes $170,000 in non-concessional contributions after downsizing her house. Her non-concessional contributions for the year are assessed at $183,000. The excess amount is $3,000. She does not choose an option to withdraw excess contributions. She must pay excess non-concessional contributions tax at 49%.

As a result, $3,000 of Sally's contributions are subject to tax at an overall rate of (49% + 49%), subject to the 95% limit.

WHAT IS A COMPULSORY RELEASE AUTHORITY?

If the Tax Office assess that a fund member has to pay excess non-concessional contributions tax, the fund member must withdraw an amount equal to the amount of this tax from their superannuation funds. This is in addition to the member's obligation to pay the tax. To withdraw the amount, a fund member must use the CRA that the Tax Office provides along with the member's notice of assessment.

A fund member must give the CRA to their fund or funds within 21 days after the date on the release authority or they will be liable to a penalty of 20 penalty units (currently $2,200).

A fund member cannot use a release authority to release an amount from a defined benefit interest.

WHAT DOES A SUPERANNUATION FUND DO WITH A COMPULSORY RELEASE AUTHORITY?

When a superannuation fund receives a CRA from its member within 90 days of the day after the issue date, they must release or pay to the member or the Tax Office the least of the following:

- the amount of excess non-concessional contributions tax stated in the release authority
- the amount the member nominates, and
- the total value of the member's balance in the fund (excluding defined benefit interests).

Even though a fund member must give the CRA to their superannuation fund within 21 days to avoid being penalised, their superannuation fund can still action a CRA that's provided after that time, as long as it's within 90 days after the release authority's issue date.

A fund cannot release money to a member unless a condition of release is satisfied. A release authority satisfies a condition of release. If a superannuation fund does not receive the release authority within 90 days after the date on the release authority, it cannot release the money.

A superannuation fund must release the amount within 30 days after receiving the release authority and send the member and the Tax Office a release authority statement within 30 days after paying the money out of the member's superannuation account.

A superannuation fund is liable for penalties if it:

- releases the wrong amount
- does not release an amount within 30 days after receiving a valid release authority, or
- does not provide the member and the Tax Office with a statement within 30 days after paying the money.

The Tax Office has issued Practice Statement PS LA 2011/24, which provides guidelines for remitting administrative penalties.

IF MONEY IS NOT WITHDRAWN USING A COMPULSORY RELEASE AUTHORITY

If a member releases less than the amount of the excess non-concessional contributions tax from their superannuation using the CRA, the Tax Office will ask the member's superannuation fund to pay the outstanding amount to them. The Tax Office will do this even if they've already paid the tax liability. The Tax Office will request the payment from the superannuation fund using an *Authority to release excess contributions tax and statement*. The Tax Office will let the member know by letter when their superannuation fund sends them any payment.

If the fund member has already paid the excess non-concessional contributions tax, the Tax Office will apply the payment from the superannuation fund against other tax debts the member may have. The Tax Office may also apply the payment against debts that the member may have with other government agencies. If a fund member has a credit after the payment has been applied against these debts, they can apply for a refund.

HOW TO PAY EXCESS NON-CONCESSIONAL CONTRIBUTIONS TAX

A member can pay their excess non-concessional contributions in any of the following ways:
- pay the tax personally and use the CRA to direct their superannuation fund to release the money to them
- use the CRA to instruct their fund to pay the money to the Tax Office on their behalf, or
- pay using a combination of these options.

However, a fund member must withdraw the full amount of their excess non-concessional contributions tax from their super, whether they use it to help them pay the tax or not.

IF EXCESS NON-CONCESSIONAL CONTRIBUTIONS TAX IS NOT PAID ON TIME

The excess non-concessional contributions tax is due and payable 21 days after a fund member receives a notice of the assessment. If the member does not pay the amount of the excess non-concessional contributions tax by the due date, General Interest Charge (GIC) will apply. However, the member can request the Tax Office to remit any GIC they incur if they do not pay by the due date. Generally, if a member gives their release authority to their superannuation fund within the time allowed for payment, and their superannuation fund makes the payment within 30 days (or any delay in payment was not within the member's control), the Tax Office will remit any GIC.

The payment made to the member is tax-free unless it is greater than their excess non-concessional contributions tax liability. If the member withdraws more money from their fund than the amount of the excess non-concessional contributions tax stated in the release authority, they may have to pay tax on the extra amount at their marginal rate and may also be liable for an administrative penalty.

IF THERE IS NOT ENOUGH SUPERANNUATION IN ONE FUND

If a member doesn't have enough money in one superannuation fund to pay their excess non-concessional contributions tax liability, they can photocopy the release authority and give it to more than one of their superannuation funds. If the member does this, they must sign each copy with an original signature.

The member must ensure that the total amount released is not greater than their excess non-concessional contributions tax liability, otherwise they will be penalised. Any additional amount released will also be counted towards their assessable income for the year that they received it.

DEFINED BENEFIT INTEREST

A member cannot use a release authority to release an amount from a defined benefit interest. However, they can use their release authority to obtain money from another superannuation fund, even if they didn't make contributions to that superannuation fund during the year.

If all of the member's superannuation is in a defined benefit interest, they won't be able to use the release authority. Instead, they will need to pay the excess non-concessional contributions tax from their own money.

19.057 EXCESS CONTRIBUTIONS TAX ASSESSMENT PROCESSES (UP TO 2012-13 YEAR)

For excess contributions tax assessment processes (up to the 2012-13 year) please refer to the *2013-14 Tax Summary* or previous editions.

19.060 TAX FILE NUMBERS AND SUPERANNUATION

Significant tax consequences on certain contributions can occur as a result of funds not holding their members' Tax File Numbers (TFN).

If a fund does not have a member's TFN:

- the fund will have to pay extra income tax on certain contributions made by the member
- the fund may not be able to accept certain other contributions from the member, and
- the member may miss out on the government co-contribution.

FUNDS WILL HAVE TO PAY EXTRA INCOME TAX

It is not compulsory for a member to give their TFN to their fund, however if they don't, the fund will be liable to pay extra income tax on certain contributions made to their account. The contributions that are most likely to be taxed in this way are:

- employer contributions, including salary sacrifice amounts, and
- personal contributions claimed as a tax deduction.

Where members who have superannuation accounts which were opened prior to 1 July 2007, and they have not provided their fund with their TFN, concessional contributions made after 1 July 2007 will be taxed an extra 31.5% (32% from 2014-15) once those concessional contributions exceed $1,000 in an income year. This includes the first $1,000.

Where superannuation accounts are opened after 1 July 2007 and have no TFN provided all concessional contributions made to that account will be taxed an extra 31.5% (32% from 2014-15).

All funds must determine whether they have to pay this extra tax at the end of each year.

INABILITY TO MAKE CERTAIN CONTRIBUTIONS

Superannuation funds are only able to accept certain contributions on behalf of the member if the member has given them their TFN (r7.04(2) SISR94). This may affect the member's eligibility to receive a government co-contribution.

Types of contributions that funds will have to reject are:

- non-concessional member contributions, and
- non-concessional spouse contributions.

QUOTING A TFN

When an employee gives their employer a *Tax file number declaration* (NAT 3092), the employer must pass the TFN on to the employee's fund.

 Members should contact their fund if they are unsure whether their TFN is recorded.

TAX OFFSETS AVAILABLE

If the TFN is provided within a four-year time frame, the fund trustee becomes entitled to a tax offset. It will be up to the trustee to claim the offset if it applies. The amount of the offset will be the sum of the amount of tax paid on the no-TFN contributions income. The offset is credited to the member's account.

The trustee cannot pay no-TFN contributions income tax for a contribution and claim a tax offset for that same contribution in the same income year. The tax offset will only be available where the member quotes their TFN in the current year, and no-TFN contributions income tax for that member's contributions was payable in one of the three most recent income years.

 Where a contribution is classified as no-TFN contributions income for the 2014-15 income year, the tax offset can only be claimed in the year the member first quotes the TFN up until the end of the 2017-18 income year, after which the right to claim the offset is lost. Trustees will need to have a process in place to identify when a TFN is provided within the four-year time frame, and another process to apply for the offset and adjust the member's account balance.

19.065 REPORTABLE SUPERANNUATION CONTRIBUTIONS

From 1 July 2009 Reportable Superannuation Contributions (RSCs) are usually taken into account in the definition of 'income' that is used to determine eligibility for government support programs such as payments for people below age pension age, family assistance, child support, superannuation co-contributions and financial and retirement savings assistance delivered through the tax system.

The RSC changes do not affect a taxpayer's assessable or taxable income; however, they may affect income tests for a range of government benefits and obligations. They can also affect the amount of income tax a taxpayer is liable to pay as they may no longer be eligible for a tax offset.

REPORTABLE SUPERANNUATION CONTRIBUTIONS

The Reportable Superannuation Contributions (RSCs) amount is the sum of:

- Reportable Employer Superannuation Contributions (RESCs) (see below), and
- personal deductible contributions (see below and 19.026).

REPORTABLE EMPLOYER SUPERANNUATION CONTRIBUTIONS

RESCs are those contributions an employer makes for an employee to the extent that the employee has influenced or might reasonably be expected to have influenced:

- the size of the contribution, and/or
- the way the amount is contributed so that his or her assessable income is reduced.

Typically, this would include contributions in addition to the compulsory contributions the employer must make under any of the following:

- superannuation guarantee law
- an industrial agreement
- the trust deed or governing rules of a superannuation fund, or
- a federal, state or territory law.

THE MEANING OF 'CAPACITY TO INFLUENCE'

If an employee enters into an arrangement with their employer, which results in the employer contributing more superannuation than is legally required, then that employee will usually be considered to have the necessary 'capacity to influence'. The employee's 'capacity to influence' will be shown by:

- the employer's relationship with the employee
- the involvement of the employee in the negotiations concerning the terms of any industrial agreement governing the superannuation contributions
- the size of the amount contributed for the employee relative to the compulsory contributions the employer is required to make
- the superannuation contribution arrangements the employer has in place for other employees, and
- any non-arm's length dealings.

Generally, an employee will not be taken to have the 'capacity to influence' the amount of superannuation contributions an employer makes where they simply vote for a collective agreement or are part of a group that negotiates a collective agreement with the employer. An employee will be taken to have the 'capacity to influence' the amount of the contributions, where they can directly negotiate or have an option to directly negotiate an employer superannuation contribution in excess of the compulsory contributions that must be paid.

 As part of an effective salary sacrifice arrangement, an employee agrees that their employer will make extra superannuation contributions for them in return for a reduced amount of salary. These extra contributions are RESCs.

Generally, where an employer makes a contribution to a superannuation fund for an employee and the amount would have otherwise been income, it is a RESC. If the employer can show that it was a compulsory contribution or it was not influenced by their employee, part or all of the contribution will not be a RESC (also see below proposed changes to the definition of a RESC).

Additional employer contributions to cover the cost of insurance premiums for an employee, because the employee chooses (by default or otherwise) a super fund to which the employer makes super contributions for the employee, will meet the definition of RESCs (ATO ID 2010/112).

Amendments to the definition of RESC contained in the *Tax Laws Amendment (2011 Measures No.4) Act* 2011 expressly exclude certain contributions to superannuation that are required by an 'industrial instrument' or rules of a superannuation fund to the extent that there is no capacity to influence the content of the requirement to make the contribution or its size. The amendments apply from 1 July 2009.

PAYMENT SUMMARIES

Payment summaries for the 2009-10 and subsequent financial years include a label to show an amount of any RESCs. An employer must include all RESCs they make for an employee on their payment summary. Anyone with a RESC amount must be issued with a payment summary.

If an employer makes a RESC, they must provide the employee with a payment summary even if they have not paid them salary or wages. If the payment of RESCs is paid by one of an employer's associates, a payment summary is still required to be issued. The payment summary must be issued by the associate.

HOW EMPLOYEES ARE AFFECTED

Although an employer must include all RESCs they make for an employee on the employee's payment summary, the employer does not include these contributions in their employee's gross income.

RESCs are not included in their employee's assessable income. However, these contributions are included in the 'income tests' that may apply to the employee for benefits and obligations the Tax Office administer, including:

- Medicare levy surcharge threshold calculation (see 3.060)
- Medicare levy surcharge (lump sum payment in arrears) tax offset
- all dependant tax offsets (see 3.110)
- senior Australian and pensioner tax offset (see 3.190)
- mature age worker tax offset (see 3.180)
- spouse contributions tax offset (see 19.074)
- government co-contributions (see 19.076)
- low income superannuation contribution (see 19.077)
- deduction for personal superannuation contributions (see 19.026), and
- Higher Education Loan Program (HELP) (see 5.510) and Student Financial Supplement Scheme (SFSS) repayments (see 5.520).

PERSONAL DEDUCTIBLE CONTRIBUTIONS

Personal deductible contributions include the total of any personal contributions an individual makes to their superannuation fund for which they can claim an income tax deduction under Subdivision 290-C of the ITAA97.

An individual can claim an income tax deduction for personal contributions made to a superannuation fund if they meet certain eligibility criteria (see 19.026).

19.070 TYPES OF CONTRIBUTIONS

All contributions received by a superannuation fund must be allocated to the member within 28 days after the end of the month in which they are received.

The form of contributions may be made in-specie (ie. in a form other than cash) (see 19.085). Where a fund receives in-specie contributions fund trustees must also ensure that the relevant anti-avoidance, in-house asset and investment provisions of the SISA93 dealing with the acquisition of assets from related parties are not breached.

Taxation Ruling TR 2010/1 explains the Commissioner's views as to the ordinary meaning of the word 'contribution' in so far as 'contribution' is used in relation to a superannuation fund, ADF or RSA in the *Income Tax Assessment Act 1997* (ITAA97). Aspects of this Ruling are also relevant to the meaning of 'contribution' in the *Superannuation Industry (Supervision) Act 1993* (SISA93) and the *Superannuation Industry (Supervision) Regulations 1994* (SISR94). However, it should be noted that the SISR94 contains a definition of 'contribution' that modifies its ordinary meaning.

19.072 EMPLOYER CONTRIBUTIONS

A fund can at any time accept employer contributions on behalf of an employee in accordance with the *Superannuation Guarantee (Administration) Act 1992* (SGAA92) (see 19.500). With the Superannuation Guarantee (SG) upper age limit of 70 removed from 1 July 2013, other awards may require contributions to be made past age 70 (ie. mandated contributions).

Providing the employee has satisfied the 'gainful employment test' (where applicable) (see 19.015), an employer can make contributions to a fund on behalf of an employee aged under 75, even if they are non-mandated employer contributions (see 19.015).

In addition to employers meeting their SG obligations, employers must also make contributions to a fund, where those contributions form part of effective superannuation based salary sacrifice arrangements.

19.073 PERSONAL CONTRIBUTIONS

Individuals make superannuation contributions in order to obtain superannuation benefits for themselves or for their dependants in the event of their own death. Certain contributions may be eligible for tax concessions.

Providing certain conditions are met, individuals who are either self-employed, or who derive only a small part of their income from employment, may be entitled to a tax deduction for their contributions (see 19.026).

Under the SISR94, an individual can only make contributions to a superannuation fund, if the fund is allowed to accept such contributions from such a person (see 19.015).

 An employer must also pay member voluntary contributions within 28 days after the end of the month in which the deduction was made from the member's salary or wage. If an employer does not pay by this date they may be liable for a penalty (s64 SISA93).

19.074 SPOUSE CONTRIBUTIONS

Eligible spouse contributions can be made for a person's working or non-working spouse so long as the spouse is:

- under age 65, or over 65 and under age 70 and satisfies the 'gainful employment test' (see 19.015), and
- not the person's employee.

A superannuation fund can accept spouse superannuation contributions for a non-working spouse provided that the trust deed allows this category of membership. Trust deeds established before spouse contributions started (in July 1997) will not mention spouse contributions. However, this will not be a problem where the trust deed contains a clause that deems any changes to the SISA93 or the SISR94 automatically becomes part of the deed. In other cases the trust deed may need to be amended so that these contributions can be accepted.

There are no restrictions on the age or employment situation of the person making the contributions. However, spouse contributions count towards the receiving spouse's non-concessional contributions cap. Therefore, their cap usage should be monitored to help the receiving spouse avoid being liable to excess contributions tax.

A person's spouse:

- includes a bona fide de facto spouse living with the person on a genuine domestic basis as the person's husband or wife, but
- excludes a spouse who is permanently living separately and apart from the person even though they are legally married.

From 1 July 2008, the definition of 'spouse' has been extended to include same-sex partners (see 19.265).

From 1 July 2009, spouse contributions include contributions by a member for the benefit of their same-sex spouse.

TAX OFFSET FOR SPOUSE CONTRIBUTIONS

The person making the eligible spouse contribution is entitled to a tax offset on the first $3,000 of spouse contributions so long as the spouse's income[1] does not exceed $10,800 (called the base income), the person making the spouse contributions can claim an 18% tax offset on the first $3,000 spouse contributions each financial year. The maximum superannuation spouse tax offset that a person can claim in an income year is $540, even if that person had more than one spouse during the year.

The $3,000 rebatable contribution limit reduces by $1 for every $1 of any amount by which the spouse's income exceeds $10,800. It therefore cuts out when the spouse's income[1] reaches $13,800.

In 2014-15 John makes a $3,000 superannuation contribution for his spouse Mary. Her income[1] is $9,000 for the year which does not exceed the base income[1] of $10,800. John can claim a tax offset on assessment of: $3,000 x 0.18 = $540.

1: 'Income' includes the spouse's assessable income (ie. before any deductions are claimed), reportable fringe benefits total and Reportable Employer Superannuation Contributions (RESCs). The reportable fringe benefits total is the grossed-up taxable value of fringe benefits for the FBT year ending 31 March that is shown on the spouse's Payment Summary for the year ending 30 June). The tax offset is claimed on the person's annual tax return and so is received on assessment as a reduction in the tax payable at the end each financial year.

TREATMENT OF SPOUSE CONTRIBUTIONS

Spouse contributions are fully preserved and form part of the tax-free component. They are treated as non-concessional contributions and are not included in the fund's assessable income.

REPORTING SPOUSE CONTRIBUTIONS

From 1 July 2009 all superannuation funds must report contributions for a same-sex spouse in the same way they currently report contributions for a different-sex spouse.

In the 'Member Information' section of the SMSF Annual Return, trustees of SMSFs will need to report contributions that are made for a member by their same-sex spouse at Label F 'spouse and child contributions amount', and not at Label G 'other family and friend contributions'. All other superannuation providers should report these contributions as 'spouse and child contributed amounts' on the member contributions statement.

RELEASING SPOUSE CONTRIBUTIONS

As spouse superannuation contributions are preserved benefits, they cannot be paid out (except as a rollover to another superannuation entity) until a condition of release occurs. Where the spouse has never been gainfully employed, they can only satisfy certain conditions of release such as reaching age 65, death, financial hardship or compassionate grounds. All other conditions of release may apply where a spouse has been gainfully employed, whether before or during the membership of the fund. For all circumstances where some or all preserved benefits can be released see 19.165.

Spouse contributions make financial sense where they are eligible for a tax offset, as it is akin to earning 18% on the first $3,000 contributions made in that year.

The other benefits of spouse contributions include:

- *allowing family superannuation assets and future retirement income streams to be more evenly divided (see also 19.075)*
- *reducing the rate of tax paid on pension income in certain instances, and*
- *it is not the subject of a 15% contributions tax.*

19.075   SUPERANNUATION CONTRIBUTIONS SPLITTING

Superannuation Contributions Splitting (SCS) allows members to split certain superannuation contributions made during a financial year to their spouse's accumulation account. It is a way for a spouse to accumulate their own superannuation, even if they have a low income or they are not working. Splitting your superannuation contributions will give you and your spouse more choices in how to prepare for your retirement. SCS is a voluntary service that may be offered by your fund.

Eligible fund members can apply to split contributions to an account held by their spouse, either within the fund, or to a different fund, RSA provider, approved deposit fund or life assurance company.

The definition of 'spouse' includes same-sex partners (see 19.265).

PARTIES TO SUPERANNUATION CONTRIBUTIONS SPLITTING

The spouse who is splitting the contributions to their spouse's superannuation account is called the 'applicant'. The spouse who is receiving the split contributions into their superannuation account is called the 'receiving spouse'. The 'receiving spouse' includes a person (whether of the same sex or a different sex) who is legally married to the 'applicant', or although not legally married to the 'applicant', lives with the 'applicant' on a genuine domestic basis in a relationship as a couple.

WHICH FUND CAN OFFER SUPERANNUATION CONTRIBUTIONS SPLITTING?

SCS is a voluntary service. Trustees can decide if the fund will offer it. If it does, it must be specified in the deed. Accumulation-style superannuation funds and RSA providers can choose to offer contributions splitting for contributions. Defined benefit-style superannuation funds can only offer contributions splitting for the accumulation interests held within the fund which is receiving contributions.

 Deciding to offer contributions splitting to members may require you to amend your trust deed.

LIMITS ON SPLITTING

The following percentages of contributions made during the relevant financial year can be split:

- up to the lesser of the concessional contributions cap or 85% of concessional contributions for *taxed splittable contributions*, and
- up to 100% of the concessional contributions cap for *untaxed splittable employer contributions* (certain employer contributions made to a public sector scheme).

TYPES OF SPLITTABLE CONTRIBUTIONS

Taxed splittable contributions are counted as assessable income and include:

- employer contributions (including salary sacrifice contributions)
- personal contributions that have been claimed or are intended to be claimed as a tax deduction
- Superannuation Guarantee (SG) entitlements transferred by the Tax Office
- Superannuation Holding Accounts Special Account (SHASA) amounts, and
- any Allocated Surplus Contribution (ASC) amounts.

Untaxed splittable employer contributions generally include:

- untaxed employer contributions made to a public sector superannuation scheme.

TIMING

A member may seek to split the contributions made to the fund during the previous financial year. This may only be sought once each financial year. Therefore members have until 30 June 2016 to ask their fund to split contributions made in the 2014-15 income year.

ROLLOVERS

The only amounts that can be split are amounts received as contributions. Contributions that are rolled over to another fund before the end of the financial year are treated as rollovers by the new fund and cannot be split to a spouse's account. Therefore if contributions to a superannuation fund are to be split in the future, this must be done before they are rolled over to a new superannuation fund. Applications can be made to split contributions made during the financial year if they form part of an entire benefit that is to be rolled over or transferred to another fund before the end of that financial year.

TREATMENT OF SPLIT CONTRIBUTIONS

Amounts split to a spouse's account are treated as a contributions splitting superannuation benefit. This means they are considered to have been rolled over into the fund.

WHEN TO MAKE A SUPERANNUATION CONTRIBUTIONS SPLITTING APPLICATION

A member can lodge a *Superannuation contributions splitting application* (NAT 15237) form to split contributions that were made into their fund. The Superannuation Contributions Splitting Application (SCSA) must be either:

- made in the following financial year (the application must be made between 1 July and 30 June following the end of the financial year in which the contributions were made), or
- made during the financial year if the entire benefit is to be rolled over or transferred before the end of that financial year.

HOW TO MAKE A SUPERANNUATION CONTRIBUTIONS SPLITTING APPLICATION

The fund should have SCSA forms for a member to complete. Each member's SCSA should specify:

- their details as the applicant
- their spouse's details (the receiving spouse) including details of the receiving fund, and
- the amount to be split from either or both of the taxed splittable contributions and untaxed splittable employer contributions.

The fund may also request the applicant for evidence to demonstrate that, at the time of application, their spouse:

- had not yet reached their preservation age (see 19.165 and 19.700), or
- is between their preservation age and age 65 and is not retired.

DEDUCTIBILITY OF SPLITTABLE AMOUNTS

Members intending to claim a tax deduction for personal contributions made to their fund during the financial year will need to lodge a *Notice of intent to claim or vary a deduction for personal superannuation contributions* (NAT 71121) approved form with their fund trustee before lodging an SCSA.

 The decision to split becomes irreversible once the SCSA is received and accepted. Therefore, if a deduction is going to be claimed for personal contributions, it is imperative that the notice of intention to claim a deduction be dated and lodged before the SCSA.

CAP IMPACT

A splittable contribution which is split between one spouse and another does not count towards the latter's (ie. the receiving spouse's) contribution caps.

19.076   GOVERNMENT CO-CONTRIBUTION SCHEME

Under the Government Co-contribution Scheme (GCS), the government may contribute towards the superannuation savings of eligible low income earners where they make eligible post-tax personal contributions into superannuation. The governing legislation for the GCS is the

Superannuation (Government Co-contribution for Low Income Earners) Act 2003 (SGCLIEA03) and its associated regulations.

Government co-contributions are explicitly excluded from the assessable income of a superannuation fund or Retirement Savings Account (RSA) provider (s295-170(1)(a)) and from the definition of a non-concessional contribution (s292-90(2)(c)(i)). Co-contributions form part of the member's tax-free component. However, the earnings on co-contributions are taxed like other fund earnings within the superannuation fund. Co-contributions are also preserved within the fund or the RSA.

 Co-contributions form part of the member's tax-free component by virtue of s307-220, which operates to treat it as part of the 'contributions segment' of that component.

From 1 July 2007, self-employed individuals are also eligible for a co-contribution under the GCS if they meet certain criteria. The following thresholds and eligibility requirements apply.

THRESHOLDS AND RATES

A maximum co-contribution payment of $500 is payable for 2015-16 and (2014-15). A lower income threshold of $35,454 ($34,448) applies and the corresponding higher income threshold is $50,454 ($49,488). An eligible person, making a non-concessional contribution of $1,000 receives the full benefit of $500, paid to the member's account, if their total income does not exceed the lower income threshold. If total income is in excess of this threshold the benefit paid is reduced by 3.333 cents for each dollar of income that is in excess of this threshold. When the level of income reaches or exceeds the higher income threshold of $50,454 ($49,488), the co-contribution amount is zero. The co-contribution matching rate for these years is currently 50%. In 2011-12 it was 100%, but was reduced to 50% for 2012-13 and subsequent years. The corresponding maximum co-contribution payable was $1,000 in 2011-12 and $500 in 2012-13..

ELIGIBILITY REQUIREMENTS OF THE GOVERNMENT CO-CONTRIBUTION SCHEME

A person is eligible to receive a co-contribution under the GCS if they meet certain criteria (s6 SGCLIEA03). To be eligible, the person must:

- make eligible personal contributions to a Complying Superannuation Fund (CSF) or a RSA they hold
- have 10% or more of their 'total income' attributable to either or both of employment related activities and the carrying on of a business
- have a 'total income' less than the co-contribution higher income threshold
- lodge an income tax return for the income year
- be under 71 years of age at the end of the income year, and
- not have held a prescribed visa at any time during the income year.

Make eligible personal superannuation contributions

A person must make eligible personal superannuation contributions during the income year. To be an eligible personal superannuation contribution it must be made by the person to a CSF or a RSA for their own benefit. The contribution cannot be:

- a rollover superannuation benefit
- a superannuation lump sum paid from a foreign superannuation fund
- a directed termination payment
- an amount transferred to the fund from a superannuation scheme which is not, and never has been, an Australian or foreign superannuation fund, was not established in Australia and is not centrally managed or controlled in Australia
- a payment from a First Home Saver Account (FHSA), or
- a government FHSA contribution.

 The definition of eligible personal superannuation contributions implicitly excludes spouse contributions.

An eligible person with a 'total income' of $31,500 makes an eligible personal superannuation contribution of $800. What government co-contribution may they expect in 2015-16 (2014-15)?

Since 'total income' is less than the lower income threshold of $35,454 ($34,488), the government co-contribution will be at the rate of $0.50 for each $1 of personal contribution up to a maximum of $500. The co-contribution is therefore $800 x 0.5 = $400 in both years.

At least 10% of total income must come from employment and or business (ie. the '10% test')

Under this test at least 10% of a person's 'total income' for the income year must be attributable to either or both of employment related activities and the carrying on of a business. This requirement means that a person who derives only passive income such as distributions, dividends, rent or interest would not be entitled to a co-contribution under the GCS.

In determining whether an individual satisfies the '10% test', 'total income' is the sum of a person's assessable income, Reportable Fringe Benefits and Reportable Employer Superannuation Contributions. 'Total income' is not reduced by the deductions that result from the carrying on of a business to ensure that self-employed individuals with low incomes or low profit margins are not disadvantaged by arbitrarily failing this test.

In working out a person's total income for these purposes, excess concessional contributions that are refunded to a person and included in their assessable income under s292-467(2)(a) are disregarded.

A member earns 'total income' from carrying on of a business of $40,000 in 2015-16, makes a personal contribution to superannuation of $1,000. What government co-contribution can the member expect?

Since the 'total income' is greater than the applicable lower income threshold in 2015-16 (2014-15) of $35,454 ($34,488), the government co-contribution will be at the rate of less than $0.50 for each $1 of eligible personal superannuation contributions up to a maximum of $1,000. The co-contribution is estimated to be about $348 ($316) in the respective years.

Jane is an Australian resident aged 36 who receives income from a religious vocation of $31,000 and passive income of $2,000 in the year. The definition of business within the meaning of the ITAA97 includes any profession, trade, employment, vocation or calling but does not include an occupation as an employee. Jane is carrying on a business for GCS purposes. The proportion of her total income from carrying on a business is nearly 94%.

As more than 10% of her 'total income' is from carrying on a business and her total income is less than the maximum threshold, Jane is eligible for a co-contribution payment if she makes eligible personal superannuation contributions.

'Total income' must be less than the higher income threshold

A person's 'total income' for the income year must be less than the higher income threshold for that year for eligibility to receive a co-contribution payment. For this test, the definition of a person's 'total income' is reduced by business deductions. Accordingly 'total income' under this test is the total of assessable income, reportable fringe benefits and RESCs less deductions from the carrying on of a business.

Although 'total income' is reduced by amounts for which an individual is entitled to a deduction for carrying on a business, these deductions do not include deductions for personal superannuation contributions. This definition of 'total income' ensures that individuals who carry on a business, and have high gross business receipts are not arbitrarily exceeding the co-contribution higher income threshold.

Ann is in a partnership and receives partnership income from carrying on a business of $50,000 for the year. Ann also receives $5,000 in passive income. Ann's partnership income is business income for GCS purposes and represents 91% of total income, thus meeting the 'more than 10%' threshold. Her total income of $55,000 exceeds the higher income threshold of $50,454 ($49,488) for 2015-16 (2014-15) so she is ineligible for a co-contribution benefit.

Lodge an income tax return for the income year

An income tax return for the person must be lodged for the income year. This applies to all persons, even those who would not normally be required to lodge an income tax return, such as those whose income is below the tax-free threshold.

 From the 2009-10 income year, taxpayers may need to complete labels F, G and H at the new adjustment item 'A3 Super co-contribution' in their income tax returns in order to receive the government co-contribution.

Be under 71 years of age at the end of the income year

At the end of the income year in which the eligible personal superannuation contributions were made, the person must be less than 71 years of age.

Not have held a prescribed visa at any time during the income year

The person must not have held a temporary visa under the Migration Act 1958 at any time in the income year, or at all times when the person held such a temporary visa during the income year, was a New Zealand citizen or holder of a visa prescribed for the purposes of s20AA(2) of the *Superannuation (Unclaimed Money and Lost Members) Act 1999.*

PAYMENT OF THE GOVERNMENT CO-CONTRIBUTION

The Commissioner must determine that a government co-contribution is payable in respect of a person for an income year if satisfied that the co-contribution is payable. The Tax Office will send the person a letter with details about the co-contribution amount after it has deposited it into the person's account.

In making a determination the Commissioner must have regard to the income tax return lodged for the person, information provided by the person's superannuation provider(s) on the relevant Member Contributions Statement(s) (MCSs), other statements given by the superannuation provider(s) and information provided in response to a request by the Commissioner. The Commissioner may pay a co-contribution to a CSF, an RSA, the person, the person's Legal Personal Representative (LPR) or the Superannuation Holding Accounts Special Account (SHASA).

Unless the person nominates a particular superannuation fund account to the Tax Office, the co-contribution will usually be paid into the account that the eligible personal superannuation contributions were paid into. The co-contribution may be paid direct to a person who no longer has a superannuation fund or RSA account because of their retirement and is already in receipt of their superannuation entitlements. In the event of the death of the person, the co-contribution may be paid to the deceased person's estate.

The SHASA will be used as a last resort option where all other avenues have been reasonably pursued, and only then used as a holding account until the Commissioner can find a superannuation fund or RSA of the person into which the co-contribution can be transferred.

The CSF or RSA provider that receives a co-contribution must credit the amount to the member's account within 28 days of the payment being made.

CALCULATING THE GOVERNMENT CO-CONTRIBUTION

The rules to work out the amount of government co-contribution paid is set out in SGCLIEA03.

- **Minimum co-contribution:** If the amount of the co-contribution for an eligible person for an income year would be less than $20, the amount of the co-contribution will be increased to $20.

- **Interest: Interest may accrue and is payable with** the co-contribution if the Commissioner fails to pay the full amount on or before the payment date. The payment date for a co-contribution is 60 days after the Commissioner has received all of the information necessary to make a co-contribution determination. The interest forms part of the actual co-contribution and is treated as such for all purposes.

CO-CONTRIBUTION TABLES

Co-contribution income thresholds

Year	Lower income threshold	Higher income threshold
2015-16	$35,454	$50,454
2014-15	$34,488	$49,488

Co-contribution lookup tables

The following tables, produced by Taxpayers Australia Ltd, indicate the level of government co-contribution support available for levels of personal non-concessional contribution and income levels for a contributor. At the time of printing the table for 2015-16 was not released by the ATO.

Contributions made in the 2015–16 income year

	$1,000	$800	$600	$500	$400	$200
And your income is:	**Your super co-contribution will be:**					
$35,454 or less	$500	$400	$300	$250	$200	$100
$36,454	$467	$400	$300	$250	$200	$100
$37,454	$433	$400	$300	$250	$200	$100
$38,454	$400	$400	$300	$250	$200	$100
$39,454	$367	$367	$300	$250	$200	$100
$40,454	$333	$333	$300	$250	$200	$100
$41,454	$300	$300	$300	$250	$200	$100
$42,454	$267	$267	$267	$250	$200	$100
$43,454	$233	$233	$233	$233	$200	$100
$44,454	$200	$200	$200	$200	$200	$100
$45,454	$167	$167	$167	$167	$167	$100
$46,454	$133	$133	$133	$133	$133	$100
$47,454	$100	$100	$100	$100	$100	$100
$48,454	$67	$67	$67	$67	$67	$67
$49,454	$33	$33	$33	$33	$33	$33
$50,454 or more	$0	$0	$0	$0	$0	$0

The following tables are released by the Australian Tax Office for earlier years.

Contributions made in the 2014–15 income year

If your personal super contribution is:

	$1,000	$800	$500	$200
And your income is:	**Your super co-contribution will be:**			
$34,488 or less	$500	$400	$250	$100
$37,488	$400	$400	$250	$100
$40,488	$300	$300	$250	$100
$43,488	$200	$200	$200	$100
$46,488	$100	$100	$100	$100
$49,488 or more	$0	$0	$0	$0

Contributions made in the 2013–14 income year

If your personal super contribution is:

	$1,000	$800	$500	$200
And your income is:	**Your super co-contribution will be:**			
$33,516 or less	$500	$400	$250	$100
$36,516	$400	$400	$250	$100
$39,516	$300	$300	$250	$100
$42,516	$200	$200	$200	$100
$45,516	$100	$100	$100	$100
$48,516 or more	$0	$0	$0	$0

Contributions made in the 2012–13 income year				
If your personal superannuation contribution is:				
	$1,000	**$800**	**$500**	**$200**
And your income is:	**Your superannuation co-contribution will be:**			
$31,920 or less	$500	$400	$250	$100
$32,920	$467	$400	$250	$100
$33,920	$433	$400	$250	$100
$34,920	$400	$400	$250	$100
$35,920	$367	$367	$250	$100
$36,920	$333	$333	$250	$100
$37,920	$300	$300	$250	$100
$38,920	$267	$267	$250	$100
$39,920	$233	$233	$233	$100
$40,920	$200	$200	$200	$100
$41,920	$167	$167	$167	$100
$42,920	$133	$133	$133	$100
$43,920	$100	$100	$100	$100
$44,920	$67	$67	$67	$67
$45,920	$33	$33	$33	$33
$46,920	$0	$0	$0	$0

NOMINATING A SUPERANNUATION FUND TO RECEIVE THE GOVERNMENT CO-CONTRIBUTION

A *Superannuation Fund Nomination form* (NAT 8676) must be completed by a fund member when they wish to nominate a particular account (other than the default) to receive superannuation entitlements including the government co-contribution.

19.077   LOW INCOME SUPERANNUATION CONTRIBUTION

NOTE: The government's pledge to abolish the Low Income Superannuation Contribution provisions was part of its policy to repeal the Mining Resource Rent Tax (MRRT) provisions and to overturn any programs reliant on the MRRT. But as part of the negotiations for the repeal of the MRRT, the LISC is to be continued until the end of 2016-17 and phased out from 1 July 2017..

From 1 July 2012, individuals with an adjusted taxable income below $37,000 are entitled to an annual additional government Low Income Superannuation Contribution (LISC). The purpose of the LISC, which will be capped at $500, is to compensate low income individuals for the 15% tax paid on their Concessional Contributions (CCs) .

The governing legislation for the LISC is in Part 2A of the *Superannuation (Government Co-contribution for Low Income Earners) Act 2003* (SGCLIEA03), which sets out the eligibility rules for the LISC and the amount that may be payable.

The LISC is in addition to the existing government co-contribution scheme (GCS) (see 19.076) and the Commissioner will make two separate determinations of entitlement. The LISC may be payable even if an individual is not entitled under the GCS as there is no age restriction for the LISC.

Harry, a low income earner, does not make any personal contributions to a superannuation fund and so is not entitled to a co-contribution. Nevertheless, if Harry's employer makes superannuation guarantee contributions to a fund on his behalf, he may be entitled to an LISC to compensate him for the 15% tax paid on those contributions. Harry would be denied a co-contribution under the GCS if he was older than 70.

WHO IS ELIGIBLE?

An individual will be entitled to the LISC if they satisfy the following conditions:

- a CC is made by or for the individual on or after 1 July 2012
- the individual's adjusted taxable income does not exceed $37,000
- at least 10% of the individual's total income for the year is derived from employment-related activities or from carrying on a business, and
- the individual is not a holder of a temporary resident visa) (a New Zealand citizen in Australia does not hold a temporary resident visa and may be eligible) (s12C).

There is no upper age limit for the LISC.

An individual does not need to lodge an income tax return for the relevant income year for eligibility. This is unlike the GCS (see 19.076), and the Commissioner may also determine eligibility based on other information.

CONCESSIONAL CONTRIBUTIONS

An individual may be eligible if CCs (see 19.020) are made for them by their employer or by themselves during the year and the contributions are made for the purpose of providing superannuation benefits for the individual (s12D). Eligible CCs include:

- superannuation guarantee contributions
- deductible personal contributions
- salary sacrifice contributions
- certain allocations from reserves, and
- notional taxed contributions for individuals with defined benefit interests.

The following would not be eligible CCs:

- the taxable component of directed termination payments
- amounts transferred from foreign superannuation funds
- roll-over amounts (19.660)
- contributions to constitutionally protected funds, and
- employer contributions to a non-complying superannuation fund.

ADJUSTED TAXABLE INCOME

To be eligible for the LISC, an individual's adjusted taxable income (ATI) for the year must not exceed $37,000. ATI is the sum of the individual's:

- taxable income
- adjusted fringe benefits total (as defined in s6(1) ITAA36; this is total reportable fringe benefits amounts x 53.5%)
- foreign income that is not taxable in Australia
- total net investment losses
- tax-free pensions and benefits (not including superannuation income stream benefits that are tax-free for an individual aged at least 60), and
- reportable superannuation contributions (as defined in s995-1(1) ITAA97, this is the amount of deductible superannuation contributions made for the individual in the year by an employer or by the individual, including salary sacrifice contributions, which are additional to the minimum contribution required by law)

less the child support or child maintenance expenditure for the year.

AT LEAST 10% OF TOTAL INCOME FROM EMPLOYMENT OR BUSINESS (THE '10% TEST')

To be eligible for the LISC, 10% or more of an individual's total income for the year must be attributable to either or both of employment-related activities and the carrying on of a business. Excess CCs that are refunded to a person and included in their assessable income under s292-467(2)(a) are disregarded.

AMOUNT OF LISC

The maximum amount of LISC for an individual for a year is $500, calculated as follows:

(a) unless either (b) or (c) applies 15% of the eligible CCs made by or for the individual during the year

(b) if the amount in (a) exceeds $500, then it is $500, or

(c) if the amount in (a) is less than $20 then the amount is nil (s12E).

 Melly's employer makes superannuation guarantee contributions of $3,150 on her behalf to her super fund. Her adjusted taxable income for the year is less than $37,000. The contributions tax paid by Melly's super fund is $472.50 ($3,150 x 15%). As an eligible taxpayer, under the LISC provisions, the ATO will make a contribution of $472.50 to Melly's super fund to reimburse her account for the contributions tax paid.

NOTE: As part of a deal to secure parliamentary passage of the repeal of the Mineral Resource Rent the government was obliged to extend the payment of LISC until to 2016-17 inclusive. It will cease for the 2017-18 year and beyond

ADMINISTRATION BY THE TAX OFFICE

The Commissioner will determine eligibility for the LISC from information in an individual's income tax return or, if the individual does not lodge a return because, for example their income is below the tax-free threshold for the year, from other information available to the Tax Office (s14(1)). This means individuals who are not required to lodge a return are not required to apply for the payment, and the Tax Office can make a payment if reasonably satisfied that the individual is eligible.

TAX CONSEQUENCES

As with a GCS, an LISC is not included in the assessable income of the superannuation fund to which it is paid, and forms part of the tax-free component when it is included in a superannuation benefit paid to the individual.

The amount will not count towards either the individual's concessional contributions cap (see 19.041) or non-concessional contributions cap (see 19.042), and will be subject to the normal preservation rules.

19.079   OTHER CONTRIBUTIONS

ARISING FROM PERSONAL INJURY PAYMENTS

The non-concessional contributions cap is subject to ongoing exemptions relating to payments for personal injuries resulting in permanent incapacity (ss292-90 and 292-95).

Where no tax deduction is claimed, contributions made from certain personal injury payments are exempt from the non-concessional contributions cap when paid into superannuation and notified using the approved form (see below).

Conditions

The personal injury payment must:

- be in the form of a structured settlement (s54-10), an order for personal injury payment or lump sum workers compensation payment
- be certified by two legally qualified medical practitioners that the person to receive the payment is unlikely to ever be able to be gainfully employed in a capacity for which they are reasonably qualified as a result of the injury, and
- be notified (see below) to the superannuation entity by the individual concerned that the contribution being made is made under this exemption before, or when, making the contribution to ensure that the superannuation entity is able to accept the contribution and does not report it against the non-concessional contributions cap.

The contribution must be paid to a superannuation fund within 90 days of whichever of the following events occurs last:

- the day the payment being received
- the day the structured settlement was entered into, and
- the day on which the court order was made.

The exemption from the non-concessional contribution cap only applies to the extent that the payment received relates to an amount for personal injury. Consequently, trustees need to have a process in place to record such notification from the member and to classify the contribution as coming within this particular exemption. They also need to ensure that members are aware of this exemption and how to claim it.

Notifications

To exclude a contribution from the non-concessional contributions cap, the *Contributions for personal injury* approved form (NAT 71162) must be lodged with the superannuation fund before or when the contributions are made.

SUPERANNUATION CONTRIBUTIONS FROM SMALL BUSINESS EVENTS: THE CGT CAP

There is a cap on the amount of Non-Concessional Contributions (NCCs) a person can make to superannuation (ss292-90 and 292-100). However, certain amounts up to a lifetime indexed limit of $1.395 million in 2015-16 ($1.355 million in 2014-15) from the disposal of qualifying small business assets will not be counted towards the individual's NCC. This amount is referred to as the CGT cap (CGTC).

Contributions allowed under the CGTC are:

- up to $500,000 of capital gains that are disregarded under the CGT retirement exemption in Subdivision 152-D
- capital proceeds from disposal of assets that qualify for the 15-year CGT exemption in Subdivision 152-B
- capital proceeds from the disposal of assets that would have qualified for the 15-year CGT exemption in Subdivision 152-B but for:
  - the disposal of the asset resulting in no capital gain or a capital loss
  - the asset being a pre-CGT asset, or
  - the asset being disposed of before the required 15-year holding period had elapsed because of the permanent incapacity of the person (which occurred after the asset was purchased).

To ensure that the superannuation provider does not report the contribution as a non-concessional contribution the individual must notify the superannuation provider that the contribution is being made under this exemption before, or when, making the contribution. Thus the contributor has a choice as to whether all or part of a contribution uses their NCC cap or CGTC. The contribution must be made no later than the day the person is required to lodge their tax return for the financial year in which the CGT event occurred or 30 days after the day the person received the capital proceeds, whichever is later.

Where an individual chooses the retirement exemption in Subdivision 152-D, the contribution required under s152-305(1)(b) can be made by transferring real property to a complying superannuation fund instead of money if the transfer satisfies the relevant provisions of the SISA93 (ATO ID 2010/217).

Where the small business CGT asset is held by a company or trust the CGTC that does not form part of non-concessional superannuation contributions can still apply provided that the necessary payment is made by the entity to a CGT concession stakeholder. The CGT concession stakeholder who chooses to make a superannuation contribution must then notify his or her superannuation fund before 31 July that the payment counts towards his or her CGTC.

Where the capital gain is made under the 15-year exemption the contribution to superannuation must not exceed the capital proceeds from that CGT event. Where the capital gain is under the retirement exemption then the contribution to superannuation cannot exceed the capital gain (s292-100).

In 2015-16 (2014-15), Sam, aged 58, sells an active asset used in his small business. Sam has owned the business for over 15 years and qualifies for the CGT 15-year exemption. The proceeds from the sale are $1.405 million and the capital gain of $350,000 is disregarded.

In 2015-16 (2014-15) and assuming that Sam wishes to contribute the entire capital proceeds to his superannuation fund, if he has not previously made any superannuation contributions or used his CGTC, he could elect to contribute $1.395 million ($1.355 million) *under the CGTC exemption and have the remaining $10,000 ($50,000) count towards his non-concessional contributions cap. This would allow him to make further NCCs of $170,000 ($130,000) in the year without exceeding his non concessional contributions cap or $530,000 ($490,000)if using the 'bring forward' option (see 19.042).*

Note: If Sam had his capital gain disregarded under the small business CGT retirement exemption he would have only been able to contribute the capital gain (up to $350,000) and not the capital proceeds under the cap exemption.

19.080 CONTRIBUTIONS TO NON-COMPLYING FUNDS

Superannuation contributions to non-complying superannuation funds are not deductible (since 30 June 2000). They are treated as assessable income and taxed in the fund at the top marginal tax rate. However an employer may be able to deduct superannuation contributions, if they had reasonable grounds to believe at the time the contributions were made, that the fund was a complying fund for that year of income (s290-75(1)(b)).

The superannuation legislation provides that contributions made to non-complying superannuation funds will not count towards the concessional contributions cap or the non-concessional contributions cap. However all contributions made from 10 May 2006 to a non-complying superannuation fund will count towards the non-concessional contributions cap in the year the fund becomes complying.

19.085 FORM OF CONTRIBUTION

A superannuation fund can receive funds in the form of cash or other assets that are permitted under the SISA93. When a contribution is received in a form other than cash it is referred to as an in-specie contribution. The Fringe Benefits Tax (FBT) implications of in-specie contributions are covered at 19.095.

Generally, trustees of SMSFs are prohibited from acquiring assets from related parties such as fund members, their family, and partners, related companies and trusts (see 19.200 and 19.202). However, there are some exceptions (see 19.205) and therefore, members of an SMSF may contribute their own assets or assets of their associates if the asset is:

- business real property used exclusively in the conduct of a business (eg. a warehouse a member conducts their business from) (see SMSFR 2009/1 which explains the Tax Office's view on the meaning and application of the term 'business real property' in relation to SMSFs for the purposes of the SISA93 and the SISR94)
- a security listed on an approved stock exchange
- an asset excluded from being an in-house asset (eg. units in a widely held unit trust or units in an eligible related private unit trust), or
- an in-house asset, providing the total market value of all in-house assets does not exceed 5% of the total market value of assets held by the fund.

 Unless it is within the 5% in-house asset limit, a member cannot transfer a residential investment property to their SMSF as it is not an excepted asset.

 Any asset transferred to an SMSF must be at market value.

The transfer of an asset in-specie is a CGT event as the transfer is a disposal and a capital gain or loss from the CGT event will be concluded in accordance with the usual CGT provisions that apply to that asset. The transfer must be at market value.

TREATMENT OF THIRD PARTY FUND EXPENSE PAYMENTS

Refer to TR 2010/1 for comment on the circumstances in which the payment of a fund expense by a third party may be considered a contribution.

19.090 OTHER AMOUNTS

TRANSITIONAL ARRANGEMENTS – 'DIRECTED TERMINATION PAYMENTS'

Transitional arrangements allow certain lump sum payments upon termination of employment to be treated as Transitional Termination Payments (TTPs) which can be rolled over into superannuation (see 11.210).

19.095 SUPERANNUATION AND FRINGE BENEFITS TAX

For commentary, please see 25.750.

19.100 SUPERANNUATION ENTITIES AND RULES

The *Superannuation Industry (Supervision) Act 1993* (SISA93) and the *Superannuation Industry (Supervision) Regulations 1994* (SISR94) provide the legislative framework for Australia's superannuation industry.

REGULATION

All superannuation entities (ie. superannuation funds, Approved Deposit Funds (ADFs), Pooled Superannuation Trusts (PSTs) and Retirement Savings Account (RSA) providers) have to comply with the SISA93 and the SISR94 if they are regulated. Only funds that are regulated are taxed concessionally and superannuation funds and PSTs have to come under one of these powers in order to be eligible for tax concessions.

THE REGULATORS

- **Australian Prudential Regulatory Authority (APRA):** APRA is the regulator of all superannuation entities other than Self Managed Superannuation Funds (SMSFs). Their info hotline number is 1300 131 060.
- **Australian Taxation Office:** The Tax Office regulates SMSFs. The superannuation helpline number is 13 10 20.

ELECTION TO BE REGULATED

If a superannuation entity wishes to be taxed concessionally, it must make an election with the regulator to be a regulated fund that complies with the SISA93. An election to be regulated under the SISA93 means the trustee must always comply with the SISA93 operating standards. The benefits gained are tax concessions that limit tax on taxable contributions and fund income (other than non-arm's length income) to 15%.

Failure to lodge the election within 60 days of establishment may result in tax concessions being lost for that financial year. Once the election is made it cannot be revoked. All new superannuation funds (both SMSFs that are regulated by the Tax Office and those regulated by APRA) lodge this election and other prescribed information with the Tax Office by completing an *Application for ABN registration for superannuation entities* (NAT 2944) approved form. The Tax Office then forwards to APRA information regarding APRA regulated funds (ie. non-SMSFs).

REGISTERING FOR AN ABN, GST AND TFN

An ABN will be allocated to new superannuation funds who lodge an *Application for ABN Registration for superannuation entities* (NAT 2944) approved form. Funds in existence prior to 1 November 1999 may also obtain an ABN by lodging the same form with the Tax Office. This form can be used to:

- elect to be a regulated superannuation fund
- apply for an ABN (see 5.100)
- register for GST (if required or desired), and
- apply for a TFN (see 5.040).

SMSFS ONLY: REGISTRATION MEASURES TO COMBAT ILLEGAL SCHEMES

From January 2010, the process of registration for SMSFs has changed as part of a Tax Office initiative to prevent certain illegal practices including Illegal Early Release (IER) of superannuation money from the superannuation system. These changes are summarised as follows:

- Improvements have been made, so that an enhanced SMSF registration process will identify and prevent sham SMSFs from operating and being displayed on Superannuation Fund Lookup (SFLU) (see 19.215). Subsequently, seven days after an ABN is issued the status of the SMSF will be shown on SFLU.

  To assist in authenticating superannuation transfers, a new category for SMSFs will be added to the SFLU. This will cover all new SMSFs, as well as existing SMSFs that have not received a Notice of Compliance (NOC). They will be allotted the new 'Registered' status category until a NOC is issued following the satisfactory lodgement of an Annual Return when the fund will be registered as 'Complying.' High risk funds will be closely investigated and excluded from SFLU.

  NOTE: SMSFs with the new 'Registered' status category will qualify for concessional tax rates and be allowed to have superannuation transferred into their fund bank account.

- Tax practitioners and their clients wishing to establish an SMSF should note:

  - It will take seven days for a new SMSF to be assessed by the Tax Office and appear on SFLU. In particular, during this period a large fund will not be able to process a rollover request by an SMSF while it is not listed on SFLU.

  - An SMSF will however still be able to access its ABN within current time frames, for establishing a bank account for the fund.

  - When processing a rollover request to an SMSF, a large fund may seek additional information from the requesting member to confirm their identity and their fund's legitimacy. It may seek copies of documents like trust deeds, investment strategies and/or bank account establishment documents. Advisers and trustees should ensure these are at hand to expedite the rollover process.

  - Ensuring that details on a request form match exactly those held on SFLU and reflect the registration details- will also assist the rollover request.

These changes are aimed at combating IER schemes using SMSFs and retain the integrity of the superannuation system.

RESIDENCY (ALL FUNDS)

In order for a superannuation fund to enjoy its tax sheltered status in an income year it must be a Complying Superannuation Fund (CSF). The CSF status of the superannuation fund requires that the superannuation fund must have also been a Resident Regulated Superannuation Fund (RRSF) at all times during the year of income. Part of the definition of a RRSF requires that the superannuation fund meet the new Australian Superannuation Fund (ASF) definition (s295-95(2)) as well as the definition of a Regulated Superannuation Fund (RSF) (s19 SISA93).

The ASF definition has a general requirement that the central management and control of the fund 'ordinarily' be in Australia. A superannuation fund will be considered 'ordinarily' in Australia even if the central management and control is temporarily outside Australia, where it is for a period of less than two years.

The Commissioner's interpretation of the definition of ASF as per s295-95(2) has been set out in TR 2008/9.

SOLE PURPOSE TEST

Superannuation funds needs to meet the 'sole purpose test' (s62 SISA93). This means a superannuation fund needs to be maintained for the sole purpose of providing retirement benefits to its members, or to their dependants if a member dies before retirement. A superannuation fund trustee needs to ensure that the superannuation fund complies with the 'sole purpose test' at all times, including when investing fund assets and paying benefits upon retirement of members. A superannuation fund needs to comply with the 'sole purpose test' to be eligible for the tax concessions available to a complying superannuation fund. The 'sole purpose test' is divided into 'core purposes'(s62(1)(a) SISA93) and 'ancillary purposes' (s62(1)(b) SISA93). A superannuation fund needs to be maintained solely for either of the following:

- one or more core purposes or
- one or more core purposes and one or more ancillary purposes.

The operation of the 'sole purpose test' has been considered in SMSFR 2008/2.

'Core purpose'

Generally, 'core purposes' are the provision of benefits for each member of a fund, on or after the:

- member's retirement from gainful employment
- members reaching the prescribed age, or
- member's death, if the death occurred before they retired from gainful employment or before they attained a prescribed age, where the benefits are provided to their dependants or legal personal representative.

'Ancillary purpose'

Generally, 'ancillary purposes' are the provision of benefits for members in the following circumstances:

- termination of a member's employment with an employer who made contributions to the fund for that member
- stopping employment due to physical or mental ill health
- death of a member after retirement, or after reaching the prescribed age where the benefits are paid to their dependants or legal personal representative, or
- other ancillary purposes approved in writing by the regulator.

This purpose lets a superannuation fund provide benefits where there is financial hardship or compassionate grounds, subject to the superannuation laws and the governing rules of the fund. From 1 November 2011, the administration of the 'Early release of benefits on specified compassionate grounds' program is now the responsibility of the Chief Executive Medicare (previously APRA).

Contravening the 'sole purpose test'

In respect to SMSFs, one of the main ways the Tax Office works out if an SMSF has contravened the 'sole purpose test' is to look at the character and purpose of the fund's investments. For example, if an SMSF member or any party directly or indirectly obtain a financial benefit when making investment decisions and arrangements (other than increasing the return to the fund), it is likely the SMSF fund will not meet the 'sole purpose test'.

Working out the purpose for which an SMSF is being maintained requires looking at all of the events and circumstances relating to the SMSF's maintenance.

When investing in collectables such as art or wine, SMSF trustees need to take care to make sure that SMSF members are not granted use of or access to the assets of the SMSF in contravention of the 'sole purpose test' (also see 19.206 for new rules that apply to SMSF investments in collectables and personal use assets from 1 July 2011). The most common breaches of the 'sole purpose test' are:

- investments that offer a pre-retirement benefit to a member or associate, or
- providing financial help or a pre-retirement benefit to someone at a financial detriment to the SMSF.

In SMSFD 2010/1, the Tax Office has determined that an SMSF is not in breach of the 'sole purpose test' where it purchases a trauma insurance policy and any benefits payable under the policy:

- are required to be paid to the SMSF
- are benefits that will become part of the assets of the SMSF at least until such time as the relevant member satisfies a condition of release, and
- the acquisition of the policy is not made to secure some other benefit for another person such as a member or a member's relative.

Penalties for contravening the 'sole purpose test'

Contravening the 'sole purpose test' is very serious and may lead to trustees facing civil and criminal penalties.

It can result in a fine of up to 2000 penalty units and/or five years imprisonment for individual trustees, and may result in the SMSF losing its complying status. Higher penalties apply to SMSF corporate trustees. The value of a penalty unit is currently $170; however for an infringement that occurred before 28 December 2012 the amount was $110.

TAX FILE NUMBERS AND SUPERANNUATION

Refer to 19.060.

NOTIFICATION OF A SIGNIFICANT ADVERSE EVENT

No later than the third business day after becoming aware of an event that has a significant adverse effect on the financial position of a superannuation fund, the trustee must give a written notice to the regulator setting out particulars of the event. This notice must be given where, before the next report to beneficiaries, the trustee cannot, or may not, be able to make payments to beneficiaries when obliged to do so (s106 SISA93).

REQUIREMENT TO GIVE INFORMATION

The regulator can require the trustee to give information, or a report on such matters, or produce any book related to the affairs of the fund, that are set out in a written notice (Part 25 SISA93).

OTHER INFORMATION TO BE PROVIDED

The trustee must provide information in writing to the regulator within the required time frame when certain events occur. These include:

- when any contact details change within one month, and
- a decision or resolution to wind up an SMSF before, or as soon as practicable after, the winding up is commenced.

COMPLIANCE TEST FOR SMSFS

The compliance test (s42A(5) SISA93) is passed if the SMSF:

- did not contravene the SISA93 or the SISR94 during the income year, or
- did contravene the SISA93 or the SISR94 but the Tax Office decides that a compliance notice should not be given for that year after taking into account:
  - the taxation consequences of treating the entity as a non-complying fund
  - the seriousness of the contravention, and
  - all other relevant circumstances.

NOTICE OF NON-COMPLIANCE ISSUED TO AN SMSF

Generally, where an SMSF fails the compliance test, a notice of non-compliance is provided to the trustee by the Tax Office. Once a notice is provided it is effective from the income year the fund first goes non-complying and subsequent years until such time as a notice of compliance is provided to the SMSF.

The Tax Office has been toughening up its stance in the past few years and rebalancing its educative role into a firmer enforcement role especially where the facts suggest a reckless or serious breach or disregard of the law. However, the Tax Office is still willing to apply a practical and flexible view where they consider it appropriate.

A lower risk of non-compliance exists if the Tax Office accepts an undertaking from an SMSF trustee to rectify a contravention.

In *Triway Superannuation Fund and FCT* (2011) AATA 302, the Administrative Appeal Tribunal (AAT) upheld the decision of the Commissioner that an SMSF should be treated as a non-complying superannuation fund and to refuse to exercise his discretion pursuant to s42A(5)(b) of the *Superannuation Industry (Supervision) Act 1993* (the SIS Act) that would allow the SMSF to be treated as a complying superannuation fund. The members and trustees of the SMSF were a husband, his wife and their son. The son had a drug addiction and took almost all of the money from the SMSF and spent it or gave it away. The son also took money from the accounts of a business conducted with his mother and lost that as well. His mother (the wife) had contributed the money to the business.

In refusing to exercise the discretion, the AAT said:

> *While tragic, the present circumstances are not those in which a discretion ought be exercised consistently with the principles governing exercise of discretionary powers. To do so would frustrate the wider objects of the SIS Act by relieving those responsible for superannuation funds of tax imposts where all of the assets of a superannuation fund are deployed inappropriately and lost as a consequence. Exercising a discretion in these circumstances is not consistent with the objects of the SIS Act.*

Factors to be considered

The Tax Office issued Practice Statement PS LA 2006/19 which stated that they will consider the following factors in determining whether a notice should be provided:

- the tax consequences if a fund was treated as a non-complying fund
- the seriousness of the contravention, and
- all other relevant circumstances.

The weight given to each factor will vary depending on the circumstances of the case. Furthermore, a decision will be determined on a case by case basis.

TRUSTEES

The SISA93 is based on the pensions and corporations power under the Constitution, and so a superannuation entity can only become regulated if the trustee is:

- a corporation, or
- individuals and the sole or dominant purpose of the fund is to provide age pensions. The fund can still offer to change benefits to a cash lump sum to members if the trust deed allows this.

Trustees of Self Managed Superannuation Funds (SMSFs)

Trustee declaration

Any trustee, or director of the corporate trustee appointed from 1 July 2007, must sign a declaration. The declaration must be in the approved form, no later than 21 days after becoming a trustee or director. The declaration aims to ensure new trustees, or directors of corporate trustees, understand their duties as trustees of an SMSF. Although the form is not required to be lodged with the Tax Office, the declaration must be readily available to the Tax Office if required. Failure to produce the signed trustee declaration at the time of a Tax Office audit or review may result in penalties being imposed. The declaration must be retained with the fund's records for at least ten years. The trustee declaration is available for download from the Tax Office web site or by ordering from the Tax Office.

All SMSFs

- it has a trust deed that meets the requirement of the SISA93, and
- no trustee, or director of a corporate trustee receives any remuneration for their services as a trustee.

SMSFs with two, three or four members

Trustee arrangements

- if the trustee of the fund is a company each director of that company is a member of the fund, or
- if the trustees of the fund are individuals each individual trustee is a member of the fund.

Membership

- the fund has two, three or four members, and
- each member is a trustee of the fund or a director of the company that is the trustee,

and

- no member is an employee of another member unless the members concerned are related.

SMSFs with one member

If the trustee of the fund is a company:

- the member is the sole director, or
- the member is one of only two directors of that company, and the member and the other director are relatives, or the member is not an employee of the other director.

If the trustees of the funds are individuals:

- the member must either be a relative or not an employee of the other trustee.

 The Tax Office has powers to manage instances where a fund fails to meet the definition of an SMSF.

SMSFs and enduring power of attorneys

If permitted by the trust deed, a person with an Enduring Power of Attorney (EPA) in respect of an SMSF member may be the trustee or director of the corporate trustee of the SMSF, in place of the member, facilitating the operation of the SMSF temporarily in the member's absence. This ensures that an entity representing the member is in place at all times as required under s17A of SISA93.

The Tax Office has issued Self Managed Superannuation Fund Ruling SMSFR 2010/2 which explains the Commissioner's view on how the EPA provisions under s17A(3)(b)(ii) apply to SMSFs. SMSFR 2010/2 expresses certain views of the Commissioner including:

- a person who holds an EPA qualifies as a Legal Personal Representative (LPR)
- the EPA must be current and accord with the relevant State or Territory legislation relating to EPAs
- the attorney must be properly appointed as a trustee or director pursuant to the terms of the SMSF's specific governing rules or corporate trustee's constitution
- a member who is a director of a corporate trustee of an SMSF may also appoint their LPR who holds an EPA as an alternative director in their place, in accordance with the corporate trustee's constitution or s201K of the *Corporations Act 2001*
- where an EPA is executed in favour of multiple attorneys, one or more of these attorneys can be appointed as a trustee or a director of the corporate trustee, in place of the member,
- where multiple members execute EPAs in favour of the same attorney, the attorney can be appointed as a trustee or director of the corporate trustee, in place of each of those members, and
- a member can execute an EPA in favour of an existing member who is a trustee, or director of the corporate trustee, in their own right.

 Section 17A(10) prevents the exceptions in s17A(3) from applying in respect of a member who is disqualified under s120 from being a trustee or a director of the corporate trustee of an SMSF.

 Where a member of an SMSF is under a legal disability due to mental incapacity, an administrator appointed by a State or Territory administration tribunal to manage the plenary estate of the member can be a trustee of the SMSF in place of that member under s17A(3)(b)(i) (see ATO ID 2010/139).

Small APRA funds

The trustee must be an approved trustee.

Tax return

All Australian resident super funds must lodge an income tax return from their establishment date, regardless of their income.

Newly registered SMSFs that have neither been legally established nor started operating in their first year of registration may not have to lodge for that first year.

Generally, non-resident funds that derive income that is taxable in Australia must also lodge a return. If a super fund has wound up, it must lodge a final income tax return. Lodgment dates are the same as for companies (see 6.700).

Rules for SMSFs

The fund income tax return, regulatory return and member contribution statement have been combined to produce a single *Self managed superannuation fund annual return* (NAT 71226). SMSFs must use this combined form to report for lodgments from 1 July 2008.

Rules for APRA-regulated funds

All superannuation funds, other than SMSFs, must complete the *Fund income tax return* (NAT 71287).

REGULATORY RETURN

All regulated superannuation funds must file an annual regulatory return.

Rules for SMSFs

The required regulatory return information is now included in the new *Self managed superannuation fund annual return* (NAT 71226). Expanded administrative penalties will be applied where an SMSF trustee fails to lodge their funds single annual return on time.

Rules for APRA regulated funds

All regulated superannuation entities other than SMSFs must lodge an annual return with APRA each year. An annual return is lodged D2A (direct to APRA) electronically, on a disk or via a 'smart' paper form if a fund cannot use D2A. It must be accompanied by a signed original trustee certificate and audit report by the due date and sent to:

> Australian Prudential Regulatory Authority
> Superannuation Statistics
> GPO Box 9836
> Sydney NSW 2001

No other documents should be sent with the return unless requested. An assessment for the supervisory levy payable will be issued by APRA. The return must be signed by the trustee for the fund to be treated as a complying fund. The Superannuation Fund Number (SFN) or Australian Business Number (ABN) should be used on all correspondence.

Annual return lodgement date is four months after year end. For funds with a 30 June year end, lodge by 31 October. A late lodgement amount is payable if a return is lodged more than 14 days late. It is included in the statement for the basic levy, forwarded to the fund by APRA and is calculated for each full or part calendar month the return is not lodged. The late lodgement amount is the greater of:

- $25, and
- basic levy amount of that return x 20% divided by 17. The minimum monthly penalty is $25.

The late lodgement amount is not tax deductible.

The supervisory levy for funds other than SMSFs and Small APRA Funds (SAFs) like ADFs and PSTs is a percentage of assets as at 30 June of the previous financial year. In 2013-14 it ranged from a minimum of $590 to a maximum of $1,786,000.

In 2012-13 and 2013-14 the SAF levy is $590 per fund, payable six weeks after the fund's annual return is lodged. A non-deductible late payment penalty of 20% pa is payable on payments which are more than 14 days late.

SUPERVISORY LEVY (SMSFS ONLY)

SMSFs must pay a supervisory levy for each year that they were a superannuation fund on 1 July. The levy is due and payable on lodgement of the fund's income tax and regulatory return each year.

Administrative changes to the method of levy collections enable the payment of the levy to be incorporated into the payment of the funds income tax liability using the new *Self managed superannuation fund annual return* (NAT 71226) with the payment brought forward a year as shown below. The late payment charge is replaced by a General Interest Charge (GIC).

Financial year	Arrangement	Amount payable
2012-13	100% of 2012-13 levy $191 *plus* 50% of the 2013-14 levy $259	$321
2013-14	50% of 2013-14 levy *plus* 100% of the 2014-15 levy $259	$388
2014-15	100% of 2015-16 levy $259	$259

NOTE: In the 2015-16 Federal Budget the Government proposed that from 1 July 2015 an increase in supervisory levies paid by financial institutions will apply to fully recover the cost of superannuation activities undertaken by the Tax Office and the Department of Human Services.

19.110   AUDIT OF ANNUAL RETURN: ALL FUNDS

Regulated funds must have their financial statements audited each year by an approved auditor.

WHO IS AN APPROVED AUDITOR?

The following can audit any fund:

- the Auditor General of the Commonwealth, a State or a Territory, or
- an auditor registered (or taken to be registered) under Corporations Law.

In addition to the above, these are approved auditors for SMSFs:

- a member of the CPA Australia
- a member of the Institute of Chartered Accountants in Australia
- a member of the Institute of Public Accountants
- a fellow or member of the Association of Taxation and Management Accountants
- a fellow of the National Tax and Accountants Association Ltd, or
- an SMSF Specialist Auditor of the SMSF Professionals' Association of Australia Limited,

up until 30 June 2013, provided the person was an approved SMSF auditor immediately before 31 January 2013. From 1 July 2013, SMSF auditors must be registered with ASIC.

NOTE: From 1 July 2013, SMSF auditors must be registered with ASIC.

Transitional arrangements

An approved SMSF auditor immediately before 31 January 2013 may continue to conduct SMSF audits until the earlier of:

- their ASIC registration, and
- 30 June 2013.

Approved SMSF auditors who lodge their registration application after 30 June 2013 are not eligible for the transitional arrangements.

WHO CANNOT BE AN APPROVED AUDITOR?

An auditor cannot have a disqualification against them (s131 SISA93).

Whilst the SISA93 does not require that an auditor be independent, members of professional accounting bodies are required, by their profession's auditing standards and ethical pronouncements to be independent when providing audit services. Thus, an auditor should be free of any interest which could be regarded as incompatible with integrity and objectivity.

A person would probably not satisfy his or her profession's standards and pronouncements of independence if:

- associated either with any member of the fund or any trustee
- involved in managing or administering the fund

- a trustee, member, or contributor to the fund
- a member of a management board, committee or other body exercising actual control over policies of the fund
- a person with actual control over the investments or administration of the fund, or
- a partner, employee or officer of the above.

TIMING OF AUDIT CERTIFICATES

After year end, an audit certificate must be provided by an approved auditor to the trustee before the fund's annual return is lodged:

- for an SMSF: the time that the *Self managed superannuation fund annual return* is lodged, and
- for any other superannuation entity: four months or the date in the trust deed if this is sooner.

Period for providing the SMSF audit report

From 1 July 2013 the trustee of an SMSF is required to appoint an auditor at least 45 days before the due date of the annual return.

REVISED GUIDANCE STATEMENT 'GS 009 (SEPT 2013)'

The Auditing and Assurance Standards Board has re-released updated *'Guidance Statement 009 Auditing Self-Managed Superannuation Funds'* (GS 009). The revised guidance statement will assist SMSF auditors in complying with the new Auditing Standards and Tax Office requirements released since GS 009 was initially issued in 2008.

AUDIT CONTRAVENTION REPORTING FOR SMSFS

Changes in the superannuation laws mean that the Tax Office now prescribe the contraventions and associated materiality levels that an SMSF auditor must report. One important consideration is reporting all prescribed contraventions, regardless of monetary value during the first 15 months of an SMSF's operation.

The *Auditor/actuary contravention report* (ACR) (NAT 11239) is the only contravention report that can be used. The ACR is event based. Auditors must report contraventions for an event. An event is something that may lead, or has led to one or more contraventions of the superannuation laws.

Auditors must apply a number of tests which will determine the sections and regulations that must be reported. They include a series of questions, the answers to which will clearly define whether a particular contravention should be reported. Auditors must report all prescribed contraventions for new funds (less than 15 months old) regardless of financial thresholds. This is one of the new tests.

The ACR requires auditors to inform the Tax Office whether the ACR is a new contravention report or a revision of a contravention report which was lodged earlier.

Contraventions should be reported as soon as possible when the auditor is of the opinion that a contravention has occurred, is occurring or may occur.

 Approved auditors and actuaries of SMSFs can lodge their ACRs online via the Tax Agent and Business Portals.

In auditing an SMSF, the auditor should adhere to:

- Auditing and Assurance Standards, and
- their professional judgment to determine to report contraventions and other important facts even if the tests do not require so.

GOVERNMENT PROPOSAL FOR SMSF TRUSTEES TO RECTIFY CONTRAVENTIONS

The government is proposing a *Stronger Super* measure that requires SMSF trustees to rectify contraventions of the superannuation legislation within a reasonable timeframe. Rectification should restore the SMSF to the same situation prior to the contravention, or ensure the SMSF is complying with the law.

PS LA 2010/2

Published on 8 July 2010, this practice statement outlines considerations for the Commissioner as Regulator of SMSFs, when deciding whether to:

- disqualify a person from being an approved auditor for the SISA93 purposes, and/or
- refer an approved auditor to their professional association.

ESAT TOOL

To help SMSF auditors complete the fund's annual compliance audit, the Tax Office have released their electronic Superannuation Audit Tool (eSAT). With eSAT an SMSF auditor can:

- identify and accurately specify contraventions
- prepare and save the ACR and lodge online
- refer to relevant case studies, topics and current legislation
- maintain notes and compliance audit history, and
- review the compliance audit outcome.

For more information about eSAT, please go to Tax Office's website at www.ato.gov.au.

19.115   POWERS OF THE REGULATOR: NON-SMSFS

The prudential regulator, APRA, can suspend or remove trustees if there is evidence that the trustee's actions are likely to lead to serious risk to the members' funds. It can appoint temporary trustees to manage the fund.

Any order appointing a temporary trustee must specify the powers, conditions (including the period of appointment) and any other terms. It can also instigate proceedings on behalf of a fund member in exceptional circumstances (ie. if it is thought to be in the public interest to recover damages for fraud, negligence, default, breach of duty or other misconduct).

POWERS OF INQUIRY

Subject to legal professional privilege the prudential regulator has investigation powers over investment managers and trustees to:

- conduct enquiries into any affairs of a fund
- investigate (or require the trustees to do so) the financial affairs of the fund
- require the external auditors to hand over any information obtained during the audit
- require the fund to provide information (ie. documents and explanations) about its affairs
- take copies or extracts of information
- have full and free access within premises to obtain relevant information
- obtain and execute search warrants, and
- conduct examinations of relevant persons.

Auditors who have been found to be unsatisfactory in carrying out their duties can be prohibited by the prudential regulator from conducting audits of superannuation entities.

RESTRICTION OF USE OF ASSETS

Limited to a period of six months, the prudential regulator can direct trustees, investment managers and others not to dispose of or otherwise deal in a fund's assets. That direction can be renewed after the six month period.

19.125   TYPES OF SUPERANNUATION FUNDS

There are five main types of superannuation funds as follows:

STANDARD EMPLOYER SPONSORED FUNDS

Standard employer sponsored funds have at least one employer who contributed for the benefit of employees under an arrangement with the trustees.

Funds with four or less members

There are two types of funds with four or less members (the four member limit includes all members with benefits in the fund including pensions):

- Self Managed Superannuation Funds (SMSFs) regulated by the Tax Office – where they satisfy the definition of an SMSF, and

- Small APRA Funds (SAFs) regulated by APRA – these funds must appoint an approved trustee. They have less prudential requirements under the SISA93 than do funds with more than four members.

PUBLIC OFFER FUNDS

Public offer funds are usually run by a professional trustee or fund manager. The fund must:

- have a corporate trustee, and

- issue applications to join, which disclose fund information to prospective members.

PUBLIC SECTOR FUNDS

As their name suggests, these funds are established for the public sector (eg. a Commonwealth Superannuation Scheme).

INDUSTRY FUNDS

Industry funds draw members from a range of employers across a single industry (or group of related industries) and are usually established under an agreement between parties to an industrial award. They are similar to corporate funds as they have standard employer sponsors and are traditionally non-public offer. They have been established in a range of industries such as construction, hospitality and health.

19.130 PRUDENTIAL RULES AND LICENSING

The prudential rules aim to safeguard members' benefits by defining the basic duties and responsibilities of trustees and investment managers. This prudential framework recognises that the primary viability and prudent operation of superannuation funds rests with the fund trustees.

ALL FUNDS EXCEPT SMSFS

These funds are subject to comprehensive and stringent prudential regulation directly by APRA. In accordance with changes to the SISA93, all trustees of APRA regulated funds must hold a Registrable Superannuation Entity (RSE) licence. Without this licence, it will be an offence to act as a trustee of a RSE or to accept contributions to a fund. The purpose of this license is to enhance the safety of members' funds in the superannuation system by requiring licensed trustees to comply with new standards covering proper governance, managing relationships with third parties, maintaining adequate resources and implementing sound risk management systems.

In April 2012, APRA released two prudential practice guides for superannuation trustees in the areas of contribution and benefit accrual standards and payment standards. The prudential practice guides (which do not introduce any new requirements for trustees) are final and are effective immediately. They are:

- Prudential Practice Guide SPG 270: *Contribution and benefit accrual standards for regulated superannuation funds*, and

- Prudential Practice Guide SPG 280: *Payment standards for regulated superannuation funds'*

SMSFS

These funds are regulated by the Tax Office and are also subject to stringent prudential regulation.

19.135   STANDARDS FOR TRUSTEES

APPLIES TO ALL FUNDS

Individual trustees or director(s) of a corporate trustee must accept appointment in writing.

Individuals and corporations cannot act as trustees of superannuation funds, ADFs and PSTs if any of the following apply:

- the individual (or a responsible officer if a company) has been:
  - convicted of fraud or has been penalised for dishonesty, or
  - is an insolvent under administration, or
  - removed or suspended by the regulator, or
- the company is in liquidation or receivers have been appointed, or it has begun to be wound up.

However the regulator can apply to the Court to have spent convictions taken into account when determining if a person (ie. individual or corporate) can be a trustee or director of a trustee company. Performing the duties of a trustee while disqualified will cause that individual or corporate trustee to be guilty of an offence.

TRUSTEE COMPANIES MUST CHECK THE CREDENTIALS OF OFFICERS

The onus is on the company to prove it had taken reasonable steps to find and check the credentials of its officers. Acts done by ineligible trustees will not be invalid only because of the individual's disqualification.

PROPOSAL IN RELATION TO A 'MINOR'

The superannuation legislation was amended so that where the trustee of an SMSF is a body corporate, a parent or guardian may be director of the body corporate in place of a member that is a minor.

19.140   TRUSTEE RESPONSIBILITIES

APPLIES TO ALL FUNDS

These duties and obligations are mandatory for all individual trustees and directors of trustee companies and cannot be excluded or modified.

HONESTY AND DILIGENCE OF TRUSTEES

- to act with the same care, skill and diligence as a prudent person would exercise when responsible for dealing with another person's property
- to act honestly in all fund matters
- to exercise power and perform duties in the best interest of the members and of the beneficiaries
- to keep the assets and money of the fund separate from that of any member, sponsoring employer or the trustee itself, and
- not to delegate responsibility (but tasks can be delegated) for any fund matter.

MEMBER ACCESS TO INFORMATION

To allow the member or beneficiary access to any information or document affecting the fund under the trustees control (but not internal working papers) unless:

- it would breach the privacy of another member, or
- it would disclose sensitive trade or commercial information damaging to the fund.

MAKING INVESTMENT DECISIONS

To formulate an investment strategy and make investment decisions based on legislative constraints (eg. in-house assets) and circumstances of the entity including:

- risk and return

- effect of composition and diversification of the fund's portfolio across asset sectors
- liquidity (in relation to cash flow requirements) and current return of the fund's investments
- projected return compared to fund's objectives, and
- the fund's existing and future obligations.
- that as part of the investment strategy trustees consider insurance for their members
- that money and other assets be kept separate from money and assets held by a trustee personally and by a standard employer-sponsor or an associate of a standard employer sponsor, and
- that assets of the fund be valued at market value for reporting purposes.

Also see *SMSF Product Ruling system* at 19.157.

SEEK ADVICE FROM QUALIFIED PERSONS ONLY

To seek legal, auditing, investment and actuarial advice from appropriately qualified and independent persons in respect of prescribed operation standards.

MAINTAIN DECLARATIONS, MINUTES, RECORDS AND REPORTS

Trustees must perform the following administrative duties:

- to lodge the required annual return
- to keep accounting records and retain them for five years (or longer if still relevant)
- to arrange an audit by an approved auditor annually
- to keep minutes of meetings, changes in trustees, consents to act as trustees and to retain these for five years (or longer if still relevant)
- to retain for inspection on request the trustee declaration, copies of notices from the regulator and general reports for ten years (or longer if they are still relevant), and
- to ensure that any engaged investment manager provides them with information on the fund's performance as well as the investment manager's financial condition.

PRODUCT DISCLOSURE STATEMENTS

These are required for all new SMSFs. However s1012D(2A) of the Corporations Act 2001 provides an exemption from this requirement where the trustee believes that a member has received or has and knows that they have access to all of the information that the Product Disclosure Statement (PDS) would be required to contain.

SIMPLE SUPERANNUATION ADVICE RELIEF FOR TRUSTEES

In July 2009, ASIC issued a class order that enables fund members to access low-cost, simple advice on their superannuation investments. The class order provides relief for superannuation trustees from the personal advice requirements of s945A of the *Corporation Act 2001* in limited circumstances.

19.145   FINANCIAL REPORTING

Each year, the trustee must prepare accounts and statements for the superannuation entity. Unless excepted by the SISR94, these must be prepared by all funds:

- a statement of financial position
- an operating statement, and
- any accounts and statements specified in the regulations.

Funds with five or more members are also required to prepare a statement of cash flows.

EXCEPTIONS

These are the situations where a statement of financial position, an operating statement and a statement of cash flows are not required:

- for defined benefit funds where in an income year the trustee prepares for the entity:
    - a statement of net assets, and

- - a statement of changes in net assets
- for superannuation funds where at year end the benefits paid to each individual member of the fund are wholly determined by reference to life assurance policies, provided that these accounts and statements are in place for the Income year:
  - - a statement that the policies are in place at the end of the year
  - - a statement on whether those policies have been fully maintained as directed by the relevant insurers
  - - the identity of those insurers
  - - the amount contributed by employers and members
  - - if not all of the amounts have been paid as premiums on the policies, the amount of premiums paid on the policies, and
  - - other expenses incurred by the fund.

The trustee must retain the accounts and statements for five years after the end of the income year for the purposes s112 of the SISA93 and Part 8 of the SISR94.

19.150   TRUST DEEDS

Superannuation funds are set up by governing rules and must have a governing trust deed or a constituent document.

SMSFS ONLY

From 1 July 2007 all new SMSF trustees must sign a 'Trustee declaration' approved form, part of which requires them to keep themselves informed of changes to the legislation relevant to the operation of their fund and to ensure that the trust deed is kept up to date, in accordance with the needs of the members and the applicable law.

OUR TRUST DEED SERVICES

Taxpayers Australia offers SMSF trust deed services through our partner Cleardocs who provide a simple, effective online system for creating and managing legal and related documents that my be suitable for readers seeking certain trust deed products.

Log on to: www.taxpayer.com.au/cleardocs for further information.

19.151   PROHIBITED ACTIONS

APPLIES IF FIVE OR MORE MEMBERS

The fund's governing trust deed must not:
- allow trustees to be directed in any matter by a party other than by law, a Court, the regulator, a member or group of members in respect of their benefits, or in special cases the employer, or
- authorise deed amendment (except for employer contributions) without the trustee's agreement
- permit returns of surplus except in special cases
- enable discretion in the deed to be exercised without the trustees consent. (This won't remove any of the members' rights or prevent the regulator exercising its powers), or
- restrict the powers of the trustees to seek advice, or be reimbursed for the cost of obtaining advice.

19.152   REMOVAL OF TRUSTEES

APPLIES IF FIVE OR MORE MEMBERS

The fund's governing deed will provide that members may remove their representative trustees as they are appointed. Independent trustees can also be removed, using the same process as for appointment.

19.155   INVESTMENT MANAGERS AND OTHERS

APPLIES TO APRA REGULATED FUNDS

Agreements between the investment manager and the trustees cannot exclude that manager from liability for negligence. Any such agreement is void.

Investment managers or a custodian of a fund's assets cannot take custody of the assets of that superannuation fund, Approved Deposit Fund (ADF) or Pooled Superannuation Trust (PST) unless they have $5 million in net tangible assets, and bank or government guarantees for a combined minimum of that amount.

Individuals and corporations are not eligible to act as investment managers of superannuation funds, ADFs or PSTs if:

- the individual or a responsible officer of the company has been convicted of fraud, penalised for dishonesty, or is insolvent, or
- the company is in liquidation or receivers have been appointed.

However, the prudential regulator can apply to the Court to have 'spent' convictions taken into account when determining if a person can be an individual or corporate trustee.

Investment managers must have a combined minimum of $5 million in net tangible assets, bank and government guarantees before being allowed to take custody of the fund's assets. The prudential regulator and the trustees must be notified immediately if the investment manager becomes ineligible.

ADDITIONAL RULES: PST MANAGERS

These additional rules apply to PSTs:

- the trustee is wholly responsible for the management of the fund
- the trustee and the manager can be the same person, and
- PSTs are wholly supervised by the prudential regulator who:
  - licences PST trustees and has the power to remove a licence, and
  - has power to issue a stop order on any advertisement or promotional material.

These PSTs are prohibited from borrowing except for short term cash flow purposes. The borrowings must not exceed 10% of the trust's assets and be for 90 days or less.

19.157   THE SMSF PRODUCT RULING SYSTEM

In August 2009 the Tax Office introduced Self-Managed Superannuation Fund Product Rulings (SMSFPRs) to provide certainty to SMSF trustees participating or potentially participating in a product. The Tax Office rules in accordance with the correct application of the law but offers no view as to the product being offered.

WHAT IS A PRODUCT?

A product refers to an arrangement in which a number of participants individually enter into substantially the same transactions with a common entity or a group of entities. For example, they may all enter into substantially the same management agreements with a manager connected with the promoter. The Tax Office will only issue an SMSFPR where it is intended for the product to be offered to SMSFs as potential investors.

The product may be described as, among other things, an investment arrangement, a tax-effective arrangement, a financial arrangement, or an insurance arrangement. Often, it is offered to the general public by way of a document such as an information memorandum or a Product Disclosure Statement (PDS), but it may be put forward to individuals on an invitation basis.

Common types of products the Tax Office is asked to provide SMSFPRs on are:

- agribusiness projects (for example, vineyards, olives, fruits, nuts)
- films, and
- financial products.

WHO IS THE PARTICIPANT?

A participant may also be referred to as an investor and is the SMSF that enters into an arrangement/product as described above.

WHO IS THE APPLICANT?

The applicant is sometimes referred to as a promoter, implementer or principal of the scheme and is the person who applies for the SMSFPR from the Tax Office on behalf of the participants or potential participants in the product. The applicant may be the responsible entity or manager of a managed investment scheme.

THE TAX OFFICE HAS POWER TO MAKE SMSFPRS

An SMSFPR is a form of SMSF advice and is not a public ruling. An SMSFPR is not, therefore, legally binding on the Commissioner. The Commissioner issues SMSFPRs under his powers of general administration of the *Superannuation Industry (Supervision) Act 1993* (SISA93) in the role of regulator of SMSFs.

 SMSFPRs are not public rulings!

An SMSFPR is written advice that is provided publicly on the prospective application of the SISA93 and the *Superannuation Industry (Supervision) Regulation 1994* (SISR94) to schemes in which the trustees of one or more SMSFs enter into substantially the same transactions with an entity or group of entities.

Though SMSFPRs are not binding on the Commissioner, they will provide certainty to SMSF trustees on the application of the SISA93 and SISR94 in relation to the specified arrangements or products. If the Commissioner later takes the view that the law applies less favourably to trustees than the SMSFPR indicates, the fact that trustees of SMSFs acted in accordance with that SMSFPR would be a relevant factor in their favour in the Commissioner's exercise of any discretion as to what, if any compliance action is to be take in response to a breach of that law. As such it is important that an SMSFPR requires a full and true disclosure by the applicant of all the relevant facts in relation to the arrangement on which the SMSFPR is sought.

 An SMSFPR will not be effective where relevant facts were not fully disclosed at the time the ruling was made.

WHAT ROLES DO SMSFPRS HAVE?

Though SMSFPRs are not legally binding on the Commissioner, they do provide trustees of SMSFs a greater level of certainty as participants or potential participants on the SISA93 and SISR94 consequences of an arrangement, provided they are carried out as described in the SMSFPR.

An SMSFPR only considers the SISA93 and SISR94 implications for SMSF participants or potential participants in relation to the specified arrangement, it does not consider tax matters. However, it is expected that an SMSFPR may include products on which a product ruling is also sought. Where a product ruling is sought and there is also a request for an SMSFPR in respect of that product then a separate SMSFPR would be issued in conjunction with the product ruling. Trustees of SMSFs should refer to both in considering the superannuation and tax issues for their fund.

 SMSFPRs do not consider taxation matters.

An SMSFPR will only be given in relation to a homogeneous group of participants, such that the SISA93 or SISR94 will apply in the same way for each SMSF participating. Additionally, an SMSFPR will not be given if it depends on an unresolved issue, for example, whether the SMSF is in business. No certainty can effectively be given in such cases.

An SMSFPR only applies to arrangements beginning on or after the date the SMSFPR is made. This means that participants are not covered by an SMSFPR if they enter into the arrangement before the SMSFPR is made.

SMSFPRs have prospective effect only.

The Tax Office does not sanction or guarantee any product as an investment and give no assurance that the product is commercially viable, that charges are reasonable, appropriate or represent industry norms, or that projected returns will be achieved or are reasonably based.

Potential SMSF participants must form their own view about the commercial and financial viability of a product. This will involve consideration of important issues, such as whether the projected returns are realistic, the 'track record' of the management, the level of fees compared with similar products and how the investment fits an existing portfolio. The Tax Office recommend a financial or other adviser be consulted for such information. Trustees of SMSFs must also ensure that all of the SMSF's investments are in accordance with the fund's properly formulated investment strategy that has regard to the whole of the circumstances of the fund and the risks associated with the investment.

The Tax Office suggest that potential SMSF participants might wish to seek assurances from applicants/promoters that the arrangement has or will be carried out in the same terms as the SMSFPR.

WHAT DOES THE TAX OFFICE EXPECT OF APPLICANTS?

A written application is required for an SMSFPR. Applicants may wish to apply for both an SMSFPR and a general product ruling using the applicable application form and checklist for each. All relevant information must accompany the application. The Tax Office provide an application form and checklist to assist applicants. It is in the interests of all applicants to obtain and use the application form and checklist, so that the Tax Office staff can be directed quickly to the relevant parts of the papers provided.

The Tax Office need to understand an arrangement and analyse the information provided before giving an SMSFPR. They will not provide an SMSFPR on insufficient information and the checklist is designed to obtain all the necessary information about an arrangement. SMSFPRs are not provided on the basis of similarities to other published SMSFPRs.

WHAT IF THE SMSFPR IS UNFAVOURABLE?

Before any SMSFPR is issued the applicant will be asked to confirm, amongst other things, that the arrangement described is correct and complete. The participant should recognise the importance of this, given that an SMSFPR applies on its terms, and will not apply in circumstances where the arrangement implemented is materially different to the arrangement on which the SMSFPR was given on.

An SMSFPR will only be published if the applicant agrees. This may mean that unfavourable SMSFPRs are unlikely to be issued. In any event, it is likely that the Tax Office would decide not to issue an unfavourable SMSFPR, as the existence of an SMSFPR, even in unfavourable terms, might be misleading to potential investors.

HOW CAN AN SMSFPR BE CHALLENGED?

The taxpayers' charter includes details on 'how to be heard' if a taxpayer believes that their legal rights or the standards outlined in the charter have not been met.

SMSFPRs are not covered by the objection and appeal provisions.

However, if an applicant wishes to challenge the position the Tax Office has taken on an SMSFPR application, the Tax Office will agree to review the decision to not issue an SMSFPR.

SMSFPR 2009/1

Published on 12 August 2009, SMSFPR 2009/1 provides the Commissioner's view on the application of the SISA93 and SISR94 to a 'scheme' or 'product' that the trustees of a number of SMSFs enter into in substantially the same way with a common entity or group of entities.

SMSFPR 2009/1 outlines the system of SMSFPRs including:

- what constitutes an SMSFPR
- the non binding status of an SMSFPR
- the consequences of how the scheme dealt with in an SMSFPR is carried out

- the extent of certainty provided by an SMSFPR, and
- when the Commissioner may refuse to issue an SMSFPR.

PS LA 2009/5

Published on 12 August 2009, PS LA 2009/5 explains:

- the forms of SMSF advice and guidance the Tax Office provides about the application of the SISA93 and the SISR94
- the weight given to the fact that an SMSF trustee has relied on SMSF advice or guidance in relation to a scheme, and
- where to find further information about procedures for developing and issuing each form of SMSF advice and guidance.

19.160 MEMBER REPRESENTATION

APPLIES IF FIVE OR MORE MEMBERS

Equal member and employer representation is mandatory for all funds with five or more members. Each individual plan (or sub-plan with five or more members in a master trust) must have a policy committee to advise the trustee, made up of equal employee and employer representatives. Alternatively, funds with between five and 49 members can opt for an independent trustee agreed to by both the employer and a majority of members.

The process for selecting representatives must be included in the fund's deed and members are to be informed in writing of that process.

POWER TO DISMISS TRUSTEES

Members have the power to appoint and dismiss those persons representing them on the board of trustees. This applies to employee representatives and to the employer sponsor(s). Members cannot overturn decisions made by the trustees but this dismissal power ensures that the representatives act in the best interests of members.

19.165 PRESERVATION OF BENEFITS

APPLIES TO ALL FUNDS

Certain superannuation benefits must be preserved until a condition of release is fulfilled. These conditions depend on whether the benefit is:

- a preserved benefit
- a restricted non preserved benefit, or
- an unrestricted non-preserved benefit.

 A trustee who knowingly or recklessly makes a payment that does not satisfy a condition of release is subject to penalties and the payment is taxed in the member's hands at their marginal tax rate.

PRESERVED BENEFITS

Preserved benefits are:

- vested benefits of employer contributions made under an award or agreement:
  - to a private sector fund after June 1986, or
  - to a public sector fund after 1 June 1990
- new or improved employer financed benefits vested in a member, arising from an arrangement made after 21 December 1986, or in the case of a public sector fund, after June 1990
- superannuation guarantee (SG) payments, including any shortfall component, made after June 1994, plus some made after June 1992

- member contributions to a private sector fund after 12 March 1989, or in the case of a public sector fund after June 1990, but before July 1994 during a period that the member did not receive employer support in that fund
- member funded deductible contributions to a self employed person's fund made after June 1994
- preserved benefits which are rolled over or transferred to a fund
- spouse contributions
- contributions for children
- superannuation contributions splitting amounts
- government co-contributions
- earnings on the above contributions
- all earnings on pre-July 1999 preserved benefits
- all post-1 July 1999 earnings and all contributions made post 1 July 1999
- employer ETPs rolled over from 1 July 2004 to 30 June 2007, and
- directed termination payments rolled over from 1 July 2007 to 30 June 2012.

Also see 19.700 for minimum retirement age and increase for people born after 30 June 1960.

CONDITIONS OF RELEASE

A preserved benefit must be held by a superannuation entity and can be released (subject to certain cashing restrictions) only when one of the following conditions or requests apply:

- the member's preserved benefits are less than $200 at the time of termination of employment
- a member's benefit is cashed in order to give effect to an excess contributions tax release authority
- a member's benefit is cashed in order to give effect to a transitional release authority
- the member is at least age 55, but less than age 60, has retired from employment for gain or reward, and does not intend to be gainfully employed ever again
- the member is at least age 60, but less than 65, if current gainful employment arrangement has changed, whether or not the member intends to be gainfully employed in the future
- the member is at least age 65, even if the member has not retired
- the member has died
- the member has a terminal medical condition (see 19.680)
- the member is permanently incapacitated
- the member is temporarily incapacitated (nb. subject to cashing restrictions that require any benefit to be paid as a non-commutable income stream for the period of incapacity)
- as from July 1 2005, an individual who has reached preservation age can access their superannuation by way of a non-commutable stream, without having to retire from the workforce (see 19.710)
- the member is experiencing 'severe financial hardship' (administered by the fund trustees, ADF or RSA provider) and has received Commonwealth income support benefits for:
  - a continuous 26 weeks and is less than 55 years, or
  - a cumulative period of 39 weeks since turning 55, and is not gainfully employed full or part time on the date of application.
    NOTE: In each 12 month period (beginning on the date of first payment), the amount released is limited to a single lump sum of not less than $1,000 (except if the amount of the person's preserved benefits and restricted non-preserved benefits is less than that amount) and not more than $10,000.

 Farm Family Support Scheme payments are now eligible income support payments for the purpose of early release of superannuation benefits on 'severe financial hardship' grounds.

- a release is made on one of these (or equivalent) compassionate grounds (previously administered by APRA, now transferred to the Chief Executive Medicare, effective 1 November 2011) to cover payments:
    - to treat life-threatening illnesses
    - to prevent foreclosure by a mortgagee or exercise of an express or statutory power of sale over the family home
    - for home and vehicle modifications to suit the needs of a severely disabled person or dependant, and
    - for medical transport, palliative care, funeral and burial expenses.

NOTE: Cashing restrictions applicable to various conditions of release are contained in Schedule 1 SISR94. Also see SMSFD 2011/1 which explains when a benefit payable with a cheque or promissory note is 'cashed' for SISR94 purposes.

Release to members who meet these tests will still be subject to the governing rules of their fund. See 19.700 for when benefits may be paid.

 A member who leaves Australia permanently cannot access preserved and restricted non-preserved benefits until one of the above conditions is satisfied. If the member is a non-resident who holds a special class of visa, he or she can access preserved benefits as a Departing Australia Superannuation Payment (see 19.670).

RESTRICTED NON-PRESERVED BENEFITS

These benefits are non-preserved (eg. undeducted contributions made before 1 July 1999 in the current employer's superannuation scheme) but they can only be paid when one of the above conditions of release is fulfilled or the member leaves the current employment.

UNRESTRICTED NON-PRESERVED BENEFITS

An unrestricted non-preserved benefit does not have to be preserved and can be paid at any time the member requests payment. Generally, these benefits are amounts that are non-preserved when termination of employment occurred, or non-preserved amounts that have previously been rolled over.

NEGATIVE INVESTMENT RETURNS

Where the fund makes a loss, the negative amount firstly reduces preserved benefits, then restricted non-preserved benefits and finally unrestricted non-preserved benefits. Future positive investment returns are all preserved benefits. This means that reductions in restricted and/or unrestricted non-preserved benefits cannot be reinstated.

MINIMUM BENEFIT STANDARDS

The fund minimum benefits to be maintained are:
- the members' own contributions plus net investment earnings
- government co-contributions plus net investment earnings
- employer contributions made to satisfy award or superannuation guarantee requirements, including any shortfall component plus net investment earnings
- all rollovers from an RSA and other rollovers or transfers treated as minimum benefits by the trustee, and
- if a member belongs to a class of employees in a defined benefit fund which has a benefit certificate, the benefit certificate amount.

PORTABILITY

Portability is the ability to transfer benefits from one fund to another. Although preservation rules require preserved amounts to be retained until a triggering event or date, a member has the right to transfer those amounts to another fund that complies with preservation requirements, unless the fund's governing rules prevent this (see 19.570).

BINDING DEATH BENEFIT NOMINATIONS

APPLIES TO ALL FUNDS EXCEPT SMSFS

A death benefit nomination that is binding on the trustee can be made in respect of accumulated superannuation benefits if the governing rules of the superannuation entity allow, or are amended to allow this to occur. The nomination can only be in favour of the member's Legal Personal Representative (LPR) and/or one or more of his or her dependants (s59(1A) SISA93 and r6.17A SISR94) (also see 19.600 & 19.720 for death benefits).

It must be in writing, signed and dated by two independent witnesses and reviewed at least every three years.

SMSFS ONLY

Section 59 of SISA93 and r6.17A of SISR94 do not apply to SMSFs and it is the SMSFs governing rules that permit members to make Binding Death Benefit Nominations (BDBNs), whether or not in circumstances that accord with the rules in r6.17A and therefore SMSF members can lodge indefinite BDBNs if their SMSF's governing rules so provide.

APPLIES TO ALL FUNDS

In ATO ID 2011/77, the Tax Office considers that a person ceases to be a 'stepchild' for the purposes of being a 'dependant' of the member under r6.22 of the SISR94, when the legal marriage of their natural parent to the member ends.

19.170   THE RIGHTS OF MEMBERS

APPLIES TO ALL FUNDS

Fund members have the right to recover any loss or damage suffered due to breaches of specific trustee obligations. However, trustees are indemnified where investments have been made in accordance with the fund's Investment Strategy (IS).

If a member becomes bankrupt, their entitlement in the superannuation entity is protected in the same way that similar benefits under a life policy are protected.

19.175   PROTECTING UNCLAIMED BENEFITS

APPLIES IF FIVE OR MORE MEMBERS

All Complying Superannuation Funds (CSFs) (other than SMSFs), ADFs, eligible rollover funds and providers of Retirement Savings Accounts (RSAs) (all referred to in this section as superannuation providers) must provide to the Tax Office regular reports in an approved format about their lost members. These reports are used to update the Lost Members Register (LMR).

What is the Lost Members Register?

The LMR is a central register of 'lost' superannuation fund members and RSA holders. The register is maintained by the Tax Office.

What is a lost member?

A lost member is a member of a superannuation provider who:

- cannot be contacted (ie. the superannuation provider may not have been advised of the member's address or mail sent to the member's last known address has been returned unclaimed)

- is an inactive member (ie. they are inactive if they joined a superannuation provider more than two years ago, but there have been no contributions or rollover amounts in the last two years), or

- transferred from another superannuation provider as a lost member and no new address has been found in the last two years.

A member can be permanently excluded from becoming a lost member if they:

- indicate by a positive act, for example deferring a benefit, that they wish to remain a member
- contact the superannuation provider and indicate that they want to remain a member, or
- belong to an SMSF.

Reports required?

There are two main lost member reports that superannuation providers must use as follows:

1. *Lost Member Report (Using Electronic Media Specification 4.0)*

   The electronic specification for this report can be downloaded from www.ato.gov.au/super. The report itself must include details of found and transferred members as follows:

   - Found members: Those who had previously been reported as lost, but have since been found.
   - Transferred members: Previously reported lost members transferred out of the fund during the half year should be reported as 'transferred'. (This excludes lost members who have been transferred to an eligible rollover fund and who have not previously been reported as lost members.)

2. *Lost members register non-lodgement advice*

   The *Lost members register non-lodgement advice* form (NAT 3797) is used to inform the Tax Office that the provider is not required to report lost members for a certain period because:

   - there are no lost members
   - lost members have a nil account balances, or
   - lost members, previously unreported, have been transferred to an eligible rollover fund.

   This form is only available to download as a paper form from the Tax Office website at www.ato.gov.au/super.

When to report

Lost member information must be reported within four months of the end of each half year as follows:

- for the half year ended 30 June, by 31 October in that year, and
- for the half year ended 31 December, by 30 April in the following year.

Methods of reporting

Lost member reporting must be in an approved electronic format as described in the Lost Members Register – electronic media specification version 4.0.

SuperReport, a software program provided by the Tax Office, can also be used to prepare lost members report in the approved electronic format. *SuperReport* can be downloaded from the Tax Office website, or can be ordered on CD-ROM by phoning the Tax Office on 13 10 20.

Penalties for not reporting

Superannuation providers who fail to provide the required information on lost members or to report on time, may be charged a penalty of up to $11,000 ($55,000 for a corporate trustee).

Accessing the LMR

The LMR is a database with search facilities. A *Lost members register enquiry form* (NAT 2476) search request can be lodged with the Tax Office, by either superannuation providers, members or the members' authorised agents. If a match is found a letter is sent to the member to let them know who may be holding their benefit. Members can also search for their lost superannuation by phoning *SuperSeeker* on 13 28 65. This phone service is available 24 hours a day, seven days a week. The search is conducted using a member's TFN and date of birth. *SuperSeeker* can also be accessed at www.ato.gov.au/super.

Lost Members Statement (LMS) paper forms

Paper versions of the LMS for Lost Members Register (LMR) reports are available in portable document format (PDF). These forms are necessary for superannuation providers or authorised suppliers of lost member information, who are required to report information about lost members or lodge paper non-lodgement advices.

They following paper forms can be downloaded:

- *Lost members statement* (NAT 71825) if you are required to
  - report information about lost members, or
  - lodge a paper non-lodgement advice
- *Member details* (NAT 71825A) if you have additional lost members.

If you are lodging for more than 100 members you must lodge the information electronically using the *Lost members statement version 5.2*. Both paper and electronic LMS now include the Non-Lodgement Advice (NLA). Completed paper forms should be sent to Australian Taxation Office, PO Box 3578, Albury NSW 2640. For more information, contact the Tax Office on 13 10 20.

19.176   UNCLAIMED MONIES

APPLIES TO ALL FUNDS

As part of the government's *Better Super* reforms, major changes were made to simplify and streamline the laws concerning the reporting and collection of unclaimed superannuation monies from private funds as from 1 July 2007. These changes to the *Superannuation (Unclaimed Money and Lost Members) Act 1999* (SUMLMA99) provide for future unclaimed superannuation monies from private sector superannuation funds to be paid to the Australian Government via the Tax Office. The amendments will assist the Tax Office in establishing a single access point for lost and unclaimed superannuation and a simpler nationalised claims process going forward. As a result, individuals will be able to seek advice directly from the Tax Office on any superannuation-related issue, without having to contact numerous government agencies.

As a result of the abolition of the 'compulsory cashing provisions' specific amendments to the definition of 'unclaimed money' have removed the requirement for a lump sum benefit to be 'immediately payable'.

The new amended version of 'unclaimed money' under s12(1) of the SUMLMA99 is an amount payable to a member of a fund if:

- the member has reached the eligibility age specified in the SISR94 (currently 65)
- the superannuation provider has not received an amount in respect of the member (and, in the case of a defined benefits superannuation scheme, no benefit has accrued in respect of the member) for at least two years, and
- after the end of a period of five years since the superannuation provider last had contact with the member, the provider has been unable to contact the member again after making reasonable efforts.

The trustee must make 'reasonable efforts' to contact the member if point 1 and 2 above are satisfied and five years have passed since last contact was made (s13(1) SUMLMA99).

 All trustees will have to change their process for identifying unclaimed money within the fund by applying the five-year requirement and removing the requirement that the benefit be immediately payable.

 If the Tax Office successfully matches an individual's details with an entry on the LMR, and the balance of the individual's lost superannuation account is less than $200, the individual may withdraw this amount from their superannuation fund tax-free regardless of their age (see 19.600).

REPORTING AND REMITTANCE OF UNCLAIMED MONIES

Superannuation providers are required to determine unclaimed monies on the 31 December and 30 June in each year. These dates are referred to as 'unclaimed money days'.

The dates for lodgement of statements and payments by superannuation providers of unclaimed monies to the Tax Office are as follows:

- for an unclaimed money day being 31 December of any year – 30 April of the following year, and
- for an unclaimed money day being 30 June of any year – 31 October of that year.

 All unclaimed superannuation money payments (including former temporary resident payments) paid to the Tax Office are lump sum superannuation benefits and are not subject to the taxing provisions in the ITAA97 and the Taxation Administration Act 1953 (TAA53). *Superannuation providers are not required to withhold tax from these payments even when they do not hold a tax file number for the member.*

PAYMENT OF SMALL AND INSOLUBLE LOST MEMBER ACCOUNTS TO THE TAX OFFICE

From 1 July 2010, the government requires superannuation providers to transfer the following accounts to unclaimed monies:

- lost accounts with balances of less than $200 (small accounts), and
- lost accounts which have been inactive for a period of five years and have insufficient records to identify the owner of the account (insoluble accounts).

Former account holders will be able to reclaim their money from the Tax Office at any time.

TAX OFFICE CONTACT INFORMATION FOR FUND MEMBERS

There are a number of ways fund members can search for their lost superannuation:

- conduct an online search using the Tax Office's online *SuperSeeker* service (As at the date of writing, regulations are being finalised which will allow individuals to use a new and simple electronic form to arrange and consolidate their super online.)
- phone the Tax Office *SuperSeeker* self-help phone service on 13 28 65. This phone service is available 24 hours a day, seven days a week
- contact the current superannuation fund and ask them to conduct a search on your behalf using the Tax Office's *SuperMatch* service, or
- download and complete a *Lost members register enquiry* form (NAT 2476) and send it to the Australian Taxation Office, PO Box 3578, Albury, NSW 2640.

USE OF TAX FILE NUMBERS

From 1 July 2011, amendments to the super law allow fund trustees and retirement savings account providers to use TFNs as a method of locating member accounts. From 1 January 2012, further changes facilitate the consolidation of multiple member accounts.

ELECTRONIC SERVICE ADDRESS

From 1 July 2015 all superannuation funds including SMSFs will need to obtain an electronic service address to be able to receive contributions and data in the SuperStream format. From 1 July 2015 employers with 20 or more employees are to use the SuperStream standard and all superfunds must receive employer contributions to their fund in this format. This will extend to employers with 19 or fewer employees from 1 July 2016, but may choose to implement this earlier.

NOTE: Contributions to an SMSF from a related party employer are exempt.

19.180   DISCLOSURE OF INFORMATION TO MEMBERS

Also see *Changes to Superannuation Return Reporting* at the end of this section.

APPLIES IF FIVE OR MORE MEMBERS

Funds must provide members with information on:

- the fund's investment strategy and details of investments accounting for 5% or more of assets
- names of trustees, investment managers, and other advisers

- the fund's earnings
- crediting rate and reserving policy
- fees, charges or other expenses deducted from a member's account
- any material matters affecting the fund's performance or management
- internal arrangements for query and complaint handling
- selection of trustee representatives
- liquidity position
- whether or not the fund has insurance cover against fraud or negligence
- details of any merger proposals where members are transferred to another fund, and
- any proposal to pay a surplus to an employer or its associate.

MEMBER STATEMENTS

APPLIES IF FIVE OR MORE MEMBERS

Under the SISR94, this information is to be given on becoming a member, annually and on leaving a fund.

TO NEW MEMBERS

- Within three months of joining, the trustees must supply a new member with a written statement showing: the contact details of the fund
- a summary of the main features of the fund or sub-plan
- a statement of financial benefits which the member may or will become entitled to
- the circumstances in which those benefits would become payable
- the method of working out those benefits
- a summary of how the fund deals with inquiries or complaints
- a copy of the most recent information given to members of the fund or sub-plan
- an outline of how fees and other costs are dealt with.

TO EXISTING MEMBERS

Within six months of the end of each year of income, the trustees must supply existing members (excluding life pensioners of the fund) with written information on events during that period:

- the member's contributions
- the amount of benefits rolled over or transferred into the fund
- the amount of withdrawals
- fees and charges deducted from the fund, and from the member's account
- the amount of any allotment of employer contributions and net earnings
- the rate of any allotment of net earnings
- the amount:
  - of bonuses that have accrued at the end of the period, on the sum assured
  - payable if the member dies:
    - at the end of the reporting period
    - at the beginning of the next reporting period, or
    - the method used to work out the amount
- details of other significant benefits including disability benefits, and
- details of outstanding contributions, and steps taken by the trustee to collect them.

TO MEMBERS LEAVING THE FUND

Within one month, the trustees must give members leaving the fund a written statement containing:

- contact details of the fund

- amount of benefit to which the member is entitled
- amount of preserved benefits, if any, and the method used to work the benefit out, and
- arrangements the fund has to deal with inquiries or complaints.

CHANGES TO SUPERANNUATION RETURN REPORTING (EXCLUDES SMSFS)

With the making of the *Corporations Amendment Regulations 2009 (No.3)* in March 2009, superannuation funds will be required to report long-term returns prominently in member statements. Specifically, superannuation funds will be required to disclose five and ten year returns in periodic member statements to help retail investors better understand their super. The measure will also:

- require returns to be disclosed at the investment option or sub-plan level in which the member is invested, and
- require the long-term returns to be highlighted, positioned and presented in a manner that will attract the member's attention.

Where a member has electronic access to personal fund information and has given permission, the fund will no longer be required to provide a written or an electronic member statement.

FUND NOTIFICATION

A proposal to increase the reporting of contribution information to members was intended to complement the 'payslips reporting' measure. This did not become law before the 2013 federal election. The current government has announced it will not proceed with the measure.

19.185   SUPERANNUATION COMPLAINTS TRIBUNAL FUNCTIONS

APPLIES IF FIVE OR MORE MEMBERS

The Superannuation Complaints Tribunal (SCT) is an independent Tribunal established under the *Superannuation (Resolution of Complaints) Act 1993* (SRCA93) to deal with complaints about:

- superannuation funds
- annuities and deferred annuities, and
- RSAs.

It does this through:

- conciliation to try to resolve the complaint, or
- formal review of the decision(s) or conduct to which the complaint relates.

The Tribunal is required to be:

- fair
- economical
- informal, and
- quick.

NOTE: SMSFs fall outside the jurisdiction of the SRCA93.

Fees

There is no application fee for lodging a complaint with the SCT, nor are any of the Tribunal's costs charged to complainant. (Any other costs are the responsibility of each of the parties to the complaint, whatever the outcome.)

Types of complaints

The SCT can deal with complaints about:

- the decisions and conduct of trustees of most superannuation funds and ADFs including the conduct and decisions of people acting on behalf of the trustee and the decisions of insurers in relation to insurance benefits provided under superannuation funds
- the decisions and conduct of life companies as providers of immediate and deferred annuities (annuity policies), including the conduct and decisions of people acting on behalf of the life company

- the decisions and conduct of providers of RSAs, including the conduct and decisions of people acting on behalf of the RSA provider and the decisions of insurers in relation to insurance benefits where the premiums are paid from the RSA.

Complaint procedures

1. First, the member should write to their fund asking them to resolve their specific problem. A copy if this letter should be kept.
2. If the complaint is not satisfactorily answered or replied to within 90 days, the member can take their complaint to the SCT. It is recommended that the member first ring the SCT, to check that their complaint is one that the SCT can deal with.
3. The member should next fill in the SCT's *Registration of Complaint* form and send it, together with a copy of their written complaint and their fund's reply, to the SCT at the address below.
4. A member can obtain the *Registration of Complaint* form from their fund or the SCT.

NOTE: The Tribunal will acknowledge a complaint within seven days of receipt. The Tribunal will then send a notice to the fund advising of the complaint.

It is possible that a Determination of the SCT could be appealed to the Federal Court. There are also some circumstances in which the Tribunal may decide not to deal with a complaint any further. In these circumstances the Tribunal will write to the complainant advising of its intention to withdraw the complaint.

19.190   WHEN FUNDS MERGE

APPLIES TO ALL FUNDS

Members' benefits are protected in all superannuation fund mergers. The merger cannot proceed without written approval of the members affected or the prudential regulator if accrued entitlements will be reduced.

In all cases where members are transferred to another scheme they must receive written advice, including the authority in the Deed for the proposal.

Also see *Optional CGT loss rollover for complying superannuation funds and ADFs* at 19.320.

19.195   WINDING UP A FUND

APPLIES TO APRA REGULATED SUPERANNUATION FUNDS ONLY

The following information applies to all types of APRA regulated funds (excludes SMSFs) when winding up, including small APRA funds, public offer funds, corporate funds, industry funds and retirement saving accounts. It lists the important tax and superannuation obligations which must be dealt with from a taxation perspective.

GENERAL AND REGULATORY OBLIGATIONS

Trustees of an APRA regulated fund must give notice in writing to APRA as soon as practicable after making the decision or resolution to wind up. This notification must be before winding up is commenced. The trustees must also ensure all outstanding obligations are met before they can wind up. These funds may have the following obligations:

- notify all members
- pay outstanding liabilities
- distribute all fund assets, and
- fulfill APRA reporting requirements.

INCOME TAX OBLIGATIONS

Check that all of their obligations under income tax legislation have been met. These include:

- lodging outstanding income tax returns, including the final return for the financial year in which the fund is wound up
- ensuring all requirements associated with paying superannuation lump sums to members have been met (see 19.600)

- lodging any outstanding business activity statements, and
- finalising any PAYGW obligations before cancelling their registration (see 19.600).

STATUTORY ADMINISTRATIVE OBLIGATIONS

Check that they have complied with other administrative obligations imposed by law. These include:

- lodging outstanding *Member Contributions Statement* (MCS) (NAT 71334) for contributing members who do not roll over to the successor fund (please note that a MCS is still required for the financial year in which the fund was wound up) complete a *Rollover benefits statement* (NAT 70944) in respect of all rollover superannuation benefits paid to other funds, including those benefits paid to successor funds
- ensuring all co-contributions and other Tax Office remittances have been either credited to member accounts prior to wind up or returned to the Tax Office using the *Superannuation payment variation advice' approved form* (NAT 8451)
- ensuring any release authorities for excess contributions tax are actioned and a *Authority to release excess contributions tax and statement* (NAT 71451) confirming the amount of contributions released has been lodged with the Tax Office (and a copy provided to the member)
- ensuring debts to the Commonwealth recognised by the Tax Office, such as overpaid co-contributions, surcharge assessments or remittances which cannot be credited to members, have been paid or otherwise resolved
- checking that the fund is up to date with reporting new lost members (see 19.175) and they report lost members transferred to successor funds, and
- ensuring a successor fund receives information sufficient to enable it to fully comply with any administrative obligations which may be transferred to them.

APPLIES TO SMSFS ONLY

WINDING UP AN SMSF

Winding up an SMSF involves trustees dealing with all of the assets of the fund so that the fund has no assets left, and completing all the reporting and other administrative obligations.

WHY TRUSTEES WIND UP SMSFS

Listed below are some common reasons why SMSFs are wound up:

- SMSFs and the law surrounding SMSFs is complex. Not everyone is ready for this when they establish a fund. To effectively manage their own super, individuals need the time and expertise. In the end, some people realise that having and managing their own fund is not for them so they decide to wind up their SMSF and transfer to, say, a public fund
- if all the members and trustees have left the SMSF (for example, they may have died), the fund needs to be wound up
- if all the benefits have been paid out of the fund, the fund needs to be wound up, and
- SMSF trustees that intend to move overseas may consider winding up their SMSF because the fund needs to meet the definition of an 'Australian superannuation fund' (s295-95(2)). The decision to continue with an SMSF when one or more members are not residing in Australia should be made very carefully.

In some cases, trustees will be able to pay benefits to members when the SMSF is wound up. In other cases, the members won't be able to, or won't want to take their benefits, so they will need to roll them over to another superannuation fund.

WHAT SMSF TRUSTEES NEED TO DO

If SMSF trustees have decided to wind up their fund, there are some key activities that they need to do such as:

- advising the Tax Office within 28 days of the fund being wound up

- dealing with the members' benefits in accordance with the superannuation laws and the trust deed – this may mean paying them a superannuation lump sum, if they are entitled, or rolling their benefits to another fund
- having a final audit of the fund undertaken, and
- completing reporting obligations with the Tax Office and paying any final liabilities.

There might also be other things that the SMSF's trust deed requires trustees to do, in order to wind up the fund.

WHAT SMSF TRUSTEES MUST NOT DO

- Do not cancel the SMSF's ABN. This will be done by the Tax Office.
- Do not assume that lodging a final income tax return and reporting wound-up information is the last contact they may need to have with the Tax Office. Trustees still need to finalise all lodgment and payment obligations before the SMSF can be wound up. Records must be kept for five years.
- Do not close the SMSF's bank accounts. SMSF trustees may still need to make payments to the Tax Office or other businesses, and may need to deposit refunds. Once closed, these bank accounts can only be re-opened by producing a new trust deed.

CONFIRMING THE SMSF HAS BEEN WOUND UP

SMSF trustees will receive written notification from the Australian Business Register when their SMSF's ABN has been cancelled. It's important to wind up the fund correctly. If they have not met all of the fund's obligations, the fund may be selected for a compliance investigation and trustees may be subject to penalties.

19.200   IN-HOUSE ASSETS

APPLIES TO ALL FUNDS

From 11 August 1999 an in-house asset is an asset of the fund that is a loan to, or an investment in a related party of the fund, or an asset of the fund subject to a lease or lease arrangement between the fund and a related party of the fund, but does not include:

- a life policy issued by a life insurance company
- a deposit with an authorised deposit-taking institution (ADI)
- an investment in a pooled superannuation trust, where the trustee of the fund and the trustee of the pooled superannuation trust acted at arm's length in relation to the making of that investment
- an asset of a public sector fund, where the asset consists of an investment in securities issued under the authority of:
  - the Commonwealth or a government of a State or a Territory, or
  - a public authority constituted by or under a law of the Commonwealth, a State or a Territory, where the public authority is not a standard employer-sponsor (or associate of a standard employer-sponsor) of the fund
- an asset which the Regulator determines by written notice given to the trustee of the fund, is not an in-house asset of the fund
- an asset which the Regulator determines is not an in-house asset of any fund; or a class of funds in which the fund is included, or
- an investment in a widely held unit trust.

APPLIES IF FOUR OR LESS MEMBERS

An in-house asset excludes:

- business real property acquired from a related party at market value and/or leased to a related party under a legally binding lease (see SMSFR 2009/1 which explains the Tax Office's view on the meaning and application of the term 'business real property' in relation to SMSFs for the purposes of the SISA93 and the SISR94) The business real property exclusion does not cover undeveloped commercial land that is not being used in a business

- company or unit trust investments that comply with certain requirements where:
  - there are no outstanding borrowings
  - there is no charge over any asset
  - no investment in or loan of money to individuals or other entities (other than deposits with authorised deposit-taking institutions eg. banks)
  - it does not conduct a business
  - it conducts all transactions on an arm's length basis, and
  - other than business real property, money and a share in a company:
    - it has not acquired an asset from a related party of the superannuation fund after 11 August 1999
    - it does not acquire an asset that had been owned by a related party of the superannuation fund in the previous three years (excluding any period of ownership prior to 11 August 1999), and
    - it does not directly or indirectly lease assets to a related party.

Also see:

- SMSFR 2009/3, which considers if an SMSF contravenes certain provisions of the SISA93 when the SMSF is presently entitled to distributions from a related trust which are not paid over to it
- SMSFR 2010/1, which explains whether an asset is intentionally acquired by a trustee or investment manager of an SMSF from a related party of the SMSF for the purposes of s66(1) of the SISA93
- SMSFR 2009/4, which explains the concepts of 'asset', 'loan', 'investment in', 'lease' and 'lease arrangement' in the definition of 'in-house asset' of an SMSF as defined in s71 of the SISA93, and
- TA 2009/10, which describes arrangements involving the non-commercial use of negotiable instruments, some of which may breach the in-house asset provisions.

TRANSITIONAL ARRANGEMENTS

Until 11 August 1999 in-house assets were defined as loans, investments or leases with the employer sponsor of the superannuation fund, or with an associate of that employer.

Transitional measures apply to particular investment arrangements in place before 12 August 1999. These are 'grandfathering' (ie. permanently exempting from the rules that apply after 11 August 1999) of:

- all investments and loans made before 12 August 1999
- assets that were subject to a lease before 12 August 1999
- leased assets where the same asset is leased to the same related party (ie. effectively a lease on that asset can be rolled over, even if this is not provided for in the original agreement)
- all investments and loans made after 11 August 1999 under legally binding contracts entered into before 12 August 1999, and
- assets subject to a lease after 11 August 1999 under a legally binding lease entered into before 12 August 1999 (while the asset continues to be leased to the same party).

INVESTMENTS MADE AFTER 11 AUGUST 1999 THAT ARE EXEMPT FROM IN-HOUSE ASSET RULES

Until 30 June 2009, funds with an investment in a related company or unit trust at 11 August 1999, could elect to use one of the following transitional provisions:

- make additional payments on partly paid shares and units or reinvest earnings, and earnings on earnings, back into the related company or unit trust. Such payments and reinvestments are excluded from the definition of in-house asset and therefore do not need to be unwound at the end of this period (ss71A and 71D SISA93), or

- in the case of SMSFs only, elect by 23 December 2000 to make additional investments in the related company or unit trust, provided their sum does not exceed the level of debt held by that related company or unit trust as at 11 August 1999 (s71E SISA93).

Also see SMSFD 2007/1 which explains when a dividend or trust distribution is 'received' before the end of 30 June 2009 for the purposes of s71D(d) of the SISA93.

NOTE: Where a superannuation fund holds units in a related unit trust, if the net income of the unit trust owed to the fund (as the unit holder) remains unpaid, there is a danger that the unpaid entitlement may be considered a 'loan' (refer SMSFR 2009/3). Where this occurred, the loan would be to a related party and therefore an in-house asset.

IN-HOUSE ASSET LIMITS

Total acquisitions of in-house assets are limited to 5% of the market value of the total assets of a superannuation fund.

A fund can not acquire a new in-house asset if that investment:

- results in in-house assets exceeding 5% of the market value of the fund's assets, or
- in-house assets already exceed the 5% limit.

In the case *JNVQ and C of T* (2009) AATA 522, the AAT upheld a Tax Office decision to issue a notice of non-compliance to an SMSF found to have contravened the five per cent limit on 'in-house assets', which occurred after the SMSF made loans to a related company to support that company's business activities.

In-house assets in excess of the 5% limit at 30 June of a financial year must be disposed of during the following financial year in accordance with a trustee's written plan.

EARNINGS RATE REQUIRED ON IN-HOUSE ASSETS

The earnings rate for in-house assets with a related party is a commercial rate of interest, determined by the trustee. These are examples of a commercial rate of return:

- the current bank overdraft interest rate, or
- the current loan FBT statutory interest rate (5.65% for the FBT year commencing 1 April 2015).

PRACTICE STATEMENT ON IN-HOUSE ASSETS

Practice Statement PS LA 2009/8 outlines the circumstances in which the Commissioner would exercise his discretion to issue a determination under s71(1)(e) of the SISA93 that an asset is not an in-house asset of an SMSF. The Tax Office subsequently issued an amendment to PS LA 2009/8, which included additional examples relating to the leasing of Water Access Entitlements (WAEs) to a related party and the circumstances where the Commissioner would consider exercising his discretion to issue a determination that the WAE is not an in-house asset.

19.202　　RELATED PARTY

In relation to a fund, the term 'related party' is relevant to the prohibition on the acquisition of assets and the in-house asset rules.

A related party of a fund covers any of the following:

- a member of the fund and their Part 8 associates (s70B to s70E SISA93), or
- a standard employer-sponsor of the fund and their Part 8 associates.

This definition operates to include a number of persons and entities that are in some way connected to the fund and its members or employer-sponsor. This would include:

- other fund members, trustee individuals and directors
- any relative of the member including grandparents through to lineal descendants and their spouses
- a partnership where the member or employer-sponsor is a partner. This includes the partners themselves, their spouses and their children, and
- any company or trust controlled by a member of the fund or employer-sponsor, including a company where the member or any associated party of the member holds a controlling interest in the company.

19.205 ACQUIRING ASSETS FROM RELATED PARTIES

APPLIES TO ALL FUNDS

A fund can only acquire (eg. by purchase or an in specie contribution) an asset from a related party including a member, if it is:

- a security listed on an approved stock exchange at its market value, such as:
  - a share in a company
  - a unit in a unit trust
  - a bond or debenture
  - a right or option, and
  - any other security
- an asset excluded from being an in-house asset, eg. units in a widely held unit trust, ie. no fewer than 20 entities holding 75% or more of fixed entitlements to its income and capital
- an asset where the acquisition occurs as the result of the relationship breakdown of a member of the fund (see 19.260)
- an asset which the Regulator by written determination, determines may be acquired by any fund or a class of funds in which the fund is included, or
- an in-house asset so long as the 5% limit is not breached.

APPLIES TO SMALL FUNDS

A fund with four or less members can use 100% of its assets to acquire business real property from a related party at market value (includes a farm of any size containing a farm house provided that no more than two hectares is used privately (s66(6) SISA93)). In-house asset rules are not affected if business real property is leased to a related party by the fund on an arm's length basis.

Also see:

- SMSFR 2010/1 which explains whether an asset is intentionally acquired by a trustee or investment manager of an SMSF from a related party of the SMSF for the purposes of s66(1) of the SISA93
- SMSFR 2009/1 which explains the Tax Office's view on the meaning and application of the term 'business real property' in relation to SMSFs for the purposes of the SISA93 and SISR94, and
- TA 2009/10 which describes arrangements involving the non-commercial use of negotiable instruments, some of which may breach the restriction on SMSFs acquiring assets from related parties.

It is the Tax Office's view that the anti-avoidance provision in s66(3) apply to participants of an arrangement that is structured so that it avoids the prohibition on the acquisition of assets from a related party of the SMSF under s66(1) (see ATO ID 2011/84).

19.206 COLLECTABLES AND PERSONAL USE ASSETS

APPLIES TO SMSFS

On 1 July 2011 new provisions were introduced into the SISA93 for SMSF investments in collectables and personal use assets for investments made by SMSFs on or after that date. Where an SMSF held an investment in a collectable or personal use asset immediately prior to 1 July 2011, it has until 1 July 2016 to comply with the rules.

Section 62A of the SISA93 provides that the regulations may make rules in relation to SMSFs making, holding and realising investments in respect to the following collectables and personal use assets:

- artwork (within the meaning of the *Income Tax Assessment Act 1997* (ITAA97))
- jewellery

- antiques
- artefacts
- coins, medallions or bank notes
- postage stamps or first day covers
- rare folios, manuscripts or books
- memorabilia
- wine or spirits
- motor vehicles
- recreational boats, and
- memberships of sporting or social clubs.

Regulation 13.18AA (1) of the SISR94 specifies the s62A assets that are taken to be collectables and personal use assets within the regulations and requires that:

- collectables and personal use assets must not be leased to any related party (see 19.202) of the funds
- collectables and personal use assets must not be stored or displayed in the private residence of any related party of the fund
- trustees must make a written record of the reasons for the decisions on where to store the collectables and personal use assets and keep the record for ten years
- trustees must ensure that collectables and personal use assets (other than a membership of a sporting or social club) are insured in the name of the fund within seven days of acquisition
- collectables and personal use assets cannot be used by any related party of the fund, and
- the transfer of ownership of collectables and personal use assets to a related party of the SMSF must be done at a market price determined by a qualified independent valuer.

19.207 VALUATION OF ASSETS

APPLIES TO SMSFS

SMSFs must use market values for all valuation purposes in relation to the purchase price of a pension and in the preparation of financial statements. Valuations should be based on reasonably objective and supportable data using a 'reasonable' process.

The current tax law does not define market value in any general provision. It is defined in the 'Definitions' part at the end of the *Income Tax Assessment Act 1997* (ITAA97), but not in a way that fixes its meaning in all contexts. As a result, 'market value' usually takes the ordinary meaning, unless specially defined or qualified in a particular provision. Business valuers in Australia typically define market value as the price that would be negotiated in an open and unrestricted market between a knowledgeable, willing but not anxious buyer and a knowledgeable, willing but not anxious seller acting at arm's length.

For further information, see ATO Superannuation Circular 2003/01 which applies only to SMSFs.

19.210 BORROWING, LENDING, FINANCIAL ASSISTANCE AND GIVING A CHARGE

APPLIES TO ALL FUNDS

Except for the in-house asset rules for private sector funds, borrowing is generally prohibited, except for short term cash flow purposes. See 19.213 for limited recourse borrowing arrangements (LRBAs). The borrowing is limited to 10% of the fund's assets and a maximum period of:

- 90 days, if a payment to a beneficiary could not be made without borrowing, and the payment was required to be made to comply with:

- the governing rules, or
- the law
- 90 days to pay the superannuation contributions surcharge, or
- 7 days, if the payment is to settle certain financial instrument acquisitions listed in s67(3)(a) of the SISA93, including bonds, debentures, shares, units and various contracts due to unforeseen circumstances when the investment was made.

Also see SMSFR 2009/2, which sets out the Commissioner's view on the meaning of 'borrow money' or 'maintain an existing borrowing of money' for the purposes of s67 of the SISA93. This Ruling applies to SMSFs only.

The superannuation legislation imposes restrictions on recognising or sanctioning a charge over or in relation to a member's benefits, or giving a charge over fund assets (r13.11 to r13.15A). In ATO ID 2011/81, the Tax Office considers that the trustee of an SMSF does not 'give a charge' for the purposes of r13.14 if the trustee purchases an asset subject to a charge that was established before the trustee purchased the asset.

THE SOLE PURPOSE TEST AND LOANS

Trustees cannot lend money to members or their relatives. This prohibition arises because the trustee must satisfy the 'sole purpose test' (s62 SISA93) (see 19.100) to provide benefits at the earlier of:

- each members retirement
- each member reaching age 65 or more (r13.18 SISR94), or
- for each member's dependants if the member dies before retirement or age 65.

Also see SMSFR 2008/2, which sets out the Commissioner's view on the application of the 'sole purpose test' in s62 of the SISA93 to the provision of benefits other than retirement, employment termination or death benefits.

FINANCIAL ASSISTANCE – SMSFS ONLY

A trustee or investment manager of an SMSF must not use the resources of the SMSF to give financial assistance to a member of the SMSF or relative of a member of the SMSF.

A member's relative includes a member's spouse or a member's (or spouse's) child. From 1 December 2008, a 'spouse' includes another person, whether of the same-sex or (see 19.265) a different sex, with whom the person is in a relationship that is registered under a law of a State or Territory, or another person who, although not legally married to the person, lives with the person on a genuine domestic basis as a couple.

The term 'financial assistance' extends beyond the provision of loans and other kinds of disposition of money or property to include the giving of a security, charge or guarantee or the taking of an obligation, or any other arrangement that can be objectively perceived as a financial accommodation. Also see SMSFR 2008/1, which sets out the Commissioner's view on the giving of financial assistance using the resources of an SMSF to a member or relative of a member that is prohibited for the purposes of s65(1)(b) of the SISA93.

Also see TA 2009/10, which describes arrangements involving non-commercial use of negotiable instruments, some of which may breach the restriction on SMSFs providing financial assistance to a member or relative of a member.

Also see TA 2010/5, which describes an arrangement where an SMSF invests funds in an unrelated trust and the trust then on lends the funds to an SMSF member or a relative of the member.

INSTALMENT WARRANTS

For instalment warrants (24th September 2007 to 6 July 2010) please see previous editions of the *Tax Summary*.

19.213   LIMITED RECOURSE BORROWING ARRANGEMENTS (APPLIES FROM 7 JULY 2010)

Arrangements entered into from 7 July 2010 are now known as Limited Recourse Borrowing Arrangements (LRBAs). From 7 July 2010, as an exception to the restriction on borrowings in s67(1), the trustee of a Regulated Superannuation Fund (RSF) may borrow money, or maintain a borrowing of money, under an LRBA covered by s67A and s67B of the *Superannuation Industry (Supervision) Act 1993* (SISA93) that replace the previous exception provided by the former s67(4A).

SMSFR 2012/1: 'LRBAS – APPLICATION OF KEY CONCEPTS'

This final Ruling (previously issued in draft form as SMSFR 2011/D1) explains how the LRBA provisions apply to an SMSF that enters into an LRBA. The key concepts explained in the Ruling are:

- what is an 'acquirable asset' and a 'single acquirable asset'
- 'maintaining' or 'repairing' the acquirable asset compared to 'improving' the asset, and
- when a single acquirable asset is changed to such an extent that it is a different (replacement) asset.

LRBAS ARE FINANCIAL PRODUCTS

Amendments to the *Corporations Regulations 2001* (CR01) provide that (LRBAs by superannuation fund trustees as permitted by the SISA93 are financial products under the *Corporations Act 2001* (CA01). This extends the CA01's consumer protections to superannuation funds when entering into LRBAs, as those dealing in (providing advice on and issuing) financial products must have an Australian Financial Services Licence (AFSL) and are legally required to provide consumer protections to their clients.

Specifically, it provides that:

- LRBAs are financial products when acquired by superannuation funds
- LRBAs are not a credit facility when acquired by superannuation funds, and
- an AFSL covering securities or derivatives is taken to also cover LRBAs.

REFINANCING

Refinancing is now expressly allowable under s67A(1)(a)(ii). This provision applies to the refinancing of a borrowing of money under an arrangement that was entered into before, on or after 7 July 2010. Refinancing is also not the only way that a new arrangement may arise. For example, a change to the terms and conditions of an arrangement that fundamentally alters the terms of the arrangement may mean that the new arrangement must comply with s67A.

 Where a fund trustee signed all the relevant documents before 7 July 2010, but does not draw down the loan until 7 July 2010 or later, the new legislation will apply.

LIMITED RECOURSE BORROWING ARRANGEMENTS UNDER S67A

A LRBA under s67A must meet the following conditions:

(a) the money is or has been applied for the acquisition of a single *acquirable asset* (see below), including:

-   expenses incurred in connection with the borrowing or acquisition, (eg. conveyancing fees, stamp duty, brokerage or loan establishment costs, as these are considered to be intrinsically linked to the purchase of the acquirable asset), or in maintaining or repairing the acquirable asset but not expenses incurred in improving the acquirable asset, and

-   money applied to refinance a borrowing (including any accrued interest on a borrowing or because of a replacement asset under s67B) in relation to the single acquirable asset (and no other acquirable asset)

(b) the acquirable asset is held on trust by a custodian trustee as the legal owner with the RSF trustee acquiring a beneficial interest in the acquirable asset

(c)   the RSF trustee has a right to acquire legal ownership of the acquirable asset by making one or more payments after acquiring the beneficial interest

(d)   the rights of the lender or any other person against the RSF trustee for, in connection with, or as a result of (whether directly or indirectly) default on the borrowing (or the sum of the borrowing and charges related to the borrowing) are limited to rights relating to the acquirable asset (for example, under condition (d), any right of a person to be indemnified by the RSF trustee because of a personal guarantee given by that person in favour of the lender is limited to rights relating to the acquirable asset)

(e)   if, under the arrangement, the RSF trustee has a right relating to the acquirable asset (other than a right described in para (c)) – the rights of the lender or any other person against the RSF trustee for, in connection with, or as a result of (whether directly or indirectly) the RSF trustee's exercise of the RSF trustee's right are limited to rights relating to the acquirable asset, and

(f)   the acquirable asset is not subject to any charge (including a mortgage, lien or other encumbrance) except as provided by para (d) or (e).

NOTE: Amendments to the law enables the asset to be retained by the bare trust after final payment is made.

'ACQUIRABLE ASSET' AND COLLECTION OF ASSETS

An asset is an 'acquirable asset' if it is not money (whether Australian or foreign currency) and the SISA93 or any other law does not prohibit the RSF trustee from acquiring the asset (s67A(2)). The term 'asset' is to be read in the **singular**, so that it is not interpreted as permitting borrowing arrangements over multiple non-identical assets.

An asset can cover a collection of assets that are identical and have the same market value (s67A(3)). Examples of a collection that can be treated as a single 'acquirable asset' include:

- a collection of shares of the same type in a single company (eg. a collection of ordinary shares in XYZ Ltd), and
- a collection of units in a unit trust that have the same fixed rights attached to them.

Examples of collections that would not be permissible include:

- a collection of shares in a single company that have different rights (eg. ordinary and preference shares), and
- a collection of units in a unit trust of different classes that have different rights attached to them or are potentially subject to differing trustee discretion.

To ensure that an 'acquirable asset' is always interpreted in the singular, the words 'collection' and 'identical' should be interpreted as ensuring that an 'acquirable asset' is one or more things that within the arrangement are seen and treated as a whole.

WHEN IS AN 'ACQUIRABLE ASSET' ACQUIRED?

An 'acquirable asset' is acquired at the time when the trustee of the holding trust (custodian trustee) gains a legal interest in the asset. At the same time, the RSF trustee gains a beneficial interest in the asset as required by s67A(1)(b). The 'beneficial interest' arises on creation of the security trust over the acquirable asset. The RSF trustee has a right to acquire the legal interest upon full repayment of the loan.

PROTECTION OF FUND ASSETS – TRUSTEE GUARANTEES AND INDEMNITY

Some lenders providing LRBAs to superannuation funds require the fund trustees, or third parties such as fund members, to provide guarantees of the borrowing to underwrite the lender's risk from the nature of the LRBA. Such an issue was raised in Taxpayer Alert TA 2008/5.

The SISA93 does not prevent a lender exercising rights under a guarantee given by a third party since the lender's rights under such guarantees are not rights against the trustee of the fund. Accordingly, the lender has rights against the guarantor's assets if there is a default on the borrowing.

The guarantor has a common law right to recover losses incurred (which may exceed the value of the asset which was the subject of the borrowing) from the principal debtor (ie. the trustee of the fund) and the trustee might then seek indemnity out of the fund's assets.

Where a guarantee is given by a trustee in a personal capacity, one issue that arises is whether a lender's entitlement to recourse against the trustee's personal assets may lead to the trustee claiming indemnity out of the fund's assets. The conditions in s67A do not explicitly refer to guarantees given the variety of ways that collateral agreements may be used to circumvent the limited recourse nature of the arrangement. However, conditions in s67A(1)(d), (e) and (f) are intended to protect fund assets from such claims by limiting the rights of the lender or any other person against the RSF trustee for, or in connection with, or as a result (direct or indirect) of a default on a borrowing or charges related to the borrowing, to rights relating to the acquirable asset.

The 'acquirable asset' under a s67A borrowing arrangement must be held in trust (s67A(1) (b)). This trust structure is a feature of traditional instalment warrants that helps to quarantine the other assets of the superannuation fund from the investment risk that the limited recourse borrowing arrangement presents.

GRANTING OF A CHARGE OTHER THAN TO THE LENDER

If the trustee of the holding trust in a LRBA grants a charge over the asset in the holding trust in favour of a person other than the lender under the arrangement, this will result in the trustee of the SMSF contravening s67(1) (ATO ID 2010/185).

PERSONAL GUARANTEES AND CONTRIBUTIONS TO THE SMSF

If a guarantor makes a payment to the lender under an arrangement where they have foregone their usual rights of indemnity against the principal debtor (the SMSF trustee) in respect of the guarantee, TR 2010/1 indicates that this may be considered a contribution to the SMSF if it satisfies a liability of the SMSF. This might happen, for example, if the guarantor paid the borrowing and the acquirable asset was transferred to the SMSF trustee under the arrangement. In contrast, there is no contribution if the SMSF trustee has exercised a right to 'walk away' from the arrangement (and has lost the acquirable asset to the lender) and has no further liability, but the lender still exercises a right to call on the guarantee for a shortfall after disposal of the original asset.

EFFECT OF UNLIMITED GUARANTEE FOR A POST 7 JULY 2010 ARRANGEMENT

If there is a third party guarantee in relation to a borrowing by an SMSF trustee that does not satisfy the requirements of s67A(1)(d) and (e), then that borrowing and the maintenance of it are in contravention of s67(1) irrespective of whether the borrowing is part of an arrangement that would otherwise satisfy the requirements of s67A. Section 67A does not by its own operation affect the rights of the parties to the guarantee.

REGULATED SUPERANNUATION FUND TRUSTEE BREACH OF DUTY

Section 67A(1)(d) and (e) do not apply to a right of a member or another trustee of the regulated superannuation fund to damages against the RSF trustee for a breach by the RSF trustee of any of the RSF trustee's duties as trustee (s67A(5), (6)). That is, members and co-trustees may pursue a claim for damages against a trustee that makes a decision to acquire an asset under a LRBA in breach of its obligations as trustee, bearing in mind that the trustee is prevented from seeking any indemnity against fund assets by SISA93 s56 and s57.

REPLACEMENT ASSET

Former s67(4A)(b) (see 19.212) previously required that a superannuation fund borrowing must be used or maintained to acquire 'the original asset, or another asset (the replacement)'. That condition created uncertainty over what constituted the replacement asset and gave rise to arrangements that could place fund assets at risk. For example, a lender could require a trustee to replace an asset within an arrangement if its value fell below a certain level, with an asset of greater value than the outstanding loan.

For borrowing arrangements under s67A, the specific circumstances permitting a replacement asset are set out in s67B(3) to s67B(8), or as prescribed by the *Superannuation Industry (Supervision) Regulations 1994* (SISR94).

REPAIRS ARE ALLOWABLE, BUT IMPROVEMENTS ARE NOT

Current legislation allows for borrowed monies in certain circumstances to be used to pay for repairs and maintenance of the relevant asset, but prohibits these monies being used for improvements (s67A(1)(a)(i)). Insight into how the Commissioner of Taxation distinguishes repairs from improvements can be obtained from TR 97/23.

TRUST DEED AND INVESTMENT STRATEGY

Trustees should ensure any asset acquisition under a LRBA is permitted by the fund's trust deed and has been taken into consideration when formulating the fund investment strategy as required by s52(2)(f).

INTERACTION WITH IN-HOUSE ASSET RULES

If an asset of a superannuation fund is an investment in a related trust (as described in s67A(1)(b)) in connection with a fund borrowing under s67A(1) and the only property of the related trust is the acquirable asset, the investment asset is an in-house asset only if the acquirable asset would be an in-house asset if it were held directly by the fund (SISA93 s71(8), (9)). This means that if the superannuation fund was considered to hold an investment in the custodian trust it would not be automatically counted against the in-house asset limit. This is to facilitate the majority of cases where the holding trust under the LRBA will be a related trust.

INSTALMENT WARRANTS – PROPOSED TAX CHANGES

The government has proposed amendments to confirm the practice of treating the investor in an instalment warrant over a single exchange traded security in a company, trust or stapled entity as the owner of the listed security for income tax purposes. The amendments will apply for assessments for the 2007-08 and later income years (see *Assistant Treasurer's Media Release No. 2010/037* dated 10 March 2010). These proposals were extended on 17 January 2011, when the government announced that these proposed income tax look-through treatments would also cover instalment warrants and receipts over direct and indirect interests in listed securities, as well as unlisted securities in widely held entities and bundles of these assets (see the Assistant Treasurer and Minister for Financial Services and Superannuation's *Media Release No. 2011/008* dated 17 January 2011).

19.215 DISCLOSURE OF INFORMATION TO THIRD PARTIES

APPLIES IF FIVE OR MORE MEMBERS

On request, third parties must be given the annual report and such information which a member can request. Funds can be charged on a reasonable cost recovery basis.

APPLIES TO ALL FUNDS

Within three days, the trustee must notify the prudential regulator of any significant adverse change in the fund's circumstances.

SUPER FUND LOOKUP

Super Fund Lookup (SFLU) contains publicly available information about superannuation funds that have an ABN. It is the central source for confirming the regulatory and compliance history of superannuation funds. It includes funds regulated by the Tax Office and APRA. The SFLU tool provides:

- real time data on the status of a superannuation fund and their contact details
- access to further information about the superannuation fund, and
- information on the taxation implications of making investments with a superannuation fund.

To reinforce the importance of SFLU in assisting the superannuation industry in managing rollovers and transfers of superannuation between funds, SFLU has been recently enhanced. Enhancements include:

- improved usability as a result of redesigning the website to make it more intuitive for users
- new functionality to support bulk download users, such as large funds and administrators, who interact with many superannuation funds on a daily basis, and
- updates to technical content.

The SFLU tool can be found at www.superfundlookup.gov.au.

Note that SFLU has replaced the decommissioned Register of Complying superannuation Funds.

19.230 ADDITIONAL RULES FOR APPROVED DEPOSIT FUNDS

APPLIES IF FIVE OR MORE MEMBERS

Approved Deposit Funds (ADFs) are wholly supervised by the prudential regulator.

REDEMPTION PERIOD

All ADFs must have a fixed stated redemption period of 12 months or less and this must be clearly disclosed on documents offered to depositors (or prospective depositors).

Any change in the redemption period can only occur by:

- resolution of 75% majority (a quorum is a minimum of 25% of those entitled to vote), or
- approval of the prudential regulator.

BUY BACK ARRANGEMENTS

There is no mandatory buy back obligation on ADFs, but failure to honour an ADF's published redemption period is treated as a serious breach of a trustee's obligations and may lead to penalties.

BORROWINGS

ADFs are not permitted to borrow funds for any purpose (although APRA, the prudential regulator can approve borrowings in exceptional circumstances).

19.235 ACTUARIAL REPORTS

A defined benefit fund is required to have an actuarial investigation at establishment or conversion, and then at least every three years. As well as other matters, that report must contain:

- a statement of the value of the assets
- whether the value of the assets is adequate to meet liabilities if members accrued benefits
- the level of contributions required to be made to the fund by the employer over the next three years
- a statement on the financial position of the fund
- if the fund has been used to satisfy superannuation guarantee obligations, and
- a solvency certificate for the next three years.

19.240 ACTUARIAL CERTIFICATES FOR FUNDS PAYING PENSIONS

APPLIES TO ALL FUNDS

Actuarial Certificates (ACs) are required for both prudential and taxation purposes.

Prudential requirements

ACs are required for purposes of the SISA93. Under the SISA93 an AC is only required for a pension that satisfies the requirements of a Defined Benefit Pension (DBP).

ACs are required for purposes of s295-385 and s295-390 of the ITAA97 to identify the fund assets that are providing pensions. However there are certain exemptions (see below).

Summary of Actuarial Certificate requirements			
	Prior to 1/7/2004	**From 1/7/2004**	**Frequency**
Allocated Pensions (APs) (segregated current pension assets)	Yes	Not required	*Prior to 01/07/2004:* Period of up to three years *From 01/07/2004:* Not applicable
Allocated Pensions (APs) (un-segregated current pension assets)	Yes	Required	Annually
Market Linked Pensions (MLPs) (segregated current pension assets)	Not applicable	Not required	Not applicable
Market Linked Pensions (MLPs) (unsegregated current pension assets)	Not applicable	Required	Annually
Defined Benefit Pensions (DBPs)	Required	Required	SAFs and SMSFs: Annually Other: Period of up to three years
		From 1/7/2007	**Frequency**
Account Based Pensions (ABPs) (segregated current pension assets)		Not required	Not applicable
Account Based Pensions (ABPs) (un-segregated current pension assets)		Required	Annually

 Where an actuarial certificate is required it must be obtained before the first tax return is lodged and be current in the subsequent income tax years.

19.245   FUNDING AND SOLVENCY CERTIFICATE

FUNDS PAYING DEFINED BENEFIT PENSIONS

A fund paying at least one defined benefit pension is required to have an actuarial funding and solvency certification with respect to the probability that the pension(s) will continue to be paid under the governing rules of the fund covering a period of one to five years. The certificate must always be current, so the first certificate must be obtained when the fund is established.

The time for obtaining further certificates is:

- by the date on which 75% of the term expires for a term of four years or less, and
- at least 12 months before the end of a term of more than four years.

19.250 PENALTIES

Illegal early release schemes undermine the Government's retirement income policy. Such schemes have commonly involved a request to a fund regulated by the Australian Prudential Regulation Authority to pay a member's superannuation benefits to the bank account of a purported SMSF that has been set up for the purpose of receiving such transfers and subsequently paying money out to participants in the scheme. Vulnerable people are exploited with promoters having taken commissions of up to 50 per cent of the member's superannuation balance.

On 18 March 2014 *Tax and Superannuation Laws Amendment (2014 Measures No. 1) Bill 2014* received Royal Assent. This bill is for an Act to amend the law relating to taxation and superannuation, and for related purposes.

While not limited to the following measures, the amendments under this bill include measures to:

- amend the *Superannuation Industry (Supervision) Act 1993* to provide that a person must not promote a scheme that has resulted in a payment being made from a regulated superannuation fund otherwise than as prescribed by payment standards and impose a civil penalty for any contravention;
- amend the *Superannuation Industry (Supervision) Act 1993* and *Taxation Administration Act 1953* to provide the power to give directions and impose administrative penalties for contraventions relating to self-managed superannuation funds.

Schedule 1 introduced civil and criminal penalties for illegal early release scheme promoters in order to discourage the promotion of such schemes. The measure was previously introduced as Schedule 1 to the *Superannuation Legislation Amendment (Reducing Illegal Early Release and Other Measures) Bill 2012* it implements recommendation 8.24 of the Super System Review.

UNLAWFUL PAYMENTS FROM REGULATED SUPERANNUATION FUNDS

Under these provisions:

(1) *A person must not promote a scheme that has resulted, or is likely to result, in a payment being made from a regulated superannuation fund otherwise than in accordance with payment standards prescribed under subsection 31(1) and provides for civil and criminal consequences of contravening, or being involved in a contravention of that subsection.*

ADMINISTRATIVE DIRECTIONS AND PENALTIES FOR CONTRAVENTIONS RELATING TO SELF-MANAGED SUPERANNUATION FUNDS

The administrative consequences of any contraventions that relate to self-managed superannuation funds under these provisions:

(a) allow the Regulator to give rectification directions and education directions, and

(b) impose administrative penalties for certain contraventions.

They provide the Regulator with the ability to give a rectification direction or an education direction where it reasonably believes that a trustee or director of a corporate trustee of an SMSF has contravened a provision of the SIS Act or *Superannuation Industry (Supervision) Regulations 1994* (SIS Regulations).

A rectification direction will require a person to undertake specified action to rectify the contravention within a specified time frame and provide the Regulator with evidence of the person's compliance with the direction.

An education direction will require a person to undertake a specified course of education within a specified time frame and provide the Regulator with evidence of completion of the course. Trustees and directors of corporate trustees will also be required to sign or re-sign the SMSF trustee declaration form to confirm that they understand their obligations and duties as a trustee (or director of a corporate trustee) of an SMSF.

The Regulator may approve courses of education for the purposes of the education direction. A fee must not be charged for an approved course, undertaken in compliance with an education direction.

A person will be liable to an administrative penalty if certain provisions of the SIS Act are contravened in relation to an SMSF. The amount of the penalty is an amount specified in the law.

An administrative penalty must not be paid or reimbursed from the assets of the fund in relation to which the administrative penalty was imposed. There are four types of penalty provisions in the SISA93. These are listed from the most serious to the least serious.

IMPORTANT: The penalties listed are those for individuals. Five times the monetary penalty for individuals can be imposed on corporate trustees. A penalty unit is currently $170. If the penalty is for an infringement that occurred before 28 December 2012, the value of a penalty unit is $110. . Some offences are punishable by up to five years imprisonment. When a natural person is convicted of an offence with a penalty of imprisonment, the court can, instead of, or as well as that penalty, impose penalty units of not more than the maximum months of imprisonment multiplied by five (for example, if an offence can incur a maximum penalty of one year of imprisonment, a maximum of 60 penalty units can be imposed (that is, 12 months x five)).

NOTE: The 2015-16 Budget includes a measure to increase the value of the penalty unit from

$170 to $180, with effect from 31 July 2015. This increase is broadly consistent with inflation since the value was last adjusted in December 2012. The Budget measure also provides for the Government to introduce ongoing automatic indexation of the penalty unit value based on the CPI. Indexation will occur on 1 July every three years, with the first indexation occurring on 1 July 2018.

1. CIVIL PENALTY

Can apply where there are serious breaches of:

- the sole purpose test (see 19.100)
- lending to members
- borrowing rules
- in-house asset rules
- prohibition of avoidance schemes
- regulator notification of the rules of significant adverse events
- arms length basis for investments rules, and
- refund of surpluses to employers.

Maximum 2000 penalty units: 'Balance of probabilities' standard of proof is required for civil convictions. Criminal prosecution can also apply where dishonestly, recklessness, intent to gain an advantage and/or fraud apply. The criminal standard of proof required for conviction is 'beyond reasonable doubt'.

2. STRICT LIABILITY

Applies regardless of fault in certain situations, for example:

- trustees who fail to comply with a direction of the regulator (Tax Office or APRA) not to accept superannuation contributions: *100 penalty units*
- failure of an acting trustee appointed by the regulator to inform members of the appointment: *Maximum penalty 50 penalty units* * Criminal standard of proof is required*
- a person other than an approved trustee who acts as a trustee of a fund with four or fewer members that is not a self managed fund: *Maximum penalty six months imprisonment (s121A SISA93)*
- failure to inform APRA or Commissioner of Taxation within a specified period (must be at least 21 days):
  - whether or not the fund was a self managed superannuation fund (SMSF)
  - if the fund was not an SMSF it is likely to become one within the period specified in the notice, and
  - if the fund was an SMSF it is likely to cease to be one (s252A SISA93)
    Maximum penalty 50 penalty units

3. FAULT LIABILITY

Covers the majority of penalty provisions. Only applies if it is proved beyond a reasonable doubt that the breach was committed intentionally or recklessly.

Penalties can be imposed for failure to comply with:

- prescribed operating standards
- lodgement of APRA annual returns
- record-keeping and fund administration requirements
- payment of unclaimed money and automatic rollover of benefit requirements
- requirements of auditors and actuaries to report breaches to trustees
- the requirement for employers to remit member contributions promptly
- inquiry or complaints resolution establishment arrangements, and
- appointment of trustees and investment managers procedures.

Penalties between six months and two years can be imposed:

- for acts of victimisation against trustees
- if disqualified persons act as trustees or investment manager
- for misleading conduct and misleading the regulator (ASIC or APRA).

FALSE OR MISLEADING STATEMENT PENALTIES EXPANDED

The law has changed to expand the false or misleading statement penalty provisions to include false and misleading statements that do not result in a shortfall amount. These changes apply to all statements made from 4 June 2010 that relate to tax and super laws administered by the Commissioner of Taxation.

The new provisions apply to all tax laws, including the following super reporting obligations:

- member contribution statements (MCS)
- lost members statements (LMS) (see 19.175)
- Departing Australia Superannuation Payment (DASP) reports (see 19.670), and
- Self-managed superannuation fund annual return.

Under the changes there is also a new penalty for making false or misleading statements to an entity other than the Tax Office if it is required or allowed to be made under tax law, for example:

- a statement made on a rollover benefit statement, and
- a notice of intent to deduct super contributions or the acknowledgment of such a notice.

Maximum penalty 600 penalty units Criminal standard of proof is required

4. CIVIL LIABILITY

Covers contraventions of the SISA93 and SISR94 which do not have any criminal liability, but which could give a statutory right of action, or require duties to beneficiaries or members. An example of civil liability is where the trustee fails to comply with statutory covenants or trustee representation rules.

There is no penalty, but there is a civil liability for the loss or damage.

19.260 SPLITTING SUPERANNUATION AND FAMILY LAW

The Family Law Act 1975 (FLA75) and the *Superannuation Industry (Supervision) Act 1993* (SISA93) and its supporting regulations provide for an interest in superannuation (superannuation interest) or a superannuation payment to be divided or split by agreement or court order in the event of a marriage breakdown. These laws also apply to de facto couples, whether of the same or opposite sex.

Couples can work out what proportion of a superannuation interest will go to each person, based on their individual circumstances. For example, separating couples can trade-off superannuation for housing where one parent needs to remain in the marital home to care for children. A superannuation agreement can be incorporated into a financial agreement so that a couple's entire financial affairs are dealt with in one agreement. Where separating couples are unable to agree, the court has the power to split the value of superannuation as part of a property settlement. Trustees of superannuation funds are required to comply with a binding agreement or a court order that provides for a division of a superannuation interest.

With the passing of the *Family Law Amendment Act 2005* the range of matters that can be the subject of private arbitration now include financial agreements and certain orders in relation to superannuation. Previously, the matters that could be the subject of private arbitration were limited to those related to property, spousal maintenance and maintenance agreements.

VALUING SUPERANNUATION INTERESTS

The regulations provide for different methods of valuing most superannuation interests depending on whether the interest is in an accumulation or a defined benefit fund.

The value of a:

- fully vested accumulation interest is the value of the interest recorded in the most recently received member statement, less any known surcharge liability

- defined benefit interest and a partially vested accumulation interest is determined actuarially, net of any known surcharge liability. The details of the information needed, and the calculations necessary are contained in the Family Law Regulations. Where the trustee considers this to be inappropriate the Minister can approve an alternative valuation method or alternative valuation factors.

Parties can defer their agreement about how a superannuation interest is to be divided, eg. if a condition of release will occur shortly (for example, retirement) at which time the actual value of the interest will be known. Where the agreement is deferred a 'flagging' agreement stops the trustee of the fund from dealing with that superannuation interest until the 'flag' has been lifted (either by further agreement or by court order should the parties be unable to subsequently agree).

FOLLOWING THE SPLIT

A proportioning rule will apply where part of a superannuation interest is paid out. This rule will also apply to family law superannuation payments to ensure that the various tax-free and taxable components of the benefit are divided fairly between each spouse. A spouse includes another person, although not legally married to the person, who lived with the person on a genuine domestic basis in a relationship as a couple (whether of the same or different sex). The general proportioning rule applies to both superannuation lump sums paid after 1 July 2007 (including rollovers) and superannuation income streams which commence after 1 July 2007.

IN-HOUSE ASSET CHANGE TO SMSFS ACQUIRING ASSETS UNDER A SPLIT

Subsection 66(2B) of SISA93 allows a trustee or investment fund manager of a regulated superannuation fund to acquire an asset from a related party of the fund where the acquisition occurs as the result of the relationship breakdown of a member of the fund. Relationship covers those in respect of marriage, and opposite-sex and same-sex de facto relationships.

Prior to these amendments Tax Office Determination SPR 2006/MB1 (repealed on 25 October 2011), relaxed the prohibition where an SMSF trustee acquires an asset from a related party following the marriage breakdown of a member. However, this Determination had a number of limitations as it did not extend to opposite-sex or same-sex de facto parties, nor did it cover transfers or roll-overs made to APRA regulated funds.

CAPITAL GAINS TAX IMPLICATIONS

CGT rollover relief is provided if a relevant CGT event happens because of a maintenance agreement made before 27 December 2000 or because of a court order.

Subsequent amendments to the *Income Tax Assessment Act 1997* (ITAA97) provide CGT rollover relief is now extended to a relevant CGT event that happens because of:

- a binding financial agreement under the FLA75 or a corresponding written agreement that is binding because of a corresponding foreign law

- an arbitral award under the FLA75 or a corresponding arbitral award under a corresponding state, territory or foreign law, or

- a written agreement that is binding because of a state, territory or foreign law relating to de facto marriage breakdowns and that, because of such a law, cannot be overridden by an order of a court except to avoid injustice.

These changes ensure that a capital gain or loss that would otherwise be made by a fund as a result of any of the above events is deferred until the transferee spouse or former spouse disposes of the CGT asset.

EXTENDING CGT ROLLOVER RELIEF ON MARRIAGE BREAKDOWN

ITAA97 provides CGT marriage breakdown rollover relief to in specie transfers of personal superannuation interests from a small superannuation fund to another complying superannuation fund under specific conditions. This enables separating spouses to achieve a 'clean break' from each other in terms of their superannuation arrangements.

The law provides CGT rollover relief on marriage breakdown for a transfer of any CGT asset reflecting the personal interest of either spouse (but not both) in a small superannuation fund to another complying superannuation fund if that transfer satisfies specific conditions. The ITAA97 amendments also allow:

- the existing CGT marriage breakdown rollover relief between small superannuation funds to extend to transfers from a small superannuation fund to another complying superannuation fund, and

- the CGT marriage breakdown rollover relief for transfers of non-superannuation assets to ensure that they apply to transfers pursuant to written agreements made under Western Australian, Tasmanian, Queensland or Northern Territory laws relating to de facto marriage breakdown.

ITAA97 enables a trustee of a small superannuation fund to access the CGT rollover relief on behalf of either spouse on marriage breakdown. However, once the trustee has obtained a CGT rollover relief for the benefit of either spouse and has transferred all of the assets reflecting the personal superannuation interest of the transferor spouse, the rollover relief is no longer available for a transfer of any asset reflecting the personal superannuation interest of the other spouse (which arises out of the same marriage breakdown). Only one spouse needs to move their personal superannuation interest for a 'clean break' to be achieved.

19.265 SUPERANNUATION AND SAME-SEX RELATIONSHIPS

Legislative changes have removed same-sex discrimination from a range of Commonwealth laws relating to super. These changes include amendments to the *Superannuation Industry (Supervision) Act 1993* (SIS Act), making it easier for regulated superannuation funds to recognise same-sex relationships. The changes have also amended taxation legislation covering superannuation death benefits and death benefit termination payments.

IN SUMMARY

- The definition of 'spouse', 'child' and 'relative' in the SISA93 and other superannuation legislation has been extended to include same-sex partners and their children.

- The definitions of 'dependant' and 'spouse' in the income tax laws have been amended to include same-sex partners and their children for anti-detriment payments made by a superannuation fund.

- Same-sex partners and their children are treated as dependants for the purposes of the taxation of superannuation death benefits and death benefit termination payments.

- Spouse contributions include contributions by a member for the benefit of their same-sex spouse.

- All superannuation funds must report contributions for a member by a same-sex spouse the same way they currently report contributions for a different-sex spouse.

In ATO ID 2011/83 the Tax Office held that although the definition of 'spouse' was only amended to include same sex couples subsequent to the relationship ceasing, the taxpayer is a 'former spouse' of the deceased superannuation fund member in terms of s302-195(1)(a) of the ITAA97.

19.270 SUPERANNUATION AND BANKRUPTCY

The *Bankruptcy Act 1966* (the Act) allows bankruptcy trustees to recover superannuation contributions made prior to bankruptcy with the intention of defeating creditors.

These legislative provisions apply to contributions made from 28 July 2006 to an 'eligible superannuation plan' (ie. a regulated superannuation fund, Approved Deposit Fund (ADF), Retirement Savings Account (RSA) or a public sector superannuation scheme). The amendments address the problems highlighted in the High Court's decision in *Cook v Benson* (2003) HCA 36 which, among other things, made it very difficult for bankruptcy trustees to recover superannuation contributions made by a person prior to bankruptcy, even where those contributions were made specifically with the intention to defeat creditors.

The Act contains substantive amendments which have the effect of rendering certain contributions void against a trustee in bankruptcy. These amendments commenced 28 July 2006. The other amendments are concerned with the recovery of void contributions.

CONTRIBUTIONS WHICH ARE RECOVERABLE

The following superannuation contributions made from 28 July 2006 to an eligible superannuation plan with the intention of defeating creditors are considered void and recoverable:

- contributions made by a person who later becomes a bankrupt where the intention was to defeat creditors, and
- contributions made by a third party for the benefit of a person who later becomes bankrupt where the person was complicit in an arrangement with that third party to defeat creditors.

The law aims to capture arrangements under which a person who later becomes bankrupt agrees that money, which would ordinarily be paid directly to them, should instead be paid to a superannuation plan for that person's benefit (eg. where the bankrupt had entered into a salary sacrifice arrangement with his or her employer to build up superannuation assets in the lead up to bankruptcy instead of other assets which would have been available to pay creditors).

RECOVERY OF VOID CONTRIBUTIONS

Superannuation account-freezing notice

The Official Receiver is given the power to issue a notice to the trustee of an eligible superannuation plan that is holding the bankrupt's contributions directing the trustee not to cash or debit, or permit the cashing, debiting, rolling over, transferring or forfeiture of the whole or part of the bankrupt's superannuation interest. The Official Receiver must give two copies of any superannuation account-freezing notice or revocation notice to the trustee of the bankrupt's estate. The trustee must give one of these copies to the bankrupt member. A member may apply to the Official Receiver in writing to request consent to the cashing, debiting, rollover, transfer or forfeiture of all or part of the member's interest where a superannuation account-freezing notice is in force in relation to that member's interest. The Official Receiver may give consent in writing (which may be subject to conditions). This written consent must be given to the trustee of the eligible superannuation plan and a copy to the member.

Rolled-over superannuation interests

The court may order payments to be made where the bankrupt has rolled over the original void contribution(s) to another eligible superannuation plan. The order is made to the trustee of the eligible superannuation plan into which the void contribution(s) have been rolled. This will ensure that a superannuation plan cannot be required to pay money which it no longer holds but will prevent an opportunity for bankrupts to avoid the operation of the new provisions.

Superannuation plan will not have to repay fees, charges and taxes

Where the trustee of a an eligible superannuation plan is required to pay an amount to the trustee in bankruptcy pursuant to a notice to recover void contributions and taxes, fees and charges have been charged in respect of those contributions, the bankruptcy trustee must pay to the fund trustee an amount equal to the amount so charged. This means that where a superannuation contribution is void, the trustee of the superannuation fund does not bear any loss resulting from fees, charges and taxes paid in respect of that contribution.

Protection of trustee

The trustee of an eligible superannuation plan who complies in good faith with a notice given by the Official Receiver is not exposed to any civil or criminal liability as a result of that compliance.

SUPERANNUATION GUARANTEE CHARGE

The SGC (see 19.530) has been afforded priority in bankruptcy under s109(1C) of the *Bankruptcy Act 1966* since 5 May 2003. The priority under s109(1C) extends to General Interest Charge (GIC) in respect to the non-payment of the superannuation guarantee charge (SGC). The SGC is included in the category of employee entitlements including salary, wages or commission.

The maximum amount subject to the priority is adjusted annually.

19.275 SUPERANNUATION & INSOLVENCY ADMINISTRATIONS

The following information sets out how superannuation affects various insolvency administrations. The Superannuation Guarantee Charge (SGC) (see 19.530) is the total of the individual employee shortfalls plus the administration component plus the nominal interest component.

Changes to the *Corporations Act 2001* mean that from 31 December 2007, employees of companies that go into liquidation, voluntary administration or receivership will stand a better chance of receiving their superannuation entitlements. Under the changes, the SGC must be paid before payments to ordinary unsecured creditors and therefore SGC obligations will rank equally with employees' entitlements for wages and superannuation contributions.

LIQUIDATION COMMENCING ON OR AFTER 31 DECEMBER 2007

With effect from 31 December 2007, s52 of SGAA92 has been repealed and the *Corporations Act 2001* has been amended to include the superannuation guarantee charge together with superannuation contributions in s556(1)(e).

SGC claims in respect of excluded employees, such as directors and their spouses, will be a priority to the extent of the first $2,000 claimed. Any amounts exceeding $2,000 will rank with unsecured creditors.

DEEDS OF COMPANY ARRANGEMENT COMMENCING ON OR AFTER 31 DECEMBER 2007

A new section in the *Corporations Act 2001*, s444DA, took effect from 31 December 2007 and impacts on Deed Of Company Arrangement (DOCA). From 31 December 2007, all DOCA are required to include a clause to the effect that 'eligible employee creditors' will enjoy a priority under the administration at least equal to what they would have received had there been a winding up. The definition of the term "eligible employee creditor" is defined to include a creditor with a liability that falls within the priority afforded by s556(1)(e) of the *Corporations Act 2001*. The Tax Office's claim for the SGC falls within this definition.

Claims by an 'eligible employee creditor' are to be paid in priority to other unsecured creditors and ahead of any priority that otherwise might be enjoyed by a charge holder.

Affected employees may vote down the inclusion of such a provision at a meeting held prior to the second meeting of creditors, provided that, with their notice of that meeting they received a written opinion from the administrator, with reasons for the opinion and other relevant information, on whether the non inclusion of that provision would be likely to result in the same or better outcome for them, as compared to what they would have received on an immediate winding up.

RECEIVERSHIP

Although not specifically legislated for, the inclusion of the SGC as a priority debt in s556(1)(e) of the *Corporations Act 2001* means that the SGC will obtain a priority in a receivership through the operation of s433(3)(c) of the *Corporations Act 2001*. The SGC will be treated in the same way as other wage related priority debts under s556(1)(e).

BANKRUPTCY

The SGC has been afforded priority in bankruptcy under s109 (1C) of the *Bankruptcy Act 1966* since 5 May 2003. The priority under s109(1C) extends to General Interest Charge (GIC) in respect to the non payment of the SGC. The SGC is included in the category of employee entitlements including salary, wages or commission.

The maximum amount subject to the priority is adjusted annually.

PART IX AND X ARRANGEMENTS

There is no legislative requirement for the SGC to be afforded a priority in arrangements made pursuant to Parts IX and Part X of the *Bankruptcy Act 1966*. However, trustees frequently address this anomaly by including a clause in the deed that gives the SGC a similar priority to that which it would have received in bankruptcy. The Commissioner may vote against a deed that does not provide priority for SGC if bankruptcy would yield a greater return.

DOUBLE PROOFS

Prior to 31 December 2007, where there were unpaid superannuation payments and the SGC was imposed and the Tax Office and superannuation fund each proved for their liabilities, the liquidator was obliged to admit both proofs. The reasoning is that the two classes of debt were legally distinct.

From 31 December 2007 external DOCA administrators are required to reject a proof of debt where such a situation arises and to reject a proof of debt for a superannuation contribution that results in a SGC (s444DB). The SGC will be preferred since it includes an interest component, providing employees a greater benefit. All DOCAs must now contain a provision to that effect.

Liquidators will also have the power under s553(1A) of the *Corporations Act 2001* to reject the whole or part of a proof of debt for superannuation where the amount has already been paid by way of the SGC or there is an admissible proof for the SGC

HOW DIVIDEND PAYMENTS ARE APPLIED

Section 64B of the SGAA92 sets out a formula for the allocation of payments received on a pro rata basis, and prior to 31 December 2007 did not allow the Tax Office to allocate shares to employees to take account of special circumstances, for example, in the case of excluded employees under Section 556(1)(a) of the *Corporations Act 2001* or s109(1)(e) of the *Bankruptcy Act 1966* in the case of an employee. Under the amendments commencing 31 December 2007 to s64B the Commissioner is now granted discretion to make the necessary adjustment.

19.280 FIRST HOME SAVER ACCOUNTS

The First Home Saver Accounts (FHSAs) scheme provides a government contribution to help first home buyers save for their first home. FHSAs can only be opened or issued after 1 October 2008. Providers of FHSAs can include trustees of Registrable Superannuation Entities (RSE) that hold a public-offer or extended public-offer RSE licence (Public-Offer Licensees) subject to being authorised to do so by APRA. SMSFs will not be able to offer the accounts as these funds are not subject to prudential regulation by APRA.

NOTE: In the 2014-15 Budget the Government announced that it will abolish the FHSA. See Abolition of the first home saver accounts (FHSA) scheme, below.

MAIN FEATURES OF THE SCHEME

- Legal nature of FHSAs. This will depend on the offeror institution, namely:
  - an FHSA opened by an ADI will be a deposit account
  - an FHSA offered by a life insurance company will be a policy, and
  - an FHSA offered by an RSE licensee will be a beneficial interest in an FHSA trust.
- Opening an FHSA. To be eligible to open an account, an individual must:
  - be aged 18 or more and under 65 years
  - have not previously owned a home in Australia in which they have lived, and
  - provide a TFN to the provider and meet standard proof-of-identity requirements
- Contributions to FHSAs:
  - there are no restrictions on who can make a contribution to an FHSA
  - all contributions must be made from post-tax income, and
  - an overall indexed account balance cap applies ($90,000 for 2013-14)
- Accessing money. To access money to purchase a first home, personal contributions of at least $1,000 must have been made in each of at least four financial years. Funds can also be accessed:
  - by way of transferring the account balance as a contribution to a superannuation fund (see below) or to a RSA provider or another FHSA, or

- by way of transferring money from the account into a genuine mortgage after the end of a minimum qualifying period (see 19.900), or
- when the holder reaches age 60, and in other limited specified circumstances.

- Government FHSA contribution:
  - this is payable in a financial year based on 17% of an individual's personal contributions of up to $6,000 (indexed) made during the 2013-14 financial year (ie. maximum payable in 2013-14 is $1,020).
  - the Commissioner determines if government FHSA contributions are payable each year and pays them into the individual's FHSA, within 60 days of receiving both the individual's tax return for the financial year that the personal contributions were made (or notice that the individual is not required to lodge a tax return) and the FHSA contributions statement from the individual's FHSA provider, and
  - government FHSA contribution is not payable for a financial year for personal contributions made in certain circumstances (eg an amount is transferred to the FHSA of a spouse or ex-spouse under a family law obligation, on transfers between FHSA providers under the FHSA portability provisions, on re-contributions to an FHSA where a home is not purchased or the occupancy requirements are not met, or where a contribution is refunded to an individual under the *Corporations Act 2001* on the grounds of an unsolicited offer, a defective product disclosure document or a cooling-off period).

- Misuse tax. If an FHSA holder does not meet conditions of eligibility, withdrawal or occupancy of the home purchased, a misuse tax applies to ensure that the person does not improperly benefit from the use of the FHSA. The misuse tax claws back government contributions paid to the FHSA, and includes a component designed to broadly neutralise the maximum benefit the holder may have obtained from having the earnings of the FHSA taxed at 15% instead of marginal tax rates.

HOW DOES THE ACCOUNT BALANCE CAP WORK?

There is an overall account balance cap on FHSAs. For the 2013-14 financial year, the cap is $90,000. The cap is indexed periodically in $5,000 increments. Once an individual's FHSA exceeds the cap, they cannot make any further personal contributions to it. However, any earnings and any outstanding government contributions can still be paid into the account. If a personal contribution will cause an individual to exceed their account balance cap, the account provider must return the amount that exceeds the cap. If the personal contribution is from a third party, the amount will be returned to the account holder, not the third party.

Megan's account balance is $90,000. On 1 May 2014, Megan makes a personal contribution of $6,000 to her first home saver account. If the account balance cap for the 2014-15 financial year is $95,000, the provider can only pay $5,000 into Megan's account and must refund $1,000 to her or pay the $1,000 into a different account for her. Megan is entitled to a government contribution on her $5,000 personal contribution. Even though Megan's account balance has reached the cap, the government contribution and any earnings can still be paid into her account. Megan can keep the account until she buys or builds her first home. However, she cannot make any further personal contributions to the account.

An individual can transfer funds from one FHSA to another, even if the closing balance of the old account is more than the cap.

IS THE ACCOUNT BALANCE CAP A LIFETIME LIMIT?

Once an individual has reached the account balance cap, they cannot make any further personal contributions into their account, even if indexation increases the cap in later years.

An account balance may also fluctuate causing an individual to move over or under the cap. For example, fees debited to an account may reduce the balance. However, once an individual exceeds the cap, they cannot make any more personal contributions.

You need to know the account balance cap for the financial year if you are likely to reach or exceed it. We publish the cap for each year.

WHAT ARE 'FIRST HOME SAVER ACCOUNT TRANSFERS' FROM THE POINT OF VIEW OF A SUPER FUND?

When a FHSA provider sends the balance of the first home saver account to a super fund, the payment is a contribution into the super system (rather than a rollover or transfer within the super system). The contribution is treated by the super fund as:

- a member contribution for the SISA93 purposes
- a non-concessional contribution and counted towards the members non-concessional contributions cap
- while similar to a personal contribution, it does not attract a super co-contribution, and
- reported only in 'all contributions' received on the Member Contribution Statement (MCS) and Rollover Benefits Statement (RBS).

HOW DOES A SUPER FUND RETURN FIRST HOME SAVER ACCOUNT PAYMENTS?

For payments of account balances received from FHSA providers, the super fund must return the payment to the payee (the FHSA provider) together with the form that accompanies the payment, either:

- *First home saver account – superannuation contribution and close account* (NAT 72537), or
- *Super contributions from a first home saver account under a family law obligation* (NAT 72629).

The super fund should provide the reason for the rejection of the payment as a notation on the form.

Where a super fund makes a payment of the FHSA government contribution originally received from the Tax Office, it needs to complete a *Superannuation payment variation advice* (NAT 8451) and send it to the Tax Office with the returned FHSA government contribution payment.

ABOLITION OF THE FIRST HOME SAVER ACCOUNTS (FHSA) SCHEME

In the 2014-15 Budget, the Federal Government announced the following changes to abolish the first home saver accounts scheme:

- new accounts created in respect of applications made from 7.30pm, Tuesday 13 May 2014 will not be able to access any concessions or the government contribution.
- eligibility for a government contribution will cease from 1 July 2014. Existing account holders will continue to receive the government contribution for personal contributions made during the 2013-14 income year.
- tax and social security concessions will cease from 1 July 2015. Existing account holders will continue to receive all tax and social security concessions associated with these accounts for the 2013-14 and 2014-15 income years.
- restrictions on withdrawals will be removed from 1 July 2015.

Once the first home saver account scheme is abolished from 1 July 2015, these accounts will be treated like any other account held with a provider.

The existing rules will continue to apply until the law is changed.

19.285 MYSUPER

The *Stronger Super* reforms introduced a simple, lower-cost default super product called *MySuper* to improve the simplicity, transparency and comparability of super products.

Leading up to 1 July 2013, super funds introduced *MySuper* products with a single investment strategy and a standard set of fees to all members. Employers may be able to negotiate a discounted administration fee and provide flexibility to offer employers with more than 500 employees for a *MySuper* product tailored to the needs of the particular workplace. These products will be able to differ from a fund's main *MySuper* product in terms of investment strategy, member services and fees.

From 1 October 2013, employer contributions for employees who have not chosen a super fund (see *Choice of fund* at 19.563) needed to be made to a fund offering a *MySuper* product to satisfy the employer's super guarantee obligations (see 19.533). Additional transitional arrangements may deal with situations involving funds nominated in enterprise agreements. Fair Work Australia was to review the default super funds named in modern awards to ensure that they offer a *MySuper* product.

By 1 July 2017, trustees of super funds (other than defined benefit funds) must have transferred all existing balances in a default member's super fund to a *MySuper* product. Members wishing to make other choices with their super will still be able to opt for an alternative product, or manage their own superannuation affairs through an SMSF.

In addition to the *MySuper* product, other parts of the *Stronger Super* package that are designed to introduce significant changes to the super system which will lead to efficiencies for members and funds include:

- make the processing of everyday transactions easier, cheaper and faster, through the *SuperStream* package of measures, and
- strengthen governance, integrity and regulatory settings of the super system, including in relation to SMSFs.

19.288 *SUPERSTREAM*

"*SuperStream* is a package of measures designed to bring the back office of superannuation into the 21st century. Its key components are the increased use of technology, uniform data standards, use of the tax file number as a key identifier and the straight through processing of superannuation transactions." *(Cooper Review, 2010)*

The *SuperStream* initiative is a comprehensive package of reforms designed to enhance the 'back office' of superannuation. It includes measures:

- to implement new data and e-commerce standards for superannuation transactions
- allowing for the use of tax file numbers (TFNs) as the primary locator of member accounts
- facilitates account consolidation and improve the treatment of contributions made without sufficient member details, and
- establishes an advisory governance body. (The SuperStream Advisory Council provides a structured forum for stakeholders to advise Government on issues for the implementation and maintenance of the protocols and data and service standards.)

Separately, measures referred to as *Securing Super* provide for better information about the amount and timing of superannuation payments to employees. It also provides notification from funds to members on whether contributions have or have not been received.

These reforms are expected to improve the productivity of the superannuation system.

The adoption of data standards should result in:

- more automated and timely processing of transactions
- improved efficiency
- a more employer friendly system
- fewer lost accounts and more timely flow of money to members' accounts, and
- the reduction in number of multiple member accounts should reduce administration fees and insurance premiums paid per member, maximising retirement benefits.

Securing Super enables employees to better monitor their contributions.

An electronic service address is required for any SMSF that receives employer contributions. A messaging provider may offer this service at a nominal annual charge. Currently some providers make available such an address at no charge. Alternatively the fund trustee may choose to engage an SMSF administrator or software provider.

SMSF trustees should ensure that their bank account is able to receive electronic contribution payments and that the fund trustee is able to receive a contribution message with information about the payments in the *SuperStream* format.

Employees should check with their employers regarding when they will commence their *SuperStream* obligations to ensure that their fund is ready for *SuperStream*.

 An Electronic Service Address arrangement is not necessary for SMSFs in receipt of employer contributions from related parties or where future contributions will not apply.

DATA AND CONTRIBUTION PAYMENTS

Under *SuperStream*, employers must make super contributions on behalf of their employees by submitting data and payments electronically in accordance with the *SuperStream* standard. This also requires that all superannuation funds, including SMSFs, must receive contributions electronically in accordance with this standard.

Employers may meet *SuperStream* obligations – either using software that conforms to SuperStream; or using a service provider who can meet the SuperStream obligations on their behalf.

TIMELINE

For companies with 20 or more employees (medium to large employers) *SuperStream* started from 1 July 2014. From that date, employers needed to start implementing *SuperStream* and they have until 30 June 2015 to meet the *SuperStream* requirements when sending superannuation contributions on behalf of employees.

The Tax Office is facilitating the implementation of *SuperStream* for employer contributions by coordinating the introduction of compliant *SuperStream* solutions. Employers will need to work with their service provider to decide when it best suits to make the change.

For companies with 19 or fewer employees (small employers), *SuperStream* starts from 1 July 2015 and employers have until 30 June 2016 to meet the *SuperStream* requirements when sending superannuation contributions on behalf of their employees.

NOTE: *SuperStream* may be voluntarily adopted from 1 July 2014 if employers are ready.

 Contributions sent to an SMSF from a related-party employer are exempt from SuperStream and can be made using existing processes.

19.300 TAXING SUPERANNUATION ENTITIES

A superannuation fund must be a Complying Superannuation Fund (CSF) to be eligible for concessional taxation treatment under Division 295 of the ITAA97.

A superannuation fund's CSF status is obtained by way of a notice issued by the Commissioner of Taxation under the SISA93, stating that the fund is a CSF. A superannuation fund will remain a CSF for tax purposes until it is notified by the Commissioner that its complying status has changed.

To obtain a complying fund notice under the SISA93 a superannuation fund:

- must be a Regulated Superannuation Fund (RSF) that is an Australian Superannuation Fund (ASF) (see 19.100) at all times during the income year that it was in existence, and
- it must comply with the regulatory provisions or, if it contravened the regulatory provisions, it must not fail the 'compliance test' (see 19.100).

A non-complying superannuation fund is a superannuation fund that fails to comply with the SISA93 conditions.

 The trading stock exception to the CGT primary code rule for complying superannuation entities for specified assets has been removed (see 19.320).

TAXABLE INCOME OF A SUPERANNUATION FUND

The taxable income of a complying superannuation fund is made up of two components:

- concessional contributions and fund earnings taxed at 15%* (with an effective rate of 10% applying to discount capital gains), and
- non-arm's length income that is taxed at 45%.

This contrasts with a Non Complying Superannuation Fund (NCSF), where its taxable income is taxed at 45%.

*From 1 July 2012 certain concessional contributions of a taxpayer whose income is in excess of $300,000, is taxed at 30%. (This rate of tax includes a contribution tax of 15% applying to concessional contributions plus a Div 293 tax of 15% that applies from 1 July 2012).

NOTE: A superannuation fund is not liable to pay Division 293 tax. It is the individual who is liable for this tax and it is paid in respect of their low tax contributions, where the sum of their income for Medicare surcharge purposes and their low tax contributions is greater than $300,000.(For low tax contributions see below.)

INCOME FOR DIVISION 293 TAX

Income used

For Division 293 Tax purposes, the individual's income tax return is used to determine:

- taxable income* (assessable income less deductions)
- total reportable fringe benefits amounts
- net financial investment loss
- net rental property loss
- amounts on which family trust distribution tax has been paid, and
- super lump sum taxed elements with a zero tax rate.

These amounts are added (except the super lump sum amount, which is subtracted) to give the income amount.

*From 1 July 2013 all concessional contributions in excess of the concessional contributions cap are included in assessable income of the taxpayer and taxed at the individual's marginal tax rate. Previously this was taxed at the top marginal tax rate (15% plus 31.5% under the ECT regime.) For individuals who are members of a defined benefit fund, Division 293 tax may be calculated on notional contributions.

LOW TAX CONTRIBUTIONS

Low tax contributions are generally contributions made in a financial year to a complying super fund in respect of the member and included in the assessable income of the superannuation fund. Excess concessional contributions are not included in the low tax contribution amount for Division 293 tax purposes, as it is included in the taxpayer's taxable income from 1 July 2013.

The member contribution statement (MCS) and/or (SMSF) annual return provide:

- employer contributed amounts
- other family and friend contributions
- assessable foreign fund amounts
- assessable amounts transferred from reserves, and
- notional employer contributions, known as defined benefit contributions, when the fund is a defined benefit fund.

CALCULATION

1. Add the income and low tax contributions.
2. Compare this amount to the $300,000 threshold. If there is any amount in excess of the threshold, this is used for working out tax amount under the Div 293 tax provisions.
3. Compare the low-tax contribution amount and the concessional cap amount. Take the lesser of the two amounts, and apply a 15% tax rate to this taxable contribution.

Benny has an income of $291,000 and low-tax contributions of $35,000. The sum of these two amounts is $326,000. The difference between this amount and the income threshold is $326,000 minus the threshold of $300,000 = $26,000. Low-tax contributions is $35,000 and the excess is $26,000. The lesser amount is $26,000. Benny has taxable contributions of $26,000. Division 293 tax is $26,000 x 0.15 = $3,900

CAPITAL GAINS

Complying superannuation funds are eligible for a one-third discount on the capital gains that are included in assessable income (where the asset was held by the fund for at least 12 months) or, in certain cases, a choice of the CGT discount or calculation of the cost base of assets with indexation frozen at 30 September 1999 (see 19.320).

The proposal that fund earnings attributable to a member in pension phase will be exempt up to $100,000 per annum, after which tax would be incurred at the 15% rate, was dropped.

CALCULATING TAX PAYABLE

The tax payable by a complying SMSF is calculated using the 'Method Statement' (s295-10(1)) as follows:

- **Step 1:** Work out the superannuation fund's no-TFN contributions income (see 19.060), and apply the applicable rates (currently at 49%) as set out in the *Income Tax Rates Act 1986* (ITRA86) to that income. (From 1 July 2014 an increase of 0.5% in the Medicare levy to fund Disability Care Australia increases the rate from 1.5% to 2%. The addition of the Budget Repair levy of 2% to the top marginal tax rate of 45%, (applying for 3 years from 1 July 2014) increases the top marginal tax rate to 47% or 49% inclusive of Medicare levy.)

- **Step 2:** Work out the superannuation fund's assessable income and deductions taking account of the special rules in Division 295 (these rules modify some ITAA97 provisions, include certain amounts in assessable income, and allow deductions and exempt amounts).

- **Step 3:** Work out the superannuation fund's taxable income as if its trustee were an Australian resident.

- **Step 4:** Work out the low tax component and non-arm's length component of the superannuation fund's taxable income.

- **Step 5:** Apply the applicable rates in the ITRA86 to the CSF's taxable income components; ie. 15% for low tax and 47% for non-arm's length or the taxable income of a NCSF. (See Step 1 above for top marginal tax rate 47%.)

- **Step 6:** Subtract the superannuation fund's tax offsets (if any) from the sum of amounts In Step 1 and Step 5.

TAXABLE INCOME

The taxable income of a fund is calculated as:

Assessable income less Allowable deductions

Allowable deductions include the following expenses:

- cost of providing death or disability cover and cost of providing terminal medical condition benefits.
  (New legislation allows super funds to also use the deductible proportion of premiums as specified by the regulations for certain types of TPD insurance policies – also see draft ruling TR 2011/D6)

- expenses incurred in deriving income (but not costs denied deductibility;
  eg. brokerage paid on the purchase or sale of shares: this forms part of the cost base of the shares)

- other expenses (apportioned between exempt and assessable income)

- any other allowable deductions, and

- current year and carry forward losses.

EXEMPT INCOME

A complying superannuation fund may reduce its assessable income under the Exempt Current Pension Income (ECPI) provisions. Under these provisions normal assessable income of a pension interest is exempt (see *Actuarial certificates* below).

Draft Taxation Ruling TR 2011/D3, finalised as TR 2013/5 and SMSFD 2013/2 considers when a Superannuation Income Stream (SIS) commences and when it ceases and, consequently, when a SIS is payable. These concepts are relevant to determining the tax consequences for both the superannuation fund and the member in relation to superannuation income stream benefits paid. The above guidance provided by the Commissioner relates to:

- a member with an accumulation interest in their taxed complying superannuation fund commences a SIS as defined in r995-1.01 of the *Income Tax Assessment Regulations 1997* on or after 1 July 2007, and

- the SIS is taken to be a pension in accordance with r1.06(1) and r1.06(9A)(a) of the *Superannuation Industry (Supervision) Regulations 1994*.

NOTE: *Income Tax Assessment Amendment (Superannuation Measures No. 1) Regulation 2013* applies from 1 July 2012 – it provides that earnings from assets supporting a pension will continue to be exempt upon the death of the member and remain exempt until the benefit is paid out, provided that this occurs within a reasonable time. This is contrary to the approach taken in TR 2011/D3 which indicates that exempt status is lost in the absence of an automatic reversionary beneficiary.

Knowing when a superannuation income stream commences is important for calculating when a member's benefits go into tax exempt 'pension phase' and for calculating the tax-free and taxable proportions of a member's SIS benefits. It is also important to know when a SIS ceases, to determine when a member's benefits cease to be in 'pension phase', for example, when a member commutes their pension.

ACTUARIAL CERTIFICATES

The income earned on the assets of a complying superannuation fund from which a pension is paid is exempt from tax. There are two methods to calculate exempt income:

- **Segregated current pension assets method**
  - Income earned on segregated current pension assets (ie. assets set aside which will discharge fully or in part, current pension liabilities as they fall due is exempt from tax (s295-385 ITAA97).
  - Section 295-385 requires an actuarial certificate to be obtained which confirms the levels of those assets.

- **Proportion of total superannuation liabilities method**
  - The proportion of income attributable to current pension liabilities is exempt from tax. It excludes taxable contributions and non-arm's length income, and is calculated as follows:

    (Value of unsegregated current pension liabilities) divided by (Value of unsegregated superannuation liabilities)

    (Note that any segregated assets covering both current and non-current pension liabilities (as certified by an actuary, s295-385 and s295-395) are excluded from the calculation.)

NON-ARM'S LENGTH INCOME

Income is non-arm's length income if the parties to a transaction or a series of transactions are not dealing at arm's length and the income derived from the transaction is greater than might have been expected had the parties been dealing at arm's length in relation to the transaction. The transactions covered may include interest on loans, rent from property, the profit on sale of assets and capital gains, and franking credits on dividends.

The 'special income' provisions under former s273 of the ITAA36 (repealed from 1 July 2007), have been replaced by equivalent 'non-arm's length income' provisions under s295-550 of the ITAA97. Taxation Ruling TR 2006/7 and TR 2006/7A, explains 'special income', and provides useful guidelines.

Non-arm's length income may include:

- private company dividends (including non-share dividends)
- certain distributions from trusts, and
- other excessive non-arm's length income that is greater than might have been expected had it been derived from an arm's length dealing.

The test for such income is a question of fact, and all of the circumstances in a relationship are relevant in determining whether the quantum of income derived from a non-arm's length dealing is greater than might have been expected had the parties been dealing at arm's length, including the commercial risks undertaken by the fund. Determining whether such income is derived from a non-arm's length dealing will include an examination of the same circumstances for an 'arm's length dealing' as outlined under non-arm's length private company dividends below.

All non-arm's length income is taxed at 47%. (From 1 July 2014 an increase of 0.5% in the Medicare levy to fund Disability Care Australia increases the rate from 1.5% to 2%. The addition of the Budget Repair levy of 2% to the top marginal tax rate of 45%, (applying for 3 years from 1 July 2014) increases the top marginal tax rate to 47%.) Each component of non-arm's length income is reduced by any deductions attributable to that income and is then taxed at the highest marginal tax rate. Allowable deductions against that income are those that relate exclusively to the non-arm's length component of income, and as much of other allowable deductions that appropriately relates to that income.

If the non-arm's length component is a loss, it should be quarantined for a future offset against income of the same class.

NON-ARM'S LENGTH PRIVATE COMPANY DIVIDENDS

An amount of ordinary income or statutory income is non-arm's length income if it is a dividend paid by a private company, or is reasonably attributable to such a dividend, unless the amount is consistent with an arm's length dealing.

In deciding whether the amount is consistent with an arm's length dealing consideration must be given to any connection between the private company and the fund, as well as any other relevant circumstance. Other relevant circumstances include:

- the value of the shares held by the fund in the company
- the cost to the fund of the shares on which the dividends were paid
- the dividend rate on those shares
- whether dividends have been paid on other shares in the company, and the dividend rate, and
- whether the company has issued shares in lieu of dividends to the fund, and the circumstances of the issue.

In *FFWX and FCT* (2009) AATA 657, the AAT held that private company dividends paid to the trustee of a super fund, in respect of four shares acquired in a private company at an undervalue, were 'special income' (ie. non-arm's length income) for the purposes of the former s273 of the ITAA36, and upheld the Commissioner's decision not to exercise his discretion in favour of the taxpayer to treat the dividends otherwise than as 'special income'. In the Decision Impact Statement released by the Tax Office in response to the decision, the Tax Office advised that the judgment is generally consistent with their view as outlined in TR 2006/7 and TR 2006/7A.

TA 2010/3: 'NON-MARKET VALUE ACQUISITION OF SHARES OR SHARE OPTIONS BY AN SMSF'

This Taxpayer Alert describes an arrangement where an individual nominates their SMSF as the acquirer of shares or share options under an employee share scheme. The trustee of the SMSF pays no consideration or less than market value consideration for the shares or the share options. One taxation issue that the Tax Office considers arrangements of this type give rise to, is whether dividend income derived by SMSFs under these arrangements is 'non-arm's length income' for the purposes of s295-550 and therefore is subject to a higher rate of tax.

NON-ARM'S LENGTH TRUST DISTRIBUTIONS

Trust distributions are non-arm's length income of a complying superannuation fund, complying ADF or PST if they are:

- distributions where the fund does not have a fixed entitlement to income from the trust (generally discretionary trusts), and

- distributions where the fund has a fixed entitlement to income from the trust and the fund acquired the entitlement to the distribution under an arrangement where the parties were not dealing at arm's length and the amount of income is more than the amount that would have been provided had the parties been dealing at arm's length.

If a fund receives a distribution from a trust, it should examine the circumstances of the distribution to determine if the income is 'non-arm's length income' as defined in s295-550 of the ITAA97.

CREDITS AND TAX OFFSETS

Tax payable on the income of the fund is the self-assessed amount that is calculated amount less:

- imputation credits

- foreign tax credits, up to the Australian tax payable on that income (excludes foreign tax credit on the net previous income prior to that year), and

- tax offsets on short term life assurance policies, where policies are held for less than ten years.

19.310 TAX RETURN LODGMENTS FOR SUPERANNUATION FUNDS

Superannuation funds must self-assess the lodgment of tax returns and payment of any tax.

The last date for lodgment of fund income tax returns (which includes the regulatory return if the fund is a self-managed fund) and rules for payment of tax for superannuation funds is the same as for companies. Non-complying superannuation funds are subject to the large businesses income tax return lodgment program.

SMSFS ONLY

The SMSFs income tax return, regulatory return and member contribution statements are now combined in the *Self managed superannuation fund annual return* (NAT 71226).

19.320 WHEN TAX IS PAYABLE BY SUPERANNUATION ENTITIES

The amount of tax payable dictates when tax is payable and tax return must be lodged (see 19.310).

Actuarial certificates are no longer required to exempt from tax, income from segregated current pension assets that form the investment base of allocated and market linked pensions, and account based pensions provided the requirements of a legislative alternative are satisfied (see 19.240).

COMPLYING FUNDS

The trustee of a superannuation fund that has made an irrevocable election to become a regulated superannuation fund under the *Superannuation Industry (Supervision) Act 1993* (SISA93) which is accepted as valid by the regulator and which is a complying superannuation fund is taxed on its taxable income in the following way:

- Employer contributions:
    - not subject to an irrevocable s295-180 election: *15%*
    - with s295-180 election: *Nil%*
- Self employed and personal concessional (ie. deductible) contributions (see 19.026): *15%*
- For 2007-08 and later income years, no Tax File Number (TFN) contributions income (see 19.060) (ie. concessional contributions taxed at the top MTR plus Medicare levy):

- - on new accounts: *(47% from 2014-15) plus Medicare levy*
  - for pre-1 July 2007 accounts after first $1,000 of no-TFN contributions income: *(47% from 2014-15) plus Medicare levy*
- Member non-concessional (ie. undeducted) contributions to:
  - an employer fund: *Nil%*
  - a personal fund: *Nil%*
- Directed termination payments (may only be permitted until 30 June 2012)
  - for 1 July 2007 to 30 June 2012 rollovers of the taxable component: *15%*
- Superannuation guarantee charge (SGC) shortfall component (see 19.530): *15%*
- Any liability attached to taxable contributions transferred from investing funds in pooled superannuation trusts: *15%*
- Income attributable to a taxed fund's liability to pay current pensions from segregated assets (see below): *Nil%*
- Income from assets invested to pay non-current pension liabilities: *15%*
- Non-reversionary life assurance bonuses: *Nil%*
- Personal injury payments: *Nil%*
- CGT cap amounts: *Nil%*
- Spouse contributions: *Nil%*
- Government co-contributions: *Nil%*
- Earnings of a taxed fund in accumulation phase (excluding non-arm's length income unreasonable private company dividends): *15%*
- Distributions from trusts (unless there is a fixed entitlement to that trust's income): *47% from 2014-15*
- Excessive non-arm's length trust distributions of income where there is fixed entitlement to income from that trust:*47% from 2014-15.*
- Excessive non-arm's length income (other): *47%*
- Excessive private company dividends: *47%.*

NOTE: From 1 July 2012, concessional contributions, up-to the concessional contributions cap, made by or in respect of individuals with an adjusted taxable income in excess of $300,000 will attract additional tax under Div 293 at the rate of 15%, payable by the individual. (see 19.300).

CAPITAL GAINS

Unlike other taxpayers, the cost base of each asset of a complying superannuation fund is either its market value as at 30 June 1988 or actual cost, which ever yields the lower capital gain or loss. (ie. no exemption for pre-CGT assets – see 12.466). Rules relating to the taxation of capital gains changed on 21 September 1999. Under the new rules, indexation of the cost base of assets was frozen at 30 September 1999. This means that the cost base of assets acquired before 21 September 1999 is not indexed beyond that date and that the cost base of assets acquired subsequent to that date are not indexed at all.

The following summarises the nominal rate of tax applied to CGT assets disposed of by a complying superannuation fund after the start time.

- Assets held for less than 12 months: *15%*
- Assets held for at least 12 months:
  - for assets acquired before 21 September 1999 the choice of the lower capital gain from:
    - the indexed cost base method, or *15%*
    - the discount method (ie. 33 1/3% discount on nominal gain): *10% (effective rate)*
  - for assets acquired after 21 September 1999:
    - only the discount method can be used (ie. 33 $1/3$% discount on nominal gain): *10% (effective rate)*

Removal of trading stock exception

The trading stock exception to the CGT primary code rule for complying superannuation entities for specified assets has been removed. This amendment ensures gains or losses on specified assets (primarily shares, units in a trust and land) are subject to CGT, consistent with CGT being the primary code for taxing gains and losses of complying superannuation entities. The measure applies with effect from 7.30 pm (AEST) 10 May 2011. However, transitional rules apply to ensure that assets held or accounted for as trading stock before that time are unaffected.

OPTIONAL CGT LOSS ROLLOVER FOR COMPLYING SUPERANNUATION FUNDS AND ADFS

A complying superannuation fund or a complying ADF can choose to roll-over capital losses and transfer revenue losses (including losses realised under the merger and previously realised losses) when they merge with a complying superannuation fund with five or more members between 24 December 2008 and 30 September 2011.

    These provisions do not apply to SMSFs.

NON COMPLYING FUNDS

- Assessed on income from all sources including realised capital gains on assets acquired after 19 September 1985, or for profit making purposes before then, employer contributions and earnings: *45% (47% from 2014-15)*
- If a fund complied in the previous year, but receives a notice of non-compliance in the subsequent year, 'net previous income in respect of previous years of income' is calculated as: Asset values – Undeducted contributions: *45% (47% from 2014-15)*

19.500 SUPERANNUATION GUARANTEE

The Superannuation Guarantee (SG) scheme is administered by the Tax Office. It requires employers to provide a minimum level of superannuation support for most employees each quarter based on the employee's Ordinary Time Earnings (OTE) (see 19.503 and 19.519). Employers must pay their SG obligations within 28 days after the end of each quarter or incur a non tax deductible Superannuation Guarantee Charge (SGC) (see 19.530). It may also include interest and penalties. The SG is imposed by the *Superannuation Guarantee (Administration) Act 1992* (SGAA92) and the *Superannuation Guarantee Charge Act 1992* (SGCA92).

Prior to the SG legislation, employer contributions were provided for some employees as award or productivity superannuation. This had its origins in a 3% wage increase being paid as superannuation following the National Wage Case in 1986. The SG legislation to provide superannuation benefits for employees works in conjunction with various industrial awards. Those contributions then count towards the superannuation support required under the SG legislation. Within this framework, an employer may pay their SG based contributions into an employee's Self Managed Superannuation Fund (SMSF) to satisfy their SG obligations.

19.501   SUPERANNUATION GUARANTEE: RECENT CHANGES

The required minimum rate of SG contributions of 9%, increased to 9.25% in 2013-14 and then to 9.5% for 2014-15.

The upper age limit of 70 for SG support was abolished from 1 July 2013.

- See 19.513 for the deductibility of SG paid to former employees.
- See 19.513 for the deductibility of SG paid for deceased employees.
- See 19.505 for the removal of the SG opt out provisions.
- See 19.525 for extending the Director Penalty Regime to SG.

19.502   SUPERANNUATION GUARANTEE: RATE

The SG rate of 9% applied from 1 July 2002, increasing to 9.25% in 2013-14 and then to 9.5% for the year 2014-15. *The Minerals Resource Rent Tax Repeal and Other Measures Bill 2014* received Royal Assent on 5 September 2014. It replaced the *Minerals Resource Rent Tax Repeal and Other Measures Bill 2013 [No. 2]* which will not proceed. This measure has the effect of fixing the SG rate at 9.5% p.a. for the years 2014-15 to 2020-21 and 10% p.a. for the year 2021-22. Thereafter incremental increases of 0.5% per year apply to achieve the rate of 12% p.a. for the year 2025-26 and for subsequent years.

SUPERANNUATION GUARANTEE RATES TABLE

Year	SG rate (%)	Year	SG rate (%)	Year	SG rate (%)
2002-03 to 2012-13	9	2017-18	9.5	2022-23	10.50
2013-14	9.25	2018-19	9.5	2023-24	11
2014-15	9.5	2019-20	9.5	2024-25	11.50
2015-16	9.5	2020-21	9.5	2025-26 & future	12
2016-17	9.5	2021-22	10		

19.503   EARNINGS BASE

From 1 July 2008 the only earnings base employers can use to calculate their SG obligations for their eligible employees will be OTE. This is the amount an employee earns for their ordinary hours of work, not including overtime. It includes over-award payments, shift allowances, commissions, and paid leave up to the maximum contributions base for the quarter.

 An upper age limit of 75 applies for the deductibility of mandated employer contributions, excluding the SG provisions that include an upper age restriction of 70 beyond which support is not provided. This will continue to apply until 30 June 2013. After 30 June 2013, the provisions extend deductibility for SG while also abolishing an upper age limit when employee eligibility for SG support ceases.

19.504   SATISFYING SUPERANNUATION GUARANTEE REQUIREMENTS

In order to satisfy the minimum SG obligations in a financial year, employers must have paid relevant SG based quarterly contributions into nominated complying superannuation funds by the due dates, with the final payment for the year made no later than 28 July of the following financial year.

NOTE: These payments are tax-deductible in the financial year in which they are made.

19.505   SUPERANNUATION GUARANTEE OPT OUT PROVISIONS

Employees with accumulated superannuation entitlements in excess of the Pension Reasonable Benefit Limit (PRBL) may elect not to receive superannuation contributions from their employers. As Reasonable Benefit Limits (RBLs) were abolished from 1 July 2007 under *Better Super*, these elections will no longer be able to be made. As these elections were irrevocable, existing elections will remain in force.

19.506   QUARTERLY SUPERANNUATION GUARANTEE CONTRIBUTIONS REQUIRED FROM 1 JULY 2003

From 1 July 2003, employers have to make superannuation guarantee contributions at least every quarter within 28 days after the end of each quarter (see 19.533). If this deadline falls on a weekend or holiday in the State or place the holiday occurs, the contribution can be made on the next working day.

19.507 EMPLOYEE SUPERANNUATION GUARANTEE REPORTING

Employers are not required under the SG legislation to provide their employees with details of SG contributions made on their behalf unless they are covered under Australian workplace legislation, awards or agreements that require them to report superannuation contributions on pay slips.

19.508 ACCEPTING MANDATED EMPLOYER CONTRIBUTIONS

Trustees of Complying Superannuation Funds (CSFs) can accept any contributions for a member if the contributions are 'mandated employer contributions' SIS r.7.04. Mandated employer contributions are contributions made by an employer to satisfy SG or Award based superannuation obligations.

19.509 SUPERANNUATION GUARANTEE CONTRIBUTIONS BELONG TO EMPLOYEES

Employer SG contributions must vest in the employee immediately and be preserved. 'Vest' means that the superannuation benefit belongs to employees when they leave the fund or Retirement Savings Account (RSA) (eg. if they change jobs or retire from work). 'Preserved' means a benefit of $200 or more, payable only when a condition of release occurs (eg. on retirement on or after preservation age (see 19.700).

19.510 PRACTICE STATEMENT ON LATE SUPERANNUATION GUARANTEE PAYMENTS

The Commissioner has released Practice Statement PS LA 2006/5 detailing how tax officers should treat superannuation contributions made by an employer for an employee after the relevant quarterly cut-off dates in the SGAA92. The relevant cut-off dates are 28 April, 28 July, 28 October and 28 January.

19.511 HOW MUCH IS PAYABLE?

Employer superannuation contribution support is currently a minimum of 9.5% for the years 2014-15 to 2020-21 and 10% p.a. for the year 2021-22. Thereafter increments of 0.5% per year raise the rate to 12% p.a. for the year 2025-26 and for subsequent years. A maximum super contribution base of $50,810 per quarter applies in 2015-16 and $49,430 per quarter in 2014-15. An employer could choose to pay superannuation guarantee on an OTE in excess of the quarterly maximum..

19.512 SUPERANNUATION GUARANTEE DEDUCTIBILITY FOR TAX PURPOSES

In addition to the employee activity, complying superannuation fund and age related conditions being satisfied, an employer must have also paid an SG contribution in order to claim it as a deduction.

19.513 SUPERANNUATION GUARANTEE DEDUCTIBILITY FOR FORMER EMPLOYEES

Contributions for a former employee may also be deductible if it reduces the employer's SG charge percentage for the employee and if made within two months of the employee ceasing employment (s290-85).

19.514 DISCLOSURE OF INFORMATION RELATING TO SUPERANNUATION GUARANTEE COMPLAINTS

The Commissioner of Taxation or an officer of the Tax Office can provide information to an employee in response to a complaint that an employer has not complied with its obligations under the Act.

19.515   WHO IS AN 'EMPLOYER'?

For SG purposes, an employer (including governments, their statutory authorities and municipal bodies) is:

- a person who pays salary or wages to another person on a full-time, part-time or casual basis. May include payments made under a contract with an individual (but not with a company, partnership or trust) that is wholly or principally (at least 50%) for that person's labour
- a non-resident employer who has employees working in Australia
- Commonwealth and tax exempt Commonwealth authorities
- tax exempt organisations, or
- family companies and trusts paying salary or wages.

19.516   WHO IS AN 'EMPLOYEE'?

Under s12(1) of the SGAA92, a person is an employee if they fall within the common law meaning or under the extended definition in SGAA92. Also see SGR 2005/1. An employee under common law is a person who receives payment in the form of salary and wages in return for work or services rendered, or payment for work under a contract that is wholly or principally for the persons labour. The person liable to make the payment is the employer.

In *Roy Morgan Research Pty Ltd and FCT* (2009) AATA 702, the AAT held that market research interviewers engaged by a market researcher were employees within the meaning of s12 of the SGAA92, either on the basis of s12(1) or s12(3). This decision was subsequently affirmed by the Full Federal Court in *Roy Morgan Research Pty Ltd v Commissioner of Taxation* (2010) FCAFC 52.

In *FCT v Newton* (2010) FCA 1440, the Federal Court of Australia held, on appeal from the AAT, that the taxpayer, who carried on the business of providing community support services to her clients, was not exempt from liability under the SGAA92 by virtue of the provisions of s12(11). It found that the services provided by the taxpayer were not provided physically or personally by the taxpayer herself but rather by employees of the taxpayer.

In *On Call Interpreters and Translators Agency Pty Ltd v FCT (No.3)* (2011) FCA 366, the Federal Court of Australia held that, in determining the taxpayer's liability to superannuation guarantee charge, the taxpayer had failed to establish that certain interpreters and translators engaged by it in its business of providing interpreting and translating services to its clients were not common law employees, and were not employees by virtue of the extended definition of employee in s12(3) of the SGAA92. In the Decision Impact Statement released in response to the decision, the Tax Office advised that the judgment is generally consistent with their own submissions and therefore the Tax Office will maintain their views as set out in SGR 2005/1.

Whether a person is an employee of another is a question of fact to be determined having regard to the key indicators expressed in various judicial decisions which have considered the issue of whether a person is a common law employee. However the classification of a person as an employee for the purposes of the SGAA92 is not solely dependent upon the existence of a common law employment relationship.

The common law meaning of employee is expanded by s12(2) to s12(11) of the SGAA92. These subsections list a number of further persons who are also to be treated as employees for the purposes of the SGAA92, even if they are not common law employees and are clearly distinguishable from common law employees.

 SGR 2009/1 explains the Commissioner's view of how the definition of 'employee' and 'employer' contained in s12(8) SGAA92 applies to sportspersons and persons providing services in connection with sporting activities.

The following are employees within the common law and expanded statutory definitions:

- an employee at common law, the main test of being the right to control how, when, where and who is to perform the work. A subsidiary test is whether a person provides services as an individual carrying on their own business (contract for services) or individually as a part of another's business organisation (contract for service)
- persons who receive prescribed payments

- Visiting Medical Officers (VMOs) if they are either common law employees or under contract to perform duties personally. However, contributions are not required if the contractors (including VMOs) are a partnership, company or trust. Also see ATO ID 2011/87, where the Tax Office held that a medical practitioner was not an employee of the medical clinic according to s12 of the SGAA92
- members of executive bodies of bodies corporate (eg. Directors (s12(2) SGAA92))
- person under contracts for labour (eg. individual contractors engaged wholly or principally (at least 50%) for their labour) (s12(3) SGAA92)
- members of Commonwealth and State Parliaments; of ACT and NT Legislative Assembly (s12(4) to s12(7) SGAA92)
- artists, musicians, sportspersons etc (s12(8) SGAA92) (for sportspersons see SGR 2009/1)
- a person who holds, or performs the duties of, an appointment, office or position under the Constitution or under a law of the Commonwealth, of a State or of a Territory (s12(9) SGAA92), and
- local government councillors and members of an eligible local governing body (s12(10) SGAA92).

Payments to an individual do not make a principal liable to provide superannuation support if another person performs the work or the individual has a contract that allows another person to perform the work (ATO ID 2001/12).

19.517 EXCEPTIONS

Superannuation guarantee contributions do not have to be provided for:
- employees paid less than $450 in a particular month (for SG calculations treat that month's wages as nil)
- employees under 18 working part time (ie. not more than 30 hours per week)
- employees paid for domestic or private work for not more than 30 hours a week (eg. a part time nanny or housekeeper) by a non-business employer (also see *Care Provider and Commissioner of Taxation* (2010) AATA 475)
- non-resident employees paid for work done outside Australia
- resident employees paid by non-resident employers for work done outside Australia
- salary as a member of the Reserve Forces which is exempt under s51-1, Item 4
- foreign executives who meet the criteria of the former Class 413 [executive (overseas)] visa or entry permit under the Migration (1993) Regulations
- partnership, company or trust contractors, or payments made to an individual if another person performs the work
- payments made under the Community Development Employment Program Scheme
- taxi drivers by taxi operators because the relationship is one of bailment, not one of employer and employee (*FCT v De Luxe Red and Yellow Cabs Co-operative (Trading) Society Ltd & Ors* 98 ATC 4466), and
- employees who have lodged an irrevocable SG opt out election with their employer prior to 1 July 2007.

19.518 EMPLOYEE'S EARNINGS BASE

An employee's earning base is the amount on which minimum superannuation contributions are payable to avoid the SGC (see 19.530). From 1 July 2008, the earnings base is determined as OTE.

VISITING MEDICAL OFFICERS

The earnings base for visiting medical officers include superannuation allowances (because they are not payments to a superannuation fund) based on:
- if for contracts for labour: the labour part of the contract, including fee for service, any hourly rate, on call allowance or call back loading, plus any earning component for background practice costs, and

- if common law employees: the whole of the payment, not just the labour component (unless there is any other earnings base).

See also SGR 2005/2.

ORDINARY HOURS OF WORK FOR EMPLOYEES COVERED BY BOTH AN AWARD AND AN AGREEMENT

Ordinary hours of work for the purposes of the definition of 'ordinary time earnings' in s6(1) of the SGAA92 for an employee who is covered by an award but has also entered into an individual agreement with the employer that requires the employee to work hours in excess of the ordinary hours contained in the award, are to be determined based on the hours of work in the agreement (ATO ID 2007/73).

19.519   ORDINARY TIME EARNINGS

Ordinary Time Earnings (OTE) is defined in s6(1) of the SGAA92. The Commissioner's explanation of the meaning of OTE as defined in s6(1) of the SGAA92 is contained in SGR 2009/2 and SGR 2009/2A1. It contains the Commissioner's explanation of the meaning of OTE as defined in s6(1) of the SGAA92. It also explains the meaning of Salary or Wages (SoW) as defined in s11(1) of the SGAA92.

PAYMENTS INCLUDED IN ORDINARY TIME EARNINGS FOR EACH EMPLOYEE

- earnings for 'ordinary' hours of work [In the case of casual workers, use actual hours worked (not minimum hours stipulated in employment contracts) re *Quest Personal Temping v FCT* (2001)
- bonuses that relate to good performance (includes Christmas bonuses)
- piece-rates where no ordinary hours of work stipulated
- over-award payments
- payments in lieu of notice made from 1 July 2009
- shift loading
- casual loading
- annual leave, sick leave or long service leave
- allowances (excluding expense allowances and reimbursements and items that are fringe benefits under the *Fringe Benefits Tax Assessment Act 1986* (FBTAA86) such as a living away from home allowance)
- commission or bonuses that relate to specific performance criteria
- government subsidies
- directors' fees
- workers' compensation and top-up payments paid in relation to hours worked
- the labour portion only of payments to a contractor who is an employee under the SGAA92 (ie. contract is wholly or principally for labour of that person)
- payments to Members of Federal and State Parliaments or the Legislative Assembly of a Territory
- payments for performance in, or provision of services relating to entertainment, sport, promotions, films, discs, tapes, TV or radio, and
- remuneration of people in the service of the Commonwealth, the States or Territories, and local government councillors who are members of eligible local governing bodies (excludes payments to elected local government officials (unless they are effectively full time employees)).

 For the Commissioner's explanation of the meaning of OTE for periods prior to 1 July 2009 use SGR 94/4W and for periods from 1 July 2009 use SGR 2009/2 and SGR 2009/2A1.

PAYMENTS NOT INCLUDED IN ORDINARY TIME EARNINGS

- ex gratia payments
- overtime payments for work performed during hours outside an employee's ordinary hours of work
- top up payments when serving on jury duty, or with reserve forces, etc
- remuneration while on parental leave
- annual leave loading
- accrued annual leave on termination of employment
- long service leave and sick leave paid as a lump sum on termination of employment
- redundancy and employment termination payments
- fringe benefits subject to fringe benefits tax
- workers' compensation and top up payments paid where no work is performed
- pensions and social security benefits
- dividends
- partnership and trust distributions
- payments for entering into a restraint of trade agreement
- payments for domestic or private work for the employment of a person for less than 30 hours a week
- allowances paid to local government councillors, unless they are effectively full time employees, and
- unused flex leave to non-ongoing employees covered by a certified agreement.

19.520 QUARTERLY CONTRIBUTIONS REQUIREMENT

CONTRIBUTION PERIOD

Superannuation Guarantee contributions made to a CSF or RSA by an employer from the first day of the current quarter until 28 days after the end of that quarter (see 19.533) are treated as current period contributions. If this deadline falls on a weekend or public holiday only for employers in the State or place the holiday occurs), the contribution can be made on the next working day.

LATE PAYMENT RELIEF

Employers are allowed to have late SG contributions offset against any SGC provided the late payment is made no later than 30 days after the SG due date. These Late Payment Offsets (LPOs) are not tax deductible (s290-95).

For further information on LPOs, see 19.534.

LIABILITY ON BACK PAYMENT OF SALARY AND WAGES

SG contributions are payable by employers on the payment of salary and wages to former employees following the termination of their employment.

SUPERANNUATION GUARANTEE PRIVACY LAW CHANGES

The Commissioner of Taxation or an officer of the Tax Office can provide information to an employee in response to a complaint that an employer has not complied with its obligations under the SGAA92.

These provisions enable the Tax Office to keep employees updated on the progress of their SG complaint by informing them on the steps and actions the Tax Office will take:

- during the investigation, and
- to recover the SGC from the employer.

The SG privacy laws do not allow the Tax Office to provide employees with information concerning the general financial affairs (including tax affairs) of their employers at any stage. However, it allows employees to be updated on the progress of their complaint by automated mail or telephone.

EMPLOYER'S SUPERANNUATION GUARANTEE REPORTING OBLIGATION

Employers whose employees are covered under Australian workplace legislation, awards or agreements must give each employee a written report showing:

- the amount of contributions made, and
- the name of the superannuation provider and, if possible, its contact phone number, and if known the employee's account or membership number.

The type of written report is left to the employer. For example, it could be:

- a letter to the employee signed and dated by the employer (or other authorised person)
- an email if the employer usually communicates with employees via email
- a notification on a payslip, or
- a copy of a receipt for contributions from the superannuation provider.

MAXIMUM EARNINGS BASE

The maximum earnings base (indexed annually by AWOTE) on which contributions must be made for each employee is $50,810 per quarter in 2015-16. In the previous two years it is $49,430 and $48,040. .

If the superannuation contributions paid fails to meet the SG rate for an employee in the contribution period any remaining shortfall is payable as a SGC. However, where the OTE exceeds the maximum earnings base, cover up to the base is required.

CALCULATING THE REQUIRED EMPLOYER SUPPORT

The required employer SG obligation is the lesser of the maximum quarterly contribution base and the employee's quarterly earnings base x 9.5% in 2015-16.

EXAMPLE: Maximum quarterly contribution base greater than earnings base
If an employee has OTE per quarter of $50,000 in 2015-16, the employer is required to contribute at the rate of 9.5% on the OTE, since this is less than the prevailing maximum quarterly contribution base of $50,810.

Employee's maximum quarterly contribution base in 2015-16 .... $50,810
Employee's quarterly earnings base.. $50,000
Minimum quarterly contribution for the employee $50,000 x 9.5% $4,750

EXAMPLE: Maximum quarterly contribution base greater than earnings base
If during a quarter in 2014-15 year the same OTE applied, given that the maximum quarterly contribution base in the previous year is $49,430, the rate of 9.5% applies to the maximum quarterly contribution base and not $50,000.

Employee's maximum quarterly contribution base in 2014-15 .... $49,430
Employee's quarterly earnings base.. $50,000
Minimum quarterly contribution for the employee $49,430 x 9.5% $4,696

MAXIMUM DEDUCTIBLE CONTRIBUTIONS

Providing certain conditions are met, an employer is entitled to a full deduction for all contributions to a CSF on behalf of an employee (see 19.022) and is subject to SG provisions if applicable.

19.521   DEFINED BENEFIT SCHEMES

A defined benefit fund is one where contributions and earnings are paid into the fund, not individual member accounts. Retiring benefits are defined and payable as either:

- a multiple of member's salary on or before retirement date, or average over a period of employment, or
- a specified amount.

The employer can satisfy SG obligations using a defined benefit scheme where the scheme is a complying superannuation scheme, and it has a current 'benefit certificate'.

19.522 SUPERANNUATION GUARANTEE DEDUCTIBILITY FOR DECEASED EMPLOYEES

Employer contributions to satisfy SG obligations, payable for an employee who is deceased, can be paid directly to the employee's estate and be treated as contributions for the deceased employee's benefit.

Deductions are available for superannuation contributions made after the death of an employee in order to satisfy an SG obligation or under a salary sacrifice arrangement. This will include payments made to the deceased employee's dependants or Legal Personal Representative (LPR).

19.523 SUPERANNUATION DOUBLE COVERAGE

Bilateral superannuation agreements remove the problem of double superannuation coverage that can occur when Australian employees are seconded to work overseas. Under these agreements, an Australian employer will be exempt from having to make compulsory contributions in the country their employee is seconded to work in, provided the employee remains covered by compulsory superannuation arrangements in Australia.

AGREEMENTS CURRENTLY IN PLACE

Australia has agreements covering double superannuation coverage with the following countries as at 6 May 2015:

Country	Start date	Country	Start date
Austria	1-Jan-12	Korea	1-Oct-08
Belgium	1-Jul-05	Latvia	1-Jan-13
Chile	1-Jul-04	fmr Yugoslav Rep of Macedonia	1-Apr-11
Croatia	1-Jul-04	The Netherlands	1-Apr-03
Czech Republic	1-Jul-11	Norway	1-Jan-07
Finland	1-Jul-09	The Republic of Poland	1-Oct-10
Germany	1-Oct-08	Portugal	1-Oct-02
Greece	1-Oct-08	Slovak Republic	1-Jan-12
Hungary	1-Oct-12	Switzerland	1-Jan-08
Ireland	1-Jan-06	United States of America	1-Oct-02
Japan	1-Jan-09		

Australian employers can obtain a *Certificate of coverage* from the Tax Office for Australian employees sent to work temporarily in another country. The employer is then exempt from paying superannuation contributions in the relevant foreign country. Where a *Certificate of coverage* has been issued by the Tax Office, the employer to whom the certificate relates, is legally obliged to make SG contributions in Australia.

Jack is an Australian resident working in Australia for an Australian employer. His employer intends to send him to the United States to work for a year. Jack's employer will be required to make compulsory social security (including super) contributions for him under United States law. In addition, Jack's employer is also required to make SG contributions for him in Australia. Before Jack leaves Australia his employer requests a Certificate of coverage from the Tax Office. This is to certify that the agreement between the United States and Australia applies to Jack's situation.

He and his employer are exempt from making contributions under United States law. However, superannuation contributions must continue to be made for Jack in Australia.

19.524 SUPERANNUATION FOR CONTRACTORS

Employers who pay contractors under a contract that is wholly or principally for labour (see below) have to pay SG. This is even if the contractor quotes an Australian Business Number (ABN). These contractors are considered employees for SG purposes pursuant to the SGAA92. Generally, a contract is principally for labour if more than half of the value of the contract is for the person's labour, which may include physical labour, mental effort, or artistic effort.

HOW DOES SG APPLY TO CONTRACTORS?

If an employer's contractors are employees for SG purposes, the employer must provide the minimum level of SG contributions. The minimum SG amount that an employer must pay is 9.5% in 2015-16 (for SG rate trajectory see 19.502) of each eligible employee's earnings base (see 19.518).

 The SG contribution should be calculated only on the labour component of the contract.

 Australian Workplace Agreements (AWAs) are employment contracts between employers and employees. This means that employers have SG and PAYGW obligations for any workers they employ under an AWA.

WHAT IS A CONTRACT THAT IS WHOLLY OR PRINCIPALLY FOR LABOUR?

A contract for labour can be made either orally or in writing.

A contract may be considered wholly or principally for labour, if the contractor:

- is remunerated wholly or principally for their personal labour and skills
- must perform the contract work personally, and
- is paid by reference to hours worked rather than completion of the contract.

If an employer makes a contract with someone other than the person who will actually be providing the labour, there is no employer-employee relationship.

The following two situations are examples of when a contract is not for the labour of the individual:

- the employer contracts with a company, trust or a partnership, or
- if the person the employer has made the contract with is free to hire other people to perform the work, even if the person ends up performing the work themselves.

If the values of the various parts of a contract (such as the provision of labour and also of assets to be used in fulfilling the contract) are not detailed in the contract, the Tax Office will accept a reasonable estimation of their market values and will take the normal industry practices into consideration. If the labour component of a contract cannot be worked out, the employer can use a reasonable market value of the labour component of the contact to represent the salary or wages of an employee.

In *Brilliant and Commissioner of Taxation* (2010) AATA 267 the Administrative Appeals Tribunal (AAT) held that a worker was an employee, not a contractor, for the purposes of the SGAA92. The AAT came to its conclusion having considered each of the indicia of control, integration, results, delegation, terms of engagement and risk. Alternatively, the worker fell within the extended definition in s12(3) of the SGAA92 as, with reference to his duties, his engagement was principally for his labour.

SUPERANNUATION GUARANTEE OBLIGATIONS AND AWARDS

Where an employer make superannuation contributions under an award, these contributions will count towards the employer meeting their SG obligations. Employers will need to check that the contributions are enough to satisfy both the award and the SG requirements.

WHAT HAPPENS IF SUPERANNUATION GUARANTEE REQUIREMENTS ARE NOT MET?

Employers who don't pay enough superannuation for their eligible contractors, or who miss the payment cut-off dates (see 19.533), will be liable to pay the SGC.

19.525   EXTENDING THE DIRECTOR PENALTY REGIME TO SG

The *Tax Laws Amendment (2012 Measures No. 2) Bill 2012* increases directors' obligations to cause their company to comply with its existing PAYGW and SG requirements. The amendments:

- extend the director penalty regime to make directors personally liable for their company's unpaid SG amounts
- ensure that directors cannot discharge their director penalties by placing their company into administration or liquidation when PAYGW or SG remains unpaid and unreported three months after the due date, and

- in some instances, make directors and their associates liable to PAYGW non-compliance tax where the company has failed to pay amounts withheld to the Commissioner.

19.530 SUPERANNUATION GUARANTEE CHARGE

Employers who fail to meet their minimum quarterly Superannuation Guarantee (SG) contributions must pay the Superannuation Guarantee Charge (SGC). Calculation of the employer's SG obligation is made on an individual employee basis. The SGC and other penalties are imposed under the *Superannuation Guarantee (Administration) Act 1992* (SGAA92), the *Superannuation Guarantee (Administration) Regulations 1993* (SGAR93) and the *Superannuation Guarantee Charge Act 1992* (SGCA92). In some instances involving statutory funds, the contribution in respect of an employee is based more generally on what is contributed overall to the scheme.

19.532   WHAT IS THE SUPERANNUATION GUARANTEE CHARGE?

The SGC is a penalty incurred by employers who fail to meet their minimum SG obligations and it is not deductible (s26-95 ITAA97).

19.533   WHEN IS THE SUPERANNUATION GUARANTEE CHARGE INCURRED?

Employers who do not meet their SG obligations by the designated quarterly cut off dates do not offer 'Choice of fund' (see 19.560) to eligible employees within 28 days, or fail to action an eligible employee's choice within two months will need to lodge a *Superannuation guarantee charge statement – quarterly* (NAT 9599) (SGC statement) and pay the SGC.

Under *Superannuation Legislation Amendment (MySuper core provisions) Act 2012 - Schedule 1* from 1 January 2014, employer contributions for all employees, including those who have not chosen a super fund (see *Choice of fund* at 19.563) must be made to a fund that offers a *MySuper* product in order to satisfy the employer's SG obligations (see 19.285).

The Tax Office has released Practice Statement Law Administration PS LA 2007/10 to outline when a default assessment can be made under s36 of the SGAA92 and the factors the Commissioner will consider in making the default assessment (see below).

Quarterly SG due dates	
SG quarter	Due date for SG payment No tax deduction available for contributions made after:
1 July – 30 September	28 October in the next quarter
1 October – 31 December	28 January in the next quarter
1 January – 31 March	28 April in the next quarter
1 April – 30 June	28 July in the next quarter

An employer who makes a required SG contribution to an approved clearing house (eg. the Superannuation Clearing House Facility – see 19.565) by the quarterly SG due date, still satisfies their obligations under the SGAA92, even if the approved clearing house fails to forward the contribution to the relevant fund by the quarterly SG due date (SGD 2005/2A1).

19.534   LATE PAYMENT OFFSET

Only late contributions paid before the employer's original SGC assessment is made are eligible for the Late Payment Offset (LPO). The LPO can only be applied against the nominal interest charge and the SG shortfall components of the SGC. The administrative fee and other interest or penalties are not available for LPOs.

LPOs are not tax deductible.

Eligible employers will generally be able to offset amounts they paid late to a superannuation fund against the SGC if they:

- have paid the late contribution to the employee's superannuation fund
- have paid the contribution before the original SGC assessment is made, and
- elect to use the LPO within four years of the original SGC assessment.

To receive the LPO, eligible employers must make an election on the *Superannuation guarantee charge statement – quarterly* (NAT 9599) (SGC statement). If they have already lodged this statement, they must complete a *Superannuation guarantee late payment offset election* (NAT 14899) instead. LPO elections cannot be revoked. LPOs are not tax deductible for income tax purposes (s290-95 ITAA97) and cannot be used as a prepayment for current or future SG periods. Alternatively, employers may be able to use a late contribution for an employee for a future quarter if the contribution is made not more than 12 months before the beginning of the quarter. If an employer chooses this option, although the contribution will be tax deductible it cannot be claimed as an LPO.

HOW TO APPLY FOR A LATE PAYMENT OFFSET

If an employer has not lodged a SGC statement or received a SGC assessment for the period for which they want to claim an LPO, they need to lodge a *Superannuation guarantee charge statement – quarterly* (NAT 9599) ensuring they complete the 'offset for late payment' section.

If an employer has paid late contributions to their employee's super fund and subsequently lodges a SGC statement or receives a SGC assessment for a quarterly period for which they want to claim an offset, they will only need to lodge a *Superannuation guarantee late payment offset election* (NAT 14899), but will need to lodge this form with the Commissioner within four years of the original assessment date.

 Frank must pay superannuation contributions for his employee, Amy. Under the SG scheme, Frank must contribute $1,000 to Amy's superannuation fund by 28 April 2015, for the quarter ending 31 March 2015. Frank makes a late payment to Amy's superannuation fund on 1 May 2014. Frank has not paid before the quarterly cut-off date, so must lodge an SGC statement and pay the SGC to the Tax Office. But as Frank paid the late contribution to the superannuation fund before his SGC assessment was made, he is eligible to apply for the LPO. Frank lodges his SGC statement, including the LPO election, on 10 May 2015. Frank pays the SGC which he has calculated less the amount of the LPO.

19.535   WHAT ARE THE SG CHARGE COMPONENTS?

The SGC is made up of three components being:

- the SG shortfall
- an administrative penalty, and
- a nominal interest component.

19.536   DETERMINING IF THERE IS A SG SHORTFALL

A quarterly SG shortfall for an employee will occur if the actual level of superannuation support provided by the employer is below the SG prescribed level. Employers subject to the SG system should use the following steps to determine if they have an SG shortfall and hence an SGC liability for the quarter:

1. Determine the Charge Percentage (CP) for the quarter (for the rate applicable see 19.502).
2. Determine the Actual Percentage (AP) level of employee support for the quarter based upon the employee's earnings base. The earnings base may not exceed the maximum quarterly contribution base, being $50,810 in 2015-16 and $49,430 in 2014-15.
3. If CP is greater than or equal to AP there is no shortfall, otherwise there is an SG shortfall. Calculate the SGC (see example below).

19.537   CALCULATING THE SUPERANNUATION GUARANTEE CHARGE

The Tax Office has released a SGC statement and calculator tool. Employers can use this tool if they are late in paying their employees' superannuation contributions. It will enable an employer to calculate their SGC liability and prepare their SGC statement for lodgment.

SGC COMPONENT 1 – SUPERANNUATION GUARANTEE SHORTFALL

An employer's SG shortfall for each employee for the quarter is calculated as the percentage difference between the CP and the AP, multiplied by the total 'Salary or Wages' (SoW) paid to the employee in the relevant quarter.

An employer's SG shortfall for an employee may be increased if the employer fails to make SG contributions in compliance with the 'Choice of fund' regime (see 19.560). SoW is defined in s11(1) of the SGAA92. Under s11(1), SoW has its ordinary or common law meaning as payments for work or services, but includes a number of specific items (see list below) and excludes other specific items (also see list below).

SGR 2009/2 and SGR 2009/2A1 contain the Commissioner's explanation of the meaning of SoW as defined in s11(1) of the SGAA92. They also explain the meaning of Ordinary Time Earnings (OTE) as defined in s6(1) of the SGAA92 (see 19.519).

SGC COMPONENT 2 – ADMINISTRATIVE FEE

Currently set at $20.00 per quarter per employee for whom a SG shortfall has occurred.

SGC COMPONENT 3 – NOMINAL INTEREST

This is currently set at 10% pa. It is a substitute for foregone fund earnings that would have accrued if the employer had met their minimum SG obligations. It is calculated by multiplying the sum of all of the employer's SG shortfalls for the quarter by the nominal interest rate of 10%, beginning on the first day of the quarter in question until the later of the SGC payment due date and the date of lodgment of the SGC statement.

Calculating the SGC resulting from a SG shortfall for the quarter ending 30 September 2014 for a single employee

Static data: SG quarter 1 July 2014 – 30 September 2014

SGC lodgement due date and actual payment date: 28 November 2014

Employer's charge percentage (CP) for the quarter	9.5%
Maximum contributions base for the quarter	$49,430
Quarterly employee earnings base (based on OTE)	$16,000
Actual wages paid during the quarter	$20,000
(Wages for quarter are less than $49,430 so full support is necessary)	
Actual contributions made for the quarter	$1,040
Administration fee	$20
Nominal interest rate	10.0%
Number of days between 1 July 2014 and 28 November 2014	151
Number of days in financial year ending 30 June 2015	365

Step 1: Determine the charge percentage (CP) 9.5%

Step 2: Determine the actual percentage (AP):
Actual level of superannuation support for the quarter
Actual percentage (AP) $1,040 x 100 divided by $16,000 .... 6.5%

Step 3: Determine if there is an SG shortfall:
Is there a SG shortfall? (ie. is AP less than CP?) .... Yes
Shortfall percentage (CP – AP) 3.0%

Step 4: Calculate SG shortfall for the quarter based on actual wages paid:
SG shortfall $20,000 x 3.0% $600.00
+ Administration fee $20.00
+ Nominal interest $600 x 10% x 151/365 .... $24.82
SGC $644.82

19.538   LODGING A SUPERANNUATION GUARANTEE CHARGE STATEMENT

An SGC statement must be lodged by the due date for each quarter where there is an SG shortfall (see table below). The statement must show:

- employer's name and postal address
- name, postal address (if known) and TFN of any employee with a shortfall
- amount of the overall shortfall
- late payment election amount (if any)
- late payment offset amount (if any)
- total of all individual shortfalls
- the amount of nominal interest
- the administrative components, and
- the SGC payable.

SGC statement due dates	
SG quarter	**Due date to lodge SG statement and pay SGC if SG not paid by due date**
1 July – 30 September	28 November in the next quarter
1 October – 31 December	28 February in the next quarter
1 January – 31 March	28 May in the next quarter
1 April – 30 June	28 August in the next quarter

19.539   RECORD KEEPING

SG records must be in writing (or convertible into writing, eg. computer records) and kept for five years, including:

- individual employee guarantee shortfalls
- interest component for each employee, and
- overall administrative component.

19.540   ADDITIONAL PENALTIES AND CHARGES

The penalties that may be imposed on employers for breaches of their SG obligations can include the following.

PART 7 ADDITIONAL SGC

Part 7 of the SGAA92 (s59 to s62A) imposes, by way of penalty, an additional SGC where an employer fails to provide when and as required:

- a SG statement for a quarter, or
- information relevant to assessing the employer's liability to pay the SGC for a quarter.

The Part 7 penalty will commonly apply in two situations:

- lodgment by an employer of an SG statement for a quarter, which is deemed by SGAA92 s35 to be an assessment of the liability for SGC, but the SG statement is lodged after the due date for lodgment, and
- default assessment for a quarter where the Commissioner assesses the employer's liability for SGC under SGAA92 s36: (a) when an employer fails to lodge an SG statement or provide information relevant to the assessment of the SGC, or (b) when an employer provides information relevant to the SGC assessment after the due date for lodgment of the SG statement.

Under Part 7, an employer is liable to pay, by way of penalty, additional SGC equal to double the SGC payable by the employer for the quarter (s59(1)). The additional SGC is worked out without taking into account the entitlement to an offset under SGAA92 s23A (ie. where an employer's late contributions are offset against their SGC liability) (s62A).

Also see PS LA 2011/28 which provides guidelines to tax officers for the remission, in whole or part, of the additional SGC imposed under s59(1) of the SGAA92.

ADMINISTRATIVE PENALTY FOR FAILING TO PROVIDE SG STATEMENT

An administrative penalty is imposed where an employer fails to lodge a SG statement by the due date and the Commissioner is required to determine the employer's tax-related liability (ie. the SGC) without the assistance of the statement (TAA53 Sch 1 s284-75(3)). The base penalty amount is 75% of the SGC penalty.

GENERAL INTEREST CHARGE

If the SGC is not paid by the due date, a deductible interest charge accrues on the total shortfall component, (excluding the administration and nominal interest components) from the original due date until payment is made. This applies even if the employer has been granted a payment extension to pay the SGC. The Tax Office can reduce this if that is fair and reasonable or there are special circumstances.

19.541   WHERE DOES THE SHORTFALL GO?

The Tax Office must notify employees in writing of their shortfall component entitlements if their entitlement is more than $20. Each employee's shortfall plus the interest calculated (but not the administration or shortfall penalty component) is paid into a CSF or RSA provider of the employee's choice, or to the Superannuation Holding Accounts Special Account (SHASA). The employee can leave the amount in the SHASA or request a trustee of a CSF or a RSA provider to collect the shortfall component.

If the amount is under $1,000, that CSF or RSA provider must have elected to protect superannuation accounts of less than $1,000. If the employee has retired permanently after preservation age or due to permanent disability the amount can be paid directly to the employee. If the employee has died the amount can be paid directly to his or her LPR.

19.542   MAKING DEFAULT SG CHARGE ASSESSMENTS

Practice Statement Law Administration PS LA 2007/10 outlines when a default assessment can be made under s36 of the SGAA92 and the factors the commissioner will consider in making the default assessment. The practice statement provides that before making s36 default assessments, the following points would be considered:

- where an employer has given the Commissioner an SGC statement that indicates that an employer has an SG shortfall for a quarter, the Commissioner cannot make a default assessment under s36 of the SGAA92. However, subject to s37 of the SGAA92, the Commissioner may amend any assessment by making any alterations or additions that the Commissioner thinks necessary. This includes an SGC statement given to the Commissioner by an employer and a previous default assessment
- with very limited exceptions, employers would be informed of the Commissioner's intention to make a default assessment, as well as the basis upon which it will be calculated, prior to the assessment being made, and
- should an employer lodge an SGC statement after they have been advised of the Commissioner's intention to make a default assessment, then a default assessment cannot be made. However, an amended assessment can be issued under s37 of the SGAA92.

19.543   RECOVERY OF SUPERANNUATION ENTITLEMENTS

FROM FAILED COMPANIES

As a result of changes to the *Corporations Act 2001* that came into effect from 31 December 2007, employees of companies that go into liquidation, voluntary administration or receivership will stand a better chance of receiving their superannuation entitlements. Under the changes, the SGC must be paid before payments to ordinary unsecured creditors. This means it will rank equally with employees' entitlements for wages as long as there are assets available for distribution to priority creditors.

FROM BANKRUPTCIES

The SGC receives priority in bankruptcy under s109(1C) of the *Bankruptcy Act 1966*. The SGC is included in the category of employee entitlements that includes salary, wages and commissions.

19.560 CHOICE OF FUND

Since 1 July 2005 under the *Choice of fund* (Choice) regime, employers have been obliged to provide most employees with the right to choose the superannuation fund into which their compulsory employer Superannuation Guarantee (SG) contributions are paid. The Choice regime is designed to complement the SG system (see 19.500).

 The Choice of fund rules do not apply to employees specifically excluded from the SG system.

Employers must identify eligible employees, and provide them with a *Standard choice form* (NAT 13080) (see 19.564) and act on the employees' choice. Eligible members have the freedom to select a superannuation fund and products for their SG contributions and to rollover their existing superannuation assets into a fund of their choice. Where an employee does not choose an eligible fund or elects a Choice fund, an employer will comply with the Choice requirements by contributing to its default fund, which must offer a minimum level of death cover insurance for its employees (see 19.563).

 The Choice of fund *rules apply to the SG portion of superannuation contribution and not necessarily additional amounts under a salary sacrifice arrangement.*

The Choice legislation is primarily contained in Part 3A of the SGAA92, which in turn provides for several key Choice measures that are prescribed under the SGAR93.

Since 1 July 2006 a larger range of employees are covered by new amendments to the Choice legislation to exercise Choice in relation to where their SG contributions were placed. This resulted from changes to workplace relations and complements the initial Choice legislation that was introduced on 1 July 2005 for those under federal awards. Under these changes employees of incorporated businesses employed under State awards may choose their superannuation fund for SG contributions.

19.562   EMPLOYEES AND CHOICE

Since 1 July 2005, many employees have been able to choose the superannuation fund or Retirement Savings Account (RSA) that will receive their superannuation contributions under the Superannuation Guarantee (SG) scheme. Choosing a superannuation fund was also extended in July 2006 to include employees working for corporations under former state awards.

ELIGIBILITY REQUIREMENTS

Employees will generally be eligible to choose a superannuation fund if:
- their superannuation is paid under a federal award or a former state award, now known as 'notional agreement preserving state award', or
- they are employed under another award or agreement that doesn't require superannuation support, or
- they are not employed under any award or industrial agreement (including contractors paid principally for their labour).

Employees may not be eligible under the SG scheme to choose a superannuation fund if:
- their superannuation is paid under a state award or industrial agreement, or
- their superannuation is paid under certain workplace agreements although choice can also be provided under these awards and agreements, or
- they are in a particular type of defined benefit fund or have already reached a certain level of benefit in that superannuation fund.

Some Federal and State public sector employees are also excluded from Choice of fund.

OPTIONS FOR ELIGIBLE EMPLOYEES

If an employee is eligible to choose a fund, their employer should give them a *Standard choice form* (NAT 13080) (see 19.564) within 28 days of when they start work. The form sets out the employee's options for choosing a superannuation fund.

If an employee receives a *Standard choice form* (NAT 13080) (see 19.564) from their employer they have two options:

- **Option 1**: Stay with the employer's superannuation fund. If an employee does not make a choice, their employer's superannuation contributions will be paid into a fund chosen by their employer.
- **Option 2**: Choose a new superannuation fund. An employee can choose the superannuation fund they want their employer superannuation contributions paid to.

 Employees may also be able to choose how their savings are invested. Some fund investment strategies offer higher returns with higher risks, while others offer greater security but with lower returns.

An employee is not obliged to choose a superannuation fund if they do not want to. If the employee does not make a choice, their employer's superannuation contributions will be paid into a fund chosen by their employer. An employer chosen fund may be suitable for the employee's current needs. Employees can choose a fund later if they like. While an employee can choose a fund at anytime, their employer is only required to act on one of the employee's choices in a 12 month period.

An employee may choose a Self Managed Superannuation Fund (SMSF) as their chosen fund.

19.563   EMPLOYER OBLIGATIONS UNDER CHOICE

Many employees are able to choose the fund into which their employer superannuation contributions are paid. From 1 January 2014, employer contributions for employees who have not chosen a super fund must be made to a fund that offers a MySuper product in order to satisfy a requirement in respect of their SG obligations (see 19.285).

REQUIRED STEPS

There are three steps that employers need to follow in order to meet their obligations when a new employee starts work.

Step 1: Identify new eligible employees

Not everyone is eligible to choose a superannuation fund. It generally depends on the type of award or industrial agreement that the employee is employed under. If an employer does not have any eligible employees, they do not need to do anything further.

 When a new member of staff is employed the employer must check their eligibility for 'choice'.

Eligibility

Employees can generally choose their superannuation fund if they are:

- employed under a federal award
- employed under a former state award, now known as a 'notional agreement preserving state award'
- employed under another award or agreement that doesn't require superannuation support, or
- not employed under any state award or industrial agreement (including contractors paid principally for their labour).

Ineligibility

An employee may be ineligible under the SG scheme to choose a superannuation fund if they are:

- paid superannuation under a state award or industrial agreement or under certain workplace agreements and collective agreements (although Choice can also be provided under these awards or agreements), or
- In a particular type of defined benefit fund or they've already reached a certain level in a defined benefit fund.

Some federal and state public sector employees are also excluded from Choice.

Step 2: Provide a 'Standard choice form' to new employees who are eligible to choose a superannuation fund

If a new employee is eligible to choose a superannuation fund, their employer should provide them with a *Standard choice form* (NAT 13080) (see 19.564) within 28 days from the day they started work.

 Although new employees are not required to complete the form if they don't want to nominate a fund, employers still have to give them the choice if they are eligible.

If an employee does not choose a fund, employers must pay that employee's superannuation contributions into the fund that the employer has identified as the employer nominated fund (see below). This fund is also known as the 'default fund'.

Employers must also provide a *Standard choice form* within 28 days if:

- an existing eligible employee asks them for a *Standard choice form* (see 19.564)
- they are unable to contribute to an employee's chosen fund, or it is no longer a CSF fund, or
- the employer changes their nominated fund.

Step 3: Act on the employee's choice

Once an eligible employee chooses a superannuation fund, employers have two months to arrange to pay contributions into that fund. After this time, any superannuation contributions must be paid to the employee's chosen fund. Employers need to start paying superannuation contributions to their employer nominated fund, if:

- an employee does not choose a fund within 28 days, or
- the employer has not accepted the employee's Choice because the employee has not yet provided all the information the employer needs.

 An employer-nominated fund must offer minimum life insurance for members.

 Employers who don't meet their obligations, including paying employee superannuation contributions to the correct fund, may face penalties (see below).

EMPLOYER-NOMINATED FUNDS

An employer-nominated fund is the fund employers pay an employee's SG contributions to if the employee does not choose a fund. The employer nominated fund must be a CSF and also offer a minimum level of life insurance (see below), as set out in the regulations (with some exceptions).

These requirements apply if employers:

- continue to make contributions to their existing nominated fund, or
- choose a new employer-nominated fund.

The funds that employers currently pay employee superannuation contributions to is likely to meet these requirements. However, employers need to make sure it does by checking with the trustee or the authorised representative of the fund. Similarly, employers who are considering a new employer-nominated fund should first check with the trustee of that fund to ensure they meet the requirements.

 It is illegal for a superannuation fund to provide benefits to employers as an incentive to use their fund as the employer's nominated fund.

INSURANCE REQUIREMENTS

An employer nominated fund must offer minimum life insurance death cover to members. The insurance cover must comply with the following requirements:

- a premium of at least $0.50 per week for those under 56 years of age, or
- the level of insurance cover must equal or exceed that shown in the table below, or
- if the contributions are made to a defined benefit fund on behalf of a defined benefit member, the cover must equal or exceed that detailed in the table below.

Age range	Level of insurance	Age range	Level of insurance
0 to 19	$-Nil	40 to 44	$20,000
20 to 34	$50,000	45 to 49	$14,000
35 to 39	$35,000	50 to 55	$7,000

NOTE: The *Superannuation Legislation Amendment Regulation 2013 (No 1)* was registered on 4 March 2013 to implement aspects of the *Stronger Super* reforms. The amendments to the *SIS Regulations and Corporations Regulations 2001* cover *MySuper* transfers and include a prohibition on self-insurance while also restricting the types of insurances that are offered within a super fund. Funds that are self-insuring at 1 July 2013 have 3 years until 1 July 2016 to set in place external insurance arrangements. Self-insurance may be continued during this period, including for new members of these funds. Accordingly, regulation 9A of the SGA Regulations, which details the requirements for insurance in respect of death, is amended. This involves a reference to actually providing death benefits in respect of *MySuper* members (other than members who are also defined benefit members), rather than merely offering death benefits (which would apply in respect of other members).

INSURANCE EXEMPTIONS

There are some instances where employer-nominated superannuation funds do not need to meet life insurance requirements, for example if employers:

- are making contributions under a federal award
- arrange insurance cover for their employees outside the superannuation system that includes death cover that is at least equivalent to the minimum insurance requirements
- are unable to obtain insurance from the fund normally used in respect of a particular employee due to the employee's health, occupation or hours worked, or
- contribute to a fund whose governing rules were in place on 11 March 2005 and determined that an amount not less than $50,000 will be payable in respect of the death of an employee.

 If an employer nominated superannuation fund does not offer the minimum life insurance for members, employers will need to arrange insurance with another insurance provider.

EMPLOYER INFORMATION AND ADVICE

Employers can provide factual information to an employee about:

- what choosing a superannuation fund is about
- their obligations in relation to choosing a superannuation fund, and
- what the employee can do to nominate a superannuation fund as their chosen fund.

 Anyone providing financial advice is generally required by law to be licensed by the Australian Securities and Investments Commission (ASIC).

RECORD KEEPING

Employers must keep records that show they have met their obligations, including:

- records showing the *Standard choice form* (see 19.564) has been provided to all eligible employees
- details of employees who do not have to be offered Choice

- receipts or other documents issued by the superannuation fund showing that the employer has made superannuation contributions to an employees' chosen fund, and
- records confirming the employer nominated fund is a CSF and meets the life insurance requirements.

 Employer records about choosing a superannuation fund must be in English and kept for at least five years.

PENALTIES

Employers who do not meet their obligations, including paying their employee superannuation contributions to the correct fund may be liable for a 'Choice liability'.

The employer's quarterly SG shortfall payable to the Tax Office may be increased by 25%, which is calculated in accordance with the following formula:

25% x [Notional quarterly shortfall less SG shortfall]

'Notional quarterly shortfall' is the amount that would have been calculated if the no choice employer contributions had not been made (s19(1) SGAA92).

The 'Choice liability', part of the Superannuation Guarantee Charge (SGC) (see 19.530), is the penalty employers have to pay if they do not meet their obligations and applies when:

- the employer has paid SG contributions to a CSF for their employee, but not to the fund chosen by the employee, or
- the employer has not given their employee a *Standard choice form* (see 19.564) in the required timeframe.

To avoid paying the SGC, it is essential employers pay enough superannuation contributions to their employee's chosen fund (or to their employer nominated fund if applicable) by the quarterly cut-off dates (see 19.533).

 Employers will also be subject to the SGC if they impose a fee on employees for implementing 'Choice of fund'.

There is a $500 cap on the amount of 'Choice penalty' for an employee. There may be a cap for either:

- a particular quarter, or
- a notice period which can consist of multiple quarters.

19.564   STANDARD CHOICE FORM

Employers are required to provide their employees with a Standard choice form (NAT 13080) that also advises of the important matters they should consider before exercising choice. In-house documents may be used, but they must include all the details covered in the standard form and may be provided in hard copy or electronic form.

Where employees fail to make a selection, the onus is on the employer to nominate a fund. The proposed fund should also be able to provide a certain minimum level of Life Cover (see above).

 If a Retirement Savings Account (RSA) is the 'default fund' it may not offer insurance cover.

The *Standard choice form* (NAT 13080) includes the employer's name and employer's fund details and must indicate the fund into which the employee contribution is to be made if it is not the employer fund. Any change-of-fund of the employer fund since the previous contribution was made must be noted together with whether the contributions exceeded the normal 9.5% rate. Employees are not limited in the number of times they seek to make a new choice of fund selection, however employers need only respond to one selection in a 12 month period.

An employer must also give an updated 'Standard choice form' to an employee if the employer discovers that the fund specified in the original 'Standard choice form' is a fund to which the employer cannot contribute for the benefit of the employee. The updated 'Standard choice form' must be given within 28 days of the employer becoming aware that the employer cannot contribute to the fund first specified. This may be the case, for example, if the assets of the employee's chosen fund are frozen by APRA.

19.565 SMALL BUSINESS SUPERANNUATION CLEARING HOUSE

The Small Business Superannuation Clearing House (SBSCH) is a free service for employers with 19 or fewer employees. It used to be run through the Department of Human Services, but as of April 2014 has transferred to the Tax Office. Employers can make their contributions as a single electronic payment to the clearing house which then distributes the payments to employees' funds.

The service is optional. It's designed to reduce red tape and compliance costs for small businesses by letting employers pay their super guarantee contributions to a single location in one simple electronic transaction.

If a small business registers to use this service:

- the super guarantee contributions are counted as being paid on the date the clearing house accepts them (so long as the fund does not reject the payments), and
- a small business has 21 days to pass an employee's choice of fund on to the clearing house.

19.570 PORTABILITY

Portability refers to the ability of employees to rollover their existing accumulated superannuation assets from one CSF to another. This is subject to some limited exceptions (see below).

EXCEPTIONS

The compulsory portability of benefit rules do not apply in the following three situations:

- to unfunded PSS schemes, SMSFs or to member benefits paid as a pension (other than an allocated pension or account based pension), or
- in respect of a defined benefit component of a superannuation interest in a defined benefit fund, if the member holds the interest as an employee of an employer-sponsor of the fund.

19.572 'PORTABILITY FORM' TO TRANSFER SUPERANNUATION BETWEEN ACCOUNTS

The *Request to transfer whole balance of superannuation benefits between funds* (NAT 71223) (also known as the 'Portability form') can be used to transfer the whole balance of a superannuation account from one fund to another, not just a part of it. When requesting the transfer, a member must provide proof of identity, such as a driver's licence or passport. The form and identity documents need to be sent to either the transferor or transferee superannuation fund. Fund members need to be aware that transferring benefits out of a fund may close that account and therefore they should first check this with the fund that they are transferring benefits from.

 This form will NOT change the fund to which an employer pays an employee's contributions.

Individuals must complete a separate *Request to transfer whole balance of superannuation benefits between funds* (NAT 71223) for each transfer. Completed and signed forms, together with certified copies of proof of identity documents, may be sent to either fund.

Before an individual decides to transfer their super, it is advisable that they consider the following:

- which account will be used for future employer contributions (Note: Individuals wishing to change the fund into which their contributions are being paid, will need to speak to their employer about Choice or complete a *Standard choice form* (NAT 13080) (see 19.564)
- will their existing entitlements cease or decrease (eg. insurance cover for death, illness or accident), and
- will they have to pay administration, exit, withdrawal or entry fees.

The fund you are transferring to must be able to accept the transfer and be a CSF.

The existing fund that is subject to a transfer request has 30 days to make the transfer. The 30 day period starts once the individual has provided all the required information to the fund. Fund trustees must follow up any incomplete member requests for transfers within ten working days after receiving the request. If that information has not been received within ten working days after making the request, the trustee must make reasonable inquiries of the member to obtain the information.

19.573 TRANSFERS TO SMSFS

The *Request to transfer whole balance of superannuation benefits between funds* (NAT 71223) may be used to transfer benefits to an SMSF. Before doing so, there are some important things an individual needs to take into account. Individuals should be aware that SMSFs are subject to the same rules and restrictions as other funds when benefits are paid out. In particular, superannuation benefits in an SMSF must be 'preserved'. This means that the individual can't access their benefits until they reach preservation age and retire or meet another condition of release (see 19.700).

 The early release of preserved superannuation benefits can only occur in very limited and tightly restricted circumstances.

 Taxpayer Alert TA 2009/1: Superannuation Illegal Early Release Arrangements *describes arrangement incorrectly offering people early release of their preserved superannuation benefits prior to retirement without meeting statutory conditions for such release. Significant penalties apply to trustees for the illegal early release of benefits. See 19.250.*

The trustee of the fund from which individuals are transferring their benefits may be able to request further information about:

- the individual's status as a member
- whether the individuals is a trustee or a director of a corporate trustee of an SMSF, and
- any multiple transfer requests to SMSFs.

 Penalties may apply for providing false or misleading information.

The *Request to transfer whole balance of superannuation benefits between funds* (NAT 71223) cannot be used to:

- transfer part of the balance of a superannuation account
- transfer benefits whose location is not known
- transfer benefits from multiple funds (separate forms must be completed for each fund from which benefits are to be transferred)
- transfer benefits where certain conditions or circumstances don't allow it, for example, if there is a 'Superannuation Agreement' under the Family Law Act 1975 in place
- open a new superannuation account in the target fund, or
- change the fund into which the employer pays contributions on the employee's behalf.

19.580 SMALL AMOUNTS OF EMPLOYER SUPERANNUATION

Superannuation entities are required to protect certain small superannuation account balances from being reduced by fund charges. Funds that do not meet the rules cannot accept, or hold small compulsory employer contributions. These rules only protect small superannuation balances of less than $1,000.

Any individual with an account balance of less than $1,000 in a superannuation fund that has arisen from superannuation guarantee or award contributions, has that balance protected from administrative fees and charges that exceed the investment earnings. Small superannuation amounts are still reduced by:

- tax and the superannuation contributions surcharge tax if applicable
- insurance premiums, and
- fund losses, including where investment earnings are not enough to pay the fund's total administration costs.

Superannuation funds can either:

- elect to protect superannuation accounts of less than $1,000, or
- not protect such amounts.

Funds which cannot protect these small superannuation amounts:

- cannot accept small superannuation payments for members, and
- must transfer existing balances of less than $1,000 to a fund which will 'member protect' (eg. to an eligible rollover fund).

Superannuation Industry (Supervision) Amendment Regulation 2013 (No. 2) was registered on 16 May 2013.

The Regulation implements a recommendation of the Super System Review to repeal the member protection standards in the *Superannuation Industry (Supervision) Regulations 1994 (SIS Regulations),* with effect from 1 July 2013.

This is necessary because MySuper, which commenced on 1 July 2013, requires that all MySuper members be charged fees on the same basis, a requirement that cannot be met at the same time as the member protection standards, which require fees for small balances to not exceed the investment earnings on the overall account.

From 1 July 2013, superannuation funds transfer small inactive accounts to the Tax Office, which will protect these accounts from being eroded by fees and charges. Interest will be paid on these accounts at a rate equivalent to Consumer Price Index measure of inflation. Members may reclaim these account balances from the Tax Office.

19.590 RETIREMENT SAVINGS ACCOUNTS

Banks, building societies, credit unions and life assurance companies (life offices) can establish Retirement Savings Accounts (RSAs) to provide superannuation services without the need for a trust structure.

RSAs must comply with the following regulations that apply to other superannuation funds:

- must be capital guaranteed
- can only be opened and maintained in the name of individual beneficiaries
- may offer life and disability cover
- are fully portable, and owned and controlled by the member
- are subject to the retirement standards including the preservation rules, and
- must offer protection for small accounts (see 19.580).

PRUDENTIAL SUPERVISION

Contributions to:

- bank RSAs form part of the bank's deposit base and balance sheet and are subject to the prudential rules
- RSAs operated by building societies and credit unions are subject to the prudential framework of the Australian Financial Institutions Commission (similar to those that operate for banks)
- life office RSAs are channelled directly into a life office statutory fund and are subject to prudential supervision and the prudential framework that currently applies to their other business.

PRUDENTIAL STANDARDS

Contributions

Employers may open RSAs for their employees to meet superannuation guarantee obligations, but only after meeting the employer obligations under choice of fund rules (see 19.560). RSAs can also accept spouse contributions including those made for non working and low income spouses (see 19.074).

Regulations have been amended to allow RSA institutions to accept personal contributions for those aged over 65 and under 70 without the individual having to meet the 'gainful employment test' (see 19.015) when they are contributing to a First Home Saver Account (FHSA) (see 19.280).

Investment restrictions

RSA account holders cannot secure loans against the assets held in an RSA account. RSAs offered by banks are not permitted to allow account linking or any interest offset arrangements. Part or all of an account balance to another RSA or superannuation fund can be transferred on the request of the account holder.

Returns and investment rules

All RSAs must be capital guaranteed (ie. the institution required to guarantee the member's capital and any returns credited to the member's account). RSA providers must provide account holders with details of the returns on RSA accounts so that they can be compared with other products. An annual report, similar to those required by other superannuation funds must also be given to RSA account holders.

Because of the lower expected returns on RSAs, the institutions must advise the account holder of alternative higher yielding superannuation investment opportunities when the RSA account balance reaches $10,000.

Benefit payment rules

Retirement benefits form part of a person's reasonable benefit limit. Payouts can only be made as lump sums or allocated pensions (see 19.660: *Rollovers*).

Disclosure to account holders

Information must be provided to account holders, including:

- annual account balance
- amount deposited
- annual and historic earnings
- crediting rates
- fees and charges, and
- point of sale information explaining main features/benefits of RSAs (including fees and charges).

Protection for small accounts

RSA fees and charges (other than tax) cannot exceed the interest credited to the account where an account has a balance of less that $1,000 (see from 19.580).

TAX TREATMENT FOR RSAS

RSAs are taxed at the same rates as superannuation funds. Employer and personal contributions for which a deduction is claimed, as well as untaxed amounts rolled over into RSAs and the net earnings of the RSA are taxed at 15%.

The financial institution must withhold the tax on behalf of the account holder and credit a periodic payment (net of expenses) to the RSA account. That tax is then remitted to the Tax Office.

RSA ACCOUNT HOLDERS

When a withdrawal is made from an RSA, the account holder is taxed on the same basis as any other person receiving retirement benefits. The financial institutions must maintain records in relation to each account holder of non-concessional contributions.

19.600 TAXATION OF SUPERANNUATION BENEFITS

The taxation treatment of a superannuation benefit depends on whether it is paid from a taxed or untaxed source, the age of the recipient, whether the benefit is paid as a lump sum or as an income stream, whether the benefit contains a tax-free or a taxable component, and whether it is paid to a dependant or non-dependant.

NOTE: As announced in the May 2015 Budget, no new superannuation taxes are proposed by the government.

A superannuation benefit paid in breach of the legislative requirements is included in the assessable income of a member and taxed at ordinary tax rates (see Brazil v FC of T *(2012) AATA192). (Also see* Benefits paid in breach of payment rules *at the end of this section.)*

For the new powers to address non-compliance and illegal early release see 19.250.

TAXATION COMPONENTS OF A SUPERANNUATION BENEFIT

A superannuation benefit may be made up of:

- a tax-free component, and
- a taxable component which may include an element
  - taxed in the fund, and/or
  - untaxed in the fund.

Superannuation funds will need to calculate these components for each benefit that is paid. The proportioning rule is generally used to calculate the tax-free and taxable components of a benefit.

THE PROPORTIONING RULE

When a superannuation benefit is paid from a superannuation interest, the benefit will include both tax-free and taxable components calculated in the same proportion that they make up the total value of the superannuation interest.

CALCULATING THE TAX-FREE COMPONENT OF A SUPERANNUATION INTEREST

The tax-free component of a superannuation interest is the total value of the following segments:

- the contributions segment, and
- the crystallised segment.

Contributions segment

The contributions segment generally includes all contributions made from 1 July 2007 that have not been included in the assessable income of the fund (non-concessional contributions)

Rollover superannuation benefits are regarded as contributions. However, the taxable component of a rollover superannuation benefit is not included in the contributions segment.

Crystallised segment

The crystallised segment includes the following existing components of a superannuation interest that are consolidated into the tax-free component:

- the concessional component
- the post-June 1994 invalidity component
- undeducted contributions
- the capital gains tax (CGT) exempt component, and
- the pre-July 83 component.

The crystallised segment is calculated by assuming that an Eligible Termination Payment (ETP) representing the full value of the superannuation interest is paid just before 1 July 2007.

When an untaxed superannuation fund crystallises these components there is no pre-July 1983 component when the taxable component consists solely of elements untaxed in the fund. The pre-July 83 component for an element untaxed in the fund is only calculated when a lump sum superannuation benefit is withdrawn or rolled over into a taxed fund.

CALCULATING THE TAXABLE COMPONENT OF A SUPERANNUATION INTEREST

The taxable component of the superannuation interest is calculated by subtracting the tax-free component from the total value of the superannuation interest. Although the taxable component can consist of an element taxed in the fund and/or an element untaxed in the fund, the taxable component of a superannuation interest in a taxed fund normally consists solely of an element taxed in the fund, whereas generally the taxable component of a superannuation benefit paid from an untaxed fund consists solely of an element untaxed in the fund.

APPLYING THE PROPORTIONING RULE WHEN PAYING A BENEFIT

When a superannuation benefit is paid from a superannuation interest, the benefit will include both tax-free and taxable components calculated in the same proportion that these components make up the total value of the superannuation interest.

Where the benefit is withdrawn as a lump sum, the proportions will be determined immediately prior to the withdrawal. However, where the benefit is withdrawn by way of an income stream, the proportions will be determined at the commencement of the income stream and continue to apply to all subsequent payments during the life of the income stream benefit.

Applying the proportioning rule when paying a benefit

Peter is 56 and withdraws a $50,000 lump sum from his taxed superannuation fund.

Just before this benefit is paid, he had a superannuation interest with a value of $400,000. The superannuation interest includes a tax-free component of $100,000, made up of a $5,000 contributions segment and a $95,000 crystallised segment.

What is the taxable component of his benefit?

Step 1: Calculate the tax free proportion of the interest.

Determine the tax-free component and value of Peter's superannuation interest just before the benefit is paid:

- *Tax-free component = $100,000; value of the interest = $400,000.*
- *The tax free proportion is $100,000/ $400,000 = 25%.*

Step 2: Calculate the taxable component of Peter's lump sum benefit

Apply the proportioning rule to the lump sum payment to determine the tax-free component of Peter's lump sum as follows:

- *Lump sum amount is $50,000, and tax free proportion is 25%.*
- *The tax-free amount of the lump sum benefit is $50,000 x 25% = $12,500.*

The taxable component of Peter's lump sum benefit is therefore ($50,000 - $12,500) = $37,500.

Modifications to the proportioning rule for a disability superannuation lump sum benefit

To determine the tax-free component of a disability superannuation lump sum benefit, a modified version of the proportioning rule is used. This approach calculates the tax free component as above, without any modification. It also calculates an amount equal to the benefit multiplied by the prospective days to retirement divided by the service period plus prospective days to retirement. The larger amount is used as per s307-145 ITAA97.

Modifications to the proportioning rule for superannuation lump sum benefits paid from an untaxed source and includes a pre-July 1983 component

To determine the tax-free component of a superannuation lump sum benefit paid from a superannuation interest that existed just before 1 July 2007, a modified version of the proportioning rule is used to take into account the crystallisation of the pre-July 83 component (s307-150 ITAA97). In this case, the tax-free component of the benefit is increased, and the element untaxed is decreased, by the lesser of the amounts in (i) and (ii) as follows:

(i)   (Original tax-free component and untaxed element) x (Number of pre-July 1983 days in service period) divided by (Total number of days in service period), and

(ii)   The amount of the element untaxed in the fund.

TA 2009/10: Non-commercial use of negotiable instruments involving SMSFs

This Taxpayer Alert describes arrangements involving the non-commercial use of negotiable instruments, some of which include the trustee of an SMSF giving a promissory note to a member to pay a benefit. The Tax Office considers such arrangements give rise to breaches of the benefit payment standards under SISA93 and SISR94.

PAYG WITHHOLDING REQUIREMENTS

Applies to all funds

A superannuation fund must withhold tax from Superannuation Lump Sum (SLS), Superannuation Income Stream (SIS) and Superannuation Death Benefit (SDB) payments in accordance with rates set out in the withholding schedules for the year. PAYGW Schedules 33 and 34 set out the rates applicable for SLSs and SISs respectively. These schedules are also relevant to SDBs.

 The failure by a member to provide a TFN can require a fund to withhold 46.5% from the taxable component of a SLS or SIS.

 Superannuation funds required to withhold an amount must do so when making the relevant payment.

Medicare levy increase to fund Disability Care Australia

From 1 July 2014, the Medicare levy rate increases from 1.5 to 2% of taxable income for the 2014-15 and later income years. This increase will also have consequential changes for legislation that reference the Medicare levy rate. The money raised from the increase will be placed into a DisabilityCare Australia Fund for ten years, which will only be drawn upon to fund the additional costs of delivering the NDIS.

The measure received Royal Assent on 28 May 2013.

Certain consequential effects of the increase in the Medicare rate include:

- super income stream benefits having a taxable portion and paid to individuals under age 60 where the taxable portion of the pension payment is taxed at marginal tax rates plus Medicare levy, with a 15% tax offset (see below)
- the tax payable on the taxable component of a super lump-sum payment to individuals under age 60 (see 19.600
- for individuals aged from preservation age, to under age 60 – the rate increases from 16.5% to 17% on the taxable component above the low rate cap amount
- the rate paid on lump sum benefits increases for taxpayers under preservation age from 21.5% to 22% on the entire taxable component
- the rate on excess non-concessional contributions will increase from 46.5% to 47%, with a further impact from the May 2014, Budget Repair levy of 2%, increasing the rate to 49%. The Budget Repair levy applies for 3 years from 1 July 2014 to 30 June 2017, and
- tax on super death benefits paid directly to non-dependents increases from 16.5% to 17%.

SMSFs only

SMSF trustees should not overlook their PAYGW obligations when paying a benefit. If an SMSF trustee does not comply with these requirements, the fund may incur a penalty.

For a fund that is required to withhold an amount from the benefit paid to a member, it needs to register for PAYGW as soon as it is known the payment will be made.

 Not all payments that an SMSF makes to a member will require amounts to be withheld or reported, as some payments are tax-free.

Where an SMSF has issued payment summaries, it also needs to lodge a payment summary annual report with the Tax Office by 14 August after the end of the financial year in which the payment(s) were made.

SMSFs can lodge their payment summary annual report in paper form using *PAYG withholding payment summary statement* (NAT 3447) or electronically.

SUPERANNUATION LUMP SUMS

Superannuation lump sums (SLSs) are superannuation benefits that are paid in the form of a lump sum. The PAYGW rate applied depends upon the age of the member, the amount of any taxed and/or untaxed elements, the quotation of a TFN and whether or not the member is suffering from a terminal illness.

Before paying an SLS, a *Superannuation lump sum pre-payment statement* (NAT 70764) form should be completed.

 The tax-free component of a SLS is Non-Assessable Non-Exempt (NANE) (see explanation below) income and not subject to PAYGW.

NOTE: NANE income is ordinary or statutory income that is expressly made not assessable income and not exempt income (s6-23 ITAA97). This income category was introduced in 2003 in order to prevent any overlap between various income categories. NANE income does not affect an individual's tax-free threshold.

The following table lists the PAYGW rates applicable to SLSs paid from the taxed and untaxed elements of the taxable component and incorporates the May 2014 Budget changes for an increase in the top marginal tax rate to 47% from 1 July 2014 and the higher Medicare levy of 2% from 1 July 2014.

Member age	Taxed element [4]	Untaxed element [4]
Any age where an eligible terminal illness	No tax withheld	No tax withheld
Below preservation age	22% for 2015-16 & 2014-15 [1,2,4]	32% for 2015-16 & (2014-15), on amounts up to the untaxed plan cap of $1.395 million ($1.355 million) [1,2,3,4] 49% for 2015-16 & (2014-15), on amounts above the untaxed plan cap of $1.395 million ($1.355 million) [1,2,3,4]
Preservation age to less than age 60	0% up to the low rate cap of $195,000 for 2015-16 ($185,000 for 2014-15) [1,2] 17% on amounts above the low rate cap of $195,000 for 2015-16 ($185,000 for 2014-15) [1,2]	17% tax up to low rate cap of $195,000 ($185,000) for 2015-16 & (2014-15). [1,2,3,4] 32% on amounts above the low rate cap of $195,000 ($185,000) for 2015-16 & (2014-15) up to the untaxed plan cap of $1.395 million ($1.355 million). [1,2,3,4] 49% for 2015-16 & (2014-15) on amounts above the untaxed plan cap of $1.395 million ($1.355 million) [1,2,3,4]
Age 60 and over	Tax-free	17% for 2015-16 & (2014-15), tax up to untaxed plan cap of $1.395 million ($1.355 million) [1,3,4] 49% for 2015-16 & (2014-15), on amounts above the untaxed plan cap of $1.395 million ($1.355 million) [1,3,4]

1: Assumes the member is a resident individual for tax purposes and subject to the Medicare levy of 2% for 2015-16 & 2014-15 (1.5% for 2013-14 and previous years).

2: If at the time of payment the member has not provided a TFN and they are under 60, the fund must withhold 49% from 1 July 2014 (46.5% for 2013-14 and previous years) from the taxable component.

3: If at the time of payment the member has not provided a TFN, the fund must withhold 49% from 1 July 2014 (46.5% for 2013-14 and previous years) from the taxable component if 60 or over.

4: A 2% Budget Repair levy applies to the top marginal tax rate for 3 years from 1 July 2014 to 30 June 2017 and a 0.5% higher Medicare levy applies for 2014-15 and subsequent years to fund NDIS (see 19.600).

TAX-FREE COMPONENT (S310-210 ITAA97)

The tax-free component of a SLS is made up of the certain components crystallised as at 30 June 2007 (the crystallised segment) and contributions made since 1 July 2007 that will not be included in the assessable income of the superannuation fund (the contributions segment).

PAYGW tax does not have to be withheld from the tax-free component even if the superannuation fund member fails to provide their Tax File Number (TFN).

TAXABLE COMPONENT (S310-215 ITAA97)

The taxable component is the balance remaining after deducting the tax-free component from the value of the SLS.

Superannuation lump sum payment

Ian and Christine are members of the Wood Family superannuation Fund (WFSF) and are aged 62 and 58 respectively. They have decided to retire and take some of their superannuation benefits as SLSs. According to their entitlements, Ian and Christine will both receive a SLS benefit of $300,000 from WFSF. Each SLS has a tax-free component of $20,000 and a taxable component taxed element of $280,000. WFSF is required to withhold an amount under the PAYGW system.

Ian and Christine have previously provided in writing their respective TFNs to WFSF.

WFSF does not need to withhold from the tax-free component of $20,000, but must withhold an amount from the taxable component taxed element of $280,000.

(a) *Amount to withhold for Ian. As Ian is over age 60, no part of his SLS payment is subject to PAYGW.*

(b) *Amount to withhold for Christine. As Christine is over her preservation age and under 60, she is entitled to the low rate cap.*

Step 1: Amount up to low rate cap $195,000 in 2015-16 ($185,000 in 2014-15), on which nil tax is payable.

Step 2: Amount above low rate cap ($280,000 – $195,000 = $85,000) in 2015-16, or ($280,000 – $185,000 = $95,000 in 2014-15) which is assessable

Step 3: Amount to withhold is 17% of $85,000 = $14,450 in 2015-16 (or 17% of $100,000 = $17,000 in 2014-15)

TAX TREATMENT FOR MEMBERS

If the marginal tax rate(s) applying to the lump sum is less than the rate of withholding applied to the payment, the member will only be taxed on their taxable component at the marginal tax rate.

If the member's marginal tax rate is higher than the rate of withholding applied to payment, the member will receive a tax offset to ensure the rate of tax on the taxable component does not exceed the rate of tax withheld.

PAYMENT SUMMARY

A superannuation fund that makes a SLS payment that is a withholding amount, must within 14 days provide a payment summary to the recipient and give a copy to the Tax Office (Schedule 1 s16-165 TAA53).

SUPERANNUATION INCOME STREAMS (SIS)

A SIS is a pension that is paid by a superannuation fund in line with legislated payment standards that apply from 1 July 2007. The relevant PAYGW rate depends on the recipient's age, the amount of the element taxed in the fund and of the element untaxed in the fund, and whether the recipient has quoted a TFN.

The tax-free component of a SIS is non-assessable non-exempt (NANE) income and not subject to PAYGW.

Taxation Ruling TR 2013/5 considers when a superannuation income stream (SIS) commences and when it ceases and, consequently, when a SIS is payable.

The following table lists the basic PAYGW requirements applicable to SISs paid from the taxed and untaxed elements of the taxable component. In some cases where tax must be withheld at Marginal Tax Rates (MTRs), but a tax-offset may be available to reduce the tax payable.

SUPERANNUATION INCOME STREAM WITHHOLDING AND TAX OFFSETS

Member age	Taxed element [4]	Untaxed element [4]
Below preservation age	Withheld at MTRs[1]	Withheld at MTRs
Preservation age to 59	Withheld at MTRs[2]	Withheld at MTRs
Age 60 and over	Tax-free	Withheld at MTRs[3]

1: 15% Tax Offset available if from a disability SIS.
2: 15% Tax Offset available.
3: 10% Tax Offset available.
4: If at the time of payment the member has not provided a TFN, fund must withhold top marginal tax rate plus Medicare levy from the taxable component.

SIS PAYEES TURNING 60

SIS payments from a taxed source are tax-free after the payee turns 60. To ensure that these payees do not have excessive PAYGW amounts withheld in the financial year they turn 60, the Tax Office has issued a withholding variation that provides:

- a formula to calculate the appropriate amount to withhold, or
- look-up tables to give the appropriate adjustment amount.

PAYMENT SUMMARY

A superannuation fund that makes a SIS payment that is a withholding amount during an income year must provide a copy of the payment summary by 14 July following the end of the financial year in which payments were made. However if a SIS recipient requests in writing for a payment summary prior to 9 June, the superannuation fund must provide a copy of the payment summary within 14 days of this request.

SUPERANNUATION DEATH BENEFITS (SDBS)

Benefits paid by a superannuation fund as the result of a member's death are called SDBs (s307-5 ITAA97). If a member dies on or after 1 July 2007, non-dependants and trustees of deceased estates may only receive Superannuation Death Benefit Lump Sums (SDBLSs). When a SDB is paid from a superannuation fund, PAYGW obligations will vary according to whether the payment is made in the form of a SDBLS or as a Superannuation Death Benefit Income Stream (SDBIS). Further variations in PAYGW obligations may occur depending on whether or not the payee meets the definition of a Death Benefit Dependant (DBD) (see next), the deceased's age, the recipient's age and the existence of any tax-free, taxed and untaxed amounts.

 Transitional arrangements apply to non-dependants who commenced a SDBIS prior to 1 July 2007. An SDBIS that was being paid to a non-dependant prior to 1 July 2007 is taxed in the same manner as a SDBIS paid to a dependant.

Surety for retirees

In the October 2012 MYEFO the government announced that it would introduce provisions to offer some surety for retirees and their dependants with the exempt current pension income (ECPI) provisions to continue to apply after the death of the member and until the death benefit was paid out as soon as practicable following the death. This has been achieved with the registration of *Income Tax Assessment (Superannuation Measures No. 1) Regulation 2013*.

Death benefits dependant

A Death Benefits Dependant (DBD) of a deceased member can be the deceased member's spouse or former spouse; or the deceased member's child aged less than 18; or any other person with whom the deceased member had an interdependency relationship or any other person who was a dependant of the deceased member just before he or she died (s302-195 ITAA97). The definition of 'dependant' for the purposes of the taxation of superannuation death benefits includes same-sex partners and their children (see 19.265).

In ATO ID 2011/83, the Tax Office held that, although the definition of 'spouse' was only amended to include same sex couples subsequent to the relationship ceasing, the taxpayer is a 'former spouse' of the deceased superannuation fund member in terms of s302-195(1)(a) of the ITAA97. The table below highlights the key PAYGW features relating to SDB payments.

Superannuation death benefits			
Age of deceased	Form of death benefit	Age of recipient	Taxation treatment
Dependant payments[1]			
Any age	Lump sum (SDBLS)	Any age	Taxable component (NANE income).
Aged 60 and above	Income stream (SDBIS)	Any age	Taxable component: Element taxed in the fund is tax-free (NANE income).
			Taxable component: Element untaxed in the fund is treated as assessable income. Dependant entitled to 10% tax offset.
Below age 60	Income stream (SDBIS)	Above age 60	Taxable component: Element taxed in the fund is tax-free (NANE income).
			Taxable component: Element untaxed in the fund is treated as assessable income. Dependant entitled to 10% tax offset.
		Below age 60	Taxable component: Element taxed in the fund is subject to MTRs and the dependant is entitled to a 15% tax offset.
			Taxable component: Element untaxed in the fund is subject to MTRs.

- SDB can be paid as a pension to a dependant if the member dies before commencing a pension. These pensions will be taxed in the same way as a reversionary pension.
- SDBs can be paid as a SDBIS to a dependant child, although when the child turns 25 the balance in the fund will have to be paid as a tax-free SDBLS unless the child has a permanent disability.

Non-dependant payments[1]			
Any age	Lump sum (SDBLS)	Any age	Taxable component: Element taxed in the fund is subject to 15% (add Medicare levy of 1.5% (2% from 2014-15) if recipient is also a resident for tax purposes).
			Taxable component: Element untaxed in the fund subject to 30% (add Medicare levy of 1.5% (2% from 2014-15) if recipient is also a resident for tax purposes).
Any age	Income stream (SDBIS)	Any age	Not applicable[2]. Income streams that had commenced prior to 1 July 2007 will be taxed as if received by a dependant.

1: The tax-free component is always tax-free.

2: From 1 July 2007 a SIS cannot revert to non-dependants as a SDB income stream. Payments to non-dependants will have to be made as a SDB lump sum.

NOTE: Medicare levy of 1.5% (2% from 2014-15)

PAYMENT SUMMARY

Superannuation death benefit lump sums

No payment summary is required where a superannuation fund makes a Superannuation Death Benefit Lump Sums (SDBLSs) to a DBD. Where a SDBLS is made to the deceased member's LPR, a payment summary should still be issued although there is no amount required to be withheld from the payment. However, the superannuation fund should still include the payment summary as part of its PAYG withholding payment summary annual report.

Superannuation death benefit income streams

The same PAYGW rules apply for Superannuation Death Benefit Income Streams (SDBISs) as for SISs.

ROLLOVERS

As a general rule, no PAYGW obligation arises from the rollover of a superannuation benefit, except where the benefit consists of an amount untaxed in the fund that is in excess of the member's untaxed plan cap of $1,395 million in 2015-16 and $1.355 million in 2014-15. The originating fund has a withholding obligation on the excess amount (Schedule 1 s12-312 TAA53) which is taxed at 49% in 2015-16 and 2014-15 inclusive of Medicare levy.

OTHER MATTERS

A superannuation fund as a benefit payer does not have to withhold tax from an amount that is exempt income or non-assessable non-exempt income (Schedule 1 s12-1(1) & (1A) TAA53).

 The taxed element of the taxable component of SLS paid after 1 July 2007 to a member over age 60 is treated as NANE income in the hands of the member recipient.

Benefits less than $200

A lump sum member benefit under $200 will be tax-free provided the following conditions are met:

- no other amount will be left in the individual's superannuation account upon payment of the lump sum, and
- the individual satisfies a condition of release, because either:
  - they were a lost member and have subsequently been found and the amount of the benefit is less than $200, or
  - they terminated gainful employment with a standard employer sponsor of the fund where their preserved benefit at the time of termination was less than $200.

 This information does not apply to payments from the Superannuation Holding Accounts Special Account (SHASA), Superannuation Guarantee Charge (SGC) payments (see 19.530) or Departing Australia Superannuation Payments (DASPs) (see 19.670).

Where an individual receives a lump sum benefit of less than $200 and satisfies the above requirements, the benefit is not assessable income and is not exempt income (ie. it is tax-free) (s301-225 ITAA97). As such, there is no requirement for the fund to withhold any tax from the payment, nor should the fund issue a payment summary and the individual is not required to report this benefit in their tax return.

Terminal illnesses (also see 19.680)

Changes have been made to the ITAA97, SISA93 and SISR94 that allow individuals with a terminal medical condition to access their benefits from their superannuation fund tax-free as from 1 July 2007.

 The Commissioner has also removed the requirement for payers to give payment summaries to eligible terminally ill members when they receive a SLS.

SUPERANNUATION LUMP SUM PRE-PAYMENT STATEMENT

A Superannuation lump sum pre-payment statement form (NAT 70764) (the statement) should be completed by a complying superannuation fund (CSF), approved deposit fund (ADF), retirement savings account (RSA) or annuity provider (the provider) if they need to inform a member that they have not met a condition for the release of funds, and need further instructions from their member about how to deal with these funds.

 A provider is not required to use this form before making a lump sum payment to a member. This statement is provided as a guide for funds on the sort of information they should be providing and receiving from their member prior to making a lump sum payment.

What parts need completing?

The provider must complete 'Part 1' of the statement by providing the amounts of each component of the superannuation lump sum. After this, the provider must send the statement to the member.

The member completes 'Part 2' of the statement by specifying whether they wish to:

- receive all or part of the superannuation lump sum in cash now, or
- roll over all or part of the superannuation lump sum
    - into a complying superannuation fund
    - into a complying ADF
    - into a RSA, or
    - to purchase a superannuation annuity.

The member should then return the completed statement to the provider.

How to complete Part 1 of the statement – Provider section

The provider should complete details about the superannuation lump sum payment, including the:

- date the calculation is valid until
- components of the lump sum, and
- preservation amounts of the lump sum.

The lump sum is made up of taxable and tax-free components. The tax-free component is made up of the contributions segment and the crystallised segment. The taxable component can be made up of:

- an element taxed in the fund, that is, the part of the taxable component that has been subject to tax in the fund, and
- an element untaxed in the fund, that is, the part of the taxable component that has not been subject to tax (for example, public sector funds or schemes established under a state act will generally have an element untaxed).

The preservation amount can include:

- preserved amounts
- restricted non-preserved amounts, and
- unrestricted non-preserved amounts.

Preserved and restricted non-preserved amounts generally cannot be taken as a cash payment. They can be rolled over into a member's superannuation account for their retirement or until they meet a condition of release and there are no cashing restrictions. The unrestricted non-preserved amount can be taken as a cash payment or rolled over into the member's superannuation account.

The provider should also complete the date the statement is issued to the member and the date the member is to return the completed statement.

 A provider does not need to send a copy of the statement to the Tax Office; however they should keep a copy of the statement for their records for a period of five years.

If a provider is instructed to:

- rollover all or part of the superannuation lump sum, they will need to fill in a *Rollover benefits statement* (NAT 70766) (see 19.660), or pay all or part of the lump sum in cash, they will need to complete a *PAYG payment summary – superannuation lump sum* (NAT 70947) approved form.

How to complete Part 2 of the statement – Member section

The member should work out how much of the lump sum they want paid as cash and write this amount at the appropriate label. If the member does not want any of the payment paid as cash they should leave this label blank.

The amount chosen to be paid as cash generally cannot be more than the unrestricted non-preserved amount on their statement.

 If a member chooses to receive their lump sum as a cash payment, they cannot change their mind to rollover this cash payment at a later stage.

If the member wishes to rollover part of their benefit, they should work out how much of the lump sum they want to rollover into a complying superannuation fund, complying ADF, RSA or to purchase a superannuation annuity. Also see 19.660 for more information on rollovers of superannuation benefits.

BENEFITS PAID IN BREACH OF PAYMENT RULES

Special taxation provisions contained in Division 304 of the ITAA97 apply when a superannuation benefit is paid in breach of the rules, so that instead of Division 301 or 302 of the ITAA97 applying, those contained in Division 304 apply in the following situations:

(a) a benefit is paid in breach of legislative requirements (see below), and

(b) a fund pays an amount in excess of the amount set out in a release authority.

The purpose of Division 304 is generally to override the concessional tax treatment that ordinarily applies to superannuation benefits if payments from complying funds are in breach of the payment rules and treat the superannuation benefit as assessable income of the member to be taxed at ordinary rates.

BENEFITS PAID IN BREACH OF LEGISLATIVE REQUIREMENTS

A superannuation benefit is included in the assessable income of a member and taxed at ordinary tax rates if:

- the member received the benefit from a complying superannuation fund, complying ADF or an RSA (or a fund or ADF that was previously complying), or the benefit is attributable to the assets of a complying superannuation fund, complying ADF or an RSA (or a fund or ADF that was previously complying), and

- when the benefit was paid, the fund was not maintained as required by s62, or the benefit was paid otherwise than in accordance with relevant payment standards prescribed under s31(1) and s32(1) (s304-10).

This could be the case, for example, if a member receives a payment without satisfying a condition of release or if the fund has not been maintained for the sole purpose of providing superannuation benefits to members.

The Commissioner has a broad discretion to decide that an amount is not to be included in a member's assessable income if satisfied that it would be unreasonable for it to be included (s304-10(4)).

In *Smith and The Commissioner of Taxation* (2011) AATA 563, the AAT affirmed the Commissioner's decision to refuse to exercise his discretion (conferred by s304-10(4) of the ITAA97), not to include super benefits which were paid to her by her SMSF (contrary to the payment standards prescribed under the SISA93), in her assessable income.

In *Mason v FC of T* (2012) AATA 133, the AAT held that a payment received by a taxpayer from an SMSF constituted an illegal early access to benefits in contravention of the SISA93. The AAT further held that the Commissioner had not acted unreasonably in refusing to exercise his discretion to exclude the payment from the taxpayer's assessable income.

19.660 ROLLOVERS

A rollover superannuation benefit that a person is taken to receive is not assessable and not exempt income (s306-5). A person is taken to have received a rollover benefit when it is made for the person's benefit or is made to another person or to an entity at the person's direction or request (s307-15).

A superannuation benefit is a rollover superannuation benefit (s306-10) if:
- it is a superannuation lump sum and a superannuation member benefit, and
- it is not a superannuation benefit of a kind specified in the regulations, and
- the benefit satisfies any of the following conditions:
  - it is paid from a complying superannuation fund or is an unclaimed money payment or it arises from the commutation of a superannuation annuity, and
  - it is paid to a complying superannuation plan or to an entity to purchase a superannuation annuity.

Where a 'roll-over superannuation benefit' is made, the paying fund must prepare a *Rollover benefits statement* (NAT 70944) approved form and send it to the receiving fund (or elsewhere if instructed) within seven days of paying the 'roll-over superannuation benefit' , and also send a copy of the statement to the individual within 30 days of paying the 'roll-over superannuation benefit' to the receiving fund. The statement may require the details of the value of the 'roll-over superannuation benefit', the tax-free component, the taxable component, the element taxed in the fund and the element untaxed in the fund. The Rollover benefits statement must be kept by the paying fund for five years. A copy does not have to be provided to the Tax Office.

 A 'superannuation member benefit' cannot be rolled over to a non-complying superannuation fund.

TAXATION IMPLICATIONS

The taxing of a 'roll-over superannuation benefit' is generally deferred until the amount is finally withdrawn from the receiving fund. Whilst held by the receiving fund, a 'roll-over superannuation benefit' that a person is taken to have received under s307-15, is generally not assessable and not exempt income under s306-5. A person is taken to receive a benefit under s307-15 when it is made for the person's benefit or is made to another person or to an entity (ie. the receiving fund) at the person's direction or request.

UNTAXED ELEMENTS

A 'roll-over superannuation benefit' is included in the assessable income of the receiving fund to the extent the benefit consists of an element untaxed in the fund and is within an individual's untaxed plan cap amount of $1,395,000 in 2015-16 and $1,355,000 in 2014-15 (Item 2 s290-190(1)).

Where an individual's 'roll-over superannuation benefit' consists of an 'excess untaxed roll-over amount' (ie. the amount above the individual's untaxed plan cap shown above, he or she is liable to pay income tax on the 'excess untaxed roll-over amount' (s306-15).

 The provisions relating to the taxing of 'excess untaxed roll-over amounts' do not apply where 'roll-over superannuation benefits' are transferred from one 'superannuation interest' to another 'superannuation interest' within the same plan (s306-15(1A)).

The paying fund (which would be an untaxed fund) is required to withhold tax on the 'excess untaxed roll-over amount' (Sch 1 s12-312 of the *Taxation Administration Act 1953*). Tax is imposed by the *Superannuation (Excess Untaxed Roll-over Amounts Tax) Act 2007* at the top marginal tax rate plus Medicare levy. Amounts that have been subject to 'excess untaxed roll-over amount tax' are not included in the assessable income of the receiving fund.

 SMSFs are not permitted to hold untaxed elements as part of a member's superannuation interest. Any untaxed element of a roll-over to the SMSF from a retail fund is subject to 15% tax in the year when it is received. The amount would

then form part of the taxed element of the taxable component for that member's accumulation superannuation interest in the fund.

RECORD KEEPING

The trustee can accept a benefit for a member directly from another superannuation fund by:

- electronic transfer, or
- a cheque from the payer solely to the nominated fund.

Rollover instructions must be given to the payer and a record of the instructions must be kept for five years (TD 98/26).

19.670 DEPARTING AUSTRALIA SUPERANNUATION PAYMENT

For Pay As You Go Withholding (PAYGW) rates and reporting obligations please see 5.200.

Under Australia's Superannuation Guarantee (SG) system, temporary resident visa holders who work in Australia will generally have superannuation contributions paid into a complying superannuation fund or Retirement Savings Account (RSA) on their behalf by their employers unless they are:

- paid less that $450 a month
- 70 years of age or over
- under 18 and working not more than 30 hours per week
- covered under a Bilateral Superannuation Agreement (BSA), or
- employed for domestic or private work for 30 hours a week or less.

Some temporary resident visa holders who have worked in Australia may be entitled to receive their superannuation benefits after they leave Australia in the form of a Departing Australia Superannuation Payment (DASP).

WHAT IS A DEPARTING AUSTRALIA SUPERANNUATION PAYMENT?

From 1 July 2007

A DASP is defined under s301-170 ITAA97 as a payment that:

- is paid in the form of a superannuation lump sum (s307-65)
- is paid to an individual who has departed Australia
- is paid in accordance with the SISA03, the *Retirement Savings Accounts Act 1997* (RSAA97), equivalent rules of an exempt public sector scheme or under s67A of the *Small Superannuation Accounts Act 1995* (SSAA95).

 Death benefits relating to temporary resident visa holders' superannuation paid by superannuation funds are not DASPs, but instead are paid under the 'death' condition of release and taxed as a death benefit superannuation lump sums (see 19.600).

ELIGIBILITY

A DASP can only be received by a person who:

- has worked in Australia while visiting as a temporary resident visa holder
- has a visa that has either expired or been cancelled, and
- has permanently departed Australia.

 Australian and New Zealand citizens, permanent Australian residents, Retirement visa holders and Investor retirement visa holders are all ineligible for a DASP, as these people have retirement options in Australia.

HOW TO APPLY FOR A DEPARTING AUSTRALIA SUPERANNUATION PAYMENT

Applying for a DASP is fairly straight forward. The applicant needs to provide the following:

- personal details such as name and date of birth
- passport number, and
- details of their superannuation fund or RSA.

(A separate DASP application must be completed by the temporary resident visa holder for each superannuation fund or RSA account held.)

The three methods of applying for a DASP are:

- using the Tax Office's online DASP system
- completing a paper application form, or
- completing an equivalent paper form from your superannuation fund or RSA provider.

When using the online system the applicants eligibility is confirmed electronically using a direct link between the Tax Office and the Department of Immigration and Multicultural and Indigenous Affairs (DIMIA). This system is free and operates 24 hours a day, seven days a week.

When a paper form is submitted, all relevant documentation to support your application must be attached. The procedure and necessary documentation to apply for a DASP differs depending upon whether or not the benefit is under $5,000 or not. A DIMIA application fee will apply for benefits greater than $5,000. Copies of the *Request for departing Australia superannuation payment – temporary resident form* (NAT 7204) can be downloaded from the Tax Offices website or by phoning the Tax Office on 13 10 20.

WHEN TO APPLY FOR A DEPARTING AUSTRALIA SUPERANNUATION PAYMENT

The earliest time that temporary resident visa holders can apply for a DASP is on the day they arrive in Australia. However, the key point is that the DASP application cannot be submitted until the applicant has departed Australia and their visa is inactive.

ROLE FOR TAX AGENTS

Duly authorised tax agents may lodge DASP applications on behalf of their clients. They must first ensure that they have also obtained access to the Tax Office's online DASP application system. As previously mentioned, the tax agent can commence the DASP application procedure for eligible clients regardless of whether their client has left Australia or is still currently working in Australia.

WHEN ARE DEPARTING AUSTRALIA SUPERANNUATION PAYMENT AMOUNTS REMITTED?

DASPs must be paid within 28 days of the super fund or RSA provider receiving a valid application.

TAXATION CONSEQUENCES

A DASP in the hands of the recipient is a superannuation benefit (s301-5), and will be subject to the normal rates of DASP withholding tax. The tax rate for the taxed element is 38% and for the untaxed element is currently 47%.

PAYGW PAYER OBLIGATIONS

For details of withholding requirements, see 5.321.

REPORTING OBLIGATIONS

By payers

A PAYGW payer must:

- report DASP payment summaries with PAYG withholding payment summaries using the *Pay as you go (PAYG) withholding payment summary annual report version 8.0* electronic report specification, and
- lodge the payment summary annual report electronically by 14 August after the end of the financial year.

By payees

As a DASP does not form part of assessable income and is treated as not assessable and non-exempt income, it does not need to be included in a temporary resident visa holder's tax return for Australian tax purposes.

 All unclaimed superannuation money payments (including former temporary resident payments) paid to the Tax Office are lump sum superannuation benefits and are not subject to the taxing provisions in the ITAA97 and the TAA53. Superannuation providers are not required to withhold tax from these payments even when they do not hold a tax file number for the member.

OTHER MATTERS

- scheduled statement due dates for lodgement and payment of temporary resident obligations are 30 April and 31 October of each year
- the DASP system is voluntary, and
- if a temporary resident visa holder's benefit is less than $200, they may be able to apply for that benefit under existing preservation rules and not use the DASP system.

 On 17 July 2014 a Registered Tax Agent on behalf of his client Mr. Wai Choy, a temporary resident visa holder aged 46, lodges an online DASP application with the Tax Office.
Mr. Choy's superannuation benefit from a taxed fund is $30,000 and consists of the following components:
- *Tax-free component: $5,000*
- *Taxable component: $25,000*

Shortly thereafter, the Tax Office electronically forwards the validated DASP application to the client's superannuation fund which in turn completes the following transactions on 10 August 2014:
- *withholds tax of $9,500 (ie. taxable component of $25,000 @ 38% PAYGW rate), and*
- *issues Mr. Choy a members benefit cheque for A$20,500.*

19.680 TERMINAL ILLNESS

A superannuation benefit paid to a person having a 'terminal medical condition' is non-assessable and non-exempt income (s303-10).

The benefit must be a lump sum superannuation member benefit which is:

- paid from a complying superannuation plan, or
- a superannuation guarantee payment, a small superannuation account payment, an unclaimed money payment, a superannuation co–contribution benefit payment or a superannuation annuity payment.

A 'terminal medical condition' exists in relation to a person at a particular time if:

- two registered medical practitioners have certified, jointly or separately, that the person suffers from an illness, or has incurred an injury, that is likely to result in the death of the person within a period (the certification period) that ends not more than 12* months after the date of the certification
- at least one of the registered medical practitioners is a specialist practising in an area related to the illness or injury suffered by the person, and
- for each of the certificates, the certification period has not ended.

The tax exemption applies if a 'terminal medical condition' exists when the person receives the lump sum or within 90 days after receiving it.

* The May 2015 Budget proposed that from 1 July 2015, the life expectancy period for full access to superannuation benefits for those with a terminal medical condition be extended from 12 to 24 months.

19.700 INCOME STREAMS

Key changes to superannuation that took effect from 1 July 2007 included the introduction of a new and more generous tax treatment of benefits received from superannuation funds and a more flexible regime associated with accessing benefits. For the taxation treatment of income streams see 19.600.

Superannuation benefits are designed primarily to provide a tax effective source of retirement income because retirees are unable to rely upon employment income for support in their old age. The minimum age when retirement can trigger access to preserved superannuation benefits is currently 55. Under transition to retirement arrangements 'limited' access to benefits is available from age 55, regardless of the member's retirement status.

PRESERVATION AGE

Preservation age is the minimum retirement age at which a superannuation fund member is normally able to access preserved benefits. The preservation age is currently 55, however as shown in the table below, it is gradually being increased so that it will ultimately be 60.

The preservation rules prevent early access to benefits. Benefits may only be accessed concessionally on reaching preservation age or if the member is terminally ill.

The progressive increase in preservation age reflects the calculus that those who were of age 35 or over on 1 July 1995 would retain the existing preservation age of 55. Those who were younger at that time would have a phased increase in preservation age as shown below. Those born on 1 July 1964 or later have a preservation age of 60. The change is such that by the year 2025, the preservation age or minimum retirement age will become 60. The table below shows birth date intervals in the range from birth dates before 1 July 1960, corresponding to a preservation age of 55 and birth dates on or after 1 July 1964 with a preservation age of 60. The corresponding preservation age ranges from 55 to 60 years.

Preservation age table	
Date of birth	Preservation age
Before 1 July 1960	55
1 July 1960 – 30 June 1961	56
1 July 1961 – 30 June 1962	57
1 July 1962 – 30 June 1963	58
1 July 1963 – 30 June 1964	59
1 July 1964 or later	60

COMPULSORY DRAWDOWN RESCINDED

Retirees may decide whether to commence taking their benefits or not, once they reach preservation age. Members holding superannuation assets may choose the manner in which the superannuation savings are managed and accessed. If being drawn down as a commutable income stream (eg. account based income stream) it may be stopped at any time after it has commenced and then converted to an accumulation account. It may then be re-commenced according to the member's needs. Note: A non-commutable income stream is generally not able to be paid out as a commutation.

FROM 1 JULY 2007

Benefits received from taxed superannuation funds by those who are age 60 or over are tax-free and classified as non-assessable and non-exempt income (also see 19.600). This applies to both existing and new pensions as well as to lump sum benefits and is of particular benefit to those in receipt of other assessable income since recipients can make use of the current individual income tax-free threshold of $18,200 and the lower marginal tax rates for such additional income They may also be able to qualify for a low income tax offset or other offsets provided through the tax system.

INCOME STREAMS

Income streams paid from retirement savings are referred to as pensions if paid by a superannuation fund and eligible annuities if paid by a life office. There are advantages for a recipient receiving retirement savings by way of income streams. When a superannuation fund account is in pension mode the earnings of the account are exempt from tax. For recipients who are at least 55 a 15% tax offset applies to the taxable or assessable income from the income stream. Upon reaching age 60 the income is tax-free however the tax free proportion of the interest is maintained for the duration of the pension (also see 19.600).

STOPPING AND STARTING AN INCOME STREAM

There are rules as to whether you are able to stop and start a superannuation income stream depending on whether you are receiving:

- an account-based superannuation income stream
- a non-account-based superannuation income stream, or
- a transition-to-retirement income stream.

If the rules allow, you can fully or partially commute a superannuation income stream to:

- stop or reduce an income stream
- purchase another income stream
- take the resulting lump-sum benefit in cash, or
- roll it back into the superannuation system.

If you commute your superannuation income stream and then decide to make further contributions to superannuation, you will be able to do so only if you are either under 65 years, or over 65 and meet the work test (see 19.015).

Also see Draft Taxation Ruling TR 2011/D3, which considers when a Superannuation Income Stream (SIS) commences and when it ceases and, consequently, when a SIS is payable.

For more information on this topic please refer to Taxpayers Australia's *DIY Superannuation Manual*.

19.710 TRANSITION TO RETIREMENT INCOME STREAMS

Transition to retirement provisions allow members who have reached their preservation age (see 19.700), to access their benefits without having to retire or leave their job. This measure permits members to access their benefits by drawing down a non-commutable income stream called a Transition to Retirement Income Stream (TRIS).

For the taxation treatment of TRISs, see 19.600.

 From 1 July 2007, new rules apply to transition to retirement income streams. Income streams which commenced before 1 July 2007 and that complied with the transition to retirement rules at the time are deemed to satisfy the new requirements and may continue to be paid under the former rules.

A TRIS commencing on or after 1 July 2007 must satisfy the following requirements:

- it must be an account-based income stream. The account balance must be attributable to the recipient of the income stream
- the payment of a minimum amount to be made at least annually (see table at 19.720)
- the total payments made in a financial year must be no more than 10% of the account balance (at commencement and then at the start of each year)
- restrictions on the commutation of the income stream (except in limited circumstances)
- there is no provision made for an amount or percentage to be left over when the income stream ceases
- the income stream can be transferred only on the death of the member to one of their dependants, or cashed as a lump sum to a dependant, non-dependant or the pensioner's estate, and
- the capital value of the income stream and the income from it cannot be used as security for borrowing.

19.720 INCOME STREAM STANDARDS

Minimum pension or annuity standards must be met for income stream payments to qualify for various tax concessions.

MINIMUM STANDARDS FOR ACCOUNT BASED PENSIONS

NOTE: Pension drawdown relief measures (see below) apply to account based pensions.

The account based pension standard provides greater flexibility than was permitted under the previous pension standards, with a lower minimum and a higher allowed maximum. The age based lower limit is less than the previous allocated pension standard for maximum flexibility. The standard requires that at least the minimum amount (subject to pension drawdown relief – see below) be withdrawn each year and in keeping with current conventions at least a single drawdown must be made each year.

The maximum drawdown is 100% or the entire account balance. Different tax consequences follow depending on the member's age.

The minimum pension payment amount is a percentage of the account balance and varies with the member's age. Due to pension relief it may also vary with the year in which it is paid.

Account based pension drawdown standards	
Age	**2015-16**
Under 65	4%
65–74	5%
75–79	6%
80–84	7%
85–89	9%
90–94	11%
95 or older	14%

Megan is 66 and retired. She has an account base pension and the account balance on 1 July 2015 is $300,000. The minimum drawdown necessary for her to meet the pension standard, can be seen in the table above. Since she is age 66, the age band of 65 to 75 applies to her situation. She must withdraw a minimum of at least 5% of the account balance for the year.

In 2015-16 she withdraws 5% of her account balance or 5% x $300,000 = $15,000.

The flexibility offered to Megan by an account based pension is highlighted by the fact that she has a wide range of income she can receive during the year from her income stream (5% to 100%) of the account balance. She can vary her income quite considerably to meet unexpected financial contingencies that might arise.

Account based pension drawdown standard-including pension relief rates				
Age	**Min drawdown as a % of account balance for 1 July 2008 to 30 June 2011**	**Min drawdown as a % of account balance for 1 July 2011 to 30 June 2013**	**Min drawdown as a % of account balance from 1 July 2007 to 30 June 2008 & post 30 June 2013**	**Max drawdown as a % of account balance**
less than 65	2%	3%	4%	100%
65 to less than 75	2.5%	3.75%	5%	100%
75 to less than 80	3%	4.5%	6%	100%
80 to less than 85	3.5%	5.25%	7%	100%
85 to less than 90	4.5%	6.75%	9%	100%
90 to less than 95	5.5%	8.25%	11%	100%
95 and over	7%	10.5%	14%	100%

Angela, aged 60, is in receipt of benefits from an account based pension.
The account balance on 1 July 2012 is $750,000. In the 2012-13 year, pension drawdown
relief applies. The minimum pension payment to be made is arrived at from the table above.
The percentage that applies is 3%. It is therefore necessary that she draws down 3% x
$750,000 = $22,500.

EXISTING NON-COMMUTABLE PENSIONS

Generally, existing complying non-commutable pensions, namely market linked pensions (MLPs) (see below) and defined benefit pensions (DBPs) (see below), must continue for the duration of their term. Such pensions may not be commuted or rolled into account based pensions. They retain any asset test exempt status that might have applied for Centrelink benefit purposes (whether 50% or 100%).

PREVIOUSLY COMMENCED ALLOCATED PENSIONS

The provisions enable any existing allocated pensions to be converted directly into account based pensions to follow the account based pension standard introduced on 1 July 2007. For pensions that were commenced earlier and where members preferred to draw down according to a previous allocated pension table, this is permitted. All old tables meet the requirements for account based pensions.

For SMSFs, the trust deed should include provisions that allow for the payment of an allocated pension to be continued to be paid as an account based pension.

DEATH BENEFITS

Paid to dependants

Following the death of a beneficiary, pension payments would only be able to revert to a single dependant, who may subsequently fully cash out the benefit or access a reversionary pension. This would be paid in line with the Account based pension rules. However if the reversion occurs from a non-commutable pension then the structure of that pension must be retained. Typically this would be a complying pension as in a defined benefit pension or a market linked pension.

Paid to non-dependants

Non-dependants may only receive superannuation benefits when they are paid as lump sum benefits. When it is paid the benefit must leave the superannuation environment with any taxes paid where applicable. For these benefits to be re-introduced into the superannuation environment they will be subject to the contributions provisions including the relevant caps.

NOTE: There are no specific provisions that allow for death benefit amounts to be retained in the fund when the pension ceases if there is no tax dependant beneficiary.

Taxation of superannuation death benefits

The taxation of death benefits is dependent on the age of the primary beneficiary and of the secondary beneficiary to whom the benefit reverts. However all lump sum payments paid to a dependant are tax-free.

The taxation of reversionary pensions is as follows:

- if the primary beneficiary was age 60 or more at the time of death then the benefits to the reversionary would be tax-free, but

- if the primary beneficiary was under 60 at the time of death then the pension would be assessable on the basis of the same tax free proportion being applied as was applicable for the primary pension if the reversionary is also under 60. If the reversionary is 60 or over at the time of the primary member's death the pension is tax-free when it reverts, with the same tax free proportion being retained.

All lump sum benefits paid to a tax-dependant are tax-free.

NOTE: Reversionary pensions may only be paid to tax-dependants of the deceased.

See 19.600 for a detailed discussion on the taxation treatment of superannuation death benefits.

MINIMUM STANDARDS FOR COMPLYING PENSIONS (IE. DEFINED BENEFIT PENSIONS)

NOTE: The pension drawdown relief measures (see above) do not apply to complying pensions.

Complying pensions fall into a class of legacy pensions with certain concessional attributes that are generally not available to a more recently commenced pension. A large number of these pensions currently continue to pay member benefits. They were essentially commenced with a view to either ensuring security of income in retirement and /or to obtain concessional taxation and Centrelink benefits.

New complying pensions may no longer be commenced from a SMSF. They could only be commenced prior to 20 September 2007, and then only from a retail fund. After that date 'new' pensions were only possible where an existing complying pension was rolled over and recommenced from a new pension provider. In most cases such an action would extinguish their Centrelink concessional treatment.

Despite the RBL provisions having been rescinded after 1 July 2007 the standard required of such pensions must be maintained where they are currently in place. A complying defined benefit pension requires:

- at least one payment annually
- the payments may be indexed or unindexed and where indexed, to a maximum of the greater of 5% or CPI + 1% (can be varied to allow payment under a payment split including reasonable fees)
- that there be no residual capital value when pension ceases, unless through reversion
- that a commutation can only occur:
  - in the first six months of the start date
  - if the primary beneficiary dies within 10 years of the start date
  - to enable payment of a superannuation surcharge liability
  - to give effect to an entitlement of a non-member spouse under a payment split
  - if the reason is to purchase another pension or annuity which satisfies the standards
- that a reversionary benefit or commuted amount cannot be more than 100% of the benefit payable immediately prior to reversion or commutation
- that it can only be transferred to:
  - a reversionary beneficiary when the primary beneficiary dies, or
  - another reversionary beneficiary
- that the capital value and income cannot be used as security for borrowing.

The term of the income stream must be for:

- a life-time and:
  - the primary beneficiary of the income stream can be any age
  - the benefit payments must be for the life of the principal beneficiary and any nominated beneficiary
  - it can have a protected term of ten years or less
- or for a fixed term, and the primary beneficiary must be Age or Service pension age, and
  - if life expectancy is less than 15 years, the term must be life expectancy, or
  - if life expectancy exceeds 15 years, the term can be from 15 years to a maximum of life expectancy rounded up to the next whole number.

MINIMUM STANDARDS FOR MARKET LINKED PENSIONS

NOTE: Pension drawdown relief measures (see above) apply to market linked pensions, and are outlined at the end of this subsection.

These pensions were available to be commenced as an original pension for only a short time from 20 September 2004 to 20 September 2007. They are now regarded as legacy pensions as they may only have been commenced in the interval mentioned above. Many currently exist and they will continue to pay benefits for a number of years into the future.

'New' market linked pensions may no longer be permitted, however any existing ones may be rolled over and recommenced as new market linked pensions from a new pension provider.

The Market Linked Pension (MLP), also called a Term Allocated Pension (TAP) or a Growth Pension (GP), meets the previous criteria set for complying pensions that enabled access to the previous Pension RBL standard when at least 50% of benefits were taken in the form of MLPs. An MLP is non-commutable and cannot be rolled into a commutable account based pension. It is essentially a fixed term pension with an annual drawdown that is set according to the account balance at the start of the financial year (or initially on commencement) and a payment factor that depends upon the remaining term for which the pension is yet to run. The term is set according to the rule below using payment factors. In each succeeding year the remaining term of the pension reduces by a year with a corresponding reduction in the payment factor. All payment factors are greater than one except in the final year of the term. It is then equal to one and the full balance must be withdrawn.

In principle the term of a MLP is based on the life expectancy of the retiree, with the duration of the pension being set according to whether the pension commenced before 1 January 2006 or after 31 December 2005 as below. The table of life expectancies may be viewed in the table on the following page, with the annual payment being dependent on both the account balance and the payment factor.

Annual payment = Account Balance/Payment Factor

The MLP was initially designed to provide a set annual amount for withdrawal in a year, depending upon the payment factor and the account balance. (The amount could be taken in a number of tranches.) A lack of flexibility in relation to the annual drawdown amount has been a major drawback. Steps were taken to improve this situation, resulting in a small improvement in flexibility available from 1 January 2006, with potentially longer terms for pensions commenced from that date and the ability to drawdown an amount that may be varied from the calculated amount by + or − 10%.

Pension commenced no later than 31 December 2005

For these market linked pensions the term was set for any duration that met the following constraints. A period in years that was equal to the life expectancy of the retiree, rounded up to the next whole number of years, but no greater than the corresponding life expectancy rounded up to the next whole number of years if the retiree was five years younger.

For reversionary pensions the same principle applied except that the longer life expectancy pensioner was the subject for purposes of determining the term of the pension.

Pension commenced no earlier than 1 January 2006

For these pensions the term could be set for any duration that met the following constraints. A period in years equal to the life expectancy of the retiree and rounded up to the next whole number of years, but no greater than the corresponding life expectancy rounded up to the next whole number of years if the retiree lived to be 100 years old.

For reversionary pensions the same principle applied as was used for market linked pensions that commenced pre-1 January 2006 except that the longer life expectancy applied for determining the term of the pension.

Allan, a retiree, commenced a market linked pension at age 65 on 1 July 2005. The account balance that paid this pension was $400,000. Allan sought to have the term of his pension set at about five years more than his life expectancy. What is his payment for the first year and for the year 2009-10? The account balance on 1 July 2009 is $500,000. From the table of life expectancies (see next page), Allan's life expectancy is seen to be 17.7 years.

This period is rounded up to 18 years and since he seeks to have a pension paid for an additional five years the term he may select is 23 years. On the basis of a 23 year term the payment factor for the period 2005-06 is determined from the table below, corresponding to a term remaining of 23 years. The payment factor is 15.62. The account balance is divided by the payment factor to obtain the annual payment amount from the following table. (In this case it represents 6.4 % of the account balance.) This amount must be withdrawn in the first year.

Drawdown for 2005-06 is $400,000/15.62 = $25,608.19 = $25,610 (rounded to nearest $10).

For the year 2009-10 the term that is remaining is represented by the original term (23 years) less the period of the pension that has elapsed (4). The remaining term is (23 – 4) years = 19 years. The corresponding payment factor is 13.71. The drawdown for that the year 2009-10 is $500,000/13.71 = $36,469.73. This is rounded to the nearest $10 giving $36,470.

Note: For this calculation the variability represented by the + or – 10% on the drawdown of $36,470 is permitted (see below).

FLEXIBILITY OF DRAWDOWNS

The original design of MLPs was based on a concept of a fixed annual drawdown based on an account balance and a payment factor determined by the life expectancy at commencement of the pension and translated into term for the pension. New provisions applied from 1 January 2006 to permit a variation of (+ or – 10%) on the calculated drawdown, irrespective of the commencement date of the pension.

Payment valuation factors for market linked income streams (term remaining = years)

Term remaining	Payment factor	Term remaining	Payment factor	Term remaining	Payment factor	Term remaining	Payment factor
70	26	52	23.8	34	19.7	16	12.09
69	25.91	51	23.63	33	19.39	15	11.52
68	25.82	50	23.46	32	19.07	14	10.92
67	25.72	49	23.28	31	18.74	13	10.3
66	25.62	48	23.09	30	18.39	12	9.66
65	25.52	47	22.9	29	18.04	11	9
64	25.41	46	22.7	28	17.67	10	8.32
63	25.3	45	22.5	27	17.29	9	7.61
62	25.19	44	22.28	26	16.89	8	6.87
61	25.07	43	22.06	25	16.48	7	6.11
60	24.94	42	21.83	24	16.06	6	5.33
59	24.82	41	21.6	23	15.62	5	4.52
58	24.69	40	21.36	22	15.17	4	3.67
57	24.55	39	21.1	21	14.7	3	2.8
56	24.41	38	20.84	20	14.21	2	1.9
55	24.26	37	20.57	19	13.71	1 or less	1
54	24.11	36	20.29	18	13.19		
53	23.96	35	20	17	12.65		

IMPORTANT: The minimum drawdown for market linked pensions may be calculated by applying the relevant 'Relief factor' from the Table below, to the minimum drawdown calculated in the usual manner. Alternatively the following three steps may be applied. This includes use of the relevant 'Multiple' from the table.

Life expectancy table at start of income stream: Annuity started since 1 January 2010

Age	Male	Female	Age	Male	Female	Age	Male	Female
50	31.43	35.17	61	21.79	25.11	72	13.33	15.82
51	30.53	34.24	62	20.96	24.23	73	12.64	15.03
52	29.63	33.31	63	20.14	23.35	74	11.96	14.27
53	28.73	32.38	64	19.34	22.48	75	11.31	13.51
54	27.84	31.45	65	18.54	21.62	76	10.68	12.78
55	26.95	30.53	66	17.76	20.76	77	10.07	12.05
56	26.08	29.61	67	16.99	19.92	78	9.48	11.35
57	25.20	28.70	68	16.24	19.08	79	8.92	10.67
58	24.34	27.79	69	15.49	18.24	80	8.38	10.01
59	23.48	26.89	70	14.76	17.42			
60	22.63	26.00	71	14.04	16.61			

IMPORTANT: The minimum drawdown for market linked pensions may be calculated by applying the relevant 'Relief factor' from the Table below, to the minimum drawdown calculated in the usual manner. Alternatively the following three steps may be applied. This includes use of the relevant 'Multiple' from the table below.

- **Step 1:** Calculate an amount by dividing the relevant Account balance by the Payment Factor that relates to the remaining term in years for the MLP, as normal.
- **Step 2:** Round the amount derived at Step 1 to the nearest $10, as normal.
- **Step 3:** Multiply the amount derived at Step 2 by the 'Multiple' for the relevant year from the Table below. This gives the minimum drawdown allowed for the MLP.

Drawdown relief table for market linked pensions		
Year	Relief factor	Multiple (for minimum payment)*
2008-09	50%	45%
2009-10	50%	45%
2010-11	50%	45%
2011-12	25%	67.5%
2012-13	25%	67.5%

* The 'Multiple' shown incorporates the 10% variation permitted for MLPs.
Relief ceases for 2013-14 and future years.

Wee Won receives income from his MLP. At the commencement of the 2010-11 year the account balance was $420,000. The term remaining on his pension was 18 years and he sought to draw down the minimum amount permitted. From the preceding table Payment valuation factors for market linked income streams, the payment factor for a term remaining of 18 years is 13.19.

Step 1:   Account balance divided by the Payment Factor = 420,000 / 13.19 = $31,842.30.

Step 2:   Amount rounded to nearest $10 gives $31,840.

Step 3:   Minimum drawdown is the amount from Step 2 multiplied by the 'Multiple' from the Drawdown relief for Market Linked Pensions table for the year 2010-11 of 45%.

The minimum drawdown is calculated as $31,840 x 45% = $14,328.

Note: If all else was the same in 2011-12 (including the term), the relevant 'Multiple' would be 67.5% and the minimum drawdown would be $31,840 x 67.5% = $21,492.

MINIMUM STANDARDS FOR ALLOCATED PENSIONS

Pension drawdown relief measures apply to allocated pensions. These are legacy pensions which have been superseded by account based pensions. As noted earlier the drawdown standard for allocated pensions falls within the envelope of account based pensions. From 1 July 2007 the account based pension standard may be used.

Allocated pensions that are continued under the pre-1 July 2007 standards require:

- at least one payment annually
- the capital value and income cannot be used as security for borrowing.
- that it can only be transferred to:
  - a reversionary beneficiary when the primary beneficiary dies, or
  - to another reversionary beneficiary, and
- minimum (subject to pension drawdown relief measures – see above) and maximum annual withdrawal limits are calculated using one of the tables below.

NOTE: The tables on the following page are provided to assist those retirees who choose to adhere to the pension standard that applied for allocated pensions. As suggested above, the applicable standard is the account based standard. This is a more liberal standard. Any drawdown conforming to a previous allocated pension automatically complies with the account based standard. For allocated pensions commenced prior to 1 January 2006 please use Table A. For allocated pensions commenced from 1 January 2006, please use Table B.

Income stream standards

Table A: Allocated pension factors to calculate annual withdrawal limits (for allocated pensions commenced prior to 1 January 2006)

Age	<=20	21	22	23	24	25	26	27	28	29	
Min	28.6	28.5	28.3	28.1	28	27.8	27.6	27.5	27.3	27.1	
Max	10	10	10	10	10	10	10	10	10	10	
Age	30	31	32	33	34	35	36	37	38	39	
Min	26.9	26.7	26.5	26.3	26	25.8	25.6	25.3	25.1	24.8	
Max	10	10	10	10	10	10	10	10	10	10	
Age	40	41	42	43	44	45	46	47	48	49	
Min	24.6	24.3	24	23.7	23.4	23.1	22.8	22.5	22.2	21.9	
Max	10	10	10	10	10	10	10	10	10	10	
Age	50	51	52	53	54	55	56	57	58	59	
Mln	21.5	21.2	20.9	20.5	20.1	19.8	19.4	19	18.6	18.2	
Max	9.9	9.9	9.8	9.7	9.7	9.6	9.5	9.4	9.3	9.1	
Age	60	61	62	63	64	65	66	67	68	69	
Min	17.8	17.4	17	16.6	16.2	15.7	15.3	14.9	14.4	14	
Max	9	8.9	8.7	8.5	8.3	8.1	7.9	7.6	7.3	7	
Age	70	71	72	73	74	75	76	77	78	79	
Min	13.5	13.1	12.6	12.2	11.7	11.3	10.8	10.4	10	9.5	
Max	6.6	6.2	5.8	5.4	4.8	4.3	3.7	3	2.2	1.4	
Age	80	81	82	83	84	85	86	87	88	89	
Min	9.1	8.7	8.3	7.9	7.5	7.1	6.8	6.4	6.1	5.8	
Max	1	1	1	1	1	1	1	1	1	1	
Age	90	91	92	93	94	95	96	97	98	99	>=100
Min	5.5	5.3	5	4.8	4.6	4.4	4.2	4	3.8	3.7	3.5
Max	1	1	1	1	1	1	1	1	1	1	1

Table B: Allocated pension factors to calculate annual withdrawal limits (for allocated pensions commenced from 1 January 2006)

Age	<=20	21	22	23	24	25	26	27	28	29	
Min	29.2	29	28.9	28.7	28.6	28.4	28.3	28.1	27.9	27.8	
Max	12	12	12	12	12	12	12	12	12	12	
Age	30	31	32	33	34	35	36	37	38	39	
Min	27.6	27.4	27.2	27	26.8	26.6	26.4	26.2	26	25.8	
Max	12	12	12	12	12	12	12	12	12	12	
Age	40	41	42	43	44	45	46	47	48	49	
Min	25.5	25.3	25	24.8	24.5	24.2	24	23.7	23.4	23.1	
Max	12	12	12	12	12	12	12	12	12	12	
Age	50	51	52	53	54	55	56	57	58	59	
Mln	22.8	22.5	22.2	21.8	21.5	21.1	20.8	20.4	20.1	19.7	
Max	12	11.9	11.8	11.8	11.7	11.5	11.4	11.3	11.2	11	
Age	60	61	62	63	64	65	66	67	68	69	
Min	19.3	18.9	18.5	18.1	17.7	17.3	16.8	16.4	16	15.5	
Max	10.9	10.7	10.5	10.3	10.1	9.9	9.6	9.3	9.1	8.7	
Age	70	71	72	73	74	75	76	77	78	79	
Mln	15.1	14.6	14.2	13.7	13.3	12.8	12.3	11.9	11.4	10.9	
Max	8.4	8	7.6	7.2	6.7	6.2	5.7	5.1	4.5	3.8	
Age	80	81	82	83	84	85	86	87	88	89	
Min	10.5	10	9.6	9.1	8.7	8.3	7.9	7.5	7.2	6.9	
Max	3.1	2.3	1.4	1	1	1	1	1	1	1	
Age	90	91	92	93	94	95	96	97	98	99	>=100
Min	6.6	6.3	6	5.8	5.5	5.3	5.1	4.9	4.7	4.5	4.4
Max	1	1	1	1	1	1	1	1	1	1	1

19.800 NON-COMPLYING SUPERANNUATION FUNDS

A non-complying superannuation fund is one that is a provident, benefit, superannuation or retirement fund for the income year but is not a complying superannuation fund for that year. The tax rules applying to a non-complying fund differ from those applying to a complying fund.

A 'non-complying' SMSF:

- is one that is not a resident of Australia, or

- has been issued with a Notice of non-compliance because it does not comply with the Superannuation Industry (Supervision) Act 1993 (SISA) regulatory provisions.

A non-complying fund can be:
- a fund that has not elected to be regulated
- a fund that is not eligible to be regulated (eg. a non-resident fund), or
- a fund where the regulator has given a written notice to the trustee stating that the fund is not a complying superannuation fund in relation to an income year specified in the notice.

The tax rules applying to a non-complying fund are different from those for a complying fund, including:
- income is taxed at the top marginal tax rate of 45% or 47% when including the 2% Temporary Budget Repair Levy for 2014-15 to 2016-17, including all contributions made by another person if the fund is a resident fund
- a complying fund that becomes non-complying is taxed at the top marginal tax rate of 45% or 47% when including the 2% Temporary Budget Repair Levy for 2014-15 to 2016-17, on the fund assets minus undeducted contributions
- Capital Gains Tax (CGT) concessions do not apply, death and disablement insurance expenses are not deductible and the exempt current pension income concessions do not apply.
- employer contributions are not tax deductible, may be subject to FBT and do not satisfy the employer's superannuation guarantee (SG) obligations.
- Member contributions are not deductible and are not rebatable. Spouse contributions are not rebatable.
- Non-complying funds do not have to lodge an annual regulatory return with the regulator but do have to lodge an income tax return (see 19.310 for dates).

 Non-complying superannuation funds are subject to the income tax return lodgement program that applies to large businesses (see calendar at 6.700).

A payment from a superannuation fund which has never been complying (ie. a continuously non-complying fund) is generally not taxable (unless it is ordinary income).

NON-RESIDENT SUPERANNUATION FUNDS

Non-resident superannuation funds are non-complying funds.

OVERSEAS PAYMENTS TO A COMPLYING FUND

Payments from an overseas superannuation fund (eligible non-resident, non-complying superannuation fund) directly into a complying fund in Australia, within six months of an individual becoming an Australian resident are tax-free and treated as an 'exempt non-resident foreign termination payment'.

If the six month rule is not met the taxpayer can make an election using *Choice to have your Australian fund pay tax on a foreign superannuation transfer* (NAT 11724) to have the assessable amount viewed as a taxable contribution to the fund. There is no tax liability arising at the individual level, but the assessable amount is taxed at the contribution tax rate of 15% in the fund. Alternatively the election may cover any proportion of the assessable amount to the fund and the balance becomes assessable in the hands of the individual. The assessable amount is a taxable contribution to superannuation (as per the election) and is deemed to be a taxable component. The non-assessable amount is a non-concessional contribution.

Contributions

Employer superannuation contributions made to a non-resident non-complying superannuation fund are either:

- non-deductible, but subject to fringe benefits tax, or
- not deductible and exempt from FBT, but only if the payment was for an 'exempt visitor' (ie. a person holding a temporary entry permit of no more than four years duration in total) to Australia, and that exempt visitor was in Australia at the end of the financial year, or has returned permanently to his or her home country.

Change of status to resident

If a non-resident superannuation fund changes its status and becomes a resident, the fund is taxed in that income year on the fund's 'net previous income in respect of previous years of income'. This claws back tax on income which may have been excluded from assessable income whilst the fund was a non-resident and is calculated as:

Asset values less Undeducted contributions

The difference between market values of assets at the end of the previous year, and current members' total contributions is taxed at:

- 15% if a non-resident fund becomes a resident complying fund, or
- 45% (47% from 2014-15) if a non-resident fund becomes a resident non-complying fund.

Any potential CGT is reduced by the asset assessed in this way.

TAX OFFSETS

Any foreign tax paid in the current or a subsequent year of income on that previous income is allowed as a foreign tax credit, up to the Australian tax payable.

Imputation credits offset the tax liability of a non-complying fund, but any unused imputation credits are not refundable and so are lost.

Retirement

20

20.000 RETIREMENT

Retirement can be a difficult time for individuals and their advisers, this chapter will deal with a number of pre-retirement and retirement issues. The reality is Australia has an ageing population (as does most of the developed world) with greater life expectancy and higher costs to government and individuals of this ageing population. Getting retirement policies right is important and the government has a number of initiatives to deal with those in retirement.

Internationally studies show that Australia consistently rates in the top 5 nations for retirement policies. Our mix of government funded means tested aged pension and superannuation system makes it one of the more affordable and flexible systems in the world.

THREE PILLARS

This mixture of government pension, superannuation and private saving is referred to as the three pillars structure for Australian retirement incomes and covers the following:

- retirement income support through Centrelink age benefits (providing means-tested government income support)
- compulsory private savings in superannuation (providing fully tax-free income from age 60), and
- voluntary private savings both within and outside superannuation.

The three pillar structure offers a significant level of flexibility, because it provides a level of income support for those with fewer means (through the first and potentially second pillars) while also providing the opportunity for individuals to increase their retirement income through additional contributions (the third pillar). The current structure is sustained by tax concessions while its risks are borne by both public and private sectors. Some tension exists between the views that it is fiscally responsible and that the concessions are skewed in favour of the wealthy. This has led more recently to re-direction of policy by government to confine certain concessions.

COVERAGE

This chapter draws on the subject matter of Chapters 3 and 19. It includes brief coverage of issues relating to superannuation, the Age Pension, the Commonwealth Seniors Health Card and other matters relevant to this demographic. It leaves aside however both the eligibility criteria and government benefits provided to pensioners who are below Age Pension age, veterans and others in receipt of family benefits or other entitlements. It does not address Aged care issues.

Having adequate funds available for retirement requires both planning and deliberate action well before retirement takes place. This chapter discusses certain aspects of taxation, transition to retirement, co-contribution, government assistance and other strategies for consideration. Transition to retirement strategies may improve after-tax outcomes prior to permanent retirement and lead to increased retirement savings through salary sacrifice to superannuation, tax rebates, differential tax rates and other matters focused on the taxpayer's after-tax position.

 This chapter considers complex and interrelated issues and provides only general guidance.

TAX FREE THRESHOLD TREBLED

A feature of the 2012-13 Federal Budget, with a potential ripple-through effect on retirement incomes was the increase in the tax-free threshold from $6,000 to $18,200 from 1 July 2012.

AGE BENEFITS

Age Pension benefits represent the first pillar of retirement support. These entitlements are available to eligible seniors, ensuring that retirees have a certain minimum level of income in retirement (see 20.410).

A benefit is paid on a needs basis. This is determined on both a senior's assets and income. The full benefit is paid where both assets and income do not exceed minimum thresholds. Where assets exceed the minimum threshold, the full benefit is reduced in proportion to the excess assets held.

Separately the full benefit is reduced if the level of income increases beyond the minimum income threshold. In all situations, if a benefit is paid it is the lower entitlement based on the two tests.

SUPERANNUATION

Currently about $1.5 trillion in savings is held in superannuation accounts demonstrating the strength of the second and third pillars for retirement savings. It is a low tax structure with income of the fund (contributions and investment earnings) taxed at 15%, with a CGT discount of one third, for assets held in excess of a year. The trade-off is that generally full access to savings is not available until an appropriate condition of release is satisfied. Partial access is however available from age 55.

Under the 'partial access' provisions, concessional, pre-retirement income streams or transition to retirement pensions may be commenced before the superannuation savings become the chief source of income in full retirement.

Superannuation benefits are also concessionally taxed in the hands of the recipient.

The concessional tax regime that applies to taxed superannuation funds results in income stream beneficiaries who are at least age 55 receiving a 15% rebate on the assessable component of the income stream until age 60. After age 60 the benefit is tax-free. For those in receipt of a transition to retirement income stream, this improves outcomes still further.

20.100 PHASES OF SUPERANNUATION

The tax-favoured nature of superannuation provides the incentive for taxpayers to build their retirement savings in superannuation within existing provisions despite constraints such as contributions caps.

There are potentially at least three phases of superannuation with distinct attributes relating to the individual taxpayer's ability to harness superannuation to advantage:

- the initial phase is a contributions only phase where access to benefits is generally not allowed
- the next phase is where contributions are still made – in all likelihood where accelerated contributions would occur, while special and limited early access to benefits is allowed under transition to retirement pensions, and
- the final phase corresponds to full retirement. No further contributions are generally allowed and the individual retiree is dependent on superannuation retirement income and/or government assistance.

Superannuation phases	Age
Contributions (generally access is not possible)	less than 55[3]
Contributions[1] and access[2] (including transition to retirement)	55[3] and less than 75
Non-contribution[2]	75 and over

1: After age 65 a work test must be met to retain eligibility for contributions to be made.
2: Access is optional.
3: Preservation age (see 19.700). Current provisions progressively increase preservation age 50 so that is 60 in 2025.

NOTE: Upon the death of a member, ongoing benefits may be paid as a reversionary income stream to dependants or otherwise paid out as a lump sum.

 These phases do not relate to the tax treatment of benefits.

20.110   CONTRIBUTIONS PHASE

This is the phase where the superannuation fund member is working and making contributions to a superannuation fund through compulsory SG payments and other contributions. Excluding exceptional circumstances there is no scope for drawing down benefits.

Contributions and net earnings of the fund provide the means for increasing a member's account balance. Contributions caps however provide a limit on the extent to which outside funds may be contributed to superannuation. Excess contributions are taxed under the excess contributions tax regime (see 19.050). During the contributions phase, taxpayers typically seek to increase their account balances through compulsory contributions, suitable investment strategies and through additional voluntary contributions.

Concessional contributions are contributions for which a tax deduction is received. They are made from gross income and taxed at the contributions tax rate of 15%*. Contributions of this kind increase wealth for the individual where marginal tax rates would otherwise exceed 15% or 30% for higher income taxpayers.

* From 1 July 2012 an additional contributions tax of 15% will apply under Division 293 for those whose income is $300,000 or more (see 19.300).

NOTE: From 1 July 2012, the low income superannuation contribution (LISC) provides taxpayers whose income is less than $37,000 with an increase of up to $500 to their superannuation savings. In effect, LISC refunds the 15% contributions tax paid by the fund on low income earner's contributions and aims to ensure they pay no tax on SG contributions. The government has put in place measures to rescind the LISC provisions. It will cease from 1 July 2017.

A non-concessonal contribution (NCC) is a contribution made by or on behalf of an individual from after-tax savings for which a tax deduction is not available. The NCC cap is set at six times the concessional cap.

The contributions phase is purely a growth phase for members' retirement savings. Ordinarily draw downs are not permitted. Arrangements such as limited recourse borrowings may be employed to enhance returns through a leveraging of asset values. During this phase, the interest expense associated with financing costs for limited recourse borrowings is generally available to offset assessable income of the fund. On the other hand during the following two phases, where exempt income is more likely to arise, there may be reduced opportunities for trustees to offset the fund income against interest expenses from limited recourse borrowings.

NOTE: Since 1 July 2007 concessional contributions have been fully deductible – either in the hands of the employer or a self-employed person or one who is deemed to be substantially self-employed (if not fully self-employed). Those considered to be self-employed must receive less than 10% of their remuneration from employment-related activities. See the 10% rule (19.026).

The elimination of age-based limits for concessional contributions and the introduction of an indexed cap improved the opportunity for younger taxpayers to increase their contributions through the direction of salary sacrificed income into superannuation. A higher transitional cap was available for older eligible taxpayers to increase their concessional contributions. However the transitional period elapsed from 1 July 2012. This together with halving the concessional contributions caps in 2009-10 has led to reduced opportunities to contribute and at the same time it increases the need for a greater focus on contributions management to ensure that taxpayers do not exceed the relevant caps or they will be penalized through the excess contributions tax regime (see 20.112).

Concessional contribution limits			
Age	2013-14	2014-15	2015-16
Under 50 years[1] (general limit)	$25,000	$30,000	$30,000
50 years and over[2]	$25,000	$35,000	$35,000
60 years and over[3]	$35,000	$35,000	$35,000

1: This concessional cap is the current contribution limit for all concessional contributions made by or on behalf of an individual to superannuation during the year. An excess contributions tax liability arises where this cap is exceeded. For those 50 and over a non-indexed transitional cap was applicable till 30 June 2012.

2: The higher cap of $35,000 applies to those aged 50 or over from 1 July 2014.

3: The government introduced a new higher cap on 1 July 2013 for those eligible and aged 60 or over.

 Jessica is in receipt of a salary of $100,000 plus $9,890 of SG contributions. She increases her contributions to super by $20,000 through salary sacrifice. The marginal tax rate increases from 30% to 37% (or 32.5% to 37% in 2012-13) above an income of $80,000.

The salary sacrifice reduces her assessable income to $80,000.

NOTE: *She turns 50 on 1 July 2014, her concessional contribution cap will be $25,000 in 2013-14, but $35,000 in 2014-15. SG is 9.25% in 2013-14 and 9.5% in 2014-15*

No salary sacrifice	2013-14	2014-15
Current salary	$100,000	$100,000
Tax on current salary	($24,947)	($24,947)
Medicare levy	($1,500)	($2,000)
Net benefit including SG	$82,803	$82,553
Salary sacrifice	2013-14	2014-15
New reduced salary	$80,000	$80,000
Tax on the reduced salary	($17,547)	($17,547)
Medicare levy on the reduced salary	($1,200)	($1,600)
Income after-tax and Medicare	$61,253	$60,853
Salary sacrificed into superannuation	$20,000	$20,000
Contributions tax and Excess Contributions Tax (ECT)[1]	($4,638)[2]	($4,140)
Net addition to superannuation	$22,762	$23,460
Net benefit including SG	$84,015	$84,313

1: ECT applies in 2013-14 as the concessional contributions cap of $25,000 is exceeded, however the higher threshold of $35,000 applies to the 2014-15 year and there is no ECT.

2: $4110 SG and $528 ECT

The benefits of salary sacrifice can be seen for each year.

Jessica is $1,962 better off through salary sacrifice of $20,000 in 2013-14 when compared to not making any salary sacrifice. Due to the lower cap of $25,000 applicable she is penalised with ECT on the 2013-14 superannuation contributions. She is $1,760 better off through salary sacrifice of $20,000 in 2014-15 when compared to not making any salary sacrifice.

NOTE: *A better outcome in 2013-14 would result from her salary sacrificing at a reduced level so her total concessional contributions do not exceed the cap of $25,000.*

CO-CONTRIBUTIONS

Co-contributions provide an avenue to augment savings via government assistance that is aimed at encouraging retirement savings. Under the provisions the government may contribute to the superannuation savings of eligible mid to low income earners who make eligible after-tax personal contributions to superannuation. The level of benefit paid is dependent on income. Below a certain lower income threshold the full benefit is paid. Above the threshold with increasing income a reduced benefit is paid, up to a higher income threshold after which no benefit is paid.

From 1 July 2007, self-employed individuals may also be eligible to benefit from the government co-contribution if they meet certain criteria. The scheme is income dependent with a sliding scale of benefits that varies with taxpayer income and level of contribution. The maximum co-contribution limit in a year is based on a member contribution of $1,000. In 2011-12, the government fully matched the equivalent after tax, taxpayer contribution. However this was reduced for 2012-13 and subsequent years, to only 50% of the previous benefit (that is the government co-contribution is capped at $500). Eligible recipients must be under 71 in the year of the eligible personal contribution. Co-contributions do not count as assessable income of a superannuation fund but form part of the member's tax-free component.

Note that the provisions have changed on a number of occasions with the level of benefit paid also having varied. For details see 19.076.

20.112   MONITORING OF CONTRIBUTIONS (ALSO SEE 19.040)

As previously noted, contributions made to an individual's superannuation savings are subject to concessional and non-concessional contributions caps, including a bring-forward arrangement. excess contributions tax (ECT) may apply where contributions exceed the caps. To ensure that an ECT liability does not arise in any year, individuals should closely monitor their superannuation contributions throughout the financial year and where necessary take appropriate steps to ensure that there are no unexpected ECT outcomes. With full deductibility of concessional contributions coupled with the ECT regime (see 19.050), the onus is on the individual to manage contributions. This is particularly relevant where a salary sacrifice of bonus is directed into superannuation.

Note that the superannuation regulations require a superannuation fund to return the excess non-concessional contribution where a single contribution exceeds the annual cap on its own. However these provisions take no account of any contributions already made in the financial year. Refer to ATO ID 2007/225.

Under the new ECT arrangements excess concessional contributions made by an individual are included in the individual's assessable income and subject to an excess concessional contribution charge (ECCC). They will be taxed at the individuals top marginal rate, while the individual will be given a non-refundable tax offset of 15%. It will also be possible for the excess contribution to be returned, if sought by the taxpayer.

Kelly is age 52 and her remuneration includes an annual SG amount of $9,000. She is paid a bonus before the end of June 2013 of $24,000. The concessional contributions cap for 2012-13 and 2013 -14 is $25,000 and for 2014-15 is $35,000.

Kelly is interested in making salary sacrifice arrangements of the bonus into her superannuation. If she sacrificed the total amount into her superannuation she would be liable for ECT. In the 2012-13 year her contributions in excess of the cap of ($33,000 – $25,000) or $8,000 give rise to an ECT liability of 31.5% x $8,000 = $2,520.

In the 2013-14 income year she would be liable under the new ECT arrangements. Her excess contributions would be taxed at her marginal rates. Her ECT would be $8,000 x her marginal tax rate 37% = $2,960. She would though get a credit for tax already paid ($8,000 x 15% = $1,200). Her total extra tax for the year would be $1,760. She would also need to pay an interest charge on top of the additional tax.

She would be better off contributing no more than $16,000 of her bonus into superannuation in order to avoid ECT in 2012-13 and 2013-14 income years.

In the 2014-15 income year she would be able to include the whole amount in her super without incurring ECT due to the higher cap of $35,000 for those 50 and over.

20.120   CONTRIBUTION AND ACCESS PHASE (AGE 55 TO LESS THAN 75)

The fact that superannuation benefits are not taxed or taxed at reduced rates means that taxpayers can take advantage of legitimate strategies to maximise their after tax income.

Since July 2007 all benefits paid from taxed superannuation funds receive tax concessions of a potential tax-free amount plus a full 15% rebate on the balance of the benefit for those who are not yet age 60. For those who have reached age 60 the entire benefit whether as a lump sum or as a pension is non-assessable, non-exempt income or tax-free income. Thus once a taxpayer attains the age of 55, the preservation age, it is generally advantageous to commence a transition to retirement (TTR) pension. It provides a concessionally taxed income stream regardless of the individual's employment status or intentions. When the individual reaches age 60, all personal income that is sourced from a (taxed) superannuation fund is tax-free. There are compelling reasons therefore to consider the use of TTR pensions. However, early access to superannuation may draw down the superannuation balance at a quicker rate. This may extinguish superannuation assets at an earlier time.

NOTE: While a superannuation interest is paying an income stream, its investment earnings arising from assets which support the pension are tax-free. This is a further reason for taxpayers to commence an income stream as soon as they are eligible.

TRANSITION TO RETIREMENT ACCESS

The process of commencing a pension or income stream from a superannuation account when the member has reached preservation age, currently 55 years of age, regardless of his or her future work intentions, is referred to as accessing retirement benefits under the transition to retirement provisions. The pension or income stream is called a transition to retirement pension or a transition to retirement income stream and may be used as part of a strategy to improve the taxpayer's financial position.

This pension on its own has the effect of increasing a taxpayer's income. But since the legislation provides for tax concessions, it results in an effective rate of tax significantly lower than the taxpayer's marginal tax rate, providing greater tax efficiency for the taxpayer.

A TTR pension can also be used in conjunction with a salary sacrifice to superannuation to maximise net benefits. This is discussed at 20.200.

TTR pensions provide a flexible source of income with a capacity to be stopped or re-started where this is necessary. At age 65 a full condition of release applies.

In summary, receipt of flexible tax effective income leads to the following possible outcomes:

- an increase in immediate income
- retention of similar level of income but working fewer hours
- increase of superannuation contributions because of the increase in income, and
- flexibility (stopping at any time and re-commencing at will to meet the individual's needs).

Since a fixed contribution tax of 15%* applies to pre-taxed or gross income directed to superannuation, contributions face lower tax provided the individual's personal marginal tax rate is in excess of 15%. Clearly there are net after-tax benefits from accessing superannuation, providing taxpayers with the opportunity to increase superannuation savings as retirement is drawing closer, and where incomes may be higher and ability to save greater. Critically however the current contributions caps serve as a strong limiter to directing additional income into superannuation.

*Commencing from the 2012-13 year:

- taxpayers with incomes up to $37,000 will receive a government contribution which effectively reimburses the contribution tax ($500 maximum) however this contribution will cease from 1 July 2017, and
- taxpayers with incomes in excess of $300,000 will be subject to a contribution tax of 30%.

It should also be noted that due to the increases to preservation age in the future, the age at which transition to retirement income streams may be commenced will gradually increase (see *Preservation age* at 19.700).

	Concessional cap (50 and over)	Concessional cap (60 and over)	Non-concessional cap
2011-2012	$50,000	$50,000	$150,000
2012-2013	$25,000	$25,000	$150,000
2013-2014	$25,000	$35,000	$150,000
2014-2015	$35,000*	$35,000*	$180,000
2015-2016	$35,000	$35,000	$180,000

* From 1 July 2014, the concessional (before-tax) contributions cap will be indexed in line with Average Weekly Ordinary Time Earnings (AWOTE), in increments of $5,000. The general concessional contributions cap is expected to reach $35,000 from 1 July 2018.

BRING FORWARD RULE FOR THOSE UNDER 65

The bring-forward rule is intended to allow for a maximum of three times the non-concessional contributions cap to be contributed by a taxpayer in a single transaction or a series of transactions over a three year period when the eligibility criteria is met. This enables a taxpayer to make a non-concessional contribution that exceeds the contributions cap for the year without penalty (see 19.402).

The bring-forward arrangement is triggered immediately the non-concessional contributions cap ($150,000 in 2013-14, $180,000 in 2014-15 and later years) is exceeded in a given year if the individual is less than 65 years of age on at least one day of the relevant financial year when the contributions cap is exceeded. Once this happens, the taxpayer may spread out the remaining contributions over the current and two future financial years.

A cap equivalent to three non-concessional caps then applies, provided the bring-forward rule has not been invoked in the previous two years. If the aggregate non-concessional contributions in the three year period exceeds three times the relevant cap ($450,000 in the period commencing, 2013-14 and previous years and $540,000 in the 2014-15 year) excess contributions tax applies. Where the bring-forward rule was triggered but the entire $450,000 ($540,000 for the 2014-15 year) was not contributed before the taxpayer reached age 65, the work test must be met for further contributions to be made as part of the bring-forward arrangements.

NOTE: The bring-forward rule is not available in respect of a particular financial year for those who are 65 or older on the first day of that financial year.

ACCOUNT BASED PENSION

This pension has a requirement that each year the member must withdraw at least the minimum annual amount. Details of this minimum standard are provided at 19.720.

20.130   NON-CONTRIBUTION PHASE

The non-contribution phase may be considered to commence once the member reaches 75 when eligibility for making contributions to superannuation generally cease. The key defining feature of the phase is its non-contributory character. It is an access-only phase* with the vast majority of superannuants typically accessing their benefits during this phase.

For taxpayers who are 65 years old or older, eligibility for making super contributions requires meeting the work test or gainful employment test. To satisfy this, the member must work for at least 40 hours during a consecutive 30-day period for financial reward. Unpaid work does not meet the definition of gainfully employed.

For members who meet the work test and are not yet 75, their fund can accept:

- mandatory super contributions made by their employer
- other types of employer contributions such as
  - voluntary contributions by their employer
  - other amounts paid by the employer to their super fund to cover administration fees and insurance premiums, and
- personal contributions made by them.

* From 1 July 2013 the upper age limit on Superannuation Guarantee (SG) support was abolished.

ACCESS NON-MANDATORY

It is not mandatory to access superannuation benefits. Therefore members may postpone access to benefits indefinitely. In the extreme they may retain their assets in superannuation until death, thus never receiving any benefits directly. Following death the members benefits must be paid out unless paid as an income stream to a dependant.

 When a superannuation interest is not in pension phase its earnings are assessable, regardless of the age of the member. Taxation is likely to be a factor when deciding whether or not to draw down benefits from superannuation.

TAX-FREE EARNINGS

As previously noted, the earnings of a superannuation interest from assets that support a pension interest are tax-free. It may be prudent during this phase to crystallise gains, particularly for assets held for long periods of time, with significant appreciation in their value.

NOTE: Since the earnings of the fund are tax-exempt there is limited ability to offset capital losses.

 Where an asset is sold and immediately repurchased or where an asset is sold to an associate so the investor's economic position is unchanged, the transaction is referred to as a 'wash sale'. Refer to Taxation Ruling TR 2008/1 for the circumstances in which the Commissioner of Taxation might apply Part IVA to a 'wash sale'. Where all fund income is exempt whilst in pension mode, Part IVA would be unlikely to have any application. However, where only some fund assets were allocated to support pension obligations the impact of Part IVA requires careful consideration.

SOME ESTATE PLANNING ISSUES

Estate planning covers a range of issues that go beyond the mere preparation of an individual's will. The objective of estate planning is to ensure that the transfer and control of assets is managed effectively to maximise the benefits available to the deceased's estate or beneficiaries. It requires an after-tax perspective of any asset transfers involved. Insurance can play an important role in estate planning; depending on the ownership of the policy, and it may be either an estate asset or the proceeds might be received outside the estate.

Estate assets are typically assets held in the will maker's name and can therefore be dealt with through the will. These assets may also include assets held as tenants in common with another entity or individual (in which case the interest transfers automatically to the surviving joint tenant). Two of the more common instances of non-estate assets are the family home held as joint tenants by the couple and retirement savings that are held as a superannuation interest by a member of a superannuation fund. Non-estate assets include life insurance policies held by an individual or entity other than the person whose life is insured. Family trust interests are also non-estate assets.

A member's superannuation benefit in a regulated superannuation fund must be cashed as soon as is practicable once the member dies (SIS Reg 6.21(1)) and the benefits paid in accordance with a binding death benefit nomination where that is current. See also 19.600.

DEATH BENEFITS

The superannuation death benefit provisions provide for the payment of benefits by way of a tax-free lump sum or a reversionary pension to death-benefit dependants of the deceased. The reversionary pension is tax-free to the beneficiary if the deceased was 60 or over or alternatively when the beneficiary reaches 60. In addition, for reversionary pensions paid to children, they must be commuted and paid out as a lump sum no later than when the beneficiary reaches age 25. The resulting lump sum benefit is tax-free.

The provisions do not allow for benefits to be retained in the fund when the member dies and where there are no dependants. In such situations benefits must be paid out as lump sum death benefits.

The tax-free component of a death benefit is tax-free when paid to a beneficiary. The taxable component is assessable at 17% including Medicare levy (and 32% to the extent the benefit is paid from the untaxed element of the taxable component of the member's account).

 While there are a number of situations in which a pension ceases, a particular condition for its cessation is when the pension member dies with no dependants. The pension exemption continues including capital gains tax exemption upon the sale or transfer of assets until the death benefits are paid; provided that this is done as soon as practicable following the member's death.

RE-CONTRIBUTION STRATEGY

Death benefit recipients are often non-dependants for tax purposes and since the taxable component of the benefit will determine the tax liability upon death, an obvious avenue open to a superannuation member during their lifetime is to increase the proportion of the tax-free component of the fund. This may be done by making (non-concessional) contributions that add to the fund's tax-free component.

An approach that does not require additional funds for contribution to superannuation is a re-contribution strategy. This is carried out by drawing cash out of the fund and then re-contributing it as non-concessional contributions. Better outcomes occur where the member is 60 or over. At this time the draw down is tax-free. If the individual is less than 65 the bring-forward rule can be invoked to maximise the amount that can be returned to superannuation in the form of a re-contribution.

NOTE: Upon reaching age 65, eligibility to contribute is dependent on meeting the work test of 40 hours in a period of 30 consecutive days.

Variations of this strategy are available however the basic principle is to draw down from a superannuation interest with a taxable component and then re-contribute as a non-concessional contribution.

Megan, age 60, retired from the workforce and was to commence an account based pension from her superannuation account. The tax-free proportion of her interest is nil because she was a late entrant to superannuation, making significant salary sacrifice contributions to superannuation with nil non-concessional contributions. Her account balance was $400,000.

She could commence drawing down from this interest and there is no tax impost on the benefit she receives because she is currently 60. All benefits would be tax-free when paid to herself. However since the tax-free proportion of the interest is 0% it would normally retain this tax-free proportion for the duration of the pension. Upon her death the residual benefit will be taxed at 17% when paid to Eric her financially independent adult son. If at a future time of her death her account balance was $300,000, Eric would receive $51,000 ($300,000 x 17%) less in a death benefit due to tax. The tax-free proportion of her interest is altered by drawing down as a lump sum the entire account balance and re-contributing it before commencing the income stream.

As the amount of $400,000 exceeds the non concessional cap of $180,000, and Megan is less than 65 the bring-forward rule would be triggered to allow contributions up to $540,000. In her case she could draw down the full $400,000 and re-contribute it. She could then commence an income stream with a full 100% tax-free proportion. Upon her death the entire residual benefit is tax-free when received by Eric.

20.200 TRANSITION TO RETIREMENT

Transition to retirement enables a person with superannuation assets to access those benefits by way of a non-commutable income stream before permanent retirement. Lump sum access is generally not permitted and a maximum drawdown in a year is limited to 10% of the opening balance of the relevant account balance. Importantly, the pension standard requires that a minimum amount must be withdrawn in the year. This is 4% (see 19.700).

FLEXIBILITY

The concept of transition to retirement was developed to enable flexibility and limit complexity when accessing superannuation benefits in advance of permanent retirement. It enables individuals who have reached preservation age to access their superannuation by way of a non-commutable income stream, without having to retire permanently from the workforce. It also allows those who have commenced an income stream to cease drawing down from it leaving the residual within the superannuation environment (see *Income stream* below). However the member is generally not permitted to commute and withdraw the balance from the account.

The flexibility of this arrangement is attractive for those reducing their hours of work, returning to the workforce and seeking to draw down some income from their superannuation savings, or using the tax concessions to improve their financial situation.

INCOME STREAMS

Any income stream available from 1 July 2005 may qualify as a transition to retirement pension product. If an allocated pension was commenced it was not commutable until the individual had retired permanently or reached age 65. This means that lump sum amounts are generally not able to be withdrawn from such pension interests even though pensions may be stopped where the rules for the pension did not prevent this. For example an allocated pension or account based pension could be stopped but not a market linked pension or a defined benefit pension.

The maximum annual draw down is 10% of the opening account balance.

An income stream that would normally permit the commutation of benefits, (that is the taking of a lump sum) may be stopped, leading to the pension account reverting to an accumulation account at the discretion of the member.

NOTE: Under current arrangements, all new earnings (such as dividends and interest) on assets supporting income streams (superannuation pensions and annuities) are tax-free.

PRESERVATION AGE

Currently preservation age is 55. It is to increase gradually to 60. Refer to 19.700.

NEED FOR FLEXIBILITY

With greater emphasis on self-funding in retirement this phase is the period when individuals most need flexibility in their affairs. It is also the last opportunity that taxpayers have to augment their superannuation savings in order to push them over the line into self-funding in retirement, particularly if they have no significant history of superannuation savings.

The period from 55 to 65 years of age might also be characterised by greater uncertainties in relation to ongoing work opportunities, health and lifestyle issues. Greater flexibility is necessary since life can be less predictable during the period immediately preceding permanent retirement. The inherent flexibility enhances the value of the transition to retirement option.

20.300 GOVERNMENT INCENTIVES

20.310 MATURE AGE WORKER TAX OFFSET

A tax offset not exceeding $500 for the year is available for certain Australian resident taxpayers aged 55 years or over who participate in the workforce. The extent of the tax offset depends on the level of income from working. As part of the 2014–15 federal Budget, the government announced that it will abolish the mature age worker tax offset from 1 July 2014.

20.315   RESTART

While the Government has abolished the MAWTO it has replaced it with the Restart program. It is a wage subsidy paid to employers which aims to assist mature age people participate in the workplace by encouraging employers to take on workers 50 years of age or older.

The full rate of the Restart subsidy is $10,000 (GST-inclusive), paid to the employer. Mature age job seekers employed for at least 30 hours per week will attract the full rate of the subsidy. Eligible job seekers employed between 15-29 hours per week will attract a pro-rata Restart subsidy.

The full rate of the subsidy is paid in four six-monthly instalments:

- $3,000 at 6 and 12 months of employment, and
- $2,000 at 18 and 24 months of employment.

WHO IS ELIGIRLE?

Job seekers who are 50 years of age or older, who have been unemployed and are on income support for six months or more, can attract a Restart subsidy for an employer.

An eligible job seeker is someone who :

- is 50 years of age or older
- has been unemployed for six months or more and has been in receipt of any of the following income support payments for six months or more:
  - Newstart Allowance; Parenting Payment; Disability Support Pension; Bereavement Allowance; Widow Allowance; Carer Payment; Special Benefit; Partner Service Pensioners; War Widows; Age Pension; Mature Age Partner Allowance; Wife Pension; Widows B Pension;
- does not have any outstanding workers' compensation claims against the employer, and
- is not an immediate family member of the employer.

The mature age worker must commence in the employment position on or after July 1, 2014.

20.320 PENSION BONUS SCHEME

Under the terms of the Budget announcement in May 2009 this scheme was closed off to new participants from 20 September 2009. Those registered before 29 June 2009 could remain in the scheme, with new entrants needing to qualify for Age Pension before 20 September 2009. Existing participants would continue to accrue entitlements under existing arrangements.

The Pension Bonus Scheme was originally intended to encourage participation in the workforce by seniors. This is now to be achieved through a new pension income test concession under the new Work Bonus scheme for age pensioners. The Pension Bonus Scheme was a voluntary scheme aimed at rewarding those who postpone claiming an age or service pension. The longer the claim was postponed the larger the bonus earned.

Eligibility was based on meeting all three of the following criteria:

- continuing to work past the date of age and residence requirements for Age Pension
- being registered as a member of the scheme, and
- meeting a flexible work test with a minimum of 960 hours for at least 12 months after registration.

No bonus is paid if any of the following applies:

- a previous payment of Age Pension or other income support (excluding carer payment) was received after reaching Age Pension age
- a bonus has already been received, or
- use is made of an International Social Security Agreement to meet the residence requirements when finally claiming a Bonus and Age Pension.

 The Pension Bonus cannot accrue after age 75.

For those intending to receive the Pension Bonus it was important to register as soon as practicable upon reaching Age Pension age. Partners were required to register individually. The Pension Bonus was to be claimed at the same time as the claim for the Age Pension or Veterans' Affairs service pension was made, but using two separate claim forms. Factors affecting the bonus paid include:

- the amount of basic age pension entitlement claimed upon leaving the workforce
- the length of time the bonus was accruing, and
- whether the taxpayer was single or partnered during the period the bonus was accruing.

Retirees who are ineligible for the basic Age Pension will not be paid a Pension Bonus. (Basic Age Pension does not include other benefits, eg. rent assistance, pharmaceutical allowance, and remote area allowance.)

To be eligible a person must have registered for the scheme prior to 1 July 2014.

Maximum bonus payable (effective 20 March 2015)		
Bonus years	Single	Partnered (each)
1 year	$1,966.20	$1,486.20
2 years	$7,864.80	$5,944.80
3 years	$17,695.80	$13,375.80
4 years	$31,459.20	$23,779.10
5 years	$49,155.00	$37,154.90

The Pension Bonus is paid as a non-taxable lump sum once the claimant applies for and receives the age pension. The payments above are a guide.

NOTE: The Pension Bonus is calculated on a pro rata basis. For example, those entitled to two thirds of the basic rate of age pension upon retirement will receive two thirds of the Pension Bonus shown above. The Pension Bonus must accrue for at least a year with a maximum accrual period of five years. Any work carried out after age 75 is not included in the accrual period.

20.330 SALARY SACRIFICE TO SUPERANNUATION

Salary sacrificing to a complying superannuation fund is a tax effective way of increasing retirement savings. It is not a fringe benefit but reduces assessable income and hence the net tax bill where an individual faces a marginal tax rate that exceeds 15%. Since contributions are taxed at 15% in the fund, those on higher marginal tax rates will benefit (including the 15% tax rate to apply to higher income earners). See 25.980 for details of salary packaging.

20.400 CENTRELINK AGE BENEFITS

20.410 AGE PENSION BENEFITS

The Age Pension is intended to ensure that Age Pension age seniors receive a level of income support in retirement. All Australian residents are eligible to apply for Age Pension entitlements. The amount of benefit paid however depends upon the applicant's financial circumstances, assessed in accordance with Centrelink measures of income and level of assets held.

For purposes of these assessments, thresholds are set and maximum benefits are paid where neither income nor assets exceeds the relevant thresholds. Higher thresholds apply for which entitlements reduce to nil. Between these thresholds a reduced entitlement is paid. The means-tested age-based entitlement is paid to eligible applicants with the maximum rate of payment set out below. The Age Pension is usually adjusted twice a year in line with increases in the cost of living. This includes the higher of the increase in the Consumer Price Index (CPI) and the increase in the new Pensioner and Beneficiary Living Cost Index (PBLCI).

NOTE 1: Veterans pensions are based on similar rules, but eligibility commences five years earlier; see Age Pension age limits below.

NOTE 2: For those who are legally blind, eligibility for the Age Pension (blind) category is independent of the income or assets test.

	Maximum benefit rates per fortnight	Pension Supplement per fortnight
	As at 20 March 2015[1]	As at 20 March 2015[2]
Single	$782.20	$63.90 [2]
Couple	$589.60 each	$96.40 combined[2]

1: The full benefit payment comprises a maximum benefit rate per fortnight adjusted downward in accordance with the assets and income tests, plus the Pension Supplement.
2: Prior to 20 September 2009 certain allowances were paid separately on a quarterly or other basis. Under present arrangements these allowances are combined and extended into a Pension Supplement and paid fortnightly. (See *Pension Supplement* below.)

RESIDENCE TESTS

To qualify for Age Pension benefits:

- the applicant must be an Australian resident living in Australia on a permanent basis and either:
    - is an Australian citizen
    - is the holder of a permanent resident visa
    - is a New Zealand citizen who was in Australia on 26 February 2001, or for 12 months in the two years immediately before that date, or was assessed as 'protected' before 26 February 2004 AND the applicant must meet the ten year qualifying Australian residence requirements, unless claiming under an International Social Security Agreement
    - claiming as a refugee or former refugee
    - the applicant was in receipt of a pension immediately before turning Age Pension age, or

-     if the claimant is a woman whose partner died while the couple were both Australian residents and the woman had two years residency immediately before claiming the Age Pension.

The ten year Australian residence requirement means that the applicant has been an Australian resident for a continuous period of at least ten years, or for a number of periods which total more than ten years, with one of the periods being at least five years.

TRANSFERRING FROM ONE TO ANOTHER BENEFIT

When transferring from one benefit type to another the recipient does not need to lodge a new claim (eg. a person receiving a disability support pension and turning Age Pension age does not need to lodge a new claim).

NOTE: Those who have lived or worked outside Australia may be eligible to claim and receive a foreign pension in Australia. Accordingly, they are encouraged to take steps to claim such pensions from the other country and Centrelink may be able to assist with such claims.

PENSION SUPPLEMENT

Previously the Age Benefit payments comprised a maximum base amount together with various allowances. Some allowances were combined and paid as a pension supplement on a fortnightly basis and others were paid on a quarterly basis. From 20 September 2009 these were rolled into a fortnightly Pension Supplement.

In particular the previous Goods and Services Tax Supplement, Pharmaceutical Allowance, Utilities Allowance, Telephone Allowance (at the higher internet rate) plus an initial increment of $2.49 per week for singles and $10.14 per week for couples combined and paid fortnightly made up the Pension Supplement.

ELIGIBILITY

Generally, people will get the supplement automatically if they are receiving:
- Age Pension
- Bereavement Allowance
- Carer Payment
- Disability Support Pension (except if you are aged under 21 and have no children)
- Widow B Pension, or
- Wife Pension.

The Pension Supplement is also automatically paid to people over age pension age who are receiving:
- Austudy
- Parenting Payment (single and partnered)
- Partner Allowance
- Special Benefit, or
- Widow Allowance.

20.420   AGE PENSION AGE LIMITS

Traditionally the qualifying age for Age Pension benefits was higher for males at 65 years, than for females. However a gradual transitional arrangement was put in place to raise the Age Pension age for women so that in a number of years the two will be the same. Legislation was passed to increase the qualifying age for the Age Pension to 65 for women over a six year period commencing 1 July 2017.

NOTE: This increase in Age Pension age will also affect seniors who apply for the Commonwealth Seniors Health Card (see 20.500 and 20.526).

A further increase to age 67 for both men and women by July 2023 will be achieved as follows.

The provisions lead to an increase of half a year in the qualifying age every two years, commencing 1 July 2017. This leads to age 67 from 1 July 2023. Refer to the table below for eligibility to meet the age criteria for Age Pension.

AGE PENSION AGE MEN AND WOMEN

Born	Women eligible for Age Pension at age	Men eligible for Age Pension at age
Between 1 July 1947 and 31 December 1948	64 and a half	65
Between 1 January 1949 and 30 June 1952	65	65
Between 1 July 1952 and 31 December 1953	65 and a half	65 and a half
Between 1 January 1954 and 30 June 1955	66	66
Between 1 July 1955 and 31 December 1956	66 and a half	66 and a half
After 1 January 1957	67	67

NOTE: If you were born before 1 July 1947, you have reached the qualifying age for Age Pension.

Min turns 60 on 5 July 2012 as her date of birth is 5 July 1952. On 5 July 2017 she will turn 65, by then, Age Pension age will be 65 years and 6 months. She would not meet her Age Pension eligibility until 5 January 2018. Alternatively, from the table above: (Note this is a transposed version of the government release.)

From the first column, determine the row in which the individual's date of birth occurs.

In our example, 5 July 1952 falls within the interval 1 July 1952 to 31 December 1953. Use this row to determine:

(a) The period during which an increase in the Age Pension age occurs (second column) in the year commencing 1 July 2017.

(b) The third column shows the prospective age for Age Pension eligibility; in this case 65 years and six months.

(c) The fourth column shows the time span during which age eligibility occurs for Age Pension under these rules.

20.430 MEANS TESTS

The level of entitlement paid to eligible seniors is determined by the outcome of both an assets test and an income test. Each test determines an amount of benefit the senior may qualify to receive and the lower benefit is the amount paid.

The amount determined under each test is arrived at by starting at the full entitlement. If the relevant threshold for full benefits is not exceeded the full benefit is payable under that test. If the level of assets or income exceeds the relevant threshold for full benefits, the benefit entitlement is 'clawed back' evenly to reflect the extent to which the assets or income exceed the relevant threshold. Each test is briefly described below with simple examples.

20.435 ASSETS TEST

Assets are items of value, including ownership or interest in property that is held by the applicant or their partner and it includes foreign assets. The assets test involves an aggregation of all assessable assets held.

Most assets are assessable in determining income support payments, with the following exceptions:

- the applicant's home
- all funds used to support an existing complying income stream that was deemed to be 100% assets test exempt, and
- 50% of funds used to support an existing complying income stream or market linked pension that was deemed to be 50% assets test exempt.

Assessable assets typically include cash, the value of bank accounts, shares, real estate, household items, motor vehicles, boats, etc. The asset value is the current market value less any outstanding debt on those assets. In addition, the value of assets gifted by the applicant, also known as deprived assets (see below), is included in the assets test.

ASSESSABLE ASSETS

- Amounts in superannuation for persons who have reached Age Pension age (including all amounts that support pensions except those shown in excluded assets below)
- Reportable superannuation contributions (typically salary sacrifice)
- Cash and the market value of financial assets held (including interest bearing deposits, fixed deposits, bonds, debentures, shares, property trust units, friendly society bonds and managed investments)
- Real estate (including a holiday home) other than a principal home
- Total net losses from rental property
- Value of businesses or farms including goodwill (where goodwill is shown on the balance sheet)
- Surrendered value of life insurance policies
- Amounts disposed of without adequate return ('deprived assets' – see *Warning* below)
- Gifts of more than $10,000 in a year (and $30,000 in five years) for an individual or couple
- The value of loans by a pensioner to family trusts, members of the family, organizations, and so on to others
- The value of motor vehicles
- The value of boats and caravans not used as homes
- Household contents and personal effects
- Collections for trading, investment or hobby purposes
- Market value of managed assets
- The value of the entry contribution to a retirement village (see next page for *Extra allowable amount for retirement village and granny flat residents*)
- The attributed value of a private trust or private company if controller of trust or company
- The value of a life interest created by the pensioner or their partner, or upon the death of the partner

 A 'garage sale' value for household assets including motor vehicles is acceptable for purposes of the assets test.

NOTE: Generally, any debt secured against an asset is deducted from the value of that asset. In such circumstances the asset value is the current market value less any outstanding debt on the asset/s.

DEPRIVED ASSETS

Assets gifted by an applicant in excess of the limits indicated are included in the calculation of the assets held by the applicant until the fifth anniversary of the date of the gifting. Gifts are also deemed to earn income in much the same way as other or normal financial assets.

In addition, assets that are gifted in the immediate five years preceding an application for benefits will also be considered for the assets test.

Non-arm's length transfers including the transfer of unit trusts or private companies at prices less than market value will result in the application gifting rules applying. Relinquishing control of a private company or trust will be seen to be potentially gifting the entire assets of the entity. Gifts to private trusts or companies that are not controlled by the retiree are also caught as are gifts to other non-related individuals, charities or relatives.

 Centrelink has indicated that in relation to the non-application of the gifting rules: 'Gifting does not include you selling or reducing your assets to meet normal expenses, for example, to buy consumer goods like a fridge or washing machine, for home maintenance/improvements, or to pay for holidays. Nor does it include payments for services received, eg. lawn mowing.'

Deprived assets are those assets that a social security recipient or applicant has gifted, in order to reduce their assessed asset level.

The rules applicable until 30 June 2002 were that amounts in excess of $10,000 per pension per year were deprived assets and remained so for a period of five years from the date of gifting. A year was measured as a calendar year. From 30 July 2002 the period is based on a financial year and although the $10,000 figure still applies in any given year, there is an additional requirement that over any rolling five year period, the amount may not exceed $30,000. This means that amounts that exceed $10,000 in a single year or the $30,000 rolling five year amount are treated as deprived assets for five years from the date of disposal.

EXCLUDED ASSETS

- Principal home (land less than two hectares)
- Life interest (not created by the pensioner, beneficiary or their partner)
- Granny flat interest
- Victorian Ministry of Housing – moveable unit
- Value of any right or interest in a sale/lease back home (if the deferred amount is greater than the difference home owner and non-homeowner allowable asset levels)
- Reversionary, remainder and contingent interest (not created by the person receiving a pension or allowance)
- Interest in an estate (not received or not able to be received)
- Medal or decoration of valor not held for investment
- $10,000 paid in advance for funeral expenses, funeral bonds, etc
- Aids for the disabled
- Gift cars from Department of Veterans Affairs
- Proceeds from the sale of a previous home that will be applied for the purposes of another home purchase in 12 months
- Amounts in superannuation where the individual is below Age retirement age
- 100% of the value of the assets supporting fully exempt defined benefit complying pensions that were commenced prior to 20 September 2004 where the individual has reached Age retirement age
- 50% of the value of the assets supporting defined benefit complying pensions commenced between
20 September 2004 and 19 September 2007 where the individual has reached Age retirement age
- 50% of the value of assets supporting a market linked pension commenced before 20 September 2007 where the individual has reached Age retirement age

NOTE: No assets test exemptions apply to new pensions commenced from 20 September 2007.

RETIREMENT VILLAGE AND GRANNY FLAT RESIDENTS

If the entry contribution for this accommodation is equal to or less than the extra allowable amount (the difference between the non-homeowner and the homeowner asset test limit which is currently $135,000) the assets test assessment is based on the non-home owner category and the entry contribution will be included for purposes of the assets test. This category of recipient may also qualify for Rent Assistance.

HARDSHIP PROVISIONS

Individuals who own assets but have limited or no income are expected to rearrange their affairs to provide for themselves. In certain circumstances this may not be possible and those facing 'severe financial hardship' may qualify for a payment from Centrelink. These assessments may use different assets and/or income tests.

ASSETS TEST RULE

An individual's total assessable assets determines the extent of benefit payable. If this amount is less than or equal to the threshold for full pension (see example following) the full benefit is payable based on the assets test.

When the level of assets exceeds the full pension threshold, a reduced age pension entitlement is based on a $1.50 per fortnight reduction for each additional $1,000 of assets above the threshold. In the 2015 Budget the Government proposed that taper rate return to $3 for every $1000 of assets above the threshold from 1 January 2017.

NOTE: No benefit is payable when the asset level is equal to or exceeds the part pension threshold.

In addition to the assets test a separate income test is also carried out. It determines the level of benefits that would be payable under the income test alone. The recipient is eligible to receive a benefit based on the lesser of the two amounts.

The asset thresholds for Age Pension benefits paid to homeowners and non-homeowners, for singles and couples follows.

Assets test for homeowners (20 March 2015)		
Family situation	**For full pension/ allowance[1]**	**For part pension limit**
Single	Assets up to $202,000	Assets less than $775,750
Partnered (combined)	up to $286,500	less than $1,151,500
Illness separated couple (combined)	up to $286,500	less than $1,433,500
One partner eligible (combined)	up to $286,500	less than $1,151,500
Assets test for non-homeowners (20 March 2015)		
Family situation	**For full pension/ allowance[1]**	**For part pension[2]**
Single	Assets up to $348,500	Assets less than $922,000
Partnered (combined)	up to $433,000	less than $1,580,000
Illness separated couple (combined)	up to $433,000	less than $1,580,000
One partner eligible	up to $433,000	less than $1,298,000

1: Assets test assets that exceed these amounts reduce pension entitlement by $1.50 per fortnight for every $1,000 above the limit (single and couple combined).

2: Limits will increase if rent assistance is paid with the pension.

As part of the Budget 2015 announcements it is proposed that from 1 January 2017 the assets test will change. The limit for full pension for house owners will increase to $250,000 for homeowner single, $375,000 for couple homeowners, $450,000 for single non-homeowners and $575,000 for couple non-homeowners.

However access to the part pension is planned to be scaled back so that the part pensions ends when assets (other than the family home) at $547,000 for single homeowners and $823,000 for couple homeowners. For non-homeowners it will reduce to $747,000 single non-homeowners and $1.023 million for couple non-homeowners.

The following examples illustrate the principle involved in determining benefits payable under the assets test.

> ***EXAMPLE 1: Assets test assessment***
> *Jack aged 68 owns his home and is assessed as having assessable assets of 142,000.*
> *He is eligible for the full Age Pension benefit of $ 782.20 per fortnight plus the Pension Supplement of $63.90 per fortnight. This is based on the assets test alone.*
> *His assessable assets do not exceed the threshold for full pension benefits of $202,000 . (An income test is also necessary to establish level of actual entitlement paid.)*

> ***EXAMPLE 2: Assets test assessment***
> *If he is gifted additional assessable assets worth $100,000, making a total of $242,000, the benefit payable would be reduced under the assets test:*
> *Excess assets = ($242,000 – $202,000 = $40,000*
> *Reduction of $1.5/$1,000 per fortnight = $60.00 per fortnight.*
> *The entitlement would be determined for purposes of the assets test as follows:*
> *($$782.20 – $60.00) per fortnight = $722.20 per fortnight plus $63.90 Pension Supplement.*
> *When the level of assessed assets equals or exceeds the maximum or part pension cut-off level of $775,750 , the benefit payable is zero.*

NOTE: The above merely demonstrates the working of the assets test. The benefit actually paid is determined after the effects of both the assets test and the income test are considered.

20.435   INCOME TEST

The income test is similar to the assets test, but compares the applicant's income against income thresholds. All income including the following is aggregated, with special rules applying for deemed and income stream income:

- salary or wage income
- rental income
- deemed income associated with investments (see below), and
- income streams (see over).

DEEMED INCOME

> ***Deemed income is calculated by way of an equivalent interest rate/s set on all financial assets (investments) and deprived assets – see Assets test at 20.435. The actual investment income is replaced by a notional or deemed amount which is calculated on the value of the relevant assets as though they were invested at the government's prescribed deeming rates of interest.***

IMPORTANT! The government has passed amendments that extend the normal deeming rules to include superannuation account-based income streams for the purposes of the pension income test to ensure all financial investments are assessed fairly and under the same rules. Standard pension deeming arrangements will apply to new superannuation account-based income streams assessed under the pension income test rules after 1 January 2015. All products held by pensioners before 1 January 2015 will be grandfathered indefinitely and continue to be assessed under the existing rules for the life of the product so no current pensioner will be adversely affected, unless they choose to change products.

The effect of deeming is to standardise the earning rates of all investments held, irrespective of how much or how little the investment actually earns. Deeming ensures that there is no advantage in respect of eligibility for a higher level of Centrelink benefits for members who hold assets in say non-interest paying bank accounts in order to reduce the income they receive to increase the benefit entitlement from Centrelink. All recipients are treated equivalently in respect of income received from investments. If retirees receive a greater income than the deemed amount then that is to their advantage. If however they receive lower incomes than the deemed amounts then clearly they are at a disadvantage.

In line with other social security parameters, the deeming rates are reviewed periodically.

The deemed income is irrelevant for income tax purposes and only has application in respect of Centrelink income tests. For income tax assessment purposes, actual investment income is assessed.

Deeming rates (20 March 2015)		
	Assets	Deeming rate
Assets threshold and deeming rate (single beneficiary)	$48,000	1.75%
Assets threshold and 2nd deeming rate (single beneficiary)	$48,001	3.25%
Assets threshold and deeming rate (couple[1])	$79,600 (combined)	1.75%
Assets threshold and 2nd deeming rate (couple[1])	$79,601 (combined)	3.25%

1: The above rates apply for a pensioner couple (both receiving a pension) or a pensioner/allowee couple (one person receiving a pension and the other receiving an allowance). If neither member of the couple is receiving a pension, the first $39,800 of the financial investments of both is deemed to earn income at 1.75% pa. Any amount over that is deemed to earn income at 3.25% pa.

The deeming rates are set jointly by the Ministers for the Department of Families, Housing, Community Services and Indigenous Affairs and the Department of Education, Employment and Workplace Relations.

WORK BONUS FOR AGE PENSIONERS

The Work Bonus was introduced from 20 September 2009 to encourage pensioners to increase their income through part-time work without the full impact of the income test claw back. It replaces the Pension Bonus Scheme that was closed to new entrants from 20 September 2009. (Those registered in the Scheme before 20 September 2009 may remain under the scheme and claim a Pension Bonus upon ceasing work and receiving entitlements.)

The Work Bonus provides an incentive for age pensioners to remain in the workforce. If an eligible person earns more than $250 per fortnight assessable employment income is reduced by $250. Earnings of less than $250 per fortnight will reduce assessable employment income to zero.

INCOME TEST FOR AGE PENSIONS

The income test allows for full benefits to be paid where a recipient's income does not exceed the lower (full payment) threshold. For incomes above this lower threshold, the benefit reduces by 50 cents for singles (25 cents for couples) for each additional dollar of income and reduces to nil at or above the maximum income threshold.

Age Pension income test thresholds (20 March 2015)		
Family situation	For full payment (per fortnight)[1]	For part payment (per fortnight)[2]
Single	up to 160*	less than $1,880.40 *
Couple (combined)	up to $284*	less than $3,724.80 *
Illness separated couple (combined)	up to $268*	less than $3,647.20 *

1: Income test assessed income that exceeds the full payment threshold results in a reduction of the benefit at a rate of 50 cents in the dollar (single) or 25 cents in the dollar each (for couples). For transitional arrangements where couples were receiving payments at 19 September 2009 a rate of 40 cents in the dollar (single) and 20 cents in the dollar each (for couples) applies.

2: These figures may be higher with rent assistance payments (see 20.524).

NOTE: A stricter Age Pension income test taper was introduced from 20 September 2009. The rate increased from 40 cents per additional dollar to 50 cents per additional dollar for single pensioners and for couples it is 25 cents per additional dollar of income.

The following example shows the application of the income test

Jack is single and a home owner, age 68 (from earlier example), with no other income or investments (deemed income is nil). The benefit payable is the full $782.20 per fortnight plus the Pension Supplement of $63.90 per fortnight. The full benefit is payable for situations of income ranging from nil to (and including) $160 per fortnight. Income above this threshold reduces the benefit by 50 cents per fortnight for each additional $1 per fortnight of (income test) income. At or above the maximum threshold of $1,880.40 per fortnight the benefit reduces to zero.

A Work Bonus for Age Pensioners may influence the result if income was derived from working.

ACTUAL BENEFIT PAID (LOWER AMOUNT FROM THE TESTS)

The benefits calculated from each test (assets and income) are compared and the lesser benefit (including a nil amount) is the benefit that is actually paid.

Jill, a single Age Pensioner and home owner, holds assets of $211,250. Her income is $9,100 pa or $350 per fortnight, comprising $150 per fortnight from part-time work, plus $200 per fortnight of deemed income. Her Age Pension entitlement is based on the full benefit of $782.20 per fortnight reduced in accordance with the asset test thresholds and taper of $1.5 per $1,000 excess assets, and the income test thresholds and taper of 50%. The Pension Supplement of $62.90 per fortnight is also paid. The lower benefit determined from these two tests is what is paid.

Assets test

Reduction in benefits per fortnight = $1.5 x ($206,000 – $196,750)/$1000 = $13.90 per fortnight.

The benefit entitlement calculated arising from the assets test is the full benefit of $782.20 less a reduction of $13.90 = $786.30 per fortnight plus the Pension Supplement of $63.90 per fortnight.

Income test

The benefit arising from the income test is the full benefit less 50% of excess income received per fortnight.

Jill can use the work bonus for Age Pensioners, (only half of the first $500 per fortnight from working is assessable). She earns $150 per fortnight from working, so half of this is exempt and the other half assessable for the income test. $75 per fortnight from part time work plus $200 per fortnight as deemed income is assessable.

A reduced figure of $275 per fortnight applies for the income test.

The benefit entitlement from the income test is the full benefit less 50% of $115 ($275 – $160) per fortnight = $782.20 – $57.50 = $724.70 per fortnight plus Pension Supplement of $63.90 per fortnight.

Benefit paid

Benefit paid is the lesser of the two, namely $724.70 per fortnight plus the Pension Supplement of $63.90 per fortnight.

Marie, age 65, owns her home and has just retired from work. Her personal effects are relatively insignificant for the purposes of this example. She is drawing down from an account based pension in a SMSF from assets valued on 1 July 2015 of $400,000, all of which comprise a taxable component of her interest. She plans to draw down $20,000 in the year 2014-15. For the Centrelink income test the annual deductible amount was determined to be $18,182 pa. (See also Centrelink tests for income streams below). She meets the age and residency tests for Age Pension eligibility.

Is she eligible for any Age Pension benefits from Centrelink?

Assets test

Marie's assets of $400,000 exceed the asset test threshold for full benefits of $202,000 while not exceeding the pension cut off threshold of $758,750. She is therefore only eligible for reduced or part pension benefits.

Under the assets test she would receive $782.20 – ($400,000 – $202,000 x $1.5/$1,000 = $485.20 per fortnight plus the Pension Supplement of $63.90 per fortnight.

Income test

Under the income test income from a superannuation income stream is the superannuation payment less the deductible amount = $20,000 – $18,182 = $1,818 pa or approximately $70 per fortnight.

The income test threshold for full benefit payment is $160 per fortnight. The income test assessment of $70 per fortnight is less than the income test threshold for full benefits. She is entitled to the full benefit under this test.

Benefit paid

The assets test entitlement yields the lower benefit so this is the relevant test. Her part pension entitlement is $485.20 per fortnight plus the Pension Supplement of $63.90 per fortnight.

For Age Pension benefit calculations, assets in superannuation are not deemed for the income test. The actual annual income stream income less an annual deductible amount is used, providing a concession for superannuation income stream beneficiaries (see Centrelink tests for income streams *below*).

CENTRELINK TESTS FOR INCOME STREAMS

These assessments are quite different from those used for income tax purposes.

INCOME TEST

Income streams from superannuation funds are assessed uniquely for Centrelink entitlements. Governments have viewed these as preferred investments for retirees from the standpoint of a long term income stream. Concessions apply through a mechanism that reduces the level of assessed income for purposes of determining the benefit a retiree may qualify to receive. A deductible amount reduces assessable 'income test income' if the retiree has reached preservation age, currently 55. The correspondingly lower income may lead to a higher benefit from Centrelink.

For account based pensions (as for other pensions) the annual deductible amount is calculated as follows:

Annual deductible amount = Purchase price/Life expectancy at commencement of pension

The income test assessment of an account based pension is determined as follows:

Income test assessed income
= Gross income payable for the year – Annual deductible amount

It must be stressed that the deductible amount calculated above is not relevant for income tax purposes.

PREVIOUSLY TWO DEDUCTIBLE AMOUNTS

Prior to the introduction of *Better Super* there were two separate calculations of deductible amounts. The first was for the determination of a social security income test as described above. The second was an annual tax-free amount, excluded from the taxable income of a beneficiary of an income stream. This was determined from the 'undeducted contributions' in the superannuation account from which the income stream was paid and calculated at the commencement of the income stream. It was an average annual amount based on the full duration of the income stream for the individual. This annual amount was tax-free in the hands of the recipient. With the introduction of *Better Super* the income stream has associated with it a proportion of income that is tax-exempt for those under 60. But for those 60 and over the benefits received are tax-free when paid from taxed superannuation funds.

ASSETS TEST FOR INCOME STREAMS

NOTE: The following information applies to pensions commenced in the past.

Retirement income streams may be divided into three distinct classes as shown below. However, there are no asset test exemptions for new income streams commenced on or after 20 September 2007.

COMPLYING STREAMS

These income streams may have been commenced prior to 20 September 2004 from SMSFs or from public offer superannuation funds prior to 20 September 2007.

NOTE: For such an income stream commenced before 20 September 2004 a 100% asset test exemption applies. Those commenced in the intervening period but before 20 September 2007 only receive a 50% asset test exemption.

ASSETS TEST

Typically complying streams are long-term streams whose asset base is assets test exempt to some degree.

INCOME TEST FOR COMPLYING STREAMS

The amount assessed is the gross income paid less an annual deductible amount. The effect of the deductible amount is to significantly reduce the assessed income for the income test.

The annual deductible amount is determined at the start of the income stream and calculated as follows:

Annual deductible amount = Amount invested / Life expectancy (in years)

EXAMPLE: Investment of $300,000 in a complying income stream, no other assets in excess of minimum asset threshold
Betty is single and a retired home owner, with an investment of $300,000 in a (100% asset test exempt) complying income stream that she made several years ago when she was 62. Her other assets have negligible market value.

Assets test
The assets of the complying pension will continue to be exempt for assets test purposes. Assessable assets are below the 202,000 assets test threshold for full benefits. She qualifies for full benefits of $782.20 per fortnight plus $63.90 per fortnight Pension Supplement.

Income test
Betty's annual income from her pension is $21,000 pa. (This is about $810 per fortnight.) Her exempt income is $12,653 pa, determined at the start of the pension. The first $12,653 of income from her superannuation benefit is not assessed under the income test. Her assessable income for purposes of the income test is therefore:
($21,000 – $12,653) or $8,347 per annum or $321 per fortnight.
The assessed income is greater than the income threshold of $160 per fortnight, for a full Age entitlement.
It is reduced as follows: Reduction rate of $0.50 for each dollar of income test assessed income in excess of $156 per fortnight.
($321 – $160) x 50% = $80.50
The reduced benefit is $701.50 per fortnight plus a Pension Supplement of $63.90 per fortnight from this test.

Benefit payable
The lower amount is payable, namely $701.50 per fortnight plus the Pension Supplement of $63.90 per fortnight or a total fortnightly payment from Centrelink of $765.40.
In total, Betty receives $765.40 per fortnight (Centrelink) + $810 per fortnight (superannuation) or $1,575.40 per fortnight income or approximately $40,960 for the year.

A 100% asset test exempt pension must have been commenced before 20 September 2004.

EXAMPLE: Investment in a market linked pension (MLP), with no other assets
Mary is retired, single and owns her home. She invested $330,000 in an MLP with a tax-free proportion of 0% and a 50% asset test exemption. The account balance is $300,000 (end June 2015) with a draw down of $15,000. The remaining term selected is 35 years. Her other assets are negligible and the exempt amount for Centrelink purposes is $13,918 pa.

Assets test

50% of the superannuation assets are assessable. This is $150,000, which is below the full pension assets test threshold of $202,000 , so the full benefit of $782.20 plus the Pension Supplement of $63.90 per fortnight is payable under this test.

Income test

Assessable income for the income test = ($15,000 – $13,918) or $1,082 pa, or about $41.62 per fortnight. This is less than the income threshold of $160 per fortnight for full entitlements. She is entitled to the full Age age pension benefit under this test of $782.20 plus the Pension Supplement of $63.90 per fortnight.

Benefit paid

The full Centrelink entitlement for the year is over $20,667 and her total annual income is approximately $36,551.40 for the year.

 EXAMPLE: Market linked pension and account based pension commenced on 1 July 2007 with no other assets

What is the situation when assessed at 1 July 2015?

Alex is a 69 year old single male retired homeowner. Following draw-downs and poor investment performance, on 1 July 2015 his market linked pension account held $280,000 with the remainder of the term being 24 years and a draw down of $17,444. His account based pension held a balance of $130,000, from which he would draw down $7,500 for the year. The annual pension exempt amounts are $18,507 and $9,253 respectively for each pension.

Assets test

The market linked pension is assessable at 50% of the value or $140,000 and the entire account based pension of $130,000 is assessable.

Assets test determination for benefits is $140,000 + $130,000 = $270,000. This exceeds the assets test threshold of $202,000 for full benefits, while being below the cut-out threshold of $775,750 . Excess benefits for a notionally full pension = $68,000.

The benefit payable under the assets test is $782.20 per fortnight less a reduction of $102. The entitlement under this test is $680.20 per fortnight plus the Pension Supplement of $63.90 per fortnight.

Income test

For purposes of the income test, the annual income from the market linked pension is the amount in excess of the exempt amount of $18,507. However the actual draw down of $17,444 is less than the exempt amount. Therefore nil excess income applies.

For purposes of the income test, the assessed account based pension, is the annual amount paid in excess of the exempt amount of $9,253. The exempt amount exceeds the actual draw down so there is nil excess income above the full benefit threshold.

The full benefit of $782.20 per fortnight plus Pension Supplement of $63.90 per fortnight is payable under the income test.

Benefit paid

The benefit paid is the lesser of the two, namely $680.20 per fortnight plus the Pension Supplement of $63.90 per fortnight or approximately $20,126.60 pa from Centrelink. Alex's total annual income is $24,944 from superannuation plus 20,126 from Centrelink = $45,070.60 for the year.

NOTE: Centrelink must be informed immediately when circumstances change in relation to income and assets. Centrelink also seeks updated information on a quarterly basis.

CENTRELINK STRATEGIES LIMITED

With the introduction of account based pensions as the new income stream standard any options in relation to mixing and matching pensions with different Centrelink assessments is now not possible for new arrangements. However the previous arrangements continue to apply for legacy products. Income test concessions are closed off for new income streams from 1 January 2015.

Existing income stream arrangements designed to optimise assets test issues should not be rolled over without seeking professional advice. The rollover could result in a pension being created that is treated under the new rules and the assets test exemption lost.

TAXATION OF FUND INCOME

An exemption applies on the investment earnings of the pension account under the exempt current pension income provisions. Superannuation funds paying either complying income streams, market linked pensions or account based income streams (previously allocated pensions) are eligible for this exemption. In addition retirees drawing down benefits from taxed superannuation funds are exempt from paying tax on the benefits if they are 60 or over. Otherwise the taxable component of the benefit is assessable, with a tax rebate of 15% applying. This rebate may be used to offset some or all of the income tax liability excluding the 2% Medicare levy.

NOTE: Excess imputation credits are refundable.

GENERAL STRATEGIES

To maximise Centrelink benefits, retirees may reduce the level of assets held that count under the assets test. Beyond a certain point this may become intrusive and generally impractical. The scope for such action may be limited, though at the margin some impact may be possible.

Retirees may bring-forward investments directed to home maintenance and renovation since the home is an exempt asset under the assets test. They may choose to reduce their incomes where possible since this would result in a lower income test assessment. These actions have at best limited application without affecting their total income and hence the retiree's well-being.

One strategy that is no longer available is the use of a superannuation fund to pay benefits. The income was previously treated concessionally for the Centrelink income test and for personal income tax purposes.

As of 1 January 2015 income stream are included under the deeming provisions. Scope still exists to use existing superannuation income streams with 100% and 50% assets test exemption to create eligibility for Centrelink benefits.

 Account based pensions do not have any assets test concessions, however the benefits are concessionally assessed for the income test.

20.500 CERTAIN OTHER CENTRELINK BENEFITS

20.516   SENIORS SUPPLEMENT

From 20 September 2009 eligible self-funded retirees gained access to a Seniors Supplement upon becoming eligible for the Commonwealth Seniors Health Card or the Department of Veterans' Affairs Gold Card with current seniors concession allowance. It incorporates existing payments of seniors concession allowance and the higher rate of telephone allowance.

The 2014-15 Budget proposed getting rid of the Seniors Supplement as of 1 July 2014. However these measures have never passed the Senate and therefore never became law. It is still government policy to get rid of the Seniors Supplement but it will require a change in policy from either the cross bench or the Greens or Labor.

From 20 March 2015 the rate of payment of Seniors Supplement is as follows:

- Single: $894.40 per annum
- Couple: $673.40 per annum each
- Couple illness separated, respite care or partner in prison: $894.40 per annum

Seniors Supplement is paid quarterly, soon after 20 March, 20 June, 20 September and 20 December. It is not taxable and not income or assets tested. It is payable when the senior qualifies for the Commonwealth Seniors Health Card and is equivalent to the minimum rate of the Pension Supplement paid to part pensioners.

Eligible seniors also receive other concessions linked to the Commonwealth Seniors Health Card. They include the Pharmaceutical Benefits Scheme for reduced costs of prescription medicines, a discounted Medicare safety net threshold, and concessional travel on the Great Southern Rail Services.

20.520   TELEPHONE ALLOWANCE

This is a non-taxable quarterly payment.

Telephone allowance	Amount per quarter
Basic rate (single or couple combined)	$27.20
Higher rate (single or couple combined)	$40.60

The telephone allowance is not subject to a separate income test or assets test and if the telephone is in joint names the amount payable is split. The telephone allowance is unrelated to any concessions or discounts offered by the telephone company or provider.

NOTE: Prior to 20 September 2009 certain allowances were paid separately on a quarterly or other basis. Under present arrangements these allowances are combined and extended into a Pension Supplement and paid fortnightly (see 20.410).

20.522   UTILITIES ALLOWANCE

The utilities allowance is a non-taxable payment that is paid to income support payment recipients (eg. age pension recipients) to assist with the payment of gas, electricity and water bills on a regular basis. The rate is $148.60 per quarter for a single person (or each member of a couple separated by illness) or $74.30 per annum per member of a couple as at 20 March 2014. The utilities allowance is adjusted in March and September each year in line with changes in the CPI.

NOTE: From 20 September 2009 the fortnightly Pension Supplement incorporates previous allowances (see 20.410).

20.523   PENSIONER CONCESSION CARD

A Pensioner Concession Card is issued annually in the month of the recipient's birth and entitles the holder to reduced costs for medicines under the Pharmaceutical Benefits Scheme plus other State and Local Government authority concessions that may include the following:

- reductions in property and water rates
- reductions in energy bills
- a telephone allowance
- reduced fares on public transport
- reductions on motor vehicle registration, and
- one or more free rail journeys within the state each year.

These concessions vary from State to State and some of these may also be available to dependants.

Entitlement to a Pensioner Concession Card is subject to the receipt of any of the following:

- a pension
  - parenting payment (single)
  - mature age allowance
  - carer payment (adult), and
  - carer payment (child)
- Newstart allowance or youth allowance (job seeker) as a single principal carer of a dependent child
- being over 60 years of age and having received one (or a combination) of the following payments continuously for more than nine months:
  - Newstart allowance
  - Sickness allowance
  - Widow allowance

- Partner allowance
- Parenting payment (partnered)
- Special benefit, or
- Assessed as having a partial capacity to work and receiving Newstart allowance, parenting payment (partnered) or youth allowance (job seeker).

NOTE: Some individuals may be eligible to keep their Pensioner Concession Card for a short time after returning to work to assist in the transition from being a Centrelink payment recipient to returning to work.

20.524 RENT ASSISTANCE

Age Pensioners may qualify for rent assistance if they:

- meet a residence test, or
- receive a pension payable under the *Social Security Act 1991* and pay more than a certain amount for:
  - rent[*] (other than for public housing)
  - service and maintenance fees in a retirement village
  - lodging (if paying for board and lodging and cannot work out the amount paid for lodging, two thirds of the amount you paid will be accepted as being for lodging)
  - fees paid to use a site for a caravan or other accommodation which is occupied as a person's principal home, or
  - fees paid to moor a vessel occupied as a person's principal home.

  [*]If paid directly to State or Territory housing authorities, the retiree is not eligible.
  In some situations sub-tenants may qualify.

Rent assistance[1] no dependants (20 March 2015)

Situation	Maximum payment per fortnight	No payment if fortnightly rent is less than	Max. payment if fortnightly rent is more than
Single	$128.40	$114.00	$285.20
Single, sharer	$85.60	$114.00	$228.13
Couple	$120.80	$185.40	$346.47
One of a couple separated due to illness[2]	$128.4	$114.00	$285.20
One of a couple temporarily separated	$120.80	$114.00	$275.07

1: Payment rates appear as a guide only, indexed to the CPI and adjusted twice annually.
2: Includes respite care and partner in prison.

RECIPIENTS WITH DEPENDENT CHILDREN

For those with dependent children, rent assistance is usually payable with family tax benefit part A. For those without dependent children and in receipt of a pension, allowance or benefit, rent assistance is normally paid with that payment.

Rent assistance[1] with dependants (20 March 2015)

Situation	Maximum payment per fortnight	No payment if fortnightly rent less than	Max. payment if fortnightly rent more than
Single parent, 1 or 2 children	$150.50	$150.08	$350.75
Single parent, 3 or more children	$170.10	$150.08	$376.88
Couple, 1 or 2 children	$150.50	$222.18	$422.85
Couple, 3 or more children	$170.10	$222.18	$448.98

1: Payment rates appear as a guide only.

Rent assistance is not payable if:

- rent is paid to a government housing authority, although in some situations sub-tenants may qualify
- the applicant resides in a Commonwealth funded nursing home or hostel, or
- the applicant is a single, disability support pensioner under 21, without dependants, living with parents, or under 25, single and living with parents.

Special rules apply to single sharers, people who pay board and lodging or live in a retirement village.

Rent Certificates are required to verify rent where a customer does not have a formal written tenancy agreement or is not named as a tenant on a formal written tenancy agreement.

Rent assistance may be payable to Austudy recipients. Eligibility applied from 1 January 2008.

20.525   ADVANCE PAYMENT FOR PENSIONERS

Those receiving Age Pension or certain other support benefits may borrow or receive an advance on their pension by way of a lump sum typically to assist with unexpected expenses. This is interest-free and repayable over 13 fortnights. Initially a maximum lump sum payment or advance on a pension of up to $500 was available. From 1 July 2010, this was increased and made more flexible, with the maximum amount linked to fortnightly basic pension rates with pensioners no longer limited to one advance per year. Part-rate pensioners also have similar entitlements. From 20 March 2015, the minimum and maximum advance amounts are $405.85 and $1,217.55 for single pensioners and $305.95 and $917.85 for each member of a couple. The amounts that can be taken over six months are:

- one advance payment of the maximum amount
- one or two advance payments greater than the minimum amount, or
- three advance payments equal to the minimum amount.

The amount available at each application will depend on whether you have received previous advance payments, and the amount taken.

Pensioners only have access to three advances over a 13 fortnight period based on the minimum amount each time. If the amount is greater than the minimum, even by a few cents, there is a risk of not having the minimum amount available next time. If more than one advance payment is taken in the 13 fortnight period, each must be repaid in the order that they were taken, however several advances may be repaid at the same time resulting in a higher deduction from each fortnightly pension.

The minimum and maximum amounts increase every 20 March and 20 September.

Advance payments are only available if they will not result in financial hardship caused by the reduction in fortnightly entitlement. Centrelink will only allow an amount the pensioner can afford to repay over the relevant 13 fortnights.

Further information on pension advance payments can be obtained from Centrelink by calling 13 2300.

20.526   COMMONWEALTH SENIORS HEALTH CARD

A number of concession cards are provided by government, one that is most sought after is the Commonwealth Seniors Health Card (CSHC), available to self-funded retirees of Age Pension age to assist with the costs of certain health and other services including the cost of prescription medicines. A senior qualifies for a CSHC by being an Australian resident, living in Australia and not being subject to the newly arrived resident's waiting period. The senior, having reached age pension age, must not qualify for any age pension benefits but should have an income below the limit outlined below in the income test. No assets test applies in determining eligibility for the CSHC.

Dependants of CSHC holders are not eligible for the concessions available for the actual cardholder.

Holders of CSHCs must notify Centrelink of any changes in their circumstances regarding eligibility (including leaving Australia temporarily) as the card is otherwise reissued automatically each year in September.

NOTE: Since a condition of eligibility for the CSHC is that the senior does not receive a Service Pension or Income Support Supplement from the Department of Veterans' Affairs or income payments from Centrelink, the receipt of any Age Pension benefit renders them ineligible.

COMMONWEALTH SENIORS HEALTH CARD RELIEF

The Government passed measures to include income from tax-free superannuation in the income test for CSHC. This was from 1 January 2015. Those who had CSHC prior to that were grandfathered to keep the CSHC, however, if they change their pension the new pension will be included.

The annual adjusted taxable income* may not exceed:

- $51,500 (singles)
- $82,400 (couples combined), or
- $103,000 (couples combined who are separated due to ill health).

The limit is increased by $639.60 for each dependant child.

* Adjusted taxable income includes taxable income, net rental property loss, target foreign income (foreign income not normally taxed in Australia including fringe benefits), employer provided fringe benefits in Australia and Reportable Superannuation Contributions (including voluntary salary sacrificed contributions and personal deductible superannuation contributions for which a personal deduction has been claimed).

COMMONWEALTH SENIORS HEALTH CARD BENEFITS

Holders of CSHCs are entitled to receive a discount on prescription medicines through the Pharmaceutical Benefits Scheme (PBS) together with a range of other benefits as follows.

SENIORS SUPPLEMENT

This is a non-taxable payment that was introduced from 20 September 2009. It is paid every three months to eligible CSHC holders to assist seniors with their regular bill payments for energy, rates, phone and motor vehicle registration fees. It replaced the Seniors Concession Allowance (see 20.516).

NOTE: The Seniors Concession Allowance has not been available since 20 September 2009.

OTHER COMMONWEALTH SENIORS HEALTH CARD BENEFITS

- Bulk-billed GP appointments. The Australian Government provides financial incentives for GPs to bulk-bill concession card holders, however the concession is provided at the discretion of the GP.
- A reduction in the cost of out-of-hospital medical expenses above a concessional threshold, through the Medicare Safety Net.
- In some instances State or Territory and local governments and private providers offer concessions at their own discretion for certain health, household, transport, education and recreation services.
- The payment of a Seniors Supplement is non-taxable and made every six months to help with bills such as energy, rates and motor vehicle registration fees not available at a concessional rate. The payment also reflects the fact that most states don't provide a full range of concessions to CSHC holders.
- The telephone allowance previously payable is now included in the Seniors Supplement. See above.

COMMONWEALTH SENIORS HEALTH CARD MEDICARE SAFETY NET

- As announced in the 2014-15 Budget, a new Medicare Safety Net is proposed. From 1 January 2016 the existing arrangements will be replaced by the new Medicare Safety Net (subject to passage of the legislation).
- The Medicare safety net enables CSHC holders to benefit from a lower threshold for accumulative, out of pocket costs associated with out of hospital services (ie. non-hospital, doctors' bills in excess of the Medicare refund) before 80% of the out

of pocket costs are refunded to patients. For the calendar year 2014 the normal threshold for Medicare cardholders is $1,248.70 whereas the threshold for CSHC holders is $624.10.

- The Medicare safety net threshold is indexed annually from 1 January and operates on a calendar year, that is from 1 January to 31 December.
- Legislation was passed granting equality of treatment under a wide range of Commonwealth laws, for same-sex couples, including being registered as a family for the Medicare safety net.
- The definition of a family for Medicare safety net purposes is:
  - a couple legally married and not separated, or a couple in a de facto partnership with or without dependent children, or
  - a single person with dependent children.

NOTE: A dependant child is a child under 16 years or a full time student under 25 years whom you support.

- All families and couples need to register, even if all family members are listed on the Medicare card.
- Those registered as a family for safety net purposes must confirm the family make-up in writing each year with Medicare before any safety net benefits can be paid for services not already claimed.
- Individuals are automatically registered so keep contact details up-to-date with Medicare. If registered as a family or couple medical costs are combined so that the threshold is reached sooner. Options include:
  - register online, or
  - download of a Medicare safety net registration form or pick-up from a local Medicare office. Completed forms can be placed in the drop box at most local Medicare offices or mailed forms sent to GPO Box 9822 in your capital city by calling 132 011.
- The services that count towards the safety net include a range of doctor visits and tests received out-of-hospital. But having surgery, seeing a doctor or having a test when you are in hospital is not covered. Some examples of services where costs count towards the safety net include:
  - GP and specialists consultations
  - ultrasounds
  - pap smear
  - blood tests
  - CT scans, and
  - x-rays.

Primary producers

21

21.000 PRIMARY PRODUCERS

A 'primary producer' is a person who carries on the business of primary production in Australia. Special tax concessions are available and income averaging provisions may apply. Access to these concessions is only available if the taxpayer is carrying on a business of primary production. The concessions are not available to hobby farmers.

All references below are to the *Income Tax Assessment Act 1997* (ITAA97) unless otherwise stated.

The main income tax concessions for primary producers include:

- 'averaging' of income for individual taxpayers by way of farm management deposit schemes and income averaging rules (21.800 and 21.900)
- a three year write off for expenditure on water facilities (see below)
- an outright deduction for 'landcare operations' under the ability to 'level' income
- special write-off provisions for new horticultural plants (where expenditure is incurred on or after 1 October 2004) (see 15.090), and
- a ten year write off period for expenditure incurred on telephone line connection or extension on land.

Primary producers, like other businesses, may elect to be a 'small business entity'. This enables a primary producer to have access to various concessions available to small business entities generally (eg. small business CGT concessions) (see 10.300).

ACCELERATED DEDUCTIONS FOR PRIMARY PRODUCERS

In the Federal Budget 2015-16, the government announced that it will allow primary producers:

- to immediately deduct capital expenditure on fencing and water facilities such as dams, tanks, bores, irrigation channels, pumps, water towers and windmills, and
- to depreciate over three years all capital expenditure on fodder storage assets such as silos and tanks used to store grain and other animal feed.

Currently, the effective life for fences is up to 30 years, water facilities is three years and fodder storage assets is up to 50 years.

The measures will apply to assets that an entity starts to hold, or to expenditure that an entity incurs, at or after 7:30pm AEST, 12 May 2015. These laws were passed on 22 June 2015.

21.005   PRIMARY PRODUCTION BUSINESS

A *primary production business* (s995-1) is carried on if the activities involve:

- cultivating or propagating plants, fungi or their products or parts (including seeds, spores, bulbs and similar things, in any physical environment (such as hydroponics)
- maintaining animals (including poultry) for the purpose of selling them or their bodily produce (including natural increase)
- the manufacture of dairy produce where the raw material was produced by the person manufacturing the dairy produce
- conducting fishing operations ie. operations relating directly to taking or catching fish, turtles, dugong, beche-de-mer, crustaceans or aquatic molluscs (but not whaling)
- conducting operations that relate directly to taking or culturing pearls or pearl shell
- planting or tending trees in a plantation or forest that are intended to be felled
- felling trees in a plantation or forest, or
- transporting trees, or parts of trees that were felled in a plantation or forest to the place where they are first to be milled or processed, or the place where they will be transported from to the place where they are to be first milled or processed.

In determining whether a taxpayer is engaged in carrying on a business of primary production, activities must have a significant commercial purpose or character (see 21.100).

Where a property or substantial part of property is used solely for agistment, a taxpayer would not be considered to be carrying on a primary production business (IT 225).

NON-COMMERCIAL BUSINESS LOSSES

The non-commercial loss provisions preclude individual taxpayers or individuals in a partnership, who incur a loss from non-commercial business activities, from deducting those losses against income from other sources unless certain conditions are met (see 14.450).

COMMENCING BUSINESS

Whether a taxpayer has commenced carrying on business or is merely intending to commence business will be determined by the facts.

In *Case Q105*, 83 ATC 171, a taxpayer and his wife who, in 1972, acquired 1,200 acres and spent several thousand dollars over a number of years to clear land, build roads, and mend fences, were held to be not carrying on a business of primary production until they bought 120 sheep in 1979.

Case 75/96, 96 ATC 677, provides an alternative view where the farmer and his wife were held to be carrying on a business of farming. In this case the farmers made immediate arrangements to stock their property once they had purchased the land and they took possession of the stock within five months.

BENEFICIARY OF A TRUST

For the purposes of the income averaging rules (see 21.900) and farm management deposit (FMD) rules (see 21.800), a beneficiary who is presently entitled to income from a trust which carries on a business of primary production will themselves be regarded as carrying on the primary production business of the trust in that year (refer: s392-20).

Where a trust has income able to be distributed, a beneficiary may become 'presently entitled' to some or all of the income of the trust estate. In a year when no trust income was available for distribution, the Commissioner adopted the practice of deeming beneficiaries of a trust which carried on a primary production business to be, themselves, primary producers. This **practice** was discontinued from 1 July 2010.

From the 2010-11 income year, the law was amended to allow a beneficiary of the trust to be deemed to be carrying on primary production business in a loss year. The requirements are as follows:

1. **Trusts with 'certain entitlements' (fixed trusts)**

   An individual beneficiary will be taken to carry on a primary production business carried on by the trust if it does not have any trust income to which a beneficiary could be presently entitled and:

   (a) at all times during the income year, the manner or extent to which each beneficiary of the trust can benefit from the trust is not capable of being significantly affected by the exercise, or non-exercise of a power ('certain entitlements'), and

   (b) if the trust had trust income for the income year the beneficiary would have been presently entitled to a share of the income.

    The trustee of the Apple Trust carries on a primary production business during the 2014-15 income year. At all times during this income year, the manner or extent to which each beneficiary of the trust can benefit from the trust is not capable of being significantly affected by the exercise, or non-exercise, of a power.

   Rob is a beneficiary of the Apple Trust. Rob's interest in the trust entitles him to receive 20% of the trust's income for the income year. In the 2014-15 income year, the Apple Trust has a loss for trust law purposes. As the trust meets the certain entitlements requirement and as Rob would have been presently entitled to a share of the trust income had the trust had some trust income for the income year, Rob is taken to carry on the primary production business carried on by the trustee of the Apple Trust for the purposes of income averaging and FMDs.

2. **Trusts with no 'certain entitlements' (non-fixed trusts)**

   Trustees of trusts without certain entitlements may, for an income year in which the trust has no trust income, choose a certain number of beneficiaries to be taken as carrying on the primary production business carried on by the trustee of the trust for that income year. The trustee may choose not more than the greater of:

- twelve beneficiaries, and
- the number of individual beneficiaries that for the previous income year were taken to carry on a primary production business carried on by the trustee for the purposes of the income averaging provisions (s392-20 and s392-22).

Beneficiaries must be nominated in writing by the trustee before the lodgement of the trust income tax return for the relevant year, unless the Commissioner of Taxation allows additional time.

Jim, David, Sue and Tom are beneficiaries of the Pear Trust. The Pear Trust does not meet the certain entitlements requirement. The trustee of the Pear Trust carries on a business of primary production during the 2014-15 income year, however, the trust has a loss for trust law purposes for this income year.

The trustee chooses Jim, David, Sue and Tom for the purposes of the income averaging provisions for the 2014-15 income year. They are therefore treated as carrying on the primary production business carried on by the trustee of the Pear Trust for the purposes of these provisions and their primary production income for the income year is nil (they do not have any primary production income from any other source).

Jim and David also hold FMDs during the 2014-15 income year. The trustee also chooses them for the purposes of the FMD provisions for the income year. They are therefore taken to carry on the primary production business carried on by the trustee of the Pear Trust for the purposes of these provisions and are able to retain their FMDs for the income year.

Sue and Tom have not been chosen by the trustee for the purposes of the FMD provisions and are therefore not taken to carry on the primary production business carried on by the trustee of the Pear Trust for the purposes of those provisions.

DIRECT FORESTRY EXPENDITURE

For details of deductions available to investors in forestry managed investment schemes see 17.460.

21.100 WHAT IS A PRIMARY PRODUCER?

There is no single test to determine whether a taxpayer is carrying on a business of primary production. Guidelines are set out in Tax Ruling TR 97/11 based on common law principles.

Owning a rural property does not automatically mean that a taxpayer will be considered a primary producer. Merely gaining rental income from the use of a property by way of primary production by another entity will not result in the land owner being considered a primary producer.

The following indicators will typically be taken into account to determine whether a business is being conducted by a taxpayer:

- a significant commercial activity
- purpose and intention of the taxpayer in engaging in the activity
- an intention to make a profit from the activity
- the activity is or is expected to be profitable
- repetition and regularity of activity
- the activity is carried on in a similar manner to that which is typically evident for the particular industry
- the activity is organised and carried on systematically and in a business-like manner
- size and scale of the activity
- the activity does not have the characteristics of a hobby, recreation or sporting activity
- a business plan exists
- commercial sales of product, and
- the taxpayer has or is developing appropriate knowledge or skills.

SIGNIFICANT COMMERCIAL PURPOSE

It will be necessary for taxpayers to show that the activity is being carried on for commercial reasons and in a commercially viable manner. This will be particularly important in the first years of any activity as there will often be initial trading losses incurred.

It is more likely that the activity will be seen as having a significant commercial character if the taxpayer:

- has drawn up a business plan
- if not an expert, has sought expert advice from other experienced farmers and agents in that field, or from other sources (eg. technical literature)
- has obtained soils and water analyses of the land to be used
- has established that the land is suitable for the activity proposed
- has considered the market and potential markets for the product (preferably a commercial market)
- has investigated capital requirements of the venture and how that capital will be obtained and used
- has conducted appropriate research including the profits that can be expected based on market prospects, the level of production and expected running costs
- has ensured the size and scale of the activity is sufficient for a commercial enterprise
- has complied with any legal requirements eg. licences, permits and registrations, and
- has an intention to make a profit (ie. a reasonable belief that the activity is likely to generate a profit in the future).

In *Thomas' case* 72 ATC 4094, the taxpayer had set out to grow avocado and macadamia trees *'on a scale much greater than was required to satisfy his own domestic needs and he expected on reasonable grounds that their produce would have a ready market and would yield...a financial return...of a significant amount... for a very long time'.* The activities were considered to constitute the carrying on of a business. Whereas, the Federal Court in *Nelson and FCT [2012]* AATA 579 held that activities undertaken over a 5-year period on a 500 acre property, such as making improvements, researching various primary production activities and preparing business plans, without generating any income did not constitute carrying on a business and were merely preparatory.

Nick was an avid fisherman who owned a 20 metre yacht. He took advantage of an opportunity to obtain a commercial fishing licence and rearranged his business affairs to enable him to spend every second weekend fishing, but trips were only made in sunny conditions.

His two sons and a few acquaintances acted as crew. Usually they were very successful and caught a lot of fish which were sold to a fish wholesaler (after the crew had taken their share). Nick did not have a business plan. He did not conduct any research into the market nor methods of fishing, and he was not worried whether his costs were covered by the sale of the fish.

Result: *Considered not to be carrying on a business as there was no intention of profit and the activity lacked the degree of organisation and system normally evident in a commercial enterprise.*

INTENTION OF THE TAXPAYER

The taxpayer must intend to make a profit from the activity being conducted. Intention is particularly related to whether the activity is preparatory or preliminary to the ultimate activity. Preparatory expenses (such as acquiring a necessary qualification) incurred prior to the actual start of an activity will not usually be regarded as carrying on a business unless those expenses result in assessable income.

Special 'blackhole expenditure provisions' (s40-880) (see 15.110) provide a deduction for certain pre-business capital expenditure. However, if a business has started, expenses incurred may be deductible even though no income is derived in the relevant income year.

PROSPECT OF PROFIT

The taxpayer must be able to demonstrate how the activity can generate a profit. This could include details of any research conducted. It is not necessary for there to be a prospect of profit in the short term, however the taxpayer must be able to demonstrate that prospect at some time in the future.

Peter used his four hectare property to cultivate 100 pawpaw trees. He believed there must be a good market for locally grown tropical fruit, but had not conducted any research nor had the soil analysed. Because of the poor soil quality he was not always able to market the limited amount of fruit able to be produced.

Result: *No business was being conducted as there was no reasonable expectation that the activity would be profitable in the future.*

REPETITION AND REGULARITY

A common feature of a business are similar activities which are repeated on a regular basis. This would involve at least the minimum activity necessary to maintain a commercial quantity and quality of product for sale. The level of that activity would depend on the type of activity being undertaken by the taxpayer.

George owned a 600 hectare property, of which 200 hectares were suitable for cultivation and the rest for open grazing. For many years after the property was acquired in 1996, the property was used to graze sheep and cattle. There were also 200 olive trees.

During 2010 to 2015, due to a legal dispute, George was unable to spend any time on the property and all stock, plant and equipment was sold to finance the legal proceedings. The olive trees were left to rot.

Result: *During 2010 to 2015, George was not carrying on a business of primary production. If the olive trees had been maintained and the produce sold, George would have continued to carry on a business of primary production.*

INDUSTRY NORMS

An activity will be more likely to be accepted as a business when it is carried on in a similar manner to other participants in the same industry. This means examining the characteristics of carrying on a business that involves that activity.

Factors which should be considered include:

- the volume of sales. Low value sales where there is no prospect of a profit are unlikely to be part of a business, however initial sales may be low in the early stages of a project due to crop development times
- types of customers the taxpayer sells the product to and the manner of marketing that product
- the type of expenses incurred
- the amount of capital invested
- the taxpayer's previous experience and the nature of any advice received from experts or research conducted, and
- how the activity compares with that of a hobby which is professionally conducted.

'BUSINESS-LIKE' MANNER

The activity should be conducted in a systematic and organised manner which conforms with ordinary commercial principles for the particular industry rather than on an 'ad hoc' basis. The mere fact that a person has poor organisational skills would not necessarily prevent them from satisfying this criteria.

SIZE AND SCALE OF ACTIVITY

The larger the scale of the activity, the more likely it is that the taxpayer will be considered to be carrying on a business. Small scale activities might be considered to constitute a business, but it would be important to be able to demonstrate that the activity was being carried on with a profit making purpose and that there was regularity and repetition of the activities.

 Kris purchased five angora goats for the purpose of carrying on a business of goat breeding. She undertook appropriate research based on authenticated sources, and found that the venture was capable of generating profit which provided a reasonable return on funds invested.

Result: *This activity may constitute a business as there was an intention to make a profit and the activity involved the degree of organisation and system normally evident in a commercial enterprise.*

HOBBY OR RECREATION?

Amounts derived from the pursuit of a hobby are not regarded as income and therefore are not assessable and expenses incurred in pursuing a hobby are not deductible.

These factors are indicative of the activity being a hobby and not a business:

- it is evident the taxpayer does not have a motive of generating profit from the activity
- losses are incurred because the activity is motivated by personal pleasure and there is no plan in place to generate profit
- there is no repetition or regularity of sales
- the activity is not carried on in a manner consistent with businesses in the same industry
- there is no system by which the activities are consistently conducted
- the scale of the activity is small, and
- the intention of the taxpayer is to carry on a hobby, recreation or a sport rather than a business.

21.200 INCOME OF PRIMARY PRODUCERS

Assessable income of primary producers includes all moneys received by a business (including government subsidies) and net capital gains from CGT events happening to CGT assets, but excludes things produced for use on a farm (eg. fodder), which is not for sale.

21.210   NORMAL GROSS RECEIPTS

Some common items of income include:

- proceeds of sale of any produce, including bartering and barter exchanges
- wool cheque (but see *Double wool clips* below)
- refund of charges or levies
- proceeds of sale of skins and skin wool
- profits from share farming
- wheat, barley or oats pool payments
- payments from packing houses for produce delivered
- bounties, subsidies, drought relief grants, etc.
- agistment fees received (note that this may not be primary production income – see IT 225)
- timber royalties
- forestry operations
- earnings from contracts, salary or wages or from cartage (not primary production income)

- amounts received by way of insurance for loss of trading stock or loss of profits, but an election available may defer the tax, and
- other assessable recoupments (see 11.005).

SUBSIDIES ARE USUALLY ASSESSABLE

When a government subsidy or rebate (eg. diesel fuel rebate) is received in relation to the carrying on of a business, s15-10 specifically taxes the receipt. The assessability of a bounty granted for capital purposes is not clear.

Amounts received which are of a capital nature for the closing down of a business are not income, however CGT may apply.

Government payments to industry to assist entities to continue, commence or cease business are assessable (see TR 2006/3).

HEDGING ON FUTURES MARKETS

If primary producers enter into hedging contracts on futures markets, income from such transactions can potentially be regarded as income from primary production. As a general rule, a sale of a futures contract by a primary producer for hedging purposes is an integral part of the primary production business where the quantity of goods specified in the contract corresponds to the estimated production and where there is a subsequent sale of goods of the kind covered by the contract. Where, as in a normal hedging operation, the futures contract is terminated by a subsequent buy-back contract, the resulting profit or loss will be accepted as arising from the primary production business

NOTE: A taxpayer may enter into a hedging transaction on a foreign futures market, if a futures market in Australia for a particular commodity does not exist. A loss resulting from such a transaction should be allowed as a deduction.

DOUBLE WOOL CLIPS

If gross income includes proceeds of a second wool clip made earlier than normal due to fire, flood or drought, s385-135 allows an election to be made to transfer the proceeds of the second clip sale (or a share coming via a trust or partnership) to the next income year (see IT 169).

The Tax Office considers that the lodgment of an election under s385-135 by a woolgrower carrying on a business in an area declared by a state authority to be a drought area may be accepted as sufficient evidence of drought conditions (IT 169). If the business is carried on by a partnership or trust, the partnership or the trustee must make the election.

CARBON SEQUESTRATION RIGHTS

CAPITAL GAINS TAX IMPLICATIONS

The States have enacted legislation allowing for the creation of a class of property rights known as carbon sequestration rights. Income may arise from the sale of rights over the carbon sequestered in the trees or CGT events may occur in relation to the right (as they constitute CGT assets).

Under State legislation, a carbon sequestration right is generally defined as a right conferred on a person by agreement or otherwise to the legal, commercial or other benefit (whether present or future) of carbon sequestration by any existing or future tree or forest on the land after 1990. CGT event D1 would occur with the creation of a carbon sequestration right by a landholder, and CGT event A1 will follow on any subsequent sale or transfer of the rights.

A capital gain made by the primary producer from granting or disposing of the right may qualify for the small business concessions (ATO ID 2004/391).

Sale of the underlying land will not result in a simultaneous CGT event in relation to the carbon sequestration right (ATO ID 2004/390).

NOTE: The carbon sink forest may be registered on the land title to ensure future owners are aware of any contractual obligation.

Andrew, a grazier, is developing a diversification strategy to improve production from current landholdings. Big Merino Ltd enters into a contract with Andrew in relation to the acquisition of a carbon sequestration right. Under the terms of the contract, Andrew must set aside and maintain a carbon sink forest of 100 hectares for 150 years. Big Merino Ltd enters the contract to obtain the rights to the legal and commercial benefits of carbon sequestered in the forest, to offset carbon emissions.

The carbon sequestration rights are created by a contractual arrangement between Andrew and Big Merino Ltd and trigger CGT Event D1.

If Big Merino sells the rights at a future date, CGT Event A1 occurs as the sale constitutes a disposal of a CGT asset.

NOTE: Any cost incurred in relation to the drawing of the contract will form part of the cost base of the rights.

DEDUCTIBLE ESTABLISHMENT EXPENDITURE

Subdivision 40-J deals with the tax treatment of costs incurred in the establishment of a carbon sink forest. From 1 July 2012, establishment expenditure will be deductible on a straight-line basis of 7% per annum, prorated to the number of days the trees were established.

The deduction will only be available to businesses that establish the trees as part of a carbon sink forest to abate greenhouse gas emissions. Managed investment schemes including both forestry and non-forestry are specifically denied a deduction (s40-1010(1)(f)).

A primary and principal purpose test ensures the deduction is only available where the trees are planted to establish a carbon sink forest and not for future felling or other commercial horticulture purposes. The deduction will only be available if the carbon sink forest achieves the following characteristics:

- at year end, the trees occupy a continuous land area of 0.2 hectares or more
- when established it is expected that the trees will attain a crown cover of at least 20% and a height of at least two metres, and
- on 1 January 1990, the forest area was clear of trees with those characteristics.

The owner of the trees must notify the details of the carbon sink forest to the Commissioner by the earlier of the due date for lodgement of the relevant return or within five months of the end of the income year. The Commissioner may seek confirmation from the government department responsible for climate change that the trees established will be able to achieve the characteristics of a carbon sink forest.

Deductible expenditure related to the establishment of a carbon sink forest may include:

- the cost of acquiring and planting of the trees or seeds
- the cost of pots and potting mixtures where the potted plants are being nurtured prior to being established in their long term growing medium, in the ground, in a permanent way
- the cost incurred in grafting trees and germinating seedlings
- the cost incurred in preparing to plant including ploughing, scarifying, contouring, top dressing, fertilising, weed spraying, stone removal, and top soil enhancement, and
- the cost of surveying the planted area.

The cost of purchasing land to be used for establishing trees in a carbon sink forest is not expenditure for establishing the trees, as the cost is attributable to the land rather than to the establishment of the trees (refer ATO ID 2009/60). Expenditure attaching to the land, such as fencing, fire breaks, roads within the forest and water facilities for the forest will not be deductible as establishment costs, but may be allowed a deduction under other capital allowance measures.

NOTE: If a forest is established for the principal purpose of harvesting or felling the trees, the activity will not fall within the carbon sink forest rules. The costs of planting and maintaining trees in forests are deductible under s8-1 ITAA97, where those forests are planted and maintained in the ordinary course of forestry activities, even if the taxpayer also carries on carbon sequestration activities (see ATO ID 2004/718). Notably, there must be an intention that the trees will be felled (see ATO ID 2004/768).

TRADABLE WATER ENTITLEMENTS

CAPITAL GAINS TAX IMPLICATIONS

The trade of temporary or seasonal water rights typically falls within the scope of ordinary income as revenue derived from a temporary transfer has the character of a lease payment. Generally, the permanent trade of water rights (licences, allocations, quotas or entitlements) will constitute the disposal of a CGT asset. In certain circumstances, a CGT roll-over may be available if a taxpayer replaces a water entitlement with one or more new entitlements pursuant to subdivision 124-R (refer below).

Although a permanent water trade would typically give rise to a CGT event, where the significant purpose was to make a profit, the Tax Office may assess the sale on revenue account. The profit-making intention does not have to be the sole or dominant purpose for the transaction only a significant purpose (s15-15).

Compensation payments for a reduction in a water entitlement that is used in the carrying on of a primary production business, are generally a payment in recognition of lost income and assessed as ordinary income.

 The Tax Office indicates that a temporary trade of rights may not have a sufficient nexus to be classified as primary production income for the purposes of such things as the taxpayer's income averaging calculations.

Where the water entitlement has been unbundled from the land, the cost base for the water rights must be apportioned on a reasonable basis (s112-25). A registered valuer may be needed to determine the market value of the water rights as at the time of unbundling.

A permanent disposal of a water right whether by assignment or sale, triggers CGT event A1. The timing of a CGT event A1 is typically the contact date or if no contract then the date on which ownership transfers.

A payment for the cancellation of the water entitlement would result in CGT event C2 (see s104-25 and TR 95/35).

A temporary disposal may also trigger CGT consequences, including:

- CGT event D1 the creation of a temporary right to the water entitlement (s104-35)
- CGT event D2 the granting of an option to use or take up the rights in the future (s104-40 ITAA97), and
- CGT event F1 the granting of a lease over a water entitlement (s104-110 ITAA97).

Some CGT events (eg. event D1) do not qualify for the 50% discount. The time of the event of both CGT event D1 and F1 will typically be the contract date. A water right may be considered to be an active asset for the purpose of the Small Business CGT concessions (see 12.525) depending on the asset's use. For discussion on the above CGT events, see 12.020.

 If a water right is purchased at the time of purchasing land, consider the allocation in the contract of the purchase price between the water right and the land.

 If the land was acquired pre 20 September 1985 and you acquired a water right with that land, it may be possible to establish that the water right has a pre-CGT status.

 Although farm land is business real property, neither a water entitlement nor a water access licence are business real property and as such can not be transferred into a self-managed superannuation fund utilising the real property exemption (see SMSFR 2009/1).

CAPITAL GAINS TAX ROLL-OVER FOR WATER ENTITLEMENTS

Subdivision 124-R has been enacted to provide CGT roll-over for taxpayers who replace an entitlement to water with one or more different entitlements. Previously, the ending of the taxpayer's ownership of a water entitlement typically triggered the realisation of a capital gain or loss.

The roll-over provisions apply for CGT events which happen in the 2005-06 and later income years. Taxpayers however will be able to choose whether or not to adopt the roll-over if the relevant transactions qualifying for the roll-over happen in the period from the 2005-06 income year to the day that the provisions were enacted (ie. 7 December 2010).

There are two types of water entitlements to which CGT roll-over provisions may apply:

(I) REPLACEMENT ASSET ROLL-OVER

This arises where a taxpayer replaces a water entitlement with one or more new water entitlements.

An automatic roll-over is available, if certain conditions are met, where the taxpayer's ownership of one water entitlement ends and they acquire one or more new entitlements (referred to as a single entitlement roll-over) (s124-1105(1)).

A taxpayer whose ownership of more than one water entitlement ends will qualify for roll-over if they acquire one or more new water entitlements as a result of the ownership of the original entitlements ending and a choice is made to obtain the roll-over (referred to as a multiple entitlement roll-over) (s124-1105(2)).

The manner in which the water entitlement ends can be by way of disposal or cancellation, etc.

A capital gain or loss may be realised to the extent that the taxpayer receives additional proceeds that do not take the form of a replacement water entitlement/s (ie. partial roll-over) (s124-1115).

Andy, Ben, Courtney, Dean and Emma each own 100 Class A shares issued by Liquid Water Irrigation Ltd (Liquid Water). Liquid Water is an operator within the Murray Darling Basin that owns a statutory licence with an 800 ML entitlement to water. Each Class A share entitles its owner to 1 ML of water, to have Liquid Water deliver the water, to one vote at the annual general meeting and the right to receive dividends.

Andy chooses to transform his 100 ML entitlement against Liquid Water. Consequently he exchanges each of his 100 Class A shares for a replacement 100 ML statutory licence and 100 Class B shares, each of which has the same rights as the Class A shares, except the right to 1 ML of water. As the replacement statutory licence and each Class B share relates to water, each asset is a water entitlement.

Andy qualifies for the single entitlement roll-over in relation to each of his 100 Class A shares.

Andy disregards any capital gains and capital losses arising from this exchange.

(II) REDUCTION ROLL-OVER

This arises where a taxpayer has a total water entitlement made up of individual entitlements and their ownership of some of those entitlements ends but the market value of those entitlements remains the same as the total market value of the original entitlements. The entitlement may include a 'conveyance loss component' which the taxpayer never receives. This conveyance loss represents water which is lost in an operator's network due to factors such as evaporation or seepage, which results in an alteration to the taxpayer's entitlement but not the amount of water to be received under that entitlement.

River Irrigation Ltd (River Irrigation) is an operator that owns a statutory licence with a 100 GL entitlement to water. River Irrigation has 100 member irrigators, each with a contractual right to water. The size of this entitlement depends on the number of shares they own in River Irrigation. Each share in River Irrigation entitles its owner to 1 ML of water.

However, each member's contractual right to water includes a conveyance component of 20%. Consequently, each member only receives up to 80% of their contractual entitlement.

Julie, a member of River Irrigation, owns 500 shares (that she acquired in 1994) and consequently has a 500 ML entitlement to water. However, due to the conveyance component Julie only ever receives up to 400 ML of water.

River Irrigation reorganises its affairs and cancels 20% of each member's shares on a pro rata basis. River Irrigation, with the agreement of its member irrigators, also cancels each member irrigator's contractual right and reissues a new contractual right without a conveyance component. This cancellation and reissue of the contractual rights qualifies for the replacement water entitlement roll-over. These transactions ensure that each member's contractual entitlement and shareholding accurately reflects the amount of water they receive.

Julie is one of River Irrigation's member irrigators. Julie has her total water entitlement reduced to 400 ML through the cancellation of 100 shares. However, as Julie continues to receive the same amount of water, the total market value of Julie's original water entitlements is the same as her retained water entitlements.

Provided that the conditions for roll-over are satisfied, Julie can disregard any capital gains or losses arising from the cancellation of her 100 shares.

CONSEQUENTIAL TRANSACTIONS – VARIATION ROLL-OVERS

Transactions which qualify for a replacement asset roll-over (refer above) may have tax implications for other taxpayers (such as the transformation of water entitlements which may impact the operator or other members). In such circumstances, the affected entities would be entitled to a roll-over (referred to as a variation roll-over) for any capital gain or loss which arises (s124-1155).

TERMINATION FEES

Termination fees in relation to the irrigation industry typically relate to any fee or charge payable to an operator for either terminating access or surrendering a water right delivery. Such costs are included in the cost base or reduced cost base of the asset as an incidental cost (s110-35(11)) (see 12.092 and 12.094). A partial roll-over will only be available to the extent that the capital proceeds include something else other than a new entitlement (eg. cash) (s124-1165). These rules apply to CGT events happening on or after 1 July 2008. However, a choice can be made not to include the termination fee in the cost base or reduced cost base.

SALE OF STANDING TIMBER

When a landholder sells standing timber by way of a right to cut that timber (assuming that the landowner is not in the business of selling such rights), the payments arising under those contracts may be assessable to the landholder.

The nature of the income will depend on the terms of the contract and the result may vary depending upon when the land was acquired and/or the granting of the right. Broadly, if a landholder grants a right to a purchaser who will derive a benefit from continued growth of the timber, then the purchaser may acquire an interest in the land. If so, the right sold may be a 'profit a prendre' and subject to the CGT provisions (CGT event D1 at the time when the right is granted). When the trees are felled by the purchaser, there is no further disposal of an asset.

If the sale is of mature timber and the purchaser acquires only that timber (rather than future rights to regrowth) then the sale would not be a 'profit a prendre'. However, any profit may be assessed if the intention was to make a profit or gain.

The mere sale of the timber growing on land acquired pre-20 September 1985 would generally not be subject to CGT. However, if the taxpayer planted trees with the view to selling the timber, the proceeds would be considered as income according to ordinary concepts. If timber is sold by reference to the cut weight, the income may be considered a royalty.

For full details on profits a prendre, easements and licenses, refer to TR 95/6.

21.260   TRADING AND PRODUCE ACCOUNTS

Trading stock includes anything produced, manufactured or acquired that is held for the purposes of manufacture, sale or exchange in the ordinary course of business and includes livestock (s70-10) (see from 14.200 and 21.400).

To calculate profits opening and closing values of produce held as trading stock are brought to account valued at cost price, market selling value or replacement cost. The opening stock value at the beginning of a new year must be the same as the closing stock value at the end of the prior year.

A value lower than the three alternatives referred to above may be used where there are special circumstances (eg. obsolescence) (see from 14.200).

GIFTS OF TRADING STOCK

Section 70-90 treats gifts of trading stock as a sale at market value for the giver, and a purchase by the recipient (if acquired in connection with the conduct of a business). Section 70-90 applies to all disposals not in the ordinary course of business (see 14.200).

If the gift of trading stock is made to a deductible gift recipient, the deduction for the donor is the market value of the stock on the day the gift was made (s30-15).

EXCLUSIONS FROM 'TRADING STOCK'

Although costs of acquisition are deductible, the following items are not included in the value of trading stock on hand at the end of the year:

- produce grown on a farm for farm feed, or purchased to feed stock, and
- grain or seeds for planting a new crop.

21.270   WOOL GROWERS

If wool is valued at cost price, include the cost of mustering, shearers' wages, stores, depreciation of shearing sheds, motor vehicle expenses, etc. If a taxpayer buys sheep heavy in wool, separate values should be specified in the agreement for the sheep and for the wool. The sheep would be brought into the livestock account at the figure specified, and a deduction allowed in the wool account for the cost of wool purchased.

Taxation Ruling 97/9 sets out the tax consequences of wool sold by auction, private treaty, forward contract, 'pooled' wool and other arrangements.

21.280   GRAIN GROWERS

Initial advances in respect of sales provided by AWB Ltd and any subsequent wheat payments are assessable income in the year they are received.

Growers returning income on an accruals basis and who sell for cash, return income in the year the grain is sold. For growers returning on a cash basis, income is included in the year the payment is received. The same basis applies for sale under contracts to sell at a previously agreed price. Drawing amounts paid to growers under an AWB pool payment agreement are loans and not income until debited against payments (see TR 2001/1).

STOCK ON HAND

If wheat or similar grains are stored in a barn, silo, etc., it is stock on hand unless held for own use (see 14.200). Standing crops or growing crops are not trading stock on hand. The crop must first be severed from the land.

Wheat does not have to be brought to account as trading stock if it is:

- delivered to the AWB Ltd (even if over quota), or
- to be used as feed or seed.

21.290   NURSERIES

A proportion of the stock held by growers may be in containers (greenstock) and not yet matured to the point of sale. Greenstock can be valued using the following methods.

- **Cost price:** The cost of materials, labour and an appropriate proportion of overheads must be taken into account in determining cost price. For greenstock in the growing stage, stock is valued at cost price, the total cost price of greenstock on hand at the end of a year may be reduced by up to 25% to anticipate plant losses (IT 33).
- **Market selling value:** The taxpayer may elect to value the stock at market selling value notwithstanding that greenstock may not have matured to a stage where it would ordinarily be sold (IT 33).

21.300   CROPS, CROP STOOLS AND TREES

Growing plants do not represent trading stock in the normal course of business. However, the sale of trading stock, standing or growing crops, crop stools or trees will be included in a taxpayer's assessable income, if they were being grown for sale in the taxpayer's business and the sale was not in the ordinary course of that business. The purchaser is allowed a deduction for the cost of the trading stock, crop stool, etc. and the cost of initial planting of annual crops.

GROWING CROPS AND CROP STOOLS

Crop stools are a *'clump of shoots or stems, springing directly or indirectly from a single seed, root or rhizome, whether or not they have emerged above the surface of the soil'* (eg. wheat; however, bananas are treated as trading stock). Crops that remain unharvested at the end of the income year are not trading stock until they are severed from the land.

21.310   ORCHARDS

The cost of initial planting is a capital cost. If existing trees are replaced due to premature death or disease, the cost of replacement is deductible. Replacing trees which have passed a point of fair economic return (eg. because of exhaustion) is a new planting and the cost is treated as a non-deductible capital expense.

21.320   PRODUCE ACCOUNTS

Primary producers are required to prepare a produce account to calculate the gross profit from sale of produce. The produce account should be retained with taxation records by the primary producer or their tax agent. It does not have to be lodged with the Tax Office.

For other produce, state nature of the product here and include their value under column 2 'Other produce'	$ Other produce	$ Wool	$ Wheat	Totals
1. **Hides and skins** 4 . . . . .7.				
2. **Fodder** . . . . 5 . . . . 8.				
3. . . . . 6 9				
GROSS SALES				
Value of produce taken for private use, for use by employees/contractors, or exchanged for goods or services				
Value of produce on hand at 30 June 2015				
Sub-total				
Less: Value of produce on hand at 1 July 2014				
Gross profit or loss				

21.400 LIVESTOCK

Opening and closing values of livestock used in a primary production business must be taken into account in determining assessable income.

WHAT IS LIVESTOCK?

Trading stock, as defined in s70-10, includes livestock. Livestock is defined in s995-1(1) which states *'livestock does not include animals used as beasts of burden or working beasts in a business other than a primary production business'*. This indicates that all animals which are part of a business of primary production are livestock and therefore trading stock. This includes insects such as bees (TD 2008/26 – also see PSLA 2008/4 (GA) for valuation principles). Livestock does not include animals that are not domesticated or tamed such as fish in the sea (see TD 93/39), animal embryos (ATO ID 2003/726) or birds on display at a tourist park (ATO ID 2009/25). Primary producers must prepare a livestock account when preparing their tax return. It does not need to be lodged with the Tax Office but must be retained by the taxpayer. It is in two parts: one has income effect items; the other shows expense effect items. The difference between the totals of those parts is the profit (or loss) on livestock.

For natural increases in livestock, taxpayers can adopt the standard values if the cost price method is used. In other cases, the value of the natural increase must be used (see 21.420).

Atlantic salmon bred in a land-based nursery as part of an aquaculture business becomes an 'animal that you hold as live stock' for the purposes of s70-55 when they reach the 'fry' stage of development (ATO ID 2011/23).

SALES, RATIONS, LOST OR DIED

- Gross sales – number and value
- Killed for rations – number and value
- Stock on hand at end – number and value
- Losses and any by death – number only (numbers are an accuracy check)

WHERE DID THEY COME FROM?

From last year, purchases and natural increase:

- Stock at start of year – number and value
- Purchases – number and value
- Natural increase – number only

OPENING STOCK ON HAND

Must be the same as used at the close of the preceding year.

KILLED FOR RATIONS

Show the value and number. If cost price is selected, use the average cost of the animal at the close of the preceding year as the per head value. If stock killed was bought during the year, it is valued at cost price. If natural increase were killed for rations, use either the cost you selected for natural increase or the market value.

BEASTS OF BURDEN

Working stock or beasts of burden are livestock only when used in a primary production business.

LOSSES BY DEATH AND THEFT

Include the number (only to make the numbers balance) but do not include them when multiplying out to get the value of stock on hand at the close of the financial year.

21.420   VALUING THE LIVESTOCK

Different rules apply when the trading stock is livestock. In valuing closing stock, the taxpayer can use either cost or market selling value or its replacement value, or a lower value in certain circumstances (see 14.200).

They are entitled to change methods on a yearly basis. The same method does not have to be used for all livestock when election is made each year (s70-45).

There are special closing valuations for horses (refer 21.490).

A small business entity (see 10.300) need only account for changes in trading stock if the value of all trading stock, including livestock, on hand at the beginning of the income year and a reasonable estimate of the value at the end of that year varies by more than $5,000.

VALUE FOR NATURAL INCREASE

For natural increases in livestock for which there is no prescribed value, primary producers must value their livestock at actual cost. The actual cost must be calculated on an absorption cost basis taking into account both the direct and indirect costs. For details of absorption costing see IT 2350.

LIVESTOCK WITH PRESCRIBED VALUE

Under ITAA97, where the primary producer has previously valued that class at cost price, choose one of:

- the greater of the last cost price used and the prescribed value
- the prescribed value, or higher Tax Office approved account, or
- the lesser of actual cost or the prescribed value.

If that class was not previously valued at cost price, the choice is:

- the prescribed value or any higher amount, or
- the lesser of actual cost or the prescribed value.

The primary producer can choose to value the natural increase at either their market value or at these rates. Only include animals which survive to the end of the year – but still include those killed for rations.

With 'cost price' the taxpayer can elect to use actual cost or these prescribed costs:

- Emus: $8
- Poultry: 35c
- Sheep: $4
- Pigs: $12
- Goats: $4
- Cattle: $20
- Horses: $20
- Deer: $20

If service fees are incurred in acquiring a horse by natural increase its cost is the greater of the actual cost, the prescribed cost, or the service fee (s70-55), ie. it cannot be less than the service fee. The lower the chosen value placed on any natural increase, the greater will be the profit on eventual sale. The decision is whether to pay more tax each year on natural increase, or be taxed all at once on large sales.

If there is no prescribed minimum value for natural increase, the taxpayer must use the greater of the cost of production (absorption cost) or the value used in the previous year of income.

Having valued natural increase, value closing stock on the 'average cost' basis by averaging the value under each of these:

- value of those on hand at start of the year
- cost of livestock bought that year, and
- natural increase of year, valued at selected price.

If able to identify the whole or a part of specific livestock on hand at year end, a taxpayer can bring the livestock to account at year end at actual cost price rather than 'average' cost. Taxpayers valuing stock on hand at cost will adopt the 'average cost' method if it is not possible to establish the actual cost of each animal.

Livestock account (cost basis elected)

Selected value for natural increase	Sheep $4		Cattle $20		Pigs $12		Other livestock type	
Section 1	Number	Value	Number	Value	Number	Value	Number	Value
Gross sales	2,800	$126,000	500	$275,000				
Killed for rations or exchanged for goods and services	5	$225	1	$400				
Stock on hand 30/6/2015 Cost/market/replacement/other value (strike out what does not apply)	10,311	$106,100	2,104	$164,480				
Losses by death, etc.	600		25					
Total number should agree with total number in Section 2 **Section 1 TOTALS**	13,716	$232,325	2,630	$439,880				
Section 2								
Stock on hand 1/7/2014 Cost/market/replacement/other value (Strike out what does not apply)	10,516	$120,060	2,300	$161,000				
Purchases at cost	200	$9,000	100	$40,000				
Natural increase selected value to be shown above	3,000		230					
Total number should agree with total number in Section 1 **Section 2 TOTALS**	13,716	$129,060	2,630	$201,000				
Deduct total value of Section 2 from total value of Section 1 **Gross profit or (loss)**	(a) $103,265		(b) $238,880		(c)		(d)	

Gross livestock profit   Net totals of (a), (b), (c) & (d) $324,145

A farmer began the year with 10,516 sheep on hand, valued at $120,060, and 2,300 cattle valued at $161,000. The farmer is not a small business entity.

During the year he purchased 200 sheep for $9,000 and 100 cows for $40,000. He uses minimum value for natural increase, in this year, 3,000 lambs and 230 calves.

At year's end, there were 10,311 head of sheep and 2,104 head of cattle on hand.

Average cost is calculated as follows:

Sheep	*Number*	*Value*
Opening stock	*10,516*	*$120,060*
Purchases	*200 @ $45*	*$9,000*
Natural increase	*3,000 @ $4*	*$12,000*
	13,716	*$141,060*

Average cost per head = $141,060 divided by 13,716 = $10.29.

Value of closing stock of sheep (10,311 head at $10.29) = $106,100.

Cattle	*Number*	*Value*
Opening stock	*2,300*	*$161,000*
Purchases	*100 @ $400*	*$40,000*
Natural increase	*230 @ $20*	*$4,600*
	2,630	*$205,600*

Average cost per head = $205,600 divided by 2,630 = $78.1749
Value of closing stock of cattle (2,104 head at $78.1749) = $164,480

21.440   INSURANCE RECOVERIES, FORCED SALES

INSURANCE RECOVERIES

Amounts received are assessable, whether as insurance against loss, or as compensation from governments on their destruction. If a loss occurs it would be taken into account in arriving at the net profit (or loss) in the livestock schedule.

FORCED SALES OF LIVESTOCK

An election can be made (s385-95 and s385-100) by primary producers carrying on business to spread or defer a profit where there is a disposal or death of livestock because of:

1. the compulsory resumption or acquisition of land under an Act
2. a State or Territory leases land for a tick eradication program
3. pasture or fodder is destroyed by fire, drought or flood and proceeds of the disposal or death will be mainly used to buy replacement stock or to maintain breeding stock to replace the livestock
4. compulsory destruction under an Australian law dealing with contamination of property, or
5. receiving an official notification under an Australian law dealing with contamination of property.

In ATO ID 2011/6, a primary producer did not satisfy the relevant conditions to elect to spread or defer profit on the disposal of livestock even though their pasture was subject to drought conditions.

The primary producer in this case sold the livestock to give financial assistance to his son's business. The ATO ID concluded that the livestock was not disposed of because of drought and that this was an incidental reason for the disposal. The decisive reason was to provide financial assistance.

The taxpayer has three options on how to account for any profit on the forced disposal or death of livestock:

- the whole amount of the proceeds of sale can be taxed in full in the income year of disposal or death
- the taxpayer can elect to spread the tax profit over five years (s385-105), or
- elect to defer the tax profit (s385-110) and to reduce the cost of replacement stock in the year of disposal and the next five years. This election can only be made if the proceeds of disposal will be mainly used to buy replacement stock or to maintain breeding stock.

SPREADING THE TAX PROFIT

If the taxpayer elects under s385-105 to spread the profit over five years, then in the year of disposal of the livestock, the taxpayer includes in assessable income the proceeds of disposal reduced by the tax profit on the disposal or death. The taxpayer then includes 20% of that profit in the year of disposal and 20% in each of the next four income years.

John owns 2,000 hectares on which he grazes 2,000 fine merino sheep. Some 1,000 hectares is resumed by the state government for the construction of a new freeway and railway corridor. This will result in John having to dispose of half of the stock due to the smaller carrying capacity of the land.

He sells the sheep for $75,000, giving him a tax profit of $25,000 (therefore $5,000 per year over five years).

John's assessable income for the year will include the proceeds of the forced disposal, which is calculated as $75,000 less $25,000 tax profit = $50,000 + $5,000 = $55,000 + other assessable income.

John will include $5,000 in the assessable income of each of the next four income years.

DEFERRING PROFIT (ALTERNATIVE ELECTION)

The taxpayer can elect under s385-110 to defer a tax profit and reduce the cost of replacement livestock. This involves the taxpayer including in assessable income in the year of disposal of the livestock the disposal proceeds reduced by the tax profit on that disposal. The tax profit is then used to reduce the cost of replacement stock in the year of disposal or any of the next five income years. The profit does not have to be used up in equal instalments; it could be used up in total in, say, the third year after the year of disposal. If any remains unused on the last day of the last of the five income years after the disposal year, that amount must be included in assessable income. The method for calculating the reduction (the reduction amount) in the purchase price of replacement stock is set out in s385-120.

> ### Replacement with same species of animal
>
> *Margaret owns land on which she grazes Hereford cattle. Due to a prolonged drought and fire which destroys remaining pasture and hay, she is forced in the 2007 income year to sell some 200 head for $80,000, resulting in a tax profit of $32,000. In the year of disposal, Margaret must include in assessable income $48,000 (ie. $80,000 less the tax profit of $32,000).*
>
> *In the 2009 income year there is good winter rain and Margaret begins restocking, spending some $22,000 to buy 100 head of Hereford cattle. The 'reduction amount' under s385-120 for reducing the purchase price is the tax profit on disposal of $32,000 ÷ 200 (the number disposed of) = $160 per head. The cost of each replacement Hereford in the 2008 income year is reduced by the reduction amount. The replacement cost is therefore $22,000 less 100 x $160 ($16,000) = $6,000.*
>
> *In the 2010 income year Margaret buys another 50 Hereford for $11,000, resulting in a replacement cost of $3,000 ($11,000 less 50 x $160).*
>
> *Margaret does not buy any more cattle until the 2014 income year which means that as at the 2012 income year (five years after the 2007 income year), $8,000 of the 2007 tax profit had not been used to reduce the purchase price of new stock (ie. $32,000 (less 150 head x $160 = $24,000) = $8,000). This would be included in assessable income for the 2012 income year.*

Note that the election under s385-110 can only be made if the proceeds will be used mainly to buy replacement livestock or maintain breeding stock. If the replacement animals are a different species than those they replace, s380-125(2) provides that the 'reduction amount' is any reasonable amount at least equal to the amount worked out under s385-120(2). This is the tax profit attributable to livestock of the species the taxpayer is replacing, divided by the number of animals of the species that you disposed of or which died.

SPREADING ASSESSABLE INSURANCE RECOVERIES

Relief is available where insurance recoveries arise for the loss of livestock that is caused as a result of drought, fire, flood, disease or any other natural disaster. In that situation the taxpayer can spread the proceeds over a five year period in equal instalments, starting with 20% in the year of receipt of the insurance recovery (see s385-130).

COMPUTING PROFIT

The profit is calculated by deducting from the amount received:

- **If the livestock were on hand at the beginning of the year:** The value at which they were taken into account at that start of the year.
- **If the livestock were acquired during the year:** The purchase price (or, if not actually purchased, the deemed purchase price).
- **If natural increase bred by the taxpayer during the year:** No deduction.

ELECTION FOR TAXPAYER'S PORTION

If income is derived from a partnership or trust, the taxpayer elects on his or her portion only. It is immaterial what others decide. Similarly, a trustee can elect for the portion assessable to the trustee.

However, if the election is in respect of the forced disposal or death of livestock, insurance for loss of livestock or trees, or double wool clips, and the business is carried on by a partnership or trust, only the partnership or trustee can make the election (s385-145). The election should be made no later than the time of lodging the return for the year during which the disposal occurred.

From 2005-06 income year, if an election was made under s385-110 to spread the profit over five years (see above) any of the following disentitling events could result in the unused tax profit being taxed immediately (s385-163):

- the taxpayer leaves Australia permanently or appears to the Commissioner to be about to do so
- the taxpayer dies
- the taxpayer becomes bankrupt, or applies for relief from debts under appropriate Acts, or
- a taxpayer (if a company) starts to be wound up.

21.450   OTHER DISPOSALS AND DONATIONS OF LIVESTOCK

If trading stock or livestock are disposed of other than in the ordinary course of business of the taxpayer (eg. a clearance sale), gifted or taken for private use, the market value on the day of disposal must be brought to account as assessable income (s70-90).

21.460   CHANGE IN PARTNERSHIP INTERESTS

When a partner enters or leaves a partnership, technically the old partnership is dissolved and a new partnership created. Without a specific provision in the law, livestock would be deemed to have been sold at market value and the profit on sale included in the assessable income of the terminating partnership.

Where the appropriate election is made, s70-100 allows livestock in a continuing business to be treated as sold for book value, provided partners who held at least a 25% interest in the terminating partnership continue to hold at least a 25% interest in the new partnership. As an anti-avoidance measure, the election to deem a sale at book values (and therefore reflect no assessable profit) is available only where, at the time of disposal, the market value is greater than the book value.

21.490 VALUING HORSES AS TRADING STOCK

TAX TREATMENT OF HORSES

If a taxpayer is carrying on a business (refer TR 2008/2 for relevant criteria), horses, including racehorses, are either:

- treated as a depreciable asset
- treated as a CGT asset, or
- treated as trading stock and included in the livestock accounts.

Horses are livestock if the sole or main purpose is to sell them, their progeny, or their bodily produce. Where the racing of a horse is incidental to selling the horse or its offspring, the horse is livestock.

Shares in stallion syndicates may be treated as livestock, but if the main purpose is to race horses, or to obtain or sell service fees, they would be treated as a depreciable asset, not livestock.

Trading stock valuation options for horses are:

- cost (see 14.200 and 21.420)
- market selling value (see 14.200 and 21.420), and
- a 'special closing value' for horse breeding stock acquired after 19 August 1992 (refer below).

SPECIAL CLOSING VALUE

Livestock is horse breeding stock only if the horse:

- was acquired by the taxpayer under a contract

- reached the age of three years before the end of the financial year (s70-65), and
- was held by the taxpayer for breeding purposes at the end of the financial year.

Section 70-60 allows a female horse which has turned 12 years before the end of the financial year to be valued at a special closing value of the greater of:

- $1, or
- opening value less 'reduction amount'.

The 'reduction amount' for a female horse less than 12 years old is calculated this way:

(Base amount divided by reducing factor) x
(Breeding days divided by total days in the income year)

Where:

- the 'base amount' is the lesser of the horse's cost price and the adjustable value at the time the horse became the taxpayer's livestock
- the 'reducing factor' is the greater of:
  - three years, or
  - 12 minus the age in whole years of the horse when first held by the taxpayer for breeding.

A seven year old female horse was purchased on 1 April for $100,000.
The reduction amount is [$100,000 divided by (12 – 7)] x (91 divided by 365) = $4,986.
The special closing value is $100,000 – $4,986 = $95,014.
The reduction amount is $20,000 in each of the next four years.
In the year the horse turns 12, it will be $15,014 which brings the special closing value to less than $1, so the special closing value will equal $1 in that and future years.

The same facts as in Example 1, except the horse is ten years old.
The reduction amount is ($100,000 divided by 3) x (91 divided by 365) = $8,310.
The special closing value is $100,000 – $8,310 = $91,690. The reduction amount is $33,333 in each of the next two years. So even though the horse turns 12, the special closing value remains above $1 due to the calculation of the reduction amount.

MALE HORSE BREEDING STOCK

Provided the horse has reached the age of three years before the end of the financial year, s70-60 allows a male horse to be valued at a special closing value of the greater of:

- $1, or
- opening value less reduction amount for the income year.

The 'reduction amount' for a male horse is calculated this way:

Base amount x nominated percentage x
(Breeding days divided by total days in the income year)

Where the 'nominated percentage' is nominated by the taxpayer (up to a maximum of 25%).

A male horse which will be three years old at the end of the year of income was purchased on 1 April for $100,000. The reduction amount (if 25% nominated percentage used) in year 1 is $100,000 x 25% x (91 divided by 365 days) = $6,233. The special closing value is $100,000 – $6,233 = $93,767.
The reduction amount will be $25,000 in years 2, 3 and 4 and $18,767 in year 5. This brings the special closing value to less than $1, so the special closing value will equal $1 in year 5 and future years.

NATURAL INCREASE

Section 70-60 values do not apply to natural increase because stock acquired through natural increase has not been 'acquired under a contract', nor does it meet minimum age requirement (three years).

The minimum value for trading stock is $20 or the cost price if this is less.

Where a service fee is incurred for natural service or artificial insemination of a female horse that results in natural increase, its cost is the greater of the actual cost of the animal, its prescribed cost (see 21.420) and the service fee attributable to acquiring the horse (s70-55(2)).

21.500 DEDUCTIONS FOR PRIMARY PRODUCERS

The tax rules for claiming general running expenses of a primary production business are generally the same as those that apply to other businesses (see 14.050), however some expenditure of a capital nature may be written off at accelerated rates (see 21.600).

ANIMAL EXPENSES

Deductions may be available for veterinary fees, shearing and crutching, licks, dips, and drenches, medicines and vaccines, breeding service fees, veterinary fees, tagging or other marking such as microchip implantation.

21.510   DECLINE IN VALUE

Depreciation is allowable on the capital cost of plant and equipment used in a primary production business. The effective life of such assets is set out in Table A beginning at 14.160. Depreciation for water facilities, horticultural plant, grapevines, landcare, electricity and telephone connections is set out at 21.600. Special depreciation rules apply to business entities that have elected to become a small business entity (see 10.300). Further, the government has announced accelerated deductions for certain primary production capital expenditure in the 2015-16 Federal Budget (see 21.000).

TRACTORS AND HARVESTERS

The effective life of tractors and harvesters used in a primary production business have a statutory cap of $6^2/3$ years (used or ready for use or after 1 July 2007).

DEDUCTION FOR TREES

A deduction is allowed for the capital costs of acquiring land carrying trees or acquisition of a right to fell trees (s70-120). If the acquisition was for land carrying trees, a proportional deduction is allowed when some or all of the trees are felled during the income year for sale, or for use in manufacture, for the purpose of producing assessable income. This also applies to trees felled under a right granted to another entity or where the market value was included in assessable income because of a disposal outside the ordinary course of business. If the acquisition was for a right to fell trees, a proportional deduction is allowed if some or all of the trees were felled during the income year for sale, or for use in manufacture, for the purpose of producing assessable income. The deduction allowable is so much of the amount paid for the land as is attributable to the trees subject to the above felling (see TR 95/6 for details).

INSURANCE

Generally, a deduction is allowed for expenses incurred in relation to loss of income, plant and equipment, livestock, fences, buildings and feed but not for the private house of the owner (unless it is provided as a fringe benefit).

INTINERANT WORKERS

Shearers and fruit pickers are employees who typically travel between various work places or have no fixed place of work but work for the same employers from year to year. The same taxation rules in relation to deductions, allowances and reimbursement for transport expenses apply to itinerant workers and employers must maintain adequate employment records (refer TR 95/34 and Chapter 11).

LEVIES BY COMMODITY AUTHORITIES

Various levies, both compulsory and voluntary, may be payable by growers. These are usually deductible, but any refund would be assessable income. Some examples of these levies are:

- cotton growers compulsory levy and voluntary levy
- wool growers
- grain growers
- pest eradication (eg. WA skeleton weed eradication levy), and
- various state levies.

LIVESTOCK LEASING

The Tax Office will allow deductions for lease payments where the residual value falls within specified ranges. Livestock leasing is acceptable under a commercial lease if the residual values (IT 213) are within:

Year 1: 65% to 80%	**Year 3:** 25% to 40%	**Year 5:** 1% to 15%
Year 2: 45% to 60%	**Year 4:** 15% to 25%	

MAINS ELECTRICITY AND TELEPHONE

The cost of connecting mains electricity (see 14.185) and a telephone to land (see 21.650) used by primary producers may be claimed over ten years.

MEMBERSHIPS

Membership of professional associations, or stud stock associations, etc. are generally deductible.

POWER, LIGHT AND FUEL

A deduction is typically available for electricity to light farm buildings (including employee's quarters) or to heat or cool them and to operate farm machinery. Claim for diesel oil, petrol, kerosene, wood, coal, coke or other fuels used in the business.

RENT OF PROPERTY AND IMPLEMENTS

A deduction is available for rent paid on the property upon which income earning activities are conducted, agistment fees paid, rent or hiring charges for farm machinery and equipment, or for a domestic residence used by employees.

A deduction is not allowable for rent paid for a taxpayer's own residence. However, if the business is carried on by an entity such as a company or trust and a rented property is provided to the shareholders/directors as employees, a deduction may be claimed, but the FBT laws would typically have application (see Chapter 25).

REPAIRS

A deduction is available for the cost of repairing any plant and equipment, including farm vehicles, buildings, employee's quarters, fences and roads – but not repairs to any residence used for private purposes (refer TR 97/23).

SALARY AND WAGES

A deduction is available for any salaries and wages for employees engaged in the normal farming operations. If family members are employed on the farm, a deduction would be available for arms-length salary paid. Excessive payments to relatives or to an 'associated person' can be fully or partly disallowed under s26-35 (see 14.120).

When checking a claim for wages paid to an 'associated person' the Tax Office will consider:

- the nature of duties performed, and where they were performed
- the time taken to perform them
- the time of day they were performed, and
- the skill, experience and qualifications of the employee.

Salary and wages incurred partly on a capital project can be apportioned by:

- time on a capital project: disallowed, but capitalised and potentially depreciable, or
- other time: deductible.

If the labour is to erect a building, the labour cost should be included in construction costs and capital allowances claimed on the total.

SEEDS, FODDERS AND FERTILISERS

A deduction is generally available for the cost of grain for seed, vegetable seeds (market gardener), fodder for all types of animals, fertilisers and similar items.

TRAVEL EXPENSES

A deduction is generally available for cost of business trips, (eg. to attend stock sales, to transport livestock to agistment, purchase farm stock or supplies, or travel between other farm properties). No deduction is allowable for travelling expenses on private or domestic matters. Expenses may be claimed in full for moving farm vehicles for business purposes. Vehicle expenses otherwise need to be apportioned on a business/private use basis.

Substantiation rules apply whether or not the owner is in business (see 14.050).

WATER EXPENSES

A deduction is generally available for expenditure in relation to water used in a primary production business (eg. irrigation of crops). Costs incurred in acquiring tradeable water rights is on capital account and is subject to the CGT regime (see 21.210 Tradeable water entitlements). A deduction is not allowable under s8-1 ITAA97 for the cost of the physical water stored on a farm where it is included as part of the cost of acquiring the primary production business (ATO ID 2013/49). This is considered to be capital in nature.

CONSERVATION TILLAGE REFUNDABLE TAX OFFSET

The conservation tillage offset is introduced as part of the carbon pricing scheme to reduce emissions and improve productivity. Qualifying primary producers may be entitled to a refundable tax offset of 15% of the cost of an eligible no-till seeder (a depreciating asset) which the taxpayer starts to use, or has installed ready for use between 1 July 2012 and 30 June 2015 (Subdivision 385-J).

In addition, to be entitled to claim the refundable tax offset, the primary producer needs to have received a research participation certificate for the relevant year.

An eligible seeder must be new. In other words, the offset is not available if the no-till seeder in question has been used, or installed ready for use, at any time before the relevant period by the taxpayer or any other entity.

IMPORTANT: Legislation was enacted in July 2014 to repeal the conservation tillage refundable tax offset one year early. This means that the offset is only available where eligible equipment has been installed and ready for use between 1 July 2012 and 30 June 2014, if all other eligibility requirements are met.

21.600 CAPITAL IMPROVEMENTS

Various provisions of the tax law may provide primary producers with accelerated deductions for capital expenditure including water facilities, horticultural plant, grapevines, Landcare, electricity and telephone connections (see 15.090).

21.630   LANDCARE

Taxpayers who carry on business for the purpose of gaining or producing assessable income from the use of 'rural land' (which is not statutorily defined) in Australia are entitled to deduct certain costs in respect of fences, including repairs and alterations (s40-630). For more details see 15.090. A full deduction is available in the income year the cost was incurred if fences are erected to help prevent land degradation.

RESTRICTIONS ON LAND USE

The business must derive its income from using the land. The deduction is available if fences are erected to separate different areas of primary production land, or of rural business land and must be erected under an 'approved whole farm plan'.

 In a primary production situation, a large paddock might be fenced off to prevent degradation of light soil, or of valuable native vegetation.

Land used for mining or quarrying is ineligible for an outright deduction of the cost of fences concerned. The land use claimable must be approved by a farm land consultant, or by a land conservation agency.

21.650   TELEPHONE LINES AND ELECTRICITY CONNECTION

ELECTRICITY CONNECTION

A deduction, spread over ten years in equal instalments, is available under s40-645 for capital expenditure on connecting, or upgrading an existing electricity connection, if at the time the expenditure was incurred:

- the taxpayer is a sharefarmer carrying on business on the land, or has an interest in the land, and
- it was intended that some or all of the electricity will be used for carrying on a business on the land or a business of sharefarming.

However, a deduction is allowable only if the power is used for a taxable purpose within 12 months of the expenditure being incurred (see s40-650).

TELEPHONE LINE CONNECTION

A deduction (under s40-645) over ten years in equal instalments is also allowable for capital expenditure for the cost of a telephone line either brought onto or extended to land if at the time the expenditure was incurred:

- a business of primary production was conducted on the land, and
- the taxpayer had an interest in the land or was a sharefarmer carrying on a business of primary production on the land.

For both electricity and telephone connections, a deduction cannot be claimed by a partnership. The costs incurred by a partnership are allocated to each partner who claims according to their proportionate interest. Any recoupment of the deductible expenditure will be included in assessable income.

21.700 MANAGED INVESTMENT SCHEMES

NON-FORESTRY AGRICULTURAL MANAGED INVESTMENT SCHEMES

The Federal Court in *Hance v FCT*; *Hannebery v FCT 2008* [2008] FCAFC 196 held that the investors were carrying on a business and entitled to claim a tax deduction for their contributions in relation to an investment in a non-forestry agricultural managed investment scheme.

 Before making their investment taxpayers should satisfy themselves that a Product Ruling (see from 4.160) has been issued by the Tax Office in respect of the scheme and there are no variations in the structure or financing of the investment compared to the arrangement upon which the ruling was based.

FORESTRY MANAGED INVESTMENT SCHEMES

Special rules apply to allow an immediate deduction for investors in a Forestry Managed Investment Scheme (FMIS) subject to Division 394 ITAA97 (see 14.700). For subsequent investors the investment acquisition cost will be on capital account, however a deduction will be available for ongoing contributions for direct forestry expenditure, provided the FMIS meets certain conditions. For those subsequent investors the investment acquisition cost will be on capital account, and a capital gain or loss recognised on disposal (see 14.700).

For an initial investor in an FMIS to retain a deduction claimed under Division 394, the law requires that a CGT event does not happen in relation to the investor's forestry interest within four years after the end of the income year in which an amount is first incurred by the investor. Division 394 prevents the deductions of investors in FMIS from being clawed back where the interest ceases to be held as a result of factors outside the control of the investor and which could not have been foreseen at the time of the investment.

21.800 FARM MANAGEMENT DEPOSITS

The Farm Management Deposit (FMD) scheme contained in Division 393 ITAA97 is designed to enable primary producers to exclude profits of a particular year from tax by paying the amount to be excluded into an FMD. This would most commonly occur in years of high profit. Amounts withdrawn from the FMD in subsequent year become assessable at that time.

OBJECT OF FARM MANAGEMENT DEPOSIT SCHEME

The object of the scheme is to provide relief for primary producers by enabling them to better manage their cash flows through profitable and unprofitable years by 'smoothing' the levels of assessable income and thereby minimising the variations in tax liability which might otherwise occur over a number of years. The scheme has the following broad features:

- taxpayers are entitled to claim a deduction for deposits into FMD accounts and will be assessed on withdrawals
- interest on deposits is set at the Commonwealth three year bond rate and paid on the investment component of the deposit
- certain financial institutions are permitted to accept farm deposits, and
- depositors are permitted to make deposits with one financial institution.

IMPORTANT: Businesses making withdrawals from the scheme will need to ensure that they have registered for an Australian Business Number (ABN) or apply for a TFN. That ABN or TFN must be provided to avoid PAYG being withheld at the top marginal rate on withdrawals. Withdrawals from an FMD account are added to the holder's PAYG instalment income for the appropriate period.

WHAT IS A FARM MANAGEMENT DEPOSIT?

Under Division 393, an FMD must be made with an 'FMD provider' (see below), such as a financial institution under an agreement that describes the deposit as an FMD. The depositor must apply to the FMD provider by completing and signing a form which states their TFN, but requires the depositor to provide any other information required by the regulations and contains a statement that the depositor has read any regulations that may apply (s393-20). The requirements for the agreement are set-out in s393-25.

Primary production business must be carried on by an individual

One key requirement is that the owner must be an **individual** who is carrying on a primary production business in Australia (see 21.100) when the deposit is made.

There are rules which apply to certain partners and trust beneficiaries as if they were individuals who carried on a primary production business. Specifically:

- **partner in a partnership:** If the taxpayer is an individual partner in a partnership which is carrying on a primary production business for the purposes of the FMD requirements, that individual is deemed to be a primary producer (s393-25(2)).

- **beneficiary of a trust:** If the taxpayer is an individual who is a beneficiary presently entitled to a share of the income of a trust, which is carrying on a primary production business, for the purposes of the FMD requirements, that person is deemed to be a primary producer (s393-25(3)).

NOTE: Provided that certain conditions are met, beneficiaries of a trust that has a loss for an income year may still be deemed to be conducting a primary production business and remain eligible for the FMD scheme (refer: 21.000).

Other requirements which must be met

Other requirements include that:

- the deposit be a minimum of $1,000 and maximum of $400,000. The sum of all deposits cannot exceed $400,000. If the deposit is less than $1,000 it must be either an immediate investment of an FMD with the same FMD provider or the extension of the term of an FMD (even if other terms such as interest is also varied).

- the deposit be made by the owner; it cannot be made in joint names or on behalf of two or more persons (companies are excluded from making deposits)

- the deposit not be made by a trustee unless the beneficiary is presently entitled to a share of the income of the trust and is under a legal disability

- the deposit can be made with one or more FMD providers from 1 July 2012 (previously a primary producer was allowed to make a deposit to one FMD provider only: see *Early access for primary producers*)

- the deposit not be transferable to another entity

- the deposit not have a charge or other encumbrance created over it

- amounts which would otherwise accrue as interest or other earnings on the deposit must not be used to reduce other liabilities which the depositor may have with the FMD provider

- the deposit not have interest or other earnings invested as an FMD with the FMD provider without first having been paid to the depositor

- the deposit must be repaid if the owner dies or becomes bankrupt; or the owner ceases to carry on a primary production business in Australia and does not start carrying on such a business again within 120 days

- be $1,000 or more, except if the entire amount of the deposit is repaid

- the FMD provider must not deduct from the deposit at any time any administrative fee or charges, and

- the FMD provider must transfer the deposit by electronic means to another FMD provider that agrees to accept the deposit as an FMD, the first FMD provider is requested by the depositor in writing to do so, and given any information or any assistance from the depositor necessary for the purpose.

NOTE: A deposit can be made with more than one FMD provider (see below for meaning). In other words, an individual can have multiple FMD accounts. Deposits cannot be made by two or more people jointly, or made on behalf of two or more people. From 1 July 2014, an eligible primary producer can consolidate deposits into a single FMD without adverse tax consequences (see below).

THE 12 MONTH REPAYMENT RULE

As a general rule, any part of a deposit repaid within 12 months after the end of the day of the deposit is not taken to be an FMD and therefore will not qualify as a tax deduction (s393-40(1)). A deposit is also not an FMD if the amount of the deposit is reduced to less than $1,000 because of one of more repayments within 12 months after the end of the day the deposit is made (s393-40(2)).

NOTE: A deposit will continue to be an FMD even if repaid on the last day of that 12-month period (ie. on the one year anniversary date of the deposit).

Where there has been a re-investing, extension of term or transferring of a deposit, the 'day that the deposit was made' is deemed to be the day that the original deposit was made (s393-40(6)).

A repayment can still be an FMD if the agreement requires that the deposit must be repaid to the depositor as a result of death, bankruptcy or the person ceases to carry on a primary production business and does not recommence such a business within 120 days (s393-40(5)).

EARLY ACCESS FOR PRIMARY PRODUCERS

The 12 month repayment rule does not apply where specific circumstances apply, including:

- if the primary producer carries on business in 'exceptional circumstances' declared areas - amongst other conditions, it would be necessary for the taxpayer to obtain an 'exceptional circumstances certificate' (see s393-40(3) ITAA97), or
- if the primary producer is affected by a natural disaster (eg. a drought, flood, etc) (as specified by by regulations). This has effect from 1 July 2010 (see s393-40(3A) ITAA97).

A deduction in relation to the deposit is still available in these circumstances. See below for comments in relation to cessation of business and death of the deposit holder.

FARM MANAGEMENT DEPOSIT PROVIDER

An FMD provider (referred to as a 'financial institution' under the former provisions) is one that:

- is an authorised deposit-taking institution under the *Banking Act 1959*
- carries on in Australia the business of banking, so long as the Commonwealth, a State or Territory guarantees the repayment of any deposit taken in the course of that business, or
- carries on in Australia a business that consists of or includes taking money on deposit, so long as the Commonwealth, a State or a Territory guarantees the repayment of any deposit taken in the course of that business.

NOTE: Inactive FMD accounts are only treated as unclaimed monies under s69 of the *Banking Act 1959* if:

- the account has been inactive for a minimum of seven years, and
- the FMD provider is unable to contact the FMD holder after reasonable efforts to do so.

CLAIMING TAX DEDUCTIONS FOR FARM MANAGEMENT DEPOSITS

A taxpayer will be entitled to an income tax deduction for an FMD provided:

- they are the owner of the FMD
- the deposit is made at a time during the year when the individual taxpayer is carrying on a primary production business in Australia
- their taxable income from non-primary production income was $100,000 or less in the year of income ($65,000 prior to 1 July 2014)
- they did not become bankrupt during the income year or cease to be a primary producer for 120 days or more (whether during the income year or not)
- the sum of FMD deductions is equal to or less than the person's taxable primary production income for the income year, and
- the minimum term of the deposit is 12 months.

Amounts deposited as FMDs are deductible in the order they were made. The amount of deductions for an FMD is limited to the person's taxable primary production income.

A person's taxable primary production income for the income year is calculated as the difference between their assessable primary production and their primary production deductions (s392-80(1)). If the amount of any deductions exceeds the amount of any assessable income the person's taxable primary production income is nil.

A person's taxable non-primary production income for the income year is the difference between their assessable non-primary production income and their non-primary production deductions (s392-85(1)). If their deductions exceed their income then their taxable non-primary production income is nil.

For the purposes of calculating both taxable primary production income and taxable non-primary production income, capital gains are excluded. Apportionable deductions are excluded from primary production deductions (s392-80(3)) and are allocated entirely to non-primary production deductions.

'Apportionable deductions' include deductible rates and land tax under s25-75, or amounts deductible under s30-15 made to certain gift recipients (subject to certain conditions) (s995-1).

ASSESSABLE FARM MANAGEMENT DEPOSITS

The taxpayer will be assessed on a repayment of an FMD provided:

- they are the owner of the FMD
- the deposit is repaid in part or in full in the year, and
- the 'unrecouped FMD deduction in respect of the deposit just before repayment' less 'any amount of the deposit remaining' is greater than nil.

'Unrecouped FMD deduction' is (a) the amount that was initially deposited (ie. the amount of the deduction) or (b) if one or more parts of the deposit has been repaid before the most recent repayment reduced by any amount included in the owner's assessable income.

 Mia makes a deposit of $3,000, all of which is deductible. The deposit's unrecouped FMD deduction just before a first repayment of $1,000 is the amount of the deduction (that is, $3,000). The deposit's unrecouped FMD deduction just before a second repayment is $2,000 (that is, the unrecouped FMD deduction immediately before the first repayment ($3,000) reduced by the $1,000 included in Mia's assessable income as a result of the first repayment).

Withdrawals of deposits for which no deduction was available would not be assessable income. Conversely, a repaid FMD that is included in a taxpayer's assessable income is assessable primary production income for that purpose (refer ATO ID 2009/26).

Non-deductible amounts are considered to have been withdrawn first when any FMD withdrawal is made. A transfer to another FMD provider, the extension of the term of an FMD or transfer of an FMD to another FMD provider is not treated as a repayment (s393-15(1)). The owner is automatically deemed to have received the repayment of the FMD if he/she dies, becomes bankrupt or ceases to be a primary producer for 120 days or more (s393-10(40)). The earnings from an FMD are assessed to the owner as they are derived.

If an FMD is repaid, in whole or in part, then the FMD provider is required to deduct PAYG withholding tax (see 5.200) at the top marginal tax rate unless the ABN or TFN of the taxpayer has been quoted. Any tax deducted at source must be remitted to the Tax Office (see dates from 45.424).

The FMD provider must forward to the Tax Office an annual payment summary (see from 5.420) statement including:

- the TFN of the owner (if quoted) or a statement that no TFN was quoted
- name and address of the depositor (if known)
- amount of the repayment, and
- amount of any deduction.

CONSOLIDATING MULTIPLE DEPOSITS

Up until 30 June 2014, if a taxpayer were to consolidate their deposits into a single deposit, the deposits are deemed to be repaid to the taxpayer and therefore included as assessable income (see *Assessable Farm Management Deposits* above).

From 1 July 2014, a taxpayer may consolidate two or more deposits into a single deposit without any tax consequences provided that, after merging the deposits, the consolidated deposit contains only amounts that the taxpayer has:

- held for at least 12 months, and
- claimed a tax deduction for.

Note that if the taxpayer consolidates multiple FMDs into a new FMD, they will need to enter into a new agreement with their FMD provider.

Having all FMDs recorded on a single account does not necessarily mean that the deposits have been consolidated into a single deposit. FMD providers may be able to offer taxpayers a single FMD account facility that records new and existing deposit. In such circumstances, all deposits and withdrawals should be shown individually on the account.

Consolidated FMDs are taken to be made on the same day as the most recent of the original deposits being consolidated. This ensures the consolidated deposit has also been held for at least 12 months.

PAYG INSTALMENTS

Under PAYG requirements, the Tax Office advise the deposit holder of an instalment rate. Instalment income is then multiplied by this rate. FMD withdrawals are included as ordinary income for instalment purposes. Instalment income for an instalment period may be reduced if a deductible FMD deposit is made during the period. Similarly, instalment income for a quarterly or annual instalment period will include any withdrawals from an FMD (see 5.200).

CESSATION OF BUSINESS

An FMD cannot be made, if after cessation of business, the taxpayer continues to receive payments from the sale of produce grown when the business was still operating. This also applies to payments received from sales generated prior to the business ceasing. This is because the rules require the owner of an FMD to be conducting a primary production business when the deposit is made. An FMD cannot be made if the taxpayer no longer carries on a primary production business.

DEATH OF DEPOSIT HOLDER

Deposits are treated as having been repaid in the year of death. To the extent to which the contributions were previously allowed as a tax deduction, they are treated as assessable income in the deceased's tax return until date of death. If the FMD is repaid within twelve months of deposit because of the death of the taxpayer it will be regarded as an FMD. However, the taxpayer will only obtain a deduction for a deposit if their death occurs after the income year in which the deposit was made.

REPORTING REQUIREMENTS

Section 395-5 of the *Taxation Administration Act 1953* outlines the reporting requirements by financial institutions which are required to be made quarterly to the Agriculture Secretary. Certain information is required to be reported before the 11th day after the end of a calendar month, to the Agriculture Secretary. That information includes:

- the number of farm management deposits held at the end of that month
- the number of depositors in respect of such deposits at the end of that month
- the sum of the balances of such deposits at the end of that month, and
- any other information, in relation to farm management deposits held by the FMD provider at any time in that month, that is required by the regulations.

There is no requirement to disclose the identity of the depositor.

21.850 FUEL TAX CREDITS

The *Fuel Tax Act 2006* (FTA06) provides a single system of fuel tax credits applicable to fuel used in vehicles used for both private and business purposes. Fuel tax credits are paid to reduce or remove the incidence of fuel tax levied on taxable fuels used by eligible taxpayers. The system may be available to those conducting a primary production business (see 28.500).

21.900 AVERAGING INCOME

Division 392 sets out the rules for the averaging of taxable incomes of primary producers by comparing taxable income with average income. Unless the taxpayer elects irrevocably to discontinue income averaging, the rules apply irrespective of whether it produces a tax advantage in relation to the particular year.

The scheme provides relief by way of a tax offset when average income is lower than taxable income, and can result in additional tax when average income of the taxpayer is higher than their taxable income.

NUMBER OF YEARS IN 'AVERAGE INCOME'

- Minimum number of years: 2
- Maximum number of years: 5

It is made up of taxable incomes which allow an offset of past losses brought forward, but no taxable income shown in it can be less than zero. Losses cannot be included to reduce the average. A loss is treated as a taxable income of zero.

AVERAGE INCOME LESS THAN TAXABLE INCOME

Where the average income is less than the taxable income, the taxpayer is entitled to a tax offset. This is calculated with the rate of tax applying to the average income being applied to the taxable income. The average income for this purpose is the average of the basic taxable income.

AVERAGE INCOME MORE THAN TAXABLE INCOME

Where the average income is more than the taxable income, the rate of tax applicable to the average income is applied to the taxable income, resulting in additional tax being paid ('extra income tax') (s392-35(3)).

MUST BE A 'PRIMARY PRODUCER' IN THE INCOME YEAR

The averaging provisions can apply to an assessment only if the taxpayer is an individual and has carried on a business of primary production in Australia for two consecutive years (the last of which is the current year).

Notwithstanding business activities in prior years, if a taxpayer was not carrying on a primary production business in an income year, averaging ceases. If a primary production business was recommenced in subsequent years, it would be necessary to begin the averaging process again. An individual in a partnership carrying on a primary production business would typically be considered to be 'an individual who carries on a primary production business' for Division 392 purposes (ATO ID 2003/359).

CEASING BUSINESS

Averaging can still apply after ceasing business if either the taxpayer's assessable income for the year was derived or resulted from carrying on that business, or a primary production business was carried on during the income year (s392-10), and averaging applied for an earlier income year.

PERMANENT REDUCTION OF TAXABLE INCOME

If a primary producer can show that because of retirement or any other cause, basic taxable income for the year is permanently reduced during that year to less than two thirds of average income, they can elect under s392-95 that averaging cease. They can subsequently elect that averaging restarts using the lower rates of income. See also *Ceasing averaging* below.

CEASING AVERAGING

A taxpayer can elect (s392-25) that averaging no longer applies to them. The Commissioner must be notified in writing. The election cannot be revoked once made.

TRUST BENEFICIARIES

Averaging will apply to a beneficiary of a primary production trust (s392-20) where:

- the beneficiary's share of income from the trust is $1,040 or more, or
- the share is less than $1,040 but only if the Commissioner of Taxation accepts that the trust distribution did not occur in order to obtain the benefit of averaging.

If the primary production trust incurs a tax loss for an income year, a beneficiary of such a trust may still be treated as conducting a primary production business notwithstanding that they are not presently entitled to any income of the trust. Subject to certain conditions, from 1 July 2010, a beneficiary of a loss trust is able to maintain their primary production status provided that certain conditions are met (see 21.005 for further information).

FIRST AVERAGE YEAR

Averaging applies to an assessment for the current year (under s392-10(1)(c)) if the taxpayer:

- is an individual
- carried on a primary production business in Australia for two or more income years in a row and the current year is the last year, and
- for at least one of those income years has basic taxable income which is less than or equal to the basic taxable income for the next income year.

If a taxpayer has a loss in a particular year, the income of that year is deemed to be nil for the purpose of calculating the average income: s392-15(2). The income of the next year will be reduced by the amount of the loss carried forward. For example, if the basic taxable income for the year ended 30 June 2014 was $30,000 and for the next year ending 30 June 2015 it is $27,000, because the basic taxable income in 2015 is lower than that in 2014, averaging cannot start. If the basic taxable income for the year ended 30 June 2015 is $30,000 or higher, then 2014 will be the first average year. The basic taxable income for two consecutive years may be 'nil', in which case averaging will commence.

A taxpayer (with no other source of income) conducted a primary production business with these results:

Income year 2010-11: loss of $4,000	Income year 2013-14: taxable income of $7,000
Income year 2011-12: loss of $3,500	Income year 2014-15: taxable income of $6,000
Income year 2012-13: loss of $3,000	

For years in which a loss occurred, taxable income is treated as 'nil' when deciding when averaging starts.

The start-up average table shows how the average table starts when there are initial losses. To find the notional primary production income for 2009-10, this is how the table will look on those sample incomes:

| 2010-11: Nil | 2012-13: Nil | 2014-15: $6,000 |
| 2011-12: Nil | 2013-14: $7,000 | |

Average taxable income $13,000 divided by 5 = $2,600. There being no tax payable on a taxable income of $2,600, there is no net tax to be apportioned across overall taxable income.

BASIC TAXABLE INCOME

For the purposes of s392-10, the basic taxable income of a primary producer is their taxable income less:

- any net capital gain, or
- income under s82-65, s82-70 or s302-145 (ie. death benefit employment termination payment or death benefit superannuation lump sum payments are excluded) (s392-15(1)(a)),

which is then reduced by any above-average special professional income under Division 405. The 'basic taxable income' for a year is nil either if there is no taxable income, or it is nil after making the reductions referred to above.

For calculations when a capital gain is derived, see TR 92/12. Note that while much terminology has changed the basic calculation approach remains the same.

TAXABLE PRIMARY PRODUCTION INCOME

The taxable primary production income of a primary producer is calculated under s392-80. Basically, this is the assessable primary production income for the year compared to primary production deductions for the year.

Primary production income requires that the primary producer is carrying on a 'primary production business' (see 21.200).

When the income is higher than the deductions, the difference is the 'taxable primary production income'. If the primary production deductions are equal to or higher than the assessable primary production income, then the primary production income is nil.

Primary production deductions are those that can be deducted against the assessable primary production income (including apportionable deductions such as rates and land tax and gifts under s30-15 – but not gifts of livestock). Non-primary production deductions for the year are the difference between the total deductions and the primary production deductions.

NOTE: Ordinary income derived by an individual from allowing wind farming infrastructure to be constructed, operated and accessed on freehold land that they own and use in carrying on a primary production business does not constitute 'assessable primary production income' of that individual (TD 2013/2). There is no causive connection between the income derived and the particular primary production business being carried on.

TAXABLE NON-PRIMARY PRODUCTION INCOME

Taxable non-primary production income for the current year is worked out by the method statement set out in s392-85(1).

- **Step 1:** Compare assessable non-primary production income for the current year with your non-primary production deductions for the current year.

- **Step 2:** If assessable non-primary production is larger than non-primary production deductions, the taxable non-primary production income is the difference between them.

- **Step 3:** If non-primary production deductions are larger than (or equal to) your assessable non-primary production income, the taxable non-primary production income is nil.

The assessable non-primary production income for the current year is the difference between basic assessable income and assessable primary production income. Non-primary production deductions are the difference between total deductions for the year and total primary production deductions. The 'taxable non-primary production income' is required to work out the 'non-primary production shade out amount'.

INCOME SUBJECT TO AVERAGING

The income of a primary producer which is subject to averaging is calculated under s392-90. The averaging component takes into account the taxable primary production income and the taxable non-primary production income.

The non-primary production shade-out amount is calculated using these formulae:

- If the taxable primary production income is more than nil, the non-primary production shade out amount is calculated:

  $10,000 – Taxable non-PP income

- If the taxable primary production amount is nil, the non-PP shade out is calculated:

  $10,000 – Taxable non-PP income – (PP deductions – Assessable PP income)

If the amount is less than nil, the non-PP shadeout amount is nil.

The following table in s390-90 is used to calculate the averaging component.

The averaging component equals			
Item	If taxable non-PP* income:	For taxable PP* income > 0	For taxable PP*income = 0
1	is nil	Basic taxable income	Nil
2	is more than nil but does not exceed $5,000	Basic taxable income	Basic taxable income
3	exceeds $5,000 but does not exceed $10,000	Taxable PP income plus non-PP shade-out amount	Non-PP shade-out amount
4	is $10,000 or more	Taxable PP income	Nil

* PP = primary production.

WHEN EXTRA INCOME TAX IS PAYABLE OR A TAX OFFSET APPLIES

Extra income tax is payable on the averaging component of the basic taxable income (excluding capital gains) if the income tax that would be otherwise payable at the 'comparison rate' is more than the amount of income tax payable at the basic rates (ie. the average income is more than the taxable income) (s392-35). A tax offset is received (for calculation see s392-60) if the income tax payable at the comparison rate is less than the amount of income tax payable at basic rates (ie. if average income is less than the taxable income (excluding capital gains)).

- The income tax payable at the 'comparison rate' is worked out by the formula:

  Basic taxable income for the current year x Comparison rate

- The 'comparison rate' is calculated under this formula:

  Income tax on average income* divided by average income

* the amount of income tax payable on average income for the current year at basic rates (s392-50).

Taxpayers do not have to calculate either the tax offset or extra income tax; these are calculated by the Tax Office.

The examples below do not include Medicare levy or any other offsets to which the taxpayer may be entitled.

Extra income tax

In the 2014-15 income year Clive carries on a business of primary production (PP) and assists a local accountant with bookkeeping for which he received wages of $4,500. He received a net PP income of $26,500. As the non-PP income is less than $5,000 it is used in calculating the basic taxable income (see table above). The average income for the year was $33,000. The extra income tax would be calculated as follows (assuming no Medicare levy payable or Low Income Tax Offset):

Tax on $31,000 taxable income at basic rates $2,432
Tax on average income of $33,000 at basic rates $2,812
Comparison rate (see formula above) $2,812 (assumed average)
divided by $33,000 = 0.0852
Tax on $31,000 x 0.0852 .... $2,642
Extra income tax is $2,642 less $2,432 .... $210
*Tax on taxable income plus extra income tax............................. **$2,642 + $210 = $2,852***

Tax offset

Assume similar facts to above except that Clive's average taxable income for the 2014-15 year is $26,000. The tax offset would be calculated as follows:

Tax on $31,000 taxable income at basic rates $2,432
Tax on average income of $26,000 at basic rates $1,482
Comparison rate (see formula above) $1,482 divided by $26,000 = 0.0570
Tax on $31,000 x 0.0570 .... $1,767
Tax offset is $2,432 less $1,767 .... $665
*Tax on taxable income less tax offset .... **$1,767– $665 = $1,102***

International taxation

22

22.000 TAXATION OF FOREIGN INCOME DERIVED BY RESIDENTS

Australian resident taxpayers are subject to income tax on Australian and worldwide income under s6-5 ITAA97.

This general rule may be modified by Australia's double taxation agreements with other countries. Furthermore, the domestic tax legislation contains various tax concessions and exemptions for specific items of foreign source income.

The deductibility of expenditure incurred in the derivation of foreign source income is determined under the general deductibility rules contained in s8-1 ITAA97 and the specific deductions provisions.

The amounts of foreign source income and related deductions taken into account for Australian tax purposes are also subject to specific integrity measures; notably, the thin capitalisation, transfer pricing and anti-tax-deferral regimes.

22.010 FOREIGN SOURCE INCOME – INDIVIDUALS

As a general rule, where foreign income is derived by an Australian resident, the gross amount must be included as assessable income and a foreign income tax offset is allowed for any tax paid overseas (see 22.400).

DIVIDENDS, INTEREST AND ROYALTIES

Dividends, interest and royalties derived from foreign sources are generally subject to income tax in Australia. Subject to any relevant double tax agreement (DTA) between Australia and the source country (see 22.200) and subject to the source country's domestic laws, the foreign payer may withhold foreign tax from the payment. In this case, the gross amount of the income (before withholding tax) is treated as assessable income for Australian tax purposes. The amount of foreign tax withheld may be creditable against Australian tax liabilities.

CAPITAL GAINS

Foreign source capital gains are generally subject to Australian income tax under the CGT regime, subject to any relevant DTA. Note that some treaties which were negotiated before the CGT measures were introduced may be silent or unclear regarding the allocation of taxing rights over capital gains.

EMPLOYMENT INCOME

Foreign source employment income derived by an Australian resident is generally assessable in Australia. Where there is a tax treaty between Australia and the source country, the other country may also have taxing rights over the income. In limited circumstances, the income may be tax exempt in Australia under s23AG or s23AF of the ITAA36.

FEES FOR INDEPENDENT SERVICES

Fees for independent services (eg. contractor fees) derived by an Australian resident from a foreign source are generally assessable in Australia unless a relevant double tax agreement between Australia and the source country allocates exclusive taxing rights over the income to the source country.

Many of Australia's DTAs contain a separate independent personal services article, such as the Australia/United States treaty. The Australia/New Zealand treaty does not include an independent personal services clause but includes such services in the expanded definition of 'business', which means that such income may now be taxed pursuant to the business profits article.

PENSIONS RECEIVED FROM OVERSEAS

Most double tax agreements provide that pensions and purchased annuities are generally assessable in the country of residence.

The Commissioner has released a number of rulings relating to specific pensions received from specific countries.

ATTRIBUTED INCOME

As well as income which is 'realised' and actually derived, an Australian resident with offshore interests in a non-resident company or trust may also be deemed to have 'derived' notional income under the attribution rules. This notional income is assessable to the Australian resident taxpayer. See 22.800.

SECTION 23AF

Section 23AF ITAA36 exempts income directly attributable to a period of service on approved foreign projects. Section 23AF requires that the taxpayer has been engaged on the project for a continuous period of 91 days or more. Certain foreign earnings are precluded from being exempt from tax under s23AF, including income which is exempt from income tax in the source country due to a tax treaty between Australia and the source country, long service leave payments and superannuation payments. Where income is exempt under both s23AF and s23AG, s23AG takes priority.

SECTION 23AG

Section 23AG ITAA36 provides a tax exemption in respect of income from foreign earnings derived by a resident of Australia in respect of foreign service if the period of foreign service is 91 days or more and if certain conditions are satisfied.

AVAILABILITY OF THE s23AG EXEMPTION

The tax exemption is only available where the continuous period of foreign service is directly attributable to a specified activity:

- work performed in relation to the delivery of Australian official aid by the employer
- work performed in relation to an international affairs deductible gift recipient operated by the employer
- work performed for an employer which is a prescribed institution exempt from income tax
- deployment overseas as a member of a Commonwealth, State or Territorial disciplined force, and
- any other activity specified in the regulations.

TR 2013/7 discusses the interpretation of certain key terms.

Within the categories listed above, the s23AG exemption will not apply if the income derived overseas is exempt from tax in the source country only because of one of the following:

- the operation of one of Australia's DTAs or a law of that country which gives effect to a DTA
- the foreign country does not tax employment income, and
- a law or an international agreement dealing with privileges and immunities of diplomats or consuls or persons connected with international organisations applies.

If the earnings would have been exempt in the foreign country for more than one reason, eg the operation of a double tax agreement and a specific agreement, and at least one of those reasons is not on the list in the legislation, then s23AG will still apply to exempt the income.

 An Australian resident volunteer aid worker (assuming that the activity is of a type which qualifies for s23AG application) has earnings in Fiji that are exempt in Fiji because of Article 21 of the Australia/Fiji DTA. The earnings are also exempt because of a Memorandum of Understanding with the Fijian Government relating to aid workers.

The earnings satisfy the tests (of s23AG(2)) because they are not tax-exempt in Fiji solely because of the DTA.

Foreign earnings that are within the scope of s23AG include allowances received in respect of expenses (eg. for purchases of household items for use in the foreign country) that are attributable to the period of foreign service (ID 2011/52).

TD 2012/8 considers what types of temporary absences from foreign service form part of a continuous period of foreign service for the purposes of s23AG. TD 2013/18 sets out the Commissioner's view that foreign earnings derived by Australian Defence Force members from a period of leave as a result of an accident or illness that occurred while deployed overseas as a member of a disciplined force are exempt under s23AG.

OPERATION OF s23AG

Refer to the Tax Office website fact sheet *Exempt foreign employment income* for a detailed explanation of the operation of s23AG.

ELLIOTT'S CASE: COMMISSIONER'S ABILITY TO AMEND ASSESSMENTS

In *Elliott v FC of T* [2012] AATA 428 (Elliott), the taxpayer disclosed amounts of (pre-1 July 2009) foreign employment income as exempt foreign employment income in his tax returns for the relevant years. The Commissioner was of the view that the income was assessable income.

A two-year amendment period applied to the taxpayer so long as the relevant item of income had been 'identified' in the lodged returns. The Commissioner argued that the two-year amendment period did not apply as the relevant item of income had not been 'identified' under the purportedly correct tax return label. However, the AAT concluded that the two-year period did apply as the item of income had been 'identified' – disclosed – in the return, regardless of whether it was treated correctly or disclosed under the correct label in the tax return. Therefore, the Commissioner was unable to amend as it was outside of the two-year period.

Note that there is no equivalent provision for expenses. Those items remain under the two-year amendment period regardless of whether they had been appropriately disclosed in the original return (unless they are subject to a 4-year period or unlimited period for another reason).

22.020   FOREIGN SOURCE INCOME – BUSINESS

Australian businesses are generally liable for Australian income tax on all foreign source income derived from overseas branches, or other overseas business, commercial or investment activities. A foreign income tax offset is usually allowed for any tax paid overseas (see 22.400).

This is subject to the allocation of taxing rights under a DTA between Australia and the country from which the income is sourced.

TAX CONCESSIONS FOR COMPANIES

Australian resident companies deriving foreign income over which Australia has taxing rights under the relevant DTA may be eligible for income tax concessions or exemptions, depending on the nature of the income. Types of foreign source income which may be subject to concessional treatment include:

- non-portfolio dividends
- foreign branch income that is non-assessable non-exempt income, and
- a capital gain or loss made from the disposal of shares in a foreign company.

NON-PORTFOLIO DIVIDENDS

Non-portfolio dividends are dividends paid to a company where that company has a voting interest (defined at s160AFB ITAA36) amounting to at least 10% of the voting power in the company paying the dividend. Under s23AJ ITAA36 a non-portfolio dividend paid to an Australian resident company is non-assessable non-exempt income provided the company does not receive the dividend in the capacity of a trustee and the company that paid the dividend is not a Part X Australian resident (which is a dual resident which is deemed to be an Australian resident solely under the DTA tie-breaker rules).

In the case *Intoll Management Pty Ltd v Commissioner of Taxation* (2012) FCAFC 179, the Full Federal Court held that s23AJ can apply to the trustee of a resident unit trust in its capacity as the 'head company' of a tax consolidated group on the basis that the trust derived the dividends in its capacity as a head company for its own benefit and not in its capacity as a trustee.

The law has been amended so that, effective from 17 October 2014, the s23AJ exemption applies:

- to returns on instruments treated as 'equity interests' under the debt-equity rules
- where a distribution flows through interposed trusts and partnerships other than corporate tax entities
- where it is received by a corporate tax entity, rather than a company; and
- in respect of distributions of a non-share dividend, which is not included in the definition of a distribution.

NON-ASSESSABLE FOREIGN BRANCH INCOME

Foreign branch income derived by an Australian resident company is non-assessable non-exempt income under s23AH ITAA36. Further, capital gains and losses made on assets which are not taxable Australian property are disregarded where the resident company used the asset wholly or mainly for the purpose of producing foreign income in carrying on a business at or through a Permanent Establishment (PE) of the company.

However, the foreign income is not assessable and the capital gains and losses are disregarded only if certain other conditions are met. In particular, foreign branch income is not assessable only if the PE passes the 'active income test' as set out in the Controlled Foreign Company (CFC) legislation and capital gains and losses are disregarded only if the disposed asset is not a 'tainted asset' (see 22.820). Other conditions depend on whether the PE is located in a listed or unlisted country.

A taxpayer is deemed to have a PE in a listed country for the purposes of s23AH at any time in an income year where an item of substantial equipment is being used in that listed country and is a deemed PE in that country for the purposes of the PE article in the treaty between Australia and that country (refer to ID 2010/204).

CAPITAL GAIN OR LOSS FROM DISPOSAL OF SHARES IN A FOREIGN COMPANY

Subdivision 768-G ITAA97 may operate to reduce the capital gain or loss made by an Australian resident company as a result of a CGT event happening in respect of a share in a foreign company. To be eligible for the concession, the Australian resident company must directly hold at least 10% of the voting rights in the foreign company. Where all necessary conditions are met, the gain or loss is reduced by the 'active foreign business asset percentage'. Broadly, this is the percentage of assets (by book value or market value) which are used by the foreign company in an active business (see Subdivision 768-G).

22.100 TAXATION OF NON-RESIDENTS

As a general rule, non-residents are liable to Australian income tax on all of their Australian sourced income, subject to the provisions of any relevant double tax agreement.

22.110 NON-RESIDENT BUSINESSES

Non-resident business entities are generally subject to Australian tax only on their Australian sourced income.

DIVIDENDS, INTEREST AND ROYALTIES

Dividends, interest, royalties and certain types of managed investment trust distributions derived by non-residents from Australian sources are generally not subject to Australian income tax by assessment, but rather, withholding tax is withheld and remitted by the Australian payer (see below).

AUSTRALIAN BRANCHES OF NON-RESIDENTS

Australia's double tax agreements typically provide that where a non-resident entity carries on business in Australia through a permanent establishment (or branch) situated in Australia, then Australia has taxing rights over the business profits attributable to that permanent establishment as though it was an independent enterprise. Generally, the permanent establishment is taxed on its worldwide income as a notional Australian resident company which is independent from its foreign head office. However, repatriations of profits from the Australian branch to the foreign head office would not be treated as dividends for Australian tax purposes.

Australian source dividends paid to a non-resident carrying on a business in Australia through a permanent establishment are exempt from withholding tax where the dividend is attributable to the permanent establishment and is not paid to the person in their capacity as trustee (s128B(3E) ITAA36). Further, such dividends are included in the assessable income of the permanent establishment and outgoings incurred in deriving such income may be deductible.

22.120 NON-RESIDENT INDIVIDUALS

In the case of individuals, non-residents are subject to higher effective tax rates than residents (see from 3.010) and are not eligible for the tax-free threshold.

Non-residents are not liable for the Medicare levy and may not claim tax offsets and rebates, including franking credits.

22.130 CAPITAL GAINS AND INVESTMENT RETURNS

A gain made by a non-resident is assessable only if it relates to 'taxable Australian property' (see 12.700), which includes real property in Australia and interests in Australian companies which have substantial holdings in Australian real property.

A capital gain made by a non-resident is taxable only if the CGT asset is 'taxable Australian property' (TAP), which includes real property in Australia and interests in land-rich Australian companies (see 12.700).

Australian residents who make interest, dividend and royalty payments to non-residents are generally required to withhold tax under the PAYG withholding rules but exemptions exist for franked dividends (see from 5.317). A DTA may provide some relief for the non-resident (see 22.210), either by limiting the withholding tax rate to a rate which is lower than the domestic rate or by providing a specific exemption. See 22.140 for detailed discussion on withholding tax.

CGT DISCOUNT FOR FOREIGN INDIVIDUALS

The ability of foreign residents and temporary residents to access the CGT discount is limited, as follows:

- the full CGT discount is available for discount capital gains to the extent the increase in value of the CGT asset occurred prior to 9 May 2012
- no CGT discount for discount capital gains accrued after 8 May 2012, and
- the CGT discount for discount capital gains is apportioned where an individual has been an Australian resident and, a foreign or temporary resident, during the period after 8 May 2012. The apportionment ensures the full 50% discount percentage is applied to periods where the individual was an Australian resident.

IMPORTANT! These limitations also apply to a non-resident individual who is beneficiary entitled to a capital gain derived by a trust in respect of a CGT asset held by the trust.

THE DISCOUNT TESTING PERIOD

The *discount testing period* is as follows:

- where the asset is held by an individual, the period from the day the CGT asset is acquired by the individual ending on the day the CGT event happens after 8 May 2012, or

- where the asset was held by a trust, the period commencing on the day the trustee acquired the CGT asset or the day the individual last became a beneficiary of the trust estate (whichever is the later), and ends on the day the CGT event happens after 8 May 2012.

CALCULATING THE DISCOUNT PERCENTAGE – ASSETS ACQUIRED AFTER 8 MAY 2012

Where an asset is acquired after 8 May 2012 and the individual is a foreign resident or temporary resident during some or all of the discount testing period, the amendments will apply to calculate the discount percentage applicable to any discount capital gain from the asset.

The discount percentage is calculated under the following formula:

$$\frac{\textit{Number of days during discount testing period that you were an Australian resident (but not a *temporary resident)}}{\textit{2 x Number of days in discount testing period}}$$

If the individual was a foreign resident or temporary resident for the entire discount testing period the discount percentage for any discount capital gain will be zero.

The explanatory memorandum to the legislation provides the following example:

EXAMPLE 1.1: Asset acquired after 8 May 2012 and the individual is a foreign resident during part of the discount testing period

XYZ Trust buys an asset on 1 January 2014 for $10,000. XYZ trust then sells the asset on 1 January 2016 for $20,000.

There are two beneficiaries of the trust, each holding a 50 per cent interest in the trust. The first is Lucas, who has been a beneficiary of the trust since 1 January 2013 and has been an Australian resident for the entire period.

The other beneficiary is Lachlan. Lachlan has also been a beneficiary of the trust since 1 January 2013. Lachlan was a foreign resident individual until 1 January 2015, when he became an Australian resident taxpayer.

The capital gains of the XYZ trust is $10,000 against which it applies the full discount percentage (50 per cent). Lucas and Lachlan are both presently entitled to $2,500 each. Applying the rules in Subdivision 115-C, both Lachlan's and Lucas's capital gains are grossed up so that they have a discount capital gain of $5,000 each.

As Lucas has not been a foreign or temporary resident during any of the discount testing period, he is not subject to the amendments. Therefore, he is entitled to the full discount percentage of 50 per cent.

Lachlan has been a foreign resident during the discount testing period and therefore is subject to sections 115-110 and 115-115. As the trust acquired the asset while Lachlan was a beneficiary, the date the asset was acquired by the trust is the relevant starting date for the discount testing period (subparagraph 115-110(2)(d)(i)).

As the asset was acquired after 8 May 2012, Lachlan must calculate the discount percentage under the formula in subsection 115-115(2). Therefore, Lachlan's discount percentage is:

$$\frac{365}{1,460} = 25\%$$

CALCULATING THE DISCOUNT PERCENTAGE: ASSETS ACQUIRED PRIOR TO 9 MAY 2012

Foreign or temporary resident on 8 May 2012 and the individual has chosen market value

Where a discount capital gain is from an asset acquired prior to 9 May 2012 and the individual was a foreign or temporary resident on 8 May 2012 and the individual chooses to use the market value approach for determining the gain which accrued prior to 9 May 2012, the discount percentage for the discount capital gain is calculated as follows:

- **Step 1** – calculate the CGT asset's excess.

  The excess is the net increase in value of the asset that has accrued prior to 9 May 2012. It is calculated as the amount by which the CGT asset's market value exceeds its cost base at the end of 8 May 2012.

  If the excess is equal to or greater than the discount capital gain from the asset, the discount percentage is 50% and no further calculation is needed.

- **Step 2** – if the excess is less than the discount capital gain from the CGT event, the discount percentage is worked out using the following formula:

$$\frac{Excess + \left[Shortfall \ x \ \dfrac{Number \ of \ apportionable \ days \ that \ you \ were \ an \ eligible \ resident}{Number \ of \ apportionable \ days} \right]}{2 \ x \ Amount \ of \ the \ *discount \ capital \ gain}$$

-   The shortfall is the net increase in the value of the asset accrued after 8 May 2012. This is calculated by subtracting the excess from the amount of the discount capital gain.
-   The number of apportionable days means the number of days after 8 May 2012 during the discount testing period.
-   The number of apportionable days that you were an eligible resident is the number of days after 8 May 2012 during the discount testing period that the individual was an Australian resident (but not a temporary resident).

The EM provides the following examples:

EXAMPLE 1.2: *Asset acquired before 9 May 2012 and market value is chosen; however, the gain at 8 May 2012 exceeds the discount capital gain: Dominic is a resident of France. On 1 January 2011 he purchased a property in Sydney for $1,000,000.*

On 8 May 2012 the property was valued at $1,100,000. On 1 July 2012 Dominic sold the property for $1,050,000.

Dominic has a discount capital gain from the disposal of the property of $50,000.

As Dominic is a foreign resident, the discount percentage applicable to the gain will be determined by reference to the amendments introduced by the bill.

For the purposes of determining the discount percentage, Dominic chooses to use the market value approach. The discount percentage is worked out as follows:

Calculate the CGT asset's excess: $1,100,000 – $1,000,000 = $100,000

As the amount of the excess is greater than the discount capital gain of $50,000 from the disposal of property the discount percentage is 50%.

EXAMPLE 1.3: *Asset acquired before 9 May 2012 and market value is chosen: Samantha is an Australian resident. On 1 July 2012, Samantha's grandmother died and Samantha inherited land in Victoria's Yarra Valley that was purchased on 1 January 2011 for $10,000,000. Samantha's grandmother was a tax resident of the United Kingdom.*

On 8 May 2012, Samantha's land was valued at $11,000,000. On 1 January 2013 Samantha sold her land for $12,000,000. Samantha has an overall discount capital gain from the disposal of the land of $2,000,000.

As Samantha is a resident for part of the discount testing period, the discount percentage will be determined by reference to the amendments introduced in this bill.

Furthermore, because item 6 of section 115-30 applies to the asset (as Samantha received the asset as the beneficiary of a deceased estate), Samantha's grandmother's residency status and previous holding are relevant for determining the discount percentage. As Samantha's grandmother held the asset on 8 May 2012, her residency status determines that Samantha must calculate the discount percentage under subsection 115-115(4) or (6).

For the purposes of determining the discount percentage, Samantha chooses to use the market value approach. The discount percentage is worked out as follows:

Step 1   *Calculate the CGT asset's excess.*

       $11,000,000 – $10,000,000 = $1,000,000

Step 2   *As the **excess** is less than the discount capital gain ($2,000,000) from the CGT event, the discount percentage is worked out using the following figures:*

-   *The **shortfall amount** is $1,000,000 ($2,000,000 less the excess)*
-   *The **number of apportionable days** Samantha was **an eligible resident** is 184 days (that is, days Samantha and her grandmother were an eligible resident)*

- The **number of apportionable days** is 237 days (that is, the number of apportionable days taking into account Samantha and her grandmother's holding of the asset), and
- Twice the **amount of discount capital gain** is $4,000,000.

Therefore, Samantha's discount percentage is:

$$\frac{\$1,000,000 + \left[\dfrac{\$1,000,000 \times 184\ days}{237\ days}\right]}{\$4,000,000} = 44.4\%$$

Individual is a foreign or temporary resident on 8 May 2012 and has not chosen market value

Where the asset is acquired before 9 May 2012 and the individual does not choose the market value approach, the discount percentage applicable to the discount capital gain is determined by the following formula:

$$\frac{Number\ of\ apportionable\ days\ that\ you\ were\ an}{Australian\ resident\ (but\ not\ a\ *temporary\ resident)}$$
$$\overline{2 \times Number\ of\ days\ in\ discount\ testing\ period}$$

The EM includes the following example:

EXAMPLE 1.5: Following on from example 1.3, if Samantha does not choose to apply the market value, then her discount percentage applicable to the discount capital gain of $2,000,000 would be:

$$\frac{184}{1,462} = 12.58\%$$

Resident individual on 8 May 2012

If an individual makes a discount capital gain from a CGT event occurring after 8 May 2012 and was:

- an Australian resident (but not a temporary resident) on 8 May 2012, and
- a foreign or temporary resident at any time during the period after 8 May 2012,

then the discount percentage is directly apportioned to reflect all days in the period of ownership before 9 May 2012 and only those days after 8 May 2012 that the individual was an Australian resident.

The following formula is used:

$$\frac{\begin{array}{c}Number\ of\ days\ in\\discount\ testing\ period\end{array} - \begin{array}{c}Number\ of\ apportionable\ days\ that\ you\ were\\a\ foreign\ resident\ or\ *temporary\ resident\end{array}}{2 \times Number\ of\ days\ in\ discount\ testing\ period}$$

The EM includes the following example:

EXAMPLE 1.6: Resident individual on 8 May 2012: XYZ Trust buys an asset on 1 January 2010 for $10,000. XYZ trust then sells the asset on 1 January 2016 for $50,000.

There are two beneficiaries of the trust, each holding a 50 per cent interest in the trust. One of the beneficiaries is Lucas, who has been a beneficiary of the trust since 1 January 2011 and was an Australian resident individual until and including 31 December 2014 (after which time he became a foreign resident).

The discount capital gain of the XYZ trust is $40,000, against which it applies the full discount percentage (50 per cent). Lucas is presently entitled to $10,000 at the end of the income year. Therefore, Lucas makes the gain on 30 June 2016.

Applying the rules in Subdivision 115-C, Lucas's capital gain is grossed up so that he has a discount capital gain of $20,000.

Lucas is subject to section 115-110 and subsection 115-115(3) as he is an individual, was a resident at 8 May 2012, has been a foreign resident individual during the discount testing period and received a discount capital gain as a beneficiary of a trust.

Lucas is subject to subsection 115-115(3) because he was an Australian resident on 8 May 2012. The relevant dates for the discount testing period are 1 January 2011 (this is the date Lucas became a beneficiary of the fixed trust) and 30 June 2016. Therefore, the following numbers are relevant:

- *the number of days in the discount testing period is 2008 days*
- *the number of apportionable days Lucas was a foreign or temporary resident is 547 days, and*
- *two times the number of days in the discount testing period is 4016 days.*

Therefore, applying subsection 115-115(3), Lucas' discount percentage is:

$$\frac{2{,}008 - 547}{4{,}016} = 36.38\%$$

The legislation and EM do not offer specific guidance on appropriate market valuations for this purpose. General guidance on market valuation approaches may be found in the Tax Office online guide *Market valuation for tax purposes* **(www.ato.gov.au).**

22.140 WITHHOLDING TAX AS A FINAL TAX

Payments of interest, dividends and royalties paid to a non-resident are subject to withholding tax prior to the transaction. Withholding tax is considered a final tax.

Interest, dividends and royalties are not included in the Australian assessable income of a non-resident. This means tax withheld from such amounts paid to (or applied on behalf of) a non-resident is a final Australian tax and there is no further tax payable (or refundable) in Australia.

WHO MUST WITHHOLD?

A person liable to pay money to a non-resident is deemed to be the person 'having control' of that money. That person is required to withhold sufficient money to pay taxes due, and is liable for any tax that should have been withheld (plus any interest and penalties on that tax) (s255 ITAA36).

These payers must withhold tax from payments to a non-resident, or when it is credited (reinvested, accumulated or otherwise dealt with) on behalf of a non-resident:

- a payer of interest or a royalty to an entity that has an address outside Australia (according to the payer's records in respect of the interest or royalty) or where the payer is authorised to pay the interest at a place outside Australia (s12-245 and s12-280 TAA). A payer must also withhold from interest paid to an Australian resident which is derived from carrying on a business at or through a foreign permanent establishment where the payee has notified the payer that withholding tax is required, and

- a resident company that pays a dividend to a shareholder whose address in its register of members is outside Australia (this also applies where shares are jointly owned and one of the addresses is outside Australia) (s12-210 TAA). A dividend is exempt from dividend withholding tax to the extent a dividend withholding tax exemption applies under s128B ITAA36.

The withholding regime (s12-315(1)(b) TAA and Division 6 of the *Taxation Administration Regulations 1976*) add further withholding obligations for:

- payments for promoting or organising casino gaming junkets at 3%

- payments for entertainment and sports activities (including activities of a performing artist or sportsperson and including payments to support staff such as art directors, body guards, coaches, hairdressers and personal trainers) – at the company tax rate where a company is involved, and at marginal rates for non-residents where the entity is an individual, and

- payments under contracts for construction, installation and upgrading of buildings, plant and fixtures and associated activities at 5%.

NOTE: The tax withheld from these is not a final tax.

Variations may be allowed with permission from the Tax Office (see also TR 2006/12).

TIMING

Withholding tax must be deducted:

- before payment of interest, a dividend or a royalty to a non-resident, or
- immediately after interest, a dividend or a royalty is received from a resident company by an Australian entity (or an Australian government agency) if a non-resident is entitled to receive the amount or have all or part of it credited to them (or otherwise dealt with on their behalf) (s12-215; s12-250 and s12-285 TAA).

PAYER'S DEDUCTIBILITY RULES

Until PAYG withholding obligations have been satisfied the payer is denied an income tax deduction for interest or a royalty paid to a non-resident which would otherwise be deductible (s26-25 ITAA97). Dividends are not deductible under general tax law.

WITHHOLDING TAX RATES

Withholding tax rates vary with the type of payment. The TAA Regs specify the default rates at which tax is to be withheld. If Australia has a double tax agreement with the income recipient's country of residence, the agreement may provide for a lower withholding rate or even an exemption from withholding tax, depending on the specific nature of the payment.

- **Dividends:** The withholding tax rate is 30%. Unless a specific exemption applies, withholding tax must be deducted from the unfranked component of the dividends paid. A withholding tax exemption applies to the franked part of a dividend. Where the recipient is a resident of a country with which Australia has entered into a relevant international tax sharing treaty or double tax agreement, the amount of tax to be withheld is calculated at the rate provided for in the treaty, which is usually lower than 30% and may be nil in certain circumstances.
- **Interest:** Withholding tax is generally limited to 10% of the gross interest. Double tax treaties reduce the rate to nil in some cases, such as interest income derived by government bodies and financial institutions in limited circumstances. The domestic law provides an exemption for interest income where it is derived by the non-resident through its Australian permanent establishment. The carve-out does not apply to partners of certain limited partnerships.
- **Royalties:** The withholding tax rate is 30%, unless a DTA applies, in which case the rate is reduced (often to 10%).

CERTIFICATES OF PAYMENT FOR NON-RESIDENTS

The Tax Office will provide certificates of payment to non-residents whose Australian sourced income is subject to interest, dividend or royalty withholding tax. The certificate provides proof of payment of Australian tax, which can be issued to payees whose country of residence has a DTA with Australia (see 22.220). The tax authorities of such countries may require the taxpayer to provide the certificate for the purposes of gaining a tax exemption or a tax credit under domestic laws on the basis that Australian tax has been paid on the income. Applications may be made to the Tax Office on the required form (NAT 6408).

DEPARTING AUSTRALIA SUPERANNUATION PAYMENT

Broadly, a departing Australia superannuation payment (DASP) is a superannuation lump sum payment made to a person who worked in Australia under certain temporary visas and who has left Australia permanently (see also 5.321 and 19.670). The current withholding tax rates for these payments are:

- 0% for the tax-free component
- 35% for the taxed element of a taxable component, and
- 45% for the untaxed element of a taxable component.

FOREIGN PENSION FUNDS

The law has been amended to ensure that foreign pension funds can access the managed investment trust withholding tax regime and the associated lower rate of withholding tax on income from eligible Australian investments. The amending legislation received Royal Assent in December 2014. The amendments apply retrospectively to fund payments made in income years starting on or after 1 July 2008, the date when the MIT withholding tax regime commenced.

REMITTANCES

WHO MUST REMIT?

PAYG withholding that has been deducted must be paid to the Tax Office by the last person holding it before it is sent overseas, or the person retaining it in Australia who is dealing with it on behalf of the non-resident.

DUE DATES FOR REMITTANCES

Amounts withheld from interest, dividends or royalty payments made to non-residents are subject to the PAYG withholding rules (see from 5.200). The due date for remittance to the Tax Office of withheld amounts is the due date that is applicable for all other PAYG withholding remittances of the paying entity (see from 5.400 and s16-75 TAA).

EXEMPTIONS

These payments are exempt from withholding tax:
- s128B(3) ITAA36 exempts dividends, interest and royalties derived by a non-resident, the incomes of which are exempt from income tax in the country in which the non-resident resides and are also exempt from Australian income tax under the following provisions of the ITAA97 (exceptions exist – see s128B(3) ITAA36):
  - s50-5: religious, scientific, charitable or public educational institutions
  - s50-10: a society, association or club established for community service purposes
  - s50-15: a trade union, or an association of employers/employees registered in Australia relating to the settlement of industrial disputes
  - s50-30: a public hospital, a hospital carried on by a society/association other than for the purpose of profit or gain to the individual members of that society or association
  - s50-40: a society/association not carried on for the purposes of profit/gain to the individual members, but established to promote the development of aviation, tourism or of the agricultural, pastoral, horticultural, aquacultural, fishing, viticultural or manufacturing of industrial resources of Australia and Australian information and communications technology resources
  - a foreign superannuation fund
- the franked part of a dividend paid by a company. If it is a partially franked dividend, the unfranked part of the dividend is subject to withholding tax (s128B(3)(ga) ITAA36) (Reg. 40 TAA Regs). Avoidance rules can apply if dividends are streamed (see 6.800 and 6.900)
- dividends that are exempt from United States tax under US law and paid to a US resident (Reg. 40 TAA Regs)
- payments in respect of:
  - non-equity shares that are considered to be debt interests for the purposes of Div 974 ITAA97, and
  - syndicated loans provided under a syndicated loan facility that has satisfied the public offer test. The legislation also enables other types of securities to be treated in this manner for the purposes of s128F and s128FA, by way of regulation. Refer: s128F and 128FA ITAA36

- income that is exempt from income tax by virtue of being a distribution to a shareholder at a time when the company is a pooled development fund (s124ZM and s128B(3)(ba) ITAA36) (see 8.200)
- income that is non-assessable income under s159GZZZZE ITAA36 Infrastructure borrowings
- resident trustees that can be assessed under s99, s99A or s102 of the ITAA36 (7.600 and 7.700)
- s215-10 ITAA97: income that consists of a non-share dividend by an ADI that is unfrankable, and
- income that consists of:
  - a dividend that is paid by a former exempting entity or a share acquired under an employee share scheme – the part of the dividend that is franked with an exempting credit, or
  - a dividend that is paid by a former exempting entity to an eligible continuing substantial member – the part of the dividend that is franked with an exempting credit, other than a dividend in respect of which a determination is made under s204-30(3)(c) or a dividend or a part of a dividend in respect of which a determination is made under s177EA(5)(6) of the ITAA36
- interest on 'nostro' settlement amounts held by Australian financial institutions with foreign banks (applies to amounts held as of 29 August 2001)
- interest derived by a non-resident carrying on business in Australia at or through a permanent establishment of that non-resident of Australia (with exceptions for partners of certain limited partnerships)
- interest to which s128EA, s128F, s128FA or s128GB of the ITAA36 apply
- an overriding provision in s128F(2) which exempts debenture interest if:
  - when the debentures were issued (and when the interest was paid) the company was a resident of Australia or carrying on business through a permanent establishment in Australia, and
  - the debenture issue satisfies the public offer test; (note that recent changes effect issues from 29 August 2001 due to amendments to s128F)
- income of a beneficiary of a trust who has not had to declare the income because ultimate beneficiary non-disclosure tax applies (see 7.300)
- an amount not declared in assessable income because family trust distribution tax applies, and
- exempt royalties including:
  - royalties paid to foreign charitable institutions, public hospitals, non-profit cultural, sporting and friendly societies that are exempt from both Australian tax and tax in their own country
  - royalties paid to certain foreign non-profit aviation, tourism, agricultural and manufacturing associations
  - royalties derived by an estate where the trustee is liable to tax
  - royalties on which family trust distributions tax has been paid, and
  - certain royalties paid to an overseas charitable institution by an Offshore Banking Unit (OBU).

PROPOSED NON-FINAL WITHHOLDING TAX ON TAXABLE AUSTRALIAN PROPERTY

On 31 October 2014, Treasury released a discussion paper in relation to the proposal to impose a 10% non-final withholding tax on the disposal, by foreign residents, of 'taxable Australian property' (with exemptions). Relevantly, such assets include Australian real property, and shares and units in land-rich entities.

Foreign residents are subject to the CGT rules only where the CGT asset is 'taxable Australian property' (refer to 12.700).

Under the proposed rules, there will be an obligation for the payer to withhold an amount equal to 10% of the proceeds from the transaction and remit it to the Commissioner. The amount withheld is a non-final payment of tax. it will be available to the foreign resident payee as a credit against their final tax liability for the relevant year.

To reduce the compliance burden on people acquiring a residential property, the government proposes an exemption where the asset is a 'residential property' valued at under $2.5 million. The measure is intended to apply from 1 July 2016.

22.200 DOUBLE TAXATION AGREEMENTS

Double taxation agreements are designed to eliminate conflict where income or gains might be subject to tax in more than one country. They allocate taxing rights over specific items of income and also provide double taxation relief.

22.210   GENERAL CONCEPTS UNDERLYING AUSTRALIA'S DOUBLE TAX AGREEMENTS

Double taxation agreements (DTAs), also known as tax treaties, entered into by Australia with various other countries are given the force of domestic law by the *International Tax Agreements Act 1953*. The ITAA36 and ITAA97 are incorporated into and must be read as part of the *International Tax Agreements Act 1953*.

The operation of the general anti-avoidance rule in Part IVA ITAA36 typically takes priority over a DTA .

   The text of the Taipei treaty is included as a Schedule to the International Tax Agreements Act 1953 but the text of all other treaties may be found online in:

- *the Tax Office website*
- *the Australian Treaty Series (DFAT website), or*
- *the Australian Treaties Library (AustLii website).*

NOTE: TR 2013/1 sets out the Commissioner's views as to the meaning of the term 'employer' for the purposes of the Income from Employment Article in Australia's tax treaties.

ALLOCATION OF TAXING RIGHTS

As a general rule, DTAs are usually negotiated whereby the taxing rights over a particular item of income are either exclusively allocated to one of the treaty countries or the taxing rights are given to both countries with provision made for relief from double taxation. The country of residence is generally required to grant relief on double taxed amounts by way of credit or exemption in accordance with its domestic laws.

If an exclusive taxing right is conferred, it is generally given to the taxpayer's country of residence. For Tax Office guidance on the interpretation of DTAs see TR 2001/13. Each tax treaty is unique but treaties entered into by Australia are based on the OECD Model Tax Convention.

The following types of income are generally taxed by the country of residence:

- remuneration derived by an employee present in the other country for less than 183 days in a year of income. This applies where the employer is a resident of the same country where the employee is resident and remuneration derived is not an allowable deduction for the employer in that other country
- income from professional services or independent activities (other than public entertainers)
- pensions and annuities
- remuneration for rendering services to government officials and bodies

- remuneration of professors or teachers present in the other country for two years or less
- payments made to students for their education or maintenance
- income derived by a resident from sources outside both countries
- profits from shipping or aircraft, and
- profits of an enterprise carried on in one country unless conducted through a permanent establishment in the other country.

Income which is generally taxed according to the source of the income includes:

- income from real property including royalties and other mining, quarrying or exploitation of natural resources
- business income derived through a permanent establishment
- public entertainers
- directors and others holding similar office
- salary or wages where the person is present in the other country for more than 183 days, and
- income derived from personal services if derived from a fixed base used by the person concerned.

Dividends, interest and royalties are taxed in various ways depending on the jurisdiction and specific circumstances (see also 22.140). Typically, the source country has the right to impose non-resident withholding tax, to be withheld and remitted by the payer before the income is paid to the non-resident. DTAs impose maximum withholding tax rates in relation to each particular type of dividend, interest and royalty income (actual rates applicable may be lower under domestic law). Withholding tax is generally a final tax in the source country.

When negotiating an alienation of property article, the Australian approach is to preserve source country taxing rights over assets with a physical connection to a country, such as interests in real property. This includes the taxation of capital gains. The position adopted by the Tax Office is that Australia's older, 'pre-CGT' DTAs which were negotiated before Australia's CGT laws came into effect do not apply to capital gains arising for a non-resident from the sale of shares in an Australian company, and therefore Australia retains its taxing rights over such capital gains. However, whilst the Federal Court in *Virgin Holdings SA v FCT* held that the pre-CGT Australia/ Switzerland DTA does apply to capital gains, neither Article 7 (business profits) nor Article 13 (alienation of property), which would allocate taxing rights to Australia, applied to the gain in question. As the other relevant clauses of the treaty did not similarly give Australia taxing rights over the gain, the capital gain was not subject to income tax in Australia.

RESIDENCY TIE-BREAKERS

Australia's tax treaties contain 'tie-breaker' rules in respect of tax residency. These rules apply where the taxpayer is a tax resident of both treaty countries under each country's domestic tax residency laws. The tie-breaker will deem the taxpayer to solely be a resident of one of the countries for the purposes of applying the other treaty articles.

Note that the treaty tie-breakers will determine residency solely for the purposes of the treaty. They have no impact on residency status under domestic laws.

Each DTA contains its own tie-breaker tests, which are typically to be applied in sequential order as set out in the relevant article. However, as a general rule, the alternative tie-breakers that apply to individuals are:

- the country in which the individual has a 'permanent home'
- the country in which the individual has a 'habitual abode'
- the country in which the individual has closer 'personal and economic relations' (also known as his or her 'centre of vital interests'), and
- the country of which the individual is a citizen or a national.

In the case of non-individual taxpayers, the place where its 'effective management' is situated is a common tie-breaker.

PERMANENT ESTABLISHMENT

All DTAs contain an Article which deals with the allocation of taxing rights over 'permanent establishments'.

Generally, an enterprise of country (A) has a permanent establishment in country (B) if it has a fixed place of business through which the business of the enterprise is wholly or partly carried on. Business profits of the country (A) enterprise which are attributable to the permanent establishment will usually be taxable in country (B).

In a typical DTA, the term 'permanent establishment' includes any:

- place of management
- branch, office, factory, workshop, mine, quarry, oil or gas well or other place of extraction of natural resources
- agricultural, pastoral or forestry property, and
- building site or construction, installation or assembly project, usually existing for six, nine or twelve months (depending on the treaty).

Some DTAs include other types of physical presence in the definition of 'permanent establishment'.

A PERMANENT ESTABLISHMENT MAY EXIST IF CERTAIN ACTIVITIES ARE UNDERTAKEN

Specified operations or activities may result in an enterprise being deemed to have a permanent establishment. Such activities include:

- carrying on supervisory activities for more than a specific period in connection with a building site or a construction, installation or assembly project, and
- substantial equipment is being used by, for or under contract with the enterprise.

Further, an enterprise of country (A) is deemed to have a permanent establishment in country (B) if there is in country (B) any person, firm or company acting on its behalf with authority to:

- conclude contracts on behalf of the enterprise (however, a permanent establishment is not deemed to exist merely because the agent purchases goods or merchandise), and
- manufacture or process goods for the enterprise (a permanent establishment exists but only in relation to goods or merchandise manufactured and processed).

EXCLUSIONS

A 'permanent establishment' typically does not exist merely because of:

- the use of facilities solely to store, display or deliver goods or merchandise belonging to the enterprise
- the maintenance of a stock of goods or merchandise belonging to the enterprise solely for the purpose of storage, display or delivery
- the maintenance of a stock of goods or merchandise belonging to the enterprise solely for the purpose of processing by another enterprise
- the maintenance of a fixed place of business solely to purchase goods or merchandise (or collect information) for the enterprise
- the maintenance of a fixed place of business solely for the purpose of activities which have a preparatory or auxiliary character for the enterprise, such as advertising or research, or
- the existence of a place where the person is carrying on business through an agent who does not have, or does not habitually exercise, a general authority to negotiate and conclude contracts on behalf of the person (eg. mere 'licence' agreements with the agent may not be enough): *Unisys Corporation v FC of T* (2002) NSWSC 1115.

 Whilst the preceding comments provide general guidance, the specific definition of 'permanent establishment' in the relevant treaty must be considered.

CONTROLLED COMPANIES

An enterprise of one country is not deemed to have a permanent establishment in the other country simply because a company that is resident of country (A) is able to control, or is controlled by, a company that is resident of country (B). Merely having a subsidiary or associated company in the other territory does not, of itself, constitute a 'permanent establishment'.

INDEPENDENT AGENT

An enterprise of country (A) is not deemed to have a permanent establishment in country (B) merely because it carries on business in country (B) through a broker, general commission agent or any other agent of independent status, if such other person, firm or company is acting in the ordinary course of their business.

PAY AS YOU GO WITHHOLDING

Non-resident businesses carrying on business in Australia through a permanent establishment that make a supply in the course of that enterprise need to quote an ABN (see 5.100) to the payer for that supply. Where an ABN is not quoted the payer must generally withhold 46.5% tax from that payment.

The payer does not need to withhold tax if:

- the non-resident is not carrying on an enterprise in Australia
- the non-resident makes the supply through an agent and quotes the agent's ABN
- the payment is exempt income (not taxable in Australia) to the non-resident
- the supply is wholly input taxed for GST
- the payment is $50 or less, or such higher amount as is specified by regulation under s29-80 of the GST Act, or
- the payment is wholly of a private or domestic nature for the payer.

DOUBLE TAXATION RELIEF

Typically, a DTA will provide double taxation relief in one of two ways (depending on the particular item of income):

- the 'exemption' method – the treaty will allocate exclusive taxing rights over the item of income to one country and the income will be exempt in the other country by grace of the treaty, regardless of its domestic laws, and
- the 'credit' method – the treaty will allocate dual taxing rights over the item of income such that both countries may tax the income under its domestic laws. The treaty will require one country (usually the country of residence) to provide a credit for the foreign tax paid in respect of that item of income, subject to the domestic laws.

22.220 AUSTRALIA'S DOUBLE TAX AGREEMENTS

The table below contains a list of the countries with which Australia currently has an effective Double Tax Agreement (DTA) and the maximum withholding tax (WHT) rates applicable under each treaty.

Where more than one WHT rate under a specific treaty is noted in respect of a particular type of income, this indicates that different maximum rates apply in relation to specific circumstances.

Following the table are summaries of the contents of the treaties which Australia has with three key trading partners: the United Kingdom, New Zealand and China.

United Kingdom agreement Under the double tax treaty signed between Australia and the United Kingdom dividend, interest and royalty payments are generally taxable in both countries. Where business profits of an enterprise resident in one country are attributable to a permanent establishment situated in the other country, generally the countries will have dual taxing rights over the permanent establishment's profits.

Country	Dividends (%)	Interest (%)	Royalties (%)	Entry into force[1]	Amending Protocol(s) in force	Concessional WHT rates on MIT distributions[2]
Argentina	10/15	12	10/15	30 December 1999		1 July 2008
Austria	15	10	10	1 September 1988		
Belgium	15	10	10	1 November 1979	Yes	1 January 2012
Bulgaria	-	-	-	Proposed		
Canada	5/15	10	10	29 April 1981	Yes	1 July 2008
Chile	5/15	5/10	5/10	27 June 2011		
China (excl Hong Kong & Macau)	15	10	10	28 December 1990		1 July 2008
Czech Republic	5/15	10	10	27 November 1995		1 July 2008
Denmark	15	10	10	27 October 1981		1 July 2008
East Timor[3]	15	10	10	20 May 2002		
Fiji	20	10	15	28 December 1990		1 July 2008
Finland	0/5/15	0/10	5	10 November 2007		1 July 2008
France	0/5/15	0/10	5	1 July 2009		1 July 2008
Germany	15	10	10	15 February 1975		1 July 2008
Greece[4]	-	-	-	7 April 1981		
Hungary	15	10	10	10 April 1992		1 July 2008
India	15	15	10/15/20	30 December 1991		1 July 2008
Indonesia	15	10	10/15	14 December 1992		1 July 2008
Ireland	15	10	10	21 December 1983		1 July 2008
Italy[5]	15	10	10	5 November 1985		1 July 2008
Japan	0/5/10	0/10	5	31 December 2008		1 July 2008
Kiribati	20	10	15	28 June 1991		1 July 2008
Korea	15	15	15	1 January 1984		1 July 2012
Malaysia	0/15	15	15	26 June 1981	Yes	1 January 2012
Malta	15	15	10	20 May 1985		1 July 2008
Mexico	0/15	10/15	10	31 December 2003		1 July 2008
Netherlands[6]	15	10	10	27 September 1976	Yes	1 July 2008
New Zealand	0/5/15	0/10	5	19 March 2010		1 July 2008
Norway	0/5/15	0/10	5	12 September 2007		1 July 2008
Papua New Guinea	15/20	10	10	29 December 1989		1 July 2008
Philippines	15/25	10/15	15/25	17 June 1980		
Poland	15	10	10	4 March 1992		1 July 2008
Romania	5/15	10	10	11 April 2001		1 July 2008
Russia	5/15	10	10	17 December 2003		1 July 2008
Singapore	0/15	10	10	4 June 1969	Yes	1 July 2011
Slovak Republic	15	10	10	22 December 1999		1 July 2008
South Africa	5/15	0/10	5	21 December 1999	Yes	1 July 2008
Spain	15	0/10	10	10 December 1992		1 July 2008
Sri Lanka	15	10	10	21 October 1991		1 July 2008

Country	Dividends (%)	Interest (%)	Royalties (%)	Entry into force[1]	Amending Protocol(s) in force	Concessional WHT rates on MIT distributions[2]
Sweden	15	10	10	4 September 1981		1 July 2008
Switzerland	0/5/15	0/10	5	14 October 2014		
Taipei (Taiwan)	10/15	10	12.5	21 October 1996		1 July 2008
Thailand	15/20	10/25	15	27 December 1989		1 July 2008
Turkey	5/15	10	10	27 June 2011	Yes	
United Kingdom	0/5/15	0/10	5	17 December 2003		1 July 2008
United States	0/5/15	0/10	5	31 October 1983	Yes	1 July 2008
Vietnam	10/15	10	10	10 December 1992		1 July 2008

1: Date of effect for withholding tax and income may be later. Pre-CGT treaties do not contain specific articles dealing with capital gains except those for Canada and USA. Subsequent amending protocols have been entered into in some circumstances.

2: Distributions of certain Australian sourced income by a managed investment trust to non-residents are subject to withholding tax. Concessional withholding rates apply in respect of recipients residing in listed jurisdictions with which Australia has effective information exchange arrangements.

3: The agreement between Australia and East Timor is the Timor Sea Treaty which provides a framework for the exploration for and exploitation of petroleum resources in a specific area. Taxes are imposed on income arising out of exploration development and exploitation of petroleum in the area. Australia applies its tax system to 10% of the income derived in the area.

4: Only an airline profits agreement

5: Plus an airline profits agreement 1976

6: Australian employers who send their employees to work temporarily in The Netherlands are now covered by an agreement dealing with double superannuation coverage. Similar agreements exist with Portugal and the US.

BUSINESS PROFITS

Profits of an enterprise of one country will be exempt in the 'other' country unless the taxpayer carries on trade or business through a 'permanent establishment' in the 'other' country (see 22.210). If there is a permanent establishment in the 'other' country, the profits to be taxed are those which might be expected to be derived if it were an independent enterprise engaged in the same or similar activities and operating at arm's length.

Where an enterprise in country (A) participates directly or indirectly in the management, control or capital of an enterprise in country (B) or the same persons participate directly or indirectly in the management, control or capital of an enterprise of both enterprises, notional profits that have not actually accrued may be subject to tax. This would arise where the two enterprises do not operate as independent enterprises dealing independently with each other and profits which may have been expected to accrue under independent dealings have not accrued by reason of this relationship. These notional profits may be included in the profits of the enterprise to which they would have accrued and are taxed accordingly.

DIVIDENDS

The rate of tax payable in country (A) on dividends paid by a company resident in country (A) to a resident of country (B) is limited to 15% but the dividends may also be taxed in country (B) under domestic laws.

Further, a limit of 5% applies to dividends where the dividend recipient is a company that directly holds at least 10% of the voting power in the company paying the dividend.

These rate caps apply to both franked and unfranked dividends, but under Australian domestic law, no dividend withholding tax applies to a fully franked Australian dividend.

No tax is payable on dividends in the source country where the dividend recipient is a company that for a 12 month period ending on the date the dividend is declared has held at least 80% of the voting power in the company paying the dividend, subject to certain conditions.

If the dividend recipient carries on a business through a permanent establishment in the source country of the dividend, but is resident in the other country, and the dividend is effectively connected with the permanent establishment, then the business profits provisions rather than the dividend provisions of the DTA apply.

Where a company which is a resident of country (A) derives profits or income from country (B), country (B) may not impose tax on any dividends paid by the company, being dividends beneficially owned by a person who is not a resident of country (B) unless the dividends are effectively connected with a permanent establishment in country (B). This does not apply to dividends paid by a company which is a resident of both Australia and the UK.

In ID 2013/17, the Commissioner concluded that a UK resident company, which beneficially owns a dividend paid by an Australian resident company to another Australian resident company as the nominee shareholder for the UK resident company, is not a company which 'holds directly' at least 10% of the voting power, as required by the DTA.

INTEREST

The rate of tax payable in country (A) on interest paid by the borrower that is a resident of country (A) to the lender that is a resident of country (B) is limited to 10% but the interest may also be taxed in country (B) under domestic laws. If the lender is carrying on a business in the borrower's country of residence through a permanent establishment and the debt from which the interest arose related to the permanent establishment, the business profits provisions rather than the interest provisions of the DTA apply. If, due to a special relationship between the lender and borrower (or between the both of them and a third party), the interest is more than the amount which might reasonably have been expected in the absence of the special relationship, the interest withholding provisions apply only to the amount reasonably expected. The excess may be taxed under the applicable domestic laws, with regard to the other DTA provisions but without the rate limitation offered by the interest withholding Article.

Interest arising in country (A) and beneficially owned by a resident of country (B) may not be taxed in country (A) if the interest is derived by:

- a government body of country (B), including a body exercising governmental functions or a bank performing central banking functions, or

- a financial institution resident in country (B) which is unrelated to and dealing wholly independently with the payer.

These provisions are subject to certain safeguards. In particular, the financial institutions exemption does not apply in the case of back-to-back loans.

ROYALTIES

Normally tax is limited to 5% on the gross amount of royalties in the country in which the payer of the 'royalties' is resident (but they may also be taxed in the country of residence of the beneficial owner of the royalties). This limitation does not apply if the beneficial owner of the royalties is resident in country (A) and carries on a business in country (B) where the royalties arise through a permanent establishment in country (B) and the right or property in respect of which the royalties are paid or credited is effectively connected with that permanent establishment. In that circumstance the business profits provisions rather than the royalty provisions of the DTA apply.

If, due to a special relationship between the payer and the beneficial owner of the royalties (or between the both of them and a third party), the amount of the royalties paid or credited is greater than the amount which might reasonably have been expected in the absence of the special relationship, the royalties provision shall only apply to the amount reasonably expected. The excess may be taxed under the applicable domestic laws, with regard to the other DTA provisions but without the rate limitation offered by the royalty withholding article.

Any amounts derived from equipment leasing (including certain container leasing) is excluded from the royalty definition. Such amounts would either be treated as profits from international transport operations (for container leasing) or as business profits (for other types of equipment leasing).

PROFESSIONAL SERVICES

Income from performing professional services (eg an architect, doctor or engineer but not as a public entertainer or athlete – which are specifically covered by another article), except where derived in the capacity of an employee, is taxable on the same basis as industrial/ commercial profits. Professional income of a resident of country (A) is taxable in country (B) only if there is a 'fixed base' (office, etc.) regularly available in country (B) and he/she is taxed there on income arising from country (B).

EXTENSION OF THE TREATY

The 2003 United Kingdom Convention extended the operation of the treaty to cover Australian tax on capital gains, Australia's resource rent tax and fringe benefits tax. Taxes remaining outside the terms of the treaty include customs and stamp duty, land tax, payroll tax and penalty taxes.

INCOME FROM EMPLOYMENT

An employee (who does not come within the ambit of the entertainers and sportspersons clause) who is a resident of country (A) who derives employment income from employment exercised in country (B) is exempt from tax on that income in country (B) if:

* the employee is in country (B) for no more than an aggregate 183 days throughout a twelve month period
* the remuneration is paid by or on behalf or an employer who is not a resident of country (B), and the remuneration is not deductible in determining taxable profits of a permanent establishment which the employer has in country (B).

If an employee is resident in a country for more than 183 days and is the recipient of fringe benefits, these are taxable in that country. See ID 2005/166.

ENTERTAINERS AND SPORTSPERSONS

The country in which services are performed has the right (but not an exclusive right) to levy tax on the income derived from the activities. This applies to entertainers (theatrical, movie, radio and television artists and musicians) and sportspersons.

GOVERNMENT SERVICES

Remuneration (but not pensions, or in respect of services rendered in connection with or trade or business carried on by the government) paid to an individual by the government of country (A) is exempt in country (B). However, if the services are rendered in country (B) and the taxpayer is a resident of country (B) and either: he/she is a national of country (B); or did not become a resident solely to render the particular services for which he/she is paid by the government concerned then the remuneration will be taxable only in country (B). This exemption does not apply to remuneration in respect of services rendered in connection with any trade or business carried on by a country or a political subdivision or local authority of that country.

VISITING STUDENTS

A student who is a resident of country (A) and is temporarily visiting country (B) solely for purposes of his or her education is exempt from tax in country (B) in relation to payments for maintenance or education if the payments come from anywhere except country (B).

PENSIONS

Where a resident of country (A) derives pensions and purchased annuities, country (A) has exclusive taxing rights over the income.

SHIPPING AND AIR TRANSPORT

Profits from operating ships or aircraft internationally are subject to tax only in the country of residence of the operating enterprise. However, where a resident of country (A) operates ships or aircraft in country (B), country (B) has taxing rights to the extent the profits are derived from ship or aircraft operations confined solely to places in that country. The treatment of shipping and aircraft leasing profits in terms of the 'substantial equipment' permanent establishment provisions of the treaty have been considered in tax ruling TR 2007/10.

NEW ZEALAND AGREEMENT

The current double tax treaty between Australia and New Zealand came into force on 19 March 2010 (effective 1 April 2010 in respect of withholding tax and fringe benefits tax and 1 July 2010 in respect of income tax other than withholding tax).

BUSINESS PROFITS

Profits derived by an enterprise that is resident in country (A) are not taxable in country (B) unless it carries on any trade or business in country (B) through a permanent establishment (see 22.210). If the enterprise carries on business through a permanent establishment in country (B), the profits of the enterprise may be taxed in country (B) to the extent they are attributable to the permanent establishment.

Note that the new treaty defines 'business' to include the performance of professional services and other activities of an independent character, thereby subjecting income derived from independent activities to the business profits article. Previously, income derived from these activities were subject to a specific independent services article.

DIVIDENDS

The rate of tax payable in country (A) on dividends paid by a company resident in country (A) to a resident of country (B) is limited to 15% but the dividends may also be taxed in country (B) under domestic laws.

Further, a limit of 5% applies to dividends where the dividend recipient is a company that directly holds at least 10% of the voting power in the company paying the dividend. These rate caps apply to both franked and unfranked dividends, but under Australian domestic law, no dividend withholding tax applies to a fully franked Australian dividend.

Where dividends are paid by a company that is resident in country (A) and the beneficial owner of the dividends is a company that is a resident of country (B) which holds, directly or indirectly, at least 80% of the voting power in the payer company for the twelve months leading up to the dividend declaration date, no tax is payable in country (A) if the recipient company satisfies certain conditions.

Dividends are also exempt from source country taxation where the beneficial owner is a government authority (including a government investment fund) of the other treaty country and it directly holds no more than 10% of the voting power in the payer company.

If the dividend recipient carries on a business through a permanent establishment in the source country of the dividend, but is resident in the other country, and the dividend is effectively connected with the permanent establishment, then the business profits provisions rather than the dividend provisions of the DTA apply.

Furthermore, if a company which is resident in country (A) derives profits or income from country (B), and dividends paid are beneficially owned by a non-resident of country (B), then country (B) has taxing rights over the dividends only to the extent that the dividends are effectively connected with a permanent establishment in country (B).

In the case of dividends paid by a company which is a dual resident, each country may tax the dividends to the extent that the dividends are paid out of profits or income sourced from that country. If the source country is country (A), and the beneficial owner of the dividends is a resident of country (B), then the withholding tax rate limitations apply as if the payer company is solely a resident of country (A).

The article contains an anti-avoidance clause which denies treaty relief where a 'main purpose' of any person connected with the relevant dividends, underlying securities or the company that is the beneficial owner is to take advantage of the article.

INTEREST

If a resident of country (A) derives interest income from a resident of country (B), both countries have taxing rights over the income. The rate of tax payable in country (B) is limited to 10%.

If the interest income recipient carries on a business through a permanent establishment in the source country of the interest, but is resident in the other country, and the interest income is effectively connected with the permanent establishment, then the business profits provisions rather than the interest provisions of the DTA apply.

No source country taxation will apply where the interest is derived by:

- a government or political body (including a government investment fund) of the other country
- a bank performing central banking functions in the other country, or
- an unrelated financial institution that is resident in the other country.

The financial institution exemption does not apply where either a payer that is subject to New Zealand approved issuer levy has not paid it or where a back-to-back loan arrangement is involved.

If, due to a special relationship between the lender and the borrower, or between them and a third party, the interest is more than the amount which might reasonably have been expected in the absence of the special relationship, the interest provisions apply only to the extent of the amount reasonably expected. The excess may be taxed under the applicable domestic laws, with regard to the other DTA provisions but without the rate limitation offered by the interest withholding article.

The article provides guidance on where interest is deemed to have arisen.

As in the case of dividends, the interest article contains an anti-avoidance clause with a 'main purpose' test.

ROYALTIES

The treaty definition of 'royalty' includes payments of any kind by a resident of country (A) to a resident of country (B) for the use of or right to use specified types of property. The rate of tax payable in country (A) is limited to 5%. However, if the beneficial owner of the royalties has a permanent establishment in country (A), and the knowledge, information, assistance, right or other property producing the royalties is effectively connected with that permanent establishment, the business profits article rather than the royalty provisions apply.

If, due to a special relationship between the payer and recipient, or between them and a third party, the royalty amount is more than the amount which might reasonably have been expected in the absence of the special relationship, the royalty provisions apply only to the extent of the amount reasonably expected. The excess may be taxed under the applicable domestic laws, with regard to the other DTA provisions but without the rate limitation offered by the royalty withholding article.

Similarly to interest, specific provisions provide guidance regarding when royalties are deemed to have arisen.

As in the case of dividends, the royalty article contains an anti-avoidance clause with a 'main purpose' test.

PENSIONS AND ANNUITIES

Pensions and purchased annuities derived from country (B) by a resident of country (A) are exempt in country (B). However, country (A) loses its taxing right where the income would not be taxable in country (B) to a resident of that country.

Lump sums relating to retirement and other causes, alimony payments and other maintenance payments sourced from country (A) and paid to a resident of country (B) are taxable only in country (A).

INDEPENDENT PERSONAL SERVICES

The current treaty does not include an independent personal services article. The definition of 'business' includes the performance of professional services and other activities of an independent character. Therefore, income derived from such services are subject to the business profits article.

INCOME FROM EMPLOYMENT AND DIRECTORS' FEES

The treaty contains separate articles dealing with income from employment and directors' fees respectively.

An individual resident of country (A) earning employment income is subject to tax only in country (A) unless the services were performed in country (B). Where the services were performed in country (B), both countries will have taxing rights over the income.

However, country (B) will not have taxing rights over the income sourced from itself where:

- the recipient is in country (B) for an aggregate 183 days or fewer in any twelve month period commencing or ending in the tax year of country (B)
- the remuneration is paid by or on behalf of an employer who is not a resident of country (B)
- the remuneration is borne by or is deductible in determining the taxable profits of a permanent establishment the employer has in country (A), and
- the remuneration is neither borne by or is deductible in determining the taxable profits of a permanent establishment the employer has in country (B).

Furthermore, income is not taxable in the source country where the individual derived it in respect of a 'secondment' to country (B) and was present in country (B) for no more than an aggregate 90 days in a twelve month period.

Directors' fees and other remuneration derived by a resident of country (A) in respect of his/her membership of the board of directors of a company which is a resident of country (B) may be taxed by both countries.

CAPITAL GAINS

Capital gains are dealt with under the law of each country, but subject to any specific provision of the agreement.

FRINGE BENEFITS

The fringe benefits article contains a tie-breaker rule in respect of a fringe benefit which is taxable in both countries.

The tie-breaker rule allocates exclusive taxing rights over the fringe benefit to the country that has the sole or primary taxing right in respect of the salary or wages to which the benefit relates.

Country (A) has the 'primary taxing right' over the employment income where both countries have taxing rights under the treaty but country (B) is required to provide double taxation relief.

ENTERTAINERS AND SPORTSPERSONS

The country in which services are performed has the right (but not an exclusive right) to levy tax on the income derived from the activities. This applies to entertainers (theatrical, movie, radio and television artists and musicians) and sportspersons. Special carve-outs apply in the case of team members of certain teams playing in a league competition played in both countries.

GOVERNMENT SERVICE

Remuneration (other than pensions or annuities) paid to an individual by the government of country (A) in respect of services rendered to country (A) is exempt in country (B).

Conversely, the exclusive taxing rights shift to country (B) if the services are rendered there and the taxpayer is a resident of country (B) and either:

- is a national of country (B), or
- did not become a resident solely to render the particular services for which he or she is paid by the government concerned.

Where one of the articles relating to employment income, directors' fees or entertainers and sportspersons also applies, the relevant article takes precedence over this article.

STUDENTS

A student or business apprentice who is or was a resident of country (A) visiting country (B) solely for the purpose of education or training is exempt from tax in country (B) in respect of payments for maintenance, education or training where the payments are sourced from outside country (B).

SHIPPING AND AIR TRANSPORT

Country (A) has exclusive taxing rights over any profit derived by a resident of country (A) from the operation of ships and aircraft in international traffic, except for profits from ship or aircraft operations confined solely to places in country (B), which may also be taxed by country (B).

TRANS-TASMAN IMPUTATION

New Zealand resident companies may elect to maintain an Australian franking account. Australian shareholders of a New Zealand resident company that has elected to maintain an Australian franking account and earns Australian sourced income will be able to access franking benefits on a pro-rata basis (in proportion to their shareholding in the New Zealand company) arising from the payment of Australian tax on that income.

Franking credits will arise in New Zealand companies' franking accounts for dividend, interest and royalty withholding taxes deducted in Australia. They will arise in addition to credits for Australian income tax and franking credits attached to dividends received. Similarly, New Zealand shareholders investing in a company resident in Australia which derives income and pays tax in New Zealand will be able to access New Zealand imputation credits on distributions on a pro-rata basis (in proportion to their shareholding in the Australian company) arising from the payment of New Zealand tax on that income.

CHINA AGREEMENT

Under the double tax treaty signed between Australia and China, dividend, interest and royalty payments are generally taxable in both countries. Where business profits of an enterprise resident in one country are attributable to a permanent establishment situated in the other country, generally the countries will have dual taxing rights over the permanent establishment's profits.

BUSINESS PROFITS

The business profits of an enterprise that is a resident of country (A) is tax-exempt in country (B) unless the enterprise carries on a 'permanent establishment' (see 22.210) in country (B). If so, country (B) may tax the profit attributable to that permanent establishment as though it were a distinct and independent enterprise.

The business profits article includes all business profits of an enterprise, but where the business profits include an item of income which is also subject to another treaty article, the business profits article specifically gives priority to the other article. This would include business profits which are in the nature of dividends, interest, rental income from real property, royalties and income from the operation of ships or aircraft.

DIVIDENDS

The rate of tax payable in country (B) on dividends paid by a resident of country (B) to a resident of country (A) is limited to 15%. The rate cap applies to both franked and unfranked dividends, but under Australian domestic law, no dividend withholding tax applies to the franked portion of an Australian dividend.

The dividend withholding provisions do not apply where the dividends are paid by a resident of country (B) to an enterprise that is a resident of country (A) which has a 'permanent establishment' in country (B) and the dividends are connected with that permanent establishment. The carve-out also applies where an individual who is a resident of country (A) performs independent personal services in country (B) through a fixed base and the dividends are connected with that fixed base.

Where a company which is a resident of country (A) derives profits or income from country (B), then country (B) cannot tax the dividends, except to the extent that the dividends are beneficially owned by a resident of country (B) or to the extent that the holding in respect of which the dividends are paid is effectively connected with a permanent establishment or fixed base situated in country (B), nor subject the company's undistributed profits to tax even if the dividends paid or the undistributed profits consist wholly or partly of profits or income arising in country (B).

INTEREST

The source country may tax interest at a maximum rate of 10%.

The term 'interest' is defined to mean interest from debt-claims of every kind, and including income from Government securities or from bonds or debentures, and all other income that is assimilated to income from money lent by the tax law of the source country.

The interest withholding provisions do not apply where the interest is paid by a resident of country (B) to an enterprise that is a resident of country (A) which has a 'permanent establishment' in country (B) and the interest is connected with that permanent establishment. The carve-out also applies where an individual who is a resident of country (A) performs independent personal services in country (B) through a fixed base and the interest is connected with that fixed base.

Where the amount of interest paid exceeds the arm's length amount, the provisions of the interest Article applies only to the arm's length amount. The excess interest above the arm's length amount shall remain taxable according to the domestic tax law of each country.

ROYALTIES

Royalty withholding tax at a rate of 10% applies for the right to use, or the use of, specified property or rights, including certain equipment. However, a rate of 0% can apply when the person beneficially entitled to the royalties is a resident of country (A) and has a permanent establishment in country (B) or performs independent personal services in country (B) from a fixed base, and the property or rights giving rise to the royalties are effectively connected with the permanent establishment or fixed place.

Where the amount of royalties paid exceeds the arm's length amount, the provisions of the royalties Article applies only to the arm's length amount. The excess royalties above the arm's length amount shall remain taxable according to the domestic tax law of each country.

INCOME FROM REAL PROPERTY

Income derived by a resident of country (A) from real property situated in country (B) is subject to dual taxing rights.

In the case of Australia, real property has the meaning which it has under Australian law, and also specifically includes a leasehold interest in land and rights to exploit or to explore for natural resources.

In the case of China, real property has the meaning which it has under Chinese law, and also specifically includes:

- property accessory to immovable property and livestock and equipment used in agriculture and forestry
- rights to which the general law provisions respecting landed property apply, and
- usufruct of immovable property and rights to variable or fixed payments either as consideration for, or in respect of, the exploitation or exploration for natural resources.

Real property, in the case of China, excludes ships and aircraft.

INCOME FROM THE SALE OF REAL PROPERTY

Income derived from the disposal of real property is subject to dual taxing rights.

Income derived from the disposal of business property of a permanent establishment, other than real property (as defined in the treaty), including income or gains from the disposal of the permanent establishment itself, is subject to dual taxing rights. The same applies to income derived from the disposal of business property of a fixed base through which an individual performs independent personal services or the disposal of that fixed base.

INDEPENDENT PERSONAL SERVICES

Where a resident of country (A) derives income from performing independent personal services, country (A) has exclusive taxing rights over that income. However, country (B) may also tax the income if the services are performed in that country and:

- the person has a 'fixed base' regularly available to him or her in country (B) for the purpose of performing those services; in such a case, only the income that is attributable to that fixed base may be taxed in country (B), or
- the person was present in country (B) for more than 183 days in aggregate in any consecutive 12-month period; in such a case, only the income that is attributable to the activities performed in country (B) may be taxed in country (B).

The term 'professional services' is defined non-exclusively and specifically includes those performed in the exercise of independent scientific, literary, artistic, educational or teaching activities. It also includes the independent activities of physicians, lawyers, engineers, architects, dentists and accountants.

DEPENDENT PERSONAL SERVICES

An employee who is a resident of country (A) and derives employment income in country (B) is subject to tax on that income in both countries.

However, the income derived from country (B) is tax-exempt in country (B) if:

- the employee is present in country (B) for fewer than an aggregate 183 days in any consecutive 12-month period
- the employer is not a resident of country (B), and
- the remuneration is not borne by a permanent establishment or a fixed base which the employer has in country (B).

Notwithstanding the above, income derived in respect of employment exercised aboard a ship or aircraft operated by an enterprise of one of the treaty countries in international traffic shall be taxable only in the employee's country of residence.

DIRECTORS' FEES

Directors' fees and similar payments derived by a person (which is defined to include an individual, a company and any other body of persons) that is a resident of country (A) in the person's capacity as a member of the board of directors of a company which is a resident of country (B) are subject to dual taxing rights.

ENTERTAINERS AND ATHLETES

Income derived by a resident of country (A) as an entertainer from their personal activities as such exercised in country (B) is subject to dual taxing rights. Where the income accrues not to that entertainer but to another person, that income is also subject to dual taxing rights.

Income derived by an entertainer who is a resident of country (A) from work performed in country (B) under a plan of cultural exchange between the governments of country (A) and country (B) is tax-exempt in country (B).

PENSIONS

Pensions in respect of past employment and social security pensions paid by country (A) to a resident of country (B) are only taxable in the source country.

GOVERNMENT REMUNERATION

Any wages, salary or similar remuneration for carrying out 'functions of a governmental nature' (other than pensions arising from such services) paid by country (A) or a political subdivision or local authority of country (A) is taxable only in country (A).

However, such remuneration is taxable only in country (B) if the services are provided in country (B) and the individual is a resident of country (B) who is a citizen or national of country (B) or did not become a resident of country (B) solely for the purposes of providing the services.

Any government pension paid by country (A) or a political subdivision or local authority of country (A) to an individual in respect of services rendered to that country or subdivision or authority is taxable only in country (A).

However, such pension is taxable only in country (B) if the individual is a resident of, and a citizen or national of, country (B).

The above provisions do not apply to remuneration or pensions in respect of services rendered in connection with any trade or business carried on by a country or a political subdivision or local authority of that country.

PROFESSORS AND TEACHERS

Where a professor or teacher who is a resident of country (A) visits country (B) for a period of no more than 2 years for the purpose of teaching or carrying out advanced study or research at a university, college, school or other educational institution in country (B), any remuneration is tax-exempt in country (B) to the extent that it is subject to tax in country (A).

The above does not apply to remuneration which a professor or teacher receives for conducting research if the research is undertaken primarily for the private benefit of a specific person or persons.

STUDENTS AND TRAINEES

A student or trainee who is a resident of country (A) or was a resident immediately before visiting country (B) and is temporarily visiting country (B) solely for purposes of his or her education or training is exempt from tax in country (B) in relation to payments for maintenance, education or training if the payments come from anywhere except country (B).

In respect of grants, scholarships and remuneration not covered by the above, a student or trainee shall be entitled during his or her education or training to the same tax exemptions, reliefs or reductions available to residents of the country which he or she is visiting.

SHIPPING AND AIR TRANSPORT

In respect of shipping, country (A) has exclusive taxing rights over any profit derived by a resident of country (A) from the operation of ships in international traffic.

In respect of air transport, there is an air transport double taxation agreement between Australia and China, signed on 22 November 1985.

CAPITAL GAINS

For Australian tax purposes, the treaty applies to capital gains.

22.230   CERTIFICATES OF RESIDENCY

If a person or entity is certified as an Australian resident for income tax purposes and receives foreign income from certain countries, they may be able to request the tax authorities of those countries to provide a tax exemption or reduce the tax liability in relation to the income.

This can be done using a tax relief form supplied by overseas authorities which is completed by the Australian resident and certified by the Tax Office. The forms will only be certified if there is a comprehensive DTA between Australia and the relevant country (see 22.220).

22.240   OTHER INTERNATIONAL AGREEMENTS

Australia has entered into other international tax agreements, which are not tax treaties. In particular, the government has recently been focusing on entering into information exchange agreements with low-tax jurisdictions to improve integrity and transparency in the international tax system.

In recent years, the Australian Government has entered into bilateral Tax Information Exchange Agreements (TIEAs) with a number of low-tax countries. Broadly, a TIEA allows the exchange of tax information between the signatory countries and is a measure used in combatting international financial and tax fraud.

As at the time of writing, there are agreements with 37 countries in force. Partner countries include Antigua and Barbuda, Bermuda, the Isle of Man, Jersey and the Netherlands Antilles. TIEAs have been signed with Brunei and Guatemala but they are not yet in force at time of writing.

Other examples of international agreements include airline profits agreements, international tax sharing treaties, the Timor Sea Treaty, the Australian-United States joint space and defence projects and in respect of Trans-Tasman business between Australia and New Zealand.

22.300   FOREIGN EXCHANGE TRANSLATION

The foreign exchange measures are contained in Division 775 ITAA97 and Subdivisions 960-C and 960-D ITAA97. See also CGT events K10 and K11 at 12.040.

22.310 CONVERSION OF FOREIGN CURRENCY AMOUNTS

For income tax purposes, foreign currency amounts are required to be translated into Australian currency. Foreign currency translation is governed by Division 960 ITAA97. This rule is known as the general translation rule.

The rules specifying the spot rate that is to be used are set out at subs960-50(6), summarised as follows:

Amount	Conversion time
Ordinary income	Earlier of derivation and receipt
Statutory income other than capital gains or losses	Earlier of inclusion in assessable income and receipt
Deductions (other than deductions in relation to depreciating assets)	Earlier of when amount is incurred and payment
Amount paid for depreciating asset	Earlier of payment and time asset starts to be 'held'
Amount in relation to capital asset	Time of transaction or event
Value of trading stock at end of year using cost method	When item became trading stock on hand
Value of trading stock at end of year using market selling method or replacement method	At end of income year
Certain withholding amounts	At time withholding required

Source: www.ato.gov.au

As an alternative to the exchange rate regime set out at s960-50(6), the *Income Tax Assessment Regulations 1997* (ITAR97) provides three different translation options. In Schedule 2 to the ITAR97, entities may use the following rates to translate an amount into Australian dollars:

- entities which prepare audited financial accounts in compliance with the *Corporations Act 2001* and use particular exchange rates to translate amounts into Australian currency for the purposes of the financial accounts may use those same exchange rates

- a daily exchange rate which is a rate appropriate to the entity's business or activities and obtained from an arm's length source, and

- an average exchange rate that is applicable during a period not exceeding 12 months.

The regulations also contain translation rules for deducting bad debts and settlement of certain spot contracts.

AVERAGE RATES

Schedule 2 to the ITAR97 allows the use of average rates in certain instances. The general effect of these regulations is that foreign currency amounts can be translated into Australian currency (or the applicable functional currency) using daily or average rates of exchange, or rates consistent with those used to prepare audited financial reports. The Tax Office has published Fact Sheets which describe the regulations and give examples.

The taxpayer may translate an amount into Australian currency using the average of rates relevant to a period (which can be less than but not more than 12 months) chosen by the taxpayer. The rate selected must reasonably approximate the rate which would apply if the spot (instant) rate applying at the specific time listed in the table above had been used. Average rates are published on the Tax Office website (www.ato.gov.au). Rates supplied by banks or other reliable published sources are also generally acceptable.

FOREIGN EXCHANGE AND WITHHOLDING AMOUNTS

Where an Australian taxpayer pays interest, dividends or royalties in foreign currency to an overseas entity, an obligation to withhold tax from the payment may arise. The withholding amount is required to be translated into Australian currency at the exchange rate which applies on the date of payment.

BANKS AND FINANCIAL INSTITUTIONS

Section 960-50 does not apply for the purposes of working out the assessable income, deductions or tax offsets of an ADI or a non-ADI financial institution.

22.320   REALISATION OF FOREIGN CURRENCY GAINS AND LOSSES

Division 775 ITAA97 contains the rules concerning the taxation treatment of foreign exchange (forex) realisation gains and losses which arise upon the realisation of assets, rights and obligations.

The foreign exchange translation provisions apply to all taxpayers except, generally, banks and similar financial institutions. Gains and losses of a private nature, or which arise in relation to exempt income, are generally not brought to account under the measures.

Foreign currency gains and losses are brought to account as assessable income and allowable deductions respectively, on the basis of realisation when a taxpayer:

- disposes of foreign currency, or a right to receive foreign currency (forex realisation event 1)
- ceases to have a right to receive foreign currency (forex realisation event 2)
- ceases to have an obligation to receive foreign currency (forex realisation event 3)
- ceases to have an obligation to pay foreign currency (forex realisation event 4)
- ceases to have a right to pay foreign currency (forex realisation event 5)

to the extent such gains or losses are attributable to a fluctuation in a currency exchange rate, or to an agreed exchange rate differing from the actual exchange rate.

To the extent that a gain or loss is brought to account for tax under both the Division 775 measures and under another provision of the tax law, Division 775 takes priority and the gain or loss will only be assessable or deductible under the forex rules.

For assets such as a foreign currency bank account and fungible rights and obligations in respect of forex events 1, 2 and 4 there is a first in first out rule (but noting the elections discussed below). Alternatively, a weighted average basis may be applied in working out these forex gains and losses.

Foreign currency gains made on payment for trading stock acquisitions can be ordinary income under s6-5: TD 2006/29. There is an exception for certain livestock.

22.330   ELECTIONS

The 12 month rule provides that the measures generally do not apply to foreign exchange gains and losses on the acquisition or disposal of depreciating assets and CGT assets where the time between that acquisition or disposal and the due time for payment is not more than 12 months.

Such gains and losses are dealt with under the CGT and/or capital allowances provisions as part of the tax treatment of the underlying asset and are not separately assessable or deductible under Division 775. In respect of the acquisition of depreciating assets, the period is extended to 24 months; forex gains or losses arising up to 12 months before and after the asset commences to be held are integrated into the treatment of the underlying asset.

The **facilities rollover election** allows the issuer of certain securities (ie. the borrower) under certain facility agreements to defer bringing to account gains or losses on the face value of such securities. The concession allows the issuer of discounted securities to defer forex gains or losses to the extent that funds are outstanding under the security. Eligible securities covered are promissory notes, bills of exchange and certain others. The taxpayer must choose to apply the rollover within 90 days after the first time a bill is issued under the security, or within 90 days after the applicable commencement date.

The **$250,000 balance election** enables taxpayers to disregard foreign currency gains and losses made as a result of forex realisation events 2 or 4 on certain foreign currency denominated bank and credit card accounts with balances below the foreign currency equivalent of A$250,000. The treatment applies from the time of election. A buffering provision exists where the limited balance of A$250,000 is exceeded for short periods. The limited balance test is provided for at Subdivision 775-D.

The **retranslation election** enables taxpayers to bring to account foreign currency gains and losses on certain foreign currency denominated bank and credit card accounts ('qualifying forex accounts') on a retranslation basis. Typically, this is a simpler methodology than the FIFO basis but unrealised gains and losses may be brought to account. The treatment applies from the time of the election. If the retranslation option is used, forex gains or losses under events 2 and 4 (and CGT events C1 and C2) are disregarded. The retranslation election is governed by Subdivision 775-E. The losses or gains deemed to be realised for Division 775 purposes are calculated in this way:

Closing account balance for the period **less** *Opening balance of account for period* **less** *Deposits to account during the period* **plus** *Withdrawals from account during the period.*

The **functional currency election** allows certain entities or parts of entities, which keep their accounts totally or predominantly in a foreign currency, to choose that foreign currency as their functional currency to work out their annual net income, which is then translated to Australian dollars. The functional currency provisions are set out at Subdivision 960-D. Entities which can so elect are:

- residents required to prepare financial reports under s292 of the *Corporations Act 2001*
- residents carrying on a business through an overseas permanent establishment
- non-residents carrying on a business through an Australian permanent establishment
- offshore banking units
- attributable taxpayers of a controlled foreign company, or
- transferor trusts.

There are special consequences where the foreign currency rules apply to consolidated groups.

22.340 FOREIGN EXCHANGE RATES

The Tax Office publishes foreign exchange rates on its website to assist taxpayers in translating their foreign currency transactions into Australian currency. There is a range of rates available, including average monthly and yearly rates and daily spot rates.

Note that the foreign currency translation legislation requires the use of the exchange rate which is 'applicable' at the relevant time but does not mandate the use of any particular benchmark rates. Apart from the Tax Office recommended rates, exchange rates published by banks operating in Australia may also be used. Other reliable published rates can be applied. Records should be kept of the rate(s) used. Taxpayers cannot, generally, supply a rate themselves or through an associate unless the Tax Office approves this.

FOREIGN CURRENCY EXCHANGE RATES FOR THE FINANCIAL YEAR ENDING 30 JUNE 2015				
Foreign currency equivalent to $1 Aust.				
Country	Average rate for year ended		Nearest actual exchange rate		Currency
	31 Dec 14[1]	30 June 15[2]	31 Dec 14[1]	30 June 15[2]	
Canada	1.0322	1.0140	0.9850	0.9885	Canadian dollar
China	5.5634	5.1837	5.0859	4.7661	Yuan
Denmark	5.2401	5.3607	5.1828	5.2718	Kroner
Europe	0.7108	0.7273	0.7040	0.7146	Euro
Fiji	1.7401	1.6919	1.6789	1.6354	Fijian dollar
Hong Kong	7.2229	6.7216	6.5666	6.1675	Hong Kong dollar
India	55.9724	52.9913	53.0430	49.8080	Indian rupee
Israel	3.3406	3.2798	3.3104	3.0102	Israeli new shekel

FOREIGN CURRENCY EXCHANGE RATES FOR THE FINANCIAL YEAR ENDING 30 JUNE 2015				
Foreign currency equivalent to $1 Aust.				
Country	Average rate for year ended		Nearest actual exchange rate		Currency
	31 Dec 14[1]	30 June 15[2]	31 Dec 14[1]	30 June 15[2]	
Japan	99.0517	99.2307	101.4300	97.7900	Yen
Kuwait	0.2645	0.2531	0.2464	0.2398	Kuwait dinar
New Cal/Tahiti	83.2198	85.1488	82.1100	85.0100	CFP franc
New Zealand	1.1183	1.1072	1.0758	1.1522	NZ dollar
Norway	5.8859	6.1524	6.3080	6.2447	Kroner
Oman	0.3694	0.3449	0.3372	0.3176	Oman rial
PNG	2.5317	2.4074	2.3512	2.1070[3]	Kina
Philippines	41.7936	38.9653	38.3610	36.2860	Philippines peso
Poland	2.9426	2.9989	2.9836	2.9797	Polish zloty
Saudi	3.4852	3.2444	3.1678	2.9692	Saudi riyal
Singapore	1.1900	1.1426	1.1280	1.0808	Singapore dollar
Solomon Is	6.9011	6.5516	6.3444	6.3097	SI dollar
Sth Africa	10.1372	9.9124	9.8062	9.7657	Rand
Sri Lanka	121.0228	113.5896	110.0400	105.4200	Sri Lankan rupee
Sweden	6.3849	6.6670	6.5382	6.5216	Kronor
Switzerland	0.8547	0.8189	0.8382	0.7396	Swiss franc
Thailand	30.0089	28.0595	27.5700	26.5600	Baht
Turkey	2.0222	2.0373	1.9401	2.1143	Turkish lira
UK	0.5686	0.5513	0.5463	0.5085	Pound sterling
USA	0.9361	0.8715	0.8511	0.8012	US dollar
Vanuatu	94.1002	90.4867	88.3000	87.4500	Vatu

1: Average and nearest exchange rates for the year ended 31 December 2014 (except for China) are as published by the Tax Office. The rates for China are calculated from the daily rates published by the RBA.

2: Average and nearest exchange rates for the year ended 30 June 2015 (except for China) are as published by the Tax Office. The rates for China are calculated from the daily rates published by the RBA.

3: The nearest exchange rate for PNG for the year ended 30 June 2015 is taken from the daily rates published by the RBA.

22.400 FOREIGN INCOME TAX OFFSETS

The Foreign Income Tax Offset (FITO) regime contained in Division 770 ITAA97 mitigates the effects of double taxation (where the taxpayer pays tax on the same item of income in Australia and another country) by allowing taxpayers to claim an offset (the FITO) in respect of the foreign tax paid on the double taxed amount against Australian tax liabilities.

22.410 ENTITLEMENT TO A FOREIGN INCOME TAX OFFSET

In order to be entitled to claim a FITO the taxpayer must have paid the foreign tax themselves or had the tax paid on their behalf.

In regard to foreign taxes paid on behalf of the taxpayer, s770-130 deems a taxpayer to have personally paid an amount of foreign tax where the tax is paid by another entity either under an arrangement with the taxpayer or under the law relating to the foreign income tax. This may commonly include foreign taxes paid by the following entities:

- the trustee of a trust of which the taxpayer is a beneficiary
- a partnership in which the taxpayer is a partner, or
- the taxpayer's spouse.

Note that foreign taxes that qualify as FITOs may be directly paid or paid by deduction or withholding (whether by the taxpayer or another entity).

 Not every payment made to a foreign authority is eligible to be claimed as a FITO. The payment must be a 'foreign tax'. Some types of social security contributions are not considered to be a 'foreign tax'. For example, the AAT concluded that compulsory contributions to an Irish Social Insurance scheme were not payments of 'foreign tax' (Confidential v Commissioner of Taxation (2014) AATA 961).

The FITO entitlement only arises once the foreign tax has been paid and must be claimed in respect of the year in which the foreign income is returned as assessable income. Where the foreign tax is paid after the relevant tax return has been lodged, it will be necessary to lodge a request for an amended assessment to claim the FITO. Section 770-190 allows amendments to be made for up to four years after the foreign tax is paid. An amendment is also required where a foreign tax amount that has been claimed as a FITO is subsequently increased or reduced (ie the foreign jurisdiction required an extra payment of tax or gave a refund).

The maximum FITO available to a taxpayer is the greater of:

- $1,000, and
- the amount calculated in accordance with the formula in s770-75, which broadly represents the amount of Australian income tax payable on all foreign source income and income on which foreign tax has been paid.

If foreign taxes paid which qualify as offset amounts total no more than $1,000 no calculation of the FITO limit is required; the taxpayer merely claims the amount actually paid. Where foreign tax paid exceeds $1,000 a taxpayer may elect to claim a FITO of only $1,000; however, the excess foreign tax paid would be lost.

Where foreign taxes are unable to be claimed as part of a FITO in a particular year, they will be lost; there is no ability to carry forward excess FITOs.

 Fred, an Australian resident, derives the following income during the year ended 30 June 2015:

Taxable income (AUD)

Australian source income	$95,000
Foreign dividends (incl foreign withholding tax paid $1,500)	$10,000
Foreign interest (incl foreign withholding tax paid $1,500)	$15,000
Total assessable income	$120,000

Less deductions

Interest (re dividend income)	$(5,000)	
Other (re Australian source income)	$(15,000)	$(20,000)
Taxable income		**$100,000**

Calculation of foreign income tax offset limit

1. *Australian tax payable on $100,000 (2014-15 rates) incl Medicare levy* $26,947
2. *Australian tax payable if the assumptions in subs770-75(4) are made:*

   Disregarded assessable income:

Foreign dividends	$10,000
Foreign interest	$15,000
Total disregarded amount	$25,000

   Disregarded deductions: No deductions are disregarded.
   Calculation: $100,000 – $25,000 = $75,000

Tax payable on $75,000, including Medicare levy	$17,422

3. | | |
   |---|---|
   | *Tax payable at step 1* | $26,947 |
   | *Less tax payable at step 2* | $(17,422) |
   | *Foreign income tax offset limit* | **$9,525** |

As the foreign tax paid of $3,000 is less than the foreign income tax offset limit ($9,525) the full offset of $3,000 is available. Had the amount of foreign tax paid exceeded the foreign income tax offset limit, the available offset would be the calculated limit.

22.420 FOREIGN LOSSES

Foreign losses are treated the same as domestic tax losses.

Carried forward foreign losses may be applied against assessable income of any source in subsequent years. Also, deductions that relate to foreign source income are not quarantined against that foreign source income and may be claimed against Australian source income.

22.500 CONDUIT FOREIGN INCOME

The conduit foreign income regime in Subdivision 802-A ITAA97 operates such that foreign income which is derived by an Australian entity free from Australian tax can be distributed to a non-resident without Australian tax. The Australian resident entity is effectively a 'conduit' for foreign income which flows into and out of Australia without attracting Australian tax.

An unfranked part of a frankable distribution that an Australian resident corporate tax entity (CTE) makes to a non-resident, is specifically exempt from dividend withholding tax to the extent that the CTE makes a declaration that the unfranked part of the distribution is 'conduit foreign income' (CFI).

Where a corporate unit trust or public trading trust that qualifies as a CTE makes a distribution to a non-resident beneficiary, the part of the distribution that is attributable to the unfranked part of a frankable distribution that the trust declares to be CFI is also exempt from withholding tax. The distributed amount which has been declared to be CFI is non-assessable non-exempt income in the hands of the non-resident (s802-15).

If an Australian CTE receives an unfranked part of a frankable distribution from another Australian CTE which has declared the unfranked amount to be CFI, the income is non-assessable non-exempt income to the recipient so long as the recipient distributes the amount and declares it to be CFI (s802-20).

An Australian CTE is (see s960-115 and s995-1 ITAA97):

- an Australian resident company
- an Australian resident corporate limited partnership
- a corporate unit trust that is a resident unit trust, or
- a public trading trust that is a resident unit trust.

The calculation of CFI is set out in the subdivision. Essentially, the CFI includes:

- income received from another Australian CTE that has been declared to be CFI by the other Australian CTE
- a distribution from a trust or a partnership to the extent that it is attributable to an unfranked distribution that is attributable to CFI
- a non-portfolio dividend that is non-assessable non-exempt income to the CTE pursuant to s23AJ ITAA36
- a capital gain that is not assessable to the CTE pursuant to any of: the participation exemption (Subdivision 768-G ITAA97), the foreign branch exemption (subs23AH(3) ITAA36) or an international tax sharing treaty, and
- an amount of foreign income on which no Australian tax is payable due to a FITO entitlement offsetting the Australian tax liability on that foreign income.

The entity's CFI amount is reduced by:

- income which is non-assessable non-exempt income of the CTE pursuant to the exemptions for income previously taxed under the CFC, FIF or transferor trust regimes (ss23AI, 23AK and 99B(2)(e) ITAA36 respectively)
- an amount of income that would be attached to the franking credits available under paragraph 802-30(4)(c) ITAA97
- a capital loss that is disregarded pursuant to any of: the participation exemption (Subdivision 768-G ITAA97), the foreign branch exemption (subs23AH(4) ITAA36) or an international tax sharing treaty

- related expenses which are not otherwise deductible under another provision of the Tax Acts, and

- a declaration that an amount of a distribution is CFI must be made on or before the day of the distribution. Note that where the CTE making the distribution is a private company, this rule brings forward the statutory deadline for giving a distribution statement. Under s202-75(3) ITAA97, a private company may give a distribution statement up to four months after the end of the year in which the distribution is made.

The CFI provisions also contain integrity measures regarding double benefits and streaming.

EXTENSION OF PART IVA

Part IVA (the general anti-avoidance provision – see 4.510) may apply to arrangements in relation to which a person had the sole or dominant purpose of reducing or eliminating a withholding tax liability on non-resident interest, dividend and royalty payments made. This may include payments to tax-exempt bodies interposed between an Australian resident payer and a non-resident recipient, or dividends consisting of bonus shares issued from the share capital account. The tax benefit which would trigger Part IVA is the amount of withholding tax that would otherwise have been payable had it not been for the scheme or arrangement.

22.550 TRUST DISTRIBUTIONS TO NON-RESIDENTS

The income tax law contains some specific provisions in relation to the taxation of particular types of distributions from Australian resident trusts to non-residents.

CAPITAL GAINS & LOSSES FOR FOREIGN RESIDENTS THROUGH FIXED TRUSTS

For the tax treatment of foreign residents who invest in fixed trusts see 12.733.

DISTRIBUTIONS TO FOREIGN RESIDENTS FROM MANAGED INVESTMENT TRUSTS

Subdivision 840-M sets out the managed investment trust withholding regime and imposes a tax liability in respect of relevant distributions. Subdivision 12-H in Schedule 1 to the TAA contains the withholding provisions.

The law provides that a distribution to a non-resident by a managed investment trust of its Australian sourced income and certain capital gains may be subject to a single non-final withholding. Subdivision 12-H requires an Australian managed investment trust or a custodian making a 'fund payment' to a foreign resident to withhold tax from the distribution. The legislation defines a 'fund payment' as a distribution made out of the trust's net income sourced from Australian source income other than dividends, interest, royalties and capital gains or losses that arises from a CGT asset that is not taxable Australian property.

Where the fund payment is made to an interposed entity that is not a managed investment trust or custodian and the interposed entity subsequently pays or credits a foreign resident an amount which is attributable to the fund payment, the withholding obligations fall on the interposed entity.

A two-tier withholding regime under which the applicable withholding tax rate depended on the country of which the non-resident recipient is a resident applies. The current rates are:

- **in respect of recipients residing in jurisdictions with which Australia has effective information exchange arrangements:** a final withholding tax at a rate of 15%, and

- **in respect of other foreign residents:** a final withholding tax at a rate of 30%.

NOTE: The reduced rate is only available to residents of countries with which Australia has effective exchange of information arrangements. This restriction exists to protect the integrity of the managed investment trust withholding tax system and also reflects Australia's commitment to using effective exchange of information arrangement to reduce opportunities for international tax evasion and avoidance. The list of countries is in the *Taxation Administration Regulations 1976*.

CLEAN BUILDING MANAGED INVESTMENT TRUSTS

The *Tax Laws Amendment (Clean Building Managed Investment Trust) Act 2012* amended the law to provide a final withholding tax rate of 10% on fund payments from eligible Clean Building MITs made to foreign residents in information exchange countries, including payments made indirectly through one or more Australian intermediaries. Where the recipient of a fund payment is not in an information exchange country, the withholding rate is 30%.

A Clean Building MIT is a MIT that holds one or more clean buildings of which construction commenced on or after 1 July 2012. The concession will be available in relation to office buildings that have obtained a 5-star Green Star rating or a predicted 5.5 star NABERS rating, and retail centres and non-residential accommodation that meet equivalent standards.

This measure will apply to fund payments from a Clean Building MIT from 2012-13.

DISTRIBUTION FROM AN AUSTRALIAN TRUST TO A NON-RESIDENT TRUSTEE BENEFICIARY

A tax obligation rests on the trustee of a resident trust which distributes to a non-resident trustee beneficiary in respect of that distribution, in line with the consequences which arise where the trustee of a resident trust distributes to a non-resident beneficiary that is not receiving the distribution in the capacity of a trustee.

The trustee of the resident trust will be liable for the income tax on assessable Australian source income (other than dividends, interest and royalties) to which the non-resident trustee beneficiary is presently entitled. The residency of the non-resident trustee beneficiary is determined at the end of the particular year of income.

The trustee of the resident trust will be liable to tax pursuant to s98(4) ITAA36.

These rules do not apply to:

- distributions attributable to conduit foreign income (which would be able to be distributed without incurring a liability to Australian tax), and
- distributions made by a resident managed investment trust to a non-resident trustee beneficiary (see above).

22.560 INVESTMENT MANAGER REGIME

In December 2010, the government proposed ATO implement a three-stage Investment Manager Regime (IMR). Some of these proposals have now been enacted.

The IMR reforms remove tax impediments to investing in Australia in order to attract foreign investment and promote the use of Australian fund managers.

Under this regime, the Commissioner would generally not be permitted to raise an assessment in respect of the relevant income, gains or losses of a 'foreign managed fund' (or a trustee or investor of the fund) that has not lodged an Australian tax return for the 2009-10 or prior income years in respect of that income, gains or losses.

Investments covered by the first stage of the reform as announced in December 2010 included:

- portfolio interests in companies, and
- portfolio interests in other entities (including units in a unit trust)

except to the extent the amount gives rise to a withholding tax liability.

The amendments to the tax law are to address concerns of foreign funds following the application of US accounting rules 'FIN 48'.

The second stage of the reforms were announced on 19 January 2011. Income from relevant investments of a foreign fund, that is taken to have an Australian permanent establishment, will be exempt from income tax. This change will align Australian rules with international practice.

The *Tax Laws Amendment (Investment Manager Regime) Bill 2012,* comprising the first two elements of the IMR, received Royal Assent on 13 September 2012.

On 12 March 2015, the government released exposure draft legislation and explanatory memorandum to implement the third element of the IMR reforms. This third element extends the IMR concession to cover investments in Australian assets (excluding real property) that are of a portfolio nature and broaden the 'widely held' test. Foreign entities will be eligible for the IMR concession if they directly invest in Australia or invest via an Australian fund manager. These amendments also simplify the operation of the existing regime and make technical changes to ensure that some entities are not inadvertently disadvantaged or excluded.

22.600 FOREIGN HYBRIDS

Foreign hybrids comprise 'foreign hybrid limited partnerships' and 'foreign hybrid companies'. Broadly, they are foreign entities which are treated as partnerships for the income tax purposes of the other country but would not be treated as partnerships for Australian tax purposes in the absences of the foreign hybrid regime. The foreign hybrid rules, contained in Division 830 ITAA97, allows the income of these entities to be taxed on a 'flow through' basis such that they are treated as partnerships.

FOREIGN HYBRID LIMITED PARTNERSHIPS

The criteria for an entity to be a foreign hybrid limited partnership are:
* it was formed outside of Australia
* the foreign country imposes its income tax on the partners and not on the limited partnership
* at all times during the year, the partnership was not a resident of any country that imposes income tax on entities on a residency basis
* it was not a resident of Australia at any time during the year
* it satisfies the requirements to be a Controlled Foreign Company (CFC) for the purposes of the CFC regime, and
* the Australian taxpayer satisfies the requirements to be an attributable taxpayer in relation to the partnership (ie. the CFC) with an attribution percentage of greater than nil, pursuant to the CFC legislation.

FOREIGN HYBRID COMPANY

The criteria for an entity to be a foreign hybrid company are:
* at all times during the year, the company was not a resident of any country that imposes income tax on entities on a residency basis
* it was not a resident of Australia at any time during the year
* it satisfies the requirements to be a CFC for the purposes of the CFC regime, and
* the Australian taxpayer satisfies the requirements to be an attributable taxpayer in relation to the company (ie the CFC) with an attribution percentage of greater than nil, pursuant to the CFC legislation.

Furthermore, the company must satisfy the relevant 'partnership treatment requirements' in order to qualify as a foreign hybrid company. The partnership treatment requirements which apply depends on whether the company is subject to particular tax treatment in the United States.

Partnership treatment requirements specific to the US:
* the company was formed in the US
* for US income tax purposes, the company is a limited liability company, and
* for US income tax purposes, either it is treated as a partnership or it is an eligible entity that is not treated as being separate from its owner.

Partnership treatment requirements specific to any foreign country:
* the company was formed in a foreign country, including the US
* for the income tax purposes of that country, the company is treated as a partnership, and
* all relevant requirements in the regulations are satisfied.

DIVISION 830 TAX TREATMENT

Foreign hybrid limited partnerships and foreign hybrid companies in respect of which an Australian partner or shareholder has made the requisite election under s485AA ITAA36 are taxed on a 'flow through' basis.

Division 830 details the tax treatment of these entities and their partners and shareholders. The provisions also contain modifications to the general operation of the tax law, including placing limits on income and capital losses of a foreign hybrid which can be deducted by a partner or shareholder against income from other sources. Also, assets of the foreign hybrid are treated for CGT purposes as assets of the partners or shareholders of the foreign hybrid.

22.700 THIN CAPITALISATION

The thin capitalisation regime is an integrity measure intended to prevent cross-border profit-shifting within multinational groups which may otherwise finance their Australian operations with uncommercially high debt levels. The thin capitalisation rules operate by setting a maximum limit on the amount of debt (relative to equity) that can be used to finance the Australian operations of a multinational business.

NOTE: The thin capitalisation rules were amended with effect from 1 July 2014.

WHEN THE THIN CAPITALISATION RULES APPLY

Division 820 applies to Australian entities including companies, trusts and partnerships that are foreign controlled and foreign entities that either invest directly into Australia or operate a business at or through an Australian permanent establishment (see definition from 22.210). These are called inward investing entities. The inward investing entity regime is further categorised into inward investment vehicles (foreign controlled Australian entities) and inward investors (foreign entities which invest in Australia). It also applies to Australian entities that control foreign entities or operate a business at or through overseas permanent establishments. These are called outward investing entities.

Within these categories, different rules apply depending on whether the entity is an authorised deposit-taking institution (ADI) or a non-ADI. Broadly, the effects of the separate measures are:

- non-ADIs – claims for debt deductions are reduced where the amount of debt used to fund an entity's Australian operations exceeds the maximum amount of debt specified in the Division (see table below), and
- ADIs – claims for debt deductions are reduced where the equity capital used to fund Australian operations is less than the minimum equity requirements specified in the Division (see table below).

A 'debt deduction' is defined in the thin capitalisation legislation at s820-40. Broadly, debt deductions are expenses incurred in relation to a 'debt interest' which are otherwise deductible (disregarding the potential application of the thin capitalisation rules which may disallow the deduction).

The meaning of 'debt interest' is found in the debt/equity rules of Division 974. A scheme gives rise to a debt interest where it satisfies the debt test set out in s974-20. Refer 6.200.

Debt deductions include:

- interest payments including an amount in the nature of interest
- discounts
- any costs incurred in connection with a debt interest
- fees, and
- the loss in respect of a repurchase agreement.

The legislation also specifies certain expenses which are not debt deductions for thin capitalisation purposes, including salaries, wages and costs incurred in hedging or managing the financial risk arising from the debt interest.

WHEN THE THIN CAPITALISATION RULES DO NOT APPLY

The thin capitalisation rules do not apply to an entity which:

- has its operations entirely confined to either within Australia or outside Australia, or
- satisfies the de minimis rule, ie the total debt deductions of the entity and its associate entities for the year do not exceed $2 million ($250,000 before 1 July 2014), or
- is an exempt special purpose (securitisation) vehicle, or
- is an outward investing entity and at least 90% the average value of the assets of the entity and its associates comprises Australian assets.

22.710 KEY FEATURES OF THE THIN CAPITALISATION RULES

The different types of investors are treated differently under the thin capitalisation rules. Investing entities are divided into the following categories:

- Non-ADI
  - outward investor (general)
  - outward investor (financial) (ie. a financial entity, other than an ADI that has a business of dealing in securities)
  - inward investment vehicle (general)
  - inward investment vehicle (financial)
  - inward investor (general), and
  - inward investor (financial).
- ADI
  - outward investing entity, and
  - inward investing entity.

Key features of the rules	
De minimis rule	The rules do not apply to a taxpayer which together with its associate entities claims $2 million ($250,000 prior to 1 July 2014) or less in debt deductions in a year of income.
Control test	There are alternative tests to determine whether an entity is 'controlled' for thin capitalisation purposes. These tests also differ depending on whether the entity being tested is Australian or foreign and on the legal form of the entity (company, trust or various forms of partnerships). Generally, control is assumed where no greater than 5 entities directly or indirectly hold at least 50% of the interests in the entity or where one single entity holds at least 40% of the interests in the entity. In some cases, actual control is an alternative test. The rules determining whether a foreign company is Australian-controlled interact with the controlled foreign company regime. Refer Subdivision 820-H.
Debt deduction: Non-ADIs investing offshore	Debt deductions proportionally disallowed if the entity's debt level exceeds its maximum allowable debt, which is the greatest of the following (Division 820-B): • safe harbour debt amount (ie safe harbour gearing limit of 1.5:1 (3:1 prior to 1 July 2014) based on average value of assets) • safe harbour debt amount in relation to on-lending to third parties by non-ADIs which are financial entities investing offshore (ie a gearing ratio of 15:1 (20:1 prior to 1 July 2014)) • arm's length debt amount applied when safe harbour test is not satisfied, or • worldwide gearing debt amount (ie. 100% (120% prior to 1 July 2014) of the gearing of the worldwide group that controls it)

Key features of the rules	
Debt deduction: Non-ADIs investing onshore	Debt deductions proportionally disallowed if the entity's debt level exceeds its maximum allowable debt, which is the greater of the following (Division 820-C): • the safe harbour gearing debt limit of 1.5:1 (3:1 prior to 1 July 2014), and • arm's length debt amount. Note: For non-ADIs which are financial entities investing onshore the safe harbour debt/equity ratio is 15:1 (20:1 prior to 1 July 2014).
Debt deduction: ADIs investing onshore and offshore	Debt deductions are proportionally disallowed if the entity's equity level is below the minimum amount, which is the lesser of the following (Divisions 820-D and 820-E): • safe harbour capital amount (6% (4% prior to 1 July 2014) of the risk-weighted assets of the Australian banking business) • arm's length capital amount, and • world wide capital amount.
Safe harbour debt amount	In practice, this is the most commonly used methodology for determining an entity's maximum allowable debt. The safe harbour gearing (or debt/equity) ratio is 1.5:1 (3:1 prior to 1 July 2014). This means that the year's total average debt cannot exceed 60% of the average value of total assets. Debt and asset values exclude specific items. The method statements for the calculation of the safe harbour debt amount for the various kinds of investors are set out in Subdivisions 820-B, 820-C, 820-D, 820-E.
Records	Australian permanent establishments of foreign entities are required to maintain certain records (Subdivision 820-L).

The thin capitalisation legislation requires asset, liability and capital values to be calculated in accordance with applicable Australian accounting standards. To mitigate potential adverse impacts that the application of International Financial Reporting Standards (IFRS) may have on taxpayers' thin capitalisation positions, taxpayers may disregard IFRS in the valuation of specific assets and liabilities for thin capitalisation purposes. Items for which this concessional treatment applies include: deferred tax assets and liabilities; assets and liabilities arising from defined benefit plans within the scope of Australian accounting standard AASB 119 Employment Benefits; and revalued intangible assets.

22.720 OUTWARD INVESTING ENTITIES

There are different rules for outward investors depending on whether the taxpaying entity is an ADI or a non-ADI. In this section we will deal only with general investors and financial investors that are non-ADIs (Subdivision 820-B).

The following rules apply to outward investors (general), which are non-banking Australian entities with offshore operations such as a foreign subsidiary or which are carrying on a business overseas through a permanent establishment in that other country.

By legislative definition (s820-85(2)), an outward investor (general) is an entity that is neither a financial entity nor an ADI at any time during the period and it is either:

- an Australian controller of at least one Australian controlled foreign entity, or
- an Australian entity that carries on a business through at least one overseas permanent establishment.
- an Australian entity that is an associate entity of another Australian entity that is an outward investing entity (non-ADI) or an outward investing entity (ADI).

The definition of an outward investor (financial) is the same except that the entity must be a financial entity.

Associates of an outward investor would only be subject to thin capitalisation rules where they are in a position to sufficiently influence the associated outward investor. The meaning of 'associate entity' is set out at s820-905.

As a general rule the rules pertaining to 'outward investing entities' take precedence over the rules for 'inward investing entities'. For example, the following rules will apply where an Australian entity has an overseas permanent establishment but is also foreign controlled.

OUTWARD INVESTING ENTITIES (GENERAL)

The thin capitalisation rules apply where the adjusted average debt of the Australian operations exceeds the maximum allowable debt under the prescribed limits (Subdivision 820-B). The limit for an Australian outward investing entity (general) that is not also an inward investment vehicle is the greatest of:

- the safe harbour debt amount
- the arm's length debt amount. This test involves the entity undertaking an analysis of the debt that an independent third party would expect to have if they undertook the same operations as the target entity, or
- the worldwide debt amount. Under this test the entity can be geared up to 100% (120% prior to 1 July 2014) of the Australian entity's worldwide group's gearing ratio.

For entities that are foreign controlled (the entity is both an outward investing entity and an inward investment vehicle) the maximum allowable debt is the greater of:

- the safe harbour debt amount, or
- the arm's length debt amount.

There is a de minimis exemption for taxpayers which, together with their associates, have total debt deductions (eg interest expenses) of below $2 million ($250,000 prior to 1 July 2014) for the year.

The thin capitalisation rules also do not apply to outward investing Australian entities (ADI or non-ADI) where at least 90% of the average value of their assets and their associates' assets (excluding domestic or private assets) comprise the values of Australian assets.

CALCULATING ADJUSTED AVERAGE DEBT

An entity's adjusted average debt for outward investing entities (non-ADI) is calculated using the following (s820-85(3)):

Step 1: Work out the average value, for that year (the relevant year), of all the debt capital of the entity that gives rise to debt deductions of the entity for that or any other income year.

Step 2: Reduce the result of step 1 by the average value, for the relevant year, of all the associate entity debt of the entity.

Step 3: Reduce the result of step 2 by the average value, for the relevant year, of all the controlled foreign entity debt of the entity.

Step 4: If the entity is a financial entity throughout the relevant year, add to the result of step 3 the average value, for the relevant year, of the entity's borrowed securities amount.

Step 5: Add to the result of step 4 the average value, for the relevant year, of the cost-free debt capital of the entity. The result of this step is the adjusted average debt.

Section 820-85 disallows all or part of each debt deduction of an outward investing entity for an income year if the entity's adjusted average debt as calculated above exceeds its maximum allowable debt.

The entity's maximum allowable debt will be the greater of:

- the safe harbour debt amount
- the arm's length debt amount, and
- the worldwide gearing debt amount.

CALCULATING THE SAFE HARBOUR DEBT AMOUNT

The safe harbour debt amount is the most common alternative used for determining an entity's maximum allowable debt amount.

The safe harbour debt amount for Australian general investors is calculated using the following method (disregarding any amount attributable to the entity's overseas permanent establishment).

Step 1: Work out the average value of all the assets of the entity.

Step 1A: Reduce the result of Step 1 by the average value, for that year, of all excluded equity interests in the entity.

Step 2: Reduce the result of Step 1A by the average value for that year of all of the associate entity debt of the entity.

Step 3: Reduce the result in Step 2 by the average value for that year of all the associate entity equity of the entity.

Step 4: Reduce the result in Step 3 by the average value for that year of all the controlled foreign entity debt of the entity.

Step 5: Reduce the result of Step 4 by the average value for that year of all the controlled foreign entity equity of the entity.

Step 6: Reduce the result of Step 5 by the average value for that year of all the non-debt liabilities of the entity. If result of this step is negative, the amount is taken to be nil.

Step 7: Multiply the result of step 6 by 60% (75% prior to 1 July 2014).

Step 8: Add to the result of step 7 the entity's associate entity excess amount.

The result is the safe harbour debt amount.

NOTE: The definition of 'excluded equity interest' set out at s820-946 requires an interest to be on issue for less than 180 days. The legislation ensures that equity interests which remain on issue for a total of 180 days or more are not 'excluded equity interests' even if they have been on issue for less than 180 days at the valuation day.

The safe harbour debt amount (or the maximum allowable debt amount calculated under another method) must then be compared with the entity's adjusted average debt. If the adjusted average debt exceeds the safe harbour amount then the entity has breached the maximum allowable debt amount. As a consequence, part of the debt deductions will be denied.

Conversely, if the adjusted average debt is lower than the safe harbour amount then there is no denial of deductions. If the amount is nil or a negative amount then the safe harbour debt amount is treated as nil.

In TR 2002/20 the Tax Office considers what is included in 'liabilities' and 'non-debt liabilities' used to calculate the maximum allowable debt a non-ADI can have for the purpose of the safe harbour debt amount. Briefly, the terms 'assets' and 'liabilities' adopt their accounting meaning and valuation must be in accordance with paragraph 4 of AASB 1001 Accounting policies. This ruling has not been amended upon the adoption of IFRS.

The following example demonstrates the calculation of the adjusted average debt and the safe harbour debt amount for outward investing entities (non-ADI) (general). The example has been sourced from the Tax Office's *Guide to Thin Capitalisation*. (**NOTE:** The example does not include the operation of step 1A in the calculation statement for the safe harbour debt amount. The Tax Office does not appear to have updated the Guide since the insertion of Step 1A. The Tax Office does not appear to have issued a numerical example which includes this step.)

IMPORTANT! At time of writing, the Tax Office guide has not been updated for the 2014 changes. The following example has been adapted from the guide and reflect the current thresholds.

Non-ADI general outward investor
(Source: adapted from the example in the Tax Office Guide to Thin Capitalisation)

Aust Co is a general entity. It has a wholly-owned foreign subsidiary (For Sub) and a wholly-owned Australian subsidiary (Ozzie Co) which is also a general entity. Aust Co has borrowed $36 million from an unrelated financial institution. It has invested $6 million as equity in For Sub and lent $9 million to For Sub.

It has invested $3 million as equity in Ozzie Co. This represents what Aust Co paid a third party for 100% of the equity in Ozzie Co. For Sub has borrowed $15 million from an unrelated financial institution and has $21 million in retained earnings. Aust Co and Ozzie Co have not formed a resident consolidated group and neither company has any overseas permanent establishments. All loans are at commercial interest rates. For the purposes of this example, Aust Co is the only entity being tested under the thin capitalisation rules. The test year is the 2014-15 income year. Following is a diagram illustrating these facts and the relevant financial information for Aust Co and Ozzie Co.

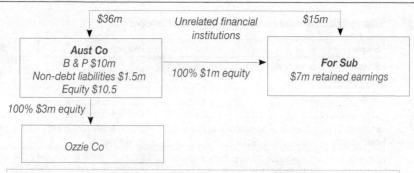

Aust Co's assets and liabilities for the year ending 30 June 2015
(average values using opening and closing balances method)

Assets	$m	Liabilities	$m
Loan to For Sub	9	Debt	36
Equity in For Sub	6	Non-debt liabilities	1.5
Equity in Ozzie Co*	3	Share capital	10.5
Building and plant	30		
	48		48

*Assume the equity investment in Ozzie Co remains valued at $1 million at all times throughout the income year.

Aust Co has $2.1 million worth of debt deductions in the 2014-15 income year and fails the debt deduction de minimis test. Assume Aust Co does not meet the asset de minimis test.

Because Aust Co and Ozzie Co have not formed a resident consolidated group, the consolidated basis for valuing assets and liabilities is not relevant.

Step 1: Calculate Aust Co's adjusted average debt

Steps	Worksheet 1		$m
Step 1: The average value of all Aust Co's debt capital that gives rise to debt deductions is $36m.	Average debt capital	(A)	36
Step 2: Aust Co does not have any associate entity debt (the loan to For Sub is not included because it is not attributable to For Sub's Australian permanent establishments or other assets held by For Sub for the purpose of producing Australian assessable income)	Average associate entity debt	(B)	0
Step 3: Aust Co's controlled foreign entity debt is the $9m loan to For Sub.	Average controlled foreign entity debt	(C)	9
Step 4: Not applicable because Aust Co is not a financial entity.			
Step 5: All of Aust Co's debt capital gives rise to debt deductions.	Average cost-free debt capital	(D)	0
Aust Co's adjusted average debt is $9m.	Adjusted average debt (A – B – C + D)	=	27

Aust Co's adjusted average debt is $27 million. This is now compared to Aust Co's maximum allowable debt, which is the greatest of its:

- safe harbour debt amount
- worldwide gearing debt amount, and
- arm's length debt amount.

Aust Co can calculate these amounts in any order it chooses and does not necessarily have to calculate all three amounts.

The calculation of the safe harbour debt amount is demonstrated below.

Step 2: Calculate Aust Co's safe harbour debt amount

Steps	Worksheet 2		$m
Step 1: *The average value of Aust Co's assets is $48 million.*	Average assets	(E)	48
Step 1A: *See note above.*			
Step 2: *Aust Co does not have any associate entity debt (see Step 2 of adjusted average debt calculation).*	Average associate entity debt (from B on worksheet 1)	(F)	0
Step 3: *The average value of Aust Co's associate entity equity is $3m (again equity invested in For Sub is not included in associate entity equity because it is not attributable to For Sub's Australian permanent establishments or other assets held by For Sub for the purpose of producing Australian assessable income).*	Average associate entity equity	(G)	3
Step 4: *The average value of Aust Co's controlled foreign entity debt is the $9m owed to Aust Co by For Sub.*	Average controlled foreign entity debt (from C on worksheet 1)	(H)	9
Step 5: *The average value of Aust Co's controlled foreign entity equity is the $6m invested in For Sub.*	Average controlled foreign entity equity	(I)	6
Step 6: *The average value of Aust Co's non-debt liabilities is $1.5m.*	Average non-debt liabilities	(J)	1.5
Step 7: *Multiply the result by 1.5/2.5.*	$(E - F - G - H - I - J) = 28.5 \times 1.5/2.5$	(K)	17.1
Step 8: *The average value of Aust Co's associate entity excess is $2.25m (calculated separately).*	Average associate entity excess amount	(L)	2.25
Aust Co's safe harbour debt amount is calculated by adding the amounts at K and L.	Safe harbour debt amount (K + L)	=	19.35

OUTWARD INVESTING ENTITIES (FINANCIAL)

For Australian financial outward investors there is a choice between two tests:

- the safe harbour debt amount, and
- the arm's length debt amount.

The safe harbour debt amount is the lesser of the total debt amount and the adjusted on-lent amount, which are calculated under the respective method statements in s820-100.

The first 6 steps for calculating the total debt amount are identical to the steps for calculating the safe harbour debt amount for Australian outward general investors. The following steps are added to derive the total debt amount. The calculation is set out at s820-100.

Step 7: Reduce the result in Step 6 by the average zero capital amount. A negative result is taken to be nil.

Step 8: Multiply the result in Step 7 by 15/16 (20/21 prior to 1 July 2014).

Step 9: Add to the result of Step 8 the average value of the zero capital amount.

Step 10: Add to the result of Step 9 the entity's average value of the associate entity excess amount.

The adjusted on-lent amount must also be calculated pursuant to s820-100(3) and compared with the total debt amount. This is the maximum amount of debt that the entity can have under the on-lending rule. This test is designed to ensure that the gearing of the entity is capped at 15:1 (20:1 prior to 1 July 2014).

22.730   NON-ADI INWARD INVESTING ENTITIES

Non-ADI inward investing entities include foreign and Australian entities but does not include banks or other ADIs. There are 4 types of inward investing entities:

- inward investing investment vehicle (general)
- inward investing investment vehicle (financial)
- inward investor (general), and
- inward investor (financial).

A summary of the rules that apply to these entities has not been included due to their length and complexity.

NOTE: The 2014 amendments introduced a new worldwide gearing debt limit for inward investing entities (and inward investment vehicles that are also outward investing), to be applied if the entity chooses, subject to an assets threshold.

22.740   ADI INWARD AND OUTWARD INVESTING ENTITIES

ADI outward investing entities and ADI inward investing entities are affected by the rules set out in Subdivision 820-D and Subdivision 820-E. Some financial entities may choose to be treated as ADIs. The operation of this choice is governed by Subdivision 820-EA.

A summary of the rules that apply to these entities has not been included due to their length and complexity.

22.750   DEBT DEDUCTIONS DISALLOWED

Where the entity's adjusted average debt exceeds the maximum allowable debt calculated under one of the tests applicable to the entity, the amount of debt deductions disallowed is determined by (s820-115):

*Debt deduction x [Excess debt / Average of the sum of
(Debt capital giving rise to debt deductions + Cost-free debt capital)]*

22.760   INTERACTION WITH CAPITAL GAINS TAX

Interest amounts which are denied a deduction under the thin capitalisation rules are not permitted to be added to the cost base of a CGT asset (refer to 12.092 on cost base).

22.770   RECORD KEEPING

If an inward investor or inward investing entity carries on business in Australia through one or more permanent establishments (PE) in Australia and total revenue attributable to those PEs is at least $2,000,000, records must be kept as follows:

- the entity may elect to keep all statements in accordance with the applicable Australian accounting standards (s820-960(1A)) – which now comprise the Australian equivalents to IFRS, or
- the entity may keep all statements in accordance with the standards (s820-960(1C)) made by the responsible body in the UK, USA, Canada, New Zealand, Japan, France, Germany or the International Accounting Standards.

22.800 ANTI-TAX-DEFERRAL REGIMES

The anti-tax-deferral regimes (also collectively known as the foreign income accruals taxation system) were designed to combat the practice of sheltering income in lower taxing countries.

Broadly, the regimes operate by attributing income derived by a non-resident entity to an Australian resident with requisite interests in the entity. The Australian resident is subject to tax on that attributed income even if the taxpayer has no actual entitlement to the income. If the attributed income is distributed to the taxpayer in a subsequent year, the provisions contain measures to eliminate double taxation of that income.

22.810 OUTLINE OF THE CURRENT ANTI-TAX-DEFERRAL SYSTEM

The anti-deferral rules are designed to protect the Australian revenue base from erosion by those taxpayers who use low-tax jurisdictions to shelter income and minimise tax.

The currently applicable regimes are:

- the Controlled Foreign Company (CFC) regime – Part X ITAA36, and
- the Transferor Trust regime – Division 6AAA of Part III ITAA36.

 The rules governing the accruals regime are very complex. Expert advice should be sought. The following serves only as a summary. Also note that these rules are undergoing reform (refer 22.840).

SUMMARY OF THE ACCRUALS TAXATION REGIMES

	Target interest	Active income exemption	Comparable tax jurisdiction concession	De minimis exemption	Computation of attributed income	Repatriation
Controlled foreign companies	Interests in foreign companies in respect of which the Australian resident has 'control' (actual or deemed)	1 July 2008 – Income and entity aspects	1 July 2008 – list of seven comparable tax countries (listed countries)	1 July 2008 – listed countries only	Unlisted countries – adjusted tainted income (if active income test failed) plus certain passive and notional amounts. Listed countries – eligible designated concession income (if active income test failed) plus certain passive and notional amounts	Participation dividend exemption; Foreign Income Tax Offsets (FITOs) for foreign tax paid; previously attributed income exempt
Transferor trusts	Australian resident 'transferors' of value to foreign trusts (mainly discretionary trusts)	No	1 July 2008 – CFC listed countries	1 July 2008 – listed countries only	Unlisted countries – net income of the trust, modified as required by legislation. Listed countries – eligible designated concession income and FIF income	FITOs for foreign tax paid

Up to 30 June 2010, the accruals taxation system also included the following regimes:

- the **Foreign Investment Funds (FIF)** regime in former Part XI ITAA36, which applied to investments in foreign resident entities where the Australian taxpayer generally is not deemed to have control over the entity. The FIF legislation attributed the foreign entity's income to the Australian investor to deter offshore accumulation of income earned by passive means, and
- the **Deemed Present Entitlement (DPE)** regime in former s96B and s96C ITAA36, under which an Australian taxpayer that holds the requisite 'interest' in a non-resident trust estate has to include a certain proportion of the trusts' net income for the year in their own assessable income.

The FIF and DPE rules were repealed with effect from 1 July 2010. For details of the former provisions, refer to 21.830 and 21.850 respectively in the *2010 & 2011 Tax Summary*.

Draft legislation (with some provisions yet to be finalised) in relation to a regime to replace the FIF rules has been introduced. At the time of writing, there is no clear indication as to when the legislation will be finalised and enacted. Refer to 22.840.

TEMPORARY RESIDENTS

Temporary residents of Australia (see 12.721) are not subject to the anti-tax-deferral regimes.

22.820 CONTROLLED FOREIGN COMPANIES

The Controlled Foreign Companies (CFC) regime focuses on situations where Australian resident taxpayers accrue income in offshore companies which the taxpayer effectively controls (or is deemed to effectively control).

IMPORTANT: The Federal Government is currently undertaking the process of reforming the anti-tax deferral regime (refer 22.840). Exposure draft legislation in relation to a reformed CFC regime has been released. At the time of writing, there is no indication as to when the legislation will be finalised and enacted.

A CFC is a company resident in a listed or unlisted country which satisfies one of these tests set out at s340 of the ITAA36:

- five or fewer Australian residents each having at least 1% controlling interest, whose collective associate-inclusive control interests in the company is at least 50% (ie there is deemed control)
- a single Australian entity has an associate-inclusive control interest of 40% or more (ie there is deemed control), so long as the company is not under the actual control of any other party, and
- five or fewer Australian entities (including associates) actually control the company, irrespective of the interests in the foreign company (ie there is actual control).

A foreign company limited by guarantee can still be a CFC – TD 2007/20.

An 'associate-inclusive control interest' is defined at s349 of the ITAA36. It includes direct and indirect interests. The control interest that an entity is taken to hold in the foreign company is the percentage that the entity holds, or is entitled to acquire, of the following (where the percentages are different, the greatest one applies):

- the total paid-up share capital
- the total voting rights
- the total rights to distributions of capital or profits upon winding-up, and
- the total rights to distributions of capital or profits in situations other than upon winding-up.

ATTRIBUTABLE TAXPAYER

Any attributable income of a CFC is only attributable to, and taxed in the hands of, an 'attributable taxpayer'.

An 'attributable taxpayer' in relation to a particular CFC is any Australian resident whose associate-inclusive control interest in the CFC is at least 10%. An Australian resident is also an attributable taxpayer where the foreign company is a CFC by virtue of the 'actual control' test (ie five or fewer Australian entities and their associates actually control the company) and the Australian resident is one of those actual controllers and holds an interest of at least 1%.

RESIDENCY – LISTED AND UNLISTED COUNTRIES

The types of income which are attributable to an Australian taxpayer depends on whether the CFC is a resident of a 'listed' country or an 'unlisted' country. Listed countries have tax systems comparable to that of Australia and they are Canada, France, Germany, Japan, New Zealand, the United Kingdom and the United States. All other countries are unlisted countries.

Pursuant to s332, a company is a resident of a listed country if it is a resident of that country under its domestic tax laws. This does not include a company which is a Part X Australian resident (being any Australian resident other than a dual resident which is deemed to be a resident of the other country for the purposes of the relevant tax treaty).

Under s333, a company is a resident of an unlisted country if it is a resident of that country under its domestic tax laws and is not also either a Part X Australian resident or a resident of a listed country. Where the company is a resident of more than one unlisted country, s333(2) allocates residency to the unlisted country in which the company was incorporated. Furthermore, the subsection provides that where the company is not a resident of any unlisted country (and not a resident of a listed country), it is deemed to have its residency in the country in which its management and control is located or in which it was incorporated (in that order of priority).

If a company is a resident of both a listed and an unlisted country, it is treated as a resident of the listed country.

CHANGE OF RESIDENCE TO A CONTROLLED FOREIGN COMPANY

Where a CFC ceases to be a resident of an unlisted country and becomes a resident of a listed country or of Australia, then the attributable income for the income year in which the change of residence occurs includes an amount calculated at the time of the change of residence (s457). However, no attribution is required if the company does not change its unlisted country of residence, but that country becomes a listed country pursuant to a change in the tax law.

ATTRIBUTABLE INCOME

The attributable income of a CFC is the CFC's taxable income for the relevant year, calculated as though the CFC is an Australian tax resident (s393). This is known as the 'residency assumption'.

The calculation of the notional Australian taxable income amount is subject to 'additional assumptions' which depend on whether the CFC is a resident of an unlisted country (s384) or a listed country (s385). The residency status is determined as at the end of the income year. The provisions also contain specific modifications to certain types of income.

In practice, attributable income is calculated by summing up the amounts (if any) referable to each type of income that is specifically included under s384 and s385, subject to applicable statutory modifications, and then deducting notional allowable deductions under the usual deductibility rules.

Subdivision B of Division 7 of Part X contains the statutory modifications to the operation of the Tax Acts that apply in the calculation of attributable income. Amongst other changes, the subdivision requires that certain regimes are disregarded, including double tax agreements, thin capitalisation, debt/equity rules and taxation of financial arrangements. Subdivision C contains the necessary modifications to the capital gains tax regime.

ATTRIBUTABLE INCOME OF CONTROLLED FOREIGN COMPANIES RESIDENT IN LISTED COUNTRIES

If the CFC is a resident in a listed country, the types of income included in the CFC's notional assessable income are:

- if the CFC fails the active income test – adjusted tainted income that is eligible designated concession income (see below)
- notional income that is attributable under the transferor trust rules
- notional trust income that has not been comparably taxed in a listed country
- notional income that is attributable under the FIF rules, and
- notional partnership income that, broadly, is of the same nature as the above items.

Eligible Designated Concession Income (EDCI) is Designated Concession Income (DCI) which is not subject to tax in the foreign country. Schedule 9 to the *Income Tax Regulations 1936* contains the list of the types of income in respect of each listed country which constitute DCI. Only listed countries have DCI (and EDCI).

A de minimis exemption exists for CFCs resident in listed countries. If the total of the attributable EDCI income and notional FIF income is less than the lessor of $50,000 and 5% of the CFC's gross turnover, then these amounts are not attributed (s385(4)).

ATTRIBUTABLE INCOME OF CONTROLLED FOREIGN COMPANIES RESIDENT IN UNLISTED COUNTRIES

If the CFC is a resident in an unlisted country, the types of income included in the CFC's notional assessable income are:

- if the CFC fails the active income test – adjusted tainted income
- notional income that is attributable under the transferor trust rules
- notional trust income
- notional income that is attributable under the FIF rules, and
- notional partnership income that, broadly, is of the same nature as the above items.

ACTIVE INCOME TEST

The 'active income test' is a quantitative test to determine whether a CFC is carrying on a sufficiently 'active' business. If the CFC fails the test, then certain amounts of income will be attributable to the Australian taxpayer where they would otherwise not have been attributable. The extra attributable types of income differ according to whether the CFC is resident in a listed or unlisted country but broadly encompass limited types of passive income which would not have been comparably taxed overseas.

This measure is designed to counter the sheltering of income in foreign structures which are not conducting a bona fide business.

The active income test has no qualitative element.

A CFC passes the test if it satisfies all of the below requirements (s432):

- it was in existence at the end of the statutory accounting period (typically the income year)
- it was a resident of a listed or unlisted country at all times during the statutory accounting period
- it has kept accounts according to commercially accepted accounting principles
- it complies with the substantiation requirements of s451 ITAA36
- it carried on business in the foreign country through a permanent establishment, and
- the tainted income ratio of the CFC is less than 5%.

The tainted income ratio is the proportion of total income which is 'tainted income', which broadly comprises passive income and income derived from related parties and Australian residents in relation to certain transactions. If 5% or more of the CFC's total income is tainted income, then the CFC's activities for the year are deemed to not have been those of a bona fide business.

TAINTED INCOME RATIO

The tainted income ratio is expressed as:

Gross tainted turnover / Gross turnover

Gross tainted turnover (s435) includes passive income (defined as s446) such as dividends, interest, royalties and capital gains arising on disposal of assets. It also includes tainted sales income and tainted services income, which comprise business income derived from related parties and Australian residents in relation to particular types of transactions.

Gross turnover (s434) refers to amounts shown in the CFC's financial accounts representing its gross revenue but excluding gross income amounts arising from the disposal of capital assets, the disposal of certain derivative contracts and foreign exchange fluctuations. The provisions specifically include in gross turnover any amounts in the accounts representing the net gains (ie total gains less total losses) arising in relation to the disposal of capital assets, the disposal of certain derivative contracts and foreign exchange fluctuations.

The active income test excludes amounts which comprise (s436):

- amounts which are otherwise assessable to the CFC outside of the CFC regime amounts derived through a permanent establishment in a listed country (other than the country of which the CFC is a resident) which have been taxed in a listed country and are not EDCI

- assessable trust distribution income
- the franked part of a distribution
- a non-portfolio dividend paid by a resident of a listed country or an unlisted country, and
- a non-resident reinsurance premium which was not deductible to the payer pursuant to s148(1).

PASSIVE INCOME

Passive income is exhaustively defined in s446. It includes:

- dividends, including unit trust dividends and other distributions taken to be dividends for tax law purposes
- tainted interest income (see s317)
- annuities
- tainted rental income (see s317)
- tainted royalty income (see s317)
- consideration for the assignment of intangibles
- income derived from carrying on a business of trading in tainted assets (see s317)
- net gains from the disposal of tainted assets (see s317 and s445)
- net tainted commodity gains (see s317 and s443), and
- net tainted currency exchange gains (see s317 and s444).

TAINTED SALES INCOME

Tainted sales income is exhaustively defined in s447. Broadly, it encompasses income derived from sales of goods where any of the following applies:

- the seller of the goods to the CFC was an Australian resident associate of the CFC
- the purchaser of the goods from the CFC was an Australian associate of the CFC
- the seller of the goods to the CFC was not an Australian resident but was an associate of the CFC and it sold the goods in the course of a business carried on through an Australian PE, and
- the purchaser of the goods from the CFC was not an Australian resident but was an associate of the CFC and it purchased the goods in the course of a business carried on through an Australian PE.

Where the income is derived from the sale of goods that have been manufactured by the CFC, the above tests apply to the purchase of the raw materials and to the sale of the manufactured goods respectively.

Income which satisfies the above criteria will not be tainted sales income if it passes the 'substantial alteration test'. This test is passed if the CFC substantially altered the goods prior to sale and a substantial part of the alteration was carried out by directors or employees of the CFC. Similarly, income derived from the sale of manufactured goods will not be tainted sales income if it passes the 'substantial manufacture test', which requires that a substantial part of the manufacture of the goods was carried out by directors or employees of the CFC.

There are also similar provisions in respect of primary production goods.

Tainted sales income does not include passive income as defined in s446.

TAINTED SERVICES INCOME

Tainted services income is exhaustively defined in s448. Broadly, it encompasses income derived from services provided by the CFC to an Australian resident (except where the services were provided to a foreign PE of the Australian resident) or to an Australian PE of a non-resident. The definition of tainted services income also includes income derived from certain types of insurance premiums.

The legislation sets out specific items of income which are not included in tainted services income at s448(2) to s448(6) and includes drinks, meals and entertainment.

Tainted services income does not include passive income as defined in s446.

EXEMPTION FOR AMOUNTS PAID OUT OF ATTRIBUTED INCOME

Under s23AI, an amount (eg. a dividend) received by a resident taxpayer from a non-resident company is non-assessable non-exempt income of the taxpayer to the extent that amount is paid out of profits of the company that have been previously attributed to the taxpayer.

Broadly, a CFC maintains an 'attribution account' and any amount included in the Australian taxpayer's assessable income pursuant to the CFC attribution rules is credited to the attribution account.

Attribution account payments include:

- a dividend
- a share of partnership net income, and
- a present entitlement to a share of the income of a trust estate.

TAXES PAID BY THE CONTROLLED FOREIGN COMPANY

Double taxation relief is available where the CFC has paid tax in respect of its income which is attributed to an Australian taxpayer which then has to pay tax on the same income.

A Foreign Income Tax Offset (FITO) is available to an attributable taxpayer in respect of taxes paid by the CFC where the requisite conditions are satisfied (s770-135 ITAA97):

- the attributable taxpayer is a company
- the attributable taxpayer has an attribution percentage in the CFC of at least 10%
- the tax was paid in respect of an amount that the attributable taxpayer included in its assessable income under the CFC attribution rules
- the tax was paid by the CFC in respect of which the income was attributed, and
- the tax paid by the CFC is an amount of foreign income tax, Australian income tax or Australian withholding tax as defined in the Tax Acts.

The testing time for the attributable taxpayer's attribution percentage is:

- where attribution occurs pursuant to s456 – at the end of the CFC's statutory accounting period, and
- where attribution occurs pursuant to s457 (upon the CFC's change in residence from an unlisted country to a listed country or to Australia) – at the time the change in residence occurs.

Section 770-135(7) provides that the FITO available to the attributable taxpayer equals the sum of all the relevant tax amounts paid by the CFC paid in respect of the underlying income multiplied by the attribution percentage.

Alpha Co. is an Australian company and is an attributable taxpayer of Beta Co., which is a CFC in an unlisted country. Alpha Co. has an attribution account surplus of $500,000 having previously been subjected to tax on attributable income. Beta Co. subsequently declares and pays a dividend of $500,000 which is subject to withholding tax of $50,000. This payment is non-assessable non-exempt income of Alpha Co. as the dividend does not exceed the attribution account surplus of Alpha Co. in relation to Beta Co.

Alpha Co. is entitled to a foreign tax offset of $50,000 for the foreign tax paid on the dividend of $500,000.

Under the CFC rules relating to the calculation of attributable income, a notional deduction is allowed in respect of foreign tax or Australian tax paid by the CFC in respect of income attributed to the Australian taxpayer (s393(1) of the ITAA36). However, the FITO regime contains a mechanism to prevent any 'double-dipping' of tax relief where the attributable taxpayer can access both the deduction and the FITO in respect of the same amount of tax paid by the CFC. The attributed income that is assessable under the CFC rules is grossed up for the amount of FITO relating to the underlying income as worked out under these rules (s770-135(8) of the ITAA97).

CFC FOREIGN LOSSES

The foreign losses regime allows a CFC to offset a revenue loss against any assessable income, including net capital gains. Losses are quarantined in the CFC that incurred them. An attributable taxpayer cannot utilise losses referable to one CFC to offset attributable income from another CFC.

RECORDS

Attributable taxpayers must keep records for five years to show the basis on which the attributable income included in their returns was calculated and their aggregate interest and attribution percentage in the CFC.

Each attributable taxpayer of a particular CFC must make its own elections and determinations. In the case of corporate taxpayers, these may be retained (except for capital gains rollover relief) until the Commissioner requires them (see 4.080).

22.830   TRANSFEROR TRUSTS

Subdivision D of Division 6AAA of Part III of the ITAA36 sets out the rules governing the accruals taxation regime which applies in relation to certain non-resident trust estates (the 'transferor trust' measures). The rules operate to attribute income derived by the trust to an Australian 'attributable taxpayer' where that taxpayer (known as the 'transferor') has transferred property or services to the trust.

IMPORTANT: The Federal Government is currently undertaking the process of reforming the anti-tax deferral regime (refer 22.840).

The transferor trust provisions may apply in respect of discretionary and non-discretionary trust estates.

ATTRIBUTABLE TAXPAYER

DISCRETIONARY TRUSTS

A resident is an attributable taxpayer in relation to a non-resident discretionary trust where:

- the trust was a discretionary trust at any time during the income year
- the trust was not a public unit trust at all times during the income year, and
- the taxpayer has transferred property or services to the trust at any time before or during the current year of income, with the exception of the following types of transfers:
    - transfers made in the ordinary course of business and at or about the same time identical or similar arm's length transfers involving ordinary clients or customers occurred
    - transfers where the transferor was not in a position to control the trust estate between the transfer time and the end of the current year of income, and
    - if the transfer was made before 7.30pm ACT time on 12 April 1989, and the trust estate was in existence and the transferor was not in a position to control the trust estate between this time and the end of the current year of income.

NON-DISCRETIONARY TRUSTS AND PUBLIC UNIT TRUSTS

A resident is an attributable taxpayer in relation to a non-resident non-discretionary trust or a public unit trust where:

- at all times during the income year, the trust was a non-resident non-discretionary trust or public unit trust
- the resident has transferred property or services to the trust estate after 7.30pm ACT time on 12 April 1989 and before or during the current income year, and
- the resident transferred the property or services to the trust for nil or less than arm's length consideration, and

- if the trust is a public unit trust the transfer was other than for the arm's length acquisition of its units.

TRANSFERORS WHICH ARE INDIVIDUALS

If the transferor is an individual (other than in the capacity of a trustee), the individual is an attributable taxpayer only if one of the following tests are satisfied:

- the individual first commenced residency sometime between 7.30pm ACT time on 12 April 1989 and the end of the current year of income, the transfer was made before the commencement of residency – and the trust was not a family trust,
- the individual did not first commence residency sometime between 7.30pm ACT time on 12 April 1989 and the end of the current year of income, or the transfer was not made before the commencement of residency – and the trust was not a family trust at all times from the 2001 income year, or
- the individual first commenced residency sometime between 7.30pm ACT time on 12 April 1989 and the end of the current year of income, the transfer was made before the commencement of residency – and the individual was in a position to control the trust at any time between the beginning of the first income year after the commencement of residency and the end of the current income year,

TRANSFERORS WHICH ARE PARTNERSHIPS AND TRUST ESTATES

Subsection 102AAT(2) clarifies that a partnership or a trust estate may be an attributable taxpayer of a non-resident trust.

TRANSFERORS IN A POSITION TO CONTROL THE TRUST ESTATE

Subsection 102AAT(4) provides that, in limited circumstances, a resident that was in a position to control the trust estate at any time after the current year of income will be deemed to be an attributable taxpayer in relation to the year of income even if the taxpayer had been carved-out pursuant to certain provisions.

ATTRIBUTABLE INCOME OF A NON-RESIDENT TRUST

The calculation of the attributable income of a trust is dependent upon whether the trust is resident in a listed country or in an unlisted country. Listed countries have comparable income taxation systems as Australia and are Canada, France, Germany, Japan, New Zealand, the United Kingdom and the United States. All other countries are unlisted countries.

To avoid confusion, the legislation specifically provides that double tax agreements are to be disregarded (s102AAV). Furthermore, a number of provisions in the Australian tax law are to be disregarded or modified – see from s102AAW to s102AAZC.

LISTED COUNTRIES

The attributable income of a trust estate that is resident in a listed country is the net income of the trust to the extent that it comprises either eligible designated concession income (EDCI) in relation to any listed country (see 22.820) or amounts which are assessable under s529 of the FIF rules (s102AAU(1)(b)) reduced by certain amounts (see below).

UNLISTED COUNTRIES

The attributable income of a trust estate that is resident in an unlisted country is the net income of the trust (s102AAU(1)(a)) reduced by certain amounts (see below).

INCOME EXCLUDED FROM ATTRIBUTABLE INCOME

Amounts excluded from the calculation of attributable income in respect of trust estates resident in both listed and unlisted countries are as follows (s102AAU(1)(c)):

- any amount taxed in the hands of a beneficiary of the trust under s97 of the ITAA36 or taxed in the hands of the trustee under s98, s99 or s99A of the ITAA36.
- income on which ultimate beneficiary non-disclosure tax is payable under Division 6D of the ITAA36

- any income paid to a beneficiary that is resident in a listed country within a 13 month period commencing the beginning of the income year and which has been subject to tax in a listed country
- the franked part of a distribution received from an Australian company or the part of a distribution franked with an exempting credit
- an amount included in assessable income under s207-35(1) or (3) relating to franked distributions received through certain partnerships and trusts
- any amount received that is attributable income of another transferor
- any amount received by a trustee that has been attributable to another taxpayer
- income subject to tax in a listed country that is not EDCI in relation to any listed country, and
- any foreign investment fund (FIF) income which is excluded due to an overlap with the CFC rules.

The attributable income is also reduced by any foreign tax or Australian tax paid by the trustee or any beneficiary on the attributable income.

As noted above, amounts paid to or applied for the benefit of the beneficiary (grossed up for any foreign tax paid) and taxable under s99B ITAA36 are excluded from attributable income. These distributions will be liable for additional tax to compensate the revenue for the deferral of taxation caused by the income being accumulated in the trust rather than being distributed yearly.

ASSESSABLE INCOME OF ATTRIBUTABLE TAXPAYER

The assessable income of an attributable taxpayer includes the whole of the trust's attributable income. If the taxpayer is resident for only part of the year, the attributable income included in assessable income is proportional to the number of days in the year during which the taxpayer is a resident.

If the attributable taxpayer and the trust estate have different years of income, the attributable income is calculated in reference to the trust's year of income and the amount of that attributable income to be included in the taxpayer's assessable income is calculated in proportion to the number of days in which the trust and the taxpayer's years of income overlap. This means that, where there are multiple attributable taxpayers, without the Tax Office exercising its discretion to reduce the assessable amount, each one can be assessed on all of the trust's attributable income.

DE MINIMIS EXEMPTION

The attributable income of one or more listed country trust estates will not be assessable income of a taxpayer that is an attributable taxpayer in relation to these trust estates if the total attributable income that is otherwise assessable to the taxpayer in relation to these trusts does not exceed the lesser of the 'de minimis' amounts:

- $20,000, and
- 10% of the total net incomes of each of the trust estates in relation to which the taxpayer is an attributable taxpayer for the year.

TRANSFEROR TRUST AND CONTROLLED FOREIGN COMPANY MEASURES

Taxation Ruling TR 2007/13 considers the application of the transferor trust and CFC measures where property or services are transferred by an Australian resident entity to a non-resident company in which a non-resident trustee has a direct or indirect ownership interest. The ruling indicates that the transfer of property or services would be considered to be made by the resident for the benefit of the non-resident trustee in terms of s102AAJ (3) and s344(3) ITAA36.

If the other requirements of the transferor trust provisions are satisfied, the resident entity would be an attributable taxpayer in respect of the non-resident trust estate (Division 6AAA).

If the other requirements of the CFC provisions are satisfied, the non-resident trustee would be a controlled foreign trust and the non-resident company a CFC. The resident entity would be an attributable taxpayer in respect of the CFC (Part X).

DEEMED RATE OF RETURN

If the taxpayer is unable to obtain the necessary information to calculate the attributable income of the trust, s102AAZD(4) provides that the amount that is assessable to the taxpayer is instead calculated in reference to a deemed rate of return on the market value (just before the time of the transfer) of the property or services transferred. That rate is set at 5% + the weighted statutory interest rate (see from 4.660).

KEEPING RECORDS

All attributable taxpayers must maintain details of how the attributable income included in their assessable income is calculated (except if calculated on the deemed rate of return basis) and why they are an attributable taxpayer.

22.840 ACCRUALS TAXATION REFORM

Since 2006, the Board of Taxation has comprehensively reviewed the anti-tax-deferral regime comprising the CFC, FIF, DPE and transferor trust rules, including undertaking public consultation. On 12 May 2009, the Board provided to the government its report, *Review of the foreign source income anti-tax-deferral regimes*, containing its final recommendations. The government has agreed to most of these recommendations in principle.

Between late 2009 and early 2011, the government released three exposure drafts and a consultation paper in relation to some of the Board's proposals. The Foreign Investment Fund (FIF) and Deemed Present Entitlement (DPE) rules have now been repealed.

BOARD RECOMMENDATIONS

The Board of Taxation's May 2009 report to the government contained ten proposals designed to improve the operation and fairness of the anti-tax-deferral regime whilst maintaining its effectiveness as an integrity measure. The key reforms include an outright repeal of the legislation governing the FIF and DPE regimes. In the absence of these specific regimes, the Board also proposes a significant rewrite of the CFC rules and the implementation of an anti-roll-up rule.

The ten recommendations are summarised as follows:

Recommendation	Summary
Recommendation 1	Retain the CFC provisions as the primary set of rules designed to counter tax deferral arrangements.
	• Rewrite the rules into the *Income Tax Assessment Act 1997*.
	• Apply the rewritten CFC rules to closely held fixed trusts.
	• Amend the rules to ensure that non-common law entities that confer ownership rights cannot avoid the operation of the CFC rules.
	Repeal the FIF and deemed present entitlement regimes.
Recommendation 2	Exempt Australian listed public companies from the rewritten CFC rules provided they satisfy at least one of the following eligibility criteria:
	• A comparable worldwide effective tax rate rule.
	• A sufficient distributions rule.
	• A maximum worldwide passive income rule.
Recommendation 3	Retain and modernise the existing legal-based definitions of passive income by addressing the constraints of the eligibility criteria as set out in paragraphs 3.37 to 3.38 [of the Report].
	Facilitate a group approach to determine eligibility for the CFC active income exemption.
Recommendation 4	Remove the base company income rules.
	Develop express integrity rules only where they are clearly needed and justified.
Recommendation 5	Exempt complying superannuation funds from the CFC rules.

Recommendation	Summary
Recommendation 6	Allow taxpayers to choose from the branch-equivalent calculation, market value or deemed rate of return attribution methods.
Recommendation 7	Retain the tax laws approach for the CFC branch-equivalent calculations.
Recommendation 8	Repeal section 404 of the *Income Tax Assessment Act 1936* and its attendant list. Amend the non-portfolio dividend exemption in section 23AJ of the *Income Tax Assessment Act 1936* by: • allowing other equity-like features to be taken into account to demonstrate ownership (including rights to dividends, capital and returns upon winding-up), and • precluding all debt-like interests.
Recommendation 9	Replace the current FIF rules with a specific anti-roll-up fund measure, with the broad design features of the measure being modelled on the principles set out in paragraph 3.90 [of the Report].
Recommendation 10	Remove the control requirement for pre-commencement and pre-resident transferor trusts. For foreign entities with multiple resident transferors, base the amount of income attributed to each transferor on the respective value of the property or services they transfer to the foreign entity and that, where it is not possible to determine this value, the transferor is deemed to hold a 100 per cent interest in the foreign entity. Consider further technical issues with the transferor trust rules as part of consultation on any draft legislation.

Source: Review of the Foreign Source Income Anti-Tax-Deferral Regimes – Report to the Assistant Treasurer and Minister for Competition Policy and Consumer Affairs

REFORM DEVELOPMENTS

1. CONSULTATION PAPER – REFORM OF THE CFC RULES

In January 2010, Treasury released for public comment a consultation paper containing the government's proposed reforms to the CFC regime. The key proposals are:

- that the attribution rules should target ordinary commercial concepts of passive income that are familiar to business and readily accessible ('prima facie passive income')
- amending the approach for defining what comprises the types of passive income that are at risk of attribution
- the calculation of 'attributable income' as being notional taxable income with modifications, add-ons and carve-outs
- the core concepts underlying the definition of 'attributable taxpayer' are 'control' and 'total participation interest'
- a simplified definition of a CFC which only requires a company to be non-resident and to have at least one attributable taxpayer
- the income attributed to a taxpayer is total attributable income multiplied by total participation interest, and
- the primary test to determine a taxpayer's 'participation interest' is referable to the taxpayer's rights to 'distributions of profits'; alternative tests are only operative where this cannot be determined.

The consultation paper also proposes reforms to the s23AJ non-portfolio dividend exemption. The key suggested changes are:

- broadening the type of income that is eligible for the tax exemption from a 'dividend' to a 'distribution' made in respect of an 'equity interest', and
- narrowing the scope of corporate taxpayers eligible for the tax exemption to those which are attributable taxpayers in the paying company under the proposed CFC rules.

Treasury received twenty submissions in response to the consultation paper. At time of writing, no draft legislation has yet been released to give effect to these reforms.

2. EXPOSURE DRAFT – ANTI-ROLL-UP RULE

In April 2010, the exposure draft for the *Tax Laws Amendment (Foreign Source Income Deferral) (No. 2) Bill 2010: Anti-roll-up rule* was released in respect of the government's proposals to implement an anti-roll-up rule in lieu of the FIF measures to be repealed.

The key concepts underlying the proposed measures are:

- the anti-roll-up rule is specifically designed to be a narrow anti-avoidance measure which targets the abusive tax deferral situations, being investments in particular foreign accumulation funds that re-invest interest-like returns

- the anti-roll-up rule should overcome some of the problems with the present widely applicable FIF regime, under which many taxpayers are subject to onerous compliance requirements without needing to attribute income

- the anti-roll-up rule applies where:

  - the Australian investor has an interest in a foreign accumulation fund

  - the investor obtains a tax deferral benefit as a result of holding that interest, and

  - the investor entered into the scheme with the dominant purpose of obtaining a tax deferral benefit

- the whole or part of the tax deferral benefit may be included in the investor's assessable income if the Commissioner makes such a determination, and

- where an amount is assessable under the anti-roll-up rule, actual distributions representing that income in subsequent years will be non-assessable non-exempt income to prevent double taxation.

3. EXPOSURE DRAFT – FOREIGN ACCUMULATION FUND RULES

A subsequent exposure draft of the anti-roll-up legislation – now known as the Foreign Accumulation Fund (FAF) rules – was released for public consultation in February 2011. The draft legislation, the *Tax Laws Amendment (Foreign Source Income Deferral) Bill 2011: Foreign accumulation funds*, was incomplete at the time of issue for consultation.

As at the time of writing, the government has not publicly announced any further developments in this area.

Below is a brief outline of the proposed Division 805.

Foreign accumulation fund

An entity is a FAF if it is a foreign resident company or non-resident fixed trust, it meets the 'investment requirement', and it meets the 'accumulation requirement'.

An entity may also be a FAF if it is of a kind prescribed by the regulations and meets the investments requirement.

Investments requirement

The investment requirement is satisfied if the market value of all debt interests held by the entity comprises at least 80% of the market value of all assets held by the entity.

The government has indicated that the aim of this requirement is to 'target entities investing to receive low-risk, interest-like returns'. As a consequence, an entity that largely invests in equity and not debt is unlikely to be within the scope of the regime.

Accumulation requirement

The accumulation requirement broadly stipulates that at least 20% of income is accumulated.

A company should distribute no more than 80% of profits and gains within the 'distribution period' (from the start of the FAF's statutory accounting period to three months after the end of that period).

For a trust, either it distributes no more than 80% of profits and gains within the distribution period or ensure no more than 80% of profits and gains is included in assessable income of one or more beneficiaries.

The profits and gains relevant to this requirement is the sum of the realised profits and gains of the non-resident entity and any unrealised profits and gains that are attributable to realised profits and gains of a controlled entity.

FAF attributable income

The exposure draft legislation does not include provisions relating to the calculation of FAF attributable income. It does state that the calculation will be based on the change in the market value of a FAF interest over the FAF statutory accounting period, plus distributions from the FAF.

Double tax relief

The new law will also contain provisions to avail taxpayers of double taxation relief through attribution credits. There will be a number of exceptions for lightly taxed entities.

4. EXPOSURE DRAFT – CONTROLLED FOREIGN COMPANY RULES

In February 2011, the government released the exposure draft of the *Tax Laws Amendment (Foreign Source Income Deferral) Bill 2011: main provisions* in conjunction with the exposure draft in relation to the proposed FAF rule. This draft legislation contains the proposed CFC regime.

At the time of writing, the government has not publicly announced any further developments in this area.

The key features of the proposed reforms are outlined below.

Active controlled foreign company test

An exemption from the attribution rules will be available where less than 5% of the CFC's accounting income has a passive character.

Active business income exemption

'Prima facie passive income' of an active character will be excluded from passive income if the income is attributable to a permanent establishment (PE) of the CFC, arises from the CFC competing in a market and arises substantively from the ongoing use of labour by the CFC. However, the income will be included in adjusted passive income if one of the three aforementioned characteristics of the income does not have a substantial connection with the country in which the PE is located.

The active business income exemption detailed in the draft legislation is different to that which was contemplated in the July 2010 consultation paper.

Rent from real property

Rent from real property is excluded from adjusted passive income. The policy rationale behind this proposal is that real property cannot be moved around for tax advantage and, also, there exists international agreement that the right to tax income from real property should rest with the country where the property is located.

Royalties

Where the CFC fails to substantially develop, alter or improve the intellectual property, the royalty income is subject to attribution.

Single controller concept

In the proposed law, 'control' will take its meaning from relevant accounting standards; in particular, AASB 127: *Consolidated and Separate Financial Statements*, and for joint control, AASB 131: *Interests in Joint Ventures*.

Where two entities each hold 50% of the equity interests in a CFC, the entities are deemed to jointly control the CFC.

Listed country approach

The listed country approach that underpins the current CFC regime will be maintained.

Attributable taxpayer

An attributable taxpayer must have either a direct or total participation interest of greater than zero in the CFC.

Calculation of attributable income

Under the new regime, the calculation of attributable income will continue to be based on a tax laws approach. However, the proposed law better targets the rules although modifications to the tax laws will still apply.

Non-portfolio participation exemption

The non-portfolio participation exemption on dividends received from foreign companies will become more accessible. Generally, the taxpayer company must hold at least 10% of the direct ordinary membership interests in the foreign company to access the exemption. Attributable taxpayers of a CFC will now be able to access the exemption regardless of the level of their equity interests in the CFC.

Other proposed changes

The proposed law includes provisions relating to CFC grouping, an Australian Financial Institution subsidiary exemption, an integrity rule, lightly taxed entity exemption and record keeping requirements.

5. LEGISLATION PASSED – REPEAL OF FIF AND DPE RULES

The *Tax Laws Amendment (Foreign Source Income Deferral) Act (No. 1) 2010* received Royal Assent on 14 July 2010. This Act gives effect to a full repeal of the FIF and DPE regimes. The main repeal provisions take effect from the day of Royal Assent but some of the supporting amendments has retrospective application from 14 September 2006.

Note that, when the repeal provisions came into effect, the FAF rule which is designed to replace the FIF regime was still in exposure draft stage. At time of writing, the replacement provisions still have not been finalised.

In June 2011, the government confirmed that the FAF regime (as yet unenacted) would not apply for 2010-11.

At the same time, in light of the stage of legislative development, the Tax Office announced that it would accept tax returns as lodged during the period up until the proposed legislation is enacted. Past year assessments will not be reviewed until the outcome of the proposed amendment is known.

In effect, investment income which previously fell within the FIF rules but which are not within the scope of the CFC, transferor trust or ordinary trust rules may receive a 'tax holiday' for 2010-11 (subject to existing integrity rules). How the government intends to address this (if at all) in the new FAF rules remains unknown.

Refer to the Tax Office page *Foreign Accumulation Fund rule* for details of the Tax Office's approach for 2010-11.

IMPORTANT: At the time of writing, the Tax Office has not advised of its approach to the 2011-12, 2012-13 or 2013-14 year. On the basis that there has been no progress in the legislative process, it may be reasonable to assume that the Tax Office will take the same approach as for 2010-11. However, affected taxpayers and tax agents are encouraged to confirm the treatment of specific circumstances with the Tax Office, in the absence of any publicly issued guidance.

6. GOVERNMENT RECOMMITMENT TO REFORM

In December 2013, the government confirmed that it will proceed with the anti-tax-deferral regimes review commenced by the previous government.

NOTE: At time of writing, there have been no further notable developments.

22.900 TRANSFER PRICING

Australia's transfer pricing regime is an integrity measure designed to protect Australian tax revenue against profit-shifting from an Australian taxpayer to a related party in a foreign country. The transfer pricing provisions have undergone recent reform. The current regime, contained in Subdivisions 815-B, 815-C and 815-D of the ITAA97, apply from 1 July 2013.

22.910 THE FORMER TRANSFER PRICING RULES (TO 30 JUNE 2013)

The former transfer pricing measures, contained in Division 13 of Part III of the ITAA36, have been repealed with effect from 1 July 2013.

Refer to 21.910 of the *2013 & 2014 Tax Summary* for an outline of the operation of Division 13.

22.920 THE CURRENT TRANSFER PRICING RULES

SUBDIVISIONS 815-B, 815-C AND 815-D

The purpose of the legislation which introduced Subdivisions 815-B, 815-C and 815-D is to modernise Australia's domestic transfer pricing rules. The provisions apply to both tax treaty and non-tax treaty cases, ensuring greater alignment between outcomes for international arrangements involving Australia and another jurisdiction irrespective of whether the other jurisdiction forms part of Australia's treaty network. The amendments also contain specific rules relating to transfer pricing documentation.

The amendments apply to income years commencing on or after 1 July 2013.

 The Tax Office has released a package of guidance dealing with transfer pricing documentation requirements under the new regime. See: TR 2014/8; TR 2014/6; PS LA 2014/2 and PS LA 2014/3.

The key aspects of the transfer pricing rules are summarised as follows:

Transfer pricing adjustments

A transfer pricing adjustment may be made under Subdivision 815-B, Subdivision 815-C, or the relevant transfer pricing provisions of a tax treaty.

Subdivision 815-B applies to certain conditions between entities and Subdivision 815-C applies to the allocation of actual income and expenses of an entity between the entity and its permanent establishment.

To the extent they have the same coverage as the equivalent tax treaty rules, an adjustment under Subdivision 815-B or Subdivision 815-C gives the same result as the transfer pricing provisions of a tax treaty.

Assessment of transfer pricing adjustments

Subdivisions 815-B and 815-C apply on a self-assessment basis.

Application of the rules to conditions between entities

Subdivision 815-B applies to conditions that satisfy the cross border test, irrespective of whether entities are associated or not and/or operating in treaty or non treaty countries.

The transfer pricing provisions of a tax treaty may apply in the event of an inconsistency with Subdivision 815-B.

Allocation of profits between entities and their permanent establishments

Subdivision 815-C applies to the allocation of actual income and expenses of an entity between the entity and its permanent establishment.

Subdivision 815-C applies to a foreign permanent establishment of an Australian resident and to an Australian permanent establishment of a foreign resident entity, irrespective of whether a tax treaty applies.

The transfer pricing provisions of a tax treaty may apply in the event of an inconsistency with Subdivision 815-C.

Arm's length principle

Subdivisions 815-B and 815-C and the tax treaty transfer pricing provisions apply the internationally accepted arm's length principle which is to be determined consistently with the relevant OECD Guidance material.

Record keeping
Subdivision 284-E of Schedule 1 TAA sets out optional record keeping requirements for entities to which Subdivision 815-B or 815-C applies.
Records that meet the requirements are necessary, but not sufficient to establish a reasonably arguable position for the purposes of Schedule 1 to the TAA.
If the documentation as specified in the Subdivision is not kept in respect of a matter, an entity is not able to demonstrate that it has a reasonably arguable position in relation to that matter for the purposes of Schedule 1 TAA.

Administrative penalties
Administrative penalties may apply if an assessment is amended by the Commissioner for an income year to give effect to Subdivisions 815-B or 815-C and the provisions of s284-145 of Schedule 1 TAA have been met.

Amendment period
An amendment to give effect to Subdivision 815-B or Subdivision 815-C can be made within seven years after the day on which the Commissioner gives notice of the assessment to the entity.
Some tax treaties impose specific time limits in relation to transfer pricing adjustments under the tax treaty.

KEY CONCEPTS

Some of the key concepts in the new provisions are discussed below.

Subdivision 815-B

Subdivision 815-B applies where an entity gets a transfer pricing benefit in an income year from conditions that operate between the entity and another entity in connection with their commercial or financial relations. In such instances, the actual conditions are taken not to operate and instead, the arm's length conditions are taken to operate for the purposes of working out the amount to which the transfer pricing benefit relates. These amounts can be the amount of an entity's taxable income, a loss of a particular sort or tax offsets for an income year, as well as withholding tax payable in relation to interest or royalties.

A transfer pricing benefit

The term 'transfer pricing benefit' describes the shortfall amount of Australian tax that an entity has as the result of its non-arm's length dealings with other entities. In the context of a self-assessed position under these rules, this tax advantage is a notional one as it would only be realised in the absence of the entity applying Subdivision 815-B.

An entity gets a transfer pricing benefit in an income year from conditions that operate between the entity and another entity in connection with their commercial or financial relations if:

- the actual conditions differ from the arm's length conditions
- the actual conditions result in a tax advantage in Australia, relative to the arm's length conditions, and
- the actual conditions satisfy the cross-border test.

While the Subdivision only operates where the entity would otherwise have received a tax advantage in Australia, it does not rely on or assume any tax avoidance purpose or motive.

Key terms

The following terms are discussed in detail in the explanatory memorandum to the amending legislation:

- commercial or financial relations
- the actual conditions
- the arm's length conditions
- a tax advantage in Australia relative to the arm's length conditions, and
- the cross-border test.

Consequential adjustments

The application of the proposed rules to determine the tax position of an entity could potentially impact the tax result of another entity, or of the same entity, in the same or a different income year. Accordingly, the Commissioner may make a consequential adjustment to ensure that taxpayers are subject to an appropriate amount of tax in Australia. The Commissioner may make a determination in order to:

- decrease the entity's taxable income for an income year
- increase the entity's loss of a particular sort for an income year
- increase the entity's tax offsets for an income year, or
- decrease the entity's withholding tax payable in respect of interest or royalties.

This example from the EM illustrates the operation of the power to make consequential amendments:

Consequential adjustment to interest withholding tax paid

Aus Co is an Australian resident company that has paid interest on a loan to a foreign resident related party. In accordance with the arm's length principle, Aus Co determines that the interest is excessive and, in order to apply the arm's length assumption, works out that it has received a transfer pricing benefit under section 815-120. Aus Co has therefore applied paragraph 815-115(2)(a), and increased its taxable income by reducing its allowable deductions.

The interest payment to the foreign resident associated entity was subject to interest withholding tax. Aus Co applies to the Commissioner under subsection 815-145(7) to make a consequential adjustment. The Commissioner determines that it is fair and reasonable to make a consequential adjustment in respect of the interest paid to the foreign company in excess of the arm's length amount that was subject to withholding tax.

To give effect to the determination the Commissioner refunds the relevant amount of interest withholding tax to the foreign resident associated entity.

Time limit for amending assessments

A transfer pricing adjustment to the tax position of an entity as a result of the application of Subdivision 815-B must be made within seven years of the day on which the Commissioner gives notice of the assessment to the entity.

This time limit does not apply to the Commissioner's ability to ascertain additional amounts of withholding tax payable under Subdivision 815-B. Also, there is no time limit for the Commissioner to make a consequential amendment.

Permanent establishments

The proposed Subdivision 815-C contains rules specific to permanent establishments to ensure that the amount brought to tax in Australia by entities operating at or through permanent establishments is not less than it would be if the Permanent Establishment (PE) were a distinct and separate entity engaged in the same or comparable activities under the same or comparable circumstances, but dealing wholly independently with the entity of which it is a part.

An entity gets a transfer pricing benefit under Subdivision 815-C in respect of the attribution of profits to a PE of the entity if:

- the actual profits attributed to the PE differ from the arm's length profits for the PE, and
- had the arm's length profits, instead of the actual profits, been attributed to the PE, the entity would have received a tax advantage in Australia.

A transfer pricing adjustment to the tax position of an entity as a result of the application of Subdivision 815-C must be made within seven years of the day on which the Commissioner gives notice of the assessment to the entity.

22.930 TREASURY DISCUSSION PAPERS

In recent years, the government has released two papers concerning the future direction of international tax laws.

ISSUES PAPER: IMPLICATIONS OF THE MODERN GLOBAL ECONOMY

The government has released an issues paper on multinational profit shifting.

In May 2013, Treasury released an issues paper, *Implications of the Modern Global Economy for the Taxation of Multinational Enterprises*, which examines the risks to the sustainability of Australia's corporate tax base from the way current international tax rules are able to be used to minimise or escape taxation. This analysis was informed by the Specialist Reference Group, comprising business representatives, tax professionals, academics and the community sector.

The paper identifies the following tax challenges posed by a changing global economy:

- the scale and complexity of international trade and foreign direct investment has substantially increased over the past decades
- the rise of the digital economy has meant that many transactions (such as retail sales) and functions (such as business services) that previously relied on a physical proximity with the market can be undertaken more or less anywhere. This has meant that an increasing proportion of economic activity has become tradeable – that is, subject to international competition – resulting in challenges and opportunities for businesses as well as substantial benefits to consumers, and
- Multinational Enterprises (MNEs) are increasingly operating as a single economic entity, rather than a collection of related separate entities.

Possible policy approaches include:

- actions countries might take on their own initiative (unilateral) and together with other countries (bilateral and multilateral)
- actions within the current international tax architecture and those that require fundamental reforms of that architecture, and
- measures taken in the short term to address current pressure areas and actions that will require consideration and implementation over the longer term.

SCOPING PAPER: RISKS TO THE SUSTAINABILITY OF AUSTRALIA'S CORPORATE TAX BASE

In July 2013, the government released a scoping paper on the risks to the sustainability of Australia's corporate tax base.

According to the government, a number of clear risks to the sustainability of the corporate tax regime have begun to emerge over the last decade. The increasing use of strategies to exploit gaps and inconsistencies in tax treaties, the increased 'digitisation' of industries and the challenges for the international community to effectively curb the harmful tax practices of some jurisdictions, have all highlighted shortcomings in the international tax framework. The paper examines such risks.

The scoping paper can be accessed on the Treasury website.

22.940 MULTINATIONAL PROFIT SHIFTING

BASE EROSION PROFIT SHIFTING

The OECD and numerous governments around the world are tackling Base Erosion Profit Shifting (BEPS) to address the worldwide issue of tax leakage and tax avoidance by multinational businesses.

In 2013, the G20 unanimously agreed to a 15-point BEPS Action Plan. This is intended to help secure Australian revenue bases by limiting the opportunities for double non-taxation and ensuring a globally coordinated approach to international tax challenges.

The G20 has also endorsed a common reporting standard for the automatic exchange of information. This will allow authorities to identify offshore income of multinationals and high wealth individuals.

Australia has committed to implementing the new reporting standard in 2017 with the first exchange a year later.

More information about the BEPS project, and periodic updates on the progress of the Action Plan, can be accessed on the OECD website (www.oecd.org).

SENATE INQUIRY

In the first half of 2015, the Senate Economic References Committee (the Committee) conducted an inquiry into corporate tax avoidance (the Inquiry).

The Inquiry examined tax avoidance and aggressive minimisation by multinational companies operating in Australia. At time of writing, the Committee has not released its report on the Inquiry.

More information about the Inquiry, including transcripts of the hearings, is available on the Parliament website (www.aph.gov.au).

AUSTRALIA'S APPROACH TO COMBATTING MULTINATIONAL TAX AVOIDANCE

In the 2015-16 Federal Budget, the Government announced a number of measures to combat multinational tax avoidance.

IMPORTANT! These measures will only apply to entities with global revenue of at least $1 billion.

The Government intends to introduce a targeted anti-avoidance law in the general anti-avoidance rule (Part IVA of the ITAA36) aimed at multinationals that 'artificially avoid having a taxable presence of Australia'.

The Government released the exposure draft of the amending legislation, the *Tax Laws Amendment (Tax Integrity: Multinational Anti-Avoidance Law) Bill 2015*, and explanatory material, on Budget night. These documents are available on the Treasury website (www.treasury.gov.au). Consultation closes on 9 June 2015.

Broadly, the measure is intended to target situations in which a foreign multinational is structured so that revenue from Australian sales are booked offshore and one of the principal purposes of the arrangements is to obtain a tax benefit under Australian law or a foreign law. The Commissioner will have the power to cancel any Australian tax benefit. There will be exemptions to protect legitimate economic activities.

NOTE: Australia is committed to cooperating with the OECD and other countries in the G20 to deal with these issues on a multilateral front. The OECD is in the process of finalising its recommendations for a global approach to multinational tax avoidance which will entail coordination between its members. At time of writing, the proposed anti-avoidance rule is only in exposure draft form. If this legislation receives passage through Parliament before the OECD provides its recommendations, then it can only be hoped that Australia's approach will not be incompatible with the OECD's recommended coordinated approaches.

In addition, the Government intends to double the maximum administrative penalties that can be applied by the Commissioner to large companies that enter into tax avoidance and profit shifting schemes.

Penalties will not change for taxpayers with a 'reasonably arguable' tax position.

Finally, the Government will implement the OECD's new transfer pricing documentation standards from 1 January 2016. Under the new documentation standards, the ATO will receive specified information on large companies that operate in Australia.

Goods and services tax: Overview

23

23.000 OVERVIEW OF GST

Goods and Services Tax (GST) applies at the rate of 10% on the supply of most goods, services and anything else, including importations, consumed in Australia.

All legislative references in this chapter are to *A New Tax System (Goods and Services Tax) Act 1999* (the GST Act) unless otherwise stated.

GST is essentially a supply tax on anything which passes from one registered entity to another entity. Accordingly, GST is a transaction-based tax.

Registered entities collect the GST on supplies they make and remit this to the Tax Office. They also pay GST for supplies they procure but are able to claim this back as a credit (with exceptions). The ultimate burden of the GST generally falls on any entity that is not entitled to claim back the GST.

GST revenue collected by the Commonwealth is channelled to the States and Territories.

 From 1 July 2015 the references in the GST Act to 'Australia' are being replaced with references to the 'indirect tax zone'.

It was announced in the 2015-16 Budget that, from 1 July 2017, digital products and other imported services supplied to Australian consumers by foreign entities (offshore intangible supplies to Australian consumers) will be subject to GST in a similar way to equivalent supplies made by Australian entities. Exposure draft legislation to give effect this announcement has been released.

23.010 HOW GST WORKS

GST is a multi-stage tax collected at all stages of production and distribution in the supply of goods and services. GST applies only to the 'value-added' component at each stage.

GST is a transaction-based tax. There is no general exemption concession for particular entities. Instead, exemption is based on the type of supplies made (ie. GST-free or input taxed supplies). Supplies will be either:

- Taxable supplies: GST is payable on these supplies.
- GST-free supplies: No GST is payable on these supplies.
- Input taxed supplies: No GST is payable on these supplies.
- Outside the scope of the GST Act: No GST is payable on these supplies.

The first three categories of supplies are identified in the GST Act.

Under s9-5, a taxable supply is such unless it is specified as a GST-free or input taxed supply. A taxable supply generally arises if the supplier is registered for GST, the supply is made for consideration, the supply is made in the course of an enterprise carried on and it is connected with Australia (to be called the indirect tax zone from 1 July 2015).

The GST is designed to ensure it does not become a cost to business. It achieves this by allowing a registered enterprise an input tax credit for the GST incurred on its creditable acquisitions and creditable importations of materials, plant, equipment and services in the course of its activities.

The GST incurred may be offset against the GST payable on the supplies made by the registered enterprise. Input tax credits may only be claimed by registered enterprises. Entitlement to claim input tax credits effectively keeps transactions between enterprises free of tax.

23.011 SUPPLIES NOT SUBJECT TO GST

GST-FREE SUPPLIES

Certain supplies made are GST-free. GST is not payable on these supplies. However, a credit (input tax credit) is available for tax paid on acquisitions (inputs) made in carrying on the enterprise that relates to making GST-free supplies (see 23.400). GST-free supplies include:

- basic food (see 23.480)
- health and medical services (see 23.430)
- educational services (see 23.441)
- childcare services (see 23.442)

- exports of goods and services for consumption outside Australia (see 23.410)
- religious services (see 23.470)
- certain charitable activities (see 23.450)
- taxes and charges imposed at all levels of government (including water, sewerage and drainage services) (see 23.490)
- supplies of retirement village accommodation (see 23.435)
- sale of a going concern (see 23.460)
- international transport and travel including international air and sea travel and domestic air travel purchased overseas by non-residents (see 23.421)
- precious metals, in some circumstances (see 23.490)
- supplies through inwards duty free shops (see 23.422)
- grants of land by governments
- sale of farm land under certain conditions (see 23.490)
- subdivisions of farm land for family residential purposes (see 23.490), and
- cars for disabled people (see 23.490).

INPUT TAXED SUPPLIES

Supplies may be 'input taxed'. GST is not payable on these supplies. However, unlike GST-free supplies, supplies acquired in making an input taxed supply are not acquired for a creditable purpose (see 23.220 for definition of creditable purpose) and therefore no input tax credit is available for GST paid on acquisitions (inputs) connected with making such supplies (see 23.300). Input taxed supplies are confined to:

- financial supplies (see 23.310)
- residential rents (see 23.320)
- sale of residential premises (excluding new premises) (see 23.330)
- precious metal (unless it is GST-free) (see 23.340)
- food at school tuckshops (if election exercised - see 23.350), and
- fund-raising activities conducted by endorsed charities (if election exercised) (see 23.360).

OUTSIDE GST SYSTEM

Some transactions may fall outside the GST system. These are not treated as taxable supplies, GST-free or input taxed. These transactions include private or domestic activities, supply made for nil consideration (eg. gifts), supplies made that are not in the course of furtherance of an enterprise, supplies made by an entity that is not registered for GST and supplies not connected with Australia.

23.100 TAXABLE SUPPLY

Anyone making a taxable supply has a liability to pay GST on that supply (s9-40).

A taxable supply is made by an entity if all these elements are satisfied (s9-5):

- there is a supply (s9-10)
- for consideration (s9-15)
- the supply is made in the course or furtherance of an enterprise (s9-20) that the entity carries on
- the supply is connected with Australia (s9-25), and
- the person making the supply is registered for GST purposes or required to be registered (s23-5).

A taxable supply does not arise if any one of the above elements is not met in respect of the supply. This means no GST is payable for that supply and no input tax credit may be claimed. However, a supply is not taxable to the extent that:

- it is GST-free under Division 38
- it is input taxed under Division 40
- a section of the GST Act or another Act states that a supply is not a taxable supply, or
- the supply falls outside the GST system.

If a supply is both GST-free and input taxed, the supply will be GST-free and not input taxed (s9-30(3)(a)).

NOTE: A supply of a right is GST-free if that right is a right to receive a supply that would be GST-free (s9-30(1)(b)). Similar provision applies to the supply of a right to receive an input taxed supply (s9-30(2)(b)).

23.110 WHAT IS A 'SUPPLY'? (s9-10)

The definition of supply for GST purposes is very broad (s9-10), being 'any form of supply whatsoever'. It goes on to specifically include the following:

- a supply of goods
- a supply of services
- the provision of advice or information
- a grant, assignment or surrender of real property
- a creation, grant, transfer, assignment or surrender of any right
- a financial supply
- an entry into, or release from, an obligation to do anything, or to refrain from an act or to tolerate an act or situation, and
- any combination of any two or more of the matters referred to above.

As a general rule, the act of providing something by one entity to another is a supply for GST purposes. Once a supply is identified, it still needs to be ascertained as to whether it is a taxable supply.

However, a supply does not include the supply of money, except where the money provided is consideration for some supply which itself is a supply of money (see 23.310).

Some provisions in the GST Act may determine when a supply is not a taxable supply, when there is no supply or when a supply is made. For example supplies that are not taxable supplies as determined by the GST Act include:

- supplies between members of a GST group (Division 48) or religious GST group (Division 49)
- settlement of a claim under an insurance policy (Division 78) or a compulsory third party scheme (Division 79)
- supply of certain type of vouchers (Division 100), and
- income tax related transactions such as transfer of unused tax losses, tax sharing agreement etc. (Division 110).

For more details of special rules relating to 'supply' see GSTR 2006/9 paragraph 47.

GSTR 2006/9 sets out the Tax Office's view of the meaning of supply. The Ruling considers each of the four subsections of s9-10 and specific provisions relating to 'supply' outside the s9-10 definition. The Ruling considers the concept of 'supply' in the context of transactions between two parties and between more than two parties (a tripartite arrangement). The Ruling sets out ten propositions to assist in identifying the supply or supplies made in a transaction between two parties. A further six propositions are set out to assist in identifying the supply or supplies in a tripartite arrangement.

The Federal Court in *Secretary to the Department of Transport (Vic) v FC of T* [2009] FCA 1209 confirmed that, in determining an entity's eligibility to the entitlement to input tax credits, the relevant perspective is the standpoint of the entity itself: the entity makes an acquisition only if the entity is the recipient of the supply, given that the GST law does not deal with tripartite arrangements except in limited circumstances.

In *Commissioner of Taxation v Qantas Airways Limited* [2012] HCA 41, the majority of the High Court held that the taxpayer did make a taxable supply and was liable to pay GST on fares when a passenger paid for airline travel but cancelled the booking or did not board the flight and did not receive a refund. The Conditions of Carriage gave rise to a legally enforceable contract between the taxpayer and the passenger. The majority of the Court concluded that the conditions did not provide an unconditional promise to carry the passenger and baggage on a particular flight. Rather, they supplied something less than that. The supply identified by the court was 'at least a promise to use best endeavours to carry the passenger and baggage, having regard to the circumstances of the business operations of the airline'. The fares were found to be consideration for that supply.

The Tax Office's Decision Impact Statement relating to the case indicates that the Commissioner's published views in relation to the interpretation issue are consistent with the High Court decision.

In FC of T v MBI Properties Pty Ltd [2014] HCA 49 the High Court pointed out that the concept of 'supply' is of 'wide import' and that the decision in FC of T v Qantas [2012] HCA 41 shows that it is wrong to consider that one transaction must always involve the making of just one supply.

The MBI case raised the question whether the purchaser of premises subject to a lease made supplies to the lessee. In holding that the purchaser did make supplies for the purposes of GST the court pointed out that in the case of a lease there will in general be a supply which occurs at the time of entering into the lease and that there will then be at least one further supply which occurs progressively throughout the term of the lease. That supply will occur by means of the lessor observing and continuing to observe the express or implied covenant of quiet enjoyment under the lease. The thing of value which the lessee thereby receives is continuing use and occupation of the leased premises.

NOTE: The Commissioner has stated that GSTR 2006/9 is being reviewed in light of the decision of the High Court in FC of T v MBI Properties Pty Ltd [2014] HCA 49 and of the decision of the Full Federal Court in ATS Pacific Pty Ltd v FC of T [2014] FCAFC 33.

In GSTR 2014/3 the Commissioner ruled that a transfer of bitcoin from one entity to another is a 'supply' for GST purposes and that the exclusion from the definition of supply for supplies of money does not apply to bitcoin because bitcoin is not 'money' for the purposes of the GST Act. Also, the supply of bitcoin is not a 'financial supply'.

NOTE: GSTR 2012/1 sets out the Commissioner's views in relation to the GST implications of certain loyalty programs, including whether a supply is made in specified circumstances.

23.111   COMPULSORY ACQUISITION OF LAND

Land compulsorily acquired by a government authority without the landowner doing anything will not be considered as 'making a supply' and compensation made to the landowner will also not be treated as consideration for any supply (GSTR 2006/9).

According to GSTR 2006/9 'to make a supply' an entity is required to take some action to cause the supply to occur. However, it is not necessary for the act to be voluntary. In Hornsby Shire Council v Commissioner of Taxation [2008] AATA 1060 the Tribunal held that CSR had made a supply on the basis that CSR entered into an obligation within s9-10(2)(g) when it requested that the taxpayer acquire the land, or by way of surrender of land within s9-10(2)(d) as a result of requesting the taxpayer to acquire the land. The facts of the case clearly demonstrated a positive action by the landowner, CSR, when it exercised its statutory right to compel the council to acquire its land.

The Tribunal affirmed the Tax Office's view that making a supply requires some positive action.

NOTE: In the decision impact statement on the decision of the High Court in FC of T v MBI Properties Pty Ltd [2014] HCA 49 it is stated that the proposition in GSTR 2006/9 that an entity must do something to make a supply is to be reviewed given the High Court's statement about it being incorrect to consider that the making of a supply must always involve the taking of some action on the part of the supplier.

In SXGX v FCT [2011] AATA 110, the taxpayer was the registered proprietor of vacant land which was identified as being in the path of a proposed busway. The taxpayer sold the land to the State of Queensland. The AAT rejected the taxpayer's argument that it did not make a taxable supply. The AAT held that, in terms of the legal requirements for the compulsory acquisition of land under the relevant Queensland legislation, the land had not been acquired by way of compulsory acquisition initiated by the relevant state authority. Instead, the AAT concluded that the taxpayer had initiated the acquisition at a time the statutory process of resumption was in prospect but it had not come to fruition. Accordingly, the AAT concluded that the sale by the taxpayer to the State constituted a supply and it was a supply for consideration.

23.120   WHAT IS 'CONSIDERATION'? (s9-15)

'Consideration' is broadly defined to include any payment, or any act or forbearance, in connection with, in response to, or for the inducement, of a supply of anything.

The fact that any of these acts might not be voluntary, rather, in accordance with an order or settlement, in relation to a matter before a court or tribunal, does not prevent it from forming consideration.

A supply is not subject to GST unless it is made for consideration. Therefore, there must be sufficient nexus between the supply and consideration in order for a supply to be a taxable supply. The term 'in connection with' used in s9-15 has been held to be broader in scope than the term 'for'. The nexus test is an objective test and requires the consideration of the true character of the transaction (GSTR 2001/6 paragraph 64-72). In *Badaoui and Konig and Commissioner of Taxation* [2011] AATA 672, the payments made by the taxpayer were purported to be consideration for a particular supply but the evidence could not conclusively support this. The Tribunal was able to develop a plausible (and, in its view, probable) alternative postulate that the payments may relate to certain other supplies. This case highlights the importance of clearly documenting the supply to which a particular amount of consideration relates.

Consideration includes more than just monetary payment for something. It also includes:

- consideration in kind
- payments by way of barter, and
- payments by someone other than the recipient of the supply.

For example, forgiving a debt in exchange for a supply would be consideration for the supply. However gifts to not-for-profit bodies would not be consideration as there is no supply.

In *Rod Mathiesen Truck Hire Pty Ltd atf The Mathiesen Family Trust v FC of T* [2013] AATA 496, the parties entered into a vendor finance arrangement, under which the purchase price was payable after settlement. The Tribunal held that all of the consideration was received at the time of settlement. Noting that the taxpayer reported GST on a cash basis, this had the effect of imposing a GST liability on the vendor for the full amount of the purchase price of the land at that time.

GSTR 2012/2 sets out the Commissioner's views on when a financial assistance payment is consideration for a supply.

In *Case 14/2009* [2009] AATA 854, the AAT held that 'cash back' payments made by a wholesaler to customers who purchase the goods from an interposed retailer do not have the effect of reducing the value of the original 'consideration' received by the wholesaler for the supply of the goods to the retailer. The Tribunal made its decision on the premise that the GST is a transaction tax applied to 'supplies'. The cash back payment, made directly from the taxpayer to the end customer, were not made in connection with either of the two supplies - the first being the supply made from the taxpayer to the retailer and the second being the supply made from the retailer to the end customer.

However, the Full Federal Court has held that In particular circumstances, rebates or incentive payments paid by manufacturers to a taxpayer can constitute consideration in respect of taxable supplies that the taxpayer makes to its customers: *A.P. Group Limited v Commissioner of Taxation* [2013] FCAFC105. This case deals with four classes of payments that are received by a motor vehicle dealership from various suppliers (manufacturers). The Tax Office has issued a ruling which is intended to provide practical guidance to the motor vehicle industry following the decision of the Full Federal Court in the *AP Group Limited* case (GSTR 2014/1).

NOTE: Salary and wages will not be consideration for a taxable supply because the payment of wages or salary to an employee does not meet the third requirement of a taxable supply, that is that the supply is made in the course or furtherance of an enterprise. An enterprise does not include an activity done by a person as an employee (s9-20(3)). However, reimbursements to employees may be treated as consideration (Div 111) (see 24.413).

NOTE: GSTD 2006/3 has determined that settlement adjustments are to be taken into account in determining the consideration for the supply or acquisition of real property.

23.121   BOOK ENTRIES

Book entries can amount to the provision or receipt of consideration for the purposes of attributing GST payable and input tax credits where the supplier and the recipient agree to discharge mutual liabilities by way of set-off. A set-off occurs if each party has made a supply to the other and each party is required to pay the other for the supply made to it.

It can also occur if the parties agree that payment is to be achieved by the supplier lending or arranging to lend the recipient the money needed to pay for the supply. In this case, the obligation to pay for the supply is replaced by the obligation to repay the loan which was lent to pay for the supply. It is important to distinguish a genuine loan from a supply made on credit. When a supply is made on credit, the consideration is made when the actual payment is eventually made (and not on the date of the book entries).

Any excess amount owed by one party to the other following the set-off may be discharged by monetary or non-monetary consideration.

There must be a binding agreement between the parties for the set off method to apply (GSTD 2004/4).

Consideration is provided or received on the date that the book entries are made, even if the obligation to pay arose at an earlier time (GSTD 2004/4).

23.122   LIABILITIES ASSUMED BY PURCHASER OF AN ENTERPRISE

An assumption of liability occurs when the purchaser agrees to assume some of the vendor's existing obligations (ie. creditors, outstanding lease payments etc). The effective assumption of liabilities, whether the liability is quantifiable or unquantifiable, by the purchaser of an enterprise forms part of the consideration for the sale of the business (GSTR 2004/9). This principle applies equally to the sale of a business that qualifies for the going concern concession under s38-325.

A computer retailer assembles computers, and sells the fully installed computers to their clients with a three year warranty. The retailer enters into an agreement to sell its enterprise to a big computer manufacturer.

In order to maintain the credibility of the retailer for the continuity of the enterprise, under the agreement the purchaser agrees to honour all warranty obligations to the vendor's clients in respect of defective products sold by the vendor prior to selling the enterprise. By referring to the prior history of claims and sale volume, the two parties agree on the estimated market value of the warranty liability to be $12,000.

The purchaser pays $488,000 in cash to the vendor and further agrees to assume another $20,000 trade creditor liability. As the parties are dealing with each other at arm's length, the total consideration should include:

Monetary consideration	*$488,000*
Assumption of quantifiable liability – trade creditors	*$20,000*
Assumption of unquantifiable liability	
– estimated market value of warranty liability	*$12,000*
Total consideration	***$520,000***

However, the consideration for the supply of the enterprise should not include any liabilities imposed by statute (eg. liability to pay long service leave) as the transfer of such liabilities is as a result of the operation of the statute and not due to the agreement between the vendor and purchaser. Hence any reduction allowed at settlement or any payment from the vendor to the purchaser in respect of a statutory liability imposed on the purchaser is considered to be a reduction to the price of the enterprise reflecting the fact that the enterprise is worth less to the purchaser as a result of the liabilities that will be imposed on the purchaser by the statute.

Note that GSTR 2004/9 does not consider the purchaser's future obligations under an ongoing agreement (such as a hire purchase agreement) assigned to the purchaser as part of the consideration for the supply of the enterprise. This is because these future payments are for the third party's ongoing performance of the agreement to the purchaser and does not have a direct connection to the supply of the enterprise by the vendor.

NOTE: This principle does not apply to a transaction, the substance of which is an assumption of another entity's liability in return for payment, where there is no supply of an enterprise.

23.123   STOLEN TAKINGS

Takings, which represent consideration for taxable supplies, that are stolen are still subject to GST. An entity's GST liability remains unaltered even if all of the takings are stolen.

23.124   SECURITY DEPOSITS, CANCELLATION FEES, DAMAGES, PENALTIES AND FINES

SECURITY DEPOSITS

Special rules concerning how to treat security deposits are set out in Division 99. The general rule is that a deposit held as security for the performance of an obligation is not treated as consideration for a supply until such time as the deposit:

- is forfeited due to failure to perform the obligation, or
- is applied as all or part of the consideration for the supply.

A deposit does not become consideration for a supply if a vendor returns the deposit to the customer. Special rules applying to security deposits are discussed in greater detail in Chapter 24 (see 24.382).

CANCELLATION FEES

Cancellation of a supply before the time of the intended supply, failing to take advantage of an arrangement by not showing up at the time of the intended supply (no show) or showing up after the time of the intended supply (late show) may incur cancellation fees.

According to GSTR 2009/3 a supply for which a cancellation fee may be consideration can be:

- an intended supply – a supply which was agreed between the purchaser and supplier but which the supplier did not avail themselves of, or
- a different supply:
  - facilitation supply – relates to all the things a supplier does to put itself in a position to make the intended supply
  - cancellation supply – relates to the supply of administration services to unwind an arrangement or make a refund, or
  - release supply – relates to creation or surrender of rights and or a release supply that occurs when an arrangement is cancelled.

If the intended supply is made but the customer does not avail themselves of it through a no show, any payment for the intended supply or cancellation fee charged representing the work done by the supplier to make the intended supply remains consideration for that supply.

If the actual supply made upon cancellation or no show is different from the intended supply, the GST status of the actual supply must be analysed to determine whether it is taxable, GST-free or input taxed.

NOTE: According to GSTR 2009/3 when a facilitation supply includes a right to receive an intended supply, the Commissioner considers the right to be the dominant part of the facilitation supply. If the right is to receive an intended supply that is either GST-free or input taxed, the facilitation supply would therefore also be GST-free or input taxed (s9-30(1)(b) and s9-30(2)(b)).

NOTE: The GST status of a release supply is not determined by the GST status of the intended supply.

The release supply discussed in GSTR 2009/3 relates only to when an intended supply has not been made at the time of release. If a supply has been made or is on a progressive basis, any termination payment or cancellation fee charged will be considered to have sufficient nexus with the earlier supply or the supply being made. Therefore, the cancellation fee or termination payment is said to be an adjustment to the consideration and is an adjustment event under Division 19 (see 24.361) and not consideration for a release supply.

NOTE: Upon cancellation of an intended supply, the forfeited security deposit can be consideration for one or more supplies and is attributed in accordance with Division 99.

PENALTIES AND FINES

Penalties and fines should be distinguished from security deposits. Penalties and fines are not subject to the special rules set out under Division 99. Such an amount is not a deposit but a penalty or liquidated damage if the amount is unreasonably high. Unless there is a greater than normal risk of significant losses involved which warrant a higher percentage of deposit to be held, an amount is normally considered to be unreasonably high if it is greater than 10% of the total amount payable. GSTR 2006/2 gives example of factors when a higher level of deposit may be required.

Penalties and fines are generally not subject to GST because they are not consideration for any supply but instead are imposed for punishment or deterrence. However, under certain circumstances where a penalty/fine or damages imposed is related to a supply the payment may be subject to GST (see 23.125).

23.125   COURT ORDERS AND OUT-OF-COURT SETTLEMENTS

The GST consequences of a court order or out-of-court settlement will largely depend on whether payment made under the order or settlement constitutes consideration for a supply. Section 9-15 defines consideration and s9-15(2A) provides that consideration can be in compliance with an order of – or settlement relating to proceedings before – a court, tribunal, or other body that has the power to make orders.

GSTR 2001/4 sets out the Commissioner's view on GST consequences resulting from court orders and out-of-court settlements. The Ruling explains the circumstances in which, because there is a link or nexus between a payment (or act or forbearance) and a supply, the payment represents consideration for a supply.

Consideration for a supply requires there to be a sufficient nexus between the supply and the payment.

A supply may include the entering into, or the release from, an obligation, and the refraining from an act. Supplies can be classified as follows:

- **Earlier supply:** Where the subject of the dispute is an earlier transaction in which a supply was made involving the parties.
- **Current supply:** A new supply may be created by the terms of the settlement.
- **Discontinuance supply:** The surrendering of a right to pursue legal action, entering into an obligation to refrain from further legal action and releasing another party from further obligations.

Where the dispute is in relation to incidents not relating to a supply, damages for such loss or injury does not constitute a supply under s9-10. Examples of such disputes are claims for damages arising out of:

- property damage
- negligence causing loss of profits
- wrongful use of trade name
- breach of copyright
- termination or breach of contract, and
- personal injury.

Where the only supply (other than a discontinuance supply) in relation to a court order or out-of-court settlement is an earlier or current supply and a sufficient nexus exists between payment made in compliance with that order or settlement and the earlier or current supply, the payment is consideration for that supply.

Where the only supply in relation to an out-of-court settlement is a discontinuance supply, the Commissioner considers there is insufficient nexus between the payment and that supply because such payment is typically a subject of a damages claim which under s9-10 does not constitute a supply.

GST AND JUDGMENT INTEREST

Pre-judgment interest provides compensation for being deprived of the use of money. The assessment of interest is over and above the awarding of damages by the court. The awarding of pre-judgment interest is separate to the cause of action and has no connection to any supply which may be the basis of the litigation.

There is no nexus between the payment of interest and any earlier supply or current supply relating to the dispute and therefore any payment of pre-judgment interest is not consideration for a supply.

23.126   NON-MONETARY CONSIDERATION

If the consideration for a supply is not consideration expressed as an amount of money, the GST is 1/11th of the GST inclusive market value of that consideration. If monetary and non-monetary considerations are received, both must be taken into account for the purposes of working out the GST liability (s9-75). GSTR 2001/6 provides principles around identifying non-monetary consideration for a supply and also considers when a non-monetary consideration can become a taxable supply.

BARTER TRANSACTION

It is common in cases of non-monetary consideration for parties to enter into multiple obligations. The act of providing non-monetary consideration may in turn give rise to the recipient of the supply making a taxable supply themselves (barter transaction). Where this happens, you need to determine the GST consequences of the supply you make. The GST inclusive market value of the consideration received for the supply you make must be determined to account for the GST payable you may now be liable for. However, you will be able to claim an input tax credit for the supply made to you.

Evan sells a computer to Philip (of whom GST registered), who provides office furniture as consideration for the computer. The GST inclusive market value of the computer and the furniture are both $5,500. Evan is making a taxable supply of the computer to Philip for non-monetary consideration. The GST payable by Evan is $500, being 1/11th of the GST inclusive market value of the furniture. Evan, however, is entitled to an input tax credit of $500 as he has acquired furniture as part of the taxable supply he has made to Philip. Philip has made a taxable supply of furniture to Evan and is liable for $500 GST being 1/11th of the GST inclusive market value of the computer.

Philip also has made a creditable acquisition of the computer and is entitled to an input tax credit of $500.

NOTE: When parties to a transaction are acting at arm's length, the goods, services or other things being exchanged are assumed to be of equal value. If this is not the case, then a reasonable GST inclusive market value of the things exchanged must be arrived at.

TRADED-IN GOODS

Goods that are traded-in for new goods are part of the consideration for those goods.

Fred runs a battery replacement service. New batteries are installed for $100 provided that Fred gets to keep the customer's old battery. If customers retain the old battery, they are charged an additional $10.

The old battery represents non-monetary consideration and must be added to the monetary consideration to arrive at Fred's GST liability for the supply of new batteries to customers.

GIFTS

A non-monetary payment is sometimes made by an entity to induce another party to make or continue to make purchases from the entity. Where the payment is truly unconditional (ie. a gift), it is not consideration for a supply by that other party.

A donor is entitled to claim an input tax credit for the cost of the gift if the acquisition of the gift is made in the course of carrying on its enterprise.

23.127   VOUCHERS (Division 100)

A voucher is any voucher, token, stamp, coupon or similar article or prepaid phone card or facility. However, a postage stamp is not a voucher (s100-25). Prepaid phone cards or facilities are treated as vouchers for the purposes of Division 100.

The Tax Office's view on GST and vouchers is set out in GSTR 2003/5.

For a voucher to fall within s100-25, it must:

- have a single function or purpose
- the presentation of the voucher must be integral to supplies on redemption, and
- upon redemption, the voucher must entitle the holder to receive supplies (GSTR 2003/5).

Further, the Commissioner has considered in ATO ID 2013/24 circumstances in which unredeemed and expired gift vouchers will necessitate an increasing adjustment for GST purposes.

A supply of a voucher is not a taxable supply if the voucher has a monetary value stated on the voucher and the holder of the voucher is entitled to supplies up to the stated monetary value and the consideration for the voucher does not exceed that monetary value (s100-5). Instead, this voucher will count as consideration in respect of a supply when it is redeemed. The dollar amount that will count toward consideration is the monetary amount for which it is redeemed. If it is fully redeemed, it is the full monetary value stated on the voucher, otherwise, it is the amount of the stated monetary value that is actually redeemed (s100-12).

A voucher that does not fall within Division 100 will be a taxable supply provided it satisfies the s9-5 taxable supplies requirements and it is neither a GST-free supply nor an input taxed supply. Such vouchers will attract GST when the voucher is sold, and not when redeemed. Examples of vouchers that do not fall within Division 100 are movie, bus or airline tickets, debit cards etc.

Section 100-18 simplifies accounting for GST on commissions and similar payments on a supply of a voucher through a distribution chain. Where a supplier enters into an arrangement (in writing) with a distributor for the supply of a voucher to a third party, and the supplier pays the distributor an amount of commission or similar payment, the supply for the commission is not a taxable supply (s100-18).

 An issuer of a prepaid phone card (voucher) sells the prepaid phone card with a stated monetary value of $44 to a retailer for $33 and the retailer subsequently sells the voucher to the consumer for $44.

On redemption of the prepaid phone card for the phone services from the issuer, the prepaid phone card is treated as consideration for the supply of the phone services. Therefore, the issuer is liable to pay GST of $4 (being 1/11th of $44) rather than $3 (being 1/11th of $33 in which it has received).

The supply from issuer to retailer is not considered to be a taxable supply under s100-18.
The supply from the retailer to the consumer is also not a taxable supply under s100-5. The only taxable supply in this instance is when the prepaid phone card (voucher) is redeemed.

23.128   SUPPLIES TO ASSOCIATES (Division 72)

Division 72 of the GST Act ensures that supplies to associates for no or inadequate consideration are brought within the GST system by applying 10% GST on the GST-exclusive market value of the goods. If the goods in question are GST-free or input taxed then there is no GST payable. Therefore supplies that would otherwise fail to be taxable supplies because of the lack of consideration provided (one of the requirements under s9-5) may be treated as taxable supplies due to the operation of Division 72.

A supply to an associate for no consideration that would be a particular kind of supply (such as a sale) if made for consideration will be taken to be such a supply.

An acquisition from an associate for no consideration that would be by way of a particular means (such as a sale) if consideration was provided will be taken to be such an acquisition.

The definition of 'associate' for GST purposes is pursuant to s318 ITAA36 and is discussed at 16.110.

NOTE: If the associate is registered for GST or required to be registered for GST and acquires the thing solely for a creditable purpose, Division 72 will not apply.

 If you are raising journal entries to reflect goods taken for personal use, then you must not neglect to account for a corresponding GST liability.

The supply of real property to an associate may interact with the Division 75 margin scheme provisions. A supply by an entity of real property that was acquired from a registered associate for no consideration (and therefore was not a taxable supply) will not be entitled to apply the margin scheme if the associate from which the entity acquired the property had previously acquired it as a taxable supply without the application of the margin scheme (s75-11(6)).

There may be consideration for the supply of real property between associates in an in specie contribution or distribution. Under such circumstances, s75-11(7) applies to ensure that the margin is calculated on the difference between the consideration and the GST-inclusive market value of the real property at the time of acquisition.

Further, consideration for the real property supplied under the margin scheme to an associate is taken to be the GST-inclusive market value of the property at the time of the supply (s75-13).

NOTE: GSTR 2009/1 on general law partnerships and the margin scheme highlights the interaction of the margin scheme with the associate provisions.

For further details on the interaction of margin scheme and the associate rules refer to 24.344.

23.129   GOVERNMENT TAXES, FEES AND CHARGES (Division 81)

Under Division 81, the payment of certain government taxes, fees and charges as determined by the Treasurer do not constitute the provision of consideration.

NOTE: Water, sewerage and drainage supplies may be GST-free under Subdivision 38-I (see 23.490).

 Reimbursement of government taxes, fees and charges by tenants leasing a commercial property may be subject to GST – see 24.341.

The principles-based legislative exemption operates as follows:
- the GST basic rules will apply to the payment of an Australian tax or Australian fee or charge in the first instance
- the payment, or the discharging of a liability to make such a payment of an Australian tax, is not treated as consideration for a supply made by the entity to which the payment is made. Such a payment will not be subject to GST
- however, regulations can be made to treat the payment of a tax, or of a type of tax, as consideration for a supply, in which case it may be subject to GST
- a payment or the discharging of a liability to make such a payment, of certain categories of Australian fees or charges is not treated as consideration for a supply made by the entity to which the payment is made. Such a payment will not be subject to GST, and
- however, regulations can be made to treat the payment of an Australian fee or charge, or of a kind of payment, as consideration for a supply, in which case it may be subject to GST (in accordance with the GST basic rules).

Regulations operate in conjunction with the principles-based legislative exemption.

23.130   WHAT IS AN 'ENTERPRISE'? (s9-20)

One of the requirements of a taxable supply is that the supply is made in the course or furtherance of an enterprise that you carry on (s9-5(b)). Further, an entity cannot be registered for GST unless it is carrying on an enterprise. Carrying on an enterprise is also a prerequisite for applying for an ABN. The term 'enterprise' is widely defined at s9-20(1) as an activity, or series of activities done:
- in the form of a business (including business-like activities that are not carried out for profit eg. associations or non-profit clubs), or
- in the form of an adventure or concern in the nature of trade (this can include a one-off adventure), or
- on a regular or continuous basis in the form of a lease, licence or grant of an interest in property, or
- by trustees of certain trusts, or
- by a trustee of a complying superannuation fund or, if there is no trustee of the fund, by a person who manages the fund, or

- by a charity, or
- by the Commonwealth or a State or Territory or by a body corporate, or corporation sole, established for a public purpose by or under a law of the Commonwealth, a State or a Territory.

'Carrying on' an enterprise includes doing anything in the course of commencement or termination of the enterprise (s195-1).

The taxpayer in *Trustee of the Family Trust v FCT* [2010] AATA 876 argued that as a trustee of the family trust, it was carrying on an enterprise because the 'economic group' to which it belonged (involving the trust and other entities and individuals) carried on an enterprise. The AAT rejected the taxpayer's argument. In the AAT's view, the enterprise must be carried out at entity level rather than the 'economic group' level.

'In the course or furtherance of an enterprise' is not defined in the GST Act. However, by reference to the Explanatory Memorandum to the *A New Tax System (Goods and Services Tax) Bill 1998* any supplies made in connection with an enterprise are deemed to be 'in the course or furtherance of', including a one-off commercial transaction with a profit-making intention. An act done for the purpose or object of furthering an enterprise, or achieving its goals, is a furtherance of an enterprise although it may not always be in the course of that enterprise. For example transactions conducted infrequently by registered entities even though they do not relate to the normal activities of a business (eg. sale of a capital asset such as a surplus company car owned by a food retailer). However, 'in the course or furtherance of an enterprise' does not include supply of private commodities.

Section 9-20(2) excludes certain activities from the definition of an 'enterprise'. This includes an activity or series of activities done:

a. by a person as an employee or in connection with earning withholding payments including: payment to employee, payment to company director, payment to office holder, and, payment under labour hire arrangement, or specified by regulations, or
b. as a private recreational pursuit or hobby, or
c. by an individual (with exceptions) or a partnership where all or most of the partners are individuals, without reasonable expectation of profit or gain, or
d. as a member of a local governing body established by or under a State law or Territory law (with exceptions).

NOTE: 'Reasonable expectation of profit or gain' is a reasonableness test and requires more than simply a possibility.

For guidance on when an entity is considered to be an enterprise see Miscellaneous Tax Ruling MT 2006/1. MT 2006/1 sets out the Tax Office's view of when an entity is carrying on an enterprise for the purpose of obtaining an ABN. GSTD 2006/6 provides that the ruling has equal application to the meaning of 'entity' and 'enterprise' for the purposes of the GST Act.

NOTE: A single entity can carry on more than one enterprise. One GST registration for that entity will cover all of its enterprises.

NOTE: GSTD 2009/1 confirms the Tax Office's view that where a discretionary trust supplies an asset that is applied in an enterprise carried on by the trust to a beneficiary of the trust upon the trustee making a resolution to make an in specie distribution to the beneficiary, the supply is made in the course or furtherance of the trust's enterprise and therefore satisfies that requirement for the supply to be a taxable supply.

23.140   WHAT IS 'CONNECTED WITH AUSTRALIA'? (s9-25)

To be a taxable supply, the supply must be connected with Australia. For example:

- goods delivered or made available in Australia to the recipient of the supply
- goods removed from or brought into Australia, and
- real property in Australia.

A supply of a thing other than goods or real property, such as services, intangible property etc. (eg. contractual rights, goodwill, copyright trademarks) is connected with Australia:

- if the thing is done in Australia, or

- the supplier carries on an enterprise through a permanent establishment (as defined) in Australia and the supply is made through that permanent establishment, or
- the thing is a right or option to acquire another thing which would be connected to Australia.

GSTR 2000/31 sets out the Tax Office's view on 'supplies connected with Australia'.

23.150   WHAT IS AN 'ENTITY'? (Division 184)

The GST Act uses the term 'you' throughout. Section 195-1 defines 'you' as applying to entities generally unless its application is expressly limited. The meaning of entity is explained at Division 184. Section 184-1 provides that an entity means any of the following:

a. an individual
b. a body corporate
c. a corporation sole
d. a body politic
e. a partnership
f. any other unincorporated association or body of persons (excluding a non-entity joint venture see definition at s995-1 ITAA97)
g. a trust, and
h. a superannuation fund.

A joint venture is not an entity. Therefore, each participant must individually account for its share of GST and input tax credits (GSTR 2004/2). However, entities that participate, or intend to participate, in a joint venture for the exploration or exploitation of mineral deposits, or for a purpose specified in subregulation 51-5.01 of the GST Regulations may apply for registration as a GST joint venture (Division 51).

In GSTR 2004/2, the Tax Office considers what is a joint venture for GST purposes (see 24.312).

 It is important to distinguish between a partnership and a joint venture and the abovementioned Ruling helps identify the status of the arrangement. Also see MT 2006/1 paragraphs 59-67.

Subsections 184-1(3) and (4) provide that a legal person can do things in multiple capacities (eg. an individual can be a sole trader and a trustee of a trust). In each of those capacities, the person is taken to be a different entity and therefore entitled to separate GST registration. A provision relating to an entity of a particular kind will relate to the entity in its capacity as that kind of entity, not in its capacity as any other kind of entity.

NOTE: As a result of s184-1(3) and (4), a partner in the capacity of a partner and on behalf of the partnership can make a supply or acquisition to and from itself in its own capacity. Similar provision applies to a trustee of a trust.

Any form of entity can conduct an enterprise. Further, an entity can carry on more than one enterprise.

NOTE: It is the entity that is entitled to an ABN and GST registration and not the enterprise.

In *AXA Asia Pacific Holdings Ltd v FC of T* [2008] FCA 1834 the taxpayer contended that NMLA invested in unit trusts of which the trustees, NMFM and NMAM, were entities within the same GST group and therefore the 'acquisition supply' is an 'intra-group' supply and must be ignored for the purpose of working out entitlement to input tax credits under s48-55.

The Court rejected this argument on the grounds that the GST Act distinguishes between an entity's personal capacity and its capacity as a trustee. NMFA and NMAM are body corporates and therefore entities in their own right, but they are also separate entities in their capacity as trustees of each of the unit trusts of which they are the trustees. NMFM and NMAM were members of the group in their personal capacities and not in the capacities of trustees of the unit trusts and therefore a supply between NMLA with NMFA and NMAM in their capacity as trustees of the unit trusts is not an 'intra-group' supply.

23.160   REGISTERED ENTITIES (Division 23)

Only entities carrying on an enterprise can be registered for GST (see 23.130 and 23.150).An entity carrying on an enterprise is required to be registered for GST if its annual turnover reaches the registration turnover threshold of $75,000 (or $150,000 for non-profit bodies). Entities carrying on an enterprise with annual turnover below the registration turnover threshold (except taxi operators) can choose whether or not to be registered for GST. Taxi operators are required to be registered for GST regardless of annual turnover (s144-5).

Division 23 sets out who is required to be registered for GST and who may register for GST. Subdivision 25-A sets out how an entity becomes registered and when the Commissioner must register an entity which has applied for registration. It also sets out the date of effect of an entity's registration and how a back-dated registration may be achieved. Subdivision 25-B sets out how and when to cancel a GST registration.

23.170   GST ON TAXABLE SUPPLIES

23.171   WHEN IS GST PAYABLE?

The accounting method a registered enterprise uses determines when the GST payable on its taxable supplies will be declared in its BAS (see 24.120).

Assessment for GST payable on a taxable importation occurs upon the goods' entry into Australia, unless the registered enterprise is entitled to use the 'GST Deferral Scheme for Imported Goods' (see 23.180 and 23.181).

23.172   GST LIABILITY

Generally, the entity making the taxable supply is liable to pay GST on that supply (s9-40), unless it falls under one of the following categories (s9-69) which may deem another entity to be liable to pay GST:

- company amalgamations – Division 153
- GST groups – Division 48 (see 24.311)
- GST joint ventures – Division 51 (see 24.312)
- offshore supplies other than goods or real property – Division 84
- non-residents making supplies connected with Australia – Division 83 (see 24.351 reverse charge mechanism)
- representatives of incapacitated entities – Division 58, and
- resident agents acting for non-residents – Division 57 (see 24.352).

23.173   DETERMINING THE GST PAYABLE

The amount of GST payable on a taxable supply is generally 10% of the value of the supply (s9-70). Consumers can work out the GST on the goods or services they are buying by dividing the purchase price by 11 (eg. displayed price of an item is $220: GST component is $20).

Where a taxable supply is partly GST-free or partly input taxed, GST is only payable on that part of the value of the supply that relates to the taxable supply (see 23.174).

Where the supply is made to an 'associate' who is not entitled to a full input tax credit, the value of the supply is the GST-exclusive market value of the supply (s72-10). This also applies to a supply for inadequate consideration (s72-70). See 23.128.

Special rules apply to gambling supplies (see 24.383) sales of second hand goods (see 24.381), sales of freehold interests in real property – margin scheme (see 24.344) and long term accommodation in commercial residential premises (see 24.341).

23.174   MIXED SUPPLIES AND COMPOSITE SUPPLIES

TAXABLE AND NON-TAXABLE

A supply may contain both taxable and non-taxable components. Such a supply will either be a mixed or composite supply. The difference in GST treatment between the two is dependent upon whether the individual parts of the supply can be identified.

MIXED SUPPLY OR COMPOSITE SUPPLY?

GST is only payable on the taxable part of a mixed supply. If it is a mixed supply and each part is taxable, you do not need to apportion the consideration for the supply as GST is payable on the whole supply. Similarly, if all of the parts of a supply are identifiable as being non-taxable, there is no need for apportionment as GST is not payable on any part of the supply.

However, where you make a supply that is a combination of separately identifiable taxable and non-taxable parts, you need to identify the taxable part of the supply. Then you can apportion the consideration for the supply, and work out the GST payable on the taxable part of the supply.

In *FC of T v Luxottica Retail Australia Pty Ltd* [2011] FCAFC 20, the Full Federal Court held that where a customer purchased discounted spectacle frames and lenses, the discount did not have to be apportioned between the frames (which are taxable) and the lenses (which are GST-free) for GST purposes.

If a composite supply is taxable, then GST is payable on the whole supply. If a composite supply is non-taxable, then no GST is payable on the supply. There is no need to apportion the consideration for a composite supply. This is why it is important to distinguish between the two types of supplies.

- **Mixed supply:** A mixed supply is a supply that must be separated or unbundled as it contains separately identifiable taxable and non-taxable parts are individually recognised. No part is integral, ancillary or incidental in relation to the whole supply. Only the taxable part of a mixed supply is subject to GST.

- **Composite supply:** If you make a supply that contains a dominant part and the supply includes something that is integral, ancillary or incidental to that part, then the supply is a composite supply. You treat a composite supply as a supply of a single thing. A composite supply is either entirely taxable or non-taxable based on the characteristics of the dominant part.

The distinction between parts that are separately identifiable and things that are integral, ancillary or incidental, is a question of fact and degree. This issue is considered by the Commissioner in ATO ID 2013/20.

GSTR 2001/8 provides the following criteria to determine whether a part of a supply is integral, ancillary or incidental to the dominant part of the supply:

a. you would reasonably conclude that it is a means of better enjoying the dominant thing supplied, rather than constituting for customers an aim in itself, or

b. it represents a marginal proportion of the total value of the package compared to the dominant part, or

c. it is necessary or contributes to the supply as a whole, but cannot be identified as the dominant part of the supply, or

d. it contributes to the proper performance of the contract to supply the dominant part.

NOTE: In GSTR 2001/8 the Tax Office provides a practical administrative solution to the problem of differentiating by allowing entities to treat something as being integral, ancillary or incidental if the consideration that would be apportioned to it does not exceed the lesser of $3.00 or 20% of the total consideration.

Healthy Ltd supplies a packet of cereal containing a sheet of stickers for $4.20. Of this consideration, 20c is for the set of stickers, and $4.00 is for the cereal.

Because the consideration for the stickers does not exceed the lesser of $3.00 or 20% of the total consideration ($4.20 x 20% = $0.80), Healthy Ltd may treat the stickers as an incidental part to the supply of cereal. The supply is treated as a supply of GST-free cereal, and no apportionment of the consideration is needed.

In some cases, a part may be recognised in its own right where a provision of the GST Act specifically requires you to recognise it, regardless of its significance and connection with the supply. For example, certain education excursions or field trips are GST-free under s38-90. However, s38-90(2)(b) specifically provides that the supply of food as part of the excursion or field trip is not GST-free under this provision. Therefore, a supply of food cannot be regarded as an incidental part of the supply of the excursion or field trip even though it satisfies the above concession.

EXAMPLES: MIXED SUPPLIES

EXAMPLE 1: Packaged deals
A 250 ml carton of flavoured milk (taxable) is supplied 'free' to the customer if a 1 litre bottle of milk (GST-free) is purchased. A coffee plunger (taxable) and a 200 gram jar of premium coffee (GST-free) are sold together at a discount price. Both supplies are examples of mixed supplies of taxable and non-taxable supplies and require apportionment of the consideration.

EXAMPLE 2: Commercial and residential premises
Roberto owns a building comprising residential and commercial premises. He leases the building to Jane who operates a small recruitment agency from the commercial premises and lives in the residential part. The supply of the residential part is input taxed. The supply of the commercial part is taxable. Roberto is making a mixed supply that is partly taxable and partly input taxed.

EXAMPLE 3: Hamper
Harry sells assorted hampers. The 'Deluxe Picnic Hamper' includes food and beverage items (bread rolls, cheese, fruit, chocolate and fruit juice), a silver handled knife and a wooden bread board. The supply of the chocolate, knife and bread board is taxable. The other items are GST-free. Each part of the supply is significant. The sale of the 'Deluxe Picnic Hamper' is a mixed supply and Harry needs to apportion the consideration for the hamper.

EXAMPLES: COMPOSITE SUPPLIES

EXAMPLE 4: Delivery of GST-free goods
A customer of 'Net-it-out' places an order for GST-free food through the internet. Net-it-out supplies the goods to the customer's doorstep for the price listed on its internet site. In this case, Net-it-out is making a supply of delivered GST-free goods, and has no liability to account for GST on the delivery of them. Delivery is an integral, ancillary or incidental part of a supply, as the supply is of delivered goods. This is a composite supply.

EXAMPLE 5: GST-free goods with ancillary item
A hearing aid is supplied with a small brush that is used as an accessory to clean the hearing aid so that it performs properly. Compared to the value of the hearing aid, the brush represents a small proportion of the value of the total package. In this case, from a common sense and objective approach, a customer who purchases the package is acquiring a hearing aid. The supply of the brush is not regarded as a part, but is merely ancillary to the supply of the hearing aid. This is a composite supply.

CALCULATING THE GST PAYABLE ON THE TAXABLE PART OF A MIXED SUPPLY (s9-80)

To work out the value of the taxable part of a mixed supply, the taxable and non-taxable parts of the supply must be identified and the consideration apportioned to each of the parts. Where a supply is a mixed supply, the value of the taxable supply is calculated as a portion of the value of the whole supply. The value of the whole supply is calculated at s9-80(2) as follows:

(Price of the actual supply x 10) divided by (10 + taxable proportion)

Taxable proportion is the proportion of the value of the actual supply that represents the value of the taxable supply (expressed as a number between 0 and 1). Price of the actual supply is the amount paid for the mixed supply.

A business makes a mixed supply for $100. The taxable portion of the mixed supply is 80% of the total amount for the mixed supply. For the purpose of calculating GST payable on the supply, the value of the whole supply is ($100 x 10) divided by (10 + 0.8) = $92.59. The value of the taxable portion is $92.59 x 80% = $74.07. The GST on the taxable portion is 10% of $74.07, which is $7.41.

23.175   GST FOREIGN EXCHANGE CONVERSIONS (s9-85)

Section 9-85 provides that consideration expressed in a currency other than Australian currency is to be treated as if it were an amount of Australian currency worked out as determined by the Commissioner.

GSTR 2001/2 provides guidelines on the manner of working out the consideration and input tax credit entitlement where amounts are expressed in a foreign currency.

As a general guide, the Commissioner will accept conversion rates determined by the following means:

- as agreed between the parties
- Reserve Bank of Australia, and
- foreign exchange organisation (eg. commercial bank).

Whichever foreign exchange conversion rate is used, it must be applied consistently.

Conversion day will depend on whether you account for GST on a cash basis or accruals basis as follows:

- **Cash basis:** You can choose one of the following as your conversion day:
  - transaction date, or
  - invoice date, or
  - day on which any of the consideration is received.
- **Accrual basis:** Conversion day is the first of:
  - day on which any of the consideration is received for the supply, or
  - transaction date/invoice date (whichever chosen) – the choice between transaction date or invoice date can be made for each supply.

23.180   IMPORTS

Goods imported into Australia will be subject to GST at the time of importation, regardless of whether or not the person who imports the goods is registered for GST purposes (Division 13). If the goods would have been GST-free or input taxed the importation does not attract GST.

Under the GST Act, anyone can make a taxable importation. There are no requirements of registration and enterprise for a taxable importation. An entity makes a taxable importation if the goods are imported and the entity enters the goods into home consumption (within the meaning of the *Customs Act 1901*).

GSTR 2003/15 sets out the Tax Office's view on the importation of goods into Australia. The Ruling provides that an entry for home consumption is the specified format in which Customs requires information to be provided in respect of imported goods. Some goods are not required to be entered for home consumption. These are still treated as taxable importations. These types of importations are set out at Division 114. An importation is not a taxable importation to the extent it is a non-taxable importation. Non-taxable importations are importations that would be GST-free or input taxed supplies if they were supplies or non-taxable importations set out at Part 3-2 (Division 42).

Division 42 non-taxable importations are classified under two categories:

- goods returned unaltered, and
- concessional goods that are exempt under the *Customs Tariff Act 1995*.

Goods that are returned unaltered can only be non-taxable importations when they satisfy the s42-10 criteria.

Some examples of non-taxable importations exempt under customs law include:

- goods of insubstantial value (see note below)
- goods imported under the Tradex scheme
- goods previously imported and later returned after repair overseas under warranty, and
- goods that are imported for repair, alteration or industrial processing followed by export.

GST payable on taxable importations is at 10% on the sum of:

- the customs value of the goods
- the amount paid or payable to transport the goods to Australia and insure them during that transportation (to the extent not included above)
- any customs duty payable on the goods, and
- any wine tax payable in respect of the local entry of the goods (s13-20). Local entry is explained at s5-30 of *A New Tax System (Wine Equalisation Tax) Act 1999*.

The GST is paid to the Australian Customs Service before goods are released from their control. Alternatively, special deferral regulations may apply to defer the GST (see 23.181).

NOTE: If an agent imports goods into Australia, it is the principal and not the agent who makes the taxable importation. Therefore, the principal is liable to pay the GST on an importation made through an agent. An agent may pay the GST on the taxable importation on behalf if its principal but it is not liable to pay the GST. The one exception to this rule applies by virtue of s57-5 which states that where a non-resident principal makes a taxable importation through a resident agent, the resident agent is liable to pay the GST in the taxable importation, not the non-resident principal (see GSTR 2003/15).

A registered enterprise or an enterprise required to be registered, that makes a taxable importation for a creditable purpose is entitled to an input tax credit of the GST paid when the goods are imported (s15-15).

NOTE: There is no GST or duty imposed on goods imported by air, sea or post where the import does not exceed the 'low value importation threshold'. The threshold is not exceeded where the total value of the consignment does not exceed $1,000 and the tax and customs duty otherwise payable do not exceed $50, unless the goods are alcohol or tobacco products. Unsolicited gifts are exempt from GST and duty if they are valued at $200 or less.

23.181 SPECIAL SCHEME TO DEFER GST ON IMPORTS

GST is generally payable by the importer at the same time as customs duty is levied. However, a special scheme allows most importers to defer paying any GST on imported goods until they lodge their next BAS. This creates cash flow benefits because it allows importers to claim their input tax credit on the importation pursuant to Division 15 at the same time as they account for their GST liability. The end result is that importers will never have to physically pay GST on the importation.

To be eligible for the scheme, you must:

- have an ABN
- be registered for GST
- lodge and pay your BAS monthly via the e-commerce lodgment process
- deal with customs electronically
- have a satisfactory compliance record with the Tax Office, and
- have approval in writing from the Tax Office to defer payment of GST on imported goods.

See the Tax Office publication 'Deferred GST schemes' to assist with deferring the payment of GST on taxable importations.

23.200 CREDITABLE ACQUISITIONS AND INPUT TAX CREDITS

Registered entities are able to recover GST paid on creditable acquisitions/importations by claiming an 'input tax credit' (Division 11).

Entitlement to an input tax credit arises if the entity makes a creditable acquisition/importation. A creditable acquisition/importation occurs where:

- the thing was acquired/imported solely or partly for a creditable purpose, and
- the supply to the entity was a taxable supply or the importation was a taxable importation, and
- the entity provides or is liable to provide consideration for the acquisition, and
- the entity is registered or required to be registered (s11-5).

The rules concerning creditable acquisitions set out in Division 11 and those concerning creditable importations (set out in Division 15) are very similar. The meaning of creditable purpose is consistent. The following analysis relates to creditable acquisitions but much is also relevant to creditable importations.

23.210   ACQUISITION (s11-10)

'Acquisition' is set out at s11-10 and is the converse of 'supply' (see 23.110). Accordingly, goods or services supplied by one party is acquired by the other.

23.220   CREDITABLE PURPOSE (s11-15)

A creditable purpose is the extent to which something was acquired/imported for the carrying on of your enterprise. However, it will not arise to the extent that something has been acquired/imported in the course of making input taxed supplies (see 23.300), or if it was acquired/imported for a private or domestic purpose.

NOTE: A creditable purpose will still arise to the extent something has been acquired/imported in the course of making GST-free supplies.

NOTE: In *Russell v FC of T* [2011] FCAFC 10, the Full Federal Court found that input tax credits were available to the taxpayer. The taxpayer had completed business plans, made financial projections, undertaken market research and taken relevant training. The Court saw these activities as being sufficient to constitute commencing an enterprise and held that the acquisitions were made for the purpose of carrying on the enterprise.

Generally, the amount of the input tax credit available to be claimed is the amount of GST included in the price, but this is reduced if the acquisition is only partly creditable (s11-30) or is a reduced credit acquisition pursuant to Division 70 (see 23.315). An acquisition may be partly creditable if the acquisition is only partly for a creditable purpose or there is only part consideration paid. In such a circumstance, you are only entitled to a credit for the part related to use for a creditable purpose.

GSTR 2008/1 discusses the meaning of 'creditable purpose'. Whether an acquisition is made in carrying on an enterprise requires a connection or link between the thing acquired and the enterprise. For example, a sole trader operating a shoe shop acquires shoes to be on-sold to customers. The shoes acquired are made in carrying on the enterprise. However, if the shoes were acquired for personal use, the acquisition was for a private purpose and therefore not for a creditable purpose.

A capital acquisition made for the carrying on of the enterprise is for a creditable purpose and therefore the entity is entitled to claim input tax credits on the acquisition. For example, an entity operating a bakery business purchases a car to deliver cakes to customers. As the car is acquired in carrying on the bakery enterprise, it is for a creditable purpose and the entity is entitled to claim input tax credits on the acquisition.

In *Rio Tinto Services Ltd v FC of T* [2015] FCA 94 the Federal Court rejected the taxpayer mining company's contention that acquisitions in providing, and maintaining, residential accommodation for its workforce in a remote location were made wholly for a "creditable purpose" because the supply of the residential accommodation was not an end commercial objective in itself but was wholly incidental to the mining operations as a necessary and essential part of those operations. The court held that the supplies were input taxed supplies. The taxpayer is appealing to the Full Federal Court from this decision.

23.221   PARTLY FOR A CREDITABLE PURPOSE

An entity needs to calculate the extent to which an acquisition has been made for a creditable purpose if the acquisition is:

- only partly used in carrying on an enterprise
- partly used to make input taxed supplies, or
- partly of a private or domestic nature.

An acquisition may be an essential prerequisite to carrying on an enterprise. However, if the acquisition is not incidental or relevant to carrying on an enterprise, it will not be made for a creditable purpose. Care must be taken in determining whether an acquisition is private in nature. It is not necessary for an acquisition that has common characteristics of a private/domestic expenditure to automatically be denied from being made for a creditable purpose. For example, a taxpayer incurs childcare costs, in order to be able to carry on his enterprise. As the acquisition is not incidental or relevant to carrying on the enterprise and is private in nature, it is not made for a creditable purpose. This does not mean that childcare costs having private/domestic characteristics are automatically denied from being made for a creditable purpose. If the childcare costs are incurred by an entity as part of a remuneration package for its employee, the expense is taken to be relevant to the carrying on of an enterprise and therefore for a creditable purpose.

NOTE: Certain acquisitions that are recreational or private in nature such as penalties, a spouse's travel expenses, entertainment expenses and non-compulsory uniform expenses, are specifically excluded from being a creditable acquisition under Division 69.

According to GSTR 2008/1 only entities that make, have made, or intend to make, input taxed supplies will need to consider whether any part of an acquisition is not for a creditable purpose due to it being partly related to making supplies that would be input taxed. It is possible that the acquisition made may relate to either past, present or future supplies made by the entity. Whether an acquisition is for a creditable purpose or not depends on the acquisition being related to supplies which, if made, would be input taxed, notwithstanding the fact that:

- the entity has not made the intended supply, has not decided on whether to proceed with making the particular supply, or that the intended supply never eventuate (future supplies), or
- the entity has ceased making those supplies (past supplies).

NOTE: When an acquisition precedes a supply, the creditable purpose will be based on the intended usage of the acquisition. There may be a requirement to make an adjustment under Division 129 at a later time to reflect the actual usage of the acquisition (see 24.263).

23.222   METHOD OF APPORTIONMENT

The method you use to establish use for a creditable purpose must be fair and reasonable. GSTR 2006/4 sets out acceptable methodologies for determining the extent of creditable purpose to calculate input tax credit entitlement, and GSTR 2006/3 sets out methodologies for calculating input tax credits and adjustments for change of use by providers of financial supplies, including extent of creditable purpose.

According to GSTR 2008/1, an acquisition may be directly related to particular taxable and input taxed supplies. In this case, apportionment is usually based on factors that directly connect the acquisition to the supplies. On the other hand, an acquisition may not be directly linked to making particular supplies, but instead it is used for all the supplies the entity makes in carrying on the enterprise and the enterprise makes both taxable/GST-free supplies and input taxed supplies. In this case, the entity may apportion the creditable and non-creditable portion on the basis of current supplies the entity makes in carrying on its enterprise. However, other apportionment methods may be used, so long as they satisfy the underlying apportionment principle of fair and reasonable.

23.223   WHOSE CREDITABLE PURPOSE?

An entity which acquires the thing may not always necessarily be the one that receives the actual thing. The entity that acquires the thing is called the recipient entity (GSTR 2008/1). It is the purpose of the recipient entity that determines whether the acquisition is made for a creditable purpose and it is the recipient entity that is entitled to claim the input tax credits.

If the entity that acquires the thing (recipient entity) made an acquisition but the acquisition is provided to another entity for the benefit of the other entity and the acquisition had no relevance to the enterprise of the recipient entity, then the acquisition is not made for a creditable purpose.

In *AXA Asia Pacific Holdings Ltd v FC of T* [2008] FCA 1834, the Court rejected the taxpayer's 'look through' argument. In this case, NMLA invested in unit trusts of which NMFM and NMAM were the trustees.

The trustees, incorporated in Australia, were within the same GST group as NMLA. The trust funds were invested wholly or substantially overseas. It was accepted that the investment of funds overseas was a GST-free supply by the relevant trustee.

The taxpayer contended that the acquisition by NMLA of units in unit trusts that invested wholly or substantially overseas was merely a 'formal mechanism' used by NMLA in order to make investments. Based on this intention, the taxpayer argued that a 'look through' approach should be applied and that NMLA had made a GST-free supply and not a financial supply (which is input taxed). As a result the general management expenses were in relation to GST-free supplies which were for a creditable purpose and therefore input tax credits on these expenses should be allowed.

The court rejected the 'look through' notion and established that the extent to which NMLA acquired the things, for which it paid general management expenses, for a creditable purpose, was answered by looking to the extent to which those things were acquired in the carrying on of NMLA's enterprise, and then to the extent that the acquisitions related, directly or indirectly, to the making of any input taxed supplies by NMLA. Neither the subjective intention of NMLA, nor the activities of the interposed unit trusts was determinative of those questions.

23.224   CHANGES IN EXTENT OF CREDITABLE PURPOSE

An adjustment may be required if there is a later change to the extent of creditable purpose (see 23.263). However, adjustments for changes in extent of creditable use are generally not necessary where the GST-exclusive amount of each acquisition is $1,000 or less.

An adjustment cannot be made after the entity is deregistered for GST because, post-cancellation, there is no tax period and therefore no adjustment period (*GOL-HUT Pty Ltd as trustee for the Helensvale Unit Trust and Commissioner of Taxation* [2013] AATA 199).

23.225   ANNUAL APPORTIONMENT OF CREDITABLE PURPOSE (Division 131)

Small businesses (those with a turnover of less than $2 million) that have not elected to pay GST by instalments or report GST annually can elect to undertake an annual apportionment of input tax credits for certain acquisitions used for a partly creditable purpose (ie. private use). Instead of adjusting the amount of input tax credit entitlement for private use in each tax period, small businesses can claim the full input tax credit in the tax period the acquisition is attributable to and later make a single increasing adjustment to its input tax credits claim to take account of private use.

The business will be able to make the relevant increasing adjustment at any time up to the end of the tax period in which it is required to lodge an income tax return to simultaneously establish the extent of business use for both income tax and GST purposes. If the business is not required to lodge a tax return, then the relevant increasing adjustment must be made in the period ending 31 December after the end of the financial year in which the acquisition was attributed to.

 An annual apportionment election cannot apply to reduced credit acquisitions or acquisitions that are not creditable at all.

NOTE: The input tax credit claimed in the period to which an acquisition is attributed will be pro-rated if the acquisitions are partly creditable due to being partly input taxed or where only part consideration is provided (see example below).

 Mary has several businesses, one of which involves renting out residential premises. Mary has chosen annual private apportionment. Mary purchases telephone services from a local telephone company. She pays $220 for these services including $20 GST and she is liable to pay the full purchase price. Mary anticipates that she will use the services 30% for regular business activities, 55% for private purposes, and 15% for renting out of residential premises.

Mary's input tax credit must take into account the extent the services relate to the supply of her rental property. The credit amount is calculated using the following formula (s131-40):

(Full GST credit) x (Extent of non-input-taxed purpose) x (Extent of consideration) = Claimable GST credit

$20 x 85% x 100% = $17

Mary can claim a GST credit of $17 in the period in which the acquisition is attributed to. If Mary had not chosen annual private apportionment, Mary would only be entitled to a GST credit of $6 (30% x $20).

As she has claimed a $17 GST credit she will need to make an annual increasing adjustment for the private use portion of $17 – $6 = $11.

23.226   INPUT TAX CREDITS FOR CAR EXPENSES

Where a car expense is incurred for a creditable purpose, there is entitlement to an input tax credit. There are no specific rules in the GST Act for calculating the extent of creditable purpose of car expenses, however GSTR 2006/4 permits the use of any fair and reasonable method to establish the extent of creditable purpose.

GSTB 2006/1 explains how you can claim an input tax credit for a car expense where the car is not used entirely for carrying on an enterprise and incorporates information on the annual apportionment of creditable purpose election contained in Division 131 (see 23.225).

 GSTB 2006/1 points out that the amount of input tax credit allowable cannot be obtained directly from the car expense claim calculated for income tax purposes (ie. you cannot claim 1/11th of your income tax claim).

NOTE: An employee's personal use of a car provided as a benefit by an employer does not affect the extent of its creditable purpose for the employer. A car provided as part of an employee's remuneration is provided in the course of an enterprise carried on by the employer and therefore has a fully creditable purpose (GSTR 2001/3).

CALCULATING EXTENT OF CREDITABLE PURPOSE (GSTB 2006/1)

The extent of creditable purpose of a car used partially in the course of an enterprise can be determined by using the following methods.

- **Formula method:** If the cents per kilometre method for income tax is used, there is no requirement to calculate an extent of business use for income tax purposes. Therefore, for GST purposes a method is required to work out the extent of creditable purpose. The following formula is one such suggested method:

    Reasonable estimate of total business kms per tax period divided by Reasonable estimate of total kms travelled per tax period

    This method is acceptable if creditable business use does not exceed 5000 kms for a year.

- **Set rate method:** This is acceptable if distance travelled for a creditable purpose does not exceed 5000 kms for a year.

Estimated kms travelled for a creditable purpose	Assumed extent of creditable purpose
0 – 1,250	5%
1,251 – 2,500	10%
2,501 – 3,750	15%
3,751 – 5,000	20%

- **One third of actual expenses method:** Both the 12% of the original value or the one third of total expense method used to calculate car expenses for income tax purposes deem a business use of 33 1/3%. This method is also acceptable for GST purposes, deeming creditable purpose to be 33 1/3%. This method can only be used if you travel over 5,000kms for a creditable purpose in the year.

- **Log book method:** The Tax Office will accept that the percentage of business use obtained for income tax purposes can be used as the extent of creditable purpose for input tax credit entitlement. If your motor vehicle is not entirely used for a creditable purpose, then you have to reduce your creditable purpose accordingly. This method can be used regardless of how much distance is travelled for creditable purpose in the year. Log books for income tax purposes are valid for five years and the Tax Office accepts that this method establishes the extent of creditable purpose for five years, provided you are not required to keep a new log book or your portion of non-creditable use does not change.

NOTE: In most cases, the business use of a car for income tax purposes is the same as its use for creditable purposes. However, business use is not the same as use for a creditable purpose where:

- some of the travel is for activities done in connection with earning certain PAYG withholding payments (eg. salary and wages, directors fees) as these activities are not part of the enterprise for GST purposes (see from 23.130), or

- some of the travel relates to making input taxed supplies, such as residential accommodation.

NOTE: It was announced in the 2015-16 Federal Budget that the statutory methods for car expense income tax deductions were to be changed for the 2015-16 and later income years.

23.227   'DE MINIMIS' RULE

Acquisitions that are used to make financial supplies may still be treated as being acquired for a creditable purpose under the 'de minimis' rule. This rule is based on the amount of input tax credits which relate to financial supplies made by a registered entity (s11-15(4)).

Under the 'de minimis' rule, a registered enterprise remains entitled to all of its input tax credits if it does not exceed the 'financial acquisition threshold' (Division 189). You will exceed the financial acquisition threshold if the total amount of your current and projected input tax credits on financial acquisitions exceeds:

- $150,000, or
- 10% of your total input tax credits to which you are entitled for all your acquisitions and importations for the year (including those attributable to making financial supplies).

The 'de minimis' rule must be satisfied each month. This effectively means constant monitoring to ensure that the entity is within the thresholds at any time during a BAS period. Financial acquisitions are acquisitions that relate to the making of a financial supply (other than a financial supply consisting of a borrowing) (s189-15). The current component relates to the input tax credits for the current month and the previous 11 months. The projected component represents the input tax credits of the current month and the next 11 months. Both components must be satisfied to be under the 'financial acquisition threshold'. The rules are similar to the current and projected GST turnover test in relation to being required to register for GST.

A registered business has enough outstanding customers' accounts to generate a substantial amount of interest income (an input taxed supply). To manage these outstanding accounts, it forms a new accounts department. It acquires goods for $220,000 to establish this department, all of which were taxable supplies. The amount of GST incurred on the acquisition of these goods was $20,000.

As the input tax credit attributable to the financial supplies is no more than $50,000, the business remains entitled to the input tax credit of $20,000 provided that this amount is no more than 10% of the business's total entitlement to input tax credits (including those attributable to making financial supplies).

Borrowing expenses can be excluded from the 'de minimis' rule to ensure most businesses are not denied input tax credits on such acquisitions unless the borrowing relates to making other input taxed supplies.

GSTR 2003/9 provides further guidance on the financial acquisitions threshold. See also 23.315.

23.230   CLAIMING INPUT TAX CREDITS

For GST purposes, the law requires input tax credits to be based on actual expenses rather than estimates. In contrast, for income tax purposes in respect of car expenses, a reasonable estimate of fuel and oil expenses is acceptable.

The accounting method used by a registered entity normally determines when and how much input tax credit they may claim (see 24.100). However, it is always subject to the requirement that a tax invoice is held at the time of lodgement of a BAS in which an input tax credit is claimed, unless it is a low value transaction. Receipts and diary entries are acceptable documentation for low value transactions (s29-80). Low value transactions are transactions that are $82.50 or less (GST-inclusive).

The amount of an input tax credit for a creditable acquisition is an amount equal to the amount of GST payable in respect of the creditable acquisition/importation. However, the amount of the input tax credit is reduced if the acquisition is only partly creditable or if it is a reduced credit acquisition. For reduced credit acquisitions the input tax credit available is a reduced input tax credit of 75% of any GST paid (see 23.315).

The Tax Office has released Taxpayer Alert TA 2012/5 which warns taxpayers to be cautious about non-commercial arrangements where large input tax credits are claimed on acquisitions of intangible items (such as rights) at grossly inflated values.

23.231 RESTRICTIONS

Generally, if goods or services are used in making input taxed supplies you will not be entitled to an input tax credit (for exceptions see 23.315).

There will be other situations where a registered enterprise has paid GST on the price of a supply in the course of its activities, but for which an input tax credit is denied. These are:

- acquisitions of freehold interests in land subject to the margin scheme (s75-20) (see 24.344)
- the amount of the input tax credit on the acquisition or importation of a car, where the GST-inclusive market value of the car exceeds the car depreciation cost limit, is limited to 1/11th of the car limit (see 15.085), and
- certain expenditure of a revenue nature made specifically non-deductible for income tax purposes (s69-5), including:
  - penalties
  - maintaining your family
  - non-compulsory uniforms
  - agreements for the provision of non-deductible non-cash business benefits
  - relatives' travel expenses*
  - recreational club expenses*
  - leisure facilities or boats*, and
  - entertainment*.

* If provided as a fringe benefit and deductible for income tax purposes, input tax credits are available.

NOTE: Input tax credits cannot be claimed for the non-deductible cost of entertainment (usually the client portion of the expense). The employee portion is usually tax deductible to the employer if the entertainment is provided as a fringe benefit and therefore an input tax credit may be claimed by the employer for providing entertainment to employees. The calculation method used for fringe benefit tax purposes is acceptable for calculating the creditable portion for claiming an input tax credit.

 Ensure you do not claim input tax credits for the non-deductible portion of entertainment expenses.

23.232 SPECIAL RULES

INPUT TAX CREDITS FOR INPUT TAX SUPPLIERS PROVIDING FRINGE BENEFITS

Special provisions may apply to input tax suppliers who provide fringe benefits to their employees (Division 71).

Certain employers making input taxed supplies in which they are wholly or partially denied input tax credits on their acquisitions may not be entitled to claim input tax credits for things acquired for the purpose of providing fringe benefits to employees (see 24.410 for specific rules).

REIMBURSEMENTS

Registered entities can claim input tax credits for reimbursements to an employee, an officer of a company or partner of a partnership for an expense they incur for an acquisition directly related to performance of their duties (Division 111). Further, registered entities can also claim input tax credits on reimbursement of an expense that constitutes an expense payment benefit (see 24.410).

The input tax credit for a creditable acquisition may be claimed by the registered entity if the tax invoice that was issued to the person who was reimbursed is held, even though the document specifies that the reimbursed person, not the entity, was the recipient.

 The requirement for a tax invoice to be held at the time the Business Activity Statement is lodged in order to claim input tax credits applies in the same manner when claiming input tax credits in relation to reimbursements.

PRE-ESTABLISHMENT COSTS

A company after it is incorporated may claim input tax credits on acquisitions made before it was incorporated (Division 60). For the pre-establishment credit entitlement to apply, all the conditions specified in s60-15 must be satisfied, that is:

- the thing acquired or imported is not applied for any purpose other than for a creditable purpose relating to a company not yet in existence, and
- the company comes into existence, and becomes registered within six months after the acquisition or importation, and
- the person that acquires the thing becomes a member, officer or employee of the company, and
- the company fully reimburses the person for the consideration provided for the acquisition.

NOTE: It is the company that is entitled to input tax credits of the pre-establishment acquisitions and not the person that has made the acquisitions. It will not be pre-establishment acquisitions for a company if the person that incurred the cost was entitled to claim the input tax credits.

23.233   TIME LIMIT IN CLAIMING INPUT TAX CREDITS

Generally you need to claim an input tax credit or notify the Tax Office of your entitlement within four years of the end of the tax period to which the entitlement relates. If you have a valid tax invoice and have not claimed the credit, the Tax Office will allow you to claim that credit in the current or any later tax period within this four year period (s105-55 TAA).

23.300 INPUT TAXED SUPPLIES

Input taxed supplies are not taxable supplies. Entities making input tax supplies have no obligation to pay GST on those supplies and are generally not entitled to claim input tax credits on acquisitions relating to making input taxed supplies. However, in some cases, acquisitions relating to financial supplies can attract a reduced input tax credit, even though no input tax credit could arise under the basic rules.

A recipient of input taxed supplies is not entitled to input tax credits as the acquisitions were not taxable supplies.

There are three major categories of input taxed supplies:

- financial supplies (see 23.310)
- residential rents (see 23.320), and
- residential premises (except 'new residential premises') (see 23.330).

Other categories of input taxed supplies are:

- precious metals (see 23.340)
- school tuckshops and canteens (see 23.350), and
- fund-raising events conducted by a charitable institution (see 23.360).

23.310 FINANCIAL SUPPLIES (Subdivision 40-A)

Section 40-5 of the GST Act provides that financial supplies are input taxed. Something is a financial supply only if it is identified as a financial supply in reg. 40-5.09 or is an incidental financial supply under reg. 40-5.10 (see GST Regulations).

You may make financial supplies in the course of carrying on your enterprise if you provide, acquire or dispose of an interest listed in the GST Regulations (see table below).

The provision, acquisition or disposal of the interest identified in regs. 40-5.09(3) or (4) must be:

- for consideration
- in the course or furtherance of an enterprise, and
- connected with Australia,

and the supplier must be:

- registered or required to be registered, and
- a financial supply provider in relation to the supply of the interest.

The GST Regulations identify supplies that are financial supplies by inclusion and exclusion. Regulation 40-5.12 has the effect of excluding things that might otherwise have been included as a financial supply by reg. 40-5.09. Regulation 40-5.12 does not exclude from being a financial supply something that is also an incidental financial supply.

NOTE: GSTR 2002/2 (note addendum) provides guidance regarding the GST treatment of financial supplies and related supplies and acquisitions.

23.311   DEFINITION OF FINANCIAL SUPPLY (regs. 40-5.09 and 40-5.10)

The supply or acquisition of a financial interest is a financial supply if it is:

- a financial supply in reg. 40-5.09(3) (see table below), regs. 40-5.09(4) and (4A), or
- an incidental financial supply. For a supply to be an incidental financial supply, the requirements of reg. 40-5.10 must be satisfied. That is, something is an incidental financial supply, if it is:
  - incidental to the financial supply, and
  - it is supplied and the financial supply is supplied at or about the same time, but not for separate consideration, and
  - it is the usual practice for the entity to supply the thing, or similar things and the financial supply together in the ordinary course of the entity's enterprise.

Item	'Financial supplies': An interest in, or under, one of the categories set out below (Reg.40-5.09(3))
1	An account made available by an Australian Authorised Deposit-taking Institution (ADI) in the course of: a. its banking business within the meaning of the *Banking Act 1959*, or b. its State banking business
2	A debt, credit or right to credit, including a letter of credit
3	A charge or mortgage over real or personal property
4	A Regulated Superannuation Fund (RSF), Approved Deposit Fund (ADF), Pooled Superannuation Trust (PST) or Public Sector Superannuation Scheme (PSSS) within the meaning of the *Superannuation Industry (Supervision) Act 1993*, or a Retirement Savings Account (RSA) within the meaning of the *Retirement Savings Accounts Act 1997*
5	An annuity or allocated pension
6	Life insurance business to which s9(1) of the *Life Insurance Act 1995*, or a declaration under s12(2) or s12A(2) of that Act applies, or related reinsurance business
7	A guarantee, including an indemnity (except a warranty for goods or for a contract of insurance or reinsurance)
7A	An indemnity that holds a person harmless from any loss as a result of a transaction the person enters with a third party
8	Credit under a hire purchase agreement (entered into before 1 July 2012) in relation to goods, if: a. the credit for the goods is provided for a separate charge, and b. the charge is disclosed to the recipient of the goods (**NOTE:** Principal component is subject to GST)
9	Australian currency, currency of a foreign country, or agreement to buy or sell the currency

Item	'Financial supplies': An interest in, or under, one of the categories set out below (Reg.40-5.09(3))
10	Securities, including: a. debenture described in paras (a)-(f) of the definition of debenture in s9 of the *Corporations Act 2001*, and b. a document issued by an individual that would be a debenture if it were issued by a body corporate, and c. a scheme described in paras (e), (i) or (m) of the definition of 'managed investment scheme' in s9 of the *Corporations Act 2001*, and d. the capital of a partnership or trust
11	A derivative

A supply (to which reg. 40-5.09(3) item 1 does not apply) by an Australian ADI for a fee of not more than $1,000 is also a financial supply under reg. 40-5.09(4) if:

(a) the item would have applied to that supply in relation to an account with the ADI (such as an electronic transfer to another Australian ADI for a person who does not hold an account with the ADI), or

(b) the fee relates to an application to the ADI that, if accepted, would result in the creation of an account by the ADI (example: loan application fee).

ATM services provided by ADIs will be input taxed as a financial supply either under reg. 40-5.09(3) item 1 or reg 40-5.09(4). However, ATM services supplied by non-ADIs do not come under financial supplies and will therefore be subject to GST. As a result reg.40-5.09(4A) was introduced so that ATM fees charged by non-ADIs are now also financial supplies and input taxed.

NOTE: Dividends are not a supply for consideration and are therefore ignored for GST purposes.

NOTE: Only the credit component of a hire purchase agreement is an input taxed financial supply. The payment of the principal component is not a financial supply and may be subject to GST if it satisfies the requirement of being a taxable supply under s9-5. For more information on hire purchase see 24.371.

 The making of a financial supply is not limited to only financial institution and does not occur only at the disposal of an interest in a financial supply. An entity can be making a financial supply even when it is acquiring an interest in a financial supply.

WHAT ARE NOT FINANCIAL SUPPLIES

Regulation 40-5.12 contains a complete list of items which are not financial supplies. The supplies of any of the following items, or interests in them, are not financial supplies and therefore taxable:

- insurance and reinsurance (other than life insurance mentioned at reg. 40-5.09(3) item 6)
- broking services
- finance leases, and
- professional services including information and advice even if in relation to a financial supply. Legal, accounting, tax and actuarial advice are therefore taxable.

Borrowing-related expenses, although relating to a financial supply, may be eligible for input tax credits so long as the borrowed money is used in connection with making taxable or GST-free supplies.

If a supply is mentioned in both regs. 40-5.09 and 40-5.12, the supply is not a financial supply. However, if a supply is both an incidental financial supply (reg. 40-5.10) and mentioned in reg 40-5.12, it is a financial supply.

In *FCT v American Express Wholesale Currency Services Pty Limited* [2010] FCAFC 122, the Full Federal Court held that the late payment fees paid by the holders of credit cards and charge cards to the issuers of the cards were 'revenue derived from input taxed supplies'. The Court said the taxpayer supplied cardholders with an 'interest' within the meaning of Reg 40-5.02 of the GST Regulations when they agreed to the cards' terms and conditions. The Full Court also believed that the term 'credit' is broader than the meanings as defined at first instance by the Federal Court, and held that the supply of the right to use a card was a supply of an interest in or under a credit arrangement or right to credit within the meaning of Reg 40-5.09. As a result, the fee payment was considered to be an input taxed supply.

The Tribunal decision in *Australian Style Investments Pty Ltd as Trustee for the Australian Style Investments Unit Trust and Commissioner of Taxation* [2013] AATA 847 sets out a comprehensive analysis of the components of the definition of a 'financial supply'; in particular, a financial supply which is 'an interest in or under... [s]ecurities'.

23.312 WHAT IS AN 'INTEREST' IN RELATION TO A FINANCIAL SUPPLY?

Regulation 40-5.02 provides that an interest in relation to a financial supply is anything that is recognised at law or in equity as any form of property. Examples include:

- a debt or a right to credit
- an interest conferred under a public or private superannuation scheme
- a mortgage over land or premises
- a right under a contract of insurance or a guarantee (GSTR 2006/1 explains how to determine whether an interest is an indemnity or guarantee)
- a right to receive payment under a derivative, and
- a right to future property.

In ID 2011/20, the Commissioner considers the issue that, when a unit holder in a unit trust enters into a contract for consideration to appoint a proxy to vote at a meeting, whether the unit holder is making a provision, acquisition or disposal of an interest in a security under item ten in the table in sub-regulation 40-5.09(3). Item ten covers securities, which include, at item 10(d), the capital of a partnership or trust.

The Commissioner believes rights created under the contract in this case could be considered to be property, and, therefore, an 'interest' in its broadest sense. Therefore, for the supplies under the contract to come within item ten in sub-regulation 40-5.09(3), it must be demonstrated that an interest in the capital of a trust is supplied by the taxpayer to Entity X. The Commissioner believes that this is not achieved by the contract. In the Commissioner's view, this arrangement may create an interest, but the interest relates to the contractual relationship between the taxpayer and Entity X and not to an interest in the capital of the trust. The taxpayer continues to hold its units, which are not diminished or disposed of under the arrangement, nor divided into separate 'voting rights' capable of on-supply.

23.313 FINANCIAL SUPPLY PROVIDER OR FINANCIAL SUPPLY FACILITATOR

The GST Regulations distinguish between a financial supply provider and a financial supply facilitator. Distinguishing between the financial supply provider and financial supply facilitator becomes important as something supplied directly by a financial supply provider to the recipient will most likely be a financial supply or an incidental financial supply and therefore input taxed.

FINANCIAL SUPPLY PROVIDER (reg. 40-5.06)

An entity is the financial supply provider of an interest if:

- the interest was the entity's property immediately before the supply (for example, if an entity sells a debenture that it owns), or
- the entity created the interest when making the supply (for example, if an entity issues a debenture).

The entity which acquires the interest supplied is also the financial supply provider of the interest, eg. in the case of someone selling shares, both the seller and purchaser are financial supply providers.

Methodologies that financial suppliers may use in apportioning their entitlements to input tax credits where they also make taxable supplies are set out in GSTR 2006/3.

FINANCIAL SUPPLY FACILITATOR (reg. 40-5.07)

A financial supply facilitator is an entity that facilitates the supply of an interest for the financial supply provider. The supply by a financial supply facilitator, in that capacity, is not a financial supply. A supply by a facilitator will be a taxable supply, unless it is not taxable under another provision of the GST Act (for example, it is GST-free or input taxed). Only the financial supply provider in relation to a particular supply can make a financial supply of that thing, as only the provider can satisfy requirements of reg. 40-5.09(1)(b)(ii).

 Norman sells shares to Fred but does so through David, a broker. Norman is making the financial supply of the shares to Fred. David is making the supply of brokerage services. The financial supply is input taxed, whilst the brokerage services are taxable.

Certain acquisitions from a financial supply facilitator qualify as reduced credit acquisitions.

23.314   DENIAL OF INPUT TAX CREDITS: NON CREDITABLE PURPOSE

Input tax credits may only be claimed for any creditable acquisition made (s11-20). Part of the requirement for an acquisition to be a creditable acquisition is that the acquisition was for a creditable purpose and that the acquisition was a taxable supply (see 23.200). Section 11-15 provides that an entity acquires or imports something for a creditable purpose to the extent that the entity acquires or imports it in carrying on its enterprise. However, the entity does not acquire or import the things for a creditable purpose to the extent that it relates to making input taxed supplies (such as financial supplies) or is of a private or domestic nature.

Therefore an entity is not entitled to input tax credits for an acquisition or importation relating to making financial supplies (even though the acquisition might have been subject to GST) because the acquisition/importation is related to making input taxed financial supplies and therefore not a creditable acquisition.

If an entity provides both input taxed financial supplies together with other services that are taxable or GST-free, then the entity will need to apportion its acquisitions for creditable acquisitions in order to arrive at the entity's entitlement to input tax credits. The Commissioner's preferred methods of apportionment in respect of financial supplies are set out in GSTR 2006/3.

Further, recipients of input taxed supplies are also not entitled to input tax credits because the acquisition is not a taxable supply (ie. not subject to GST), and therefore not a creditable acquisition.

23.315   EXCEPTIONS TO THE DENIAL OF INPUT TAX CREDITS

There are several exceptions to the general rule for acquisitions or importations that relate to making input taxed financial supplies set out above, that enable you to claim an input tax credit or a reduced input tax credit.

The major exceptions include:

- 'reduced credit acquisitions' (Division 70) – certain specified acquisitions (also known as reduced credit acquisitions) that relate to making financial supplies can give rise to an entitlement to a Reduced Input Tax Credit (RITC). The GST Regulations specify the acquisitions that are reduced credit acquisitions, and provide that the RITC claimable is 75% of any GST paid on acquisitions. GSTR 2004/1 provides guidance on which acquisitions are reduced credit acquisitions that entitle a financial supply provider to a RITC under Division 70
- the acquisition or importation relates to a supply consisting of a borrowing (and the borrowing relates to making supplies that are not input taxed) (s11-15(5)), and
- 'de minimis' rule – if you do not exceed the financial acquisitions threshold, anything you acquire or import will be for a creditable purpose to the extent you import or acquire it in carrying on your enterprise (s11-15(4)) – see 23.227.

REDUCED INPUT TAX CREDITS (Division 70)

In some cases, acquisitions that relate to making financial supplies may attract an RITC, even though no input tax credit would arise under the general rules. These acquisitions are reduced credit acquisitions and are listed in reg. 70-5.02. An RITC only applies to acquisitions relating to financial supplies.

GSTR 2004/1 provides guidance on what acquisitions are reduced credit acquisitions and therefore qualify for an RITC.

 The RITC only applies to acquisitions made to make financial supplies and does not apply to other inputs related to taxable supplies or input tax supplies which are not financial supplies (ie. residential rents).

A registered superannuation fund incurs brokerage of $110 inclusive of $10 GST in relation to the acquisition of some publicly listed shares. The acquisition of shares is a financial supply and the brokerage fee is a reduced credit acquisition under item 9 of the table in reg. 70-5.02. Therefore, the superannuation fund can claim back $7.50 (75% of $10 GST) as an RITC.

NOTE: Apportionment of RITC claimable for reduced credit acquisitions is required in certain circumstances. For example:

- the acquisition is a mixed supply in which part of it is a reduced credit acquisition and the other part is not (GSTR 2004/1), and
- a reduced credit acquisition is not wholly related to making a financial supply but was partially used to make other input taxed supplies (eg. residential rents), GST-free supplies or even taxable supplies (GSTR 2006/3).

FINANCIAL ACQUISITIONS THRESHOLD (Division 189)

You exceed the financial acquisitions threshold during a particular month if your 'current' or 'projected' input tax credits related to making those financial supplies exceed:

- $150,000, or
- 10% of the total amount of input tax credits to which you would be entitled for all acquisitions and importations.

The 'current' component measures acquisitions made or likely to be made in the 12-month period ending at the end of that month plus the previous 11 months.

The 'projected' component measures acquisitions made or likely to be made in the 12-month period starting from the start of that month plus the next 11 months.

'Financial acquisitions' are acquisitions that relate to the making of a financial supply (other than a financial supply consisting of a borrowing) (s189-15).

If you exceed either of these levels, you will have exceeded the financial acquisitions threshold and therefore not entitled to claim any input tax credits on acquisitions relating to making financial supplies. However, you may be entitled to claim RITCs of 75% of GST paid on reduced credit acquisitions.

If you do not exceed the financial acquisitions threshold, you will be entitled to full input tax credits under Division 11 for acquisitions relating to making financial supplies. Under such circumstance, you are not entitled to claim RITCs on reduced credit acquisitions as you will be able to claim full input tax credits under Division 11 for such acquisitions.

Financial acquisitions threshold is explained in greater detail in GSTR 2003/9.

Other aspects of the financial supply provisions are:

- Australian ADIs who make financial supplies consisting of a borrowing through the provision of deposit accounts are not able to claim input tax credits for acquisitions that relate to the financial supply consisting of a borrowing, even where the borrowing relates to making supplies that are not input taxed
- input tax credits on acquisitions made under a hire purchase agreement are available to cash basis taxpayers as if they had accounted on a non-cash basis for that transaction. This means that input tax credits are available upfront, and
- supplies or acquisitions of goods or credit made under a hire purchase agreement are not supplies or acquisitions made on a progressive or periodic basis.

23.316   GST AND SUPERANNUATION FUNDS

Essentially most acquisitions made by superannuation funds do not qualify for input tax credits under the basic rules as the acquisitions are connected with investments which are input taxed activities. This makes the acquisitions non-creditable acquisitions.

Unless the fund has direct property investments by which the fund may make a taxable supply, the only way it can obtain some relief from GST charged on its acquisitions is through the RITC provisions.

The RITCs claimed will be in addition to input tax credits claimed under the basic rules relating to any taxable or GST-free supplies. Knowing what these entities are entitled to under the RITC provisions will be critical information in deciding whether it is cost effective to register for GST and funds that are already registered, to maximise existing credit entitlements.

SUPERANNUATION FUND-SPECIFIC REDUCED CREDIT ACQUISITIONS

Particular categories of acquisitions for which an RITC will be available which are relevant to superannuation funds are as follows (reg. 70-5.02):

  a.   Securities transaction services – item 9

  b.   Funds management services – item 23, and

  c.   Fund administration functions – item 24.

NOTE: Accounting practitioners will need to itemise services they have provided on their invoices. If some of the services do not qualify as reduced credit acquisitions the invoice will need to be apportioned.

Some accountants perform most of the administrative duties for the fund and in this case not all of their fee will be eligible for RITCs. General accounting for the fund, tax and auditing do not qualify for RITCs. However, records relating to fund members and associated accounting do qualify for RITCs.

An acquisition of management services of a client's asset portfolio involves the ongoing services of professional management of an entity's investment portfolio to maximise return. A fundamental characteristic of this service is that the entity supplying the investment management services exercises control or authority over the asset portfolio in carrying out its obligations. This service involves more than the mere provision of advice to be acted upon by the client. An acquisition of advice, by itself, is not a reduced credit acquisition under item 23(a) of reg. 70-5.02.

Fees charged by a registered tax agent for the following **do not** give rise to an RITC:

- preparation and lodgement of tax returns and any other form/statement required by the Tax Office
- representing clients in connection with any audit activities instigated by the Tax Office
- provision of taxation advice
- business activity statements
- instalment activity statement
- preparation and lodgement of member contribution statements for super surcharge purposes
- audit fees
- specific investment advice not in the course of portfolio management, and
- purchase of a computer or software application to manage an investment portfolio.

Hazel Super Fund is a SMSF and is registered for GST. Hazel Super Fund has made the following purchases (amounts include GST):

- *repairs to residential property: $6,600*
- *repairs to commercial property: $13,200*
- *management of investment portfolio: $1,320 (50% relates to financial investment, 30% relates to residential property investment and 20% relates to commercial property investment)*
- *maintenance of member records and associated accounting (excluding auditing and tax services): $880 (50% relates to financial investment, 30% relates to residential property investment and 20% relates to commercial property investment)*
- *brokerage on share sale: $440.*

Financial acquisitions the fund made are:

- *50% of the investment portfolio management*
- *50% for maintaining member records and associated accounting, and*
- *100% brokerage on share sale.*

Total GST credits on financial acquisitions =
[($1,320+$880) x 50% x 1/11] + [$440 x 100% x 1/11] = $140

Total GST credits that the fund could claim (including financial acquisitions) =
[$13,200 + ($1,320 x 70%) + ($880 x 70%) + $440] x 1/11 = $1,380.

Although the amount of input tax credits relating to financial acquisitions does not exceed $150,000, the fund has still exceeded the financial acquisitions threshold as its total GST credits on financial acquisitions exceeds 10% of the total GST credits the fund could claim ($140 / $1,380 x 100% = 10.14%). Therefore the 'de minimis' exemption does not apply.

Hazel Super Fund is not entitled to claim input tax credits for GST paid on acquisitions that relate to the making of an input taxed supply of residential rent, which are input tax credits of:

* *$600 relating to repairs to residential property*
* *$36 relating to portion of the management investment portfolio that are related to the residential property, and*
* *$24 relating to portion of the maintenance of members records and accounting fees that are related to the residential property.*

Providing a commercial property by way of lease is a taxable supply and hence input tax credits on acquisitions in relation to making this supply are claimable. The input tax credit entitlement relating to this supply is calculated as: [$13,200 + ($1,320 x 20%) + ($880 x 20%)] x 1/11 = $1,240.

Fifty per cent of fees paid to manage the fund's investment portfolio and maintaining its member records and associated accounting as well as 100% brokerage fee are all purchases that relate to making financial supplies. The fund can claim RITCs for these purchases because these items are listed in the GST Regulations as reduced credit acquisitions. Therefore, the fund can claim RITCs for:

* *portfolio management: $45 ($1,320 x 50% x 1/11 x 75%)*
* *records maintenance and associated accounting: $30 ($880 x 50% x 1/11 x 75%), and*
* *brokerage costs: $30 ($440 x 100% x 1/11 x 75%).*

The total reduced GST credit they can claim is $45 + $30 + $30 = $105.

Therefore, the total input tax credits Hazel Super Fund is entitled to is $1,240 + $105 = $1,345 (rounded).

23.320 RESIDENTIAL RENTS (Subdivision 40-B)

A supply of residential premises by rental is input taxed to the extent that the supply is of residential premises used predominantly for residential accommodation (s40-35). The supplier of the premises cannot claim any input tax credits for GST included in the price of supplies acquired for the rental property (eg. insurance, repairs, agency commission).

'Residential premises' is defined to mean land or a building that is occupied as a residence or for residential accommodation or is intended to be occupied, and is capable of being occupied, as a residence or for residential accommodation, regardless of the term of the occupation or intended occupation.

GSTR 2012/5 deals with the term 'predominantly for residential accommodation'. This term indicates that premises that are residential premises are capable of use for purposes other than residential accommodation.

The function of this term is to differentiate the GST treatment of any portions of residential premises that are commercial. This would apply, for example, to a house that has been partly converted for use as a doctor's surgery. Several parts of the house may still be used predominantly for residential accommodation, such as bedrooms, bathroom, kitchen, living rooms and gardens, while other areas are not, having been converted to office and consulting room space, and storage for the surgery. In this case these commercial parts are excluded from the input-taxed treatment of the rest of the property and may be a taxable supply if all requirements under s9-5 are satisfied.

Whether or not a particular room or part of residential premises is to be used predominantly for residential accommodation, as opposed to commercial purposes, is a question of fact and degree. A home office in a house will not generally be sufficiently separate from the rest of the residential premises to distinguish its use and its predominant use will still be residential accommodation.

GSTR 2012/5 considers that it is their physical characteristics that mark them out as a residence. In turn, these characteristics determine when the use or proposed use is for residential accommodation.

To be used for 'residential accommodation' or to be 'occupied as a residence', premises do not have to be a home or a permanent place of abode. To be residential premises as defined, a place need only provide sleeping accommodation and the basic facilities for daily living, even if for a short term.

NOTE: A display home leased to a builder is an input taxed supply. A display home comprises a house that has all the usual physical characteristics that enable it to be used for residential accommodation.

 If a property is a retail outlet with a residence on top of the store, only the rent for the store is taxable as the supply of residential premises is input taxed only to the extent that the premises are used predominantly for residential accommodation. The supplier in this case will need to apportion its entitlement to input tax credits which will only apply to the proportion relating to the commercial rents. GSTR 2006/4 assists with determining the extent of creditable purpose for claiming input tax credits.

For more details on GST and real property see 24.340.

23.330 SALE OF RESIDENTIAL PREMISES (Subdivision 40-C)

Subject to two major exceptions, the supply of residential premises such as houses or units by way of sale or long term lease is input taxed (s40-65). That is, no GST is payable on the sale. The sale of residential premises is only input taxed to the extent that the premises are to be used predominantly for residential accommodation. Land alone, although zoned as residential, is not capable of being residential premises and will be a taxable supply if it satisfies all the requirements in s9-5.

The definition of 'residential premises' in s195-1 is as follows:

Residential premises means land or a building that:
- is occupied as a residence for residential accommodation, or
- is intended to be occupied, and is capable of being occupied, as a residence or for residential accommodation,

regardless of the term of the occupation or intended occupation, and includes a floating home.

Sellers of residential property will not be entitled to input tax credits for GST included in the expenses associated with the sale of the input taxed residential property. If residential property is purchased by an investor for rental, there will be no input tax credit entitlement for any GST included in the price. Similar treatment applies to occupancy related costs and the denial of input tax credits. However, the GST inclusive cost is included as part of deductible costs for income tax purposes.

There are however two major exceptions which effectively treat the sale of residential premises as taxable rather than input taxed. These are:
- the sale of new residential premises other than those used for residential accommodation before 2 December 1998, and
- the sale of commercial residential premises.

NEW RESIDENTIAL PREMISES

If the residential premises are new, the sale will not be input taxed. The definition of 'new residential premises' is therefore important.

Residential premises are new residential premises, as defined in s40-75(1), if they:
- have not previously been sold as residential premises (other than commercial residential premises) and have not previously been the subject of a long-term lease, or
- have been created through substantial renovations of a building, or
- have been built, or contain a building that has been built, to replace demolished premises on the same land.

These categories are not mutually exclusive. Provided residential premises satisfy any one of the categories, they are new residential premises.

Residential premises will not be sold as new residential premises if they have been previously sold as residential premises (other than commercial residential premises) or the subject of a long-term lease, unless they have been substantially renovated or built to replace demolished premises.

Section 40-75(2) provides that premises are not new residential premises if for five years after they have become new residential premises, they have only been used for making input taxed supplies of residential rent under s40-35(1)(a). See 24.342 for more detail on what is considered to be new residential premises.

NOTE: The five year rule will not apply if new residential premises have been applied for a dual purpose (eg. owner rents out the new residential premises but has an intention to sell the property when he is able to find a buyer) or if it has been used, other than for making input taxed supplies of residential rent during that five year period or more. GSTR 2003/3 considers the five year period must be a continuous period and not broken by short periods between tenancies in which the property is actively marketed for rent. The new residential property will remain new and therefore will qualify as an input taxed supply.

NOTE: If residential premises are new residential premises because they have been substantially renovated or built to replace demolished premises on the same land, the new residential premises include the land of which the new residential premises are part.

23.340 PRECIOUS METAL (Subdivision 40-D)

The first supply of precious metals by a refiner to a dealer of precious metals is GST-free (s38-385) (see 23.490). Any other supply of precious metals that does not qualify to be GST-free will be input taxed (s40-100). For example, subsequent supply of the precious metal by a dealer of precious metal will be an input taxed supply.

A 'precious metal' is:

- gold of at least 99.5% fineness
- silver of at least 99.9% fineness
- platinum of at least 99% fineness, or
- any other substance prescribed by regulation (s195-1).

In each case, the metal must be in an investment form.

23.350 FOOD SUPPLIED THROUGH SCHOOL TUCKSHOP
OR CANTEEN (Subdivision 40-E)

A non-profit body providing food through a school tuckshop or canteen of a primary or secondary school can choose to have the food treated as input taxed supplies.

However, this choice cannot be revoked within 12 months of when it is made and vice versa; the choice cannot be made within 12 months after a previous choice was revoked.

23.360 FUND-RAISING EVENTS BY CHARITIES ETC (Subdivision 40-F)

An endorsed charity, a gift-deductible entity or a government school may choose for supplies made in connection to a fund raising event to be input taxed.

The kinds of fund-raising events which can be treated as input taxed include:

- a fête, ball, gala show, dinner or similar event
- events comprising sales of goods (eg. flowers, chocolates) where the consideration received does not exceed $20 and the sale is not a normal part of the charity's business – exclude events involving sale of alcohol or tobacco products, or
- an event decided by the Commissioner to be a fund-raising event (on application in writing by fundraiser).

The Commissioner may only determine that an event is a fund-raising event if it is satisfied that the supplier is not in the business of conducting such events and the proceeds from the event are to directly benefit the supplier's charitable purpose.

23.400   GST-FREE SUPPLIES (Division 38)

Registered entities making GST-free supplies have no obligation to pay GST on the supplies they make, but they remain entitled to claim input tax credits for things they acquire in the course of carrying on their enterprise. Entities making GST-free supplies need to lodge a BAS to claim input tax credits.

 Entities supplying GST-free supplies should consider registering for GST and lodging their BAS on a monthly basis in order to bring forward the receipt of input tax credits.

23.410 EXPORTS (Subdivision 38-E)

The consumption of goods and other things outside Australia is generally GST-free. The circumstances in which the supply of goods for consumption outside Australia will be GST-free are set out at s38-185(1).

23.411   GOODS

For goods to be consumed outside of Australia, they must be physically transported out of Australia. The export of goods is GST-free if the supplier exports the goods from Australia within 60 days of receiving any consideration or issuing an invoice, whichever happens first.

NOTE: The GST meaning of goods is any form of tangible personal property (s195-1).

If consideration is to be invoiced and received in instalments, the 60 days start from the earlier of:

* the issue of an invoice for the final instalment, or
* when any of the final instalment is received.

The time at which goods are exported is the time at which the ship or aircraft with the goods on board departs its final Australian port or airport and clears the territorial limits of Australia. However, in practice, this time may not be known by the supplier. Therefore, the Commissioner accepts that the 60 days requirement is met when the supplier hands over possession of the goods to an international transport provider or delivers the goods to the ship or aircraft operator before or within the 60 day period (GSTR 2002/6).

 Taxpayers should keep records (eg. shipping documents such as airway bills, bills of lading, Customs Office paperwork) to prove that the timing requirements for exports to be GST-free have been met. The entity exporting the goods will lose its GST-free status if the export is not made within the 60 day period. An increasing adjustment will then be required if the GST-free status was claimed in an earlier tax period.

Excluding recipient exported goods, goods will be treated as exported by a supplier where:

* the supplier is responsible for delivering the goods on board a ship or to an aircraft operator, and
* that ship or aircraft operator has been engaged, either by the seller or the buyer (or by another party acting on behalf of the seller or buyer), to carry those goods to an overseas destination.

See GSTR 2002/6 for further explanation of when supplies of goods are GST-free exports including where the supplier contracts with an international carrier for the transportation of the goods to a destination outside Australia.

A supply of goods is GST-free if the supplier exports the goods from Australia to an associate for no consideration.

NOTE: Eligible supplies of boats used for recreational purposes are GST-free if the boats are exported within 12 months. The rule applies to supplies of ships made under contracts entered into on or after 1 July 2011 and which are not made pursuant to rights or options granted before 1 July 2011.

23.412   RECIPIENT EXPORTED GOODS

It is common for the Australian supplier to supply the goods to an overseas purchaser who takes delivery whilst in Australia and organises the export.

The Australian supplier can treat such a supply as a GST-free export only if the following conditions are met (s38-185(3)):

- the overseas purchaser is not GST registered nor required to be registered but is responsible for exporting the goods
- the goods have been entered for export
- the goods will not be altered or used in any way by the overseas purchaser (except to the extent necessary to prepare them for export), and
- the Australian supplier has documentary evidence that the purchaser actually exported the goods.

Unless all of the above are satisfied, GST will be payable on the supply. Australian suppliers will be at risk as they are reliant on the purchaser to provide documentary evidence to prove goods were exported.

23.413   OTHER GOODS

The following exports of goods are also GST-free:

- export of aircraft or ships (s38-185(1) item 3 and 4)
- export of goods that are to be consumed on international flights or voyages where the destination is outside Australia whether or not part of the flight involves journey between places in Australia (s38-185(1) item 5) – see GSTR 2003/4 for more information
- export of new recreational boats
- goods used to repair, renovate, modify or treat imported goods whose destination is outside Australia (s38-185(1) item 6), and
- goods exported by travellers as accompanied baggage (s38-185(1) item 7) - see 23.423 under *Tourist Refund Scheme*.

Goods exported by travellers are GST-free only if the traveller qualifies as a 'relevant traveller'. The GST provisions adopted the meaning of 'relevant traveller' used in the *Customs Act 1901*. The AAT held that a sale of goods was not GST-free because the supplier could not prove that the goods were sold to relevant travellers in *Sogo Duty Free Pty Ltd v FC of T* (2010) AATA 111.

For goods used to repair, renovate, modify or treat imported goods which are then exported overseas to be GST-free, the goods used must be attached to the imported goods, or become unusable as a direct result of the repair. For example, the spare parts used to repair a car will be GST-free under s38-185(1) item 6 if it is used to repair a car imported from Japan which is intended for export to New Zealand. However, the tools used for this repair will not be GST-free. The repair services may be GST-free – see 23.416. This exemption will not apply if the work done has resulted in the creation of new goods (GSTR 2005/2). However, the new goods may be GST-free under item 1 of s38-185(1) if it meets the requirement of exported goods.

23.414   LEASE OF GOODS USED OVERSEAS

Leasing or hiring out of goods used outside Australia will be GST-free (s38-187).

23.415   TOOLING

Supplies of tooling (certain machine tools) to non-residents who are neither registered for GST nor required to be registered for GST can be GST-free if the tooling is to be used in Australia solely to manufacture goods for export (s38-188).

23.416   THE SUPPLY OF THINGS OTHER THAN GOODS OR REAL PROPERTY
        (s38-190)

The supply of things other than goods or real property (ie. services, rights etc) for consumption outside of Australia may be GST-free if certain criteria are met.

When the supply is not a good or real property, s38-190(1) is the operative section which taxpayers must satisfy in order for the supply to be treated as GST-free.

Subsection 38-190(1) sets out five items which are things other than goods or real property for consumption outside Australia and are GST-free unless ss38-190(2), (2A) or (3) apply (anti-avoidance provisions).

Supplies of things, other than goods or real property, for consumption outside Australia		
Item	Topic	These supplies are GST-free
1	Supply connected with property outside Australia	A supply that is directly connected with goods or real property situated outside Australia.
2	Supply to non-resident	A supply that is made to a non-resident who is not in Australia when the thing supplied is done, and: • the supply is neither a supply of work physically performed on goods situated in Australia when the work is done nor a supply directly connected with real property situated in Australia, or • the non-resident acquires the thing in carrying on the non-resident's enterprise, but is not registered or required to be registered.
3	Supplies used or enjoyed outside Australia	A supply: • that is made to a recipient who is not in Australia when the thing supplied is done, and • the effective use or enjoyment which takes place outside Australia • other than a supply of work physically performed on goods situated in Australia when the thing supplied is done, or a supply directly connected with real property situated in Australia.
4	Rights	A supply that is made in relation to rights if: • the rights are for use outside Australia, or • the supply is to an entity that is not an Australian resident • and is outside Australia when the thing supplied is done.
5	Export of services used to repair etc. imported goods	A supply that is constituted by the repair, renovation, goods modification or treatment of goods from outside Australia whose destination is outside Australia.

 Items (2) and (3) will not be GST-free if the supply under an agreement entered into, directly or indirectly, with a non-resident, is provided (or the agreement requires for the supply to be provided) to another entity in Australia (s38-190(3) and (4)).

SUPPLY THAT IS MADE IN RELATION TO RIGHTS

In *Travelex Ltd v FCT* [2010] HCA 33 the High Court affirmed the lower courts' decision that the supply of foreign currency was not GST-free. The phrase 'supply that is made in relation to rights' under s38-190(1) item 4 should be construed as meaning a supply of rights by way of the creation, grant, transfer or assignment of the rights or a supply by way of the surrender of the rights. In this case, the taxpayer, Travelex contended that the supply of Fijian currency resulted in the holder obtaining rights to spend the note in Fiji. Therefore, the supply of Fijian currency was made in relation to the rights that arose by reason of the passenger being the holder or owner of bank notes issued by the Reserve Bank of Fiji and that those rights were for use outside Australia within the meaning of s38-190(1) item 4(a) and should be classified as a GST-free supply. Both the taxpayer and the Commissioner agreed that the supply of Fijian currency is a financial supply under s40-5(2) and therefore an input taxed supply. However, under the operation of s9-30(3)(a) to the extent a supply is both GST-free and input taxed, the supply will be GST-free and not input taxed.

The court held that s38–190(1) item 4 only applied to a supply if the essential character or substance of the supply, or a separately identifiable part of the supply, was one of rights. It did not apply where the supply of rights was merely integral, ancillary or incidental to another dominant part of the supply, the supply being characterised by the dominant part. A supply that did not bind the parties in some way was not a supply that was made in relation to rights.

The supply of brokerage services that facilitates the sale or purchase of financial products on overseas securities or futures exchanges is a GST-free supply under para (a) of item 4 in the table in subs 38-190(1) (GSTD 2015/1).

'DIRECTLY CONNECTED WITH GOODS OR REAL PROPERTY' (ITEMS 1 TO 3 OF S38-190(1))

GSTR 2003/7 gives guidance as to the interpretation of 'directly connected with goods or real property'. If a supply is directly connected with goods or real property, it is treated, for the purposes of s38-190(1), as being consumed where the goods or real property are located. The Commissioner's interpretation of the expression 'directly connected with' in the context of s38-190(1) contemplates a very close link or association between the supply and the goods or the real property. The supply must have a direct effect (or have the purpose of having a direct effect) upon the goods or real property.

In determining whether there is a direct connection between a supply and specific goods or real property, the location of the recipient of a supply is not relevant.

A close link or association between the supply and particular goods or real property exists where:

- the supply changes or affects the goods or real property in a physical way, or
- there is a physical interaction with the goods or real property but without changing the goods or real property, or
- the supply establishes the quantity, size, other physical attributes or the value of the goods or real property, or
- the supply affects (or its purpose is to affect) or protects the nature or value (including indemnity against loss) of the goods or real property, or
- the supply affects, or is proposed to affect, the ownership of the goods or real property including any interest in, or right in or over goods or real property.

EFFECTIVE USE OR ENJOYMENT TAKES PLACE OUTSIDE AUSTRALIA

GSTR 2007/2 explains when 'effective use or enjoyment' of the supply may 'take place outside Australia' in respect of s38-190(1) item 3(b) of the GST Act to a supply. The Ruling explains:

- how to determine when effective use or enjoyment of a supply takes place, or does not take place, outside Australia, and
- the apportionment required if effective use or enjoyment of the supply takes place in part outside Australia.

'A SUPPLY OF WORK PHYSICALLY PERFORMED ON GOODS' (s38-190(1) item 3)

According to GSTR 2003/7, a supply of work physically performed on goods requires a closer connection with the goods that are 'directly connected with goods or real property'. It requires a physical intervention with the goods. For example, a supply affecting a transfer of title to goods is directly connected with goods but it is not a supply of work physically performed on goods as there is no physical intervention with the goods.

A supply is a supply of work physically performed on goods where something is done to the goods to change them or to otherwise affect them in some physical way. In contrast, where activities do not change or affect goods in a physical way there is no supply of work physically performed on goods. For example, a supply of transporting goods is not work physically performed on goods because the supply only changes the location of the goods, not the goods themselves.

The work physically performed does not have to bring about a fundamental change to the attributes of the goods. For example, cleaning goods is a supply of work physically performed on goods even though the cleaning does not make them into fundamentally different goods - the change is simply the difference between dirty goods and clean goods. Other examples of work physically performed on goods include supplies that maintain or restore the function of goods. Repairs to machinery used in a manufacturing business falls into this category. Painting a ship is also a supply of work physically performed on goods: the purpose of the supply is to preserve the physical condition of the vessel.

SUPPLIES TO OFFSHORE OWNERS OF AUSTRALIAN RESIDENTIAL PROPERTY

Under subs38-190(2A), services you supply (directly or indirectly, partly or wholly) to a non-resident owner of an Australian residential property became subject to GST if the owner makes or intends to make a supply of the property by:

- renting the property, or
- selling the property (excluding the sale of new residential premises).

Services commonly supplied may include, but are not limited to:

- repairs and maintenance
- rent collection ensuring the rental property is properly maintained and secured
- obtaining tenants
- signing lease agreements on behalf of non-resident owners, and
- arranging a tradesperson to repair and/or maintain the rental property.

NOTE: You need to include GST on tax invoices you provide to non-resident property owners and report the GST to be paid on your activity statement.

23.420 GST AND TRAVEL

Goods and services consumed by tourists in Australia, such as meals and hotel accommodation, are subject to GST as such supplies have the necessary connection with Australia (see 23.140).

Paragraph 9-25(5)(c) ensures the supply of a right or option to acquire something in which the thing would have been connected to Australia would have the necessary connection with Australia. This means that components of Australian travel packages such as car hire, meals, entertainment, domestic transfer, etc. made by registered foreign travel operators are subject to GST (see NAT 13904).

Certain telecommunication supplies for global roaming in Australia which are provided to subscribers of a non-resident telecommunication supplier while the subscribers are visiting Australia are GST-free.

23.421 INTERNATIONAL TRANSPORTATION (Subdivision 38-K)

International air travel and sea travel are GST-free, as well as any domestic travel purchased whilst overseas by non-residents. Domestic air and sea travel is also GST-free if it is part of international travel and the domestic leg forms part of an international ticket or was cross-referenced to an international travel ticket.

Other supplies relating to international transportation that are GST-free include:

- international travel insurance including the domestic component if the domestic component forms part of the international travel (s38-355 item 6 and GSTR 2000/33)
- services to arrange transport or insurance in relation to GST-free travel – eg. travel agent's fee in arranging international air ticket and travel insurance (s38-355 item 7)
- travel agent services in relation to arranging for supplies in which its effective use or enjoyment is to take place outside Australia – eg. travel agent's fee for arranging overseas accommodation (s38-360)
- international transportation of goods to, from Australia or between destinations outside Australia
  (s38-355 item 5). Note if the transportation of goods to and from Australia includes a domestic component, the domestic component is GST-free only when the domestic transportation is provided by the same supplier that supplies the international transportation, and
- insurance and associated loading and handling services in relation to international transportation of goods (s38-355 item 6 and 7).

Further:

- the cost of domestic transport is added to the 'value of taxable importation' which is used to calculate the GST liability on importation, and

- subcontracted domestic services that are part of the domestic leg of an inbound or outbound international transport service is made GST-free when made to a non-resident not in Australia.

23.422 INWARD DUTY FREE PURCHASES (Subdivision 38-M)

Airport shop goods such as tobacco, alcoholic beverages, perfume etc. purchased by passengers or crew members that have arrived in Australia on an international flight from an inwards duty free airport shop are GST-free (s38-415).

23.423 TOURIST REFUND SCHEME (TRS) (Division 168)

Tourists and Australian residents (except for operating air and sea crew) going overseas can recover GST paid on some goods purchased in Australia which they take with them when they leave. This is limited to purchases totalling $300 and above from the same retailer, as an aggregate of multiple invoices, and purchases must be made within 60 days of departure. When the person exports the goods when they leave Australia, they can claim a GST refund, and a WET refund if applicable, at the TRS facility at any international airport or seaport.

NOTE: The TRS does not apply to goods that are consumed or partly consumed in Australia such as food. However, other goods such as clothing and electrical appliances purchased in Australia and used in Australia prior to departure are also eligible for TRS.

TRS also does not apply to tobacco or tobacco products and alcoholic beverages (except for wine on which WET has been paid). Unaccompanied goods such as freight or posted goods will not be eligible for TRS.

Refunds are claimed at TRS booths at airports and require the traveller to produce the following:

- the original tax invoices totalling $300 or more (inclusive of GST)
- their passport
- their international boarding pass, and
- their goods (unless it is liquid, aerosol or gel which is forbidden by aviation security measure).

NOTE: Residents of Australia's External Territories (including Norfolk, Cocos (Keeling) and Christmas Islands) can claim GST refunds under the TRS if they can prove that the goods have been exported to the External Territory within the required timeframes.

The Sealed Bag Scheme (SBS) allows international travellers to purchase goods, tax-free (excise or customs duty, GST or WET) from duty free stores and certain retail stores. Goods purchased through the SBS are placed in a sealed bag which remains sealed to ensure that the traveller takes the goods out of the country so that the goods cannot be consumed in Australia, and therefore are not subject to Australian taxes. Goods must be acquired within 60 days of departure.

23.430 HEALTH GOODS AND SERVICES (Subdivision 38-B)

23.431 MEDICAL SERVICES (s38-7)

Medical services are GST-free if supplied by, or on behalf of, a medical practitioner or an approved pathology practitioner. The definition of 'medical practitioner' is as per the *Health Insurance Act 1973*. It includes general practitioners and specialists such as radiologists, anesthetists and oncologists. The service must also be generally accepted in the medical profession as being appropriate and necessary for the treatment of the recipient of the supply, or for which a Medicare benefit is payable. Note that preventative medicine such as childhood immunisation program is considered to be necessary and appropriate treatment.

NOTE: A medical report supplied is only GST-free where a Medicare benefit is payable for it.

NOTE: Medical check-ups performed by or on behalf of a medical practitioner such as pap smear, breast cancer screening, vaccination, etc. are generally accepted as being necessary and appropriate treatment for patients and are therefore GST-free.

A medical practitioner contracted and paid by a third party to supply medical services to a patient does not fall under GST-free medical services as the recipient of the medical services is the third party and not the patient even though it is the patient receiving the treatment. The medical service is not seen as necessary and appropriate treatment to the recipient of the supply. For example, where an employer pays a medical practitioner to perform a medical examination on potential employees, the supply is not one of GST-free medical services.

Goods supplied in the course of supplying GST-free medical services such as bandages, dressings and antiseptics made at the premises at which the medical services are supplied will also be GST-free (s38-7(3)).

NON-GST-FREE MEDICAL SERVICES

Medical services rendered where no Medicare benefit is payable is not a GST-free supply despite it being provided by a medical practitioner. This generally covers services that are purely for cosmetic purposes. Further, certain professional services supplied within the meaning of regulation 14 of the Health Insurance Regulations made under the *Health Insurance Act 1973* such as removal of tattoo or injection of prescribed substances in the management of obesity are excluded from being GST-free.

23.432   OTHER HEALTH SERVICES (s38-10)

The GST-free exemption also applies to other recognised health professionals who provide the following health services in which the supply is generally accepted in the profession as being necessary for the appropriate treatment of the recipient of the supply:

- Aboriginal or Torres Strait Islander health
- Acupuncture
- Audiology, audiometry
- Chiropody
- Chiropractic
- Dental
- Dietary
- Herbal medicine (including traditional Chinese herbal medicine)
- Naturopathy
- Nursing
- Occupational therapy
- Optometry
- Osteopathy
- Paramedical
- Pharmacy
- Psychology
- Physiotherapy
- Podiatry
- Speech pathology
- Speech therapy, and
- Social work.

23.433   DRUGS AND MEDICINAL PREPARATIONS (s38-50)

Drugs and medicinal preparations are GST-free if:

- the supply is on a prescription and the supply is restricted and can only be made on prescription,
- the drug or medicine is on prescription and is a pharmaceutical benefit
- supplied by a medical practitioner, dental practitioner, pharmacist or other person permitted by law

- eligible analgesic as determined by the Health Minister to be GST-free in GST-free supply (Drugs and Medicinal Preparations) Determinations, and
- supplied under Special Access Scheme for example in circumstances where a person has a life-threatening or other serious condition and products that are approved under the Australian Register of Therapeutic Goods that are available at that time are found unsuitable.

A supply of drug or medicinal preparation is GST-free only if it is for human consumption and the supply is to an individual for private or domestic use or consumption. Therefore, drugs acquired to be on-supply such as the supply of drugs from a manufacturer/supplier to a pharmacist will not be GST-free because it is not supply made to an individual for private use.

23.434   OTHER GST-FREE MEDICAL AND HEALTH RELATED SERVICES

These supplies are also treated as GST-free:
- ambulance service in the course of treatment of the recipient (s38-10(5))
- other government funded health services in connection with GST-free medical services (s38-7) or other health services (s38-10) as determined by the Health Minister in writing (s38-15)
- a supply of hospital treatment and a supply of goods if supply is directly related to supply of hospital treatment (main exceptions: cosmetic treatments that do not qualify for Medicare benefits (s38-20))
- supplies of residential, community and flexible care specified in the *Aged Care Act 1997* (ss38-25, 38-30 & 38-35) – see 23.435
- services described as accommodation, community support, community access or respite provided by a supplier who receives funding under the *Disability Services Act 1986* (s38-40)
- medical aids and appliances covered in Schedule 3 of the GST Act designed for people with an illness or disability and is not widely used by people without an illness or disability (eg. wheelchairs, crutches, artificial limbs and modifications to cars) – supplier and recipient of such supply can together agree to not treat these supplies as GST-free (s38-45)
- private health insurance and insurance against liability to pay for ambulance services (s38-55), and
- the supply of other health goods as determined by the Health Minister to be GST-free under GST-free Supply (Health Goods) Determination 2005 – supplier and recipient of such supply can together choose not to treat these supplies as GST-free (s38-47).

The supply of a car to a disabled veteran or other disabled individuals may be GST-free (Subdivision 38P) (see 23.490).

Certain supplies made to health insurers in the course of settling health insurance claims are GST-free.

NOTE: Non-medical care items such as food served in hospital cafeterias and rented television sets etc. are subject to GST.

A supply made by a health care provider to:
- an insurer
- a statutory compensation scheme operator
- a compulsory third party scheme operator, or
- a government entity

is treated as a GST-free supply to the extent that the underlying supply from the health care provider to an individual is a GST-free health supply from 1 July 2012.

23.435   GST-FREE RESIDENTIAL CARE SERVICES AND ACCOMMODATION
     (s38-25)

A supply of residential care services is GST-free if the services are of a kind covered by Schedule 1 to the *Quality of Care Principles 1997* and provided by:

- an approved residential care provider through a residential care service (within the meaning of the *Aged Care Act 1997*)
- a government funded body to one or more aged or disabled people, or
- a private facility to an aged or disabled person in a residential setting; and includes daily living activities assistance or nursing services that are only provided to people who require them.

Further, the supply of retirement village accommodation by an endorsed charitable institution or endorsed charitable fund may also be GST-free under s38-260 (see 23.450).

The Aged Care Minister has issued the *GST-free Supply (Residential Care – Non-Government Funded Supplier) Determination 2000* that sets out the circumstances in which certain supplies are of a kind covered by Schedule 1 to the *Quality of Care Principles 1997*.

- A supply of residential premises consisting of a serviced apartment in a retirement village by way of lease, hire, licence, freehold or under a share arrangement is GST-free if: the premises are supplied to a resident who requires daily living activities assistance or nursing services, and
- the premises are supplied in connection with the supply of care services and other services, such as meals, laundry and cleaning, that meet the requirements outlined above to be GST-free.

Daily living activities assistance and nursing services are set out in Items 2.1 and 3.8 of Schedule 1 to the *Quality of Care Principles 1997*, which is available on the Department of Health and Ageing website at www.health.gov.au.

A retirement village is residential premises in which:

- accommodation is intended for people who are at least 55 years old or older, and
- there are communal facilities for use by the residents of the premises.

The Commissioner released Taxpayer Alert TA 2010/7 which describes an arrangement in which a retirement village operator requires residents to buy electricity which the operator has purchased from an electricity supplier.

Where the residential accommodation is GST-free, retirement village operators are not entitled to claim GST credits on the costs of supplying that accommodation. However, under the arrangement described in TA 2010/7, the retirement village operator is able to claim GST credits by treating its supply of electricity to residents as a taxable supply, separate from the non-taxable supply of residential accommodation.

In a separate media release, the Commissioner warned retirement village operators that the Tax Office will review these arrangements where they sell services, such as electricity, to residents in an attempt to gain a tax advantage.

The Commissioner believes that these arrangements appear artificial and contrived in their design and execution. In his view, it is unlikely these operators would begin supplying electricity under a separate contract if it was not for the GST credits they believe they will gain from the arrangement. As such, the Commissioner emphasised that the Tax Office will examine these arrangements and any others that attempt to take advantage of the GST provisions contrary to the intention of the law.

In GSTR 2012/3, the Commissioner expresses his views in relation to when supplies of care services and supplies of accommodation to residents in privately funded nursing homes and aged care hostels or serviced apartments in a retirement village are GST-free.

23.440   EDUCATION AND CHILDCARE

23.441   EDUCATION (Subdivision 38-C)

The supply of an 'education course' is GST-free. Education courses provided by all recognised pre-school, primary school, secondary school and tertiary institutions (including a college, TAFE, university or other recognised institutions that leads to a degree, diploma, certificate or similar qualification) are GST-free. The Minister for Education is able to make a course GST-free by Ministerial Determination. For the purposes of the GST Act 'education course' is defined in s195-1.

NOTE: By Ministerial Determination, Language Other Than English (LOTE) courses provided by an approved non-profit ethnic school, where its primary aim is to teach languages other than English and has close links with a community whose first language is not English, will be GST-free.

These education-related supplies are GST-free (see also GSTR 2000/27; GSTR 2000/30; GSTR 2001/1; GSTR 2003/1):

- supply of an educational course (includes tuition, facilities and other curriculum related activities)
- supply of administrative services (eg. school library fees) directly related to the supply of an educational course, if provided by the supplier of the course
- supply of course material
- supply by way of lease or hire of curriculum-related goods to a student by the supplier of the education course (provided ownership remains with the supplier)
- supply of an excursion, but only if the excursion is directly related to the curriculum and is not predominantly recreational
- assessment or issue of qualification carried out by the relevant body (eg. an education institution, Commonwealth authority, professional association, etc.) for the purpose of access to education, membership of a professional/trade association, employment or registration or licensing for a particular occupation
- supply of student accommodation by the supplier of the course to students undertaking a primary or secondary course, and/or attending a 'special school'
- if the accommodation is provided in a hostel, the primary purpose of which is to provide accommodation for students from rural or remote locations undertaking such courses, and
- supply of cleaning and maintenance, electricity, gas, heating, telephone, television or any other similar thing as part of the provision of student accommodation which is GST-free.

NOTE: Cancellation fees as a result of withdrawal from a GST-free course after the course has started or even before the commencement of the course will also be GST-free as the payment made is connected to a GST-free course. For more information see 23.124 and GSTR 2009/3.

These educational services are also GST-free:

- lifesaving and first aid courses provided by approved entities, principally involving training individuals in first aid, resuscitation or other similar life saving skills (including personal aquatic survival skills but not swimming lessons), surf life saving and aero-medical rescue (see NAT 10336 and NAT 10920)
- professional or trade courses where they are an essential prerequisite to entry or commencement of employment in a trade, profession or occupation but not a course for a qualification which may be required by a particular employer
- an English language course for overseas students
- special education course designed specifically for children with disabilities or students with disabilities
- an adult and community education course as determined by the Education Minister, and
- tertiary residential college course supplied in connection with a tertiary course at premises that are used to provide accommodation to students undertaking tertiary courses.

The following supplies are **not** GST-free:

- uniforms, sports clothes, musical instruments, equipment or textbooks
- supply of any food as part of an excursion
- supply of food as part of student accommodation
- accommodation provided as part of an excursion in relation to a tertiary course, tertiary residential college course or professional or trade course
- supply by way of sale of goods other than course material
- supply of membership to a student group, and

- hobby or personal development and recreational courses and courses undertaken to keep abreast of developments in a professional field and short occupational courses to maintain skills.

School tuckshops are not required to charge GST on the goods they sell if they choose to be input taxed, which means they are unable to claim input tax credits on their acquisitions (Subdivision 40-E) – see 23.350.

23.442   CHILDCARE (Subdivision 38-D)

Childcare provided at a recognised facility receiving government funding, or by a registered carer for the purposes of the Childcare rebate, is GST-free, whether the childcare is long day care, short day care (before and/or after school), family day care, occasional care, vacation care or any other type of care determined by the Childcare Minister. All directly related goods and services supplied by, or on behalf of, the supplier of the child care are also GST-free.

NOTE: Child care services provided by an unregistered/unrecognised entity eg. a private baby sitter is not GST-free. However, in most cases the supply is not subject to GST as the entity will not be registered for GST.

NOTE: Pre-school courses are GST-free under Subdivision 38-C 'Education' see 23.441.

23.450   CHARITABLE ACTIVITIES (Subdivision 38-G)

Generally, non-commercial activities of endorsed charities are GST-free.

A supply by an endorsed charity, a gift deductible entity or a government school is GST-free if:
- For a supply other than accommodation, the consideration must be:
  - less than 50% of the GST inclusive market value of the supply, or
  - less than 75% of the consideration provided by the charity for acquiring the thing supplied. (The consideration the supplier provided for acquiring capital assets that diminish in value over time can be taken into account, to the extent the consideration provided reasonably relates to that supply: GSTD 2013/4.)
- For a supply of accommodation, the consideration must be:
  - less than 75% of the GST-inclusive market value of the supply, or
  - less than 75% of the cost to the supplier to provide the accommodation.
- For a supply of second-hand goods
  - those goods were supplied to the institution as a gift, or
  - by way of a supply that was GST-free for any of the above reasons.

NOTE: However, if the donated goods have been transformed from their original character, they will be subject to GST (s38-255).

The above non-commercial activities of charities are not GST-free where the supply is made by a gift-deductible entity endorsed as a deductible gift recipient unless:
- the supplier is an endorsed charity, or
- the supplier is a government school, or
- the supplier is a fund, authority or institution of a kind referred to in s30-125(1)(b) ITAA97, or
- each purpose to which the supply relates is a gift-deductible purpose of the supplier.

The meaning of 'charitable institution' is set out in TR 2011/4. See also TR 2005/22 for companies controlled by exempt entities. Note in *Commissioner of Taxation v Word Investments Limited* [2008] HCA 55, the Full High Court held that an institution could be charitable even where it did not engage in charitable activities beyond making profits that were directed to charitable institutions which did engage in charitable activities.

 In the aftermath of the Word Investments *decision, the government proposed a number of reforms to the not-for-profit sector, including the introduction of a statutory definition of 'charity'. The new definition is contained in the Charities Act 2013 which commenced on 1 January 2014. The Act, among other things:*

- *defines charity and charitable purpose for the purposes of Commonwealth law*

- *describes 12 categories of charitable purposes derived from principles in common law, and*

- *allows charitable funds to retain their charitable status for the purposes of Commonwealth law where they provide benefits to an entity that would be a charity except that it is a government entity.*

23.460 SUPPLY OF A GOING CONCERN (Subdivision 38-J)

Supplies that satisfy the going concern requirements of the GST Act are GST-free (s38-325).

A supply of a going concern arises where the supply is for consideration, the recipient is registered or required to be registered for GST purposes and both the supplier and the recipient have agreed in writing that the supply is of a going concern.

 The written agreement must be in place at or before the time of the supply: see Brookdale Investments Pty Ltd & FC of T *[2013] AATA 154* and Re Nitram Consulting Pty Ltd & FC of T *[2008] AATA 1119.*

NOTE: A proposal that the GST-free status of supplies of going concerns be replaced with a reverse charge mechanism has been abandoned.

The Tribunal has held that the written agreement need not necessarily be written into the contract of sale. In *SDI Group Pty Ltd & FC of T* [2012] AATA 763, it was held that other documentation, a tax invoice and a particular type of statutory declaration provided the necessary written evidence that the going concern exemption had been adopted.

The supplier must supply all of the things that are necessary for the continued operation of an enterprise and the supplier must carry on (or will carry on) the enterprise until the day of supply. The Tax Office's interpretation of the requirements is contained in GSTR 2002/5.

NOTE: This ruling is being reviewed in the light of the decision of the High Court in *FC of T v MBI Properties Pty Ltd* [2014] HCA 49.

The Federal Court decision in *Aurora Developments Pty Ltd v FC of T* [2011] FCA 232 confirms that the conditions required for the going concern provisions to be satisfied, that is, (i) in supplying 'all things necessary' and (ii) maintaining the same enterprise until the day of supply, are strictly interpreted by the courts. The Court believed that it was not sufficient that the purchaser selected or had been supplied with only the things they regarded as necessary to undertake their enterprise. In terms of the 'day of supply', the Court noted that the settlement day for the contract was to occur 60 days from the date the taxpayer gave notice to the purchaser of the satisfaction of the contractual conditions. In the Court's view, this meant that settlement was treated by the taxpayer and the purchaser as the day of supply. It was therefore necessary that the relevant enterprise continue until that day.

A 'thing' is considered to be necessary for the continued operation of an 'identified enterprise' if the enterprise could not be operated by the recipient in the absence of the thing. The supplier must supply all of the things necessary for the continued operation of an enterprise so that the recipient is in a position to carry on the enterprise, if the recipient chooses. However, the intended or actual use of the things by the recipient is not relevant in determining whether a particular supply is a 'supply of a going concern'.

 An entity acquiring a GST-free going concern will need to make an adjustment to remit GST to the Tax Office for any private or input taxed use of the going concern –see 23.264.

 Buying an enterprise (eg. a business or tenanted commercial building) under the going concern exemption will enable the purchaser to avoid unnecessary stamp duty as the purchase price is a GST-exclusive amount rather than a GST-inclusive price. Also, the purchaser will not need to finance the GST component and then have to wait to receive the input tax credit.

 Where the vendor agrees to the GST-free going concern concession to apply, this will advantage the purchaser as noted above. The vendor should obtain from the purchaser an indemnity against the possibility that for one reason or another it turns out that the concession does not apply.

Where the identified enterprise forms part of a larger enterprise, the supplier can still use the going concern exemption so long as all of the things necessary to continue the operation of that part of the enterprise as an independent enterprise are supplied (eg. where an owner of a chain of retail bakeries sells off one of its bakeries in a particular suburb).

If the item in question is merely an asset used in the supplier's enterprise, it will not qualify as supply of a going concern.

In some circumstances, it may not be possible for a supplier to transfer some of the things necessary for the continued operation of an enterprise. Where the asset is incapable of assignment (eg. statutory licence, permit, quota or franchise agreement), the Tax Office view is that the surrender of the relevant asset is, in substance, enough to satisfy the requirements of the going concern exemption in circumstances where it is highly probable that the asset will be automatically reissued by the relevant third party.

If the enterprise has goodwill which is capable of being supplied, that goodwill must be supplied as one of the things necessary for the continued operation of that enterprise. If the goodwill arises from the personal attributes of an individual, it will be sufficient compliance, with the requirement that goodwill be supplied, for the supplier to agree to introduce existing customers to the recipient.

Staff are not capable of being supplied, therefore all that a vendor must do is take all reasonable steps to facilitate the transfer of particular skills and knowledge of key employees.

Where a supplier occupies premises pursuant to a mere tenancy at will (eg, during a brief holding over upon expiration of a lease) and pays no rent, the supplier is unable to supply those premises because a tenancy at will is not capable of assignment. If the premises occupied under a tenancy at will are a thing necessary for the continued operation of the relevant enterprise, the supplier is not able to make a supply of a going concern. But, if upon expiration of a lease, the tenant is allowed to continue in possession pursuant to a short term periodic tenancy, the new periodic tenancy may be capable of assignment. Care is clearly needed in these kinds of case.

ID 2012/54 sets out the Commissioner's view that an entity can supply something that is being utilised in its enterprise, which is not necessary for its continued operation, independently of the arrangement under which the business is sold to the same recipient as a going concern. A thing is considered to be supplied independently of the arrangement if:

- it is supplied under a separate, independent agreement whose terms are not dependent upon any other agreement under which the entity's business is sold to the same recipient as a GST-free going concern, and
- it is not identified as being a part of the arrangement in a written agreement entered into by the parties for the purposes of the going concern provisions, or in any other written agreement that describes the arrangement under which the entity's business is sold to the recipient as a GST-free going concern.

To qualify for the going concern exemption, the supplier must carry on the enterprise until the day of supply. All activities of the enterprise must be active and operating on the day of supply. The day of the supply is the date the recipient assumes effective control and possession of the enterprise (usually settlement date). It is important that the enterprise being supplied must not only be carried on but also operating. An enterprise that is in the process of selling off its assets and terminating its activity is considered to be carrying on an enterprise but not active and operating and could therefore not be a supply of a going concern.

NOTE: For the interaction of the GST-free going concern and the margin scheme see 24.344.

SUPPLY OF A LEASING ENTERPRISE

GSTR 2002/5 accepts that the enterprise of leasing can be the subject of the supply of a going concern. Accordingly, the sale of leased premises can be the supply of a going concern.

NOTE: All things necessary for the continued operation of an enterprise consisting solely of the leasing of a property include the property and the lease covenants. Therefore, an owner of an enterprise consisting solely of the leasing of a property cannot make a 'supply of a going concern' when supplying the real property to the current tenant of the property because the owner is incapable of supplying the tenant the benefit of the lease covenants.

With respect to a temporarily vacant commercial property, if the building was previously leased to a tenant, it will remain as an enterprise during a period of temporary vacancy when a new tenant is being actively sought by the building owner. If certain floors of a building are unavailable for lease temporarily while repairs, refurbishment or other activities requiring vacancy take place, the requirement that the vacant floors be actively marketed will not apply to those floors for the period during which the activities take place. However, where a building has not previously been leased but is actively being marketed, an enterprise of leasing is not in operation until the activity of leasing actually commences. Therefore, under such circumstance the enterprise cannot be the supply of a going concern until a time where an agreement to lease the property is entered into.

A purchaser of a going concern will need to make an increasing adjustment for the extent of the going concern that is not used to make taxable or GST-free supplies (see 24.264). A residential lease is an input taxed supply. Therefore, for any part of a going concern used to make a supply of residential premises, the purchaser will need to make an increasing adjustment equivalent to the GST amount payable had the part relating to residential premises not been subject to the going concern exemption.

SUPPLY OF A GOING CONCERN AND PARTNERSHIP

The supply of an interest in a partnership is not a supply of a going concern as the enterprise is not carried on by the partner. However, the partnership can sell part of its enterprise or all of its assets to another entity under the going concern exemption.

A single entity (ie. sole trader) that takes a partner into its business results in the formation of a partnership and an acquisition of an interest in the partnership by each partner. If the supply of the enterprise meets all the other requirements of the going concern exemption, it can also be GST-free as a supply of a going concern.

Similarly, a partnership can make the supply of a going concern to another partnership comprising some of the same partners as the partnership making the supply.

SUPPLY OF A SINGLE ENTERPRISE TO TWO RECIPIENTS

An owner/occupier of business premises can effectively retain the premises while still selling the business conducted from those premises. This can be achieved by entering into a lease agreement with the recipient of the enterprise as part of the sale of that enterprise. On entering into a lease agreement with the recipient of the enterprise as part of the sale of that enterprise, the supplier will commence and carry on an enterprise of leasing. A sale of the leased premises with the benefit of the lease to the recipient of the business enterprise will be the supply of an enterprise of leasing. The supplier can then sell the premises to a third party as a going concern.

Steven owns an art studio from which he operates an art school. Steven wants to sell both his premises and business, but has trouble selling them together.

Steven can sell his business to one of his former students who in turn leases the art studio from Steven.

Steven can then sell the art studio with a lease to a third party as a going concern as well as being able to sell the business with the lease intact as a going concern.

SUPPLY OF TWO ENTERPRISES TO ONE RECIPIENT

Where there are two related entities, one of which owns the land from which the other operates a business, the supply of each enterprise to a single purchaser will be two supplies of going concerns. The Tax Office accepts that the recipient of a supply of an enterprise who takes over the leased premises from which the enterprise operates simultaneously acquires those premises from an entity which carried on a business of leasing the premises.

Sharon operates a motel business from leased premises owned by another entity (Fred). A purchaser wants to acquire both the business consisting of goodwill, plant and equipment, forward bookings etc and the premises.

Fred can sell the premises as a going concern provided the premises are sold with the lease intact. Sharon can sell the business as a going concern if she assigns the lease to the purchaser. Both transactions can occur simultaneously.

In *Debonne Holdings Pty Ltd & FC of T* [2006] AATA 886, the AAT considered whether the sale of a business and the sale of the land on which the business operated, sold in two separate contracts, was the sale of a going concern. The AAT considered the going concern was the subject of both contracts because the sale of the business was dependent upon the land on which the hotel was situated as the hotel enterprise could not be conducted without the land. The Tribunal placed weight on the fact that the two contracts required simultaneous settlement.

The supply of all of the shares in a company that conducts an enterprise is not the supply of a going concern as the supplier of the shares is not the entity that conducts the enterprise. If the entity is a trust, the trustee can make a supply of a going concern as the trustee is conducting the enterprise on behalf of the trust.

NOTE: The going concern ruling GSTR 2002/5 states that the following transactions will not qualify as the sale of a going concern:

- sale and lease back arrangements on a commercial property, and
- sale of a commercial property to its sole tenant.

23.470   RELIGIOUS SERVICES (Subdivision 38-F)

The supply of religious services by a religious institution is GST-free if integral to the practice of that religion (s38-220).

According to TR 92/17, for a body to be regarded as a religious institution its objects and activities must reflect its character as a body instituted for the promotion of some religious object and the beliefs and practices of the members of that body must constitute a religion.

The two most important factors for determining whether a particular set of beliefs and practices constitute a religion are:

- belief in a supernatural Being, Thing or Principle, and
- acceptance of canons of conduct which give effect to that belief, but which do not offend against the ordinary laws.

23.480   GST ON FOOD (Subdivision 38-A)

Most food for human consumption is GST-free (except where explicitly specified as taxable).

This includes food and beverages such as fruit and vegetables, meat, eggs, bread, cheese, soup, milk, tea, coffee, fruit and vegetable juices (with 90% minimum by volume of juice), breakfast cereals, infant formula and sugar. Ingredients for food, some beverage ingredients, goods to be mixed with or added to food such as condiments, spices and flavourings, as well as fats and oils for culinary purposes are also GST-free.

The definition of food as set out at s38-4 excludes:

- unprocessed cow's milk
- live animals (other than crustaceans or molluscs)
- any unprocessed grain, cereal or sugar cane, or
- plants under cultivation (eg. herbs in a pot, vegetables growing in the ground).

Food marketed for animals is not GST-free as it is not for human consumption.

The following items, although falling within the definition of food, are specifically excluded from being GST-free:

- food consumed on the premises or the grounds surrounding the premises in which it is supplied (eg. cafés, restaurants, food courts, football grounds)
- hot food for consumption away from those premises
- most food and beverages listed in Schedule 1 of the GST Act including:
  - prepared food including pizzas, quiches, hamburgers, hot dogs, sandwiches, platters of food and food marketed as 'prepared meals'
  - confectionery eg. lollies, chocolates, muesli or 'health food' bars, popcorn, crystallised fruit
  - savoury snacks including potato chips, processed seeds or nuts and caviar
  - bakery products including cakes, cheesecakes, muffins, pavlovas, pastries, scones, doughnuts, croissants, pies (meat, vegetable or fruit), sausage rolls,

   - pastries and bread with a sweet filling or coating. **NOTE:** Bread, including savoury bread, is GST-free
   - ice cream foods including ice cream cakes, frozen yoghurt, soft serves, flavoured ice blocks, and
   - biscuits including cookies, pretzels, crackers, wafers and cones.

All beverages and ingredients for beverages are taxable unless they are in one of the following GST-free categories as listed in Schedule 2 of the GST Act:

- milk products, lactose, soy milk and rice milk, but not including flavoured milk
- preparations for the making of beverages:
   - tea
   - coffee
   - coffee essence
   - chicory essence
   - malt
   - malt extract for drinking purposes
   - similar preparations marketed as substitutes for these
   - dry preparations marketed for the purposes of flavouring milk
- fruit and vegetable juices if they consist of at least 90% by volume of juices of fruits or vegetables
- non-alcoholic carbonated beverages, if they consist wholly of juices of fruits or vegetables
- non-alcoholic non-carbonated beverages, if they consist of at least 90% by volume of juices of fruits or vegetables
- non-carbonated natural water without any other additives, and
- beverages and ingredients for beverages marketed as food for infants or invalids.

In *JMB Beverages Pty Ltd v FC of T* (2010) FCAFC 68, the Full Federal Court held that particular alcohol-removed wine products could not be classified as GST-free under the relevant items of the list in Schedule 2.

The Federal Court, in *Lansell House Pty Ltd & Anor v FC of T* [2010] FCA 329, held that for the purposes of classifying food for GST purposes, the overall impression of a product must be taken into account. In the present case – whether Mini Ciabatte was a 'cracker', 'biscuit' or 'bread' - this included appearance, manufacturing, ingredients, end use and comparability to other products. The Court decided that Mini Ciabatte was not food of a kind specified in item 32, namely food that was, or consisted principally of, crackers. The Court held that an expert's evidence was irrelevant in determining the meaning of ordinary words such as those under consideration. Furthermore, the Court determined that a supplier's label on the product's packaging does not influence the classification of the product for GST purposes. The Full Federal Court dismissed the taxpayer's appeal in *Lansell House Pty Ltd & Anor v FC of T* [2011] FCAFC 6.

Food that is a combination of food that is GST-free and one or more of the above taxable categories is not GST-free. For example, a snack pack containing cheese (GST-free) and biscuits is not GST-free. However, Items in a hamper are taxed individually as this supply is considered to be a mixed supply (see 23.174). The basic premise of these rules is relatively simple – all basic food is GST-free unless specifically excluded.

'PREMISES' USED TO SUPPLY FOOD

Food for consumption on the premises from which it is supplied is subject to GST. Therefore, for the purpose of determining whether goods are subject to GST, the definition of premises becomes very important.

Premises are defined as set out at s38-5 (and explained further in GSTD 2000/4) to mean:

- the place where the supply takes place and includes:
   - the grounds surrounding a cafe or public house
   - shops in caravan parks or camping grounds

- canteens in hospitals, offices or factories
- other outlets for the supply of the food, or
- the whole of any enclosed space, eg. football ground, garden, showground, amusement park, exhibition halls, gyms, golf courses, racecourses, zoos, galleries or similar area with a clear boundary,

- but does not include any part of a public thoroughfare unless it is an area designated for use in connection with supplies of food from an outlet for the supply of food (presumably this would catch vendors selling food outside football grounds).

MEANING OF 'CONSUMED' (GSTD 2000/5)

GSTD 2000/5 considers when a supply of food for consumption on the premises from which it is supplied, occurs. Food vendors need to distinguish between their 'dine-in' and 'take-away' customers, as this determines whether the food they sell is GST-free or taxable (s38-3).

If the food vendor is able to make this distinction, all 'dine-in' food is subject to GST, regardless of whether it is otherwise GST-free. If the distinction cannot be made, only hot 'take-away' food is taxable and food that would otherwise be GST-free remains so if:

- it is served in its original or take-away form, and
- it is not served in circumstances indicating that consumption will take place on the premises.

A supplier will be able to identify take-away food from dine-in food if the supplier:

- has separate ordering and serving processes for dine-in and take-away customers
- provides different packaging for dine-in and take-away customers, or
- has different menus or product lines for dine-in and take-away customers.

Schedules showing GST-free and taxable food and drink are shown below. A more detailed, searchable list is available on the Tax Office website: www.ato.gov.au. If a product is not listed in this food index, the Tax Office can be contacted to confirm GST status. Alternatively, manufacturers and other suppliers can rely on 'EANnet' GST classifications for food and grocery products. EANnet is an online catalogue of unique numbers and barcodes used for identifying products, and also identifies their GST status. The Tax Office says that where suppliers rely on EANnet GST classifications, there will be no risk of penalties or of unfavourable retrospective adjustments to their GST liability. The EANnet listing covers over 35,000 products. The Tax Office provides a link from the Tax Office Food Industry home page to the EANnet listings.

NOTE: Where an item is shown as GST-free, it loses this status if it is sold for consumption on the premises, it is a hot takeaway or is part of a prepared meal.

Food and drink that is GST-free	
Food	**GST-free unless excluded by s38-3**
Live animals	Live crustaceans and molluscs (eg. lobsters, oysters and crabs) for human consumption.
Meat products	Raw and processed meat (eg. beef, kangaroo, lamb, chicken etc. either whole or pieces/strips) Edible offal (eg. liver, kidney, brain, tongue) where supplied as food for human consumption Smallgoods such as cold meats (ham, salami), frankfurts, bacon, paté, etc. Soup bones supplied as food for human consumption Meats in marinade, stir fry mix (eg. beef in black bean sauce sold in butcher shops) kebabs, shaslicks
Seafood	Fresh and frozen whole fish and fillets, smoked fish products (eg. salmon, kippers and eels), prawns, seafood kebabs
Grains, cereals and sugar cane	Grains, cereals or sugar cane that has been processed or treated resulting in an alteration of its form, nature or condition and which are food for human consumption (eg. wild rice which has had impurities removed and packaged for sale)

Food and drink that is GST-free	
Food	**GST-free unless excluded by s38-3**
Plants under cultivation	Herbs sold in bunches and not as part of a living plant
Fruit and vegetables	Raw, frozen, and dried fruits and vegetables Salads including fruit salads Wine grapes and table grapes Pre-cooked frozen potato products that only require re-heating in the oven or deep frying
Prepared food	Food not considered to be a prepared meal: • frozen vegetables (chopped or whole) • uncooked pasta products (noodles) • baby food, baked beans, tinned spaghetti, and tinned Irish stews • dims sims, spring rolls, fish cakes, meatballs where sold frozen or fresh (if not supplied hot) • frozen pizza bases • fish fingers, crumbed fish fillets or mollusc meat such as scallops (However if marketed as a prepared meal, it will be subject to GST)
Confectionery	Candied peel, glucose, unfilled chocolate dessert cups
Savoury snacks	Unshelled nuts and unsalted raw nuts (including macadamia nuts)
Bakery products	Plain bread and rolls, (white, wholemeal or multigrain) sesame/poppy seed rolls Cheese topped bread, cheese and bacon breads (rolls) Bread with unsweetened toppings other than cheese Pumpkin bread, garlic bread, herb bread Hamburger buns, damper, sour dough bread, rye bread Bread that has ingredients mixed with the dough before baking including fruit Loaves without a coating or filling (a glaze is not considered to be a coating) Traditional hot cross buns (with cross baked into the dough and glazed) Plain or flavoured focaccias (including pumpkin, garlic, herb and olive topped) Tortillas, unleavened bread, gluten free or yeast free bread Pita, Lebanese or lavash bread Bread type breakfast muffins, crumpets
Ice-cream food	Frozen whole fruit
Cereal	Breakfast cereal
Condiments	Goods to be mixed with or added to food for human consumption including spreads eg. jam, honey, marmalade, mustard, pickles, etc, spices, seasonings, breadcrumbs, yeast extracts, flavouring and thickening agents
Dry ingredients	Rice and pasta preparations Cake and muffin mixes Soup mixes (canned and dry) Dry cereal, dessert and potato preparations Jelly crystals Custard powder
Other ingredients for food or beverages	Sugar, salt, pepper, spices Preservatives and colouring Fats and oils marketed for culinary purposes Sauces such as tomato, BBQ, tartare, apple, marinating, etc Salad dressing

Food and drink that is GST-free

Beverage	GST-free unless excluded by s38-3
Milk products	Milk, skim milk or buttermilk: liquid, powdered, concentrated or condensed Casein Whey, whey powder or whey paste Unflavoured beverages consisting of any of the above, or a combination thereof, to at least 95% Lactose Processed cow's milk Goats milk (processed or unprocessed)
Soy milk and rice milk	Beverages consisting principally of soy milk or rice milk, coffee, etc.

Beverage	GST-free unless excluded by s38-3
Tea, coffee, etc	Tea (including herbal tea, fruit tea, ginseng tea and similar beverage preparations) Coffee and coffee essence Chicory and chicory essence Malt and malt extract if it is marketed principally for drinking purposes Preparations for drinking purposes that are marketed principally as tea preparations, coffee preparations, or preparations for malted beverages Preparations marketed principally as substitutes for the above two items Dry preparations marketed for the purpose of flavouring milk
Fruit and vegetable juices	Concentrates for making non-alcoholic beverages, if at least 90% juices or fruits Non-alcoholic carbonated beverages if they consist wholly of juices of fruits or vegetables Non alcoholic non-carbonated beverages if at least 90% of juices of fruits or vegetables
Beverages for infants or invalids	Beverages, and ingredients for beverages, of a kind marketed principally as food for infants or invalids
Water	Non-carbonated natural water without any additives (including spring and mineral water)

Food and drink that is taxable

Food	Taxable
Live animals	Live cows, sheep, pigs and poultry
Meat products	Carcasses and other animal products not supplied for human consumption Spoiled or rotten meat sold as pet food Soup bones sold as pet bones, or not for human consumption
Seafood	Live fish Hot, cooked seafood Any seafood that is marketed as a prepared meal (eg. sushi)
Grains, cereals and sugar cane	Unprocessed grains, cereals, sugar cane Processed grains, cereals and sugar products which are not food for human consumption
Plants under cultivation	Potted herbs
Fruit and vegetables	Rotten fruit and vegetables not supplied as food for human consumption Seed potatoes

Food and drink that is taxable	
Food	**Taxable**
Prepared food	Quiches Sandwiches (any type of bread or roll) Pizzas, pizza subs, pizza pockets and similar food Food marketed as a prepared meal, (but not soup) eg.: • prepared meals such as curry and rice, mornays and similar dishes sold cold by a takeaway or supermarket that only need reheating to be ready for consumption • fresh or frozen prepared lasagne • sushi • cooked pasta dishes sold complete with sauce • frozen TV dinners • fresh or frozen complete meals eg. single serves of a roast dinner including vegetables and low fat dietary meals • platters, etc. of cheese, cold cuts, fruit, vegetables and other arrangements of food • hamburgers, chicken burgers and similar food • hot dogs
Hot food	Hot food supplied for consumption away from the premises. 'Hot food' means food that has been heated above room temperature or above the generally surrounding air temperature for consumption.
Food supplied for consumption on premises (cafés, restaurants, snack bars)	All food and drink supplied for consumption on the premises where it is supplied. 'Premises' means more than just the place where the food is sold and includes the surrounding grounds or other enclosed spaces.
Confectionery	Confectionery and food marketed as confectionery, including chocolate Food marketed as ingredients for confectionery Food consisting principally of confectionery, confectionery novelties Popcorn Food known as muesli bars, health food bars, breakfast bars etc (including 'energy' bars) Crystallised fruit, glace fruit and drained fruit Crystallised ginger and preserved ginger Edible cake decorations Milk crumb Confectioner's glaze
Savoury snacks	Potato crisps, sticks or straws, corn crisps or chips, bacon or pork crackling or prawn chips Seeds or nuts that have been processed or treated by salting, spicing, smoking or roasting, or in any other similar way Food similar to either of the above, whether or not it consists wholly or partly of any vegetable, herb, fruit, meat, seafood or dairy product or extract and whether or not it is artificially flavoured Caviar and similar fish roe Food consisting principally of any of the above

Food and drink that is taxable	
Food	**Taxable**
Bakery products	Cakes, slices, cheesecakes, pancakes, waffles, crepes, muffins and puddings
	Pavlova and meringues
	Pies (meat, vegetable or fruit), pasties and sausage rolls
	Tarts and pastries
	Doughnuts and croissants
	Pastizzi, calzoni and brioche
	Scones and scrolls
	Bread and buns with a sweet filling or coating
	Pikelets
	Iced hot cross buns
	Panettone (traditional Italian Christmas cake)
	Rice pudding
	Christmas pudding
	Steamed puddings
	Self-saucing puddings
	Tapioca pudding
Ice-cream food	Ice-cream, ice-cream cakes, ice-creams and ice-creams substitutes
	Frozen confectionery, frozen yoghurt, and frozen fruit products
	Flavoured ice blocks (whether or not marketed in a frozen state)
	Any food similar to the above
Biscuit goods	Food that is, or consists principally of, biscuits, cookies, crackers, pretzels, cones or wafers
Dry ingredients	Vitamins and minerals (liquid, tablet and capsule form)
Beverage	**Taxable**
Milk products	Flavoured milk beverages
Soy milk and rice milk	Flavoured soy or rice milk beverages
Tea, coffee, etc.	Tea, coffee etc beverages marketed in a ready to drink form such as packaged iced coffee or tea or takeaway coffee or tea
Fruit and vegetable juices	Sports drinks unless the concentrates consist of at least 90% by volume of juices or fruits
Water	Soda water
	Packaged and bulk ice

NOTE: A more detailed list is available in the GST food guide (NAT 3338) which can be found on the Tax Office website at www.ato.gov.au. If a product is not listed in this food index, contact the Tax Office to confirm GST status.

23.490 OTHER GST-FREE SUPPLIES

Other GST-free supplies include:

- water supply is GST-free if it is not supplied in a container or transferred into a container that has a capacity of less than 100 litres (s38-285)
- sewerage services, storm water drainage services, and the emptying of septic tanks (ss38-290, 38-295 and 38-300)
- the supply of potential residential land if the land is sub-divided from land on which the supplier has carried on a farming business for at least five years and that supply is made to an associate without consideration for less than the GST-inclusive market value (s38-475)
- the supply of land on which a farming business has been carried on for at least five years and the recipient intends that a farming business be carried on the land (s38-480). **NOTE:** A proposal that the GST-free status of supplies of farm land supplied for farming be replaced by a reverse charge mechanism has been abandoned.
- the first supply of precious metal by a refiner of precious metal after its refining by, or on behalf, of the supplier, to a dealer in precious metal (s38-385) – see 23.340
- international mail (s38-540)
- the supply of a car (including parts) to a disabled veteran for his or her personal transportation (s38-505), and
- the supply of a car to a disabled individual and he or she intends to use the car in his or her personal transportation to or from gainful employment (s38-510).

NOTE: The supply of a car to a disabled veteran or other disabled individuals is GST-free only to the extent the GST-inclusive market value of the car does not exceed the car depreciation limit ($57,466 for 2014-15 and 2013-14). The GST-inclusive market value of the car excludes any value that is attributable to modifications made to the car solely for the purpose of adapting it for driving by the individual or adapting it for transporting the individual.

NOTE: Certain government taxes, fees and charges (Division 81) as determined by the Treasurer are not subject GST (see 23.129).

NOTES

Goods and services tax: Administration and special topics

24

24.000 REGISTRATION, TAX PERIODS AND GST ACCOUNTING

The GST turnover of an entity is important to determine:

- whether an entity is required to be registered for GST
- the entity's tax period, and
- the attribution of GST and input tax credits to the relevant tax period.

If an entity meets its GST turnover threshold, it is required to register for GST purposes (see 24.210). Entities that are not required to register may voluntarily register. Transactions conducted by unregistered entities that are not required to be registered are not subject to GST.

An entity may report for GST purposes either on a monthly, quarterly or annual basis subject to turnover – its 'tax period' (see 24.110).

GST is reported either on a cash or accruals basis. To be eligible to account for GST on a cash basis, an entity's GST turnover needs to be below a certain threshold (see 24.120).

An entity must hold a tax invoice at the time it is claiming the input tax credits, unless the GST inclusive purchase price is $82.50 or less. Tax invoices are discussed in greater detail at 24.230.

BOARD OF TAXATION REVIEW OF THE APPLICATION OF GST TO CROSS-BORDER TRANSACTIONS

The Board of Taxation undertook a review of the application of the GST to cross-border transactions. The report, *Review of the application of GST to cross-border transactions*, was publicly released in May 2010.

The review revealed that the main issues that arise in the application of GST to cross-border transactions are the following:

- the GST system is overly inclusive of non-residents, which results in unnecessary compliance costs on non-residents and embedded taxation for enterprises carrying on business in Australia
- significant compliance costs for non-residents that register in the GST system, and
- inefficient collection of GST associated with enforcing compliance on non-residents outside Australia's jurisdiction.

The Board's report contains fourteen recommendations which aim to simplify the cross-border rules, improve the balance between reducing the unnecessary inclusion of non-residents and ensuring the GST tax base is maintained.

The table below outlines the Board's recommendations.

No.	Board of Taxation recommendations
1	**Amend the GST law to limit the application of the connected with Australia provisions for the supplies by a non-resident of services and intangibles** Such supplies that are done in Australia should not be connected with Australia if the supply is made to a business that has a presence in Australia that is registered for GST and the non-resident supplier either has no business presence in Australia or has a business presence in Australia but does not use it in making the supply.
2	**Amend the GST law to limit the application of the connected with Australia provisions for the supplies of goods by a non-resident** Such supplies should not be connected with Australia if the supply is made to a business that has a presence in Australia that is registered for GST and the non-resident supplier either has no business presence in Australia or has a business presence in Australia but does not use it in making the supply.
3	**Amend the GST law to limit the application of the connected with Australia provisions for the certain supplies of goods within Australia between non-residents** If the non-residents carry on the enterprise outside Australia, supplies of goods that are already in Australia would not be connected with Australia if the recipient continues the underlying lease of those goods to a business that has a presence in Australia that is registered for GST.
4	**Amend the GST law to expand the existing compulsory reverse charge provisions to include goods** Division 84 should be broadened to complement the proposed changes to the connected with Australia rules.

No.	Board of Taxation recommendations
5	**Amend the GST law to make GST-free supplies made to a non-resident but provided to a registered business in Australia or employee or office holder** A supply of services or intangibles should be GST-free where the supply is provided to a registered business in Australia, an employee or office holder of a registered business in Australia or an employee or office holder of an unregistered non-resident business and the acquisition by the non-resident is for a fully creditable purpose.
6	**Amend the GST law to make GST-free supplies of warranty services made to a non-resident but provided to an Australian warranty holder** The supply of warranty services, including replacement parts, to an unregistered non-resident warrantor should be GST-free if the goods are supplied under a warranty agreement and either the goods were subject to GST as a taxable supply, subject to GST as a taxable importation, GST-free or not subject to GST.
7	**Amend the GST law to expand the non-resident agency provisions to broaden their application beyond common law agency relationships** The expansion of the provisions would allow a non-resident without a business presence in Australia to appoint a resident commission agent. Both parties would have to agree for the agency provisions to apply.
8	**Amend the GST law to remove the requirement for non-resident registration under the agency provisions** Non-residents would not be required to register for GST if the only taxable supplies made by the non-resident are made through at least one resident agent.
9	**Amend the GST law to remove the requirement for non-residents to register if they only make GST-free supplies** Non-residents making only GST-free supplies should not be required to register for GST. If the non-resident also makes supplies that are not GST-free, the GST-free supplies should count towards the GST registration threshold.
10	**Streamline the registration process for non-residents** Where a non-resident is not entitled to an ABN, they should be able to register for GST only by providing documentation to show registration with an ASIC equivalent and a letter issued by the revenue authority of a comparable taxing regime to show that the entity exists in their records and carries on an enterprise.
11	**A direct refund system is not required at this time** However, the Board recommends that this issue be reviewed after the other recommendations have been implemented and operational for an appropriate period of time.
12	**Introduce options for calculating the transport and insurance cost to include in the value of taxable importations** All registered importers should be allowed to calculate the transport and insurance costs as the actual amount paid or payable, or alternatively, use an uplifted percentage or predetermined rates.
13	**The low value importation threshold of $1,000 is appropriate** It is not currently administratively feasible to bring non-resident supplies of low value goods and services into the GST system.
14	**The Commissioner should improve taxpayer awareness and education regarding the circumstances that no entity is entitled to claim back the GST on the importation of goods** The Commissioner should ensure that this issue is avoided and provide guidance as to how it can be avoided.

In February 2011, the Government released a discussion paper outlining the following proposed changes:

- limiting the application of the connected with Australia provisions for the supplies by a non-resident of services and intangibles
- limiting the application of the connected with Australia provisions for the supply of goods by a 'non resident'

- limiting the application of the connected with Australia provisions for certain supplies of goods within Australia between non-residents
- expanding the existing compulsory reverse charge provisions to include goods
- allowing supplies made to a non-resident but provided to a registered business in Australia or employee or office holder to be GST-free
- allowing supplies of warranty services made to a non-resident but provided to an Australian warranty holder to be GST-free
- expanding the non-resident agency provisions so that they apply more broadly than to common law agency relationships
- removing the requirement for non-resident registration under the agency provisions
- removing the requirement for non-residents to register if they only make GST-free supplies, and
- introducing options for calculating the transport and insurance cost to include in the value of taxable importations.

In the 2012-13 Federal Budget, the Government announced that the package will take effect from the first quarterly tax period following Royal Assent of the amending legislation. In addition, the Government will make a number of other changes, including:

- changes to the proposed measures for the supply of goods by non-residents
- not proceeding with the proposed measures relating to the non-resident agency provisions, and
- clarifying and narrowing the definition of permanent establishment for GST purposes.

In December 2013, the Government indicated that it will proceed with the intended amendments. The commencement is to be deferred until the first quarterly tax period following assent to the amending legislation.

24.100 HOW TO ACCOUNT FOR GST

GST liabilities are worked out at the end of each tax period. Depending on your circumstances, this period can be either quarterly, monthly or annually (see 24.110).

Attribution rules determine the timing of when the GST payable (including increasing adjustments) needs to be declared, and when input tax credits (and decreasing adjustments) may be claimed, to work out your net amount of GST for a tax period. There are two ways to account for the GST: the 'cash basis' and the 'other than cash basis' (usually referred to as the 'accruals basis').

24.110   TAX PERIODS (Division 27)

The general rule is that a tax period is each period of three months ending on 31 March, 30 June, 30 September and 31 December. However, one month tax periods apply where:

- the GST turnover of the enterprise is $20m or more, or
- the Commissioner is satisfied that the period for which the person will be carrying on an enterprise in Australia is less than three months, or
- the Commissioner is satisfied that the person has a history of failing to comply with their tax obligations, or
- you elect to lodge monthly.

A taxpayer may withdraw from the monthly tax period by notifying the Commissioner in an approved form, provided that the taxpayer has been using the monthly periods for at least 12 months and that the taxpayer's GST turnover is not $20m or more. However, the Commissioner may exercise discretion for taxpayers that have voluntarily elected to be on a monthly tax period to revoke this election within 12 months of using the monthly tax period, if a revocation request is made by the taxpayer in an approved form.

Entities which register voluntarily (ie. are not required to be registered) and did not elect to pay GST by instalments may elect to have annual tax periods pursuant to Division 151. This applies to entities with GST turnover of less than $75,000 ($150,000 for non-profit entities), but does not apply to taxi operators and entities that are not required to be registered for GST because offshore supplies of rights or options have been disregarded in calculating their GST turnover. For eligible entities, an election needs to be made to the Commissioner in an approved form by:

- 21 August if currently reporting GST monthly
- 28 October if currently reporting GST on a quarterly basis, or
- for newly registered entities (ie. entities with current GST lodgement record of six months or less) that became eligible to make an annual tax period election after 28 October, any dates on or before the date their next GST return is due.

An annual election once made continues on indefinitely (ie. there no need to make an annual election each year) until one of the following occurs:

- the taxpayer revokes the election in an approved form – the revocation applies in the year of revocation if made on or before 28 October. Revocation after 28 October will become effective the following year, or
- the Commissioner disallows the election on the grounds of bad compliance history, or
- the taxpayer becomes required to be registered as at 31 July in a financial year.

 If on 31 July of a financial year you become required to register (eg. GST turnover exceeds the registration turnover threshold) your annual tax period election will cease. You will be required to inform the Tax Office when this occurs.

24.111   CONCLUDING TAX PERIODS (Section 27-40)

Your last tax period ends at the following specified time:

- at the end of the day before you die or become bankrupt or the entity goes into liquidation or receivership or ceases to exist
- at the end of the day you cease your enterprise, or
- at the end of the day on which your GST registration cancellation takes effect (the cancellation date).

 The concluding tax period for an entity with annual tax period, that becomes bankrupt, goes into liquidation or receivership is according to s27-40 the day before the entity becomes bankrupt, goes into liquidation or receivership. However, in the event of death, cessation of enterprise or cancellation of GST registration, the entity's annual tax period will continue until the end of that financial year.

24.120   CASH AND ACCRUALS BASIS (Division 29)

It is compulsory for an entity to account for GST using the accruals basis unless it is eligible to use the cash basis and chooses to do so.

Only the following entities are entitled to elect to use the cash basis (s29-40):

- a small business entity (other than because of s328-110(4) ITAA97) for the income year in which they make the choice
- an entity that does not carry on a business and their GST turnover does not exceed the cash accounting turnover threshold of $2 million
- an endorsed charity, a gift-deductible entity or a government school (regardless of annual turnover) – see Division 157
- entities using cash basis for income tax purposes, and
- enterprises carried on that have been approved by the Commissioner as being able to adopt a cash basis. (The determination will cover enterprises belonging to a certain class, kind, or type and the application for approval is made by industry groups on behalf of their members and not by individual entities).

Ineligible entities can also seek independent approval to enable them to use the cash basis (s29-45). You must apply for this approval and the Commissioner has provided guidelines in GSTR 2000/13. The Commissioner may approve your application to use the cash basis if after consideration of the nature and size of your enterprise that you carried on as well as the accounting systems used it is decided that it is appropriate to do so. Examples of some factors that are taken into consideration are:

- whether the supplies are on a cash or credit basis
- value and volume of the supplies
- reliance on circulating capital or consumables
- capital items used, and
- credit policy and debt recovery policy.

A small business entity is defined in s328-110 ITAA97 (see 10.200). You will be a small business entity if:

a) you carry on a business in the current year, and

b) one or both of the following applies:

   i) you carried on a business in the income year before the current year (the previous year) and your aggregated turnover for the previous year was less than $2 million, and/or

   ii) your aggregated turnover for the current year is likely to be less than $2 million.

NOTE: Division 188 sets out the meaning of GST turnover (see 24.211).

24.121 CASH BASIS (Division 29-B)

TAXABLE SUPPLIES

If you account for GST on a cash basis, you must attribute GST payable on a taxable supply to the tax period in which you receive consideration for the supply, but only to the extent that the consideration is received in the tax period.

Gordon runs a small print shop. He accounts for GST on a cash basis and has quarterly tax periods. Sam orders a print job for 500,000 forms at a total cost of $3,300.
Sam pays Gordon $2,200 on 10 December 2015 and $1,100 on 2 February 2016.
GST payable on the taxable supply is:
- *for the period ending 31 December 2015: 1/11 x $2,200 = $200*
- *for the period ending 31 March 2016: 1/11 x $1,100 = $100*

CREDITABLE ACQUISITIONS

The input tax credit for a creditable acquisition is attributable to the tax period in which you provide consideration for the acquisition.

Gordon purchases stock for his print shop on 28 September 2015 for $5,500. On the same day he pays $3,300 and is issued with a tax invoice asking for payment of the balance within 60 days.
Gordon is entitled to an input tax credit of $300 (1/11 x $3,300) attributable to the tax period ending 30 September 2015 as he obtained a tax invoice before lodging his BAS.

You are not entitled to attribute an input tax credit to a tax period unless you have a tax invoice for the acquisition when you lodge your BAS for that period.

NOTE: GSTR 2000/13 sets out the Tax Office's view on how to account for GST on a cash basis.

24.122 ACCRUALS BASIS (Division 29-A)

TAXABLE SUPPLIES

Attribute all of the GST payable on a taxable supply to the earlier of the tax period in which:
- any of the consideration for the supply is received, or
- an invoice for the supply is issued.

If you supply on credit terms you may have to account for GST payable before actually receiving payment for the supply.

NOTE: An 'invoice' is defined in s195-1. It is not necessarily a tax invoice. An invoice is a document notifying an obligation to make a payment and does not necessarily contain all the information required for it to be a tax invoice (see GSTR 2000/34). For more information see 24.220.

CREDITABLE ACQUISITION

All the input tax credits for an acquisition are attributable to the earlier of the tax periods in which:

- you provide any of the consideration, or
- an invoice is issued for the acquisition.

This means that you will be entitled to an input tax credit before paying the consideration, provided you have a tax invoice for the acquisition when you lodge your BAS for that tax period.

PROGRESSIVE SUPPLIES (Division 156)

If an entity operates on an accruals basis, there is a special rule which applies to agreements where both the supplies and the payment are made progressively or for a period. An agreement of this nature is treated as a series of separate supplies over each instalment period.

The normal attribution rules apply to each instalment. If they did not, the entity would have been required to attribute all the GST and input tax credits to the tax period in which the first payment was made or invoiced.

The special progressive supplies rules apply to things like leases or maintenance contracts, long term construction contracts and other similar agreements.

Ted, who accounts for GST on an accruals basis, grants a lease on a shop to Arthur. The lease is for a term of 12 months with lease payments of $1,100 per month.

Division 156 treats each periodic component (each monthly payment) as a separate supply and therefore Ted attributes GST payable of $100 to each monthly tax period, or $300 to each quarterly tax period.

Supplies or acquisitions made under a hire purchase agreement are not supplies or acquisitions made on a progressive periodic basis.

Although each component is treated as a separate supply, it is not necessary to issue a separate tax invoice for each of those supplies. A single invoice covering all the supplies can suffice if it identifies the price of each component of the supply (GSTR 2013/1). A lease agreement for example can be a tax invoice covering all the monthly tax periods provided it contains all the information and criteria necessary for it to be a tax invoice.

Where an invoice for the whole supply or a number of components of the supply is issued prior to any payment of consideration, the effect of attributing GST and input tax credits in accordance with the accruals basis under Division 29-A would be that attribution would occur at the time the invoice issued. However, this is inconsistent with the intended operation of Division 156, and specifically s156-10 operates to modify the basic attribution rules for accruals basis to apply only where an invoice is issued for a particular component. Where no invoice which is particular to a component of the supply or acquisition can be identified, then attribution will occur when a payment is made which relates to a particular component (GSTR 2000/35).

24.123   HOLDING A TAX INVOICE

If an entity (regardless of whether accounting on a cash or accruals basis) does not hold a tax invoice for a creditable acquisition when a GST return is lodged for the tax period in which the input tax credit would otherwise be attributable, the input tax credit is not attributable to that tax period but is instead attributable to the first tax period for which the entity lodges a GST return taking into account the input tax credit when the tax invoice is held (ss29-10(3) and (4)). Accordingly, an entity can postpone the attribution of an input tax credit to any tax period after it holds a tax invoice. There is no requirement to lodge an amended GST return for the tax period in which it should have claimed the input tax credit. See 24.230 and 24.251 for further information.

The Commissioner is of the view that subs29-10(4) does not prevent an entity from revising a GST return for an earlier tax period so as to take into account an input tax credit in the net amount for that tax period. If a GST return for the earlier tax period is revised, subs29-10(4) does not apply (ATO ID 2011/76).

NOTE: For GST returns and assessments lodged or issued, and revisions to GST returns and revised assessments issued or made, after 7.30pm (AEST) on 12 May 2009, input tax credits must be claimed within a four-year period.

Regardless of the accounting method used, a tax invoice must be held at the time the Business Activity Statement is lodged in order to claim input tax credits.

24.124   CHANGING METHODS (Division 159)

There are transitional rules when an entity changes its attribution basis, to ensure that transactions are not taxed twice (ie. if it changed from accruals to cash) or not taxed at all (if the change is from cash to accruals).

24.130 SPECIAL RULES ON ATTRIBUTION

24.131   ATTRIBUTION UNDER COMMISSIONER'S DETERMINATION

Section 29-25 provides that the Commissioner may determine particular tax periods to which a specified kind of taxable supply, input tax credits and adjustments are attributable. GSTR 2000/29 sets out how the Commissioner can determine, under s29-25, particular tax periods different to the tax periods that would otherwise apply under the basic or special rules.

GSTR 2000/29 alters the operation of the basic attribution rules for specific taxable supplies and creditable acquisitions including the following:

a) **Contracts subject to statutory 'cooling off' period:** GST and input tax credit entitlement is attributed to the tax period in which the cooling off period ends.

b) **Supplies made through banknote and coin-operated machines or similar devices:** GST payable on these supplies is attributed in the tax period in which the notes or coins are removed rather than when they are deposited in the machine.

c) **Supplies and acquisitions made through agents:** (see 24.330)
   - for entities on an accruals basis, GST is attributable to the tax period in which you become aware that:
     - any of the consideration for the supply has been received, or
     - an invoice relating to the supply has been issued,
   - for entities using the cash basis, GST is attributable to the tax period in which you become aware that consideration for the supply has been received. Corresponding rules apply to the attribution of input tax credits and adjustments.

d) **Retention of consideration (only applies for accruals basis):** If a contract allows for the recipient of the supply to retain part of the consideration, the GST is only attributable to the tax period in which the supplier receives it. GST is deferred until the tax period in which it is actually received or an invoice relating to it is issued, whichever is earliest. Likewise, the input tax credit entitlement is attributable to the tax period in which the recipient pays the amount. An example would be the 'retention amount' in the construction industry.

e) **Total consideration unknown:** If, in a tax period, you receive any consideration for a taxable supply before you can determine the total consideration, attribute GST on the taxable supply to the tax period to the extent that you received the consideration in that tax period. When the final consideration is determined, any GST adjustment should be attributed to the tax period in which the supplier first knew the amount of total consideration but only to the extent the GST has not been attributable to the earlier tax period.

24.132   ATTRIBUTION ON LAND SALES

GSTR 2000/28 outlines the Tax Office's position on the taxable supply of land under a completed standard land contract. The ruling states that you attribute the GST payable to the tax period in which settlement occurs, irrespective of whether you use the cash or accruals basis.

A deposit under a standard land contract displays the essential characteristics of a Division 99 deposit. Therefore, payment of a deposit will not trigger attribution of GST payable or input tax credits at the time the deposit is paid. There will be attribution when there is a forfeiture of the deposit because of a failure to perform the obligation or when it is applied as part of the consideration for the supply of the land (GSTR 2000/28A, also see 24.382). Nor is attribution triggered by the early release of the deposit prior to completion of the contract which is permissible in certain states such as Victoria. The Tax Office does not consider a standard land contract to be an invoice for GST purposes and therefore will not trigger attribution of GST at the time the contract is entered into.

As a supplier making a taxable supply of land under a completed standard land contract, you attribute the GST payable in the tax period in which settlement occurs.

NOTE: The Ruling does not cover the sale of land on terms or by instalments whereby the purchaser is entitled to possession of the land before becoming entitled to a transfer or conveyance of land. The Tax Office's position on such arrangements is uncertain.

24.133 ATTRIBUTION ON LAY-BYS

Under GSTR 2000/12, the attribution of lay-bys is determined by the accounting method used:
- **If cash:** Attribution occurs upon each payment, and
- **If accruals:** Attribution occurs upon payment of the final instalment.

24.134 ATTRIBUTION ON OTHER SALES

In GSTR 2000/29, the Tax Office stated that the normal attribution rules will apply in relation to supplies and acquisitions made under:

a) **Supply of goods on approval or on 'sale or return' terms:** 'Ownership' of the goods remains with the supplier until the recipient accepts the goods. The recipient of the supply will not usually be invoiced or make any payment before title in the goods is transferred. Therefore, no attribution of GST payable on the supply or input tax credits for the acquisition occurs before title in the goods passes to the recipient. See 24.332 for consignment sales.

b) **Floor plan arrangements:** Usually a dealer takes possession of the goods but is not invoiced and does not pay for the goods until a customer is found. The dealer pays regular bailment fees for such an arrangement. Ownership and title to the goods remain with the manufacturer, distributor or financier, while possession only (and the obligation to return the goods if unsold) is granted to the dealer.
There are two separate taxable supplies under this arrangement:
- a supply of rights to display the goods for sale for which the consideration is the bailment fee, and
- a supply of goods by way of sale for which the consideration is the amount paid for the goods.

If using the accruals basis, GST is attributable to the earlier of the tax period in which you are issued an invoice or receive any part of the consideration for the goods from the dealer. This usually occurs when the dealer acquires title to the goods, having secured a customer for them. The delivery documentation accompanying the physical removal of the goods to the dealer would not be an invoice as it is not an obligation to make a payment.

If you account for GST on a cash basis, attribute GST payable to the tax period in which you receive payment.

NOTE: Manufacturers/importers in the motor vehicle industry often make a payment to their retailers called the holdback payment. These payments according to GSTD 2005/4 are not consideration for a supply as no supply is provided in return for these payments. Note that the Commissioner has reviewed this determination in the light of the decision of the Full Federal Court in *AP Group Limited v FC of T* [2013] FCAFC 105.

c) **Hire purchase:** Under hire purchase agreements, the purchaser has possession of, and right to use, the goods, as well as an option to purchase the goods, exercisable at or before the end of the hire period. For GST attribution purposes, a hire purchase agreement is to be regarded as a sale of goods. If using the accruals basis, attribute all the GST payable under the agreement to the tax period in which you enter the agreement. Likewise, if you make a payment on an invoice issued in the tax period in which you enter a hire purchase agreement, attribute all the input tax credit under the agreement to the tax period in which you enter the agreement. The supply or acquisition of goods under the hire purchase agreement is not a supply or acquisition on a periodic or progressive basis and therefore Division 156 does not apply. If using the cash basis, the normal rules apply.

 If you are using the cash basis for GST, hire purchase is not the best option as entities will only be able to claim 1/11th of the principal component of each payment over the term of the agreement.

24.135   CONSIDERATION: WHEN IS IT PROVIDED/RECEIVED?

For attribution purposes it is important to establish when you have provided or received consideration for a supply. The Tax Office has issued GSTR 2003/12 which provides guidelines on when this occurs for the various payment instruments that may be used in transactions. The Ruling does not deal with financial supplies. Some of the more common payment instruments and the Ruling's guidelines are set out below:

- **Cash:** When cash is tendered.
- **Payment made by cheque:** When payment is made by cheque, the recipient of the supply provides consideration when the cheque is either handed or posted to the supplier. Consideration is received by the supplier when the cheque is received, not when it is banked or cleared.
  NOTE: When payment is with a post-dated cheque, consideration is provided and received on the date stated on the cheque. The bank however can process the post-dated cheque as soon as it is drawn, although the bank is not obliged to pay on a post-dated cheque before the date specified on the cheque.
  If the cheque is dishonoured and you are on the accruals basis, then this will not be an adjustment event. Relief will be provided when a debt is written off.
- **Payment by credit card:** When a payment is made by credit card in person, consideration is provided and received when the recipient of the supply signs the docket to authorise the transaction. Where a credit card payment is made over the telephone or internet, consideration will be provided or received when the cardholder gives their details.
- **Debit card (EFTPOS):** The consideration is received when the transaction is accepted by the system.
- **Direct credit/Inter-bank transfer:** Consideration is received when payment is authorised and the payment is credited to the supplier's account.
- **Direct debit:** Consideration is received at the time of transfer.
- **Traveller's cheque:** Consideration is received when the cheque is countersigned.
- **Voucher:** Where the payment for the supply is made using a voucher which entitles the holder to receive supplies up to a monetary value stated on the voucher, consideration is provided and received when the voucher is redeemed (see 23.127).
- **Line of credit or overdraft:** If the supplier provides a line of credit or overdraft facility which accrues interest, and if the payment for the supply is reflected by an increase in the amount owing on the debt facility, the consideration is both provided and received at the time the supplier or other person who provides the debt facility records the increase.

NOTE: Where the supply is made on credit (eg. 30 days credit terms, no interest payable), the credit is not considered to be a loan for the purposes of paying the consideration. Consideration is provided and received when actual payment is made and this is determined by the payment instrument used.

24.200 ADMINISTRATION

An entity will only have GST liabilities and is entitled to claim input tax credits if it is in the GST system. In order to be in the GST system, an entity must be carrying on an enterprise and be registered for GST. Certain entities are required to be registered for GST (see 24.210).

An entity's GST liabilities are worked out at the end of each tax period – either monthly, quarterly or annually (see 24.110) and the entity will be required to give the Commissioner a GST return for each tax period (see 24.240). A tax invoice plays an important role in the GST system – see 24.230. Without it, an entity will not be entitled to claim input tax credits on acquisitions.

Other than accounting for GST on sales and input tax credits on acquisitions, the GST return can also include adjustment and correction of errors. See 24.250 and 24.260.

SELF-ASSESSMENT

As a result of amendments made by the *Indirect Tax Laws Amendment (Assessment) Act 2012*, the self-actuating system that had applied for GST and other indirect taxes was replaced (very broadly from 1 July 2012) with a system under which liabilities and entitlements are dependent on an assessment (see Division 155 Sch 1 TAA).

It was not expected that these amendments would have any practical impact on the way in which taxpayers lodge their returns.

The self-assessment system allows the majority of taxpayers to self assess their tax-related liabilities and tax-related entitlements through the lodgment of the relevant return for a tax period. On lodgment, the Commissioner is treated as having made an assessment for the reported tax period and the return is deemed to be the notice of assessment for that tax period. The assessed amount is worked out in accordance with the information set out in the return.

The Commissioner is also deemed to have made an assessment of the amount of GST payable on an importation when a taxpayer lodges an import declaration or a self assessed clearance declaration with the Australian Customs and Border Protection Service (Customs). Customs issues an import declaration advice or a self assessed clearance declaration advice respectively. The two documents are together deemed to be a notice of assessment.

As part of establishing an assessment system, there is a four-year period of review during which the assessment may be amended. The period of review commences on the day the taxpayer is issued with a notice of the assessment (in most cases, this will be the same day the taxpayer lodges his or her return) and ends four years after the day after lodgment. The period of review may be extended in certain circumstances.

An amended assessment gives rise to a refreshed period of review of four years commencing on the day after notice of the amended assessment is provided or is taken to have been provided. The refreshed period of review only applies in relation to the amended particular and is subject to restrictions.

As a consequence of the removal of time limits on the recovery of liabilities and entitlements, taxpayers ceased to be entitled to credits if they have not been taken into account in an assessment of the net amount during the period of four years after the date the return was required to be lodged for the tax period to which the credit would be attributable under the GST Act.

24.210 REGISTRATION

The GST Act uses the term 'you' throughout. Section 195-1 defines 'you' as applying to entities generally unless its application is expressly limited.

The meaning of an entity is set out in Division 184. 'Entity' means any of the following:

- a) an individual
- b) a body corporate
- c) a corporation sole
- d) a body politic
- e) a partnership
- f) any other unincorporated association or body or persons
- g) a trust, or
- h) a superannuation fund.

An entity is required to register for GST if it is carrying on an enterprise (see 23.130) and has a GST turnover of $75,000 or more. The registration turnover threshold for not-for-profit clubs, societies and associations is $150,000 (s23-15). Registration is optional for entities that do not meet these thresholds; it is up to the entity to decide whether it is in its interest to register. However, taxi operators must register regardless of turnover (Division 144).

Non-profit sub-entities may access the GST concessions available to their parent entity (such as charitable institutions). All non-profit sub-entities will be able to access the higher registration turnover threshold that applies to non-profit bodies (ie. $150,000).

A non-profit sub-entity will be taken to be a body of the type of its parent if the parent entity is one of the following:

- a non-profit body
- charitable institutions, trustees of a charitable fund or gift deductible entities
- government schools
- endorsed charitable institutions or endorsed trustees of charitable funds
- gift-deductible entities endorsed as deductible gift recipients under s30-120 ITAA97, and
- funds, authorities or institutions of a kind referred to in s30-125(1)(b) ITAA97.

The GST Act provisions for which the non-profit sub-entity will be treated as being a body of the same type as the parent entity are in relation to:

- gifts to non-profit bodies not for consideration (s9-15(3)(b))
- a supply covered by Subdivision 38-G (activities of charitable institutions etc)
- school tuck shops and canteens (Subdivision 40-E)
- fund-raising events conducted by charitable institutions etc (Subdivision 40-F)
- reimbursements of volunteers' expenses under s111-18
- gifts made to gift deductible entities (s129-45), and
- the accounting basis of charitable institutions etc (Division 157).

The non-profit sub-entity of the parent entity can choose to access these provisions, even if the parent entity has not chosen to apply those provisions to its own activities.

NOTE: Only entities that are carrying on an enterprise or intend to carry on an enterprise can be registered for GST (s23-10).

Division 23 sets out who is required to be registered for GST and who may register for GST. Division 25 sets out how an entity becomes registered and when the Commissioner must register an entity which has applied for registration. Division 25 also sets out the date of effect of an entity's registration and how a back-dated registration may be achieved.

If an entity does not register and is not required to do so, it will not be required to pay GST on its supplies nor will it be able to claim input tax credits on its acquisitions. However, as well as the penalty for failing to register when required to do so, entities which have not registered when required to will also be liable for 1/11th of the value of supplies backdated to the point when the entity's annual turnover reached the registration turnover threshold. The Tax Office will also allow input tax credits to be claimed from this point, provided tax invoices have been kept.

A registered entity must lodge a GST return for each tax period. The return will form part of the BAS (see 5.800 and 24.240).

An entity must have been registered for 12 months before it can cease to be registered (unless it has ceased business). The Tax Office has discretion to cancel the GST registration before the 12 months have expired. The Commissioner can also in certain circumstances backdate a cancellation to 1 July 2000.

24.211   CALCULATION OF GST TURNOVER

To calculate an entity's GST turnover, the entity needs to look at both its current and projected GST turnover. 'Current GST turnover' is the value of all supplies made or likely to be made during the current month and supplies made during the previous 11 months (Division 188). 'Projected GST turnover' is the value of all supplies made during the current month and all supplies likely to be made for the next 11 months.

Don't forget! 'Value' refers to the GST-exclusive price.

Current GST turnover and projected GST turnover are calculated by adding the value of all the supplies you make, or are likely to make, but excludes the value of the following supplies:
- input taxed supplies
- supplies that are not made in connection with an enterprise you carry on
- supplies made between members of the same group
- supplies not connected with Australia (including those connected with Australia pursuant to s9-25(5(c))
- insurance settlements, and
- supplies for no consideration (unless made to associates pursuant to Division 72).

In working out your current GST turnover, you also disregard any supply of a right or option to use commercial accommodation in Australia, that is not made in Australia and that is made through an enterprise that the supplier does not carry on in Australia. This applies to any supply that has not already been disregarded by virtue of not being connected with Australia (including connected with Australia pursuant to s9-25(5)(c)).

As well as the above exclusions, an entity excludes from projected GST turnover any of the following supplies made or likely to be made:
- transfer of ownership of capital assets, and
- any supply as a consequence of ceasing an enterprise or substantially and permanently reducing the size or scale of the enterprise.

Accordingly, where an entity supplies a capital asset by way of transfer or where an enterprise is winding down or ceasing and supplies are made as a consequence (such as capital assets being sold), the supply of those assets is not included in the calculation of the projected GST turnover. This provision is set out at s188-25. Assistance with the application of s188-25 can be found in GSTR 2001/7.

 You must include the value of GST-free supplies in your turnover calculation.

If the current GST turnover reaches the registration turnover threshold and the entity believes that projected GST turnover is below this threshold, the entity may not be required to register (s188-10). The following examples are based on the examples found in GSTR 2001/7.

 Ceasing to carry on an enterprise

Fred, a grazier, aged 72, decides to retire from his farming activities. He holds a clearing sale and sells all his livestock, machinery and various tools to a number of buyers. Proceeds from these activities total $80,000, which will be included in his current GST turnover. Fred is not registered for GST as his normal annual turnover from selling livestock is usually $35,000pa. Although Fred would normally have sold some of the livestock in his day to day operations, the whole herd has been sold at this time solely as a consequence of ceasing to carry on his enterprise and is therefore excluded from his projected GST turnover. Fred's projected GST turnover will be below the registration turnover threshold as he intends to cease business. Although his current GST turnover is above the threshold, his projected GST turnover is below the threshold and therefore his GST turnover does not meet the registration turnover threshold. Fred is not required to register for GST.

 Sale of a capital asset

Peter, a retiree, owns all three shops located next to a suburban railway station. Each shop is rented to tenants whose weekly tenancies are to terminate on 14 December 2015. The rent payable for each of the three shops is $200 per week.

The railway department is planning an expansion of the station. Peter sells the shops with vacant possession to the railway department for $200,000. Peter's only enterprise is renting the shops. He is not registered for GST. He is not intending to carry on any other enterprise in the next 12 months. Settlement is to take place on 20 December 2015.

Peter's current GST turnover is 50 weeks rent of $600 per week (up to 14 December 2015) plus the $200,000 from the sale of the shops; that is, a total of $230,000. Peter's current GST turnover is above the registration turnover threshold. Peter's projected GST turnover is the *sum of the values of all the supplies that Peter has made or is likely to make in December 2014 and up to 30 November 2015. Peter has made or will make supplies of two weeks rent of $600 per week (up to 14 December 2014) plus the $200,000 from the sale of the shops. His projected GST turnover calculated under s188-20 is $201,200.*

In selling the shops, however, Peter will dispose of a capital asset in addition to ceasing to carry on his enterprise, which means that those proceeds according to s188-25 are excluded when calculating projected GST turnover. Peter can disregard the $200,000 from the sale of the shops. Peter's projected GST turnover is $1,200. As Peter has calculated his projected GST turnover on a reasonable basis to be below the registration turnover threshold, his GST turnover does not meet that particular turnover threshold. He is not required to register for GST.

24.212   REGISTRATION PROCEDURES

If an entity is required to be registered for GST, it must apply for registration within 21 days of becoming required to do so, that is when the entity carrying on an enterprise first meets the registration turnover threshold (s25-1). Note that the definition of carrying on an enterprise includes anything done in the course of commencement.

An entity needs to have an ABN in order to be able to register for GST. GST registration can be done at the same time that an entity is applying for an ABN through the Australian Business Register website www.abr.gov.au (see 5.120). Alternatively, if you already have an ABN, you can register for GST by completing *Add a new business account form* (NAT 2954) which can be downloaded from the Tax Office website www.ato.gov.au. Another option of registering for GST is via the business portal (or tax agent portal).

24.213   CANCELLATION OF REGISTRATION

The cancellation of a GST registration is governed by the provisions of Subdivision 25-B. The Commissioner is not required to cancel a GST registration if the registration is less than 12 months old. The application to cancel a GST registration must be made in the approved form and the Commissioner must be satisfied the applicant is not required to be registered.

BUSINESS CEASES

If you cease carrying on any enterprise, you need to cancel your GST registration within 21 days after such cessation (s25-50). The definition of enterprise, however, includes all the things you do in the course of terminating it. The effect of cancellation will be that the entity will have a concluding tax period (see 24.111) up to the end of the day on which the cancellation takes place (for an annual GST reporter it will be until the end of the financial year in which the cancellation occurs).

 If the entity still holds assets on which it has previously claimed input tax credits at the time of cessation of registration, it will need to include an increasing adjustment in its concluding tax period. The amount of the adjustment will be 1/11th of the GST inclusive market value of the asset just before cancellation. This is calculated pursuant to Division 138 (see 24.264).

BANKRUPTCY, RECEIVERSHIP, LIQUIDATION

A representative of an incapacitated entity (eg. the liquidator of a company) is required to be registered in that capacity if the incapacitated entity is registered or required to be registered (s58-20). The representative will have the same tax periods as the entity it represents. The representative needs to notify the Commissioner in an approved form within 21 days after ceasing to represent the incapacitated entity, and the Commissioner must cancel the representative's registration if satisfied that the representative is no longer required to be registered.

Division 58 ensures that a representative of an incapacitated entity is responsible for the GST consequences that arise from supplies, acquisitions and importations made during its appointment. The Tax Office has released a Decision Impact Statement which sets out its approach to the administrative treatment in relation to this matter.

Note the following IDs:

- ID 2012/6 confirms that a representative of an incapacitated entity is entitled to claim input tax credits on administration fees paid to itself in its capacity as an insolvency practitioner, and

- ID 2012/7: a representative of an incapacitated entity will not be liable for GST when the representative receives consideration in respect of a taxable supply made by the incapacitated entity prior to the appointment of the representative.

Division 105 operates to the exclusion of Division 58 where a creditor makes a supply of a debtor's property in satisfaction of a debt (eg where a mortgagee exercises a power of sale). This, for example, allows mortgagees in possession or control of property of corporations to continue to report and account for their GST obligations under a single registration. This applies to all circumstances where a representative of an incapacitated entity is a creditor of that incapacitated entity, and the representative makes a supply of the incapacitated entity's property in satisfaction of a debt that the incapacitated entity owes to the representative.

The Explanatory Memorandum to the relevant legislation contains the following example:

EXAMPLE 2.1 (from the EM)

Company MCH borrows money from a finance provider, PLB Bank, to purchase a property. A mortgage is registered over the property with PLB Bank as the mortgagee. The terms and conditions of the mortgage deed allow the mortgagee to take control or possession of the property and to exercise the power of sale to recover any outstanding debts owed by MCH. MCH defaults on the loan repayments and PLB Bank takes possession of the property and subsequently exercises its power of sale as mortgagee and sells the property to a third party. The sale proceeds are applied towards the satisfaction of the outstanding debt owed by MCH to PLB Bank. If MCH had sold the property, the sale would have been a taxable supply for GST purposes.

PLB Bank is a controller, as defined in section 9 of the Corporations Act 2001, and is therefore a representative, (as defined in section 195-1 of the GST Act), for the purposes of Division 58. When PLB Bank sells the property by exercising its power of sale as mortgagee it is making a supply of a kind covered by paragraph 105-5(1)(a).

Section 58-95 of the GST Act ensures that Division 105 applies to this arrangement to the exclusion of Division 58. More specifically, Division 105 overrides Division 58 to the extent that the representative PLB Bank makes supplies covered by paragraph 105-5(1)(a).

BUSINESS OWNER DIES

If an individual owner of a registered business dies, this will require cancellation of the GST registration. As noted above, cancellation of GST registration can potentially cause increasing adjustments for assets which remain in existence at the time of cancellation. If a GST registered estate trustee continues the business of the deceased then it will not trigger these increasing adjustments. The same applies if a GST registered estate beneficiary decides to take over the running of the business from the trustee.

An increasing adjustment may arise where the estate trustee distributes a deceased's estate asset to a beneficiary for private purposes. The trustee under these circumstances will be liable for an increasing adjustment pursuant to Division 139.

24.220   DIFFERENCES BETWEEN AN 'INVOICE' AND A 'TAX INVOICE'

An 'invoice' is a document notifying an obligation to make a payment and can be in electronic form. A 'tax invoice' must contain certain information unnecessary in an 'invoice' and must be held to claim input tax credits (GSTR 2000/34).

The issue of an 'invoice' is relevant if using the accruals basis in determining the correct tax period to attribute GST payable or an input tax credit. When using the cash basis the issue of an 'invoice' is irrelevant because the attribution of GST payable or an input tax credit is based on when the consideration is paid or received.

Therefore, if using the accruals basis and none of the consideration has been received to attribute GST payable to a tax period, it is sufficient to hold an 'invoice' rather than a 'tax invoice'.

An 'invoice' is issued at the date when it is electronically transmitted, posted, couriered, hand delivered or similar. Under the accruals basis, it is this issue date, and not the date the document is prepared or the date shown on the document, that determines which period GST payable or input tax credits are attributable to (GSTR 2000/34 and *Tavco Group Pty Ltd v FCT* [2008] AATA 843).

NOTE: However, regardless of whether the cash or accruals method is used, a 'tax invoice' must be held at the time the input tax credit is claimed.

GSTD 2005/1 clarifies that a Recipient Created Tax Invoice can be an invoice for the purposes of the attribution rules.

GSTD 2005/2 has determined that an invoice posted on a website is 'issued' for the purposes of the attribution rules.

24.230   TAX INVOICES (Subdivision 29-C)

A tax invoice for a transaction will normally need to be held for an input tax credit in respect of the transaction to be claimed (s29-10).

A tax invoice can usually only be issued by the entity that made the taxable supply. The supplier must issue a tax invoice within 28 days of a request to do so, unless it is an approved recipient created tax invoice.

Tax invoices are not required where the GST-exclusive value of the transaction does not exceed $75 (ie. a GST-inclusive price of $82.50) or if it falls under one of the exceptions (see 24.234).

Pursuant to subs29-70(1), a tax invoice must:

- be issued by the supplier, unless it is a recipient created tax invoice
- be in the approved form
- contain the supplier's identity and ABN
- identify what is supplied, including the quantity and price
- include detail of the extent to which each supply is a taxable supply
- display the date of issue
- show the amount of GST (if any) payable in relation to each supply
- if the tax invoice was issued by the recipient and GST is payable – indicate that the GST is payable by the supplier
- contain any other details as required by the regulations, and
- clearly show that the document was intended to be a tax invoice or, if it was issued by the recipient, a recipient created tax invoice.

Further, the document must show the recipient's identity or ABN if either of the following applies:

- the total price of the supply or supplies is at least $1,000 (or higher, as specified by the regulations), or
- the document was issued by the recipient.

GSTR 2013/1 sets out the information requirements for a tax invoice. It also explains when a document is in the approved form for a tax invoice and the discretions that are available to the Commissioner in the event that there is an element of non-compliance.

Section 48-57 broadly allows a document which does not identify the recipient to be a tax invoice if the recipient is a member of a GST group. This concession is available if the document identifies the GST group, the representative member or another member of the GST group to which the recipient belongs. Furthermore, the recipient may still request that the tax invoice identifies the recipient.

TAX INVOICE ISSUED BY THE TRUSTEE OF A TRUST

A tax invoice for a supply made by a trustee in the capacity of a trustee of a trust must show the trustee's ABN (GSTR 2013/1).

Although an entity is defined to include a trust, a trust has no legal personality and so will not be registered in its own right on the Australian Business Register. Rather, the trustee of the trust will be registered and will be issued with an ABN in its capacity as trustee.

The trustee's identity and ABN must be clearly ascertainable from a tax invoice issued by the trust. The ruling notes that information sufficient to identify the trustee would include the legal name for the trustee – for example, The Trustee for the XYZ Family Trust or XYZ Pty Ltd as Trustee for the XYZ Family Trust. It is interesting to note that the ruling, unlike its predecessor, does not mention that the requirement can be satisfied with either:

- the name of the trustee – for example, XYZ Pty Ltd, or
- the trading name of the enterprise carried on by the trustee – for example, XYZ Plumbing Services.

However, the ruling does indicate that such indicators of the trustee's identity may be relevant in the Commissioner considering whether to exercise his discretion to treat a document as a tax invoice that is provided under subs29-70(1B).

According to GSTR 2008/3 under a bare trust arrangement, it is the beneficiaries of a trust and not the trust that makes the taxable supply or creditable acquisition and therefore it is the beneficiary that is entitled to input tax credits or liable to pay GST. Normally, it is the supplier (in the case of a bare trust this would be the beneficiary) that is required to issue the tax invoice and the tax invoice will need to include the beneficiary's ABN and name. However, the Commissioner can exercise discretion under GSTR 2008/3 to treat an invoice issued by the trustee of a bare trust with the trustee's ABN and name as a valid tax invoice.

24.233   CERTAIN TYPES OF DOCUMENTS QUALIFY AS TAX INVOICES

PROGRESSIVE SUPPLIES

GSTR 2013/1 provides guidelines on tax invoice requirements for taxable supplies that are:
- made for a period or on a progressive basis, and
- made for consideration that is provided on a progressive or periodic basis.

Each progressive or periodic component of the supply is generally treated as a separate supply. GSTR 2013/1 states that a single document can be a tax invoice for all components of the supply if it satisfies the tax invoice requirements and shows the price of each component of the supply. A lease document therefore can be used as a tax invoice for each monthly rental so long as all the requirements are satisfied. As a supplier you therefore do not have to issue separate tax invoices for each component of the supply.

NOTE: If there are price variations for supplies made on a periodic or progressive basis (eg. lease payments adjusted for CPI or lease payments that include an amount for outgoings), and the taxpayer needs to rely on other documents, the exercise of the Commissioner's discretion is relevant.

 If you use direct debit facilities, it would be advantageous for all parties to ensure that the lease document meets the requirements of a tax invoice to avoid the need to issue a separate tax invoice for each periodic payment.

CORPORATE CREDIT CARD STATEMENTS

Normally, to claim input tax credits you need to hold a tax invoice which is issued by the supplier of the goods or services. In the case of a corporate credit card statement, as it is not being issued by the actual supplier of the goods or services, it would not normally qualify as a tax invoice. However, the Tax Office has issued a Ruling (GSTR 2000/26) that allows businesses to claim input tax credits based on corporate credit card statements from approved corporate credit card providers where certain conditions are satisfied. GSTR 2000/26 sets out details a corporate credit card statement must contain to be sufficient to claim an input tax credit for a creditable acquisition without holding a tax invoice. VISA, AMEX, Diners, Qantas and Mastercard have been approved as corporate card providers. Approved corporate credit card providers are identified by determination – Waiver of Tax Invoice Determination. These are available from the Tax Office website www.ato.gov.au.

The credit card statement can only be used to claim the input tax credit where the supplier is making a taxable supply (ie. it is not a mixed supply) and the GST is exactly 1/11th of the supply. If the supply is a mixed supply or a taxable supply where GST is not 1/11th of the price, you need to obtain a tax invoice to substantiate the input tax credit for the supply. You will need to ask the supplier for a tax invoice before you attribute an input tax credit to a tax period.

 A condition required is that you have an effectively regulated corporate credit card policy which makes adjustments for circumstances when the card is used for private or personal expenditure.

OFFER DOCUMENTS

Subscriptions and renewals may be treated as tax invoices even though they are issued before a supply is made (GSTR 2013/1).

The Commissioner will allow such offer documents to be treated as a tax invoice if they:

- meet the requirements of subsection 29-70(1) in respect of the total of all supplies being offered when issued by the supplier
- indicate which supplies have been accepted, the total price and amount of GST payable in relation to what is supplied when completed by the prospective recipient, and
- include the following or similar statement: This document will be a tax invoice for GST when fully completed and you make a payment.

24.234   TAX INVOICE OR ADJUSTMENT NOTE IS NOT ALWAYS REQUIRED

Recipients who have made a creditable acquisition or have a decreasing adjustment generally must not claim an input tax credit or decreasing adjustment if they do not hold a valid tax invoice or adjustment note. There are, however, exceptions to this rule as follows:

- if the GST exclusive value of the taxable supply or the amount of the decreasing adjustment is $75 or less (s29-80)
- if you import goods (customs documentation may evidence GST paid)
- if the Commissioner determines in writing that the requirement does not apply (s29-10(3), GSTR 2013/1, GSTR 2004/1)
- if second-hand goods have been acquired from a registered seller and you have made a record of the acquisition (s66-17), or
- if creditable acquisitions are made of 'reverse charged' supplies made by non-residents (s83-5).

24.235   SUPPLIERS' OBLIGATIONS TO PROVIDE TAX INVOICES

Suppliers of taxable supplies are obliged to issue tax invoices and adjustment notes to recipients within 28 days after the recipient requests them (s29-70(2)). Suppliers who fail to issue a tax invoice or adjustment note as required are liable to an administrative penalty under s288-45 of Schedule 1 to the TAA. If a tax invoice or adjustment note is not provided by the supplier as a normal incident of the transaction, the recipient should make genuine reasonable attempts to request one. The emphasis is on genuine reasonable attempts. The recipient is not required to go to extraordinary lengths to pursue a supplier for the tax invoice.

If a tax invoice or adjustment note is not received within 28 days after the request, the recipient should contact the Tax Office for assistance, providing details of the transaction and any attempt(s) to request the document. In the event that the recipient is unable to obtain a valid tax invoice after making all reasonable attempts, the Commissioner may exercise a discretion to treat another document as a tax invoice (see 24.236).

NOTE: It is advisable for the supplier to keep a copy of the tax invoice issued as evidence of compliance with the requirement to issue a tax invoice.

24.236   COMMISSIONER'S DISCRETION TO TREAT A DOCUMENT
AS A TAX INVOICE (PS LA 2004/11)

Practice Statement PS LA 2004/11 deals with how the Commissioner will exercise his discretion to treat a document as a tax invoice or as an adjustment note.

The Commissioner has the discretion to treat as a tax invoice an adjustment note (s29-70(1B); 29-75(1)) a particular document that does not meet the requirements for being a tax invoice. In deciding whether to exercise the discretion, the Tax Office needs to be satisfied that there is sufficient evidence of the recipient making a creditable acquisition (under Division 11 of the GST Act) or having a decreasing adjustment (under Division 19 of the GST Act). To substantiate the correct input tax credit entitlement, Tax Officers should verify the price of the relevant goods or services, the amount of GST included in the price, and the names, addresses and ABNs of each party to the transaction.

An entity is able to treat a document as a tax invoice where that document does not contain the required information in certain circumstances. This rule exists in conjunction with the Commissioner's discretion to treat such a document as a tax invoice.

The main situations covered by PS LA 2004/11 involve recipients who are claiming an input tax credit or decreasing adjustment, but do not hold the necessary tax invoice or adjustment note.

In deciding whether to exercise the discretion or not, different considerations apply if the input tax credit or decreasing adjustment has not yet been claimed, compared with the situation where a claim has already been made. To acknowledge the different circumstances, the Tax Office adopts a separate approach for each situation. Flowchart A (see following) summarises the approach where the recipient has already claimed the input tax credit or decreasing adjustment. Flowchart B (see following) summarises the approach for cases where the recipient has not claimed the input tax credit or decreasing adjustment.

IN WHAT CIRCUMSTANCES WOULD IT BE REASONABLE TO EXERCISE THE DISCRETION FOR THE RECIPIENT?

If there is a creditable acquisition or decreasing adjustment, and the recipient has made a genuine attempt (in their circumstances) to comply, the discretion should be exercised. The key focus here is whether the recipient, through their actions in the circumstances, has made a genuine attempt to meet the requirements to hold a tax invoice or adjustment note. If not, it may be reasonable to refuse to exercise the discretion. Tax Officers should consider the recipient's circumstances, including the practical and commercial realities of record keeping.

PS LA 2004/11 sets out factors to consider relating to the document held by the recipient, such as the kind of defect that makes the document invalid as a tax invoice. It also sets out factors to consider in respect of the recipient's circumstance. These factors plus others must be considered by Tax Officers in determining whether it is appropriate for the Commissioner to exercise his discretion.

PS LA 2004/11 also considers situations of lost or destroyed tax invoices and adjustment notes, making enquiries of third parties (such as suppliers) and where parties may be in dispute over an aspect of a transaction.

RECIPIENT HAS NOT YET CLAIMED INPUT TAX CREDIT OR DECREASING ADJUSTMENT

If the recipient has not yet claimed an input tax credit or decreasing adjustment, the Tax Officers will need to follow the decision making process outlined in the flowchart below.

The recipient of a taxable supply needs to call or write to the Tax Office requesting advice because they have made a creditable acquisition or have a decreasing adjustment but they have not been able to obtain a valid tax invoice or adjustment note from the supplier. The situation could also arise during Tax Office verification activities, such as a field visit.

Tax Officers need to follow the steps below in deciding whether to exercise the discretion.

- **Step 1.** Has the recipient made a reasonable attempt to request the tax invoice or adjustment note from the supplier? If YES, go to step 2. If NO, Tax Officers must advise the recipient to make a reasonable attempt to request a valid document from the supplier (see paragraph 25 of PS LA 2004/11 for a discussion of what constitutes a 'reasonable attempt').
    - If the recipient obtains a tax invoice or adjustment note, they can claim the input tax credit or decreasing adjustment in the next or a subsequent activity statement.
    - If the supplier has failed or refused to provide the requested document, or the recipient was unable to locate or contact the supplier, go to step 2.
- **Step 2.** Is it reasonable to conclude from the available evidence that the recipient has made a creditable acquisition or has an adjustment from an adjustment event? If YES, exercise the discretion, go to step 3. If NO, the discretion will not be exercised, go to step 4.
- **Step 3.** Exercise the discretion to treat a particular document as a tax invoice or adjustment note. If there is sufficient evidence to establish a creditable acquisition or decreasing adjustment, there will be some document on which the discretion can operate. Tax Officers must advise the recipient to claim the input tax credit or decreasing adjustment in the next or a subsequent activity statement, provided the other requirements for attribution have been met. Tax Officers should refer details of the case to the relevant compliance area for possible action in respect of the supplier's behaviour.
- **Step 4.** If the answer at step 2 was NO, Tax Officers may not exercise the discretion and advise the recipient of the decision and the reasons for the decision.

FLOWCHART A: RECIPIENT HAS NOT YET CLAIMED INPUT TAX CREDIT OR DECREASING ADJUSTMENT *(Source: PS LA 2004/11)*

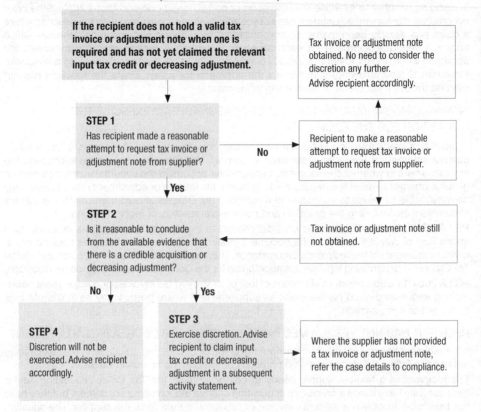

RECIPIENT HAS CLAIMED INPUT TAX CREDIT OR DECREASING ADJUSTMENT

If the recipient has already claimed an input tax credit or decreasing adjustment, the decision making process is outlined in the flowchart below.

- **Step 1.** Is it reasonable to conclude from the available evidence that the recipient has made a creditable acquisition or has an adjustment from an adjustment event. If YES, go to step 2. If NO, the discretion will not be exercised and the recipient must be advised accordingly. Amend the activity statement to disallow the input tax credit or decreasing adjustment.

- **Step 2.** In the circumstances is it reasonable to exercise the discretion? The key focus here is whether the recipient, through its actions, has made a genuine attempt to meet the requirements to hold a tax invoice or adjustment note. Tax Officers should consider all relevant circumstances, and not irrelevant circumstances when reaching a decision. If YES, exercise the discretion, go to Step 3. If NO, do not exercise the discretion, go to Step 4.

- **Step 3.** If the answer at step 2 was YES, exercise the discretion to treat a particular document, that was held at the time the relevant activity statement was lodged, as a tax invoice or adjustment note.

  - If there is sufficient evidence to establish a creditable acquisition or decreasing adjustment, there will be some document on which the discretion can operate (for example, invalid tax invoice, normal invoice, contract, etc).

  - The recipient will be taken to have held a tax invoice or adjustment note at the time of giving the GST return in which the credit or decreasing adjustment was claimed. If the other requirements for attribution have been met, the recipient will have made a valid input tax credit claim or decreasing adjustment and there is no need to take any further action in respect of this claim.

- The recipient must be given clear advice about the requirements to hold a tax invoice or adjustment note and be advised to take steps to avoid similar problems in future. If the tax invoice or adjustment note problems are caused by the supplier, and the supplier does not comply in the future, the recipient should approach the Tax Office in the first instance, before claiming an input tax credit or decreasing adjustment.

- If the supplier has not issued a valid tax invoice, consider whether to refer details to compliance for possible follow-up action.

- **Step 4.** If the answer at step 2 was NO, do not exercise the discretion. Tax Officers must:
  - amend the activity statement to disallow the input tax credit or decreasing adjustment
  - advise the recipient to keep and retain adequate records of their GST transactions and indicate that failure to do so could lead to an administrative penalty
  - advise the recipient to make a reasonable attempt to obtain a tax invoice or adjustment note from the supplier (see paragraph 25 of PS LA 2004/11 for what constitutes a reasonable attempt)
  - advise that, if a tax invoice or adjustment note is subsequently obtained, the input tax credit or decreasing adjustment can be claimed in a later activity statement
  - advise that if the recipient makes a reasonable attempt to request a tax invoice or adjustment note, but is not able to obtain one, they may make a new request for the exercise of the discretion. The recipient's new request should be considered as if the input tax credit or decreasing adjustment had not been claimed before (see Flowchart A), and
  - consider whether to refer details of the supplier's actions to compliance for possible follow-up action.

FLOWCHART B: RECIPIENT HAS CLAIMED INPUT TAX CREDIT OR DECREASING ADJUSTMENT *(Source: PS LA 2004/11)*

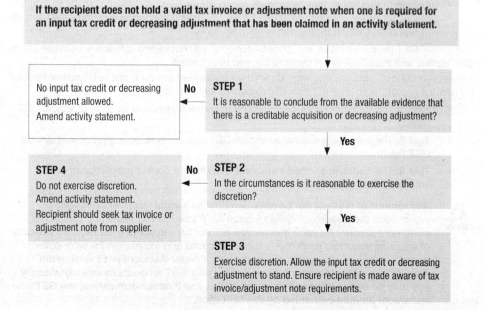

24.240   GST REMITTANCES AND REFUNDS

Section 31-5 requires that an entity that is registered or required to be registered must give the Commissioner a GST return for each tax period. The GST return is incorporated into the BAS (see 5.800). Registered enterprises with an annual turnover of less than $20 million can prepare and lodge their GST return on either a monthly or quarterly basis. This is also known as remitting a GST return. A voluntary monthly remitter can not revert back to a quarterly basis within a 12 month period (see 24.110).

A monthly remitter must lodge a return for each monthly tax period by the 21st day of the month following the end of the preceding month.

Registered enterprises with an annual turnover of $20 million or more must remit on a monthly basis. They must lodge their BAS and make payments electronically.

Quarterly returns must be lodged by 28 October, 28 February, 28 April, and 28 July.

Small businesses and non-profit organisations that have voluntarily registered for GST are allowed to report and pay GST on an annual basis (see 24.110).

The Tax Office is required to pay refunds directly to bank accounts. Interest is payable if a refund is not paid within 14 days from the lodgement of your BAS.

When completing the BAS, a registered enterprise will work out a net amount by subtracting the input tax credits on creditable acquisitions from the GST payable on the taxable supplies made for the tax period ie:

Net amount = GST payable – input tax credits

A net amount greater than 0 means an amount is owing to the Tax Office. A net amount less than 0 is the amount owed by the Tax Office.

If you have not nominated your bank details you will not receive a refund as the Tax Office will only credit directly into a bank account.

Monthly remitters must apply the standard method to report and pay GST, that is to report and pay (or claim) actual GST amount monthly.

Quarterly remitters have three choices in the way they report and pay GST, as set out below.

- **Option 1:** Report and pay (or claim) actual GST amounts quarterly together with required statistical data.

- **Option 2:** Report and pay (or claim) actual GST amounts quarterly and lodge statistical data as part of an annual GST information report.

- **Option 3:** Eligible entities (principally those whose turnover is less than $2 million) can pay a Tax Office calculated GST instalment quarterly and lodge an annual GST return to report and adjust for the actual GST amounts.

The annual GST return for those who choose option 3 will require any difference between actual GST liability and total GST instalments to be paid or refunded.

Those who choose option 3 can vary down their instalment amount, but risk underestimation penalties if any of the following 3 mutually exclusive tests are breached:

- **Test 1:** The total paid (including instalment payments) is at least 85% of annual GST liability.

- **Test 2:** The taxpayer's estimated annual GST amount is at least 85% of their annual GST liability.

- **Test 3:** The taxpayer's varied instalment amount is a correct proportion of their estimated annual GST amount.

Any refunds of GST will not be refunded until an annual statement is lodged if you choose the instalment option (option 3). If you use the Tax Office calculated instalment amount for each quarter you will not be subject to a penalty. The process of ensuring you meet each test is so complicated and the margin for error before penalties apply is so small that it represents a major disincentive to varying the Tax Office instalment amount. If you expect your GST amounts to vary significantly you may be better off choosing to use option 1 or 2 rather than varying the GST instalment amount calculated by the Tax Office.

NOTE: Primary production businesses or certain individuals who are eligible to average their income for tax periods (ie. authors, artists, sportspersons) will be eligible to pay only 2 not 4 instalments each year. The two instalments are to be payable at the end of the 3rd and 4th quarter. See 5.800 for further guidance regarding these options and how each are reflected in relevant activity statements.

An overpaid refund under s35-5 is treated as an amount due and payable from the date of the overpayment.

It is not mandatory to apply a payment, credit or RBA surplus against a tax debt that is a business activity statement amount (eg. GST payable) unless that amount is due and payable. The Commissioner may decide not to apply a payment or credit against a tax debt that is due but not payable including a tax debt that is a BAS amount.

24.241 BUSINESSES IN A NET REFUND POSITION MAY CONTINUE TO USE THE GST INSTALMENT SYSTEM

From 1 July 2013, small businesses in a net refund position may choose to access the GST instalments system, with an instalment amount each quarter of zero. Any refund or liability due to the taxpayer will be reconciled in their annual GST return. Only those businesses already using the GST instalment system will be allowed to continue to use it if they move into a net refund position.

Entities that are eligible to elect to have annual tax periods and have done so will lodge their GST returns and pay their GST or receive refunds of GST on an annual basis. An entity that has made an annual tax period election must lodge its GST return for the annual tax period no later than the date required to lodge its annual income tax return. If you are not required to lodge income tax returns, you must lodge a GST return on or before 28 February in the financial year following the end of the relevant annual tax period.

This change benefits those taxpayers that temporarily move into a net refund position and those taxpayers normally in a net refund position who consider that the compliance cost advantages of submitting their BAS annually outweigh the cash flow cost of delayed refunds.

24.242 COMMISSIONER'S DISCRETION TO WITHHOLD REFUNDS

The Commissioner is entitled to hold tax refunds for verification prior to payment. Section 8AAZLGA of the TAA operates as follows:

Scope

The TAA provides the Commissioner with a legislative power to retain an amount pending refund integrity checks of a taxpayer's claim.

It applies where a taxpayer has given the Commissioner a notification (such as a GST return) that affects, or may affect, the amount that the Commissioner is required to refund to the taxpayer.

In circumstances where it would be reasonable to require verification of information provided by the entity relating to a refund, the Commissioner may retain that refund. The Commissioner may also retain an amount if the entity requests that the Commissioner retain the amount for verification purposes.

When deciding whether to retain the amount, the Commissioner must have regard to a number of factors, including, but not limited to:

- the impact on the entity's financial position
- the impact on the revenue, and
- the likelihood that there is fraud or evasion, intentional disregard or recklessness as to the operation of a taxation law.

If the Commissioner retains the amount, the taxpayer must be notified within 14 or 30 days depending on whether the amount relates to an RBA surplus or alternatively, a credit in the entity's favour.

Time frame for verification

Broadly, the Commissioner may retain a refund until the earliest of the following:

- the day it would be no longer be reasonable to require verification of the information
- if the Commissioner failed to notify the taxpayer of the decision to retain the refund – the day after the required timeframe for notification, and
- the day the Commissioner amended an assessment relating to an amount or, in relation to tax periods commencing prior to 1 July 2012, has made or amended an assessment under Division 105 of Schedule 1 to the TAA.

Review rights

A taxpayer may object under Part IVC TAA to the Commissioner's decision to retain the refund.

Delayed refund interest

Delayed refund interest is payable by the Commissioner for the withholding of refunds.

EXAMPLE (from the explanatory memorandum)

Duncan runs a shoe shop and is registered for GST. On 28 July 2014, Duncan lodges his GST return for the tax period ending 30 June 2014. Duncan's net amount for that period is a refund of $15,000. The RBA interest day would be 11 August 2014. Duncan's past compliance history has been poor and at times he has been found to have been reckless when lodging his GST returns. On this occasion, his claim for a refund does not correspond with his recent lodgement activity. As a result, the Commissioner is satisfied that it would be reasonable to require the amounts in Duncan's GST return to be verified and on 8 August 2014 informs Duncan that he has decided to retain the refund under ss8AAZLGA(1).

On 8 September 2014, the Commissioner requests additional information from Duncan. Duncan provides this information to the Commissioner on 30 October 2014.

In investigating the correctness of the amount claimed by Duncan in his return, the Commissioner discovers that the acquisitions to which the refund claim relates are part of a complex supply chain.

Having regard to the complexity involved and the likelihood that Duncan may again be acting recklessly, the Commissioner is satisfied that it would be reasonable to continue to retain the refund after 9 November 2014 (60 days from the RBA interest day plus the 30 days Duncan took to provide the requested information to the Commissioner). The Commissioner is required to notify Duncan of this decision by 23 November 2014.

If by 23 November 2014, the Commissioner still has not refunded the amount, made an assessment of Duncan's net amount or informed Duncan of the decision, Duncan may object to the Commissioner's decision to retain the amount under Part IVC TAA53.

NOTE: PS LA 2012/6 explains when the discretion may be exercised by the Commissioner to retain an amount for verification purposes.

24.243   REFUNDING EXCESS GST

Division 142 of the GST Act governs the refund of excess GST for tax periods starting on or after 31 May 2014. It effectively replaced s105-65 of Schedule 1 to the TAA (24.256), which applies to tax periods starting before 31 May 2014 (24.256).

Under Division 142, a supplier self-assesses their entitlement to a refund of an amount of excess GST according to specific criteria. The object of the Division 142 is to ensure that excess GST is not refunded if this would give rise to an entity receiving a windfall gain. Generally, the Division operates so that a supplier is not entitled to a refund of an amount of excess GST where the supplier has passed on the GST to another entity (the recipient), and has not reimbursed that other entity for the passed-on GST. Where a supplier is uncertain whether it has passed on the GST or reimbursed, it may apply for a private ruling.

'Excess GST' is an amount of GST that has been taken into account in an entity's assessed net amount and is in excess of what was payable by the entity in the relevant tax period prior to taking into account or applying the provisions of Division 142.

Excess GST does not include:

- an amount of GST that was correctly payable but is later subject to a decreasing adjustment, and
- an amount of GST that is payable but is correctly attributable to another tax period.

Division 142 may apply regardless of how the excess GST arose. For example, excess GST can arise as a result of a mischaracterisation, a miscalculation, or a reporting or administrative error. An amount of excess GST will only be refundable if:

- it has not been passed on to the recipient, or
- it has been passed on to the recipient, and the recipient has been reimbursed.

If the excess GST has not been passed on, the supplier may, subject to the period of review, request an amendment to their assessment for the relevant tax period to reduce the amount of GST attributable to that tax period.

If the excess GST has been passed on to the recipient, s142-10 applies to treat the excess GST as always having been payable, and payable on a taxable supply, until the excess GST has been reimbursed to the recipient. Once s142-10 ceases to apply, the supplier can claim a refund of the excess GST.

If s142-10 applies (that is, where a supplier has passed on the excess GST and has not reimbursed the recipient), the supplier may request that the Commissioner exercise the discretion (under s142-15) to treat s142-10 as not applying.

The Commissioner has issued a ruling which explains his view on the meaning of the terms 'passed on' and 'reimburse' for the purposes of Division 142 (GSTR 2015/1).

24.250   CORRECTING GST MISTAKES

Under s17-20, the Commissioner can make a determination that allows a net amount for a tax period to include the correction of an error made in a preceding tax period. The Tax Office has issued two fact sheets providing the Commissioner's guidelines for when a business can use a later BAS to correct mistakes made on an earlier BAS: 'Correcting GST errors', with effect from 10 May 2013 (NAT 4700) and 'Correcting GST mistakes before 10 May 2013', for mistakes made before 10 May 2013 (the former NAT 4700).

Appendix C to the former guide contains a summary outlining the key differences between the two guides.

NOTE: Correcting GST mistakes only applies to errors and mistakes, not adjustment events (see 24.260).

24.251   INPUT TAX CREDITS CLAIMABLE ON AN EARLIER BAS

If you were entitled to claim input tax credits on a previous BAS, but for some reason you did not (eg. you were not aware you were holding a tax invoice), then you can claim it on any following BAS after you hold the tax invoice. There is no time limit for claiming input tax credits that were never claimed.

For GST returns and assessments lodged or issued, and revisions to GST returns and revised assessments issued or made, after 7.30pm (AEST) on 12 May 2009, input tax credits must be claimed within a four-year period.

Claiming input tax credits that could have been claimed in a prior BAS is not affected by the correction limits or time limits set out in the fact sheets on correcting GST mistakes.

24.252 OTHER CORRECTIONS

GUIDELINES ON CORRECTING GST MISTAKES

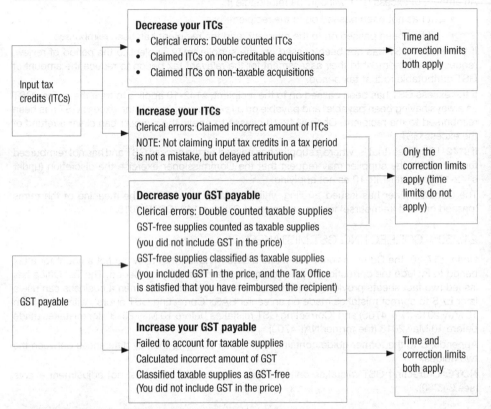

In all other cases, there are limits to the amount of the correction, and in some instances there is a time limit on when you can make the correction on a later BAS.

For errors requiring a decrease in GST payable (ie. overpaid GST or under-claimed input tax credits in an earlier BAS), corrections can be made in a current or later BAS provided the amount is within the correction limits (see table in 24.253) and the correction is made within the 4 year period set out in Subdivision 105-C TAA.

For errors requiring an increase in GST payable (ie. underpaid GST or over-claimed input tax credits in an earlier BAS), corrections can be made in a current or later BAS provided:

- the correction is made within the time limits (see table in 24.254), and
- the amount is within the correction limits (see table in 24.253).

If the error falls outside of these conditions, you have no alternative but to revise the earlier BAS containing the error. Revising an earlier BAS may result in a liability to pay interest where GST has been underpaid. Division 105-C of the TAA sets out time limits on credits, refunds and recovering amounts.

The Commissioner is able to make a determination that a taxpayer can correct errors for a preceding BAS on their current BAS.

24.253 CORRECTION LIMITS

The correction limits below reflect the Commissioner's determination Goods and Services Tax: Correcting GST Errors Determination 2013 which applies in working out a net amount for a tax period for which you give the Commissioner your GST return on or after 9 May 2013. The determination does not apply in working out a net amount for a tax period that started before 1 July 2012.

Annual turnover	Correction limits
Less than $20m	Less than $10,000
$20m to less than $100m	Less than $20,000
$100m to less than $500m	Less than $40,000
$500m to less than $1b	Less than $80,000
$1b and over	Less than $450,000

You can make corrections to increase or decrease your GST payable or your input tax credits on your next BAS, only if their net effect (ie. the total GST effect of all the errors) is within the correction limits which vary depending on the size of your enterprise. The correction limits are the net effect of the total of all errors occurring in earlier BASs. They are the maximum amount of corrections you can make on a later BAS. It is not 'per BAS' or 'per mistake' limit.

In working out whether your corrections are within these limits, you can offset total overpayments against total underpayments.

24.254   TIME LIMITS

Annual turnover	Time limit in which you can correct errors
Less than $20m	Up to 18 months (18 monthly BASs, 6 quarterly BASs or 1 annual GST return)
More than $20m	Up to 3 months (3 monthly BASs)

Corrections which increase your GST payable, or reduce your input tax credits can be corrected on a later BAS only if the errors fall within the time limits applicable to the size of your enterprise. Where the mistakes fall outside of these time limits, you must revise the original BAS in which the mistake occurred.

NOTE: Section 105-50(1) of Schedule 1 to the TAA has the effect that the GST ceases to be payable four years after it becomes payable by the taxpayer. However, s105-50(3) TAA provides that this provision does not apply to the extent that within those four years the Commissioner has required payment by serving a notice to the taxpayer. The decision in *Cyonara Snowfox Pty Ltd and Commissioner of Taxation* [2011] AATA 124 confirmed that the notice issued in this case was valid, regardless of the fact that it did not require payment of the correct amount.

An enterprise with an annual turnover of $2 million incorrectly included six taxable supplies on its previous two quarterly BASs. The GST-inclusive amount of these supplies was $11,000 each (totalling $66,000), with GST of $1,000 payable on each (totalling $6,000).

The total amount overpaid on the earlier BASs and needing correction is $6,000, which exceeds the limit of $5,000, even though the amount of each mistake was below the limit.

If the same taxpayer also overstated input tax credits of $2,000 for an acquisition on an earlier BAS, the net effect of all the corrections above would be a reduction in GST of $4,000 (ie. $6,000 – $2,000), which is within the correction limit. Therefore, this business could correct these mistakes on its current BAS.

However, note that the correction on the overstated input tax credits of $2,000 is also subject to a time limit of up to 18 months because it is a correction that decreases the input tax credits claim. The correction to the overstated input tax credits need to be made within 18 months from the time the error was included in a BAS.

24.255   ANNUAL GST PREPARERS

If you are a small business that pays GST by instalments for a full year, you will account for GST on an annual basis and report GST in an annual GST return. Where you make an error in that return, subject to the correction limits, you will be able to correct that error in your next annual GST return. Correcting your mistakes in this way may inflate your Commissioner notified GST instalment amount for the next year.

24.256   TIME LIMITS ON GST REFUNDS

IMPORTANT: For tax periods commencing on or after 31 May 2014, see also 24.243.

Your entitlement to claim unpaid net amounts, refunds, credits and other amounts (including any relevant GIC) (Subdivision 105-C of the TAA) is subject to a four-year time limit. The four-year time limit generally expires four years after the end of the tax period or the date of importation. For example if you have a quarterly tax period that ends on 30 June 2012, the four-year limit expires on 30 June 2016.

In order to be within the four-year time limit, you must either:

- lodge your refund claims in relation to the refund or credit amount, or
- notify the Tax Office of the entitlement before the four year limit expires.

In *Australian Leisure Marine Pty Ltd v FC of T* [2010] AATA 620, the taxpayer lodged a revised Activity Statement for the relevant tax period (June 2005) increasing its claims for input tax credits on creditable importations. The AAT held that a taxpayer was not entitled to claim the additional ITCs on the basis that the lodgment of the notice (ie. the revised Activity Statements) on 6 August 2009 was outside the four year time frame. Whilst it was accepted the taxpayer gave a valid notice to the Commissioner, the AAT noted that the notice was not given within the required timeframe of four years. In the AAT's view, s105-55 has substantive effect in that the expiry of the four-year time limit extinguishes the right of a taxpayer to notify the Commissioner of an entitlement to an ITC. In addition, the AAT was of the view that the Commissioner did not have the discretion to extend the four year time period.

Note however that for tax periods starting before 1 July 2012, this four year time limit does not apply to input tax credit entitlement arising from a tax invoice for a purchase in which no GST credit was ever claimed before. Input tax credits arising under such circumstances can be claimed in any following BAS after the tax invoice is held, subject to certain conditions. This exception does not apply to tax periods starting on or after 1 July 2012. If you choose to claim such credits by revising an earlier activity statement, the revision is limited to a tax period that has ended not more than four years ago.

For more information see NAT 11645 *Time Limit on GST Refunds*.

For taxpayers who have incorrectly overpaid their GST liability on the mistaken belief that a supply they have provided is a taxable supply, the Commissioner can deny the refund on the overpaid amount if:

- the Commissioner is not satisfied that the taxpayer will reimburse the recipient for the amount of GST overpaid, or
- the recipient is not registered or not required to be registered for GST (s105-65 Sch 1 TAA).

In ID 2013/56, the Commissioner confirms that he will not be satisfied that an amount of overpaid GST has been reimbursed to a recipient when the supplier merely makes a journal entry in its accounts, unless the journal entry offsets a pre-existing liability owed by the recipient to the supplier.

NOTE: The law applies to overpaid amounts of GST on the basis of a mistaken belief that there was a taxable supply regardless of whether or not there was a supply subsequently.

Further, the Commissioner may at any time make an assessment of a taxpayer's net amount (ie. GST payable less input tax credits that may be claimed) for a tax period and may amend an assessment at any time (ss105-5 and 105-25 TAA). An amendment of an assessment is a reviewable indirect tax decision which may be objected against. Similarly, the Commissioner's assessment is subject to a four year time limit (Subdivision 105-A Schedule 1 of the TAA) and any amount payable as a result of an assessment (including general interest charge) will cease to be payable four years after it became payable (Subdivision 105-C Schedule 1 of the TAA).

However, the four year limit does not apply to GST payable where:

- within those four years the Commissioner has required payment of the amount by giving a notice to the taxpayer, or
- the Commissioner is satisfied that the payment of the amount was avoided by fraud or evasion.

 The time limit issues relating to entitlements for GST refunds are complicated by the legislative changes that came into effect on 1 July 2008 and 1 July 2012.

Taxpayers that are contemplating amending prior year GST returns and are uncertain about their entitlements or the relevant time limits may find it useful to refer to the Tribunal's analysis in Swanbat Pty Ltd and Commissioner of Taxation [2013] AATA 891.

NOTIFICATION FOR THE PURPOSE OF CREDITS OR REFUND ENTITLEMENT

There is no prescribed form for the purposes of a notification under section 105-55, informing the Tax Office of an entitlement to a refund or credit. Notification of entitlement to GST refund form (NAT 11719) can be used but is not necessary. However, the notification should be in writing and must be received on or before the fourth year after the end of the relevant tax period or the date of importation.

MT 2009/1 outlines what constitutes notification by an entity for the purpose of section 105-55. The following are valid notifications:

- an activity statement or revised activity statement which includes the relevant entitlement in the relevant tax period
- an application for a private indirect tax ruling, an objection or other correspondence from an entity that asserts the entity has an entitlement, and
  - provides a description of the nature of the entitlement to a refund, other payment or credit, which is sufficient to bring to the Commissioner's attention the basic factual and legal basis for the entitlement, and
  - specifies the tax period(s) or importation(s) to which the entitlement relates.

It is only required that the entitlement is clearly defined but not necessary for it to be quantified. Correspondence that is speculative in nature is not accepted as a valid notification of an entitlement to a refund or credit. Correspondence purported to be a valid notification but lacking in information will not be accepted as a valid notification. However, if at a later time further information is provided and, together with the earlier correspondence, it is sufficient to make a valid notification, the Tax Office accept the time a valid notification is provided to be the time the later information is provided.

24.257   CORRECTION APPLIES ONLY TO GENUINE ERROR

The Commissioner's guidelines in the superseded version of NAT 4700, which applies to mistakes made before 10 May 2013, only apply to mistakes that are genuine and reasonable. If you correct such mistakes within the time and correction limits there will be no penalties or interest.

If you are attempting to manipulate your affairs, you will be unable to use these arrangements and you will need to revise each BAS in which an error occurred. This could have GIC ramifications (ie. the business would need to amend its BASs for the earlier quarters and will be subject to interest from the due dates of those earlier BASs). In addition, the Commissioner can withdraw the right to use the arrangements in the future.

If you establish a regular pattern of correcting mistakes by adjusting your current BAS for amounts that are at the upper end of the correction limits then this may be considered taking advantage of the arrangements in the fact sheet, unless the mistakes are genuine and occur in the normal course of your business.

Every correction that would increase an entity's GST payable or that would decrease its input tax credits should be made as soon as possible after the mistake is found. Either make the correction in the next BAS if the correction is within the guidelines, or revise the original BAS in which the mistake occurred.

To delay the correction until the last tax period before the time limit runs out would be considered by the Commissioner as a deliberate manipulation of an entity's affairs.

EXAMPLE: Source – former NAT 4700

Chand Associates has a turnover of $2 million. It reports and pays GST on a quarterly basis and lodged four quarterly BASs for the 2009-10 income year. After completing its income tax return on 31 October 2010, Chand Associates realises that it made the following mistakes:

- *July – September 2009 BAS: overclaimed $800 in input tax credits (as an acquisition was only 50% creditable)*

- *October – December 2009 BAS: underpaid $400 in GST (from incorrectly recording a taxable supply as GST-free)*
- *January – March 2010 BAS: underpaid $800 in GST (from incorrectly recording a taxable supply as GST-free)*
- *April – June 2010 BAS: underpaid $1,400 in GST (from incorrectly recording a taxable supply as GST-free)*
- *July – September 2010 BAS: underpaid $1,400 in GST (from incorrectly recording a taxable supply as GST-free).*

Chand Associates fixes their incorrect classification of the taxable supply from 1 October 2010 so that this error does not recur from that date. Chand Associates wish to correct all of the errors that occurred in the 15 month period in its October – December 2010 BAS. The Commissioner would consider that all of the above mistakes made by Chand Associates are genuine and reasonable since they are made in legitimate circumstances and the business has not deliberately manipulated its affairs to take advantage of the arrangements in the fact sheet.

The total of Chand Associates' errors in the 15 month period from July 2009 to September 2010 is $4,800. As this is below the correction limit threshold for Chand Associates, and they wish to correct their mistakes within the time limit threshold, Chand Associates may make this correction in their October – December 2010 BAS.

NOTE: PS LA 2006/2 explains the administration of shortfall penalties for false or misleading statements. Correcting GST mistakes is considered within this practice statement.

IMPORTANT! The current NAT 4700 (which applies from 10 May 2013) does not contain any commentary regarding genuine and reasonable mistakes. However, under the new guide, the error cannot be made as a result of recklessness or intentional disregard of a GST law.

Intentional disregard of a GST law (Source – current NAT 4700)

Duck and Dodge Co is facing a cash flow problem and deliberately under-reports GST on its sales by $10,000 when lodging its activity statement for the November 2013 reporting period. As the debit errors (the under-reporting of GST payable) result from Duck and Dodge Co intentionally disregarding the GST law, the errors cannot be corrected on a later activity statement.

24.260   ADJUSTMENTS

Events will occur where adjustments need to be made to the amount of GST paid or input tax credit claimed in a previous tax period. An adjustment is not a correction in error. An adjustment arises as a result of changes to transactions or the entities operations that result in an over/under payment of GST or an over/under claiming of input tax credits.

An 'increasing adjustment' is where too little GST was paid or too much credit was claimed.

A 'decreasing adjustment' is where too much GST was paid or too little credit claimed.

There are three main circumstances that will give rise to adjustments:

- adjustment events (Division 19) – see 24.261
- bad debts or overdue debts (Division 21) – see 24.262, and
- a change in the extent of creditable purpose (Division 129) – see 24.263.

Adjustments also arise under the following circumstances (see 24.264):

- goods are applied solely to private or domestic use – increasing adjustment arises (Division 130)
- a supply of something acquired, imported or applied for a purpose that is not fully creditable – decreasing adjustment arises (Division 132)
- where a payment is made to a third party relating to a thing that the payer has supplied to another entity and which the payee subsequently acquired, indirectly reducing the amount the payer receives for the supply – decreasing adjustment arises (Division 134)
- where a going concern has been acquired and some supplies made in running the concern will not be taxable or GST-free – increasing adjustment arises (Division 135)
- where stock is on hand at the time of registration, or becoming required to be registered – decreasing adjustment arises (Division 137)

- where a GST registration ceases – increasing adjustment arises (Division 138)
- where distributions for private consumption are made from a deceased estate – increasing adjustment arises (Division 139), and
- where a person holds a Tradex order and the goods are dealt with contrary to the Tradex Scheme – increasing adjustment arises (Division 141).

NOTE: Miscellaneous Taxation Ruling MT 2010/1 considers the application of s105-65 of Schedule 1 to the TAA, which provides for restrictions on GST refunds, to certain situations. Specifically, this Ruling explains:

- whether s105-65 of Schedule 1 to the TAA applies to overpayments of luxury car tax (LCT), wine equalisation tax (WET) and to taxable importations
- the meaning of 'overpaid'
- the meaning of 'treated' as a taxable supply
- the meaning of 'to any extent'
- the operation of s105-65 where the wrong entity remits the GST
- the meaning of the Commissioner need not 'give' a 'refund of an amount'
- the circumstances in which the Commissioner may exercise the discretion to refund where s105-65 applies
- the amount of any refund that is given
- the ability of the Commissioner to recover amounts refunded without regard to s105-65, and
- whether the operation of s105-65 must be taken into account in working out an entity's net amount.

MT 2010/1 sets out the Tax Office view of the issue as it relates to the supplier. Practice Statement PS LA 2013/3 (GA) is concerned with the recipient's ability to retain the input tax credits.

24.261   ADJUSTMENT EVENT (Division 19)

An adjustment event arises where:

- all or part of a supply or acquisition is cancelled (eg. return of goods)
- the consideration for a supply or acquisition is altered (eg. discounts, rebates)
- a supply becomes or stops being taxable, or
- an acquisition becomes or stops being creditable.

GSTR 2000/19 explains the Commissioner's view on the operation of Division 19. In the Ruling the Commissioner considers that a foreign currency gain or loss is not a change in consideration and therefore not an adjustment event. Further, the Ruling provides that a correction of an error in a lodged BAS is not an adjustment event.

Entity A sells goods to entity B for $11,000. Entity A pays GST of $1,000 to the Tax Office. Entity B discovers one month later that some of the goods are faulty and receives a refund of $2,750 from Entity A.

Entity A needs to make a decreasing adjustment of $250 in its next return whilst entity B needs to make an increasing adjustment of $250 for the overclaimed input tax credit.

A supplier should give the recipient of a supply an adjustment note where there is an adjustment event relating to a taxable supply. The adjustment note must be issued within 28 days of the earlier of:

- the supplier becoming aware of the adjustment, or
- the time the recipient requested the adjustment note.

This applies unless any tax invoice relating to the supply would have been a recipient created tax invoice, in which case the adjustment note must be issued by the recipient.

The required contents of an adjustment note are set out in s29-75 and in GSTR 2013/2. An adjustment note is not required if the GST-exclusive value of the decreasing or increasing adjustment does not exceed $75.

An adjustment note is a document that complies with the following requirements:

- it is issued by the supplier of the taxable supply
- it sets out the ABN of the entity that issues it

- it is in the approved form, and
- it meets the information requirements that the Commissioner has determined. This requires that an adjustment note contains the following information, or enough information to enable the following to be clearly ascertained:
  - that the document is intended as an adjustment note and the effect of the adjustment
  - the identity of the supplier or the supplier's agent
  - the identity or ABN of the recipient, the recipient's agent, or another member of the recipient's GST group, if the adjustment note:
    - relates to a tax invoice showing the total price for the supply or supplies is at least $1,000 (or such higher amount as regulations), or
    - arises out of an adjustment event where a supply that was not taxable becomes taxable and the price of the supply is at least $1,000 (or such higher amount as the regulations specify)
  - the issue date of the adjustment note
  - a brief explanation of the reason for the adjustment
  - the amount of the adjustment to the GST payable, and
  - the difference between the price of the supply before the adjustment event and the price of the supply after the adjustment event. If the supply is not a wholly taxable supply, the price of the supply is referable to that part of the supply that is affected by the adjustment event and that is, or becomes, taxable (s29-75(1): GSTR 2013/2).

 You can combine a tax invoice with an adjustment note (eg. where a tax invoice shows the terms of a settlement or prompt payment discount). The tax invoice must show the amount of the reduction in the price that is available to the recipient. The document will become an adjustment note when the settlement or prompt payment discount is taken up by the recipient.

Any adjustment is to be reflected in the BAS. Generally, an adjustment is attributed to the tax period when a registered enterprise becomes aware of the adjustment event (s29-20). However, if you account on a cash basis and the adjustment arises from an adjustment event as a result of which you are liable to provide consideration, then the adjustment is attributable in the tax period when consideration is provided.

Regardless of the accounting method used, the adjustment note must be held at the time the BAS is lodged.

TRADE REBATES/OFFSETS

Rebates and/or trade incentive payments may also be known as trade discounts, trade price rebates, volume rebates, promotional rebates, incentive rebates, or co-operative advertising allowances. Some of these incentives will affect the price for which the goods were sold (price adjustments which give rise to an adjustment event) while others will not (separate taxable supply of services).

For a rebate to reduce the price of goods sold, it must relate to the sale and the selling price of the goods, so as to bring about a reduction in the price of the goods. A rebate that is paid to subsidise, compensate or reimburse a purchaser for advertising expenditure undertaken on behalf of the supplier, does not reduce the price of goods and therefore does not constitute an adjustment event.

An objective assessment of the intention of the parties in light of all the circumstances is required to determine whether the rebate is an adjustment event or consideration for a separate supply. Certain factors are relevant in determining whether rebates are adjustment events or consideration for a separate taxable supply (see GSTR 2000/19).

The intention of the parties is objectively assessed by looking at:

- written evidence of the obligations and expectations of each party to the contract, and
- the actions or conduct of the parties in relation to their dealings with the goods.

Relevant written evidence may include:

- the contract of sale, including supporting documentation relating to the terms of trade

- promotional plans drawn up by the parties
- reports relating to the conduct of or monitoring of promotional activities
- minutes of meetings between the supplier and the retailer
- details of the calculation of the amount of the rebate, and/or
- relevant invoices, claim forms or credit notes.

Relevant actions or conduct may include:

- whether other rebates are paid
- the actual promotions undertaken by the retailer
- the degree of monitoring by the supplier of promotions undertaken by the retailer
- any influence exerted by the supplier in relation to promotional activities undertaken by the retailer, and
- the accounting treatment of the payment in the financial records of the supplier and the retailer.

Not all agreements between parties are included in a written contract. The written contract may incorporate certain terms and conditions. However, there may exist other understandings, evidenced in other documents or in the conduct of the parties that place an obligation on one or other of the parties.

REBATES THAT ARE ADJUSTMENT EVENTS

Adjustment event rebates relate to the sale and selling price of the goods which result in a reduction in the consideration for the relevant goods. Examples of rebates that adjust the price of goods or services include:

- volume rebates and deferred credits (suppliers may pay rebates to customers who reach certain levels of purchases), and
- settlement or trade discount (after a supply occurs, a discount may be granted for early payment).

Where the actions and written documents clearly show that the rebate relates to a change in the selling price, the rebate will be considered an adjustment event.

Farmland Pty Ltd supplies eggs to Ritches Supermarket. The price per dozen is $2.20. Ritches purchases 10,000 dozen for the month of August 2014 and is invoiced $22,000 for that month, payable by 30 September 2014. Since this is the third month that Ritches has purchased at least 10,000 dozen, it receives a rebate of $0.20 per dozen, which is shown on the invoice for the month of September 2014. Ritches pays the invoice on 20 September 2014 and receives a 5 per cent discount for early payment and, therefore, pays $19,000. The rebate and discount are changes in the consideration for the supply of eggs, and therefore, are treated as an adjustment event.

How to account for GST: Farmland Pty Ltd accounts for GST on a non-cash basis and has monthly tax periods. In the month of August 2014, Farmland will account for GST of $2,000 for the supply of eggs to Ritches Supermarket. In September 2014, the actual amount of GST attributable is $1,727.27 ($19,000 x 1/11). In this example, an adjustment event has occurred, the GST was attributable in an earlier tax period and the previously attributed GST ($2,000) has changed. Therefore Farmland has an adjustment event and must issue an adjustment note for the amount of $272.73 to Ritches.

Where there is an adjustment to the price (as in the above example) there is an adjustment event. If there is an adjustment event in relation to a taxable supply, an adjustment note must be issued.

You cannot offset the adjustments against the taxable supplies. They must be separately identified on the adjustment note or tax invoice or the combined document.

REBATES WHICH ARE CONSIDERATION FOR A SEPARATE TAXABLE SUPPLY OF SERVICES

Some rebates do not adjust the price of goods but are made as a result of the purchaser doing something for the supplier such as advertising, promotion, warehousing, distribution or other marketing activities, accounting, bookkeeping or debt collection functions or allowing the supplier a right to use the purchaser's premises or equipment for these activities.

These payments are commonly referred to as promotional rebates. Common examples include:

- co-operative rebates
- co-operative allowances
- co-operative payments
- advertising rebates, and
- advertising allowances.

Promotional rebates that provide a commercial advantage to the supplier by maximising sales are treated as consideration for a supply of services by the recipient. The supply of these services by the recipient is made for consideration equal to the amount of the rebate. Despite the form taken by the rebates, they are directed at an end other than the reduction of the selling price and do not vary the consideration for a supply.

Where the rebates are consideration for a separate taxable supply of services, the supplier of those services must issue a tax invoice in relation to these supplies (unless it is a recipient created tax invoice in which case the recipient will need to issue an invoice for the supply). From a practical perspective, the purchaser's remittance payment could also be a tax invoice if it has all the things necessary for it to be a tax invoice. A tax invoice is not required if the GST-exclusive value of the supply is less than $75.

24.262   BAD DEBTS (Division 21)

Where an entity does not account for GST on a cash basis, an adjustment may be required where the entity writes off a bad or overdue debt after 12 months. Writing off a bad debt may give rise to a decreasing adjustment.

To qualify for a decreasing adjustment of 1/11th of the amount written-off:

- there must have been a taxable supply
- the whole or part of the consideration for the supply was not received, and
- the entity writes off as bad the whole or part of the debt, or the whole or part of the debt has been owing for 12 months or more.

If the debt is later recovered, an increasing adjustment must be made which will be 1/11th of the amount recovered. Also, if the bad debt arises in relation to a mixed supply, the adjustment only arises to the extent that the original supply was taxable. Where an entity receives a payment under an insurance policy for non-payment of customer debts, this will not cause an increasing adjustment.

A bad debt adjustment also arises when an entity makes a creditable acquisition and subsequently the debt relating to the acquisition is written-off as bad or has been overdue for over 12 months. This adjustment will be an increasing adjustment if the following criteria are met:

- there is a creditable acquisition and an input tax credit has been attributed to a tax period
- the whole or part of the consideration for the acquisition has not been paid, and
- the supplier of things you acquired writes off the debt as bad or the debt has been overdue for 12 months or more.

If the debt is subsequently repaid, a decreasing adjustment must be made on the amount repaid for the creditable use portion.

An adjustment for a bad debt is attributed to the tax period in which the entity becomes aware of it, that is:

- if the debt is written-off, when you become aware that the debt is written-off, or
- if it has not been written-off, the tax period in which you become aware the debt has been overdue for 12 months.

NOTE: A bad debt adjustment does not require an adjustment note because it is not an adjustment event under Division 19.

GSTR 2000/2 explains the Commissioner's view on the adjustment for bad debts.

24.263   CHANGE IN EXTENT OF CREDITABLE PURPOSE (Division 129)

GST registered entities are entitled to claim an input tax credit to the extent that an acquisition is made for a creditable purpose. For example, if the acquisition was partly used for making taxable or GST-free supplies and partly for private purposes or for input taxed activities, the extent of creditable use would be limited to the part used to make taxable or GST-free supplies only. The entitlement to the input tax credit in these circumstances will be based on the planned business use of the acquisition at that time. If the extent of creditable purposes subsequently changes, under Division 129 taxpayers are required to make adjustments in the relevant adjustment periods to reflect either an increasing or decreasing GST adjustment. This ensures that GST included in the acquisition is only claimed as an input tax credit up to the extent of creditable purpose following its acquisition. This imposes a requirement to annually review the use of partly creditable acquisitions in order to assess whether an adjustment is necessary. The adjustment, if required, is made annually.

Section 129-5 provides than an adjustment for an acquisition or importation can arise under Division 129 in respect of any adjustment period for the acquisition or importation. Division 129-B sets out the meaning and application of adjustment periods.

ADJUSTMENT PERIODS

Adjustment periods usually start 12 months after the end of the tax period in which the input tax credit was claimed, but are made in the tax period that ends on 30 June. Adjustment periods are the periods during an acquisition's lifetime when the taxpayer must review their usage of an acquisition and make an increasing or decreasing adjustment if necessary to reflect change in use.

 A GST registered taxpayer makes a partly creditable acquisition on 5 July 2014. Assuming that this taxpayer is a quarterly lodger, the input tax credit will be attributable to the tax period ending on 30 September 2014.

If the planned use of the acquisition changes, the first adjustment period will be the period ending 30 June 2016, being the first 30 June tax period 12 months after the tax period in which the input tax credit is claimed.

NOTE: If a company provides a benefit to an employee, it will still have a 100% creditable purpose, as it will be subject to FBT and therefore no GST adjustment will be necessary. For more information see 24.410.

The number of adjustment periods you have for an acquisition depends on the GST-exclusive amount paid for the acquisition (see table below). For acquisitions that do not relate to making financial supplies, no adjustments are required in relation to the changes in the extent of creditable purpose where the GST-exclusive value is $1,000 or less (or $10,000 if acquisition relates to making financial supplies that are not partly used for private or domestic purposes).

GST-exclusive amount of consideration for the acquisition	Number of adjustment periods
$1,000 or less	None
$1,001 to $5,000	2
$5,001 to $499,999	5
$500,000 or more	10

There will be no further adjustments required for any changes to the creditable use that occurs after the last adjustment period.

 Sam, a GST registered sole trader, purchases a PC for less than $1,000. He intends on using the PC 80% of the time for business use. Sam is entitled to claim 80% of the GST as an input tax credit.

Sam will not have to make any future adjustments even if his actual business use differs from his planned business use as the GST-exclusive amount is less than $1,000.

 Peter, a GST registered sole trader, purchases a car for $42,000 and estimates his planned business use is 70%. As the car costs between $5,000 and $499,999, the number of adjustment periods will be five. The car was purchased in February 2013. The first adjustment period for the acquisition of the car will be 30 June 2014 and the last adjustment period will be 30 June 2018.

Peter will have to annually review his business usage of the car up to 30 June 2017 to see whether actual use has differed from planned use. Thereafter it will not matter if there are changes in use as no adjustments under Division 129 are necessary.

If the acquisition that gave rise to partial input tax credit is lost, stolen or destroyed then the next tax period that ends on 30 June in any year will be the last adjustment period required.

If the taxpayer dies or the entity ceases or cancels its GST registration, then the next tax period ending on 30 June does not apply and the adjustment under Division 129 need to be taken up in the entity's concluding tax period.

CALCULATION OF THE ADJUSTMENT

Section 129-40 sets out a method statement to help work out whether there is an increasing or a decreasing adjustment in relation to the change in extent of creditable purpose of an acquisition. Note no adjustment is required for an acquisition where the GST-exclusive value is $1,000 or less. GSTR 2000/24 provides guidance regarding how to calculate an adjustment under Division 129.

In determining the amount of each subsequent adjustment, you must take into account the actual total use since purchase, not just the actual use since the last adjustment.

METHOD STATEMENT (S129-40)

- **Step 1:** Work out the extent (if any) to which you have applied the thing acquired or imported for a creditable purpose during the period of time:
    - starting when you acquired or imported the thing, and
    - ending at the end of the adjustment period.
    This is the actual application of the thing.

- **Step 2:** Work out:
    - If you have not previously had an adjustment under Division 129 for the acquisition or importation – the extent (if any) to which you acquired or imported the thing for a creditable purpose (intended application of the thing), or
    - If you have previously had an adjustment under Division 129 for the acquisition or importation – the actual application of the thing in respect of the last adjustment (former application of the thing).
    This is the intended or former application of the thing.

- **Step 3:** If the actual application of the thing is less than its intended or former application, you have an increasing adjustment, for the adjustment period, for the acquisition or importation.

- **Step 4:** If the actual application of the thing is greater than its intended of former application, you have a decreasing adjustment, for the adjustment period, for the acquisition or importation.

- **Step 5:** If the actual application of the thing is the same as its intended or former application, you have neither an increasing adjustment, nor a decreasing adjustment, for the adjustment period, for the acquisition or importation.

Division 129 adjustment results in an accumulative measurement of its use, starting from the time the taxpayer acquired it and finishing at the end of the relevant adjustment period, expressed as a percentage. Therefore, one adjustment may result in changes to the cumulative measurement of its use resulting in adjustments in the remaining adjustment periods even where no changes have occurred thereafter (see following example).

GSTR 2006/4 outlines direct and indirect methods which are available (but taxpayers are not limited to) to calculate the actual use to which an acquisition has been put. A direct method applies data from records reflecting actual use, such as a vehicle log-book or floor space of a building. An indirect method uses an input or output based approach based on estimated usage of acquisitions.

 Fred is a sole trader registered for GST and is a quarterly lodger. Assume he acquires a second hand car on 30 September 2013 for $22,000 and at that point he estimates his business usage as 20%. Fred's input tax credit entitlement for the acquisition of the car will

be $400 (20% of $2,000 being the GST component) which is attributed in the tax period ending 30 September 2013.

As the GST-exclusive value of the car is $20,000 (between $5,001 and $499,999), there will be five adjustment periods in relation to this acquisition. The first adjustment period will be the quarter ending 30 June 2015 and the last adjustment period will be the quarter ending 30 June 2019.

There is no actual change in business use before 30 June 2015 which represents the first adjustment period, therefore no adjustment is required. For year ended 30 June 2016 Fred's business use increases to 30%, an adjustment under Division 129 is necessary, which will be reflected in the tax period ending 30 June 2016.

Calculation of the adjustment for the quarter ending 30 June 2016

Step 1: Applying these facts to the method statement results in an actual application of the car of 23.6% which has been calculated as follows:

A. Date acquired: September 2013

B. End date of adjustment period 30 June 2016. Period held = A – B = 33 months

C. Period during which extent of creditable use is 20% is from September 2013 – June 2015 = 21 months. Therefore, (21 months divided by 33 months) x 20% = 12.7%

D. Period during which extent of creditable use is 30% is from July 2015 – June 2016 = 12 months

Therefore, (12 months divided by 33 months) x 30% = 10.9%

D + C = average creditable use of the car = 12.7 + 10.9 = 23.6 %

Step 2: Intended application of things = 20%

Step 4: As the actual application is greater than the intended application of the thing a decreasing GST adjustment will result. Steps 3 and 5 are ignored.

Decreasing adjustment = Full input tax credit x (actual application – intended application) = $2,000 x (23.6% – 20%) = $2,000 x 3.6%

Decreasing adjustment = $72

For the adjustment period ending 30 June 2016, a decreasing adjustment of $72 needs to be made.

Calculation of the adjustment for the quarter ending 30 June 2017

Step 1: Applying these facts to the method statement results in an actual application of the car of 25.3% which has been calculated as follows:

A. Date acquired: September 2013

B. End date of adjustment period 30 June 2017. Period held = A – B = 45 months

C. Period during which extent of creditable use is 20% is from September 2013 – June 2015 = 21 months

Therefore, (21 months divided by 45 months) x 20% = 9.3%

D. Period during which extent of creditable use is 30% is from July 2015 – June 2017 = 24 months.

Therefore, (24 months divided by 45 months) x 30% = 16%

D + C = average creditable use of the car = 9.3 + 16 = 25.3 %

Step 2: As there was previous Division 129 adjustment, the former application of things is the actual application of things in the last adjustment = 23.6%

Step 4: As the actual application is greater than the former application of thing a decreasing GST adjustment will result. Steps 3 and 5 are ignored.

Decreasing adjustment = Full input tax credit x (actual application – intended application) = $2,000 x (25.3% – 23.6%) = $2,000 x 1.7% Decreasing adjustment = $34

For the adjustment period ending 30 June 2015, a decreasing adjustment of $34 needs to be made.

 Even if the actual application of the thing remains at the same level for the rest of the adjustment periods, an adjustment under Division 129 is still required. This is due to the fact that the actual application of the asset is expressed as an average from when the asset was acquired.

An adjustment may not be necessary if an adjustment occurs because there is a change in the extent to which the acquisition is used in making financial supplies due to the operation of the 'de minimis' rule.

ADJUSTMENT FOR CHANGES IN EXTENT OF CREDITABLE PURPOSE FOR NEW RESIDENTIAL PROPERTY

Ruling GSTR 2009/4 (addendum exists) deals with Division 129 adjustments in relation to new constructed residential property for sale but subsequently rented out.

An entity applies a thing for a creditable purpose to the extent that the entity applies it in carrying on its enterprise (subs129-50(1)). However, according to subs129-50(2), the entity does not apply a thing for a creditable purpose to the extent that the application relates to making supplies that are input taxed or for private or domestic use. The term 'apply' is therefore central to determining the extent to which an acquisition has been applied for a creditable purpose and whether or not an adjustment under Division 129 arises.

Section 129-55 defines the term 'apply' in relation to a thing acquired or imported to include:
- supply the thing, and
- consume, dispose of or destroy the thing, and
- allow another entity to consume, dispose of or destroy the thing.

In accordance with the s129-55 definition of 'apply', a thing will be applied in carrying on an entity's enterprise when it is sold or otherwise disposed of in the course of the entity's enterprise.

Further, as noted in GSTR 2009/4 the definition of 'apply' in s129-55 is an inclusive definition. Therefore, in addition to the specific reference incorporated in the provision, the term 'apply' also encompasses the ordinary meaning which includes 'to put to use; employ' or 'to devote to some specific purpose' or 'make use of as relevant or suitable; employ'. Accordingly, a thing will have been applied in the entity's enterprise if it has been allocated or dedicated to a particular use(s) in the enterprise. As such, GSTR 2009/4 concluded that the sale of a newly constructed residential premises, holding the newly constructed premises for sale or the renting of the newly constructed premises are all considered to have applied the newly constructed premises in the entity's enterprise.

The Ruling has also made distinction between things held for the purpose of sale or exchange as part of an enterprise being carried on by an entity (eg. trading stock) and things used by an entity in carrying on an enterprise (eg. business plant). The Ruling lists factors distinguishing between the two. Newly constructed residential property held for sale (even though the sale has not eventuated) is considered to have been applied for a creditable purpose. On the other hand, new residential premises applied by an entity carrying on a leasing enterprise is considered to have been in relation to making input taxed supply and therefore applied for a non-creditable purpose.

Furthermore, there may be situations where during the relevant period an entity may have applied the premises to a dual concurrent application. For example, an entity may apply new residential premises for the creditable purpose of sale where the premises are being held for sale as part of the entity's enterprise, whilst concurrently applying the new residential premises for the non-creditable purpose of making input taxed supplies of leasing under s40-35.

NOTE: An entity's planned use needs to be supported by evidence of the objective assessment of all relevant facts and circumstances.

When there is dual concurrent application, a taxpayer will be required to apply reasonable methods of apportionment to apportion creditable purpose. GSTR 2009/4 gives examples of some reasonable methods of apportionment in relation to new residential premises that are held for sale but are subsequently rented out.

If the property is applied partly for a creditable purpose of sale and partly for a non-creditable purpose of making input taxed supplies during the relevant period and the premises are sold prior to the end of the adjustment period, the consideration for the input taxed rent and the consideration for the sale will be known at the time of the adjustment. Therefore, the Ruling considers a reasonable method of apportionment in this case to be an output based indirect method. The formula is as follows:

Actual consideration for the taxable supply of the premises divided by
Actual consideration for the taxable supply of the premises plus
Actual consideration for the input taxed rent

If the premises remain unsold at the end of the relevant adjustment period, the actual consideration for the sale will not be known. Under such circumstances, the Commissioner consider using an estimated consideration for the taxable supply of the premises on sale in the output based indirect formula as follows:

Estimated consideration for the taxable supply of the premises divided by
Estimated consideration for the taxable supply of the premises plus
Actual consideration for the input taxed rent

A further time based apportionment needs to be introduced to modify the output based indirect formula when during the whole relevant period there are parts that are fully creditable, parts that are fully non-creditable and parts that are for dual application. See the following example (adapted from Example 11 in GSTR 2009/4):

John is registered for GST and has quarterly tax periods. He constructed new residential premises for the purpose of sale and was entitled to full input tax credits on his acquisitions. One particular acquisition of construction services was made on 1 October 2013 for $55,000 (GST inclusive). The premises were completed on 1 February 2014. John continued to hold the premises for the purpose of sale but also commenced renting the premises for residential accommodation on 1 April 2014. John received rental income of $2,500 per month and expected to sell the premises for $500,000. John has continued to retain the dual concurrent application since 1 April 2014. However, on 1 January 2015 John decided to hold the premises solely for the purpose of leasing.

Therefore for the 15 months from 1 October 2013 to 31 December 2014 John applied the premises for a creditable purpose to some extent. John works out the extent of creditable purpose for part of that relevant period in two steps.

First, John uses an output based indirect method (using estimated sales consideration) as follows:

$500,000 divided by ($500,000 + $37,500) = 93.02%

John now needs to undertake a further apportionment to reflect the fact that the premises were not held for the purpose of sale for the entire adjustment period. This is calculated by adjusting the above percentage by the relevant proportion of the relevant period for which the premises were being held for the purpose of sale:

93.02% x 15 months / 21 months = 66.44%

From 1 January 2015 until 30 June 2015, John applied the premises solely in relation to making input taxed rent. Therefore, the extent of creditable purpose for this 6 months is 0%.

Therefore, the total percentage of creditable purpose for the period between 1 October 2013 until 30 June 2015 (a span of 21 months) is equals 66.44% + 0% = 66.44%.

This percentage is the actual application of the thing for the purposes of step 1 of the method statement in subsection 129-40(1).

INTERACTION BETWEEN DIVISION 129 AND THE '5 YEAR RULE' IN S40-75(2)

GSTR 2009/4 also considers the interaction between Division 129 and the 'five year rule' in s40-75(2). Subsection 40-75(2) provides where new residential premises have been used solely for making supplies that are input taxed under s40-35(1)(a) for a period of at least five years since they became new residential premises, they will not be new residential premises any more. Subsequent sale of the residential premises will be input taxed and not a taxable supply (as it is no longer 'new').

This Ruling interprets the meaning of 'used' in s40-75(2) and 'apply' in Division 129 to be consistent. This means that if an entity has applied new residential premises for a creditable purpose in accordance with Division 129, eg. held for sale, the premises will also have been used other than for making supplies that are input taxed under s40-35(1)(a). Therefore, the requirements for subs40-75(2) will not be satisfied.

The AAT has accepted the Commissioner's view in the ruling that an apportionment method based on the effective life of premises is not considered to be fair and reasonable for the purposes of Division 129 (*A Taxpayer and Commissioner of Taxation* [2011] AATA 160).

24.264 OTHER TYPES OF ADJUSTMENTS

GOODS APPLIED SOLELY FOR PRIVATE OR DOMESTIC USE (Division 130)

An increasing adjustment needs to be made where an input tax credit has been claimed on an acquisition that was solely for a creditable purpose and is subsequently used solely for private or domestic purposes (Division 130). For example, a clothing sole trader took some clothing item from their trading stock for their own personal use. The net effect is that previously claimed input tax credits are reversed when the goods are applied to a private use.

For Division 130 to apply, the goods must be applied solely to private or domestic use. The application of this Division depends on the meaning of the word 'solely' and whether goods that have been applied to a business or enterprise use can be subsequently applied 'solely' for private and domestic use.

In GSTR 2003/6 the Tax Office established their view that Division 130 can operate in relation to goods (trading stock, plant, building materials, office equipment, etc.) that have been previously applied to a business or enterprise use. Per the Ruling, the Commissioner considers that the reference to application of the goods solely to private or domestic use in s130-5(1)(c) is a reference to the point in time when goods are removed from an enterprise. Past applications of the goods are not relevant for the purposes of s130-5(1)(c).

The application for private or domestic use for the purpose of Division 130 must be by the entity carrying on the enterprise (GSTR 2003/6 paragraph 55) and not the subsequent application by the recipient of the supply.

SALE OF THINGS USED PARTLY FOR A CREDITABLE PURPOSE (Division 132)

There will be a decreasing adjustment if an entity subsequently sells a thing it has previously acquired for which it was not entitled to claim full input tax credits because it was partly applied to make input taxed supplies or for a private purpose.

Melissa runs a florist business and is registered for GST. She purchased a station wagon for $5,500 (GST inclusive) to be used 80% for her florist business and 20% for private use. She is only entitled to claim input tax credits of $400 (80% of $500) in relation to the purchase of the station wagon.

Subsequently, Melissa sold the station wagon for $4,400. As the station wagon was used in the carrying on of her florist enterprise, it will be subject to GST and she will have to remit GST on 1/11th of the sale price, being $400.

However, as the station wagon was not entitled to full input tax credits because 20% of it was for private use, there will be a decreasing adjustment for the portion for which she is not entitled to input tax credits.

The decreasing adjustment is calculated as follows:

1/11 x Sale price x (1 – input tax credits claimed / full input tax credits)

= 1/11 x $4,400 x (1 – $400 / $500)

= $80

NOTE: The input tax credits claimed takes into account any previous adjustments such as adjustments under Division 129.

NEWLY REGISTERED ENTITIES (Division 137)

A decreasing adjustment occurs when an entity becomes registered for GST and at the time of registration the entity held stock for the purpose of sale, exchange or use as raw materials to be used in the carrying on of the entity's enterprise.

As the stock was acquired prior to registration, the entity would not have been entitled to input tax credits. However, when the stock is subsequently sold (after the entity is registered for GST), it will be subject to GST. Therefore, Division 137 allows a decreasing adjustment to reduce an entity's GST liability for the amount of input tax credit an entity would have been entitled to claim had it been registered for GST when acquiring the stock.

NOTE: This adjustment is only available for trading stock and not capital assets.

NOTE: Further, this adjustment is only available for a re-registered entity if the entity has previously claimed input tax credits on stock and made adjustment pursuant to Division 138 (see following) when it cancelled its GST registration.

CANCELLATION OF GST REGISTRATION (Division 138)

An entity will have an increasing adjustment if its GST registration is cancelled and immediately before the cancellation, the entity still had assets for which it has previously been entitled to claim input tax credits. Generally, the adjustment will be attributed to the entity's concluding tax period.

The amount of adjustment is calculated as follows:

1/11 x Actual application of the asset x Applicable value

where 'Actual application' is the percentage for which the asset was used for a creditable purpose from the time of purchase until the date of GST cancellation.

Applicable value is the lesser of:

- the GST inclusive market value of the asset immediately before cancellation, or
- the amount of consideration provided or liable to be provided for the acquisition of the asset.

There will be no adjustment for assets held immediately before the cancellation of GST registration under Division 138 if the last adjustment period pursuant to Division 129 (see 24.263) has ended.

James runs a plumbing business and is registered for GST from 1 July 2013. On 1 January 2014, he purchased a station wagon for $11,000 (GST inclusive) to be used 100% in his plumbing business and claimed input tax credit of $1,000 on this acquisition in his BAS ending 31 March 2014.

Subsequently James cancels his GST registration and the cancellation takes effect from 1 July 2017. Immediately prior to cancellation of his GST registration, he still had his station wagon and the market value of the station wagon was $7,700.

As the station wagon's GST-exclusive amount at the time of acquisition was between $5,001 and $499,999, he will have five adjustment periods, with the first period starting 30 June 2014 and the last period ending 30 June 2019.

He cancels his GST registration prior to the last adjustment period. Therefore he will have an increasing adjustment under Division 138.

His increasing adjustment is calculated as follows:1/11th x 100% x $7,700 = $700.

NOTE: Adjustment under this Division does not apply to cancellation of GST as a result of the death of a taxpayer where the executor or trustee or beneficiaries of the deceased estate is registered or required to be registered for GST and continue to carry on the enterprise.

Further, if an entity accounts for GST on a cash basis and immediately before cancellation of its GST registration, there was GST on taxable supplies and input tax credits on creditable acquisitions which had not been attributed to a tax period, these GST and input tax credits will be attributable in the entity's concluding tax period (s138-15).

ACQUISITION OF A GOING CONCERN OR FARMLAND NOT USED TO MAKE TAXABLE OR GST-FREE SUPPLIES (Division 135)

There will be an increasing adjustment in the event where an entity acquires a going concern under s38-325 GST-free exemption but then uses the enterprise to make input taxed or private or domestic supplies.

The increasing adjustment is calculated as follows:

1/10 x Supply price of the going concern x Proportion of non-creditable use

where 'Proportion of non-creditable use' is the proportion of all the supplies made through the enterprise that are neither taxable nor GST-free supplies, expressed as a percentage worked out on the basis of the prices of those supplies.

The intention of Division 135 is to provide for one or more adjustments to ensure that a recipient of a GST-free supply of a going concern accounts for GST to the extent that the going concern is used for non-creditable purposes.

Alfred purchased a leasing enterprise which consists of a leased residential property and a leased commercial property with the leases on both these properties being transferred together with the properties. All the requirements under s38-325 are met and therefore the acquisition of the leasing enterprise is a GST-free going concern. He paid a total of $800,000 for the going concern.

However, as Alfred will continue to lease the residential property, there will be an increasing adjustment because rent from a residential property is input taxed.

Assuming the lease from the residential property makes up 30% of the enterprise's supply, the increasing adjustment is calculated as: 1/10 x $800,000 x 30% = $24,000

NOTE: Supply of residential premises with leases intact can be an input taxed supply under s40. However, it can also be supplied under s38-325 as GST-free going concern if all requirements in that section are satisfied.

Accordingly, when a supply is both input taxed and GST-free, s9-30(3)(a) provides that the supply is GST-free and not input taxed. See GSTR 2002/5. A supplier of such a supply will be entitled to claim input tax credits for acquisitions (eg. legal fees) related to making the GST-free supply.

The same adjustment will apply to the acquisition of farmland that is GST-free under s38-480.

There will be subsequent adjustments under this Division (s135-10) if:

- the enterprise was acquired GST-free under the going concern or farmland exemptions
- it makes supplies that are neither taxable nor GST-free, and
- the actual proportion of supplies that are neither taxable nor GST-free is different from the intended proportion.

The adjustment under such circumstances will be similar to methods worked out under Division 129. See also ID 2007/180.

PAYMENTS MADE TO THIRD PARTIES (Division 134)

Under Division 134, where an entity (the payer) supplying things for re-sale makes a monetary payment to a third party (the payee) in connection with the payee's acquisition of those things, the payer will be entitled to a decreasing adjustment reflecting the difference between the GST remitted on the original supply and the GST which would have been payable had the consideration been calculated net of the third party payment.

The following conditions must be met for a decreasing adjustment to arise:

- the supply by the payer must be a taxable supply
- the payment must have a connection with (or be in response to, or for the inducement of) the payee's acquisition of the thing, and
- the payment must not be consideration for a separate supply to the payer.

The payee will be entitled to a corresponding increasing adjustment if the acquisition was for a creditable purpose.

These adjustments can occur even if there is more than one interposed entity in the supply chain.

The payer must issue a third party adjustment note within 28 days of the earlier of becoming aware of the adjustment or a request by the payee for a copy of the note. The decreasing adjustment for the payer will be attributable to the tax period in which the payer first holds a third party adjustment note. The third party adjustment note requirement does not apply to decreasing adjustments not exceeding the adjustment notes threshold, which is $75.

A third party payment adjustment takes priority over any other adjustment event which the payment may also fall within.

The following example is extracted from the Explanatory Memorandum to the amending legislation.

EXAMPLE (from EM): Retail third party rebate

Fascam Ltd, a manufacturer, sells a camera to Choice Cameras Ltd, a retailer, for $660. Choice Cameras sells the camera to a customer, Irene, for $880 at a time when Fascam is offering a cash-back incentive to retail customers to boost its sales. Irene applies for and receives a cash-back payment of $110 from Fascam.

Under section 134-5 Fascam is entitled to a decreasing adjustment with regard to the cash-back payment.

The decreasing adjustment is calculated as follows:

(A) *GST payable on supply to Choice Cameras:* $A = \$660 \times 1 / 11 = \$60$

(B) *GST which would have been payable had the consideration been reduced by the amount of the payment to the payee:* $B = (\$660 - \$110) \times 1 / 11 = \$50$

$A - B = \$60 - \$50 = \$10$

Fascam is entitled to a decreasing adjustment of \$10.

(As the decreasing adjustment is for an amount less than \$50, Fascam is not required to issue a third party adjustment note).

Choice Cameras is not affected by the decreasing adjustment to which Fascam is entitled. Choice Cameras's GST liability remains as follows:

GST payable on sale – input tax credits on acquisition = GST liability:

$(\$880 \times 1 / 11) - (\$660 \times 1 / 11) = \$80 - \$60 = \$20$

If Irene is registered for GST as a professional photographer and has purchased the camera for use in her business, the acquisition of the camera is a creditable acquisition. She therefore has an increasing adjustment under section 134-10.

The increasing adjustment is calculated as follows:

(C) *Input tax credit entitlement arising from the acquisition from the other entity (Choice Cameras):*

$C = \$880 \times 1 / 11 = \$80$

(D) *Amount of input tax credits to which the payee would have been entitled had the consideration for the acquisition been reduced by the amounts of the payer's payment:*

$D = (\$880 - \$110) \times 1 / 11 = \$70$

$C - D = \$80 - \$70 = \$10$

Irene has an increasing adjustment of \$10. If Irene is not registered for GST, this increasing adjustment does not arise.

If Irene is registered for GST but intends to use the camera 50 per cent for private purposes and 50 per cent for creditable purposes she is entitled to an input tax credit of 50 per cent of the full input tax credit.

The increasing adjustment is calculated as follows:

(C) *Input tax credit entitlement arising from the acquisition from the other entity (Choice Cameras).*

$C = \$880 \times 1 / 11 \times 0.50 = \$40$

(D) *Amount of input tax credits to which the payee would have been entitled had the consideration for the acquisition been reduced by the amounts of the payer's payment:*

$D = (\$880 - \$110) \times 1 / 11 \times 0.50 = \$35$

$C - D = \$40 - \$35 = \$5$

Irene has an increasing adjustment of \$5.

NOTE: The third party adjustments enabled by Division 134 will arise where the relevant parties in the supply chain are members of the same GST group, GST religious group or GST joint venture.

NOTE: The law has been amended to ensure the third party payment adjustment provisions operate appropriately where there are third party payments relating to a supply by the payer that is not taxable or a supply to the payee that is GST-free, not connected with Australia or subject to a GST refund under the Tourist Refund Scheme. The Tax Office has released information regarding its administrative treatment in relation to these changes.

24.300 SPECIAL TOPICS

This section covers some of the special rules that apply in specific circumstances.

24.310 GST GROUPS AND JOINT VENTURES

Special rules under the GST groups and GST joint ventures provisions allow:

- one nominated party of the GST group or GST joint venture to account for GST liability, and
- GST on transactions between GST group members or between GST joint venture operator and participants to be ignored.

24.311   GST GROUPS (Division 48)

By using the GST grouping rules, related businesses will be able to remove the need to charge GST and claim input tax credits on related transactions within the group. That should also assist in removing the cash-flow differences and timing issues that would have been caused if all GST transactions between related entities were required to be accounted for individually.

If the GST group provisions apply, a GST group is treated as a single taxpayer. One company, being the GST group representative member, will be liable for GST on supplies made by the group and entitled to input tax credits for acquisitions by the group. There will be no liability to account for GST on inter-group transactions. A representative member of the group must be appointed to lodge GST returns accounting for all taxable supplies from the group, and to claim the group's input tax credit entitlements.

NOTE: All members of the GST group are jointly and severally liable for GST payable by the group.

NOTE: It is the time of attribution that is relevant in determining who – the member itself or the representative of the group – is required to account for the GST on taxable supplies and input tax credits on creditable acquisitions of the member and not the time when the supplies or acquisitions are made.

 In The Taxpayer v FCT *[2010] AATA 497, the AAT held that the GST system does not have a 'single entity' style rule (akin to the single entity rule for income tax in the tax consolidations regime) for GST grouping purposes. This decision of the AAT will likely impact other GST arrangements. For example in GSTR 2005/4, the Commissioner states that in calculating the margin under s75-10(2) in a group situation, the consideration for the acquisition should be the consideration for the supplying group member's acquisition and not the consideration for the acquiring group member's acquisition. Putting aside any Division 165 implications, the AAT effectively rejects the single entity rule adopted by the Commissioner in this ruling.*

GST GROUPING RULES

The underlying requirement of the grouping rules is that each entity wishing to group must first be registered for GST before that entity can become a member of the GST group. Each member of the group must also have the same tax periods and accounting basis as the other members.

Related companies, trusts (including superannuation funds), partnerships, not-for-profit bodies and government bodies who satisfy the membership requirements set out in Division 48 of the GST Regulations can group for GST purposes. There are slightly different membership requirements for different entities wanting to join/form a GST group.

Companies within a 90% owned group can be approved as a GST group (s48-1). Two companies are members of the same 90% owned group if one of the companies has at least a 90% stake in the other company, or a third company has at least a 90% stake in each of the two companies (s190-1). Comparable rules apply to partnerships and all kinds of trusts (including superannuation funds).

Partnerships that share common partners, fixed trusts that are members of the same 90% owned group, and trusts with common family members as beneficiaries are able to access

GST grouping arrangements. Individuals can also join a GST group, consisting of a company, partnership or trust, subject to certain conditions being met.

Entities are able to self-assess their eligibility to form, change or dissolve a GST group and to change the GST group representative member. Entities may undertake such changes at any time during a tax period.

Notice is to be given to the Commissioner in relation to decisions made under self-assessment. Failure to give notification within prescribed timelines will result in a requirement to obtain the Commissioner's approval for the date of effect of the change.

Members of a GST group may enter into an indirect tax sharing agreement with the representative member of the GST group. This enables an entity to leave a GST group clear of indirect tax liabilities for a tax period if it leaves before the group lodges a GST return for the period.

24.312   GST JOINT VENTURES (Division 51)

A joint venture is not an entity for GST and ABN purposes and cannot itself make supplies or acquisitions. It is usually the participants that are individually registered for ABN and GST and therefore account for their respective GST and input tax credits. However, entities engaged in a joint venture may apply to the Commissioner under Division 51 of the GST Act to be treated as a GST joint venture if the requirements for approval are satisfied. Forming a GST joint venture will simplify GST accounting for the entities involved.

The effect of forming a GST joint venture is that one member (the nominated joint venture operator) pays the GST and is entitled to the input tax credits on supplies, acquisitions and importations it makes on behalf of the other joint venturers for the purpose of the joint venture. The joint venture operator will also be responsible for any adjustments relating to these supplies, acquisitions and importations (though other rules apply when a participant leaves a GST joint venture).

Supplies made by the joint venture operator to a participant in the GST joint venture for the purpose of the joint venture will not be subject to GST. However, transactions between joint venture participants where the supplier does not make the supply in its capacity as the joint venture operator are subject to the usual GST rules. This is in contrast to the approval of a GST group where most intra-group transactions are treated as if they are not taxable supplies.

WHAT IS A JOINT VENTURE?

According to GSTR 2004/2, a joint venture is an arrangement between two or more parties, characterised by the following features:

- each participant receives an agreed share of the product or output and deals with their share of output or product accordingly in their own right. Sharing of jointly earned profit from the sale of the output may indicate a partnership
- a contractual agreement between the participants establishing the operation, management and joint control of the joint venture
- joint control
- a specific economic project with a finite life in which the joint venture ends at the completion of the specified project, and
- cost sharing where the costs of the joint venture are met by participants individually (ie. each participant incurs its own expenses and liabilities and raises its own finance).

ELIGIBILITY TO BE A GST JOINT VENTURE

A joint venture needs to meet all requirements in Division 51-A (ss51-5 and 51-10) in order to be approved by the Commissioner to be a GST joint venture. Entities that participate, or intend to participate, in a joint venture for the exploration or exploitation of mineral deposits, or for a purpose specified in sub-regulation 51-5.01 of the GST Regulations, may apply for registration as a GST joint venture.

The activities listed in subregulation 51-5.01 qualify for registration as a GST joint venture.

For a joint venture to be eligible to become a GST joint venture, it cannot be a partnership. The following table taken from GSTR 2004/2 summarises the differences between a partnership and a joint venture.

Partnership	Joint venture
Joint entitlement to profit or income	Sharing of product or output in defined portions
A continuing business	Specific economic project
One partner's actions may bind all of the partners	Joint control of the venture
Partners have indirect undivided interests in the partnership assets (a partner can individually deal with its interest in the partnership but not the underlying partnership assets.)	Well-defined separation of interests, rather than a joint undivided interest, in assets contributed to the venture
Partners in a partnership are agents of the other partners and are ordinarily jointly and severally liable for the expenses of the partnership	Joint venture participants are usually liable for their own debts which they incur individually as principals

Further, all participants of the joint venture must each satisfy the participation requirements in s51-10 and must jointly apply to the Commissioner to be a GST joint venture. In the application, a participant of the joint venture or another entity must be nominated to be the joint venture operator, which will account for the joint venture's GST obligations.

For an entity to satisfy the participation requirements under s51-10 it must:

- participate in, or intend to participate in, the joint venture
- is a party to a joint venture agreement with all the other entities participating in, or intending to participate in, the joint venture
- is registered for GST purposes, and
- accounts for GST on the same basis as all the other participants.

NOTE: Where the joint venture operator is an entity other than a party to the joint venture agreement, the joint venture operator must nevertheless be registered for GST purposes and account for GST on the same basis as the participants in the joint venture.

The Commissioner must approve two or more entities as participants in a GST joint venture if it is to satisfy all criteria under Division 51-A. The notification of approval must be made in writing to the nominated joint venture operator.

Entities are able to self-assess their eligibility to form, change or dissolve a GST joint venture and to change the joint venture operator. Entities may undertake such changes at any time during a tax period.

Notice is to be given to the Commissioner in relation to decisions made under self-assessment. Failure to give notification within prescribed timelines will result in a requirement to obtain the Commissioner's approval for the date of effect of the change.

Members of a GST joint venture may enter into an indirect tax sharing agreement with the representative member of the joint venture operator. This will enable an entity to leave a GST joint venture clear of indirect tax liabilities for a tax period if it leaves before the joint venture lodges a GST return for the period.

24.320   PARTNERSHIPS

For GST purposes a partnership is a separate entity from the partners who make up the partnership. A partner is an associate of the partnership. As an entity for GST purposes, a partnership may register for GST and be liable for GST on taxable supplies as well as have an entitlement to input tax credits for creditable acquisitions it makes.

A partner does not carry on an enterprise as a partner in a partnership. As a result, a partner cannot register for GST purely as a result of being a partner of a partnership. Under general law however, a partnership is not recognised as an entity distinct from its partners. As a consequence of this, GST will have application to transactions between the partners and the partnership which will not reflect the general law treatment of those transactions. For GST purposes, transactions involving the acquisition, disposal or changes in the level of interests held in a general law partnership are considered in the context of input taxed financial supplies.

24.321 TAX LAW PARTNERSHIPS AND GENERAL LAW PARTNERSHIPS

For tax law purposes there are two kinds of partnerships, general law partnerships and tax law partnerships. A partnership for tax purposes including GST, is defined in s995-1 ITAA97 as follows. Partnership means:

- an association of persons (other than a company or a limited partnership) carrying on a business as partners or in receipt of ordinary income or statutory income jointly, or
- a limited partnership.

The first limb of the definition ('an association of persons carrying on a business') refers to a general law partnership (GSTR 2003/13) and the second limb ('an association of persons in receipt of ordinary income or statutory income jointly') refers to a tax law partnership (GSTR 2004/6).

24.322 TAX LAW PARTNERSHIPS (GSTR 2004/6)

For GST purposes, an association of persons in receipt of income jointly is a tax law partnership. It comes into existence from the time that the association of persons jointly commence an activity from which the income is or will be received jointly.

Most tax law partnerships arise in situations involving the leasing of co-owned property. At general law, joint tenancy, tenancies in common, joint property or part ownership do not, in themselves, create a partnership in respect of anything that is so held. Neither does the sharing of any profits from the use of such property result in a partnership.

The GST Act treats partnerships as an entity separate from its partners. An entity in a tax law partnership is a partner for the purposes of the GST Act, and can make supplies and acquisitions as a partner.

A tax law partnership does not have capital. Partners in a tax law partnership have neither interests in the capital of a partnership, nor interests in the partnership. The only interest that a partner in a tax law partnership has is an interest in the property, coupled with a right to a share of the net income or losses in accordance with that interest. On this basis, a supply of a financial interest (ie. input taxed financial supply) under item 10(d) of sub-regulation 40-5.09(3), does not arise in situations involving tax law partnerships.

ENTERPRISE CARRIED ON BY THE PARTNERSHIP (ENTERPRISE PARTNERSHIP)

A tax law partnership is capable of carrying on an enterprise. GSTR 2004/6, which considers tax law partnerships and co-owners of property, refers to a tax law partnership carrying on an enterprise as an 'enterprise partnership'. Carrying on an enterprise includes doing anything in the course of the commencement or termination of an enterprise. A tax law partnership may make supplies or acquisitions in carrying on its enterprise. Supplies and acquisitions made by or on behalf of a partner in the partnership as partners, are taken to be supplies and acquisitions made by the partnership. For GST purposes, an enterprise partnership can have assets and liabilities. Things that are acquired by partners, as partners, in an enterprise partnership, are acquisitions of the partnership. Those things can become assets of the partnership.

The enterprise partnership itself may register for GST, and must register if it meets the registration turnover threshold. However, the partners of an enterprise partnership cannot register for GST, nor can they acquire an ABN in relation to the enterprise carried on by the partnership. They may be registered in relation to a separate enterprise that they carry on in their own right (see below). A partner may make a supply in their own right to an enterprise partnership in which they are a partner. The supply is a taxable supply if the partner is registered (or required to be registered) and it meets the requirements of s9-5. A registered partnership may make supplies to a partner that are taxable. The supply is a taxable supply if it satisfies the requirements of s9-5. The partnership may also make supplies that are GST-free or input taxed.

ENTERPRISE CARRIED ON BY PARTNERS

A tax law partnership may not be the entity carrying on the enterprise. A tax law partnership may still exist but an enterprise is being carried on by each co-owner in their own right.

In such circumstances, the GST laws apply separately in respect of the respective interests of the partners and not to the tax law partnership. Each co-owner may register for GST, make supplies or acquisitions, be liable to pay GST and be required to lodge an activity statement. Indicators as to whether an enterprise is being carried on by a tax law partnership or co-owners in their own right are set out in GSTR 2004/6 and summarised in the following table:

Enterprise carried on by tax law partnership	Enterprise carried on by co-owners in their own right
Joint tenants	Tenants in common
There may be an oral or written agreement determining the mutual rights and obligations of the parties.	There may be an agreement between co-owners not to form a partnership nor jointly carry on an enterprise.
The income producing property is jointly acquired by the co-owners under a single contract. Therefore, it can only be disposed jointly.	Each co-owner's acquisition and disposal of their interest in property is made separately.
Income from and/or expenses relating to the income producing property is paid into/from a joint bank account of the co-owners.	The income is not paid into and the expenses are not paid out of a joint bank account in the co-owners names – rather a trust account may be used.
The co-owners of the income producing property jointly appoint a manager or agent. The appointed manager or agent will account to co-owners jointly.	Each co-owner acts independently with respect to appointment of a manager or agent (however the appointed manager or agent may be the same person). The appointed manager or agent accounts to each co-owner separately.
Co-owners act for the mutual benefits of all co-owners and a co-owner may act, with authorities from all other co-owners, on behalf of them in regards to the activities of the enterprise.	The co-owners act independently in relation to the making of decisions about their respective investments and are primarily concerned with securing and enhancing return on their own investment (and not mutual benefits).
Co-owners fund their acquisition of the property out of joint borrowings or funds.	Co-owners independently fund the acquisition of their share of the investment.

TERMINATION OF AN ENTERPRISE PARTNERSHIP

An enterprise partnership terminates if the association of persons is no longer in receipt of income jointly. Circumstances that may lead to the termination of a tax law partnership include:

- the sale of an income producing property that is the sole source of income
- the property or properties are no longer used for an income producing purpose
- a change of persons comprising the association of persons in receipt of income jointly, and
- the partitioning of land (GSTR 2009/2) in which co-owners of land become the owner in severalty of a specifically ascertained part(s) of the land.

A tax law partnership cannot be reconstituted. If one or more of the co-owners of the income producing property dispose of their interest in that property, this constitutes a change in the association of persons. A tax law partnership cannot be treated as continuing in these circumstances.

The sale of an interest in an income producing property will often mean a substantial change in the ownership of the partnership's asset(s) and for this reason the Tax Office takes the view that a tax law partnership cannot be reconstituted.

A tax law partnership that is registered for GST at termination must apply for cancellation of its registration, and may have an increasing adjustment under Division 138 in respect of previously claimed input tax credits on assets in existence on cancellation. It is possible that some of the partners from the old partnership form a new partnership with new co-owners. Under such circumstances, it is considered to be a new partnership and the new partnership must apply for a new ABN and GST.

Unlike general law partnerships, a tax law partnership does not involve a partnership agreement. Accordingly, there is no continuity clause.

SUPPLY OF AN INTEREST MADE BY THE ENTERPRISE PARTNERSHIP

Any sale of a property or interest in a property which is used in carrying on an enterprise by a partnership is a supply by the partnership and not by the co-owners. There will be GST consequences if the partnership is registered. For instance, the supply may be a taxable supply if the requirements of s9-5 are met, or the supply of a going concern that is GST-free if it meets the requirements of s38-325.

An enterprise partnership can make a supply of a going concern under s38-325(2). A supply by an enterprise partnership of all the interests in leased property, that is, all the co-owners as partners selling their respective interests in the leased property, may be the supply of all things necessary for the continued operation of the enterprise.

SUPPLY OF AN INTEREST MADE BY CO-OWNERS IN THEIR OWN RIGHT

Supply of an interest in the income producing asset can be made by co-owners in their own right. In this case, GST consequences apply to the individual co-owner that made the supply. A new tax law partnership will be formed when the new co-owner/partner enters into an agreement to acquire an interest in the income producing property.

24.323   GENERAL LAW PARTNERSHIPS (GSTR 2003/13)

A general law partnership is defined as an association of persons carrying on business as partners. It does not include a company. A general law partnership is formed when persons commence carrying on business together with a view of profit under an agreement, either written or oral. The 'association' is one that arises under an agreement.

Under general law, a partnership is not an entity. The general law regards the business as being carried on by the persons that are in partnership. The term 'partnership' is merely descriptive of the relation between persons carrying on a business with a view of profit.

The position under the GST Act is different. The definition of an entity includes a partnership. A consequence of this is that the GST Act applies to partnership transactions, in particular dealings between partners and the partnership in a manner that does not reflect the general law treatment of those transactions. GSTR 2003/13 explains how GST applies to transactions involving general law partnerships.

As an entity, a general law partnership may register for GST. It is liable for GST on taxable supplies that it makes, and is entitled to input tax credits for creditable acquisitions it makes. Supplies and acquisitions that are made by or on behalf of partners in their capacity as partners are treated as supplies and acquisitions by the partnership. Subsection 184-5(1) states that a supply, acquisition or importation made by or on behalf of a partner of a partnership in his or her capacity as a partner:

- is taken to be a supply, acquisition or importation made by the partnership, and
- is not taken to be a supply, acquisition or importation made by that partner or any other partner of the partnership.

Whether a partner makes a supply or acquisition in their capacity as a partner is a question of fact. Factors (set out in GSTR 2003/13) that may indicate that a supply is made by a partner in that capacity include:

- the consideration for the supply is paid to a common fund, or to all the partners
- the supply is of a kind typically made in the type of enterprise carried on by the partnership, and
- the invoice or tax invoice shows the firm or business name, or the names of all the partners as supplier.

Factors that may indicate that an acquisition is made by a partner in that capacity include:

- the acquisition is used in the enterprise of the partnership
- the acquisition is made with the consent of all the partners
- the acquisition is paid for out of partnership profits or from a partnership account, and
- the invoice or tax invoice shows the firm or business name, or the names of all the partners as recipient.

SUPPLIES AND ACQUISITIONS MADE BY THE PARTNERSHIP ON FORMATION

When a partnership is formed, the partners acquire interests in the partnership. The consideration for those interests can include capital contributions and the mutual obligations that each partner undertakes, including promises to provide labour, skills or services in the conduct of the partnership business.

An in-kind contribution from a partner is consideration for the supply of the partnership interest. However, the acquisition by the partnership relates to the actual operation of the partnership and, therefore, relates to the making of supplies by a partnership in the course of the partnership's ordinary or general business. Any claim, therefore, for input tax credits is determined by reference to the use of the in-kind capital contribution in the partnership's business activities and will be a creditable acquisition if the requirements of s11-5 are met.

INTERESTS IN A PARTNERSHIP

Upon a partnership coming into existence, its partners hold interests in the partnership. A partner's interest in the partnership may increase or decrease over time. A partner's interest is extinguished if the partner exits the partnership, unless the partner sells or assigns their interest to another entity. No interests in the partnership are held once the partnership ceases to exist.

An interest in a partnership includes a right to a proportion of any surplus after the realisation of the assets and payment of the debts and other liabilities of the partnership, and is inclusive of a partner's entitlement to a share in the capital of the partnership.

For GST purposes, transactions involving the acquisition, disposal, or changes in the level of interests held in a partnership are considered in the context of financial supplies. If a partnership makes supplies to the partners or their associates in the course or furtherance of its enterprise without consideration or for inadequate consideration, Division 72 may apply. Division 72 ensures that supplies to, and acquisitions from, associates without consideration are brought within the GST system, and that supplies to associates for inadequate consideration are properly valued for GST purposes. As a partnership and its partners are associates under the GST Act, Division 72 may apply to supplies between a partnership and its partners.

Division 72 will not apply if the acquirer is both registered and makes the acquisition for a solely creditable purpose (see 23.223).

TRADING STOCK TAKEN BY PARTNER

In GSTD 2009/2, the Tax Office expresses its view that when a partner in a partnership takes goods held as trading stock for private or domestic use, there is a supply by the partnership to the partner in the course or furtherance of the partnership's enterprise.

Furthermore, the Tax Office considers that an *in specie* distribution of trading stock by a partnership to a partner is made for consideration, the consideration being a proportionate reduction of the partner's entitlement to a distribution of any surplus remaining upon the winding up of the partnership after the realisation of assets and payment of liabilities of the partnership. Where the other s9-5 requirements are satisfied, the supply of the trading stock will be a taxable supply.

SUPPLY OF A GOING CONCERN

A general law partnership can make a supply of a going concern under subs38-325(2).

A general law partnership may make the supply of a going concern to another partnership comprising some of the same partners as the partnership making the supply. This may occur where a partner supplies their interest in the partnership to an incoming partner, or the existing partners.

The supply of an interest in a partnership is not, of itself, a supply of a going concern. However, if a supply of an interest in a partnership results in the general dissolution and wind-up of the existing partnership (rather than a technical dissolution and reconstitution), this has the effect of transferring the entire enterprise from the old partnership to the new partnership. The sale of an interest in a partnership under this arrangement results in the supply of a going concern by the 'old' partnership to the 'new' partnership, which may be GST-free if the requirements of subs38-325(1) are met. See 23.460 and 24.324.

Upon the supply of a going concern by the old partnership to the new partnership, the old partnership is dissolved and is required to cancel its GST registration. The new partnership must apply for GST registration.

24.324   DISSOLUTION OF A GENERAL LAW PARTNERSHIP

At general law, dissolution of a partnership may be brought about in a number of different ways, including by a change in its membership or by a cessation of its business. Where the partnership no longer carries on a business, it is dissolved and wound up. However, on the departure of a partner the partnership is either wound up or the continuing partners agree that the business or firm may be carried on by the continuing partners, with or without new partners. In the latter situation, there may be no change in the outward appearance of the partnership business or firm.

A dissolution leading to the winding up of the partnership is called a general dissolution. A dissolution that does not result in the winding up of a partnership is called a technical dissolution. A technical dissolution occurs where the assets and liabilities of the partnership are taken over by the continuing partners (and any new partners) and the partnership business is continued without any apparent break.

GENERAL DISSOLUTION

A general dissolution of a partnership may be brought about in a number of ways. These include:
- by mutual agreement between the partners
- upon the expiration of time if the partnership is for a fixed period of time
- by the death or bankruptcy of a partner, and
- on the permanent cessation of the business carried on.

GST CONSEQUENCES OF A GENERAL DISSOLUTION

Some or all of the partners may continue to carry on the enterprise of the partnership during its winding up. The definition of 'carrying on an enterprise' at s195-1 includes doing anything in the course of the termination of the enterprise. This includes the final distribution.

SUPPLIES MADE BY A PARTNERSHIP ON WINDING UP

Realising business assets as part of winding up a partnership involves the partnership making supplies in the course or furtherance of an enterprise that it carries on. Those supplies are taxable supplies if all the requirements of s9-5 are satisfied.

Following the payment of the partnership debts and other liabilities after realisation of assets, any available surplus is applied in making distributions to the partners. Where not all of the assets of the partnership are required to be sold in order to meet the debts and other liabilities of the partnership, remaining assets may be distributed to the partners. Where the partnership makes an in-kind distribution to a partner in satisfaction of a partner's interest in the partnership, for GST purposes it is something done in the course of the termination of the partnership's enterprise.

An in-kind distribution to a partner as part of the final distribution is made without consideration. There is no payment, act or forbearance in connection with the supply. The partner's interest in the partnership is extinguished when the distribution is made rather than surrendered back to the partnership as consideration.

As the supply of the in-kind distribution is made to an associate without consideration, Division 72 may apply.

   An in-kind distribution to a partner may be a taxable supply.

FINAL DISTRIBUTIONS TO THE PARTNERS

At the time of making the final distributions of a partnership, all of the partners' interests in the partnership are extinguished. The partnership ceases to exist. No GST consequences arise in respect of the extinguishment. The final distribution by the partnership means the partners' interests are surrendered to the partnership.

Supplies made by a partnership to the partners on winding up

Tony and Sue decide to retire and wind up their GST registered partnership. The partnership plant and equipment are sold to another entity. The supply of plant and equipment is made to the other entity in the course or furtherance of the partnership's enterprise, and is a taxable supply by the partnership.

However, not all of the partnership assets need to be sold to meet the debts and other liabilities of the partnership. The partnership is left with $6,000 in money, and a motor vehicle with a GST-inclusive value of $5,500. The partnership's final distribution to Tony consists solely of the vehicle.

Tony's interest in the partnership is extinguished upon the making of the final distribution to him. The supply of the vehicle, though made in the course or furtherance of the partnership's enterprise, is made without consideration. As Tony is an associate of the partnership and is not GST registered, Subdivision 72-A applies to the supply. As a result, the supply by the partnership to Tony is a taxable supply. As the GST-exclusive market value of the vehicle is $5,000, the partnership has a GST liability of $500. After discharging this liability, the partnership has $5,500 in money.

The partnership makes a final distribution of the remaining $5,500 in money to Sue. This is not a supply for GST purposes pursuant to s9-10(4).

SUPPLIES MADE BY THE PARTNERS ON WINDING UP A PARTNERSHIP

If, after payment of debts and other liabilities of the partnership, there is a surplus, the partners ordinarily would not make any supplies to the partnership. Where the partnership has a deficiency upon winding up, the partners may contribute money or other assets to ensure that the partnership meets its debts and other liabilities. In this case, the partners' interests in the partnership are not extinguished until the partnership has met its debts and other liabilities.

The contribution of money by a partner to make good a partnership deficiency is not a supply. The supply of other assets by a registered partner to the partnership, if made in the course or furtherance of their separate enterprise, is a taxable supply if all the requirements of s9-5 are met. The partnership acquires the assets in the course of the termination of its enterprise, that is, in carrying on its enterprise. It therefore makes a creditable acquisition of the asset supplied by the partner.

TECHNICAL DISSOLUTION/CONTINUITY CLAUSES

Under general law, any change in the membership of a general law partnership leads to its dissolution. However, the dissolution may not lead to the winding up of the partnership. The continuing partners and any new partner may conduct the business of the partnership without any break in its continuity. This is referred to as a reconstituted partnership. Whether or not there is a reconstituted partnership depends on the intention of the parties and the terms and conditions of the partnership agreement.

A written partnership agreement may expressly provide for the continuation of the firm or business in the event of a change in the membership of the partnership. This provision is often referred to as a continuity or non-dissolution clause. In the absence of a written agreement, such a clause may be implied by the conduct of the partners following the retirement or death of a partner, or introduction of a new partner.

The Courts have, however, distinguished between a technical dissolution and a general dissolution. They have shown a reluctance to order a partnership to be wound up on a change of members where there is an express or implied continuity clause, and it is clear that the firm continues. GSTR 2003/13 considers the GST consequences of both kinds of dissolution.

To regard a change in the membership of a partnership as leading to a winding up of an existing partnership and the formation of a new partnership would lead to administrative and compliance difficulties for the partnership and its partners. This would be the case particularly for partnerships that experience frequent membership changes. Every change in membership would require cancellation of the partnership's GST registration (and ABN), and the re-application for a new GST registration (and ABN) by the continuing partners.

For GST purposes, it is open and appropriate for the Commissioner to accept that a change in membership does not necessarily result in the general dissolution and winding up of the partnership. For GST purposes, a continuity clause (whether express or implied) is effective.

The view that there can be continuity of a partnership for GST purposes means that the partnership is dissolved only as far as a retiring or deceased partner is concerned. The retiring or deceased partner's interest in the partnership crystallises as a debt owing by the partnership to that partner. The reconstituted partnership continues as far as the continuing partners are concerned.

For a partnership to be treated as reconstituted, there needs to be an express or implied continuity clause in the partnership agreement, and there should be no break in the continuity of the enterprise or firm.

CHANGE IN THE MEMBERSHIP OF A TWO-PARTNER PARTNERSHIP

A partnership can be a reconstituted partnership only where two or more partners remain. In a two-partner partnership, the departure of one through retirement or death will normally lead to a general dissolution and winding up of that partnership. However, a two-person partnership can be reconstituted where a partner in a two-partner partnership sells or assigns an interest in the partnership to an incoming partner, or where a partner dies and the partnership agreement allows for continuity of the partnership with either the executor, trustee or beneficiary of the deceased partner's estate. The continuity clause may be express, or implied by way of conduct. Where this happens and the firm continues without any break in the continuity of the enterprise, it will be considered that there is a change in members and a reconstituted partnership.

GST CONSEQUENCES OF A TECHNICAL DISSOLUTION (RECONSTITUTION)

A reconstituted partnership retains its GST registration despite the change in its membership. As there is no winding up of the partnership, the change in membership does not give rise to any supplies or acquisitions from one partnership to another partnership.

The GST consequences of a reconstituted partnership for the partners will depend on the circumstances of the reconstitution. A reconstitution may result from a partner selling or assigning their interest in the partnership. Alternatively, a change in membership may occur without any sale or assignment by a partner of their interest in the partnership.

SALE OR ASSIGNMENT OF AN INTEREST IN A PARTNERSHIP – PARTNER TO PARTNER TRANSACTION

A sale or assignment of an interest in a partnership may be made by a continuing partner to an incoming partner, or by an outgoing partner to either a continuing or an incoming partner. The supply is a partner-to-partner transaction and does not involve the creation or supply of any new interest by the partnership. Such a sale or assignment is a supply by the partner of a financial interest, and is a financial supply if the requirements of sub-regulation 40 5.09(1) are satisfied. If the partner making the supply is unregistered, or the supply is not made in the course or furtherance of an enterprise carried on by the partner, no GST consequence arises in relation to the supply.

NO SALE OR ASSIGNMENT OF INTERESTS – PARTNERSHIP TRANSACTION

A reconstituted partnership may also involve the creation and supply by the partnership of a new interest in the partnership, rather than the supply of an existing interest by a partner. The GST consequences of such a reconstitution for the partnership, the outgoing partner and the incoming partner are as follows:

- **Outgoing partner and partnership:** For a retiring or deceased partner (the outgoing partner), the crystallisation of their interest in the partnership as a debt is not as a consequence of a supply of any new financial interest by the partnership. A partner's interest in a partnership includes a right to share the surplus (if any) after repayment of debts and other liabilities. This right is acquired when the partnership is formed, or when the partner joins the partnership. The crystallisation is of a right that the partner already has, and is not a new right that is acquired.
  The crystallisation of the interest in the partnership as a debt results in the extinguishment of the outgoing partner's interest in the partnership. Following this extinguishment, there is an increase in each of the continuing partners' fractional interest in the partnership. This increase is a consequence of the extinguishment of

the outgoing partner's interest and does not involve a supply of any new or additional interests in the partnership by the partnership.

- **Incoming partner and partnership:** Where a reconstitution results from the addition of a new partner (the incoming partner), there is a supply of a new interest in the partnership by the partnership to the incoming partner. It is a supply of a financial interest in the course or furtherance of the enterprise carried on by the partnership. If the other requirements of sub-regulation 40-5.09(1) are satisfied, it is a financial supply.

  Consideration for the supply of the new interest is the capital contribution made by the incoming partner or the promise to provide labour, skills or services in the conduct of the partnership business.

  In these circumstances, there will be a reduction, by way of extinguishment, in the interests of the continuing partners, which does not involve a supply by them.

CHANGE IN LEGAL OWNERSHIP OF PROPERTY HELD BY THE PARTNERSHIP ON A TRANSFER OF A PARTNERSHIP INTEREST

As partnerships are not recognised as separate legal entities, legal title in partnership property is held by the partners. Regardless of legal title, each partner has a beneficial interest in each and every partnership asset. The partner or partners holding legal title do so on trust for themselves and the other partners on behalf of the partnership.

A supply of an interest in a partnership by a partner may require the outgoing partner to effect a change in legal title or interest in partnership assets. The acquiring partner acquires the beneficial and legal interests under the supply of the interests in the partnership. For GST purposes, the transfer of the legal interest does not involve any separate supply by the outgoing partner. Any supply of partnership property would be by the partnership. Therefore, where property stays in the partnership, there is no supply as the supply and acquisition would be by the partnership.

GST LIABILITIES AND OBLIGATIONS OF PARTNERS BEFORE AND AFTER RECONSTITUTION

Retiring partners are only responsible for the GST liabilities and obligations of the partnership before reconstitution and not for any after its reconstitution. Similarly, new partners are only responsible for the GST liabilities and obligations of the partnership after its reconstitution and not for any liabilities and obligations before its reconstitution. However, the continuing partners are responsible for the GST liabilities and obligations of the partnership both before and after reconstitution.

The acceptance of a reconstituted partnership and the fact that it retains its existing GST registration makes it prudent for a reconstituted partnership and the retiring partner or partners to inform the Commissioner of the change in the membership of the partnership. Where there is a failure to notify the Commissioner of a change in the membership of a general law partnership, recovery action may be contemplated against a retired partner for any unpaid GST liabilities arising after the reconstitution of the partnership.

The notification may be made by the retiring partner, the personal representative of a deceased partner, or the continuing partners and any incoming partner, or by a person authorised by those parties to deal with the Commissioner in relation to their GST affairs. In the case of a large partnership, a managing partner with the consent and authorisation of all partners, retiring, continuing or incoming, may make the notification.

ONE PARTNER ACQUIRES ALL INTERESTS IN THE PARTNERSHIP AND CONTINUES AS SINGLE ENTITY

Where one partner takes over the business of the partnership, this is usually achieved by the purchase of the other partners' interests in the partnership. It makes no difference whether the sale or assignment of an interest in a partnership by an outgoing partner is to either an incoming or a continuing partner. Therefore, where one partner acquires the partnership interests of all the other partners, the outgoing partners make supplies of financial interests to the acquiring partner. The supplies by the outgoing partners, and the acquisition-supply by the acquiring partner, will be financial supplies if the requirements of sub-regulation 40-5.09(1) are met.

By acquiring all of the other partnership interests, the acquiring partner effectively takes over all of the assets and liabilities of the partnership and carries on the enterprise in its own right. Upon the supply of all the other interests in the partnership to the acquiring partner, the partnership is dissolved. Since the partnership is no longer carrying on the enterprise, the partnership GST registration (and ABN) must be cancelled. The purchaser may apply for a new GST registration (and ABN) and must do so if it is required to be registered.

24.325   GENERAL LAW PARTNERSHIP AND THE MARGIN SCHEME

GSTR 2009/1 considers whether the margin scheme can apply to the following circumstances:
- an in specie contribution of real property by partners into a partnership
- reconstitution of a partnership, and
- general dissolution that results in an in specie distribution of real property.

This Ruling accepts that the supply of real property as a capital contribution is a sale and therefore accords with the meaning of 'selling' for the purpose of s75-5(1). Hence, the 'margin scheme' (refer 24.344) may apply to a capital contribution of real property to a general law partnership in exchange for consideration being the supply of an interest in the partnership. The Commissioner takes the view that a partnership through the acts of a partner in the capacity of partner, may enter into a transaction with itself in its own capacity. Thus, when a partnership acquires real property contributed by a partner in its own capacity, the property becomes partnership property notwithstanding the fact that there is no change in legal ownership.

NOTE: Contributions by partners to a partnership most of the time may not consists of a taxable supply because the partner might not be registered for GST in its own capacity or the supply may not be made in the course or furtherance of an enterprise carried on by the partner. In this case, the contribution will not be subject to GST and the margin scheme will be irrelevant.

The vice versa applies when an in specie distribution of real property by a general law partnership to a partner as a result of general dissolution takes place. The real property is supplied to the partner in its own capacity by the partner in the capacity of partner in the partnership in so far the property is no longer partnership property. The in specie distribution is a supply for consideration and in the Commissioner's view it is in accordance with the meaning of 'selling' for the purpose of s75-5(1). Therefore, if all other requirements under s75-5 are met, the margin scheme may be applied in working out the GST on the supply.

NOTE: In the case of a general law partnership reconstitution, as mentioned in an earlier section, although there may be a change in legal ownership, however for GST purposes the real property remains in the partnership and therefore there is no supply or acquisition from one partnership to another. Accordingly, there is no supply to which the margin scheme can apply.

Supply between partners and the partnership are supplies between associates. The margin for supplies made between associates (partner and partnership) is calculated pursuant to s75-11(6) and (7) unless any other subsections in s75-11 apply. Section 75-11 takes precedence over s75-10(2) and (3).

In the case of an in specie capital contribution by a partner and an in specie distribution by the partnership in the event of a general dissolution, it is already established that the supply is a supply for consideration. Therefore, s75-11(6) is not applicable as it is regarding supply to associates for nil consideration.

24.330 AGENCY RELATIONSHIPS AND CONSIGNMENT SALES

24.331   SELLING ON A 'SALE OR RETURN' BASIS OR AS AN AGENT?

GSTR 2000/29 distinguishes between supplies/acquisitions on 'sale or return' terms and supplies/acquisitions made through an agent.

In most situations, consignment sales are 'sale or return'. In this arrangement, title in the goods stays with the owner until a buyer is found. The sale to the buyer then involves two transactions – a sale of the goods by their owner to you, and then an immediate sale of the goods by you to the new owner.

On the other hand, agency sales involve the sale of goods by the owner to the buyer via you as an agent.

Factors which indicate that you are selling consignment goods on a sale or return basis include:

- the amount you pay to the owner when a buyer is found is pre-agreed (this can often evidence an agreement for you to purchase and then resell the goods)
- any amount over and above this pre-agreed amount is yours to keep
- you set the sale price of the goods
- you are entitled to keep secret from the owner of the goods the final selling price and details of your remuneration or profit on the transaction
- you are required to provide a warranty on the goods
- you are required to guarantee title to the goods
- you are prevented by a state law from selling goods as an agent – this is common in the motor vehicle industry, and
- you do not bear any commercial risk – if the goods are not sold, you are not obligated to purchase them.

Many businesses refer to themselves as an agent in the relationship they have with various suppliers. Whether you are an agent or not is a question of fact. Factors which indicate that you are acting as an agent for the owner of the consigned goods include:

- you do not set the sale price of the goods
- you receive either a flat rate or percentage commission on completion of the sale
- you do not hold the goods out in your own right, and
- you and the owner of the goods agree that you will act as an agent.

An agent is normally an intermediary authorised to act on behalf of another party. The party who authorises an agent to do something on that party's behalf is called the principal. At common law, an agent is a person who is authorised by a principal to act for that principal so as to create or affect legal relations between the principal and third parties.

The principles of the general law of agency are to be followed in applying GST law to agency relationships. However the GST Act provides some flexibility in its application. If you are an agent then your principal will be responsible for the GST when you make the sale on the principal's behalf.

An entity that facilitates supplies or acquisitions for another entity may utilise the simplified accounting procedures so long as the principal and the intermediary agree that the intermediary will take responsibility for using such procedures in relation to certain transactions.

24.332   CONSIGNMENT SALES

If your business sells goods on consignment, you will need to look at the nature of the contractual arrangement you have with your customer(s) so that you can determine how to correctly account for GST on such sales.

Goods sold 'on consignment' refer to an arrangement where a business agrees to sell goods without first buying those goods from the owner. Typically, the agreement will specify that the business sells the goods on behalf of the owner as an agent, or that the business will agree to purchase the goods for an agreed price when it finds a buyer, otherwise, the goods may be returned to the owner.

IS GST PAYABLE ON GOODS SOLD ON CONSIGNMENT?

If your business is registered for GST and you sell goods on consignment, you will have to account for GST on the sale of those goods if the agreement stipulates that you will buy the goods from their owner when a buyer is found for those goods. This type of consignment arrangement is known as 'sale or return'. Effectively, you are selling the goods to the customer in your own right. To do this, you acquire title to those goods at the time that you make the sale. You are making an acquisition of the goods – from the owner – at the same time as you are making a supply to the purchaser.

If you sell consigned goods on behalf of the owner as his or her agent, GST is payable on the supply only if the owner is registered for GST and is making the supply in the course of their enterprise. This means that if you are acting as an agent, you will need to establish whether or not the owner is registered for GST and whether the goods are being sold in the course of their business or in their capacity as private consumers. If you are registered for GST, you will need to include GST on the commission you charge to the owner of the goods (see 24.333).

Chris is a landscaper who is registered for GST. Chris decides to sell one of his lawn mowers and engages a second-hand equipment dealer for that purpose. The equipment dealer is registered for GST and agrees to sell the mower as an agent for Chris.

The equipment dealer will earn a commission from Chris for selling the mower. Because Chris is registered and is making the supply of the mower in connection with his landscape enterprise, GST will be payable by Chris on the full payment for the mower. Chris will also be charged GST on the commission he pays to the equipment dealer and will be entitled to an input tax credit.

For attribution purposes, there are two separate supplies made under arrangements for the supply of goods on approval, or on 'sale or return' terms:

- a supply of a right to display the goods for sale, for which no consideration is paid, and
- a supply of goods by way of sale, which occurs when the goods are accepted or on-sold.

INPUT TAX CREDITS ON CONSIGNED GOODS

If your business sells goods on a sale or return basis, you will be entitled to an input tax credit if the owner of the goods is registered for GST and the supply of the goods to you is a taxable supply. This is because you will make an acquisition of those goods in the tax period in which you sell them and the acquisition will be a creditable acquisition.

Most goods sold by consignment, however, are secondhand goods owned by individuals not registered for GST. The GST Act allows you to claim an input tax credit on any secondhand goods you acquire for the purpose of selling or exchanging in your business, even if that acquisition was from a supplier who was not registered for GST. Second-hand goods are explained in further detail at 24.381.

24.333   GST AND AGENCY RELATIONSHIPS (Division 153)

For GST purposes, when an agent makes a supply on behalf of the principal, it is the principal that is making the supply and therefore the principal that is liable to pay GST. In the same way, an acquisition made by an agent on behalf of a principal is taken to be an acquisition by the principal and therefore it is the principal that is entitled to claim input tax credits.

NOTE: Whether there is an obligation to pay GST or claim input tax credits is dependent on whether the principal is registered or required to be registered for GST, and not the agent's registration status. Therefore, a supply made by a principal that is not registered for GST through an agent who is registered for GST, is not subject to GST and there will be no entitlement to input tax credits on acquisition.

GSTR 2000/37 considers how to treat GST payable and input tax credits in relation to agency relationships and transactions occurring under agency arrangements.

Where a principal makes a taxable supply or creditable acquisition through an agent, the normal GST rules apply with respect to the attribution of the GST payable and the input tax credit entitlement.

The application of the basic attribution rules may impose an unreasonable burden where the principal does not have information about when the consideration is provided or when an invoice is raised etc. The Commissioner however has made a determination to alter the normal attribution rules for principals who rely on an agent for information required to account for GST: *GST (A New Tax System (Goods and Services Tax) (Particular Attribution Rules for Supplies and Acquisitions made through Agents) Determination (No. 1) 2000).*

A copy of this determination is attached to GSTR 2000/29 as Schedule 4.

The determination basically allows flexibility to the attribution rules so that the principal is only liable for any GST payable on a taxable supply, and gets any input tax credit arising from a creditable acquisition based on when the principal becomes aware of the information. It is therefore acceptable for principals to attribute a transaction after the end of a relevant tax period if the principal did not obtain the information at the time.

Whatever the circumstances are, an input tax credit is only claimable in the period in which a tax invoice is held. A tax invoice is taken to be held by the recipient in the context of an agency relationship when either the principal or agent holds the relevant tax invoice (s153-5).

An obligation to issue a tax invoice for a taxable supply made through an agent arises when the recipient of a supply makes a request either to the principal or the agent. This obligation to issue a tax invoice is complied with if the agent issues a tax invoice on behalf of the principal (s153-15). The tax invoice can have either the principal's or the agent's ABN to be compliant. However, the principal and agent must not both issue separate tax invoices in relation to a supply. Doing so will attract a penalty. PS LA 2007/3 sets out guidelines for Tax Office staff in respect of the remission of penalties imposed where both a principal and an agent issue separate tax invoices or adjustment notes contrary to the GST legislation.

24.334   AGENCY RELATIONSHIP AND DISBURSEMENTS

Agents may incur expenses as an agent on behalf of their principal and/or incur expenses in the ordinary course of providing their services to the principal. Whether it is the former or latter will determine if the reimbursement will be subject to GST or not. The former is a reimbursement / recovery. The latter is an on-charge. For more information see 24.384.

Disbursement made by a solicitor

If a disbursement is made by a solicitor and incurred in the solicitor's capacity as a paying agent for a particular client, no GST is payable by the solicitor on subsequent reimbursement by the client.

The following common fees and charges, for which a client (principal) is liable, may be paid for by a solicitor (agent) as a paying agent of the client but will not attract GST on subsequent reimbursement by the client:

- application fees
- registration fees
- court fees
- incorporation fees
- probate fees
- barrister's fees when barrister engaged by client, and
- fines, penalties, stamp duty and taxes.

Examples of common disbursements that can be incurred by the solicitor and then reimbursed by a client that will attract GST on the subsequent reimbursement by the client to the solicitor include:

- search fees
- municipal search fees
- witness fees
- fees for recording court proceedings, and
- service of document fees.

Examples of costs that a solicitor may incur in carrying on the business of providing a legal service to the client on which GST is payable on any subsequent payment by the client include:

- telephone
- postage
- photocopying
- travel, and
- typing.

OTHER REIMBURSEMENTS

Division 111 provides that input tax credits may be claimed in respect of some reimbursements made to agents for expenses they incur. Section 111-5(1)(a) provides that if an agent is reimbursed for an expense they incur that is related directly to their activities as an agent, the reimbursement is treated as consideration for an acquisition made from the agent. The fact the supply to the principal is not a taxable supply does not prevent the acquisition from being a creditable acquisition. However, the acquisition:

- is not a creditable acquisition to the extent:

- the agent is not entitled to an input tax credit for acquiring the thing acquired in incurring the expense, or,
- the acquisition would not, because of Division 69 (an acquisition is not a creditable acquisition to the extent it is a non-deductible expense), be a creditable acquisition if made by the principal, and
- is not a creditable acquisition unless the supply of the thing acquired by the agent was a taxable supply, and
- is not a creditable acquisition if the principal, because of Division 71 (suppliers making input taxed supplies may not be entitled to input tax credits for acquisitions made to provide fringe benefits) would not have been entitled to an input tax credit if they had made the acquisition made by the agent.

24.335   AGENT TREATED AS A SEPARATE SUPPLIER/ACQUIRER

Subdivision 153-B provides an alternative way for agents and principals to account for GST by allowing an option for entities to enter into an arrangement under which an agent is treated as a separate supplier. The general effect of entering into these arrangements in respect of both supplies and acquisitions, is that the principal and its agent are treated as acting as two principals. These GST arrangements do not impact on the common law contractual obligations between the parties.

GSTR 2000/37 considers the application of such an arrangement. To enter into this arrangement there must be a written agreement under which:

- the agent arranges to make supplies and/or acquisitions to or from third parties on behalf of the principal
- the kinds of supplies and/or acquisitions to which the arrangement applies are specified
- the agent is treated for the purposes of GST law as a principal in making supplies or acquisitions
- the agent will issue all tax invoices and adjustment notes relating to those supplies to third parties in the agent's name and the principal will not issue such documents, and
- both parties must be registered.

A taxable supply made to a third party is taken to be a taxable supply made by the agent. In addition, the principal is taken to have made a taxable supply to the agent of the same thing that the agent is taken to have supplied. The agent has made a creditable acquisition in its own right.

As the supply by the principal to the agent is a taxable supply, the principal is required to account for the GST payable on the supply, usually being 10% of the value which is the amount the agent is actually required to pay the principal. This amount is normally the price charged to the third party, less the amount the agent is permitted to keep as commission. Under these circumstances, the agent's supply of services is not a taxable supply and the principal is not entitled to claim input tax credits relating to the commission.

Chasers (principal) supplies a sporting good at a price of $220 to Fred (third party) through Metro (agent). Metro is entitled to receive commission of $22 from Chasers for selling the good. Both Chasers and Metro have entered into written arrangements to treat their dealings as separate supplies.

For GST purposes, Chasers is taken to have made a taxable supply to Metro with the value of the supply being the price of the sporting good that was sold to Fred less the commission payable to Metro ie. value = 10/11 x ($220 − $22) = $180.

Chasers is liable to pay $18 GST on the taxable supply to Metro (ie. 10% of $180). Metro in turn makes a taxable supply to Fred and is liable to pay GST of $20 (1/11 x $220). Metro however is entitled to the input tax credit of $18 for the GST included in the acquisition from Chasers.

Chasers is not entitled to any input tax credit on the commission component.

24.340 GST AND REAL PROPERTY

Summary of GST status for sale of real property		
Type of property	**Example**	**GST treatment**
Residential premises	Existing residence	Input taxed
New residential premises	Newly built or substantially renovated or built to replace	Taxable*
Commercial residential	Hotel, motel, boarding house	Taxable*
Commercial property	Factory, office	Taxable*
Farm land	Sale to farmer	GST-free if sold on the basis that it will continue to be used as farm land
Going concern	Sale of property as part of an enterprise	GST-free if conditions satisfied
Commercial residential:		
• short-term	Hotel	Taxable*
• long-term	Boarding house/on site caravan	Input taxed/concessional (Division 87)
Commercial property	Factory, office	Taxable*
Lease for more than 50 years	Lease for 100 years	Treated as a sale (see above table)

* Taxable provided s9-5 taxable supply requirements are all satisfied.

 The sale of a property used for leasing purposes by an entity carrying on a leasing enterprise is excluded from the calculation of its projected GST turnover as the property is a capital asset of the enterprise and not trading stock. In such circumstances, an entity may not be required to be registered for GST at all and therefore the sale of the property will not be subject to GST because all the requirements under s9-5 for a taxable supply are not met. For calculation of GST turnover see 24.211.

24.341   GST IMPLICATIONS OF LEASING REAL PROPERTY

In *FC of T v MBI Properties Pty Ltd* [2014] HCA 49 the High Court held that the purchaser of premises subject to a lease made supplies to the lessee. The court pointed out that in the case of a lease there will in general be a supply which occurs at the time of entering into the lease and that there will then be at least one further supply which occurs progressively throughout the term of the lease. That supply will occur by means of the lessor observing and continuing to observe the express or implied covenant of quiet enjoyment under the lease. The thing of value which the lessee thereby receives is continuing use and occupation of the leased premises. The Commissioner has issued a decision impact statement on the High Court's decision.

The Commissioner has issued a ruling which considers the GST consequences of development lease arrangements with government agencies (GSTR 2015/2).

LEASING OF RESIDENTIAL PROPERTY (Division 40-B)

A supply of residential premises for rental is input taxed to the extent the supply is of residential premises used predominantly for residential accommodation (s40-35). The rent will not be subject to GST. The supplier of the premises cannot claim any input tax credits for GST included in the price of supplies acquired for the rental property (eg. insurance, repairs, agency commission).

'Residential premises' is defined (s195-1) to mean land or a building that is occupied as a residence or for residential accommodation or is intended to be occupied, and is capable of being occupied, as a residence or for residential accommodation, regardless of the term of the occupation or intended occupation. A floating home is included.

The Full Federal Court has held that vacant land does not come within the definition of 'residential premises' (*Vidler v Commissioner of Taxation* [2010] FCAFC 59).

GST Ruling GSTR 2012/5 considers how Subdivision 40-B and Subdivision 40-C of the GST Act applies to the supply of residential premises. The ruling does not consider new residential premises (refer to GSTR 2003/3) or commercial residential premises (refer to GSTR 2012/6).

GSTR 2012/5 deals with the term 'predominantly for residential accommodation'. This term indicates that premises that are residential premises are capable of use for purposes other than residential accommodation. The function of this term is to differentiate the GST treatment of any portions of residential premises that are commercial. This would apply, for example, to a house that has been partly converted for use as a doctor's surgery. Several parts of the house may still be used predominantly for residential accommodation, such as bedrooms, bathroom, kitchen, living rooms and gardens, while other areas are not, being turned over to office and consulting room space, and storage for the surgery. In this case these commercial parts are excluded from the input-taxed treatment of the rest of the property.

EXAMPLE 8 from GSTR 2012/5

Shannon decides to partly modify her house to use in her profession as a doctor. She modifies an area of the house to provide office and consulting room space, an operating theatre, a waiting room and storage for the business. A sealed car park is also added to the property. Significant physical modifications are made to these areas, including the removal and alteration of walls, and the addition of lighting, hygiene facilities and security to meet industry standards. The existing lounge room is used as the patients' waiting room. An existing bedroom is used for storage. No physical modifications are made to the lounge room or bedroom.

The modifications result in the part of the premises consisting of the office, consulting room, operating theatre and car park no longer being residential premises to be used predominantly for residential accommodation. Objectively, part of the premises is still designed predominantly for residential accommodation, comprising bedrooms (including the bedroom used for storage), bathroom, kitchen, living room, lounge room and gardens .

If Shannon later sells or leases the premises, she will need to apportion the value of the supply between the taxable and input taxed parts of the supply

Whether or not a particular room or part of residential premises is to be used predominantly for residential accommodation, as opposed to commercial purposes, is a question of fact and degree. A home office in a house will not generally be sufficiently separate from the rest of the residential premises to distinguish its use and its predominant use will still be residential accommodation. GSTR 2012/5 states:

> *'Residential premises' are not limited to premises suited to extended or permanent occupation. Residential premises provide 'living accommodation', which does not require any degree of permanence. It includes lodging, sleeping or overnight accommodation.*
>
> *To satisfy the definition of residential premises, premises must provide shelter and basic living facilities. Premises that do not have the physical characteristics to provide these are not residential premises to be used predominantly for residential accommodation.*

NOTE: A display home leased to a builder is an input taxed supply. A display home comprises a house that has all the usual physical characteristics that enable it to be used for residential accommodation.

If a property is a retail outlet with a residence on top of the store, only the rent for the store is taxable as the supply of residential premises is input taxed only to the extent that the premises are used predominantly for residential accommodation. The supplier in this case will need to apportion its entitlement to input tax credits which will only apply to the proportion relating to the commercial rents. GSTR 2006/4 assists with determining the extent of creditable purpose for claiming input tax credits.

In *Commissioner of Taxation v Gloxinia Investments Ltd atf Gloxinia Unit Trust* [2010] FCAFC 46, the Full Federal Court confirmed that the assignment of a lease of a unit in a proposed residential development is an input taxed supply.

In January 2011, the Government released a discussion paper in relation to proposed amendments to restore the intended policy outcome for the GST treatment of residential premises. The inherent policy approach is that sales or long-term leases of new residential premises by a registered entity are taxable supplies and that sales or long-term leases of residential premises (other than new residential premises) are input taxed supplies. See also 24.342. The decision of the Full

Federal Court in the *Gloxinia* case has been overcome by amending legislation. Reference may be made to the Commissioner's decision impact statement on the decision in the *Gloxinia* case. Taxpayer Alert TA 2009/5 indicates that the Tax Office is examining arrangements where an entity engages an associate to construct (or arrange for the construction of) residential premises which are to be leased by the entity in order for the entity to claim input tax credits for the costs of construction while deferring the corresponding GST payable (sometimes indefinitely). This deferral is possible because the associate does not request payments from the entity until the premises are sold. Subsequent to the release of the Taxpayer Alert, the Tax Office issued GSTR 2010/1 which outlines the possible tax consequences that may arise from arrangements covered by TA 2009/5:

- where the only activity of the associate is constructing, or arranging the construction of, the residential premises for the entity – the associate is deemed to not be carrying on an enterprise and is not entitled to any input tax credits
- where the associate is carrying on an enterprise separate from the construction of the residential premises – the associate may not be entitled to input tax credits for the acquisitions made in respect from the construction, or the arrangement of the construction, of the residential premises
- where the entity makes a payment or act that involves the associate – this may be deemed to be consideration for the supply of the construction services and the entity's GST liability may be attributable to the tax period when the deemed consideration is received rather than when the residential premises are sold
- where there is no payment or act by the entity that involves the associate prior to the sale of the residential premises – the supply of the construction services may be treated as a taxable supply and the GST is attributable to the associate in the tax period in which the supply first becomes a supply that is connected with Australia, or
- the anti-avoidance provisions in Division 165 may apply.

For the Commissioner's views on the issues raised by TA 2009/5, see GSTR 2010/1.

LEASING OF COMMERCIAL RESIDENTIAL PREMISES

Supplies of accommodation in commercial residential premises (eg. hotels, motels, etc.) on the other hand are subject to GST as they do not have the same character as residential premises. Generally, GST is calculated under the basic rules at 1/11th of the price of the supply (unless it is a long term accommodation – see below).

'Commercial residential premises' is defined in s195-1 as:

a) *a hotel, motel, inn, hostel or boarding house, or*
b) *premises used to provide accommodation in connection with a school, or*
c) *a ship that is mainly let out on hire in the ordinary course of a business of letting ships out on hire, or*
d) *a ship that is mainly used for entertainment or transport in the ordinary course of a business of providing ships for entertainment or transport, or*
e) *a marina at which one or more of the berths are occupied, or are to be occupied, by ships used as residences, or*
f) *a caravan park or a camping ground, or*
g) *anything similar to residential premises described in paragraphs (a) to (e).*

GSTR 2012/6 considers how the GST Act applies to commercial residential premises. The ruling lists the following characteristics of commercial residential premises:

- a commercial intention
- accommodation is the main purpose
- multiple occupancy
- occupants have status as guests
- holding out to the public
- central management
- provision of or arrangement for services, and
- management offers accommodation in its own right (rather than as an agent).

LONG TERM ACCOMMODATION

If however the commercial residential premises is supplied as long term accommodation to an individual for a continuous period of 28 days or more, you have a choice of:

- applying the special rules which reduce the value upon which the GST is payable under Division 87, or
- treating it as an input taxed supply under s40-35.

If the supplier chooses to apply the special rules under Division 87, its GST liability for the long term accommodation is calculated as follows:

- if the premises are 'predominantly for long term accommodation', the value of the supply of accommodation for 28 days or longer is reduced to 50% of the price of the total stay, and
- if the commercial residential premises are not 'predominantly provided for long term accommodation', the 50% reduction only applies from the 28th and each additional day thereafter.

Commercial residential premises are 'predominantly for long-term accommodation' if at least 70% of the individuals who are provided with commercial accommodation in the premises are provided with long term accommodation (s87-20).

Long term accommodation in commercial residential premises are discussed in GSTR 2012/7.

In *Meridien Marinas Horizon Shores Pty Ltd v FC of T* [2009] FCA 1594, the Federal Court ruled that a supply of marina berths was not eligible for the 50% reduction.

Premises predominantly for long-term accommodation
Riverside Caravan Park provides predominantly long-term accommodation to its guests. The usual rate per caravan is $44 per night inclusive of GST.

Jonathan and his wife stayed in the caravan park for one night. As the stay is classified as a short-term accommodation, GST is calculated using the normal method of 1/11th of the price. Therefore, Jonathan needs to pay $44, of which the GST component is $4 being 1/11th of this amount.

Annie on the other hand lives in a caravan for long term. The caravan park operator has elected for Division 87 to apply in calculating the GST liability on long-term accommodation. Therefore, the value of the supply to Annie per night is 50% of the price = 50% x $44 = $22. GST is calculated 10% on the value of the supply, being $22 x 10% = $2.20. Therefore, the actual price charged per night should be the GST-exclusive rate plus GST calculated using the concessional method under Division 87 which is $40 + $2.20 = $42.20.

A simple method to calculate the GST amount is to multiply the GST-exclusive rate by 5.5%. For example, $40 x 5.5% gives GST of $2.20.

Premises not predominantly for long-term accommodation
Sunrise Hotel in Sunshine Coast Queensland usually provides short-term accommodation to its guests. The usual rate per room is $220 per night inclusive of GST. Elsie who was on a long vacation stayed in Sunrise Hotel for 60 days. For the first 27 days of her stay, Elsie is charged the normal rate of $220 per night (inclusive of $20 GST). From the 28th day onwards, the GST of 10% is calculated on 50% of the price = $220 x 50% x 10% = $11. Therefore, the actual price charged from the 28th day onwards is $200 + $11 = $211 per night.

If you choose not to apply the concession in Division 87, the supply of long term stays is input taxed. In this case, if you also provide short term accommodations, you will need to apportion input tax credits for overhead costs between short term accommodation that is a taxable supply and long term accommodation that is input taxed.

LEASING OF COMMERCIAL PROPERTY

Leasing of commercial properties such as factories and offices are neither GST-free nor input taxed and will be subject to GST if all requirements in s9-5 are met.

An entity leasing commercial property can be registered for GST. However, registration for GST is not compulsory unless GST turnover of the entity exceeds the registration turnover threshold. Therefore, for an entity below this threshold, it can choose not to be registered for GST and therefore will not need to charge

GST on rent and will not be entitled to any input tax credits on acquisitions. In this case, the input tax credit component can be claimed as a deduction for income tax purposes.

OUTGOINGS PAYABLE BY A TENANT UNDER A COMMERCIAL LEASE

There is a GST Determination (GSTD 2000/10) on the treatment of outgoings under a commercial property lease. Where the tenant is liable to meet an outgoing, meeting that outgoing is not part of the consideration for the supply of the premises. Where the tenant meets outgoings for which the landlord is liable, the payment of the outgoing is part of the consideration for the premises.

Obligations imposed under a lease for the tenant to reimburse the landlord are all treated as part of the consideration payable under the lease if the payment is for a service that would normally be expected to form part of the supply of the premises. For example, if the landlord incurs local rates, land tax or water charges which are not taxable supplies because of Division 81 or are GST-free because of Subdivision 38-I, the landlord needs to include GST on such outgoings when seeking reimbursement by the tenant, as the reimbursement forms part of the consideration relating to the taxable supply of the commercial lease.

Other obligations imposed under the lease for the tenant to reimburse the landlord, or to pay costs for which the landlord is liable, will also form part of the consideration for the supply of the premises (eg. insurance, promotional levies, and reimbursement of the landlord's costs of repairs and maintenance).

Bart leases commercial premises to Philip. The consideration under the lease agreement consists of $1,000 rent plus reimbursement of Bart's outgoings on the premises including council rates, water rates and cleaning and maintenance. Bart pays council rates of $200, water rates of $400 and cleaning and maintenance expenses of $330.

Rates are a tax, fee or charge specified in the Division 81 determination and therefore do not constitute a taxable supply by the local authority. The water rates represent a supply of water to Bart and are GST-free under Subdivision 38-I even though the water usage is metered to Philip, as it is incidental to and cannot be separated from the supply of the premises.

Cleaning and maintenance fee of $330 is subject to GST of $30. Bart is entitled to claim input tax credits on this expense as it is in relation to making a taxable supply of a commercial rent.

Bart will need to provide a tax invoice to Philip for $2,090 which consists of:

Base rent	*$1,000*	
*Cleaning and maintenance (net of input tax credit)**	*$300*	
Council rates	*$200*	
Water rates	*$400*	*$1,900*
plus GST		*$190*
Total		*$2,090*

*In calculating consideration for the commercial rent, the reimbursement of outgoings should exclude input tax credit claimable otherwise it will result in a windfall gain for the landlord.

Bart will then need to remit GST of $190 to the Tax Office relating to the supply of commercial rent. He is also entitled to claim GST of $30 for repair expenses. There is no entitlement to any input tax credits on the council and water rates as they were not subject to GST when supplied to Bart.

WHAT IF TENANT PAYS OUTGOINGS DIRECTLY TO THE LANDLORD'S SUPPLIER?

The GST treatment of reimbursements for non-taxable supplies or GST-free supplies does not change even if the tenant makes a payment directly to the entity levying the tax, fee or charge as the Commissioner still considers the payment to be consideration relating to the supply of the commercial property.

Tenant pays the rates directly to the local authority on behalf of the landlord. The landlord is liable for 1/11th of rates paid directly by the tenant to the local authority because it is part of the supply to the tenant so GST must be charged on the supply in order to recover the GST payable. The payment of the rates by the tenant is treated no differently to the consideration payable under the lease.

24.342   BUYING AND SELLING PREMISES (Division 40-C)

Whether a sale of property is subject to GST will be dependent on a number of factors. The sale of real property must be made in the course or furtherance of an enterprise before it is brought into the GST system.

 Fred, a sole trader in business as a butcher and who is registered for GST, decides to sell a block of land he has held for many years for personal purposes. He would not be liable for GST on this transaction as the sale was not made in the course or furtherance of his butcher enterprise. If however Fred sold the premise that was used for his butcher business, the disposal is a disposal of a capital asset that is connected to his enterprise. As he is registered for GST and the property is a commercial property, the sale will be subject to GST. It may not be in the ordinary course of Fred's butchery business to sell the property. But it is still considered to be in the course or furtherance of his enterprise to dispose of a capital asset.

An entity's GST registration status will also determine whether a sale of real property is subject to GST. An entity not registered and not required to be registered for GST will not be required to charge GST on the sale of the property.

 It should be noted that a single activity of developing and selling a property could be sufficient to require a person to be registered as they may be considered to be carrying on an enterprise for GST purposes (an adventure in the nature of trade). Mere realisation of assets will not however be considered an enterprise. The Tax Office will generally take a narrow view of what amounts to a mere realisation. See MT 2006/1 for guidance and examples of what may and may not constitute an enterprise in respect of buying and selling real property. The Ruling considers a number of examples of property development.

If the entity that owns real property derived rental income from such property but was not required to register for GST as it was under the registration threshold, it is not required to register for GST when it sells the property on the basis that it is a sale of a capital asset (ie. the property was never acquired to re-sell at a profit). Capital assets are excluded from the calculation of projected GST turnover for GST registration purposes (see 24.211).

NOTE: The Commissioner has ruled (in GSTD 2014/3) that payments made to a purchaser of real property by the vendor when the rent received falls below the rental yield guaranteed by the vendor of the real property for a specified period, give rise to an adjustment event for the purposes of Division 19 when certain conditions are met, including that the payments are made pursuant to a bilateral agreement between the vendor and the purchaser of the real property and that the purchaser allows the vendor to act as its letting agent.

SALE OF A RESIDENTIAL PROPERTY (S40-65)

The sale of residential premises is an input taxed supply to the extent that the property is residential premises to be used predominantly for residential accommodation. However, the sale of 'new residential premises' (other than those used for residential accommodation before 2 December 1998) and the sale of 'commercial residential premises' are taxable supplies if all the other conditions required for there to be a taxable supply (s9-5) are met. See below for an explanation of new residential premises and commercial residential premises.

No GST is payable on the sale of input taxed residential premises and there will be no input tax credit entitlement for the seller arising from acquisitions relating to making such sale. The purchaser of the residential property will also not be entitled to any input tax credits as there is no GST component charged on the sale. According to GSTD 2012/1, the Commissioner is of the view that following a sale of residential premises that are subject to a lease, there is a continued supply of the premises by way of lease which remains an input taxed supply. This view has been confirmed by the decision of the High Court in *FC of T v MBI Properties Pty Ltd* [2014] HCA 49.

The sale of residential premises is only input taxed to the extent that the premises are to be used predominantly for residential accommodation. Land alone, although zoned as residential is not capable of being residential premises and will be a taxable supply if sold by a registered entity. Pursuant to s195-1, the definition of 'residential premises' is as follows:

Residential premises means land or a building that:

(a) *is occupied as a residence or for residential accommodation, or*

(b) *is intended to be occupied, and is capable of being occupied, as a residence or for residential accommodation (regardless of the term of the occupation or intended occupation)*

and includes a floating home.

By virtue of the definition, the following are input taxed supplies:

- short-term letting of strata titled units such as serviced apartments by owners to guests
- leasing of strata titled units to hotel operators or similar operators, and
- leasing of display homes and provision of certain short-term employee accommodation.

However, a distinction needs to be made between residential premises and commercial residential premises. Supply of accommodation provided to individuals in commercial residential premises by an entity that owns or controls the premises remains subject to GST. For example, a sale of one or several units in a hotel complex will not constitute a supply of commercial residential premises. This is because the sale of a single unit or several units in, for example, a hotel or motel is not a supply of a hotel or motel. A supply comprising only the accommodation units in a hotel complex, without other parts of the hotel, such as the reception, is also not a supply of commercial residential premises but instead a supply of residential premises.

On the other hand, a sale or lease of the whole of a hotel complex will be a supply of commercial residential premises, whether or not the hotel complex is strata titled.

Whether a sale or lease of anything less than the whole of a hotel complex (eg. not all of the rooms within the complex or not all of the hotel infrastructure such as lobby, kitchen or pool areas) would constitute a supply of commercial residential premises, will depend on the facts of each case.

SUBJECTIVE V OBJECTIVE TEST

In *Sunchen Pty Ltd (as Trustee of the Sunchen Family Trust) v FC of T* [2008] AATA 838 the Tribunal considered whether the property in that case was residential premises 'to be used predominantly for residential accommodation (regardless of the term of occupation)'. The taxpayer purchased a residential property and claimed an input tax credit on the acquisition on the basis that it was intending to develop it for sale. At the time of acquisition the property was subject to a continuing tenancy agreement and was also the subject of an approval for a development of a five storey residential flat building with strata subdivision. By the time of hearing (about two years after the acquisition), the property was still leased to residential tenants and the taxpayer had done very little to obtain finance, construction certificates or anything towards his intention of developing the land.

The taxpayer argued its case based on the decision in *Toyama Pty Ltd v Landmark Building Developments Pty Ltd* [2006] ATC 4160, that is the test must be considered subjectively. It was only necessary to have regards to events at the date of completion of the sale and not events that occurred after that.

The Tribunal however held otherwise and agreed with the Commissioner that what occurred afterwards was relevant in so far as it threw light on the situation at completion (that is, based on the authority of *Marana Holdings Pty Ltd v Commissioner of Taxation* [2004] FCAFC 307 that the test must be considered objectively).

The decision of the Tribunal was upheld by the Full Federal Court in *Sunchen Pty Ltd v FC of T & Anor* [2010] FCAFC 138. The Full Federal Court held that the definition of 'residential premises' looks to an existing state of fact. The second limb of the definition (is intended to be occupied, and is capable of being occupied), notwithstanding the phrase 'intended to be occupied', is looking to the characteristics or nature of the property, rather than the intention of any person. The Tax Office has released a Decision Impact Statement in relation to the case.

RESIDENTIAL PREMISES – CHATTELS

The GST treatment of chattels included in the sale of residential premises can vary depending on whether chattels are included in the sale of residential premises and the vendor has used those chattels solely in connection with its input taxed supply of the residential premises. If this is the case the chattels will form part of the supply of the input taxed residential premises.

If however, the enterprise consists of renovating and selling old houses, the supply of chattels will be a separate taxable supply from the input taxed supply of residential premises. The supply of chattels is not integral, ancillary or incidental to the supply of residential premises and therefore the vendor is making a mixed supply. The vendor will need to apportion consideration as GST is payable on the taxable supply of the chattels.

NEW RESIDENTIAL PREMISES

If the residential premises are new, the sale will not be input taxed. The definition of 'new residential premises' therefore becomes all-important.

Residential premises are new residential premises, as defined in s40-75(1), if they:

(a) have not previously been sold as residential premises (other than commercial residential premises) and have not previously been the subject of a long-term lease, or

(b) have been created through substantial renovations of a building, or

(c) have been built, or contain a building that has been built, to replace demolished premises on the same land.

These categories are not mutually exclusive. Provided residential premises satisfy any one of the categories, they are new residential premises.

Residential premises will not be sold as new residential premises if they have been previously sold as residential premises (other than commercial residential premises) and have not previously been the subject of a long-term lease, unless they have been substantially renovated or built to replace demolished premises (see below).

NOTE: '... (other than commercial residential premises)' was inserted into the GST Act as a result of the Marana decision – see above. The amendment was made to ensure that residential premises, even if previously sold as commercial residential premises, when first sold as residential premises would still be a taxable supply pursuant to s40-75(1)(a).

For supplies of residential premises on or after 21 March 2012, premises that become new residential premises because of substantial renovations or because they have been built to replace demolished premises cease to be new residential premises once they are sold or supplied by way of long-term lease.

In relation to supplies of residential premises on or after 27 January 2011, the following apply:

- the subdivision of existing residential premises that are not new residential premises does not result in the subdivided premises becoming new residential premises

- the 'wholesale supply' of residential premises under certain arrangements is disregarded in determining whether the subsequent supply of the premises is a supply of new residential premises. The earlier 'wholesale supply' is also a supply of new residential premises which will be a taxable supply if made by a GST registered entity, and

- the strata titling and grant of a strata-lot lease over newly constructed residential premises does not of itself cause these premises to cease to be new residential premises and not subject to GST when sold to home buyers and investors.

Subsection 40-75(2) provides that premises are not new residential premises if for five years after they have become new residential premises, the premises have been solely used to make input taxed supplies under s40-35(1)(a) (ie. supply of residential premises by way of lease). GSTR 2003/3 considers the five years must be a continuous period and this period will not be broken by short periods of vacancies between tenancies where the property is actively marketed for rent. However, this continuous period of five years does not include when premises were used for private purposes or left vacant with no attempt to lease it.

NOTE: According to GSTR 2009/4 new residential premises that are held for sale but are subsequently rented (dual concurrent purpose) will not meet the five year rule because the property will not have been used solely to make input taxed supply under s40-35(1)(a). See 24.263.

NOTE: The supply of new residential premises supplied for the first time since they were built is not treated as a taxable supply where the supply is made within a GST group or between certain members of a GST joint venture (s40-75(2A)).

NOTE: If residential premises are new residential premises because they have been substantially renovated or built to replace demolished premises on the same land, the new residential premises include land of which the new residential premises are a part (s40-75(3)).

Effective 27 January 2011, sales by developers of residential premises constructed under certain arrangements (development lease arrangements) will be taxable supplies of new residential premises. This will be the case even though, under the terms of the arrangement, there may have been an earlier 'wholesale supply' of the newly built premises to the developer (s40-75(2B)). Transitional arrangements apply.

CHANGES IN THE SIZE OF THE LAND

Where land that contains a residential building changes in size, to determine whether there are new residential premises, it is necessary to consider whether the land and residential building together have previously been sold as residential premises, or been the subject of a long-term lease.

Subdivision of land will not create new residential premises in respect of the land itself.

In deciding whether land and buildings have previously been sold as residential premises or been the subject of a long-term lease, it is necessary to consider the land and building together (GSTR 2003/3).

Where land with a residential building has previously been sold as residential premises, or been the subject of a long-term lease, and the area of land is reduced in size, the subsequent sale of that land with the residential premises is not a sale of new residential premises. The reduced land area and building, as a 'package', have previously been sold as residential premises, or been the subject of a long-term lease and are not therefore 'new residential premises' as defined. The supply of the vacant land may however be a taxable supply in its own right (GSTR 2003/3).

Fred, a property developer, is registered for GST. He purchases residential premises on a large block of land and subdivides the land into two blocks. The land at the time of purchase was on a single title. One block of land contains the existing residential premises and Fred erects a house on the vacant block of land. Both residential premises are sold.

The first block of land, now reduced in size (ie. the block containing original house), is not new residential premises as that house and land together have previously been sold as residential premises.

The second block of land containing the newly built house is new residential premises as the block of land and new house have not previously been sold. The supply of the block with the newly built house is a taxable supply when sold in the course of Fred's enterprise. Fred is entitled to claim input tax credits on acquisitions relating to new residential premises, but not those relating to the previously existing premises.

Where the area of land with a residential building has previously been sold as residential premises, or been the subject of a long-term lease, and is subsequently increased, there is a different residential premises 'package'. The residential premises 'package' after the increase in land comprise of two parts. One part of the package is the land and residential building that has previously been sold as residential premises or been the subject of a long-term lease. This part is not new residential premises and therefore would be input taxed. The other part of the package is the additional land area that had not previously been sold or been the subject of a long-term lease as part of the earlier residential premises 'package'. This part is excluded from the input taxed treatment and its sale may be a taxable supply. When the whole property inclusive of the new land is subsequently sold together for a single price, an apportionment of the consideration between the building and previous land area, and the new land, may be required (GSTR 2003/3).

NOTE: The Tax Office provides guidance on acceptable methods of apportionment in GSTR 2001/8.

NEW RESIDENTIAL PREMISES WHERE BUILDING RELOCATED

A residential building may be relocated on the same land on which it was purchased together as a 'package', but it would still not be considered new residential premises because the 'package' (land and building) have previously been sold as residential premises (GSTR 2003/3).

NOTE: It may also be necessary to consider whether the supply of the now vacant land after the removal of the building is a taxable supply in its own right. The vacant land is not residential premises.

A house is located in the centre of 1600 sq m of land. The house and land have previously been sold together. The house is moved so that it is wholly located within one half of the allotment to enable the land to be subdivided into two 800 sq m blocks. The house and the 800 sq m of land on which it now sits have previously been sold as residential premises and therefore are not new residential premises. The subdivided land however is not residential premises and therefore may be subject to GST on disposal (provided the subdivision activity is part of carrying on an enterprise).

Where a residential building is relocated from one block of land to a different vacant block, the building and new block of land become new residential premises. The land and building, as a 'package', have not previously been sold together, or been the subject of a long-term lease (GSTR 2003/3).

 Additional residential buildings built on land with existing residential premises

Sandra lives in the family home located on 40 acres of land adjacent to a National Park. These premises have not been substantially renovated since Sandra bought the house from her parents in 1990.

Sandra decides to sell the whole property, and to maximise her return, she builds one residential chalet on the property. She has registered for GST and has claimed input tax credits relating to construction costs. She sells the property as a whole. Prior to the construction of the chalet Sandra's property is residential premises. It is land and a building occupied as a residence.

When Sandra later builds one chalet, additional residential premises are created. Land previously part of the original residential premises is now used in conjunction with the chalet, and forms part of the additional residential premises. When the additional residential premises are supplied by Sandra (as part of her overall sale) they will not previously have been sold as residential premises and will therefore be new residential premises.

Sandra makes a supply that comprises a taxable part and an input taxed part. The taxable part is the supply of the residential chalet and its surrounding land. The input taxed part is the supply of her home and the remainder of the land, being residential premises.

Any reasonable method of apportionment in relation to the taxable and non-taxable parts of Sandra's supply will be appropriate. For various acceptable methods of apportionment see GSTR 2001/8.

RESIDENTIAL PREMISES PREVIOUSLY SOLD AS COMMERCIAL RESIDENTIAL PREMISES/COMMERCIAL PROPERTY

Premises previously sold as 'commercial residential premises' or 'commercial property' are not considered to have been sold as residential premises and therefore may still be sold as 'new residential premises' and be treated as a taxable supply.

 Commercial residential premises not previously sold as residential premises

Jackie purchased a motel, then strata titled it and sold each unit separately. There was no need for any substantial renovation. The units are considered to be 'new residential premises' as it was previously sold as 'commercial residential premises' and not as 'residential premises'. Strata titling itself does not create 'new residential premises' – see below.

 Residential premises not previously sold as residential premises

Evan, a builder who is registered for GST, acquires a 1940s style commercial warehouse in August 2010. Evan substantially renovates the building and converts the building into a residence that he sells in February 2015.

The land and building are new residential premises as they have not previously been sold as residential premises nor previously been the subject of a long-term lease. In addition, the residential premises which have been created by substantial renovations of the building are new residential premises.

The new residential premises have not been used only for making input taxed supplies (ie. residential rental) for at least 5 years since the premises first became residential premises. The supply of the residential premises is a taxable supply when the premises are sold by Evan in the course of his enterprise.

SUBDIVISION OF APARTMENTS INTO STRATA TITLE UNITS

The process of strata titling an apartment block does not, by itself, create new residential premises under s40-75(1)(a). When the newly strata titled units are subsequently sold, the supplies of those units are not sales of new residential premises, if the land and the building together have previously been sold as residential premises, or been the subject of a long-term lease. Physically, the combination of land and the building as residential premises remains basically the same. It is only the nature of the legal interest which has changed. If the process of strata titling is accompanied by works on the building, it is then a question of whether the works constitute substantial renovations.

Peter sells the block of flats on one title to a developer who, as part of his enterprise, strata titles and sells the individual units. The sale of each unit is not a sale of new residential premises for the purpose of s40-75(1)(a), as the residential premises have previously been sold.

An exception would be where those residential premises become new residential premises again, for example because the developer substantially renovates the premises (see below), and the five year rule does not apply. This is because the premises have not been rented continuously for five years since completion of the substantial renovations.

Effective 27 January 2011, the law was amended to clarify that the subdivision or strata-titling of new residential premises, on its own, does not mean that the premises are no longer new residential premises. Similarly the subdivision or strata-titling of existing residential premises, on its own, does not cause the premises to become new residential premises (s40-75(2AA)).

COMPANY TITLE CONVERTED TO STRATA TITLE

Under company title, a company owns the building, and the company's shares are divided into a number of blocks or classes, each block or class entitling the owner of the shares to exclusive occupation of a particular part of the building. This right of exclusive occupation is not a proprietary interest in the freehold, but is rather a contractual right against the company or sometimes a right to be granted a lease. Under company title, the company holds the title to the building. The company may be the first owner having built the building (that is, it has never been sold) or it may have purchased the building (in which case it has previously been sold).

The company issues shares that contain certain rights. The rights attached to the shares include an entitlement to occupy a unit in the building owned by the company. Following conversion of the title, in some cases, the newly created strata titled units will be transferred to the existing shareholders for nominal consideration or in exchange for shares in the company.

Where the company is the first owner of the building, the supply of the residential units by the company to the individual shareholders is a supply of new residential premises under s40-75(1)(a) as they have not previously been sold. It is only shares in the company that have previously been sold. The supply of the units may be a taxable supply by the company. However, where the residential units have been used for residential accommodation before 2 December 1998 (s40-65(2)(b)), the transfer of the newly strata titled units by the company to the shareholders is not a taxable supply, provided ss40-75(1)(b) or (c) do not apply.

Where the shareholder returns the shares to the company in exchange for the unit, the supply of the shares is a financial supply and may be an input taxed supply under Subdivision 40-A. Any subsequent sale of a unit by the new owner will not be a sale of new residential premises under s40-75(1)(a).

TENANTS IN COMMON

Residential premises, for example a block of units, may be developed by two or more owners as tenants in common and converted to strata title. The strata titling does not, by itself, involve a transfer of any interest. All that results is that the residential premises are held under a different title by the same owners.

The newly created strata titled units may then be transferred between the individual participants so that each becomes the sole owner of specified units. For example, A and B are tenants in common in equal shares of land and enter into a joint venture to construct 6 units. A transfers his interest in three units to B and B transfers his interest in three units to A. In this case, the transfer of each participant's interest as tenant in common to the other is not a sale of residential premises. Given the definition of 'residential premises' in s195-1, the interest sold is not occupied or capable of being occupied as a residence. What is sold is merely part of the interests in the whole of the units. Therefore, it is necessary to consider the application of s9-5 to determine if the supply of the interest is a taxable supply. This consequence may be different if A and B were a partnership for the purposes of the GST Act and the units were assets of the partnership. In this case there may be a sale of residential premises by the partnership to each partner.

However, where the newly strata titled individual units are subsequently sold by the individual participants together, in this case there will be a sale of new residential premises.

NOTE: GSTR 2009/2 considers whether the partitioning of land is a taxable supply.

NEW RESIDENTIAL PREMISES CREATED THROUGH SUBSTANTIAL RENOVATIONS

New residential premises may be created through substantial renovations of a building (s40-75(1)(a)). Where, however, the substantial renovations occurred before 2 December 1998 and the premises have been used for residential accommodation before that date, sale of the premises is not a taxable supply. It is an input taxed supply.

The term substantial renovations is defined in s195-1 as follows:

> ... 'substantial renovations' of a building are renovations in which all, or substantially all, of a building is removed or is replaced. However, the renovations need not involve removal or replacement of foundations, external walls, interior supporting walls, floors, roof or staircases.

This definition requires consideration of the cumulative work that has been done to the building since it was acquired by the current owner. A building comprises a number of components, which can be termed either structural (ie. the foundations, external walls, interior supporting walls, floors, roof, etc.) or non-structural (including fixtures, fittings, plumbing, mechanical, fire systems, electrical, lifts, air conditioning, etc). Whether renovations are substantial is to be determined in the light of all the facts and circumstances.

According to GSTR 2003/3, for substantial renovations to occur for the purposes of the GST Act, the renovations need to satisfy the following criteria before it is necessary to make further inquiry to establish whether the renovations are substantial:

- the renovations need to affect the building as a whole, and
- the renovations need to result in the removal or replacement of all or substantially all of the building.

Where one of the above criteria is not satisfied substantial renovations have not occurred and no further inquiry needs to be made.

SUBSTANTIAL RENOVATIONS NEED TO AFFECT THE BUILDING AS A WHOLE

Whether substantial renovations have occurred should be based on consideration of the building in its entirety, that is the building as a whole, and not by reference to specific or individual rooms in the building. For renovations to be substantial they must directly affect most rooms in a building (GSTR 2003/3). The renovation of only one part of a building, without any work on the remaining parts of the building, would not constitute substantial renovations.

The owner of a large four bedroom house removes the wall between two bedrooms for the purpose of creating a large bedroom with ensuite. The former door to one of the bedrooms is removed and replaced with gyprock so that the newly created larger bedroom can only be entered by one doorway. The room is repainted and recarpeted. Although significant, the work does not constitute substantial renovations as only one area is affected.

Work associated with the renovations, but not directly attributable to the building itself, for example, landscaping and beautification of surrounding land, is not renovations of a building.

Additions that are undertaken with renovations are not included in determining whether a building has been substantially renovated. However, if it is determined that a building has been substantially renovated and new residential premises created, all additions to the building form part of the new residential premises.

WHEN IS THE SALE OF REAL PROPERTY THE SALE OF NEW RESIDENTIAL PREMISES?

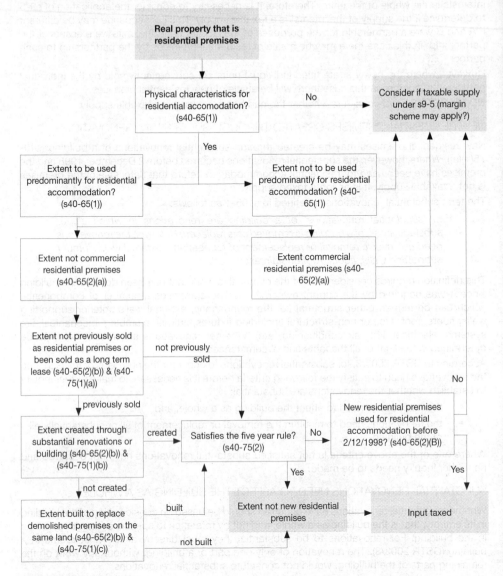

NOTE: For a further explanation of new residential premises, including the meaning of substantial renovations, see GSTR 2003/3.

REMOVAL OR REPLACEMENT OF ALL OR SUBSTANTIALLY ALL OF THE BUILDING

The extent to which parts of a building are removed or replaced will determine whether the above criterion is satisfied. The definition of substantial renovations states that it is not necessary for foundations, external walls, interior supporting walls, floors, roof or staircases to be removed or replaced for renovations to be substantial.

This criterion is satisfied where there is a removal or replacement of a substantial part of the:
- structural components of the building, or
- non-structural components of the building (GSTR 2003/3).

Structural work may give rise to substantial renovations in its own right. Structural work includes:
- altering, or replacing of, foundations

- replacing, removing or altering of floors or supporting walls, or parts thereof (interior or exterior)
- lifting or modifying of roofs, and
- replacing existing windows and doors such that it is necessary to alter brickwork (eg. replacing a single door with a double sliding door).

Structural work is also undertaken in the course of building an extension to a house or adding new bedrooms to a house. Where a substantial part of the structural components of a building is removed or replaced this will often mean that a substantial part of the non-structural components is also removed or replaced.

However, substantial renovations may also occur where a substantial part of the non-structural components is removed or replaced but the structural components are not substantially affected. For example, in a unit, it is not essential that both components are substantially removed or replaced for substantial renovations to have occurred.

Non-substantial renovations – a large part of the building not affected

Anne, a property speculator who is registered for GST, acquires a large two storey, four bedroom Victorian terrace house with a separate kitchen, lounge room, music room and bathroom on the ground floor. Anne regularly buys, renovates and sells houses (usually two a year on average). She employs a builder to undertake the following work.

The old kitchen is replaced with beech panelled cupboards, which have expensive granite benchtops, and stainless steel appliances. The kitchen walls and ceiling are repainted and new linoleum is added to replace the existing floor covering. A small bathroom that existed off the kitchen is removed and a new bathroom is constructed in one of the upstairs bedrooms. The two walls between the former bathroom and kitchen are removed so that the kitchen is much larger and can now also be used as a dining room. Anne replaces the door and back window of the kitchen with French doors that open out onto the courtyard. The removal of the bathroom and addition of the French doors have opened up the back part of the ground floor of the house and the courtyard is now more accessible. The dilapidated slate roof of the house is replaced with a new tile roof. The floorboards, joists and bearers in all of the ground floor rooms are also replaced due to water damage. The ceilings in most of the downstairs rooms are replaced due to cracking and mould damage.

Although the renovation work is significant, the renovations are not substantial renovations. The house in its entirety has not been substantially renovated, as a number of rooms have not been affected. The four bedrooms upstairs are untouched with the exception of one room which has become a bathroom. If Anne was to sell the house, she would be making an input taxed supply. However, where the changes described above are combined with further renovations such as the creation of a larger lounge room by removing a wall between the existing lounge room and music room, and the modernisation of the upstairs bedrooms by replacing the existing plaster on the walls and ceiling with gyprock, installing skylights, repainting, and replacing old carpets with parquetry and cupboards with new walk-in robes, substantial renovations have occurred.

After the renovations, Anne puts the house on the market for $480,000. If Anne sells the residence in the course of her enterprise after undertaking the extra work described she would be making a taxable supply.

New residential premises created through substantial renovations of a building – rented for over five years

Steve, a property speculator who is registered for GST, acquired a 1950s style one-bedroom fibro weekender in September 2008 with the intention of renovating, renting and eventually selling the property.

Steve extensively modifies the interior and exterior of the weekender. The fibro exterior of the house is replaced by brick, some interior walls are removed and flooring throughout the house is completely replaced by polished hardwood floors. Air conditioning is installed, the existing kitchen is removed and a new extended kitchen is installed. The existing bathroom is removed and a new bathroom including a spa bath is installed. The building is repainted both inside and outside. The work is completed in March 2009 and the weekender is rented for six years immediately following the modifications, but there are short periods between tenancies while the property is being advertised for rental. Steve sells the weekender in June 2015.

At the time of sale, Steve will have to decide whether it is a sale of 'new residential premises'.

To do this he will have to decide whether substantial renovations have occurred, and if yes, has the property been used for making input taxed supplies of residential rental for at least five years since it was substantially renovated.

The work done amounts to substantial renovations of the building. New residential premises were created through substantial renovations in March 2009. As the residential premises have been used solely to make input taxed supplies of residential rental for a continuous period of at least five years since the premises were last substantially renovated, the premises are no longer new residential premises. The sale of the residential premises is not a taxable supply. The sale of the property is an input taxed supply. Short breaks where the premises are not tenanted between tenancies are not treated as a break in the continuous period. However, substantial breaks between tenancies and using the premises for personal use is a break in continuous period.

 Even though the sale of residential premises is input taxed, costs incurred in selling the property, such as agent's commission, fees charged by solicitors and advertising will be subject to GST irrespective of whether the property is newly constructed or existing.

24.343   CALCULATING GST ON TAXABLE SUPPLY OF REAL PROPERTY

Where the sale of real property by a registered entity is a taxable supply and subject to GST, the following two methods are potentially available for calculating the GST:

     A.   Normal rules: 10% GST is added to the value, and

     B.   Margin Scheme.

NOTE: The sale of real property may be exempt from GST:

- under Subdivision 38-J 'supply of a going concern' if property is sold as part of an enterprise
- under Subdivision 38-O 'supply of a farmland' (see 23.490).

 As stamp duty is levied on the GST-inclusive value of the supply, where possible sell the property under a GST exemption to avoid stamp duty on the GST component. Stamp duty is non-refundable and forms part of the cost base.

24.344   SALE OF FREEHOLD INTEREST USING MARGIN SCHEME (Division 75)

The sale of real property by an entity which is registered, or required to be registered, becomes taxable if it is 'new residential', commercial residential or commercial property, unless it is sold under the GST-free exemption using either the going concern or farmland concessions. As an alternative to working out the GST under the normal method by applying 10% to the value of the property, the supplier and the recipient may agree for the margin scheme to apply to work out the GST payable. For the margin scheme to apply the parties must agree in writing that it apply (see further below).

ELIGIBILITY

To be eligible to apply the margin scheme for property acquired after 30 June 2000, it must be acquired:

- from an unregistered vendor, or
- from another GST registered entity who used the margin scheme, or
- under an input taxed sale.

 You cannot use the margin scheme if you acquired the interest in real property where the vendor calculated the GST under the normal method.

If a property was acquired from a fellow member of a GST group, the margin scheme will only potentially apply in relation to the property if the group member who first acquired the property from a party that is outside the GST group was eligible to apply the margin scheme. Similar measures apply to supplies between joint venture operators and joint venture participants as well as supplies that were inherited from a deceased person.

The written agreement between the supplier and the recipient that the margin scheme apply must be made on or before the making of the supply (unless the Commissioner allows a further period) (s75-5(1A)).

NOTE: Effective 1 July 2013, the law was amended such that when determining the margin for a taxable supply of an interest, unit or lease where the real property supplied has been subdivided from land or premises previously acquired by the supplier, the margin can be determined by reference to the corresponding proportion of (as applicable):

- the consideration for the acquisition or supply (depending upon the specific statutory requirements) of the interest, unit or lease
- the approved valuation of that interest, unit or lease as at the specified date, or
- the GST inclusive market value of that interest, unit or lease as at the specified day or time (s75-15).

REAL PROPERTY ACQUIRED GST-FREE

A supply of real property is ineligible for the application of the margin scheme if:

- the property was acquired GST-free under the going concern provisions (Subdivision 38-J) or the farmland provisions (Subdivision 38-O), and
- at the time of acquisition the vendor was registered for GST (or was required to be registered), and
- the vendor had acquired the entire interest, unit or lease through a taxable supply where the margin scheme was not applied (s75-5(3)(e) and (f)).

A similar provision applies to supplies made to registered associates without consideration: s75-5(3)(g).

Therefore, a supply that was ineligible for the margin scheme continues to be ineligible for the margin scheme after it is supplied as part of a GST-free supply of a going concern or GST-free supply of farmland or is supplied to a registered associate for no consideration. If, however, an eligible supply (eg. a supply that has calculated GST using the margin scheme) was subsequently supplied as part of a GST-free supply of a going concern or farmland, or a non-taxable supply to a registered associate without consideration to you, and you then re-supply it to another party, this re-supply will still be eligible for the margin scheme. Nonetheless, the margin for such re-supply is calculated by looking-through the prior GST-free or non-taxable supply in order to avoid the reduction of a GST liability as a result of resetting the margin by way of interposing these GST-free supplies or non-taxable supplies.

Hence, the margin will be the difference between the selling price and either one of the following (depending on when the entity supplying you the property was registered and when it acquired the property):

- approved valuation of the property on the date the entity you acquired the property from acquired the interest, on the date it became registered for GST or 1 July 2000
- GST-inclusive market value on 1 July 2000, at the time of acquisition or when it became registered for GST, and
- consideration paid by the entity you have acquired the property from (only applicable if the interest was acquired on or after 1 July 2000 and at the time of acquisition the entity was registered or required to be registered) (s75-1(5) and (6)).

You should obtain the vendor's acquisition cost or valuation of the property when acquiring a real property from an unrelated party under the GST-free going concern or farmland provisions. The valuation date of the property is dependent on the vendor's GST registration and when the property was acquired pursuant to s75-11(5). This information is needed to calculate the margin on which GST liability is determined when you choose to sell the property.

(Modified from Tax Law Amendment (2008 Measures No. 5) Bill 2008 – Explanatory Memorandum)

Mark is registered for GST, and held a vacant block of land before 1 July 2000. Mark sells the vacant land to Highlands Pty Ltd, a property developer (who is also registered for GST) for $165,000. Highlands Ltd. did not choose for the margin scheme to apply as it wishes to be entitled to claim input tax credits on the purchase. Therefore, GST on this supply of land was *calculated using the basic GST rule ($165,000 x 10/11). Mark will be required to remit $15,000 of GST to the Tax Office and Highlands will be entitled to claim $15,000 in input tax credits.*

Highlands Pty Ltd then begins to build two units on the block of land. Highlands Pty Ltd ran out of funds and decided to sell the partly constructed unit development together with all necessary arrangements for the construction to continue to Landrich Development Pty Ltd (which is also registered for GST) for $440,000. Highlands and Landrich agreed in writing that the supply is a supply of a going concern. Therefore, the supply is not subject to GST. Landrich is also not entitled to claim any input tax credits on the acquisition. Eventually, Landrich completed the construction and sold both the units for $660,000 to Jack, a private individual who is not registered for GST. As the supply is a supply of new residential premises it is a taxable supply and therefore subject to GST.

Under the margin scheme provisions as presently enacted the supply of the units by Landrich to Jack is ineligible for the margin scheme. This is because (s75-5(3)(e)):

- *the property was acquired by Landrich as part of a GST-free supply of a going concern, and*
- *Highlands, the entity Landrich acquired the property from was registered for GST at the time of the transaction with Landrich, and*
- *Highlands acquired the property from a former seller, Mark, as a taxable supply without applying the margin scheme.*

Therefore, the full GST will apply. Landrich will be required to remit GST being 1/11th of the price to the Tax Office (1/11th x $660,000 = $60,000). Jack is not entitled to claim any input tax credits because he is not registered for GST and has acquired the units for private purposes.

The Commissioner considers that for the sale of a freehold interest or stratum unit, the supply and the acquisition is made at settlement as this is when the purchaser (or the purchaser's agent) obtains unconditional possession of a registrable instrument of transfer or an instrument of transfer that would be registrable once stamped (GSTR 2006/7).

The following supplies are not affected by the provisions:
- supplies made using the margin scheme prior to the date of commencement, and
- supplies that were acquired as part of a going concern or farmland, or from a registered associate for no consideration, where the acquisition was prior to the date of commencement.

Supplies that were acquired as part of a going concern or farmland, or from a registered associate for no consideration, where the acquisition was on or after the date of commencement will be subject to the new rules – provided that the written agreement relating to the GST-free going concern or farmland supply, or the supply from a registered associate for no consideration specifies that the consideration has not been paid prior to the commencement date.

HOW TO CALCULATE THE 'MARGIN'

If using the margin scheme, the GST payable on real property becomes 1/11th of the margin for the supply. The 'margin' for GST purposes is the difference between the tax inclusive sale price and the original purchase price paid, or a valuation amount, as at 1 July 2000, of the property where it was held before 1 July 2000. The valuation point may not necessarily be as at 1 July 2000 if the entity was not required to be registered at that date (s75-10). The principle behind this is that GST is only to be charged on any increase in value from that date. Any improvements (ie. development or construction costs) are not taken into account to reduce the margin (s75-14). Incidental costs such as stamp duty, solicitors' costs, etc which form part of the cost of acquiring the interest in the real property are also not included as part of the cost of acquiring the property for GST margin calculation purposes (s75-14). Instead, the vendor is entitled to claim any GST credits on incidental or improvement costs as they arise in the tax period the acquisitions are attributable to.

NOTE: If the property was acquired before 1 July 2000, but you were not registered, or required to be registered at 1 July 2000, the valuation of the property is at the date you become registered (or were required to become registered).

NOTE: In the case *The Taxpayer v FCT* [2010] AATA 497, the AAT concluded that the anti-avoidance provisions under Division 165 (refer 24.430) should not apply to supplies on or after 17 March 2005.

The AAT was of the view that because of the existence of the 2005 year amendments to the margin scheme, the taxpayer was entitled to use a valuation as at 1 July 2000 to calculate the margin and therefore was merely applying a provision offered by the legislation. In the circumstances there would be no 'GST benefit' for the purposes of the anti-avoidance provisions.

The valuations do not have to be physically undertaken on the date as specified in the GST Act (see table in s75-10(3)) but should reflect the market value of the property at that date. The Tax Office allows the valuation to be made no later than the end of the tax period in which the GST payable is attributable, ie. when a supplier must account for the GST on the supply in their BAS.

In *Brady King Pty Ltd v FCT* (No 2) [2008] FCA 1918, the Court was required to consider whether the valuation obtained by the taxpayer complied with the requirement of s75-10(3) of the GST Act. According to s75-35, a valuation made in accordance with the requirements determined by the Commissioner in writing by legislative instrument is an approved valuation. The legislative instrument laying out the requirements for making valuations under the margin scheme are in the form of a series of Margin Scheme Valuation Requirements Determinations (MSVs).

The taxpayer, Brady King, adopted method 1 in MSV 2000/2 which deals with valuations for partly completed buildings. Specifically, method 1 of MSV 2000/2 is the valuation of partly completed buildings as determined by a professional valuer. The Court in reaching its decision held that the method applied by the taxpayer was in fact the appropriate method. However, in reaching the final valuation, the professional valuer had deviated from the method of valuation dictated by the terms of the Determination. Therefore, the Court found that the valuation method applied by the taxpayer did not comply with the requirements of s75-10(3) and held the valuation to be invalid.

 If using the margin scheme, do not take development costs into account when calculating the margin as this will grossly understate GST liability resulting in penalties and interest.

 Fred, a property developer who is registered for GST, purchases a block of land with an old house on it from an unregistered vendor on 10 September 2006 for $150,000. Fred spends a further $220,000 (GST inclusive) developing the block by demolishing the existing building and constructing a new house which he then sells for $450,000 (GST inclusive). For GST margin scheme calculation purposes, the margin is $300,000 (ie. $450,000 – $150,000). Fred is entitled to claim input tax credit of $20,000 (1/11th of $220,000) on the development cost in the tax period the cost is attributable to.

The margin is not $100,000 (ie. $450,000 – $150,000 (cost of land) – $200,000 (GST exclusive cost of developing the land)).

Fred's GST liability on the sale of the property using the margin scheme is one eleventh of the margin = 1/11 x $300,000 = $27,272.72. The builder's gross profit on the sale:

Cost of land	*$150,000.00*
Development costs	*$220,000.00*
Less input tax credits on development costs	*($20,000.00)*
Total cost	*$350,000.00*
Net proceeds after remitting GST component to the Tax Office ($450,000 – $27,272.72)	*$422,727.28*
Gross profit: *Net proceeds less total cost (net of GST)*	***$72,727.28***

NOTE: The developer would have had to sell the property for $465,000.50 under the normal method to achieve the same gross profit result had he not calculated the GST under the margin scheme. This highlights the benefit of using the margin scheme as the developer has been able to sell the property at a lower price, which is more attractive to potential purchasers. Further, there would also be stamp duty benefits as the stamp duty is calculated on the GST-inclusive value of the supply. A supply applying the margin scheme will have a lower GST-inclusive amount as compared to the supply applying the normal rule.

 GSTR 2006/7 sets out how to apply the margin scheme to the supply of property made on or after 1 December 2005 for supplies acquired prior to 1 July 2000. GSTR 2000/21 sets out how to apply the margin scheme to the supply of property made prior to 1 December 2005 for supplies acquired prior to 1 July 2000. GSTR 2006/8 sets out how to apply the margin scheme for supplies of real property acquired on or after 1 July 2000.

In MSV 2009/1, the Tax Office outlines its valuation requirements for calculating the margin for taxable supplies of real property made on or after 1 March 2010. The four acceptable valuations discussed are:

- the market value as determined by a professional valuer
- a valuation based on the consideration received by the supplier under the contract of sale
- the most recent value determined by the State or Territory Government department before the valuation date for rating or land tax purposes, and
- the Commissioner's valuation in certain circumstances.

MSV 2005/3 provides that the valuation must be made by the due date for lodgment of the supplier's Activity Statement for the tax period to which the GST on the supply is attributable. However, if the Commissioner has allowed a further period under s75-5(1A)(b) for the supplier and recipient to agree in writing that the margin scheme is to apply in working out the GST on the supply, the valuation must be made by the later of:

- eight weeks from the further period that the Commissioner has allowed under s75-5(1A)(b), or
- eight weeks from the date of the Commissioner's decision to extend the further period under s75-5(1A)(b).

In relation to taxable supplies of real property made before 1 March 2010, refer to previously issued determinations as follows:

- taxable supplies of real property made on or after 1 December 2005 and before 1 March 2010 – MSV 2005/3
- taxable supplies of real property made after 1 July 2005 under contracts entered into before 1 July 2005 – MSV 2005/2, and
- taxable supplies of real property made before 1 December 2005 – MSV 2005/1.

IMPACT OF MARGIN SCHEME ON PURCHASER

There is no entitlement to an input tax credit for the purchaser of real property where GST has been calculated using the margin scheme (s75-20). However, the purchasing entity can choose to apply the margin scheme when making a subsequent taxable supply of the property.

NOTE: The supplier of real property does not have to provide a tax invoice to the purchaser for the sale where the margin scheme was used to calculate the GST liability (s75-30). The purchaser does not need one in any case as there is no entitlement to an input tax credit for purchases made under the margin scheme.

SPECIAL RULES OF THE MARGIN SCHEME

The margin on a supply by an entity that has acquired the property from another member of the GST group to a party outside the group, is the difference between the consideration for the supply, and

- the consideration paid by the member of the GST group when first acquiring from an outside party if the acquisition from an outside party occurs on or after 1 July 2000.
- the valuation of the property as at 1 July 2000 if the acquisition from a party outside the group occurs prior to 1 July 2000 (s75-11). **NOTE:** Similar measures apply to GST joint ventures.

Where the margin scheme is applied to a supply between associates, the consideration for the purpose of the calculation of the margin is treated as if it were the GST-inclusive market value at the time of the supply (s75-13).

For the purposes of calculating the margin under the margin scheme, where the consideration for the acquisition of the property has not been paid in full at the time of the subsequent supply, the consideration for the acquisition is reduced by the unpaid amount (s75-12). A subsequent payment may result in a decreasing adjustment (s75-27). Where real property has been acquired from a deceased estate, the consideration will be the consideration for the supply to the deceased if known, or an approved valuation as at the latest of:

- (if the deceased was unregistered), 1 July 2000, the day the property was inherited or the first day you were registered or were required to be registered, or

- (if the deceased was registered), 1 July 2000 or the first day the deceased was registered or was required to be registered.

Where real property was acquired but only part of the property was eligible, the margin scheme will still apply to a subsequent sale. However, an increasing adjustment must be made to reflect input tax credits incorrectly claimed (s75-22).

NOTE: GSTD 2014/2 confirms that where real property is acquired following the exercise of a call option, the call option fee does not form part of the consideration for the acquisition for the purposes of the margin scheme. The supply of the call option and the supply of the real property are two separate supplies.

SUBDIVIDED LAND

From 1 July 2013, taxpayers are able to use:

- the consideration method
- the valuation method, or
- the GST-inclusive market value method,

whichever is appropriate, when calculating the margin on a taxable supply of subdivided land. This would maintain consistency throughout Division 75 by allowing taxpayers to use the most appropriate method for calculating the GST payable, as well as reducing costs for taxpayers complying with their GST obligations.

The following examples are taken from the explanatory memorandum.

EXAMPLE 1.1: Using the consideration method to calculate the margin on subdivided land

Caroline carries on a property development enterprise and is registered for GST. In July 2012, Caroline makes a taxable supply of real property when she sells a newly developed residential lot to Emily for $450,000. The residential lot sold to Emily was subdivided from land and premises that Caroline acquired from Pat, an unregistered home owner, in June 2011 for consideration of $600,000.

Caroline and Emily agreed in writing that the margin scheme is to apply to Caroline's sale of the residential lot to Emily. Subsection 75 10(2) of the GST Act applies for the purposes of calculating the margin for the supply. The margin for the supply is equal to the difference between the sale price of $450,000 and the relevant proportion of the $600,000 consideration that Caroline provided for her acquisition of the land and premises she acquired from Pat, and from which the residential lot was subdivided.

The buildings on the land and premises that Caroline acquired from Pat were demolished and the remaining land was subdivided. Assuming the remaining land was subdivided into three residential lots of equal size and value, the margin for the sale of the single residential lot to Emily may be calculated as being equal to $450,000 – $200,000 (ie. $600,000 divided by 3) = $250,000.

EXAMPLE 1.2: Using an approved valuation to calculate the margin on subdivided land

Pearce Development Pty Ltd (PD) is a property development company and is registered for GST. On 6 July 2012, PD makes a taxable supply of real property when it sells a newly developed residential lot to Lisa for $500,000.

The residential lot sold to Lisa is referred to as Lot 42 in the registered plan of subdivision and was subdivided from land that PD held as at 1 July 2000. An approved valuation of the land held by PD as at 1 July 2000 was $36,000,000.

PD and Lisa agreed in writing that the margin scheme is to apply to the sale of Lot 42 to Lisa. Subsection 75-10(3) applies for the purposes of calculating the margin for the supply. The margin for PD's supply of Lot 42 to Lisa is equal to the difference between the sale price of $500,000 and the relevant proportion of the $36,000,000 approved valuation of the land held by PD as at 1 July 2000, and from which Lot 42 was subdivided.

Assuming the land that PD held as at 1 July 2000 was subdivided into 120 residential lots of equal size and value, then the margin for the sale of Lot 42 to Lisa may be calculated as being equal to $500,000 – $300,000 (ie. $36,000,000 divided by 120) = $200,000.

GUIDE FOR TAXABLE SUPPLIES OF REAL PROPERTY UNDER THE MARGIN SCHEME

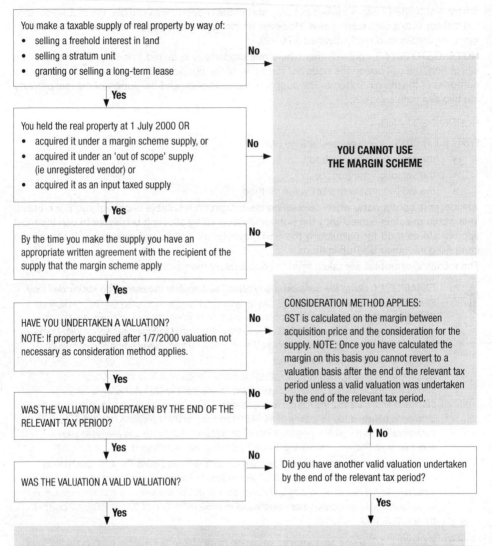

You make a taxable supply of real property by way of:
- selling a freehold interest in land
- selling a stratum unit
- granting or selling a long-term lease

No →

Yes ↓

You held the real property at 1 July 2000 OR
- acquired it under a margin scheme supply, or
- acquired it under an 'out of scope' supply (ie unregistered vendor) or
- acquired it as an input taxed supply

No →

Yes ↓

By the time you make the supply you have an appropriate written agreement with the recipient of the supply that the margin scheme apply

No →

Yes ↓

HAVE YOU UNDERTAKEN A VALUATION?
NOTE: If property acquired after 1/7/2000 valuation not necessary as consideration method applies.

No →

Yes ↓

WAS THE VALUATION UNDERTAKEN BY THE END OF THE RELEVANT TAX PERIOD?

No →

Yes ↓

WAS THE VALUATION A VALID VALUATION?

No →

Yes ↓

YOU CANNOT USE THE MARGIN SCHEME

CONSIDERATION METHOD APPLIES:
GST is calculated on the margin between acquisition price and the consideration for the supply. NOTE: Once you have calculated the margin on this basis you cannot revert to a valuation basis after the end of the relevant tax period unless a valid valuation was undertaken by the end of the relevant tax period.

No ↑

Did you have another valid valuation undertaken by the end of the relevant tax period?

Yes ↓

VALUATION METHOD APPLIES:
GST is calculated on the margin between the valuation and the consideration for the supply.
NOTE: Any valid valuation you have undertaken by the end of the relevant tax period, and used as the basis to calculate the margin, cannot be replaced after the end of the relevant tax period:
- by another valuation or valuation method
- by a calculation based on consideration under s75-10(2)
- by reverting to a supply under the basic rules and not made under the margin scheme.

24.350 GST AND NON-RESIDENTS

GST registration rules apply in the same way to non-residents as they do to residents, that is:
- if a non-resident is not required to register for GST they may still do so provided they are carrying on an enterprise, either in Australia or elsewhere, and
- if a non-resident is carrying on an enterprise and its GST turnover meets the registration turnover threshold of $75,000 ($150,000 for non-profit bodies), it is required to be registered for GST. Note that the turnover threshold tests exclude supplies that are not connected with Australia, that are not made in Australia and that are made through an enterprise that is not being carried on in Australia.

Taxable supplies covered by a reverse charge agreement (see 24.351) are excluded from the calculation of non-resident GST turnover for GST registration purposes (s83-25).

As there is no requirement that the enterprise be carried on in Australia, a non-resident entity that satisfies the conditions for GST registration and makes creditable acquisitions in Australia, is entitled to GST registration. Once registered for GST, the entity can seek a refund of input tax credits for the GST paid on creditable acquisitions.

There are several mechanisms implemented in the GST legislation to assist the Tax Office in collecting GST on supplies made by non-residents. These include:
- Division 83 on reverse charges when the recipient pays GST liabilities on behalf of non-resident suppliers, and
- Division 57 where resident agents that are acting on behalf of a non-resident will be liable for the non-residents GST obligations.

24.351 REVERSE CHARGE (Division 83)

In some circumstances, an overseas supplier can avoid having to register for GST if the supplier and the recipient agree the recipient is liable for the GST to be paid on the supply. This is a reverse charge. Where a non-resident makes taxable supplies, practical difficulties can arise in respect of paying the GST to the Tax Office where the non-resident does not have a physical presence in Australia.

Division 83 enables suppliers and recipients to agree the GST on a taxable supply is payable by the recipient where:
- the supplier is a non-resident, and
- the supplier does not make the supply through an enterprise that the supplier carries on in Australia, and
- the recipient is registered or required to be registered, and
- the supplier and recipient agree that the GST on the supply be payable by the recipient.

This provision does not apply to:
- a supply that is a taxable supply under Division 84 (which is about offshore supplies other than goods or real property), or
- a taxable supply made by a non-resident through a resident agent, or
- a supply that is disregarded under s188-15(3)(b) or (c) or s188-20(3)(b) or (c) (which are about supplies of rights or options).

A non-resident is not required to be registered for GST where their GST turnover would not meet the registration turnover threshold but for the inclusion of taxable supplies covered by a reverse charge agreement.

Tax invoices are not required for reverse charged supplies made by non-residents.

24.352 RESIDENT AGENTS ACTING FOR NON-RESIDENTS (Division 57)

The GST Act imposes the GST obligations on resident agents acting for non-residents, as it is easier from a tax administration viewpoint to enforce the GST obligations on entities that are resident in Australia. The agent, through whom non-residents make taxable supplies or creditable acquisitions, is the responsible entity for GST purposes.

An agent resident in Australia that acts for a non-resident is required to register for GST if the non-resident is required to register. See GSTR 2000/37 for the registration requirements for resident agents acting for non-residents. It is the resident agent (instead of the non-resident) that is required to on behalf of the non-resident:

- pay GST on taxable supplies
- entitled to input tax credits on acquisitions that it makes on behalf of non-residents
- make adjustments (if any), and
- lodge GST returns – rule allowing to lodge 'nil' return over the phone is not applicable to an agent acting on behalf of a non-resident unless the non-resident did not make any sales or acquisitions through the agent during that tax period.

NOTE: If a non-resident belongs to a GST group, the GST group representative member is liable for all the non-resident's GST obligations and *not* the agent acting on behalf of the non-resident.

NOTE: GSTR 2000/37 sets out the Commissioner's view on GST and agency relationships. This includes consideration of resident agents acting for non-residents. (See 24.333 for GST and agency relationships.)

Rugs Galore is a Fijian company that sells rugs in Australia through its agent, Australian Rugs P/L. If Australian Rugs P/L sells the rugs as the resident agent for Rugs Galore, Australian Rugs P/L is liable for the GST on the taxable supply when the rugs are sold in Australia.

If the importation of the rugs is done through Australian Rugs P/L as the resident agent of Rugs Galore, Australian Rugs P/L is liable for the GST payable on the taxable importation and is also entitled to the input tax credits for the creditable importation.

Agency services supplied by a resident agent to the non-resident are a separate supply to the transactions being undertaken as resident agent on behalf of the non-resident.

The agent acting on behalf of the non-resident will need to keep good accounting records of both its own business dealings and those it undertakes on behalf of the non-resident, especially where it acts on behalf of a number of non-residents.

NOTE: A resident agent who ceases to act for a non-resident must notify the Commissioner within 14 days. Notification of cessation must contain details as set out in GSTR 2000/37.

24.360   SIMPLIFIED ACCOUNTING METHODS (Division 123)

Some retailers may choose to apply simplified accounting methods, approved by the Tax Office, to meet their GST compliance obligations in relation to trading stock.

Simplified accounting methods under Division 123 apply to entities which:

- are specified retailers which include retailers that sold food or endorsed charities making GST-free supplies under Subdiv. 38-G (non-commercial activities)
- are small business entities (see from 10.200 for definition of small business entities), and
- do not constitute a business but meet the $2 million 'small business entity enterprise turnover threshold'.

The Commissioner has released a number of simplified accounting method determinations – SAM 2001/1, SAM 2004/1, SAM 2005/1, SAM 2006/1 and SAM 2007/1. (**NOTE:** SAM 2005/1 sets out a method available to supermarkets and convenience stores – the sales percentage method).

The simplified accounting methods available and outlined below are explained in the above determinations and the Tax Office booklet *Simplified Accounting Methods for food retailers*.

The simplified accounting methods are:

- **Snapshot method:** based on a 'snapshot' of sales and purchases to estimate the GST-free amounts.
- **Purchases snapshot method:** based on a 'snapshot' of the retailer's purchases to estimate the GST-free components.
- **Stock purchases method:** the percentage of GST-free sales will be the same percentage of GST-free purchases.

- **Business norms:** method where the retailer can use standard percentages which can be applied to their sales and purchases to estimate the amount of GST-free sales and purchases.
- **Sales percentage method:** where you calculate the percentage of GST-free sales you made in a tax period and apply this percentage to estimate your GST-free purchases. Applies to supermarkets and convenience stores where at least 95% of the sales are in unchanged form.

WHO CAN USE THE VARIOUS METHODS?

The Tax Office guide provides that a food retailer is eligible to use a simplified GST accounting method if:

- they are registered for GST, and
- are a retailer who sells both taxable and GST-free food at the same premises (unless they wish to use the purchases snapshot method), and
- their annual turnover is not more than $2 million.

It does not matter whether a cash or non-cash basis of accounting is used.

There are also specific eligibility criteria that must be met for each type of simplified GST accounting method. See following table. (Source: *Simplified Accounting Methods for food retailers*.)

Eligibility criteria for simplified GST accounting methods					
Your business's profile	Business norms	Stock purchases	Snapshot	Sales percentage	Purchases snapshot
Your annual turnover is $2 million or less, and you are a reseller[1].	Y	Y	Y	Y	Y
Your annual turnover is $2 million or less, and you are a converter[2] and your conversions make up less than 5% of your total sales.	Y	N	Y	Y	Y
Your annual turnover is $2 million or less, and you are a converter[2] and your conversions make up 5% or more of your total sales.	Y	N	Y	N	Y

1: A reseller resells stock without converting it into different products.
2: A converter buys GST-free goods and converts them into taxable goods. A business that converts as well as re-sells (such as a snack bar) is treated as a converter (eg. a business buying bread to make sandwiches).

These methods can only be used for supplies and acquisitions of trading stock. Goods or services such as rent, telephone or non-stock or capital items will still need to be accounted for in the normal manner.

24.361   SNAPSHOT METHOD

This method is available to retailers with inadequate point-of-sale equipment.

The snapshot method enables a retailer to take a 'snapshot' of their trading twice each year to determine GST-free sales and/or GST-free purchases. Under this method, a snapshot must be done twice a year over a continuous two week period for sales and a continuous four week period for purchases. The retailer must keep a daily worksheet to record all sales and stock purchases, showing taxable and GST-free sales and detail commonly sold categories (eg. confectionery cakes).

The results of the snapshot can be used as the basis for determining all GST-free sales and GST-free stock purchases during the following tax periods:

Snapshot period	Used for tax periods
1 June to 31 July	July to December
1 December to 31 January	January to June

A corner store owner decides to use the snapshot method and, during the respective two week and four week record keeping periods, the following details are recorded:

Total sales	*$35,000*
Total GST-free sales	*$15,400*
Percentage of GST-free sales ($15,400 / $35,000)	*44%*
Total purchases	*$21,000*
Total GST-free stock purchases	*$11,520*
Percentage of GST-free stock purchases ($11,520 / $21,000)	*55%*

The owners would use these percentages to determine:

GST-free sales	*44%*
GST-free stock purchases	*55%*

24.362   STOCK PURCHASES METHOD

This method is only available to small food retailers without adequate point-of-sale equipment and not converting GST-free ingredients that they purchase into taxable items – ie. reseller (eg. a fish and chip retailer who buys GST-free potatoes and makes french fries would not be entitled to use this method).

Businesses that convert their GST-free purchases into taxable sales can only use either the business norms method or the snapshot method. Businesses using the stock purchases method need only calculate the percentage of their purchases that are GST-free during a snapshot period and use this percentage to calculate their GST-free sales and GST-free stock purchases. This assumes that the retailer is not converting any stock purchases, so percentage of sales to purchases remains constant.

Under this method, the retailer can choose to calculate their GST-free stock purchases either:

- each tax period, or
- for two 4 week periods (the periods are the same as for the snapshot method).

Once the percentage that GST-free purchases are of total purchases is arrived at, this becomes the basis to calculate not only GST-free purchases but also GST-free sales for each period.

5% GST-FREE STOCK ESTIMATION BASIS

For food retailers with only a small amount of GST-free purchases, the Tax Office has simplified the stock purchases method even further, developing the 5% GST-free stock estimation basis.

This estimation basis can be used for GST-free goods such as bottled water, pure fruit juice, milk or fresh fruit that are purchased GST-free and sold GST-free.

To be eligible to use the 5% GST-free stock estimation basis, purchases of GST-free items must be less than 5% of total purchases.

Rather than examining all your purchases for a four-week period, you only have to track GST-free goods you purchase. This will simplify accounting as it reduces the number of purchases to be monitored.

The 5% GST-free stock method allows an estimation to be made of GST-free sales by using the amounts of GST-free purchases, and adding mark-up to that amount, to provide the total GST-free sales for the tax period. This will simplify accounting for sales as there will be no need to identify and record GST-free sales.

A video hire shop which is eligible to use this method records its total GST-free purchases for the tax period as:

Item and cost	*Mark up*	*Estimate: GST-free sales*
Bottled water: $1,500	*40%*	*$2,100*
Pure fruit juice: $2,250	*30%*	*$2,925*
		$5,025

The video shop simply applies the respective mark-up to each of the product lines to estimate total GST-free sales, which in this case totals $5,025.

24.363　BUSINESS NORMS METHOD

Under the business norms method, the retailer can apply standard percentages to total sales and purchases for every tax period to estimate GST-free sales and purchases.

This method is only available to retailers who:
- have an annual turnover of less than $2 million
- do not have adequate point of sales equipment, and
- is a type of business listed in the following table.

These percentages are applied to the retailer's total sales and total stock purchases to determine GST-free sales and purchases. The standard percentages for the type of business are shown below.

PERCENTAGES: BUSINESS NORMS METHOD (source: *Simplified Accounting Methods for food retailers* – NAT 3185)

Type of retailer	GST-free sales	GST-free stock purchases
Hot bread shops	50%	75%
Convenience* stores that prepare takeaway food but do not sell fuel or alcohol	22.5%	30%
Convenience* stores that do not prepare takeaway food and do not sell fuel or alcohol	30%	30%
Continental delicatessens (that do not sell hot foods or prepared meals)	85%	90%
Cake shops	2%	95%
Health food shops	35%	35%
Fish shops (that sell fresh fish)	35%	98%
Pharmacies (with both taxable and GST-free food sales)		
• Dispensary: non-claimable	98%	0%
• Over the counter	47.5%	2%
Rural convenience* stores		
• Converters	22.5%	30%
• Non-converters	30%	30%

* A convenience store is generally a business that sells milk, bread, soft drinks, cigarettes, confectionery, ice creams or groceries. A convenience store can sell take-away food such as sandwiches. However, if the take-away food sales are the dominant source of sales, it is not a convenience store and not eligible for the above concessional percentages.

A hot bread retailer has sales in the tax period 1 July to 30 September of $180,000. Total stock purchases in this tax period were $40,000.
- *GST-free sales (50% of $180,000): $90,000*
- *GST-free stock purchases (75% of $40,000): $30,000*

These components must be separately identified on the retailer's Business Activity Statement.

24.364　SALES PERCENTAGE METHOD

The sales percentage method is designed for retailers that are almost exclusively resellers.

This method may be used if the retailer:
- has an annual turnover of $2 million or less
- has adequate point-of-sale equipment
- operates a supermarket or convenience store (not a petrol station), and
- converts 5% or less of their goods into taxable products.

The total sales in each tax period are examined and the GST-free percentage of total sales worked out. This percentage is applied to purchases made (trading stock only) for the tax period to estimate GST-free purchases.

The sales percentage method assumes that if you only resell goods that you purchase, the percentage of your GST-free sales will be similar to the percentage of your GST-free purchases. This method is provided for in determination SAM 2005/1.

24.365   PURCHASES SNAPSHOT METHOD

The purchases snapshot method is similar to the snapshot method except it only applies to trading stock purchases. This is the accounting method set out in SAM 2006/1. GST liability on sales and input tax credit entitlement on purchases that are not trading stocks are worked out using the normal rules.

When using this method, you must monitor your trading stock purchases over two four-week sample periods each financial year and work out the percentage of GST-free trading stock purchases you make. Each four week sample period should represent the usual amount of trading stock purchases you make.

This method is eligible to the retailers who operate a restaurant, café or catering business with annual turnover of $2 million or less. It does not matter whether you have adequate or inadequate point-of-sale equipment.

24.366   OTHER USEFUL RESOURCES

In addition to *Simplified Accounting Methods for food retailers* (NAT 3185), the Tax Office have released the following useful guides:

- *GST – completing your activity statement – purchases snapshot method* (NAT 15978)
- *GST – completing your activity statement – business norms percentages method* (NAT 16013)
- *GST – completing your activity statement – snapshot method* (NAT 16014)
- *GST – completing your activity statement – stock purchases method* (NAT 16015), and
- *GST – completing your activity statement – sales percentage method* (NAT 16016).

24.370 HIRE PURCHASE AND LEASES

Leases are not input taxed financial supplies pursuant to Regulations 40-16 Item 6. Hire purchases have been treated as wholly taxable supplies (if they satisfy all requirements under s9-5) since 1 July 2012.

24.371   HIRE PURCHASE

Hire purchase agreements essentially represent financing arrangements which facilitate the sale and purchase of goods. Prior to 1 July 2012, the supplier of a hire purchase agreement made a mixed supply that consisted of a taxable supply and an input taxed supply. The interest component was treated as an input taxed supply. Therefore, acquisitions relating to making a hire purchase agreement needed to be apportioned and entitlement to input tax credits arose only in relation to the taxable component.

All components of a hire purchase transaction are treated as taxable supplies, for agreements entered into on or after 1 July 2012.

Normal attribution rules apply to hire purchase agreements. Liability for GST under a hire purchase agreement arises at the start of the agreement and not continuously throughout the period of the agreement (ie. a hire purchase is not treated as a progressive supply).

IF RECIPIENT ACCOUNTS FOR GST ON ACCRUAL BASIS

All the input tax credit on a creditable acquisition under a hire purchase agreement is attributable to the tax period in which the agreement is entered into as this is normally when the recipient makes a payment or an invoice is issued. The recipient can therefore claim 10% of the principal component if the supply of the goods is a taxable supply.

IF RECIPIENT ACCOUNTS FOR GST ON CASH BASIS

Under s158-5, a cash basis taxpayer is treated as though they do not account for GST on a cash basis, in relation to an acquisition they make under a hire purchase agreement. This rule applies to hire purchase agreements entered into on or after 1 July 2012. Therefore, the input tax credits may by wholly claimed upfront.

CLAIMING INPUT TAX CREDITS BY SUPPLIER OF A HIRE PURCHASE ARRANGEMENT

Input tax credits on acquisitions are claimable to the extent of the acquisitions creditable purpose (see 23.221).

The Tax Office has released Practice Statement PS LA 2008/1 (GA) regarding the acceptable approach in apportioning input tax credit entitlement for acquisitions relating to making supplies under a hire purchase agreement. The practice statement points out that no supplies made under a hire purchase agreement entered into on or after 1 July 2012 are financial supplies, regardless of whether the credit provided under the agreement is charged separately and disclosed to the recipient of the goods.

A credit charge that is separately identified and disclosed under a hire purchase agreement. entered into on or after 1 July 2012, is consideration for a supply separate from the underlying supply of goods, and is a taxable supply if the underlying supply is taxable. If the credit charge is not separately disclosed, the total consideration under the agreement relates to the supply of the goods. This is more fully explained in GSTR 2000/29.

It follows that acquisitions that relate both to the supply of goods and the supply of credit made under hire purchase agreements entered into on or after 1 July 2012 are not made partly for a creditable purpose.

24.372   LEASES

Generally, leases (irrespective of whether they are finance, operating or novated leases) will be subject to GST as they are not input taxed financial supplies (Regulations 40-16 item 6). For GST purposes, leases are treated as progressive supplies and the normal attribution rules apply to each component of the supply (ie. each lease payment). This differs from hire purchase agreements that are treated as a one-off supply rather than progressive supplies.

If the lessee accounts for GST on the cash basis, the lessee will be entitled to an input tax credit when the lease payment is made.

If the lessee accounts for GST on an accruals basis, Division 156 will apply to deem each payment component to be a separate supply and the lessee will be entitled to an input tax credit for each of the component under the normal attribution rule that is the earlier of when.

- any of the consideration for the supply is received, or
- an invoice for the supply is issued.

See 24.122 and GSTR 2000/35 for more information on how Division 156 applies.

24.373   TERMINATION OF LEASES

Termination of a lease often requires the payment of a termination payment or the sale and/or purchase of the leased asset. GSTD 2001/2 sets out how to treat the sale of goods by a lessor on the termination of a lease agreement.

The sale of the goods by a lessor is a separate supply to the supply by way of lease, regardless of whether the lessor sells the goods to the lessee or to a third party.

As a sale of the goods by the lessor is a separate supply, the sale of the goods on or after 1 July 2000 will not be a GST-free supply even if the supply of goods by way of lease may be GST-free under the transitional rules. If the lessee accepts an offer from the lessor under which it can acquire the asset, the lessor will be making a taxable supply and will be liable for 1/11th of the consideration.

NOTE: If the lease agreement gives the lessee the right or obligation to purchase the goods on termination of the lease, the agreement will be considered a hire purchase agreement rather than a lease agreement.

It is not uncommon for the lessee to acquire the goods on expiry of the lease for an amount equal to the residual value. The important thing is that the lessee does not acquire the goods under the terms and conditions of the original lease but under a separate or collateral agreement that is separately negotiated between the parties.

Assuming that the lessor can recover the GST from the lessee (which will depend on the contractual terms of the lease), the lessee will be entitled to an input tax credit on the payout of the lease residual if registered. If the lessee returns the goods to the lessor, the GST treatment of the shortfall or surplus on termination needs to be considered.

If your existing lease does not qualify for GST-free treatment under the transitional arrangements, the following treatment applies:

- **sale proceeds less than the residual value:** If the lessee is required to make a further payment because the sale proceeds are less than the residual value, the lessee will have a decreasing adjustment. The lessee will be able to claim an input tax credit on the shortfall so long as an adjustment note or tax invoice has been provided from the lessor. The lessor will be liable for additional GST as the adjustment event results in an increasing adjustment to the lessor
- **sale proceeds exceed the residual value:** Where the lease agreement provides for the lessor to pay the difference to the lessee, the excess received by the lessee will be an increasing adjustment. An adjustment note issued by the lessor effectively reduces previous input tax credits claimed by the lessee, while the lessor gets an input tax entitlement for the amount paid.

NOTE: Leases that are GST-free under the GST transitional rules do not give rise to adjustment events for any shortfall or excess on the guaranteed residual value. No input tax credit was claimed on the monthly lease payments and hence no adjustment event arises on termination.

EARLY TERMINATION OF A LEASE

Early termination of a lease can result from the following events:

- a right to terminate in accordance with the original terms of the lease
- a mutual agreement by the parties to terminate the lease agreement early, whether under the terms of the contract or a separate agreement
- a default by the lessee
- a casualty occurrence, or
- a statutory right to terminate early.

Early termination of a lease often requires the payment of a termination payment. Some terminations of leases require the payment of a termination payment where the termination may result in damages or loss of future profits to the lessor. A compensating payment for this loss or damage (a termination payment) does not constitute consideration for a taxable supply. In such cases, the proportion of consideration in relation to this component will not be a taxable supply. Lessees will therefore be making payments in connection with leases with no entitlement to input tax credits as these payments will not represent consideration for a taxable supply by the lessor.

GSTR 2003/11 sets out the Commissioner's view on GST and early termination of a lease of goods.

EARLY TERMINATION BY AGREEMENT IN ACCORDANCE WITH THE ORIGINAL TERMS OF THE LEASE

GSTR 2003/11 considers the GST consequences of early termination as a result of a party, usually the lessee, exercising a right to terminate in accordance with the original terms of the lease which allows for early termination at the option of that party without any default or other event occurring.

Where the lease is terminated in these circumstances, the termination payment is considered to change the consideration for the earlier supply of the goods by way of lease. Accordingly, there is an adjustment event in relation to that earlier supply.

A payment made on early termination in accordance with the original terms of the lease may consist of a number of components. These components may include:

- a payment of arrears of lease instalments and, as such, part of the consideration for the original supply of goods by way of lease

- a payment in return for transferring title to the goods to the lessee on termination. A payment in return for a supply of title to the goods is consideration for the supply of title to the goods. This supply is subject to GST where the other requirements of a taxable supply are met, and

- where the goods are sold to a third party on termination, under the terms of the lease the lessee may be liable for, or entitled to, the difference between the net sale proceeds and the residual value of the goods and future rental (commonly adjusted to present values). If the sale proceeds are less than the adjusted residual value and future rental, so that a shortfall payment is required, there is an adjustment event in relation to the earlier supply of the goods by way of lease. This adjustment event gives rise to an increasing adjustment for the lessor where the supply is a taxable supply. Where the lessee's acquisition of the goods by way of lease was a creditable acquisition, the lessee has a decreasing adjustment.

Where the sale proceeds exceed the adjusted residual value and future rental and the lessor is required under the lease to pay the difference to the lessee, there is an adjustment event in relation to the original supply of goods by way of lease. The lessor has a decreasing adjustment where the supply of the goods by way of lease is a taxable supply. Where the acquisition of the leased goods by the lessee was a creditable acquisition, the lessee has an increasing adjustment.

EARLY TERMINATION AND PAYMENT AS A RESULT OF MUTUAL AGREEMENT

This occurs where the lessor and the lessee terminate the lease early on a consensual basis.

The payment received on early termination is 'consideration for a supply' where it is given in return for releasing the lessee from its contractual obligations. The lessor supplies a release of the lessee's contractual obligations under the lease. This supply is made in return for payment. As such, a sufficient nexus exists between the payment and the supply. Therefore, the part of a payment given on early termination in return for this supply is subject to GST.

Where payment is made on early termination as a result of a mutual agreement, the payment may be given for current or earlier taxable supplies between the parties. For example, part of the payment may be given in satisfaction of arrears of lease instalments due for the supply of the goods under the lease prior to early termination. This part of the payment is consideration for the earlier supply by way of lease. GST is payable on this supply.

Part of the payment may also be given in return for transferring title to the goods to the lessee on termination. Any such sale of the goods is a new transaction separate from the earlier supply by way of lease. Payment given in return for a current supply of title to the goods is 'consideration for a supply' and GST is payable on this supply. Alternatively, where the goods are sold to a third party on termination, the lessee may be liable for, or entitled to, the difference between the net sale proceeds and the residual value of the goods. This payment alters the amount of consideration for the earlier supply of the goods by way of lease.

The GST consequences of the adjustments arising from such a payment are set out above in respect of early termination in accordance with the original terms of the lease. See examples below.

Mutual agreement – shortfall between termination amount and sale proceeds: Finance lease

Fred seeks a voluntary early termination of his truck lease and Easy Finance agrees to this. At the termination date, the termination amount is $25,000. This amount comprises $15,000 for the present value of the future lease payments and $10,000 for the present value of the residual goods.

Easy Finance obtains possession of the truck and manages to sell it for $20,000 to a third party. Fred must make a payment of $5,000 (the difference between termination amount and sale price) to Easy Finance.

The $5,000 consideration made by Fred is in respect of two supplies:
- *the original supply of the truck by way of lease, and*
- *the release from Fred's obligations to Easy Finance under the lease.*

An adjustment event arises for Easy Finance in relation to the above supplies.

This adjustment event gives rise to an increasing adjustment for Easy Finance of $5,000 x 1/11 ($454.54).

Easy Finance will be required to issue an adjustment note to Fred. Fred will also have an adjustment event and will be entitled to a decreasing adjustment of $5,000 x 1/11 ($454.54).

EARLY TERMINATION AND PAYMENT AS A RESULT OF A DEFAULT BY THE LESSEE

Early termination as a result of a default by the lessee occurs where a lease is unilaterally terminated by the lessor due to the lessee's failure to properly perform (or to be ready and willing to perform) its contractual duties.

Early termination may flow from a default by the lessee, which results in the lessor exercising its common law right to terminate and recover damages (default termination).

Where a lease is terminated early because of a default by the lessee, termination occurs without any mutual agreement of the parties. As such, payment is often made to compensate the lessor for any loss or damage suffered because of the early termination. This loss or damage cannot be characterised as a supply made by the lessor, because the loss or damage does not in itself constitute a supply under s9-10.

The payment received to compensate the lessor's loss or damage flowing from early termination as a result of a default by the lessee is not 'consideration for a supply'. There is no liability for GST because no supply is made in connection with the payment. Similarly, interest paid by the lessee as a consequence of default in the payment of lease instalments is not 'consideration for a supply'. There is no liability for GST because no supply is made in connection with the payment of the interest.

After a default termination, a separate agreement may be made for the payment of damages (as opposed to being specified in a liquidated damages clause in the original lease agreement). The fact that a payment is made under such an agreement does not, in itself, mean that it is consideration for a taxable supply. A separate agreement as to damages payable has a different character to a mutual agreement for early termination. A separate agreement for damages records the terms upon which compensation is paid following an early termination as a result of a default.

A payment made on early termination due to the lessee's default may have more than one purpose. For example, in the context of a finance lease, part of the payment may be made in connection with an earlier or current taxable supply between the parties. Where the payment has a sufficient nexus with one or more taxable supplies, and is also partly for a purpose not connected with any supply, the payment must be apportioned between those parts and the GST payable or input tax credits attributed to the relevant tax period.

The following examples illustrate the GST implications of early terminations arising out of default by the lessee.

> ### Default – residual shortfall: Finance lease
>
> *Fred is in arrears for four lease payments when Easy Finance terminates the lease because Fred has defaulted on his monthly payments. Easy Finance takes possession of the truck and sells it for $20,000.*
>
> *At the termination date, the termination amount is $25,000 which is comprised of $15,000 for the present value of the future lease payments and $10,000 for the present value of the residual goods.*
>
> *Under the agreed damages clause the following amounts are payable:*
>
> - *arrears of 4 x $880 (monthly payments under the lease are $880) = $3,520, and*
> - *amount by which the termination amount exceeds the sale price = $5,000.*
>
> *The arrears of $3,520 are in respect of the earlier taxable supply of the truck under the lease.*
>
> *The amount of $5,000 is apportioned for the following purposes:*
>
> - *to the extent that the payment is to be apportioned against the residual, it represents the residual shortfall and is connected with the original taxable supply of the truck by way of lease, and*
> - *to the extent that the payment is to be apportioned in respect of future lease payments which is in the nature of damages for a loss of bargain which is not connected with any taxable supply.*

Step 1: *Easy Finance works out the amount of the residual shortfall by making the following apportionment:*

> *Residual shortfall = Total shortfall payment x (Residual value divided by Total termination amount)*
>
> *= $5,000 x ($10,000 divided by $25,000) = $2,000*

In respect of the residual shortfall, an adjustment event arises for Easy Finance in relation to the supply of the truck under the lease. This adjustment event gives rise to an increasing adjustment for Easy Finance of $2,000 x 1/11 ($181.82).

Easy Finance will be required to issue an adjustment note to Fred. Fred will also have an adjustment event and will be entitled to a decreasing adjustment of $2,000 x 1/11 ($181.82).

Step 2: *Easy Finance subtracts the amount of the residual shortfall from the termination shortfall amount so as to calculate the amount of damages for its loss of the lease.*

> *Damages = termination shortfall amount – residual shortfall amount*
>
> *= $5,000 – $2,000 = $3,000 (this amount is not connected with any taxable supply)*

The lessee will be required to pay $5,000, of which only $2,000 represents a taxable supply for which there will be an input tax credit entitlement. The lessor will need to provide a tax invoice for this mixed supply and show that GST has only been included on the taxable termination component of the supply.

Termination by default – sale proceeds exceed termination amount (GSTR 2003/11)

Dustin is in arrears for four lease instalments when Finco exercises its right under the lease to terminate the lease because of Dustin's default. Finco takes possession of the truck and sells it to a third party for $33,000. Finco makes a taxable supply of the truck to the third party and is liable for GST of 1/11 of the selling price (that is, $3,000). The net sale proceeds are $30,000.

At the termination date, the termination amount is $25,000 exclusive of GST. This amount comprises $15,000 for future rental and $10,000 for the residual value, both adjusted to present values.

Under the agreed damages clause of the lease, Finco is entitled to arrears of 4 x $700 = $2,800 plus GST. The arrears of $2,800 are in respect of the earlier taxable supply by Finco to Dustin of the truck by way of lease. As such, the payment is part of the consideration for a taxable supply by Finco under the lease and must be grossed up for GST in accordance with the terms of the lease. Therefore, Dustin pays Finco $2,800 x 11/10 = $3,080 (being the arrears of rent grossed up for GST). Finco is liable for GST of 1/11 of that amount (that is, $280) and Dustin has a corresponding input tax credit of $280.

Dustin must also pay interest on the arrears of $2,800 (plus GST) x 10% per annum = (say for example) $90. This amount is paid as consideration for a financial supply. As such, it is consideration for an input taxed supply. As the net sale proceeds exceed the termination amount, any loss Finco may have suffered because of the early termination, has been wholly mitigated.

Under the agreed damages clause, Finco must pay to Dustin the difference between the net sale proceeds and the termination amount. This requirement gives rise to an adjustment event in relation to the supply of the truck by way of lease because it changes the consideration for that earlier supply. The payment must be grossed up for GST in accordance with the terms of the lease.

Therefore Finco pays Dustin $5,000 x 11/10 = $5,500 (being the difference between the GST exclusive termination amount and the net sale proceeds, grossed up for GST).

Finco has a decreasing adjustment of $5,500 x 1/11 (that is, $500). Finco is required to issue an adjustment note to Dustin. Dustin has an increasing adjustment of $5,500 x 1/11 (that is, $500).

Under the lease, Dustin must pay Finco $3,080 + $90 = $3,170 and Finco must pay Dustin $5,500. The parties may agree to net these amounts off, so that Finco ultimately pays Dustin $5,500 – $3,170 = $2,330. Whether or not the parties come to such an arrangement, their GST liabilities arising from the payments made under the lease agreement are as outlined above.

EARLY TERMINATION AND PAYMENT AS A RESULT OF A CASUALTY OCCURRENCE

Early termination as a result of a casualty occurrence occurs where an external event frustrates proper performance of the parties' contractual duties.

A casualty occurrence is usually beyond the parties' control; or example, where the leased goods are:

- stolen by a third party and not recovered
- totally destroyed as a result of a natural disaster, such as fire, or
- compulsorily acquired by a government agency.

The lessee is usually liable to pay an amount to the lessor on early termination resulting from a casualty occurrence. For example, the lease may require the lessee to pay to the lessor the full insurable value of the goods or, if the lessor requires, an amount equivalent to the remaining lease payments and the specified residual value of the goods, both adjusted to present values. As such, payment may be made to compensate the lessor for its loss of a lease or damage suffered because of the early termination. This loss or damage cannot in itself be characterised as a supply made by the lessor.

The payment received to compensate the lessor for its loss or damage flowing from early termination as a result of a casualty occurrence is not 'consideration for a supply'. There is no GST liability because no supply is made in connection with the payment. This outcome is not altered by the inclusion or omission in the lease of a mechanism for calculating the amount payable on early termination.

However, a payment made on early termination as a result of a casualty occurrence may have more than one purpose. Therefore, where the payment made on early termination has more than one purpose, it must be apportioned as to its relevant parts. For example, part of the amount paid on termination may be rent relating to a period prior to the casualty occurrence. That part has a sufficient nexus with an earlier taxable supply and GST is payable on the supply.

Casualty occurrence – finance lease

The truck leased by Fred is stolen and is not recovered. At the termination date, the termination amount is $25,000. Fred receives $22,000 insurance proceeds from his insurer which he passes on to Easy Finance. Under the lease, he is also required to pay another $3,000. There are no lease instalments in arrears.

Neither of the above payments is connected with a taxable supply. Easy Finance does not have an increasing adjustment and therefore does not have to issue a tax invoice. Fred therefore receives no input tax credit for payment made.

TERMINATION PURSUANT TO A STATUTORY RIGHT UNDER STATE OR TERRITORY CONSUMER CREDIT LEGISLATION

The Consumer Credit Code regulates certain consumer leases relating to goods. The Code confers statutory rights on the lessee which cannot be excluded by agreement between parties. It also contains procedural requirements.

Part 10 of the Code regulates certain leases where a natural person or strata corporation hires goods and does not have a right or obligation to purchase those goods.

Where a lease is covered by Part 10 of the Code, a statutory right is conferred on the lessee, which may be exercised at any time, to terminate the lease early by returning the goods.

The amount payable by a lessee on exercising this statutory right, is the lesser of:

- the amount payable under the lease on such a termination, or
- the amount determined in accordance with the principles (if any) set out in the regulations.

A lease covered by Part 10 of the Code may be terminated in circumstances where the lessee exercises the statutory right to terminate early upon making a termination payment provided for in the original terms of the lease. In these circumstances, the payment is considered to change the consideration for the earlier supply of the goods by way of lease. Accordingly, there is an adjustment event in relation to that earlier supply. Any part of a payment given in satisfaction of arrears of lease instalments is consideration for the supply of the goods by way of lease. This supply is subject to GST where the other requirements of a taxable supply are met. Interest paid by the lessee as a consequence of default in the payment of lease instalments is not consideration for a supply.

An adjustment event arises where the goods are sold to a third party on termination and the lessee is liable for, or entitled to, the difference between the net sale proceeds and the residual value of the goods. Payment of the shortfall or excess alters the amount of consideration for the earlier supply of the goods by way of lease.

24.380 SPECIAL GST RULES

Special GST rules apply in some circumstances to determine when GST or input tax credits are attributable, in some cases how GST is determined as well as who is liable to pay GST/ entitled to input tax credits.

24.381 SECOND-HAND GOODS (Division 66)

If a registered entity buys second-hand goods from an unregistered entity there will be no GST in the price. Registered entities can, however, claim a notional input tax credit provided the second-hand goods (other than livestock or plants) are acquired as trading stock and the subsequent supply of those goods is a taxable supply. This concession only applies to second-hand goods that were purchased for the purpose of sale or exchange. It does not apply to second-hand goods acquired to be used as capital assets or as raw materials for manufacture.

What constitutes second-hand goods and when they are acquired for the purposes of sale or exchange in the ordinary course of business has been considered by the Commissioner of Taxation in draft determination GSTD 2013/D2.

NOTE: Repair or minor renovation to the second-hand goods prior to re-supply is not considered to be used for manufacture.

This concession to enable a notional input tax credit to be claimed will not apply to second-hand goods if:

- the entity imported the goods
- the supply of the goods was by way of hire
- the acquisition of the goods was a GST-free supply
- the acquisition was a taxable supply (in this case the entity is entitled to the actual GST input tax credit)
- the entity makes a subsequent supply of the goods that is not a taxable supply, or
- the acquisition of second-hand goods that are divided up for re-supply (see global method below).

In *LeasePlan Australia Limited v DFC of T* [2009] FCA 1309, employees of the taxpayer sold their motor vehicles to the taxpayer. The vehicles were leased back to the employees. Under the agreements, LeasePlan sold the vehicles at the end of each lease. If the sale price was greater than the agreed residual value, the taxpayer paid the difference to the employee. If the sale price was lower than the residual value, the employee paid the difference to the taxpayer. LeasePlan claimed input tax credits under Division 66 in relation to the purchases of the vehicles from the employees.

The Tax Office assessed the taxpayer on the basis that it was not entitled to the input tax credits on the basis that the vehicles were not acquired for the purpose of sale, which is a requirement under s66-5(1). The taxpayer objected to the assessments. Its objections were disallowed and the taxpayer appealed to the Federal Court against the objection decision.

The Federal Court held that the legislative requirement was satisfied because one of the taxpayer's purposes of the acquisitions was the purpose of sale. The existence of another purpose, such as leasing, under the 'composite transaction', did not prevent the s66-5(1) requirement from being met. The Court ordered that the decision to disallow the taxpayer's objections to the assessments be set aside.

Subsequent to the Court's decision, the Tax Office issued a Decision Impact Statement and amended GSTR 2005/3 (which discusses the exploitation of second-hand goods provisions to obtain input tax credits) to reflect the *LeasePlan* decision. Taxpayers are also advised that they may seek a refund of any overpaid GST on transactions which are comparable to those considered in the case. However, the Tax Office also cautions that it does not consider the case to be authority for the broader proposition that input tax credits would be available in any situation where there exists an intention that the goods will ultimately be sold, on the basis that the Court specifically noted that the present case was decided on the evidence.

NOTE: This concession does not apply to acquisitions of second-hand goods by an unregistered entity as the subsequent supply by the unregistered entity is not a taxable supply.

Where consideration for the acquisition is $300 or less, the amount of notional input tax credit available will be equal to 1/11th of the consideration provided for the acquisition.

Where the consideration for the acquisition is more than $300, the amount of notional input tax credit claimable will be the lesser of:

- 1/11th of the consideration provided for the acquisition, or
- 1/11th of the amount of any taxable supply subsequently made in respect of the acquisition.

Accordingly, the credit cannot be more than the amount of the GST you charge when you later sell the item.

The input tax credit for acquisitions of $300 or less can be claimed using the normal attribution rules (see 24.120), that is generally in the period the purchase occurred. Where the value of the acquisition is $300 or more, the tax period in which the input tax credit can be claimed is linked to the tax period in which consideration is received for the subsequent taxable supply of the second-hand goods. If the entity making the subsequent supply accounts on a non-cash basis (ie. accruals), the relevant tax period will be the earlier of when consideration is received or when a tax invoice is issued for the taxable supply (s66-15). The entity still needs to prepare a document similar to a tax invoice to substantiate the credit claim.

A private motor vehicle is traded in to a used car dealer for $6,600 (not subject to GST). The dealer then sells the car for a GST-inclusive price of $9,900. The dealer will be entitled to a notional input tax credit of $600 (ie. 1/11th of the acquisition price) when it sells the traded vehicle.

GLOBAL METHOD OF ACCOUNTING (SUBDIVISION 66-B)

A global method of accounting can be used where it is expected that more than one supply will be made from one acquisition. This may occur where parts of an acquisition are physically broken down (eg. a wrecker buys a car, dismantles it and sells the parts).

The global method allows all of the input tax credits to be offset against all of the GST on supplies made from this pool of acquisitions. No GST will be payable on all the individual supplies until all of the notional input tax credits have been absorbed. This approach does not apply where the consideration for the acquisition is less than $300 unless the entity chooses to apply it.

24.382   SECURITY DEPOSITS (Division 99)

The GST Act has a special rule dealing with the treatment of security deposits. A security deposit is a deposit held as security for the performance of an obligation. Examples of security deposits include chattel hire, advance bookings and deposits under standard contracts of sale.

WHAT IS CONSIDERED TO BE A 'SECURITY DEPOSIT'?

According to GSTR 2006/2, for a payment to be considered a 'security deposit' for the purposes of Division 99, it should have the following characteristics:

- be held as a security for the performance of an obligation
- the contract, conduct and intent of the parties to the contract must be consistent with the payment being a security deposit
- be at risk of forfeiture upon failure to perform the obligation, and
- be a reasonable amount.

Distinction must be made between a deposit and a part (instalment) payment. A deposit is commonly described by the Courts as an 'earnest' that is paid to bind the bargain. Division 99 only applies to deposits. The normal attribution rules apply for part payment, unless the entity accounts on an accruals basis in which the part payment is for a progressive supply. In this case, Division 156 applies (see from 24.122).

Further a deposit must be a reasonable amount. This amount is usually in the vicinity of 10% of total amount payable but may be varied based on the circumstances of the case (eg. a higher deposit may be required if there is a long period between the contract time to when the final payment is being made therefore increasing the risk arising out of default). This requirement is for the purpose of distinguishing between a deposit and liquidated damages/unenforceable penalty. Division 99 does not apply to payments that are liquidated damage/unenforceable penalty. Liquidated damages are payments of an amount of damages in advance and must be a genuine pre-estimation of the loss likely to be suffered by the injured party on termination.

Where the deposit is not a reasonable amount it will not be a security deposit and as such will be consideration for a supply. Accordingly, the GST payable or creditable acquisition will be attributed to the tax period in which the deposit – considered to be other than a security deposit – was paid /received.

WHEN IS A 'SECURITY DEPOSIT' CONSIDERATION FOR A SUPPLY?

Under s99-5 a deposit held as security for the performance of an obligation is not treated as consideration for a supply unless the deposit:

- is forfeited due to failure to perform the obligation, or
- is applied as all or part of the consideration for the supply.

NOTE: Mere payment and subsequent refunding of a security deposit will not give rise to GST consequences.

Where forfeiture or application occurs, there are specific GST attribution rules which apply. GST will be attributable by an entity to the tax period during which the deposit:

- is forfeited, and
- is applied as all or part of the consideration for a supply.

The ordinary attribution rules that apply depending on whether you are a cash or non-cash GST remitter are overridden by the specific attribution rules under Division 99 that apply to security deposits.

The entity making a security deposit is not entitled to an input tax credit unless the deposit is forfeited or applied to the consideration for a supply.

You do not need to remit GST at the time when you receive a deposit. You will only need to remit GST on the deposit when it is either forfeited or applied as all or part of the consideration for the supply. Therefore, when taking a deposit, it is not necessary to include GST on the deposit. However, bear in mind that in the event of a default and a security deposit is forfeited, you will have a GST liability of 1/11th of the deposit amount. You will need to finance the GST out of the forfeited deposit unless it is stated in the contract that there is a right to recover this amount. Therefore, it is advisable when taking a security deposit to base it on a GST inclusive amount.

In *Commissioner of Taxation v Reliance Carpet Co Pty Ltd* [2008] HCA 22, the High Court concluded that the forfeited deposit was a consideration for a supply and was attributable in the period of forfeiture pursuant to Division 99. The High Court overturned the Federal Court's decision that when the contract to supply the real property did not eventuate, there was no supply and therefore there cannot have been a consideration for a supply as a supply did not exist. The High Court however held that upon the exchange of contracts for the supply of the real property, there was a supply of several things, one of which was a contractual right exercisable over the actual piece of real property, in particular the right to require the property upon completion of the sale. The supply of this right constitutes a supply pursuant to s9-10(2)(d). As a result, GSTR 2000/28 and GSTR 2006/2 have been amended to take account of the High Court's decision in this case.

Fred hires a hall for $550 and pays $110 as a security deposit. When returning the keys, Fred paid the whole $550 and the $110 deposit was returned to him. The consideration for the hall hire is the $550 Fred paid when he returned the keys. The $110 deposit returned to him is not counted as consideration. Had Fred only paid $440 and allowed the deposit to be offset against the outstanding balance, the deposit would become part of the consideration for the hall hire.

If the deposit was non-refundable upon cancellation and Fred cancelled his booking, the deposit would also become consideration and subject to GST.

Also see GSTR 2009/3 regarding the interaction of cancellation fees and security deposits (see 23.124).

24.383   GAMBLING AND LOTTERIES (Division 126)

Gambling and lotteries are gambling supplies and are subject to GST. Gambling supplies include the supply of lottery, raffle or similar tickets, or the acceptance of bet relating to the outcome of a gambling event. A gambling event includes the conducting of a lottery or raffle or similar undertaking, or a race, game, sporting event, or any other event for which there is an outcome.

Special rules under Division 126 apply to the calculation of GST payable on gambling supplies. Effectively, GST is levied on the operator's margin on those activities and not on the value of prizes paid out. This would, in effect, be a 10% margin tax calculated on the difference between total ticket sales or bets taken and the value of prizes paid.

Amounts that the operator is liable to pay out on bets that are GST-free, such as prize monies payable to entities outside Australia, are excluded from total monetary prizes amounts.

The thresholds for tax periods and accounting method are calculated on the basis of the gambling margin rather than the gross amounts gambled (s188-32).

NOTE: Most office footy tipping and lotto pool arrangements will not be subject to GST or come under this Division as they are an informal arrangement amongst staff for private purposes and not in relation to the carrying on of an enterprise.

24.384   RECOVERY AND ON-CHARGE

Entities may incur expenses on behalf of a customer (as agent) or as a principal in the ordinary course of providing their services to the customer.

Where the cost is incurred as principal, the entity may seek to build that expense into the fee charged to the customer. This is referred to as 'on-charging'. Where the cost is absorbed into the consideration paid for the supply and 'on-charged' to the customer, its GST treatment is dependent on the supply which it is built into. For example GST-free council rates being reimbursed by a tenant to a landlord for a commercial rent is taken to form part of the consideration on the supply of the commercial rent and therefore is subject to GST (see 24.341). This expense incurred is treated as an input into the service or supply made by the entity. The entity incurring the cost is entitled to claim input tax credits if the acquisition is a creditable acquisition.

On the other hand, where the cost is incurred on the customer's behalf, the entity may seek reimbursement for that amount from the customer. This is referred to as 'recovery' or reimbursement. In this case, it is the principal that is entitled to the input tax credits because the acquisition was made on the principal's behalf relating to the carrying on of the principal's enterprise. The reimbursement to the agent itself is not subject to GST. For more information on GST and agency relationship see 24.330.

Where a financial supply facilitator incurs costs in providing the taxable supply of its services and passes on the costs as part of its fee for service (on-charging), the entire fee will be taxable. The facilitator may also incur expenses on behalf of the financial supply provider, and recover those expenses. The recovery will have the same character as the expense incurred on behalf of the financial supply provider.

24.410 GST AND FRINGE BENEFITS

For GST purposes, a fringe benefit is governed by the meaning given in s995-1 ITAA97 but specifically includes exempt benefits. This inclusion has significant consequences, as exempt benefits would not otherwise have fallen into the GST regime. The *Fringe Benefits Assessment Act 1986* specifically excludes exempt benefits from the definition of a fringe benefit. See also 25.150.

GST Ruling GSTR 2001/3 *GST and how it applies to supplies of fringe benefits* details the interaction of GST and the fringe benefit regime.

A provision of a fringe benefit to an employee, or an associate of an employee, can be a supply. However, for GST purposes, the supply of fringe benefit can only be a taxable supply if the recipient (employee) makes a form of payment or contribution to the employer for the benefit provided (ie. consideration for supply). This is the only form of consideration that is taken into account for calculating the employer's GST amount payable.

Services provided by employees in exchange for the benefit is not taken to be consideration for GST purposes, and therefore the provision of the benefit in these circumstances will not be a taxable supply.

Philip is provided with a car fringe benefit. He contributes $100 out of after tax dollars to his employer per week towards its cost to reduce the FBT taxable value. The $100 is treated as a recipient's payment and constitutes consideration for the taxable supply by the employer for the use of the car fringe benefit.

The employer is liable for the GST portion of the employee contribution – which is considered to be GST-inclusive. The employer will be liable for (1/11 x $100 = $9.09).

Employee payments made for benefits with no FBT value or for exempt fringe benefits will also be subject to GST. Therefore, it would be far better to salary sacrifice an exempt benefit as this is not consideration for GST purposes.

Where the employee makes a recipient contribution or recipient's payment to reduce the FBT liability by journal entry, the Tax Office will accept that consideration for the supply of the fringe benefit is received at the time of making the journal entries, to the amount of the offset that those journal entries reflect. It has long been established for FBT purposes that journal entries in the employer's accounts are a payment of a recipient's contribution and those journal entries can be made at the time the books of accounts are written up for income tax purposes.

Evan has a car provided as a fringe benefit in respect of which the FBT liability is $5,500. The accountant who prepares the income tax return for the year ended 30 June makes the necessary journal entries in September to reduce the FBT liability to nil. The reduction in the FBT liability of $5,500 is a recipient payment and the GST payable by the employer of $500 will be attributable to the September quarter.

Even though the employer will be required to remit GST of $500, this amount does not affect the employer's FBT liability on the car fringe benefit. The full amount of $5,500 will be deducted in calculating the taxable value of the car fringe benefit.

24.411 CAR-RELATED FRINGE BENEFITS

In relation to car fringe benefits, it is not always the whole amount of the recipient's payment that is used in working out the amount of GST payable by the employer. Employees can reduce the FBT value for a car fringe benefit by either making payments directly to employers or to third parties as consideration for supplies by third parties to the employee. Payments to third parties are not consideration for the supply of car fringe benefit by the employer. Instead, these third party payments are counted as consideration for supplies from the third party.

Andrew is provided with a car benefit of $3,300, calculated using the statutory method. Andrew contributes $1,100 in the form of payments to his employer but is also liable for the fuel cost, which is $400.

Even though the recipient payment and contribution total $1,500, which is the amount of the reduction in the taxable value of the car fringe benefit, only $1,100 will be subject to GST by Andrew's employer.

Andrew's payments directly to third parties will not be counted as consideration for the taxable supply of the car fringe benefit but is consideration for supplies from other suppliers.

24.412 SUPPLY OF FRINGE BENEFITS THAT ARE GST-FREE OR INPUT TAXED

Recipients' payments or contributions made for the supply of a fringe benefit that is GST-free or input taxed will not create a GST liability as there is no GST payable on these supplies.

If a private school provided discounted education to children of teachers, it is a fringe benefit. As the supply of education in this case is GST-free, no GST is payable on the supply of this fringe benefit for any recipient contribution or payments received by the school. Similarly, if residential houses are provided for senior executives to live in on an ongoing basis, no GST liability will arise on the supply of this benefit, as it is an input taxed supply.

24.413 REIMBURSEMENTS

An employer reimbursement of an expense payment benefit to the employee will not trigger a GST obligation on the employer. Instead, the employer is treated as if the reimbursement was consideration for an acquisition it has made and may be entitled to an input tax credit. The employer will only be entitled to the credits if the employee themselves is not entitled to claim it.

If the employee makes a contribution to the expense payment benefit, this should be treated as a reduction of the consideration for the acquisition which will result in an increasing adjustment event for the employer.

24.414 INPUT TAX CREDITS ENTITLEMENT FOR THE PROVISION OF FRINGE BENEFITS

With respect to input tax credits on the provision of fringe benefits to employees, the general rule is that they are acquired in carrying on the enterprise and will be available to be claimed. Employers who do not make any input taxed supplies will generally be in a position to claim all input tax credits on acquisitions acquired to provide employees with fringe benefits.

NOTE: Fringe benefits provided to employees in respect of employment in an enterprise is considered to be in connection with the enterprise carried on by the employer and will not be considered private or domestic even if the acquisition is used by the employee for personal purposes. For example, the provision of a car by an employer for the private use of an employee will not make the acquisition non-creditable.

For employers who provide fringe benefits but also make input taxed supplies, the GST position becomes less straightforward. Division 71 provides that suppliers of input taxed supplies may not be entitled to input tax credits on acquisitions made to provide fringe benefits. Acquisitions made to provide fringe benefits with no FBT value are not subject to Division 71. To ascertain the GST position, GSTR 2001/3 introduces two concepts, namely 'work benefit' and 'remuneration benefit'. These concepts will determine input tax credit entitlements for entities that make both input taxed supplies and provide fringe benefits.

These terms are not in the GST Act. These concepts cannot be read into the meaning of what is contained in the Act.

REMUNERATION BENEFITS

Remuneration benefits are benefits provided to employees in return for employee services. Suppliers of input taxed supplies are entitled to claim input tax credits on acquisitions that relate to providing remuneration benefits to employees. The fact that the employer makes input taxed supplies to customers will not make the acquisitions that relate to providing these remuneration benefits input taxed.

Ajax Credit Union acquires a car by way of lease for the purposes of providing it to an employee as a remuneration benefit. The supply of the car will be a taxable supply but Ajax will be entitled to an input tax credit for the lease payments and the car running costs.

However if the acquisition relates to the provision of remuneration benefits that itself is an input taxed supply such as residential housing, there will be no entitlement to an input tax credit.

WORK BENEFITS

In contrast, work benefits are not provided for consideration in the form of the employee's services because the purpose of the benefit is to serve genuine and legitimate ends of the employer's enterprise and any incidental advantage to the employee is disregarded as a minor outcome. Examples of work benefits include:

- provision of a car to an employee to use for work activities
- business travel and accommodation
- uniforms, and
- use/benefit of work property on work premises for work activities.

Acquisitions that result in work benefits are treated on the same basis as any other acquisitions that the entity makes. Connection between the acquisitions and the supplies made need to be established in order to determine the portion of input tax credit entitlement.

Home Loans Credit Union has a lending division. It has calculated that acquisitions that the credit union makes in this division relate 80% towards making input taxed supplies.

Any acquisitions, including work benefits, will be limited to 20% input tax credit entitlement for the lending division.

PART REMUNERATION, PART WORK BENEFIT

Where an acquisition is made to provide a fringe benefit that is in part a remuneration benefit and in part a work benefit that has a connection with making input taxed supplies, Division 71 will disallow the whole of the input tax credit.

Home Loans Credit Union acquires a fleet of vehicles by way of lease to use in the lending division. The vehicles are allocated to employees who are allowed to garage the vehicle at their homes.

FBT is payable on the vehicles due to the fact that employees are allowed to garage them. In this scenario, Division 71 will deny any input tax credit entitlement on the lease of motor vehicles as the vehicles have been acquired partly for (input taxed) enterprise activities and partly for private use by employees.

NOTE: Employers who make input taxed supplies need to be very careful how they classify their fringe benefits.

24.420 GST AND INCOME TAX

Generally, the GST component of income or expenditure is ignored for income tax purposes. However, there are exceptions, particularly where there has been a change in planned use.

The effect of GST on assessable income are:
- the GST payable in respect of taxable supplies is excluded from assessable income, and
- a decreasing adjustment is included in assessable income. (This can arise as a result of a change in the extent of creditable purpose [eg. when something is acquired for use in making an input taxed supply but its use changes to be applied to making taxable supplies]).

In respect of decreasing adjustments, an enterprise would have claimed an allowable deduction for an amount that includes the GST on the acquisition which was not claimed as an input tax credit to the extent the acquisition was not a creditable acquisition.

Therefore, by claiming the decreasing adjustment in a BAS, the over-claimed income tax deduction needs to be reduced by declaring the decreasing adjustment as assessable income.

NOTE: As unregistered enterprises do not make taxable supplies they will need to include the full amount of their supplies as assessable income.

The effect of GST on allowable deductions are:
- the input tax credit claimable in respect of creditable acquisitions and creditable importations is excluded from allowable deductions, and
- an increasing adjustment is included as an allowable deduction.

In respect of increasing adjustments, the enterprise would not have claimed an allowable deduction for an amount which was claimed as an input tax credit.

Therefore, by declaring the increasing adjustment in a BAS, the under-claimed allowable deduction needs to be taken into account by claiming increasing adjustment as an allowable deduction.

Where the adjustment relates to increased private or domestic use of the item, the increasing adjustment will not be deductible.

NOTE: Registered entities making acquisitions relating to input taxed supplies (ie. residential rents) will not be entitled to claim any input tax credits under the GST operations, however the GST component of the acquisition is included together with the acquisition and claimed as deductible expenditure.

Unregistered entities can claim the GST component of deductible outgoings including the cost of depreciable plant, CGT assets and trading stock.

NOTE: For income tax purposes, depreciable assets are depreciated over a period of time. However, for a registered entity the GST component of a depreciable asset is claimed outright at the time of attribution (subject to adjustments if there is a change in the extent of creditable purpose) and not over a period of time.

Where an input tax credit is not claimed by a registered entity, no income tax deduction is available for the portion of the expense that would otherwise be an input tax credit.

XYZ, a registered entity, receives a non-compliant tax invoice for $110 inclusive of GST. XYZ decides not to pursue the supplier for a compliant tax invoice. XYZ can only claim a tax deduction for $100 as it is entitled to an input tax credit for $10. The onus is on XYZ to request a compliant tax invoice from its supplier.

Division 27 ITAA97 sets out the effect of GST on deductions.

24.430 ANTI-AVOIDANCE

Division 165 of the GST Act contains the general GST anti-avoidance rules.

Under s165-5, the provisions of Division 165 operate if:
- an entity (known as the avoider) gets a GST benefit from a scheme (broadly defined)
- the GST benefit is not attributable to any entity making a choice, election, application or agreement that is expressly provided for by the GST law, the wine tax law or the luxury car tax law, and
- taking into account the matters in s165-15, it is reasonable to conclude that either:
  - an entity that, whether alone or with others, entered into or carried out the scheme, or part of the scheme, did so with the sole or dominant purpose of that entity or another entity getting a GST benefit from the scheme, or
  - the principal effect of the scheme, or of part of the scheme, is that the avoider gets the GST benefit from the scheme directly or indirectly.

Division 165 has no territorial limitations; it applies whether the scheme, or any part of the scheme, was entered into or carried out inside or outside Australia.

SCHEME

A scheme, defined in s165-10 inclusively, is:
- any arrangement, agreement, understanding, promise or undertaking – whether it is express or implied and whether or not it is legally enforceable, or
- any scheme, plan, proposal, action, course of action or course of conduct.

GST BENEFIT

An entity gets a GST benefit from a scheme if any of the following applies (s165-10):
- an amount of GST payable by the entity is, or could reasonably be expected to be, smaller than it would be apart from the scheme or a part of the scheme
- an amount of GST receivable by the entity is, or could reasonably be expected to be, larger than it would be apart from the scheme or a part of the scheme
- an amount of GST payable is, or could reasonably be expected to be, payable later than it would be apart from the scheme or a part of the scheme, or
- an amount of GST receivable is, or could reasonably be expected to be, receivable earlier than it would be apart from the scheme or a part of the scheme.

A GST benefit can arise even if there is no economic alternative that would have produced an effect equivalent to the effect of the scheme or part of the scheme.

GST DISADVANTAGE

A GST disadvantage is defined as (s165-45(2)):

- an amount of GST payable is, or could reasonably be expected to be, larger than it would be apart from the scheme or a part of the scheme
- an amount of GST receivable is, or could reasonably be expected to be, smaller than it would be apart from the scheme or a part of the scheme
- an amount of GST payable is, or could reasonably be expected to be, payable earlier than it would be apart from the scheme or a part of the scheme, or
- an amount of GST receivable is, or could reasonably be expected to be, receivable later than it would be apart from the scheme or a part of the scheme.

MATTERS TO BE CONSIDERED

Section 165-15 lists the matters to be taken into account in considering an entity's purpose in entering into or carrying out a scheme and the effect of the scheme:

- the manner in which the scheme was entered into or carried out
- the form and substance of the scheme (legal, economic and commercial)
- the purpose or object of the GST Act, the *Customs Act 1901* and any relevant provision of either Act
- the timing of the scheme
- the period over which the scheme was entered into and carried out
- the effect that the GST Act would have in relation to the scheme
- any change in the avoider's financial position that has resulted, or may reasonably be expected to result, from the scheme
- any change that has resulted, or may reasonably be expected to result, from the scheme in the financial position of a connected entity (the connection may be of a family, business or other nature)
- any other consequence for the avoider or a connected entity
- the nature of the connection between the avoider and a connected entity, including the question of whether the dealing was at arm's length
- the circumstances surrounding the scheme, and
- any other relevant circumstances.

CONSEQUENCES OF APPLYING DIVISION 165

Where Division 165 applies, s165-40 allows the Commissioner to negate a GST benefit the avoider got from the scheme, by making a declaration stating either or both of the following:

- the avoider's net amount for a specified tax period that has ended, and
- the amount of GST on a specified taxable importation that was made by the avoider.

Where the Commissioner considers that another entity (the loser) got a GST disadvantage from the scheme, and he considers that it is fair and reasonable that the loser's GST disadvantage be negated or reduced, s165-45 allows the Commissioner to negate or reduce the GST disadvantage by making a declaration stating either or both of the following:

- the loser's net amount for a specified tax period that has ended, and
- the amount of GST on a specified taxable importation that was made by the loser.

An entity may give the Commissioner a written request to make such a declaration (at his discretion).

In making a declaration in respect of either the avoider or the loser, the Commissioner may:

- treat an event that actually happened as not having happened
- treat an event that did not actually happen as having happened, and

- treat a particular event that actually happened as having happened at a different time or having involved particular action by a particular entity.

A single declaration may cover several tax periods or taxable importations.

NOTE: The High Court considered the operation of the anti-avoidance provisions in Division 165 in *Commissioner of Taxation v Unit Trend Services Pty Ltd* [2013] HCA 16. Whilst the relevant events occurred primarily before a change to the law which applied from 17 March 2005, the judgment contained generally applicable comments regarding how the exception for GST benefits arising from a '*choice, election, application or agreement that is expressly provided for by the GST law*' should be interpreted.

Fringe benefits tax

25

25.000 FRINGE BENEFITS TAX: OVERVIEW

Fringe benefits tax (FBT) is imposed pursuant to the *Fringe Benefits Tax Assessment Act 1986* (the FBT Act) and is payable by employers who provide taxable fringe benefits to employees, or associates of employees, in respect of their employment. FBT is payable at the top marginal rate of tax on the grossed-up taxable value (GST-inclusive cost) of benefits provided, with the amount of tax payable being assessed annually. The FBT year commences 1 April and ends 31 March each year.

All references are to the FBT Act unless otherwise stated.

25.001   DETERMINING THE FBT LIABILITY OF AN EMPLOYER

The following approach should be adopted to determine whether or not an FBT liability exists.

1: DETERMINE WHETHER OR NOT A FRINGE BENEFIT EXISTS

Pursuant to ss136(1), a fringe benefit will arise where all of the following conditions are satisfied:

- a benefit has been provided by an employer, an associate of an employer, or by a third party (an arranger) under an arrangement with the **employer** or an associate of the employer to an **employee** or an **associate** of the employee **'in respect of the employment'** of the 'employee', and is not specifically excluded.

The following items are specifically excluded from the definition of fringe benefit:

- salary and wages
- benefits made specifically exempt under the FBT Act
- benefits under certain employee share schemes
- superannuation contributions to complying superannuation funds
- employment termination payments
- capital payments in the nature of restrictive covenants or compensation for personal injury, and
- deemed dividends.

'Benefit' is defined broadly in ss136(1) FBT Act to include any type of benefit, including any right (including a right in relation to, and an interest in, real or personal property), privilege, service or facility, except for those specifically designated as being exempt.

2: DETERMINE THE TAXABLE VALUE OF THE FRINGE BENEFIT

Divisions 2 to 12 of the FBT Act categorise fringe benefits into thirteen different categories. Each category has its own rules for determining its taxable value:

Category	Division	Category	Division
Car	2	Board	9
Debt waiver	3	Meal entertainment	9A
Loan	4	Tax exempt body	10
Expense payment	5	Car parking	10A
Housing	6	Property	11
Living-away-from-home allowance	7	Residual	12
Airline	8		

3: APPLY ANY EXEMPTIONS/REDUCTIONS IN TAXABLE VALUE

FBT may be reduced or exempted altogether due to the application of specific provisions contained within the FBT Act (see 25.200 for list of exemptions and reductions available).

4: GROSS-UP THE TAXABLE VALUE OF THE FRINGE BENEFIT

The taxable value is grossed-up using either the:

- **Type 1 rate:** where the provider has an entitlement to an input tax credit (ITC) in respect to the provision of the fringe benefit, or
- **Type 2 rate:** where no ITC is available

For the FBT year commencing 1 April 2016, the Type 1 and Type 2 gross-up rates have increased due to the increase in the FBT rate (see below). The change in gross-up rates is summarised below:

Gross-up rate	2014-15 FBT year	2015-16 FBT year	2016-17 FBT year
Type 1	2.0802	2.1463	2.1463
Type 2	1.8868	1.9608	1.9608

5: CALCULATE THE FBT LIABILITY

The Step 4 amount is multiplied by the current FBT rate of **49%** to determine the amount of FBT. This is the employer's total FBT liability for the FBT year (exclusive of any instalments which have been remitted in respect of the FBT year).

The current FBT rate of 49% applies **for** the FBT year commencing 1 April 2015. The rate has increased from 47% (the rate that had applied from 1 April 2014) as a consequence of the imposition of the Temporary Budget Repair Levy on high income individuals from 1 July 2014 until 30 June 2017. This levy applies at a rate of 2% of an individual's taxable income in excess of $180,000 per annum. In order to maintain the relationship between the top personal marginal rate of tax and the rate of FBT, FBT has increased from 47% to 49% until 31 March 2017. Consequently, the Type 1 and Type 2 gross-up rates are also impacted by the rate change. This will ultimately affect the grossed-up taxable value of fringe benefits provided. The Type 1 and Type 2 gross-up rates for the 2015-16 and 2016-17 FBT years are 2.1463 and 1.9608 respectively.

Certain income tax exempt employers may either be entitled to an FBT rebate or a full FBT exemption (see 25.005 for the calculation of the FBT liability for such employers).

Reportable fringe benefit amounts will be grossed-up by the Type 2 gross-up rate also for the relevant period (see 25.300).

25.002 'EMPLOYEE', 'INDEPENDENT CONTRACTORS' AND 'ASSOCIATES'

EMPLOYEE

The definition of employee for FBT purposes is widely defined.

A current employee is defined in s136 FBT Act as a person who receives, or is entitled to receive, certain payments that are subject to PAYG withholding obligations, including payments of salary or wages and remuneration paid to a director.

NOTE: The term 'employee' also includes a future or former employee. This is designed to ensure that benefits provided to induce a person to become an employee and benefits provided after a person has ceased to be an employee (recognising past service) will be subject to FBT.

Importantly, s137 FBT Act extends the definition of employee to include persons who receive non-cash remuneration for services rendered in circumstances where, had they received a cash payment, they would have been considered a current employee. *Miscellaneous Tax Ruling MT 2019* provides an example of a director of a company who receives no cash remuneration for their services but is provided with non-cash benefits in connection with those services and therefore the FBT provisions have application. This treatment recognises that directors are considered to be 'employees' for FBT purposes.

The Full Federal Court in *Commissioner of Taxation v Indooroopilly Childrens Services Pty Ltd* [2007] FCAFC 16 considered it necessary to identify a particular employee in respect of whose employment a benefit has been provided before a fringe benefit can exist. Where an employer provides a benefit for employees generally, such as contribution to an employee benefit trust without reference to particular employees, it should follow that no FBT liability will arise.

LOCAL GOVERNMENT REPRESENTATIVES

Benefits received by elected representatives (councillors) are not automatically subject to FBT as they are not employees. Councillors may however elect unanimously (s446-5 of the *Tax Administration Act 1953*) to be treated as employees. If they do, the Commissioner must publish the election in the Government Gazette and FBT applies to any 'benefits' provided. These are then income tax exempt. The election can only be rescinded by another unanimous vote.

EMPLOYEE OR INDEPENDENT CONTRACTOR?

As a liability to FBT can only arise where an employment relationship exists, it is important to correctly distinguish an employee from an independent contractor. This can be a complex issue and is to be determined in light of the circumstances of each individual case. However there are established generic factors which will typically be relevant, with no one factor necessarily being conclusive.

Factors to consider in determining whether an individual is an employee or a contractor include:

1. **Performance of the work** – an employee performs duties within the business of their employer; an independent contractor conducts their own business, entering into contracts with others to perform agreed works and has the ability to delegate or subcontract work to another party.

2. **Degree of control** – in an employment situation the recipient of the services would typically have the power to control the delivery of services, whereas an independent contractor would carry out the work in a manner of their choosing with an intention of achieving a given result.

3. **Risk** – an employee would usually bear no risk in respect of the duties they perform, however an independent contractor bears various commercial risks flowing from the work they are engaged to carry out.

4. **Entitlements** – an employee would be entitled to annual leave, sick leave and long service leave which accrue to employees whereas a contractor would not be entitled to benefits of this type.

5. **Place of work** – an employee would usually perform their duties at the premises of the employer or at another location directed by the employer; an independent contractor would maintain their own place of business and perform services at the location of their customer/client when the contractor considered it necessary to do so.

6. **Tools and equipment** – an employee is likely to be provided with tools of trade from their employer; an independent contractor would provide their own tools and equipment.

Where it is determined that an individual is a contractor, benefits provided to the individual are not 'fringe benefits' as the required employer/employee relationship does not exist.

NOTE: The fact that an individual has obtained an Australian Business Number does not automatically rule out the possibility of that person being considered an employee. All factors relevant to distinguishing contractors from employees must be examined. The issue of workers being incorrectly classified as contractors rather than employees is a common area of review by the ATO and other revenue authorities.

VOLUNTEERS

For FBT purposes, an employee is a person who receives (or is entitled to receive) salary or wages, or a benefit that has been provided in respect of their employment. Generally, volunteers are not paid for work. Reimbursing a volunteer for out-of-pocket expenses does not cause them to be defined as an employee. Accordingly, benefits provided to volunteers do not attract FBT. FBT may apply, however, if an organisation provides non-cash benefits to workers in lieu of salary and wages.

BENEFITS PROVIDED TO AN 'ASSOCIATE'

The term 'associate' is important to the operation of the law. The FBT Act adopts the definition of associate contained in s318 ITAA36 subject to minor variations in s159 to deem authorities of the Commonwealth to be associates of each other, with the same applying for State authorities.

The term 'associate' is widely defined and in the case of an employee typically includes:

- a relative (see s995-1 ITAA97)
- a spouse or child
- a partner
- entities such as trusts under which the employee or an associate of the employee could benefit directly or indirectly, and
- companies more than 50% owned by the employee and/or associates and partnerships which are associates of similar entities or of natural persons. Partners

and partnerships are associates of reconstituted partnerships or partnerships which no longer exist.

A third entity can be an associate of a primary entity (see ATO ID 2006/196 for an example).

 Same sex partners are deemed to be associates pursuant to ss148(2) FBT Act.

RELATED COMPANIES

A company is related to another if:
- one company is a subsidiary of the other, or
- each of the companies is a subsidiary of the same company (ie. there is a holding company).

A 'subsidiary company' is defined in ss158(2).

THIRD PARTY PROVIDERS AND ARRANGEMENTS

An employer can be liable for FBT even if (directly or indirectly) the benefits are provided by third parties, or by an associate of the employer.

Arrangements to which these provisions might apply would include employees of retailers receiving benefits directly from the suppliers of those products which they sell – however, it would be necessary for the employer to be party to the arrangement, having knowingly participated in or facilitated the provision of the benefit for an FBT liability to arise.

The mere acquiescence by an employer to the provision of benefits in these circumstances may be sufficient to result in it being considered an arrangement for FBT purposes. Accordingly employers will be liable to FBT if they actually knew that they were involved in a manner described above in the provision of the benefit. Even if the employer did not know, a benefit still arises however if it is reasonable to conclude that they should have known that arrangements of the type described above resulted in the provision of the benefit (eg. where it is common industry practice for employees of retailers to receive incentive awards from manufacturers).

An employer would not be liable for FBT if they did not know of the arrangement and could not reasonably be expected to have known of the arrangement.

ARRANGER PROVISIONS AND MEAL ENTERTAINMENT

An employer is not necessarily liable for FBT for meal entertainment where the employer merely allows an employee (with or without leave) to, for example, go out to lunch with a client (where the client provides the meal entertainment) or attend a function provided by a third party.

Taxation ruling TR 97/17 however confirms that an employer is deemed to have entered into an arrangement where an employee is provided with an entertainment benefit if the employer knows of, or consents to, the provision of the entertainment to the employee by a third party, such that:
- the meal entertainment was provided under an agreement between the employer and the third party, or
- the employer knowingly participated in the provision or receipt of the meal entertainment (eg. by providing the drinks for a function organised by the third party), or
- the employer knowingly facilitated the provision or receipt of the meal entertainment (eg. by making premises available for a function organised by the third party), or
- the employer promoted, participated in or facilitated a scheme under which the meal entertainment was provided by the third party, (eg. by encouraging sales staff to participate in a product promotion organised by the third party under which they would be eligible for prizes consisting of meal entertainment).

 Heather is employed by an accountancy practice which provides taxation advice to many AFL footballers. The footballers often arrange free tickets for Heather and her partner to attend AFL matches and the corporate functions which precede them on match days. The partners of the practice encourage Heather to take up these offers as they provide an opportunity to network for new business opportunities. Might an FBT liability arise for the accountancy practice in these circumstances?

It is likely that a benefit has been provided, by a third party, which arises in respect of Heather's employment, which would make the benefit subject to the FBT provisions, resulting in her employer having an FBT liability.

25.003   'IN RESPECT OF EMPLOYMENT'

For a benefit to be a fringe benefit, it must be provided 'in respect of employment'. The link to employment must be substantive and material (see: *J & G Knowles & Associates v FCT* 2000 ATC 4151).

A 'benefit' as defined in ss136(1) includes any right, privilege, service or facility and must be provided *in respect* of the employment of the employee. A benefit arises when provided to an employee (or associate) by the employer of the employee (or an associate of the employer). A benefit may also arise if provided under an arrangement between the employer and a third party (see *Third party providers and arrangements* above).

Subsection 148(1) provides that a benefit will be 'in respect of employment' even though the benefit may also be provided in respect of, by reason of, by virtue of, or in relation directly or indirectly to, any other matter or thing.' Consideration of this provision occurs most often in situations where benefits accrue to the 'owners' of a business.

 Roger is an employee who is employed under the provisions of a particular industry award. The award requires Roger's employer to reimburse him for his home internet rental expenses. Roger's employer reimburses him, but only because they are required to do so under the award provisions.

If Roger wasn't an employee, the reimbursement would not have been made. The reimbursement is therefore a benefit provided in respect of employment and, consequently, it is a fringe benefit for the purposes of the FBT Act.

NOTE: The 'otherwise deductible rule' might apply to reduce to reduce the taxable value of the fringe benefit.

A specific reimbursement of legal costs incurred by an employee in a dispute concerning termination of employment will not have a sufficient or material connection to the former employment to fall within the meaning of 'fringe benefit' (TR 2012/8).

SITUATIONS WHERE FBT IS NOT PAYABLE

Miscellaneous Tax Ruling MT 2016 lists a number of specific examples of benefits which are considered outside the scope of FBT law:

- the value of meals and accommodation provided in the family home where children of a primary producer work on the family farm
- the value of board provided free in the family home to a child apprenticed to his/her parent as a motor mechanic
- a birthday present given to a child who works in a business run by the parents
- a wedding gift given by parents to an adult child who had some years earlier worked after school in the family business
- an interest-free or concessional loan given to such a child for the purpose of buying a matrimonial home
- the rental value of a farm homestead occupied by a family whose private company conducts the farming business in which they work and holds the title to the homestead, and
- the administration costs of an employer in providing fringe benefits (also see ATO ID 2001/333).

For legislative FBT exemptions and reductions see 25.200.

SHAREHOLDERS

Many shareholders in family companies allow their loan accounts to 'move' from credit to debit balances through the year. If the loan account is in credit (that is, the company owes the shareholder money) there cannot be a loan fringe benefit (see debt/equity rules at 6.200).

Similarly, should the company incur any expenses on behalf of the employee/shareholder or provide any taxable benefits, and an entry equivalent to the taxable value authorised by the employee/shareholder is debited to a loan account in credit, no FBT liability can arise (see also 25.150). But if the account becomes a debit loan account, consideration has to be given to whether a 'deemed dividend' arises under Division 7A ITAA36.

If, for example, a loan account has been in debit for the majority of a financial year but converts to credit immediately prior to year end (perhaps by declaration of a dividend), a loan benefit may arise. If the benefit arose from 'ownership' rather than employment however no fringe benefit would arise.

The Federal Court has held, in considering the meaning of 'in respect of the employment of the employee' that 'it must be established whether there is a sufficient or material, rather than a causal connection or relationship between the benefit and the employment.' It is not sufficient that there is some causal connection (eg. a director authorises the provision of a benefit to him/herself). There needs to be 'some discernible and rational link' and that connection must be 'material' (see *J & G Knowles and Assoc v C of T* [2000] FCA 196).

LOANS AND PAYMENTS AS DEEMED DIVIDENDS

When a journal entry turns an account into a debit loan account (or the loan account was in debit before the entry was made) a deemed dividend may arise unless certain conditions are complied with (see 6.300, 6.350 and 25.450).

Division 7A ITAA36 provides that a deemed dividend may arise in respect of a payment or loan to a shareholder (or associate), or from the forgiveness of a debt owed to the company by a shareholder (or associate) notwithstanding that the event occurs in consequence of the person's employment.

If the benefit being derived is either a loan or a debt forgiveness, the Division 7A rules will always apply, even if the contention by the lender is that the loan was made to the person in their capacity as an employee. That is, the FBT rules will not apply to such loans and Division 7A cannot be avoided by paying FBT. However, Division 7A will not apply to a payment made to a shareholder, or their associate, if the payment is made in their capacity as an employee (as defined in the FBT Act) or an associate (ss109ZB(3) ITAA36). An associate for this purpose is defined in s318 ITAA36. This means that such things as the payment of a shareholders business related expenses (eg. hotel costs while travelling for the business), the provision of an exempt benefit such as superannuation, will fall for consideration under the FBT rules, not Division 7A.

FBT is not payable on a loan made to an employee where the employee is a shareholder and no assessable dividend arises for Division 7A purposes because the company does not have a distributable surplus (s109Y limits deemed dividends to the distributable surplus). The loan is precluded from being a loan fringe benefit under the definition of 'fringe benefit' (see ATO ID 2011/33).

Note that while a loan may, for FBT purposes, have the 'otherwise deductible rule' applied, this rule does not apply for Division 7A purposes.

From 1 April 2007 any loan which meets the conditions in s109N ITAA36 (relating to the terms of the loan) will not result in a fringe benefit where the loan arises in respect of employment and no interest is payable in the first year ie. from the date of the loan to 30 June (see 6.300).

BENEFITS IN CONNECTION WITH EMPLOYMENT

A clear distinction is drawn by the Tax Office between benefits of the type described above (ie provided to shareholders in their capacity as shareholders), and those which form an integral part of the carrying out of duties for the employer.

Where a benefit is provided to a shareholder/employee of a family company in connection with the performance of his or her duties as an employee, it will be taken to be provided in respect of the person's employment (eg. a car owned by a family company is used by a shareholder/employee both in the course of employment as well as being available for private use).

FBT NOT PAYABLE IN THESE SITUATIONS

The employer would not generally be liable for FBT in the following examples involving family private companies (adapted from MT 2019).

Company A has two director/ shareholders, a husband and wife. The company's only asset is a house used as the private residence of the shareholder/directors. The company has no income from any source. Rent has not been paid on the house and all expenses – rates, repairs, maintenance etc have been paid for directly by the director/shareholders.

 Company B is the trustee of a family trust. Its directors are a husband and wife who, together with their children, are also the beneficiaries of the trust and reside in a house owned by the trust. The trust instrument provides for the beneficiaries to have a life tenancy in the house.

SUPERANNUATION INCLUDING IN-SPECIE CONTRIBUTIONS

Employer contributions of money made to a complying super fund in respect of an employee are exempt from FBT where the payment is made in money (paragraph 136(1)(j)). This exemption applies to contributions made to satisfy a super guarantee or award obligation, voluntary additional employer contributions and contributions made under an effective salary sacrifice arrangement (see 25.980). In specie contributions are specifically exempt from 1 July 2007.

25.004   PERSONAL SERVICES INCOME

For the Tax Office view on the interaction of FBT with the PSI rules see TR 2003/10 (also see from 16.100).

25.005   CATEGORIES OF EMPLOYERS

Depending upon the type of organisation, certain benefits provided to employees may receive concessional FBT treatment. The specific categories of employers that may receive concessional treatment for FBT purposes include:

- wholly exempt (for certain employees)
- partially exempt
- rebatable, and
- fully taxable.

WHOLLY EXEMPT EMPLOYERS – S57

Religious institutions are wholly exempt employers in respect of benefits provided to a person (or their spouse or children) where the benefit is principally provided in relation to pastoral duties or any other duties directly related to the practice, study, teaching or propagation of religious beliefs. Religious institutions are not required to report benefits provided to a religious practitioner (including their family) on that person's Annual Payment Summary.

Where benefits are provided to other employees of a religious institution, the institution will be taxed as a rebatable employer in respect of those benefits. See TR 92/17 for more information.

PARTIALLY EXEMPT EMPLOYERS – S57A

The FBT law provides an exemption for fringe benefits provided up to a specified amount per employee. Generally referred to as partially exempt employers, for the 2015-16 FBT year they are:

- Cap of $17,667 (grossed-up):
  - public hospitals
  - public ambulance services
  - not-for-profit hospitals, and
- Cap of $31,177 (grossed-up):
  - endorsed public benevolent institutions (PBI), and
  - endorsed health promotion charities.

NOTE: With the introduction of a three year Temporary Budget Repair Levy on high income individuals of 2%, the FBT rate has increased to 49% with effect from 1 April 2015 until 31 March 2017. To protect the cash value of benefits received by employees of certain FBT exempt and rebatable employers the annual FBT caps will be increased. For the 2015-16 and 2016-17 FBT years, the $30,000 and $17,000 caps will increase to $31,177 and $17,667 respectively.

Although in these cases the liability for FBT is reduced, the total value of the reportable benefits must appear on the individual's payment summary (s135Q). Benefits in excess of the caps are subject to the normal FBT rules.

Michael is employed by a Public Benevolent Institution (PBI) and during the 2015-16 FBT year packaged the following benefits:

	Taxable value	Grossed-up taxable value
Type 1 Benefits (@ 2.1463)	$6,000	$12,878
Type 2 Benefits (@ 1.9608)	$10,000	$19,608
Total	$16,000	$32,486

As the PBI is not subject to FBT on the first $31,177 of grossed-up benefits provided to Michael, the FBT payable in respect of Michael's benefits will be (($32,486 – $31,177) x 49%) = $641.41).

Michael's reportable fringe benefits on his 2016 Payment Summary will be $31,373. (ie. $16,000 x 1.9608)*

*The lower gross-up rate is always used to calculate RFB amounts.

VALUE OF CAPPING LIMITS

2014-15 FBT year

What value of benefits equals $17,000 when grossed-up?	What value of benefits equals $30,000 when grossed-up?
$9,009 (where 1.8868 is used) – Type 2	**$15,899** (where 1.8868 is used) – Type 2
$8,172 (where 2.0802 is used) – Type 1	**$14,421** (where 2.0802 is used) – Type 1

2015-16 & 2016-17 FBT years

What value of benefits equals $17,667 when grossed-up?	What value of benefits equals $31,177 when grossed-up?
$9,010 (where 1.9608 is used) – Type 2	**$15,900** (where 1.9608 is used) – Type 2
$8,231 (where 2.1463 is used) – Type 1	**$14,526** (where 2.1463 is used) – Type 1

The caps are maximised for the employee where Type 2 benefits are provided (such as mortgage repayments made on behalf of employees).

NOTE: In the May 2015 Federal Budget it was announced that a $5,000 per employee grossed up capping threshold will be introduced on certain meal entertainment and entertainment leasing facility expense ('EFLE') benefits provided by certain not for profit organisations under salary packaging arrangements. A salary packaging arrangement is one involving a benefit provided in exchange for a reduction in salary, or where it is reasonable to conclude that the salary would be higher if the benefit was not provided. This change, if it is passed by Parliament, will become effective from 1 April 2016. Such benefits provided in excess of this threshold will be subject to FBT at the full rate. However, an employee can apply their existing cap (ie the $31,177 or $17,667) to reduce the FBT on the excess meal entertainment and EFLE benefits. These benefits will also become reportable benefits for Payment Summary purposes.

BENEFITS EXCLUDED FROM THE CAPPING RULES

Some benefits referred to as 'excluded fringe benefits' are not required to be included in the cap calculation. Benefits excluded from the capping rules are:

* meal entertainment (see note above)
* car parking fringe benefits, and
* entertainment facility leasing expenses (eg. use of corporate box) (see note above).

Scott is the marketing manager of a well-known Public Benevolent Institution (PBI). The PBI as the employer is exempt from FBT where the total grossed-up value of certain fringe benefits for each employee during the 2015-16 FBT year is $31,177 or less.

As a marketing manager, Scott is entitled to receive the following benefits during the FBT year ended 31 March 2016:

	Taxable value	Grossed-up value
Car benefit	$4,659	$10,000
Expense payments	$6,989	$15,000
Meal entertainment	$13,352	Nil
Total cost	**$25,000**	**$25,000**

Assume the employer can claim input tax credits for all of the benefits. The employer offers Scott two options for his remuneration package:

1. Total salary of $105,000 (excl. superannuation guarantee), or

2. Salary of $80,000 (excl. superannuation guarantee) plus fringe benefits of $25,000.

From the employee's perspective:

	Option 1	Option 2
Taxable income	$105,000	$80,000
Less income tax	$26,797	$17,547
Less Medicare levy (@ 2%)	$2,100	$1,600
Income after tax	$76,103	$60,853
Less expenses the employee has to pay	$25,000	Nil
Net disposable income	$51,103	$60,853
Reportable amount	NIL	$25,000

(Calculations are based on the 2015-16 tax rates. Assume Scott has his own private health insurance. The reportable amount is the taxable value grossed-up by Type 2 factor - excluding meals as they are excluded from reporting). Note that with the proposed introduction of a $5,000 gross up cap on meal entertainment effective 1 April 2016, the result will be considerably different in the 2016-17 FBT year.

REBATABLE EMPLOYERS – S65J

Rebatable employers are certain non-government, non-profit organisations and are eligible for a rebate of 49% (increased from 48% in the 2014-15 FBT year) of the amount of FBT that would otherwise be payable. The organisations that may qualify for the rebate include:

- certain religious, scientific or public educational institutions
- endorsed charitable institutions
- trade unions and employer associations
- non-profit organisations established for the purpose of:
  - encouragement of music, the arts, science or literature
  - encouragement or promotion of a game, sport or animal race
  - community services purposes
  - promoting the development of aviation or tourism, and
  - promoting the development of the agricultural, pastoral, horticultural, viticultural, manufacturing or industrial resources of Australia.

The Commissioner of Taxation has indicated that charitable funds, as distinct from charitable institutions, cannot be rebatable employers for the purposes of s65J (refer to TR 2011/4). A charitable fund is typically established under a trust instrument or will.

The rebate is effectively capped at $31,177 (grossed-up) per employee per year, and therefore if the total grossed-up value of the fringe benefits provided to an individual employee exceeds $31,177, the rebate cannot be claimed for the FBT liability on the excess.

Graeme is employed as the finance manager at an endorsed charitable institution. During the 2015-16 FBT year, he has salary packaged the following benefits:

	Taxable value	Grossed-up taxable value
Type 1 benefits (@ 2.1463)	$6,000	$12,878
Type 2 benefits (@ 1.9608)	$10,000	$19,608
Total	**$16,000**	**$32,486**
FBT payable before rebate	$32,486 x 49%	$15,918
less rebate	49% x $31,177 x 49%	($7,486)
FBT payable after rebate		$8,432

As noted above, the May 2015 Federal Budget announced the introduction of an additional capping threshold which will become effective from 1 April 2016. The cap will be a $5,000 per employee grossed up capping threshold imposed on meal entertainment and entertainment leasing facility expense (EFLE) benefits provided by certain not for profit organisations under salary packaging arrangements. Such benefits provided in excess of this threshold will be subject to FBT at the full rate. However, an employee can apply their existing cap (ie the $31,177 or $17,667) to reduce the FBT on the excess meal entertainment and EFLE benefits.

25.050 FBT ADMINISTRATION

25.051   LODGMENT OF AN FBT RETURN

The FBT year runs from 1 April to 31 March in the following calendar year. Annual FBT returns for the year ending 31 March are generally due to be lodged by the first business day after 21 May each year, unless lodged through a tax agent, in which case the lodgement date is typically 28 May each year, or a later Tax Office approved date. Extended lodgment dates may apply to tax agents who lodge FBT returns electronically.

Tax agents can send clients' FBT returns directly to the Tax Office via the electronic lodgement service (ELS), in the same way they lodge income tax returns electronically. Alternatively, if a paper return is being lodged it must be signed and mailed to the Tax Office.

An annual FBT return is not required to be lodged if an employer's fringe benefits taxable amount for the FBT year is nil. However, if the employer is registered for FBT purposes but is not required to lodge an FBT return the employer must complete a *Fringe benefits tax - notice of non-lodgment*.

25.052   FBT INSTALMENTS

FBT instalments are not required to be paid where:
* an employer has not previously paid FBT
* lodged an FBT return, or
* if the FBT liability in the previous FBT year was less than $3,000.

These employers need only pay on an annual basis on lodgement of their FBT return.

For employers whose FBT was greater than $3,000 in the prior FBT year, FBT quarterly instalments are payable throughout the year via the employer's Business Activity Statement (BAS) or Instalment Activity Statement (IAS) (see 5.700). The FBT instalments will be printed on the June, September, December and March BAS or IAS sent by the Tax Office and are required to be paid by the due date for payment of the BAS or IAS, which is generally the 21st of the following month for monthly BAS lodgers and the 28th of the following month for quarterly BAS or IAS lodgers.

The amount of each FBT instalment for each quarter is normally a quarter of the FBT liability for the previous year (known as the notional tax amount), unless varied by the employer. Some small employers who are not required to be registered for GST can pay annually.

Where additional FBT is to be paid after the quarterly instalments have been made, any final payment is required to be made before the lodgment date of the FBT return for the year. Where the FBT return is lodged on or before the due date, any balancing payment can be made upon lodgment of the annual FBT return. Conversely, if the employer's instalments are more than the annual FBT liability and no other taxes are outstanding, the difference will be refunded.

VARYING INSTALMENTS

Where an employer estimates that their FBT payable will be less than the notional tax amount (ie. based on the prior year's FBT liability), an employer may vary their quarterly instalment on their BAS or IAS if the BAS or IAS is lodged by the due date.

To vary, the employer must disclose on the BAS or IAS the estimated amount of tax payable for the whole year, the varied FBT instalment and a reason code for the variation. The amount payable as a varied instalment is a quarter of the estimated FBT liability for the year.

 Caution should be exercised when varying an instalment amount as the employer may incur a general interest charge (GIC) where an underpayment of FBT liability arises for the FBT year.

25.053   'SELF-ASSESSMENT' AND FBT

As FBT is a 'self-assessed' tax, annual returns are not assessed. Instead, the FBT taxable amount, and tax payable reported on the return is treated as if a notice of assessment had been served on the employer on the date the return was lodged.

There is no 'grouping' of employers as commonly occurs with state based payroll tax. Each entity must register and lodge an FBT return. Consolidated entities are therefore required to lodge individual FBT returns. The FBT file number is the same as the employer's Tax File Number (TFN), regardless of whether the employer is a company, sole trader, trust or partnership.

DEFAULT ASSESSMENTS MAY BE ISSUED

If an FBT return is not lodged, an assessment may be issued (a default assessment) to show the taxable amount, and the FBT due.

PENALTIES

Failure to lodge a return by the due date may incur one 'penalty unit' up to a maximum of five units, for each 28 day period (or part) that lodgment is late. One penalty unit is currently equal to $170 ($180 from 31 July 2015). For a medium entity the penalty is multiplied by two and for a large entity by five. Making a false or misleading statement may incur a penalty of up to 200% of the tax avoided. Details as to how the Tax Office will apply penalties can be found in Practice Statement Law Administration PS LA 2012/5. Late payment of FBT due, or an instalment may result in a GIC being applied (see 4.660).

25.054   OBJECTIONS AND APPEALS

Similar rules apply to FBT objections and appeals as those which apply to income tax assessments (see 4.200 and 4.300). If a refund arises from an objection, interest on overpayments is receivable (see 4.265). Briefly, an objection must be in writing and state in full the grounds of the objection. The objection must be made within four years of either the date of assessment or self-assessment. However, if you are objecting to an amended assessment, this must be done within the later of:

- four years of the date of the notice of assessment that you are objecting to, or
- 60 days of the notice of that amended assessment.

Further reviews may be lodged with the Administrative Appeals Tribunal or the Federal Court. This is usually required within sixty days of the notice of decision on the objection being served on the taxpayer.

25.100   TAXING FRINGE BENEFITS

FBT liability is calculated on the grossed-up 'taxable value' of the benefits provided to employees (and their associates). The cost of the benefit and any FBT payable is tax deductible to the employer unless the FBT liability arises in the course of generating income which is not assessable.

In calculating the amount of FBT payable, the employer is required to:

(i)   identify and aggregate all Type 1 and Type 2 benefits provided

(ii) reduce the taxable value by any reductions, concessions or exemptions available

(iii) gross-up the taxable value(s) by the relevant gross-up rates (see below), and

(iv) apply the current FBT rate.

The introduction of the GST means that two separate gross-up rates are used in order to calculate the taxable value of fringe benefits – a higher (Type 1) gross-up rate and a lower (Type 2) gross-up rate. For FBT year commencing 1 April 2015, the Type 1 and Type 2 gross-up rates are 2.1463 and 1.9608, respectively.

These rates apply depending upon whether the provider of the benefit (ie. the employer). has an entitlement to input tax credits. The grossing-up of fringe benefits using the two different rates was introduced with the intention of restoring the similarity in tax treatment between salary and fringe benefits to the employee.

If the employee incurs and pays their own cost the before-tax cost is calculated this way:

Expense incurred x [1 divided by (1 – the employee's marginal tax rate)]

For an employee on the highest marginal tax rate of 49% (for 2015/16 including 2% Medicare levy) the equivalent pre-tax ratio is **1.9608**.

 During the 2015-16 FBT year, a $10,000 benefit that is not a GST creditable benefit is paid under a salary sacrifice arrangement.

Company employer	Paid as benefit	Salary
Salary	–	$19,608
Fringe benefit value	$10,000	–
FBT cost ($10,000 x 1.9608 = $19,608 x 49%)	$9,608	–
Total value	$19,608	$19,608
less tax deduction for payments made @ 30%	$5,882	$5,882
After-tax cost to employer (rounded to nearest $)	$13,726	$13,726

THE GROSS-UP FACTOR

The gross-up factor represents the amount of FBT payable on the grossed up value of the benefit. For all concessionally taxed employers, the exemption thresholds ($17,667 and $31,177 for the 2016 FBT year) do not include exempt benefits (such as superannuation) or excluded benefits. Excluded benefits are:

- car parking fringe benefits
- meal entertainment (ie. provision of food or drink) and benefits associated with that entertainment such as travel and/or accommodation, and
- entertainment facility leasing (eg. corporate box).

If the employer is a rebatable employer (see 25.105), the excluded fringe benefits are deducted from the individual grossed-up amount before the $31,177 cap is applied (refer to the previous note regarding the changes announced in the May 2015 Federal Budget regarding the imposition of a $5,000 grossed up cap on meal entertainment and entertainment facility leasing expenses). For PBIs (not a hospital) $31,177 is deducted from the 'individual grossed-up non-exempt amount' of fringe benefits. For example, if an employee has $45,000 in taxable benefits, deduct the $31,177 cap from the total. FBT payable is $13,823 x 49% = $6,773. When the employer is a not-for-profit organisation or a public hospital, the $17,667 cap is subtracted from the individual grossed-up non-exempt amount.

The gross-up position of a fully taxable employer is as follows:

*During the 2015-16 FBT year, an employer reimbursed $10,000 of various expenses of an
employee. All expenses are taxable supplies and a tax invoice is supplied for each expense.*

*The employee lodged a declaration with the employer claiming that under the 'otherwise
deductible' rule that $1,000 of those expenses would have been allowed as a tax deduction
to the employee.*

The FBT payable by the employer is calculated:

Expense benefits paid or reimbursed.. $10,000.00
less expenses under 'otherwise deductible' rule ....($1,000.00)
Taxable value of benefits... $9,000.00

*The fringe benefit gross-up factor is 2.1463 because the employer can claim
a GST input credit for all of the invoices reimbursed.*

Grossed-up value of benefits 2.1463 x $9,000 .... $19,316.70
FBT payable @ 49%** **$9,465.18

NOTE: See 25.150 for further details on the gross-up rates.

25.101   DEDUCTIBILITY OF FBT

Generally, employers can claim a tax deduction for the FBT incurred.

For 30 June balancing employers, FBT is deductible on this basis (see TR 95/24 for details):

**Actual FBT liability for FBT year ended 31 March less FBT instalment for June quarter
of the previous FBT year plus the instalment for the June quarter of the current year**

Employers who cannot claim their FBT liability as a tax deduction include not-for-profit bodies,
some of which are:

- entitled to the 49% rebate of FBT payable, or

- partly or wholly exempt from FBT, or

- assessed only on non-member income and the FBT is not related to that assessable
  income.

*A not-for-profit club derived assessable income from investments of $3,000. It provided
HELP and entertainment fringe benefits to employees of $1,600. No deduction is allowed for
the FBT liability as it was not incurred in deriving the assessable income of the entity.*

25.102   CONCESSIONALLY TAXED EMPLOYERS

Some employers are exempt from FBT while others are entitled to a 49% rebate (for the 2015-16
FBT year) against their FBT liability (see 25.105). In all cases the extent of the concession is limited
by a cap that is applied to benefits provided to each employee.

The value of concessionally taxed benefits for the employees of public and private non-profit
hospitals is limited to a grossed up value of $17,667 per employee. A $17,667 cap also applies
to employees of public ambulance services where the employee is predominantly involved in
connection with the provision of those services. If an employee is provided with grossed-up
benefits in excess of $17,667, full FBT is payable on the balance.

The value of FBT-free benefits for the employees of public benevolent institutions (other than
a hospital) is limited to a grossed-up value of $31,177 per employee. This also applies to
charitable institutions whose principal activity is to promote the prevention or control of diseases
in humans (a 'health promotion charity'). If the grossed-up benefits provided to an employee
exceed $31,177, the excess is subject to full FBT. Neither the $17,667 nor $31,177 limits are
pro-rated for part year employment and the cap applies to each employer of the employee.

All other benefits in excess of the above amounts will be taxed at 49% on their grossed-up value
for FBT years commencing from 1 April 2015.

25.103   NOT-FOR-PROFIT BODIES

Income tax-exempt organisations and those that are only assessable on their non-mutual
income generally pay FBT on the benefits they provide to their employees, or associates of
their employees. Some, however, have an exemption threshold of either $17,667 or $31,177

per employee (see 25.102 and 25.105 and the table at 25.987). Non-profit organisations that are neither exempt nor rebatable (see below) pay FBT on the grossed-up GST-inclusive value of taxable fringe benefits they provide, for example, entertainment expenses (see 25.920) or car fringe benefits (25.350).

The rules outlined below apply to employers which are:

- wholly exempt from income tax (see examples at 11.910), and
- partially exempt from income tax (includes not-for-profit clubs, societies and associations who derive income from member and non-member sources, but are taxed only on their non-member income).

25.105 REBATABLE ORGANISATIONS

A charity has to be endorsed and have an ABN if it wants to use the charity tax concessions available under the FBT legislation. Instructions for endorsement can be found in the Tax Office publications NAT 10651 and 10652.

NOTE: Charitable institutions of the Commonwealth, a State or a Territory, are not able to claim an FBT rebatable employer status.

The following not-for-profit bodies are exempt from income tax and are entitled to a 49% rebate of the amount of FBT they would otherwise have to pay. The total grossed up value of benefits that can be provided to each employee is however capped at $31,177 per FBT year. If the grossed up value of benefits to an employee exceed $31,177, the rebate cannot be claimed on the excess over that amount. The cap is not apportioned for an employee who is not employed for the full year. If the employee has more than one rebatable employer, the $31,177 cap applies to each employer. The relevant not-for-profit bodies include:

- religious institutions
- non-government scientific, charitable or public educational institutions
- non-government not-for-profit schools (includes pre-schools, but not tertiary institutions)
- trade unions
- associations of employers or employees registered under the law of the Commonwealth, State or Territory relating to settlement of industrial disputes
- a not-for-profit society, not-for-profit association, or not-for-profit club established for:
  - musical purposes, or the encouragement of music, art, science or literature
  - the encouragement or promotion of a game of sport
  - the encouragement or promotion of animal races
  community service purposes (not being for political or lobbying purposes), or
- a not-for-profit society, or association established for promoting the development of:
  - aviation or tourism
  - agricultural, pastoral, horticultural, viticultural, aquaculture, fishing, manufacturing or industrial resources of Australia, and
  - Australian information and communications technology.

A non-government scientific institution provides Type 2 taxable fringe benefits totalling $80,000 to its employees during the 2015-16 FBT year, but no individual employee exceeds the $31,177 cap.

Grossed-up taxable value of benefits is $156,864 ($80,000 grossed-up by 1.9608).

FBT payable ($156,864 @ 49%)	*$76,863.36*
less Rebate (49% of tax payable)	*($37,663.05)*
Net FBT payable	**$39,200.31**

NOTE: In the May 2015 Federal Budget it was announced that a $5,000 per employee grossed up capping threshold will be introduced on certain meal entertainment and entertainment leasing facility expense ('EFLE') benefits provided by certain not for profit organisations under salary packaging arrangements. A salary packaging arrangement is one involving a benefit provided in exchange for a reduction in salary, or where it is reasonable to conclude that the salary would be higher if the benefit was not provided. This change will become effective from 1 April 2016.

Such benefits provided in excess of this threshold will be subject to FBT at the full rate. However, an employee can apply their existing cap (ie the $31,177 or $17,667) to reduce the FBT on the excess meal entertainment and EFLE benefits.

REBATABLE EMPLOYERS – EMPLOYEE BENEFITS OF SALARY SACRIFICING

While the costs to the employer of an employee salary sacrificing FBT is tax neutral (assuming the employee is required to package any FBT cost), there can be benefits for employees. In determining any benefits to the employee, it is necessary to consider their marginal tax rate, the fringe benefits packaged and the employee's personal circumstances which may be impacted by reportable fringe benefit disclosures.

An employee has a total remuneration package of $100,000. He entered into a salary sacrifice arrangement to package a car under a novated lease for three years from 1 April 2015, and the details include:

- *Lease value: $30,000*
- *Statutory formula method is used to calculate the taxable value - the statutory fraction is 20%*
- *Total costs (including lease costs): $11,000 including GST per annum*
- *Superannuation guarantee is in addition to total remuneration and is excluded for the purposes of this example*
- *Medicare levy: 2%*
- *Cash salary is equal to taxable income*
- *Assume marginal tax rates for the 2014-15 year apply*
- *The employer is rebatable employer for FBT purposes.*

	Benefit not packaged	Benefit fully packaged
Total remuneration	$100,000	$100,000
Taxable value of car benefit	0	($6,000)[1]
Costs of car above taxable value	0	($5,000)[2]
FBT payable	0	($3,218)[3]
Input tax credit	0	$1,000
Cash salary	$100,000	$86,782
Income tax	($24,947)	($20,056)
Medicare levy @2%	($2,000)	($1,736)
After-tax cash in hand	$73,053	$64,990
After-tax costs of the car	($11,000)	0
Cash in hand	$62,053	$64,990
Benefit of packaging		$2,937[4]

*1: Taxable value = $30,000 * 20% statutory fraction = $6,000*
2: $11,000 (assumed costs per facts) – $6,000 taxable value = $5,000
*3: $6,000 * 2.1463 * 49% = $6,310. Less 49% rebate of $3,092 = FBT payable of $3,218*
4: Difference in cash in hand to the employee (ie. $64,990 – $62,053) = $2,937

In certain circumstances, employee contributions (ie. car expenses incurred from after-tax income) may reduce the FBT liability further. This would increase the 'cash in hand' available to the employee where the employee's personal marginal tax rate is less than the top marginal rate.

25.106   REDUCING THE VALUE OF FRINGE BENEFITS

There are a number of exemptions and a range of concessions available within the FBT Act.

EXEMPTIONS

Broadly, the categories of exempt fringe benefits include:
1. general benefit exemptions
2. specific benefit exemptions

3. certain relocation expenses
4. work related items (s58X), and
5. exempt minor benefits (s58P).

See *FBT exemptions* at 25.200 for further details.

REDUCTIONS

A reduction in the taxable value of a fringe benefit may occur because of:

- **Employee contributions (also referred to as recipient's payments)**
- **The otherwise deductible rule:** Benefits can usually be reduced to the extent that the employee would be entitled to a once-only tax deduction had the employee incurred the cost themselves.

JOINT BENEFITS

Where a benefit is provided to an employee and their associate(s) jointly (which includes loan fringe benefits, expense payment benefits, property benefits and residual benefits), the benefit is deemed to have been provided to the employee only (s138(3)). This means that the 'otherwise deductible rule' would will only operate to reduce the taxable value of a fringe benefit to the extent the employee's share of the fringe benefit is used for income producing purposes of the employee. The taxable value would not be reduced under the otherwise deductible rule in respect of the associate's share.

- **Certain exemptions:** For example, the first $1,000 of in-house benefits and concessions (eg. discount for travel in respect of employees in the travel industry). See 25.200 and 25.880. This reduction may not be available under certain salary packaging arrangements where the benefit is provided on or after 22 October 2012 (see 25.862).
- **Personal Services Income:** Where the provider of a fringe benefit (either an individual or a Personal Services Entity (PSE)) is not able to claim a deduction for the provision of the benefit because of the personal services income rules, the value of the benefit is reduced by the amount that is non-deductible to the provider. See 25.354.

An employee declaration is usually required before an employer can reduce the value of a benefit. The 'otherwise deductible' rule (see 25.555 and 25.826) does not allow a reduction in value for a benefit provided to an associate of the employee.

EMPLOYEE CONTRIBUTIONS

The taxable value of a fringe benefit may be reduced by the amount of any payment or contribution made by an employee or recipient of a fringe benefit towards the cost of providing that benefit (typically from their after-tax income). Such payments are known as employee contributions (or recipient's contributions).

The payment is not considered to be a recipient's contribution if an employee is provided with an expense payment fringe benefit in relation to the payment proportion of interest incurred on a loan granted to them by their employer (ATO ID 2012/88). See 25.550 for expense payment fringe benefits.

CONTRIBUTIONS BY JOURNAL ENTRY

Journal entries are evidence of an employee (recipient's) contribution only if all of the following conditions are met:

- the employee is under an obligation to make a contribution to the employer
- the employer has an obligation to make a payment to the employee, and
- the employer and employee agree to set-off the employee's obligation against that of the employer's obligation to the employee.

If payment of the employee's contribution is to be by journal entry, the entries must be made at the time the books of account are written up for income tax purposes (see MT 2050).

EXCESS CONTRIBUTIONS FOR A CAR FRINGE BENEFIT

The taxable value of a car benefit is reduced by employee contributions, both by way of payment of unreimbursed car expenses (fuel, maintenance and repairs) and cash paid to the employer. If contributions exceed the taxable value of the benefit, the excess cannot be carried forward to another FBT year, and cannot be used to reduce the taxable value of other benefits. The exception to this is if there is a remuneration agreement in place between the employee and employer to make recipients payments under sub-paragraph 9(2)(e)(i) to the extent of the taxable value of the fringe benefit; excess amounts may be set aside for a later FBT year (see ATO ID 2005/210).

An employer provides an employee with a fringe benefit that has an FBT taxable value of $1,100 and which is a GST taxable supply. The employee contributes $440 towards the cost of the benefit. This amount is paid directly to the employer.

Employer's position

- *$40 GST ($440 x 1/11th) is the amount the employer must pay in respect of the employee contribution received.*
- *$400 is included in employer's assessable income.*

FBT taxable value reduced to $660 ($1,100 – $440).

Only contributions made by the recipient of the benefit reduce the taxable value.

Employer's income tax and amount of employee's payment or contribution			
Taxable supply for GST purposes	**Amount included in employer's assessable income**	**Input tax credit available?**	**Employer's tax deduction**
Yes	GST exclusive value (ie. 10/11th of payment or contribution)	Yes	GST exclusive value (ie. 10/11th of amount)
No	Full payment or contribution	No	Full amount paid

REIMBURSEMENTS

An employer reimbursement to an employee for an expense payment benefit will not trigger a GST obligation for the employer. For GST purposes, an employer is generally only liable for GST if the employee makes some form of payment or contribution (consideration) to the employer for the benefit provided (supply). If the employee only provides their services in exchange for the benefit, this is not 'consideration' for GST purposes. Therefore, the provision of the benefit in these circumstances will not be a taxable supply.

Division 111 *A New Tax System (Goods and Services Tax) Act 1999* (GST Act) however treats payments to employees in the form of expense payment benefits as consideration for an acquisition made by the employer so that the employer is entitled to an input tax credit as if the employer had acquired the thing directly from a supplier.

NOTE: It does not matter if the employer reimburses the employee or makes a direct payment to the supplier of the goods on behalf of the employee.

An employer reimburses one of its employees for gym membership fees of $330 GST inclusive. Under Division 111 GST Act, the employer will be entitled to an ITC of $30 (1/11th of $330). As there is an ITC entitlement, this is a Type 1 benefit and the higher gross-up rate applies.

For the 2015-16 FBT year, Jill spends $440 (GST inclusive) on hotel accommodation when she is away on her employer's business. Her husband Claude accompanies her and does not work for her employer. Jill's employer reimburses her the full $440 ($110 of which is applicable to Claude). Jill's employer can claim a full GST ITC of $40 ($440/11). Employer's tax deduction is $400 (10/11 x $440). FBT payable = $110 x 2.1463 x 0.49 = $115.69.

25.150 FBT AND GST

25.151 FBT AND GST RATES

A GST of 10% applies on most goods and services supplied in Australia and imported into Australia. GST affects the classification of benefits as either type 1 or type 2 benefits and also affects the calculation of an employer's FBT liability.

As outlined above, the higher, type 1 gross-up rate is used by an employer to calculate their FBT liability where they (or other providers) are entitled to input tax credits for GST paid on goods or services acquired to provide benefits. Conversely, the lower type 2 gross-up rate is used where there is no entitlement to an ITC.

Where an employee makes a contribution or payment towards the cost of the fringe benefit provided, this may be treated as consideration for a taxable supply for GST purposes.

The Tax Office has issued two rulings on the interaction of GST and FBT. TR 2001/2 is entitled *FBT: the operation of the new fringe benefits tax gross-up formula to apply from 1 July 2000* and GSTR 2001/3 is entitled *GST and how it applies to supplies of fringe benefits* (see 24.410).

FBT liability is calculated on the grossed-up taxable value of the benefits provided to employees (and their associates). The cost of the benefit and any FBT payable is typically tax deductible to a tax paying employer.

There are two gross up rates depending on whether or not the benefit is a GST creditable benefit (ie. the employer is entitled to recoup some or all of the GST input tax credits). The current FBT rate (49% for the 2015-16 FBT year) results in the gross up rates shown below. Specifically:

- **From 1 April 2014 to 31 March 2015:** The Type 1 gross up rate is 2.0802 and Type 2 gross-up rate is 1.8868.
- **From 1 April 2015 to 31 March 2016:** The Type 1 gross up rate is 2.1463 and Type 2 gross-up rate is 1.9608.

25.152 EFFECT OF GST ON FBT

If there are supplies which include GST but for which no tax deduction is available, an input tax credit cannot be claimed. However, if they are provided as fringe benefits they are generally deductible for income tax purposes and the input tax credit can be claimed. Examples include:

- travel expenses for relatives where an employee undertakes business travel
- recreational club expenses to obtain membership rights to enjoy facilities of a recreational club, and
- entertainment expenses.

All of the above acquisitions, if provided as fringe benefits (ie benefits on which FBT arises) and therefore deductible for tax purposes, will entitle the provider to an ITC. The test for determining which gross-up rate to use is whether the acquisition of the thing used to provide the benefit resulted in an entitlement to an ITC to the provider.

If the benefit has neither been acquired nor imported (eg. manufactured) it cannot be a type 1 benefit.

 If the benefit provided was an in-house property fringe benefit (see 25.860), the provider would treat the provision of such a benefit as a Type 2 benefit as it was not acquired.

A provision of a fringe benefit which is GST-free or input taxed will not entitle the provider to any ITCs. As no ITC is available to the provider, these benefits will be classified as type 2 benefits. Examples include:

- **Input taxed fringe benefit:** long-term residential accommodation and private credit card debts where no specific invoices are provided, and
- **GST-free fringe benefit:** school fees.

GST-INCLUSIVE OR EXCLUSIVE

Irrespective of whether a benefit is Type 1 or Type 2, for calculating the taxable value of a fringe benefit, the GST-inclusive value of the fringe benefit is used when calculating the taxable value of a fringe benefit. When calculating the taxable value of a fringe benefit, the value of a recipient's payment or a recipient's contribution will also be the GST-inclusive value.

Where the otherwise deductible rule applies (see 25.555 and 25.826), the calculation of the taxable value of a fringe benefit is reduced by the deduction to which the employee would have been entitled had the employee incurred the expense personally. In these situations, the employer takes into account the GST-inclusive value, as applicable.

For the purposes of calculating the taxable value of a car fringe benefit, there are two methods available, either the statutory method or the operating cost method. Both methods use the GST-inclusive value of the car. For the operating cost method, running cost expenses will also be the GST-inclusive value.

25.200 FBT EXEMPTIONS

Some benefits provided to employees (or their associates, see 25.002) are exempt from FBT. With the exception of car expense reimbursement benefits paid using the cents-per-kilometre method, exempt benefits are exempt from both FBT in the hands of the employer and income tax in the hands of the employee. Some benefits are exempt because of the nature of the employer, some because they are 'minor' and others are specifically exempt.

 Where an employer applies any of the following concessions and reduces the taxable value of a fringe benefit, the employer should maintain appropriate documentation.

25.201   FBT-EXEMPT EMPLOYERS

Some or all of the benefits provided by these employers are exempt from FBT.

 The reportable fringe benefit rules still apply unless the benefit is an exempt benefit (eg. a minor benefit) or an excluded fringe benefit (see 25.305).

PUBLIC BENEVOLENT INSTITUTIONS

Benefits provided to employees of non-hospital public benevolent institutions are exempt to a maximum grossed up amount of $31,177 per employee (see 25.100 and 25.103).

PUBLIC AND NON-PROFIT HOSPITALS ETC

Public hospitals (including government public hospitals) and not-for-profit hospitals are limited to a capped exemption per employee of a grossed up amount of $17,667 (see 25.100 and 25.102).

HEALTH PROMOTION CHARITIES

An exemption applies to benefits provided by a charitable institution, the principal activity of which is promoting the prevention or control of disease in humans. The exemption is subject to the $31,177 grossed up limit per employee (see 25.100 and 25.102).

HOUSING BENEFITS FROM CHARITIES AND NON-PROFIT HOSPITALS IN REGIONAL AREAS

An exemption from FBT applies for housing benefits provided by these employers located at least 100 kilometres from a population centre of 130,000 or more.

PUBLIC AMBULANCE SERVICES

Fringe benefits provided to an employee are exempt from FBT subject to a cap of $17,667 per annum per employee, grossed up taxable value. The exemption applies to an employee where the employer provides public ambulance services or services to support those services and the employee is predominantly involved in connection with the provision of those services.

HOUSING BENEFITS PROVIDED BY PUBLIC AMBULANCE SERVICES

The remote area housing exemption applies to benefits provided by a public ambulance service or services that provide those services. The employee must be predominantly involved in connection with the provision of those services. A remote area for this purpose is a one that is at least 100 kms from a population centre of 130,000 people.

LIVE-IN RESIDENTIAL CARE WORKERS

Accommodation and meals etc. provided by government bodies, religious institutions and not-for-profit companies are exempt when provided to employees caring for elderly or disadvantaged persons (s58).

- 'Disadvantaged' means intellectually, psychiatrically or physically handicapped, or in necessitous circumstances.
- 'Elderly' means people over 60 years of age.

RELIGIOUS INSTITUTIONS

FBT is not payable on benefits (including those provided to an employee's spouse or child), if the employee is a religious practitioner or full-time member (or a student training to become a member) of a religious order and the benefit is provided principally in respect of pastoral duties or other duties related directly to the practice, study, teaching or propagation of religious beliefs.

As long as the religious practitioner's duties are of a religious nature, the exemption extends to any accommodation and food provided to that employee (including their spouse and child) by religious institutions (s57).

This exemption applies even though the practitioner is not a common law employee.

If the benefit is provided principally in respect of duties that are not directly related to pastoral duties or the study, teaching or propagation of religious beliefs, the exemption is limited to the lesser of an employee's reportable fringe benefit amount (see 25.300) and $31,177.

Benefits provided in respect of duties that are not religious in nature are subject to FBT but are rebatable even when provided by a religious institution (see 25.105).

 Use of a motor car for private purposes, or where the car is provided principally on account of employment in a school.

INTERNATIONAL ORGANISATIONS

FBT is not payable by international organisations exempt from income tax and other taxes by the operation of the *International Organisations (Privileges and Immunities) Act 1963.*

Also exempt are organisations established under international agreements to which Australia is a party and which oblige Australia to grant the organisation general exemption from taxes.

25.202   SPECIFIC FBT EXEMPTIONS

MEDICAL TREATMENT

All employer payments for workers' compensation and payments by workers' compensation insurance are exempt from FBT. Medical services provided on site through first aid posts and medical clinics are exempt if principally for treating any work-related injuries and illnesses.

WORK-RELATED HEALTH CARE

Work-related preventative health care is an exempt benefit under s58M. The care must be available to all employees of the employer at risk of suffering from similar work related trauma, who work in close proximity to the employees suffering from the trauma and who performs similar duties. For example, a flu injection provided to all employees of an employer would be exempt (see ATO ID 2004/301).

Where an employee undergoes a medical examination prior to the commencement of a new employment position with the same employer, the benefit will also be accepted as a work-related medical examination that is an exempt fringe benefit.

Where an employer has arranged for a fitness program to be made available to its employees for the purpose of assisting them with managing their health, fitness and stress by learning to eat better, exercise properly and the employer allocates time during the working day, the Tax Office concedes that the employer would have an objective, plan or policy in place to improve or maintain the quality of their employees' performance which would qualify as an exempt benefit under s58M. The program should be limited to only educating employees on how to eat healthier and exercise correctly.

The subsidising of private health premiums was not considered to be an exempt expense payment fringe benefit under s58M in *Lake Fox Limited and Commissioner of Taxation* [2012] AATA 265. The Tribunal was of the view that the expenditure did not constitute either work-related medical examination costs, medical screening, preventative health care or counselling expenditure.

RELOCATION AND RECRUITMENT COSTS

The following expenses are exempt:

- employee and family travel costs to the new work location, including accommodation and meals to break the journey, and accident insurance
- removal and storage of household goods and effects as part of the relocation
- temporary accommodation (for time limit see *Temporary accommodation when relocating*), and
- costs of sale or purchase of houses owned by an employee on job relocation – such as stamp duties, legal fees and commissions.

An employee who is required to live 3,000 kilometres away from their usual place of residence is still entitled to an exemption for expenses reimbursement for removal and storage of household goods notwithstanding that the employer does not require the employee to change their residence (ATO ID 2013/8).

Visa costs incurred by an employer in respect of an employee who has already in Australia to extend that employee's stay is not an exempt benefit (as relocation transport) (see ATO ID 2013/35).

CERTAIN OVERSEAS MEDICAL TRAVEL

Where the employee is posted to a foreign country, there is no FBT on the cost of travel of either the employee or family members when solely for the purpose of getting suitable medical treatment at either the nearest place it is available, or where it can be obtained at the least cost.

EMERGENCY ASSISTANCE

FBT is not payable for emergency assistance given to an employee if the assistance is, for example, health care, food, clothing, accommodation or transport etc. following a natural disaster.

 The health care exemption only applies if given to an employee of the employer.

EMPLOYEE TRANSPORT

If an employer is in the business of providing transport to the public, and the employee is employed in that business, there is no FBT on the provision of free or discounted travel:

- to or from work, or
- on a scheduled metropolitan service.

NOTE: This exemption is available in respect of in-house fringe benefits. This exemption is not available where provided under a salary packaging arrangement on or after 22 October 2012 (see 25.862).

USE OF BUSINESS VEHICLES

An exemption from FBT exists for incidental use of some business vehicles. See 25.350.

TAXI TRAVEL

Taxi travel provided to employees is exempt from FBT:

- if provided for travel when due to illness or injury, between any of work, home or other necessary or appropriate place, and
- when the travel either began or ended at the employee's place of work. The travel must be a single trip (eg. if an employee travels by taxi from work to a concert, and then by taxi to home, only the fare from work to the concert is exempt).

Taxis provided on other occasions can also be exempt as minor benefits if provided on an irregular and infrequent basis (see minor benefits below). While there is no need to retain receipts or other declarations, employers must be able to produce reasonable records to show the taxi travel satisfied these conditions.

EXEMPT LOAN BENEFITS

Loan benefits are exempt from FBT when provided to employees and:

- the employer is engaged in the business of money lending and the loan made to the employee was fixed at a rate equal to a rate available to members of the public
- the employer is in the business of money lending and the rate is variable but is never less than the arm's length rate
- the employer advances money to the employee to meet employment-related expenses which will be incurred within the next six months. The expenses must be accounted for and any excess refunded or offset, and
- an advance which is repayable within 12 months is used by the employee as a security deposit for accommodation. Applies only where the accommodation is also an exempt benefit.

'PROPERTY' CONSUMED ON BUSINESS PREMISES

Goods provided to, and consumed by employees on a working day on the employer's business premises are exempt from FBT. Examples include:

- meals and drinks (see 25.900, 25.920 and 25.940) except those provided under 'meal card' arrangements, and
- private telephone calls (including those made from employer provided mobile phones).

This exemption does not apply to such benefits where they are provided under a salary packaging arrangement.

USE OF BUSINESS PROPERTY

Any private use of plant located on the business premises used principally for business purposes is exempt from FBT (excludes use of an employer's 'motor car' (see 25.350)).

BENEFITS PROVIDED ON EMPLOYER'S PREMISES

Some benefits provided to employees are exempt where they are provided on the employer's premises for the benefit of the employees, including:

- recreational facilities (even if provided on the business premises of a related company in a wholly owned company group)
- child care facilities located on business premises of the employer or a related company
- the provision of health care being medical treatment, first aid, physiotherapy, diagnostic services, health counselling and provision of drugs in an in-house health care facility (s58K).

The clinic or facility must be operated principally for health care relating to work-related injuries of employees and must be on the employer's premises. The exemption will also apply if the services are provided off-premises by a member of staff of the facility to an employee.

For what constitutes 'business premises' see 25.353 and TR 2000/4.

TEMPORARY ACCOMMODATION WHEN RELOCATING

If an employee is provided with temporary accommodation (including household goods) when changing his/her usual place of residence in the course of their employment (or starting new employment) the benefit may be reduced to nil. The exemption takes two forms:

- **Accommodation at former location:** An exemption applies for a maximum of 21 days for temporary accommodation at the employee's former locality. This applies where the house is no longer available (eg. sold) or it is unsuitable for residential use due to removal of furniture or other matters caused by the change in employment.

- **Accommodation at new locality:** After starting work at the new locality the employee must make sustained, reasonable efforts to obtain permanent accommodation. The maximum exemption period is usually four months, starting seven days before starting the new employment, and ending when it could reasonably be expected that the new residence would be occupied. The exemption period can increase to six months where the employee gives to the employer a declaration which details efforts made to find permanent accommodation. The exemption can extend to 12 months if a similar declaration is made and the employee sold his/her residence at the previous locality within six months of starting the new employment.

RELOCATION

Many of the costs associated with relocation of an employee (both new and existing) are exempt from FBT if they are required to change their job locations. This exemption applies to:

- costs of removal and storage of household effects (including pets), including removal, storage, packing, unpacking and insurance of household effects. The removal must take place within 12 months of starting employment duties at the new location

- costs associated with the sale of a house, including stamp duty, advertising, legal fees, agent's commission, discharge of a mortgage, and expenses of borrowing provided:
  - the sale is made solely because the employee changed his/her usual residence to carry out the employment duties
  - the house was owned by the employee before being notified of the required change in location
  - the house was the employee's usual place of residence and the sale contract was made within two years of commencing duties at the new location

- costs associated with the purchase of a house at the new location provided:
  - the employee owned a home at the former location
  - the purchase was made solely because of the relocation
  - the new home will become the usual place of residence,
  - the purchase contract is made within four years of starting employment at the new location, and
  - the employee must either sell their old dwelling, or propose to sell it.

- when an employee purchases a dwelling at a new location without having sold their dwelling at their old location, the employer is still able to get the FBT exemption for costs incidental to the purchase of the new dwelling, provided that the employee sells their dwelling at the old location within two years of commencing their new employment. The date at which an employee enters into a contract for the new dwelling is the date of the contract. The existing four year limit referred to above is retained. However, if the employee fails to sell their old dwelling within two years of commencing duty at the new location, the benefit becomes subject to FBT in the year in which two years after that commencement occurs.

- cost of connecting electricity, gas and telephone if they are connected within 12 months of starting work at the new location

- employees and family members' transport costs (including meals and accommodation en route). This exemption includes employer paid travel costs to arrange accommodation prior to actual employment relocation provided that the employee has already accepted an offer to transfer (see ATO ID 2004/293).

If a car reimbursement is on a cents-per-km basis, the value of the payment is reduced by the amount that would have been applicable if deductions were claimed on a cents-per-km basis, and

- the cost of engaging a relocation consultant under an arm's length arrangement to assist in the relocation of an employee where the employee moves residence as part of their employment.

  The benefit must be an expense payment or residual benefit (eg. the consultant obtains removalists quotes, negotiates leases etc.) but the exemption does not extend to payments that the consultant makes on behalf of the employee (full conditions are set out in 58AA(1)(c)).

ACCOMMODATION AWAY FROM HOME

A unit of accommodation provided to employees who are required to live away from home to perform their employment, or who are travelling in the course of their employment duties, may be exempt provided the employee gives the employer an approved declaration. Where the employee is living away from home the potential exemption is very limited and subject to a number of criteria being satisfied (see 25.840).

The same declaration can be used where, rather than paying a Living-Away-From-Home (LAFH) Allowance (see 25.840) to an employee, the employer reimburses or pays the accommodation expenses of the employee required to live away from his/her usual home.

WORK-RELATED ITEMS – S58X

Any of the following benefits provided by an employer to an employee in respect of the employee's employment is an exempt benefit:

- an expense payment benefit where the recipient's expenditure is in respect of an eligible work-related item
- a property benefit where the recipient's property is an eligible work-related item
- a residual benefit where the recipient's benefit consists of the making available of an eligible work-related item

Each of the following is an *eligible work related item* if it is primarily for use in the employee's employment:

- a portable electronic device (such as a laptop computer, tablet computer, personal digital assistant (PDA), etc)
- an item of computer software
- an item of protective clothing
- a briefcase, and
- a tool of trade.

However, the exemption is restricted to one item per FBT year per employee. This means that an employer can provide an employee with one portable device, one item of computer software, and one briefcase which will each be eligible for the exemption. However, if an employer provides an employee with two portable electronic devices that have a substantially identical function, only one of the portable devices will be eligible for the exemption. If the second portable device is provided to the employee as a replacement item (ie. the first one was stolen) the second portable device would then also be eligible for the exemption.

The exemption applies only to an employee – such benefits provided to an associate of the employee are not exempt.

NOTE: In the May 2015 Federal Budget it was announced that the FBT concessions for work-related portable electronic devices would be extended for small businesses (ie those businesses with an aggregated annual turnover of less than $2 million). With effect from 1 April 2016 small businesses will not be subject to the limitation of one qualifying work-related portable electronic device, where the items have substantially similar functions. However, it is important to note that the requirement that each device be provided primarily for employment remains in place.

MEMBERSHIP FEES

Membership fees and subscriptions paid or provided to employees are exempt if they are:

- a subscription to a trade or professional journal
- an entitlement to use a corporate credit card, and
- entitlement to use an airport lounge membership (eg. Qantas Club).

IN-HOUSE BENEFITS

The first $1,000 of the taxable value of in-house benefits may be exempt (see 25.860). Note however that this reduction may not be available where in-house benefits are provided under a salary packaging arrangement on or after 22 October 2012 (see 25.862).

CAR EXPENSES

Car expense payments where the employee is reimbursed for the use of his/her personal car using the cents-per-km method, are exempt from FBT. They are unique because they are the only benefits which are assessable in the hands of the employee.

This particular exemption does not apply if the reimbursement of the car expense is for any of the following, but a part or full exemption from FBT may apply under particular provisions:

- holiday transport from a remote area
- overseas employment holiday transport
- relocation transport (see *Relocation*)
- transport:
  - to attend an employment interview or selection test
  - to attend work-related medical examinations, preventative health care, medical screenings, counselling and migrant language training, or
  - provided after the employee has ceased to perform the duties of that employment.
    Note that if the employer supplies the employee with petrol from his/her own car, a property fringe benefit may result. If the employer pays the employee for petrol actually purchased, there may be an expense payment fringe benefit.

Certain cars are also exempt benefits because of the alienation of personal services income rules (see Chapter 16 and 25.354).

CAR PARKING EXEMPTION

A car parking benefit provided to an employee is exempt pursuant to s58GA if:

- the car is not parked at a commercial parking station, and
- the employer is not a public company or a subsidiary of a public company, and
- the employer's gross ordinary and statutory income for the year ending before the start of the FBT year is less than $10 million or alternatively, the taxpayer constitutes a 'small business entity' pursuant to Division 328 ITAA97 (aggregate annual turnover is less than $2 million).

Employers commencing business during the FBT year must make a reasonable estimate of their ordinary and statutory income and if under $10 million, the exemption will still apply.

MINOR BENEFITS

FBT is not charged on benefits which have a notional taxable value of under $300 and satisfy the s58P criteria listed below. The employer will be denied a tax deduction for the expenditure if it is entertainment (see 25.903). TR 2007/12 outlines the Tax Office's views on the application of the minor benefit exemption.

 If the taxable value of a fringe benefit exceeds the threshold, the whole amount is subject to FBT, not just the amount over the threshold (the value of the benefit being $300 or more means the entire amount is subject to FBT).

Some benefits are excluded (ss58P(1)(b) and (c)) from being exempt as a minor benefit. These are airline transport fringe benefits, and expense payment, property or residual fringe benefits which are in-house fringe benefits. The minor benefits exemption does not apply to benefits that are provided to an employee under a salary sacrifice arrangement. If an employer and their employees jointly purchase a gift for an employee, only the employer's contribution is considered in determining whether the minor benefit exemption applies (ATO ID 2005/366).

Section 58P specifies criteria for deciding whether it is unreasonable to treat the minor benefit as a fringe benefit. It is necessary to look at the nature of the benefit and give due weight to each of the following criteria:

- the infrequency and irregularity with which identical or similar benefits to the minor benefit are provided. Infrequent and irregular does not mean 'isolated or rare' and will depend on the circumstances. The more often and regular the provision of the benefit, the less likely this criterion is satisfied. The term 'identical benefit' is considered to mean another benefit that is the same in all respects except for minimal differences

- the total taxable value of the minor and similar benefits. The greater the value of the minor benefit and identical or similar benefits, the less likely it will qualify as a minor benefit. Benefits provided in the past and current FBT years, as well as those likely to be provided in the future are taken into account

- the taxable value of associated benefits. This considers the value of associated benefits provided in connection with the minor benefit. For example, a meal provided in connection with accommodation

- the practical difficulty in determining the value. This includes consideration of the difficulty for the employer in keeping the necessary records. TR 2007/12 notes that an employer must keep records that explain all transactions, and

- the circumstances in which minor benefits and associated benefits are provided. This requires consideration as to whether the benefit was provided as a result of an unexpected event or is principally in the nature of a reward for services.

The Tax Office considers that 'infrequent and irregular' does not mean 'isolated or rare' and will depend on the circumstances (TR 2007/12). However, the more often and regular the benefits are provided, the less likely the criterion will be satisfied. The term 'identical benefit' is considered to mean another benefit that is the same in all respects except for minimal or insignificant differences. TR 2007/12 also sets out detailed examples, such as Christmas parties etc., which would constitute exempt minor benefits. In considering the frequency of benefits the Tax Office considers it inappropriate to set a number, but points out that the more often and regular that benefits are provided, the less likely the provision of the benefit would be considered 'infrequent and irregular'.

Some examples of exempt minor benefits set out in TR 2007/12 include:

- a one-off welcome gift (eg. food hamper) for a new employee
- meals provided on an ad-hoc basis a few times a year
- tolls provided via an e-tag facility on an ad-hoc basis (but not if part of a salary sacrifice arrangement)
- occasional use of employer's car for a special purpose (eg. use for three days during a public transport strike)
- a short-term advance to help an employee pay unexpected debts
- recovery of overpaid salary by instalments
- stationery for private use
- use of office staff to type essays or assignments, and
- permitting staff to take waste materials of a business such as packing boxes or fabric remnants.

TAX-EXEMPT EMPLOYERS AND ENTERTAINMENT

There are two circumstances where an income tax-exempt organisation can take advantage of the minor benefit rule in relation to entertainment (s58P). For entertainment rules see from 25.900.

1. The entertainment is incidental to the provision of entertainment to persons who are not employees (or associates of employees) of the employer, and the entertainment does not consist of, nor is provided in connection with, the provision of a meal other

than light refreshments. For example, a school provides morning tea for visiting academics from overseas and some of the staff attend the function merely to talk to the visitors. However, if a meal was provided, whether on the school premises or at an outside restaurant, the minor benefit exemption rule does not apply.

2. The entertainment is provided to an employee (or associate) on the employer's premises or a place where the employee performs their employment duties and the purpose of the entertainment is solely to recognise the special achievements of the employee in a matter relating to the employment of the employee. The Tax Office gives as an example a meal given to the family of a professional footballer in the club's dining room to mark selection in a representative team. The benefit can only be an exempt minor benefit if the sole purpose of the meal is to recognise the award and the entertainment takes place on the employer's premises. It would not be an exempt benefit if the footballer had another employer who gave the dinner (eg. the footballer was also employed by a stockbroker).

25.203   EMPLOYEES ON SERVICE OVERSEAS

An exemption from income tax for foreign remuneration (of salary/wages) is given by s23AF and s23AG ITAA36 (see 22.010). Because the definition of 'fringe benefit' in ss136(1) has the effect that only activities related to salary/wages taxable in Australia are subject to FBT, no FBT is payable on benefits provided to an employee who is exempt under s23AF or s23AG ITAA36. However, from 1 July 2009 the availability of the s23AG exemption was significantly reduced (see 22.010). This will result in many situations arising where employees temporarily working overseas receive fringe benefits which are no longer exempt from FBT.

25.204   OTHER EXEMPTIONS

Other examples include:
- newspapers and goods consumed by employees on the business premises on a working day
- genuine safety awards made to an employee in an FBT year up to a total value of $200, but over $200 the whole amount is subject to FBT
- certain road tolls and e-tag expenses (see 25.600)
- long service awards for service of more than 15 years. Threshold is $1,000 for 15 years of service and $100 for each additional year. If the employer provides another benefit following additional years of service, the benefit is exempt if it is no more than $100 per year for each year of service in excess of those years for which a benefit was previously provided. If in excess of either the $1,000 or $100 limits, no exemption applies. The Tax Office accepts that employee contributions are usually not counted towards the value of the benefit. A separate benefit provided by work colleagues in an arm's length situation would not be subject to FBT
- if an employee has been posted overseas:
  - 50% of the cost of one return holiday per year for the employee and family
  - there is no fringe benefits tax on the cost to the employer of children's education
- superannuation contributions paid in cash to a superannuation fund by the employer, and gratuitous retirement benefits (see 25.750) made for an employee of the contributor. The person making the payment must have reasonable grounds for believing the fund was a complying superannuation fund for the purpose of making superannuation contributions for the employee. The contribution is exempt from FBT if made in specie from 1 July 2007. Contributions made by an employer for the benefit of an associate of an employee (eg. employee's spouse) are subject to FBT
- the making of a contribution to a foreign superannuation fund for the purpose of providing superannuation benefits for an employee who is a temporary resident when the payment is made
- payments to non-employer childcare centres to secure priority access for employee's children
- payments for priority access to childcare centres under the Childrens' Services program

- compassionate travel by employees while travelling or living away from home on employment duties to attend the funeral of a close relative or to visit a close relative who is seriously ill, and
- disabled persons car parking (see 25.404).

25.250 RECORD KEEPING FOR FBT

Employers paying FBT must keep sufficient records (in English, or in a readily accessible form that is convertible to English) to enable the liability for FBT to be calculated and audit-checked.

Employers must retain for five years after completion of the transaction, records or copies of documentary evidence received (including employee declarations) from the date of assessment, or any dispute on the assessment has been finalised (also see 4.700).

Associates of employers must:

- keep records for five years, and
- provide a copy of those records to the employer by 21 April each year.

Employers who keep records on computers must be able to demonstrate that the records are both secure and accurate. For full details of Tax Office requirements see TR 2005/9 in relation to electronic records.

Employee declarations must be obtained by the employer by the due date for FBT return lodgment (see 25.051).

If a fringe benefit is provided by an associate of the employer, a copy of the relevant information must be given to the employer within 21 days of the end of the FBT year. If a fringe benefit is provided by another entity under an arrangement, the employer of the employee must take reasonable steps to obtain details from the provider of the benefit.

25.251   RELIEF FROM RECORD KEEPING

Under substantiation rules (see 13.100) the Commissioner has the power to accept the taxable value of certain fringe benefits without full substantiation. This power can only be exercised by the Tax Office under s123B when:

- reviewing the affairs of the employer (normally occurring as part of an audit or review of the taxpayer's assessment), or
- when considering an objection, or request for amendment or review of the assessment lodged by the employer. For the purposes of this discretionary power, the Tax Commissioner is deemed to have made an assessment even if the taxpayer's taxable income is nil, or if no tax is payable on the assessment.

The substantiation rules do not apply in relation to a benefit if the quality and nature of the evidence held satisfies the Tax Office that the taxable value of the benefit is not greater than the taxable value specified in the FBT return.

Typical substantiation would be documentary evidence required to reduce a car benefit eg. employee's petrol expenses. 'Documentary evidence' is defined in ss136(1).

25.252   RECORD KEEPING EXEMPTION FOR SMALL BUSINESS

The Record Keeping Exemption Arrangements (RKEA) are intended to simplify FBT record keeping for small business. RKEA applies to employers whose fringe benefits do not exceed a threshold amount. The exemption threshold for the FBT year commencing 1 April 2015 is $8,164 – see TD 2015/5.

AGGREGATE FBT AMOUNT

All employers providing aggregate benefits below the threshold of $8,164 can use the exemption, except for employers who are:

- government bodies (ie. Commonwealth, a State, a Territory or an authority of the Commonwealth, State or Territory), or
- exempt from income tax on all their income at any time during the year.

To qualify for RKEA, an employer must satisfy two conditions:

1. The year immediately before the current year was a base year, or some other FBT year was a base year and the aggregate FBT amount is calculated using the most recent base year instead of the current year.
2. The employer has not been given a written notice by the Tax Office requiring the resumption of record keeping during the FBT year.

THE BASE YEAR

The base year can be the FBT year ended 31 March 1997 or any later year.

The FBT year will be a 'base year' for an employer if:

- the employer carried out business operations for all of the FBT year
- the employer had lodged an FBT return for the year by the due date (note: an employer is not eligible for RKEA if an FBT return is not lodged, even if that is because aggregate fringe benefits are nil as a result of employee contributions)
- all records that are required to be kept and retained (see above) under FBT law have been kept and retained for the FBT year. An employer could still treat an FBT year as a base year when they are relying on s132A (ie. evidence being obtained within a reasonable time of lodgement of the FBT return for the year), and
- the aggregate fringe benefits for the FBT year do not exceed **$8,164** for the FBT year commencing 1 April 2015.

However, if having established a base year, an employer then chooses to calculate their FBT liability based on aggregate fringe benefits for the current year, the base year originally established can no longer be used.

To qualify for RKEA again, a new base year must be established. The 'current' year used could be a new base year, provided the conditions for a base year are complied with.

CONSEQUENCES OF QUALIFYING FOR RKEA

If an employer qualifies in a current FBT year for RKEA, the employer:

- will not have to keep or retain FBT records for that year (subject to exceptions below), and
- their FBT for the current year will be determined from an aggregate amount of an earlier year when FBT records were kept.

 The Tax Office may issue a written notice in a current year requiring an employer to resume keeping and retaining records. The requirement will apply from the date of the notice. Such a notice will issue where the Taxation Office believes that the benefits being provided have increased above the limit allowed and the employer has insufficient records to refute the notice.

WHEN FBT INCREASES

The RKEA will cease to apply if the employer's aggregate fringe benefits amount for the current year exceeds the most recent base year by more than 20%, unless the difference is $100 or less.

 The aggregate fringe benefit amount was $100 for the most recent base year and $180 for the current year. That is 80% greater, but RKEA can still apply because the difference ($80) is less than $100.

Because employers who qualify under RKEA are not required to keep FBT records, the onus of proof lies with an employer as to whether the 20% test is failed. Special rules apply to 'assist' employers in determining their current year fringe benefit amount, even though records have not been kept. These are purely administrative rules which apply to retention of statutory evidentiary documents and valuation of car benefits.

STATUTORY DOCUMENTS

Section 123 provides that if an employer has failed to retain, for the required period, statutory documents given to them (eg. employee declarations) they are deemed to have never received the documents. For RKEA purposes, this rule is disregarded in determining the appropriate fringe benefits in a current year.

CAR BENEFITS

Special rules apply in calculating the taxable value of car fringe benefits to ascertain whether the 20% test has been failed.

If the statutory formula has been used to determine the FBT payable, the taxable value of the car can be determined by using the 'statutory fraction' used in the first year the benefit was provided, so long as the annualised kilometres travelled in the current year are at least 80% of the (annualised) kilometres travelled in the first year that the car was provided.

If the 'operating cost' method is used, the employer can use the business use percentage for the 1st year that the car benefit is provided (this can also be the base year), provided that the business percentage for the current year is no more than 20 percentage points lower than the business percentage for the first year.

An employer qualified for RKEA when the business percentage was 70%. In a later FBT year the business use percentage drops to 55%.

Because the business use percentage has dropped by only 15 percentage points compared to the base year, the 70% can be used to calculate the FBT for the current year.

CEASING BUSINESS DURING THE YEAR

If an employer has qualified for RKEA, but ceases to carry on business during the current year, the FBT liability is calculated as a proportion of aggregate fringe benefits in the most recent base year.

An employer has been using RKEA using base year aggregate fringe benefits of $4,800 and business ceases after 146 days in the year.

The 20% variation tolerance is calculated as (146 divided by 365) x $4,800 x (120 divided by 100) = $2,304.

RECORDS

While RKEA generally exempts an employer from keeping records in the circumstances set out above, copies of records provided by associates must always be kept for five years. Records must also be kept when the Tax Office issues a written notice requiring the resumption of record keeping during the FBT year.

While an employer may be exempt from record keeping under these rules, an obligation still exists to include details of reportable fringe benefits (see 25.300) on an employee's payment summary (see 5.422).

25.300 REPORTABLE FRINGE BENEFITS

Reporting fringe benefits on the payment summaries of employees, called the reportable fringe benefits amount, affects the way employers are required to maintain their FBT records. The amount of reportable fringe benefits may affect the employee's entitlement to certain income tested deductions and tax offsets. It can also affect Higher Education Loan Program (HELP) repayments, the amount of child support payable and the Medicare levy surcharge liabilities of an affected employee.

Employers are required to include the grossed-up amount of reportable fringe benefits on the payment summaries of their employees. That amount is not included in the employee's assessable income, but is taken into account for the purposes of certain income tests including:

- assessing liability for the Medicare levy surcharge (applies to individuals and couples) (see 3.060)
- mature age worker tax offset and the seniors and pensioners tax offset (see 3.180 and 3.190)
- determining entitlement to a deduction for personal superannuation contributions (see 13.400)

- determining entitlement to a tax offset for contributions to a spouse's superannuation (see 19.074)
- determining entitlement to a superannuation co-contribution (see 19.076), and
- calculating a taxpayer's liability in respect of (HELP) repayments
- child support obligations, and
- income-tested government benefits.

The reportable fringe benefits total is calculated by applying a gross-up rate of **1.9608** (ie Type 2 rate for 2015-16 FBT year) to those benefits which must be reported.

25.301   INDIVIDUAL FRINGE BENEFITS AMOUNT

An employee's individual fringe benefits amount (or quasi-individual fringe benefits amount where the employer is exempt from FBT) is his or her share of the taxable value of each fringe benefit provided in respect of his or her employment, other than 'excluded fringe benefits'.

If benefits are provided to an associate of an employee in respect of that employee's employment, the value is allocated to the employee, not the associate.

25.303   REPORTABLE FRINGE BENEFITS AMOUNT

There is a reportable fringe benefits amount where an employee's individual fringe benefits amount (ie. non-grossed up) is **more than** $2,000.

The threshold is not apportioned if an employee is only employed for part of the FBT year and applies per employee per employer and is not subject to any grouping requirements.

 The value of benefits that are exempt from FBT (see from 25.100) are also exempt from reporting requirements. However, if the benefit is exempt solely because the person is an employee of a public benevolent institution and/or is a live-in residential care worker, the notional taxable value must be allocated to the employee. This is of significance for Religious Practitioners deriving benefits which are exempt because the benefit relates principally to their pastoral duties. Such benefits are not reportable.

CALCULATING REPORTABLE FRINGE BENEFITS AMOUNT

The gross up rate is always the lower Type 2 rate, calculated as:

Individual fringe benefits amount x 1.9608 (for the 2015-16 FBT year)

In practice, the amount reported for the FBT year ended 31 March 2016 should not be less than $3,924 ($2,001 x 1.9608).

The reportable fringe benefits amount for employees with an individual quasi-fringe benefit amount is calculated as:

Individual fringe benefits amount + Individual quasi-fringe benefits amount divided by 1 – FBT rate of tax (ie. 49% for the 2015-16 FBT year)

 Toni is a nurse with a taxable employer who during the 2015-16 FBT year supplies her with a car for her own use (taxable value $3,000). She also works part-time with a public hospital and salary sacrifices some of her wages to pay her mortgage. While the hospital does not have to pay FBT (see 25.080) on the benefit (taxable value $6,500) it is reportable.

> *Employer 1: $3,000 x 1.9608* *$5,882*
> *Employer 2: $6,500 x 1.9608* *$12,745*
> **$18,627**

The income tax year and the reportable fringe benefits period are not aligned and employers are required to calculate the reportable fringe benefits for every employee for the FBT year. The reportable fringe benefits period is the FBT year and starts from 1 April and ends on 31 March. The income year commences on 1 July and ends on 30 June.

25.304   REPORTABLE FRINGE BENEFITS TOTAL

An employee's reportable fringe benefits total is the sum of the employee's reportable fringe benefits amounts from all his or her employers for an income year (s135N).

IF THE EMPLOYER AGGREGATES FRINGE BENEFITS

Employers providing fringe benefits that do not exceed the exemption threshold can aggregate fringe benefits (s135A) under the record keeping exemption arrangements (see 25.252).

Employers aggregate the fringe benefits amount for an earlier year of tax in working out the current year's tax liability and the employer determines the employee's individual fringe benefits amount in writing. However, for reportable fringe benefits purposes this must equal the aggregate fringe benefits amount used for working out the employer's liability to pay tax for the year. This means that there cannot be any excluded fringe benefits.

A reasonable apportionment must be made if there are two or more employees.

CALCULATING THE EMPLOYER'S AGGREGATE FRINGE BENEFITS AMOUNT

An employer's aggregate fringe benefits amount for an FBT year can be calculated using these steps:

- **Step 1:** Work out the individual fringe benefits amount for the FBT year for each of the employer's employees.

- **Step 2:** Add up all the individual fringe benefits amounts worked out in Step 1.

- **Step 3:** Add up the taxable value of every excluded fringe benefit relating to an employee of the employer, the employer and the FBT year.

- **Step 4:** Add the Step 2 and Step 3 totals. **NOTE:** The Step 4 total is generally the employer's aggregate fringe benefits amount unless there are amortised[1] or reducible[2] fringe benefits in relation to the employer.

- **Step 5:** Add the amortised amount for the tax year of each amortised fringe benefit[1] (if any) relating to an employee of the employer, the employer and any tax year to the Step 4 total.

- **Step 6:** Subtract the reduction amount for the tax year of each reducible fringe benefit[2] (if any) relating to an employee of the employer, the employer and the tax year from the Step 5 total.

  1: Relates to remote area residential property benefits and option fees.
  2: relates to remote area home repurchase schemes.

25.305   EXCLUDED FRINGE BENEFITS

Certain benefits are not included on a payment summary as reportable fringe benefits. However, they may still be required to be included as part of the FBT calculation from the employer's perspective.

The following (non-exhaustive) list of excluded fringe benefits do not form part of the individual's fringe benefits amount and therefore are not required to be allocated to individual employees or reported on employees' payment summaries:

- provision of meal entertainment (regardless of whether the employer has elected to calculate FBT using the 50/50 split or the amount worked out from a 12 week register kept by the employer – see 25.906).
  The exclusion includes travel and accommodation associated with the meal entertainment (see chart at 25.940 for what is/is not reportable)

- a car parking fringe benefit but excluding car parking expense payments (see 25.400)

- a benefit prescribed by Regulation as excluded, (eg. where the compliance costs exceed the equity objectives of this measure)

- one whose taxable value is wholly or partly attributable to entertainment facility leasing expenses

- a remote area housing fringe benefit (see 25.700 and 25.800)

- remote area residential fuel under s59 (see 25.657)

- remote area housing under s60 (see 25.807)
- occasional travel to a major population centre in Australia for employees and family members residing in a location that is not in or adjacent to an eligible urban area
- emergency or other essential health care given to an employee (or associate) who is either an Australian citizen or permanent resident, whilst working outside Australia and Medicare benefits are not available, and
- car benefits for employees utilising a pooled or shared car which is employer provided and shared at the directive of the employer (see comments on pooled or shared cars below).

NOTE: An eligible urban area is a location that, by the shortest practicable surface route, from the centre of an eligible urban area is less than:

- 40 kilometres, if the census population is less than 130,000, or
- 100 kilometres, if the census population is not less than 130,000.

NOTE: The census refers to the 1981 Census.

The following may, depending on the circumstances, be either an excluded or exempt benefit:

- certain car benefits in respect of travel between home and work by police and ambulance officers, and firefighters when using marked emergency vehicles,
- housing benefits provided to employees of a public not-for-profit hospital, police service or charitable institution when located more than 100kms from a town with a population exceeding 130,000, and
- a pool or shared car that is provided by an employer for the use of two or more employees.
  Note that for this exclusion to apply there needs to be a car benefit, meaning the exclusion can only apply where the definition of 'car' is satisfied. This means a utility truck designed to carry a load of one tonne or more will not be excluded due to the sharing or pooling of the utility truck.

NOTE: In the May 2015 Federal Budget it was announced that a $5,000 per employee grossed up capping threshold will be introduced on certain meal entertainment and entertainment leasing facility expense ('EFLE') benefits provided by certain not for profit organisations under salary packaging arrangements. This change will become effective from 1 April 2016. These benefits will become reportable benefits for those employees impacted by the proposed changes.

LIVING-AWAY-FROM-HOME ALLOWANCE BENEFITS FOR COMMONWEALTH EMPLOYEES EXCLUDED

A reportable fringe benefit amount arising from the provision of living-away-from-home allowance fringe benefits to certain Commonwealth employees is excluded under regulation (see *Fringe Benefits Tax Amendment Regulation 2013 (No. 1)*).

Specifically, a benefit that is provided to a Commonwealth employee on or after 1 October 2012 is a benefit that is excluded from being a reportable fringe benefit if the benefit is any of the following:

- a living-away-from-home allowance dealt with under Division 7 of Part III FBT Act (25.840)
- an expense payment benefit which is not exempt under s21 FBT Act; and relates to accommodation that is required solely because the duties of the person's employment require the person to live away from the person's normal residence (25.550), or
- a residual benefit that is not exempt under ss47(5) FBT Act; and relates to accommodation that is required solely because the duties of the person's employment require the person to live away from the person's normal residence (25.820).

A 'Commonwealth employee' means an employee of the Commonwealth and includes defence force members and police officers.

25.306   SHARED FRINGE BENEFITS

Where benefits are provided to a number of employees but there is only one calculation of taxable value any allocation of benefits must reasonably reflect the benefit(s) received by each employee. To avoid potential problems the employer and employee should take into account the usage by each employee and agree on a reasonable method of apportionment prior to the employee receiving a fringe benefit. See the reporting exclusion above for a pool or shared car.

An employer owns a motor launch which is used by three employees during the 2015-16 FBT year: A for 14 days, B for 21 days and C for 28 days (ie. total of nine weeks).

The employer determines that the appropriate value for FBT purposes is the arm's length value if the employees were to hire the boat themselves. The value is $2,000 per seven day period: 9 x $2,000 = $18,000.

The reportable fringe benefits amount and the grossed up taxable value would be:

A: $4,000 x 1.9608 .... $7,843
B: $6,000 x 1.9608 .... $11,765
C: $8,000 x 1.9608 .... $15,686

As the reportable fringe benefits amount (ie. not grossed up) is more than $2,000 in the year, the grossed up amount is included in the payment summary of each employee.

25.307   PART-YEAR EMPLOYMENT

Where employment ceases between 1 April and 30 June and the employee received fringe benefits with a taxable value (pre-gross-up) of over $2,000, the grossed-up taxable value of those benefits is reported on the payment summary for the following income year.

If a former employee requests their payment summary in writing, the employer can be required to issue it unless the employee will have a reportable fringe benefits amount. In this case, the employer is not required to issue a payment summary prior to the required date (14 July 2015 for the current year). For example, if received between April and June 2015, it will be reported on the 2016 payment summary.

25.308   AMENDMENT OF A REPORTABLE FRINGE BENEFIT

Where there is an understatement of a reportable fringe benefits amount in an employee's payment summary which is $195 or less, the Tax Office does not require an amendment (Practice Statement PS LA 2002/7).

25.350 CAR BENEFITS

FBT is payable if cars owned or leased by an employer are made available (or deemed to be available) for private use by employees (or their associates). The employer can choose to calculate the taxable value of a car fringe benefit by using either the statutory formula method or the operating cost method.

The car fringe benefit is calculated on a daily basis and arises when the employee (or associate) uses the car for private purposes, or it is available or deemed to be available, to the employee or associate for private purposes (eg. garaged at or near the employee's home or even if the car is left in a long-term car park at an airport).

25.351   WHAT IS A 'CAR'?

A car fringe benefit will only arise where the vehicle provided is a 'car' as defined under the FBT Act (which derives its definition from s995-1 ITAA97) as follows:

A car is any motor powered road vehicle designed to carry a load of less than one tonne and fewer than nine passengers and typically includes passenger vehicles,(including four wheel drives), station wagons, panel vans, utility trucks or other similar vehicles.

Motorcycles and vehicles designed to carry a load of greater than one tonne or greater than nine passengers are not 'cars', as defined and accordingly, the provision of such vehicles to an employee will not constitute a 'car fringe benefit' however may in certain circumstances constitute a residual fringe benefit.

WHAT IS 'PRIVATE USE'?

Private use arises where any use of the car is not exclusively in the course of producing the employee's assessable income. A prime example of private use is travel between home and the employee's place of employment.

Difficulties may arise in identifying private usage in respect to:

- multiple places of employment/business
- duties such as a commercial traveller
- a business related activity on the way to or from work, and
- travel involving the transport of bulky equipment.

Refer to MT 2027 for examples.

Travel by an employee from home to an employer (employer B) in a car provided by an unrelated employer (employer A) is considered not to be 'work-related travel' (see ATO ID 2013/34).

25.352   AVAILABLE FOR PRIVATE USE?

A car will be deemed to be 'available for private use' irrespective of whether it is actually used by the employee (or associate) for private purposes in the following circumstances:

- where the car is garaged or kept at or near the place of residence of the employee (or associate)

Margaret, the national sales manager of a cosmetics company, travels interstate for ten days to attend a marketing strategy seminar. During this time, Margaret leaves the car garaged at home. The car is not used by any of her associates.
The car will be deemed to be available for private use given that it is garaged at or near the employee's place of residence. The fact that it hasn't actually been used for private purposes is irrelevant.

NOTE: In the case of *Jetto Industrial Pty Ltd and Commissioner of Taxation* (2009) AATA 374, the tribunal determined that a car was garaged 'at or near a place of residence of the employee' where the employee's home was adjacent to the business premises.

or

- the car is not at the business premises of the employer and either:
  - the employee (or associate) is entitled to apply the car to a private use, or
  - the employee (or associate) is not performing the duties of his or her employment and has custody or control of the car.

The Tax Office considers that a car, which has been left at an airport car park whilst the employee flies interstate or overseas, is still available for private use. Where however the employee has left the keys with the employer, the car is no longer considered to be in the employee's custody and control and therefore not available for private use, to the extent that there exists a consistently enforced prohibition on the use of the car for private purposes (refer to TD 94/16). Class Ruling CR 2009/3 further indicates that a car may no longer be in the custody and control of an employee where the keys are surrendered to the car park operator.

NOTE: A car held in a workshop for a long period for (non routine) major repairs will not be considered to be available or applied for private use. Similarly, if a car is provided by an employer to an employee and because of employment duties the car is parked overnight at or near the employee's temporary accommodation (hotel, motel, etc.) the car is considered to be available for private use (see ATO ID 2004/852).

25.353   'BUSINESS PREMISES'

Premises are usually business premises if a person owns the premises or has exclusive occupancy rights as lessee and activities conducted at the premises include those undertaken in the ordinary course of carrying on a business or those having a commercial character. For full details refer to TR 2000/4.

25.354   EXEMPT CAR BENEFITS

'WORK RELATED' TRAVEL IN COMMERCIAL CARS

A car benefit will be an exempt benefit where the vehicle constitutes a taxi, panel van, utility or other road vehicle designed to carry a load of less than one tonne (other than a vehicle designed for the principal purpose of carrying passengers) and the employee's private use of the car is limited to:

- 'work-related' travel (ie. travel between home and work, or which is incidental to travel in the course of employment duties), or
- private use which is minor, infrequent and irregular (eg. delivery of domestic rubbish to the tip).

It should be noted that the transporting of family members in a vehicle may impact whether or not a respective trip satisfies the definition of business or work related travel (see ATO Interpretative Decisions 2012/96, 2012/97 and 2012/98. Accordingly, care should be taken in such circumstances.

CARS USED FOR EMERGENCY SERVICES

Cars used for emergency services which are garaged or kept at or near an employee's (or associate's) residence are exempt car benefits (ss7(2A)), where the car:

- is used by a police, ambulance or fire fighting service, and
- is fitted with a flashing warning light and siren, and
- has exterior markings which indicate its use.

NOTE: The exemption only applies in the above situation. If the car is provided in another situation for private use, a car benefit will arise.

UNREGISTERED CARS

A car benefit will be an exempt benefit where at all times during the year of tax when the car was held by the provider, the car was unregistered and the car was wholly or principally used directly in connection with business operations of the employer (eg. a farm vehicle).

CARS SUPPLIED BY PERSONAL SERVICES ENTITIES

As a personal services entity is unable to deduct car expenses for more than one car utilised by an individual (pursuant to s86-60 ITAA97), a car benefit in respect of a second car is an exempt benefit in relation to an FBT year.

25.356   VEHICLES OTHER THAN CARS

Motor cycles and vehicles designed to carry at least one tonne are not 'cars' and accordingly, the car benefit valuation rules do not apply.

 Panel vans and utilities designed to carry a load of at least one tonne do not meet the definition of a 'car', therefore the 'car' rules do not apply to calculate FBT. Instead, the arm's length value of the benefit is taxed as a residual benefit if the private use (other than 'work-related' travel – see 25.354) is more than minor, infrequent and irregular.

Dual cab vehicles are variants of commercial vehicles, often having additional seating positions. A dual cab that is designed to carry a load of less than one tonne may qualify as a car benefit eligible for the work-related use exemption only if the vehicle is not designed for the principle purpose of carrying passengers.

MT 2034 lists dual cab, single cab and four wheel drives and vans eligible for exemption when use is limited to 'work related' travel. It also indicates that one method to value the benefit is to multiply the number of private kms by a set rate per km, but this can only be used where there is extensive business use of the vehicle.

To calculate FBT payable, multiply the following appropriate rate by the number of private kilometres travelled in the FBT year commencing 1 April 2015 (TD 2015/6). See TD 2014/6 for 2014-15 rates.

Vehicle engine capacity	Rates / km: FBT year 2014-15	Rates / km: FBT year 2015-16
Up to 2,500cc	50 cents/km	51 cents/km
Over 2,500cc	60 cents/km	61 cents/km
Motorcycles	15 cents/km	15 cents/km

If a 3,000cc, one tonne utility travelled 1,000 private kms in use that was not minor, infrequent and irregular and there was extensive business use of the vehicle, the value of the benefit (which is a GST creditable benefit, ie. employer entitled to ITC's) is 1,000 x $0.61 = $610. FBT payable by a taxable company for the 2015-16 FBT year is $610 x 2.1463 x 49% = $641.53.

ALTERNATIVE VALUATION METHOD

Alternatively, the valuation of the benefit can be calculated by using the operating cost method (see 25.380). However, both the cents per kilometre and operating costs methods assume that the vehicle is supplied on a fully maintained basis. If the cents per kilometre method is used and the employee is responsible for supplying petrol, then the Tax Office accepts that in the absence of specific records, the rate can be reduced by an amount calculated by multiplying the private kilometres by an estimate of fuel costs per kilometre based on average fuel prices and average fuel consumption. The Tax Office accepts average fuel prices published by the Australian Automobile Association.

Any motor vehicle can be subject to FBT. If it is an 'exempt car' (see 25.354) and is not used in an exempt way, FBT is charged as a car benefit. If it is not a car as defined, such as an over one tonne utility, FBT is charged as a residual benefit.

25.357   HIRE CARS AND TAXIS

Subsection 7(7) provides that a car is not 'held by a person' if it is a taxi or a hire car and is not valued as a car benefit unless there is substantial continuity in the hiring of the car. The Tax Office considers that anything less than 12 weeks is considered to be short term hire. Note that the hiring will be valued as a residual benefit (see 25.820).

25.360   VALUING CAR BENEFITS

The employer can, for each car, choose whether to value the car benefit using the (i) statutory formula method or (ii) operating cost method. An employer has until the due date of lodgement of the FBT return, or the date lodged if earlier, in which to make the election. If no election is made, the statutory formula method automatically applies. The election is made in relation to each car and is revocable each FBT year. There is no requirement to notify the Tax Office of the chosen method as the disclosure in an employer's FBT return and supporting documentation evidence suffices.

Even if the employer chooses the operating cost method, the statutory method will apply (ss10(5)) if it results in a lower FBT liability for that car, or the aggregate of all cars provided to employees (or their associates).

25.370   USING THE STATUTORY FORMULA METHOD

The taxable value of a car fringe benefit calculated using the statutory formula method (ss9(1)) is valued by applying a statutory percentage by the cost of the car at the date of purchase or lease. The employer's liability is reduced by the number of days the car was not used or available for private use and any after-tax employee contributions made towards the running and maintenance costs of the car (refer to *Employee contributions* at 25.106).

The following formula is used to calculate the taxable value of a car fringe benefit using the statutory formula method:

Statutory formula method = (A x B x C/D) – E
where:

- A = the base value of the car
- B = the statutory fraction (see 25.374)
- C = the number of days during that year of tax on which the car fringe benefits were provided (ie. available for private use)
- D = the number of days in FBT year (365 or 366 in a leap year), and
- E = the amount of any employee contribution to the employer or provider in consideration for the benefit.

25.371   BASE VALUE OF THE CAR

Pursuant to ss136(1), 'cost price' comprises the following elements:

1. WHERE THE CAR IS OWNED BY THE PROVIDER

Costs which are directly attributable to the acquisition and delivery of the car excluding insurance, registration and stamp duty costs. GST and luxury car tax where actually paid are included, however it is not reduced by the amount of any customs duty concessions.

For the purposes of determining 'cost price', the Commissioner has previously indicated the following:

- The cost of a new car warranty is included, however not the cost of an extended warranty (ATO ID 2006/253). The cost price is the arm's length wholesale value (including GST) where the provider is the manufacturer of the car (ATO ID 2003/585). Where the associate of the provider is a foreign car company that manufactured the car, the transport costs, customs duty and import duty do not form part of the wholesale price of the car and therefore are not included in the cost price (ATO ID 2006/253).
- A car held under a hire purchase arrangement is deemed to be purchased (s7(6)).

TR 2011/3: Cost price of a car

TR 2011/3 sets out the Commissioner's view that the following reduce the cost price of a car:

- the trade-in value of a car provided by an employee directly to a car dealer who directly sells a car either to the employer or the lessor
- any cash payment made by an employee to either the car dealer or the employer to assist with the purchase of the car
- any fleet discounts, or any other incentives or discounts that are applied by a car dealer to reduce the purchase price of a car, and
- manufacturer rebates paid to purchasers, or applied at their direction or on their behalf, to reduce the purchase price of the car.

Where it is the employer that provides a trade-in vehicle as part of an acquisition, the cost price will not be reduced by the value of the trade-in as the cash and trade-in are both assets of the employer and make up the total amount of the expenditure incurred by the employer.

Where no expenditure is incurred or the parties are not dealing with each other at arms-length, then s13 may apply to deem the cost price to be the market value of the car.

2. WHERE THE CAR IS LEASED BY THE PROVIDER

The 'leased car value' at the earliest time that the car is held by the provider or associate, which is the cost price of the car to the lessor (calculated in accordance with the approach described above). Where however the car was not leased at about the time that car was purchased by the lessor, the leased car value is the market value of the car at the time that the lease was entered into (ss136(1). The cost price is determined by reference to the original lease agreement where the car has been previously provided to an employee under an earlier lease agreement (ATO ID 2004/528).

3. THE COST OF ANY NON-BUSINESS ACCESSORIES FITTED TO THE CAR AT OR ABOUT THE TIME THAT THE CAR WAS FIRST ACQUIRED, REDUCED BY THE AMOUNT OF ANY EMPLOYEE CONTRIBUTION.

'Non-business accessory' is defined in ss136(1) to mean an accessory fitted to the car, whether at the factory where the car was assembled or at some other place, other than an accessory required to meet the special needs of any business operations in relation to which the car is used.

 ATO ID 2006/253 states that expenditure incurred on the purchase of an extended car warranty does not form part of the cost price of a car as the expenditure is not directly attributable to the acquisition or delivery of the car.

ATO ID 2011/47 also affirms the Commissioner's view that the following are each a 'non-business accessory':

- paint protection
- fabric protection
- rust protection, and
- window tinting.

Other examples include:

- air conditioning (MT 2021)
- water proofing (FBT States and Territories Industry Partnership minutes 17 March 2009)
- a stereo (MT 2021), and
- customised wheels.

25.372   ELECTION TO USE STATUTORY FORMULA

There is no need to lodge an election with the Tax Office to use this method. The Tax Office accepts that employers are able to demonstrate that election on the FBT annual return itself.

25.373   BASE VALUE AFTER FOUR YEARS

Under the statutory formula method only, the base value of the car is reduced by one third after it has been owned or leased for at least four years on 1 April of the FBT year (ie. four full FBT years) (see TD 94/28). The car does not have to have been held continuously by the employer for the entire four year period (see ATO ID 2004/527).

That reduction applies only once in the life of the car:

- if the car was acquired on 1 April: on the fifth anniversary of its acquisition
- if acquired on some other date: on 1 April after the fourth anniversary of its acquisition

 The reduction does not apply to non-business accessories added to the car after it was acquired.

 A car was purchased on 1 May 2010 for $42,000 (including GST) and used for private purposes by an employee. The employer can reduce the base value by one third ($14,000) in the FBT year beginning 1 April 2015. The reduced base value of the car for subsequent FBT year is $28,000 (ie. two thirds).

25.374   STATUTORY FRACTION

The statutory fraction determines the extent that car is used for business purposes. For car fringe benefits that were provided under financial commitments entered into prior to 7.30pm on 10 May 2011, this statutory fraction was based on the distance travelled by the vehicle. A flat 20% rate applies to car fringe benefits provided under financial commitments commenced after that time (subject to certain transitional rules) irrespective of the distance travelled.

COMMITMENTS ENTERED INTO PRIOR TO 7.30PM ON 10 MAY 2011

For commitments entered into prior to 10 May 2011 (and there has been no material change to the arrangement), the statutory fraction is determined by the annualised kilometres travelled by the vehicle for the FBT year. For these commitments, the following statutory fractions apply:

Total kms travelled in year	Statutory rate
Under 15,000	0.26
15,000 to 24,999	0.20
25,000 to 40,000	0.11
Over 40,000	0.07

ANNUALISED NUMBER OF KILOMETRES

Where a car is not held for the whole FBT year, the kilometres travelled will need to be annualised in order to calculate the equivalent number of kilometres the car would have travelled if it had been held for the full FBT year. The following formula is applied to calculate the annualised kilometres (paragraph 9(2)(d)):

$$\frac{A \ x \ C}{B}$$

where:

A = number of kms travelled in the period during the FBT year when the car was owned or leased by the employer

B = number of days in that period, and

C = number of days in the FBT year.

A car was purchased and made available to an employee on 1 May 2010. The car was sold on 30 April 2014. For the FBT year ended 31 March 2015, the car travelled 2,000 kilometres. The annualised kilometres for the FBT year ended 31 March 2015 are calculated as follows:

$$\frac{2,000 \ x \ 365}{30}$$

= 24,333 kilometres

The statutory rate is therefore 0.20.

The annualisation applies to the days held, not the days available for private use. Any period not available for private use is reflected in an apportionment. A car would still be held even if awaiting sale at an auctioneer's premises on the basis that it is still 'available for private use'.

COMMITMENTS ENTERED INTO AFTER 7.30PM ON 10 MAY 2011

The statutory rate is a single rate of **0.2** which applies regardless of the distance travelled. The change applies to all car fringe benefits provided after 7.30pm, AEST on 10 May 2011, except where an employee, employer or their associate had committed to the acquisition of the car that was the subject of a car benefit (for a specified period of time) prior to 7.30pm, AEST on 10 May 2011, and there has been no material changes to that arrangement.

Important transitional rules applied to such car benefits from 10 May 2011 to 31 March 2014, so as to phase in the 20% rate: The rates phased in over four years were as follows:

STATUTORY RATE				
Distance travelled during the FBT year (1 April – 31 March)	New contracts entered into after 7.30pm (AEST) on 10 May 2011			
	From 10 May 2011	2012-13 FBT year	2013-14 FBT year	2014-15 FBT year
0 – 14,999 km	0.20	0.20	0.20	0.20
15,000 – 24,999 km	0.20	0.20	0.20	0.20
25,000 – 40,000 km	0.14	0.17	0.20	0.20
Over 40,000 km	0.10	0.13	0.17	0.20

- The rate of 0.2 applies from 1 April 2014 regardless of the kilometres travelled.
- All car benefits are covered by the new rules unless it can be proved that an agreement was in place prior to 7.30pm, AEST on 10 May 2011, committing to the transaction. The car benefit does not need to have been delivered by 10 May 2011, but the commitment needs to be financially binding on one or more of the parties.

- Changes made after 7:30pm, AEST on 10 May 2011 to commitments made prior to 7:30pm, AEST on 10 May 2011, such as re-financing a car, altering the duration of an existing contract or changing employers, are new commitments meaning the car benefits are subject to the new arrangements.

- If the new rules begin to apply part way through a year (because of a change in commitment), the changes commence from the beginning of the next FBT year.

- Employers and employees who seek to end existing contracts early and immediately enter into new contracts, in order to obtain a benefit from adopting the new arrangements, may be caught by the general anti-avoidance provisions.

- The requirement to annualise kilometres where applicable continues under the revised rules.

The following two examples are extracted from the Explanatory Memorandum (EM) .

Tim is provided with a salary sacrificed car on a lease contract that lasts the sooner of two years or 40,000kms, commencing 1 January 2010. On 17 August 2011, as Tim is nearing the 40,000kms, he gets the contract changed to allow for 50,000kms. This would be considered a new commitment, and from 1 April 2012, the contract and car benefit would move to the new arrangements (under the transitional arrangements). (Since the amendments begin to apply part way through an FBT year in relation to a car that was available from 1 April, the new arrangements will apply from 1 April 2012.)

James enters into a novated lease arrangement on 1 July 2012 for a car with a base value of $35,000. The lease on the car is for three years, running until 30 June 2015. In the FBT period from 1 July 2012 to 31 March 2013, James drives 35,000kms. From 1 April 2013 to 31 March 2014, James drives 42,000kms in the car. From 1 April 2014 until the end of the lease, James drives 10,500kms.

From 1 July 2012 until 31 March 2013, the annualised kilometres driven would be 35,000 × 366 / 275 = 46,582kms. As such, the statutory rate applied to the car fringe benefits would be 0.13.

From 1 April 2013 to 31 March 2014, when James drives 42,000kms, the statutory rate of 0.17 would apply. From 1 April 2014 until the end of the lease, the annualised kilometres driven would be 10,500 × 365 / 91 = 42,115kms. The statutory rate applying to the lease would be 0.20.

25.375   REDUCING THE TAXABLE VALUE

DAYS AVAILABLE FOR PRIVATE USE

The full year taxable value calculated under the statutory formula method is reduced in proportion to the number of days (between 1 April and 31 March) that the car was not available for private use. Note that total days is 366 for a leap year.

EMPLOYEE CONTRIBUTIONS (RECIPIENT'S PAYMENT)

The taxable value of the car fringe benefit is reduced by any (unreimbursed) payment by the employee (out of after-tax dollars) to the employer or provider of the car fringe benefit in consideration for providing the car. The payment does not have to be made during the FBT year and the Tax Office accepts a payment that is made between the end of the FBT year and the lodgment of the FBT return for the purposes of reducing the taxable value. It is possible to effect an employee contribution by journal entry – refer to MT 2050 (see 25.106 for employee contributions and below for comment).

25.377   EMPLOYEE'S COSTS

The taxable value of the car benefit is reduced by the following GST inclusive costs incurred by the employee **during** the relevant FBT year (but reduced by any reimbursement received by the employee):

- a 'car expense' including:
  - registration or insurance

- repairs or maintenance (including car cleaning costs, but subject to documentary evidence – see s136(1) and Division 900E ITAA97
- fuel, and
- membership fees for road service entitlement.

The employee must provide to the employer by the due lodgment date of the FBT return, or if an FBT return does not have to be lodged, 21 May:

- if the expenses were for fuel and oil, either:
  - a declaration of those expenses in the format approved by the Tax Office, or
  - documentary evidence of the expense.
- for other expenses, (ie. not fuel or oil) written evidence (see also 13.120).

The declaration must be obtained by the employer before the due date for lodgement of the FBT return. If this is not done the relevant expenses cannot be treated as an employee contribution.

Documentary evidence of expenses incurred means a receipt, invoice or similar document, prepared in English (or, if incurred outside Australia, in the language of that country) showing the:

- date the expense was incurred
- name of supplier
- amount of expense
- nature of the goods or services, and
- date the document was prepared.

 Any direct employee contribution is consideration for making a taxable supply (ie. provision of the car benefit) and consequently the employer must remit to the Tax Office 1/11th of the contribution as part of their GST obligations (GST registered employers only). However, if the contribution is by way of direct payment of fuel, repairs etc. such a contribution is not consideration for a taxable supply.

 Where a car is provided by an employer to an employee, the employee cannot claim any deductions for the car (ie. for business use). This also applies to depreciation expense even where the car is owned by the employee and leased to the employer (s51AF ITAA36 and s28-13 ITAA97).

25.380 USING THE OPERATING COST METHOD

An employer can choose to calculate the taxable value of a car fringe benefit using the operating cost method by lodging an election under ss10(1). Where this method is adopted, the taxable value is based on the private usage proportion of the total costs of either owning (or leasing) and operating the car during the FBT year.

 An election can be made in relation to each individual car and can be changed each year. The election is evidenced by the presentation of the FBT return.

This method requires the employer to determine:

- the total operating costs (including a deemed depreciation and interest component where the car is owned by the employer)
- the percentage of private use during the year (or part year), and
- the costs paid by a person other than the employer (including the employee or an associate contributions).

The following formula is used to calculate the taxable value of a car fringe benefit under the operating cost method:

Taxable value = [C x (100% – BP) – R]

where:

C = the total operating costs of the car during the holding period

BP = the business percentage use of the car, and

R = the employee contribution (otherwise known as the recipient's payment) in consideration for the benefit.

25.381   OPERATING COSTS

The total operating costs of a car include actual costs (such as running expenses) and deemed costs (such as depreciation and interest, where the car is owned). The GST-inclusive amount of a cars operating costs (eg. petrol) incurred by an employee or associate are included, as appropriate. Determining total operating costs depends on whether the car is owned or leased. Under ss10(3) 'operating costs' include the following items:

- For all cars, operating expenses (GST-inclusive) as follows (refer to TR 2001/2):
    - repairs (but not reimbursements met by an insurance company for accidents etc.)
    - maintenance
    - fuel
    - registration and insurance (applicable to the period the car was available for private use), and
    - extended car warranty (ATO ID 2006/253).
- For cars owned by the employer:
    - deemed depreciation (from 1 April 2008 calculated at 18.75% for cars acquired between 1 July 2002 and before 10 May 2006 and 25% for cars acquired on or after 10 May 2006). The rate is calculated on diminishing balance, irrespective of whether the car is luxury or non-luxury and is calculated by multiplying the depreciation value of the car at the start of the FBT year by the deemed depreciation rate that applied at the time the car was purchased.

 If the car was not used for the full FBT year, apportion the depreciation to reflect the period it was used.

    - Since 1 July 2000 the 'cost' of the car includes GST (TR 2001/2). If the cost of the car exceeds the depreciation cost limit ($57,466 for the 2014-15 income year; 2015-16 cost limit is not yet available) the actual purchase price is used.
    - deemed interest, calculated by multiplying the depreciated value (s11) of the car by the statutory FBT benchmark interest rate of 5.65% for the 2015-16 FBT year (TD 2015/8) (5.95% for the 2014-15 FBT year). As for depreciation, the deemed interest is apportioned to reflect the period the car was used to provide the fringe benefit.

 Deemed depreciation and interest is calculated on non-business accessories fitted to the car after its purchase.

- For leased cars:
    - leasing costs attributable to the holding period (ie. based on that part of the year when the car was available for private use).

NOTE: If the car is neither owned by, nor leased to, the provider, include the amount of depreciation and interest which would be deemed to have been incurred had the provider purchased the vehicle at that time for consideration equal to its leased car value.

 A car held on hire-purchase is deemed to have been purchased by the hirer (at the time the person first took the car on hire).

DETERMINING THE BUSINESS PERCENTAGE

To establish the applicable business percentage of a car (or conversely the private use percentage which is the difference between 100 and the percentage of business use) a log book must be maintained for a continuous 12 week period (which is representative of the use for the full FBT year).

The test for determining the business percentage for FBT purposes is the same as that which applies under the income tax law to determine the extent to which expenses incurred in operating a car are deductible under s8-1 ITAA97 (MT 2027, paragraph 11).

The percentage of business use is calculated as follows:

$$\frac{A \times 100\%}{B}$$

where:

A = the employer's estimate of business kilometres travelled during the year, and

B = the total kilometres (business and private) travelled during the year (ie. from odometer records).

NOTE: Specific relief from the substantiation provisions, when considering a log book, exists in s127B. For details as to how the Tax Office will exercise this discretion see TR 97/24 and ATO ID 2003/1099.

 While an employer can use the operating cost method for a particular year for which a log book has not been maintained, there is no reduction in the operating cost of the car for any business journeys made (see ATO ID 2004/385).

 Business use by associates: If a car is provided by an employer to an associate (usually the spouse) of the employee, any use by the associate for business purposes or for producing assessable income is still regarded as being for private purposes and accordingly, is not included in business kilometres under 'A' in the formula above (see MT 2027).

 The depreciated value of a car as at 1 April 2015 is $62,170 (depreciation for the year to 31 March 2016 is $15,542 @ 25%). It is used 60% privately for the year (as established by the log book). GST inclusive operating costs for the year for petrol, maintenance, insurance and registration are $9,000. The employee made a contribution of $1,500 toward the cost of the benefit direct to the employer. The statutory interest rate is 5.65% for 2015-16 (deemed interest $3,513 ($62,170 x 5.65%)).

> *Actual and deemed costs .... $28,055 (ie. $15,542 + $9,000 + $3,513)*
> *Business use 40%*
> *Private use... 60%*
> *Contribution paid by employee... $1,500*

Applying the operating cost method of (C x (100% – BP)) – R (where C is operating costs, BP is business use percentage and R is recipient's contribution) the taxable value is as follows:
> *($28,055 x (100% – 40%) – $1,500*
> *= ($28,055 x 60%) – $1,500*
> *Taxable value = $15,333*

25.383 LOG BOOK YEAR

A new log book must be maintained for a continuous period of 12 weeks:

- in the first year the employer chooses to use the actual operating cost method
- after every five years
- if you obtain an additional car (not a replacement car) for which you want to use the log book method, and
- if the Tax Office requests a log book.

The 'log book' must be recorded in English and contain the relevant information.

If a car is replaced during the year, and the same business percentage is maintained, a 'new' log book is not required but the employer must record for both cars before 28 April:

- the make, model and registration number
- the date of replacement.

A log book entry must be entered in respect of each journey undertaken in the car during the selected continuous 12 week period. Each entry must set out for each journey (multiple journeys are treated as a single journey):

- the date the journey began and ended
- odometer readings of the car at the start and end
- number of kilometres travelled by the car, and
- the purpose of the travel.

 The Administrative Appeals Tribunal in Latif v FCT (2008) AATA 675 held that the description 'meeting' was insufficient description of the business nature of a trip for the purposes of the log book requirements.

Where a log book period is started within 12 weeks of the end of the FBT year, the log book can be used for both years, provided the 12 weeks have been completed. The log book will establish the estimated business usage of the car. The estimate should take into account the log book and odometer records, any other records kept by the employee and variations in business usage during the years, eg. holidays.

For each FBT year, odometer readings of the car must be maintained at the start and end of the FBT year to enable the total kilometres travelled to be calculated.

The Tax Office accepts that high integrity electronic devices, other than the motor vehicles own odometer, may be used in lieu of a written logbook. Such a system would employ a high integrity global positioning system to record distances, locations, dates etc. (see ATO ID 2002/925).

Odometer readings must also be recorded when the car ceases to be used as a fringe benefit.

The following information does not need to be recorded in either the log book or odometer records:

- the name of the driver
- the date the entry was made, or
- the signature of the entry maker.

Both the log book and odometer records must be given to the employer, who is required to estimate the percentage of business use of the car. Although the business use of the car has been established in the log book year, the employer must estimate the business use of the car for each FBT year. This requirement is separate and distinct from maintaining the log book. The employer must estimate the number of business kilometres travelled during the full FBT year to determine the percentage of business use for that FBT year.

The percentage of business use is:

> *A divided by B x 100%*

where:

A = the employer's estimate of business kms travelled during the year

B = the total kms (business and private) travelled during the year (ie from odometer records).

NOTE: A specific relief from the substantiation provisions, when considering a log book, exists in s127B. For details as to how the Tax Office will exercise this discretion see TR 97/24 and ATO ID 2003/1099.

 While an employer can use the operating cost method for a particular year for which a log book has not been maintained, there is no reduction in the operating cost of the car for any business journeys made (see ID 2004/385).

 Business use by associates: If a car is provided by an employer to an associate (usually the spouse) of the employee, any use by the associate for business purposes or for producing assessable income is still regarded as being for private purposes and is not involved in business kilometres under 'A' in the formula above (see MT 2027). However, if the associate used the car to carry on a business of the employee, these would be regarded as business kilometres.

25.384   EMPLOYEE CONTRIBUTIONS

The taxable value of the car benefit may be reduced by any employee contributions (paid out of after-tax salary, ie. not salary sacrificed) such as fuel (the GST inclusive amount) or cash paid to the employer. Refer *Employee contributions* at 25.106.

25.390 LEASED CARS

For GST-registered entities entitled to a full input tax credit, lease payments other than those under non-reviewable pre-8 July 1999 leasing contracts include GST and any expense from 1 July 2000 is at its GST-inclusive value.

25.391   GST AND LEASED CARS

Where a car is provided as a car fringe benefit by an employer registered for GST, GST applies to lease fees from 1 July 2000 so input tax credits are available to GST-registered employers, or other GST-registered providers, from that date. Therefore the Type 1 gross-up rate should be used for any car fringe benefit provided on or after 1 July 2000 (see 25.000).

25.392   EMPLOYER-PURCHASED VEHICLES

Many employers provide employees with leased cars as part of their terms of employment and subsequently acquire those cars at the end of the lease period. If the car continues to be provided by the employer to an employee as a car benefit, the base value of the car for the purposes of the statutory formula method of valuation will continue to be the original lease value of the car. In some cases the employer may on sell the car to an employee. If the property was acquired by the employer under an arm's length arrangement, the property's taxable value is its cost to the employer. If a vehicle is acquired at the end of a lease period by the employer and sold to the employee for its residual value, no FBT is payable on that transaction (TD 95/63).

 When a lessee disposes of a car acquired from the lessor, any profit made on disposal may still be assessed (ss20-100 to 20-160 ITAA97). A similar outcome will arise for motor vehicle lease novations where depreciation has been claimed by any person in respect of that vehicle.

This Determination requires the arrangement between the lessor (the finance company) and the lessee (the employer) to:
- be an arm's length transaction
- be based on the minimum residual values (IT 28), and
- not contain any express or implied agreement that ownership of the property will pass to the lessee at the end of the lease period.

To avoid FBT when a previously leased vehicle is sold to an employee, the employer must:
- enter into a genuine lease with the lessor (ie. one that complies with IT 28)
- acquire the vehicle by paying out its residual value including GST, and
- transfer the vehicle to the employee for an amount equivalent to the residual value at the completion of the lease.

The Tax Office accepts that where an employee acquires a car for its residual value at the end of a lease, the taxable value of the fringe benefit may be reduced to nil, provided the lease is a 'bona fide lease' (refer to TD 95/63). That is, where the residual value is equal to or exceeds the minimum residual values outlined in Taxation Ruling IT 28 (for cars acquired prior to 1 July 2002) and ATO ID 2002/1004 (for cars acquired from 1 July 2002).

25.395 CALCULATING THE FBT LIABILITY

Regardless of the election (if any) made, the method which results in the lowest taxable value will be used to calculate FBT liability. See car FBT calculation at 25.395.

 A car purchased on 1 April 2013 for $38,000 is used by an employee solely for private purposes for the year ended 31 March 2016. The employer elected to use the operating cost method. The employee travelled 26,500kms during the year and contributed $2,600 to the employer. The car is otherwise fully maintained by the employer.

Statutory formula method

Base value of car $38,000
Taxable value = ($38,000 x 0.2 x 365 divided by 365) – $2,600 .... **$5,000**

Note: The statutory fraction of 0.2 applies as this is a post-11 May 2010 commitment –
phase-in rates no longer apply from 1 April 2014 and as a result kilometres travelled are not
relevant for the purposes of working out the statutory fraction.

Operating costs method

These costs were incurred by the employer.

Operating costs (GST inclusive)

Registration and insurance.. $1,250
Repairs[4].. $500
Maintenance... $1,780
Fuel $4,500
Depreciation (WDV of $21,375 @ 25%[1]) $5,344
Deemed interest (5.65%[2] of $21,375) $1,208
Value of car benefit.. **$14,582**
less recipient's contribution $2,600
Taxable value.. **$11,982**

*Therefore, use the **statutory formula method**.*

FBT liability on this car for the 2015-16 FBT year: $5,000 (taxable value) x 2.1463 x 49% =
$5,258 [3]

One eleventh of $2,600 employee contribution or $236.36 GST is payable by the employer
(see 24.410).

1:   The cost of the car is used if purchased during the FBT year. If the car is purchased on or after 1
     April 2008, use 25%.
2:   The benchmark interest rate is 5.65% for 2015-16 (TD 2015/8).
3:   If the employer is a rebatable employer this would be reduced by 49%.
4.   But not crash repair expenses paid by an insurance company legally responsible for such
     damage to the car.

25.400 CAR PARKING BENEFITS

Car parking on the employer's business premises or private parking at commercial car parks
which is paid or reimbursed by the employer may be subject to FBT. Taxation Ruling TR 96/26
explains the various provisions in full.

25.401   WHAT IS A CAR PARKING BENEFIT?

A car parking fringe benefit arises only if **ALL** of the following conditions are satisfied:

- a car is parked on premises or associated premises of the provider
- a commercial car parking station is located within a 1 kilometre radius of the premises at
  which the car is parked
- the lowest fee charged by the operator of any commercial parking station located within
  a 1 kilometre radius for 'all-day parking' on the first 'business day' of the FBT year is
  more than the 'car parking threshold'. This amount is **$8.37** for the 2015-16 FBT year
  (see TD 2015/11), up from **$8.26** for the 2014-15 FBT year (see TD 2014/11).

 Two commercial car parking stations within 1 kilometre charge the lowest fees at
1 April 2015 of $8.00 and $9.00. The condition is satisfied because the lowest fee
charged by one of the operators on 1 April 2015 exceeds the $8.37 threshold.

- the car is parked on the premises for more than four hours between 7am and 7pm
  (times in that day are cumulative) on the day the car is used for travel between home
  and work at least once on that day
- the provision of the parking facility is in respect of the employment of the employee
- the car is owned by, leased to, or otherwise under the control of the employee, and

- the employee has a primary place of employment on that day and the parking is at or in the vicinity of that primary place of employment.

While a benefit will not arise for workers who work shifts outside the above hours, a benefit still arises for those who work on weekends, even if it is overtime work or not normal business hours. If the benefit provided is neither an expense payment benefit (see 25.550) nor a car parking benefit as defined, it is not subject to FBT.

WHAT IS A 'COMMERCIAL PARKING STATION'?

A commercial parking station is defined in ss136(1) FBT Act as any permanent commercial (ie. run with a view to profit) car parking facility where car parking spaces are available in the ordinary course of business to members of the public for all-day parking on payment of a fee and does not include meter or ticket parking on a public street, road, lane, thoroughfare or footpath.

In *Commissioner of Taxation v QANTAS Airways Ltd* [2014] FCAFC 168, the Full Federal Court considered the issue of what is a commercial car park in the context of airport car parks. It held that an airport car park could be a commercial parking station even though it was not available in the ordinary course of business to members of the public due their use was restricted to airline passengers only. **NOTE:** Employers in close proximity to airport car parks should exercise caution in identifying commercial car parks.

WHAT IS 'ALL-DAY' PARKING?

'All-day parking' is defined in the FBT Act with reference to the parking of a single car for a continuous period of six hours or more during a daylight period on the particular day. A fee charged by the operator of the commercial parking station for vehicles entering the station from 1 p.m. is not a fee for 'all-day parking' (ATO ID 2014/2). The ID states that after 1 p.m. it is impossible to park for a continuous period of six hours of more during a 'daylight period' on that day. A 'daylight period' ends before 7.00 p.m. on that same day.

REPRESENTATIVE FEE

A fee is not representative if, on a particular day, it is substantially different to the lowest average fee usually charged to a member of the public for all day parking. To check this, the employer compares the fee for a particular day, with the average fee charged during the four week periods either before or after that day.

THE 'ONE KILOMETRE' RULE

A commercial parking station is within one kilometre of the business premises only if a car entrance to the commercial station is within one kilometre, measured by the shortest practicable route, from the carpark entrance to the business premises. This route can be travelled on foot, by car, train, boat etc. whichever produces the shortest route including the use of any legal access such as laneways or shopping arcades etc. – but not a route which would involve an illegal act (eg. trespass) or that involves walking through a store or other business or private premises (TR 96/26).

BUSINESS PREMISES

Employers are taxed on the value to employees of car parking provided on business premises located within one kilometre of a commercial car park. Some small business are exempt (see below). Special rules apply to value the amount of the benefit to be included (see *Exemptions* below and *Taxable value* from 25.410).

BUSINESS DAY

A 'business day' means a day that is not a Saturday, a Sunday or a public holiday in the place concerned. From June 2011, this definition is contained in the Acts Interpretation Act 1901 with the former definition in the FBT Act being repealed (noting however that the definition itself did not change).

IN THE VICINITY OF

The Full Federal Court in the case of *Virgin Blue Airlines Pty Ltd v FC of T* [2010] ATC 20 considered the statutory interpretation of the phrase 'in the vicinity of' and concluded that the parking provided was not 'in the vicinity of' the employee's place of employment. In the view of the Full Court, concepts such as 'functional space' bore no relevance to the question and that such a construction would actually result in anomalies as regards employer provided car parking located say two kilometres from the employee's principal place of employment within a large functional space eg. an airport or hospital versus employer provided car parking located the same distance from the employee's principal place of employment within a much narrower functional space such as the CBD.

25.402   EXEMPT ORGANISATIONS

Certain organisations are exempt from FBT where car parking facilities are provided to employees or an employee's costs are paid or reimbursed by the employer (ss58G(2) and (3) FBT Act). These specified organisations are:

- a scientific organisation (but not one carried on by a company, society or association for profit or gain to its individual shareholders or members)
- a religious institution
- a charitable institution
- a public educational institution
- a government body in relation to an employee who is employed exclusively in connection with a public educational institution.

25.403   SMALL BUSINESS EXEMPTION

A car parking benefit provided to an employee is exempt pursuant to s58GA FBT Act where:

- the car is not parked at a commercial parking station, and
- the employer is not a public company or a subsidiary of a public company, and
- the employer is not a government body, and
- the employer's gross ordinary and statutory income for the year ending before the start of the FBT year is less than $10 million or alternatively, the taxpayer constitutes a 'small business entity' pursuant to Division 328 ITAA97 (where aggregate annual turnover is less than $2 million).

Employers starting business during the FBT year may make a reasonable estimate of their ordinary and statutory income for the purposes of the exemption.

In the 2014-15 income year, Tuan carried on a business as an engineer and had an aggregated turnover of $1.98 million. For that year he is a small business entity because the aggregated turnover is less than $2 million. For 2015-16 Tuan will still be a small business entity because the 2014-15 aggregated income was less than $2 million.

25.404   DISABLED CAR PARKING

The provision of car parking fringe benefits to disabled employees is exempt where the following conditions are satisfied:

- the employee is the driver or passenger in the car
- that person is entitled to use a disabled persons' car parking space (if a public car parking area and designated for the exclusive use of disabled persons) under a State or Territory law, and
- a valid disabled persons' car parking permit is displayed on the car.

25.405   CAR PARKING COSTS PAID OR REIMBURSED BY EMPLOYER

FBT is payable on an employee's private car parking if the employee contracts personally with a car parking facility to provide a car park and the employer pays or reimburses that expense. Such payment is however classified as a car parking expense payment fringe benefit as opposed to a car parking fringe benefit.

Accordingly, the taxable value of the benefit will be calculated under the expense payment fringe benefit rules pursuant to Division 5 FBT Act and the employer will be liable to FBT on the grossed-up value of the benefit paid to the car parking facility or reimbursed to the employee less any contribution made by the employee.

The reimbursement of parking fees to an employee constitutes an exempt fringe benefit under s58G(1)(a) where the fees are incurred to park the employee's car at the local airport whilst the employee is working interstate at a remote location (ATO ID 2012/18).

25.410 TAXABLE VALUE OF A CAR PARKING BENEFIT

In calculating the taxable value of a car parking fringe benefit, an employer must determine both the number of benefits provided (ie. the number of times a car parking fringe benefit arose) and the value of each car parking space provided. For either determination, the employer may apply one of the five methods described below.

25.411 COMMERCIAL CAR PARKING STATION METHOD

The commercial car parking station method is calculated using the lowest all day parking fee charged by a commercial parking station located within a one kilometre radius of the employer's premises, on each day that a parking benefit was provided, multiplied by the actual number of benefits providing during the FBT year.

25.412 MARKET VALUE METHOD

The market value method is determined by an arm's length qualified valuer providing a report in an acceptable form as to the value of the car parking spaces available. The taxable value is calculated by multiplying this amount by the actual number of benefits provided during the FBT year.

INDEPENDENT VALUATION

Where the independent valuation method is adopted, the FBT taxable value of the car parking fringe benefit is based on the cost the employee could expect to pay under an arm's length transaction for similar parking.

The employer must elect to use this method and:

* the valuation must be obtained from a suitable qualified arm's length valuer
* the valuation report must be in a form approved by the Tax Office, and
* the FBT return must be based on that valuation report (ie. as far as it relates to the taxable value of the benefit).

The valuation method requires that the employee and the provider of the parking be treated as in an arm's length situation. The valuer cannot take into account any employment related conditions which may, prima facie, affect the benefit's value. The onus of proving that a person has expertise in a particular field will rest in each case with the taxpayer (employer).

The employer must be able to produce, if required, details of the basis on which the valuation was determined. That information may be set out in a separate valuer's report. No election is required if this method is used.

25.413 AVERAGE COST METHOD

The average cost method is calculated using an average of the lowest all day parking fee charged by commercial parking station operators within a one kilometre radius of the premises in which the car is parked, on the first and last days of the FBT year. The taxable value is calculated by multiplying this amount by the actual number of benefits providing during the FBT year. The average fee is found by adding the lowest fee for the first and last days and dividing by two. The lowest fee can be based on that charged at any commercial car parking facility within the one kilometre radius. It does not have to be based on the fee charged at the employer provided facility.

 John parked his car on his employer's premises between 1 April 2015 and 31 March 2016. A commercial car park charges as its lowest fee during that time, $12 per day. Another operator (also located within one km) charged $8.00 on 1 April 2015 and $9.00 on 31 March 2016. FBT for 2015-16 will be charged on the average of $8.50.

25.414   STATUTORY FORMULA (SPACES) METHOD

Statutory formula (spaces) method deems that a car parking space provided to an employee will be used 228 days during a full FBT year. The total taxable value of the employer's car parking fringe benefits is calculated using the following formula:

*Daily rate amount x (number of days in availability period
in relation to the space/366*) x 228*

*366 days is used whether a leap year or not.

where:

- the daily rate amount is determined using either the commercial parking station method, the market value method or the average cost method, and

- the number of days in the availability period in relation to space means the number of days beginning on the first day and ending on the last day in the FBT year on which there is a car parking benefit for the space for an employee covered by the election.

Where the employer elects to use the statutory spaces method, the total value (GST inclusive) of car parking benefits for all employees is covered by an election. Thus the written election must specify whether the election applies to all employees, a class of employees, or specific employees. If the number of spaces exceeds the number of employees, the statutory benefit is multiplied by:

Average number of employees divided by Average number of eligible spaces

An employer elects to use the statutory formula (spaces) method to determine the taxable value for 50 employees. The employer provides 60 car parking spaces, but the benefits are provided for only half of the FBT year. Employees contributed $10,000. Average cost of car parking within one kilometre is $15.

The taxable value for each car parking space is $1,710 (ie. $15 x 228 days x 183/366).

For the 50 employees, the total taxable value is $75,500 (($1,710 x 60 spaces x 50/60) – $10,000).

Employers contemplating this method should be wary as it may result in a higher FBT liability, because the statutory formula is based on the parking space being available for 228 days. This may not necessarily adequately account for public holidays, sick days, Rostered Days Off (RDOs) or when the employee is away on business travel.

12 WEEK REGISTER METHOD (ELECTION REQUIRED)

Under this method, the employer keeps a register of the actual number of car parking fringe benefits provided during a continuous 12 week period. The total taxable value of the employer's car parking benefits for employees covered by the election for an FBT year is calculated using the following formula:

*[Total value of car parking benefits (register) x 52/12] x number of days
in car parking availability period/366*

where:

- the total value of car parking benefits is equal to the number of benefits per register multiplied by the value of the car parking fringe benefit calculated using either the commercial car parking station method, the market value method or the average cost method, and

- number of days in car parking availability period means the number of days beginning on the first day and ending on the last day in the FBT year on which there is a car parking benefit for an employee covered by the election.

After keeping a register for 12 weeks, an employer elects that the 250 car parking benefits be valued per day at $8 each (or $480 for the 12 weeks) using the 'lowest fee charged' method. The car parking spaces were available for the whole FBT year. The taxable value is 250 spaces x $480 x 52/12 = $520,000.

Using the facts in the first example, the spaces were available only to employees from 1 October onwards. The taxable value is reduced to 250 spaces x $480 x 52/12 x 182/366 = $258,578.

The number of benefits calculated under this method continues to apply in future years until the number of car parking spaces (or the number of employees allowed to park, if that is less) increases by more than 10% over the base log book year. If the employer fails to satisfy the 10% rule, a new log book must be maintained in the next FBT year if the employer wishes to continue using the 12 week sample method.

If more than one register is kept within a year, the later one applies. This applies if no election is made.

25.415   RECORD-KEEPING

Irrespective of which method the employer chooses to calculate the taxable value of car parking benefits provided to employees on the employer's business premises, records must be maintained showing how those benefits are calculated (but see 25.250).

Car parking benefits records must be in English, be kept in a readily accessible form, and retained for five years for the FBT year starting from:

* the date the FBT return is lodged, or
* the due date for lodgment of the FBT return.

25.416   DECLARATION BY THE EMPLOYER

Before lodging FBT returns, all employers providing car parking benefits should complete a declaration stating:

* the number of car parking spaces available for employees and/or their associates, ie. the number of spaces which could be taken up by a car, which do not have to be physically marked as such
* the daily value of those spaces (see 25.414)
* the number of business days in the year, and
* the method of valuation used.

If only that basic information is maintained, the taxable value of the parking is on the basis that all parking spaces were occupied once for more than four hours on each business day of the year and employees did not make a contribution.

VACANT CAR SPACES

If there are more spaces available than employees who park in them, an additional declaration can be made to the effect that a certain number of parking spaces are not occupied by employees or associates for four hours or more between 7am and 7pm. If that information is not provided, FBT will be imposed on the basis that a parking benefit arose for each spot on each business day.

25.417   REPORTING SYSTEMS

If the actual number of car parking benefits provided to employees is more or less than would be the case if all available car parking spaces were occupied by one car on every business day, to demonstrate the actual benefits provided, an employer may adopt one or both of the following reporting systems.

THE EXCEPTION OR ADDITION SYSTEM

The basic records described above (see 25.416) should be maintained. In addition, records may be kept which note the occasions when no parking benefits arise for a car parking space because an employee who would normally occupy the space was absent. Records should also be kept of those occasions when a parking benefit arises on a day which is not an ordinary business day (eg. weekends). In compiling information on staff absences under this system, other records may be relied on, such as personnel records (to verify staff absences) records of travel arrangements or a register of absences.

A more detailed register could be kept as an alternative to the two systems above.

 A company provides on-site parking for 200 senior staff at their building which is within one kilometre of a commercial parking station charging more than the car parking threshold (see 25.401). The value of each benefit is $16 (GST inclusive). Based on 200 staff and 250 business days, the taxable value is $800,000 (ie. 200 x 250 x $16). However, an administrator

in each area notes in a diary the days during the year when senior staff who use the on-site parking facilities are absent for the entire day. The collated results identified 10,000 days in which a parking benefit did not arise.

The taxable value is therefore reduced by $160,000 (ie. $16 x 10,000 days) to $640,000.

An employer may use the exception reporting system in conjunction with the system of reporting permanently vacant car parking spaces (see *Vacant car spaces* above).

THE REGISTER SYSTEM

The register system, although available to any employer, would mostly be used by those who operate a pool of vehicles (available for employees to travel to and from work), or when employees use their own vehicles, but the day and time parked at the employer's premises vary. If the register system is used, in all cases the register should be compiled for vehicles under the control of an employee or associate who parks in the space provided.

The person responsible for making entries in the register must do so as soon as practicable after details are known.

NOTE: A register is not valid if it contains an entry that is false or misleading in a material particular.

The register must be representative for the first FBT year for which it is valid. If the 12 week period begins in one FBT year and ends in another, the register is valid only for the latter year and the next four years.

The register, which must be representative of benefits provided over a full year of tax, should be compiled over a continuous period of 12 weeks. A new register is required every five years.

The information will form the basis of assessment for the current and following tax year.

Where an employer uses the 12 week register method for determining the taxable value of a car parking fringe benefit, the act of changing the location of the car parking facilities will not invalidate the original register.

The employer must complete another register if the level of car parking benefits provided increases by 10% or more. To ensure the 10% is not exceeded, the employer must monitor the car parking spaces provided.

25.450 LOAN BENEFITS

A loan benefit arises where a loan is made by an employer (or associate) to an employee (or an associate, see definition at 25.005) either without interest or at a rate lower than the benchmark statutory rate is 5.65% for the FBT year commencing 1 April 2015 (see TD 2015/8). GST does not affect the taxable value of these benefits.

If the loan is used by the employee to derive assessable income, the taxable value of the loan benefit is reduced by the amount of interest that would have been tax deductible in the hands of the employee had the employee incurred the cost (only once-off notional deductions can be taken into account). Further loan benefits can arise if the employer does not require the payment of interest on time, or defers payment of the interest indefinitely.

25.451   WHAT IS A LOAN FRINGE BENEFIT?

The definition of a loan is very wide and includes:

*   an advance of money (see also *Company loan debit accounts* at 6.300 and 6.350)
*   the provision of credit (or other form of financial accommodation)
*   the repayment of an amount owing (whether express or implied), and
*   a transaction (whatever its terms or form which in substance effects a loan of money).

The unpaid amount of a debt is treated as a loan if an employee owes a debt to an employer, but the employer does not enforce payment after the debt becomes due. Further loan benefits will arise for the amount of any unpaid interest.

The Tax Office also considers that, where an employee is given time to repay an overpaid salary, a loan fringe benefit arises. The minor benefit exemption may however apply (see TD 2008/10 and 25.200).

If the whole or part of the principal remains unpaid after the due date, another loan benefit is created.

The deemed interest rate is the rate accruing on any unpaid amount (under the terms of the loan) or nil, if there is no default rate. This can create a compounding effect if the principal, or part of it, remains unpaid. A 'deferred interest loan' arises if a loan is made to an employee under terms that allow for interest payments to be made less frequently than every six months and all or part of the interest remains unpaid. The 'new loan' will be deemed to have a nil rate of interest and the period of the loan is from the end of that six months until the interest is paid. A debt waiver benefit arises if the employer releases the employee from the obligations to repay the loan (see 25.500).

 If an employer allows an employee to salary sacrifice (ie. to repay the debt from pre-tax dollars) the amount is treated as a debt waiver (see 25.500).

25.452   BENCHMARK INTEREST RATES

The statutory interest rate is set by reference to the 'large bank housing lenders variable rate for housing for owners/occupiers' published by the Reserve Bank immediately prior to the start of the FBT year.

The benchmark interest rate used to calculate the taxable value of all types of loans provided by employers for the 2015-16 FBT year is **5.65%** (TD 2015/8) and for the 2014-15 FBT year is **5.95**% (TD 2014/5).

25.453   TAXABLE VALUE OF LOAN FRINGE BENEFIT

The taxable value of a loan benefit (or a deferred loan benefit) is the difference between:

- the notional interest, ie. the interest that would have accrued to the loan if the statutory benchmark rate had applied to the outstanding daily balance, and
- the interest (if any) which actually accrued.

The taxable value is grossed-up by 1.9608 (loans are input taxed for GST purposes and accordingly, the FBT type 2 gross up applies: see 25.100).

 *On 1 April 2015, an employee was given a $50,000 loan at 5% interest (payable six monthly). The employee used the loan to build an extension to his main residence. No repayments of principal are required until 1 April 2016. The benchmark rate for the year commencing 1 April 2015 is **5.65%**.*

Notional interest ($50,000 x 5.65%)	*$2,825*
less actual interest incurred @ 5%	*($2,500)*
Taxable value	*$325*
Grossed-up amount ($325 x 1.9608)	*$637*
***FBT payable** ($637 x 49%)*	***$312.13***

25.454   EXEMPT LOAN BENEFITS

The value of a loan benefit is exempt from FBT in the following circumstances.

EMPLOYER IN THE BUSINESS OF MONEY LENDING

- **Fixed interest loans:** In this situation, there will be no benefit to the employee (or associate) if the interest rate on the loan is at least equal to the interest applicable to loans made to a member of the public in the ordinary course of business when the loan was made to the employee.
  The rate of interest must be specified in a document in existence when the loan was made and the rate must not be variable. The exemption for such loans remains for the duration of the loan.
- **Variable loans:** An exemption is available in this case if the rate of interest charged on the loan is not less than the arm's length rate charged to the public for a similar loan. Exemption must be determined each FBT year.

DEEMED DIVIDENDS

Division 7A ITAA36 specifically provides that a deemed dividend may arise in respect of a loan made to a shareholder (or associate of a shareholder), notwithstanding that the loan is made to a person in the capacity of an 'employee'. FBT does not apply to a loan which is taken to be a deemed dividend under Division 7A ITAA36.

If an interest-free loan is made to an employee/shareholder and only a part of the loan is deemed to be a dividend under Division 7A because the deemed dividend is limited to the amount of the distributable surplus, FBT is not payable on the balance (see also 6.310).

EMPLOYMENT-RELATED EXPENSES

If an employer advances money to an employee solely to meet the requirements of employment-related expenses in relation to that employer, the loan is exempt from FBT if:

- the expenses are incurred within six months of the advance
- the advance is not substantially in excess of the estimated expenses
- the employee accounts for the expenses met from the loan, and
- any unspent money is repaid.

NOTE: When calculating the 'otherwise deductible' amount allowed for self-education expenses, both the substantiation requirements and the non-deductibility of the first $250 are ignored (see 13.100 and 13.700).

TEMPORARY ADVANCE TO COVER SECURITY DEPOSIT

A temporary advance is exempt from FBT if it is:

- repayable within 12 months, and
- made to an employee solely to pay a security deposit (eg. rental bond, temporary accommodation or telephone, gas or electricity deposits).

25.455   'OTHERWISE DEDUCTIBLE' RULE

The taxable value of a loan benefit may also be reduced if the borrowed funds are used to derive assessable income by the employee. This concession ensures that only the private use of the loan benefit is subject to FBT.

The reduction in the taxable value of the loan benefit is calculated using this method.

- **Step 1:** Calculate the taxable value of the loan benefit as if no interest was paid (or payable) on the loan (ie. nominal interest).
- **Step 2:** Calculate how much of the interest would have been tax deductible to the employee (ie. the theoretical claim).
- **Step 3:** Calculate how much of the interest paid (or payable) is allowable as a real tax deduction to the employee.
- **Step 4:** Deduct Step 3 from Step 2. The result is the 'otherwise deductible amount' (ie. the amount by which the taxable value of the loan benefit may be reduced).

On 1 April 2015, an employee of a financial institution was provided with a low interest loan of $100,000. The loan was an interest-only loan for a five year period. It is the employer's policy to charge interest on all staff loans at 2%. Interest is charged every six months. The benchmark interest rate for the FBT year commencing 1 April 2015 is 5.65%. The employee used $90,000 to purchase a small rental property and the remaining $10,000 was spent on a holiday.

Step 1:	*Notional interest ($100,000 x 5.65%)*	*$5,650*
	less actual interest charged ($100,000 @ 2%)	*($2,000)*
		$3,650
Step 2:	*Theoretical tax deduction ($5,650 x 90%)*	*$5,085*
Step 3:	*Actual tax deduction ($2,000 x 90%)*	*($1,800)*
Step 4:	*Loan benefit reduction ($5,085 – $1,800)*	*$3,285*

The 'otherwise deductible' amount is $3,285.

Taxable value of loan benefit.. $3,650
less 'Otherwise deductible amount'..($3,285)
Taxable value.. $365
Grossed-up amount ($365 x 1.9608) $715.69
FBT liability ($715.69 @ 49%).. **$350.69**

The use of the 'otherwise deductible' rule must be supported by an employee declaration. That declaration must be obtained from the employee before the employer lodges their FBT return and must be in an approved format. The need for that declaration is waived where:

- the loan is used solely to enable the employee to acquire shares in the employer company and the shares are owned by the employee throughout the period of the FBT year when the loan is outstanding, or

- the loan consists of the provision of credit by the employer in respect of a sale to the employee of goods or services that are used exclusively in the employer's employment (eg. the sale of a company uniform on interest-free credit terms).

The 'otherwise deductible' rule applies only to loans made to employees. If the loan is made to an associate of the employee, there is no reduction under this rule (TD 93/90). Where a loan is made jointly to an employee and their associate to jointly acquire income-producing property, the reduction under the otherwise deductible rule only applies to the employee's share and not the associate of the employee's share (s138(3)).

25.500 DEBT WAIVER FRINGE BENEFITS

A debt waiver fringe benefit arises upon the waiving or forgiving of a debt owed by an employee (or associate) to their employer (or associate). The waiver must occur in connection with the debtor's employment. The release of the employee's obligation to pay or repay an amount owing to the employer (eg. for the sale of goods or the balance of an outstanding loan) (see **Loan fringe benefits** at 25.450) gives rise to a fringe benefit.

The word 'waive' was considered by the Court in *Banning v Wright* (1972) 2 All ER 987 where it was held to mean the giving up or abandoning of some right.

A debt owed by an employee that is written off as a genuine bad debt is not a debt waiver fringe benefit.

FBT will not apply to a private company's forgiveness of a debt owed by a person (who is a shareholder or associate of a shareholder) in their capacity as an employee. The deemed dividend rules in Division 7A ITAA36 will apply to such debt forgiveness (see ss109ZB(2) ITAA36).

25.501   TAXABLE VALUE OF DEBT WAIVER FRINGE BENEFITS

The taxable value of a loan fringe benefit is the amount of the debt released, plus any interest unpaid and waived. If an employer does not require an employee to repay a $5,000 loan, and releases the debt when $420 of the interest is overdue, the taxable value of the debt waiver is $5,420. See also 25.450 about salary sacrifice to repay debt.

25.502   EXEMPTIONS FOR DEBT WAIVER FRINGE BENEFITS

There are no specific exemptions for debt waiver fringe benefits in the FBT Act. However, a debt waiver fringe benefit may be an exempt benefit where the minor benefit exemption in s58P FBT Act can be applied.

25.550 EXPENSE PAYMENT BENEFITS

An expense payment fringe benefit arises where an employer (or associate or third party under an arrangement) makes a payment to discharge an obligation of an employee (or associate) or reimburses an employee (or associate) for expenditure incurred.

NOTE: Car expenses reimbursed on a cents-per-kilometre basis are not subject to FBT. The amount is assessable income of the employee.

 To be able to claim input tax credits employers need to hold a tax invoice and make reimbursements for particular expenses (see 25.150 and GSTR 2001/3).

25.551   TAXABLE VALUE OF EXPENSE PAYMENT FRINGE BENEFITS

The taxable value of an expense payment fringe benefit depends upon whether the benefit is an external or in-house expense payment fringe benefit. Each valuation rule however allows for the taxable value to be reduced by the amount of any employee contribution and/or the otherwise deductible rule (see 25.558).

 If an expense payment fringe benefit satisfies the criteria to be classified as a minor benefit, it may be exempt.

NOTE: It is a question of fact whether GST is included. If it is, the taxable value of the benefit is the GST inclusive value reduced to the extent to which the expenditure would have been deductible, had the expense been met by the employee or an employee contribution.

EXTERNAL EXPENSE PAYMENT FRINGE BENEFITS

External expense payment fringe benefits are those other than in-house expense payment fringe benefits. That is, the goods or services provided by the employer to the employee are not ordinarily provided to the general public in the ordinary course of the employer's business.

The taxable value of external expense payment fringe benefits is the amount of expenditure incurred by the employee which is paid or reimbursed by the employer, less any employee contributions made.

 An employer who is in the retail industry pays for certain employee's private health insurance at a cost of $2,300 per annum. As the benefit provided is not of a type that is sold or provided to the general public in the ordinary course of the employer's business, the benefit is an external expense payment fringe benefit and has a taxable value of $2,300.

IN-HOUSE EXPENSE PAYMENT FRINGE BENEFITS

In-house expense payment fringe benefits arise where the employer reimburses an employee for the purchase of goods or services of a kind that the employer sells to customers in the ordinary course of business. There are two types and each have concessional valuation rules, as follows:

- **in-house property expense payment:** the amount that would have been the valuation of an in-house property fringe benefit if the expense payment fringe benefit were a property fringe benefit (see 25.862), and

- **in-house residual expense payment:** is the amount that would have been the valuation of an in-house residual fringe benefit if the expense payment fringe benefit were a residual benefit (see 25.862).

 An employer manufactures glassware which is sold though independent retailers. An employee of the retailer buys $500 of glassware and the employer reimburses $200. The retailer paid $350 for the goods. The taxable value is $350 – ($500 – $200) = $50. Assuming this is the only in-house fringe benefit the employee receives, the taxable value may be reduced to nil by applying the $1,000 per employee, per FBT year, reduction.

 Consider the $1,000 exemption per employee, per FBT year, to reduce the taxable value of each employee's aggregate in-house fringe benefit. This concession may not be available for in-house benefits provided on or after 22 October 2012 under a salary packaging arrangement (see 25.862).

25.552   CLAIMING INPUT TAX CREDITS FOR EXPENSE PAYMENT FRINGE BENEFITS

In order to claim input tax credits, employers must hold a valid tax invoice and make reimbursements for particular expenses (see GSTR 2001/3).

Division 111 GST Act provides for an employer to claim an input tax credit for reimbursements to an employee in respect of expenses incurred, notwithstanding that the relevant tax invoice may be in the name of the employee. Specifically, the division provides that:

- the fact that the supply to the employer from the employee is not a taxable supply is irrelevant. The original supply to the employee, associate etc. must however have been a taxable supply for it to be creditable, and

- no input tax credit is available to the extent that the employee, associate, officer etc. is entitled to an input tax credit in their own right, or the acquisition would not be creditable if it had been directly incurred by the employer (eg. because it is non-deductible and non-creditable under Division 69 GST Act).

25.553   REDUCTIONS IN TAXABLE VALUE

The taxable value of an expense payment fringe benefit may be reduced by application of the otherwise deductible rule. This rule may be applied to reduce the taxable value by the amount that would have resulted in a one-off deduction (in full or part) to the employee if the employee had themselves incurred the expenditure.

 A reduction in the taxable value of an expense payment fringe benefit is not available where the benefit is provided to an associate of the employee.

 The otherwise deductible rule does not apply to deductions for the decline in value of depreciating assets (ie. depreciation), except when the cost is less than $300. The otherwise deductible rule only applies where the employee would have been entitled to a once only deduction.

Documentary evidence of the type required to substantiate expenses claimed as income tax deductions is generally required for FBT purposes.

Further, the first $1,000 of in-house expense payment fringe benefits provided to an employee during an FBT year are exempt. Where the fringe benefit may be subject to another concession, such as the otherwise deductible rule, the other concession is applied before the $1,000 threshold exemption. Note that the concession may not be available where provided under a salary packaging arrangement.

See 25.682: *Changes to in-house fringe benefits*.

25.554   EXEMPT EXPENSE PAYMENT FRINGE BENEFITS

Whilst not exhaustive, the following benefits are exempt expense payment benefits:

- expense benefits in respect of which there is a 'no private use' declaration
- expenditure in respect of accommodation costs incurred because the employee is required to live away from their usual place of residence in order to perform their employment duties; refer s21 (exempt accommodation expense benefits)
- reimbursement of an employee's car expenses based on the distance travelled (typically cents per kilometres) provided the car is owned or leased by the employee and the travel is in connection with the employee's duties; refer s22 FBT Act
- long service awards, where all criteria within the s58Q are satisfied
- payment or reimbursement of certain relocation expenses, and
- expense payment benefits falling within the general exemption provisions, including:
  - minor benefits, s58P
  - eligible work related items, s58X
  - membership fees and subscriptions associated with employment duties, s58Y, and
  - taxi travel, s58Z.

25.555   SUBSTANTIATION RULES

In order to reduce the taxable value of an expense payment fringe benefit under the otherwise deductible rule, both documentary evidence, substantiating the expenditure incurred or reimbursed and declarations, completed by the employee substantiating the extent to which the expense is 'otherwise deductible', are required.

EXCEPTIONS

Receipts etc. need not be provided if the employee:

- supplies the employer with a declaration that the expenses (other than interest) were incurred exclusively in gaining or producing the employee's salary (eg. if employer reimburses employee for taxi fares to visit a client's premises), or
- is paid or reimbursed by the employer for:
  - reasonable costs of accommodation, meals or other incidentals for travel exclusively in the course of their employment – within Australia (regardless of duration), and outside Australia for less than six nights – which do not require substantiation because the amounts claimed are considered reasonable (see 13.160 and 13.190), or
  - overtime meal expenses that would not have required substantiation had they been met out of a reasonable overtime meal allowance (see 13.140).

DOCUMENTATION

Generally, expense payment fringe benefits are evidenced by invoices, receipts or the like showing the following details:

- date the expense was incurred
- date of the receipt
- name of the supplier of the goods and services
- nature of the good and services, and
- the amount paid.

DECLARATIONS

In order to reduce the taxable value of an expense payment fringe benefit, the employer is required to obtain a declaration (by the due date for lodgement of the employer's FBT return), from the employee (set out in an approved form) detailing the particulars of the expense. There are two types of employee declarations:

a.   'Recurring fringe benefit declaration', and

b.   'No private use declaration' (expense payments).

25.556   EMPLOYEE'S CAR EXPENSES

If car expenses (other than borrowing or leasing costs) are met by an employer in respect of a car owned by the employee, the taxable benefit is reduced to the extent a deduction would have been allowed to the employee had he/she paid the costs. Additional rules apply to the reimbursement of car expenses relating to a car owned or leased by an employee.

There are three methods of establishing the hypothetical deductions that would have been allowable as a tax deduction to the employee:

- substantiation by log book, odometer or car records, and an employee declaration
- estimated business use percentage established by an employee declaration (maximum estimated percentage allowed is $33^1/3\%$), or
- a deemed $33^1/3\%$ business use, provided the car travelled on average a minimum of 96 kms per week (or 5,000 kms per year). An employee declaration is required to substantiate the kilometres.

See 25.558.

CAR EXPENSES REIMBURSED PER KILOMETRE

If an employer compensates an employee on the basis of the cents per kilometres method for the cost of operating a car owned or leased by the employee, the payment is not subject to FBT. The employee must declare the full amount received in their income tax return and claim expenses they have incurred if calculated on the employment-related kilometres travelled. The cents per kilometre method may only be used where the business related travel is less than or equal to 5,000 kilometres. When more than 5,000 business kms are travelled, the employee's claim is limited to 5,000 kms.

The employee's claim is calculated by multiplying:

> *Business kms travelled in the income year (limited to 5,000 kms)*
> *x Rate based on car's engine capacity*

An 'allowance' is assessable to the employee, who must substantiate claims for deductions. There will be no FBT payable on money spent by the employee on their car.

25.557   BUSINESS TRAVEL RATES

The rates for income-producing travel in a privately owned car for the 2013-14 and 2014-15 years are as follows:

Engine capacity		Rate per km 2013-14 & 2014-15
Normal engine	**Rotary engine**	
Up to 1,600cc	Up to 800cc	65c
1,601 to 2,600cc	801 to 1,300cc	76c
2,601cc and over	1,301cc and over	77c

NOTE: In the May 2015 Budget the Federal Government announced its intention to introduce a single cents per km rate of 66 cents, regardless of engine capacity, from 1 July 2015. This is not yet enacted at the time of writing.

> *In 2014-15 Joan uses her own car (normal engine with capacity 2000cc) to travel 6,000 employment-related kilometres.*
>
> *Her employer compensates her for that use at 76c per kilometre. In her tax return Joan includes $4,560 (6,000 x 76c) as assessable income. However, if she uses the cents per kilometre method her maximum deduction is $3,800 (5,000 x 76c) (see 13.230).*

25.558   'OTHERWISE DEDUCTIBLE RULE'

The taxable value of an expense payment benefit provided to an employee (but not an associate of the employee) can be reduced by the amount that would have been deductible to the employee if the employee had themselves incurred the expenditure. Documentary evidence of the type required to substantiate expenses claimed as income tax deductions (see 13.100) is generally required for FBT purposes.

The employee is also required to set out in an approved declaration the particulars of the expense. There are two types of employee declarations:

- a *Recurring fringe benefit declaration*, and
- a *No private use declaration* (expense payments).

All employee declarations must be in an approved form and must be given to the employer before the due date for lodgement of the employer's FBT return. If no FBT return is required, the declaration must still be given no later than 28 May.

The *Recurring fringe benefit declaration* may be lodged where the employee receives a series of expense payment benefits that are essentially the same except for the value of the benefits or the proportion of business use of the benefits. By completing this declaration the employee does not need to complete a separate declaration for each and every separate expense benefit. Once made, the declaration applies for five years unless it is revoked earlier by the employee.

Benefits are treated as being identical for declaration purposes if the deductible proportion of the expense does not differ by more than ten percentage points.

An employer regularly reimburses an employee for the cost of home telephone expenses. The employee gives the employer a recurring fringe benefit declaration that sets out that 80% of the expenses qualify under the 'otherwise deductible' rule. That declaration will remain in force for the next five years provided the employee does not lodge another declaration or the employment related component does not increase to above 90% or below 70%. In that case a new declaration is required.

The *No private use declaration* covers all expense payment benefits where the taxable value of the benefit is nil (ie. the entire amount of the benefit would have been tax deductible if it had been incurred by the employee). This declaration must be lodged each FBT year.

25.600   ROAD TOLL AND E-TAG EXPENSES

A fringe benefit will usually arise if the car is being used for private purposes and the employer pays for the toll or provides the electronic tag.

Private travel is usually travel to and from work, and all other usage not associated with work purposes. If an employer either pays for an employee's road toll, or allows the employee to use the employer's electronic toll tag (e-tag), a benefit arises. This will be either an expense payment fringe benefit (25.550) or a residual fringe benefit (25.820). However an exemption may apply.

25.601   EXPENSE PAYMENTS

If an employee incurs a road toll expense when using either their own car or a car held by their employer, and:

- the purpose for the travel is private
- the e-tag is held in the name of the employee and/or the employee makes cash payments at a toll booth, and
- the employer reimburses the employee for the expense of the e-tag or cash payment,

the reimbursement is an expense payment fringe benefit and the taxable value is the amount reimbursed.

25.602   RESIDUAL FRINGE BENEFITS

If an employee incurs a road toll expense when using their own car or a car held by their employer, and:

- the purpose for the travel is private
- the e-tag is held in the name of the employer, and
- the employer pays the e-tag account,

then each road toll recorded is a residual fringe benefit. The taxable value is the total paid by the employer, less any contribution made by the employee to the employer.

All road tolls incurred while undertaking private travel are subject to FBT and the e-tag statements provide sufficient details to identify the tolls relating to that car. The taxable value is the total costs of the tolls shown on the statements.

25.603   EXEMPTIONS

If an exemption applies, no FBT is payable, and the amount does not have to be included on the employee's payment summary. The possible exemptions are:

- the minor benefits exemption (refer to 25.202), and
- the benefit relates to an exempt car benefit (refer to 25.354).

An employee's use of a taxi, panel van, utility or other commercial vehicle (one that is not designed principally to carry passengers) is exempt from FBT if private use of the vehicle is restricted to:

- travel between home and work
- travel that is incidental to travel when undertaking employment duties, and
- non-work related use that is minor, infrequent and irregular (eg. occasional use of the vehicle to remove rubbish from their home).

25.605   VALUATION OPTIONS AVAILABLE

The Tax Office offers practical options to determine the taxable value of fringe benefits provided as road tolls. Although these options can be used to value the road tolls applicable for each employee, the employer can use any approach that gives a reasonably based measure of the taxable value of the benefits.

- **Actual value**

  The taxable value of road toll benefits is the amount that the employer pays for each road toll. The private use percentage can be used to determine the taxable value of the road tolls.

- **Diary records**

  If a diary or similar record of road toll usage is kept over a representative four week period which establishes the business/private usage of road tolls over that period, the percentage of use calculated can be used for the entire FBT year.

- **Other records**

  If records such as car logbooks, odometer records and running sheets record car travel and establish the business/private use in an FBT year, then the private use established for an FBT year from these records can be applied to total road toll expenditure for the year. Logbooks which comply with the car fringe benefit operating cost method may only need to be completed every five years.

- **Employee's usual road toll expenditure**

  If the employer has difficulty working out the road toll expenditure for a pool car, then the employee's usual private road toll expenditure in a normal working week can be applied to the employee's working year. E-tag records, running sheets and employee attendance records can be used to support the calculation.

An employee has a salary sacrificed car and on work days travels from home to work on a toll road. The car is used as a pool car by a number of employees during the day when it is used by a number of employees. The car is available for private use at all other times (during which road tolls may be incurred).

An e-tag in the name of the employer is attached to the car and this records all road toll expenditure for that car. Each road toll recorded in relation to an employee is a residual benefit and the employer must determine the taxable value of residual fringe benefits provided to the employee who has entered into the salary sacrifice arrangement.

The employer must review the information available to confirm which road tolls are incurred while the car is used as a pool car (eg. using the e-tag statement). These can be subtracted from total road toll expenditure because they would generally be incurred for business purposes and are 'otherwise deductible'.

The employer can use factors such as the days and times the employee generally arrives at work and returns home, the days the employee is on holiday or which road tolls would generally be incurred on the private trip home to determine when the tolls are incurred for private purposes. The taxable value will be the total expenditure on road tolls for private travel.

25.650 HOUSING BENEFITS

A housing fringe benefit arises when an employer provides an employee, including family members, the right to occupy or use a 'unit of accommodation' as their usual place of residence. Residential premises are usually GST input taxed when supplied under a lease or licence, or they are hired, so the employer pays no GST. A payment for use of commercial residential premises or short-term accommodation may have some GST input tax credits (see GSTR 2000/20).

Although accommodation can be public (eg. hotel, motel, etc.) a housing fringe benefit does not arise for overnight or short term accommodation while the employee is travelling in the course of producing assessable income. If the accommodation is not the employee's usual place of residence, a residual benefit may arise.

25.651   'UNIT OF ACCOMMODATION'

A 'unit of accommodation' is broadly defined to include:

- a house, flat or home unit
- accommodation in a house, flat or home unit
- accommodation in a hotel, motel, guest house, hostel, caravan or mobile home, bunkhouse or other living quarters
- accommodation in a ship or other vessel or floating structure, and
- a caravan or mobile home.

25.652   VALUING ACCOMMODATION PROVIDED TO EMPLOYEES

Valuation rules generally rely on a market rental value of the right to occupy the accommodation, disregarding any special employment conditions or associated expenses relevant to the occupant, reduced by any contribution paid by the employee. The market value does not include gas/electricity/water etc paid for by the employer (if these are paid for by the employer as part of the right to occupancy, the market value should reflect that value), or any onerous conditions specific to the occupant's employment (for example, being on call for duty).

25.653   TAXABLE VALUE

The taxable value of housing fringe benefits are measured by reference to the market value of the right to occupy a unit accommodation reduced by any rent or other consideration paid by the employee.

The taxable value depends upon whether the housing benefit is provided within or outside Australia and whether it is located in a remote or non-remote area. Where the accommodation giving rise to a non-remote housing benefit is a hotel, motel, guesthouse etc and it is supplied by a person in the business of providing such accommodation, special rules apply to calculate the taxable value.

The following table summarises the taxable value of house fringe benefits.

Taxable value of housing fringe benefits	
Location	**Taxable value**
Within Australia	**Accommodation provided in hotel, motel, hostel, guesthouse, caravan or mobile home:** • Provider is the employer and identical or similar accommodation is offered to the public: *75% of the market value (see below) less recipient's rent* • Provider is the employer and the accommodation provided is not identical or similar to that offered to the public: *market value (see below) less recipient's rent* • Provider is not the employer: *market value (see below) less recipient's rent* **All other accommodation:** AB/C – D A = statutory annual value of housing right B = number of whole days in the tenancy period C = number of days in the FBT year D = recipient's rent
Within Australia, but remote location	Exempt housing benefit
Outside Australia	Market value less recipient's rent

MARKET VALUE

The valuation of housing fringe benefits generally rely on the market rental value of the right to occupy the accommodation (that is, what it would command for rent in an open market situation), disregarding any special employment conditions or associated expenses relevant to the occupant. Specifically, the market value does not include gas/electricity/water etc paid for by the employer (if these are paid for by the employer as part of the right to occupancy, the market value should reflect that value), or any onerous conditions specific to the occupant's employment (for example, being on call for duty).

Statutory annual value

Where the current year of tax is the base year of tax = AB/C

- A = market value
- B = number of days in the current year of tax
- C = number of whole days in the tenancy in the tenancy period

In any other case = AB

- A = the prior year statutory annual value
- B = the indexation factor in respect of the current year of tax in respect of the State or Territory in which the recipient's unit of accommodation is situated. The indexation factors for the 2013-14 and 2014-15 FBT years are as follows:

Non-remote area housing indexation factors		
State/Territory	2014-15 (TD 2014/3)	2015-16 (TD 2015/4)
New South Wales	1.037	1.032
Victoria	1.020	1.020
Queensland	1.022	1.022
South Australia	1.024	1.020
Western Australia	1.067	1.028
Tasmania	1.010	1.011
Northern Territory	1.076	1.043
Australian Capital Territory	1.017	0.989

NOTE: A new *base year* is to be determined where:

- the current year of tax is the tenth year after the last base year, or
- there has been a material alteration to the unit of accommodation resulting in either a 10% increase or decrease to its market value, or
- there has been a break of least twelve months where the unit of the accommodation has not been provided as a housing fringe benefit.

25.654   EXEMPT HOUSING BENEFITS

REMOTE AREA HOUSING BENEFITS

Section 58ZC of the FBT Act exempts remote area housing benefits for all employers.
A benefit is a remote area housing benefit if during the whole of the period of tenancy:

- the accommodation was not located in or adjacent to an 'eligible urban area', and
- for the whole of the tenancy period, the recipient of the benefit was a current employee (of the employer providing the benefit) and the usual place of employment of that employee is in the remote area.

For accommodation to be in a remote area, it must either be located:

- at least 40 kilometres from a town with a population of 14,000 to less than 130,000, or
- 100 kilometres or more from a town with a 1981 Census population of 130,000 or more.

EXAMPLE: Modified from the Explanatory Memorandum
Gulpilil Island is 80 kilometres, by the shortest practicable surface route, from the centrepoint of an inland eligible urban area with a population of 140,000. It is also situated 45 kilometres by the shortest practicable surface route, from the centre point of an eligible urban area with a population of 20,000.

The shortest practicable surface route to the island involves travel by road of 40 kilometres, and travel by sea of 40 kilometres. Gulpilil Island is now considered to be remote as it would be taken to be 120 kilometres from the eligible urban area by the shortest practicable surface route. This would be calculated: 40kms (by land) plus 2 x 40 kms (by water) = 120 kms.

If the benefit also includes the provision of 'residential fuel' (gas or electricity) only the housing benefit is exempt under s58ZC (see 25.657). However, if free water is provided to an employee under a residential tenancy agreement between the employer and employee, the water forms part of the housing benefit on which the remote area housing fringe benefit is based. In this instance the water is also exempt from FBT.

ADDITIONAL TESTS TO BE SATISFIED

- the employer must provide or arrange free or subsidised accommodation for employees because:
    - the employer's business is such that employees are liable to be frequently required to change their places of residence, or
    - in the area in which the employee is being employed, insufficient suitable residential accommodation is available at or near the place of employment,
- the benefit must not be granted under either:
    - a non-arms length arrangement, or
    - an arrangement entered into by any of the parties to the arrangement for the purpose of enabling the employer to obtain the benefit of the exemption (s58ZC(2)(C)). This exemption does not apply to either the reimbursement or payment of rent where an employee (or associate) incurs that expenditure.

The Commissioner has a discretion to apply the exemption to persons who live in an 'eligible urban area' if persons who live or work near that person are outside the area.

The inclusion of a housing benefit in a salary sacrifice arrangement does not automatically mean that the employer and employee have entered an arrangement for the purpose of enabling the employer to benefit from the application of the section.

A police officer salary sacrifices for provision of accommodation at the back of a rural police station. This does not prevent the remote area housing exemption applying, as that concession applies because of the nature of the employee's duties.

Taxpayer Alert TA 2002/9 focuses on arrangements where the employee owns a remote area property and leases it to their employer who allows the employee to live there rent free. Such arrangements seek to gain a tax deduction for the employee whilst receiving an FBT exempt benefit (see also TD 2004/26 and ATO ID 2001/761).

25.655   REMOTE AREA HOUSING RENTAL

A fringe benefit arising from either the reimbursement or payment of rent when a current employee (not associates) incurs that expenditure, is reduced by 50% when:

- the benefit provided was a housing fringe benefit, it would be a remote area fringe benefit
- the employee occupied or used the accommodation as the usual place of residence
- the benefit was not provided under a non-arm's length arrangement or an arrangement entered into to enable the employer to get the benefit.

For full details of the conditions refer to s60 and also see 25.807 regarding housing assistance.

25.656   HOUSING EXEMPTION FOR CERTAIN REGIONAL EMPLOYERS

Housing benefits are exempt from FBT when provided in an area at least 100 kilometres from a town with a census population of 130,000 or more, and the employer is:

- a public hospital which is not a government hospital

- a public hospital which is a public benevolent institution
- a hospital carried on by a non-profit society or non-profit association
- a charitable institution
- a government body if the employee performs duties exclusively in or in connection with a public hospital
- a police service, or
- public ambulance services where the employer provides public ambulance services (or services that support those services) and the employee is predominantly involved in connection with the provision of those services.

25.657   RESIDENTIAL FUEL EXPENSES

The market value of accommodation does not include expenses of occupancy such as gas, water or electricity which are incurred by the occupant but paid for by the employer. Such payments are valued as expense payment fringe benefits (see 25.550). If the right of occupancy of the accommodation provides gas and water etc without charge (ie. the value is effectively included in the rent) the market value of the rent should reflect that right.

IF IN A 'REMOTE AREA'

If the unit of accommodation is in a designated remote area, the provision of residential fuel (including electricity) qualifies for a 50% discount on taxable value.

25.700 BOARD AND MEALS

Board fringe benefits arise when an employer provides an employee with accommodation and meals. The taxable values are 'statutory values' and are unaffected by GST (TR 2001/2).

25.701   WHAT IS A BOARD FRINGE BENEFIT?

A board fringe benefit arises when an employer provides an employee with accommodation and:
- the employee is:
    - entitled under the provision of an industrial award to the provision of two meals per day, or
    - under an employment arrangement is ordinarily provided with at least two meals per day, and
- the meals are supplied by the employer (or related company)
- the meals are cooked or prepared on the premises of the employer (or related company) or on a worksite or place adjacent to it, or
- the meals are supplied on the employer's premises (or related company).

Except for employees at a restaurant, hotel or motel, the meals must not be provided in a dining facility open to the public. If employee's meals are 'contracted out' commercially, they are treated as having been provided by the employer.

25.702   TAXABLE VALUE

For meals given, the taxable value **per meal** is:
- each person 12 years or over before 1 April: $2 per meal
- each person 11 years or younger before 1 April: $1 per meal

 This does not apply to meals at a party, or a special function, or meals prepared in a facility used principally to prepare meals for a particular employee.

25.703   REDUCTIONS

If the employee would have been entitled to a tax deduction if he or she had paid for the meal, the taxable value is nil under the otherwise deductible rule.

For information about resolving whether benefits are provided to employees or family members, see 25.003.

25.704   EXEMPTIONS

A specific exemption exists for board meals provided to employees who are employed in a primary production business located in a remote area.

25.750 SUPERANNUATION AND FBT

From 1 July 2007 all eligible superannuation contributions, including in specie contributions, paid by an employer for an employee are exempt from FBT when paid to a complying superannuation fund.

Whether made in cash or in-specie, the employer entity making the contribution must have reasonable grounds for believing that the fund is a complying superannuation fund for the purpose of providing superannuation benefits for the employee. The entity making the payment must have a written statement from the trustee that the fund is a regulated superannuation fund.

A complying superannuation fund is one that complies with all of the requirements of the *Superannuation Industry (Supervision) Act 1993*. Complying fund status is restricted to resident regulated superannuation funds.

 Employer contributions to a non-complying superannuation fund are not tax deductible (s290-10(2)) unless the employer reasonably believed that the fund was a complying fund (s290-75(b)). Contributions to a non-complying fund are therefore both non-deductible and subject to FBT unless the employer reasonably believed the fund to be a complying fund, in which case no FBT is payable and a tax deduction is allowed for the contribution.

 Contributions made for the benefit of an associate of an employee (eg. spouse of the employee) are subject to FBT.

25.800 EMPLOYEES IN REMOTE AREAS

For details of remote area accommodation, see *Housing benefits* (at 25.650), including specific details on accommodation provided and employer-reimbursed housing fuel costs.

FBT law recognises the extra assistance employers must provide to employees in remote locations by giving special exemptions or concessions.

25.805   'FLY-IN-FLY-OUT' ARRANGEMENTS

If it is not feasible for employees to live near the work site, any costs involved in regular travel to the site is exempt.

OIL RIGS AND OFF-SHORE JOBS

Although employees must live for long periods on the rig, there is no FBT on the cost of similar travel to and from oil rigs and other off-shore installations.

Under the existing FBT legislation, the provision of transport by an employer between the usual place of residence of an employee and his or her usual place of employment in a remote area or on an oil rig or other installation at sea is an exempt benefit pursuant to s47(7) of the FBT Act. From 1 July 2009, the exemption under s47(7) is expanded to apply to domestic fly-in fly-out arrangements in respect of Australian residents working in remote areas overseas. This measure ensures that Australians working in similar circumstances either domestically or internationally are taxed consistently as well as removing the potential for double taxation on such benefits received by Australians working in remote locations overseas. This exemption applies where employees cannot live anywhere other than in employer-provided accommodation at or near the work site, and no reasonable alternative accommodation is available.

25.806   HOLIDAY TRAVEL FROM A REMOTE AREA

Remote area employees who take annual leave usually receive return fares or transport to the city or town from which they were originally engaged. The taxable value otherwise used for FBT purposes is discounted by 50% if the travel is provided for extended recreation leave (of more than three days) for employees and their families.

If a reimbursement of such travel costs is made by the employer, evidence of the expenditure must be provided.

If car expenses are reimbursed, the taxable value is:

* the amount of car expenses calculated on the relevant per-kilometre rate (see 25.556), but discounted for the remote area to 50%, plus
* the excess of the actual reimbursement over the per-kilometre amount.

25.807   ASSISTANCE TO BUY HOUSING

An employer may assist with housing by subsidising the purchase price, the interest due, or a combination of both. If the employer gives a low interest loan (or sells on low interest terms) for housing in a remote area, the taxable value is reduced by 50% provided:

* it is customary for employers in that industry to provide housing assistance, and
* the employer's assistance is necessary.

A 50% reduction in the taxable value of any eligible benefit is allowed if certain conditions are satisfied. The 50% reduction in the taxable value applies if the employer makes a reimbursement to the employee for costs incurred in:

* acquiring land on which a house exists (or on which one will be built), or
* constructing or extending an existing house.

To be eligible, construction must begin within six months and the house must be occupied by the employee within 12 months.

Remote area housing benefits that receive concessional treatment include:
* *payments or reimbursement of rent (ID 2003/159)*
* *payment or reimbursement of interest (ID 2003/157)*
* *payment or reimbursement of the costs of acquiring land and/or house, or*
* *extensions etc. (ID 2003/160).*
However, the Tax Office considers that remote area mortgage repayments do not qualify for the concession because the expenditure incurred by the employee is not wholly to enable the employee to acquire land on which there is a dwelling (ID 2003/158).

OPTION FEES

This reduction of 50% in the taxable value otherwise used operates if:

* a home-ownership scheme is operating in a remote area, and
* fees are reimbursed to an employee as part of an agreement made on or before the property was acquired by the employee.

Conditions apply when the fee is for an option to repurchase the property, and the employee agrees to retain the property for a minimum of five years.

REMOTE AREA HOME OWNERSHIP AND SPREADING OF FBT

Some remote area housing scheme fringe benefits can be spread over a number of years. The FBT liability can be spread only if the employee agrees to retain the property for at least five years and will sell only to the employer. The amortisation period is basically no less than five years, and no more than seven years. The maximum period of seven years is raised to fifteen years if certain conditions are made, and an amended assessment can be issued to diminish past FBT liabilities.

Amortising the liability: The periods are expressed in months, and the part subject to FBT in the current year is:

Overall taxable value x whole months in this year of the full amortisation period divided by months in amortisation period

On 3 July 2006, an employee acquired a house in a remote area.

Cost of house	$85,000
Employee paid only	($31,700)
Gross benefit	$53,300
Taxable value (discounted by 50%, being in a remote area)	$26,650

Contract obligation is to retain the housing for seven years, so the taxable benefit is spread over 84 months.

Applying the formula above involving whole or part months in each year, the taxable value in these FBT periods is:

2006-07 FBT year (9/84ths)	$2,855
2007-08 through to 2013-14 (each FBT year 12/84ths)	each $3,807
2014-15	$953

LOSS ON REPURCHASE BY THE EMPLOYER

If, under a 'buy back' agreement of a remote area home, the employer has an obligation to repurchase the employee's house and does so at below market value, 50% of that loss can be deducted from the employer's total taxable values in the FBT year in which the loss is incurred.

An employee entered into a remote area home ownership scheme and resigns two years later. At that time the market value of the house is $70,000 and the employer purchases the house for $66,000. The reduction amount is 50% of the loss amount of $4,000 or ($70,000 – $66,000) = $2,000.

There is no carry forward or carry back if the loss exceeds the taxable benefit.

PROFIT ON REPURCHASE BY EMPLOYER

If the employer later repurchases the house (under an obligation) and the consideration exceeds the market value at that time, the taxable value is reduced by 50%. Avoidance provisions apply if the consideration exceeds both the market value and the CPI indexed purchase price.

25.820 RESIDUAL FRINGE BENEFITS

A residual fringe benefit is any fringe benefit that is not covered under a specific category of the FBT Act (eg. the provision of free or discounted services, the use of property, provision of vehicles that are not cars for use on a regular basis for private purposes (eg. a truck) and general benefits which flow to employees (eg. trauma insurance which covers all employees). A residual fringe benefit includes any right, service or facility provided in respect of employment.

25.821　TYPES OF RESIDUAL BENEFITS

There are two types of residual benefits:
- **In-house residual benefits:** provided by the employer (or their associate) which consist of, or includes the provision of, identical or similar benefits to 'outsiders' (ie. the public), eg. an architectural firm provides free design services to employees.
- **External residual benefits:** any benefit which is not an in-house benefit (usually of a kind which would not be provided by the employer in the ordinary course of their business, eg. a building contractor arranges with a clothing company for employees to buy work clothing at a discount).

25.822   WHEN IS A BENEFIT RECEIVED?

The benefit is generally provided when received or over the period actually provided, for example:

- free car servicing provided to an employee by a car retailer: *benefit arises when the car is serviced*
- employee of a law firm receives legal advice at a discounted fee: *benefit arises when the employee is billed for the service*

25.823   GST TAXABLE VALUE

The taxable value of a residual benefit is the GST-inclusive value or GST-exclusive value depending on whether GST is payable (GSTR 2001/2). See 25.150.

Where an employee makes an employee contribution towards the residual fringe benefit, the value of that employee contribution will be the GST-inclusive value.

25.824   VALUATION RULES

The taxable value of an in-house residual fringe benefit is 75% of the lowest amount paid by the public, in an arm's length transaction, at or about the same time for an identical benefit, reduced by any amount paid by the employee. If identical benefits have not been provided to the public around the same time, the value is 75% of what a purchaser could have been expected to pay.

The taxable value of an external residual fringe benefit is either of:

- if the employee paid an arm's length price for the benefit: *that amount less any employee contribution*
- in any other case: *the amount the employee would have paid at about the same time had they paid for the service themselves, less any employee contribution*

 The above concession and the exemption for the first $1,000 of the taxable value of in-house (including in-house residual) benefits per employee is not available where the benefit is provided under a salary packaging arrangement on or after 22 October 2012 (see 25.862)).

25.825   TAXABLE VALUE OF MOTOR VEHICLES OTHER THAN 'CARS'

The private use of a vehicle other than a 'car' (as defined in the FBT Act) may give rise to a residual fringe benefit.

 Panel vans and utilities designed to carry a load of at least one tonne do not meet the definition of a 'car', therefore the 'car' rules do not apply to calculate FBT. Instead, the arm's length value of the benefit is a residual benefit if the private use (other than work-related travel) is more than minor, infrequent and irregular.

There are two methods for valuing these residual fringe benefits:

1. operating cost method – this is the same as the calculation for car fringe benefits (see 25.380), or
2. cents per kilometre basis – this method can only be used where there is extensive business use of the vehicle.

CENTS PER KILOMETRE METHOD – MOTOR VEHICLES OTHER THAN 'CARS'

Motor vehicle engine capacity	Rates per km: 2014-15 FBT year (TD 2014/6)	Rates per km: 2015-16 FBT year (TD 2015/6)
Up to 2,500cc	50 cents/km	51 cents/km
Over 2,500cc	60 cents/km	61 cents/km
Motorcycles	15 cents/km	15 cents/km

25.826   OTHERWISE DEDUCTIBLE RULE

The 'otherwise deductible rule' applies when the recipient of the benefit is an employee of the employer providing the benefit (but the rule cannot apply to an associate, see TD 93/90). The taxable value is reduced if the employee would be entitled to a once-only tax deduction had they paid for the benefit/service themselves. This rule prevents a deduction for depreciation that is over a period longer than one year.

An employee of an equipment hire company leases equipment from his employer for $600 at a 50% discount on the lowest price of $1,200 available to the public.

The equipment is used 40% for tax deductible purposes in a business conducted by the employee.

The benefit is calculated:

Taxable value $1,200 (public cost) x 75%	*$900*
Hypothetically tax deductible amount of 40%	*$360*
Actually deductible (40% of actual contribution of $600)	*$240*
Deductible amount	*$120*
***Taxable value** = $900 – $600 – $120*	***$180***

The 'otherwise deductible' rule can only be used if substantiation is obtained from the employee prior to lodgement of the FBT return.

OTHERWISE DEDUCTIBLE RULE AND EMPLOYEE CARS

The rule may be applied where the employer has met costs relating to a car which an employee either owns or leases. Such costs may be loan, expense payment, property or residual benefits (see 25.555, 25.826, and 25.860).

25.827   EXEMPTIONS

Road tolls and E-tag expenses (see 25.600 for the treatment of road tolls and E-tag expenses as either expense payment or residual fringe benefits).

25.828   DOCUMENTATION

For travel within Australia involving more than five nights, where the travel was not exclusively for the purpose of performing employment duties, or the travel was for more than five nights overseas, a travel diary must be obtained from the employee.

An employee declaration is always required unless:

- the benefit is used exclusively for performing employment duties (eg. tools)
- the benefit is one for which a recurring fringe benefit declaration exists (ie. a declaration in respect of identical benefits including the value and deductible percentages).

Both the *Residual benefit declaration* and the *Recurring fringe benefit declaration* are required in the Tax Office approved format.

25.840 LIVING-AWAY-FROM-HOME ALLOWANCE

A living-away-from-home allowance (LAFHA) arises when an employer pays an allowance to an employee as compensation for additional expenses (not being deductible expenses) and other additional disadvantages incurred by the employee because the employee is required to live away from his or her usual place of residence in order to perform the duties of their employment. These FBT rules do not apply to expenses where the employee would be entitled to a tax deduction (eg. an employee travelling in the course of performing employment duties). GST does not affect the taxable value of these allowances.

A LAFHA can only be provided by an employer. An allowance paid by an associate or by a third party to an employee (or an associate) who is required to live away from home will not give rise to a LAFHA fringe benefit.

LAFH ALLOWANCE RULES FROM 1 OCTOBER 2012

Amended LAFH allowance rules have applied since 1 October 2012 (with some transitional rules in place – see 25.845 below). These amendments reduce the concessional FBT treatment that may be available from the provision of such allowances compared with the former rules.

Under the new provisions, the concessional treatment for LAFH allowances and benefits is limited to employees (other than those working on a fly-in fly-out (FIFO) or drive-in drive-out basis (DIDO)) who:

- maintain a home in Australia (at which they usually reside) for their immediate use and enjoyment at all times while required to live away from that home for employment purposes
- it is reasonable to expect, will resume living at that home when they are no longer required to live away from home for employment purposes
- incur expenses for accommodation and food or drink for a maximum period of 12 months while living away from home at a particular work location, and
- have provided their employer with a declaration that they are living away from home.

25.841   WHO IS CONSIDERED TO BE LIVING AWAY FROM HOME?

The new law now states that such a LAFH allowance or benefit will arise where the person's employment duties requires them to live away from their 'normal residence'.

NORMAL RESIDENCE

'Normal residence' is defined as:

- the employee's 'usual place of residence' if that is in Australia, or
- if the employee's usual place of residence is not in Australia, either:
  - the employee's usual place of residence, or
  - the place in Australia where the employee usually resides while in Australia.

The change from 'usual place of residence' to 'normal residence' means that a LAFH allowance fringe benefit can now arise regardless of the location of the employee's usual place of residence, whether that is a home in Australia or overseas.

USUAL PLACE OF RESIDENCE

An employee's usual place of residence will generally be regarded as their former residence, being the residence from which they have temporarily vacated in order to perform their employment related duties. It is not a requirement that the employee own their residence in the former location for it to be considered their usual place of residence.

INDICIA OF AN EMPLOYEE LIVING AWAY FROM HOME

Whether an employee is living away from home is a question of fact. Some of the factors to be considered include (but are not limited to):

- the intention of the employee in returning to his/her former place of residence (place of residence is defined in s136 to mean a place at which the person resides or a place at which the person has sleeping accommodation, whether on a permanent or temporary basis and whether or not on a shared basis)
- the contractual agreement between the employee and employer, for example, whether the position is for an agreed period of time or indefinite, including extensions thereto
- the nature of the work undertaken, for example, itinerant or cyclical workers
- the type of profession and industry
- whether the employee has relocated family members and personal belongings
- the temporary or permanent nature of the residence to which the employee has relocated
- the status of the employee's usual residence ie. is it being looked after by relatives or friends, is it being rented out to a third party or has it been sold

- the type and length of visa held, for international assignees
- practical matters such as the cancellation or suspension of memberships, whether a new driver's licence has been issued and whether or not electoral roll details have been updated
- lifestyle of the employee, and
- any other factors relevant in determining the living away from home status of the employee.

Miscellaneous Tax Ruling MT 2030 indicates that a period away from home in excess of 21 days may satisfy the requirements to be considered 'living away from home'. It should be emphasised that this is merely a 'rule of thumb'.

As a general rule, the Tax Office considers that the maximum length of time domestic and international employees are considered to be living away from home is two and four years respectively. However, as this is not legislated, it is only a guide and should be considered along with all other relevant factors. It should be noted that although the Tax office has this rule of thumb, under the new LAFHA rules, the FBT concession only applies for the first 12 months of the period of living away from home.

NOTE: The Federal Court has confirmed allowances paid to employees working on oil and gas rigs are subject to FBT (see *Maretech CMDL Pty Ltd v C of T* 97 1110 FCA 1).

LAFHA VERSUS RELOCATION

For an employee to be living away from home there is an intention or expectation that they will return to their former location, being their usual place of residence as the arrangement is temporary. Conversely, an employee will have 'relocated' when they are required to change their usual place of residence and permanently relocate to another location in order to perform their employment duties. The arrangement is more permanent in nature, often having an open ended employment contract and no intention to return to the former location.

LAFHA VERSUS TRAVEL ALLOWANCES

Where a LAFHA constitutes a taxable fringe benefit, it is subject to FBT pursuant to the FBT Act. In contrast, a travelling allowance is not a fringe benefit but rather it forms part of the employee's assessable income and accordingly, this distinction is important.

LAFHA differs from a travelling allowance which is paid to an employee to compensate for costs incurred during travel in the course of performing his or her employment duties. The Tax Office considers that the following criteria should be used in determining whether an employee is travelling in the course of performing their job:

- the nature of the duties performed
- whether the employee is accompanied by dependents, and
- the length of time spent away from home (on the basis that travel allowances are generally paid for relatively short periods).

The Tax Office has also indicated that where the period away from home does not exceed 21 days, then it is likely that the employee would be considered to be travelling (refer MT 2030 and TD 96/7). It should be noted, however, that the 21 day period referred to is only a general guide.

An allowance which is not a LAFHA is taxable in the hands of the employee and not subject to FBT. These allowances are not LAFHA:

- travelling allowances paid to employees who are away from home for up to 21 days for business related purposes. These allowances are assessed to the employee as salary or wages, with deductions allowed for expenses incurred (MT 2030)
- allowances paid to certain occupations where it is necessary to accept regular transfers from one place to another (eg. police, defence forces, teachers) (MT 2030)
- location allowance paid to all employees at a location to attract employees to live in, or remain in a particular location. It is assessable to the employee as income according to ordinary concepts (TD 94/14)
- allowances described as either LAFHA, subsistence, location or living allowances which are paid to a foreign national working in Australia on a working holiday maker visa have

previously been considered by the Tax Office to not be a LAFHA and therefore treated as income. The official view is as set out in MT 2030

- a 'hardlying' allowance paid to offshore oil and gas workers (ID 2004/706 and AAT case *Crane v F C of T* (supra)), and
- a LAFHA paid to oil rig workers to compensate them for their living conditions was held by the AAT to be subject to FBT (AAT 2007 AATA 1185).

Amounts which are described as 'hardlying allowance' are generally assessable income to the employee and not considered to be a LAFHA fringe benefit (*Crane v FC of T* [2005] AATA 872) and ATO ID 2005/314.

Amounts received by an electrician from his employer under a fly-in, fly-out arrangement were properly characterised as a living-away-from-home allowance and not a travel allowance (*Hancox v Commissioner of Taxation* [2013] FCA 735). The taxpayer was not entitled to claim tax deductions with respect to work-related travel costs. The costs of accommodation and travel was incurred because the taxpayer chose to reside away from his place of employment.

NON-CASH BENEFITS

The LAFH allowance amendments do not solely apply to cash allowances paid to the employee. Like the former rules, the provision of non-cash LAFH benefits may be exempt for the following benefits provided to employees:

- accommodation expense payment fringe benefits (s21) – for example, the reimbursement of an employee's accommodation expenditure
- provision of food fringe benefits (s63 FBT Act), and
- residual fringe benefits consisting of the provision of accommodation to the employee.

The provision of such benefits will be exempt to the extent that the employee either:

- satisfies the requirements about maintaining a home in Australia during the first 12 month period, or
- is working on a FIFO or DIDO basis.

It would be necessary in either case to determine whether the employee is living away from their 'usual' or 'normal' place of residence (see below for discussion). A declaration is required to be provided by the employee in either case by the requisite date.

25.843   TAXABLE VALUE OF LAFHA BENEFITS

FORMER RULES: PRE-1 OCTOBER 2012

Under the former rules, the taxable value of a LAFHA is the amount of the allowance paid less:

- any exempt accommodation component, and/or
- any exempt food component.

See below for meaning of 'exempt accommodation component' and 'exempt food component'.

 In order for an employer to reduce the taxable value of a LAFHA by the exempt accommodation and/or food components, the employer is required to obtain from the employee, prior to the lodgment of the FBT return, a declaration in the approved form.

CURRENT RULES – POST-1 OCTOBER 2012

Under the current rules, the calculation of the taxable value of the LAFH benefit depends on the circumstances of the employee receiving the benefit. There are three scenarios in which a different taxable value arises:

- **Scenario 1:** the employee maintains a home in Australia at which they usually reside and the fringe benefit relates to the first 12-month period
- **Scenario 2:** the employee is working on a Fly-In, Fly-Out (FIFO) or Drive-In, Drive-Out (DIDO) basis, and
- **Scenario 3:** all other cases.

Scenarios 1 and 2 represent concessional methods for calculating the taxable value.

SCENARIO 1: EMPLOYEE MAINTAINS HOME IN AUSTRALIA

The concessional FBT treatment is limited to a 12 month period at the one location where the employee 'maintains a home in Australia'. An employer can calculate the taxable value of a LAFH allowance fringe benefit by taking the dollar amount of the fringe benefit and subtracting:

- any exempt accommodation component, and/or
- any exempt food component.

In order for the employee to calculate the taxable value under this scenario the following conditions must be satisfied:

Condition (i): Home maintained in Australia for immediate use at all times

The employee maintains a home in Australia (at which they usually reside) for their immediate use and enjoyment at all times whilst they are away from it (and it must be reasonable to expect that the employee will subsequently resume living at that home).

Key terms under this requirement are explained as follows:

- **Home in Australia:** This includes a 'unit of accommodation' such as a house, flat, home unit, caravan or accommodation in living quarters.
- **Maintaining a home in Australia:** The employee, or their spouse, is required to have an 'ownership interest' in their home in Australia. It must also be reasonable to expect that the employee will resume living in that home once they have completed the work that required them to be away.
- **Ownership interest:** A person would typically have an 'ownership interest' in their home if they either own or rent the property. Adult children who reside in the family home would generally not be considered to have an 'ownership interest' in the home and therefore are not considered to be 'maintaining a home'.
  An employee who lives with their parents or a sibling may fall into this category.
- **Home available for employee's immediate use and enjoyment at all times:** This means that the home cannot be rented out or sublet while the employee is living away from it unless the terms of the arrangement enable the employee to eject the tenant and immediately resume occupancy when desired.
  It is possible for an employee to sublet or rent a part of their home whilst they are living away from it. A typical example is where a bedroom is rented to a person with access to general living areas. Employees who choose to sublet or rent their home in this manner must be able to access their home for their immediate use and enjoyment at all times.

Condition (ii): Benefit relates to first 12 months

The fringe benefit relates to the first 12 months of the employee living away from that home in Australia for employment purposes. Key features of this requirement include:

- The benefit must relate to all or part of the first 12 months that an employee is living away from home in Australia for employment purposes.
- It may be possible for the employee to choose to pause the 12 month period. This may include times when they take annual leave, long service leave or sick leave. The exempt accommodation and food components will not reduce the taxable value of the fringe benefit during the pause period. That is, the employer would be subject to FBT on the full taxable value of allowances paid during this period.
- A new 12-month period applies if the employee moves to another location to perform their employment duties. It must also be unreasonable to expect the employee to commute to the new location from the earlier location in providing a LAFH allowance benefit.
- A change in nature of the employee's employment arrangement does not affect the 12 month period (eg. a promotion or change in job title). This includes situations where the employee takes up employment with an associate of the employer (eg. following a corporate restructure).

Condition (iii): Employee provides approved declaration

An approved declaration is required to be provided by an employee in receipt of a LAFH allowance benefit. Employers must obtain all employee declarations no later than the day on which the FBT return is due to be lodged or, if a return is not required to be lodged, by 21 May. The Tax Office has released pro-forma declarations on its website.

SCENARIO 2: EMPLOYEE MAINTAINS HOME IN AUSTRALIA

The taxable value of a LAFH fringe benefit for FIFO or DIDO (or equivalent) employees is calculated in a similar manner to Scenario 1 above. An employee is eligible to access the concessions under scenario 2 if all the following are satisfied:

The employee:

- has residential accommodation at or near the usual place of employment
- is considered to be working on a FIFO or DIDO basis (see below), and
- provides the employer with a declaration about living away from home (see above).

It is not necessary for the employee to 'maintain a home in Australia' which they live away from under this scenario as would be the case under Scenario 1. The 12-month period does not apply to restrict the concession as long as the employee is working on a FIFO or DIDO basis.

When is an employee working on a FIFO or DIDO basis?

An employee is considered to be working on a FIFO or DIDO basis if the following are satisfied:

- The employee works for a number of days and has a number of days off which are not the same days in consecutive weeks on a regular and rotational basis. A standard five day working week and weekend does not satisfy this requirement. The employee returns to their normal residence during the days off. For the purposes of this condition, an employee is considered not to be working on a regular and rotational basis where (during the period of their employment tenure) they work for five and half days and remain on call on the seventh day (ATO ID 2013/43).
- It is customary in the industry in which the employee works for employees performing similar duties to work on a rotational basis and return home during days off (eg. employees in the mining industry working on a rotational basis).
- It is unreasonable to expect the employee to travel between work and their normal residence on a daily basis given the locations of the employment and their home, and
- It is reasonable to expect that the employee will resume living at the normal residence.

SCENARIO 3: TAXABLE VALUE ANY OTHER CASE

The taxable value of the fringe benefit is the full amount of the allowance where an employer provides a LAFH fringe benefit to an employee who is neither:

- maintaining a home in Australia (Scenario 1), nor
- working on a FIFO or DIDO (or equivalent) basis (Scenario 2).

Exempt accommodation component

The exempt accommodation component of a LAFH allowance represents the amount of compensation for expenses incurred in respect of accommodation for the employee and 'eligible family members' whilst the employee is required to live away from home. **Eligible family members** includes the employee's spouse and children living with the employee.

The exempt amount is equal to the actual expense incurred by the employee and must be substantiated (see *Substantiation requirements for employees* below).

Under the former rules, it was only necessary to work out a reasonable amount for accommodation costs. There was no statutory amounts or guidance given to determine the amount. Rather, this was done on a case by case basis taking into account circumstances, such as:

- the employee's current living standards
- the position held and seniority of the employee within the organisation
- the location of the employee's accommodation and place of employment

- family size and whether family members will accompany the employee
- duration of the temporary employment, and
- whether the accommodation is furnished.

Exempt food component

The exempt food component represents the amount of compensation for expenses actually incurred by the employee (in respect of the employee and eligible family members) for food or drink whilst the employee is required to live away from home, less the applicable statutory food total for that period. See meaning of 'eligible family member' above.

The statutory food total is:

- $42 per week for adults, and
- $21 for children under 12 years of age.

An 'adult' for the purposes of these rules is a person who had attained the age of 12 years before the beginning of the FBT year. The statutory food total represents an assumed amount for the value of food and drink costs that would be consumed by the employee (and any accompanying family members) if they were living at home.

For example, the statutory food total for an employee who relocates from home with their spouse and two children under 12 years of age would be $126 (ie. [$42 x 2] + [$21 x 2]).

There are substantiation requirements for the exempt food component where the expenditure exceeds the amount that the Commissioner considers reasonable (see TD 2013/4 and Substantiation requirements below). These rules are similar to that under the former rules where the employee is required to substantiate their expenses in respect of the exempt food component.

25.844   SUBSTANTIATION REQUIREMENTS FOR EMPLOYEES

Under the new rules, the employee must substantiate both the exempt accommodation and food components. This also includes those working on a FIFO or DIDO basis. This means that:

- **accommodation expenses:** incurred by the employee must be substantiated in full, and
- **food and drink expenses:** will require substantiation only where the expenses incurred while living away from home exceed reasonable amounts as determined by the Commissioner of Taxation.

REASONABLE AMOUNTS

The reasonable amounts for the 2015-16 FBT year are set out in TD 2015/7 (TD 2014/9 for the 2014-15 FBT year). These tax determinations show the reasonable amounts for locations within Australia and overseas.

The table below sets out the weekly amounts the Commissioner considers to be reasonable food and drink amounts for a LAFHA paid to employees living away from home within Australia for the FBT year commencing on 1 April 2014 and 2015 respectively. These amounts are for the total of food or drink expenses and include any amounts that may have been allowed for home consumption.

FROM TD 2015/7: Exempt food component – within Australia

Jasper, his wife and their two children (both under 12 years of age) temporarily move to Brisbane from Sydney for a period of five months (from 1 May 2015 to 30 September 2015; 21 weeks and 6 days) for Jasper to work on a project for his employer. Jasper receives a LAFHA from his employer.

Jasper does not need to substantiate his family's food and drink expenses during the five month period if his total expenses do not exceed $10,579 ($484 per week multiplied by 21 6/7 weeks).

If Jasper's family's total food and drink expenses for the period exceed $10,579, Jasper will have to substantiate all of the expenses incurred, or his employer will be liable to FBT on the amount of LAFHA paid to Jasper that is in excess of $10,579.

Reasonable food components ($ per week)	2014-15 FBT year (TD 2014/9)	2015-16 FBT year (TD 2015/7)
One adult	$236	$241
Two adults	$354	$362
Three adults	$472	$483
One adult and one child	$295	$302
Two adults and one child	$413	$423
Two adults and two children	$472	$484
Two adults and three children	$531	$545
Three adults and one child	$531	$544
Three adults and two children	$590	$605
Four adults	$590	$604
Each additional adult	$118	$121
Each additional child	$59	$61

ITEMS TO BE PROVIDED

In substantiating these expenses, the employee must provide their employer with either:

- documentary evidence (such as receipts or credit card statements detailing the expense), or
- a declaration setting out information about the expense.

It is necessary that the employee retain the relevant documents for a period of five years if a declaration is made. The five year period is triggered when the declaration is made. This requirement is not necessary however if actual documentation has already been provided to the employer.

Jim is employed by Pear Ltd (Pear) as a computer programmer in Sydney. He has been asked to temporarily go to Melbourne with his family to co-ordinate the development of a new Mapping app for Pear's smartphone. Jim owns a home with his wife in Sydney. They have a new born baby and three year old child. The length of the assignment is for 12 months commencing from 1 April 2015. Jim is expected to return to his home in Sydney upon completion. Jim's family go with him to Melbourne for the period of his assignment and they leave their Sydney home vacant whilst in Melbourne.

Jim is paid a LAFH allowance to compensate for his accommodation costs and total food and drink expenditure.

He is paid a weekly allowance of $850 which is to compensate for the following:

- *accommodation expenses (per lease agreement): $400, and*
- *compensation for total food and drink (including home food costs): $450*

Calculation of taxable value for FBT purposes

The benefit provided to Jim is a LAFH allowance fringe benefit. The taxable value of the benefit is calculated under s31 (see Scenario 1 above) as Jim is maintaining a home in Australia which continues to be available for his use while living away from home and the benefit relates to the first 12-months of him and his family being away from that home. The taxable value is:

Total allowance	*$850*
Less exempt accommodation component	*($400)*
Less exempt food component	*($324)**
Taxable value	*$126*

*The exempt food component in this case is the food component less the statutory food amount for Jim and his family (ie. $484 – [($42 x 2) + ($21 x 2)].) The taxable value in this case is made up of the statutory food amount of $126.

This outcome may be avoided if Pear had agreed only to compensate Jim for food costs which are additional to the statutory food amount. This would need to be carefully documented.

NOTE: The concessional treatment of the LAFH allowance would not be available for any part of the assignment which extended beyond 12 months.

Declaration and substantiation requirements

It would be necessary for Jim to provide a declaration in an approved form to Pear before the due date of the company's FBT return for the 2015-16 FBT year. Jim would be required, in substantiating the accommodation and food and drink expenses, to:

- *Accommodation expenses: Provide a receipt or bank statements showing that he has paid the accommodation expenses in accordance with the lease agreement.*
- *Food and drink expenses: Jim is not required to substantiate his food and drink expenditure. The amount that Pear pays Jim for food and drink costs as part of his LAFH allowance does not exceed the reasonable food amount outlined TD 2015/7. In this case, the amount for two adults and two children is $484 whilst the allowance paid was $450.*

25.845   TRANSITIONAL RULES

Transitional rules applied to limit the impact of the new rules on existing employment arrangements with a LAFH component that were in place before 7.30pm AEST on 8 May 2012 (ie. Budget time). The rules differed depending on whether the employee is a permanent resident or temporary or foreign resident. The transitional rules ceased to apply with effect from 1 July 2014, meaning that all LAFHAs provided in the 2015-16 FBT year are governed by the new rules.

(i) If the employee is a permanent resident

The requirements that the employee must maintain a home in Australia and that the fringe benefits must relate to the first 12 months the employee is living away from home do not apply until 1 July 2014. This deferral will apply as long as:

- there was an existing employment arrangement before Budget time, and
- the employment arrangement was not materially varied (see below) or renewed between Budget time and 1 October 2012.

The new rules will also apply if there is a 'material variation' or renewal of the employment arrangement between 1 October 2012 and 1 July 2014. The new rules start from the time that such a variation or renewal occurs.

What constitutes a 'material variation'?

Transitional rules will not apply if there has been a material variation or renewal of an existing employment arrangement.

- An annual salary review is not a material variation to an employment arrangement.
- Changes to an employment arrangement to reflect other annual adjustments, such as the food component of a LAFH allowance, do not constitute a material variation.

In the case of promotions it will depend on the circumstances in each case. For example, if an employee is promoted and the underlying terms of their employment arrangement do not change, it is unlikely that there would be a material variation in the employment arrangement. The employment arrangement has been the subject of a material variation however if there are fundamental differences to the employment arrangement arising from the promotion.

Application of 12 month period

The 12 month period is taken to notionally apply from 1 October 2012. This means that if there is no material variation, the transitional rules apply to 30 June 2014. If there is a material variation however the concessional period will stop if such treatment has already applied for at least 12 months from 1 October 2012. For example, if there is a material variation of an existing employment arrangement on 1 November 2013, then the concessional period will apply from 1 October 2012 until that time.

If concessional treatment has not applied for at least 12 months, then it will only continue to apply for the balance of the 12 month period. For example, if there was material variation of an existing employment arrangement on 1 January 2013, then concessional treatment will apply until 30 September 2013 provided that the employee is maintaining a home in Australia that they are living away from.

(ii) If the employee is a temporary resident or foreign resident

The transitional rules for a temporary or foreign resident are less accommodating than those for an employee who is a permanent resident.

The requirement that the fringe benefits must relate to the first 12 months the employee is living away from home does not apply until 1 July 2014. The deferral will apply as long as:

- the employment arrangement was not materially varied or renewed between Budget time and 1 October 2012, and
- the employee is maintaining a home in Australia for their immediate use and enjoyment at all times whilst they are away from it performing their employment duties.

The new rules will apply if there is a 'material variation' or renewal of the employment arrangement between 1 October and 1 July 2014.

NOTE: The terms 'temporary resident' and 'foreign resident' have the same meaning as that in the ITAA97. A temporary resident, amongst other things, would typically satisfy this meaning where such a person holds a temporary visa (eg. a 457 visa). A foreign resident is defined under s6(1) ITAA36 and rely on common law principles.

25.860 PROPERTY BENEFITS

A property fringe benefit arises where an employer (or associate or a third party arranger), provides property to an employee or associate of an employee free or at a discount (s40 FBT Act).

KEY CONCEPTS

The FBT Act defines property as follows:

- **tangible property** includes tangible goods (including animals, fish and electricity and gas (unless supplied through a reticulation system)).
- **intangible property** includes real property (land and buildings), a chose in action and any other kind of property other than tangible property, however, it does not include a right arising under a contract of insurance or a lease or licence in respect of real property or tangible property.
- **money** has also been held to constitute property for the purposes of the FBT law (see *Caelli Constructions (Vic) Pty Ltd v FCT* (2005) 60 ATR 542; ATO ID 2007/204). Although money is property for the purposes of the FBT Act, it does not meet the definition of 'tangible property' under FBT law. Money will however satisfy the definition of 'intangible property' under FBT law (see ATO ID 2010/151).

All other in-house benefits are treated as property, residual or expense payment benefits.

PROVIDE

The term 'provide' contemplates the provider of the benefit disposing of their interest in the property requiring something more than the provider merely giving up possession of the property.

 Where an employer has made a contribution to its employee's social club, the contribution will not be a property fringe benefit. This is because at the time of the contribution no particular employee has been identified as the beneficiary of that contribution.

When property is provided as a fringe benefit, the value is the GST-inclusive value or the GST-exclusive value depending on whether GST is payable (GSTR 2001/2).

25.862   TAXABLE VALUE

The taxable value of a property fringe benefit will be dependent upon whether the benefit is an external or in-house property fringe benefit and whether provided by the employer or by a third party. Each valuation rule however allows for the taxable value to be reduced by the amount of any employee contribution and/or the otherwise deductible rule (see 25.868).

EXTERNAL FRINGE BENEFITS

An external property fringe benefit is any property fringe benefit that is not an in-house property fringe benefit. An external property fringe benefit will arise, for example, where the property provided does not constitute goods or services that are similar or identical to those sold by the employer in the ordinary course of their business.

The taxable value of external property fringe benefits provided under the following circumstances is calculated as follows:

- Where the employer or associate provides the property and it was purchased under an arm's length transaction at or about the provision time:
  Taxable value = cost price – recipient's contribution
- Where a third party provides the property on an arm's length basis:
  Taxable value = arm's length amount paid – recipient's contribution
- In any other case:
  Taxable value = the notional value[1] – recipient's contribution

  1: The 'notional value' is the amount that the recipient could reasonably be expected to have paid to acquire the property under an arm's length transaction. Refer TD 93/231.

 Where an early payment discount is received, for example, a 5% discount is given where payment is made within a certain time frame, the discounted price is used for determining the taxable value.

IN-HOUSE FRINGE BENEFITS

Broadly, an in-house benefit arises where tangible property is provided by an employer (or associate or a third party under an arrangement) to an employee (or associate) in one of the following situations:

- the benefit is provided by an employer who carries on a business which includes the provision of identical or similar property to outside parties in the ordinary course of business
- the benefit is provided by a third party under an arrangement whereby:
  - the provider purchases the property from the employer (or associate), and
  - the provider and the seller carry on a business which includes the provision of identical or similar property to outside parties.

NOTE: Identical benefits are the same in all respects except for any differences that are minimal or insignificant, or that relate to the value of the benefits.

In-house benefits are generally valued on a concessional basis. In addition, there is a $1,000 per annum exemption applied to the total of all in-house benefits provided to each employee each year.

The taxable value of in-house property fringe benefits provided under the following circumstances is calculated as:

- where the employer (or associate) manufactured, produced, processed or treated the property
- where identical property is sold in the ordinary course of business to manufacturers, wholesalers or retailers (that is, not direct to the public):
  Taxable value = the lowest arm's length selling price of the goods – recipient's contribution

   A manufacturer of white goods provides a fridge to an employee. The fridge is identical to goods sold to wholesalers. The manufacturer sells the item for $1,200 (including GST) to wholesalers. The invoice provided allows for a discount of 5% for early payment, if the invoice is paid within seven days.

  Therefore, if the wholesaler pays within seven days, they will pay $1,080 for the fridge. However, if the wholesaler doesn't pay within seven days, they will pay $1,200 for the fridge.

  The lowest arm's length selling price in this example is $1,080.

- where identical property is sold to members of the public:

Taxable value = 75% of the lowest arm's length selling price – recipient's contribution
- where the property manufactured is similar but not identical to property sold as part of the employer's ordinary business, eg. seconds or damaged stock:
Taxable value = 75% of the notional value of the property – recipient's contribution

NOTE: The 'notional value' means the amount that the employee could reasonably be expected to have been required to pay to obtain the property from the provider under an arm's length transaction (on the basis of age, type and condition). The Tax Office accepts the following ways of obtaining the notional value:

- the price of comparable goods advertised in local newspapers and/or relevant magazines or similar publications
- the price paid for comparable goods at a public auction
- the price paid for comparable goods at a secondhand store, or
- the market value of the goods determined by a qualified valuer (TD 93/231).

- where the property was purchased for resale and sold as part of the ordinary course of business by the employer (or associate): Taxable value of the property will be the lesser of:
    - the arm's length price of the property paid by the employer (or associate), or
    - the notional value of the property, or
    - less recipient's contribution.

- in any other case:
Taxable value = 75% of the notional value of the property – recipient's contribution

A lounge suite normally sold to the public for $4,900 is sold for $2,000 to an employee. It is the employee's only purchase for the FBT year from the employer.

75% of normal $4,900 retail price	*$3,675*
less amount paid by employee	*($2,000)*
less general exemption for in-house benefits of $1,000	*($1,000)*
Taxable value of fringe benefit	**$675**

IN-HOUSE FRINGE BENEFIT PROVIDED UNDER A SALARY SACRIFICE ARRANGEMENT (ON OR AFTER 22 OCTOBER 2012)

The above noted concessional valuation treatment, including the $1,000 exemption, is not available for in-house benefits provided under salary packaging arrangements made **on or after 22 October 2012,** and from 1 April 2014 for in-house benefits provided under any salary packaging arrangements.

MEANING OF 'SALARY PACKAGING ARRANGEMENT'

The term 'salary packaging arrangement' is defined as an arrangement where the employee receives a benefit:

- in return for a reduction in salary or wages that would not have happened apart from the arrangement, or
- as part of the employee's remuneration package, and the benefit is provided in circumstances where it is reasonable to conclude that the employee's salary or wages would be greater if the benefit were not provided.

This commonly covers two types of situations:

- **A negotiated salary packaging arrangement:** where the employee enters into an agreement with their employer to have their salary and wages reduced (or 'sacrificed') in order to receive a benefit (such as in-house goods).
- **An 'implicit' salary packaging arrangement:** where a reduction in salary may not have been negotiated but the employee is given a benefit as part of their employment contract and, it is reasonable to assume that the salary and wages they would have received would have been greater without that benefit being provided. For example, an employer gives an employee in-house goods however that person's salary is reduced by the notional value of the goods.

CHANGES TO IN-HOUSE FRINGE BENEFITS PROVIDED UNDER SALARY PACKAGING ARRANGEMENTS

The changes to the concessional FBT treatment of in-house benefits provided under such arrangements on or after 22 October 2012 is summarised as follows:

(i) 75% lowest price valuation not available

Concessions that apply to the valuation rules in respect to in-house expense payment benefits, in-house property benefits and in-house residual benefits do not apply to benefits where the employee accesses the benefit under a salary packaging arrangement. Instead, the taxable value of the benefit is based on the 'notional value' of the benefit (ie. its market or arm's length value) and not 75% of the lowest price paid.

EXAMPLE from explanatory memorandum

Kane works at the Geelong Meat Works abattoir and as part of his annual remuneration negotiations agrees to a reduction in his salary in exchange for a meat pack for Christmas which includes hams, steaks and other choice cuts. This meat pack is an in-house property fringe benefit.

The taxable value of the benefit would have previously been 75% of the lowest price paid for the meat, which would have been the wholesale price. However, under this measure the taxable value of the benefit provided to Kane would be the notional value of the meat, which is its market value. As Kane is not a wholesaler the taxable value would therefore be the retail price of the meat.

(ii) Specific exemption for public transport travel removed

The specific exemption that applies to residual benefits in respect to private home to work travel through public transport (where the employer and associate are in the business of providing transport to the public) does not apply where the benefit is provided in-house and where the employee accesses the benefit under a salary packaging arrangement.

(iii) $1,000 reduction to taxable value of certain fringe benefits removed

The annual reduction of aggregate taxable value of $1,000 does not apply to in-house benefits where the employee accesses the benefit under a salary packaging arrangement. The in-house benefit FBT concessions still have application provided that the benefits are not accessed by way of salary packaging arrangements.

EXAMPLE from explanatory memorandum

Ronita works for an electricity and gas provider and receives two types of in-house benefits. The first is an in-house residual expense payment benefit in respect to her quarterly electricity bill. The taxable value of the benefit is $500 a year and it is provided under a salary packaging arrangement. The second benefit is the provision of bottled gas and is an in-house property benefit. The taxable value of the benefit is $500 and it is not provided under a salary packaging arrangement.

Under this measure, Ronita's employer would not reduce the aggregate taxable value of the electricity bill benefit because it is provided under a salary packaging arrangement and therefore would only reduce the aggregate taxable value of the gas bottle benefit to zero (as the sum of the taxable value of the non-salary packaged in-house benefits is less than $1,000).

25.868   OTHERWISE DEDUCTIBLE RULE

The taxable value of a property fringe benefit can be reduced under the 'otherwise deductible rule' by the amount of any once-off income tax deduction to which the employee (but not an associate of the employee) would have been entitled.

The otherwise deductible rule can only be applied where the recipient of the benefit is the employee (the rule cannot apply to an associate, see TD 93/90).

To obtain the benefit of the otherwise deductible rule, the employee must provide a declaration to the employer showing the otherwise deductible percentage. However, there is relief from the requirement for the employee to provide a declaration in respect of certain benefits, see 25.869 below).

OTHERWISE DEDUCTIBLE RULE IN RELATION TO CARS

Special rules apply in relation to a car owned or leased by an employee where the employer has met some or all of the operating costs and the 'otherwise deductible' rule applies.

There are three different methods of calculating the amount of the expense that hypothetically would have been tax deductible to the employee. The differences arise due to the extent to which the car is used for business purposes, and/or the type of evidence available to substantiate the use.

The three methods of calculating the hypothetical expense deductible to the employee are:

1. An estimated percentage of business use substantiated by records (12 week log book, odometer etc.) and an employee declaration. The employer calculates the relevant percentage.

2. An estimated percentage of business use substantiated only by an employee declaration. Estimated business use cannot exceed 33^1/3%.

3. A deemed percentage of business use of 33^1/3% provided the car travelled at least 5,000 business kilometres during the year. An employee declaration is required to substantiate the business kilometres travelled.

In each case, the deemed deductible amount is reduced by the actual deductible amount, with the net amount then reducing the taxable value of the fringe benefit.

Estimated business use percentage established by an employee declaration (maximum estimated percentage allowed is 33^1/3%).

A deemed 33^1/3% business use, provided the car travelled on average a minimum 96 kms per week (or 5,000 kms per year).

An employee declaration is required to substantiate the kms.

REDUCTION IN TAXABLE VALUE

IN-HOUSE PROPERTY BENEFITS

The first $1,000 of the taxable value of in-house property fringe benefits provided to an employee are excluded from FBT if the benefits are goods or services of a kind sold or provided in the course of the employer's business. The maximum reduction is $1,000 which is applied on an individual employee basis once per FBT year.

IMPORTANT: The annual reduction of aggregate taxable value of $1,000 does not apply to in-house benefits where the employee accesses the benefit under a salary packaging arrangement. This applies to benefits provided on or after 22 October 2012 (subject to transitional rules). See 25.862.

EXEMPT PROPERTY BENEFITS

If an employer provides property benefits to a current employee on a working day on the business premises of the employer, and that property is consumed by the employee on that working day, the benefit is an exempt benefit.

The benefit would not only apply to a tangible property, but would extend to use of equipment (eg. computer) and facilities such as private phone calls.

Tomoko owns a restaurant and because the employees work long shifts she provides them with meals which are consumed during their work-breaks. These are exempt benefits. Tomoko also provides meals to staff at a 50% discount if they buy meals at her restaurant on their days off. The benefit is not exempt but subject to the other valuation rules in this chapter.

BIG Ltd provides senior employees with a voucher that entitles each employee to receive massage services during a working day on the employee's premises. This is not an exempt benefit because the benefit is not consumed by the employee (see ATO ID 2005/109).

25.869   DOCUMENTATION

Documentary evidence must be maintained, and include a tax invoice or receipt etc showing:

- date the expenditure was incurred

- name and address of the provider/supplier
- nature of the goods or services
- date of the document, and
- amount of the expense.

A declaration in a form approved by the Commissioner is required before lodgement date of the FBT return and applies to all benefits with the exception of:

1. Recurring fringe benefits
2. Exclusive employee fringe benefits, and
3. Extended travel fringe benefits.

25.880 AIRLINE TRANSPORT FRINGE BENEFITS

FBT is payable where free or discounted air travel in a passenger aircraft is provided to employees (or their associates) of an airline or a travel agent. Normal valuation rules apply unless the employees travel under the conventional standby arrangements. Changes to the valuation of airline fringe benefits apply from 8 May 2012.

Standby travel is available to employees (or associates) in the airline industry or travel agents when no members of the general public want available seats. Free or discounted air travel not subject to the standby rules is a residual fringe benefit.

25.881   GST AND TAXABLE VALUE

The taxable value of domestic air fares is their GST inclusive value. Note that transport to, from or outside Australia (ie. non-domestic) is GST-free. Accordingly, domestic air fares, which have GST payable on them are classified as Type 1 fringe benefits and are grossed-up at the higher gross-up rate. GST-free travel, such as international travel is classified as Type 2 fringe benefits and gross-up at the lower gross-up rate.

25.882   STANDBY TRAVEL

Stand-by airline travel restrictions customarily apply in the airline industry and is travel in which seating on the aircraft is subject to availability and is not guaranteed for the employee or associate of the employee. This means that employees or associates of the employee may be displaced from a flight at any time up to the point of departure.

From 8 May 2012 the method of determining the taxable value of 'airline transport fringe benefits' is aligned with the in-house fringe benefit provisions.

Specifically:

- The taxable value of an airline transport fringe benefit is aligned with the in-house benefit valuation method and is calculated as 75% of the stand-by airline travel value of the benefit, less the employee contribution.
- **For domestic travel:** The stand-by airline travel value is 50% of the carrier's lowest standard single economy airfare for that route as publicly advertised during the year of tax.
- **For international travel**: The stand-by airline travel value is 50% of the lowest of any carrier's standard single economy airfare for that route as publicly advertised during the year of tax.

25.883   FREQUENT FLYERS

Benefits received by an employee due to membership of a frequent flyer club or similar consumer award-based incentive program (see 11.100) are not treated as fringe benefits (TR 1999/6 and *Payne v FCT* [1996] 66 FCR 299; [1966] 32 ATR 516) with one exception. FBT applies when the person with the personal contract is an employer and provides a flight reward to an employee.

25.884   NON-STANDBY TRAVEL

Non-standby airline travel does not satisfy the meaning of standby airline travel (see 25.882).

This is a residual fringe benefit. The taxable value subject to FBT is 75% of the lowest arm's length price that the public is charged less any payment made by the employee.

25.885   'OTHERWISE DEDUCTIBLE' RULE

The taxable value of airline benefits can be reduced (under the 'otherwise deductible' rule) by the percentage which the employee could otherwise have claimed as a once-only income tax deduction.

TRAVEL DIARY IS REQUIRED

Employees must generally keep a diary or similar document for all overseas or domestic travel of more than five nights away from home.

The entries should be made at the time of, or as soon as reasonably practicable after, the activity. The documents must be given to employers before the FBT return is lodged. This requirement does not apply to aircrew.

25.886   EXEMPTIONS

This involves a separate checking of facts for each employee for the FBT year.

If the taxable value of all 'in-house' airline fringe benefits for an employee (or associate of the employee) is under $1,000, no FBT is payable on them. This applies to in-house benefits provided after 8 May 2012 also. The reduction to taxable value however will not be available where the benefits are provided under a salary packaging arrangement.

25.900 ENTERTAINMENT

Entertainment provided to an employee or an associate of an employee may be subject to FBT. Depending upon the circumstances, the employer may or may not be entitled to claim an income tax deduction for the cost of the entertainment or any FBT liability. Entertainment, other than sustenance, provided to clients is neither tax deductible nor subject to FBT.

25.901   WHAT IS THE PROVISION OF ENTERTAINMENT?

There is no specific 'entertainment fringe benefit' category within the FBT Act. The provision of entertainment may take many forms, such as food and drink or recreational entertainment and can be classified as one of a number of different fringe benefit types, such as meal entertainment, expense payment, property or residual fringe benefits.

25.902   MEAL ENTERTAINMENT

A meal entertainment fringe benefit arises where an employer provides:
- entertainment by way of food or drink
- accommodation or travel in connection with, or for the purpose of facilitating, entertainment by way of food or drink, or
- the payment or reimbursement of expenses incurred in providing something covered by (a) or (b) above.

This is the case:
- regardless of whether or not business discussions or business transactions occur, or
- there is any connection with the working of overtime or otherwise in connection with the performance of the duties of any office or employment, or
- for the purposes of promotion or advertising, or
- at or in connection with a seminar.

This type of fringe benefit only occurs where the employer is the provider of the benefit (s37AE). If the employer is not the provider, another type of benefit may arise (s37AG).

The entertainment may be classified as one of a number of fringe benefit categories depending upon the circumstances in which the entertainment is provided by the employer or third party.

NOTE: Car parking fees reimbursed to an employee by an employer for travelling to a venue for meal entertainment is considered an expense incurred in providing the employee with travel. This is because the fees were incurred as part of the employee's journey to the venue. These expenses therefore form part of meal entertainment for FBT purposes (ATO ID 2014/15).

EXAMPLES OF ENTERTAINMENT

- Meal entertainment benefit – food and drink provided either on or off business premises to employees, directly or in connection with entertainment
- Expense payment benefit – reimbursement of an employee's restaurant bill by the employer.
- Property benefit – meals provided to an employee at a restaurant
- Residual benefit – use of recreational assets owned by the employer, such as accommodation in connection with the entertainment, and
- Tax-exempt body entertainment benefit – specifically applies to income tax exempt employers.

The benefits in the nature of entertainment may be treated as meal entertainment benefits if the employer elects to do so. This provides the opportunity to adopt the 12 week register or 50/50 split method in respect of those benefits (see below).

FOOD AND DRINK – IS IT ENTERTAINMENT?

Not all food and drink provided by an employer to its employees gives rise to an entertainment fringe benefit.

In making this determination the following factors should be considered:
- Why is the food or drink being provided?
- What food or drink is being provided?
- When is the food or drink being provided?
- Where is the food or drink being provided?

25.903   EXEMPTIONS AND CONCESSIONS

The following exemptions and concessions may apply to reduce the taxable value of entertainment fringe benefits.

ENTERTAINMENT CONSUMED ON BUSINESS PREMISES

The provision of food or drink which is consumed by current employees on the employer's business premises on a working day results in an exempt property benefit. The exemption does not however extend to associates of employees. Furthermore, the exemption does not apply if such benefits are provided to an employee under a salary packaging arrangement.

The provision of light meals and refreshments, including morning and afternoon teas, will not result in a taxable fringe benefit. The Tax Office is of the view however that, if excessive alcohol is provided, the benefit is likely to take on the characteristic of entertainment. Note that the exemption for 'on-premises' consumption may still apply.

MINOR BENEFITS

In general, benefits provided by employers that are less than $300 (GST inclusive) are exempt from FBT, if any other identical or similar benefits are provided infrequently and irregularly.

 The minor benefit exemption is not available to employers using the 50/50 split or 12 week register method to establish the taxable value of meal entertainment benefits.

See TR 2007/12 for the Commissioner's views on the treatment of minor benefits.

OTHERWISE DEDUCTIBLE RULE

Where the employee would have been entitled to a one-off income tax deduction in respect of the entertainment provided (for example, for attending a seminar) had the expenditure been incurred by the employee directly (not reimbursed by the employer), the otherwise deductible rule may apply to reduce the taxable value of the fringe benefit partly or wholly.

Note that meals taken while on deductible work-related travel in most cases are not considered to be entertainment. This is so even if the travelling employee has a meal with a customer. It should also be noted that, unlike the definition of entertainment for income tax purposes (see 13.500) recreation is not included in the FBT definition of meal entertainment.

If the employer uses the 50/50 split method or the 12 week register method:

- no benefit will arise to an employer where the same benefit arises to another employer, and
- a fringe benefit may arise where the employer has not provided the benefit, or where the employer has provided the benefit but the benefit is a fringe benefit in relation to another employer.

25.904   TAXABLE VALUE

Where certain fringe benefits are classified as meal entertainment fringe benefits, an employer has to classify all fringe benefits arising from the provision of meal entertainment during the FBT year as meal entertainment fringe benefits.

The three valuation methods which may be available (for both taxable and tax-exempt employers) include:

- the '50/50 split method'
- the '12 week register method', and
- the 'actual cost method'

MEAL ENTERTAINMENT AND GST CREDITS

GST input tax credits in respect of meal entertainment or entertainment facility leasing are available to the extent that income tax deductions are allowable when elections are made under the:

- 50/50 split method (see 25.905)
- 12 week register method (see 25.906), and
- 50/50 split entertainment facility leasing rules (GSTR 2001/3).

ENTERTAINING EMPLOYEES AND NON-EMPLOYEES

When an employer provides entertainment to both employees and non-employees (eg. at a corporate function), difficulties may arise in determining the amount subject to FBT. The Tax Office accepts that, if the part of the benefit which relates to employees only is not easily ascertained from the available information, the employer may use a per-head apportionment (TD 94/25).

TIPS AND ENTERTAINMENT

The Tax Office considers that a genuine tip (ie. paid voluntarily) can be treated as entertainment. As such a tip is not subject to GST. However, if an employer reimburses an employee for entertainment, including a genuine tip, the reimbursement is a type 1 benefit grossed up at 2.0647. If the employee is reimbursed separately in relation to a genuine tip, the benefit is a type 2 benefit grossed up at 1.8692.

25.905   50/50 SPLIT METHOD

This method ensures that FBT applies to half of the total expenditure incurred by an employer in providing meal entertainment benefits to its employees, their associates and non employees, regardless of whether the expenditure would be deductible for tax purposes.

The taxable value of meal entertainment provided to employees by an associate or a third party under the arranger rules is not included in the taxable value of meal entertainment benefits. Those benefits are assessed for FBT under the relevant existing rules, ensuring that an employer cannot avoid paying FBT on entertainment provided to employees by another who would be entitled to an income tax deduction for the relevant expenditure.

The taxable value of meal entertainment benefits cannot be reduced by the application of the 'otherwise deductible' rule, but the cost of providing the meal entertainment is reduced by unreimbursed employee or associate contributions. Under these rules, an income tax deduction is allowed for 50% of meal entertainment expenses where the employer has elected to use this method. No other deductions are available to the employer for the same expenditure.

An employer incurs $200,000 expenditure on meal entertainment in the FBT year - being provided to both employees and non-employees. If the employer elects to use the 50/50 split method, $100,000 will be subject to FBT and can be claimed as an income tax deduction (and GST input tax credits claimed). The other 50% or $100,000 will not be subject to FBT, cannot be claimed as an income tax deduction and there is no entitlement to an input tax credit).

By adopting the 50/50 method, the employer is electing to pay FBT (and be entitled to income tax deductions) on 50% of ALL meal entertainment regardless of whether on an individual transaction basis the amount may have been exempt from FBT. See the tables at 25.940 to find whether or not particular transactions are 'meal entertainment'. In some situations, this may result in FBT being payable on expenditure that was never subject to FBT. If not using the 50/50 method, expenditure in respect of a client would be non-deductible with no FBT payable. This type of expenditure is included in the 50/50 split. Employers should carefully consider their circumstances before adopting this method.

25.906 12 WEEK REGISTER METHOD

Under the 12 week register method, the taxable value of the meal entertainment fringe benefits for the employer is:

> *Total meal entertainment expenditure x Register percentage*

The register percentage is:

> *(Total value of meal entertainment fringe benefits provided in 12 week period divided by Total value of meal entertainment in 12 week period) x 100%*

The register must be kept for a continuous period of at least 12 weeks throughout which meal entertainment is provided by the employer, and this period must be representative of the first FBT year for which it is valid. If the register does not meet this requirement, it will not be valid. The register is valid for an FBT year in which the 12 week period starts and finishes, and the four subsequent years. If the 12 week period straddles two FBT years, it will only be valid for the second year and the four subsequent FBT years. The register ceases to be valid if the total expenses incurred by the employer in providing meal entertainment for the FBT year is more than 20% higher than the corresponding total for the first FBT year for which the register was valid.

DETAILS IN THE REGISTER

The register must include the following details:

- the date the employer provided meal entertainment
- for each recipient of meal entertainment, whether the person is an employee or an associate
- the cost of the meal
- the kind of meal entertainment provided
- where the meal entertainment was provided, and
- if on the premises, whether in an in-house dining facility.

The person responsible for making entries in the register must make the entry as soon as practicable after he or she knows the details required.

Under these rules, the amount which will be deductible to the employer will include expenditure that relates to meal entertainment fringe benefits and also other deductible entertainment expenditure incurred by the employer in the FBT year, multiplied by the register percentage.

An employer incurs total expenditure on food and drink of $200,000 in the FBT year. This includes meal entertainment fringe benefits of $170,000 and other deductible entertainment (eg. employee meals while travelling) expenditure of $30,000. The employer has maintained a register which shows 30% of his meal entertainment expenditure was provided as a fringe benefit.

If the employer elects to use the 12 week register method, $51,000 (ie. $170,000 x 30%) is subject to FBT.

The employer is entitled to an income tax deduction for $51,000 and $30,000, a total of $81,000.

The remaining $119,000 (ie. $170,000 x 70%) will not be subject to FBT and cannot be claimed as an income tax deduction.

25.907   ACTUAL COST METHOD

If either the 12 week register or 50/50 split method is not used, the taxable value of the entertainment is determined by the valuation rules applicable to the type of benefit, ie:

- expense payment benefit (see 25.550)
- property benefit (see 25.860)
- residual benefit (see 25.820), or
- tax-exempt body entertainment benefit.

Where the actual cost method is used to value meal entertainment, the minor benefit rule and the 'on business premises' rule may be applied to reduce the taxable value of the benefits provided.

25.908   RECREATIONAL ENTERTAINMENT

Recreational entertainment is generally not meal entertainment. Examples include:

- sports and leisure time pursuits, such as tickets to sporting events and the theatre
- conference 'day trips', including joy fights and harbour cruises
- sponsorship tickets, and
- holiday travel.

TAXABLE VALUE OF RECREATIONAL ENTERTAINMENT

The taxable value of recreational entertainment is generally equal to the cost of the activity; for example, the entry fee for a golf day, and is calculated using the respective valuation rules according to the classification of the benefit as expense payment, property or residual fringe benefits.

The minor benefit rule may apply to reduce the taxable value of recreational entertainment fringe benefits where the conditions for application of the minor benefit rule are satisfied.

25.909   ENTERTAINMENT FACILITY LEASING EXPENSES

Entertainment Facility Leasing Expenses (EFLEs) are expenses incurred by an employer in hiring or leasing:

- a corporate box
- boats or planes for entertainment, and
- other premises or facilities for providing entertainment.

Expenses that are not considered EFLEs include:

- expenses attributable to providing food or drink, and
- expenses attributable to advertising that would be an allowable income tax deduction.

CORPORATE BOXES ETC.

Corporate boxes and other similar hospitality arrangements are not 'business premises' (see 25.353). Food and drink consumed by employees and their associates on those premises will be subject to FBT.

The 50/50 split method may be applied to leasing or hiring costs of corporate boxes, boats or aircraft and other similar hospitality arrangements to determine what portion of these leasing or hire costs is subject to FBT. Expenses attributable to providing food or drink or advertising (that would be tax deductible) are not entertainment facility leasing expenses. Where an employer elects to apply the 50/50 split method to corporate box leasing or hire costs, a deduction equal to 50% of those expenses will be allowable as a deduction in the year incurred. If the 50/50 split method is not chosen (see TD 92/162 about the deductibility of corporate box entertainment), the Tax Office according to the TD accepts that 5% of the total cost represents a proportion applicable to advertising, and 95% of the total cost is in respect of entertainment.

25.910   REPORTING REQUIREMENTS

Meal entertainment is defined as an 'excluded benefit' and is therefore not a reportable fringe benefit. That is, entertainment by way of food or drink, and benefits associated with that meal entertainment, such as travel and accommodation are excluded benefits for reporting purposes and are therefore not disclosed on employee's reportable fringe benefits amount on their payment summary. Similarly, EFLEs are also an 'excluded benefit' and as such are specifically excluded for reporting purposes. See 25.300.

Other types of recreational entertainment, such as tickets to sporting events and musicals are subject to the reporting requirements as they are considered recreational entertainment as opposed to meal entertainment.

NOTE: In the May 2015 Federal Budget it was announced that a $5,000 per employee grossed up capping threshold will be introduced on certain meal entertainment and entertainment leasing facility expense ('EFLE') benefits provided by certain not for profit organisations under salary packaging arrangements. This change will become effective from 1 April 2016. These benefits will become reportable benefits.

25.920 ENTERTAINMENT: FBT AND INCOME TAX

The Tax Office considers that entertainment has been provided only when the food and drink confers entertainment on the recipient (TR 97/17).

This should be established by an objective analysis of all of the circumstances surrounding the provision of the food and drink, taking into account:

- **The type of food provided**: Morning and afternoon tea provided to staff on a work day on the employer's premises or worksite, or a light working lunch do not constitute entertainment. More elaborate meals, such as working lunches, may confer entertainment and therefore fall within the definition of entertainment in s51AE.

- **When the food and drink is provided**: Provision of food during work time, overtime or whilst travelling are less likely to have the character of entertainment, as this type of meal usually does not go beyond providing mere sustenance.

- **Where the food and drink is provided**: Food and drink provided on work premises is less likely to have the character of entertainment, whilst food and drink provided at a hotel, restaurant, etc., or consumed with other forms of entertainment is more likely to have such a character.

- **Why the food and drink is provided**: The purpose test requires an evaluation of the reason for the provision of the relevant food and drink. Where the purpose is to entertain, the food and drink will adopt the character of entertainment.

An element of entertainment is required before the provision of food and drink becomes an 'entertainment meal'.

25.940 'ENTERTAINMENT' OR 'NON-ENTERTAINMENT'

The following chart is a Tax Office checklist of situations of whether food and drink constitute an 'entertainment meal' or 'non-entertainment meal' (see TR 97/17). This table provides a quick reference to the FBT and income tax treatment of each circumstance.

Y/N = depending on what is provided, food or drink may or may not amount to provision of meal entertainment.

Circumstances in which food or drink provided	ME [1] Y/N	R [2] Y/N	Taxable employer FBT Y/N	Taxable employer Ded'n Y/N	Tax-exempt body FBT Y/N
a. Food or drink consumed on the employer's premises ...					
(a) ... by employees					
1. at a social function	Y	N	N	N	Y
2. in an in-house dining facility – not at a social function	Y/N	N	N	Y	N
3. in an in-house dining facility – at a social function	Y	N	N	N	Y
4. morning and afternoon teas and light lunches	N	N	N	Y	N
(b) ... by associates					
1. at a social function	Y	N	Y	Y	Y
2. in an in-house dining facility – not at a social function	if Y	N	Y	Y	Y
	if N	Y	Y	Y	Y
3. in an in-house dining facility – at a social function	Y	N	Y	Y	Y
4. morning and afternoon teas and light lunches	N	Y	Y	Y	Y
(c) ... by clients					
1. at a social function	Y	N	N	N	N
2. in an in-house dining facility – not at a social function	If Y	N	N	N#	N
	If N	N	N	Y	N
3. in an in-house dining facility – at a social function	Y	N	N	N	N
4. morning and afternoon teas and light lunches	N	N	N	Y	N
b. Food or drink consumed off the employer's premises ...					
... at a social function or business lunch					
• by employees	Y	N	Y	Y	Y
• by associates	Y	N	Y	Y	Y
• by clients	Y	N	N	N	N
c. Alcohol					
1. employee travelling – wine accompanies evening meal	N	N	N	Y	N
2. alcohol provided at conclusion of CPD seminar with finger foods	N	N	N	Y	N
d. Food or drink consumed by employees while travelling					
1. employee travels and dines alone	N	N	N	Y	N
2. two or more travelling employees dine together	N	N	N	Y	N
3. travelling with client and dine together	N	N	N	Y	N
4. as in 3. except employer pays for all meals					
• employee's meal	N	N	N	Y	N
• client's meal	N	N	N	Y	N
5. dines with client who is travelling separately	N	N	N	Y	N
6. dines with employee not travelling					
• only employee's meal provided	N	N	N	Y	N
• both employees' meals provided					
- travelling employee's meal	N	N	N	Y	N
- non-travelling employee's meal	Y	N	Y	Y	Y

| Circumstances in which food or drink provided | ME [1] Y/N | R [2] Y/N | Taxable employer | | Tax-exempt body |
			FBT Y/N	Ded'n Y/N	FBT Y/N
7. dines with client who is not travelling					
• only employee's meal provided	N	N	N	Y	N
• employee's and client's meal provided					
- employee's meal	N	N	N	Y	N
- client's meal	Y	N	N	N	N
e. Employees dining with other employees of the same employer or with employees of associates of the employer					
1. employee entertains another employee and is reimbursed by the employer	Y	N	Y	Y	Y
2. employee entertains an employee of an associated company of the employer and is subsequently reimbursed					
• employer's employee (expense payment)	Y	N	Y	Y	Y
• associate's employee (property)	Y	N	Y	Y	Y
* = associate; ** = employer			*	**	
f. Meal consumed by employees while attending a seminar					
1. provided incidental to a seminar that satisfies s32-35 and is not held on the employer's premises	Y/N	N	N	Y	N
2. light breakfast provided at a CPD seminar that does not satisfy s32-35	N	N	N	Y	N
3. light refreshments incl. moderate amount of alcohol provided immediately after a CPD seminar that does not satisfy s32-35	N	N	N	Y	N
g. Food or drink consumed by employees at promotions					
function not held on employer's premises; open to general public	Y	N	Y	Y	Y
h. Meals provided under an arrangement					
client does not facilitate or promote an arrangement where its employee is taken out to lunch by another employer					
• client's employee	N	N	N	N	N
• employee of other employer	Y	N	Y	Y	Y
i. Use of corporate credit card					
employees dine together at a restaurant and the meal is paid for with the credit card	Y	N	Y	Y	Y
j. Restaurant discount cards					
employee who holds a restaurant discount card entertains client					
• employee – 1/2 total discounted price	Y	N	Y	Y	Y
• client – 1/2 total discounted price	Y	N	N	N	N
k. Meals for accompanying spouses					
with employee travelling on business; employer pays for all meals					
• employee	N	N	N	Y	N
• spouse	Y	N	Y	Y	Y
l. Food or drink provided by tax-exempt bodies					
1. 'non-deductible' meal entertainment provided to employees, whether or not on employer's premises	Y	N	N/A	N/A	Y
2. meals provided to employees in an in-house dining facility	Y/N	N	N/A	N/A	N
3. non-meal entertainment provided to employees on employer's premises	N	N	N/A	N/A	N

1: ME = Meal entertainment   2: R = Reportable fringe benefit

\# An income taxable employer has the option to claim a deduction for the cost of the meal and include $30 in their assessable income (s32-70 ITAA97)

25.960 TAX-EXEMPT BODY ENTERTAINMENT

A tax-exempt body fringe benefit only arises where the expenditure would not be deductible for income tax purposes. Where a tax-exempt body provides entertainment to an employee or an associate, a fringe benefit arises, even if it would qualify as a 'minor benefit' (see 25.202). This rule includes entertainment benefits provided in connection with meals. The employer may elect for Division 9A to apply. Accordingly, the 50/50 split method and the 12 week register methods are available.

The taxable value of tax-exempt body entertainment is the amount incurred by the employer and therefore disregards any employee contributions. The taxable value of such benefits is the GST-inclusive value.

25.961   WHAT IS A TAX-EXEMPT BODY ENTERTAINMENT FRINGE BENEFIT?

Where a tax-exempt body provides entertainment to an employee or an associate, a fringe benefit arises, even if it would qualify as a 'minor benefit'. This rule includes entertainment benefits provided in connection with meals. The employer may elect for Division 9A FBTAA to apply, in which case the 50/50 split method and the 12 week register methods are available to value tax-exempt body entertainment.

A tax-exempt body fringe benefit only arises where the expenditure would not be deductible for income tax purposes. Even though the grossing-up rules treat expenditure in providing a fringe benefit as tax deductible to a taxpaying employer, the expense is treated as non-deductible in relation to tax-exempt bodies.

25.962   WHO IS A TAX-EXEMPT BODY?

A tax-exempt body is an organisation whose income is either:
- wholly exempt from income tax (for example, a club that earns income from members only), or
- partially exempt from income tax (eg. a club that earns income from both members and non-members).

 In order for a charity to be income tax-exempt it must be endorsed.

25.963   TAXABLE VALUE

The taxable value of tax-exempt body entertainment is the amount Incurred by the employer in providing the entertainment. Employee contributions are disregarded and therefore do not reduce the taxable value of tax-exempt body entertainment benefits. The taxable value of such benefits is the GST inclusive value. Tax-exempt bodies calculate the taxable value of meal entertainment fringe benefits in the same way as income tax paying bodies (see 25.904).

MINOR BENEFITS

In addition to the general criteria for determining whether the minor benefits exemption applies to a particular fringe benefit (see 25.202), for tax-exempt bodies the exemption is only available where:
- the provision of the entertainment is incidental to the provision of entertainment to outsiders and does not consist of a meal, other than light refreshments, or
- a function is held on the employer's premises solely as a means of recognising the special achievements of the employee in a matter relating to the employment of the employee.

25.964   RECREATIONAL ENTERTAINMENT

Recreational entertainment includes amusement, sport and similar leisure time pursuits, such as playing golf, providing theatre or movie tickets, a joy flight or a harbour cruise (see 25.908).

25.965 ENTERTAINMENT FACILITY LEASING EXPENSES

Entertainment facility leasing expenses (EFLEs) are exempt from FBT when incurred by PBIs, HPCs, public hospitals, non-profit hospitals and public ambulance services (see 25.909).

NOTE: In the May 2015 Federal Budget it was announced that a $5,000 per employee grossed up capping threshold will be introduced on certain meal entertainment and entertainment leasing facility expense ('EFLE') benefits provided by some not for profit organisations under salary packaging arrangements. A salary packaging arrangement is one involving a benefit provided in exchange for a reduction in salary, or where it is reasonable to conclude that the salary would be higher if the benefit was not provided. This change, if it is passed by Parliament, will become effective from 1 April 2016. Such benefits provided in excess of this threshold will be subject to FBT at the full rate. However, an employee can apply their existing cap (ie the $31,177 or $17,667) to reduce the FBT on the excess meal entertainment and EFLE benefits. These benefits will also become reportable benefits for Payment Summary purposes.

25.966 REPORTING REQUIREMENTS

The reporting requirements for tax-exempt bodies are the same as for tax-paying bodies. That is, meal entertainment (ie. food and drink) and benefits associated with that entertainment, as well as EFLEs are 'excluded benefits' for reporting purposes. Accordingly, they are not included on the employee's reportable fringe benefits amount on their payment summaries (see 25.910). See the note above regarding the proposed amendment regarding meal entertainment and EFLEs.

 Other types of recreational entertainment, such as tickets to sporting events and musicals are subject to the reporting requirements as they are considered recreational entertainment as opposed to meal entertainment.

25.967 FBT IMPLICATIONS OF TAX-EXEMPT BODIES PROVIDING MEAL ENTERTAINMENT

The table below summarises the FBT implications of tax-exempt bodies providing food and drink.

Circumstances in which food or drink provided (either on or off business premises)	Meal entertainment Y/N	Fringe benefits tax arises?		
		For employees Y/N	For associates Y/N	For clients Y/N
At a social function (eg. a staff Christmas party)	Y	Y	Y	N
In an in-house dining facility (not at a social function)	N	N	Y	N
In an in-house dining facility (at a social function)	Y	Y	Y	N
Morning and afternoon teas and light lunches	N	N	Y	N
At a social function or business lunch	Y	Y	Y	N
Employee on business travel overnight and dining by themselves or with an employee, employee of an associate or client who is also on business travel overnight (regardless of who pays)	N	N	Y	N
Employee on business travel overnight dining with employee not on business travel overnight (employer pays for all meals): • travelling employee's meal • non-travelling employee's meal	 N Y	 N Y		

25.980 SALARY SACRIFICE ARRANGEMENTS

A Salary Sacrifice Arrangement (SSA) arises when an employee agrees contractually to forego part of the remuneration otherwise receivable as salary or wages, in return for the employer or employer's associate providing benefits of an agreed value. Where the arrangement is made for future benefits, the employee is taxed on the reduced salary or wages and the employer may be liable to pay FBT on the benefits provided. Taxation Ruling TR 2001/10 discusses effective SSAs.

25.981   DERIVING INCOME

Taxation Ruling TR 2001/10 accepts that employees do not derive ordinary or statutory income from their employment until the income either has been received, or is taken to have been received (by ss6-5(4) or ss6-10(3)) ITAA97. However, once an employee has earned an entitlement to receive an amount of 'salary or wages', the amount is taxed to the employee as 'salary or wages' income when the employer deals with the amount in any way on the employee's behalf.

25.982   RETROSPECTIVE ARRANGEMENTS

A SSA is not effective where the arrangement applies retrospectively (eg. where a bonus already earned is applied to employer superannuation contributions). Therefore benefits paid under retrospective SSA's are 'salary or wages' and the employer must generally withhold PAYG from the gross amount (see from 5.200).

25.983   PROSPECTIVE ARRANGEMENTS

Prospective SSA's are effective, even if they reduce salary or wages below the minimum entitlement under industrial law. This means that benefits provided to, or at the direction of, employees under prospective salary sacrifice arrangements, are not assessable income of the employees.

These are examples of acceptable prospective SSAs:

- an entitlement to a bonus or other performance remuneration, provided the arrangement is entered into before the employee gains a presently existing entitlement to the bonus
- annual and long service leave that will accrue from the provision of future services
- employer superannuation contributions under prospective SSA's to complying superannuation funds on behalf of their employees. These contributions are accepted to be employer contributions to the superannuation fund for the purposes of the *Superannuation Guarantee (Administration) Act 1992* and ss82AAC – 82AAF ITAA36 (see 13.400).

Where the arrangement allows that any residual amount not taken as benefits can be paid as cash, any such cash payments would be assessable as salary or wages to the employee when they are paid.

Where there is an effective prospective SSA, employers do not have to withhold PAYG from the payments – however, FBT may be payable. Where FBT is payable the amount may need to be reported on the employee's payment summary (see 25.300).

NOTE: Otherwise deductible rule and interaction with non-commercial loss rules

The otherwise deductible rule does not apply to a salary sacrifice strategy which attempts to negate the application of the non-commercial loss rules and in particular the $250,000 income test (14.450). This involves high income employees salary sacrificing expenses (by way of reimbursement) in relation to an unrelated business venture (eg. hobby farm). The Commissioner in TR 2013/6 and TD 2013/20 considers that it would be necessary to hypothetically determine whether the business expenditure incurred by the individual would have been deductible absent the salary sacrifice arrangement. For the purposes of the otherwise deductible rule, a 'once-only deduction' is considered not to apply and therefore, FBT would be imposed on the taxable value of the reimbursement by the employer. See TR 2013/6 and TD 2013/20 for details.

25.986   THE EMPLOYEE CONTRIBUTION METHOD

Where an employee's marginal tax rate for income tax purposes is less than the FBT rate (currently 49%), the employee may consider making an employee contribution:

- by making an after-tax contribution to reduce the taxable value of the benefit, or
- paying for specific expenses, such as running costs of a car, out of after tax dollars.

Where an employee makes a contribution equal to the taxable value of a concessionally treated fringe benefit, the portion of the benefit that would have been taxed at the FBT rate is effectively transferred to the employee's income and is taxed at the marginal income tax rate. The difference between the taxable value and the total cost of the benefit will not be subject to FBT or income tax.

Employee contribution method

Natalie has a total remuneration package of $100,000. She entered into a novated car lease for three years on 1 April 2015. The lease value of the car is $30,000.

The total costs for the car (including lease costs) is $11,000 (GST-inclusive) per annum.

The statutory formula method is used to calculate FBT payable.

Superannuation is ignored for this example.

Medicare levy is 2% of cash salary .

It is assumed that Natalie has adequate private health cover and therefore, is not subject to Medicare Levy Surcharge.

Assume cash salary = taxable income.

	Not packaged	Fully packaged	ECM
Total remuneration	$100,000	$100,000	$100,000
Taxable value of car benefit		($6,000)[1]	-
Costs of car above taxable value		($5,000)	($5,000)
FBT payable		($6,310)[2]	-
Input tax credit		$1,000	$455[3]
Cash salary	$100,000	$83,690	$95,455
Income tax	($24,947)	($18,912)	($23,265)
Medicare levy (@ 2%)	($2,000)	($1,674)	($1,909)
After-tax cash in hand	$73,053	$63,104	$70,281
After-tax costs of the car	($11,000)	-	($6,000)
Cash in hand	$62,053	$63,104	$64,281
Total benefit compared to not packaging		**$1,051**	**$2,228**

1: $30,000 x 0.2 = $6,000
2: $6,000 x 2.1463 x 49% = $6,310
3: $5,000 x 1/11 = $455

Payroll tax

26

26.000 PAYROLL TAX

Payroll tax is imposed by each State and Territory on wages paid or payable to employees and is administered in accordance with the individual State and Territory Payroll Tax Acts. The payroll tax rate varies as does the amount of the threshold entitlement available to employers. Payments made to contractors can be subject to payroll tax and all States and Territories include fringe benefits paid to employees (and all persons taken to be employees) as taxable wages.

Payroll tax is only payable where the employer's 'wages' (as defined) exceeds certain thresholds during the financial year. These thresholds vary between the States and Territories (see 26.300). State and Territory Governments agreed to improve inter-jurisdictional consistency of payroll tax and adopted uniform provisions for eight key areas. These are:

- timing for the lodgment of returns
- the treatment of services performed outside Australia
- the motor vehicle allowances exemption
- the accommodation allowances exemption
- the treatment of fringe benefits
- the treatment of employee share acquisition schemes
- grouping provisions, and
- superannuation contributions.

Victoria and New South Wales introduced new Payroll Tax Acts from 1 July 2007 to harmonise payroll tax arrangements for both States. Tasmania adopted the uniform Victorian/New South Wales legislation from 1 July 2008. Queensland and Australian Capital Territory harmonised key aspects of the New South Wales/Victorian legislation from 1 July 2008. The Northern Territory and South Australia adopted the uniform provisions for the abovementioned eight key areas from 1 July 2008 and harmonised their payroll tax provisions from 1 July 2009 with those of New South Wales, Victoria and Tasmania with the exception of rates, thresholds and a few minor jurisdictional specific areas. The Australian Capital Territory introduced a new payroll tax Act (*Payroll Tax Act 2011*) from 1 July 2011 to harmonise further payroll tax provisions, with the exception of rates, thresholds and Australian Capital Territory specific provisions.

In Western Australia, legislation was introduced to improve inter-jurisdictional consistency of payroll tax between Western Australia and the other states. The *Payroll Tax Assessment Amendment Bill Act 2010* containing the above amendments received Royal Assent on 25 June 2010 and included two new exemptions announced in the 2009-10 Budget in relation to parental or adoption leave, and specified emergency services volunteers as well as a number of other measures. The Act also contains new nexus provisions that govern where tax is to be paid when services are provided in more than one jurisdiction in a month.

26.010 DEFINITION OF WAGES

All States (except Western Australia) have extended the definition of wages to include payments made to contractors.

For the purposes of the respective Payroll Tax Acts the general definition of wages in the New South Wales, Northern Territory, Queensland, Victorian, Tasmanian, Australian Capital Territory and South Australian Acts is:

- wages (including apprentice and trainee wages but see 26.200 for exemptions)
- remuneration (including payments to company directors)
- salary (including annual, long service and sick leave)
- commission
- bonuses, or
- allowances (but see 26.020), and
- paid or payable to an employee.

Wages also include:

- an amount paid or payable by way of remuneration to a person holding an office under the Crown or in the services of the Crown

- an amount paid or payable under any prescribed class of contracts to the extent to which that payment is attributable to labour
- an amount paid or payable by a company by way of remuneration to, or in relation to a director or member of the governing body of that company
- an amount paid or payable by way of commission to an insurance or time-payment canvasser or collector, and
- an amount or benefit that is included as or taken to be wages by any other provision of the Act.

The following are also taken to be wages under the Acts:

- employer (pre-tax) superannuation contributions including:
  - superannuation guarantee payments
  - salary sacrifice contributions, and
  - the value of non-monetary contributions
- fringe benefits, within the meaning of the *Fringe Benefits Tax Assessment Act 1986 (Cth)*
- the value of shares and options granted to employees, directors, former directors and some contractors
- payments to contractors in certain circumstances
- payments by employment agencies arising from employment agency contracts to on-hired workers, and
- employment termination payments and accrued leave paid on termination.

The definition of wages includes those that are paid or payable at piece work rates or otherwise and whether paid or payable in cash or in kind. The abovementioned wages are liable to payroll tax based on the amount paid or payable in any month. Each State also includes an expanded definition to include other payments made by employers that are connected to the service of employees or deemed employees.

More details can be found at 26.350: *Payments liable for payroll tax*.

TAXING OF EMPLOYEE BENEFITS

The definition of wages for payroll tax purposes includes any fringe benefits as defined in the *Fringe Benefits Tax Assessment Act 1986* (FBTAA) and therefore, as a general rule, benefits that are taxable under the FBTAA are also taxable under the Payroll Tax Act and must be declared as wages for payroll tax purposes (with an exception being tax-exempt body entertainment fringe benefits as defined in the FBTAA).

From 1 July 2008, all States except Western Australia (in Victoria and New South Wales from 1 July 2007) and Territories include the value of benefits as calculated under the FBTAA and require employers to include the total of the type 1 and type 2 aggregate amount of the fringe benefits grossed up using the factor for 'Type 2 benefits' specified in the FBTAA. See 26.350 for a summary of the differences in the taxing of employee benefits between the States and Territories.

The *Payroll Tax Assessment Act 2010* (WA) amended the provisions of the *Payroll Tax Assessment Act 2002 (WA)* to require (consistent with the other States and Territories) that only the type 2 factor is used when calculating the taxable value of fringe benefits.

The following payments are also liable for payroll tax:

- employer contributions to industry redundancy funds, portable long service leave funds and employee share/option plans (Western Australia)
- employer contributions to industry redundancy funds, portable long service leave funds and employee share/option plans, but not the Construction & LSL Building Industry fund (South Australia)
- living away from home allowances – reasonable motor vehicle and accommodation allowances are exempt to the extent of the prescribed limits (see from 26.350). (In Western Australia a living away from home allowance (LAFHA) is defined as a fringe benefit for the FBTA Act purposes from 1 July 2009 onwards), and
- prescribed benefits (eg. contributions to employee share acquisition scheme) (Western Australia and from 1 July 2005 the Australian Capital Territory).

In Queensland, employer contributions to an approved industry redundancy fund or to an approved portable long service leave fund are not liable for payroll tax.

In Western Australia the 'otherwise deductible rule' (see 25.455) is taken into consideration when calculating the value of fringe benefits for payroll tax purposes. (From 1 July 2009, the otherwise deductible rule is not added back when calculating the value of fringe benefits for payroll tax purposes).

EMPLOYER SUPERANNUATION CONTRIBUTIONS

All employer-funded (before income tax) superannuation contributions paid or payable in respect of an employee, deemed employee or made to or in connection with, directors, members of a corporation's governing body are liable wages. This includes the super guarantee levy, salary sacrifice arrangements and any additional payments paid on behalf of employees and persons taken to be employees into any form of superannuation, provident or retirement fund or scheme. The value of any non-monetary employer-funded superannuation contribution is taxable for payroll tax purposes.

In South Australia, a superannuation contribution includes the crediting of an account of an employee or the debiting of any other account where it increases the employee's entitlement (ie. contribution holidays where interest or capital increases employee entitlements is taxable). Since 1 July 2009, the value of any superannuation contribution has been liable for payroll tax purposes.

SHARES AND OPTIONS

The value of the grant of a share or option to an employee or deemed employee, a director or former director or member (or former member) of the governing body of the company is subject to payroll tax.

The 'granting' of a share or an option occurs if a person acquires a share or, in the case of an option, a right to the share.

The value of the share or option is recognised on the 'relevant day'. The employer can elect to treat the relevant day as either the date that the share or option is granted to the employee or the 'vesting date'.

The vesting date for a share is the date when any conditions which apply to granting the share have been met and the employee's legal or beneficial interest in the share cannot be rescinded. The vesting date for a share is the earlier of either the date as defined above or the date at the end of the seven years from the date on which the share is granted to the employee.

The vesting date for an option is the earlier of one of three dates:

- when the share to which the option relates is granted to the employee, or
- when the right under the option to have the relevant share transferred, allotted or vested is exercised by the employee
- at the end of the period of seven years from the date on which the option is granted to the employee.

If the granting of a share or option constitutes wages, the amount of wages is the value of the share or option on the relevant day, less any consideration paid or given by the employee for the grant (excluding consideration in the form of services rendered).The value of a share or an option is the market value or the amount determined as provided for in section 83A-315 of the *Income Tax Assessment Act 1997* (Commonwealth) and Division 83A of the *Income Tax Assessment Regulations 1997* of the Commonwealth.

If an employer does not include the value of a grant of a share or option in its taxable wages for the financial year in which the grant occurred, the wages constituted by the grant are taken to have been paid or payable on the vesting date of the share or option.

Where the employer elects the relevant date as the vesting date, the seven year vesting date is the latest date for vesting unless the other specified vesting events occur before the end of the seven years.

The employer may reduce the taxable wages declared by the value of any previously declared share or option value, if the grant of a share or option was rescinded because the vesting conditions were not met. This reduction in the taxable wages would not apply in circumstances where the employee decided not to exercise the option.

If the grant of a share or option is withdrawn, cancelled or exchanged before the vesting date for some valuable consideration other than a share or option, the date on which that occurs is deemed to be the vesting date and the taxable amount is taken to be the value of the consideration.

The seven year vesting date applies to shares and options that have been forfeited or lapse prior to seven years from the grant date if the other specified events have not occurred. However, as such shares / options have been forfeited or lapsed prior to seven years from the grant date, the value of the shares / options at the seven year vesting date is regarded as being nil because the share / option does not exist at that time.

If a share or option granted is classified as a fringe benefit under the *Fringe Benefits Tax Assessment Act 1986* (Commonwealth), it is treated as a fringe benefit for payroll tax purposes.

TERMINATION PAYMENTS

Termination payments are generally subject to payroll tax. They comprise two components:

- the value of an employment termination payment, and
- the value of all paid out annual and long service leave.

Employment termination payments (ETPs), previously known as eligible termination payments include payments in lieu of notice, severance pay, redundancy payments, paid out unused sick leave and compensation for loss of income. The value of an ETP for payroll tax purposes is that part of an ETP payment that would be included in the assessable income of that employee (or a person taken by this Act to be an employee) if the whole of the ETP had been paid to the employee or person taken to be an employee.

Persons taken to be employees include directors, members of a corporation governing body, persons who perform services under employment agency contracts and contractors whose payments are taken to be wages under the Act.

The value of paid out annual and long service leave is liable to payroll tax irrespective of when it was accrued.

In Queensland, a payment arising from the termination of employment may constitute either a genuine redundancy payment under the ITAA or an early retirement scheme payment under the ITAA. Such payments are exempt from payroll tax to the extent that they are exempt from income tax.

In Western Australia from 1 July 2009, the term 'eligible termination payment' was replaced with 'employment termination payment'. The *Pay-roll Tax Assessment Amendment Act 2010* also includes a provision (consistent with other jurisdictions) to impose payroll tax in Western Australia on amounts paid by a company as a consequence of the termination of the services or office of a director (including members of the governing body of the company).

DEFENCE FORCE PAYMENTS

Payroll tax does not apply to payments made to employees while in the Australian Defence Force, provided no work is done for the employer in that period (see Payroll tax exemptions above).

PAYROLL TAX ON GROSS WAGES

Payroll tax is payable on the gross wage even if an amount is deducted from an employee's gross wage for board and quarters, superannuation, tax instalments or other items.

PAYMENTS TO NON-WORKING DIRECTORS

Payroll tax is payable in respect of remuneration, superannuation contributions, shares and options and termination payments for all directors.

In Western Australia the *Pay-roll Tax Assessment Amendment Act 2010* contains amendments that specifically clarify that payroll tax is imposed on superannuation contributions made on behalf of non-executive directors.

Payment received by a non-working director in the form of allowances for travelling, entertaining, etc. is not subject to payroll tax. However in Western Australia if the payments fall within the definition of directors remuneration they will be subject to payroll tax. Any benefits provided to non working directors are subject to FBT and as such will also be subject to payroll tax.

PAYMENT TO EXECUTIVE DIRECTORS

For directors who are employees and directors, payroll tax is payable on their remuneration plus any allowances, superannuation contributions, benefits, shares and options in the same manner as ordinary employees.

Any payment made by an employer in connection with the work or appointment of any director is a wage even if paid to a third party, for example a director's corporation.

PAYMENTS FOR MATERNITY/PARENTAL AND ADOPTION LEAVE

In the Australian Capital Territory wages paid or payable to an employee on maternity leave, adoption leave or primary carer leave are exempt from payroll tax for a maximum of 14 weeks leave for any one pregnancy, birth or adoption.

In Victoria, wages paid or payable to employees on maternity or adoption leave are exempt from payroll tax. The exemption applies to all wages other than fringe benefits and is limited to a maximum of 14 weeks pay. The exemption can be pro-rated for full-time employees who take leave for more than 14 weeks at less than full pay, but not part-time employees. From 1 July 2012, the exemption can be pro-rated for part-time employees who take leave for a period of more than 14 weeks at a reduced rate of pay.

In New South Wales wages paid or payable to employees on maternity or adoption leave are exempt from payroll tax. The exemption applies to all wages other than fringe benefits and is limited to a maximum of 14 weeks pay. This is in line with the harmonisation process with Victoria. From 1 July 2010 wages paid or payable to employees on paternity leave are exempt from payroll tax.

In South Australia, Queensland, Tasmania and in the Northern Territory wages paid or payable to employees for maternity or adoption leave (and paternity leave in Queensland and the Northern Territory) are exempt from payroll tax. The exemption does not apply where the leave is a fringe benefit and the exemption is limited to a maximum of 14 weeks pay. This is in line with the harmonisation process with Victoria and New South Wales. The exemption does not apply to paid sick leave, annual leave, long service leave or similar leave taken in connection with an adoption, pregnancy or the birth of the employee's child. In Queensland, surrogacy leave is also exempt from payroll tax for a maximum equivalent of 14 weeks pay. From 16 April 2011, the Queensland exemption for part-time employees includes leave taken over a longer period for wages equivalent to 14 weeks at the part-time rate of pay.

PAYMENTS FOR PAID PARENTAL LEAVE

Payments to employees under the Commonwealth Government's Paid Parental Leave (PPL) scheme (effective from 1 January 2011) do not constitute wages and are not liable to payroll tax as they are not paid by the employer in respect of services provided by the employee (or in anticipation of future services to be provided by the employee).

The PPL Scheme provides eligible working parents of children born or adopted on or after 1 January 2011 with a maximum of 18 weeks of government funded paid parental leave at the National Minimum Wage. PPL payments are not taxable for payroll tax because they are Commonwealth Government payments that employers pay on behalf of the Commonwealth Government and are not paid by employers in respect of services provided by their employees (or in anticipation of future services to be provided by their employees).

VOLUNTEER EMERGENCY DUTIES

In all States and Territories except the Australian Capital Territory, payments made to employees, not otherwise on leave, who are released to undertake certain emergency work as a volunteer, eg. for fighting bushfires (refer to *Payroll tax exemptions* above) are exempt from payroll tax.

In the Australian Capital Territory, payments made to a person who takes part in activities under the *Emergencies Act 2004* as volunteer firefighters, emergency service volunteers and other volunteers are exempt from payroll tax. However wages that are paid or payable as annual leave, long service leave or sick leave for such volunteers are not exempt wages.

In Western Australia a payroll tax exemption applies to wages paid in the first two years of employment of new employees with a disability. It applies to businesses that hire new employees with a disability (on or after 1 July 2012) for whom they are in receipt of a Commonwealth

Disability Employment Service wage subsidy or who are eligible for any form of Western Australian Disability Services Commission Support.

In New South Wales the Jobs Action Plan is a rebate scheme which is designed to give businesses an incentive to employ new workers. Under the Plan businesses that increase the number of New South Wales full time equivalent employees for a period of at least two years will receive a payroll tax rebate. The scheme applies to new jobs created after 1 July 2011.

In Western Australia, small to medium businesses are eligible to receive a full rebate of payroll tax for wages paid to new indigenous employees, hired on or after 1 July 2013, over the first two years of employment. Eligibility criteria apply.

ALLOWANCES

Allowances are generally liable for payroll tax in all States and Territories, but different rules apply to motor vehicle allowances, accommodation allowances and living away from home allowances which may be fully or partially exempt in certain circumstances. Details of exempt motor vehicle and accommodation allowances are shown at 26.350. See Revenue Ruling PTA005 *Exempt Allowances: Motor Vehicle and Accommodation (Version 2)* for further information regarding the treatment of such allowances.

There is a distinct difference between:

- an allowance (the money belongs to the employee, even though some or all of it must be spent as the employer directs), and
- a reimbursement of a precise amount of expenses (or advance of money, requiring the employee to return any change) paid by the employee but incurred in the employer's business.

NOTE: Even if the allowance is based on distance travelled in a car, with or without a lump sum added for basic costs, it is still regarded as an 'allowance' (see *Payments liable for payroll tax* at 26.350).

26.020 PAYROLL TAX EXEMPTIONS

In certain circumstances wages paid by some organisations may be exempt from payroll tax.

The following lists typical exemptions that may apply. Please note that this list is not exhaustive and may not necessarily apply to all States and Territories. It is therefore necessary to consider the definition of wages, both inclusions and exclusions, in each relevant State or Territory.

NOT FOR PROFIT ORGANISATIONS

Non-profit organisations having as their 'sole' (for Victoria 'whole') or dominant purpose a charitable, benevolent, philanthropic or patriotic purpose (not including schools, educational institutions, educational companies or State instrumentalities), for wages paid to persons engaged exclusively in work of a charitable, benevolent, philanthropic or patriotic nature are exempt from payroll tax. There are qualifications on payroll tax exemptions available to organisations engaging in commercial activities.

Even though the exemption requires the organisation to have as its 'sole' (for Victoria 'whole') or dominant purpose a charitable purpose, an organisation that has some non-charitable purposes will qualify for the exemption so long as those non-charitable purposes are merely incidental or ancillary to its charitable purposes. (In South Australia and Queensland, philanthropic and patriotic purposes are not recognised) (this does not wholly apply in Western Australia).

In Western Australia, 'fourth limb' charities that have been established and carried on for the promotion of trade, industry, or commerce can no longer claim a charitable exemption unless the sole or dominant purpose of that charity is the relief of poverty, the advancement of education or the advancement of religion. An organisation or body liable to payroll tax which is a relevant body as defined under section 42A of the *Payroll Tax Assessment Act 2002* will not qualify for a charitable exemption unless a beneficial body determination is in place for that relevant body.

Other not for profit organisations that are exempt from payroll tax on wages include:

- Public benevolent institutions (for Victoria – not including an instrumentality of the State), for wages paid to persons engaged exclusively in work of a public benevolent nature.
- Religious institutions, for wages paid to persons engaged exclusively in religious work of that institution.
- Non-profit non-government schools, for wages paid to persons providing education at or below secondary level.
- Public hospitals, for wages paid to persons engaged exclusively in the work of the hospital.
- Non-profit private hospitals, for wages paid to persons engaged exclusively in the work of the hospital.
- Wages paid to persons engaged exclusively in work of a health care service provider, namely an ambulance service, a community health centre, denominational hospital, multi-purpose service, public health service, public hospital and the Victorian Institute of Forensic Mental Health (does not apply in South Australia or Western Australia). For New South Wales see Schedule 2 of the *NSW Payroll Tax Act 2007* for 'Health Care Service provider' definition. For Queensland equivalent, wages paid by Hospital and Health Services established under the *Hospital and Health Board Act 2011 (Qld)* are exempt from payroll tax.
- Councils, other than wages paid or payable for or in connection with specified activities such as the supply of electricity or gas, water, sewerage, conduct of abattoirs, public markets and parking stations, cemeteries or crematoria, hostels, public transport or other prescribed activities. This does not apply in Tasmania.

OTHER EXEMPTIONS

- Compensation payments to injured workers (eg. WorkCover and TAC payments) but not amounts paid in excess of the amounts prescribed as compensation (eg. make-up pay is taxable).
- The income tax-free portion of bona fide redundancy or early retirement payment.
- Maternity and adoption leave unless paid as part of a form of other leave.
- Paid parental leave amounts.
- Paternity leave unless paid as part of a form of other leave (New South Wales, Queensland and Northern Territory provision).
- Payments to employees while they are on leave to work in the Defence Forces.
- Wages paid or payable to employees who are volunteer emergency workers who are absent from work to volunteer as firefighters or respond to other emergencies (includes honorary ambulance officers in Queensland). (See also *Volunteer emergency duties.*)
- Wages paid or payable to aboriginal persons who are under an 'employment project' through the Community Development Employment Project (which is funded by the Commonwealth Department of Employment) or the Torres Strait Regional Authority (this does not apply in Western Australia).

NORTHERN TERRITORY-SPECIFIC EXEMPTIONS

- From 1 July 2015, exemptions do not apply to wages paid to employees which perform services in connection with any commercial or competitive activity carried on by the entity.
- Political parties, industrial associations and non-profit organisations that have a purpose of the promotion of trade, industry or commerce are also not eligible for the exemption.

QUEENSLAND-SPECIFIC EXEMPTIONS*

- Apprentice and trainee wages are exempt from payroll tax under certain conditions and are to be excluded from wages (see also 26.210 *Apprentice wages, rebates and grants*).
- Surrogacy leave unless paid as part of a form of other leave.

- Wages paid or payable to employees who are volunteer emergency workers and including honorary ambulance officers who are absent from work to volunteer as firefighters or respond to other emergencies (includes in Queensland) (see also *Volunteer emergency duties*)
  - Apprentice and trainee wages that meet certain conditions.
  - Wages paid by government departments but not including wages paid by commercialised business units.

* In Queensland, philanthropic and patriotic purposes are not recognised.

VICTORIA-SPECIFIC EXEMPTIONS

- Wages paid by State school councils within the meaning of the *Education and Training Reform Act 2006*
- Wages paid by approved not for profit group training organisations to apprentices that satisfy funding requirements as a new entrant.

NEW SOUTH WALES-SPECIFIC EXEMPTIONS

- Wages paid to an employee who is employed by a non profit organisation approved by the Director General of the Department of Education and Training and in accordance with a group apprenticeship scheme.

SOUTH AUSTRALIA-SPECIFIC EXEMPTIONS*

- Specific exemptions are provided in respect of wages paid or payable by:
  - the Sexual Health Information Networking and Education South Australia Incorporated
  - non-profit child care centres and kindergartens
  - non-profit health services providers
  - a University College affiliated with the University of Adelaide or the Flinders University of South Australia, and
  - a motion picture production company, being wages paid or payable to a person who is involved in the production of a feature film in South Australia, where the Minister is satisfied that:
    - the film will be produced wholly or substantially within South Australia
    - the production of the film will involve or result in the employment of South Australian residents, and
    - the production of the film will result in economic benefits to the State of South Australia.

* In South Australia, philanthropic and patriotic purposes are not recognised.

WESTERN AUSTRALIA-SPECIFIC EXEMPTIONS*

- Wages paid in the first two years of employment of new employees who are hired with a disability on or after 1 July 2012, if they are in receipt of a Commonwealth Disability Employment Service wage subsidy or who are eligible for any form of Western Australian Disability Services Commission support.
- Wages paid to apprentices and trainees are exempt under certain conditions.

* In Western Australia, 'fourth limb' charities that have been established and carried on for the promotion of trade, industry, or commerce can no longer claim a charitable exemption unless the sole or dominant purpose of that charity is the relief of poverty, the advancement of education or the advancement of religion. An organisation or body liable to payroll tax which is a relevant body as defined under section 42A of the *Payroll Tax Assessment Act 2002* will not qualify for a charitable exemption unless a beneficial body determination is in place for that relevant body.

AUSTRALIAN CAPITAL TERRITORY-SPECIFIC EXEMPTIONS

- From 2013-14 to 2014-15 financial years a $4,000 payroll tax concession is available to eligible employers who employ recent school leavers with a qualifying disability.

26.040   IN WHICH JURISDICTION IS PAYROLL TAX PAYABLE?

Where an employee provides services wholly in one Australian State or Territory (jurisdiction), payroll tax will continue to be paid in the jurisdiction where those services are performed irrespective of where the wages were paid.

RULES FROM 1 JULY 2009

From July 2009, all jurisdictions amended the rules in respect of payroll tax on wages paid to employees that perform services in more than one jurisdiction or one or more jurisdictions and overseas in a given month, ensuring that an employer does not become liable to payroll tax on the same wages twice. The payroll nexus rules that apply in all Australian jurisdictions are outlined below.

SERVICES ARE PERFORMED WHOLLY IN ONE JURISDICTION

In these circumstances, payroll tax will continue to be paid to the jurisdiction where those services are wholly performed. This looks at the place where services are performed by the employee in the month that the wages are paid even if that place is not where the employee usually performs services.

SERVICES PERFORMED IN MORE THAN ONE AUSTRALIAN JURISDICTION AND/OR PARTLY OVERSEAS

If the services performed by an employee in a month are performed in more than one jurisdiction or in one or more jurisdictions and overseas, the new provisions provide a tiered test for determining the payroll tax liability as follows.

THE PAYROLL TAX NEXUS RULES

These rules apply where wages are paid to employees who provide their services in more than one Australian jurisdiction or partly in more than one Australian jurisdiction and partly overseas in a calendar month. There is a four tier test used to determine a payroll tax liability where the employee provides services in more than one Australian jurisdiction and/or partly overseas.

(1) **Employee's principal place of residence:** Payroll tax is to be paid to the jurisdiction where the employee's Principal Place of Residence (PPR) is located.

(2) **Employer's ABN address or principal place of business:** If the worker does not reside in Australia, payroll tax is to be paid to the jurisdiction where the registered Australian Business Number (ABN) address of the employer is located. If the employer does not have a registered ABN address, or has two or more ABN addresses in different jurisdictions, payroll tax is payable in the jurisdiction where the employer has their Principal Place of Business (PPB).

(3) **Where wages are paid or payable:** If the employee does not have a PPR in any Australian jurisdiction and the employer does not have an ABN address or PPB in any Australian jurisdiction, payroll tax is payable in the jurisdiction where the wages are paid or payable in that calendar month. If wages are paid or payable in a number of jurisdictions, payroll tax is paid in the jurisdiction where the largest proportion of wages is paid.

(4) **Services performed mainly in one Australian jurisdiction:** If both the employee and the employer are not based in any Australian jurisdiction and wages are not paid in Australia, a payroll tax liability arises in the jurisdiction where the services are mainly performed in that calendar month (that is, if the work performed in that jurisdiction during that month is greater than 50 per cent).

WHERE ARE THE WAGES PAID?

The provisions in each of the Payroll Tax Acts deem wages to have been paid where a cheque or other instrument is received. If wages are paid into an employee's bank account, they are deemed to have been received in the State in which the employee holds his or her bank account. A typical clause in a State Act reads:

For the purposes of this section, where a cheque, bill of exchange, promissory note, money order or a postal order issued by a post office, or any other instrument, is sent or given by an employer to a person (or his agent) at a place within Australia in payment of wages, those wages shall be deemed to have been paid at that place.

If a liability to pay wages has arisen but the wages are not yet paid by the end of the month, wages can be 'deemed' to have been payable at the place where wages were last paid by the employer to the employee or if wages were not previously been paid, the place where the employee last performed services in respect of the employer before the wages became payable.

OVERSEAS WORK

Where an employee is working in another country or countries for a period of six months or less, a payroll tax liability arises in the jurisdiction where the wages are paid or payable. Where an employee is working in another country or countries for a continuous period of more than six months, then the wages paid or payable to that employee for the whole period will be exempt from payroll tax including the first six months.

The six month period must be a continuous period but need not be in the same financial year. Should an employee who is working in another country return to Australia, it will not be considered to be a break in continuity of their overseas employment if the employee returns for a holiday or to perform work that exclusively relates to the overseas assignment for a period of less than one month provided that the employee returns immediately to that country to continue their overseas employment.

Where an employee is performing services offshore, ie. outside all Australian jurisdictions, but not in another country, the wages are taxable in the Australian jurisdiction in which wages are paid or payable. The exemption available for employees working in another country or countries would not apply in this instance. See Revenue Ruling PTA039 *Payroll tax nexus provisions* for further information.

26.050 OBJECTIONS AND APPEALS

If an employer is dissatisfied with an assessment of their payroll tax liability or with certain other decisions, they may object in writing within 60 days of the date of service of the assessment or decision. Similarly, appeals must also be lodged within a specified time where an employer is dissatisfied with a decision on an objection.

In South Australia, objections must be lodged with the Minister for Finance and appeals made to the Supreme Court. In Tasmania, taxpayers dissatisfied with a Commissioner's decision on an objection may seek a review by the Magistrates Court (Administrative Appeals Division) or lodge an appeal with the Supreme Court. In the Northern Territory the appeal must be made to the Tribunal or Supreme Court. In Queensland a taxpayer can only object to an assessment or to a reassessment (limited) and may apply to the Queensland Civil and Administrative Tribunal (QCAT) for a review of the objection decision or lodge an appeal with the Supreme Court. In Western Australia, a taxpayer can object to an assessment and may apply to the State Administrative Tribunal for a review of the objection decision. In New South Wales, Victoria, South Australia and Tasmania, if an objection is successful a refund applies.

The Commissioner pays the refund amount with interest at the market rate applying from time to time calculated from the date the tax relating to the objection was first paid. On the other hand, if the objection is disallowed, interest may accrue on any unpaid amount of tax. As with successful objections, any refund following a successful appeal, is paid with interest at the market rate applying from time to time calculated from the date the tax was paid. A summary of the relevant time limits for objections and appeals is as follows:

State/Territory	Number of days: Objections	Appeals
New South Wales	60^1	60^1
Queensland	60^1	60^5
South Australia	60^2	60^4
Western Australia	60^1	60^1
Tasmania, Victoria	60^1	60
Australian Capital Territory	60^1	28
Northern Territory	60^1	60^3

1: Extension of time may be granted.

2: Extension may be granted by the Minister but no later than 12 months after the decision / assessment.

3: Extension may be granted by the Tribunal or Supreme Court.

4: Extension may be granted by the Supreme Court but no later than 12 months after the Minister's determination of the objection.

5: QCAT cannot extend the period in which the taxpayer may apply for a review of the Commissioner's objection decision.

26.060 DUE DATE FOR RETURNS

A registered employer has to file monthly returns and an annual reconciliation by the due date as specified by the respective State or Territory.

In Queensland, New South Wales, Victoria, Tasmania, South Australia and Australian Capital Territory, monthly returns must be lodged by the seventh of the month after that in which wages were paid (except in the Australian Capital Territory for December which has a due date of 14 days after end of month). Even if there is no payroll tax liability for a month, the employer must still lodge a return recording a 'nil' liability. However, if the estimated tax payable by an employer is relatively low, the employer may apply to the State Revenue Office for approval to pay annually except in Queensland, where an employer can only apply to lodge half-yearly returns.

In New South Wales, Victoria, Australian Capital Territory, Queensland, South Australia and Tasmania, employers must lodge an electronic annual reconciliation incorporating June's wages by 21 July each year. The annual reconciliation reconciles the tax payable for the financial year and incorporates the wages for the month of June. There is no separate payroll tax return for the month of June in Queensland, Victoria, New South Wales, South Australia and the Australian Capital Territory.

For the Northern Territory, each monthly return and any payment must be lodged by the 21st of the month after that in which wages were paid, unless the Commissioner has given approval to pay tax annually. In general, the Commissioner will approve this only if the estimated tax payable in a financial year is less than $8,400, in which case the employer will only be required to lodge an Annual Adjustment return. The annual adjustment return must be lodged and paid by all registered employers by 21 July each year. An approved designated group employer can lodge returns on behalf of group members.

In Western Australia, a liable employer must register for payroll tax. If registered a monthly return must be lodged unless exempted from doing so, in which case an annual or quarterly return must be lodged. Monthly returns are available electronically on the 7th of each month and must be lodged with payment by the 7th of the following month. Quarterly lodgments of returns are available in Western Australia if lodgment and payment are made electronically. Businesses that have a (expected) liability of $100,000 per annum must lodge and pay a monthly return via the online portal. Following the passing of the *Pay-roll Tax Assessment Amendment Act 2010* the lodgment and payment of the June return and the reconciliation return are due by 21 July.

In the Australian Capital Territory, the Northern Territory, Queensland, Victoria, Western Australia, South Australia and Tasmania employers must provide Australia-wide wages figures to enable annual reconciliations to be made.

In Victoria and Tasmania, two or more group members may lodge a scheduled group return (if approved). This is called a single lodger group in New South Wales.

26.070 GROUPING OF EMPLOYERS

Grouping provisions apply throughout Australia. They were designed to prevent taxpayers using a number of businesses to avoid or diminish payroll tax liabilities. As a result of grouping, wages paid by group employers are added together and a single deduction is given to the designated group employer on behalf of the group. The remaining group members are required to pay payroll tax on their wages without any deduction.

The common grouping provisions include:
- consistent provisions relating to related corporations under the *Corporations Act 2001*
- consistent provisions relating to common or inter-used employees
- consistent test of controlling interest of more than 50%
- adopting the tracing provisions, and
- consistent exclusion provision.

LODGING RETURNS

Even though a number of employers may be grouped for payroll tax purposes, each employer must register separately and lodge returns. To obtain the deduction in New South Wales, Victoria, South Australia, Queensland, Western Australia, the Northern Territory and the Australian Capital Territory, a member of the group is nominated by the members, or selected by the Commissioner to be the Designated Group Employer (DGE).

In New South Wales the group or the Chief Commissioner may nominate only one designated group employer who either pays more than $750,000 (for the 2014-15 financial year) in Australian wages per annum, or one member of the group may be nominated as the group single lodger, by the other members of the group, or the Chief Commissioner, if the group's Australian wages exceed $750,000 (for 2014-15 financial year).

In Tasmania, a member of the group can be nominated to receive the deduction, otherwise each member is entitled to a proportion of the deduction.

In Queensland, the group members may nominate a Queensland registered employer as the DGE.

In the Northern Territory, an approved designated group employer may lodge a return on behalf of all of the group members.

In the Australian Capital Territory, an approved designated group employer may make application to be a joint return lodger for itself and other Australian Capital Territory members within the group.

In South Australia, an approved designated group employer, with the Commissioner's approval, can lodge a joint return on behalf of specific members of the group.

In Victoria, one member who is designated by the group (the designated group employer) is entitled to claim a deduction on behalf of the group. The other members (the ordinary members) are not entitled to claim any deduction and must pay payroll tax on their Victorian wages.

In Western Australia, the DGE receives the threshold on behalf of the group. All other ordinary members are not entitled to claim a monthly threshold. However, if the DGE does not utilise all of the threshold, any remaining threshold is apportioned to all other ordinary members based on their taxable wages upon final reconciliation. The DGE is responsible for submitting the interstate wages of all other ordinary members in conjunction with their reconciliation return.

IMPORTANT: Only one deduction is available to each group. If wages are paid in more than one State or Territory the deduction is adjusted in each State or Territory. See 26.345 for the formula.

BUSINESS GROUPING RULES

The grouping provisions have the effect of adding together the wages paid by group employers and allowing only the designated group employer to claim the deduction.

A group will exist where any of the following four circumstances applies:
- employers are related bodies corporate under section 50 of the *Corporations Act 2001*
- one or more employees of an employer perform duties in connection with another business or businesses.
- the same persons have controlling interests in a number of businesses (whether conducted by persons, partnerships, corporations or trusts) and which are carried on by separate legal entities, or

- an entity (ie. a person or set of associated persons) has a direct, indirect or aggregate controlling interest in a corporation.

However, in addition to the above, Western Australia also provides that two businesses constitute a group if one is a branch, agency or subsidiary managed by a head or parent business.

RELATED COMPANIES

Companies are related if:
- two companies are a holding company and a subsidiary, or
- two companies are both subsidiaries of the same holding company.

For those purposes, a company is deemed to be a subsidiary of another company if:
- the composition of its Board is controlled by another company
- more than half the voting rights are controlled by another company, or
- more than half the share capital is controlled by another company.

For the grouping of companies, a subsidiary of a subsidiary is deemed to be a subsidiary of the ultimate holding company. This grouping relationship also applies to Australian subsidiaries of an overseas parent corporation.

COMMON EMPLOYEES

An employer and any other person constitute a group if:
- any employee performs duties for or in connection with a business carried on by the employer and another person
- any employee is employed solely or mainly to perform duties for or in connection with a business carried on by another person, or
- an agreement, arrangement or undertaking exists between an employer and another person in respect of the common use of employees between businesses.

The term 'business' includes:
- a trade or profession
- any other activity carried on for a fee, gain or reward
- employing one or more persons who perform duties in connection with another business
- the carrying on of a trust, and
- holding any money or property used for or in connection with another business whether carried on by one person or two or more persons together.

COMMONLY CONTROLLED BUSINESSES

Businesses constitute a group under this test if the same person(s):
- has the right to instruct the majority of corporate directors, or controls more than 50% of the voting rights at meetings of the directors of the corporation
- can control the exercise of more than 50% of the voting power attached to voting shares
- owns more than 50% of the partnership capital or is entitled to more than 50% of any profits
- is the beneficiary (beneficiaries) of more than 50% of the value of the interests in the trust
- constitutes more than 50% of the board of management or control the composition of the board of the body corporate or unincorporate, and
- is the sole proprietor/s.

In New South Wales, Victoria, Western Australia, Australian Capital Territory, South Australia, Tasmania, Northern Territory and Queensland any beneficiary of a discretionary trust is deemed to have more than 50% of the value of the interests in the trust.

In Western Australia, South Australia and the Australian Capital Territory, businesses may also be grouped if the head or parent business exercises administrative, financial or procedural control over a branch, agency or subsidiary.

TRACING OF INTERESTS IN CORPORATIONS

In New South Wales, Victoria and Tasmania an entity and a corporation form part of a primary group if the entity has a controlling interest in the corporation. A controlling interest in a corporation is where the entity has a direct, indirect or aggregate interest in the share capital of the corporation greater than 50%. An entity can be a person or a group of associated persons. The meaning of 'associated person' is defined in the legislation.

From 1 July 2008, the Northern Territory, Australian Capital Territory, Queensland, South Australia and Tasmania adopted the New South Wales/Victoria tracing provisions. In Western Australia, the *Pay-roll Tax Assessment Amendment Act 2010* includes tracing provisions from 1 July 2012 when other amendments to the grouping provisions commenced.

GRANTING EXCLUSION FOR A GROUP

All States and Territories may exclude a member from a group if it is satisfied that the business is carried on independently of and is not connected with the carrying on of a business carried on by any other member of the group, except if the member is a body corporates and deemed to be related under the *Corporations Act 2001*.

Application for exclusion from grouping should be in writing, together with supporting information/ documentation substantiating the claim that the businesses are carried on independent of and not connected with one another, taking into consideration the nature and degree of ownership and control of the businesses, the nature of businesses and any other relevant matters.

26.100 PAYMENTS TO CONTRACTORS

Victoria, New South Wales, the Australian Capital Territory, Tasmania, Queensland (from 1 July 2008), South Australia and the Northern Territory have extended the definition of 'wages' to include payments made under certain 'relevant contracts'. Also, employers resident in other States must be cautious if they make payments there for services rendered by 'contractors'.

In Western Australia, payment by a principal to a contractor for work performed under a contract for services may not be taxable; the liability is determined by the facts. A payment to a 'contractor' might be taxable, if the person is in fact an employee. Payments to contractors are liable for payroll tax if an employer/employee relationship between the principal and the worker exists.

Broadly, the question of whether a payment is taxable depends on the circumstances of the engagement, the working arrangements between the principal and each 'contractor' and the essential nature of the payment. Under the 'contractor' provisions which exist in some States and Territories, certain payments are taken to be 'wages' where a contractor or sub-contractor provides labour or services exclusively or primarily to a person under a 'relevant contract', but some specific exemptions exist.

Contractor provisions in Victoria, New South Wales, South Australia, Queensland, Tasmania and the Northern Territory are identical. The requirements in the Australian Capital Territory are somewhat broader than in Victoria, and the extent of any exemptions are more limited.

Payroll tax is generally not payable on payments made to contractors who are genuinely offering their services to the public. In the Australian Capital Territory, the contractor must be rendering their service(s). However, many of the situations caught involve people who were with the same organisation as employees, and who (for income tax or for some other reason) have changed their status.

In New South Wales, payroll tax could be required to be paid by a principal contractor (hiring business):

- if that person enters into a contract for carrying out of work by another person (sub-contractor) and employees of that sub-contractor (ie. relevant employees) are engaged in carrying out the work and the work is carried out in connection with a business undertaking of the principal contractor, and

- if any payroll tax payable by the sub-contractor in respect of wages paid to relevant employees during the financial year for work done in connection with the contract/s has not been paid and no signed bona-fide statement/s is/are available. The principal contractor will be jointly and severally liable with the sub-contractor, unless they secure a signed statement from the sub-contractor stating that they don't need to register for payroll tax, or are up to date with their payroll tax liabilities. The signed statement/s will need to be available for auditing by 60 days after the end of each financial year.

EXEMPT CONTRACTS

In New South Wales, Victoria, Tasmania and Queensland, payments to contractors who are owner/drivers, insurance agents and door-to-door sellers are exempt unless there is a contrived arrangement to avoid payroll tax. South Australia and the Australian Capital Territory laws contain similar provisions. From 1 July 2015, the Northern Territory only provides an exclusion to owner/drivers.

HOW THE SYSTEM WORKS

Payroll tax is payable on payments made to contractors or sub-contractors unless an exemption applies: Typical situations that are caught include:

- an employee ceases to be an employee and becomes a subcontractor working exclusively for the person or firm who was the former employer, and
- an employee forms a family company or family trust. The company or trustee then contracts with the employer to provide the services of the 'employee' to the firm.

Under the contract provisions contractors are taken to be 'employees' and the payments made to them, excluding goods and services tax (GST), are taken to be wages.

The legislation has a wide definition and has been framed to give the term 'relevant contract' as wide a meaning as possible, with only specific exclusions to limit its effect.

'Relevant contracts' are those where a person, in the course of a business:

- supplies to another person services for (or in relation to) the performance of work (eg. plumber providing services to a business or household, or a farm enters into a contract with a company, or some other entity to supply the services of a professional person, tradesman or artist)
- is supplied with the services of another person for or in relation to the performance of work, or
- gives out goods to individuals for work to be performed by those individuals in respect of those goods, and for re-supply of the goods to the first mentioned person (eg. outworkers or contractors working at home on piece rates).

The term 'contractor' is a generic one, which includes sub-contractors, consultants and out-workers. The provisions apply regardless of whether the contractor provides services via a company, trust, partnership or sole trader.

The contractor provisions contain several exemptions and if any one applies to a particular contract, the arrangement is not a relevant contract and therefore not taxable. These provisions allow the Commissioner to disregard, and treat as taxable, an arrangement that exists only to reduce or avoid payroll tax.

EXCLUSIONS FROM THE CONTRACTOR PROVISIONS

The following are applicable in Victoria, New South Wales, South Australia, Tasmania, Queensland, the Australian Capital Territory and the Northern Territory which limit the scope of those payments to contractors liable to payroll tax. These are not necessarily applicable in Western Australia.

1. Labour is ancillary to supply of goods or use of goods provided by the contractor

This is for arrangements under which the supply of materials or equipment is fundamental to the contract.

A contract is entered into for the supply of a crane and driver. This would be exempt where the supply of the crane is the significant and fundamental object of the contract. In other words, the supply of a driver is ancillary to the supply of the crane itself.

2. Services a business does not ordinarily require and is supplied by someone who normally provides such services to the public generally

The second category of contract exempt from payroll tax is one under which the services provided are:

- of a type which are not ordinarily required in the course of a person/firm's ongoing business, and
- provided by a person who ordinarily performs services of a similar kind to the public generally.

Many business transactions are contracts for services which are not part of the mainstream of a person/firm's business (ie. it is not work normally required by the business in an ongoing sense).

 A business which operates retail shops engages a firm of shop fitters to refit the interior of premises. This would not be regarded as a regular requirement of the business as the shopfitter provides his services to shopkeepers generally. By contrast, payroll tax is payable if a large chain store engages a shopfitter permanently on contract (or on a series of contracts), because its operations required ongoing shopfitting.

3. Contractor provides services of a type ordinarily required by a business for less than 180 days in a financial year

Businesses may require various ad hoc services allied to the mainstream of the business's work. For services of any one type, a statutory limit is imposed of 180 days in a financial year.

NOTE: The 180 day rule does not apply in the Australian Capital Territory or in Western Australia.

 A contract is excluded if a contract plumber is engaged by a building firm which ordinarily requires plumbing services for less than 180 days in a year. A 'day' is one on which any work at all of the particular type is done. Each financial year is treated separately. If any work under two or more contracts (even by different people) is done on the same day, that day is counted only once.

 If a contract plumber were engaged for 140 days, and later (on completion of that contract) another contract is entered into (even with the same plumber) for another 100 days, it would be taken that the services of that type were required for 240 days and the exemption does not apply. That would apply even if the services are required for only four hours each day.

 If two contract plumbers are engaged to perform similar services, and those services are provided during the same period (eg. for 140 days) it would be accepted that the type of service is required for only 140 days as only 140 days and the exemption would apply.

Even though a person or firm receives a particular type of service for 180 days or more in a financial year, and the contractor payments are not exempt under this provision, an exemption may be available under one of the subsequent clauses.

4. Contractor provides services for up to 90 days in a financial year

There is no payroll tax on payments made under a contract under which services are provided to the person by the same contractor on no more than 90 days in total in a financial year.

NOTE: The 90 day rule does not apply in Western Australia and the Australian Capital Territory.

If the services provided exceed 90 days, the exemption vanishes for the whole financial year for that contractor.

In the Australian Capital Territory, if a contractor is employed through an employment agency the period is 8 days in a calendar month. Affected persons should contact the Australian Capital Territory SRO for more information.

The exemption does not apply elsewhere if:

- the contractor (whether an individual, a partnership or a company) provides similar services to the same person for more than 90 days under this and any other contract in that financial year, and
- the person/s doing the actual work has (have) performed similar work for the same person/firm on more than 90 days in the same financial year.

 A construction firm engages a plumber under contract in a period of high activity. If a contractor was engaged by the same construction firm for a 20 day period, and then either earlier or later in that same financial year that same contractor was engaged by the firm under another contract which ran for more than 70 days, payroll tax would be payable on both contracts.

If the contractor provides his/her services to the same person or firm for another period in the same financial year (maybe by way of a different entity, eg. another company or trust) the exclusion test would not be satisfied as it is a test based on the number of days on which services are provided by the person who actually performs the work.

Payments for casual labour on a short term basis are liable for payroll tax, and always have been. The above exclusion doesn't override that.

5. If contractor engages labour to do work or to help with it

Payments under contracts are exempt (except in the Australian Capital Territory) if one or more of these conditions are met:

- a corporation engages two or more persons to perform the actual work required under the contract, or a partnership of natural persons where the work is performed by one or more partners and also by one or more persons (not in partnership) or two or more persons none of whom is a partner, and
- a natural person engages one or more persons to perform the work under the contract.

The exemption is restricted to persons engaged to perform the work required under contract. Anyone engaged to perform administrative and accounting services for the contractor cannot be treated as persons engaged to perform the actual work under the contract.

6. If work is normally done for the public

The Commissioner can exclude payments if the contractor ordinarily performs services of that kind to the public generally in the same financial year. Evidence of actually being paid to perform such work within the year in question is required, or documented evidence of attempts to gain such work, such as copies of tender applications that were lodged by the contractor with multiple businesses.

ANTI-AVOIDANCE POWER OF THE COMMISSIONER

The Commissioner may disregard any arrangements and deem the payments made to a partnership, trust or company to be wages where the arrangement provides for a natural person to perform the services where the effect of the arrangement was to avoid or reduce payroll tax.

IF A CONTRACTOR: WHO IS LIABLE?

If a contract for labour is not excluded under any of the provisions above, it is a 'relevant contract' and payments to contractors will be taxable. The business receiving the services is the person taken to be the employer (the designated person).

PERSON TAKEN TO BE THE EMPLOYER

A person taken to be the employer is a person receiving services (or one who gives goods to another for re-supply).

PERSON TAKEN TO BE THE EMPLOYEE

A person taken to be the employee is a person who performs work for, or in relation to services which are supplied to another person, or any natural person (or company in South Australia) who re-supplies goods to the 'employer'.

NOTE: Western Australia does not have relevant contract legislation.

AMOUNTS TAKEN TO BE WAGES

Amounts taken to be wages are amounts paid or payable or benefit provided by a person taken to be an employer during a financial year in relation to services provided (or re-supply of goods) under a 'relevant contract'. These amounts include superannuation contributions and the value of any share or option.

In all States and Territories the taxable wages exclude any GST component attributable to the service provided.

EMPLOYMENT AGENCY ARRANGEMENTS AND CONTRACTS

An employment agency is taken to be the employer and will generally be liable for payroll tax on payments made to contractors and employees that it on-hires to end-users.

Wages paid under an employment agency contract include:

- any amount paid or payable to or in relation to the on-hired worker in respect of the provision of services under the employment agency contract
- the value of any fringe benefits provided to the on-hired worker, and
- any payment that would be a superannuation contribution if made in relation to the on-hired worker.

The exemptions under the contractor provisions do not apply to employment agency contracts.

However for payroll tax purposes where the worker is on-hired to an exempt employer, the employment agency is exempt on those wages, provided a declaration is obtained from the exempt clients. This exemption is not available in the Australian Capital Territory and Western Australia.

Note that for Western Australia, the payments made by the agent to the worker are wages for payroll tax purposes, but the worker is taken to be neither the employee of the agent nor the agent's client.

26.160 REDUCING 'AMOUNTS TAKEN TO BE WAGES'

In certain circumstances and industries, payroll tax will be charged on a net figure after deducting a prescribed amount.

Deductions apply if the contractor provides materials and equipment. The amount of the permitted reduction in 'wages' differs between the States. If a (sub) contractor supplies tools, any equipment and materials (not bought from the deemed employer) payroll tax is calculated using the following labour content percentages of the contractor payments. These deductions apply if materials and/or equipment are provided by the contractor and no specific exemptions (see from 26.130) apply.

In Victoria, New South Wales, South Australia, Queensland, Northern Territory and Tasmania, application can be made to the Commissioner if a contractor operates in a profession or trade not listed.

Contractor	Percentage of labour content*	Contractor	Percentage of labour content*
Architects	95%	Engineers	95%
Blind fitters	75%[3]	Fencing contractors	75%
Bricklayers	70%	Painters	85%[2,3]
Building supervisors[1]	75%	Plumbers	75%
Cabinetmakers/Kitchen fitters	70%[3]	Roof tilers	75%
Carpenters	75%	Tree fellers	75%
Carpet layers	75%	Wall and ceiling plasterers	80%
Computer programmers	95%	Wall and floor tilers	75%[3]
Draftspersons	95%	Vinyl layers	63%[3]
Electricians	75%[3]		

*Australian Capital Territory, New South Wales, Northern Territory, Queensland, South Australia, Tasmania, Victoria

1: Providing their own vehicles and visiting more than six sites per week.

2: A rate of 70% if the painter provides the paint

3: No general determination in South Australia.

NOTE: There is no general determination in Queensland.

26.200   APPRENTICE WAGES, REBATES AND GRANTS

26.210   QUEENSLAND

APPRENTICE/TRAINEE WAGES

Wages paid to apprentices and trainees (subject to certain conditions) are excluded from taxable wages for the duration of the apprenticeship or traineeship where the apprenticeship or traineeship is under the Further Education and Training Act 2014 (or before 30 June 2014, the *Vocational, Education, Training and Employment Act 2000*.

An incentive rebate for employers who employ apprentices and trainees will apply during the 2015-16, 2016-17 and 2017-18 financial years. If the apprentice or trainee wages are exempt from payroll tax, a rebate (4.75% of 25% of the exempt wages) is available to employers. The rebate amount is applied to reduce the payroll tax otherwise payable on the employer's taxable wages.

26.220   SOUTH AUSTRALIA

SMALL BUSINESS PAYROLL TAX REBATE

A two year payroll tax rebate payment is provided to eligible employers with a taxable Australian payroll of less than or equal to $1.2 million.

NOTE: As part of the 2015-16 State Budget, the Government announced that the South Australian Small Business Payroll Tax Rebate, introduced in the 2013-14 State Budget, will also be available in 2015-16. See PTASA002(v2).

26.230   TASMANIA

A payroll tax rebate (EISPR3) is available to employers for new positions created on or after 10 December 2012 and on or before 30 June 2014. To be eligible, new positions must be created between 10 December 2012 and 30 June 2014 and maintained until at least 30 June 2015. The rebate can be claimed from 1 July 2013 to 30 June 2015 for wages paid to eligible positions. Current payroll tax registrants have until 21 July 2014 to register for EISPR3.

A fact sheet detailing eligibility criteria and registration details can be obtained from www.sro. tas.gov.au

26.240   VICTORIA

From 1 January 2005 the only exemption provided is for wages paid by approved group training organisations to apprentices who are new entrants. The list of approved group training organisations is available on the Victoria SRO's website.

26.250   NEW SOUTH WALES

From 1 July 2008, there is an exemption for wages paid to an employee who is employed by a non profit organisation that is approved by the Department of Education and Training and in accordance with a group apprenticeship scheme or a group traineeship scheme also approved by the Department. A rebate scheme is available for all other employers for wages paid to apprentices and trainees as defined in the *Apprenticeship and Traineeship Act 2001*. An employer is not entitled to the rebate in respect of wages paid to a trainee who has been continuously employed by the employer for more than 3 months full time or 12 months casual or part-time immediately prior to commencing employment as a trainee.

26.260   WESTERN AUSTRALIA

Wages paid to apprentices (including trainees) under a training contract registered under the *Vocational Education and Training Act 1996*, Part 7, Division 2 are excluded from taxable wages and therefore exempt from payroll tax.

Section 40(2)(m) now ties a payroll tax exemption to 'an apprentice under a training contract registered...', so in order to qualify for exemption three criteria must now be met:

- the employee must be an apprentice, and
- there must be a training contract in place, and
- the contract must be registered.

Note that under the new provisions there is no mention made of 'trainee' or 'probationer'. However, 'apprentice' means a person who is named in a training contract as the person who will be trained under the contract whether the person is termed an apprentice, trainee, cadet, intern or some other term (Section 60A, Division 1 of Part 7 *Vocational Education and Training Act 1996*).

As a 'trainee' falls within the definition of 'apprentice', the exemption for trainees still applies.

A 'probationer' is no longer catered for by s40(2)(m) and is therefore no longer exempt.

In broad terms a 'training contract' is a training contract taken out between the employee and the employer. The contract must be registered with the Department of Training and Workforce Development. 'Training contract' is also defined in the *Vocational Education and Training Act*.

In order to qualify for a payroll tax exemption under s40(2)(m), the wages must be paid or payable:

- in relation to an 'apprentice' (as defined)
- who must be party to a contract signed between the employee/employer, and
- the contract is registered with the Department of Training and Workforce Development.

26.270   NORTHERN TERRITORY

From 1 July 2015, the only exemption provided is for wages paid to persons employed under the Community Development Employment Project.

26.280 AUSTRALIAN CAPITAL TERRITORY

A new starter employed for the first time in an industry or occupation, who is receiving eligible training that is approved training as described for the purposes of the *Training and Tertiary Education Act 2003* for work in that industry or occupation and commences training within the first 12 months of employment and continues with that training for no more than 12 months is exempt from payroll tax.

Approved Group Training Organisations are exempt from paying payroll tax on wages of trainees and apprentices for the full term of an approved training contract, which can be up to three or four years.

26.300 PAYROLL TAX RATES AND THRESHOLDS

Most employers do not pay wages outside their home State or Territory and are not grouped to other employers, so we print a scale of taxes, rather than a scale of rates. The scales take into account statutory deductions and any surcharge payable at the appropriate level of wages. In some States and Territories, the annual tax must be calculated over two separate periods. The unused deduction in one period is not transferable to the other period of the year. Do not use this section if wages are paid outside your State.

The following taxes have been computed to be based on gross wages (ie. without calculating the deduction) but only apply if:

- all wages are subject to payroll tax within the same State or Territory, and
- the employer is not linked with others (so that in this case the deduction would not be varied by rules in another jurisdiction).

NEW SOUTH WALES

28 Day Month: From 1 July 2013

Gross wages in the period	up to $57,534	Nil
	over $57,534	5.45%

30 Day Month: From 1 July 2013

Gross wages in the period	up to $61,644	Nil
	over $61,644	5.45%

31 Day Month: From 1 July 2013

Gross wages in the period	up to $63,699	Nil
	over $63,699	5.45%

Annual payroll tax: From 1 July 2013

Gross wages in the year	up to $750,000	Nil
	over $750,000	5.45%

WESTERN AUSTRALIA*

Monthly payroll tax: From 1 July 2012 to 30 June 2014

Gross wages in the month	up to $62,500	Nil
	$62,500 and over	5.5%

Annual payroll tax: From 1 July 2012 to 30 June 2014

Gross wages in the year	up to $750,000	Nil
	on excess over $750,000	5.5%

Monthly payroll tax: From 1 July 2014 to 30 June 2016

Gross wages in the month	up to $66,667	Nil
	$66,667 and over	5.5%

Annual payroll tax: From 1 July 2014 to 30 June 2016

Gross wages in the year	up to $800,000	Nil
	on excess over $800,000	5.5%

Monthly payroll tax: From 1 July 2016 onward

Gross wages in the month	up to $70,833	Nil
	$70,833 and over	5.5%

Annual payroll tax: From 1 July 2016 onward

Gross wages in the year	up to $850,000	Nil
	on excess over $850,000	5.5%

* In Western Australia, a diminishing payroll tax exemption threshold is expected to apply as of 1 July 2015. This is consistent with the approach taken by Queensland and the Northern Territory. The exemption threshold is $800,000 p.a. The benefit of the threshold will gradually phase out for employers or groups of employers with annual taxable wages in Australia between $800,000 and $7.5 million. Large businesses with taxable wages of $7.5 million or more will not receive any threshold and will be liable for payroll tax on their total taxable wages. Please note that this amendment has not yet received Royal Assent.

NORTHERN TERRITORY

Annual payroll tax: 2011-12 and 2012-13

	Tax rate	Exemption threshold*		Range for deduction	
		monthly	yearly	monthly	yearly
Gross wages in the year	5.5%	$125,000	$1,500,000	$125,000 to $625,000	$1,500,000 to $7,500,000

* From 1 July 2011, the exemption threshold was increased to $1,500,000. Similar to the method adopted by Queensland the exemption operates as a deduction from an employer's taxable wages where the deduction reduces by $1 for every $4 of taxable wages over the exemption threshold of $1,500,000. Thus, no deduction is available where taxable wages exceed $7,500,000.

TASMANIA

28 Day Month: From 1 July 2013

| Gross wages in the period | up to $95,890 | Nil |
| | over $95,890 | 6.1% |

30 Day Month: From 1 July 2013

| Gross wages in the period | up to $102,740 | Nil |
| | over $102,740 | 6.1% |

31 Day Month: From 1 July 2013

| Gross wages in the period | up to $106,164 | Nil |
| | over $106,164 | 6.1% |

Annual payroll tax: From 1 July 2013

| Gross wages in the year | up to $1,250,000 | Nil |
| | over $1,250,000 | 6.1% |

QUEENSLAND*

| Financial year | Tax rate | Exemption threshold* | | Range for deduction | |
		monthly	yearly	monthly	yearly
2012–13 to 2014-15	4.75%	$91,666	$1,100,000	$91,666 to $458,333	$1,100,000 to $5,500,000

* The current exemption threshold is $1,100,000. The deduction for payroll tax liability is based on the exemption threshold. The deduction reduces by $1 for every $4 of taxable wages over the exemption threshold of $1,100,000 and therefore no deduction is available where taxable wages exceed $5,500,000.

SOUTH AUSTRALIA

Monthly payroll tax: From 1 July 2012 and subsequent years

| Gross wages in the month | up to $50,000 | Nil |
| | over $50,000 | 4.95% |

Annual payroll tax: From 1 July 2012 and subsequent years

| Gross wages in the year | up to $600,000 | Nil |
| | over $600,000 | 4.95% |

AUSTRALIAN CAPITAL TERRITORY

Monthly payroll tax: From 1 July 2014 and subsequent years

| Gross wages in the month | up to $154,167 | Nil |
| | over $154,167 | 6.85% |

Annual payroll tax: From 1 July 2014 and subsequent years

| Gross wages in the year | up to $1,850,000 | Nil |
| | over $1,850,000 | 6.85% |

VICTORIA

Monthly payroll tax: From 1 July 2014 and subsequent years

| Gross wages in the month | up to $45,833 | Nil |
| | over $45,833 | 4.85% |

Annual payroll tax: From 1 July 2014 and subsequent years

| Gross wages in the year | up to $550,000 | Nil |
| | over $550,000: On excess over $550,000 | 4.85% |

26.345 DEDUCTION FOR INTERSTATE EMPLOYERS

If an employer pays wages in more than one State or Territory, the deduction for each jurisdiction is diminished on a pro rata basis. As the payroll tax thresholds differ from State to State and Territory, the total deduction allowed may not add up to the normal deduction provided in the home State or Territory.

For monthly returns, the deduction in each State or Territory is diminished according to the anticipated annual level of 'wages' paid throughout Australia. Any discrepancy is adjusted in the annual reconciliation returns (in the Australian Capital Territory a statement of wages) when the final figures are known. In South Australia any discrepancy is adjusted on lodgment of the annual return when the final figures are known. The deduction allowed on an annual basis in each State/Territory is:

(Wages in the State or Territory in which the return is lodged) divided by (Total wages paid in Australia) multiplied by (Threshold in that State or Territory)

In Queensland, a variation of the above formula is used. Once the annual wages exceed the exemption threshold of $1,100,000, the maximum deduction allowed of $1,100,000 reduces by $1 for every $4 of wages over the exemption threshold. When taxable wages are more than $5,500,000, the deduction will be $0.00.

Similarly, in the Northern Territory, once the annual wages exceed the threshold of $1,500,000, the maximum deduction allowed of $1,500,000 reduces by $1 for every $4 of wages over the threshold. When taxable wages are more than $7.5M, the deduction will be $0.00.

GROUP EMPLOYER'S RETURNS

Employers which form a group must register and lodge separate returns in Western Australia and Queensland. In the Northern Territory, Tasmania and the Australian Capital Territory an approved designated group employer may lodge returns on behalf of group members.

In South Australia, employers in a group must register and lodge separate returns, however, an approved designated group employer, with the Commissioner's approval can lodge a joint return on behalf of the group.

Generally, a deduction (based on the group wages) available in the Territory or State is allowed only to the designated group employer. The deduction allowed on an annual basis in each State/Territory is calculated as:

(Wages in the State or Territory of the group in which the return is lodged) divided by (total wages of the group paid in Australia) multiplied by (threshold in that State or Territory)

3 STEP FORMULA

Step 1: $\dfrac{\text{State wages}}{\text{Total Australian wages}}$ x State Payroll Tax threshold = State threshold entitlement

Step 2: State wages – State threshold entitlement = State taxable wages

Step 3: State taxable wages x Payroll Tax rate % = State Payroll Tax liability

Step 1: $\dfrac{\$1,000,000 \ (Vic \ wages)}{\$2,000,000 \ (Total \ Aust \ wages)}$ *x $550,000 (Vic Payroll Tax threshold)*

            = $275,000 (Vic threshold entitlement)

Step 2: *$1,000,000 (Vic wages) – $275,000 (Vic threshold entitlement)*
            = $725,000 (Vic taxable wages)

Step 3: *$725,000 (Vic taxable wages) x 4.85% (Payroll Tax rate from 1 July 2014)*
            = $35,162.50 (Vic Payroll Tax liability)

That calculation is done for each State and Territory to find the threshold entitlement available to the designated group employer.

In Queensland, a variation of the above formula is used. Once the annual wages exceed the exemption threshold of $1,100,000, the maximum deduction allowed of $1,100,000 reduces by $1 for every $4 of wages over the exemption threshold. When taxable wages are more than $5,500,000, the deduction will be $0.00.

Similarly, in the Northern Territory, once the annual wages exceed the threshold of $1,500,000, the maximum deduction allowed of $1,500,000 reduces by $1 for every $4 of wages over the threshold. When taxable wages are more than $7,500,000, the deduction will be $0.00.

In Western Australia, once the annual wages exceed $800,000, the maximum deduction of $800,000 gradually reduces based on the following calculation:

(Annual threshold amount – [(total Australian taxable wages – annual threshold amount) x tapering value)] x (total WA taxable wages / total Australian taxable wages)

The tapering value for the 2015-16 financial year is 8/67.

26.350 SUMMARY OF PAYMENTS LIABLE FOR PAYROLL TAX

Y – Yes, N – No, C – depends on circumstances (see the following page). F – Yes, but taxability is determined according to FBT rules (see from 25.000). Also refer to notes on following pages.

Type of payment	NSW	Vic	Qld	SA	WA	Tas	NT	ACT	See note
Accident pay	Y	Y	Y	Y	Y	Y	Y	Y	1
Allowances: general	Y	Y	Y	Y	Y	Y	Y	Y	2
Allowances: aldermen/councillors	N	N	N	N	N	Y	N	N	2
Back pay	Y	Y	Y	Y	Y	Y	Y	Y	–
Bonuses	Y	Y	Y	Y	Y	Y	Y	Y	–
Commissions	Y	Y	Y	Y	Y	Y	Y	Y	3
Compensation: sickness	Y	Y	Y	Y	Y	Y	Y	Y	4
Compensation State Compensation	N	N	N	N	N	N	N	N	4
Defence Force payments	N	N	N	N	N	N	N	N	5
Directors' fees	Y	Y	Y	Y	Y	Y	Y	Y	6
Discounts on staff purchases	F	F	F	F	F	F	F	F	7
Dividends	N	N	N	N	N	N	N	N	–
Employee share options	Y	Y	Y	Y	Y	Y	Y	Y	8
Fringe benefits	Y	Y	Y	Y	Y	Y	Y	Y	17
Gifts as business expense	F	F	F	F	F	F	F	Y	9
Holiday pay: continuing service	Y	Y	Y	Y	Y	Y	Y	Y	10
Holiday pay: on termination	Y	Y	Y	Y	Y	Y	Y	Y	10
Holidays for employees: free or subsidised	F	F	F	F	F	F	F	F	11
Housing	F	F	F	F	F	F	F	F	12
Low interest loans	F	F	F	F	F	F	F	F	13
Long service leave: continuing service	Y	Y	Y	Y	Y	Y	Y	Y	14
Long service leave: on termination	Y	Y	Y	Y	Y	Y	Y	Y	14
Maternity/paternity & adoption leave	C	C	C	C	C	C	C	C	15
Meals and sustenance	F	F	F	F	F	F	F	F	16
Motor car: work-related	F	F	F	F	F	F	F	F	19
Motor car: personal use	F	F	F	F	F	F	F	F	17
Overtime	Y	Y	Y	Y	Y	Y	Y	Y	–
Paid Parental Leave	N	N	N	N	N	N	N	N	18
Payments and benefits for employees	F	F	F	F	F	F	F	F	19
Payments to contractors	C	C	C	C	C	C	C	C	20
Pensions	N	N	N	N	N	N	N	N	–
Piece work payments	Y	Y	Y	Y	Y	Y	Y	Y	–
Prizes	F	F	F	F	F	F	F	F	21
Professional advice	F	F	F	F	F	F	F	F	22
Reimbursements of work expenses	N	N	C	N	N	N	N	N	28
Relocation expenses	F	F	F	F	F	F	F	F	23
Salaries	Y	Y	Y	Y	Y	Y	Y	Y	–
Sick pay	Y	Y	Y	Y	Y	Y	Y	Y	10

Type of payment	NSW	Vic	Qld	SA	WA	Tas	NT	ACT	See note
Study expenses	F	F	F	F	F	F	F	F	25
Superannuation	Y	Y	Y	Y	Y	Y	Y	Y	26
Termination payments	C	C	C	C	C	C	C	C	24
Trust distributions	N	N	N	N	N	N	N	N	29

NOTE: For remote area FBT exemptions see explanatory note 27.

EXPLANATORY NOTES: PAYMENTS LIABLE FOR PAYROLL TAX

On a State by State basis, further information on the potential liability of some payments made to employees or benefits provided to them is outlined below.

1. Accident/sickness pay

Payments made to an employee off work for sickness or injury following an accident are liable to payroll tax unless the payments are made under the provisions of a relevant WorkCover or Workers Compensation Act. If an employer pays 'make-up pay' (ie. difference between employee's regular salary and compensation payments), it is liable to payroll tax.

In Queensland, wages paid by employer for the day of injury are taxable.

2. Allowances

Allowances are generally liable to payroll tax in all States and Territories, although any exact reimbursements to employees for expenses incurred on behalf of employers are not liable for payroll tax anywhere (unless subject to FBT). A clear distinction must be drawn between:

- allowances (liable)
- reimbursements of business expenses incurred (not liable), and
- advances to an employee, such as a petty cash advance (not liable).

The amount is not an allowance if the employee incurs the cost on behalf of the employer (ie. the costs are not for the private expenditure of the employee).

In Western Australia, the FBT elements of living away from home allowances are subject to payroll tax but reasonable motor vehicle and accommodation allowances are exempted. The accommodation allowance exemption refers to the 'lowest salary band/lowest capital city.' rate that is updated annually by the Tax Office.

In Victoria and South Australia, a living away from home allowance is a fringe benefit and the value to be declared for payroll tax purposes is the value determined in accordance with the FBT Act. If the allowance does not qualify as a living away from home allowance under the FBT Act, it will be treated in the same manner as an overnight accommodation allowance.

Travel or accommodation allowances paid to employees in Tasmania, South Australia, Queensland, New South Wales, Victoria, Northern Territory and Western Australia are not liable to payroll tax if within prescribed limits (see below). Where the employer pays the accommodation component, meals and incidental allowances paid to employees are exempt from payroll tax where paid to an amount up to the Tax Office substantiation rate per day.

In all States and Territories the following rates apply:

- Motor vehicle allowance rate per kilometre: 77c (from 1 July 2014)
- Accommodation allowance rate per night*: $253.25

*Applies for the 2014-15 financial year and will be tied to relevant Tax Office rates.

NOTE: Allowances paid to elected aldermen or city councillors, or other voluntary workers or members of an association are not liable to payroll tax as they are not paid to an 'employee'.

In Tasmania the allowances are liable to payroll tax where the persons are members of the governing body of a council which is a body corporate.

3. Commissions

Commissions paid to any insurance or time-payment canvasser or collector are liable to payroll tax. Payroll tax is payable on commissions of insurance agents only if they operate on a door-to-door basis to collect premiums and canvass new business. That was confirmed in *General Accident Fire and Life Assurance Corporation Ltd v Comm. of Payroll Tax* (NSW) 82 ATC 4077.

In Victoria, South Australia, New South Wales, Queensland and Tasmania, commissions paid to contractors who are life insurance agents, and door to door sellers (selling goods for domestic purposes) are exempt.

Commissions paid to an employee (where an employer/employee relationship exists) are taxable.

4. Compensation payments

Payments of wages made to sick or injured workers are wages under all State Acts, but payments of compensation (including compulsory excess) under WorkCover or Workers Compensation Act are not subject to payroll tax. If an employer pays 'make-up pay' (ie. difference between employee's regular salary and compensation payments), it is liable to payroll tax.

In Queensland, wages paid by employer for the day of injury are taxable.

5. Defence Force payments

Payments are exempt from payroll tax if made by an employer to an employee's pay while absent from employment to perform defence force activities. This includes make-up pay.

6. Directors' fees and allowances

Directors' fees (whether executive or non-executive directors) being remuneration are liable for payroll tax. Benefits provided to directors that are subject to FBT are also liable to payroll tax.

In Queensland, some allowances and benefits provided to non-working directors may be liable to payroll tax.

Payroll tax is payable if such allowances are paid or benefits provided to working directors.

In New South Wales, Victoria, Queensland, South Australia and the Northern Territory indirect payments made to company directors, and members of the governing body of a company, are wages for payroll tax purposes. This includes payments made to a director's personal company or superannuation fund.

7. Discounted staff purchases

All States and Territories include the FBT taxable value of discounted staff benefits (see from 25.860) and include the grossed-up value of fringe benefits provided to employees (and their associates) in determining 'wages' for payroll tax purposes.

8. Employee share plans or options

The issue of company shares to employees, if taxable as a fringe benefit, is liable for payroll tax in South Australia and Western Australia.

The granting of shares or options to an employee is subject to payroll tax nationwide.

Employers in Western Australia are able to elect the day of liability for payroll tax between the grant date and the vesting day. Provisions are included to allow for a refund of payroll tax paid on a grant on shares or options that do not vest in an employee, except when the employee has chosen not to take up the shares.

In New South Wales and Victoria, the grant of a share or option to an employee, a director (including for the appointment of a director), or deemed employee that is an ESS interest (as defined in the ITAA97) constitutes wages. An ESS interest is defined as shares or options in the employer company or its parent company.

Such wages are taken to be paid or payable on the relevant day, which is the day on which a share or option is granted to the employee or the date it vests with them. Employers can choose to declare the taxable value when shares or options are granted or when the share vests with the employee or director. Shares or options are taken to vest at the end of seven years after the grant of the share or option, if vesting has not occurred before that date.

The taxable value of the share or option is the market value on the relevant day, less the consideration (if any) paid or given by the employee for the grant of the share or option (other than consideration in the form of services performed or rendered). All other shares and options will be taxable as fringe benefits, which means the grossing up provisions apply for the purpose of determining their taxable value.

In Queensland, the value of the share or option is the market value or the amount worked out under s83A-315 *Income Tax Assessment Act 1997*.

9. Gifts to employees

A gift will generally be liable for payroll tax if it is made to the person in his or her capacity as an employee and the employer treats the cost as a business expense.

In Victoria, a gift will be taxable if it has a taxable value for FBT purposes.

10. Holiday pay

Payments of annual leave and sick pay are subject to payroll tax where it is received by an employee continuing in service with the employer. Where accrued annual leave or sick pay is paid on ceasing employment, it is subject to payroll tax if it represents a reward for service that existed before the employment ceased. Holiday pay is taxable on a monthly basis based on the jurisdiction in which the last services were performed.

In NSW all accrued annual leave will be liable on ceasing employment. Accrued sick leave is also subject to payroll tax to the extent it forms part of an employment termination payment.

Victoria, Queensland, South Australia, Tasmania and Western Australia include all leave on termination of employment as wages for payroll tax purposes.

11. Holidays: Free or subsidised

The cost to the employer is subject to payroll tax in all States and Territories; the taxable value is the taxable value for FBT purposes and the grossed-up value of fringe benefits provided to employees (and their associates) is included in determining 'wages' for payroll tax purposes.

The Northern Territory, Victoria, New South Wales, Queensland, Tasmania and the Australian Capital Territory apply the Type 2 gross-up rate to both Type 1 and Type 2 benefits. In South Australia, only the lower gross-up factor (Type 2) under the FBT legislation is used. In Western Australia, only the Type 2 factor is used.

12. Housing

Employee housing is generally caught for payroll tax. All States and Territories include the FBT value of those benefits. If remote area housing, exempt in all states other than Queensland where it is taxable. In Queensland, this is calculated using the lower Type 2 FBT gross-up factor.

13. Low interest loans

In all States and Territories, payroll tax is payable on the benefit to an employee of a low interest loan if provided in relation to employment, and has a taxable value as calculated under the FBTAA for FBT purposes (see 25.450).

All states will exempt a benefit that was exempt under the 100% 'otherwise' deductible rule.

In Queensland, this is calculated using the lower Type 2 FBT gross-up factor.

14. Long service leave

Long service leave is subject to payroll tax where received by an employee continuing in service with the employer. Where long service leave is paid on ceasing employment, it is subject to payroll tax if it represents a reward for service that existed before the employment ceased. If an employee travels overseas and is paid overseas their wages are taxable in the last jurisdiction in which they provided services in Australia.

15. Maternity and adoption leave

Wages paid to an employee (but not normal leave entitlements) as maternity or adoption leave is exempt from payroll tax nationwide. The exemption is limited to a maximum of 14 weeks (or equivalent if paid as a lump sum) and can be pro-rated for full-time employees who take leave for more than 14 weeks at less than full pay, and in Victoria for part-time employees who take leave for a period of more than 14 weeks at a reduced rate of pay. The exemption does not apply to wages that are fringe benefits or to paid annual leave, long service leave or similar leave. In New South Wales the exemption also applies to paternity leave.

In Queensland wages paid or payable to employees on parental or adoption leave are exempt from payroll tax, limited to a maximum of 14 weeks pay and does not include paid leave and fringe benefits. Surrogacy leave is also exempt from payroll tax for a maximum equivalent of 14 weeks pay.

16. Meals and sustenance

The grossed up FBT value of meals and sustenance is to be included (to the extent it is taxed under the FBTAA) for all States and Territories. As noted earlier, South Australia, Queensland, Tasmania, Victoria, New South Wales and the Northern Territory will only use the lower gross-up factor (Type 2) under the FBT legislation.

17. Motor vehicles

In all States and Territories, payroll tax liability for a vehicle provided for personal use of an employee (or 'associate' of the employee) is based on the amount calculated for FBT purposes (see 25.200).

18. Paid parental leave (PPL) payments

PPL payments are Commonwealth Government payments that employers pay on behalf of the Commonwealth Government. They do not constitute wages and are not taxable as they are not paid by the employer in respect of services provided by the employee (or in anticipation of future services to be provided by the employee).

19. Payments made by employer on behalf of an employee

All States and Territories include FBT taxable value of those benefits (see 25.500) in determining the payroll tax liability. In all States and Territories the grossed-up value of fringe benefits provided to employees (and their associates) is included to determine 'wages' for payroll tax purposes.

The Northern Territory, the Australian Capital Territory, South Australia, Queensland, Tasmania, Victoria and New South Wales apply the Type 2 gross-up rate to both Type 1 and Type 2 benefits. Examples of payments liable for payroll tax include:

- Health insurance: Fund membership dues, or other payments relating to the medical and/or health costs of the employees and their families.
- School fees: Fees and related costs paid on behalf of an employee including those paid by a scholarship trust set up by an employer.
- Life assurance premiums: Premiums an employer pays on life assurance policies in which the employee (or family members) have a beneficial interest.
- Subscriptions to clubs and associations: Liable for payroll tax if not 'otherwise deductible'.
- Home telephone expenses.

20. Payments to contractors

Victoria, New South Wales, South Australia, Tasmania, the Australian Capital Territory, Queensland and the Northern Territory have each extended their definition of 'wages' to include payments to some contractors. Full details are given at 26.100. Payments to contractors are liable wages when the contract is liable as a relevant contract. If an employer-employee relationship exists between the parties the contractor provisions and their exclusions do not apply.

21. Prizes

The grossed-up value of these benefits (using the Type 2 gross-up factor) for FBT purposes is included for payroll tax purposes. In Queensland, this is calculated using the lower Type 2 FBT gross-up factor.

22. Professional advice

The FBT grossed-up value of this benefit must be included. Generally this is calculated using the lower Type 2 FBT gross up factor.

23. Relocation expenses

If amounts paid or reimbursed to the employee are subject to FBT, the value of those amounts is included for payroll tax purposes. If the benefit is FBT exempt (eg. relocation consultants from 1 April 2006) it is exempt. Allowances paid to employees are subject to payroll tax throughout Australia, with no offset allowed for costs incurred.

24. Termination payments

Except in South Australia and Queensland, payments of superannuation and golden handshakes to ex-employees are not taxable provided the payment is made after termination of employment and does not include accrued benefits. Unused sick leave is not taxable on termination.

In Victoria, NSW, Western Australia, Tasmania, South Australia, Queensland and the Northern Territory the following are included on termination of employment as wages for payroll tax purposes:

- all accrued annual leave and long service leave (see also 11.260 and 11.270)
- all employment termination payments (ETP) (see 11.210) (except bona fide redundancy payments ie. 'lump sum D' amounts)
- the excess amount above the bona fide redundancy and early retirement scheme thresholds (see 11.240).

Any termination payment which represents a reward for service that existed before ceasing employment is subject to payroll tax.

Employment termination payments, previously known as eligible termination payments, contain payments in lieu of notice, severance pay, redundancy payments, paid out unused sick leave and compensation for loss on income. The value of an ETP for payroll tax purposes is that part of an ETP payment that would be included in the assessable income of that employee (or a person taken by this Act to be an employee) if the whole of the ETP had been paid to the employee or deemed employee.

Persons taken to be employees include directors, members of a corporation governing body and contractors whose payments are taken to be wages under the Act.

The value of paid out annual and long service leave is liable irrespective of when it was accrued. Payroll tax is payable in all States and Territories on the taxable value of any Australian ETP paid as a consequence of the retirement or termination of any office or employment (see 11.210 and 11.220).

25. Study expenses

Include the FBT value of study expenses for all States and Territories. Generally this is calculated using the lower Type 2 FBT gross-up factor.

26. Superannuation contributions

Superannuation contributions made by an employer for the benefit of an employee (or by a company for a director of the company) to a retirement savings account within the meaning of the *RSA Act 1997*, the Superannuation Holding Accounts Special Account (SHASA) or any other form of superannuation fund or scheme) are included as wages for payroll tax purposes.

27. Remote area FBT exemptions

The FBT Act provides exemptions or concessional treatment for fly in/fly out transport and accommodation, residential fuel and holiday transport for employees in remote areas. For Western Australian payroll tax purposes, fly in/fly out arrangements are not included as wages. In addition, a full exemption is provided for residential fuel, housing assistance, domestic water, holiday transport (limited to return economy airfare to the capital city of the workplace if the employee does not travel to their home town), and education costs (limited to education expenses for a dependant required to live away from home on a full-time basis and the place of education is not within a reasonable distance of the remote place of employment.

28. Reimbursements

If in the course of work an employee incurs an expense and is reimbursed for that expense against receipts, the payment is not salary or wages. Employers must be able to account for the payments either as an advance which is later adjusted against receipts or payments against receipts. Payments, which have no documentation (eg. meal allowances) are not accepted as reimbursements. In Queensland, reimbursements are taxable if they are subject to FBT.

29. Trust distributions

Trust distributions in all States and Territories are not liable to payroll tax (but may be liable in South Australia and Queensland if it can be shown it is for the provision of services). See 26.010.

NEED MORE INFORMATION ON PAYROLL TAX MATTERS?

Each State Revenue Office has a website where more in-depth information can be obtained including rates and thresholds, forms and circulars and public rulings.

SRO	Website	Email	Phone
VIC	www.sro.vic.gov.au	sro@sro.vic.gov.au	13 21 61
NSW	www.osr.nsw.gov.au	payrolltax@osr.nsw.gov.au	1300 139 815
		prtnewclient@osr.nsw.gov.au	(02) 9761 9366
QLD	www.osr.qld.gov.au	payrolltax@osr.qld.gov.au	1300 300 734
SA	www.revenuesa.sa.gov.au	payrolltax@sa.gov.au	(08) 8204 9880
WA	www.finance.wa.gov.au	www.osr.wa.gov.au/PayrollEnquiry	(08) 9262 1300
TAS	www.sro.tas.gov.au	taxhelp@treasury.tas.gov.au	(03) 6166 4400
ACT	www.revenue.act.gov.au		(02) 6207 0028
NT	www.revenue.nt.gov.au	ntrevenue@nt.gov.au	1300 305 353

Land tax

27

Note: No land tax in Northern Territory

27.100 ACT LAND TAX

Web: www.revenue.act.gov.au   Telephone: 02 6207 0047

Land tax is imposed under the *Land Tax Act 2004*. The marginal rates used to calculate land tax are determined under the *Taxation Administration Act 1999*.

LIABILITY

An applicable land owner is subject to land tax on 'rateable land'. An owner for land tax purposes in the ACT is generally the registered proprietor that has been granted a long term lease by the Territory or the Commonwealth. The liability to land tax is generally imposed under s9 *Land Tax Act 2004*. Land tax is no longer levied on Commercial properties (this commenced 1 July 2012). A liability for land tax is imposed for a quarter on rateable land. Subject to some exceptions, 'rateable land' that triggers a liability is comprised of two main types of land:

- rented residential land, or
- residential land owned by a corporate trustee (whether it is rented or not).

If a landowner, other than the Commonwealth or Territory, has an interest in residential property that is rented, they are liable for land tax on that property. This also applies to boarding houses and multiple dwellings, including dual occupancies and granny flats that are rented. Rent can include cash, services or any other valuable consideration earned in respect of a property for which any form of tenancy arrangement exists.

ASSESSMENT OF TAX

The assessment of the land to determine land tax occurs on 1 July, 1 October, 1 January and 1 April of the relevant year. From 1 July 2014, land tax for a particular quarter is based on a fixed charge and marginal rate that is applied to a three year average unimproved land value using the formula:

$$\frac{(Fixed\ charge\ x\ (determined\ rate\ x\ average\ unimproved\ value)\ x\ number\ of\ days\ in\ quarter)}{Days\ in\ year}$$

Average unimproved value (defined in *Rates Act 2004*) has the following three meanings:

- On a parcel of land not previously classified as 'rateable land' the unimproved value of the land,
- On a parcel of land classified as 'rateable land' for less than three years, the average unimproved value over those years, and
- On a parcel of land that has been 'rateable land' for longer than three years, the average unimproved value over the previous three years.

Determined rate (defined in s139 *Taxation Administration Act 1999*) is a marginal rate that is reproduced below:

DETERMINED RATES OF TAX FROM 1 JULY 2014

Average unimproved value	Tax rate/Charge
Residential land	
Fixed charge	$945.00
$1 - $75,000	0.41%
$75,001 - $150,000	0.48%
$150,001 - $275,000	0.61%
$275,001 and over	1.23%

NOTE: At the time of writing the 'Determined rate' of land tax had not been changed from the previous year. Readers should check the relevant 'disallowable instruments' published on the ACT Revenue Office website to verify the rates have not been amended.

LATE PAYMENTS

The penalty interest is currently 10.75% pa and is charged and compounds on a monthly basis on any amount that remains unpaid by the due date.

Compounding interest charges, which may be subject to change during the year, are calculated and imposed on unpaid amounts on the 16th of each month.

PENALTIES

The *Land Tax Act 2004* requires taxpayers to advise the Commissioner for ACT Revenue within 30 days of any changes in circumstances that may render any such property liable for land tax. Penalties as high as 90% may be imposed on property owners for failing to provide required information or for providing false or misleading information.

NOTE: Any information regarding land tax liability must be notified in writing.

EXEMPTIONS

There are several exemptions from land tax in the ACT that apply:

- Residential land used as a retirement village, nursing home, or owned by a religious institution is exempt from land tax. Other exemptions from land tax include land used for rural purposes, broad-acre subdivision, residential land owned by a trustee under a will of a deceased person and occupied by a life tenant, and residential land owned by a not-for-profit housing corporation.
- Exemption from land tax on residential land owned by a building or land development corporation can apply for two years from the first quarter after the date of ownership if used to construct new residential premises that are to be sold when finished.
- An exemption on compassionate grounds may be available for up to one year on a residential property that is rented where the Commissioner for ACT Revenue is satisfied that the owner (a natural person) is temporarily absent because of a compelling compassionate reason.

27.200 VICTORIAN LAND TAX

Web: www.sro.vic.gov.au   Email: sro@sro.vic.gov.au   Telephone: 13 21 61

LIABILITY

Land tax is an annual tax levied on the owners of land in Victoria as at midnight on 31 December of the year preceding the year of assessment (ie. 2015 assessment is based on land holdings at 31 December 2014). The general threshold is $250,000.

The Principal Place of Residence (PPR) is exempt from land tax if it is owned and occupied by natural persons. The PPR exemption is also available for land owned by certain trustees (eligible trustee) where a vested beneficiary of the trust uses the land as their PPR.

TRUST SURCHARGE

For land held in trusts, the threshold is $25,000 (excluding exempt land) and a surcharge applies. The surcharge applies to the Victorian landholding of trusts with a total taxable value between $25,000 and $3 million. It is 0.375% for landholdings between $25,000 and $1.8 million and tapers away between $1.8 million and $3 million. Landholdings valued above $3 million are not affected by the surcharge.

The SRO has been proactive in requesting confirmation of properties that may be held on trust, and offering reduction on penalties for non-disclosure errors or omissions.

LAND HELD BEFORE 31 DECEMBER 2005

A trustee that holds non-exempt land purchased before 31 December 2005 will not be required to pay the surcharge if they have nominated a beneficiary (in the case of a discretionary trust) or have notified of the respective unit holders or beneficiaries (for unit trusts and fixed trusts) before the specified time allowed under the legislation.

FIXED AND UNIT TRUSTS WITH LAND HELD AFTER 1 JANUARY 2006

Trustees of unit trusts or fixed trusts which only hold post-2006 land (ie. land acquired after 1 January 2006), can notify the State Revenue Office (SRO) of unit holders or beneficiaries of the trust. The trustee will be assessed at the general land tax rates and the beneficiary will also be assessed on the trust lands together with any other lands owned at the general land tax rates subject to a deduction for the tax payable by the trustee. The notification will take effect for the tax year following the year in which the notice was lodged.

DISCRETIONARY TRUSTS WITH LAND HELD AFTER 1 JANUARY 2006

The trustee of a discretionary trust (where trustee holds discretion regarding distribution) which acquires land after 31 December 2005 (post-2006 land) will be taxed on that land at the trust surcharge rate, unless there is a nominated principal place of residence beneficiary for a particular land.

NOMINATION OF PRINCIPAL PLACE OF RESIDENCE (PPR) BENEFICIARY

Trustees of discretionary or unit trusts may nominate a PPR beneficiary so that a trust land is not subject to the surcharge and is assessed on a single landholding basis if the land is used by the nominated PPR beneficiary (provided a substantial business activity is not being conducted on the land). There can only be 1 PPR beneficiary for each trust.

NOTE: The trustee of a unit trust can either lodge a notification of unit holders or a nomination of a PPR beneficiary but not both. The trustee of a discretionary or unit trust is not liable for the surcharge on trust land occupied by a nominated beneficiary as his/her PPR.

EXEMPTION FROM THE SURCHARGE

The surcharge does not apply to land that is exempt under the existing provisions and land that is held for an excluded trust or an administration trust (where the testator died on or after 12 December 2007). In these situations the trustee is assessed at the general land tax rates.

A trust may qualify as an excluded trust if it is:

- a charitable trust
- a concessional trust
- a public unit trust scheme
- a wholesale unit trust scheme
- a trust for a club
- a trust established by a will where the testator died before 12 December 2007, or
- a superannuation trust.

An administration trust is a trust under which the assets of a deceased person are held by a personal representative for a specified period, which is the earlier of the date that the administration of the estate is completed or three years from the death of the testator (or a longer period approved by the Commissioner). This definition applies where the testator died on or after 12 December 2007.

The personal representative of a deceased estate that has land in Victoria must lodge a written notice with the SRO within one month after the administration of the estate commences or is completed. Failure to lodge a notice may lead to the trustee being liable to pay penalty tax.

If land which is held in a trust is exempt from land tax under the Act (eg. land used for primary production) the land will remain exempt and will not be included for the calculation of the land tax liability of the trust.

IMPLIED OR CONSTRUCTIVE TRUST

Land owned by a trustee of an implied or constructive trust is separately assessed at general rates as if the land were the only land owned by the trustee. Where the trustee holds land for more than one implied or constructive trusts for the same beneficiary or beneficiaries, the lands held for those trusts are assessed on a aggregated land holding basis.

OWNER OF LAND

The owner of land as at midnight on 31 December of the year preceding the year of assessment is liable for land tax if his/her total landholdings exceed the applicable threshold. For example, for the 2015 assessment year, ownership is determined as at midnight on 31 December 2014. An owner includes:

- a person who holds the freehold title to land
- a person who leases Crown land either directly from the Crown or indirectly via a Committee of Management such as a statutory body
- a person deemed to be the owner because he or she is in possession of the land. This includes a right to occupy the land and a right to income and profits derived from the land
- a person deemed to be the owner because he or she is nominated as a beneficiary or notified unit holder of certain trusts
- a person who occupies land subject to a life estate, and
- certain licensees of Crown land whether the land is licensed directly from the Crown or indirectly via a Committee of Management such as a statutory body.

Every person who acquires land in Victoria must lodge a Notice of Acquisition with Land Victoria, together with the Transfer of Land document and Certificate of Title. The information contained in the notice of acquisition is used to update details of ownership for land tax purposes.

Where land is transferred without valuable consideration (eg. gifted) but the transfer remains unregistered, the transferee is deemed to be the owner if the Commissioner is satisfied that the transfer was made in good faith and the transferee has taken possession of the land on or before 31 December in the year preceding the tax year.

NOTE: In a land sale, if a minimum payment of 15% of the purchase price is paid and possession has been given under the contract of sale, the purchaser is deemed to be the owner of the land.

Where a contract for the sale of land does not meet these requirements, the vendor will remain the owner of the land. Documentary evidence may be requested in certain cases including transfer of land forms, contracts of sale and bank statements.

TAXABLE VALUE OF LAND

The taxable value of land which is used for land tax purposes is the site value or unimproved value of the land.

Site valuations are generally carried out by the Municipal Council but may in some cases be carried out by the Valuer-General. Councils conduct general valuations every two years. Valuations for the 2015 and 2016 years are based on the 2014 municipal general valuation. Where a municipal valuation has not been made for a property, a valuation is obtained from the Valuer-General.

CALCULATION AND ASSESSMENT OF LAND TAX

The actual amount of land tax payable is calculated by selecting the appropriate land tax rate from the scale of rates (see *Rates of Tax* table below) and applying this to the total taxable value of land, excluding any exempt land. Lands owned by a trustee subject to the trust surcharge are assessed at the appropriate surcharge rate (see *Surcharge Rates* table below).

The assessment must be paid by the due date shown on the assessment. Taxpayers may elect to pay the tax in four equal instalments over 37 weeks.

OBJECTIONS TO ASSESSMENTS

Objections to assessments must be lodged in writing within 60 days of the date after service of the assessment. The grounds for the objection must be stated in full and in detail.

OBJECTIONS TO VALUATIONS

Taxpayers are able to object to their land valuation either on receipt of their municipal rates notice or receipt of their land tax assessments. To object to the site values shown on a rate notice, taxpayers need to contact the relevant municipal council. To object to the site values shown on a land tax assessment notice, taxpayers should lodge their objections with the State Revenue Office (SRO). For a taxpayer to object to a valuation used in the assessment, the objection must be lodged within two months after service of the assessment. However, if an objection has been previously lodged with the rating authority for the same valuation, a further objection cannot be made within 12 months of that objection.

Where the Valuer-General has made a valuation for an item of land, taxpayers may lodge an objection with the Commissioner. Taxpayers have 60 days from the date of service of the land tax assessment notice to lodge an objection.

PENALTY TAX

Taxpayers are required to notify the SRO of certain errors and omissions in their assessment. Notification to the SRO is required within 60 days from the date the assessment was issued if:

- any additional land owned has not been included in the assessment
- any additional land jointly owned by two or more owners had not been included in the joint assessment, or
- an exemption is received for which the land is not eligible.

Failure to notify the SRO of these errors and omissions may lead to a penalty tax.

Trustees are required to lodge a notice with the SRO within one month of acquiring trust land, disposing trust land, change in the type of trust, change in beneficial interest in a fixed trust or change in the unit holdings in a unit trust. Failure to lodge a notice may lead to the trustee being liable to pay a penalty tax.

RELATED CORPORATIONS

All land owned by related corporations, is aggregated and assessed as if owned by a single corporation.

A corporation is related to another corporation if:

- that corporation holds more than 50% of its issued share capital, or controls the composition of its board of directors, or effectively controls more than 50% of its voting rights. The term 'issued share capital' excludes shares held under the terms of any debenture, shares carrying no right to participate beyond a specified amount of profit or capital and shares held by money lenders and held as a security over a transaction entered into
- a person (or persons) has a controlling interest in each corporation (ie. if the person holds more than 50% of its issued capital or controls the composition of its board of directors, or effectively controls more than 50% of its voting rights, or a combination thereof), or
- the first corporation and its shareholders together own more than 50% of the second corporation's issued capital. (This only applies if the portion of issued share capital of the second corporation held by the shareholders of the first corporation is greater than the difference between 50% and the proportion of the issued share capital of the first corporation held by the second corporation.)

The assessment of related corporations is issued to:

- all corporations named in the assessment
- to a corporation nominated by all parties to the assessment, or
- to a corporation nominated by the Commissioner. Notice of the issue will be sent to all other parties to the assessment.

NOTE: Related corporations for the purposes of land tax grouping can include corporations that do not own land in Victoria.

IF TWO OR MORE HOLDING COMPANIES HAVE SUFFICIENT SIMILARITY OF SHAREHOLDINGS

If more than half of the 'issued ordinary share capital' in a holding company is held by, or on behalf of, shareholders of another holding company, the landholdings not only of the two holding companies, but also of their subsidiary companies, may be aggregated and taxed jointly.

NOTE: 'Issued ordinary share capital' does not include any capital represented by shares which have no right to participate beyond a specified amount in the distributions of either profits or capital. (Any participating preference shares would appear to be regarded for these purposes as ordinary capital.) 'Shareholder' includes all persons on whose behalf a share in the company is held by a trustee or by any other person.

WHEN COMPANIES ARE JOINTLY ASSESSED

If companies are jointly assessed, they are jointly and individually liable for the land tax payable by the group, but have such rights of contribution or indemnity between themselves as is just.

RATES OF TAX

The following rates apply if non-exempt land is owned as at 31 December 2014.

Total taxable value	Tax rates
2015 General rates	
$0 to less than $250,000	Nil
$250,000 to less than $600,000	$275 plus 0.2% for each dollar over $250,000
$600,000 to less than $1,000,000	$975 plus 0.5% for each dollar over $600,000
$1,000,000 to less than $1,800,000	$2,975 plus 0.8% for each dollar over $1,000,000
$1,800,000 to less than $3,000,000	$9,375 plus 1.3% for each dollar over $1,800,000
$3,000,000 and over	$24,975 plus 2.25% for each dollar over $3,000,000
2015 Surcharge rates for trusts	
Less than $25,000	Nil
$25,000 to less than $250,000	$82 plus 0.375% for each dollar over $25,000
$250,000 to less than $600,000	$926 plus 0.575% for each dollar over $250,000
$600,000 to less than $1,000,000	$2,938 plus 0.875% for each dollar over $600,000
$1,000,000 to less than $1,800,000	$6,438 plus 1.175% for each dollar over $1,000,000
$1,800,000 to less than $3,000,000	$15,838 plus 0.7614%* for each dollar over $1,800,000
$3,000,000 and over	$24,975 plus 2.25% for each dollar over $3,000,000

* The surcharge phases out for landholdings in excess of $1.8 million.
  For landholdings valued at or over $3 million, the surcharge is zero and the normal marginal rate applies.

SPECIAL LAND TAX

Special land tax is a 'once only' tax calculated at a rate of 5% of the taxable value of the land. It is payable when certain exempt lands cease to be exempt.

Where the land loses its exemption immediately upon, or within 60 days of, a change in ownership, special land tax is payable by the person who was the owner immediately before that change of ownership. In all other cases, special land tax is payable by the person who is the owner at the time the exemption ceases.

Special land tax does not apply to primary production land which ceases to be exempt on or after 1 May 2007. However, landowners are still required to notify the State Revenue Office (SRO) when primary production activities cease, as land tax at the general rates will still apply.

Special land tax does not apply to land which ceased to be exempt land because it was compulsorily acquired by an authority under a compulsory acquisition law (Victorian or Commonwealth).

Special land tax is not imposed on land previously owned by a public statutory authority if it has a taxable value of less than $250,000 and is to be used exclusively as the principal place of residence of the new owner.

EXEMPT LAND

Land tax is assessed each calendar year – and while all land owners (other than trustees) will not pay land tax if their taxable land holdings are below the $250,000 threshold in 2015, they may be entitled to further exemptions, as outlined below.

PRINCIPAL PLACE OF RESIDENCE EXEMPTION

A Principal Place of Residence (PPR) exemption is available to natural persons for the land which they use and occupy as their principal place of residence. This means that an individual is not required to pay land tax if their principal residence, which they occupy, is the only land they own in Victoria. This exemption extends to trustees of certain trusts (excluding discretionary and unit trusts) where one or more of the vested beneficiaries use the land as their PPR. However, the PPR exemption is only intended to apply where the beneficiary has a present vested interest in the trust land. In addition, where not all of the beneficiaries under the trust use and occupy the land as their PPR, only a partial exemption may apply.

Any jointly-owned land which is the PPR of any one of the joint owners, who is a natural person, is also exempt from land tax in the primary assessment. However, those joint owners who do not occupy the property as their principal residence may be taxable for their share of the property.

The exemption is available for only one residence regardless of where it is located in Australia and is not available for companies and other entities (apart from certain trusts – see above).

Where a substantial business activity is conducted on the land used as the PPR, land tax is imposed on the portion of the property attributable to the business use.

Where the individual owner or the resident beneficiary of an eligible trust, who was using the land as their PPR, has died, the PPR exemption will continue to apply for up to three years from the date of that person's death or the interest of the owner is given to another beneficiary or the date the land was sold or transferred, whichever comes first.

A refund of land tax paid may be available to an owner where unoccupied land is subsequently used as the owner's PPR provided no other PPR exemption has been claimed.

RIGHT TO RESIDE

The PPR exemption is available for land used and occupied by a natural person who has a right to reside granted under a will or testamentary instrument. The exemption only applies where the right was granted on the death of the person previously occupying the land; the right was granted in writing under a will and was not granted in exchange for monetary consideration. The exemption does not apply to a right to occupy land as a lessee or as a beneficiary of a discretionary trust or a unit holder of a unit trust scheme. In addition, the land is not exempt unless immediately before the person who has a right to reside on the land was granted the right, the land was exempt as a PPR. Further, the person who has the right to reside must not be entitled to the PPR exemption for any other land in Victoria or any equivalent exemption in any other State or Territory.

LAND USED FOR PRIMARY PRODUCTION

Land used for primary production may be exempt from land tax.

Land can be classified as 'used for primary production' if it is primarily used for:

- the cultivation of the land for the purposes of selling the produce of cultivation
- the maintenance of animals or poultry for the purposes of selling them or their natural increase or bodily produce
- the keeping of bees for the purpose of selling their honey
- commercial fishing (including preparation for such fishing, or the storage or preservation of fish or fishing gear), or
- the cultivation or propagation for sale of plants, seedlings, mushrooms or orchids.

IMPORTANT: If the land is within greater Melbourne and is wholly or partly within an urban zone under a planning scheme under the *Planning and Environment Act 1987*, the exemption applies only if that land is used primarily for the business of primary production and the owner, or one of the owners or a relative of the owner(s) is normally engaged in a substantially full-time capacity in the business of primary production (of the type carried out on the land). If the land is owned by a company or trust the principal business of the entity must be primary production of the type carried on on the land and at least one of the shareholders or beneficiaries must be normally engaged in a substantially full-time capacity in the business of primary production (of the type carried out on the land).

CHARITABLE INSTITUTIONS

Any portion of land used by a charitable institution exclusively for charitable purposes is exempt and therefore no ownership test is required.

OTHER EXEMPTIONS

There are specific exemptions that may be available for land held by a particular body and used for a specific purpose. These may include land owned by the following:

- the Crown
- public statutory authorities

- armed service personnel associations
- friendly societies
- agricultural shows
- non profit bodies that provide or promote sporting, outdoor recreation or outdoor cultural activities, and
- mines.

Land or part of land owned by a public statutory authority is not exempt land if the land or part is leased or occupied for any business purposes by a person or body other than a public statutory authority, non-profit bodies that provide or promote sporting, outdoor recreation or outdoor cultural activities, municipal councils, armed service associations and friendly societies.

Land is also exempt if it is used as a caravan park, for aged care facilities, nursing homes, supported residential services, rooming houses, retirement villages, residential services for people with a disability and certain health centres and services.

CONCESSIONAL TAX RATE

Tax is limited to a rate not greater than 0.357% of the taxable value of the land or part owned and solely occupied by any society, club or association not carried on for the profit or gain of individual members and exclusively used for one of these purposes:

- providing for social, cultural, literary, educational or recreational interests of its members, or
- promoting or controlling pony racing, horse racing or harness racing in Victoria.

CROWN LAND HELD BY A LESSEE

Lessees of Crown land are deemed to be the owner for land tax purposes. Crown land held by a lessee is aggregated with their freehold land to calculate land tax payable.

TRANSMISSION EASEMENTS

Land tax is payable on transmission easements held by electricity transmission companies. The taxable land valuations used to calculate the tax payable are provided by the Valuer-General.

HARDSHIP RELIEF

Any land owner who would either suffer serious hardship from payment of land tax, or is in necessitous circumstances, may apply for relief. Applications cannot be considered if the land tax has been paid.

ASSESSMENTS OF JOINT HOLDINGS

Where land is owned jointly by a number of owners and the total taxable value of that land exceeds the general exemption, an assessment notice will be issued. The joint owners collectively are deemed to be the 'primary taxpayer'. The assessment will be issued to one joint owner nominated to receive that assessment where a written request has been made by all joint owners, or one of the joint owners nominated by the Commissioner.

ASSESSMENT OF EACH JOINT OWNER

The joint owners together are called the 'primary taxpayer' and are assessed as if they are one owner. All joint owners are jointly liable for the land tax payable by the primary taxpayer.

Each joint owner is deemed to be the secondary taxpayer. An assessment is raised on the taxable value of all the land owned by the secondary taxpayer (either solely or jointly). To prevent double taxation a deduction is allowed in the joint owner's assessment ('secondary assessment') if tax is payable in the 'primary assessment'. The deduction is the lesser of either the individual owner's share of the tax paid in the 'primary assessment' or the amount of tax calculated in the 'secondary assessment' for the share of the jointly owned land.

27.300   NSW LAND TAX

Web: www.osr.nsw.gov.au   Email: landtax@osr.nsw.gov.au   Telephone: 1300 139 816

Land tax is a tax levied on the owners of land in NSW as at midnight on 31 December of each year. In general, your principal place of residence (your home) or land used for primary production (a farm) is exempt from land tax.

You may be liable for land tax if you own or part-own:

- vacant land, including vacant rural land
- land where a house, residential unit or flat has been built
- a holiday home
- investment properties
- company title units
- residential, commercial or industrial units, including car spaces
- commercial properties, including factories, shops and warehouses, or
- land leased from state or local government.

2015 RATES OF TAX

GENERAL RATES

Total taxable land value	Tax rates
Up to $432,000	Nil
$432,000 up to $2,641,000	$100 + 1.6% of the value exceeding $432,000
Over $2,641,000	$35,444 + 2.0% of the value exceeding $2,641,000

NON-CONCESSIONAL COMPANIES AND SPECIAL TRUSTS

Total taxable land value	Tax rates
Up to $2,641,000	1.6% of the value exceeding $432,000
Over $2,641,000	$42,256 + 2.0% of the value exceeding $2,641,000

In 2015 the non-concessional companies and special trusts rate is 1.6% of each dollar of land value up to $2,641,000 and 2% on the land value exceeding $2,641,000.

DATE OF LODGMENT OF RETURNS

If an owner becomes liable for the first time, a registration form will be required. The due date for 2015 was 31 March 2015. An assessment will be calculated and forwarded by the Office of State Revenue.

CHANGE IN LAND HOLDINGS OR USE

If the circumstances have changed and the taxpayer is liable for 2015 land tax, a 2015 Variation Form (or Registration Form) must be lodged. This can be completed online at www.osr.nsw.gov.au.

DATE OF OWNERSHIP LIABILITY

Ownership is determined for NSW land tax purposes as at midnight on 31 December immediately preceding a tax year that commences on 1 January.

BASIS OF VALUATIONS

Land values are determined by the Valuer-General each year at 1 July (ie. six months before the land tax year).

AVERAGING VALUES

For 2007 and later years, valuations are averaged over three years. The average land value used for a 2015 land tax assessment will be the average of the 2015, 2014 and 2013 land values determined for that land.

SUBDIVISIONS AND AMALGAMATIONS

Where a parcel of land was only recently created, eg. subdivision or amalgamation and did not exist at either or both of the previous taxing dates, the average value will be based only on the land values for those taxing dates when the land did exist.

EXEMPT LAND

There is a comprehensive list of land specifically exempt from land tax and a further list of land conditionally exempt, depending on use.

RESIDENTIAL LAND

Principal Places of Residence (PPRs) (not owned by a company or a trustee) are, in general, exempt from land tax. However, a family, including dependents under 18 years, can claim the PPR exemption for only one property. Where more than one residence is used, simultaneously an election can be made of which property will be treated as the family PPR.

ACQUIRING A NEW PRINCIPAL PLACE OF RESIDENCE

A land owner can claim the PPR exemption for two properties for one tax year. If a new residence is purchased within the six months leading to the relevant taxing year with the intention that this new residence will be occupied as a PPR and the former residence has not been sold at the relevant taxing year both residences are exempt.

Previously the owner had to sell the former residence by 30 June following the relevant taxing year and occupy the new residence by the following 31 December for the concession to apply. The amendment removes the requirement that the former residence must be sold. The only requirement is that the new residence must be used and occupied as the PPR by the following taxing date. The concession applies for only one tax year.

LAND INTENDED AS PRINCIPAL PLACE OF RESIDENCE

This exemption applies to residential land that is intended to be used and occupied as the owner's PPR. This exemption cannot apply if an owner is using and occupying another property that they own.

The exemption applies:

- for the four tax years following the year in which the property was acquired, or
- if the owner did not occupy the land after it was first acquired (eg. it was rented for residential purposes), the concession will apply for the four tax years following the date the actual work commenced to rebuild the residence.

When the residence is completed the owner must physically occupy the property for a period of at least six months. If not, the exemption will be revoked.

TEMPORARY ABSENCE FROM PRINCIPAL PLACE OF RESIDENCE

An owner may be absent from their PPR for up to six years but still retain the PPR exemption, provided the property is not leased for more than six months during a tax year. Owners may retain the exemption if they are absent from their home for an extended period of time.

Before 2014 the concession only applied if the person used and occupied other land that was not owned by the person as a PPR during their absence. After 2014 the requirement that an absent owner live in another property as their PPR on the taxing date to qualify for the exemption has been removed. It will be sufficient that the person does not own any other land used and occupied by the person as a PPR.

DECEASED ESTATES

Exemption applies in cases where land was used and occupied by a deceased person as the principal place of residence. The exemption will notionally continue after the person's death until the earlier of:

- the second anniversary of the death, or
- the land is transferred to any person other than beneficiary or executor under the will.

Exemption is also available for:

- a person using and occupying a property under a right of occupancy created under the will of the owner of the property
- a person (not a tenant) who resided with the deceased owner immediately before his or her death, and who continues to reside on the property with the permission of the deceased person's personal representative, or
- from 2007, a person to whom the ownership of the land has been transferred as beneficiary may provide permission to a person living with the deceased at the time of death to continue to reside in the premises.

MIXED LAND USE

A reduction in the land value is made for an owner-occupied residence in a building on the land if part of the building(s) or land is used or occupied for other purposes.

BOARDING HOUSES AND LOW COST ACCOMMODATION

An exemption is available to boarding houses throughout NSW and land used to provide accommodation to low income persons. Application for exemption must be made. Refer to Revenue Ruling *LT 95 Land Used & Occupied Primarily for a Boarding House* and Revenue Ruling *LT96 Land used and occupied primarily for low cost Accommodation*.

REGISTERED RETIREMENT VILLAGES, AGED CARE ESTABLISHMENTS AND NURSING HOMES

Exempt for land held from 31 December 1990 onwards. A pro rata reduction applies if only part of the land is used as a registered retirement village or nursing home.

RESIDENTIAL PARKS PRIMARILY USED AND OCCUPIED BY RETIRED PERSONS

Exempt for land held from 31 December 2002 onwards. Refer to Revenue Ruling LT-71 for exemption criteria.

RURAL LAND WITH DOMINATE USE BEING PRIMARY PRODUCTION

Generally, primary production land that has a dominant use of primary production, is exempt from tax. Land not zoned as rural land must be dominantly used for a primary production use that has a significant and substantial commercial purpose.

SPORTS AND GAMES CLUBS

Land owned by, or held in trust for non-profit sports and games clubs (eg. tennis, cricket, horse racing and motor racing etc.) is generally exempt from land tax.

CHARITABLE BODIES

Institutions are exempt from land tax if they are carried on solely for charitable or educational purposes. This measure makes it clear that the exemption also applies to bodies corporate, societies, institutions or other bodies carried on solely for charitable or educational purposes.

CHILD CARE CENTRES

From 1 January 2012, a new National Law commenced operation under the Children (Education and Care Services) National Law (NSW), and replaced the licensing processes for child care services with provision for approval of providers and services, and certification of supervisors of services. This amendment updates the land tax exemption for child care centres for consistency with the National Law.

OBJECTIONS TO ASSESSMENTS

Objections against assessments must be lodged with the Chief Commissioner within 60 days of receiving the assessment by fully setting out the grounds of objection. Any objection to land value, including valuation allowances and concessions, must be lodged with the Valuer-General. If dissatisfied with the Chief Commissioner's decision, a taxpayer may lodge an application with the Supreme Court or the Civil Administrative Tribunal of NSW (NCAT) to have the decision reviewed. Application for such a review must be lodged within 60 days of the Chief Commissioner's decision.

ASSESSMENT PENDING APPEAL

Even though an objection may have been made, land tax may be recovered (including late payment interest) on the basis of the assessment made.

LAND TAX CLEARANCE CERTIFICATES (SECTION 47 CERTIFICATE)

An amount is payable on each separate application of the purchaser, vendor or mortgagee (ie. in respect of each parcel of land separately valued) seeking details of the land tax charged on the land. Valuation certificates may also be obtained. This may be paid by cash or cheque in person, or by cheque in the mail. Certificates may also be obtained electronically through Client Service Providers.

SHAREHOLDERS IN HOME-UNIT COMPANIES

Owners of shares which give exclusive right to occupy a unit for residential purposes (company title units) are regarded as owners of that unit and are assessed for land tax as if the unit was a strata title. Exemption is available if the unit is the shareholder's PPR. The value of the land is attributed to shareholders on the basis of the proportion of shares held by each shareholder in the company.

To calculate the value of a unit:

(Total value of land) multiplied by (Shares held by the owner) divided by (Total shares)

Unless the unit is exempt because it is the owner's principal place of residence, that value is aggregated with other taxable land owned by that person.

JOINT OWNERSHIP OF LAND

SINGLE ASSESSMENT OF LAND JOINTLY OWNED

Joint owners of land (except those whose interests are exempt) will be assessed and liable in respect of the land owned by them jointly as if it were owned by a single person.

ASSESSMENT OF EACH PERSON

Each joint owner may also be liable and assessed separately in respect of:

- the individual interest in jointly owned land
- any other land owned severally, and
- the individual interests in any other land.

PREVENTION OF DOUBLE TAXATION

Joint owners are deemed to be the 'primary taxpayer' and each joint owner individually is the 'secondary taxpayer'. If a taxpayer has interests in land (such as joint ownership of land, assessed firstly as though owned by a single person) relief is given to the individual taxpayer as a 'secondary taxpayer'.

The deduction is the lesser of (a) or (b):

a. *[Interest (share of land value) of individual in joint ownership] divided by [total land value of joint ownership] multiplied by [tax on joint ownership]*

b. *[Interest (share of land value) of individual in joint ownership] divided by [total land value of individual] multiplied by [tax on individual]*

CROWN LAND ETC.

The Crown, statutory authorities and local councils are exempt. Lessees of land from the Crown are liable, but only in respect of leases entered into from or renewed after 1 January 1987.

Lessees of land from public authorities, county and local councils are liable, but only in respect of leases entered into from or renewed after 1 January 1991.

RELATED COMPANIES

SELECTION OF ONE COMPANY TO RECEIVE THRESHOLD

The Chief Commissioner classifies only one related company as a 'concessional company' which is entitled to the tax free threshold. The others are regarded as non-concessional companies. Non-concessional companies are taxed at a flat 1.6% where the total group land value is under $2,641,000 or 2.0% where the total group value exceeds $2,641,000 (2015 tax year rates).

A company is related to another company if:

- that other company controls the make-up of the board of directors, controls more than 50% of the voting power or that other company holds more than half the issued share capital of the other
- in respect of each company, the same persons control the make-up of the board of directors, control more than 50% of the voting power or hold more than half the issued share capital of each company
- more than half the issued share capital is held jointly by that other company and its shareholders, provided that the percentage of issued share capital (of the first company held by shareholders of the second company) is more than the difference between 50% and the percentage of issued share capital of the first company held by the second company, or
- one company is related to a company to which the other company is related.

'SPECIAL TRUSTS'

Non-exempt land held by 'special trusts' is taxed at a flat 1.6% where the total value is between $6,250 and $2,641,000, and 2.0% on the value exceeding $2,641,000. A trust is a 'special trust' if the property includes land, the trustee (of the trust) is the only legal owner of the land (the beneficiaries are not considered to be owners) and the trust is not a fixed trust.

When land is owned by a trust on behalf of a superannuation fund and the fund complied with the *Superannuation Industry (Supervision) Act 1993* in the preceding year, it will not be regarded as a 'special trust' if it is:

- a fund which has elected to be a regulated fund and was a complying fund
- a complying approved deposit fund, or
- a pooled superannuation trust.

UNIT TRUSTS

A High Court decision in 2005 resulted in the trust status of unit trusts changing from 'fixed' to 'special' for 2006. A concession for unit trusts was included in the NSW 2006 Budget. If a unit trust was assessed as fixed in the past, provided that 95% of the units are held by members of the same family and the land value is $1,000,000 or less as at 31 December 2005, the unit trust is assessed as a family unit trust under Schedule 1AA for 2006 and subsequent years.

Any unit trust can restructure into a fixed trust. A restructured trust will receive the benefit of the threshold for the following year in which it was restructured. A liability to duty may not be applicable in these cases. From 2014, for a unit trust to not be treated as a special trust it can only issue one class of units and each unit provides the holder with an entitlement to both the income and capital of the trust fund which is fixed and in the same proportion.

27.400   QUEENSLAND LAND TAX

Web: www.qld.gov.au/landtax   Email: landtax@osr.qld.gov.au   Telephone: 1300 300 734

Land tax is a tax on freehold land.

For land tax purposes 'land' includes:

- vacant land
- land that is built on
- lots in building unit plans
- lots in group title plans
- lots in a time share scheme, and
- lots owned by a home unit company.

Land tax is assessed on the total taxable value of landowners' freehold land owned at midnight on 30 June each year. The taxable value is reduced by any exemptions that have been claimed.

LAND TAX CLEARANCE APPLICATIONS

Unpaid land tax represents a first charge over land. This charge may or may not be registered on the title, it has priority for payment over any mortgage and will continue as a charge on land if it is transferred.

An applicant is usually an intended purchaser who will receive either notification of the amount of land tax payable or a 'Clearance Certificate'. A land tax 'Clearance Certificate' provides that there is no identified land tax payable on the land as at the anticipated date of possession. It provides protection to the purchaser from recovery of land tax that may subsequently be identified. However the issue of a 'Clearance Certificate' will not remove any additional debt owed or that may become payable by the vendor.

Applications may be made:

- **Online:** Application fees for electronically lodged forms with an online service provider will be at their discretion, and
- **Mail:** $36.70 from 1 July 2014 when the application is lodged with the Queensland Office of State Revenue (OSR).

ASSESSMENTS

Assessments are issued automatically from 1 August each year, based on information held in the OSR. Landowners not receiving an assessment should notify OSR if liability is suspected

Land tax is levied on the total taxable value of all non-exempt freehold land owned in Queensland as at midnight 30 June each year.

OWNERSHIP

The relevant land tax rate is determined by the type of owner as follows:

Unimproved freehold land thresholds	2012-13, 2013-14 and 2014-15
Absentee owners	$350,000
Trustees	$350,000
Companies	$350,000
Managers of timeshare schemes	$350,000
Other resident owners	$600,000

NOTE: A trustee is assessed on land in their capacity as trustee separately from land holdings they have in another capacity. A beneficiary's interest in a trust (other than a deceased estate) is not included in their landholdings. For more information see Public Ruling LTA020.

TOTAL TAXABLE VALUE

The total taxable value is the aggregate of all freehold land owned in Queensland less exemptions.

The 'taxable value' for a financial year is the lesser of the following amounts:

1. *Land Valuation Act 2010* (LVA) value of land at 30 June as determined by the Valuer-General and other relevant departments.
2. Average value of the land at 30 June which is defined as either:
   - The average value of the land for the current and two previous financial years, or
   - If the property has not been valued for all these years, the current value multiplied by the LVA averaging factor (factor is 0.99 for June 2014)

LAND TAX RATES AND THRESHOLDS

Land tax assessments for the 2014-15 financial year will be based on the following rates.

Taxable value of land owned at 30 June	Tax rate
Companies, absentee owners and trustees	
Up to $349,999	Nil
$350,000 to $2,249,999	$1,450 plus 1.7 cents for each $1 over $350,000
$2,250,000 to $4,999,999	$33,750 plus flat rate of 1.5 cents for every $1 over $2,250,000
$5,000,000 and above	$75,000 plus 2 cents for every $1 over $5,000,000
Taxable value of land owned at 30 June	**Tax rate**
Individuals	
Up to $599,999	Nil
$600,000 to $999,999	$500 plus 1 cent for each $1 over $600,000
$1,000,000 to $2,999,999	$4,500 plus 1.65 cents for each $1 over $1,000,000
$3,000,000 to $4,999,999	$37,500 plus 1.25 cents for each $1 over $3,000,000
$5,000,000 and above	$62,500 plus 1.75 cents for each $1 over $5,000,000

UNPAID TAX INTEREST

Unpaid tax interest applies at the annual rate of 10.69% for the 2015-15 year. For late payments it will accrue weekly until the amount payable is received in full.

PENALTY TAX

Penalty tax of up to 90% may apply.

OBJECTIONS

A taxpayer who is dissatisfied with their assessment may lodge an objection. The objection must:
- be in writing
- state the grounds for the objection
- include copies of relevant material, and
- be lodged within 60 days of the assessment notice being issued.

PAYMENTS

The payment of land tax can be made by credit card (using BPOINT), telephone banking, over the internet, direct payment, electronic funds transfer or cheque and money order.

EXTENDED PAYMENT OPTION

A land owner may elect to pay a 2015-16 assessment in three instalments. These instalments will be due 45, 90 and 150 days after the assessment notice is issued. This election can only be made where the taxpayer agrees within 21 days of the issuing of the relevant assessment notice that they will pay by direct debit. Alternatively, land tax will be due in one lump sum 90 days after the assessment notice is issued.

EXEMPTIONS

Depending on the use of the land and ownership, the landowner may be eligible for a land tax exemption. Generally, once a successful claim is made, the exemption will continue – the landowner does not need to apply each year. Penalties may apply for failing to notify the OSR in writing after they becoming ineligible to receive an exemption. It is an offence not to do so. Further information on exemptions is available on the relevant website.

EXEMPTION FOR LAND USED AS A HOME

This exemption is available only to qualifying Queensland resident individuals, deceased estates and trustees. Companies are not eligible for this concession.

An exemption is available for a parcel of land, a lot in a Building Unit Plan or a Group Title Plan used as the landowner's home/Principal Place of Residence. An owner can only have one home as at 30 June each year.

A full exemption will apply to certain working arrangements which are incidental to residential use and where there is limited letting of the premises. A partial home exemption/deduction may apply where land is used as a home and for another substantial non-exempt purpose.

The home exemption covers owners who are absent due to illness, care requirements or undertaking substantial renovations. Public Ruling LTA000 1.2 and LTA041 1.2 clarify this exemption.

NOTE: Companies are not eligible for the home exemption.

PRIMARY PRODUCTION

If all or part of a landowner's land is used solely for the business of primary production (agriculture, pasturage or dairy farming), the landowner may apply for a primary production exemption as follows:

- **If the land owned by a resident individual, a relevant proprietary company or exempt charitable institution:** The exemption will apply to that part of the taxable value of the land used for the business of agriculture, pasturage or dairy farming.
- **If the land is owned by a trustees of a trust:** Providing all the beneficiaries are either Australian resident individuals, relevant proprietary companies or exempt charitable institutions, the exemption will apply to the relevant portion of land.

NOTE: If the business is not being conducted by the owner of the land further evidence will be required. For more information see LTA053 1.1 and LTA053 2.1.

DECEASED ESTATES

For the trustees of a trust or deceased estate, an exemption may be made for the land owned where all the beneficiaries of the trust use that land as their home. Where land is held by a trustee, administrator, executor or personal representative for a deceased estate, enquiries should be made regarding land tax liability to the OSR.

AGED CARE FACILITIES

An exemption applies for land on which an aged care facility is located. The exemption only applies if residential care is provided by an approved provider in accordance with the *Aged Care Act 1997* (Cwlth). More information can be found at **www.qld.gov.au/landtax**.

SUPPORTED ACCOMMODATION SERVICES

An exemption applies for land used for a supported accommodation service. This exemption applies to a residential service defined in section 4 of the *Residential Services (Accreditation) Act 2002* (RSAA) and accredited at Level 3 under section 34 of the RSAA.

RETIREMENT VILLAGES

An exemption may be available if the land is used for premises or facilities for residents of a retirement village which are registered under the *Retirement Villages Act 1999*.

MOVEABLE DWELLING PARKS

An exemption applies for moveable dwelling parks where:
- the land is used predominantly as a moveable dwelling park, and
- more than 50% of sites in the park are occupied, or solely available for occupation, for residential purposes for periods of more than six weeks at a time.

A movable dwelling park is a place where a caravan or manufactured home sites are leased or rented. See LTA054 1.1.

NON-PROFIT ORGANISATIONS

An exemption may be available where land owned, or held on trust for a non-profit organisation. For an exemption to apply there must be a building on the land.

CHARITABLE INSTITUTIONS

An exemption may be available if the land is owned or held in trust by a charitable institution* and used for a qualifying exempt purpose, for example:

- public benevolence
- charity
- education
- religion
- relief of poverty, and
- provision of care.

* A charitable institution refers to an institution registered under the *Taxation Administration Act 2001*, part 11A.

27.500 SOUTH AUSTRALIAN LAND TAX

Web: www.revenuesa.sa.gov.au   Email: landtax@sa.gov.au Telephone: (08) 8204 9870

Land ownership, site value and land use as at midnight 30 June each year is used to determine the land tax for the forthcoming financial year. Land tax revenue assists in the provision of public services such as education, health and public safety.

RevenueSA is responsible for the collection of land tax under the *Land Tax Act 1936*, the *Taxation Administration Act 1996* (TAA) and associated Regulations. Details of land transfers are obtained from the Land Titles Office.

PENALTIES AND INTEREST

The TAA allows for a flat penalty tax of 75% of the unpaid land tax to be imposed in instances of the deliberate non-payment (default) of land tax, or 25% for any other situation. The penalty tax may be adjusted in the following situations:

- if the taxpayer made a sufficient disclosure of the tax default while not subject to a tax audit – the penalty tax is to be reduced by 80%
- if the taxpayer made a sufficient disclosure of the tax default while subject to a tax audit – the penalty tax is to be reduced by 20%, and
- if the taxpayer engaged in obstructive conduct while subject to a tax audit – the penalty tax may be increased by the Commissioner by 20%.

The Commissioner may, at the Commissioner's discretion, remit penalty tax payable by a taxpayer by any amount. The TAA also allows for interest to be imposed on unpaid tax on a daily basis from the due date until the date the land tax is paid.

WHO IS LIABLE FOR PAYMENT OF LAND TAX?

The owner of the property as at midnight 30 June is liable to pay the land tax assessed for the forthcoming financial year. Where a property is sold after 30 June, the vendor (seller) is still liable for the land tax.

It is a common practice (although not a legal requirement) for land conveyancers to arrange a proportional adjustment between the purchaser and the vendor of land, for any applicable land tax at the time of land settlement. This adjustment should be calculated as if the property being sold is the only taxable property owned.

OBJECTIONS

Objections against an assessment or decision of the Commissioner must be lodged with the Minister for Finance within 60 days of either the date on which the notice of assessment was served on the taxpayer or the date on which the taxpayer was notified of the decision. The grounds of an objection must be stated fully and in detail in the notice of objection. Unsuccessful objections to a tax assessment or decision may be appealed to the Supreme Court within 60 days of the Minister's determination of the objection, or if the objection has not been determined, within 90 days of its lodgement. Objections against a valuation must be in writing to the State Valuation Office, within 60 days of the receipt of the first rates notice from any statutory authority that advises of your site value (Council, RevenueSA or SA Water), and must contain a full and detailed statement of the grounds on which the objection is based.

Any objection to an assessment or valuation does not mean payment of land tax can be withheld pending the outcome of the objection. Land tax is due and payable by the due date and the tax may be recovered as if no objection were pending, including penalty tax and interest accruing.

LAND FOR WHICH A TRANSFER HAS NOT BEEN REGISTERED

If a land transfer is not registered by 30 June of the financial year in which the change in the ownership occurred, the taxpayer must notify the Commissioner in writing, providing satisfactory documentary evidence, on or before the following 31 July.

LAND JOINTLY OWNED

Land owned by more than one person is taxed separately from other land, which may be held by any one of the joint owners individually.

SHACK SITES

Shack site lessees of privately owned land are deemed to be the owner where:

- the shack site is situated on or adjacent to the banks of the River Murray, a tributary of the River Murray, or a lake or lagoon connected with the River Murray or a tributary of the River Murray, and
- a registered lease existed as at midnight 30 June 1989 over the land, and
- the term of the lease is at least 40 years.

Further, the occupier of land in a defined shack-site area is similarly deemed to be the land tax owner. Shack-site areas are regions of land located within certain council areas where the land has been deemed to be a shack-site area by the Governor through a proclamation in the Government Gazette.

LAND HELD AS A REPRESENTATIVE

Land held by a taxpayer in a representative capacity may be taxed separately from other land held by the taxpayer in their individual right. The taxpayer must give notice in writing together with any such evidence as required by the Commissioner within the financial year for which the tax is to be calculated (thus recognition of a representative capacity cannot be recognised for years prior to the year in which notice is given).

MINOR INTERESTS IN LAND

Minor interest provisions were introduced into the *Land Tax Act 1936* with effect from 30 June 2008 to address the practice where owners of more than one piece of land avoid paying higher marginal rates of land tax by structuring their ownerships so that another party (or parties) hold a minor interest in an individual piece of land thereby creating different legal ownerships.

'Minor interest' of five per cent or less

Where land is owned by two or more persons and one or more of those persons hold an interest in the land of five per cent or less (the 'minor interest'), the person or persons holding the minor interest will be taken not to be an owner of the land for the purposes of the Act. In such cases, the land tax payable in respect of the relevant land will be assessed, and is payable, as if the land were wholly owned by the owner or owners of the land who do not hold the minor interest.

The relevant land will therefore be aggregated with any other land owned by the owner or owners for the purposes of assessing land tax.

The owner or owners may apply to the Commissioner in writing, to request that the minor interest not be disregarded for the purposes of the Act, on the basis that the minor interest was created solely for a purpose, or entirely for purposes, unrelated to reducing the amount of land tax payable in respect of any land. Where an application is made and the Commissioner is satisfied that there is no doubt that the minor interest was created solely for a purpose, or entirely for purposes, unrelated to reducing the amount of land tax payable in respect of any land, the minor interest will not be disregarded by the Commissioner for the purposes of assessing land tax.

Minor interest between five per cent and 50 per cent

Where a person or persons hold an interest in land of greater than five per cent but less than 50 per cent the interest will be disregarded for the purposes of assessing land tax only if the Commissioner forms the opinion that the purpose or one of the purposes for the creation of the interest was to reduce the amount of land tax payable in respect of any land.

ADDITIONAL INFORMATION

The Commissioner may have regard to the following criteria to determine whether a minor interest should or should not be disregarded for the purposes of the Act:

- the nature of any relationships between the owners of the relevant land, or between the owners of two or more pieces of land
- the lack of consideration, or the amount, value or source of the consideration, provided in association with the creation of the interest
- the form and substance of any transaction associated with the creation or operation of the interest, including the legal and economic obligations of the parties and the economic and commercial substance of any such transaction
- the way in which any transaction associated with the creation or operation of the interest was entered into or carried out, and
- any other matter the Commissioner considers relevant.

An interest in land will not be disregarded if the effect of disregarding the interest is to decrease the amount of land tax payable in respect of any land. An interest may be disregarded by the Commissioner regardless of whether it was created before or after the commencement of the provisions.

A person who is dissatisfied with a decision of the Commissioner may lodge a written notice of objection with the Minister for Finance.

Where a minor interest in land has been disregarded under the *Land Tax Act 1936*, the holder of the disregarded interest is not eligible for an exemption.

TENANT LIABILITY

The *Retail and Commercial Leases Act 1995* prohibits the inclusion, in any retail shop lease, of provisions requiring the lessee to pay or reimburse land tax. However the landlord under a lease governed by the *Retail and Commercial Leases Act 1995* may take into account land tax when assessing rent. The *Residential Tenancies Act 1995* requires a residential tenancy landlord to bear the cost of land tax.

RATES OF LAND TAX

The rates and thresholds for the 2015-16 financial year are as follows:

Total taxable site value	Rate
Up to $323,000	Nil
$323,001 to $593,000	$0.50 for each $100 or part thereof over $323,000
$593,001 to $862,000	$1,350 plus $1.65 for every $100 or part thereof over $593,000
$862,001 to $1,078,000	$5,788.50 plus $2.40 for every $100 or part thereof over $862,000
Over $1,078,000	$10,972.50 plus $3.70 for every $100 or part thereof over $1,078,000

NOTE: No tax is payable if the amount is less than $20.

Land tax is calculated on the basis of the total taxable site value of all land owned (by an owner or a group of owners) as at midnight 30 June. Where land is owned jointly, a person holding a minor interest may be taken not to be an owner.

Where an owner owns more than one taxable property, land tax is apportioned to each taxable property within the ownership based on the taxable site value of each taxable property.

EXEMPTION OF LAND USED AS OWNER'S PRINCIPAL PLACE OF RESIDENCE

Where the land was the principal place of residence of the owner as at midnight 30 June:

(a)   a full exemption is available where:

- the land is owned by a natural person (whether or not he/she is the sole owner of the land)
- the buildings on the land have a predominately residential character, and
- less than 25% of the total floor area of all buildings on the land are used for any business or commercial purpose (other than the business of primary production).

(b)   a partial exemption is available where the first two full exemption criteria mentioned above are met and between 25% and 75% of the total floor area of all buildings on the land are used for any business or commercial purpose (other than the business of primary production). A sliding scale of exemption exists in these circumstances, ranging from 25% to 75% reduction in the taxable value of land. In this situation a Notice of Land Tax Assessment will indicate a taxable site value that is correspondingly less than the site value of the land as determined by the Valuer-General.

The exemption, or partial exemption, extends to hotels, motels, sets of serviced holiday apartments and other similar accommodation. To be wholly exempted from land tax more than 75% of the total floor area of all buildings on the land must be used as the person's principal place of residence. To be partially exempted from land tax 25% or more of the total floor area of all buildings on the land must be used as the person's principal place of residence. The area used for the hotel, motel, set of serviced holiday apartments or other similar accommodation will be taken to be the area used for business or commercial purposes.

Relief may be available where a person has ceased to occupy their principal place of residence because it has been destroyed or rendered uninhabitable by an occurrence for which they were not responsible, or which resulted from an accident, provided certain criteria are met.

It is an offence not to forthwith inform the Commissioner in writing when circumstances change so that:

- proper grounds for the exemption cease to exist, or
- proper grounds for the exemption continue to exist but a lesser exemption than the one actually given applies.

From 30 June 2015, a full exemption is available where land constitutes the principal place of residence of the primary beneficiary of land held in a Special Disability Trust.

LAND TAX RELIEF WHERE OCCUPATION COMMENCES DURING FINANCIAL YEAR

Where the land becomes the principal place of residence of the owner after 30 June (ie. between 1 July and 30 June in the year of assessment), a waiver (similar to the exemption described in 1(a) or (b) above) or a refund, may be available in any of the following circumstances:

- where at 30 June a person owns land on which a home is either to be constructed or is in the process of being constructed and where owner occupation has occurred during the financial year for which the exemption is sought. If an exemption has been granted on another property, then that property must be sold during the financial year for an exemption to be considered within the same financial year for their new principal place of residence
- where a person is in the process of selling a home and as a result owns two properties at 30 June:
    - one of which is the current principal place of residence (and eligible for exemption) and the other is the intended but not yet occupied principal place of residence (and liable for land tax), or

- one of which was their principal place of residence (and liable for land tax) and the other is now their principal place of residence (and eligible for an exemption)
- relief will be made available on both properties provided no rental income or other consideration is received from either property (when not occupied by the owner) during the period that the homes are owned concurrently and the former residence is sold prior to the end of the financial year in which the exemption on the new residence is sought
- where a person purchases a property as their principal place of residence which was taxable in the ownership of the vendor and in accordance with contractual arrangements, the land tax payable is apportioned between the vendor and purchaser as part of the settlement process.

Where a minor interest in land has been disregarded under the Act, the holder of the disregarded interest is not eligible for an exemption.

EXEMPTION OF LAND USED FOR PRIMARY PRODUCTION (OUTSIDE THE DEFINED RURAL AREA)

If the land is situated outside the 'defined rural area' of the State (ie. predominately outside the greater metropolitan areas of Adelaide and Mount Gambier), a primary production exemption is available if:

- the land is 0.8 hectare or greater in area, and
- the Commissioner is satisfied that the land is used wholly or mainly for the business of primary production.

It is an offence not to forthwith inform the Commissioner in writing when proper grounds for the exemption cease to exist.

EXEMPTION OF LAND USED FOR PRIMARY PRODUCTION (INSIDE 'DEFINED RURAL AREA')

If the land is situated inside the 'defined rural area' of the State, a primary production exemption may apply if:

- the land is 0.8 hectare or greater in area
- the Commissioner is satisfied that the land is used wholly or mainly for the business of primary production, and
- the Commissioner is also satisfied that the principal business of the owner of the land is:
  - primary production of the type for which the land is used, and the land is used to a significant extent for that business, or
  - processing or marketing primary produce, and the land is used to a significant extent for that purpose.

In determining if the principal business of the owner/s of the land is that of primary production, one of the following categories must be satisfied:

- the sole owner of the land is a natural person who is engaged on a substantially full-time basis (either on his or her own behalf as an employee) in a relevant business
- the land is owned jointly or in common by two or more natural persons at least one of whom is engaged on a substantially full-time basis (either on his or her own behalf or as an employee) in a relevant business and any other owner who is not so engaged is a relative of an owner so engaged
- the land is owned solely, jointly or in common by a retired person and the following conditions apply:
  - the retired person was, prior to his or her retirement, engaged on a substantially full-time basis (either on his or her own behalf or as an employee) in a relevant business
  - the co-owner or co-owners of the land (if any) are relatives of the retired person, and
  - a close relative of the retired person is currently engaged on a substantially full-time basis (either on his or her own behalf or as an employee) in a relevant business.

- the land is owned solely or by tenancy in common by the executor of the will, or the administrator of the estate, of a deceased person and the following conditions are satisfied:
  - the deceased person was, prior to his or her death, engaged on a substantially full-time basis (either on his or her own behalf or as an employee) in the relevant business
  - the co-owner or co-owners of the land (if any) are relatives of the deceased, and
  - a close relative of the deceased person is currently engaged on a substantially full-time basis (either on his or her own behalf or as an employee) in a relevant business.
- the land is owned by a company, or by two or more companies, or by a company or companies and one or more natural persons, and the main business of each owner is a relevant business.
- the land is owned by a company and one of the following conditions is satisfied:
  - a natural person owns a majority of the issued shares of the company and is engaged on a substantially full-time basis (either on his or her own behalf or as an employee) in a relevant business
  - two or more natural persons own in aggregate a majority of the issued shares of the company and each of them is engaged on a substantially full-time basis (either on his or her own behalf or as an employee) in the relevant business, or
  - two or more natural persons who are relatives own in aggregate a majority of the issued shares of the company and at least one of them is engaged on a substantially full-time basis (either on his or her own behalf or as an employee) in the relevant business.

A relevant business means a business of primary production of the type for which the land is used or is a business of producing or marketing primary produce, and the land or the produce of the land is used to a significant extent for the purposes of that business.

A person is a close relative of another if:

- they are a spouse or domestic partner
- one is a parent or child of the other, or
- one is brother or sister of the other.

A person is a relative of another if:

- they are spouses or domestic partners
- one is an ascendant or descendant of the other or of their spouse or domestic partner
- one is a brother or sister of the other or of their spouse or domestic partner, or
- one is an ascendant or descendant of a brother or sister of the other or of their spouse or domestic partner.

Applications, including supporting documentation, should be made prior to the due date on the *Notice of Land Tax Assessment*. Applications should be made using the appropriate Revenue SA form.

It is an offence not to forthwith inform the Commissioner in writing when proper grounds for an exemption cease to exist.

OTHER EXEMPTIONS FROM LAND TAX

Subject to certain conditions, other exemptions from land tax include:

- land used for religious, hospital or library purposes
- land owned, let to or occupied by an association whose objects are or include supplying assistance to necessitous or helpless persons
- land owned, let to or occupied by an association which receives an annual grant or subsidy from money voted by Parliament, and in the Commissioner's opinion is used solely or mainly for the purposes for which the grant or subsidy is made

- land owned by an association whose object(s) is/include the conservation of native fauna or flora, and is used solely or mainly as a reserve for the purpose of conserving native fauna or flora
- land owned or occupied without payment by a person or association carrying on an educational institution not for profit, and is used solely or mainly for such an institution
- land owned by an association established for a charitable, educational, benevolent, religious, or philanthropic purpose
- land owned by specific types of sporting or racing associations; an ex-servicemen (or their dependents) association; an employer or employee industrial association; an association for the recreation of the local community; an association for the hosting of agricultural shows or similar exhibitions; or an association for the preserving of buildings or objects of historical value on the land and the whole of the net income from the land is used in furtherance of the objects of the association
- land owned by a prescribed body and used for the benefit of the Aboriginal people
- land that is a supported residential facility and licensed as such under the *Supported Residential Facilities Act 1992*
- land may be wholly or partially exempted from land tax if the land is used wholly or partially for the provision of residential care by an approved provider. 'Approved provider' and 'residential care' have the same meaning as in the *Aged Care Act 1997* of the Commonwealth
- land that is a caravan park
- land within a retirement village if:
    - the land constitutes a residential unit that is:
        - ° occupied, under a residence contract, by a natural person as his or her principal place of residence, or
        - ° available for occupation, under a residence contract, by a natural person as his or her principal place of residence and likely to be so occupied at some time during the ensuing 12 months
    - the land is appurtenant to such a residential unit, or
    - the land is a facility provided under the retirement village scheme for the exclusive use of residents (and their guests)
- land within a retired persons' relocatable home park if:
    - the land constitutes the site for a relocatable home and:
        - ° there is a relocatable home on the site owned by a natural person and occupied by the natural person as his or her principal place of residence, or
        - ° it is likely that within the ensuing 12 months there will be a relocatable home on the site owned by a natural person and occupied by the natural person as his or her principal place of residence
    - the land is appurtenant to such a site, or
    - the land is a facility provided by the owner of the land for the exclusive use of residents (and their guests).

Applications including supporting documentation should be made prior to the due date on the Notice of Land Tax Assessment using the appropriate RevenueSA form. It is an offence not to inform the Commissioner in writing when proper grounds for an exemption cease to exist.

27.600 WEST AUSTRALIAN LAND TAX

Web: www.osr.wa.gov.au   Telephone: 08 9262 1200

Land tax is an annual tax based on the ownership and usage of land at midnight on 30 June. It is levied in respect of the financial year immediately following that date.

Land tax is based on the aggregated taxable value of all land owned at 30 June which is not exempt land. The taxable value for land is based on the unimproved value as determined by the Valuer-General and from 2009-10, increases have been capped at 50% of the previous year value for land tax purposes. The unimproved value of land is its market value under normal sales conditions assuming that no structural improvements have been made. Land within both the Perth Metropolitan Region and townsites throughout Western Australia is assessed on the 'site value' basis which includes merged improvements with examples including draining, filling, excavation, grading and retaining walls.

Each year, the Valuer-General determines the unimproved values of all land in the State.

OBLIGATIONS

The owner(s) of land who receives a land tax assessment notice must notify the Office of State Revenue of any error or omission in the notice. Failure to do so before the due date of the notice may result in the imposition of additional tax in the form of penalties and retrospective assessments of tax. Payment of a land tax liability must also be made by the due date shown on an assessment notice. Failure to do so without making alternative payment arrangements may also result in the imposition of additional penalty tax for late payment.

CERTIFICATE OF LAND TAX CHARGES

APPLICATION FEES FOR CERTIFICATES OF LAND TAX CHARGES

- Paper advice of sale: $35
- Electronic advice of sale: $35

RATES OF LAND TAX 2014-15

Aggregated taxable value of land	Tax rates
Up to $300,000	Nil
$300,000 to $1,000,000	0.11 cent for each $1 in excess of $300,000
$1,000,000 to $2,200,000	$770 plus 0.58 cent for each $1 in excess of $1,000,000
$2,200,000 to $5,500,000	$7,730 plus 1.51 cents for each $1 in excess of $2,200,000
$5,500,000 to $11,000,000	$57,560 plus 1.80 cents for each $1 in excess of $5,500,000
Over $11,000,000	$156,560 plus 2.67 cents for each $1 in excess of $11,000,000

METROPOLITAN REGION IMPROVEMENT TAX

Land situated within the Perth metropolitan region that is liable for land tax, is also liable for Metropolitan Region Improvement Tax (MRIT) at 0.14% (14c per $100) of the taxable value of the land in excess of the exemption threshold of $300,000. If land is not liable for land tax, it will not be liable for MRIT.

At the time of writing, the West Australian State Budget had not been handed down (14 May 2015) and therefore it is not known whether any rate changes will occur.

EXEMPT LAND

An exemption removes the liability to pay land tax in relation to the whole or to part of the taxable value of a lot or parcel of land. Certain classes of land are exempt from assessment and taxation as specified in Part 3 of the *Land Tax Assessment Act 2002* subject to the qualifications specified in Part 3.

The following are examples of the more common concessions or exemptions from land tax that are available.

RESIDENTIAL EXEMPTION

A residential exemption from land tax is available for private residential property owned as at 30 June where all the owners use the land as their primary (sole or principal) residence. A partial residential exemption is also available where not all of the owners use the land as their primary residence, or where the land is used for both residential and business or commercial purposes.

Subject to eligibility criteria, a residential exemption may also be available for land or, classes of owners of land in other circumstances including:

- owners who are in the process of constructing or refurbishing their primary residence can apply for exemption for two years of assessment prior to taking up residence on the land
- a residence held by an executor or administrator under a will where a beneficiary has a life tenancy or right of residence under the will
- a residence owned by a husband and wife or by partners who have lived in a de facto relationship for at least two years (whether or not they still live on that basis), if either one of them uses the land as their primary place of residence, or
- parents, grandparents or siblings who provide a residence for a disabled family member.

The following land is *not* eligible for residential exemption:

- land owned by a company and used by its shareholders as their primary place of residence, or
- any land to the extent that it is held in trust, except where it is used by a disabled beneficiary of the trust as their primary place of residence.

TWO RESIDENCES OWNED AT 30 JUNE

A land tax exemption may also be available for an owner who owns two residences at 30 June. This can be two existing residences, or an existing residence and a vacant lot on which a new residence is to be constructed.

This exemption is subject to a number of eligibility conditions being fully satisfied, including:

- no income can be derived from either property while both are owned
- the new residence must have been acquired during the financial year before 30 June, and
- the original residence must be sold within one year after 30 June (or up to two years if building or refurbishing a new residence).

PRIMARY PRODUCTION EXEMPTION

New legislation amending the *Land Tax Assessment Act* received Royal Assent on 25 February 2015 and is effective for the 2014-15 land tax assessment year.

The amendments provide that the land tax primary production exemption will apply, even when the primary produce is sold in a processed or converted state. For competitive neutrality reasons, the exemption will apply to land used to grow the produce but will not apply to the portion of land used to process the produce. Where land is used for both primary production and secondary processing as part of an integrated business, a partial exemption will apply.

The amendments have abolished the one-third income test (and 50% concession for those failing the one-third income test) and replaced it with a more flexible business test.

The criteria in the legislation for the business test are based upon well established common law indicators used to determine whether an activity constitutes the carrying on of a business. No single criterion is decisive, and there is often an overlap in criterion. The Commissioner will consider all of the criteria to determine whether the use of the land indicates that a primary production business is being carried out, however the weighting to be given to each criterion may vary from case to case.

The amendments have also replaced the Commissioner's discretion to exempt land with defined exemption criteria that expands the owner-user rule to include certain related entities. This allows the owner to qualify for the exemption when, for example, a related entity of the owner or family member, uses the land for a primary production business. The expanded owner-user rule is largely based on the definition of a family member in the *Duties Act 2008.*

Further information about eligibility requirements can be obtained from the Office of State Revenue on 9262 1200 or the website www.osr.wa.gov.au

CONCESSION FOR PROPERTY DEVELOPERS

From 2009-10, a concession has been available for land resulting from a subdivision in the previous financial year and still held by the subdivider at 30 June. This concession allows land tax and MRIT to be paid on the lower undeveloped (or 'englobo') value of the individual land (ie. the value prior to subdivision), rather than the full value of the subdivided lots. The concession applies for one year of assessment following the creation of the lot.

CARAVAN PARKS

An exemption is available for land used as a licensed caravan park or camping ground. Retrospective assessment of land tax may occur for up to ten years where land in receipt of this exemption is subdivided.

OTHER EXEMPTIONS AND CONCESSIONS

Other land tax exemptions and concessions include:
- land owned by, vested in or held in trust for religious or educational bodies and used for religious or educational purposes
- land used for public or religious hospitals
- land owned by, vested in or held in trust for public charitable or benevolent institutions and used for the public charitable or benevolent purposes for which the institution was established. (Amendments to this exemption are effective 9 March 2015 - refer website for further details: www.osr.wa.gov.au)
- land owned by, vested in or held in trust for various non-profit associations, and used in whole or in part in attaining the objectives of the association. (Minor amendments to this exemption are effective 25 February 2015 - refer website for further details: www.osr.wa.gov.au).
- land used for, or available to be used for, residential premises in retirement villages within the meaning of the *Retirement Villages Act 1992. (S39 of the Land Tax Assessment Act in respect to this exemption, has been replaced effective 25 February 2015 - refer website for further details: www.osr.wa.gov.au).*
- land used as an aged care facility for the provision of a residential care service certified under the *Commonwealth Aged Care Act 1997. (Minor amendments to this exemption are effective 25 February 2015 - refer website for further details: www.osr. wa.gov.au).*
- land used solely or principally for the conservation of native vegetation and subject to an approved conservation covenant
- land owned by or vested in the Crown, local government or an agency of the Crown and not leased to other parties
- land dedicated to a zoological garden, an agricultural show or other similar public purposes, and
- land held as a mining tenement.

ANTI-AVOIDANCE PROVISIONS

Sections 45A and 45B of the *Land Tax Assessment Act* enable the Commissioner to make a determination that a Minor Interest in a lot or parcel of land can be disregarded for the purposes of assessing land tax. The Commissioner can only make a determination to disregard an interest in a lot or parcel of land if the interest is a minor interest and the Commissioner is of the opinion that the purpose, or one of the purposes, of the creation of the interest was to reduce the amount of land tax payable on that, or any other, lot or parcel of land.

27.700 TASMANIAN LAND TAX

Web: www.sro.tas.gov.au Email: taxhelp@treasury.tas.gov.au Telephone: (03) 6166 4400 / 1800 001 388

Land tax is payable by anyone who owns property at 1 July each year, unless the land is:
- classified as the owner's principal place of residence
- classified as primary production, or
- exempt under the *Land Tax Act 2000*.

For the period 1 July to 30 June, land tax is assessed on the aggregate assessed land value of all property owned as at 1 July of that year, with the exclusion of exempt land and a person's principal place of residence or primary production land which both attract zero land tax.

RATES OF LAND TAX

The applicable rates of land tax from 1 July 2010 are as follows:

Aggregated land value	Tax scale
$0 – $24,999	Nil
$25,000 – $349,999	$50 plus 0.55% of value above $25,000
$350,000 and above	$1,837.50 plus 1.5% of value above $350,000

DATE OF OWNERSHIP LIABILITY

An owner at 1 July is liable for tax for the financial year commencing on that date.

The registration of title transfer with the Recorder of Titles represents an ownership change with the purchaser becoming the taxpayer for land tax purposes effective from the date of settlement.

ADJUSTMENT FACTORS

As land values in each municipality are not subject to general revaluation each year, an annual adjustment factor is applied to account for value movements since the last general valuation. The annual adjustment factor is used to arrive at an assessed land value for land tax purposes. The Valuer-General determines the annual adjustment factors which reflect the general value of land preceding the tax year within each municipality.

Land tax is calculated on the assessed land value and this is determined annually by the Valuer-General using one of the two methods below:

1. In municipalities where a revaluation is undertaken, the new land values are determined and a Notice of Valuation is sent to the property owner. Generally, approximately a third of Tasmania is revalued every two years.

2. In non-revaluation municipalities, adjusted land values are assessed using market-based adjustment factors. The rate of land tax increases in increments with the total value of land owned as shown in the table above.

EXEMPT LAND

Land may be exempt where it is:
- owned by the Crown
- owned by any charitable or religious organisation and used for those purposes
- owned by a community service organisation
- owned by a school
- subject to a conservation covenant
- used principally for Aboriginal cultural activities and is Aboriginal land
- used to operate a retirement village, or for related purposes
- used as a medical establishment or convalescent home
- owned by a local authority or other local governing or statutory public body and is a park or garden in public recreational use

- owned and used by a day procedure centre, a private hospital or a residential care service, or
- owned by the YMCA, YWCA, CWA, Boy Scouts, Girl Guides, Police Boys and Girls, or by the Returned Soldiers' League of Australia.

This list is not exhaustive; call the SRO for further information on (03) 6166 4400 or taxhelp@treasury.tas.gov.au.

GROUPING OF RELATED COMPANIES

Land held by related companies is aggregated for the purpose of calculating land tax. Two companies are related if the same person or persons control both companies, one company is related to another company to which the other is related or the companies are related under the *Corporations Act 2001*.

PRINCIPAL PLACE OF RESIDENCE

A Principal Place of Residence (PPR) classification may be applied to land on which a dwelling is erected and which is occupied and used by the owner as their main place of residence as at 1 July of each financial year. This classification cannot be applied to:

- holiday homes
- rented houses or units
- vacant land, or
- commercial land.

In order to qualify for a principal residence classification, the applicant must own at least 50 percent of the land and the residence must be occupied:

- by that person, or their spouse or former spouse
- the beneficiary of the estate of a deceased owner
- a beneficiary of a trust appointed by a court, or
- the beneficiary of a Special Disability Trust.

SPECIAL DISABILITY TRUST

From 7 December 2011, a Special Disability Trust may be eligible for a zero land tax rate (meaning that land tax may not be payable on eligible property) for the principle place of residence of a beneficiary of this type of trust. Please read the exemption guide on the relevant website.

Land is classified as principal residence land if, on 1 July in the relevant year, it was the PPR of the home owner (or through strata title) and occupied by the following people:

- the owner
- one or more of the owners who singly or jointly own 50 % or more of the property, or
- (in the case of single or joint ownership) the spouse (or former spouse) of the owner or any one of the joint owners who own 50% or more of the property.

DISASTER RELIEF

From 1 July 2013, where land is subject to fire, flood or similar disaster, the owner of the property may apply a PPR classification for up to 2 financial years following the disaster. This applies even if the property is not being used as an owner's principle place of residence.

PART APPORTIONMENT OF PRINCIPAL RESIDENCE LAND

Land can be apportioned and classified as part principal residence land if only a part of the land is partially used as an owner's principal residence. A percentage of the land will be classified as principal residence based on the usage of the land.

DECEASED ESTATE OR TRUSTEE OF A TRUST

Where the owner is a registered trustee company; the executor, administrator, guardian, committee, receiver or liquidator; the trustee appointed by a court or trustee; or the trustee of a special disability trust, the principal residence on the land must be occupied by at least one of the beneficiaries.

HOME UNIT COMPANIES

Land held by a home unit company may also receive the benefit of PPR classification where a person owning shares in the company occupies a unit as their PPR. However not all land owned by such a company qualifies. The portion of the total land value which qualifies is determined according to the value established on the floor area of the unit, compared with the total floor area of all units capable of being separately occupied. Unless separately exempt, any land not qualifying would be assessable under the general rate scales.

A person occupying residential premises in a retirement village is unable to claim principal place of residence classification on another property.

PRINCIPAL RESIDENCE ON COMPANY OWNED LAND

The land may still qualify if the dwelling is occupied as their principal residence by a person who owns at least 50% of the shares in the company, and the property is an asset of that company.

HOME BUSINESS CONCESSION

If a qualifying home business is conducted from an owner's home, land tax will not be payable on the portion of the property from which the home business is operated. Not all home businesses will qualify, please see further conditions on the website, sro.tas.gov.au

REBATES

TWO RESIDENCES OWNED IN TRANSITIONAL CIRCUMSTANCES

If an owner purchased a new principle place of residence before 30 June and has not sold the their original principle place of residence by 30 June of that year both properties may be claimed as a principle place of residence subject to a number of conditions.

NEW HOME BUILDERS

New home builders may be eligible for a land tax rebate for a financial year subject to a number of conditions.

PRINCIPAL RESIDENCE LAND REBATE

A land tax rebate is available for newly constructed principal residences where the owner did not own other principal residence land either in Tasmania or any other State or Territory, as at 1 July and the owner occupies the newly constructed dwelling before the end of the financial year. Where an owner owns two principal residences as at 1 July (for example, where the purchase of a new principal place of residence has been completed prior to 1 July and the sale of the previous principal place of residence had not been completed as at 1 July) a transitional circumstances rebate may be available (conditions apply – contact the SRO for details. Additional information is available at www.sro.tas.gov.au).

PRINCIPAL RESIDENCE RATE SCALE

Since 1 July 1996 principal residence land has been zero rated for land tax purposes.

PRIMARY PRODUCTION

Land is categorised under this classification if on 1 July in the relevant year, it was used substantially for a business of primary production which is carried out in a business-like manner with a reasonable expectation of profit.

The business of primary production includes any substantial agricultural, horticultural, viticultural, forestry, orcharding, pastoral or dairy farming, horse breeding, poultry farming or apicultural undertaking.

PRIMARY PRODUCTION LAND RATE SCALE

Since 1 July 1996 primary production land has been zero rated for land tax purposes.

PRIMARY PRODUCTION CLASSIFICATION

The primary production classification includes land:
- which is used in conjunction with commercial fishing and aquaculture activities
- that has been declared as a private timber reserve under the *Forest Practices Act 1985*
- that is permanent timber production zone land within the meaning of the *Forestry Management Act 2013*
- that has been declared as a State Forest under the *Forestry Act 1920*, or
- subject to a forest practices plan certified by the Forest Practices Authority in accordance with the State Permanent Forest Estate Policy.

PART PRIMARY PRODUCTION

Land can be classified as part primary production if the land is only partially used for substantial primary production activities.

CONSERVATION COVENANTS

Land which is subject to a conservation covenant under Part 5 of the *Nature Conservation Act 2002* as at 1 July of the financial year will be eligible for a land tax exemption.

SPORTING BODIES

Sporting bodies with land owned and used for sporting purposes may have the land tax reduced to a flat rate of 0.4 percent.

SALE OR TRANSFER OF LAND

Outstanding land tax is payable at the time of a land sale or transfer. Where a property is sold by a council under the *Local Government Act 1993* the proceeds of sale are first applied to meet the council's selling costs and then any balance is apportioned between any outstanding land lax and rates. If more than one parcel of land is owned, a proportion of total tax liability is payable. For more information visit www.sro.tas.gov.au.

NOTES

Duties and other taxes

28

28.000 DUTIES

Much like the Federal system, State governments levy a number of duties and taxes on the general population as well as specific business groups. The Duties that apply predominately to the general population are largely made up of Stamp Duties on the conveyance of land and motor vehicles. The following sections provide some detail regarding these obligations imposed by each state however, should specific guidance be required (for instance regarding surcharges for land held on trust) please contact the respective State Revenue Office.

28.010 AUSTRALIAN CAPITAL TERRITORY DUTIES

Australian Capital Territory (ACT) duties website: www.revenue.act.gov.au/duties
Telephone: 02 6207 0028

DUTIABLE PROPERTY

In the Australian Capital Territory, 'dutiable property' includes:
- land in the ACT
- a Crown lease
- a land use entitlement
- a commercial lease with a premium
- an option to purchase land in the ACT

A liability to Duty is determined under the *Duties Act 1999* and administered under the *Taxation Administration Act 1999*. Partnerships that have an indirect interest in the above listed 'dutiable property' will also be liable notwithstanding the fact that property is held by the partners in a partnership rather than the partnership itself. Goods in the ACT will also be considered to be 'dutiable property' if the subject of the arrangement that includes a dutiable transaction is considered to be 'dutiable property' pursuant to s10 of the *Duties Act 1999*.

DUTIES

Dutiable property	Rate
For land in the ACT based on the greater of the consideration or unencumbered value of the land	Conveyance rates
Partnership interest	At the rate applicable to the assets on the proportion of the unencumbered value of dutiable assets of the partnership
Goods in the ACT that involve dutiable property	At the rate applicable to the assets used solely for business purposes (until 30 June 2006)

It is immaterial whether or not a dutiable transaction is affected by a written instrument.

Liability arises when a transfer of 'dutiable property' occurs. This can take the form of an agreement of sale, declaration of trust, grant of Crown lease or when a Commercial lease is first executed. Duty is payable within 90 days after the liability arising.

DUTIABLE BUSINESS ASSETS/PARTNERSHIP INTERESTS

Duty is not chargeable on the acquisition of core business assets which are not real property and involve:
- the goodwill of a business
- intellectual property, and
- a statutory licence or permission under Commonwealth or Territory law.

Duty was also abolished on 1 July 2006 for the transfer of goods (but not if involving the transfer of land, a crown lease, land use entitlements, unquoted marketable securities or units in a unit trust). If the assets include property or vehicles the duty is payable at the rate applicable for those assets on the portion of the unencumbered value of dutiable assets conveyed.

MOTOR VEHICLES

VEHICLE REGISTRATION AND TRANSFERS

Duty is payable on the dutiable value (the greater of consideration or market value) in relation to a motor vehicle. The determined rate is $3 for every $100 or part of $100. For passenger vehicles designed to carry up to 9 occupants which have a dutiable value of more than $45,000, the rate is $1,350 plus $5 for every $100 or part of $100 in excess of $45,000.

Duty is imposed on an application for registration if a vehicle has not previously been registered in the ACT, or the name of the person in whose name the vehicle is to be registered is different to the last registration. Duty is payable by the applicant at the time the vehicle is registered. Duty is not payable under the *Duties Act 1999* for applications to register or transfer registration of a caravan or camper trailer. Duty remains payable on applications to register and transfer all other trailers that are not camper trailers.

EXEMPTIONS

Chapter 9 of the *Duties Act 1999* imposes duty on the application for registration and the transfer of motor vehicle registration and allows for certain exemptions. For more information relating to motor vehicle duty exemptions refer to Revenue Circular DAA009.

GREEN VEHICLE RATING

Additional duty is payable on motor vehicles based on the vehicle performance rating adjusted for environmental pollution impact.

A Green Vehicle Rating only applies to a new motor vehicle that has not previously been registered under:

- the *Road Transport (Vehicle Registration) Act 1999* or another Territory law, or
- a law of the Commonwealth, a State, another Territory or a foreign country.

The meaning of a new motor vehicle includes demonstrator vehicles. In order to qualify for the differential rates of duty applicable to green vehicles, a demonstrator vehicle must be sold or otherwise disposed of within one year of the date it first became a registered motor vehicle. Demonstrators that do not meet the definition of demonstrator under this instrument and are not disposed of by a licensed vehicle dealer within one year, will not qualify for the differential rates of duty applicable to green vehicles.

The duty payable for vehicles with a Green Vehicle Rating is calculated in accordance with Tables 1, 2 and 3 below.

For the purpose of charging duty, a Green Vehicle Rating for a new motor vehicle means a rating of A, B, C, or D corresponding to the vehicle's environmental performance score as determined in the Green Vehicle Guide (www.greenvehicleguide.gov.au). The environmental performance score for a motor vehicle is the total of the air pollution rating and the corresponding greenhouse rating for the vehicle.

Table 1 lists the Green Vehicle Ratings and environmental performance scores.

Table 1: Green vehicle ratings and environmental performance scores	
Green vehicle rating	**Environmental performance score**
A	16 or more
B	14 or more but less than 16
C	9.5 or more but less than 14
D	Less than 9.5
Table 2: Amounts payable	
Green vehicle rating: Motor vehicle valued at $45,000 or less	**Amount payable**
A-rated vehicle	Nil
B-rated vehicle	$2 for each $100, or part of $100, of the dutiable value of motor vehicle
C-rated vehicle and non-rated vehicle	$3 for each $100 or part of $100, of the dutiable value of motor vehicle
D-rated vehicle	$4 for each $100, or part of $100, of the dutiable value of motor vehicle

NO GREEN VEHICLE RATING

Non-rated motor vehicles are those that are currently registered or have previously been registered, or those that are not rated under the Green Vehicle Guide.

The duty payable for non-rated motor vehicles is the same rate of duty as C-rated motor vehicles in Table 2 above.

The duty payable for a non-rated passenger motor vehicle constructed primarily to carry no more than nine people and with a dutiable value of more than $45,000 is the same rate of duty as C-rated motor vehicles in Table 3 below.

However, the duty payable for certain vehicles with a dutiable value of $45,000 or more, such as a two to three seater cab chassis with equipment attached (eg. tray, tipper, garbage compactor), a motorcycle, buses for more than nine people including the driver, an invalid conveyance, or a hearse; is the same rate of duty as C-rated motor vehicles in Table 2 above. Table 2 lists the amount payable, which applies to all motor vehicles not included in Table 3. Table 3 lists the amount payable, which applies to passenger motor vehicles constructed primarily for carriage of not more than nine occupants and valued at more than $45,000.

Table 3: Amounts payable	
Green vehicle rating **Motor vehicle valued at more than $45,000**	**Amount payable**
A-rated vehicle	nil
B-rated vehicle	$900, plus $4 for each $100, or part of $100, of the dutiable value of the motor vehicle that is more than $45,000
C-rated vehicle and non-rated vehicle	$1,350, plus $5 for each $100, or part of $100, of the dutiable value of the motor vehicle that is more than $45,000
D-rated vehicle	$1,800, plus $6 for each $100, or part of $100, of the dutiable value of the motor vehicle that is more than $45,000

For further information regarding the administration and payment of duty on the registration or transfer of registration of a motor vehicle, refer to Revenue Circular DAA005.3 and DAA009.

DOCUMENTATION AND COMPLIANCE

The purchaser must give to the Road Transport Authority their details, the details of the vehicle purchased and a notice of disposal from the former owner. The *Road Transport (Vehicle Registration) Act 1999* provides that a person who purchases a vehicle is required to transfer the registration within 14 days of purchase.

CONVEYANCE AND TRANSFER OF REAL PROPERTY

In the Australian Capital Territory, a Crown lease represents 'real property'.

Duty is imposed on real property and includes the following:

- the grant of a Crown lease or Commercial lease
- the agreement to sell or transfer dutiable property
- a declaration of trust over dutiable property, and
- the transfer (or agreement to transfer) a land use entitlement.

DUTY AT THE GENERAL RATE

The duty (often referred to as conveyance rates) is based on the higher of the consideration or the unencumbered value of the land transferred (or agreed to be transferred) at the determined rate:

Duty payable: Transaction dates from 3 June 2015	
Land value	**Rate**
Up to $200,000	$20 or $1.80 per $100 or part thereof, (whichever is greater)
$200,001 to $300,000	$3,600 plus $3.00 per $100 or part thereof by which the value exceeds $200,000
$300,001 to $500,000	$6,000 plus $4.00 per $100 or part thereof by which the value exceeds $300,000
$500,001 to $750,000	$14,600 plus $5.00 per $100 for each $100 or part thereof by which the value exceeds $500,000
$750,001 to $1,000,000	$27,100 plus $6.50 per $100 for each $100 or part thereof by which the value exceeds $750,000
$1,000,001 to 1,454,999	$43,350 plus $7.00 per $100 for each $100 or part thereof by which the value exceeds $1,000,000
$1,455,000 and over	A flat rate of $5.17 per $100 applied to the total transaction value

'OFF THE PLAN' PURCHASES

Liability for duty on residential property purchased under an 'off the plan' agreement arises if at least one of the following events occurs:

- the agreement is completed
- any of the purchaser's interest is assigned, or
- the following period, beginning on the date of the agreement, ends:
  - for a purchase agreement for a declared affordable house and land package: two years
  - for any other 'off the plan' purchase agreement: one year, and
- a certificate of occupancy is issued.

HOME BUYER CONCESSION

The Home Buyer Concession Scheme (HBCS) is an Australian Capital Territory Government initiative administered by the Australian Capital Territory Revenue Office to assist persons in purchasing a residential home or residential vacant land by charging duty at a concessional rate. The concession ceased for the purchase of an established property as of 1 September 2012.

The lodgment for assessment of duty of interdependent land and building contracts will continue to be assessed as off the plan agreements.

The HBCS applies to property where the transaction date, which is the date of grant, transfer, or agreement for transfer (whichever is first) occurs between 1 January 2015 and 30 June 2015. This is the date of first execution of an agreement or transfer, not the settlement date. The concession applies to new or substantially renovated properties for transactions dated 3 June 2015 to 31 December 2015 (total gross income threshold is $160,000 from 5 June 2013). For previous years concessions see past Tax Summary guides.

Further details on the application of this scheme can also be found at www.revenue.act.gov.au/duties.

PENSIONER DUTY CONCESSION

The Pensioner Duty Concession Scheme (PDCS) is to assist eligible pensioners to move to accommodation more suited to their needs (eg. from a house to a townhouse) but who may find the duty involved to be a significant impediment. Such persons are assisted to purchase a residential home or residential vacant land by paying duty at a concessional rate. The PDCS has been extended for a further year in the Budget 2015-16.

The lodgment for duty of interdependent land and building contracts will continue to be assessed as off the plan agreements. For further information see *Off the plan agreements, assessment of duty*.

For the purposes of determining the application of the PDCS it is necessary to determine the transaction date, which is the date of grant, transfer, or agreement for transfer (whichever is first). Different rules apply where the transaction date is in the period:

- 1 January 2013 to 30 June 2013
- 1 July 2013 to 31 December 2013
- 1 January 2014 to 3 June 2014
- 4 June 2014 to 31 December 2014, and
- 3 June 2015 to 31 December 2015

OVER 60s DUTY CONCESSION

The 'Over 60s Duty Concession Scheme' (O60DCS) is to assist eligible non-pensioners move to accommodation more suited to their needs (e.g. from a house to a townhouse) but who may find the duty involved to be a significant impediment. The O60DCS is available to all people aged 60 years or older. The scheme commences 3 June 2015 and runs for two years (2014-15 and 2015-16).

Eligible applicants are assisted to purchase a residential home or residential vacant block by paying duty at a concessional rate. The Home Bonus Scheme applies to properties where the transfer of dutiable property occurs between 3 June 2015 and 31 December 2015. This is the date of execution not settlement.

The rate of Concessional duty payable for both Pensioner's concession and over 60s scheme from 3 June 2015 – 31 December 2015 for both residential homes and vacant land is as follows:

Concessional duty payable			
Residential homes		**Vacant land**	
Dutiable value	**Concessional duty payable**	**Dutiable value**	**Concessional duty payable**
$625,000 or less	$20 (minimum duty)	$332,100 or less	$20 (minimum duty)
More than $625,000 but less than $807,000	$16.90 for each $100 or part thereof by which the dutiable value exceeds $625,000 ($20 minimum duty)	More than $332,100 but less than $391,700	$17.20 for each $100 or part thereof by which the dutiable value exceeds $332,100 ($20 minimum duty)
$807,000 or more	No concession	$391,700 or more	No concession

See www.revenue.act.gov.au/duties for further details.

LAND RENT

The Land Rent Scheme is part of the Australian Capital Territory Government's Affordable Housing Action Plan. The Land Rent Scheme gives a lessee the option of renting land through a land rent lease rather than purchasing the land to build a home. The *Land Rent Act 2008* is administered under the *Taxation Administration Act 1999.*

Under the scheme, purchasers of a single dwelling residential block (previously unleased land) sold by the Land Development Agency (LDA) have the option of applying for the crown lease to be issued as a land rent lease. The advantage for potential lessees in taking up this option is the reduction of the up-front costs associated with owning a house. That is, lessees will not need to finance the cost of the land, only the costs associated with the transfer of the land (such as duty) and the construction of the home.

Land rented under a land rent lease is subject to payment of an annual land rent charge. In addition, the lessee will be liable to duty on the grant of the land rent lease, rates, and, if applicable, land tax. Duty is payable on the land rent lease on the same basis as applies to the grant of a nominal crown lease. The dutiable value is not reduced by virtue of the lessees taking a land rent option.

As of 1 October 2013, entrance to the Land Rent Scheme is restricted to low to moderate income earning households eligible for the discount land rent rate of 2%. The standard 4% rate will no longer be provided to new entrants to the scheme. The relevant date of the transaction is the contract date.

For Land Rent leases where the Crown lease was first granted under a contract entered into on or after 1 October 2013, and for any subsequent transfers of such a block, applicants must meet the discounted land rent eligibility criteria:

- income: threshold of $160,000 applies and is calculated on a household basis (that is, the income of all lessees and their domestic partner). The income threshold is increased by $3,330 for each dependent child up to a maximum of five
- lessees who enter into the Land Rent Scheme cannot own any other real property at any time while leasing a land rent block, and
- at least one participant in the scheme must reside in the property built on the block.

Lessees who have entered into arrangements prior to 31 October 2013 will not be affected. Applicants for a land rent lease are encouraged to seek legal advice.

LAND RENT AMOUNT: PRE-31 OCTOBER 2013

The discount land rent rate is 2% of the unimproved value of the leased land while the standard land rent rate is 4% of the unimproved value of the leased land.

When a land rent lease is granted, lessees will commence on the standard land rent rate. Lessees who are eligible for the discounted land rent rate must apply to the Commissioner for ACT Revenue (the Commissioner).

GENERAL INSURANCE

Duty is payable on the amount of premium paid in relation to a contract for general or life insurance. Normally this duty is paid by policyholders to insurance companies. Insurance companies then submit returns and payments on or before the 21st of each month to the Revenue Office.

Amateur sporting and community not-for-profit bodies may be exempt from duty on public liability insurance and other prescribed general insurance required to hold a public event. Organisations must apply to the Commissioner to determine eligibility for exemption. Further details are provided in duty exemption guidelines available at www.revenue.act.gov.au/duties.

DUTY AMOUNT

The amount of duty payable will depend on the type and value of insurance policy. From 1 July 2014 the rates of insurance duty are as follows:

- duty on general insurance contracts (including disablement or sickness policies) is calculated at the rate of 4% of the net premiums received.
- duty on life insurance policies that are term, temporary, or insurance rider policies is calculated at the rate of 2% of the first year's premium.
- duty on life insurance contracts is 40 cents on the first $2,000 or part thereof $2,000 of the total sum insured and 8 cents for every $200 or part of $200, of the sum insured that is more than $2,000.
- Disability income insurance duty is 6% of the relevant amount.

Further details are provided in the Online Return Form that is available at www.revenue.act.gov.au/duties.

SPECIAL APPLICATION FOR REFUND OF GENERAL INSURANCE DUTY

Following a 2009 NSW Court decision, the Australian Capital Territory Revenue Office will refund duty paid on certain general insurance policies. The special duty refund arrangement applies only where:

- the policy was provided by persons who were not registered or authorised insurers under the *Duties Act 1999*, and
- the duty was paid during 1 March 1999 to 17 May 2006 as part of a general insurance premium.

To make an application for a refund of insurance duty use the Special Application Refund Form.

REFUNDS

Where a premium is returned, a refund is available for the amount of duty paid on the returned premium.

Following a 2009 NSW Court decision, the Australian Capital Territory Revenue Office will refund duty paid on certain general insurance policies. The special duty refund arrangement applies only where:

- the policy was provided by persons not registered or authorised insurers under the *Duties Act 1999*, and
- the duty was paid during 1 March 1999 to 17 May 2006 as part of a general insurance premium.

OTHER LEVIES AND TAXES

AMBULANCE SERVICE LEVY

The ambulance service levy, as defined under the *Emergencies Act 2004*, is payable by private health insurance companies to offset the cost of providing ambulance services in the Territory.

For the reference months January 2015 to December 2015, the levy is calculated at the rate of $2.26 per person per week and $4.52 per family per week. Private health insurers are required to lodge returns by the 15th day of each month.

Contributions by some people are exempt from the ambulance service levy.

FIRE AND EMERGENCY SERVICES LEVY

The Fire and Emergency Services Levy in 2014-15 is imposed on all rateable properties as follows:

- Residential and Rural: Fixed charge $130.00, and
- Commercial: AUV x Marginal Rates as follows:

$1 - $300,000	0.6097%
$300,001 - $2,000,000	0.7153%
$2,000,001 and above	0.8209%

The amount imposed for the Fire and Emergency Levy for each property, together with the payment options, are detailed on 2014-2015 Rate Assessment Notice. Payment in full will attract a 3% discount, payment in quarterly installments will not. Pensioners eligible for a general rates pensioner rebate receive a rebate of 50% of the levy.

CITY CENTRE MARKETING AND IMPROVEMENTS LEVY

The *Rates Amendment Act 2006 (No 2)* was passed by the Legislative Assembly on 6 March 2007. The Act provides the collection mechanism for the City Centre Marketing and Improvements Levy. The revenue collected from the levy is used to promote, maintain and improve the amenity of the Civic area. The levy is imposed on rateable commercial land within a prescribed collection area. The collection area will be divided into two zones with differential percentage rates to apply. These percentage rates, and the collection area, are determined by two disallowable instruments. The CCMIL in 2014-15 is imposed on rateable commercial properties within the prescribed collection area as follows:

- Area A – Retail Core   AUV x 0.2992%, and
- Area B – Non Retail Core AUV x 0.2161%.

See www.revenue.act.gov.au/ for further information.

UTILITIES (NETWORK FACILITIES) TAX

Effective from 21 December 2006 under the *Utilities (Network Facilities Tax) Act 2006*, this tax is imposed upon the owners of any network facility on land in the Australian Capital Territory. A network facility is any part of the infrastructure of a utility network not fixed to land subject to either a lease, a license granted by the Territory or any right prescribed by regulation.

Utility networks include networks for transmitting and distributing electricity, gas, sewage, water and telecommunications. Examples of network facility include power lines or pipes over or under land, and telecommunications cabling.

Registered owners of utility networks in the Australian Capital Territory provide an annual return accompanied by payment, before 31 May of each year. For the year ending 31 March 2015, the determined rate is $992.

ENERGY INDUSTRY LEVY

The Energy Industry Levy is used to recover the costs of regulating utilities and is applied to four energy sectors:

- electricity distribution
- electricity supply
- gas distribution, and
- gas supply.

Energy utilities providing services in the Australian Capital Territory are required to register with the Commissioner. This must be done within 90 days after commencing the provision of services.

LEVY AMOUNT

Australian Capital Territory regulatory costs are determined each year and apportioned between the four energy sectors. The fixed and variable amounts vary according to the reference year and sector type. These amounts are displayed in the online return form.

LODGMENT OF RETURNS

Registered utilities are required to lodge annual returns. Annual returns for each year must be lodged with the Commissioner by 31 October in the same financial year. Use the Online Energy Industry Levy Return to lodge the annual return and make payment by EFT or BPay.

28.020 NORTHERN TERRITORY DUTIES

Website: www.revenue.nt.gov.au   Email: ntrevenue@nt.gov.au   Telephone: 1300 305 353

The *Stamp Duty Act 2002* imposes duty on dutiable instruments and transactions. The instruments liable to duty are generally described in Schedule 1 to the Act. Exempt instruments and transactions are generally described in Schedule 2 to the Act.

Following is a general overview of the documents and transactions liable to stamp duty including dutiable property, rates, concessions and exemptions. For further detail reference should be made to the Act.

DUTIABLE PROPERTY

A conveyance or an agreement to convey dutiable property is liable to stamp duty. Where dutiable property is acquired without being evidenced by a dutiable document, the person acquiring the property is required to complete a statement detailing the transaction.

Dutiable property includes land (including leases, mining tenements, exploration rights and fixtures), goodwill, intellectual property, trade names and licences, patents, options (to purchase property or an interest in it), and chattels included as part of the property (and an estate or interest, including a partnership interest, in dutiable property) but not trading stock, livestock, registrable motor vehicles, cash and deposits at call and negotiable instruments.

RATES OF DUTY

Duty is calculated on the purchase price or unencumbered value of the dutiable property (including agreements to transfer and convey and surrenders of dutiable property), whichever is the greater, as follows:

On the greater of the value of the property or the consideration expressed:

- For values up to $525,000, the duty is calculated as $D = (0.06571441 \times V^2) + 15V$, where:

    D = the duty payable in Australian dollars

    V = the dutiable value divided by 1,000

    eg. if the value of the property is $500,000, $D = [(0.06571441 \times 500 \times 500) + (15 \times 500)] = \$23,929$

- For dutiable values over $525,000 but under $3 million, a rate of 4.95% applies to the total amount.
- For dutiable values of $3 million or more, a rate of 5.45% applies to the total amount.

HOME INCENTIVE SCHEMES

FIRST HOME OWNER GRANT

The First Home Owner Grant replaced the First Home Owner Concession from 4 December 2012. The dutiable property it applies to is determined with reference to the date of the transaction and the value of the transaction as follows:

Commencement date	Transaction eligibility threshold
After 1 January 2015	No threshold applies
From 4 December 2012 to 1 January 2015	$600,000
From 1 January 2010 to 3 December 2012	$750,000
Prior to 1 January 2010	No threshold applied

The amount of the grant is the lesser of the consideration actually paid for the eligible transaction, or:

Commencement date of eligible transaction	New home	Established home
From 1 January 2015	$26,000	Nil
From 13 May 2014 to 31 December 2014	$26,000	• Urban area $12,000 • Elsewhere $25,000
From 4 December 2012 to 12 May 2014	$25,000	• Urban area $12,000 • Elsewhere $25,000
Prior to 3 December 2012	$7,000	$7,000

Further details can be found at www.revenue.nt.gov.au.

PRINCIPAL PLACE OF RESIDENCE REBATE

The Northern Territory Government provides a stamp duty concession to persons purchasing a home or land on which to build a home that is to be their principal place of residence. The concession is available to all persons other than those eligible for the First Home Owner Grant or the stamp duty Senior, Pensioner and Carer Concession.

The scheme is not means tested.

From 4 December 2012, the Principal Place of Residence Rebate is $7,000 off the duty payable but is now only available to persons who are purchasing a new home or land on which a new home will be built.

SENIOR, PENSIONER AND CARER CONCESSION

The Northern Territory Government provides a stamp duty concession for non-first home buyers aged at least 60 years or buyers who hold a Northern Territory Pensioner and Carer Concession Card and purchase a home or land on which to build a home that is to be their principal place of residence. The scheme is not means tested, however eligibility ceases if the dutiable value of the home is more than $750,000 and $385,000 for vacant land on which a home is to be built. For vacant land, there is no limit on the cost of construction of the home.

From 28 April 2015, a concession of up to $10,000 off the duty payable may be claimed, which represents the duty on approximately the first $292,300 of the property's value. For transactions before 28 April 2015, the amount of the concession was up to $8,500.

PARTITION OF LAND

Duty of $20 is payable where it is an equal partition and no consideration for the conveyance is given. If consideration is given, or agreed to be given, or if the partition is unequal, based on only the difference in the value, duty is charged at conveyance rates but only on the amount of the difference or if all or part of the consideration is not ascertainable at the time of the grant, the higher of the ascertainable consideration or the unencumbered value of the land.

IF IMPROVEMENTS DONE BY OR FOR TRANSFEREE

When calculating the value on which duty is payable, the Northern Territory Revenue Office can exclude the value (as at the date on which conveyance is executed) of any improvements on the land claimed by the conveyee to have been effected by him/her, or at his/her expense.

TRANSFERS FOLLOWING A STAMPED AGREEMENT

Duty of $5 is payable where conveyance made subsequent to, and in conformity with, a duly stamped agreement for such conveyance. Duty of $5 is also payable where conveyance is not in conformity with a duly stamped agreement, where the purchaser named in the agreement and the transferee under the transfer are 'related' (as defined) and valuable consideration is not provided by the transferee to the purchaser.

ACQUISITIONS IN CERTAIN CORPORATIONS AND UNIT TRUST SCHEMES ENTITLED TO LAND

Any conveyance of a marketable security resulting in an acquisition of a significant interest, or a further interest, in certain land owning corporations or unit trusts: duty on a conveyance for the Northern Territory land of the corporation or unit trust (including its share of Northern Territory land held by 'linked entities').

The legislation is directed at companies and trusts (including those listed on a recognised financial market such as the Australian Securities Exchange) which own land in the Northern Territory (whether directly or through holdings in 'linked entities') with an unencumbered value of not less than $500,000.

'Land' comprises land in the Northern Territory and includes an estate or interest in land, a lease of land or a mining tenement (including exploration rights) and anything fixed to land (irrespective of whether it would be regarded as a fixture at common law).

A person has a 'significant interest' if that person would have an entitlement to either:
- 90% of the property of a publicly listed corporation or publicly listed unit trust scheme, or
- for other corporations and unit trust schemes, 50% or more of all the property of the corporation or scheme.

if the corporation or trust was to be wound up immediately after acquisition of the interest.

If the listing is, or is part of, a tax avoidance scheme, the threshold is 50%.

Special rules apply to mergers of land holding entities. For precise details of the land-holding provisions, refer to Part 3, Division 8A of the *Stamp Duty Act* and relevant Revenue Circulars.

EXEMPTIONS

- Conveyance of company property on a distribution in specie to a shareholder following liquidation proceedings where the distribution is not part of a scheme to avoid stamp duty.
- Appointment or replacement of a trustee if no beneficial interest in the property is conveyed.
- Conveyance to the Territory, Commonwealth or to an authority of the Commonwealth.
- Exemptions for public benevolent institutions, religious institutions, public hospitals, and schools now include all non-profit organisations that have a sole or dominant purpose that is benevolent, charitable, philanthropic or patriotic (other than commercial activities); the exemption does not apply where the property is used in a manner that competes with another entity's business irrespective of how the entity uses any funds derived from this use.
- Conveyance from a trustee to a beneficiary not made for valuable consideration.
- Conveyance from a trustee of a discretionary trust to a beneficiary is only exempt if that beneficiary is a natural person who takes the property in a non-fiduciary capacity and the conveyance is not made for valuable consideration.
- A conveyance to a Special Disability Trust where no valuable consideration is given.

DEED (NOT OTHERWISE CHARGEABLE UNDER ANOTHER PART)

Stamp duty of $20 is payable on deeds not otherwise chargeable with conveyance duty that constitute a trust, vary a trust in any way, deal with actual, potential or contingent interests or entitlements under a trust or extinguishes a trust. All parties to the Deed are jointly liable for the payment of the duty.

FORECLOSURE ORDER

On the dutiable value of the property in the order, the same duty is levied as on a conveyance.

INSURANCE: LIFE POLICIES

From 1 July 2015, life insurance policies relating to a person residing in the Northern Territory are no longer dutiable. 'Life insurance riders' (ie. policies that are packaged with life insurance and provide additional cover for further specified events and contingencies, such as trauma, illness or income protection policies) are however, subject to general insurance duty. Transitional provisions apply to life insurance policies issued before 1 July 2015, or for group life insurance policies where members joined a group prior to that date. For further information on this reform, please refer to Revenue Circular RC-SD-004 2015-16 Budget Measures - Life Insurance Duty (Abolition).

GENERAL INSURANCE POLICIES

General insurance policies that relate to property or risk that may occur in the Northern Territory are liable to stamp duty at a rate of 10% of the premium paid for the policy. Where the policy also relates to a risk or property outside of the Territory, the premium is apportioned accordingly (refer to Commissioner's Guideline CG-SD-006 for details).

DUTY PAYABLE ON MONTHLY RETURNS

Where an Australian insurer effects the policy, the insurer must register (using form F-SD-016) and remit duty generally by monthly return. The insurer usually passes the cost of the duty on to their customers. Where an overseas insurer effects the policy, the insured is required to lodge a return (F-SD-018) and remit the duty.

EXEMPTIONS

- Any insurance cover-note in pursuance of which a duly stamped policy is issued within three months of the date of the cover-note.
- The insurance of goods or merchandise or the freight of goods or merchandise carried by sea, land or air.
- A policy of medical benefits insurance issued by a person registered as a private health insurer under Part 4-3 of the *Private Health Insurance Act 2007 (Cth)*.
- Any policy of insurance issued to the original insured (or to the insured's personal representative) in pursuance of a cover-note which has been duly stamped as a policy.
- Any policy of insurance taken out as a requirement of the *Workers Rehabilitation and Compensation Act*.
- A life policy issued by a life insurer.
- Residential building insurance policies and fidelity certificates required under the *Building Act*.

LEASE OF LAND IN THE TERRITORY (OR A FRANCHISE AGREEMENT)

The grant of a lease also remains dutiable at conveyance rates set out above if valuable consideration (eg. a premium) in addition to, or instead of, rent is given for the lease (other than a lease that is a residence contract under the *Retirement Villages Act*, which remains exempt from duty).

Duty is calculated on the amount or value, of the consideration payable.

MOTOR VEHICLE CERTIFICATE OF REGISTRATION

Stamp duty is payable on the issue or transfer of a motor vehicle certificate of registration. Duty is calculated at the rate of $3 per $100 (or part thereof) of the purchase price of the vehicle including additional equipment and accessories fitted to the vehicle if the transaction is made on normal commercial terms. In any other case, duty is calculated on the greater of the market value (including additional equipment and accessories) at the time of the transaction or at the time the application for registration or transfer is made.

EXEMPTIONS

- Any vehicle registered in a State or Territory of the Commonwealth in the name of the present owner (which had not been transferred since then to some other person) providing duty has been paid under any law in force in the Commonwealth, a State or Territory.
- A motor vehicle certificate of registration issued following a transfer:
  - to a person who is the spouse, de facto partner, parent or child of the person in whose name the vehicle was last registered (whether in the Territory or elsewhere) before the issue of the motor vehicle certificate of registration, or
  - to or from the spouse, de facto partner, parent, child or stepchild jointly with that person, if the transfer is wholly by way of gift.
- A motor vehicle certificate of registration issued to a person who is engaged solely or principally in the business of agricultural or pastoral production other than in respect of a vehicle designed primarily and principally for the transport of persons.
- A motor vehicle certificate of registration issued to a person to give effect to a change in that person's name or a change in the name of the business carried on by that person.
- A motor vehicle certificate of registration issued to a person:
  - who is the executor or administrator of, or the person administering, the estate of a deceased person for the purpose of transferring the vehicle to a person beneficially entitled to the vehicle
  - who is the executor or administrator of, or the person administering, the estate of a deceased person for the purpose of sale in the course of winding up the estate of the deceased person, or
  - who is beneficially entitled to the vehicle under the estate of the deceased person.
- Registration or transfer of a vehicle by a veteran eligible to receive an Extreme Disablement Adjustment (EDA) pension under s22(4) of the *Veterans' Fntitlements Act (Cth)* or a special rate of pension (ie. TPI pension) under s24(2) of the *Veterans' Entitlement Act (Cth)* and the vehicle is for non-commercial use.
- The registration or transfer of a vehicle pursuant to a Family Law Court settlement or the breakdown of a de facto relationship.
- A duplicate motor vehicle registration certificate.
- A motor vehicle certificate of registration issued on an application by the Territory, by a Government Business Division declared by regulation to be a Government Business Division for the purpose of this item or by a person acting on behalf of the Territory other than a Government Business Division.
- A motor vehicle certificate of registration issued to a person who, in the opinion of the Commissioner, is engaged principally in the business of buying and selling motor vehicles in respect of:
  - a vehicle acquired by the motor vehicle trader for the purposes of resale by the motor vehicle trader in the ordinary course of business, or
  - a new motor vehicle used solely or principally by the motor trader to sell new motor vehicles of the same class, other than:
    * a vehicle used solely or principally by the motor vehicle trader, a member of staff or of the trader's family, or
    * a vehicle used for general purposes in the motor vehicle trader's business.

- Motorised wheelchairs.
- Experimental or research vehicles with no readily ascertainable market value.
- Vehicles brought into the Territory to take part in a specific event.
- A classic motor vehicle, an individually constructed vehicle or a street rod (ie. an enthusiastic vehicle as defined in *Motor Vehicles (Fees and Charges) Regulations*).
- Vehicles registered in the name of a public hospital, public benevolent institution, religious institutions, public education institutions or non-profit school bodies or a non-profit organisation having as its sole or dominant purpose a charitable, benevolent, philanthropic or patriotic purpose.
- A motor vehicle registration, issued solely to correct an error on a previously paid registration.
- A non-motorised trailer, such as a caravan, that has a gross vehicle mass of not more than 4.5 tonnes.

28.030 VICTORIAN DUTIES

The *Duties Act 2000* commenced on 1 July 2001.
Website: www.sro.vic.gov.au/ Email: sro@sro.vic.gov.au Phone: 13 21 61

TRANSFER OF PROPERTY AND ACQUISITION OF LAND-USE ENTITLEMENTS

Duty is calculated on the greater of:
- the market value of the property, or
- the consideration – including any GST.

The purchaser or transferee is liable to pay the duty within 30 days of the transaction.

The rates of duty differ depending on the date of the contract. The following standard duty rates apply to a transfer of property for contracts entered into on or after 6 May 2008:

Property value	Rate
Up to $25,000	1.4%
$25,001 to $130,000	$350 + 2.4% of the surplus over $25,000
$130,001 to $960,000	$2,870 + 6% of the surplus over $130,000
Over $960,000	5.5%

NOTE: Amounts are rounded to the nearest whole dollar for these transactions.

PRINCIPAL PLACE OF RESIDENCE CONCESSION

A duty concession for the purchase of a Principal Place of Residence (PPR) is available where the property is valued at more than $130,000 and less than $550,000. The rates of duty are applicable as follows:

Dutiable value of PPR	Reduced rate of duty	Standard rate of duty	Difference
More than $130,000	$2,870 plus 5% of amount over $130,000	$2,870 plus 6% of amount over $130,000	Rate reduction of 1%
More than $440,000 to $550,000	$18,370 plus 6% of amount over $440,000		Duty reduction of $3,100

If a contract of sale has been entered into for the purchase of a PPR, the purchaser may be entitled to the PPR concession if the contract was entered into on or after 6 May 2008 and the purchaser intends to use and occupy the property as their PPR for a continuous period of at least 12 months within 12 months of becoming entitled to possession of the property. Where there are two or more purchasers, at least one of them must satisfy the above requirements. If these requirements are not met, duty will be reassessed at the standard rate.

Land will not be considered as being able to be occupied as a PPR unless there is a building affixed to the land that, in the Commissioner's opinion, is designed and constructed primarily for residential purposes and may lawfully be used as a PPR.

A duty reduction of 50% for the purchase of a PPR valued up to $600,000 is available for first home buyers of both newly constructed and established homes for transactions that occur on or after 1 September 2014.

The rates of duty are applicable as follows:

Dutiable value of PPR	Reduced rate of duty	Standard rate of duty
Up to $25,000	1.4% less 50%	1.4%
$25,001 to $130,000	$350 plus 2.4% of amount over $25,000 less 50%	$350 plus 2.4% of the amount over $25,000
$130,001 to $440,000	$2,870 plus 5% of the amount over $130,000 less 50%	$2,870 plus 6% of the amount over $130,000
$440,001 to $550,000	$18,370 plus 6% of the amount over $440,000 less 50%	
$550,001 to $600,000	$28,070 plus 6% of the amount over $550,000 less 50%	

For more information regarding the duty eligibility requirements, please visit www.sro.vic.gov.au or contact the SRO on 13 21 61.

FIRST HOME BUYERS

In addition to the PPR concession, first home buyers may also be eligible for the First Home Owner Grant (the Grant). For contracts entered into on or after 1 July 2013, the Grant is only payable for first home buyers who enter into a contract to purchase or build a new home and the price of purchase or construction of the home does not exceed $750,000. The exception to this requirement is where the contract relates to a home that is on, or to be built on, primary production land.

NOTE: The First Home Owner Bonus (the Bonus) and the Regional First Home Bonus (the Regional Bonus) ceased to apply for contracts entered into on or after 1 July 2012. The Grant on the purchase of an established home concludes on 1 July 2013. First home buyers may be eligible to receive the PPR concession in addition to the Grant.

First home buyers with at least one dependent child, who enter into a contract to purchase their first home may be entitled to a full or partial exemption or concession from duty if the dutiable value of the property does not exceed $200,000. In order to be eligible for the exemption, the home buyer must have at least one child under the age of 18 prior to or within 11 months of the contract date. However, this duty relief cannot be granted if either the home buyer or their spouse or partner has previously held an estate in fee simple in land on which a dwelling was erected which was used and occupied as their PPR anywhere in Australia.

The value of the exemption/concession decreases as the value of the property increases.

Value	Duty
Up to $150,000	Exemption
$150,001 to $200,000	Concession
$200,001 or more	No exemption or concession

Where an eligible first home buyer with a dependent child also qualifies for the Grant, the Bonus and Regional Bonus (if the contract was entered into before 1 July 2012), they must elect to receive either the exemption or concession from duty or the Bonus and Regional Bonus, they cannot receive both.

An eligible first home buyer with a dependent child will automatically receive the PPR duty concession.

Please note that the formulae for calculating the concession is too complicated to include in this publication. Contact the SRO for more details on 13 21 61.

PENSIONER EXEMPTION OR CONCESSION FROM DUTY

An exemption or concession from duty may apply to any pensioner eligible to receive benefits under the *State Concessions Act 2004*. This includes Department of Social Security, or Department of Veterans' Affairs Pensioner Concession Cards, Commonwealth Health Cards and Commonwealth Seniors Health Cards.

The exemption or concession is based on the dutiable value of the property (and of any goods sold with it) where the contract has been entered into on or after 1 July 2011. Note that other thresholds apply prior to this date.

Value	Duty
Up to $330,000	Exemption or refund
$330,001 to $750,000	Concession or partial refund
$750,001 or more	No exemption or concession

Where an eligible pensioner also qualifies for the Grant, the Bonus and Regional Bonus (if the contract was entered into before 1 July 2012), they must elect to receive either the exemption or concession from duty or the Bonus and Regional Bonus, they cannot receive both.

Please note that an eligible pensioner will automatically receive the PPR duty concession.

Pensioners who elect to receive the exemption or concession from duty must apply to the SRO after settlement.

OFF THE PLAN SALES

Where a person enters into a contract of sale for the purchase of a land and building package or the refurbishment of an existing building and the construction or refurbishment has not commenced or is incomplete at the date the contact was entered into, duty concessions apply in respect of the post-contract construction or refurbishment costs.

PARTITION OF LAND

Duty is payable on any excess in value of property received over the value of the original entitlement at the same rates as for Transfers of Property.

INSURANCE BUSINESS: GENERAL

General insurers who insure property or risks in Victoria must register and lodge monthly returns (by the 21st day of each month) in respect of all general insurance unless it is exempt insurance or life insurance. The amount of duty payable is 10% of the amount of any premiums paid.

INSURANCE ARRANGED WITH A PERSON WHO IS NOT A REGISTERED INSURER

If a person/firm takes or renews general insurance outside Victoria (with a company, firm or person who is not registered in Victoria) to insure property in Victoria or against any risk, contingency or event occurring in Victoria, within 21 days of obtaining the cover, the insured person must lodge a return. The amount of duty payable is 10% of the amount of any premiums paid.

LIFE INSURANCE POLICY RIDERS

Life insurance was abolished effective from 1 July 2014.

Effective from 1 July 2014 *all* life insurance policy riders are to be treated as general insurance and not life insurance by providing that:

- If a life insurance policy offers the payment of benefits on events that do not relate to or depend on life, then this *additional insurance* is taken to be general insurance and not life insurance
- Insurance duty will apply to the *additional insurance* offered by *life insurance policy riders* regardless of whether:
    - the life insurance and additional insurance are separate or distinct matters; and
    - payment of a benefit under the *additional insurance* component of the life insurance policy will or may reduce the benefit payable under the life insurance component of the policy or terminate the policy

- Where no separately identifiable part of the premium payable in respect of the policy is attributable to the *additional insurance*, or in the Commissioner's view, the identified part of the premium attributable to the *additional insurance* is not reflective of the *additional insurance*, the Commissioner may determine the amount or proportion of the premium attributable to the *additional insurance* for the purposes of calculating the duty payable.

The duty chargeable on the premium paid in relation to a contract of insurance is 10% of the amount of the premium.

EXEMPTIONS

The *Duties Act 2000* provides several exemptions. Some examples include (but are not confined to):

- insurance against damage by hail to cereal and fruit crops
- insurance on any premiums covering transit risks associated with all goods carried by land, sea, air, or on insurance on the hull of a floating vessel used for commercial purposes
- all health insurance business
- risks outside Victoria
- WorkCover
- policies of re-insurance from one registered insurer to another provided duty has been paid on the premium
- Private Fidelity Insurance schemes, and
- insurance carried out by Registered Friendly Societies.

INSURANCE: LIFE

Life insurance has been abolished since 1 July 2014. However certain life insurance riders may be dutiable as general insurance (see above).

LEASE, AGREEMENT FOR LEASE OR ASSIGNMENT OF LEASE

Under the lease provisions, duty is charged on the grant of a lease for which any consideration other than rent reserved is paid or agreed to be paid, either in respect of the lease or the acquisition of certain rights or interests pertaining to the underlying land. Duty is also charged on the transfer or assignment of a lease for which consideration is paid or agreed to be paid, either in respect of the transfer or assignment or the acquisition of certain rights or interests pertaining to the underlying land. Such rights include a right to purchase the land or a right to a transfer of the land, an option to purchase the land or an option for a transfer of the land, a right of first refusal in respect of the sale or transfer of the land or any other lease, licence, contract, scheme or arrangement by which the transferee or assignee, or associated person, obtains any right or interest in the land that is the subject of the lease other than the leasehold estate.

Under such leasing arrangements, the rights and benefits obtained by the lessee are viewed as being equivalent to the rights and benefits obtained by a person who acquires the land directly. Essentially, the lessee acquires rights over the land equivalent to ownership. The consideration paid, or agreed to be paid, is for the acquisition of these valuable rights and is in contrast to the rent payable under the lease, which is often minimal.

The lease provisions apply in respect of the grant of a lease entered into on or after 21 November 2008 for which consideration other than rent reserved is paid or to be paid. The provisions also apply in respect of the transfer or assignment after 21 November 2008 of a lease entered into before or after that date if consideration is paid or to be paid for that transfer or assignment. Similarly, the surrender after 21 November 2008 of a lease entered into before or after that date and for which consideration was paid or to be paid would be dutiable. However, no duty is payable on the surrender after 21 November 2008 of a lease for which no consideration was paid in respect of its grant, transfer or assignment.

The lease provisions apply broadly and potentially include the grant, transfer, assignment or surrender of a lease for which consideration is paid in respect of any Victorian land whether used for residential or commercial purposes. Residential leases include, for example, leases of caravan park sites and caravans, leases of alpine apartments and resorts, leases of apartments in golf resorts and eco-resorts where these types of arrangements do not constitute land use entitlements.

All leases of commercial property would fall within the lease provisions where consideration is paid or to be paid for the grant, transfer or assignment of the lease or for a right or option to acquire the underlying land. For example, duty would be payable in respect of the transfer or assignment of a lease of commercial property in consideration of the payment of a premium and an annual peppercorn rental.

However, the grant of a lease under the *Retail Leases Act 2003* would generally not be dutiable because the *Retail Leases Act 2003* prohibits the payment of 'key money', being money payable by a tenant by way of a premium in consideration of, for example, a lease being granted, an agreement to grant a lease, an option for the renewal of a lease or consent being given to the assignment of a lease or to the sub-leasing of premises. Arrangements that circumvent this prohibition may result in such leases being dutiable under the lease provisions. Where consideration is paid for the transfer or assignment of a lease under the *Retail Leases Act 2003* duty may be payable.

MOTOR VEHICLES

Duty is payable on an application for registration or an application for transfer of the registration of a motor vehicles (as defined under the *Road Safety Act 1986*).

Duty is calculated on the dutiable value of the motor vehicle. This is defined as the greater of the price at which the vehicle might reasonably have been sold, free from encumbrances, in the open market, or the purchase price (including GST). Duty on an application for the registration of a motor vehicle is payable by the applicant. Where a motor vehicle is purchased from a Licensed Motor Car Trader (LMCT), the purchaser and the LMCT are jointly and severally liable to pay the duty.

REGISTRATION OF A MOTOR VEHICLE THAT IS A PASSENGER CAR
(excludes vehicles with nine or more seats, motor cycles, utilities and panel vans)

Dutiable value range	Not previously registered		Previously registered
	Passenger	Non-passenger	
Up to $63,184:	$6.40 per $200 (or part thereof)	$5.40 per $200 (or part thereof)	$8.40 per $200 (or part thereof)
Over $63,184:	$10.40 per $200 (or part thereof)		

TRANSFER OF REGISTRATION OF CERTAIN DEMONSTRATOR OR TRADING STOCK VEHICLES

The following rates apply in respect of an application for the registration or transfer of registration of a motor vehicle previously registered to a LMCT where:
- the vehicle is a 'passenger car'
- the vehicle is acquired within 60 days of the initial LMCT registration, and
- no duty has been paid on or since the initial LMCT registration of the vehicle.

Value	Rate
Up to $63,184: For each $200 (or part of $200)	$6.40
Over $63,184: For each $200 (or part of $200)	$10.40

SALE OF LIVESTOCK

When cattle, sheep or goats (or their carcasses) are sold, duty is payable on the sale price excluding GST.

If sold through an approved agent, the agent is liable to pay the duty but may pass the cost on to the vendor. Duty on sales by approved agents is paid to the State Revenue Office by way of a monthly return. Vendors selling on their own behalf are required to pay duty direct to the State Revenue Office by way of statement.

The rates for calculating duty on the sale of livestock under the *Livestock Disease Control Act 1994* are as follows:

Value	Rate
Live cattle	5c per $20 value or part thereof (maximum amount of duty of $5 per head)
For cattle carcasses: • weight up to and including 250kg • weight over 250kg	 90c $1.30
Calves	0.15c
Sheep, goats or carcass	0.12c
Swine	$0.02 for every $5 or part thereof (maximum of $0.16)

ESTABLISHMENT OF TRUST

Duty is charged upon the declaration / establishment of a trust regardless of whether there is dutiable property associated with that declaration or not. The rates of duty are as follows:

Value	Rate
On each declaration of trust over non-dutiable or unidentified property	$200
On each declaration of trust over dutiable property	Transfer of property rates apply

28.040 NEW SOUTH WALES DUTIES

Website: www.osr.nsw.gov.au   Email: duties@osr.nsw.gov.au   Telephone: 1300 139 814

Under the *Duties Act 1997* 'dutiable property' includes land and goodwill and is defined in Section 11 of the *Duties Act 1997*.

The duty is calculated on the dutiable value of the property which is the higher of:
- the consideration (if any) for the property (which may be money and/or liabilities assumed), and
- the unencumbered value of the property.

Duty on the transfer of business assets (other than land) licences, permissions and poker machine entitlements was announced to be abolished on 1 July 2013 however it has been deferred for an unspecified timeframe.

The *Duties Act 1997* generally allows three months from the date a liability arises (for example, three months from the date of first signing a dutiable document) to pay the duty without penalty. If duty is not paid by the due date, interest and penalty tax may be imposed by the *Taxation Administration Act 1996*.

AGREEMENT OR MEMORANDUM

If not specifically charged elsewhere: Is not subject to duty and does not require stamping.

CONVEYANCES AND TRANSFERS OF PROPERTY

TRANSFERS BETWEEN SPOUSES

Exemption depends on a breakdown of marriage, de-facto relationship or domestic relationship, or on transfer which results in the principal place of residence being held by a married (or de facto) couple as joint tenants or tenants in common in equal shares.

SALE OR EXCHANGE: TRANSFER DUTY*

Value	Rate
Up to $14,000	1.25%
Over $14,000 to $30,000	$175 plus 1.5% of the excess over $14,000
Over $30,000 to $80,000	$415 plus 1.75% of the excess over $30,000
Over $80,000 to $300,000	$1,290 plus 3.5% of the excess over $80,000
Over $300,000 to $1,000,000	$8,990 plus 4.5% of excess over $300,000
Over $1,000,000 to $3,000,000	$40,490 plus 5.5% of excess over $1,000,000
Over $3,000,000**	$150,490 plus 7% of excess over $3,000,000

* When calculating the percentage, round up any excess to the next hundred dollars.

** Applies to residential land.

Residential land is defined in section 32A of the *Duties Act 1997*. Non-residential properties continue to attract 5.5%.

PARTITION OF LAND IN NSW

Under s30 of the Act a concessional duty applies for partitions of land in NSW. If the partition is equal in unencumbered value, each transfer is liable to fixed duty of $50. If the partition is unequal in unencumbered value, duty on transfer of the land is charged on the more valuable unencumbered parcel of land, the other parcel is subject to the fixed $50 charge.

PRINCIPAL INSTRUMENT AND OTHERS

Where there are several instruments for completing the title of either party:

Instrument	Rate
Principal instrument	Transfer duty
Any other instruments	$50

DUTY FOR FIRST HOME BUYERS

From 1 January 2012, the First Home – New Home scheme replaced the First Home Plus scheme. Contracts to buy first homes that are new homes, or land to build a first home are exempt if the dutiable value (consideration or unencumbered value) is no more than:

First home	Threshold
With new home	$550,000
Vacant block	$350,000

The duty is 'phased in' above these thresholds up to $650,000 (home) and $450,000 (vacant land).

From 1 May 2007, First Home Plus allows eligible purchasers to buy property with other parties and still receive a concession. To qualify, the eligible purchasers must buy at least 50% of the property. The value limits and other eligibility criteria of First Home Plus still apply. Transfer duty is calculated with reference to the proportion of the property purchased by the other parties. However, this interest is disregarded if it is not more than 5%.

A home is a new home if it has not previously been sold as a place of residence, nor occupied as a place of residence.

NEW HOME GRANT SCHEME

From 1 July 2012, a $5,000 grant is available to buyers of new homes, whether off the plan or newly built, with a value up to $650,000 and to buyers of vacant land that is intended to be the site of a new home valued up to $450,000.

Applications for the grant must be made within three months of the date of execution of the agreement for sale or of the transfer (where there is no agreement).

A purchaser under the scheme can be any entity, including a natural person, a company or a trustee of a trust and is available to investors as well as owner occupiers.

The payment of the grant will be administered by way of applying the amount of the new home grant as a credit against liability for duty on the agreement for sale or transfer. However, if the total amount of duty is paid, or there is a balance of grant owing, a payment will be issued by cheque upon completion of the purchase (ie. the registration of the change of title).

EXEMPTIONS AND CONCESSIONS

Items that do not attract duty when buying a business in NSW include:

- goods that are stock-in-trade
- materials held for use in manufacture
- goods under manufacture
- goods held or used in connection with land used for primary production
- livestock
- a registered motor vehicle, and
- a ship or vessel.

Refer to Revenue Ruling DUT004 for more information on transactions relating to goods and other property.

DECLARATION OF TRUST

A Declaration of trust over dutiable property in NSW is a dutiable transaction. This declaration of trust is any declaration (except by will) that identifies property vested in or to be vested in a person making the declaration or is to be held in trust.

Such a dutiable transaction is subject to ad valorem duty as if it were a transfer of the vested property in the declarant. The duty is payable by the person declaring the trust.

- Any instrument declaring that a person (in whom dutiable property is vested or will be vested as apparent purchaser) holds the property in trust for the person who actually paid or will pay the purchase money: $50.
- A declaration that any identified dutiable property vested (or to be vested) in the person executing the declaration of trust is (or shall be) held in trust for the person(s) or purpose(s) stated, notwithstanding that the beneficial owner/ person entitled to appoint such property may not have joined therein, or assented to it: Transfer rates.

A fixed duty is payable on declaration of trust where:

- the same trusts are declared as having been declared in respect of the same property by an instrument on which duty was paid: $10
- the trusts declared are the same trusts as those upon (or subject to which) the same property was transferred to the person declaring the trust by an instrument duly stamped with ad valorem duty: $10
- any instrument executed in NSW declaring a trust over non-dutiable NSW property: $500, and
- any instrument executed in NSW declaring that any property not identified in it is to be vested in the person executing the document is to be held in trust: $500.

DEED

A deed is not specifically chargeable with duty. Thus, if a deed is not otherwise chargeable with duty (whether ad valorem or nominal) it does not require stamping.

DUPLICATE OR COUNTERPART OF ANY INSTRUMENT

A duplicate or counterpart of an instrument chargeable with duty is charged at the duty rate of $10.

The person liable for duty is the person liable for duty on the original instrument.

EXCHANGE

When an instrument effects an exchange of any property, or any instrument partly effects such an exchange, the dutiable value of the property is the greater of the unencumbered value and the consideration. Duty is charged at the general rate, the same as for a conveyance.

FORECLOSURE ORDER

Duty is calculated on the unencumbered value of the property included in the order not on the value of the debt secured by the mortgaged property. Duty is the same as for a transfer of the property.

INSURANCE: LIFE POLICIES

TEMPORARY OR TERM INSURANCE

Of the first year's premium: 5%.

OTHER LIFE INSURANCE POLICIES

Based on the sum insured:

Value	Rate
Up to $2,000	$1
Over $2,000	$1 + 20c per $200 (or part) on the amount in excess of $2 000

TRANSFER OR ASSIGNMENT OF LIFE POLICY

On the value: Is not subject to duty and does not require stamping.

INSURANCE (GENERAL)

Where the property or risk is in NSW see the Act for details. Duty is payable on premiums paid:

Premium	Rate
Type A (all general insurance other than Type B or C)	9%
Type B (motor vehicle, aviation, disability income, occupational indemnity, hospital and ancillary benefits)	5%
Type C (crops and livestock)	2.5%

LEASES

RENT ON LAND/BUILDINGS

- **For leases executed on or after 1 January 2008:** Duty is abolished on leases first executed from 1 January 2008. Stamping is not required unless the document falls under one of the following categories:
  - a lease or agreement for lease in respect of which a premium is paid or agreed to be paid (not including any premium paid or payable for a lease of premises in a retirement village within the meaning of s5 of the *Retirement Villages Act 1999*)
  - a lease entered into pursuant to an option if an amount is paid or payable for the grant of the option
  - a transfer or assignment of lease, or
  - a surrender of lease.

  Such transactions remain subject to transfer duty. For transactions before this date refer to previous volumes of the Tax Summary.

MORTGAGE DUTY

From 1 July 2013 mortgage duty was due to be abolished but this has been deferred for an unspecified time period. Mortgage duty is payable as follows:

Value	Rate
Up to $16,000	$5
Over $16,000 – for each $1,000 (or part of $1,000)	$4 (plus an additional fixed amount of $5 is payable)

COLLATERAL MORTGAGES

A collateral mortgage is chargeable with a minimum duty of $50.

NOTE: In some circumstances a collateral mortgage will form part of a multi state mortgage package.

CERTAIN MORTGAGES

Caveat protecting interest under a mortgage or charge where has been paid on the mortgage or charge: $50.

EXEMPTIONS AND CONCESSIONS

- Mortgages associated with owner occupied housing (borrower must be a natural person).
- Mortgages associated with investment housing (borrower must be a natural person).
- Refinanced loans where the amount secured does not exceed the maximum amount secured by the previous security and where the borrowers are the same and the securities are substantially the same as for the previous security. A cap of $1 million applies except where land is used for primary production or aquaculture.
- A mortgage created solely for the purpose of providing security imposed on grant of bail in criminal proceedings.
- A mortgage taken by a non-profit organisation in conjunction with a lease.
- Mortgage of any ship or vessel, or of any part, interest, share or property of or in any ship or vessel.
- A mortgage given by the Government of the Commonwealth or a Government of a State or Territory or by any public statutory body constituted under a law of a State or Territory.
- A mortgage under the Liens on Crops and Wool and *Stock Mortgages Act 1898*.
- A charge over land that is created under an agreement for the sale of the land if any part of the deposit or balance of the purchase price is paid to the vendor before completion.

UNLISTED SHARES OR UNITS

For every $100 (or part thereof): *60c of the dutiable value of the shares or units.*

The dutiable value is the greater of the market value or consideration paid for the shares or units. A minimum duty of $10 per transfer applies. The transferee is the person liable to pay the duty.

Duty must be paid within three months of the date of first execution of the agreement or transfer. The abolition of duty on the transfer of unlisted securities which was intended to occur on 1 July 2013, has been deferred.

TRANSFERS BETWEEN SPOUSES

See exemptions under *Conveyances* (only on breakdown of marriages and other relationships).

FOREIGN COMPANIES

Duty is payable if the share is kept on the Australian register kept in New South Wales.

LANDHOLDER DUTY

Acquisition of interests in landholders apply to relevant acquisitions in private landholders and in public landholders. Where a company or unit trust scheme holds land in NSW valued at $2,000,000 or more, an acquisition of shares in the company or units in the unit trust scheme may attract duty at the general rate as if it were an acquisition of the land and goods held by such entity.

The concessional rate of duty for acquisitions in public land holders is 10% of the transfer duty on a transfer of all the landholdings and goods (other than exempt goods) of the landholder in NSW.

To be a landholder, the company or unit trust must have land holdings in NSW with a threshold value of $2,000,000 or more.

If a land holding consists of an estate in fee simple in land, the value of the land (as determined under the *Valuation of Land Act 1916*), rather than the unencumbered value of the land, is used to determine whether the $2,000,000 threshold is met. (However, once a liability arises, duty will still be calculated with reference to the unencumbered value of the land holdings in NSW).

A person who has an interest in a landholder has a significant interest in the landholder if the person, in the event of a distribution of all the property of the landholder immediately after the interest was acquired, would be entitled to:

- in the case of a private landholder: 50 per cent or more of the property distributed, or
- in the case of a public landholder: 90 per cent or more of the property distributed.

TRANSFERS TO VEST RIGHTS IN SHARES

If the transfer of shares includes a right to shares (and the transfer is correctly stamped in respect of such rights), on the transfer necessary to vest the rights: *Exempt.*

EXEMPTIONS

Any transfer of shares effecting a share buy back in accordance with the *Corporations Act 2001.*

ACQUISITION OF BONUS SHARES

If a duly stamped transfer of shares is not registered and, due to it not being registered, bonus shares (or rights) accrue to the registered owner, on any transfer necessary to vest those other shares (or rights) in the transferee: Exempt.

MOTOR VEHICLE CERTIFICATE OF REGISTRATION

In New South Wales duty is payable on an application to register a motor vehicle when:

- it is new and is being registered for the first time
- registration is being transferred to another person, and
- an imported second hand vehicle is first registered in NSW.

Duty is primarily payable by the person in whose name the certificate is issued and based on the value of the motor vehicle.

Value*	Rate
For each $100 (or part of $100)	$3
For passenger vehicles of $45,000 or more	$1,350 plus $5 for every $100 (or part thereof) on the amount in excess of $45,000

* If GST is payable, duty is calculated on GST-inclusive full value on new vehicles, or sale price or market value of a used vehicle.

SUPERANNUATION

Duty payable on	Rate
Instrument creating or amending a complying superannuation fund deed	No duty
Instrument where employer agrees to participate in complying superannuation fund	No duty
Transfer of property between complying funds (as a result of transfer of members)	Maximum $500 (conveyancing rules also apply) If dutiable property transferred or agreed to be transferred is a marketable security: Duty is $10.

Duty of $50 applies to certain transfers from members to the trustee of their self managed superannuation fund. See section 62A of the *Duties Act 1997.*

28.050 QUEENSLAND DUTIES

Website: www.osr.qld.gov.au Telephone: 1300 300 734

Transfer duty is calculated on the dutiable value of a transaction under the *Duties Act 2001*. Generally, this is the greater of the consideration paid for, or the unencumbered value of, the property acquired.

INSURANCE DUTY

Insurance duty (ie. relating to general, life and accident insurance) is charged on premiums, however the time it is payable may vary according to the type of insurance.

GENERAL INSURANCE

The rates of duty for general insurance depend on the class of insurance and when the insurance contract was entered into as follows:

Class	Rate (entered into before 1 August 2013)	Rate (entered into on or after 1 August 2013)
Class 1	7.5% of premium paid	9% of premium paid
Class 2	5% of premium paid	9% of premium paid

Class 1 general insurance is general insurance other than Class 2 general insurance or Compulsory Third Party (CTP) insurance. Class 2 general insurance is insurance for, or relating to, any of the following:

- professional indemnity
- personal injury to a person relating to the person's travel on an aircraft
- a motor vehicle, other than CTP insurance
- a home mortgage that is a first mortgage, or
- a life insurance rider.

Duty on CTP insurance is imposed at the rate of 10c per premium.

LIFE INSURANCE

The rate of insurance duty imposed on a contract of life insurance that affects temporary or term insurance is 5% of the first year's premium. The rate of insurance duty imposed on another contract of life insurance is:

Sum insured	Rate
If the sum insured is not more than $2,000	0.05% of the sum insured
If the sum insured is more than $2,000	0.05% of the first $2,000 and 0.1% of balance of sum insured

ACCIDENT INSURANCE

Accident insurance is imposed on WorkCover premiums at the rate of 5% on the net premiums charged.

NOTE: Some exemptions from insurance duty are available.

TRANSFERS OF DUTIABLE PROPERTY

Dutiable value of dutiable property is calculated on the consideration or the unencumbered value, whichever is greater. Consideration may also include liabilities assumed or debts extinguished as part of the transaction. If the transfer is by way of partial interest, duty is payable on the additional interest passing.

If the consideration, or any part of the consideration, for a dutiable transaction on which duty is imposed consists of an amount payable periodically and the total amount, including any interest, to be paid can be ascertained, the consideration or part of the consideration is the total amount.

NOTE: Duty must be calculated on the GST-inclusive amount when GST is a component of a particular transaction.

TRANSACTIONS ENTERED INTO FROM 1 AUGUST 2013

Value	Rate
Not more than $5,000	Nil
$5,001 to $75,000	$1.50 for each $100* on the excess over $5,000
$75,001 to $540,000	$1,050 plus $3.50* for each $100* on the excess over $75,000
$540,001 to $1,000,000	$17,325 plus $4.50* for each $100* on the excess over $540,000
More than $1,000,000	$38,025 plus $5.75* for each $100* on the excess over $1,000,000

*Calculated for each $100 or part of $100

BUSINESS ACQUISITIONS

When you acquire a Queensland business or a Queensland business asset you are required to pay transfer duty, regardless of whether or not a written agreement is entered into to formalise the transaction. If two or more business assets are acquired, the dutiable values are aggregated and transfer duty is calculated on the total. Once the transaction has taken place, an approved Form 2.2, together with the instrument or Form 2.3, must be lodged with the Office of State Revenue within 30 days of the date of the acquisition or the unconditional date or with a legal representative who can in most cases assess the transaction.

Business assets include goodwill, a statutory license or the right to use a statutory business license to carry on a business, the business name used to carry on a business, a right under a franchise arrangement used to carry on a business, a debt of a business (if the debtor resides in Queensland), a supply right of a business, intellectual property used for carrying on a business and personal property in Queensland of a business. Standard transfer duty rates apply.

CONCESSIONS FOR HOMES

The Queensland Government provides home buyers with a concession for transfer duty to minimise the cost of acquiring a home and to make home ownership more attainable. The requirements of the concessions for home and first home are outlined in Part 9 of the Duties Act 2001 and information sheets, approved forms and concessional rates of transfer duty can be found on the website: www.osr.qld.gov.au.

A concession is also available to individuals who are at least 18 years of age and are acquiring vacant land to build their first home and occupy it as their principal residence. For details of the First Home Vacant Land Transfer Duty Concession and the qualifying circumstances, please refer to the information sheet available on the website, www.osr.qld.gov.au.

HOME CONCESSION RATES

Purchase price / Value	Duty rate
Up to $350,000	$1.00 for each $100*
$350,001 to $540,000	$3,500 plus $3.50 for every $100* over $350,000
$540,001 to $1,000,000	$10,150 plus $4.50 for every $100* over $540,000
More than $1,000,000	$30,850 plus $5.75 for every $100* over $1,000,000

*Calculated for each $100 or part of $100

TRANSFER OF MARKETABLE SECURITIES (SHARES)

Certain acquisitions of shares may be subject to landholder duty or corporate trustee duty.

TRANSFER OF MORTGAGE

Transfer duty is applicable for the transfer of a mortgage that is solely over land in Queensland, whether the transfer is absolute or by way of security or of an ancillary security: $5.00 per mortgage.

TRANSFER DUTY EXEMPTIONS

Exemptions for transfer duty are outlined in Chapter 2 (Part 13) and Chapter 10 of the Duties Act 2001.

- **Family Law Act:** Certain transactions under Part VIII and Part VIIA of the *Family Law Act* are exempt.
- **Superannuation:** Concessions or exemptions from transfer duty may apply to the following dutiable transactions:
  - transfer of dutiable property between superannuation funds to effect a merger of two or more superannuation funds, or splitting of a superannuation fund into two or more superannuation funds.
  - creation of a trust of dutiable property because of the variation or reconstitution of a superannuation fund.
  - transfers between a superannuation fund and a custodian as part of a limited recourse borrowing arrangement.

The merger concession depends on whether the superannuation fund will become a complying superannuation fund within one year after the merger, split or creation of the trust. Where the concession is allowed, the amount of transfer duty imposed is $20.00.

TRUST ACQUISITION

Standard transfer duty rates apply. Trust acquisitions occur when a person becomes a beneficiary of a trust whether on its creation or otherwise or, a person who is a beneficiary of the trust increases their interest in the trust other than by the surrender of another beneficiary's trust interest in the trust for which transfer duty has been paid.

A trust interest is a person's interest as a beneficiary of a trust other than a life interest. For discretionary trusts, only beneficiaries who can take in default of an appointment by the trustee can have a trust interest. For a trust that is a superannuation fund, a member of the fund has trust interest in the fund.

TRUST CREATION

Standard transfer duty rates apply. A creation of a trust is when a person who has acquired dutiable property in a capacity other than as a trustee commences to hold the property as trustee, or, when a person who holds dutiable property on trust commences to hold that dutiable property as trustee for another trust.

TRUST SURRENDER

Standard transfer duty rates apply. A trust surrender occurs if the person surrenders a trust interest in a trust which holds dutiable property or has an indirect interest in dutiable property.

TRUST TERMINATION

Standard transfer duty rates apply. A trust of dutiable property is terminated if the person who held the property in their capacity as a trustee commences to hold the property other than as a trustee.

TRUST EXEMPTIONS

Duty exemption may apply to trusts under the following circumstances:

- change of trustee
- particular vestings of dutiable property
- trust acquisition or surrender in family trust
- trust acquisition or surrender in superannuation fund, and
- trust transfers for people under legal disability.

For further information relating to exemptions for trusts, please refer to Part 13 of the *Duties Act 2001*. For information on public unit trusts refer to s68-79 of the *Duties Act 2001*.

VEHICLE REGISTRATION DUTY

A person is required to pay vehicle registration duty on an application to register a vehicle, or on an application to transfer a vehicle's registration from one person to another. Duty payable is calculated on the vehicle's dutiable value (other than for 'special' vehicles). The dutiable value of a vehicle that has not previously been registered, whether in Queensland or another State, and for which there is a list price, is the total of the vehicle's list price, and the price of all items of optional equipment not included in the list price.

The dutiable value of a vehicle previously registered in Queensland or another State, or for which there is no list price, is the greater of the total amount payable by the purchaser including any deposit, trade-in allowance and the price of all optional equipment, or the market value of the vehicle.

The rates for vehicle registration duty are (other than for 'special' vehicles*):

- for hybrid vehicles (with any number of cylinders) and electric vehicles: $2 for each $100 and each part of $100 of the dutiable value of the vehicle
- for vehicles with one to four cylinders or two rotors or a steam vehicle: $3 for each $100 and each part of $100 of the dutiable value of the vehicle
- for vehicles with five or six cylinders or three rotors: $3.50 for each $100 and each part of $100 of the dutiable value of the vehicle
- for vehicles with seven or more cylinders: $4 for each $100 and each part of $100 of the dutiable value of the vehicle.

The rate of duty for 'special' vehicles*: $25.00.

* A special vehicle is mobile machinery (other than trust based) or a vehicle that has been conditionally registered for limited use under the *Transport Operations (Road Use Management – Vehicle Registration) Regulation 2010*, section 12(2).

Certain vehicle registrations are exempt. Refer to the relevant sections of the *Duties Act 2001* or the website, www.osr.qld.gov.au for details of the exemptions.

28.060 SOUTH AUSTRALIAN DUTIES

Website: www.revenuesa.sa.gov.au Email: stamps@sa.gov.au Phone: (08) 8226 3750 / 1800 637 778

In South Australia (SA) duty is charged on certain documents and transactions at either a flat rate or an ad valorem rate (based on the value of the transaction) depending on the particular document or transaction under the *Stamp Duties Act 1923*.

As part of the 2015-16 State Budget handed down on 18 June 2015, the following stamp duty measures were announced:

- abolition of duty on non-quoted marketable securities (see below under Transfer of Shares);
- abolition of duty on transfers on non-real property;
- phased abolition of duty on commercial land;
- abolition of duty on transfers of units in a unit trust; and
- removal of the $1 million landholder threshold.

CONVEYANCE OF LAND

Subject to certain exemptions and concessions, stamp duty is charged on either the market value or consideration (whichever is the greater), when there is a conveyance of land situated in South Australia.

Land, whether referred to as land, real property or property when it is constituted by land, includes (but is not limited to):

- An estate or interest in land;
- A right In relation to land;
- A mining tenement;
- An interest conferred by a forest property (vegetation) agreement;
- An option to acquire land;
- A right to acquire an estate or interest in land and
- Any other right or interest prescribed by the regulations.

Non-real property comprises property that is not land and buildings. Transfers of statutory leases and licences, such as fishing licences, taxi licences, gaming machine licences and entitlements, together with most forms of business assets including goodwill, trading stock (other than land), and intellectual property will obtain the benefit of the abolition of stamp duty on non-real property transfers.

CONVEYANCE OF NON-RESIDENTIAL, NON-PRIMARY PRODUCTION LAND

Stamp duty on non-residential, non-primary production real property transfers will be phased out over a three year period commencing 1 July 2016. Duty rates will be reduced by a third from 1 July 2016, a further third from 1 July 2017, before the duty is abolished from 1 July 2018. See Information Circular No: 76.

CONVEYANCE OF UNITS IN A UNIT TRUST

Stamp duty on the issue, redemption and transfer of units in unit trusts will be abolished from 1 July 2018. From 18 June 2015, duty is only payable where the unit trust owns land in SA.

CERTAIN INSTRUMENTS DEEMED TO OPERATE AS A VOLUNTARY DISPOSITION INTER VIVOS

Any instrument that relates to land or a unit under a unit trust scheme (or an interest in any of those), that effects, acknowledges, evidences or records:

- a transfer of property to a person who takes it as trustee, or
- a declaration of trust, or
- the creation of an interest in property subject to a trust, or
- the transfer of an interest in property subject to a trust, or
- the surrender or renunciation of an interest in property subject to a trust, or
- the redemption, cancellation or extinguishment of an interest in property subject to a trust,

is deemed to be a voluntary conveyance inter vivos whether or not consideration is given (Sections 71(3) & (4) of the Act). Further, an instrument under which a person who is entitled to share in the distribution of an estate of a deceased person disclaims or assigns or transfers an interest in the estate is taken to be a voluntary conveyance inter vivos, whether or not consideration is given (Section 71AA).

EXEMPTIONS

Numerous instruments, whilst belonging to one or other of the categories described above, are nevertheless deemed not to be a voluntary conveyance inter vivos and give rise to exemptions. Refer to: Section 71(5) of the *Stamp Duties Act 1923*.

Other specific exemptions and concessions

- Section 71(7)(d): Exemption on the transfer of community title land to a beneficiary pursuant to a trust.
- Section 71(7a): Exemption on the transfer of property from a custodian trustee to the trustee of a SMSF.
- Section 71A: Exemption where an executor distributes property in specie to a beneficiary under a will in lieu of converting property to money.
- Section 71C: Concessional duty for first home buyers, where a conveyance gives effect to a contract entered into, or relates to land where the construction of a dwelling house has commenced, before 5 June 2008.
- Section 71CA: Exemption for the transfer of property pursuant to a Family Law agreement (as defined) or a Family Law order between the parties to the marriage (or the former marriage) or former de-factor relationship and no other person.
- Section 71CAA: Exemption for a transfer of a disabled person's principal place of residence into a Special Disability Trust for no consideration.
- Section 71CB: Exemption for transfer of an interest in a shared residence or registration of a motor vehicle between spouses or domestic partners, or between

former spouses or former domestic partners where the instrument has been executed as a result of the irretrievable breakdown of the parties' marriage or relationship.

- Section 71CBA: Exemption in respect of a transfer of property, pursuant to a certified domestic partnership agreement or a property adjustment order, between the parties to the former domestic relationship if the domestic relationship has broken down irretrievably and the domestic partners (as defined in the Domestic Partners Property Act 1996) lived together continuously for at least three years.
- Section 71CC: Exemption for the transfer of farming land or farming land and farming goods between family members, where the land is used wholly or mainly for the business of primary production and is not less than 0.8 hectares, a business relationship existed between the transferor and the transferee for at least 12 months immediately before the date of the transfer, the principal business of the transferor is primary production, and the document transfers land between natural persons who are specified relatives, or trustees of the specified relatives.
- Section 71CD: Exemption for the transfer of property from the Official Trustee in Bankruptcy or a registered trustee under the *Bankruptcy Act 1966* to the bankrupt or former bankrupt where property of the bankrupt or former bankrupt had vested in the Official Trustee or the registered trustee.
- Section 71D: Concessional duty applies to a transfer of an exploration tenement or an interest in an exploration tenement where the consideration or a part of the consideration consists of an undertaking by the transferee to engage in or contribute to exploratory or investigatory operations within the tenement.
- Section 71DA: Concessional duty applies, subject to certain conditions, on the transfer of property between superannuation funds, from a superannuation fund to a pooled superannuation trust, and from a pooled superannuation trust to a superannuation fund or another pooled superannuation trust at the direction of the superannuation fund.
- Section 71DB: Concessional duty applies, subject to certain conditions, on purchases of off-the-plan apartments within certain areas. See Circular No. 48 and 65.
- Part 4AA: Exemption for corporate group restructuring transactions. See Information Circular No. 77.

TRANSACTIONS EFFECTED WITHOUT CREATING A DUTIABLE INSTRUMENT

Transactions that result in a change in the ownership of a legal or equitable interest in land are chargeable with duty as though the transaction had been effected by a dutiable instrument. A Section 71E Statement, available on the RevenueSA website, must be completed. Stamp duty is payable on the statement as if it were a conveyance effecting the transaction to which it relates.

LANDHOLDER DUTY (APPLIES FROM 1 JULY 2011)

An acquisition of shares or units may be chargeable with duty as though the acquisition was a conveyance of an interest in the South Australian land and goods owned (directly or indirectly) by the company or unit trust.

If a person or a group acquires an interest of 50% or more of the shares or units of a private company or trust and that entity holds, directly or indirectly, local land assets of $1 million or more, ad valorem rates will apply. If a person or group acquires 90% or more of the shares or units of a listed company or public unit trust scheme duty will apply at a concessional rate of 10 % of the duty amount determined at ad valorem rates.

An entity is a land holding entity if the unencumbered value of the underlying local assets of the entity is $1 million or more. A local land asset is a land asset consisting of an interest in land in South Australia. The underlying local land assets of an entity include the land assets held beneficially by the entity and its notional interests in the land assets of related entities.

A *Section 102B Return – Acquisition Statement*, available from the RevenueSA website, must be completed.

For further information refer to Information Circular No: 29.

NOTE: The $1 million landholder threshold will be removed from 1 July 2018.

RATES OF DUTY

If the value or the consideration inclusive of GST for the sale is:

Value	Rate
Up to $12,000	$1 for every $100 or part of $100
$12,001 to $30,000	$120 plus $2 for every $100 or part of $100 over $12,000
$30,001 to $50,000	$480 plus $3 for every $100 or part of $100 over $30,000
$50,001 to $100,000	$1,080 plus $3.50 for every $100 or part of $100 over $50,000
$100,001 to $200,000	$2,830 plus $4 for every $100 or part of $100 over $100,000
$200,001 to $250,000	$6,830 plus $4.25 for every $100 or part of $100 over $200,000
$250,001 to $300,000	$8,955 plus $4.75 for every $100 or part of $100 over $250,000
$300,001 to $500,000	$11,330 plus $5 for every $100 or part of $100 over $300,000
Over $500,000	$21,330 plus $5.50 for every $100 or part of $100 over $500,000

EXEMPTIONS (NOT EXHAUSTIVE)

- Grants of land from the Crown
- Conveyances (whether on sale or otherwise) to the Crown, and to any person on behalf of the Crown.
- Transfers and conveyances of a mortgage (or interest in a mortgage) including the transfer of debt secured by that mortgage.
- Conveyance on sale of any debenture, debenture stock, bond, note or other security of a government, municipal or other corporation, company or society.

TRANSFER OF SHARES

Stamp duty on transfers of non-quoted marketable securities (also known as share duty) will be abolished from 18 June 2015.

For transfers of non-quoted marketable securities before 18 June 2015 duty payable is 60 cents per $100 (or part thereof) of the market value or consideration, whichever is the greater.

INSURANCE

Every insurer which carries on any insurance business in South Australia must be registered with the Commissioner. An insurer carries on insurance business in South Australia if the insurer grants or issues in the State:

- life insurance or personal accident insurance for a person whose principal place of residence is in the State at the time that the policy providing the insurance is issued, or
- general insurance for an insurance risk within the State

(whether the head office or principal place of business of the insurer is in the State or elsewhere).

Insurance business under the Act is of two distinct types of risks, risks relating to general insurance, and risks relating to life insurance. See *South Australian property, risk, contingency or event insured outside South Australia.*

Insurers are required to lodge a relevant Statement and pay relevant duty equivalent to the amount of premium received (or credited to an account but not received that the insurer chooses to include). Premium means an amount paid or payable for insurance and includes an insurer's liability for GST, a levy charged to a policy holder, an instalment of premium or part of a premium.

RISKS RELATING TO GENERAL INSURANCE

General insurers, including those deriving motor vehicle third-party premiums, are required to lodge a monthly statement (even if no duty is payable) and pay duty equivalent to 11% of premiums by the 15th day of the following month.

General insurance includes personal accident insurance.

Premium for general insurance purposes does not include stamp duty received or charged in respect of a premium. Further, the following amount of premium is not to be taken into account:

- premium refunded during the month
- premium paid for insurance risk outside the State (other than a personal accident insurance risk), or
- premium paid for personal accident insurance for a person whose principal place of residence was not in the State at the time the policy was issued.

INCLUSIONS TO GENERAL INSURANCE

Premiums include commission and discounts.

DEDUCTIONS FROM GENERAL INSURANCE

Premiums exclude:

- stamp duty received or charged
- reinsurance effected in South Australia
- refunds, and
- insurance risks outside South Australia.

RISKS RELATING TO LIFE INSURANCE

Life insurers are required to lodge an annual statement (even if no duty is payable) equivalent to 1.5% of premiums of the previous calendar year by 31 January each year.

'Life insurance' means insurance of a contingency that is dependent on the duration of human life, but does not include personal accident insurance (which is insurance covering personal accident or workers' compensation or a policy complying with Part 4 of the *Motor Vehicles Act 1959 (SA)*, or insurance in respect of trauma, or a disabling or incapacitating injury, sickness, condition or disease).

Premium for life insurance purposes does not include stamp duty received or charged in respect of a premium, and is a reference to net premium, with any commission or discount not to be taken into account. Further, the following amount of premium is not to be taken into account:

- premium paid for life insurance for a person whose principal place of residence was not in the State at the time the policy was issued, and
- premium refunded during the year.

EXEMPTIONS FROM GENERAL AND/OR LIFE INSURANCE

Premium exempt from duty is premium received or charged:

- in respect of reinsurance
- under a private guarantee fidelity insurance scheme promoted amongst and sustained solely for the benefit of the officers and servants of a particular public department, company, person or firm and not extended, either directly or indirectly, beyond such officers and servants
- under a scheme in the above paragraph promoted amongst and sustained solely for the benefit of the officers and members of a friendly society or branch thereof and not extended, either directly or indirectly, beyond such officers and members
- for life insurance in respect of investment and not in respect of a risk insured by the policy under which the premium is paid
- in respect of a life or personal accident insurance risk where the principal place of residence of the insured person is in the Northern Territory and the policy under which the premium is paid is registered in a registry kept in the Northern Territory pursuant to the *Life Insurance Act 1995* (Cth)
- under a policy of workers compensation insurance where the premium is referable to insurance against liability to pay workers compensation in respect of workers under the age of 25 years
- under a policy of insurance by a body registered under Part 4-3 of the *Private Health Insurance Act 2007* (Cth) where the premium is referable to insurance against medical, dental or hospital expenses

- in respect of life insurance providing for the payment of an annuity to the person insured, and
- in respect of the insurance of the hull of a marine craft used primarily for commercial purposes or in respect of the insurance of goods carried by railway, road, air or sea or of the freight on such goods.

SOUTH AUSTRALIAN PROPERTY, RISK, CONTINGENCY OR EVENTS INSURED OUTSIDE SOUTH AUSTRALIAN

Where a company, person or firm that is not required to be registered obtains, effects or renews, outside the State, a policy of insurance wholly or partly in respect of property in the State, or a risk, contingency or event occurring in the State, not being life insurance, relevant stamp duty must be paid to RevenueSA. In this situation the responsibility for payment of the stamp duty rests with the company, person or firm effecting the insurance.

A relevant company, person or firm must, within one month of obtaining, effecting or renewing the policy, lodge a return Statement and pay duty equivalent to 11% of any premium paid to the insurer. A rebate is allowed on the proportion of a premium properly attributable to property outside the State or a risk, contingency or event occurring outside the State.

MOTOR VEHICLE REGISTRATIONS AND TRANSFER APPLICATIONS

Duty is payable on an Application to Register a new motor vehicle or an Application to Transfer the Registration of a second hand motor vehicle within 14 days of purchase. The duty is payable by the person or firm applying to have the vehicle registered or transferred into their name.

DEFINITION OF 'NEW VEHICLE' VALUE

The manufacturer's recommended retail list price or market value (if no list price) plus retail price of optional transmission or power steering (if fitted and not included in list price), or (if there is no list price of those options) the actual value of the options. Value is inclusive of GST.

DEFINITION OF 'SECOND HAND' VALUE

Whichever is greater – the consideration for the sale, or the market value. If the transfer is not a sale, market value applies. Values are inclusive of GST.

A. The registration component

For vehicles which are not commercial vehicles or primary producers' tractors or trailers: this component is based on the value (and not necessarily the actual GST inclusive selling price):

Value	Rate
Up to $1,000	$1 for each $100 or part of $100 with a minimum of $5 payable in all cases
Over $1,000 to $2,000	$10 plus $2 for each $100 or part of $100 over $1,000
Over $2,000 to $3,000	$30 plus $3 for each $100 or part of $100 over $2,000
Over $3,000	$60 plus $4 for each $100 or part of $100 over $3,000

For commercial vehicles and primary producers' tractors or trailers: this component is based on the value (and not necessarily the actual GST inclusive selling price):

Value	Rate
Up to $1,000	$1 for each $100 or part of $100 with a minimum of $5 payable in all cases
Over $1,000 to $2,000	$10 plus $2 for each $100 or part of $100 over $1,000
Over $2,000	$30 plus $3 for each $100 or part of $100 over $2,000

Duty may be refunded if:
- within three months, the vehicle is returned to the seller and is accepted by that person, or
- the registration or transfer of registration was made in error.

EXEMPTIONS FROM THE REGISTRATION COMPONENT

- Exemption 1: By a person who carries on the business of selling motor vehicles if in the ordinary course of that business or for demonstrating that motor vehicle to prospective purchasers.
- Exemption 2: For a previously registered motor vehicle previously registered to a dealer if made for the purpose of the resale by the dealer and the resale is in the ordinary course of the business of the dealer.
- Exemption 3: By a person or body which is entitled to registration of that vehicle without fee.
- Exemption 4: For a trailer (other than a trailer that is constructed or adapted solely or mainly for the carriage of goods and has a gross vehicle mass of more than 3 tonnes).
- Exemption 5: By the Crown or a statutory body or authority holding its assets on behalf of the Crown or any such body or authority.
- Exemption 6: To the extent ad valorem duty has been paid on another instrument transferring the property in the vehicle.
- Exemption 7: By the executor or administrator of a deceased estate if made only to transfer the motor vehicle to the beneficiary(ies) or for the sale of the motor vehicle in the course of winding up the estate.
- Exemption 8: By an owner who has repossessed the vehicle pursuant to a hire purchase agreement or by an owner in pursuance of the return of the vehicle to that owner by the hirer voluntarily where the vehicle is the subject of a hire purchase agreement or upon the termination of a hiring agreement (not being a hire purchase agreement).
- Exemption 9: For a vehicle used solely or predominantly to carry passengers for hire or reward (seating capacity of not less than 12 adult passengers).
- Exemption 10: By a local council as defined in the *Local Government Act 1999*, or a subsidiary of a local council under that Act.
- Exemption 10A: For a conditional registration under section 25 of the *Motor Vehicles Act 1959* (eg. historic vehicles, left-hand drive vehicles manufactured before 1974, vehicles used between farm blocks).
- Exemption 11: By a person entitled under section 38 of the *Motor Vehicles Act 1959* to have registration at a reduced fee and is not receiving the benefit of this exemption on any other vehicle (ie. incapacitated ex-service personnel).
- Exemption 12: By a licensed interstate motor vehicle dealer for the purpose of resale in another State or Territory in the ordinary course of business of that person.
- Exemption 13: : By an owner where as a consequence of the loss of use of one or both of their legs they are permanently unable to use public transport, and are not enjoying the benefit of this exemption on any other vehicle owned by them.
- Exemption 14: Where vehicle rights have passed by assignment to a person under the rights of a hire purchase agreement.
- Exemption 15: For a vehicle previously registered by the applicant in another State or Territory and the applicant was a resident of or carried on business in that State or Territory.
- Exemption 16: By the East Torrens Country Board of Health constituted under the *Health Act 1935*.
- Exemption 17: By a mortgagee who under the *Consumer Transactions Act 1972* has taken possession of the vehicle in pursuance of a consumer mortgage or to whom the vehicle has been voluntarily returned by the mortgagor in pursuance of that Act.
- Exemption 18: For a tractor or item of agricultural machinery owned by a primary producer.
- Exemption 19: By a beneficiary(ies) of the estate of a deceased person in order to give effect to a will or the rules of intestacy, and Sections 71CB or 71CBA – Transfer between parties who are spouses or former spouses, or domestic partners or former domestic partners.
- Exemption 20: By a parent or legal guardian of an incapacitated person who is a minor where the vehicle is used to transport the minor.

B. *The insurance component (Compulsory third party insurance)*

For a period of:	Rate
12 months	$60
3 months	$15

EXEMPTIONS FROM THE INSURANCE COMPONENT

- Exemption 1: By a person or body entitled to registration without fee.
- Exemption 2: For a trailer that is not a heavy vehicle.
- Exemption 3: By the Crown or by any statutory body or authority.
- Exemption 4: For a vehicle used solely or predominantly to carry passengers for hire or reward (seating capacity of not less than 12 adult passengers).
- Exemption 5: By a council as defined in the *Local Government Act 1934* or a subsidiary of a council.
- Exemption 5A: A conditional registration under section 25 of the *Motor Vehicles Act 1959* (eg. historic vehicles, left-hand drive vehicles manufactured before 1974, vehicles used between farm blocks).
- Exemption 6: By a person entitled under s38 of the *Motor Vehicles Act 1959* to have registration at a reduced fee and is not receiving the benefit of this exemption on any other vehicle (ie. incapacitated ex-service personnel).
- Exemption 7: A single policy of insurance by an owner who has lost the use of one or both legs for a vehicle to transport that person.
- Exemption 8: By a person who is the owner of the vehicle and is entitled as the holder of a State concession card issued by the Department of Community Welfare or a pensioner entitlement card issued under any Act or law of the Cth to travel on public transport in South Australia at reduced fares.
- Exemption 20: By a parent or legal guardian or an incapacitated person who is a minor where the vehicle is used to transport the minor.

GENERAL EXEMPTIONS FROM ALL STAMP DUTIES

- Wills, testamentary instruments and letters of administration.
- Agreement or memorandum of agreement made on or after 1 September 1992, not under seal, and not otherwise specifically charged with duty.
- Certificates of title issued from the Lands Titles Office.
- Customs bonds.
- Administration bonds.
- Bonds to the Crown.
- Conveyances of bills, bonds, debentures or other securities issued by a public statutory body constituted under a law of the Cth or of any State or Territory, not being a prescribed statutory body or a statutory body of a prescribed class.
- Bond on appointment of a special bailiff.
- Memorandum of association, articles of association and rules and regulations of any incorporated company, association or society.
- Marriage settlements.
- Mortgage bonds guaranteed by the Government of South Australia.
- Articles or indentures of apprenticeship and assignments of articles or indentures of apprenticeship.
- Leases to the Crown and to any person on behalf of the Crown.
- A power of attorney (or any other instrument in the nature of a power of attorney).
- Grant of land from the Crown.
- Conveyance, whether on sale or otherwise, to the Crown or to any person on behalf of the Crown (not being a surrender to the Crown, or any such person, of a lease or

other interest in land in order that the Crown may grant to a person other than the surrender or a lease of, or other interest in, the same land or any part thereof).

- Any transfer of any fire, personal accident, fidelity, guarantee, livestock, plate glass or marine insurance or assurance policy.

- Any cemetery leases.

- Bills, bonds, inscribed stock, debentures, deposit receipts and other securities issued by the Government of the State, and coupons or interest warrants issued in connection with any such bills, bonds, stock, debentures, deposit receipts or other securities, and any transfer of, or document relating to, the purchase or sale of any such bills, bonds, stock, debentures, deposit receipts or other securities.

- Conveyance or transfer of a financial product by the personal representative of a deceased person to another person entitled under the will of the deceased person, or on intestacy, to have the financial product conveyed or transferred to him or her.

- Conveyance or transfer of a financial product if the conveyance or transfer is made for the purpose of effectuating the appointment of a new trustee or the retirement of a trustee and all duty chargeable on any instrument for the appointment of the new trustee or the retirement of the trustee, as the case may be, has been duly paid.

- Conveyance or transfer of a financial product if the conveyance of transfer is made in pursuance of any deed of settlement or deed of gift and all duty chargeable on the deed of settlement or deed of gift, as the case may be, has been duly paid.

- Any conveyance, transfer or mortgage to which a prescribed person is a party and which is executed or entered into in connection with the purchase or gift of any land on which the prescribed person resides or intends to reside shall be exempt from stamp duty on so much of the amount on which the duty is chargeable as does not exceed two thousand four hundred dollars, but a conveyance, transfer or mortgage shall not be exempt under this paragraph unless the Commissioner is satisfied by such evidence as he requires:

  (a) that the purchase or gift is made for the purpose of enabling the prescribed person to become the owner, or lessee from the Crown, of a dwelling house in which he resides or intends to reside

  (b) that a conveyance, transfer or mortgage to which the prescribed person was a party and which was executed or entered into in connection with any other purchase or gift of land on which the prescribed person resided or intended to reside has not previously been exempt from stamp duty pursuant to this paragraph or any enactment relating to advances for homes.

- A conveyance or transfer of a financial product made solely for the purpose of a security lending transaction of a kind that would qualify for relief under section 26BC(3) of the *Income Tax Assessment Act 1936* (Cth).

- A declaration of trust by the Public Trustee for the benefit of a child under the age of 18 years who has received a payment under the *Victims of Crime Act 2001* or a corresponding previous law.

- An instrument executed by a trustee of a regulated superannuation fund within the meaning of the *Superannuation Industry (Supervision) Act 1993* (Cth) in the ordinary course of administering the fund for the purpose of effecting or acknowledging, evidencing or recording:

  (a) the creation of an interest in the property of the superannuation fund on account of a person becoming a member of the fund, or

  (b) the redemption, cancellation or extinguishment of an interest in the property of the superannuation fund on account of a person ceasing to be a member of the fund, but not so as to exempt any conveyance or transfer of property into or out of the fund.

- An instrument of discharge or partial discharge of a mortgage or charge.

- A conveyance (other than a conveyance operating as a voluntary disposition inter vivos) for effectuating the appointment of a new trustee or the retirement of a trustee.

- A conveyance of a kind for which no specific charge, or basis for charging duty, is fixed.

- A deed or transfer of a kind for which no specific charge, or basis for charging duty, is fixed.
- A conveyance of a carbon right created under an Act of the Commonwealth.
- A conveyance of a renewable energy certificate under the *Renewable Energy (Electricity) Act 2000* of the Commonwealth.

28.070 WESTERN AUSTRALIAN DUTIES

Website: www.osr.wa.gov.au   Web Enquiry: www.osr.wa.gov.au/DutiesEnquiry   Telephone: (08) 9262 1100

The relevant legislation is the *Duties Act 2008*.

APPOINTMENT OF TRUSTEE

An instrument evidencing the appointment of a trustee is not a dutiable transaction, however, the transfer of dutiable property as a result of the appointment of a trustee is generally chargeable with nominal duty, subject to the conditions imposed by s119 *Duties Act*.

BUSINESS ASSET TRANSFER

Any transaction by which a business asset is acquired or which establishes the right or option to acquire a business asset (whether it is transferred by formal instruments or not) gives rise to transfer duty.

Business assets include goodwill, a restraint of trade, a business identity, a business licence, a right of a business under an uncompleted agreement to supply commodities or provide services, intellectual property and things that a business has that are in the nature of rent rolls and client lists.

CHANGE OF CONTROL OF CERTAIN LAND OWNING CORPORATIONS AND UNIT TRUSTS

If a person (includes a corporation) makes a relevant acquisition in a corporation or unit trust scheme that is a landholder, an acquisition statement must be lodged with the Commissioner of State Revenue within two months of the acquisition occurring and duty at the general rate of transfer duty will apply.

A relevant acquisition is an acquisition of a significant interest (ie. 50% or more of an unlisted corporation or unlisted unit trust scheme or 90% or more of a public listed corporation or public listed unit trust scheme) or a further interest.

A corporation or unit trust scheme is a landholder if it is entitled to land in Western Australia, and the value of that land is $2 million or greater.

ENTITY RESTRUCTURING

The entity restructuring exemptions apply to certain transactions involving related corporations and/or unit trust schemes. An exemption is available for a relevant transaction that is either a relevant consolidation transaction (landholder acquisition) or relevant reconstruction transaction (certain dutiable transactions).

An application for exemption is required to be lodged with the Commissioner of State Revenue within 12 months after the transaction. A person can also request the Commissioner to determine whether an exemption would be granted in relation to a proposed transaction. Once an exemption is granted, there is an obligation for three years following the relevant transaction to notify the Commissioner of certain transactions that occur that may affect the entity structure.

The Commissioner also has the ability to revoke an exemption if the Commissioner is of the opinion that it was part of a scheme or arrangement to avoid duty on another transaction or to avoid another tax.

DUTIABLE PROPERTY

Dutiable property is:
- land in Western Australia
- a right

- chattels in Western Australia, and
- Western Australian business assets.

RATES OF TRANSFER DUTY

Following are the rates of duty in Western Australia effective 1 July 2008.

General rates	
Up to $80,000	$1.90 for each $100 or part thereof
$80,001 to $100,000	$1,520 + $2.85 per $100 or part thereof above $80,000
$100,001 to $250,000	$2,090 + $3.80 per $100 or part thereof above $100,000
$250,001 to $500,000	$7,790 + $4.75 per $100 or part thereof above $250,000
$500,001 and above	$19,665 + $5.15 per $100 or part thereof above $500,000
Residential rate	
Up to $120,000	$1.90 for each $100 or part thereof
$120,001 to $150,000	$2,280 + $2.85 per $100 or part thereof above $120,000
$150,001 to $360,000	$3,135 + $3.80 per $100 or part thereof above $150,000
$360,001 to $725,000	$11,115 + $4.75 per $100 or part thereof above $360,000
$725,001 and above	$28,453 + $5.15 per $100 or part thereof above $725,000
Principal residence or business property (concessional rate s147)	
Up to $100,000	$1.50 for each $100 or part of $100
Over $100,000 to $200,000	$1,500 + $4.39 for each $100 or part of $100 on excess over $100,000

REBATE OR REFUND TO ELIGIBLE FIRST HOME BUYERS

First home owners who have been, or will be, paid a first home owner grant may be entitled to the first home owner rate of transfer duty on the transfer, or agreement to transfer, in respect of the acquisition of the home or vacant land to which the grant relates. First home owners who receive property as a gift or for no consideration, or first home owners that are residents of the Indian Ocean Territories, may also be entitled to the First Home Owner Rate of duty.

The rebate also applies where the first home owner grant is paid to a person who is not listed as purchaser on a contract, but acquires the land due to a substituted transferee or where the purchaser was acting as an agent.

To be eligible for the First Home Owner Rate of duty the unencumbered value of the property must not exceed $530,000 for the purchase of an established home or $400,000 for the purchase of vacant land. The threshold will apply based on the date of agreement to purchase the property or date transfer of land is executed.

The First Home Owner Rate of duty also applies to the purchase of a further interest in a property by an eligible first home buyer who enters into a shared equity arrangement with the Department of Housing and Works on or after 1 July 2004.

Value		Rate
Established home	Up to $430,000	Nil
	$430,001 to $530,000	$19.19 per $100 or part thereof above $430,000
Vacant land	Up to $300,000	Nil
	$300,001 to $400,000	$13.01 per $100 or part thereof above $300,000

APPLICATIONS FOR FIRST HOME OWNER REFUNDS (FHOR)

An application for the First Home Owner rate of duty may only be made within the period beginning on the commencement date of the eligible transaction to which the grant relates, and ending on the later of the day that is within 12 months after the completion date of the eligible transaction (eg. settlement date), or within three months after the day on which the grant is paid.

GIFTS OF DUTIABLE PROPERTY

Duty is charged using transfer duty rates and is payable by the donee. No duty is payable where the donee is an exempt body.

EXEMPTIONS AND NOMINAL DUTY

- Transfer of a residential property between spouses or de facto partners
- Special disability trust transactions
- Family farm transactions, and
- Cancelled transactions:
    - No longer reduction of duty if matter not carried into effect
    - Transactions will either be cancelled or not, with no partial reduction.
    - Duty will be chargeable if a transaction is cancelled to allow for a replacement or subsale transaction. A replacement transaction is:
        - ° between all of the same parties as the cancelled transaction, and
        - ° substantially similar in effect to the cancelled transaction, and
        - ° in the Commissioner's opinion, is a scheme or arrangement with the sole or dominant purpose of avoiding, reducing or deferring payment of duty.

    A subsale transaction is another dutiable transaction which results in a beneficial interest in the dutiable property the subject of the cancelled transaction being held by:
    - ° a person who is not a party to the cancelled transaction, a result which is provided for under the cancelled transaction, or
    - ° a person who is not a party to the cancelled transaction, a result which is substantially similar to the effect of the cancelled transaction, or
    - ° another person as a result of an agreement, arrangement or understanding between a person liable to pay duty on the cancelled transaction and any other person.
- Where a transaction is cancelled the application for an exemption must be made within five years of the original assessment of duty, or within one year after the date transaction is cancelled, whichever is later.
- A transfer, or agreement for the transfer of dutiable property to a superannuation fund, between superannuation funds, or from a superannuation fund to a member of the fund may be chargeable with nominal duty if certain conditions are satisfied.

CONVEYANCE OF PROPERTY BETWEEN SPOUSES

Duty is not chargeable on the transfer of property between spouses or de facto partners of two years where:

- the transferor is the sole owner of the property
- the property is used solely or dominantly as the ordinary place of residence of the transferor and the transferee at the time of the transaction, and
- the result of the transaction is that the property will be owned by the transferor and the transferee as joint tenants or tenants in common in equal shares.

DECLARATION OF TRUST

- A declaration of trust that is not over dutiable property is not a dutiable transaction.
- A declaration of trust over dutiable property: Will be chargeable with transfer duty at the general rate or nominal duty pursuant to s117 *Duties Act 2008*.
- No double duty will apply to a declaration of trust that declares the same trusts as those upon and subject to which the same dutiable property was transferred, or agreed to be transferred, to the person declaring the trust if the transfer, or agreement, is duty endorsed.

INSURANCE DUTY

Duty chargeable on the premium paid in relation to a contract of insurance is payable by:

- the insurer: if the insurer is a general insurer, or
- the insured person: if the insurer is not a general insurer.

A general insurer, being a person who is:

- a person authorised under the *Insurance Act 1973*, or
- a person registered under the *Life Insurance Act 1995*

must lodge a monthly return and pay duty in respect of any premiums or instalments of premiums received during the month. To calculate the dutiable amount, the total premium is reduced by the duty component. The amount of duty payable on a premium, or an instalment of a premium, is 10% of the amount of the premium, or instalment, that is attributable to general insurance: s215 *Duties Act 2008*.

ADDITIONAL POLICIES

A life insurance policy, where the insured person resides in Western Australia, that also provides for the payment of a benefit upon an event that does not relate to or depend upon a life or lives, is taken to be a general insurance policy to the extent of the additional insurance.

LEASE OR AGREEMENT FOR LEASE

Lease duty is not chargeable under the *Duties Act 2008*. If there is no consideration paid for:

- the grant of a lease (ie. a premium)
- the transfer of, or an agreement for the transfer of a lease, and
- the surrender of a lease

there is not a dutiable transaction and documents should not be presented to the Office of State Revenue for endorsement. Duty on the premium: Transfer duty based on the premium.

Where a premium is paid for the grant of a lease or there is consideration paid by the lessor for the surrender of the lease, transfer duty will be assessed on the amount of the premium or consideration paid.

TRANSFER OR ASSIGNMENT OF A LEASE

Where there is consideration for the transfer or assignment, transfer duty is assessed on the amount of the consideration. If no consideration payable for the transfer or assignment of a lease, the transaction is non dutiable.

If the grant of a lease includes rent that is in excess of the fair market rent, that amount is included in the dutiable value for the transaction.

MATRIMONIAL INSTRUMENTS OR MARRIAGE BREAKDOWNS

Section 113 provides that duty is not chargeable on a dutiable transaction to the extent that it is effected by a matrimonial instrument mentioned in ss129(b) or (c) or a de-facto relationship instrument referred to in ss130(a) of the *Duties Act 2008*.

Nominal duty is chargeable on a dutiable transaction to the extent that it is in accordance with a matrimonial instrument mentioned in ss129(b) or (c) or de-facto relationship instrument referred to in ss130(a) *Duties Act 2008*.

Nominal duty is chargeable on a dutiable transaction to the extent that it is effected by a matrimonial instrument mentioned in ss129(a) or (d) or de-facto relationship instrument referred to in ss130(b) *Duties Act 2008*.

MORTGAGES

Mortgages are not dutiable under the *Duties Act 2008*. However, a transfer of a security interest for consideration less than its market value remains dutiable under the *Duties Act 2008* and will be charged at the general rate of duty.

NON-HEAVY MOTOR VEHICLE LICENCE OR TRANSFERS (GROSS VEHICLE MASS LESS THAN 4.5 TONNES)

Transfer of a licence under a Will or upon intestacy to a person entitled to that vehicle in the Will or intestacy: $20.

Dutiable: From 1 July 2008	Value rate
$0 to $25,000	2.75% of dutiable value (DV)
$25,001 to $50,000	[2.75% + {(DV − 25,000) divided by 6,666.66}%] of dutiable value (DV) (rounded to two decimal places)[1,2]
$50,000 and upwards	6.50% of dutiable value

HEAVY MOTOR VEHICLES LICENCE OR TRANSFERS (GROSS VEHICLE MASS MORE THAN 4.5 TONNES)

Dutiable: From 1 July 2008	Value rate
$0 to $400,000	3.00% of dutiable value
$400,001 and upwards	$12,000

EXEMPTIONS

- To a dealer for re-sale
- To a dealer for demonstration purposes
- To certain classes of users who do not pay a traffic licence fee
- Where a vehicle in the applicant's name has previously been registered in another State/Territory in Australia or another Country, and
- A licence granted or transferred for a caravan or a camper trailer, that is, a trailer permanently fitted for human habitation in the course of a journey.

PARTITION

For any transaction causing the partition of any property: The minimum amount of duty payable is $20.

DUTIABLE VALUE

The dutiable value of partitioned land is calculated by a formula and is the greater of the proportionate amount of the sum of any consideration paid for the partition by any of the parties, or the proportionate amount of a person's excess entitlement. Duty is charged on the transfer using transfer duty rates.

Richard and Natallia own a block of land which has an unencumbered value of $100,000 and a houseboat that has an unencumbered value of $300,000. The total value of the property being partitioned is $700,000 and Richard and Natallia are each entitled to $350,000. Natallia is taking the land by way of partition although the value exceeds her entitlement by $50,000. Natallia will be assessed to duty and the dutiable value of the land will be as follows:

$50,000 (excess entitlement) x $400,000 (value of dutiable property) divided by $700,000 (value of all property).

The dutiable value for the transfer of land to Natallia is $28,571.

RELEASE OR RENUNCIATION

Release or renunciation of any dutiable property or any right or interest in it as a gift or sale: is chargeable with transfer duty.

VESTING OR TERMINATION OF A DISCRETIONARY TRUST

- Transfer of, or an agreement for the transfer of dutiable property to a taker in default on the vesting or termination of the trust: nominal duty is chargeable provided there is, or will be, no consideration for the transaction: s114 *Duties Act 2008*.
- Transfer of, or an agreement for the transfer of dutiable property to a beneficiary of a discretionary trust in the exercise by the trustee of a power of appointment over property: Nominal duty subject to s115 *Duties Act 2008*.

28.080 TASMANIAN DUTIES

Website: www.sro.tas.gov.au/ Email: dutyhelp@treasury.tas.gov.au Phone: (03) 6166 4400

Duty (previously known as 'stamp duty') is a form of taxation charged by the State Government, under the *Duties Act 2001*, levied on an interest in property. Normally, duty must be paid by the transferee within three months of the date of the transfer of the property.

The Act applies to instruments executed or transactions effected on or after 1 July 2001.

DUTIABLE PROPERTY

Duty in Tasmania is levied on dutiable transactions, the most common being the transfer of dutiable property; a declaration of trust over dutiable property and grant or surrender of an interest in land in Tasmania. Dutiable property includes land and fixtures, mineral tenements, land use entitlements and goods if subject of an arrangement that includes other dutiable property. The Duties Act also levies duty on a relevant acquisition of shares or units in a land-rich private corporation and the acquisition of shares that confer land use entitlement.

LIABILITY FOR DUTY

Duty is payable by the transferee, in the case of a declaration of trust the transferee is the person declaring the trust. The liability for duty arises upon the transfer of dutiable property or when the declaration is made over property. A tax default does not occur if duty is paid within three months from the date the liability arises. Interest and penalty tax may be applied to tax defaults depending on the circumstances leading to the default.

DUTY CONCESSIONS

Subject to the conditions set out in the *Duties Act 2001*, a concessional rate of duty may apply to the transfer of dutiable property under the following circumstances:
- change of trustee (s37)
- transfer from or to a responsible entity of a managed investment scheme (s38) property vested in an apparent purchaser(s39)
- transfers back from a nominee (s40)
- property passing to beneficiaries (s41)
- establishment of a trust relating to unidentified and non-dutiable property (s42)
- instrument relating to managed investment scheme (s43)
- transfer of property from one superannuation fund to another (s45)
- transfers between trustees and custodians of superannuation funds or trusts (s46)
- certain transfers from deceased estates (s47)
- conversion of lots to strata title (s48)
- if there is no change in beneficial ownership (s49), and
- transfers to shareholders during the course of a company wind up (s50).

DUTY EXEMPTIONS

Subject to the conditions set out in the *Duties Act 2001*, the following are some of the more common circumstances under which a transfer of dutiable property would be exempt from duty:
- transfers relating to liquidation, bankruptcy or receivership (s52)
- transfers that give effect to the incorporation or amalgamation of an association (s53)
- certain transfers of real property to councils (s53)
- an assent given under the *Administration and Probate Act 1935* vesting real estate (s53)
- transfers effecting gifts for charitable, religious or educational purposes (s53)
- certain transfers to partners in a marriage or relationship (s55)
- transfer of property resulting from a break-down of marriage or termination of relationship (ss56, 56A & 57), and
- intergenerational rural transfers of land used for primary production (s225).

Transfer of certain property to councils can offer a full or partial exemption (s57A).

Duty is not payable on duplicate instruments if duty has been paid on the original instrument (s219).

DUTIABLE VALUE

Duty is assessed on the greater of the consideration for the dutiable transaction or the unencumbered value of the dutiable property being transferred.

DUTY RATES

The liability date is used to determine which rates apply, the liability is the date on which the transfer is affected, generally for most land conveyance transactions this is the date of settlement.

Dutiable value	Duty
Rates/thresholds from 1 October 2012 to 20 October 2013	
Dutiable value not more than $1,300	$20
More than $1,300 but not more than $25,000	$20 plus $1.75 for every $100 or part by which dutiable value exceeds $1,300
More than $25,000 but not more than $75,000	$435 plus $2.25 for every $100 or part by which dutiable value exceeds $25,000
More than $75,000 but not more than $200,000	$1,560 plus $3.50 for every $100 or part by which dutiable value exceeds $75,000
More than $200,000 but not more than $375,000	$5,935 plus $4.00 for every $100 or part by which dutiable value exceeds $200,000
More than $375,000 but not more than $725,000	$12,935 plus $4.25 for every $100 or part by which dutiable value exceeds $375,000
More than $725,000	$27,810 plus $4.50 for every $100 or part by which dutiable value exceeds $725,000
Rates/thresholds from 21 October 2013 onward	
Not more than $3,000	$50
More than $3,000 but not more than $25,000	$50 plus $1.75 for every $100, or part, by which the dutiable value exceeds $3,000
More than $25,000 but not more than $75,000	$435 plus $2.25 for every $100, or part, by which the dutiable value exceeds $25,000
More than $75,000 but not more than $200,000	$1,560 plus $3.50 for every $100, or part, by which the dutiable value exceeds $75,000
More than $200,000 but not more than $375,000	$5,935 plus $4.00 for every $100, or part, by which the dutiable value exceeds $200,000
More than $375,000 but not more than $725,000	$12,935 plus $4.25 for every $100, or part, by which the dutiable value exceeds $375,000
More than $725,000	$27,810 plus $4.50 for every $100, or part, by which the dutiable value exceeds $725,000

INSURANCE: LIFE POLICIES

Insurance duty is imposed on contracts of General and Life insurance. The duty is charged on the amount of the premium paid in relation to a contract that effects general insurance and on a policy of life insurance.

TEMPORARY OR TERM INSURANCE

5% of the first year's premium.

OTHER LIFE INSURANCE POLICIES

Based on the sum insured:
- up to $2,000: 10c per 200 (or part thereof): $1, and
- over $2,000: $1.00 plus 20c per $200 (or part thereof) by which sum exceeds $2,000.

TRANSFER OR ASSIGNMENT OF LIFE POLICY

No duty payable.

EXEMPTIONS

An exemption applies to the public liability component of insurance premiums in some circumstances. To qualify for this exemption either:
- the insurance policy covers public liability only, or
- the premium payable (in relation to the public liability component of a package of insurance) is separately itemised on the policy.

The exemption, in relation to a package of insurance, does not apply to a domestic policy covering home and/or contents insurance.

Other less common exemptions are available (detailed s190 of the Act) on specific types of policies or policies insuring the interest of specific entities.

INSURANCE: GENERAL

Duty is imposed where the property or risk is in Tasmania; see the *Duties Act 2001* for details. Duty is calculated at the rate of 10% of any premiums paid on or after 1 October 2012.

EXEMPTION ON GENERAL INSURANCE

Duty may be exempted from public liability component of insurance premiums in some circumstances. For more information consult the website.

MOTOR VEHICLE: APPLICATION TO REGISTER OR TRANSFER REGISTRATION

Duty is imposed on the following:
- an application to register a motor vehicle
- an application to transfer the registration of a motor vehicle,
- a notice of change of beneficial ownership of a motor vehicle, and
- a notification of a 'change of purpose' lodged by a motor vehicle dealer who did not pay duty when the vehicle was acquired because it was purchased for resale.

RATE OF DUTY

The rate used to calculate the duty payable on a transfer of vehicle registration (or other dutiable motor vehicle transaction or event) depends on:
- the dutiable value of the vehicle
- the type of vehicle (Passenger, Heavy or Other), and
- whether the vehicle was purchased with a manufacturers fleet discount.

The minimum amount of duty payable on a dutiable transaction is $20.00 (regardless of the dutiable value of the vehicle, the type of vehicle or whether the vehicle was purchased with a manufacturers fleet discount) – s197(3).

Vehicles purchased with a manufacture's fleet discount (except heavy vehicles) attract duty at a rate of $3.50 per $100 (or part thereof) of the dutiable value – s197(3A). Heavy vehicles attract duty at a rate of $1.00 per $100 (or part thereof) of the dutiable value – s197(3B).

Passenger vehicles attract duty at the rates shown in the table – s197(2).

Dutiable value	Rate of duty
$600 or less	$20
$601 to $35,000	$3 per $100 or part thereof
$35,001 to $40,000	$1,050 plus $11 for each $100 or part thereof, of the value that exceeds $35,000
$40,001 or greater	$4 per $100 or part thereof

All other vehicles attract duty at a rate of $3.00 per $100 (or part thereof) of the dutiable value – s197(1).

EXEMPTIONS

There are exemptions for certain individuals and organisations; check with the SRO. Additional information is available on the SRO website or contact the SRO on (03) 6166 4400 or dutyhelp@treasury.tas.gov.au.

28.100 OTHER TAXES

The introduction of GST on 1 July 2000 was accompanied by a series of other tax measures, including a Wine Equalisation Tax (WET) and a Luxury Car Tax (LCT). In addition to the WET and LCT, a Fuel Tax Credits (FTC) scheme was introduced to replace the Energy Grant Credits Scheme (EGCS) effective from 1 July 2006.

28.200 LUXURY CAR TAX

Since 1 July 2000, an LCT of 25% applied on all taxable supplies and importations of luxury cars. Effective 1 July 2008, the increased LCT rate of 33% applies to certain vehicles over the luxury car tax threshold. This tax is in addition to any GST payable and is payable on the amount that is in excess of the 'luxury car threshold'. Registered entities making a taxable supply of a luxury car must include any luxury car tax as part of their BAS. In theory, this tax replaces the 45% Wholesale Sales Tax that formerly applied to luxury cars.

The luxury car tax rules are governed by *A New Tax System (Luxury Car Tax) Act 1999* (LCT Act).

28.220 WHAT IS A 'LUXURY CAR'?

A 'luxury car' is a motor vehicle designed to carry a load of less than two tonnes and fewer than nine passengers, with a GST-inclusive price that exceeds the luxury car tax threshold. For 2014-15, the GST-inclusive LCT threshold is $61,884 and the fuel efficient car limit is $75,375.

Year	Luxury car tax threshold	Depreciation limit for motor vehicles
2014-15	$61,884	$57,466
2015-16	$63,184	$57,466*

*Preliminary calculations using Australian Bureau of Statistics – *Motor vehicle sub-group of the Consumer Price Index – weighted average of the eight capital cities* – indicate that there is no indexing of the car limit for 2015-16. The ATO has yet to confirm the car limit in a Tax Determination at the time of writing.

 Luxury car limit for depreciation purposes is different from the luxury car tax.

A luxury car is a car whose luxury car tax value exceeds the luxury car tax threshold, but excludes:

- a. a vehicle that is specified in the regulations to be an emergency vehicle, or that is in a class of vehicles that are specified in the regulations to be emergency vehicles, or
- b. specifically fitted out for transporting *disabled people seated in wheelchairs (unless the supply of the car is *GST-free under Subdivision 38-P of the *GST Act), or
- c. a commercial vehicle that is not designed for the principal purpose of carrying passengers, or
- d. a motor home or campervan.

28.230 AMOUNT OF LUXURY CAR TAX

From 1 July 2008, LCT is imposed at the rate of 33% on that part of the GST-exclusive price that exceeds the LCT threshold. The luxury car value includes the value of any parts, accessories or attachments supplied or imported at the same time as the car. The LCT only applies to supplies of luxury cars by entities registered for GST. It does not apply to unregistered activities such as a private sale.

LIABILITY FOR LUXURY CAR TAX

LCT is only payable on the taxable supply of a luxury car. Section 5-10 of the LCT Act provides that:

(1) *You make a taxable supply of a luxury car if:*
   (a) *you supply a luxury car, and*
   (b) *the supply is made in the course or furtherance of an enterprise that you carry on, and*
   (c) *the supply is connected with Australia, and*
   (d) *you are registered, or required to be registered.*

(2) *However, you do not make a taxable supply of a luxury car if:*
  (a) *the recipient quotes for the supply of the car, or,*
  (b) *the car is more than 2 years old, or*
  (c) *you export the car in circumstances where the export is GST-free under Subdivision 38-E of the GST Act.*

WHEN LUXURY CAR TAX DOES NOT APPLY

Subsection 5-10(2) LCT Act, the luxury car tax does not apply in the following three circumstances:
- where the recipient quotes for the supply (ie. holds an ABN and is registered for LCT)
- where the car is more than two years old, and
- the car was exported GST free under Subdivision 38-E GST Act.

RECIPIENT QUOTES

The LCT applies in addition to any GST and no input tax credit is allowed for any LCT paid regardless of whether the car is used for business or private purposes. A quoting system applies for those cars that are held as trading stock. Under this system registered dealers can quote their ABN to ensure that they do not pay the LCT on the cars to be held as trading stock. The LCT will eventually be borne by the purchaser. Cars held for hire or lease will attract LCT and the person acquiring the car is not entitled to quote their ABN to avoid paying the LCT.

THE CAR IS MORE THAN TWO YEARS OLD

A car is not subject to LCT when it is considered more than two years old at the time of a supply, this is the case (under ss5-10(3) LCT Act) where:
- for a car that has not been imported – the car was manufactured more than two years before the time of the supply, or
- the car was entered for home consumption more than two years before the time of the supply.

GST-FREE EXPORT UNDER SUBDIVISION 38-E GST ACT

Generally GST-free exports occur where the supply is not to be consumed in Australia. Where an export is GST-free because of this division no LCT will apply.

CALCULATING LUXURY CAR TAX

The formula for calculating the LCT is set out at s5-15 of the LCT Act:

(Rate of Luxury Car Tax) x (10 divided by 11) x [Luxury car tax value – Luxury car tax threshold]

The terms in the above formula are as follows:
  (a) Rate of LCT is 33%
  (b) Luxury car tax value is the value as determined under s5-30 LCT Act. Generally the 'Luxury car tax value' is equal to the price of the car excluding both:
   - the LCT that is payable on the vehicle (as this is what is being calculated by the formula), and
   - any other Australian Tax or Australian fee or charge with the exception of the GST

   In other words for the purposes of the formula the GST inclusive value (net of other taxes and charges) is what is used to determine the LCT payable on a car. Note that a number of modifications apply to the 'Luxury car tax value' as follows:
   - where the car is GST-free under Subdivision 38-P GST Act
   - supply of cars to associates
   - additional supplies and modifications for cars
   - modifications for disabled people, and
   - supply of cars by way of lease or hire.

   These are discussed more fully in s5-20 LCT Act.
  (c) Luxury car tax threshold is $61,884 for 2014-15

Because the 'Luxury car tax value' is the price of the car excluding any LCT payable on the supply and any other Australian tax payable other than GST, no customs duty will be included in this item of the formula. Furthermore, the price of the car will also exclude stamp duty, transfer fees, registration, compulsory third party insurance and extended warranties. However both dealer delivery charges and standard and statutory warranties as well as GST will be included in this figure.

 A taxpayer buys a car in August 2014 from a registered car dealer with a GST-inclusive price of $88,000. This amount includes the GST but excludes the LCT on the supply.

The amount of LCT is $7,835 being 33% x (10 divided by 11) x ($88,000 − $61,884).

The total amount payable by the taxpayer for the car is:

Cost of the car	*$80,000*
GST	*$8,000*
LCT	*$7,835*
Total amount payable	*$95,835*

NOTE: The formula to calculate LCT has a term (ie. 10/11) that adjusts for the formula using the GST-inclusive value of the car on the price of the luxury car that exceeds the LCT limit in order to ensure that the LCT does not apply on the GST payable by the recipient of the supply (ie. tax on tax).

Section 5-15 of the LCT Act provides that the amount of LCT payable is reduced by the sum of all LCT that was payable for any previous importation or supply of the car. This effectively ensures that no more LCT is payable unless the value of the car increases. The liability to pay LCT rests with the supplier (and not the recipient) of a taxable supply of a luxury car in the same way the liability to pay GST rests with the supplier of a taxable supply.

Useful guides provided by the Tax Office regarding the LCT include:

- *Luxury car tax – how to meet you luxury car tax (LCT) obligations* (NAT 3394), and
- *Luxury car tax – how to complete your activity statement* (NAT 7391).

28.240   LUXURY CAR TAX AND GST

Input tax credits on luxury cars are restricted for end consumers by the car depreciation limit. For the 2014-15 financial year, the maximum GST credit claimable for the purchase of a car which exceeds the depreciation limit of $57,466 is 1/11th of that limit or $57,466 = $5,224 under s69-10 GST Act.

Under s27-80 ITAA97 the definition of 'cost' under income tax laws in respect of depreciating assets is reduced to exclude input tax credits. This means when comparing a depreciating asset's cost to the car limit for income tax purposes it is done on a GST-exclusive basis under s40-230 ITAA97. Thus a car's GST exclusive cost is reduced to the car limit for the purposes of obtaining an income tax deduction for depreciation. However this is not the case for GST, the GST Act clearly states that a GST credit of up to 1/11th of the car limit is available.

 EXAMPLE

GST-inclusive cost of car	*$62,690*
Less available ITCs: 1/11th of $57,466	*$5,224*
Depreciation car limit	**$57,466**

If creditable use of the car is not 100%, then the input tax credit claimable will be the maximum amount of input tax credit available being $5,224 multiplied by the proportion of creditable use.

The restriction on input tax credits claimable only applies to cars that fall within the definition of 'luxury car' (see 28.120) and are subject to the LCT. The input tax credit restriction does not apply to vehicles that exceed the LCT limit but are not luxury cars such as:

- an emergency vehicle
- a commercial vehicle not designed for the principal purpose of carrying passengers
- a motor home or campervan
- a car in circumstances where it is a GST-free export, or
- a vehicle specifically fitted out for transporting disabled people seated in wheelchairs (unless the sale of the car was GST-free).

The restriction also does not apply to cars for which the taxpayer is entitled to quote their ABN and not pay LCT (ie. cars held as trading stock, but do not include cars held for hire or lease).

NOTE: The LCT paid does not attract an input tax credit. If a car is leased, input tax credits may be claimed if the GST is included in each lease payment, based on the amount the car is used in carrying on the business.

On 2 September 2014 Darren purchased a new car for $96,660 (including $8,000 GST and $8,660 luxury car tax). Darren plans to use the car 100% in carrying on his business. As the car limit for the 2014-15 financial year is $57,466, the maximum GST credit Darren can claim is 1/11 x $57,466 = $5,224.
If Darren planned to use the car only 50% in carrying on his business, he would be entitled to claim 1/11 x $57,466 x 50% = $2,612.
Darren cannot claim a credit for the LCT paid on the car.

28.250   LUXURY CAR TAX CONCESSIONS

The Government has also amended the LCT legislation to introduce concessions to the LCT.

PRIMARY PRODUCERS AND TOURISM OPERATORS

Primary producers and tourism operators may be eligible to claim refunds of the additional 8% LCT payable on certain luxury cars up to a maximum of $3,000 per car. To be eligible for the concession, a primary producer or a tourism operator must have an ABN and be registered for GST. Eligible taxpayers can claim refunds by completing an *Application for luxury car tax refund for primary producers and tourism operators form* (NAT 72601).

NOTE: Primary producers can only claim a refund for one eligible car per income year. Tourism operators may claim a refund for all eligible cars.

Primary producers and tourism operators can only claims refunds for cars that are either four wheel drive or all wheel drive and are either a 'passenger car' with a ground clearance of at least 175 mm or an 'off road passenger vehicle'.

FUEL-EFFICIENT CARS

The fuel-efficient car limit for the 2015-16 financial year is $75,375. Vehicles with fuel consumptions below 7 litres per 100 kms are considered as fuel efficient cars.

ENDORSED PUBLIC MUSEUMS AND ART GALLERIES

In the 2011-12 Budget the Australian Government announced it would amend the LCT legislation to allow eligible entities, such as endorsed public museums and art galleries, to import cars free from the LCT. At the time of writing no legislation has been enacted.

28.300 WINE EQUALISATION TAX

The Wine Equalisation Tax (WET) is levied on the wholesale sale value at a rate of 29% on all wine products including non-grape wines, cider, perry, mead and sake.

A quotation system similar to the one that applies for luxury cars also applies to ensure that the WET is only applied to the last wholesale sale price of wine in Australia. WET is payable by wine manufacturers, wine wholesalers and wine importers and is remitted as part of the BAS for an entity for each tax period. A WET rebate is available for wine producers. WET is governed by *A New Tax System (Wine Equalisation Tax) Act 1999* (WET Act).

Generally exports of wine are GST-free and are not subject to WET.

28.310   WINE EQUALISATION TAX-RELATED BEVERAGES

Generally, WET applies to assessable dealings of:
* grape wine (ie. table wines, sparking wines, fortified wines and dessert wines)

- grape wine products which contain between 8% and 22% by volume of ethyl alcohol such as marsala, vermouth and wine based cocktails
- fruit or vegetable wines
- cider and perry
- mead, and
- sake.

However, WET does not apply to:

- beverages that do not contain more than 1.15% by volume of ethyl alcohol
- beer
- spirits, liquors or spirituous liquors, or
- beverages containing beer, spirits, liqueur or spirituous liquors.

28.320 ASSESSABLE DEALINGS

Dealings which attract WET are called assessable dealings and can include selling wine, making wine or making a local entry of imported wine at the customs barrier. WET is imposed on all assessable dealings with wine unless an exemption applies (ss5-5(2)).

There are four broad instances of assessable dealings where the tax is imposed:

1. **Sale:** The most common assessable dealing is a wholesale sale followed by retail sales including royalty-inclusive sales and indirect marketing sales. Some assessable retail sales include cellar door sales or retail sales of repackaged bulk wine.

   For a royalty-inclusive sale to exist the following conditions are necessary:
   - the sale is a retail sale
   - the sale occurs in the ordinary course of business
   - the sale is not covered by any other category of assessable dealing, and
   - the seller (or an associate) incurs a royalty that is paid or payable in connection with the wine.

   An indirect marketing sale is a retail sale by an entity which is not the manufacturer of the wine and occurs when a sale is made by the seller through another entity (other than through an employee).

2. **Application to own use:** An application to own use includes consumption, gifts, transferring property in wine under a contract that is not a contract of sale, granting any right or permission to use the wine, and using wine as materials in the manufacture or processing or treatment of wine. Some of the common examples of wine being applied for own use are:
   - wine used for tastings and promotions
   - wine donated to charity
   - wine given as samples
   - wine given to staff, and
   - wine taken for personal consumption.

3. **Local entry:** Local entry only applies to imported wine. Section 5-30(5) of the WET Act sets out the situations that amount to a local entry of imported wine for the purposes of the WET.

4. **Removal from customs area:** Removal from customs clearance area applies in limited situations such as inward bound travellers where they exceed the traveller's exemption limit.

EXEMPTIONS

In some circumstances, an assessable dealing with wine is exempt from WET. The following situations are exempt:

- GST-free supplies including exports, religious services and some treatments in hospitals
- where a quotation has been made allowing the tax to be deferred until a later assessable dealing, and
- if wine has already been taxed (eg. while in bond).

28.330 TAXABLE VALUES

The following table sets out the methods to calculate the taxable value of each assessable dealing.

Wine equalisation tax: Calculating the taxable value of each assessable dealing		
Assessable dealing		**Taxable value**
Wholesale sale	• by manufacturer	Price (excluding GST and wine tax) for which the wine was sold
	• by non-manufacturer	Price (excluding GST and wine tax) for which the wine was sold
Retail sale	• by manufacturer	Notional wholesale selling price. Use either method.
	• by non-manufacturer (obtained under quote)	Notional wholesale selling price. Use half retail price method
Assessable dealing		**Taxable value**
Royalty-inclusive sale		Amount that would be the notional wholesale purchase price if manufacturer had incurred eligible royalty costs
Indirect marketing sale		Notional wholesale selling price
Untaxed wine sale by non-manufacturer		Notional wholesale selling price
Goods for own use: non-manufacturer & manufacturer		Notional wholesale selling price
Goods for own use by non-manufacturer - but obtained by quote		Purchase price (excluding GST)
Royalty-inclusive goods for own use		Amount that would be the notional wholesale selling price if the manufacturer had incurred the eligible royalty costs
Removal of airport shop wine		Price for which the wine was purchased by the traveller

Under the notional wholesale selling price, where retail sales are made by the manufacturer or the wine is applied for own use there is a choice:

- half price method (50% of the price of the sale), or
- average wholesale price method (using the weighted average of prices after excluding WET and any GST).

NOTE: The average wholesale price method is only available if at least 10% of all sales by value, of all grape wine of the same vintage and produced from the same grape variety, are wholesale sales.

Half price method An entity makes retail sales of grape wine at $140 per dozen. The taxable value is calculated at $70 per dozen.

Average wholesale price method During a particular tax period, 70% of the wholesale sales of grape wine of a particular vintage and variety are made to a distributor at $80 per dozen. The remaining 30% are distributed to hotels and restaurants at $90/dozen. The weighted average price for all wholesale sales during the period is (70% of $80) + (30% of $90) = $83 per dozen.

28.340 WINE EQUALISATION TAX CREDITS

Wine equalisation tax credits may be claimed by the person who paid the WET for which the credit is sought. The credits may be claimed in a number of different circumstances including:

- where the producer rebate is available
- overpaid WET
- avoidance of double taxation
- export-related credits
- import-related credits, and
- bad debts.

28.350   WINE PRODUCER REBATE

As a general rule, the producer rebate scheme entitles wine producers to a rebate of 29% of the wholesale value of eligible domestic sales up to a maximum of $500,000 each financial year, If the eligible taxpayer belongs to a group of associated producers, this limit applies to the whole group. The producer rebate available to producers who:

- manufacture wine from grapes, other fruit, vegetables or honey the producers produce or purchase, or
- provide grapes, other fruit, vegetables or honey to a contract winemaker to be made into wine on your behalf.

From 1 July 2005 the WET tax rebate was extended to cover New Zealand wine producers, whose wine is exported to the Australian market. WETR 2006/1 (note addendum) explains how the wine tax producer rebate operates for New Zealand wine producers exporting to Australia. The operation of the producer rebate for non-New Zealand participants is described in WETR 2009/2. Generally, eligible taxpayers can claim the producer rebate on wine they have to pay WET on when it's sold in Australia or applied to their own use. Eligible taxpayers can also claim the producer rebate on their wine sales even if they didn't have to pay WET because the purchaser quoted their ABN, but only if they indicated on the quotation form that they didn't intend to make a GST-free supply of the wine. The producer rebate is assessable for income tax purposes, and it needs to be declared in the tax return.

As of 10 December 2012, the government amended the *A New Tax System (Wine Equalisation Tax) Act 1999* to ensure that wine producers who buy wine for blending or further manufacture must now reduce the amount of their rebate claim by any earlier amount of rebate attributable to the wine. To be able to claim a rebate on the total amount of wine used in manufacture, you must have a notification from your supplier that they are not entitled to claim the rebate.

If you do not receive a notification from your supplier, you must assume the supplier has claimed the full rebate on the wine sold to you and subtract that amount from your total claim. The amount to subtract is 29% of the GST exclusive price of the purchased wine.

28.400   CARBON TAX

The carbon tax commenced from 1 July 2012. The scheme imposes a price on carbon dioxide with liable entities required to purchase permits (categorised as 'units') for each tonne of the greenhouse gas produced. This measure was repealed on 17 July 2014, with effect from 1 July 2014. For further information, refer to the *Tax Summary 2014 & 2015*.

28.500   FUEL TAX CREDITS

The *Fuel Tax Act 2006* (FTA06) provides a single system of fuel tax credits applicable to fuel used in vehicles used for both private and business purposes. Fuel tax credits are paid to reduce or remove the incidence of fuel tax levied on taxable fuels used by eligible taxpayers.

The scheme allows eligible taxpayers to claim the fuel tax credit via Business Activity Statements (BAS) in the same manner as other indirect taxes such as GST and wine equalisation tax. The fuel tax credit must be included as assessable income for income tax purposes. Any fuel tax credit received must be included in the taxpayer's BAS as part of the PAYG instalment income calculation. However, the credit is not subject to GST. Generally, business will claim the fuel tax credit. However, rules apply to households using fuel for domestic electricity generation and non-profit organisations using emergency vehicles.

Note that where an entity has omitted to claim a fuel tax credit in an earlier activity statement, it can choose to revise its earlier activity statement to include the credit, or include the credit in a subsequent activity statement (ATO ID 2014/4).

REGISTRATION AND ELIGIBILITY

Only businesses registered for GST are eligible to claim the fuel tax credit. Taxpayers registered for GST that were previously registered for the EGCS are automatically registered for fuel tax credits. Otherwise registration is required by contacting the Tax Office.

Certain businesses must also meet environmental criteria (for diesel vehicles) or the Greenhouse Challenge Plus (GCP) programme criteria. Businesses claiming fuel tax credits in excess of $3 million in any one financial year must join the GCP or the fuel tax credit refund will be capped to $3 million.

To make a claim the registered business must use fuel to undertake an eligible business activity such as:

- **Primary production:** Agriculture, fishing, forestry, and
- **Non-primary production:** Road transport, marine transport, rail transport, generation of electricity, mining, non-fuel use, nursing or medical.

In ATO ID 2010/107, an entity was held to be entitled to a fuel tax credit under s41-5 FTA06 for taxable fuel for use in a refrigerated container with an integral mechanically-driven compressor while being transported by a vessel (which relates to marine transport). Similarly, in ATO ID 2008/66, an entity that acquires taxable fuel for use in a clip-on generator set to power a refrigerated container is entitled to a fuel tax credit under s41-5 FTA06. To be eligible, the owner of the fuel must acquire the fuel; refer s41-5(1) FTA06. ATO ID 2007/152 considers whether a fisherman owns fuel where a commercial fishing operation provides a share of the value of the catch less an amount to cover the costs of the fishing expedition to that contracted fisherman. The Commissioner decided that the fisherman had not acquired the fuel for the purposes of s41-5(1) FTA06 and therefore was not eligible to the fuel tax credit.

Domestic electricity generation

Garry lives on a sheep station in central Queensland. He uses a diesel-powered generator to produce electricity for two homes on the property - the family home and the shearers' quarters. He is entitled to claim a fuel tax credit for the diesel acquired to use in the generator because the fuel is acquired for use in domestic electricity generation (see s42-5 FTA06).

Garry uses another diesel generator to power the shearing shed and several other outbuildings used in the primary production business. Garry is also entitled to claim a fuel tax credit for the diesel acquired for use in this generator because he has acquired the fuel in an eligible activity.

The availability of a fuel tax credit in a vehicle or equipment hire arrangement is considered in FTR 2009/1.

WORKING OUT YOUR FUEL TAX CREDIT

The calculation of the fuel tax credit involves a three step process:
- **Step 1:** Calculate the number of eligible litres of fuel used in the business
- **Step 2:** Determine the fuel tax credit rate applicable to the business activity
- **Step 3:** Multiply the eligible litres by the applicable fuel tax credit rate.

CALCULATING THE ELIGIBLE LITRES

The Tax Office provides alternative ways for calculating the eligible litres:
- Basic methods
- Percentage use calculation method, and
- Small claimants method.

The basic methods adopt alternative approaches being a constructive calculation or a deductive calculation. The constructive method involves adding up the litres of each eligible fuel type intended for use in eligible activities. The deductive method involves subtracting the litres of ineligible fuel from total fuel acquired to determine the eligible litres.

The percentage use calculation method relies upon a consistent usage pattern over time. Businesses that adopt the percentage use calculation method, must maintain a detailed record of fuel usage for at least 12 weeks, using either the constructive or the deductive basic methods. The 12 week record must reflect the continuing operations. Separate percentages are calculated for activities entitled to different fuel tax credit rates. The percentage can be used for five years provided the pattern of use remains substantially the same and the fuel tax credit entitlement is less than $10,000 in any financial year. If the business operations change in a way that substantially affects the percentage of eligible fuel purchases, the percentage use must be recalculated.

Small business operators or eligible taxpayers that only use a small scale of eligible fuel may estimate the fuel tax credit using the small claimants method. However, the estimate must be reasonable and the claimant must be able to demonstrate how the estimate was established.

Small claimant's method

Thomas and Lilly own an eight tonne tray truck, used on their farm. Thomas and Lilly in the prior year received $4,500 in fuel tax credits. Their farming business has not changed significantly and they expect their total claim for fuel tax credits this year will not exceed $5,000. Using the small claimant's method, they will report the claim for fuel tax credits on the annual BAS.

The amount of a taxpayer's fuel tax credit entitlement may be reduced by a cleaner fuel grant or the road user charge. Different rates apply for the road user charge depending on whether the fuel was acquired, manufactured or imported into Australia on or after 1 July 2009 or before that date (see ATO ID 2011/17).

APPORTIONMENT

FTD 2010/1 states that apportionment can be used in working out the net fuel amount that the taxpayer is entitled to claim that is attributable to a period. The Commissioner states that this must be determined by using a 'fair and reasonable' principle. In working out the net fuel amount, a taxpayer is required to perform a separate calculation so that applying a fair and reasonable basis of apportionment is achieved where there is:

- one type of taxable fuel for use in multiple activities that either attract no fuel tax credit, a full fuel tax credit, or a half fuel tax credit, or the amount of the taxpayer's fuel tax credit entitlement may be reduced by a cleaner fuel grant or the road user charge
- more than one type of taxable fuel for use in the same activity, or
- more than one type of taxable fuel for use in multiple activities that either attracts no fuel tax credit, a full fuel tax credit, or a half fuel tax credit, or the amount of the taxpayer's fuel tax credit entitlement may be reduced by a cleaner fuel grant or the road user charge.

FUEL TAX CREDIT RATES

For fuel tax credit rates which applied up to 30 June 2014, see the *Tax Summary 2014 & 2015* at 28.500.

TABLE 1: FUEL TAX CREDIT RATES FOR LIQUID FUELS ACQUIRED FROM 1 JULY 2014, 10 NOVEMBER 2014 AND 2 FEBRUARY 2015

Business use	Eligible liquid fuel	Rate for fuel acquired from 1 July 2014	Rate for fuel acquired from 10 November 2014	Rate for fuel acquired from 2 February 2015
In a heavy vehicle* (including emergency vehicles) for travelling on public roads	Liquid fuels – for example, diesel or petrol	12.003**	12.46**	12.76**
All other business uses – such as on private roads, off public roads and non-fuel uses	Liquid fuels – for example, diesel or petrol	38.143	38.6	38.9
To power auxiliary equipment of a heavy vehicle* travelling on public roads – such as fuel used to power a refrigeration unit or a concrete mixing barrel	Liquid fuels – for example, diesel or petrol	38.143	38.6	38.9
Packaging fuels in containers of 20 litres or less for uses other than in an internal combustion engine	Mineral turpentine, white spirit, kerosene and certain other fuels	38.143	38.6	38.9
Supply of fuel for domestic heating	Heating oil and kerosene	38.143	38.6	38.9

* A heavy vehicle is a vehicle with a gross vehicle mass (GVM) greater than 4.5 tonnes. Diesel vehicles acquired before 1 July 2006 can equal 4.5 tonnes.

** This rate accounts for the road user charge (which is subject to change) and applies to fuel used in a heavy vehicle for travelling on public roads.

TABLE 2: FUEL TAX CREDIT RATES FOR GASEOUS FUELS ACQUIRED FROM 1 JULY 2014, 10 NOVEMBER 2014 AND 2 FEBRUARY 2015

Business use	Eligible gaseous fuel	Rate for fuel acquired from 1 July 2014	Rate for fuel acquired from 10 November 2014	Rate for fuel acquired from 2 February 2015
In a heavy vehicle* (including emergency vehicles) for travelling on public roads	Duty paid LPG, LNG or CNG – transport	0.0**	0.0**	0.0**
All other business uses – such as on private roads, off public roads and non-fuel uses	Duty paid LPG – transport	10.0	10.1	10.2
	Duty paid LNG or CNG – transport	20.9 cents/kg	21.2 cents/kg	21.3 cents/kg
	LPG, LNG or CNG – non-transport	0.0	0.0	0.0
To power auxiliary equipment of a heavy vehicle* travelling on public roads – such as fuel used to power a refrigeration unit or a concrete mixing barrel	Duty paid LPG – transport	10.0	10.1	10.2
	Duty paid LNG or CNG – transport	20.9 cents/kg	21.2 cents/kg	21.3 cents/kg
Supplying LPG: • by filling cylinders of 210kg capacity or less for non-transport use	Duty paid LPG – transport	10.0	10.1	10.2
• in tanks for residential use	LPG – non-transport	0.00	0.00	0.00

* A heavy vehicle is a vehicle with a gross vehicle mass (GVM) greater than 4.5 tonnes. Diesel vehicles acquired before 1 July 2006 can equal 4.5 tonnes.

** This rate accounts for the road user charge (which is subject to change) and applies to fuel used in a heavy vehicle for travelling on public roads. The road user charge currently exceeds the rate of duty paid for gaseous fuels.

TABLE 3: FUEL TAX CREDIT RATES FOR STANDARD FUEL BLENDS ACQUIRED FROM 1 JULY 2014, 10 NOVEMBER 2014 AND 2 FEBRUARY 2015

Business use	Eligible blended fuel	Rate for fuel acquired from 1 July 2014	Rate for fuel acquired from 10 November 2014	Rate for fuel acquired from 2 February 2015
In a heavy vehicle* (including emergency vehicles) for travelling on public roads	B5 (5% biodiesel / 95% diesel)	12.003**	12.46**	12.76**
	B20 (20% biodiesel / 80% diesel)	12.003**	12.46**	12.76**
	E10 (10% ethanol / 90% petrol)	12.003**	12.46**	12.76**
	E85 (85% ethanol / 15% petrol)	0.0**	0.0**	0.0**
All other business uses – such as on private roads, off public roads and non-fuel uses***	B5	38.143	38.6	38.9
	B20	38.143	38.6	38.9
	E10	38.143	38.6	38.9
	E85	5.72145	5.79	5.835
To power auxiliary equipment of a heavy vehicle* travelling on public roads – such as fuel used to power a refrigeration unit or a concrete mixing barrel	B5	38.143	38.6	38.9
	B20	38.143	38.6	38.9
	E10	38.143	38.6	38.9
	E85	5.72145	5.79	5.835

* A heavy vehicle is a vehicle with a gross vehicle mass (GVM) greater than 4.5 tonnes. Diesel vehicles acquired before 1 July 2006 can equal 4.5 tonnes.

** This rate accounts for the road user charge (which is subject to change) and applies to fuel used in a heavy vehicle for travelling on public roads. The road user charge currently exceeds the rate for E85.

*** Does not include packaging fuels in containers of 20 litres or less.

Index

M